Oxford Dictionary of
National Biography

Volume 12

Oxford Dictionary of National Biography

IN ASSOCIATION WITH
The British Academy

From the earliest times to the year 2000

Edited by
H. C. G. Matthew
and
Brian Harrison

Volume 12
Clegg–Const

OXFORD
UNIVERSITY PRESS

OXFORD

UNIVERSITY PRESS

Great Clarendon Street, Oxford OX2 6DP

Oxford University Press is a department of the University of Oxford.
It furthers the University's objective of excellence in research, scholarship,
and education by publishing worldwide in

Oxford New York

Auckland Bangkok Buenos Aires Cape Town
Chennai Dar es Salaam Delhi Hong Kong Istanbul Karachi
Kolkata Kuala Lumpur Madrid Melbourne Mexico City Mumbai Nairobi
São Paulo Shanghai Taipei Tokyo Toronto

Oxford is a registered trade mark of Oxford University Press
in the UK and in certain other countries

Published in the United States
by Oxford University Press Inc., New York

British Library Cataloguing in Publication Data
Data available

Library of Congress Cataloging in Publication Data
Data available: for details see volume 1, p. iv

ISBN 0-19-861362-8 (this volume)
ISBN 0-19-861411-X (set of sixty volumes)

Text captured by Alliance Phototypesetters, Pondicherry
Illustrations reproduced and archived by
Alliance Graphics Ltd, UK
Typeset in OUP Swift by Interactive Sciences Limited, Gloucester
Printed in Great Britain on acid-free paper by
Butler and Tanner Ltd,
Frome, Somerset

LIST OF ABBREVIATIONS

1 General abbreviations

AB	bachelor of arts
ABC	Australian Broadcasting Corporation
ABC TV	ABC Television
act.	active
A$	Australian dollar
AD	*anno domini*
AFC	Air Force Cross
AIDS	acquired immune deficiency syndrome
AK	Alaska
AL	Alabama
A level	advanced level [examination]
ALS	associate of the Linnean Society
AM	master of arts
AMICE	associate member of the Institution of Civil Engineers
ANZAC	Australian and New Zealand Army Corps
appx *pl.* appxs	appendix(es)
AR	Arkansas
ARA	associate of the Royal Academy
ARCA	associate of the Royal College of Art
ARCM	associate of the Royal College of Music
ARCO	associate of the Royal College of Organists
ARIBA	associate of the Royal Institute of British Architects
ARP	air-raid precautions
ARRC	associate of the Royal Red Cross
ARSA	associate of the Royal Scottish Academy
art.	article / item
ASC	Army Service Corps
Asch	Austrian Schilling
ASDIC	Antisubmarine Detection Investigation Committee
ATS	Auxiliary Territorial Service
ATV	Associated Television
Aug	August
AZ	Arizona
b.	born
BA	bachelor of arts
BA (Admin.)	bachelor of arts (administration)
BAFTA	British Academy of Film and Television Arts
BAO	bachelor of arts in obstetrics
bap.	baptized
BBC	British Broadcasting Corporation / Company
BC	before Christ
BCE	before the common (*or* Christian) era
BCE	bachelor of civil engineering
BCG	bacillus of Calmette and Guérin [inoculation against tuberculosis]
BCh	bachelor of surgery
BChir	bachelor of surgery
BCL	bachelor of civil law
BCnL	bachelor of canon law
BCom	bachelor of commerce
BD	bachelor of divinity
BEd	bachelor of education
BEng	bachelor of engineering
bk *pl.* bks	book(s)
BL	bachelor of law / letters / literature
BLitt	bachelor of letters
BM	bachelor of medicine
BMus	bachelor of music
BP	before present
BP	British Petroleum
Bros.	Brothers
BS	(1) bachelor of science; (2) bachelor of surgery; (3) British standard
BSc	bachelor of science
BSc (Econ.)	bachelor of science (economics)
BSc (Eng.)	bachelor of science (engineering)
bt	baronet
BTh	bachelor of theology
bur.	buried
C.	command [identifier for published parliamentary papers]
c.	*circa*
c.	*capitulum pl. capitula*: chapter(s)
CA	California
Cantab.	Cantabrigiensis
cap.	*capitulum pl. capitula*: chapter(s)
CB	companion of the Bath
CBE	commander of the Order of the British Empire
CBS	Columbia Broadcasting System
cc	cubic centimetres
C$	Canadian dollar
CD	compact disc
Cd	command [identifier for published parliamentary papers]
CE	Common (*or* Christian) Era
cent.	century
cf.	compare
CH	Companion of Honour
chap.	chapter
ChB	bachelor of surgery
CI	Imperial Order of the Crown of India
CIA	Central Intelligence Agency
CID	Criminal Investigation Department
CIE	companion of the Order of the Indian Empire
Cie	Compagnie
CLit	companion of literature
CM	master of surgery
cm	centimetre(s)

Cmd	command [identifier for published parliamentary papers]
CMG	companion of the Order of St Michael and St George
Cmnd	command [identifier for published parliamentary papers]
CO	Colorado
Co.	company
co.	county
col. *pl.* cols.	column(s)
Corp.	corporation
CSE	certificate of secondary education
CSI	companion of the Order of the Star of India
CT	Connecticut
CVO	commander of the Royal Victorian Order
cwt	hundredweight
$	(American) dollar
d.	(1) penny (pence); (2) died
DBE	dame commander of the Order of the British Empire
DCH	diploma in child health
DCh	doctor of surgery
DCL	doctor of civil law
DCnL	doctor of canon law
DCVO	dame commander of the Royal Victorian Order
DD	doctor of divinity
DE	Delaware
Dec	December
dem.	demolished
DEng	doctor of engineering
des.	destroyed
DFC	Distinguished Flying Cross
DipEd	diploma in education
DipPsych	diploma in psychiatry
diss.	dissertation
DL	deputy lieutenant
DLitt	doctor of letters
DLittCelt	doctor of Celtic letters
DM	(1) Deutschmark; (2) doctor of medicine; (3) doctor of musical arts
DMus	doctor of music
DNA	dioxyribonucleic acid
doc.	document
DOL	doctor of oriental learning
DPH	diploma in public health
DPhil	doctor of philosophy
DPM	diploma in psychological medicine
DSC	Distinguished Service Cross
DSc	doctor of science
DSc (Econ.)	doctor of science (economics)
DSc (Eng.)	doctor of science (engineering)
DSM	Distinguished Service Medal
DSO	companion of the Distinguished Service Order
DSocSc	doctor of social science
DTech	doctor of technology
DTh	doctor of theology
DTM	diploma in tropical medicine
DTMH	diploma in tropical medicine and hygiene
DU	doctor of the university
DUniv	doctor of the university
dwt	pennyweight
EC	European Community
ed. *pl.* eds.	edited / edited by / editor(s)
Edin.	Edinburgh
edn	edition
EEC	European Economic Community
EFTA	European Free Trade Association
EICS	East India Company Service
EMI	Electrical and Musical Industries (Ltd)
Eng.	English
enl.	enlarged
ENSA	Entertainments National Service Association
ep. *pl.* epp.	*epistola(e)*
ESP	extra-sensory perception
esp.	especially
esq.	esquire
est.	estimate / estimated
EU	European Union
ex	sold by (*lit.* out of)
excl.	excludes / excluding
exh.	exhibited
exh. cat.	exhibition catalogue
f. *pl.* ff.	following [pages]
FA	Football Association
FACP	fellow of the American College of Physicians
facs.	facsimile
FANY	First Aid Nursing Yeomanry
FBA	fellow of the British Academy
FBI	Federation of British Industries
FCS	fellow of the Chemical Society
Feb	February
FEng	fellow of the Fellowship of Engineering
FFCM	fellow of the Faculty of Community Medicine
FGS	fellow of the Geological Society
fig.	figure
FIMechE	fellow of the Institution of Mechanical Engineers
FL	Florida
fl.	*floruit*
FLS	fellow of the Linnean Society
FM	frequency modulation
fol. *pl.* fols.	folio(s)
Fr	French francs
Fr.	French
FRAeS	fellow of the Royal Aeronautical Society
FRAI	fellow of the Royal Anthropological Institute
FRAM	fellow of the Royal Academy of Music
FRAS	(1) fellow of the Royal Asiatic Society; (2) fellow of the Royal Astronomical Society
FRCM	fellow of the Royal College of Music
FRCO	fellow of the Royal College of Organists
FRCOG	fellow of the Royal College of Obstetricians and Gynaecologists
FRCP(C)	fellow of the Royal College of Physicians of Canada
FRCP (Edin.)	fellow of the Royal College of Physicians of Edinburgh
FRCP (Lond.)	fellow of the Royal College of Physicians of London
FRCPath	fellow of the Royal College of Pathologists
FRCPsych	fellow of the Royal College of Psychiatrists
FRCS	fellow of the Royal College of Surgeons
FRGS	fellow of the Royal Geographical Society
FRIBA	fellow of the Royal Institute of British Architects
FRICS	fellow of the Royal Institute of Chartered Surveyors
FRS	fellow of the Royal Society
FRSA	fellow of the Royal Society of Arts

FRSCM	fellow of the Royal School of Church Music		ISO	companion of the Imperial Service Order
FRSE	fellow of the Royal Society of Edinburgh		It.	Italian
FRSL	fellow of the Royal Society of Literature		ITA	Independent Television Authority
FSA	fellow of the Society of Antiquaries		ITV	Independent Television
ft	foot *pl.* feet		Jan	January
FTCL	fellow of Trinity College of Music, London		JP	justice of the peace
ft-lb per min.	foot-pounds per minute [unit of horsepower]		jun.	junior
FZS	fellow of the Zoological Society		KB	knight of the Order of the Bath
GA	Georgia		KBE	knight commander of the Order of the British Empire
GBE	knight or dame grand cross of the Order of the British Empire		KC	king's counsel
GCB	knight grand cross of the Order of the Bath		kcal	kilocalorie
GCE	general certificate of education		KCB	knight commander of the Order of the Bath
GCH	knight grand cross of the Royal Guelphic Order		KCH	knight commander of the Royal Guelphic Order
GCHQ	government communications headquarters		KCIE	knight commander of the Order of the Indian Empire
GCIE	knight grand commander of the Order of the Indian Empire		KCMG	knight commander of the Order of St Michael and St George
GCMG	knight or dame grand cross of the Order of St Michael and St George		KCSI	knight commander of the Order of the Star of India
GCSE	general certificate of secondary education		KCVO	knight commander of the Royal Victorian Order
GCSI	knight grand commander of the Order of the Star of India		keV	kilo-electron-volt
GCStJ	bailiff or dame grand cross of the order of St John of Jerusalem		KG	knight of the Order of the Garter
			KGB	[Soviet committee of state security]
GCVO	knight or dame grand cross of the Royal Victorian Order		KH	knight of the Royal Guelphic Order
			KLM	Koninklijke Luchtvaart Maatschappij (Royal Dutch Air Lines)
GEC	General Electric Company		km	kilometre(s)
Ger.	German		KP	knight of the Order of St Patrick
GI	government (*or* general) issue		KS	Kansas
GMT	Greenwich mean time		KT	knight of the Order of the Thistle
GP	general practitioner		kt	knight
GPU	[Soviet special police unit]		KY	Kentucky
GSO	general staff officer		£	pound(s) sterling
Heb.	Hebrew		£E	Egyptian pound
HEICS	Honourable East India Company Service		L	lira *pl.* lire
HI	Hawaii		l. *pl.* ll.	line(s)
HIV	human immunodeficiency virus		LA	Lousiana
HK$	Hong Kong dollar		LAA	light anti-aircraft
HM	his / her majesty('s)		LAH	licentiate of the Apothecaries' Hall, Dublin
HMAS	his / her majesty's Australian ship		Lat.	Latin
HMNZS	his / her majesty's New Zealand ship		lb	pound(s), unit of weight
HMS	his / her majesty's ship		LDS	licence in dental surgery
HMSO	His / Her Majesty's Stationery Office		*lit.*	literally
HMV	His Master's Voice		LittB	bachelor of letters
Hon.	Honourable		LittD	doctor of letters
hp	horsepower		LKQCPI	licentiate of the King and Queen's College of Physicians, Ireland
hr	hour(s)		LLA	lady literate in arts
HRH	his / her royal highness		LLB	bachelor of laws
HTV	Harlech Television		LLD	doctor of laws
IA	Iowa		LLM	master of laws
ibid.	*ibidem*: in the same place		LM	licentiate in midwifery
ICI	Imperial Chemical Industries (Ltd)		LP	long-playing record
ID	Idaho		LRAM	licentiate of the Royal Academy of Music
IL	Illinois		LRCP	licentiate of the Royal College of Physicians
illus.	illustration		LRCPS (Glasgow)	licentiate of the Royal College of Physicians and Surgeons of Glasgow
illustr.	illustrated			
IN	Indiana		LRCS	licentiate of the Royal College of Surgeons
in.	inch(es)		LSA	licentiate of the Society of Apothecaries
Inc.	Incorporated		LSD	lysergic acid diethylamide
incl.	includes / including		LVO	lieutenant of the Royal Victorian Order
IOU	I owe you		M. *pl.* MM.	Monsieur *pl.* Messieurs
IQ	intelligence quotient		m	metre(s)
Ir£	Irish pound			
IRA	Irish Republican Army			

m. *pl.* mm.	membrane(s)	ND	North Dakota
MA	(1) Massachusetts; (2) master of arts	n.d.	no date
MAI	master of engineering	NE	Nebraska
MB	bachelor of medicine	*nem. con.*	*nemine contradicente*: unanimously
MBA	master of business administration	new ser.	new series
MBE	member of the Order of the British Empire	NH	New Hampshire
MC	Military Cross	NHS	National Health Service
MCC	Marylebone Cricket Club	NJ	New Jersey
MCh	master of surgery	NKVD	[Soviet people's commissariat for internal affairs]
MChir	master of surgery		
MCom	master of commerce	NM	New Mexico
MD	(1) doctor of medicine; (2) Maryland	nm	nanometre(s)
MDMA	methylenedioxymethamphetamine	no. *pl.* nos.	number(s)
ME	Maine	Nov	November
MEd	master of education	n.p.	no place [of publication]
MEng	master of engineering	NS	new style
MEP	member of the European parliament	NV	Nevada
MG	Morris Garages	NY	New York
MGM	Metro-Goldwyn-Mayer	NZBS	New Zealand Broadcasting Service
Mgr	Monsignor	OBE	officer of the Order of the British Empire
MI	(1) Michigan; (2) military intelligence	obit.	obituary
MI1c	[secret intelligence department]	Oct	October
MI5	[military intelligence department]	OCTU	officer cadets training unit
MI6	[secret intelligence department]	OECD	Organization for Economic Co-operation and Development
MI9	[secret escape service]		
MICE	member of the Institution of Civil Engineers	OEEC	Organization for European Economic Co-operation
MIEE	member of the Institution of Electrical Engineers		
		OFM	order of Friars Minor [Franciscans]
min.	minute(s)	OFMCap	Ordine Frati Minori Cappucini: member of the Capuchin order
Mk	mark		
ML	(1) licentiate of medicine; (2) master of laws	OH	Ohio
MLitt	master of letters	OK	Oklahoma
Mlle	Mademoiselle	O level	ordinary level [examination]
mm	millimetre(s)	OM	Order of Merit
Mme	Madame	OP	order of Preachers [Dominicans]
MN	Minnesota	op. *pl.* opp.	opus *pl.* opera
MO	Missouri	OPEC	Organization of Petroleum Exporting Countries
MOH	medical officer of health	OR	Oregon
MP	member of parliament	orig.	original
m.p.h.	miles per hour	OS	old style
MPhil	master of philosophy	OSB	Order of St Benedict
MRCP	member of the Royal College of Physicians	OTC	Officers' Training Corps
MRCS	member of the Royal College of Surgeons	OWS	Old Watercolour Society
MRCVS	member of the Royal College of Veterinary Surgeons	Oxon.	Oxoniensis
		p. *pl.* pp.	page(s)
MRIA	member of the Royal Irish Academy	PA	Pennsylvania
MS	(1) master of science; (2) Mississippi	p.a.	per annum
MS *pl.* MSS	manuscript(s)	para.	paragraph
MSc	master of science	PAYE	pay as you earn
MSc (Econ.)	master of science (economics)	pbk *pl.* pbks	paperback(s)
MT	Montana	*per.*	[during the] period
MusB	bachelor of music	PhD	doctor of philosophy
MusBac	bachelor of music	pl.	(1) plate(s); (2) plural
MusD	doctor of music	priv. coll.	private collection
MV	motor vessel	pt *pl.* pts	part(s)
MVO	member of the Royal Victorian Order	pubd	published
n. *pl.* nn.	note(s)	PVC	polyvinyl chloride
NAAFI	Navy, Army, and Air Force Institutes	q. *pl.* qq.	(1) question(s); (2) quire(s)
NASA	National Aeronautics and Space Administration	QC	queen's counsel
NATO	North Atlantic Treaty Organization	R	rand
NBC	National Broadcasting Corporation	R.	Rex / Regina
NC	North Carolina	*r*	recto
NCO	non-commissioned officer	*r.*	reigned / ruled
		RA	Royal Academy / Royal Academician

RAC	Royal Automobile Club
RAF	Royal Air Force
RAFVR	Royal Air Force Volunteer Reserve
RAM	[member of the] Royal Academy of Music
RAMC	Royal Army Medical Corps
RCA	Royal College of Art
RCNC	Royal Corps of Naval Constructors
RCOG	Royal College of Obstetricians and Gynaecologists
RDI	royal designer for industry
RE	Royal Engineers
repr. *pl.* reprs.	reprint(s) / reprinted
repro.	reproduced
rev.	revised / revised by / reviser / revision
Revd	Reverend
RHA	Royal Hibernian Academy
RI	(1) Rhode Island; (2) Royal Institute of Painters in Water-Colours
RIBA	Royal Institute of British Architects
RIN	Royal Indian Navy
RM	Reichsmark
RMS	Royal Mail steamer
RN	Royal Navy
RNA	ribonucleic acid
RNAS	Royal Naval Air Service
RNR	Royal Naval Reserve
RNVR	Royal Naval Volunteer Reserve
RO	Record Office
r.p.m.	revolutions per minute
RRS	royal research ship
Rs	rupees
RSA	(1) Royal Scottish Academician; (2) Royal Society of Arts
RSPCA	Royal Society for the Prevention of Cruelty to Animals
Rt Hon.	Right Honourable
Rt Revd	Right Reverend
RUC	Royal Ulster Constabulary
Russ.	Russian
RWS	Royal Watercolour Society
S4C	Sianel Pedwar Cymru
s.	shilling(s)
s.a.	*sub anno*: under the year
SABC	South African Broadcasting Corporation
SAS	Special Air Service
SC	South Carolina
ScD	doctor of science
S$	Singapore dollar
SD	South Dakota
sec.	second(s)
sel.	selected
sen.	senior
Sept	September
ser.	series
SHAPE	supreme headquarters allied powers, Europe
SIDRO	Société Internationale d'Énergie Hydro-Électrique
sig. *pl.* sigs.	signature(s)
sing.	singular
SIS	Secret Intelligence Service
SJ	Society of Jesus

Skr	Swedish krona
Span.	Spanish
SPCK	Society for Promoting Christian Knowledge
SS	(1) Santissimi; (2) Schutzstaffel; (3) steam ship
STB	bachelor of theology
STD	doctor of theology
STM	master of theology
STP	doctor of theology
supp.	supposedly
suppl. *pl.* suppls.	supplement(s)
s.v.	*sub verbo / sub voce*: under the word / heading
SY	steam yacht
TA	Territorial Army
TASS	[Soviet news agency]
TB	tuberculosis (*lit.* tubercle bacillus)
TD	(1) *teachtaí dála* (member of the Dáil); (2) territorial decoration
TN	Tennessee
TNT	trinitrotoluene
trans.	translated / translated by / translation / translator
TT	tourist trophy
TUC	Trades Union Congress
TX	Texas
U-boat	*Unterseeboot*: submarine
Ufa	Universum-Film AG
UMIST	University of Manchester Institute of Science and Technology
UN	United Nations
UNESCO	United Nations Educational, Scientific, and Cultural Organization
UNICEF	United Nations International Children's Emergency Fund
unpubd	unpublished
USS	United States ship
UT	Utah
v	verso
v.	versus
VA	Virginia
VAD	Voluntary Aid Detachment
VC	Victoria Cross
VE-day	victory in Europe day
Ven.	Venerable
VJ-day	victory over Japan day
vol. *pl.* vols.	volume(s)
VT	Vermont
WA	Washington [state]
WAAC	Women's Auxiliary Army Corps
WAAF	Women's Auxiliary Air Force
WEA	Workers' Educational Association
WHO	World Health Organization
WI	Wisconsin
WRAF	Women's Royal Air Force
WRNS	Women's Royal Naval Service
WV	West Virginia
WVS	Women's Voluntary Service
WY	Wyoming
¥	yen
YMCA	Young Men's Christian Association
YWCA	Young Women's Christian Association

2 Institution abbreviations

All Souls Oxf.	All Souls College, Oxford
AM Oxf.	Ashmolean Museum, Oxford
Balliol Oxf.	Balliol College, Oxford
BBC WAC	BBC Written Archives Centre, Reading
Beds. & Luton ARS	Bedfordshire and Luton Archives and Record Service, Bedford
Berks. RO	Berkshire Record Office, Reading
BFI	British Film Institute, London
BFI NFTVA	British Film Institute, London, National Film and Television Archive
BGS	British Geological Survey, Keyworth, Nottingham
Birm. CA	Birmingham Central Library, Birmingham City Archives
Birm. CL	Birmingham Central Library
BL	British Library, London
BL NSA	British Library, London, National Sound Archive
BL OIOC	British Library, London, Oriental and India Office Collections
BLPES	London School of Economics and Political Science, British Library of Political and Economic Science
BM	British Museum, London
Bodl. Oxf.	Bodleian Library, Oxford
Bodl. RH	Bodleian Library of Commonwealth and African Studies at Rhodes House, Oxford
Borth. Inst.	Borthwick Institute of Historical Research, University of York
Boston PL	Boston Public Library, Massachusetts
Bristol RO	Bristol Record Office
Bucks. RLSS	Buckinghamshire Records and Local Studies Service, Aylesbury
CAC Cam.	Churchill College, Cambridge, Churchill Archives Centre
Cambs. AS	Cambridgeshire Archive Service
CCC Cam.	Corpus Christi College, Cambridge
CCC Oxf.	Corpus Christi College, Oxford
Ches. & Chester ALSS	Cheshire and Chester Archives and Local Studies Service
Christ Church Oxf.	Christ Church, Oxford
Christies	Christies, London
City Westm. AC	City of Westminster Archives Centre, London
CKS	Centre for Kentish Studies, Maidstone
CLRO	Corporation of London Records Office
Coll. Arms	College of Arms, London
Col. U.	Columbia University, New York
Cornwall RO	Cornwall Record Office, Truro
Courtauld Inst.	Courtauld Institute of Art, London
CUL	Cambridge University Library
Cumbria AS	Cumbria Archive Service
Derbys. RO	Derbyshire Record Office, Matlock
Devon RO	Devon Record Office, Exeter
Dorset RO	Dorset Record Office, Dorchester
Duke U.	Duke University, Durham, North Carolina
Duke U., Perkins L.	Duke University, Durham, North Carolina, William R. Perkins Library
Durham Cath. CL	Durham Cathedral, chapter library
Durham RO	Durham Record Office
DWL	Dr Williams's Library, London
Essex RO	Essex Record Office
E. Sussex RO	East Sussex Record Office, Lewes
Eton	Eton College, Berkshire
FM Cam.	Fitzwilliam Museum, Cambridge
Folger	Folger Shakespeare Library, Washington, DC
Garr. Club	Garrick Club, London
Girton Cam.	Girton College, Cambridge
GL	Guildhall Library, London
Glos. RO	Gloucestershire Record Office, Gloucester
Gon. & Caius Cam.	Gonville and Caius College, Cambridge
Gov. Art Coll.	Government Art Collection
GS Lond.	Geological Society of London
Hants. RO	Hampshire Record Office, Winchester
Harris Man. Oxf.	Harris Manchester College, Oxford
Harvard TC	Harvard Theatre Collection, Harvard University, Cambridge, Massachusetts, Nathan Marsh Pusey Library
Harvard U.	Harvard University, Cambridge, Massachusetts
Harvard U., Houghton L.	Harvard University, Cambridge, Massachusetts, Houghton Library
Herefs. RO	Herefordshire Record Office, Hereford
Herts. ALS	Hertfordshire Archives and Local Studies, Hertford
Hist. Soc. Penn.	Historical Society of Pennsylvania, Philadelphia
HLRO	House of Lords Record Office, London
Hult. Arch.	Hulton Archive, London and New York
Hunt. L.	Huntington Library, San Marino, California
ICL	Imperial College, London
Inst. CE	Institution of Civil Engineers, London
Inst. EE	Institution of Electrical Engineers, London
IWM	Imperial War Museum, London
IWM FVA	Imperial War Museum, London, Film and Video Archive
IWM SA	Imperial War Museum, London, Sound Archive
JRL	John Rylands University Library of Manchester
King's AC Cam.	King's College Archives Centre, Cambridge
King's Cam.	King's College, Cambridge
King's Lond.	King's College, London
King's Lond., Liddell Hart C.	King's College, London, Liddell Hart Centre for Military Archives
Lancs. RO	Lancashire Record Office, Preston
L. Cong.	Library of Congress, Washington, DC
Leics. RO	Leicestershire, Leicester, and Rutland Record Office, Leicester
Lincs. Arch.	Lincolnshire Archives, Lincoln
Linn. Soc.	Linnean Society of London
LMA	London Metropolitan Archives
LPL	Lambeth Palace, London
Lpool RO	Liverpool Record Office and Local Studies Service
LUL	London University Library
Magd. Cam.	Magdalene College, Cambridge
Magd. Oxf.	Magdalen College, Oxford
Man. City Gall.	Manchester City Galleries
Man. CL	Manchester Central Library
Mass. Hist. Soc.	Massachusetts Historical Society, Boston
Merton Oxf.	Merton College, Oxford
MHS Oxf.	Museum of the History of Science, Oxford
Mitchell L., Glas.	Mitchell Library, Glasgow
Mitchell L., NSW	State Library of New South Wales, Sydney, Mitchell Library
Morgan L.	Pierpont Morgan Library, New York
NA Canada	National Archives of Canada, Ottawa
NA Ire.	National Archives of Ireland, Dublin
NAM	National Army Museum, London
NA Scot.	National Archives of Scotland, Edinburgh
News Int. RO	News International Record Office, London
NG Ire.	National Gallery of Ireland, Dublin

NG Scot. — National Gallery of Scotland, Edinburgh
NHM — Natural History Museum, London
NL Aus. — National Library of Australia, Canberra
NL Ire. — National Library of Ireland, Dublin
NL NZ — National Library of New Zealand, Wellington
NL NZ, Turnbull L. — National Library of New Zealand, Wellington, Alexander Turnbull Library
NL Scot. — National Library of Scotland, Edinburgh
NL Wales — National Library of Wales, Aberystwyth
NMG Wales — National Museum and Gallery of Wales, Cardiff
NMM — National Maritime Museum, London
Norfolk RO — Norfolk Record Office, Norwich
Northants. RO — Northamptonshire Record Office, Northampton
Northumbd RO — Northumberland Record Office
Notts. Arch. — Nottinghamshire Archives, Nottingham
NPG — National Portrait Gallery, London
NRA — National Archives, London, Historical Manuscripts Commission, National Register of Archives
Nuffield Oxf. — Nuffield College, Oxford
N. Yorks. CRO — North Yorkshire County Record Office, Northallerton
NYPL — New York Public Library
Oxf. UA — Oxford University Archives
Oxf. U. Mus. NH — Oxford University Museum of Natural History
Oxon. RO — Oxfordshire Record Office, Oxford
Pembroke Cam. — Pembroke College, Cambridge
PRO — National Archives, London, Public Record Office
PRO NIre. — Public Record Office for Northern Ireland, Belfast
Pusey Oxf. — Pusey House, Oxford
RA — Royal Academy of Arts, London
Ransom HRC — Harry Ransom Humanities Research Center, University of Texas, Austin
RAS — Royal Astronomical Society, London
RBG Kew — Royal Botanic Gardens, Kew, London
RCP Lond. — Royal College of Physicians of London
RCS Eng. — Royal College of Surgeons of England, London
RGS — Royal Geographical Society, London
RIBA — Royal Institute of British Architects, London
RIBA BAL — Royal Institute of British Architects, London, British Architectural Library
Royal Arch. — Royal Archives, Windsor Castle, Berkshire [by gracious permission of her majesty the queen]
Royal Irish Acad. — Royal Irish Academy, Dublin
Royal Scot. Acad. — Royal Scottish Academy, Edinburgh
RS — Royal Society, London
RSA — Royal Society of Arts, London
RS Friends, Lond. — Religious Society of Friends, London
St Ant. Oxf. — St Antony's College, Oxford
St John Cam. — St John's College, Cambridge
S. Antiquaries, Lond. — Society of Antiquaries of London
Sci. Mus. — Science Museum, London
Scot. NPG — Scottish National Portrait Gallery, Edinburgh
Scott Polar RI — University of Cambridge, Scott Polar Research Institute
Sheff. Arch. — Sheffield Archives
Shrops. RRC — Shropshire Records and Research Centre, Shrewsbury
SOAS — School of Oriental and African Studies, London
Som. ARS — Somerset Archive and Record Service, Taunton
Staffs. RO — Staffordshire Record Office, Stafford

Suffolk RO — Suffolk Record Office
Surrey HC — Surrey History Centre, Woking
TCD — Trinity College, Dublin
Trinity Cam. — Trinity College, Cambridge
U. Aberdeen — University of Aberdeen
U. Birm. — University of Birmingham
U. Birm. L. — University of Birmingham Library
U. Cal. — University of California
U. Cam. — University of Cambridge
UCL — University College, London
U. Durham — University of Durham
U. Durham L. — University of Durham Library
U. Edin. — University of Edinburgh
U. Edin., New Coll. — University of Edinburgh, New College
U. Edin., New Coll. L. — University of Edinburgh, New College Library
U. Edin. L. — University of Edinburgh Library
U. Glas. — University of Glasgow
U. Glas. L. — University of Glasgow Library
U. Hull — University of Hull
U. Hull, Brynmor Jones L. — University of Hull, Brynmor Jones Library
U. Leeds — University of Leeds
U. Leeds, Brotherton L. — University of Leeds, Brotherton Library
U. Lond. — University of London
U. Lpool — University of Liverpool
U. Lpool L. — University of Liverpool Library
U. Mich. — University of Michigan, Ann Arbor
U. Mich., Clements L. — University of Michigan, Ann Arbor, William L. Clements Library
U. Newcastle — University of Newcastle upon Tyne
U. Newcastle, Robinson L. — University of Newcastle upon Tyne, Robinson Library
U. Nott. — University of Nottingham
U. Nott. L. — University of Nottingham Library
U. Oxf. — University of Oxford
U. Reading — University of Reading
U. Reading L. — University of Reading Library
U. St Andr. — University of St Andrews
U. St Andr. L. — University of St Andrews Library
U. Southampton — University of Southampton
U. Southampton L. — University of Southampton Library
U. Sussex — University of Sussex, Brighton
U. Texas — University of Texas, Austin
U. Wales — University of Wales
U. Warwick Mod. RC — University of Warwick, Coventry, Modern Records Centre
V&A — Victoria and Albert Museum, London
V&A NAL — Victoria and Albert Museum, London, National Art Library
Warks. CRO — Warwickshire County Record Office, Warwick
Wellcome L. — Wellcome Library for the History and Understanding of Medicine, London
Westm. DA — Westminster Diocesan Archives, London
Wilts. & Swindon RO — Wiltshire and Swindon Record Office, Trowbridge
Worcs. RO — Worcestershire Record Office, Worcester
W. Sussex RO — West Sussex Record Office, Chichester
W. Yorks. AS — West Yorkshire Archive Service
Yale U. — Yale University, New Haven, Connecticut
Yale U., Beinecke L. — Yale University, New Haven, Connecticut, Beinecke Rare Book and Manuscript Library
Yale U. CBA — Yale University, New Haven, Connecticut, Yale Center for British Art

3 Bibliographic abbreviations

Adams, *Drama*	W. D. Adams, *A dictionary of the drama*, 1: *A–G* (1904); 2: *H–Z* (1956) [vol. 2 microfilm only]
AFM	J O'Donovan, ed. and trans., *Annala rioghachta Eireann / Annals of the kingdom of Ireland by the four masters*, 7 vols. (1848–51); 2nd edn (1856); 3rd edn (1990)
Allibone, *Dict.*	S. A. Allibone, *A critical dictionary of English literature and British and American authors*, 3 vols. (1859–71); suppl. by J. F. Kirk, 2 vols. (1891)
ANB	J. A. Garraty and M. C. Carnes, eds., *American national biography*, 24 vols. (1999)
Anderson, *Scot. nat.*	W. Anderson, *The Scottish nation, or, The surnames, families, literature, honours, and biographical history of the people of Scotland*, 3 vols. (1859–63)
Ann. mon.	H. R. Luard, ed., *Annales monastici*, 5 vols., Rolls Series, 36 (1864–9)
Ann. Ulster	S. Mac Airt and G. Mac Niocaill, eds., *Annals of Ulster (to AD 1131)* (1983)
APC	*Acts of the privy council of England*, new ser., 46 vols. (1890–1964)
APS	*The acts of the parliaments of Scotland*, 12 vols. in 13 (1814–75)
Arber, *Regs. Stationers*	F. Arber, ed., *A transcript of the registers of the Company of Stationers of London, 1554–1640 AD*, 5 vols. (1875–94)
ArchR	*Architectural Review*
ASC	D. Whitelock, D. C. Douglas, and S. I. Tucker, ed. and trans., *The Anglo-Saxon Chronicle: a revised translation* (1961)
AS chart.	P. H. Sawyer, *Anglo-Saxon charters: an annotated list and bibliography*, Royal Historical Society Guides and Handbooks (1968)
AusDB	D. Pike and others, eds., *Australian dictionary of biography*, 16 vols. (1966–2002)
Baker, *Serjeants*	J. H. Baker, *The order of serjeants at law*, SeldS, suppl. ser., 5 (1984)
Bale, *Cat.*	J. Bale, *Scriptorum illustrium Maioris Brytannie, quam nunc Angliam et Scotiam vocant: catalogus*, 2 vols. in 1 (Basel, 1557–9); facs. edn (1971)
Bale, *Index*	J. Bale, *Index Britanniae scriptorum*, ed. R. L. Poole and M. Bateson (1902); facs. edn (1990)
BBCS	*Bulletin of the Board of Celtic Studies*
BDMBR	J. O. Baylen and N. J. Gossman, eds., *Biographical dictionary of modern British radicals*, 3 vols. in 4 (1979–88)
Bede, *Hist. eccl.*	*Bede's Ecclesiastical history of the English people*, ed. and trans. B. Colgrave and R. A. B. Mynors, OMT (1969); repr. (1991)
Bénézit, *Dict.*	E. Bénézit, *Dictionnaire critique et documentaire des peintres, sculpteurs, dessinateurs et graveurs*, 3 vols. (Paris, 1911–23); new edn, 8 vols. (1948–66), repr. (1966); 3rd edn, rev. and enl., 10 vols. (1976); 4th edn, 14 vols. (1999)
BIHR	*Bulletin of the Institute of Historical Research*
Birch, *Seals*	W. de Birch, *Catalogue of seals in the department of manuscripts in the British Museum*, 6 vols. (1887–1900)
Bishop Burnet's History	*Bishop Burnet's History of his own time*, ed. M. J. Routh, 2nd edn, 6 vols. (1833)
Blackwood	*Blackwood's [Edinburgh] Magazine*, 328 vols. (1817–1980)
Blain, Clements & Grundy, *Feminist comp.*	V. Blain, P. Clements, and I. Grundy, eds., *The feminist companion to literature in English* (1990)
BL cat.	*The British Library general catalogue of printed books* [in 360 vols. with suppls., also CD-ROM and online]
BMJ	*British Medical Journal*
Boase & Courtney, *Bibl. Corn.*	G. C. Boase and W. P. Courtney, *Bibliotheca Cornubiensis: a catalogue of the writings … of Cornishmen*, 3 vols. (1874–82)
Boase, *Mod. Eng. biog.*	F. Boase, *Modern English biography: containing many thousand concise memoirs of persons who have died since the year 1850*, 6 vols. (privately printed, Truro, 1892–1921); repr. (1965)
Boswell, *Life*	*Boswell's Life of Johnson: together with Journal of a tour to the Hebrides and Johnson's Diary of a journey into north Wales*, ed. G. B. Hill, enl. edn, rev. L. F. Powell, 6 vols. (1934–50); 2nd edn (1964); repr. (1971)
Brown & Stratton, *Brit. mus.*	J. D. Brown and S. S. Stratton, *British musical biography* (1897)
Bryan, *Painters*	M. Bryan, *A biographical and critical dictionary of painters and engravers*, 2 vols. (1816); new edn, ed. G. Stanley (1849); new edn, ed. R. E. Graves and W. Armstrong, 2 vols. (1886–9); [4th edn], ed. G. C. Williamson, 5 vols. (1903–5) [various reprs.]
Burke, *Gen. GB*	J. Burke, *A genealogical and heraldic history of the commoners of Great Britain and Ireland*, 4 vols. (1833–8); new edn as *A genealogical and heraldic dictionary of the landed gentry of Great Britain and Ireland*, 3 vols. [1843–9] [many later edns]
Burke, *Gen. Ire.*	J. B. Burke, *A genealogical and heraldic history of the landed gentry of Ireland* (1899); 2nd edn (1904); 3rd edn (1912); 4th edn (1958); 5th edn as *Burke's Irish family records* (1976)
Burke, *Peerage*	J. Burke, *A general [later edns A genealogical] and heraldic dictionary of the peerage and baronetage of the United Kingdom* [later edns *the British empire*] (1829–)
Burney, *Hist. mus.*	C. Burney, *A general history of music, from the earliest ages to the present period*, 4 vols. (1776–89)
Burtchaell & Sadleir, *Alum. Dubl.*	G. D. Burtchaell and T. U. Sadleir, *Alumni Dublinenses: a register of the students, graduates, and provosts of Trinity College* (1924); [2nd edn], with suppl., in 2 pts (1935)
Calamy rev.	A. G. Matthews, *Calamy revised* (1934); repr. (1988)
CCI	*Calendar of confirmations and inventories granted and given up in the several commissariots of Scotland* (1876–)
CClR	*Calendar of the close rolls preserved in the Public Record Office*, 47 vols. (1892–1963)
CDS	J. Bain, ed., *Calendar of documents relating to Scotland*, 4 vols., PRO (1881–8); suppl. vol. 5, ed. G. G. Simpson and J. D. Galbraith [1986]
CEPR letters	W. H. Bliss, C. Johnson, and J. Twemlow, eds., *Calendar of entries in the papal registers relating to Great Britain and Ireland: papal letters* (1893–)
CGPLA	*Calendars of the grants of probate and letters of administration* [in 4 ser.: *England & Wales, Northern Ireland, Ireland*, and *Éire*]
Chambers, *Scots.*	R. Chambers, ed., *A biographical dictionary of eminent Scotsmen*, 4 vols. (1832–5)
Chancery records	chancery records pubd by the PRO
Chancery records (RC)	chancery records pubd by the Record Commissions

CIPM	*Calendar of inquisitions post mortem*, [20 vols.], PRO (1904–); also *Henry VII*, 3 vols. (1898–1955)
Clarendon, *Hist. rebellion*	E. Hyde, earl of Clarendon, *The history of the rebellion and civil wars in England*, 6 vols. (1888); repr. (1958) and (1992)
Cobbett, *Parl. hist.*	W. Cobbett and J. Wright, eds., *Cobbett's Parliamentary history of England*, 36 vols. (1806–1820)
Colvin, *Archs.*	H. Colvin, *A biographical dictionary of British architects, 1600–1840*, 3rd edn (1995)
Cooper, *Ath. Cantab.*	C. H. Cooper and T. Cooper, *Athenae Cantabrigienses*, 3 vols. (1858–1913); repr. (1967)
CPR	*Calendar of the patent rolls preserved in the Public Record Office* (1891–)
Crockford	*Crockford's Clerical Directory*
CS	Camden Society
CSP	*Calendar of state papers* [in 11 ser.: domestic, Scotland, Scottish series, Ireland, colonial, Commonwealth, foreign, Spain [at Simancas], Rome, Milan, and Venice]
CYS	Canterbury and York Society
DAB	*Dictionary of American biography*, 21 vols. (1928–36), repr. in 11 vols. (1964); 10 suppls. (1944–96)
DBB	D. J. Jeremy, ed., *Dictionary of business biography*, 5 vols. (1984–6)
DCB	G. W. Brown and others, *Dictionary of Canadian biography*, [14 vols.] (1966–)
Debrett's Peerage	*Debrett's Peerage* (1803–) [sometimes *Debrett's Illustrated peerage*]
Desmond, *Botanists*	R. Desmond, *Dictionary of British and Irish botanists and horticulturists* (1977); rev. edn (1994)
Dir. Brit. archs.	A. Felstead, J. Franklin, and L. Pinfield, eds., *Directory of British architects, 1834–1900* (1993); 2nd edn, ed. A. Brodie and others, 2 vols. (2001)
DLB	J. M. Bellamy and J. Saville, eds., *Dictionary of labour biography*, [10 vols.] (1972–)
DLitB	Dictionary of Literary Biography
DNB	*Dictionary of national biography*, 63 vols. (1885–1900), suppl., 3 vols. (1901); repr. in 22 vols. (1908–9); 10 further suppls. (1912–96); *Missing persons* (1993)
DNZB	W. H. Oliver and C. Orange, eds., *The dictionary of New Zealand biography*, 5 vols. (1990–2000)
DSAB	W. J. de Kock and others, eds., *Dictionary of South African biography*, 5 vols. (1968–87)
DSB	C. C. Gillispie and F. L. Holmes, eds., *Dictionary of scientific biography*, 16 vols. (1970–80); repr. in 8 vols. (1981); 2 vol. suppl. (1990)
DSBB	A. Slaven and S. Checkland, eds., *Dictionary of Scottish business biography, 1860–1960*, 2 vols. (1986–90)
DSCHT	N. M. de S. Cameron and others, eds., *Dictionary of Scottish church history and theology* (1993)
Dugdale, *Monasticon*	W. Dugdale, *Monasticon Anglicanum*, 3 vols. (1655–72); 2nd edn, 3 vols. (1661–82); new edn, ed. J. Caley, J. Ellis, and B. Bandinel, 6 vols. in 8 pts (1817–30); repr. (1846) and (1970)
DWB	J. E. Lloyd and others, eds., *Dictionary of Welsh biography down to 1940* (1959) [Eng. trans. of *Y bywgraffiadur Cymreig hyd 1940*, 2nd edn (1954)]
EdinR	*Edinburgh Review, or, Critical Journal*
EETS	Early English Text Society
Emden, *Cam.*	A. B. Emden, *A biographical register of the University of Cambridge to 1500* (1963)
Emden, *Oxf.*	A. B. Emden, *A biographical register of the University of Oxford to AD 1500*, 3 vols. (1957–9); also *A biographical register of the University of Oxford, AD 1501 to 1540* (1974)
EngHR	*English Historical Review*
Engraved Brit. ports.	F. M. O'Donoghue and H. M. Hake, *Catalogue of engraved British portraits preserved in the department of prints and drawings in the British Museum*, 6 vols. (1908–25)
ER	The English Reports, 178 vols. (1900–32)
ESTC	*English short title catalogue, 1475–1800* [CD-ROM and online]
Evelyn, *Diary*	*The diary of John Evelyn*, ed. E. S. De Beer, 6 vols. (1955); repr. (2000)
Farington, *Diary*	*The diary of Joseph Farington*, ed. K. Garlick and others, 17 vols. (1978–98)
Fasti Angl. (Hardy)	J. Le Neve, *Fasti ecclesiae Anglicanae*, ed. T. D. Hardy, 3 vols. (1854)
Fasti Angl., 1066–1300	[J. Le Neve], *Fasti ecclesiae Anglicanae, 1066–1300*, ed. D. E. Greenway and J. S. Barrow, [8 vols.] (1968–)
Fasti Angl., 1300–1541	[J. Le Neve], *Fasti ecclesiae Anglicanae, 1300–1541*, 12 vols. (1962–7)
Fasti Angl., 1541–1857	[J. Le Neve], *Fasti ecclesiae Anglicanae, 1541–1857*, ed. J. M. Horn, D. M. Smith, and D. S. Bailey, [9 vols.] (1969–)
Fasti Scot.	H. Scott, *Fasti ecclesiae Scoticanae*, 3 vols. in 6 (1871); new edn, [11 vols.] (1915–)
FO List	Foreign Office List
Fortescue, *Brit. army*	J. W. Fortescue, *A history of the British army*, 13 vols. (1899–1930)
Foss, *Judges*	E. Foss, *The judges of England*, 9 vols. (1848–64); repr. (1966)
Foster, *Alum. Oxon.*	J. Foster, ed., *Alumni Oxonienses: the members of the University of Oxford, 1715–1886*, 4 vols. (1887–8); later edn (1891); also *Alumni Oxonienses … 1500–1714*, 4 vols. (1891–2); 8 vol. repr. (1968) and (2000)
Fuller, *Worthies*	T. Fuller, *The history of the worthies of England*, 4 pts (1662); new edn, 2 vols., ed. J. Nichols (1811); new edn, 3 vols., ed. P. A. Nuttall (1840); repr. (1965)
GEC, *Baronetage*	G. E. Cokayne, *Complete baronetage*, 6 vols. (1900–09); repr. (1983) [microprint]
GEC, *Peerage*	G. E. C. [G. E. Cokayne], *The complete peerage of England, Scotland, Ireland, Great Britain, and the United Kingdom*, 8 vols. (1887–98); new edn, ed. V. Gibbs and others, 14 vols. in 15 (1910–98); microprint repr. (1982) and (1987)
Genest, *Eng. stage*	J. Genest, *Some account of the English stage from the Restoration in 1660 to 1830*, 10 vols. (1832); repr. [New York, 1965]
Gillow, *Lit. biog. hist.*	J. Gillow, *A literary and biographical history or bibliographical dictionary of the English Catholics, from the breach with Rome, in 1534, to the present time*, 5 vols. [1885–1902]; repr. (1961); repr. with preface by C. Gillow (1999)
Gir. Camb. opera	*Giraldi Cambrensis opera*, ed. J. S. Brewer, J. F. Dimock, and G. F. Warner, 8 vols., Rolls Series, 21 (1861–91)
GJ	*Geographical Journal*

Gladstone, *Diaries* — *The Gladstone diaries: with cabinet minutes and prime-ministerial correspondence*, ed. M. R. D. Foot and H. C. G. Matthew, 14 vols. (1968–94)

GM — *Gentleman's Magazine*

Graves, *Artists* — A. Graves, ed., *A dictionary of artists who have exhibited works in the principal London exhibitions of oil paintings from 1760 to 1880* (1884); new edn (1895); 3rd edn (1901); facs. edn (1969); repr. [1970], (1973), and (1984)

Graves, *Brit. Inst.* — A. Graves, *The British Institution, 1806–1867: a complete dictionary of contributors and their work from the foundation of the institution* (1875); facs. edn (1908); repr. (1969)

Graves, *RA exhibitors* — A. Graves, *The Royal Academy of Arts: a complete dictionary of contributors and their work from its foundation in 1769 to 1904*, 8 vols. (1905–6); repr. in 4 vols. (1970) and (1972)

Graves, *Soc. Artists* — A. Graves, *The Society of Artists of Great Britain, 1760–1791, the Free Society of Artists, 1761–1783: a complete dictionary* (1907); facs. edn (1969)

Greaves & Zaller, *BDBR* — R. L. Greaves and R. Zaller, eds., *Biographical dictionary of British radicals in the seventeenth century*, 3 vols. (1982–4)

Grove, *Dict. mus.* — G. Grove, ed., *A dictionary of music and musicians*, 5 vols. (1878–90); 2nd edn, ed. J. A. Fuller Maitland (1904–10); 3rd edn, ed. H. C. Colles (1927); 4th edn with suppl. (1940); 5th edn, ed. E. Blom, 9 vols. (1954); suppl. (1961) [see also *New Grove*]

Hall, *Dramatic ports.* — L. A. Hall, *Catalogue of dramatic portraits in the theatre collection of the Harvard College library*, 4 vols. (1930–34)

Hansard — *Hansard's parliamentary debates*, ser. 1–5 (1803–)

Highfill, Burnim & Langhans, *BDA* — P. H. Highfill, K. A. Burnim, and E. A. Langhans, *A biographical dictionary of actors, actresses, musicians, dancers, managers, and other stage personnel in London, 1660–1800*, 16 vols. (1973–93)

Hist. U. Oxf. — T. H. Aston, ed., *The history of the University of Oxford*, 8 vols. (1984–2000) [1: *The early Oxford schools*, ed. J. I. Catto (1984); 2: *Late medieval Oxford*, ed. J. I. Catto and R. Evans (1992); 3: *The collegiate university*, ed. J. McConica (1986); 4: *Seventeenth-century Oxford*, ed. N. Tyacke (1997); 5: *The eighteenth century*, ed. L. S. Sutherland and L. G. Mitchell (1986); 6–7: *Nineteenth-century Oxford*, ed. M. G. Brock and M. C. Curthoys (1997–2000); 8: *The twentieth century*, ed. B. Harrison (2000)]

HJ — *Historical Journal*

HMC — Historical Manuscripts Commission

Holdsworth, *Eng. law* — W. S. Holdsworth, *A history of English law*, ed. A. L. Goodhart and H. L. Hanbury, 17 vols. (1903–72)

HoP, *Commons* — *The history of parliament: the House of Commons* [*1386–1421*, ed. J. S. Roskell, L. Clark, and C. Rawcliffe, 4 vols. (1992); *1509–1558*, ed. S. T. Bindoff, 3 vols. (1982); *1558–1603*, ed. P. W. Hasler, 3 vols. (1981); *1660–1690*, ed. B. D. Henning, 3 vols. (1983); *1690–1715*, ed. D. W. Hayton, E. Cruickshanks, and S. Handley, 5 vols. (2002); *1715–1754*, ed. R. Sedgwick, 2 vols. (1970); *1754–1790*, ed. L. Namier and J. Brooke, 3 vols. (1964), repr. (1985); *1790–1820*, ed. R. G. Thorne, 5 vols. (1986); in draft (used with permission): *1422–1504, 1604–1629, 1640–1660,* and *1820–1832*]

IGI — *International Genealogical Index*, Church of Jesus Christ of the Latterday Saints

ILN — *Illustrated London News*

IMC — Irish Manuscripts Commission

Irving, *Scots.* — J. Irving, ed., *The book of Scotsmen eminent for achievements in arms and arts, church and state, law, legislation and literature, commerce, science, travel and philanthropy* (1881)

JCS — *Journal of the Chemical Society*

JHC — *Journals of the House of Commons*

JHL — *Journals of the House of Lords*

John of Worcester, *Chron.* — *The chronicle of John of Worcester*, ed. R. R. Darlington and P. McGurk, trans. J. Bray and P. McGurk, 3 vols., OMT (1995–) [vol. 1 forthcoming]

Keeler, *Long Parliament* — M. F. Keeler, *The Long Parliament, 1640–1641: a biographical study of its members* (1954)

Kelly, *Handbk* — *The upper ten thousand: an alphabetical list of all members of noble families*, 3 vols. (1875–7); continued as *Kelly's handbook of the upper ten thousand for 1878* [1879], 2 vols. (1878–9); continued as *Kelly's handbook to the titled, landed and official classes*, 94 vols. (1880–1973)

LondG — *London Gazette*

LP Henry VIII — J. S. Brewer, J. Gairdner, and R. H. Brodie, eds., *Letters and papers, foreign and domestic, of the reign of Henry VIII*, 23 vols. in 38 (1862–1932); repr. (1965)

Mallalieu, *Watercolour artists* — H. L. Mallalieu, *The dictionary of British watercolour artists up to 1820*, 3 vols. (1976–90); vol. 1, 2nd edn (1986)

Memoirs FRS — *Biographical Memoirs of Fellows of the Royal Society*

MGH — Monumenta Germaniae Historica

MT — *Musical Times*

Munk, *Roll* — W. Munk, *The roll of the Royal College of Physicians of London*, 2 vols. (1861); 2nd edn, 3 vols. (1878)

N&Q — *Notes and Queries*

New Grove — S. Sadie, ed., *The new Grove dictionary of music and musicians*, 20 vols. (1980); 2nd edn, 29 vols. (2001) [also online edn; see also Grove, *Dict. mus.*]

Nichols, *Illustrations* — J. Nichols and J. B. Nichols, *Illustrations of the literary history of the eighteenth century*, 8 vols. (1817–58)

Nichols, *Lit. anecdotes* — J. Nichols, *Literary anecdotes of the eighteenth century*, 9 vols. (1812–16); facs. edn (1966)

Obits. FRS — *Obituary Notices of Fellows of the Royal Society*

O'Byrne, *Naval biog. dict.* — W. R. O'Byrne, *A naval biographical dictionary* (1849); repr. (1990); [2nd edn], 2 vols. (1861)

OHS — Oxford Historical Society

Old Westminsters — *The record of Old Westminsters*, 1–2, ed. G. F. R. Barker and A. H. Stenning (1928); suppl. 1, ed. J. B. Whitmore and G. R. Y. Radcliffe [1938]; 3, ed. J. B. Whitmore, G. R. Y. Radcliffe, and D. C. Simpson (1963); suppl. 2, ed. F. E. Pagan (1978); 4, ed. F. E. Pagan and H. E. Pagan (1992)

OMT — Oxford Medieval Texts

Ordericus Vitalis, *Eccl. hist.* — *The ecclesiastical history of Orderic Vitalis*, ed. and trans. M. Chibnall, 6 vols., OMT (1969–80); repr. (1990)

Paris, *Chron.* — *Matthaei Parisiensis, monachi sancti Albani, chronica majora*, ed. H. R. Luard, Rolls Series, 7 vols. (1872–83)

Parl. papers — *Parliamentary papers* (1801–)

PBA — *Proceedings of the British Academy*

Pepys, *Diary* — *The diary of Samuel Pepys*, ed. R. Latham and W. Matthews, 11 vols. (1970–83); repr. (1995) and (2000)

Pevsner — N. Pevsner and others, Buildings of England series

PICE — *Proceedings of the Institution of Civil Engineers*

Pipe rolls — *The great roll of the pipe for . . .*, PRSoc. (1884–)

PRO — Public Record Office

PRS — *Proceedings of the Royal Society of London*

PRSoc. — Pipe Roll Society

PTRS — *Philosophical Transactions of the Royal Society*

QR — *Quarterly Review*

RC — Record Commissions

Redgrave, *Artists* — S. Redgrave, *A dictionary of artists of the English school* (1874); rev. edn (1878); repr. (1970)

Reg. Oxf. — C. W. Boase and A. Clark, eds., *Register of the University of Oxford*, 5 vols., OHS, 1, 10–12, 14 (1885–9)

Reg. PCS — J. H. Burton and others, eds., *The register of the privy council of Scotland*, 1st ser., 14 vols. (1877–98); 2nd ser., 8 vols. (1899–1908); 3rd ser., [16 vols.] (1908–70)

Reg. RAN — H. W. C. Davis and others, eds., *Regesta regum Anglo-Normannorum, 1066–1154*, 4 vols. (1913–69)

RIBA Journal — *Journal of the Royal Institute of British Architects* [later *RIBA Journal*]

RotP — J. Strachey, ed., *Rotuli parliamentorum ut et petitiones, et placita in parliamento*, 6 vols. (1767–77)

RotS — D. Macpherson, J. Caley, and W. Illingworth, eds., *Rotuli Scotiae in Turri Londinensi et in domo capitulari Westmonasteriensi asservati*, 2 vols., RC, 14 (1814–19)

RS — Record(s) Society

Rymer, *Foedera* — T. Rymer and R. Sanderson, eds., *Foedera, conventiones, literae et cuiuscunque generis acta publica inter reges Angliae et alios quosvis imperatores, reges, pontifices, principes, vel communitates*, 20 vols. (1704–35); 2nd edn, 20 vols. (1726–35); 3rd edn, 10 vols. (1739–45), facs. edn (1967); new edn, ed. A. Clarke, J. Caley, and F. Holbrooke, 4 vols., RC, 50 (1816–30)

Sainty, *Judges* — J. Sainty, ed., *The judges of England, 1272–1990*, SeldS, suppl. ser., 10 (1993)

Sainty, *King's counsel* — J. Sainty, ed., *A list of English law officers and king's counsel*, SeldS, suppl. ser., 7 (1987)

SCH — Studies in Church History

Scots peerage — J. B. Paul, ed. *The Scots peerage, founded on Wood's edition of Sir Robert Douglas's Peerage of Scotland, containing an historical and genealogical account of the nobility of that kingdom*, 9 vols. (1904–14)

SeldS — Selden Society

SHR — *Scottish Historical Review*

State trials — T. B. Howell and T. J. Howell, eds., *Cobbett's Complete collection of state trials*, 34 vols. (1809–28)

STC, 1475–1640 — A. W. Pollard, G. R. Redgrave, and others, eds., *A short-title catalogue of . . . English books . . . 1475–1640* (1926); 2nd edn, ed. W. A. Jackson, F. S. Ferguson, and K. F. Pantzer, 3 vols. (1976–91) [see also Wing, *STC*]

STS — Scottish Text Society

SurtS — Surtees Society

Symeon of Durham, *Opera* — *Symeonis monachi opera omnia*, ed. T. Arnold, 2 vols., Rolls Series, 75 (1882–5); repr. (1965)

Tanner, *Bibl. Brit.-Hib.* — T. Tanner, *Bibliotheca Britannico-Hibernica*, ed. D. Wilkins (1748); repr. (1963)

Thieme & Becker, *Allgemeines Lexikon* — U. Thieme, F. Becker, and H. Vollmer, eds., *Allgemeines Lexikon der bildenden Künstler von der Antike bis zur Gegenwart*, 37 vols. (Leipzig, 1907–50); repr. (1961–5), (1983), and (1992)

Thurloe, *State papers* — *A collection of the state papers of John Thurloe*, ed. T. Birch, 7 vols. (1742)

TLS — *Times Literary Supplement*

Tout, *Admin. hist.* — T. F. Tout, *Chapters in the administrative history of mediaeval England: the wardrobe, the chamber, and the small seals*, 6 vols. (1920–33); repr. (1967)

TRHS — *Transactions of the Royal Historical Society*

VCH — H. A. Doubleday and others, eds., *The Victoria history of the counties of England*, [88 vols.] (1900–)

Venn, *Alum. Cant.* — J. Venn and J. A. Venn, *Alumni Cantabrigienses: a biographical list of all known students, graduates, and holders of office at the University of Cambridge, from the earliest times to 1900*, 10 vols. (1922–54); repr. in 2 vols. (1974–8)

Vertue, *Note books* — [G. Vertue], *Note books*, ed. K. Esdaile, earl of Ilchester, and H. M. Hake, 6 vols., Walpole Society, 18, 20, 22, 24, 26, 30 (1930–55)

VF — *Vanity Fair*

Walford, *County families* — E. Walford, *The county families of the United Kingdom, or, Royal manual of the titled and untitled aristocracy of Great Britain and Ireland* (1860)

Walker rev. — A. G. Matthews, *Walker revised: being a revision of John Walker's Sufferings of the clergy during the grand rebellion, 1642–60* (1948); repr. (1988)

Walpole, *Corr.* — *The Yale edition of Horace Walpole's correspondence*, ed. W. S. Lewis, 48 vols. (1937–83)

Ward, *Men of the reign* — T. H. Ward, ed., *Men of the reign: a biographical dictionary of eminent persons of British and colonial birth who have died during the reign of Queen Victoria* (1885); repr. (Graz, 1968)

Waterhouse, *18c painters* — E. Waterhouse, *The dictionary of 18th century painters in oils and crayons* (1981); repr. as *British 18th century painters in oils and crayons* (1991), vol. 2 of *Dictionary of British art*

Watt, *Bibl. Brit.* — R. Watt, *Bibliotheca Britannica, or, A general index to British and foreign literature*, 4 vols. (1824) [many reprs.]

Wellesley index — W. E. Houghton, ed., *The Wellesley index to Victorian periodicals, 1824–1900*, 5 vols. (1966–89); new edn (1999) [CD-ROM]

Wing, *STC* — D. Wing, ed., *Short-title catalogue of . . . English books . . . 1641–1700*, 3 vols. (1945–51); 2nd edn (1972–88); rev. and enl. edn, ed. J. J. Morrison, C. W. Nelson, and M. Seccombe, 4 vols. (1994–8) [see also *STC, 1475–1640*]

Wisden — *John Wisden's Cricketer's Almanack*

Wood, *Ath. Oxon.* — A. Wood, *Athenae Oxonienses . . . to which are added the Fasti*, 2 vols. (1691–2); 2nd edn (1721); new edn, 4 vols., ed. P. Bliss (1813–20); repr. (1967) and (1969)

Wood, *Vic. painters* — C. Wood, *Dictionary of Victorian painters* (1971); 2nd edn (1978); 3rd edn as *Victorian painters*, 2 vols. (1995), vol. 4 of *Dictionary of British art*

WW — *Who's who* (1849–)

WWBMP — M. Stenton and S. Lees, eds., *Who's who of British members of parliament*, 4 vols. (1976–81)

WWW — *Who was who* (1929–)

Clegg, Sir Alexander Bradshaw [Alec] (1909–1986), schoolteacher and educationist, was born on 13 June 1909 in Sawley, Derbyshire, the only son and youngest of five children of Samuel Clegg, headmaster of Long Eaton Grammar School, and his wife, Mary Bradshaw. Alec, as he was known, attended his father's school before going on to the Quaker Bootham School, York, at the age of fifteen. He studied modern languages at Clare College, Cambridge, where he obtained a second class (division one) in all three of his examinations—part one (French) in 1929, part one (German) in 1930, and part two (1931). He then qualified as a teacher at the London Day Training College.

Clegg served as an assistant master at St Clement Danes Grammar School in London, where he taught languages and football. In 1936 he was appointed an administrative assistant to the Birmingham education committee. His notebooks of that period show a meticulous regard for the details of administrative procedures, which he was sometimes later at pains to conceal. In 1939 he became assistant education officer to Cheshire, before being appointed in 1942 as deputy education officer to Worcestershire. He became deputy education officer to the West Riding, one of the largest education authorities in the country, in January 1945. Within a few months the chief education officer moved to Lancashire and Clegg was appointed in his place. In later years he attributed this to the fact that the clerk to the West Riding, himself legally qualified, discovered that the preferred candidate also had a legal qualification. So began a remarkable career in creative educational administration.

Clegg concentrated on the essentials. Early on he established a number of specialist colleges for teachers: in 1949 Bretton Hall for teachers of the arts, and in 1952 Woolley Hall as the first in-service residential college. Others followed. Bringing teachers together, thinking with them, and learning from them, was a matter of personal commitment throughout Clegg's career. He had a gift for expressing complex ideas simply. He wrote *Ten Years of Change* (1953), which was the first of four major reports to the West Riding education committee. Unlike most such reports, it pointed sharply, with accompanying photographs, to the failures of the system as well as to its successes. As regards secondary schools, Clegg believed they should take responsibility for children of all abilities but insisted that there was no one way of achieving this. Local communities in the West Riding were encouraged to shape schools to their needs. So some comprehensive schools were large, some small; some had sixth forms, others did not. What worked was the test. Clegg had no interest in uniformity. He was one of the main architects of the comprehensive system of education.

In 1959 Clegg served on the Central Advisory Council for Education, chaired by Sir Geoffrey Crowther, which dealt with the education of fifteen- to eighteen-year-olds, but his main interests lay with the changing primary school. After widespread discussion with teachers, he came to the view that a middle-school system would combine the best practices of the primary school with the needs of eleven- and twelve-year-olds. His reasoning convinced the secretary of state and enabling legislation was passed in 1964.

In 1964 the West Riding published his *The Excitement of Writing* to show what could be achieved by young children if the opportunity was given to them to express themselves freely. In 1963 he was invited to serve on the inquiry chaired by John Newsom, whose report, *Half our Future* (1963), concluded that most children in secondary modern schools were undervalued, a view he shared. He was knighted in 1965, the year in which he became president of the Association of Chief Education Officers. In 1968 his most influential book, written with Barbara Megson, *Children in Distress*, was published. In 1970 he was invited by the Department of Education and Science to deliver the lecture in Central Hall, Westminster, to commemorate one hundred years of state education. In that lecture, published in *About our Schools* (1980), he examined the failure over that period to achieve genuine educational opportunities for the disadvantaged and pointed to the disturbing social and economic consequences of this. After retiring from the West Riding in March 1974, he became chairman of the Centre for Information and Advice on Educational Disadvantage, a post he held between 1976 and 1979.

Clegg was awarded honorary degrees by Leeds (1972), Loughborough (1972), and Bradford (1978), and was made a fellow of King's College, London (1972), and an honorary fellow of Bretton Hall (1981). The inspirational qualities which he brought to his achievements in the West Riding and elsewhere were remarkable. He was proud of his ability to pick and then trust colleagues of high quality. Informality mixed with firmness of purpose, good humour, and approachability were characteristics of his style. Absolute integrity and a commitment to put the interests of children above all else were at the heart of his achievement. In 1940 he married Jessie Coverdale, daughter of Thomas Phillips, teacher; they had three sons. Clegg died in York on 20 January 1986.   PETER NEWSAM, *rev.*

Sources U. Leeds, Lawrence Batley Centre, Clegg MSS · *Bramley Occasional Papers*, 4 (1990) · personal knowledge (1996) · private information (1996) · *CGPLA Eng. & Wales* (1986)

Archives National Arts Education Archive, corresp. and papers as chief education officer, West Yorkshire · U. Leeds, Lawrence Batley Centre

Wealth at death £73,895: probate, 24 July 1986, *CGPLA Eng. & Wales*

Clegg, Sir (John) Charles (1850–1937), football administrator, was born in Sheffield on 15 June 1850, the eldest son of William Johnson Clegg (d. 1895) and his wife, Mary (née Sykes). His father was an ambitious solicitor and politician, active in the temperance movement, who became mayor of Sheffield. Charles's first public appearance was alongside his father on a temperance platform at the age of seven. He was educated in Sheffield and later at Gainford School, Darlington, alongside many other sons of well-to-do northerners. Clegg soon displayed unusual athletic talents and after returning to Sheffield in 1866 to train as a solicitor established himself as an unbeatable quarter-mile runner. He seems to have thought nothing of

Sir (John) Charles Clegg (1850–1937), by Elliott & Fry, 1900

competing (usually successfully) for several different events on the same afternoon. Clegg later implied that it was the prevalence of betting that drove him out of local athletics, and football, then in its first few years as an organized sport, became his sole sporting passion. He and his brother William (W. E.) Clegg (1852–1932) were among the first local players to earn wider renown, by playing for Sheffield Wednesday and various representative sides. Charles was even chosen for the first ever football international, England v. Scotland in 1872: but it was a bitter experience. Clegg scarcely got a kick and became convinced that his mostly old school and varsity team mates were deliberately not passing to him: as he recalled, 'Some members of the England eleven were awful snobs and not much troubled about a "man fra' Sheffield"' (J. A. H. Catton, *Wickets and Goals*, 1926, 171).

The year 1872 was important for Clegg in other ways. He qualified as a solicitor, joined his father's firm, and married a young woman from Manchester, Mary Sayles (d. 1933). He followed his father into the temperance movement, became a stern opponent of gambling, and served as a Liberal city councillor in the late 1870s and early 1880s. But it was his brother William who was to emulate the father's political successes. Charles took up a more daunting challenge: that of imposing his own vision on the new and increasingly complex phenomenon of a mass

sport. The original gentlemanly and clerical patrons of football had seen it wholeheartedly embraced by the populace. At local level this infused the game with more traditional popular habits, including betting and brawling. At higher levels gate money was being taken and the players expected to be at least compensated for giving up work to play. Clegg's rise through the ranks of those controlling the sport was rapid. He refereed in 1882 the first Football Association (FA) cup final to feature a team of working-class *de facto* professionals. In 1886 he forced through the amalgamation of Sheffield football associations and became president of the resultant Sheffield and Hallamshire Football Association (SHFA). This position brought him a seat on the national FA council. The gentlemen of the football establishment could no longer ignore the 'man fra' Sheffield': if the game were to be controlled perhaps a tough northerner with a sharp legal mind, undaunted either by gentleman or player, might be the man to do it.

As a football administrator Clegg became identified with his favourite dictum, 'No-one gets lost on a straight road'. But he was more flexible and pragmatic than his reputation allows. A hardline opponent of professional football when it appeared in the early 1880s, he had no problems adapting when the FA recognized professionalism in 1885. Indeed he was a director when the Wednesday turned professional in 1887, was instrumental in the establishment of a second local professional club, Sheffield United, in 1889, and when in 1890 professionalization edged Major Marindin into quitting as FA president, Clegg was elected to the resultant vacancy as FA chairman—the most powerful position in football.

Clegg's belief was that while professionalism was there to stay, the financial side of the game should be tightly controlled so as to preserve something of the old amateur spirit and to ensure that serious corruption did not destroy the game, as he had seen happen to Sheffield athletics. He responded to evidence that Manchester City had been involved in trying to bribe opponents in 1905–6 by conducting a thorough and scrupulous investigation: the ensuing punishments were exemplary and paid no regard to the fame or status of the miscreants. He supported the maximum wage and disliked the Players' Union (PU), with its arguments that players' wages should be fixed by the market instead. Clegg believed that the maximum wage stopped the wealthy clubs from enticing all the best players their way—which to some extent it did—but also clearly felt there was something distasteful in the idea of players getting paid like popular entertainers rather than as sporting artisans. The FA remained firmly opposed when the PU threatened to strike in 1909: the union eventually received some concessions but the strike was averted and the maximum wage survived.

Clegg was equally tough when some southern football associations challenged the FA's authority in the cause of amateurism by demanding the right to exclude professionals. Clegg held the FA firm and by 1914 the amateurs were suing for terms: another victory for the 'man fra' Sheffield' over the old school. The latter had their final fling against him when, after the outbreak of war, the football authorities agreed that the professional season should continue. The reaction of various mostly southern clerics and sportsmen so recently dispatched by Clegg in pursuit of a different-shaped ball was swift and hysterical: professional football, they alleged, was encouraging potential military recruits to loaf around on football terraces instead. Clegg was shaken but held firm: it was falling gate receipts rather than moral pressure that eventually persuaded professional football to suspend operations. To his relief George V, who had delighted the FA by attending the 1914 cup final, was indifferent to the controversy and was back in the royal box, when health permitted, in the post-war finals too. Finally, it was under Clegg that the FA and county equivalents established a number of disciplinary committees to deter betting, violence among players and spectators, and lesser irregularities. Clegg was actively involved on these committees. His was a forbidding presence: hair and moustache the colour of high-grade Sheffield steel, clear blue eyes, firm jaw; many players reported that facing him on these committees was always worse than any subsequent punishment.

When Lord Kinnaird died in 1923, Clegg succeeded him as FA president, a less active position. Still president of the SHFA and on the Sheffield United and Wednesday boards, his attendance at committee meetings became more sporadic. He was in his seventies. He was bowed by personal tragedies. His eldest son, William, who had joined the family law firm, died young in 1927. Clegg himself seems to have had a stroke the same year. His younger son Colin died in 1929. His wife's death in 1933 was a particularly severe blow. But despite these setbacks he retained a massive moral influence over the game. He was knighted in 1927 for 'services to the Board of Trade and the Ministry of Labour'. This could have been for work with local youth and employment committees: most assumed that Baldwin had recommended football's first knighthood.

Clegg's approach to football was of a piece with his Methodist beliefs and commitments. He and Lady Clegg were temperance activists: he was secretary and later president of the British Temperance League. As late as the 1940s, accordingly, Sheffield United players seeking to make a living outside the game as publicans were being driven out of the club. He remained a fierce opponent of gambling: hence football's unavailing attempts to prevent gambling on the game. He was a regular chapel-goer and inaugurated a special annual service for footballers. He was a magistrate and widely respected official receiver in bankruptcy for Sheffield. Sir Charles Clegg died at his home, Clifton House, 32 Cavendish Road, Sheffield, on 26 June 1937, and was buried four days later in Fulwood churchyard.

One of Clegg's last appearances in public life had been to defend a match between England and the Nazi-sponsored German team near Jewish parts of north London. His view that 'politics' should be kept out of sport was looking out of touch. By the time of his death other horrors—a rejuvenated Players' Union, the football pools—were clearly not going to go away. But the game still, and for years later, reflected Clegg's flinty image. It was neither amateur nor fully commercialized. It was neither democratic—Clegg's autocratic attitude to committee meetings and debates invited and received comparisons with Napoleon—nor élitist. It was popular but respectable enough to be endorsed by royalty and prime ministers. Not for decades was the maximum wage finally removed, a deal with the pools done, or players given freedom of contract. Clegg may have been more pragmatic than he liked to let on, but that he so successfully stamped his own values on the first modern mass sport remains one of the unlikelier phenomena of twentieth-century British society.

NICHOLAS FISHWICK and ROLAND FISHWICK

Sources *The Times* (28 June 1937) · *The Times* (1 July 1937), 19 · *WWW* · N. Fishwick, *From Clegg to Clegg House* (1986) · N. Fishwick, *English football and society: 1910–1950* (1989) · A. Gibson and W. Pickford, *Association football and the men who made it*, 4 vols. [1905–6], vol. 3, pp. 132–5

Likenesses Elliott & Fry, photograph, 1900, Empics Sports Photo Agency, Nottingham [*see illus.*] · Elliott & Fry, photograph, *c.*1905, repro. in Gibson and Pickford, *Association football*, facing p. 17 · photograph, repro. in Fishwick, *From Clegg to Clegg House*, p. 48

Wealth at death £24,834 10*s*. 2*d.*: probate, 17 Aug 1937, *CGPLA Eng. & Wales*

Clegg, Hugh Anthony (1900–1983), journal editor, was born on 19 June 1900 at St Ives, Huntingdonshire, the third in the family of four sons and three daughters of the Revd John Clegg, headmaster of the local grammar school, and his wife, Gertrude, daughter of John Wilson of Hull. He won a king's scholarship in classics to Westminster School, London, and thence an exhibition to Trinity College, Cambridge, where he obtained a senior scholarship in natural sciences. He took first-class honours in part one of the natural sciences tripos in 1922, and qualified MRCS and LRCP from St Bartholomew's Hospital medical school, London, in 1925. He became MB BCh in 1928 and MRCP in 1929.

After junior hospital appointments Clegg joined the *British Medical Journal* in April 1931 as sub-editor; he became deputy editor in 1934 and was editor from 1947 to 1965. Clegg was also active in international medico-politics, helping to establish the precursor of the British Council's medical department and the World Medical Association. After his retirement in 1963 he became the first director of the international relations office of the Royal Society of Medicine and the first editor (1971–2) of its journal, *Tropical Doctor*.

Clegg's career spanned immense changes in medicine—from few useful therapeutic drugs to antibiotics in profusion, and from the disorganized health-care system which preceded the National Health Service to the later co-ordinated network of district general hospitals and health centres. As the editor of one of Britain's two principal medical journals he was well placed to influence events. For some years before he became titular editor, moreover, he had had this role owing to the inertia and ill health of his predecessor. His first task was to recover editorial freedom from the British Medical Association (BMA) officers, to whom it had latterly been so lightly relinquished. Next he had to create policy (for both the *BMJ* and the BMA) in response to the novel proposals for a national health service—given that, until the mid-1930s at any rate, the BMA was more a gentleman's club than a streamlined trade union.

Ultimately policy arose out of the mixture of reports of debates, correspondence, and particularly editorials in the *BMJ* in the run-up to the National Health Service Act of 1946. But editorials did not arise in a vacuum and even before the war Clegg was playing a prominent part in the discussions about the future organization of medicine. He was careful to allow free debate within the journal; nobody knew all the answers and under Clegg the correspondence columns assumed a leading place in the *BMJ*, where anybody could express his or her opinions provided these were well argued. BMA medico-politicians might not like these views or those in the editorials but their plaints were brushed aside, as were the calls (both then and subsequently) to discipline or even dismiss Clegg. Some have portrayed the *BMJ* of this time as reactionary, implacably opposed to any health service, and poles apart from its sister weekly, the liberal *Lancet*. Little could be further from the truth: the BMA, its journal, and Clegg had favoured a health service all along, but they foresaw that the details were as important as the principle. And with his sixty editorials, almost all of them written by himself, Clegg did affect the details—the independence of the family doctor was one direct result.

Nevertheless, Clegg's *BMJ* had a clinical and scientific aspect as important as its political one, and in particular his warm personal and professional relationship with Tony (Sir Austin) Bradford Hill ensured that the journal spearheaded the important breakthroughs in medical statistics and epidemiology that occurred just after the war. At one time a frequent contributor to *The Lancet*, Hill had quarrelled with Robbie (Sir Theodore) Fox over some swingeing changes made to his draft of an unsigned leading article, and switched his allegiance to the *BMJ*—a defection made all the more easy because both he and Clegg then lived at Great Missenden and throughout the war commuted together to Bloomsbury in London every day. Under Clegg the *BMJ* came to publish the first report of the first randomized clinical trial (of streptomycin in pulmonary tuberculosis, in 1948) and seminal epidemiological papers such as the demonstration of the link between cigarette smoking and cancer of the lung.

Clegg was not an easy man to get to know or to retain as a friend. Outside politics and literature he had few interests, though he returned to reading the classical Greek and Latin authors during his retirement. Stocky and neat, with a military moustache, he hated pomposity, and had an endearing tendency to wear brown shoes with blue suits. His greatest regret was that he had been born too late to fight in 1918, and his greatest pride was to have organized the first world conference on medical education. *Sub specie aeternitatis* neither matters, but three other achievements do: his re-creation of an independent inter-

national journal, designed by Stanley Morison and Eric Gill; his creation of specialist journals for complex research topics; and his co-authorship with the secretary of the Finnish Medical Association of the declaration of Helsinki, an epoch-making event in medical ethics.

Elected FRCP in 1944, Clegg received the honorary degrees of MD from Trinity College, Dublin, in 1952, and DLitt from the Queen's University, Belfast, in 1962, as well as the gold medal of the BMA in 1966, the year he was created CBE.

In 1932 Clegg married Baroness Kyra Engelhardt, of Smolensk, Russia, only daughter of Baron Arthur Engelhardt; they had a daughter and a son. Clegg died in London on 6 July 1983.   STEPHEN LOCK

Sources *BMJ* (5 July 1982) · *The Times* (7 July 1983) · *BMJ* (16 July 1983), 220–21 · *The Lancet* (16 July 1983) · Munk, *Roll* · private information (2004) · personal knowledge (2004) · *WWW* · *Old Westminsters*, vol. 3
Likenesses photograph, 1980, Hult. Arch. · M. Evans, portrait, priv. coll.
Wealth at death £9560: probate, 13 Feb 1987, *CGPLA Eng. & Wales* (1985)

Clegg, Hugh Armstrong (1920–1995), industrial relations expert, the fourth child and third son of Herbert Hobson Clegg, a Wesleyan minister, and his wife, Mabel Duckering, was born at Parkvedras House in Truro, Cornwall, on 22 May 1920. Educated at Kingswood School, Bath, the renowned Methodist public school, he reacted against his background, becoming an atheist and a member of the Communist Party as a teenager. This independence of mind, and his ability, were demonstrated by his election to the top scholarship (demyship) in classics at Magdalen College, Oxford, while insisting that he be allowed to read philosophy, politics, and economics, in which he took a first class in 1947 after five years of military service. In the army he showed his grasp of practicalities at the shop-floor level in becoming a skilled telephone engineer. On 28 June 1941 he married (Mary) Matilda Shaw (b. 1918/19), the elder daughter of George Shaw, a retired bank manager, and Mary Magowan; they had two sons and two daughters, and Clegg was a devoted and conscientious father.

Demobilized in 1945, Clegg soon found his communist faith undermined, crucially by his philosophy tutor, the redoubtable T. D. Weldon. By 1949, when he was elected a fellow of Nuffield College, Oxford, he was essentially a disillusioned empiricist, whose watchword he described, with some exaggeration, as being that 'an ounce of fact is worth a pound of theory' (*The Guardian*). His early books were a mixture of the monographic and wider studies, on nationalization and industrial democracy, which revealed a touch of the surviving theoretician. From 1955 he was in demand as a candid friend of the unions in a series of public inquiries into disputes, and he also presided at Nuffield over convivial gatherings of employers, politicians, and union leaders in a search for the elusive consensus.

In his heyday Clegg was the most persuasive advocate of collective bargaining in the voluntarist tradition as a better answer than legislative interference to the problem of damaging relations between capital and labour. His greatest success came as a member of the Donovan commission on trade unions and employers' associations (1965–8). He was largely responsible for its massive research and, by threatening a minority report, inveigled his colleagues into abandoning legal restraints in favour of trying to improve collective bargaining. The commission's modest proposals reassured the unions and modified the attitude of many employers; but during a turbulent decade they were not welcomed by most politicians, who became committed increasingly to legislative interference. Clegg's public service ended in 1980 as chairman of the committee on pay comparability. His last recommendations were reluctantly accepted by the Thatcher government and the committee was abolished.

In 1967 Clegg was appointed founding professor of industrial relations at Warwick University, which offered him novel scope and enhanced backing. He soon displayed his talents as an academic entrepreneur. Having helped to launch the new business school, he presided over the labours of capable assistants as director of the Industrial Relations Research Unit, who produced work which was, as he said too modestly, 'of some use to someone' (*The Guardian*). But the strain of years had begun to tell, and he resigned his chair in 1979. Long into retirement, however, he kept in touch with his creation, the most respected centre of his favourite studies in the country, cycling in from Kenilworth whenever he could.

Clegg now concentrated on completing a long-delayed project, *A History of British Trade Unions since 1889*. The first volume, to 1910 (with A. Fox and A. F. Thompson), had been published in 1964; the second (1911–33) followed in 1985, and the third (after 1933) in 1994, when his health was failing. This was a monumental achievement and remains pre-eminent in its detailed coverage of the whole range of trade-union development over a lengthy period. Here and elsewhere, Clegg has sometimes been criticized for failing to deal adequately with the social and political background to his masterly treatment of the institutional, procedural, and legal aspects of the subject. His mastery is also displayed in the other of the most important among his many books, *The System of Industrial Relations in Great Britain*, originally published in 1953 and revised in 1970 and 1979. Regarded for a generation and more as the indispensable textbook, it is voluminous and completely authoritative.

Clegg had an incisive, retentive mind, apparent in everything he attempted, on paper and in person. Once sure of his views, after weighing the evidence and the opinions of those he respected, he worked quickly, preferably alone, and wrote with a straightforward clarity in a field not noted for stylistic niceties. He could seem dour, even forbidding, but was essentially considerate and warm-hearted—as became evident when he proved an excellent Oxford tutor and a fine supervisor of graduate students. Immensely loyal himself, he attracted loyalty from others, and was an engaging and often convivial colleague. (*Who's Who* recorded his recreations as 'walking and beer'.) Impressively agile in committee, he was an outstanding manager of seminars but curiously pedestrian as a lecturer. Growing infirmity meant shorter walks and less of his cycling into Warwick. He never learned to drive and his lifestyle was remarkably simple. Mourned by everyone who knew him, he died in Warwick Hospital on 8 December 1995 of a cerebrovascular infarction.

A. F. THOMPSON

Sources MS fragment of autobiography, covering the years up to 1949, priv. coll. [A. F. Thompson] · *The Times* (13 Dec 1995) · *The Guardian* (12 Dec 1995) · *The Independent* (15 Dec 1995) · *Daily Telegraph* (27 Dec 1995) · personal knowledge (2004) · private information (2004) · *WWW* · b. cert. · m. cert. · d. cert.
Archives U. Warwick Mod. RC, research material concerning industrial relations
Likenesses photograph, repro. in *The Times* · photograph, repro. in *The Independent*
Wealth at death under £145,000: probate, 21 March 1996, *CGPLA Eng. & Wales*

Clegg, James (1679–1755), Presbyterian minister and physician, was born on 20 October 1679 in Shawfield, near Rochdale, Lancashire, the son of James Clegg (1655–1737), clothier, and his wife, Ann Livesay (1654/5–1730), the daughter of a dissenter of Berkle, Lancashire. In his autobiography Clegg reveals that he was able to read and write by the age of four, when he was sent to a school run by Joseph Whitworth, a dissenting minister, at Falinge, Lancashire. From there he went to the free school at Rochdale, and then to James Lawton's dissenting school at Oldham, Lancashire. His maternal grandfather marked him down for the ministry and financed his education from the age of ten, sending him first, in 1689, to Jeremiah Barlow's academy at Blackley, Lancashire, and then to the Revd Richard Frankland's academy at Rathmell, near Settle, Yorkshire. When Frankland died in 1698 Clegg moved to Manchester, and studied with John Chorlton, Presbyterian minister and tutor. Clegg admitted that he led a wild life in Manchester, and to reform his ways he moved to lodge with Joseph Dawson, a dissenting minister in Rochdale. While there he preached his first sermon at Bispham, on the Fylde, Lancashire, taking as his text Romans 14: 12. By this time he was beginning to reject the Calvinist doctrine, a trend which was to continue. In a sermon preached at Chinley, Derbyshire, on 7 November 1734 he maintained that Calvin's doctrine was contrary to nature and the perfection of God. In July 1702 he was asked to preach an approbation sermon to a Presbyterian congregation founded by William Bagshaw at Malcoff, near Chapel-en-le-Frith, Derbyshire. The congregation unanimously accepted him as their pastor and he moved to Ford Hall, Derbyshire, where he received free board and lodgings in return for teaching Samuel Bagshaw's sons. He was ordained at Malcoff on 25 August 1703.

At Ford, Clegg met Ann Champion (1682–1742) of Edale, Derbyshire, and married her in February 1704. They were to have nine children, eight of whom survived to adulthood. His diary reveals his love for her, and the loneliness he felt after her death. Eventually, on 2 August 1744, he was married to Sarah Eyre, *née* Jones (d. 1748), a widow of Macclesfield, Cheshire.

Not only was Clegg minister at Malcoff but he preached to congregations across the north-west. Relationships with the established church in this area were not always cordial. He and Samuel Bagshaw were often engaged in disputes with the local clergy, and the vicar of Hope, Derbyshire, tried to persuade Clegg to conform. Although Clegg worked mainly within the Presbyterian system he adopted some practices from the Independents, ministering to a gathered congregation rather than to all Christians. His diary shows that he took sole responsibility for admitting new members to the Lord's supper and for excluding wrongdoers from it. The diary also reveals that he relied completely on God and his belief in the spiritual value of prayer.

In 1711 Clegg moved to Stoddard Hall, Malcoff, Derbyshire, where he rented a farm to help support his growing family. In the same year a new chapel at Chinley, Derbyshire, was opened. To further supplement his income, with the assistance of Dr Adam Holland of Macclesfield he took up medicine, but after treating some of the wealthier families of the district he was threatened with prosecution for practising without a licence. In October 1729 he was awarded a *diploma medicum in absentia* by the University of Aberdeen on the testimonials of three medical doctors. He became one of the foremost medical practitioners in north-west Derbyshire, treating all types of illness. His diary records accurate observations of symptoms and how they were treated.

With the Revd John Ashe, Clegg edited William Bagshaw's *Essays on a Union unto Christ* in 1703. He also published *A Discourse on the Covenant of Grace* in 1721, a sermon entitled *The Continuation of the Christian Church* preached at the ordination of John Holland in 1731, and the text of a sermon preached in Nottingham entitled *The Things that Made for Peace and Edification amongst Christians* in 1738, and edited seventeen sermons by John Ashe in 1741. He remained active until the end of his life, but his later years were marred by attacks on Chinley Chapel and the desecration of the tomb of his wives and children. He died at Stoddard Hall on 5 August 1755 and was buried at Chinley with his wives and children. His will, made during an illness in 1753, left bequests to his children and grandchildren, and set up a trust vested in a piece of ground to go towards the salary of a minister for Chinley Chapel and pay school fees for poor children. He also left six volumes of *The Morning Exercise* to be chained to the south side of the chapel. E. LORD

Sources *The diary of James Clegg of Chapel en le Frith, 1708–1755*, ed. V. S. Doe, 3 vols., Derbyshire RS, 2–3, 5 (1978–81) · chapel register, 1755, Chinley Chapel, Derbyshire, PRO, RG 4/96 [burial] · P. J. Anderson, ed., *Officers and graduates of University and King's College, Aberdeen, MVD–MDCCCLX*, New Spalding Club, 11 (1893) · W. B. Bunting, *Chapel-en-le-Frith: its history and its people* (1940)
Wealth at death £260 plus goods and chattels: will, *The diary of James Clegg*

Clegg, John (b. c.1714, d. in or after 1746), violinist, was born in Dublin, probably the son of William Clegg, a state musician in that city until 1723. He is said to have received early instruction from his father and William Viner, master of the Dublin Castle band, and later to have studied with the virtuoso violinist Dubourg in Dublin, and with Giovanni Bononcini in London, presumably for composition. His musical development must also have been further enhanced when, as Hawkins reports, he travelled in Italy with Lord Ferrers.

In a notice for Clegg's first public performances at a concert in Dublin in March 1723 he is described as 'a boy of about nine years of age' (*Harding's Weekly Impartial News-Letter*, 20 March 1723). Since Viner died in November 1716 it would appear either that young Clegg had taken to the violin at an exceptionally early age or that his extreme youth had been somewhat exaggerated. Nevertheless, such was Clegg's precocious talent that his London début concert, which took place on 23 May 1723, was later judged by Burney to have been one of the two most memorable musical events of that year.

By the early 1730s Clegg had established himself as one of the leading executants resident in London. Burney records that there was 'no concert now without a solo on the violin by Veracini or Clegg' (Burney, *Hist. mus.*, 4.657), and Hawkins attests to the strength of his tone, the rapidity and distinctness of his execution, and his excellence as an orchestral leader. However, Burney was correct in his assertion, contradicting Hawkins, that it was Festing rather than Clegg who was appointed to succeed Pietro Castrucci as leader of the opera orchestra at the King's Theatre in 1737.

In 1730, 1733, and 1737 Clegg made return visits to Dublin, where he gave concerts in collaboration with his sister, Miss Clegg (Mrs Davis from c.1733), a prominent Dublin soprano. Clegg's solo repertory seems to have focused on the Italian school, Vivaldi and Geminiani in particular, but in some programmes compositions of his own are featured. One of these was published, alongside minor works by Handel, Geminiani, and Quantz, in *Forty-Five Airs and New Variations* (1748).

Clegg's last known solo engagement was in March 1741 at a concert given in London in aid of the 'Fund for Decay'd Musicians' (later the Royal Society of Musicians), established in 1738. Though he was not a founder member, Clegg's name appears in the society's lists of subscribers in 1739, 1742, and 1744.

Early in 1744 Clegg's career was cut short by mental illness brought on, according to Hawkins, by 'intense application and incessant practice' (Hawkins, 5.362). He was a patient in Bethlem Hospital from 21 January until 20 July 1744, when he was considered to be 'well', but had to be readmitted on 15 December. Clegg was encouraged to play the violin at Bethlem, where, as Burney deftly puts it, he attracted many visitors 'in hopes of being entertained by his fiddle or his folly' (Burney, *Hist. mus.*, 4.659). He was finally released from the hospital uncured in October 1746 and seems to have died not long afterwards, probably in London. IAN BARTLETT

Sources Burney, *Hist. mus.*, vol. 4 · J. Hawkins, *A general history of the science and practice of music*, 5 (1776) · E. L. Avery, ed., *The London stage, 1660–1800*, pt 2: *1700–1729* (1960) · A. H. Scouten, ed., *The London stage, 1660–1800*, pt 3: *1729–1747* (1961) · O. E. Deutsch, *Handel: a* *documentary biography* (1955) • B. Boydell, *A Dublin musical calendar, 1700–1760* (Dublin, 1988) • T. J. Walsh, *Opera in Dublin, 1705–1797: the social scene* (1973) • B. Matthews, ed., *The Royal Society of Musicians of Great Britain: list of members, 1738–1984* (1985) • Grove, *Dict. mus.* (1927) • R. McGuiness, ed., *The Royal Holloway College computer register of musical data in London newspapers, 1660–1750* [forthcoming] • High-fill, Burnim & Langhans, *BDA*, vol. 3 • [J. S. Sainsbury], ed., *A dictionary of musicians*, 2 vols. (1825) • A. Rees and others, *The cyclopaedia, or, Universal dictionary of arts, sciences, and literature*, 45 vols. (1819–20), vol. 8 • private information (2004) [P. Allderidge] • I. Bartlett, 'John Clegg: a burning talent', *The Strad*, 111 (2000), 1076–80

Clegg, John Atherton (1913–1987), physicist, was born on 15 May 1913 at 6 Moor Close, Middleton, Manchester, the son of Albert Clegg, a compositor, and his wife, Mabel Webster. He was educated at Queen Elizabeth's Grammar School, Middleton, before completing an honours degree in physics at the University of Manchester in 1935. He qualified as a secondary school teacher the following year, and took up (after a succession of temporary posts) a job as physics master at Middlesbrough high school. In 1940 he was recruited to work at the Telecommunications Research Establishment (TRE), the major site of British radar development. The rapid expansion of the chain home coastal radar system relied on the training of staff, and after two years of radar research Clegg's teaching skills were mobilized as deputy head of TRE's teaching school. In 1943 Clegg married Marjorie Fuller (d. 1986). He finished the war at the Ministry of Aircraft Production headquarters in London.

As the Second World War was ending, many scientists returned to the universities armed with new techniques, equipment, and useful government and industrial contacts. Clegg, after preliminary arrangements to work on cosmic rays at Birkbeck College, was persuaded to join Professor Patrick M. S. Blackett's physics department in Manchester. On his return to his city of birth in 1946, Clegg, an expert on aerials, began work at Jodrell Bank, a Cheshire outpost of Blackett's department where Bernard Lovell was assembling ex-military equipment and staff to investigate radar echoes of unclear origin. The Jodrell Bank team soon identified the radar echoes with the trails of meteors. Since their technique of investigation was relatively undisturbed by the sun, the radar team soon found and published details about previously unsuspected daytime meteor showers. Clegg used his knowledge of radio wave propagation, learned during his wartime work, to assist the team's efforts to calculate orbital information from meteor trail reflections. Jodrell Bank's use of this information to claim that sporadic meteors were not of interstellar origin was one of the first interventions of radio techniques into astronomy.

Clegg was elected a fellow of the Royal Astronomical Society in 1950. With Lovell he published *Radio Astronomy*, one of the first books on the subject, in 1952. He played a major part in designing and building the first elements of Jodrell Bank's pioneering radio telescope in 1946–7, but he did not publish on any observations made with it.

Reminiscing in the 1970s Clegg recalled that his enjoyment of radio astronomy at Jodrell Bank diminished as the research station grew and the work became more routine and team orientated. Troubled also by his health, Clegg moved back to the physics laboratories in Manchester in 1951 to assist Blackett with his investigations of rock magnetism. Blackett was interested in the possibility that a massive rotating body could possess a magnetic moment independent of any electric currents within it. The extremely sensitive magnetometer he designed to measure the effect was also suited to measuring the magnetic field trapped in rock. A paper published by Clegg with Mary Almond (who had also worked at Jodrell Bank in the early years) and P. H. S. Stubbs in 1954 claimed that measurements from rocks collected from sites across the United Kingdom showed that the land mass had rotated clockwise by over 30° since the Triassic period. Such claims bolstered the emerging theory of continental drift.

When Blackett left Manchester in 1953 to be appointed professor at Imperial College, Clegg went with him, continued the research on rock magnetism, and took up the post of lecturer in physics. He was promoted to senior lecturer in 1956, and reader the following year. In 1961 he was given leave of absence and seconded to Ibadan, Nigeria, as professor of physics; however, he once again suffered ill health, this time a viral complaint. On return to London he began teaching again, and was senior tutor of Imperial College physics department from 1967 to 1974. Contemporaries remember him as an excellent pedagogue, and he passed on this experience in his later years as an education consultant for the Institute of Physics. He retired in 1977 and died at 42 Shelley Road, Worthing, of heart failure on 28 August 1987.   JON AGAR

Sources A. C. B. Lovell, *Quarterly Journal of the Royal Astronomical Society*, 29 (1988), 403–9 • J. A. Clegg, taped interview, JRL • B. Lovell, *The story of Jodrell Bank* (1968) • D. Edge and M. Mulkay, *Astronomy transformed* (1976) • b. cert. • d. cert.
Archives JRL, Jodrell Bank archive | SOUND JRL, Jodrell Bank archive, taped interview [made for D. Edge and M. Mulkay, *Astronomy transformed* (1976)]
Wealth at death £104,010: probate, 13 Oct 1987, CGPLA Eng. & Wales

Clegg, Samuel (1781–1861), civil engineer, was born at Manchester on 2 March 1781. He received a scientific education under the care of John Dalton, tutor at the Manchester Academy (1793–9). He was then apprenticed to Boulton and Watt, at whose Soho factory in Birmingham he witnessed many of William Murdock's early experiments in the use of coal gas. He left in 1805 to set up as a gas engineer on his own account and was soon engaged by Henry Lodge to adapt a new gas lighting system to his cotton mills at Sowerby Bridge, near Halifax.

To purify gas Clegg developed a wet-liming process, which was widely used for some forty years. After removing to London, in 1813 he lighted with gas Rudolph Ackermann's fine-art establishment in the Strand. Meanwhile he had joined (1812) the newly founded Chartered Gas Company and in 1814 was appointed engineer. He left in 1817 after a pay dispute and in the same year installed gas at the Royal Mint, with Frederick Accum, incorporating a self-activating wet meter of his own design. For some years he was engaged in the construction of gasworks, or in advising on the formation of new gas companies. Unwisely, as it turned out, he joined an engineering firm at Liverpool, and lost everything he possessed. In 1836, with his son, Samuel [see below], he was employed by the Portuguese government as an engineer. In that capacity he reconstructed the mint at Lisbon, and executed several other public works.

On Clegg's return to England, railway works engaged his attention, and he became obsessed with the atmospheric system then being developed for locomotives. In this, a piston in a wide tube was connected through a continuous sealed slot to the leading carriage. The pipe in front of the piston was exhausted of air by a series of stationary pumping engines at intervals along the track. Isambard Kingdom Brunel was one of its advocates, introducing it on the South Devon Railway in 1844. Unfortunately, in the end it proved one of the most costly failures in the history of engineering up to that time.

Clegg played no further part in railway construction but he was appointed by the government as one of the surveying officers for conducting preliminary inquiries on applications for new gas bills, and he contributed to the exhaustive treatise on the manufacture of coal gas published by his son in 1850. He became a member of the Institution of Civil Engineers in 1829, and took a prominent part in its proceedings. He died of chronic bronchitis and asthma at his home, Fairfield House, 39 Adelaide Road, Haverstock Hill, Hampstead, on 8 January 1861.

Clegg's only son was **Samuel Clegg** (1814–1856), civil engineer, born at Westminster on 2 April 1814. He studied engineering at University College, London (1830–33), and was employed as an assistant engineer on the Greenwich, Great Western, and Eastern Counties (afterwards the Great Eastern) railways and as a resident engineer on the Southampton and Dorchester Railway in 1844. Before this, he was employed on a number of occasions in Portugal. His first visit took place in 1836–7, when he and his father made a trigonometrical survey of part of the Algarve. In 1849, he was appointed professor of civil engineering and architecture at the College for Civil Engineers, Putney, and in the same year he became a lecturer on civil engineering to the officers of the East India Company's engineers at Chatham, which latter post he held until his death. In 1855 he was sent by the government to Demerara, to report on the sea walls there and to superintend the works for their restoration. After returning home he became engaged in elaborating a plan for removing all the gas manufactories in London to a single site outside the city in Essex. He was author of a comprehensive treatise on coal gas in 1850. A contemporary described him as an amiable man of considerable ability, acquirements, and cultivated taste. He died at Putney on 25 July 1856, leaving a widow and a young family.

G. C. BOASE, rev. TREVOR I. WILLIAMS

Sources PICE, 16 (1856–7), 121–4 • T. I. Williams, A history of the British gas industry (1981) • A. Elton, 'Gas for light and heat', A history of technology, ed. C. Singer and others, 4: The industrial revolution, c. 1750 to c. 1850 (1958), 258–75 • Boase, Mod. Eng. biog.
Likenesses portrait, Sci. Mus.
Wealth at death £600: probate, 28 Feb 1862, CGPLA Eng. & Wales

Clegg, Samuel (1814–1856). See under Clegg, Samuel (1781–1861).

Cleghorn, George (1716–1789), physician, born at Granton, near Edinburgh, on 18 December 1716, was the youngest of five children of a farmer who died when George was three years old. He was educated in the grammar school of his native parish of Cramond, before being sent to Edinburgh in 1728 to learn Latin, French, Greek, and mathematics. He entered the University of Edinburgh as a student of physic under Alexander Monro in 1731, and lived in his house. In that same year, Cleghorn met John Fothergill and they became friends and correspondents for life. He also participated in the formation of the Royal Medical Society at Edinburgh.

In 1736 Cleghorn was appointed, on the recommendation of Dr St Clair, as surgeon to the 22nd regiment of foot, then stationed in Minorca; he remained in that island until his regiment was ordered to Dublin in 1749. Cleghorn corresponded in Latin with Fothergill on the medical observations which he made in Minorca, and on his return from the Mediterranean he was persuaded by his friend to collect and arrange the contents of these letters. The work was ready for the press in 1750, and while Cleghorn was superintending its publication in London he attended the anatomical lectures of William Hunter.

The book appeared in 1751 under the title Observations on the Epidemical Diseases in Minorca from the Year 1744 to 1749. It began with an introduction, in which Cleghorn gave a general account of the climate, local inhabitants, and natural history of the island, with meteorological tables and lists of plants and animals, together with the native names of several species. In the following seven chapters Cleghorn summarized his observations on the diseases of the local population and of the British troops. He distinguished between ship and Mediterranean fever, and his extensive observations rendered the book essential reading for those going to practise in Minorca. The book went through four editions in Cleghorn's lifetime, and a fifth was published in 1815. The author made many postmortem examinations, and Matthew Baillie's copy of the book, which was deposited in the library of the Royal College of Physicians, contains annotations which indicate the value he placed on it.

Cleghorn recognized the fact that many otherwise inexplicable statements in the Hippocratic writings became clear when studied by the light of clinical observations on the Mediterranean coasts. There, both acute and chronic diseases were modified in a way rarely seen farther north, owing to the concurrence of malarial fever. Although the pathology of enteric fever and acute pneumonia was unknown in Cleghorn's time, his book gives a clear account of the course of enteric fever complicated with tertian ague, with dysentery, and with pneumonia.

Because Cleghorn kept so strictly to what he observed, the validity of his observations was not impaired by beliefs later found to be erroneous.

Cleghorn settled in Dublin in 1751 and began to give lectures in anatomy; a few years later he was made the first lecturer on anatomy in the university, and afterwards he was appointed professor of anatomy. The index of his lectures shows that they were not confined to details of human anatomy, but included both comparative and surgical anatomy and the general principles of physiology (*Index of an Annual Course of Lectures*, 1756).

Cleghorn was successful in practice, though in his later years he spent much of his time on his farm near Dublin. Due to declining health he spent more and more time away from the city, finding the pleasures of the outdoor life more rewarding. In 1784 Cleghorn was elected a member of the College of Physicians of Ireland; he was also one of the original members of the Royal Irish Academy. He was made a fellow of the Royal Medical Society in Paris in 1777.

Cleghorn was married but had no children of his own, caring instead for the nine children of a deceased brother. One of these, William Cleghorn, took the degree of MD at Edinburgh in 1779. In 1786 Cleghorn was still delivering anatomical lectures at Dublin. He was unwilling to retire from the professorship until one of his nephews was in a strong position to apply for the vacant chair. Cleghorn died in Dublin three years later, in December 1789.

NORMAN MOORE, rev. CLAIRE E. J. HERRICK

Sources *Memoirs of the life and writings of the late John Coakley Lettsom*, ed. T. J. Pettigrew, 3 vols. (1817), vol. 3, pp. 210, 364–8 · N. Cantlie, *A history of the army medical department*, 1 (1974), 109, 246; 2 (1974), 391–2 · J. J. Keevil, J. L. S. Coulter, and C. Lloyd, *Medicine and the navy, 1200–1900*, 3: *1714–1815* (1961), 110, 333 · A. Peterkin and W. Johnston, *Commissioned officers in the medical services of the British army, 1660–1960*, 1 (1968), 8 · J. C. Lettsom, *Memoirs of Fothergill, Cleghorn, and others* (1786) · G. Cleghorn, *Index of an annual course of lectures* (1756) · H. J. Rose, *A new general biographical dictionary*, ed. H. J. Rose and T. Wright, 12 vols. (1853) · A. Chalmers, ed., *The general biographical dictionary*, new edn, 32 vols. (1812–17) · B. Hutchison, *Biographica medica*, 2 vols. (1799)
Archives TCD, anatomy lectures
Likenesses C. Sherwin, stipple (after drawing), BM, NPG; repro. in Lettsom, *Memoirs* · oils, TCD
Wealth at death considerable estates in co. Meath; lucrative practice in Ireland

Cleghorn, Hugh (1752–1837), colonial administrator, was born on 21 March 1752 at The Society, Edinburgh, the only son of John Cleghorn (*d.* 1774), merchant and brewer, and his wife, Jean (1712–1791), daughter of William Scott, professor of Greek at Edinburgh University, and Jean Fairbairn. The Cleghorn's only other child was a daughter, Magdalene. Hugh Cleghorn's family represented a solid alliance between well-to-do brewers and influential academics, among whom were William Hamilton, principal of Edinburgh University, and William Cleghorn, professor of moral philosophy there. William Cleghorn gave his 'dying voice' for Adam Ferguson, one of the outstanding personalities of the Scottish Enlightenment, to be the next professor of moral philosophy at Edinburgh. Hugh Cleghorn was to be a student of Ferguson's at the university; he went there in 1764, at the age of twelve, because he wanted to study Greek and could not do so at the Edinburgh high school, where he began his education. Cleghorn's mind was thus formed by and imbued with the challenges of the Scottish Enlightenment and of Edinburgh at its most brilliant period in the eighteenth century. His own inclination was at first towards academic life: in 1773 he was appointed professor of civil history at the University of St Andrews. On 2 February 1774, in Old Greyfriars parish, Cleghorn married Rachel McGill (*d.* 1821), daughter of John McGill, and a relative of Adam Smith, who left the young Cleghorns £400 in his will. It was early in their marriage that their two sons and five daughters were born; both the sons eventually followed careers in Madras.

Sixteen years in St Andrews proved to Cleghorn that it was too narrow a stage for his abundant energy and 'bigness of mind', as his friend William Adam phrased it (Clark, 283). A passionate desire to travel led him to seize the opportunity to see Europe as 'bear leader' to the tenth earl of Home. One of the most important results of this tour (1788–90) was the friendship he formed in Neuchâtel with the comte de Meuron, whose mercenary Swiss regiment had been hired by the Dutch East India Company to guard Colombo and other Dutch garrisons in Ceylon. Cleghorn also acquired an appetite for politics, and his fertile mind was busy with schemes for an alliance between Britain and the Swiss cantons, which, if they launched an attack on the eastern frontier of France, might restrain the French from invading the Netherlands. These schemes brought him to the notice of Henry Dundas, the most influential government minister in Scotland, who, as president of the Board of Control, was able to ensure that the East India Company gave jobs to the many young Scots he recommended. Dundas found Cleghorn's intelligence reports valuable, and regarded him as another instrument to be used in furthering British interests in India.

Cleghorn wanted the government to safeguard Madras by extending British control to Ceylon. When de Meuron confided in Cleghorn how dissatisfied he was with the Dutch as paymasters, and when the French revolutionary armies invaded the Netherlands and William V of Orange fled to England, the opportunity arrived for Britain to get Ceylon into its sights, for William, in his 'Kew letter', ordered all commanders of Dutch forces to hand over forts under their command to the British. Dundas agreed with Cleghorn that, as de Meuron's Swiss regiment in Colombo constituted the only reliable force there, if these troops could be persuaded to change sides, Ceylon could be won without, in Cleghorn's words, 'great effusion of blood'. So he and de Meuron were authorized in 1795 by the British government to go to Madras with all possible speed to bring about the transfer of the allegiance of the Swiss regiment to the British, and to end Dutch rule in Ceylon. Cleghorn hoped the element of surprise would add to Dutch confusion, so he tried to stop the comte boasting too loudly about his new rank of major-general during their journey to India. Once there, Cleghorn did go so far as to write to a friend, 'I am not here merely to eat mangoes' (Clark, 127). In the event, the plan worked: the Swiss obeyed their colonel's instructions, the Dutch governor surrendered after a token resistance, and the British army entered Colombo.

Cleghorn's return to Britain took him through Europe, and set his ever eager mind to planning how to frustrate Napoleon's drive into Italy. His plan impressed Dundas, who read it over with Pitt at Walmer Castle, although the treaty of Campo Formio made it irrelevant. In 1798 Dundas sent a reluctant Cleghorn back to Colombo as secretary of state under the governorship of Frederick North: Dundas, under pressure to exchange Ceylon for the Cape, wanted to keep both, and needed someone who shared his views on the spot. But the personal antipathy between Cleghorn and North, and the failure of the pearl fishery of which Cleghorn had been put in charge, led to his leaving Ceylon after only two years, with a charge of stealing pearls hanging over him. The charge was unfounded, as the official inquiry established, but it meant the end of Cleghorn's public career.

Cleghorn retired to Fife and set himself to 'improve' his estates and enjoy his friends and his grandchildren, as far as his financial worries would permit. He had put the £5000 given him by the East India Company for his first enterprise in Ceylon towards buying Stravithie, an estate in Fife just south of St Andrews, and had little spare capital and a somewhat meagre government pension. To add to his difficulties, William Campbell, a writer to the signet and the husband of Cleghorn's second daughter, Jane, attempted to avert his own financial ruin by using Cleghorn's name as security. Cleghorn accepted responsibility for the debt, but was so mortified by his own carelessness over money that he made Stravithie in its entirety over to his surviving son, Peter (1783–1863), registrar-general to the supreme court in Madras. From 1831 Hugh Cleghorn lived on his pension in the family house, Wakefield, Stravithie, Dunino, Fife, where he died on 19 February 1837. He was buried in Dunino churchyard.

In the second half of the twentieth century Cleghorn's name acquired some notoriety in Sri Lanka (as Ceylon became in 1972). On his first visit in 1795 he had undertaken a tour of the northern coastal region, writing to Dundas, 'At present we are as ignorant of Ceylon as we are of Japan' (Clark, 138). He had had much conversation with Dutch settlers, officials, and lawyers, and after eight months as secretary of state, he set down what he had learned from them of 'the administration of justice and of the revenues under the Dutch government' in a minute to Dundas of 1799. In 1954 the Tamils, looking for ammunition to sustain their claims to a separate homeland in the north and east of the island, seized on some phrases in Cleghorn's minute to justify them. For example, he asserted that 'Two different nations, from a very early period, have divided between them the possession of the island.

First the Sinhalese, inhabiting the interior of the country in its southern and western parts. … and secondly the Malabars [Tamils] who possess the northern and eastern districts. These two nations differ entirely in their religion, language and manners' (de Silva, appx B). Throughout his life Cleghorn's enthusiasm for learning, from whatever situation he found himself in, remained undimmed. Whether he was exhorting his St Andrews students to read Adam Smith and John Millar, analysing his observations on Europe at war for Pitt and Dundas, or putting into practice scientific methods of farming on his own estate in Fife, he was always forward-looking and his ideas sparkled with 'bigness of life'. AYLWIN CLARK

Sources A. Clark, *An enlightened Scot* (1992) · K. M. De Silva, *The 'traditional homelands' of the Tamils: separatist ideology in Sri Lanka*, 2nd edn (1994) · G. de Meuron, *Le regiment Meuron, 1781–1816* (1982) · U. St Andr. L., Cleghorn MS 53 · correspondence between Secretary Dundas and Hugh Cleghorn relating to Ceylon, 1795–1800, NA Scot., GD51/17/71 · F. North to the court of directors, East India Company, CKS, U471 C29/2 · Henry Smith to secret committee of the court of directors, East India Company, BL OIOC, F/4/129 · correspondence between Hugh Cleghorn and William Adam, NA Scot. · minutes of the United College, U. St Andr. L., UC 400, vol. 1 · H. Cleghorn, letter to Dundas, 1790, Duke U., Perkins L. [incl. a copy of his paper on the Swiss cantons addressed to the duke of Leeds] · parish register (births), Edinburgh, March 1752 · NA Scot., RS27/213 · catalogue of graduates, U. Edin. L.
Archives NA Scot., letters · PRO, letters relating to Ceylon, WO1/361 P8138 · U. St Andr. L., MSS | BL, letters to Lord Melville, Add. MS 69097 · CKS, Frederic North MSS · Duke U., corresp. with Evan Nepean · NA Scot., letters to Dundas · NA Scot., corresp. with Lord Melville and papers relating to Ceylon · NA Scot., Adam Smith's will · NL Scot., letters to Adam Ferguson · NL Scot., letters to John Lee · NL Scot., letters to Alexander Walker · PRO, Dundas's secret service accounts, AO 1/2122/6 · PRO, letters relating to comte de Meuron, HO 50/452 H338L
Likenesses A. Skirving, pastel drawing, 1790, priv. coll.
Wealth at death gave estate of Stravithie to second son in 1831 (est. value £40,000 in 1825): U. St Andr. L., MS 53, box 2, envelope no. 11

Cleghorn, Isabel (1852–1922), educationist, was born on 14 March 1852 at King Street, Rochester, Kent, the fifth child and second daughter of Alexander Cleghorn (*d.* 1893), custom house officer, and his second wife, Mary Ann Robinson (*d.* 1904). The family moved to Tyneside and Cleghorn was educated at the North Shields middle class elementary school. She became a pupil teacher at the Jarrow Chemical Company's School at South Shields before attending Stockwell Training College with a first-class queen's scholarship. After teaching in Scarborough and Thetford, in 1880 she became head of the girls' department at the Sheffield school board's newly opened Heeley Bank School.

Cleghorn was headmistress at Heeley for thirty-eight years. In her early years at the school she worked by correspondence course for the St Andrews University LLA, which she was awarded in 1888. A year later she was appointed teacher of sewing at the Sheffield Pupil Teacher Centre, and her interest in this subject was reflected in her development of the Sheffield Needlework Scheme and in the publication of her *Needlework for Scholarship Students* in 1896. Her meticulously kept school logbook reveals that during the 1880s she was also beginning to broaden her interests outside the classroom. She joined the committee of the Sheffield branch of the Teachers' Benevolent and Orphan Fund, whose girls' home was at Page Hall in Sheffield, and served as chairman of its house committee for three years. She remained a firm supporter of the fund throughout her life. She was also a member and the first woman president of both the Sheffield Teachers' Association and of the Sheffield Head Teachers' Association. She was a co-opted member of the Sheffield education committee for fifteen years and was appointed to the consultative committee to the Board of Education in 1907 and subsequently to various departmental committees. From 1900 she regularly attended the annual conferences of the National Union of Women Workers (later the National Council of Women) and became a member of its national council.

Cleghorn was also a member of the local branch of the National Union of Teachers and on the national executive committee from 1895 to 1919. She was vice-president of the union in 1910–11 and served with distinction as the first woman president in 1911–12. During her year of office she was awarded honorary MAs by the University of Wales and by the University of Sheffield on whose court of governors she served as the Sheffield teachers' representative.

Cleghorn, who was unmarried, retired from teaching at the end of March 1918 and marked her retirement by giving 178 books from her personal reference library to her school. In 1919 she joined the Sheffield committee of the Women's Citizens' Association, which encouraged women to participate more widely in local government in the post-war period. In 1922 she was elected to represent Heeley ward on the Ecclesall Bierlow board of guardians. She lived at 89 Meersbrook Park Road, Sheffield, for over twenty years and died there on 4 December 1922 from ovarian cysts and cancer of the stomach. She was buried three days later at Ecclesall parish church.

Cleghorn made a significant contribution to educational development, particularly through her campaigning on such issues as teachers' pay, class sizes, curriculum development, nursery schooling, continuation classes, and the school-leaving age. She believed very strongly in the importance of education and in equality of opportunity, but adopted a pragmatic attitude which was no doubt engendered by teaching for thirty-eight years in a predominantly working-class community in a northern industrial city:

> Education should be an effective preparation for life … Experience tells us that the bulk of our children are destined for industrial work, and yet we send them out of our schools absolutely unprepared for such work … It is also quite as necessary, if not more so, to educate our girls for the duties of the home. (*National Union of Teachers Annual Report*, 1911)

While not as militant on suffrage issues as some of her colleagues in the National Union of Women Teachers, she was through her own example and achievements a pioneer for women within the teaching profession. As the inscription on her grave recognizes, 'Her works do follow her'.   SYLVIA DUNKLEY

Sources *Sheffield Daily Telegraph* (6 Dec 1922) · logbook, Heeley Bank School girls' department, Jan 1880–March 1903, April 1903–Oct 1934, Sheff. Arch. · *The Schoolmaster* (9 July 1910) · *The Schoolmaster* (16 July 1910) · *The Schoolmaster* (22 April 1911) · *The Schoolmaster* (29 April 1911) · *The Schoolmaster* (8 July 1911) · *The Schoolmaster* (15 July 1911) · *The Schoolmaster* (9 Sept 1911) · *The Schoolmaster* (14 Oct 1911) · *The Schoolmaster* (18 Nov 1911) · *The Schoolmaster* (16 Dec 1911) · *The Schoolmaster* (6 Jan 1912) · *The Schoolmaster* (13 Jan 1912) · *The Schoolmaster* (20 Jan 1912) · *The Schoolmaster* (16 March 1912) · *The Schoolmaster* (13 April 1912) · *The Schoolmaster* (18 May 1912) · *The Schoolmaster* (22 June 1912) · *The Schoolmaster* (30 March 1918) · *The Schoolmaster* (8 Dec 1922) · *The Schoolmaster* (15 Dec 1922) · *National Union of Teachers Annual Report* (1911) · W. Odom, *Hallamshire worthies* (1926) · *Sheffield Independent* (18 April 1911) · *Sheffield Independent* (13 June 1911) · J. H. Bingham, *The Sheffield School Board, 1870–1903* (1949) · school management sub-committee minute book, 59, 1917–18, Sheff. Arch., Sheffield Education Committee · H. Kean, *Deeds not words: the lives of suffragette teachers* (1990) · *Sheffield and District Who's Who* (1905) · d. cert. · b. cert.
Archives U. Warwick Mod. RC, National Union of Teachers archives · Women's Library, London, National Union of Women Teachers archives
Likenesses D. Beresford, oils, repro. in *Sheffield Independent* (18 April 1911) · Haines, group photograph, repro. in *The Schoolmaster* (16 July 1910) · double portrait, photograph (with next president of NUT), repro. in *The Schoolmaster* (13 April 1912) · photograph, repro. in *Sheffield and District Who's Who*
Wealth at death £4530 2s. 2d.: probate, 12 Jan 1923, CGPLA Eng. & Wales

Cleghorn, James (1778–1838), actuary and author, was born at Duns, Berwickshire. Although lame from birth, he was for some time a farmer, but in 1811 he moved to Edinburgh where he edited the *Farmer's Magazine*. In 1817 William Blackwood appointed Cleghorn and Thomas Pringle editors of his new *Edinburgh Monthly Magazine*, which he intended should counter the views expressed in the *Edinburgh Review*. Blackwood soon realized that the articles which Cleghorn and Pringle published were in fact supporting the opinions of the *Review*, and he accordingly dismissed them within the year, after which the *Edinburgh Monthly* was transformed into *Blackwood's Magazine*, under his own editorship. Cleghorn succeeded Robert Brown as editor of the *Scots Magazine* until its closure in 1826. Cleghorn's major essay, 'The depressed state of agriculture', was published in 1822. In it, he examined the present and past effects brought about by the various corn laws, the weather, and other economic factors both at home and abroad, and their consequences for landowners and labourers. The essay received favourable reviews in the agricultural press, and the Highland Society of Scotland awarded him a piece of plate worth 50 guineas. Cleghorn also contributed the article on agriculture to the seventh edition of the *Encyclopaedia Britannica*.

Cleghorn founded the Scottish Provident Assurance Company, and was its manager. He was also actuary of the Edinburgh National Security Savings Banks, and proposer of a widows' scheme for the Faculty of Advocates. He enjoyed a high reputation as an actuary and accountant, and published several pamphlets on that topic. He died unmarried on 27 May 1838. ANITA McCONNELL

Sources J. A. Symon, *Scottish farming* (1959), 308 · *DNB* · B. W. Crombie and W. S. Douglas, *Modern Athenians: a series of original portraits of memorable citizens of Edinburgh* (1882), 178
Archives NL Scot., corresp. with Archibald Constable

Cleghorn, William (1718–1754), moral philosopher and university teacher, was probably born in Edinburgh, the son of Hugh Cleghorn (d. 1734), a brewer and burgess of Edinburgh, and his wife, Jean Hamilton. He entered Edinburgh University in 1731 and graduated MA in 1739. He was probably intended for the ministry, and must have also studied divinity. It appears that he was licensed to preach, but never held charge of a parish. In 1739 and 1740 he was tutor to Sir Henry Nisbet of Dean, who died while still a minor.

In 1742 the continued absence of the Edinburgh professor of moral philosophy, John Pringle, on war service in Flanders, led the senatus of the university to appoint Cleghorn among others to conduct his classes while he was away. Pringle finally resigned from his post on 27 March 1745, and Cleghorn was appointed to the position on 5 June, after the Edinburgh clergy exercised their right to block a rival candidate, David Hume. Family connections may have played a part in the appointment. Cleghorn's grandfather William Hamilton had been principal of the university from 1730 to 1732, and one of his uncles, Gavin Hamilton, was a member of Edinburgh town council, which controlled university appointments. Cleghorn's appointment was also a victory for the squadrone political faction over the Argathelians in their ongoing battle for control of Scotland. In addition, it is probable that Cleghorn, a Presbyterian and whig, was considered a more appropriate candidate for the post than Hume, whose religious views had already attracted suspicion, and whose political position sometimes caused him to be suspected of Jacobitism (Sher, 106, 108). Cleghorn's commitment to the whig and Presbyterian cause was amply evident in his conduct during the Jacobite rising of 1745–6. He was a member of the college company of Edinburgh, volunteers formed to defend the city, and undertook to call upon the volunteers to join Sir John Cope's forces if the defence of Edinburgh were abandoned. Soon after the conflict he is said to have published a pamphlet entitled *Address to some Gentlemen Immediately after the Rebellion*, but no copies appear to be extant. He was also a member of the Revolution Club, which was dedicated to the protestant and anti-absolutist principles of the revolution of 1688.

Cleghorn held the moral philosophy chair for the remainder of his short life. He seems to have spent all his time in Edinburgh, apart from a brief visit to Huntingdon in 1750 and a possible tour of the highlands with Adam Ferguson. He never made any published contribution to moral philosophy, but a large collection of student lecture notes is preserved in Edinburgh University Library. Examination of these notes by modern scholars suggests that his political opinions inclined to classical republicanism

and the views of Machiavelli, Harrington, and Algernon Sidney. He was a confirmed opponent of monarchical absolutism and despotism, and may have preferred republicanism to monarchy as a form of government (Nobbs, 584, 586). His general view of moral philosophy also appears to have been heavily influenced by the thought of Cicero, particularly as expressed in *De officiis* (Stewart-Robertson, 33–4). Although not a major figure in eighteenth-century Scottish political and philosophical thought, Cleghorn apparently influenced no less a figure than Ferguson, who was commended by Cleghorn on his deathbed and who later held the moral philosophy chair. In 1754 Cleghorn's declining health led him to visit Lisbon, but he was soon back in Scotland. His condition led him to resign his chair on 21 August 1754, and he died at Edinburgh, apparently unmarried, two days later, at the age of thirty-six. ALEXANDER DU TOIT

Sources D. Nobbs, 'The political ideas of William Cleghorn, Hume's academic rival', *Journal of the History of Ideas*, 26 (1965), 575–86 · R. B. Sher, 'Professors of virtue: a social history of the chair of moral philosophy at Edinburgh', *Studies in the philosophy of the Scottish Enlightenment*, ed. M. A. Stewart (1990), 87–126 · E. C. Mossner and J. V. Price, introduction, in D. Hume, *A letter from a gentleman to his friend in Edinburgh, 1745*, ed. E. C. Mossner and J. V. Price (1967), vii–xxxv · R. L. Emerson, 'The "affair" at Edinburgh and the "project" at Glasgow: the politics of Hume's attempts to become a professor', *Hume and Hume's connexions*, ed. M. A. Stewart and J. P. Wright (1994), 1–22 · M. A. Stewart, *The kirk and the infidel: an inaugural lecture at Lancaster University* (1994) · J. C. Stewart-Robertson, 'Cicero among the shadows: Scottish prelections of virtue and duty', *Rivista Critica di Storia della Filosofia*, 38 (1983), 25–49 · A. Grant, *The story of the University of Edinburgh during its first three hundred years*, 1 (1884), 277; 2 (1884), 337–8 · A. Bower, *The history of the University of Edinburgh*, 3 vols. (1817–30)
Archives U. Edin., signature and notes on lectures, Da.2.1p61; Dc.3.3.6

Clein [Cleyn], **Francis** [*formerly* Franz Klein] (d. 1658), painter and tapestry designer, was born at Rostock in Germany, possibly the son of a goldsmith, Hans Klein. Apart from date of birth and parentage, Clein's life up to 1642–3, when details seem to have been obtained from Clein himself by Thomas Fuller, was published in Fuller's *History of the Worthies of England* (1662), in the section on tapestry manufacture at Mortlake in Surrey. Fuller stated that Klein was born in Rostock; bred at the Danish court; travelled to Italy, living in Venice, where he first met Sir Henry Wotton, the English ambassador; and endeavoured to unite perfections of the Dutch and the Italians 'in this Mystery' (art: possibly tapestry design). Moreover, that from Denmark, Klein was invited to England by Charles, prince of Wales; but arriving when the prince was in Spain, was sent back by James I with a letter asking Christian IV to relinquish Klein to serve the prince. Fuller himself transcribed this letter, dated 8 July 1623, 'out of a Copy compared with the Original', publishing it in full. 'But the K. of Denmark', Fuller continued, 'detained him all that Summer' to complete some work: 'This ended, then over he comes, and settled with his Family in London', receiving a gratuity of £100 per annum paid 'until the beginning of our Civil Wars' (Fuller, *Worthies*, 77–8).

Independent evidence corroborates most of Fuller's

statements. Drawings survive inscribed by Clein 'in Rostock' (*Diana and Actaeon*; priv. coll.) and 'in Copenhagen 1617' (*Apollo and Marsyas*; Royal Print Room, Statens Museum for Kunst, Copenhagen). Sketches, some with Dutch subjects, having calculations in Netherlandish currency on the back, substantiate implied studies in the Netherlands (BM and Statens Museum for Kunst, Copenhagen). Richard Symonds, visiting Clein in the 1650s, learned that he had spent four years in Italy, which, to coincide with Wotton's appointments, must have included years between 1604 and 1612, or 1616. A portrait of Christian IV dated 1611 attributed to Clein does not date his presence in Denmark: as that painting is now accepted as a copy, the date may belong to the original. Clein's work for the Danish king is recorded in treasurer's accounts of 1617 to 1625 and includes history and ornamental painting, landscapes, portraits, various designs, and teaching one of Christian IV's illegitimate sons. Regardless of the type of work, Clein was called 'portrait painter', which makes it less strange that his two most successful pupils in England, William Dobson and Richard Gibson, painted portraits. From 1617 to 1623 Clein was paid for large allegorical oil paintings, part of a decorative scheme for the great hall in Christian IV's new palace, later called Rosenborg. Some of these paintings survive (moved to Kronborg Castle, Elsinore), including two signed by Clein and one, depicting fireworks, named in a payment of May 1619. Some paintings in the king's writing cabinet at Rosenborg, and others ascribed to Clein by Francis Beckett, have since been reassessed by Thomas Campbell and Meir Stein.

Fuller implied that Clein settled in London in late 1623: in September 1624, however, Christian IV paid Clein for two views of Copenhagen. Possibly this payment was belated, as another, dated November 1625, must have been, unless Clein sent his design for a table cover to Denmark from England, where he was by then established. In May 1625 Clein's gratuity was granted or confirmed, and he was denizened along with Philip de Maecht, director of weavers at Mortlake since 1620. In November 1625 Clein's son Francis was baptized at Mortlake. Clein's bill to Charles I for eighteen items totalling £483, headed 'March A[nn]o 1625' (not passed for payment until April 1631: £200 paid in August 1632), covered a protracted and uncertain period involving work connected with the new reign—designs for the great seal, the privy purse, and a triumphal arch—and much in London, at Inigo Jones's house, the Tower, and Somerset House where Clein worked with two assistants for seven months (PRO, E 404/153 pt 1, fols. 9, 10; E 403/1746). His ceiling and frieze in the Queen's Cabinet Room, described admiringly by Edward Norgate, date probably from about 1628–30, when Matthew Gooderick painted the more mundane components and repetitive grotesque panelling. Of the £483 bill, £130 was for copying two of Raphael's cartoons for *The Acts of the Apostles*, the subjects of Ananias and Elymas—work also possibly done in London, for these two cartoons were noted by Abraham van der Doort at Whitehall Palace in 1639, while the other five had been sent to Clein at Mortlake. Besides making faithful copies, Clein was entrusted with creating an eighth cartoon, *The Death of Sapphira*. His border designs, differing for each tapestry, in a set of Mortlake *Acts* woven for Charles I (Mobilier National, Paris) were once attributed to Van Dyck.

Charles I purchased from Sir Francis Crane at Mortlake three sets of *Hero and Leander* (one in Drottningholm, Sweden) and two of *Grotesco*, the series of *The Senses* as at Haddon Hall, Derbyshire, woven from Clein's designs of the 1620s; also, from Richard Crane, two sets of *The Horses* designed *c.*1635. The popular *Hero and Leander* series and *The Horses* were named as Clein's designs when Sir Sackville Crow was recommending tapestries to the countess of Rutland in 1670. After Charles I acquired the workshops, allotting Clein, 'nowe designer of all patternes used in the said worke', £250 per annum for himself and an assistant in June 1638 (PRO, E 351/3415), Clein adapted tapestry designs by Giulio Romano and Bernaert van Orley, adding new subjects to form the series *The Naked Boys* and *The Hunters' Chase*. Embellishing all Clein's tapestries were inventive, striking border designs, some containing cartouches with additional scenes in miniature.

Clein worked in England in various media and for several employers. He drew illustrations engraved by Salomon Savery for George Sandys's *Ovid's Metamorphosis English'd* (1632). William Sanderson wrote of painting in the German manner, in fresco, on the outer walls of houses, at Crane's Stoke Park, Northamptonshire (1630s), 'done by claine', at Carey House, Parsons Green, Middlesex, and (intended, before 1638) at Wimbledon House, Surrey (Sanderson, 24). The gallery at Hanworth, described by its owner, Sir Francis Cottington, in 1629 as by a second Titian, was thought by Vertue to be Clein's work: but this is uncertain, as is the work that Walpole assumed to be by Clein at Holland House, Kensington, both interior decoration and the design for shell-backed chairs of Italianate form. These great houses have all been destroyed. Decorative paintings from the last twenty years of Clein's life survive at Ham House, Surrey. Damaged overmantle and overdoors in the North Drawing Room are the 'fixed pictures' of 'Decline' inventoried in 1683. In tempera on paper in the Green Closet, ceiling (figures in clouds) and cove (four scenes adapted from paintings by Polidoro da Caravaggio acquired by Charles I in 1638) show Clein's expertise in this medium. Also recorded as by 'Decline' is a portrait in oils at Kingston Lacy, Dorset, of a son of Sir John Bankes with his tutor, Sir Maurice Williams, inventoried in 1659.

Much local work could be done from Clein's house at Mortlake across the road from the manufactory, by the parish church; owned by Crane, it comprised hall, parlour, kitchen, four chambers, two garrets, and a little garden plot. Five children were baptized at the church: Francis (1625), Charles (1627), John (1629), Sarah (1630), and Magdalen (1632). Burials recorded in Mortlake's erratic registers named Sarah and Ann 'Clyant', daughter and wife of Francis, on 3 October 1633; Magdalen (1634); Charles 'Cline', son of Francis and 'Mary' (1638). In records of the Dutch church, Austin Friars, Clein's wife was named Johanna Cleyn when godmother at Mortlake baptisms of 1628–30. No records of Clein's marriages are known; but his wife between 1636 and 1642 was named Anna when she stood godmother to eleven children of weavers. Clein himself was godfather to another eleven between 1628 and 1646, demonstrating his excellent relations with the tapestry makers.

Among Clein's godsons, presumably his pupil, was Josias English (1635–1705) who etched several of Clein's works including *Variae deorum ethnicorum effigies* (1654) and a now lost painting of a toper (1656). Clein's sons Francis and John, also his pupils, were praised by John Evelyn in *Sculptura* (1662) for work 'never yet exceeded by mortal men' (Evelyn, 111), seven large ink drawings (AM Oxf.) after Raphael's cartoons, dated 1640, 1645, 1646, two signed by John. In *Sculptura* Evelyn stated that both sons were dead. Vertue paid 5d. to search the register of St Paul, Covent Garden, finding the younger Francis buried on 21 October 1650. No evidence exists of a daughter, Penelope, to whom Vertue and Walpole ascribed two miniatures signed P. C. (possibly Peter Cross) dated 1677 and 1683.

In the 1640s, when Mortlake's fortunes were too low to require new tapestry designs, Clein designed and etched sets of prints—*Varii zaphori figuris animalum ornati* (1645), *Septem liberales artes* (1645), *Quinque sensuum descriptio … (grottesche)* (1646)—and several frontispieces, including one for Fuller's *A Pisgah-Sight of Palestine* (1650). Clein paid rates at Mortlake until 1648–9, and in Henrietta Street, Covent Garden, London, from 1650 to 1658. The move was possibly to be near John Ogilby, for whose lavishly illustrated publications—*Aesop's Fables* (1651), *Virgil (Eclogues, Georgics, Aeneid)* (1655)—Clein supplied many narrative and ornamental designs, most engraved by Wenceslaus Hollar and Pierre Lombart. Symonds, visiting Clein in Covent Garden, found him working on the *Virgil* at 50s. each drawing (two survive in the Ashmolean). Francis Clein had begun work on Ogilby's *Iliad* (1660) and was supervising new cartoons for Mortlake when he died. He was buried in the churchyard of St Paul, Covent Garden, London, on 23 March 1658. No will has been found. Of the many portraits recorded of him, there remains only an engraving by Thomas Chambars for Walpole's *Anecdotes of Painting* (repr. 1762, 2.127) that appears to copy a self-portrait. Clein's contemporaries rated him highly. A hyperbolical inscription, 'Il Famoss[issi]mo Pittore Francesco Clein. Miracolo dell Secolo … 1646', was noted by Vertue (Vertue, *Note books*, 1.117). Sanderson prophesied that Clein's tapestry designs 'will eternize his aged body' (Sanderson, 20); Fuller described them as 'the soul … of that Mystery' (Fuller, *Worthies*, 78). Edward Norgate praised his friend Clein for his 'soe great varietie, soe rare Invencon', 'indefatigable industry', and 'vertuous Life', 'for any to copy that ever means to be good workman or good man' (Norgate, 63).

WENDY HEFFORD

Sources Richard Symonds's notebook, BL, Egerton MS 1636, 89v. • bill headed March 1625, with warrant 13 April 1631, PRO, E 404/153 pt 1; fols. 9, 10; PSO 5/5; payment, 18 August 1632, E 403/1746 • indenture, Mortlake weavers with Charles I, PRO, E 351/3415 • survey of Limner's House, Mortlake, PRO, E 317/Surrey/37 • parish register, Mortlake, Surrey HC • Mortlake rate books, Surrey HC, MS 2397/6/1 and 2 • parish registers, St Paul, Covent Garden, 1653–, City Westm. AC, register I, pt 2 • rate books, St Paul, Covent Garden, City Westm. AC, H.1–2, H.433–9 • register of baptisms (including those at Mortlake), Dutch church, Austin Friars, GL, MS 7382 • Fuller, *Worthies*, 77–8 • E. Norgate, *Miniatura, or, The art of limning*, ed. M. Hardie (1919), 62–3 • W. Sanderson, *Graphice* (1658), 20, 24 • J. Evelyn, *Sculptura* (1662); ed. C. F. Bell (1906), 111–12 • Vertue, *Note books*, vols. 1, 2, 4 and 5 • H. Walpole, *Anecdotes of painting in England … collected by the late George Vertue, and now digested and published*, 2 (1762), 127–30 • F. R. Friis, *Samlinger til Dansk bygnings- og kunsthistorie* (1872–8), 30, 35–6 • F. Beckett, 'The painter Frantz Clein in Denmark', *Mémoires de l'Académie Royale des Sciences et des Lettres de Danemark, Section de Lettres*, 7th ser., 5/2 (1936), 1–16 • M. Stein, *Christian den Fjerdes billedverden* (1987), 21–55, 73–81, 141–7 • *Christian IV and Europe* (1988), cat. entries 98, 208, 210–11, 217–18, 295–6, 357–72, 391, 396, and ten illustrations [exhibition catalogue, nineteenth art exhibition of the Council of Europe, Denmark] • W. G. Thomson, *Tapestry weaving in England* (1914) • E. Croft-Murray and P. H. Hulton, eds., *Catalogue of British drawings*, 2 vols. (1960) • E. Croft-Murray, *Decorative painting in England, 1537–1837*, 1 (1962) • E. Hodnett, 'Francis Cleyn and John Ogilby', *Francis Barlow: first master of English book illustration* (1978), 73–88 • P. Thornton and M. Tomlin, 'Franz Cleyn at Ham House', *National Trust Studies 1980* (1979), 21–34 • D. B. Brown, *The earlier British drawings* (1982), vol. 4 of *Catalogue of the collection of drawings in the Ashmolean Museum* • T. P. Campbell, 'A consideration of the career and work of Francis Clein', MA diss., Courtauld Inst., 1987 • A. Laing, 'Sir Peter Lely and Sir Ralph Bankes', *Art and patronage in the Caroline courts: essays in honour of Sir Oliver Millar*, ed. D. Howarth (1993), 107–31 • A. Griffiths and R. A. Gerard, *The print in Stuart Britain, 1603–1689* (1998), 118–24, 172–3, 185–8 [exhibition catalogue, BM, 8 May – 20 Sept 1998]

Likenesses T. Chambars, line engraving (after self-portrait by Clein, seventeenth century), repro. in Walpole, *Anecdotes of painting*, 127

Cleland, James (1770–1840), statistician and civic administrator, was born in Glasgow on 28 January 1770 and spent his early career as a cabinet-maker in his father's firm. He was educated at the high school in Glasgow, and completed his training in London in the late 1780s. In 1791 he returned to Glasgow as his father's partner. He was a successful businessman and urban property developer, and was first appointed to civic office in 1794, when he was elected collector to the Incorporation of Wrights. In 1800 he was appointed member of the town council, and he became a bailie of Glasgow in October 1803. He was authorized to superintend the building of a new tollhouse in 1804, and in 1807 his plan for the building of a new grammar school was adopted by the city. He was convener of the Trades' House in 1809, treasurer to the city in 1812, and in 1814 was appointed superintendent of public works, a post which he held until 1834, when he was ousted from office by a post-reform administration. He was also superintendent of statute labour to the city of Glasgow between 1814 and 1818.

Cleland's flair for statistics was first revealed in a modest pamphlet of the early 1790s entitled *Tables for Showing the Price of Packing-Boxes of Sundry Dimensions and Thicknesses*, which was widely employed among tradesmen and established his interest in the standardization of weights, measures, and prices. His first substantial publication was *The Annals of Glasgow* (1816), a meticulous account of the history and conditions of the city, which illustrated the author's concern with such issues as population growth, commercial advance, and the state of the poor. On behalf of the town council, Cleland undertook in 1819 the most extensive and sophisticated local census that had ever been conducted in Britain at that time. The results were published by the city authorities in 1820 under the title *Rise and Progress of the City of Glasgow*. He was also responsible for drawing up the bills of mortality for Glasgow from 1820 to 1834. Several of Cleland's pioneering approaches to census taking and demographic statistics were adopted by British government officials for the national censuses of 1821 and 1831. His contributions to statistical enquiry received wide recognition in Britain and Europe as a result of his numerous publications, public lectures, and membership of learned societies.

As superintendent of public works, Cleland was responsible for the building of a new fruit market in 1817, a cattle market in 1818, and a number of city-owned churches, including St David's, to accommodate the growing population. He was also responsible for the redevelopment of Glasgow Green, for the construction of new bridges across the Clyde, and for the new parliamentary roads. In the mid-1820s he played a major role in the investigations that led to the introduction and monitoring of standardized weights and measures in Glasgow. James Cleland's contributions to statistical enquiry and to the advance of his native city were recognized in 1826 when the University of Glasgow conferred on him the honorary degree of LLD. He died on 14 October 1840 at Glasgow.   STANA NENADIC

Sources 'James Cleland, LLD, 1770–1840', *Glasgow Chamber of Commerce Journal* (July 1971), 289–91 · J. C. Burns, 'A memoir of Dr Cleland', *The history of the high school of Glasgow*, ed. J. C. Burns (1878), 7–16 · *Corrections and additions to the Dictionary of National Biography*, Institute of Historical Research (1966)
Archives U. Edin., New Coll. L., letters to Thomas Chalmers
Wealth at death £5955 6s. 5d.: inventory, 1841

Cleland, John (*bap.* 1710, *d.* 1789), novelist, was baptized on 24 September 1710 in Kingston upon Thames, Surrey, the first of the three children of William *Cleland (1673/4–1741) and his wife, Lucy (*d.* 1763), daughter of Samuel DuPass, a wealthy Anglicized Dutch Jewish merchant, and his wife, Dorothy. William Cleland, born in Edinburgh to an ancient Scottish family, was an army officer and then a civil servant in Scotland and England, and a friend of Alexander Pope. Lucy Cleland moved in fashionable circles and was known to Bolingbroke, Lord Chesterfield, and Horace Walpole. In January 1721 Cleland entered Westminster School, but was withdrawn for unknown reasons only two years later. From August 1728 until 1740 Cleland worked for the East India Company in Bombay, rising from foot soldier through the ranks of the civil service until recalled to London by his ailing father, who died in September 1741, a month after Cleland's arrival.

After William Cleland's death his wife was granted control of the family estate, and during the 1740s Cleland's fortunes began to decline. His protracted attempts to interest Portuguese officials in the creation of a Portuguese East India Company proved fruitless. In February 1748 he was arrested for non-payment of debts of £840, on the charges of two creditors, and detained for more than a year in the Fleet prison. Here he completed his famous erotic novel, *Memoirs of a Woman of Pleasure*, published in two instalments, in November 1748 and February 1749. He later claimed, in a conversation with Boswell, to have written most of the novel in Bombay, in his early twenties, in order to show his colleague at the East India Company, Charles Carmichael, that it was possible to write about a prostitute without using vulgar language. In this he was remarkably successful: *Memoirs of a Woman of Pleasure* is a stylistic *tour de force*, employing a dazzling variety of metaphors for parts of the body and for sexual acts, with a series of sly comic puns animating the delicately periphrastic prose.

Released from prison in March 1749, Cleland was briefly detained again in November that year, when a warrant was issued to seize the author, printer (Thomas Parker), and publishers (Ralph Griffiths and his brother Fenton Griffiths) of *Memoirs*. It seems that Fenton Griffiths was not found at the time, but the other three appeared in court, charged with producing an obscene work, and were found guilty. Cleland himself renounced the novel as 'a Book I disdain to defend, and wish, from my Soul, buried and forgot' (Foxon, *Libertine Literature*, 54). *Memoirs of a Woman of Pleasure* was withdrawn, at least officially, from circulation, and remained an illicit, although best-selling, work until the 1970s. In response to a request by Ralph Griffiths, Cleland prepared a heavily expurgated version, *Memoirs of Fanny Hill*, published in March 1750. It too, however, became the object of government prosecution, although Cleland had taken pains to make the abridgement as anodyne as possible. The prosecution seems to have been eventually dismissed or withdrawn, since Griffiths continued to advertise the abridged *Fanny Hill* openly in the *Monthly Review*. In his obituary notice in the *Gentleman's Magazine*, John Nichols claims that Cleland was 'rescued from the like temptation' of writing other obscene works by a government pension of '£100 per year, which he enjoyed to his death' (Nichols, 180).

Whatever the truth of this delightful but improbable story, Cleland experienced financial distress for the remainder of his life. Between 1749 and 1769 he was a highly productive but unsuccessful author, working in a variety of genres. He published at least two more novels—*Memoirs of a Coxcomb* (1751) and *The Woman of Honor* (1768)—as well as a collection of romances, *The Surprises of Love* (1764). *Memoirs of a Coxcomb*, which contains a scurrilous parody of Lady Mary Wortley Montagu, depicted as Lady Bell Travers, attracted much attention but was never completed. He tried his hand at play writing, hoping for support from his friend David Garrick, but neither his tragedy, *Titus Vespasian* (1755), nor his comedies, *The Ladies Subscription* (1755) and *Tombo-Chiqui, or, The American Savage* (1758), were ever produced on stage. His other writings included two verse satires, *The Times!* (1760–61), addressed to the reforming Roman emperor Titus Flavius Vespasian, who was also the subject of his tragedy; two cantankerous medical treatises, *Institutes of Health* (1761) and *Phisiological*

Reveries (1765), supporting his boast that he 'understood the nerves better than any doctor in Europe' (*Boswell Laird of Auchinleck*, ed. J. W. Reed and F. A. Pottle, 1977, 77); and three eccentric linguistic treatises (1766, 1768, 1769), exploring the Celtic roots of English words, postulating links between Welsh and Hebrew, and in one case plagiarizing an account of Sanskrit by an earlier writer. Among his miscellaneous productions were translations from French and Italian, with substantial prefaces; burlesques, such as *The Oeconomy of a Winter's Day* (1750), parodying Robert Dodsley's *The Oeconomy of Human Life*; adaptations, including a popular *Dictionary of Love* (1753) based on a French original; a history of Madame de Pompadour, mistress of Louis XV (1760); and political and critical treatises. Cleland also wrote more than thirty book reviews for the *Monthly Review*, from its foundation by Griffiths in May 1749 until 1774, and, from 1757 until 1787, more than 200 letters for the *Public Advertiser*, under the pseudonyms A Briton, A Parlementarian, and Modestus. These political squibs have long lost their currency, and as Nichols justly remarked, when Cleland 'touched politics, he touched it like a torpedo, he was cold, benumbing, and soporific' (Nichols, 180).

In his later years Cleland, repeatedly disparaged for his authorship of *Memoirs*, as well as for deistic views (despite his nominal Anglicanism), became increasingly embittered. Before his mother's death in 1763 he repeatedly denounced her for refusing to support him financially. He quarrelled with Garrick, whom he blamed for failing to produce his plays, and with Sterne, whom he accused, with some audacity, of writing pornography. Boswell described him in 1772 as 'a fine sly malcontent' and in 1778 found him at home, 'a coarse, ugly old woman for his servant', his books 'in confusion and dust'. Cleland 'had a rough cap like Rousseau, and his eyes were black and piercing' but 'there was something *genteel* in his manner amidst this oddity' (*Boswell for the Defence*, ed. W. K. Wimsatt and F. A. Pottle, 1960, 84; *Boswell in Extremes*, ed. C. McC. Weis and F. A. Pottle, 1970, 316). In 1781, Josiah Beckwith found it 'no wonder' that Cleland 'should pass under the Censure of being a Sodomite, as he now does, and in Consequence thereof Persons of Character decline visiting him, or cultivating his Acquaintance' (Merritt, 306). The rumour might have had a factual basis, or it could have evolved because of an explicitly homosexual passage in *Memoirs of a Woman of Pleasure*.

Cleland died, unmarried, at his house in Petty France, Westminster, on 23 January 1789, and was buried on 27 January in the nearby St Margaret's churchyard. In his obituary, Nichols praised Cleland's conversational powers and knowledge of modern languages, but deplored the 'poisonous contents' of the novel that 'brought a stigma on his name, which time has not obliterated' (Nichols, 180). Yet time has obliterated the stigma; *Memoirs of a Woman of Pleasure* is now the most celebrated erotic novel in English and has finally brought its author not infamy but fame.   PETER SABOR

Sources W. H. Epstein, *John Cleland: images of a life* (1974) · R. Lonsdale, 'New attributions to John Cleland', *Review of English Studies*, new ser., 30 (1979), 268–90 · J. G. Basker, '"The wages of sin": the later career of John Cleland', *Études Anglaises*, 40 (1987), 178–94 · J. Nichols, *GM*, 1st ser., 59 (1789), 180 · D. Foxon, *Libertine literature in England, 1660–1745* (1965) · W. H. Epstein, 'John Cleland', *British novelists, 1660–1800*, ed. M. C. Battestin, DLitB, 39/1 (1985), 101–12 · H. Merritt, 'A biographical note on John Cleland', *N&Q*, 226 (1981), 305–6 · J. Cleland, *Memoirs of a woman of pleasure*, ed. P. Sabor (1985) · J. Cleland, *Fanny Hill, or, Memoirs of a woman of pleasure*, ed. P. Wagner (1985) · P. Sabor, 'The censor censured: expurgating *Memoirs of a woman of pleasure*', *'Tis nature's fault: unauthorized sexuality during the Enlightenment*, ed. R. P. Maccubbin (1987), 192–201 · D. Foxon, 'The reappearance of two lost black sheep', *Book Collector*, 14 (1965), 75–6 · P. Wagner, *Eros revived: erotica of the Enlightenment in England and America* (1988)

Archives Bodl. Oxf., corresp., MS Ind. Misc. d. 3 · PRO, corresp., SP 36/111/151–152 | Morgan L., corresp., mainly with Edward Dickinson · V&A NAL, Forster Collection, corresp. with David Garrick, F. 48, F. 28

Cleland, William (1661?–1689), army officer and poet, was the son of Thomas Cleland, gamekeeper to the marquess of Douglas. His father's occupation suggests that he was born and brought up near Douglas Castle in Lanarkshire, where the marquess had his chief residence. He was educated at the university of St Andrews, where he entered St Salvator's College in 1676, and matriculated on 2 March 1677. By this date William, his brother James Cleland, and their likely brother-in-law John Haddoway, chamberlain to the marquess of Douglas, had been charged with attending conventicles. In 1678 he accompanied the Revd John Blackadder to Fife. He was present at Drumclog Moor on 1 June 1679 when John Graham of Claverhouse's attempt to disperse a conventicle ended in military victory for the covenanters commanded by Cleland, 'a youth extraordinary in warlike affairs and promising, a great philosopher, physician and divine, very sober and pious' (*Memoirs*, 107). Cleland then joined the covenanting army assembled near Hamilton and acted as one of the captains at Bothwell Bridge later that month. After the battle a proclamation was issued denouncing among others William and James Cleland and John Haddoway. Cleland escaped to Holland, and on 4 October 1680 entered Leiden University, probably studying civil law, for in 1684 he published *Disputatio juridica de probationibus*. He was present at the meeting held at Amsterdam on 17 April 1685 to concert the earl of Argyll's invasion of Scotland. He was sent to Lanarkshire and Ayrshire ahead of Argyll, and after the defeat of the rebellion he spent some time in hiding in Scotland. On 23 February 1686 he married at Cambusnethan, Lanarkshire, Margaret Steil (b. 1657) before returning to Holland.

Cleland was commissioned by the Scottish exiles to visit Scotland in advance of William of Orange's invasion in 1688. In the following year he must have been one of the minority of covenanters who at a meeting held on 29 April in Douglas church agreed to form a regiment to 'resist Popery and Prelacy' (Cowan, 143). Cleland was commissioned lieutenant-colonel of this regiment under the earl of Angus (heir to the Douglas marquessate), and later known as the Cameronians. This may explain why, according to the extreme covenanting party, Cleland was regarded as 'though once with us', yet 'afterwards a great opposer of our testimony, and a reproacher of Mr James Renwick and our faithful brethren both at home and abroad' (*DNB*). The regiment arrived too late to fight against Graham of Claverhouse (now Viscount Dundee) at the battle of Killiecrankie, but it arrived at Dunkeld on 17 August 1689 to be faced by the Jacobite forces now commanded by General Cannon. On 21 August Cleland organized his forces into defensive positions, but he 'at the beginning of the action going up and down encouraging his men, was shot in the head, and immediately died' (Crichton, 1.224). His men, however, won an important victory and prevented the rebellion from gaining further momentum. In October 1689 his brother-in-law Thomas Steil, chamberlain of Jedburgh Forest, was detailed to look after his affairs.

A collection of several poems and verses, composed upon various occasions, by Mr William Cleland, lieutenant-colonel to my Lord Angus's regiment was published in 1697. The first piece in this volume, 'Hullo, my fancie, whither wilt thou go?', was only partly authored by Cleland; the last nine stanzas were written by him as an eighteen-year-old college student. The original song had achieved popularity twenty years before his birth. Other important pieces in this volume are 'Mock poem on the expedition of the highland host who came to destroy the western shires in winter 1678', and 'Mock poem on the clergie when they met to consult about taking the test in the year 1681'.

T. F. HENDERSON, *rev.* STUART HANDLEY

Sources *The exact narrative of the conflict at Dunkeld* (1689) · J. Howie, *Faithful contendings displayed* (1780) · *Memoirs of Mr. William Veitch and George Brysson written by themselves*, ed. T. McCrie (1825) · A. Crichton, *The life and diary of Lieutenant-Colonel John Blackader* (1824) · D. Irving, *The history of Scottish poetry*, ed. J. A. Carlyle (1861) · R. Wodrow, *The history of the sufferings of the Church of Scotland, from the Restauration to the revolution*, 1 (1721) · E. Peacock, *Index to English speaking students who have graduated at Leyden University*, Index Society, 13 (1883), 20 · *IGI* · E. W. M. Balfour-Melville, ed., *An account of the proceedings of the estates in Scotland, 1689–1690*, 1, Scottish History Society, 3rd ser., 46 (1954) · *Reg. PCS*, 3rd ser., vols. 6, 11, 14 · I. B. Cowan, *The Scottish covenanters, 1660–1688* (1976)

Cleland, William (1673/4–1741), friend of Alexander Pope, was of Scottish birth and held the rank of major. He studied at Utrecht, served in Spain under Lord Rivers, and after the peace became a commissioner of customs in Scotland until 1714, and from May 1724 to July 1738 of the land tax and house duties in England. He lived in St James's Place and associated with the Scottish tory peers and Pope's circle. He was dismissed from his office (worth £500 per annum). His wife was Lucy (*d.* 1763), daughter of Samuel DuPass, a wealthy Anglicized Dutch Jewish merchant.

Cleland is known chiefly from his connection with Pope. Pope presented a portrait of himself by Jervas, and a copy of his Homer, to Cleland, with the inscription, 'Mr. Cleland, who reads all other books, will please read this from his affectionate friend, A. Pope' (Carruthers, 260). A letter, obviously written by Pope, but signed William Cleland (dated 22 December 1728 from St James's), was prefixed to the enlarged edition of *The Dunciad*. Pope may also have made use of Cleland to write a letter to Gay in

contradiction of the report that 'Timon' was intended for James Brydges, duke of Chandos.

A note by Pope on the *Dunciad* letter is the chief authority for the facts of Cleland's life; some writers at the time of its first publication, including the critic John Dennis, even denied his existence. There is no doubt of the facts mentioned, but other statements about Cleland are contradictory. He has been described as the son of Colonel W. Cleland, which is impossible, as Colonel Cleland was born about 1661. He is also said to have been the prototype of Steele's Will Honeycomb, which is improbable from a consideration of dates. Neither can he be identified with a Colonel Cleland with whom Swift dined on 31 March 1713. He and Mrs Cleland are mentioned in Swift's correspondence by Mrs Kelly and Mrs Barber as known to Swift.

In November 1730 Pope asked Lord Oxford to recommend Cleland's son Henry, who was then at Christ Church, having been elected from Westminster in 1728. Another son was John *Cleland, the novelist who was also at Westminster in 1722, and who was mentioned in his lifetime as the son of Pope's friend. His father's portrait, in the fashionable costume of the day, is said always to have hung in the son's library. Cleland died on 21 September 1741, aged sixty-seven.   [ANON.], *rev.* FREYA JOHNSTON

Sources R. Carruthers, *The life of Alexander Pope*, 2nd edn (1857) · Nichols, *Lit. anecdotes*, vol. 2 · *GM*, 1st ser., 11 (1741), 500 · *GM*, 1st ser., 59 (1789), 180 · J. Welch, *The list of the queen's scholars of St Peter's College, Westminster*, ed. [C. B. Phillimore], new edn (1852) · *The correspondence of Jonathan Swift*, ed. H. Williams, 3 (1963) · *The correspondence of Alexander Pope*, ed. G. Sherburn, 3 (1956) · A. Pope, *The Dunciad*, ed. J. Sutherland (1943), vol. 5 of *The Twickenham edition of the poems of Alexander Pope*, ed. J. Butt (1939–69)

Clemens Scottus [Clemens Scotus] (*fl. c.*814–826), grammarian, was an Irish teacher at the court of Louis the Pious (*r.* 814–40). Born presumably in Ireland in the second half of the eighth century, he joined the band of *Scotti peregrini*, Irish migrants to Francia, toward the end of Charlemagne's reign (if there is any truth to the tale relayed by Notker Balbulus in his *Gesta Karoli*) and taught at the palace school at least until 826. His pupils included boys of all social classes, among them the future emperor, Lothar, to whom he dedicated a grammar. Ratger, abbot of Fulda from 802 to 817, sent him several monks for training in Latin grammar. Clemens is mentioned in poems about the court of Louis the Pious by Theodulf of Orleans and Ermoldus Nigellus. Whether he was one of the Irishmen whose influence at the court Alcuin decried, as an older generation of scholars claimed, is uncertain. Ermoldus depicts Clemens in attendance at the baptism of the Danish king, Harold, in the year 826. After that event he disappears from view; an entry in the Würzburg necrology records his death on 29 May in an unspecified year. It is assumed that he died while on a pilgrimage to the shrine of St Kilian, the Irish founder of the monastery at Würzburg.

Clemens's literary activity is if anything fraught with greater uncertainty than his biography. His name is linked with various grammars in three ninth-century manuscripts. The attribution to him by a later hand in

Bern, Burgerbibliothek MS 123, of a grammar now known as *Donatus Ortigraphus* may be discounted at once. The evidence points more strongly in the direction of a treatise largely in the form of a florilegium on barbarisms, solecisms, and figures of speech, covering much the same ground as the third book of the celebrated *Ars maior* by the mid-fourth-century Roman grammarian Aelius Donatus. Four manuscripts, all from ninth-century France, are known: Bamberg, Staatliche Bibliothek, Msc. Class. 30, fols. 56v–70v; Leiden, Bibliotheek der Rijksuniversiteit, Bibl. Publ. Lat. MS 135, fols. 87r–93v; Leiden, Bibliotheek der Rijksuniversiteit, Vossius Lat. MS Q.33, fols. 160r–171r; Valenciennes, Bibliothèque Municipale, MS 393 (formerly 376), fols. 112v–123r. The title—*Pauca de barbarismis collecta de multis* ('A few [words] about barbarisms assembled from amongst many [sources]')—is echoed in the first line of a short poem placed at the end of the work in the Bamberg manuscript:

> Pauca tibi, Caesar, de multis, magne Hlothari,
> Iure tuus Clemens saepe legenda dedi.
> ('Your Clemens, great Lothar, has presented you with these few words from among many, for your perusal.' 'Ad Hlotharium regem', 670, poem XXIV, ll. 1–2)

The attribution of *Pauca de barbarismis* to Clemens thus seems assured.

For many decades, however, a different work has gone under Clemens's name: a grammar dealing with the eight parts of speech which draws heavily upon the *Ars Ambianensis*, among other sources, and is prefaced by an account of philosophy and its parts based on Alcuin's *De vera philosophia*. It is this grammar which was published under Clemens's name in 1928, edited by J. Tolkiehn, as *Clementis Ars grammatica*, and to which allusions to 'Clemens's grammar' in recent secondary literature refer. An overhasty interpretation of an inscription in the Bamberg manuscript is the cause of this misattribution. Two grammatical treatises precede Clemens's *Pauca de barbarismis*: the treatise on the parts of speech just mentioned and a short tract on metrical feet. The first has (sub-)titles beginning with a favourite Irish incipit, *Pauca de ...*, like the treatise on barbarisms, but lacks any attribution, while the second has no title at all. On the same line as the colophon of the first work is a heavily abbreviated inscription—C G P A HL F D HV IM—tentatively interpreted by Elias Steinmeyer (*Die althochdeutschen Glossen*, 4.539) as a dedication by Clemens to Lothar: *Clemens grammaticus principi augustissimo Hlothario filio domni Hludovici imperatoris* ('Clemens the grammarian to the most august prince Lothar, son of the emperor, lord Louis'). Despite the fact that dedicatory inscriptions normally *precede* the work to which they relate, it has been assumed that it was the foregoing work, the treatise on the parts of speech, which was by Clemens. Far more plausible, as Manitius and Barwick observed long ago, is that it was meant to precede the treatise on barbarisms, but that the brief tract on metrical feet came to intervene through one of those accidents to which medieval manuscripts are all too prone.

V. A. LAW

Sources 'Clementis ars grammatica', ed. J. Tolkien, *Philologus: Supplement*, 20/3 (1928) [whole issue] · C. Scottus, 'Ad Hlotharium regem', *Poetae Latini aevi Carolini*, ed. E. Dummler, MGH Poetae Latini Medii Aevi, 2 (Berlin, 1884), 670 · M. Manitius, *Geschichte der lateinischen Literatur des Mittelalters*, 1 (1911), 456–8 · K. Barwick, review, *Gnomon*, 6 (1930), 385–95 · *Donatus Ortigraphus: ars grammatica*, ed. J. Chittenden (Turnhout, 1982), xxv–xxix · DNB · E. von Steinmeyer and E. Sievers, *Die althochdeutschen Glossen*, 5 vols. (Berlin, 1879–1922) · Würzburg necrology

Archives Bibliothèque Municipale, Valenciennes, MS 393, fols. 112v–123r · Bibliotheek der Rijksuniversiteit, Leiden, Bibl. Publ. Lat. MS 135, fols. 87r–93v; Vossius Lat. MS Q.33, fols. 160r–171r · Staatliche Bibliothek, Bamberg, Msc. Class. 30, fols. 56v–70v

Clement (*fl.* 744–747), alleged heretic, was a cleric in Francia during the time of St Boniface (*d.* 754); he claimed to be a bishop, implying probably the status of a chorbishop or Irish-style bishop rather than governance of a diocese. Although said to have been Irish by birth, he is never called Clemens Scottus, and should not be so termed. The little that is known about him comes from a small cluster of references in Boniface's correspondence and related texts. In June 744 Pope Zacharias wrote to Boniface, largely summarizing the text of a letter (now lost) that Boniface had written to him earlier in the year about heresy and other problems; the views ascribed to one unnamed heretic are identical with those later attributed to Clement. Boniface evidently linked Clement with another 'heretic', a Frank named Adalbert who was condemned by name at the Council of Soissons in March 744: Adalbert enjoyed popular following for a cult which included the worship of crosses set up in the open and a belief in his own sanctity and ability to communicate directly with heaven. Clement, who is consistently given less space than Adalbert, was said to have had two sons by a concubine and to have claimed to be a bishop nevertheless, citing the Old Testament precedent of the Levites; he advocated a brother's marrying his deceased brother's wife, again on Old Testament authority; and he taught that Christ had released all from hell on his descent there, leaving none behind.

In October 745 a synod met in Rome under Zacharias. The synodal protocol, preserved in Boniface's letter collection, records the reading out of a letter from Boniface about Adalbert and Clement by his representative Denehard, and the synodal response. From this some additional details emerge: Boniface had deprived them of ordination and had imprisoned them; but they had not remained in penance, continuing to seduce the people. The charges of the previous year were repeated, and in addition Clement was said to preach views on predestination contrary to the Catholic faith, and to reject the authority of the canons and of the fathers Jerome, Augustine, Gregory, and Ambrose. Boniface asked for the synod to instruct the mayor of the palace, Carloman, to imprison Clement and so prevent his spreading these beliefs. This implies that Clement's field of action was the eastern part of the Frankish realm, where Boniface was to clash with other Irish clerics besides Clement.

Neither the condemnation of 744 in Francia nor the confirmation of this by the Roman synod of 745 seems to have been particularly effective, for in January 747 Zacharias wrote to Boniface asking that the cases of Adalbert and Clement be heard again, and that they be sent on to him should they continue to maintain their innocence. This is the last mention of Clement, though a canon law collection associated with Boniface's circle (Würzburg, Universitätsbibliothek, MS Mp.th.q.31) includes a number of rubrics which clearly refer to Clement's case and imply that his rejection of the fathers was coupled with a belief that it was possible to understand the Bible directly, without teachers or treatises. The clash between Boniface and Clement may exemplify a contrast between 'Roman' and 'Irish' forms of Christianity; but it is just as likely that Boniface's attack on Clement, a married cleric with heterodox views, was an indirect criticism of contemporary Frankish clerics with lax sexual practices and inadequate education. TIMOTHY REUTER

Sources M. Tangl, ed., *Die Briefe des heiligen Bonifatius und Lullus*, MGH Epistolae Selectae, 1 (Berlin, 1916) · N. Zeddies, 'Bonifatius und zwei nützliche Rebellen: die Häretiker Aldebert und Clemens', *Ordnung und Aufruhr im Mittelalter: historische und juristische Studien zur Rebellion*, ed. M. T. Fögen (Frankfurt am Main, 1995), 217–63 · J. B. Russell, 'Saint Boniface and the eccentrics', *Church History*, 33 (1964), 235–47 · J. Jarnut, 'Bonifatius und die fränkischen Reformkonzilien (743–748)', *Zeitschrift der Savigny-Stiftung für Rechtsgeschichte, Kanonistische Abteilung*, 65 (1979), 1–26 · A. Nürnberger, 'Über die Würzburger Handschrift der irischen Canonensammlung', *Archiv für katholisches Kirchenrecht*, 60 (1888), 3–84

Clement (d. **1258**), Dominican friar and bishop of Dunblane, was of Scottish, English, or, least probably, French birth. He may have been the Father Clement Rocha, who owned a manuscript now in Edinburgh; Rocha could be the Scottish name Rock. He had entered the Dominican order by the later 1220s and knew Edmund of Abingdon (to whom he wrote a tribute) before becoming bishop. He presumably studied at Paris or Oxford—he is once called master—and a sermon by Friar Clement surviving in a Dominican collection was probably by him.

The Dominican order spread slowly in England, having only five houses by 1230, when it was said to have gone to Scotland. That may be an anticipation, for no foundation is attested before 1233. The see of Dunblane, traditionally in the patronage of the earls of Strathearn, had fallen vacant in 1231–2, and on this occasion, perhaps because the only chapter was a dilatory diocesan synod, the pope was able to delegate nomination to three Scottish bishops. They chose Clement, who was consecrated by Bishop William Malveisin of St Andrews, at Stow in Wedale, on 4 September 1233. Whether he was a Scot, whence he came (Oxford or another house), and why a Dominican in general and Clement in particular was chosen, are unanswered questions. The choice of the first friar-bishop in the churches in Britain can only be called daring.

Clement found his see in a state of extreme dilapidation, and in his twenty-five years in it he probably began or built the transeptless cathedral which has lent Gothic architectural touches to many later Scottish kirks; he established a cathedral chapter after a visit to the pope in 1237, as a result of which religious houses with revenues from the diocese were persuaded to yield some of them; and he held at least two diocesan synods, in 1235 and 1239. There is no evidence of his promulgating diocesan canons, but, in the wake of the legate Otto's visit in 1239, such activity is likely. Clement contributed evidence to the dossier for the canonization of Edmund of Abingdon in 1241–2 and was one of those appointed to inquire into the saintliness of Queen Margaret, leading to her canonization about 1249; he granted indulgences to those from his diocese visiting the shrines of St Cuthbert at Durham and of St Edmund at Pontigny. And he was appointed, as Dominicans often were, as collector of taxation of the church for the Holy Land in 1247.

The diocese of Argyll, lacking a bishop from 1241, was placed in Clement's charge, as a result of which he probably persuaded the pope to commission him in 1248 to move its cathedral from Lismore to the mainland, and to secure a new bishop. This charge explains why he urged Alexander II to make an expedition to Argyll, and accompanied him there, persuading the king to endow the episcopal *mensa* of Argyll on the day of his death there, 8 July 1249. In the following years Clement was active in ecclesiastical business, but not prominent in political debates, despite which he was associated with the Comyn ascendancy of 1251–5, and, with many others, was on 20 September 1255 excluded from the council for seven years by the young Alexander III, himself prompted by Henry III. Clement died in 1258 and his death was remembered on 19 March, so it probably occurred on that day.

Clement was the first of a number of friar-bishops, usually Dominicans and usually in the less important and wealthy sees in the church in Scotland, but he stands out from the rest by the energy of his efforts to advance the organization of the church within his diocese, and in that of Argyll. His reputation as a preacher and teacher must have been more than posthumous *pietas* among his brethren, for in May 1250 a general chapter of the Dominicans at London decreed that when he died a special mass was to be said for his soul throughout the order. Whether Clement was present then or not—and he was surely at Dunfermline for the translation of St Margaret on 19 June 1250—he clearly enjoyed a reputation far wider than his domestic accomplishments alone would explain. He represents the occasional triumph of the ideal of reform of church life over the careerism which generally motivated thirteenth-century clergy. A. A. M. DUNCAN

Sources J. Dowden, *The bishops of Scotland … prior to the Reformation*, ed. J. M. Thomson (1912), 196–8 · D. E. R. Watt, *A biographical dictionary of Scottish graduates to AD 1410* (1977) · J. H. Cockburn, 'Friar Clement, OP', The society of friends of Dunblane cathedral, 7 (1956), 86–93 · W. A. Hinnebusch, *The early English Friars Preachers* (1951)
Likenesses portrait, U. Durham L., Durham dean and chapter archives, Misc. Ch. 820, 823

Clement of Llanthony. *See* Llanthony, Clement of (d. after 1169).

Clement Scotus I. *See* Clement (*fl.* 744–747).

Clement, Caesar (1561–1626), Roman Catholic priest, was born in Louvain, Brabant, the illegitimate son of Sir Thomas Clement (*fl.* 1559–1600), and was thus a grandson of the physician and exile Dr John *Clement (*d.* 1572). When very young he was sent to the English College, Douai, and in 1578 he was one of four students sent to Rome when the rest of the college removed to Rheims. He was ordained priest in the Lateran on 7 September 1586, with dispensation for illegitimacy. He left Rome for England in October 1587, but after arriving at Rheims on 1 December he instead travelled to his father in Flanders. From 1589 he received a royal pension in Flanders and in 1595 the archduke Ernest appointed him chaplain of the oratory at the court in Brussels. He visited Spain and Italy in 1598. Within the next few years he was appointed protonotary apostolic and vicar-general to the Spanish army of Flanders, with responsibility for appointing and disciplining all the regimental chaplains. His Spanish translation of Philip Numan's account of the miracles at Scherpenheuvel in Brabant was published at Brussels in 1606 as *Historia de los milagros*. In 1607 he was appointed to a canonry in the collegiate church of St Gudula in Brussels, becoming dean of the chapter in 1617.

Clement took a leading part in procuring an establishment for the English canonesses (St Monica's) at Louvain in 1609, and in 1622 donated £200 towards their church. In 1612 he had carried out a visitation of the English College, Douai, with Robert Chambers, and together they drew up new statutes for the seminary. The historian Charles Dodd possessed 'a great many original letters' from which he deduced that Clement was 'a common arbitrator' of the difficulties arising among the English exile community (Dodd, 2. 388–9). He died in Brussels on 18 August 1626 and was buried in the church of St Gudula. By his will he made bequests to many of the English houses in Flanders, including St Monica's in Louvain, the Benedictine nuns in Brussels, and the English College, Douai, as well as to relatives, friends, and the poor.   PAUL ARBLASTER

Sources G. Anstruther, *The seminary priests*, 1 (1969), 79 · T. F. Knox and others, eds., *The first and second diaries of the English College, Douay* (1878), 26, 218, 359 · E. H. Burton and T. L. Williams, eds., *The Douay College diaries, third, fourth and fifth, 1598–1654*, 1, Catholic RS, 10 (1911), 116–21 · C. Dodd [H. Tootell], *The church history of England, from the year 1500, to the year 1688*, 2 (1739), 388–9 · will, National State Archives, Brussels, fonds sint Goedele, 269, fols. 128–37 · residency licence, National State Archives, Brussels, papieren van staat en audiëntie, 1398/7 · J. A. Rombaut, *Het Verheerlyckt of Opgehelderd Brussel* (1777), 125–6 [epitaph] · H. R. Hoppe, 'Dr Caesar Clement, chaplain to the archduke Albert', *Recusant History*, 7 (1963–4), 263–4 · L. Antheunis, 'Quelques exilés anglais célèbres', *Mededelingen van de Geschied — en Oudheidkundige Kring voor Leuven en omgeving*, 1 (1961), 33–8 · A. Hamilton, ed., *The chronicle of the English Augustinian canonesses regular of the Lateran*, 1 (1904) · A. J. Loomie, *The Spanish Elizabethans* (1963), 245–6
Likenesses J. Francquart, portrait, repro. in J. Francquart, *Pompa funebris … Alberti … archiducis Austriae* (1623), pl. 5, far right
Wealth at death see will, National State Archives, Brussels, fonds sint Goedele, 269, fols. 128–37

Clement, Gregory. *See* Clements, Gregory (*bap.* 1594, *d.* 1660).

Clement, John (*d.* 1572), physician, was probably a native of Yorkshire. He was educated at John Colet's newly established St Paul's School under William Lily, and possibly for a time at Oxford. He made an early acquaintance of Sir Thomas *More, who took him into his family, made him tutor to his children, and treated him with great kindness. He accompanied More on his Flanders embassy of 1515 and appears in the discussion that introduces *Utopia*:

> John Clement, my pupil-servant, was also present at the conversation. Indeed, I do not allow him to absent himself from any talk which can be somewhat profitable, for from this young plant, seeing that it has begun to put forth green shoots in Greek and Latin literature, I expect no mean harvest some day. (More, *Utopia*, 41)

In April 1518 Clement passed into the service of Cardinal Wolsey. On learning of this, Erasmus, whom he had met while in More's household, sent him a warning not to overwork, and not to write at night if he could; if he must, he must learn to do so standing up (*Correspondence*, 5.392). He did not remain with the cardinal in person, but was sent to Oxford, where he settled at Corpus Christi College as reader in rhetoric and humanity, a post Wolsey had just created. Michaelmas 1518 saw Clement lecturing, a proud More informed Erasmus, 'to a larger audience than anyone has ever had before; it is remarkable how popular he is', even impressing Thomas Linacre with his learning (*Correspondence*, 5.215). In 1519, however, Clement devoted himself to medicine. He travelled to Louvain in Brabant, where he graduated MD on 30 March 1525. While on the continent he went to Italy, visiting Erasmus at Basel in 1522 on his way. He stayed there for several years, for some of the time working with Thomas Lupset, his successor at Oxford, on the Aldine Greek edition of Galen's works from April to August 1524.

Clement returned to England in 1525 and moved into More's old house, The Barge, in Bucklersbury, London. That year he obtained the minor court title of sewer of the chamber. In 1526 he married Margaret Giggs (1508–1570) [*see* Clement, Margaret], More's adopted daughter whom he had taught while tutor to the family. By 1528 he was receiving regular half-yearly payments of £10 from the court as a 'phisicion'; and he was one of the physicians sent by Henry VIII to Wolsey when the cardinal lay languishing at Esher in 1529. On 1 February 1528 Clement was admitted a member of the London College of Physicians. On 16 April following he became an elect, and was consiliarius from 1529 to 1531 and in 1547.

Clement was imprisoned with More in the Tower of London in 1535 for refusing to take the oath of supremacy. Margaret, his wife, was a devout Catholic who secretly took food to the priors of the Charterhouse when they were chained in the Tower for the same reason. When More was executed she was the only one of his household to attend the execution and it was she who retrieved the headless corpse for burial. Clement was released after a while and his fortunes seem to have suffered no long-term harm. His royal payments as physician continued until

1540, and in 1544 he was elected president of the College of Physicians.

Under Edward VI, Clement was less fortunate. In July 1549 he fled abroad to Louvain, where he was joined in October by his wife, and in December by his daughter Winifred (b. 1527) and her husband William Rastell, More's nephew. He remained in the colony of English religious exiles supported by Antonio Bouvisi in Louvain until 19 March 1554, when he returned to England. During Mary's reign he practised at Marshfoot in Essex, but in 1562, four years after Elizabeth's accession, he again left the country.

Clement and his family next lived for a time at Bergen, before moving to Malines where he became one of the English colony's most important members. He died at his house in Blockstraate in St John's parish, Louvain, on 1 July 1572, and was buried the next day near the high altar of the cathedral church of St Rumbold, close to his wife, who had died on 6 July 1570. In addition to Winifred, Clement had a son, Thomas, who was a godson of More, and two other daughters: Dorothy, who became a Poor Clare in 1571 at Louvain, and Margaret, who entered St Ursula's Convent there.

Clement was not a prolific writer, but he did translate several religious works from Greek into Latin, including 'The epistles of Gregory Nazianzen', 'The homilies of Nicephorus Calixtus concerning the Greek saints', and 'The epistles of Pope Celestine I to Cyril, bishop of Alexandria'. In this work he was assisted by Margaret, his wife.

PATRICK WALLIS

Sources Munk, *Roll* · M. McDonnell, ed., *The registers of St Paul's School, 1509–1748* (privately printed, London, 1977) · *The correspondence of Erasmus*, ed. and trans. R. A. B. Mynors and others, 22 vols. (1974–94) · A. W. Reed, 'John Clement and his books', *The Library*, 4th ser., 6 (1925–6), 329–39 · *The correspondence of Sir Thomas More*, ed. E. F. Rogers (1947) · St Thomas More, *Utopia*, ed. E. Surtz and J. H. Hexter (1965), vol. 4 of *The Yale edition of the complete works of St Thomas More* · R. W. Chambers, *Thomas More* (1935) · P. Gwyn, *The king's cardinal: the rise and fall of Thomas Wolsey* (1990) · *Hist. U. Oxf.* 3: *Colleg. univ.* · Wood, *Ath. Oxon.* · *DNB*

Clement [Clemmet], **Joseph** (*bap.* **1779**, *d.* **1844**), engineer, was baptized on 13 June 1779 at Great Asby, Westmorland, one of several children of Thomas Clemmet, a hand-loom weaver, and his wife, Sarah, *née* Elliotson. The village school taught him only to read and write, but he learned from his father, who had a taste for natural history and mechanics and had built himself a lathe. Joseph first worked alongside his father as a weaver, then as a slater, and devoted his spare time to metalworking skill, taking lessons from the local blacksmith and building his own lathe. On this he turned various woodwind instruments, which he also learned to play.

By 1805 Clement (it is not known when he adopted this form of his name) had decided to earn his living by engineering, and was making looms at a factory in Kirkby Stephen, moving to Foster & Sons, Carlisle, then in 1807 to Glasgow where he took drawing lessons from Peter Nicholson and became a competent draughtsman. Later he was with Leys, Masson & Co. of Aberdeen, where in 1812–

13 he found time to attend lectures in natural philosophy given by Professor Copland at Marischal College.

Having saved £100, Clement moved in 1813 to London, then the world's foremost centre for engineering. His rare combination of mechanical and drawing skills enabled him to progress rapidly to the top; from a humble beginning with Galloway at Holborn, he soon rose to be works manager for Joseph Bramah at Pimlico and by 1815 he was chief draughtsman at the leading firm of Maudslay, Son, and Field. His experience at these two renowned firms was to prove invaluable. In 1817 Clement set up his own business, specializing in technical drawing and the manufacture of high-precision machinery, working from premises behind his house at 21 Prospect Place, Southwark. Turnover was modest until in 1823 Charles Babbage employed Clement on his project to design and construct the complex 'difference engine', a large mechanical calculating device. Clement was required to build large, highly accurate machine tools, the best-known of which was his planing machine, built in 1831. According to general practice, the cost of building workshop tools was chargeable to the project but they were considered to be the property of their maker. Clement's machinery was, however, so much larger and more costly than the tools usually considered under this head that he fell out with Babbage on this score, and they eventually parted company. These tools brought him a good income for many years for customers were attracted by his skill and the quality of his products, despite his justifiable reputation for charging remarkably high prices.

Clement was an outstanding toolmaker and draughtsman. He introduced both headless and fluted screw-cutting taps and was one of those urging the adoption of a standard system of screw threads. His works was regarded as one of the best schools for practical mechanics; and perhaps the most distinguished engineer to be employed there was Joseph Whitworth. From 1815 Clement provided technical drawings for the publications of the Society for the Encouragement of Arts, and he was awarded three medals by the society for his various tools and inventions.

Clement never lost his Westmorland accent and was described by the engineering historian Samuel Smiles as 'a heavy-browed man without any polish of manner of speech' whose head was 'a complete repertory of inventions' and who liked nothing better than a 'tough job' (Smiles, 245, 257).

In his later years Clement returned to his old love of music and constructed an organ, which Smiles reported as sounding very well. He died unmarried at 31 St George's Road, Southwark on 28 February 1844. The major bequest in his will was the legacy of Bank of England stock valued at £4000 to his natural daughter Sarah Clement, daughter of Agnes Esson of Tanfield, Durham. Sarah was also to receive his gold watch and two of the medals awarded him by the Society of Arts. Other bequests went to the offspring of his four brothers and sisters, while his machine tools and the contents of his workshop, which he valued at £4000, were to be offered to his nephew Joseph, son of his sister, Barbara Wilkinson, at that price. Joseph Wilkinson did take up this offer, and he continued Clement's business, but only for a short time.

ANITA McCONNELL

Sources S. Smiles, *Industrial biography: iron-workers and tool-makers* (1863) • A. Hyman, *Charles Babbage: pioneer of the computer* (1982) • L. T. C. Rolt, *Tools for the job: a short history of machine tools* (1965) • will, proved, London, 20 March 1844, PRO, PROB 11/1944 • G. Ramsden, *Correspondence of two brothers: Edward Adolphus, eleventh duke of Somerset and Lord Webb Seymour* (1906), 306 • 'Clement', Sci. Mus., Rhys Jenkins Collection • committee of correspondence and papers, 1811–19, RSA • d. cert.
Wealth at death under £12,000: will, PRO, PROB 11/1944

Clement [Clements; *née* Giggs], **Margaret** (1508–1570), adopted daughter of Sir Thomas More, is of obscure parentage. She was described by the biographer of her daughter Margaret as having been 'a gentleman's daughter of Norfolk' (Durrant, 183); a family named Giggs lived in a building adjoining Bucklersbury in London, at first the home of Thomas *More and thereafter of the physician John *Clement (*d.* 1572) after his marriage to Margaret in 1526. In the portrait of the More family by Holbein, Margaret Giggs is described as 'cognata', a relative, so it seems to be in that capacity that she was adopted to keep More's eldest daughter, also a Margaret, company. More spotted her intelligence and piety, and she was taught in his 'school' along with his other daughters and close friends. Her teacher in Greek, for a time, was her future husband. She had a reputation for having a sense of humour, and Vives praised her Greek.

Margaret Giggs acted as More's almoner when he was lord chancellor and looked after his objects of personal piety, including his hair shirt. When More was in the Tower, Margaret lent him her 'algorism stone', a slate for calculations or, in his case, for jotting down thoughts best kept from prying eyes. Margaret was one of the few eyewitnesses to his execution and the only member of his household present. As promised, the king permitted her to recover the body for burial; she was also one of those to whom the emperor, Charles V, conveyed condolences on More's death.

By the time that Margaret Giggs married John Clement he was rapidly making his reputation as a doctor. The matrimonial home held a portrait of Thomas More, and it was full of books in Greek and Latin as well as glasses and 'earthern painted pots' with medicines inside. Margaret's first child was born in 1527 and her last (the eleventh) in 1540. Amid the rigours of childbirth Margaret found time, in May 1537, to minister to the Carthusians who were imprisoned in Newgate without trial and chained to a post without access to food or sanitation. Margaret bribed the gaoler and for a time kept them fed and clean until their very survival alerted the king to the succour they were receiving.

The Clements had to flee on the accession of Edward VI, first to Bruges and Louvain but ultimately to Malines. In the reign of Mary they made a brief return to England both to reclaim their confiscated property (carefully listed by Margaret) and to attempt to regain possession of their houses in London and Hornchurch. The reign of Elizabeth saw them in exile again and Margaret died in Malines on 6 July 1570. She was buried in the cathedral of St Rumbald. Two of her daughters entered the religious life, while her eldest married William *Rastell. Her gifts were directed to serving her family, the religious, and the poor. A drawing of her by Holbein, inscribed Mother Jak, probably for Mother Jack or John (Clement), suggests a thoughtful and rather serious woman.

MARGARET BOWKER

Sources C. S. Durrant, *A link between Flemish mystics and English martyrs* (1925) • T. Stapleton, *Life of Sir Thomas More*, trans. P. E. Hallett (1928) • A. W. Reed, 'John Clement and his books', *The Library*, 4th ser., 6 (1925–6), 329–39 • F. G. Murray, 'Feminine spirituality in the More household', *Moreana*, 7/27 (1970), 92–101 • L. M. Martz, *Thomas More: the search for the inner man* (1990) • P. Hogreve, *The Sir Thomas More circle* (1959) • R. M. Warnicke, *Women of the English Renaissance* (1983) • R. W. Chambers, *Thomas More* (1935) • Emden, *Oxf.*, 4.121
Likenesses H. Holbein, charcoal sketch, 1530, Royal Collection • H. Holbein, group portrait, oils (with More family), Kunstsammlung, Basel

Clement, William Innell (1779/80–1852), newspaper proprietor, was born probably in London, of humble parents, and received only a scanty education. However, he soon became one of the leading newsvendors in London, and in 1814 extended his press activities when he bought *The Observer*, which had been founded in 1791. Two years later he was accepting moneys from the government in return for supporting them, and for distributing free copies of the paper. Clement aimed at making *The Observer* the leading Sunday newspaper—'a seventh-day paper'; and by not printing until four o'clock on Sunday morning he was able to provide the latest news.

In 1819 Clement's deputy publisher, George Goodger, revealed that *The Observer* sold 10,850 copies on a Sunday, plus a further 2000 of its Monday print, all of which were stamped. However, he believed that 10,000 other copies, unstamped, were given away, under the pretence of being specimen copies. Postmen were each sent approximately 200 copies of the paper, and were asked to distribute them without charge. One postman said he 'was given two or three shillings for his trouble. He delivered them to the lawyers, doctors and gentlemen of the town' (Griffiths, 154). Clement himself admitted that free distribution of *The Observer*, on behalf of the government, extended to Bath and Dublin.

Apart from owning *The Observer*, Clement was by this time also the publisher of William Cobbett's *Weekly Register*, but it proved not to be a happy relationship: Cobbett, upon the suspension of the Habeas Corpus Act in 1817, fled to America and remained there until 1819. In the summer of 1820 Clement, based at 192 Strand, London, sold the property and his newsvending business to W. H. Smith, and the following year, upon James Perry's death, he bought the *Morning Chronicle* for £42,000, retaining John Black as editor. However, the purchase of the *Chronicle* was not a success, and he had been obliged to raise the greater portion of the money by bills. Through these transactions he became involved with Messrs Hurst and Robinson, upon whose bankruptcy he suffered greatly.

To make *The Observer* an even more popular and influential paper, Clement continued to spend money on the title, and he was fortunate that in Lewis Doxat he had a most successful editor-manager. Doxat, who served the paper for fifty-three years, revelled in the fact that 'he never wrote an article on any subject whatever'. During those years, Clement believed in 'a well-paid and well-informed staff', and as a result, with the use of new typography and woodcuts, the contents of the paper improved greatly—especially at the time of the Cato Street conspiracy in 1820, when circulation doubled. However, Clement overreached himself when, ignoring the express injunction of the lord chief justice who presided over the trials of the Cato Street conspirators, he 'unlawfully and contemptuously' published in *The Observer* an account of the trials of Thistlewood and Ings. Clement was fined £500 for contempt of court, but the fine was never paid.

In 1824 or 1825 Clement bought *Bell's Life in London*, which was to become the leading sporting paper and extremely prosperous; during the next twenty years he saw its circulation rise from 3000 to more than 30,000. The editor was Vincent George Dowling, who remained in charge until his death in October 1852. Dowling was also the chief reporter on *The Observer*, and in the pay of the Home Office. During those years Lord Palmerston wrote editorials for the paper in support of his foreign policy, and he paid Clement from secret service funds. At his peak, in 1828, Clement owned four major London titles: *The Observer*, the *Morning Chronicle*, *Bell's Life in London*, and *The Englishman*. But, within six years, despite support from the whigs, he was forced to sell the loss-making *Chronicle* to Sir John Easthope for an estimated £16,500. William Clement remained in charge of *The Observer* until his sudden death from apoplexy at Hackney, Middlesex, on 24 January 1852. He was buried at Kensal Green cemetery on 31 January.   D. M. GRIFFITHS

Sources D. Griffiths, ed., *The encyclopedia of the British press, 1422–1992* (1992) · J. Anstey and J. Silverlight, *The Observer observed* (1991) · C. Wilson, *First with the news: the history of W. H. Smith, 1792–1972* (1985) · *DNB* · A. Aspinall, *Politics and the press, c.1780–1850* (1949) · Boase, *Mod. Eng. biog.* · d. cert.
Likenesses two portraits, The Observer Newspaper, London

Clementi, Sir Cecil (1875–1947), colonial governor, was born on 1 September 1875 at Cawnpore in India, the eldest child of Colonel Montagu Clementi (1839–1919), judge advocate-general in India, and his wife, Isabel Collard (1850–1930). He was educated at St Paul's School in London and at Magdalen College, Oxford, where he was elected a demy. Studying classics and Sanskrit, he received a first class in classical moderations in 1896, the Boden Sanskrit scholarship in 1897, a second class in *literae humaniores* in 1898, and the chancellor's Latin essay prize in 1899.

In 1899 Clementi came fourth in the competitive examination for posts in the home, India or colonial civil service and selected Hong Kong as his first choice. He was appointed a Hong Kong cadet that year and on arrival in Hong Kong was sent up to Canton (Guangzhou) to learn Cantonese. Unrest on the Chinese mainland resulted in his return to Hong Kong in July 1900. He was to spend the

Sir Cecil Clementi (1875–1947), by Walter Stoneman, 1931

next twelve years working in the administration there, with the exception of two secondments, to India in 1902 and to Kwangsi (Guangxi) province in 1903. From 1903 to 1906 he had the arduous task of registering land titles in the New Territories in Hong Kong. On 16 April 1912 he married (Marie) Penelope Rose Cobbold Eyres (1889–1970), the beautiful daughter of an admiral based in Hong Kong. They had four children; Clementi adored Penelope, and she was a constant support throughout his career.

Clementi was sent to British Guiana as colonial secretary in 1913. He remained there until 1922, administering the government on three occasions during his tenure. From there, he was posted to Ceylon as colonial secretary and also administered the government once. In October 1925 he was appointed governor of Hong Kong, only the second cadet to achieve this position. The colony was at that point in a state of extreme civil unrest. A general strike and boycott was paralysing the colony's trade and relations between Hong Kong and China had rarely been worse. Clementi immediately instigated informal talks with the authorities in Canton. His negotiating stance was stern but open and within a year the boycott was over and diplomatic relations repaired. Overcoming the major physical and economic threats from China throughout 1925 and 1926 was an undoubted victory for Clementi. An extremely active governor, he also introduced effective measures to counteract further communist penetration of the unions and brought in important public health, factory, and employment legislation. He also took steps to improve Hong Kong's water supplies following the severe drought of 1928–9. Other achievements during his tenure included the nomination of the first Chinese member to the executive council and improving the balance in the annual budget. Clementi's major disappointment in Hong Kong was his lack of success in persuading the London government to extend land leases in the New Territories beyond 1997. In 1930 Britain returned Weihaiwei in north China to the Chinese and Clementi argued that this rendition should have been used as a bargaining counter to secure Hong Kong for Britain beyond 1997.

In 1930 Clementi was transferred to the governorship of the Straits Settlements following the sudden retirement of the previous incumbent on health grounds. The post, which incorporated the duties of high commissioner of the Malay states, was one of the most important in the empire. The administrative organization he inherited was complex and unwieldy and he decentralized the administration whenever possible in moves he hoped would eventually defederalize the states. He also introduced administrative posts for members of the indigenous population and supported Malayan culture and language in his reorganization of the education system. Many of these moves were unpopular with the Chinese and Malay populations and at times, notably in his educational and administrative reforms, Clementi was forced to compromise. With hindsight, his undiluted reforms would probably have been the better option for the region. In Singapore he developed diabetes and as a result was forced to retire in 1934, his work in the area unfinished.

Clementi was tall and slim and it was the opinion of his peers that he was both hard-working and extremely intelligent. Despite his sometimes controversial approach to colonial administration and his propensity for giving notice of his gubernatorial actions retrospectively to London, he was highly rated within the Colonial Office. He was appointed CMG in 1916, KCMG in 1926, and GCMG in 1931 for his services. A fine negotiator who was charming in private, he preferred academic pursuits to parties and found great joy in travelling. He travelled to all of the Chinese provinces and took every opportunity to explore the countries in which he worked. His twin beliefs of equality of opportunity and education determined many of his actions as a governor. A scholar who was fluent in several Chinese dialects, his translations of Chinese love poems are charmingly phrased. His two publications on British Guiana remain important sources of information on the area.

Clementi was closely associated with the foundation of the University of Hong Kong and was chancellor from 1925 to 1930. He was awarded an honorary LLD by the institution in 1926. His support included writing the anthem (in Latin verse) for the university in 1912, gifting an important collection of Chinese books, and raising funds for the study of Anglo-Chinese cultural relationships. He spent his retirement in Britain writing and studying. He died of heart failure at Holmer Court, Holmer Green, near High Wycombe, on 5 April 1947; his ashes were buried in Penn Street church, Buckinghamshire.

A creative administrator in the Straits Settlements and one of Hong Kong's most distinguished governors, a reassessment of Clementi's historical importance during the height of British imperialism is long overdue. In his own lifetime he was acknowledged as one of Britain's brightest and most able colonial officers. However, his proposals for reforms in Hong Kong and the Straits Settlements frequently caused conflict with the local populations. Many of his ideas on equality and education were decades ahead of colonial policy but his interventionist tendencies have been criticized by historians writing since his death.   SHIONA M. AIRLIE

Sources PRO, CO 129 · A. L. Mills, *British rule in eastern Asia: a study of contemporary government and economic development in British Malaya and Hong Kong* (1942) · N. Miners, *Hong Kong under imperial rule* (1987) · J. Keay, *Last post: the end of the empire in the Far East* (1997) · *DNB* · George Watson's College, Edinburgh, Stewart Lockhart collection · matriculations and admissions register, 1891–1900, Magd. Oxf. · A. Abbas, *Hong Kong: culture and the politics of disappearance* (1997) · B. Harrison, ed., *University of Hong Kong: the first 50 years, 1911–1961* (1962) · H. Lethbridge, *Hong Kong: stability and change* (1978) · private information (2004) [family] · *CGPLA Eng. & Wales* (1947) · d. cert. · S. Airlie, *Reginald Johnston, Chinese mandarin* (2000)
Archives Bodl. RH, papers incl. reports and diary letters relating to services in Hong Kong · Bodl. RH, papers as governor of Malaya · NL Scot., letters · PRO, CO 129 | Bodl. RH, corresp. with Sir Matthew Nathan
Likenesses W. Stoneman, photographs, 1931, NPG [*see illus.*] · A. Schuster, oils, University of Hong Kong · photograph, George Watson's College, Edinburgh, Stewart Lockhart collection
Wealth at death £3983 19s. 2d.: probate, 9 Sept 1947, *CGPLA Eng. & Wales*

Clementi, Muzio (1752–1832), composer, pianist, and teacher, was born on 23 January 1752 in Damaso, Rome, the eldest of seven children of Nicolo Clementi (1720–1789), a silversmith, and his wife, Magdalena, *née* Kaiser (d. 1785). He received the standard musical training of a church organist from various teachers in Rome, and became organist in his local church at thirteen. His playing attracted the attention of Peter Beckford (1740–1811), cousin of the novelist William Beckford (1759–1844), who in 1766 contracted with Clementi's father to 'buy' his son's services for seven years, taking him back to his country estate in Dorset. Though isolated from the mainstream of musical life, Clementi laid important foundations for his future career as a musician and virtuoso, spending hours at the harpsichord and studying scores by older composers such as Handel, Domenico Scarlatti, J. S. Bach, and C. P. E. Bach. He dedicated his first set of six sonatas, op. 1, to Beckford.

Leaving Beckford's service in 1774, Clementi travelled to London. Although he published a set of bravura variations, *The Black Joke*, as 'M. C.' in 1777, he made his reputation as a virtuoso with the publication of his op. 2 sonatas in 1779. Typically, this was a set of six sonatas, three to be accompanied by a violin or flute, and the remainder for piano solo. The second, which became well known as 'the celebrated octave lesson', epitomized the virtuosic style that became associated with Clementi. At this time the piano was still in its infancy and had not yet supplanted the harpsichord. As the piano developed, so did

Muzio Clementi (1752–1832), by Henry R. Cook, pubd 1833 (after James Lonsdale, exh. RA 1817)

Clementi's style, and he gradually blended his bravura writing with a more expressive style, eminently suited to the piano.

Clementi went on the first of his continental travels in 1780, performing in Paris and in Vienna, where he took part in the famous 'competition' against Mozart, who acknowledged but derided his virtuosity in a now famous letter to his father. Paradoxically, Clementi's sonatas opp. 7–10, written at this time, mark a turning away from empty virtuosity and reveal more depth in his musical style. After returning to London he was noted by 1785 not just as a performer but also as a composer: his symphonies were performed in 1786 and 1787, but they could not stand comparison with those of his famous contemporary Haydn. He conducted his own symphonies until 1796, but made his last concert appearance as a pianist in 1790, after which he turned instead to teaching. This appeared to be a reasonably lucrative pursuit, and Clementi attracted good pupils, including J. B. Cramer, John Field, and Theresa Jansen. The 1790s were a period of prolific composition of solo and accompanied sonatas as well as sonatinas for younger players; the latter are still played and enjoyed. Clementi's pedagogical interests of this time are also reflected in his *Introduction to the Art of Piano Playing* (1801), which is as interesting for its selection of 'lessons' by a variety of composers as it is as a guide to contemporary pianism.

Clementi was as much a businessman as a musician, being involved with music publishing and piano manufacture. In 1798 he took over the firm Longman and Broderip with a partner, James Longman, who left in 1801, when Clementi took over with several partners at 26 Cheapside; additional premises were acquired in 1806 at 195 Tottenham Court Road.

Clementi travelled extensively from 1802 to 1810, penetrating as far as eastern Europe and St Petersburg in order to sell his instruments and to court various composers for their compositions. Accompanying him was Field, whom he took first to Vienna in 1802, and then to St Petersburg, where Field remained. During this time Clementi attracted other pupils, notably Alexander Klengel and Ludwig Berger. Clementi's letters to his chief partner, Frederick William Collard, reveal an astute businessman who nevertheless seemed in constant need of money. Keenly conscious of competition from other London makers such as Broadwood and Tomkison, he bullied his way from dealer to dealer, venting his frustration at his partners' occasional mistakes by quoting Virgil—'let us not *renovare dolorem*' (Clementi to Collard, 17 Aug 1803)—and generally adopting a hectoring tone. The letters reveal a keen, highly literate man, with a flair for languages and with a certain dry humour. It was probably due to Clementi's considerable acumen that the firm remained successful even after a disastrous fire in 1807.

Letters of this period reflect the frenetic pace of Clementi's life. While in Berlin on 18 September 1804 he married Caroline Lehmann, the eighteen-year-old daughter of a noted Berlin musician. The marriage ended tragically less than a year later when she died shortly after giving birth to a son, Carl. Clementi wrote of his 'fatal and irreparable loss … God alone can give me strength to bear it' (Clementi to Collard, 31 Aug 1805). Throwing himself into his business, he announced in a letter of April 1807 his conquest of 'that haughty Beauty, Beethoven', who agreed to let him publish several of his works, though the arrangement was bedevilled by communication problems between the composer and the firm. After returning to London in the summer of 1810, Clementi swiftly made amends for whatever mistakes had occurred, issuing first editions of ten works.

Clementi married Emma Gisborne (*bap.* 1785), a contemporary of his first wife, on 6 July 1811; they had four children. In 1813 he was invited to become a director of the newly formed Philharmonic Society, which offered a forum for the performance of his own symphonies. In December 1814 he was elected to the Swedish Royal Academy of Music. His public success in England prompted him to set off again for the continent, this time to promote his own symphonies in Paris and in Leipzig.

Clementi's most important work of this period, and indeed of his life, was the aptly named *Gradus ad Parnassum*. Far more than just a collection of exercises for the piano, the three-volume *Gradus* encompasses a variety of genres and styles of keyboard composition; it is a vast compendium of Clementi's works for the piano written over many years, and published between 1817 and 1826. It is a monument to a composer who was called 'the father of the pianoforte'; though he was not the first composer to write for the piano, his contribution to its development was inestimable. Indefatigable to the end, he retired to

Lichfield in 1830, and died in Evesham, possibly at Elm Lodge, on 10 March 1832. He was buried with full honours in the cloisters of Westminster Abbey on 29 March.

DOROTHY DE VAL

Sources L. Plantinga, *Clementi: his life and music* (1977) · *Quarterly Musical Magazine and Review*, 2 (1820), 308–16 · 'Memoir of Muzio Clementi', *The Harmonicon*, 9 (1831), 183–6 · M. Unger, *Muzio Clementis Leben* (1914) · M. Clementi, *Works for pianoforte solo*, ed. N. Temperley, 5 vols. (1984–7) · A. Tyson, *Thematic catalogue of the works of Muzio Clementi* (1967) · D. de Val, '*Gradus ad Parnassum*: the pianoforte in London, 1770–1820', PhD diss., U. Lond., 1991 · letters from Clementi to Collard, 1801–8, and balance sheets of the firm of Clementi & Co., 1811, priv. coll. · J. S. Shedlock, 'Clementi correspondence', *Monthly Musical Record*, 32 (1902), 140–44 · J. S. Shedlock, 'Muzio Clementi', *Monthly Musical Record*, 24 (1894), 171–3 · *Mendelssohn and his friends in Kensington: letters from Fanny and Sophy Horsley, written 1833–36*, ed. R. B. Gotch (1934)
Archives Archivio Vaticano | Yale U., Wiltshire MSS
Likenesses H. R. Cook, engraving (after J. Lonsdale, exh. RA 1817), NPG; repro. in W. Jerdan, *National portrait gallery* (1833) [*see illus.*] · E. Hader, portrait; copy, photograph, Yale U., Institute of Sacred Music · D. Orme, engraving, Yale U., Institute of Sacred Music

Clementina [Maria Clementina Stuart, *née* Sobieska] (1702–1735), consort of James Francis Edward, Jacobite claimant to the English, Scottish, and Irish thrones, was born Maria Clementina on 18 July 1702. She was the third and youngest daughter of James Sobieski, prince of Poland, and his wife, Hedwig Elizabeth of Neuberg. Clementina's grandfather was the Polish hero-king John III, who turned the Turks back at the gates of Vienna in 1683, but the Polish crown was not hereditary and her father failed to be elected king on John's death. However, James retained powerful royal connections through his wife, whose sisters were Holy Roman empress and queen of Spain, and Clementina's sisters in turn married well; the elder, Casimira, was betrothed to James Francis Edward's cousin, the duke of Modena, while Charlotte married the powerful duc de Bouillon, great chamberlain of France and regular drinking and gambling partner of Louis XV.

To the alarm of many Jacobites, by 1718 *James Francis Edward (1688–1766) had reached the age of thirty without wife or heir, and had been rejected by the daughter of the duke of Modena. Finding a bride would be a delicate task, partly because he was a king without a throne, but also because the government in London was expected to put every obstacle in the way of a Stuart marriage. James ordered Charles Wogan, a passionately loyal Irish adventurer, to scour the courts of central Europe in search of a suitable bride, adding as an afterthought that he should enquire about the Sobieski prince's daughters 'if they fall in your way or be not much out of it' (*Stuart Papers*, 5.284–5). Wogan found the princesses at Ohlau, and was enchanted with the youngest, sixteen-year-old Clementina, who was pious and beautiful, with large glowing eyes, brown hair, and a passionate desire to become queen of Britain one day. The pope was her godfather and she would bring a large dowry. James proposed at once and was accepted.

George I prevailed upon the holy Roman emperor to

Clementina [Maria Clementina Stuart] (1702–1735), by Francesco Trevisani

arrest Clementina as she travelled through Austria on her way to Italy, and the young princess was detained in the Schloss Ambras at Innsbruck during winter 1718–19. Wogan again came to James's rescue by spiriting his bride out of the castle disguised as a maid, and after a nightmare journey over the snowbound Brenner Pass, Clementina reached Bologna in April 1719. No bridegroom awaited her; James had departed for Spain to lead what became another ill-fated Jacobite rising, but had left instructions for a proxy marriage ceremony to be performed as soon as his bride arrived. Following this ceremony on 9 May, Clementina continued her journey to Rome, where she was fêted as the British queen. Four months later, after the failure of the 1719 rising, Clementina met her husband for the first time on 2 September at Montefiascone, and on the same day a second marriage ceremony took place in the cathedral there. Clementina and James settled in the Palazzo Muti, a small palace in Rome which the pope made over to them, and here, to the great joy of the Jacobite world, their first child, *Charles Edward, was born on the last day of the year 1720. A second son, *Henry Benedict, followed five years later on 6 March 1725.

Clementina's happiness was short-lived; even before the birth of Charles it was becoming evident that the marriage was not the success she or Jacobite followers had hoped for. James was twelve years older than his wife, and his 'dour, stoical, pragmatic approach to life failed to strike a chord in her romantic soul' (McLynn, 13). The drab Palazzo Muti offered none of the fun of her father's court at Ohlau, while her husband closeted himself away, writing endless letters and plotting to regain his crown. With a mounting sense of exclusion, it soon became evident to Clementina, that while she might be called queen of Britain in Rome, she would never reign in that country.

The peace of the Muti was broken by frequent quarrels, which led to tantrums on the part of Clementina and cold withdrawal by James. According to John Hay (later Jacobite earl of Inverness): 'Their tempers are so very different that, although they are never of the same opinion on the smallest trifles, the one will not yield an inch to the other … which must end in something very dismal' (Hay to earl of Mar, 21 April 1722, Stuart papers, 64/93). They argued fiercely whenever they were together, yet missed one another when apart. Clementina wrote on the last day of July 1722:

> I am trying now to overcome my bad temper so as to appear to you in the future as the best girl in the world … I shall know no rest or quietude until I am in the arms of my Carissimo.   (ibid., 61/64)

Ever solicitous of his wife's feelings, James intercepted correspondence from Ohlau to cushion the blow when her mother was dying, and he diverted her by taking her to watch the palio and visit religious houses at Bologna and Lucca.

Charles Edward's development towards boyhood introduced more serious causes for dissent. Both parents were utterly devoted to him, but for different reasons: Clementina to compensate for her husband's neglect, and James because the child was heir to his royal line. Protestant nurses were appointed to care for the child, but the earl of Mar proposed Mrs Sheldon, a Roman Catholic, as governess. Clementina, now lonely and miserable, fell under the influence of this domineering woman, who inflamed new quarrels over the child's education. Sheldon resented every protestant at court and spread rumours that James was having an affair with Hay's wife. Gossip, encouraged by Hanoverian spies, suggested that Charles was a sickly child and that Clementina could never bear a second child. According to rumours, Pope Clement XII was 'commonly supposed' to be her lover (*The Complete Letters of Lady Mary Wortley Montagu*, ed. R. Halsband, 3 vols., 1965–7, 2.228).

As the young prince grew up he became aware of his father's cold withdrawals from family life and his mother's tantrums. As early as the age of three he could be wilful and disobedient, mortifying the court once by refusing to kneel when presented to Pope Benedict XIII. In November 1725 James decided the boy needed a firmer hand, so he took him away from Mrs Sheldon and female nurses and handed him over to male governors, first Andrew Michael Ramsay and later James Murray of Stormont, with Thomas Sheridan as under-governor. Although it has generally been assumed that this was done simply because James wanted a stronger masculine influence around his son, it has been suggested that in the eighteenth century there was a fear among aristocratic parents that children left in the care of females might be sexually molested (McLynn, 13). The truth may lie somewhere in between, and apart from personal dislike of Mrs Sheldon, James was certainly blinkered by a lack of understanding of women. The appointment of Murray and Sheridan could not have come at a worse time, since in March Clementina had proved the gossips wrong by giving the Stuarts a second prince, Henry Benedict. By now, however, she was suffering from some form of hysteria, in all probability post-puerperal depression (State papers, Italian States, quoted in McLynn, 14). Abetted by Mrs Sheldon, Clementina may have seen this thrusting of her firstborn into the charge of so many men as an attempt to cut her off from her beloved Charles.

Clementina now prayed and brooded by turns, storming at her husband that he must get rid of Hay and his wife, as well as Murray, and Winifred, countess of Nithsdale, who had been given charge of Prince Henry. James refused, and dismissed Mrs Sheldon. On 15 November 1725 Clementina drove out of the palace with Sheldon and her other ladies and sought sanctuary in the convent of St Cecilia, where she poured out her marital woes to the nuns. The pope, fearing the Stuarts might abandon the Roman Catholic faith to regain their throne, took Clementina's part and reduced James's allowance. While Clementina wrote 'wronged wife' letters to the king of France and the queen of Spain, her husband wrote to his wife's relatives, at one stage suggesting to her father that she should be sent back to Ohlau (James Francis Edward to Prince James Sobieski, 16 Nov 1725, Stuart papers, 87/81). He visited her at the convent, but no reconciliation resulted, and neither talked afterwards of what was discussed. The quarrel turned into a grim internecine war which left supporters of the movement in Britain and throughout Europe greatly demoralized. By playing on the pope's fear that Prince Charles might abandon his Roman Catholic faith, Cardinal Giulio Alberoni, outwardly Jacobite but in the pay of London, ensured that Clementina remained in the convent and reconciliation proved next to impossible. While James blamed his old enemy, the earl of Mar, Clementina railed against the Dunbar–Hay clique, who were hated even by fellow protestant Jacobites. All this dissent caused irreparable damage to James's cause.

Although the Hays left James's service in spring 1727, Clementina still refused to leave the convent, and in June, when George I died, her husband set out for France to seek help from Louis XV to mount an invasion of Britain. With tragic mistiming Clementina chose that moment to leave the convent and join her sons at Bologna. She had been separated from husband and children for two years, but now poured out her love to her boys only to abandon them again for long periods to go on pilgrimages. She refused to join James at Avignon, nor would she be reconciled on his return to Italy early in 1728, and she continued to keep Mrs Sheldon at her side. In despair James told Hay:

> She leads a singular life … and when she is not at Church or at Table, is locked up in her room and sees no mortal but her maids or so; she eats meat this Lent, but fasts to the degree that I believe no married woman that pretends to have

children ever did; I am very little with her. I let her do what she will.   (James to Hay, 7 Feb 1728, Stuart papers, 114/16)

Clementina spent her time fasting and kneeling in prayer in cold, damp churches for such long periods that her health became damaged permanently, and she refused to accompany her family to Albano that summer. Now a deeply pious recluse, she no longer ate with her family, but kept her own little table, where James watched helplessly as she toyed with her food and grew weaker. She also suffered from asthma and manic depression as well as some allergy condition (see correspondence in *The Scotsman*, 15, 22, 26 April 1988, and H. Douglas, *The Private Passions of Bonnie Prince Charlie*, 1998, 45–6). Her health deteriorated alarmingly.

During 1728 Clementina again fell pregnant but, hardly surprisingly, lost the child. There were rumours of other pregnancies, but the plain fact is that the couple rarely slept together and James lived much of the time at Albano while Clementina remained in Rome. She still showed great love for her children, however. When Charles was sent off to gain military experience with the Spanish army then besieging Gaeta in southern Italy in 1734, she became terrified for his safety and rushed off to church to pray for him. By the end of that year, when the prince attained his fourteenth birthday, it was evident that his mother was dying. Although it is difficult to diagnose at this distance in time and without fuller detail of her medical condition, she now was almost certainly suffering from some form of lung disease, probably tuberculosis. On 12 January 1735 Clementina received the last rites of the church, but remained perfectly lucid and asked to see her sons to plead with them never to abandon their Roman Catholicism for all the kingdoms in the world. On 18 January 1735 she died at the Palazzo Muti, Rome, and was laid to rest in St Peter's.

Historians have expressed the view that Clementina was quite unfitted to be the wife of an exile such as James, and Sir Charles Petrie goes so far as to say that, had the Pretender been restored to the throne during her lifetime, she must of necessity have become as much his evil genius as Henrietta Maria had been of his grandfather, and more than Mary of Modena had been of his father. As it was, Petrie claimed, she exercised no influence upon the course of the Jacobite movement. That verdict cannot be sustained: the conduct of Clementina and inept response of her husband caused irreparable damage to the Jacobites at a time when their cause was already at a low ebb. As for her son, those frequent withdrawals of a mother's love and abandonment during his formative years lay at the root of Charles Edward's inability to establish lasting stable relationships with men or women; this later played an important part in the failure of the Jacobite cause which he came in time to lead.   HUGH DOUGLAS

Sources C. Wogan, *Narrative of the detention, liberation and marriage of Maria Clementina Sobieska styled queen of Great Britain, etc.*, ed. J. Gilbert (1894) • Royal Arch., Stuart papers, 61/64; 64/93; 87/81; 114/16 • P. Miller, *A wife for the pretender* (1965) • P. Miller, *James* (1972) • L. Frati, *Maria Clementina Sobieska in Italia* (1908) • F. J. McLynn,

Charles Edward Stuart: a tragedy in many acts (1988) • C. Petrie, *The Jacobite movement* (1932) • *Memorial of the chevalier de St George on the Princess Sobieska's retiring into a nunnery* (1726) • H. Tayler, ed., *Jacobite epilogue* (1941) • H. Tayler, ed., *The Jacobite court at Rome in 1719*, Scottish History Society, 3rd ser., 31 (1938)

Likenesses O. Hamerani, bronze medal, 1719, NPG • oils, *c*.1719, Scot. NPG • oils, *c*.1719, NPG • attrib. G. Pesci, oils on copper, *c*.1721, Bodl. Oxf. • G. Pesci, double portrait, oils, *c*.1722 (with her son), Stanford Hall, Leicestershire • oils, *c*.1722, Lennoxlove, Lothian region; version, Versailles • F. Chereau, line engraving (after F. Trevisani), BM • A. David, oil type, LPL • P. Drevet, line engraving (after A. David), BM • A. Masucci, group portrait, oils (*Solemnization of marriage of James Francis Stuart and Maria Clementina Sobieska at Montefiascone, September 1719*), Scot. NPG • A. Miller, mezzotint (after F. Trevisani), BM • F. Trevisani, oils, Prado, Madrid; on loan to Spanish Embassy, Lima, Peru [*see illus.*] • by or after F. Trevisani, oils, Scot. NPG • enamel, Scot. NPG • medals, Scot. NPG • oils (after L. G. Blanchet), Scot. NPG

Clements, Gregory (*bap.* **1594**, *d.* **1660**), politician and regicide, was baptized at St Andrew's, Plymouth, on 21 November 1594, the son of John Clement, a local merchant who became mayor of the town in 1614, and his wife, Judith Sparke. Clements's formal education may have been minimal and he followed his father into trade, but although he 'had no good elocution, yet [he] was of a good apprehension and judgement' (Ludlow, 245). By 1616 he was a factor for the East India Company; he subsequently worked in India, where he remained, on a salary of £100, until he was dismissed in 1630, having been fined for engaging in illegal interloping trade. After his return to England and his marriage to Christian Barter at St Dunstan and All Saints, Stepney, on 25 June 1630, Clements emerged as a prominent 'new merchant' alongside Maurice Thompson, trading with the New England colonies. Although their interloping was controversial, they secured royal letters of reprisal for the loss of ships to Dunkirk privateers and Spanish ships in 1637. By the late 1630s Clements was a well-established merchant figure, and lived in a substantial property in the parish of St George's, Botolph Lane. Ludlow later estimated that his fortune may have peaked at £40,000.

Clements supported the parliamentarian cause during the 1640s, although his service was financial rather than administrative or military in nature. In June 1642 he joined a mercantile consortium which offered ships to help deal with the Irish rising, and he subsequently invested almost £10,000 in the Irish adventure, entitling him to some 13,500 acres of land, eventually drawn in King's county. He and Thompson also lent substantial sums to the Adventurers Committee for goods and artillery, although it remains unclear whether Clements ever recovered the £2000 which he provided. By 1647 Clements was also one of the backers of the colonial venture in the Bahamas.

Clements was returned to parliament in July 1648 as recruiter MP for Fowey in Cornwall, having sought to exploit the influence of a kinsman, John Rashleigh, who had been ejected from the seat for royalism. He made no recorded appearance in the Commons before Pride's

Purge (6 December 1648), but thereafter he took his dissent from the vote of 5 December, indicating his opposition to further negotiations with Charles I, and was named to a number of important standing committees, including the army committee, the committee for compounding, and the committee for plundered ministers. Having been appointed to the high court of justice for the trial of the king, Clements attended all four sessions, although he was less assiduous in attending the meetings of the commissioners in the painted chamber. He signed the death warrant, although the circumstances are obscure, since his signature was placed over one of the erased names [see also Regicides]. During the Rump he was active in the house on matters which reflected his own personal interests and expertise: Ireland; trade and the colonies; relations with the City of London; and the sale of crown, church, and delinquents' lands. Clements himself acquired property in Greenwich, and paid over £8000 for the manor of Potterne, Wiltshire, formerly owned by the bishopric of Salisbury. By early 1652, however, he had probably aroused the hostility of radicals, who seized an opportunity to orchestrate his removal from the house. Information was submitted against Clements in February 1652 and following a protracted investigation he was discharged from the house on 11 May for carriage 'offensive and scandalous', which apparently related to improper sexual relations with a maidservant. Clements withdrew from public life thereafter, although he continued to seek repayment of money loaned in relation to Irish affairs for the remainder of the 1650s.

As a regicide Clements faced arrest in 1660 and went into hiding in a 'mean house in Purple Lane near Gray's Inn', although he was quickly discovered. Although not recognized by the searchers, a blind man happened to identify his voice, which was 'somewhat remarkable' (Ludlow, 154). He was dispatched to the Tower and excepted from pardon. At his indictment in October 1660 Clements pleaded not guilty, but later changed this plea at the importuning of his family in the hope of saving his estate, if not his life. He was executed at Charing Cross on 17 October 1660; accounts vary widely as to his demeanour on the scaffold.   J. T. PEACEY

Sources JHC, 6–7 (1648–59) · CSP dom., 1636–62 · C. H. Firth and R. S. Rait, eds., Acts and ordinances of the interregnum, 1642–1660, 3 vols. (1911) · R. Brenner, Merchants and revolution: commercial change, political conflict, and London's overseas traders, 1550–1653 (1993) · CSP col., vols. 4, 6–7 · State trials, vol. 5 · E. Ludlow, A voyce from the watch tower, ed. A. B. Worden, CS, 4th ser., 21 (1978) · M. Coate, Cornwall in the great civil war and interregnum, 1642–1660 (1933) · Fourth report, HMC, 3 (1874) · Fifth report, HMC, 4 (1876) · CSP Ire., 1647–60 · T. C. Dale, ed., The inhabitants of London in 1638, 2 vols. (1931)
Likenesses group portrait, line engraving (The regicides executed in 1660), BM · line engraving, NPG

Clements, Sir John Selby (1910–1988), actor and theatre manager, was born on 25 April 1910 at 1 Carlton Terrace, Childs Hill, Hendon, Middlesex, the only child of Herbert William Clements, barrister, and his wife, Mary Elizabeth Stephens. He was educated at St Paul's School, and spent one term at St John's College, Cambridge. He was forced to withdraw from the college, where he had begun to study

history, because sudden financial loss meant his family could no longer afford the fees. His mother's great friend Marie Löhr gave him his first job at the age of twenty at the Lyric Theatre, Hammersmith. In 1931 he joined the Shakespearian Company run by Sir Ben Greet, and at twenty-five, in 1935, was sufficiently confident to found the Intimate Theatre, Palmers Green, as a weekly repertory company which he managed, directed, and acted in until 1940. In the first year he produced forty-two plays there, playing thirty-six leading parts.

In 1936 Clements married his first wife, Inga Maria Lillemor Ahlgren. They had no children and the marriage was dissolved ten years later. In 1946 he married the actress Kay Hammond, whose real name was Dorothy Katherine, daughter of Sir Guy Standing KBE of the Royal Naval Volunteer Reserve. Kay was formerly the wife of Sir Ronald George Leon, third baronet, and was the mother of Sir John Leon, fourth baronet, later better known as the actor John Standing. She and Clements had no children.

During the Second World War, Clements produced many plays for Entertainments National Service Association (ENSA) and also organized a revue company to entertain the troops at out-of-the-way places. John Clements and Kay Hammond together became one of the best-known theatrical couples of their day. In 1944 they acted at the Apollo in *Private Lives*, by Noël Coward, an enchanting production with which Coward was delighted. In 1946 Clements appeared as the earl of Warwick in *The King-maker* at the St James's Theatre, which he himself managed. He presented and directed *Man and Superman* in 1951 at the New Theatre, playing the role of John Tanner.

In addition to his many productions and performances, Clements was a successful broadcaster on the radio, taking part with Kay Hammond in the weekly discussion programme *We Beg to Differ*. Their comic rivalry on the air delighted audiences. From 1955 Clements was adviser on drama for Associated Rediffusion, one of the first independent television companies, for which he was contracted to produce a number of television plays. In July 1955 he joined the board of directors of the Saville Theatre, the management of which came under his personal control.

In 1960 Kay Hammond became paralysed after a stroke and was confined to a wheelchair for the remaining twenty years of her life. Clements joined the Old Vic Company in 1961, making his first appearance in New York in the title role in *Macbeth* in 1962. In 1966 he took on the challenge of directing the Chichester festival theatre when Sir Laurence Olivier left to found the National Theatre. His boundless enthusiasm and love of the theatre overcame any initial reluctance on the part of the actors he approached for his first season at Chichester to join him 'in the wake of Larry'. He was able to recruit Celia Johnson and Bill Fraser and splendid supporting casts, who were very loyal to him. His seasons were independent and enterprising, and he was always encouraging, calm, and resourceful in times of crisis.

As a director Clements was businesslike, almost prosaic, and very logical, never selfish and always courteous. Six feet tall, with a handsome face and slightly 'jug' ears, he had kind eyes and excellent hands. He was one of the last actor–managers in the country. In Chichester he was not only the director of four plays each summer season, but also played, among other parts, Macbeth, Antony, and Prospero, as well as two of Jean Anouilh's heroes, the general in *The Fighting Cock* and Antoine in *Dear Antoine*. It was his appreciation of the literary tradition of drama that gave him the courage to present *The Fighting Cock*, a great success in its original French version in Paris. *Heartbreak House*, in which he played Shotover, was one of his most memorable productions. Clements also acted in a number of films, including *Things to Come* (1936), *South Riding* (1937), *The Four Feathers* (1939), *Oh What a Lovely War!* (1969), and *Gandhi* (1982). He was appointed CBE in 1956 and knighted in 1968. A member of the council of Equity in 1948–9 and vice-president in 1950–59, he was also a popular trustee of the Garrick Club.

Clements left Chichester in 1973 to spend more time with his wife, for they were a devoted couple. She died in 1980. Clements died on 6 April 1988 at Pendean Convalescent Home near Midhurst, Sussex, where he had spent the last two years of his life. BESSBOROUGH, *rev.*

Sources WWW · *The Times* (8 April 1988) · *The Times* (21 April 1988) · personal knowledge (1996)
Likenesses photographs, *c*.1938–1944, Hult. Arch.
Wealth at death £117,750: administration with will, 30 June 1988, *CGPLA Eng. & Wales*

Clements, Michael (*b.* in or before **1735**, *d. c.***1797**), naval officer, is of unknown origins. Between 1748 and 1749 he served in the *Syren* in the East Indies. His lieutenant's passing certificate (PRO, ADM 107/4, p. 334) gives his age in December 1755 as 'twenty and upwards'. In May 1757 he was first lieutenant of the frigate *Unicorn* when she engaged and captured the *Invincible*, a large Malouin privateer. Captain Thomas Graves of the *Unicorn* was killed, and Clements, after conducting the fight to a successful issue, brought the prize into Kinsale and went out again in pursuit of the privateer's consort, which he also captured and brought in. For this good service Clements was immediately promoted to the command of the buss *London*, and four months later (29 September) to post rank and the command of the frigate *Actaeon*. Clements continued in her, attached to the Channel Fleet, until June 1759, when he was moved into the *Pallas* (36 guns), also with the fleet blockading Brest and Quiberon Bay, and specially employed, with the other frigates, in cruising against the enemy's privateers and in communicating with the home ports. By a fortunate accident, the *Pallas*, in company with the *Aeolus* and *Brilliant*, put into Kinsale in the last days of February 1760, just as a message came from the duke of Bedford, lord lieutenant of Ireland, that Thurot's squadron was at Belfast. They immediately put to sea again, and, coming off Belfast on the morning of 28 February, succeeded in capturing all Thurot's ships with little loss. The *Pallas* continued on the same service until the end of the year, and was then sent to the Mediterranean, where she remained until after the peace, and returned to England in December 1763.

Michael Clements (*b.* in or before **1735**, *d. c.***1797**), by Nathaniel Hone

On paying off this ship Clements refused to give a certificate to the master, whom he reported as 'inattentive to his duty'. The master in revenge laid an accusation of waste and malversation of stores against his captain. After an inquiry at the Navy Office the charge was, in November 1765, pronounced groundless and malicious. In 1769 he commanded the *Dorsetshire* (70 guns) guardship at Portsmouth, which in 1770 was sent to the Mediterranean as part of the British fleet watching the French at Toulon. In March 1778 he was appointed to the *Vengeance* (74 guns), which he commanded in the action off Ushant on 27 July and in the October cruise under Admiral Augustus Keppel. He was afterwards a witness for the defence in the admiral's trial, and spoke very strongly in the admiral's favour. A few months later he was compelled to resign his command owing to poor health, and he never received another. In July 1780 he applied for leave to go abroad with his family, his residence (since at least 1767) having been Weybridge, Surrey. Clements chose Tuscany and finally asked for a passport for himself, his wife, and daughter for Ostend. 'When my health shall be re-established', he added, 'I shall be happy to return and follow my profession with every zeal to regain that reputation which at present appears to me so much sullied.' His name continued on the list of captains until 1787, when there was a very large retirement. Then, or a year or two later, he was made a rear-admiral on the superannuated list; he is believed to have died about 1797.

J. K. LAUGHTON, *rev.* CHRISTOPHER DOORNE

Sources J. Charnock, ed., *Biographia navalis*, 6 (1798) · R. Beatson, *Naval and military memoirs of Great Britain*, 2nd edn, 2 (1804) · commission and warrant books, May 1751–June 1779, PRO, ADM 6/18;

6/19; 6/20; 6/21 • *The private papers of John, earl of Sandwich*, ed. G. R. Barnes and J. H. Owen, 4 vols., Navy RS, 69, 71, 75, 78 (1932–8) • W. L. Clowes, *The Royal Navy: a history from the earliest times to the present*, 7 vols. (1897–1903); repr. (1996–7), vol. 3 • Steel's navy lists, 1796–7 • personal correspondence, NMM, Clements MSS • PRO, ADM 107/4, p. 334
Archives NMM, logbooks and papers
Likenesses N. Hone, oils, NMM [*see illus.*]

Clements, Nathaniel (1705–1777), Treasury official and property developer, was the fifth son of Robert Clements (1664–1722) of Rathkenny, near Cootehill, co. Cavan, a second-generation squire of Cromwellian origins, and Elizabeth (d. 1742), daughter of General Theophilus Sandford of Moyglare, co. Meath. Clements married, on 31 January 1730, Hannah (1705–1781), daughter of William Gore, dean of Down. Like her husband, she was poor but well connected, being a cousin of most of the celebrated 'nine Gores' who sat in the Irish House of Commons in the middle of the eighteenth century. His wife's connections were to have a major bearing on Clements's career in a variety of ways. They had three sons and four daughters.

Accumulation of offices The connections of Clements's own family were with officials in the Irish administration rather than with prominent parliamentarians. Clements's father, Robert, was teller of the Irish exchequer until his death in 1722 and was succeeded by his eldest son, Theophilus, who also acted as agent for the civil and military pensioners on the Irish establishment. Nathaniel Clements was brought into the teller's office by Theophilus as soon as, or even before, he came of age. In 1728, when Theophilus died young, Nathaniel succeeded him, and in 1731 he also obtained the coveted and lucrative recommendation to be agent to the pensioners. He owed these swift promotions in part to the influence of William Conolly, speaker of the Irish House of Commons from 1715 to 1729, and in part to that of a distant family connection, Luke Gardiner, deputy vice-treasurer from 1725 to 1755. Gardiner had ingratiated himself with the watchdog of the so-called 'English interest' in Ireland, Archbishop Hugh Boulter of Armagh. Boulter regarded Gardiner as a trustworthy Irishman, and extended this indulgence to Clements. Otherwise, neither Gardiner nor Clements would have been able to penetrate the Irish administration in the second half of the 1720s when, following the débâcle of Wood's halfpence, Irishmen were more than ever objects of English suspicion. Between the mid-1720s and the mid-1750s, the 'Irish interest' was at its low-water mark, which is why Gardiner's and Clements's successful partnership in office is a unique phenomenon.

Clements became an official pluralist on a staggering scale. In addition to the tellership, which he held until 1755, the deputy vice-treasurership, which he held from 1755 until his death, and the agency for the pensioners, which he or one of his sons held until 1793, he acted as agent for the regiments on the Irish establishment serving abroad from 1756, a function which was formalized into an office conferred on one of his sons in 1772. Along with his other agency activities Clements acted as private banker to nearly every lord lieutenant of the period 1749–

77. This brought him into early association with all the lords lieutenant for whom he acted, while the agency for the pensioners brought him many influential contacts, including members of the royal family and, still more important, royal mistresses such as the countess of Yarmouth. His official functions were also very lucrative. As agent for the pensioners alone, his profits may have been as much as £1500 p.a. in the mid-1740s, rising by 1750 to over £2500. The agency for the foreign regiments was worth £800 p.a. in the mid-1770s. The tellership also gave him major opportunities for putting public money to his private advantage: in his last years as teller, the mid-1750s, his income from all official sources was reckoned as £8000 p.a., a huge sum for that period, and more than Clements was ever again to earn. Measures were taken to clip his wings in 1755. On Gardiner's death in 1755 Clements was appointed to the more prestigious deputy vice-treasurership, and in 1757 he was sworn of the Irish privy council. But the emoluments of the office were reduced to £1149 p.a., which he alleged was £1161 less than Gardiner had enjoyed, and the opportunities to use public money for private investment did not recur after 1755 on the same scale as before, though they never disappeared entirely.

Clements's numerous other offices were semi-sinecures, and some of them places of dignity rather than great profit. He was clerk of the wool accounts (1736–47); searcher, packer, and gauger of Dublin port (1738–77; deputy constable of Dublin Castle (1738–77); customer and collector of Carrickfergus (1742–8); register of forfeitures (1750–60); and ranger of Phoenix Park (1751–77). These grants were mostly purchased, as was the pension of £3000 p.a. which Clements bought for £9500 in 1743 (when it had six and a half years to run), from the countess of Chesterfield. Clements's office-holding career shows that, in the then current state of the Irish economy, offices and pensions were an attractive form of investment.

Acquisition of land and political patronage Land had the superior attraction of bringing with it political influence, usually in county elections. Most of Clements's purchases were made with this end in view. His earliest, however, were involuntary and a consequence of his role in clearing up the financial mess which his eldest brother, Theophilus, left behind him in 1728. In 1735 an act of parliament was passed authorizing the sale of Theophilus's estates to meet the claims of creditors, and between 1730 and 1740 Clements bought for about £4000 Theophilus's long-leasehold estate of Ashfield, near Rathkenny, co. Cavan. Clements's next theatre of operation was co. Donegal. In 1744 he bought from his feckless friend and cousin by marriage Gustavus Hamilton, second Viscount Boyne, property comprising nearly 9000 Irish acres, with a rental of £900 p.a. Following Boyne's death in 1746 Clements acquired—mainly via a mortgage he already held on the property—Boyne's much larger manor of Kilmacrenan, a leasehold estate under Trinity College, Dublin, comprising nearly 17,500 acres, for which he paid £6250. This transaction led to litigation with Boyne's heirs which eventually went to the British House of Lords, and was not terminated, in Clements's favour, until 1766. In 1749 Clements transferred his attention to co. Leitrim, where he bought first the approximately 6000 acre Mohill estate of the first Lord Conway; then the Glenboy estate situated beside Manorhamilton; and finally, in 1759, the 5400 acre Manorhamilton estate itself, for which he paid nearly £22,000. There was a pattern to these transactions: all the vendors, with the exception of Lord Conway, were financially embarrassed Gore or Hamilton cousins of Mrs Clements; and nearly all the land, including Lord Conway's, was poorish and/or in undesirable locations. Nevertheless, his net rental income was over £6000 by 1760.

Following his acquisition of landed property totalling c. 85,000 statute acres in three counties, and the purchase about 1760 of the political patronage of the borough of Carrick-on-Shannon, co. Leitrim, Clements became possessed of a significant political interest in the Irish House of Commons, independent of the influence he already enjoyed as office-holder and financier. He had been returned by purchase for the borough of Duleek, co. Meath, in 1727, and therefore had to continue as MP for Duleek for the duration of George II's Irish parliament. In 1760–1 he was an unsuccessful candidate for co. Donegal. The senior branch of his family, Theophilus's nephew and successor at Rathkenny, controlled one seat for the borough of Cavan, which Clements occupied from 1761 to 1768. At the 1768 general election he was elected unopposed for co. Leitrim, and then returned himself for Carrick-on-Shannon (1776–7). During his lifetime his sons Robert and Henry Theophilus between them sat for co. Donegal (1765–8 and 1776–83), Carrick-on-Shannon (1768–76), Cavan borough (1769–76), and co. Leitrim (1776–83). The marriages of three of his daughters further strengthened his political interest in co. Cavan, co. Donegal, and co. Leitrim. From the 1760s, when he acquired a parliamentary borough and his sons became county MPs, he was an obvious candidate for a peerage. None was conferred on him, or as far as is known solicited by him, for a peerage would hardly have been appropriate to a Treasury official and miscellaneous agent. After his death his elder surviving son, Robert, was created earl of Leitrim in 1795.

Architectural influence Through another component of his portfolio of estates, his Dublin city property, Clements became a significant figure in the history of Irish architecture. His patron, Gardiner, had acquired in the late 1720s extensive property in undeveloped north Dublin, and proceeded to lay out a series of fashionable streets and squares, using as his architects the very best available in Ireland at the time, Sir Edward Lovett Pearce and Richard Castle. Under Gardiner's influence, Clements built between 1733 and 1744 four grand houses in the smartest enclave in the Gardiner development, Henrietta Street, probably designed by Castle, and two more, in the 1750s and 1760s, in Sackville (now O'Connell) Street. Gardiner was keeper of the Phoenix Park, and had employed Pearce to rebuild the keeper's lodge; and the ranger of the park from 1736 to 1751, General Sir John Ligonier, was another Pearcean in his architectural taste. During the fourth earl of Chesterfield's lord lieutenancy (1745–6) Phoenix Park

was landscaped and turned into a place of fashionable resort. Ligonier was abroad on active service so the remodelling of the park was carried out by Clements, who occupied the ranger's lodge by agreement with Ligonier. In 1748–9 Ligonier transferred his ambitions and his residence to England; Clements succeeded him (by purchase) as ranger in 1751, and between 1752 and 1757 replaced the ranger's lodge with a new Palladian building, erected at public expense and subsequently the official residence of the lords lieutenant, viceroys, governors-general, and presidents of Ireland.

On the strength of the ranger's lodge, which was a very influential building, and in the absence of resident architects in succession to, and of the stature of, Pearce and Castle, Clements has been credited with the role of skilful and prolific amateur architect. However, the houses which have been attributed to Clements were at best specimens of his taste and strategic advice rather than proofs of his skill as an architect. He almost certainly had nothing to do with some of them—for example, Woodville, Lucan, co. Dublin; and Williamstown, Carbury, co. Kildare. But there is a strong probability that he advised on Beauparc, near Slane, co. Meath (c.1753–5), and a strong possibility that he advised on Newberry Hall, Carbury, co. Kildare (c.1765), and, towards the end of his life, Lodge Park, near Straffan, in the same county (1775–7). Clements's principal significance lies in the fact that, through the example of the ranger's lodge and through the leading position which he occupied in Dublin society, he popularized among fashionable people in Ireland a small-scale but sophisticated type of Palladian villa-farm which has no obvious English counterpart.

Politics and finance The early 1750s were the high-water mark of Clements's career. Following early and middle years of uninterrupted success he found himself pitched into two successive crises in the years 1753–5 and 1759–60 respectively. The first was the so-called 'money bill dispute', which was really a power struggle between George Stone, archbishop of Armagh, and the veteran Irish political manager Henry Boyle, speaker of the House of Commons. Clements found himself, like it or not, on the side of Boyle and the 'patriot' opposition, the side on which 'the nine Gores' were ranged, two of whom had been brought into parliament at Clements's expense. Moreover one of the leaders of the opposition, Anthony Malone, was married to another of Mrs Clements's Gore cousins. Clements himself either voted for the government in key divisions, or stayed away. But Stone, and the chief secretary, Lord George Sackville, argued in their representations to London that a leading office-holder should have done more than this and indeed have brought all his and the Treasury's connections over to the government side. Instead Clements had in practice been financing the opposition, since it was notorious that he had lent Boyle and other leading patriots considerable sums of money from public funds. In September 1753 and October 1754 Clements was summoned to London to be sternly lectured by Henry Pelham and the duke of Newcastle who, as successive first lords of the Treasury, technically had authority over the teller of the Irish exchequer. But these repeated interviews manifestly had a much wider political significance. In January 1754 Stone unwisely made the dismissal of Clements the touchstone of the British government's support for its Irish counterpart, but ministers drew back from so extreme a step: in April 1755 Dorset and Sackville were superseded; Stone was relegated to the sidelines; and, when Gardiner died soon afterwards, Clements was promoted to the deputy vice-treasurership.

Clements was forced to accept a lower income in his new office, which was further lowered by the subsequent reduction of the recurrent surplus in the Treasury, the nominal cause of the 'money bill dispute'; by the end of the Seven Years' War the surplus was to become a deficit. Clements had in the past come close in practice to acting as a private banker; and in 1758, in order to regain access to the level of funds on which his investment activities depended, he formally opened a private bank in Dublin in partnership with Anthony Malone, now chancellor of the exchequer, and another of Mrs Clements's cousins, John Gore, the first counsel to the revenue commissioners. The bank attracted numerous customers, and the envy of most other banks, by lending money at as low a rate of interest as 2½ per cent. Clements, Malone, and Gore were thought to have set it up partly to reduce the rate of interest which they themselves paid on money borrowed to finance the purchase of estates; and, from a number of circumstances, it looks as if the bank did indeed finance Clements's purchase of the Manorhamilton estate in 1759. It was later asserted by the lord president of the council in Great Britain, Earl Granville, that the bank 'had stopped the circulation of near £300,000 for some years' (William Blair to Clements, 28 Feb 1760, TCD, MS 1742/63).

In November 1759 the crash came and the bank stopped payment. Its debts seem to have totalled about £75,000, for which the three partners were jointly and severally liable. As the bank's assets were wholly inadequate to meet this liability, an act of parliament (33 Geo. II c. 4) was required to establish a phased plan of repayment by the partners and to give the creditors the security of the partners' private estates. For a time it was touch-and-go whether this act would pass the British privy council, and also whether Clements would be allowed to retain the deputy vice-treasurership. In the end his office was saved by the intervention of his most influential pensioner, Lady Yarmouth, and of the lord lieutenant, the fourth duke of Bedford. Clements seems to have raised the money to pay his third share of the debt by calling in a loan of about £10,000 made in 1747–8 and by selling three of his Henrietta Street houses and other Dublin property. The rest he seems to have paid out of income over time. The worst was over by 1765, and in 1773 his private estates and those of his partners were released from the trusteeship set up by the act of parliament. Because of the lesser liquidity of his partners, this was mainly achieved by borrowing from alternative sources; the debt of about £75,000 was not in fact discharged until 1805. The bank crash in 1759 seems to have consumed most of his disposable capital, and significantly, he made only one more, fairly modest, purchase of land.

Death and legacy The other problem which beset Clements in his later years was the succession to his offices of business, for which he groomed all three of his sons in turn. In the event, he died in harness. It may be conjectured that this was partly because he enjoyed the work, and mainly because he wanted to clinch the succession. Robert acted as agent for the pensioners (1755–c.1766), but found the work uncongenial and was apparently not on good terms with his father. In any case a peerage for the eldest son must already have been an object of family ambition. The middle brother, William, a former banker, was associated with his father in the Treasury (1760–8), but his health failed and he died at Bath in 1770. The third son, Henry Theophilus, who was a colonel in the army, was made to switch careers and was appointed to the agency for the foreign regiments in 1772. When Clements died at the ranger's lodge, Phoenix Park, on 26 May 1777 the lord lieutenant successfully recommended H. T. Clements to succeed him as deputy vice-treasurer and agent for the pensioners.

A portrait of Nathaniel Clements painted in middle life shows a handsome man of benign appearance, and gives little inkling of the astuteness which lay below the surface. It was probably an ingredient in his success that he had the good fortune to be underestimated by all who judged him superficially. He was an elegant and lavish host and, clearly, the best of company on social occasions. Although a good attender in parliament, he was not a speaker: his contribution to public affairs was administrative and made behind the scenes. In the absence of an Irish pay office, the Treasury had responsibility for paying the army on the Irish establishment and thus for a major component of the British and imperial war machine; in the absence, except in name, of a chancellorship of the Irish exchequer, the deputy vice-treasurer performed much of the role of a minister of finance. Moreover, for about fifteen years before he actually became deputy vice-treasurer, Clements had been doing most of the work of that office on Gardiner's behalf.

Clements was very unusual in obtaining and holding a position of near-indispensability in Dublin Castle at a time when Irishmen were 'very narrowly ... watched'. His influence declined somewhat between 1755 and the early 1760s, but he soon re-established himself as a leading servant and supporter of government, and died in an aura of elder statesmanship. He had been at the centre of the financial administration of Ireland for the half-century between 1726 and 1777, spinning from within the Treasury a web of obligation and intrigue, and most unusually (for an Irishman) being the subject of personal lobbying and solicitation by two successive British prime ministers. He was essentially a harmonizer of British and Irish interests, but he adhered to the latter when a choice had to be made in 1753–5.

A. P. W. MALCOMSON

Sources Clements papers, priv. coll. [Killadoon, Celbridge, co. Kildare] · NL Ire., Clements MSS 36010–36022, 36025, 36029, 36030/4–5 · TCD, Clements MSS 1741–1743, 7258–7360 · A. P. W. Malcomson, *The indispensable Irishman: Nathaniel Clements (1705–77)* [forthcoming] · D. FitzGerald, 'Nathaniel Clements and some eighteenth-century Irish houses', *Apollo*, 84 (1966), 314–21 · L. M. Cullen, 'Landlords, bankers and merchants: the early Irish banking world, 1700–1820', *Economists and the Irish economy from the 18th century to the present day*, ed. A. E. Murphy (1984) · E. M. Johnston-Liik, *History of the Irish parliament, 1692–1800*, 6 vols. (2002) · J. Walton, ed., *The king's business: letters on the administration of Ireland, from the papers of Sir Robert Wilmot* (1996) · PRO NIre., Wilmot MSS, T 3019 · PRO NIre., O'Hara MSS, T 2812, esp. T 2812/91 · C. L. Falkiner, ed., 'Correspondence of Archbishop Stone and the duke of Newcastle', *EngHR*, 20 (1905), 376–7 · L. Pilkington, *Memoirs of Laetitia Pilkington*, ed. A. C. Elias, 2 vols. (1997) · NL Ire., Heron MS 13035 · *Eighth report*, 3 vols. in 5, HMC, 7 (1881–1910)

Archives NL Ire. · priv. coll. · TCD, corresp. and ledgers | BL, corresp. with earl of Liverpool, Add. MSS 38207–38208, 38306 · Cornwall RO, letters to Richard Edgcumbe · Derbys. RO, letters to W. G. Hamilton; corresp. with Sir Robert Wilmot · PRO NIre., Wilmot MSS

Likenesses attrib. S. Slaughter, portrait, *c.*1750, priv. coll.

Clemo, Reginald John [Jack] (**1916–1994**), poet and novelist, was born on 11 March 1916 at Goonamarris, St Stephen, St Austell, Cornwall, the second child of Reginald Clemo (1890–1917), clay quarry worker, and his wife, Eveline, *née* Polmounter (1894–1977), whose first child died at five weeks old. His parents and grandparents were Cornish land or mine workers.

Clemo was born on the edge of the clay mining area of mid-Cornwall and soon became aware of the tense inheritance of his mother's piety and his father's dissolute nature. His father died on active service in the First World War. Clemo suffered a bout of blindness when he was five and attacks returned again at intervals. At six he enrolled in Trethosa council school, attending intermittently to the age of twelve.

At thirteen Clemo rebelled against his religious upbringing and for years wandered around the clay dumps engaging in erotic daydreams, fuelled by provocative letters he fired off to the county press. At the age of nineteen he was overcome by deafness. His intense personal struggles were finally resolved in a conversion which allied him with his mother's unswerving faith and he emerged by 1938 an orthodox Calvinistic Christian. The mystical trait in him produced convictions that he should be a writer and that he carried a divine vocation for marriage.

Clemo's first novel, *Wilding Graft*, was published in 1948 and won the Atlantic award. It portrayed the turmoil of private and spiritual passions played out in the narrow village life of the Cornish china clay world during the war years of the 1930s and 1940s. His autobiography *Confession of a Rebel* was published in 1949.

In 1951 Clemo's sequence 'The Wintry Priesthood' won the Festival of Britain poetry prize and his first book of verse, *The Clay Verge*, was published. His early poetry is infused with an erotic view of the barren clay landscape of his home and God's just demand for the surrender of the personal soul. He praised the industrial invasion of the natural world as God's grace claiming his own. Though he

derided nature, his verse has a haunting beauty of expression and the challenge of a personal, honest voice. In 1953 he suffered a cerebral paralysis and a year later blindness enveloped him. Though he remained blind and deaf for the rest of his life, the cause of his disabilities was never identified.

Each attempt Clemo made to pursue his vocation to marry ended in failure. The effort of it was compounded by the necessity for all correspondence to him to be traced, letter by letter, onto the palm of his hand. This his mother did for him. In 1955, with his mother typing to his dictation, he wrote his credo, *The Invading Gospel*, 'after a lapse into paganism'.

On 26 October 1968 Clemo married Ruth Grace Peaty (*b.* 1923) who had started writing to him the previous year. Just before his mother died she published a memoir in which she describes the fulfilment of God's promise through the life of her son. Clemo owed an incalculable amount to the love, devotion, and patience of his mother as well as to her tenacity of spirit and faith. At her death, his wife took on the roles his mother had performed, adding an almost telepathic understanding of her husband and becoming his eyes and ears as she communicated the world around him. *The Marriage of a Rebel*, the second volume of Clemo's autobiography, was published in 1980. That year his early life was the subject of a BBC television drama documentary, *A Different Drummer*.

In 1984, after Clemo had suffered a crippling attack of ill health, he and his wife moved to Weymouth, leaving behind the tiny granite cottage, beleaguered by the encroaching clay works, which had been his home since birth. In Weymouth his health improved and his poetry took on a more measured, calmer tone, taking in the Dorset landscape and engaging with characters from his Braille readings. Clemo and his wife attended Weymouth Baptist Church. The story of their marriage is told in Sally Magnusson's book *Clemo: a Love Story* (1986). His second novel, *The Shadowed Bed*, appeared in 1986. The influence of T. F. Powys and Thomas Hardy can be discerned in his novels, while Robert Browning was a lifelong fascination which commenced with Clemo's early identification with his evangelical zeal and the story of his 'creed-bedded marriage'.

In 1987 Clemo visited Venice and in 1993, Florence. These trips opened up a sudden, final flowering of verse, combining landscape and love with Christian faith, and weaving the personal into the history of European literature. *Selected Poems* was published in 1988, followed by *Approach to Murano* in 1993.

Clemo was awarded a civil-list pension for services to literature in 1961. In 1970 he was crowned *prydyth an pry* (poet of the clay) at the Cornish gorsedd, and in 1981 received an honorary DLitt from the University of Exeter.

Clemo was of short stocky build. The striking and sombre effect of dark glasses and black beret was offset, close up, by an impish face and corresponding sense of fun which was easily roused.

Jack Clemo died on 25 July 1994 at Weymouth, of cancer, and was buried in Weymouth cemetery on 1 August. The

Arts Centre Group of London instituted a biennial Jack Clemo poetry competition. A collection of poems, *The Cured Arno*, was published in 1995 and a novel, *The Clay Kiln*, was published in 2000. Trethosa Methodist Chapel, where he was baptized, married, and where he and his wife attended together, opened a memorial room to his memory in 2001.

Charles Causley, who was best man at his wedding, called him 'one of the best landscape poets of his generation'. In spite of his disabilities, Clemo's love poems, an important part of his output, are as vivid as his landscape verse. He was also, in that long and rich, central English tradition, one of the finest Christian poets of the twentieth century. MICHAEL SPINKS

Sources J. Clemo, *Confession of a rebel* (1949) · J. Clemo, *The marriage of a rebel*, revised edn (1988); original edn (1980) · J. Clemo, *The invading gospel*, rev. edn (1972); original edn (1958) · E. Clemo, *I proved thee at the waters: the testimony of a blind writer's mother* (c.1976) · S. Magnusson, *Clemo: a love story* (1986) · private information (2004) [Ruth Grace Clemo, widow; sister-in-law; foster sister; Alan M. Kent; Michael Williams; Charles Causley] · b. cert. · m. cert. · d. cert.
Archives Trethosa Methodist Chapel, Cornwall, Jack Clemo Memorial Room · University of Exeter Library, notebooks and papers · Wheal Martyn China Clay Heritage Centre, near St Austell, MSS and printed material | Ransom HRC, Derek Parker papers · University of Exeter, Charles Causley collection · University of Exeter, A. L. Rowse collection · Wheaton College, Illinois, Norman Stone collection · Yale U., Beinecke L., Donald Davie collection | FILM BFI NFTVA, *A different drummer*, BBC TV film (1980) | SOUND BL NSA, BBC radio broadcasts · Harvard U., recordings of Clemo reading his own poems · Wheaton College, Norman Stone collection, audio tapes relating to BBC TV film, *A different drummer*, broadcast 1980
Likenesses L. Miskin, double portrait, tempera and pastel, 1958, Royal Institution of Cornwall, Truro; repro. in A. M. Kent, *The literature of Cornwall* (2000) · L. Miskin, oils, 1959, repro. in J. Clemo, *Selected poems* (1988); priv. coll. · B. Penver, oils, 1970, priv. coll. · T. Porter, double portrait, photograph, 1975 (with his wife), NPG · T. Porter, photograph, 1975, NPG · M. Spinks, pen-and-ink drawing, 1980, priv. coll. · H. Spears, pencil sketches, 1992, priv. coll.

Clench, Andrew (d. 1692), physician and victim of murder, was the son of Edmund Clench of Ipswich. He matriculated from St Catharine's College, Cambridge in 1663, and was created MD at Cambridge by royal mandate on 29 March 1671. Clench was admitted a candidate of the College of Physicians on 22 December 1677, and a fellow on 23 December 1680; he had become a fellow of the Royal Society in April of that year. Between 1682 and 1687 Clench came into conflict with the College of Physicians over his criticism of the college and its fellows, and because of his friendship with the empiric Samuel Haworth.

Clench lived in Brownlow Street, Holborn, London. He was murdered between nine and eleven o'clock on the night of Monday, 4 January 1692. 'This week', wrote John Evelyn in his diary:

> a most execrable murder was committed on Dr Clench, father of that extraordinary learned child whom I have before noticed. Under pretence of carrying him in a coach to see a patient, they strangled him in it, and sending away the coachman under some pretence, they left his dead body in the coach, and escaped in the dusk of the evening.

A swindler named Henry Harrison, to whose mistress Clench had lent money, was convicted of the murder and hanged on 15 April 1692. Clench and his wife, Rose, had two sons, Edmund and John. From his will, we learn that he possessed property in Norfolk and Suffolk.

GORDON GOODWIN, rev. MICHAEL BEVAN

Sources Munk, *Roll* · Venn, *Alum. Cant.* · H. Harrison, *The arraignment, tryal, conviction and condemnation of Henry Harrison for the barbarous murther of Dr Andrew Clenche* (1692) · H. Harrison, *The last words of a dying penitent* (1692) · N. Luttrell, *A brief historical relation of state affairs from September 1678 to April 1714*, 2 (1857) · H. Harrison, *The tryal of John Cole for the murther of Dr Andrew Clenche* (1692) · R. Rowe, *Mr Harrison proved the murtherer* (1692) · H. J. Cook, *The decline of the old medical regime in Stuart London* (1986) · *Diary and correspondence of John Evelyn*, ed. W. Bray, new edn, ed. [J. Forster], 4 vols. (1850–52)
Wealth at death left property in Norfolk and Suffolk

Clench, John (c.1535–1607), judge, was the son of John Clench of Wethersfield, Essex, and Jane, daughter of John Amyas of the same county. His grandfather, also John Clench, came from Leeds in Yorkshire. He was admitted to Lincoln's Inn in 1556, called to the bar in 1563, and served as reader of Furnival's Inn for three years from 1566 to 1569; these readings were on the Statutes of Wills and the statute *De conjunctim feoffatis*. In 1570 he was called to the bench of Lincoln's Inn, where he delivered a reading in 1574 and was treasurer from 1578 to 1579. He became recorder of Ipswich in 1575. In 1580 he was created serjeant-at-law, his patrons at the ceremony being the earl of Oxford, Lord Wentworth, and Sir William Cordell. A year later, on 27 November 1581, he was appointed one of the barons of the exchequer, and on 29 May 1584 he was translated to the queen's bench.

Clench married Katherine, daughter of Thomas Almot of Creeting All Saints, with whom he had five sons and eight daughters. It was said that Elizabeth I referred to him as 'her good judge', but he was never knighted. By 1602, being 'so decrepit that he could not well travel outside his country' (Yale U., law school, MS G. R29.15, fol. 31), he was discharged from attendance at court; and on 17 September 1602 he was granted a pension. He died on 18 or 19 August 1607 at Holbrook, Suffolk, where he was also buried, and where there is a large monument bearing his effigy in robes. A three-quarter-length portrait in oils formerly existed in a number of versions, and was the basis of the quarter-length etching by Hollar dated 1664 for Dugdale's *Origines juridiciales*. Clench was a reporter of cases from 1571 to 1592. His autograph reports, never published, together with notes of his Furnival's Inn readings, are now in the British Library (Harley MS 4556); and there is an incomplete copy at Yale. His eldest son, Thomas (d. 1624), followed his father as a barrister of Lincoln's Inn and reader of Furnival's Inn; he served as member of parliament for Suffolk in 1620. Another son, Robert, was principal of Clifford's Inn from 1624. J. H. BAKER

Sources Foss, *Judges*, 5.474–5 · W. P. Baildon, ed., *The records of the Honorable Society of Lincoln's Inn: the black books*, 1 (1897) · Baker, *Serjeants*, 173, 434, 505 · Sainty, *Judges*, 30, 122 · BL, Harley MS 4556 · J. H. Baker, *English legal manuscripts in the United States of America: a descriptive list*, 2 (1990), nos. 1496, 1500, 1506 · PRO, C142/658/93 · N. Bacon, *The annalls of Ipswche*, ed. W. H. Richardson (1884), 301 ·

G. R. Clarke, *The history and description of the town and borough of Ipswich* (1830), 41 • Yale U., law school, MS G. R29.15, fol. 31 • W. A. Copinger, *The manors of Suffolk*, 7 vols. (1905–11), vol. 6, pp. 65–6 **Archives** BL, notes of his readings, and law reports, Harley MS 4556 **Likenesses** attrib. I. Oliver, miniature, 1583, priv. coll. • I. Oliver, miniature, 1583, Buccleuch estates, Selkirk • oils, 1602 • effigy on monument, *c*.1607, Holbrook church, Suffolk; repro. in R. L. Cron, *Justice in Ipswich* (1968), 14, 17 • W. Hollar, etching, 1664 (after oil painting, 1602), BM; repro. in W. Dugdale, *Origines juridiciales* (1666)

Clendining [*née* Arnold]**, Elizabeth** (*bap.* 1767, *d.* 1799), singer, was baptized at St Peter's, Stourton, Wiltshire, on 13 January 1767, the daughter of John Arnold (*bap.* 1746, *d.* 1774/5) and his wife, Mary (*d.* in or after 1785). Her father had been educated as a boy chorister at Salisbury Cathedral and became a vicar-choral at Wells Cathedral in 1768. He was a soloist in Thomas Linley's concerts at Bath, where he was praised by the castrato Ferdinando Tenducci. The family moved to Dublin in 1773 when Arnold became a leading cathedral singer there, but he died less than two years later.

Elizabeth Arnold remained in Dublin with her mother and in 1785 performed as the second chief vocalist at the Rotunda summer concerts, receiving 60 guineas. That year she married William Clendining (*d.* 1793), an Irish surgeon with landed property in co. Longford, and she then retired from public performance for six years. Her husband's 'professional inattention' and '*indiscriminate* hospitality' (Haslewood, 2.379) led to his imprisonment in Dublin for debt, and in December 1791 Mrs Clendining went to London with her young family in an attempt to earn money as a professional singer. Despite the help and hospitality of the soprano Elizabeth Billington, whom she had met in Dublin, she failed to obtain singing engagements. She went to Bath, and there the flautist Andrew Ashe, a fellow performer at the Dublin Rotunda, introduced her to the castrato Venanzio Rauzzini, who had become an admired singing teacher and was in charge of the concerts there. After lessons from him, she appeared first at Ashe's benefit concert, and then in Rauzzini's 1792 passion week oratorios. The noblemen and gentlemen of the Bath Catch Club engaged her for their concerts and were the patrons of her benefit on 2 May 1792, at which she raised enough money to release her husband from debtors' prison. Clendining became surgeon of the frigate *Inconstant* but died at Portsmouth on 27 April 1793.

Mrs Clendining made her first stage appearance at Covent Garden on 3 November 1792, when she played Clara in *Hartford Bridge*, a part specially composed for her by William Shield. Her first song was encored, and 'the depth and fullness of her middle and lower tones, and the sweetness of the upper ones were acknowledged and admired' (Haslewood, 2.384). Mrs Clendining sang at Covent Garden for six seasons in English operas, musical afterpieces, and pantomimes. The author of *Candid and Impartial Strictures* summed her up as 'A sweet singer with a tolerable person, and pleasing countenance', but added, 'The least we say of her acting the better' (p. 65). On 2 January 1795 she could not appear because she had dislocated her

shoulder and collar-bone, but she was performing again before the end of the month. Michael Kelly, who heard her at the Plymouth theatre in summer 1796, noted that she 'had a very good voice, and was a favourite with the town, in spite of a most implacable Irish brogue' (Kelly, 2.123). In summer 1797 she sang with success in Dublin opposite the tenor Charles Incledon. She returned to London that autumn for what proved her final Covent Garden season. Her health was declining, and she made her last appearance at her benefit on 24 May 1798, when her daughter played Little Bob in the afterpiece *The Poor Sailor* by John Bernard and Thomas Attwood. Mrs Clendining was engaged at the Edinburgh theatre for winter 1798–9, but illness often prevented her appearing. A charitable gentleman, previously unknown to her, 'hearing of her distressed situation, administered every sort of sustenance and medical assistance to her during her illness, and she was buried very decently at his expense' (*Monthly Mirror*, 120). She died in Edinburgh on 16 July 1799, and her benefactor is reported to have provided for her two children.

OLIVE BALDWIN and THELMA WILSON

Sources C. B. Hogan, ed., *The London stage, 1660–1800*, pt 5: *1776–1800* (1968) • *Bath Chronicle* (29 March 1792) • *Bath Chronicle* (26 April 1792) • B. Boydell, *Rotunda music in eighteenth-century Dublin* (Dublin, 1992) • T. J. Walsh, *Opera in Dublin, 1705–1797: the social scene* (1973) • [J. Haslewood], *The secret history of the green rooms: containing authentic and entertaining memoirs of the actors and actresses in the three Theatres Royal*, 3rd edn, 2 (1795) • *Candid and impartial strictures on the performers belonging to Drury-Lane, Covent-Garden, and the Haymarket theatres* (1795) • *The thespian dictionary, or, Dramatic biography of the eighteenth century* (1802) • M. Kelly, *Reminiscences*, 2 (1826) • J. Roach, *Roach's authentic memoirs of the green room* (1796) • *Monthly Mirror*, 8 (Aug 1799), 120 • *GM*, 1st ser., 69 (1799), 718 • J. H. Ellis, ed., *The registers of Stourton, County Wilts from 1570 to 1800* (1887) • private information (2004) [archivists of Salisbury and Wells cathedrals] • *European Magazine and London Review*, 23 (1793), 400 [death notice of Mr Clendining]

Clennell, Luke (1781–1840), artist and wood-engraver, was born on 8 April 1781 at Ulgham, near Morpeth, Northumberland, and baptized there on 11 May, the second of the seven children of John Clennell, farmer. His powerful natural gifts as a draughtsman were evident from an early age. After attending Ulgham village school he was placed briefly with his uncle, a grocer and tanner in Morpeth. His graphic talent is said to have so impressed the young Lord Morpeth, son of the earl of Carlisle, that an introduction was made to Thomas Bewick (1753–1828), to whom he was indentured for seven years on his sixteenth birthday, 8 April 1797 [*see* Bewick, Thomas, apprentices]. Bewick was at the height of his powers, having just put to press his first volume of the celebrated *British Birds*. Clennell was fortunate in the timing of his training and before long was contributing to the production of the second volume of the *Birds*. His tailpiece vignettes are distinctive in the vigour of their cutting and are clearly the work of a confident hand; some are of his own design and some exquisitely finished preliminaries survive in private hands; these anticipate his success as a watercolourist during his later brief career in London.

During the latter part of Clennell's apprenticeship Bewick's workshop had been engraving blocks for James

Wallis, a London bookseller who was publishing editions of Shakespeare's plays and Hume's *History of England*. Charlton Nesbit, a former apprentice by then working in London, had also been commissioned by Wallis, and he may have been the spur to Clennell's move south. Here Clennell flourished, securing the full fee for work from which his master had previously deducted half. He was soon introduced to a wider circle of artists and engravers and on 27 August 1809 married, at St Pancras Church, Elizabeth, the daughter of Charles *Warren, a leading metal-engraver employed by the book- and printsellers. They lived in London first at 9 Constitution Row, Gray's Inn Lane, and then in 1813 moved to 33 Penton Place, Pentonville. Among his commissions were wood engravings for *The Hive of Ancient and Modern Literature* (1806), William Falconer's *Shipwreck* (1808), William Beattie's *The Minstrel* (1808), John Lawrence's *The History and Delineation of the Horse* (1809), *The Antiquarian Itinerary* (1815), and *Recreations in Natural History* (1815). For the latter, and for some of the illustrations in Mrs Barbauld's edition of the *British Novelists* (1810), copperplates were engraved by various hands after Clennell. There are thirty of his drawings for the novels of Smollett, Sterne, and others, in the Victoria and Albert Museum, London, and his lively figures and the vigorously expressed narrative content show a marked contrast to the more staged and delicate work of the other illustrators of the day such as Richard Corbould and Richard Westall. His name is often remembered for the cuts he engraved after drawings by Thomas Stothard, for Samuel Rogers's *Pleasures of Memory* (1810), although these are no more than very sensitively worked reproductive engravings in the black-line manner.

Clennell's powers as a painter were recognized by Benjamin West, whose motif for the Highland Society of London's diploma he had engraved on wood in 1809, and it is said that it was West who encouraged him to move away from engraving. He was soon exhibiting with the various societies of painters in watercolours and in 1812 was elected an associate of the Society of Painters in Water Colours.

By 1814 Clennell had produced sixty-eight large drawings for most of the plates in Scott's *Border Antiquities* engraved by Storer and Greig. Examples are to be seen in the Laing Gallery, Newcastle upon Tyne, and in the Victoria and Albert Museum. They show all his skilful freedom in handling and effect, and much of the influence of Peter DeWint, and of François Francia and Thomas Girtin. His colouring is generally rich and sombre and his rustic figures are particularly characteristic, often with gesturing hands and prominent thumbs, and possibly reflecting what may have been his own sturdy build. Other examples of his work are rare, but some are to be found at the Paul Mellon Center for British Art, New Haven, Connecticut, the British Museum, the Natural History Society of Northumbria, Newcastle upon Tyne, and in private hands. He was given to signing his engravings and drawings within and as part of his designs, as for example on a packhorse's load or on an inn sign or turnpike notice,

either simply with initials or with his name in a running hand.

Clennell had also taken to painting in oils. His first major subject, *Sportsmen Taking Refreshment at the Door of a Country Ale House*, was exhibited at the British Institution in 1813. His fine *The Baggage Waggon in a Thunderstorm* was shown at the Royal Academy in 1816, based on an earlier watercolour of 1810; versions of this subject can now be seen at the Laing Gallery and at the Paul Mellon Center for British Art, New Haven. In the same year he won a premium from the British Institution for his *Final Charge of the Life Guards at Waterloo*, a composition 'full of fire and furious movement' (Dobson, 196).

The most substantial work of Clennell's career brought it to a tragic end. In 1814 a banquet was held at London's Guildhall to celebrate what was thought to be the end of the Napoleonic wars, and the earl of Bridgewater commissioned Clennell to make a record of the occasion. The canvas measured 4 ft 2 in. by 6 ft 3 in. and was to contain the portraits of more than a hundred of the guests. Sketches had to be made of them, accommodating all their foibles and vanities as sitters. In 1817, when this had been accomplished and the composition established, a depression seems to have descended on Clennell, who became more and more dejected; eventually he turned the picture to the wall and refused to discuss it. He was shortly afterwards, at thirty-six, committed to a London asylum. A print of the *Final Charge of the Life Guards* engraved by W. Bromley was published in 1819, from which a subscription was raised to support Clennell's wife and four children. The incomplete picture of the 1814 banquet was later finished by other hands and is now after a long period of misattribution restored to Clennell's name in the Guildhall, London. By 1827 Clennell was living with relatives in Northumberland before his uncontrolled insanity led to his incarceration in a Newcastle asylum. He died on 9 February 1840 and was buried in St Andrew's churchyard, Newcastle upon Tyne.

Two self-portraits exist, one a sketch in the Laing Gallery, the other in oils as a figure in the Guildhall painting. They show a strong head but little of Clennell's figure, which the engraver Edward Willis described as 'small and in-kneed', adding that Clennell had 'a peculiar look with his eyes' (MS records for Chatto's *Treatise on Wood Engraving*, 1839, London Library). William Bell Scott described Clennell's son Luke as 'a short man of Herculean build and bluff face, full of energy and possessed of an impulsive mental force which I feared from the first moment I saw him'; Scott went on to tell of the son's decline into insanity at the same age as his father (*Autobiographical Notes*, 198–201). It may be reasonable to suppose that the son's sturdy frame was inherited. A further, unnamed, witness spoke of how much he loved Clennell: 'he was always so mild, so amiable, in short, such a GOOD fellow' (Dobson, 200).

Some of Clennell's watercolours for tailpiece subjects are in the British Museum and the Natural History Society of Northumbria, Newcastle upon Tyne. The Victoria and Albert Museum and the Laing Art Gallery hold many of his landscape and genre watercolours, including, in the latter, several for Scott's *Border Antiquities* (1814). Examples of his oils are in the Laing Art Gallery, the Yale Center for British Art, New Haven, Connecticut, and the Guildhall Art Gallery, London. Some of his original woodblocks are in the Newberry Library, Chicago, the Central Library, Newcastle upon Tyne, and in private collections.

IAIN BAIN

Sources V. Knight, 'Luke Clennell at the Guildhall', *Apollo*, 138 (1993), 234–41 · *Autobiographical notes of the life of William Bell Scott: and notices of his artistic and poetic circle of friends, 1830 to 1882*, ed. W. Minto, 2 vols. (1892) · *A memoir of Thomas Bewick, written by himself*, ed. I. Bain, rev. edn (1979) · R. Robinson, *Thomas Bewick: his life and times* (1887) · M. Postle, 'Luke Clennell, 1781–1840', MA report, Courtauld Inst., 1981 · J. Brown, *Ulgham: its story continued, a study of a Northumbrian village in its parish setting* (1986) · H. Miller, ed., *Memoirs of Dr Robert Blakey* (1879) · R. Welford, *Men of mark 'twixt Tyne and Tweed*, 3 vols. (1895) · A. Dobson, *Thomas Bewick and his pupils* (1884) · *IGI*
Archives Tyne and Wear Archives Service, family and business corresp., incl. the Beilby–Bewick account books showing wages and progress through apprenticeship
Likenesses L. Clennell, self-portrait, oils, Guildhall Art Gallery, London · L. Clennell, self-portrait, pencil drawing, Laing Gallery, Newcastle upon Tyne

Clenock [Clenocke], **Maurice** (*c*.1525–1580?), Roman Catholic ecclesiastic and administrator, was probably born in Clynnog Fawr, Caernarvonshire. He was educated at Oxford, possibly at Christ Church, proceeding BCL in 1548 after more than twelve years of study, by his own account. He lectured there on civil law for six years. He claimed to have studied law for a further eight years in Louvain (as well as theology for two years), Bologna and Padua, probably after he left England in 1559. He compounded for the rectorship of Gatcombe, Isle of Wight, to which Sir Geoffrey Pole had presented him, on 4 September 1554. He had become prebendary of Botevant in York Minster by 22 July 1556, but almost certainly never resided and resigned on 25 February 1561. Cardinal Pole appointed him dean of Shoreham and Croydon on 31 August 1557, after Clenock had obtained the rectory of Shoreham through other means, as well as that of Orpington, Kent, from Pole. Clenock was then identified as Pole's chaplain and domestic. He alleged that Pole made him chancellor of the prerogative court of Canterbury and dean of Canterbury peculiars, as well as legatine auditor, confessor to Pole and his household, and the cardinal's almoner and personal secretary, but only the first (between about August and October 1558) can be documented and Clenock was unusually called 'custos'; most of the rest seems unlikely, since Pole never identified him as anything more than chaplain, whether in an act of December 1557 or in his will, which Clenock witnessed.

Thomas Goldwell, bishop of St Asaph, presented Clenock to the rectory of Corwen or Curr Owen on 20 November 1556. He was probably the 'Mr Maurice' who had a room in Lambeth Palace at Pole's death in 1558. At about that time he was nominated bishop of Bangor, but was never consecrated. When Elizabeth came to the throne he is said to have surrendered his preferments and

to have had a licence to leave the realm, but he was certainly deprived of Orpington, perhaps not until 27 December 1566. Although in 1560 he accompanied Pole's former agent, Vincenzo Parpaglia, on an abortive mission to Elizabeth, by the following year he was urging Cardinal Morone, protector of England, to induce Philip II to depose the queen. Thereafter he went first to Louvain and then to Rome, about 1563, perhaps in company with Goldwell, although they very quickly came to head opposing factions there. Probably after his arrival in Rome an anonymous reporter judged him 'a good man, but … no preacher' and suitable for Bangor, should the pope decide to fill the see.

Once in Rome, Clenock became Morone's client. By 1564 he had entered the English Hospice, and in the following year became its warden; he kept rooms there until 1578. He almost immediately found himself in conflict with a faction of the hospice led by Nicholas Morton, which was backed by Goldwell. An attempt to depose Clenock in 1565 was thwarted by Parpaglia and Morone's auditor. Elected warden again in 1567 Clenock refused and became a chamberlain instead, a position which he held again in 1569–71 and 1573, at which time he was said to be without means of subsistence. His catechism, *Athravaeth Gristnogaul* ('Christian teaching'), with an introduction by Gruffydd Robert, appeared in Milan in 1568.

In 1575 and 1576, probably in co-operation with Owen Lewis, Clenock drafted several detailed plans for an invasion of England. He also proposed that Lewis be made a cardinal. During the discussions of these plans in Rome the decision was taken to convert the hospice into a college, and on 26 May 1576 Clenock again became warden. Within a year a proposal was floated that the Jesuits take over. The English students quickly rebelled against Clenock's government, alleging among other things that he favoured Welshmen. Morone firmly backed Clenock, separating hospice and college and extending Clenock's term as warden of the latter to two years and then making him perpetual rector in 1578, assisted by two (later three) Jesuits. Clenock traced the origins of his terminal difficulties to his refusal to remove Goldwell from his rooms at the hospice. Morone, in tandem with Lewis, tried to quash the rebellion, but the English party with backing from the Jesuit Robert Persons induced Pope Gregory XIII to remove Clenock, probably on the grounds that he was interfering with their missionary vocation. Clenock retired to Rouen and, embarking thence for Spain, was drowned at sea, probably in 1580.

T. F. MAYER

Sources Pole's register, LPL, fols. 27v – 28r · Biblioteca Apostolica Vaticana, Vatican City, MS Vat. lat. 12159, fols. 98r–v, 122r, 130r – 131r, 135r – 140v · 'The memoirs of Father Persons', ed. J. H. Pollen, *Miscellanea, II*, Catholic RS, 2 (1906), 12–218 · National Library of Malta, Arch. 17, Zammit Gabarretta, document 25 · *CSP Rome, 1572–8* · PRO, PROB 11/42A, fols. 107r – 108r · PRO, PROB 29/10, fol. 98r · PRO, SP 12/1, fols. 20r – 29r · A. Kenny, 'From hospice to college', *The Venerabile*, 21 (1962), 218–73 [sexcentenary issue: *The English hospice in Rome*] · J. M. Cleary, 'Dr Morys Clynnog's invasion projects', *Recusant History*, 8 (1965–6), 300–22 · *DWB* · *Dodd's Church history of England*, ed. M. A. Tierney, 5 vols. (1839–43), vol. 2, pp. cccxlvi–ccclxxiii · Wood, *Ath. Oxon.: Fasti* (1815), 126, 208 ·

Foster, *Alum. Oxon.* · Gillow, *Lit. biog. hist.*, 1.501–5 · C. Kitching, 'The prerogative court of Canterbury from Warham to Whitgift', *Continuity and change: personnel and administration of the Church of England, 1500–1642*, ed. R. O'Day and F. Heal (1976), 191–214, esp. 200 · G. M. Griffiths, 'St Asaph episcopal acts, 1536–1558', *Journal of the Historical Society of the Church in Wales*, 9 (1959), 32–69, esp. 46, 50 · *Fasti Angl., 1541–1857*, [York] · J. C. H. Aveling, *Catholic recusancy in the city of York, 1558–1791*, Catholic RS, monograph ser., 2 (1970) · PRO, E 334/4

Archives Archivio Vaticano, Vatican City, Misc. Arm. 64:28, fols. 51r, 68r, 274r · Westm. DA, Anglia II, no. 25, pp. 105–10

Clephan, James (1804–1888), journalist, was born on 17 March 1804 in Monkwearmouth, co. Durham, the second son and child of ten children born to Robert Clephan (1777?–1857), a baker, and his wife, Elizabeth Bails (1780?–1851). Robert Clephan had gone to England from Edinburgh and shortly after James's birth moved to Stockton-on-Tees, where his bakery, specializing in ship's biscuits, expanded into ship chandlery.

Robert and Elizabeth Clephan had belonged to the Church of Scotland, but in Stockton the family joined the Unitarian congregation meeting in the Presbyterian Chapel, High Street. Largely drawn from families of small tradesmen and working men, the congregation had declined from its once flourishing state and indeed was closed in 1817–20 in a dispute with a minister who had returned to orthodoxy and refused to give up the chapel. The Unitarians nevertheless remained a lively force in the culture of Stockton, a place for which James Clephan retained an abiding affection.

Apprenticed to a Stockton printer, in 1825 Clephan sought work in Edinburgh, where his father's family could offer support and where he greatly improved his skill. He returned to Stockton in 1827 and in October 1828 became a journeyman printer for the *Leicester Journal*, serving also as sub-editor. He was active in the Unitarian congregation at Great Meeting and in the Leicester Mechanics' Institute. In 1838 he was appointed editor of the *Gateshead Observer*, a weekly of recent foundation, which he edited (being as well sub-editor and reporter) until his retirement in 1859. The *Observer* was already a lively and hard-hitting paper when Clephan joined it but, in an age when newspapers borrowed heavily from each other, his incisive, witty, and quotable commentary brought it a national reputation. On his retirement his fellow journalists in the area presented him with a silver inkstand and a cheque for £250.

On 16 July 1832 Clephan married Jane Pringle (b. 1801/2) of Stockton, who died on 10 March 1849; there were no children. After his retirement he returned to Stockton, but in 1861 was lured back into newspaper work, freelancing for the *Newcastle Daily Chronicle* and for the *Weekly Chronicle*, with which he maintained a connection after his second retirement in the mid-1870s. His essays for the *Chronicle* newspapers drew on his deep literary and antiquarian knowledge and his memories of the social revolution—from stagecoach to railway and from sail to steam—through which he had lived. In his later years his friends received privately printed Christmas volumes made up of his essays and poems. A list of his separately published

works appears at the end of the sketch in Richard Welford's *Men of Mark 'twixt Tyne and Tweed* (1895); two series of manuscript letters, which he transcribed and somewhat abridged and which were later deposited in the Northumberland Record Office, offer delightful glimpses into a closely knit family in a provincial town.

Clephan was a staunch Liberal and reformer. He steadily opposed capital punishment and was a strong advocate of sanitary reform, notably in a series of articles in the 1850s calling attention to three earlier visitations of cholera to Gateshead and reprinted in *The Three Warnings* (1854). He was a dedicated supporter of the Gateshead Mechanics' Institute and the Gateshead Dispensary, and of the Newcastle Literary and Philosophical Society, the Newcastle Antiquarian Society, and the Unitarian congregation in Newcastle, meeting first in Hanover Square and later as the Church of the Divine Unity.

At the beginning of the 1880s Clephan withdrew from all journalistic work, except for occasional articles for the Unitarian *Christian Life*, and thereafter was largely confined by ill health to his room. He remained his charming, congenial self, however, until his death from bronchitis at his home, 9 Picton Place, Newcastle, on 25 February 1888; he was buried in Jesmond old cemetery in Newcastle on 28 February.   R. K. WEBB

Sources *Newcastle Daily Chronicle* (27 Feb 1888) · R. Welford, *Men of mark 'twixt Tyne and Tweed*, 2 (1895), 593–6 · Northumbd RO, Clephan papers · *Christian Life* (3 March 1888) · *Leicester Daily Mercury* (27 Feb 1888) · registers, High Street Chapel, Stockton-on-Tees, PRO · *Two hundred years: a short account … of the Society of Protestant Dissenters … at Stockton-on-Tees* (1888) · A. Temple Patterson, *Radical Leicester: a history of Leicester, 1780–1850* (1954) · *Gateshead Observer* (1838–59) · d. cert.

Archives Northumbd RO, Newcastle upon Tyne

Likenesses photograph, repro. in *Archaeologia Aeliana*, 3rd ser., 10 (1913) · wood-engraving, repro. in Welford, *Men of mark*, 594

Wealth at death £610 10s. 6d.: probate, 28 March 1888, CGPLA Eng. & Wales

Clephane, John (1701/2–1758), physician, was born in Scotland, probably the eldest of the three sons and two daughters of Colonel William Clephane (d. 1727), a Jacobite who escaped after the 1715 rebellion, and Elizabeth, daughter of James Cramond, priest of the Scottish Episcopal church. Between 1716 and 1724, suspected of being a Jacobite, he took a full arts and divinity course at St Andrews University. He then matriculated in the faculty of letters at Leiden in 1724 and studied medicine under Boerhaave, with whom he later corresponded. About 1725 he joined his father in Antwerp but returned to Scotland after his father's death. On 29 May 1729 he received an MD at St Andrews, with testimonials from Adam Murray MD, Thomas Carmichael, and James Blair.

In 1731 Clephane was in Groningen, supervising the studies of Lord Sherard Manners, and between 1731 and 1737 he travelled as tutor to the younger sons of the duke of Rutland, lords Robert and Charles Manners. In 1735, living in the Rutland house in Cavendish Square, London, he is said to have been engaged to Lady Diana Grey, but in 1736 she married George Middleton and Clephane remained a bachelor. In 1739 Clephane travelled with Lord

Maunsel to Italy and set out in October 1740 on a similar journey as tutor to John Bouverie; their time in Florence was recorded in letters from Horace Mann to Horace Walpole. Clephane was again in Italy in 1744 with Lord Montrath.

By 1746 Clephane was practising medicine in London, and through Lord Sandwich he was appointed on 16 April as physician to the force, under General Sinclair, that failed to destroy the French East India Company stores at Port L'Orient, Brittany. He also met the philosopher and historian David Hume, Sinclair's secretary, who was to become a lifelong friend. On 8 January 1747 Clephane was elected FRS, and was described by Richard Mead as 'well skilled in Natural History, Chemistry and other branches of useful knowledge' (Royal Society, fellowship certificate). Four months later Lord Sandwich found him employment as physician to the army hospital at Osterhout, Flanders, after which in 1749 he was briefly superintendent of the army hospital at Ipswich.

Placed on half pay and back in London, on 8 May 1751 Clephane was appointed physician to St George's Hospital. By 1752 he was living in Golden Square, and on 25 June he became a licentiate of the Royal College of Physicians. He was soon involved in disputes between the licentiates and the college, and in July 1752 he took out a writ against the college to recover the fees that, possibly illegally, he had been forced to pay for his licence. The college, fearing to lose the case, repaid the fees in December and the case was withdrawn. As a doctor, Clephane was interested in the possible connection between weather and disease, but his records were never published. He was an original member of the Society of London Physicians, founded in 1754, and published articles in its *Medical Observations and Inquiries* (vol. 1, 1757) on the successful treatment of lockjaw and the history of gout powder.

Although unwell, Clephane was recalled to military service in 1758 as physician to a force assembled in the Isle of Wight to destroy French ports. At the beginning of August he was taken ill on his ship, which was lying off Cherbourg, and he returned to the Isle of Wight, where he died on 11 October; his place of burial is not known. A classical scholar with interests outside medicine, he had correspondents in Britain and on the continent. Far from wealthy, he helped his relations financially when he could. His sister Elizabeth, married to Hugh Rose of Kilravock, administered his estate and was residuary legatee, and a collection of Clephane's papers are among those of the Roses of Kilravock at Register House, Edinburgh. William Hunter sent Elizabeth a copy of *Medical Observations and Inquiries*, praising Clephane's 'knowledge both natural and acquired' and 'his amiable and conciliating temper' that preserved harmony in the society (Innes, 462). Elizabeth may have given Clephane's medical papers to Hunter; they were later in the Hunterian Library, Glasgow University. Clephane is now mainly known as a correspondent of David Hume, through the publication of Hume's letters to him by J. H. Burton in his *Life of David Hume* (1846). No letters from Clephane to Hume are known.

HELEN BROCK

Sources C. Innes, *A genealogical deduction of the family Rose of Kilravock etc.* (1848), 412, 414, 415, 421–4, 445–65 · NA Scot., Rose MSS · *A letter from a physician in town to his friend in the country concerning the disputes* (1753) [Library R. C. P.] · U. St Andr. L. · RS · St George's Hospital, London, archives · Royal College of Physicians, committee books · H. Barlow, *Descriptive catalogue of the legal and other documents in the archives of the Royal College of Physicians of London* (1924) · G. Clark and A. M. Cooke, *A history of the Royal College of Physicians of London*, 2 (1966), 556–7 · *The letters of David Hume*, ed. J. Y. T. Greig, 2 vols. (1932) · Walpole, *Corr.*, 17.63, 67, 70–71, 97, 100, 116–17, 146, 154; 18.479; 33.169; 43.235 · U. Glas., Clephane medical MSS · Fortescue, *Brit. army*, 2nd edn, 2.156, 348 · *GM*, 1st ser., 28 (1758), 504 · J. Ingamells, ed., *A dictionary of British and Irish travellers in Italy, 1701–1800* (1997)

Archives NA Scot., corresp. and papers · U. Glas., Hunterian collection | BL, letters to Thomas Birch, Add. MS 4302, fols. 260–84

Wealth at death in credit £122; £50 owed him not to be claimed, furniture, 15 Aug 1758: St George's Hospital, London, archives

Clérisseau, Charles-Louis (*bap.* 1721, *d.* 1820), architect and architectural draughtsman, was baptized in Paris on 28 August 1721, the son of Jean Clérisseau, seller of perfumed gloves, and his wife, Jeanne Rosselet. By 1745 he was attending the Académie Royale d'Architecture as a pupil of the architect Gabriel-Germain Boffrand. In 1746 he won the grand prix, which led to three years' study in Rome as *pensionnaire* of the Académie Française. He arrived in Italy in 1749, and stayed there until 1767. On 1 December 1763 he married Thérèse, daughter of the sculptor Pierre L'Estache (*c.*1688–1774).

Clérisseau was one of a succession of young architects and artists in Rome who, since the early 1740s, had been sowing the seeds of neo-classicism. He found his métier (and lifelong bread and butter) in the production of views, mainly in gouache, of real or idealized classical ruins. His contacts included friendships with Giovanni Battista Piranesi and Johann Joachim Winckelmann. While in Italy he acted as architectural mentor to Sir William Chambers, and, more significantly, to Robert and James Adam, thus profoundly influencing the course of neo-classicism in Britain. His contact with Chambers, datable to between 1751 and 1754, is recorded only in a lost drawing, begun by Chambers and finished by Clérisseau, and some gossip from Robert Adam: 'I have also got acquaintance with one Clérisseau who draws in architecture delightfully in the free manner I wanted.' Chambers, he wrote, 'owes all hints and notions to this man with whom he differed and to whom he behaved ungratefully' (McCormick, 23). On arriving in Italy in 1755, Adam had placed himself entirely in Clérisseau's hands. Clérisseau both selected objects for study and taught Adam to draw in his characteristically picturesque manner. Adam saw that Clérisseau's draughtsmanship could be useful for the publications essential to future success. A plan for a revised edition of A.-B. Desgodetz's *Edifices antiques de Rome* came to nothing, but in 1757, the year in which he left Italy, Adam engaged Clérisseau on a regular basis for the production of most of the drawings and the arrangements for engraving his *Ruins of the Palace of the Emperor Diocletian in Spalatro in Dalmatia*, published in 1764. In 1760–61 James Adam also studied under Clérisseau. By this time Robert's relationship with Clérisseau had turned from one of admiring friendship to that of employer and employee—Clérisseau was refused extra money and proper recognition for his work on *Spalatro*.

In 1767 Clérisseau left for France, and in 1769, as 'painter of architecture', became a member of the Académie Royale de Peinture et de Sculpture. In 1771 he moved to Britain, according to Edward Edwards at the invitation of Robert Adam, but also perhaps to be nearer the British patrons who were the principal admirers of his pictures. He exhibited four pictures, a bath and a sepulchral chamber 'composed after the manner of the Ancients', a view of the Forum of Nerva, and a triumphal arch, at the Royal Academy in 1772 (when living at Great Marlborough Street) and also exhibited at the Society of Artists in 1775, 1776, and 1790. Of design activities there is less evidence. There are drawings of ornament (RIBA) made by pupils, perhaps those of Robert Adam, but corrected by Clérisseau. In 1774 he designed for Lansdowne House (an Adam project) a gallery (not executed), and an aedicule for the garden. Although his movements after 1771 are uncertain, Clérisseau was certainly back in Paris by 1775, where he carried out schemes of interior decoration. In 1775 he designed a 'Roman house' and a triumphal arch (unexecuted) for Catherine the Great, who made him her *premier architecte*. The Russian designs are among the 1170 Clérisseau drawings bought by Catherine (The Hermitage, St Petersburg). The next largest collection is at Sir John Soane's Museum, London. In 1778 he designed his only major executed building, the Palais de Justice at Metz. In 1815 he was made a member of the Légion d'honneur, but his last twenty-five years were inactive. He died at his home, 14 rue Molière, Auteuil, outside Paris, on 19 January 1820, leaving an exceptional architectural library. Clérisseau's difficult character and proud and prickly behaviour while doing business may account for the failure of many of his schemes.   MICHAEL SNODIN

Sources T. J. McCormick, *Charles-Louis Clérisseau and the genesis of neo-classicism* (1990) [citing many other sources] · J. Lejeaux, 'Charles-Louis Clérisseau, architecte', *L'Architecture*, 41/4 (1928), 115 · P. J. Mariette, *Abécédario*, 1 (1853), 378 · E. Edwards, *Anecdotes of painters* (1808); facs. edn (1970), 73
Archives NA Scot., Clerk of Penicuik papers, Adam MSS
Likenesses P. L. Ghezzi, pen-and-ink caricature, 1751, Gabinetto delle Stampe, Rome · P. L. Ghezzi, pen-and-ink caricature, 1752, BM · J. Fischer, fresco, *c*.1772, Schloss Wörlitz · crayon drawing, 1809, Musée Carnavalet, Paris · probably J. Fischer, crayon drawing, priv. coll. · crayon drawing (after Légrand), Musée Carnavalet, Paris · engraving, priv. coll.

Clerk. *See also* Clark, Clarke, Clerke.

Clerk, Sir Dugald (1854–1932), mechanical engineer, was born at Glasgow on 31 March 1854, the eldest son of Donald Clerk, machinist, of Glasgow, and his wife, Martha Symington, second daughter of John Brown, of Glasgow. He was about fifteen years old when he began his training in the drawing office of H. O. Robinson & Co., of Glasgow, and in his father's works, also attending classes at Anderson's University, Glasgow. From 1871 to 1876 he studied at Anderson's University and the Yorkshire College of Science, Leeds, under the chemist T. E. Thorpe, who made him one of his assistants and set him to work on the fractionation of petroleum oils. He had intended to become a chemical engineer, but after seeing a Lenoir gas engine at work in a joiner's shop in Glasgow, this and other forms of the internal combustion engine became the leading interest of his life.

After his return to Glasgow, Clerk was for a short time assistant to E. J. Mills, the Young professor of technical chemistry at Anderson's University; he then devoted himself to research on the theory and design of the gas engine, first with the Glasgow firm of Thomson, Sterne & Co., from 1877 to 1885, then with Messrs Tangyes, of Birmingham. Clerk married, in 1883, Margaret (*d.* 1930), elder daughter of Alexander Hanney, of Helensburgh.

Sir Dugald Clerk (1854–1932), by Archibald Standish Hartrick, 1906

In 1888 Clerk joined his friend George Croydon Marks in the firm of Marks and Clerk, consulting engineers and patent agents; this partnership lasted for the rest of his life. From 1892 to 1899 he was engineering director of Messrs Kynoch, of Birmingham, for whom he designed machinery for the manufacture of ammunition, and from 1902 he was a director and from 1929 until his death chairman of the National Gas Engine Company, of Ashton under Lyne.

Clerk began his work on the gas engine at the end of 1876. His first patent, taken out in 1877, was followed by a second in 1878, and in 1881 he patented an engine working on what became known as the Clerk (two-stroke) cycle, in which the main crankshaft received an impulse at each revolution, in contrast to the Otto (four-stroke) engine in which there was one impulse for each two revolutions. Engines of the Clerk type were manufactured in considerable numbers, but their popularity waned for a time after the lapse of the Otto patent in 1890. The Clerk cycle, however, came into extensive use for gas engines of the larger sizes.

Clerk's assiduous researches on the internal combustion engine, the specific heat of gases, and the explosion of gaseous mixtures won him an international reputation. He embodied his results in a book, *The Gas Engine* (1886), which subsequently appeared as *The Gas, Petrol and Oil Engine* (1909), and in many communications to scientific and technical societies, particularly the Institution of Civil Engineers, to which, between 1882 and 1928, he contributed five papers and two James Forrest lectures (1904 and 1920). The second of these lectures dealt with coal conservation in the United Kingdom and followed the theme of his Thomas Hawksley lecture to the Institution of Mechanical Engineers in 1915 on the world's supplies of fuel and motive power. In 1917 he delivered the first Trueman Wood lecture to the Royal Society of Arts.

During the First World War, Clerk was director of engineering research at the Admiralty (1916–17) and served on many committees concerned with the war effort. He was also chairman of the water power resources committee of the conjoint board of scientific societies (1917) and a member of the water power resources committee appointed by the Board of Trade in 1918. Other activities included chairmanship of the delegacy of the City and Guilds College, South Kensington, London (1918–19), and membership of the University Grants Committee and the Carnegie Trust for Scotland. He was frequently a judge at the reliability trials which were fashionable in the early days of the motor car.

Clerk, who was appointed KBE in 1917, received honorary degrees from the universities of Glasgow, Leeds, Liverpool, Manchester, and St Andrews. The Royal Society of Arts awarded him the Albert medal in 1922, and the Royal Society, of which he was elected a fellow in 1908, a royal medal in 1924. For the papers which he read before the Institution of Civil Engineers he received the Watt medal (1882), Telford prize (1882 and 1886), and Telford gold medal (1907). Ill health dogged his latter years; he died at his home, Lukyns, Ewhurst, Surrey, on 12 November 1932.   H. M. Ross, *rev.* John Bosnell

Sources H. R. R., *Obits. FRS*, 1 (1932–5), 101–2 • *The Engineer* (18 Nov 1932) • *Engineering* (18 Nov 1932) • *PICE*, 235 (1932–3), 507–9 • W. A. Tookey, 'Sir Dugald Clerk and the gas engine', *Journal of the Institution of Civil Engineers*, 12 (1938–9), 246–7 [lecture, abridged report] • *Institution of Mechanical Engineers: Proceedings*, 123 (1932) • *Nature*, 130 (1932), 953–4 • *CGPLA Eng. & Wales* (1933)
Likenesses A. S. Hartrick, pencil, crayon, and watercolour drawing, 1906, Scot. NPG [*see illus.*] • H. Speed, oils, 1910, Inst. CE • W. Stoneman, three photographs, 1917–27, NPG • photograph, repro. in H. R. R., *Obits. FRS*, facing p. 101
Wealth at death £54,412 9*s.* 11*d.*: probate, 10 Feb 1933, *CGPLA Eng. & Wales*

Clerk, Sir George, of Penicuick, sixth baronet (1787–1867), politician, was the elder son of James Clerk of the East India Company and his wife, Janet, daughter of George Irving of Newton, Lanarkshire, and grandson of Sir George Clerk *Maxwell; he was born on 19 November 1787, and educated at the high school, Edinburgh, and at Trinity College, Oxford, where he was admitted on 21 January 1806. His father died in 1793, and in 1798 he succeeded his uncle, Sir John Clerk, as the sixth baronet. He was admitted an advocate in 1809, and created a DCL of Oxford on 5 July 1810. At a by-election in July 1811, supported by the Melville family interest, he was elected MP for Midlothian (Edinburghshire), for which he sat until 1832. From a family strongly tory, Clerk was on 5 March 1819 appointed one of the lords of the Admiralty in the Liverpool administration. He held this post until May 1827, when he became clerk of the ordnance. He was gazetted one of the council of the duke of Clarence, the lord high admiral, on 4 February 1828, but upon the duke's resignation was reappointed a lord of the Admiralty. On 5 August 1830 he became under-secretary for the Home department for the few remaining months of the Wellington administration.

At the first general election after the passing of the Reform Bill, which took place in December 1832, Clerk lost his seat for Midlothian, being defeated by Sir John Dalrymple, the whig candidate, by 601 to 536. He was re-elected, however, in January 1835 for his old constituency, but at the next general election, in August 1837, was defeated by William Gibson Craig. In April of the following year he was elected unopposed for the borough of Stamford, which he also represented in the succeeding parliament. In July 1847 Clerk was returned for Dover—despite opposition from an extreme protestant—but, after unsuccessfully contesting that constituency in July 1852 and March 1857, made no further attempt to re-enter parliament. He held the post of secretary to the Treasury in Sir Robert Peel's administration from December 1834 to April 1835, and from September 1841 to February 1845. On 5 February 1845 he was appointed vice-president of the Board of Trade, and was at the same time sworn of the privy council. In the same month he was made master of the Royal Mint on the retirement of W. E. Gladstone. Clerk held both these offices until July 1846, when Sir Robert

Peel's second administration came to an end. For many years he was an able and zealous supporter of the tory party, and particularly of Peel, a friend from his Oxford days. He was an earlier convert to free trade than the majority of his party (*Hansard 3*, 83.1420–39), and continued to belong to the Peelite section until it was finally broken up.

On 13 August 1810 Clerk married Maria (*d.* 7 Sept 1866), second daughter of Ewan Law of Horsted Place, Sussex, with whom he had eight sons and four daughters. He was president of the Zoological Society 1862–7, FRS, chairman of the Royal Academy of Music, an elder of the Church of Scotland, and a deputy lieutenant of Midlothian. He died on 23 December 1867, at Penicuik House, near Edinburgh, in his eighty-first year. He was succeeded in the title by his eldest son, James; James Clerk Maxwell was his great-nephew.   G. F. R. BARKER, *rev.* H. C. G. MATTHEW

Sources HoP, *Commons* · *GM*, 4th ser., 5 (1868), 246–7 · *The Times* (25 Dec 1867) · J. B. Conacher, *The Peelites and the party system* (1972) · Burke, *Peerage*
Archives NA Scot., corresp. and papers | BL, corresp. with W. E. Gladstone, Add. MSS 44355–44527 · BL, corresp. with Sir Robert Peel, etc., Add. MSS 40348–40601 · NA Scot., corresp. with Lord Dalhousie
Likenesses W. Dyce, oils, 1830, Penicuik House, Midlothian · J. Watson-Gordon, oils, exh. RA 1857, Penicuik House, Midlothian

Clerk, Sir George Russell (1800–1889), administrator in India, was born at Worting House, Hampshire, in 1800, the eldest son of John Clerk (1759–1842) and his wife, Anne (*d.* 1820), daughter of Carew Mildmay of Shawford House, Hampshire. In 1815 he was nominated to the Bengal civil service and entered the East India Company's college at Haileybury.

Clerk arrived in Bengal in February 1818 and initially appeared destined for a career in the secretariat; as early as 1822 he was first assistant to the secretary in the secret and political department. Some time in the 1820s, however, he began an affair with Mary, wife of Colonel Stewart, but was unable to marry her until Stewart died some years later. When Calcutta society refused to receive Mary, Clerk, who had been disinherited by his father over the affair, opted for a career on Bengal's far-flung western frontier.

In 1829 Clerk became first assistant to the resident in Delhi; in 1831, political agent at Ambala; in March 1840, agent to the governor-general for the affairs of the Punjab; and, finally, in October 1842, envoy to the court of Lahore. He effectively controlled British relations with Lahore from 1831 until 1843, and, in contrast to Auckland's pro-Afghanistan policy, advocated the construction of a strong Sikh buffer state in the Punjab to break what he saw as the chain of Islam running from central Asia to Hindustan.

In 1843 Clerk was appointed lieutenant-governor of the North-Western Provinces. Distrustful of the social-engineering objectives of the utilitarians, he briefly interrupted the levelling land revenue policies then in vogue in the North-Western Provinces, before being promoted in

November 1844 to a seat on the executive council in Calcutta. In January 1847 he was appointed governor of Bombay, but was forced by ill health to retire early the following year.

Back in England, Clerk declined the governorship of the Cape of Good Hope, but went instead to South Africa in 1853 as a commissioner to negotiate the boundaries of the Orange Free State. In 1857 he became secretary of the India board and in 1858 permanent under-secretary of state for India. In May 1860 he again accepted the governorship of Bombay but two years later, as before, was compelled by ill health to resign. In 1863 he was appointed to the secretary of state's council for India, which position he retained until his retirement in 1876.

Clerk was a Conservative, who trusted to experience and common sense rather than political theorizing. He disapproved, on both financial and moral grounds, of the annexations of Sind, the Punjab, and Oudh, arguing that the rebellion of 1857 was largely the result of Britain breaking faith with her former allies. He disliked evangelicalism and was scathing about missionary hopes of universal Christianization.

Clerk was made a KCB in 1848, KCSI in 1861, and GCSI in 1866. He died at his home, 33 Elm Park Gardens, Middlesex, on 25 July 1889 and was buried at Bournemouth. He was survived by his three sons: the eldest, Claude, who was born in 1833 and became tutor to the nizam of Hyderabad; General Sir Godfrey Clerk (1835–1908); and Colonel John Clerk (*d.* 1919). Mary Clerk had died in 1878.

KATHERINE PRIOR

Sources M. E. Yapp, *Strategies of British India: Britain, Iran and Afghanistan, 1798–1850* (1980) · H. T. Prinsep and R. Doss, eds., *A general register of the Hon'ble East India Company's civil servants of the Bengal establishment from 1790 to 1842* (1844) · *East-India Register* · F. C. Danvers and others, *Memorials of old Haileybury College* (1894) · *DNB* · BL OIOC, Haileybury MSS · BL, Clerk MSS · H. T. Lambrick, *Sir Charles Napier and Sind* (1952) · *The Times* (27 July 1889), 7 · I. Krishen, *An historical interpretation of the correspondence of Sir George Russell Clerk, political agent, Ambala and Ludhiana, 1831–43* (1952) · Burke, *Gen. GB* (1937)
Archives BL OIOC, corresp. and papers, MS Eur. D 538 · BL OIOC, corresp. relating to India | BL OIOC, corresp. with J. C. Melvill, MS Eur. B 137 · Government RO, Lahore, Pakistan, Ambala and Ludhiana agency records · priv. coll., Cathcart MSS · PRO, corresp. with Lord Ellenborough, PRO 30/12 · W. Yorks. AS, Leeds, letters to Lord Canning
Wealth at death £11,995 9*s.* 2*d.*: probate, 16 Sept 1889, *CGPLA Eng. & Wales*

Clerk, Sir George Russell (1874–1951), diplomatist, was born on 29 November 1874 in India, the only son of General Sir Godfrey Clerk (1835–1908), army officer, later commandant of the rifle brigade and groom-in-waiting to Queen Victoria and Edward VII, and his wife, Alice Mary, daughter of William Edward Frere, of the Bombay civil service; his grandfather was Sir George Russell *Clerk (1800–1889), East India Company servant. He was educated at Eton College and at New College, Oxford, where he received a third class in *literae humaniores* (1897). After studying foreign languages abroad, he passed the Foreign Office entrance examination in December 1898.

Clerk served in March–April 1901 as acting third secretary to the duke of Abercorn's special mission to the courts of northern Europe, announcing the accession of Edward VII. In April 1903 he was posted, at his own request, to Abyssinia, where the British agency was no more than a group of round tuguls with thatched roofs and mud and wattle walls. He was twice left in charge and learnt Amharic before being recalled owing to ill health. He was promoted to second secretary in February 1907 and to assistant clerk in May 1907, and again served at the Foreign Office from May 1907 to October 1910. In the latter month he was promoted to first secretary and posted to the embassy at Constantinople, and in his spare time learned Turkish. In February 1912 he returned to the Foreign Office, where he was promoted in October 1913 to senior clerk and head of the Eastern department. On 16 June 1908 he had married (Janet) Muriel Whitwell, an accomplished artist, and daughter of Edward Robson Whitwell, of Yarm-on-Tees, Yorkshire. They had no children.

At the outbreak of war in 1914 Clerk was appointed head of the Foreign Office's new war department, which combined the pre-war regional departments covering Europe. He was promoted counsellor in December 1916. He worked closely with the secretary to the war cabinet, Maurice Hankey, forming one of his most important official relationships. In January 1917 he attended the conference in Rome at which the allies' overall campaign strategy for the year was planned. Later that month he accompanied Lord Milner on his mission to Russia. From January to September 1919 he was private secretary to Lord Curzon, the acting foreign secretary, and, with many of the senior officials in attendance at the Paris peace conference, he was in effect under-secretary. In August 1919 he was himself sent to Paris to serve as secretary to the foreign secretary, Sir Arthur Balfour.

In September 1919 Clerk was appointed the first British minister to the new Czechoslovak state. First, however, he was sent on a special mission by the peace conference to Bucharest and Budapest, to secure the evacuation of the Romanian army from Hungary. During a stay in Budapest from October to December 1919, he witnessed the removal of the Romanian army, which in turn opened the way for the entry of the White forces under Admiral Horthy. Clerk's anti-Bolshevism made him tolerant of Horthy and the 'White terror' he unleashed upon Hungary, and his association with the admiral became controversial. In his defence, it was argued that his attitude was dictated by necessity since there was little choice but to use these forces if order was to be restored in the country.

Throughout the war Clerk had advocated the dismemberment of the Habsburg empire and had been sympathetic to the views of the *New Europe* group led by R. W. Seton-Watson. This connection led him to become acquainted with many of eastern Europe's future leaders. The decision to send him to Prague was inspired in part by his good relations with President Masaryk. Clerk did

much to establish a good diplomatic atmosphere in Prague, and he was one of the few British ministers to sympathize with the Czechoslovaks over their efforts to handle the minorities question. He was less successful in his aspiration to make Czechoslovakia a centre for British influence in central Europe, when Curzon decided to swing away from Prague to Budapest. Arguments with the British ministers to Budapest and Vienna over policy also marked Clerk's tenure.

In November 1926 Clerk was appointed ambassador to Turkey and once again he was called upon to improve a strained diplomatic relationship. He succeeded in bringing about a rapprochement in Anglo-Turkish relations, damaged not only by the First World War but also by Britain's subsequent support for Greece's invasion in 1919 and compounded by a longer-lasting distrust of the Turkish leader, Kemal Atatürk. Clerk could have expected a major embassy, such as Berlin, as his next posting, but he received instead the minor embassy at Brussels, in October 1933. A few months later, however, in April 1934, he was the surprise choice to become ambassador to Paris in succession to Lord Tyrrell. Clerk's tenure of the Paris embassy witnessed the prelude to the Second World War. Acting upon instructions Clerk played an important role during the Spanish Civil War when, in a meeting with the foreign minister, Yvon Delbos, on 7 August 1936, he helped to convince the French government to adopt the British policy of non-intervention. None the less, Clerk was one of the group of ambassadors, including Horace Rumbold and Eric Phipps, who were alive to, and warned of, the threat from Germany. As ambassador he was a notable host and particularly enjoyed entertaining members of the French aristocracy at the Jockey Club in Paris. Lady Clerk, with whom his relationship was often strained, preferred informality as much as her husband preferred formality.

Clerk retired from the diplomatic service in April 1937 and became an active member of the Royal Geographical Society, serving as president during the difficult war years of 1941–5. He played an important role in overseeing the transition from the age of exploration to that of the scholarly study of detail. A cigar smoker, he was a passionate fisherman, stag hunter, polo player, card player, and lover of books. Harold Nicolson, who served under him, observed that the habitually tidy Clerk 'was impervious to disturbance; he would have mounted the scaffold with the same imperturbability as he mounted the steps of the Turf Club, his spats and monocle shining in the summer air' (Nicolson, 859). An apparent dilettantism masked a forceful personality which enabled Clerk either to smooth previously ruffled feelings, as he did in Prague and Turkey, or to implement difficult policies, as he did in Budapest, or to see to the efficient administration of a wartime department, as he did during the First World War. He was appointed CMG (1908), CB (1914), KCMG (1917), PC (1926), and GCMG (1929). He held the grand cordon of the Légion d'honneur from France and decorations from Italy, Russia, and Czechoslovakia. He died at 29 Cleveland Gardens,

Paddington, London, on 18 June 1951. A funeral service was held at Golders Green, and a memorial service at St Margaret's, Westminster, London.   ERIK GOLDSTEIN

Sources DNB · H. Seton-Watson and C. Seton-Watson, *The making of a new Europe: R. W. Seton-Watson and the last years of Austria-Hungary* (1981) · H. Rumbold, Bodl. Oxf., MSS Add. · Bodl. Oxf., MSS Lord Simon · H. Nicolson, 'Marginal comment', *The Spectator* (29 June 1951), 859 · *GJ*, 117 (1951), 369–70 · G. Protheroe, 'Sir George Clerk and the struggle for British influence in central Europe, 1919–26', *Diplomacy and Statecraft* [forthcoming] · T. Hohler, *Diplomatic petrel* (1942) · M. Peterson, *Both sides of the curtain: an autobiography* (1950) · R. Barclay, *Ernest Bevin and the foreign office, 1932–1969* (1975) · J. Dreifort, *Yvon Delbos at the Quai d'Orsay* (1973) · M. Thomas, *Britain, France, and appeasement: Anglo-French relations in the popular front era* (1996) · *WWW, 1951–60* · Burke, *Peerage* · FO List · CGPLA Eng. & Wales (1951)
Archives FILM BFI NFTVA, news footage
Likenesses W. Stoneman, two photographs, 1931–47, NPG · C. Sheridan, bronze head, Gov. Art Coll.
Wealth at death £25,654 17s. 3d.: probate, 17 Oct 1951, CGPLA Eng. & Wales

Clerk, John (1481/2?–1541), diplomat and bishop of Bath and Wells, was probably one of several sons of Clement Clerk of Much Livermere, Suffolk, and very likely the John Clerk of Norwich diocese dispensed in 1501 to hold a benefice despite being aged only nineteen.

Early career in diplomacy Having graduated BA from Cambridge in 1498, and MA in 1502, Clerk went to study law at Bologna, where he became a doctor of canon law in 1510 (he was generally, and probably rightly, credited with the doctorate of both laws). He took service in the household of Cardinal Bainbridge at Rome, and was briefly chamberlain of the English Hospice in Rome, but returned to England after the cardinal's death in 1514. Having transferred to the service of Cardinal Wolsey, he was appointed dean of the Chapel Royal in 1516, and by now had a clutch of parochial benefices as well, though it is not always possible to be certain that a benefice held by one of the many John Clerks was actually held by him. He certainly held the rectories of Rothbury, Northumberland (1512–23); Portishead, Somerset (1513–19); Ditcheat, Somerset (resigned by 1519); Ivychurch, Kent (1514–23); and South Molton, Devon (1519–23). To these he added the archdeaconry of Colchester and the deanery of St George's, Windsor, in 1519.

John Clerk occupied a prominent place in English politics throughout the chancellorship of Cardinal Wolsey, to whose patronage he owed his choicer ecclesiastical preferments, including, as he later remarked with gratitude, his promotion as bishop of Bath and Wells in 1523. At first his role was essentially that of the confidential intermediary between the king and the cardinal. In 1519 he was appointed a judge in Star Chamber, and he would often figure as judge or arbitrator thereafter, for example between the marquess of Dorset and Lord Hastings in 1527. Indeed, for just under a year, from 20 October 1522, he was master of the rolls. But it was as a diplomat that he found his métier. In 1519 he embarked upon the first of many missions, dispatched back to Rome (and *en route* putting in an appearance at the court of Louise of Savoy).

Attendance at the Field of Cloth of Gold in 1520 was perhaps hardly diplomacy of the highest order, but in his second mission, once more to Rome (1521–2), he was entrusted with the prestigious task of presenting to Pope Leo X a fine copy of Henry VIII's refutation of Luther, the *Assertio septem sacramentorum*, with verses personally inscribed by the king. The ceremony itself, on 2 October 1521, was in secret consistory rather than in the glare of publicity for which he had hoped. But he made the best of it, and marked the occasion with a lengthy oration which was subsequently printed and bound with the *Assertio* when it was generally released early next year.

Clerk's third mission to Rome followed in 1523–5. At an early stage he was provided to the see of Bath and Wells, succeeding his patron, Wolsey, and took advantage of the opportunity to be consecrated bishop in Rome itself in 1523. Having left Rome in December 1525, he served as ambassador at the French court from July 1526 to September 1527, and again from March to November 1528. John Clerk was manifestly an able and effective diplomat. The frequency with which he served in this capacity is perhaps sufficient testimony, but to this we can add the quality of his dispatches, which were regular and packed with information. Moreover, he got results. Henry VIII was delighted with the papal title *Fidei defensor* which Clerk wheedled out of Leo X (and preserved through Leo's death and the election of his successor, Adrian VI). And he continued to serve his patron as well as his king. It was Clerk who secured the series of bulls in the early 1520s which conceded to Wolsey unprecedented powers as papal legate in England.

The price of resistance Clerk's political career was stopped in its tracks by the king's Great Matter. Despite the lead of his patron and the example of most of his colleagues in the cardinal's service, Clerk affiliated himself at an early stage to the camp of Katherine of Aragon. When Henry VIII was trying to win over Sir Thomas More to his cause, the king gave More some papers to guide his thoughts, and then suggested that Clerk and Cuthbert Tunstall should look over them with him. Although this has been interpreted as meaning that Clerk and Tunstall were intended to persuade More, the latter's subsequent excuse to the king, that neither he nor the others were really competent to judge of the issues raised, shows that all three were in the same boat, as men whom Henry wished to have on his side. Both Tunstall and Clerk were to be among the counsel appointed for Queen Katherine in the tribunal which convened at Blackfriars in 1529 to adjudicate on the validity of the marriage. For the tribunal itself Clerk composed a treatise on the queen's behalf, but it is not known to have survived—Clerk himself and More are known to have burnt copies. Clerk's involvement in the divorce proceedings was not limited to his evident contacts with More. His chaplain was in contact with Queen Katherine via the latter's almoner, and he also discussed the case with John Fisher. When the opinions of foreign universities were presented to the House of Lords in 1531, and Henry's advisers spoke in their support, Clerk made a formal protest. And finally, when in April 1533 convocation was asked to deliberate on whether or not the pope had power to dispense for marriages such as Henry's, Clerk was one of the few who dared vote in favour of papal authority. This consistent record of opposition is enough to render entirely incredible earlier suggestions that he assisted Cranmer in producing works on the divorce and the supremacy.

Clerk paid literally as well as metaphorically for his temerity in opposing the king. His obvious loss of favour is reflected in the fact that no further use could be found for his manifest diplomatic talents in the 1530s. When in autumn 1529 Henry VIII pushed three bills through parliament encroaching upon ecclesiastical privilege, Clerk joined Fisher and Nicholas West of Ely in appealing to the pope against these statutes—and was briefly imprisoned with them for his pains. Not only did his diocese contribute substantially to the £100,000 subsidy which convocation had voted to the king in January 1531, but later that year Clerk himself was mulcted of £700 for the escape of seven prisoners from the episcopal gaol—the conventional penalty but one usually remitted.

There were limits to Clerk's resistance. He bowed to pressure in 1533, and not only attended the coronation of Anne Boleyn himself, but joined with Gardiner and Tunstall in urging Thomas More to do likewise (in vain). He and the canons of Wells subscribed to the royal supremacy on 6 July 1534. Having signed a formal renunciation of papal authority on 10 February 1535, he was assiduous thereafter in enforcing the royal supremacy. He even wrote to Cromwell to excuse one of his canons, who through a slip of the tongue had prayed for Katherine of Aragon instead of Anne Boleyn—though this should also be seen as a sign of the fear and anxiety which then prevailed: Clerk was obviously concerned as much to protect his own back as his canon's. He also found it expedient to offer Cromwell a pension on one of his best manors as a Christmas present. Cromwell clearly had a complete ascendancy over Clerk, whose letters to Cromwell are abject and subservient. Cromwell and Henry VIII picked some of Clerk's ecclesiastical plums in the later 1530s. Not only did Henry take away the gift of the archdeaconry of Wells in 1537, but he also forced Cromwell upon him as dean of Wells—the appointment of Cromwell as a lay dean must have stuck in Clerk's throat. Clerk's brother Thomas turned the situation to his advantage. Soon after Cromwell's appointment as dean, Thomas Clerk is found described as a servant of Cromwell, and he acquired a respectable share of former monastic property. John Clerk, though, found himself on the wrong end of redistribution, as Henry took a bite out of the bishop's estates. Like many of his colleagues, Clerk was persuaded to surrender his London residence (Bath Place) into the king's hands, receiving in exchange the former convent of Franciscan nuns in Aldgate.

Conservative bishop For most of the 1520s Clerk was scarcely a model bishop. Fully occupied with diplomatic or conciliar business, he was not resident in his diocese,

which he cannot be shown to have entered prior to September 1530. It was managed in his absence by administrators who had already grown accustomed to doing without their bishop for nearly twenty years. The temporalities of the diocese were from the start largely managed by Thomas Clerk, who accumulated a substantial position in Somerset, resided at an episcopal palace in Wookey, and, having served in Edward VI's first parliament as MP for Wells, died a wealthy esquire in 1555. Wolsey's political eclipse and John Clerk's personal commitment to the cause of Katherine of Aragon combined to cause the bishop to spend far more of his time in his diocese in the 1530s. Curiously, the surviving episcopal register for Clerk's episcopate terminates in June 1534, at just about the time when other sources show Clerk beginning to take a serious interest in his diocese. Rough notes kept by his vicar-general show Clerk conducting a thorough visitation of his diocese in July—perhaps some sort of general stocktaking exercise. It looks as though Clerk was packed off to his diocese in 1534 primarily in order to oversee the enforcement of the oath to the succession, and with a general hint that there was no need for him to hurry back to London. Presumably a fresh register was commenced to mark the new diocesan regime, and it may have been lost because it remained with the bishop rather than at Wells: Clerk died away from his diocese. There is no reason to believe that the absence of a surviving register denotes administrative failings. Clerk's capacity was trusted enough for him to be put in charge of the ecclesiastical valuation of Somerset early in 1535, a task which he completed on time in September. Records survive of his visitation of Glastonbury Abbey in 1538, and the impression derived from the fragmentary documentation of his personal episcopate is that of a diligent pastor.

Clerk's political marginalization in the 1530s was not helped by his well-known religious conservatism. He had made no secret of his contempt for Lutheran teachings in his oration to Leo X, and he was occasionally involved in heresy proceedings in England. Early in 1526 he was one of those bishops deputed by Wolsey to hear the case of Robert Barnes, one of whose answers in court so displeased Clerk that he colourfully told him he would see him fry for it (though he had to wait nearly fifteen years for this dénouement). In April 1529 he took part in proceedings against John Tewkesbury, and he took cognizance of some accusations of heresy during his visitation in 1534. His general religious conservatism remained in evidence throughout the 1530s. He was one of the bishops who signed a statement in favour of pilgrimage, probably early in 1537 in the context of the preliminary discussions which were to lead towards the Bishops' Book (*The Institution of a Christian Man*), during which he was noted by Alexander Alesius as speaking on the conservative side. However, although his name appears in the Bishops' Book, he had no direct role in its composition (when he wrote to Cromwell in October 1537 to thank him for sending a copy, it was evidently the first he had seen of it). In 1539 Clerk was involved in the passage of the Act of Six Articles, and in the same year he led a commission, with bishops Sampson of Chichester and Rugg of Norwich, to look into reports of heresy in Calais.

The conservative backlash in religion which set in during 1539 marked not only the beginning of the end for Cromwell, but also a new political dawn for Clerk, whom the fiasco of the Cleves marriage in 1540 brought back to the centre of events. He was chosen to take the news of the annulment of that marriage to the duke of Cleves, hardly an easy mission—Clerk himself remarked on the inconsistencies in the case against the marriage, but it was doubtless welcome for what it signified, namely Cromwell's fall. But the dawn proved false. Clerk fell ill at Dunkirk on his way back from Cleves, and made his will there on 27 September. There were the usual rumours of poison, but as one of his servants on the voyage had fallen ill and evidently later died, the less romantic explanation of infectious disease seems more probable. Clerk apparently expected to die soon, as he provided for burial at Calais. He bequeathed £180 for doles, obits, and masses for his soul, besides a 'remembraunce' of £100 for King Henry and gifts for bishops Tunstall and Gardiner. Clerk recovered enough to make the crossing to England, but he died in London on 3 January 1541 at his residence in Aldgate, and was buried in St Botolph's Church there.

RICHARD REX

Sources CEPR letters, vols. 17–18 · G. M. Bell, A handlist of British diplomatic representatives, 1509–1688, Royal Historical Society Guides and Handbooks, 16 (1990) · P. M. Hembry, The bishops of Bath and Wells, 1540–1640 (1967) · H. Maxwell-Lyte, ed., The registers of Thomas Wolsey … John Clerke … William Knyght … and Gilbert Bourne, Somerset RS, 55 (1940) · D. S. Chambers, Cardinal Bainbridge in the court of Rome, 1509 to 1514 (1965) · LP Henry VIII · W. Roper, The life of Sir Thomas More, ed. E. V. Hitchcock, Early English Text Society, original ser., 197 (1935) · P. Gwyn, The king's cardinal: the rise and fall of Thomas Wolsey (1990) · M. Bateson, ed., Grace book B, 2 vols. (1903–5) · Emden, Cam., 139 · F. W. Weaver, ed., Somerset medieval wills, 3, Somerset RS, 21 (1905) · HoP, Commons, 1509–58 · Matricule de l'Université de Louvain, vol. 4 (Brussels, 1961)

Clerk, John (d. 1552), author, is of obscure early life and education; Anthony Wood claimed that he studied at the University of Oxford, but this is doubtful. Clerk was employed at Kenninghall as the tutor for Henry Howard, earl of Surrey, until the latter's residence in Windsor from about 1530, and remained with Surrey's father, the duke of Norfolk, as his secretary. Upon the duke's imprisonment in 1546 Clerk appears to have searched for another patron, dedicating a portion of his work to Charles Stourton. Clerk was apparently conservative in matters of religion, 'an open enemy to the gospel and all godly preachers' according to martyrologist John Foxe (Acts and Monuments, 8.634) although Bale simply calls him 'pius ac christiane doctus' ('learned in matters of the faith'; Bale, Index, 193).

Clerk's works are largely showcases for his linguistic ability, and document his search for patronage. His translation from the French of a Spanish treatise on courtly behaviour, Lamant mal traicte de samye (1543?), dedicated to Surrey, acknowledges Surrey's own skill as a translator while advertising Clerk's facility in capturing 'thintencion of thauthor'. Better known is his Opusculum

plane divinum de mortuorum resurrectione et extremo juditio (1545). In this Catholic redaction of biblical accounts of the general resurrection of the dead and the last judgment Clerk urges Christians to ensure their salvation by performing the traditional corporal works of mercy described in Matthew. Unlike a growing number of his reformist contemporaries, who saw in Rome's primacy signs of the approaching second coming of Christ, Clerk asserts only that, since the time of the parousia is unknown, all Christians should heed the gospel admonition to be prepared. A second edition followed in 1547, shorn of the dedication to Surrey (recently executed for treason) but containing a set of grammatical tables in French and Italian, and dedicated to Stourton, a young aristocrat perhaps as much in need of a tutor as Clerk was of a patron.

In 1552 Clerk was examined by the council for 'lewd prophecies and slanders' and books of necromancy found in his rooms. He was sent to join his former patron the duke of Norfolk in the Tower, where he committed suicide by hanging himself, on 10 May 1552.

SEYMOUR BAKER HOUSE

Sources Bale, Index · Tanner, Bibl. Brit.-Hib. · STC, 1475–1640 · The acts and monuments of John Foxe, ed. S. R. Cattley, 8 vols. (1837–41), vol. 8, p. 634 · Emden, Oxf., vol. 4 · DNB · N. Williams, Thomas Howard, fourth duke of Norfolk (1964) · APC, 1552–4

Clerk, Sir John, of Penicuik, first baronet (1649/50–1722), landowner and coal owner, was born probably at Penicuik in Edinburghshire, the son of John Clerk (1611–1674) and Mary, the daughter of Sir William Gray of Pittendrum. Clerk's father traded profitably as a merchant in Paris between 1634 and 1646, when he returned to Scotland and lived as a country gentleman. In 1646 he bought the barony of Penicuik, and had his son educated at home to prevent him acquiring immoral or profligate habits. Clerk succeeded his father as laird of Penicuik in 1674, and it was in that year that he married his first wife, Elizabeth, daughter of Henry Hendersone of Elvingston (Haddingtonshire), a doctor of physic. Clerk subsequently extended his estates in Edinburghshire by purchasing further land, including the barony of Lasswade (adjacent to Penicuik) from Sir John Nicolson in 1696. He was a member of the Scottish parliament (separate from that of England until 1707) for Edinburghshire from 1690 to 1702, served as a lieutenant-colonel in the militia, and (after 1707) was a justice of the peace for the shire. He was created a baronet on 24 March 1679.

Clerk was a traditional landowner, but he was also an exponent of new agricultural organization and techniques, notably the consolidation of landholdings, soil improvements, and the commutation of payments in kind to money rents. To pay off the large debt incurred to buy the Lasswade estate, he began more systematically to exploit its extensive coal deposits. In consequence of dealing with the technical problems of extraction he also sought to increase output in an uncertain and competitive industry through new patterns of work discipline. In response to shortages of skilled labour in the coal and salt industries, a statute of 1606 (not repealed until 1799) had

Sir John Clerk of Penicuik, first baronet (1649/50–1722), by William Aikman, 1700

bound Scottish colliers for life to the owner of the coal, giving them the legal status of serfs but at the same time making them difficult to control by purely economic means such as wages. The special status of the colliers, and certain prominent cultural features such as shared leisure, contributed to their strong sense of identity.

As a coal owner Clerk treated his workers well in spite of their servile position. He insisted that his overseers and other tenants dealt fairly with the colliers and he provided housing for the workers and education for their children. Relations between Clerk and his employees were a good deal more amicable than those which obtained under the second baronet. However, in return Clerk demanded regular hard work coupled with adherence to strict Calvinist tenets of sobriety and morality. Himself an ardent Calvinist, apparently untroubled by doubt about his own rectitude, he waged a tireless campaign with the help of the local church against what he saw as the colliers' wanton idleness, their fondness for drink, their profane and brutal behaviour, and their dishonesty in exploiting the perquisites of their employment. One of his first acts as the new feudal lord of Lasswade was to proscribe sabbath breaking, profanity, and drunkenness among all his workers and tenants. He himself gave up alcohol around 1710 to help his gout and other ailments. Clerk took a close personal interest in mineral exploitation and was a source of advice to fellow coal owners in the Forth basin where most contemporary pits were located.

Clerk and his wife, Elizabeth, had seven children, including his heir, the second baronet, Sir John *Clerk of Penicuik (1676–1755). After Elizabeth's early death at the

age of twenty-five he remained a widower for nearly a decade. He then married Christian, daughter of the Revd James Kilpatrick of Carrington (Edinburghshire), with whom he had nine more children. Having managed his affairs with great frugality, on his death he was a substantial landowner in the richest part of Scotland and had provided well for his surviving children. Immediately after his death his heir began to construct a large Palladian mansion at Penicuik.

In his *Memoirs* the second baronet wrote that his father had 'left a great many journals and writings under his hand which will, I hope, bear testimony to the regard he always had for religion, vertue and honesty' (*Memoirs*, 8). Although a man with 'no great humour of talking', these manuscripts reveal that, in Clerk's desire systematically to generate profits and regenerate men, he combined different strands of early modern Scottish life. A product of his age in his religious and moral outlook, he was also an important transitional figure in terms of the regulatory framework that he sought to impose on his labour force (and akin to the iron manufacturer Abraham Crowley (1658–1713)). A small but well-built man, Sir John Clerk died peacefully at Penicuik House in March 1722, aged seventy-two.   R. A. HOUSTON

Sources *Memoirs of the life of Sir John Clerk of Penicuik*, ed. J. M. Gray, Scottish History Society, 13 (1892) · J. Hatcher, *Before 1700: towards the age of coal* (1993), vol. 1 of *The history of the British coal industry* (1984–93) · F. Oukham, *A history of the Scottish coal industry, 1700–1815* (1970), vol. 1 of *A history of the Scottish coal industry* · G. Marshall, *Presbyteries and profits: Calvinism and the development of capitalism in Scotland, 1560–1707* (1980) · Clerk of Penicuik muniments, NA Scot., GD 18
Archives NA Scot., journals, corresp., and papers
Likenesses W. Aikman, portrait, 1700, priv. coll. [*see illus.*]

Clerk, Sir John, of Penicuik, **second baronet** (1676–1755), politician and antiquary, was born at Edinburgh on 8 February 1676, the second child and eldest son of Sir John *Clerk of Penicuik, first baronet (1649/50–1722), landowner and coal owner, and his first wife, Elizabeth Hendersone, who died aged twenty-five leaving seven children. With his second wife the first Sir John had a further nine children. Clerk's merchant grandfather had bought the estate of Penicuik, Edinburghshire, and the first baronet had developed the coal reserves there. Clerk was educated at Penicuik parish school and Glasgow University, before being sent for legal study to Leiden in the Netherlands. After three years there, during which he developed considerable skill on the harpsichord and became a close friend of Herman Boerhaave, he went on a two-year European tour. He spent considerable periods of time in Vienna, Rome, and Paris, and acquired an enthusiasm for Italian music and Roman antiquities.

On returning to Scotland, Clerk was admitted advocate in 1700, and on 23 February 1701 married Lady Margaret Stewart, eldest daughter of the third earl of Galloway. She died in childbirth within the year, leaving him with a son who died aged twenty-one. The marriage brought Clerk into politics as a firm supporter of the proposed Hanoverian succession and an adherent of the Church of Scotland. He represented Whithorn in the Scottish parliament

(1703–7), a constituency under the control of his father-in-law, and came into the political circle of the second duke of Queensberry. In 1703–4 Clerk served on a commission to examine the public accounts; he was one of a small group who made a thorough investigation into the leakage of public money, and he wrote the commission's report. He thus gained a reputation for public finance, which led to his appointment in 1706 as one of the thirty-one Scottish commissioners for the treaty of union with England. His *Memoirs* (not published until 1892) are one of the few historical sources for the treaty negotiations. It was Clerk who checked the calculation for the Equivalent, the recompense to be paid to Scotland for accepting the burden of a share in the interest payments on the English national debt. He served as one of the Scottish members for the first parliament of Great Britain in 1707, and was involved in the transfer to Scotland of the exchequer bills for the Equivalent and the return of the retired notes. He retired from politics in 1708, having been appointed a baron of the newly created court of the exchequer in Scotland, a semi-sinecure which gave him £500 a year. His second marriage, on 15 November 1709, was to Janet Inglis (d. 1760), daughter of Sir John Inglis of Cramond, baronet; they had nine sons, including John *Clerk of Eldin (1728–1812), naval writer, and seven daughters.

Clerk inherited the family estate and the baronetcy in 1722. His income, talents, interests, and occupation gave him opportunities for cultured leisure activities. He improved his estate, planting trees and modernizing the tenancies, gave advice to landed neighbours on their coalmines, and designed and commissioned the construction of a new house, Mavisbank, at Loanhead, Edinburghshire. Clerk wrote and played music, and cultivated literary figures, the most notable of whom was the poet Allan Ramsay (1686–1758). Clerk was one of the earliest and most constant patrons of Ramsay, who used to spend a portion of each summer under his roof. The premature death of Clerk's first son in 1722 was made the occasion for an elegy by Ramsay. After the poet's death an obelisk was erected in his memory at Penicuik.

Clerk followed up his enthusiasm for Roman remains and the classics with excavations, and made a collection of Roman finds. At Penicuik House he accumulated a valuable collection of antiquities, which brought him membership of the Society of Antiquaries in 1727. He served on the board of trustees for manufactures from its start, was made a fellow of the Royal Society in 1729, and was also president of the Edinburgh Philosophical Society. He died on 4 October 1755, at Penicuik House.

Clerk published a number of works on political and antiquarian themes, and many other writings were still in manuscript form at his death. *An Essay upon the Intended Limitations* (1703) was a response to criticisms of the union with England; and it was followed by two further pamphlets, *A Letter to a Friend Giving an Account of how the Treaty of Union has been Received* (1706) and *An Essay upon the XV. Article of the Treaty of Union* (1706). A manuscript entitled 'Observations on the present circumstances of Scotland', comprising a balanced review of the economy, was first published

by the Scottish History Society only in 1965 (*Miscellany*, 10). With the chief baron of the exchequer he wrote *A Historical View of the Forms and Powers of the Court of Exchequer in Scotland*, published in 1820. Two short papers by Clerk also appeared in *Philosophical Transactions of the Royal Society*: in 1731 'De stylis veterum et diversis chartarum generibus', and in 1738 'An account of the observation of the late solar eclipse made at Edinburgh on February 18th 1736–7'. In 1750 he published *Dissertatio de monumentis quibusdam Romanis in Boreali Magnae Britanniae parte detectis anno MDCCXXI*. He wrote over many years a long Latin paper, 'De imperio Britannico', a history of English-Scottish relations. It was summarized and translated and published for the Scottish Historical Society in 1973. His musical compositions, mostly pieces for chamber orchestra, almost entirely remain in manuscript.

Clerk's *Memoirs* give a view of the culture of Scottish landed society, especially at the time of the union with England; they also provide perceptive comments on the economy. Although not published until 1892, the editor noted that 'the passages, in particular, which deal with his two interviews with Queen Anne, if they want the dignity of formal history … bring us close to the time and the scenes' (*Memoirs*, 15).   ROSALIND MITCHISON

Sources *Memoirs of the life of Sir John Clerk of Penicuik*, ed. J. M. Gray, Scottish History Society, 13 (1892) · M. D. Young, ed., *The parliaments of Scotland: burgh and shire commissioners*, 2 vols. (1992–3) · J. Purser, *Scotland's music: a history of the traditional and classical music of Scotland from earliest times to the present day* (1992) · J. G. Dunbar, *The historic architecture of Scotland* (1966) · GEC, *Baronetage* · D. McElroy, 'The literary clubs and societies of eighteenth-century Edinburgh', PhD diss., U. Edin., 1952 · Register of baptisms, General Register Office for Scotland, Edinburgh · G. Marshall, *Presbyteries and profits: Calvinism and the development of capitalism in Scotland, 1560–1707* (1980) · *Scots Magazine*, 17 (1755), 461 · J. Clerk, *History of the union of Scotland and England*, ed. and trans. D. Duncan, Scottish History Society, 5th ser., 6 (1993) · I. G. Brown, 'Sir John Clerk of Penicuik (1676–1755): aspects of a virtuoso life', PhD diss., U. Cam., 1980 · I. G. Brown, *The hobby-horsical antiquary* (1980) · I. G. Brown, *The Clerks of Penicuik: portraits of taste and talent* (1987) · I. G. Brown, 'Modern Rome and ancient Caledonia: the Union and the politics of Scottish culture', *The history of Scottish literature*, ed. C. Craig, 2: *1660–1800*, ed. A. Hook (1988), 33–49
Archives NA Scot., journals, corresp., and papers · NL Scot., 'The practice of the court of exchequer in Scotland'
Likenesses W. van Mieris, pencil drawing, *c*.1695–1697, Penicuik House, Midlothian · W. Aikman, oils, Penicuik House, Midlothian; copy, Scot. NPG · W. Aikman, oils, Penicuik House, Midlothian · J. B. Medina, oils, Penicuik House, Midlothian

Clerk, John, of Eldin (1728–1812), naval writer, was born at Penicuik, Edinburghshire, on 10 December 1728, the seventh son of Sir John *Clerk of Penicuik, second baronet (1676–1755), politician and antiquary, and his second wife, Janet, *née* Inglis (d. 1760). His wealthy family background encouraged an open-minded attitude. He was educated at Dalkeith grammar school and started medical studies at Edinburgh University, though he did not complete them. He entered the world of business, and in 1733 there was a mention of him as a merchant in Edinburgh. He was also involved in the coalmining industry and showed considerable interest in geology, which he studied at university

John Clerk of Eldin (1728–1812), by Sir Henry Raeburn, *c.*1800

with a fellow student, James Hutton. A true child of the Enlightenment, Clerk was also active in the mid-eighteenth-century Edinburgh élite, including Adam Smith, Adam Ferguson, Hugh Blair, and David Hume. In 1753 he married Susannah, the daughter of William Adam of Maryburgh and the youngest sister of the architects Robert, John, Adam, and William. John and Susannah had four daughters and a son, John *Clerk, Lord Eldin.

Clerk displayed a passion for harbours and shipbuilding in his youth. His interest in the navy grew in the 1770s when he had frequent contact with Captain Alexander Edgar, who had taken part with John Byng in the battle of Minorca (1756). The American War of Independence was the actual starting point of his work on naval tactics. He improved his knowledge of major battles by reading histories, newspaper articles, and logbooks which enabled him to reconstruct battles. He then put his analyses to the test with the aid of cork models floated on water, an original method distinct from the abstract conceptions favoured by French tacticians such as Bigot de Morogues and Bourdé de la Villehuet. In the late 1770s Clerk spoke of his work to Richard Atkinson, a friend and secretary to Admiral George Rodney. In an account written in 1804 Clerk also claimed he had given a memorandum to Rodney advising him on the tactical devices he might employ. Disappointed not to see his ideas implemented, Clerk decided to publish his research himself. He was further stimulated by the British defeat at Yorktown when a larger home force lost to the strategy of the French navy.

In 1790 Clerk published part one of *An Essay on Naval Tactics*. The study was distinctive as one of the first British accounts of tactics, as opposed to a work in French translation, and for its criticism of the current Royal Naval practice of looking more to signal books to the detriment of fighting instructions. Clerk's focus on practical tactics, developed during the course of the 1790s, sought to redress this habit; parts two, three, and four of the *Essay* were published in 1797.

Clerk died on 10 May 1812. After his death there arose a tremendous controversy regarding the true origin of the manoeuvre he is said to have devised: an attack on the enemy's lee side and breakthrough of their battle line, as Admiral Rodney had done at the battle of the Saints (12 April 1782). In an article published in the *Quarterly Review* (1829) Howard Douglas, the son of Rodney's flag officer, Sir Charles Douglas, maintained that his father, not Clerk, had invented this tactic. The claim triggered a response from Clerk's supporters in the *Edinburgh Review* (1830), where it was alleged that Rodney and Douglas had read Clerk's report, passed on by Richard Atkinson, on the morning of the battle. In 1832 Howard Douglas asked why the first part of Clerk's *Essay* had not included a reference to the manoeuvre, and accused Clerk of appropriating Rodney's innovation as his own and of plagiarizing Paul Hoste's *Art des armées navales* (1697). Clerk himself had maintained in 1804 that his ideas were not fully developed at the time of the battle of the Saints, and that his thinking had not finally come together until the late 1790s, when he published details of the manoeuvre.

Clerk's abilities as a tactician may have been overrated by friends and disputed by his critics. Nevertheless, he remains an author of the highest order, who attempted to understand manoeuvres while looking for effective ways to bring the battle to a decisive conclusion. Clerk's *Essay* certainly helped to inspire a later generation of naval officers, notably Admiral Adam Duncan at the decisive battle of Camperdown (11 October 1797), and was subsequently translated into French, Portuguese, Russian, and Dutch.

MICHEL DEPEYRE

Sources DNB · H. Douglas, *Naval evolutions: a memoir by Major General Sir Howard Douglas, bart* (1832) · C. Ekins, *Naval battles from 1744 to the peace in 1812, critically reviewed and illustrated* (1824) · T. White, *Naval researches, or, A candid inquiry into the conduct of admirals Byron, Graves, Hood and Rodney … being a refutation of the plans and statements of Mr Clerk*, *Mariner's Mirror*, 20 (1934), 475–95 · M. Depeyre, *Tactiques et stratégies navales de la France et du Royaume-Uni, 1690–1815* (Paris, 1998) · B. Lavery, *Nelson's navy: the ships, men, and organisation, 1793–1815* (1989) · B. Tunstall, *Naval warfare in the age of sail: the evolution of fighting tactics, 1650–1815*, ed. N. Tracy (1990)
Archives NA Scot., corresp. and papers · priv. coll., corresp. | priv. coll., corresp. with William Creech
Likenesses H. Raeburn, portrait, *c.*1800, Currier Gallery of Art, Manchester, New Hampshire [*see illus.*] · Cow, portrait, BM · H. Raeburn, portrait, priv. coll. · J. Saxon, oils, Scot. NPG

Clerk, John, Lord Eldin (1757–1832), judge, was born in April 1757, the eldest son of John *Clerk of Eldin (1728–1812), the author of *An Essay on Naval Tactics*, and his wife, Susannah Adam, sister of the celebrated Adam brothers, the architects. Though originally intended for the Indian Civil Service, he was apprenticed to a writer of the signet. His interest as a young man in debating and essaying upon literary, philosophical, and political topics can be inferred from his election to the recently established Speculative Society of Edinburgh during its 1777–8 session. He appears to have been an active member and was elected a president for the 1782–3 session. After serving his articles he practised for a year or two as an accountant, and eventually was admitted a member of the Faculty of Advocates on 3 December 1785.

Clerk soon made his mark at the bar, where he acquired so extensive a practice that, it is said, at one period of his career he had nearly half the business of the court in his hands. As a pleader he was remarkable, both for his acuteness and for his marvellous powers of reasoning, as well as for his fertility of resource. Possessed of a rough, sarcastic humour, he delighted in ridiculing the bench, and was in the habit of saying whatever he liked to the judges without reproof. When appearing as defence counsel for the co-accused in the sensational trial of Deacon William Brodie in 1788, he gained notoriety for his intemperate exchanges with the trial judge, Robert Macqueen, Lord Braxfield. On another celebrated occasion, probably between 1819 and 1823, after a prolonged wrangle, he was compelled by the court to apologize to Sir William Miller, Lord Glenlee, for a fiery retort. Even then, the apology was scornful: 'since *your Lordships insist upon't*, I now make an apology to Lord Glenlee, IN RESPECT OF YOUR LORDSHIPS' COMMANDS!!' (*Journal*, 2.210). Apart from the trial of Deacon Brodie, his other prominent court appearances included appearing for the defence alongside his fellow advocates Francis Jeffrey and Henry Cockburn in the so-called state trials for sedition in 1817.

In politics Clerk was a keen whig. He made a notable contribution to the movement for burgh reform in the 1780s, serving on the standing committee which promoted (unsuccessfully) two parliamentary bills which addressed the reform of burgh government and parliamentary representation. On 11 March 1806 he was appointed solicitor-general for Scotland in the Grenville administration, where he played a leading role alongside Henry Erskine, the lord advocate, in attempting to reform the moribund court of session, sponsoring a radical parliamentary bill in 1807. Although the attempt failed owing to the fall of the ministry, it enshrined principles which provided the basis of the reforms of the subsequent two decades.

Clerk's practice at the bar had been for some time falling off, and his health had already begun to fail, when on 10 November 1823 he was appointed an ordinary lord of session in the place of William Macleod Bannatyne, Lord Bannatyne. Assuming the title Lord Eldin, he took his seat on the bench on 22 November. As a judge he was not a success; his temperament was not a judicial one, and his poor health rendered him unfit for the office. After five years of judicial work he resigned in 1828, and was succeeded by John Fullerton, Lord Fullerton.

Clerk had a considerable taste for fine arts, and occasionally amused himself in drawing and modelling. In appearance he was remarkably plain, and paid no attention to his dress. One of his legs was shorter than the other, leading to the anecdote that when walking down High Street one day from the court of session he overheard a young lady saying to her companion rather loudly, 'There goes Johnnie Clerk, the lame lawyer.' Upon which he turned round and said, 'No, madam, I may be a lame man, but not a lame lawyer.' Henry Cockburn remembered his 'very bushy eyebrows, coarse grizzly hair, always in disorder, and firm projecting features', which 'made his face and head not unlike that of a thoroughbred shaggy terrier' (Cockburn, *Life of Lord Jeffrey*, 1.200). He also described him as 'honest, warm-hearted, generous and simple' (ibid.) but suffering from 'infantine self-deification' (ibid., 1.201). His consulting room was overrun by his collection of art, literature, and animals: 'all manner of trash, dead and living, and all in confusion' (ibid., 1.204).

Clerk died unmarried at his house in Picardy Place, Edinburgh, on 30 May 1832. His collection of pictures and prints was sold by auction at his house in March 1833, a serious accident occurring when the floor gave way. It is reputed that the sale lasted fourteen days owing to the immense size of the collection.

G. F. R. BARKER, rev. A. M. GODFREY

Sources J. Kay, *A series of original portraits and caricature etchings … with biographical sketches and illustrative anecdotes*, ed. [H. Paton and others], new edn [3rd edn], 2 (1877), 438–42 · G. Brunton and D. Haig, *An historical account of the senators of the college of justice, from its institution in MDXXXII* (1832), 551–2 · *Memorials of his time, by Henry Cockburn* (1856), 272–3, 407–8 · H. Cockburn, *Life of Lord Jeffrey, with a selection from his correspondence*, 1 (1852), 199–205 · *Journal of Henry Cockburn: being a continuation of the 'Memorials of his time', 1831–1854*, 2 vols. (1874) · J. Anderson, *A history of Edinburgh* (1856), 428–9 · *Edinburgh Evening Courant* (2 June 1832) · *Edinburgh Magazine and Literary Miscellany*, 92 (1823), 760 · W. F. Gray, *Some old Scots judges* (1914), 211–26 · W. Ferguson, *Scotland: 1689 to the present* (1968), 245, 280 · N. Phillipson, *The Scottish whigs and the reform of the court of session, 1785–1830*, Stair Society, 37 (1990), 20, 22, 89 · B. D. Osborne, *Bratfield* (1997), 170–80
Archives NL Scot., roll-book of cases · NRA, priv. coll., family corresp.
Likenesses J. Kay, caricature, etching, 1810, NPG; repro. in J. Kay, *A series of original portraits and caricature etchings … with biographical sketches and illustrative anecdotes*, ed. H. Paton and others, new edn [2nd edn], 2 (1842) · H. Raeburn, oils, c.1815, Scot. NPG · W. Bewick, chalk drawing, 1824, Scot. NPG · A. Geddes, oils, Scot. NPG · S. Joseph, plaster bust, Scot. NPG · C. Smith, oils, Parliament Hall, Edinburgh, Faculty of Advocates
Wealth at death art collection

Clerk [Clarke], **Josiah** [Josias] (*bap.* 1639?, *d.* 1714), physician, may have been the son of Josias Clerk baptized at Romford, Essex, on 4 January 1639. He was educated at Bishop's Stortford, Hertfordshire, and was admitted as a pensioner of Peterhouse, Cambridge, on 1 May 1656, and took the two degrees in medicine, MB in 1661, MD on 3 July 1666. He was admitted a candidate of the College of Physicians on 26 June 1671, a fellow on 29 July 1675, and was appointed censor in 1677 and 1692. On the death of Sir Thomas Witherley he was named elect on 16 April 1694, delivered the Harveian oration in 1708, was consiliarius in 1707, 1709, 1710, 1711, and 1712, and was elected to the presidentship, void by the death of Dr Edward Browne, on

Josiah Clerk (*bap.* 1639?, *d.* 1714), by unknown artist, *c.*1690

13 September 1708, being re-elected at the general election of officers on the 30th of the same month. Clerk 'being indisposed by many bodyly infirmityes, and also aged', was unable to act; he accordingly resigned on 18 December, and Charles Goodall was appointed on 23 December 1708. Clerk had been chosen treasurer on 16 April 1708, and retained that office as long as he lived. Clerk died at his house in Fenchurch Street, London, in the autumn of 1714, in the seventy-fifth year of his age. In the annals of the college cited by Munk the date of Clerk's death is given as 8 December, which is erroneous. His will (PRO, PROB 11/542/188) was proved on 14 October. He desired 'to be decently, tho' very privately, buried by night in the vault in St. Olave Hart Street Church, where my honoured mother and my children lye, if it may be done with conveniency'. He was survived by his wife, Abigail, and their daughter, Elizabeth, who was married to Richard Wilshaw.

GORDON GOODWIN, *rev.* MICHAEL BEVAN

Sources Munk, *Roll* · IGI · Venn, *Alum. Cant.*
Likenesses oils, *c.*1690, RCP Lond. [*see illus.*]

Clerk, Matthew (1659–1735), Presbyterian minister, was born near Kilrea, co. Derry, of parents who are unknown. His early years are obscure but he was an officer in Derry during the siege (1688–9), and received a bullet wound on the temple, leaving a sore, over which he wore a black patch to the end of his days. It was not until after the siege that he began his studies for the ministry. He was ordained in 1697 by the Route presbytery as minister of

Kilrea and Boveedy, co. Derry. In 1721 he was the sole dissentient from the synod's 'charitable declaration', an attempt to reach a compromise with the minority of clergymen who opposed subscription to the Westminster confession of faith. Next year he, with two others, entered a strong protest against making any concessions to the non-subscribing party. This party attacked him in his own presbytery, but though the matter was referred to the synod the non-subscribers were too much occupied in defending themselves to proceed with it. Clerk's literary contribution to the controversy, *A Letter from the Countrey, to a Friend in Belfast, with Respect to the Belfast Society* (1722), was the first on either side which appeared with the author's name. His friends considered his manner of writing not sufficiently grave in tone. 'I don't think', wrote Livingstone of Templepatrick to Wodrow on 23 June 1723, 'his reasoning faculty is despisable, but I wish it were equal to his diverting one, for I think he is one of the most comical old fellows that ever was' (*DNB*).

On 29 April 1729 Clerk resigned his charge and emigrated to New Hampshire. On landing he found that James Macgregor, formerly minister of Aghadowey, and founder of the township of Londonderry on the Merrimac, had died on 5 March. He succeeded him as minister, and also engaged in educational work. Clerk had already been twice married, of which no details are known, and eventually married Macgregor's widow as his third wife. He was a strict vegetarian, but his abstemious diet did not subdue his violent tendencies. Among the anecdotes told of him is one of his criticizing St Peter: 'He only cut off a chiel's lug, and he ought to ha' split doun his heid' (*DNB*). Clerk died on 25 January 1735. He was carried to his grave by old comrades at the Derry siege.

ALEXANDER GORDON, *rev.* I. R. McBRIDE

Sources J. W. Kernohan, *The parishes of Kilrea and Tamlaght O'Crilly in a sketch of their history, with an account of Boveedy congregation* (1912) · J. McConnell and others, eds., *Fasti of the Irish Presbyterian church, 1613–1840*, rev. S. G. McConnell, 2 vols. in 12 pts (1935–51) · E. P. Parker, *The history of Londonderry, comprising the towns of Derry and Londonderry N. H.* (Boston, MA, 1851) · W. B. Sprague, *Annals of the American pulpit*, 7 vols. (New York, 1857–61) · R. S. Wallace, 'The Scotch-Irish or provincial New Hampshire', PhD diss., University of New Hampshire, 1984

Clerk, Simon (*d.* 1489). *See under* Wastell, John (*d. c.*1518).

Clerk, William (*d.* 1655), civil lawyer, was admitted as a scholar to Trinity Hall, Cambridge, in 1605. By its statutes Trinity Hall was committed to the study of the civil law, which was derived from Roman law and governed ecclesiastical, maritime, and international affairs. Clerk was a fellow of the college from 1609 to 1634, taking the degrees of LLB in 1610 and LLD in 1629. In 1631 he published a pamphlet entitled *An Epitome of Certaine Late Aspersions Cast at Civilians*. This was a contribution to the continuing defence of the civil law against the encroachments of the common lawyers, and aimed to refute criticisms of the civil law made in the preface to Sir John Davies's *Primer report des cases & matters en ley* (1615).

By the 1620s Clerk was seeking to become established as a practitioner in the civil law courts. In 1624 he was appointed as joint commissary of the exchequer and prerogative court of York, but never assumed the post. He obtained full membership of Doctors' Commons in 1629, and probably by 1634 had become official of the archdeacon of London. From 1635 until 1640 he was active as an advocate in the London courts, and was also appointed to a number of commissions for piracy.

Although parliament abolished the ecclesiastical courts in 1646, there was still a need for the expertise of civil lawyers. From 1647 Clerk served as a judge in the court of admiralty, and was also president of Doctors' Commons. The outbreak of war with the Dutch in the spring of 1652 led to a considerable increase in the business being handled by the admiralty court, and in recognition of this Clerk's salary was set at £200 per annum.

As a judge Clerk frequently had to deal with cases of international importance. The most celebrated of these was the trial of Don Pantaleone Sa, the brother of the Portuguese ambassador, for his involvement in the murder of an innocent bystander during a street disturbance. Don Pantaleone claimed he had authority to act as ambassador in his brother's absence, and thus had diplomatic privilege, even though the crime of which he was accused was against the law of nations. Clerk was one of a committee of six judges appointed to consider whether Don Pantaleone could be tried. The committee decided that a trial was permissible, and a special commission of three common law judges, three civil law judges, including Clerk, and three laymen was appointed to hear the case, with a mixed English and foreign jury. In spite of his claim to ambassadorial status Don Pantaleone was found guilty, and executed on 10 July 1654.

Clerk was buried on 3 August 1655, and appears to have continued working until his death, which probably took place in London. He left a wife, Mary (d. 1674), and a daughter, Elizabeth. His achievement was to help in keeping the civil law alive in the unsettled political conditions of the civil war and interregnum.   SHEILA DOYLE

Sources B. P. Levack, *The civil lawyers in England, 1603–1641* (1973), 219 · *CSP dom.*, 1634–5, 429; 1652–3, 92; 1653–4, 360–62; 1654, 156, 169 · E. R. Adair, *The extraterritoriality of ambassadors in the sixteenth and seventeenth centuries* (1929), 147–52 · F. A. Inderwick, *The interregnum (A. D. 1648–1660)* (1891), 296–308 · G. D. Squibb, *Doctors' Commons: a history of the College of Advocates and Doctors of Law* (1977), 64, 117, 174 · grant of administration de bonis non in estate of William Clerk, 1674, PRO, PROB 6/49, fol. 174v · S. R. Gardiner, *History of the Commonwealth and protectorate, 1649–1656*, new edn, 4 vols. (1903), vol. 3, pp. 79–81

Clerke, Agnes Mary (1842–1907), writer on astronomy, born at Skibbereen, co. Cork, on 10 February 1842, was the younger daughter of John William Clerke (1814–1890), and his wife, Catherine (1818–1897), daughter of Rickard Deasy of Clonakilty, co. Cork, and sister of Rickard Deasy, an Irish politician and judge. Her elder sister was Ellen Mary *Clerke (1840–1906). Her only brother, Aubrey St John Clerke, (1843–1923), after a brilliant career as a scholar and medallist in mathematics and science at Trinity College, Dublin, became a Chancery barrister in London. The father, a classical scholar and graduate of Trinity

Agnes Mary Clerke (1842–1907), by Hayman Selig Mendelssohn

College, Dublin, was manager until 1861 of a bank at Skibbereen, owned land in the district, and practised astronomy as a recreation. From 1861 to 1877 he was registrar to his brother-in-law at the court of the exchequer, Dublin.

Interested as a child by her father in astronomy, Agnes Clerke was highly educated at home. In 1861 she moved with her family to Dublin. She and her sister, Ellen Mary, spent the years 1867–77 in Italy, chiefly in Florence, where Agnes studied in the libraries and wrote her first article of astronomical interest, 'Copernicus in Italy', published in the *Edinburgh Review* in July 1877. A total of fifty articles mainly on scientific themes, both contemporary and historical, appeared in the *Edinburgh Review* between that year and her death. In 1877 the family settled in London, which was thereafter Agnes Clerke's home. A paper in the *Edinburgh Review* on 'The chemistry of the stars' in 1880 was followed in 1885 by her first book, *A Popular History of Astronomy during the Nineteenth Century* (4th edn, 1902). Nothing of the kind had appeared since 1852, when the *History of Physical Astronomy* was published by Robert Grant. In the interval the spectroscope had been applied to astronomy and the science of astronomical physics established. Agnes Clerke's work, which at once became the standard work in its field, was especially valuable for its wealth of references. In 1888 she had the opportunity of practical astronomical work during a two months' visit to Sir David and Lady Gill at the observatory at the Cape of Good Hope. Soon after her return she was offered, but declined, a post at the nominal rank of computer at the Royal Observatory, Greenwich. In 1890 her second book, *The System of the Stars* (2nd edn, 1905), which shows clear evidence of Gill's influence, maintained her reputation. The third and last of her larger works, *Problems in Astrophysics*, came out in 1903. Smaller volumes were *The Herschels and Modern Astronomy* (1895) in the Century Science series, edited by Sir Henry Roscoe, *Astronomy* (1898) in the Concise Knowledge series, and *Modern Cosmogonies* (1905). Each annual volume of the *Observatory Magazine* from 1886 until her death contained reviews by her of books or descriptions of new advances in astronomy. She contributed many articles, including those on Galileo, Laplace, and Lavoisier, to the *Encyclopaedia Britannica* (9th edn). In the 11th edition (1910) she was the author of the main article on the history of astronomy as well as of numerous biographies of astronomers. For the *Dictionary of National Biography* she wrote 150 entries, which include almost all the lives of astronomers from the first volume to the supplementary volumes in 1901. In 1893 the governors of the Royal Institution awarded to Agnes Clerke the Actonian prize of 100 guineas for her writings on astronomy. She was commissioned to write the Hodgkins Trust essay on 'Low temperature research at the Royal Institution 1893–1900', published in 1901 (*Proceedings of the Royal Institution*, 16.699–718). This substantial essay, and her *Modern Cosmogonies*, reveal her interest in her later years in new developments in physics and chemistry. In 1903 she was elected an honorary member of the Royal Astronomical Society, a rare distinction among women, shared at the time with Lady Huggins; it had been accorded previously only to Mary Somerville, Caroline Herschel, and Ann Sheepshanks.

Clerke's devotion to science never lessened her interest in literature and cultural matters generally, on which she wrote from time to time in the *Edinburgh Review*, as, for example, in her essays on Don Sebastian (1882) and the letters of Edward Fitzgerald (1894). In 1892 she published *Familiar Studies in Homer*, which illustrated her breadth of learning. She was also an accomplished musician. In private life she was shy and unpretentious. 'No purer, loftier and yet sweetly unselfish and human soul has lived', was Lady Huggins's appraisal of her character. Never particularly robust, her health declined in the last few years of her life, though she worked to the very end. She died of pneumonia at her residence, 68 Redcliffe Square, London, on 20 January 1907, and was buried three days later in Brompton cemetery.

Agnes Clerke's active years spanned a period of exceptionally rapid development in astronomy. Her meticulous *Popular History of Astronomy in the Nineteenth Century*, with its abundance of references to the work of minor as well as of major figures, remains a valuable chronicle of that important era. *The System of the Stars*, with its assertion as 'a practical certainty' that 'the entire contents, stellar and nebular, of the entire sphere belong to one mighty aggregation' represents the generally accepted view of the universe at the turn of the century.

H. P. HOLLIS, rev. M. T. BRÜCK

Sources M. L. Huggins, *Agnes Mary Clerke and Ellen Mary Clerke: an appreciation*, printed for private circulation (1907) · M. T. Brück, *Agnes Mary Clerke and the rise of astrophysics* (2002) · M. T. Brück, 'Agnes Mary Clerke, chronicler of astronomy', *Quarterly Journal of the Royal Astronomical Society*, 35 (1994), 59–79 · M. T. Brück, 'Ellen and Agnes Clerke of Skibbereen, scholars and writers', *Seanchas Chairbre*, 3 (1993), 23–43 · M. T. Brück, 'Agnes Clerke's work as a scientific biographer', *Irish Astronomical Journal*, 24 (1997), 193–8 · *The Times* (22 Jan 1907) · *Nature*, 75 (1906–7), 299–300 · *The Observatory*, 30 (1907), 107–8 · *Monthly Notices of the Royal Astronomical Society*,

67 (1906–7), 230–31 · *Popular Astronomy*, 15 (June–July 1907), 323–6 · *WW*

Archives U. Cam., department of history and philosophy of science | California Institute of Technology, Hale MSS · CUL, Cape/ RGO archives, Gill MSS · U. Cal., Santa Cruz, Lick Observatory, Mary Lea Shane archives, Holden MSS · University of Chicago, Yerkes Observatory, Hale MSS · University of Exeter Library, J. N. Lockyer MSS · University of Wisconsin, Holden MSS

Likenesses Barraud, photograph, repro. in H. McPherson, *Astronomers of today* (1905) · Elliott & Fry, photograph, repro. in *Knowledge and Scientific News* (Feb 1907) · H. S. Mendelssohn, photograph, repro. in Huggins, *Agnes Mary Clerke and Ellen Mary Clerke* · H. S. Mendelssohn, photograph, NPG [*see illus.*]

Wealth at death £6164 4s. 2d.: probate, 1 March 1909, CGPLA Eng. & Wales

Clerke, Bartholomew (*c*.1537–1590), civil lawyer, was the son of John Clerke (*d.* 1573), of Wells, Somerset, a notary public and proctor of the arches, and Anne, daughter of Henry Grantoft of Huntingdonshire. He was educated at Eton College (*c*.1550–1554) and King's College, Cambridge, where he was elected scholar on 23 August 1554 and proceeded BA in 1559. Appointed professor of rhetoric *c*.1563, Clerke was proctor in 1564 and took part in the public disputation for doctors' degrees in philosophy that was held in the presence of the queen on her visit to the university. Rumours circulated of his unsoundness in religion—perhaps explained by his letter of December 1565 to William Cecil as chancellor of the university complaining of those who, 'though otherwise good and religious men', were too fond of wrangling about trifles, and 'feigned to themselves unheard of laws of conscience', notably in respect of the wearing of the surplice in ministration and the use of the traditional priest's square cap, both of which they rejected as popish. Clerke dubbed them 'fanatici superpellicani & galeriani' ('surplice and cap fanatics') who 'infected many with their venom, not to say anabaptistical principles' (Strype, *Parker*, 197, bk 3, appx 43).

Clerke's studies, meanwhile, embraced both modern languages and the law, and at some stage they took him to France, where he was offered but declined a public readership at Angers. In 1568 he was recommended by Cecil and others to succeed Roger Ascham as Latin secretary to the queen, but the office was already promised to another, and in 1569 Clerke again served as university proctor. Through the influence, in all probability, of the poet turned statesman Thomas Sackville, Lord Buckhurst, Clerke was elected member for Bramber in the parliament of April 1571, and shortly thereafter accompanied his patron to Paris on an embassy to congratulate Charles IX on his marriage. On his return he resided for some months in Buckhurst's household where he worked on a much admired translation into Latin of Castiglione's *Il cortigiano* ('The courtier'), a series of discourses expounding the humanist values of the Italian Renaissance in which scholarship was allied to refinement and gentility. As elsewhere in Europe, the book became fashionable reading for the aristocracy, and Clerke's version went through three further editions in Elizabeth's reign (1577, 1579, and 1585). It was prefaced with letters of commendation from Edward de Vere, the earl of Oxford (to whom, it appears, Clerke had been tutor), Buckhurst, and John Caius.

Clerke proceeded LLD in 1572. His legal studies made him the ideal choice when Archbishop Parker heard that Burghley was looking for a scholar to refute Nicholas Sander's attack (*De visibili monarchia ecclesiae*) on the legitimacy of the queen's title. Parker reported that 'for his more estimation I have honested him with a room in the Arches … and he shall not want my advice and diligence' (Bruce and Perowne, 411). His work was forwarded to Burghley for approval and published in 1573 (*Fidelis servi subdito infidelio responsio, una cum errorum et calumniarum examine quae continentur in septimo libro a Nicholao Sandero conscripto*). In January of that year Clerke became a member of Doctors' Commons, and in May, by Parker's patronage, succeeded Thomas Yale as dean of the arches. The queen ordered Parker to rescind the appointment, on the pretence that he was too young to hold the post, but Clerke refused to be intimidated, pointing out that others had been preferred as young as he was and that to dismiss him would be to discredit him in his profession; he challenged a trial of his competence, and repeated that 'he would rather render his life than the office' (ibid., 417–32). Parker respectfully held his ground, the appointment stood, and other offices followed. In November 1573 Clerke was member of a commission to visit the church, city, and diocese of Canterbury; in 1577 he was appointed a master in chancery and in 1578 became a judge of the court of audience. According to Aylmer he was one of the few lawyers who was 'painful' and who did not 'follow his private gain' (Strype, *Aylmer*, 62).

Clerke figures prominently in the judicial records of the period 1572–89. In December 1585 Clerke and Henry Killigrew were sent as members of the earl of Leicester's council of state to the Netherlands. Clerke's links were with the peace faction represented by Lord Burghley and the earl of Sussex, and Leicester would have preferred someone else, describing him as having 'good will, and a pretty scholar's wit', but 'no great stuff in him—he is too little for these big fellows' (Bruce, 33). Clerke for his part was pessimistic as to the outcome of the expedition. In a series of letters to Burghley he wrote that 'here all is full of jealousies and mislikes' (*CSP for.*, 1586–7, 75). The financial support of the states was much less than they had been led to expect, and there were tensions between the states and the earl. He found his work uncongenial and the climate unhealthy. His diligence, however, earned him Leicester's belated respect, and in October he was dispatched back to England on a special mission to the queen. In a memorandum of November 1586 he gave his opinion 'on the Queen's proceedings in the Low Countries', advising that a limited campaign of defending the four provinces was the only realistic option (ibid., 247–9). By April 1587 he was back at The Hague to assist Buckhurst and Sir John Norris in exploring the possibility of a peace settlement with Spain and to allay Dutch discontent at Leicester's conduct. On neither count was the mission successful, and in July, much to his relief, he was again recalled to England.

In 1573 Clerke inherited, along with his brother Francis, the lease of his father's farm at Merton in Surrey. He married, at some date after 1575, Eleanor Haselrigge (*d.* 1594), widow of Thomas Smith of Mitcham in Surrey, where they lived until 1583, when he bought the manor of Clapham. On his death in Clapham on 12 March 1590 Clerke left the manor, together with leases of land at Grantchester, Waddon Mills, the parsonage of Ashe, and meadowland at Vauxhall to his son, Francis, his wife having in all cases a life interest. Provision was also made in his will for his daughter, Cecily (he hoped, God willing, that she would marry someone of his own name), his stepchildren and 'the poor children' of his wife's brother John. Among several items of jewellery mentioned is a 'great cross of diamonds and rubies I had of the Lady Frances, Countess of Sussex'. Clerke wanted a simple funeral, but left money for the building of a small chapel 'close to Clapham Chancel north window' to contain a family tomb. The present church of St Paul's has preserved all that remains of this—the figure of his son, kneeling, and the epitaph on Clerke and his wife. P. O. G. WHITE

Sources J. Strype, *Annals of the Reformation and establishment of religion … during Queen Elizabeth's happy reign*, 3rd edn, 4 vols. (1731–5) · J. Strype, *The life and acts of Matthew Parker* (1711) · *CSP for.*, 1585–7 · *CSP dom.*, *addenda*, 1547–80 · *APC*, 1572–89 · *Correspondence of Matthew Parker*, ed. J. Bruce and T. T. Perowne, Parker Society, 42 (1853) · J. Bruce, ed., *Correspondence of Robert Dudley, earl of Leycester*, CS, 27 (1844) · W. Cole, 'A history of King's College, Cambridge', BL, Add. MS 5815, 2, fols. 91–7 · will, 1590, PRO, PROB 11/75, sig. 21 · will, 1573, PRO, PROB 11/55, sig. 1 [John Clerke] · O. Manning and W. Bray, *The history and antiquities of the county of Surrey*, 3 vols. (1804–14) · Cooper, *Ath. Cantab.*, 2.70, 544 · HoP, *Commons*, 1558–1603 · DNB · J. Strype, *The history of the life and acts of … Edmund Grindal* (1710) · J. Strype, *Historical collections of the life and acts of … John Aylmer* (1701) · will, PRO, PROB 11/84, sig. 56 [Eleanor Clerke]

Archives BL, Lansdowne MSS · Bodl. Oxf., Tanner MSS · Inner Temple Library, London, Petyt MSS

Wealth at death lands; significant collection of jewellery: will, PRO, PROB 11/75, sig. 21

Clerke, Charles (1743–1779), naval officer and circumnavigator, was born in Weatherfield, Essex, the son of Joseph Clerke, a farmer. He had a brother, Sir John Clerke, and a sister who married Paul Henry Maty. He entered the navy in 1755 as captain's servant and midshipman in the *Dorsetshire*, served continuously during the Seven Years' War, and was on board the *Bellona* when she captured the *Courageux* on 13 August 1761. During the action Clerke was stationed in the mizen-top, and when the mizen-mast was shot away fell with it into the sea. After the peace he was appointed able seaman and midshipman in the *Dolphin*, and sailed with Commodore the Hon. John Byron on his voyage round the world in 1764 to 1766. On his return he communicated to Matthew Maty, secretary of the Royal Society, an account of the great height of the Patagonians, among whom he says they saw 'hardly a man less than eight feet; most of them considerably more'. The letter was read to the society on 12 February 1767, and published in the *Philosophical Transactions* for 1767 (57, 1768, 75–9). In 1768 he was appointed as master's mate to the *Endeavour*, with Captain Cook, and again sailed round the world on that expedition in 1768 to 1771. During the *Endeavour*'s stay in Tahiti, Clerke was associated with a girl known as Mrs

Tate. He was ordered by Cook to act as lieutenant in a vacancy on 27 May 1771, during the voyage, as he was 'a young Man extremely well quallified for that station' (*Journals*, 1.472) and was confirmed in that rank on the expedition's return to England on 31 July 1771. He sailed as second lieutenant of the *Resolution* in Cook's second voyage round the world in 1772 to 1775.

On his return to England, Clerke was advanced to the rank of commander on 26 August 1775, and when Cook's third expedition was fitting out in 1776, Clerke was appointed to command the *Discovery*. Before the *Discovery* sailed, Clerke was committed to the king's bench prison for debt, having apparently made himself security for his brother Captain Sir John Clerke RN, who had sailed for the East Indies without discharging his debts. Eventually Clerke managed to extricate himself from prison and rejoin the *Discovery* in Plymouth, catching up with Cook in Table Bay. On the death of Captain Cook on 14 February 1779, Clerke succeeded to the command of the expedition, which, however, he did not long enjoy, dying six months later of tuberculosis he had contracted in prison. During these six months he had given proofs of his ability, energy, and devotion. In accordance with Cook's orders he had taken the expedition once again through Bering Strait into high latitudes in an attempt to return to England by the north-west passage or failing that the north-east passage. Being obstructed by pack ice he was forced to turn back, realizing that any further attempt would not only be fruitless, but also dangerous. The climate proved extremely trying to his condition and he died on 22 August 1779 within sight of Kamchatka and was buried with full military honours on 30 August under a tree, on rising ground in a valley on the north side of the Russian settlement of Petropavlovsk in Avacha Bay.

J. K. LAUGHTON, *rev.* ANDREW C. F. DAVID

Sources *The journals of Captain James Cook*, ed. J. C. Beaglehole, 4 vols. in 5, Hakluyt Society, extra ser., 34a, 35, 36a–b, 37 (1955–74), vols. 1–3 • J. King, *A voyage to the Pacific ocean*, 3 (1784) • H. Wallis, 'The Patagonian giants', in *Byron's journal of his circumnavigation, 1764–1766*, ed. R. E. Gallagher, Hakluyt Society, 2nd ser., 122 (1964), 185–213 • *Byron's journal of his circumnavigation, 1764–1766*, ed. R. E. Gallagher, Hakluyt Society, 2nd ser., 122 (1964) • H. B. Carter, *Sir Joseph Banks, 1743–1820* (1988)
Archives BL, original log kept on Cook's second voyage, Add. MSS 8951–8953 • BL, second copy of fair log kept on Cook's second voyage, Add. MSS 8961–8962 • Hydrographic Office, Taunton, Admiralty Library, journal, MS 74/8 [extract] • PRO, corresp. to Admiralty Secretary, ADM 1/1611 and 1/1612 • PRO, corresp. to Navy Board, ADM 106/1233 • PRO, journal kept on Cook's first voyage, ADM 51/4548 • PRO, fair log kept on Cook's second voyage, ADM 55/103 • PRO, log and observations kept on Cook's third voyage, ADM 51/4561 • PRO, log kept on Cook's third voyage, ADM 55/124 • PRO, log and proceedings kept on Cook's third voyage, ADM 55/22 and 23 • S. Antiquaries, Lond., corresp., mainly letters to his sister | British Columbia Archives and Records Service, Victoria, Canada, instructions from Cook, log of HMS *Resolution* [copy] • Mitchell L., NSW, corresp. to Joseph Banks relating to Cook's second and third voyages
Likenesses N. Dance, oils, *c.*1776, Government House, Wellington, New Zealand; repro. in Beaglehole, ed., *Journals*, vol. 3 • J. Taylor, wash drawing, 1776, U. Cal., Los Angeles, University Research Library, special collections; repro. in Beaglehole, ed., *Journals*, vol. 2

Clerke, Ellen Mary (1840–1906), translator and writer, was born on 26 September 1840 at Skibbereen, co. Cork. She was the eldest of three children of John William Clerke (1814–1890), classical scholar, graduate of Trinity College, Dublin, and manager of a bank in Skibbereen, and his wife, Catherine (1818–1897), daughter of Rickard Deasy of Clonakilty, co. Cork.

Her sister, Agnes Mary *Clerke (1842–1907), whose middle name, like Ellen's, was an indication of the Clerke family's devout Catholicism, was born two years later. Neither married and the Clerke sisters were to be close companions throughout their lives. Their younger brother, Aubrey St John Clerke, became a Chancery barrister in London. Both women were very intelligent and had wide-ranging interests. They were educated to an exceptionally high degree at home and grew up to share a taste for literature, science, and music. Their father initially taught them astronomy, of which he was a keen amateur student. Both Clerke sisters later wrote about astronomy and Agnes became an eminent authority on the subject—it remained a subsidiary interest for Ellen.

The Clerke family moved to Dublin in 1861 and then, in 1863, back to co. Cork to the small port of Queenstown (renamed Kobh after 1922), presumably in connection with John Clerke's work. By 1867, when Ellen was twenty-seven, they had settled in Italy where they remained for ten years, living mostly in Florence. During her time in Italy, Ellen, ever keen to enlarge the horizons of her knowledge, became fluent in the Italian language. She began to study Italian literature and to translate Italian texts for English publication. She also wrote critiques of Italian literature, samples of which can be read in Richard Garnett's *History of Italian Literature* (1897). Her *Fable and Song in Italy*, which was eventually published by Grant Edwards in 1899, and which was dedicated to Garnett, gathered together some of her earlier essays which had first appeared in periodicals such as the *Dublin Review* and the *Gentleman's Magazine*. It also included line-by-line verse translations of poets such as Boiardo, a fifteenth-century Tuscan.

Shortly after the family's return from Italy to settle in London, where John Clerke died in 1890, Ellen had published in 1881 by W. Satchell & Co. a volume entitled *The Flying Dutchman and other Poems*. It contains some of her own ballads, early and miscellaneous poems, along with some translations from Italian. Like most of her writing, the style, to the modern ear, is too controlled and self-consciously accurate to evince any real passion, though the range of mythological and literary subjects shows a formidable breadth and depth of learning.

Once she had taken up residence in London, Ellen also embarked on a weekly leader column in *The Tablet* which she kept up for twenty years. Always a woman of eclectic interests she wrote monographs on Jupiter and on Venus, published by Edward Stanford in 1892 and 1893 respectively. She also wrote occasional pieces for *The Observatory*, the journal of the Royal Astronomical Society, founded by William Christie in 1877, though her sister Agnes wrote many more of these.

Ellen was sixty-two before her novel *Flowers of Fire* was published by Hutchinson in 1902. It is a well enough written romance, in her usual careful prose, set in the cosmopolitan upper strata of Italian society which she knew so well. Its quaint formality has not worn well, though the physical description of the eruption of Vesuvius in chapter 24 imaginatively and effectively evokes the horror of the flames and fear as the heroine and her lover flee to safety while everyone else in the party perishes.

Ellen Mary Clerke died from bronchitis on 2 March 1906 at 68 Redcliffe Square in Kensington, the home she shared with Agnes, who outlived her by only ten months. Although she had written a great deal and achieved much, she seemed all her life to be overshadowed by her younger and better known sister. When *The Times* published its 400-word obituary of Agnes on 22 January 1907 it dismissed her sister with the words: 'Her sister Miss EM Clerke, who died a few months ago, also wrote on astronomical matters, though in a far more humble way.' *Agnes Mary and Ellen Mary Clerke: an Appreciation* was printed for private circulation in 1907. It was written by Lady Huggins, wife of the eminent scientist Sir William Huggins, with a foreword by Aubrey St John Clerke.

SUSAN ELKIN

Sources 'Clerke, Agnes Mary', *DNB* · *The Times* (22 Jan 1907) [obit. of Agnes Mary Clerke] · d. cert.
Wealth at death £3318 10s. 6d.: administration, 7 May 1906, *CGPLA Eng. & Wales*

Clerke, Francis (*fl.* 1564–1594), civil lawyer and jurist, whose origins are unknown, spent most of his professional career as a proctor in the courts of the archbishop of Canterbury in London and also in the admiralty courts. In a preface to a work written in the 1590s, he made known that he had been active in the court of arches during the previous thirty-six years. As was customary, he would first have spent some years in the equivalent of pupillage, since the contemporary records of the courts show his formal admission as a proctor in 1564. In 1583 a Francis Clerke was admitted to Gray's Inn; it was not unusual for a civil lawyer to be so welcomed by the common lawyers. If this is the same person, he came from Stevenage. It has also been suggested that he was related to Bartholomew Clerke (*d.* 1590), dean of the court of arches, but again the possibility rests only on the coincidence in profession and name. Unlike advocates, proctors commonly entered practice after leaving university without having taken a degree or even without having attended a university at all, and one of these was evidently the path Clerke took. However, he supplicated for, and received, the BCL from Oxford in 1594, professedly so that he could lay claim to that distinction on the title-page of his soon to be published book, the earliest copies of which, though all in manuscript, date from the mid-1590s.

Most of what can be known about Clerke must be derived from his two works, which were used by practitioners as long as the courts about which he wrote flourished. Lord Hardwicke later described him as 'an author of undoubted credit' (*Sir Henry Blount's case*). Clerke's close familiarity with the courts and his stated goal of helping practising civil lawyers overcome the limitations of academic training lend credence to the description. The longer of his works, *Praxis in curiis ecclesiasticis*, was published after Clerke's death, in Dublin in 1666, and in London in 1684. However, it circulated widely in manuscript beforehand, and many manuscript copies have survived in local and diocesan archives—testimony to its utility in understanding the procedure employed in all English ecclesiastical courts. The Latin is unvarnished, and substantive law is related to its discussion of procedure. Unfortunately, the long gestation period of a printed edition led to the introduction of errors, and no satisfactory edition has ever been produced. It was largely overtaken by Henry Conset's *Practice of the Spiritual or Ecclesiastical Courts* (1684), which itself relied heavily on Clerke's work.

Many similar works were written during this period by continental jurists. They combined descriptions of the special features of particular courts with more general treatments of procedural law in the *ius commune*. Typically, they moved through the steps in litigation, from citation to sentence and appeal. Clerke followed that model but, unlike most continental writers, he provided no citations to the works of learned jurists. Many manuscript copies carry marginalia, made later by the proctors and advocates who did provide them.

Clerke's second and shorter work, *Praxis curie admiralitatis Angliae*, is similar in approach to the first. The admiralty courts used the same basic procedure as the church's courts, but they varied it, as for example in allowing *in rem* attachments of vessels appropriate to general maritime law. This work enjoyed a longer currency, perhaps because of a lack of effective competition. The first edition, published in London in 1667, was reprinted in 1679. Other editions, some produced with facing translations, appeared in 1722, 1743, 1798, and 1829, the second of these edited by Francis Hargrave. John Elihu Hall translated the text and added American notes in a version published in Baltimore, Maryland, in 1809. No trace of Clerke's will has survived, and even the date of his death is unknown.

R. H. HELMHOLZ

Sources J. D. M. Derrett, 'The works of Francis Clerke, proctor', *Studia et Documenta Historiae et Iuris*, 40 (1974), 52–66 · J. H. Baker, *Monuments of endlesse labours: English canonists and their work, 1300–1900* (1998), 71–6 · W. Senior, 'Early writers on maritime law', *Law Quarterly Review*, 37 (1921), 328–9 · R. H. Helmholz, *Roman canon law in Reformation England* (1990), 128–32, 196–7 · Sir Henry Blount's case, 1 Atk. 295, Ch. 1737 · D. M. Owen, *The medieval canon law: teaching, literature and transmission* (1990), 47–53 · M. J. Prichard and D. E. C. Yale, eds., *Hale and Fleetwood on admiralty jurisdiction*, SeldS, 108 (1993), cxxxii–iv

Clerke, Gilbert (*bap.* 1626, *d. c.*1697), mathematician and theologian, was born at Uppingham, Rutland, and baptized there on 19 March 1626. He was a son of John Clerke, headmaster of Uppingham School. He was educated at Geddington, Northamptonshire, and from 1637 at Oundle School. In 1641 he entered Sidney Sussex College, Cambridge; he graduated BA in 1644–5 and took his MA in 1648, when he was elected to a fellowship. He was the first fellow of Sidney to be nominated as proctor, serving in 1652–3. He took Presbyterian orders in 1651, but in 1655 resigned his fellowship and left Cambridge because of religious scruples. He later claimed to have been one of those who introduced the teaching of mathematics and of the new philosophy at Cambridge.

Clerke's earliest published writings, *De plenitudine mundi* (1660) and *Tractatus de restitutione corporum* (1662), reveal that he was a convert to Descartes's philosophy. They defend the Cartesian theory of matter, concentrating on Descartes's denial that a vacuum might exist in nature. Clerke criticized the alternative theories of Bacon, Ward, and especially Hobbes, whose linguistic critique of Descartes and denial of the reality of the spring of air he derided. Although he was familiar with Torricelli's findings and with Boyle's air-pump experiments (which indicated the existence of a vacuum), he believed that these exemplified the action of a subtle ether that could penetrate glass and that filled all space. In the *Tractatus* he was nevertheless also critical of Boyle's Jesuit opponent Francis Line (Linus).

Tractatus de restitutione corporum was dedicated to Sir Justinian Isham, second baronet, a pupil of Clerke's father who became his patron during the 1660s. After leaving Cambridge, Clerke moved eventually to a moated house, Bleakhall, outside Loddington, Northamptonshire, which he filled with elegant objects, and where he established a small pipe works. This was a short distance from the Isham estate at Lamport, where Clerke was a frequent visitor, acting as mathematical tutor to the Isham children. Between 1677 and 1683 he lived chiefly at Lamport, managing the estate for his former pupils Sir Thomas Isham, third baronet, and Sir Justinian Isham, fourth baronet, during their long absences abroad and in London. He was an efficient steward, who warned of the dangers posed by youthful profligacy. With the Ishams, Clerke pored over accounts of reflecting telescopes in the Royal Society's *Philosophical Transactions* and experimented with one of Morland's speaking trumpets. At Lamport he observed the comet of 1681, and made precise calculations of latitude that were later used by Morton to establish the boundaries of Northamptonshire. In 1682 he published *Oughtredus explicatus*, an edition of Oughtred's *Clavis*, dedicated to Sir Justinian Isham, fourth baronet. This edition, which was criticized by John Collins, represented the culmination of work begun by Clerke in the early 1660s. He advised local gentlemen on the manufacture and setting up of dials, the subject of his *Astronomica specimina* (1682) and *The Spot-Dial* (1687).

Clerke shared the Ishams' interest in cases of witchcraft and spirit possession. His account of a haunted house near Daventry in 1658 was later included by Glanvill and More in *Saducismus triumphatus* (1681); subsequently he investigated disturbances at Brixworth and Bowden. He remained sceptical about the true causes of such phenomena, and was critical of the treatment of the children who were said to have been bewitched at Bowden in February 1673. In 1681 he corresponded with Richard Baxter on subjects raised by Baxter's disputes with Stillingfleet, expressing his sympathy for the writings of Socinus and discussing the nature of the Trinity, the atonement, and original

sin. He stressed his independence in religion, writing that he could neither subscribe to the Thirty-Nine Articles nor to Socinus's opinions concerning the Trinity. These matters were taken up in the anonymous *Tractatus tres* (1695), to which Clerke contributed the first two treatises. He was concerned to demonstrate the pre-eminence of God the Father, arguing that the interpretation of the Trinity found in the Nicene creed was a result of the corruption of Christianity by Platonism. He suggested elsewhere that this corruption had been predicted in the books of Daniel and Revelation.

Clerke was not an original theologian but relied heavily on the writings of Sandius and Zwicker. The theologian George Bull argued that he had misrepresented Clement of Alexandria. At his brother's invitation, Clerke moved from Lamport to Stamford Baron, Northamptonshire, about 1683. There he continued to teach and practise mathematics, one of his pupils being the young William Whiston. Clerke was among the first readers of Newton's *Principia*, and wrote to its author in 1687 to criticize the book's obscure terminology. From his brother he inherited an estate at Luffenham, Rutland, worth £40 a year. He is thought to have died about 1697.

SCOTT MANDELBROTE

Sources *The diary of Thomas Isham of Lamport (1658–81)*, ed. G. Isham, trans. N. Marlow (1971) · DWL, R. Baxter MSS · J. Glanvill, *Saducismus triumphatus, or, Full and plain evidence concerning witches and apparitions*, trans. A. Horneck, pt 2 (1681), 263–8 · *The correspondence of Isaac Newton*, ed. H. W. Turnbull and others, 2 (1960), 485–500 · R. Nelson, *The life of Dr George Bull* (1713), 497–510 · G. Bull, *Some important points of primitive Christianity*, ed. R. Nelson, 3 vols. (1713), 3.915–1064 · J. Morton, *The natural history of Northamptonshire* (1712), 2 · W. Whiston, *Memoirs of the life and writings of Mr William Whiston: containing memoirs of several of his friends also* (1749) · J. Bridges, 'Collections on Northamptonshire', Bodl. Oxf., MS Top. Northants. f. 1, 65 · Venn, *Alum. Cant.* · G. M. Edwards, *Sidney Sussex College* (1899), 136 · S. P. Rigaud and S. J. Rigaud, eds., *Correspondence of scientific men of the seventeenth century*, 1 (1841), 470–74 · parish register, Uppingham, 19 March 1626, Leics. RO [baptism] · *The grounds and occasions of the controversy concerning the unity of God* (1698), 17

Archives DWL, Baxter MSS · Massachusetts Institute of Technology, Cambridge, Burndy Library, Newton MSS · Northants. RO, Isham MSS

Wealth at death over £40 p.a.; also estate at Luffenham, Rutland: Nelson, *Life of Dr George Bull*, 510

Clerke, Henry (1621/2?–1687), physician, was one of several children of Thomas Clerke (1580–1663) of Willoughby, Warwickshire. He matriculated at Magdalen Hall, Oxford, in 1638, when his age was entered as sixteen, and spent the remainder of his life within Magdalen College, where he obtained a demyship, graduated BA in 1641, and proceeded MA in 1644. From 1642 to 1667 he held a fellowship, submitting to the parliamentary visitors' examination in 1648 and having no trouble retaining his position in 1660 when the surviving expelled fellows returned. He was reader in logic in 1643, bursar in 1653, 1656, and 1662, and vice-president in 1655 and again in 1663.

Clerke was created BM in January 1648, admitted to practise medicine the following February, and took the

MD by accumulation in 1652, being incorporated in Cambridge in 1673. From 1652 to 1671 he deputized for William Petty as Tomlins reader in anatomy. He was admitted a candidate of the College of Physicians in 1658 and elected fellow in 1669. Clerke was one of the group of virtuoso-physicians who gathered at Petty's house from 1649 and, after his departure, at John Wilkins's lodgings at Wadham College, to perform dissections and discuss apothecary matters and other scientific topics. John Evelyn, Henry Oldenburg, and Robert Boyle were among their visitors. In 1657 the group migrated to Boyle's house where they had access to his scientific apparatus. Clerke was an early member of the Royal Society, and the first from Magdalen, being elected on 24 October 1667, but he paid his subscription only for 1667–9 and played no part in its London meetings.

Following the death of Thomas Pierce, president of Magdalen College, Clerke was elected in his place on 5 March 1672, and in order to fully qualify for the office he soon afterwards took holy orders. He was appointed vice-chancellor on 9 October 1676. He married, probably in the 1660s, Catherine (1635/6–1669), fourth daughter of William Adams of Charwelton, Northamptonshire. They had a son, Henry, who died in the same year as his mother, and a daughter, Catherine, known around the college as the Infanta, possibly because of the haughty air she adopted as the president's daughter. She married in 1682 Richard Shuttleworth (1666–1687) of Gawthrop (or Gawthorpe) Hall, near Burnley, Lancashire, at that time a gentleman commoner of Trinity College and considerably younger than his wife—he was still in his minority at the time of his father-in-law's death, by which time they had three children. In the summer of 1685 Clerke went on a tour of Yorkshire with his daughter and son-in-law, calling on the way back at Willoughby and Nottingham.

Clerke died at Gawthrop Hall on 24 March 1687, allegedly aged sixty-eight, and on 9 April was buried with his ancestors at Willoughby. He left the furniture and linen in his college lodgings to one of his sisters and her daughter, who may have been looking after him there. He made generous bequests to his immediate family, part of this to come from the sale of his books; to his college the sum of £50 to buy a gilded bowl and cover to be placed on the altar; and lesser sums to various parishes. The college erected and subsequently restored a monument in the church at Willoughby commemorating him as a great benefactor.   ANITA McCONNELL

Sources J. R. Bloxam, *A register of the presidents, fellows … of Saint Mary Magdalen College*, 8 vols. (1853–85), vol. 5, pp. 154–8 · Munk, *Roll*, 1.358–9 · Magd. Oxf., MSS 427, 684 · will, U. Oxf., chancellor's court wills, archives · M. Hunter, *The Royal Society and its fellows, 1660–1700: the morphology of an early scientific institution* (1982) · *Hist. U. Oxf.* 4: *17th-cent. Oxf.* · Foster, *Alum. Oxon.* · parish registers, 9 April 1687, Willoughby, Warwickshire [burial]
Likenesses oils, Magd. Oxf.

Clerke, Richard (*fl.* **1572–1596**), navigator and privateer, claimed to have been born at Buckhurst, Essex, but is generally referred to as 'of Weymouth'. He presumably learned his trade in the ships of the latter port, being master of the *Pilgrim* between Weymouth and Bordeaux in 1572. Part at least of the next ten years was evidently spent in the Newfoundland fishing trade, as he developed a specialist knowledge of the waters round that island. He entered the service of Henry Oughtred of Southampton, a major international merchant and shipowner. In command of Oughtred's *Susan Fortune* he accompanied the *Popinjay* of Sir John Perrot to Newfoundland in 1582. Oughtred claimed he had suffered losses in Spain and employed Clerke to help recover them from Spanish (in fact Portuguese) vessels in Newfoundland. At Fermeuse the two English vessels attacked and robbed three Portuguese vessels, lading their catch and goods into the *São João*, which they brought back to Southampton, presumably dividing the returns between Perrot and Oughtred. Masters of English ships at Fermeuse were shocked at this disruption of a peaceful fishing community. The Portuguese took an action against Clerke in the high court of admiralty, supported by testimonies from an English ship's master who had been at Fermeuse, though no conclusion to the action has been found.

When, later in 1582, Sir Humphrey Gilbert was preparing an American colonizing expedition, Clerke entered his service and, between June and August 1583, served as master of his flagship, the *Delight*, first under William Winter as captain and then under Maurice Browne. The *Delight* met with opposition at St John's harbour from the mixed fishing community, but on sight of the queen's commission the squadron was admitted, and Gilbert went through the ceremony of annexing Newfoundland to England and issuing passes to non-English vessels to fish there. Clerke had a shallop built for exploration of the harbours of south-eastern Newfoundland, and fortunately it remained on tow when the ships left for the mainland. Off Sable Island—Clerke maintained as the result of a changed order from Gilbert—the *Delight* went aground, losing most of her men and all the data so far collected. Clerke bravely secured the shallop and with fifteen men contrived to sail northward to Newfoundland. Without stores or adequate sails they suffered great hardships, but eventually arrived in south-west Newfoundland, where Clerke knew the French Basques had fishing stations. They took his men, restored them to health, and brought them safely to Pasaje, where they were nearly taken by the Spanish, but eventually they reached England at the end of 1583 to find that Edward Hayes, whose *Golden Hind* was the only vessel to survive, accused Clerke of having cast away the *Delight*. Clerke made a technical and convincing reply, illustrating his knowledge of these waters. Richard Hakluyt printed both versions of the disaster in 1589.

Clerke presumably returned to the Newfoundland fishery, as he is not found in the Armada lists. He was still involved in the fishery in 1596, when he took the *Pilgrim* of Newport, Isle of Wight, into St John's harbour to purchase additional salt. He was received in a friendly fashion by the master of a French Basque ship of St Jean-de-Luz, who then turned on him, imprisoned him and his men, and stripped the *Pilgrim* of all but a minimum of food and sails. Clerke had to make his way home with such limited resources but succeeded in doing so successfully. He then fades out of the records.   DAVID B. QUINN, *rev.*

Sources R. Hakluyt, *The principall navigations, voiages and discoveries of the English nation*, 3 vols. in 2 (1589); facs. edn, Hakluyt Society, extra ser., 39 (1965) · D. B. Quinn, A. M. Quinn, and S. Hillier, eds., *New American world: a documentary history of North America to 1612*, 3–4 (1979)

Clerke, Richard (*d.* 1634), Church of England clergyman, was born in London, the son of George Clarke (*d.* 1607). He matriculated as a pensioner from Christ's College, Cambridge, in December 1579 and graduated BA in early 1583. Elected that year as a fellow, he proceeded MA in 1586. As a leader of the minority conformist faction in this generally puritan college, in 1590 he came to blows with the strongly Calvinist George Downame, later bishop of Derry. That October, Clerke and a colleague, John Powell, wrote to Lord Burghley complaining that they had not been promoted within Christ's because 'we do not favour the party of those who through portents of new opinions and treading down of all laws would attack the jugular of the college' (Bondos-Greene, 200). Burghley effected a reconciliation in November, but in the fellowship elections of 1596 Clerke, who had proceeded BTh in 1593 and who was that year Lady Margaret preacher, encountered further trouble when he opposed the candidature of Thomas Rainbow, whom he considered a 'schismatic'.

In 1597 Clerke was instituted as vicar of Minster, in the island of Thanet, and the following year, having proceeded DTh, he relinquished his fellowship. Within a short time he married; his wife's name is unknown, but a son, Martin, perhaps their eldest child, who graduated from Christ's early in 1621, was probably born before 1602. On 8 May 1602 Clerke was collated to the office of six-preacher in Canterbury Cathedral; regular baptisms and burials of members of his family suggest that from at least early 1605 he was often resident in the city. A learned Hebraist, he was chosen as one of the translators of the Authorized Version of the Bible and worked on the first section from Genesis to Kings. He sufficiently impressed the king to become the latter's apparently preferred candidate to succeed Edmund Barwell (*d.* 1609) in the mastership of Christ's College, but at the last minute James I ordered the earl of Salisbury to institute Valentine Cary on the stated grounds that Cary was unmarried and childless. Compensation came to Clerke successively in the form of the Kentish rectory of Shargate and vicarage of Monkton with Birchington, which he held with Minster respectively from 1609 to 1611 and from 1611 until his death.

Having given birth to at least ten children, Clerke's wife died, and was buried in Canterbury Cathedral on 8 October 1620; most of the children also predeceased their father. Having married again, Clerke died in 1634 and was buried in the cathedral on 29 September. His will gave little to his two 'unkinde sonnes', Martin and James; his daughter Katherine, who was under nineteen, was left to the guardianship of her maternal relatives, including her great-aunt, 'the elder Lady Oxinden'. Other beneficiaries included his widow, the hospitals of St John's, Canterbury, and St Nicholas, Harbaldown, the schools of St Paul's, London, and Christ Church, Canterbury, and Christ's College. He also confirmed a deed of 1625 setting aside £120 for loans to farmers at Minster to improve their stock. Seventy-four of his sermons were edited by Charles White and published as *Sermons Preached by that Reverend and Learned Divine Richard Clerke* (1637). According to William Prynne's account in his *Canterburies Doome* (1646) of the testimony given by White at Archbishop William Laud's trial, Laud's chaplains and licensers made extensive alterations to Clerke's text, purging much of his anti-Catholicism and seeking to give his moderate Calvinism an Arminian gloss. Passages affirming the pope to be Antichrist, attacking the mass, and criticizing monks and clergy were removed, while his restriction of salvation to an elect few was replaced by a doctrine approaching universal grace. However, taken at face value Clerke's collected works still represent not so much full-blown Laudian ceremonialism as 'a Whitgiftian (but distinctly pre-Laudian) Conformist churchmanship' (Collinson, 183). Visitation sermons apart, their message was generally non-controversial, valuing equally prayer, preaching, sacraments, and the decency of actions such as kneeling at communion. Such a message sits reasonably comfortably with the anti-puritanism of his younger days.

VIVIENNE LARMINIE

Sources Venn, *Alum. Cant.* · S. Bondos-Greene, 'The end of an era: Cambridge puritanism and the Christ's College election of 1609', *HJ*, 25 (1982), 197–208 · A. Milton, *Catholic and Reformed: the Roman and protestant churches in English protestant thought, 1600–1640* (1995) · P. Collinson, 'The protestant cathedral', *A history of Canterbury Cathedral*, ed. P. Collinson, N. Ramsay, and M. Sparks (1995), 183, 186 · R. Hovenden, ed., *The register booke of christeninges, marriages, and burialls within the precinct of the cathedrall and metropoliticall church of Christe of Canterburie*, Harleian Society, register section, 2 (1878) · *Fasti Angl., 1541–1857*, [Canterbury], 27 · E. Hasted, *The history and topographical survey of the county of Kent*, 2nd edn, 10 (1800), 285, 293 · will, CKS, PRC 32/50/322

Clerke, Sir Thomas Henry Shadwell (1792–1849), army officer and military journalist, was born at Bandon, co. Cork. Intended for the army, a profession also adopted by his brothers, St John Augustus Clerke, who died a lieutenant-general and colonel in the 75th foot on 17 January 1870, and William Clerke, afterwards a major in the 77th foot, he was sent to the Royal Military College, Great Marlow, where he distinguished himself, and was appointed to an ensigncy without purchase in 1808. As a subaltern in the 28th and 5th foot he served through the Peninsular campaigns until he lost his right leg in the engagement at Redinha in 1811 and was incapacitated for further active service. On the recommendation of Lord Wellington he was promoted to a company in the 1st garrison battalion, with which he served until its reduction in 1814. He afterwards served with the 2nd battalion 57th, and on the army depot staff. He was promoted to a majority unattached in 1830, and was made KH in 1831.

Clerke became first editor of *Colburn's United Service Magazine* in January 1829, and so continued until July 1842. On the death of Colonel Gurwood, he was entrusted with the task of seeing through the press the last volume of *Selections from the Wellington Despatches*. Although his name does not appear as the author of any scientific or other works, he was an active member of the British Association and of various learned societies. At the time of his death he was a fellow of the Royal Society (elected 10 April 1833), a vice-president of the Royal United Service Institution, of which he had been one of the founders, and a fellow of the Royal Astronomical and Geological societies; for a short time he had been honorary foreign secretary of the Royal Geographical Society. Clerke died at his residence in Brompton Grove, London, of 'paralysis', on 19 April 1849.

H. M. CHICHESTER, rev. JAMES LUNT

Sources Hart's Army List · T. H. S. Clerke, editorial, *United Service Magazine*, 2 (1842), 401 · *Colburn's United Service Magazine*, 2 (1849), 138–9 · *Abstracts of the Papers Communicated to the Royal Society of London*, 5 (1843–50), 888–9
Likenesses W. Drummond, lithograph, pubd 1835 (after E. U. Eddis), BM, NPG

Clerke, William (*fl.* 1575–1594), writer, matriculated as a sizar of Trinity College, Cambridge, in June 1575. He became a scholar of that house and in 1578–9 proceeded BA. In 1581 he was elected a fellow of his college and in 1582 he commenced MA. He may also have been the William Clerke of St Paul's School who received money from Robert Nowel's estate on 3 June 1579 and 20 February 1580 for attendance at Cambridge. In 1594 Clerke published *The triall of bastardie … annexed at the end of this treatise, touching the prohibition of marriage, a table of the levitical, English, and positive canon catalogues, their concordance and difference*. He may also have written *Polimanteia, or, The meanes lawfull and unlawfull, to judge of the fall of a common-wealth against the frivolous and foolish conjectures of this age* (1595), the author of which is identified as 'W. C.' in the dedication to Robert Devereux, earl of Essex.

THOMPSON COOPER, rev. ELIZABETH GOLDRING

Sources Cooper, *Ath. Cantab.*, vols. 1–2 · Venn, *Alum. Cant.* · R. B. Gardiner, ed., *The admission registers of St Paul's School, from 1748 to 1876* (1884) · W. T. Lowndes, *The bibliographer's manual of English literature*, ed. H. G. Bohn, [new edn], 6 vols. (1869) · ESTC

Clerke, Sir William Henry, eighth baronet (1751–1818), Church of England clergyman, was born on 25 November 1751 in Jamaica, the second son of Francis Clerke (1724–1760) of Weston, Oxfordshire, and Susannah Elizabeth Ashurst. He matriculated at Christ Church, Oxford, in December 1769; he was subsequently a member of All Souls College, Oxford, and he took his BCL degree in October 1778. In 1778 Clerke succeeded to the baronetcy on the death of his elder brother, Francis, the favourite aide-de-camp to General John Burgoyne in North America, who was mortally wounded at Saratoga. When he was dying Francis asked Burgoyne to endeavour, on his return to England, to procure preferment for William, who had taken orders. The twelfth earl of Derby—at the prompting, no doubt, of General Burgoyne, who had married the earl's aunt—presented Clerke to the rectory of Bury, Lancashire, to which he was instituted on 6 February 1778.

Clerke's religious and political views appear to have been those of a conventional high-church tory. He was well received on his arrival in Bury and as rector was remembered as good natured and charitable to the poor. In particular, he paid much attention to the physical health of his parishioners; he vaccinated the children of the local poor and for a considerable time even travelled to Rochdale once a week to perform the same operation. On the occasion of an outbreak of fever he issued, in 1790, *Thoughts upon the means of preserving the health of the poor by prevention and suppression of epidemic fever*, a pamphlet advocating the use of quarantine, improved cleanliness, and extensive lime whitewashing as a means of controlling the disease. These suggestions, perhaps partly inspired by Clerke's own extensive involvement in the lime trade, were supported by an appeal for paternalistic involvement on the part of employers of labour and by a long letter on the pamphlet's subject matter by the philanthropic Dr Thomas Percival.

In May 1792 Clerke married Byzantia (*d.* 1815), daughter of Thomas Cartwright of Aynho; they had three sons and one daughter. The eldest son, William Henry (1793–1861), became ninth baronet and he served in the Peninsular War and at Waterloo. The two younger sons both went into the church and the youngest, Charles Carr, became archdeacon of Oxford and a canon of Christ Church. At a time when a French invasion was feared Clerke printed *A sermon preached in the parish church of Bury on the 18th October 1798, on the occasion of the colours being presented to the Bury Loyal Association* and *A Serious Address to the People of this Country*. Appended to the sermon was the speech made on the reception of the colours by the lieutenant-colonel commandant of the Bury Volunteers, the first Sir Robert Peel, whose second wife was Clerke's sister. Another of Clerke's publications is his undated *Penitens, or, The dying tradesman, extracted from the books of a late pious writer: to which is added prayers*.

In addition to the manufacture of lime, Clerke involved himself energetically in a number of agricultural pursuits and enterprises. These included farming the extensive rectory lands, often taking a turn at the plough and participating in the harvest. He built his own corn mill and became a significant dealer in both corn and malt. Unfortunately Clerke's enthusiasm for business exceeded his aptitude, and he borrowed extensively, sometimes at high rates of interest, to support his enterprises and he suffered from the dishonesty of some of his associates. Eventually, his financial embarrassments grew to such an extent that his living was sequestered for the benefit of his creditors. He died on 10 April 1818, in the Fleet prison, where he was incarcerated for debt, his wife having died three years previously on 30 April 1815.

MARK SMITH

Sources B. T. Barton, *History of the borough of Bury and neighbourhood in the county of Lancaster* (1874) · E. Baines and W. R. Whatton, *The history of the county palatine and duchy of Lancaster*, new edn, ed. J. Croston and others, 3 (1890) · Foster, *Alum. Oxon.* · private information (1887) [C. W. Sutton] · Burke, *Peerage* (1970)
Wealth at death see Baines and Whatton, *The history of the county palatine*

Clerkington. For this title name *see* Scott, Sir William, of Clerkington, Lord Clerkington (*d.* 1656).

Clermont. For this title name *see* Fortescue, Chichester Samuel Parkinson-, Baron Carlingford and second Baron Clermont (1823–1898).

Clery, Sir Cornelius Francis (1838–1926), army officer, was born at 2 Sidney Place, Cork, on 13 February 1838, the fourth son of James Clery, wine merchant, of Cork, and his wife, Catherine Walsh. After being educated at Dublin and at the Royal Military College, Sandhurst, he was commissioned ensign in the 32nd foot in March 1858. He was promoted lieutenant in June 1859 and captain in January 1866. From 1868 to 1870 he studied at the Staff College. In 1871 he was appointed an instructor of tactics at Sandhurst, where he proved an immediate success, and in September 1872 was appointed professor of tactics. On completing his term of office in May 1875 he published *Minor Tactics*, the result of his Sandhurst teaching, which for thirty years was a leading and influential textbook.

Clery left Sandhurst in 1875 in order to join the administrative staff at army headquarters in Ireland; from there he was transferred to Aldershot in April 1877. A year later he was sent to the Cape on special service as a major on half pay. On the outbreak of the Anglo-Zulu War in January 1879 he was appointed operational staff officer to Colonel R. T. Glynn's column, and later adjutant-general to the flying column. He was present at the battle of Ulundi (4 July). After the war he returned home, and was promoted brevet lieutenant-colonel for his services. In August 1882 he went to Egypt as brigade major in Wolseley's army. After the battle of Tell al-Kebir (13 September), Clery remained in Egypt on the headquarters staff, and subsequently acted as chief of staff in the Suakin expedition under Major-General Sir Gerald Graham in 1884, taking part in the actions at al-Teb (29 February) and Tamai (13 March). In these he was conspicuous, as he refused to wear the new khaki uniform, choosing instead a smartly cut scarlet jacket. For his services he was promoted brevet colonel in May 1884 and was made CB.

Clery served as deputy adjutant and quartermaster-general in the Gordon relief expedition, and was appointed chief of staff of the army of occupation in Egypt in March 1886. Having shown he was a fighting soldier, and no mere theorist, Clery was appointed commandant of the Staff College in August 1888. After five years there he reverted to half pay until promoted major-general in December 1894. In 1896 he was appointed deputy adjutant-general at the War Office.

Clery remained there until, on the outbreak of the Second South African War in October 1899, he was appointed to command the 2nd division in Natal. This he led throughout the campaign to relieve Ladysmith (28 February 1900) and the subsequent invasion of the eastern Transvaal. In October 1900 the Natal army was broken up to garrison the territory it had captured. Without a command Clery, like many others, returned to England. The

Sir Cornelius Francis Clery (1838–1926), by Bassano

reason for his recall was the subject of many rumours: indecisiveness in command, ill health, or personal considerations in high places that had no connection with his professional ability. He was created KCB in 1899 and KCMG in 1900, and retired in February 1901. A dandy of the old school, who dyed his whiskers and dressed impeccably even on campaign, Clery was a brave soldier. He died, unmarried, at his home, 4 Whitehall Court, Westminster, London, on 25 June 1926.

H. DE WATTEVILLE, rev. M. G. M. JONES

Sources *Army List* · *The Times* (26 June 1926) · L. S. Amery, ed., *The Times history of the war in South Africa*, 3 (1905) · L. S. Amery, ed., *The Times history of the war in South Africa*, 4 (1906) · T. Pakenham, *The Boer War* (1979) · D. R. Morris, *The washing of the spears* (1966) · *DSAB* · personal knowledge (1937)

Likenesses Bassano, photograph, NPG [*see illus.*] · Cumming, photograph, repro. in C. N. Robinson, *Celebrities of the army* (1900)

Wealth at death £68,946 0s. 8d.: probate, 6 Aug 1926, CGPLA Eng. & Wales

Clery, William Edward [*pseud.* Austin Fryers] (1861–1931), trade unionist and writer, was born in Ireland but emigrated to London in 1877 taking with him, as he later recalled, little more than his brogue. In 1888 he passed the civil service examination and became a sorter at the chief post office in St Martin's-le-Grand in the City of London. At the same time he began to write plays and to publish articles in the *Gentleman's Magazine* under the *nom de plume* 'Austin Fryers', which he used for the rest of his life.

This was the period which saw the founding of numerous 'new' unions, including for the various grades of Post

Office workers, and involvement in union activities frequently resulted in dismissal, especially in the very traditionally minded Post Office. Clery's impulsive character brought him to the fore when the 'Fawcett Scheme Committee' in April 1889 obtained support from London sorters by arguing that W. E. Gladstone's postmaster-general Henry Fawcett had promised in 1881 to improve their conditions to the level of those of telegraphists.

Clery published *An Exposition of the Fawcett Scheme* (1889), which brought a summons to meet tory postmaster-general Henry Raikes. Subsequently the authorities considered but did not accept the demands of the sorters while acknowledging the right to combine within the service. On 10 February 1890 the first number of the sorters' journal, *The Post*, appeared with Clery as editor and the Fawcett Association (FA) began with Clery as secretary.

The first trial for the new association came in July 1890 when the London postmen struck in defence of their union which was run by an 'outsider', J. L. Mahon. Clery did not want to get involved and initiated the sorters' decision to 'follow official routine' (Clinton, *DLB*) as the Postmen's Union was destroyed and 400 strikers were dismissed. After this defeat, postal workers achieved little in the following months. Clery then urged FA members to lobby candidates in the July 1892 general election, despite an explicit Post Office ban against such representations. Clery argued that they were only calling for an inquiry. However, when Postmaster-General Sir James Fergusson returned from the polls where the Conservatives were defeated, he dismissed Clery and his union colleague W. B. Cheesman for the crime of proposing and seconding the resolution advocating lobbying.

Clery and Cheesman immediately became full-time officials of the Fawcett Association, respectively as chairman and secretary, but they never got their jobs back, despite furious lobbying and many parliamentary discussions. In the next period while Cheesman ran the FA, Clery represented it on the London Trades Council, the Trades Union Congress, and elsewhere. He became interested in parliamentary representation, which he thought should be through the Liberal Party. He led the FA into becoming an early affiliate of the Labour Representation Committee in 1900. In 1902 he was adopted as Liberal–Labour candidate for Deptford.

By this time, however, Clery's other interests were impinging on his trade union activities. He was an effective chairman of the FA during the 1890s, leading its rather conservative membership in many new directions. On 20 June 1897 he married the actress Elva Dearen. The FA tolerated Clery's extra-mural activities, but concern grew when his mounting personal debts were visited on the association itself in August 1902. In 1903 after a series of bitter and difficult disputes, Clery's Deptford candidature was repudiated and he lost his position in the FA.

During the following years, Clery continued to write plays, novels, and books about the theatre. These included *A Pauper Millionaire* (1899), *A Guide to the Stage* (1904), *A New Rip Van Winkle* (1905), and also a popular life of Henry Irving (1906). Clery became ill in 1911, and the FA awarded

him a pension, an arrangement continued by the Union of Post Office Workers after 1920. He then disappeared from view, and was found in extreme poverty in February 1930. He wrote some articles about his early struggles and died on 20 October 1931 at 81 Lupus Street, Westminster, London. He was survived by his wife and a stepson. At his pauper's funeral, there was no representative of the trade union organizations which he had done so much to build. A pioneer of and 'martyr' for Post Office trade unionism, Clery was also a journalist (he edited the *Crystal Palace Magazine*), popular novelist, playwright and actor–manager. His achievements in his many activities were tragically squandered and the admiration and loyalty he won were lost by dishonesty and self-deception. Yet after his death there was a moving obituary in *The Post*. G. H. Stuart-Binning, a former general secretary of the Postman's Federation, wrote that 'his courage was abundant to the point of recklessness … his personal fascination was amazing. Men would go to meetings determined to oppose him and come away having agreed to all he proposed' (Clinton, *DLB*).

ALAN CLINTON

Sources A. Clinton, 'Clery, William Edward', *DLB*, vol. 7 · A. Clinton, *Post Office workers: a trade union and social history* (1984) · H. G. Swift, *A history of postal agitation*, rev. edn (1929) · W. E. Clery, 'Memoirs', *The Post* (Aug–Sept 1930) · H. St J. Raikes, *The life and letters of Henry Cecil Raikes* (1898) · *The Post* (1890–1931) [available at Union of Communication Workers House, London] · d. cert.
Archives Post Office, London, records · U. Warwick Mod. RC · Union of Communication Workers, London

Cleveland. For this title name *see* Wentworth, Thomas, earl of Cleveland (1591–1667); Palmer, Barbara, countess of Castlemaine and *suo jure* duchess of Cleveland (*bap.* 1640, *d.* 1709); FitzRoy, Charles, second duke of Cleveland and first duke of Southampton (1662–1730); Vane, William Harry, first duke of Cleveland (1766–1842).

Cleveland, Augustus. *See* Clevland, Augustus (1754–1784).

Cleveland, John (*bap.* 1613, *d.* 1658), poet, was baptized on 20 June 1613 at Loughborough, the son of Thomas Cleveland (*d.* 1652) and Elizabeth Hebbe (*d.* 1649). He was the second of their eleven children, not all of whom survived, and their eldest son. Thomas Cleveland was then assistant to the rector of the parish church as well as usher at Burton's Grammar School. In 1621, however, he became vicar of Hinckley.

Cleveland's education continued with his admission to Christ's College, Cambridge, on 4 September 1627. He was enrolled as a lesser pensioner and his fees were therefore £50 a year, a substantial sum in those days and one indicating that his family had become financially comfortable since the time when his father had been trying to glean an adequate income from two jobs. John's tutor at Christ's was William Siddall, who stood high in seniority—perhaps second—among the fellows.

The years at Cambridge were distinctly productive for Cleveland with regard to both academic achievement and the writing of poems. In September 1629 he was selected to deliver the Latin speech of welcome to the earl of Holland, who was chancellor of the university. The earl was

For weighty Numbers, sense, misterious wayes
Of happie Wit, Great Cleauland claimes his Baies.
Sepultus Colleg: Whitintonij. 1. May Anᵒ: 1 6 5 8.

John Cleveland (*bap.* 1613, *d.* 1658), by unknown engraver

accompanied by the French ambassador. Later, though perhaps while he was still an undergraduate, John acted as 'father' (that is, master of ceremonies) at the Cambridge revels. If his having been selected to make the Latin speech to the university chancellor suggests the esteem accorded his Latinity and his rhetorical skills, his appointment as father of the revels implies that he was not merely well liked by students and fellows but also esteemed for his wit. Aubrey described him as 'a comely plump man, good curled haire, darke browne' (*Brief Lives*, 1.174–5).

In any event, although John's role as father may not strictly count as one of his academic achievements, there were certainly others. He graduated BA early in 1632, was elected to the Hebblethwaite fellowship at St John's College in 1634, and proceeded MA in 1635. Two of the students under his guidance were Samuel Drake and John Lake; they compiled the 1677 edition of his works. Anthony Wood's claim that John proceeded MA from Oxford as well as from Cambridge remains unsubstantiated. It should be added that, although fellows of St John's College were obliged to take holy orders within six years of their elections, John did not. He was admitted to the law

line in 1640. Between 1635 and 1637 he became rhetoric reader. His duties involved writing orations and also letters on behalf of St John's, for example to the archbishop of Canterbury and to Lord Herbert of Cherbury. In 1636 he delivered an address to Charles Lewis, son of Frederick, the elector palatine, and of King Charles's sister. In March 1642 he addressed the king himself. The king apparently liked the speech and ordered that a copy be sent him after his departure that evening from the university. Cleveland also contributed verses to two university miscellanies. One of these was an elegy for the death of Edward King, and was published in the same volume as fellow Christ's man John Milton's 'Lycidas' (*Juxta Edouardo King*, 1638). It is among the earliest of Cleveland's datable poems, but reveals qualities to be seen throughout his verse as a whole. Writing in the tradition of the 'literature of tears' (primarily though not solely a religious literary tradition in seventeenth-century English verse), Cleveland portrays his grief as being a virtual re-enactment of King's death.

> My tears will keep no channells, know no laws
> To guide their streams; but like the waves, their cause,
> Run with disturbance, till they swallow me
> As a description of his miserie.
> (*Juxta Edouardo King*, ll. 13–16)

Such hyperbole and catachresis (an extravagant metaphor using words in an alien or unusual way) recur in many of Cleveland's poems. Sometimes he uses the figures to indicate intense anger, as in his political poems; sometimes to indicate wonder in celebration of the ineffable, as in poems extolling the king; sometimes, as in various erotic poems, he uses them for comic effect. The elegy also shows John Donne's influence on Cleveland: notably in the tendency to paradox and epigram.

It has been argued that many of Cleveland's amatory and non-political poems were written while he was still at university—June 1642 is the last sure date that marks his presence there. They show him fully engaged in the social and political upheavals of the times, with mocking denunciation of the king's enemies running through the verses. In 1640 Cleveland opposed Oliver Cromwell's campaign for election to the Long Parliament. As Samuel Drake and John Lake later described the event:

> When *Oliver* was in Election to be Burgess for the Town of *Cambridge*, as [Cleveland] engaged all his Friends and Interests to oppose it, so when it was passed, he said with much passionate Zeal, That single Vote had ruined both Church and Kingdom. (Drake and Lake, foreword, sig. Abv)

More vigorous political action on Cleveland's part would follow, and it is as political satirist that he is chiefly famous. In 'Upon the Kings Return from Scotland', for example, he represents Charles I as a godlike figure, a sun king who is also the soul of the state (ll. 1–8), and the guarantor of both its peace and of its established religion (ll. 35–40). 'To P. Rupert', in harmony with that poem, portrays the prince as mysteriously the embodiment of past, present, and future heroic virtue (ll. 55–70), standing between the state and those who would confound it (ll. 155–72). Drawing upon the resources of royalist polemic and adding to them, the poems suggest that law and religion, reason and virtue are centred on the monarchy. The enemies of the crown are presented as men who would undo the law, who promote a parody of true religion, and who are (often wilfully) self-deluding creatures driven by unreason and expediency. They are the instigators of anarchy, who would turn the world upside down and so erase all decorum. In 'A Dialogue between two Zealots, upon the &c. in the Oath', for example, two puritan divines construct a crazy, self-interested, apocalyptic fantasy around the ampersand in the so-called etcetera oath of 1640 legitimizing the new ecclesiastical canons. Another satire, 'Smectymnuus, or, The Club-Divines', continues Cleveland's portrait of the puritan grotesque in its depiction of the five ministers who under that name published anti-episcopal pamphlets in 1641.

Some time after June 1642 Cleveland left Cambridge, which was a difficult place for an outspoken royalist to live, as violent hostilities had begun between parliamentary supporters in the town and members of the university. He joined the king at his headquarters, established at Oxford in November. There John wrote 'The Rebell Scot' and *The Character of a London-Diurnall*. The former, a satirical poem against the Scots, is now perhaps the best-known poem in the Cleveland canon; certainly it is the most famous of his verse satires. The speaker of the satire derides the Scots as being the bestial inhabitants of a wilderness whose wretched poverty drives them abroad as mercenaries. Early in the poem the speaker is quick to suggest the unnaturalness of a Scottish threat to England and his fury at such a prospect (ll. 3–7). He thereafter says:

> Nature her selfe doth Scotch-men beasts confesse,
> Making their Countrey such a wildernesse:
> A Land that brings in question and suspense
> Gods omnipresence, but that CHARLES came thence:
> But that *Montrose* and *Crawfords* loyall Band
> Atton'd their sins, and christ'ned halfe the Land.
> (ll. 47–52)

The Scots are pictured as creatures whom nature has excluded from civil life (elsewhere in the poem they are portrayed as having no sense of the common weal; see ll. 63–80). They and their country have been definitely brought into the divine order of things only because of the English monarch's recent visit to Scotland and the redemptive, military power of his representatives. *The Character of a London-Diurnall*, a prose satire ridiculing the London newsbooks, was published anonymously early in 1645. The London newsbooks reported lies, Cleveland's speaker declared, not news, and inflated their accounts of parliamentary victories. 'A Diurnal is a puny Chronical', Cleveland wrote,

> scarce Pin-feather'd with the wings of Time. It is History in Snippets: The English Iliads in a Nutshel: The Apochryphal Parliament's Book of Maccabees in single sheets.
> (J. Cleveland, *The Character of a London-Diurnall*, 1645, 108)

The satire also contains a vigorous caricature of Cromwell. The publication of the pamphlet was noted by Marchamont Nedham in *Mercurius Britannicus* on 10 February, though Nedham waited until the following week to print his attack. Many other newsbooks printed their responses, and three pamphlets were published attacking *The Character* in three weeks. A later 'character' continued

the attack. With Nedham's *Mercurius Politicus* (1650) in his sights, Cleveland suggested: 'It is time that we had our State-scold to the Ducking-stool' (quoted in J. Raymond, *The Invention of the Newspaper*, 1996, 219).

From approximately spring 1645 to that of the following year Cleveland served as judge advocate with the royal garrison at Newark. His appointment was noticed by the opposite faction in the *Kingdome's Weekly Intelligencer*:

> But to speak something of our friend Cleveland, that grand malignant of Cambridge, we hear that now he is at Newark, where he hath the title of advocate put upon him. His office and employment is to gather all college rents within the power of the king's forces in those parts, which he distributes to such as are turned out of their fellowships at Cambridge for their malignancy. (*Kingdome's Weekly Intelligencer*, no. 101, 27 May 1645, 811)

The king left Newark just before the city was besieged by the Scots in November 1645 and it was Cleveland who wrote in refusal of a demand for the city's surrender. However, on 5 May 1646 the king surrendered himself to the Scots at Southwell, not far from Newark. The Scots' demand for the city's surrender was agreed to by the king and surrender was made on 6 May. There seems little evidence to support a story that, after the surrender, Cleveland was tried and disdainfully dismissed by David Leslie, commander of the Scottish forces.

Following the popularity of *The Character of a London-Diurnall* (ESTC notes four variants of the 1645 edition), Cleveland published *The Character of a London-Diurnall: with Several Select Poems* (1647). This was the first time that many of the poems had been published, and it shows how Cleveland's political satires helped to secure his place in popular taste. Eight different variants of this edition exist from 1647. In the same year another volume of mixed prose and poetry was published, *The Character of a Moderate Intelligencer with Some Select Poems*. Cleveland's works proved tremendously successful. *Poems by J. C. with Additions*, first published in 1651, was reprinted in 1653, 1654, 1656, 1657, 1659, 1661, 1662, 1665, and 1669. Other volumes of his poetry and prose were published in 1658, 1659, 1677, and 1687. Yet another indication of his popularity is the many works not by Cleveland that were published under his name by booksellers keen to exploit his fame.

Not much seems to be known about what happened to Cleveland after the war. There has been a reasonable assumption that, in Berdan's words, '[l]ike the great majority of the unfortunate cavaliers, he wandered about in complete dependence upon his more fortunate friends' (*Poems*, ed. Berdan, 39). He may sometimes have worked on royalist newspapers in London but that remains uncertain. It is certain, on the other hand, that when he was arrested on 10 November 1655 he admitted to having been in London about a year beforehand. His arrest probably took place at Norwich, where he was living in the house of an Edward Cooke. He claimed to be Cooke's private tutor but those who arrested him seem to have been uneasy about the claim, for Cooke was well known as a royalist sympathizer who drew other such folk about him; moreover, Cleveland's genteel garb but lack of funds, along with his role at Newark and his acknowledged abilities, excited suspicion. Consequently he was imprisoned at Great Yarmouth for three months, whereupon he wrote to Cromwell and obtained his release (the exact date of which is not known). The letter to Cromwell has been admired for the way in which its author pleads his cause without demeaning that of his party.

After his release Cleveland appears to have had no fixed abode. There is a likelihood that from the latter half of 1657 he lived at Gray's Inn, London, and that he received financial support from a John Onebye who came from Hinckley, where the poet's father had been vicar. Cleveland died in London of an intermittent fever on 29 April 1658. He was buried on 1 May at the church of St Michael Royal, College Hill, London, and the preacher at his funeral was Dr John Pearson, one of his contemporaries at Cambridge.

In 1675 Edward Phillips described Cleveland's high standing as a poet: 'a Notable High soaring Witty Loyalist … he appear'd the first, if not only, Eminent Champion in verse against the *Presbyterian* Party'. He also noted that some 'Grave Men' declared Cleveland to be 'the best of English Poets' (E. Phillips, *Theatrum poetarum*, 1675, 104–5). But the decline of his reputation, so high during Cleveland's lifetime, had already begun by this point. His use of catachresis, and the influence of that use, were attacked in Dryden's *An Essay of Dramatick Poesie*, 'that which the world has blam'd in our satyrist Cleveland; to express a thing hard and unnaturally, is his new way of Elocution'. Dryden also observed that Cleveland expressed 'common thoughts in abstruse words' (J. Dryden, *Essay of Dramatick Poesie*, 1668, 42–4). The disparagement just quoted is, however, almost immediately followed by praise for lines 63–4 of 'The Rebell Scot'. Samuel Johnson famously added to Dryden's dispraise of Cleveland in his 'Life of Cowley'. The revival of Cleveland's reputation in more recent times effectively dates from Berdan's edition of the poems in 1903.　　　　A. D. COUSINS

Sources The poems of John Cleveland, ed. J. Berdan (1903) • S. V. Gapp, 'Notes on John Cleveland', *Publications of the Modern Language Association of America*, 46 (1931), 1075–86 • S. Drake and J. Lake, foreword, in *Clievelandi vindiciae*, ed. S. Drake and J. Lake (1677) • The poems of John Cleveland, ed. B. Morris and E. Withington (1967) • L. A. Jacobus, *John Cleveland* (1975) • Brief lives, chiefly of contemporaries, set down by John Aubrey, between the years 1669 and 1696, ed. A. Clark, 2 vols. (1898) • Venn, *Alum. Cant.* • Fuller, *Worthies* (1662) • Wood, *Ath. Oxon.*, 1st edn • J. Cleveland, *Poems* (1651)
Archives Yale U., Beinecke L., letters and verses
Likenesses engraving, BM, NPG; repro. in Cleveland, *Poems*, frontispiece • etching, NPG [see illus.]

Cleveley family (*per. c.*1747–1809), marine painters, came to prominence with **John Cleveley the elder** (*c.*1712–1777), the son of Samuel Cleveley, a joiner of Newington Butts, Southwark, who was already dead when, perhaps aged about fourteen, his son was apprenticed on 3 November 1726 to another joiner, Thomas Miller. Later he was turned over to John Hall, a shipwright and Deptford boat builder. He first appears in the Deptford rate books (St Paul's parish) in July 1742, for a house in or near Slade's Court, and on 9 June 1743 was sworn a freeman of the

Shipwrights' Company on the testimony of Hall and William Houlder, shipwright, although he must then have been long out of indentures. Cleveley's main career was spent as a shipwright in the royal dockyard at Deptford. He lived in King's Yard Row, Dogg Street, at least from 1747, died there in May 1777, and was buried on 21 May at the parish church of St Paul's, Deptford. Letters of administration granted to his widow, Sarah, on 14 June 1778 refer to him both as lately of that parish and as 'Carpenter belonging to his Majesty's Ship the *Victory* in the pay of his M[y]'s Navy' (General Register Office for England, AA 1777 Farrant). *Victory* was held in ordinary (reserve) at Chatham from her launch in 1765 until first commissioned for sea in March 1778, so Cleveley may latterly have been attached to her in some capacity, although not as her regular carpenter.

How Cleveley learned to paint is unknown, although it may have been through association with ship painters, whose opportunities increased from 1704 when the Admiralty reduced carved ship decoration in favour of painting. The earliest date yet found on his work is 1747, and he specialized in shipping and Thames shipbuilding and launching scenes, especially at the Deptford yard. He also produced other marine views (including of shipbuilding in East Anglia), Hanoverian comings and goings in the royal yachts, sea fights, and ship portraits. The last tend to be repetitive, often with little more than a change of name. Little of the artist's work was engraved, but he contributed shipping to the prints of Sheerness, Chatham, and Plymouth dockyards (1755–6) by Thomas Milton, and possibly those of Deptford, Woolwich, and Portsmouth (1753–4) in the same set. Cleveley was a good draughtsman and colourful painter. His art combines a valuable historical record with much human detail and at its best has an unpretentious grandeur. While not the equal of Samuel Scott, he must have known the latter's work and perhaps that of Canaletto's English period (1746–55). He exhibited at the Free Society from 1764 to 1776, but confusion at the time with his son John [see below] makes it unclear how many of the forty-three pictures listed under his name for those years may have been by the younger man. His work is widely dispersed, but the National Maritime Museum, Greenwich, has sixteen paintings, the most impressive being a fictitious placing of the *Royal George* (launched in 1756) off Deptford at the launch of the *Cambridge* in 1755. This too was a composition he repeated. No portrait of Cleveley is known, but he sometimes seems to have included himself in his work: a view of the *Buckingham* on the stocks at Deptford (dated 1752 and also at Greenwich) shows a sturdy, respectably dressed figure drawing the scene depicted.

Cleveley and his wife, Sarah (1722–1798), had seven known children: John and Hannah (*bap.* 1744 and 1747) presumably died in infancy. Another Hannah was baptized in 1750 and Rebecca in 1754. A younger son, James (*bap.* 29 June 1752), was a ship's carpenter and served as such under Captain Cook in the *Resolution*, on Cook's third Pacific voyage (1776–80).

The couple's other two children were **John Cleveley**

the **younger** (1747–1786) and **Robert Cleveley** (1747–1809), twin sons born at Deptford on 25 December 1747 and baptized on 7 January 1748 at St Paul's, Deptford, as were all their siblings. John was apprenticed to his shipwright father on 3 May 1763 but did not complete this training. Instead, probably through his father's artistic connections, he learned to paint in watercolours and do tinted drawings from Paul Sandby, then the drawing instructor at the Royal Military Academy in nearby Woolwich. He was presumably taught oil painting by his father, and was arguably a better painter, but he was known primarily as a watercolour painter and draughtsman, winning a premium for this from the Society of Arts. Many of his drawings were also engraved. While his father signed his paintings 'I. Cleveley', he signed as 'Jnᵒ Cleveley, Junr.' at least until 1782. He first exhibited two drawings at the Free Society in 1767, but, of the oil paintings listed under his father's name there up to 1776, some were probably his, as were all twenty-one from 1778 to 1783. All thirty-eight works credited to John Cleveley at the Royal Academy from 1770 to 1786 were presumably his. After first showing drawings there in 1770–71 he was appointed draughtsman to (Sir) Joseph Banks's expedition to Iceland in 1772, and he exhibited two drawings of Iceland at the Royal Academy in 1773. He is widely reported to have been on Captain Phipps's Arctic expedition, which sailed in the *Racehorse* and *Carcass* on 3 June 1773, an error springing from his various drawings of it, including those engraved in Phipps's published account and elsewhere. It is now known that these were done at home from sketches brought back by Midshipman Philippe d'Auvergne, later last duc de Bouillon (1754–1816). Cleveley's views of this subject are mainly in the British Museum, the Victoria and Albert Museum, and the National Maritime Museum, but which were the pair exhibited at the Royal Academy in 1774 is uncertain. On 23 June 1773 Cleveley himself was present at George III's review of the fleet at Spithead; he exhibited two drawings of it at the academy in each of the years 1774 and 1775, of which three are now in the National Maritime Museum. He also painted this in oils. In 1774 he moved from Deptford to Brewer Street, Golden Square, and from 27 August 1775 to January 1776 he made a voyage to Lisbon. This also produced exhibited views, and a bound-up volume of thirty-seven watercolour and wash drawings from it was sold at Sothebys in 1983 and subsequently dispersed. A number of later watercolours, one shown at the academy in 1781 (and a painting of 1784), were of episodes on Captain Cook's last Pacific voyage (1776–80) and four engraved in aquatint by Francis Jukes were advertised as being based on sketches brought back by his brother James, in the *Resolution*.

John Cleveley the younger's exhibited oil works show a broad range of marine subjects, mostly of British and north European situation, but there are few in public collections: the National Maritime Museum has only one confirmed example, with drawings, which are more widely encountered. He died in London on 25 June 1786, probably in Pimlico, which was his Royal Academy exhibiting address from 1783. Nothing has emerged to support the *Dictionary of National Biography* inference that he may have died in Deptford, whence he had last sent a picture to the academy in 1781—probably from his mother's house, since she remained at King's Yard Row until her death in March 1798.

Robert Cleveley was John Cleveley the younger's twin brother. There is no report of his being taught, as John was, by Paul Sandby, although opportunity and his fine watercolour style make this possible, and he, too, probably learned oil painting from his father. In 1795 a Deptford Dockyard official told Joseph Farington that 'when young he was bred as a Caulker', but disliked it, was laughed at for working in gloves, and gave it up (Farington, *Diary*, 2.308). Probably through his father, he instead gained the 'interest' of Captain William Locker, a significant naval patron of artists. On 4 October 1770 he volunteered for the navy in London, and on 23 October was appointed Locker's clerk in the frigate *Thames*. He remained in her when George Vandeput took over command in 1773 and that December followed him into the *Asia*, which sailed for the North American station until 1777. According to Farington, Vandeput was 'his great friend' (ibid.) in career terms, and on his return he was appointed purser of the storeship *Camel* (on 31 October 1777), then of the *Monsieur* (in July 1780). In July 1783 Cleveley was with Vandeput when he took Prince William (later duke of Clarence and William IV) to Hanover, in the royal yacht *Princess Augusta*, and sailed with him on her again in June 1786 when princes Ernest, Augustus, and Adolphus were sent to Göttingen University. On both occasions he was officially mustered as 'assistant to the Clerk of the Kitchen' in the royal entourage. He was also purser of the *Melampus* (from August 1783), the *Portland* (December 1783), the *Swiftsure* (July 1802), and the *Sussex* (from January 1805 until his death). Most of these ships were stationed in home ports—the *Portland* 'in ordinary' and on harbour service at Portsmouth throughout his nearly eighteen years in her, and the *Sussex* a hospital ship at Sheerness. This explains both how he also sustained a painting career and why he was sometimes referred to as an artist 'of the Royal Navy' at least until 1795. His will, dated 1808, names him as purser of the *Sussex* and circumstantially confirms that he was the Robert Cleveley who married Catherine Collett or Collitt at St Pancras on 31 January 1787.

Although Robert Cleveley produced shipping and coastal views at home and abroad, he was best-known as a painter of the naval actions of the American War of Independence and the French Revolutionary Wars, of which many were engraved. He exhibited fifty-one works, including drawings, at the Royal Academy from 1780 to 1803, but not in all years. This was as an 'Honorary Exhibitor' from 1780 to 1786 and as 'of the Navy' from his second appearance in 1782 until 1788, when he sent pictures from the first of three Westminster addresses. Two huge and admired paintings of the beginning and end of Lord Howe's victory at the battle of 1 June 1794 were shown at the premises of the printseller A. C. de Poggi, at 91 New Bond Street, in 1795–6, from which T. Medland and B. T.

Pouncy engraved large subscription prints. A separate text booklet includes Cleveley's large fold-out plan of the battle, probably the most detailed of the period. The oils remained together until auctioned at Sothebys in 1981. In 1796 J. F. Rigaud also employed Cleveley to 'retouch' the shipping in his painted ceiling of the court room at Trinity House (now destroyed). From 1791 or 1792 Cleveley was marine draughtsman to the duke of Clarence, and he also became marine painter to the latter's elder brother, the prince of Wales. There are four paintings by him in the National Maritime Museum, which also has drawings and prints, and many elsewhere. In his will, dated 4 April 1808, he gave his address as 'late of Devonshire Street, Portland Place'. He died on 28 September 1809 after accidentally falling 25 feet down a cliff at Dover while visiting a relative there with his wife. A half-length portrait of Cleveley in civilian dress, stipple-engraved by Freeman after Sir William Beechey, was published in the *Monthly Mirror* in 1810.   PIETER VAN DER MERWE

Sources rate books, Deptford, Lewisham Local History Library · parish registers, Deptford, St Paul's, LMA, PAU/75/1 [baptism, burial] · artist's file notes (incl. data from PRO naval musters), NMM · General Register Office for England, administrations, AA 1777 Farrant · C. H. Ridge, *Records of the Worshipful Company of Shipwrights*, 2 vols. (1939–46), vol. 1, p. 43 · Graves, *Soc. Artists* · Graves, *RA exhibitors* · A. Savours, 'The younger Cleveley and the Arctic, 1773–4', *Mariner's Mirror*, 69 (1983), 301–4 · P. van der Merwe, 'The glorious first of June: a battle of art and theatre', *The glorious first of June 1794: a naval battle and its aftermath*, ed. M. Duffy and R. Morriss (2001), 132–58 · *British drawings and watercolours* (1983), lot 51 [sale catalogue, Sothebys, 17 Nov 1983] · Farington, *Diary*, vols. 2, 10 · R. Quarm and S. Wilcox, *Masters of the sea: British marine watercolours* (1987) · S. F. D. Rigaud, 'Facts and recollections of the XVIIIth century in a memoir of John Francis Rigaud', ed. W. L. Pressly, *Walpole Society*, 50 (1984), 1–164 · E. H. H. Archibald, *The dictionary of sea painters of Europe and America*, 3rd edn (2000) · *DNB* · *IGI* · R. Joppien and B. Smith, 'The Cleveley problem', *The art of Captain Cook's voyages*, 3, 216–21 · PRO, ADM 36/10207 and 10674 (*Princess Augusta* musters 1783 and 1786) · will, PRO, PROB 11/1504, sig. 737 [Robert Cleveley]
Likenesses Freeman, stipple engraving (R. Cleveley; after W. Beechey), repro. in *Monthly Mirror* (1810)

Cleveley, John, the elder (*c*.1712–1777). *See under* Cleveley family (*per. c*.1747–1809).

Cleveley, John, the younger (1747–1786). *See under* Cleveley family (*per. c*.1747–1809).

Cleveley, Robert (1747–1809). *See under* Cleveley family (*per. c*.1747–1809).

Cleverdon, (Thomas) Douglas James (1903–1987), bookseller and radio producer, was born on 17 January 1903 in Bristol (he retained all his life a faint trace of a Bristol accent), the elder son (there were no daughters) of Thomas Silcox Cleverdon, master wheelwright, and his wife, Jane Louisa James. The only book in the house in those days was his mother's Welsh Bible. He was educated at Bristol grammar school, where he learned his love of books from the headmaster, Ted Barton. While still an astonishingly good-looking schoolboy in a cap and blazer he went for a week to London, and walked into Francis Birrell's and David Garnett's new bookshop. He was fêted by Clive Bell and Roger Fry, and introduced to the latest work in painting, engraving, and printing.

Cleverdon published his first catalogue as an undergraduate at Jesus College, Oxford, immediately establishing his reputation as a lover of fine printing and exquisitely illustrated books. He became part of what he himself later called the 'typographical renaissance' made possible by Stanley Morison's reintroduction of great typefaces of the past and Eric Gill's sculptural lettering, and became a close friend and disciple of both. At Oxford he obtained a second class in classical honour moderations (1924) and a third in *literae humaniores* (1926).

In 1926 Cleverdon opened his own bookshop in Charlotte Street, Bristol. Roger Fry painted the hanging sign, bought from an old pub, with Athena's owl perched on a pile of books, and Eric Gill painted the fascia over the shop window in sans-serif capitals. Cleverdon asked him for a copy of the alphabet, and it was from this that Morison commissioned the famous 'Gill Sans-serif'. At this time he also began publishing, with Gill's *Art and Love* (1927), printed in a limited edition, including thirty-five copies on full vellum, and S. T. Coleridge's *The Rime of the Ancient Mariner* (1929), for which he commissioned ten copper-engravings, and an introduction from David Jones. This venture was brought to an end by the economic depression, but Cleverdon continued to sell books until the end of the 1930s, when he was persuaded by Francis Dillon to begin working part-time for the BBC. In 1939 he worked for *Children's Hour* and in the same year became a west regional features producer. In 1940, as he himself put it, 'a bomb fell on the bookshop, and I was with the BBC for thirty years'. In 1943 he became a features producer in London. He was to bring to radio all his skills as a publisher: inspired commissioning of new work; patient encouragement and direction of writers, musicians, and actors; perfectionism in editing and production; and all the craftsmanship he had learned from Morison and Gill, and in his father's workshop.

It was shortly before the Second World War that Cleverdon met (Elinor) Nest, former head girl of the Clergy Daughters School in Bristol, and daughter of James Abraham Lewis, canon, of Cardiff. They eventually married in 1944, though John Betjeman referred to her ever afterwards as 'Douglas's child bride'. They were to have two daughters, the elder of whom, born in 1948, died immediately, and three sons, the eldest of whom died at birth in 1952. Cleverdon, busy, bustling, chuckling, with sparkling blue eyes and a slightly irregular smile, would greet almost everyone as 'my dear' to save himself from having to remember names. He was a small man, but even so it was said that he towered over his wife. She was to be his strength and stay.

Cleverdon's main achievement of the war years was *The Brains Trust*, which he devised with Howard Thomas, and which reached an audience of twelve million. He was sent briefly to Burma in 1945 as a BBC war correspondent, and on his return began by developing the already existing *Radio Portrait* series for the Third Programme. He dramatized David Jones's *In Parenthesis* (1948) and *The Anathemata*

(1953), using the voices of Richard Burton and Dylan Thomas. He also launched Henry Reed's satirical *Hilda Tablet* series in 1953, broadcast the poems of Sylvia Plath, Ted Hughes, Thom Gunn, Wole Soyinka, John Betjeman, Siegfried Sassoon, and Stevie Smith, and produced the work of David Garnett, Rose Macaulay, Compton Mackenzie, and Jacob Bronowski. He also travelled to Rapallo to record a series of broadcasts with Max Beerbohm.

Cleverdon produced programmes of folk-song with A. L. Lloyd and Alan Lomax, and commissioned new music from Humphrey Searle, Alan Rawsthorne, Lennox Berkeley, Aleksandr Tcherepnin, Peter Racine Fricker, and Mátyás Seiber. He was the first to engage Michael Flanders and Donald Swann for the radio. His most famous commission was *Under Milk Wood*, broadcast in 1954, which he succeeded in wringing out of Dylan Thomas shortly before his death in 1953.

Cleverdon retired from the BBC in 1969, and, as well as organizing poetry festivals, returned to publishing, with his own Clover Hill Editions, called after the Old English meaning of his own name. His printer was his old friend Will Carter of the Rampant Lions Press, Cambridge. He preserved the same standards he had set himself as a young man, with beautifully produced work by Reynolds Stone, Michael Ayrton, and David Jones, and *The Story of Cupid and Psyche*, an unprinted Kelmscott Press book with wood blocks by William Morris after Sir Edward Burne-Jones. Cleverdon died on 1 October 1987 at his home at 27 Barnsbury Square, London. JOHN WELLS, *rev.*

Sources D. Cleverdon, *Fifty years* (1983) · [N. Barker], *Book Collector*, 32 (1983), 7–21 · *The Times* (3 Oct 1987) · private information (1996) · personal knowledge (1996) · *CGPLA Eng. & Wales* (1988)
Wealth at death £210,221: probate, 27 Jan 1988, *CGPLA Eng. & Wales*

Cleverley, Samuel (*d.* 1824), physician, was the son of William Cleverley, a shipbuilder of Gravesend, Kent. After some schooling at Rochester he appears to have been apprenticed to the Rochester surgeon William Cowper in 1787 before spending two years at the borough hospitals of Guy's and St Thomas's in London. He then moved to Edinburgh, where he took the degree of MD on 24 June 1797 (his inaugural essay was entitled 'De anasarca'). Cleverley next travelled to the continent to carry out further study, and visited Halle, Göttingen, Vienna, and Paris. He was held prisoner in France for eleven years, being confined successively at Fontainebleau, Verdun, and Valenciennes, where he spent the greater part of his detention and where on his arrival he found the prisoners in great need of medical assistance. 'He accordingly proposed to the Committee of Verdun to give them his gratuitous care, which was gladly accepted, and a Dispensary was, in consequence, established, though not without great difficulties, from the French military authorities' (*Authentic Memoirs*, 481–2). Cleverley was allowed to return home in 1814, when he received for his services at Valenciennes the grateful thanks of the managing committee of Lloyd's. Cleverley eventually settled in London, where he was admitted a licentiate of the Royal College of Physicians,

on 22 December 1815, and appointed one of the physicians to the London Fever Hospital. He died at his house in Queen Anne Street, Cavendish Square, on 10 November 1824. GORDON GOODWIN, *rev.* MICHAEL BEVAN

Sources Munk, *Roll* · *GM*, 1st ser., 94/2 (1824), 645 · *Authentic memoirs, biographical, critical, and literary, of the most eminent physicians and surgeons of Great Britain*, 2nd edn (1818), 481–2 · P. J. Wallis and R. V. Wallis, *Eighteenth century medics*, 2nd edn (1988)

Clevland, Augustus (1754–1784), East India Company servant, was born in London on 19 September 1754, the son of John *Clevland (1706–1763), MP and secretary to the Admiralty, of Tapley, Devon, and his second wife, Sarah (*fl.* 1749–1763), daughter of Richard Shuckburgh of Longborough, Gloucestershire. His eldest half-brother, John Clevland (1734?–1817), followed his father into the Admiralty and was the MP for Barnstaple from 1766 to 1802. Augustus was one of the younger of John Clevland's seven surviving children and was still a child when his father died in 1763, heavily in debt to the Admiralty, but the Clevlands were well connected, and in 1770, after a brief course of financial instruction in Greenwich, Augustus secured a writership in the East India Company's Bengal establishment. His patron among the company's directors, Frederick Pigou (1711–1792), former chief supercargo of Canton, was the patron also of his relation and intimate friend John Shore (1751–1834), later first Lord Teignmouth and governor-general of Bengal.

Clevland arrived in India about 1771 and was appointed assistant collector of Bhagalpur; he was promoted to collector in 1775. Bhagalpur was a jungly district to the west of Bengal proper, agriculturally rich along the plains which straddled the Ganges, but bordered on the southeast and west by the Rajmahal and Kharakpur hills respectively. The hills were the preserve of aboriginal peoples—'tribals'—who were incorporated only loosely into the political and religious life of the plains, and who gave the district its ancient reputation for 'refractoriness'. As collector, Clevland understood that he would never get more revenue from those who lived on the plains until he proved that the British could contain the hill peoples who frequently raided them. In spite of initial government scepticism, he persisted with a plan to conciliate the hill chiefs and their followers by creating a militia or corps of hill rangers which respected the internal authority of the chiefs and shielded them from the interference of the company's regular courts. Hill chiefs who joined Clevland's corps were rewarded with honours, cash, feasting, uniforms, and, eventually, firearms. The landlords of the plains mostly welcomed the initiative and the revenue collections increased accordingly, but some, such as the Rani Serbissery of Sultanabad, correctly perceived in Clevland's taming of the hills the loss of their own autonomy as well and turned themselves into outlaws rather than submit to company control. For the most part, however, Clevland's experiment was regarded as a triumph. The hill peoples entered British Indian imperial lore as the first in a long line of stereotypical 'loyal savages', while

Clevland amassed increased authority on the strength of their pacification, including the exclusive right to oversee the administration of justice by the hill chiefs.

Clevland's other notable achievement was the creation of the first invalid *thana*, a settlement of invalided soldiers from the Bengal army designed to colonize marginal lands, thus extending the boundaries of company influence while also boosting the land revenue. Credit for the idea belongs to Captain James Browne, an officer in charge of the jungle tarai, but it was to Clevland that, in 1779, Warren Hastings, the governor-general, entrusted the first experiment. He began by settling over 180 retired Indian sepoys on the fringes of the Rajmahal hills, parcelling out to each settler a substantial tract of land, the size of which was determined by the rank he had attained in the army. Under his watchful eye, the newcomers soon formed a well-armed and disciplined buffer between the cultivators in the plains and the raiders of the hills. It was another, vital step in Clevland's mission to tame the hill frontier, and invalid *thanas* were soon established on other frontiers: they had become 'the vanguard of colonial expansion westwards' (Alavi, 101–2).

Clevland was a brilliant administrator who combined ambition and seriousness of purpose with considerable personal charm and generosity. He quickly became a favourite of Warren Hastings, and Hastings's wife, Marian, descended on him for weeks at a time in his magnificent riverside mansion. Another visitor to enjoy Clevland's hospitality, and also his munificent patronage, was the painter William Hodges, who immortalized Clevland's hill rangers in paint and the 'ingenuity, address, and humanity' (Hodges, 90) of Clevland himself in his published reminiscences, *Travels in India* (1793).

The support of Hastings and also of John Shore, who was emerging as Bengal's foremost authority on land revenue, ensured that Clevland's demands for further powers were rarely disappointed. In 1783 he made his most far-reaching proposal yet, a request to be personally granted the revenue-collecting contract for the whole of Bhagalpur which, if allowed, would have turned him into a jungle king of *Heart of Darkness* proportions. The court of directors had explicitly forbidden revenue farming by company employees, but such was Clevland's reputation that Hastings's council agreed to ask the directors to waive the prohibition in his case. Before they could rule, however, Clevland sickened with fever and dysentery. In early 1784 he boarded the *Atlas*, bound for the Cape of Good Hope, but died at sea on 13 January 1784. He was twenty-nine. His body was returned to Calcutta and interred there on 30 January 1784 in the South Park Street burial-ground, where Hastings subsequently had a substantial monument erected to him at public expense. Shore penned a monodic lament on his lost cousin, and his estate, including twenty-one paintings by Hodges, was eventually sold off for funds to be remitted to his sisters and their children in Britain. He had never married. The most famous memorial to him, however, was the cairn erected at Bhagalpur out of Rs28,000 subscribed by local landlords. Forty

years later, Bishop Heber found both the monument and local memory of Clevland intact; indeed, the longevity of Clevland's reputation acquired historical importance in itself. With his death, Bhagalpur's drift to personal rule was halted and the company gradually imposed more rigorous controls on the aspiring rajas in its service, but for advocates of a paternalistic, socially conservative imperialism, Clevland's example shone forth as the perfect means to conciliate a rude and savage people. The belief that his memory lived on in Bhagalpur was as reassuring to them as it was to the hill peoples who had originally accepted him as their overlord.   KATHERINE PRIOR

Sources Bengal revenue consultations, 1780–84, BL OIOC, P/50/24–P/50/52 · writers' petitions, BL OIOC, J/1/8, fols. 66–8 · Bengal wills and administrations, 1784–6, BL OIOC, L/AG/34/29/5 · S. Alavi, *The sepoys and the company* (1995) · C. J. Shore, second Baron Teignmouth, *Memoir of the life and correspondence of John, Lord Teignmouth*, 2 vols. (1843) · HoP, *Commons, 1754–90*, vol. 2 · K. K. Basu, 'The early Europeans in Bhagalpur', *Bengal Past and Present*, 56 (1939), 81–97 · list of Clevland's estate, *Calcutta Gazette* (9 Jan 1794); repr. in W. S. Seton-Karr, *Selections from Calcutta gazettes*, 2 (1865), 570–71 · W. Hodges, *Travels in India, 1780–83* (1793) · R. Heber, *Narrative of a journey through the upper provinces of India*, 2 vols. (1828) · *The Bengal obituary, or, A record to perpetuate the memory of departed worth*, Holmes & Co. (1848)

Archives BL OIOC, Bengal revenue consultations, official corresp.

Wealth at death over £10,000: will, 3 Feb 1784, BL OIOC, Bengal wills and administrations, 1784–6, L/AG/34/29/5, no. 13

Clevland, John (1706–1763), naval administrator and politician, was born in Saltash, Cornwall, the eldest of eight children born to Captain William Clevland (*d.* 1735) of Lanarkshire, naval officer and controller of the storekeeper's accounts at the Navy Office (1718–32), and his wife, Anne (*fl.* 1703–1720), daughter of John Davie of Orleigh in Devon. John Clevland's career well illustrates the acceleration given by war to an administrator raised in naval traditions of duty and service which attracted powerful patronage and facilitated his family's social elevation.

Clevland's father had received his first naval command, the *Discovery*, in 1692 and thereafter was employed in catching privateers in the channel and off the Irish coast (1695–7) and in convoying merchants from Jamaica in 1703 in the *Mountague* (60 guns). He acquired an estate, Tapeley Park in Westleigh, near Bideford, Devon, and married Anne Davie on 6 January 1704. He later participated in the capture of Gibraltar and the battle of Malaga (1704), and in 1716, while commanding the *Shrewsbury*, he was appointed 'Commander in Chief of the Ships on the Coast of Norway on 12 Octo^r 1716' by Sir John Norris. As a 'reward for his long and faithful services', in April 1718 he became controller of the storekeeper's accounts at the Navy Office, a post he held until his pensioned retirement in May 1732. He died on 9 June 1735.

While his father was at the Navy Office, John Clevland attended Westminster School from 1718 to 1722. His first post was clerk to the storekeeper's accounts in September 1722. In December 1726 he became chief clerk to his father, with a salary of £100 a year, and in 1731 clerk of the cheque at Plymouth Dockyard. About this time he married Elizabeth, coheir of the banker Sir Caesar Child, second baronet, of Woodford, Essex, an exceptionally advantageous union for a naval clerk. At Plymouth the couple had seven children: Anne, John, and William, born in 1731 and 1732, all of whom died young; and Hester, John, Archibald, and Elizabeth who were born before 1741. Following Elizabeth's death during the 1740s Clevland married his second wife, Sarah (*fl.* 1749–1763), daughter of Richard Shuckburgh of Longborough, Gloucestershire. His three surviving children from this marriage—George (1749–1765), Augustus *Clevland (1754–1784), and Matilda Shore (*b.* 1758)—were christened at St Martin-in-the-Fields, Westminster. His surviving daughters from his first marriage also married at St Martin-in-the-Fields: Hester married William Saltern-Willet, a new naval captain, in 1747, and Elizabeth married John Ibbetson in 1757.

In 1741 Clevland was elected MP for the Admiralty seat of Saltash which he vacated in March 1743. A month later he became clerk of the acts in London with an annual salary of £500. In August 1746 he exchanged posts with Robert Osborn, deputy secretary of the Admiralty, becoming second secretary, a post revived to assist secretary Thomas Corbett, now too old to cope with extra wartime business. He was paid £600 a year, increased to £800 in the autumn, and also received a share of office fees. Clevland's rapid elevation has prompted naval historians such as Daniel Baugh to ask 'Who was responsible for Clevland's nomination to the Admiralty seat at Saltash in 1741 and his subsequent rise from Clerk of the Cheque at Plymouth to the Navy Board in 1741 (a big step)?' (Baugh, 82). Although his success probably owed much to George Anson, with whom Clevland corresponded during the 1740s, his first patron (while Anson was a mere lieutenant) was Thomas Corbett. Corbett had preceded Clevland at Westminster School and was an Admiralty clerk in 1715. Corbett's brother William, secretary to Sir George Byng, had also served with Clevland's father in the Baltic (1716–17). As deputy Admiralty secretary from 1728 and MP for Saltash from 1734, Corbett was sufficiently powerful to select his protégé for Admiralty and parliament. When he died in April 1751 Clevland succeeded him as secretary to the Admiralty with a salary of £800 plus £300 as secretary to the marine department and half the Admiralty fees. Clevland earned over £2000 a year from fees and perquisites as secretary (a total figure greater than that received by Admiralty lords) and underwrote government loans: £2000 for the 1746 land tax and £10,000 for a war loan in 1760.

As secretary Clevland was able to decide whether incoming letters should be discussed by the Admiralty board or with a single Admiralty lord. He replied directly to the four-fifths of letters not presented to the board (sent to naval, dockyard, and colonial officers and other government departments), authorizing the immediate dispatch of provisions to admirals abroad. 'Every expression of the secry's Public Letters always contains or implies their Lordp^s- Orders, & is Capable of no other meaning, & has been always so understood by the Officers of the Navy'

(PRO, ADM 3/47, 7 Jan 1744). In addition to these responses Clevland initiated the board's decisions which were summarized on the 'turnover' page, from which a clerk prepared the reply for his signature. As the source of the largest fount of government patronage Clevland now commanded considerable respect in naval and political circles. After resigning the Treasury, for example, the duke of Newcastle wrote requesting that 'we may continue the same friendship and that you would now and then come and take a dinner with us here; nobody can be more welcome'. Lord Halifax would not agree to become first lord until 17 June 1762, 'assur'd from Clevland that he would continue Secretary during the war' (Namier, 42). As secretary Clevland also exercised an executive role. In 1756 he suggested tactics in the West Indies to Anson and a year later he provided documents which allowed Lord Hardwicke to defend ministerial policy in the Mediterranean in the wake of Admiral Byng's execution. In the same year he identified British ships convoyed to the West Indies which surreptitiously landed beef at St Eustatius, supplying French ships and enabling them to put to sea. In 1759, at the request of the Treasury secretary, he placed £20,000 of Spanish and Portuguese *specie*, urgently needed in Massachusetts, on a ship bound for New York and Boston.

In November 1756 Clevland's dutiful service was rewarded by early promotion for his son Archibald, a lieutenant in 1755, to captain of the *Gibraltar*. The move incensed Fanny Boscawen, wife of Admiral Edward Boscawen and a regular correspondent with Clevland:

> T'other day his son Archibald was made a Captain and John Clevland told me Lord Anson had done it unasked by his father … The boy is but 18 I believe. It looks as though Clevland really has that influence which people give him over our superior. (Aspinall-Oglander, 209)

The minimum age for such promotion was twenty. Archibald died on the Guinea coast in 1766 aged twenty-nine. Clevland was also able to advance the career of his other surviving son from his first marriage, John, who became clerk to the clerk of the acts (1744–6), extra clerk at the Admiralty (December 1751), and clerk on £100 a year from 1753 to 1766, when he resigned. Between 1754 and 1762 the younger John was also deputy judge advocate of the fleet, as well as accountant at the sixpenny office (1762), second clerk at the marine department (1755–60), agent of marines (1763–7), and commissioner for the sale of prizes and director of Greenwich Hospital. Further instances of Clevland's influence include the advance of his son-in-law John Ibbetson, from second clerk in the Admiralty office (1755), to clerk two years later; in 1782 Ibbetson became deputy secretary and in 1783 second secretary, a position he held until his resignation in 1795.

Clevland had re-entered parliament as MP for the Admiralty seat of the Cinque ports (1747–54), and thereafter he sat for Sandwich (1754–61) and finally Saltash from 1761 until his death. In 1754 he was paid £1000 by the government to promote ministerial interests at Barnstaple where his family had connections and to where his son John was returned from 1766 to 1802. In 1760 the 'State of Cornish Burroughs from Lord Edgcumbe' described Saltash as being, through Clevland's influence, 'very secure in the Admiralty or Navy interest'. In 1761 he advised the duke of Newcastle to declare a candidate to replace him at Sandwich or risk 'a friend of your Grace's not being chose there' (Namier, 302, 141).

In 1762 Clevland petitioned George III for a pension for his second wife, Sarah, claiming that

the extensive and arduous operations of the present war have brought such an increase of business on the office of Secretary of the Admiralty, that Mr. Clevland's health and eyesight is greatly impaired by incessant application to the faithful discharge of his trust. (BL, Add. MS 32945, fol. 449)

Clevland died in office on 19 June 1763, and was buried in his vault at the parish church of Westleigh, Devon. His will, made in 1762, reveals an extensive fortune. To the younger John he bequeathed printed and manuscript books, and the estate and farm at Tapeley Park. Other lands around Bideford, Barnstaple, and Saltash were to be managed or invested in government securities to provide incomes for his family. He also provided 'for any profession or in the purchase of any Military Commission or Commissions in order to gain their advancement in the world' for his two youngest sons (PRO, PROB 11/889, fol. 294). The younger John died childless in 1817, and was succeeded by his sister Hester's grandson, Augustus Saltern-Willett, who assumed the name Clevland.

Namier describes Clevland as 'a hard-working hungry Scot who acquired unrivalled knowledge of Admiralty matters, and thereby rose to a position of considerable importance' (Namier, 39). His portrait suggests a man more comfortable than hungry.

ANN VERONICA COATS

Sources PRO, ADM 1/925, 3/45, 3/47, 3/48, 3/49, 3/51, 3/54, 3/55, 3/62, 3/67, 3/68, 3/69, 3/71, 3/74, 6/16, 7/810, 7/811, 7/812, 7/813, 7/861, 8/14, 98/5, 106/3532; PROB 11/726, fol. 322v; PROB 11/889, fols. 289v–294v; T 1/319 · Royal Naval Museum, Portsmouth, admiralty library and manuscript collection, MS 127/1, MS 247/1 · D. A. Baugh, British naval administration in the age of Walpole (1965) · J. M. Collinge, Navy Board officials, 1660–1832 (1978) · J. C. Sainty, ed., Admiralty officials, 1660–1870 (1975) · L. Namier, The structure of politics at the accession of George III (1963) · C. Aspinall-Oglander, Admiral's wife (1940) · 'Boscawen's letters to his wife, 1755–1756', ed. P. K. Kemp, The naval miscellany, ed. C. Lloyd, 4, Navy RS, 92 (1952), 163–256 · N. A. M. Rodger, The wooden world: an anatomy of the Georgian navy (1986) · F. B. Wickwire, 'Admiralty secretaries and the British civil service', Huntington Library Quarterly, 28 (1964–5), 235–54 · IGI · J. Charnock, Biographia navalis, 3 (1795), 66–70; 4 (1796), 158 · D. Syrett and R. L. DiNardo, The commissioned sea officers of the Royal Navy, 1660–1815, rev. edn, Occasional Publications of the Navy RS, 1 (1994) · E. Cruickshanks, 'Clevland, John', HoP, Commons, 1715–54
Archives BL, memorial, Add. MS 32945, fol. 449 | BL, corresp. with the duke of Newcastle, Add. MSS 32718, fol. 19; 32858, fol. 263; 32860, fol. 5; 32861, fol. 1; 32864, fols. 343, 506; 32865, fols. 7, 366; 32866, fols. 101, 322; 35193, fols. 15, 18–20, 37; 36132, fol. 84 · PRO, ADM 1/925 · PRO, ADM 2/717, ADM 2/538 · PRO, ADM 3/31, ADM 3/36, ADM 3/45, ADM 3/47, ADM 3/48, ADM 3/49, ADM 3/51, ADM 3/54, ADM 3/55, ADM 3/67, ADM 3/68, ADM 3/69, ADM 3/71, ADM 3/74, ADM 3/137 · PRO, ADM 6/14, ADM 6/16 · PRO, ADM 7/810, ADM 7/811, ADM 7/812, ADM 7/813 · PRO, ADM 106/3532 · PRO, C 66/3586, C 66/3612 · PRO, PC 2/86 · Royal Naval Museum, Portsmouth, admiralty library and manuscript collection, MSS 127/1, 247/1
Likenesses W. Collins?, oils, Gov. Art Coll. · portrait, NMM

Wealth at death at least £13,600 in bequests; plus manor and farm at Tapeley, near Westleigh, Devon; manors of Dolton and Chembeer in Dolton and Saunton Court in Braunton, Devon; estates in Bideford and George Ham; land in Saltash, Cornwall: will, PRO, PROB 11/889, fols. 289v–294v

Cleworth, Thomas Ebenezer (1854–1909), religious educationist, eldest survivor of the seven sons and five daughters of Enoch Cleworth of Tyldesley, near Manchester, and Mary Sykes of Heywood, was born at Westminster on 2 April 1854, his father at that date being a London city missionary. Cleworth was educated at the West Ham Pelly Memorial School, and was for some years a teacher there. About 1871 he began mission work under the Evangelisation Society and attached himself to the American missioner D. L. Moody, for whom he addressed meetings in Dublin and Cork. In 1874 his health broke down. In 1879 he entered St John's College, Cambridge, where he graduated as a passman in 1882. He was stroke of one of the college boats. Ordained deacon and priest in 1881, he served in the Cambridge long vacations as curate of Kirk German, Isle of Man.

In 1882 Cleworth joined the staff of the Church Parochial Mission Society under Canon Hay Aitken, and in 1884, on the nomination of the trustees, he became vicar of St Thomas, Nottingham. In the same year he married Edith Annie, daughter of Alfred Butterworth JP, of Oldham and Andover. Cleworth's father-in-law presented him in 1888 to the rectory of Middleton, Lancashire. In 1899 Dr James Moorhouse, bishop of Manchester, created him rural dean of Middleton and Prestwich, and in 1902 an honorary canon of Manchester. At Middleton he organized many missions and 'instruction services' held after the Sunday evening service in Lent. His parochial schools, on which he spent much time as well as money, were of unusual efficiency. The renovation of the parish church was another focus of Cleworth's endeavours, and the chancel was restored in his memory after his death.

Convinced that the efficiency of church life ultimately depended on the schools, Cleworth actively devoted himself to educational controversy, especially resisting, during the discussion of the Education Bill of 1902, every proposal to diminish the absolute control of the church over the religious teaching of its schools. In November 1903 he formed the Church Schools Emergency League, for the maintenance of church schools as such and of religious education by church teachers and clergy in school and church during school hours. Cleworth acted as secretary and treasurer of the league, which opposed with effect much of the Board of Education's policy touching church schools, and attacked the passive attitude of the National Society. Ultimately Cleworth's policy, while maintaining the *status quo* of the church schools, claimed that church teaching should be given in council schools by a church teacher on the staff, with parallel rights for nonconformists. He was a member of the Middleton local education authority, a member of the standing committee of the National Society, and a leader of the 'no surrender' party in 1906; he was largely responsible for the great demonstrations in Lancashire and London against the Liberal government's Education Bill of 1906, which the House of Lords rejected. A constant speaker throughout the country, he compiled the first eighty-four leaflets of the Emergency League (which were afterwards bound in seven volumes), besides contributing largely to the Manchester and London press, including *The Times* and the *Church Family Newspaper*. He published a volume on the education crisis in 1906 jointly with the Revd John Wakeford. Cleworth died on 5 April 1909 at Middleton rectory, Lancashire. 'In days of fluid convictions and wavering beliefs Canon Cleworth was pre-eminently "justus ac tenax propositi vir"' (Dr Knox, bishop of Manchester, in *Manchester Diocesan Magazine*, May 1909). He was survived by his wife, two sons, and two daughters.

J. E. G. DE MONTMORENCY, *rev.* M. C. CURTHOYS

Sources private information (1912) · emergency leaflet no. 85 · *The Times* (7 April 1909) · *Treasury* (March 1905) · Venn, *Alum. Cant.*
Likenesses photograph, repro. in *Treasury*
Wealth at death £1072 11s. 10d.: probate, 22 April 1909, CGPLA Eng. & Wales

Cleyn, Francis. *See* Clein, Francis (d. 1658).

Cleypole. For this title name *see* Claypole, John, appointed Lord Cleypole under the protectorate (1625–1688).

Cleypole, Elizabeth. *See* Claypole, Elizabeth (*bap.* 1629, d. 1658).

Clibborn, Catherine Booth- [*called* La Maréchale] (1858–1955), evangelist, was born on 18 September 1858 at Gateshead, the third of eight children and the eldest daughter of the Revd William *Booth (1829–1912), then a minister in the Methodist New Connexion, and his wife, Catherine *Booth, *née* Mumford (1829–1890). She had three brothers, including (William) Bramwell *Booth, and four sisters. Her mother began preaching when Catherine (Katie to her family) was aged two; in 1862 William Booth resigned from the Gateshead circuit and the family lived as itinerant evangelists, finally settling in London in 1865. Catherine Booth distrusted schools, so Katie was initially tutored at the Booths' Gore Road home. It was proof of the young Catherine's determination that she persuaded her mother to allow her to attend school for a time to learn French and German.

During her childhood Katie was particularly close to William Booth's secretary, George Scott Railton (1849–1913), who lived with them for ten years and acted as her spiritual mentor. Already saved by the age of thirteen, she began preaching at the age of fifteen and shared the platform with her father at the East London Christian Mission's annual conference in 1876. It was at this time that Katie proved herself as a preacher, earning the nickname Blücher from her father—a tribute to her ability to rescue a failing meeting. She was the natural choice to begin Salvation Army operations in France, viewed as a particularly difficult and hostile country, and began work there in March 1881; her future husband, the converted Quaker Arthur Sydney Clibborn (1855–1939), was sent to Paris in October as her chief of staff. Arthur was the son of James Clibborn, co-founder of the model mills at Bessbrook in co. Armagh. Even before their marriage on 8 February 1887 Arthur actively supported Catherine's desire to ignore orders from army headquarters at variance with her own convictions. When they attempted to extend Salvation Army operations to Switzerland in 1882–3 she ignored her father's pleas for moderation, deliberately flouted a decree against holding army meetings, and was arrested outside Neuchâtel. She was tried, acquitted, and deported from Switzerland.

Catherine returned to France in October 1883 to find public opinion in her favour and the army began to flourish there. After fifteen years in France the Booth-Clibborns were sent to command army operations in Holland and Belgium. Confrontations with army headquarters continued over the necessity of social work (Catherine felt it to be a mistake and diversion), the interpretation of the Bible (especially those passages relating to holiness and physical healing), and the restrictive nature of the army's military style of government. Following the birth of their tenth child, Catherine and Arthur resigned from the Salvation Army in January 1902. At Arthur's wish, Catherine and the children travelled with him to the cult leader John Alexander Dowie's 'Zion City', a township about 40 miles north of Chicago. Catherine did not believe Dowie's grandiose claims—in 1901 he declared himself the prophet Elijah the Restorer, and in 1904 the first apostle of Jesus Christ—and was offended by his criticism of her father even though her resignation had made her an outcast from both her family and the army. For the rest of her life she had almost no contact with her father or with those siblings who remained in the army.

After a few months at Zion City they returned to the continent where Arthur began preaching Dowie's beliefs; in 1905 he was seriously injured while preaching in Paris and never fully recovered. Catherine supported her family by speaking and, with the help of her son Theo, built an impressive international reputation as a preacher. Her last major speaking tour was made in her ninetieth year, after which she retired to her home, The Haven, Ilsington, near Newton Abbot, Devon. She died there of double pneumonia on 9 May 1955, and was buried in Highgate cemetery, Middlesex.

Despite a preaching career lasting three-quarters of a century, comparatively few of Catherine's sermons and addresses were printed. Those that were strongly advocated a non-formulaic but demanding and apostolic Christianity. When writing and speaking about women, she concentrated on their spiritual rights, duties, and possibilities rather than on their political status. A charismatic and persuasive speaker, had she stayed in the army, Catherine Booth-Clibborn might well have been its first woman general.

L. E. LAUER

Sources C. Scott, *The heavenly witch* (1981) · C. Booth-Clibborn, *They endured* (1934) · J. Butler, *The Salvation Army in Switzerland* (1883) · F. Dingman, 'La Marechale: young Catherine Booth', *New Frontier* (8 Jan 1997), 4–5 · J. Strahan, *The Marechale* (1934) · CGPLA Eng. & Wales (1955)

Archives Salvation Army International Heritage Centre, London, papers
Likenesses G. Cederstrom, oils, Art Museum, Gothenburg, Sweden · photographs, Salvation Army International Heritage Centre, London
Wealth at death £3696 7s. 11d.: probate, 9 July 1955, *CGPLA Eng. & Wales* · £3187—net: *Nottingham Evening Post* (22 July 1955)

Clibborn, Stanley Eric Francis Booth- (1924–1996), bishop of Manchester, was born in London on 20 October 1924. He was the grandson of the eldest daughter, Catherine, of General William Booth, the founder of the Salvation Army, and was the son of the Revd John Eric Booth-Clibborn (1895–1924), Church of England clergyman, and his wife, Lucille, *née* Leonard (1903–1989). Educated at Highgate school, Middlesex, he was drafted into the Royal Artillery (1942–5) and the Royal Indian Artillery (1946–7), in which he became a temporary captain. After military service he read modern history at Oriel College, Oxford, receiving a second-class degree in 1950, and then prepared for ordination at Westcott House, Cambridge. He served as curate of Heeley in the Sheffield diocese of Bishop Leslie Hunter from 1952 to 1954, and subsequently in the Attercliffe parishes (then at the heart of the steel industry) from 1954 to 1956.

In 1956 Booth-Clibborn made a major move to become training secretary of the Christian Council of Kenya (until 1963) and, after that, chief editor of East African Venture Newspapers (1963–7). At a time when the Church of England was still dominant in the Anglican communion, Africa gave him a refreshingly different slant on the church in England in his later ministry, as it had to face great changes in its position both at home and overseas. His years in Africa in an ecumenical job reinforced his commitment to the ecumenical movement for both the unity and renewal of the churches and for its emphasis on the cause of the poor and marginalized. He saw the urgency of preparing Christians in Kenya for leadership as the British empire was dismantled. This meant their taking politics seriously. His outspoken newspapers offended the more evangelical Christians who regarded politics as a dirty business, and also the colonial administrations, which the papers frequently criticized. For a time one of them was suppressed. When Booth-Clibborn realized that he would not again get editorial freedom he returned to the UK. However, Africa remained a continual concern for him and his family. On 15 February 1958 he had married Anne Roxburgh Forrester (*b.* 1926), the daughter of Professor William and Margaret Forrester, both influential members of the Church of Scotland, and this increased his ecumenical concern. His wife later became deputy chair of Christian Aid in the UK, with special responsibility for Africa. They had two sons and two daughters.

On his return to the UK, Booth-Clibborn was asked to take charge of the Lincoln Centre Team ministry, but three years later he was called to the university church, Great St Mary's, Cambridge, which had a vigorous ministry to the town but also to students, particularly with its late Sunday evening service, to which speakers of

Stanley Eric Francis Booth-Clibborn (1924–1996), by unknown photographer

national and international significance came. He maintained its vigour for nine years. By now his energy, communication skills, and leadership qualities were well known, and it was no surprise that in 1979 he was nominated to the see of Manchester, a diocese whose importance was equalled by its problems. The world's first industrial city was now the centre of a conurbation which was a northern metropolis, a dynamic city, with a rapidly changing industrial and commercial base. But the diocese included all the poorer areas and few of the more prosperous ones, except the city centre; and most of those who worked there lived outside the diocesan boundary. Of the just over 300 parishes, two-thirds were shortly to be classed as urban priority areas, or almost so, an indication of the problems of unemployment, crime, and vandalism which they faced. The church had inherited too much plant from the Victorian expansion, much of it inflexible and unsuitable, and many parishes were having a hard struggle. Booth-Clibborn liked Manchester but he could not in one diocese solve the wider problems of the Church of England. He reorganized his diocese into three episcopal areas, each of just over 100 parishes, which made it more efficient in terms of the existing structures of the Church of England and also more pastorally cared for. On a wider scale he played a full part in the general synod and its standing committee, and he took his membership of the House of Lords very seriously, hard as it was to fit it in with diocesan duties. He was a public figure, often called upon by the media for comments, especially in the early years, when little of public interest was said by the then archbishops of Canterbury and York. He always expressed himself clearly without evasions. His arrival in Manchester coincided with the Thatcher years in politics, and those who approved of them regarded him as a dangerous radical, but in fact he stood for the kind of consensus which was associated with the earlier post-war years. Broadly his theology and social ethics were those associated with William Temple, and were acceptable not only to the Labour Party, of which he was a member, but also to most Liberals and a considerable number of Conservatives, often called 'wets' by the new protagonists in that party. His one book, *Taxes: Burden or Blessing?* (1991), was mainly a reasoned defence of direct taxation as a way of discharging civic responsibility, hostility to which was characteristic of the Thatcher years.

Booth-Clibborn was a keen advocate of women's ministry and was the first moderator of the Movement for the Ordination of Women (1989–92). During his time in Manchester he also retained his connection with Africa, making several visits to Namibia and establishing a special relationship between that diocese and the Manchester diocese. Ill health dogged his retirement, after 1992, but his work in Manchester, which had already been recognized by Manchester Polytechnic in 1989, was further honoured by the conferment of the degree of DD by Manchester University in 1994. He died in Edinburgh (to where he and his wife had retired), following major heart surgery and a stroke, on 6 March 1996. He was cremated in Edinburgh on 12 March and his ashes were interred in Manchester Cathedral on 29 March. He was survived by his wife and four children.   RONALD H. PRESTON

Sources private information (2004) [Mrs A. Booth-Clibborn] · personal knowledge (2004) · *The Times* (8 March 1996) · *The Independent* (8 March 1996) · *Daily Telegraph* (8 March 1996) · WWW · Crockford
Archives Man. CL, diocesan records · U. Edin. L., African collection | Women's Library, London, movement for ordination of women
Likenesses photograph, priv. coll. [*see illus.*] · photograph, repro. in *The Times* · photograph, repro. in *The Independent* · photograph, repro. in *Daily Telegraph*
Wealth at death £78,295.11: confirmation, 29 May 1996, NA Scot., SC/CO 922/43

Cliderhou, Robert de. *See* Clitheroe, Robert (*d.* 1334).

Clidro, Robin (*fl.* 1547), Welsh-language poet and minstrel, lived near Ruthin, Denbighshire. Although his surname suggests that he was of English extraction, persons bearing the name Cliderowe had lived in the area from the early part of the fourteenth century.

Although little is known of Robin Clidro, the subsidy roll of 1547 shows that he paid £10 10s. in tax on land, which suggests that he was a gentleman rather than a member of the yeoman class. Indeed his independent means may well explain the cavalier manner in which he cocked a snook at the established bardic tradition in many of his poems. However, despite his social status, Clidro is associated with a sub-literary culture stretching back to the fourteenth century.

Even before the Caerwys eisteddfod of 1567, the evidence of the courts of great sessions suggests that the authorities were clamping down on 'vagraunt and idle persons, naming theim selfes mynstrelles, rithmers and barthes' (Suggett, 170). Clidro himself appeared before such a court in Flintshire in 1547 together with a motley band of rhymesters, dancers, and musicians. As well as being a performing poet Clidro was also a piper and fiddler.

Clidro's extant output is limited, comprising seven odes, seven *cywyddau*, and seventeen shorter works. In language, tone, and subject matter, his poetry contrasts strikingly with the work of the professional bards of the period. He wrote in the idiom of ordinary folk, using the rich dialect of the Vale of Clwyd. The most characteristic feature of his work is its lively narrative and ribald humour. While the recognized bards wrote elegies to people of substance, in 'Awdl y gath' ('Ode to a Cat') he mourns the passing of a tomcat; while they eulogize, he vilifies, and while they jealously protect their dignity, Clidro exults in self-denigration. Lawyers, sheriffs, mayors, and parsimonious clerics all feel the lash of his tongue.

Living in the Vale of Clwyd, one of the bastions of Welsh poetry and culture, Clidro was well acquainted with the mores of the bardic tradition—its propensity to praise, its preferred subjects, its deference to lineage, its exalted language, its traditional metres, and, above all, its general sobriety. All these characteristics become the targets of Clidro's humour and there is evidence to suggest that even in his own idiosyncratic form of alliteration he is thumbing his nose at the intricacies of *cynghanedd*, the very bedrock of the formal poetic tradition.

To contemporaries and later generations Clidro was an object of ridicule and was judged to be the epitome of poetic incompetence. He should not, however, be viewed as a late medieval William McGonagall, but rather as one of the last representatives of the *clêr*, those inferior poets who are satirized in the Red Book of Hergest for soliciting among the lower orders of society but who are deemed to have been an important influence on such distinguished poets as Dafydd ap Gwilym. The distinctive metre in which Clidro wrote some of his most memorable odes was once thought to have been the creation of his fertile imagination, but is now known to have been used from the early fourteenth century onwards by the unqualified wandering poets of medieval Wales whose characteristic satire and vituperation were eschewed by more respectable practitioners of the art.

With the accelerating breakdown of the formal bardic order in the sixteenth century, the dividing line between the professional poets and the *clêr* became more blurred. There is evidence in Clidro's work that lighter forms of verse and minstrelsy were welcomed in the houses of the less conservative nobility, and one of the most distinguished poets of the period, Siôn Tudur, wrote a light-hearted elegy to Clidro even while the subject was still alive. Fortunately enough of Robin Clidro's work has been preserved to give a taste of a genre which, by its ephemeral oral nature, was rarely recorded in the manuscripts of the period.   CENNARD DAVIES

Sources C. Davies, 'Robin Clidro a'i Ganlynwyr', MA diss., U. Wales, 1964 · B. Rees, *Dulliau'r Canu Rhydd, 1550-1650* (1952) · T. H. Parry-Williams, *Canu rhydd cynnar* (1932) · H. M. Evans, 'Iaith a Ieithwedd y Cerddi Rhydd Cynnar', MA diss., U. Wales, 1937 · H. M. Edwards, *Dafydd ap Gwilym: influences and analogues* (1996) · R. Suggett, 'Yr Iaith Gymraeg a Llys y sesiwn Fawr', *Y Gymraeg yn Ei Disgleirdeb*, ed. G. H. Jenkins (1997), 151–79 · C. Davies, 'Early free metre poetry', *A guide to Welsh literature*, ed. R. G. Gruffydd, 3: *c.1530–1700* (1997), 75–99 · D. J. Bowen, 'Y Cywyddwyr a'r Dirywiad', *BBCS*, 29 (1980–82), 453–96 · E. Roberts, *Gwaith Siôn Tudur* (1980)

Cliff, Clarice (1899–1972), ceramic designer and art director, was born on 20 January 1899 at 19 Meir Street, Tunstall, Staffordshire, one of eight children of Harry Thomas Cliff, iron-moulder, and his wife, Ann (*née* Machin). Her parents were working-class and of Staffordshire descent. Though not a family of pottery workers, her aunt ran the decorating shop at Alfred Meakin Ltd which the young Clarice visited regularly.

Cliff was educated at the High Street elementary school, and later at Summerbank Road School, Tunstall. At thirteen, she was apprenticed as a painter to Lingard Webster & Co. Ltd, and moved to Hollinshead and Kirkham Ltd as an apprentice lithographer in 1915. She also began attending evening classes at the Tunstall School of Art. In 1916 she joined the Burslem earthenware manufacturers Arthur J. Wilkinson Ltd, a larger firm offering better prospects. Cliff continued her lithographic training at Wilkinsons, completing this in 1920. At this time, her artistic abilities were noticed by the decorating manager Jack Walker, brother-in-law of Arthur Colley Austin Shorter (1882–1963), the firm's managing director. As a result, Cliff was placed in the design studio. Between 1924 and 1925 she attended evening classes at the Burslem School of Art.

Until 1925 Cliff had lived in the family home. In that year, though still unmarried, she moved into her own flat at 40 Snow Hill, Hanley. Cliff was a round-faced young woman who, though perhaps not a natural beauty, was fashionable in the style of the period. At about this time, Cliff's relationship with Colley Shorter, who was married with two daughters, developed beyond the purely professional. This distanced her from the other employees and those members of Shorter's family who ran the firm. Cliff's social life at the time appears to have been limited, and she devoted herself both to her work and to her relationship with Shorter. This relationship provided her with opportunities of which she was fully able to take advantage. In 1925 she was given her own studio in the adjacent Newport pottery, which Wilkinsons had acquired in 1920. In 1927 she attended a training course at the Royal College of Art. The same year she travelled to Paris to study art.

On her return, Cliff developed a range of brightly coloured geometrical patterns, with the assistance of apprentice Gladys Scarlett. These were initially used to decorate surplus stock from the Newport pottery. In July

Clarice Cliff (1899–1972), by unknown photographer

1928 Cliff coined the name 'Bizarre' for the range. Like much of Cliff's work of the late 1920s and 1930s, these designs were art deco in character, and were produced at a time when the style was only beginning to appear in England. Despite the low expectations of Wilkinsons salesmen, 'Bizarre' was an immediate success. Later in 1928 Cliff produced the 'Crocus' pattern, a simple design made up of a few brushstrokes. Developed from an earlier lithographic design, 'Crocus' became an enduring favourite, was adapted to a variety of different pottery shapes, and remained in production until 1963.

In 1929 Cliff began designing new pottery shapes for 'Bizarre'. These were severely geometrical and modernistic. Of the principal shapes, 'Conical' appeared in 1929, 'Stamford' in 1930, and 'Le bon jour' and 'Biarritz' in 1933. Often inspired by designs illustrated in the French journal *Mobilier et Décoration*, certain shapes derived from Jean Tétard silver, the designs having initially been used without his knowledge or consent.

Between 1929 and 1936 Cliff designed numerous patterns, including abstract designs, stylized flowers or fruit, and landscapes. Bold and lively, these were normally composed of solid areas of bright enamel colour. They were issued in ranges under titles including 'Bizarre', 'Fantasque', and 'Appliqué'. Other more limited ranges, such as 'Inspiration' and 'Latona', relied on particular glaze-effects. On occasion, Cliff is known to have borrowed patterns from outside sources, as well as from employees in her workshop. Besides tableware and other functional wares, she produced ornamental masks and figures, most notably *Age of Jazz* (1930).

Throughout the early 1930s, Cliff's pottery achieved enormous success, and the entire Newport factory was devoted to its production. The wares were sold through department stores and other retail outlets throughout the country, as well as being exported widely. In 1931 she was appointed art director. Cliff was adept at creating publicity, and the 'Clarice Cliff' name became an important marketing device. Its use as a backstamp was sometimes indiscriminate—a fact which angered the influential designer and educator Gordon Forsyth when it was placed on a range of pottery designed by contemporary artists during 1933–4.

From 1935 the popularity of 'Bizarre' (by then used to describe all Clarice Cliff pottery) waned considerably. In the later 1930s her designs became increasingly conservative, using muted colours or relief-moulded decoration. Wartime restrictions on the production of decorated pottery left her without a major role at the factory. On 21 December 1940 Cliff married Shorter, following the death of his first wife. The marriage was kept secret for almost a year. Following the Second World War, Cliff produced fewer designs, spending most of her time at Chetwynd, their Staffordshire home. She did not have children. By 1960 Shorter's health was failing, and he died in 1963. Cliff sold Wilkinsons the following year to W. R. Midwinter Ltd, and went into retirement. A retrospective exhibition of her work was held at the Brighton Museum and Art Gallery in 1972, to which she contributed catalogue notes. On 23 October that year, Cliff died in Staffordshire of heart failure. Her work has since enjoyed a considerable revival among collectors and students of art deco pottery. Small collections of her work can be seen in the Victoria and Albert Museum, London, and in the Brighton Museum and Art Gallery.

Cliff has often been derided by modernist design critics who consider her work to fail their criteria for good design. She has also been accused of achieving success only through Shorter. Nevertheless, and notwithstanding her occasional plagiarism, Cliff produced and publicized many striking and adventurous designs. She challenged accepted women's roles through her design of pottery shapes, and achieved success without the benefit of a privileged background. Her major talent was perhaps not as a design originator, but lay in her ability to assemble a range of pottery which captured the mood of the period and the imagination of the public.   ALUN R. GRAVES

Sources C. Buckley, 'What the ladies think!', *Potters and paintresses: women designers in the pottery industry, 1870–1955* (1990), 96–133 · L. Griffin, L. K. Meisel, and S. P. Meisel, *Clarice Cliff: the Bizarre affair* (1988) · *Clarice Cliff* (1972) [exhibition catalogue, Brighton Museum and Art Gallery] · P. Wentworth-Shields and K. Johnson, *Clarice Cliff* (1976) · H. Watson and P. Watson, *The colourful world of Clarice Cliff* (1992) · I. Hopwood and G. Hopwood, *The Shorter connection: a family pottery, 1874–1974* (1992) · L. R. Griffin,

'Cliff, Clarice', *The dictionary of art*, ed. J. Turner (1996) · b. cert. · m. cert. · *CGPLA Eng. & Wales* (1972)
Archives Hanley Library, Stoke-on-Trent, Wilkinson collection
Likenesses photograph, 1931, Hanley Library, Stoke-on-Trent, Wilkinson collection · photograph, priv. coll. [*see illus.*]
Wealth at death £76,051: probate, 13 Nov 1972, *CGPLA Eng. & Wales*

Cliff, Henry de. See Cliffe, Henry (*c.*1280–1334).

Cliff, Tony [*formerly* Ygael Amnon Gluckstein] (**1917–2000**), Trotskyist leader, was born on 20 May 1917 at Zikhron Yaakov in Turkish Palestine, the youngest of four children of Akiva Gluckstein, a prosperous building contractor, and his wife, Esther, who had emigrated from Russian Poland in 1902. Akiva went bankrupt shortly after Ygael was born; his upbringing was not prosperous. The family were staunch Zionists. At fifteen he joined the youth section of the Zionist Mapai party, moving two years later to the left-wing Poale Zion. Radicalized by the treatment accorded young Arabs and Hitler's rise in Germany, he became a Trotskyist after a brief flirtation with Stalinism. The Poale Zion Trotskyists around the paper *Kol Hama'amed* ('Workers' Voice') coalesced with German refugees and members of Haschomer Hazair, the socialist Zionist kibbutz movement, to form the Revolutionary Communist Alliance. In 1938 contact was established with the American Socialist Workers' Party; Gluckstein's earliest work in English appeared in their journal *New International*. His studies at the Hebrew University, Jerusalem, were disrupted in 1939 when he was imprisoned at Acre for twelve months by the British authorities, and he spent the next five years working full-time to build the Fourth International in Palestine.

In February 1945 Gluckstein married Chanie Rosenberg, a South African socialist and his lifelong political collaborator. They had two daughters and two sons. The couple travelled to Britain via Paris where they met the leaders of the Fourth International. In London, where he was transformed from Ygael Gluckstein to Tony Cliff, he joined the Revolutionary Communist Party. But his stay was fleeting: late in 1947 he was ordered to leave the country. He spent the next four years in Dublin, visiting Britain only briefly. He studied at Trinity College but, seeing little prospect of developing Trotskyism in Ireland, focused on Britain. In 1950–51, after the demise of the Revolutionary Communist Party, he assembled a small group of supporters working in the Labour Party around the journal *Socialist Review*. It argued that the USSR was not, as Trotsky had claimed and as the Fourth International still accepted, a degenerated workers' state but a state capitalist society where accumulation of capital was driven by competition with the West.

First enunciated in the Revolutionary Communist Party in 1947, this theory was expounded in successive editions of Cliff's book *Stalinist Russia: a Marxist Analysis* (1955) and in other work in the 1950s: *Stalin's Satellites in Europe* (1952) and *Mao's China* (1957). It was applied in the refusal of *Socialist Review* to support either Moscow or Washington in the Korean War, and was complemented by the recognition, which again distinguished the group from most orthodox Trotskyists, that capitalism was temporarily thriving and the post-war boom was fuelled by arms expenditure. Whatever the inadequacies of this approach, and they were argued fulsomely by its Marxist opponents, it demonstrated an ability to engage with a changing world, stimulated realism, and emphasized the working class, rather than a variety of insubstantial substitutes, as the bearer of socialist change. Through the 1950s Cliff worked with different political currents and moved away from Trotskyism towards a libertarian Marxism. He concluded in an eponymous book of 1959 that Rosa Luxemburg provided an exemplar for revolutionaries superior to Lenin.

Despite an impressive new journal, *International Socialism*, and an agitational paper, *Labour Worker*, membership of the International Socialists, as the group became known, reached only 200 in 1964 and 1000 in 1968. By that date it had left the Labour Party, and *Labour Worker* became *Socialist Worker*. Cliff, always the dominant force, turned back towards orthodoxy, impressed by the growth of industrial militancy in Britain and the insurgency of May 1968 in France. The group's eclectic and variegated politics were replaced by Leninism, its open federal structure by democratic centralism.

Between 1968 and 1972, Cliff's organization added to its intellectuals a small but significant group of shop stewards. The process was facilitated by his books on incomes policy and productivity deals, and the International Socialists were able to develop rank-and-file caucuses in trade unions. As the climate hardened with the initial success of the Labour government's 'social contract' in 1974, he became impatient with the orientation towards experienced trade unionists and conservative elements inside the International Socialists. A faction fight in 1975 deprived the group of important members, and the decline in industrial militancy led him to theorize about 'a downturn in class struggle' which was to last two decades. Nothing daunted, if against the grain of developments, the group, with fewer than 4000 members, declared itself in 1977 the Socialist Workers' Party. Cliff took up the evasive discourse of 'build the party' as the answer to political difficulties. To this end he busied himself with political biographies of Lenin (four vols., 1975–9) and Trotsky (four vols., 1989–93).

In the late 1970s and 1980s the Socialist Workers' Party animated influential campaigns, notably the Anti-Nazi League, indulged in unsuccessful electoral interventions, and wound up its rank-and-file caucuses. Cliff was energetic in constraining feminist trends in the organization and in constructing an international tendency reflecting the Socialist Workers' Party's politics. The radicalization in the Labour Party between 1978 and 1984 passed the Socialist Workers' Party by, and it lost out to the militant group in the anti-poll tax campaign. None the less, by the mid-1990s, with some 6000 members, Cliff had outstripped his competitors. He continued to deny the need for any formal programme. Together with minimal internal democracy and the Socialist Workers' Party's self-imposed isolation, this denial strengthened his status as an oracle, although his later pronouncements—the 1990s were a slow-motion re-run of the 1930s, capitalism was hurtling towards economic crisis, the election of the Blair government would produce significant working-class insurgency—were wide of the mark.

Chronicling Cliff's life means narrating his political life: his other interests hardly existed. When he died at Homerton Hospital, Hackney, London, on 9 April 2000 of pleurisy which led to heart failure, it was with a sense of fulfilment. He had seen the fall of Stalinism, the collapse of the Communist Party, and his own creation, the Socialist Workers' Party, emerge as the biggest far-left organization in Britain. The retreat of socialism and his own strategies ensured that it possessed limited influence. Cliff was survived by his wife and their four children. He was a man of charm and humanity, an incessant, humorous, inspiring exponent of socialist ideas and a relentless, intolerant prosecutor of his own politics. These had the strengths and weaknesses of the outsider. If he surpassed most other Trotskyist leaders, in the final analysis he shared many of their deficiencies.   JOHN MCILROY

Sources T. Cliff, *A world to win: life of a revolutionary* (2000) · J. Higgins, *More years for the locust: the origins of the SWP* (1997) · J. Callaghan, *British Trotskyism: theory and practice* (1984) · I. Birchall, *The smallest mass party in the world* (1979) · *The IS–SWP tradition*, Workers Liberty (1996) · J. McIlroy, 'The Trotskyists in the trade unions', *British trade unions and industrial politics*, ed. J. McIlroy and others (1999) · Y. Sarneh, 'A revolutionary life', *International Socialism*, 87 (2000) · R. Kuper, ed., *The Fourth International, Stalinism and the origins of the International Socialists* (1971) · E. Mandel, *Readings on state capitalism* (1973) · J. Rees, 'Tony Cliff: theory and practice', *International Socialism*, 87 (2000) · 'Tony Cliff: optimism of the will', *Socialist Review* (May 2000) · *The Guardian* (11 April 2000) · *The Independent* (15 April 2000) · d. cert.

Archives U. Warwick Mod. RC, Barker papers, Hyman papers, Jefferys papers, Kuper papers, Tarbuck papers, MSS

Likenesses photograph, repro. in *The Guardian* · photograph, repro. in *The Independent* · photograph, repro. in 'Tony Cliff: optimism of the will', 13 · portrait (as a young man), repro. in Cliff, *A world to win*, facing p. 112

Cliffe [Clyffe], **Henry** (*c*.1280–1334), administrator, was probably born at Cliffe near Selby. An MA by 1307, possibly of Oxford, in 1329 he attested the conveyance of a messuage, La Oriole, which gave its name to Oriel College, Oxford. Between 1316 and 1319 he occurs as chancellor of the Winchester diocese, but his life's interest was to be in royal service. A chancery clerk, he first appears as a temporary keeper of the great seal in 1318 and continued as such at intervals until 12 December 1324. He was also appointed to audit petitions at the York parliament of October 1318 and to respond to them at the Westminster parliament of 1320. A clerical proctor in various parliaments, he represented the dean and chapter of York five times between 1324 and 1332. After serving as keeper of the privy seal from April until July 1325 he was appointed keeper of the chancery rolls, an office he retained until the end of Edward II's reign. Following Isabella's coup in 1326 he was a keeper of Edward II's great seal—by a legal fiction affixed in the name of the 'keeper of the realm'—and was with her at Hereford to receive the captured chancery rolls. During Edward III's reign, apart from minor intervals, he remained in office and with custody of the rolls until 8 January 1333, being by virtue of his clerkship attached to the household of Queen Philippa.

Cliffe's first benefice (1307) was Collingtree rectory with Melton (Northamptonshire). Royal patronage brought others in various counties but, as a chancery clerk, he could not have been forced to reside in any of his rectories. Dean of Tamworth between 1317 and 1319, he subsequently held canonries of York (with Apesthorpe prebend), Salisbury, Wells, and Chichester, being treasurer of the last by 1333. Regularly described as 'clerk', he doubtless did not proceed to higher orders. In 1325 he secured a mortmain licence for a chantry in St Gregory's Priory, Canterbury. The proving of his will in 1334 is the only evidence for the date of his death. It includes bequests to his brother John and John's wife, Emma, and their seven young sons, as well as £20 for the marriage portion of their daughter Isabella. John was also to receive the stock at Apesthorpe and there was a bequest for the parishioners there. Cliffe left £2 apiece to the Dominican, Franciscan, Carmelite, and Augustinian friars of both York and London and other sums to the nunneries of Stratford (also to Alice de Clyffe, a nun there), Clerkenwell, Haliwell, and the Minories outside Aldgate. He wished his body to be buried in the Augustinian priory of Drax, near Cliffe.

J. A. HAMILTON, *rev.* ROY MARTIN HAINES

Sources register of wills, 1321–1493, York Minster Library, fols. 13–14 · BL, Cotton MS Galba E.111, fol. 184v · Rymer, *Foedera*, new edn, 2.i-ii · F. Palgrave, ed., *The parliamentary writs and writs of military summons*, 2 vols. in 4 (1827–34) · Chancery records · CEPR letters, vol. 2 · R. M. Haines, *A calendar of the register of Adam de Orleton, bishop of Worcester, 1327–1333*, Worcestershire Historical Society, 10 (1979) · Emden, *Oxf.*, 1.438–9 · *Fasti Angl., 1300–1541*, [Salisbury] · *Fasti Angl., 1300–1541*, [Bath and Wells] · *Fasti Angl., 1300–1541*, [Chichester] · *Fasti Angl., 1066–1300*, [York] · J. H. Denton and J. P. Dooley, *Representatives of the lower clergy in Parliament* (1987) · J. C. Davies, *The baronial opposition to Edward II* (1918) · Tout, *Admin. hist.*, vols. 2, 3, 5–6 · J. L. Grassi, 'Royal clerks from the archdiocese of York in the fourteenth century', *Northern History*, 5 (1970), 12–33 **Wealth at death** bequests incl. £20 for daughter's marriage portion, and more than £10 to religious foundations: will, York Minster Library, register of wills, 1321–1493, fols. 13–14

Clifford, de. For this title name *see* Russell, Edward Southwell, twenty-sixth Baron de Clifford (1907–1982).

Clifford, Anne [*known as* Lady Anne Clifford], **countess of Pembroke, Dorset, and Montgomery** (1590–1676), noblewoman and diarist, was born at Skipton Castle in Craven in the West Riding of Yorkshire on 30 January 1590, the only surviving child of George *Clifford, third earl of Cumberland (1558–1605), and his wife, Lady Margaret (1560–1616) [*see* Clifford, Margaret, countess of Cumberland], youngest daughter of Francis *Russell, second earl of Bedford. She was brought up in her father's houses at the Charterhouse and in Clerkenwell and at the homes of her mother's Russell relatives, Chenies in Buckinghamshire and North Hall in Hertfordshire. She was educated by her mother and her Russell relatives, all intellectually gifted, her governess Anne Taylor, and until 1602 her tutor, the author Samuel Daniel. The composer Jack (John)

Anne Clifford, countess of Pembroke, Dorset, and Montgomery (1590–1676), by William Larkin, 1618

Jenkins taught her to play the lute in 1603. She had a dancing master, Stephen, and performed in masques at James I's court.

Lady Anne's mother was her mentor and remained her exemplar. She and Daniel in particular inspired in their pupil a love of literature, history, the classics, and religious works and fostered her precocious autodidactism and critical bent. To them she owed her piety and biblical knowledge, though she eschewed their puritan convictions. Reading (more often being read to) was for her a lifelong pleasure and a solace in periods of trouble and depression. Having inherited her mother's library, she built up, to quote her officer George Sedgewick, 'a library stored with very choice books, which she read over, not cursorily, but with judgement and observation'. Her breadth of knowledge surprised John Donne, who remarked that 'she knew well how to discourse of all things, from predestination to slea-silk'. Bishop Edward Rainbow attests that her conversation could be not only 'useful and grave, but also pleasant and delightful' (Spence, *Lady Anne Clifford*, 189–90, 14, 223).

Lady Anne's life was dominated by the great inheritance dispute caused when her father in 1605 bequeathed his estates (for financial reasons) to his brother Francis *Clifford, fourth earl of Cumberland, leaving her instead a £15,000 portion. Countess Margaret, as her guardian, initiated claims on Anne's behalf to both the Cliffords' baronial titles, which the earl marshal's court refused in 1606, and the estates. Her archival researches demolished Earl

Francis's case for all the estates in the court of wards in 1607, the judges deciding the Skipton properties (though not the other Craven manors) were rightfully Anne's, although her uncle kept possession.

Lady Anne married, on 25 February 1609, Richard Sackville, Lord Buckhurst, third earl of Dorset (1589–1624), with whom she had three short-lived sons and two daughters, Margaret and Isabella. From 1612 her husband Dorset took charge of her lawsuits, complicating the issues because he stood out for the maximum gain, but in 1615 the court of common pleas decided that he and Anne could have the Skipton and Westmorland estates or the portion, but not both. After her mother's death in May 1616 Anne was isolated, refusing to yield her claim on all the estates despite unpleasantness from Dorset and incessant pressure from James I's courtiers. She suffered a period of ill health and withdrawal. Worse followed when she refused to accept the king's award in February 1617 which settled the dispute by giving all the estates to Earl Francis and his male heirs and £17,000 in compensation to Dorset and Anne, which her husband then pocketed.

Countess Anne's marriage had been deeply scarred by the bitter quarrels with Dorset—over the estates, his profligacy, and his infidelities. She became perforce far more independent-minded, self-reliant, and worldly-wise. She helped with cash her uncle's Westmorland tenants who opposed him in the law courts and supported his political opponents in the north-west. She also indulged her artistic and literary tastes by erecting monuments to her cousin Lady Frances Bourchier in Chenies church, to her mother in Appleby church, and in 1620 to Edmund Spenser, a favourite author, in Westminster Abbey. Her burgeoning interest in her family's history and her father's achievements led her to commission an illustrated volume of his sea enterprises and the antiquary St Loe Kniveton to write up her mother's legal archives in two books. Her own diary for these years has survived in part.

Dorset's death in 1624 made Countess Anne wealthy, with a generous jointure of £2000 a year landed income in Sussex and Essex, and independent. Her daughters' welfare and her claim for the estates were her overriding concerns, hence her purchase of their wardships from the crown. Besides living with her relatives, she frequented the court, with an eye to Lady Margaret's marriage and her own. The suitable match for Lady Margaret was John, Lord Tufton, later second earl of Thanet (1609–1664), the wedding being celebrated on 21 April 1629. The countess added to the Sussex manors provided by Dorset for Lady Margaret's portion several from her own jointure holding. Feeling the need for greater financial security and political support in her campaign for the estates because Earl Francis's heir, her cousin Henry *Clifford, had been elevated to the Lords, she married, on 3 June 1630, Philip *Herbert, earl of Montgomery and fourth earl of Pembroke (1584–1650), Charles I's lord chamberlain. He brought her great wealth, power, royal influence, and a life at court, what she needed to counter 'the envie, malice and sinister practices' of her enemies Henry Clifford and her brother-in-law Edward, fourth earl of Dorset, who

resented her occupying so much Sackville property (Spence, *Lady Anne Clifford*, 94).

With Henry Clifford lacking male heirs, Countess Anne could anticipate the king's award taking effect at his death. She reached an agreement with Pembroke in December 1634 which ensured her possession of the Westmorland lordships while he would hold Skipton on a life interest and raise £5000 there towards her daughter Lady Isabella's portion. Soon after they had a great quarrel—over the estates or his infidelities—and he banished her from London. For eight years she and Lady Isabella lived at his Wiltshire houses, although he joined with her in making formal claims to the estates. On the outbreak of the civil war in 1642 Pembroke requested her to reside in his Baynard's Castle in London to safeguard his rich household belongings, which he moved there. She did not leave for six years and negotiated from there Lady Isabella's marriage on 5 July 1647 to James Compton, third earl of Northampton (1622–1681), the portion being Sussex manors Dorset had assigned Isabella in 1624.

Although the hostilities prevented Countess Anne from entering her estates following Henry Clifford's death in December 1643, she appointed officers in Westmorland and also in Craven, Pembroke's interest notwithstanding. His death in January 1650, six months after she had ridden north, brought her a second jointure estate, in Kent, worth £2000 a year in rents, adding to her now great landed wealth. Moreover, she now had the freedom of action to overthrow the king's award. In Westmorland the issue was the rate of entry fines set by the award. Determined and abrasive, she was successful in November 1656 after years of costly litigation and ejections of tenants in a manner which tarnishes her image. Her object in Craven was to oust Henry Clifford's heirs, Richard Boyle, earl of Burlington (1612–1698), and his countess, Elizabeth, from the properties awarded Earl Francis in 1607. Their Skipton town and her own Silsden tenants bore the brunt of her litigation until she conceded defeat in 1657. But she widened her campaign by championing her Clifford fee as a liberty separate from Staincliffe wapentake which was in Burlington's hands. This alarmed the Yorkshire political establishment who, fearing her love of controversy and lawsuits, blocked her by resort to the courts. Burlington's retaliation, invoking the financial safeguards of the award, threatened not just Countess Anne's Sussex jointure estates but also the Dorsets', Thanets', and Northamptons' interests in them. It appears to have succeeded in curbing Countess Anne's claims to Burlington's Craven properties. She was particularly intransigent during the 1660s, exploiting her powers as hereditary sheriff of Westmorland to defy court orders over paying rents to Sackville College, the East Grinstead almshouses she and Dorset had founded.

The last thirty years of Countess Anne's life, starting at Baynard's in 1646, were immensely creative. She commissioned there two copies of the great triptych, one for each daughter, an exaltation of her noble family and her right to the inheritance (painted by Jan van Belcamp and possibly Peter Lely). She had Kniveton's volumes rewritten and expanded, with contributions from the antiquary Roger Dodsworth, into three great books of record (three copies), a documentary assertion of her title. At Skipton Castle in 1652 she inserted in them her summary of the lives of her forebears and thereafter entered yearly a memorial of her life. Subsequently, she added to her collections two histories of her forebears compiled by the judge and antiquary Sir Matthew Hale, two copies of Earl George's voyages, a book of heraldry, genealogies, and a volume of her mother's letters, which, with the numerous legal documents, mark her as a family historian of special note.

Countess Anne has an outstanding reputation as a builder, restorer, and conservator, a passion indulged on her ancestral estates from 1650 as a very wealthy landowner with about £8000 gross yearly income. In Westmorland she repaired her four castles: Appleby, Brougham, which had been damaged in the civil war, Brough, which had burnt down in 1521, and Pendragon, destroyed by the Scots in 1341. In Craven she restored Skipton Castle so far as she was allowed, following its slighting by parliament in 1648, and Barden Tower, which had been disroofed by the combatants. Her restoration of churches helped revitalize religious observance on her estates, where she defiantly continued to use the proscribed Book of Common Prayer through the 1640s and 1650s, and, unlike her castles, the churches are all still standing. In Westmorland her work is visible at St Lawrence and St Michael's, Bongate, Appleby, at St Wilfrid's and St Ninian's (Ninekirks), Brougham, at St Mary's Chapel, Outhgill, Mallerstang, and at her oratory at Appleby Castle. Her renovations at Holy Trinity, Skipton, and the chapel of Barden Tower were extensive. In 1632 she had, with Pembroke's help, completed the building and endowing of her mother's Beamsley almshouses near Skipton. Between 1651 and 1653 she erected almshouses in Appleby, St Anne's Hospital, initially a retirement home for her women attendants. Plaques on all her buildings publicized her inherited rights to her father's lands and titles. Even more illuminating of her sense of ancestral pride and title were the coats of arms on the triptychs, the inner walls of the hospital, and her fine monuments in Skipton church to her father and in Appleby church to herself. The last also bear uncompromising inscriptions. Her most public demonstration was the shields and inscription on the Countess's Pillar, which she erected near Brougham in 1654 to mark her last parting from her mother. Her other monuments commemorated Samuel Daniel, in Beckington church, Somerset, and her clerk of works, Gabriel Vincent, who directed all her building, in Brough church.

Countess Anne spent the last twenty years of her life as a grand lady, dressed in her favourite black. Her brown eyes and, when young, brown hair worn waist length, complemented a shapely figure, of which she was very proud. In spite of her small stature—less than 5 feet tall—she had a formidable presence, and the strength of will which was a frequently remarked facet of her complex personality is revealed in portraits of her from her middle twenties in a stubbornness about the mouth and chin. Latterly she progressed from castle to castle, receiving in audience a stream of titled relatives and friends who came to pay their respects to her. Living frugally herself, she kept rigorous account of her finances. Her household was a place of piety, charity, and hospitality, her regime beneficent, religious, and, in the best sense of the term, baronial. It ended on 22 March 1676, in Brougham Castle. She was buried on 14 April in the vault she had built for herself in St Lawrence, Appleby.   RICHARD T. SPENCE

Sources R. T. Spence, *Lady Anne Clifford: countess of Pembroke, Dorset and Montgomery, 1590–1676* (1997) · R. T. Spence, 'Lady Anne Clifford, countess of Dorset, Pembroke and Montgomery (1590–1676): a reappraisal', *Northern History*, 15 (1979), 43–65 · G. C. Williamson, *Lady Anne Clifford* (1922) · J. P. Gilson, *Lives of Lady Anne Clifford, countess of Dorset, Pembroke and Montgomery (1590–1676), and of her parents* (1916) · *The diaries of Lady Anne Clifford*, ed. D. J. H. Clifford (1990) · J. W. Clay, 'The Clifford family', *Yorkshire Archaeological Journal*, 18 (1904–5), 354–411, esp. 400–11 · M. A. Holmes, *Proud northern lady: Lady Anne Clifford, 1590–1676* (1984) · *DNB* · GEC, *Peerage*
Archives Appleby Castle, Appleby triptych · Cumbria AS, Kendal, accounts and papers; corresp. and papers · Cumbria AS, Kendal, Great Books of Record, Book of Heraldry, 'A brief relation …' (voyages of her father, Earl George), Hothfield MSS, WD/Hoth · Yale U., Beinecke L., account book | BL, copies of her now lost diary, Harley MS 6177; Portland MS 24, Longleat · Bodl. Oxf., copies of notes from papers · CKS, Sackville and Tufton MSS · Cumbria AS, Carlisle, letters to Sir John Lowther · Dalemain, Cumbria, 1676 day book · PRO NIre., diary, D3044/G/5 · W. Yorks. AS, Leeds, Yorkshire Archaeological Society, Skipton MSS and Beamsley Hospital records
Likenesses attrib. P. Lely, oils, c.1605 (after portrait), priv. coll. · attrib. I. Oliver, miniature, c.1608–1609, priv. coll. · attrib. W. Larkin, oils, c.1610, Knole, Kent · W. Larkin, oils, 1618, Knole, Kent [*see illus.*] · attrib. P. van Somer, oils, c.1619, priv. coll. · oils, c.1619–1620, priv. coll. · H. T. Fattorini, oils, 1620 (after Van Somer) · attrib. G. Honthorst, oils, c.1629, priv. coll. · A. Van Dyck, group portrait, oils, 1636 (with the earl of Pembroke's family), Wilton House, Wiltshire · attrib. J. van Belcamp, oils, c.1648 ('Appleby Triptych'), Appleby Castle; version, NPG · attrib. P. Lely, oils, c.1648, priv. coll. · obverse, silver gilt medal, after 1649, BL · J. Bracken, oils, c.1675, Abbot Hall Art Gallery, Kendal, Cumbria · J. Bracken, oils (after oil painting by P. Lely?, c.1648); copies · R. White, line engraving (aged thirteen), BM
Wealth at death perhaps the wealthiest noblewoman in later Stuart England; £8000 p.a. gross rents, incl. jointure estates; £80,000 heritable estates at twenty years' purchase; £6400 lent, in bonds; est. £1500 chattels: Spence, *Lady Anne Clifford*, pp. 83, 111, 210–16

Clifford, Arthur (1777–1830), family historian, was born on 5 July 1777, the fourth son of the nine children of Thomas Clifford (1732–1787), fourth son of Hugh Clifford, third Lord Clifford of Chudleigh (1700–1732). His mother was Barbara Aston (1744–1786), youngest daughter and coheir of James, fifth Lord Aston of Forfar (1723–1751); through her the estate of Tixall, in Staffordshire, came into the Clifford family. With his twin brother, Lewis (*d.* 1806), Arthur Clifford became a pupil at the English College at Douai in September 1786; when the college was taken over by French revolutionary forces, both were imprisoned, with the professors and other students. After their release, they returned to England, and reached London in March 1795; Lewis later wrote a brief account of their captivity. After spending a term at Stonyhurst College, Arthur Clifford rejoined some of his former fellow prisoners at St Edmund's College, Old Hall Green, near Ware, in late 1795. In May or June 1809 he married Eliza Matilda (d. 1827), daughter of Captain John Macdonnell of Leagh, Inverness-shire; the couple had one daughter and two sons, the eldest of whom, Arthur Lewis (1818–1841), became a Jesuit.

In 1809 Clifford published *The State Papers and Letters of Sir Ralph Sadler* (2 vols.); Sadler's granddaughter Gertrude had married Sir Walter (later Lord) Aston (1584–1639) and Clifford drew his materials from original manuscripts found at Tixall. Allegedly stored in an old oaken box and preserved by female members of the family from destruction, the papers had been deciphered, copied, and generally prepared for publication by John Kirk (1760–1851) in the 1790s. Thus Clifford's part in the preparation of the collection for publication must have been relatively small, as Sir Walter Scott wrote both the memoir of Sadler's life and the historical notes that accompanied the work. These tasks interrupted Scott's writing of *Marmion* (1808), and involved the poet in correspondence with the Durham antiquary Robert Surtees (1779–1834). *The State Papers and Letters* received an unfavourable review in the *Edinburgh Review*, where the critic opined that 'its inaccuracy is still more remarkable than its beauty … the whole publication bears the marks of great negligence and precipitancy on the part of all concerned' (*EdinR*, 16, August 1810, 461). Nevertheless, it was a far more complete publication than the earlier 1720 collection of Sadler's papers.

At Tixall, Clifford also found letters and papers relating to the family of Sir Walter Aston; this discovery led to his publication in 1813 of *Tixall Poetry*, a collection of poems either written or transcribed by members of the Aston family, concluding with Clifford's own verses. Among these was his 'Midnight Meditation among the Ruins of Tixall', also published separately. *Tixall Poetry* was the subject of two complimentary essays in Nathan Drake's *Evenings in Autumn* (2 vols., 1822). Of more note, however, was Clifford's collection *Tixall letters, or, Correspondence of the Aston family and their friends during the seventeenth century* (1815), which sheds light on the family life of the seventeenth-century Catholic gentry. It includes interesting correspondence relating to Walter Aston's conversion to Roman Catholicism and the courtship by his son Herbert (promoted avidly by his sister Constantia) of his future wife, Catherine Thimelby, as well as the letters of Winefred Thimelby, an abbess in Louvain, to Herbert. Clifford also published *Collectanea Cliffordiana* (1817), a miscellany of material relating to his family, including a tragedy from his own pen; in the same year he also published, with his elder brother Sir Thomas Hugh Constable Clifford, *A Topographical and Historical Description of the Parish of Tixall*.

Both these works were published in Paris: Clifford's unfortunate experiences during the revolutionary years do not seem to have prejudiced him against France, as he lived and wrote for many years in the French capital. In addition to editing a paper for the French publisher Galignani, he also wrote guides for him to Paris (n.d.), France (1822), Italy (1823), and Switzerland (1823). He also seems to have acted as editor of the *Antiquities and Anecdotes of the City of Paris* (n.d.). Clifford also published (in Oxford) several works on the teaching of languages, especially Greek and Latin. He died at Winchester on 16 January 1830.   ROSEMARY MITCHELL

Sources Gillow, *Lit. biog. hist.* · Burke, *Peerage* (1907) · Burke, *Gen. GB* · *GM*, 1st ser., 100/1 (1830), 92, 274 · P. R. Harris, ed., *Douai College documents, 1639–1794*, Catholic RS, 63 (1972) · H. Chadwick, 'Seizure of the English College, Douai and imprisonment at Doullens, 1793–4: a contemporary narrative', *Recusant History*, 8 (1965–6), 147–57 · *The letters of Sir Walter Scott*, ed. H. J. C. Grierson and others, centenary edn, 12 vols. (1932–79), vols. 1–2, 12 · [M. Napier], 'Sadler's state papers', *EdinR*, 16 (1810), 447–64 · N. Drake, *Evenings in autumn*, 2 vols. (1822), 1.139–95 · J. Kirk, *Biographies of English Catholics in the eighteenth century*, ed. J. H. Pollen and E. Burton (1909) · G. Oliver, *Biography of the Scotch, English and Irish members of the Society of Jesus* (1845)
Archives William Salt Library, Stafford, collections relating to Tixall

Clifford, Sir Augustus William James, **first baronet** (1788–1877), naval officer and court official, was born abroad on 26 May 1788, the illegitimate son of William *Cavendish, fifth duke of Devonshire (1748–1811), and Lady Elizabeth Foster (1757–1824) [see Cavendish, Elizabeth Christiana], daughter of the fourth earl of Bristol and wife of John Thomas Foster MP (d. 1796); she married Cavendish on 19 October 1809. He was educated at Harrow School (1796–9). Throughout his career he benefited from the generosity of his half-brother, the sixth duke, who settled £2000 a year on him on their father's death in 1811, and an even more generous settlement at his marriage in 1813. He entered the navy as a midshipman in May 1800, under the auspices of Earl Spencer, then first lord of the Admiralty, and was promoted to a lieutenant in 1806. He served at the capture of St Lucia and Tobago in 1803, and throughout the operations in Egypt during 1807, and was involved in the capture of a convoy in the Bay of Rosas in 1809 (for which he received a medal), and in the operations on the coast of Italy in 1811 and 1812. After this, as captain, he was for many years actively employed in naval duties, being several times mentioned in the *London Gazette* for his courage in cutting-out expeditions and on other occasions. For some time he was in attendance on the lord high admiral, the duke of Clarence (afterwards William IV), and in 1828 he took Lord William Bentinck as governor-general to India. This was his last service afloat, and he was not actively employed after 1831.

Clifford obtained the rank of rear-admiral in 1848, vice-admiral in 1855, admiral of the blue on 7 November 1860, and admiral of the red in 1864, becoming retired admiral on 31 March 1866. He was whig MP for the duke of Devonshire's Irish pocket boroughs: Bandon Bridge (1818–20), Dungarvan (1820–22), and Bandon Bridge again (23 July 1831 to 3 December 1832). He was nominated CB on 8 December 1815, knighted on 4 August 1830, and created a baronet on 4 August 1838.

The duke of Devonshire, then lord chamberlain, appointed Clifford on 25 July 1832 gentleman usher of the black rod, which office he held, much to his satisfaction, until his death. On various occasions between 1843 and 1866 he acted as deputy lord great chamberlain of England, in the absence of Lord Willoughby d'Eresby. He was a patron of the arts, and formed a collection of paintings, sculpture, etchings, engravings, and *bijouterie*. He died at his residence, Royal Court, in the House of Lords on 8 February 1877.

On 20 October 1813, Clifford had married Lady Elizabeth Frances Townshend, sister of John, fourth Marquess Townshend. She was born on 2 August 1789, and died at Nice on 10 April 1862. They had three sons and two daughters; Captain William John Cavendish Clifford RN (1814–1882) succeeded his father as second baronet. The baronetcy became extinct in 1895.

G. C. BOASE, *rev.* ROGER MORRISS

Sources P. J. Jupp, 'Clifford, Augustus William James', HoP, *Commons* · O'Byrne, *Naval biog. dict.* · *The Times* (9 Feb 1877), 5 · *The Times* (12 Feb 1877), 8 · *The Graphic* (24 Feb 1877), 172, 179 · *ILN* (17 Feb 1877), 167 · *ILN* (24 Feb 1877), 171, 181 · Boase, *Mod. Eng. biog.* · *CGPLA Eng. & Wales* (1878)
Archives Bodl. Oxf., MS 'Sketch of the life of the sixth duke of Devonshire' · NMM, logbook
Likenesses W. Gillier, mezzotint, pubd 1844 (after F. R. Say), BM, NPG · G. Hayter, group portrait, oils (*The christening of HRH Prince of Wales*, 1842), Royal Collection · Lacretelle, etching, NPG · portrait, repro. in *The Graphic* · portrait, repro. in *ILN*, 70 (17 Feb 1877), 167 · wood-engraving, repro. in *ILN* (24 Feb 1877), 171, 181
Wealth at death under £200,000: resworn probate, Feb 1878, *CGPLA Eng. & Wales*

Clifford, Sir Bede Edmund Hugh (1890–1969), colonial governor, was born on 3 July 1890 on his father's sheep farm in the South Island of New Zealand. He was the third and youngest son of William Hugh Clifford (1858–1943), later tenth Baron Clifford of Chudleigh, and his wife, Catherine Mary, daughter of R. Bassett, a New Zealander. His mother died when he was very young, and he moved with his father from one unsuccessful farm to another. At an early age he displayed outstanding intelligence with an unorthodox bent. Although he entered a Melbourne boarding-school at the age of ten without knowing the alphabet, he became the star pupil. After a brief spell at Melbourne University he joined a firm of surveyors in Western Australia, but eventually signed on as fourth officer on a tramp steamer, of which his brother was the navigating officer, in order to reach England. He took the opportunity to master the use of the sextant for solar and stellar observations.

On the outbreak of war in 1914 Clifford enlisted in the Royal Fusiliers and soon gained his commission. He was gassed and invalided and in 1917 was appointed aide-de-camp to Sir Ronald Munro-Ferguson (later Viscount Novar), governor-general of Australia. He was quickly promoted to the more congenial position of private secretary (1918–20) and was therefore privileged to meet with many famous figures. He accompanied Admiral Jellicoe on an inspection of the outlying defences of Australia, and for his services during the visit of the prince of Wales was appointed MVO. In 1921 Clifford was selected by Lord Milner as secretary to Prince Arthur of Connaught,

governor-general of South Africa. J. C. Smuts, the prime minister, quickly appreciated Clifford's ability and consulted him on imperial problems.

In 1924 Clifford was appointed secretary to Prince Arthur's successor, the earl of Athlone; but in the same year he became imperial secretary to the South African high commission. The protectorates of Bechuanaland, Swaziland, and Basutoland being under his jurisdiction, he immediately carried out a detailed tour. In 1925 he married Alice Devin (*d.* 1980), daughter of John Murton Gundry, an eminent banker, of Cleveland, Ohio. His very beautiful and highly talented wife played a most important role in helping him in their arduous public life. They had three daughters famous for their beauty and wit.

In 1928 Clifford became the first white man to cross the Kalahari Desert, a fine feat of navigation. In 1929 and 1931 he surveyed the boundaries and determined the size of the Great Makarikari salt lake for a possible railway route from Southern Rhodesia to Walvis Bay. In the meantime J. B. M. Hertzog had applied for Clifford to be appointed (1928) first representative of the United Kingdom to the Union of South Africa. He was able to persuade Hertzog to defer constitutional changes until after he had attended the prime ministers' conference; and by subtle argument he persuaded the government to join in financing the Imperial Airways link with South Africa in spite of strong German competition. For his services in South Africa, Clifford was appointed CMG in 1923 and CB in 1931.

At the end of 1931 Clifford was appointed governor of the Bahamas, the youngest governor in the colonial service. Owing to his imagination and initiative in encouraging the development of the tourist industry the prosperity of the islands was greatly increased. He was promoted KCMG in 1933. In 1937 a visit to Germany convinced Clifford that war was inevitable. In the same year he was appointed governor of Mauritius, and during a visit to Diego Suarez *en route*, he made a careful study of the harbour defences which helped in its eventual capture.

On arrival in Mauritius, Clifford stimulated research for the improvement of the sugar and pineapple industries. In case of war, he laid in large stocks of coal, so that the railways could be maintained. He developed the hydroelectric and irrigation resources: a lasting contribution. He provided machinery for the regulation of wages and working conditions. His handling of industrial disputes was unorthodox but effective. When the docks were picketed to prevent the loading of sugar for export Clifford had a labour force recruited from the plantations. The men were transported in closed railway wagons into the port area with sufficient equipment and supplies to be self-supporting, and the strike was broken.

In 1942 Clifford was appointed governor of Trinidad, a very sensitive area in the U-boat campaign. His principal task was to resolve friction which had arisen between the resident British and American admirals, and this he was able to do with tact and firmness. In appreciation he was awarded the Legion of Merit by the United States government. He was able also to negotiate a most satisfactory agreement with Venezuela over the demarcation of the sea bed of the gulf between the two countries for oil exploration and exploitation. Clifford was most solicitous for the large numbers of survivors from vessels sunk by U-boats and at times up to four and five hundred were in the clearing stations.

Clifford was appointed GCMG in 1945 and in the next year his medical advisers told him that he should cease to work in the tropics. In his retirement he loved travelling. He enjoyed being his own builder and electrician and designed and partly built the small house in which he and his wife lived. He was an insatiable reader, his favourite author being Herodotus. In 1964 his autobiography *Proconsul* was published. In addition he advised and edited *For my Grandchildren* by Princess Alice, countess of Athlone (1966). He was writing a radio play, 'Cyrus the Great', and a history of the Clifford family at the time of his death. He died at Queen Anne Farm, Jacob's Well, Guildford, on 6 October 1969 and was buried in the family vault at Ugbrooke Park, Chudleigh, Devon.   H. A. SMITH, *rev.*

Sources B. Clifford, *Proconsul* (1964) · private information (1981) · *WWW* · *The Times* (8 Oct 1969) · Burke, *Peerage* · personal knowledge (1981)
Archives NRA, priv. coll., corresp. and papers | NL Aus., corresp. with Viscount Novar
Likenesses A. F. M. Clifford, oils

Clifford, Camilla Antoinetta [Camille] (*c.*1885–1971), actress, was born in Belgium, the daughter of Reynold Clifford. She was brought up in New York and became a chorus girl, appearing in 1902 in the musical comedy *The Defender* at the Herald Square Theater in New York. In 1903 she won a beauty contest to find a Miss New York, organized by Charles Dana Gibson, the popular illustrator, whose drawings of 'the American Girl' from 1890 onwards had idealized American womanhood and had led millions of young women to copy her 'look'. When *The Prince of Pilsen*, a musical comedy by Frank Pixley, opened at the Broadway Theater, New York, in March 1903, Camille Clifford appeared in the chorus representing New York in 'The American Girl', also known as 'The Song of the Cities', in which a succession of girls paraded across the stage, each representing a different American city: they became known as the 'Gibson girls'.

When *The Prince of Pilsen* opened at the Shaftesbury Theatre in London in May 1904, Camille Clifford, with her hourglass figure (and reputedly an 11 inch waist) was a sensation: after the show closed at the end of September and the company returned to the United States she remained in London to join the cast of *The Catch of the Season* by Seymour Hicks and Cosmo Hamilton. A musical comedy based on the story of Cinderella, this had opened a few weeks earlier at the Vaudeville Theatre. The characters included a Mr. William Gibson and his ten tall daughters, who paraded across the stage singing:

Seeing we were proving a sensation
We thought we might become a bigger one
By walking in single file
In the Dana Gibson style.

We realize the pictures, tall and divinely fair,
By society invited, we go everywhere,

We've copied every detail, dress, stately walk, and curls
And everybody calls us 'Dana Gibson Girls'.

Wearing very beautiful clothes designed by Lady Duff-Gordon following the fashions sketched by Charles Dana Gibson, and made by her firm, Mme Lucille of Hanover Square, the Gibson Girls became the most popular feature of the show when Camille Clifford took on the role of Miss Sylvia Gibson, appearing in a number, 'The Gibson Girl', written specially for her. Although her singing voice was non-existent, she was given a few lines to speak, and a new song, which declared:

As she comes strolling down she sets their hearts in a whirl
She is the cutest little pearl, Sylvia, the Gibson Girl.

The Catch of the Season was followed in 1906 by a new musical comedy, *The Belle of Mayfair* by C. H. Brookfield and Cosmo Hamilton, a modern *Romeo and Juliet*, which opened at the Vaudeville Theatre in April 1906. In a part written specially for her Clifford played the Duchess of Dunmow, the American wife of an English duke, and was given a song 'Why do they Call me a Gibson Girl', and also sang 'I'm a duchess'. Her billing as 'the Original Gibson Girl' attracted so much publicity that the leading lady, Edna May, walked out of the show.

Camille Clifford retired from the stage at the end of 1906 after touring in *A Grand Flying Matinee*, and on 11 October 1906 married the Hon. Henry Lyndhurst Bruce (1881–1914), eldest son of Henry Campbell Bruce, second Baron Aberdare. They had one daughter, Margaret, born in 1909, who died in infancy. A captain in the 3rd battalion, the Royal Scots, her husband was killed in action in December 1914. After his death she returned briefly to the stage, appearing in the music-hall *The Girl of the Future* in 1916, but retired again in 1917 on her marriage on 9 August 1917 to Captain John Meredyth Jones Evans MC (*b.* 1894), of the Royal Welch Fusiliers, son of Owen Lloyd Jones Evans of Broom Hall, Caernarfon. She was a widow when she died on 28 June 1971 at her home, Wishanger Lodge, Headley, near Alton, Hampshire.   ANNE PIMLOTT BAKER

Sources K. Gänzl, *The encyclopedia of the musical theatre* (1994) · K. Gänzl, *The British musical theatre*, 1 (1986) · E. V. Gillon and H. C. Pitz, *The Gibson Girl and her America* (1969) · Burke, *Peerage* · F. Downey, *Portrait of an era: as drawn by C. D. Gibson* (1936) · d. cert. · m. cert. [Henry Lyndhurst Bruce] · F. Gaye, ed., *Who's who in the theatre*, 14th edn (1967) · CGPLA Eng. & Wales (1971)
Likenesses three postcard photographs, 1906, repro. in www. collectorspost.com, 7 Oct 2002
Wealth at death £118,494: probate, 6 July 1971, CGPLA Eng. & Wales

Clifford, Sir Conyers (*d.* 1599), soldier and president of Connacht, was the eldest son of George Clifford of Bobbing Court in Kent and his wife, Ursula, daughter of Roger Finch. William, Richard, Thomas, and Conyers Clifford went to Ireland as a family group in the 1570s (the precise relationship between them is unknown), and settled in co. Roscommon under the auspices of the Connacht presidency. William was sufficiently well established as a landowner by 1585 to be allowed concessions in the 1585 composition agreement. Conyers was attached to Roscommon Castle while serving with Sir Nicholas Malby during the early 1580s. However, his military experience was limited and was gained mainly while serving in Europe, usually under the earl of Essex. He was taken prisoner at Lisle in September 1588 but was exchanged for a Spanish prisoner. He was praised for his 'forwardness and good directions' when serving as a captain under Essex during the siege of Rouen in 1591 and was knighted in that year. Through his association with Essex, Clifford represented Pembroke borough in the parliament of 1593. Together with his brother Nicholas he was conferred with the degree of MA by the University of Cambridge at a special congregation in 1594/5. He married, after 1594, Mary, daughter of Francis Southwell, of Wymondham Hall, Norfolk, widow of Thomas Sydney of Kent and of Nicholas Gorges of London (d. 1594). They had two sons, Henry and Conyers, and a daughter, Frances, who died young. Clifford's wife survived him, and subsequently married Sir Anthony St Leger; she died on 19 December 1603, aged thirty-seven.

Clifford again served with Essex in 1596 during the Spanish siege of Calais. He was sergeant-major in the expedition against Cadiz later in the same year, had charge of the *Dreadnaught* with Alexander Clifford, and served on the council. His share of the plunder, £3256, was among the highest recorded. The Nine Years' War was in progress in Ireland when Clifford was appointed chief commissioner of Connacht on 2 December 1596. Having arrived in Dublin on 4 January 1597, he was dispatched to Connacht on 8 February to replace the suspended Sir Richard Bingham. He was effective in limiting the impact on Connacht of the war in Ulster, although hampered by the numbers of Irish in the ranks of his soldiers. He was respected by the Irish as 'better and more faithful to his promises' than Bingham had been (Ó Clérigh, 1.133). He recaptured Sligo Castle from O'Donnell in March 1597, but was defeated at Ballyshannon in July–August in an attempted two-pronged military offensive on Ulster.

Officially appointed president of Connacht with effect from 1 January 1598 (by letters patent dated 4 September 1597), Clifford was normally based at Athlone Castle thereafter. His annual fee was £140 and he had a lease of the manor and demesnes of Athlone and Ballymote, and of the abbey of Boyle. He regarded his instructions for the civil government of Connacht as impractical until military victory had been achieved in Ulster. In summer 1599 he led a military expedition north towards Collooney to relieve O'Connor Sligo, then being besieged by Hugh O'Donnell. On 5 August 1599 Clifford was fatally shot by O'Donnell's supporters in an ambush in the Curlew Mountains just north of Boyle, co. Roscommon. Over 200 of his soldiers were killed in the ambush. His body was buried in the monastery at Trinity Island in Loch Lough, but his head was taken to Collooney by Brian Oge O'Rourke to be displayed before O'Connor Sligo as a trophy. The King family erected a small tower to mark the spot where Clifford died in the townland of Garroo.

BERNADETTE CUNNINGHAM

Sources CSP Ire., 1596–1600 • The Irish fiants of the Tudor sovereigns, 4 vols. (1994) • L. Ó Clérigh, The life of Aodh Ruadh Ó Domhnaill, ed. P. Walsh and C. Ó Lochlainn, 2 vols., ITS, 42, 45 (1948–57) • R. Lascelles, ed., Liber munerum publicorum Hiberniae … or, The establishments of Ireland, 2 vols. [1824–30] • T. Cronin, 'The Elizabethan colony in co. Roscommon', ed. H. Murtagh, Irish Midland Studies (1980), 107–20 • Venn, Alum. Cant., 1/1 • HoP, Commons, 1558–1603, 1.615–16 • W. B. Devereux, Lives and letters of the Devereux, earls of Essex … 1540–1646, 2 vols. (1853) • C. Falls, Elizabeth's Irish wars (1950) • T. Coningsby, 'Journal of the siege of Rouen, 1591', ed. J. G. Nichols, Camden miscellany, I, CS, 39 (1847), 64 • CSP dom., 1581–90 • A. M. Freeman, ed., The compossicion booke of Conought (1936) • PRO, SP/63 • W. A. Shaw, The knights of England, 2 vols. (1906) • DNB

Clifford, Francis, fourth earl of Cumberland (1559–1641), nobleman, was born on 30 October 1559 at Skipton Castle in Craven in the West Riding of Yorkshire, the younger son of Henry *Clifford, second earl of Cumberland (1517–1570), and his second wife, Anne (c.1538–1581), youngest daughter of William Dacre, third Baron Dacre of Gilsland. He was privately tutored. In 1576 he roomed at Clifford's Inn and in 1583–4 was admitted to Gray's Inn but by his own confession was 'unlearned in the Lawes of this Realme' and could not 'reade or understand any lattyn conveyance' (Spence, *Privateering Earl*, 37).

In 1580 Clifford inherited widespread properties in Yorkshire and Derbyshire but sold most of his manorial lands in the latter county to meet his expenses accompanying his spendthrift courtier brother George *Clifford, third earl. However, in 1587 he assured his social status by purchasing from his brother the reversion of Londesborough and other East Riding manors which he already held on a life interest from his father. In June 1589 he married Grissell (bap. 1559, d. 1613), elder daughter of Thomas Hughes of Uxbridge, Middlesex, and widow of Edward Neville, Lord Bergavenny. He built Londesborough House for her, which remained his family's seat until 1643. They had four children, George (b. 1590), Henry *Clifford, fifth earl, Margaret, who married Sir Thomas Wentworth, and Frances, second wife of Sir Gervase Clifton of Clifton, Nottinghamshire, from whom the latter's family descended.

Clifford was busily employed in his brother's financial and estate affairs and as his steward in Craven. He was a justice of the peace in the East Riding from 1592, sheriff of Yorkshire in 1600, member of the council in the north from 1601, and joint constable and steward of Knaresborough from 1604. He sat in the Commons as member for Westmorland in 1584–7 and for Yorkshire in 1604–5 and was created knight of the Bath on 6 January 1605. Succeeding to the earldom in 1605 brought him a *damnosa hereditas* of his brother George's great debts, impaired estates, and a costly twelve-year dispute over the inheritance with Anne Herbert (née Clifford). He restored the Clifford houses, revitalized estate management—both neglected by his brother—and developed coal, iron, and lead mining. He demonstrated his standing as the north's premier resident nobleman with feasting at Londesborough and Skipton Castle, and especially by entertaining James I and his court in August 1617 at Carlisle and his own Brougham Castle, the famous Brougham feast. His ultimate success in the inheritance quarrel was a pyrrhic victory because the king's award settlement in 1617 required him to pay

£17,000, which incurred a burden of new debts from which he, and his son Henry, never escaped.

The earl was heavily engaged in northern administration, as *custos rotulorum* of Cumberland and hereditary sheriff of Westmorland from 1606, joint lord lieutenant of Cumberland from 1607, and of Northumberland, Westmorland, and Newcastle upon Tyne from 1611. He helped complete the work started by the third earl in pacifying the borders, supporting his fellow lieutenant George Hume, earl of Dunbar (*d.* 1611), and the middle shires commissioners. Complementary to this was his firm control of the long-disordered crown border properties which his brother George and he purchased or held in lease. This raised land values and brought prosperity. In 1611 he claimed with pride that he had 'helpt to beare the Brunt of the day' (*CSP dom.*, 1611–18, 24). He exercised parliamentary patronage in Westmorland and Appleby and Carlisle boroughs. In 1619 his heir, Henry, took over their joint lieutenancy responsibilities.

Cumberland was a tall, dark-haired, slender man, reserved by nature and rather colourless. He had literary interests, some of his inscribed books surviving in the Devonshire collections. His passion was music and drama. He was a patron of the composers William Byrd and Thomas Campion, and supported from their youth the composer George Mason and organist and composer John Hingeston, both members of his own small orchestra. He warmly welcomed travelling groups of players. Indeed, Campion described Londesborough as 'the Muses Pallace' (Spence, 'A royal progress', 59). Cumberland died at Skipton Castle on 28 January 1641 and was buried with noble ceremony in Holy Trinity Church, Skipton. No monument was erected to him. There is a full-length portrait of him by Augustine Harrison (1610).　RICHARD T. SPENCE

Sources R. T. Spence, *The privateering earl* (1995) · R. T. Spence, *Lady Anne Clifford: countess of Pembroke, Dorset and Montgomery, 1590–1676* (1997) · R. T. Spence, 'The pacification of the Cumberland borders, 1593–1628', *Northern History*, 13 (1977), 59–160 · R. T. Spence, 'A royal progress in the north: James I at Carlisle Castle and the feast of Brougham, August 1617', *Northern History*, 27 (1991), 41–89 · R. T. Spence, 'The backward north modernized? The Cliffords, earls of Cumberland, and the socage manor of Carlisle, 1611–1643', *Northern History*, 20 (1984), 64–87 · R. T. Spence, 'Mining and smelting in Yorkshire by the Cliffords, earls of Cumberland, in the Tudor and early Stuart period', *Yorkshire Archaeological Journal*, 64 (1992), 157–83 · R. T. Spence, 'Mining and smelting by the Cliffords, earls of Cumberland, in Westmorland in the early seventeenth century', *Transactions of the Cumberland and Westmorland Antiquarian and Archaeological Society*, [new ser.,] 91 (1991), 101–17 · W. Yorks. AS, Leeds, Yorkshire Archaeological Society, Skipton MSS · Chatsworth House, Derbyshire, Devonshire collections, Londesborough MSS · *CSP dom.*, 1603–18 · T. D. Whitaker, *The history and antiquities of the deanery of Craven, in the county of York*, 3rd edn, ed. A. W. Morant (1878) · J. P. Cooper, ed., *Wentworth papers, 1597–1628*, CS, 4th ser., 12 (1973) · J. W. Clay, 'The Clifford family', *Yorkshire Archaeological Journal*, 18 (1904–5), 354–411

Archives U. Hull, Brynmor Jones L., accounts | Chatsworth House, Derbyshire, Devonshire collections, Bolton MSS · Chatsworth House, Derbyshire, Devonshire collections, Currey MSS · Chatsworth House, Derbyshire, Devonshire collections, Hardwick MSS · Chatsworth House, Derbyshire, Devonshire collections, Londesborough MSS · W. Yorks. AS, Leeds, West Yorkshire Archaeological Society, Skipton MSS

Likenesses A. Harrison, oils, 1610, Skipton Castle, Yorkshire · A. Harrison, portrait, 1610, priv. coll.

Clifford, Frederick (1828–1904), journalist and legal writer, was born at Gillingham, Kent, on 22 June 1828, the fifth son of Jesse Clifford and his wife, Mary Pearse. After private schooling he engaged in provincial journalism, but settled in London in 1852, and joined the parliamentary staff of *The Times*, of which his elder brother George was already a member. He retained his connection with the provinces by acting as London correspondent of the *Sheffield Daily Telegraph*, and in 1863 he became its joint proprietor with William Christopher Leng (1825–1902). In 1866 he went to Jamaica to report for *The Times* on the royal commission of inquiry into the conduct of the governor, Edward Eyre. He helped in 1868 to found the Press Association, an institution formed to supply newspaper proprietors of London and the provinces with home and foreign news, and he acted as chairman of the committee of management during two periods of five years each, finally retiring in 1880. In 1877, owing to the failing health of the editor, John Thaddeus Delane, Clifford was transferred by *The Times* from the reporters' gallery of the House of Commons to the central offices at Printing House Square, and he acted as assistant editor until his health obliged him to resign in 1883.

Clifford also pursued a career as a legal writer. He was admitted to the Middle Temple on 3 November 1856, and was called to the bar on 10 June 1859. With Pembroke S. Stephens KC, he published *The Practice of the Court of Referees on Private Bills in Parliament* (1870), which became the standard textbook on the subject. It also brought him work at the parliamentary bar. The historical aspect of the practice especially interested him, and he later published *The History of Private Bill Legislation* (2 vols., 1885–7). This was a valuable and painstaking account, which revealed the largely public aims of private bill legislation over the course of more than three centuries. It remained the most significant work in its field until O. C. William's *Historical Development of Private Bill Procedure* (1948). Clifford took silk in 1894, and was elected a bencher of his inn on 18 May 1900.

Early in his career Clifford co-operated with Edward Bulwer-Lytton, Charles Dickens, and other men of letters and artists in forming the Guild of Literature and Art, which was incorporated by private act of parliament in 1858. Clifford was a member of the council. The guild did not succeed in its aims, and Clifford and Sir John Richard Robinson, the last surviving members of the council, wound up its affairs in 1897. Clifford was an active member of the Royal Botanic Society, and a student of agricultural questions, publishing *The Agricultural Lockout of 1874* (1875) and a small treatise on the Agricultural Holdings Act of 1875 (1876). He was also a collector of fans and other works of art.

Clifford married Caroline (*d.* 1900), third daughter of Thomas Mason of Hull, in 1853. He died at his residence, 24 Collingham Gardens, South Kensington, London, on 30

December 1904; four sons and two daughters survived him. His library formed a three days' sale at Sothebys (5–7 May 1905).   C. E. A. BEDWELL, *rev.* JOSEPH COOHILL

Sources *The Times* (31 Dec 1904) · *The Times* (2 Jan 1905) · *Sheffield Daily Telegraph* (31 Dec 1904) · *Men and women of the time* (1899) · [S. Morison and others], *The history of The Times*, 2 (1939), 513–15 · J. Foster, *Men-at-the-bar: a biographical hand-list of the members of the various inns of court*, 2nd edn (1885) · D. L. Rydz, *The parliamentary agents: a history* (1979)
Archives Bodl. Oxf., corresp. and papers
Likenesses E. Mortwell, portrait, priv. coll.
Wealth at death £191,373 18s. 5d.: probate, 22 Feb 1905, *CGPLA Eng. & Wales*

Clifford, George, third earl of Cumberland (1558–1605), courtier and privateer, was born on 8 August 1558 in Brougham Castle, Westmorland, the eldest son of Henry *Clifford, second earl of Cumberland (1517–1570), and his second wife, Anne (*c.*1538–1581), daughter of William, third Baron Dacre. He spent his early years on his father's estates near his birthplace, and at Skipton Castle in Yorkshire; his education at this stage was Roman Catholic. In January 1570 his father died and George inherited the title and estate, although since he was under age he became a ward of the crown. The wardship was granted to Francis Russell, second earl of Bedford, with whom George's father had already been in negotiations concerning the boy's marriage to one of Bedford's daughters. George therefore went to live among the devoutly protestant Russells at Chenies in Hertfordshire. In 1571 he became a student at Trinity College, Cambridge, with the master and future archbishop of Canterbury, John Whitgift, as his tutor. According to his daughter Anne *Clifford, who was his first biographer, it was his love of mathematics which led him to take an interest in navigation. Having graduated MA at Cambridge in 1576, he may also have undertaken a more informal course of study at Oxford.

Husband and courtier On 24 June 1577 in the church of St Saviour, Southwark, in the presence of the queen, Cumberland wed Lady Margaret Russell [see Clifford, Margaret, countess of Cumberland (1560–1616)], the daughter of his guardian, the earl of Bedford. This marriage had long been planned by the families. They had a daughter, Anne, and two sons, Francis and George, both of whom died young. The marriage is reckoned not to have been happy, although the evidence of letters the earl wrote from time to time to his 'sweet Meg' suggests that this was not always the case. The countess worried about the immense debts her spendthrift husband built up and described her life as 'a dance to the pilgrimage of grief' (Williamson, *George, Third Earl of Cumberland*, 285), which suggests a depressive character. The earl had at least two illegitimate children with different mistresses. At some point in the 1590s the couple began to live apart, although a reconciliation was effected as Clifford lay dying and after he had written begging his wife's forgiveness.

His education and marriage complete, Cumberland became a courtier of Queen Elizabeth. He was never a major political figure under Elizabeth, and was not given a

George Clifford, third earl of Cumberland (1558–1605), by Nicholas Hilliard, *c.*1590

place on her privy council; he did not receive, to his chagrin, a military command under the queen, nor could he be described as one of her most powerful favourites. Nevertheless, he was a most loyal courtier and played an important ceremonial role at court. He enjoyed royal favour, and the distinction of a royal nickname; he was Elizabeth's 'rogue'. It seems likely that the queen underestimated Clifford's abilities, but it is understandable perhaps that she should. His most important promotion at court was achieved in 1590, when he was made the queen's champion, a position he held until her death. The main duties involved in this post were to perform at the jousts, especially those held annually to commemorate the queen's accession, when he also gave a speech, some examples of which have survived. Clifford entered enthusiastically into the rich life of a courtier. To quote his puritanical daughter, who perhaps was remembering her mother's views on this: he had 'an extreme love for horse races, tiltings, bowling matches and shooting … and hunting, and all such expensive sports did contribute the more to the wasting of his estate' (Williamson, *George, Third Earl of Cumberland*, 17). He played a more serious role in affairs from time to time, sitting in 1586 on the commission which tried Mary, queen of Scots, and attending her execution the following year at Fotheringhay.

Privateer It was partly to recoup some of his losses as a gambler and a courtier that in 1586 Cumberland began his career as a privateer. The war with Spain was just beginning, and Cumberland was also keen to do his patriotic duty and win honour and glory in the maritime sphere, which had interested him since his student days. The first privateering venture he financed he did not himself accompany. Four ships, including two which he had just purchased, the *Red Dragon* and the *Bark Clifford*, sailed from Gravesend under Robert Withrington, with instructions to emulate Drake and sail round the Horn to the south seas, where much valuable plunder was to be had. Instead the small fleet turned back without leaving the Atlantic, and gained a few minor prizes off Brazil at the loss of a number of lives. The venture was a considerable waste of money.

The escalating conflict with Spain allowed Cumberland to gain his first personal taste of naval action. In 1587 he sailed across the channel in an attempt to help protect Sluys from the duke of Parma. He arrived too late to prevent the fall of Sluys and instead visited the earl of Leicester's camp at Bergen-op-Zoom. Cumberland played a brave part in the Armada campaign of 1588, offering his two ships for service in the English fleet, and serving himself on board a royal ship, the *Elizabeth Bonaventure*. He was included in Howard's council of war, fought courageously at the battle off Gravelines, and after the Spanish had retreated north of Harwich he was sent by the admiral to report to the queen at Tilbury. He then returned to the fleet, to help guard against any attempt by Parma to invade from the Netherlands. The earl completed this eventful year by setting out on the first privateering voyage which he himself accompanied, commanded, and financed. The queen lent two royal ships for this expedition, which was intended to intercept enemy shipping in the channel. Cumberland took one insignificant prize, but the royal ship the *Golden Lion* lost its mast while at anchor in a storm.

During the next ten years Cumberland engaged, either as commander or as promoter, in a privateering voyage every year. The expedition of 1589 was, unusually, a financial success, although with more luck it might have been much more lucrative still. Cumberland commanded the *Victory*, a royal ship, and took three of his own. He was accompanied by two professional naval commanders, Christopher Lister and William Monson, the latter a man with whom he was to work on other occasions, and with whom he later quarrelled violently. They sailed for the Azores, but narrowly missed intercepting both the Portuguese carracks returning from the East Indies and the Spanish silver fleet sailing from the West. They did take one very rich prize, worth apparently £100,000, but it sank in a storm in Mount's Bay, off Cornwall, as it was being escorted home. Nevertheless, some of its cargo was salvaged, and this, together with the other vessels taken and the proceeds from pillaging Santa Cruz, in the Azores, enabled Cumberland to make a profit on this expedition. He showed his bravery during the voyage, being wounded in an action at St Marie in the Azores, and sharing the considerable suffering of his men as they struggled home with low stocks of water and the wind against them.

In 1590 Cumberland financed two small privateering ventures, which sailed without him and probably broke even financially. The expedition of 1591 he accompanied himself. It involved an attempt to blockade the coast of Spain, while Lord Thomas Howard patrolled the Azores awaiting the Portuguese carracks. Cumberland did not show a profit on this expedition, although his action in dispatching one of his ships to warn Howard of the approach of a Spanish fleet saved much of the Royal Navy from danger. In 1592 Cumberland, undaunted by his previous financial failures, planned to take an expedition across the Atlantic and to harry the Spanish West Indies. He was held up at Plymouth for three months by bad weather, thus missing the chance to cross the ocean, and when the fleet departed with the more limited goal of the Azores, he did not accompany it; it was led instead by John Norton. It joined up with a royal fleet under Sir John Burgh, and together they captured the great Portuguese carrack the *Madre de Dios* and her cargo of spices, silks, and jewels, estimated to be worth £500,000. Much of the profit from the voyage was lost, plundered by the sailors, and the queen claimed the main share of what was left. This led to a rather bitter dispute between Elizabeth and Cumberland, which ended in the earl's recovering £36,000, which eased his financial position a little while tempting him to continue to try his luck as a privateer.

The following year Cumberland understandably set off for the Azores again, hoping to net another carrack. The voyage was cut short, however, by the earl's illness. He was close to death and his life was only saved by Captain Monson, at great personal risk, securing a cow from the island of Corvo in order to supply him with milk. The bulk of the fleet turned for home to enable their leader to recover his health. In 1594 Cumberland, who from now on worked increasingly closely with syndicates of London merchants, dispatched another fleet to the Azores. It came tantalizingly close to capturing two great carracks, the *Cince Chagas* of 2000 tons, and the *San Felipe* of 1500 tons; but the first ship sank after being set on fire in the fight, and the second fought off the privateers. The losses to the earl on this expedition were considerable. Undaunted by this reverse, he commissioned late in 1594 the building at Deptford of the largest ship ever built by an English subject, the 600 ton *Malice Scourge*, which cost £6000. The expedition of 1595 was a somewhat limited affair, which the earl did not accompany, but the *Malice Scourge* was at least given her sea trials.

Weighed down with debts, Cumberland suffered two further barren years. Efforts to prosecute a successful expedition early in 1596 were frustrated when the queen ordered him to return to England to station himself off Dover for defensive purposes as the Spanish attacked Calais. The following year his voyage was cut short again, this time when the *Malice Scourge* lost her main mast in a storm no more than 40 leagues out at sea, and was forced to limp home for repairs.

Puerto Rico, 1598, and last years In 1598 Cumberland set out on his last and most glorious expedition, financed by him and his London merchant backers. He took a substantial fleet of twenty vessels, six of which he owned himself, with 1000 seamen and 700 soldiers. After taking a few prizes on the way, the fleet arrived in the West Indies, where Cumberland succeeded in taking San Juan de Puerto Rico. This town had been previously attacked unsuccessfully in 1595 by Drake. Cumberland displayed considerable military skill in devising a successful means of capturing this strongly defended town. He entered the thick of the fighting and would have drowned, having fallen in full armour into a defensive moat, had he not been rescued by one of his officers. The capture of the port proved to be of no great value, however. Like many English strategists, Cumberland had high hopes of establishing a permanent settlement in the West Indies from which to attack the Spanish. But the reality was very different. His men began to die of dysentery in increasing numbers, and in the end he was forced to abandon his conquest and sail home, with very little plunder to show for his expensive investment. He had, however, succeeded in disrupting the economy of the great Spanish empire: as a result of his raid the plate fleet did not sail to Spain in 1598. Although this was the last privateering expedition of the earl, he continued to take an interest in maritime matters; in 1601, when the East India Company was founded, he was one of the original members, and his ship the *Malice Scourge* was commissioned as one of the first merchantmen employed by the company.

Cumberland's last years were spent in desperate efforts to clear his debts. He seems to have become, rather late in life, more responsible, surprising his friends with a new restraint as a gambler. He began a concerted effort with his estate officials to recover some control over his lands. A process of renegotiating the terms on which his property was leased began, in the course of which large sums of money were raised, which were then used to pay off his debts. He remained active in the life of the court at the end of Elizabeth's reign, sitting on the commission which condemned his friend the earl of Essex in 1601. He was able to transfer his loyalty successfully from Elizabeth to James I. In 1603 he rode north to welcome the new king into his kingdom. James was quick to recognize the value of Cumberland, and appointed him to his privy council. The earl was given an important role to play in the new Stuart settlement of the Anglo-Scottish border. He was appointed warden of the west and middle marches and applied himself assiduously to the pacification of this area, a project which was greatly assisted by the union of the two crowns, and in which as a landowner on the border he had a personal stake.

Cumberland had lived a full and unhealthy life. He died from 'a bloody flux' (Spence, 215)—probably dysentery—on 29 October 1605 at the duchy house by the Savoy in London. Not being survived by any of his sons, in his will he left his lands and titles to his brother Francis *Clifford, which would be the cause of a major dispute when his daughter Anne questioned this settlement. He was buried on 29 December 1605 in the family vault at Holy Trinity, Skipton.

There are many portraits of Cumberland, which show him resplendent as a dazzling aristocratic courtier. Perhaps the best example hangs in the National Maritime Museum; the work of Nicholas Hilliard, it depicts Cumberland as the queen's champion, his hat adorned with the jewelled glove given to him by Elizabeth as a token. Two centuries ago the great antiquary William Whitaker took a look at his embalmed body in the crypt of Skipton church and reported with relish that the portraitists had none of them shown the three warts on his cheek. The judgement of Whitaker on the character and achievements of Cumberland has left its mark on his later biographers. He was 'a great but unamiable man' whose story 'admirably illustrates the difference … between fame and virtue' (Whitaker, 2.354). Whitaker acknowledged the earl's military prowess but condemned him as an unkind father, a faithless husband, and a poor manager of his estates. What Whitaker neglected to weigh in the balance was Cumberland's pious commitment to his family's tradition of absolute loyalty to the Tudor crown. His estate and his marriage were to some degree sacrificed to this.

PETER HOLMES

Sources DNB · R. T. Spence, *The privateering earl* (1995) · G. C. Williamson, *George, third earl of Cumberland* (1920) · T. D. Whitaker, *The history and antiquities of the deanery of Craven, in the county of York*, 3rd edn, ed. A. W. Morant, 2 (1878) · H. Clifford, *The house of Clifford* (1987), 93–105 · K. R. Andrews, *Elizabethan privateering* (1964), 70–82 · Cooper, *Ath. Cantab.*, 2.413–21 · GEC, *Peerage* · W. W. Rouse Ball and J. A. Venn, eds., *Admissions to Trinity College, Cambridge*, 2 (1913), 85 · Venn, *Alum. Cant.*, 1/1.355 · T. A. Walker, *A biographical register of Peterhouse men*, 1 (1927), 265–6 · Foster, *Alum. Oxon.*, 1500–1714, 1.291 · Wood, *Ath. Oxon.: Fasti* (1815), 260, 427 · R. T. Spence, 'The pacification of the Cumberland borders, 1593–1628', *Northern History*, 13 (1977), 59–160 · *The diaries of Lady Anne Clifford*, ed. D. J. H. Clifford (1992), 1–27, 98–9 · *The naval tracts of Sir William Monson*, ed. M. Oppenheim, 5, Navy RS, 47 (1914), index · J. K. Laughton, ed., *State papers relating to the defeat of the Spanish Armada, anno 1588*, 1, Navy RS, 1 (1894), 16; 2, Navy RS, 2 (1894), 6, 59, 69, 84, 95, 195, 211, 297, 338 · S. Purchas, *Hakluytus posthumus, or, Purchas his pilgrimes*, bk 16 (1625); repr. Hakluyt Society, extra ser., 29 (1906), 5–106; bk 17 (1625); repr. Hakluyt Society, extra ser., 30 (1906), 263; bk 18 (1625); repr. Hakluyt Society, extra ser., 31 (1906), 371, 375; bk 19 (1625); repr. Hakluyt Society, extra ser., 32 (1906), 240–41; bk 20 (1625); repr. Hakluyt Society, extra ser., 33 (1907), 91 · R. Hakluyt, *The principal navigations, voyages, traffiques and discoveries of the English nation*, 10 vols. (1927–8), 1.10; 2.386; 4.163, 305, 355–80; 5.21–43, 61, 68; 7.62; 8.132–53, 171 · T. Fuller, *The worthies of England*, ed. J. Freeman, abridged edn (1952) · G. C. Williamson, *Lady Anne Clifford* (1922), 25–42, 456–7

Archives Cumbria AS, Kendal, corresp.; papers of and relating to individual accounts of voyages · LPL, book of voyages [copy] | BL, Sloane MSS, papers · Chatsworth House, Derbyshire, Bolton MSS · W. Yorks. AS, Leeds, Yorkshire Archaeological Society, Skipton MSS

Likenesses N. Hilliard, miniature, c.1580–1594, NPG · portrait, 1588, NPG · N. Hilliard, miniature, 1589 · W. Rogers, engraving, c.1589, BM · N. Hilliard, miniature, c.1590, NMM [*see illus.*] · N. Hilliard, miniature, 1591, Nelson-Atkins Museum of Art, Kansas City · N. Hilliard, miniature, 1597, NPG · group portrait, oils, c.1600, Sherborne Castle, Dorset · J. van Belcamp, group portrait, oils, 1646 (with his family), Abbot Hall Art Gallery, Kendal · group portrait, oils, 1649 (with family), Cumbria AS, Carlisle · T. Cockson, engraving, BM · R. Vaughan, line engraving, BM, NPG · line engraving, BM · oils (after N. Hilliard), NPG; version, Bodl. Oxf.

Wealth at death supposedly died £80,000 in debt: will, PRO, PROB 11/108, fols. 3r–4v; Spence, *The privateering earl*, 211

Clifford, Henry, tenth Baron Clifford (1454–1523), magnate, was the eldest son of John *Clifford, ninth Baron Clifford (1435–1461), and his wife, Margaret Bromflete (d. 1493). A pillar of the house of Lancaster, John Clifford was killed in 1461, on the day before the battle of Towton, and was subsequently attainted, his family's lands being mainly granted to the Nevilles and Stanleys. But there is no evidence, later stories to the contrary notwithstanding, that the seven-year-old Henry Clifford was ever pursued by vengeful Yorkists, and the legend of the Shepherd Lord first recounted by Edward Hall in the mid-sixteenth century—telling of the young fugitive brought up among remote sheepfolds, so that he never learned to read, while his younger brother Richard was smuggled overseas, where he died—hardly stands up to scrutiny. Henry Clifford was later to be not just literate but even bookish, owning volumes on law and medicine, and developing a taste for astronomy and alchemy, while his brother is recorded in England as late as 1499. It may be that the Clifford heir thought it prudent to keep a low profile, but the fact that in 1466 Henry Harlington of Craven could bequeath him a sword and a silver bowl suggests that even then he stood in no perceptible danger. The possibility that he would recover his inheritance arose briefly in 1470–71, during the readeption of Henry VI, when John Neville, Marquess Montagu, was granted the Clifford lordship of Skipton specifically during Henry Clifford's minority. But though this prospect disappeared when Montagu, with his brother the earl of Warwick, was killed at Barnet on 14 April 1471, Clifford was no more imperilled by his Lancastrian connections than he had been before, and on 16 March 1472 Edward IV granted him a formal pardon.

The king's clemency did at least give Clifford the prospect of succeeding to his mother's hereditary estates, based on Londesborough in the East Riding of Yorkshire, but she lived until 1493, and there is no evidence as to how he passed the years from 1472 to 1485, beyond engaging in at least one liaison which brought him an illegitimate son. The overthrow of Richard III on 22 August 1485 changed Clifford's position at once. In September he was appointed a commissioner in Yorkshire and a JP in Westmorland, and in November he successfully petitioned parliament for the reversal of his father's attainder, so obtaining restoration of the Clifford lands and title. Henry VII needed loyal supporters in the north of England, his predecessor's power base, and he built up the position of the new Lord Clifford accordingly. In May 1486 he was granted the offices of chief steward of the lordship of Middleham and bailiff of the franchise of Richmond, and about the end of that year he married Anne St John (d. 1508), daughter of the king's mother's half-brother. In 1494 Clifford was dubbed a knight of the Bath. He remained almost unfailingly loyal to the crown, campaigning against the Scots in 1497 and leading a force at Flodden in 1513, and perhaps acting as a member of the council headed by Archbishop Thomas Savage, through which Henry VII endeavoured to extend his power in Yorkshire. But at the same time he used royal service as a means of rebuilding his family's position in the north.

Clifford's activities on his own behalf were not always well received. In April 1486 he notified the authorities in York that he intended to come to that city, there 'to mynistre as myn auncistres haith done here to fore in all thinges that accordith to my dewtie …' (Attreed, 479–80), only to be firmly informed by the city fathers that no member of his family had ever exercised authority there. In spite of this rebuff, when Yorkist rebels approached York in June 1487 in the name of Lambert Simnel, Clifford was forward to defend the city, although in the event his performance was somewhat inglorious, since he was defeated in a night-time skirmish and lost his baggage. In 1488 he and his wife joined York's Corpus Christi Guild, but he was still regarded with suspicion there, for in May 1489 the citizens refused to admit him to the city, on the grounds that his claims represented a threat to the rule of the mayor and aldermen. They were probably right to suspect his intentions; in 1513 Clifford demanded the leadership of the city's troops, and was once more refused.

Clifford was more successful on his home territory, in the West Riding of Yorkshire and in Westmorland. He moved round properties where no Clifford had been seen for a quarter of a century, staying in castles that he repaired or rebuilt; his works at Skipton and Barden were particularly extensive. To raise money Clifford exploited his feudal rights of wardship and marriage—in 1518, for instance, selling the marriage of the heir to Askham in Westmorland for 100 marks—and applied himself to the improvement of his own estates, on one occasion provoking a suit to the council against his enclosures. Such was his success that by 1496 a year's revenue from the lordship of Skipton amounted to little less than £300, and at his death his total annual income was assessed at £1332 2s. 4d., placing him in the top third of the English nobility for wealth. Full coffers gave Clifford the means to make friends and form alliances in circles lay and ecclesiastical. He was a benefactor to the monasteries of Shap, Bolton, Guisborough (where in 1508 he and his wife were enrolled in the priory's confraternity), and above all Mount Grace, which benefited substantially from his munificence. He established links with northern gentry families both through marriage alliances, for instance bestowing his daughters Margaret and Dorothy on Cuthbert Radcliffe and Hugh Lowther respectively, and through retaining fees. In 1493 he indented to pay Ralph Eure, the son of Sir William Eure, 10 marks yearly for services done and to be done. And no doubt he hoped to win approval through lavish hospitality, like the 'great Christmas' recorded as held at Brough in 1521, shortly before a fire largely destroyed the castle.

Restoring his lordship was not an easy business for Henry Clifford, whose frequent abrasiveness as landlord and neighbour several times prompted or threatened disorder, and so led to royal disapproval, at a time when the king was paying a good deal of attention to the extension of his authority and the maintenance of order in the north. Henry VII may have hoped to bring Clifford under closer control by a *quo warranto* action challenging the latter's hereditary shrievalty of Westmorland, and although Clifford was eventually confirmed in his family's traditional rights, he appears to have fallen foul of the king again by leading resistance to royal taxation in Yorkshire, and was heavily fined. None the less Clifford attended Henry VII's funeral in 1509, and lent 1000 marks to Henry VIII in 1522. The fact that his wife was the king's kinswoman by marriage had not saved Clifford from royal displeasure, indeed, it may have served to lower him in Henry VII's eyes, for his marriage to Anne St John proved unhappy, thanks at least in part to Clifford's infidelity (he had two or three illegitimate children), and by 1499 a separation was being mooted. In the end the couple remained together until Anne died in 1508. By July 1511 Clifford had remarried; his new wife was Florence Pudsey (d. 1558), widow of Sir Thomas Talbot. This marriage, too, turned out badly, culminating in a suit which Florence brought in the church court at York, demanding restitution of her conjugal rights. Her husband's riposte was to accuse her of adultery with one of his household officers. Even so, Lord Clifford's second marriage, like his first, was to endure.

In addition to his marital difficulties, Henry Clifford also found himself at loggerheads with his son and heir, another Henry *Clifford, who was born about 1493, and brought up at court with the future Henry VIII. Some time after 1511 Lord Clifford complained of his son's unruliness and extravagance, not least the way in which he paraded in cloth of gold, 'more lyk a duke than a pore baron's sonne as hee ys' (Whitaker, 327). If the son had ideas above his station, the responsibility was largely his father's, who not only placed him at court but also set about marrying him into the high aristocracy. A union with the Talbots was brought to nothing by the bride's early death, but late in 1512 arrangements were successfully made for Henry Clifford to marry Margaret Percy, daughter of the earl of Northumberland. The son's wild ways may also have been prompted by frustration at his father's longevity. By September 1522, however, when Lord Clifford was described as 'feebled with sickness' (LP Henry VIII, 2.2, no. 2524), young Henry did not have long to wait for his inheritance. Lord Clifford died on 20 April 1523, and was buried in the following year at either Bolton or Shap. From his first marriage he left two sons and four daughters, from his second marriage a single daughter. His heir's elevation to be earl of Cumberland in 1525 owed much to Henry Clifford's labours to revive the fortunes of his family.

HENRY SUMMERSON

Sources Cumbria AS, Kendal, WD/Hoth/Books of Record 2, 487–545 · Bodl. Oxf., MSS Dodsworth, 70, 74, 83 · Coll. Arms, Arundel MS 33, fol. 303r–v · LP Henry VIII, vols. 1–3 · Chancery records · R. T. Spence, The shepherd lord of Skipton Castle (1994) · T. D. Whitaker, The history and antiquities of the deanery of Craven, in the county of York, 3rd edn, ed. A. W. Morant (1878) · A. G. Dickens, ed., Clifford letters of the sixteenth century, SurtS, 172 (1962) [1962 for 1957] · L. C. Attreed, ed., The York House books, 1461–1490, 2 vols. (1991) · RotP, 6.280 · A. Raine, ed., York civic records, 3, Yorkshire Archaeological Society, 106 (1942), 40–41 · R. W. Hoyle, ed., Early Tudor Craven: subsidies and assessments, 1510–1547, Yorkshire Archaeological Society, record ser., 145 (1987) · M. K. Jones and M. G. Underwood, The king's mother: Lady Margaret Beaufort, countess of Richmond and Derby (1992), 163–4 · R. W. Hoyle, 'The earl, the archbishop and the council: the affray at Fulford, May 1504', Rulers and ruled in late medieval England: essays presented to Gerald Harriss, ed. R. E. Archer and S. Walker (1995), 239–56 · GEC, Peerage, new edn, 3.294–5

Archives BL, corresp., Add. MS 48965 · Cumbria AS, Kendal, WD/Hoth

Wealth at death £1332 2s. 4d. p.a.: Coll. Arms, Arundel MS 33, fol. 303r–v

Clifford, Henry, first earl of Cumberland (c.1493–1542), magnate, was the elder son of Henry *Clifford, tenth Baron Clifford (1454–1523), magnate, and his first wife, Anne (d. 1508), daughter of Sir John St John of Bletsoe, Bedfordshire, and his wife, Alice. He had a brother, Sir Thomas Clifford (d. 1543), a notable soldier, who acted on his behalf as constable of Carlisle between 1525 and 1529 and captain of Berwick, Northumberland, until 1538, four sisters, and a surviving half-sister. According to his great-granddaughter, Anne *Clifford, countess of Pembroke, Dorset, and Montgomery (1590–1676), he was 'bred up for the first part, in his childhood and youth, with the said king [Henry VIII] … Which engrafted such a love in the said Prince towards him that it continued even to the very end' (Dickens, 140). There is indeed evidence that he was educated at court.

Clifford was made KB at the coronation of Henry VIII on 23 June 1509. He was not, however, one of the king's circle of chivalric companions or 'minions', nor does he ever seem to have sought a military reputation. As a young man he was criticized by his father for his ostentation, dressing 'more like a duke than a poor baron's son as he is', for assaults on Lord Clifford's servants, and for extorting leases of tithes from unwilling monastic houses (T. D. Whitaker, The History and Antiquities of the Deanery of Craven, 3rd edn, 1878, 327). He married Margaret (d. in or before 1516), daughter of George *Talbot, fourth earl of Shrewsbury, and his first wife, Anne. She died only a year or two after the marriage and there were no children. Clifford married for a second time about 1516. His wife was Margaret (c.1492–1540), first daughter of Henry Percy, fifth earl of Northumberland, and his wife, Catherine. They had two sons, Henry *Clifford, second earl of Cumberland (1517–1570), and Sir Ingram Clifford (1518?–1578/9), and four daughters. In 1517 Clifford was imprisoned for a time in the Fleet prison for unknown offences. He succeeded his father on 20 April 1523, when he was said to have been about thirty, and was created earl of Cumberland on 18 June 1525 as part of a reorganization of the government of the north. At the same time the king's bastard son, Henry Fitzroy, was created duke of Richmond and earl of Nottingham, and Thomas Manners, twelfth Baron Ros, earl of Rutland. Cumberland was then in October appointed deputy warden of the west marches against Scotland under Richmond over the claims of William Dacre, third Lord Dacre of Gilsland. This experiment was not seen to be a success. Despite the title adopted for their earldom, the Clifford heartlands were in the West Riding of Yorkshire, around Skipton, and in the Eden valley, Westmorland, where they had castles at Brougham and Appleby. Cumberland had little standing in Cumberland or on the west marches, and found himself compelled to compete for offices and authority against Dacre. In late 1527 he was allowed to surrender the wardenship and Dacre was appointed in his place before 26 June 1528. Cumberland however remained in charge of Carlisle until August 1529, impairing Dacre's effectiveness as warden and provoking Dacre-inspired riots in the city.

Cumberland supported Henry's divorce from Katherine of Aragon and, with other nobles, signed a letter to Clement VII, asking him to grant it, on 13 July 1530. In 1534, in ways that are not clear, he was complicit in the fall of Dacre and in the charges of treasonable communication with the Scots brought against him by Sir William Musgrave. Dacre was acquitted at a trial by his peers in July but subsequently fined £10,000 and deprived of his offices by the king. Cumberland was appointed warden of the west marches for a second time in September and again his record was mixed. He could not secure the co-operation of the Dacres and once more was forced to compete for the monastic and crown stewardships that were held by them as adjuncts of the warden's office. Dacre also maintained that Cumberland had purloined his goods after his arrest: this grievance was still a sore point between the families as late as 1554. The tensions between the Clifford and Dacre factions were made plain when Richard Dacre attempted to stab Musgrave in the presence of Cumberland's son, Henry, Lord Clifford, in Carlisle on 9 December 1536. As a result Cumberland, Musgrave, and Dacre and their various supporters were severely admonished by Henry VIII in a letter of 24 January 1537. Cumberland's friends on the privy council urged him on 31 January to take the opportunity to surrender the wardenship, reminding him of his reluctance to accept the office in the first place. He wrote to the king offering to resign, but seems to have remained titular warden until the end of his life. The day-to-day responsibilities passed to Thomas Wharton. There is little evidence to suggest that Cumberland sought what was almost certainly an unattractive office on the borders. Rather he was used as an alternative at moments when the Dacres were politically out of favour. His own interests seem to have lain entirely in expanding his family's influence in the West Riding. It is striking that neither he nor his heir took the opportunity to acquire monastic lands in Westmorland, many of which (including Shap, where the tenth Lord Clifford may have been buried) were purchased by Wharton.

Cumberland's loyalty to the king is seen most clearly during the Pilgrimage of Grace in 1536–7. He was initially instructed to lead a force to Hexham, Northumberland, where the monks had barricaded themselves in the monastery in defiance of the commissioners sent to suppress it. He appears to have attempted to reach Hexham about 16–17 October 1536, but to have been beaten back to Skipton. He took refuge in his castle and faced a short siege from a party of the Richmondshire commons who deviated to Skipton on their way to Pontefract, West Riding, apparently with the aim of recruiting Cumberland to their cause. The force he had gathered (probably to lead to Hexham) melted away and he was left to defend Skipton with household servants alone. A party of Clifford women including Eleanor Clifford, *née* Brandon (1519–1547), Cumberland's daughter-in-law, were stranded at Bolton Priory and were led back through the rebels' lines by the earl's steward and cousin, Christopher Aske, brother of Robert Aske, the grand captain of the pilgrims. Cumberland was impotent to influence the course of the pilgrimage. While he made much of his defiance, the truth is that he was in fact trapped in his castle by an insurrection of his own tenants, who attacked his houses and killed his deer. A delegation was sent to him to try and persuade him to attend the York conference on 22 November but his refusal to lend any weight to the Pilgrimage of Grace was total. Henry, Lord Clifford managed the defence of Carlisle against the Cumberland commons. In the new year Cumberland appears to have tried to implement the king's instruction to seize the captains of the rebellious commons. His attempt to seize their leaders around Kirkby Stephen, Westmorland, prompted a renewal of the conflict in Westmorland and Cumberland. A second attempt to besiege Carlisle failed after the castle garrison under Cumberland's bastard, Thomas Clifford (d. in or after 1555), issued from the town and, with the aid of a force led by Sir Christopher Dacre, routed the commons on 16 February 1537. Henry's gratitude made it impossible for Cumberland to be dismissed from the wardenship, hence the arrangement where Wharton took over the duties but was denied the title. Cumberland was elected to the Order of the Garter on 23 April 1537 to reward his loyal service.

When Cumberland had livery of his lands on 18 July 1523, they had a gross annual rental of £1332. He had already acquired the manor of Carleton in Craven in 1514 but made no further acquisitions until he secured the Craven manors of Marton Priory by purchase from Charles Brandon, first duke of Suffolk, in 1541. In April 1542 he was granted by letters patent the Craven estates of Bolton Priory—a house with which the Cliffords were traditionally associated as founders—worth nearly £400 per annum, in reward for royal service. The augmented estates were valued at £1720 per annum in the earl's inquisition post mortem. As a landlord, Cumberland needs to be defended against the assertions that he was raising the cornage rents of his tenants in Westmorland and that he was rapacious in his treatment of tenants in Craven. He was, however, a notable encloser. Some of his Craven enclosures were destroyed in riots in May 1535, and his new fences in the Eden valley were thrown down in the unsettled conditions of the winter of 1536. Thomas Howard, third duke of Norfolk, was particularly critical of Cumberland's estate policies: 'he must be brought to change his conditions, that is to say, not to be so greedy of getting money of his tenants and others under him' (*LP Henry VIII*, 12/1, no. 919). His predatory manner may also be seen in his dealings with Furness Abbey over their manor of Winterburn in Craven. Cumberland clearly coveted this manor. He later claimed to have a lease from 1531, but it was known from 1536 onwards that this was a forgery, made after some of the monks, during the vacancy of 1531, broke into a chest and applied the convent seal to some blank parchments. While the facts were well established, Cumberland insisted on the validity of this lease and persistently ejected the manor's tenants.

Cumberland died on 22 April 1542 and was buried on 2 May at Skipton, where his tomb may still be seen in the parish church. His will, dated 2 April 1542 and proved on 4 June 1543, suggests orthodox religious tastes: he left money to pay for the singing of a requiem and dirge by every curate in Westmorland and Craven willing to do so, and for an obit to be established in Skipton parish church. His wife predeceased him, dying on 25 November 1540 at Skipton. R. W. HOYLE

Sources M. E. James, 'The first earl of Cumberland (1493–1542) and the decline of northern feudalism', *Northern History*, 1 (1965), 43–69 · R. W. Hoyle, 'The first earl of Cumberland: a reputation reassessed', *Northern History*, 22 (1986), 63–94 · A. G. Dickens, ed., *Clifford letters of the sixteenth century*, SurtS, 172 (1962) · R. W. Hoyle, ed., 'Letters of the Cliffords, lords Clifford and earls of Cumberland, c.1500–1565', *Camden miscellany, XXXI*, CS, 4th ser., 44 (1993), 1–189 · J. W. Clay, 'The Clifford family', *Yorkshire Archaeological Journal*, 18 (1905), 375–9
Archives BL, corresp., Add. MS 48965 · W. Yorks. AS, Leeds, Yorkshire Archaeological Society, deeds, family and estate papers, DD121 | Chatsworth House, Derbyshire, Devonshire collections, Bolton MSS; Cury Papers

Clifford, Henry, second earl of Cumberland (1517–1570), magnate, was the eldest of the six children of Henry *Clifford, first earl of Cumberland (c.1493–1542), and his second wife, Margaret (c.1492–1540), daughter of Henry *Percy, fifth earl of Northumberland. He was educated at home and then at court, where he spent much of his youth. He also attended the duke of Richmond in the latter's household at Pontefract Castle, and was made knight of the Bath at Queen Anne's coronation in 1533. In June 1535 he married Henry VIII's niece Eleanor (1519–1547), daughter of Charles Brandon, duke of Suffolk, and Mary, daughter of Henry VII and widow of Louis XII of France. His father built for them the octagonal tower and long gallery extension at Skipton Castle. Clifford escorted Lady Mary Tudor at the funeral of Queen Jane at Windsor on 12 January 1537, and represented his father when Henry VIII met Anne of Cleves in January 1540. That year he served in the king's chamber, as a carver.

Clifford was prominent in the military crises of Henry VIII's later years. In 1536 he rallied the Carlisle townsmen to stand firm against the rebels. He played some part in the defence of the west march in 1541, and from September 1542 until 1544, following his father's death, he was continually employed mustering his Yorkshire tenants and leading them on the borders. He was proposed as warden-general for all the marches, but the king preferred a more experienced man, in John Dudley, Viscount Lisle. Instead, Clifford was appointed to the council of the borders, and was rewarded in 1544 by being added to the council in the north. He repeated this service during Elizabeth I's Scottish campaign of 1559–60. It was his military outlay, rather than court life, which forced him to sell lands during the 1540s. Even so, the rental from his estates at his death amounted to some £2000 per annum.

Clifford was tall, slender, and dark-haired, a learned man with a fine library whose interests were alchemy, astrology, and distilling. These he indulged after Countess Eleanor's death in 1547, a blow which so prostrated the earl that he was laid out for dead, according to family tradition recovering his strength by sucking milk from a woman's breasts; thereafter he retired to his northern castles, rarely visiting the court. He was instrumental with William Ermysted in founding Skipton grammar school. A testimony to his cultural concerns and pride in his royal marriage is the organ he presented to Carlisle Cathedral in 1542. The organ case, of Italian design, displays on its heraldic panels the coats and supporters of the Cliffords and Brandons. The oldest in England, it is now in St Lawrence's, Appleby.

Clifford's absence from court exposed him to political intrigue. His parliamentary patronage in Westmorland and friends in the privy council enabled him to obstruct Thomas, Lord Wharton's bills in 1549 and 1558 to deprive him of his hereditary sheriffwick of Westmorland and punish his servants. He was potentially dangerously exposed in 1553 when his only child, Margaret, heiress to the great Clifford inheritance and with a claim to the throne, was drawn by John Dudley, now duke of Northumberland, into his schemes to achieve his own dynastic ambitions and perpetuate the protestant regime. But Northumberland's proposal, that Margaret should marry his own son Lord Guildford Dudley, came to nothing, and on Mary Tudor's accession Clifford was swift to extricate himself by demonstrating his loyalty to her. His inheritance worries only ceased well after his second marriage in 1554 to Anne (c.1538–1581), daughter of William, third Baron Dacre of Gilsland, with the birth in 1558 of George *Clifford, the future third earl (1558–1605). (His second son was Francis *Clifford (1559–1641), eventually the fourth earl.) This marriage also served to heal a long-running dispute between the Dacres and the Cliffords.

Clifford's initial support for Queen Mary was unequivocal. A traditionalist in matters of religion, he welcomed her restoration of Catholicism and used his electoral patronage in Westmorland to return members of like mind, but he became disenchanted with her later policies. Under Elizabeth he was accused of protecting popish priests in the north. However, the agreement he reached in 1565 for George's marriage with Margaret, daughter of Francis Russell, second earl of Bedford, signalled his alignment with the strongly protestant group at court under Robert Dudley, earl of Leicester. At the time of the 1569 uprising he was suspected of sympathy, at the very least, with the rebels, but again demonstrated his loyalty to the Tudor crown by holding Brougham Castle for the queen. He died there on 8 January 1570 and was buried in Holy Trinity Church, Skipton. RICHARD T. SPENCE

Sources R. T. Spence, *The privateering earl* (1995) · A. G. Dickens, ed., *Clifford letters of the sixteenth century*, SurtS, 172 (1962) · J. W. Clay, 'The Clifford family', *Yorkshire Archaeological Journal*, 18 (1904–5), 354–411 · C. C. Stopes, *Shakespeare's environment* (1918) · Chatsworth House, Derbyshire, Devonshire collections, Bolton MSS, Londesborough MSS · W. Yorks. AS, Leeds, Yorkshire Archaeological Society, Skipton MSS · T. D. Whitaker, *The history and antiquities of the deanery of Craven, in the county of York*, 3rd edn, ed. A. W. Morant (1878) · J. Bain, ed., *The Hamilton papers: letters and papers illustrating* the political relations of England and Scotland in the XVIth century, 1, Scottish RO, 12 (1890) • LPL, Shrewsbury MSS 695, 696 • H. Miller, Henry VIII and the English nobility (1986) • D. M. Loades, The reign of Mary Tudor: politics, government and religion in England, 1553–58 (1979) • M. A. R. Graves, The House of Lords in the parliaments of Edward VI and Mary I (1981) • S. J. Gunn, Charles Brandon, duke of Suffolk, c.1484–1545 (1988) • court of wards, miscellaneous books, PRO, WARD 9/140, fols. 291–4

Archives Stonyhurst College, Lancashire, corresp. and papers • W. Yorks. AS, Leeds, executorship papers | Chatsworth House, Derbyshire, Devonshire collections, Bolton MSS; Londesborough MSS • Cumbria AS, Kendal, Hothfield MSS • LPL, Shrewsbury MSS • W. Yorks. AS, Leeds, Yorkshire Archaeological Society, Skipton MSS

Wealth at death approx. £2000 net rental, excl. tithes and income from wardships and timber: PRO, WARD 9/140, fols. 291–4

Clifford, Henry, fifth earl of Cumberland (1592–1643), local politician and royalist army officer, was born on 28 February 1592 at Londesborough in the East Riding of Yorkshire, the second, surviving son of Francis *Clifford, fourth earl of Cumberland (1559–1641), and Grissell (bap. 1559, d. 1613), elder daughter of Thomas Hughes of Uxbridge, Middlesex, and widow of Edward Neville, Lord Bergavenny. He was educated at first privately and then, until about 1606, at Dean John Higgins's school at Well, near Ripon. He matriculated at Christ Church, Oxford, in January 1606, and graduated BA in 1609; and in 1610 he was admitted to Gray's Inn, London. He was created knight of the Bath on 3 June 1610. After his marriage on 25 July 1610 at Kensington to Lady Frances Cecil (1594–1644), daughter of Robert *Cecil, earl of Salisbury, he spent a year at M. de Pluvinel's academy in Paris.

Clifford was a tall, dark-haired, scholarly man, a lutenist and poet, skilled in mathematics and architecture, and accomplished in field sports. Although, because of his family's financial problems, he could not, in Clarendon's words, 'live with the lustre of his ancestors' (Clarendon, Hist. rebellion, 2.286), his conviviality towards the Yorkshire gentry gave him the social leadership of the county. He was a patron of musicians and players, planning the songs and masque when Earl Francis entertained James I at Brougham Castle in August 1617, and staging the first full-text presentation of Milton's Comus at Shrovetide 1637 in Skipton Castle where, in 1628, he had converted the outer gatehouse into a showpiece neo-Platonic grotto. He is credited with designing the monument to Countess Grissell, commissioned in 1631 from Nicholas Stone, in All Saints', Londesborough. From 1631 to 1638 he maintained in his household the Dutch painter Hendrick de Keyser the younger. His poems survived in manuscript among his family papers but are lost except for his 'Poetical Translations of some Psalms and the Song of Solomon', now in the Bodleian Library.

At court Clifford jousted, carried banners at royal funerals, and escorted foreign dignitaries into the king's presence. With his son-in-law Richard *Boyle, Lord Dungarvan, he met the Dutch lords at Thames wharf on 1 January 1641 to negotiate a marriage between William of Nassau and Princess Mary. In 1614 and 1621 he was elected MP for Westmorland and on 17 February 1628 he was summoned to the Lords as Baron Clifford. Having taken over

from his ageing father from 1621, he dispensed his family's political patronage in Westmorland and the boroughs of Appleby and Carlisle. By 1619, when he was appointed to the council in the north, he had become the active lord lieutenant first of Cumberland and then Westmorland and Northumberland (offices jointly held with Earl Francis and the Howards, earls of Suffolk), and governor (with Earl Francis) of Carlisle Castle; and from 1641 he was hereditary sheriff of Westmorland. His responsibilities embroiled him in factional rivalry with Lord William Howard of Naworth.

Clifford was prominent in the bishops' wars. Having been appointed governor of Newcastle on 20 February 1639, he completed Sir Jacob Astley's work in preparing its defences and recruited a well-equipped cavalry troop. Given command in Cumberland and Westmorland on 26 March by the lieutenant-general, the earl of Essex, he speedily raised the trained bands to garrison Carlisle, where a Scottish incursion was feared imminent. He saw to their replacement by Sir Francis Willoughby's veteran Irish levies and the safe delivery of ordnance and ammunition sent by sea from Cornwall. Later he raised the trained bands again to secure the frontier defences. However, acting as a conduit between Lord Deputy Wentworth and the court at Berwick and working to prevent the dismembering of Willoughby's force undermined Clifford's position. The lord general, the earl of Arundel, replaced him with his son Sir William Howard, but Clifford refused before Charles I to yield Carlisle Castle to him.

Clifford's disgruntlement did not diminish his commitment during the Second Bishops' War (1640). But it may have given the king's opponents expectations of gaining his support in 1642: on 9 February they nominated the earl of Cumberland (as he had become on his father's death the year before) lord lieutenant of Westmorland. These expectations were unrealistic because Cumberland was a committed royalist who abhorred alike 'all manner of poperye and sismatticall opinions' (Clay, 389). However, he showed some ambiguity after Charles I, responding to the majority gentry views, appointed him commander in Yorkshire in July. During August Clifford acted with urgency, seizing the key castles of Pontefract, Sandal, and Knaresborough and appointing Colonel Sir Philip Musgrave commander in Westmorland. At his own expense he readied Skipton Castle for war and began to recruit in Craven a company of foot and a cavalry troop. Yet he strove to keep Yorkshire at peace, negotiating a truce, the treaty of Rothwell, on 29 September, with his near neighbour Ferdinando, Lord Fairfax, and other roundhead leaders in the county, only to see it broken by Sir John Hotham in Hull, and by intransigent parliamentarians in Whitehall.

As Sir Philip Warwick commented, Cumberland's 'genius was not military' (Warwick, 257). He had little military experience and relied on his subordinates such as Sir Thomas Glemham who, lacking adequate forces, suffered reverses which put the whole county at risk. Negotiations with the earl of Newcastle to come to their aid were done with Clifford's cognizance, although he yielded his command in December with reluctance. He retired to

Skipton Castle, appointing as governor there in January 1643 Colonel Sir William Mallory, one of his officers in the First Bishops' War. He continued to finance recruitment and also took some part in administration. Following the royalists' defeats in Lancashire in May, he moved to Sir William Robinson's house, Minster Yard, York, where he died of a fever on 11 December, aged fifty-one. His cortège had a military escort to Skipton, with a parade and cannon salute before his interment on 31 December in Holy Trinity Church, Skipton. His countess died at York on 4 February 1644 and was buried in the minster.

By Cumberland's death the Cliffords' earldom of Cumberland became extinct. The barony of Clifford (1299) fell to Lady Anne *Clifford but that of 1628 passed to Clifford's sole surviving child, Elizabeth, Lady Dungarvan, countess of Cork (and later countess of Burlington). His estates were divided between them in accordance with the terms of the king's award of 1617 which settled the family's great inheritance dispute. An original portrait of him by Mytens is in the Devonshire collections. His daughter commemorated him prominently in 1644 by placing his shield on Clifford's Tower, York, beneath the coat of arms of Charles I.   RICHARD T. SPENCE

Sources R. T. Spence, *Skipton Castle in the great civil war, 1642–1645* (1991) · R. T. Spence, 'Henry, Lord Clifford and the first bishop's war, 1639', *Northern History*, 31 (1995), 138–56 · Chatsworth House, Derbyshire, Devonshire collections, Bolton MSS · J. W. Clay, 'The Clifford family', *Yorkshire Archaeological Journal*, 18 (1904–5), 354–411 · R. T. Spence, 'A noble funeral in the great civil war', *Yorkshire Archaeological Journal*, 65 (1993), 115–23 · R. T. Spence, *Lady Anne Clifford: countess of Pembroke, Dorset and Montgomery, 1590–1676* (1997) · J. P. Cooper, ed., *Wentworth papers, 1597–1628*, CS, 4th ser., 12 (1973) · *DNB* · *CSP dom.*, 1610–43 · T. D. Whitaker, *The history and antiquities of the deanery of Craven, in the county of York*, 3rd edn, ed. A. W. Morant (1878) · R. T. Spence, 'A royal progress in the north: James I at Carlisle Castle and the feast of Brougham, August 1617', *Northern History*, 27 (1991), 41–89 · G. Radcliffe, *The earl of Strafforde's letters and dispatches, with an essay towards his life*, ed. W. Knowler, 2 vols. (1739) · N. Canny, *The upstart earl: a study of the social and mental world of Richard Boyle, first earl of Cork, 1566–1643* (1982) · J. Nichols, *The progresses, processions, and magnificent festivities of King James I, his royal consort, family and court*, 4 vols. (1828) · *Brief lives, chiefly of contemporaries, set down by John Aubrey, between the years 1669 and 1696*, ed. A. Clark, 2 vols. (1898) · P. Warwick, *Memoirs of the reign of King Charles the First* (1813) · Clarendon, *Hist. rebellion*, 2.286 · parish register, Londesborough, East Riding of Yorkshire [baptism]
Archives U. Hull, Brynmor Jones L., accounts | BL, Althorp MSS, Add. MSS · Chatsworth House, Derbyshire, Devonshire collections, Bolton MSS · Chatsworth House, Derbyshire, Devonshire collections, Bolton MSS, Bolton additional series · Chatsworth House, Derbyshire, Devonshire collections, Currey MSS · Chatsworth House, Derbyshire, Devonshire collections, Hardwick MSS · Chatsworth House, Derbyshire, Devonshire collections, Londesborough MSS · Sheff. Arch., letters to Lord Strafford · Sheff. Arch., letters to Thomas Wentworth · W. Yorks. AS, Leeds, Yorkshire Archaeological Society, Skipton MSS
Likenesses D. Mytens, oils, 1631, Chatsworth, Derbyshire · C. Johnson, oils, 1640 (Henry Clifford?) , Abbot Hall Art Gallery, Kendal, Cumbria · oils, c.1720 (after D. Mytens), Holkham Hall, Norfolk · W. Kent?, oils, 1730 (after D. Mytens), Chiswick House, London · Johnson, repro. in *The Walpole Society*, 10 (1922), pl. 77
Wealth at death £5028 in debt, with other unspecified debts not secured: Chatsworth House, Derbyshire, Devonshire collections, Londesborough MS, 1/95 · estate rental £5500 gross, £4500 net:

R. T. Spence, 'The Cliffords, earls of Cumberland, 1579–1646 …', PhD diss., U. Lond., 1959, 359–60

Clifford, Henry (1768–1813), Roman Catholic layman and lawyer, was born on 2 March 1768, the second of the eight sons of Thomas Clifford (1732–1787) of Tixall, Staffordshire (brother of Hugh, fourth Baron Clifford), and his wife, Barbara (d. 1786), youngest daughter and coheir of James, fifth Baron Aston. His mother was the niece of Thomas and Edward, eighth and ninth dukes of Norfolk respectively, and of George, fourteenth earl of Shrewsbury. His elder brother was Sir Thomas Hugh Clifford, topographer and botanist. He was educated at the English Jesuit Academy at Liège, and admitted to Lincoln's Inn on 23 January 1788. He was called to the bar in February 1793, soon after the passage of the Catholic Relief Act of 1791.

Clifford was a prominent activist on behalf of the Catholic Committee and claimed personally to have collected the signatures of 1300 'loyal Catholics' to the committee's protestation (1789) which denounced the theory that the pope could dispense from civil oaths and explicitly denied papal infallibility. In his *Reflections on the Appointment of a Catholic Bishop to the London District* (1791) he criticized the appointment of John Douglass as vicar apostolic, urging the rival claims of Joseph Berington, a candidate more acceptable to the liberal aristocracy and gentry. When the Catholic Committee was reconstituted as the Cisalpine Club he chaired its first meeting in April 1792, and was its secretary and treasurer for three years.

Clifford deployed his eloquence and legal learning in the cause of civil liberties, achieving popular fame as the champion of the 'O.P.' (Old Price) demonstrators in the autumn of 1809. When the rebuilt Covent Garden Theatre opened to the public in September 1809, the increase in the price of tickets and the extension of private boxes provoked rowdy protests. Clifford joined the demonstrators and took a successful action against the theatre manager, whom he sued for wrongful arrest. His victory in the courts in December forced the proprietor, John Kemble, to yield to the demands of the pit, and Clifford was hailed as 'another Hampden in the cause of disenthralment' (*The Covent Garden Journal*, 1.92).

In January 1813 Clifford married Anne Teresa, youngest daughter of Edward Ferrers, of Baddesley Clinton, Warwickshire. He died three months later at Bath on 22 April 1813.   THOMPSON COOPER, rev. G. MARTIN MURPHY

Sources B. Ward, *The dawn of the Catholic revival in England, 1781–1803*, 2 vols. (1909) · J. J. Stockdale, *The Covent Garden journal*, 2 vols. (1810) · Gillow, *Lit. biog. hist.* · E. Duffy, 'Ecclesiastical democracy detected [pt 2]', *Recusant History*, 10 (1969–70), 309–31, esp. 318 · Watt, *Bibl. Brit.* · R. Trappes-Lomax, 'Boys at Liège Academy, 1773–91', *Miscellanea, VIII*, Catholic RS, 13 (1913), 202–13, esp. 204
Likenesses coloured drawing; copy, priv. coll.

Clifford, Sir Henry Hugh (1826–1883), army officer, third son of Hugh Charles *Clifford, seventh Baron Clifford (1790–1858), and Mary Lucy (1799–1831), only daughter of Thomas *Weld of Lulworth Castle, Dorset, was born on 12 September 1826 at Irnham Hall, Lincolnshire. He was educated at Prior Park, near Bath, Stonyhurst College, and the University of Fribourg, and commissioned as a second lieutenant in the rifle brigade on 7 August 1846. He served in South Africa, fighting in the Cape Frontier War (1846–7), and then against the Boers at the battle of Boomplaats (29 August 1848). On the outbreak of a war against the Basuto in 1852 he again went to Africa, where he was present at the battle of Berea Mountain (20 December 1852). He left in November 1853. He also served in the Crimean War, and was appointed aide-de-camp to Colonel Sir George Buller, brigade commander in the light division. He was present at Alma and Inkerman, and for his bravery at the latter was awarded the Victoria Cross. In May 1855 he was appointed deputy assistant quartermaster-general, and remained in the Crimea until the end of the war. He was then promoted brevet major, and awarded the légion d'honneur and the Mejidiye (fifth class). He married on 21 March 1857 Josephine Elizabeth (d. 1913), only child of Joseph *Anstice of Madeley Wood, Shropshire, professor at King's College, London; they had six daughters and three sons.

Clifford was sent to China on the outbreak of hostilities, and as assistant quartermaster-general was present at the operations between December 1857 and January 1858 which resulted in the capture of Canton (Guangzhou). For his services he was promoted brevet lieutenant-colonel. On his return to England he began a long term of service on the staff; he was assistant quartermaster-general at Aldershot (1860–64) and at headquarters (1865–8), aide-de-camp to the duke of Cambridge (1870–73), and assistant adjutant-general at headquarters (1873–5). In April 1879 Clifford was sent by Cambridge to South Africa to reorganize army transport and repair relations between the military and civil authorities. He was successful in this task, although his own relationship with the field commander, Lord Chelmsford, was frosty. His labours were fully acknowledged by Sir Garnet Wolseley. He was gazetted a CB on 2 June 1869 and a KCMB on 19 December 1879, and was major-general of the eastern district of England from April to September 1882. Sir Henry died of cancer at his home, Ugbrooke Park, near Chudleigh, Devon, on 12 April 1883, and was buried at the chapel there.

G. C. BOASE, rev. M. G. M. JONES

Sources H. Clifford, *Henry Clifford VC: his letters and sketches from the Crimea* (1956) · Burke, *Peerage* · C. R. Low, *Soldiers of the Victorian age* (1880), 208–21 · *The Graphic* (12 April 1879), 372 · *The South African journal of Sir Garnet Wolseley, 1879–1880*, ed. A. Preston (1973) · *DSAB* · I. Knight, *Brave men's blood: the epic of the Zulu War, 1879* (1990) · D. R. Morris, *The washing of the spears* (1966) · T. Day, *But burdens shouldered: Anglo-Zulu war graves and memorials in the United Kingdom* (Zulu Study Group, Victorian Military Society, 1995)
Archives Devon RO · priv. coll., Crimean war journal and letters | NAM, letters and telegrams to Lord Chelmsford
Likenesses photograph, c.1855, repro. in Clifford, *Henry Clifford VC* · Fradelle, photograph, repro. in T. E. Toomey, *Heroes of the Victoria cross* (1895) · Fradelle, photograph, repro. in *The register of the Victoria cross* (1981) · F. Podesti, oils, Ugbrooke Park, Devon · J. Ramsay, oils, Ugbrooke Park, Devon · photographs, NAM · portrait, repro. in *The Graphic*, 372
Wealth at death £1188 0s. 6d.: probate, 8 Sept 1883, *CGPLA Eng. & Wales*

Clifford, Hugh Charles, seventh Baron Clifford of Chudleigh (1790–1858), aristocrat, eldest son of Charles, sixth Baron Clifford (1759–1831), and Eleanor Mary (d. 1835), daughter of Henry Arundel, eighth Baron Arundell of Wardour, was born at New Park, Somerset, on 22 May 1790, the eldest boy in a family of twelve. The family were Roman Catholics and he was educated at Stonyhurst, and in 1814 attended Cardinal Consalvi to the Congress of Vienna. He served as a volunteer through a large portion of the Peninsular campaigns. He succeeded his father in 1831 and took his seat in the House of Lords, the first of his family to do so since 1678. He supported the whigs, but seldom took part in the debates except on questions connected with Roman Catholicism. In his later years he lived chiefly in Italy, near Tivoli. On 1 September 1818 he married Mary Lucy (1799–1831), only child of Thomas (afterwards Cardinal) *Weld of Lulworth Castle, Dorset; they had two daughters and four sons. The eldest son, Charles Hugh Clifford, became eighth baron; the third was Sir Henry Hugh *Clifford. The other sons took orders in the Roman Catholic church, and one daughter became a nun of the Sacré Cœur. Clifford was the author of a number of political pamphlets on Ireland, India, and the corn laws. He died at Rome on 28 February 1858 of the effects of a wound in the ankle, and was buried beside his father-in-law, Cardinal Weld, in Rome, on 2 March 1858.

T. F. HENDERSON, rev. K. D. REYNOLDS

Sources GEC, *Peerage* · *GM*, 3rd ser., 4 (1858), 551
Archives NRA, priv. coll., corresp. and papers | Devon RO, letters to Sir T. D. Acland · Lpool RO, letters to Lord Stanley · W. Sussex RO, letters to duke of Richmond
Likenesses J. Green, chalk drawing, 1819, Ugbrooke Park, Devon · J. Ramsay, oils, 1829, Ugbrooke Park, Devon
Wealth at death under £60,000: resworn probate, July 1859, *CGPLA Eng. & Wales* (1858)

Clifford, Sir Hugh Charles (1866–1941), colonial governor and author, was born in London on 5 March 1866, the eldest son of Major-General Sir Henry Hugh *Clifford (1826–1883) and grandson of the seventh Baron Clifford of Chudleigh. His mother was Josephine Elizabeth (d. 1913), only child of Joseph Anstice, of Madeley Wood, Shropshire, a professor of classics at King's College, London. A member of a west country recusant family, he was educated at Woburn Park under Mgr William Joseph Petre. Although he passed for Sandhurst, reduced family circumstances following the death of his father resulted in his taking immediate employment offered by a kinsman, Sir Frederick Weld, who was governor of the Straits Settlements.

Clifford arrived in Malaya in 1883 aged seventeen. The British then administered the colony of the Straits Settlements while in the west coast Malay states residents were establishing an 'advisory system' to disguise British control under a cloak of Malay sovereignty. Clifford's first posting outside Singapore was as secretary to Hugh Low, the venerable resident of Perak. In 1887 Weld dispatched Clifford on a mission to the east coast state of Pahang, where he successfully persuaded its ruler to accept British control of external affairs. Clifford was then appointed British agent in Pahang, but his powers were limited and within a year Sir Cecil Clementi-Smith, Weld's successor as governor, compelled the sultan to upgrade the British

Sir Hugh Charles Clifford (1866–1941), by Bassano, 1915

agent to resident. A senior official, John Rodger, was appointed to this position while Clifford sailed to England with acute dysentery. He returned in 1890 as superintendent of Ulu Pahang (the interior), where between 1891 and 1895 he led the suppression of armed resistance. Once this was settled, Clifford was advanced to resident of Pahang, which in 1896 became part of the Federated Malay States. For Clifford adventure gave way to administration as he moved from the frontier to the secretariat. In 1900 he was seconded to the British North Borneo Company and served as governor of North Borneo until a dispute with the directors led to his resignation. He returned briefly to Malaya, but in September 1901 sickness once again overwhelmed him. Poisoning was suspected and he sailed for England, apparently broken in health.

During 1901–3 he slowly recuperated in his mother's grace-and-favour apartment in Hampton Court palace and supplemented his half pay by writing. Clifford had become fluent in Malay, recorded his observations, and assiduously collected data on indigenous peoples. He presented papers to learned societies, such as the Royal Geographical Society, and produced *Further India: being the story of exploration from the earliest times in Burma, Malaya, Siam, and Indo-China* (1904). He also contributed articles on topical subjects to the press and wrote semi-autobiographical short stories, the first collection being published as *East Coast Etchings* (1896) and in a revised form as *In Court and Kampong* (1897). Other stories followed in *Macmillan's Magazine*, *Temple Bar*, *Cornhill Magazine*, and *Blackwood's Magazine*; and further collections appeared: *Studies in Brown Humanity* (1898), *In a Corner of Asia* (1899), and *Bushwhacking and other Sketches* (1901). His first novel, *Since the Beginning*, came

out in 1898. Thus, when ill health obliged him to write for a living, he was building on an established reputation and within a literary circle which included Joseph Conrad. His stories cover the poignant interaction of Europe and Asia, illustrated by the predicament of the political officer alone in an alien and potentially hostile environment or the fatal impact of modernization upon Malays. For example, Saleh, the eponymous hero of two novels, is educated in England but rejected by the English when he woos his host's daughter. On his return to his father's court he dies while leading an armed rising. In the foreword to *Saleh: a Sequel* Clifford spells out the dangers of the British 'endeavouring to impose on their Oriental brethren education of a purely Occidental type', which the fictional British officer endorses with the lament: 'May God forgive us for our sorry deeds and for our glorious intentions!'

In the autumn of 1903 Clifford was passed fit for tropical service, but was not restored to Malaya. As colonial secretary in Trinidad (1903–7) and Ceylon (1907–12) he managed well-established bureaucracies, but, when he was promoted to governorships in west Africa, he encountered rudimentary ones. As governor of the Gold Coast (1912–19) he overhauled the administration, reformed the legislative council, invested in public works, and vastly improved the living conditions and hence the morale of public servants. In doing so he paved the way for developments under his successor, Sir Gordon Guggisberg. When he was promoted governor of Nigeria (1919–25) Clifford set about rectifying what he condemned as the administrative chaos of Sir Frederick Lugard's amalgamation of Northern and Southern Nigeria. Superhuman stints in the office and extensive tours of the countryside resulted in voluminous dispatches, addresses, and memoranda. He revelled in the written and spoken word, shifted paper at speed, made systems, and made them work. In each territory he was indefatigable, bringing to administration the same vigour that had characterized his youthful exploits on the frontier and usually applying to the problems of 'native administration' the yardsticks of Malaya. But his manic energy and occasional bouts of depression exhausted subordinates and worried superiors.

Hugh Clifford was twice married: first in 1896 to Minna, daughter of Gilbert à Beckett. They had one son and two daughters. Their son was killed on the Somme in 1916, as was Clifford's younger brother. Minna died following an accident in Trinidad in 1907. In 1910 he married Elizabeth Lydia Rosabel (1866–1945), daughter of Edward Bonham and widow of Henry de la Pasture. Writing as Mrs de la Pasture she was a popular novelist; her daughter from her first marriage published under the name of E. M. Delafield.

In 1925 Clifford was promoted to Ceylon, where he remained just two years until Malaya became vacant, but long enough to set in train a major constitutional review carried out by the Donoughmore commission (1927–8). For Clifford the years spent away from Malaya had been years of exile, but his governorship of Malaya (1927–9) is more remarkable as the last chapter in a personal odyssey than for its impact on the country. Ironically, his greatest administrative achievements had been outside Malaya, particularly in west Africa. By now he was over sixty, exhausted, and on the verge of breakdown. Some say it was the agony of trying to reconcile modern Malaya with the land of his youth that precipitated collapse; but the demands of more than forty years of overseas service had taken their toll, resulting in increasingly eccentric behaviour. Signs of mental imbalance cut short his term, and in October 1929 he departed Malaya for ever. It was a distressing end to a major proconsular career. Instead of enjoying a respected retirement—it was rumoured that a peerage might have been added to his GCMG (1921) and GBE (1925)—he was eventually confined to The Priory at Roehampton, where he died of broncho-pneumonia on 18 December 1941, ten days after the start of the Japanese invasion of Malaya.

Well over 6 feet tall and bald from early adulthood, Clifford was an imposing man with strong emotions and an almost theatrical physicality. His exploits were legendary, while his disputes assumed a magnificence that obscured their frequently petty origins. Personal magnetism and a self-indulgent charm earned him the reputation of a ladies' man and revealed a romanticism touched with tragedy which permeated his life and cast a cruelly pathetic shadow over his last years. A. J. STOCKWELL

Sources H. A. Gailey, *Clifford: imperial proconsul* (1982) · J. de V. Allen, 'Two imperialists: a study of Sir Frank Swettenham and Sir Hugh Clifford', *Journal of the Malaysian Branch of the Royal Asiatic Society*, 37/1 (1964), 41–73 · A. J. Stockwell, 'Sir Hugh Clifford's early career (1866–1903) as told from his private papers', *Journal of the Malaysian Branch of the Royal Asiatic Society*, 49/1 (1976), 89–112 · A. J. Stockwell, 'Sir Hugh Clifford in Malaya, 1927–9: *Pinang pulang ka-tampok*', *Journal of the Malaysian Branch of the Royal Asiatic Society*, 53/2 (1980), 21–44 · private information (2004) · Hugh Clifford MSS, priv. coll. [c/o Mr Hugo Holmes] · *DNB* · H. Clifford, *The house of Clifford* (1987) · d. cert.
Archives Bodl. RH, Colonial Records collection · National Archives of Malaysia, Kuala Lumpur, Pahang diaries · NRA, priv. coll., corresp. and papers · PRO, Colonial Office country series | Bodl. Oxf., corresp. with Lewis Harcourt · Bodl. RH, letters to Sir William Gowers · News Int. RO, corresp. with Lord Astor, etc. · U. Leeds, Brotherton L., letters to Edward Clodd · U. Lond., Institute of Commonwealth Studies, corresp. with Theodor L. Clemens · Wilts. & Swindon RO, corresp. with Viscount Long | FILM BFI NFTVA, actuality footage
Likenesses Bassano, photograph, 1915, NPG [*see illus.*] · photographs, priv. coll.

Clifford, James (*bap.* 1622, *d.* 1698), Church of England clergyman and musician, son of Edward Clifford, a cook, was born at Oxford, in the parish of St Mary Magdalen, where he was baptized on 2 May 1622. He had three brothers and two sisters. He was a chorister at Magdalen College from 1632 to 1642 and was educated in the choir school, but he took no degree at Oxford. On 1 July 1661 Clifford was appointed tenth minor canon of St Paul's Cathedral, London, where he later became sixth minor canon (1675), senior cardinal (1682), and sacrist (1682). He was for some years curate of St Gregory by St Paul's, a post he seems to have resigned before September 1695, in which

month he was succeeded by Charles Green. He was also chaplain to the Society of Serjeants' Inn, Fleet Street.

In 1663 Clifford published the first edition of the work for which he is best known, *The divine services and anthems usually sung in the cathedrals and collegiate choires in the Church of England*. This is a collection of the words of 172 anthems by composers ranging from William Byrd and Thomas Tallis of the Elizabethan period to Henry Lawes and William Child, both of whom were active church musicians until the prohibition of choral services during the civil war. In 1664 Clifford published a second edition with many additions, which took the total to 406 anthems and included brand new works by Matthew Locke, Pelham Humfrey, and John Blow. *The Divine Services* also contains 'Brief directions for the understanding of that part of the divine service performed with the organ in S. Pauls Cathedral', a 'Scale or basis of musick' by Ralph Winterton, regius professor of medicine at Cambridge, and a 'Psalm of Thanksgiving', sung by the children of Christ's Hospital, set to music by Thomas Brewer. The book is a valuable record of Restoration choral regeneration.

In 1694 Clifford published *A catechism containing the principles of Christian religion … with a preparation sermon before the receiving of the holy sacrament of the Lord's supper*. He was twice married. His first wife's name is unknown, but on 30 May 1667 he obtained a licence for his marriage at St Dunstan-in-the-West, or the chapel of Serjeants' Inn, with Clare Fisher of the parish of St Gregory by St Paul's. His son was baptized at St Gregory's on 2 May 1679 and buried there in 1684. Clifford died in September 1698. His will (dated 16 June 1687) was proved on 26 September by his widow, who after her husband's death lived with her daughter in Wardrobe Court, Great Carter Lane, where the two women kept a school for small children. By his will Clifford left all his music to be divided among the minor canons of St Paul's.

W. B. SQUIRE, *rev.* PETER LYNAN

Sources J. R. Bloxam, *A register of the presidents, fellows … of Saint Mary Magdalen College*, 8 vols. (1853–85), vol. 1, pp. 39–40, 56 · Wood, *Ath. Oxon.*, new edn, 4.597 · I. Spink, *Restoration cathedral music, 1660–1714* (1995) · J. Hawkins, *A general history of the science and practice of music*, new edn, 3 vols. (1853); repr. in 2 vols. (1963), vol. 2, pp. 690–91

Clifford, John, ninth Baron Clifford (1435–1461), soldier and magnate, sometimes known as 'the Butcher', was born at Conisbrough Castle in the West Riding of Yorkshire on 8 April 1435, the eldest son of Thomas *Clifford, eighth Baron Clifford (1414–1455), and his wife, Joan Dacre (*b.* before 1424, *d.* before 1455). Conisbrough was the dower house of his great-aunt Maud, countess of Cambridge, who was one of John's godparents, and later left him twelve silver dishes in her will. Nothing else is known of his childhood and youth, and it is in keeping with the rest of his short adult life that he should be next recorded on 24 August 1453, supporting the Percys, allies of the Cliffords since the 1390s, in their confrontation with the Nevilles, equally long-term adversaries in north-west England of the Cliffords, on Heworth Moor near York. In the following year he became a father. His wife was Margaret (*d.*

1493), daughter and heir of Henry Bromflete, Lord Vescy, and their marriage appears to have formed part of Thomas Clifford's programme of expanding his interests in parts of the north relatively free from Neville domination. Husband and wife would later join the York Corpus Christi Guild.

On 22 May 1455 Thomas Clifford was killed in battle with the duke of York and the Nevilles at St Albans. John Clifford was still a few months under age, and not until 5 July 1456 did he enter into his inheritance. To an already prolonged contest with the Nevilles for pre-eminence in the north-west he brought additional bitterness arising from a desire for vengeance. For a while the conflict was precariously contained by Yorkist control of government, and by the efforts of king and council to make peace. On 24 March 1458 it was arranged in King Henry's name that Richard Neville, earl of Warwick, should pay 1000 marks (£666 13s. 4d.) to John Clifford and his brothers and sisters, in compensation for their father's death. But the fact that Clifford, ominously described as one of 'the yong lordes whoos fadres were sleyne at Seynt Albonys' (English Chronicle, 77), had earlier arrived in London alongside the sons of the earl of Northumberland, also killed at St Albans, at the head of a force of 1500 men, forcibly underlines the difficulties facing any would-be peacemaker. The king's settlement, and the ceremonious 'loveday' that followed it, had little effect. Queen Margaret became ever more dominant in government, and Clifford's energy made him an increasingly important supporter of the Lancastrian cause—a propaganda poem of 1458 names him as one of the components of the 'well good sayle' of the ship of state (Robbins, 192–3).

Clifford became increasingly active away from the court. A JP in Westmorland since 1456, in July 1458 he was also appointed to the bench for the West Riding of Yorkshire. Summoned to the Coventry parliament of November 1459, he took the oath of allegiance to the king, queen, and Prince Edward on 11 December. Eight days later he was granted the honour and castle of Penrith, forfeited by the earl of Salisbury; the Nevilles' control of Penrith had been particularly obnoxious to the Cliffords, thanks to its proximity to their own lordship in north Westmorland and their castle at Brougham. On 8 April 1460 Clifford was appointed warden of the west march, another office recently monopolized by the Nevilles. The fact that he was ordered to raise men in Cumberland, Westmorland, and Northumberland to resist the duke of York and other rebels indicates how he was expected to use the resources of his wardenry. On 8 October 1460, following the Yorkist victory at Northampton, Clifford was ordered to surrender Penrith to Salisbury. Two days later the duke of York claimed the throne, precipitating an all-out dynastic conflict.

Clifford had been summoned to the parliament that was to debate York's claims, but does not appear to have attended it. He had probably remained in the north, where he was one of the lords who assembled at Hull to meet with Queen Margaret, and subsequently gathered in council at York, before setting out to destroy the tenants of the duke of York and earl of Salisbury. Clifford was himself later said to have engaged in pillage, and also to have recruited men by 'moost drad proclamations' (RotP, 6.20). On 31 December 1460 the Lancastrians overwhelmed York and his men at Wakefield. Clifford was knighted by the duke of Somerset immediately before the battle, which subsequently brought him considerable notoriety, much of it first reported only several decades after the event. It is John Leland, writing in the years around 1540, who reports that Clifford 'for killing of men at this bataill was caullid the boucher' (Itinerary, 1.41). To Leland's general attribution of slaughter and mayhem has been added a more specific charge, the slaying of the young Edmund, earl of Rutland, York's second son. This is first ascribed to Clifford in the Annales of William Worcester, a contemporary source. But whereas Worcester records baldly that Clifford killed Rutland on Wakefield Bridge as he fled from the battle, Edward Hall, in his Union of the Two Noble and Illustre Famelies of Lancastre & Yorke, completed about 1532 and published in 1548, provides an altogether more circumstantial account of the deed (later heavily drawn upon by Shakespeare). Here Rutland, his age reduced from seventeen to twelve, and accompanied by a tutor, pleads voicelessly for mercy, 'for his speache was gone for feare', but is pitilessly struck down by Clifford, with the words 'By God's blode, thy father slew myne, and so wil I do the and all thy kyn' (Hall, 250–51). This may indeed have been how Clifford felt towards York and his family, but whether he actually voiced his feelings thus may be doubted.

Following their victory at Wakefield, the Lancastrians moved south, Clifford among them. He fought at the second battle of St Albans, on 17 February 1461, and it was reportedly in his tent that Henry VI was afterwards reunited with Queen Margaret and Prince Edward. But the Lancastrians lost the initiative by failing to capture London, and retreated north, with the Yorkists in slow pursuit. On 28 March there was a sharp contest for the passage of the Aire at Ferrybridge. A force led by Clifford captured the bridge, but was itself attacked in the flank by Yorkists who had crossed the river upstream, and Clifford was killed—according to tradition he fell at Dittingdale, near Castlebridge, struck in the throat by a headless arrow. His body seems to have been cast into a common burial pit. Following the shattering defeat of the Lancastrians at Towton on the following day, Clifford was attainted and his lands forfeited; his Westmorland estates were later granted to the earl of Warwick. The tribulations undergone by his young heir, Henry *Clifford, the so-called Shepherd Lord, appear to be mythical, but the ruin of the family was for the time being complete. John Clifford left two sons and two daughters. His widow, who lived until 1493, married Sir Lawrence Threlkeld, a Westmorland landowner, with whom she had one son and two daughters.

HENRY SUMMERSON

Sources Cumbria AS, Kendal, WD/Hoth/Books of record, 2, 437–85 · chancery, inquisitions post mortem, PRO, C139/159 nos. 16, 20; C139/162 no. 30 · J. S. Davies, ed., *An English chronicle of the reigns of Richard II, Henry IV, Henry V, and Henry VI*, CS, 64 (1856) · J. Gairdner, ed., *The historical collections of a citizen of London in the fifteenth century*, CS, new ser., 17 (1876) · J. Gairdner, ed., *Three fifteenth-century chronicles*, CS, new ser., 28 (1880) · J. Stevenson, ed., *Letters and papers illustrative of the wars of the English in France during the reign of Henry VI, king of England*, 2/2, Rolls Series, 22 (1864) [incl. William Worcester's *Annales*] · R. Flenley, ed., *Six town chronicles of England* (1911) · J. Stow and E. Howes, *Annales, or, A generall chronicle of England … unto the end of this present yeere, 1631* (1631), 414 · R. H. Robbins, ed., *Historical poems of the XIVth and XVth centuries* (1959), 192–3 · *The itinerary of John Leland in or about the years 1535–1543*, ed. L. Toulmin Smith, 11 pts in 5 vols. (1906–10), vol. 1, p. 41 · *Hall's chronicle*, ed. H. Ellis (1809) · *Chancery records* · *RotP*, vols. 5–6 · *RotS*, vol. 2 · *Reports … touching the dignity of a peer of the realm*, House of Lords, 4 (1829) · R. H. Skaife, ed., *The register of the Guild of Corpus Christi in the city of York*, SurtS, 57 (1872), 61 · [J. Raine], ed., *Testamenta Eboracensia*, 2, SurtS, 30 (1855), 118–24 · V. J. C. Rees, 'The Clifford family in the later middle ages, 1259–1461', MLitt diss. University of Lancaster, 1973, 163–70 · GEC, *Peerage*, new edn, 3.293–4 · C. L. Kingsford, *Prejudice and promise in XVth century England* (1925), 52 · R. T. Spence, *The shepherd lord of Skipton Castle* (1994) · H. Summerson, M. Trueman, and S. Harrison, *Brougham Castle, Cumbria* (1998) · R. A. Griffiths, *The reign of King Henry VI: the exercise of royal authority, 1422–1461* (1981) · R. L. Storey, *The end of the house of Lancaster* (1966) · J. W. Clay, 'The Clifford family', *Yorkshire Archaeological Journal*, 18 (1904–5), 354–411 · BL, Harley MS 5177, fol. 103 · J. Watts, *Henry VI and the politics of kingship* (1996) · H. T. Riley, ed., *Registra quorundam abbatum monasterii S. Albani*, 1, Rolls Series, 28/6 (1872)

Archives BL, Harley MS 5177, fol. 103 · Cumbria AS, Kendal, WD/Hoth

Wealth at death estates in Yorkshire and Westmorland valued at £374 14s. 7½d.: Clay, 'The Clifford family'

John Clifford (1836–1923), by George Charles Beresford

Clifford, John (1836–1923), minister of the New Connexion of General Baptists, was born at Sawley, Derbyshire, on 16 October 1836, the eldest of the seven children of Samuel Clifford, a warp-machine worker, and his wife, *née* Mary Stenson. His father's family were Methodists and his mother's family were Baptists, three of his uncles being Baptist preachers. He went to Baptist schools in Sawley and Lenton, and Wesleyan and national schools in Beeston. At eleven he started work in a lace factory, with a sixteen-hour working day. By the age of thirteen he could read while working his machine, and first began to absorb Emerson's *Essays*, which was to be in his hands the week he died. He regarded Emerson as 'one of the most potent forces in shaping my life' (Marchant, 12), because he learned from him the value of ideas.

In November 1850 Clifford experienced conversion in the General Baptist chapel at Beeston, and after being accepted for membership on 29 April 1851 he was baptized on 16 June 1851 by Richard Pike. After two years as a lay preacher in Nottingham, he was recommended by his church to the Midland Baptist College in Leicester, where he began his course in September 1855. Like many other theological students he questioned the historical truth of Christianity, the teaching of Christ, and the place of miracles in the life of the world. Although some of his contemporaries found that they could be more open to biblical criticism as Unitarian ministers, Clifford adopted a broad-based evangelical theology, believing that God's self-revelation was progressive and that geology compelled a reappraisal of Genesis. He became senior student in his third year when the college moved to Nottingham, and accepted an invitation to Praed Street Baptist Church,

Paddington, on condition that he could continue his studies at University College, London. He began his ministry on 17 October 1858 and remained there until he retired on 29 August 1915. He married Rebecca (d. 1919), daughter of Dr Thomas Carter of Newbury, on 14 January 1862, and they had four sons and two daughters. Clifford took his BA in 1861, BSc in 1862 (with honours in logic, moral philosophy, geology, and palaeontology), MA in 1864 (when he was first in the year), and LLB in 1866 (with honours in the principles of legislation). He was elected a fellow of the Geological Society in 1879. He received an honorary DD from Bates' College, Maine, in 1883 and from the University of Chicago in 1911, and an honorary LLD from McMaster University, Toronto, in 1911. His interest in geology reflected his sense of the urgency of reconciling the claims of religion and science, and his study of the principles of legislation indicated his concern for social reform, to be achieved through parliament.

When Clifford went to Praed Street the church had just over sixty members; by the turn of the century there were over a thousand. He believed that the church existed 'not only for our spiritual improvement, but also and specially for saving the souls and bodies of the people in the neighbourhood in which we are located' (Marchant, 40), and this characterized his ministry. A Mutual Economical Benefit Society was established in 1861 to provide sickness insurance, and then a Mutual Improvement Society. The growth of the church made it necessary to build a new chapel a mile away in Westbourne Park Place. Built in early Gothic style it cost £15,000 and was opened on 30 September 1877. Charles Spurgeon preached at a special service the following Tuesday (as he had done when the previous chapel was enlarged in 1872). Clifford's work was especially effective among young men, who formed the backbone of the Westbourne Park Institute, which offered such extensive educational and recreational opportunities that it was called a 'people's university'. Some twenty-three of 'Clifford's boys' entered the Baptist ministry. The church also opened a home for young women moving to London in 1885, and Clifford's Inn, a public house without beer, in 1908. There were the usual Sunday schools and children's organizations (such as the Band of Hope, Girls' Life Brigade, and Christian Endeavour) as well as a Pleasant Sunday Afternoon Fellowship inaugurated in 1902.

Clifford was brought up in the New Connexion of General Baptists, a product of the eighteenth-century evangelical revival centred in the midlands. As a minister in London he became a national leader and was editor of the *General Baptist Magazine* (1870–84). He was president of the General Baptist Association in 1872 and again in 1891, when the association formally joined with the Baptist Union of Great Britain and Ireland, a moment for which Clifford had worked hard for many years. He was president of the London Baptist Association in 1879, and of the Baptist Union in 1888 and 1899. When the first Baptist World Congress was held in London in 1905, attended by delegates from nearly thirty countries, it was resolved to form the Baptist World Alliance, and Clifford was unanimously elected president. In 1908 he chaired the first European Baptist Congress in Berlin, and in 1911 presided at the second Baptist World Congress in Philadelphia. He spoke at the second European Congress in Stockholm in 1913, and presided over the meeting in London in 1920 to organize assistance for European Baptists who had suffered from the war.

Clifford was open to new directions in theology, while preserving the centrality of the person of Christ. This is seen in books such as *The Inspiration and Authority of the Bible* (1892), *The Christian Certainties* (1894), and *The Ultimate Problems of Christianity* (1906). As vice-president of the Baptist Union in 1887–8 he found himself involved in the downgrade controversy. Spurgeon (a lifelong friend) had accused members of the Baptist Union of abandoning doctrines which he held dear, and resigned from the union. Clifford was involved in the attempts at reconciliation, but was determined to avoid the pressure for a new credal statement as a basis for membership. Instead he drafted a declaratory statement which was approved by the Baptist Union Assembly in 1888. His presidential address on that occasion, 'The great forty years', set out his own view of primitive Christianity. Clifford's emphasis on the incarnation was characteristic of the period. His twin emphases on a personal relationship to Christ and freedom of conscience have led to criticisms that he had a 'diminished ecclesiology'. He regarded ecclesiology as a branch of sociology, which is why he believed that Christians had to be committed to transforming the whole of society.

Clifford was therefore inevitably a public figure. His concern for social questions began in his childhood factory and memories of Chartism, but later found theological justification. His autumn address to the Baptist Union in 1888 was on the primitive Christian faith as a social gospel, balancing the doctrinal emphasis of his spring address. Hence he supported the London dock strike of 1889 and the Progressive Party on the London county council. Though a lifelong Liberal he was also a member of the Fabian Society: two of his addresses were published as Fabian pamphlets. Clifford is most widely remembered for his involvement in the education controversy. He successfully opposed the imposition of religious tests on board school teachers in London in 1893–4. His campaign against rate assistance for denominational schools in the 1902 Education Act was unsuccessful, and he became leader of the passive resistance movement which refused to pay education rates because they infringed freedom of conscience.

Clifford's contribution to nonconformist life generally was recognized by his presidency of the National Council of the Evangelical Free Churches (1898–9). Although a keen opponent of the Second South African War, his influence was important in securing Free Church support for the First World War in 1914. After retirement he was president of the Brotherhood Movement (1916–18) and the World Brotherhood Federation (1919–23). In the new year's honours list of 1921 Clifford was one of the first Free Churchmen to become a Companion of Honour. Though rather short Clifford was of striking appearance, with a full beard (originally red, later grey) and moustache compensating for his bald head, and always a twinkling smile. He died at a meeting of the Baptist Union council at Baptist Church House, Southampton Row, London, on 20 November 1923, and was buried in Kensal Green cemetery. His wife had died on 23 August 1919.

DAVID M. THOMPSON

Sources J. Marchant, *Dr John Clifford, CH: life, letters and reminiscences* (1924) · C. T. Bateman, *John Clifford: Free Church leader and preacher* (1904) · J. H. Y. Briggs, *The English Baptists of the 19th century* (1994) · D. M. Thompson, 'John Clifford's social gospel', *Baptist Quarterly*, 31 (1985–6), 199–217 · E. A. Payne, *The Baptist Union: a short history* (1959) · M. T. E. Hopkins, 'Spurgeon's opponents in the downgrade controversy', *Baptist Quarterly*, 32 (1987–8), 274–94 · M. Hopkins, 'The down grade controversy: new evidence', *Baptist Quarterly*, 35 (1993–4), 262–78 · H. J. Cowell, *John Clifford as I knew him* (1936) · G. W. Byrt, *John Clifford: a fighting Free Churchman* (1947) · A. G. Gardiner, *Prophets, priests and kings* · E. M. Jeffs, *Princes of the modern pulpit*

Archives NRA, priv. coll. | BLPES, corresp. with E. D. Morel · Bodl. Oxf., Asquith MSS · Regent's Park College, Oxford, Baptist Union Council archives, corresp. with Herbert Asquith

Likenesses J. Collier, oils, 1906, Baptist Church House, London · J. Collier, oils, 1906; replica, 1924, NPG · E. Kapp, drawing, 1913, Barber Institute of Fine Arts, Birmingham · G. C. Beresford, photographs, NPG [*see illus.*] · R. Haines, print, postcard, NPG

Wealth at death £2162 8s. 2d.: probate, 8 Jan 1924, *CGPLA Eng. & Wales*

Clifford, Sir Lewis (c.1330–1404), soldier and suspected heretic, 'far from being of the north-country baronial family was a cadet of the Cliffords of Devonshire, such small fry that their pedigree is difficult to trace' (McFarlane, 162). He was probably born in the early 1330s. His military career began inauspiciously as one of the Calais garrison captured at the battle of St Georges in June 1351. He had entered the service of Edward, the Black Prince, by 1360, first as a yeoman, but was an esquire by 1364. He was knighted in 1368, whereafter he received an annuity of 100 marks from the prince and by 1378 (when that was confirmed) a further £100 p.a. for life as keeper of Cardigan Castle, as well as gifts indicating a personal friendship. After the prince's death, on 8 June 1376, Clifford became a trusted servant of his widow, Joan of Kent (d. 1385), mother of Richard II. In spring 1377 she employed him to reconcile John of Gaunt, duke of Lancaster (d. 1399), with the Londoners, who disliked the latter's support of John Wyclif (d. 1384) against their bishop and his attack on the city's liberties; in 1378, again ostensibly on behalf of the popular Joan but probably at Gaunt's request, he intervened to seek an end to Archbishop Sudbury's trial of Wyclif. Neither incident can of itself suggest Clifford's own religious sympathies.

Between 1370 and 1372 Clifford married Eleanor, daughter of John (II) *Mowbray, Lord Mowbray of Axholme, and Joan of Lancaster, and widow of Roger, Lord de la Warr (1326–1370), from whom she brought a large jointure as well as her own descent from Henry III. Before her early death in June 1387 Clifford had prudently renegotiated the settlement with her son, so as to give himself a life interest in a large estate in Ewyas Harold, Herefordshire. He acquired holdings in six other counties to add to valuable life tenancies received from the Black Prince and Joan, but curiously never established a perpetual estate, perhaps because his son, Lewis, predeceased him.

In 1367 Clifford had fought in Spain under the Black Prince; in 1373–4 he took part in John of Gaunt's unsuccessful campaign in France, and in 1378 concluded his soldiering with Gaunt's expedition to Brittany. He was elected to the Garter in 1377 or 1378, doubtless—as his services in the home crisis had also indicated in those years—with the approval of both Gaunt and the young king's domestic circle, an unusual consensus. His personal service to Princess Joan evidently kept him out of the political mainstream in the early 1380s, and that was to prove fortunate. In June 1385 Clifford was commanded by the king to be in continual attendance on his failing mother; in August he was named as one of her executors; in September he received livery of mourning. Richard II naturally confirmed Clifford in everything he had held of Joan.

Clifford visited France in 1385–6. Perhaps now, but certainly by 1396, Clifford was elected to the Passion, an international crusading order based in France. After the political crisis that overwhelmed Richard II's regime in 1386–8 Clifford became one of the most frequent attenders on the king's council between 1389 and 1393, a knight of the chamber, and a member of many commissions—clearly a trusted and prestigious contributor to the king's determined restoration of his authority. Clifford's experience and his personal standing in France made him a natural choice for missions in February 1391 and 1393 preparing the way for peace talks, and in 1396 he helped negotiate the king's marriage to Princess Isabella. Despite his earlier links with Gaunt it is not surprising that Clifford enjoyed no favour from Henry IV after Richard's deposition; although originally ratified in his holdings, he was deprived of two major estates (Princes Risborough, Buckinghamshire, and Mere, Wiltshire) on alleged legal grounds in 1404.

When he was in France in 1385–6, Clifford met the poet Eustache Deschamps, who (like Froissart) admired him and called him l'amoreux. He brought back one of Deschamps's works for Geoffrey Chaucer, to whose son Lewis he may have been godfather—the Treatise on the Astrolabe was written for either this boy or Clifford's own son. Chaucer also addressed a poem to Sir Philip la Vache, the second husband of Clifford's daughter, Elizabeth. (Sir Philip had, incidentally, received a gold goblet from Princess Joan as a wedding present.) Clifford and la Vache, always close associates, are found frequently in the public and private company of those household knights of the Black Prince and Richard II whom the chroniclers Knighton and Walsingham identified as supporters of, and even adherents to, Lollardy [see Lollard knights]. Like Clifford, some were notably cultured, some especially interested in crusading. Clifford himself was said by Walsingham to have encouraged the audacious publication of the twelve conclusions of the sect in London in January 1395. Walsingham also claimed that in 1402 Clifford recanted (informally) and submitted a memorandum of seven radical beliefs held by his sectarian associates. Although prudence may have persuaded Clifford to forswear under the new, unsympathetic, regime, his sympathies remained. He had been an overseer to the highly idiosyncratic will of Sir Thomas Latimer (d. 1401), a determined supporter of Wycliffite teaching, and repeated the key sentiments in his own will (like Latimer's and, unusually, in English) on 17 September 1404; he chose as executors Sir John Cheyne (d. 1414), Sir John Oldcastle (d. 1417), and the equally suspect Richard Colefax, a brazen selection when viewed with hindsight. The fact that probate of his will was granted on 12 December 1404 indicates that he had died soon after making it. PETER FLEMING

Sources K. B. McFarlane, Lancastrian kings and Lollard knights (1972) • W. T. Waugh, 'The Lollard knights', SHR, 11 (1913–14), 55–92 • Chancery records • M. C. B. Dawes, ed., Register of Edward, the Black Prince, 4 vols., PRO (1930–33) • M. D. Legge, ed., Anglo-Norman letters and petitions from All Souls MS 182, Anglo-Norman Texts, 3 (1941) • L. C. Hector and B. F. Harvey, eds. and trans., The Westminster chronicle, 1381–1394, OMT (1982) • The chronicle of Adam Usk, 1377–1421, ed. and trans. C. Given-Wilson, OMT (1997) • P. McNiven, Heresy and politics in the reign of Henry IV (1987) • A. Hudson, The premature reformation: Wycliffite texts and Lollard history (1988) • J. Dahmero, William Courtenay, archbishop of Canterbury, 1381–96 (1966)

Clifford [née Lane], (**Sophia**) **Lucy Jane** [pseud. John Inglis] (**1846–1929**), writer, was born in Camden Town, London, on 2 August 1846, the daughter of John Lane and Louisa Ellen, née Gaspey (d. 1901). At a very early age, however, she started to present herself as a few years younger than she really was, eventually being entered by her son-in-law, upon her death, as seventy-two when in fact she was ten years older. She seems also to have supported the myth that she was born in Barbados, since she approved of some of the biographical entries on her husband in which this erroneous fact is noted. She met William Kingdon *Clifford (1845–1879), the brilliant professor of applied mathematics at University College, London, in the early 1870s, and they married on 7 April 1875. When his health and his

(**Sophia**) **Lucy Jane Clifford** (1846–1929), by Lafayette, 1926

prospects still appeared to be excellent, W. K. Clifford renounced his father's inheritance to the benefit of the latter's second, much younger family. He could not have foreseen that he was to fall ill and die quite soon after this gesture, leaving his wife and two small daughters almost penniless. Clifford's friends organized a testimonial fund which helped the young widow for a short while but she soon decided to take matters into her own hands, resuming her career as a writer and continuing the salon which had enjoyed such a distinctive reputation during her marriage. Regular visitors of Clifford's at-homes were Leslie Stephen, Frederick Pollock, John Collier, Frederick Macmillan, and, for a while, the controversial 'Vernon Lee' (Violet Paget). At this time Henry James became one of Lucy Clifford's most prized friends, and their correspondence was extensive.

Lucy Clifford's first publications were printed anonymously in *The Quiver* in the early 1870s. In tales such as *The Dingy House at Kensington*, *Queen Madge*, *Against Herself*, and *The Troubles of Chatty and Molly* she tends to portray young, female protagonists who experience an emotionally painful intermezzo before they can marry the man of their dreams, their purity and goodness remaining unquestioned. After the death of her husband most of her books were published under the name Mrs W. K. Clifford. Her first relatively successful work, however, was a collection of children's verses, *Children Busy, Children Glad, Children Naughty, Children Sad* (1881) signed L. C., which was erroneously attributed by some to Lewis Carroll. Real fame came

in 1885 with the anonymous publication of *Mrs Keith's Crime*. This novel is the harrowing, personal narrative of a young widow who first loses her eldest child and then has to cope with the imminent death from tuberculosis of her small daughter. When the family doctor predicts that she herself will die first, she decides to kill the child so that she will not have to suffer a lonesome death. The novel paved the way for a writing career in which books such as *Love Letters from a Worldly Woman* (1891) and *Aunt Anne* (1892) seem to have been the highlights after 1885.

Lucy Clifford's novels contain a great number of autobiographical elements. The central characters are usually women, mostly young women, who have to prove their strength and will-power in the face of adversity. Mother–daughter relationships are extremely important, often with the mother sacrificing herself for her daughter. She also wrote a few successful plays in the 1890s and the first decade of the twentieth century. *The Likeness of the Night*, for instance, was first produced at the Royal Court Theatre, Liverpool on 18 October 1900 and then went to London the following year. The most enduring of her writings, however, have been two short stories, 'The New Mother' and 'Wooden Tony', which have been repeatedly included in anthologies of children's tales. 'The New Mother', especially, has drawn a good deal of critical comment because of the unexpected callousness of the mother towards her children and the horrifying aspect of the new mother herself. Lucy Clifford was also a sporadic contributor to a variety of journals. She wrote a great number of gossip items for *The Athenaeum*, and she was on the staff of *The Standard* for fourteen years.

After the First World War, Lucy Clifford's fame declined and she found it extremely hard to get her books published. She remained a feisty, enterprising woman until the very end of her life, even going to Spain to learn Spanish in 1920 when she was seventy-four years old (Meynell, 22–4). She died at her home, 7 Chilworth Street, Paddington, London, on 21 April 1929 of pneumonia, and was buried in Highgate cemetery, next to her husband. The two Clifford daughters survived their mother. Little is known of Margaret (1877–1932), the younger of the two, but Ethel Clifford (1876–1959) was a poet and celebrated beauty in her youth. She became Lady Dilke in 1905 when she married Sir Fisher Dilke (1877–1944), Sir Charles Wentworth Dilke's nephew.   MARYSA DEMOOR

Sources *Henry James: letters*, ed. L. Edel, 4 vols. (1974–84) · *Vernon Lee's letters*, ed. I. C. Willis (privately printed, London, 1937); repr. (1970) [microfilm] · V. Meynell, ed., *The best of friends: further letters to Sydney Carlyle Cockerell* (1956) · M. Demoor, 'Self-fashioning at the turn of the century: the discursive life of Lucy Clifford (1846–1929)', *Journal of Victorian Culture*, 4.1 (1999), 102–17 · 'Bravest of women and finest of friends': Henry James's letters to Lucy Clifford, ed. M. Demoor and M. Chisholm (1999) · private information (2004) [R. Chisholm, R. Farwell, M. Chisholm] · b. cert. · m. cert. · d. cert. · *CGPLA Eng. & Wales* (1929)

Likenesses Lafayette, photograph, 1926, NPG [*see illus.*] · photograph, repro. in *Bravest of women*, ed. Demoor and Chisholm, frontispiece

Wealth at death £275—limited to settled land: probate, 1 Nov 1929, *CGPLA Eng. & Wales*

Clifford [*née* Russell], **Margaret, countess of Cumberland** (1560–1616), noblewoman, was born at Bedford House, Exeter, on 7 July 1560, the youngest child of Francis *Russell, second earl of Bedford (1526/7–1585), and Margaret (*d.* 1562), daughter of Sir John St John of Bletsoe. Following her mother's death in August 1562 she lived for seven years with her aunt Mrs Elmes of Lillford, Northamptonshire, and afterwards at Woburn, receiving an extensive education, judging by the wide-ranging scholarly interests she later displayed.

On 24 June 1577 at St Saviour's, Southwark, Lady Margaret married George *Clifford, third earl of Cumberland (1558–1605), her father's ward. Although her affection towards him remained undiminished, his courtier profligacy and infidelity led to their separation in 1600. The early death of both their sons caused the countess anguish and thereafter she devoted herself to the welfare of her surviving child, Lady Anne *Clifford (1590–1676). Lady Anne describes her mother as having a 'very well favoured face with sweet and quick gray eyes and a comely personage' (Williamson, *Lady Anne Clifford*, 36–8). Intelligent with many practical as well as intellectual interests, Countess Margaret was an exceedingly pious lady, a zealous puritan who helped foster the spread of her beliefs from the earl's Skipton Castle in the West Riding of Yorkshire. When building Beamsley Hospital, the almshouse she founded for widows near Skipton in 1593, she stressed the centrality of religious devotion by choosing the style of the round Romanesque churches.

Countess Margaret was extremely well-read, patronized the translation of foreign authors, and attracted dedications, especially from puritan writers. Her marital plight inspired verse letters from Samuel Daniel and perhaps Fulke Greville, and her piety was praised in Emilia Lanier's religious poems. Part of her revealing biographical letter survives. She also had a scientific and entrepreneurial bent. She practised alchemy, distilled medicines, and invested in lead-mining in Craven and in experiments to smelt iron with coal. Emulating her husband, she invested in the East India Company. She erected a monument in Hornsey church, Middlesex, to Richard Cavendish, her lead-mining associate who died in 1601.

'Her Spirit', Lady Anne rightly said of Countess Margaret, 'never yielded to ill fortune or opposition' (Williamson, *Lady Anne Clifford*, 38). When Earl George excluded Anne from his inheritance in favour of his brother Francis *Clifford, fourth earl, the countess amassed documentary evidence with the aid of the antiquary St Loe Kniveton which in 1607 undermined Earl Francis's pleas in the court of wards. This archive formed the core of the three great books of record of the Clifford family that Lady Anne later compiled. Furthermore, she vigorously overcame by litigation the opposition of her Westmorland jointure tenants. According to Lady Anne, she was worldly-wise, Sir William Wentworth correctly judging her 'much experienced and verie pollitique' (Cooper, 30). Countess Margaret died aged fifty-five, on 24 May 1616, at Brougham Castle, Westmorland. She was buried on 7 July

in Appleby church, where her daughter erected a fine monument to her with a lifelike effigy, attributed to Maximilian Colt.

RICHARD T. SPENCE

Sources R. T. Spence, *Lady Anne Clifford: countess of Pembroke, Dorset and Montgomery, 1590–1676* (1997) · R. T. Spence, *The privateering earl* (1995) · G. C. Williamson, *George, third earl of Cumberland (1558–1605): his life and voyages* (1920) · G. C. Williamson, *Lady Anne Clifford* (1922) · J. P. Gilson, *Lives of Lady Anne Clifford, countess of Dorset, Pembroke and Montgomery (1590–1676), and of her parents* (1916) · *The diaries of Lady Anne Clifford*, ed. D. J. H. Clifford (1990) · J. W. Clay, 'The Clifford family', *Yorkshire Archaeological Journal*, 18 (1904–5), 354–411 · *DNB* · T. D. Whitaker, *The history and antiquities of the deanery of Craven, in the county of York*, 3rd edn, ed. A. W. Morant (1878) · R. T. Spence, 'Mining and smelting in Yorkshire by the Cliffords, earls of Cumberland, in the Tudor and early Stuart period', *Yorkshire Archaeological Journal*, 64 (1992), 157–83 · A. Lanyer [E. Lanier], *Salve deus rex Judaeorum* (1611) · J. P. Cooper, ed., *Wentworth papers, 1597–1628*, CS, 4th ser., 12 (1973) · G. Blakiston, *Woburn and the Russells* (1980)

Archives Alnwick Castle, Northumberland, Syon MSS · Cumbria AS, Kendal, Hothfield MSS [copies, Longleat House, holograph letters] · W. Yorks. AS, Leeds, Yorkshire Archaeological Society, Skipton MSS

Likenesses oils, 1585, Gorhambury, Hertfordshire; version, NPG · G. Gower, oils, 1586; copies · L. Hilliard, miniature, 1603–5, V&A · M. Colt?, alabaster effigy on monument, 1617, Appleby church, Cumbria · triptych, oils, *c.*1648 (after G. Gower), Appleby Castle, Cumbria

Wealth at death approx. £500 in land, excl. jointure estate; approx. £500 in jewels, plate, and other goods: will, Clay, 'The Clifford family', 393–6

Clifford, Martin (*c.*1624–1677), headmaster and author, eldest son of Henry Clifford, gentleman, and his wife, Cecily (*bap.* 1600), daughter of Bishop Martin *Fotherby of Salisbury and his wife, Margaret Winter, was presumably born in London. His parents were married in All Hallows Church in Lombard Street, London, on 17 December 1623 and his younger brother, Francis, died as a baby in 1625. By the time his sister, Mabel, died in 1639 at the age of ten, his father was already dead.

Clifford attended Westminster School as a king's scholar and liberty boy. In 1640 he entered Trinity College, Cambridge, where he was a contemporary of the duke of Buckingham and of Abraham Cowley, with whom he would conduct a lifelong friendly and learned correspondence. Like most eldest sons of the gentry, he did not graduate, but he had acquired 'good learning, and might have been eminent had not the wars hindred his progress' (Wood, *Ath. Oxon.*, 3.999). What became of him during the civil war is not known. According to Warren's contemporary life, he was 'always loyal to his King' (Warren, 144) and it seems that he followed the court into exile. A letter from Abraham Cowley to the duke of Ormond on 26 December 1659 suggests that at that time Clifford was in Brussels.

After the Restoration, Clifford became Buckingham's secretary and lived at the Savoy. As an unrepentant drinker and talented and biting poet, Clifford was much sought after among the court wits. In May 1669 he mocked in verses Edward Howard's prolix and bombastic heroic poem 'The Brittish princes', while in four defamatory letters, probably written between January 1671 and July 1672 (Winn, 579), he charged John Dryden with plagiarism. The latter circulated by transcripts until their posthumous publication as *Notes upon Mr. Dryden's Poems in Four Letters* (1687). It was said that he had a hand, along with Cowley, Thomas Sprat, and Edmund Waller, in producing the famous 'Rehearsal' by Buckingham, and according to Evelyn he was involved with Buckingham, Sprat, Waller, and Evelyn himself in promoting a society aimed primarily at the improvement and the polishing of the English tongue (J. Evelyn, *Diary and Correspondence*, ed. W. Bray, 1906, 3.455–6).

In 1671 Clifford was elected master of the Charterhouse, probably through the influence of Buckingham. His meagre salary was raised by the mediation of the earl of Shaftesbury. During the years of his mastership he loved conversing on poetry, religion, and human nature with Dame Sarah Cowper (1640–1719), who wrote that 'Because he treated Fools according to their Folly, it gott him the Character of ill Nature; but I never knew him other than Compassionate, Charitable, generous and Just'. In spite of her assertion that he was, 'no Contemner of Religion, or such as maintain the principles of it, but wou'd express great Veneration for B^p Wilkins Dr Tillot: Dr Barrow and the like' (Herts. ALS, D/EP F30, fol. 131), and although his office demanded adherence to the established church, Clifford seems to have been a covert deist.

In 1674 Clifford published anonymously in London *A Treatise of Humane Reason*, which stirred up a ten-year controversy by advancing the hypothesis of salvation even for an honest erring conscience. It was frequently reprinted. Not long after its publication Bishop Benjamin Laney of Ely dined with many 'persons of quality' in the Charterhouse, when he was asked about his opinion on that book. Undoubtedly unaware that he was in the presence of its author, the bishop answered that 'twas no matter if all the copies were burnt and the author with them, knowing by what he had read in the book that the author makes every man's private fancy judge of religion' (Wood, *Ath. Oxon.*, 3.999).

On 10 December 1677 Clifford died at Sutton's Hospital in the Charterhouse, 'not much lamented by the Pensioners' (Warren, 144), and was buried on the 13th in the chancel of St Margaret's, Westminster. His funeral was attended by many lords including the duke of Buckingham. In 1682 the Unitarian author William Popple (1638–1708) published a French translation of Clifford's treatise introduced by a longer preface justifying the opinions in it, with the title *Traité de la raison humaine traduit de l'anglois* (1682). This aroused great interest among the Huguenot refugees in Holland.   GIOVANNI TARANTINO

Sources G. Tarantino, *Martin Clifford, 1624–1677: deismo e tolleranza nell'Inghilterra della Restaurazione* (Florence, 2000) · T. Sprat, *An account of the life and writings of Mr Abraham Cowley written to Mr M. Clifford*, in *The works of Mr Abraham Cowley*, ed. T. Sprat (1668) · GL, MS 17613, fols. 14v, 52v, 102v, 105r · Wood, *Ath. Oxon.*, new edn · Venn, *Alum. Cant.* · A. Pritchard, 'Six letters by Cowley', *Review of English Studies*, new ser., 18 (1967), 253–63 · A. Warren, *An apology for the discourse of humane reason, written by Ma. Clifford, Esq; being a reply to plain dealing, with the author's epitaph and character* (1680) · Herts. ALS, Cowper (Panshanger) MSS D/EP F29, fol. 90; F30, fols. 98, 131; F32, fol. 114 · PRO, SP 44/36; MS 30/24/6A · BL, Add. MS 5866, fol. 58r; Add. MS 27872, fols. 8–9 · J. A. Winn, *John Dryden and his world* (1987) · *Jean Le Clerc: epistolario*, ed. M. G. Sina and M. Sina, 1 (Florence, 1987), 125, 127, 138, 141, 158, 168 · L. Simonutti, 'Un acteur et témoin du débat sur la tolérance: William Popple, marchand, écrivain et poète de la liberté', *Q/W/E/R/T/Y. Arts, Littérature et Civilisations du Monde Anglophone*, 8 (1998), 267–72 · J. Nichols, ed., *A select collection of poems*, 8 vols. (1780–82) · 'Life', E. Waller, *Poems, &c.*, written upon several occasions and to several persons, 9th edn (1712) · A. H. Nethercot, *Abraham Cowley: the muse's Hannibal* (1931) · J. Welch, *The list of the queen's scholars of St Peter's College, Westminster*, ed. [C. B. Phillimore], new edn (1852) · 'The session of the poets (1666)', *Poems on affairs of state: Augustan satirical verse, 1660–1714*, ed. G. de F. Lord and others, 1 (1963), 327–37, esp. 328–9 · parish register, St Margaret's, Westminster, 13 Dec 1677 [burial] · H. Love, 'How personal is a personal miscellany? Sarah Cowper, Martin Clifford and the "Buckingham commonplace book"', *Order and connexion: studies in bibliography and book history* [Cambridge 1994], ed. R. C. Alston (1997), 111–26

Archives BL, Add. MS 5866 · BL, Add. MS 27872 · GL, MS 17613 · PRO, MS 30/24/6A · PRO, SP 44/36 | BL, Harley MS 6862 · Charterhouse School, London, Godalming, ref. 170/2/4 · Herts. ALS, Cowper (Panshanger) MSS · Yale U., Beinecke L., Osborne shelves, Buckingham

Likenesses M. Vandergucht, line engraving, BM, NPG; repro. in Sprat, *An account*

Clifford, Richard (*d.* 1421), bishop of London and administrator, had a brother, Robert (*d.* 1423), who was an esquire of Tonbridge, Kent, and was a kinsman of Thomas Fishbourne, anchorite and first confessor to the new Bridgettine nunnery at Syon, Middlesex. This is the total of firm evidence about the bishop's family, despite repeated and extensive efforts to link him with the great northern baronial family and with Sir Lewis Clifford (*d.* 1404), the Wycliffite, who was of an established Devon family. The future bishop, Sir Lewis, and Thomas, sixth Lord Clifford, were all in Richard II's household in the 1390s. Fishbourne and Robert Clifford both had some landholdings in the north. There is some inconclusive heraldic evidence. If Richard was indeed kin to the baronial family, there is no indication that this was significant in his career. A second Richard Clifford, who was archdeacon of Middlesex between 1418 and 1422, and received considerable patronage from the bishop, was almost certainly a close kinsman, but there is no evidence that he was the bishop's nephew.

The elder Richard Clifford was a graduate: a master by 1397 and bachelor of civil and canon laws by March 1398, perhaps of Oxford, where he later proposed to found a college. On 23 July 1380 he appears as a king's clerk, when he was presented by the crown to the mastership of the free chapel of Jesmond, Northumberland, a county where his brother had lands. By 1394 he held or had held six rectories and sixteen other preferments, most of them by royal nomination. Clifford was at the heart of the household, being clerk of the chapel and close to the king. He performed no external commissions. In April 1387 the king wrote to the pope on behalf of his 'dear clerk' (Perroy, 50–51). Probably he remained with the king in the midlands throughout this year. He was with him at Woodstock on 11 October 1387 as Richard prepared to face the lords appellant, and was detained by them in the Tower of London on 8 February with a view to being tried in parliament. In the event, he was probably not charged, but he was released, by mainprise of three leading border knights, on condition of appearing in the next parliament, living in his own house, and having no contact with the king.

Once the king recovered his authority, Clifford was recalled promptly to his side and became keeper of the great wardrobe on 28 November 1390. Alongside his many preferments, he obtained the farm of the alien priory of Burstall in Holderness on 12 January 1392, bringing his brother in as co-beneficiary a year later. On 29 August 1394 he became archdeacon of Ely. On 1 December 1395 he was elected, presumably with Richard II's support, to the see of Salisbury, but the pope had already translated Bishop Richard Medford of Chichester, who had at least as long and serious claims to the king's sympathy, and was accordingly successful. On 23 February 1397 Clifford exchanged his archdeaconry of Ely for the more prestigious one of Canterbury. On 28 March 1398 he was admitted as dean of York. Apart from these three dignities, Clifford held no fewer than six further preferments at some time between 1394 and 1401. Throughout his career Clifford shuffled his pack to increasing self-advantage. On 14 October 1399 Henry IV would ratify his tenure of the deanship, the archdeaconry, four prebends, and one mastership of a hospital. At least half the bishoprics in England were worth less than these. Accordingly, since Clifford wanted to be a bishop, it was reported that he was even intriguing to oust Ralph Erghum, the veteran servant of John of Gaunt, duke of Lancaster, from the see of Bath and Wells in the late 1390s. In January 1398 Clifford took pains to obtain a prebend in Wells as a base.

On 14 November 1397 Richard II appointed Clifford as keeper of the privy seal, as part of his extension of firm personal control over all arms of the government after his coup against his major enemies. This may well have saved Clifford's career. He was appointed an executor of the king's will on 16 April 1399, and an attorney for several of the leading figures accompanying the king's expedition to Ireland. He himself remained behind to help govern England in the king's absence, but he was not among the king's intimates at the heart of this caretaker regime. Accordingly, if still remarkably, he was not only able to survive the king's fall, but was reappointed without a break by Henry IV as keeper of the privy seal on 30 September. Furthermore, ostensibly by petition of the Commons in parliament, he was declared loyal on 10 November, notwithstanding his exclusion from the general pardon issued by Richard II's opponents back in 1388. He remained uncontentiously in office, and is found being summoned to the king at Leeds Castle, Kent, on 5 April 1400 to explain an existing treaty with the duke of Gueldres.

So confidently had Clifford adapted to the new dynasty that he continued his campaign to gain Bath and Wells. Once Erghum had at last died, Clifford gained papal provision on 12 May 1400. However, the king was supporting Henry Bowet, once as formidable a Ricardian careerist as Clifford, but one who had transferred into John of Gaunt's service and shared Henry's own exile. Bowet had gained

election by the chapters. Deadlock ensued. On 2 March 1401, the Commons in parliament urged Clifford's cause, as having failed to gain Salisbury in 1395 and as an excellent keeper of the privy seal. The king responded that both candidates were excellent, and he would work for both of them. This is so rare an entry by either house in parliament into an episcopal appointment that the possibility that it was stage-managed must be considered. The Cistercian monk Tideman Winchcombe, formerly Richard II's all-night drinking partner and physician and reputedly also a magician, died on 1 June, leaving the see of Worcester available. Quite likely this event had been as long expected as it was universally welcomed. The king sent the monks a licence to elect on 20 June, and Clifford became their choice seven days later. He received custody of the temporalities five days later (2 July), albeit forfeiting at the rate of £100 p.a. on 6 August to the royal household. The papal translation was issued briskly on 17 August. He received the bulls in London on 20 September, the temporalities the next day, and was consecrated in St Paul's on 29 October. Worcester was just about sufficient for Clifford in terms of income and status. Bowet, of course, took up Bath and Wells.

Clifford resigned as keeper of the privy seal at once, on 3 November 1401, as was often customary at this time, but he seems to have remained active as a counsellor around the government. Apart from January–April 1403 (during which visit he was enthroned on 4 February), July–August 1403, September–December 1404, and March–September 1407, he was absent from his diocese. During his spell of residence in 1404 he appointed proctors to the parliament at Coventry, having a rash of white spots all over his body and being quite unable to ride. On 6 May 1402 he had left London as an escort of Princess Blanche to her marriage (6 July) with the son of Ruprecht, king of the Romans. He returned to London on 29 July. In March 1404 he was appointed a member of the council, but was not included in its next formal reconstitution on 22 May 1406. It is possible that he was, at least by now, identified with Archbishop Thomas Arundel in politics.

On 22 June 1407 Clifford was translated to the see of London. He received the papal bulls on 13 October and the temporalities seven days later. He was engaged in extending the truce with Scotland in this year, but otherwise seems to have been little involved in government affairs. His only commission of any note was to hear an appeal from the court of admiralty on 22 August 1409. However, when Archbishop Arundel was restored to power in 1412, Clifford subsequently reappeared in attendance at meetings of the royal council. He also acted as an assessor at the trial of the heretic Sir John Oldcastle on 23 September 1413.

Clifford's public career was now in its twilight, and the accession of Henry V confirmed this. None the less, he retained full health. On 9 April 1416 he was even appointed to reinforce the delegation of the province of Canterbury to the Council of Constance, with letters of protection on 9 July. On 20 July he was also named as a delegate of the crown, an interesting piece of evidence that Henry V believed that Clifford would respond loyally to his policy of bringing the English 'nation' to heel under collective episcopal leadership. Clifford arrived at Constance on 7 October 1416, and made such an impression that he was even considered as a possible choice for papacy. In the event, it was he who nominated Odo Colonna on 11 November 1417, and conducted his coronation as Martin V.

The mayor and aldermen of London, with whom he enjoyed good relations, urged Clifford to come home as soon as he could. Their reasons are unknown, but some oblique light might be cast on their appeal by the fact that his diocesan administration was in unusual disarray, with no fewer than five vicars-general in succession during his absence. As for himself, he gained licence on 19 April 1418 from Martin V to be allowed to appoint coadjutors should he become too weak or old to administer his diocese. He probably travelled from Constance to join Henry V in France, although his whereabouts there are unknown. On 20 June 1418 he was granted letters of attorney by the king in France because he was 'going abroad' (that is, out of the Lancastrian realm). He is then to be found in Cologne in November 1418 and still in February 1419, presumably on royal business and once more dealing with the former Princess Blanche.

Clifford was still absent from his diocese on 10 May 1419 but had returned by 9 June. His public life was over. Martin V wrote to him on 27 April 1421, to express both friendship and anxiety for news of his good health. Perhaps the pope was moved by knowledge that Clifford's health was far from good. However, the bishop did not change the uncomplicated will he had made on 20 August 1416 when setting out for Constance, which suggests that his final illness was sharp. His burial was to be in St Paul's Cathedral or whatever 'honest' place God pleased. Saints Peter, Paul, and Earconwald were invoked as special patrons. The bishop designated £100 for his funeral and a marble stone, £100 for paupers on his estates, £100 for paupers in hospitals and prisons, and 1000 marks for poor scholars at his proposed college in Oxford—which was currently just Burnell's Inn—with £40 to the master and fellows. His brother, Robert, was left plate and bedding, and was also named as principal executor, with instructions to reward the bishop's household and then distribute the rest of his possessions for the good of his soul. Clifford died on 20 August 1421 and was buried in the cathedral, on the site where the shrine of St Earconwald had formerly stood. There are many signs from throughout his career that his personal reputation stood far higher than official records alone indicate.   R. G. DAVIES

Sources R. G. Davies, 'The episcopate in England and Wales, 1375–1443', PhD diss., University of Manchester, 1974, 3. xcv–c · register for Worcester, Worcs. RO, b716.093–BA.2648/5(i) · register for London, GL, MS 9531/4, fols. 37–191v · Emden, *Oxf.*, 1.440–42 · E. F. Jacob, ed., *The register of Henry Chichele, archbishop of Canterbury, 1414–1443*, 2, CYS, 42 (1937), 224–6 · *The diplomatic correspondence of Richard II*, ed. E. Perroy, CS, 3rd ser., 48 (1933) · St Paul's Cathedral archives, MS WD 13, fol. 79v

Archives GL, register, MS 9531/4, fols. 37–191v · Worcs. RO, register, b716.093–BA.2648/5(i)

Clifford, Robert, first Lord Clifford (1274–1314), soldier and magnate, was born about the beginning of April 1274, the son of Roger de Clifford the younger (d. 1282) and his wife, Isabella de Vieuxpont (d. 1291), coheir with her sister Idonea to the lordship of Westmorland. The Cliffords had previously been a family powerful in the Anglo-Welsh marches. The Vieuxpont marriage led to their becoming one of the most important northern baronial dynasties. Aged only eight when his father was killed in Wales, Robert Clifford's wardship appears to have been granted to Edmund of Cornwall, the king's brother, but to have been effectively disposed of by Robert's mother, who entrusted the upbringing of her son to Gilbert de Clare, earl of Gloucester (d. 1295); only in 1291 did Edmund recover the custody. In 1294 Clifford was said to be in the king's wardship, and he was with Edward I in Wales in the spring of 1295. He had livery of his estates on 3 May 1295, but was still trying to recover usurpations suffered during his lengthy minority more than fifteen years later. The task was complicated by the demands of war and public office in Scotland and the north of England, almost as soon as Clifford entered upon his inheritance. In 1296 he accompanied the king to Scotland, and in July 1297 he was appointed captain of the king's castles in Cumberland. At the end of that year he led a destructive raid into Annandale which defeated the local levies and burnt ten villages. In the following February another raid left Annan in ashes.

On 22 July 1298 Clifford fought at Falkirk as a household banneret, and after the victory, on 25 November, he was made captain and king's lieutenant in north-west England and in Scotland to the boundaries of Roxburghshire, an office he still held in the following July. Nor was this the only responsibility entrusted to him, for on 7 July 1298 he became keeper of Nottingham Castle and justice of the forests north of the Trent, positions he would occupy to the end of the reign. As a reward for his labours, on 26 September 1298 Edward I granted Clifford Caerlaverock Castle and the lands of Sir William Douglas, in the process initiating a feud between the Cliffords and the Douglases which would last for a century. A series of personal summonses to parliament which began on 29 December 1299 has led to his being styled Lord Clifford. In 1300 he accompanied the king on the Caerlaverock campaign. He engaged himself to serve in Scotland over the winter of 1301–2, and accompanied the king there in 1304, participating in a successful attack on the Scots near Peebles about 1 March. Later that year he joined the forces of the prince of Wales, and with them took part in the siege of Stirling Castle. But though he remained close to Prince Edward, who in August 1305 described him as 'our dear and well loved knight' (*Letters of Edward, Prince of Wales*, 92), he also continued to serve the king, on whose behalf he was keeper of the see of Durham in 1302–3 and 1305–7, and by March 1306 he was back in Scotland, as keeper of Selkirk. Shortly afterwards he was one of the English captains ordered to attack the rebellious Robert Bruce, and in

February 1307 is recorded as pursuing Robert in Galloway. He was unable, however, to prevent James Douglas from capturing Douglas Castle and massacring the garrison that Clifford had placed in it.

Loyal and energetic service to Edward I did not hinder Clifford from safeguarding and extending his own interests in the north of England. In May 1306 he was granted Hart and Hartlepool in the bishopric of Durham, forfeited by Robert Bruce, and in February 1307 the king gave him lands in Cumberland forfeited by Sir Christopher Seton. But Westmorland remained fundamental to his regional standing and authority, and he enhanced his position there by adding to his estates (he acquired the manor of Brough Sowerby in 1298), by building up a loyal following among the gentry of the region, several of whom served repeatedly under his leadership in Scotland, and by the prestige to be had from large-scale architectural projects. In the years around 1300, possibly as a result of a visit in that year by Edward I and his court, Clifford made substantial additions to Brougham Castle, finally gaining the seal of royal approval in the form of a licence to crenellate in 1309.

Trusted by Edward I and close to Prince Edward, Clifford was one of four leading barons whom the former on his deathbed is said to have begged to have the prince crowned as soon as possible, and to keep Piers Gaveston out of England—'and thai grantede him with god wille' (*Brut: England*, 1.202–3). Early in the new reign Clifford was appointed marshal of England, and presumably organized Edward II's coronation on 25 February 1308. He had already subscribed to the declaration issued by a number of barons at Boulogne on 31 January, undertaking to preserve the rights of the crown, thereby suggesting his willingness to support the new king in the face of mounting baronial discontent. On 12 March 1308 he was relieved simultaneously of the marshalcy, Nottingham Castle, and his forest justiceship, but this can hardly be construed as resulting from loss of favour at court, for on 20 August he was appointed captain and chief guardian of Scotland. On 13 October, moreover, it was 'by the command of our lord the king' (books of record, 2.66–7) that he concluded negotiations with his maternal aunt Idonea and her second husband, John Cromwell, which resulted in his reuniting the lordship of Westmorland, divided since the mid-1260s. More probably Edward II had decided to build up Clifford's position in the north of England, at a time when the English position in Scotland was coming under growing pressure. It is likely to have been for the same reason that a sequence of three royal grants made between March and September 1310 gave him the castle and honour of Skipton in Craven in Yorkshire. He subsequently carried out important works on Skipton Castle. That his daughter Idonea should have married Henry Percy, second Lord Percy, with whose father Clifford many times campaigned against the Scots, is a pointer to the extent to which he came to identify himself with the nobility of northern England.

Clifford served regularly in Scotland and on the Scottish borders in the early years of Edward II's reign. On 26 October 1309 he was appointed keeper of the Carlisle march, and on 20 December following was ordered to act as warden of Scotland, with a force of 100 men-at-arms and 300 foot soldiers. He had relinquished that office by 1 April 1310, but on 17 July received a protection as he was about to set out for Scotland, and was said to have parleyed with King Robert at Selkirk in December. On 4 April 1311 he was appointed keeper of Scotland south of the Forth, with his headquarters at Berwick, and in November led a raid upon the Scots in which eleven of his knights lost their horses. But he was increasingly distracted from his duties in the north by his involvement in English politics, particularly as these were directed against Piers Gaveston. Clifford may have been influenced in this by the grant to Gaveston of the honour of Penrith in December 1310, perhaps fearing that Gaveston might become his rival for preeminence in north-west England. But as Gaveston had formerly held the more valuable lordship of Skipton, subsequently granted to Clifford, the latter had arguably gained more from royal favour, and it is likely that Clifford was moved principally by the general baronial hostility towards the favourite, and by his own undertaking to the king's father. He was not one of the ordainers, and Edward II probably regarded him as basically well disposed; when Skipton was resumed under the ordinances on 21 October 1311, it was restored to Clifford on 13 November following.

Nevertheless, Clifford was active against Gaveston in 1312, holding the borders to prevent his seeking Scottish aid, and later besieging him in Scarborough Castle. Though not involved in Gaveston's death, he appears to have taken some of the valuables that the king and Gaveston abandoned in Newcastle—some jewels were later returned to Edward from Clifford's London house. Gaveston was executed on 19 July 1312, and for over a year Clifford was continually active as an intermediary on behalf of the earls of Lancaster and Warwick in their negotiations with the king, receiving a series of safe conducts and letters of protection. On 14 October 1313 the barons responsible for Gaveston's death received pardons, and two days later Clifford himself obtained a general pardon. Although the reconciliation between the king and his leading opponents was superficial, it allowed Edward II to turn his attention to Scotland. Summoned to attend a muster at Berwick on 10 June 1314, Clifford took part in the campaign that culminated in the battle of Bannockburn. On the day before the main engagement, he was one of two leaders of an English force that tried to get behind the Scottish force drawn up in front of Stirling Castle, either to cut off its retreat or to make contact with the castle garrison. But his men could not break the ranks of the enemy infantry, and were eventually scattered; Clifford's own withdrawal was regarded by one chronicler as shameful—he had been 'disgracefully routed' (*Vita Edwardi secundi*, 51). Perhaps anxiety to recover his honour made him over-impetuous, for on the following day, 24 June, he charged into action in the English vanguard and was killed.

The Scottish king demanded no ransom for the return of Clifford's body, which was taken to Carlisle, and almost certainly interred at Shap Abbey, where Clifford had founded a chantry for his parents. By 1295 he had married Maud, daughter of Thomas de Clare of Thomond, the brother of the earl of Gloucester in whose household Clifford was brought up. The marriage brought the Cliffords Irish estates of greater potential than actual value. Robert and Maud Clifford had two sons, Roger (d. 1322) and Robert (d. 1344), both minors at their father's death. A daughter, Margaret (d. 1382), married Peter (V) *Mauley, third Lord Mauley [see under Mauley family]. Roger Clifford became the ward of Sir Bartholomew Badlesmere, whose influence doubtless helped carry him into opposition to the crown. A committed Lancastrian, in 1322 Roger fought in the baronial army at Boroughbridge, where he was wounded and captured. He was hanged at York on 23 March. The Clifford estates, forfeited for Roger's treason, were restored in 1327 to his brother Robert, with whose descendants the Clifford line continued. Maud Clifford, forcibly abducted in 1315 by Jack the Irishman, the keeper of Barnard Castle, married Sir Robert Welle, one of her rescuers, and died in 1325. Her first husband seems to have been widely trusted and admired. His martial prowess was acknowledged by the Scots: for John Barbour he was 'The lord clyffurd that wes so stout' (Barbour, 1.277). And the *Song of Caerlaverock* (admittedly a work that Clifford may have sponsored himself) praises his wisdom and prudence, describes his 'much honoured banner', and declares that 'If I were a young maiden I would give him my heart and person, so good is his fame' (*Roll of Caerlaverock*, 12).   HENRY SUMMERSON

Sources Cumbria AS, Kendal, WD/Hoth/Books of record, 2.23–143 · Cumbria AS, Kendal, WD/Hoth/A988/11, 31, 33, 59 · V. J. C. Reer, 'The Clifford family in the later middle ages, 1259–1461', MLitt diss., University of Lancaster, 1973, 30–58 · *Chancery records* · *RotS*, vol. 1 · *CDS*, vols. 2–3, 5 · exchequer, king's remembrancer, inquisitions *post mortem*, PRO, E 149/1 no. 27(2) · GEC, *Peerage*, new edn, 3.290–91 · *CIPM*, 5, nos. 533, 561 · F. W. D. Brie, ed., *The Brut, or, The chronicles of England*, 2 vols., EETS, 131, 136 (1906–8), vol. 1, pp. 202–3 · N. Denholm-Young, ed. and trans., *Vita Edwardi secundi* (1957) · J. Stevenson, ed., *Documents illustrative of the history of Scotland*, 2 (1870) · *Thomae Walsingham, quondam monachi S. Albani, historia Anglicana*, ed. H. T. Riley, 2 vols., pt 1 of *Chronica monasterii S. Albani*, Rolls Series, 28 (1863–4), vol. 1, pp. 141–2 · *The roll of Caerlaverock*, ed. T. Wright (1864) · J. Barbour, *The Bruce*, ed. W. W. Skeat, 2 vols., EETS, extra ser., 11, 21 (1870–79) · *The chronicle of Walter of Guisborough*, ed. H. Rothwell, CS, 3rd ser., 89 (1957) · F. Palgrave, ed., *The parliamentary writs and writs of military summons*, 2 vols. in 4 (1827–34), vol. 1/2, p. 536; vol. 2/3, pp. 687–8 · E. B. Fryde, ed., *Book of prests of the king's wardrobe for 1294–5* (1962) · *Letters of Edward, prince of Wales, 1304–1305*, ed. H. Johnstone, Roxburghe Club, 193 (1931) · G. W. S. Barrow, *Robert Bruce and the community of the realm of Scotland*, 3rd edn (1988) · N. Denholm-Young, *History and heraldry, 1254 to 1310* (1965) · J. R. S. Phillips, *Aymer de Valence, earl of Pembroke, 1307–1324: baronial politics in the reign of Edward II* (1972) · J. R. Maddicott, *Thomas of Lancaster, 1307–1322: a study in the reign of Edward II* (1970) · M. Prestwich, *Armies and warfare in the middle ages* (1966), 44 · H. Summerson, M. Trueman, and S. Harrison, *Brougham Castle, Cumbria* (1998)
Archives Cumbria AS, Kendal, WD/Hoth
Wealth at death lands in Yorkshire, Durham, and Westmorland: *CIPM*

Clifford, Sir Roger de (b. c.1221, d. in or before 1286), baron and soldier, was the son of Roger de Clifford of Tenbury Wells, Worcestershire (d. 1230/1231), younger son of Walter de *Clifford, lord of Clifford, near Hay, Herefordshire, and of Sybil (fl. c.1221–1253), daughter of Robert of Ewyas and widow of Robert de Tregoz and William of Newmarch. A minor at his father's death, Roger was in the custody of his uncle Walter, lord of Clifford, until he came of age, probably in 1242. He inherited lands in Worcestershire, Herefordshire, and Berkshire from his father, held predominantly from his cousin, another Walter de Clifford. In 1248 he was granted a weekly market and annual fair at Tenbury. He spent the early part of his career as a knight of Richard de Clare, earl of Gloucester. In 1248 he went on pilgrimage with the earl, and in 1254 he travelled with him to join Henry III in Gascony.

By the end of 1258 Clifford had joined the new political grouping which grew up around the Lord Edward, but in 1262 he was associated with Roger of Leybourne, who was accused of misappropriating funds from Edward. At this time Clifford, together with many of Edward's former intimates, abandoned the prince and joined the supporters of Simon de Montfort, and in May 1263, as a representative of the lords of the Welsh marches, wrote to the king urging him to uphold the provisions of Oxford. That August he and his fellows were forbidden to take part in tournaments, or to take up arms without royal licence, but despite this he was given command of the castles of Marlborough and Ludgershall. During 1263 Clifford campaigned in the Welsh marches with Roger of Leybourne and others, but by August they had been reconciled with the king and Edward. Clifford was pardoned for his activities, and in December was appointed sheriff of Gloucester, thereafter remaining loyal to Henry III. On 5 April 1264 he was present at the siege of Northampton, where he captured Simon de Montfort the younger. Himself taken at the battle of Lewes on 14 May, Clifford was released with the other marcher lords on condition that he would attend parliament when summoned, but he failed to do so. In October he besieged the castle at Hanley of Gilbert de Clare, earl of Gloucester (son of his former lord).

In January 1265 Clifford was among those offered safe conducts to withdraw to Ireland for a year, but remained in England where he took part in negotiations between the Lord Edward and the barons. He fought for the king at Evesham, and played a role in the subsequent pacification of England. In August he was appointed justice of the forest south of the Trent, an office he held for the next sixteen years, and keeper of the peace in Westmorland. At this time he also served as constable of Gloucester and in various minor offices, and was twice sent to the marches to hear complaints on the king's behalf. He received substantial rewards for the services he performed for Henry III and his son. In 1261 he was granted a pension of 50 marks a year, and three years later Edward granted him land worth 100 marks in the honour of Monmouth. After Henry III's victory at Evesham he was given lands of rebels in Warwickshire, Leicestershire, and elsewhere, and was pardoned a debt of nearly £400. He also received the custody of Isabel, eldest daughter and coheir of the former rebel Robert de Vieuxpont, and married her to his own son Roger.

In 1270 Clifford joined the Lord Edward's crusade, and was one of the executors of the will made by him at Acre in 1272. After he took the cross he was promised the next available wardship worth more than £500 p.a., because he had 'borne himself laudably in the king's service' (*CPR, 1266–72*, 448). While returning from the crusade through France he married a lady mysteriously designated the countess of Lerett, or Lauretania, whose identity remains obstinately impenetrable. It would seem that all that can be said of her is that she outlived her husband and was buried in Worcester Cathedral after her death in 1301. His first wife had probably been Hawisia, widow of John de Boterel, whose marriage was granted to Clifford's father for his son's use in 1230. In 1274 he negotiated a truce with Llywelyn ap Gruffudd and in 1275 he acted as Edward I's proctor at the *parlement* of the king of France. In the following year he temporarily lost the custody of Eardisley Castle, when his bailiffs there threw the king's writ in the face of a royal messenger and threatened to kill him unless he left immediately. Between 1277 and 1280 he served as a justice on eyre for the forest, and in 1279 he was appointed justice of Wales. In 1282 Clifford was dragged from his bed and taken prisoner after a surprise attack on his castle of Hawarden by the Welsh prince Dafydd ap Gruffudd. His son, Roger the younger, was killed in the same year during an assault on Anglesey.

Clifford was still alive in 1284, when he granted £10 to Westwood Priory, Worcestershire, and settled the manor of Severn Stoke on his younger grandson, another Roger. It may have been at this time that he founded a chantry in the parish church at Tenbury. He seems to have suffered some financial difficulty in his later years, for in the late 1270s he sold property in London to the city for 300 marks, and in December 1283 he and his heirs were pardoned half his outstanding debts to the king. He was dead by 3 April 1286 when his goods were impounded on account of debts owed to the crown, although the private property of his widow was exempted from this order. He was succeeded by his grandson, Robert *Clifford (1274–1314), who inherited substantial property in Westmorland from his mother, Isabella de Vieuxpont (*d*. 1291), and was the first member of his family to receive a personal summons to parliament. KATHRYN FAULKNER

Sources Chancery records · VCH Worcestershire · The historical works of Gervase of Canterbury, ed. W. Stubbs, 2 vols., Rolls Series, 73 (1879–80) · Ann. mon., 1–4 · Chronicon Henrici Knighton, vel Cnitthon, monachi Leycestrensis, ed. J. R. Lumby, 2 vols., Rolls Series, 92 (1889–95) · M. Prestwich, Edward I (1988) · DNB

Clifford, Roger, fifth Baron Clifford (1333–1389), magnate, was born at Brougham Castle in Westmorland on 20 July 1333, the second son of Robert Clifford, third Lord Clifford of Westmorland (1305–1344), and Isabel, daughter of Maurice, Lord Berkeley. His elder brother, Robert Clifford, died early in 1346, married but without an heir of his body, leaving the twelve-year-old Roger heir to the Clifford lands and title; on 17 March Roger's wardship was entrusted to Thomas Beauchamp, earl of Warwick, whose daughter Maud (*d*. 1403) he was subsequently to marry. It was doubtless under Warwick's guidance that Clifford, still in his teens, fought in the sea battle of 1350 known as 'les Espagnols sur Mer'; in 1355 he accompanied Warwick to France in the first division of the army led by Edward, the Black Prince. By then he had attained his majority; he was granted livery of most of his lands on 14 May 1354, though not then quite of full age, and proved his age on 10 August following.

Clifford was to have trouble recovering his family's position in the north of England. To the normal difficulties resulting from an extended minority were added those arising from his mother's second marriage, to Sir Thomas Musgrave of Musgrave, who even after Isabel's death in 1362 tried to keep Clifford out of his mother's dower lands at Skipton, and was dislodged only by litigation in king's bench in 1366. His problems may have helped make Clifford a careful manager of his estates, which he augmented where possible—he acquired lands at Lamonby, in south Cumberland, and in Appleby. In 1357 he settled Hart and Hartlepool in the bishopric of Durham on himself and his wife, and in 1373 did the same with Brougham, which would be his widow's dower house. In addition he conveyed estates to his eldest son and his brother, both named Thomas. Clifford also speculated in the wardship and marriage market. In 1371 he agreed to pay £240 per annum for nearly three years for the wardship of Ralph, heir to the barony of Greystoke, while in 1388 he paid 500 marks (£333 6s. 8d.) for the marriage of the son and heir of Lord Ferrers of Groby [see Ferrers family (*per. c.*1240–1445)]. Moreover he strengthened his local position by retaining members of the Cumbrian gentry; in 1368, for instance, he retained Sir Robert Mowbray, lord of Bolton in Allerdale, for £10 per annum in peacetime and £33 6s. 8d. in time of war, but then replaced the peacetime fee with a lease of the manor of Skelton at a highly favourable rent.

Clifford needed retainers like Mowbray, for he was continually involved in national affairs. In 1359–60 he served in Edward III's expedition to France, and went to France again in the king's retinue in 1369; as part of his preparations for the latter campaign he made an indenture at Brougham with Sir Richard Flemyng of Coningston on 10 July 1369, retaining Flemyng for war in the king's army. Clifford had considerable estates in Ireland, and was more than once ordered to go there to help uphold the English position against native attacks. Finally in September 1379 he was retained by Edmund Mortimer, earl of March, to serve in Ireland for a year with a force of five knights, thirty-four esquires, and forty mounted archers; whether he actually went is uncertain. Clifford was first summoned to parliament on 15 December 1357, and thereafter was regularly summoned to parliaments and councils. He was a trier of petitions in 1363, 1373, 1376, and in both the parliaments of 1377; in November 1381 he was among the lords who demanded the repeal of manumissions granted during the peasants' revolt.

But Clifford was above all, and to an increasing extent, involved in the defence of the north of England against the Scots. He was first ordered to be ready to defend the borders in November 1356, and received his first commission as a march warden in May 1366. Altogether he received twenty-four such commissions, usually for the west march alone, but on three occasions for the whole of the English border area, and also a number of other appointments relating to the security of the north. In August 1374, for instance, he was one of the commissioners appointed to try to settle the long-running dispute between the Percys and the Douglases over Jedworth Forest. In spite of the fourteen-year truce of 1369 (to which Clifford was one of the English signatories) the borders were never truly at peace. In the autumn of 1372 Clifford was licensed to send an attorney to parliament, so that he could take precautions against a threatened Scottish attack, while after 1377, when the Scots ceased to pay David II's ransom, he became ever more active on the marches. Sheriff of Cumberland in 1377–8, in February 1379 he was made a commissioner of array to enable him to resist invasion. In March 1380 he was instructed to remain on the west march with forty men-at-arms and fifty mounted archers, and in November that year he was one of the deputies of John of Gaunt, duke of Lancaster, appointed to hold a march day with Sir Archibald Douglas. In 1382 he was one of the lords ordered to stay at home in the north for its defence, and on 29 May he was appointed to keep Carlisle Castle for a year.

Efforts to keep the peace continued; in April 1383 Clifford attended a march day with the earl of Douglas. But the imminence of open war led in December 1383 to an order for the sheriffs of Cumberland and Westmorland to supply masons to carry out repairs to Clifford's castles, and on 2 February 1384 the truce expired. Clifford was at Appleby in October that year, and acted as one of the commanders of the English army's rearguard when Richard II invaded Scotland the following summer. As part of his contribution to the defence of the north-west, he carried out substantial works on Brougham Castle, attested by a stone inscribed 'Thys Made Roger' which was originally placed over the entrance to the great hall, but is now set above the gatehouse arch. But political dissension weakened the English defences, and in August 1388 a Scottish invasion penetrated into north Westmorland and devastated a number of Clifford's estates, including Brougham, Brough, and Appleby. Clifford may not have been there at the time; in May 1388 he had joined the earl of Arundel's expedition to Brittany, possibly as a gesture to take pressure off his eldest son, Thomas *Clifford, who was out of favour with the lords appellant, of whom Arundel was one.

In January 1389 Clifford was appointed a warden of the west march for the last time; he appears to have retreated to Skipton, where he is recorded on 8 May, and it was most likely there that he died of a stroke, on 13 July 1389, having restored his family to a place in the forefront of the northern baronage. He was justly remembered by his descendants as 'one of the wysest and gallantest men of all the

Cliffords of his race' (books of record, 2.293). Recorded as a benefactor of the nuns of Arthington, Roger Clifford was probably buried at Bolton Priory, of which he was the patron. His wife, Maud, survived him, dying on 28 February 1403. They had two sons, Thomas, who succeeded as Baron Clifford, and William, who married Anne, daughter of Thomas, Lord Bardolf, and who contrived to flourish under both Richard II and Henry IV, in spite of his support for the Percys in all three of their rebellions against the latter king. They also had two daughters, Katherine, who married her father's ward, Ralph *Greystoke, third Baron Greystoke [see under Greystoke family (per. 1321–1487)], and Margaret, who married Sir John Melton. A son Roger, mentioned in a deed of 1365, may have been illegitimate, or may have predeceased his father.

HENRY SUMMERSON

Sources Cumbria AS, Kendal, WD/Hoth/Books of record, 2.211–12, 246–94 • V. J. C. Rees, 'The Clifford family in the later middle ages, 1259–1461', MLitt diss., University of Lancaster, 1973, 81–106 • Bodl. Oxf., MSS Dodsworth 70, 82 • Chancery records • RotS • CDS, vol. 4 • RotP, vols. 2–3 • Reports … touching the dignity of a peer of the realm, House of Lords, 4 (1829) • W. Yorks. AS, Leeds, Yorkshire Archaeological Society, MS DD121/31/12, fols. 23–24v • CIPM, 10, no. 202; 16, nos. 827–45 • Rymer, Foedera, new edn, vol. 3 • L. C. Hector and B. F. Harvey, eds. and trans., The Westminster chronicle, 1381–1394, OMT (1982) • special collections, ancient petitions, PRO, SC8/191, no. 9512 • [J. Gaunt], John of Gaunt's register, 1379–1383, ed. E. C. Lodge and R. Somerville, 2, CS, 3rd ser., 57 (1937), 384–6 • Chronicon Galfridi le Baker de Swynebroke, ed. E. M. Thompson (1889), 129 • Chroniques de J. Froissart, ed. S. Luce and others, 4 (Paris, 1873), 90, 136 • Chroniques de J. Froissart, ed. S. Luce and others, 15 (Paris, 1975), 17 • F. Devon, ed. and trans., Issue roll of Thomas de Brantingham, RC (1835) • H. Summerson, M. Trueman, and S. Harrison, Brougham Castle, Cumbria (1998)
Archives Cumbria AS, Kendal, WD/Hoth
Wealth at death see CIPM, 16; W. Yorks. AS, Leeds, Yorkshire Archaeological Society, MS DD121/31/12, fols. 23–24v

Clifford, Rosamund [called Fair Rosamund] (b. before 1140?, d. 1175/6), royal mistress, was the daughter of Walter Clifford and Margaret, daughter of Ralph de Tosny, and was born probably before 1140. She is linked to *Henry II by a grant, recorded in the hundred rolls of 1274, made by the king of the manor of Corfham to Walter Clifford, 'for the love of Rosamund his daughter' (Rotuli hundredorum, 2.93–4); but her time living openly as the king's mistress was short indeed. Gerald of Wales, writing just before 1200, said that soon after Henry II had been reconciled with his sons (1174), he imprisoned his wife, Eleanor, and 'having long been a secret adulterer, now openly flaunted his mistress, not that rose of the world [rosa-mundi] of false and frivolous renown, but that rose of unchastity [rosa-immundi]' (Gir. Camb. opera, 4.21–2). Elsewhere Gerald says that Rosamund was still young when she died, and his contemporary Roger Howden states that, for the love of her, Henry II bestowed many benefits on the convent of Godstow (on the Thames just north of Oxford), where she was buried, and adds that the king gave the convent, which was previously impoverished, many valuable endowments including 'noble buildings'. These grants are well documented in the pipe rolls and Godstow's cartulary: they include two churches at Wycombe and Bloxham and substantial sums of money for building materials from 1175/6 to 1177/8, suggesting that Rosamund died in the first of those accounting years. At about the same time Walter Clifford granted valuable assets to the abbey including several mills and a meadow for the souls of his wife and his daughter Rosamund. And about 1180, according to the English register of Godstow, Bernard de St Valéry granted the king the patronage of the abbey 'by a silken thread [cloth] whereof was made a chasuble' (Clark, 1.129–30), so that Rosamund's resting-place was henceforth a royal foundation. The results of this patronage became apparent to Hugh, bishop of Lincoln, when he visited Godstow Abbey in 1191. Here he found Rosamund buried in a magnificent tomb adorned with hangings, lamps, and wax candles, and set in the middle of the church choir in front of the high altar. Disgusted at such profanation he gave orders for her body to be disinterred and reburied outside the church. Higden and others say that she was placed in the chapter house, where her tomb had the inscription:

> This tomb doth here enclose the world's most beauteous Rose,
> Rose passing sweet erewhile, now nought but odour vile.
> (Speed, 471)

As the rhyme suggests, by the fourteenth century Rosamund Clifford had become a figure of romance and legend, much of it associated with her death. In the earliest account of this, in the mid-fourteenth-century *Croniques de London*, Queen Eleanor (who is here confused with Eleanor of Provence, the wife of Henry III) causes Rosamund to be bled to death in a hot bath at Woodstock, after which the king has her body interred at Godstow. Higden, in his colourful *Polychronicon*, describes how at Woodstock 'King Henry had made for her a house of wonderful workmanship, a labyrinth of Daedelian design' (*Polychronicon*, 8.52). But in spite of Henry's efforts to hide her from the jealousy of the queen, Eleanor tracked Rosamund down by following her silken embroidery through the maze. What happened next Higden did not know, only that Rosamund's death followed. Still later sources, of the sixteenth and early seventeenth centuries, filled this gap in the story, representing the queen as confronting her beautiful rival and offering her the choice of death by poison or the dagger. Rosamund chose the poisoned bowl, and the grieving king buried her at Godstow. Here the bones of the real Rosamund may have remained until the Reformation, when John Leland (d. 1552), as cited by Dugdale, recorded that 'Rosamund's tomb at Godstow nunnery was taken up a-late. It is a stone with this inscription: *Tumba Rosamundae*' (Dugdale, 4.365). Leland's near contemporary Thomas Allen, who died in 1632 at the age of ninety, said that before its destruction her tomb had contained 'enterchangable weavings drawn out and decked with roses red and green, and the picture of the cup out of which she drank the poison, given her by the queen, carved in stone'. Thomas Hearne, who preserved Allen's account, also recorded local tradition as still pointing out Rosamund's stone coffin in his own time (c.1711),

although Hearne himself regarded it as 'no more than a fiction of the vulgar' (Hearne, 3.739).

A sketch of Everswell, adjoining Woodstock Palace, made by John Aubrey in the seventeenth century shows a complex of buildings with pools, a cloister, and a garden. Woodstock was a favourite residence of Henry II and the pipe rolls record that substantial sums were expended on the palace, grounds, and spring during his reign. The spring was known later as 'Rosamund's well', and nearby was a building first called 'Rosamund's chamber' in a pipe roll of 1231. It is likely that much of the villa complex in this area, including its cloister and pools, was laid out by Henry II, perhaps inspired by the rural pavilions of the Norman kings of Sicily. Another influence may have been the romance of Tristan and Isolde, a version of which was probably written for the king. Tristan and Isolde meet in secret in an orchard, and communicate by dropping twigs into the stream that runs through her chamber. Everswell's buildings included a similar orchard, spring, and bower for the secret meetings of Rosamund and Henry II.

T. A. ARCHER, *rev.* ELIZABETH HALLAM

Sources Gir. Camb. opera · Chronica magistri Rogeri de Hovedene, ed. W. Stubbs, 4 vols., Rolls Series, 51 (1868–71) · William of Newburgh, Chronica, ed. T. Hearne (1719) · Polychronicon Ranulphi Higden monachi Cestrensis, ed. C. Babington and J. R. Lumby, 9 vols., Rolls Series, 41 (1865–86) · A. Clark, ed., The English register of Godstow nunnery, EETS, 129, 130, 142 (1905–11) · VCH Oxfordshire, vol. 2 · R. Brown, H. M. Colvin, and A. J. Taylor, eds., The history of the king's works, 1 (1963) · Pipe rolls, 21–25 Henry II · [W. Illingworth], ed., Rotuli hundredorum temp. Hen. III et Edw. I, 2 vols., RC (1812–18) · Dugdale, Monasticon, new edn, vol. 4 · W. L. Warren, Henry II (1973) · G. J. Aungier, ed., Chroniques de London, CS, 28 (1844) · J. Speed, The history of Great Britaine (1611) · R. W. Eyton, Court, household, and itinerary of King Henry II (1878)

Clifford, Thomas, sixth Baron Clifford (1362/3–1391), magnate, was the eldest son of Roger *Clifford, fifth Baron Clifford of Westmorland (1333–1389), and his wife, Maud Beauchamp (d. 1403). His father started providing for Thomas's future when he was still an infant, in 1365 granting him the Westmorland manor of King's Meaburn for life. Then in 1373 arrangements were made for his marriage, to Elizabeth, daughter of Thomas, Lord Ros of Helmsley, which had taken place by 2 November. It was apparently a condition of the match that Roger Clifford should settle lands worth £100 on the couple—he conveyed estates worth 40 marks in 1379, and lands in Brough in 1383. By then Thomas Clifford had entered public life. On 26 October 1379 his father, preparing to go to Ireland, and presumably wishing to ensure that his Cumbrian retainers had Clifford leadership in the event of a Scottish invasion, made an indenture with John Lowther, under which Lowther was to wait upon Thomas, and take him to battle should war break out.

At that date Thomas Clifford had also started to attend the court—on 4 May 1379 he secured a pardon for a Yorkshireman's killer. In October 1382 he was one of three 'king's kinsmen and young knights' licensed to hunt in the royal forests (*CPR, 1381–5*, 176), and in December that year he was described as one of the king's chamber knights. On 23 October 1385 he received an annual grant of 200 marks, which was converted first into the custody of four manors in the south-west, and then, on 9 January 1387, into the keepership of the forests north of the Trent. Clifford was not allowed, probably did not wish, to forget his northern interests. On 16 December 1384 he was granted the custody of Carlisle Castle for life—an office he shared with John Neville (*d.* 1388)—and in March 1386 he was appointed a warden of the west march. When the appellants took power at the end of 1387, Thomas Clifford was one of a number of Richard II's friends who were ordered to leave the court, with the proviso that they be ready to appear before the next parliament. If Clifford did leave, he soon returned, since in September 1388 he was master of the king's horses, and was again described as a chamber knight in May 1389.

Soon afterwards, on 13 July, Clifford's father died. Aged twenty-six, Thomas was the only Clifford to succeed to his peerage title as an adult before 1523. On 9 October he reaped the benefits of royal favour when he was pardoned the relief due from his lands. On 6 December he was summoned to parliament as a peer. Thomas Clifford was a war-like and adventurous man. In July 1386 he had challenged Sir Jacques de Boucicault, a notable practitioner of chivalry, to joust; in 1387 he was licensed to perform feats of arms in the Anglo-Scottish borders; in 1388 he jousted at Calais. In 1390 (presumably between 26 May and 16 June, dates on which he is recorded in England) he took part in the international tournament held at St Inglevert near Calais, 'honourably and valorously', according to Froissart (Froissart, 2.436), and another French chronicle also describes him as participating in the crusade against Mahdiyya in north Africa later that year. By the end of 1390 he was back in England, and he was at Skipton on 19 January 1391. He was already planning to go abroad again, for on 11 January it was granted that should Clifford die overseas, his attorneys were to have the profits from his estates for a year to pay his debts.

In the middle of February 1391 Clifford set off for the Baltic, with other young English nobles. During the summer, while he was at Königsberg, he became involved in a quarrel with Sir William Douglas, an illegitimate son of the earl of Douglas. The two men were old adversaries. Their families had been at feud since 1298, when Edward I granted the Douglas lands in Scotland to the first Lord Clifford. It was doubtless in connection with this that some time before 1390 Clifford challenged Douglas to combat, and that on 6 June 1390 Douglas received a safe conduct to come to England for a suit against Clifford in the English military court. Their encounter in Königsberg led to a furious brawl in the city streets in which Douglas was killed. Clifford seems to have been overcome by remorse, for he set off for Jerusalem and died on the way there, on an unidentified Mediterranean island, in a state of deep penitence. The exact date is uncertain—English sources favour 4 October 1391.

Thomas Clifford had apparently been a happily married man—he was later referred to by his widow, who lived until 26 March 1424, as 'my most dear lord and husband' (books of record, 2.329). They had two children, a son,

John Clifford (*d.* 1422), aged two at his father's death, who succeeded to the lordship, and a daughter, Maud, who was married successively to John Neville, Lord Latimer, from whom she was divorced, and to Richard, earl of Cambridge, executed for treason in 1415. Maud lived until 1446, and remembered her nephew, Thomas *Clifford, and great-nephew, John *Clifford, in her will.

HENRY SUMMERSON

Sources Cumbria AS, Kendal, WD/Hoth/Books of record, 2.297–348 • V. J. C. Rees, 'The Clifford family in the later middle ages, 1259–1461', MLitt diss., University of Lancaster, 1973, 107–17 • Bodl. Oxf., MS Dodsworth 70 • *Chancery records* • *CPR, 1381–5*, 176 • *CIPM*, 16, nos. 827–45; 17, no. 10–24 • *RotS*, vol. 2 • *Reports ... touching the dignity of a peer of the realm*, House of Lords, 4 (1829) • *Knighton's chronicle, 1337–1396*, ed. and trans. G. H. Martin, OMT (1995), 428 [Lat. orig., *Chronica de eventibus Angliae a tempore regis Edgari usque mortem regis Ricardi Secundi*, with parallel Eng. text] • *Thomae Walsingham, quondam monachi S. Albani, historia Anglicana*, ed. H. T. Riley, 2 vols., pt 1 of *Chronica monasterii S. Albani*, Rolls Series, 28 (1863–4), vol. 2, pp. 172–3 • A. M. Chazaud, *La chronique du bon duc Loys de Bourbon* (Paris, 1876), 222, 238, 249 • L. Bellaguet, ed. and trans., *Chronique du religieux de Saint-Denys*, 1 (Paris, 1839), 676–7 • L. C. Hector and B. F. Harvey, eds. and trans., *The Westminster chronicle, 1381–1394*, OMT (1982), 455–7, 475–7, 481 • F. R. H. Du Boulay, 'Henry of Derby's expeditions to Prussia, 1390–1 and 1392', *The reign of Richard II: essays in honour of May McKisack*, ed. F. R. H. Du Boulay and C. M. Barron (1971), 153–72, 170–71 • F. W. Ragg, 'Hetton Flechan, Askham and Sandford of Askham', *Transactions of the Cumberland and Westmorland Antiquarian and Archaeological Society*, new ser., 21 (1920–21), 174–233, esp. 189–90 • PRO, CIPM 47/9/37 • J. Froissart, *Chronicles of England, France, Spain, and the adjoining countries*, trans. T. Johnes, 2 (1839), 436
Archives Cumbria AS, Kendal, WD/Hoth
Wealth at death £324 16s knight's fees: PRO, C 47/9/37; *CIPM*, 17

Clifford, Thomas, eighth Baron Clifford (1414–1455), magnate, was born at Skipton Castle on 20 August 1414, the son of John, seventh Baron Clifford (1388/9–1422), and his wife, Elizabeth Percy (*d.* 1436). Thomas was not quite eight when his father was killed in France, on 13 March 1422, leaving him heir to the baronies of Westmorland, centred upon Appleby, and Skipton in Craven, in the West Riding of Yorkshire. In February 1423 his mother and grandmother (Elizabeth Ros, widow of Thomas *Clifford, sixth Baron Clifford) paid 800 marks for his marriage and wardship, and on 1 August 1424 entered into an agreement with Thomas, Lord Dacre, whereby Thomas Clifford was to marry Dacre's daughter Joan (*b.* before 1424, *d.* before 1455). The match maintained a political alignment originating in John Clifford's minority, linking the Cliffords with the Percys and the offspring of the first marriage of Ralph *Neville, first earl of Westmorland (who included Thomas Dacre's wife, Philippa), in opposition to the children of Westmorland's second marriage, headed by Richard *Neville, earl of Salisbury.

John Clifford had been only two when his father died in 1391. In 1396 Richard II granted the lordship of Penrith, at the southern end of Cumberland, to Ralph Neville, in 1397 made Neville earl of Westmorland, and early in 1398 gave him the shrievalty of the latter county, in flagrant disregard of the Cliffords' hereditary right in that office. Three months later this last grant was revoked, as a result of opposition which may well have been led by the Percys, but Clifford suspicion of Neville ambitions in the north-west, so close to their own power base, persisted. In 1404 the first earl of Northumberland, acting with the consent of John Clifford's mother, married John to his own daughter Elizabeth, in the process overriding a grant of John's marriage made in August 1403 to Joan Beaufort, the earl of Westmorland's second wife and the earl of Salisbury's mother. When the elder Elizabeth Clifford died in 1424, it can have done nothing to appease Clifford fears that the lordship of Brough, part of her dower, should during her grandson's minority have been awarded to Salisbury, to help him maintain himself in the office of warden of the west march. Two years later Thomas Clifford's mother remarried; her new husband was Ralph *Neville, second earl of Westmorland, who was then engaged in a bitter dispute with Salisbury over the first earl's estates.

Under the indenture of 1424 Thomas Clifford was brought up by his father-in-law, Lord Dacre, who in February 1434 was ordered to bring him before the king's council. He was now twenty years old, and it may have been decided to send him to France—'The sonne and heire of the lord Clifford, after lord Clifford' was said to have been a member of the duke of Bedford's retinue before the latter's death in the following year (Stevenson, 2.435). In 1435 he came of age and had livery of his lands, including Brough. On 1 May 1436, no doubt under compulsion, Clifford made a release for wastes perpetrated on his lands to the earl of Salisbury, who in the meantime had been confirmed in his office of steward of the lordship of Kendal. However, Clifford's own resources increased when his mother died on 16 October 1436, giving him possession of her dower. He also began to take part in public affairs. In August 1436 he was a commissioner to resist the Scots when they attacked Berwick and Roxburgh. On 10 December he received his first summons to parliament. From 1437 he was regularly a JP and a commissioner in Westmorland and the West Riding of Yorkshire. But unlike his father and grandfather, he did not risk dissipating his strength in campaigns and other adventures overseas—reports of his military prowess in France in the sixteenth-century writings of Polydore Vergil and Edward Hall are unsubstantiated by contemporary records, and can be discounted.

Instead Clifford made strenuous efforts first to recover and then to maintain his family's position in the north-west. In 1437 he is recorded as carrying out substantial works on Skipton Castle—which explains why he spent that year at Conisbrough Castle, the dower house of his aunt Maud, countess of Cambridge. When Maud died in 1446, her bequests to her nephew included a bed which was to remain forever at Skipton. Clifford also financed a new hall and chapel at Appleby Castle, completing the work in 1454. His political activities between 1437 and the early 1450s are not in general well documented, but their pattern is clear enough. He continued to resist the earl of Salisbury, in the process allegedly countenancing, or even instigating, some of the disorders which troubled the peace of Cumbria during these years, and he maintained his alliances with the senior line of Nevilles and with the

Percys. When on 8 August 1444, in two separate transactions, he conveyed his principal estates to two groups of feoffees, one group was headed by Sir John Neville, the second earl of Westmorland's brother, and the other by the earl of Northumberland. One of his daughters, Anne, married Sir Richard Tempest, and another, Elizabeth, married successively Robert Plumpton (d. 1450) and William Plumpton (d. 1461), sons of Sir William Plumpton (d. 1480); both the Tempests and the Plumptons had close links with the Percys.

In 1448–9 there was a sharp outbreak of Anglo-Scottish hostilities. Clifford was among the northern lords sent to defend the marches, and thanked for their services afterwards. And once the fighting was over, he was several times commissioned to negotiate truces with the Scots, and to maintain them once they were agreed upon. Yet although his interests always lay primarily in the north, Clifford did not neglect to maintain links with the court and central government. He was regularly summoned to parliament, though he did not always come—in 1454 he was fined £40 for failing to attend. In 1444 he accompanied the earl of Suffolk to France to bring Margaret of Anjou to England. In 1448 he was a supplementary feoffee for the duchy of Lancaster estates under Henry VI's will. He was also a feoffee for the first duke of Buckingham, and an executor for John Talbot, later second earl of Shrewsbury. His sons Roger and Robert married into the Courtenay and Berkeley families respectively.

Although it is possible that he had shown hitherto underappreciated military or organizational skills in the war against the Scots, his contacts with the court and southern nobility may provide one explanation for Clifford's appointment in March 1452 to assemble ships and sailors for the relief of Calais, threatened by the French. Another may lie in a growing involvement with north-east England, especially with the East Riding of Yorkshire. In 1451 he was granted the subsidy and alnage on cloths in Yorkshire, York, and Hull, and in the early 1450s he was among the noblemen cultivated by the townsmen of York and Hull. Above all, some time before 1454 his eldest son, John *Clifford, married Margaret, daughter and heir of Henry Bromflete, Lord Vescy, an important landowner in the East Riding. Perhaps Clifford hoped to give himself greater freedom for manoeuvre by expanding into a region where the Nevilles were considerably less powerful than the Percys.

Although Clifford was among the lords who confronted the duke of York at Dartford in February 1452, in this he was probably showing loyalty to the king rather than a personal hostility towards the duke. There can be little doubt, however, about his animus towards the earl of Salisbury, as he showed in October 1453, when he joined the Percys in a confrontation with the Nevilles at Topcliffe which only just failed to turn into outright battle. In January 1454 he was reported to be in alliance with the duke of Exeter and Thomas Percy, Lord Egremont, in enmity to the Nevilles. Perhaps he had doubts about the wisdom of associating with Egremont, for when York became protector on 27 March 1454, Clifford was prepared to act with him in a commission of oyer and terminer in Yorkshire, and was even instructed to act against Egremont's 'misgovernance and assembles' in Westmorland (*Proceedings … of the Privy Council*, 6.194–5), though he cannot be shown to have done so. But when York's protectorate ended in January 1455, Clifford continued to be associated with the court. He was present when his enemy Salisbury resigned as chancellor on 7 March, and was among the king's supporters when they confronted York and the Nevilles at St Albans on 22 May. Indeed, he played a leading part in the battle, so much so that attempts were made afterwards to blame him for its having taken place. When the fighting began he 'kept so strongly the barreres of the same towne' (*John Vale's Book*, 192) that the Yorkists were forced to make a flank attack to break into the town. But when they did so Clifford was killed, perhaps the victim of Neville score-settling, though once the battle was lost his prominence in the fray was such as to place him in great peril. His body, which was at first left lying in the street, was later buried in the lady chapel of St Albans Abbey church. His wife Joan Dacre, by family tradition, 'dyed butt a litle before him' (books of record, 2.432). They had four sons—John, Roger, Robert, and Thomas—and five daughters—Elizabeth (who married, in succession, the brothers Robert and William Plumpton [*see under* Plumpton family]), Maud, Anne, Joan, and Margaret.

HENRY SUMMERSON

Sources Cumbria AS, Kendal, WD/Hoth/Books of record, 2.393–436 · V. J. C. Rees, 'The Clifford family in the later middle ages, 1289–1461', MLitt diss., University of Lancaster, 1973, 143–62 · Cumbria AS, Carlisle, MS Hill 3, 47 · Chancery records · N. H. Nicolas, ed., *Proceedings and ordinances of the privy council of England*, 7 vols., RC, 26 (1834–7), vols. 3–4, 6 · *RotS*, vol. 2 · J. Stevenson, ed., *Letters and papers illustrative of the wars of the English in France during the reign of Henry VI, king of England*, 2, Rolls Series, 22 (1864), 435 · *CDS*, vols. 4–5 · *Report of the Lords committees … for all matters touching the dignity of a peer of the realm*, 4 (1829) · [J. Raine], ed., *Testamenta Eboracensia*, 2, SurtS, 30 (1855), 118–24 · *VCH Yorkshire City of York*, 59, 64 · *VCH Yorkshire East Riding*, 1.23 · N. H. Nicolas, ed., *Testamenta vetusta: being illustrations from wills*, 1 (1826), 21–4 · *The Paston letters, 1422–1509 AD*, ed. J. Gairdner, new edn, 3 vols. (1872–5); repr. in 4 vols. (1910), vol. 1, pp. 264, 332 · M. L. Kekewich and others, eds., *The politics of fifteenth-century England: John Vale's book* (1995), 192 · H. T. Riley, ed., *Registra quorundam abbatum monasterii S. Albani*, 1, Rolls Series, 28/6 (1872), 175–8 · *Three books of Polydore Vergil's 'English history'*, ed. H. Ellis, CS, 29 (1844), 65–6 · *Hall's chronicle*, ed. H. Ellis (1809), 190–91 · J. S. Roskell, 'The problem of the attendance of the lords in medieval parliaments', *BIHR*, 29 (1956), 153–204, esp. 190 · R. A. Griffiths, *The reign of King Henry VI: the exercise of royal authority, 1422–1461* (1981) · R. L. Storey, *The end of the house of Lancaster* (1966) · H. Summerson, M. Trueman, and S. Harrison, *Brougham Castle, Cumbria* (1998)

Archives Cumbria AS, Kendal, WD/Hoth 436

Clifford, Thomas, first Baron Clifford of Chudleigh (1630–1673), politician, was born at Ugbrooke Park, Devon, on 1 August 1630, and baptized at the nearby parish church of Chudleigh on 12 August. He was the second child and eldest son of Hugh Clifford, a relatively obscure minor gentleman who led a cadet branch of the great medieval house of Clifford and died on 12 February 1640 leaving an estate worth £374. His mother was Mary, eldest daughter of Sir George *Chudleigh of Ashton, Devon.

Thomas Clifford, first Baron Clifford of Chudleigh (1630–1673), by Sir Peter Lely, late 1660s

Early life Nothing more is known of Clifford until his matriculation at Exeter College, Oxford, on 21 May 1647, a place which he quitted after only a year; almost certainly because he was expelled for royalist and Anglican views in the purge of the university conducted in 1648. His devout Anglicanism—together with his taste for classical poets and Ben Jonson—is proved by the commonplace book which he began to keep at university, and his mother's family had become prominent royalists. He seems to have moved directly from Oxford to the Middle Temple, and may have travelled in Europe thereafter; if so, however, his experiences must have been negative, because he never learned another modern language and his attitude towards foreigners was almost consistently hostile.

Clifford married Elizabeth (d. 1709), eldest daughter of William Martyn of Lindridge, his immediate neighbour, on 27 June 1650. It was clearly a love match and the union was an outstanding success, productive of lasting close affection and seven sons and eight daughters. It also seems to have significantly augmented Thomas's wealth, for by 1659 his estate was worth £1490.

Restoration MP During the whole of the 1650s Clifford seems to have lived at Ugbrooke in domestic bliss and political quarantine, being kept out of any employment by the regimes of the interregnum. It is wholly appropriate, therefore, that his first engagement with public life was in an action which helped to pull down the republic: his prominent role in a meeting of Devon gentry at Exeter in January 1660 which demanded the readmission of the secluded members to the Long Parliament. When that readmission brought about the dissolution of the parliament, he was elected to the convention which succeeded it for the nearby borough of Totnes, and reoccupied the same seat in the Cavalier Parliament of the next year. With the Restoration his pent-up energy and ambition was released. He became one of a clique of young gentlemen from Devon and Cornwall who formed around the comptroller of the household, Sir Hugh Pollard, and could be relied upon to defend the court interest, especially in the Commons. Rewards came swiftly, in an appointment as an extraordinary gentleman of the privy chamber on 21 December 1660 and in a lease of crown land in 1662. It was apparently through Pollard that he formed a friendship—fast by late 1662—with Sir Henry Bennett, subsequently Lord Arlington, who became a powerful and consistent patron to him.

Most of Clifford's early speeches in parliament have been lost, but it is possible to discern a pattern whereby he supported not merely royal policy but toleration for Catholics and protestant dissenters; the latter stance mirrored that of Arlington, but also seems to have reflected his own interest in the reconciliation of rival forms of Christianity. He also demonstrated a quick temper, most dramatically by coming to blows with Andrew Marvell in the House of Commons itself during a break between business.

The Second Anglo-Dutch War Clifford's real rise to prominence in the house, and in national life, came about in the debates preceding the outbreak of the Second Anglo-Dutch War of 1665–7. He emerged as one of the most passionate and persuasive of the speakers who, in the course of the year 1664, led the Commons into supporting an aggressive royal policy towards the Dutch and voting enormous supplies for operations against them. Appreciation for his services came in the form of a knighthood during the summer, and a further lease of crown land and a share in the farm of wine and liquor licences in Ireland during the early part of 1665. He also obtained further honour, employment, and profit from the administrative machinery set up to fight the war, being made one of the commission set up to care for sick and wounded sailors and prisoners of war on 27 October 1664, and a sub-commissioner for prizes on 4 January 1665. On 18 January he was appointed, in addition, to the commission which managed the estates of the king's son, the young duke of Monmouth. All this testifies to a belief in his financial acumen and capacity for industry, and he acquitted himself so well as a sub-commissioner that on 28 June the value of a whole prizeship was awarded to him in recognition of the money which he had made and saved the government.

This achievement is the more remarkable in that for most of the summer Clifford was on active service with the fleet, as a volunteer. He was present at the great battle off Lowestoft on 3 June 1665 and the less successful attack on the Dutch ships in the harbour at Bergen on 2 August, in which he played a prominent part as an agent in the complex negotiations with the Danish governor. The courage and energy which he displayed in these actions, and the clarity and impartiality of the reports which he

sent back to Arlington, caused him to be appointed on 29 August as an ambassador-extraordinary to the crowns of Denmark and Sweden. The period from September until January was consumed in this mission to negotiate an alliance against the Dutch, which was rendered fruitless by wider European developments.

Upon his return to England, Clifford recommenced his duties as a commissioner and rejoined the fleet for the opening of the 1666 fighting season. He witnessed its two main clashes, the four-day battle of 1–4 June and the St James's day fight of 25 July, and won the especial regard of Prince Rupert. The latter recommended him for a command on 1 July and chose him to carry the official report of the victory on the 25th to the king. During August and September he divided his time between patrolling with the navy and acting as a commissioner for sick and wounded ashore. Pepys noted him as 'much set by at court for his activity in going to sea, and stoutness everywhere, and stirring up and down' (Pepys, 17 Sept 1666).

This fine reputation, and the continued support of Arlington, earned Clifford a major office on 28 November 1666, when he succeeded to Pollard's post as comptroller of the household. On 5 December he was sworn of the privy council, and on 22 May 1667 he was placed on the newly established commission to manage the Treasury, a body of men chosen specifically for their skill in fiscal affairs. His particular ability in that regard was recognized again upon 14 June 1668, when he was promoted treasurer of the household. Clifford had thus become one of the leading figures of the court, and in the process became famed both for the munificence of his hospitality and for his patronage of writers. The greatest of these was Dryden, who repeatedly expressed gratitude to him and later gave him the dedication of his tragedy *Amboyna*; it seems very likely that it was Clifford who obtained Dryden the office of poet laureate in 1670. Clifford's own patron during this period remained Arlington, who was now the king's chief minister, and he continued to follow the latter's inclinations in parliament—abstaining during the attack on Clarendon in 1667 and arguing for religious toleration in 1668. The only point at which his views departed from those of his benefactor was over the triple alliance of 1668 in which England joined with its recent enemies, the Dutch. Clifford's detestation of the latter, expressed to such effect in 1664, had become instinctual, and he could never bring himself to speak well of the partnership with them.

The secret treaty of Dover This being so, Clifford must have been mollified by a new employment to which he was put in 1669, as secretary in the clandestine negotiations with the French which were to culminate in the secret treaty of Dover in May 1670. Clifford's appointment to this post must have owed much to the fact that Arlington was the only minister involved in the negotiations. He was in some respects very badly equipped for it, having no knowledge of the French language and regarding France itself with a suspicion which he accorded to all foreign nations, and which was only too patent to the French ambassador, Colbert de Croissy. In others, however, he was ideal. He was totally devoted to the service of his royal master—something indicated by the manner in which he had repeatedly defended the king's prerogative whenever it had become a matter for debate in the Commons. His dedication and discretion in a highly dangerous and secret negotiation could be deemed absolute; and the truth of this is proved by the manner in which the English copy of the secret treaty, and the working papers of the talks, remained hidden at his seat of Ugbrooke until the nineteenth century. Clifford also possessed technical abilities suited to the work, most of all his ability to draft documents swiftly and accurately. It must have counted for a great deal, moreover, that the two central aspects of the agreement with the French were both very congenial to his own views. One was an alliance against the Dutch, whose power was finally to be broken in a sudden joint attack. The other was an undertaking by Charles II that, if given French financial assistance, he would declare himself to be a Roman Catholic and so attempt to lead his subjects back to the Church of Rome.

This was a course upon which Clifford's own feet were now set—probably by the time that the overture to France was made, and certainly by that of the completion of the treaty on 22 May 1670, when he acted as one of the signatories. His commonplace book, kept faithfully since his time as an undergraduate, shows a gradual, if undated, shift from an interest in Anglican devotional works to those more suited to a Catholic. To describe him as a convert at this stage, however, would be seriously misleading; he was, rather, an Anglican who wished to reconcile his church with that of Rome by a process of negotiation and compromise. The secret treaty had stipulated that Charles's declaration of Catholicism would precede the attack on the Dutch, and Clifford accordingly gave thought to the practical details of how it might be effected. He advised the king to repair key fortresses and place them and his guard regiments in safe hands, while preparing a promise of liberty of conscience to all of his subjects who did not feel able to follow his change of faith. At the same time he drafted instructions for an envoy to be sent to the pope to acquaint him with the venture and secure his co-operation; and he worked with a prominent English Benedictine, Hugh Cressy, to draw up possible terms for the reunion of the faiths, by which the pope would write off all land formerly confiscated from the church in England, agree to toleration of protestants, and accept compromise over the questions of the liturgy, communion, reordination, and clerical marriage. All these efforts were in vain, for Charles himself never showed any interest in them. It seems likely, indeed, that his profession of interest in conversion had been a diplomatic ploy to win the friendship of France and to get money from there, and it gradually became eclipsed by preparations for the war with the Dutch.

The stop of the exchequer and the declaration of indulgence Clifford was certainly given ample recompense for these valuable and delicate services, and for those which he continued to give in his official duties in the household and Treasury. In 1669 he obtained a valuable lease of crown land in Buckinghamshire, which was given to his heirs in perpetuity in 1671. In the latter year, also, he was given an annual pension out of the estates of the dean and chapter of Exeter. By this time he had become one of the most important of royal councillors, sitting on the select committee for foreign affairs, which (despite its name) functioned as the principal body for the making of policy in all areas. Although his most obvious expertise was in financial matters, he contributed fully to all debates and played a key part in two celebrated initiatives upon the eve of the war. One was the stop of the exchequer on 2 January 1672, by which all payments to government creditors were suspended in order to release the full income of the state for military measures. There seems to be little doubt that the idea for it was Clifford's own, and its bold and ruthless nature has the full stamp of his character; it is equally obvious why, despite much argument, it was accepted by the rest of the privy council, for it provided such a simple and effective solution to the acute short-term problem of how to equip a fleet for a surprise attack. Clifford also supported the second dramatic measure, the declaration of indulgence on 15 March which licensed public worship for protestant dissenters and private worship for Catholics. It was so completely in harmony with the views that he had expressed consistently for ten years that his enthusiasm for it is hardly surprising; what is worth emphasizing is that this was shared by all the rest of the committee for foreign affairs, with the sole exception of Charles himself, who was persuaded into it only with difficulty.

On 22 April 1672 Clifford was elevated to the peerage with the title of Baron Clifford of Chudleigh as part of the general round of creations and promotions accorded to the king's chief minister and councillors to encourage them at the outset of the war. In May he made a last attempt to persuade Charles to form plans for his declaration of allegiance to Rome, and then turned his energies to the prosecution of the war, this time at the level of high financial administration and policy making. In June, when the Dutch seemed to be ready to sue for peace, he outstripped all other members of the foreign affairs committee in pressing for harsh terms, involving either the dismemberment of the Dutch state or the annexation of part of it by England. His colleagues agreed upon a much more moderate package, and it was Arlington, sent as one of the plenipotentiaries, who ensured that it was more moderate still. Despite this it was rejected, but the difference in attitudes to the Dutch between Clifford and his old benefactor, which had briefly opened over the matter of the triple alliance, had reappeared in much more glaring form. This may have been assisted by the growing friendship between Clifford and a still more powerful figure, the heir presumptive to the throne, James, duke of York. The latter had travelled in parallel with him in an increasing sympathy for the Church of Rome and support for a royal declaration of reconciliation to it. During the summer of 1672 the connection between the two men became obvious, as Clifford effectively looked after James's affairs while the royal duke commanded at sea.

Lord treasurer By autumn the switch of allegiance had become obvious, and was dramatically illustrated on 28 November when Charles formally dissolved the Treasury commission and vested ultimate control of state finances in Clifford, with the revived office of lord treasurer. James later claimed the credit for having persuaded his brother into the choice, and indeed it can be argued that of all Charles's leading servants he was the best qualified for the job. Arlington, however, saw things differently. He had been expecting to receive the post himself, only to see it awarded to somebody whom he had himself helped to power. His sense of betrayal, and of ingratitude upon the part of a former client, made a complete and lasting rupture in relations between the two men. At this cost, Clifford accepted the office and set about it with the systematic hard work which he had brought to all his previous duties. Each Saturday he personally drew up lists of all the moneys to be paid out by the Treasury, and his care is visible in every other department of its activities. A story often repeated by historians, that at his suggestion the fleet was kept at sea all winter because the government could not afford to pay it off after the summer campaign, is a political libel. In fact the sailors were paid in full during the autumn, and—due in large part to French subsidies and a trade boom but also to sound management—the government actually concluded the first year of war in financial surplus.

In the winter of 1672–3 Clifford reached the apogee of his career. He was now both in office and influence one of the great ministers of state, and has traditionally been grouped with Arlington, Buckingham, Ashley, and Lauderdale in a government known (from the first initials of their titles) as the Cabal. The perception of their preeminent importance is correct, but at no time did they function as a group; the last three were all allied against Clifford and Arlington, while these were divided by their quarrel in November, and Clifford was closest to the duke of York, who was by definition not a minister or court official but clearly an important figure in policy discussions at this time. On the other hand, apart from the pleasing coincidence of the initials, there is one good reason for applying the nickname to the ministry: that Clifford himself used it, although in a different spelling and in the common contemporary sense of a small group of people engaged in secretive business. In a letter to Lauderdale in 1672 he referred to the leading royal advisers as 'the caball' (BL, Add. MS 23135, fol. 203).

Clifford was now adopting the lifestyle of a magnate as well as the responsibilities of a minister. He commenced the emparking and rebuilding of his ancestral home of Ugbrooke, purchased fine Dutch and Flemish paintings, commissioned portraits and landscape scenes from artists such as Lely and Dankers, and had tapestries of New Testament scenes made at the Pointz factory in Hatton Garden; several of these works survive at Ugbrooke. His whole position, however, was to be destroyed by a single financial circumstance: that the government had only half the money needed to send the navy out against the Dutch in the approaching summer of 1673. The remainder could be obtained only by a parliamentary grant, and the members of the Cabal, including Clifford, made strenuous efforts to canvass MPs with whom they had ties in preparation for the spring session. All were in vain; when that session opened in February, the Commons, deeply suspicious and resentful of the crown's policy towards religion, made the vital grant conditional upon the recall of the declaration of indulgence and the passage of a statute, which became known as the Test Act, to make the holding of public office conditional upon the taking of Anglican communion.

Clifford, accompanied by York, Ashley (now earl of Shaftesbury), and Lauderdale, urged the king vehemently to sacrifice the taxes, and the Dutch war, rather than agree to these demands. Arlington and lesser advisers, supported by the French, counselled the opposite course, and it seems likely that Charles's own natural inclinations, which had been against the declaration of indulgence, were upon their side. At any rate he withdrew the declaration on 8 March, an act which expedited the grant of supply but did nothing to slow the progress of the bill for a religious test. Charles himself seems to have regarded this without alarm, and even encouraged its progress to please the Commons—apparently because he believed that it would actually have the effect of pushing his brother, and Clifford, back into the Anglican fold. Clifford himself, who must already have been facing the opposite likelihood, became the only minister to oppose the bill, delivering a speech of frantic denunciation when the measure reached the House of Lords in mid-March. With the king seeming to countenance the measure, and Shaftesbury overtly doing so with the prestige of the office of lord chancellor, these efforts were unavailing, and the bill passed into law at the end of the month.

Resignation and death The Test Act supplied Clifford with a succeeding interval of two months in which to reach a decision upon his response. To state that the act exposed him as a Roman Catholic would be false; rather, it forced him to make a formal conversion. Until this point his position had remained that of an Anglican who, in the words of his friend John Evelyn, jotted down in 1671, was 'a little warping to Rome' (Evelyn, 3.577, 17 May 1671). On 17 July of that year a chapel had been consecrated at Ugbrooke according to the rites of the Church of England, although dedicated to Cyprian, proponent of the unity of Christendom. The chapel at Clifford's London residence as lord treasurer was also Anglican, and on 8 April and 18 June 1673 he attended the successive weddings of his two eldest daughters there, conducted by a minister of the Church of England. He postponed the resignation of his offices for the longest possible duration permitted by the Test Act, until 19 June; and only after that did he commence, and adhere to, the open practice of Catholic worship. It seems very likely that his loyal and straightforward nature would have dictated his resolution once the reunion of the churches seemed to be indefinitely postponed and he had come to regard that of Rome as the essential one. It may also be argued, however, that his decision was influenced to some extent by that of his great friend and patron the duke of York, who took the same course and resigned his own posts on the preceding day.

It was now perfectly possible for Clifford to remain a prominent figure at the royal court, relieved of the burdens of office while enjoying the new financial and social position which they had bequeathed. He chose instead to retire completely from public life, and prepared for a resumption of that relaxed existence of provincial seclusion which he had known in the 1650s. Even this, however, was to be denied to him by destiny, for he died at Ugbrooke on 17 October, and was interred in the chapel there two days later. Some mystery and controversy hangs over the circumstances of his end. It is clear that his health had been declining for years under the strains of his public position and duties. By September 1671 he was already expressing fatigue, and envy for ministers who had retired honourably from office. In the summer of 1672 he was seriously ill and obliged to take the waters at Bath to assist a recovery. Writing to Sir Joseph Williamson at that time, he commented that 'I am ever in pain' (*CSP dom.*, 1672, 414). Immediately after his resignation in the following year he was found taking another rest-cure at a spa, this time Tunbridge Wells. No doubt the terrible emotional pressures which preceded that event had taken their toll, but it is also beyond doubt that he was suffering from a real complaint, subsequently diagnosed as urinary stones. He made his will ten days before he died, suggesting the recognition of a mortal illness. On 13 October a correspondent in London confirmed that his doctors 'expect nothing but his death' and that the cause was indeed an exceptionally severe attack of stones (Christie, 2.40).

There would therefore be no question over the manner of Clifford's end, and a persistent if subdued rumour that he had committed suicide could be dismissed as religious rancour, were it not for the remarkably circumstantial account of his death by self-induced strangulation recorded by Evelyn. It must be noted, however, that Evelyn's source seems to have been at least secondhand, and that he himself thought the matter 'not confidently affirm'd' (Evelyn, 4.21, 18 Aug 1673). It seems likely, therefore, that the story was a libel.

Assessment Clifford's talents as an administrator and minister are undoubted. The lucidity of the reports which he made to Arlington and others during his service at sea and as a diplomat is as patent to the historian as it was to his recipients. The letters which he wrote as a financial officer are equally fluent and shrewd, and his acumen in monetary matters is as obvious as his industry and dedication in them. He enjoyed a reputation for probity in office even among his enemies; after his resignation an observer of metropolitan affairs could say that all thought him 'an exact honest man and uncorrupted' (Christie, 1.46). Pepys considered that he spoke 'very well and neatly' in the House of Commons (Pepys, 5.294, 11 Oct 1664).

Clifford's self-discipline in business was balanced, however, by an exceptionally quick temper and passionate nature, well expressed in the leonine features and stubborn mouth which are displayed in his portraits. Colbert de Croissy, who generally thought well of him, rued his 'excessive ardour' (Croissy to Louis, 17 April 1673, Correspondance politique, Angleterre, 106). It was a combination of the total dedication with which he pursued practical tasks, the emotional fervour with which he invested ideological causes, the utter lack of flexibility or moral relativism with which he viewed the world, and an ingrained natural piety which made him such an impressive figure and ultimately led to his political ruin. He was succeeded in his title and estates by his fourth son, Hugh, and perhaps his most enduring achievement may be accounted his foundation of one of England's most remarkable noble Catholic families.

RONALD HUTTON

Sources Ugbrooke Park, Devon, Clifford family MSS · BL, Add. MS 65138 · W. A. Shaw, ed., *Calendar of treasury books*, 1–4, PRO (1904–9) · *CSP dom.*, 1660–73 · Evelyn, *Diary*, vols. 1, 3–4 · Pepys, *Diary* · W. D. Christie, ed., *Letters addressed from London to Sir Joseph Williamson*, 2 vols., CS, new ser., 8–9 (1874) · BL, Add. MS 23135 · *The works of Sir William Temple*, 2 vols. (1720), vol. 2 · correspondance politique, Angleterre, Archives du Ministère des Affaires Étrangères, Paris · PRO, SP 104/176–7 · Longleat House, Wiltshire, Coventry MSS 64–5 · C. H. Hartmann, *Clifford of the Cabal* [1937] · R. Hutton, *Charles the Second: king of England, Scotland and Ireland* (1989) · J. P. Ferris, 'Clifford, Thomas', HoP, *Commons, 1660–90*, 2.91–4 · Bodl. Oxf., MS Ashmole 436, fol. 58 · GEC, *Peerage*

Archives BL, letter-book · BL, papers, Add. MSS 65131–65141 · NL Ire., papers relating to Ireland · NMM, naval papers · Ugbrooke Park, Devon, MSS

Likenesses P. Lely, oils, 1666–9, Ugbrooke Park, Devon [*see illus.*] · S. Cooper, watercolour miniature, Ugbrooke Park, Devon · P. Lely, oils, second version, NPG

Clifford [later **Constable**], **Sir Thomas Hugh, first baronet** (1762–1823), topographer and botanist, was born on 4 December 1762 in London, the eldest son of Thomas Clifford (1732–1787) (fourth son of Hugh, third Baron Clifford of Chudleigh) and Barbara Aston (d. 1786), youngest daughter and coheir of James, fifth Lord Aston of Forfar. He belonged to a well-established Roman Catholic family with strong French connections and was educated in the academy opened at Liège by the English ex-Jesuits after their expulsion from Bruges. He continued his studies at the college of Navarre, in Paris, after which he travelled on foot over Switzerland. After the death of his mother he settled at Tixall in Staffordshire, the estate of the Astons, which he inherited from her. On 17 June 1791 he married Mary Macdonald (d. 1825), second daughter of John Chichester of Arlington, Devonshire. They had one son, Sir Thomas Aston Clifford, second baronet.

During periods of residence at Bath, Clifford gave a cordial welcome to the loyalist exiles from France, and when Louis XVIII visited that city in 1813, a few months before the restoration of the French monarchy, he twice invited him to his table. By patent dated 22 May 1815 Clifford was created a baronet at the special request of Louis XVIII. In 1821 he succeeded to the estates of Francis Constable of Burton Constable, Yorkshire and Wycliffe Hall, Oxfordshire and took the name of Constable only. With his brother Arthur *Clifford he published *A Topographical and Historical Description of the Parish of Tixall* (1817), to which he appended his *Flora Tixalliana* (reissued separately in the following year). Some of his devotional reflections were published privately, at his own expense, in 1814. His works were published under the surname Clifford. He appears to have resided at Paris towards the end of his life, and his *Description of Tixall* was issued there. A zealous Roman Catholic, he is said to have been a follower of the Abbé Carron (1760–1821), an influential French cleric active in London between 1799 and 1814. He died at Ghent on 25 February 1823.

THOMPSON COOPER, rev. ALEXANDER GOLDBLOOM

Sources GM, 1st ser., 93/1 (1823), 470 · Burke, *Peerage* · Gillow, *Lit. biog. hist.* · *Annuaire Nécrologique* (1824), 337 · L. G. Michaud and E. E. Desplaces, eds., *Biographie universelle, ancienne et moderne*, new edn, 8 (Paris, 1854) · Desmond, *Botanists*, rev. edn · narrative of his [Clifford's] relations with Louis XVIII, 1809–1814, BL, Add. MS 41648 · GEC, *Peerage*

Archives BL, narrative of his relations with Louis XVIII, Add. MS 41648 · East Riding of Yorkshire Archives Service, Beverley, corresp. and papers · U. Hull, Brynmor Jones L., family letters

Clifford, Walter de (d. 1190), landowner and soldier, was the son of Richard fitz Pons and Maud, the daughter of Walter of Gloucester. Richard was still alive in 1128 but had died by 1138, when Walter de Clifford exchanged his manor of Glasbury for that of 'Esleche' held by Gloucester Abbey. By that same year Walter held Clifford Castle and the Herefordshire Domesday reports that he held it in the 1160s, along with the manors of Hampton, Hamnish, Rochford, Dorstone, 'Burchstanestone', 'Roenoura', Hanley, and 'Madme'—all lands which his uncle Drew fitz Pons had held in 1086. By 1116 Richard fitz Pons had established a castle at Llandovery from which he dominated Cantref Selyf in central south Wales. Walter de Clifford inherited this castle but lost it in a resurgence of Welsh power about 1140. From c.1143 to 1155 he was a prominent member of the retinue of Roger, earl of Hereford, and worked to assist Roger's ambitions in the southern march. In 1158 his position in south Wales was restored. The *Brut y tywysogyon* reports that in that year Clifford raided the lands of Rhys ap Gruffudd, the Lord Rhys (d. 1197), who, after his complaint about this to Henry II went unheeded, retaliated by besieging and capturing the castle. Clifford clearly continued to be active in southern Wales, for the pipe roll for 1160 reports that £44 7s. 6d. was paid to troops in Cantref Bychan through him. In 1163 he killed Cadwgan ap Maredudd. The *rapprochement* reached between Henry II and Rhys in 1171 gave the latter possession of Cantref Bychan and deprived the Cliffords of their foothold there.

The children of Walter de Clifford and his wife, Margaret de Tosny, who was probably the daughter of Ralph de Tosny, included another Walter, who may have been the eldest son, Richard, and Rosamund *Clifford (b. before 1140?, d. 1175/6). Rosamund lived openly with Henry II as his mistress in the mid-1170s. It was probably because of this relationship that the king granted the Shropshire manor of Corfham to Clifford in 1177. He held this from the king in chief for the service of one knight's fee. After

Walter de Clifford's death in 1190, Richard inherited Clifford. He may have died in 1199, for the younger Walter succeeded to Corfham and other lands in that year.

FREDERICK SUPPE

Sources R. W. Eyton, *Antiquities of Shropshire*, 12 vols. (1854–60) · I. J. Sanders, *English baronies: a study of their origin and descent, 1086–1327* (1960) · J. E. Lloyd, *A history of Wales from the earliest times to the Edwardian conquest*, 3rd edn, 2 vols. (1939); repr. (1988) · V. H. Galbraith and J. Tait, eds., *Herefordshire domesday, circa 1160–1170*, PRSoc., 63, new ser., 25 (1950) · T. Jones, ed. and trans., *Brut y tywysogyon, or, The chronicle of the princes: Red Book of Hergest* (1955) · J. Williams ab Ithel, ed., *Annales Cambriae*, Rolls Series, 20 (1860) · *Pipe rolls*, 7 Henry II · J. H. Round, ed., *Ancient charters, royal and private, prior to AD 1200*, PRSoc., 10 (1888) · I. J. Sanders, *Feudal military service in England* (1956) · D. Walker, ed., 'Charters of the earldom of Hereford, 1095–1201', *Camden miscellany, XXII*, CS, 4th ser., 1 (1964), 1–75

Clifford, William (bap. 1594, d. 1670), Roman Catholic priest, was baptized on 10 November 1594 at Louth, Lincolnshire, the son of Henry Clifford of Brackenborough, Lincolnshire, and Elizabeth Thimelby (1565–1642) of Irnham, Lincolnshire, who after the death of her husband became a professed canoness of St Augustine at Louvain. He was descended from the family of the barons Clifford, to which he may have become male heir in 1643, but his humility prevented him from asserting an erroneous claim to the barony. He was educated in St Alban's, the English college at Valladolid, where he was ordained priest and after a short stay at Douai he was sent to England. In May 1630, after ten years work on the mission, he was sent by Bishop Richard Smith, the vicar apostolic of England, to become vice-president and procurator of the English College at Lisbon. He left in 1634 for Rome, from where he returned to England in 1636. He was made a member of the chapter in 1638 and then in 1640 was appointed superior of the Collège de Tournai at Paris, which Cardinal Richelieu had founded for the higher education of the English clergy. Between 1655 and 1658 he was recommended to become vicar apostolic but he declined this honour. During the latter years of his life he resided in the Hôpital des Incurables at Paris, where he spent the greater part of his time in ministering to the wants of the poor inmates. He died there on 30 April 1670, and was buried in the churchyard belonging to the hospital. A copy of the inscription on his tomb is preserved in the archives of the archbishop of Westminster.

Clifford wrote two works of spiritual direction, *Christian Rules Proposed to the Vertuous Soul* (1655) and *A Little Manual of the Poor Man's Dayly Devotion* (1669) as well as a translation of the *Spiritual Combat* of Lorenzo Scupoli.

THOMPSON COOPER, rev. G. BRADLEY

Sources G. Anstruther, *The seminary priests*, 2 (1975), 62 · M. Sharratt, ed., *Lisbon College register, 1628–1813*, Catholic RS, 72 (1991), 32, 111 · Gillow, *Lit. biog. hist.*, 1.514–15 · E. Henson, ed., *The registers of the English College at Valladolid, 1589–1862*, Catholic RS, 30 (1930), 114 · E. H. Burton and T. L. Williams, eds., *The Douay College diaries, third, fourth and fifth, 1598–1654*, 1, Catholic RS, 10 (1911), 183, 189; 2, Catholic RS, 11 (1911), 533 · A. F. Allison, 'Richard Smith's Gallican backers and Jesuit opponents [pt 1]', *Recusant History*, 18 (1986–7), 329–401 · A. F. Allison, 'Richard Smith's Gallican backers and Jesuit opponents [pt 2]', *Recusant History*, 19 (1988–9), 234–85 · A. F.

Allison, 'Richard Smith's Gallican backers and Jesuit opponents [pt 3]', *Recusant History*, 20 (1990–91), 164–205
Wealth at death left interest of £200 for publication of his 'Poor man's manual': Gillow, *Lit. biog. hist.*, vol. 1, p. 515

Clifford, William Joseph Hugh (1823–1893), Roman Catholic bishop of Clifton, was born on 24 December 1823 at Irnham, Lincolnshire, the second surviving son of Hugh Charles *Clifford, seventh Baron Clifford of Chudleigh (1790–1858). His mother was Mary Lucy Weld (1799–1831), the only child of Thomas *Weld, who as a widower took holy orders and subsequently became a cardinal. Clifford was educated at Hodder Place, near Stonyhurst; at Prior Park, near Bath; and at the Collegio degli Nobili Ecclesiastici, Rome. On 15 August 1840, at the age of sixteen, he delivered a Latin panegyric in honour of the Virgin Mary before Pope Gregory XVI.

Ordained priest in 1850 at the pro-cathedral, Clifton, by Bishop Hendren, Clifford returned to Plymouth, where he took charge of the mission at Stonehouse. He was secretary to the first provincial synod of the English bishops, which was held at Oscott College in 1852, and was elected vicar capitular of the diocese when Bishop George Errington became coadjutor archbishop of Westminster (1855). In 1856 Clifford returned to Rome to study canon law at the Collegio Pio.

While Clifford was there Pope Pius IX personally appointed him third bishop of Clifton, and consecrated him in the Sistine Chapel on 15 February 1857. At thirty-three he was the youngest bishop to be appointed in England since the Reformation. Throughout his thirty-six years at Clifton he showed great personal generosity towards the impoverished diocese, contributing funds for the re-purchase of Prior Park as a seminary and for the embellishment of the pro-cathedral. He opened no fewer than twenty-eight churches and chapels during his episcopate, and at the time of his death the diocese's pastoral and financial future were secure.

Clifford's adroit exposition of the unpopular 'Syllabus of errors' (1864), just eight days after the death of Cardinal Wiseman in 1865, led to his being seen by Acton and other liberal Catholics as an ideal successor at Westminster. However, in a joint letter to Rome, Clifford and Thomas Grant of Southwark asked not to be considered, but suggested that Errington be appointed, despite his having been removed from automatic succession by the pope himself. The letter so angered Pius IX that, according to Frederick Neve, cardinals had to be summoned to restrain him: accordingly, Henry Edward Manning was appointed.

Clifford made several lengthy interventions at the First Vatican Council (1869–70). These concerned clerical discipline and a proposed catechism for the universal church. His outstanding contribution, however, was to express strong misgivings over the proposed definition of papal infallibility, which was largely instigated by Manning. He argued that there had been no consultation of clergy and laity prior to the council, that protestants sympathetic to the church would be antagonized, and that it would create a theological imbalance between the see of Rome and the other bishops who—as successors of the apostles—were not rubber stamps for papal initiatives. It would also be a betrayal of the undertaking given to the British government in the 'Protestation' of 1789. Newman shared these reservations.

The definition took place in Clifford's absence, but he loyally accepted it. He was vindicated by the limited scope of the final text defining papal infallibility, and more strikingly by the document 'Christus dominus' of the Second Vatican Council (1962–5).

In the 1880s Clifford wrote an acclaimed series of articles in the *Dublin Review* seeking to interpret the Mosaic account of creation in Genesis in terms of a liturgical hymn. He successfully lobbied in Rome on behalf of the English bishops in their dispute with the religious orders ('Romanos pontifices', 1881). For many years he had tried unsuccessfully to secure church agreement for Catholic students to attend the universities.

Popular but diffident by nature, and with a slight impediment of speech, Clifford was said to be a more accomplished speaker in Italian than in English. He was a member of various local archaeological societies. He underwent an operation at Prior Park in July 1893 and died there seven weeks later, on 14 August, aged sixty-nine. His funeral oration was delivered by Bishop Hedley and his interment, next to Errington, took place on 18 August in the chapel precincts. After Manning and Newman, Clifford deserves to rank with Ullathorne as the outstanding prelate of the late nineteenth-century church.

J. A. HARDING

Sources J. A. Harding, 'Dr William Clifford, third bishop of Clifton', PhD diss., U. Lond., 1991 · H. Clifford, *The house of Clifford* (1987) · J. Murch, *Biographical sketches of Bath celebrities, ancient and modern* (1893) · *The Tablet* (26 Aug 1893) · T. S. Holmes, 'Bishop Clifford', *Proceedings of the Somersetshire Archaeological and Natural History Society*, 39 (1893), 140–46 · G. Oliver, *Collections illustrating the history of the Catholic religion in the counties of Cornwall, Devon, Dorset, Somerset, Wilts, and Gloucester* (1857), 264, 265 · parish register (baptism), Irnham Hall, St Mary's, near Colsterworth, Lincolnshire, Nottingham Roman Catholic diocese, Wilson House, Nottingham, diocesan archives · J. Shepherd, *Reminiscences of Prior Park* (1894)
Archives Bristol RO · Clifton Roman Catholic diocese, Bristol · priv. coll. | Venerable English College, Rome, Italy, Talbot MSS
Likenesses F. Podesti, oils, *c.*1857, Ugbrooke Park, Chudleigh, Devon; repro. in Clifford, *House of Clifford* · oils, 1865–70, St Ambrose, Leigh Woods, Bristol · photograph, repro. in C. Butler, *The life and times of Bishop Ullathorne* (1925), 1

Clifford, William Kingdon (1845–1879), mathematician and philosopher of science, was born on 4 May 1845 at Exeter, the eldest son of William Clifford, a justice of the peace who died in 1878. His mother, whose maiden name was Kingdon, died not long after he was born. Clifford's studies at Mr Templeton's school in Exeter prepared him for entrance in 1860 to King's College, London, where he pursued a wide range of classical, literary, and scientific subjects. He developed an interest in mathematics and obtained a scholarship at Trinity College, Cambridge, in 1863. He won the college declamation prize in 1866 for an oration on Sir Walter Raleigh and in November of that year he was elected to a university debating club, the Cambridge Conversazione Society, also known as the Apostles.

A common memory of his friends from student days was of Clifford's gymnastic feats. Though slight, he demonstrated considerable dexterity and strength; he could, for example, do pull-ups with only one hand on the horizontal bar. In the Apostles, Clifford met a fellow third-year student, Frederick Pollock, who was studying the classical curriculum and who became one of Clifford's closest friends. Pollock's introduction to Clifford's *Lectures and Essays* (1879) is a principal source of biographical information about him and, in particular, tries to document what little is known about Clifford's seemingly gradual movement away from his high-church upbringing. A major influence in this direction came from reading the authors that Clifford and Pollock most often discussed: Charles Darwin, Herbert Spencer, Benedict de Spinoza, and Giuseppe Mazzini.

In 1867 Clifford was ranked second wrangler in the university mathematical tripos and was second Smith's prizeman. His friends were surprised at his doing so well in the face of all his non-mathematical activities and the small amount of time he appeared to put into studying for the examination. The following year he was elected a fellow of Trinity College and gave his first public discourse to a large audience, 'On some of the conditions of mental development', at the Royal Institution in London. This talk, which applied Herbert Spencer's ideas on biological evolution to the development of the mind, established him as an effective and popular speaker on scientific topics. Until 1875, when failing health curtailed his public speaking, Clifford addressed general audiences on topics such as the history of the sun, the evidence for an ether, the relation between science and poetry, and Charles Babbage's calculating machines.

In 1870 Clifford received his MA and went on the English expedition to observe the solar eclipse of December that year in the Mediterranean. In spite of the wreck of his ship near Catania, Italy, this trip gave Clifford a taste for travel and a love of the Mediterranean region. He moved from Cambridge in 1871 to take up the professorship of applied mathematics at University College, London. In 1874 he was elected fellow of the Royal Society for, among other things, his distinction in 'the metaphysics of geometrical and physical science' (RS archives, election certificate, 1874). On 7 April 1875 he married Lucy [*see* Clifford, (Sophia) Lucy Jane (1846–1929)], daughter of John Lane. They had two daughters. Clifford's friends described him as having an amicable attitude towards everyone but enjoying himself most when planning children's parties and joining in the entertainment. Although he practised his athletic abilities beyond his student days, he was not particularly careful about his health and was known to stay up all night on occasion in order to complete a mathematical project. In 1876 he had symptoms of a pulmonary disease and reluctantly took a six-month leave of absence. His friend Leslie Stephen, later to become editor of the *Dictionary of National Biography*, began a subscription to pay for a trip to the warmer climate of Spain and Algiers. This mitigated Clifford's continuing weakness but in early 1878 his condition worsened to such an extent that, following medical advice, he and his wife travelled to the Mediterranean. Again he seemed improved on his return but the next year a relapse caused them to journey to Madeira where he remained for the last few months of his life.

Clifford's years of illness were at the same time among the most mathematically productive of his short life, and he was encouraged to continue by some of the leading

William Kingdon Clifford (1845–1879), by John Collier, 1878

mathematicians of the day. Olaus Henrici reported on 26 June 1878 (Royal Society Library, RR.8.84) on a paper submitted by Clifford to the Royal Society, entitled 'Classification of locii', that the work was a 'very important one and the simplicity of the methods used … fully worthy of the genius of Clifford'. Although, 'owing to the bad state of health of its author' the work was still 'fragmentary and under ordinary circumstances' not publishable, he nevertheless recommended that it 'be printed as it stands, with the addition perhaps of one or two explanatory notes' since Clifford was in no condition to correct the manuscript. Such notes supplied by Henrici and others to this and other works in the *Mathematical Papers* (1882) are a useful, indeed essential, adjunct to Clifford's original presentations.

On his death, Clifford's wife gave his unfinished manuscripts to those of his colleagues who were willing to complete them and see to their publication. One such manuscript, for a book concerned with the bases of pure and applied mathematics, was completed by Karl Pearson and published in 1885 as *The Common Sense of the Exact Sciences*. Though Clifford intended the work to be readable by the layperson, it was more than a popularization of mathematics since it contained many original ideas. Bertrand Russell, in a preface for the 1946 edition, described his enthusiasm in reading the book at the age of fifteen in 1887. Russell had been puzzling over Euclid's geometry and was delighted to find that there was a rationale for geometry, and mathematics generally, that he found lacking in Euclid's presentation.

Most of Clifford's mathematical work centred on geometry which, considered as the study of space, he regarded as an empirical science. He believed that Immanuel Kant's argument for an a priori, universal component in mathematics was justified by discoveries about human development, perception, and language made since Kant's time by Darwin, Spencer, and Max Müller. Clifford readily adapted to his own use the work on invariant theory by the leading British mathematicians of the time, Arthur Cayley and James Joseph Sylvester. His discovery of a generalization of quaternions, which he termed 'biquaternions', and of the algebra associated with them (and later named after him), was built upon the work of the Irishman William Rowan Hamilton, who discovered quaternions, and of the German Hermann G. Grassmann, whose ideas Clifford helped to propagate in the English-speaking world. Clifford also used Hamilton's quaternions in his *Elements of Dynamic: an Introduction to the Study of Motion and Rest in Solid and Fluid Bodies* (1878). Though quaternions themselves did not continue to play such a direct role in physics, the notions Clifford derived from them, such as the divergence of a vector, and the vector and scalar products, continued to be useful in twentieth-century physics. Clifford's biquaternions, on the other hand, found applications (unanticipated by Clifford) in the representation of the wave function in quantum physics.

Invariant theory and biquaternions, though algebraic topics, have strong connections in Clifford's work to geometry and in particular to the non-Euclidean geometries that were discovered earlier in the nineteenth century but became incorporated into the main body of mathematics only during his lifetime. Intrigued by the possibility that one of these new geometries could describe the physical world better than the traditional Euclidean geometry, he made new discoveries concerning all of them but singled out as his favourite candidate the elliptic geometry. He discovered a surface (since named the 'Clifford surface') in elliptic space with the unexpected property of supporting parallel lines ('Clifford parallels'). In an abstract for proposed work in 1870 he posited that motion of matter could be explained by the variation of the curvature of space. This anticipation of one of the features of Albert Einstein's general theory of relativity forty years later came from his reading of the German mathematician Georg Friedrich Bernhard Riemann, whose key work in this area Clifford translated into English ('On the hypotheses which lie at the bases of geometry').

Many of Clifford's popular lectures and writings strongly upheld scientific reasoning over religious dogma. His lively, aphoristic style and authoritative and wide-ranging knowledge made him an influential spokesman for a certain view of the scientific spirit of the late nineteenth century. His creed expressed in 'The ethics of belief' (1876), that 'it is wrong always, everywhere, and for anyone, to believe anything upon insufficient evidence' (Clifford, *Lectures*, 1.186), was approvingly cited by others such as the psychologist William James in his *Will to Believe* (1897). Scientific progress for Clifford was made by having doubts, not faith. His anti-religious stance was so rigorous that, as James Sully expressed it in a review of *Lectures and Essays*, Clifford had a 'religious abhorrence of religion' and thus could be said to have adopted a dogmatism comparable to that of his high-church upbringing (*The Academy*, 17, 1880, 133–4). Clifford was the basis for William Hurrell Mallock's young materialist, Mr Saunders, in *The New Republic* (1877), an unflattering caricature that Mallock moderated somewhat in the version that appeared shortly after Clifford's death. One of the tenets of Clifford's alternative to the usual religious views was his version of a psychological atomism that asserted that 'Reason, intelligence, and volition are properties of a complex which is made up of elements, themselves not rational, not intelligent, not conscious' (Clifford, *Lectures*, 2.87). Twentieth-century theories of self-organization may have made Clifford's notion scientifically more acceptable, but his views undoubtedly appeared rather extreme in his time.

Clifford sought to formulate an ethic consistent with his philosophical and scientific positions and, like Spinoza, one that had geometrical certainty. He felt that the theory of evolution, when applied to societies, provided the best available scientific foundation for ethical beliefs and that the theory implied that the survival of the community depends on how well it treats its members. Ethics is thus a matter for the community, not for 'self-regarding' individuals, and happiness is desirable only if it makes for a more efficient citizen. Society must support creative activity and the search for truth by an individual, wherever that may lead, since a knowledge of the truth has great social importance. The formality of his ethics, however, contrasted with his more flexible and open personal manner: 'All this, by the way', he wrote to Frederick Pollock's wife, 'is only theory; my practice is just like other people's' (Clifford, *Lectures*, 1.49).

Clifford died at Madeira on 3 March 1879. He was buried in Highgate cemetery, Middlesex. His friends began a subscription for a pension to benefit his family which otherwise would have been without income. His wife, Lucy, maintained their social circle and became a confidante of literary figures such as George Eliot, James Russell Lowell, and Henry James. She wrote a number of novels, her first and best known being *Mrs Keith's Crime* (1885). She died on 21 April 1929 and was also buried in Highgate cemetery.

ALBERT C. LEWIS

Sources F. Pollock, 'Introduction', in W. K. Clifford, *Lectures and essays*, ed. L. Stephen and F. Pollock (1879) · W. K. Clifford, *Mathematical papers*, ed. R. Tucker (1882), xiii–xxix, xxxi–lxx · *DNB* · E. A. Power, 'Exeter's mathematician. W. K. Clifford, F.R.S., 1845–79', *Advancement of Science*, 26 (1970), 318–28 · N. G. Annan, *Leslie Stephen: the godless Victorian*, rev. edn (1984) · *CGPLA Eng. & Wales* (1879) · *The Times* (17 March 1879), 6f · M. Chisholm, *Such silver currents: the story of William and Lucy Clifford, 1845–1929* (2002)
Archives UCL, letters
Likenesses J. Collier, oils, 1878, RS [*see illus.*] · J. Collier, oils, 1899 (after his oil painting, 1878), NPG · C. H. Jeens, line engraving (after photograph by Barraud and Jerrard), repro. in Clifford, *Lectures and essays*, 1, frontispiece · photograph, repro. in Clifford, *Lectures and essays*, 2, pasted-in frontispiece
Wealth at death under £450: administration, 18 June 1879, *CGPLA Eng. & Wales*

Clift, William (1775–1849), museum curator and scientific illustrator, was born at Burcombe, near Bodmin, Cornwall, on 14 February 1775, and was baptized (as William Cleft) in the Bodmin parish church on 12 April that year. He was the youngest of the seven children (Elizabeth, Joanna, Robert, Thomas, John, one of unknown name, and William) of Robert Clift (1720–1784), a miller, whose death left his wife, Joanna, *née* Coutts (*bap.* 1733), a seamstress, and family in poverty. Clift was sent to school at Bodmin, and his abilities at illustration drew the attention of Walter Raleigh Gilbert of The Priory, Bodmin (one of the gentlemen of the bedchamber to George III), and his wife, Nancy Hosken, 'a lady of great accomplishments'. Mrs Gilbert had been a schoolfellow of Anne Home, who married the celebrated surgeon John *Hunter (1728–1793) in 1771. Mrs Gilbert recommended Clift as an apprentice to Hunter to replace his former anatomical assistant, William Bell, emphasizing his abilities as an artist. Clift arrived in London in the company of the Gilberts on 14 February 1792, and was accepted by Hunter as his apprentice for a six-year period without the payment of the standard apprenticeship fee, on the understanding that he was to make drawings, copy dictation, and assist in the care of the anatomical museum which Hunter had created on the property between his two residences on Castle Street and Leicester Square.

While Hunter lived this arrangement proved satisfactory to both of them: Clift assisted Hunter with his dissections and wrote from his dictation from early morning until late at night. Hunter's sudden death on 16 October 1793 passed his two residences to his wife, Anne, and his son John and daughter Agnes. His massive collection of 18,682 anatomical preparations was willed to his son-in-law Everard Home and assistant, Matthew Baillie, with instructions to offer it for sale to parliament. Wartime economies made parliament reluctant to purchase it, however, and during negotiations for sale Clift was engaged during 1793–9 by Hunter's executors to watch over the collections, living with an old housekeeper in Hunter's residence on Castle Street; for this he received a meagre income. He was solely responsible for the safety and preservation of the collection, and guarded it with zeal. Fearing for its safety Clift copied out for private keeping nearly half of Hunter's unpublished manuscripts (thus saving this material from Home's intentional destruction of the main body of the original manuscripts in 1823). Clift was a tireless curator and when parliament agreed to purchase the collection in 1799 it was reported to be in a better state than at its owner's death. The Company of Surgeons, incorporated in 1800 as the College of Surgeons of England, was asked by parliament in 1799 to assume the charge of the collection, to which it agreed in December that year.

One of the first acts of the trustees of the new college was to retain Clift's services, dignifying him with the title of conservator of the Hunterian Museum at a salary of £80 per annum. From that date his time and talents were devoted to the collection. Under his supervision Hunter's collections were twice moved without damage, first in 1806 from their Castle Street location to a temporary warehouse on Lincoln's Inn Fields, where they remained until 1813 while the original College of Surgeons buildings were constructed, and again during the rebuilding of the museum and college in 1834–7. Clift was a scrupulous record-keeper and his surviving diaries covering the years 1811 to 1842 supply a detailed insight into the workings of the College of Surgeons, the Hunterian Museum, and London scientific life generally. He lived to see the museum enriched and enlarged to become the foremost museum of comparative anatomy in the world. On 21 January 1801 Clift married Caroline Harriet Pope (1775–1849) at St Martin-in-the-Fields, London. His only son, William Home *Clift (1803–1832), a fine illustrator whom Clift was preparing as his successor, died on 17 September 1832 from injuries sustained in a carriage accident. His only daughter, Caroline Amelia Clift, was born in September 1801 (*bap.* 10 January 1802) and died on 7 May 1873. She married Clift's assistant Richard *Owen (1804–1892) at St Pancras New Church on 20 July 1835; their only child, William (1837–1886), left one son, Richard Startin Owen.

Clift's dedication to science and his reputation for care and thoroughness gave him a standing in the scientific community that went beyond his limited scientific publications. He was praised by the surgeon John Flint South,

Sir Benjamin Brodie the elder (1783–1862), Sir Joseph Banks, William Wollaston, and Humphry Davy, and through the influence of the latter was elected FRS on 8 May 1823. He was also a member of the Society for Animal Chemistry, a small London scientific association created as an assistant society of the Royal Society of London in 1809, and drawn from members of the Royal Institution and the College of Surgeons. This group was dedicated to the study of physiology and animal chemistry, communicating results through publications in the *Philosophical Transactions of the Royal Society*. It died out in 1825.

Clift was also interested in palaeontology and geology and was a fellow of the Geological Society. His knowledge of palaeontological and geological issues was acknowledged by Gideon Mantell, Georges Cuvier, and Charles Lyell. Clift's skills as an anatomical illustrator were early displayed in print in Matthew Baillie's *A series of engravings … to illustrate the morbid anatomy of some of the most important parts of the human body* (1799–1803), for which he was the unnamed illustrator. Similarly, many of the 320 illustrations in Home's 100 papers on anatomical subjects in the *Philosophical Transactions* were by Clift. Clift himself contributed papers to the *Philosophical Transactions* for 1815 and 1823, to the *Edinburgh New Philosophical Journal* for 1831, and to the *Transactions of the Geological Society* in 1829 and 1835. His paper 'On the fossil remains … found on the left bank of the Irawadi' in the *Transactions of the Geological Society* for 1829 was reprinted in an appendix to John Crawfurd's *Journal of an Embassy from the Governor General of India to the Court of Ava* (1829). Richard Owen published in 1861 two volumes of *Essays and Observations on Natural History, Anatomy, &c., by John Hunter*, drawn in the main from the private copies made by Clift of Hunter's manuscripts between 1793 and 1800. Clift himself had contemplated their publication and drawn up some notes for that purpose, but never carried this out. Some of these had been previously published in part in Owen and Clift's *Descriptive and illustrated catalogue of the physiological series of comparative anatomy contained in the museum of the Royal College of Surgeons* (1833–1840), but the whole collection was not placed in Owen's hands until a short time before Clift's death. With Owen's assistance, Clift was also the primary compiler of the *Catalogue of the Hunterian Collection of the Museum of the Royal College of Surgeons of London* (1830–31).

In 1842 Clift retired from full-time duties at the museum and moved with his wife to Stanhope Cottage, Mornington Crescent, Hampstead Road; he was replaced as curator by his son-in-law. Caroline Clift died on 8 May 1849 and Clift himself died of unspecified causes at his home shortly afterwards, on 20 June 1849. Both were buried in Highgate cemetery. His esteem in the scientific and medical communities is indicated by several laudatory obituaries that appeared on his death in such periodicals as *The Lancet* and the *Proceedings of the Royal Society of London*.

Clift's personal effects were sold at auction in August 1849, and his papers were either retained by the College of Surgeons, were passed to Owen, or were acquired at auction. Those in the possession of Owen, including the main

collection of the Clift correspondence, are now in the Natural History Museum as part of the Owen papers. An additional collection of manuscripts was obtained by the College of Surgeons in 1945 from materials that had been in the possession of Thomas Madden Stone, assistant librarian to the college from 1832 to 1853.

PHILLIP R. SLOAN

Sources RCS Eng., Clift papers • NHM, Richard Owen MSS • J. Dobson, *William Clift* (1954) • W. Le Fanu, 'Clift, William', *DSB* • Z. Cope, *The Royal College of Surgeons of England: a history* (1959) • V. G. Plarr, *Catalogue of manuscripts in the library of the Royal College of Surgeons of England* (1928) [annotated version in RCS Eng.] • J. Dobson, 'The architectural history of the Hunterian Museum', *Annals of the Royal College of Surgeons of England*, 29 (1961), 113–26 [annotated version in RCS Eng.] • *Richard Owen's Hunterian lectures in comparative anatomy: May–June 1837*, ed. P. R. Sloan (1992) • A. Desmond, *The politics of evolution: morphology, medicine and reform in radical London* (1989) • *The Lancet* (23 June 1849), 685 • *GM*, 2nd ser., 32 (1849), 209–10 • C. R. Weld, *A history of the Royal Society*, 2 vols. (1848), vol. 2, pp. 237–43

Archives BL, family corresp. and papers, Add. MSS 39954–39955 • NHM, corresp. and papers • NHM, corresp. mainly with his wife and sisters • RCS Eng., corresp. and papers; museum diary, family corresp. • Wellcome L., corresp. | NHM, corresp. with Sir Richard Owen

Likenesses F. Chantrey, pencil sketch, 1831, BM • W. H. Clift, three pencil drawings, c.1831, BM • H. Schmidt, oils, 1833, RS • marble effigy, 1845, RCS Eng. • Bosley, line engraving, 1849 (after daguerreotype), BM • A. A. Claudet, daguerreotype, 1849, probably RCS Eng. • plaster bust, RCS Eng.

Wealth at death £3000: Dobson, *William Clift*, 128

Clift, William Home (1803–1832), museum curator, was born on 20 May 1803 at the home of the late John Hunter, 13 Castle Street, Leicester Square, London, the second of two children of William *Clift (1775–1849), natural scientist and first conservator of the Hunterian Museum, and his wife, Caroline Harriet, née Pope (1775–1849) of Mells, Somerset. William Home was named after his godfather, Sir Everard Home, the surgeon and anatomist, who was Hunter's executor and brother-in-law. The Clift family moved into accommodation at the Royal College of Surgeons of London in Lincoln's Inn Fields when buildings to house the museum were completed in 1811. In 1813 Clift was attending a private academy run by a Mr Williams, but of other schooling nothing is known except that Home dissuaded Clift's father from sending him to public school. Consequently, he spent most of his life at the college, trained up from an early age to assist in the museum, where it was expected he would eventually succeed his father as conservator. From the college records it is evident that he was already working in 1818 and in January 1823 he was officially appointed assistant conservator. His most lasting and important work was the preparation of catalogues which were a necessary complement to Hunter's collection.

The catalogues had become a matter of controversy. Home had insisted that he should prepare the catalogues but in 1823 he told Clift's father that he had burned Hunter's papers, without which they could not be compiled. After some months Clift's father brought the matter to the notice of the board of curators but following prolonged investigations the affair was dropped. Fortunately, Clift's father had made copies of many of the manuscripts between Hunter's death in 1793 and 1800 when Home caused them to be removed into his keeping, but the appropriation of the papers and subsequent destruction of them led to a long delay. Thus, in 1829 Clift was asked by the board of curators to arrange and catalogue the osteological section of the collection. The original minutes of the board show that Clift completed the first edition of this catalogue in 1830 and he received a gratuity of £50. (In his digest of the minutes, written in the 1920s, Arthur Keith mistakenly states that Clift was relieved of the project in March 1831.) In 1831 Clift's catalogue, *Monsters and Malformed Parts*, was published and he was working on further lists at the time of his death in 1832. Biographers of both Hunter and Richard *Owen, who was appointed second assistant in the museum in 1827, subsequently attributed the preparation of these catalogues, which entailed the description of nearly 3000 specimens, to Owen. Clift's work, therefore, has been totally unacknowledged. Owen married Clift's sister, Caroline Amelia, in 1835 and this, coupled with the fact that he eventually succeeded Clift's father as conservator, may help to account for Clift's contribution to the work of the museum being overlooked.

Of Clift's personality little would be known were it not for the letters he wrote to his parents and sister on brief holidays away from the museum, including one to Scotland when he visited museums and collections. He was a likeable young man with a great sense of fun and zest for life. His interests included music and the theatre and among his many friends was the journalist Eugenius Roche, whose portrait he drew. His letters display Regency wit and style and are sprinkled with pencil sketches. He was a considerable artist and left a useful collection of portraits of some of the eminent natural scientists and surgeons of his time. Late on 11 September 1832 he was seriously injured when alighting from a cabriolet in Chancery Lane and was taken to St Bartholomew's Hospital, where he was attended by Owen. He died on 17 September. As a token of respect the museum was closed until after the funeral, which took place at Bunhill Fields cemetery on 22 September 1832. FRANCES AUSTIN

Sources J. Dobson, *William Clift* (1954) · *The letters of William Home Clift, 1803–1832*, ed. F. Austin (1983) · minute books of the board of curators of the Hunterian Museum, London, RCS Eng. · W. Clift, diaries, RCS Eng. · F. Austin, ed., *The Clift family correspondence, 1792–1846* (1991) · A. Keith, 'Abstract of minutes of the museum committee, 1800–1907', 1908, RCS Eng.
Archives NHM · RCS Eng. | NHM, corresp. with Richard Owen

Clifton, Arthur. *See* Corri, (Philip) Antony (1784?–1832), *under* Corri family (*per. c.*1770–1860).

Clifton, Francis (d. 1736), physician, was the fourth and youngest son of Josiah Clifton, merchant, of Great Yarmouth, Norfolk, and his wife, Mary, only child of Thomas Fenne of the same town. Choosing to join the medical profession, he entered Leiden University on 23 May 1724, and graduated as doctor of medicine there in September of the same year. His inaugural dissertation, 'De distinctis et confluentibus variolis', was later published.

Clifton afterwards settled in London, where his classical and scientific learning won him the friendship of many eminent men, among them Sir Hans Sloane, on whose proposition he was elected a fellow of the Royal Society on 22 June 1727. The same year he published *Hippocratis Coi operum quae extant omnium secundum leges artis medicae dispositorum, editionis novae specimen*, and in 1732 he published a proposal to print a new edition of the works of Hippocrates; however, lack of sufficient subscriptions meant that it never appeared. Clifton received the honorary degree of MD from Cambridge on 26 April 1728, during the visit of George II; he was admitted a candidate of the Royal College of Physicians on 23 December in the same year and a fellow on 22 December 1729, and gave the Goulstonian lectures in 1732. He also held the appointment of physician to the prince of Wales, which he resigned in 1734, when he abruptly left London for Jamaica.

Writing to Sir Hans Sloane from Kingston, Jamaica, on 3 June 1736, Clifton says: 'My misfortunes came so fast upon me, and my brother's provocations were so frequently repeated, that I was hurried in a manner to death about 'em' (BL, Sloane MS 4041, fol. 9). He died there a few weeks afterwards, leaving a widow, Sarah Banckes, daughter of a merchant in Leadenhall Street, London. There were no children of the marriage. In the letters of administration granted on 6 November 1736 to his widow, Clifton is described as 'late of the parish of St George, Hanover Square, Middlesex, but at Kingston in Jamaica, deceased'. His widow survived until 1747, and was buried in the parish church of St Andrew Undershaft (will, PRO, PROB 11/754, sig. 145).

At the time of his death Clifton was engaged in drawing up an account of the diseases of Jamaica, but left it unfinished. Among his other works was *The State of Physick, Ancient and Modern, Briefly Considered*, in which he maintained that Hippocrates had anticipated Newton in his idea of the system of gravitation. A French version by the Abbé Desfontaines was published at Paris in 1742.

GORDON GOODWIN, rev. PATRICK WALLIS

Sources R. W. Innes Smith, *English-speaking students of medicine at the University of Leyden* (1932) · C. J. Palmer, *The perlustration of Great Yarmouth*, 3 vols. (1872–5) · Munk, *Roll* · M. Neuburger, 'Francis Clifton and William Black: eighteenth century critical historians of medicine', *Journal of the History of Medicine and Allied Sciences*, 5 (1950), 44–9 · Nichols, *Lit. anecdotes*, 2.14–15 · will, PRO, PROB 11/587, sig. 191 [Josiah Clifton] · will, PRO, PROB 11/633, sig. 295 [Mary Clifton] · Sloane MS, BL, MS 4041, fol. 9 · will, PRO, PROB 11/754, sig. 145 [Sarah Clifton]
Archives BL, letters, Sloane MS 4041

Clifton, Francis (*fl.* 1716–1724), printer, of unknown parentage, seems to have been educated at Oxford University despite being of the Roman Catholic faith. Between 1716 and 1724 he was notorious in London as a printer of cheap, seditious broadsheets espousing the Jacobite cause. He was involved in the production of three newspapers, the *Oxford Post* (December 1717 to 1719), the *Weekly Medley, or, The Gentleman's Recreation* (1718–19), and briefly the *Orphan Revived* (1720) for Elizabeth Powell, another printer. Clifton's wife, Catherine, was also active in his printing business. Little is known of their married life, although

Clifton described his wife as being pregnant in April 1720 (PRO, SP 35/23/37(3)), and later in that year, 'lame', while he portrayed himself as 'weak and consumptive' (PRO, SP 35/24/75(5)). His evidence, however, is not wholly reliable as he was at that time pleading for sympathy from government officials investigating him for his treasonable printing activities.

Francis Clifton was variously described as printing in Black House Alley, Fleet Street (1718), 'near the Ditchside' (1718), at the Old Bailey (1719 and 1720), in 'the Libertys of the Fleet [prison]' (1719 and 1720), in Waterman's Lane (1723), and in Little Wild Street. His frequent changes of premises reflect the precarious nature of his business, being often pursued for debt as well as for political reasons.

Clifton was probably the most active and persistent of a number of printers making a living by producing cheap broadsheets and pamphlets of an anti-Hanoverian and often Jacobite content at a time when, in the aftermath of the Jacobite rising of 1715, George I's ministers were desperately concerned to stamp out any signs of support for the Pretender. Clifton had the ability to exploit the market for scurrilous popular ballads and verses which were reputedly cried about the capital in large numbers. One magistrate, Sir John Fryer, warned that Clifton's works, 'tho' they are silly ridiculous things, yett they do much hurt among the common people' (PRO, SP 35/18/35). A more sympathetic account is given by Clifton's journeyman, Thomas Gent, later himself a prominent printer in York, who noted his employer's 'poor circumstances' and difficulties over debts, but presented a graphic picture of Clifton's busy enterprise carried on within the Fleet:

> Some time in extreme weather, have I worked under a mean shed, adjoining to the prison wall, when snow and rain have fallen alternately on the cases; yet the number of wide-mouthed stentorian hawkers, brisk trade, and very often a glass of good ale, revived the drooping spirits of the workmen. I have often admired at the success of this person in his station; for … advantageous jobs so often flowed upon him, as gave him cause to be merry under his heavy misfortune. (*Life*, 85, 86–7)

At least fourteen Jacobite broadsheets can be positively identified as having been produced by the Cliftons between 1716 and 1724, although this list is certainly incomplete. Thomas Gent records that on one occasion Clifton was secretly employed by the Jacobite Francis Atterbury, bishop of Rochester. Clifton's works included two broadsides on the death of the nineteen-year-old Jacobite John Matthews in 1719, the last printer to be executed in Britain. It is hard to assess how many copies of each of his pieces Clifton printed, perhaps between several dozen and several hundred, but these works were usually intended to be sung or declaimed to a wider audience in alehouses and gin shops, or on street corners.

Much of the evidence for the importance of the Cliftons in this period comes from the careful attention paid to them by authorities keen to clamp down on a dissident press: they were a prime target for informers, and raids on their establishments and several arrests followed. In 1719 Clifton was taken up for an edition of the *Oxford Post*, and in 1720 was jailed as a result of a series of vehement accusations of treasonable work made by Richard Burridge, a hack writer and business rival. From prison Clifton wrote pleading letters to Charles Delafaye, the under-secretary of state responsible for his case, and even to a disdainful archbishop of Canterbury. He remained in custody until late March 1721 when he was finally allowed bail, the Treasury solicitor concluding that there was insufficient evidence against him to warrant prosecution. Another informer, Richard Shaw, continued to complain of Clifton's work, which was sustained despite the dangers of government action—including the breaking up of his print by government messengers—and Clifton's supposed ill health. In 1722 Clifton was again jailed, this time on suspicion of printing 'lines' on the arrest of the bishop of Rochester.

Clifton's Jacobitism was certainly persistent despite adversity. However he showed little solidarity with other Jacobite printers, offering to give information against those he clearly saw as business rivals if it would get him off the government hook, and denying that he ever received funding from Jacobite sources. He claimed that he was unfairly treated because of his Catholicism. Thomas Gent, growing disillusioned with his employer, portrayed Clifton as having an 'obstinate', violent, and 'ungovernable' temper, and as 'ill-respected'. The last work which can be attributed to him with any certainty was in 1724, after which, according to Gent, he 'proved himself a villain, in moving off to France with the money of a brewer to whom he was a steward, & left his bondsmen to answer for what damage he had done thereby' (*Life*, 112). Clifton is thought to have died in France, although the date of his death is unknown.

PAUL CHAPMAN

Sources state papers, domestic, George I, PRO, SP 35 · *The life of Mr Thomas Gent … written by himself*, ed. J. Hunter (1832) · P. M. Chapman, 'Jacobite political argument in England, 1714–66', PhD diss., U. Cam., 1983 · P. K. Monod, *Jacobitism and the English people, 1688–1788* (1989)
Archives PRO, domestic, George I, SP 35

Clifton, John Charles (1781–1841), music teacher, was born in London on 7 November 1781. His father intended him to become a merchant, but his early talent for music was such that he was placed in the care of a relative, Richard Bellamy, with whom he studied music for five years. He then became a pupil of Charles Wesley, and eventually decided to follow music as a profession, giving up a position as a clerk in the Stationery Office which he had held for about two years.

Clifton's first professional engagement was at Bath, where he conducted the Harmonic Society. In 1802 he went to Dublin and became a music master, and in 1816 he produced there a successful piece, *Edwin and Angelina* (after Goldsmith), written with Sir John Stevenson. He also organized, with Stevenson, a large-scale concert in aid of famine relief in Ireland. About 1816 he invented an instrument to aid sight-singing called the 'Eidomusicon', which does not appear to have been patented. About the same time he finished a plan of music education detailed in his *Theory of Harmony Simplified*, and about 1817 lectured in Dublin on both the plan and the invention. In 1818 Clifton moved to London in order to have his ideas published, but the project proved too expensive and impractical. He then adopted the Logierian system of musical instruction, and for some years was a teacher of repute in London; he also became an associate of the Philharmonic Society. He married the proprietress of Teresa House, a ladies' boarding-school in Hammersmith, where the last years of his life were spent, and where he taught singing and the piano for a time. His compositions consist chiefly of songs and glees, one of which gained the prize offered by the Manchester Glee Club.

Around 1838 Clifton's mental health deteriorated and he became possessed with the idea that he was enormously wealthy; the delusion grew to such an extent that it was found necessary to place him under a gentle restraint. The *Musical World* (25 November 1841) described how, 'even during this time, the generosity of his heart was made manifest by his anxiety to make very handsome presents to his friends and acquaintances'. He died at Teresa House on 18 November 1841.

W. B. SQUIRE, *rev.* DAVID J. GOLBY

Sources *Musical World* (25 Nov 1841), 344 · J. C. Kassler, *The science of music in Britain, 1714–1830: a catalogue of writings, lectures, and inventions*, 1 (1979), 203 · J. C. Clifton, 'Letter to the editor', *The Harmonicon*, 6 (1828), 73–5 · [Clarke], *The Georgian era: memoirs of the most eminent persons*, 4 (1834), 529 · *GM*, 2nd ser., 17 (1842), 112 · Grove, *Dict. mus.*

Clifton, Richard (c.1553–1616), separatist minister in the Netherlands, was born at Normanton, Derbyshire, the eldest son of Thomas Clifton of Normanton and his first wife. On 12 February 1585 Clifton was instituted to the vicarage of Marnham near Newark, Nottinghamshire. On 11 July 1586 he was instituted to the rectory of Babworth, near Retford, in the same county. That September he married Anne (c.1555–1613), daughter of I. Stuffen of Warsop, Nottinghamshire. The couple had at least three sons born at Babworth: Zachary (12 May 1589), Timothy (29 September 1595), and Eleazer (1 November 1598). Three daughters, also born at Babworth, died in infancy.

In May 1591 Clifton was charged in the Nottingham archdeaconry court with various misdemeanours, including failure to read the injunctions, to announce saints' days, to wear the surplice, and to use the cross in baptism. No punishment seems to have been imposed. However, on 15 March 1605, having been warned several times, Clifton was presented in the court of chancery at York for nonconformity to the new canons. He was ordered to confer with William Palmer, chancellor of York Minster, and in the hope of his future conformity was respited until 12 April. Then, in a hearing before Archbishop Matthew Hutton, he was deprived of his living and suspended from the ministry. On 6 March 1607 he was cited in the chancery court for continuing to preach unofficially, as the 'pretended minister' or curate at Bawtry, a village near Scrooby, in south Yorkshire. William Bradford, first governor of Plymouth, New England, recalled having enjoyed his 'illuminating ministry' in this period (Burgess, 90).

Clifton did not answer the charge; he was excommunicated on 20 March, but five days later this was suspended in the hope of his appearance; on 24 April he failed to attend and the sentence was reimposed.

By this time Clifton had formally separated from the Church of England. Although undoubtedly leader of the Scrooby group, which supplied the nucleus of the Pilgrim Fathers, he was associated by this time with John Robinson and John Smyth, the future Baptist, of nearby Gainsborough. Clifton appears to have had differences with both men, even before all three took ship for the Low Countries. On arrival in Amsterdam in August 1608, he can only have been about fifty-five, but he appeared as 'a grave and fatherly old man … having a great white beard' ('A dialogue or summe', *Publications of the Massachusetts Colonial Society*, 22, 139). In the factional disputes developing among the émigrés, Clifton soon aligned himself with the separatist 'Ancient church' of Francis Johnson and Henry Ainsworth. In spring 1609, John Robinson, weary of internecine conflict, decamped to Leiden with his followers. These included most of the original Scrooby members, but not Clifton, who remained with Johnson in Amsterdam. Meanwhile, Smyth had embraced believer's baptism, and in early 1610 Clifton issued *A Plea for Infants and Elder People* against him. In December, when Ainsworth abandoned the Ancient church, Clifton replaced him as its teacher. It seems that he was not ordained to this position, perhaps because Johnson felt that the Dutch synods would have interpreted the reimposition of hands upon him as a denial of the legitimacy of his English episcopal ordination. It was in his capacity as teacher of the church that Clifton issued *An Advertisement Concerning a Book* (1612) against his predecessor. According to the family Bible, his wife, Anne, died in Amsterdam on 3 September 1613, 'aged fifty-eight'. Richard Clifton died on 20 May 1616, also at Amsterdam, 'aged sixty-three', and was buried in the South Church there. Their sons Timothy and Eleazer died in the city on 7 June 1663 and 18 January 1669 respectively.

STEPHEN WRIGHT

Sources R. Marchant, *The puritans and the church courts in the diocese of York, 1560–1642* (1960) · W. Burgess, *John Robinson* (1920) · 'Plymouth church records', *Publications of the Massachusetts Colonial Society*, 22 (1920) · family Bible, U. Oxf., Taylor Institution
Archives U. Oxf., Taylor Institution, family Bible

Clifton, Robert Bellamy (1836–1921), physicist, was born at Gedney in Lincolnshire on 13 March 1836, the only son of Robert Clifton, a landowner, and his wife, Frances Gibbons. After schooling in Peterborough and Brighton he studied at University College, London, and in 1855 entered St John's College, Cambridge. His position as sixth wrangler in the tripos in 1859 was seen as disappointing, but he was second Smith's prizeman and became a fellow of his college. In 1860 he was appointed the first professor of natural philosophy at Owens College, Manchester. There he lectured successfully and in 1862 married Catharine Elizabeth Butler (d. 1917) of Brighton. They had three sons and a daughter.

Clifton's application for the new chair of experimental

philosophy at Oxford in 1865 was supported by testimonials from Henry Roscoe, William Thomson, James Prescott Joule, William Whewell, George Gabriel Stokes, and J. C. Adams, as well as from Robert Bunsen and Gustav Kirchhoff of Heidelberg, who had met Clifton during a visit to Manchester in 1862. This support and his record at Cambridge and Manchester set him comfortably ahead of the only other applicant, George Griffith, an Oxford graduate and part-time schoolmaster at Winchester College, who had deputized as professor of experimental philosophy during the protracted incapacity of the Revd Professor Robert Walker. After arriving in Oxford in 1866 Clifton began his tenure of the chair promisingly. More than a decade after its foundation, the school of natural science had achieved respectability, and the opening of the university museum in 1860 had further advanced the interests of science in the university. The flow of students seeking laboratory instruction immediately rendered the space for experimental philosophy in the museum inadequate, and Clifton began a campaign for the new laboratory that was to constitute his greatest single contribution to the discipline and to Oxford.

Although Clifton's case rested on a belief in the importance of training in experimental technique that most progressive physicists would have shared, it appeared initially to have little chance of success. But it carried the day when the trustees of the funds arising from the bequest of the great-grandson of the earl of Clarendon offered £10,700 for the erection of what was to be the first purpose-built physics laboratory in the world. The Clarendon Laboratory, as it soon came to be called, was completed in 1872 at a total cost of £12,000.

The internal design and fitting out of the Clarendon reflected Clifton's concern for detail and his vision of the laboratory as a leading centre for teaching and research in the physics of precise measurement. Conscious of the delicacy of much of the equipment, he devoted each room to a specific range of experiments, so that the students, rather than the equipment, moved about the building. Fear of the harm that could befall apparatus in inexperienced hands also made him cautious about releasing it from the locked cupboards in which it was kept when not in immediate use. These attitudes discouraged all but the most committed students, and few chose to specialize in physics for the honour school. In 1887 Clifton's failure to develop the subject at the honours level had its inevitable consequences when convocation rejected his request for £4800 for the construction of an electrical laboratory. This defeat, allied to the persistent neglect of his case for the appointment of other professors (in particular, of someone who would teach electricity, in which he had little competence), appears to have undermined Clifton's will to fight for his subject, and in 1895 he reallocated his personal laboratory for the purposes of teaching. In fact, the decision to relinquish his laboratory had few consequences, for Clifton had published only one substantial scientific article since arriving in Oxford.

The last two decades of Clifton's career, until he retired in 1915, were marked by the undiminished fastidiousness of his teaching but also by tensions. The long-awaited appointment of a second professor, J. S. E. Townsend, in 1900 brought him more unhappiness than relief. He and Townsend never worked well together, and Townsend consistently attracted the larger share of serious students and of material support, notably for a new and quite separate electrical laboratory, opened in 1910.

For much of his career Clifton was active in the wider world of science. As a fellow of the Royal Society, to which he was elected in 1868, he served three times on the council and was vice-president from 1896 to 1898. He was also president of the Physical Society from 1882 to 1884 and maintained friendships in the discipline, notably with Stokes. But he was a reserved and at times difficult colleague. Although a fellow of Merton College (from 1869) and an honorary fellow of Wadham, he took little active part in college life and never secured the allies that his discipline needed within the university. He was best known, in fact, for quiet domestic hospitality, offered at his home in Oxford until his wife's death in 1917.

Clifton's involvement in public life beyond science tended to be concentrated in his earlier years in Oxford. In the late 1860s and 1870s he was an informative witness before the Devonshire commission on scientific instruction and other inquiries, and from 1879 to 1886 served on the royal commission on accidents in mines, for which he performed experiments and even designed a new safety lamp. A more enduring and, in the years of agricultural depression, burdensome commitment was his supervision of the property in Gedney that he inherited on his father's death in 1873. It was typical of Clifton that his activities were so dispersed and that he invested so much energy in each of them. Despite his thin record in research his life was full and, not least because of his curious habit of working from midnight until the early morning before sleeping for a couple of hours and appearing in the laboratory at 11 a.m., quietly productive. He died at his home, 3 Bardwell Road, Oxford, on 22 February 1921. The obituaries that followed convey the impression of someone whose personal dignity and achievements as a teacher were valued more highly than the subsequent, generally critical assessments of him would suggest.

ROBERT FOX

Sources R. T. G. [R. T. Gunther], *PRS*, 99A (1921), vi–ix · *Nature*, 107 (1921), 18–19 · G. J. N. Gooday, 'Precision measurement and the genesis of physics teaching laboratories in Victorian Britain', PhD diss., University of Kent at Canterbury, 1989 · St John Cam., Archives · Oxf. UA, University Museum archives · correspondence, CUL, Add. MS 7656 · d. cert.
Archives CUL, letters to Sir George Stokes · Oxf. U. Mus. NH, letters to Sir E. B. Poulton
Likenesses photographs, Clarendon Laboratory, Oxford
Wealth at death £158,441 4s. 10d.: probate, 10 May 1921, *CGPLA Eng. & Wales*

Clifton, Robert Cox (1810–1861), Church of England clergyman, the son of Robert Cox Clifton, a clergyman who was many years British chaplain at Bruges, was born at Gloucester on 4 January 1810. The earlier part of his education was received under his father's care at Worcester, and in 1827 he went to Oxford, where he matriculated at Worcester College. He proceeded BA in 1831 and MA in 1834, and was ordained in 1833 by the bishop of Oxford. In 1833 he was elected fellow of his college. Before taking his first curacy, which was in Berkshire, he spent some time in Oxford as a tutor.

In 1837 Clifton was appointed to the office of clerk in orders at the Manchester collegiate church, and on 6 December 1843 was elected to a fellowship by the collegiate chapter. When the church was made a cathedral, he became a canon there. In 1843 he became rural dean and rector of Somerton in Oxfordshire, which benefice he held, with his Manchester preferment, until his death.

Clifton took a very active part in the administration of public charities and religious societies in Manchester, and was a trustee of Owens College. Clifton was an admirable man of business and an influential and useful member of the cathedral chapter. He was active in the division of the parish of Manchester in 1850 and published a pamphlet on it. He also published several occasional sermons and other pamphlets, including *A Letter to the Rev. Dr Hook on the Subject of National Education* (1846). He died at his rectory at Somerton on 30 July 1861, his wife, Charlotte Hornsby Clifton, surviving him.

C. W. SUTTON, rev. H. C. G. MATTHEW

Sources *Manchester Guardian* (3 Aug 1861) · *Manchester Courier* (3 Aug 1861) · Foster, *Alum. Oxon.* · W. R. Ward, *Religion and society in England, 1790–1850* (1972) · *CGPLA Eng. & Wales* (1861)
Wealth at death £2000: probate, 19 Oct 1861, *CGPLA Eng. & Wales*

Cline, Henry (1750–1827), surgeon, born in London, was educated at Merchant Taylors' School, London. His sister, Frances, was the mother of the surgeon Joseph Henry *Green (1791–1863). At the age of seventeen Cline was apprenticed to Thomas Smith, one of the surgeons to St Thomas's Hospital, London, and during his apprenticeship he frequently lectured for Joseph Else, then lecturer on anatomy. On 2 June 1774 Cline obtained his diploma from Surgeons' Hall. In the same year he attended a course of John Hunter's lectures, and as a result became a strong supporter of Hunter. In 1775 Cline took a house in Devonshire Street, and married a Miss Webb, lecturing on the day of his marriage. They had at least one son and one daughter. When Else died in 1781, Cline bought his preparations from his executors, and was appointed to lecture on anatomy. Three years later, on the death of his old master, Smith, Cline succeeded him as a surgeon to St Thomas's.

According to Astley Cooper, who became his pupil in 1784, Cline was 'in surgery cool, safe, judicious, and cautious; in anatomy sufficiently informed for teaching and practice' (Cooper, 1.98). Despite such ability, Cooper considered that Cline liked 'other things better than the study or practice of his profession' (ibid.). A democrat at a time when the term was synonymous with 'subversive', Cline was a friend of Horne Tooke and John Thelwall, visiting the former when he was confined in the Tower and giving evidence for the latter at his treason trial in 1794. For years

afterwards Cline held an annual dinner at his house in Lincoln's Inn Fields to commemorate Horne Tooke's acquittal. Cline also used his influence to secure Astley Cooper's safety during his stay in Paris in 1792. A patriot in the true sense of the word, and a deist in religion, Cline was a man of integrity. His character, said Astley Cooper, 'was that of Washington; he would have devoted himself to what he considered to be the advantage of his country, and surrendered whatever distinction he might have attained when he had accomplished his object' (Cooper, 2.338). After living for some years in Jefferies' Square, 12 St Mary Axe, Cline moved in 1796 to Lincoln's Inn Fields, where he remained for the rest of his life.

In 1796 Cline was elected a member of the court of assistants of the Surgeons' Company; but the fact that his election took place at a meeting when neither of the two governors was present (one having just died) was found to have contravened the act of incorporation.

In 1808 Cline, having become interested in agriculture, bought some land at Bounds Green in Middlesex. This venture, together with his interest in politics, lost him the chance to increase his income. Although Cline earned about £10,000 in 1810, Astley Cooper considered that it could have been far more, had he devoted himself to cultivating his practice. In 1810 Cline became an examiner at the Royal College of Surgeons, and in 1812 resigned his appointments at St Thomas's, to be succeeded as surgeon by his son Henry (d. 1820). In 1815 he became master of the College of Surgeons, and in the following year delivered the Hunterian oration (never published); he gave the oration again in 1824. In 1823 Cline was president of the college, the title having been changed from that of master in 1821. He died at his home at Lincoln's Inn Fields on 2 January 1827, a short time after catching an ague. His only publication was *On the Form of Animals* (1805).

MICHAEL BEVAN

Sources B. B. Cooper, *The life of Sir Astley Cooper*, 2 vols. (1843), vol. 1, p. 98; vol. 2, p. 338 · Mrs Thelwall, *The life of John Thelwall* (1837) · *Memorials of John Flint South*, ed. C. L. Feltoe (1884), 198–208 · S. C. Lawrence, *Charitable knowledge: hospital pupils and practitioners in eighteenth-century London* (1996) · *GM*, 1st ser., 97/1 (1827), 90 · *DNB*
Archives RCS Eng., lecture notes · U. Birm. L., lecture notes · Wellcome L., lecture notes
Likenesses F. Chantrey, bust, c.1812, St Thomas's Hospital Museum · F. Chantrey, marble bust, 1825, RCS Eng. · F. Chantrey, drawing, NPG

Clint, Alfred (1807–1883), marine painter, was the fifth and youngest son of George *Clint ARA (1770–1854), painter and engraver, and his first wife. He was born in Alfred Place, Bedford Square, London, on 22 March 1807. A pupil of his father, Clint also studied from life with a society of students meeting first in Drury Lane and later at the Savoy. He was also at one time a member of the Clipstone Street Artists' Society, a sketching club. Ottley states that Clint initially painted portraits, as did his father, but that an unstated health problem compelled him to take up landscape painting, in which he was self-taught.

Clint exhibited for the first time in 1828 at both the Society of British Artists' galleries in Suffolk Street, London, and the British Institution. In the following year his *Study from Nature* was accepted for exhibition at the Royal Academy. By the close of his career he had exhibited in excess of 400 landscapes and coastal views at these three institutions and others, by far the majority having been shown at Suffolk Street. Clint proved a capable administrator: he was elected a member of the Society of British Artists in 1843 and for some years held the office of secretary. He succeeded Frederick Yeates Hurlstone as president in 1869 and on retiring in 1881 was made honorary president. With others, he instigated both the Artists' Amicable Fund and the short-lived Institute of Fine Arts.

Clint is now best-known as a marine painter, especially of views taken on the south coast of England and the Channel Islands. He also painted views of the British countryside, accompanying the actor George John Bennett on the second of his Welsh journeys, and contributed twenty etchings to Bennett's *The Pedestrian's Guide through North Wales*, published in 1838. Paintings bearing Welsh titles were exhibited at Suffolk Street and the Royal Academy in 1839 and 1840. His *Hampstead from the South-East* (*c.*1852–3) is in the Tate collection, and *Morning: London from Highgate* of 1841 is in the Walker Art Gallery, Liverpool. These two London scenes are quiet and contemplative in mood, but frequently the groups of figures included by Clint animate the landscapes, while shipping and rough seas enliven the coastal views. In 1855 Clint wrote *Landscape from Nature*, being the second part of John Samuelson Templeton's *The Guide to Oil Painting* in a series published by George Rowney & Co., suppliers of artists' materials.

For the last five years of his life Clint was forced to give up painting owing to failing eyesight. He died at his home, 54 Lancaster Road, Westbourne Park, London, on 22 March 1883, his seventy-sixth birthday. He was buried in the same grave as his father in Kensal Green cemetery and his remaining works were sold by Christies in February 1884. R. E. GRAVES, *rev.* PAUL A. COX

Sources Bryan, *Painters* (1866) · *The Athenaeum* (31 March 1883) · *The Times* (28 March 1883) · Graves, *RA exhibitors* · Graves, *Brit. Inst.* · J. Johnson, ed., *Works exhibited at the Royal Society of British Artists, 1824–1893, and the New English Art Club, 1888–1917*, 2 vols. (1975) · *CGPLA Eng. & Wales* (1883) · Redgrave, *Artists*
Likenesses A. Miles, two portraits, exh. Society of British Artists 1862–70 · attrib. A. Clint, self-portrait, miniature, NPG · wood-engraving (after photograph by W. Croydon), repro. in *ILN* (7 April 1883)
Wealth at death £692 17s. 5d.: resworn probate, June 1884, *CGPLA Eng. & Wales* (1883)

Clint, George (1770–1854), theatrical genre painter and engraver, was born in London at Brownlow Street, Holborn, on 12 April 1770, the son of Michael Clint, a hairdresser in Lombard Street, and his first wife. The family came from Hexham in Northumberland. Clint received a simple education in Yorkshire. He had several false starts before taking up painting, first as a fishmonger's apprentice, then in an attorney's office, and finally as a house-painter. During this period he married his first wife, the daughter of a small farmer in Berkshire, with whom he had five sons and four daughters. Clint began as a miniature painter with a painting room in Leadenhall Street, London. From Edward Bell, the nephew of John Bell the

publisher, a mezzotint engraver best-known for his plates after George Morland, Clint learned the technique of mezzotint engraving that he practised throughout his career. Among his early engravings are *The Frightened Horse* after George Stubbs, and *The Death of Nelson* after W. Drummond. The precise date when Clint embarked on an artistic career is uncertain, but from the path of his development and the date of his first oil painting exhibited at the Royal Academy (1802) it can probably be assigned to the mid-1790s. From his wife's approach to Sir William Beechey for an opinion on his first attempt at oil painting, a portrait of his wife, a lasting friendship grew between Clint and Beechey. At about this time Clint's friend Samuel Reynolds, the mezzotint engraver, advised him to take up watercolour portraiture. Clint eked out his income by painting copies of prints after Morland and David Teniers, and many copies of *The Enraged Bull* and *The Horse Struck by Lightning* by Stubbs. Sir Thomas Lawrence was impressed by Clint's engraving skills and gave Clint several of his portraits to engrave. A misunderstanding over the engraving of Lawrence's portrait of Lord Ellenborough which Clint believed had been promised to him but which Lawrence disposed elsewhere led to a rupture in their relationship that damaged Clint's engraving practice.

A significant event in Clint's career was his engraving of G. H. Harlow's theatrical painting *The Trial Scene from 'Henry VIII'* with portraits of the Kemble family, published in January 1819. Harlow's picture was an attempt to raise the status of theatrical genre painting to that enjoyed by history painting. Clint's engraving of this work established his reputation for treating theatrical subjects. Clint practised as a portrait painter throughout his career, but is chiefly remembered for his theatrical scene paintings. He also painted numerous theatrical portraits. His principal patrons were Lord Egremont and the celebrated actor Charles Mathews the elder. Between 1802 and 1817 the Royal Academy catalogues show that he frequently changed his studio address (all in London), suggesting that his commissions during this period were haphazard and uncertain. From 1817 he remained for over twenty years at 83 Gower Street, London. Throughout the 1820s he exhibited at the Royal Academy a number of theatrical scenes with portraiture from a scene in *The Clandestine Marriage* (1819) to a scene from *Love, Law and Physic* (1830; both Garrick Club, London). The most ambitious of these works is his large painting of Edmund Kean in *A New Way to Pay Old Debts* (1820; Garrick Club), which approaches the scale of a history painting, but he did nothing else in the same vein. His works of this period generally derive from ephemeral comedies and farce. Clint was elected an associate of the Royal Academy in 1821 presumably on the strength of his scene from *Lock and Key* (Garrick Club), exhibited in the same year.

In the 1830s Clint's theatrical scenes changed to subjects from Shakespearian comedy painted without portraiture and so distanced from the working stage. Typical of those scenes are the three works painted for Lord Egremont exhibited at the Royal Academy in 1833: *The Carousing Scene* and *The Duelling Scene* from *Twelfth Night*, and *Falstaff Relating his Gadshill Adventure* from *1 Henry IV* (Petworth House, Sussex). This change of style was not to a purely literary representation of dramatic subjects since the spatial and compositional restrictions of the stage remained. Clint was a painter of the comic. His only scene from tragedy was from the working stage: *Mr. Young in 'Hamlet'* (V&A), shown at the Royal Academy in 1831. In his colouring Clint was influenced by the work of seventeenth-century Netherlandish masters, including Van Dyck. The largest collection of Clint's theatrical works is in the Garrick Club, London, which owns six of his scene paintings and ten theatrical portraits.

Full membership of the Royal Academy was an important goal for Clint. His failure to achieve this led to his resignation from the academy in 1836. In that year he gave evidence hostile to the Royal Academy to the House of Commons select committee on arts and manufactures. He seems to have had a difficult temperament. While he was not directly involved in current debates on the direction and content of the visual and dramatic arts, Clint's work stands at the intersection of painting and the theatre and is emblematic of those debates.

The poverty Clint knew for most of his life was eased by some property that came to him with his second wife, which helped to augment his income from painting and engraving. He retired to 1 Albert Cottages, Montpellier Road, Peckham, Surrey, and moved near the end of his life to 32 Pembroke Square, Kensington, where he died, a widower, on 16 May 1854. Clint had a pupil, (Robert) William Buss, who was the author of his obituary in the *Art Journal* (July 1854). Of his sons, Scipio *Clint (1805–1839) became a medallist, and Alfred *Clint (1807–1883) became a marine painter. A. NISBET

Sources R. W. Buss, 'George Clint ARA', *Art Journal*, 16 (July 1854), 212–13 · Redgrave, *Artists* · G. Ashton, *Pictures in the Garrick Club*, ed. K. A. Burnim and A. Wilton (1997) · D. Shawe-Taylor, *Dramatic art: theatrical paintings from the Garrick Club* (1997) [exhibition catalogue, Dulwich Picture Gallery] · R. D. Altick, *Paintings from books* (1985) · G. Ashton, *Catalogue of paintings at the Theatre Museum, London*, ed. J. Fowler (1992) · W. L. Pressly, *A catalogue of paintings in the Folger Shakespeare Library* (1993) · d. cert. · will, PRO, PROB 11/2194 · census returns, 1851
Archives W. Sussex RO, Petworth House archives, letters to members of the Wyndham family
Likenesses G. Clint, self-portrait, oils, c.1800, NPG · G. Clint, group portrait, oils, 1820, Garr. Club · T. Lupton, mezzotint, pubd 1854 (after self-portrait by G. Clint), NPG · E. Bell, pen-and-ink drawing, BM · J. H. Robinson, etching (after W. Mulready), BM; repro. in J. Pye, *Patronage of British art* (1845)
Wealth at death £1500–£2000; bequeathed approx. £1200 cash; plus paintings, drawings, and other personal possessions: will, PRO, PROB 11/2194

Clint, Scipio (1805–1839), medallist and sculptor, was one of the nine children of the portrait painter and engraver, George *Clint ARA (1770–1854). He was awarded a gold medal at the Society of Arts in 1824 and 1826. On 20 August 1828 he married at St Clement Danes, Westminster, Ann Randall Anderson, with whom he had four children. He was appointed medallist to William IV in 1831 and seal engraver to Queen Victoria in 1838. Among his medals are

one commemorating the abolition of the Test Act in 1830; three of Sir Thomas Lawrence; a medal of Cardinal Wiseman, dated 1836; and one of the prize medals for Winchester College, which depicts on the obverse the head of William IV, and on the reverse the tomb of William of Wykeham. His medals are signed Clint or S. Clint. Examples can be seen at the Ashmolean Museum, Oxford, and the British Museum, London.

He also carved marble busts, including those of Margaret Watson and Mrs Robert Graves, shown at the Royal Academy in 1835 and 1837 respectively. Clint was secretary to a Roman Catholic society established to support a government plan of education. He died on 6 August 1839 at the age of thirty-four, before his career had fully developed.

W. W. WROTH, rev. AMANDA GIRLING-BUDD

Sources L. Brown, *A catalogue of British historical medals, 1760–1960*, 1 (1980) · L. Forrer, ed., *Biographical dictionary of medallists*, 1 (1902); 7 (1923), 1923 · Redgrave, *Artists* · R. Gunnis, *Dictionary of British sculptors, 1660–1851* (1953); new edn (1968) · J. R. B. Taylor, *The architectural medal: England in the nineteenth century: an annotated catalogue ... based on the collection ... in the British Museum* (1978) [incl. biographies of architects and medallists] · IGI

Clinton, Charles (1690–1773), surveyor and landowner, was born in Corbay, co. Longford, the grandson of an officer of Charles I's army who had settled in Ireland. He married Elizabeth Denniston (*d.* in or after 1773), who was of Scots-Irish descent, some time before the family left for America in May 1729. The couple had seven children, three of whom were born in Ireland; two died during the voyage to America. The family's decision to leave Ireland was prompted by the religious intolerance of the dominant Anglican landowners toward their Presbyterian faith. In 1729 Clinton leased his land to Lord Granard and chartered a ship, the *George and Anne*, to carry four hundred relatives and friends to Philadelphia. Clinton landed at Cape Cod in early October after a passage that saw ninety deaths from a measles epidemic. Clinton's diary record of the crossing was published in the fourth volume of *Olde Ulster* (1905–14).

In the spring of 1731 Clinton moved to Ulster county, New York, where he purchased land at Little Britain, about 8 miles from the Hudson River. An educated man who was learned in mathematics and literature, Clinton was employed by the New York surveyor-general, Cadwallader Colden, to assist in his survey of the province. Colden later recommended Clinton to a distant relation, Governor George Clinton, who in turn nurtured the early career of Clinton's youngest son, George *Clinton (1739–1812).

On 24 March 1758 Charles Clinton was appointed lieutenant-colonel of James De Lancey's force, and he served in the Anglo-American expedition against Fort Frontenac on Lake Ontario in August that year. In 1769 he became first judge of the Ulster county court of common pleas, an appointment he held until his death in Little Britain on 19 November 1773. Of his surviving children, James (1736–1812) served as a revolutionary military officer and was the father of De Witt Clinton (1769–1828), later New York's mayor and state governor. George Clinton became governor of New York and was vice-president of the United States between 1804 and his death in 1812.

H. M. CHICHESTER, rev. PHILIP CARTER

Sources American Magazine of History, 2 (1858), 118–19 · E. W. Spaulding, His Excellency George Clinton, 2nd edn (1964) · J. P. Kraminski, George Clinton: yeoman politician of the new republic (1993)

Clinton, Charles John Fynes (1799–1872), Church of England clergyman, born on 16 April 1799, was the third son of the Revd Charles Fynes, later Fynes Clinton (1747?–1827), prebendary of Westminster, and his wife, Emma, née Brough (d. 1831); Henry Fynes *Clinton, the chronologist, was his brother. He was educated at Westminster School and at Oriel College, Oxford, graduating BA in 1821. He was ordained priest in 1824, and was appointed vicar of Orston in 1827 and rector of Cromwell in 1828; both were in Nottinghamshire, the livings being owned by his relative, the duke of Newcastle. He held Orston until 1855 and Cromwell until his death. In 1842 he published Twenty-One Plain Doctrinal and Practical Sermons (which suggest an evangelical turn of mind) and in 1853 edited and completed for publication An Epitome of the Civil and Literary Chronology of Rome and Constantinople, which had been left unfinished by his brother Henry. In 1854 he edited and published the Literary Remains of his brother. He married, first, in 1826, Caroline, née Clay (d. 1827), and second, in May 1829, Rosabella, née Matthews (d. 1871). His second marriage produced seven sons. He died at 3 Montague Place, Russell Square, London, on 10 January 1872, three weeks after his second wife.

H. C. G. MATTHEW

Sources Men of the time (1865) · Crockford (1870) · Foster, Alum. Oxon. · Burke, Peerage [Newcastle] · CGPLA Eng. & Wales (1872) · CGPLA Eng. & Wales (1875) · DNB
Wealth at death under £2000: resworn probate, Sept 1875, CGPLA Eng. & Wales (1872)

Clinton, Edward Fiennes de, first earl of Lincoln (1512–1585), military commander, was the only son and heir of Thomas Fiennes de Clinton, eighth Baron Clinton and Saye (c.1490–1517), and his wife, Joan, illegitimate daughter of Sir Edward *Poynings (1459–1521). Thomas, whose seat was at Folkestone Manor, served Henry VIII as a captain at Tournai in 1515. He succeeded his father as eighth baron the same year, but held the title for only two years: after his death on 7 August 1517 his five-year-old son's wardship was granted to Poynings. Edward, ninth Baron Clinton, was granted possession of his father's lands in November 1535, aged twenty-three. On 27 April 1536 he was summoned to parliament by a writ addressed to 'Edwardo Fenys de Clynton et Say'.

Marriages and military service In the early 1530s Edward acquired a Lincolnshire estate through marriage to Elizabeth, daughter of Sir John Blount and widow of Gilbert, Lord Tailboys, who had settled his Lincolnshire estate upon her [see Blount, Elizabeth (c.1500–1539×41)]. Clinton and Elizabeth had three daughters, one of whom, Bridget,

Edward Fiennes de Clinton, first earl of Lincoln (1512–1585), by unknown artist, 1584

married Robert *Dymoke (d. 1580) [see under Dymoke family (per. c.1340–c.1580)]. Elizabeth, a former mistress of Henry VIII, was also mother of the king's illegitimate son, Henry Fitzroy, duke of Richmond. Through the marriage Clinton appears to have won the king's favour. He attended Henry VIII at Boulogne and Calais in 1532, acted as a cup-bearer at the coronation of Anne Boleyn in 1533, and was present at Anne's trial in May 1536. Later that year, when most Lincolnshire gentlemen rebelled against the king in the Pilgrimage of Grace, Clinton raised 500 of his servants and tenants against them, joining forces with the royal army to suppress the rebels. Clinton was rewarded by the grant of the house and site of the dissolved monastery of Sempringham, Lincolnshire, which he made his principal residence, and, in addition, the houses and sites of the dissolved priories of Haverholme, Lincolnshire, Folkestone, Kent, and Flitcham, Norfolk. In June 1541 a further grant of lands was made to Clinton, but jointly with his second wife, Ursula (d. 1551), daughter of William, seventh Baron Stourton, and his first wife, Elizabeth, daughter of Edmund Dudley and sister of John Dudley, the future duke of Northumberland. Clinton had two daughters and three sons with Ursula. The eldest son was Henry (1540–1616), later tenth Baron Clinton and second earl of Lincoln. In 1544 Clinton served in Hertford's Scottish expedition under the command of his wife's uncle, John Dudley, then Viscount Lisle and lord admiral. Clinton participated in the burning of Edinburgh and Leith, and was knighted on 11 May at Leith by Hertford. Shortly afterwards he accompanied Lisle to France; he arrived in Boulogne on 28 July with 900 men, and assisted in the siege of Boulogne, entering the town on 18 September.

The reign of Edward VI After the accession of Edward VI, when the Hertford–Lisle coalition dominated the regency council, Clinton's military association with the two, strengthened by his marriage to Lisle's niece, paid dividends. Under the 'unfulfilled gift clause' of Henry VIII's will, Hertford (now Protector Somerset) directed to Clinton a grant of confiscated Howard lands in Lincolnshire worth about £52 per annum. In June 1547 Somerset appointed Clinton admiral of the fleet that went on to co-operate with the land forces in the invasion of Scotland and in the decisive English victory over the Scots at the battle of Pinkie. Clinton was then given responsibility for the surrender of Broughty Castle and for supervising its fortification as an English garrison. He was again rewarded with a further grant of lands, mainly in Lincolnshire, worth £61 5s. 6d. per annum. By April 1549 he was governor of Boulogne, defending the garrison until the treaty of Boulogne was signed on 24 March 1550 and then supervising the English withdrawal from the town. He was rewarded by his appointment on 4 May 1550 as a privy councillor and as lord high admiral of England for life, with an annuity of 200 marks. Clinton's living was deemed insufficient to maintain him in such high office and so, on 11 May, the privy council granted him an additional £200 in land and made him a gentleman of the king's privy chamber. Clinton was also elected a knight of the Garter in April 1551 and was installed on 30 June. Later that year he was granted the former Howard estate at Tattershall, Lincolnshire, worth £83 0s. 9d. per annum, which he made his principal seat, with Sempringham as his second residence.

In October 1551 Clinton represented the king at the baptism of Henri II's son, Édouard Alexandre, duke of Angoulême, and received the formal ratification of the marriage treaty between Edward VI and Henri's daughter, Princess Elizabeth. On 15 April 1552, 'in consideration of his expenses in his late journey in France', he received a grant of lands worth £70 per annum (*CPR, 1550–53*, 363). Ursula, Lady Clinton, had died in the previous year and in 1552 Clinton married for the third time. His new wife was Elizabeth (1528?–1589) [see Clinton, Elizabeth Fiennes de], widow of Sir Anthony Browne and youngest daughter of Gerald *Fitzgerald, ninth earl of Kildare. They had no children.

Philip and Mary Despite his remarriage Clinton maintained his allegiance to his second wife's uncle, now duke of Northumberland. After Edward VI's death on 6 July 1553, Clinton seized the Tower in support of Northumberland's plot to exclude the Catholic Mary from the succession and to place Lady Jane Grey on the throne. Imprisoned after the plot failed, Clinton begged Queen Mary for forgiveness and was pardoned on 27 July, compounding for £6000. The queen would not allow him to continue as lord admiral, but Clinton was a skilful politician and within a few months had won her trust. In January 1554, hearing that Sir Thomas Wyatt's Kentish rebels

threatened the capital, Clinton and the earl of Pembroke promptly raised a force of 5000 or 6000, confronting the rebels at Temple Bar. Clinton was then appointed lieutenant-governor of London and its neighbourhood, with 'troops and ample powers' (*CSP Spain*, 1554, 140). Two years later he was granted lands in Lincolnshire worth £60 per annum in consideration of his service.

Clinton attended Philip of Spain on his arrival in England in July 1554 and was rewarded with a pension from Philip of 1000 crowns per annum. That autumn Mary sent Clinton to invest the duke of Savoy with the Order of the Garter, instructing him to visit Philip in Brussels on his return journey. In April 1556 Clinton was again Mary's envoy, travelling to Blois to congratulate Henri II on the truce of Vaucelles between France and Spain. The truce was short-lived. The following March Philip sought military assistance; Henri II's support of English rebels in France provoked a declaration of war against France on 7 June 1557. Pembroke and Clinton's expeditionary force was transported to France to assist in the duke of Savoy's siege of St Quentin: it reached the town after the turning point of the siege, but joined with Philip's forces in the final assault on 27 August.

After the surprise French attack on Calais, which fell in early January 1558, Philip tried to persuade the privy council to retake the town immediately. The council refused, but Clinton, with typical political skill, overtly supported Philip's plan. Proclaiming his confidence in Clinton, Philip advised Clinton's reappointment as lord high admiral. Duly reappointed on 12 February 1558, Clinton was also named to Mary's privy council because 'he is in favour with the Queen and knows more about military affairs than the others' (*CSP Spain*, 1554–8, 349–50), and was appointed to the newly formed council of war. On 1 May the Spanish ambassador told Philip that 'I have always found the Admiral full of goodwill' (ibid., 378). Two weeks later he stressed the importance of the admiral's presence in council for the progress of the war: 'Although the Admiral is a double-dealer and principally concerned with his own interests, he has more authority than anyone else in these particular affairs, and feels more obligation towards your Majesty' (ibid., 385–7). Clinton's task was made more difficult, however, by Mary Stuart's marriage to the French dauphin: the already demoralized council was aggrieved that while Philip was demanding English contributions to his war effort, he refused to sever his own relations with Scotland. The Spanish ambassador reported that the council had 'even reproached the Admiral for not having … told you how much feeling there is about it', but that 'the Admiral says he did not mention it … because he only likes to tell people things they will be glad to hear' (ibid., 394–6).

Despite the council's misgivings, Clinton agreed to make the English fleet available throughout the summer to assist the Spanish campaign in France. In July 1558 a joint English and Flemish fleet attacked the Breton coast, aiming at Brest, but the 7000 men landed by Clinton met with unexpected resistance. Abandoning their attempt, the fleet returned to Portsmouth, where Clinton learned of French preparations to transport troops to Scotland. Sending Vice-Admiral Winter to intercept them on their voyage north, Clinton took the rest of the fleet to Normandy; he attempted a landing, but the fleet became fogbound, losing the advantage of surprise. The fleet returned to Portsmouth, bringing the unsuccessful summer campaign of 1558 to an end.

The accession of Elizabeth Within four days of Mary's death in November 1558, Clinton was appointed a member of Elizabeth's privy council. His wife, Elizabeth, had been brought up with the queen and became a member of her privy chamber, attending her between 1559 and 1585. Clinton further strengthened his position by remaining on good terms with both William Cecil and Lord Robert Dudley, siding with each at different times, depending upon the issue. In July 1559, with a renewed threat of French military intervention in Scotland after François II's accession to the French throne with Mary Stuart as queen, Clinton advocated early action. The queen and most councillors were uncertain but, when the French reached Leith, it was agreed to send a fleet to the Firth of Forth, with Clinton (as lord admiral) directing the operation. By early May 1560 the English had failed to end French resistance in Leith, and Clinton advocated additional forces to end the siege, passionately proclaiming his readiness to risk his own life in this venture. In early June, Clinton was at sea with the fleet, planning to intercept French reinforcements. There was no confrontation, since the French fleet was lost in a storm. The French war effort soon crumbled. Clinton again led the English fleet against the French in summer 1563, to relieve English troops besieged in Le Havre, but arrived two days after the garrison had surrendered.

On 24 November 1569 Clinton and Warwick were appointed lieutenants-general of the forces to suppress the rising of the northern earls. Clinton's troops set out from Lincoln on 1 December, marching north and uniting with the forces raised by Warwick and the earl of Sussex, lord president of the council of the north. When the royal army approached Darlington on 17 December the rebels fled to Scotland. Clinton was rewarded for his service when, on 4 May 1572, he was created earl of Lincoln in recognition of 'his service to Henry VIII, Edward VI and Queen Mary, and to the present Queen, particularly during the late rebellion in the North; and for his service as High Admiral both to the present Queen and Queen Mary'. The following month Lincoln was sent to Paris to ratify the treaty of Blois, signed on 19 April and marking a new Anglo-French defensive alliance against Spain. This was the last major service that Lincoln (now aged sixty) performed, although he continued in the office of lord admiral and remained at court and a member of the privy council until his death.

In his will dated 11 July 1584 Lincoln bequeathed Tattershall Castle to his son and heir, Sir Henry Clinton, and Sempringham to his wife, Elizabeth, for life. Correctly anticipating that Elizabeth might have 'some trouble or disturbance' from Henry over the will, Lincoln made detailed provisions against it. Henry contested the will,

but in March 1587 it was confirmed by sentence. Lincoln died in London on 16 January 1585, aged seventy-two. He was buried in St George's Chapel, Windsor, where an ornate monument commemorates his life and the Lincoln chapel was named in his honour.   ANNE DUFFIN

Sources A. Austin, *The history of the Clinton barony, 1299–1999* (privately published, 1999) · *DNB* · GEC, *Peerage* · will, PRO, PROB 11/68/26 · *CSP Spain, 1554–8* · *LP Henry VIII* · *LP Henry VIII, addenda* · *CSP for., 1547–74* · *CSP Scot.* · G. A. J. Hodgett, *Tudor Lincolnshire* (1975) · T. Glasgow, 'The navy in Philip and Mary's war, 1557–1558', *Mariner's Mirror*, 53 (1967), 321–42 · C. S. L. Davies, 'England and the French war, 1557–9', *The mid-Tudor polity, c.1540–1560*, ed. J. Loach and R. Tittler (1980), 159–85 · A. Weikel, 'The Marian council revisited', *The mid-Tudor polity, c.1540–1560*, ed. J. Loach and R. Tittler (1980), 52–73
Likenesses H. Holbein the younger, chalk drawing, c.1534–1535, Royal Collection · attrib. E. Worth, oils, c.1550, AM Oxf. · oils, c.1560–1565, NPG · attrib. H. Eworth, oils, 1562, AM Oxf. · oils, c.1570–1575, NMM · oils, 1584, NPG [*see illus.*] · alabaster and porphyry effigy, 1585, St George's Chapel, Windsor · M. Gheeraerts senior, group portrait, etching (*Procession of knights of Garter 1576*), BM · M. R. Sheppard, engraving (after Holbein), priv. coll.
Wealth at death Tattershall Castle; Sempringham; extensive lands in Lincolnshire: will, PRO, PROB, 11/68/26

Clinton [*née* Knevitt], **Elizabeth, countess of Lincoln** (1574?–1630?), noblewoman and writer, was the daughter and coheir of Sir Henry Knevitt (Knyvett; *d.* 1598) of Charlton, Wiltshire, and Elizabeth, daughter and heir of Sir James Stumpe. Some time after 21 September 1584 (when the earl of Huntington wrote that he hoped the match would soon be settled) she married Thomas Clinton (otherwise Fiennes), Lord Clinton (1567/8–1619). The early years of the marriage were not easy. In August 1597, writing on the occasion of the recovery of his daughter-in-law, the privy council wrote to the earl of Lincoln reminding him 'what it is for young folks to want'. Prompted by the queen, they asked him to provide 'some convenient house where the young lord and lady may live with their children' (HoP, *Commons, 1558–1603*). Elizabeth writes of having had eighteen children; at least nine survived infancy (five daughters and four sons).

Clinton succeeded his father as third earl of Lincoln in 1616, and died three years later at his castle at Tattershall, Lincolnshire, on 15 January 1619. He in turn was succeeded by his third, but first surviving son, Theophilus (c.1600–1667), who married Bridget (*d.* 1675), daughter of William Fiennes, first Viscount Saye and Sele in 1620. At the time of the third earl's inquest (1620), the countess and her three younger sons were living at Sempringham, Lincolnshire.

In 1622 the dowager countess published a short tract on breastfeeding, *The Countesse of Lincolnes Nurserie*. She dedicated the work to her daughter-in-law, who, she writes, 'doe goe on with that loving act of a loving mother' (*Nurserie*, sig. A2r). She herself had not nursed any of her babies, and writes in contrition, having been 'partly … overruled by anothers authority, and partly deceived by some ill counsell, & partly I had not so well considered of my duty' (ibid., 16). She confesses that she believes 'the death of one or two of my little Babes came by the defalt of their nurses' (ibid., 18). Unpretentious in tone and unpreachy, firmly anchored in biblical sources, the dowager countess justifies her writing straightforwardly:

> Because it hath pleased God to blesse me with many children, and so caused me to observe many things falling out to mothers, and to their children; I thought good to open my minde concerning a speciall matter belonging to all childe-bearing women, seriously to consider of.   (ibid., 1)

She discusses numerous worthy biblical women who nursed their children, and sets forth rather individual interpretations of biblical precepts and of God's works as proofs of her thesis. She ends by asserting that it is the duty of older women to exhort younger ones:

> Thinke alwaies, that having the child at your breast, and having it in your armes, you have *Gods blessing* there. For children are Gods blessings. Thinke again how your Babe crying for your breast, sucking hartily the milke out of it, and growing by it, is the *Lords owne instruction*, every houre, and every day, that you are suckling it, instructing you to shew that you are his *new borne Babes*, by your earnest desire after his word; & the syncere doctrine thereof.   (ibid., 20)

Clinton describes the *Nurserie* as 'the first worke of mine that ever came in print' (sig. A2r), and it is her only known work. It was reprinted in 1628. In 1625 Theophilus brought a suit in chancery against his mother in her capacity as guardian of the three younger sons. She probably died in 1630.   BETTY S. TRAVITSKY

Sources V. Fildes, ed., *Women as mothers in pre-industrial England* (1990) · P. Crawford, 'The construction and experience of maternity in seventeenth-century England', *Women as mothers in pre-industrial England*, ed. V. Fildes (1990), 3–38 · V. Wayne, 'Advice for women from mothers and patriarchs', *Women and literature in Britain, 1500–1700*, ed. H. Wilcox (1996), 56–79 · GEC, *Peerage* · HoP, *Commons, 1558–1603* · G. Ballard, *Memoirs of several ladies of Great Britain* (1752) · B. S. Travitsky, *Mothers' advice books* (1998), vol. 8 of *The early modern Englishwoman: a facsimile library of essential works*

Clinton, Elizabeth Fiennes de [*née* Lady Elizabeth Fitzgerald], **countess of Lincoln** [*other married name* Elizabeth Fiennes Browne, Lady Browne; *called* Fair Geraldine] (1528?–1589), noblewoman, was the second daughter of Gerald *Fitzgerald, ninth earl of Kildare (1487–1534), and his second wife, Lady Elizabeth Grey. Her mother, the daughter of Thomas Grey, marquess of Dorset, and granddaughter of Edward IV's queen, Elizabeth Woodville, was Henry VIII's first cousin. Lady Elizabeth's early childhood was spent in her father's great household at Maynooth, which was wealthy, cultivated, and devout, the seat of Kildare ascendancy in Ireland. In October 1533 Lady Kildare returned to England, followed by her husband in February 1534, in response to a royal summons. In their absence, official threats to Kildare supremacy precipitated the rebellion of Lord Offaly ('Silken Thomas'), Lady Elizabeth's half-brother, and culminated in the destruction of the house of Kildare. The title was forfeited, the estates confiscated, and the family proscribed. The countess withdrew with her children—except Gerald, who was in exile—to Beaumanor, Leicestershire, the estate of her brother Lord Leonard *Grey, who was himself executed in 1541. In the late 1530s Lady Elizabeth joined the household of her royal cousins, the princesses Mary and Elizabeth, and by June 1539 had entered the service of Princess Elizabeth.

Elizabeth Fiennes de Clinton, countess of Lincoln (1528?–1589), by unknown artist

At visits of the princesses' household to Hunsdon, Hertfordshire, and Hampton Court, Henry Howard, the poet earl of Surrey, first saw Lady Elizabeth. He wrote a sonnet, 'From Tuscan cam my ladies worthi race', to 'Geraldine', praising her descent, her education with a 'kinges child', and her beauty of form and spirit:

> Bewty of kind, her vertues from above;
> Happy ys he that may obtaine her love.
> (Howard, *Poems*, 9)

Surrey's father, the third duke of Norfolk, had offered support at court to the earl of Kildare in the early 1530s, and now Surrey offered chivalrous protection to the earl's daughter in the shipwreck of her family. Another sonnet, 'The golden gift that nature did thee geve', was, in the second edition of Richard Tottell's *Songes and Sonnettes* (1557, known as Tottell's Miscellany), addressed to 'Garret'. There Surrey, or his poetic persona, wrote as 'thy frende … who seekes alway thine honour to preserve', and offered a cautionary warning: since her gifts were divinely given

> Do not deface them than wyth fansies newe,
> Nor chaunge of mindes let not thy minde infect.
> (ibid., 8)

On 12 December 1542 Lady Elizabeth married Sir Anthony *Browne (*c*.1500–1548), master of the horse, one of the grandest and wealthiest of Henry VIII's courtiers. She used the influence that this marriage gave her to restore the fortunes of her family; writing in July 1547 for a command in Scotland for her brother Edward, and arranging the marriage of her stepdaughter Mabel to her brother Gerald. Gerald Fitzgerald returned to England, was received into favour by Edward VI, and was knighted and restored to his Irish estates in April 1552. Sir Anthony Browne died in 1548. Lady Elizabeth bore him two sons, Edward and Thomas, who both died in infancy, and never bore another child.

In 1552 Lady Elizabeth married Edward Fiennes de *Clinton, ninth Baron Clinton and Saye (1512–1585), lord high admiral. He was created earl of Lincoln in 1572. In 1569 Gerald, eleventh earl of Kildare, his brother, Edward, and three sisters, Margaret, Elizabeth, and Cecily, petitioned the queen, successfully, to be restored to their blood and lineage. Suits to the countess of Lincoln show that she was believed to have influence with Queen Elizabeth. In his will of July 1584 Clinton made his wife executor, but also attempted to guard her from attempts by his son Lord Henry Clinton to dispute the will. Three days before his father's death on 16 January 1585 Henry Clinton wrote to Lord Burghley complaining of the machinations of the countess to deprive him of his inheritance, and of her maligning him to the queen. Elizabeth, countess of Lincoln, died in March 1589 and was buried beside her second husband in St George's Chapel, Windsor, where she had already erected an elaborate monument to his memory.

Elizabeth Fiennes de Clinton had been a figure of some political influence, with a compelling pride in her Fitzgerald blood, but her posthumous reputation was as the Fair Geraldine, the object of the earl of Surrey's Petrarchan adoration. In Thomas Nashe's *The Unfortunate Traveller* (1594) Surrey is seen writing her love poetry in the tradition of courtly love and, travelling in Italy, challenging all comers in defence of the beauty of his Fair Geraldine. Both the journey and the challenge were fictive. Michael Drayton used Nashe's fiction in *Englands Heroicall Epistles, Henry Howard Earle of Surrey to Geraldine* (1597), and told of Surrey's love for Geraldine. Sir Walter Scott followed Nashe's tale of Surrey's consultation of Cornelius Agrippa in Venice and his sight of Geraldine in a magic mirror in his 'Lay of the Last Minstrel' (canto 6, stanzas 16–20).

SUSAN BRIGDEN

Sources *LP Henry VIII* · *State papers published under … Henry VIII*, 11 vols. (1830–52) · J. Graves, *A brief memoir of the Lady Elizabeth Fitzgerald known as the Fair Geraldine* (1874) · R. Hughey, ed., *The Arundel Harington manuscript of Tudor poetry* (Ohio, 1960) · *The works of Henry Howard, earl of Surrey, and of Sir Thomas Wyatt, the elder*, ed. G. F. Nott, 2 vols. (1815–16) · H. Howard [earl of Surrey], *Poems*, ed. E. Jones (1964) · W. A. Sessions, *Henry Howard, the poet earl of Surrey: a life* (1999) · *The works of Thomas Nashe*, ed. R. B. McKerrow (1904–10); repr. with corrections and notes by F. P. Wilson (1958); repr. (1966) · Marquess of Kildare, *The earls of Kildare and their ancestors* (1858) · F. Madden, *Privy purse expenses of the Princess Mary, daughter of King Henry the Eighth* (1831) · *CSP dom.*, 1547–53; 1581–90 · J. S. Brewer and W. Bullen, eds., *Calendar of the Carew manuscripts*, 1: 1515–1574, PRO (1867) · will, PRO, PROB 11/75, fols. 160r–161v

Likenesses portrait, NG Ire. [*see illus.*] · portrait, second version, Carton House, Maynooth

Wealth at death see will, PRO, PROB 11/75, fols. 160r–161v

Clinton, Geoffrey of (d. c.1133), administrator, came of a family originating at Semilly in the Cotentin, which after 1066 seems to have acquired certain English possessions, notably Glympton (*Clintona*) in Oxfordshire. Clinton may have been among those taken into the service of the future king, Henry I, while he ruled the Cotentin in the 1090s, but the first trace of him in royal service is in an attestation of 1110 to an act of King Henry's at Woodstock. The fall of Herbert the chamberlain in 1118 brought Clinton into a more prominent position in the administration of the king's treasure. He took Herbert's place, and probably in 1121 obtained in addition the shrievalty of Warwick. His acquisition of the office of sheriff was for a purpose. In 1124, Roger, earl of Warwick, was compromised in the rebellious schemes of his cousin, Waleran, count of Meulan, and at the same time Clinton acquired seventeen fees from the earl. The transfer of lands from earl to sheriff must have been a forced enfeoffment designed to lessen the king's ill will against Earl Roger, by an act of patronage towards Clinton, the king's servant. The foundation chronicle of Biddlesden Abbey notes just such another enfeoffment in his favour, on this occasion by a Bedfordshire baron who needed his support when trying to escape the consequences of a forest offence. The king enhanced his local power by grants of royal demesne at Kenilworth near Warwick. He then underlined his local dominance by the building of a castle and priory there in 1124. It was doubtless at this time of royal favour that Clinton acquired his collection of fees from several magnates: the earl of Gloucester, and the Stafford and Ferrers families, among others. In 1129 he further consolidated his local position when his nephew Roger obtained the see of Coventry (on Clinton's payment of 3000 marks, as it was alleged).

In the meantime Clinton had brought into Warwickshire a number of Normans from the Cotentin as his tenants. The pipe roll compiled at Michaelmas 1130 gives a picture of him at the height of his power. His exemptions from danegeld reveal a great landed estate of at least 578 hides concentrated in the south and west midlands. It also illustrates why he has been taken by modern writers as the archetype of Henry I's 'new man'. He held numerous wardships, of individuals and the abbey of Evesham; he had taken up debts and farms of royal manors. During the years before 1130 he had been active as a justice in seventeen counties. He was everywhere involved in business, manipulation, and making money. No wonder that he had enemies. These engineered his temporary downfall at Easter 1130, when he was arrested at Woodstock for alleged treason. Those who charged him were not named, but are suggested to have been members of Roger of Warwick's family, which returned to royal favour in the course of 1129. Clinton escaped the charges by heavy bribes, and continued to appear in the royal entourage until 1133. He died before 1135; a late writ of Henry I survives referring to his death.

By 1124 Clinton was married and had sons. He was succeeded by the younger Geoffrey of Clinton, who was a minor, as appears from an account of a deathbed grant in the Kenilworth cartulary. A measure of continuing royal favour after 1130 is that the younger Geoffrey was given to his uncle, William, in wardship; he ran into trouble at some time in 1137 or 1138, when the earl of Warwick attempted to reclaim the lands extorted from him by Geoffrey's father. The problem was eventually solved by a marriage treaty, by which Geoffrey married Agnes, the earl's young daughter, and received his lands back at preferential terms, with a concession of the hereditary possession of the shrievalty of Warwick. He died about 1175. Clinton also had another son, Robert (mentioned in a charter of the younger Geoffrey), and at least one daughter, Lescelina, for whom he bought the manor of Wolfhamcote, Warwickshire, as an endowment.

DAVID CROUCH

Sources cartulary of Kenilworth, BL, Harley MS 3650 · R. W. Southern, *Medieval humanism and other studies* (1970) · C. W. Hollister, 'The origins of the English treasury', *EngHR*, 93 (1978), 262–75 · D. Crouch, 'Geoffrey de Clinton and Roger, earl of Warwick: new men and magnates in the reign of Henry I', *BIHR*, 55 (1982), 113–24 · J. A. Green, *The government of England under Henry I* (1986) · BL, Harley MS 4714, fol. 1 · *Reg. RAN*, 2.1933

Clinton, George (1686–1761), naval officer and colonial governor, was born in Stourton Parva, Lincolnshire, to Francis Clinton, sixth earl of Lincoln (c.1635–1693), and his second wife, Susanna (d. 1720), daughter of Anthony Penyston or Penniston. As second son of a nobleman Clinton had little hope of inheriting his father's peerage or estates, and so he joined the Royal Navy in 1708 to make a living. He advanced to captain in 1716 but he never showed much ability, losing his ship in a storm in 1720. Because his sister-in-law was sister of Thomas Pelham-Holles, first duke of Newcastle, Clinton enjoyed the duke's patronage, obtaining postings that included commodore-governor of Newfoundland, in 1731, and commodore of the Mediterranean Fleet, in 1736–8. He was promoted rear-admiral in 1743. However, naval officials never assigned him to any profitable wartime commands.

Clinton by 1740 was embarrassingly in debt. By that time he had married Anne (d. 1767), daughter of Major-General Peter Carle, and they had six children, including Sir Henry *Clinton (1730–1795). Clinton's half pay as an inactive officer was inadequate, and throughout the 1730s he solicited Newcastle for more profitable posts. In July 1741 Newcastle secured his appointment as governor of New York. Clinton arrived in the colony in September 1743.

The neophyte governor turned to James DeLancey, the colony's leading merchant, councillor, and judge, for advice. DeLancey persuaded Clinton to accept his salary from the assembly for one year only instead of the five years that his instructions specified. The assembly gave him an extra £1000 in exchange but held the governor's salary ransom. However, by April 1745 Clinton had become angry that the assembly was demanding more power over appropriations and frustrating his plans for military defence. The house resolved that the legislature, not the governor, would make estimates on fortification repairs. Clinton dissolved the assembly and the voters re-elected nearly all the assemblymen who had opposed him. Clinton, now deciding that he should try to escape this unhealthy and unprofitable colony, failed to find a lucrative wartime command or a buyer for his governorship. He plunged into further political difficulty when in the spring of 1746 he and DeLancey had an inebriated quarrel and his former adviser led the council into opposition. DeLancey also used his influence to obtain a commission as lieutenant-governor. Clinton in 1746 took as his principal adviser Cadwallader Colden, long-time councillor, who wrote several speeches for the governor. By 1752 Clinton, with the aid of British officials, finally got a majority of his supporters appointed to the council.

Clinton had much less success in controlling the colony's assembly. He managed to obtain most of the defence measures he wanted and he established good relations with the Iroquois confederacy through William Johnson but he was too insistent on curtailing the assembly's powers and privileges from 1746 until the end of his term. In 1746–7 the assembly asserted control over disbursements for military purposes by giving that authority to commissioners of its choosing. During 1747 it baulked at providing additional support for troops. It blamed Clinton undeservedly for mismanagement of American Indian affairs. It criticized his use of the unpopular Colden as adviser and speech writer. The result was another dissolution in November 1747. Assembly members pledged to unite to get every assemblyman re-elected so that in the new assembly of 1748 Clinton confronted firm opposition.

Clinton's tactic with the newly chosen delegates was to accept some important bills but insist on a five-year salary bill, in what appears to have been an attempt to bring about intervention from London. The assembly refused adamantly and passed no support bill for the next two years. Clinton again tried a dissolution in July 1750. He and Colden thought that they could organize a party to elect some supporters but they failed for the governor and his ally were too unpopular. Clinton resigned himself to one year's support in November 1750. The assembly paid his back salary, signalling that it would be accommodating if its powers were not challenged. After again asserting its privileges in November 1751 the assembly was dissolved once more. Clinton in early 1752 was so weary of the battles with the legislature that he prepared to return to England without permission. He was warned not to do so and instead remained in New York and turned to land acquisitions so that he would have something to show for his governorship. He was finally replaced in May 1753 and left the colony in DeLancey's hands in November.

No successes came his way in his remaining years. The Admiralty turned down his request for wartime command; he purchased a seat in parliament in the 1754 election, as member from Saltash, Cornwall, but contributed little. His wife's mental condition deteriorated after 1757. Clinton predeceased her, on 10 July 1761, owing £1500 in debts, having been unsuccessful at managing either ships or governments.

BENJAMIN H. NEWCOMB

Sources S. N. Katz, *Newcastle's New York: Anglo-American politics, 1732–1753* (1968) · P. Ranlet, 'Clinton, George', *ANB* · P. U. Bonomi, *A factious people: politics and society in colonial New York* (1971) · D. A. Baugh, *British naval administration in the age of Walpole* (1965) · L. W.

Labaree, 'Clinton, George', *DAB* • W. B. Willcox, *Portrait of a general: Sir Henry Clinton in the war of independence* (1964) • B. H. Newcomb, *Political partisanship in the American middle colonies, 1700–1776* (1995) • W. Smith, *The history of the late province of New-York*, [another edn], 2 (1829); (New York, 1974) • E. B. O'Callaghan and B. Fernow, eds. and trans., *Documents relative to the colonial history of the state of New York*, 15 vols. (1853–87), vol. 6 • *Journal of the votes and proceedings of the general assembly of the colony of New York from 1766 to 1776*, 2 (1776) • 'Lincoln', GEC, *Peerage*, new edn, vol. 7 • *IGI*

Archives New York Historical Society, papers • NMM, letterbook • U. Mich., Clements L., papers | BL, corresp. with duke of Newcastle, Add. MSS 32691–33055, *passim* • BL, Newcastle papers • New Jersey Historical Society, Newark, Robert Hunter Morris papers

Wealth at death owed £1500: Ranlet, 'Clinton, George'

Clinton, George (1739–1812), revolutionary and politician in the United States of America, was born on 26 July 1739 in the hamlet of Little Britain, Ulster county, New York, one of two sons of Charles *Clinton (1690–1773), landowner and surveyor, and Elizabeth Denniston (*d.* in or after 1773). He was a lifelong Presbyterian. George Clinton was not a member of colonial New York's landed aristocracy. None the less, his birth placed him well for a political career. His father led a sizeable group of Irish Presbyterians from co. Longford to New York in 1731, settling in sparsely populated Ulster county. The elder Clinton attracted the attention of the imperial placeman Cadwallader Colden, who linked him to his distant relative George Clinton, governor of the province. The admiral complimented the migrant leader by naming young George as clerk of the Ulster county court in 1748 (when George was nine), to take office when the incumbent died. He succeeded to the position in 1759 and held it until his death.

Clinton had no formal schooling, but he did receive tutoring as a boy. He served briefly on a privateer during the Seven Years' War, and took subaltern's rank in a militia unit in 1760, serving under both his brother (a captain) and his father (a lieutenant-colonel). After the war ended he studied law in the New York city office of William Smith jun., future chief justice of British-controlled New York during the American War of Independence and subsequently of Canada. Smith provided both as good a legal education and as powerful a set of political connections as could be had in New York at the time. Clinton acquired more political connections with his marriage to Cornelia Tappan (1744–1800) on 7 February 1770.

In 1768 Ulster county chose Clinton as one of its two delegates to the provincial assembly. He served in that body until the independence crisis seven years later. Assembly politics were structured by rivalry between the mercantile De Lancey family of New York city (who would become loyalists) and the land-owning Livingstons of the Hudson valley, who chose independence but who were not in sympathy with the popular dimensions of the growing revolutionary movement. Clinton aligned himself with the Livingstons, but he also displayed strong sympathy for the street politician Alexander McDougall when the assembly majority imprisoned McDougall for writing his blistering broadside *To the Betrayed Inhabitants of the City and Colony of New York* (1769).

George Clinton (1739–1812), by John Trumbull, 1791

Despite his early favour from Cadwallader Colden (who was lieutenant-governor of New York during its final British years) and from his namesake the colonial governor, and despite the politics of his one-time teacher, loyalism was never an option for Clinton. By 1775 he was both a brigadier-general in the revolutionary militia and a member of the second continental congress. He was quicker than most New York leaders to favour breaking the tie with Britain, but with an invasion of his home state imminent he left congress to command his militia brigade before the Declaration of Independence was signed. Preferring military service to politics, he took no part in drafting New York's new state constitution, which came into force in 1777. Thanks to his colonial-era public record and to his considerable popularity among ordinary soldiers, he won both the governorship and the lieutenant-governorship of the state in the subsequent election (he resigned the latter post). He won successive three-year terms as governor until 1795 and held the office again from 1800 until he assumed the vice-presidency in 1805.

The governor's immediate concern in 1777 was the state's survival. British forces occupied Manhattan, Long Island, Staten Island, and the lower part of Westchester county, on the mainland. In the north-eastern part of the state, territory that had been disputed between New York and New Hampshire declared its own independence as the state of Vermont. In the west there was civil war that involved the Iroquois and white settlers on both sides. Even in the Hudson valley there was very considerable loyalism. Major-General John Burgoyne counted on all these factors as he developed his plan to split the revolution by leading a major army from Montreal to Albany while other forces converged on the same city from the west and the south. Burgoyne's defeat at Saratoga in October, combined with the failure of the other two forces, effectively scuttled British hopes of victory. Clinton's own part during the crisis was to attempt a defence of forts at the Hudson River highlands, pitting his small force of inexperienced militia against unstoppable British professionals sent up from New York city. He was nearly captured in the rout, but the failure of the larger British strategy meant that he did have a state to govern.

Clinton has a historical reputation as leading an internal revolution against New York's traditionally aristocratic politics which coincided with the larger American movement for independence. His election to the governorship certainly surprised his former teacher William Smith jun., who was under patriot house arrest, and the magnates' candidate Philip Schuyler, who thought Clinton's 'family and connections' did not merit 'so distinguished a predominance' (Kaminski, 25). But Clinton was no supporter of popular militancy for its own sake. He opposed Vermont's claim to separate statehood so strongly that he always called it a 'pretended state' and its people 'revolted subjects'. In 1781 he threatened to prorogue the state legislature rather than watch it consider Vermont's independence. Five years later, confronted with the fact of Shays's rebellion in neighbouring Massachusetts, he proclaimed his own state's active disapproval.

None the less, Clinton moved from casting himself as willing to co-operate with anybody who supported American independence and New York's integrity to the undoubted leadership of one political group among several. His shift began in 1779. Confronted with a crisis that was compounded out of paper-currency inflation, short supplies, and growing hostility towards the state's policy of attempting to bring loyalists over to the patriot side, he advised the legislature to pay heed to popular demands for price controls and for stringent anti-loyalist legislation. The result was that his name became associated with state-level policies that nationally oriented and fiscally conservative figures came to loathe. After the return of peace and the British evacuation of the state's 'southern district' in 1783 he made no attempt to stop persecution of former loyalists (despite the terms of the treaty of peace). He also endorsed New York's two rejections (in 1784 and 1786) of proposals to give an independent taxing power to the confederation congress, a weak body that provided what central government there was over the independent states.

Within New York, Clinton's political position was unassailable by then. His outright opponents, men such as John Jay, Philip Schuyler, and the rising Alexander Hamilton, turned together with their kind in other states to national-level politics, developing the project of creating a strong central government that would undercut the power that men such as Clinton held. Clinton himself recognized that some reform was necessary, and he did not oppose the choice of Hamilton as one of New York's delegates to the constitutional convention that met in Philadelphia in 1787. He was suspicious of the project, however, and New York's other two delegates, John Lansing and Robert Yates, were men of Clinton's sort. When the convention produced the present United States constitution Clinton took a very active role in the hard-fought campaign as to whether New York would ratify. He is generally credited with writing the Cato letters, which rank among the foremost anti-federal writings. Presiding over the state's ratifying convention in 1788, he led the very large majority of delegates opposed to the constitution. Ratification by ten other states (one more than the requisite nine) changed the issue from whether the constitution would take effect to whether New York would participate in the new republic. Confronted with that, and with a threat of secession by highly pro-constitution New York city, Clinton's forces conceded and the state became 'the eleventh pillar'.

The remainder of Clinton's time as governor was less successful. His ally Robert Yates switched sides and ran a hard campaign against him in 1789. His re-election in 1792 required machine-style politics and electoral fraud. Facing defeat, he did not run in 1795. It was a sign of his partisanship that in 1794 his daughter Cornelia married 'Citizen' Edmond Genet, the French revolutionary diplomatist who attempted to go over the head of President Washington in regard to relations between the American and French republics. His return to the governorship in 1800 was more as a supporter of Thomas Jefferson's bid for the presidency than in his own right, a point confirmed when Jefferson picked him as vice-presidential candidate in 1804. Despite his one-time opposition to the constitution, his political life shifted to Washington, DC, and his nephew De Witt Clinton assumed leadership of the Clintonian political group. Ironically, given their origins, the Clintonians became associated with the upper class within their state's tangled politics. George Clinton sought the presidency itself in 1808, losing to James Madison, but keeping the vice-presidency. His relations with the new president were so cool that he did not even attend Madison's inauguration. He died of pneumonia in Washington on 20 April 1812 and was buried next day in the congressional cemetery at the Washington navy yard.

EDWARD COUNTRYMAN

Sources J. P. Kaminski, *George Clinton: yeoman politician of the new republic* (1993) · E. W. Spaulding, *His Excellency George Clinton: critic of the constitution* (1938) · A. F. Young, *The democratic republicans of New York, the origins, 1763–1797* (1967) · *Public papers of George Clinton*, ed. H. Hastings, 10 vols. (1899–1914) · E. S. Lafuse, 'Clinton, George', *ANB*

Likenesses J. Trumbull, portrait, 1791, Art Commission of City of New York [*see illus.*] · portrait, repro. in Kaminski, *George Clinton*, facing p. 113

Clinton, Sir Henry (1730–1795), army officer, was born on 16 April 1730, the second of the three surviving children of

Sir Henry Clinton (1730–1795), by John Smart, c.1777

George *Clinton (1686–1761), naval officer, governor of New York, and MP, and his wife, Anne (d. 1767), the daughter of General Peter Carle.

Education and early service To an unusual extent, Henry Clinton's early development was shaped by his father and his father's family. Captain George Clinton, a diffident man and a marginally successful naval officer, was at sea for nearly all of his son's childhood. In 1741 Captain Clinton turned to his brother's brother-in-law, the powerful first duke of Newcastle, for help with his career and mounting debts. Newcastle arranged to have him promoted admiral and appointed royal governor of New York. So it was that Henry Clinton, whose childhood had been spent in the company of a strong-willed mother and two sisters, was transported in 1743 to a remote provincial capital to live among colonists who resented his privileged status. Young Clinton was intelligent and he had the benefits of a sound, basic education—perhaps through tutors and travel, probably through the Revd Samuel Seabury's school at Hempstead, Long Island. But his appearance—he was not handsome—and early experiences seem to have encouraged what his father described as a family disposition towards diffidence. He never gained the confidence in himself or the skill in working with others to match his considerable intelligence.

Clinton's career in the army was also shaped by his father and his father's family. In 1745 Admiral Clinton obtained his son a lieutenancy in an independent company of infantry at New York and a tour of duty with a detachment sent to occupy the French fortress of Louisbourg on Cape Breton. By the autumn of 1748 Captain-Lieutenant Henry Clinton was asking for leave 'to go to France'—presumably to study his profession (23 Oct 1748, 23 June 1749, PRO, WO 25/3191). His leave granted, and having been promoted captain, Clinton sailed for England in the summer of 1749. It seems likely that he then went to France. If so, he returned to find that the duke of Newcastle had secured him a commission in the élite Coldstream Guards (as lieutenant and then as captain, 1751–8) and, eventually, appointment as aide-de-camp to Field Marshal Sir John Ligonier. Following further promotion, as captain and then lieutenant-colonel in the 1st foot guards (1758–62), he accompanied his new regiment to Germany in June 1760 to serve against the French as a volunteer and aide-de-camp with the celebrated young commander Prince Charles of Brunswick. Clinton saw action at Korbach and Kloster Kamp in 1760, won Prince Charles's admiration, and was promoted colonel (1762). He went home after being wounded in late August 1762. Brief as his active service had been, Clinton emerged from the Seven Years' War with a reputation as a brave and knowledgeable officer and a student of the art of war.

Secondary commands, 1769–1778 During the years between the Seven Years' War and the American War of Independence, Clinton advanced steadily in the army, entered parliament, and enjoyed a happy, if brief, marriage to Harriet Carter (1747–1772), the daughter of Thomas and Martha Carter, of St James's, Westminster, and Penn, Buckinghamshire. The couple were married on 12 February 1767. Clinton was colonel of the 12th foot from 1766 to 1778, took part in summer manoeuvres in 1767, accompanied his regiment to Gibraltar, where he served as second in command in 1769, and was promoted major-general in 1772. He also sat in parliament on the interest of his cousin, the second duke of Newcastle, for Boroughbridge (1772–4) and, later, Newark (1774–84). But on 29 August 1772 his wife died after giving birth to her fifth child in five years of marriage. Clinton was profoundly depressed by Harriet's death. Her parents and two sisters moved into his house in Weybridge, Surrey, to care for his children—two of whom, William Henry *Clinton (1769–1846) and Henry *Clinton (1771–1829), became generals in the Napoleonic era. Clinton then sought to escape his grief by accompanying fellow officers to observe the Russo-Turkish War in 1774 and by accepting appointment as third in command of British forces in North America in February 1775.

Clinton reached Boston on 25 May 1775 to start three years of frustrating service under generals Thomas Gage and William Howe. He made sound plans for defeating the rebellious colonists, but he was rarely successful in advocating or carrying out those plans. At Boston in 1775 he failed to dissuade Gage from launching a costly frontal attack on rebel forces on Charlestown Neck, the battle of Bunker Hill. The following year, after becoming second in command and leading an abortive expedition to the Carolinas, he also failed to persuade Howe, the new commander-in-chief, to accept plans for trapping and destroying the continental army at New York. And in 1777, after a brief winter's leave in England, during which he learned the government's plans, Clinton was unable to convince Howe that he was expected to co-operate with a British army advancing south from Canada in a summer campaign along the Hudson. Howe, ignoring Clinton's arguments and the government's plans, took his army to Pennsylvania by way of Chesapeake Bay. He left Clinton to hold New York city and to do what he could to favour the British forces from Canada. When in early October Clinton made a bold dash up the Hudson, Howe promptly stripped him of the troops he was employing to open the river. Clinton, thoroughly frustrated with Howe, asked to resign as soon as he learned that the Canadian army had surrendered.

Commander-in-chief Rather than accept his resignation, the British government decided during the winter of 1777–8 to make Clinton commander-in-chief and to adopt a new strategy for ending the rebellion: the surrender of the Canadian army and Howe's own wish to resign had changed matters. To carry on the war with depleted regular forces, the government proposed to rely on the Royal Navy and loyal colonists to end the rebellion. Clinton was to try to engage the continental army in a decisive battle. Failing that, he was to withdraw from Philadelphia and co-operate with the navy in raiding the coasts of New England and sending a detachment of 7000 men to Georgia to join loyalists there in restoring royal government throughout the southern colonies.

Before he could carry out this new strategy, France intervened on the side of the rebels, and Clinton had temporarily to subordinate the American war to a wider war with France. In late March 1778, after France announced it had concluded a treaty with the United States, the British government ordered Clinton to send 5000 men to capture the French island of St Lucia in the West Indies and an additional 3000 to reinforce the Floridas. He was then to evacuate Philadelphia and use his remaining forces to defend British posts from New York to Newfoundland. Clinton received these instructions at Philadelphia in May, when he became commander-in-chief. He evacuated Philadelphia in June, marched and fought his way through New Jersey (engaging the continental army inconclusively at Monmouth), and co-operated with the British navy against a French squadron that ranged along the Atlantic seaboard from July to November. Not until November, when he had at last sent a detachment to St Lucia and the French squadron had gone, was Clinton able to concentrate on ending the American rebellion.

But, in pursuing the government's new strategy of relying on the navy and loyalists to restore royal government, Clinton was markedly more cautious than he had been while serving under Howe. In late November 1778 he made a tentative start on recovering the south, sending some 3000 regulars to assist loyalists in restoring royal government in Georgia. When that start proved unexpectedly successful, he considered detaching more regulars to capture Charles Town. But he wasted nearly five months during the spring and summer of 1779 awaiting reinforcements, in mounting a diversionary raid in the Chesapeake, and in trying to lure the continental army into a decisive battle along the Hudson river at Stony and Verplancks points, 40 miles north of New York city. By the time that a reinforcement of 3300 sickly men arrived in late August, a French squadron was on its way to North America. Clinton withdrew his forces from Stony and Verplancks points, as well as Rhode Island, and prepared to meet the French at New York.

Charles Town and the south, 1780–1781 That winter, after the French had left American waters, Clinton undertook an expedition to South Carolina. He went south to take pressure off his forces in Georgia by capturing Charles Town and enlisting loyalists in pacifying South Carolina. On reaching Charles Town in February 1780 he saw an opportunity to do more than he had planned—to capture at Charles Town the principal American army in the south and to carry his offensive well beyond South Carolina and Georgia. He proceeded cautiously: surrounding, besieging, and capturing (on 12 May) Charles Town with its garrison of 3371 men and 300 cannon. He then moved quickly to exploit his greatest victory. He established armed camps in the interior of South Carolina, raised loyalist units, and called upon all colonists to swear allegiance to the crown. But he was all too quick to assume that he had ended the rebellion in South Carolina and that his second in command, Charles, Earl Cornwallis, would be able with relatively few regular troops—about one-quarter of the army in America—to restore royal government from Georgia to Virginia.

Clinton returned to New York in June 1780 to seek a decisive battle with the continental army and to resume raiding warfare in the north—indeed, to make his principal effort there. Yet in the year following his return to New York, a year in which he became paralysed by the arrival of a French squadron at Rhode Island and by disagreements with his naval counterpart, Admiral Marriot Arbuthnot, he gradually shifted his army to the south and allowed Virginia to become the seat of the war. He did so because he lacked the confidence to control Cornwallis, who had the enthusiastic support of the British government. Clinton had ordered Cornwallis to restore royal government gradually, establishing loyalists in one province before going on to another. When Cornwallis chose instead to secure South Carolina by invading North Carolina, and when he suffered defeats and called for help, Clinton began sending reinforcements. Between October 1780 and May 1781 he made four separate detachments to the Chesapeake. But even then, even after three-fifths of his army was in the southern colonies, he still did not intend to concentrate there. And he was angry to learn in late May 1781 that Cornwallis had, unilaterally, taken his small army to Virginia, leaving the interior of South Carolina exposed to the rebels.

Clinton was not angry—or confident—enough to take command of Cornwallis's forces or to pursue his own strategy during the critical summer of 1781. Knowing that the French were sending a powerful fleet to America and that British forces in the Chesapeake would be vulnerable to such a fleet, he had decided to leave only a small contingent of regulars in Virginia and to attack either Philadelphia or Newport. Yet when Cornwallis met his request for troops by threatening to withdraw from Virginia, Clinton allowed him to keep all of his forces and to establish a base at Yorktown. Once he had made these concessions to Cornwallis and to the British government's preference for concentrating in the Chesapeake, he had to forgo his own plans and to rely on the Royal Navy to preserve Cornwallis from the Franco-American forces gathering in Virginia. The navy tried and failed to open the Chesapeake in early September, and on 19 October Cornwallis surrendered, the victim of his own insubordination and of Clinton's inability to exercise authority.

Reputation Cornwallis's surrender effectively ended the American war and Clinton's command—indeed, his active military service. He returned to England in June 1782 to devote the remainder of his life to redeeming his reputation, enjoying the pleasures of a complicated domestic life, and performing occasional duties as colonel of the 84th foot (1778–82) and 7th dragoons (1779–95); he was promoted lieutenant-general (1777) and general (1793). Finding that he was widely blamed for British defeat and that the king was unwilling to reward him for his American service, beyond having created him knight of the Bath on 11 April 1777, he undertook a prolonged, lonely defence of his command. He entered a destructive pamphlet war with Cornwallis and other, anonymous, opponents; he tried and failed to get an Irish viscountcy (the government offered a barony, which he declined); and he worked intermittently on his apologia, a long manuscript history of the American rebellion that did not see publication until 1954. But he also had the good sense to enjoy his families and friends. He installed his children and sisters-in-law at Portland Place, London, and Orwell Park, Suffolk, and set up his mistress from the American war, Mary Baddeley, *née* O'Callaghan, the wife of Captain Thomas Baddeley (d. 1782), with their five children in Paddington. He also had an illegitimate daughter from his former liaison with a Mrs Preussen. Somehow he managed, after delicate introductions, to divide his time between these households and excursions abroad to Europe. By the 1790s other friends from the American war—the second duke of Northumberland and Clinton's second cousin, the third duke of Newcastle—had found him a seat in parliament (for Launceston, 1790–94), an offer of active service (which he declined), and the governorship of Gibraltar (1794–5). He died, before going to Gibraltar, at Portland Place, on 23 December 1795.

Clinton's reputation rests almost entirely on his service in the American War of Independence. His performance was sometimes energetic and inspired, usually sound, and almost always marred by his inability, by what historians have come to see as a disordered personality, to work well with other generals and admirals and to carry out his own plans. He clearly understood the war as a whole: the importance of gradually enlisting the support of the American people; of gaining control of lands that could provide food, fuel, and shelter for British forces; and of maintaining control of the seas about the colonies. He also understood the importance of avoiding costly defeats, of pursuing strategies and tactics that minimized risks to British regular forces. Yet he was so unsure of himself, so hesitant in exercising authority, that he could not translate his insights into British victory. Nor could he avoid being blamed for Lord Cornwallis's climactic defeat at Yorktown. Clinton was a brave, knowledgeable officer who was unsuited by temperament to high command—especially in the long, difficult American War of Independence.   IRA D. GRUBER

Sources W. B. Willcox, *Portrait of a general: Sir Henry Clinton in the war of independence* (1964) · I. D. Gruber, 'Britain's southern strategy', *The revolutionary war in the south*, ed. W. R. Higgins (1979), 205–38 · I. D. Gruber, 'The education of Sir Henry Clinton', *Bulletin of the John Rylands University Library*, 72 (1990), 131–53 · I. D. Gruber, 'George III chooses a commander in chief', *Arms and independence: the military character of the American Revolution*, ed. R. Hoffman and R. J. Albert (1984), 166–90 · *The American rebellion: Sir Henry Clinton's narrative of his campaigns, 1775–1782*, ed. W. B. Willcox (1954) · M. Stern, *Thorns and briars: bonding, love, and death, 1764–1870* (1991) · F. Wickwire and M. Wickwire, *Cornwallis: the American adventure* (1970) · P. H. Smith, *Loyalists and redcoats* (1964) · J. Brooke, 'Clinton, Henry', HoP, *Commons, 1754–90* · W. Stokes, 'Clinton, Sir Henry', HoP, *Commons, 1790–1820* · I. D. Gruber, 'British strategy: the theory and practice of eighteenth-century warfare', *Reconsiderations on the revolutionary war*, ed. D. Higginbotham (1978), 14–31 · R. A. Bowler, 'Sir Henry Clinton and army profiteering', *William and Mary Quarterly*, 31 (1974), 111–22 · R. Kaplan, 'The hidden war: British intelligence operations during the American Revolution', *William and Mary Quarterly*, 47 (1990), 115–38

Archives JRL, MSS · U. Mich., Clements L., corresp. and papers | Alnwick Castle, Northumberland, Percy MSS · BL, letters to Lord Auckland, Add. MSS 34416–34460, *passim* · BL, corresp. with Sir Frederick Haldimand, Add. MSS 21807–21808 · Hunt. L., Hastings MSS · Norfolk RO, corresp. with earl of Buckinghamshire · PRO, official corresp. with the American secretary, CO 5/95–104 · PRO, corresp. with Lord Amherst, WO 34 · PRO, corresp. with Guy Carleton, PRO 30/55 · PRO, corresp. with Lord Cornwallis, PRO 30/11 · PRO, corresp. with Lord Rodney, PRO 30/20 · U. Hull, Brynmor Jones L., letters to Sir Charles Hotham-Thompson · U. Mich., Clements L., Germain and Knox MSS · U. Mich., Clements L., corresp. with John Simcoe · U. Nott. L., letters to Charles Mellish; corresp. with duke of Newcastle

Likenesses oils, *c*.1760, NAM · J. Smart, miniature, *c*.1777, NAM [*see illus.*] · T. Day, miniature, 1787, repro. in Willcox, *Portrait of a general*, frontispiece · S. Addington, miniature, 1793, V&A · Ritchie, engraving, repro. in G. A. Billias, ed., *George Washington's opponents* (1969), following p. 78

Wealth at death left £400 in annuities from estates in Shropshire; £5800 in bequests; £5000 invested for his children; £4194 for Carter-Clinton children from marriage settlement; remainder of estate left to his sons by Harriet Carter: will, PRO, PROB 11/1271, fols. 117–19; Willcox, *Portrait*, 21, 449, 489

Clinton, Sir Henry (1771–1829), army officer, was born on 9 March 1771 in Weybridge, Surrey, the younger son of General Sir Henry *Clinton (1730–1795) and his wife, Harriet (1747–1772), daughter of Thomas Carter. Henry and his elder brother, Sir William Henry *Clinton, were brought up by their aunt, Elizabeth Carter, following the premature death of their mother at the age of twenty-six. In 1782, while his father was commanding the British forces in the United States, Henry was sent to Eton College, where he joined his brother. In 1785 Henry left Eton with William, and soon after entering the army on 10 October

1787 as an ensign in the 11th regiment took leave and set off for France and Germany. In January 1788 he was at Tours, then joined his brother in Valenciennes, where he remained from February until April. After a visit to Brussels he met up with his brother at Koblenz and from there made excursions to Mayen, Bonn (where he was presented to the elector of Cologne), Aachen, Dusseldorf, and Maastricht, among other places. In October 1788 he became a volunteer in the Brunswick corps raised by Lieutenant-General Riedesel, his father's old comrade, which was acting with the Russian army in the Netherlands. In March 1791 he was transferred to the Grenadier Guards, promoted captain into the 15th regiment in April, and transferred back to the Grenadier Guards in November 1792. In January 1793, at the beginning of the war with France, he was appointed aide-de-camp to the duke of York (a post his brother was to hold three years later) and served on his personal staff throughout the disastrous campaigns in Flanders, being promoted brevet major on 22 April 1794. On 10 May he was severely wounded at Campin. He remained with the duke until he was promoted to the lieutenant-colonelcy of the 66th regiment on 30 September 1795, at which time he went to join his regiment in the West Indies.

Clinton was present at the landing in St Lucia under Sir Ralph Abercromby and at the siege and surrender of Morne Fortuné. In 1796, after having exchanged back into the Grenadier Guards, he sailed to England from San Domingo but *en route* was captured by a French cruiser and did not arrive home until the summer of 1797. In the following year he was made aide-de-camp to Lord Cornwallis in Ireland and was present at the surrender of the French force under General Humbert. He was attached to Lord William Bentinck's mission with General Suvorov in Italy during April 1799 when he was present at the battles of the Trebia and of Novi. On 23 December 1799 he married the Hon. Susan Charteris (1774–1816), second daughter of Francis, seventh Lord Elcho; they had no children. She insisted on following him to Switzerland when he was appointed military assistant to William Wickham in 1800. In that year he was also employed on a mission to the Austrian army in Swabia and was present at the battles of Eugen and Moeskerch. He was appointed assistant adjutant-general in the eastern district in June 1801 and adjutant-general in India in January 1802, and was promoted colonel on 25 September 1803. George III at this time praised him and his brother as soldiers of 'uncommon abilities'.

While in India, Clinton did good service in commanding the right wing at the battle of Laswari, but he left in March 1805. He next acted as military commissioner with the Russian general Kutuzov in the campaign of Austerlitz, and in July 1806 he embarked for Sicily as commander of the flank companies of the guards. He commanded the garrison of Syracuse from December 1806 to November 1807, during which time he met Sir John Moore, who became a close friend. Clinton was promoted brigadier-general in January 1808 and, as such, accompanied Moore to Sweden. On 21 August following he arrived in Portugal as adjutant-general to Sir Harry Burrard, but on the next day found himself under a new commander, Sir Hugh Dalrymple, whom he later described as 'unfit' for the post (H. Clinton to W. H. Clinton, 17 Oct 1808). When at last the command fell to Moore, Clinton was delighted, although he did not favour his friend's strategy in the Peninsula. Under Moore he proved himself a decisive deputy, but his imperiousness as a disciplinarian made him unpopular with some. According to one victim of Clinton's anger, Captain Cochrane, Clinton, in the presence of several other officers, 'loaded me with such a torrent of abuse as could not have been merited by the most "worthless" individual in the army' (*Proceedings of a General Court Martial*, 8). In May 1809 Clinton unsuccessfully prosecuted Cochrane in a court martial for disobedience and neglect of duty, although his real motive was to clear himself of charges of unreasonable conduct towards Cochrane following the latter's complaint against him. Clinton took charge of the embarkation procedures on arrival at Corunna, but two days before the battle he was taken ill with dysentery and was replaced by his deputy, Colonel Anderson. After Moore's death he was the first person to defend Moore's proceedings, in a pamphlet entitled *A few remarks … explanatory of the motives which guided the operations of the British army during the late short campaign in Spain*, which, along with two other publications by him, appeared in 1809. In that year he also acted as adjutant-general in Ireland. Before leaving for Sweden he had joined his brother as the duke of Newcastle's MP for Boroughbridge, Yorkshire, having the previous year failed as Lord Elcho's candidate for the Haddington burghs. When present (which was not often) he voted with ministers, and against parliamentary reform and Roman Catholic relief, until his resignation from the Commons in 1818. (He never spoke in debate.)

After his promotion to the rank of major-general on 25 July 1810, Clinton asked to be sent to the Peninsula for active service. His request was granted, and in October 1811 he joined the duke of Wellington and was given the command of the 6th division. Although lacking the military abilities of Thomas Picton or Lowry Cole, he nevertheless made a competent general of division. After attacking the forts of Salamanca in June 1812, he played a conspicuous part in the battle that ensued on 22 July, when his division took the Arapiles valley following the failure of Pack's Portuguese troops. When Wellington went on to march against Joseph Bonaparte at Madrid, Clinton was entrusted with that section of the army that remained behind on the River Douro. He afterwards co-operated in the costly and unsuccessful siege of Burgos in the autumn of 1812. He was made a local lieutenant-general in April 1813 and on 29 July was created a KB for his services at the battle of Vitoria. In the early spring of 1813 he showed the first signs of the mysterious illness which was to plague him until his death. After a short period of convalescence in England he returned in time to command his division at the battles of the Nive, Orthez, and Toulouse, and the affairs of Cáceres and Tarbes.

At the conclusion of the war Clinton's services were

amply rewarded. He received a gold cross and one clasp, and the order of the Tower and the Sword; was made colonel of the 1st battalion, 60th regiment; was promoted lieutenant-general on 4 June 1814; and was appointed inspector-general of infantry. On Napoleon's escape from Elba, Wellington applied for Clinton, who took command of the 3rd division, which was posted on the right centre at the battle of Waterloo on 18 June 1815. In this position he suffered as much from the French artillery as did the other divisions in the centre, and he also had to resist many cavalry charges. After the battle he was made a knight of the orders of Maria Theresa, of St George of Russia, and of William of the Netherlands, and on 9 August 1815 he was made colonel of the 3rd regiment (the Buffs). Two months earlier his elder brother William had applied to the marquess of Hertford for a peerage for Clinton, in the process waiving his own claims for a barony. However, his words fell on deaf ears. During the occupation of France, Clinton commanded a division of the British contingent, and in the autumn of 1815 William visited him in Paris, where he regretted that his brother's former 'open cordiality' towards him had been replaced by a formal 'courteous manner', which he attributed to Clinton's lengthy career as a commander of men.

On 20 May 1816 the Commons, for the third time, thanked Clinton for his military service—on this occasion for his part at Waterloo—and he was again present to acknowledge this honour. However, following the death of his devoted wife, Susan, on 17 August, his health deteriorated rapidly and he became a recluse. In the spring of 1817 he was said to be 'very ill' at Lyons, and by 1819 his elder brother held out little hope for his recovery. In the previous year he had already resigned his seat on the grounds of ill health. The exact nature of his affliction is hard to determine, but he is known to have been severely asthmatic. He died at his country seat of Ashley Clinton, near Lymington, Hampshire, on 11 December 1829 and was buried with his wife in the parish church at Barkway, Hertfordshire. A memorial to him was erected in the church, alongside memorials to other members of the Clinton family.   H. M. STEPHENS, *rev.* R. M. HEALEY

Sources M. Stern, *Thorns and briars: bonding, love and death, 1764–1870* (1991) · *United Service Journal*, 1 (1830), 303–5 · W. B. Willcox, *Portrait of a general: Sir Henry Clinton in the war of independence* (1964) · W. Stokes, 'Clinton, Henry', HoP, *Commons* · W. F. P. Napier, *History of the war in the Peninsula and in the south of France*, rev. edn, 6 vols. (1851) · M. Glover, *Wellington's army in the Peninsula, 1808–1814* (1977) · C. Oman, *Sir John Moore* (1953) · H. Clinton, *A few remarks … explanatory of the motives which guided the operations of the British army during the late short campaign in Spain* (1809) · J. E. Cussans, *History of Hertfordshire*, 35 · *GM*, 1st ser., 86/2 (1816), 376 · Clinton MSS, JRL · D. W. Davies, *Sir John Moore's Peninsular campaign, 1808–1809* (1974) · C. Hibbert, *Corunna* (1967), 169 · *Proceedings of a general court martial … on charges preferred by Brigadier General Henry Clinton … against the Hon. W. E. Cochrane* (1809) · statement of the service of Brigadier General Henry Clinton, PRO, WO 25/744 2768
Archives BL · JRL, corresp. and papers · NAM, letter-books · NAM, letters describing Abercromby's campaign in the West Indies · Yale U., Beinecke L., corresp., journals, and papers | BL, corresp. with Sir Hudson Lowe, Add. MSS 20113–20114, 20162–20165, 20192–20197 · Hants. RO, corresp. with William Wickham · Royal Military College, Sandhurst, letters to Le Marchant · U. Nott.

L., corresp. with Lord William Bentinck · U. Southampton L., Wellesley MSS
Likenesses aquatint, 1817, BM · S. W. Reynolds senior, mezzotint, pubd 1827 (after S. W. Reynolds junior), NPG · H. Edridge, watercolour miniature, priv. coll.

Clinton, Henry Fiennes Pelham-, ninth earl of Lincoln and second duke of Newcastle under Lyme (1720–1794), politician, was born Henry Fiennes Clinton on 16 April 1720, either at Stourton, Lincolnshire, or at Westminster, London, and baptized on 24 April at St James's, Westminster, the second son of Henry Clinton, seventh earl of Lincoln (1684–1728), a ministerial and household office-holder, and Lucy (1692–1736), daughter of Thomas, first Baron Pelham. He succeeded his elder brother, George, who had become the eighth earl in 1728, as ninth earl on 30 April 1730. He was educated at Eton College from 1733, tutored by John Hume (later Bishop Hume), and in 1737 entered Clare College, Cambridge, where in 1749 he was made a doctor of laws. After travelling on the continent, he returned to England in late 1741 and charmed George II, who called him '*the handsomest man in England*' (Walpole, *Corr.*, 30.31).

Having come of age, Lincoln took his seat in the Lords on 1 December 1741 and followed the political lead of his mother's brothers, Henry *Pelham and Thomas Pelham-*Holles, duke of Newcastle upon Tyne, who both served as prime minister. A haughty and loose-living man, Lincoln was described by his friend Horace Walpole as 'a very dark thin young nobleman, who did not look so much of the Hercules, as he said he was himself' (Walpole, *Corr.*, 30.1). He was compared to the comte de Guise and depicted in the study 'Patapan, or, The Little White Dog' by Walpole, who also composed verses to 'Little Peggy', the daughter born in 1743 to Lincoln and his mistress of humble birth, Peggy Lee (ibid., 30.38, 76–7, 294, 307). Despite having been deeply enamoured of Lady Sophia Fermor (1721–1745), he married, on 3 October 1744, his first cousin (his uncle Henry's daughter), Catherine Pelham (1727–1760), which occasioned a quarrel between the brothers about the future control of the family's estates. Lincoln, who had already in 1742 been appointed lord lieutenant of Cambridgeshire, which he remained until 1757, and had become a lord of the bedchamber in January 1743, received from his uncles a series of lucrative offices: he was made master of the jewel office in 1744, cofferer of the household in 1747 (which he held until 1754), joint comptroller of the customs of London in 1749, and auditor of the exchequer in 1751. He was nominated a knight of the Garter on 13 March and installed on 4 June 1752.

That Lincoln was destined to be heir to his childless uncle Thomas was confirmed on 13 November 1756, when Newcastle was additionally created duke of Newcastle under Lyme, with a special remainder to Lincoln. Yet, although the touchy Newcastle required constant attention and selfless loyalty, Lincoln was increasingly impatient with him and relations between them deteriorated. In 1757 Lincoln opposed the formation of the Pitt–Newcastle coalition and in 1762, after Newcastle had left office, he only reluctantly resigned as a lord of the bedchamber to George III. Thereafter, as Walpole wrote, ministers 'never had much reason to complain of Lord Lincoln's hostilities. His exceeding pride kept him excluded from the world, and rarely did he appear either at court or in parliament'. He soon attached himself to William Pitt, earl of Chatham, 'with constant derision of, and insult to, his uncle', who bitterly resented the 'open ingratitude' of his favourite nephew (Walpole, *Corr.*, 30.178–9). It is possible that the death of the countess of Lincoln, to whom the duke of Newcastle had been very attached, diminished his loyalty to the Pelham cause. The final breach came at the general election of 1768, when Lincoln used his influence at Newark, where Newcastle had already made over property to him, to promote his own interest at the expense of his uncle's. On 17 November 1768 he succeeded as second duke of Newcastle under Lyme, and by royal licence on 1 December that year he took the additional surname of Pelham. He was also appointed steward of Sherwood Forest and lord lieutenant of Nottinghamshire, where he inherited his predecessor's estates and extensive electoral patronage, and he was sworn of the privy council on 16 December 1768.

Newcastle was the only peer to pronounce Elizabeth Chudleigh, duchess of Kingston, 'guilty erroneously, but not intentionally' (*State trials*, 20.624–5) when she was convicted of bigamy in the House of Lords on 22 April 1776. He preferred the pleasures of sport and the country to a life of politics, although he held several local offices, including (from 1759) the high stewardship of Westminster. He died, following a paralytic stroke, at his London house in Palace Yard, Westminster, on 22 February 1794 and, although having lived mostly at Oatlands, near Weybridge, Surrey, chose to be buried in the family vault at Bamber, Lincolnshire. By his will (dated 11 May 1793) he passed over his elder son, Thomas Pelham-Clinton, the third duke (1752–1795), of whose marriage he disapproved, in favour of his grandson Henry (1785–1851), who the following year became the fourth duke of Newcastle under Lyme.

S. M. FARRELL

Sources GM, 1st ser., 64 (1794), 279–80 · Walpole, *Corr.* · *State trials*, 20.624–5 · R. Browning, *The duke of Newcastle* (1975) · L. B. Namier, *England in the age of the American revolution*, 2nd edn (1961) · IGI

Archives U. Nott. L., corresp. and papers, MSS NeC2, 230–234, 495 | BL, corresp. with first duke of Newcastle, Add. MSS 32692–33072 · U. Nott. L., letters to third duke of Portland

Likenesses G. Kneller, portrait, *c*.1721 (with first duke of Newcastle), NPG · F. Bartolozzi and S. Alken, group portrait, pubd 1792 (after *The return from shooting*, stipple by F. Wheatley), BM · W. Hoare, replica portrait, NPG · C. Warren, print, line (after W. H. Brown), NPG

Clinton, Henry Fynes (1781–1852), classical scholar, was born at Gamston, Nottinghamshire, on 14 January 1781, the first of the three sons of Charles Fynes (1747?–1827), rector of Gamston and Cromwell, and his wife, Emma (*d.* 1831), daughter of Job Brough of Newark. Charles Fynes became prebendary of St Peter's, Westminster, in 1788 and minister of St Margaret's, Westminster, in 1797. He assumed the additional name of Clinton on 26 April 1821 by royal licence for himself and his issue in recognition of descent from Henry Clinton, second earl of Lincoln (*d.*

1616). Henry Fynes was educated at Southwell grammar school (1789–96), where Magnus Jackson instilled in him habits of intellectual discipline, and at Westminster School (1796–99). He matriculated at Christ Church, Oxford, in April 1799. He later wrote that at Oxford then 'Greek learning was perhaps at the lowest point of degradation' (*Hist. U. Oxf.* 5: *18th-cent. Oxf.*, 524), and that he was inadequately taught and gained more from discussions with friends than from his official teachers. He read voraciously and prodigiously in Greek literature and conceived the love of classical scholarship which became the passion and solace of his life. He graduated BA in March 1803 and MA by examination in 1805, and remained in Oxford until 1806 as private tutor to Francis, Lord Gower, son of George Granville Leveson-Gower, second marquess of Stafford. In 1825 he deplored the low state of classical education at Oxford and compared English research unfavourably with German.

Fynes abandoned a planned career in the church in response to the wish of his kinsman and benefactor Isaac Gardiner of Saffron Walden, Essex, that he should become 'a country gentleman'. (On Gardiner's death in 1811 he inherited landed property in Bedfordshire, Buckinghamshire, Cambridgeshire, Essex, and Middlesex and so acquired 'a comfortable independence'.) He was studying at Oxford when Henry Pelham, fourth duke of Newcastle, another distant relative, returned him to parliament for Aldborough, Yorkshire, by arrangement with his father at the general election in November 1806. 'Astonished at finding himself called to the duties of a Member of Parliament' and feeling himself to be 'unprepared and unqualified for such a situation', he studied history and economics in a conscientious attempt to qualify himself for a political career (*Literary Remains*, 19, 45). At first he 'diligently attended the business of the House' and was 'not without the ambition of becoming a speaker', but his 'natural reserve' and 'lack of readiness of expression' defeated him; his only known contribution to debate in almost twenty years was a brief one on election petition procedure on 25 May 1821 (ibid., 25, 31). Uncompromisingly hostile to Catholic relief, like Newcastle, he opposed the short-lived Grenville ministry and supported its successor under the duke of Portland, whose offer to appoint him to a place at the Admiralty board in March 1807 was declined for him by Newcastle. He came in unopposed for Aldborough at the general elections of 1807, 1812, and 1818 and was successful in a token contest in 1820. In 1807 he published *Solyman, a Tragedy*, of which hardly fifty copies were sold.

On 22 June 1809 Fynes married Harriott, the eldest daughter of the Revd Charles Wylde, rector of St Nicholas, Nottingham. She died in premature childbirth on 2 February 1810 and the child, a boy, lived for only a few hours. Grief temporarily kept him from parliament, but he resumed attendance late in the year to support the administration of Spencer Perceval, whom he admired, on the regency question. On 6 January 1812 he married Katherine (*d.* 25 April 1871), third daughter of Henry William *Majendie (1754–1830), bishop of Bangor; they had two sons, who predeceased him, and nine daughters, seven of whom survived him. His son Charles Francis Fynes Clinton, BA of Christ Church, Oxford, served in the Christina army in Spain, was British arbitrator under the Anglo-Portuguese anti-slavery treaty, and died at Luanda on 5 June 1844. In 1812 Henry Fynes bought the mansion and estate of Welwyn in Hertfordshire, where he chiefly lived for the rest of his life.

Fynes's parliamentary attendance became more sporadic as his literary pursuits increasingly consumed his time and interest. He gave general support to Lord Liverpool's ministry, but cast a few wayward votes on economy and taxation in 1816. He voted consistently against parliamentary reform. By the end of 1819 he had 'entirely abandoned' any idea of making a mark in politics and, shunning the notion of taking office, which he thought would 'impair my health, waste my spirits, and withdraw me from that literature by which I am best able to be useful to myself and others', concluded that he was 'destitute of political ambition' (*Literary Remains*, 140–41). A convinced believer in a revealed religion, he claimed in 1822 to be able to 'look with philosophical indifference upon the vain pursuits of ambition, and to appreciate justly the value of that safe mediocrity of station and fortune in which I am placed'. Yet in February 1824 he got Newcastle to try to obtain for him a place at one of the public boards, preferably customs or excise, but Liverpool could not oblige him. He consoled himself with the observation that 'the loss of a lucrative post is the less to be regretted, because the possession of it would have been accompanied with a sacrifice, in part at least', of his 'two great objects' of giving his children a decent education and of advancing 'learning and moral and religious truth' (ibid., 205, 221–2). At the dissolution in June 1826 he retired from parliament, reflecting that he had been, 'as far as public speaking is concerned, an inefficient Member' (ibid., 247). The greatest disappointment of his life was his failure to secure the principal librarianship of the British Museum in December 1827, when he was passed over in favour of Henry Ellis, the long-serving keeper of printed books. An application on his behalf by Newcastle for the receiver-generalship of Nottinghamshire in 1832 also came to nothing.

Fynes Clinton achieved some measure of happiness with his literary studies, his 'consolation and peace and security against my own passions, and in the midst of many tribulations' (*Literary Remains*, 292–3). Resuming them after the death of his first wife, he turned them to good account by directing his reading towards the production of works on Greek and Roman chronology. The first part of his *Fasti Hellenici: the Civil and Literary Chronology of Greece* was published by the Clarendon Press in January 1824 and favourably reviewed. Further instalments appeared in 1830 and 1834. His publications included articles in the classical journal *The Philological Museum*. His *Fasti Romani: the Civil and Literary Chronology of Rome and Constantinople* was published in two volumes in 1845 and 1850. *Epitome of the Civil and Literary Chronology of Greece* came out in 1851, and he was compiling a companion work on Rome

until a fortnight before his death at Welwyn House, Hertfordshire, on 24 October 1852. It was completed and published in 1853 by his only surviving brother, the Revd Charles John Fynes *Clinton, who also edited and published in 1854 his *Literary Remains*, which contains his autobiography (written in 1818), his literary journal (1819–52), and some essays on theology; his other brother, Clinton James Fynes Clinton (1792–1833), had replaced him as member for Aldborough. Fynes Clinton applied a more exacting and critical scholarship to ancient chronology than had earlier chronologists and included a 'literary chronology' with evidence for the dating of ancient authors. His major work was of long-lasting importance, though today it is rarely consulted.   D. R. FISHER

Sources *Literary remains of Henry Fynes Clinton*, ed. C. J. Fynes Clinton (1854) · W. Stokes, 'Clinton', HoP, *Commons, 1790–1820*, vol. 3 · D. R. Fisher, HoP, *Commons, 1820–32* [draft] · *GM*, 2nd ser., 39 (1853), 315–16 · *Annual Register* (1852), 94, 323 · *DNB* · M. L. Clarke, *Greek studies in England, 1700–1830* (1945) · *Hist. U. Oxf.* 6: *19th-cent. Oxf.* · Foster, *Alum. Oxon.* · Burke, *Peerage*
Archives Herts. ALS, letters to E. Bulwer Lytton · NL Wales, Harpton Court MSS, letters to Sir G. Cornewall Lewis
Wealth at death under £7000: PRO, death duty registers, IR 26/1928/863

Clinton, Henry Pelham Fiennes Pelham-, fourth duke of Newcastle under Lyme (1785–1851), landowner and politician, was the elder son of Thomas Pelham-Clinton, third duke of Newcastle under Lyme (1752–1795), and his wife, Lady Anna Maria Stanhope (1760–1834), fifth daughter of William Stanhope, second earl of Harrington. He was born at Walton, Essex, on 30 January 1785. His father held the dukedom from 22 February 1794 to his death, 17 May 1795, when Henry succeeded him. He was educated at Eton College (1796–9), where he was appalled by its irreligion; in 1829 he founded the Newcastle scholarship there as a prize for divinity and classics. In 1803 he was abroad with his mother and stepfather when war with France was resumed; he was taken prisoner and detained at Tours for three years. After his return to England in 1806 he married, on 18 July 1807 at Lambeth Palace, Georgiana Elizabeth (1789–1822), second daughter and heir of Edward Miller Mundy of Shipley, Derbyshire, and his wife, Georgiana, widow of Lord Middleton. She brought him a sum of £190,000 and £12,000 p.a. They had twelve children and she died aged thirty-three giving birth to twins, on 26 September 1822. Her death seems to have removed a stabilizing influence.

Newcastle was appointed to the usual offices appropriate to his station: lord lieutenant of Nottinghamshire in 1809, and in 1812 knight of the Garter and steward of Sherwood Forest and of Folewood, Nottinghamshire. But he was 'a manic-depressive, prone in periods of euphoria to see himself as the saviour of his country and to take impetuous initiatives only subsequently to lapse into long periods of despondency and inaction' (Wolffe, 23). From about 1826 he was one of the leaders of the tory 'ultras' and a fervent opponent of Catholic emancipation, consequently condemning Wellington's government in 1829 and behaving like a radical agitator in trying to bring a

Henry Pelham Fiennes Pelham-Clinton, fourth duke of Newcastle under Lyme (1785–1851), by Henry William Pickersgill, exh. 1835

crowd to Windsor to frighten the king with an anti-Catholic petition. He published a *Letter to Lord Kenyon* (1829) on this subject. He saw the reform proposals of 1830 as literally catastrophic, and became the most notorious of the opponents of the government's bill. In October 1829, when reproached for evicting tenants who voted against his candidate, he wrote publicly: 'Is it presumed then that I am not to do what I will with my own?' (Brock, 63), a remark he repeated in the Lords on 3 December 1830. He was reported as making further politically motivated evictions in September 1830, which led to the rebuke from *The Times* (29 September 1830) that his actions did much more to justify reform than to prevent it. Newcastle was already unpopular in Nottingham for leasing land only to members of the Church of England. On 10 October 1831, in one of several local incidents, a crowd burnt to the ground his mansion, Nottingham Castle (never rebuilt); he fortified his house at Clumber, and the windows of his London house in Portman Square were broken by a crowd. He complained bitterly at not being a member of the special commission to inquire into the Nottingham episode. Newcastle was one of twenty-two peers to vote against the Reform Bill on its third reading on 4 June 1832. He published his views of the catastrophe in *An Address to All Classes and Conditions of Englishmen* (1832). As a result of the bill he lost the patronage and interest of six boroughs, worth, he believed, about £200,000.

Newcastle had used his patronage in the cause, as he saw it, of establishmentarian protestantism. After 1832 he

maintained this objective. On his son Lord Lincoln's recommendation he gave the young tory W. E. Gladstone his first seat—Newark, which was still effectively a nomination borough. He strongly opposed the grant to Maynooth College, and when Gladstone voted for the grant in 1845, withdrew the nomination, though they continued to share a detestation of concurrent endowment. He presented Protestant Association petitions to the Lords and vehemently opposed the Diplomatic Relations [with Rome] Bill in 1848. In Nottinghamshire he was equally energetically establishmentarian and in 1839 was dismissed as lord lieutenant following his behaviour over the appointment of two nonconformists as magistrates.

Newcastle had no more success as a landowner than as a reactionary. His estates, though in a prosperous and burgeoning county, declined and he left his heir a wasting inheritance. In 1833 he paid £70,000 for an estate in Cardiganshire and in 1839 £370,000 for Worksop Manor, which proved a bad investment. In two years in the 1830s he spent £450,000, most of it borrowed, on land in Nottinghamshire. He ended his life estranged from most of his children, including his heir, Henry Pelham Fiennes Pelham-*Clinton, fifth duke of Newcastle and colonial secretary. Suffering from typhus in January 1851, he is said narrowly to have escaped being buried alive when in a coma. He died at Clumber Park, Nottinghamshire, on 12 January of that year and was buried in nearby Markham Clinton church on 21 January, having gained the reputation of representing all that was worst about the English aristocracy. H. C. G. MATTHEW

Sources GEC, *Peerage* · *The Times* (15 Jan 1851) · *GM*, 1st ser., 92/2 (1822), 370 · *GM*, 2nd ser., 35 (1851), 309–10 · J. Wolffe, *The protestant crusade in Great Britain, 1829–1860* (1991) · M. Brock, *The Great Reform Act* (1973) · M. I. Thomis, *Politics and society in Nottingham, 1785–1835* (1969) · J. Golby, 'A great electioneer and his motives: the fourth duke of Newcastle', *HJ*, 8 (1965), 201–18 · Gladstone, *Diaries* · *DNB*
Archives JRL, corresp. · Royal College of Physicians of Edinburgh, diary of his last illness · U. Nott. L., corresp., diaries, and papers | BL, letters to Stanley Lees Gifford, Add. MS 56368 · BL, corresp. with W. E. Gladstone, Add. MS 44261 · BL, corresp. with second earl of Liverpool, Add. MSS 38256–38328, 38572, 38578, *passim* · BL, corresp. with earls of Liverpool, loan 72 · BL, corresp. with Sir Robert Peel, Add. MSS 40346–40558 · Derbys. RO, corresp. with John Chambers, estate agent at Clumber · Lpool RO, letters to Lord Stanley · NRA Scotland, priv. coll., letters to tenth duke of Hamilton · NRA, priv. coll., letters to Eldon · St Deiniol's Library, corresp. with Sir John Gladstone relating to Newark election · U. Nott. L., corresp. with fourth duke of Portland · U. Southampton L., letters to first duke of Wellington · W. Sussex RO, letters to fifth duke of Richmond
Likenesses J. Nollekens, marble sculpture, exh. RA 1815, Newark town hall, Lincolnshire · J. Doyle, pencil caricatures, 1829–40, BM · C. Turner, mezzotint, pubd 1830 (after T. Lawrence), BM, NPG · H. W. Pickersgill, oils, exh. 1835, Palace of Westminster, London [*see illus.*] · W. Behnes, sculpture, 1843, Eton · attrib. I. Cruikshank, group portrait, pencil and wash (*Members of the House of Lords*), NPG · S. W. Reynolds, mezzotint, BM

Clinton, Henry Pelham Fiennes Pelham-, fifth duke of Newcastle under Lyme (1811–1864), politician, was born on 22 May 1811 at 39 Charles Street, Berkeley Square, London, the third child but eldest son of Henry Pelham Fiennes Pelham-*Clinton, fourth duke of Newcastle

Henry Pelham Fiennes Pelham-Clinton, fifth duke of Newcastle under Lyme (1811–1864), by Frederick Richard Say, 1848

under Lyme (1785–1851), and his wife, Georgiana Elizabeth (1789–1822), daughter of Edward Miller Mundy of Shipley, Derbyshire. Styled the earl of Lincoln until 1851, he was educated at Eton College (1824–8), and in 1829 proceeded to Christ Church, Oxford, where he took a BA degree in 1832. While at Oxford he became a close friend of William Ewart Gladstone; both belonged to the Union Debating Society, each serving as president, and both were members of the Essay Club, founded as an Oxford equivalent to the Cambridge Apostles. He also shared Gladstone's high-church Anglicanism.

Peelite politician Both Lincoln and Gladstone entered parliament as Conservatives in December 1832 through the influence of the fourth duke of Newcastle, the former, without a contest, for South Nottinghamshire and the latter for Newark. On 27 November 1832, shortly before his election, Lincoln married Susan Harriet Catherine (1814–1889), daughter of Alexander Douglas-*Hamilton, tenth duke of Hamilton, granddaughter of William *Beckford, and sister of William Douglas-*Hamilton, later the eleventh duke, an Eton and Oxford friend of Lincoln. He served as a lord of the Treasury from 31 December 1834 to 20 April 1835 in Sir Robert Peel's first ministry. It was at this time that a lasting bond of friendship was established between Peel and his young subordinate colleagues, whom he had introduced to official life.

Lincoln became first commissioner of woods and forests on 15 April 1841 when Peel formed his second administration. As commissioner he performed a myriad of tasks, including providing more public accessibility to royal buildings and parks; enacting the major recommendations of the metropolitan improvements commission, over which he served as chairman; enlarging Buckingham Palace; and superintending the work of the British Geological Survey. Following Gladstone's resignation over the Maynooth College grant early in 1845, Peel appointed Lincoln to the cabinet; and on 14 February 1846 he was made chief secretary for Ireland in Peel's reconstituted administration. The potato famine had become catastrophic by the time he arrived in Ireland. Despite opposition to large-scale state assistance from Treasury officials, especially Charles Edward Trevelyan, he helped to set in motion famine relief measures that included a programme of public works to create employment to enable the Irish people to purchase imported grain. He also became a principal proponent for larger measures to stimulate economic growth and reconstruct Irish society. Although modest, the famine relief measures prevented exceptional suffering during the first half of 1846; but his tenure as chief secretary ended when the Peel ministry resigned in June 1846.

By the time of his appointment as chief secretary Lincoln had modified his earlier protectionist views and was in complete agreement with Peel over the necessity of repealing the corn laws. Peel acknowledged the support he received from Lincoln during the contest over corn law repeal, and the obloquy and sacrifice which this had involved. He suffered his father's wrath for supporting repeal, having already angered him by his support for the Maynooth grant. When he had to seek re-election for his South Nottinghamshire seat on accepting the Irish chief secretaryship, he was defeated by a protectionist candidate backed by his father. His father-in-law, however, helped to find him a seat, Falkirk burghs, for which he was elected in May 1846. The crisis strengthened his devotion to Peel and separated him irrevocably from many of his earlier political positions, as well as from his father.

During the late 1840s Lincoln and the other leading Peelites tried unsuccessfully to get Peel to resume leadership of a moderate political party. Following Peel's death in 1850 Lincoln's own political ambitions were raised. His devotion to public service and his capacity for hard work earned him recognition, and a few prominent individuals, including Prince Albert, the prince consort, encouraged him to seek the leadership of a coalition of Peelites and liberal whigs. Although Lord Aberdeen, rather than Lincoln, was selected to head the coalition government when it was formed in December 1852, many regarded him as the major spokesman of Peelite political philosophy and the most likely successor of Lord Aberdeen as prime minister. A series of misfortunes, however, including his tragic marriage, prevented him from fulfilling his political ambitions and left him with shattered health and a damaged official reputation.

Divorce, peerage, and the Crimean War Lady Lincoln [see Opdebeck, Lady Susan Harriet Catherine], who bore him four sons and a daughter, had a series of affairs, which led to several separations and reconciliations between the couple. After a period of reconciliation during 1844–7, she finally left on 2 August 1848 and travelled on the continent in the company of Lord Horatio Walpole, with whom she had a child a year later. This, and the failure of Gladstone's mission to Italy in the summer of 1849 to persuade Lady Lincoln to return to her husband and children, obliged Lincoln to seek a divorce. On 14 August 1850 the marriage was formally dissolved by act of parliament (with Gladstone giving evidence). Lincoln's father, from whom he had also become estranged, died early in the following year, and he succeeded (12 January 1851) both to the title, as fifth duke of Newcastle, and to estates which were encumbered with debt.

Newcastle was secretary for the colonies in Aberdeen's administration from December 1852 until June 1854, when the outbreak of the Crimean War necessitated the creation of a separate department for administering military affairs. His administrative difficulties began when he took over this newly created office as secretary of state for war. Newcastle laboured indefatigably throughout the summer and autumn to see that the army was as well equipped and prepared as the capabilities of the country allowed, knowing all the while that the system of military administration was in a hopeless state of disorganization and confusion. Despite these problems and administrative shortcomings, the army at the time of the Crimean invasion was more than sufficiently supplied and equipped. Nevertheless, circumstances largely beyond Newcastle's control brought near disaster to the British army in the Crimea during the winter of 1854-5. Although the duke cannot be exonerated completely, an objective review of his administration of the War Office clearly reveals that no individual was solely responsible for the failures. The mistakes and miscalculations of the civilian authorities in London were compounded by those of the military men in the Crimea. However, it was more a failure of strategy and military execution than one of logistics that nearly lost the army; and it was Newcastle's misfortune to be placed at the head of a weak and corrupt system without sufficient authority or opportunity to make it more workable. For his failures he suffered the wrath of the nation early in 1855. He resigned in disgrace on 1 February 1855.

Even before his resignation Newcastle had effected, perhaps belatedly, many of the measures that would rectify the difficulties for the army in the Crimea, including the construction of the Balaklava railway, establishment of the Land Transport Corps, and the appointment of the hospitals commission. Lord Panmure candidly stated that 'the barometer was steadily on the rise' (Munsell, *Unfortunate Duke*, 216) when he took over the War Office from the duke and that he had little to add to the measures that had already been initiated by his predecessor for improving the condition of the army. Yet Panmure and Lord Palmerston, the new prime minister, received all the credit for the improvement of the army, and the duke continued to be pilloried by the press and subjected to parliamentary censure for conducting the war without sufficient care and forethought. Rather than remain in England to resist the motion of censure, the duke accepted Palmerston's invitation to go to the East to report on the state of the army in the Crimea and the hospitals in Turkey.

Colonial secretary Much of the rancour against Newcastle had disappeared by the time of his return to England late in 1855. None the less, still bitter over his past treatment, he semi-retired from politics. His close friend Lady Frances Waldegrave promoted him as a possible Liberal leader to succeed Palmerston; for his part Newcastle looked to Lady Waldegrave, then married to a third, elderly husband, as a possible second wife. In the event neither objective was achieved. He was also distracted by domestic worries. His eldest son rebelled against his strict upbringing and turned out a wastrel, fleeing the country to escape vast gambling debts. Newcastle's determination to prevent his daughter, Susan, from inheriting the characteristics of her mother, merely drove her into an elopement with a drunken and violent husband, Lord Adolphus Vane. His third son, Arthur, deserted from the navy in 1864 and died in 1870 while awaiting trial on charges of indecency in the case involving Ernest Boulton and Frederick Park. With the exception of his second son, Edward (who became master of the queen's household), Newcastle's record as a father was disastrous.

In June 1859 Newcastle joined the Palmerston cabinet as colonial secretary, a position for which he was well suited. As a decided imperialist who administered the empire with tact and understanding in an innovative way, he became a highly regarded colonial secretary. He greatly accelerated the transfer of governmental responsibility to the settlement colonies of North America, Australia, and New Zealand, a process which he believed was necessary to save the empire. To him it was in the best interests of Great Britain to foster communities overseas (he was a member of the Canterbury Association) and to tie them to the mother country with 'bonds of mutual sympathy and mutual obligation' (Munsell, *Unfortunate Duke*, 243). His administration of the Colonial Office provided many valuable precedents that were extremely important in the evolutionary process from empire to Commonwealth.

In 1860 Newcastle served as an official adviser and leader of the entourage accompanying the prince of Wales to British North America and the United States. The duke also chaired the royal commission on popular education (1858-61), the recommendations of which were partially incorporated in the revised code of 1862 and the Education Act of 1870. Other offices and honours that Newcastle held or received included high steward of Retford (1851), lieutenant-colonel commandant of the Sherwood rangers (1853), lord lieutenant of Nottinghamshire (1857), lord warden of the stannaries (1862), honorary DCL of Oxford (1863), councillor to the prince of Wales (1863), and a knight of the Garter (1860).

Contemporary assessments of Newcastle varied widely. To the duke of Argyll, a fellow Peelite and ministerial colleague, 'Newcastle was an industrious and conscientious worker, but he had no brilliancy and little initiative' (G. Douglas, eighth duke of Argyll, *Autobiography and Memoirs*, 2 vols., 1906, 1.380). Frederic, Lord Blachford, longtime under-secretary of state for the colonies, described the duke as 'an honest and honourable man' who in political administration was 'painstaking, clear-headed and just', but whose abilities were far too insufficient 'for the management of great affairs—which, however, he was always ambitious of handling'. Newcastle was also stand-offish and overcritical of others, and although he respected other people's positions, he was always sensible of his own. 'It was said of him', Blachford added, 'that he did not remember his rank unless you forgot it', an expression that aptly described the duke's relations to subordinates (Rogers, 225).

Despite these judgements, Newcastle was highly regarded by some of the most prominent of his contemporaries, including the prince consort, a close friend. In the early 1850s Gladstone and Lord Aberdeen believed that the duke would some day head a government. Gladstone always respected Newcastle and sought his opinions on political and religious matters. Only towards the end of the duke's life did Gladstone see a decline in the abilities that he believed had distinguished the duke more as a statesman than as an administrator. Lord Palmerston regarded Newcastle as an excellent colonial secretary; in 1864, when failing health forced the duke to retire, Palmerston waited as long as he could before accepting his letter of resignation.

Suffering a rapid deterioration of health following his resignation from office in the spring, Newcastle died at Clumber Park, Nottinghamshire, his principal residence, from a cerebral haemorrhage on 18 October 1864. He was buried in the family mausoleum at Markham Clinton. He left his estates in financial disarray, which Gladstone and Frederick Ouvry, as executors and trustees, spent years disentangling. The fortitude with which Newcastle had borne accumulated misfortune and torturing disease touched those who knew him. Gladstone believed that the life of the unfortunate duke was so tragic that it was best forgotten. Fortunately, however, historians in the late twentieth century have rescued Newcastle from obscurity to place both his failures and accomplishments into historical perspective. Earlier accounts that were overly critical of his career, particularly his administration of the War Office, have been corrected, and he has now been allowed to take his place in history as an important political figure during the period of the 1840s through the early 1860s and as one of the most effective colonial secretaries of the nineteenth century.   DARRELL MUNSELL

Sources F. D. Munsell, *The unfortunate duke: Henry Pelham, fifth duke of Newcastle, 1811–1864* (1985) · J. Martineau, *The life of Henry Pelham, fifth duke of Newcastle, 1811–1864* (1908) · V. Surtees, *A Beckford inheritance: the Lady Lincoln scandal* (1977) · F. D. Munsell, 'Charles Edward Trevelyan and Peelite Irish famine policy, 1845–1846', *Societas*, 1/4 (1971), 299–315 · C. C. Eldridge, 'The Lincoln divorce case: a study in Victorian morality', *Trivium*, 11 (1976), 21–39 · N. Gash, *Mr Secretary Peel: the life of Sir Robert Peel to 1830* (1961) · Gladstone, *Diaries* · J. B. Conacher, *The Aberdeen coalition, 1852–1855* (1968) · *Letters of Frederic Lord Blachford*, ed. G. E. Marindin [F. Rogers, Baron Blachford] (1896) · G. Smith, *Reminiscences* (1910) · W. P. Morrell, *British colonial policy in the mid-Victorian age* (1969) · J. M. Ward, *Colonial self-government: the British experience, 1759–1856* (1976) · P. Gibbs, *Crimean blunder* (1960) · GEC, *Peerage*

Archives St Deiniol's Library, Hawarden, corresp. and papers · U. Nott. L., corresp. and papers | Archives New Zealand, Wellington, corresp. with Sir T. G. Browne · Auckland Public Library, letters to Sir George Grey · BL, corresp. with Lord Aberdeen, Add. MS 43197 · BL, letters to Mrs Gladstone, Add. MS 46227 · BL, corresp. with Sir Robert Peel, Add. MSS 40405–40594 · Bodl. Oxf., corresp. with fourth earl of Clarendon · Bucks. RLSS, letters to duke of Somerset · Flintshire RO, Hawarden, Gladstone–Glynne MSS · Lpool RO, corresp. with fourteenth earl of Derby · NRA, priv. coll., corresp. with Sir George Cathcate · NRA, priv. coll., letters to duke of Hamilton · NRA, priv. coll., letters to Lord Houghton · NRA, priv. coll., letters to Lord Wemyss · PRO, corresp. with Lord John Russell, PRO 30/22 · Som. ARS, letters to Lady Waldegrave and Chichester Fortescue · U. Nott. L., corresp. with J. E. Denison · U. Southampton L., corresp. with Lord Palmerston · U. Southampton L., letters to first duke of Wellington · Wilts. & Swindon RO, corresp. with Sidney Herbert

Likenesses J. Hayter, oils, 1836, Newcastle estate office, Warminster · F. R. Say, oils, 1848, NPG [*see illus.*] · G. Richmond, chalk drawing, 1856, NPG · J. Brown, stipple, 1866, NPG · F. Thed, marble bust, 1887 (after A. Munro), National Gallery of Canada, Ottawa · Caldesi, Blanford & Co., photograph, NPG · A. W. Cox, oils, Castle Art Gallery, Nottingham · J. Doyle, two caricatures, BM · J. Gilbert, group portrait, pencil and wash (*The Coalition Ministry, 1854*), NPG · J. W. Gordon, portrait · G. Hayter, group portrait, oils (*The House of Commons, 1833*), NPG · H. N. O'Niel, oils, Keele University · J. Partridge, group portrait, oils (*The Fine Arts Commissioners, 1846*), NPG · G. Zobel, mezzotint (after J. W. Gordon), NPG; version, BM · photograph, repro. in *ILN* (22 Dec 1860)

Wealth at death under £250,000: double probate, March 1866, *CGPLA Eng. & Wales* (1865)

Clinton, William, earl of Huntingdon (d. 1354), soldier and magnate, was the second son of John Clinton, of Maxstoke (d. 1315), and Ida, daughter and coheir of William de Odingsells of Maxstoke, through whom the family inherited the castle and manor of Maxstoke. Clinton was born in the early years of the fourteenth century; he was knighted by 1324 and was summoned to serve in Gascony in 1325. He evidently supported the coup of Queen Isabella and Roger Mortimer in 1327, and was rewarded for his services on 18 September 1327 with a grant of the castle, manor, and hundred of Halton, Cheshire, and the rank of knight-banneret. In November 1327 he conducted William, count of Hainault, and his daughter Philippa to the English court for the latter's marriage to Edward III. For these and similar services he received his first personal summons to parliament in September 1330 and was appointed justiciar of Chester by October. However, Clinton would appear to have defected from the queen's cause, for he supported the young king's surprise attack on Mortimer at Nottingham in November 1330. The strong bond of friendship between the two men is suggested by events at the Dartford tournament in the spring of 1331, when the king himself fought under Clinton's standard.

Recognizing Clinton's special worth, Edward appointed him constable of Dover Castle and warden of the Cinque Ports on 14 December 1330 and made him admiral of the western fleet, a post he held from 16 July 1333 to January 1335. Clinton was among those nominated in the parliament of January 1333 to advise on the projected invasion of Scotland and gave active service in the campaigns that followed; he was present at the siege of Berwick and served with a retinue of sixty-six men at arms and forty mounted archers in the summer campaign of 1335. In his capacity as warden of the Cinque Ports, however, he was also much involved in the defence of the south coast from projected French and Flemish attacks, and in 1332 and 1334 he also undertook diplomatic missions to France.

On 10 March 1337, in parliament at Westminster, Clinton was created earl of Huntingdon and promised 1000 marks a year in lands or rents to support his new dignity. He subsequently secured the valuable Lincolnshire manor of Kirton as part of this settlement. His was one of six new comital creations deliberately designed to restock the ranks of the English nobility in preparation for war with France. Clinton was promptly dispatched to Valenciennes on an important mission to build up a scheme of alliances with the princes and towns of the Low Countries. In March 1338 the earl was nominated as the leader of an expedition to Gascony, but this campaign was called off in June and Clinton was instead appointed a member of the regency council that would rule England during the king's absences over the following two years: closely associated with the Black Prince's council from 1337, he was a natural choice as personal guardian to the young regent and in 1340 was recommended, along with Archbishop John Stratford, as chief councillor in the domestic administration. He also led the force supplied by the Cinque Ports at the battle of Sluys on 24 June 1340.

Clinton's role in the political crisis of 1340–41 is difficult to disentangle. On the king's return from the Low Countries in December 1340, the earl was one of those appointed to inquire into the misdemeanours of royal agents in the shires; he was also nominated as a member of the lords' committee established to investigate the king's charges against Archbishop Stratford in the parliament of April–May 1341. On the other hand there are signs that the king's treatment of the archbishop aroused disaffection in Clinton. He did not serve on the Scottish campaign of 1341–2, excused himself from the important tournament held at Dunstable in 1342, declined to participate personally in the king's expedition to Brittany in 1342–3, and gave up the office of warden of the Cinque Ports on 3 December 1343. Not surprisingly, then, it has been suggested that his political career was permanently affected by the crisis of 1340–41: the fact that he was omitted from the membership of the Order of the Garter, founded by Edward III in 1348, certainly suggests that there had been a cooling of the relationship between king and earl.

This, however, is very far from saying that Clinton was an exile from either the court or the council. During the 1340s he continued a busy career as an ambassador: he undertook a mission to Hainault to treat with the French in August 1341, was nominated to serve at the peace talks in Avignon in 1343 and with the Flemings in 1348, and took an active role in negotiations at Calais in 1349, 1351, and 1354. He was regularly appointed to commissions in the shires and was made keeper of the king's forests south of the Trent in 1344. He served again as admiral of the western fleet between 12 June 1341 and 3 April 1342, and

took some part in the great campaign of 1346–7, returning home after the sack of Caen with a copy of the recently discovered French plan of 1338 for an invasion of England and, after attending a great council in March 1347, rejoined the king's forces at the siege of Calais. In December of the same year he was promised £824 as a gift for good service in the wars. By this stage he was clearly a wealthy man: in 1349 he was able to lend Sir John Pulteney the considerable sum of 2000 marks. If Clinton's career was at all compromised in the 1340s, it may in fact have had as much to do with ill health (he was reported to be sick in 1343 and 1346) as with loss of royal favour.

Clinton married, between 17 August and 17 October 1328, Juliana *Leybourne (1303/4–1367), who brought him a life interest in her major landed estate in Kent. The couple had no children. Possibly because of this Clinton chose to concentrate his building projects and religious benefactions at Maxstoke, the seat of his nephew and heir, John, Lord Clinton. In 1330 he purchased the advowson of the parish church at Maxstoke with the intention of establishing a college of secular priests there; by 1336 or 1337 he had abandoned this plan and assigned the church to the upkeep of a house of Augustinian canons. The new priory buildings were dedicated on 8 July 1342, and the foundation was confirmed by the pope in 1344. The parish church at Maxstoke was also rebuilt around this time. Then, in 1345, the earl secured a licence to crenellate the manor house of Maxstoke on behalf of his nephew; the well-preserved remains, though remodelled in the fifteenth century, represent one of the best examples of mid-fourteenth-century castle architecture. Finally, in 1350 Clinton petitioned the pope for licence to build a chapel at the castle, stating that he and his wife and their household spent much time at the manor and were frequently prevented from getting to the parish church since the connecting road ran through woods and was frequently flooded in winter.

Clinton died on 25 August 1354, having made his will two days before. He specified that his body should be buried at Maxstoke Priory, where, under the terms of the foundation, bread was distributed to 100 poor people of the parish every year at his anniversary. Clinton's family had prospered through his connections: his brother John (d. 1335) had been summoned to parliament from 1332 and his nephew had an active career in politics and government during the second half of the fourteenth century. The comital title, however, became extinct on William Clinton's death and the senior line of the family maintained its baronial status as the lords Clinton and Saye.

W. M. ORMROD

Sources GEC, *Peerage* · PRO · C. Given-Wilson, *The English nobility in the late middle ages* (1987) · R. Nicholson, *Edward III and the Scots: the formative years of a military career, 1327–1335* (1965) · J. Sumption, *The Hundred Years War*, 1 (1990) · J. Vale, *Edward III and chivalry: chivalric society and its context, 1270–1350* (1982) · D. Knowles and R. N. Hadcock, *Medieval religious houses, England and Wales*, new edn (1971) · VCH Warwickshire · *Adae Murimuth continuatio chronicarum. Robertus de Avesbury de gestis mirabilibus regis Edwardi tertii*, ed. E. M. Thompson, Rolls Series, 93 (1889) · *CEPR letters*, vol. 3 · E. B. Fryde, *William* *de la Pole, merchant and king's banker* (1988) • W. Dugdale, *The antiquities of Warwickshire illustrated*, rev. W. Thomas, 2nd edn, 2 vols. (1730)

Clinton, Sir William Henry (1769–1846), army officer and administrator, was born on 23 December 1769 in Lyons, France, the elder son of General Sir Henry *Clinton (1730–1795) and his wife, Harriet, daughter of Thomas Carter. William and his younger brother, Sir Henry *Clinton, spent their early childhood at the family home in Weybridge, Surrey, where, following the premature death of their mother in 1772 at the age of twenty-six, they were cared for by their aunt, Elizabeth Carter, who with her sister moved into the family home. In 1780, while his father was commanding the British forces in the United States, William was sent to Eton College. His brother joined him in 1782 and both left in 1785. Meanwhile, on 22 December 1784 William had been gazetted cornet in his father's regiment, the 7th light dragoons, and thereafter, thanks to his father's wealth and influence, promotion quickly followed. In 1786 he accompanied his father on a short tour of France and Switzerland. On 29 August they set off for the continent and early in the following month arrived at the home, near Neuchâtel, Switzerland, of Monsieur Traytorrens, a member of an illustrious family who had been patrons of Rousseau. Under the care of Traytorrens, Clinton spent a year in mainly rustic pursuits, though he was frequently entertained at the homes of neighbouring English residents and travellers, who included Mark Beaufoy and his wife. He also perfected his French, began to study German, and recorded the days' events in the journal that was to run almost unbroken for nearly sixty years. From Neuchâtel, Clinton travelled north to Valenciennes where, apart from a short break in England, he spent a further eight months, partly in the study of fortification. On 1 May 1788 he headed eastwards, visiting Brussels, Liège, Aachen, Cologne, Bonn, Koblenz, and Mayen, among other places. For much of his tour he was accompanied by his younger brother Henry, and the two travellers discovered that the influence of their famous father opened many doors, including those of several German electors and Count Metternich, father of the illustrious Austrian statesman. On 7 March 1787, while in Switzerland, Clinton had been promoted lieutenant. He was subsequently promoted captain into the 45th regiment on 9 June 1790 and captain in the 1st Grenadier guards on 14 July 1790. In 1793 Clinton saw his first action in the campaign in Flanders, and on his return in the following year he succeeded his kinsman Thomas Pelham Clinton as tory member for East Retford in Nottinghamshire. He retained his seat until 1796 but is known to have spoken only once in the Commons—on the Flanders campaign, on 5 February 1795. Meanwhile, on 29 December 1794 he had been promoted lieutenant-colonel, and in August 1795 he accompanied General Doyle on his abortive campaign to the coast of France. On his twenty-sixth birthday Clinton succeeded his father in the family property and soon afterwards, in January 1796, was appointed aide-de-camp to the duke of York, in which capacity he acted, apart from a spell of duty

in Ireland, until June 1799. On 14 March 1797 he had married Lady Louisa Dorothea Holroyd (1777–1854), daughter of John Baker *Holroyd, first earl of Sheffield. They had two sons, Henry and Frederick, both of whom became army officers, and four daughters, Lou, Anna, Maria, and Harriot.

In 1799 Clinton was on the continent with Colonel Ramsay and accompanied him on a secret mission to the Russian generals Korsakov and Suvorov, returning to England in October to resume his association with the duke of York at The Helder. It was Clinton's duty to bring home the news of the Alkmaar armistice. In June 1800 he was appointed acting deputy quartermaster in Egypt, on 1 January 1801 was promoted colonel by brevet, and was soon afterwards made inspector-general of foreign corps. In June of that year he was chosen to command a secret expedition, and on 23 July he took possession of Madeira, which he governed as a brigadier-general until the conclusion of the peace of Amiens in 1802. He then resumed his duties as inspector-general of foreign corps until that post was suppressed in December 1802. His success at this time prompted George III to recommend him for further employment, and he and his brother Henry were praised as soldiers of 'uncommon abilities' who were 'well respected in their profession'. In April 1803 he resumed his duties with the duke of York, this time as his military secretary. He returned to Ireland on 26 July 1804 as quartermaster-general but declined an invitation to join Lord Harrington's mission to Berlin in December 1805, informing Prime Minister Pitt that he felt unqualified for the task. He re-entered parliament in 1806, this time on the duke of Newcastle's interest at Boroughbridge in Yorkshire, and when present gave silent support to the Portland and Perceval ministries.

In May 1807 Clinton was sent on a secret mission to Charles XIII of Sweden but arrived too late to prevent the signing of an armistice with France. He nevertheless took the opportunity of meeting the king, visiting Malmö, Stralsund, Memel, and Copenhagen (among other places), and being thoroughly briefed by the British envoy, Lord Hutchinson. He was promoted major-general on 26 April 1808 but despite frequent applications to serve abroad was neglected for nearly four years. At the beginning of 1812 he was sent to Sicily, and while commanding the division at Messina he was seriously wounded. At the end of September 1812 he proceeded to Alicante to take command of the troops on the east coast of Spain until replaced in December by Major-General James Campbell, who was in his turn superseded by Sir John Murray. On his return from leave in April 1813 Clinton commanded the 1st division at the battle of Castalla, but fell out with Murray. In June 1813 the ineffectual Murray was himself replaced by Lord William Bentinck, who in September gave the command-in-chief back to Clinton. During the autumn and winter campaigns of 1813–14 he had no great difficulty in keeping Maréchal Suchet's forces in check and in forming the blockade of Barcelona that enabled Ferdinand VII of Spain to return. Part of Clinton's success was undoubtedly due to his humanitarianism as a general and especially to his fervent opposition to corporal punishment, which he later claimed to have reduced markedly among his troops in Spain, and afterwards in Portugal.

Clinton had been made lieutenant-general in 1813 and colonel of the 55th regiment in 1814. On his return to England in that year, unsuccessful efforts were made to obtain a barony for him, as well as the governorship of Gibraltar. However, on 2 January 1815 he was made a GCB and in June astonished the marquess of Hertford by stating that he now waived his own claims to a peerage in favour of the superior claims of his brother Henry. But Henry too was passed over, and this neglect rankled with Clinton for the rest of his life. In September 1815 he journeyed to Paris with Thomas Murdoch FRS in the hope of obtaining employment from the duke of Wellington. He returned to England empty-handed and for the next ten years (he failed to obtain the governorship of Nova Scotia in October 1819) remained without employment. During this period he took a more active part in politics, attending the Commons regularly and giving silent support to Lord Liverpool's ministry. In 1818 his patron transferred him to a seat for Newark and persuaded him, against his wishes, to stand again in 1820. In 1821 Henry Bathurst, secretary for war and the colonies, proposed him for the governorship of Barbados, which he failed to get.

Clinton's life took a new turn in November 1823, with his removal from Sheffield Lodge, on his father-in-law's east Sussex estate, to the much grander Cokenach at Barkway, near Royston, Hertfordshire, the property of Sir Francis Willes, a kinsman. He now saw himself as a gentleman farmer and, though only a leaseholder, began to invest heavily in a hitherto neglected estate. His appointment in 1825 to the lucrative post of lieutenant-general of the ordnance enabled him to continue his programme of improvement, and when, on Willes's death in 1827, he became the new owner of Cokenach he began to draw up ambitious plans for the mansion, which came to fruition in the extensive additions and alterations of 1833–6 by Henry Harrison. Meanwhile, in December 1826 he had received the command of 600 men who were sent to Portugal to keep the peace against the Miguelist and Spanish threat. His personal popularity was such that he was offered, but declined, the command-in-chief of the Portuguese army. Eventually, after over a year of occupation, the troops were brought home by their commander in April 1828.

While in Portugal Clinton was offered the governorship of Mauritius but declined it. Soon after his return to England the finance committee voted to abolish his office at the ordnance. In February 1829 he resigned from the Commons. Although his promotion to general in July 1830 and the offer of the governorship of Madras in the same year were doubtless meant as compensation, he reserved bitter words in his journal for Wellington and his cabinet. Madras had to be declined due to ill health, and his rancour increased in 1835 when, for the second time, he was passed over for the governorship of Gibraltar. In retirement he was seldom idle, as he divided his time between

Hertfordshire and London. He regularly visited and entertained, read French and German daily, rode, planted trees, and kept his (by now) voluminous journal. In 1842, at the age of seventy-three, he became lieutenant-general of Chelsea Hospital in London. He had been a commissioner at the Royal Military College at Sandhurst for many years, and it was while attending the general examination at Addiscombe College in 1845 that he caught a chill that led eventually to his death, at Cokenach on 16 February 1846. He was buried on 24 February at the parish church at Barkway, Hertfordshire.   R. M. HEALEY

Sources M. Stern, *Thorns and briars: bonding, love and death, 1764–1870* (1991) · W. B. Willcox, *Portrait of a general: Sir Henry Clinton in the war of independence* (1964) · *Colburn's United Service Magazine*, 1 (1846), 479–80 · W. Stokes, 'Clinton, William Henry', HoP, *Commons* · R. Macaulay, *They went to Portugal too*, ed. L. C. Taylor (1990), 232–45 · Clinton papers, Yale U., Beinecke L., Osborn collection · journal, JRL, Clifton Family Archive · D. W. Davies, *Sir John Moore's Peninsular campaign, 1808–1809* (1974) · C. Hibbert, *Corunna* (1967), 169
Archives BL · Herts. ALS, letters to his wife · JRL, military and other papers and letters · NAM, letter-book, account book, corresp. · PRO, statement of the service of General Henry Clinton, WO 25/744.2768 · Yale U., Beinecke L., Osborn collection, corresp. with his brother | NAM, corresp. with Sir George Nugent · Nationaal Archief, The Hague, letters to Lord Reay
Likenesses H. Edridge, miniature watercolour, priv. coll.

Clipston [Clipstone], **John** (d. c.1378), prior of Nottingham and theologian, joined the Carmelite order in Nottingham. He studied at Cambridge, where he incepted as DTh and lectured in the university. On 7 December 1349 he was granted permission to hear confessions in the Ely diocese. He was prior at Nottingham for some years and died there c.1378. Clipston was a noted scripture scholar and preacher, but sadly none of his works survives. Bale preserves the titles and incipits of ten of his compositions, which include a 'large work' describing the personages of the Bible in alphabetical order. About 1550 Bale saw five volumes of his sermons which had once been in the possession of the monastery at Syon.   RICHARD COPSEY

Sources J. Bale, Bodl. Oxf., MS Bodley 73 (SC 27635), fols. 40, 118v · J. Bale, BL, Harley MS 3838, fols. 77r–v, 180 · Bale, *Cat.*, 1. 484 · Bale, *Index*, 193 · J. Stevens, *The history of the antient abbeys, monasteries, hospitals, cathedral and collegiate churches*, 2 (1723), 162 · Emden, *Cam.*, 142 · J. Bale, *Illustrium Maioris Britannie scriptorum … summarium* (1548), 250

Clissold, Augustus (1797?–1882), Swedenborgian activist, the son of Augustus Clissold of Stonehouse, near Stroud, Gloucestershire, matriculated from Exeter College, Oxford, on 6 December 1814, the same day as his elder brother, Henry Clissold. He took the ordinary BA degree in 1818, proceeding MA in 1821. He was ordained deacon in 1821 and priest in 1823. He held for some time the curacies of St Martin-in-the-Fields and St Mary, Stoke Newington, but withdrew from the ministry about 1840, although he remained nominally connected with the Church of England to the end of his life. Having become an enthusiastic student of the writings of Emanuel Swedenborg, he joined, in 1838, the Swedenborg Society as a life member, and in the same year was placed on the committee. In 1840 he was elected chairman of the annual meeting. In addition to publishing numerous theological and eschatological works of his own, Clissold translated and printed at his own expense Swedenborg's *Principia rerum naturalium* (2 vols., 1845–6) and *Oeconomia regni animalis* (edited by J. J. Garth Wilkinson, 2 vols., 1846), both of which he presented to the Swedenborg Association. The association, of which he was chosen president, was founded in 1845 for the publication of Swedenborg's scientific works, and later merged with the larger Swedenborg Society.

In 1854 Clissold purchased for the use of the society a seventy years' lease of a house at 36 Bloomsbury Street, London, which later became the depot of New Church literature. During the stormy time through which the Swedenborg Society passed in 1859 and 1860 Clissold assisted it liberally with money, and by his will he bequeathed to it the sum of £4000. In 1870 he assisted financially in the publication of *Documents Concerning the Life and Character of Emanuel Swedenborg*, translated and edited by R. L. Tafel (2 vols., 1875–7), and during the last two years of his life he similarly made possible the publication of Swedenborg's posthumous work *The Brain* (1882), which formed a portion of the *Regnum animale perlustratum*. After resigning his second curacy Clissold continued to live at Stoke Newington, making occasional visits to his country house at 4 Broadwater Down, Frant, Sussex, near Tunbridge Wells. He died there on 30 October 1882.

GORDON GOODWIN, *rev.* TIMOTHY C. F. STUNT

Sources Foster, *Alum. Oxon.* • Crockford (1823–40) • *Men of the time* (1879) • *The Times* (2 Nov 1882)
Wealth at death £34,048 7s. 4d.: resworn probate, July 1883, CGPLA Eng. & Wales (1882)

Clissold, Stephen (*bap.* 1789, *d.* 1863), Church of England clergyman and writer, was born at Reading and baptized there on 25 September 1789, the son of Stephen Clissold of Hill House, Gloucestershire, and his wife, Diana Mortimer. He matriculated from Clare College, Cambridge, in 1815, proceeding BA in 1819 and MA in 1822. He was admitted to Lincoln's Inn on 11 May 1819. However, he abandoned the law for the church, being ordained priest in 1828. He was rector of St Nicholas, Wrentham, Suffolk, from 1830 to 1853, and honorary canon of Norwich Cathedral. Clissold dabbled in political economy, publishing *Letters of Cincinnatus* (1815), *Considerations on the Trade, Manufacture, and Commerce of the British Empire* (1820), and *National Piety the Source of National Prosperity* (1828). He also published the *Official Account of the Parochial Charities … Belonging to the Blything Union, Halesworth* (1838). On 17 June 1824 Clissold married Charlotte Matilda Gooch (1798–1852), with whom he had at least two sons, Edward and Stephen. He died at Wrentham on 12 May 1863 and was buried in the parish churchyard there.

FRANCIS WATT, *rev.* H. C. G. MATTHEW

Sources *GM*, 3rd ser., 14 (1863), 801–2 • *GM*, 3rd ser., 15 (1863), 108 • Venn, *Alum. Cant.* • *IGI* • Clergy List (1850) • Clergy List (1863) • www.gravestonephotos.com/suffolk/wrentham.htm
Wealth at death under £60,000: probate, 10 June 1863, CGPLA Eng. & Wales

Clitheroe. For this title name *see* Assheton, Ralph, first Baron Clitheroe (1901–1984).

Clitheroe, James Robinson [Jimmy] (1921–1973), comedian, was born on 24 December 1921 at 58 Wilkin Street, Clitheroe, Lancashire, the son of James Robert Clitheroe, cotton weaver, and Emma, *née* Pye (d. 1973). He was brought up and went to school in the nearby village of Blacko, near Nelson. Clitheroe, unlike the surname of Eric 'Morecambe' and George 'Formby', was not an invented stage name. Trained as a dancer, he joined the Winstanley Babes, a juvenile troupe, and soon included roller-skating, female impersonation, and accordion and saxophone playing among his contributions to touring revue. He then began the hard slog of variety, with good pantomime and summer season dates and bit-part film appearances with top-liners such as Old Mother Riley, George Formby, Vera Lynn, and Frank Randle.

Glandular disablement stopped Clitheroe's growth at eleven and he never reached puberty; because of his stunted growth he assumed a 'little boy' persona and remained a stage juvenile until his death. He thereby followed in the tiny footsteps of Wee Georgie Wood, but whereas his predecessor had adopted a rather well-articulated Eton-collared choirboy image Jimmy Clitheroe was much more the mischievous and knowing brat, a sort of working-class 'Just William'. They were alike in adopting stage mothers, with Renee Houston, Patricia Burke and, most famously, Mollie Sugden playing the role for Clitheroe that Dolly Harmer had performed for Wee Georgie Wood.

Clitheroe came to attention, especially in the north of England, in concert with Albert Burdon: beginning in revue at the South Pier, Blackpool, in the summer of 1945, they became noted partners in variety and pantomime. This led to radio work from Manchester in *The Mayor's Parlour* and *Call Boy*, and then James Casey, the BBC light entertainment producer and son of the comedian Jimmy James, decided that Jimmy Clitheroe should star in his own series. *The Clitheroe Kid*, a showcase for his precociously insolent exploits, normally against a domestic background, ran from 1958 to 1972, making history as the longest-running radio comedy programme. In 1959 Jimmy Clitheroe took part in the royal command variety show and he also starred in the television series *Holiday Hotel*. His catch-phrase—'some mothers do 'ave 'em'—proved very popular. Against the canvas of the purportedly 'swinging sixties', the rather dated and superficial concert-party sketch approach of *The Clitheroe Kid* may appear an anachronistic success. The vaguely northern, working-class imagery of the characterization seems to have preserved its appeal, and it may have resonated with the 1950s proletarian anti-heroes of the Sillitoe, Amis, Osborne, or Braine mould: in the perhaps overblown dramatic terms of that age, where Wee Georgie Wood had been 'french windows', Jimmy Clitheroe was 'kitchen sink'.

The 'cheeky boy' routine was a staple of variety and

film, as witnessed by the success of Will Hay and his classroom cameos, or of Hollywood's *Our Gang*. Contemporary with Jimmy Clitheroe, the popular radio programme *Educating Archie*, featuring the ventriloquist Peter Brough and his brash juvenile doll, Archie Andrews, exhibited a similar character; what was different was that Jimmy Clitheroe was a child impersonator. A diminutive 4 feet 2 inches and weighing only 5 stone, he found, as Wee Georgie Wood could have testified, that, even with the fortunate outlet of theatre to assist, life for those branded abnormal was not too sweet. As *The Guardian* reported at the time of his death, 'he was always acutely conscious of his stature and would never allow it to be discussed in his presence' (*The Guardian*, 7 June 1973). Although he had one strong friendship with a woman, Clitheroe felt he should not marry, given that he could not have children. He lived as something of a recluse, behind high walls, in Bispham Road, Blackpool. His health failed by the early 1970s and in April 1973 he was found unconscious in a Plymouth hotel bedroom, but recovered in Freedom Fields Hospital, Plymouth. On 6 June 1973, the day of the cremation of his mother, with whom he had always lived and who had been a major personal and professional support, Jimmy Clitheroe was found unconscious in bed by relations arriving to attend the funeral. He died the same day in the Victoria Hospital, Blackpool. The inquest was told that he had swallowed at least four barbiturate sleeping pills and seven brandies; a verdict of accidental death was recorded. It was only then that the mystery of his age was clarified, for it was widely believed that he was born in 1916 and was fifty-seven (not fifty-one). His fortune of £102,000, intended for his mother, went, after some small bequests, to the Cancer Research Campaign. It would appear that his may have been the last of the 'boy-man' characterizations.   ERIC MIDWINTER

Sources R. Busby, *British music hall: an illustrated who's who from 1850 to the present day* (1976) · Covent Garden, London, Theatre Museum collections · Lancashire, Burnley District Central Library collections · b. cert.
Archives FILM BFI NFTVA, performance footage | SOUND BL NSA, documentary recordings · BL NSA, performance recordings
Likenesses portraits, Trinity College of Music, London, Jerwood Library of the Performing Arts, Mander and Mitchenson Theatre Collection
Wealth at death £102,306: probate, 25 Oct 1973, *CGPLA Eng. & Wales*

Clitheroe [Cliderhou], **Robert** (*d.* 1334), administrator, came of a family originating at Clitheroe, Lancashire. He held the nearby manor of Bailey, and had licence in 1330 to alienate it to the abbot and convent of Cockersand, for the provision of two chaplains to celebrate divine service daily, in the chapel of St John the Baptist at Bailey, for the souls of Robert and his parents, who are identified by Whitaker as Jordan de Cliderhou and his wife, Cicely. At his trial in the autumn of 1323 it was stated that Clitheroe had been a clerk of the king's chancery for thirty years. This strengthens the case for his identification with the Robert Cliderhou summoned as one of sixteen clerks of the council to the parliament which was called to meet at Lincoln in July 1312, but which actually met at Westminster in August. The trial also identified him as an escheator north of the Trent; he was appointed on 19 February 1315 and was succeeded by Robert Sapy on 27 September 1316. He was also probably the Robert Cliderhou empowered to examine and correct the assessment of the fifteenth in the city of York in September 1316. The name Robert Cliderhou occurs as that of a judicial commissioner of assize or oyer and terminer in various counties between 1310 and 1331, and a Robert Cliderhou was joint keeper of the bishopric of Worcester from 21 October 1313 to 17 February 1314, but it is not certain that these are all references to the same person.

Clitheroe was instituted as rector of Wigan on 22 September 1303; his death caused a new presentation to be made on 15 June 1334. The court of king's bench sat at Wigan in October and November 1323, in the aftermath of the rebellion of Thomas, earl of Lancaster. Jurors found Clitheroe guilty of sending, at his own expense, two well-mounted men-at-arms (one of them his son Adam) and four footmen, armed with swords, knives, and bows and arrows, to aid Lancaster against the king, and also of preaching publicly in his church at Wigan in support of the earl, calling his enterprise lawful and the king's unlawful, and promising to absolve from their sins those willing to go to the earl's aid, charges which he denied. He was committed to prison, and subsequently bailed, and he paid a fine of £200. Later, in an undated petition attributed to Edward III's reign, he sought redress of grievances arising from these circumstances, but was told that nothing could be done because he had voluntarily agreed to the fine. The episode is a rare illustration of political intervention from the pulpit, and seems to need explanation, since even after his rebellion, Clitheroe continued in royal employment and protection, being still described as king's clerk, for example, in October 1330. One suggestion for the cause of Clitheroe's discontent is that in 1322 he was smarting over accusations made in 1320 that he had committed extensive peculation during his period as escheator.   HELEN M. JEWELL

Sources G. Tupling, *South Lancashire in the reign of Edward II as illustrated by the pleas at Wigan recorded on coram rege roll no. 254*, Chetham Society, 3rd ser., 1 (1949), 71–3 · *Chancery records* · F. Palgrave, ed., *The parliamentary writs and writs of military summons*, 2/2 (1830), 73 · *RotP*, 2.406 · E. Baines and W. R. Whatton, *The history of the county palatine and duchy of Lancaster*, rev. edn, ed. J. Harland and B. Herford, 2 (1870), 177 · T. D. Whitaker, *An history of the original parish of Whalley*, rev. J. G. Nichols and P. A. Lyons, 4th edn, 2 (1876), 83, 471 · J. R. Maddicott, *Thomas of Lancaster, 1307–1322: a study in the reign of Edward II* (1970), 309 · Foss, *Judges*, 3.246–7 · W. Farrer, ed., *Final concords of the county of Lancaster*, 1, Lancashire and Cheshire RS, 39 (1899); 2, Lancashire and Cheshire RS, 46 (1903) · W. Farrer, ed., *The chartulary of Cockersand Abbey of the Premonstratensian order*, 3, Chetham Society, new ser., 56–7, 64 (1905–9), pt 3, 1109 · W. A. Hulton, ed., *The coucher book, or chartulary, of Whalley Abbey*, 4 vols., Chetham Society, 10–11, 16, 20 (1847–9), vol. 4

Clitherow, Sir Christopher (1577/8–1641), merchant and politician, was the only son of Henry Clitherow (*d.* 1608), a merchant, of the parish of St Andrew Undershaft, London, and his first wife, Bridget, the daughter of Thomas Hewett. He was presumably descended from Richard or William Clitheroe, both of whom migrated to London and

Sir Christopher Clitherow (1577/8–1641), by unknown artist

Kent towards the end of the fourteenth century from the Lancashire town from which they took their name. His paternal grandfather became a junior warden of the Merchant Taylors' Company in 1521, while his father, who traded in cloth, wine, and cordage and invested in privateering, achieved the distinction of being elected master of the Ironmongers' Company on four separate occasions.

Education and early career Clitherow entered St John's College, Oxford, in 1593 at the age of fifteen, and followed his father into the Ironmongers' Company in 1601. In the same year he was admitted to the newly formed East India Company, in which he invested £240, and from which he undoubtedly made a handsome profit. Membership of the revived but short-lived Spanish Company (1604) soon followed, and after his father's death he joined the Virginia (1609), French (1611), and North-West Passage (1612) companies. It is not known when he entered the Eastland, Muscovy or Russia, and Levant companies, but he served as one of the Levant Company's assistants in 1616. The only major trading company to which Clitherow did not subscribe was the Company of Merchant Adventurers, whose interests he opposed; he joined instead the New Company of Merchant Adventurers in 1615, the body briefly established in its place by Sir William Cokayne. Both his marriages were to daughters of fellow merchants. Catherine Rowland (d. 1606), whom he had married by 1601, was the daughter of Thomas Rowland (d. 1593), a London draper. Sir Thomas Cambell, to whose daughter Mary (d. 1646) Clitherow was married by 1608, was a leading figure in the Ironmongers' and East India companies.

Although Clitherow was obliged to disburse more than £215 towards settlement of the Muscovy Company's debts in 1624 and lost whatever money he sank into the ill-fated Virginia Company, trade evidently made him rich. In 1615 he bought the Essex manors of Highams and Follifaunts for £1680, and in 1630 he purchased the Oxfordshire manor of Bensington for £386. Further acquisitions included the Middlesex manor of Ruislip, with a house at Pinner, and the lease of various tenements in Finsbury from the corporation of London, on which he may have spent as much as £600 in making improvements. His London properties also included a town house in Leadenhall Street, for which he paid £60 a year in rent. The house served as his normal residence—it was where at least ten of his twelve children were born—and from 1638 until his death it provided the venue for meetings of the board of directors of the East India Company at an annual fee of £150. Income from rents, and the profits of commerce, enabled Clitherow to raise fairly substantial sums in cash. In 1640 he provided the king with £500 as part of a larger City loan, while in the following spring he contributed £1000 towards a second City loan to pay off the defeated English army in the north.

Political life Clitherow's commercial success was reflected in the fact that he was often called on to hold office in the companies of which he was a member. Elected warden of the Ironmongers' Company in 1611, he became master in 1618 and again in 1624. In 1615–16 he served as treasurer of the New Company of Merchant Adventurers. Perhaps his most prestigious appointments were in the East India Company, where he achieved office as deputy governor (1624) and governor (1638). He also served as governor of the hardly less significant Eastland Company (from at least 1632). James I considered him suitable to fill the post of treasurer of the Virginia Company in May 1622, despite the fact that he initially failed to contribute towards the Palatine benevolence, but though he stood for election he was trounced by Henry Wriothesley, third earl of Southampton.

As a leading figure in the City, Clitherow was naturally involved in its government. At parish level he served as churchwarden of St Andrew Undershaft in 1612 and was one of the feoffees of the parish until at least 1617. He was a governor of Christ's Hospital by 1616, and was elected its president in 1637 after Sir Thomas Moulson declined to serve. A member of common council by 1623, he served as sheriff in 1625–6 and was admitted to the aldermanic bench in 1626. His promising career in City government was seemingly placed in jeopardy in February 1628, when his opposition to the forced loan prompted London's citizens to elect him to parliament in preference to the corporation's nominees, even though he had never served as mayor and was not then of knightly status. However, his commercial interests made him an ideal spokesman for the City's diverse mercantile interests. He had grown particularly concerned at the ailing Danish war effort and the concomitant increase in imperial power in the Baltic, and when on 26 March the secretary of state, Sir John Coke, advanced a fourteen-point plan for military action to bolster the Danes, Clitherow, who was in communication with Coke over Baltic affairs, offered his warm support. In his maiden speech, delivered on 4 April, he drew on his own experience of the Eastland and Muscovy trades to argue that nothing 'more nearly concerns us ... than ... the King of Denmark and the defence of the Baltic sea' (Johnson and others, 2.305). Though his claim that English merchants would be 'altogether confined to our own country' (ibid.) were the Baltic to fall into the hands of the holy Roman emperor was undoubtedly exaggerated, he correctly pointed out that maintaining access to the Baltic was vital for the continued supply of naval stores, such as pitch, tar, and cordage. It was therefore reasonable to suppose that, if the emperor succeeded in dominating the Baltic, 'he will master us all' (ibid., 2.300).

Perhaps Clitherow's most important speech to the house, because it touched on the interests and fears of every shipowning merchant and not just those trading to the Baltic, was delivered on 9 June. Speaking immediately after Moulson, his fellow member for London, Clitherow informed his listeners that 'I have been desired by the merchants of London to inform you of the miserable losses at sea' (Johnson and others, 4.200). He then proceeded to detail the loss of valuable shipping and cargoes to the Dunkirk privateers over the last few years, illustrating his case with the example of one vessel laden with masts worth £80,000 which had been recently captured. Complaining that the merchant marine was afforded inadequate protection, he also observed that the navy served only to worsen the situation by its heavy demands for mariners and ships. In view of all these difficulties, he added, it was hardly surprising that 'all merchants are disheartened' (ibid., 4.201). Despite the importance of Clitherow's contribution to the trade debate, he appears to have been added to the committee appointed to prepare a schedule of lost shipping only as an afterthought. This schedule was included in the remonstrance submitted by the house to Charles I on 17 June, but Clitherow was aware that action rather than mere words would be needed if commerce was not to suffer further depredations, and he was therefore dismayed to learn that the king intended to prorogue parliament. In his final speech to the house, delivered on 24 June, he asserted that 'Now is the time to think on trade', and he warned that, if parliament went into recess, 'I fear not a decay only but an utter extirpation' (ibid., 4.456). Parliament was powerless to act, however, and the war with Spain was not brought to an end until 1630.

Mercantile matters During the later 1620s and throughout the 1630s Clitherow and his fellow directors of the East India Company came under attack from a number of disgruntled shareholders for the losses sustained by the company. In the course of the 1628 parliament, Clitherow, who was the senior member of the company in the Commons, endeavoured to counter a petition presented by the aggrieved shareholders. He later proved a loyal ally of the governor, Sir Maurice Abbot, whom he replaced on the latter's resignation in 1638. He was appointed a royal commissioner in 1628 to collect the arrears owed by various City companies towards the cost of the Algiers expedition

of 1620–21, and was named a commissioner to raise contributions for the repair of St Paul's Cathedral in 1633. He served as lord mayor of London in 1635–6, and was knighted during his term of office (15 January 1636). A leading member of London's élite, he evidently entertained a low opinion of Charles I, and refused to admit one man to the Eastland Company despite the king's letter of recommendation. When the man's brother-in-law told Clitherow that Charles had promised to do the company a favour in return for the man's admission, Clitherow is said to have replied 'in an unseemly, slighting manner, that they all knew well enough what the king's good turns were when they came to seek them, or words to that effect' (CSP dom., 1637–8, 549–50). In January 1641 Clitherow, as governor of the East India Company, was bullied by Charles into ordering the withdrawal of a petition to parliament complaining of the activities of one of his favourites, Endymion Porter, whose associates had allegedly committed acts of piracy in the Red Sea in 1630. Despite the obvious strain in relations between Clitherow and the king, the former may have shared the latter's conservative religious leanings, as a Paul's Cross sermon was dedicated to Clitherow while lord mayor by the Arminian preacher John Gore in 1635. Moreover, during the mid-1630s Clitherow's daughter Rachel married one of the king's chaplains, Dr William *Paule, later bishop of Oxford. In 1668 the royalist writer David Lloyd recalled Clitherow as being 'a great stickler for the Church', and 'a great honourer of clergymen in the best of times, to whom some of his nearest relations were married in the worst'. It has been suggested that Clitherow was 'probably part of a ... London group of Arminian sympathisers' (Tyacke, 221) which included his brother-in-law and fellow aldermen Henry Garway and Anthony Abdy.

Clitherow drew up his will on 14 April 1640, died at his house in Pinner on 11 November 1641, and was buried seven days later at St Andrew Undershaft, where a monument was erected in his memory. Although he had at least seven sons, only his son James prevented the various branches of his family from becoming extinct in the male line. His daughter Judith married Thomas *Cory (d. 1656).

ANDREW THRUSH

Sources A. Thrush, 'Clitherow, Sir Christopher', HoP, Commons · Miscellanea Genealogica et Heraldica, 5th ser., 3 (1918–19), 170–71 · CSP col. · R. C. Johnson and others, eds., Proceedings in parliament, 1628, 2–4 (1977–8) · E. B. Sainsbury, ed., A calendar of the court minutes ... of the East India Company, [1–2]: 1635–43 (1907–9) · C. T. Carr, ed., Select charters of trading companies, AD 1530–1707, SeldS, 28 (1913) · K. R. Andrews, ed., English privateering voyages to the West Indies, 1585–1595, Hakluyt Society, 2nd ser., 111 (1959); repr. (1986), 50 · PRO, PROB 11/111, fols. 83–4 [father's will] · P. Croft, The Spanish Company, London RS, 9 (1973), 11 · R. Brenner, Merchants and revolution: commercial change, political conflict, and London's overseas traders, 1550–1653 (1993) · CSP dom., 1627–40 · V. Harding and P. Metcalf, Lloyd's at home (1986), 61 · grant book 2, Corporation of London, fols. 52v–53v · RCE sales book, 1628–31, Corporation of London · R. W. K. Hinton, The Eastland trade and the common weal in the seventeenth century (1959), 219 · PRO, SP28/162 [Robert Bateman's account] · The manuscripts of the Earl Cowper, 3 vols., HMC, 23 (1888–9), vol. 1, p. 331 · Ironmongers' Company minute books, GL, MS 16367, vols. 2 and

3 · admission to freedom of Ironmongers' Company, GL, MS 16978, fol. 48 · court minutes of Christ's Hospital, GL, MS 12806, vols. 3 and 4 · St Andrew Undershaft, miscellaneous book, GL, MS 4115 · St Andrew Undershaft, miscellaneous items, GL, MS 23737/13, nos. 13 and 17 · parish register, St Andrew Undershaft, GL, MS 4107/2 · GL, MS 25475/1, fol. 12 · D. Lloyd, *Memoires of the lives … of those … personages that suffered … for the protestant religion* (1668), 632 · S. M. Kingsbury, ed., *The records of the Virginia Company of London*, 1–3 (1906–33) · N. Tyacke, *Anti-Calvinists: the rise of English Arminianism, c.1590–1640* (1987) · PRO, SP14/127/48; SP14/156/14 [regarding 1622 benevolence] · A. Hughes, *List of sheriffs for England and Wales: from the earliest times to AD 1831*, PRO (1898); repr. (New York, 1963) · W. A. Shaw, *The knights of England*, 2 (1906), 205 · H. L. Hopkinson, *Report on the ancient records in the possession of the Guild of the Merchant Taylors* (1915), 117 [Clitherow's grandfather] · will, PRO, PROB 11/187, sig. 140

Archives GL, Ironmongers' Company records · GL, St Andrew Undershaft records

Likenesses M. Garrard, oils, *c*.1635; last known at Boston House, Brentford, Middx, 1903 · oils, Christ's Hospital, Horsham, West Sussex · portrait; Sothebys, 9 March 1988, lot 27 [see illus.]

Clitherow [*née* Middleton], **Margaret** [St Margaret Clitherow] (**1552/3–1586**), Roman Catholic martyr, was born in York, the youngest of the four children of Thomas Middleton (*d.* 1567), wax chandler and freeman of York, and his wife, Jane (*c*.1515–1585), daughter of Richard Turner, innkeeper. She was almost certainly baptized at the church of St Martin, Coney Street, where her father was churchwarden between 1555 and 1558. She was eighteen when she married John Clitherow, a widower with two sons, on 1 July 1571. Clitherow, a prosperous butcher who had become a freeman in 1560, was elected a chamberlain in 1574. Upon her marriage Margaret moved to the Shambles, the butchers' street in York, where she assisted her husband with his business. Although John Mush, the priest who wrote the biography which is the principal source for her life, described her as 'a plentiful mother' (Morris, 368), the number of children she had is unknown. In addition to her stepsons William (1563–1636) and Thomas (*d.* 1604) we know of Henry (*b.* 1572) and Anne (1574–1622). In 1576 she was reportedly pregnant, and in 1581 she was released from prison to give birth, but the names of these children and their survival are uncertain.

Margaret Clitherow's life changed immeasurably when she took the bold step of converting to Catholicism about 1574. She was apparently drawn towards the faith by stories of the heroic suffering of priests and lay people for their beliefs. Inspired by their example Margaret accommodated fugitive priests and provided her neighbours with facilities for regular access to the Catholic sacraments. The high incidence of recusancy in her parish of Christ Church during the 1570s and 1580s perhaps reflects her missionary success. Inevitably her actions drew official censure, and from 1576 John Clitherow incurred regular fines for her recusancy. He remained a protestant, and is said to have railed against Catholics when drunk at a banquet, upsetting his wife. He then tried to reassure Margaret that he was not referring to her, since she was a good wife in all but two things—her excessive fasting, and her refusal to go to church with him. Margaret was imprisoned several times for her nonconformist behaviour, serving three separate terms in York Castle (August 1577 – February 1578; October 1580 – April 1581; March 1583 – winter 1584). In prison she learned to read, and apparently relished the semi-monastic regime of prayer and physical deprivation that incarceration offered.

Despite this punishment and increasingly punitive anti-recusancy legislation, which in 1585 made harbouring clergy a capital felony, Margaret Clitherow maintained her activities. On 10 March 1586 the Clitherow premises were searched and a frightened child revealed the priests' secret room, replete with items of Catholic worship. The priest was safely hidden in the house next door, thus avoiding capture. Margaret was taken to prison and on 14 March appeared at the assizes, charged with harbouring. Although repeatedly asked to plead, she refused trial by jury, thereby incurring the penalty of *peine forte et dure*. During the next week she was visited by protestant preachers and kin, who in vain urged her to submit, or to admit that she was pregnant and thereby obtain a stay of execution. On 25 March 1586 Margaret was taken to the toll-booth on Ouse Bridge and pressed to death under 7 or 8 hundredweight. Six weeks later John Mush and other friends found her body and buried it in an unknown location in accordance with Catholic rites.

Margaret Clitherow maintained that she died for the Catholic faith, attributing her refusal to plead as a device to prevent her children and servants having to testify against her, and to protect the souls of the jury which would find her guilty. It is more likely that she wanted to shield other recusants who had assisted her, whose identity would inevitably have been revealed in her trial. However, her biographer affirmed that she was also attracted to martyrdom, which she believed would secure her salvation. Her apparent calm, even joy, at the prospect of death, led some contemporaries to suggest she was mad. Indeed she was not without her detractors, including her stepfather, Henry May, the lord mayor of York, who accused her of committing suicide, and fuelled rumours of an improper relationship with her confessor. Most people could not comprehend her apparent disregard for her husband and children. To counter such views she sent her hat to her husband in acknowledgement of his authority, and her hose and shoes to her daughter, Anne, as a signal that she should follow her mother's virtuous steps.

After Margaret's execution John Clitherow remarried, still a protestant. However, the children inherited their mother's recusant legacy. Anne Clitherow ran away from home and was imprisoned at Lancaster on account of her religion in 1593. She became a nun at St Ursula's in Louvain in 1598. Henry Clitherow studied at the English colleges in Rheims and Rome, and temporarily joined the Capuchins in 1592, then the Dominicans, dying either insane or unconvinced of his vocation. Of her stepsons, William became a seminary priest in 1608, and Thomas, a draper, was imprisoned for his recusancy, and died in Hull prison in 1604.

Margaret Clitherow was beatified in 1929 and canonized

on 25 October 1970 as one of the forty English martyrs. A relic, said to be her hand, is held at the Bar Convent in York. CLAIRE WALKER

Sources 'Mr John Mush's life of Margaret Clitherow', *The troubles of our Catholic forefathers related by themselves*, ed. J. Morris, 3 (1877), 333–440 · J. Mush, *An abstracte of the life and martirdome of mistres Margaret Clitherowe* (1619) · M. Claridge [K. Longley], *Margaret Clitherow, 1556?–1586* (1966); completely revised edn as K. Longley, *Saint Margaret Clitherow* (1986) · J. C. H. Aveling, *Catholic recusancy in the city of York, 1558–1791*, Catholic RS, monograph ser., 2 (1970) · K. M. Longley, 'The "trial" of Margaret Clitherow', *Ampleforth Journal*, 75 (1970), 335–64 · J. Wadham, 'Saint Margaret Clitherow: her "trial" on trial', *Ampleforth Journal*, 76 (1971), 9–22 · Gillow, *Lit. biog. hist.*, 1.517–19 · A. Hamilton, ed., *The chronicle of the English Augustinian canonesses regular of the Lateran*, 1 (1904), 22–3, 33–4, 119–20, 168 · G. Anstruther, *The seminary priests*, 2 (1975), 64 · R. Challoner, *Memoirs of missionary priests*, rev. edn (1924), 119–20 · H. J. Coleridge, *St Mary's Convent, Micklegate Bar, York* (1887), 384–5 · C. Cross, 'An Elizabethan martyrologist and his martyr: John Mush and Margaret Clitherow', *Martyrs and martyrologies*, ed. D. Wood, SCH, 30 (1993), 271–81

Likenesses illustration of martyrdom, repro. in R. Verstegan, *Theatrum crudelitatum haereticorum nostri temporis* (1587) · steel engraving (of Clitherow?), repro. in Longley, 'The "trial" of Margaret Clitherow', 334

Clive [*née* Wigley; *later* Meysey-Wigley], **Caroline** [*known as* Mrs Archer Clive; *pseud.* V.] (**1801–1873**), novelist and poet, born at Brompton, London, on 30 June 1801, was the second daughter of Edmund Wigley (1758–1821)—who later changed his surname to Meysey-Wigley—barrister and, for a short time, MP, and his wife, Anna Maria Meysey (*d.* 1835), the daughter and heir of Charles Watkins Meysey. She was brought up at Shakenhurst in Worcestershire, the home which her mother had inherited. At the age of two she contracted a disease, possibly poliomyelitis, which left her permanently disabled. She was educated by governesses, and after the deaths of her brother Edmund and her mother she became a wealthy heir. On 10 November 1840 she married the Revd Archer Clive, rector of Solihull, near Birmingham, the second son of Edward Bolton Clive MP. She had been in love with him for nine years and had lived alone at Solihull for five years in order to be near him. They had two children: a son, Charles Meysey Bolton, and a daughter, Alice. In 1845, following the death of his father, Archer Clive inherited Whitfield, the family estate in Herefordshire, and in 1847 he took his family to live there.

Caroline Clive's first book, a slim volume of religious meditations entitled *Essays on the Human Intellect as Constructed by God …*, had been published in 1827 under the pseudonym Paul Ferrol. Earlier, signing herself George Ferrol and P. Ferrol, she had sent poems first to Isaac D'Israeli, then to the philosopher Dugald Stewart, who passed them on to the poet Thomas Campbell. Campbell's response was encouraging, but it was not until 1840, a few months before her marriage, that her first book of verse, *IX Poems by V.*, made its appearance. Appreciatively noticed by Henry Nelson Coleridge in 'Modern English poetesses', an article in the *Quarterly Review* (September 1840), as well as by other reviewers, the book established her reputation

as one of the leading female poets of the day. A second edition, with nine additional poems, came out in 1841. Most of the poems are conventional late Romantic lyrics, gloomy and graceful, but George Saintsbury, in *A History of Nineteenth Century Literature* (1876), which remained in print until well into the twentieth century, remembered them as 'really good' (Saintsbury, 310). Over the next twelve years she had five long poems published, as well as *Saint Oldooman: a Myth of the Nineteenth Century* (1845), a prose satire on Newman's *Lives of the Saints*. The best and most admired of the poems was *The Queen's Ball: a Poem by V.* (1847), based on a report that 150 dead people had been invited to a ball given by Queen Victoria; the poem contains a few good lines and many poor ones. 'V.', the pseudonym which Clive adopted for nearly all her poetic works, was short for Vigolina, Archer Clive's dog-Latin translation of Wigley, her maiden name. In 1847 she met both Mary Russell Mitford and Elizabeth Barrett Browning but was not impressed with either; Browning spoke slightingly of Clive's poetry and personality.

Clive's minor celebrity as a poet was spectacularly eclipsed by the fame and notoriety resulting from her first novel, *Paul Ferroll: a Tale by the Author of 'IX Poems by V.'*, published in 1855. A forerunner of the sensation novel, it shocked many readers by its apparent amorality. The eponymous hero not only murders his first wife without any perceptible qualms of conscience but also shoots down a rioting workman in cold blood; yet his doting daughter from his marriage to his second wife does not recoil from him when she hears of the murder of the first, and the author herself, in describing the two killings, shows no sign of repugnance towards the killer. Clive was perhaps trying to imitate the 'cynicism' of Balzac, whose novels she read avidly; the fact that she had on several earlier occasions used Ferroll or Ferrol as her *nom de plume* suggests that she identified closely with the hero of her novel, just as Balzac identified with his character Vautrin. In both *Paul Ferroll* itself and its sequel, *Why Paul Ferroll Killed his Wife* (1860), the hero is even credited with the authorship of well-known poems by Clive herself. *Paul Ferroll* was translated into French twice, in 1858 and 1859, and into Russian in 1859. *Why Paul Ferroll Killed his Wife*, probably written partly in the hope of appeasing readers who had been scandalized by *Paul Ferroll* itself, explains that just before he murdered her Ferroll had found out that his first wife had tricked him into marrying her by telling him, falsely, that the woman he really loved—who later became his second wife—had gone off with another man. Clive's only other published works of fiction, *Year after Year: a Tale* (1858) and *John Greswold* (1864), aroused much less interest than *Paul Ferroll* and its sequel. Collections of her poems were issued in 1856 and 1872; after her death a further collection appeared in 1890, with an introduction by her daughter Alice Greathead.

Accidents in 1860 and 1863 left Clive permanently confined to a wheelchair, and in 1865 she suffered a stroke. She died on 14 July 1873 from injuries received two days before when her dress caught fire in her library at Whitfield. She was survived by her husband. New editions of *IX*

Poems by V. and *Paul Ferroll* were published in 1928 and 1929, both with introductions by Eric Partridge. *Paul Ferroll* was reissued in the Oxford Popular Fiction series in 1997, with an introduction by Charlotte Mitchell.

P. D. Edwards

Sources *Caroline Clive: from the diary and family papers of Mrs Archer Clive, 1801–1873*, ed. M. Clive (1949) · C. Mitchell, 'Introduction', in C. Clive, *Paul Ferroll* (1997) · [H. N. Coleridge], 'Modern English poetesses', *QR*, 66 (1840), 374–418 [review] · G. Saintsbury, *A history of nineteenth century literature, 1780–1895* (1910) · M. R. Mitford, *Recollections of a literary life*, 3 vols. (1852) · *The letters of Elizabeth Barrett Browning to Mary Russell Mitford, 1836–1854*, ed. M. B. Raymond and M. R. Sullivan, 2 (1983) · *CGPLA Eng. & Wales* (1874) · d. cert.
Archives priv. coll., diaries and family MSS · Shakespeare Birthplace Trust RO, Stratford upon Avon, legal documents · Solihull Central Library, diaries kept jointly with her husband [microfilm] | Worcs. RO, Shakenhurst MSS
Wealth at death under £300: resworn probate, 15 June 1874, *CGPLA Eng. & Wales*

Clive [née Raftor]**, Catherine** [Kitty] (**1711–1785**), actress, was born on 5 November 1711, according to a letter she wrote to a fellow actress, Jane Pope, in 1782. According to William Chetwood's *General History of the Stage* (1749), Clive was the daughter of William Raftor, a Kilkenny lawyer of considerable estate who ruined his fortunes by aligning himself with James II during the latter's campaign in Ireland in 1690. After a period of exile, he was pardoned and returned to London to marry a Mrs Daniel, 'Daughter to an eminent Citizen on Fishstreethill with whom he had a handsome Fortune' (Chetwood, 126). Chetwood further claims that the couple had numerous children, but the names of these brothers and sisters are unknown, except for James (d. 1790), who joined Kitty in a stage career, and a sister whose married name was Mrs Mestivyer. There is evidence that Kitty Clive supported her father once she was working, so whatever handsome fortune was in place when her parents married evidently dwindled over time.

Early career Chetwood also tells the story of the actress's advent to the stage in 1728, when he was serving as prompter at Drury Lane. A friend of Jane Johnson, the first wife of Theophilus Cibber, Kitty was introduced to both Cibber and Chetwood. They, in turn, impressed with her 'infinite Spirits, with a Voice and Manner in singing Songs of Pleasantry peculiar to herself' (Chetwood, 127), recommended her to Colley Cibber, who added her to his list of performers at Drury Lane. Chetwood indicates that she had a few minor appearances in the spring of 1728, but once the full 1728–9 season opened she began appearing regularly in increasingly large and important roles. Throughout that season and those that followed she moved from supporting roles in tragedy to singing in afterpieces and playing the first-ranking characters in the farces popular in the period.

The fashion of musical comedy and burlesque suited Kitty's vocal and comic talents perfectly, and she shone in parts such as Nell in Charles Coffey's *The Devil to Pay*, in which she portrayed a cobbler's wife transformed into the lady of the manor. Henry Fielding wrote several parts for her that highlighted her skills, including Chloe in *The Lottery* and Lappet in an adaptation of Molière's *The Miser*. In

Catherine Clive (1711–1785), by Jeremiah Davison, 1735

the summer of 1732 she was given the most sought-after female role in musical comedy, Polly in John Gay's *The Beggar's Opera*, and received a tribute to her portrayal from the *Daily Journal*, which called her the 'Darling of the Age' (25 July 1732).

During the rebellion of the players in 1733, Kitty remained with John Highmore's company at Drury Lane. One of the most popular actresses to do so, she earned the ire of hack writers who supported the alternative company at the Haymarket. Their squibs provide some insight into her character and to the position she had attained on stage. *The Theatric Squabble* (1733) described her as:

> A pleasing Actress, but a Green-Room Scold
> Puffed with Success, she triumphs over all
> Snarls in the Scene-Room, Curses in the Hall.

Henry Fielding, who also remained loyal to Drury Lane, praised her acting talents and the alternative view of her character. In his preface to *The Intriguing Chambermaid* (1734), in which she played the title role, he compliments her as 'the best Wife, the best Daughter, the best Sister, and the best Friend' (Fielding). Although to some degree both descriptions are coloured by their authors' intentions, they do indicate the personality traits and acting skills which would remain consistent throughout her long career. Kitty Clive was both quick-witted and quick-tempered. She would prove a generous friend but a dangerous enemy. She maintained a reputation for chastity in her personal life, yet she sparkled on stage when 'personating the foolish and vitious' (Fielding) of her sex. Her best roles were particular comic types: the silly country miss, the wiser and more fashionable version of the same, and the pert and resourceful servant. These remained her strong suit for much of her career.

Marriage and the 'Polly war' Few details are known about Catherine Raftor's marriage to George Clive (d. 1780), a barrister and second cousin to Robert Clive 'of India', but she appeared as Mrs Clive in the bills for the first time in October 1733. The name change suggests that the pair had just married or had done so during the summer, when she would not have been performing regularly. Evidence about the couple's married life is also slight, but the two did not live together for very long, separating some time in 1735. Chetwood, ostensibly declining to comment on marital affairs, declares, 'I never could imagine she deserved ill Usage' (Chetwood, 128), implying that was just what she received. Years later, in a letter to David Garrick, Clive herself commented, 'You are very much mistaken if you imagine I shall be sorry to hear Mr. Clive is well; besides, it is so long ago since I thought he used me ill, that I have quite forgot it' (Highfill, Burnim & Langhans, *BDA*). George Clive was less forgiving and, in his will, made a point of excluding her from any benefit at his death, 'it being my will and intention that she have nothing to do with my executors & representatives nor they with her' (ibid.).

Although Clive herself did not contribute to the pamphlet war during the theatrical rebellion of 1733, in 1736 she had reason to believe that the acting manager, Theophilus Cibber, was trying to claim some of her roles for his second wife, Susannah. Clive published her side of the controversy in the press in order to defend her position on the stage. The question of which actress was to play Polly in *The Beggar's Opera* provoked a storm in the papers, and the dispute received regular mention in the *Daily Gazetteer*, *London Evening-Post*, *Grub Street Journal*, and *London Daily Post and General Advertiser*. This 'Polly war' also inspired a farce, *The Beggar's Pantomime, or, Contending Columbines*, which was performed regularly at Lincoln's Inn Fields. Given its long run, the afterpiece probably made more money for its producers than the original's limited revival at Drury Lane, regardless of who played Polly.

It seems likely that Theophilus Cibber, a notorious puffer, was behind some of the attacks against Clive, who, by 1736, was a well-established comic actress and vocalist. At the same time she did not shy away from defending herself in print and on the stage:

> It is my consolation to think, that as I have always endeavor'd to please them [the town] as an Actress, to the best of my Abilities, whatever has been urged to the contrary by the Malice of my Enemies, will have no weight or Influence upon my Friends. (*London Daily Post and General Advertiser*, 19 Nov 1736)

When Clive's appearance as Polly was finally presented, she addressed herself to the house, apologizing for the disturbance and offering to play the secondary part of Lucy instead. This apologetic tone and willingness to appease her audience secured both her popularity and the role of Polly until she herself was ready to bestow it on a younger actress of her own choosing in 1745.

Although publicly Clive decried and apparently regretted bringing theatrical matters notoriety in the press, the lesson she learned during the Polly war served her well in 1744. After the failure of Charles Macklin and David Garrick to open a third theatre to break the monopoly held by the patentees, Clive found herself unemployed. Rather than relying on others to defend her position and livelihood, that October she printed a pamphlet, *The Case of Mrs. Clive Submitted to the Publick*, explaining her position and that of other performers. Particularly galling to her was the loss of her annual free benefit, a privilege she had held for nine years, and how she discovered her lack of a job—by finding other actresses listed in her roles in the bills. This 'unprecedented Act of Injustice' (*The Case of Mrs. Clive*, 14) did not allow her the time to find work in Dublin, where she had met with success during the summer of 1741. Following the publication of her pamphlet, Clive held a benefit concert at the Haymarket on 2 November by command of Frederick, prince of Wales, and Augusta, princess of Wales. The royal couple had commanded Clive's benefits in the past, and their continued patronage of her expressed their personal dismay at the lord chamberlain's ruling in favour of the patentees. Theophilus Cibber confirmed that the audience at the benefit had been a notable one, by describing the affair as having 'many Persons of the first Distinction ... in the Pit and Boxes' (Cibber, 76). The manager, John Rich, no fool, recognized Clive's drawing power, and rehired her the next month at Drury Lane, although not at the salary level she had previously attained. As in the Polly war, Clive found that humble approaches to the theatregoing public could push theatrical management to some semblance of civility towards players. At the same time there was some cost to her reputation, and she maintained the dubious distinction of being a demanding and even temperamental actress. Samuel Foote best described the equivocal nature of her character and defended her actions: 'This lady has now and then perhaps ... expressed herself behind the Scenes in too loud and forcible a Manner ... But ... this Vehemence is assumed in order to procure a more decent Entertainment' (Foote, 42–3).

Stability Once David Garrick attained the patent for Drury Lane in 1747, Clive's career settled down considerably. Printed appeals to the public were no longer necessary, except for a skirmish with the actor Ned Shuter over benefit performances in 1761. She continued to shine in her best venue, the stage. She retained many of the parts that she had made famous, including Nell in *The Devil to Pay*, but moved out of *ingénue* roles into those more suited to her maturing voice and figure. Flora in Susanna Centlivre's *The Wonder*, Mrs Cadwallader in Foote's *The Author*, the Fine Lady in Garrick's *Lethe*, and Lady Wishfort in William Congreve's *The Way of the World* were typical of these later roles. Comedy remained her forte, but she also continued her facility in speaking prologues and epilogues. Garrick was especially proficient at presenting aspects of her reputation in these short speeches, which provoked the audience to laughter. During the competition between

Drury Lane and Covent Garden over *Romeo and Juliet*, Garrick wrote an epilogue for Clive, although she held no role in the production; 'What! All these janglings and I not make one!' highlighted her irascible reputation and was typical of these short pieces in which the actress essentially played herself. Clive's comic opera song, in which she made fun of Italian singers and their exorbitant salaries, continued to please audiences. Although she was never successful in tragedy, her Portia in *The Merchant of Venice*, in which she imitated the speech and mannerisms of the lord chief justice, William Murray, Baron Mansfield, was popular with audiences but disdained by critics.

A dedicated performer, and one with full appreciation for the transience of theatrical life, Clive continued to seek new roles for herself and new ways to supplement her income. She tried her hand at writing farces, which became a feature of her benefits. Her first, *The Rehearsal, or, Bays in Petticoats*, was first presented at her benefit in 1750. There were scattered additional performances, and it was eventually published in 1753. Clive wrote at least three more farces, *Every Woman in her Humour*, *A Fine Lady's Return from a Rout*, and *The Faithful Irishwoman*, but none received even the limited fame that her first had done and none was published. Indeed, the second of these was rebuked in the *Theatrical Review* as 'Vile!' and 'Execrable!' (*Theatrical Review*, 146) after its presentation in April 1763. These farces survive in manuscript at the Huntington Library, San Marino, California.

Throughout her long career Clive remained a London actress, and except for the two seasons at Covent Garden (1743–5) she was loyal to Drury Lane. However, at some point in the 1740s it is apparent that she moved her primary residence to Twickenham and lived in lodgings in London during the theatrical season. In that small community, she and Horace Walpole became close friends. In 1749 she wrote to him requesting advice about a gardener, 'for th'o I am now representing women of qualitty and Coblers wives &c &c to Crowded houeses, and flattering applause; the Charecture I am most desierous to act well is; a good sort of Countrey gentlewoman at twickenham' (Walpole, *Corr.*, 40.61). Soon afterwards she had become a visible and cheering presence in his correspondence, and he gave her a small house on his property. Reading through the correspondence makes it clear that Walpole and Clive developed a strong, enduring, and almost certainly platonic friendship. He evidently relished her company and her insight into the theatrical world, while she enjoyed the amusing variety of company, their conversation, and the card games central to his social circles. There are jokes about the ruddiness of her complexion—which also received notice in theatrical gossip—and compliments to her good nature and good humour. Their relationship was misinterpreted in a *Town and Country Magazine* tête-à-tête in December 1769, much to Walpole's amusement. His friends such as Etheldreda, Viscountess Townshend, Isabella Seymour-Conway, countess of Hertford, and Lady Anne Connolly included the actress on an excursion to see George III's coronation, while George

Montagu's Christmas gift of venison left her 'up to her elbows in currant jelly and gratitude' (Walpole, *Corr.*, 10.241). Through Walpole, but because of her vibrant personality, Clive successfully moved into a social milieu that transcended the purely theatrical.

Retirement In 1768 Walpole mentioned to a friend that Clive was preparing to leave the stage, and the bill for her benefit in April 1769 advertised that it would be the 'last time of her appearing on the Stage' (Stone, 3.1401). She performed some of her favourite roles: Flora in *The Wonder* and the Fine Lady in *Lethe*. After more than forty successful years on the stage, Clive had earned enough to support herself comfortably in her retirement. In her published *Case* in 1744 she revealed that she had been making £300 annually, plus her benefit, which in her most successful years could almost double that salary—in 1750, for example, her benefit brought her just over £250. In 1765, in a letter to David Garrick, she commented that her salary remained £300 a year. Although much of her income would have gone to support her professional life (she spent considerable sums on singing lessons and appropriate clothes) she had evidently managed her money wisely. Her pay places her among the very best actresses of her generation, although she would complain that her tragic counterparts such as Susannah Cibber earned twice as much for working fewer nights in the theatrical week. Still, both her income and the popularity she achieved over her long career prove her star quality and her comic ability. She was easily one of the most talented and most famous actresses of her generation.

Her own correspondence, along with that of Walpole and David Garrick, reveals Clive's retirement to have been carefree, except for bouts of illness and occasional trouble from footpads and tax collectors. Her brother James and sister lived with her, and were, according to Jane Pope, supported by her. She busied herself with 'Routs either at home or abroad every night [and] all the nonsense of having my hair done time enough for my parties as I used to do for my parts with the difference that I am losing money instead of getting some' (Highfill, Burnim & Langhans, *BDA*). Her periods of illness—self-described jaundice—eventually grew more frequent, and after catching a chill at the funeral of Lieutenant-General Henry Lister, she died on 6 December 1785. She was buried in Twickenham churchyard on 14 December. Horace Walpole dispersed her personal possessions among her friends and relatives.

K. A. CROUCH

Sources Highfill, Burnim & Langhans, *BDA* • W. R. Chetwood, *A general history of the stage, from its origin in Greece to the present time* (1749) • *The case of Mrs. Clive submitted to the publick* (1744) • C. Clive, letters, Folger • Walpole, *Corr.* • *The private correspondence of David Garrick*, ed. J. Boaden, 2 vols. (1831–2) • *The letters of David Garrick*, ed. D. M. Little and G. M. Kahrl, 3 vols. (1963) • H. Fielding, 'An epistle to Mrs Clive', *The intriguing chambermaid* (1734) [preface] • S. Foote, *Roman and English comedy considered* (1747) • *London Daily Post and General Advertiser* (13 Nov 1736) • T. Cibber, 'Romeo and Juliet', a tragedy, revis'd and alter'd from Shakespear … to which is added, 'A serio comic apology, for part of the life of Mr. Theophilus Cibber' [1748] • Mr Lun, jun. [H. Woodward], *Beggars pantomime, or, Contending Columbines: a new comic interlude* (1736) • D. Garrick, 'An epilogue spoken by Mrs Clive', *GM*, 1st ser., 20 (1750), 472 · *Town and Country Magazine*, 1 (1769) · F. Gentleman, *The dramatic censor*, 2 vols. (1770) · *Theatrical examiner: an inquiry into merits and de merits of English performers in general* (1757) · *The old maid* (1755–6) · *Theatrical Review, or, Annals of Drama* (1763) · G. W. Stone, ed., *The London stage, 1660–1800*, pt 4: *1747–1776* (1962)

Archives Folger, letters | Bodl. Oxf., letters to Jane Pope · V&A NAL, corresp. with David Garrick

Likenesses P. van Bleeck, painting and engraving, 1735 (as Philida) · J. Davison, oils, 1735, Longleat House, Wiltshire [*see illus.*] · W. Verelst, oils, 1740, Garr. Club · J. Brooks, miniature engraving, 1750 · C. Mosley, engraving, 1750 (after van Bleeck), Harvard TC · A. van Haecken, engraving (after J. Van Haecken), Harvard TC · sometimes attrib. Hogarth, oils (as the Fine Lady in *Lethe*), Garr. Club · attrib. J. Richardson, oils, NG Ire.

Wealth at death personal possessions dispersed among her friends and relatives: Walpole, *Corr.*

Clive, Sir Edward (1704–1771), judge, was the eldest son of Edward Clive of Wormbridge, Herefordshire, and Aldermanbury, London, and his wife, Sarah Key, daughter of a Bristol merchant. He was admitted to Lincoln's Inn in 1719, and to University College, Oxford, in 1722, and was called to the bar by the former in 1725. His first legal appointment seems to have been as steward of Newcastle under Lyme in 1724, a position which he held until 1740. In 1741 he became deputy justice of Carmarthen, and member of parliament for Mitchell, Cornwall, in the interest of Thomas Scawen. He remained in parliament until his appointment to the bench in 1745.

During this period he sought a patent of precedence from Lord Hardwicke, without success, and he made a similar unavailing application through John Carteret, Earl Granville, with the support of Chief Justice Willes. Nevertheless, in 1745 on Hardwicke's recommendation he was appointed a baron of the exchequer, in place of Sir Laurence Carter, and in 1753 succeeded Sir Thomas Burnet as a puisne justice of the common pleas, whereupon he was knighted. In 1761 he suggested to Hardwicke that Chief Baron Parker should succeed Sir John Willes as chief justice of the common pleas, and that he might himself succeed Parker, with the explanation that 'The honour, and the ease in point of spring circuits are the temptations to me, as I am now on the worst side fifty years of age, tho' I thank God not yet sensible of any great infirmities' (BL, Add. MS 35596, fol. 92). This proposed arrangement was not, however, adopted.

In 1745 Clive married Elizabeth, daughter of Richard Symons of Mynde Park, Herefordshire. Elizabeth died in 1762, and the following year he married Judith, daughter of his cousin, the Revd Benjamin Clive; she died in 1796 at Wormbridge. There were no children from either marriage.

Clive retired from the bench in February 1770 with a pension of £1200 a year, and was replaced by Sir William Blackstone. He died the following year, on 16 April 1771. He has been identified as the subject of one of the cruel caricatures in William Hogarth's sketch *The Bench*, which was engraved in 1758, though this is open to considerable doubt. Clive had a London residence in Ormond Street.

After his death his Wormbridge residence passed to the great-grandson of Clive's eldest uncle, Robert Clive, and remained in the family until recent times.

J. H. BAKER

Sources E. Cruickshanks, 'Clive, Edward', HoP, *Commons, 1715–54* · BL, Yorke correspondence, Add. MSS 35587, fols. 21, 25; 35588, fol. 47; 35596, fol. 92 · H. Walpole, *The memoirs of the reign of George III*, 1 (1847), 189 · W. Musgrave, *Obituary prior to 1800*, ed. G. J. Armytage, 1, Harleian Society, 44 (1899) · Sainty, *Judges* · *GM*, 1st ser., 41 (1771), 239 · Baker, *Serjeants* · Foster, *Alum. Oxon.* · W. R. Williams, *The history of the great sessions in Wales, 1542–1830* (privately printed, Brecon, 1899)

Likenesses W. Hogarth, caricature, engraving, 1758, FM Cam.

Clive, Edward, first earl of Powis (1754–1839), administrator in India, was born in Queen Square, London, on 7 March 1754, the first of the four surviving children of Robert *Clive, first Baron Clive of Plassey (1725–1774), and his wife, Margaret *Clive (1735–1817), daughter of Edmund Maskelyne of Purton, Wiltshire. He was educated at Eton College between 1762 and 1770 and matriculated at Christ Church, Oxford, on 28 February 1771. His education was completed by a period spent in Geneva with a tutor.

The death of his father in November 1774 meant that Clive inherited a significant territorial and political presence in Shropshire and the border counties. The wealth acquired by Robert Clive as a result of his activities in India had been used to purchase estates and electoral power. In particular, Clive's influence had eclipsed that of Henry Arthur Herbert (c.1703–1772), who had been created earl of Powis (second creation) in 1748. Herbert had inherited the estates of the marquesses of Powis, which included property in Shropshire and Montgomeryshire, and had acquired political influence in the region. Relations between the Clive and Herbert families, which had been shaped by political and financial considerations, were cemented on 7 May 1784, when Edward Clive married Lady Henrietta Antonia Herbert (1758–1830), daughter of the earl of Powis.

Clive was MP for Ludlow between 1774 and 1794, served as lord lieutenant of Shropshire from 1775 to 1798 and from 1804 to 1839 and of Montgomeryshire between 1804 and 1830, and was recorder of Shrewsbury and Ludlow. In the House of Commons he supported the North administration and, following the dismissal of the Fox–North coalition in 1783, he went into opposition. He was, however, anxious to improve upon the Irish title given to his father and therefore transferred his support to Pitt. He was rewarded with the creation of a British peerage (Baron Clive of Walcot) in 1794.

Although Clive's experience of public office at the national level had been limited to his appointment in 1793 to the board of agriculture, he was appointed to the governorship of Madras in 1797 and took up the post in August 1798. The appointment seems to have owed much to Clive's need for additional income and to the Clive family's connection with India. Arthur Wellesley described him at this time as a 'mild, moderate man, remarkably reserved, having a bad delivery, and apparently a heavy understanding' (Archer, 25). Shortly after his arrival Clive was involved in preparations for the attack upon Tipu Sultan of Mysore, which culminated in the successful assault on Seringapatam in May 1799. The resulting settlement of Mysore greatly extended British influence in the region, and during the remaining years of his governorship Clive continued to provide able support for the policy of consolidation and expansion of the British position in south India which was promoted by the governor-general, Lord Wellesley. The East India Company took over the administration of Tanjore in 1799 and that of the territories of the nawab of Arcot in 1801; in 1803 a decisive victory was won over Maratha forces at Assaye. Clive resigned his governorship, which appears to have been conducted very much under Wellesley's aegis, in August 1803, although he had almost done so earlier on account of a perception that he had lost the confidence of the directors of the company.

On his return to England Clive was able to add the numerous Indian curiosities that he and Lady Clive had acquired to the collection formed by his father. Clive and his wife shared an interest in natural history and collected animals, seeds, and plants. The death of Lady Clive's unmarried brother, the earl of Powis, in 1801 without an heir further strengthened the union of the Clive and Herbert families, since the Powis estates passed to Clive's eldest son, who in 1807 took the name of Herbert instead of Clive. On 14 May 1804 Clive was created earl of Powis of the third creation.

Although nominated as lord lieutenant of Ireland in 1805, Clive did not take up the post. He died at his home, 45 Berkeley Square, London, on 16 May 1839, and was buried at Bromfield, Shropshire, nine days later. His wife having died in 1830, he left two sons, including Edward *Herbert, second earl of Powis, and one daughter. Another daughter predeceased him.   D. L. PRIOR

Sources BL OIOC, Clive MSS, MS Eur. G 37 · BL OIOC, Sutton Court MSS, MS Eur. F 128 · BL, Powis MSS · BL, Wellesley MSS · East India Company records, BL OIOC · HoP, *Commons, 1754–90* · HoP, *Commons, 1790–1820* · M. Bence-Jones, *Clive of India* (1974) · M. Archer, *Treasures from India: the Clive collection at Powis Castle* (1987) · GEC, *Peerage*
Archives BL OIOC, corresp. and papers relating to India, MS Eur. G 37 · NL Wales, corresp. · NL Wales, corresp. and papers · Powis Castle, Montgomeryshire, collection of Indian curiosities · Shrops. RRC, corresp. and papers, SRO 552 | BL, letters to Lady Powis, Add. MS 64105 · BL, corresp. with Lord Wellesley, Add. MSS 13621–13628, 37280–37310 · BL OIOC, Sutton Court collection, corresp. with Sir Henry Strachey, MS Eur. F 128 · Bucks. RLSS, corresp. with Lord Hobart · Devon RO, corresp. with Lord Sidmouth · PRO, letters to John Ashby, C109
Likenesses T. Gainsborough, oils, c.1763, Powis Castle, Montgomeryshire · H. D. Hamilton, pastels, 1788, Powis Castle, Montgomeryshire · ivory miniature, c.1800, Powis Castle, Montgomeryshire · vellum miniature, c.1800, Powis Castle, Montgomeryshire · W. Hoare, oils, Eton · R. B. Parkes, mezzotint (after T. Gainsborough), BM, NPG

Clive [née Maskelyne], Margaret, Lady Clive of Plassey (1735–1817), society figure, was born on 24 October 1735 at Kensington Gore in London, the fourth of the four children of Edmund Maskelyne (1698–1744), a civil servant, and his wife, Elizabeth, née Booth (d. 1748). After the death of her mother Margaret lived with relatives in Wiltshire and attended the school run by Mrs Saintsbury at Cirencester in 1749. The Maskelyne family pursued a number of scholarly endeavours, and Margaret's brother Nevil *Maskelyne later became astronomer royal. From an early age Margaret herself developed a close interest in astronomy, music, and poetry, and at school she became proficient in the French language. The Maskelyne family also had strong connections with the East India Company, and by the late 1740s Margaret's brother Edmund was stationed at Madras, where he became a close friend of Robert *Clive (1725–1774). In 1751 Edmund encouraged Margaret to sail to India after Clive, according to legend, had become captivated by her beauty as represented in a miniature portrait. By the time Margaret arrived in India in 1752, Clive had become a military hero and, after a six-month courtship, the couple were married at Madras on 18 February 1753. A month later Margaret and her new husband sailed for Britain.

The course of the Clives' marriage was determined by two further periods of service undertaken by Robert in India. On the first occasion, between 1755 and 1760, Robert was accompanied by Margaret, who gave him devoted and affectionate company as he established the British military and political position in Bengal. The Clives returned to Britain in 1760, fabulously wealthy and much envied. In spite of Robert's best efforts, however, the Clives were not fully accepted into polite society, which was deeply suspicious of the new wealth accumulated by company 'nabobs'. Their time together was often devoted to music and they were regular attenders at concerts and operatic events. When Robert, now Baron Clive of Plassey, was reappointed as governor of Bengal in 1764, Margaret, who was pregnant, stayed in Britain. She spent much of her time at a rented house at Westcombe, near Blackheath, Kent, where she kept a small circle of friends around her, but she also played an active role in supervising her husband's political and financial affairs. Although she lived a quiet life, devoting much attention to astronomy, music, and the learning of Italian to improve her understanding of opera, Margaret maintained a public profile when it was necessary to sustain Robert's political ambitions. She attended court in 1765, and in the same year she organized a remarkable soirée at the Clive home in Berkeley Square, where the young Mozarts, then visiting London, appeared with the popular Italian castrato Manzuoli.

Robert Clive returned to Britain in 1767. Margaret then accompanied him to France for an eight-month visit the following year as he endeavoured to recover from a bout of depressive illness. Clive was also now beset by political problems, and over the next five years he was forced to defend his reputation and private fortune. Margaret remained in the background, content with the company of her four children and several close companions. Robert's actions in India were subjected to searching parliamentary inquiry in 1772–3, but he eventually escaped with his honour intact. He died unexpectedly in November 1774, having suffered a seizure after taking a large dose of opium to relieve acute discomfort caused by illness. Margaret recovered from the shock of this devastating tragedy and picked up the threads of a quiet, almost reclusive existence. She lived out the rest of her life at Oakly Park, one of the Clive family homes in Shropshire, where she followed her hobbies surrounded by her extensive collections of telescopes, globes, and cats. Her interest in Anglo-Indian affairs was renewed in 1797, when Edward *Clive, first earl of Powis (1754–1839), the eldest of her children, was appointed governor of Madras. She died at Oakly Park on 28 December 1817. H. V. BOWEN

Sources BL OIOC, MS photo. Eur. 287 [two boxes of photocopied correspondence owned by Mr N. Arnold-Foster of Basset Down, Wiltshire] · BL OIOC, Clive MSS, MS Eur. G 37 · NL Wales, Powis 1990 deposit [esp. box 1, letters to Lady Clive] · M. Bence-Jones, *Clive of India* (1974) · I. Woodfield, 'New light on the Mozarts' London visit', *Music and Letters*, 76 (1995), 187–208 · *GM*, 1st ser., 87/2 (1817), 633
Archives BL OIOC, collection, MS Eur. G 37 · BL OIOC, corresp., MS photo. Eur. 287 | BL OIOC, Ormathwaite collection, corresp., MS Eur. D 546 · BL OIOC, Sutton Court collection, corresp., MS Eur. F 128 · NL Wales, corresp., Powis 1990 deposit
Likenesses N. Dance, portrait, c.1770, Powis Castle, Montgomeryshire · N. Dance, portrait, c.1770, Basset Down, Wiltshire · W. Owen, oils, Powis Castle, Montgomeryshire · W. Owen, oils, Oakly Park, Shropshire · W. Owen, oils (after portrait), Basset Down, Wiltshire · miniature, Powis Castle, Montgomeryshire

Clive, Robert, first Baron Clive of Plassey (1725–1774), army officer in the East India Company and governor of Bengal, was born on 29 September 1725 at Styche Hall, Moreton Say, near Market Drayton in Shropshire, the eldest of the thirteen children of Richard Clive (c.1693–1771), lawyer and MP, and his wife, Rebecca, daughter of Nathaniel Gaskell of Manchester.

Early years and education, 1725–1743 Although his family had been long established as members of the Shropshire gentry, Clive experienced a somewhat peripatetic childhood and he spent much time away from his parents, who were struggling to cope with a large number of children. Between the ages of three and seven he lived with his aunt and uncle, Elizabeth (d. 1735) and Nathaniel Bayley, of Hope Hall, Eccles, Lancashire. He then attended a series of schools and educational establishments around the country: Dr Eaton's at Bostock, Cheshire; the grammar school at Market Drayton; Merchant Taylors' School, London (1737–9); and finally Mr Sterling's at Hemel Hempstead, Hertfordshire (1739), where he learned bookkeeping procedures. Clive was no more than an average scholar, and contemporary reports suggest that he was a boisterous and at times aggressive child who engaged in a wide range of adventurous pursuits. As early as 1728 Nathaniel Bayley reported that Clive was 'out of measure addicted' to fighting, and in his dealings with his five-year-old nephew he was endeavouring to 'suppress the hero, that I may help forward the more valuable qualities of meekness, benevolence, and patience' (Malcolm, 1.33). Clive's youthful activities and feats of daring in Market Drayton, most notably his climbing of the local church tower, earned him a certain amount of notoriety which in later years gave rise to a number of colourful local myths and legends about his

Robert Clive, first Baron Clive of Plassey (1725–1774), by Nathaniel Dance, c.1770

adolescent behaviour. No doubt by nature and temperament unsuited to follow his father into the law, Clive's future career path was marked out for him on 15 December 1742, when, at his father's prompting, he was appointed to serve at Madras as a writer or clerk in the East India Company. Clive left London for India in March 1743 but his voyage, which was an unusually lengthy and hazardous one, lasted for almost fifteen months and was interrupted by an enforced visit to Brazil, during which time he learned the rudiments of the Portuguese language.

India, 1744–1753 By the 1740s the East India Company had established three coastal footholds in India at Bombay, Calcutta, and Madras. Each of these presidencies was administered by a governor and council, who supervised the company's 'servants' as well as a small number of licensed private merchants. Not yet a territorial power, the company was dedicated almost exclusively to the pursuit of commercial objectives and the procurement of local goods for export. Only a small number of armed men were deployed to defend the company's main fortified settlements against incursions from unfriendly local rulers or other European trading organizations. In particular, Anglo-French rivalries caused problems for those in Madras, and by the time Clive began his first term of company service the political situation on the Coromandel coast was already inflamed to the point that it threatened the stability of the entire region.

Clive arrived in Madras in June 1744, impoverished by debts incurred during the journey and without any connections or acquaintances in the small British settlement of Fort St George. These circumstances made for a miserable existence, and in February 1745 Clive confessed that 'I have not enjoyed one happy day since I left my native country' (Malcolm, 1.145). It was around this time that he attempted to commit suicide, his life being saved by the fact that his pistol twice misfired. Although Clive appears to have believed that fate had marked him out for higher things, such aspirations to greatness were not shared by his colleagues, many of whom found him to be a difficult individual, prone to fits of black depression and melancholy. As several serious disputes and quarrels indicate, he had already developed the capacity to make lifelong enemies, and he distanced himself from all but a few of his immediate circle. Clive's official duties were initially of a secretarial nature, but in 1746 he transferred to the accountant's office, where he acquired a wide range of technical skills while dealing with the company's commercial affairs. He also sought to improve himself and broaden his education in other ways. He made regular use of the well-stocked Fort St George Library, and developed the capacity to think independently and absorb large amounts of factual information.

A rather tedious life of routine industry was rudely interrupted by events which, after the outbreak of war in Europe, saw Madras fall to the French in September 1746. Following the sacking of the city by the forces of Joseph Dupleix, Clive escaped south to Fort St David, where he assisted with defensive duties. He formally entered the company's military service, having been awarded an ensign's commission after catching the eye of the local authorities. Clive soon enhanced further his reputation when, under the command of Major Stringer Lawrence, he helped with the successful defence of Cuddalore against Dupleix's forces in June 1748. Then later the same year, following the arrival of artillery reinforcements from Britain led by Admiral Boscawen, he performed capably and acted bravely during an ill-judged and poorly executed attempt to capture the fortified French settlement of Pondicherry.

These actions, which represented a testing military apprenticeship, earned Clive promotion to lieutenant in the company's forces in March 1749, and helped him to forge a close working relationship with Lawrence. This partnership was strengthened during the Tanjore expeditions of 1749, when British forces were deployed in support of a displaced Maratha prince who offered the company the port of Devakottai in return for assistance with the return of his throne. Two attempts were made to take Devakottai. The first, a small-scale overland expedition in which Clive took part, ended in some disarray; the second, a seaborne operation, was successful, with Clive leading the troops who, not without considerable difficulty and losses, eventually stormed the town's fortifications. Clive,

with some luck and considerable bravery, played a pivotal role in the action, prompting Lawrence later to comment that Clive's 'early genius' suggested that he had been 'born a soldier', with 'courage and judgement much beyond what would be expected from his years' (Malcolm, 1.103–4). His reward was to be appointed as Lawrence's quartermaster when Madras was returned to the English company by the French under the terms of the treaty of Aix-la-Chapelle of 1748.

By the end of 1749 Clive had returned to civil employment, although he was fortunate to obtain, through Lawrence's patronage, the lucrative position of commissary for the supply of provisions to the company's troops. The profitable opportunities opened up by the levying of commission on all goods purchased on the army's behalf were considerable, and in a short period of time Clive was able to lay the foundations of his private fortune. His entrepreneurial activities were interrupted, however, in early 1750 by illness and nervous disorders of the type that were to punctuate the remainder of his life. Intense physical pain was coupled with depression which necessitated frequent recourse to medication, and on this occasion Clive undertook a first visit to Bengal, where he recuperated in Calcutta.

By the time Clive returned to Madras the East India Company was once more engaged in hostilities with its French counterpart, both having become embroiled in a struggle for military and political supremacy in southern India after backing local rival claimants for the position of nawab of the Carnatic. As a result, Clive resumed his company military career with the rank of captain in July 1751. His first actions were to accompany convoys and reinforcements from Madras to Trichinopoly, which, although in the hands of the British ally Muhammad Ali, was being threatened by the French-backed Chanda Sahib. The British, whose strategy was being planned by Governor Thomas Saunders of Madras, decided that relief for besieged Trichinopoly could best be effected by a diversionary action. It was agreed that a march on Arcot, the capital of the Carnatic, offered the best opportunity for such an operation. Clive, whose role in the development of the final plan is a matter for debate, volunteered to command the small, inexperienced body of troops allotted to the task.

Clive's force of 800 men left Madras on 26 August and arrived five days later at an undefended, hastily evacuated fort at Arcot. The dilapidated fort was occupied, and Clive began to prepare it for a siege, this work only being interrupted by raids into the surrounding countryside, to where the garrison had fled. Clive's tactics had the desired effect, and Chanda Sahib was soon obliged to send a detachment of troops from Trichinopoly to Arcot. These troops, joined by French soldiers from Pondicherry, occupied the city of Arcot on 23 September, and a blockade of the fort began. The ensuing siege lasted for fifty days until it was lifted on 14 November, by which time the defenders had overcome heavy odds to prevent the enemy from breaching the walls of the fort. That the company's force was able to withstand such a lengthy assault in the face of overwhelming numbers owed much to Clive's leadership and organizational skills, and he proved able to command loyalty from his Indian and British troops alike. The final outcome was determined by stubborn resistance and the approach of a relieving force, as much as by any fighting, but Clive acquired the status of a hero and his actions did much to raise the standing of the British in the region. Building on his success at Arcot, Clive then went on in quick succession to take a number of forts, defeat the enemy at the battle of Arni, twice recapture Conjeeveram, rout a small French force during a night-time engagement at Kaveripak, and lay waste to the town of Dupleix Fatihabad.

These actions, all important but hardly decisive in their own right, were only a prelude to a major expedition mounted to relieve Muhammad Ali, who was still besieged at Trichinopoly. Clive was recalled to Fort St David from his roving campaign to lead the expedition, which was reinforced by troops from Bengal. Because Stringer Lawrence had recently returned from Britain, however, Clive eventually found himself acting as a willing deputy to his mentor. On 16 April 1752 the company's forces began to engage the enemy troops, besieging the fort of Trichinopoly, and by fighting off relieving troops, blockading the besiegers, and capturing key positions to the north of the fort, they finally compelled the enemy to surrender on 13 June. Clive had again not only made several telling tactical contributions to the victory but, more importantly and to greater effect, had always been in the thick of the action. According to contemporary reports, he narrowly escaped death on several occasions. He often appeared to be blessed with good fortune, and this served only to enhance his growing reputation as a bold and successful commander.

Clive remained well to the fore in the operations that followed the Trichinopoly campaign, but his health once more deteriorated quite rapidly and by the end of the year he had decided to return to Britain. Before he did so, however, he married Margaret Maskelyne (1735–1817) [see Clive, Margaret, Lady Clive of Plassey]. His new wife, the seventeen-year-old sister of his close friend Edmund, had recently arrived at Fort St David and, according to legend, Clive had been captivated by her beauty as displayed in a miniature portrait. The marriage took place at Madras on 18 February 1753. The couple sailed for Britain on 23 March, two days after Clive had arranged for all of his estate in India to be invested in diamonds.

Britain, 1753–1755 Clive received a warm welcome in London upon his return in October 1753, and he accepted gifts from a grateful East India Company as well as accolades from public figures. His private wealth stood at £40,000, a sum that was substantial enough to support his political and social ambitions, but it began to attract attention and criticism from those who envied his success. Clive was generous towards his friends, but at this stage of his life his spending was never reckless, and outgoings were closely monitored in meticulously kept personal accounts. Family debts were paid, including much of the £8000 mortgage on Styche Hall; allowances were settled on relatives; and property was purchased, before Clive began to seek an entry into parliamentary politics. He was fortunate that a general election was called in April 1754, and he was afforded active support by the influential though unpopular earl of Sandwich, who was patron of Margaret Clive's brother Nevil Maskelyne, the future astronomer royal. Clive stood for one of the two seats for the borough of Mitchell in Cornwall which, under the control of the Sandwich–Scawen interest, had been represented by his cousin Edward between 1741 and 1751. Clive and his fellow Sandwich-sponsored candidate John Stephenson were returned after a hotly contested poll of the fifty or so voters, but their position was threatened immediately when the result was disputed following protests from the candidates standing on the rival government interest.

The Mitchell petition struggle was a complicated, long-drawn-out parliamentary episode which was not resolved until 24 March 1755, when Clive and Stephenson were finally unseated following a vote in the Commons which divided the house along partisan lines. Not only were Clive's immediate political ambitions thwarted by this set-back, but his electioneering had been a considerable drain on his financial resources. Perhaps with this in mind, he had already welcomed several approaches from the company about a possible return to India. With further hostilities likely against France, Clive had been offered the position of second-in-command (with a royal commission) of an expedition to be mounted from Bombay against the French-backed nizam of Hyderabad. The company's offer, made before the vote in the Commons, also included the governorship of Fort St David, a position which, by placing him as deputy to the new governor of Madras, meant that he would in due course become governor of the presidency. These were offers too good to refuse before the age of thirty, and Clive signed his commission at the end of March 1755. A couple of weeks later he and Margaret sailed for India at the end of a short and ultimately unsatisfactory sojourn in Britain.

India, 1755–1760 When Clive arrived at Bombay in October 1755 he found, somewhat to his surprise, that the Hyderabad expedition had been abandoned by the local authorities. Instead, the combined forces assembled under Admiral Watson were deployed against the pirate fortress of Gheria, which surrendered after two days of heavy naval bombardment. Clive and Watson then sailed on to Madras, and Clive formally took up his position as governor of Fort St David on 22 June 1756. He did not have long, however, to enjoy his return to familiar surroundings. In mid-August news arrived that the young nawab of Bengal, Siraj ud-Daula, fearing the growth of European strength in the region, had seized the city of Calcutta, which contained the company's settlement of Fort William. The nawab's success had been followed by the notorious 'black hole' incident in which forty or so British prisoners died during the course of a cramped and stifling overnight confinement in a small room.

The British response was to mount a relieving expedition, led by Watson and Clive, which eventually set sail from Madras on 16 October. This combined operation was hampered by disagreements over tactics, and by disputes over prerogative between Clive, still a company soldier, and the regular naval officers serving in Watson's squadron. Clive confided to a friend in early January 1757 that 'I cannot help regretting that I ever undertook this expedition' (Malcolm, 1.156). Nevertheless, Clive's troops, after meeting resistance at Budge-Budge, recaptured Calcutta without a struggle on 2 January 1757, but then had to confront a major assault on the city from a large army led by the nawab. The effectiveness of a boldly conceived night-time counter-operation was undermined by several misjudgements made by Clive, but the action of his forces was robust enough to persuade the nawab to withdraw and open negotiations with the British. Clive, now in a position of some advantage but racked by increasingly characteristic battlefield indecision, hesitated before pressing for acceptance of his terms. Agreement was reached on 9 February 1757, when, by the treaty of Calcutta, the nawab restored to the British the position they had held before the outbreak of hostilities, and he also granted them reparations and important new privileges.

Although arrival of news of the outbreak of the Seven Years' War suggested that Clive would soon return to Madras to meet an anticipated French offensive, continuing fears for the security of Calcutta dictated that he remain in Bengal, not least to try and prevent any alliance from being formed between the nawab and the French. Acknowledging the threat posed by the French forces stationed at Chandernagore, Clive attacked the settlement on 13 March 1757, but the arrival of Watson's ships ten days later made the decisive contribution to victory. The nawab, much alarmed by this turn of events, was in a vulnerable position, and he was also threatened by a conspiracy among followers who were aiming to remove him from power. Now fast emerging as the main power brokers in the region, the British were drawn into the conspiracy when offered the prospect of peace and stability which could be strengthened by their own active sponsorship of an acceptable candidate as nawab. After much political manoeuvring, Clive and the British authorities in Calcutta became involved in negotiations with such a candidate, Mir Jafar [see Bengal, nawabs of], who was a general in the nawab's army. Acting as a go-between in the negotiations, but not trusted by the British, was the Calcutta merchant *Amir Chand, who had previously enjoyed a close relationship with the nawab. Amir Chand made heavy financial demands which he wished to have settled during the course of any coup, and he appeared to be taking advantage of his influential position by insisting that these demands were met in any treaty drawn up between the British and Mir Jafar.

These uneasy circumstances formed the background to the infamous episode in which Clive ordered two treaties to be drafted. One fictitious treaty was destined for Amir Chand and contained a clause detailing a large payment to be made to him in the event of any transfer of power, while the authentic treaty placed before Mir Jafar mentioned no such sum of money. If this action was in itself duplicitous and offered considerable ammunition to later generations of Clive's critics, then so too was the forging on the fictitious treaty of the signature of Watson, who was seemingly reluctant to put his own hand to the document.

In whatever moral context these actions may be set, they paved the way for the overthrow of the nawab, which occurred at the battle of Plassey on 23 June 1757. In military terms, the battle was a rather desultory affair with relatively few casualties. Clive, although again courageous, was once more hesitant in the field and did not greatly distinguish himself as a tactician, even though the nawab, surrounded by disloyal officers, was defeated. The aftermath of the battle saw the British triumphant in their new role as king-makers, and Siraj ud-Daula was, as planned, replaced as nawab by Mir Jafar. In July 1757 Clive was able to report to the company's directors that 'this great revolution, so happily brought about, seems complete in every respect' (Malcolm, 1.271).

The transfer to British-backed power in Bengal was accompanied, according to local custom, by lavish gifts or 'presents' worth over £1.2 million which were bestowed upon leading British figures by the new nawab, and the company itself was also compensated for the sacking of Calcutta. Clive was generously rewarded by a grateful Mir Jafar and, although his reasons for sanctioning the overthrow of Siraj ud-Daula in the first place cannot be ascribed to the narrow motives of personal financial gain, he certainly took full advantage of circumstances and was able greatly to enrich himself. He received presents worth £234,000 in 1757, and two years later, following the successful defence of Bengal against invasion by the son of the Mughal emperor, Mir Jafar bestowed upon Clive a much solicited jagir, a grant of land revenue worth around £27,000 a year to the recipient. These sums represented substantial personal gains which allowed Clive to invest £30,000 in Golconda diamonds at Madras in 1757, and during the aftermath of Plassey he was also able to negotiate the purchase of £230,000 bills to be drawn on the Dutch East India Company. Such actions later encouraged others to follow Clive's example and seek similar rewards, and they also began to attract considerable attention from those in Britain who were becoming increasingly uneasy about the ill-gotten gains being obtained by rapacious company servants, or 'nabobs' as they became known. Indeed, Clive was to spend the rest of his life seeking to preserve both his reputation and his jagir.

It had originally been intended that after the defeat of Siraj ud-Daula Clive would return to Madras, which was once more threatened by the French. In the event, however, he became de facto chairman of a newly appointed governing council in Calcutta before he received news in November of his appointment as governor of the presidency of Bengal. He spent his time in office dispatching troops to beleaguered Madras and attempting to bolster the British position in Bengal, a process which, as he reported, involved 'Bullying and Keeping under the Black fellows' (Clive to Sir George Pocock, 25 Aug 1759, BL OIOC,

MS Eur. G 37, box 3). In November 1759 he sanctioned Francis Forde's destruction at Badara of threatening Dutch troops who were advancing as reinforcements towards their settlement at Chinsura.

During 1756–7 Clive had been presented with a set of circumstances in which any British conquest of Bengal was far from inevitable or unavoidable. His actions and decisions nevertheless determined an outcome which not only restored the British position after the initial loss of Calcutta but also saw company power and authority then quite systematically extended and consolidated in Bengal. As part of that process the British, through Clive, had first established political control over the nawab, and one important consequence of this was a great expansion of inland trading activity. Clive had then sought to eliminate the threat posed by the French and Dutch, and this left the British, for the time being, in a position of uncontested supremacy in the region. Neither Clive nor anybody else in the company had sought, in premeditated fashion, such an outcome, but there is no doubt that, as events unfolded before him, he had taken advantage of opportunities to establish considerable economic, political, and strategic advantages for the company. He was certainly aware of the implications of what he was doing, and this suggests that he had developed a clearer vision of the company's long-term future than many of his contemporaries.

Clive also began to take a wider view of British interests in India. He outlined his ideas in a letter to William Pitt in 1759, and suggested that the British government should now take a fuller responsibility for the territories now under the company's control. Declaring that 'so large a sovereignty may possibly be an object too extensive for a mercantile Company', he asked Pitt to consider whether the nation would derive greater long-term advantage from the Indian territories if they were brought under the management of the state (Forrest, 2.175–7).

Clive made significant progress towards his aims during his time as governor of Bengal. At the same time he found himself steadily becoming embroiled in acrimonious disputes not only with some of those in India, such as the regular army officer Eyre Coote, but also with the company's directors, many of whom he felt had been insufficiently swift to acknowledge his success and endorse his elevation to the position of governor. From this time on he retained a low opinion of those directors who were not members of his personal following. In particular, and despite outward displays of friendship, he came to regard the director Laurence Sulivan as a great rival whom in time he was prepared to 'hurt', 'if he attempts to hurt me' (Malcolm, 2.195). It was in these increasingly troubled circumstances that Clive resolved to return to Britain, and he set sail from Bengal with his wife in February 1760.

Britain, 1760–1764 Clive arrived in Britain in July 1760, in possession of a fortune worth about £300,000 and his *jagir* income, having been lauded by William Pitt in 1757 as a 'heaven-born general' (Richard Clive to Clive, 6 Dec 1757, BL OIOC, MS Eur. G 37, box 4). Once more he received a hero's welcome and numerous official honours. Even so,

he was disappointed in his attempt to secure an English peerage, receiving instead an Irish barony (as Baron Clive of Plassey) in March 1762. Two years later he was made knight of the Bath.

Clive again devoted much of his time to politics, and was obliged in particular to defend himself within the East India Company against the charge that his *jagir* had been obtained against the company's best interests. Although Clive eventually managed to have his right to the *jagir* confirmed and then extended for ten years, this deeply contentious issue soon translated itself into a bitter ongoing struggle for control of the company. This saw the votes of Clive's supporters regularly being deployed in ballots and elections against those commanded by his great rival Sulivan. As a result, throughout the 1760s events at East India House, together with a vigorously contested propaganda war fought out in pamphlets and newspaper articles, regularly captured public attention and held the centre of the national political stage.

Clive also sought a return to the House of Commons and, having had the ground prepared for him by his father during his absence in India, he was elected unopposed as MP for Shrewsbury in April 1761. He then built up around him a small group of followers, including his father (MP for Montgomery since 1759) and John Walsh, a close company associate who had been elected MP for Worcester. After initially supporting the duke of Newcastle (who had obtained his barony for him), he threw in his hand with George Grenville, prime minister in 1763–5, in return for assistance with the campaign to secure the *jagir*.

Clive again took great trouble to look after the well-being of his family and close friends. He did this through a series of generous gifts and settlements, providing a new house for his parents on the Styche estate. Although for a while Clive and his family lived in an enormous house at Condover near Shrewsbury, he also began to acquire a number of substantial new properties which enabled him to consolidate both his political and social position. These included a modest Irish estate, which was renamed Plassey to mark Clive's greatest triumph. Lord Montfort's 7500 acre Shropshire estate was bought for £70,000 in 1761, and the nearby 6000 acre Walcot estate and house were purchased for £92,000 in 1763. A fashionable town house, 45 Berkeley Square in London, was rented from Lord Ancram, and this too was eventually acquired for an outlay of £10,500.

Still afflicted by ill health, Clive spent his time outside politics in a state of semi-retirement, often at Bath, but he and Margaret displayed great enthusiasm for concerts, operas, and plays. In early 1764, however, the arrival of news from India of several serious military set-backs experienced by the company at the hands of Indian forces prompted calls for his reappointment as governor of Bengal and commander-in-chief of the army. With a strong tide of popular support from a majority of the company's stockholders running behind him, Clive took advantage of the situation to assert his supremacy over Sulivan and secure his *jagir*. Then, accepting the task of restoring the company's fortunes, Clive was charged with both settling external relations with Indian powers and bringing order to confused and corrupt internal affairs. Central to the first aim was the need to regulate private trading activity, a cause of conflict which had drawn the company into war with local rulers, notably Mir Kasim, who, with British support, had replaced Mir Jafar as nawab of Bengal in 1760. The second objective was to be achieved largely, and most controversially in view of Clive's earlier career, through the prohibition of present taking by company servants. To help him overcome any resistance from disaffected company servants in Calcutta, a new five-man select committee was established and empowered to overrule the Bengal council whenever necessary. Clive set sail for India, without his wife and children, on 4 June 1764. He was determined, as he later put it, to cleanse 'an Augean stable' (Forrest, 2.257) which, with an irony that was not lost on many contemporaries, his own earlier activities and example had in large part served to create.

Bengal, 1765–1767 Clive's voyage to India again took longer than usual, and he was much delayed at Rio de Janeiro. By the time he arrived in India, reaching Madras on 10 April 1765 and Bengal on 3 May, the company's hitherto precarious military position had been transformed. This had been achieved largely as a result of the battle of Buxar, fought on 22 October 1764. The company's forces, led by Hector Munro, had secured a decisive victory over the combined armies of Mir Kasim (who the previous year had been overthrown when Mir Jafar had once more been installed as nawab of Bengal by the British), Shuja ud-Daula, the wazir of Oudh, and Shah Alam II, the Mughal emperor. Accordingly, not only did the company find itself firmly in control of Bengal, but it had been presented with the opportunity of a military advance as far as Delhi, the seat of the emperor. With the young Najm ud-Daula (recently installed as nawab of Bengal following the death of Mir Jafar) and the much weakened Shuja ud-Daula now seeking British support to prevent invasion of their territories by marauding Afghan and Maratha forces, there seemed every prospect that the company might extend its influence across much of northern India.

Clive firmly rejected any ambitious expansionist schemes, preferring instead to consolidate the company's economic and political position in Bengal. To this end, the treaty of Allahabad, signed by Clive on 12 August 1765, contained a settlement which, among other things, saw the imperial authority of Shah Alam acknowledged by the British. The company was granted the lucrative office of *diwan*, or revenue collector, in the Mughal provinces of Bengal, Bihar, and Orissa in return for military support and a 'tribute' payment of 26 lakhs of rupees a year to the emperor. With the *diwani* transferred from the nawab to the company, the British gained direct access to the considerable wealth of Bengal, which enabled them to sustain the growth of their armed forces and increase the annual investment in goods for export to Britain. The nawab was almost entirely dependent upon the company even though, for the sake of outward appearances, he retained some independent control over local police and judicial functions. The collection of revenues also remained in Indian hands, but company officials closely monitored the entire operation. This division of governing responsibilities in Bengal established by Clive gave rise to what became known as his 'dual system' of government, an administrative scheme of arrangement which survived until it was superseded by reforms engineered by Warren Hastings during the early 1770s. Few contemporaries were in any doubt, however, that Clive's settlement had enabled the company firmly to secure *de facto* control of Bengal and its adjacent territories.

Clive's success had a profound effect upon the company's status and fortunes in Britain as well as India. Most notably, when news of the acquisition of the *diwani* was received in London in April 1766, city speculators began to take a close interest in steadily rising East India stock prices. Clive himself played an important part in fuelling this increasingly frenzied activity, which in the long run inflicted considerable damage on the company's financial position. In September 1765 he had made use of his inside knowledge of developments in Bengal to advise friends in Britain to buy company stock, and he ordered his own London attorneys to raise large loans, liquefy his assets, and make substantial purchases on his behalf. These instructions were followed with great zeal, and by the beginning of 1767 Clive owned £75,000 India stock, although the full extent of these stock market transactions was partially concealed from public scrutiny (and later parliamentary examination) by the use of nominee holding accounts. Clive secured a generous profit from enhanced dividend payments and the timely sale at a high price of half of his accumulated stock in the spring of 1767. Thereafter he continued to conceal his East India holdings so that 'the World may not know what sum or sums of money I have in that stock' (Clive to George Clive, 9 Aug 1767, NL Wales, Clive MS 58, p. 21). Once more he demonstrated his avaricious appetite for private gain from company or public service, but he later robustly denied any wrongdoing when his stock market transactions were examined by a House of Commons committee of inquiry. Clive was not unlike many of his contemporaries when he attempted to exploit his official position and increase his personal fortune, but the extent to which he sought to line his own pockets through actions such as these gave substance to rumours about his fabulous wealth that were by now in circulation.

As far as the company's internal affairs were concerned, Clive's second governorship of Bengal was characterized by a programme of rigorous, wide-ranging reforms. This he deemed to be necessary because he had found the company's civil and military affairs to be in a 'state of confusion beyond what I had even Reason to expect' (Clive to Robert Palk, 4 May 1765, BL OIOC, MS Eur. G 37, box 3). He aimed primarily to eliminate among his colleagues 'Rapacity and Luxury; the unreasonable desire of many to acquire in an instant' (Forrest, 2.257), his view being that substantial financial rewards from Indian service should be forthcoming only for those such as himself who had given long, meritorious service to the company. He set the general tone of his administration on 9 May 1765, when, in an action which caused considerable resentment, he insisted that, as previously instructed by the directors, members of the Bengal council sign covenants which prohibited present taking by company servants. This firmness, together with Clive's sustained and at times vindictive attempts to punish those he believed to have been recently involved in extorting presents from the new nawab, caused bitter, long-running feuds with several senior company servants. These included the councillors John Burdett, George Gray, John Johnstone, and Ralph Leycester, who, along with others, were either suspended or obliged to resign from company service. These disaffected individuals all returned to Britain nurturing deep grievances, determined to pursue personal vendettas against Clive. Moreover, in order to fill the gaps created in the council, Clive sought replacements from Madras, and this caused considerable affront to the British community in Calcutta.

Clive's unpopularity increased yet further when, at the behest of the directors, he began to regulate the private trading activity of company employees. In the summer of 1765 reform of the 'inland' trade in salt, tobacco, and betel nut was effected through the creation of a monopolistic Society of Trade developed by William Sumner. The aim was to eliminate abuses, and with fixed prices for commodities it was hoped that the local population would no longer suffer from extortion at the hands of unscrupulous private British traders. Duties on the goods traded by the society would be paid to the company, and a fund was to be established from which regular and generous salaries could be paid to senior company officials in an attempt to dissuade them from engaging in trade on their own account. The scheme had some merits from the company's point of view, but it nevertheless served only to cause disaffection among those, especially in the lower ranks, who felt that perquisites were being denied to them without the provision of adequate compensation. At the same time it appeared that Clive and his favourites were profiting from monopoly arrangements, a charge which gained greater substance when the directors, generally uneasy about involvement in the inland trade, ordered the abolition of the Society of Trade in 1766.

As far as the company's military forces were concerned, Clive, who had given detailed thought to the matter when last in Britain, set about reorganizing and redeploying the army in an attempt more effectively to meet a new set of defensive priorities. Serious problems were encountered, however, when Clive tackled the issue of financial retrenchment and the rationalization of the army's pay and allowance structure. In particular, an attempt to reduce field allowances for officers met with stiff opposition from those who already felt that their financial position had been undermined by the restrictions imposed upon private trade. During the early months of 1766 discontent within the company's officer corps translated itself into a campaign of active resistance against the reforms. A leading figure in this campaign was Sir Robert Fletcher, commander of a brigade stationed at Monghyr, who reported to Clive that all of his junior officers were planning to resign their commissions unless the old rate of allowance was reinstated. Having sent for additional officers from Madras, Clive tackled this dangerous situation by travelling to confront the mutineers at Monghyr on 15 May. He appealed directly to the loyalty of the company's European and Indian troops stationed there and, having won them over, reinstated most of the rebellious officers, one exception being Fletcher who was court-martialled and cashiered. Clive's actions, which were brave but also characterized by a brutal efficiency, had the effect of defusing the situation. The officers' mutiny, which had been threatening to spread throughout the army, was contained and then extinguished. Again, however, one important long-term consequence was that a number of embittered enemies returned to Britain, where, like others, they embarked on a vigorous campaign to clear their names and blacken Clive's reputation.

Clive's time as governor was devoted to politics and administration. He spent £11,000 on 'table' expenses during his second governorship, but was often ill at ease and withdrawn in social gatherings unless they took the form of concerts, when he enjoyed listening to the works of Handel and Corelli. Indeed, he only ever relaxed and conversed freely in the company of his closest friends such as his private secretary Henry Strachey, his physician Samuel Ingham, and Edmund Maskelyne, or Mun, who was now serving as his aide-de-camp. Consequently, his countenance often seemed dark and brooding, and his appearance was increasingly defined by a heavy brow and gains in weight. Clive paid close attention to his appearance, carefully choosing his clothing and wigs, but although he was often accused of extravagance he does not seem to have indulged in ostentatious displays of his private wealth in Bengal. A contemporary Indian observer offered a general description of Clive during his times in India, and he contrasted the simplicity of his lifestyle with that of senior French figures in India, reporting that Clive 'always wore his regimentals in the field, was always on horseback, and never rode in a palanquin. ... He never wore silks but in town' (Malcolm, 3.384). Clive never mastered local languages, but he did become an enthusiastic if not always discriminating collector of daggers, swords, and oriental art. He also took a collector's interest in animals, and he arranged for several different species to be shipped to Britain.

In a hostile political climate Clive could not be seen to be profiting from present taking or private trade. Thus, in order to avoid any further charges of double standards, he gave away large sums of money to his friends, and the substantial bequest of 5 lakhs of rupees made to him in Mir Jafar's will was used to establish a fund to provide financial relief for disabled or impoverished company soldiers. 'With regard to myself', he claimed, 'I have not benefited or added to my fortune one farthing, nor shall I; though I might, by this time have received £500,000' (Clive to Richard Clive, 25 Sept 1765, NL Wales, Clive MS 236, p. 39). Even so, during his second governorship Clive was still able to remit home over £160,000, a sum arising from *jagir* payment arrears and the final settlement of his Indian affairs.

Clive's private papers and letter-books from this period reveal him to be a man who was engaged in the single-minded pursuit of his domestic and Indian political ambitions. He would not accept criticism or alternative points of view from anyone, and at times this was translated into extreme forms of high-handedness and arrogance. Thus while he always remained deeply affectionate and loyal towards his family and inner circle, he was often withering in his assessment of those whose qualities he deemed to be limited or flawed. He had a vengeful streak within him, and in his correspondence he often rejoiced at the political and personal misfortunes of his enemies. At the same time he displayed all the characteristics of a determined self-publicist, and he took great care to ensure that news of his successes was spread far and wide.

During the summer of 1766 Clive continued actively to settle the company's affairs, but in the autumn he again fell ill, once more exhibiting the symptoms of acute nervous and physical disorder. He admitted to the directors that the combined effects of the climate and hard work had 'destroyed' his constitution and reduced his body and mind to a 'state of imbecility' (Clive to the directors, 6 Dec 1766, BL OIOC, MS Eur. G 37, box 3). Only large doses of opium relieved the agony, but Clive was entirely incapacitated and in much distress for several months before, having made a slight recovery, he left India for the last time, setting sail from Calcutta on 29 January 1767.

Last years and death: Britain, 1767–1774 Clive arrived back in Britain in July 1767 and was once more honoured with many official marks of gratitude. He estimated that his personal fortune now stood at just over £400,000, but public condemnation of his private wealth, as well as criticism of his actions as governor, began ever more to force him onto the defensive. His cause was not helped by the fact that, as a foretaste of things to come, in early 1767 the East India Company had been subjected to the first parliamentary inquiry into its affairs, and this had focused attention on recent developments in Bengal.

Now a man without an official role in public life, Clive did not at once seek to play an active part in Westminster and company politics. Instead, having received George III's encouragement, he hoped to act as a detached, statesmanlike figure who would advise the government and company on East Indian affairs. This was far from easy, however, because the supporters of Laurence Sulivan and others had further fuelled hostility towards him within the higher echelons of the company. Clive in turn made no secret of his contempt for many of the directors, even though he sought to liaise with them over the development of further detailed plans for reform of the company's army. Pursuit of his political ambition was also hampered by the fact that his patron George Grenville was now in opposition. Perhaps more importantly, the return of illness eventually obliged him to seek recovery, first at Bath in late 1767 and then on the continent in 1768.

Even so, an eight-month absence in France did not prevent Clive, through his representatives John Walsh and Henry Strachey, from playing a prominent part in the general election of 1768. A variety of schemes were floated and a large amount of money was spent in an attempt to try and increase the size of his following in the House of Commons. His £30,000 purchase, from Walter Waring, of another Shropshire estate in November 1767 had given Clive complete control over both seats at Bishop's Castle. In March 1768 an estate at Usk and Trellech was bought from Clive Morris for £43,000 in an ultimately unsuccessful attempt to establish a parliamentary interest in Monmouthshire. Clive later made several smaller purchases of land totalling £5400 in the Usk area, but then, wishing to concentrate his attention on Shropshire and Montgomery politics, he abandoned his Monmouthshire venture in 1772. Always seeking to drive a hard bargain, he was nevertheless able to make a handsome profit from his brief foray into Monmouthshire when he sold all his property in the county to Lord Beaufort for £57,000. As far as the general election of 1768 was concerned, heavy expenditure was not matched by results and only three members were added to the Clive group in the Commons. Clive himself was returned, in his absence, for Shrewsbury in the face of a stern challenge from John Johnstone's brother William Pulteney.

Clive did not seek to involve himself in parliamentary politics, often declaring that he was now above party or faction. Even so, on 27 February 1769 he took a prominent part in a Commons debate about the renewal of an agreement established with the company in 1767. Steadfastly opposing the policy of the directors and the terms of their agreement with ministers, Clive made a notable speech, during the course of which he outlined his personal view of recent events in India. He also advanced plans for the root-and-branch reform of the company's affairs. His speech was well received but did not influence the new settlement in any way, an outcome which served only to increase his hostility towards many of the company's directors. This hostility had also developed to the point that from 1768, contrary to many claims of a lack of interest in internal company politics, he renewed his efforts to carve out a position of strength for himself and his followers in the general court and court of directors. There was an urgent need to do this because of Laurence Sulivan's continuing influence within the company. At the same time Clive had to counter the increasingly concerted efforts of company factions and those individuals who were seeking to restore their reputations and once more challenge Clive's right to the *jagir*, the term of which had been extended by a narrow majority of stockholders in September 1767. As a result, Clive devoted considerable time and energy to alliance making within the company, notably with the banker Sir George Colebrooke, and his financial resources were channelled once more into company electioneering on a grand scale.

Election expenditure was not so great, however, that it prevented Clive from spending £25,000 in 1769 on the purchase of the Claremont estate in Surrey from the widow of the duke of Newcastle. Two years later the Oakly Park estate (with its electoral influence at Ludlow) was bought from Lord Powis, and he also purchased the Okehampton estate in Devon. Indeed, Clive's wealth was now such that he sanctioned the demolition of the old, and to his mind uncomfortable, Vanbrugh-designed Palladian mansion at Claremont. In its place was built a rather more simple house designed by Capability Brown and Henry Holland.

The struggle for supremacy within the East India Company during the late 1760s did not produce a decisive outcome, but there was a need to put the company's affairs in order. This became only too apparent during the early summer of 1769, when reports arrived in London of serious military set-backs suffered in the Carnatic at the hands of the forces of Haidar Ali of Mysore. In May this news caused a fall in company stock prices, which had remained buoyant since 1766. At a stroke many of the leading figures within the company were ruined because vote creation activity had resulted in their being caught with stock in their possession which had been bought at a high price with borrowed money the previous autumn. Clive did not get his fingers burnt to any great degree, but he did now reluctantly acknowledge the need to negotiate with Laurence Sulivan in an attempt to secure agreement on ways of addressing the company's serious problems in India. The favoured way forward, much discussed during the summer of 1769, was for the company to dispatch 'supervisors' to India in an attempt to secure compliance with the directors' orders. Clive advocated the appointment of a governor-general, but eventually a three-man supervisory commission was established, including Clive's close friend Luke Scrafton and a representative of the Sulivan 'interest', Henry Vansittart, the former governor of Bengal, who was hoping to repair his and Sulivan's recently shattered personal finances. The third member of the commission was Francis Forde, who was supposed to exert a mediating influence but was in fact well disposed towards Clive and his followers. The supervisory commission thus offered Clive the opportunity to reassert some degree of direct control over Indian affairs. But any hopes that he might have entertained about this were dashed when the frigate carrying the supervisors to India disappeared after leaving Cape Town at the end of December 1769.

The loss of the supervisors represented a heavy blow to the company in its efforts to put its own affairs in order. The company's difficulties then mounted when, contrary to the expectations raised by Clive's settlement of 1765, its financial position worsened markedly during 1771 and 1772. At the same time news began to arrive in Britain about the devastating effects of the Bengal famine of 1769–70, and this heightened unease about company misrule. Clive, held by some to have been responsible for establishing the economic preconditions for the famine, was now routinely condemned along with other 'nabobs' in print and cartoons. Demands were also made for inquiry and reform, and it was against this background that Lord North and his ministers began to address the East Indian problem.

Clive now found himself in a difficult political position, and he became rather isolated as friends and allies either died or were abandoned. Scrafton had been lost in 1769, George Grenville and Richard Clive died in 1770 and 1771 respectively, while old associates from India such as Stringer Lawrence and Robert Orme had long been alienated from him. Clive was gradually forced into retreat by enemies who took advantage of the prevailing public mood and pressed home legal and literary attacks upon him. The pressure increased when the directors, acting on information passed on to them by Clive's enemies, attempted to secure repayment from him of money they believed was owed to the company from the salt duties collected by the Society of Trade in Bengal during 1765 and 1766. In an attempt to set the record straight, Clive, who had been assiduously gathering materials to use in his own defence, considered writing a history of his governorship, but he was warned against this by close friends. He was, however, also being courted by ministers who welcomed his expert advice on Indian affairs, and, following the death of George Grenville, he and his followers began to gravitate towards Lord North, the new prime minister. North, through the former Grenvillite Alexander Wedderburn, made approaches to Clive during the second half of 1771 asking for his views and opinions on company matters.

In early 1772 the company acknowledged the need for reform of its affairs and prepared a parliamentary bill which was designed to improve the administration of British justice in Bengal. When, on 30 March 1772, Laurence Sulivan announced his intention to introduce the bill into the Commons, it became clear that many MPs were not prepared to discuss any measure without a thorough inquiry into the company's affairs and recent history. Clive took advantage of these proceedings to offer a detailed defence of his conduct in Bengal, and his two-hour speech included trenchant criticism of the directors and all of his enemies. He argued that he had followed the correct course of action in 1765 and that it was absurd for him to be held in any way responsible for the Bengal famine of 1769–70. The speech was well received, and Clive's oratorical skills were widely praised, but the critics were not silenced and the house eventually agreed to establish a select committee of inquiry under the chairmanship of John Burgoyne. The terms of reference of the inquiry were such that the committee, which included Clive as one of its thirty-one members, undertook a close examination of the company's history since 1756. The committee proceedings did not take the form of a witch hunt, although Clive and many of his former allies were called as witnesses and subjected to searching interrogation. Because of this, Clive later complained in the Commons that he had been treated like a 'sheep stealer' and the committee had attempted to 'mark him' (Cobbett, *Parl. hist.*, 17, 1772, cols. 852–3), but the published reports in fact offered a reasonably objective view of events and Clive's career. The committee's proceedings dragged on for months, offering Clive the opportunity to present lengthy, if at times selective, accounts of his conduct.

While Clive's tone was usually measured and controlled, he did occasionally combine defiance with attempts to claim the moral high ground from his detractors. There was no better example of this than when, recalling the riches offered to him by Mir Jafar in 1757, he made his famous remark, 'Mr Chairman, at this moment I stand astonished at my own moderation!' (Spear, 189).

During the summer and autumn of 1772 the company lurched towards bankruptcy, a development which saw, as a prelude to government reform, a second inquiry into East Indian affairs launched in the form of a secret committee of the House of Commons. Clive received some much needed relief from his personal troubles, being at last installed as knight of the Bath in June, and he was then appointed lord lieutenant of both Shropshire and Montgomery during the autumn. But although he emerged relatively unscathed from the select committee proceedings and reports, politicians and the public continued to express concern about the state of British India. It was against a background of sustained hostility towards the East India Company that during the early months of 1773 Lord North and his ministers began to prepare regulatory legislation.

By May 1773 a tense political atmosphere had developed. Burgoyne chose this moment to act upon the findings of his select committee, and by doing so he mounted an attack upon Clive and other 'nabobs'. On 10 May he made three motions in the Commons, two of which condemned present taking and the appropriation of money by the authorities in Bengal, and he listed the crimes perpetrated by company servants. Clive's conduct was defended with some success by Wedderburn, but Burgoyne's motions were passed and the house agreed further to consider the committee's reports. This was eventually done on 19 May, when, amid great excitement, Clive spoke for over an hour in his own defence and presented a straightforward account of his career. This action was very necessary because Burgoyne had indicated that he would make a motion declaring that Clive had illegally acquired £234,000 after the battle of Plassey. The proceedings were adjourned, however, until 21 May, when Clive made a further short speech which ended with the dramatic and celebrated plea 'leave me my honour, take away my fortune' (BL, Egerton MS 247, 131–4). Clive then left the house, and a lengthy debate took place on Burgoyne's motion. During the course of this debate it became clear that a majority of MPs were now sympathetic towards Clive, and it was eventually resolved that, although he had indeed received £234,000, he had not abused his powers to do so. Sensing the changing mood in the house, Wedderburn then pressed home Clive's advantage. He made the motion that 'Robert Clive did at the same time render great and meritorious service to this country' (JHC, 34.331), to which members assented almost unanimously during the early hours of the morning.

Such an outcome represented a remarkable triumph for Clive, and it was widely assumed that he had bought his way out of trouble. This was nonsense. Clive's success was based upon his own robust and sustained defence of his conduct, and Wedderburn's techniques of backstairs parliamentary management and alliance building. Indeed, the campaign had been so successful that his reputation was enhanced at the very time that many assumed and eagerly anticipated that he would be humiliated.

Following the high drama of these proceedings, the East India Company was reformed by a series of legislative actions, most notably Lord North's Regulating Act of 1773. Clive did not wholeheartedly endorse these measures, but he took a full part in the debates which shaped their final form. This was not the response of a man broken by recent events, and historians have tended to exaggerate the damaging effects that the parliamentary proceedings had upon him. Well used to hostile criticism, Clive did not withdraw from public life, and he continued to play an active part in East Indian politics. In particular, he spent some considerable time advising members of the recently appointed supreme council of Bengal, especially Philip Francis, on Indian policy. Whatever Clive's intentions, however, the outcome of this intervention was damaging to the company in the long run because Francis, when drawing on Clive's advice in India, directed a sustained campaign of criticism and obstruction against the governor-general, Warren Hastings.

Clive spent much of the winter of 1773–4 in Italy in the company of several companions but not his wife. The purpose of the trip was twofold: to escape harsh weather and to procure works of art for the new house at Claremont, which was now approaching completion at a cost of around £30,000. The summer of 1774 was then spent in Shropshire, where guests were entertained and preparations were made for the forthcoming general election. In early November, however, Clive fell ill, as a common cold steadily worsened. He travelled first to Bath for the waters and then moved on to London. By the time he arrived at Berkeley Square on 20 November he had been in considerable pain for some time, and his old ailments had returned with a vengeance. He resorted to large doses of opium, which brought some respite, but on 22 November, having abandoned a game of cards being played with friends, he was found dead on the floor of an adjoining room.

Mystery long surrounded the circumstances of Clive's death, and both contemporary and historical accounts offer a variety of often lurid versions of his final minutes. Most modern biographers, drawing on contemporary rumour and speculation, have argued that he died by his own hand, having sought escape from acute pain by plunging a penknife into his throat. However, a recent well-documented and convincing counter-claim (Prior, 345–7) suggests that Clive, in great discomfort, took an excessively large dose of opium which led ultimately to a fatal seizure or epileptic fit. The arrangements for his funeral were conducted along normal lines, which does not suggest that the family entertained any great concern about the religious consequences of death by suicide. Clive was buried inside the parish church of St Margaret at Moreton Say on 30 November, and his presence there was marked by a small plaque bearing the words 'Primus in Indis'.

With assets worth over £500,000 at the time of his

death, Clive left his family well established as members of the landed élite, and by securing this he had undoubtedly achieved one of his major ambitions. He was survived by his wife, who lived until 1817, and by two sons and two daughters. His eldest son, Edward *Clive (1754–1839), later became governor of Madras and earl of Powis.

Clive's career and achievements were matters for great debate during his lifetime, and a process of re-evaluation and revision has continued ever since. Always a figure of great controversy, his reputation has changed as the tides of British imperial fortunes have ebbed and flowed, and as attitudes towards the empire have altered over the last 200 years or so. Adopting often quite different moral perspectives and critical standards, successive generations of biographers from diverse historiographical traditions have seldom been neutral in their attitudes towards him. Their verdicts have ranged from wholehearted praise for the bold man of action through to outraged condemnation of his greed, corruption, and double standards. If these contradictory views reveal anything at all, they demonstrate that he was simultaneously a man of many qualities and shortcomings who was very much a product of his time and the unique situation in which he found himself. These views have also ensured that he has remained prominent in popular consciousness, a position sustained through fictional and cinematic representations of his life. That his thoughts and actions were decisive in shaping the early expansion of British India is beyond any doubt, but so too responses to the events of 1756–9 and 1765–7 served to determine imperial attitudes and policy long after his death. For these reasons Clive was more than simply a soldier and statesman: he was an architect of empire whose influence has cast a lengthy shadow over the history of Britain and India.   H. V. BOWEN

Sources M. Bence-Jones, *Clive of India* (1974) • P. Spear, *Master of Bengal: Clive and his India* (1975) • J. Malcolm, *The life of Robert, Lord Clive, collected from the family papers communicated by the earl of Powis*, 3 vols. (1836) • G. Forrest, *The life of Lord Clive*, 2 vols. (1918) • A. M. Davies, *Clive of Plassey: a biography* (1939) • T. B. Macaulay, *EdinR*, 70 (1840), 295–362 • B. Lenman and P. Lawson, 'Robert Clive, the "black jagir" and British politics', *HJ*, 26 (1983), 801–29 • H. V. Bowen, 'Lord Clive and speculation in East India Company stock, 1766', *HJ*, 30 (1987), 905–20 • H. V. Bowen, *Revenue and reform: the Indian problem in British politics, 1757–1773* (1991) • P. J. Marshall, *East Indian fortunes: the British in Bengal in the eighteenth century* (1976) • M. Archer, C. Rowell, and R. Skelton, *Treasures from India: the Clive collection at Powis Castle* (1987) • HoP, *Commons, 1754–90*, 2.223–8 • BL OIOC, Clive MSS, MS Eur. G 37 • NL Wales, Clive papers • D. L. Prior, 'The career of Robert, first Baron Clive, with special reference to his political and administrative career', MPhil diss., U. Wales, 1993 • parish register, Moreton Say, Shrops. RRC, 4257/Rg/2 [burial]

Archives BL OIOC, corresp. and papers, MS Eur. G 37 • BL OIOC, corresp., journals, papers, Home misc. series • Herefs. RO, letters from various Indian rulers [copies] • NL Wales, corresp. and papers • Shrops. RRC, estate papers • Shrops. RRC, papers | BL, letters to George Grenville [microfilm] • BL, letters to Warren Hastings, Add. MS 29131 • BL, corresp. with duke of Newcastle, etc., Add. MSS 32685–32987, *passim* • BL, letters to Robert Orme, Add. MS 44061 • BL OIOC, corresp. with John Carnac, MS Eur. F 128 • BL OIOC, Ormathwaite MSS, MS Eur. D 546 • BL, Sutton Court MSS, MS Eur. F 128 • BL OIOC, corresp. with Henry Strachey, MS Eur. F 128 • BL OIOC, corresp., mostly letters to Harry Verelst, MS Eur. E 231 • BL OIOC, corresp. with Harry Verelst, MS Eur. F 218 • BL OIOC, letters to Harry Verelst, MS Eur. K 016 • BL OIOC, corresp. with John Walsh and J. Fowke, MS Eur. D 546 • PRO, letters to John Ashby, C109 • University of Minnesota, Minneapolis, Ames Library of South Asia, letters to Sir George Pocock

Likenesses P. Scheemakers, marble statue, 1764, BL OIOC • J. van Nost and C. G., silver medal, 1766, NPG • N. Dance, oils, *c.*1770, Powis Castle, Montgomeryshire [*see illus.*] • N. Dance, oils, *c.*1772–1774, NPG • J. E. Thomas, marble bust, 1845, Powis Castle, Montgomeryshire • J. Tweed, statue, 1912, 'Clive Steps', King Charles Street, London • J. Macardell, mezzotint (after T. Gainsborough), NPG • oils, NAM

Wealth at death over £500,000: will, 1773, PRO, PROB 11/1003, sig. 426; abstracts and legal opinions, BL OIOC, MS Eur. E 285; Bence-Jones, *Clive of India*

Clive, Sir Robert Henry (1877–1948), diplomatist, was born in London on 27 December 1877, the third and youngest surviving son, and fourth of the five surviving children, of Charles Meysey Bolton Clive JP (1842–1883), gentleman, of Whitfield, Herefordshire, and his wife, Lady Katherine Elizabeth Mary Julia, *née* Feilding (d. 1882), daughter of William Basil Percy Feilding, seventh earl of Denbigh. His father was a first cousin four times removed of Clive of India. A younger brother died in infancy. Educated at Haileybury College and Magdalen College, Oxford, where he graduated with a pass degree in classics in 1899, Clive entered the diplomatic service in January 1902. He was posted to Rome in February 1903 and promoted third secretary in April 1904. He was transferred to Tokyo in June 1905 and promoted second secretary in August 1908. On 10 July 1905 he married Magdalen Agnes Muir Mackenzie (1884–1971), third and youngest daughter of Kenneth Augustus Muir *Mackenzie, Baron Muir Mackenzie, permanent secretary to the lord chancellor from 1880 to 1915. They had two sons, Peter Julian (b. 1906) and Robert Wilfred Kenneth (b. 1909), and a daughter, Amy Catherine (b. 1913).

In April 1909 Clive was posted as second secretary to Cairo. Robert Vansittart, who served with him there, wrote that 'he was a man so modest that he might easily be overlooked', who represented a new type of diplomat without court or political connections (Vansittart, 84). From Cairo, Clive was transferred to Bern in October 1911 and to Stockholm in October 1913, becoming a first secretary in August 1915 and acting on several occasions as chargé d'affaires.

In June 1919 Clive was transferred to the Foreign Office and appointed CMG. In January the following year he became counsellor in Peking (Beijing), remaining there until July 1923, when he was appointed consul-general at Munich. He was sent to inquire into the separatist movement which had succeeded in establishing itself in Bavaria, then under French occupation. His tact and perspicacity in carrying out this mission were an important contributory factor in the eventual restoration of order. He was present in Munich in November 1923 when Adolf Hitler and the nascent Nazi party tried unsuccessfully to overthrow the Bavarian government. He reported to the Foreign Office that 'If Hitler had stayed in power for even one day, I do not believe that there would have been a French officer alive in Munich' (PRO, FO 371/8818, 9 Nov 1923). It was a tribute to his skill that the French authorities raised no objection when, in October the following year, he was appointed consul-general at Tangier. As the first British representative on the committee of control, he helped substantially to launch the new international regime set up by the convention of 1923 and to harmonize the interests of the signatory powers. Clive's five years as minister at Tehran, from October 1926 to September 1931, covered a period of increasing Persian nationalism and xenophobia, and his efforts to conclude a commercial and a general treaty were frustrated. His patience and the objectivity of his judgement were nevertheless of great value during this difficult period in Anglo-Persian relations. He was promoted KCMG in 1927.

After a short time as minister to the Holy See from March 1933 to May 1934, Clive was appointed ambassador in Tokyo, and was sworn of the privy council. Japan was no longer the country he had known in the heyday of the Anglo-Japanese alliance. The termination of the alliance in 1922, naval rivalry, Japan's conquest of Manchuria, and her withdrawal from the League of Nations in 1933 had estranged the two countries, while Japanese military ambitions were beginning to threaten British interests in China and the Far East. Clive's task was in the circumstances a difficult one, but he responded with his usual determination. He reduced tension, but he had few illusions about the dangers of the situation and his reports to the government were models of clarity and good sense. He was promoted GCMG in 1936. It was not until after his departure that Japan took the irrevocable step of attacking mainland China.

When Clive arrived in Brussels as ambassador in July 1937, Great Britain had lately renewed her guarantee to Belgium. That little progress was made towards the more specific understandings desired by his government was not for want of pertinacity on Clive's part, for he again displayed patience and clear-headedness. But he was unable to persuade King Leopold to abandon his 'policy of independence', reporting in January 1939 that the Belgian monarch wanted peace at almost any price, and would not agree to staff talks with the French because he feared that these would provoke the Germans. Clive told the Foreign Office that the Belgians doubted whether France had any spare troops to defend them or wished to make any military commitments to another state. He retired from the diplomatic service at the end of 1939.

Clive was characteristic of the best in the diplomatic service: reliable, modest, sensitive, but dispassionate. A devoted career diplomat, he was undeterred by the succession of difficult and frustrating posts to which he was assigned. He had many outside interests, had a gift for both drawing and poetry, and was a connoisseur of furniture, oriental porcelain, and rugs, of which he was a keen collector. He was a man of distinguished appearance, faultlessly dressed but lacking in personal vanity. His obvious interest in his fellow human beings made him a stimulating companion and inspired affection in all those who

served with him. He died at his home, Cherry Orchard, Forest Row, Sussex, on 13 May 1948. He was survived by his wife and their three children.

ASHLEY CLARKE, *rev.* PETER NEVILLE

Sources *Documents on British foreign policy*, 3rd ser., 4 · R. Keyes, *Outrageous fortune: King Leopold of the Belgians*, 1: *1901–1940* (1990) · R. Lamb, *The drift to war* (1989) · Lord Vansittart, *The mist procession* (1958) · earl of Avon [A. Eden], *Facing the dictators* (1962) · D. Cameron Watt, *How war came* (1989) · PRO, FO 371/8818 · *The Times* (14 May 1948) · *FO List* (1939) · *WWW*, *1941–50* · Burke, *Peerage* · Burke, *Gen. GB* · personal knowledge (1959) · private information (1959)
Likenesses W. Stoneman, photograph, 1933, NPG
Wealth at death £35,352 7s. 4d.: probate, 6 Sept 1948, *CGPLA Eng. & Wales*

Clod, Frederick (*b.* 1625x35, *d.* in or after **1661**), physician and alchemist, was born between 1625 and 1635 in Holstein in Germany, where his father, Johann Clod (an itinerant experimenter), had agricultural interests. Clod had travelled widely in Germany and the Low Countries before arriving in London, probably early in 1652, when he became acquainted with Samuel Hartlib. On 18 August 1652 he was co-signatory (with Hartlib and the ecclesiastical negotiator John Dury) of the *Christianae societatis pactum*, a manifesto for a protestant fraternity devoted to the reformation of religion and the 'rational sciences'. In the summer of 1653 he married Hartlib's daughter Mary (with whom he had a son, born early in 1655). Early in 1654 Clod established a 'goodly laboratory' in the kitchen of his father-in-law, dedicated to alchemical and iatrochemical experiments. The 'Laboratorium Clodianum' was to be a centre for medical and pharmaceutical reform, dedicated to public health including the distribution of medicines to the poor. It was part of a scheme to establish a 'general chymical council' with his friend and correspondent Sir Kenelm Digby, who promised to provide £600 of funding per year for the venture, and Robert Boyle was approached to sponsor a new and larger laboratory. Clod was a regular scientific correspondent of Boyle, Digby, Joachim Polemann, Johann Morian, Peter Staehl, and other English and continental chemists and physicians, with whom he exchanged information on alchemical processes and chemical and herbal medicines. His medical and alchemical knowledge seems to have been well-regarded by some of his peers, but he developed bad relations with his competitor George Starkey. In addition strong doubts about his character were expressed by John Evelyn and Henry More: Evelyn later dismissed him as 'a profess'd adeptus, who by ... pretence of extraordinary arcana insinuated himselfe into acquaintance of his father-in-law' (*Diary of John Evelyn*, 3.391). Evelyn's judgement may reflect Clod's fraudulent dealings with patients. In 1653, on More's recommendation, Clod treated Anne, Viscountess Conway, for debilitating headaches, and also promised to convey a portrait of her to her brother John Finch in Padua. According to More, Clod received sixteen pieces of gold for his services but purloined the picture and provided the viscountess with an ineffectual or dangerous medicine. He was, according to More, a 'snap' (swindler), a 'misshapen monster' whom it was 'impossible ever to prove honest', and 'as accurs'd a

Raskall as ever trod on English ground' (*Conway Letters* and Hutton, 88, 94–5). Clod's shady reputation persisted. In May 1661 Dury wrote to Hartlib during the latter's last, fatal illness, lamenting 'the continuance of your son Clod's misdemeanours' which made him 'incapable of the love of honest friends who will not … trust or assist him.' On the other hand, writing only a few weeks earlier, Hartlib had commented to John Worthington that William Brereton 'would use no other physician but Clodius' (*Diary and Correspondence of Dr John Worthington*, 1.304). Clod's subsequent fortunes and the date and place of his death are not known for certain, but he may have died during the plague of 1665. STEPHEN CLUCAS

Sources *Diary of John Evelyn*, ed. W. Bray, new edn, ed. H. B. Wheatley, 4 vols. (1879) · *The Conway letters: the correspondence of Anne, Viscountess Conway, Henry More, and their friends, 1642–1684*, ed. M. H. Nicolson, rev. edn, ed. S. Hutton (1992) · R. E. W. Maddison, *The life of the Honourable Robert Boyle, FRS* (1969) · G. H. Turnbull, *Hartlib, Dury and Comenius: gleanings from Hartlib's papers* (1947) · C. Webster, *The great instauration: science, medicine and reform, 1626–1660* (1975) · W. R. Newman, *Gehennical fire: the lives of George Starkey, an American alchemist in the scientific revolution* (1994) · *The diary and correspondence of Dr John Worthington*, ed. J. Crossley and R. C. Christie, 2 vols. in 3, Chetham Society, 13, 36, 114 (1847–86) · *The works of the Honourable Robert Boyle*, ed. T. Birch, 5 vols. (1744)

Clodd, Edward (1840–1930), banker and popular anthropologist, was born at Queen Street, Margate, Kent, on 1 July 1840, the eldest child of Edward Clodd and his wife, Susan Parker. Of his six brothers and sisters four died in infancy and two did not survive childhood. His father was a Trinity House pilot, and in early life was captain and part owner of a brig. Born at Aldeburgh, Suffolk, he had lived for a time at Margate, from where his brig traded with the north, but he returned to Aldeburgh soon after his son's birth. From his mother Clodd early acquired a love of reading. His parents, of Suffolk farming and fishing background, were Baptists, and Edward was intended for the ministry. After receiving instruction at a dame-school, he attended Aldeburgh grammar school, of which Joseph Buck was master. During a visit to London at the age of fourteen, Clodd obtained work as a clerk and settled there. Initially employed in an accountant's office in Cornhill, he subsequently worked for two other firms, one of which was James Coster & Co., Fountain Court, before he became a clerk at the London Joint Stock Bank in 1862; ten years later, he was appointed secretary. On 20 August 1861 he married Eliza Sarah, the daughter of a surgeon, Cornelius Garman, of Bow, London.

From his early days in London Clodd attended the Birkbeck Institute, read assiduously in the free libraries, and heard lectures. On Sundays he listened to the best-known preachers of every denomination and followed the controversies with lively interest. His Baptist creed was exchanged for Congregationalism and Unitarianism, and he soon became friendly with many of the more liberal leaders of religious thought. The debates generated by biblical criticism and evolutionary theories instilled in him an interest in science. In 1869, with the help of William Huggins, he was admitted to the Royal Astronomical Society. Here he met Richard Anthony Proctor, who

Edward Clodd (1840–1930), by Emil Otto Hoppé, *c.*1909

invited him to contribute to the weekly scientific periodical *Knowledge*. During Proctor's lecture tours in the USA and Australia in the 1880s Clodd acted as sub-editor, and he gave occasional lectures on science and literature.

In 1873 Clodd published his first book, *The Childhood of the World*. Written as a primer on evolutionary anthropology, it introduced children to the latest information on prehistoric man. It quickly passed through four editions and was translated into six European and two African languages. Two years later he expanded his analysis with the *Childhood of Religions*. This marked his foray into folklore. His address of the same year to the Sunday Lecture Society, entitled 'The birth and growth of myth, and its survival in folk-lore, legend, and dogma', ultimately culminated in his *Myths and Dreams* (1885). One of the six men who constituted the 'great team' of British folklorists, Clodd was a self-proclaimed 'anthropological folklorist' (Dorson, 202–65). In 1877 he joined the unconventional Century Club, where he met Samuel Butler, W. K. Clifford, John Tyndall, E. B. Tylor, and many other men of distinction in science and letters. In 1878 he resigned from the Royal Astronomical Society and joined the Folk-Lore Society. Although a departure from his earlier theistic writings, his *Jesus of Nazareth* (1880) was pronounced 'one of the best of its kind in the language' by the Unitarian *Inquirer* (McCabe, 47). It won for Clodd the friendship of T. H. Huxley, York Powell, John Collier, Frederick Pollock, Leslie Stephen, Mrs Lynn Linton, and other well-known people.

Clodd's success had been laboriously won. Long hours of reading, after an average of ten hours a day at work in the bank, resulted in recurrent bouts of insomnia and neuralgia. His *Story of Creation* (1888), a popular study of evolution, sold five thousand copies in three months, and publishers began to court him. At this time, under the influence of James Cotter Morison, he had leanings towards the Positivist Society, but he found a corrective in his friendship with the novelists Grant Allen and George Meredith.

Clodd had, as Thomas Hardy (who knew him well) noted in 1915, 'a genius for friendship' (Haddon, 185). From 1878 he used his weekend home in Aldeburgh, Strafford House, for annual Whitsuntide gatherings of eminent intellectuals. In addition to the friends already mentioned, J. B. Bury, Sir Ray Lankester, Sir James Frazer, Sir Alfred Lyall, Sir Mortimer Durand, and George Haven Putnam were often there. In 1900 thirty-four friends, including Herbert Spencer, W. Holman Hunt, Edmund Gosse, and Clement Shorter, presented him with a carved oak table as a sixtieth birthday gift. Historically, Clodd continues to be remembered for his friendships. His letters and diaries have provided insight into the lives and intellectual careers of Thomas Hardy, James Frazer, George Gissing, and W. B. Yeats. Meredith called Clodd 'Sir Reynard', perhaps because of his shrewd expression, but on his native heath he looked like a sailor and radiated a bluff benevolence. According to contemporaries, he was essentially a man of generous and sociable disposition, who devoted unremitting attention to his guests, and showed himself a zealous humanitarian on all public issues.

In 1881 Clodd was elected to the Savile Club; he was an original member of the Johnson Club and the Omar Khayyam Club, founded in 1884 and 1892 respectively. President of the Omar Khayyam Club in 1895, Clodd adopted the epicurean philosophy of the Persian poet from his fiftieth year onwards. In the true Huxleyan sense of the word, Clodd had become an agnostic. His presidential addresses of 1895 and 1896 to the Folk-Lore Society demonstrated the implications of his agnosticism for the study of folklore and embroiled him in controversy. W. E. Gladstone, an original member of the society, resigned in protest against what he regarded as Clodd's offensive remarks, and the Catholic Truth Society responded with a 24-page pamphlet. Clodd became notorious for his condemnation of the culturally atavistic superstitions behind spiritualism and 'dogmatic' Christian theology and ritual. Through lectures and numerous journal articles and reviews, he established himself as a prolific popularizer of scientific naturalism. From 1906 to 1913 he served as chairman of the Rationalist Press Association and, upon the founding of the Secular Education League in 1907, he was appointed to its general council. Through the character of Edwin Dodd in *Boon* (1915), H. G. Wells provided a trenchant satirization of Clodd, the rationalist. According to Boon, Dodd 'looked under his bed for the Deity, and slept with a large revolver under his pillow for fear of a revelation' (Wells, 45). In the early twentieth century, Clodd vociferously objected to another threat to rationalism: psychoanalysis.

Clodd's first wife, from whom he was separated, died in 1911. He confided in his diary that he was pleased to be a widower. Three years earlier, Arnold, one of their eight children (six sons, two daughters), had died. He, in turn, had been predeceased by two brothers, who died in infancy. On 18 December 1914 Clodd married 27-year-old Phyllis Maud Rope. The daughter of a farmer, Arthur Mingay Rope, of Leiston, Suffolk, she was a student of biology at the Royal College of Science. The following year, on Clodd's seventy-fifth birthday, he retired from the Joint Stock Bank, and proceeded to write his *Memories* (1916) at his now permanent residence in Aldeburgh. A 'shrewd and excellent handler of credit', the *Investors' Review* said of him on his retirement. He was still vigorous in mind and body, lecturing at the Royal Institution in 1917 and 1921, and writing much on folklore and occultism. After 1922 he suffered occasional illness, sometimes severe. In May 1928 he had a stroke, and for more than a year he suffered from aphasia, and could not read owing to cataract. He seemed to recover, but in the spring of 1930 he contracted bronchial asthma. 'I die, I die' (McCabe, 215), he murmured minutes before the end. He died fully conscious on 16 March 1930 at Strafford House, 33 Crag Path, Aldeburgh. In accordance with his wishes his body was cremated at Ipswich four days later and the ashes were scattered upon the sea off Aldeburgh. He had no children by his second marriage. He was survived by his wife.

E. S. P. HAYNES, rev. J. F. M. CLARK

Sources J. McCabe, *Edward Clodd: a memoir* (1932) • E. Clodd, *Memories* (1916) • A. C. Haddon, 'In memoriam: Edward Clodd (1840–1930)', *Folk-Lore*, 40 (1929), 183–9 [with bibliography of his works and articles] • R. M. Dorson, *The British folklorists: a history* (1968) • *The letters of George Gissing to Edward Clodd*, ed. P. Coustillas (1973) • *Investors' Review* (3 July 1915), 4–5 • F. J. Gould, *The pioneers of Johnson's Court: a history of the Rationalist Press Association from 1899 onwards*, rev. edn (1935) • [C. Shorter], 'A literary letter', *The Sphere* (14 July 1900), 56 • D. Tribe, *100 years of freethought* (1967) • [H. G. Wells], *'Boon', 'The mind of the race', 'The wild asses of the devil' and 'The last trump'* [1915] • G. Brennan, 'Yeats, Clodd, *Scatalogic rites* and the Clonmel witch burning', *Yeats annual*, ed. W. Gould, 4 (1986), 207–15 • E. Royle, *Radicals, secularists and republicans: popular freethought in Britain, 1866–1915* (1980) • B. Lightman, *The origins of agnosticism: Victorian unbelief and the limits of knowledge* (1987) • M. Seymour-Smith, *Hardy* (1994) • b. cert. [Phyllis Maud Rope] • m. certs. • d. cert.
Archives Duke U., Perkins L., letters and papers • priv. coll., diaries • U. Leeds, Brotherton L., letters and papers | BL, Macmillan Archives • Folklore Society Library, London, MS material pasted into books from his personal library • U. Leeds, Brotherton L., corresp. with Sir Edmund Gosse
Likenesses E. O. Hoppé, photograph, *c*.1909, NPG [*see illus.*] • J. Collier, oils, 1914, Rationalist Press Association Library, London; repro. in Gould, *Pioneers of Johnson's Court*, 43 • H. Bedford, chalk drawing, 1928, NPG • H. G. Wells, pen-and-ink drawing, repro. in Wells, *Boon, the mind of the race*, 52 • photograph, repro. in Shorter, 'A literary letter' • photograph, repro. in Haddon, 'In memoriam', pl. 3 • photograph, repro. in J. McCabe, *Edward Clodd*, frontispiece • photograph, repro. in *Letters of George Gissing to Edward Clodd*, ed. Coustillas, following p. 56
Wealth at death £11,020 3s. 9d.: probate, 12 Aug 1930, *CGPLA Eng. & Wales*

Clodius Albinus, Decimus (d. 197), Roman governor of Britain, was reportedly born into a noble family at Hadrumetum in the province of Africa Proconsularis (modern Tunisia). Albinus held a major military command in Dacia, on the lower Danube, early in the 180s, and possibly served as governor of Lower Germany before being appointed governor of Britain in 191 or early in 192. He thus held one of the major military commands in the Roman empire at a time of serious political crisis following the assassination of the emperor Commodus, the last, and unworthiest, representative of the Antonine dynasty. Commodus was struck down on the last day of 192. The strict and senior general, Publius Helvius Pertinax, was hailed as emperor, but only three months later was removed and replaced by Didius Julianus, a wealthy senator. His election was not generally popular and three months later he was killed in his deserted palace. The most powerful provincial governors had been notably unimpressed by the choice of Didius Julianus. The initiative was seized by Lucius Septimius Severus, the governor of Pannonia Superior on the upper Danube. He, Clodius Albinus in Britain, and Pescennius Niger, governor of Syria, held three of the greatest military commands; the civil wars which followed were fought out by these three and their armies.

Septimius Severus was the swiftest to act. Twelve days after the removal of Pertinax he had been hailed as emperor by his troops. In the search for potential allies he was bound to look to the forces under the command of Clodius Albinus in Britain. Albinus was offered the rank of Caesar, a position promptly accepted as an earnest of what it might lead to. Having thus neutralized, for the present, the threat on his western flank, Severus could turn his attention to his eastern rival, Pescennius Niger, eliminating him in 195. Albinus was now isolated but still retained possession of a formidable army. Severus gave clear notice of his intentions by renaming his eldest son Marcus Aurelius Antoninus, a reference to the dynasty which had died with Commodus. Clodius Albinus Caesar was a redundant figure in the emerging Severan order and was declared an enemy of the state.

Nothing is known of Albinus's activities between the early months of 193 and the winter of 195, when the final breach with Severus was effected. In 196 he crossed to Gaul, taking with him a substantial part of the army of Britain, no doubt hoping to gather additional military forces there. He was proclaimed emperor, issued his own coins, and won some successes in the field, defeating in the course of these actions one of Severus's generals, Virius Lupus. He took possession of Lugdunum (Lyons) in this campaign and prepared to face the army of Severus close to that city early in 197. The issue was contested on 19 February of that year in a hard-fought battle, in which Albinus's forces acquitted themselves well. But the army of Severus proved too strong and broke their opponents' line. When defeat was certain, Albinus took his own life. The battle was destructive of life to both sides and may have been followed by confiscation of property of those who had supported Albinus.

Very little is known of Albinus's personal life and circumstances aside from his origins in the urban élite of Africa. He was married, but nothing is recorded of relatives or descendants.   MALCOLM TODD

Sources Dio's Roman history, ed. and trans. E. Cary, 9 (1927), lxxvi [epitome] · D. Magie, ed. and trans., 'Clodius Albinus', Sciptores historiae Augustae, 1 (1921) · A. R. Birley, Septimius Severus (1971) · P. Salway, Roman Britain (1981)
Likenesses bust (contemporary), Petworth House, West Sussex

Cloëté, Sir Abraham Josias (1794–1886), army officer, second son of Peter Laurence Cloëté, member of the council of the Cape of Good Hope, was born in Cape Town on 7 August 1794. He was educated in Holland and at the Royal Military College, Marlow. Appointed to a cornetcy in the 15th hussars on 29 January 1809, he was promoted successively lieutenant (1810), captain (1812), brevet-major (1822), lieutenant-colonel (1837), colonel (1851), major-general (1856), lieutenant-general (1863), and general (1871). Joining the 15th hussars in England soon after its return from Corunna, Cloëté served with it during the Burdett riots of 1810 and the Luddite disturbances in the midlands and Lancashire of the following years.

On 28 October 1813 Cloëté exchanged to the 21st light dragoons at the Cape, and returned as aide-de-camp to the newly appointed governor, Lord Charles Somerset. He commanded a military detachment of volunteers from regiments at the Cape, sent to occupy the desert island of Tristan da Cunha soon after the arrival of the emperor Napoleon at St Helena. Leaving the detachment there, Cloëté resumed his duties as aide-de-camp. In 1817 Cloëté accompanied his regiment to India, and served with a squadron employed as a field force in Cuttack, on the frontiers of Orissa and Bihar, during the Pindarri war of 1817–19. The 21st dragoons (a party at St Helena excepted) was disbanded in England in May 1819, and Cloëté was placed on half pay. In 1820 he was employed, with the rank of deputy assistant quartermaster-general, in superintending the landing and settling on the eastern frontier of the Cape Colony, in the districts of Albany and Somerset, of a large body of government immigrants, known as the 'settlers of 1820'. In 1822 he was sent home with important dispatches, after which he was appointed town-major of Cape Town, a post he held until 1840. He served in the Cape Frontier War of 1834–5. In 1836 he was made KH, and at the time of his death was the last surviving knight companion of the Royal Guelphic Order in the Army List.

In 1840 Cloëté was appointed deputy quartermaster-general at the Cape, and retained the post until 1854. In 1842 he was sent with reinforcements from Cape Town to relieve a small force under Captain Smith, 27th Inniskillings, which was besieged by Boers near Durban, when his firm and judicious action not only prevented a war with the Boers but also prepared the permanent settlement of the colony of Natal. He was quartermaster-general in the Cape Frontier War of 1846–7 and was mentioned in dispatches, and in 1848 was made CB. He was chief of the staff with the army in the field in the Cape Frontier War of 1850–53, including the operations in the

Basuto country, and the battle of the Berea, where he commanded a division. He was mentioned in dispatches in the *London Gazette* (4 May 1852), and knighted for his services in 1854. As major-general on the staff he commanded the troops in the Windward and Leeward islands from 1855 to 1861. He was made colonel 19th foot (later the Princess of Wales's Own Yorkshire regiment) in 1861, and KCB in 1862. He was placed on the retired list in 1877.

Cloëté had married on 8 May 1857 Anne Woollcombe Louis (*d.* 1906), granddaughter of Rear-Admiral Sir Thomas Louis, bt; they had a son and a daughter. As a young man, he had fought a duel with the surgeon James Barry over his future wife's aunt. He died at his home, 88 Gloucester Terrace, Hyde Park, London, on 26 October 1886.   H. M. CHICHESTER, *rev.* LYNN MILNE

Sources J. C. Chase, *Cape of Good Hope*, ed. J. S. Christophers (1843) · H. Cloëté, *Five lectures on the emigration of the Boers* (1856) · J. G. Romer, 'Cloete, Sir Abraham Josias', *DSAB* · *The Times* (28 Oct 1886) · *Colburn's United Service Magazine*, 2 (1876) · J. Foster, *The peerage, baronetage, and knightage of the British empire for 1882*, 2 vols. [1882] · Burke, *Peerage* (1939) · *CGPLA Eng. & Wales* (1886)
Archives Cape Archives, Cape Town, Acc 457 | Rhodes University, Grahamstown, South Africa, Cory Library for Historical Research, corresp. with Sir Benjamin D'Urban · Wellcome L., corresp. with John Hall
Likenesses oils, Africana Museum, Johannesburg
Wealth at death £21,609 3*s.* 9*d.*: probate, 18 Nov 1886, *CGPLA Eng. & Wales*

Clogie, Alexander (1614–1698), Church of England clergyman and biographer, was born in Scotland and may have attended Trinity College, Dublin. He was admitted to holy orders by Bishop William Bedell of Kilmore in 1636 and collated to the vicarage of Dyne, co. Cavan, on 12 November 1637. The same month he married Bedell's stepdaughter Leah Mawe, daughter of a recorder of Bury St Edmunds and his wife, also Leah Mawe, but she died within a few weeks. On 7 May 1640 Clogie became vicar of Urney or Cavan. Resident at the episcopal palace at Kilmore, by his own account he assisted Bedell with his translation of scripture into Irish. Following the outbreak of the 1641 rising Clogie, together with the bishop and several others, was seized by the insurgents in December 1641 at Kilmore and conveyed to the nearly ruinous castle of Cloughoughter, where the party was kept for three weeks in severe winter weather. Released in a prisoner exchange, they remained in the area residing at the home of a clergyman, Denis O'Sheridan. Bedell became seriously ill and Clogie remained with him until his death on 7 February 1642. After officiating at Bedell's funeral he joined refugees who departed Cavan for protestant-held Drogheda in June 1642. He moved on to Dublin and later reported that he had served for fifteen months as a deputy commissary to Sir Philip Perceval, responsible for the receipt of bread and biscuit from the Dublin bakers. In late 1643 he travelled to England with the troops dispatched by the marquess of Ormond to serve the king, acting as chaplain to the cavalry. By September 1646 he was minister at Beely, in Worcestershire, and by the following year was officiating as minister at Wigmore, in Herefordshire, a living in the hands of the parliamentarian Harley family.

Clogie remained at Wigmore for the rest of his life. His early praise for the populace seems to have been reciprocated, for in 1650 inhabitants of the parish successfully petitioned in his favour against an act banishing Scots from England. He married Susanna Nelme (*d.* 1711), the daughter of John Nelme, at Ludlow on 11 December 1655, and the baptism of two sons and four daughters of their marriage are recorded at Wigmore between 1656 and 1671. At some point before 1679 he wrote *Speculum episcoporum, or, The apostolique bishop, being a brief account of the lyfe and death of that reverend father in God, D. William Bedell*. Though it was the foundation for the much more influential life of Bedell published by Bishop Gilbert Burnet in 1685, Clogie's work was not published until 1862, then again in 1902. He published *Vox corvi, or, The Voice of a Raven* (1694, perhaps with a first edition in 1691), a sermon prompted by an incident where his grandson heard a raven 'that thrice spoke these words distinctly; "Look into Colossians the 3rd, and 15th"' (Jones, 219), a command which Clogie related to a family dispute in the parish. He died in 1698 at Wigmore, where he was buried.

A. C. BICKLEY, *rev.* KARL S. BOTTIGHEIMER

Sources *A true relation of the life and death of ... William Bedell*, ed. T. W. Jones, CS, new ser., 4 (1872) · E. S. Shuckburgh, ed., *Two biographies of William Bedell, bishop of Kilmore, with a selection of his letters and an unpublished treatise* (1902) · *The manuscripts of his grace the duke of Portland*, 10 vols., HMC, 29 (1891–1931), vol. 5 · *Report on the manuscripts of the earl of Egmont*, 2 vols. in 3, HMC, 63 (1905–9), vol. 1

Cloncurry. For this title name *see* Lawless, Valentine Browne, second Baron Cloncurry (1773–1853).

Clonmell. For this title name *see* Scott, John, first earl of Clonmell (1739–1798).

Clontarff. For this title name *see* Rawson, John, Viscount Clontarff (1470?–1547?).

Clopton, Hugh (*c.*1440–1496), merchant, mayor of London, and civil benefactor, was the younger son of John and Agnes Clopton, of Clopton, near Stratford upon Avon, where the family had been settled since the thirteenth century. Apprenticed to John Roo, mercer of London, in 1456/7, he became a member of the company in 1463/4, serving as warden in 1479, 1484, and 1488. He was elected alderman for Dowgate ward on 15 October 1485, and had moved to Bread Street by 1495. He was elected sheriff of London in 1486, and mayor in 1491. After serving with the delegation sent by Edward IV to Archduke Maximilian in Flanders in 1482, he was also elected one of four members for the City of London in the parliament which sat from 20 January to 18 February 1483. Contrary to previous assertions, Clopton was never knighted, describing himself in his will as 'citizen, mercer and alderman' (Shakespeare Birthplace Trust, ER 1/121).

Although he made his career in London and abroad as mercer, stapler, and venturer, Clopton retained close links with Stratford upon Avon, where he built a 'praty howse of brike and tymbar', later known as New Place and purchased in 1597 by William Shakespeare. Leland also credits him with the building of the stone bridge over the river at Stratford which still bears his name, replacing

'The bridge ther of late tyme … very smaulle and ille, and at hygh waters very harde to passe by' (*Itinerary*, 2.49). He is also said to have repaired and improved the highway from London near Aylesbury. Hugh Clopton died, unmarried, in London on 15 September 1496 and was buried, according to his directions, in the chapel of St Katherine in the church of St Margaret's, Lothbury.

Clopton made two wills, one dated 8 March 1496 and enrolled in the husting court of London, and the other dated 14 September 1496 and proved in the prerogative court of Canterbury on 14 February 1497. The wills provided, in addition to conventional pious bequests to the poor and to religious houses in and around London and Warwickshire, 200 marks for the marriage of twenty poor maidens in London and the same number in Stratford. Clopton also endowed three exhibitions for five years for poor scholars at Oxford, and the same at Cambridge; and ensured the completion of building work—the nave, tower, and porch—at the chapel of the Guild of the Holy Cross, Stratford, for which 'of late I have bargayned with oon Dowland and divers other masons' (Shakespeare Birthplace Trust, ER 1/121). The amount bequeathed for this work is unspecified, but a sum of £50 was also left towards the building of a cross aisle in the parish church of Holy Trinity, Stratford. His regular travels between London and Stratford may be deduced from his bequests towards the 'repayring and amending of perilous bridges and weyes within the space of x myles of Stratford upon Avon' (Shakespeare Birthplace Trust, ER 1/121), and the fact that, at the time of his election as mayor of London, he was 'nowe in Warwickshire' when the Mercers' Company determined that twenty-four of their number should meet and escort him the last 10 miles into the city (Lyell and Watney, 220). Total financial bequests and provisions came to more than £1700 and in addition real estate was devised in Stratford and Wilmcote in Warwickshire and at Calais in France. The separately enrolled husting will bequeathed a freehold tenement in Bow Lane, Vintry, to Whittington College, for the benefit of the testator's soul, with a request that preference should be given to a graduate of Oxford for any vacancy in the mastership. The inquisition *post mortem*, taken at Stratford on 1 November 1497, specifies nine properties in Stratford upon Avon, together with the manors of Little Wilmcote and Clopton, which he may have held as guardian of his great-nephew William, whose father, John, son of Thomas, Hugh's elder brother, had died in 1486. The wardship of William was granted in 1498 to Hugh Clopton's executors. William, aged fifteen in 1497, was served heir to his great-uncle on 20 July 1504.

M. R. MACDONALD

Sources L. Lyell and F. D. Watney, eds., *Acts of court of the Mercers' Company, 1453–1527* (1936) · will, PRO, PROB 11/11, sig. 2 [transcript in Shakespeare Birthplace Trust Record Office, ref. ER 1/121] · Mercers' Hall, London, wardens' accounts, 1390–1463 · Clopton cartulary, Folger, Vb88 · R. R. Sharpe, ed., *Calendar of letter-books preserved in the archives of the corporation of the City of London*, [12 vols.] (1899–1912), vol. L · A. B. Beaven, ed., *The aldermen of the City of London, temp. Henry III–[1912]*, 2 vols. (1908–13) · journals, CLRO, 9–10 · CLRO, husting rolls, 224/15 · letter-books, CLRO, K and L · J. Stow, *A survey of London*, rev. edn (1603); repr. with introduction by C. L.

Kingsford as *A survey of London*, 2 vols. (1908); repr. with addns (1971) · P. E. Jones, ed., *Calendar of plea and memoranda rolls preserved among the archives of the corporation of the City of London at the Guildhall*, 6: 1458–1482 (1961) · *The itinerary of John Leland in or about the years 1535–1543*, ed. L. Toulmin Smith, 11 pts in 5 vols. (1906–10)

Archives CLRO, letter-books K and L

Wealth at death see will, PRO, PROB 11/11, sig. 2; CLRO, husting rolls, 224/15; inquisition post mortem, microfilm SBTRO PR 54/14

Clopton, Walter (*d.* 1400), justice, was probably a member of a family established at Clopton, near Crewkerne in Somerset, and which also held lands elsewhere in Somerset and in Dorset. Little is known about his early career, but he was appointed a king's serjeant in 1376. A patent was issued for his appointment as one of the justices of the king's bench on 27 November 1377, but for reasons that are not clear the appointment did not take effect, and he continued as a king's serjeant until 1388. He served as a justice of assize and gaol delivery on the south-western circuit between 1377 and 1380, and on the home circuit between 1382 and 1387. He was on the commission of the peace in the south-western counties in the early 1380s, and he also served as a commissioner of array in Somerset in 1377 and 1380. He had links with William, earl of Salisbury, acting as one of his feoffees in 1381 and 1382. In these years he acquired more property in Somerset and Dorset—a life tenancy of the manor of Shepton Beauchamp (Somerset) and the manor of Kingston Russell (Dorset); he also held land at Long Sutton (Somerset) and Bromley (Dorset). By grant of Margaret, countess of Devon (*d.* 1391), he was tenant of the manor of Corston, Somerset, for her life, and in 1385 he acted as a feoffee for her grandson, Edward, earl of Devon. By the 1390s he was sufficiently wealthy to make a loan to the king of 500 marks in August 1396, and he was required to contribute a further 500 marks to Richard II's forced loan in October 1397.

In the political crisis of November–December 1387 the chief justice of the king's bench, Sir Robert Tresilian, was appealed of treasons by the lords appellant, and on 31 January 1388 Clopton was appointed chief justice in his place. He was created knight-banneret in the following April. He presided over the impeachment in the Merciless Parliament (February–June 1388) of four of Richard's closest associates, Simon Burley, John Beauchamp of Holt, James Berners, and John Salisbury, and pronounced sentence of death on them. Despite Clopton's part in the condemnation of his friends, Richard II reappointed him as chief justice of the king's bench when he resumed power in May 1389. During the 1390s Clopton's gaol delivery work was increasingly concentrated on Newgate prison, but he was still appointed from time to time as a justice of the peace and commissioner of gaol delivery in his native west country. As chief justice of the king's bench he was regularly summoned to parliament, and served as a trier of petitions in every parliament until his death. In the parliament of September 1397 the earl of Arundel was arraigned on a charge of treason for his part in the opposition of the lords appellant to Richard II between 1386 and 1388. Arundel pleaded a royal pardon, but was told that the pardon had been obtained by deceit and was null and void. The king then ordered Clopton to warn the earl of the penalty he faced if he could make no better plea, and Clopton went on to inform Arundel that if he had nothing else to say he would be convicted and attainted. The earl's conviction and execution duly followed.

When the second session of this parliament opened at Shrewsbury on 28 January 1398, its first business was to annul the proceedings of the Merciless Parliament of 1388 and to reaffirm the validity of the judges' answers of 1387, which Clopton's predecessor, Tresilian, had helped to formulate and which had constituted one of the counts against him at his trial in 1388. William Thirning, chief justice of the common pleas, was asked his opinion of the answers, and replied that declaration of new treasons was a matter for parliament, but if he had been a lord or peer of parliament and had been asked his opinion he would have replied in the same manner. Clopton, when asked his opinion, offered the same tactful if evasive reply. Clopton was evidently confirmed in office at the accession of Henry IV (though the confirmation was not enrolled), and in the first parliament of the new reign (October–November 1399) he was involved in the inquiry into the circumstances surrounding the death of the duke of Gloucester at Calais in September 1397. On 17 October John Hall was brought before parliament and interrogated by Clopton about a statement he had made admitting his complicity in Gloucester's murder. Hall was condemned to death and executed the same day, but there remains much doubt about the truthfulness of his confession. On the following day (18 October) Clopton was required to cross-examine his fellow judge Sir William Rickhill about the latter's part in obtaining the duke of Gloucester's confession. Rickhill maintained that when he was ordered to go to Calais he believed that the duke was already dead, and that in interviewing him and receiving his confession he was doing no more than the king and the captain of Calais, Thomas (I) Mowbray, had required of him. He was duly exonerated.

Clopton died on 21 October 1400. He and his wife, Edith, had no surviving heirs, and his brother Robert, aged over fifty, was named as his heir. He was succeeded as chief justice of the king's bench by Sir William Gascoigne.

ANTHONY TUCK

Sources Baker, *Serjeants* · G. O. Sayles, ed., *Select cases in the court of king's bench*, 7 vols., SeldS, 55, 57–8, 74, 76, 82, 88 (1936–71), vols. 6–7 · J. R. Maddicott, 'Law and lordship: royal justices as retainers in thirteenth- and fourteenth-century England', *Past and Present*, suppl. 4 (1978) · C. Given-Wilson, ed. and trans., *Chronicles of the revolution, 1397–1400: the reign of Richard II* (1993) · L. C. Hector and B. F. Harvey, eds. and trans., *The Westminster chronicle, 1381–1394*, OMT (1982) · *RotP* · *Chancery records* · *CIPM*, 19, nos. 922–3 · exchequer of receipt, issue and receipt rolls, PRO, E 403, E 401 · *DNB*

Clore, Sir Charles (1904–1979), businessman, was born on 24 December 1904 in Mile End, London, penultimate child of five sons and two daughters of Israel Clore, a Russian immigrant, and his wife, Yetta Abrahams. After a local education, Clore worked in his father's textile business before leaving for South Africa at the age of twenty.

On his return to London in 1927 Clore bought the South African rights to a cinema film of a world championship boxing match, and resold these at a profit in South Africa. In 1930 he bought a derelict skating rink in Cricklewood and leased the Prince of Wales Theatre. Later he developed numerous industrial premises, and invested in Lydenburg Estates, a lucrative South African gold mining company. He was described as 'a well-known dealer in property' (21 Feb 1939) when *The Times* reported his leadership of a syndicate which had bought the London Casino (formerly the Prince Edward Theatre) for £250,000. During the war Clore was partly occupied in building government premises. Afterwards he was well placed to expand his interests.

In 1946 Clore bought a coachworks at Park Royal, textile mills in Yorkshire, the thirty dress shops of the Richards Shops retail chain, and the Heelas department store in Reading. In 1951 he bought for £4 million Furness Shipbuilding (sold in 1969 to Swan Hunter). Many other acquisitions followed. The most important, in 1953, was his purchase of 70 per cent of the equity of J. Sears (Tru-Form Boot) Company, which owned 900 footwear shops and several factories. This was a contested bid, made without prior consultation with the company, appealing to the cupidity of its shareholders against its directors' wishes. Clore pioneered this contentious technique, which suited the brutality in his character. His contested bids forced boards of directors to recognize that they must maximize the assets for which they were responsible if they were to prevent control of their companies from passing to what Brendan Bracken in 1953 (reflecting a widespread prejudice) called 'the invading Israelites' (Cockett, 152).

In 1955 Clore became chairman of a reconstructed company called Sears Holdings. He acquired other shoe retailers, such as Dolcis (with 250 shops, bought for £5.8 million in 1956), combining these into the British Shoe Corporation, which with 2000 shops in the 1960s controlled almost one-quarter of the British retail shoe trade. The pre-tax profits of Sears rose from £1.4 million in 1953 (the year of Clore's acquisition) to over £90 million in 1979–80 (the year of his death).

Clore's other deals included the acquisition of the Mappin and Webb jewellery group in 1957, the heavily contested acquisition of the Lewis's Investment Trust (controlling Selfridges and other department stores) in 1965, and the acquisition of the William Hill bookmakers group for £20 million in 1971. His most ambitious bid, for the brewers Watney Mann in 1959, was defeated. He was also rebuffed when he tried to buy the Savoy Hotel in 1953; but his property company, City and Central Investments, then spent eight years in acquiring land near Park Lane and obtaining planning permissions to build a skyscraper hotel, for which in 1960 he signed a contract with the American hotelier Conrad Hilton.

In 1960 City and Central Investments merged with City Centre Properties run by Jack Cotton and later with a company called Murrayfield Properties. The new company of City Centre endured many internal troubles until in 1963 Clore ruthlessly marginalized Cotton. Clore's ambition to become a dominating force in property development was nevertheless frustrated, and after City Centre merged in 1968 with Land Securities Investment Trust, he relinquished participation in publicly quoted property companies. In 1964 he acquired 14 per cent of the equity of the merchant bank of M. Samuel and joined its board.

Clore married in 1943 Francine Rachel (who received the Croix de Guerre for war work in the French Resistance), daughter of Henri Jules Halphen, company director, of Paris. Clore and his wife, who had a son and daughter, were described in 1953 by Henry Channon as 'a nice couple, abundantly rich, and highly ambitious socially' (*Chips*, ed. James, 479). Clore liked to move among the gentile aristocracy, though he regarded them (as he did most people) with contempt. His sexual pride and furious possessiveness were outraged by the breakdown of his marriage, which was dissolved in 1957. He thereafter embarked on a libidinous rampage that lasted almost until his death. He was virile, sexually gluttonous, often crude and impatient. For some years Janet, marchioness of Milford Haven, acted as his social companion.

Clore farmed at Stype Grange in Berkshire, and in 1961 bought 16,627 acres in Herefordshire, which he sold for £20.5 million a few months before his death. His horses won several important races, notably the Oaks in 1966 (Valoris). He collected fine paintings and *objets d'art*, guided by 'a natural taste and a fine eye' (*The Clore Gallery*, 10). He was a benefactor of Jewish causes, and reputedly gave a cheque for £1 million to Zionist fund-raisers on the outbreak of the Six Day War in 1967. Having made other large charitable donations, he was displeased at waiting until 1971 for his knighthood. He retired as chairman of Sears in 1976 to enter tax exile at Monte Carlo, and died of cancer on 26 July 1979 at the London Clinic, Devonshire Place, London. Shortly before his death he discussed with the Tate Gallery the possible involvement of the Clore Foundation, which he had founded for philanthropic purposes, in finding a solution to the long-standing problem of the housing and display of J. M. W. Turner's bequest of his paintings to the nation. After Clore's death the Clore Gallery was built at the Tate to house the Turner bequest.

A small, elegant man with cold eyes, Clore detested weakness but always probed for it in others. 'All his life, he had the feeling of divine right, that he was superior, that he was a special person', his friend Charles Gordon wrote (Gordon, 43). His relationships were almost all mutually vigilant and calculating. He declared that he was always unhappy and had never known anyone who could truthfully say they were happy. Though luxury and power gratified him, money was his only passion.

RICHARD DAVENPORT-HINES

Sources personal knowledge (2004) · private information (2004) · C. Gordon, *The two tycoons* (1984) · *The Times* (21 Feb 1939) · R. Cockett, ed., *My dear Max* (1990), 152 · '*Chips': the diaries of Sir Henry Channon*, ed. R. R. James (1967), 479 · C. King, *Diary, 1965–1970* (1972), 260 · E. L. Erdman, *People and property* (1982) · O. Marriott, *The property boom* (1967) · L. Sainer, 'Clore, Sir Charles', *DBB · DNB* · R. Hamlyn, *The Clore Gallery: an illustrated account of the new building for the Turner Collection* (1987) · *Daily Telegraph* (27 July 1979)
Archives Wellcome L., corresp. with Sir Ernst Chain

Likenesses photograph, 1943 (with wife), Hult. Arch. · photograph, 1963, Hult. Arch. · G. Sutherland, pencil and crayon drawings, 1967, NPG · oils, Tate collection
Wealth at death tax exile in Monte Carlo

Close, Sir Barry, baronet (1756–1813), army officer in the East India Company and political officer in India, was born on 3 December 1756 at Elm Park, co. Armagh, the third son in the family of four sons and five daughters of Maxwell Close (*d.* 1793) and his wife and cousin, Mary, daughter of Captain Robert Maxwell of Fellows Hall, co. Armagh. The protestant ascendancy family had come to Ireland from Yorkshire under Charles I. After early education in Ireland he was entered as a cadet in the Madras army in 1771 at the age of fifteen, and was commissioned an ensign in the Madras native infantry on 3 September 1773. He was appointed adjutant of the newly formed 20th battalion in 1777, which joined the British garrison of Tellicherry on the Malabar coast, to be attacked and besieged by the forces of Mysore under Haidar Ali in 1780. Close's personal courage and talent for leadership were revealed in this action, and his treatment of the sepoys' followers and families ensured that his battalion remained steady when adjacent battalions mutinied after promises over leave and allowances were broken. The 1780 mutiny and subsequent inquiry prepared him for later experiences in an army whose loyalty was notoriously volatile. He acquired a reputation as an excellent linguist, invariably conducting his business with the sepoys in their own language.

In 1781 Close was appointed aide-de-camp to Major-General James Stuart, the commander-in-chief of the Madras army, and saw that officer summarily dismissed by the governor, Lord Macartney, for refusing to accept orders concerning the deployment of troops of the king's army against the French. Close was in attendance on the one-legged general throughout the drama of his arrest and forcible embarkation for England on 17 September 1783. His diplomatic handling of these highly contentious events enhanced his reputation among the British community in Madras. Gazetted a captain on 18 December 1783, he was selected to conduct boundary negotiations with the representatives of the new ruler of Mysore, Tipu Sultan. His career as a staff officer continued as deputy adjutant-general of the Madras army under Lord Cornwallis during the Third Anglo-Mysore War (1790–92), against Tipu Sultan. On his return to Madras he was appointed adjutant-general and gazetted a lieutenant-colonel on 29 November 1797.

Barry Close was an active member of the European community in Madras, gaining the respect of his fellows for speaking out against inflated food prices, bad roads, and general street lawlessness. He was instrumental in the formation of a permanent police committee on 29 December 1797, and in the establishment of the Madras military fund for the relief of widows and children.

Lord Wellesley's policy of aggressive expansion once more brought the Madras army, in combination with elements from Bombay and the nizam of Hyderabad, to the gates of Seringapatam in May 1799. Close, as adjutant-general, played the leading role in the planning and conduct of the successful assault in which Tipu Sultan died and the substantial kingdom was brought under British control. He was appointed to the commission which supervised the partition of Mysore, and drafted the subsidiary treaty which defined the terms under which the ancient Hindu dynasty of Mysore rulers would be restored to the throne from captivity. The governor-general, Wellesley, described Close as

> by far the ablest man in the army of Madras, and few more able officers exist in the world. He was the life and soul of the campaign. In addition, he is the ablest scholar in Persian, and in several of the native dialects. He is a man of extraordinary general knowledge and talents. His integrity is irreproachable; and he is a very amiable and pleasant man, with a rather warm temper.   (Ingram, 170)

Close was appointed the first resident at the Mysore court, with the task of supervising the young raja and settling the new state. But, before this could be achieved, he was dispatched to negotiate the annexation of all the territories in the Carnatic ruled by the nawab of Arcot, who was accused of having secretly plotted with Tipu against the British. During the negotiations (15 July 1801), the nawab died, and Close's mission was extended to settle the disputed succession. His mission successfully completed, in the same year he was appointed resident at the court of the peshwa at Poona in anticipation of further British expansion under Wellesley. He was responsible for concluding the treaty of Bassein with the peshwa on 31 December 1802 which permitted British intervention on the latter's behalf to coerce the princes of the Maratha confederacy. Subsequently, the initial subordination of the confederacy was completed by Arthur Wellesley's victory over Daulat Rao Sindhia at the battle of Assaye in 1803.

Close was promoted colonel of the 20th Madras native infantry on 27 August 1805 and, while nominally still resident at Poona, held a roving commission to maintain the uncertain peace among dissident elements within the Maratha states by negotiation and swift military action. But perhaps his most significant contribution to the East India Company's affairs was to intervene in the mutiny of British officers which paralysed the Madras army for eight months in 1809. In July that year his personal exhortation to the officers not to defy the Madras authorities, and, in their own language, to the sepoys not to follow their dissenting officers, caused the disaffected Hyderabad regiments to give up their protest and eventually led to the collapse of the mutiny throughout south India.

Close returned to Britain on leave in 1810 after almost forty continuous years of service in India. He was immediately promoted major-general (25 July 1810) and, through the influence of the earl of Buckinghamshire (then president of the Board of Control), was created a baronet by the prince regent on 12 December 1812. He died, unmarried, in London on 12 April 1813, and was buried on 23 April with full company honours in Marylebone church, Middlesex. His baronetcy became extinct.

Barry Close gained neither the fame nor the fortune

which came to later soldier administrators in India, such as Sir John Malcolm and Sir Thomas Munro, who profited from the consequences of the Wellesley period of intervention and expansion. Rather, he was representative of those men who enabled the East India Company to transform itself from an armed merchant to the agent of empire. It was a substantial change, which relied upon the uncertain talents of an expatriate community where the necessary skills were not imbued by formal training, but were found to a lesser or greater extent in the character and personal abilities of those on the spot who had sufficient ambition to respond to the demands of the moment.   NIGEL CHANCELLOR

Sources J. Burke and J. B. Burke, *A genealogical and heraldic history of the extinct and dormant baronetcies of England, Ireland, and Scotland* (1838) · Burke, *Gen. GB* (1837) · *GM*, 1st ser., 83/1 (1813), 496–7 · H. D. Love, *Vestiges of old Madras, 1640–1800*, 4 vols. (1913), vol. 3 · biographical series, personal records, BL OIOC, o/6/4, fol. 85 · biographical series, personal records, BL OIOC, o/6/13, fols. 42, 176, 271 · biographical series, personal records, BL OIOC, o/6/11, fol. 496 · records of service, Madras officers, 1771–1846, BL OIOC, L/Mil/11/38–49 · *East-India Register and Directory* (1813) · S. C. Hill, ed., *Catalogue of the home miscellaneous series of the India Office records* (1927) · J. Philippart, *East India military calendar*, 2 (1824) · BL, Wellesley MSS, 1756–1842, Add. MSS 13593, 13596, 13597, 13599, 13725 · M. Wilks, dedication, *Historical sketches of the south of India, in an attempt to trace the history of Mysoor*, 1 (1810) · Viscount Sidmouth, 'Notes', *Journal of the Society for Army Historical Research*, 46 (1968), 246–7 · R. D. Choksey, *A history of British diplomacy at the court of the peshwas, 1786–1816* (1951) · J. Mill, *The history of British India*, ed. H. H. Wilson, 5th edn, 10 vols. (1858) · W. J. Wilson, ed., *History of the Madras army*, 1–3 (1882–3), vols. 1–3 · E. Ingram, ed., *The private correspondence of Mr Dundas and Lord Wellesley, 1798–1801* (1969)

Archives BL, corresp. and papers, Add. MSS 13593, 13596–13599, 13669, 13725, 13770 · BL OIOC, letter-book and papers, Eur. MS D 1053 · BL OIOC, corresp. relating to India, home misc. series | BL OIOC, corresp. with Sir Arthur Wellesley, Eur. MS E 216 · NL Scot., corresp. with Alexander Walker · U. Southampton L., corresp. with Sir Arthur Wellesley

Likenesses J. Stuart, miniature, 1794, repro. in Sidmouth, 'Notes', facing p. 247; Christies, 25 June 1968 · T. Hickey, chalk drawing, 1801, Stratfield Saye, Hampshire · Moore, oils (after unknown artist), Oriental Club, London · M. A. Shee, oils, Man. City Gall.

Close, Sir Charles Frederick Arden- (1865–1952), surveyor and geographer, was born on 10 August 1865 at St Saviour's, Jersey, the eldest of the eleven children of Captain (later Major-General) Frederick Close (1830–1899) and his second wife, Lydia Ann Stevens. He was educated at a dame-school in Rochester, then at Thompson's school, Jersey, and at a crammer, passing second into the Royal Military Academy, Woolwich, in 1882. He excelled in mathematics, and in 1884 he passed out first, with the Pollock memorial medal, was commissioned in the Royal Engineers, and joined the School of Military Engineering, Chatham. After a year (1886) in Gibraltar he was first attached to and later commanded the balloon section at Chatham (1887–8). He was next posted to India where he served one year on battery construction for the Hooghly defences and then four years (1889–93) with the survey of India, engaged on topographic work in Upper Burma and geodetic triangulation on the Mandalay primary series

Sir Charles Frederick Arden-Close (1865–1952), by Walter Stoneman, 1939

(Toungoo-Katha) and the Mong Hsat secondary series up to the Siam border.

Returning to Chatham, Close was sent in the next year (1895) to west Africa to survey the boundary between the Niger Coast Protectorate and the German Cameroons. On his return he was appointed to the Ordnance Survey and in 1898 was made British commissioner to delimit the frontier of British Central Africa and Northern Rhodesia with German East Africa for over 200 miles between lakes Nyasa and Tanganyika. He collaborated with David Gill, HM astronomer at the Cape, in relation to longitude fixation of points on the German frontier. He was appointed CMG in 1899. Next year he led a small survey detachment for the Second South African War, for which practically no maps existed. It is claimed that this survey unit produced the first multicoloured map to be printed by lithography in the field by the British army. In 1902–5 he was chief instructor in surveying at Chatham. There he introduced new methods and revised his earlier work, *Text Book of Military Topography*, part 2 (1898), to produce the *Text Book of Topographical and Geographical Surveying* (1905) which, with later revisions, remained the standard work for the next half-century.

By 1905 Close had very wide practical experience of surveying, both geodetic and topographic, in three continents, as well as firsthand knowledge of international boundary surveys and settlements. In that year he became head of the topographical (from 1907 geographical) section, general staff, at the War Office, of which a major concern was overseas maps. He pressed, with success, for the formation of the colonial survey committee (August 1905) and for surveying in British colonies. Close and his directors in MI4, having experienced in South Africa the disadvantages of waging war without maps, took the unprecedented step of preparing maps of a probable European theatre of war. He was to recall that:

> it was whilst we were drawing these maps that Mr Haldane, the Secretary of State, came round the GSGS. When he saw the maps of France and Belgium he turned to me and said 'You will never want those'.   (Institution of Royal Engineers, May 1933)

Thanks to the foresight of the geographical section, the British army entered the First World War better supplied with maps than in any previous conflict. An even wider project was the Carte Internationale du Monde au Millionième—first proposed in 1891 and exhaustively discussed later but with little progress. With support from the War and Foreign offices, Close arranged a meeting of the newly formed international map committee at the Foreign Office in 1909, attended by delegates of the great powers, at which concrete proposals were made. The large number of maps eventually published on this system is a tribute to Close's driving power.

Close was appointed director-general of the Ordnance Survey on 18 August 1911. He found the organization 'rather out of touch with the scientific world'. He proceeded with a second geodetic levelling of the United Kingdom, creating 'fundamental' bench marks which have been of lasting value. He also established three mean-sea level tidal stations—at Dunbar, Newlyn, and Felixstowe, of which the second remains in operation. Close also turned his attention to the cartography of the Ordnance Survey with the intention of revolutionizing the appearance of the one-inch map. His first attempt, the *Killarney District* map (1913), was crowned with success. For artistic achievement in colour printing it remains unsurpassed by the Ordnance Survey. But the processes involved were too expensive in post-war Britain, and a simpler model was adopted for the one-inch map. This new style lacked the coloured layers, hill-shading, and hachures of the Irish sheet, but, with a smaller contour interval and revised road classification system, it set the pattern for all subsequent one-inch series. In 1919, Close secured the appointment of a civilian archaeology officer, O. G. S. Crawford, resulting in a highly acclaimed series of historical maps of which the first was *Roman Britain* (1924). In 1913 Close had married Gladys Violet (d. 1953), daughter of Theodore Henry Percival, formerly of the India Office. They had one daughter and two sons. Close had become a parent in later life but, even in his late fifties and early sixties, was always ready to play football with his sons. This thoughtfulness for the well-being of others extended from his own family—he had been constant in giving financial help to his mother and siblings—to those in his employ. He was affectionately known as Pa Close in the army, and he instituted the system of staff rewards for innovative ideas in the Ordnance Survey.

In 1914 Close delivered the Halley lecture at Oxford which was incorporated in his 'Notes on the geodesy of the British Isles' (Ordnance Survey professional paper no. 3). During the First World War the Ordnance Survey printed 32 million maps for the armies in France and elsewhere. Close, who had been promoted major (1901), lieutenant-colonel (1908), and colonel (1912), periodically visited the western front. After the war Close had the disagreeable task of implementing drastic cuts in the Ordnance Survey establishment which had been recommended by the Geddes committee. A direct result of this was that the large-scale plans fell massively into arrears by the 1930s.

Close retired in 1922, and in the many productive years still before him he devoted himself to his family and to work on geographical and kindred matters. In 1911 he had been president of section E (geography) of the British Association, giving a controversial address in which he stated that much of the subject matter then studied by geographers was more properly the province of other disciplines ('Report 18', *British Association*, 1911, 436–43). It was regarded by his professional geographical contemporaries as 'geographical heresy' (RGS, Close MSS, 1911). However, he served on the council of the Royal Geographical Society (1904–40), and was Victoria gold medallist (1927) and president (1927–30). He was chairman of the national committee for geography and general secretary of the International Geographical Union, being president in 1934–8. He was first treasurer (1919–30) then chairman of the Palestine Exploration Fund (1930–45), and president of the Hampshire Field Club (1929–32 and 1935–6). In 1927, when president of the Geographical Association, he addressed that body with a lecture entitled 'Population and migration'. He was the author of about fifty publications on topics ranging from geodesy and map projections, history of cartography, and meteorology to population studies. Among these were: *The Early Years of the Ordnance Survey* (1926), *The Map of England* (1932), 'A fifty years retrospect', *Empire Survey Review* (vol. 1, 1932, and vol. 2, 1933–4), and 'Our crowded island', *Eugenics Review* (April 1948). He was president of the International Union for the Scientific Investigation of Population Problems in 1931–7. He also taught mathematics at Winchester College during the Second World War, standing in for staff who were employed on military service.

Close was elected FRS in 1919; received an honorary ScD from Cambridge (1928); and was an honorary member of the Russian, German, Belgian, Dutch, Spanish, and Swiss geographical societies. He was appointed CB in 1916 and KBE in 1918; he was an officer of the order of Leopold, and a member of the Afghan order of Astaur. He changed his name to Arden-Close by deed poll in 1938 in order to comply with the terms of a bequest. Arden-Close died at the Enniskerry Nursing Home, Sleepers Hill, Winchester, on 19 December 1952. His contribution to the cartography and history of the Ordnance Survey was recognized in 1980 with the formation of a society named after him: The Charles Close Society for the Study of Ordnance Survey Maps.   J. De Graaff-Hunter, *rev.* Yolande Hodson

Sources T. W. Freeman, 'Charles Frederick Arden-Close, 1865–1952', *Geographers: biobibliographical studies*, 9, ed. T. W. Freeman (1985) · C. I. M. O'Brien, 'A man for his time' Sir Charles Arden-Close, 1865–1952', *Sheetlines*, 34 (1992), 1–7 · RGS, Close MSS · 'The history of the formation and work of MI4 war office/geographical section of the general staff', Institution of Royal Engineers, class no. 355.486 [a file of papers and corresp.] · Y. Hodson, 'The ordnance survey popular edition one-inch map of England and Wales, 1919–1942: a cartographic study', PhD diss., U. Lond., 1995 · *The Times* (22 Dec 1952) · M. N. M., 'Colonel Sir Charles F. Arden-Close', *Royal Engineers Journal*, new ser., 67 (1953), 91–3 · *Eugenics Review* (April 1953) · M. N. M., 'Colonel Sir Charles F. Arden-Close', *GJ*, 119 (1953), 251–2 · *GJ*, 119 (1953), 257 · J. de Graaff-Hunter, *Obits. FRS*, 8 (1952–3), 327–39 · T. Owen and E. Pilbeam, *Ordnance Survey: map makers to Britain since 1791* (1992) · W. A. Seymour, ed., *A history of the Ordnance Survey* (1980) · private information (1971, 2004) · personal knowledge (1971) · *CGPLA Eng. & Wales* (1953)
Archives Ordnance Survey Library, Southampton, MSS relating to projections · RGS, corresp. and papers relating to Royal Geographical Society · Royal Engineers, Brompton barracks, Chatham, Kent, MSS relating to ballooning | Bodl. Oxf., letters to O. G. S. Crawford · Bodl. Oxf., corresp. with J. L. Myres · Palestine Exploration Fund, corresp. with Palestine Exploration Fund relating to Samaria
Likenesses W. Stoneman, photographs, 1917–39, NPG [*see illus.*] · photograph, *c.*1919, RS; repro. in *Obits. FRS* · photograph, *c.*1930, ordnance survey · group portrait, photograph, 1930–39 (with family), repro. in Freeman, 'Charles Frederick Arden-Close'; priv. coll.
Wealth at death £1436 13*s.* 2*d.*: administration with will, 24 Aug 1953, *CGPLA Eng. & Wales*

Close, Francis (1797–1882), dean of Carlisle, was born at Corston, near Bath, on 11 July 1797, the youngest of four boys and five girls of the family of the agriculturist the Revd Henry Close (1753–1806) and Mary Waring (1754–1843). Close was educated at Midhurst grammar school (1806–8) and Merchant Taylors' School (1808–12). In 1813 he experienced an evangelical conversion during his four years as a private pupil of the Revd John Scott of Hull. Close entered St John's College, Cambridge, where he continued to identify himself with evangelicalism and came under the influence of Charles Simeon, whom he described as 'my affectionate father, my generous patron, and my wise and helpful counsellor' (manuscript at Ridley Hall, Cambridge). He graduated BA in 1820 and MA in 1824; he was awarded a Lambeth DD in 1856. In 1820 Close married Anne Diana Arden (1791–1877); they had a family of five boys (one of whom died in infancy) and four girls.

Close was ordained deacon in 1820 and priest in 1821. He was successively curate of Church Lawford, near Rugby (1820–22), Willesden and Kingsbury (1822–4), and Holy Trinity Church, Cheltenham (1824–6). On the sudden death of Charles Jervis, Simeon appointed Close to succeed him as perpetual curate of Cheltenham parish church. He was also chaplain to Lord Decies from 1828, and rector of Hatford, Oxfordshire (1832–5). Close consolidated and expanded the work of Jervis, and as Cheltenham increased in population from 13,396 in 1821 to 35,051 in 1851 he developed the spa town into a leading evangelical centre, which Simeon described as 'a heaven upon earth' (W. Carus, *Memoir of Charles Simeon*, 1847, 783). Close

Francis Close (1797–1882), by John Jabez Edwin Mayall

erected four district churches each with its own infant and national schools. In 1853, with other evangelicals who objected to the outlook of the National Society, Close formed the Church of England Education Society. Educational establishments in Cheltenham were founded (like Cheltenham College in 1841) or revived (like Cheltenham grammar school) while Close was incumbent; he was actively involved in their running, considering them to be 'his right hand and his left hand' (A. Harper, ed., *The History of the Cheltenham Grammar School*, 1856, 43). Close was chairman of the directors of Cheltenham College, and its evangelical stance was lost only after the constitution was changed in 1862. After his death the Dean Close Memorial School (opened in 1886) continued the evangelical tradition no longer evident at Cheltenham College. Close's greatest and most lasting achievement was in the provision of teacher training. By the mid-1840s several hundred teachers had been trained in the Cheltenham schools, and in 1847 the Church of England Training School was opened. Three years later it moved into purpose-built premises which had been financed by fund-raising engagements mainly conducted by Close.

Close appointed evangelicals as curates, as incumbents to the district churches, and as members of staff in the educational establishments. This brought a critical response: Alfred Tennyson, who lived for a short time in Cheltenham, called Close a parish pope, and those who objected to the activities of Close and his military friends referred to 'the Lieutenant-General Close brigade' (*Cheltenham Free Press*, 25 Dec 1847). Yet the town became known as one of the most sober and religious places in the whole of the United Kingdom. Close had the support of at least half of the inhabitants, and his forceful preaching attracted large congregations and numerous female admirers. Many of his sermons were published (the first anonymously in 1822) and several of them were highly critical of Romanism within and outside the Church of England, most notably *The Restoration of Churches is the Restoration of Popery* (1844) and his five November sermons, *The Footsteps of Error* (1863). Close supported missions at home and overseas, was a convinced sabbatarian (particularly opposing Sunday trains), and was an outspoken critic of horse-racing and the stage.

After a boating accident in Switzerland in 1855 Close became slightly paralysed and, in addition, suffered from gout, but in 1856 he was appointed dean of Carlisle in succession to A. C. Tait. In Carlisle Close took on a new lease of life and extended many of his earlier concerns, apart from education. As dean he worked with bishops Henry Montagu Villiers and Samuel Waldegrave, and they made Carlisle the most protestant of the English dioceses. In the city Close regarded himself as the 'rector of Carlisle' and as such took a lead in its affairs. He was concerned with the spiritual destitution of the poor and opened mission rooms and a temporary wooden church. He erected two city churches (St John's and St Mary's) and was involved in the erection of a third. At Cheltenham he had been known as the poor man's friend and, in Carlisle, alarm at the effects of drink among the working classes turned him into a convinced teetotaller. His concern for total abstinence earned him the sobriquet of the teetotal dean. His opposition to Anglo-Catholicism continued, and much of his energy was directed against the English Church Union. At the cathedral he dismissed the precentor, and in the city he led a movement to close an Anglo-Catholic oratory. He was an active member of the Church Association, and like his more conservative contemporaries was critical of the early Keswick Movement.

Close was a big man, tall with a commanding voice. He modelled his preaching and teaching on those of Simeon and constantly expressed his indebtedness to him. Close had a good sense of humour and was extremely fond of his pets. Though he was much criticized, contemporaries admired his staunch commitment to the gospel in Cheltenham and Carlisle.

On 22 December 1880 Close married Mary Antrim Hodgson (1806–1899), daughter of John Mabanke and widow of David Hodgson. He resigned as dean in August 1881 and settled in Penzance at Morrab House, where he died of heart failure on 18 December 1882. He was buried in Carlisle cemetery and a marble effigy was erected in the cathedral in 1885. A. F. MUNDEN

Sources *The Times* (19 Dec 1882) · *The Times* (25 Dec 1882) · [R. Glover], *The golden decade of a favoured town* (1884) · G. Berwick, 'Close of Cheltenham: parish pope', *Theology*, 39 (1939), 193–201,

276–85 · M. Hennell, *Sons of the prophets* (1979), 104–21 · A. F. Munden, 'Evangelical in the shadows: Charles Jervis of Cheltenham', *The Churchman*, new ser., 96 (1982), 142–50 · A. F. Munden, 'Radicalism versus evangelicalism in Victorian Cheltenham', *Southern History*, 5 (1983), 115–21 · A. F. Munden, *A Cheltenham Gamaliel: Dean Close of Cheltenham* (1997) · O. Ashton, 'Clerical control and radical response in Cheltenham Spa, 1838–48', *Midland History*, 8 (1983), 121–47 · C. More, *The training of teachers, 1847–1947* (1992) · private information (2004)

Archives LPL, letters to A. C. Tait

Likenesses J. P. Papera, bust, 1836, Dean Close School, Cheltenham · J. R. Jackson, mezzotint, pubd 1850 (after H. W. Phillips), BM · Armstead, marble monument, 1885, Carlisle Cathedral · Day & Son, lithograph, NPG · J. J. E. Mayall, photograph, NPG [*see illus.*] · D. J. Pound, stipple (after photograph by Mayall), BM, NPG · portrait, Cheltenham Art Gallery and Museum · portrait, Cheltenham parish church · two portraits, Dean Close School, Cheltenham

Wealth at death £1764 3*s.* 11*d.*: probate, 13 Jan 1883, *CGPLA Eng. & Wales*

Close [*married name* Neame], **Ivy Lilian** (1890–1968), beauty queen and film actress, was born in Stockton-on-Tees, co. Durham, on 15 June 1890, the elder daughter and one of four children of John Robert Close, a jeweller in Stockton, and his wife, Emma (*née* Blackburn). Her birthplace, 19 Durham Street, was two doors away from the house where, in 1888, the film star Will Hay was born.

On 4 May 1908 it was announced she was winner of the *Daily Mirror*'s International Beauty Competition, Britain's first national beauty contest, organized as a response to the *Chicago Tribune*'s assertion that the winner of the 1907 American Beauty Contest was 'the most beautiful woman in the world'. Over 15,000 women entered the British contest, which was judged by a committee of distinguished artists. As a prize, Ivy received a Rover car, and her portrait was painted by Arthur Hacker and exhibited at the Royal Academy's 1908 summer show.

After a long engagement, Ivy Close married on 26 December 1910 (Stuart) Elwin Neame (1886–1923), a portrait photographer who had been commissioned by the *Mirror* to photograph entrants to the beauty contest. He also experimented with moving pictures, and in 1912 directed her in her first film, *Dream Paintings*. They were signed by Cecil Hepworth, who released—among others—*The Sleeping Beauty* (1912) and *Myfanwy: a Tragedy* (1913) under the name Ivy Close Films. Elwin's artistic approach was epitomized in his 1914 film *Ivy's Elopement*, in which she posed as figures from famous paintings. That year Ivy starred in her first feature film, *The Lure of London*, directed by Bert Haldane. In May 1916 she sailed for the USA to star in a series of comedy shorts for the Kalem company. Interviewed by *Pictures and the Picturegoer* before leaving, she stated she 'could not have enough excitement' and that her favourite hobby was 'motorcycling' (*Pictures and the Picturegoer*, 204–5). During 1917, back in Britain, she appeared in four films for Broadwest, including the documentary *The Women's Land Army* with Violet Hopson. In 1918 she played Nelson's wife in Maurice Elvey's propaganda film *Nelson*. Her most significant role was in the French director Abel Gance's pioneering film *La roue*

Ivy Lilian Close (1890–1968), by unknown photographer

(1920), set in a Marseilles railway marshalling yard and the Alps.

Elwin Neame was killed in a motor accident in 1923, leaving Ivy to bring up their two sons. Although she still played small roles, her career declined, and in 1930 the *North-Eastern Daily Gazette* described her predicament under the headline 'Stockton girl cursed by beauty'. In 1934 she was interviewed by the BBC, with other silent movie stars, such as Dorothy and Lilian Gish and Mary Pickford, about the early days of film. Her elder son, Ronald Neame (*b.* 1911), went on to a successful career as cinematographer, film producer, and director.

Ivy Close died at a nursing home in Goring, Oxfordshire, on 4 December 1968. In its obituary, the *Daily Mirror* described her as a 'pioneer', and quoted her son Ronald saying that 'in her time she was one of the top five British stars'.   MARK ROWLAND-JONES

Sources 'Ivy Close joins Kalem', *Pictures and the Picturegoer* (3 June 1916), 204–5 · 'Miss Ivy Lilian Close', *Daily Mirror* (4 May 1908), 1 · 'Stockton girl cursed by beauty', *North-Eastern Daily Gazette* (13 Feb 1930), 1 · R. Low, *The history of the British film, 4: 1918–1929* (1971) · K. Brownlow, *The parade's gone by* (1968) · 'A living poem', *The Bioscope* (3 Oct 1912), 171 · 'The *Mirror*'s first glamour girl is dead', *Daily Mirror* (7 Dec 1968), 3 · I. Close, 'How to become beautiful', *Woman's Life* (29 May 1909), 920 · b. cert.

Archives Green Dragon Museum, Stockton-on-Tees, scrapbook | FILM BFI NFTVA, performance footage | SOUND BBC WAC, oral history interview

Likenesses A. Hacker, oils, 1908, repro. in Cassell, *RA pictures* (1908), 152 · E. Neame, photograph, 1908, repro. in 'Miss Ivy Lilian Close', *Daily Mirror*, 1 · E. Neame, portraits, Green Dragon Museum, Stockton-on-Tees · photograph, Green Dragon Museum, Stockton-on-Tees [*see illus.*]

Close, John [*called* Poet Close] (1816–1891), writer of doggerel, was born at Gunnerside, Swaledale, Yorkshire, and baptized there on 11 August 1816. He was the son of Jarvis Close (*d.* 1853), a butcher and Wesleyan preacher, and his wife, Elizabeth. While assisting his father in the butchery trade, Close began to issue verse-tracts and fly-sheets in the 1830s, including *The Satirist, or, Every Man in his Humour* (1833). In 1846 he established himself as a printer in Kirkby Stephen, and *The Poetical Works … of John Close* appeared in 1860.

Close's assiduity in writing verse about people and affairs in his neighbourhood attracted the patronage of the local nobility, despite his lack of any real literary talent. Owing to the support of Lord Carlisle, Lord Lonsdale, and other gentlemen, in April 1861 Close was awarded a civil-list pension of £50 on the recommendation of Lord Palmerston. The award provoked a question in the House of Commons (*Hansard 3*, 162, 2 May 1861, 1375–6), and much amused comment in the London press; on 3 June 1861 it was cancelled, and by way of compensation Close received £100 from the Royal Bounty Fund.

Close was married, and had a daughter and two sons. After the events of 1861 he continued to issue 'pamphlets of metrical balderdash, interspersed with documents relating to his wrongs' (*DNB*), selling them from a bookstall at Bowness-on-Windermere. Among his subsequent works were *The Wise Man of Stainmore* (1864) and *Bowness Church Bells and other Poems* (1872). He died at Kirkby Stephen, Westmorland, on 15 February 1891, and was buried in the local cemetery. He is referred to as Poet Close in 'Ferdinando and Elvira, or, The Gentle Pieman', one of W. S. Gilbert's *Bab Ballads* (1869).   DOUGLAS BROWN

Sources Boase, *Mod. Eng. biog.* · *DNB* · J. Close, *Poet Close and his pension* (1861) · J. Close, *The poetical works … of John Close* (1860) [with a biographical sketch of the poet by 'Delta'] · *The Times* (17 Feb 1891) · *ILN* (21 Feb 1891) · *Penrith Observer* (17 Feb 1891) · *Penrith Observer* (24 Feb 1891) · *Daily News* (17 Feb 1891) · *Daily News* (18 Feb 1891) · *Yorkshire Post* (17 Feb 1891) · *Yorkshire Post* (18 Feb 1891) · *Newcastle Leader* (17 Feb 1891) · *Newcastle Leader* (18 Feb 1891) · *St James's Gazette* (17 Feb 1891) · *St James's Gazette* (18 Feb 1891) · *IGI*
Archives Mitchell L., Glas., Glasgow City Archives, documents relating to grant of a Royal Literary Fund pension
Wealth at death £41 18s. 1d.: probate, 24 March 1891, *CGPLA Eng. & Wales*

Close, Maxwell Henry (1822–1903), geologist and man of science, born on 23 October 1822 at 7 Merrion Square East, Dublin, the eldest son among the eight sons and three daughters of Henry Samuel Close, later of Newtown Park House, co. Dublin, and his wife, Jane, daughter of Holt Waring of Waringstown, co. Down, the dean of Dromore. His father was a partner in Ball's Bank, Dublin. Major-General Sir Barry Close was his great-uncle, his brother Major George Champagné Close served in the Abyssinian expedition of 1868, and another brother, Captain Arthur Richard Close, was killed in 1865 during the New Zealand wars.

After education by private tutor and at a school in Weymouth, Dorset, Close entered Trinity College, Dublin, in June 1840; he received his BA in 1846, the divinity testimonium in 1847, and his MA in 1867. In 1847 he took holy orders and he was ordained priest in the Church of England the following year. He served as curate of All Saints, Northampton, from 1847 to 1849, and as rector of Shangton, in Leicestershire, from 1849 to 1857, but he resigned that living on conscientious grounds because he no longer felt able to hold a benefice obtained through lay patronage. He served as curate of Waltham on the Wolds, Leicestershire, from 1857 to 1861, but, as his father had recently died, he returned to Dublin in 1861 to live the life of a gentleman scholar, although he occasionally performed clerical duties. He is not known to have been married.

Close devoted himself to the affairs of such bodies as the Royal Dublin Society (he long served on the council), the Royal Geological Society of Ireland (president between 1877 and 1879), the Fortnightly Club (council member), and the Royal Irish Academy. He was elected a member of the academy on 13 May 1867 and served as its treasurer from 30 November 1878 until 16 March 1903. It was generally understood that had he not been afflicted by increasing deafness, he would have been elected to the academy's presidency.

Close contributed to astronomy, Pleistocene geology, mathematics, physics, and the study of the Irish language. The results of his acute geological field investigations were incorporated in three important papers read to the Royal Geological Society of Ireland between May 1864 and May 1870, and in an essay on the glaciation of Iar-Connaught written in collaboration with George Henry Kinahan and published in 1872. His studies demonstrated that Ireland had formerly been covered by an ice-cap centred over co. Fermanagh, that local glaciers had once existed in the Irish uplands, and that many lake-basins in co. Kerry were ice-excavated.

A gentle, genial, modest, and retiring man, Close published a work on physics (1884, 2nd edn, 1886) and another on astronomy (1894) under the pseudonyms of John O'Toole and Claudius Kennedy respectively, in order to divert attention away from himself. He died on 12 September 1903 in the bachelor apartments which had long been his at a hotel at 38 Lower Baggot Street, Dublin, and was buried in Dean's Grange cemetery. His keen interest in the Irish language is reflected in his will where he left £1000 towards the printing cost of an Irish-language dictionary to be published by the Royal Irish Academy.

GORDON L. HERRIES DAVIES

Sources *Irish Naturalist*, 12 (1903), 301 · *Geological Magazine*, new ser., 4th decade, 10 (1903), 575–6 · A. Geikie, *Quarterly Journal of the Geological Society*, 60 (1904), lxxi–lxxiv
Likenesses oils, Royal Irish Acad.
Wealth at death £10,750 9s. in England: Irish probate sealed in England, 11 Nov 1903, *CGPLA Eng. & Wales*

Close, Nicholas (d. 1452), bishop of Coventry and Lichfield, was probably a member of a minor Westmorland family, and most likely began his ecclesiastical career in the diocese of Carlisle. Stephen Close, a master of arts of Cambridge and a chaplain of Bishop Lumley of Carlisle in 1448, who acted as Nicholas's proctor in Rome in respect of both his episcopal promotions, was surely a kinsman.

Close's career was established during his time at Cambridge University, where he was acting as a proctor in 1433–5 and obtained the degrees of BTh by March 1441 and DTh by 1445. More especially, he was nominated on 13 February 1441 by Henry VI as one of the first six fellows of King's College. The accounts of the college show Close's heavy personal involvement in the consolidation of the new foundation, and in 1447 he became its official master of works. On 22 March 1446 he had actually been appointed warden of the older King's Hall, remaining so until 1452, but on 30 November that year was appointed warden of King's College, or at least granted the reversion. By 22 March 1446 he had been appointed a royal chaplain, a sign of favour he still held on 9 January 1448, when the pope described him as 'continually commensal' with the king (*CEPR letters*, 10.11). In early July 1449 Close was serving as chancellor of the university when he was commissioned to treat for a truce with the Scots. Probably on 30 January 1450 he was granted arms by the king 'for the laudable services rendered by him in many diverse ways, both in the work of building our college royal and in other matters' (Bouch, 117).

Close was admitted as vicar of St Zachary's, Cambridge, on 16 May 1445. On 22 March 1446 he was granted the wardenship of St Nicholas's Hospital, Carlisle, for life, and he was archdeacon of Carlisle by 9 January 1448. The then bishop, Marmaduke Lumley, an impressive treasurer of the realm, was already being vigorously supported by the government for promotion to some greater see, at this time London. It can be no coincidence that Close was made archdeacon of Colchester in that diocese on 15 February 1449. Given the king's personal favour, his own local birth and preferment, and perhaps even the personal goodwill of his predecessor, Close's papal provision to Carlisle on 30 January 1450, when Lumley finally secured Lincoln, is no surprise. The temporalities were restored on 14 March, and his metropolitan, Cardinal Kemp, consecrated him at York House in Westminster on the following day.

Close had secured permission from the pope to make formal visitations of his diocese by deputy for life and to receive procurations in cash, 'he being much hindered by the service of [the king], that he cannot do so in person, and it being more burdensome to be visited by the bishop than by his officials' (*CEPR letters*, 10.57). If the second reason was brazenly disingenuous, the first may have been rendered redundant by circumstances even before the bull was issued, although Close's service to the king had not been political. A satirical ballad of the summer of 1450 calls upon the bishop of Carlisle to 'sing *Credo* full sore, "to such false traitors come foule ending"', but possibly its author still had Lumley in mind (Wright, 2.234). Close's

whereabouts during 1450 are quite unknown; there is no sign of him in Cambridge, his diocese, or with the king. The loss of his Carlisle register hides his whereabouts throughout his episcopacy. In 1451, however, he was appointed a commissioner to investigate the performance of the conservators of the truce with Scotland, which suggests that he would be at least visiting his diocese.

It is clear, however, that the king retained a high opinion of Close, who on 30 August 1452 was translated to the more considerable see of Coventry and Lichfield, with restitution of temporalities being made as early as 8 September. In the event, he barely lived to enjoy his advancement, and again no evidence survives of his initial administrative arrangements. He died on 24 November 1452, intestate. King's College none the less came to possess his library. As he had already given it a number of valuables, this would no doubt have been to his satisfaction. It had been the corner-stone of his achievement.

RICHARD K. ROSE

Sources *Chancery records* · Emden, *Cam.*, 142 · C. M. L. Bouch, *Prelates and people of the lake counties: a history of the diocese of Carlisle, 1133–1933* (1948) · M. Harvey, *England, Rome, and the papacy, 1417–1464* (1993) · *Fasti Angl., 1300–1541*, [St Paul's, London] · *Fasti Angl., 1066–1300*, [York] · *Fasti Angl., 1300–1541*, [Coventry] · *CEPR letters*, vol. 10 · T. Wright, ed., *Political poems and songs relating to English history*, 2, Rolls Series, 14 (1861), 234

Close, Thomas (1796–1881), antiquary, was born in Manchester on 12 February 1796, the son of John Close, a Manchester merchant, and his wife, Mary. He was a keen antiquary who specialized in genealogy and heraldry. He drew up elaborate pedigrees of the Tattershall, Wahe, and other prominent families. In several peerage cases he gave important evidence, including that of the Shrewsbury and Talbot succession in 1856–8. In 1866 he published *St. Mary's Church, Nottingham: its probable architect and benefactors, with remarks on the heraldic window described by Thoroton*. Close was a fellow of the Society of Antiquaries, a chevalier of the order of Leopold in Belgium, and a member of other foreign orders. He was also grand master of the masonic province of Nottingham, and one of the founders and original members of the Reform Club (1836). For many years he served as the auditor of the London and South Western Railway. He died at his home in St James's Street, Nottingham, on 25 January 1881, three days after the death of his wife.

W. W. WROTH, rev. MICHAEL ERBEN

Sources *The Times* (31 Jan 1881) · Boase, *Mod. Eng. biog.* · Allibone, *Dict.* · *CGPLA Eng. & Wales* (1881) · parish register, Manchester Cathedral, Man. CL, Manchester Archives and Local Studies
Archives V&A NAL, MS of work on Clarendon's 'Rebellion'
Wealth at death under £60,000: probate, 4 March 1881, *CGPLA Eng. & Wales*

Close, William (1775?–1813), antiquary, was reputedly born on 25 May 1775 at Field Broughton, Cartmel, Lancashire. His father, John Close, variously described as farmer and molecatcher, subsequently moved to the Isle of Walney, off the Furness coast, before settling by 1795 at Dalton in Furness. Until he was ten, Close attended the chapel school on the Isle of Walney, where the only book was *Lilly's Grammar*. He recalled supplementary study under an ash tree in the chapel yard, and apparently desired originally to be a sailor. But in 1790 he was apprenticed to Mr Parkinson, a surgeon at Burton in Kendal. In 1796–7 Close attended lectures at the Royal Infirmary and the university in Edinburgh. Shortly afterwards, having apparently obtained a diploma, he joined Thomas Brockbank in medical practice at Dalton in Furness. On 30 October 1803 he married Isabel, daughter of Robert Charnock, a blacksmith, and his wife, Isabella; a son was born in 1805, and a daughter in 1806.

For sixteen years Close devoted himself to professional duties while also studying music, drawing, natural philosophy, and the history of the Furness area. He showed awareness of medical advances: in 1799 he experimented with vaccination against smallpox; children in the village of Rampside were inoculated at his own expense and with supposed success. In 1805 he produced a new edition of Thomas West's *Antiquities of Furness*, with a supplement of eighty-six pages. Among other topics, he added local detail on Dalton, a biography of George Romney, the portrait painter (born in Dalton in Furness), engravings, and lists of plants. Between 1805 and 1813 he prepared a topographical work, *An Itinerary of Furness and the Environs*. The historian T. A. Beck later tried arranging Close's unfinished notes into a continuous narrative, and the subsequent manuscript survives at Manchester Central Library. The work contains descriptions of country seats, picturesque scenery, and other local sights, supplemented by transcripts of documents and epitaphs and observations on recovering land from Walney Channel.

Between 1800 and 1805 Close contributed to William Nicholson's *Journal of Natural Philosophy*. From youth, he had also performed music, which he initially taught to Dalton children. By 1798 he was contemplating improvements to wind instruments. In 1809 he sent proposals to the Society of Arts for improving the range of trumpets by using tubular appendages. His techniques were also adaptable to the french horn and the bugle. After commissioning trials, a committee recommended Close for the society's gold medal, but he was offered only a silver medal. Close declined the award (the society's minutes suggested controversy) and he was also asked to relinquish patent rights. During 1812 he published a treatise and on 14 April was granted a patent for improvements to 'polyphonian trumpets'. He subsequently sold the rights to Thomas Percival, a London dealer. Close died from consumption at Dalton in Furness on 27 June 1813; he was buried at Walney chapel on the 29th.

One writer described Close as 'a little slender man, very clever but rather changeable and fond of riding on horseback' (Gaythorpe). His medical colleague William Harrison mentioned his 'natural irritability', while estimates of his medical and academic work have varied. Although some of his interests seemed eccentric, later scholars utilized and generally admired his writings. However, the contemporary diarist William Fleming of Pennington (possibly because of academic rivalry) was often contemptuous of his personality, appearance, music playing, and

editorial ability. Certainly his musical innovations were quickly superseded by later advancements. But during his lifetime Close was probably the most active personality in the intellectual life of the Furness area.

AIDAN C. J. JONES

Sources H. Gaythorpe, 'William Close, surgeon, apothecary, historian, musician', *Proceedings of Barrow Naturalists Field Club*, 17 (1903–4), 166–80 · William Fleming of Pennington, diaries, 1805–13, Barrow Central Library · *GM*, 1st ser., 83/2 (1813) · *Lancaster Gazette* (3 July 1813) · Royal Society for the Encouragement of Arts, Manufactures & Commerce, London, minutes of the committee of mechanics, 18 Jan 1810, 14 March 1811, 28 March 1811, 11 April 1811 · Royal Society for the Encouragement of Arts, Manufactures & Commerce, London, society minutes, 17 April 1811, 24 April 1811, 22 May 1811 · matriculations, 1796–7, U. Edin. L., university archives · F. Evans, *Furness and Furness Abbey* (1842), 143 · C. M. Jopling, *A sketch of Furness and Cartmel* (1843), 192 · R. Casson, *A few Furness worthies* (1889), 9–10 · parish register, Dalton in Furness, Cumbria AS, Barrow · parish register, Walney, Cumbria AS, Barrow
Archives Cumbria AS, Barrow, MSS · Man. CL | Cumbria AS, Barrow, Harper Gaythorpe MSS

Closse, George (*fl.* 1571–1621), Church of England clergyman, is of unknown origins. First recorded in 1571, when he matriculated as sizar at Trinity College, Cambridge, he was incorporated as BA from Oxford and proceeded MA in 1579. In 1581 he attempted to become vicar of Cuckfield, Sussex. This benefice had recently been the subject of much controversy, culminating in the deprivation of its incumbent, who was also Bishop Curteys's brother. Closse tried to take advantage of this by persuading Archbishop Grindal to present him on the grounds of the living's vacancy, even though Curteys had already presented one Alexander Southwick. Grindal's chancellor instituted Closse on 14 June 1581, but he was unable to take effective possession, and by 14 September 1582 he had been deprived, having also been summoned before the privy council. It is probable that Closse's next move was to the relatively wealthy parish of Black Torrington, Devon, in 1582, although his payment of first fruits did not commence until 1586. In the intervening years he appears to have been preacher at St Magnus the Martyr, London. Called upon at short notice to preach at Paul's Cross on 6 March 1586, Closse took the opportunity to reprove the lord mayor, Sir Wolstan Dixie, for partiality in a cause which he had been instrumental in placing before Dixie the previous Friday. Dixie summoned Closse to answer for this at Guildhall, and it was concluded that a complaint should be laid before Archbishop John Whitgift, who ordered Closse to preach again on 27 March to make submission.

Before a large auditory Closse explained that his previous attack on bribery did not apply to the city magistrates, and explained the cause of his earlier outburst. He was seeking to help the wife of a Flemish resident who wanted to retain her servant boy, whom his mother wished to reclaim by sending a city officer to seize him: violent actions and words had ensued and with Closse's help all parties had gone to the magistrate's house, where the mother's case was upheld. It was this seeming injustice which had aroused Closse's earlier wrath, and he made no real apology in this later sermon. Although the six examining clergy agreed there was no further case against Closse, Dixie took the matter to privy council, which after some prompting judged that Closse had indeed insulted him and should be suspended from preaching in London diocese for a year. Closse's own account of the affair, prepared for a new edition of Holinshed's *Chronicles*, claims that he would have accepted the council's wish for a private reconciliation, but that Dixie insisted on pursuing the matter.

In October 1585 Closse's wife bore him a daughter, who, however, died in June 1586; following this loss and his suspension, the couple retreated to his Devon parish, where eight more children were born, three of them dying in infancy. In 1606 Closse published a pamphlet, *The Parricide Papist*, describing a Catholic son's murder of his protestant father at Padstow. He also became incumbent of the neighbouring parish of Bradford in 1591, and offered employment there to another clergyman, William Rickard, allegedly as a bribe: Closse wished him to deny that while Rickard was a prisoner in Exeter gaol Closse had entered the prison in disguise to consort with Jane Beaton, another prisoner. Many statements were made in Star Chamber over this and related matters between 1608 and 1621. There were accusations by Closse at an assize sermon of venality among the judges and false charges against him aided by falsified letters, charges that Jane Beaton had a child by Closse, who had bought drugs to kill it. The result was Closse's deprivation and degradation in 1615 while in the Fleet prison under a two-year sentence. No more is known of Closse after his final answers in Star Chamber in 1621. While there are no proven links between the Cambridge graduate, the intruder at Cuckfield, the Paul's Cross preacher, and the minister of Black Torrington, the name and provocative behaviour would seem to be a common factor.   R. A. CHRISTOPHERS

Sources G. Closse, 'A sermon preached at Paules Crosse the 27 day of March 1586', Cranston Library, Reigate, MS item 1592, fols. 46–92 • state papers, domestic, Elizabeth I, PRO, SP 12/149, 180–82 • *CSP dom.*, 1581–90, 24 • *APC*, 1585–7, 60, 150, 188–9 • *Holinshed's chronicles of England, Scotland and Ireland*, ed. H. Ellis, 4 (1808), 888–91 • F. Peck, ed., *Desiderata curiosa*, 1 (1732), bk 6, after p. 51 • Star Chamber proceedings, James I, PRO, STAC. 8/17/19, STAC. 8/49/3, STAC. 8/97/19, STAC. 8/91/6, STAC. 8/33/8 • Venn, *Alum. Cant.*, 1/1 • Cooper, *Ath. Cantab.*, vol. 2 • parish register, Black Torrington, Devon RO • parish register, Bradford, Devon RO • parish register, St Magnus the Martyr, GL • H. F. Williams, 'Notes on the parish of Black Torrington', 1964, Devon Local Studies Library, Exeter • H. F. Williams, 'Notes on the parish of Bradford', 1963, Devon Local Studies Library, Exeter • exchequer, first fruits and tenths office, composition books, PRO, E. 334/10 • PRO, C. 66/1218 [*CPR*, 1580–82] • *STC*, 1475–1640 • J. H. Cooper, 'The Elizabethan vicars of Cuckfield', *Sussex Archaeological Collections*, 44 (1901), 11–27

Archives St Mary's Church, Reigate, Cranston Library, text of sermon, MS item 1592

Closterman, John (1660–1711), history and portrait painter, was born in Osnabrück, a prince-bishopric in north Germany, from 1648 ruled alternately by a Roman Catholic bishop and a Hanoverian Lutheran prince. 'Mr. Tiburing', a fellow townsman, gave George Vertue Closterman's place and year of birth (Vertue, *Note books*, 1.44). Houbraken stated in his biography of 'Kloosterman' that he was born at Hanover in 1656 (Houbraken, 3.284). This may be the birth date of John Baptist Closterman [*see below*], John's brother, also a painter, who was alive in 1713 when Houbraken visited England.

Family and early years In his outline biography of John Closterman, Vertue gives his death date as '171.' and only once cites 'Bapt. Closterman <face painter>', as a subscriber to the 1711 London Academy (Vertue, *Note books*, 2.140, 6.168). Certainly after Houbraken's biography John and John Baptist Closterman were conflated. This became apparent only in 1964 with the publication of John's will leaving the bulk of his estate to 'my Deare and Loveing Brother John Baptist' (Stewart, 'John and John Baptist Closterman', 307).

John Closterman was the 'son of a painter' (Vertue, *Note books*, 1.44), perhaps Hermann Cloisterman, elected burgher of Osnabrück on 22 December 1656, who died on 27 January 1682 and whose wife died on 14 June 1669. Tiburing and John Closterman went 'in … 1679. to Paris, where they staid about 2 years & wrought for de Troyes [François de Troy]'; 'by some of [Closterman's] portraits done after his first coming into England, it is very apparent he had much studied [de Troy's] manner' (ibid., 1.44, 3.29). In de Troy's *Marie-Anne de Bourbon, Princesse de Conti* (Musée des Augustins, Toulouse), we see the draperies with flickering highlights, ivory flesh tones, and an elegant sprightliness, all characteristics of Closterman's best early English work.

Doubtless Closterman and Tiburing went to England because of the death of Sir Peter Lely, principal painter to Charles II. Vertue states that they came in 1681 (Vertue, *Note books*, 1.61). He also mentions Closterman's portrait of John Saunders, master of the Painter–Stainers' Company, London, dated 1680, implying that the painter may have arrived late in that year (ibid., 2.30; Rogers, no. 84). The picture survives, but is in poor condition. A signed pair of oval busts of an unknown man and woman of 1682 (ibid., nos. 109, 120) and the three-quarter-length *Sir William Petty* (c.1683; no. 76) show the impact of the dourness of late works by Lely.

Partnership with John Riley Closterman went into partnership with John Riley: 'had not Riley died [in 1691] he [Closterman] might have been in debt & the other grown rich because Riley did 10 heads to one whole lenght. or two half lenghts. & for each head Closterman was only to have 30 shillings for the Drapery' (Vertue, *Note books*, 1.61). This garbled account seems improbable. Closterman knew the portraiture market, and later displayed a shrewd head for business. There are independent works by him through the 1680s; and in 1688–9 the painter Jacques Parmentier (1658–1730) did work (presumably drapery painting) for him (ibid., 3.46).

Yet the partnership seems confirmed by the composite character of portraits like the three-quarter-length of Katherine Elliott (d. 1688)—in the Royal Collection—described in a Queen Anne inventory as 'Ryley ye Head Closterman ye Drapery' (Millar, no. 331). Also in the Royal

Collection is the remarkable full-length of another royal servant, Bridget Holmes (1686), waving a broom at a backstairs page-boy, who dodges behind a curtain. The humour recalls Dutch genre pictures. The *Bridget Holmes* bears a strengthened Riley 'signature', yet as Christopher Lloyd has noted: 'the drawing is unusually accurate for [Riley]' (Lloyd, no. 33). The figures have volume and weight and move easily in space whereas Riley's signed three-quarter-length portrait of a scullion (Christ Church, Oxford) shows a flat, cramped static figure. The *Bridget Holmes* also contains an urn with a relief of dancers borrowed from Polidoro da Caravaggio, and an unidentified relief of Roman soldiers on the plinth below it.

The composition, forms, learned allusions, and humour of the *Bridget Holmes* seem beyond Riley's powers. But they are found in Closterman's works, such as his mid-1680s full-length *1st Earl Poulett* (Paul Mellon Center for British Art, New Haven, Connecticut; Rogers, no. 78). Dressed elegantly like the royal page, Closterman's smiling boy stands in a landscape, nonchalantly cradling a flint-lock musket, his dog at his side. The picture recalls Lely's Arcadian child portraiture, but Closterman uses contemporary dress. Yet the classical portico behind suggests that the painter also knew the mythological origin of hunting: 'Game and hounds are the invention of gods, of Apollo and Artemis' (Xenophon, 367).

Closterman's three-quarter-length *John Dryden* (priv. coll.) was painted about 1683. Behind the bulky, powerfully modelled, smiling sitter is a relief of Poetry being garlanded, an adaptation from Cesare Ripa's allegorical handbook *Iconologia*. The painting was engraved as a small illustration in a 1709 edition of Dryden's *Virgil* (nearly a decade after Dryden's death) as the work of Riley. But its quality, style, and learned accessories seem more consistent with Closterman.

Closterman's first piece 'that gain'd much Credit' was his three-quarter-length portrait of Grinling Gibbons, the woodcarver, and his wife, Elizabeth (Vertue, *Note books*, 1.61), now known only from John Smith's mezzotint (1691; Rogers, no. 38). It is a complex composition, with an elaborate curtain, dramatically foreshortened columns, and a relief of putti (whose meaning is enigmatic). Yet there is lively informality in the crossing diagonal poses of the sitters.

An oblong three-quarter-length (an unusual format) portrait of Mary Morrice, wife of Sir John Carew, bt (Antony House, Cornwall), presently attributed to Riley, is surely also by Closterman. The lighting, drapery forms, learned accessories, and diagonal pose recall the Gibbons portrait. Lady Carew leans on a draped funeral urn carved with cupids, one caressing a dog (symbol of faith); she grasps part of a cupid-and-dolphin (the latter a symbol of resurrection) fountain at the right. Her mourning posture and the images of consolation suggest that the portrait was commissioned after her husband's death in 1692.

Eminence The three-quarter-length portrait of Sir Christopher Wren (Royal Society, London) was once attributed to Riley. But its easy, dynamic composition, elegant drapery forms, firm modelling, and (again enigmatic) putto relief proclaim it as Closterman's work of the mid-1690s. Closterman's portrait of Henry Purcell is lost, but known from an engraving of 1698 and a powerful black chalk, life-size head study (NPG), the only identifiable drawing by Closterman. The large-scale head study was reintroduced into England by Kneller in the 1680s, and Closterman's use of this type shows contact with his studio. Both artists came from north Germany; and by 1692, symbolic of his new eminence, Closterman had moved into The Piazza, Covent Garden, where Kneller also rented a house from 1682 to 1703.

In 1689 Riley was nominated steward of the St Luke's Club feast, an occasion founded by Van Dyck 'for men of the highest character in Arts and Gentlemen Lovers of Art' (Vertue, *Note books*, 3.120). But Riley 'then being much indisposed of an illness of which he died [March 1691; his place] was supplyd by his friend and companion Mr. John Closterman' (Vertue, BL, Add. MS 39167B, fol. 75).

Closterman inherited much of Riley's clientele, including Charles Seymour, sixth duke of Somerset, who, says Vertue, 'took Closterman with him [to auctions] to have his judgment on the pictures' (Vertue, *Note books*, 4.21). On Closterman's advice the duke bought a Guercino for 200 guineas 'when Guineas was raising [from 20] to 26 shillings a piece' (ibid.). When the picture was delivered the auctioneer demanded more money, which the duke refused to pay. Closterman himself bought the painting but Somerset 'became his greatest enemy and from him went to [Michael] Dahl' (ibid.). Of the duke and his duchess (the latter with a child) Closterman painted full-lengths, and also a large, lively group portrait of their children (Petworth House, Sussex; Rogers, nos. 89, 90, 92). Although these works have been said to be of the mid-1690s, they must have been completed by 1694, the year the guinea peaked in value.

Of 1696 is Closterman's *Children of John Taylor* (NPG; Rogers, no. 97), a picture of rhythmic grace and ravishing colour: harmonies of green and gold, deep orange and silver, mauve and grey. The colour shows Closterman's French training but the composition reflects Van Dyck's *Pembroke Family*. The picture illustrates the family motto: 'Fame is sweeter than a white rose'. The oldest boy, Brook, is seated at the left (the heraldic right), being crowned by two sisters who hold trumpets of fame; another sister distributes white roses. Brook Taylor holds a recorder, doubtless an allusion to his grandfather Nathaniel Taylor, recorder (judge) of Chester. The Taylor group demonstrates the period's love of witty allegory, and Closterman's light-hearted brilliance at expressing it.

In 1699 Samuel Pepys named only two artists for his proposed gift of a picture of the mathematician Dr Wallis to the Bodleian Library, Oxford, 'Sir Godfry Kneller' and 'Cloysterman' (*Letters and the Second Diary*, 274). (In the event, Kneller was chosen.) Closterman's eminence in literary-artistic circles is further demonstrated by his subscription to Dryden's *Virgil* (1697). The 100 first subscribers, mostly nobility and gentry, paid 5 guineas, and each received the dedication of a plate inscribed with his name and arms. Plate 85 was dedicated to 'Mr John

Closterman'; his 'arms' (which also appear on his 1702 bookplate; Franks Collection, BM) show a unicorn rampant. They were perhaps 'canting' arms, wittily alluding to the painter's name and place of birth. Closterman (literally cloistered man) is close to the word *Closterbruder*, German for monk, whose vow of chastity would make the unicorn an appropriate emblem. Yet the unicorn, save for its horn, recalls the heraldic white horse of Hanover. Kneller was the only other artist who was a first subscriber. Both were 'gatherers' of second subscribers, being indebted to Dryden for publishing his *Parallel between Painting and Poetry* together with his own translation of Roger De Piles's French version of C.-A. Du Fresnoy's *De arte graphica* in 1695. Second subscribers paid 2 guineas and just had their names listed.

Visit to Spain and Italy According to Vertue, 'having a desire further to distinguish himself in the Art [Closterman] went to Spain' (Vertue, *Note books*, 2.139), the first artist from England to go there. He is documented in Madrid between November 1698 and April 1699 in letters from his host, the British resident, the Hon. Alexander Stanhope, to his son James, afterwards Earl Stanhope (Stewart, 'John and John Baptist Closterman', 307). (As 'Col. J. Stanhope' he was a second subscriber to Dryden's *Virgil*.) As a present for James, Closterman painted the father, full-length in Spanish court dress, with a page (compositionally a re-working of the *Bridget Holmes*). Through the resident Closterman gained introduction to court, where he painted, in competition with Luca Giordano, a dwarf, and full-lengths of Carlos II and his queen, Maria Aña of Neuberg, 'in a rich hunting dress, a gun in her hand', a present for his host (ibid.). Sadly only the portrait of Alexander Stanhope survives (Chevening, Kent). Also missing are letters which Closterman wrote to Richard Graham 'concerning paintings in Spanish palaces' (Vertue, *Note books*, 5.61).

From Madrid Closterman travelled to Rome, stopping at Florence, where he wrote on 19 August 1699 to Lord Ashley, a friend of James Stanhope's, and also a second subscriber to Dryden's *Virgil*. Ashley had asked Closterman to obtain statues of virtues for a monument, probably to his grandfather, the first earl of Shaftesbury. Closterman said that he had been unable to find anyone 'in all Lombardy … for your purpose' because 'the[y] all want drawing'. However, he hoped to be in Rome 'the first of october where I shall in mediatly see for a master for your ocasion … I hope to stay in rome six mounths and to see them [the statues] done' (O'Connell, 159).

Closterman wrote to Lord Ashley again from Rome ('where I did long for these manny years'), enclosing drawings of Prudence and Justice by the sculptor Domenico Giudi, but was lukewarm about them. The painter confessed that 'my eyes see so many noble things of the ancients that I cant like nothing else', although he was also enthusiastic about Bernini's works. Ashley had evidently written 'his thoughts for a family pictor, and that I shall perform it as sune I come home … and to goe into the contry is better still then we shall have howly our thought together' (Wind, 67–8).

In Rome, Closterman met the leading painter Carlo Maratta (perhaps through Kneller, who had studied with him in the 1670s) and painted Maratta's portrait (Richard Graham's sale, 6 March 1712; Rogers, no. 63). Closterman gained access to Maratta's drawings collection, which included 1800 sheets by Domenichino (then considered to be a second Raphael) and drawings by the Carracci and Raphael himself. Furthermore, Closterman negotiated the purchase of this remarkable collection for a deposit of 1000 scudi, and 4000 scudi on receipt of the drawings. By a dramatic *avviso* (28 April 1703) Pope Clement XI (Albani) bought the drawings himself, refunding the deposit to the 'inglese'. Houbraken told the story in 1718, stating that Closterman was acting for an 'English Lord' (probably either the second duke of Devonshire or Lord Somers; Houbraken, 2.236–7); Jonathan Richardson also published an account in 1724. Despite his failure Closterman deserves great credit for his enterprise in furthering the taste for old master drawings, then still relatively novel in England. In 1762 James Adams bought the Albani collection for George III, since when it has been one of the great jewels of the Royal Collection.

John Closterman is recorded on 23 July 1700 in the day book of the third earl of Shaftesbury (as Lord Ashley had become in November 1699) at his Dorset estate, Wimborne St Giles. Vertue says that Closterman:

> went to Italy returned to England brought over several fine pictures. & went again to Italy. & made an additional Collection to his Pictures. came back & livd with great splendor at his house in Covent Garden haveing improvd his Fortune <considerably>. (Vertue, *Note books*, 2.139–40)

Closterman's second Italian trip is confirmed by an auction catalogue of a sale of eighty-nine lots of pictures on 26 December 1702 at the painter's house in Covent Garden. Had Closterman brought the pictures from Rome in 1700, it is inconceivable that he would have waited for nearly two years to sell them. To obtain the latter collection of pictures, he must have gone to Rome again, probably in the summer of that year.

Later works John Closterman was doubtless at Lord Shaftesbury's Dorset estate in July 1700 to paint the 'family pictor' referred to in the painter's letter from Rome, a double full-length portrait of the earl and his brother Maurice (NPG; Rogers, no. 86) dressed in neo-Greek tunics and caps. The brothers' pose derives from the Hellenistic sculpture of Castor and Pollux (mythical twins of transcendent virtue), now in the Prado, Madrid, but then in the Odeschalchi collection, Rome.

Closterman also painted separate full-lengths of Lord Shaftesbury and his brother (priv. coll.; Rogers, nos. 87, 5). The earl in a gown, representing contemplative life, holds a book; Maurice (active life) appears in a landscape, flintlock in hand, with a groom below holding a horse. The portraits are linked by a figure behind Shaftesbury carrying the peer's parliamentary robes, illustrating the Neoplatonic doctrine that 'active righteousness is only the prerequisite of contemplative illumination' (E. Panofsky, *Studies in Iconology: Humanistic Themes in the Art of the Renaissance*, 1962, 192). The robes may commemorate a rapid journey to London which the earl made in February 1701 to vote on the second partition treaty. Shaftesbury leans on a plinth on which are more volumes, two labelled Plato, and another Xenophon, who wrote treatises in praise of hunting (noted above), but also on horsemanship and statesmanship (the *Cyropodeia*, which Maurice had translated). The twin portraits develop a theme begun in England with Van Dyck's *Lords Digby and Russell* (also indebted to the *Castor and Pollux*) which Closterman must have known.

Another picture, also possibly painted for Lord Shaftesbury, is the three-quarter-length Lady Ashe as St Cecilia (priv. coll.; Rogers, no. 4), startling in its grisaille colouring—sober greys and browns, subtly relieved by pinks. Vertue says that 'about the beginning of Queen Annes Reign [Closterman] lost him self much; especially as to colouring. for from a strong lively manner. he fell into a grey uncertain colour entirely disagreeable' (Vertue, *Note books*, 3.29). Actually Closterman was following Pliny the younger's doctrine of a restricted palette—an idea cited with approval in the seventeenth century by Junius, Kneller, and Lord Shaftesbury, and later by Benjamin Haydon. Yet among English baroque painters, only Closterman seems to have applied the doctrine consistently throughout a whole painting.

In his fourth treatise Shaftesbury revealed his unbounded enthusiasm for Closterman. He dismissed the 'face painter … (as Cooper, Sir Godfrey Kneller, Riley, etc.)', because the patron (supposedly saw everything—'nothing when their back is turned':

> But when a subject is given to a real painter, a heroic great subject: Good heavens! what toil! What study! … What restless nights! What … *rabiosa silentia* [mad silences]! Here remember what said of Michelangelo. Domenichino … so my painter [Closterman] going into his picture when in the dark and standing long before it.   (Shaftesbury, *Second Characters* 131–2)

Vertue says that:

> being a Man of great Ambition. [Closterman] was by some disgust against Sir G Kneller. sett up by a party of his [Closterman's] Freinds in Opposition. & recommended to … Queen [Anne]—<at Guildhall a large Picture painted by him> the *Duke of Marlbro'* <a large Picture on Horseback with Aligrioriall figures> whose pictures he drew & many other people of Quality.   (Vertue, *Note books*, 2.139)

The London Guildhall commission was won in May 1702 in competition with four other painters, including Kneller and Jonathan Richardson. Perhaps because of Closterman's second Italian trip, the painting was not delivered until February 1703 (Stewart, 'John and John Baptist Closterman', 308–9). It is known only from a three-quarter-length studio version (NPG) and John Faber junior's mezzotint. From these it seems to have been a stiff, even clumsy composition, showing the queen standing in robes, holding the sceptre and orb. Yet it impressed the Dutch painter J. C. Weyerman, who was in England in 1709 and later wrote enthusiastically that the viewer 'heard the golden fabrics and other costly silk stuffs crackle' (Weyerman, 3.190).

In October 1703 Kneller nearly lost another commission to Closterman. The diarist Luttrell noted that the archduke Charles was visiting and 'Mr. Closterman, the famous picture-drawer, is goeing to Portsmouth to take his picture' (Stewart, 'John and John Baptist Closterman', 309). In the event the archduke sat to Kneller (the portrait is in the Royal Collection), but the fact that it could even be mooted that this distinguished visitor would be painted by anyone other than the principal painter shows the seriousness of Closterman's rivalry.

The equestrian *Duke of Marlborough* cited by Vertue was engraved (head and shoulders only) with the date 1705 and is now at the Chelsea Royal Hospital, London, having been given first in 1852 to the London Drapers' Company by 'Mr William Lyle', when it was stated to have been painted for 'a Duke of Buckingham' (Rogers, no. 66). Perhaps this was the second duke of Buckingham and Chandos (son of a daughter of the last duke of Chandos) who went bankrupt in 1848 and sold many of his possessions at Stowe. The 1725 inventory of Cannons, the Chandos house, lists only one picture on the staircase wall, 'the Duke of Marlborough by Closterman' (Simon, *English Baroque Sketches*), almost certainly the equestrian portrait.

The design of the *Marlborough* derives partly from Rubens's *George Villiers, Duke of Buckingham* (owned by Closterman's client Sir Francis Child) though vertical, rather than horizontal, and more open and airy. The colour, much of it pale, anticipates the rococo, although the handling of paint has none of the brilliance of Kneller's at this date. Above at the right of Marlborough flies Fame; directly above him is an eagle with a laurel wreath; at the left is Victory, extending a palm to the duke and a profile medallion of Queen Anne. The last motif was a French practice, known as *le portrait en tableau* (a portrait in a painting).

About 1705 Closterman painted the *Unknown Hunter* (priv. coll.; Wilton, no. 22), a full-length wrongly inscribed as by Kneller, and representing the duke of Marlborough. The design is a reworking of the portrait of Maurice Shaftesbury, but the pose is more energetic and the lighting more dramatic. The sublime, wild, brightly lit rocky scenery derives from Salvator Rosa, whom Closterman had copied in Italy for Sir John Cropley. Similar rocky backgrounds occur in Closterman's *Duke of Argyll* (1704; priv. coll.) and another three-quarter-length, of about the same date, identified as his work only towards the end of the twentieth century, probably representing Sir Richard Temple, afterwards Lord Cobham (Fairfax House, York).

The enthusiasm for Rosa may have been inspired by Henry Cooke (c.1642–1700), who had been Rosa's pupil. Cooke made his 'loveing friend John Closterman' an executor of his will; Closterman in turn named Henry Cooke junior an executor of his own will. Closterman's sale in 1702 included three Rosas, two of which, nos. 17 and 26, because of the subjects and sizes, are almost certainly the *Drunkenness of Noah* (priv. coll.; Salerno, no. 223) and *Landscape with Bathers* (Yale University Art Gallery, New Haven, Connecticut; Salerno, no. 147). In furthering the taste for Rosa, Closterman was again in the van; Rosa was to become extremely popular with English collectors as the century progressed.

On 6 August 1705 Closterman advertised that:

being obliged at Christmas next to go to Hanover, and afterwards to several Courts of Germany; so that it is uncertain whether he will ever return to England. Such Persons of Quality and others, as have lately sat to him, are desired to take notice, that their pictures will be finished out of hand, and deliver'd as they shall best please to order them.
(*Daily Courant*, 6 Aug 1705; Ashton, 281)

In April 1706 Closterman advertised again that he, 'being oblig'd to leave England very suddenly, will sell all his pictures by Auction' (ibid.).

Closterman's decision to go to Hanover may have been connected with events there. In August 1705 the duke of Celle died, his heir being his nephew George Louis, the elector prince of Hanover, whose increased income led to further artistic patronage. As a Hanoverian, Closterman may have hoped for a share of this. Whether he went, and for how long, is unknown.

However, Closterman did paint Richard Newdegate, who had died aged less than a year on 18 March 1706. The child is shown at length, asleep on a cushion, with angels' heads above (priv. coll.; Rogers, no. 71). The design appears to derive from an engraving by Pieter Jode the younger, after Artemisia Gentileschi's *Child Sleeping* (Bissell, fig. 113).

In 1708 Closterman acted again as steward for the St Luke's Club feast (Vertue, BL, Add. MS 39167, fol. 75*v*). One of Closterman's latest datable pictures is a portrait of Mathew Prior (priv. coll.), presently called *School of Kneller*. It is a sombre-coloured yet boldly lit work, showing the poet in cap and open-necked shirt, with his hand on an upright volume labelled 'PRIOR', presumably his *Poems on Several Occasions* (1709). He continued his picture-dealing career, advertising a sale for as late as 28 February 1711 (Ashton, 281).

Death Closterman's last days were tragic, something hinted at by Vertue: 'sometime before he died he was a little delirious & <not rightly in his senses>' (Vertue, *Note books*, 2.140). Closterman had buried his wife, Hannah, on 27 January 1702. Later, according to J. C. Weyerman, he took a beautiful mistress who, while he was away in the country, robbed him of his valuables and disappeared, actions which drove the painter into madness. He was buried in St Paul's Church, Covent Garden, on 24 May 1711. His will of 19 August 1710 was probated on 11 June 1711. It shows that he had a sister 'Margareta Catherina Gruter', wife of his 'Servant' (assistant) 'Philipus ffranciscus fferdinandus Gruter'. Probably the Gruters lived in the Closterman house in Covent Garden. Another sister, 'Anna Maria Muino', was 'liveing at the Hague' (Stewart, 'John and John Baptist Closterman', 306). John Closterman left his assistant £100 and each sister £500, the residue of the estate going to his brother **John Baptist Closterman** (*b.* 1656?, *d.* in or after 1713), painter.

John Baptist Closterman is known from two full-lengths, *1st Duke of Rutland* (*c.*1703), signed 'J. Baptist Closterman', and the portrait of the second duke, signed

'J. Baptista Closterman, Pinxit Ano 1703' (both priv. coll.). The draperies of the former are painted in a coarsened version of John Closterman's style, and neither shows the sense of structure or handling of space seen in John Closterman's work. John Baptist was clearly a very inferior painter.

Several other documents mention John Baptist Closterman, the earliest recording him in July 1700, with his brother, at Wimborne St Giles. With Margaret, his wife, he had a daughter, Catherine, who was baptized at St Paul's, Covent Garden, on 15 November 1711. The month before, in Amsterdam, Egbert and Abraham Edens, art dealers, were instructed by 'Jan Baptiste Closterman painter' of London to go to the house of Matheus Crackau, open some boxes left there for safe keeping by 'Mons. Frans de Gruter also painter at London', and make a list of the contents (Bredius). The pictures listed are mostly copies after Poussin and Jacques Courtois, known as Borgognone, and Closterman portraits. The latter included a copy of a portrait of the 'dead Closterman'. This was perhaps after one of the self-portraits recorded by Vertue: 'Mr John Closterman his picture painted by himself in the hands of Mr. Cope. Another in possession of Mr. Tiburin' (Vertue, *Note books*, 1.29). No portrait of either brother is known to have survived.

Reputation John Closterman's tragic end presaged that of his reputation. For over 250 years his identity and *œuvre* were conflated with those of his brother. John Closterman's early partnership with John Riley further confused the situation. From late twentieth-century research it is clear that John Closterman was an extremely fine painter, with considerable range. The *1st Earl Poulett*, the Shaftesbury portraits, and the *Unknown Hunter* are equal to Kneller's best full-lengths. The Chelsea *Duke of Marlborough* is the only equestrian portrait of the period to rival Kneller's, while Closterman's *Children of John Taylor* is undoubtedly the finest group portrait of the period. Closterman also deserves recognition for his enterprise as an art dealer, especially for furthering an English taste for Salvator Rosa, and for his near acquisition of the Maratta drawings collection.   J. DOUGLAS STEWART

Sources M. Rogers, 'John and John Baptist Closterman: a catalogue of their works', *Walpole Society*, 49 (1983), 224–79 · J. D. Stewart, 'John and John Baptist Closterman: some documents', *Burlington Magazine*, 106 (1964), 306–9 · [M. Rogers], *John Closterman: master of the English baroque* (1981) [exhibition catalogue, NPG, 24 July – 4 Oct 1981] · J. D. Stewart, review of *John Closterman: master of the English baroque*, *Burlington Magazine*, 123 (1981), 689–90 · J. D. Stewart, *Sir Godfrey Kneller and the English baroque portrait* (1983) · Vertue, *Note books* · A. Houbraken, *De groote schouburgh der Nederlantsche konstschilders en schilderessen*, 3 vols. (1718–21); repr. P. T. A. Swillens, ed. (1943) · J. C. Weyerman, *De levens-beschryvingen der Nederlandsche konst-schilders en konst-schilderessen*, 4 vols. (The Hague, 1729–69) · O. Millar, *The Tudor, Stuart and early Georgian pictures in the collection of her majesty the queen*, 2 vols. (1963) · C. Lloyd, *The queen's pictures: royal collectors through the centuries* (1991) [exhibition catalogue, National Gallery, London, 1992] · A. Wilton, *The swagger portrait: grand manner portraiture in Britain from Van Dyck to Augustus John, 1630–1930* (1992) [exhibition catalogue, Tate Gallery, London] · *Letters and the second diary of Samuel Pepys*, ed. R. G. Howarth (1932); repr. (1933) · Xenophon, *Scripta minora*, trans. E. C. Marchant (1962) · W. H. Hunt, ed., *The registers of St Paul's Church, Covent Garden, London*, 1, Harleian

Society, register section, 33 (1906), 152 · L. Salerno, *L'opera completa di Salvator Rosa* (1975) · G. C. Brooke, *English coins from the seventh century to the present day*, 3rd edn (1950) · J. Simon, *English baroque sketches: the painted interior in the age of Thornhill* (1974) [exhibition catalogue, Marble Hill House, Twickenham] · Covent Garden poor rate books, Westminster Public Library, London · G. Vertue, BL, Add. MS 39167B, fol. 75 · Franks collection, John Closterman's 1702 bookplate, BL, Brighton series no. 354 · C. A. Du Fresnoy, *The art of painting*, trans. J. Dryden (1716) [incl. R. G. [Richard Graham], *A short account of the most eminent painters both ancient and modern*] · C. H. C. Baker, *Lely and the Stuart portrait painters: a study of English portraiture before and after van Dyck*, 2 vols. (1912) · J. D. Stewart, 'Portraiture in the reign of Louis XIV', *Apollo*, 147 (May 1998), 51–2 [review of *Visages du grand siècle: le portrait française sous le règne de Louis XIV, 1660–1715*] · E. Wind, 'Shaftesbury as a patron of art: with a letter by Closterman and two designs by Guidi', *Hume and the heroic portrait: studies in eighteenth-century imagery*, ed. J. Anderson (1986), 64–73 · J. Ashton, *Social life in the reign of Queen Anne*, reissued 1968 (1883) · Anthony, earl of Shaftesbury, *Second characters, or, The language of forms*, ed. B. Rand (1914) · J. K. Westin and R. H. Westin, *Carlo Maratti and his contemporaries: figurative drawings from the Roman baroque* (University Park, PA, 1975) [exhibition catalogue, Museum of Art, Pennsylvania State University, 19 Jan – 16 March 1975] · D. Mannings, 'Shaftesbury, Reynolds and the recovery of portrait painting in eighteenth-century England', *Zeitschrift für Kunstgeschichte*, 48 (1985), 319–28 · R. Hatton, *George I: elector and king* (1978) · R. W. Bissell, *Artemisia Gentileschi and the authority of art* (1999) · A. Bredius, ed., *Künstler-Inventare*, 8 vols. (The Hague, 1915–22), vol. 3, p. 869 · I. Pears, *The discovery of painting: the growth of interest in the arts in England, 1680–1768* (1988) · S. O'Connell, 'Lord Shaftesbury in Naples, 1711–1713', *Walpole Society*, 54 (1988), 149–218, esp. 159

Likenesses J. Closterman, self-portrait; formerly in possession of Mr Cope · J. Closterman, self-portrait; formerly in possession of Mr Tiburing

Wealth at death very wealthy; however, will possibly made before mistress robbed him

Closterman, John Baptist (*b.* 1656?, *d.* in or after 1713). *See under* Closterman, John (1660–1711).

Clotworthy, John, first Viscount Massereene (*d.* 1665), politician, was the son and heir of Sir Hugh Clotworthy (*d.* 1630), descended from the Devon family of that name, and Mary, daughter of Roger Langford of co. Antrim, Ireland. His father, a soldier–adventurer of Massereene, co. Antrim, served as sheriff of the county, and his mother was the 'worthy matron' from whom Clotworthy appears to have inherited his religious principles (Adair, 191). Nothing is known of his education but he was a representative of the new generation of settlers in Ireland and was knighted in 1626. He was closely associated with the plantation of Ulster and his kinsmen Edward Rowley and Tristram Beresford were two of the leading agents for the investment of the guilds of London. Clotworthy himself owned a 61-year lease of the Drapers' proportion, and possessed an extensive estate in Antrim, which county he represented in the Dublin parliament of 1634. Before 1643 he married Margaret (*fl.* 1638–1683), daughter of Roger Jones, first Viscount Ranelagh. This union confirmed his position among the New English opponents of Viscount Wentworth, lord deputy of Ireland. His father-in-law was a close political ally of Richard Boyle, earl of Cork. His wife, like Sir John himself, was a presbyterian, and suffered imprisonment at the lord deputy's hands for her beliefs. Clotworthy was a leading patron of hardline protestant

John Clotworthy, first Viscount Massereene (*d.* 1665), by unknown artist, after 1648

ministers, and was said to have once remarked that 'the conversion of the papists in Ireland was only to be effected by the Bible in one hand and the sword in the other' (*DNB*). His close friendship with leading Scottish preachers and planters, and his refusal to relinquish his private monopoly of licensing taverns, wines, and whiskey in counties Down and Antrim, set him and Wentworth further at odds. Their differences only deepened when the lord deputy refused to grant Clotworthy a commission in the company of horse previously commanded by his father, aggravating a long-running grievance which Clotworthy nurtured in the face of repeated failure on the part of the government to make good on promises of a military command. So uncomfortable was his situation by 1635 that Clotworthy apparently discussed emigration to Massachusetts with John Winthrop's son. In 1637 he put together a bid for control over the Londonderry plantation which had been forfeited to the crown in 1635. Blocked by Wentworth nothing came of it, and ultimately Clotworthy found himself stripped of his interest in the Drapers' lands to boot.

Clotworthy's landed interests in Ireland brought him into close contact with Scottish presbyterian interests, and it was reported by Wentworth in 1638 that when Clotworthy went to the king to promote his scheme for the resettlement of Londonderry he had in fact travelled first to Edinburgh 'to see what becomes of the kirk' (Donald, 191). Clotworthy's sister was married to John Pym, and it would appear that he acted as a conduit between the Scottish covenanters and the puritan circles in England organizing the opposition to the personal rule. When eventually he made it to London, he wrote letters of intelligence—and, at the behest of his English contacts, advice and encouragement—to his friends at Edinburgh, some of which were intercepted. Clotworthy was back in Dublin in August 1639 and in the following year he was returned to the Short Parliament for the Cornish borough of Bossiney (perhaps on the interest of Francis Russell, earl of Bedford). In September 1640 he took a prominent role in organizing the circulation of the petition of the twelve peers calling on the king to summon a new parliament. In November he took his seat in the Long Parliament as one of the representatives for the Essex borough of Maldon, possibly on the interest of the local magnate Robert Rich, the earl of Warwick. In February and March 1641 he lobbied hard for the appointment of Warwick's half-brother, the earl of Holland, as lord deputy of Ireland in place of Wentworth, now the earl of Strafford.

Within days of the Long Parliament's sitting, on 3 November 1640 Clotworthy had seconded his kinsman Pym's motion for the appointment of a committee of the whole house to consider Irish affairs, and had given a speech alerting parliament to the dangers threatening from Ireland, warning that a popish army was 'ready to march where I know not' (D'Ewes, 13–14). He 'became the principal intermediary between the English, Scottish and Irish malcontents' (Ohlmeyer, 'Strafford', 226) and was very prominent in the attack on Strafford, helping to orchestrate the case against him while testifying himself several times, particularly in connection with Strafford's attempt to improve Irish linen manufacture. Archbishop Laud dubbed him 'a firebrand brought from Ireland to inflame this kingdom' (ibid.). The Irish plot to seize Dublin Castle was discovered when an attempt was made to recruit Clotworthy's own servant, Owen O'Connolly. Sir John adventured £1000 for the recovery of Ireland and in 1645 he sat on the parliamentary committee for the relief of that kingdom. He fought against the rebels in person at the head of his own regiment in 1642–3, relieving the English held captive at Moneymore, co. Londonderry, and capturing Mountjoy, Tyrone. His men were also involved in an atrocity which was investigated at the Restoration, when Clotworthy justified the execution of 100 MacDonnell rebels on the grounds that many of his troops were Campbells, the clan's sworn and unswerving enemies.

In 1643 Clotworthy moved the inclusion of Ireland within the solemn league and covenant. But having helped engineer the Anglo-Scottish alliance he became disaffected from the war party leadership when command of the British forces in Ireland was entrusted to the Scotsman Robert Monro. From 1645 Clotworthy sat on the committee of both kingdoms and took part in the prosecution of Laud, goading the former archbishop on the very scaffold where he died. In October 1646 he went to Dublin to negotiate with Ormond for the city's surrender to parliament, but returned unsuccessful in February 1647. He was a commissioner to negotiate with the army that spring. It was he who brought to the Commons a copy of the soldiers' petition which led to the declaration of dislike and the New Model Army's entry into politics. His association with the presbyterian faction at Westminster brought down on him charges of embezzlement, obstructing the lord lieutenancy of Viscount Lisle, and treacherous dealings with Ormond, as part of the army's impeachment of the eleven members. Clotworthy and his fellow targets sought unsuccessfully to vindicate themselves. Taking flight for the Netherlands, he was intercepted just outside Calais by a frigate under parliamentary command and brought back to Dover. However, he was then 'dismissed, and reached the Continent in safety' (Reid, 2.81). On 28 January 1648 he was disabled from sitting in the Commons any longer. But his expulsion, and the election of a successor, Henry Mildmay, were reversed on 26 June amid the presbyterian revanche which coincided with the second civil war and Clotworthy's return to England. Purged once more in December, his expulsion was renewed and he was subsequently placed under arrest on a charge of complicity in the Scottish invasion the previous summer. He remained a prisoner until November 1651, and after his release lay very low. In 1653 he was living at St Martin-in-the-Fields, and that year over 11,000 acres of the forfeited estates of the marquess of Antrim were allotted to him in requital of his original investment in the Irish adventure. He then promptly doubled his landholdings, principally in the baronies of Massereene and Dunluce, by the purchase of further lots in the latter. In all, he spent £5441 acquiring the greatest estate in the county. On 6 August 1654 Cromwell appointed him one of the committee established to determine differences among the adventurers for Irish land, and in the same year Clotworthy personally interceded with Fleetwood and the council at Dublin on behalf of the presbyterian ministers of Antrim and Down. This initiated a series of talks which resulted, after the arrival of Henry Cromwell, in the ministers' acceptance of government salaries in November 1655. The tide of affairs now turned. Clotworthy resumed prominence on the county benches of Antrim and Down. In 1655 his presentation to livings in Antrim marked the revival of lay patronage in the appointment of ministers in Ireland. In 1656 he proposed the establishment of a college at Antrim—perhaps a reflection of his association with the fringes of the Hartlib circle—to be headed by a prominent Scottish presbyterian.

Clotworthy was instrumental in promoting the Stuart restoration. Elected to represent co. Antrim in the Irish convention, in March 1660 he was sent to England (where the council of state had itself appointed him a commissioner for the government of Ireland) to represent the interests of the adventurers and the soldiers settled in the kingdom. He proposed an act confirming all estates of soldiers and adventurers as they stood on 7 May 1659. The order that he return to Ireland to take up his responsibilities there was a rebuff for this proposal. Back in Dublin he obtained a new appointment as a messenger to England. Once there he sought to influence the drawing of the convention's Act of Indemnity and Oblivion in order to exclude from its provisions all Catholic rebels in Ireland, thereby tying the hands of a monarch he and others rightly suspected of a desire to indulge influential papists in Ireland such as the marquess of Antrim. On 21 November 1660 Clotworthy was created Viscount Massereene and Baron of Loughneagh. On 1 December he entered the Irish privy council. He was a commissioner for the court of claims, but was unable to prevent a ruling in 1663 restoring Antrim's estates to him. Riots in the region of Dunluce ensued, possibly instigated by Massereene's kinsman Tristram Beresford. Massereene remained resolute in his opposition to the restoration of episcopacy 'though he knew well that his vote would signify nothing towards it' (*DNB*), and staunchly defended the presbyterians of Ulster before his colleagues in the privy council at Dublin. Clarendon commended his sincerity, which was unquestionable, as also his 'generous and jovial' character, and his loyalty to the royal service (*DNB*). Massereene was *custos rotulorum* in co. Londonderry in 1663, and became a fellow of the Royal Society on 20 May that year. He and the earl of Anglesey held a contract for the reclamation of marsh lands around Dublin, and shortly before his death Massereene secured for the town of Antrim the right to hold fairs, and to return two burgesses to the Irish parliament. He died at Dublin on 23 September 1665; his widow was still alive in 1683. Their only child, Mary, married Sir John Skeffington, bt, to whom the title of Massereene descended in 1665.   SEAN KELSEY

Sources *DNB* • GEC, *Peerage*, 8.543–4 • P. Adair, *A true narrative of the rise and progress of the Presbyterian church in Ireland (1623–1670)*, ed. W. D. Killen (1866) • J. S. Reid and W. D. Killen, *History of the Presbyterian church in Ireland*, new edn, 3 vols. (1867) • *The journal of Sir Simonds D'Ewes from the beginning of the Long Parliament to the opening of the trial of the earl of Strafford*, ed. W. Notestein (1923) • Keeler, *Long Parliament* • T. Barnard, *Cromwellian Ireland* (1974) • M. Perceval-Maxwell, 'Protestant faction, the impeachment of the earl of Strafford and the origins of the Irish civil war', *Canadian Journal of History*, 17 (1982), 235–55 • H. Kearney, *Strafford in Ireland: a study in absolutism* (1989) • P. Donald, *An uncounselled king: Charles I and the Scottish troubles, 1637–1641* (1990) • J. H. Ohlmeyer, *Civil war and Restoration in the three Stuart kingdoms: the career of Randal MacDonnell, marquis of Antrim, 1609–1683* (1993) • J. H. Ohlmeyer, 'Strafford, the "Londonderry business" and the "New British History"', *The political world of Thomas Wentworth, earl of Strafford*, ed. J. F. Merritt (1996), 209–29 • G. Radcliffe, *The earl of Strafforde's letters and dispatches, with an essay towards his life*, ed. W. Knowler, 2 vols. (1739)
Likenesses oils, after 1648, NPG [*see illus.*]

Clough, Anne Jemima (1820–1892), college head and promoter of women's education, was born in Liverpool on 20 January 1820, the third child and only daughter of James Butler Clough (1784–1844), cotton merchant, and his wife, Anne (*d.* 1860), daughter of John Perfect. In 1822 the family moved to Charleston, South Carolina, as her father endeavoured to build up his business; Anne wrote vividly of a lonely childhood there in recollections set down for the memoir of her brother, the poet Arthur Hugh *Clough (1819–1861). When the family returned to Liverpool in 1836 she settled into the conventional pattern of visiting the poor and assisting at local day and Sunday schools. In 1841 the failure of her father's business led her to try keeping a small girls' school on a more systematic basis.

Anne Jemima Clough (1820–1892), by Sir William Blake Richmond, 1882

Anne Clough herself had been educated entirely at home by her mother. In part because of this, she developed a passionate and lifelong concern with processes of teaching, a concern in which her brother encouraged her, although when working with younger children she doubted her capacity to keep either order or her temper. In 1849 she spent three months in London as an observer, at first the Borough Road and then the Home and Colonial training schools. She would have liked to remain in London but her mother clung to familiar surroundings, and Anne returned to Liverpool to work with an informal, domestic group of middle-class pupils. In 1852 they moved to the Lake District, to Eller How just outside Ambleside. Once again Anne gathered round her a group of pupils, including Mary Arnold, the future novelist Mrs Humphry Ward. The group developed gradually the more formal structure of a school, with between twenty and thirty pupils, mostly day, with boys as well as girls to the age of eleven, and girls to the age of sixteen. Anne was joined by an assistant, Mrs Fleming, who took over the school when she left; it continued at least until the end of the century.

Mrs Clough died in 1860. A legacy from her brother to Anne had removed financial anxieties, but family duty of another kind now intervened. The early death of Arthur Hugh Clough in November 1861 left his widow, Blanche, with three small children, and in 1862 Anne gave up the house by Ambleside and went to live with her sister-in-law to help with the upbringing of the children.

The main family bases were the Clough house in London

and Combe Hurst in Surrey, the house of Blanche's parents, the Samuel Smiths; this brought Anne into contact not only with the great cousinage of Smiths, Nightingales, and Bonham Carters but also with the Langham Place circle, who all encouraged her in her educational schemes. She was a signatory of the memorial asking the schools inquiry commission to investigate girls' schools as well as boys' and submitted to them a note of suggestions for action, which she then expanded into a brief article for *Macmillan's Magazine* in 1866. While acknowledging the force of traditional arguments for educating girls either at home or in small schools—the school as home model—she contended that there was 'always a need of superior guidance and the excitement of collective instruction and companionship to call forth the higher intellectual powers' (A. Clough, 'Hints on the organization of girls' schools', *Macmillan's Magazine*, 14, 1866, 438). To raise standards and mobilize resources economically she advocated combination between schools to share specialist teachers, and suggested that these local networks might also arrange courses of lectures by distinguished visitors, 'as a means of creating a taste for higher studies and collective instruction' (ibid.).

In 1867 Anne Clough chose Liverpool as her base for a pilot project on these lines. It rapidly became clear that specialist lectures would command more support than attempts to persuade schools to combine; the North of England Council for Promoting the Higher Education of Women, of which Anne was a founder member and secretary in 1867–70, brought together associations in five cities, Liverpool, Manchester, Sheffield, Leeds, and Newcastle, to commission a first course of lectures on astronomy from James Stuart, fellow of Trinity College, Cambridge.

Having inspired a host of associated and competing enterprises and sown the seed of the university extension movement, the council, under Anne's presidency in 1873–4, wound up its activities. By then she herself was fully engaged in the enterprise which brought together all her aspirations, enthusiasms, and energies. In May 1871 she accepted an invitation from the philosopher Henry Sidgwick to take charge of a house which he had rented in Cambridge where five young women who wished to come from a distance to attend the recently established lectures for women were to reside. Demand rapidly outstripped supply, and a larger house and then a second one were leased. In October 1873 Anne Clough opened negotiations with St John's College to lease a field on which to build, and she and the committee of management who supported her turned themselves into a limited company, the Newnham Hall Company, to raise funds. The new hall admitted its first students in October 1875. Such was the buoyancy of demand that more building was soon contemplated; in 1879 the Newnham Hall Company and the association which had launched the lectures combined forces to form the Newnham College Association for Advancing Education and Learning among Women in Cambridge to build, to organize lectures and teaching, and to raise and administer funds for scholarships and

bursaries. The gestation of Newnham College was complete, and Anne Clough became its first principal, serving throughout without a salary.

Raising money was hard and unremitting work, but more straightforward than dealing with the other newly founded women's college, Girton, or the hostility with which many members of the university regarded the women. Despite the quickness of her temper, Anne Clough was temperamentally opposed to confrontation, always soothing, and infinitely creative in seeking ways round difficulties. She was not a good draughtswoman, often began an argument in the middle, and seemed to fuss; but this of itself was disarming, and her own modest view of her capacities made it easier for her to draw heavily on the strategic guidance of Henry Sidgwick and the administrative and financial abilities of Eleanor Balfour, who became his wife. Together they did much to secure the formal admission of women to university examinations in 1881, and in 1887 the grand opening of the third Newnham hall, Clough Hall, was graced by the prince and princess of Wales with the royal children and the prime minister, Lord Salisbury, Eleanor Sidgwick's uncle.

Anne Clough's lack of self-consciousness and pretension also eased her relationships with students. She could and did admit frankly to her mistakes, whether of policy or of human relations. Some were initially disconcerted by her homeliness or made fun of her lack of style: as her niece Blanche Clough put it, she 'dressed like a bundle' (BL, Add. MS 72830B, fol. 53). Her most striking features were her great dark eyes, framed by hair which had turned prematurely white. In repose her eyes were hooded and she might seem tired. The full force of her gaze was startling in its penetration and few failed ultimately to respond to the transparent sincerity and warmth which lay behind it. As Blanche again wrote, 'she showed to innumerable people the sort of tender, understanding kindness which only a few people can show to more than a few' (Clough, *Memoir*, 211).

Nor was Anne Clough uncertain or unclear about her fundamental objectives. Newnham, unlike Girton, did not immediately insist on its students going through the same academic hoops as the men. Some of the earliest students came for less than three years—or stayed for longer—doing work at a level which matched their particular situations. She argued successfully for the retention of this flexibility longer than Sidgwick had initially thought appropriate from a sharp, first-hand awareness of the variability of the education offered to girls in the first three-quarters of the century. However, in 1889, drafting a reply to Alfred Marshall who was fussing about the implications of a meeting held at Newnham to discuss the suffrage, she was clear that her work and that of the college was directed 'towards the opening out of new careers & a broader life for women' (A. J. Clough MSS).

Anne Clough was wholehearted too in her commitment to Newnham's absence of religious affiliation. Having endured her own period of intense evangelical self-examination in the 1840s and watched with distress her brother's agonies of doubt she developed a considerable distaste for denominational rivalries, and her bequest to Newnham was conditional upon its non-sectarian status. She was not, however, agnostic. She died from heart disease in her rooms at Newnham on 27 February 1892 and was buried, by her own wish, in the churchyard at Grantchester on 5 March 1892, following a service in King's College chapel.   GILLIAN SUTHERLAND

Sources B. A. Clough, *A memoir of Anne Jemima Clough* (1897) · A. J. Clough MSS, Newnham College, Cambridge · BL, Clough–Shore Smith MSS · B. Clough, ed., *The poems and prose remains of Arthur Hugh Clough*, 2 vols. (1869) · *The Times* (29 Feb 1892), 6f
Archives Newnham College, Cambridge, MSS | Balliol Oxf., A. H. Clough MSS · BL, Clough–Shore Smith MSS · Bodl. Oxf., A. H. Clough MSS · King's AC Cam., letters to Oscar Browning · U. Reading L., letters to George Bell
Likenesses W. B. Richmond, oils, 1882, Newnham College, Cambridge [*see illus.*] · J. J. Shannon, oils, 1890, Newnham College, Cambridge · cabinet photographs, NPG · photographs, Newnham College, Cambridge · photographs, BL · portrait, repro. in *ILN* (12 March 1892), 322
Wealth at death £14,508 7s. in UK: probate, 9 April 1892, *CGPLA Eng. & Wales*

Clough, Arthur Hugh (1819–1861), poet, was born on 1 January 1819 at 5 Rodney Street, Liverpool, the second son of James Butler Clough (1784–1844), a Liverpool cotton merchant of Welsh extraction, and Anne Perfect (*d.* 1860), the daughter of a Yorkshire banker. In December 1822 the Cloughs, with their four children, emigrated to Charleston, South Carolina. The family continued to reside in America until 1836, but Arthur was taken back to England in 1828 and for a year attended a school in Chester. In 1829, with his elder brother Charles, he entered Rugby School; there he formed a great admiration for the headmaster, Thomas Arnold, who welcomed him into his family circle where he formed lifelong friendships with the two eldest boys, Matthew and Thomas. He was taught by Arnold to take life with great seriousness and imbued with a sensitivity of conscience which in later life he came to regard as excessive. During his time at Rugby he lived up to Arnold's ideals, working hard in class and winning many prizes, editing a school magazine, and taking a significant part in school government, and in spite of a frail constitution achieving renown in football, swimming, and running.

University life: religion and politics In November 1836 Clough won a scholarship to Balliol and went into residence in October 1837. Balliol was now beginning to compete with Oriel as the centre of academic distinction in Oxford, and Clough had as fellow students Arthur Stanley, Benjamin Brodie, Benjamin Jowett, John Duke Coleridge, and Frederick Temple. Among his tutors were A. C. Tait and W. G. Ward; the latter became a very close and possessive friend during his undergraduate days. Partly through Ward, Clough was attracted by the Oxford Movement and fell for a while under the influence of John Henry Newman. He had been brought up in an evangelical tradition by his mother, and had imbibed liberal Christianity at Rugby, and it was the devotional and ascetic rather than the dogmatic and sacerdotalist aspects of Tractarianism that attracted him. His diaries at this time show the great

Arthur Hugh Clough (1819–1861), by Samuel Rowse, 1860

strain caused by enduring the pull of conflicting theological traditions, and by bearing with patience the intellectual and emotional demands of Ward. Though he kept up an increasingly lively social life, and was active in student societies such as the Union and the Decade, Clough's academic work suffered; he postponed his final examinations, and when he sat them in 1841 he obtained only a second class. He walked to Rugby to tell Arnold that he had failed.

While a schoolboy Clough had written copious but indifferent verses, publishing many of them in the *Rugby Magazine* over the alias T. Y. C. (Tom Yankee Clough). He began to write again with greater maturity in his second year at Balliol, and submitted competent poems in two successive years as entries for the university's English verse prize. During his undergraduate years he also wrote a number of shorter verses in a variety of metrical forms. They display the influence of Wordsworth, particularly a sequence entitled 'Blank Misgivings of a Mind Moving in Worlds not Realised' which follows the theme and imitates the diction of the immortality ode. Most of these early verses are of biographical rather than poetic interest.

In November 1841 Clough sat the examination for a Balliol fellowship, but was again disappointed. However, two things brought him comfort during the academic year: Matthew Arnold was now a scholar at Balliol, and his father, Thomas Arnold, was lecturing in Oxford as regius professor of history. In March he sat examinations again, this time for the great prize of an Oriel fellowship; and this time he was successful, being elected on 1 April 1842.

His happiness during the succeeding months came to an abrupt end when, in June, Arnold was struck down by a heart attack. Clough tried to console himself by a month of solitary walking in Wales. By Easter term 1843 his spirits had recovered somewhat, and his diary records him enjoying, with the two Arnold brothers, the Oxfordshire excursions later described so engagingly in Matthew's 'Scholar-Gipsy'.

At Oriel, Clough found himself a colleague of Newman, but by this time he had ceased to feel any attraction to the Tractarian movement, which had now reached a point of crisis. In 1841 Newman had published *Tract XC*, which claimed that it was possible to subscribe to the Thirty-Nine Articles of the Church of England (as Oxford undergraduates and MAs were obliged to do) without rejecting anything of Catholic belief. Hebdomadal council condemned the tract, and at the behest of the bishop of Oxford, Newman brought the series of tracts to an end. Ward, at Balliol, wrote pamphlets in defence of the tracts and as a result had to resign his tutorship. Clough had his own problems with the Thirty-Nine Articles: if he was to proceed to his MA he would have to subscribe to them once again, and by 1843 he had begun to feel that subscription was a crippling bondage. In 1844 he did sign, stifling his doubts, but they were not suppressed for long. He may have been encouraged to subscribe by the need to support his family: his brother George had died in November 1843 and his father in October 1844.

Meanwhile Ward, having written a Romanizing book that gave great scandal, was degraded by the university in 1845, and resigned his Balliol fellowship in order to marry. He and his new wife became Roman Catholics in June, and Newman followed shortly afterwards. Many liberals in Oxford found Newman's departure a liberation; but Clough, partly under the influence of Carlyle and German biblical scholarship, had now moved so far from orthodoxy as to find the Anglicanism even of post-Tractarian Oxford burdensome. He began to seek alternatives to his Oriel tutorship, even though Matthew Arnold had joined him as a fellow in spring 1845. During his years as a tutor he was a conscientious teacher, and in the summer vacations he took reading parties of his pupils to Braemar and Loch Ness in Scotland.

In the years following 1845 Clough's attention turned to political matters. He wrote a number of letters in 1846 on political economy, which were published in a journal called *The Balance*. In the same year he made his first continental tour, visiting Germany, Switzerland, and the Italian Lakes. In 1847 he wrote a pamphlet on the Oxford Retrenchment Association urging, in spite of *laissez-faire* economists, that conspicuous consumption in England, and especially in Oxford, should be curtailed in order to help the Irish poor during the famine. By the end of his time at Oriel he had acquired a reputation as a political radical.

Clough's religious doubts, especially about the historicity of the gospels, persisted and increased, despite the patient but uncomprehending remonstrances of Provost Hawkins of Oriel. To the disturbing influence of Carlyle

was added that of Emerson, whom he first met in November 1847. At the beginning of 1848, while his fellowship still had eighteen months to run, he resigned his tutorship, telling Hawkins that he could no longer adhere to the Thirty-Nine Articles.

1848 was a year of revolution throughout Europe. 'Citoyen Clough' spent the spring in Paris, witnessing the French revolution at first hand. Emerson was there too, and they saw each other daily during May and June. When Emerson left Liverpool for America in July, Clough saw him off. He lamented his departure: Carlyle, he complained, had led everyone out into the desert and left them there. Emerson, in reply, laid his hand on Clough's head, and told him he was to be bishop of all England.

The Bothie Clough's next act, however, took both his Anglican and his Emersonian friends by surprise. He spent the summer writing, not a religious or socialist tract, but a narrative poem 1700 verses long, entitled *The Bothie of Toper-na-Fuosich* (changed in later editions to *The Bothie of Tober-na-Vuolich*). The poem was published in November: in the previous month Clough had finally resigned his fellowship at Oriel.

The poem is set in the context of a Scottish reading party, in which the tutor and his pupils bear a strong resemblance to Clough and his young friends. The characters are skilfully differentiated, and the holiday exuberance of youth is vividly portrayed; the poem is rich in colourful descriptions of natural scenery. The student hero is a radical poet, Philip Hewson, who combines a belief in the dignity of labour with a keen susceptibility to feminine beauty. After two abortive flirtations, he falls in love with a crofter's daughter, Elspie, and emigrates with her to New Zealand, whither, in reality, young Tom Arnold had emigrated in the previous December. The poem contains some pointed criticism of the relationship between the sexes and the classes in Victorian Britain, but it is at the same time a nostalgic farewell to the life of an Oxford tutor.

The Bothie is written in hexameter verses, in an imitation of the metre of Homer, but with the feet measured by stress, in accordance with the conventions of English verse, instead of by length, as in Greek. In most positions in a verse of this kind, the poet is free to place either one or two syllables between each stressed syllable, and this allows the kind of flexibility that Gerard Manley Hopkins later claimed for his newly invented sprung rhythm. Clough exploited the possibilities by writing in a variety of registers, ranging from colloquial and slangy dialogue, through lyrical natural description, to abstract political and philosophical theorizing. He imitated Homer not only in metre but also in features of style: the use of identifying epithets and stylized repetition, for instance, and the positioning of powerful, self-standing, similes at key points in the narrative.

Though some critics judged the narrative too inbred an Oxford production, and others found the hexameters too rough and irregular, most reviewers acclaimed *The Bothie* from the outset. The poem sold well and quickly established its author's reputation as a poet. Hard on its heels followed a second publication: in January there appeared *Ambarvalia*, a collection of verse by Clough and his Cambridge friend Thomas Burbidge.

This collection contained Clough's choice of the poems written during the years at Balliol and Oriel. Most are short poems, recalling the trials of student years and the journeys of the religious doubter. '*Qui laborat, orat*', admired by Tennyson, expresses the tension of prayer to a God who is ineffable; 'The New Sinai' dramatizes the conflict between religion and science. There are poems of love and friendship in various moods and metres, and there is a surprisingly frank celebration of fleeting sexual impulse in '*Natura Naturans*'.

Italian influences From April to August Clough was in Rome where, since the expulsion of Pius IX in 1848, Mazzini had presided over a short-lived Roman republic. Clough's letters give a vivid account of Garibaldi's defence of the city against the besieging French army under General Oudinot. With astonishing speed he exploited this experience in poetical form, writing an epistolary novel in five cantos, *Amours de voyage*. This poem, which is the most enduringly popular of his works, tells the story of Claude, a supercilious Oxford graduate who is initially contemptuous of Rome, and of a young English woman he meets on the grand tour, Mary Trevellyn. By the end of the story Claude has fallen in love both with Mary and with the Roman republic, only to lose them both, as the Trevellyns travel north without him and the French restore the rule of the pope. The first draft was finished shortly after his return to England, but the final version was not published until 1858 when it appeared in an American journal, the *Atlantic Monthly*.

Like *The Bothie*, the greater part of *Amours de voyage* is written in hexameters; Clough is now more at home with the metre, and there are fewer of those rugged lines which bring the reader up short, uncertain where to place a stress. Each canto is preceded and followed by a short poem in an English approximation to an elegiac distich. The characterization is not as vivid as in *The Bothie*, but there is a dramatic energy in the narration of episodes in the siege of Rome. The personality of the anti-hero, and the downbeat ending of the poem, puzzled some contemporary readers (including Emerson) but gave it an unusual appeal to twentieth-century taste.

In summer 1848 Clough visited Naples. While there he wrote the most successful of his poems on religious topics, 'Easter Day'. It is an unblinking denial of the resurrection of Jesus, the central Christian doctrine, in words taken from the Christian scriptures themselves; it accompanies the denial with an unflinching vision of the hopes that are given up by one who abandons Christianity. Believers and unbelievers alike have admired its emotional and intellectual power.

In October of the same year Clough became the head of University Hall, London, a non-sectarian collegiate institution for students attending lectures at University College. He was not happy there, finding it no easier to accommodate himself to the principles of the Unitarians and Presbyterians who governed it than to the articles of the Church of England which had troubled him at Oriel. His principal consolation at this period was the friendship of Carlyle. From 1850 he held simultaneously a professorship of English language and literature at University College, and wrote a number of lectures on poets and poetical topics which have survived and were published posthumously.

The most productive period of these years was a visit to Venice in 1850 in which he started a dramatic poem, *Dipsychus*. This is a Faust-like dialogue between a tormented youth, in two minds (Dipsychus) about his future career, and a spirit (named in one version Mephistopheles) who represents the temptations of the world, the flesh, and the devil. The scenes of the dialogue are set, often not very convincingly, in different locations in Venice; the text was often revised but never completed, and there has been little agreement among posthumous editors about the best way of presenting its fragments. None the less, in its unfinished and uneven state it contains the most impressive embodiment of Clough's mature thought on religious topics. The dialogue is conducted in many different metres, from solemn quasi-Shakespearian blank verse to Gilbertian patter-songs.

Family life and later work At the end of 1851 Clough left University Hall. He applied in vain for a professorship of classics in Sydney. It had become important for him to find alternative employment, because he was now in love with Blanche Mary Shore Smith (b. 1828) of Combe Hall, Surrey, a cousin of Florence Nightingale, to whom he became engaged in 1852. In October 1852 he sailed with W. M. Thackeray to America, where he spent nine months in a vain search for a suitable job. He was warmly welcomed by Emerson, Longfellow, Charles Eliot Norton, and other members of the Boston literary society that he described vividly in letters to his fiancée and to Carlyle. He undertook some private tutoring and worked on a revision of Dryden's translation of Plutarch, but had no success in finding a permanent job.

Meanwhile, however, Clough's friends in England found him a post as examiner in the education office, which enabled him to marry Blanche on 13 June 1854. She was a devoted wife, and bore him at least four children, including Blanche Athena *Clough (1861–1960), college principal and educational administrator, but she never fully entered into his aesthetic and intellectual concerns. In 1860 Clough's mother died; he remained close to his sister Anne Jemima *Clough (1820–1892), later to become the first principal of Newnham College, Cambridge. What time he had to spare from his exertions in the education office was now spent in assisting Florence Nightingale in her campaign to reform military hospitals. It was he who had escorted her to Calais in 1854 on her first voyage to the Crimea.

By 1861 Clough's health had broken down, and he was given sick leave for a foreign tour. He went to Greece and Constantinople, and began to write his last long poetical venture, a series of tales entitled *Mari magno*. In this work a young Englishman, a returning American, a lawyer, and a clergyman entertain each other on an Atlantic crossing by telling stories that illustrate different conceptions of marriage and the relationship between the sexes. The seven tales of this suite, though they contain a few skilful and moving passages, in both content and expression fall far short of the standard set by the hexameter poems of 1848–9.

After a few weeks at home in June 1861 Clough went abroad again, and spent some time in the Pyrenees with the Tennysons. The attempt to recover his health was vain, and he died on 13 November in Florence, where he was buried in the protestant cemetery. His death was mourned by Matthew Arnold in his elegy *Thyrsis* which, like 'The Scholar-Gipsy', recreates the Oxford companionship of the two poets.

Afterlife Besides *Dipsychus* and *Mari magno* many of Clough's best shorter poems remained unpublished at his death. Among them are a number of biblical lays based on the book of Genesis, a Browning-like monologue on Louis XV ('Sa majesté très Chrétienne'), and the two poems most often anthologized, 'Say not the struggle naught availeth' and 'The Latest Decalogue'.

An edition of Clough's poems was published by his wife in 1862, with a memoir by F. T. Palgrave in England, and one by C. E. Norton in Boston. In 1865 a volume of *Letters and Remains* contained the first printing of *Dipsychus* and of 'Easter Day'. A new collection, *Poems and Prose Remains*, appeared in 1869 with a memoir by his wife.

Critical response to these posthumous publications was mainly very favourable. From the 1860s it was not uncommon to regard Clough as an equal partner of a poetic fraternity whose other members were Tennyson, Browning, and Arnold. A reaction against his poetry, however, set in during the 1890s, with Swinburne and Saintsbury. In the first half of the twentieth century Lytton Strachey sniggered at Clough's association with Florence Nightingale, and Leavis exalted the talents of Hopkins above all four of the original Victorian quartet.

In 1941 Winston Churchill, anxious to secure American co-operation in the fight with Hitler, broadcast some lines from 'Say not the struggle naught availeth' which ended 'Westward, look, the land is bright'. This brought some at least of Clough's poetry back to the national consciousness, and in the post-war years several critics were willing to hail him as the most modern of Victorian poets. The first modern edition of the poems appeared in 1951, and a fuller, critical edition, in 1974. The 1960s and 1970s saw a series of biographies and literary studies appear on both sides of the Atlantic. Changing fashions in English departments in universities have led, since 1980, to comparative neglect of Clough's *œuvre*, though popular editions of the principal poems have continued to appear regularly. The start of the twenty-first century has seen welcome signs of a renewed interest in this most intelligent of Victorian poets.   ANTHONY KENNY

Sources *The poems of Arthur Hugh Clough*, ed. F. C. Mulhauser, 2 vols. (1974) · *Correspondence of Arthur Hugh Clough*, ed. F. L. Mulhauser, 2 vols. (1957) · *The Oxford diaries of Arthur Hugh Clough*, ed. A. Kenny (1990) · R. K. Biswas, *Arthur Hugh Clough: towards a reconstruction* (1972) · C. Ricks, ed., *The new Oxford book of Victorian verse* (1987) · M. Thorpe, ed., *Clough: the critical heritage* (1972) · R. M. Gollin, W. E. Houghton, and M. Timko, *Arthur Hugh Clough: a descriptive catalogue* (1966) · *Selected prose works of Arthur Hugh Clough*, ed. B. B. Trawick (1966)

Archives Balliol Oxf., journals and papers · Bodl. Oxf., corresp. and drafts of poems · LUL, letters · UCL, letters | BL, corresp. with Florence Nightingale, Add. MS 45795 · Harvard U., Norton MSS · LMA, papers as secretary of Nightingale Fund council · Oriel College, Oxford, letters to Dr Hawkins · Wellcome L., memo of conversations with Florence Nightingale

Likenesses S. Rowse, chalk drawing, 1860, NPG [*see illus.*] · T. Woolner, marble bust, 1863, Rugby School · S. Laurence, portrait (after S. Rowse, 1860), Oriel College, Oxford; copy of drawing, Oriel College, Oxford · Richmond, portrait, Oriel College, Oxford · F. W. de Weldon, bust (after early etching), Charleston city hall, South Carolina · death mask, Balliol Oxf. · drawing, NMG Wales · plaster bust (after marble bust by T. Woolner, 1863), NPG

Wealth at death £4000: probate, 18 Feb 1862, *CGPLA Eng. & Wales*

Clough, Blanche Athena (1861–1960), college head and educational administrator, was born at Combe Hurst in Surrey on 5 August 1861, the fourth child and second daughter of Arthur Hugh *Clough (1819–1861), poet and civil servant, and his wife, Blanche Mary Shore (b. 1828), daughter of Samuel Smith. She never saw her father, who was travelling in Europe in a vain attempt to restore his health when she was born; he died at Florence in November of that year. Her early upbringing was in the hands of her mother, supported by her father's only sister, Anne Jemima *Clough, and her maternal grandparents, energetic members of the great cousinage of Shore Smiths, Nightingales, and Bonham Carters. The family's life was divided between the Clough house in London and the Samuel Smiths' home at Combe Hurst.

After tuition at home Blanche Athena attended Miss Metcalfe's school in Hendon, where her schoolfellows included the Jex-Blake sisters. She entered Newnham College, Cambridge, of which her aunt was principal, in 1884. She read classics, although taking no tripos examinations, and in 1888 became secretary to her aunt, enabling Anne Jemima to continue as principal as her health began to fail. Following her aunt's death in 1892, Blanche Athena turned to support the second principal, Eleanor Sidgwick, as assistant secretary and treasurer of the college, while preparing a *Memoir* of her aunt which was also an account of Newnham's foundation, published in 1897. In 1896 she became one of three vice-principals, who performed a tutorial as much as an administrative role; in 1917, under the reorganization of college government following the granting of a charter, she became sole vice-principal, being elected principal in 1920.

The public picture is one of quintessentially safe hands. In private Blanche Athena engaged in periodic bouts of savagely destructive self-criticism. The burdens of service at the shrines of two icons, her father and her aunt, were heavy, especially for someone with a strong depressive streak. Her sense of her own inadequacy led her to decline the Newnham council's invitation to succeed Eleanor Sidgwick as principal in 1911. She allowed herself to be drafted in 1920 only when the governing body, conducting an election for the first time, had got itself into a muddle

Blanche Athena Clough (1861–1960), by Sir William Nicholson, 1924

over competing candidates, while simultaneously facing a difficult situation outside over the proposals to admit women to full membership of the university.

Blanche Athena's own view of the forces that kept her at work was characteristic: 'when I see a mess I want to clean it up. … I am driven on always by shame and fear of consequences … all these things produce a habit of not shirking very much' (Clough-Shore Smith MSS, BL, Add. MS 72830E, fol. 39). Yet the public poise and performance were always impeccable. Known to her peers and seniors as Thena, she was rather reserved and statuesque in manner, with the Clough dark eyes and a deep voice. She was nevertheless an excellent listener and her rare remarks were informed by a wry, sharp sense of humour. Her students felt absolutely secure in the unfailing and intelligent support of B.A., as they called her among themselves. These qualities served her particularly well at the end of the war when she had first to uphold and then to rethink the crumbling structures of undergraduate discipline, including chaperonage.

Blanche Athena was a fine draughtswoman; her memoranda and minutes are marked by a spare, plain, admirably clear style. She also had a sharp ear. The letters written to her mother in the winter of 1899–1900, when she travelled half way around the world in the company of Philippa Fawcett, her mathematician colleague and friend, form a vivid travel diary. The research that underpinned her *Memoir* of Anne Jemima Clough was meticulous, thorough, and sensitive: it involved for her not only an exploration of her aunt's life and work but also a journey towards her father.

Black self-doubts notwithstanding, Blanche Athena Clough played a major role in the transformation of Newnham College from a small, informal, rather inward-looking enterprise to a large public institution. She herself dated the beginnings of change from the end of the 1880s, when the numbers of students rose sharply and more formal internal procedures became essential. The reconstruction of college government was a more complex issue. At first the college had been essentially a limited company, run by a council largely composed of external members, the employer of the lecturers and tutors. The Cambridge college model, however, was one of a self-governing academic corporation. From 1889 a small number of lecturers were invited to serve on the council. In private Blanche Athena was unsure whether 'oligarchy is the best organization' (Clough-Shore Smith MSS, BL, Add. MS 72829, fol. 84), but she was fully alive to the importance of becoming like the rest of Cambridge. In 1911, as president of the Associates, an energetic group of former students, she initiated discussions which resulted eventually in the granting of a royal charter (1917) and statutes. This limited the number of outside council members to three and brought together all lecturers and tutors, now styled fellows, into the first governing body of the college. In the five years that this took to achieve, Blanche Athena worked closely with Katharine Stephen, as principal, in lengthy negotiations both within college and with the privy council, while also spending time in London contributing to the organization of women's war work.

As principal, Blanche Athena had to maintain the morale and dignity of the college when proposals for women's full membership of the university were defeated in 1920 and successive half-loaf schemes ran into trouble. She led the college's celebration of its fiftieth birthday in the summer of 1921. Yet she had also to stand and watch on the night of 20 October 1921 when male undergraduates celebrating the defeat of one of the schemes for improving the women's position used a handcart as a battering ram against the bronze gates constructed as a memorial to Anne Jemima Clough. Throughout, Blanche Athena held the fellowship together, maintained complete accord with Girton, whose mistress was now her schoolfriend Katharine Jex-Blake, and liaised closely with supporters in other colleges, prominent among them J. M. Keynes and A. D. McNair. She also advised on the best way to handle the issue of the university's treatment of women before the royal commission on Oxford and Cambridge, on which she herself was serving as the token Cambridge woman. With the token Labour member, Will Graham, she signed a note of reservation to the final report in 1922, arguing that public funds should not go to an institution of which women were not full members.

By mid-1923 Blanche Athena judged the situation had stabilized sufficiently, if unsatisfactorily, to allow her to retire, taking great pleasure in the election of her friend and colleague Pernel Strachey to succeed her as principal.

For most of the remainder of her long life she lived at Burley Hill, near Ringwood in Hampshire. A devoted bird-watcher and naturalist, her common sense and administrative skills remained in demand on a variety of bodies. She served as an external member of Newnham's governing body until 1944, when her eyesight began to deteriorate and an accident curtailed her energetic walking. She was a member of several school governing bodies and took a share both in the government of the Women's University Settlement and that of the National Society for Women's Service. She died at 95 Howards Lane, Putney, London, on 14 June 1960 and was cremated on 17 June at Putney Vale crematorium. GILLIAN SUTHERLAND

Sources [A. B. White and others], eds., *Newnham College register, 1871–1971*, 2nd edn, 1 (1979) · M. G. Burton, C. D. Rackham, and E. E. H. Welsford, 'In memoriam Miss Blanche Athena Clough', *Newnham College Roll Letter* (1961), 38–45 · BL, Clough–Shore Smith MSS · Newnham College, Cambridge, B. A. Clough MSS · Newnham College, Cambridge, Council and governing body MSS · *The Times* (15 June 1960) · *The Times* (18 June 1960) · B. A. Clough, *A memoir of Anne Jemima Clough* (1897) · 'Report', *Parl. papers* (1922), vol. 10, Cmd 1588 [royal commission on Oxford and Cambridge universities] · *CGPLA Eng. & Wales* (1960)

Archives Newnham College, Cambridge | BL, Clough–Shore Smith MSS · Newnham College, Cambridge, council and governing body MSS

Likenesses A. J. Pertz, oils on board, 1897?, Newnham College, Cambridge · W. Nicholson, oils, 1924, Newnham College, Cambridge [*see illus.*] · W. Rothenstein, black and white chalk drawing, 1927, Newnham College, Cambridge · photographs, Newnham College, Cambridge · photographs, BL, Clough–Shore Smith MSS

Wealth at death £11,685 8s. 1d.: probate, 19 Dec 1960, *CGPLA Eng. & Wales*

Clough, Charles Thomas (1852–1916), geologist, was born in Huddersfield on 23 December 1852, the third of four sons and fifth of six children of Thomas William Clough, solicitor and later an alderman, of South Parade, Huddersfield, and his wife, Amelia Jane, daughter of James Ibeson, surgeon. He was educated at Rugby School and at St John's College, Cambridge, where he graduated first class in the natural sciences tripos in 1874, proceeding MA in 1878. On graduating he joined the Geological Survey in 1875, working in the Teesdale and Cheviot districts until 1884, when he was posted to the survey's Edinburgh office. In 1881 he married Anne Mary, daughter of Thomas Durham Usher, gentleman. They had a son and two daughters.

On Clough's appointment in Scotland he formed part of a group of geologists who, in the period before the First World War, were internationally without parallel for their original insights into metamorphic and igneous rocks and the intricate problems of structural geology. On his promotion to district geologist in 1902, he became the leader of that group. He made major contributions to the geology of Dalradian rocks along the highland border between Callander and Loch Lomond and in the Cowal district of Argyll. In Wester Ross, western Inverness-shire, and on Skye he unravelled the intricate metamorphic and structural history of the Moine schists and Lewisian gneisses, and on Mull he demonstrated complicated, intrusive, igneous relationships in the Tertiary Igneous Complex.

Clough's particular strength lay in the meticulous detail in which he recorded field data. His contemporaries considered him a master of geological field-mapping techniques and his original maps of many parts of Scotland confirm his observational skills and his ability to locate himself in the wilderness with astounding accuracy. However, his passion and concern for minutiae may have diminished the impact that his work had on his contemporaries and successors. The detail recorded on his maps was extended into his writings, where his conclusions about many geological relationships, later taken for granted but then original and often fundamental, were hidden in a mass of detailed evidence and justification.

The obscuring by detail of some of Clough's more fundamental and original conclusions may have resulted in formal recognition of his contributions coming rather late in his life, although he was awarded the Murchison medal of the Geological Society in 1906 and was president of the Geological Society of Edinburgh from 1908 to 1910. It was not until the year of his death that he was elected a fellow of the Royal Society of Edinburgh and awarded an honorary LLD by St Andrews University.

Clough was small with disproportionate strength and powers of endurance. He had golden-brown hair and beard and a voice high in pitch but rich in timbre. He had dogged determination and was of undeviating rectitude, although without well-defined religious beliefs. He had a profound influence at a personal level on his contemporaries. Clough died at Edinburgh Royal Infirmary on 27 August 1916 of injuries sustained three days earlier in a railway accident while examining rocks in a narrow cutting. He was buried on 30 August in Lasswade churchyard. He was commemorated by creation of the Geological Society of Edinburgh's Clough memorial medal, awarded annually to geologists who have done significant original work in Scotland or northern England.

A. L. HARRIS, *rev.*

Sources Archives of the Geological Society of Edinburgh · Archives of the Geological Survey, Edinburgh · W. Yorks. AS, Kirklees · E. Greenly, *A hand through time*, 2 vols. (1938) · *Geological Magazine*, new ser., 6th decade, 3 (1916), 525–7 · *Proceedings of the Geological Society*, 73 (1917), lx–lxi

Archives BGS, notebooks | BGS, letters to F. L. Kitchin; letters to Herbert Thomas

Wealth at death £77,926 11s. 9d.: confirmation, 5 April 1917, *CCI*

Clough, Prunella. *See* Taylor, (Cara) Prunella Clough- (1919–1999).

Clough, Richard (*d.* 1570), merchant, was the fifth and youngest son of Richard Clough, a Denbigh glover, who by two advantageous marriages, first to the daughter of Humphrey Holland and then to a Whittington of Chester, rose in fame and fortune. Of the younger Richard's early life little is known apart from certain possibly apocryphal stories. In his boyhood he allegedly went to be a chorister in the city of Chester, but lacking an outlet for his musical talents there, made his way, probably in his early teens, to London. From there, in the fervour of youthful zeal, he is said to have made a pilgrimage to Jerusalem, where it is

Richard Clough (*d.* 1570), by unknown artist, *c.*1550

related he was created a knight of the Holy Sepulchre, a title which, if actually awarded, he probably never used in the atmosphere of religious intolerance which pervaded the London to which he returned possibly about 1545. As an apprentice mercer in London from about 1545 to 1552 Clough seems to have developed a protective façade, presenting himself when required as that deferential and rather pedestrian creature who from 1552 moved easily in the circles of the newly appointed royal agent in the Netherlands, Thomas Gresham.

Clough's appointment to the 'House of Gresham' was occasioned by the departure of Robert Berney, who, having served William Read and then Gresham faithfully at Antwerp for at least ten years, in 1552 decided to establish his own mercantile house. In taking up residence at Antwerp, Clough thus became the new boy in a long-established network of factors and agents serving Gresham in his joint capacities as merchant and financial agent for the crown. His counterpart at the opposite end of the Antwerp–London axis, which formed the main highway for the house's business transactions, was John Elliot, who continued during the years 1552–7 to oversee the firm's business at its London office in Lombard Street. They were assisted by Francis Tomazo, who from 1549 to 1554 carried the company's dispatches between the two commercial centres, and William Bindlowe and John Spritewell, who from 1547 to 1554 and from 1550 to 1555 respectively were entrusted with the much more delicate task of accompanying supplies of bullion and armaments

during their often illicit passage from Antwerp to London.

From 1557 changing circumstances raised Clough's position within the firm. Against a background of major personnel changes, which made him one of the longest serving members of the team, the temporary closure of Gresham's Seville office brought the Anglo-Netherlands trade to the forefront of the firm's commercial activities. His position was strengthened by the subordination of that trade to Gresham's increasingly important financial business on behalf of the crown. In the aftermath of the 1557 imperial bankruptcy, Antwerp's money markets underwent a major transformation. The city was no longer subject to the depredations of the Habsburgs, who henceforth secured their funds from dealings on the Sevillian-Genoese financial axis, and its financial prosperity now rested on the provision of commercial investments. Clough's mercantile connections, developed in his capacity as both private merchant and factor for the House of Gresham, could now be exploited by his master in his commercial and in his financial dealings. They could also be used and extended by Gresham's mentor, Sir William Cecil, as from 1558 he began to build an intelligence network to report on political conditions in the increasingly troubled Low Countries. Clough was rapidly becoming the central figure in a completely remodelled network. His new counterpart at the opposite end of the Antwerp–London axis, along which now passed a flow of political intelligence as well as news of mercantile-financial transactions, was Richard Candeler, a member of a respectable Norfolk family, who from 1557 to 1566 acted as Gresham's factor in the English capital. The two men utilized the services of another of Gresham's servants, John Spritewell, the company's carrier of dispatches. Gresham thus had at the core of his business a formidable team, headed by Clough, which was quite capable of handling not only his increasingly important financial business on behalf of the crown but also his residual commercial activities in the city on the Scheldt. As the House of Gresham became a front for Cecil's intelligence operations, Clough became a key figure in an extended network of agents scattered throughout the Low Countries.

The years 1557 to 1569 thus witnessed Clough's assumption of a central role in the operations of the House of Gresham. They also saw a growing intimacy pervade his relations with his master. Yet at no stage during these years did he display any executive abilities in the work he undertook for Gresham. In his continuing capacity as an independent mercer-adventurer he performed small commercial favours for his master or the latter's political patrons. No more taxing were his duties as bookkeeper in relation to his master's increasingly important financial business on behalf of the crown. On occasion he was required to store at Antwerp munitions and other items bought from the proceeds of loans, but their subsequent transmission to England was undertaken on Gresham's personal responsibility. In relation to Clough, as with his other servants, Gresham was singularly incapable of devolving managerial responsibilities. It is thus surprising to find that in 1560, having undertaken preliminary negotiations for a loan worth some £75,000 with Hans Keck, the agent of Herzog Christoff Albrecht of Mansfeld, Gresham dispatched Clough to Saxony to conclude the deal. His factor's singular inability to perform this task, and Gresham's resulting discomfiture, ensured that the latter would never again entrust the hapless Clough with such weighty responsibilities. Throughout the final decade of his employment by Gresham, Clough was restricted to the pedestrian duties associated with the running of his master's Antwerp office.

For fifteen years (1552–67) Clough thus served his master, and latterly Sir William Cecil, with diligence but little imagination, and in due course was suitably rewarded for his efforts. He obtained in 1564 a substantial grant of leaseholds in Wales to augment the income from those Denbigh properties on which he had commenced to build the mansion at Bachegraig and the smaller but more elegant Clough Hall (Plas Clough), which were both completed in 1567. By his mid-thirties he had become a man of substance in his native country, his newly acquired wealth giving him some degree of independence and allowing him to dispense with that façade which he had so carefully constructed some twenty years earlier. 1567 saw the romantic, sensitive young man of the stories reappear to public view as he commenced on a completely uncharacteristic course of action. In three short weeks, between 16 April and the 7 May 1567, this pedestrian servant was transformed. He made only a cursory duty call on Gresham before departing post-haste for Wales where, after a whirlwind romance, he married the beautiful and recently widowed Katherine Tudor (d. 27 Aug 1591), the sole daughter and heir of Tudor ap Robert Fychan of Berain and his wife, a granddaughter of Henry VII. The couple then immediately left for London, pausing briefly at Gresham House before continuing their journey to Antwerp. Over the next three years, whether acting as Gresham's factor at Antwerp (May 1567–March 1569) or serving in an independent capacity the following year as deputy of the Company of Merchant Adventurers at their new Hamburg mart, to which the English traders had moved on being ejected from Antwerp, Clough found his lifestyle utterly changed. His household in these cities, presided over by the beautiful Katherine, included Richard and Winefrid Clough, whom their father mentions as his 'base children, forren born', and Thomas Dutton and Thomas Denne, kin-related 'gossips' of the principal factor. It was augmented as Katherine gave birth in rapid succession to two daughters—Anne in 1568 and Mary in the early part of the ensuing year. Supported by a loving wife and revelling in the company of his children and associates, Clough in his actions during the last three years of his life manifested a personality change. His correspondence, previously controlled and somewhat pedantic in character, now displayed a marked volatility in style related to his rapidly changing moods. Thus, laid low during a serious illness shortly after his return to Antwerp in December 1567, he was certainly prepared for the first time to neglect his work and excuse himself to his master on the grounds of his health. On the occasion of his next and final illness, during the period February–March 1570, he did not even bother to excuse himself when important diplomatic dispatches went missing. These were difficult times when his letters to Cecil were uniformly dark and mysterious. There were also good times, however, as when in September 1568 he declared he was 'in right good health and merry'.

Yet the past was not easily swept away, as the compilation of Clough's will reveals. First composed on 20 September 1568, when he was enjoying both good health and considerable prosperity, the document reflected his present concerns, as, in a happy frame of mind, he left his possessions to his wife and children. Yet health and cheerfulness were but transient states, and, as from February 1570 his health finally deteriorated, something of his associated change of mind may be discerned in the proliferation of codicils and the creation on the 26th of that month, with death imminent, of a new document. In his adversity the past weighed heavily on him and, forgetting his recent happiness and remembering 'the time of [his] service under and with [his] master', he disinherited his family and gave to Gresham all his moveable goods. He died in Hamburg in March 1570 and was buried there. To Gresham's credit, he renounced the last will, allowing the earlier will to be proved to the benefit of Clough's family.

IAN BLANCHARD

Sources CSP for., 1547–65 • Fuller, Worthies (1662) • T. Pennant, A tour in Wales, 1770 [or rather 1773], 2nd edn, 2 vols. (1784) • J. W. Burgon, The life and times of Sir Thomas Gresham, 2 vols. (1839) • wills, PRO, PROB 11/52, sig. 23 and sig. 37
Archives BL, state papers, letters • Bodl. Oxf., state papers, letters • PRO, state papers, letters | BL, Harley MS 1971
Likenesses portrait, c.1550, priv. coll. [see illus.] • J. Basire, line engraving (after M. Griffith), BM, NPG

Clouston, Arthur Edmond (1908–1984), air force officer, was born in Motueka, New Zealand, on 7 April 1908, the eldest of the four sons and five daughters of Robert Edmond Clouston (1874–1961), a mining engineer, gold-mine manager, and forest ranger, and his wife, Ruby Alexander Scott (1886–1943). Although he received no formal education beyond the primary level in Motueka, he mastered such outdoor skills as hunting, shooting, and fishing. He intended to become a master mariner, but a year of seasickness forced him ashore and in 1924 he started a garage and second-hand car business in Westport, 80 miles south-west of Motueka.

In September 1928 Charles Kingsford Smith landed in Christchurch to complete the first successful aerial crossing of the Tasman Sea, and Clouston, suitably inspired and moderately prosperous, learned to fly during the following year. He went to England in 1930 to seek a short-service commission in the RAF. Having failed a medical examination three times because of high blood pressure, he made himself known to a fellow countryman, Wing Commander Keith Park, who arranged for him to have yet another examination; this time he passed. Park, wrote

Arthur Edmond Clouston (1908–1984), by Hay Wrightson

Clouston, 'was my friend and saviour and I owe my career in flying entirely to him' (Orange, 53–4).

Clouston proved to be a natural pilot, and in 1931 he was posted to an élite unit—25 fighter squadron, at Hawkinge in Kent—where he performed spectacular aerobatics at the annual Hendon air display and learned to navigate exactly. He was promoted flying officer, but refused an extension of his commission in 1935 because he thought civil aviation in New Zealand might offer better pay and career prospects. In response, the Air Ministry created a new position which he accepted: permanent civilian test pilot in the aerodynamics section at the Royal Aircraft Establishment, Farnborough, Hampshire.

'Try it and see', wrote Clouston, was Farnborough's motto for pilots testing novel designs (including the helicopter's forerunner) with numerous experimental features (Clouston, 22). One test programme calling for repeated acts of great bravery was to fly deliberately into the middle of black thunderclouds and carefully record the effects of icing on engines, wings, and control surfaces. Another was to fly, equally deliberately, into wires and even steel cables hanging from parachutes to see if low-flying bombers could survive collision with barrage-balloon cables. For these endeavours, which helped scientists to devise solutions to serious problems, Clouston was awarded the AFC in 1938.

Interspersed with his Farnborough duties, Clouston sought fame and fortune in air races and long-distance flights. He bought (second-hand) a small single-seat, single-engined Miles Hawk to compete for a £10,000 prize in a race from Portsmouth to Johannesburg in September 1936. He crash-landed some 400 miles north of his destination, founding a reputation and earning valuable experience, but he received only the cost of a sea passage home. In 1937 he bought and had rebuilt the wreck of a famous aeroplane: the de Havilland Comet, named *Grosvenor House*, a twin-engined two-seater that won the MacRobertson air race to Australia in 1934. With Flight Lieutenant George Nelson as co-pilot, he took part in August 1937 in a race from Marseilles to Paris via Damascus. He enhanced his reputation, gained more experience, but won only a small bronze plaque. However, his third major flight, with Mrs Betty Kirby-Green, a newly qualified pilot who put up the necessary money, was a triumph. In November 1937 they flew the Comet, now named *Burberry* (after their principal sponsor), from Croydon to Cape Town (via Cairo, Khartoum, and Johannesburg) and back in a flying time of 45 hours (outward) and 57 hours (homeward). They spent under six days (including two nights and a day in Cape Town) on the round trip, more than three and a half days better than the previous record. Huge crowds welcomed them and they became instant media celebrities. Clouston was awarded both the Segrave and Britannia trophies; Mrs Kirby-Green received the Segrave medal.

In February 1938 Clouston attempted to fly the Comet, renamed *Australian Anniversary*, from Gravesend to Sydney to mark the 150th anniversary of that city's foundation. Victor Ricketts, air correspondent of the *Daily Express*, was in the back seat and, like Mrs Kirby-Green, was able to relieve Clouston from time to time. After delays in Turkey and damage to the Comet in Cyprus, they returned to England and made a fresh start from Gravesend on 15 March. They reached Sydney (via Cairo, Basrah, Allahabad, Singapore, and Darwin), received a tumultuous welcome, and flew on to New Zealand and an equally enthusiastic reception in Blenheim, where Clouston had first learned to fly. They landed at Croydon on the 26th, after a round trip lasting just under eleven days, covering 26,000 miles at an average speed of 187 m.p.h.: 'nobody has travelled from England to New Zealand as fast before and nobody has come back as fast' wrote C. G. Grey, the editor of *The Aeroplane*, on 30 March; Clouston and Ricketts 'deserve full credit for having made the World's greatest flight—so far' ('The world's greatest flight', 379).

Clouston was recalled to RAF service in September 1939 with the rank of squadron leader. He continued to serve at Farnborough on test duties, but managed to fit in several attacks on enemy aircraft. He earned a bar to his AFC in 1941 for testing a variety of airborne searchlights to help both night fighters and bombers hunting U-boats. In 1943 he was promoted wing commander and appointed commanding officer of 224 squadron, equipped with four-engined consolidated B-24D Liberators, at St Eval in Cornwall. His efforts during that year earned him a DSO and a DFC. In February 1944 he was promoted group captain and took command of a new station at Langham, on the Norfolk coast, to supervise attacks on German shipping in the North Sea and air–sea rescue patrols.

In June 1945 Clouston accepted a permanent commission and was sent to Bückeburg, Germany, headquarters of the British air forces of occupation, to organize air transport for all three services. In 1947 he went to New Zealand on a two-year attachment to the Royal New Zealand Air Force and commanded a base at Ohakea, near Palmerston North. He returned to Farnborough as commandant of the Empire Test Pilots' School (1950–53) and then, on promotion to air commodore, served as head of Far East command Singapore (1954–7). He was appointed CB in 1957. He ended his service career as commandant of the Aeroplane and Armament Experimental Establishment at Boscombe Down, Wiltshire (1957–60).

Clouston married Elsie Turner, the daughter of Samuel Turner, an engineer, of Farnborough, on 4 December 1937; they had two daughters. He was a tall, dark man with a ready smile enhanced by a thick moustache, but his direct gaze quickly discouraged unwelcome familiarity. He died at his home, Wings, Constantine Bay, St Merryn, Padstow, Cornwall, on 1 January 1984. 'Of all the splendid and remarkable men (and women) who have come from these delightful islands in the Pacific', wrote Alex Henshaw, himself a famous test pilot and long-distance aviator, 'none will have carved a greater niche in the history of our Nation than Arthur Clouston' (*Aeroplane Monthly*, Feb 1984, 68).   VINCENT ORANGE

Sources A. E. Clouston, *The dangerous skies* (1954) • H. Penrose, *Ominous skies* (1980) • 'The world's greatest flight', *The Aeroplane* (30 March 1938), 379–80 • D. Middleton, 'Test pilot profile, no. 4: A. E. Clouston', *Aeroplane Monthly*, 10 (1982), 548–53 • *Aeroplane Monthly*, 12 (1984), 610–11 • *Flight* (25 Nov 1937), 501 • *Nelson Evening Mail* (5 Jan 1984) • V. Orange, *Sir Keith Park* (1984) • m. cert. • d. cert.

Archives Nelson Provincial Museum, Nelson, New Zealand, MSS |FILM BFI NFTVA, documentary footage • New Zealand National Film Archive, news of Clouston's arrival in Blenheim, March 1938 [copy at Motueka Museum] |SOUND IWM SA, oral history interview

Likenesses H. Wrightson, photograph, NPG [*see illus.*] • photograph, repro. in C. Winchester, ed., *Wonders of world aviation*, 25 (Aug 1938)

Wealth at death £29,557: probate, 13 April 1984, *CGPLA Eng. & Wales*

Clouston, Sir Thomas Smith (1840–1915), asylum physician, was born on 22 April 1840 at Nisthouse, Orkney, the youngest of the four sons of Robert Clouston, an Orkney laird, and Janet Smith of Stromness. He was educated at West End Academy in Aberdeen, studied medicine at Edinburgh University, and graduated MD in 1861, receiving a gold medal for his thesis on the nervous system of the lobster. He worked initially as an assistant physician with Dr David Skae at the Royal Edinburgh Asylum, before his appointment as medical superintendent of the Cumberland and Westmorland Asylum in Carlisle in 1863. He became LRCP (Edin.) in 1860 and was elected a fellow in 1873. On 27 April 1864 he married Harriet Segur Williamson (*b.* 1834/5), a widow, the daughter of Reuben Storer of New Haven, Connecticut; they had two sons and a daughter. One son, Storer Clouston, became a humorous writer.

The ten years at Carlisle were formative for Clouston, and he spent his time learning the practicalities of asylum management and writing a steady stream of articles for medical journals. In 1870 he was awarded the Fothergillian gold medal for his paper on the use of medication in the treatment of insanity. In 1872 he became co-editor with Henry Maudsley of the *Journal of Mental Science*. The following year he was appointed superintendent of the Royal Edinburgh Asylum, and he remained in this post until 1908. Clouston embarked on a bold rebuilding programme designed to improve patient care. His most ambitious scheme achieved fruition in 1894 with the opening of Craighouse, a large Gothic mansion catering for upper-class patients. Clouston saw insanity as representing a loss of self-control, and held that it was the role of the asylum, in the form of a strict and ordered regime, to help patients regain mastery over their unruly behaviour.

In 1879 Edinburgh University appointed Clouston as its first lecturer in mental disease, a post which contemporaries judged he occupied with ability and flair. Clouston was also a prolific author, producing a wide range of material for medical journals, textbooks, asylum reports, pamphlets, and newspapers. He wrote two clinical books, *Clinical Lectures on Mental Diseases* (1883) and *The Neuroses of Development* (1891), and four popular works: *The Hygiene of Mind* (1906), *Unsoundness of Mind* (1911), *Before I Wed* (1913), and *Morals and Brain* (1914). His numerous clinical papers appeared regularly in all the leading British journals and also, to a lesser extent, in the American and European ones. His work embraced every major nineteenth-century psychiatric concern, including alcoholism, general paralysis, asylum management, and medico-legal matters. Many of his peers felt that Clouston's most significant contribution to psychiatry was his description of the 'insanity of adolescence', which he defined as an inherited developmental disease arising in early adult life and often leading to mental deterioration in later years. Clouston's concept was later overshadowed by Kraepelin's delineation of 'dementia praecox', a condition subsequently renamed schizophrenia.

From his initial empirical studies Clouston increasingly moved to consider the wider implications of mental disease for society. He used his annual asylum reports, which were widely reported in the national press, to speak directly to the population. Greatly influenced by the prevailing climate of scientific naturalism, he outlined the 'laws' of human existence, and in his later books he fused religious and scientific precepts to exhort the public to healthy living. Clouston took a prominent part in the establishment of a council of public morals in Scotland and was interested in eugenics and marriage. His book *Before I Wed* was said to contain 'sound and practical advice of a much needed character' (*The Lancet*, 937). In 1910 he gave evidence on behalf of the British Medical Association before the royal commission on divorce and matrimonial causes. However, although recognized by his peers as a highly efficient asylum manager who had transformed the psychiatric care at Morningside, by the end of his tenure it was also recognized that a less regimented approach was now more appropriate for the needs of the patients. Likewise his writings, which provided a bold and populist synthesis of the leading currents of Victorian thought, are today largely unread and are viewed by historians as representing little more than the conventional codes of morality expressed in the language of 'science'.

Clouston was elected president of the section of psychology of the British Medical Association in 1886 and 1898, president of the Medico-Psychological Association of Great Britain in 1888, Morison lecturer of the Royal College of Physicians of Edinburgh in 1890, and president of the Royal College of Physicians of Edinburgh between 1902 and 1904. He was awarded an LLD degree from the University of Aberdeen in 1907, made a freeman of the burgh of Kirkwall, Orkney, in 1908, and elected a corresponding member of the Societé de Psychiatrie de Paris in 1911. In the same year he was awarded an LLD degree from the University of Edinburgh and also received a knighthood.

A thin, wiry, bearded man, Clouston was described by contemporaries as an energetic, driven clinician who expected high standards from both himself and others. His pastimes were shooting, fishing, and golf. He died suddenly from a stroke on 19 April 1915 at his home at 26 Heriot Row in Edinburgh. A funeral service was held on 22 April at St Cuthbert's Church, Edinburgh, after which his body was interred at Dean cemetery.

ALLAN BEVERIDGE

Sources A. Beveridge, 'Thomas Clouston & the Edinburgh school of psychiatry', *150 years of British psychiatry, 1841–1991*, ed. G. E. Berrios and H. Freeman, [1] (1991), 359–88 · *Journal of Mental Science*, 61 (1915), 333–8 · *BMJ* (24 April 1915), 744–5 · *The Lancet* (1 May 1915), 936–7 · J. S. Clouston, *The family of Clouston* (1948) · A. Beveridge, 'Madness in Victorian Edinburgh: a study of patients admitted to the Royal Edinburgh Asylum under Thomas Clouston, 1873–1908', *History of Psychiatry*, 6 (1995), 21–55, 133–57 · M. Thompson, 'The mad, the bad & the sad: psychiatric care in the Royal Edinburgh Asylum (Morningside)', PhD diss., University of Boston, 1984 · M. Thompson, 'The wages of sin: the problems of alcoholism and general paralysis in nineteenth century Edinburgh', *The anatomy of madness*, 3, ed. W. F. Bynum, R. Porter, and M. Shepherd (1988), 313–40 · D. K. Henderson, *The evolution of psychiatry in Scotland* (1964) · parish register, Harray, Orkney, 22 April 1840 [birth] · m. cert.
Archives Orkney Islands Council, Orkney Library, family papers · priv. coll., family papers · U. Edin., Lothian Health Board special collection, clinical papers
Likenesses G. F. Watt, oils, 1909, Royal Edinburgh Hospital · Adtard & Son, photograph, repro. in *Journal of Mental Science* · G. F. Watt, oils, Royal College of Physicians of Edinburgh · caricature, repro. in *Student: the Edinburgh University Magazine* (1907) · double portrait, photograph (with his wife), U. Edin., Lothian Health Board special collection · group portrait, photograph (with assistant physicians), U. Edin., Lothian Health Board special collection · photograph, U. Edin., Lothian Health Board special collection · photograph (at time of knighthood), U. Edin., Lothian Health Board special collection
Wealth at death £27,453 1s. 2d.: confirmation, 13 Aug 1915, CCI

Cloutt, Thomas. *See* Russell, Thomas (c.1781–1846).

Clover, Joseph (1725–1811), veterinary surgeon and farrier, son of a blacksmith, was born in Norwich on 12 August 1725. He benefited from some early schooling and learned his trade working alongside his father. When he was seventeen his father died and Joseph took over the family business, providing support for his mother and three siblings. About 1750 he attracted the notice of Kirvin Wright, an eminent physician, by whom he was encouraged to apply himself to the investigation and treatment of the diseases of horses. By dint of extraordinary application he mastered Latin and French and was able to read the best contemporary authors on farriery and horse medicine, particularly Vegetius and Étienne La Fosse. He also became a good mathematician, and was a member of the Bilbean Society of Norwich where 'men of original minds and with small incomes [met], for improvement in mathematics, experimental philosophy' (*GM*, 191), natural history, and botany, under the direction of Peter Bilby.

From 1765 Clover devoted himself entirely to veterinary practice. In this he was assisted by many well-known medical men, especially Benjamin Gooch, the surgeon, who inserted in his *Cases and Practical Remarks in Surgery* a letter from Clover which gave his description and drawing of a machine he had invented for the cure of ruptured tendons and fractured legs in horses. As early as 1753 he had discovered the manner in which the larvae of bots are conveyed from the coat of the horse into the stomach and intestines, and he had demonstrated this fact at several meetings of the Bilbean Society.

Gooch, writing in his *Chirurgical Works*, gave Clover an excellent testimonial: 'Mr Clover's character, by all who know him, is that of having a great superiority of knowledge in his profession, and his moral character is not less excellent'. Clover was tall and with 'a strong muscular frame of body' (*GM*, 192). However, for many years he suffered from giddiness and head pains. He died, aged eighty-five, at Norwich, on 19 February 1811.

GORDON GOODWIN, rev. LINDA WARDEN

Sources *GM*, 1st ser., 81/2 (1811), 191–2 · B. Gooch, *The chirurgical works of Benjamin Gooch*, 3 vols. (1792) · B. Gooch, *Cases and practical remarks in surgery* (1758)
Archives Norfolk RO, corresp. and papers

Clover, Joseph Thomas (1825–1882), anaesthetist and surgeon, was born on 28 February 1825 at home, over his father's shop, at 6 Market Place, Aylsham, Norfolk, the third of the five children of John Wright Clover (1780–1865), draper, and his second wife, Elizabeth Mary Anne Peterson (1791–1883), property owner. He was educated at Grey Friars' Priory School, Norwich, and at the age of sixteen he was apprenticed to a local surgeon, Charles Mends Gibson, and enrolled as a dresser at the Norfolk and Norwich Hospital. His apprenticeship was interrupted by ill health, almost certainly tuberculosis. In 1844 he proceeded to University College Hospital, London, where his fellow students included Joseph Lister and Henry Thompson. His claim, made many years later, that he was present on 21 December 1846 when Robert Liston amputated a leg under the first general anaesthetic to be given in England, though not supported by his diary, was confirmed by the fellow student who gave the ether, William Squire.

Clover qualified MRCS, LSA, in 1847, and in 1848 he was appointed to the onerous post of apothecary, renamed resident medical officer in 1851, at University College Hospital. Here he operated, administered anaesthetics by a

Joseph Thomas Clover (1825–1882), by Joseph Clover

method of his own devising, and taught students. He attained the fellowship of the Royal College of Surgeons on 11 April 1850. In 1853 he entered private practice and moved with his parents to 44 Mortimer Street, renamed 3 Cavendish Place in 1860, where he lived for the rest of his life. Here, in his own workshop, he made the prototypes of his many inventions, most of which were produced commercially by Mayer and Meltzer and Coxeter & Sons. Clover had become a skilled lithotritist, and went on to design improved blades and to invent a bladder syringe to facilitate the removal of the crushed fragments of stone. He also designed the Clover crutch, to hold the patient in the lithotomy position, and a gas cautery. But the greater part of his professional life was spent as an anaesthetist.

Appreciating the importance of knowing, and having control over, the concentration of chloroform vapour being inhaled by the patient, about 1860 Clover set about designing an inhaler free from the problems caused by cooling or breath-holding that were inherent in all contemporary vaporizers. The result was a more practical application of an idea first tested by John Snow, who had occasionally acted as anaesthetist for Clover. It consisted of a very large reservoir bag that was filled with a known concentration of vapour before the start of the operation. This established a safe maximum, which could be diluted by admitting air at the facepiece. The contents of such a bag would have lasted some fifteen minutes. By hanging this cumbrous device on his back to keep it out of the way of the surgeon, Clover initiated the fashion that required the well-turned-out Victorian anaesthetist to appear with pieces of apparatus suspended about his person. He exhibited the inhaler at the International Exhibition of 1862,

and the official report described it as 'undoubtedly, the safest instrument which has yet been devised for the administration of chloroform, [which] would surely be generally adopted if it could be rendered a little less cumbersome. It is, however, admirably suited for hospital use' (Traer, 148–9). The administration of chloroform by this apparatus became the approved method at St Mary's Hospital, the Great Northern, Guy's, and the Westminster. The quest for latent heat of vaporization continued throughout Clover's life. It resulted in his counter-current inhaler, and in vaporizers designed to be worn in the anaesthetist's axilla, and on the top of his head; this latter was rejected because of the discomfort caused by pressure on the scalp.

In 1863 the Royal Medical and Chirurgical Society, disturbed by the number of chloroform deaths, set up a committee of inquiry. No practising anaesthetist was included among its members, but Clover, who was a fellow of the society, played a great part in its experimental investigations, which were carried out in the physiology laboratory of University College. It was widely thought that he drafted its report and was largely responsible for its recommendations ('Report of the committee appointed … to inquire into … chloroform', *Medico-Chirurgical Transactions*, 47, 1864, 323–442). The investigation confirmed that 5 per cent chloroform vapour was the safe upper limit, and showed conclusively that when strong mixtures were inhaled the pulse became impalpable well before the heart ceased to beat. From this came the recommendation that the pulse should be monitored continuously. The photograph of Clover demonstrating the use of his chloroform bag shows him with a finger ostentatiously on the pulse, and he was always critical of any apparatus that did not allow the anaesthetist to keep one hand free for this purpose.

Clover's principal appointments were at University College, London, where he was lecturer on anaesthetics, and at the Dental Hospital. In October 1864 he was offered an attachment at the Westminster, but this, and his sessions at Guy's, lasted less than three years. Much of his private work was in dental anaesthetics. He was a very active member of the Odontological Society of Great Britain, to which several of his more important papers were read. Until the process of antisepsis allowed the body to be subjected to more extensive surgical interventions, it was in anaesthesia for dentistry that the advances were being made. Clover was much in demand by dentists. Unlike deaths in the anonymity of the hospital, a death in the dental chair was a death in the community, and dentists contrasted the pleasure of operating with Mr Clover, when they had not the slightest passing uneasiness, with their anxiety when the patient's own doctor volunteered to give the chloroform, when, as they said, they were often frightened out of their wits. Clover, with a few quiet words of explanation, was able to gain the confidence of the most nervous patient, and of the dentist too.

Clover prepared the official report when the use of nitrous oxide ('laughing gas') was demonstrated at the

Dental Hospital by T. W. Evans in 1868 (J. T. Clover, 'Anaesthesia in dentistry by protoxide of nitrogen', *BMJ*, 4 April 1868, 337–8). He immediately recognized its advantages for dental anaesthesia and rapidly adapted his own apparatus for its use. But the apparatus for which Clover is best known is his portable regulating ether-inhaler, the subject of several modifications, and illustrated in every textbook of anaesthetics for the next fifty years (J. T. Clover, 'Portable regulating ether-inhaler', *BMJ*, Jan 20 1877, 69–70). Its portability made it very popular with the peripatetic jobbing anaesthetists of the period. Oddly, it was the one he least liked to use himself.

Clover kept a careful record of his cases. His continual search for safety led him to try, and to reject, other anaesthetic agents. Realizing that some deaths were caused by the inhalation of vomit, he campaigned against the surgical practice of dosing the patient with alcoholic stimulants before operation. He insisted that the patient fast for six hours before the anaesthetic, and preferred to anaesthetize before breakfast or at two o'clock in the afternoon.

Clover's other contributions to the instrumentation of the specialty were a nosepiece for dental anaesthetics, a spring-loaded dental prop, an oral airway, a device for the rapid performance of laryngotomy, and 'funnel-shaped india-rubber tubes for conveying the anaesthetic to the back of the mouth during operations on the jaw'. These, together with a plenum vaporizer supplied by a foot-operated bellows, and a 'down-draught dilutor', which he was still developing at the time of his death, were shown at the 1881 congress (J. T. Clover, 'On apparatus for giving anaesthetics with precision', *Transactions of the International Congress of Medicine*, 1881, 2.390–92).

Clover worked with the leading surgeons of the day, and often with the urologist Sir Henry Thompson; among their patients was the deposed Napoleon III of France. Clover also anaesthetized Alexandra, princess of Wales, Princess Beatrice, Florence Nightingale, and Sir Erasmus Wilson. He enjoyed a rich social life, and made many friends. Among them were Tennyson, the Terrys, Holman Hunt, Burne-Jones, Ruskin, Coventry Patmore, Carl Rosa, and Brunel. He very likely participated in Sir Henry Thompson's celebrated dinner parties for eight, the 'octaves'. In 1869 he married Mary Anne Hall (1839–1929), artist and musician. Of their five children, three sons and a daughter survived to adult life.

Clover was indisputably the leading British anaesthetist of his day. He did not publish a textbook, but spread his ideas at meetings, through lectures and the journals, and by example. His well-received articles on anaesthetics, artificial respiration, and resuscitation, in Sir Richard Quain's *Dictionary of Medicine* (1882), appeared posthumously.

Clover died at 3 Cavendish Place, Cavendish Square, on 27 September 1882, of the tuberculosis that had troubled him for most of his life. Many tributes were paid to his professional and personal attributes. He is depicted as the supporter on the sinister side of the coat of arms of the Royal College of Anaesthetists, and a biennial Clover lecture is delivered in his memory. He was buried on 30 September in the Brompton cemetery in London.

David Zuck

Sources Wellcome L., Clover MSS, WMSS 1684–1686, 6942–6951 · Wellcome L., Clover/Buxton MSS, WMSS 5461 · Wellcome L., Macintosh MSS, PP/RRM/A4, E5–6 · V. G. Plarr, *Plarr's Lives of the fellows of the Royal College of Surgeons of England*, rev. D'A. Power, 1 (1930) · *The Lancet* (7 Oct 1882) · *British Journal of Dental Science*, 25 (1882), 1021–3 · *Journal of the British Dental Association*, 3 (1882), 555–7 · *Medico-Chirurgical Transactions*, 66 (1883), 14–17 · *BMJ* (30 Sept 1882), 656 · C. H. M. Woollam, 'Joseph T. Clover (1825–1882)', *Current Anaesthesia and Critical Care*, 5 (1994), 53–61 · A. K. Adams, 'More about Joseph Thomas Clover', *Proceedings of the History of Anaesthesia Society*, 7 (1990), 7–10 · A. D. Marston, 'The life and achievements of Joseph Thomas Clover', *Annals of the Royal College of Surgeons of England*, 4 (1949), 267–80 · B. Duncum, *The development of inhalation anaesthesia* (1947) [repr. 1994] · K. B. Thomas, 'The Clover/Snow collection', *Anaesthesia*, 27 (1972), 436–49 · R. S. Atkinson and T. B. Boulton, 'Clover's portable regulating ether inhaler (1877)', *Anaesthesia*, 32 (1977), 1033–6 · W. R. Merrington, *University College Hospital and its medical school: a history* (1976) · *London and Provincial Medical Directory* (1850–82) · W. Squire, *The Lancet* (14 Oct 1882), 649 · J. R. Traer, 'Notices of … the International Exhibition of 1862', *Medical Times and Gazette* (9 Aug 1862), 148–9 · parish register (baptism), Aylsham, PD 602/4 · Norfolk RO, PD 602/9 · *British Journal of Dental Science*, 12 (1869), 584 · burial register, Brompton cemetery

Archives Norfolk RO · Nuffield Oxf., medical notebooks · RCS Eng. · Royal College of Anaesthetists, London · University of British Columbia, Woodward Biomedical Library, corresp. and papers · Wellcome L., corresp. and papers | Association of Anaesthetists of Great Britain and Ireland, London, King MSS · Wellcome L., Macintosh MSS

Likenesses J. Clover, oils, 1844, Royal College of Anaesthetists, London · J. T. Lucas, photographs, 1869?, Wellcome L. · J. Clover, portrait, RCS Eng. [*see illus.*] · Keturah-Collinge, photograph, Royal Society of Medicine · daguerreotype, Frenchay Hospital, Bristol; repro. in Duncum, *Development of inhalation anaesthesia*

Wealth at death £27,932 14s. 2d.: probate, 18 Nov 1882, CGPLA Eng. & Wales

Clowes, Butler (*d. c.*1788), engraver and print seller, lived, and kept a printshop, in London at 18 Gutter Lane, Cheapside, from about 1760 until his death (his address has been recorded on prints by James Watson and others). The business was subsequently carried on by a John Clowes, presumably his son, at the same address. Clowes engraved a number of small-scale, modest mezzotint portraits after his own designs, which usually show the sitter half-length and enclosed in an oval or roundel. These include a self-portrait in a cap of 1771, and portraits of John Glas, founder of the Sandemanian sect, of the jeweller Thomas Liddiard, of a Mr Atwood, writing master to Christ's Hospital, and of other 'middling' folk drawn from his family, acquaintance, or general social milieu.

Larger, more ambitious mezzotints by Clowes consist of theatrical scenes and fancy pictures. His best-known theatrical subject is probably the portrait of the playwright Charles Dibdin, *Mr Dibdin in the Character of Mungo, in the Celebrated Opera of The Padlock*, after his own design, published in 1769 and later retouched and republished by Carington Bowles. Clowes's fancy pictures include a Chardinesque *School Boy* at a table with writing instruments, after William Elmer of Dublin, and a female figure on a terrace engaged in *Domestick Employment, Starching* of

Butler Clowes (*d. c.*1788), self-portrait, 1772

1769, probably after, or at least reminiscent of, the works of Henry Morland. A large mezzotint after Colson of a man firing a miniature cannon, entitled *The Engineer*, is described in a pencil note on the print as 'very scarce'; an impression is held in the British Museum. At the Free Society of Artists, between 1768 and 1773, Clowes exhibited a total of sixteen mezzotints of a largely comical or theatrical content, such as *The Hen-Pecked Husband* and *The Dying Usurer, or, The Wife the Physician*, after William Dawes (both 1768), and *The Female Bruisers*, after John Collet (1771), as well as portraits (1771, 1772, 1773), a print after Heemskerck (1772), and a scene from rural life (1769).

According to a contemporary trade directory, Mortimer's *Universal Director* of 1763, before his activity as a mezzotint engraver from the late 1760s, Clowes seems to have been known primarily as an 'engraver of heraldry, ornaments &c', and the production of furniture designs and engraved ornament continued to occupy him at least until the late 1770s. He etched the majority (forty-one of fifty-three plates) of untitled designs for carved furniture by Thomas Johnson (1758); this collection was later reissued by Robert Sayer under the misleading title *One Hundred and Fifty New Designs* (1761). The influence of Johnson's vivid, spiky rococo style is very obvious in a set of nine heraldic bookplates designed and etched by Clowes about 1760 for the dukes of Beaufort, Bolton, Cleveland, Grafton, Leeds, Norfolk, Richmond, St Albans, and Somerset. In 1762 Clowes etched nine plates for carvers' pieces for the third edition of Chippendale's *The Gentleman and*

Cabinet-Maker's Director, and a decade later he produced, after his own designs, a set of eight plates with six monograms (AA-ZA) each. In a complete stylistic departure (together with a J. A. Clowes), he engraved a set of twenty small-scale designs, moderately neo-classical and relatively simple, for chimney-pieces after the sculptor Richard W. Westmacott (*d.* 1808), which were published in 1777.

Clowes married Susanna Matthews on 7 January 1753. He died about 1788. A copy after his 1771 self-portrait shows 'a man past the prime of life, with a round, jovial, and doubtless rubicund countenance' (*DNB*). Henry Bromley's unfavourable account of Clowes's work, published soon after the latter's death, influenced the majority of nineteenth-century critics—with the notable exception of John Chaloner Smith—who considered Clowes's mezzotints amateurish and incompetent; his engraved ornament (and thus his brilliant etching technique and his versatility) were ignored. ANNE PUETZ

Sources Graves, *Soc. Artists* · Thieme & Becker, *Allgemeines Lexikon* · J. C. Smith, *British mezzotinto portraits*, 1 (1878), 138 · I. Maxted, *The London book trades, 1775–1800: a preliminary checklist of members* (1977) · *Katalog der Ornamentstichsammlung der staatlichen Kunstbibliothek Berlin*, Staatliche Kunstbibliothek, Berlin (Berlin, 1939), nos. 1228, 5323 · *Engraved Brit. ports.*, 6.590 · H. Bromley, *A catalogue of engraved British portraits* (1793) · Redgrave, *Artists* · Bryan, *Painters* (1886–9) · G. K. Nagler, ed., *Neues allgemeines Künstler-Lexikon*, 22 vols. (Munich, 1835–52) · Bénézit, *Dict.*, 3rd edn · G. J. Armytage, ed., *The registers of baptisms and marriages at St George's Church, Mayfair* (1889) · land tax assessment books, GL, Farringdon within Ward, MS 11316/184 (1760–61) to 268 (1788–9) · *DNB*

Likenesses B. Clowes, self-portrait, mezzotint, 1772, BM [*see illus.*] · stipple, pubd 1802, BM, NPG · stipple and etching, pubd 1802 (after B. Clowes), V&A

Clowes, John (1743–1831), Church of England clergyman and Swedenborgian preacher, was born at Manchester on 20 October 1743 and baptized at St Ann's Church there on 17 November, the fourth son of Joseph Clowes, barrister, and Catherine, daughter of the Revd Edward Edwards, possibly curate of Llanbedr, near Ruthin. Clowes was only seven or eight years old when his mother died but she laid the foundation of his religious education, which was continued by his equally devout father. He was subsequently schooled at the Revd John Clayton's academy at Salford, and possibly also at the grammar school there. At the age of eighteen, in 1761, he was admitted to Trinity College, Cambridge, where his tutor was Dr Richard Watson, future bishop of Llandaff, with whom he remained on friendly terms in later life. In January 1766 he graduated BA. During the next three years, while working as a private tutor, he took two prizes for Latin essays and was elected fellow of Trinity; he proceeded MA in 1769. Having abandoned his original idea of entering his father's profession he had prepared for holy orders and was ordained in 1767 by Bishop Richard Terrick. Illness meant that he could no longer continue tutoring, and when on 13 August 1769 he was offered the rectorship of St John's, Manchester, a position he had previously rejected, he accepted. St John's Church had only recently been built by his relative Edward Byrom, son of the poet John Byrom.

Still in delicate health Clowes felt himself unprepared for his vocation in other ways. In this diffident state of mind he one day came across a copy of William Law's *Christian Perfection*. The book had a profound effect on him and led him to study Law's other works as well as the writings of sundry English, French, and German mystics. In 1773 he was introduced to the writings of Emmanuel Swedenborg by Richard Houghton of Liverpool, who advised him to purchase a copy of Swedenborg's *True Christian Religion*. Through Houghton, Clowes became acquainted with the Revd Thomas Hartley, rector of Winwick, Northamptonshire, and the earliest translator into English of any of Swedenborg's works. The study of Swedenborg's writings proved a lifelong commitment for Clowes and he spent many years translating them. His first published translation was the *Vera Christiana religio* (1781), which was followed by four other works.

Soon after his conversion Clowes consulted with Hartley in London as to the propriety of remaining an Anglican clergyman. This was the only meeting in person between the two men and Hartley urged him to remain in the Church of England. Clowes followed his advice and remained rector of St John's, in spite of occasional opposition from his own curate, among others. Several pamphlets were published against him, and finally an appeal was made in 1783 to his bishop, Dr Beilby Porteus. The bishop dealt very gently with Clowes and dismissed him with a friendly caution to be on his guard against adversaries. However, Clowes remained involved in controversies over his Swedenborgian doctrines throughout his life. As well as preaching these doctrines from his pulpit he organized twice-weekly meetings, from which there sprang up in the manufacturing towns and villages around Manchester many popular Swedenborgian societies. In 1782 he founded a Society of Gentlemen, renamed the Manchester Printing Society in 1801 (which still exists as part of the North of England New Church House), for the purpose of printing and circulating the writings of Swedenborg and tracts on his teaching.

In 1787 at a meeting in London the followers of Swedenborg resolved to separate from what they called the old church and in 1792 the New Jerusalem Church in Peter Street, Manchester, was opened. This action was taken against Clowes's wishes and he made several trips to London to speak against it, but it did not prevent him from continuing to hold communion with his fellow believers. He became closely associated with the meeting at Hawkstone Park, Shropshire, held from 1806 by those who chose not to separate from the established church. He was a firm monarchist, who believed that 'governors should derive their rank and authority, not from the people whom they govern, but from the Head under which they govern' (Compton, 167). He was thus indignant when Abbe Barruel identified Swedenborgianism with Jacobinism; Clowes wrote his *Letters to a Member of Parliament* (1799) specifically to refute this claim. In 1804 he declined a bishopric offered to him by William Pitt on the recommendation of Baron Graham, although he did accept the chaplaincy of the Manchester Volunteers. The fiftieth anniversary of his induction to St John's was commemorated by the erection in the church of a bas-relief tablet, sculptured by John Flaxman, himself a Swedenborgian and a personal friend of Clowes, and by the painting of a portrait by John Allen, which was placed in the vestry.

Clowes was taken ill in 1823 while visiting Birmingham and was unable to return to Manchester. He died at Leamington on 29 May 1831 in his eighty-eighth year, and was buried at St John's, Manchester, on 9 June. The records of the Manchester Printing Society in 1828 showed that nearly 200,000 copies of sermons, pamphlets, and tracts by Clowes had been published. Among them were many reflecting his early interest in the Sunday schools movement. Many of his tracts for children were collected together as *Religious Instruction for Youth* (1812).

JON MEE

Sources *A memoir of the late Rev. John Clowes ... written by himself*, 2nd edn (1849) · T. Compton, *The life and correspondence of the Revd John Clowes*, 3rd edn (1898) · E. Fletcher, *Autobiography of Mrs Fletcher of Edinburgh* (1875), 40–44 · D. K. McCallum and M. McCallum, *New Church House and its origins, 1792–1982* (1982) · R. Hindmarsh, *Rise and progress of the New Jerusalem Church in England, America, and other parts*, ed. E. Madeley (1861) · *The collected writings of Thomas De Quincey*, ed. D. Masson, new edn, 14 vols. (1889–90)
Archives Chetham's Library, Manchester, autobiography
Likenesses J. Allen, oils, Chetham's Library, Manchester · J. Flaxman, plaster relief for monument, UCL · J. Flaxman, sculpture, St John's Church, Manchester · R. Westmacott, marble monument, St John's Church, Manchester

Clowes, William (1543/4–1604), surgeon, born at Kingsbury, Warwickshire, was the son of Thomas Clowes and his wife, Emma Beauchamp. He described himself in 1585 as being then forty-one years old. Of his early life nothing is known, and although for much of his life he practised in London his career did not follow the usual pattern of apprenticeship to a member of the Company of Barbers and Surgeons, followed by examination and a licence to practise within the City and suburbs. He eventually became a member of the company on 8 November 1569, but it was by translation from another, unknown company, and his subsequent relations with the Barbers' Company were far from harmonious.

Clowes is now regarded as one of the most eminent surgeons of his day as well as an outstanding writer on this topic. He wrote, abandoning precedent, in English, and from the many incidental remarks in his works it seems he was at odds with the surgical establishment which he tended to despise. His deepest criticism, and also his strongest invective, was, however, reserved for the ignorance of quack surgeons and the generally deplorable standards of surgical practice of his day. He was in addition, perhaps because of his lack of formal qualifications, highly sensitive to adverse comment, which he thought arose from envy or malice, and by way of defence gave details of his life, achievements, and methods which incidentally provide much insight into the surgical world of his day. Clowes became part of the shift towards Paracelsianism in the writings of surgeons during the period 1570–90. He went on to become 'a leading proponent of chemical therapy' and, along with George Baker and John Banister, one of the leaders of the profession who 'not only advocated chemical therapy but also projected themselves as allies of the Paracelsian' (Webster, 327).

Clowes claimed to have studied surgery under a George Keble, also a physician, of whom nothing is known. Clowes praised him highly, and states specifically that he (Clowes) had studied and practised surgery since 1563, asserting that this was 'well known to most men'. In that same year, when he was only nineteen, he served as a surgeon in Warwick's expedition to Le Havre, where he met John Banister, acknowledging their long friendship in an introduction to the latter's *An Antidoterie Chyrurgical* in 1589. On his return in 1564 and until about 1570 he served as a naval surgeon in Portsmouth, where he acquired a fund of experience and skills which he was able to communicate to his younger colleagues in his subsequent books. Clowes is known to have served on the *Aide*, which escorted in 1570 the emperor's daughter through the channel on her way to marry Philip II of Spain, and he describes an operation on this voyage to remove a splinter of bone from the lung of the boatswain's mate whose ribs had been fractured. The patient made a full recovery by the tenth day, an impressive achievement on a small vessel at sea.

Clowes was then in his own words 'employed in the hospitals in London', but it was not until March 1576 that he secured a permanent post as one of the surgeons at St Bartholomew's Hospital at a salary of £20 yearly. His previous service and devotion to his patients were acknowledged in his appointment, and a happy relationship lasted until March 1585 when he resigned with the goodwill of the governors to join, for nine months, Leicester's expedition to the Low Countries. From 1576 Clowes also treated sick children at Christ's Hospital as apothecary-surgeon, and although he appears to have maintained a harmonious relationship with both hospitals this was certainly not the case with the Company of Barbers and Surgeons. The company's minutes record continuous friction with the governors and other members, leading on one occasion to a commitment to ward for some misdemeanour and at least two accusations of taking money from patients without a cure, though to be fair to Clowes this was, at that time, a common occurrence. In February 1575 there was a complaint that he had abused the masters 'with scoffing words and jests', but not for the first time he was forgiven on the promise to conduct himself properly in future. These incidents culminated in March 1577 when he fought with George Baker, one of the queen's surgeons, in Moorfields, and the court once again 'pardoned this great offence in the hope of amendment'. The dispute must soon have been forgotten as Baker and he remained on friendly terms thereafter. Clowes's behaviour was therefore tolerated, probably because he was too important a man to ignore, but it was not until July 1588 that he was finally taken into the assistance, or governing body of the company, and it is noteworthy that while he rose to middle warden in 1584 he never became master. Clowes

was granted a bishop's licence to practise in 1580 at the direct request of the queen.

About 1586 Clowes was appointed surgeon to the fleet and also one of the queen's surgeons, an honour which he claimed occurred solely through the queen's 'favour and good-liking'. It was, in his own mind, a vindication against his enemies: 'I am not so barren or gross-witted or unlearned in the art', he said, 'as some have termed me to be'. He was appointed by Howard to serve on his flagship the *Ark Royal* during the Armada campaign, though he left no record of his activities during this period, probably because there were few casualties resulting from engagement with the enemy. The more pressing need in 1588 was for physicians to deal with sickness and disease caused by poor sanitation and bad food. This was a common problem on all sea voyages, and Clowes from his experience was well aware that there was little the naval surgeon could do for such cases as he could by law treat only external injuries and was prohibited from practising internal medicine. He therefore believed naval surgeons should have some knowledge of physic and the right to practise it as they 'cannot always have physicians at the elbows to counsel them'. A highly principled man he would use all means, lawful or otherwise, rather than allow his patient to perish through want of help.

As a naval surgeon Clowes encountered the ravages of scurvy which he rightly associated with the seaman's diet and as a preventative, long before Cook's use of lime juice, recommended fresh fruit and vegetables, watercress, or scurvy grass though he could not legally prescribe them. Scurvy was not, however, exclusively a maritime complaint and he noted that it was prevalent among the children at Christ's Hospital where he treated twenty or thirty cases at a time. He recognized also the tendency of gunshot wounds to become gangrenous and advised amputating where possible well above the affected area to avoid the spread of infection. His advice on the technique of amputation, using the tourniquet as tightly as possible as an anaesthetic as well as to minimize the flow of blood, remained standard for many years. So too did his technique for closing wounds. He was always ready to adopt the recommendations of others, and, for example when Guillemeau in 1594 advised tying the arteries to reduce blood loss after amputation, he was the first in this country to adopt the technique.

For the remainder of his professional life Clowes was in practice in London, where, as he pointed out, he encountered the best and most skilful surgeons. He was certainly successful enough to acquire two houses in Fenchurch Street and an estate in West Ham, then becoming a fashionable suburb, to which he later retired, describing himself as a gentleman. He married twice, but in both cases the dates are unknown and little is known of his first wife except that she came from the Godwin family of Kent and had two sons. The first, William *Clowes (1582–1648), also a surgeon, benefited from the bequest of his father's surgery chest with its pewter boxes, a silver salvatory and plaster box, and his instruments and books. The other son, Richard, was left only £20 in Clowes's will and then only after his daughters had received their legacies on majority or marriage. His second wife, Katherine, *née* Smith, had another son by him, Henry, later described as 'of Cornhill', who was admitted to the company in January 1626. There were also two daughters of this marriage, Katherine and Marie. Three other daughters are also mentioned in his will, though it is not clear from which marriage: Margaret, Friswith, and Johanne, who married a William Gregorie. The last was left a clock in Clowes's will, and £3 10s. 'which I owe him'.

Clowes died in 1604 at West Ham, reportedly of the plague, and was buried in the parish church. He was survived by his wife. In his lifetime a successful career followed from his energy, practical skill, and great experience, though his aggression towards those who, he believed, envied and wished to discredit him 'as though I had spent all the days of my life in the rude woods or wild forests of ignorance' would not have made him a popular figure, except among his patients, and those of his contemporaries he admired. Undoubtedly a difficult man he was driven nevertheless by the highest motives, principally the welfare of his patients and the need to improve the status of the profession by adherence to the best clinical practice based on past experience and teaching. He would not, he said, refuse anything that would benefit his patients from whatever quarter, even infidel, but be thankful for it.

Well read in Latin and French, Clowes was not an innovator but in many ways a conventional figure, who looked back for guidance to Galen 'prince of physicians and surgeons', Hippocrates, Vigo, and de Chauliac, and, in his own day, the Frenchman Ambroise Paré, whose influence survived until well into the eighteenth century. He should also be remembered as an early advocate of Paracelsianism in England. A further mission was to remove the abuses perpetrated by incompetent surgeons, mountebanks, and quacks who did so much harm and lowered the standing of the profession in the public eye. During Leicester's expedition he believed that there were more killed by the ignorance and incompetence of surgeons than by the enemy, and he was especially enraged by naval surgeons who, once appointed, absconded with their imprest money, given to buy surgical supplies, which could amount to £40.

The first of Clowes's published works was *A short and profitable treatise touching the cure of the disease called morbus gallicus, by unction*, first published in 1579. Years of practice at St Bartholomew's and in the navy had led to a thorough acquaintance with syphilis and its treatment; he estimated that 50 per cent of those who entered the hospital suffered from the disease and that he and three colleagues treated a thousand cases a year. His second publication, and the most influential, was *A Proved Practice for All Young Surgeons*, published in 1588. Its aim, as its title suggests, was practical guidance for the young practitioner based on what was known, by experience, to be successful, and it included a series of case studies with methods of treatment as well as various compounds and preparations, some of them his own which he generously shared with the reader and some inherited from his master, Keble. Both books ran to several editions. Towards the end of his life, in 1602, he published a work on struma, or the king's evil.

Clowes published these works 'for the good of the country', and the tenor of his writing shows him to be immensely patriotic with a strong sense of nationhood and belief in his country's religion and constitution. Perhaps for these reasons he wrote in vigorous and usually colourful English, pointing out that the great writers of the past had always written in their native tongues while those who criticized him for doing so feared only that the art would become 'too common, whereby every bad man and lewd woman is become a surgeon'. In other words, Clowes believed that surgery was too exclusive, concealing its mystery in the Latin in which most of the literature was written and which few could read. Clowes's importance perhaps lies in his vigorous attempts to impose higher professional standards and open up the profession to a broader spectrum of the public by the use of plain English. In doing so he no doubt incurred the hostility of which he complained so often.   I. G. MURRAY

Sources F. N. L. Poynter, *Selected writings of William Clowes* (1948) · J. J. Keevil and others, *Medicine and the navy, 1200–1900*, 1: *1200–1649* (1957) · S. Young, *Annals of the Barber Surgeons* (1890) · J. Banister, *An antidoterie chyrurgical* (1589) · court minutes, 1551–86, Barbers' Company archives, CB/1/D · Journal no. 2, 1567–86, Archives of St Bartholomew's Hospital [board of governors' minutes] · wills proved at Chelmsford, Essex RO, D/AER 18/98, pt 1 · C. Webster, 'Alchemical and Paracelsian medicine', *Health, medicine, and mortality in the sixteenth century*, ed. C. Webster (1979), 301–34
Likenesses portrait, 19th cent. (of Clowes?), Wellcome L.
Wealth at death wealth lay in property; legacies to children amounting to approx. £300 to be paid from houses in London and estate in West Ham: will, Essex RO

Clowes, William (1582–1648), surgeon, was the son of the distinguished surgeon William *Clowes (1543/4–1604). He was apprenticed to his father and admitted to the Barber-Surgeons' Company of London on 22 January 1605. When called to the livery of the Barber–Surgeons' Company on 13 December 1615 he was already surgeon to the prince of Wales and because of his royal duties was allowed to attend lectures and company functions only when convenient to him. He became sergeant-surgeon to the king on the prince's accession as Charles I in 1625 and subsequently declined to serve as renter warden (in seniority, the fourth warden of the Barber–Surgeons' Company), considering the office to be too lowly for a king's surgeon.

The records that survive of Clowes's career mainly concern matters of controversy. In 1626 he was chosen to be master of the Barber–Surgeons but his election was called into question because by convention it was the turn of a barber that year. The election was allowed to stand, but the wardens of the company's yeomanry were fined for not carrying the standing cups before him, suggesting that some opposition remained.

One of the duties of the king's surgeon was to examine all persons brought to be cured by the royal touch and in this capacity Clowes complained of a man called Leverett, a gardener, who claimed to be able to cure the king's evil (scrofula). Clowes was directed by the court of Star Chamber to refer the matter to the College of Physicians of London, and Leverett appeared at the college on 3 November 1637, claiming to be able to cure just by touch a range of diseases. When Leverett failed to cure cases given to him Clowes presented a memorial stating that Leverett slighted the king's sacred gift of healing, enticed lords and ladies to buy the sheets he had slept in, and deluded the sick with false hopes. Clowes also produced further evidence that Leverett was an impostor, including the proof that he was a fourth, not a seventh son. The college duly reported its findings to the Star Chamber.

Clowes's second term as master, in 1638, also began controversially. The election was unable to proceed because the first set of barber electors could not agree and were therefore discharged. Six more electors were chosen but two refused to serve. After fresh electors were chosen Clowes and the new wardens were sworn in. Just prior to Clowes's mastership the famous anatomy theatre designed by Inigo Jones had been added to the company's building in Monkwell Street. Clowes was a substantial contributor to the building fund. The new theatre was required because of the increased demand for lectures and dissections, stimulated by William Harvey's discovery of the circulation of the blood, as well as advances in surgery.

In April 1641 it was reported in the court minutes of the Barber-Surgeons that Clowes, following a complaint by one of the wardens, had been ordered to acknowledge that in his anger and passion he had spoken 'some words to the wrong' of the court. Later in the same year, on 30 September, Clowes was one of the seven examiners in surgery who made various orders concerning the reading of lectures, perhaps aimed at raising or maintaining standards; these included the requirement that surgery lectures were to be read by approved surgeons only, and that the lecturers were to have a month's notice to prepare. Clowes's last appearance in the Barber-Surgeons' Company was on 14 September 1648 and he died later that year. By his will of 28 March 1630 he left his property to Sara, his wife, and to his three children, James, Ann, and Sara.

ANDREW GRIFFIN

Sources S. Young, *The annals of the Barber-Surgeons of London: compiled from their records and other sources* (1890) · records of the Barber-Surgeons' Company, Barber-Surgeons' Hall, London · annals, RCP Lond., vol. 3 · *DNB*

Clowes, William (1779–1847), printer, was born on 1 January 1779 at Chichester, Sussex, the elder of the two children of William Clowes (1738–c.1782), schoolmaster in Chichester, and his wife, Elizabeth Harraden (d. 1816), schoolmistress. At the age of ten William was apprenticed to Joseph Seagrave, printer, in Chichester and in 1802 he went to London as a journeyman.

While working as a compositor for Henry Teape at George Street, Tower Hill, Clowes met William Winchester, a cousin of his mother, who took an interest in him. Winchester was a stationer in the Strand who had become one of the principal contractors to the government for the

William Clowes (1779–1847), by unknown artist

supply of stationery and printing of all kinds. Clowes borrowed money from his mother and from Winchester to start up his own business and on 21 October 1803 he began to trade on his own in 22 Villiers Street, Strand, employing just one man. His first book appears to have been *A full and genuine history of the inhuman and unparalleled murders of Mr. William Galley, a custom-house officer, and Mr Daniel Chater, a shoemaker, by fourteen notorious smugglers*, printed by Clowes for J. Seagrave and Longman and Rees. Through Winchester, he gained a share of government printing work. In December 1804 Clowes married Winchester's niece, Mary Winchester (1774/5–1836); they were to have four daughters and four sons. Her dowry enabled him to take more rooms in Villiers Street and to employ three more men and buy more equipment. Three years later the firm moved to larger premises in Northumberland Court, Charing Cross, which allowed him to bind books on site and to take on twenty more staff.

Clowes's early ventures proved successful. By 1813 he was dealing directly with a number of government departments, printing the casualty lists of the Peninsular War, stationery for the militia, and the *Navy List*, as well as work for the Religious Tract Society, British and Foreign Bible Society, and Royal Academy of Arts. At the time of Waterloo he opened a military bookshop at 14 Charing Cross and issued *Cannon's Historical Records of the British Army*. His financial position was so secure that when that same year he suffered a fire at his Northumberland Court premises and was forced to rebuild he was in a position to buy the freehold of the property.

In 1823 Clowes installed a powered press specially

designed by Applegarth and Cowper on the site, digging a well and installing a steam engine in the building. His neighbour the duke of Northumberland brought an action for nuisance caused by his machinery. Although the duke lost the action, he bought out William who, having lost an estimated £25,000 after the failure of Archibald Constable had rocked the industry in 1826, was then able to move in the following year to take over Applegarth's business premises in Duke Street, Blackfriars, where he formed what became the largest printing works in the world. By 1839 the London Union of Compositors reported 186 compositors working for Clowes, 86 more than Hansard, the second largest employer. (A description of the works, including the unique on-site type and stereotype foundries, was published in the *Quarterly Magazine* in December 1839.) Although Clowes suffered another financial set-back in 1840, the firm recovered its financial footing and by 1843 he employed twenty-four Applegath and Cowper perfectors and twenty-four hand-presses to print 1500 reams a week.

Clowes was constantly looking for technical improvements and innovative working practices which would improve his business. For instance in 1820 he was one of the first employers to start a benevolent fund for his workforce and he also was probably the first to use double sheets in bookwork, which became common after 1828. He experimented with the printing, in 1840, of the Mulready envelopes for the Post Office and he also produced the works of all the major book and magazine publishers of the day including George Henry Bohn, John Murray, Rivington, Routledge, and Longman and Rees. However, perhaps his most famous technical achievement was the printing, with Thomas De La Rue, of the gold coronation edition of *The Sun* published on 28 June 1837.

Clowes believed that steam-powered presses opened the way to cheapen the production of books and expand the market for the printed product. Working closely with Charles Knight, one of the leading figures concerned with the Society for the Diffusion of Useful Knowledge (SDUK), he printed from 1832 the *Penny Magazine* and the *Penny Cyclopaedia*, among other publications. They held similar beliefs in the importance of the new developments:

> What the printing press did for the instruction of the masses in the fifteenth century, the printing machine is doing for the nineteenth. Each represents an æra in the diffusion of knowledge; and each may be taken as a symbol of the intellectual character of the age of its employment,

stated Knight in the first number of the *Printing Machine* (1834), printed by Clowes. The great contribution of Clowes was the unprecedented level of accuracy, speed, and output from his presses; it was this that gained the admiration of Samuel Smiles, who held him up as an icon of energy and enterprise in his biographical sketches *Men of Invention and Industry* (1884).

In 1824 Clowes was honoured by his native town when he became a freeman of Chichester, although until the year before his death he lived in Parliament Street, Westminster, London. He died in London on 26 January 1847 at his home, 68 Wimpole Street, Marylebone, and was buried in Norwood cemetery. In 1839 he had changed the name of the firm to William Clowes & Sons, and at his death he left his three sons, William *Clowes (1807–1883), Winchester (1808–1862), and George (1814–1886), to run the business. ALEXIS WEEDON

Sources W. B. Clowes, *Family business, 1803–1953* (1953) · S. Smiles, *Men of invention and industry* (1884), 208–19 · private information (2004) · 'A visit to Mr. Clowes's printing office, 1833', *Penny Magazine* (30 Dec 1833), suppl.; repr. in *B. S. L. Pamphlets*, 2 · F. B. Head, review, *QR*, 65 (1839–40), 1–30 · E. Howe and H. E. Waite, *The London Society of Compositors: a centenary history* (1948) · *GM*, 2nd ser., 28 (1847) · *Sussex Agricultural Express* (30 Jan 1847) · *The Times* (28 Jan 1847), 7b · *The Athenaeum* (9 June 1883), 733 [obit. of William Clowes, the younger] · *The Times* (14 June 1824), 2e · *The Bookseller* (1 June 1870) [J. W. Parker] · G. Pollard, 'Notes on the size of the sheet', *The Library*, 4th ser., 22 (1941–2), 105–37 · G. Dodd, *Days at the factories* (1843), 326–60 · *DNB* · d. cert.

Archives Museum and Archive, Beccles, Suffolk · St Bride Institute, London, St Bride Printing Library · UCL, MSS · UCL, own and son's business letters to the Society for the Diffusion of Useful Knowledge

Likenesses portrait, repro. in Clowes, *Family business*, frontispiece · portrait, William Clowes Museum of Print, Beccles, Suffolk [*see illus.*]

Wealth at death left business to sons: *The Athenaeum* (9 June 1883), 733

Clowes, William (1780–1851), a founder of the Primitive Methodist Connexion, the son of Samuel Clowes, potter, and Ann, daughter of Aaron Wedgwood (a member of the illustrious ceramics family), was born at Burslem, Staffordshire, on 12 March 1780, and employed during his early years as a potter. He was considered one of the finest dancers in his neighbourhood and for many years led a dissipated life, but on 20 January 1805 he was converted during a prayer meeting. He soon established a prayer meeting in his own house, became the leader of a Wesleyan Methodist class, and joined a society which endeavoured to promote the keeping of the sabbath. He was one of the attendants at the first camp meeting ever held in England, at Mow Cop, near Harriseahead, on 31 May 1807, and was joined in this meeting by Hugh and James Bourne and others. In October 1808 he preached his trial sermon near Ramsor on the Staffordshire–Derbyshire border and was duly appointed a local preacher with the Wesleyan Methodists, but, continuing to associate with the Bournes and to attend camp meetings, his name was omitted from the preachers' plan in June 1810. In September his quarterly ticket as a member of the society was withheld from him by the Burslem Wesleyan authorities, who were angered by his 'irregular' methods of evangelism.

After this Clowes made common cause with the Bournes and James Crawfoot, and with them was one of the founders of the Primitive Methodist Connexion, which dates its commencement from 14 March 1810. From this time he became one of the best-known, most forceful, and confident preachers of the new society, and his vigorous labours in most of the northern counties of England, as well as in London and Cornwall, were most successful in adding members to the church. In 1819 he visited Hull, where Primitive Methodism was as yet unknown, and

William Clowes (1780–1851), by Samuel Freeman, pubd 1854

such was the impact of his preaching that within six months 300 people had joined the society. Hull became one of the major centres of Primitive Methodism. On 10 June 1842 he was placed on the superannuation fund, but still continued his ministry as before, and was at his work until a day or two before his death, from paralysis, which took place at Hull on 2 March 1851. He was buried at Hull. Clowes, who was twice married (he left his first wife after an argument with his mother-in-law), was a man of strong common sense and of great persuasive powers.

G. C. BOASE, rev. W. J. JOHNSON

Sources J. T. Wilkinson, *William Clowes, 1780–1851* (1951) · G. Herod, *Biographical sketches of some of those preachers whose labours contributed to the origination and early extension of the Primitive Methodist Connexion* [n.d., c.1855] · J. Petty, *History of the Primitive Methodist connexion* (1864) · W. Clowes, *The journals of William Clowes, a Primitive Methodist preacher* (1844) · H. B. Kendall, *The origin and history of the Primitive Methodist church*, 2 vols. [n.d., c.1906] · J. S. Werner, *The Primitive Methodist connexion: its background and early history* (1984) · J. Davison, *The life of the venerable William Clowes* (1854) · *Primitive Methodist Magazine*, 32 (1851), 249

Archives JRL, Methodist Archives and Research Centre, notebooks

Likenesses S. Freeman, engraving, repro. in Davison, *Life of the venerable William Clowes* [see illus.] · oils, Methodist Publishing House, London · portrait, repro. in Petty, *History of the Primitive Methodist connexion* · portraits, repro. in *Primitive Methodist Magazine* · portraits, JRL, Methodist Church archives · steel, repro. in Kendall, *Origin and history of the Primitive Methodist church*, vol. 1, p. 43

Clowes, William, the younger (1807–1883), printer, was born on 15 May 1807, the eldest son of the eight children of William *Clowes (1779–1847) and his wife, Mary Winchester (1774/5–1836). He entered his father's printing business in 1823 and later worked alongside his brothers Winchester (1808–1862) and George (1814–1886) in the firm. He married Emma Lett in 1835 and they had four sons and five daughters.

Around 1840 Clowes became interested in the possibilities of mechanical composition and bought the patent of a Polish invention for a typesetting machine. Two years later he endeavoured to print the *Family Herald* on a Young–Delcambre composing machine, but the experiment was not a success. By 1875 the technical difficulties had largely been resolved and Clowes installed Hooker's electric typesetting machine linked to a distributing machine in the Duke Street factory. It was one of the first composing machines to be of practical use, yet, although he installed four more, they were never popular with other printers. He soon realized that the United States was ahead of Britain in their development and he sent his nephew Edward Arnott Clowes (1851–1911) to America to bring back the most modern machinery. The Monotype machines which followed were widely used among British book printers and the firm became renowned for its expertise in composition. William Clowes made improvements especially in music printing and the firm became experts in printing in a range of different alphabets and languages.

In 1839 Clowes's father changed the name of the firm to William Clowes & Sons. His sons, William and his brother George, added to their father's impressive client list, which included the government and the military, the Council of Law Reporting, and the Royal Academy, as well as all the major book and magazine publishers. Their biggest coup was to win the contract for the official catalogues of the Great Exhibition (1851), which was a considerable logistical exercise as they had to co-ordinate and typeset the entries from the various exhibitors from different countries around the world and to print the illustrative colour plates and engravings. The firm became a recognized authority and was consulted by the organizers of many exhibitions. This success was followed, in 1881, by the *General Catalogue of Printed Books in the British Museum Library*, which took nineteen years to complete. The firm also took a leading role in the production of *Hymns Ancient and Modern*, which originally came out in 1859 and was revised and enlarged several times before the popular 1875 edition.

While Clowes ran the business in London, his eldest son, William Archibald Clowes (1843–1904), and his nephew William Charles Knight Clowes (1838–1917), independent of the main firm, went into partnership with William Moore of the Caxton Press at Beccles, Suffolk, a small concern valued at less than £5000 with four power presses. When Moore suddenly disappeared with all the money leaving considerable debts, the firm was re-established as Clowes and Clowes. It prospered and by 1876 was valued at over £20,000 and had fifteen power printing presses. Four years later Clowes and Clowes and William Clowes & Sons, the Beccles and London firms, were amalgamated and a limited company was formed.

William Clowes was well known for his benevolent and

active interest in the welfare of printers and craftsmen. In 1844 he became a trustee and nine years later the treasurer of the Printers' Pension Corporation and was concerned in the building and endowment of the printers' almshouses at Wood Green, London. He died on 19 May 1883 at his home, 51 Gloucester Terrace, Hyde Park, London, and was buried in Norwood cemetery.

ALEXIS WEEDON

Sources W. B. Clowes, *Family business, 1803–1953* (1953) · private information · 'The right royal opening of "The Colinderies"', *Punch*, 90 (1886), 231–3 · *DNB* · A. Weedon, 'A quantitative survey: George Bell & Sons', *Publishing History*, 33 (1993), 5–35 · *Printers' Register* (6 June 1883) · *The Athenaeum* (9 June 1883), 733 · *Publishers' Circular* (15 June 1883) · *The Times* (18 March 1851), 5f · *The Times* (28 April 1880), 14c · E. Howe and H. E. Waite, *The London Society of Compositors: a centenary history* (1948) · *CGPLA Eng. & Wales* (1884)
Archives Museum and Archive, Beccles, Suffolk · St Bride Institute, London, St Bride Printing Library | GL, Butterworth collection, corresp. with authors
Wealth at death £47,302 1s. 10d.: resworn probate, Aug 1884, *CGPLA Eng. & Wales* (1883)

Clowes, Sir William Laird [*pseud.* Nauticus] (1856–1905), writer on naval issues, born at Hampstead, London, on 1 February 1856, was the eldest son of William Clowes, sometime registrar in chancery and part editor of the fifth edition (1891) of Seton's *Forms and Judgments*. The younger Clowes was educated at Aldenham School at Elstree in Hertfordshire and at King's College, London, and began studying at Lincoln's Inn, London, on 16 April 1877. He had already, in 1876, published *Meroë*, an Egyptian love tale in verse, and on 11 March 1879 left Lincoln's Inn for journalism. He was employed at first in the provinces but returned to London in 1882, marrying that year Ethel Mary Louise, second daughter of Lewis F. Edwards of Mitcham, Middlesex; they had one son, Geoffrey S. Laird (*b.* 1883).

In London Clowes gained his first insight into naval affairs on the staff of the *Army and Navy Gazette*. Concentrating on naval questions, he accompanied the Home Fleets during the manoeuvres as special naval correspondent successively of the *Daily News* (1885), *The Standard* (1887–90), and *The Times* (1890–95). His reputation for expert naval knowledge was soon established. Articles by him, some under the pseudonym Nauticus, on such topics as the role of torpedo boats in war, the gunning of battleships, and the use of the ram, were widely translated and apparently influenced expert opinion in many countries. His anonymous articles on 'The needs of the navy', in the *Daily Graphic* in 1893, were credited with substantially increasing the naval estimates.

Naval interests did not monopolize Clowes's attention. In autumn 1890 he paid one of many visits to the USA, commissioned by *The Times* to study racial difficulties in the southern states. He published articles on this subject in *The Times* in November and December 1890, and then in 1891 in *Black America: a Study of the ex-Slave and his Master*, foretelling a terrible race war in the USA. An excellent linguist, in his later years he contributed frequently to reviews in England, France, and Germany. Besides historical and technical books he wrote many tales, mainly of

the sea, and some verse. He was part author of *Social England* (6 vols., 1892–7) and founded in 1896, and for some years edited, the *Naval Pocket Book*. He also edited *Cassell's Miniature Cyclopaedia* (1898) and did much to promote the issue of cheap reprints of standard literature; he was advisory editor in 1901 of the Unit Library.

Clowes gradually gave up journalism for research in naval history. Between 1897 and 1903 he compiled *The Royal Navy: its History from the Earliest Times* (7 vols.) in collaboration with Sir Clements Markham, A. T. Mahan, W. H. Wilson, and others. Its value was generally recognized and it continues in use. He also published other works of naval history. He was knighted in 1902 but because of ill health lived abroad, for some years at Davos, Switzerland. He was granted, in 1904, a civil-list pension of £150. He was awarded the gold medal of the United States Naval Institute in 1892, was an associate of the Institution of Naval Architects, and in 1896 was elected an honorary member of the Royal United Service Institution, where he gave several lectures. In 1895 he was elected a fellow of King's College, London. He died at his home at Eversleigh Gardens, St Leonards, Sussex, on 14 August 1905. A civil-list pension of £100 was granted to his widow on 30 November 1905.

S. E. FRYER, *rev.* ROGER MORRISS

Sources *WW* · *The Times* (16 Aug 1905) · *The Standard* (15 Aug 1905) · *Army and Navy Gazette* (18 Aug 1905) · *Men and women of the time* (1899) · D. C. Gilman and others, eds., *The new international encyclopaedia*, 20 vols. (New York, 1910)
Archives NMM, papers

Clowne, William (*d.* 1378), abbot of Leicester, was a canon of the Augustinian abbey of St Mary de Pratis, Leicester, and abbot of that house from 1345 to 1378. His parentage and the place and date of his birth are unknown, though the date of his election suggests that he is unlikely to have been born later than 1315. He probably took his name from Clowne in Derbyshire, rather than Clun in Shropshire, with which he has sometimes been identified. A William Cloune was bailiff of the honour of Leicester in 1329–32, and mayor of Leicester in 1338–9, but has no known connection with the abbot.

Clowne's fame rests upon the encomium of his career and merits which appears in the chronicle written by his fellow canon Henry Knighton. Knighton's portrait of the benign, wise abbot, revered and admired by his neighbours, and affably regarded by the king, has made him one of the best-known members of the higher English clergy in the later middle ages.

Clowne was elected abbot in October 1345 in succession to Richard Towers. In 1346 he sat as a papal judge-delegate in a dispute over a presentation, and he was appointed to examine the qualifications of a papal notary in 1349. An indult granted in 1350 allowed him to appoint his own confessor. He also discharged the normal run of royal warrants, providing safe keeping for the king's prise of wool in Leicestershire in 1347, and acted as a commissioner for array in 1360. In 1371 he was appointed to the commission that collected the subsidy of 116s. then levied on every parish.

Leicester Abbey was effectively a Lancastrian house, even though its patronage had been reserved to the crown when Simon de Montfort received the lands of the earldom of Leicester. Henry of Grosmont, earl, and later duke, of Lancaster, was a natural friend and protector: in 1352 he furthered the abbey's petition to impropriate the churches of Humberstone and Hungarton, Leicestershire, and in the same year he allowed the abbot to impark his wood at Anstey, and arranged for it to be stocked with beasts from Leicester Forest.

It was probably Clowne's zest for hunting that particularly commended him to Edward III, though he very properly told Knighton that he set no store by such distractions, and cultivated the company of the great only for the good of the house. The first mark of royal favour came in February 1352, when the chancery acknowledged that the abbot did not hold by barony and was exempt from attendance at parliaments. A curious episode followed, in which the abbey's temporalities were seized because Clowne had withdrawn from the king's council without permission. The lands were restored in October 1352, and any cloud soon dispersed. The king and Prince Edward hunted regularly in Leicestershire, and Clowne's prowess at coursing was much admired. It may be significant that although hunting was forbidden by Benedict XIII's ordinances for the Augustinians, the general chapter of 1346, which met at Leicester, merely observed that hounds ought not to be fed regularly in the conventual kitchens. In 1363, during a visit to Leicester, Edward granted the abbey the keeping of its own lands during a vacancy. The privilege was confirmed by Richard II in 1378, only a few days before Clowne's own death.

Although Knighton speaks warmly of Clowne's excellent relations with his neighbours, the abbey had on occasion to preserve its rights against encroachment, both by minor tenants, as in a dispute at Belgrave in 1357, and by members of the gentry, such as Sir John Arden, at Bearwood and Curdworth, Warwickshire, in 1360. In 1376 Clowne was named with two of his canons as participant in a brawl over a fishery at Wanlip, Leicestershire. On that occasion he may have contributed moral rather than physical force to the dispute, but such episodes were the small change of lordship. It seems likely that Knighton's references to Clowne's love of peace and distaste for conflict reflect a role as an arbiter in the community of the shire.

Clowne died at Leicester Abbey in January 1378; Knighton gives the date as 22 January, a Friday, but subsequently speaks of it as a Sunday, presumably 24 January. His successor, William Kereby (1378–93), was blessed by the bishop of Lincoln on 27 March. The abbey prospered under Clowne, who enlarged and developed its estates despite the disruptive effects of plague and depression. Four canons were chosen as the heads of other houses during his time, and Philip Repyndon was sent to study in Oxford. Knighton's work suggests also that the abbey library was respectably stocked and used. It is a measure of Clowne's posthumous fame that he should have been seen as a model for Chaucer's Monk: the association is unlikely, but in his lifetime he was unmistakably an abbot.

G. H. MARTIN

Sources *Knighton's chronicle, 1337–1396*, ed. and trans. G. H. Martin, OMT (1995) [Lat. orig., *Chronica de eventibus Angliae a tempore regis Edgari usque mortem regis Ricardi Secundi*, with parallel Eng. text] · A. H. Thompson, *The abbey of St Mary of the Meadows, Leicester* (1949) · *Chancery records* · *CEPR letters*, vol. 3 · A. K. McHardy, ed., *Clerical poll-taxes of the diocese of Lincoln, 1377–1381*, London RS, 81 (1992)

Clubbe, John (c.1703–1773), satirist and Church of England clergyman, was one of the sons of the Revd George Clubbe (d. 1711), rector of Whatfield, Suffolk. Clubbe entered King's College, Cambridge, as a sizar in 1721, and took his BA in 1725. Ordained deacon in September of the same year, he was priested two years later. His subsequent clerical career was unexciting: vicar of St Clement's, Ipswich (1729), vicar of Debenham, Suffolk (1730), and rector of Whatfield (1735). (Whatfield had been held by his father from 1703 until his death in 1711.)

Clubbe's most impressive work was the anonymously published *History and Antiquities of the Ancient Villa of Wheatfield* (1758). Ostensibly aimed at Philip Morant's *History and Antiquities of … Colchester* (1738), Clubbe's main target was, in fact, a whole genre of contemporary writing. Clubbe burlesqued the solemn self-importance of Georgian local historians and topographers: 'The ancient villa or parish of Wheatfield lies in the South-west part of the county of Suffolk, in the 52d Degree, 12 minutes of Northern Latitude, and distant from London 66 miles' (Clubbe, *History*, 15). He also poked delicious fun at prim morality. Viewing the classical 'Scamna or Benches' in the parsonage garden at Whatfield, he noted that they used to have on them 'many imperfect Letters and Words … which more than hint to us that [the] obscene God Priapus had a Statue erected to him in one of the Fruit Quarters' (ibid., 19). The offending words, Clubbe assures the reader, have been removed by the current rector.

Clubbe's other works—all of them ephemeral—were published in two volumes of *Miscellaneous Tracts* (1770). The best of these was 'A letter of free advice to a young clergyman'. Ahead of its time, 'A letter' breathed a spirit of real social sensitivity and concern: 'carry not a rich man into the church, and read over him the whole burial service, and huddle a poor man into his grave with a small portion of it' (Clubbe, *Miscellaneous Tracts*, 2.27). Clubbe married Susannah Beeston on 8 August 1732. He had twelve children, eight of whom survived him. Among the survivors were John Clubbe, an Ipswich physician, and William *Clubbe (bap. 1745, d. 1814), a cleric and poet.

Clubbe kept his sense of humour to the end. The night before his death he was visited by his doctor, who remarked that his pulse was much more even than it had been on his last visit. 'My dear friend, if you do not already know, or have not a technical expression for it, I will tell you what it beats—it beats *the Dead March*' (Nichols, 2.378). Clubbe died on 2 March 1773; his wife survived him.

PETER VIRGIN

Sources [J. Clubbe], *The history and antiquities of the ancient villa of Wheatfield* (1758) · J. Clubbe, *Miscellaneous tracts*, 2 vols. (1770) ·

P. Morant, *The history and antiquities of the most ancient town and borough of Colchester in the county of Essex* (1748) · Nichols, *Lit. anecdotes* · Venn, *Alum. Cant.*

Clubbe, William (*bap.* 1745, *d.* 1814), Church of England clergyman and poet, was the seventh son of the Revd John *Clubbe (*c.*1703–1773), rector of Whatfield, Suffolk, and his wife, Susannah, *née* Beeston. He was baptized at Whatfield on 16 April 1745, and attended schools at Lavenham and at Hackney, Middlesex. He matriculated in 1762 at Gonville and Caius College, Cambridge, where he was a scholar from 1762 to 1768 and graduated LLB in 1769. In the same year he was instituted to the rectory of Flowton, and in the following year to the vicarage of Brandeston, both in Suffolk. He married Mary, daughter of the Revd William Henchman of Brandeston; they did not have any children.

In addition to performing his pastoral duties, Clubbe also composed poetry, and his works include: *The Emigrants* (1793), *Six Satires of Horace* (1795), and *The Epistle of Horace to the Pisos on the Art of Poetry; Translated into English Verse* (1797), as well as other miscellaneous translations from the classics, and translations of English works into Latin. He also produced a miscellany entitled *The omnium; containing the journal of a late three days tour in France; … and other miscellaneous pieces, in prose and verse* (1798), and published two works on education, *A Plain Discourse on the Subject of National Education* (1812) and *A Plain Discourse on the … Establishment of a Sunday School* (1812).

Clubbe continued to live at Brandeston until the death of his wife in 1808, when he moved to the home of his youngest brother, Nathaniel, an attorney at Framlingham. Clubbe died on 16 October 1814 at Framlingham and was buried in the churchyard at Brandeston.

THOMPSON COOPER, *rev.* REBECCA MILLS

Sources Venn, *Alum. Cant.*, 2/2.73 · *The Suffolk garland, or, East country minstrel* (1818), 365–7 · H. R. Luard, ed., *Graduati Cantabrigienses*, 6th edn (1873), 104 · A. Page, *A supplement to the Suffolk traveller* (1844), 82 · [J. Watkins and F. Shoberl], *A biographical dictionary of the living authors of Great Britain and Ireland* (1816) · [D. Rivers], *Literary memoirs of living authors of Great Britain*, 1 (1798), 103 · *GM*, 1st ser., 40 (1770), 280 · *GM*, 1st ser., 84/2 (1814), 507 · Allibone, *Dict.* · Watt, *Bibl. Brit.*, 1.241 · IGI

Archives BL, Add. MSS 19167, fol. 78; 19209, fol. 160b · BL, travel journal, verses, and translations, Add. MSS 19197, 19201

Cluer, John (*d.* 1728). *See under* Dicey family (*per.* c.1710–c.1800).

Clugston, Beatrice (1827–1888), philanthropist, was born in Barony parish, Glasgow, on 19 September 1827, the eldest of five children of John Clugston and his wife, Mary Mackenzie. John Clugston was apparently by profession an accountant but he was also the owner of the firm John Clugston & Co. (Bleachers) of Avonbank, Larkhall, southeast of Glasgow.

Beatrice Clugston became the doyenne of Glasgow philanthropists. Her achievement as a supporter of charities and a fund-raiser was the more remarkable because she was not from a wealthy family: she wrote that she had spent the first nine years of her life 'in the midst of the working classes and when too young to understand sorrow herself, her heart was trained to sympathy by parents whose delight it was to minister to the poor and afflicted' (Morrison, 83). From these early years she seems to have derived a deep spring of sympathy for the poor. Possibly by 1860 Beatrice Clugston, resident in Glasgow again after the death of her father, at the age of thirty-two started her 'professional' career as a prison visitor. This work taught her the importance of convalescence for those who were recovering from illness and who, after discharge from hospital, had no option but to return to the inner wynds and closes of Glasgow.

Miss Clugston was the major sponsor of the Glasgow Convalescent Home (originally opened in Bothwell in 1866, but transferred to new premises in Lenzie in 1873), the Scottish National Institution for the Relief of Incurables (at Broomhill and Lanfine hospitals, Kirkintilloch, opened in 1876), and Dunoon Convalescent Home (opened in 1869). Other charities with which she was associated, and for which she raised money, included Lochburn House (the Glasgow Magdalene Institution, in Maryhill), the Dorcas Society of the Glasgow Royal Infirmary (1864), the Samaritan Society of the Western Infirmary, and the Sick Children's Hospital, Glasgow.

Of all her contemporaries, Beatrice Clugston was the one who could marshal the aristocracy to her cause and persuade them to patronize the grandest of grand bazaars held in aid of her various charities. In the City Hall, Glasgow, on 1–4 November 1871, at the pre-Christmas bazaar in aid of the West of Scotland Convalescent Homes, Dunoon, Miss Clugston had no less than thirty-one patrons, headed by Princess Louise, Queen Victoria's daughter, who had married the marquess of Lorne, the heir to the duke of Argyll. Of the patrons, more than twenty were titled; they included the duke and duchess of Argyll and the duke and duchess of Roxburghe.

In 1876 Miss Clugston held a bazaar in the Kibble Palace which raised £14,000; with further donations this was increased to £24,000, and enabled the Broomhill estate, Kirkintilloch, to be bought. The success of her fundraising enabled her to launch bigger schemes which gave Glasgow and the west of Scotland a range of large-scale facilities which were second to none.

Beatrice Clugston impoverished herself by her charitable projects: in 1876 she had no option but to accept a gift of money, and later friends provided her with an annuity. She moved, with her mother, to Lenzie (which was convenient for the Incurables Home at Kirkintilloch) in her later years. Her mother was, she said, pleased with the removal out of Glasgow, for in Glasgow 'her daughter Beatrice was constantly bringing in the halt, the lame, and the blind to be fed and clothed with the consequence that her cupboards were kept bare and her carpets lasted no time' (Morrison, 84).

Beatrice Clugston, who never married, died suddenly, on holiday, intestate, on 5 June 1888, at 3 Arran Place, Ardrossan, Ayrshire, and was buried in the Auld Aisle cemetery, Kirkintilloch, where an elaborate tombstone bears a bas-relief depicting charity, mercy, and humility. The legend 'Dunoon Homes, Glasgow Convalescent Home and Broomhill Home' is carved around the edge of the memorial.   OLIVE CHECKLAND

Sources O. Checkland, *Philanthropy in Victorian Scotland, social welfare and the voluntary principle* (1980) · A. G. Tough, *Medical archives of Glasgow and Paisley* (1993) · T. Watson, *Kirkintilloch, town and parish* (1894) · A. A. Morrison, *The story of Free St David's (now St David's United Free Church, Kirkintilloch, 1843–1926* (1926) · *Glasgow Herald* (6 June 1888) · *Glasgow Herald* (15 Dec 1964) · *Kirkintilloch Herald* (22 July 1891) · *Kirkintilloch Herald* (23 Dec 1891) · *Kilsyth, Campsie and Cumbernauld Press* (6 June 1891) · T. Martin, *Kirkintilloch local history, sixty years ago* (1909) · *Evening News and Star* (5 May 1879) · parish register (birth), Glasgow, Barony parish, 19 Sept 1827 · parish register (baptism), Glasgow, Barony parish, 14 Oct 1827
Archives Mitchell L., Glas., Greater Glasgow health board institutional MSS

Clulow, William Benton (1802–1882), Congregational minister and author, was a native of Leek, Staffordshire, and, after receiving a preliminary education in the grammar school there, entered Hoxton Academy. He became pastor of the Congregational church at Shaldon, Devon, where he remained for twelve years. In 1835 he became classical tutor at Airedale College, Bradford, but in 1843 he left in consequence of a disagreement with some influential supporters of the institution. He turned to writing, and published *Aphorisms and Reflections, a Miscellany of Thought and Opinion* (1843), *Essays of a Recluse, or, Traces of Thought, Literature and Fancy* (1865), and his most successful work, *Sunshine and Shadows, or, Sketches of Thought Philosophic and Religious* (1863), which ran to three editions over the next twenty years. After residing at Bradford for forty years he retired to Leek, where he died on 16 April 1882.

THOMPSON COOPER, rev. K. D. REYNOLDS

Sources *Congregational Year Book* (1883), 269
Wealth at death £586 10s. 9d.: probate, 3 Aug 1882, *CGPLA Eng. & Wales*

Clunes, Alexander de Moro Sherriff [Alec] (1912–1970), actor and theatre manager, was born at 2 Western Road, Brixton, London, on 17 May 1912, the son of Alexander Sherriff Clunes, actor, and his wife, Georgina Ada Sumner, actress. He was educated at Cliftonville, Margate. Although he came of stage stock on both sides, he did not originally intend to adopt his parents' profession, but earned his living in advertising and journalism while keeping his inherited acting talent to enliven his leisure time. He was, however, a natural player and after considerable and valuable experience with leading amateur groups he found the urge to turn professional too strong for him. By 1934 he was touring with Sir P. Ben Greet and later in the same year joined the Old Vic Company. His progress thereafter was steady, and the parts he was called upon to play, both in the classics and in contemporary drama, grew in importance until in 1939 he was one of the leaders of the company at the Shakespeare Memorial Theatre at Stratford upon Avon, playing Petruchio, Richmond, Iago, Benedick, and Coriolanus. He was now firmly established and what was more his work during the Malvern festival of 1938 had caught the eye and ear of George Bernard Shaw who in 1940 gave him the part of Godfrey

Kneller in *In Good King Charles's Golden Days* at the New Theatre in London. In 1941 Clunes toured with the Old Vic Company, during its wartime exile, playing Young Marlow, Malvolio, and Taffy in *Trilby*; but he left them in order to embark, in the following year, upon a project of his own which was to prove his most important contribution to the theatre and carry him to the peak of his career.

This was the foundation, in May 1942, of the Arts Theatre Group of Actors, a body which Clunes served as leading spirit, manager, director, and actor for the next ten or eleven years. Some movement of the kind was badly needed at the time; for although in a general way the theatre was prosperous during and after the last years of the war, the taste of the emergent new playgoing public was for revivals of established favourite plays rather than for new work. One of Clunes's best claims to respect during his time at the Arts Theatre Club was his readiness to help high-aspiring new dramatists. He subsidized Christopher Fry during the writing of *The Lady's not for Burning*, and then staged the play (1948) with himself in the lead. And he accepted John Whiting's obscure *Saint's Day* (1951) at a time when it was unlikely that any of the regular theatre managers would have taken the risk. In all, he was responsible for the production of more than 100 plays at this little theatre, and the artistic standard at which he aimed was always impressively high.

Clunes's work at the Arts Theatre was very much to his credit and might well have carried him to the topmost rank in his profession; but this did not quite happen. The reason was not easy to see, for in every technical respect he was an exceptionally well-graced actor. He had a good stage presence, a fine voice which he knew very well how to use, an impressive sense of character, and a lively intelligence. All these qualities were well in evidence when in 1945 he played Hamlet; while the performance was going on it was possible for a critic to rate it among the best Hamlets of the day. Yet somehow when the final curtain was down there was a feeling that his Hamlet had been addressed to the intellect rather than to the emotion of its audience, and it did not have much hold upon the memory.

So the later years of Clunes's stage career seemed to be tinged with disappointment: his varied natural talent and intensive experience had not availed to put him among those leaders of his profession whom the public acclaimed. He lacked, perhaps, that personal magnetism popularly known as 'star quality'. For instance, when he succeeded Rex Harrison as Professor Higgins in *My Fair Lady*, his performance was striking; yet it was Harrison's image that lived more vividly in the memory. Luckily for him, Clunes had other interests. He collected prints and drawings and owned and ran a bookshop. In 1964 he published a handsomely produced volume, *The British Theatre*.

In 1956 Clunes married Daphne Acott, with whom he had one son and one daughter. An earlier marriage, in 1949, to Stella Richman, had been dissolved in 1954. Clunes died in London on 13 March 1970. His son Martin also became an actor.   W. A. DARLINGTON, rev.

Sources J. C. Trewin, *Alec Clunes* (1958) · *The Times* (14 March 1970) · *Daily Telegraph* (14 March 1970) · personal knowledge (1981) · b. cert. · *CGPLA Eng. & Wales* (1970)
Archives FILM BFI NFTVA, performance footage
Wealth at death £39,179: probate, 2 Nov 1970, *CGPLA Eng. & Wales*

Clunie, John (*c*.1757–1819), Church of Scotland minister and songwriter, was educated for the Church of Scotland and licensed by the presbytery of Edinburgh on 29 December 1784. He then became schoolmaster at Markinch, Fife, where possessing a fine voice and some musical skill he acted as precentor in the parish church. In 1790 he was presented by the duke of Buccleuch to the parish of Ewes, Dumfriesshire, and on 12 April 1791 to that of Borthwick, Edinburghshire; he was also chaplain of the eastern regiment of Edinburghshire volunteer infantry. On 31 October 1790, at Ewes, he married Mary, daughter of Alexander Oliphant, minister of Bower. He and Mary soon began a family.

Clunie's reputation for the rendering of Scottish songs led to an acquaintanceship with Burns, who highly appreciated his singing. Clunie also composed several songs of his own to the old tunes, but did not take the trouble to publish them. The first two stanzas of the song 'I lo'e na a laddie but ane' are attributed to him by Burns, a better authority than Ritson, who in his *Collection of Scotch Songs* prefixes to them the initials J. D.; the four supplementary stanzas beginning with 'Let others brag weel o' their gair' were added by Hector MacNeil. The song 'Ca' the yowes to the knowes' was taken down by Stephen Clarke when he and Burns were spending a night with Clunie in 1787. Writing to George Thomson in September 1794, Burns says: 'I am flattered at your adopting "Ca' the yowes to the knowes", as it was owing to me that it ever saw the light. About seven years ago, I was well acquainted with a worthy little fellow of a clergyman, a Mr. Clunzie, who, sang it charmingly; & at my request, Mr. Clarke took it down from his singing' (*Complete Letters*, 655). Burns added two stanzas to the song and made several alterations in the old verses; these old verses, as taken down by Clarke, are printed in Stenhouse's edition of Johnson's *The Scots Musical Museum*. Clunie was the author of the account of his parish in Sinclair's *Statistical Account of Scotland*. He died at Greenend, near Edinburgh, on 13 April 1819, in his sixty-second year. T. F. HENDERSON, *rev.* JAMES HOW

Sources IGI · Anderson, *Scot. nat.* · M. F. Conolly, *Biographical dictionary of eminent men of Fife* (1866) · Irving, *Scots.* · J. D. Ross, *Who's who in Burns* (1927) · *The complete letters of Robert Burns*, ed. J. A. MacKay (1987)

Clutterbuck, Henry (1767–1856), physician and medical writer, was born at Marazion, Cornwall, on 28 January 1767, the fifth child of Thomas Clutterbuck (1728–1781), a solicitor, and his wife, Mary, daughter of Christopher Masterman, a merchant of Truro. After attending the local grammar school Clutterbuck was apprenticed to James Kempe, a surgeon in Truro, whence, aged twenty-one, he entered the United Hospitals of Guy's and St Thomas's in

Henry Clutterbuck (1767–1856), by John Cochran, pubd 1840 (after Henry Room)

London. On 7 August 1790 he passed as a member of the Company of Surgeons and settled to general practice at Walbrook in the City of London, where he soon prospered. This was helped by his publishing the *Medical and Surgical Review* between 1794 and 1807. In the journal, which appeared in alternate months, he 'proposed to give a summary view of all the books in the different branches of medicine in Great Britain and Ireland' (1794, 1.v). About twelve books were reviewed in each issue, and all the editorial work was done by Clutterbuck himself. In appearance Clutterbuck was above middle height with a striking florid complexion. He married, in 1796 at Walbrook church, Harriet Matilda (*d.* 1852), daughter of William Browne, a solicitor of Kirby Street, Hatton Garden. They had ten children, of whom four survived infancy.

Wishing to leave general practice and become a physician Clutterbuck spent 1802 studying in Edinburgh, but then transferred to Glasgow, where he graduated MD on 16 April 1804. He returned to London, setting up in practice at 17 St Paul's Churchyard. He wrote much about fevers, which he considered to be primarily an affection of the brain. His doctoral thesis was 'Tentamen pathologicum inaugurale quaedam de sede et natura febris proponens' (1804), and he followed this with other books on the nature of fevers. Among his other writings was a youthful *Account of a New Method of Treating Affections which Arise from the Poison of Lead* (1794), *Remarks on some of the Opinions of the Late Mr John Hunter Respecting the Venereal Disease* (1799), and memoirs on Nathaniel Hulme (1810) and George Birkbeck (1842).

On 1 October 1804 Clutterbuck was admitted licentiate

of the Royal College of Physicians and because of the regulations had to pay £22 to disenfranchise himself from Surgeons' Hall. He moved to 1 The Crescent, New Bridge Street, Blackfriars, in 1808, and the next year was elected physician to the General Dispensary, Aldersgate Street, where he started a lucrative career as lecturer in medicine and materia medica. *The Lancet* (1850, 2.213) described his style as 'plain, forcible and unadorned'. It is said that one year his lecturing earned him more than £1000. With the foundation of the Aldersgate school of medicine in 1826 he transferred his lectures there, several of which were subsequently published. These included *On the Proper Administration of Blood-Letting for the Prevention and Cure of Disease* (1840) and *Series of Essays on Inflammation* (1846).

An individualist, in his youth Clutterbuck resigned from the Aldersgate dispensary when the governors tried to remove some voting privileges of the physicians. In 1809 he led a group that objected to the presidency of the Medical Society of London being perpetual, and late in life he declined a fellowship of the Royal College of Physicians on the grounds that many worthy people had not been elected.

Clutterbuck was very friendly with Lettsom, and inherited much of his practice. This flourished among the merchants and middle classes of London. He also attended several dispensaries and the Peckham Lunatic Asylum. Lettsom introduced him to the Medical Society of London, of which he was a member for more than fifty years and which he served as librarian and council member, and as president on three occasions. He was a model debater, who said nothing that he could not substantiate, who treated young members well, and who never lost his temper. On leaving the anniversary meeting of the society on 8 March 1856 he was run over in the street and died at his home at New Bridge Street, Blackfriars, on 24 April 1856. He was buried at Kensal Green cemetery.

G. C. Boase, *rev.* J. M. T. Ford

Sources T. J. Pettigrew, *Medical portrait gallery: biographical memoirs of the most celebrated physicians, surgeons … who have contributed to the advancement of medical science*, 4 vols. in 2 [1838–40], vol. 2, pp.1–10 · Munk, *Roll* · *Medical Circular and General Medical Advertiser* (1853), 496 · *The Lancet* (17 Aug 1850), 210–14 · *The Lancet* (3 May 1856), 490–91 · *The Lancet* (10 May 1856), 526 · *People's and Howitt's Journal*, 3 (1850), 245–7 · [W. MacMichael and others], *Lives of British physicians*, [2nd edn] (1857), 403 · Boase & Courtney, *Bibl. Corn.* · G. C. Boase, *Collectanea Cornubiensia: a collection of biographical and topographical notes relating to the county of Cornwall* (1890) · W. C. Taylor, *The national portrait gallery of illustrious and eminent personages, chiefly of the nineteenth century: with memoirs*, 4 vols. in 2 [1846–8], vol. 2 · *ILN* (17 May 1856), 523 · US Army, *Index-catalogue of the library of the surgeon-general's office*, 3 (1882), 234 · T. Hunt, *The Medical Society of London* (1972) · *GM*, 2nd ser., 45 (1856), 663 · *Medical Times and Gazette* (17 May 1856), 505 · d. cert.

Likenesses J. Cochran, stipple, pubd 1840 (after H. Room), BM, NPG [*see illus.*] · Mayall, engraving (after daguerreotype), repro. in *The Lancet*, 2, 216 · C. Measom, engraving, repro. in *People's and Howitt's Journal*, 244 · C. Measom, line engraving and etching, NPG · Smyth, engraving, repro. in *Medical Circular* · oils, Medical Society of London

Clutterbuck, Richard Lewis (1917–1998), army officer and counter-insurgency and anti-terrorism expert, was

Richard Lewis Clutterbuck (1917–1998), by Frank Herrmann, 1981

born on 22 November 1917, 'fourteen days after the Communist Revolution in Russia' (Clutterbuck, 3), at 30 West Park, Eltham, London, the son of Major Lewis St John Rawlinson Clutterbuck, Royal Artillery officer, and his wife, Isabella Jessie, *née* Jocelyn. He was educated at St Ronan's preparatory school, Worthing (1926–31); Radley College, Abingdon (1931–5); the Royal Military Academy, Woolwich (1936–7); and Pembroke College, Cambridge (1937–9), where he graduated with a second class degree in mechanical sciences in 1939. He rowed in the Radley first and Pembroke second eights.

Clutterbuck was commissioned second lieutenant, Royal Engineers, in August 1937. In the Second World War, promoted lieutenant in August 1940 and subsequently holding wartime acting ranks, he served in France (and was evacuated from Dunkirk), the Sudan, Ethiopia, the western desert (including Alamein), and Italy. Promoted captain in August 1945, he served in Germany at the end of the war, then in Trieste, where he witnessed the effects of ethnic conflict and terrorism. In 1946–7 he served in Palestine during the Zionist terrorism. He was GSO2 staff duties at the War Office (1947–51) and in 1948 attended the Staff College, Camberley. He married on 15 May 1948 Angela Muriel, aged twenty, daughter of Lieutenant-Colonel Bernard Cole Barford, Royal Artillery officer; they had three sons, Peter, Robin, and Julian. Promoted major in August 1950, he commanded 4th field squadron, Royal Engineers, in the 7th armoured division in Germany (1951–3), and was an instructor at the Staff College, Camberley, from 1953 to 1956.

From 1956 to 1958 Clutterbuck served in Malaya on the director of operations' staff, based at Kuala Lumpur and co-ordinating army and police, in the classic successful campaign against communist guerrillas. He became fascinated with counter-terrorism, and his Malayan experience largely laid the foundation of his later career. Promoted brevet lieutenant-colonel in July 1956, he accompanied foot patrols. In 1958 he was appointed OBE. Promoted lieutenant-colonel in September 1958, he commanded in that year 32nd regiment, Royal Engineers, during nuclear tests on Christmas Island. After them he took his regiment to Ripon, Yorkshire, as part of the strategic reserve. In 1961 he was assigned to double Royal Engineers recruitment in eight months; he trebled it. He was an instructor at the US Army Staff College, Fort Leavenworth, Kansas (1961–3), moved to the War Office, and then in 1965 had a sabbatical year studying at the Imperial Defence College, London. Promoted brigadier in March 1966, he was chief engineer, Far East land forces (1966–8) based at Singapore. In northern Thailand he applied his evolving counter-terrorist philosophy, linking vulnerable isolated villages by roads: 'There's a Latin American guerrilla saying that when the bus comes along it's time for the guerrilla to move out', he said (*The Guardian*, 9 Jan 1998). Promoted major-general in April 1968, he was engineer-in-chief (army) at the Ministry of Defence (1968–70), then senior army instructor (1970–72) at the Royal College of Defence Studies (formerly the Imperial Defence College). In 1968 he enrolled at London University, and in 1971 gained his PhD in political science. Made a CB in 1971, he was colonel commandant of the Royal Engineers from 1972 to 1977.

Upon retiring from the army in 1972, Clutterbuck became senior lecturer and reader in political conflict at Exeter University, a post he held until 1983. Despite some initial undergraduate suspicion, his courses became popular, and he was noted for his enthusiasm, the quality of his lectures, his concern for his students, and such minor eccentricities as colour-coded spectacles and a tape-repaired wallet. When he retired he was made an honorary research fellow. He broadcast on radio and television; taught on police, business, American, and Foreign Office courses; and carried out consultancies for governments and multinational corporations: the last, in 1990 in Moscow, was on international co-operation against drug-trafficking and terrorism. In 1975 he became a member of the BBC General Advisory Council: his role included reviewing controversial programmes and assisting in selecting candidates for the council. From 1977 to 1987 he was a director of the company Control Risks, which grew to be the market leader in political risk and security consultancy.

An internationally recognized authority in his field, Clutterbuck published numerous articles in British and American journals, and twenty books. His first was a novel, under the pen-name Richard Jocelyn, *Across the River* (1957), based on his experience in the Italian campaign. Possibly his best was *The Long Long War* (1966), on the Malayan emergency, in which he argued the ineffectiveness in counter-insurgency warfare of aerial bombing— 'any villages so attacked would never have co-operated with the government again' (Clutterbuck, 161)—and the importance of intelligence. He also criticized the conduct of the Vietnam War, and claimed that each stage of Mao Zedong's guerrilla-war plan could have been effectively countered. His *Riot and Revolution in Singapore and Malaya, 1945–1963* (1973) considered the attempted urban revolution in Singapore and the last years of the emergency. Based on his own experience and on available research

findings, his works attempted practical solutions to crucial problems. His *Protest and the Urban Guerrilla* (1973) emphasized, among other things, how tiny and unrepresentative a minority were the hard core of student activists, and that they were predominantly bourgeois, not working-class. His *Living with Terrorism* (1975) warned that 'everyone today lives under the threat of terrorist violence' (Clutterbuck, *Living with Terrorism*, 1975, 15) and covered kidnapping, assassination, blackmail, bombs, and hijacking. His other works included *Kidnap and Ransom* (1978), *The Media and Political Violence* (1981), and his last book, *Families, Drugs and Crime* (1998). Repeatedly he argued for a firm, measured response and warned against over-reaction. He wrote that 'In the long run it never pays to give way to blackmail. In the short run this principle is easier to enunciate than to practise' (Clutterbuck, *Living with Terrorism*, 1975, 145).

Clutterbuck's recreations included sailing, canoeing, and hill-walking. In his last years he suffered from heart trouble. He died of coronary atherosclerosis on 6 January 1998 at his home, Thorverton House, 7 Silver Street, Thorverton, Devon. He was survived by his wife, Angela, and their three sons.   ROGER T. STEARN

Sources *The Guardian* (9 Jan 1998) · *The Times* (12 Jan 1998) · *Daily Telegraph* (21 Jan 1998) · WW (1998) · b. cert. · m. cert. · d. cert. · *St Peter's College, Radley, register, 1847–1933* (1933) · records of Pembroke College, Cambridge, Pembroke Cam. · *Army List* (1937); (1941); (1945–6); (1957); (1960); (1965); (1967); (1970) · R. Clutterbuck, *The long long war: the emergency in Malaya, 1948–1960* (1966)
Archives CAC Cam., notes, lectures, and papers relating to international terrorism | SOUND BL NSA, oral history interview
Likenesses F. Herrmann, photograph, 1981, News International Syndication, London [*see illus.*] · photograph, repro. in *The Guardian* (9 Jan 1998) · photograph, repro. in *Daily Telegraph* (21 Jan 1998)

Clutterbuck, Robert (1772–1831), local historian and landowner, was born and baptized at Watford House, High Street, Watford, in Hertfordshire, on 28 January 1772. He was the eldest surviving son of Thomas Clutterbuck the younger (1744–1791) and Sarah Thurgood (1749–1788), daughter of Robert and Sarah Thurgood, brewers of Baldock, also in Hertfordshire. Clutterbuck was educated at Harrow School and was gentleman commoner of Exeter College, Oxford, from 1791 until 1794, when he graduated BA. Admitted to Lincoln's Inn, London, in 1791, he was described as being a member in 1794. However, he abandoned law for chemistry and painting, taking lessons in the latter from James Barry (1741–1806), and possibly living in London until his marriage, on 10 January 1798, to Marianne (1774–1856), eldest daughter of James Capper (1743–1825), a retired East India Company colonel. Clutterbuck and his wife were living at Cathays, near Cardiff, when their children Robert and Marianne were born, in October 1798 and March 1800 respectively. In 1799 the Thurgood brewery at Baldock, with eleven inns and beer-houses, which Clutterbuck had inherited from his grandfather, was sold for £8842. From July 1801, when another son was born, the Clutterbucks' home was at Watford House, which was set in spacious grounds with a maltings nearby (the family brewery was at Stanmore, Middlesex). Between 1817 and 1830 Clutterbuck travelled in Europe,

Robert Clutterbuck (1772–1831), by William Bond (after William Henry Hunt, c.1815)

making many sketches. In 1823–4, as a magistrate and deputy lieutenant, he helped to unravel the mysterious murder of William Weare.

Clutterbuck's claim to fame is his monumental work *The History and Antiquities of the County of Hertford*, published, in three massive volumes, in 1815, 1821, and 1827. Thomas Leman supplied the early history in volume 1 (pp. vi–xvii); three volumes of Thomas Blore's manuscripts, acquired in 1811, proved invaluable. The subtitle of Clutterbuck's history claimed that the text was 'compiled from the best printed authorities and original records preserved in public authorities'; it is vast and comprehensive. J. E. Cussans used the text for reference when visiting churches to research for his *History of Hertfordshire*, but claimed that Clutterbuck 'visited but few of the parishes he describes. … He trusted entirely to assistants of greater or less accuracy' (Deacon and Walne, 39). Since much of both histories consists of inscriptions on church memorials this is important. Branch Johnson alleged that 'if the most austere in manner Clutterbuck is the most lavish in production' (p. 9), and the *Gentleman's Magazine* claimed that 'the plates have never been surpassed in similar productions; several were from sketches of his own'. Some were by Thomas Blore's son, Edward. While Clutterbuck produced a monumental record of manors, churches, and the landed gentry before the early nineteenth century, 'the short and simple annals of the poor will be looked for in vain' (Johnson, *Local History*, 9). In 1828, however, Clutterbuck published *An Account of the Benefactions to the Parish of Watford*.

Robert Clutterbuck died at Watford House on 25 May 1831, following a sudden 'inflammation in the stomach before medical aid could be obtained' (*GM*, 566). He was buried on 1 June in the family vault at Watford House. There is an extraordinary claim by Cussans that Clutterbuck 'committed suicide by cutting his throat', for which there is no supporting evidence (Deacon and Walne, 39). At his death he owned land in Aldenham, Ashwell, Bushey, and Hinxworth, in addition to the family property at Watford. This was all left to his wife, Marianne, with reversion to his sons. His will mentioned eight shares in the Sun insurance company, £800 in 3 per cent bank annuities, and a debt of £2400 for enclosing Hinxworth. According to one historian of Watford 'He stood 6′6″, was of imposing presence, looking what he was—a gentleman' (Jones, 21).

LIONEL M. MUNBY

Sources GM, 1st ser., 101/1 (1831), 565–6 · W. B. Johnson, introduction, in J. E. Cussans, *History of Hertfordshire*, 1 (1972), v–xiv, esp. vi–vii, 140 · will, PRO, PROB 11/1786, sig. 320 [proved 24 June 1831] · W. T. J. Gun, ed., *The Harrow School register, 1571–1800* (1934), 54 · Foster, *Alum. Oxon.* · W. P. Baildon, ed., *The records of the Honorable Society of Lincoln's Inn: admissions*, 1 (1896), 539 · will, PRO, PROB 11/1205 [T. Clutterbuck the younger, proved 9 June 1791] · *VCH Hertfordshire*, 3.236, 237, 479 · A. Deacon and P. Walne, 'A professional Hertfordshire tramp': John Edwin Cussans (1987), 39–40, 103 · K. R. Jones, *More about Watford* (1973), 14, 21–2 · *A complete history: murder of Mr Weare* (1824), 4, 25, 39; appx 15, 61, 66, 67, 69, 75, 166, 167, 169, 202 [adjourned trial] · M. Cornell, 'Simpson's of Baldock', *Hertfordshire's Past*, 46 (spring 1999), 2–14 · Nichols, *Illustrations*, 6.437, 447–8 · H. Poole, *Here for the beer* (1984), 7, 55 · *DNB* · Herts. ALS, calendar vol. 20, Accessions, 28489, 28490 · parish register, Watford, St Mary's Church, HRO, D/P117/1/21, 1 June 1831 [burial] · W. B. Johnson, *Local history in Hertfordshire* (1964), 8–9 · N. Connell, 'Robert Clutterbuck of Watford: county historian and topographer', *Hertfordshire's Past*, 53 (Aug 2002)

Archives Cardiff Central Library, travel diaries · Herts. ALS, corresp.; working papers, MS history of Hertfordshire, illustrations, and accounts, misc. M8 46432, 46433, 46434, 46470–46475, 46477

Likenesses lithograph, 1818, BM · W. Bond, stipple (after W. H. Hunt, c.1815), BM; version, NPG [*see illus.*] · J. E. Clutterbuck, mezzotint (after G. F. Joseph), NPG · R. J. Lane, lithograph, NPG · portrait, repro. in J. E. Cussans, *History of Hertfordshire*, 3 (1972), facing p. 140

Wealth at death estate not valued; left main estate to wife, with reversion to sons; Watford House property covered over 100 acres; also owned land in other parishes; will mentions land in Aldenham and Bushey; four shares in Sun; four shares in Sun Life Assurance; £800 in 3 per cent annuities; £2400 in debt: will, PRO, PROB 11/1786, sig. 320; Jones, *More about Watford*

Clutton, Henry (1819–1893), architect, was born on 19 March 1819, the third son of Owen Clutton (1776–1834) of Walworth, Surrey, and Elizabeth Goodinge (d. 1846), formerly of Tunbridge Wells. The Cluttons originally came from Cheshire, but branches of the family settled in Surrey and Sussex during the eighteenth century. Henry Clutton, who inherited the Surrey property, should not be confused with Henry Clutton (1814–1895), a partner with Messrs Clutton of 8 Whitehall Place, London. On the death of his father the fifteen-year-old Henry was articled to Edward Blore, in whose office he remained for a decade. Having assisted Blore in his architectural practice, Clutton succeeded him as William Dugdale's architect at Merevale, Warwickshire, in 1845. Between 1845 and 1856 Clutton's career advanced with commissions for country houses, Anglican churches, schools, and colleges. He became prominent in architectural circles, as a founder member of the Architectural Museum, a member of the Ecclesiological Society, and fellow of the RIBA, and as the author of articles in *The Builder* (1854–5) and *The Ecclesiologist* (1850, 1855–6). His major publication, *Remarks with illustrations on the domestic architecture of France from the accession of Charles VI to the demise of Louis XII* (1853–6), drew attention to the distinction of fifteenth-century French domestic buildings, establishing Clutton as an authority. Clutton and William Burges travelled to France in 1851, researching for Clutton's book. Their collaboration culminated in competition designs for Lille Cathedral in the thirteenth-century French Gothic style. Clutton and Burges were awarded the first premium (1856), but national and religious prejudice prevented the execution of their designs. A row in May 1856 ended the partnership.

Clutton's reception into the Roman Catholic church in 1857 was the turning point of his career. Thereafter, commissions from the Anglican establishment ceased and he relied instead on the patronage of country house clients, the dukes of Bedford, and the Roman Catholic hierarchy. As a result of Clutton's marriage on 17 October 1860 to Caroline Alice Ryder (1841–1934), daughter of George Dudley Ryder, another convert, H. E. Manning became Clutton's brother-in-law, and J. H. Newman a family friend. As converts, the family felt socially ostracized; indeed, Clutton himself gives the impression of a person solitary in manner, a man without warmth. Of his nine children, four became Roman Catholic nuns or priests.

Clutton's mastery of thirteenth-century French Gothic architecture was demonstrated in the churches he designed for poor Roman Catholic congregations such as St Francis of Assisi, Pottery Lane, London (1859–60). He produced sophisticated designs for the Jesuits' chapel in Farm Street, London (1858–60), and an Italian Renaissance cloister for the Oratorians at Edgbaston, Birmingham (1872–3). Clutton's country houses varied in style from Hatherop House, Gloucestershire (1848–56), an Elizabethan mansion for Lord de Mauley, to Minley Manor, Hampshire (1858–62), an exuberant interpretation of a fifteenth-century French château for Raikes Currie.

The climax of Clutton's career was to have been the new Roman Catholic Westminster Cathedral. He was appointed architect in 1867 and spent six years on designs before the project ran aground; the cathedral was eventually executed by J. F. Bentley, Clutton's former pupil. Clutton suffered several professional disappointments: Lille, Salisbury, and Westminster cathedrals, the Oxford Oratory, dismissal from the restoration of All Souls College chapel, and the rejection of his prize-winning design for Brompton Oratory. In 1881 blindness forced his retirement, whereupon remaining work for the duke of Bedford in Covent Garden, London, was entrusted to Clutton's assistant Alfred J. Pilkington. Clutton died at Brookside, Yiewsley, West Drayton, Middlesex, on 27 June 1893 and was buried in the family tomb at Mortlake, Surrey.

PENELOPE HUNTING

Sources P. Hunting, 'The life and work of Henry Clutton (1819–93)', PhD diss., U. Lond., 1979 · G. McHardy, 'Henry Clutton and his early ecclesiastical work', MA diss., Courtauld Inst., 1969 · S. Welsh, 'Henry Clutton: a biographical note and list of principal works', 1973, RIBA BAL · priv. coll. · *Building News*, 64 (1893), 886 · *Journal of Proceedings of the Royal Institute of British Architects*, new ser., 9 (1892–3), 460 · *The Times* (29 June 1893) · P. Hunting, 'From Gothic to red brick: the planning of Westminster Cathedral', *Country Life*, 167 (1980), 580–82 · m. cert.
Archives Archives Historiques, Lille, Lille Cathedral designs, 1856 · Archives of the British Province of the Society of Jesus, London · Beds. & Luton ARS, Duke of Bedford's estate office archives ·

Duke of Bedford's estate office, London, Bedford office annual reports · LMA
Likenesses photograph, priv. coll.
Wealth at death £99,026 19s. 5d.: probate, 25 Aug 1893, *CGPLA Eng. & Wales*

Clutton, Henry Hugh (1850–1909), surgeon, born on 12 July 1850 at Saffron Walden, Essex, was the third son of Ralph Clutton (1804/5–1886), vicar of that parish, and his wife, Isabella Ellice. Clutton was educated at Marlborough College from 1864 to 1866, when he left on account of ill health. He entered Clare College, Cambridge, in 1869, and graduated BA in 1873, MA and MB in 1879, and MCh in 1897. He commenced clinical studies at St Thomas's Hospital, London, in 1872, and was appointed resident assistant surgeon in 1876, assistant surgeon in 1878, and full surgeon in 1891. While assistant surgeon he took charge of the department for diseases of the ear. Clutton's other appointments in London were as surgeon to the Victoria Hospital for Children at Chelsea from 1887 to 1893, consulting surgeon to Osborne House, and treasurer of the Medical Sickness Annuity and Life Assurance Society and of the Convalescent Homes Association. He was also on the executive committee of the Imperial Cancer Research Fund and a visitor for the King Edward's Hospital Fund.

Clutton was admitted a member of the Royal College of Surgeons in 1875, and a fellow in 1876; he served on the council from 1902 until his death, and sat on the senate of the University of London as the college representative. In 1905 he was president of the Clinical Society of London. He married in 1896 Margaret Alice, third daughter of Canon Young, rector of Whitnash, Warwickshire.

Clutton was an early supporter of antiseptic and aseptic methods, and of surgery for middle-ear disease. He wrote over sixty-five papers, mainly in the *Transactions of the Pathological and of the Clinical Society*, and in *St Thomas's Hospital Reports*, demonstrating an especial interest in bone and joint diseases. One paper in *The Lancet* (13 March 1886, 516), described symmetrical swellings of the knees in children with congenital syphilis. This condition became known as 'Clutton's joints'. Clutton wrote on pyaemia in T. Holmes's and J. W. Hulke's *A System of Surgery* (1883), and on diseases of the bones and the surgery of deformity in F. Treves's *System of Surgery* (1895); he translated material from the German F. von Esmarch's *The Surgeon's Handbook on the Treatment of Wounded in War* (1878). He designed urethral sounds and bougies which were known by his name and employed until the 1960s.

In his younger days, Clutton was a fell walker and fisherman, visiting Scotland and Ireland. He read widely on history, art, and architecture, and enjoyed travel. His remarkable endurance and capacity was sapped twelve years before his death by two episodes of septicaemia due to wound infections. After a long illness, alleviated temporarily by an operation, Clutton died at his house, 2 Portland Place, London, on 9 November 1909, and was buried in Brompton cemetery. He was survived by his wife and daughter. An old friend commented:

> He was a patient, careful and skilled observer; no trouble was too great for him, whether it was required in the pursuit of

purely scientific knowledge or in sifting the signs and symptoms at the bed-side … He was a clear and admirable teacher … always followed by a keen and appreciative crowd of students. (*St Thomas's Hospital Gazette*, 19, 1909, 157–60)

D'A. POWER, rev. JOHN KIRKUP

Sources *St Thomas's Hospital Gazette*, 19 (1909), 157–60 • *The Lancet* (20 Nov 1909), 1552–6 • *BMJ* (20 Nov 1909), 1504–5 • V. G. Plarr, *Plarr's Lives of the fellows of the Royal College of Surgeons of England*, rev. D'A. Power, 1 (1930), 248–9 • personal knowledge (1912) • private information (1912) • Venn, *Alum. Cant.* • b. cert. • *CGPLA Eng. & Wales* (1910)
Likenesses Elliott & Fry, photograph, repro. in *BMJ*, 1504 • photograph, repro. in *St Thomas's Hospital Gazette*, 157
Wealth at death £51,475 16s. 8d.: resworn probate, 4 Jan 1910, *CGPLA Eng. & Wales*

Clutton, John (1809–1896), surveyor, was born at Hartswood, Reigate, Surrey, the third of the four sons and six daughters of William Clutton (1745/6–1839) of Hartswood and his second wife.

John Clutton's grandfather, also William Clutton (1740–1826), was the third son of Ralph Clutton (1695–1761), vicar of Horsted Keynes, Sussex. This grandfather married Sarah, only surviving child of Robert Chatfield (1698–1780), of Cuckfield, Sussex, surveyor, and later took over his father-in-law's practice, which included the agency for the Sussex estates of Henry Smith's Charity. This business was conducted from William Clutton's home, the Jacobean house Ockenden, Cuckfield, which he leased from the Burrell family, one of the trustees of the charity; in the next generation it was moved to Hartswood, an estate of several hundred acres purchased by John Clutton's father.

John Clutton was educated at Cuckfield grammar school, of which he remarked in later life 'at this place I learnt little good' (Clutton, 3); it was intended that he should be articled to a solicitor but in 1826 he was called home to join his father's firm, whose affairs had fallen into confusion. His elder brother Robert (1801–1877), who had been formally articled to a surveyor in Maidenhead, was called back at the same time; he sorted out the muddled accounts, put the practice back on its feet, and remained in charge of the original family business for the rest of his life. John's next brother, Ralph (1804–1886), became vicar of Saffron Walden, Essex; his younger brother, Henry (1814–1895), was articled to the architect Decimus Burton, but his tastes were more agricultural than architectural and about 1856 he gave up his architecture in order to join John's independent surveying business.

In 1837 John Clutton married Elizabeth, daughter of George Spencer Smith, and moved to London to set up in practice on his own account. The move was helped by the legacy of £3000 which he received on his father's death, but it was prompted, and indeed necessitated, by the sudden growth of a large volume of surveying business negotiating land purchases for railway construction, business in which a location close to parliament where railway bills were determined was most desirable. His introduction to railway land purchasing came from the South Eastern Railway, whose line originally started from Reigate; eventually he was responsible, as chief land agent, for acquiring all the land and house property for the entire 120 miles of its route. Similar work for the London, Brighton, and South Coast Railway, which also passed through Reigate, followed, but by this time he and his wife had set up house in Parliament Street, London, which also served as his office. By the late 1830s his reputation as a skilful valuer, negotiator, and arbitrator in railway business was growing. He acted for other companies, notably the Eastern Counties Railway, and in 1845 was a key expert witness before the select committee of the House of Lords on compensation for lands taken by railways, from which stemmed the important procedural legislation of the Land Clauses Consolidation Act and the Railway Clauses Consolidation Act in 1845.

Two strokes of good fortune enabled Clutton to diversify. In 1845 he became agent for the Kensington estate of Henry Smith's Charity on the death of the architect George Basevi, who had been the surveyor appointed to lay out that estate for building development (the agency of the country estate remaining with Robert and the Reigate office). Two years earlier Decimus Burton had introduced him to Charles Knight Murray, secretary to the newly established ecclesiastical commissioners, who commissioned Clutton to handle the first case under the Ecclesiastical Leases Act of 1842 of a proposal to grant a building lease of church land. From this followed, in 1845, the commission to conduct a survey, valuation, and report on all the lands and properties of the ecclesiastical commissioners in the southern half of England and Wales. When completed over the next decade this survey formed the first systematic and comprehensive description and account of church lands since the interregnum. It also made Clutton the obvious choice as regular agent for the southern estates of the church, an agency retained by the firm into the 1990s. The work quickly assumed a gigantic character, so that Clutton took on a staff of assistants (one of them Edward James Smith, who later became principal agent for the northern estates of the ecclesiastical commissioners, and president of the Institution of Surveyors, 1876–8) and clerks. His greatly enlarged office moved from Parliament Street to 8 Whitehall Place. The new premises, to which the adjoining no. 9 was soon added, for a time served as the family home as well, but in 1859 the family took a house in fashionable Bayswater, at 3 Sussex Square. Clutton found the daily walk to the office and back very good for his health, while saying that the house 'is rather too expensive, for it is not probable that I shall have such continued success' (Clutton, 5).

The 'continued success' referred to the addition of crown estate business to that of the ecclesiastical commissioners. Clutton seems to have owed his connection with the crown estate to the influence of James White Higgins, with whom he had formed a close friendship when they were both engaged in land purchase negotiations for the South Eastern Railway. Higgins introduced Clutton to Alexander Milne, second commissioner of woods and forests, in 1848 when a select committee on woods, forests, and the land revenues of the crown was being set up. Clutton was at once commissioned to report on the condition of New Forest and the Forest of Dean, and gave evidence to the select committee. His grasp of the intricacies of rights and encroachments in royal forests, and of the business of woodland management, was impressive. In 1850 he was appointed crown receiver (agent) for Surrey, and this extended the following year to the receivership for all the midland and southern English counties, to which Norfolk and Suffolk were later added. Clutton thus became the reigning woodland expert of the day, with the agency for 47,000 acres of crown lands which he held until 1889; his last public act was to give evidence to the 1890 select committee on woods, forests, and land revenues of the crown. On his advice the disafforestations of Hainault (1852), Whittlewood (1856), and Wychwood (1857) were carried out, policies which were strongly criticized with the hindsight of the 1880s and 1890s for creating unwanted extra agricultural acreage at great expense, although at the time grubbing up neglected and mismanaged woodland seemed the best course.

Coupled with some large commissions for acquiring land for camp sites and training areas for the War Office, Clutton's career was thus largely in the public service, although he was always remunerated by percentage commissions and never became a salaried civil servant. He kept some private clients and these became relatively more important to the firm of Cluttons, as it was styled from the 1850s, after his retirement. With an income approaching £20,000 a year by the early 1870s John Clutton was a wealthy man, at the head of his profession in wealth as well as in reputation. He became a member of the Royal Agricultural Society in 1838, was elected to the exclusive Land Surveyors' Club in 1839, and was recruited as an associate of the Institution of Civil Engineers in 1848. In March 1868 he took the lead in arranging a meeting of influential surveyors at the Westminster Palace Hotel, favourite rendezvous of railway valuers and arbitrators, which led to the foundation of the Institution of Surveyors, of which he was elected first president.

Clutton recorded little about his wife beyond writing that 'my marriage has been one of unvaried good, and my good wife is a pattern to all women' (Clutton, 5). He was wealthy enough to send all his four sons to Harrow. The youngest, Hubert (1850–1905), became a solicitor, while the other three entered the firm. The eldest, Robert George (1839–1907), more or less gave up going to the office after his father died, and retired to the south of France, but the other two, Ralph (1843–1912) and John Henry (1844–1927), were competent and diligent surveyors who maintained the family business as one of the leading firms in the country. John Henry, who was in charge of the country estates of both church and crown, unfortunately fell out with the Liberal president of the Board of Agriculture and Fisheries, Lord Carrington, in 1906, by telling him to his face that he had a misguided enthusiasm for small-holdings. As a result the crown receivership for the southern agricultural estates was taken away from Cluttons and given to Carter Jonas, Lord Carrington's own

agent. Later one of John Clutton's grandsons, Brian Clutton (1884–1938), more than made amends by securing the firm's appointment as surveyors for the crown's London estates in 1927. John Clutton's only daughter, Katherine, also helped to sustain the continuity of the family firm, as her grandson Bernard Marr-Johnson (1871–1945), was articled to Cluttons in 1892 and became a partner in 1901, to be followed into the firm in turn by his own son, Kenneth Marr-Johnson. In the 1990s several of Clutton's direct descendants were partners in the firm, including two of his great-grandsons.

Clutton was an unassuming, unpretentious, but firm-willed man. Lacking in eloquence himself, and neither speaking nor writing with fluency or ease, he paid scant attention to the rhetoric of expert witnesses or counsel when acting in arbitration cases. He disliked the atmosphere of parliamentary committee rooms, where he frequently appeared, because of the dominance of rhetoric over reason, and sometimes showed his impatience. The story runs that on one occasion in cross-examination (although this cannot be traced in any of the printed proceedings of the select committees to which he gave evidence) he was asked: 'Are you infallible, Mr Clutton? Do you never make mistakes?' 'Oh yes,' he replied, 'more than most men.' And, after a pause, 'but then, I do more business than most men' (Rogers, 495).

> What he did possess, and that to an extraordinary degree, was the solid practical business faculty, in union with a calm temperament, great sobriety of judgment, a firm will, and a large amount of natural caution; these were the principal qualities which he brought to the building up of his vast business. (Rogers, 495)

Clutton told the 1845 select committee on compensation for lands taken by railways: 'I do not know of any process by which you can prevent a rich man taking advantage of his position' ('Select committee … public railways', 124–7). He himself took little advantage of his own position as a rich man until he was into his sixties, when he eased up on work and took to renting some of the best shooting in Scotland, and at other times sporting seats and large residential houses in England, notably Tyringham House, Newport Pagnell. He acquired a farm at Flanchford, on the River Mole near Reigate, and was at his happiest in these rural surroundings walking over his land and going round his farm buildings. He died there, at his home, Woodhatch House, on 1 March 1896.

F. M. L. THOMPSON

Sources 'Cluttons 1765–1965', 1965, Messrs Cluttons, 45 Berkeley Square, London [typescript] · *Cluttons: some historical notes put together in 1948* (privately printed, 1950) · J. C. Rogers, 'Memoir of John Clutton', *Transactions of the Surveyors' Institution*, 28 (1895–6), 478–97 · J. Clutton, *Memoranda as to his life* (privately printed, 1896) · F. M. L. Thompson, *Chartered surveyors: the growth of a profession* (1968) · *The Times* (5 March 1896) · 'Select committee … on compensation to owners … whose lands may be compulsorily taken for construction of public railways', *Parl. papers* (1845), 10.417, no. 420 · 'Select committee on the ecclesiastical commission', *Parl. papers* (1847–8), 7.523, no. 645 · 'Select committee on woods, forests, and land revenues of the crown', *Parl. papers* (1849), 20.1, no. 513; 20.559, no. 574; (1890), 18.677, no. 333 · 'Select committee of the House of Lords to consider episcopal and capitular estates',

Parl. papers (1851), 13.311, no. 589 · 'Select committee on the management and condition of crown forests in England', *Parl. papers* (1854), 10.429, no. 377 · d. cert. · d. cert. [William Clutton]
Archives Messrs Cluttons, 45 Berkeley Square, London, archives
Likenesses M. Wagmüller, bust, 1871, Royal Institution of Chartered Surveyors · oils, c.1880, Messrs Cluttons, London · F. Grant, oils, Royal Institution of Chartered Surveyors
Wealth at death £148,997 3s. 8d.: probate, 18 May 1896, *CGPLA Eng. & Wales*

Clux, Sir Hartung van. *See* Klux, Sir Hartung von (*d.* 1445).

Clyde. For this title name *see* individual entries under Clyde; *see also* Campbell, Colin, Baron Clyde (1792–1863).

Clyde, James Avon, **Lord Clyde** (1863–1944), judge, was born at Dollar, Clackmannanshire, on 14 November 1863, the second son of James Clyde LLD and his wife, Elizabeth Rigg, of Whitehaven, Cumberland. His father was a distinguished teacher of the classics, first at Dollar Academy and later for many years at the Edinburgh Academy. Young Clyde himself entered the latter school and after being *dux* of all his classes and of the school proceeded to the University of Edinburgh, where his career was equally brilliant. He graduated with first-class honours in classics in 1884, won the Gray scholarship in that year, and graduated LLB in 1888. During his university days he was a prime mover in the establishment of a students' representative council and a students' union; he learned to debate at the Speculative Society, training ground of many famous lawyers, and was successively librarian and president of that body, of which he became an honorary member in 1921. In 1910 he was made honorary LLD of Edinburgh University, and in 1923 received the same distinction at St Andrews.

Clyde passed advocate in 1887. He had no influence, but his contemporaries at the 'Spec' and elsewhere were convinced that he would go straight to the top. And this, after one or two lean years, he proceeded to do. In addition to great natural ability he was a tireless worker, and once he had secured a hearing the easy maturity of his style made such a strong impression that work flowed in. Well armed at every point as an advocate, he had established the heaviest junior practice at the bar by 1901, when he became a KC. Thereafter he carried all before him, and the House of Lords reports attest the almost universal sweep of his activities as counsel. He became solicitor-general in 1905 during the closing months of the Unionist government, and later returned to office as lord advocate from 1916 (when he was sworn of the privy council) to 1920. He had become dean of the Faculty of Advocates in 1915, and on his appointment as lord advocate his brethren paid him the unique distinction of asking him to continue in office as dean in spite of his new duties. He resigned the deanship in 1919; he was elected honorary bencher of Gray's Inn in the same year. Of all the many celebrated cases in which Clyde appeared perhaps the most noteworthy was that heard in 1918 by the judicial committee of the privy council regarding the ownership of the unalienated lands of Southern Rhodesia. Clyde led for the British South Africa Company, and in a galaxy of counsel which included many of the leaders of the English bar, among

James Avon Clyde, Lord Clyde (1863–1944), by Walter Stoneman, 1924

them Sir F. E. Smith, there was general agreement that Clyde's performance was easily the finest.

A lifelong Unionist in politics, Clyde became member for West (subsequently North) Edinburgh in 1909, and retained his seat until his elevation to the bench in 1920. With one noteworthy exception, his contributions to the work of the House of Commons were almost wholly those of an efficient law officer. The exception occurred in August 1919, when he replied to strictures on the lord advocate and his department for failing to prosecute in a case of fraud at Renfrew aerodrome. A member present wrote that 'Clyde's answer did not contain a violent or a bitter word; but throughout it there ran an undercurrent of mockery, which was gentle and playful—and deadly' (private information). Hopes that he would thereafter take a more prominent part in the business of the house were ended in 1920 by his appointment, with the judicial title of Lord Clyde, as lord justice-general of Scotland and lord president of the Court of Session in succession to Lord Strathclyde.

Clyde's fifteen years as head of the court in Scotland constitute the most important chapter in the story of his life. A sound lawyer, he was never afraid to enunciate general principles, and his judgments, ranging over every department of Scots law, increasingly provided material to writers, advocates, and judges in their work. The burden of the court fell heavily on Clyde's shoulders during his period of office, since with some noteworthy exceptions his immediate colleagues were not distinguished for ability or teamwork. His extempore judgments were always impressive, assisted as they were by his fine presence, good voice, and easy flow of English. They were as finished and well expressed as the written judgments of others. In his reserved judgments there was a tendency to over-elaboration, but all were written out first in his own hand, and were therefore free from the verbosity born of dictation. He once deprecated 'unreceptive judicial silence', and certainly did not indulge in it himself. But his interventions made for a high standard of pleading, and he had a stimulating influence on all who appeared before him. He loved battle, and like a good fighter he was always prepared to take as good as he gave. Throughout his career, and into old age, he was always the dominant figure in any gathering. His appearance, his manner, even his walk, suggested, as was the fact, that he was endowed with an immense store of vitality and power.

No account of Clyde's presidency would be complete without reference to two heavy outside tasks undertaken by him during its currency. In 1926 he became chairman of the royal commission appointed to report on the Court of Session and the office of sheriff-principal. The labour involved was immense, and the report, an exhaustive one, advised drastic reforms in procedure, which were partly carried out by statute in 1933. Clyde deplored the transfer of the Advocates' Library to the nation in 1925, but as an *ex officio* member of the new board of trustees he played an indefatigable part in seeing the new institution through its teething troubles. From 1936 he was chairman of the board and its main driving force.

In 1895 Clyde married Anna Margaret McDiarmid (*d.* 1956), daughter of Peter Wallwork Latham, Downing professor of medicine at Cambridge; they had two sons, of whom the elder, James Latham McDiarmid *Clyde, became lord justice-general of Scotland and lord president of the Court of Session in 1954. Always a lover of the country, Clyde retired in 1935 to his home at Briglands, Rumbling Bridge, Kinross-shire, literally 'to cultivate his garden', for he was a great rose-grower. He became lord lieutenant of Kinross-shire and when the war came took an active part in organizing the war savings of the county, with results remarkable for an agricultural community. When still lord president, he had found time to publish, in two volumes, his own translation of Sir Thomas Craig's *Jus feudale* (1934). He followed this up in his retirement by the publication, in two volumes (1937–8) for the Stair Society, of Sir Thomas Hope's *Major Practicks, 1608–1633*. Finally, again for the Stair Society, he published (1943) an edition of the *Acta dominorum concilii, 1501–1503*. It may be regretted that to these works of scholarship he did not add his personal reminiscences, for he had, in informal talk, a great gift of vivid and racy characterization. Clyde died in Edinburgh after a short illness on 16 June 1944.

T. B. SIMPSON, *rev.*

Sources *The Times* (17 June 1944) · *The Scotsman* (17 June 1944) · personal knowledge (1959) · private information (1959) · *CGPLA Eng. & Wales* (1944)
Archives HLRO, corresp. with Andrew Bonar Law

Likenesses W. Crooke, photograph, *c.*1920, NPG · W. Stoneman, photographs, 1924–38, NPG [*see illus.*] · R. S. Forrest, watercolour drawing, Parliament Hall, Edinburgh

Clyde, James Latham McDiarmid, Lord Clyde (1898–1975), judge, was born on 30 October 1898 at 17 Heriot Row, Edinburgh, the elder son (there was no daughter) of James Avon *Clyde (1863–1944), later lord justice-general of Scotland, and his wife, Anna Margaret McDiarmid (*d.* 1956), daughter of Professor Peter Wallwork Latham of Cambridge. His parents were formidable personalities. Having, as a small boy, saved his pocket money to buy his mother a scarf for her birthday, he was sharply told to take it back: he had bought it at a shop owned by supporters of the Liberal Party. Although he later followed almost every step of his father's career, he did so under constant pressure to succeed without the advantage of his father's majestic presence, intellect, or self-confidence. His stern upbringing may explain a certain insensitivity to the feelings of others less resilient than himself which he sometimes displayed on the bench, particularly in criminal appeals.

Clyde was educated at the Edinburgh Academy, Trinity College, Oxford, and the University of Edinburgh. He was commissioned in the Royal Garrison Artillery towards the end of the First World War. He obtained a third class in *literae humaniores* at Oxford in 1921 but a pass with distinction in the LLB examination at Edinburgh in 1924. In 1928 he married Margaret Letitia (*d.* 1974), daughter of Arthur Edmond DuBuisson, barrister; they had one son, James John (the third Lord Clyde on the Scottish bench, lord of appeal in ordinary, 1996–2001), and one daughter, Margaret Ann (Lady Butler).

Clyde was admitted to the Scots bar in 1924 and was counsel in three *causes célèbres* of the period. As junior to Craigie Aitchison he appeared for John Donald Merritt at his trial for the murder of his mother in 1927, and for Oscar Slater at his appeal in 1928. In 1932 he appeared in the House of Lords in *Donoghue v. Stevenson*. He took silk in 1936 and became one of the leaders of the bar, retained in particular by the City of Edinburgh. The uncertain life of an advocate attracted him because, as he said, he loved living on the edge of a precipice. Like most advocates in those days he took an active part in politics, and became Conservative MP for North Edinburgh (1950–54). Appointed lord advocate and sworn of the privy council in 1951, he became lord justice-general and lord president in 1954. Slight of build and exceptionally agile in body and mind, he was rarely at rest. Like his father, he did not practise unreceptive judicial silence. Hitching of his gown, which was always falling off his shoulders, and faster twiddling of his pencil, meant that counsel would be wise to move on. Further argument was profitless when he started shuffling his notes for the judgment which he would, in almost every case, deliver without hesitation or correction as soon as counsel sat down.

Clyde was not popular with some sections of the legal profession and of the press, which suggested that his appointment to high office was due more to birth and political influence than to legal talent. But his shortcomings (of which he was engagingly aware) reflected those very traits of character which made him, in the words of *The Times* obituary, a great public servant and a most lovable man. He was decisive and never wasted time on second thoughts. His deceptively simple judgments dealt only with the essential points, stated the law tersely and clearly, and rarely provoked dissent. Although (or perhaps because) his filing system consisted of used envelopes and a blunt pencil, his court administration was quick, simple, and efficient. An agenda was something to be got through, not discussed. He had a deep contempt for the bureaucratic mind and took particular delight in circumventing bureaucratic obstruction. The backlog left by his predecessor (Baron Cooper of Culross) was soon cleared and was not allowed to build up again. He sought out (he did not summon) those he wished to consult, and if persuaded would act at once. Under his guidance Parliament House was transformed from a nineteenth-century warren into a modern court house and nothing gave him greater pleasure than to explore, and share with others, its secrets and treasures.

Known to everyone as Hamish, Clyde was quite without side (he refused a peerage), and off the bench, and sometimes on it, he had the charm and endless curiosity of a small boy. (His appearance on the bench was nicely caught in a caricature by David Langdon.) He loved Scotland, its countryside, its history, its monuments, and its books. He was happiest in old clothes, with a pipe in his mouth and his much loved wife at his side, gardening, tending trees, reading, or playing with his model railway, at Briglands, the house at Rumbling Bridge, Kinross-shire, designed for his father by Sir Robert Lorimer. He served for twenty years as vice-chairman of the National Library of Scotland. With the chairman, David Lindsay, earl of Crawford and Balcarres, he worked tirelessly for the library at a critical period in its history. He was appointed a deputy lieutenant of Kinross-shire in 1964, and was awarded the honorary degree of LLD by the universities of Edinburgh (1954), St Andrews (1955), and Aberdeen (1960). Clyde died at home in Rumbling Bridge on 30 June 1975.

DAVID EDWARD, rev.

Sources *The Times* (8 July 1975) · private information (1993) · personal knowledge (1993) · *DNB* · *WWW*
Likenesses D. Langdon, caricature
Wealth at death £46,778.26: confirmation, 20 Jan 1976, *CCI*

Clydesmuir. For this title name *see* Colville, (David) John, first Baron Clydesmuir (1894–1954); Colville, Ronald John Bilsland, second Baron Clydesmuir (1917–1996).

Clyffe, William (d. 1558), civil lawyer, is of unknown parentage. He was educated at Cambridge, where he graduated LLB in 1514 and LLD in 1523. Clyffe had an active legal career. He was admitted as an advocate of Doctors' Commons on 15 December 1522, and was commissary of the diocese of London between 1522 and 1529. He built a reputation as an expert on the law of marriage and divorce, and convocation sought his advice regarding Henry VIII's divorce from Katherine of Aragon in 1533. He continued to take similar cases throughout his career, and was named in several royal commissions and grants to hear and determine divorce cases, such as that between John and Elizabeth Atherton, alongside other notable civil lawyers, such as Henry Harvey, master of Trinity Hall, Cambridge, and Richard Cox.

Clyffe also became the subject of some controversy as well, however. Thomas Cranmer, archbishop of Canterbury, wrote to Sir Thomas Cromwell, principal secretary and vicegerent in spirituals, in October 1533 asking him to summon Clyffe for retaining the registers of the late Nicholas West, bishop of Ely. According to the complaint of Dr William May, Cranmer's vicar-general in the diocese of Ely, Clyffe hindered him from administering justice. In 1533 he was involved in litigation with Thomas Stanceby and Elizabeth Lutton, who claimed that Clyffe had wrongfully interfered with their case before the court of chancery. Clyffe was granted a preferment to the deanery of Chester and was immediately thrown into the Fleet prison at the instance of Sir Richard Cotton, comptroller of the king's household, because he refused to lease chapter lands to him at a rate far below their worth. He was released only after he changed his mind.

Clyffe held several ecclesiastical posts and, in addition, was among the authors of the celebrated treatise on *The Godly and Pious Institution of a Christian Man*, commonly known as the Bishops' Book, and published by the authority of the king in 1537. He was instituted as prebend of Twyford in the diocese of St Paul, London, in 1526; was appointed archdeacon of London three years later; and held the prebend of Fenton in the archdiocese of York in 1532. In 1533 he resigned the archdeaconry of London to take up the post of archdeacon of Cleveland, Yorkshire. He became precentor of York in 1534, treasurer of York in 1538, and in 1547, when that office was suppressed, he was made dean of Chester. He was prebend of Noxton, Middlesex, from 1548. Clyffe died on 13 December 1558.

JOHN F. JACKSON

Sources J. Strype, *Ecclesiastical memorials*, 2/2 (1822), 198–203 · *LP Henry VIII*, 6.1340; 15.737 · G. D. Squibb, *Doctors' Commons: a history of the College of Advocates and Doctors of Law* (1977), 140 · [C. Coote], *Sketches of the lives and characters of eminent English civilians, with an historical introduction relative to the College of Advocates* (1804), 9, 19 · Wood, *Ath. Oxon.: Fasti* (1815), 27 · J. Strype, *Ecclesiastical memorials of Thomas Cranmer*, 1 (1822), 77, 113 · Cooper, *Ath. Cantab.*

Clyn, John (d. 1349?), Franciscan friar and annalist, is said by John Bale and James Ussher to have been born in Leinster. There is a Clinstown near Kilkenny, and variant spellings of the surname Clyn can be found in the Kilkenny area. The same name can also be found in the Somerset area: an indenture of 1413 relating to the earl of Ormond was witnessed by a John Clyne, mayor of Bristol.

Clyn is the author of the *Annalium Hiberniae chronicon, ad annum MCCCXLIX*, which is a compilation until 1332 and thereafter original. The original manuscript was at one time in the possession of Sir Richard Shee of Kilkenny and later with David Rothe, bishop of Ossory in the first half of the seventeenth century, but is no longer extant. The four main seventeenth-century transcripts state that the annals were taken from the community book of the Franciscans of Kilkenny. Although unquestionably a Franciscan annal, information regarding the order is minimal; perhaps the presence of the annal within the community book made it seem unnecessary to duplicate Franciscan material in the former. Clyn probably began writing in 1333; three transcripts agree that there was a second heading in the original manuscript at that date. From the years 1333 to 1349 each year is entered only once; and the annals also expand in detail and personal comment from that year.

Nearly all that is known of Clyn is recorded in or can be deduced from the annals, or from later annotations on them. A note in Ussher's hand names Clyn as 'doctor'; according to Sir James Ware, the seventeenth-century Irish antiquary, Dublin University created three friars doctors of divinity at an unspecified date not long after its foundation in 1320, and Clyn may have been one of these. Entries in the annals for 1331 and 1332 concerning Dublin might indicate Clyn's presence there, particularly as he does not report a chapter held in Kilkenny in 1332. According to the annals, Clyn was the first guardian of the friary of Carrickbeg, near Carrick-on-Suir, in 1336. He probably left Carrickbeg after 1338 when the donor, the earl of Ormond, died; building did not commence there until 1347. A rough seventeenth-century transcript of the annals claims that Clyn was guardian of the friary of Kilkenny.

Clyn may have attended the general chapter of the Franciscans at Marseilles in 1343. Apart from his notice of a general chapter in 1313, the one at Marseilles is the only other referred to by him. There is a lack of precise dating in the annals at this period and the entries following 1343 include items concerning Fortanerius Vassali, King Robert of Jerusalem and Sicily, the plague and Tripoli prophecy in Avignon, and the rise of Cola di Rienzo (who was at Avignon in 1343). Entries like these relating to continental Europe are uncommon in the annals and might have been prompted by a journey to Marseilles in 1343.

The annals are famous for a dramatic firsthand account of the black death in Ireland in 1349, during which Clyn identifies himself as the author of the annals. It has been assumed that Clyn died of plague. However, following his report of the epidemic, he has two further entries: the first reports the price of corn and ginger, the second relates the death of Fulk de la Freigne. Clyn's main interest was the military society of the area surrounding Kilkenny. He exhibits a personal knowledge of various members of the Mac Gilla Pátraic family, whose later principal stronghold and residence was at Cullahill, about 10 miles from Clinstown. All the internal evidence would suggest that Clyn was a member of a knightly family, albeit of a minor rank. He reports the knightings of local military personnel and the interrelationship of a hierarchy of knights. He had a special relationship with the Freigne family and especially with Fulk, the dominant personality in Clyn's narrative. One mile from Clinstown is Foulksrath, Fulco's Rath, which was named after its earlier proprietors, the Freignes. Clyn's greatest praise in his annals

is reserved for Fulk and for other members of his family, and it is with great sorrow that in his last entry Clyn reports the death of Fulk in 1349. Immediately following the notice of this death the four main manuscripts contain the words, *Videtur quod author hic obiit* ('Here it seems the author died').

According to Bale, Clyn also wrote *De regibus Anglorum*, *De custodiis provinciarum*, and *De Franciscanorum cenobeis et eorum distinctionibus*. Ware adds *Catalogum sedium episcopalium, Angliae, Scotiae et Hiberniae*; none of these works is known to survive.

BERNADETTE A. WILLIAMS

Sources The annals of Ireland by Friar John Clyn and Thady Dowling: together with the annals of Ross, ed. R. Butler, Irish Archaeological Society (1849) · TCD, Ussher MS 790, fol. 61r · TCD, MSS 402, 574 [Clyn, guardian of Kilkenny] · Bale, Cat., 1.244 · The whole works of Sir James Ware concerning Ireland, ed. and trans. W. Harris, 3/1 (1746), 84 · W. Carrigan, The history and antiquities of the diocese of Ossory, 2 (1905); repr. (1981), 199 · E. Curtis, ed., Calendar of Ormond deeds, 6 vols., IMC (1932–43), vol. 1, no. 269; vol. 3, no. 7 · The Red Book of Ormond, ed. N. B. White (1932), 35, 68 · H. G. Richardson and G. O. Sayles, eds., Parliaments and councils of mediaeval Ireland, IMC, 1 (1947), 133, 176 · E. W. W. Veale, ed., The Great Red Book of Bristol, [pt 2], Bristol RS, 8 (1938), 207 · E. W. W. Veale, ed., The Great Red Book of Bristol, [pt 3], Bristol RS, 16 (1951), 34 · D. O. Shilton and R. Holworthy, Wells city charters, Somerset RS, 46 (1932), 136, 139 · B. Jennings, ed., Wadding papers, 1614–38, IMC (1953), 551 · E. B. Fitzmaurice and A. G. Little, eds., Materials for the history of the Franciscan province of Ireland, AD 1230–1450 (1920) · E. St J. Brooks, Knights' fees in counties Wexford, Carlow and Kilkenny, 13th–15th century, IMC (1950), 182–8

Archives TCD, MSS 402, 574; Ussher MS 790, fol. 61r

Clynes, John Robert (1869–1949), trade unionist and politician, was born at Oldham, Lancashire, on 27 March 1869, the elder of two sons, and one of seven children of Patrick Clynes, an illiterate Irish farmworker, and his wife, Bridget Scanlan. His father had been evicted in 1851 and emigrated to Lancashire, where he gained employment as a gravedigger.

Clynes stated later that he hated his years at the local elementary school, and eagerly became a 'half-timer' at the age of ten, working as a 'little piecer' in a textile mill from six in the morning until noon for half-a-crown a week and continuing at school in the afternoon. At the age of twelve he left school altogether and was earning 10s. a week at the mill. Out of his early wages he bought a tattered dictionary for 6d. and Cobbett's *Grammar* for 8d. He received 3d. a week for reading regularly to three blind men, whose discussions of the political news aroused his interest. He paid 8d. for tuition on two nights a week from a former schoolmaster.

By 1883 Clynes was a 'big piecer' earning 17s. 6d. a week, and was reading the works of Carlyle, Ruskin, Mill, Emerson, and Renan. Attracted to the skills of debate, Clynes practised oratory with a workmate in a disused quarry outside the town. He began to contribute to the local press under the pen-name Piecer, describing the conditions of child life in the mill, and writing on trade unionism, socialism, and labour representation. He successfully

John Robert Clynes (1869–1949), by Walter Stoneman, 1924

rebelled against having to clean and oil machinery without pay, and organized a Piecers' Union, for piecers had no direct representation in the Spinners' Union. In 1891, at the invitation of Will Thorne (1857–1946), he left the mill to serve as a district organizer at 30s. a week for one of the first organizations for unskilled workers, the National Union of Gasworkers and General Labourers, which Thorne had inaugurated in 1889.

Described in his obituary in *The Times* as 'short in stature, slight in build, not a powerful voice', and without a forceful personality, Clynes gained respect by the very reasonableness and gentleness of his approach. It was said of him in 1901 that he was a man of peace who thought that what was mostly wanted was a sense of humour. His methods were often seen by contemporaries to have achieved results when the more aggressive tactics of some of his colleagues had failed. On 13 September 1893 he married a cardroom hand, Mary Elizabeth, daughter of Owen Harper, watchmaker, of Oldham. They had two sons and a daughter.

Clynes was president of the Oldham Trades Council in 1892 and its secretary from 1894 to 1912. At this time he also began to be involved in socialist politics on a wider front: he attended the foundation conference of the Independent Labour Party at Bradford in 1893, and in the same year was a delegate to the International Socialist Congress at Zürich. A twenty weeks' lock-out in the cotton trade during this period emphasized in his mind the need for working-class political organization. Representing his

union at the Belfast Trades Union Congress in 1893, he supported nationalization as a principle. He was appointed secretary for the Lancashire district of his union in 1896. His union was one of the strongest proponents of independent labour political action and Clynes represented it at the Plymouth Trade Union Congress in 1899 when it was decided to form the Labour Representation Committee, destined from 1906 to become the Labour Party. At the inaugural conference in London in February 1900 he again attended for his union, and in 1904 was elected to represent the affiliated trades councils on the national executive; from 1909 to 1939 he was consistently elected to the trades union section. He was chairman of the party organization in 1908, presiding over the Portsmouth conference in 1909.

Clynes's parliamentary career began in 1906 when he was returned for the North-Eastern (later Platting) division of Manchester as a member of the first Parliamentary Labour Party, and he lived to be the last survivor of this group. He represented the constituency until defeated in October 1931. He made various journeys abroad, among others to attend the 1909 Toronto convention of the American Federation of Labor as fraternal delegate from the British Trades Union Congress.

In 1915 Clynes opposed the entry of Labour into the Asquith coalition in which three of his colleagues had appointments; but after the formation of the Lloyd George coalition he served on the food commission in 1917 and in the same year joined David Alfred Thomas, Lord Rhondda, food controller, as parliamentary secretary. A system of rationing was gradually introduced and a consumers' council set up, of which Clynes was chairman. He became a privy councillor in 1918 and succeeded Rhondda as food controller when the latter died in that year. When the war ended Clynes opposed the withdrawal of the Labour Party from the government, sharing the view of his colleague, G. N. Barnes, that Labour should assist in the formulation of the peace treaties; but when the party decided against that policy, Clynes, unlike Barnes, conformed, and resigned his office.

Clynes was returned unopposed as MP for Platting at the general election in 1918. Elected vice-chairman of the parliamentary party, he became chairman in 1921 after the resignation of William Adamson, and led the party in the general election of 1922. In the election for chairman of the parliamentary party which followed, he was defeated by Ramsay MacDonald by five votes, and accepted the vice-chairmanship. In January 1924 he moved the successful vote of no confidence which brought about the defeat of the Baldwin government and led to MacDonald's first Labour administration in which Clynes himself was lord privy seal and deputy leader of the House of Commons.

Opposed to the principle of a general strike, in 1926 Clynes and others in the parliamentary party sought to conciliate between the Miners' Federation, the mine owners, and the government. Nevertheless, when the strike took place Clynes supported the miners throughout the dispute, which cost his union £200,000 in strike pay. As home secretary in MacDonald's second government of

1929, Clynes was active in the area of prison reform and took great interest in an inquiry into the cotton trade. He was also responsible for refusing Trotsky permission to settle in England. In 1931 Clynes introduced an electoral reform bill providing for the alternative vote, and also abolishing university representation, a clause which was deleted by four votes in the committee stage in the House of Commons. The bill was drastically amended in the House of Lords and soon afterwards the economic situation brought the Labour government to an end.

On the formation of Ramsay MacDonald's 'national' government, Clynes refused the party leadership which went to Arthur Henderson. In the ensuing general election Clynes lost his seat and devoted himself to the work of his union, of which he had been president since 1912. The union, which was by then known as the National Union of General and Municipal Workers, had become one of the largest in the country, and when Clynes retired from the presidency in 1937 it covered nearly half a million members in a wide range of industries. Clynes received the honorary degree of DCL from the universities of Oxford and Durham in 1919.

In 1935 Clynes returned to parliament as MP for Platting and was content to be counted an elder statesman of the labour movement generally. Contemporaries greatly respected his judgement, sincerity, and loyalty. In 1945 he retired on reaching the parliamentary age limit set by his union and lived quietly and frugally, on the pension which it gave him, in his Putney home. In 1947 Clynes wrote to *The Times* and other journals complaining of his circumstances and the insufficiency of his union pension, and a fund was raised by his parliamentary colleagues and friends. Many close to him were disappointed by these complaints, which they felt to be unjustified, and thought they indicated how his wartime and other trials had affected him (his wife became an invalid after sustaining serious air-raid injuries in the Second World War). Clynes died at his home, 41 St John's Avenue, Putney Hill, London, on 23 October 1949. He was cremated at Putney Vale crematorium on 27 October. His wife survived him, but died shortly afterwards.

J. S. MIDDLETON, *rev.* MARC BRODIE

Sources J. R. Clynes, *Memoirs*, 1 [1937] · J. R. Clynes, *Memoirs*, 2 [1937] · *The Times* (25 Oct 1949) · *The Times* (28 Oct 1949) · *Manchester Guardian* (25 Oct 1949) · personal knowledge (1959) · WWBMP · *Dod's Parliamentary Companion*
Archives Labour History Archive and Study Centre, Manchester, corresp. and papers | BLPES, corresp. with the independent labour party · HLRO, corresp. with David Lloyd George | FILM BFI NFTVA, news footage
Likenesses photographs, 1906–37, repro. in Clynes, *Memoirs* · W. Stoneman, photograph, 1924, NPG [*see illus.*] · M. Hicks, photograph, Woodstock College, Surbiton, Surrey · photograph, repro. in *The Times* (25 Oct 1949) · photograph (with Will Thorne), NPG; repro. in *Daily Herald*
Wealth at death £9816 8s.: probate, 3 Feb 1950, *CGPLA Eng. & Wales*

Clynnog, Morgan (*b.* 1558?, *d.* in or after 1619), Roman Catholic priest, the nephew of Maurice *Clenock

(*d.* 1580?), was most probably born in the parish of Clynnog Fawr in Caernarvonshire. Clenock had been elected in 1578 as rector of the English College in Rome, and Morgan followed in his uncle's footsteps to that city. Clenock was soon criticized for favouring his nephew and other Welsh students, with the result that he had to resign in 1579 under pressure from the English students. This motivated Morgan Clynnog to take the missionary oath as soon as he could, and this happened on 23 April 1579 before his uncle left for Spain.

Ordained as a priest, Morgan Clynnog returned home in 1582 to live the devout Catholic life in the hidden world of Elizabethan Catholic Wales. There is ample evidence that he and his colleague Phillip Williams were active in the 1580s and 1590s in hearing masses in Llandeilo, Kidwelly, and the villages of Llangyndeyrn and Llanegwad in the Carmarthenshire countryside. The masses were held in houses, and in particular in the home of Jane Lloyd at Llandeilo in the Tywi valley. Roman Catholics could not have their children baptized legally in the Catholic rite by a priest, but that did not deter the wife of David Delahay, a gentleman of Llanegwad, from travelling 40 miles through Llandeilo to an old chapel, near the home of David ap Jevan between Margam and Aberafan, to have their child baptized by Morgan Clynnog. On this occasion there were twenty people participating in the mass, six of them being women. In the same year, 1591, nine recusants from Margam were convicted and fourteen from the neighbouring parishes of Pyle and Kenfig-with-Cornelly, all of them the flock of Morgan Clynnog. Between 1591 and 1596 he stayed with the family of Jenkin Turberville of Pen-llin, Glamorgan, a family which was continually persecuted. In 1587 Cecilia Turberville, the wife of Jenkin, submitted to the authorities as the act of that year exposed families to the loss of their chattels and two-thirds of their land. But within a few years she and Anne Rees of Lysworney in the Vale of Glamorgan, near Bridgend, had returned to recusancy.

Clynnog is next heard of in Pen-llin in 1596. His presence on that occasion led to the conviction of twelve recusants, ten of them members of the Turberville family at whose house he was hidden. Like Robert Jones in Monmouthshire Morgan Clynnog was described as a 'firebrand', and his ministry led to the conviction of a number of Catholic believers. He left Pen-llin in 1602 for Monmouthshire, where he became friendly with David Baker (1575–1644) of Abergavenny. When Baker returned to his home town from the continent in 1606 as a Benedictine he was instrumental in convincing a number of his family and friends to accept the Roman Catholic faith. However, his father, William Baker, a pioneer in horticulture and a magistrate of distinction, was more than he could manage. So he brought in Morgan Clynnog. William Baker made his confession to Clynnog, and received the blessed sacrament. When William's health declined, he asked for the sacrament of extreme unction. Morgan Clynnog was called upon to administer it, which he did in a hurried manner, and was consequently reprimanded by William Baker. The rebuke did not deter him from ministering for at least another thirteen years in south Wales. He had excellent relationships with both the Jesuits and the secular clergy. Clynnog also prepared young men to be trained at Douai and Valladolid seminaries. He was chosen as an assistant to the archpriest in 1600, and when last heard of, on 2 December 1619, he had been promoted as the chief assistant. This indicates the respect shown towards him by his fellow Catholics in Wales as well as in England for at least thirty-seven years. Clynnog was a remarkable priest, who has been too long in the shadow of his more celebrated uncle.   D. BEN REES

Sources M. Cleary, 'Morgan Clynnog', *Y bywgraffiadur Cymreig, 1941–1950*, ed. [R. T. Jenkins, E. D. Jones, and W. L. Davies] (1970), appx, 73 · J. H. Pollen, ed., *Unpublished documents relating to the English martyrs*, 1, Catholic RS, 5 (1908), 43 · J. H. Pollen, ed., 'Recusants and priests, March 1588', *Miscellanea, XII*, Catholic RS, 22 (1921), 120–29, esp. 127 · R. C. Baigent, ed., 'The Catholic registers of the Brambridge (afterwards Highbridge) mission in Hampshire, 1766–1869', *Miscellanea, XIV*, Catholic RS, 27 (1927), 1–52, esp. 20 · E. Henson, ed., *The registers of the English College at Valladolid, 1589–1862*, Catholic RS, 30 (1930), 68 · J. McCann and H. Connolly, eds., *Memorials of Father Augustine Baker and other documents relating to the English Benedictines*, Catholic RS, 33 (1933), 91–2 · E. G. Jones, *Cymru a'r hen Ffydd* (1951) · G. Bowen, 'Morys Clynnog (1521–1580/1)', *Transactions of the Caernarvonshire Historical Society*, 27 (1966), 73–97 · G. Williams, 'Morris Clynnog', *National Library of Wales Journal*, 9 (1955–6), 79

Cnut [Canute] (*d.* 1035), king of England, of Denmark, and of Norway, was the son of *Swein Forkbeard (*d.* 1014), king of England and of Denmark, and a sister of Boleslav of Poland, possibly widow of King Erik of the Swedes. He was the brother of Harald, probably king of the Danes, and a number of sisters, including Santslaue and Estrith, wife of, first, Earl Ulf and, second, Robert (I), duke of Normandy.

Birth and early campaigns The poem *Knútsdrápa*, composed for Cnut by the Icelandic skald Ottar the Black, says that Cnut started his military career unusually young, and mentions an attack on Norwich perhaps identifiable with that by his father in 1004. If so, Cnut might have been born in the early 990s or a little before; if not, his earliest campaigns may have been in 1013 and 1014, which would suggest a birth date of *c.*1000. The thirteenth-century Icelandic *Knytlinga saga*, which wrongly states that he ruled England for twenty-four years, reports that he was thirty-seven when he died.

The author of the encomium of *Emma of Normandy (*d.* 1052), writing in St Omer *c.*1040–42, states that Cnut was the elder son of Swein and encouraged his father to attack England. There is no doubt that he accompanied Swein thither in 1013, although the fact that Harald was left to rule in Denmark may confirm the statement of other sources that Cnut was really the younger of the two. They forced King Æthelred II into exile and when Swein died, on 3 February 1014, the army recognized Cnut as his successor. However, the English invited Æthelred to return, and although Cnut made some sort of military alliance with the people of Lindsey, he remained at his base at Gainsborough until Easter (25 April), and was then expelled when an English attack found him unprepared.

Cnut (*d.* 1035), drawing

Before sailing for Denmark he touched at Sandwich to land hostages given to his father, after cutting off their hands, ears, and noses. According to the encomiast, Cnut asked his brother to divide Denmark between them, while offering him the eventual choice of Denmark or England if he would assist in conquering the latter; but Harald refused both requests and Cnut assaulted England alone. This may contain some truth, for the earliest Scandinavian coins inscribed 'CNVT REX DÆNOR' ('Cnut, king of Danes') seem to have been struck from dies probably made in Lincoln no later than 1015, and thus hint that he did put forward a claim to the Danish throne. However, according to the contemporary German bishop Thietmar of Merseburg, Harald accompanied Cnut to England.

The conquest of England Cnut's campaign began in September 1015, when he appeared at Sandwich, sailed for the mouth of the Frome, and faced little opposition in ravaging Dorset, Wiltshire, and Somerset; Æthelred was now sick, and his son Edmund Ironside at loggerheads with the powerful ealdorman of Mercia, Eadric Streona. The latter then joined Cnut, together with forty ships of Scandinavian mercenaries probably commanded by Thorkill the Tall, and by Christmas the people of Wessex had recognized Cnut as king, given hostages, and supplied his army with horses. During the Christmas festival he crossed the Thames into Mercia and ravaged Warwickshire, and when Edmund and Earl Uhtred of Northumbria raised troops Cnut made for York, where Uhtred and the Northumbrians were obliged to submit. Uhtred was executed, and replaced as earl by Cnut's brother-in-law, the Norwegian Earl *Erik of Hlathir. By Easter (1 April) Cnut had returned to his ships, and soon after, on 23 April, Æthelred died and Edmund was elected king by the chief men present in London. The chronicler John of Worcester, writing c.1120, believed that other English magnates concurrently elected Cnut king and swore fidelity to him at Southampton. He then moved to assault London, but the city resisted successfully, despite being closely invested by enemies who passed London Bridge by bringing their vessels through a canal which they dug to the south of it. Cnut subsequently divided his forces, some fighting Edmund in Wessex at Penselwood, Somerset, and Sherston, Wiltshire, probably on 25 June, after which Edmund drove the rest from London and defeated them after crossing the Thames at Brentford. Cnut renewed the siege when Edmund attempted to raise more men in Wessex, but was again unsuccessful, and was eventually pursued by Edmund into Kent after a battle at Otford; Ealdorman Eadric now forsook him. He then crossed the Thames estuary into Essex and proceeded to ravage in Mercia, and was doubtless returning to his ships when Edmund overtook him at the hill called 'Assandun' (Ashingdon or Ashdon, Essex). Here, on 18 October 1016, he defeated Edmund in a fight in which the Anglo-Saxon Chronicle says that the flower of the English fell; Eadric and his men were the first to flee. There may have been a further battle near the Forest of Dean, but finally Cnut and Edmund met at Alney in Gloucestershire and agreed to divide the country, Edmund taking Wessex while Cnut received Mercia and probably Northumbria, in addition to the promise of a payment to his army. The Londoners came to terms too, also offering the Danes money and winter quarters, which were accepted. But on 30 November Edmund died and Cnut succeeded to the entire kingdom.

Such is the story drawn largely from the contemporary account in the Anglo-Saxon Chronicle. The encomiast thought that Cnut occupied London briefly after Æthelred's death, and rejected an offer of single combat by Edmund; Thietmar of Merseburg that he was accompanied by his brother Harald, had a fleet of 340 ships (the encomiast gives 200, some versions of the Anglo-Saxon Chronicle 160), and that he demanded £15,000 to guarantee the safety of Queen Emma when she was besieged in London. None of these writers mentions that he had also taken as his consort, perhaps partly for political reasons, *Ælfgifu of Northampton, daughter of Ælfhelm, ealdorman of Northumbria (of a Mercian family, and murdered, possibly at Eadric's instigation, in 1006), and that

by 1017 she had borne him two sons, Swein and Harold Harefoot [see Harold I].

King of the English John of Worcester says that after Edmund's death Cnut held a meeting in London and asked the witnesses of the Alney agreement whether it had there been settled that Edmund's brothers and sons were entitled to succeed him. They replied that no claim had been left to the brothers and that Edmund had wanted Cnut to protect his sons until they were old enough to rule, and also swore that they wished to elect Cnut king, obey him, and make a payment to his army; finally, they completely rejected Edmund's male relatives and denied that they were kings. Whether or not they lied in describing Cnut's agreement with Edmund, as John of Worcester says, this attempt by Cnut to legitimize his position suggests that right of conquest was not thought title enough, and the meeting may have led directly to the coronation of Cnut in London by Archbishop Lyfing (Ælfstan) of Canterbury, which is reported by Ralph of Diceto, a twelfth-century dean of St Paul's. It is perhaps indicative of the special importance of Cnut's coronation that his earliest coin type, 'quatrefoil', is the first since the reign of Edgar to show a king wearing a crown.

Cnut divided the country into four in 1017, keeping Wessex for himself and giving East Anglia to Earl Thorkill the Tall, Mercia to Ealdorman Eadric, and Northumbria to Earl Erik of Hlathir. Probably intended to provide an interim military government during the collection of the very large sum to be given to his army, this move would also have given his chief supporters the impression that their efforts were going to be well rewarded. This impression was illusory in Eadric's case, for although undoubtedly powerful, nobody had been able to rely on his loyalty during the previous year, and at Christmas 1017 Cnut had him killed in London. Nor did the executions end there: the Mercian Northman, son of Ealdorman Leofwine, was also eliminated, along with the important West Saxons Æthelweard and Brihtric; perhaps others too. Eadwig, described as 'king of the ceorls' (which may indicate his leadership of some sort of peasant revolt) was banished, as was the atheling Eadwig, Æthelred's last surviving son with his first consort, Ælfgifu. John of Worcester reports that Cnut had schemed unsuccessfully to have Eadwig killed, as he eventually was when he returned to England in circumstances which are thoroughly obscure. Edward Ætheling and Edmund, infant sons of Edmund Ironside, also went into exile; again, an alleged attempt by Cnut to have them murdered came to nothing. Of Cnut's rivals for the throne of England, this left Edward (the Confessor) and Alfred Ætheling, Æthelred's sons with Emma, who were in Normandy. Cnut may well have feared an attempt by Richard (II), duke of Normandy, to reinstate them, and countered this by marrying Emma himself, in mid-1017. Her encomiast suppressed the inconvenient fact that she had previously been Æthelred's wife, and tells how Cnut's men searched far and wide for a suitable bride, who insisted that any son she might bear would have precedence in the succession over his existing offspring. By the end of 1017 Cnut had removed a great many of the immediate threats to his position.

Consolidation in England and Denmark, 1018–1024 The following year the English paid £72,000 to Cnut and his men, while the Londoners gave £10,500. These figures, if accurate, denote an extraordinarily high level of taxation; collection had probably been under way ever since Cnut's agreement with Edmund late in 1016. Doubtless he used much of the money to pay off his men, many of whom returned to Scandinavia, while forty ships remained in his service. Perhaps it was this force which he employed, according to Thietmar of Merseburg, to defeat the crews of thirty pirate vessels during 1018. He then proceeded to a meeting at Oxford where 'the Danes and the English reached an agreement' (*ASC*, s.a. 1018). Its nature is unknown, but may well signify that a formal end to hostilities had been made possible by the payment of tribute. The evidence of royal land charters suggests that he spent the rest of the year in the south-west, and that by Easter (29 March) 1019 he was in Winchester. Later, he sailed for Denmark, where he remained over the winter.

Events there are obscure at this time. It is likely that Cnut's brother Harald had exercised some sort of control over the country, but he was perhaps dead by the winter of 1019. At any rate, he is not heard of again, and Cnut sent a communication to the English from Denmark which described how he had gone there because he had heard that they were threatened by a great danger, which he had succeeded in dispelling. He returned to England in the spring of 1020 and at Easter (17 April) a large meeting was held at Cirencester which outlawed Æthelweard, ealdorman of Wessex. Clearly, there had been unrest in the area during Cnut's absence, although of what sort is unknown, unless it was connected with the return of the atheling Eadwig. Later in the year, probably on the anniversary of the battle which had taken place on 18 October 1016, he went to 'Assandun' for the consecration of a new church there to commemorate the recent battle. Henceforth, knowledge of Cnut's activities, always scanty, deteriorates. His sole recorded action in 1021 is the outlawing on 11 November of his old associate Earl Thorkill of East Anglia, who then went to Denmark. This probably reflects considerable political difficulties with the powerful figure to whom he may have owed much of his victory in 1016, and shows that Cnut's position was now strong enough for Thorkill to be dealt with; if he had reckoned that he could dominate the young king to his own advantage, then he had miscalculated.

According to the Anglo-Saxon Chronicle, in 1022 Cnut sailed out with his ships to 'Wiht'. This almost certainly means the Isle of Wight, although why he should have needed a fleet there at this date is unclear. Sandwich was better situated to meet a threat from Scandinavia; Wight implies a connection with the south or west, and perhaps particularly Normandy. Even so, Cnut's relations with the duchy are not known to have worsened until after the death of Duke Richard (II) in 1026, and it is quite possible that he was awaiting a piratical attack of the sort that had occurred in 1018. It is also conceivable, however, that the 'Wiht' of the chronicle here denotes an area known as Witland, which lay in what is now north-east Poland, and that Cnut was therefore fighting on the southern shores of the Baltic, presumably to reinforce his position in Denmark. However that may be, he was certainly in Denmark early in 1023, making terms with Thorkill, whose position there had strengthened since his expulsion from England to the extent that Cnut chose to leave it in his care and exchanged sons with him. Reliable sources do not mention Thorkill again, and it is probable that he disappeared shortly thereafter. On his return to England, Cnut appears to have been accompanied by Gerbrand, bishop of Roskilde, who was included among the witnesses to a charter in favour of Ely Abbey, which perhaps received a royal visit at this time to deal with trouble involving the abbot, who had recently taken his case to Rome. By early June 1023 Cnut was in London for the translation from St Paul's to Canterbury of the relics of St Ælfheah. His only known act in the following year is the grant of land in Dorset to his Scandinavian follower Urki. Meanwhile, across the North Sea, events were building to a crisis.

Conflict over Norway In his later years, Swein Forkbeard had ruled Norway through his son-in-law Earl Erik of Hlathir and the latter's brother Swein. However, while Erik was assisting Cnut in England in 1015–16, Swein was defeated by the wealthy Norwegian chieftain Olaf Haraldsson at the battle of Nesjar and died shortly afterwards. His nephew, Erik's son Hákon, made his way to England, and Olaf became king of Norway, where he was a champion of Christianity and was revered as a saint after his death. Doubtless Cnut intended to reconquer Norway eventually, but Olaf struck first, in alliance with King Anund Jacob of Sweden, who like Olaf may have felt threatened by the strength of Cnut's position in England and Denmark. It was during the ensuing campaign that Cnut fought the Swedes at the battle of Holy River, usually identified with that still known as Helgeå, which enters the sea near Kristianstad in southern Sweden and lay roughly on the eastern border of what was then the Danish province of Skåne. The battle is something of a puzzle. The E text of the Anglo-Saxon Chronicle enters it under 1025 and says that many of Cnut's men, both Danes and English, fell there, and that the Swedes had possession of the place of slaughter. In other words, one would think that Cnut was defeated. However, Ottar the Black's poem *Knútsdrápa* says that Cnut threw back the Swedes there, and certainly he was successful in the campaign as a whole. Another *Knútsdrápa*, by the poet Sighvat, reports that Olaf and Anund's attack on Denmark failed. In his letter sent to England in 1027, Cnut writes of the defeat of the peoples who had attempted to deprive him of both kingdom and life (*English Historical Documents*, 1, 416–18). Unless the fighting was protracted, this may indicate that the battle of Holy River was in 1026, not 1025. Cnut uses the title 'king of all England and Denmark and the Norwegians and of some of the Swedes' in the letter, although it exists only in twelfth-century copies in which the title may have been altered to suit conditions later in the reign (Cnut did not become king of the Norwegians until 1028). Nevertheless, it is not impossible that part of Sweden did come under his control, either immediately after Holy River or at some subsequent date: historians cannot agree on the significance of coins minted in his name, but not necessarily with his authority, in Sigtuna (on Lake Mälar, near modern Stockholm).

Pilgrimage to Rome After the fighting Cnut went on pilgrimage to Rome, where he was present at the coronation as Roman emperor of Conrad II at Easter (26 March) 1027. In the letter of 1027, Cnut emphasizes the pious reasons for which he had undertaken the pilgrimage, and how he was received with honour by Pope John XIX and Conrad, and given costly presents, including vessels of gold and silver and silken robes. He also negotiated a reduction in the tolls payable by English merchants and pilgrims travelling to Rome, and the pope agreed to discontinue the practice which demanded the payment of large sums by archbishops visiting the apostolic see to obtain the pallium. Cnut seems to have travelled from Rome to Denmark, with the intention of concluding a peace with his enemies; but he was now determined to destroy Olaf Haraldsson of Norway, and returned to England to marshal his resources.

King of the Norwegians The C text of the Anglo-Saxon Chronicle says that in 1028 Cnut sailed from England to Norway with fifty ships, while other versions add that he drove Olaf away and took it for himself. Poetry is more informative. Sighvat, who was in Olaf's service at the time, names Earl Hákon, son of Erik of Hlathir (*d. c.*1023), as acting with Cnut, and speaks repeatedly of money offered to Olaf's men, a detail confirmed by John of Worcester. After assembling his ships in the Limfjord in Jutland, Cnut sailed north along the Norwegian coast to Trondheim. Olaf, deserted by many of his followers (who had been seduced by his enemy's cash and angered, according to Adam of Bremen, by his tendency to apprehend their wives for sorcery), could mount no effective resistance, and withdrew, while Cnut put Norway under Hákon's control. It may also have been at this time that he gave authority in Denmark to one of his sons, probably *Harthacnut, his child with Queen Emma. In 1029 he returned to England, but Earl Hákon drowned not long afterwards and was replaced in Norway by Cnut's consort Ælfgifu of Northampton and their son Swein. Meanwhile, Olaf had returned and been killed by his countrymen at the battle of Stiklestad, near Trondheim, on 29 July 1030.

Other foreign relations The D and E versions of the Anglo-Saxon Chronicle record that Cnut visited Rome and Scotland in 1031. It is not impossible that he travelled to Rome twice, for there is later hagiographical evidence, of questionable reliability, for a journey in which he went there, not from Scandinavia, as in 1027, but from England; but it is more likely that the chronicle entry has been misdated, 1031 being a scribal error for 1026, when the 1027 journey may well have started. Cnut no doubt had important relations with Scotland, but they are obscure. The chronicle E text says that in 1031 he went there and received the submission of three kings, Malcolm II (*d.* 1034), Mælbæth, and Iehmarc. Mælbæth may be Shakespeare's Macbeth, who deposed Malcolm II's grandson Duncan in 1040, and who seems to have ruled an area around the Moray Firth *c.*1030; Iehmarc could have been Echmarcach Ragnallson, who perhaps controlled part of Galloway and the Isle of Man. The continental chronicler Ralph Glaber, writing before *c.*1030, says that Cnut fought a long war against Malcolm and the Scots, that they were eventually reconciled through Emma and Richard of Normandy, and that he received Malcolm's (otherwise unknown) son from the baptismal font. If correct, this must refer to events before Richard's death in 1026, and perhaps to those following the battle of Carham, a Scots victory over the English on the Tweed probably early in Cnut's reign. However, unless the 1031 visit to Scotland has been misdated, it looks as though he undertook a further campaign, perhaps connected with a verse by Sighvat, seemingly composed after 1030, which says that famous princes had brought their heads to him from Fife to buy peace.

Probably Cnut also had contacts of some sort with the Welsh and the Irish. Emma's encomiast lists *Brittania* among his dominions, and a verse attributed to Ottar the Black greets the ruler of the Danes, Irish, English, and Island-dwellers. Further evidence is hard to come by, but it may be that the plundering of Wales by the Dubliners and English, recorded by the Irish annals of Tigernach under 1030, was a joint expedition by the forces of Cnut and the Hiberno-Norse ruler of Dublin, Sihtric Silkenbeard (*d.* 1042). Cnut had a powerful military machine at his disposal, and may have used it to establish his lordship just as effectively in the British Isles as he did in Scandinavia. Indeed, it is unlikely that any English king before this time had been as concerned as was Cnut with foreign policy. Germany, too, attracted his attention, partly because of its border with Denmark, partly because he was eager to imitate the imperial style of the German emperors. Nothing is known of any connection with the emperor Heinrich II (*d.* 1024), but it has already been noted that Cnut attended the coronation of Conrad II in Rome, and Adam of Bremen says that Conrad sought the marriage of his son (the future emperor Heinrich II) to Cnut's daughter with Emma, Gunnhild, and ceded Schleswig and territory north of the River Eider as a token of their treaty of friendship. Gunnhild was betrothed to Heinrich in 1035 and the marriage took place in 1036; she died of pestilence in Italy in 1038.

Another politically important union was that of Cnut's sister Estrith to Robert (I), duke of Normandy from 1027 until 1035, which ended in Robert's divorce of her. The necessity for this match suggests that in the later part of Cnut's reign his marriage to Emma was not alone thought sufficient to keep the Normans friendly, and this proved to be the case when Robert began to champion the cause of the athelings Edward and Alfred. The Norman chronicler William of Jumièges says that Robert treated them as brothers and asked Cnut to restore them to their own. On his refusal, a large fleet was assembled at Fécamp, which sailed against England but was driven back by a gale; nevertheless, Cnut, who was gravely ill, now offered the brothers half his kingdom. The latter part of this story, at least, is unlikely to be true, but Norman charter evidence shows that Edward was being accorded the title king by 1033, and it may be that some sort of expedition was mounted on his behalf; both he and Alfred led troops against England soon after Cnut's death.

Administration and taxation in England Cnut's conquest of England was not marked by a removal of the native aristocracy on the scale that followed the battle of Hastings, and for a number of reasons. Not all his powerful Scandinavian henchmen proved completely trustworthy (Thorkill the Tall, for example), while significant numbers of English nobles, including some doubtless disillusioned by the unsatisfactory rule of Æthelred II, were willing to throw in their lot with his regime: Godwine, earl of Wessex, and Leofric, earl of Mercia, became two of his major English followers. Also, Cnut was able to use the powerful English taxation system to reward his victorious army with money rather than land, with the result that many returned willingly to Scandinavia. All the same, some did settle in England. Erik of Hlathir became earl of Northumbria and Osgod Clapa and Tovi the Proud are known to have received estates fairly widely and to have become powerful figures. Erik's son Hákon received lands in Worcestershire and held the office of earl in the area, while Herefordshire was controlled by Earl Hrani and Gloucestershire connected with Earl Eilaf. Sources also tell of soldiers being established in this region, no doubt because of the need for defence against the Welsh. However, there is little reason to suppose that Scandinavian landowners were ever anything more than a minority there; or elsewhere: charter evidence reveals a number—Urki, Bovi, and Agemund—who received estates in Dorset, but again they were almost certainly outnumbered by English landowners, and the same was probably true of the many other areas from which no worthwhile evidence survives.

This is not to say that the English found Cnut's rule easy. If, as the Anglo-Saxon Chronicle reports, £82,500 really was paid to the Scandinavians in 1018, it must be stressed that much, if not all, of this must have derived from taxation on a colossal scale, and that heavy taxation probably remained one of the most notable features of his reign. His exploits abroad were probably often funded largely by English money. It served, too, to pay mercenary troops. He retained forty ships in his service in 1018, and from their crews the soldiers known as housecarls and lithsmen may have originated. Lithsmen are usually to be found connected with ships, and those based in London participated in the succession dispute after Cnut's death. Housecarls, who were not necessarily always distinct from them, nevertheless appear in a wider range of contexts. They formed a probably élite corps in the army, and (in Harthacnut's time, at least) also acted as tax collectors, while some (Bovi and Urki, for example) received land. The Danish historians Sven Aggeson and Saxo Grammaticus, writing c.1200, have much to say about them, but the bulk of it is probably fictitious, and more reliable evidence is hard to come by. However, the hagiographer Osbern gives a late-eleventh-century account of how housecarls were on hand to oppose native opposition to the removal of St Ælfheah's relics from London to Canterbury in 1023, and the mention in Domesday Book of 15 acres 'where the housecarls used to be' (*Domesday Book*, 1.56b) in the strategically important town of Wallingford may hint at the existence of housecarl garrisons, there and elsewhere. Mercenary troops were almost certainly a vital element in Cnut's control of the country: early-eleventh-century England had a sophisticated administration which allowed kings to tap its considerable wealth through taxation; this in turn paid for soldiers who safeguarded Cnut's position and could be used coercively to increase his administrative power even further, at the same time as acting as a counter-balance to that of the great nobles.

The forty ships retained in 1018, if paid at the rate of 8 marks a rowlock given to Harthacnut's crews in 1041, would have cost nearly £14,000 a year, while the sixteen ships said to have comprised Cnut's standing fleet later in the reign would have required just over £5000 a year. The taxation necessary to support such forces has left marked traces in the records. It is known that defaulters were likely to find their lands being given to those who could pay the money due on them. Churches sometimes melted down precious objects and mortgaged land to obtain the necessary money; but such expedients did not always suffice, and estates were certainly lost: records from the archbishopric of Canterbury, the bishopric of Worcester, and the abbeys of Glastonbury, Malmesbury, and Peterborough all refer to difficulties caused by taxation. The extraordinary levy of 1018 was also reflected in the coinage. Cnut took over an advanced and complex coinage system, which produced large numbers of silver pennies from mints scattered throughout the country, thus facilitating both trade and ready payment of royal fiscal demands. The first type struck in his name, known today as 'quatrefoil', may have achieved a volume of approximately 47 million coins. If so, it was the largest of the late Anglo-Saxon period, presumably because of the need to produce pennies in quantity for the 1018 payment. The two succeeding types, 'pointed helmet' and 'short cross', were struck in fewer numbers by a smaller group of moneyers. All were minted to low weight standards which may reflect a shortage of silver. Cnut's awareness of the importance of coin is also shown by the extension of the Danish coinage during his reign: eight mints eventually struck for him there, but with nothing like the uniformity that characterized the English system.

Law codes It is difficult to understand the operation of Cnut's administration of England, despite the survival of several law codes. These, which comprise a document prepared for the Oxford meeting of 1018 and two further texts known as I and II Cnut, were all written by Wulfstan, archbishop of York, who had produced similar material for Æthelred II. It is doubtful, however, whether the 1018 document really reflects the business transacted at the

Oxford meeting, while I Cnut is concerned solely with ecclesiastical matters and II Cnut probably presents an unduly favourable view of his methods of government. This is because Wulfstan did his best to alleviate the harsh social conditions of the period, which partly resulted from oppressive royal action. Accordingly, he penned texts infused with sermonizing, piety, and concern for the church, in which kings seem very concerned to act justly; then he secured royal approval and perhaps publication of his work. Thus, on taxation, for example, he did not say that defaulters' land was liable to be confiscated, a method of which he almost certainly disapproved, but simply that those who had met the public burdens on their estates were to have undisputed possession of them. As a result, Wulfstan's texts may make Cnut's administration look far more benevolent now than it did to contemporaries. Cnut himself was no doubt eager to appear before his people in as favourable a light as possible, as the letters he sent to England in 1019–20 and 1027 and his relations with the English church show, and he was probably happy to be associated with and to publicize the promises of good government made by Wulfstan on his behalf. But how far he sought to put them into practice is much more difficult to determine, not least because it would have involved a king who was often absent from the country exercising close control over local officials who were often guilty of corruption.

Cnut and the English church Cnut's relations with Wulfstan really form part of his links with the English church as a whole, about which more is known than other aspects of his rule because of the relatively good survival of church records. This is a political, and not purely a religious, matter. By Cnut's time English monarchs were closely associated with the church, which secured promises of good government in return for anointing them on their accession. It expected them to prove its patrons and protectors in return for considerable ideological support: for example, in tenth-century England, as in Germany, there was an increasing tendency to stress the Christ-like attributes of kings, thus drawing a sharp and significant distinction between them and other laymen. Cnut was very willing to profit from what the church offered in this respect. His piety was of a very ostentatious type—his wife's encomiast claims to have been an eyewitness to his lavish gifts to the monasteries and poor of St Omer when on his way to Rome, and of the tears and breast beating which accompanied them. Similarly, he is said to have walked barefoot for 5 miles before reaching the church of St Cuthbert in Durham. There may even be a factual basis behind the famous story, not recorded until the twelfth-century works of Henry of Huntingdon and Gaimar, of how he attempted to turn back the waves and then used his failure to demonstrate to his courtiers the weakness of his power compared with that of God. It was the suffering Christ with which kings were encouraged to identify themselves, and thus, paradoxical as it may seem, Cnut's acts of humility were really statements about the elevated nature of his power.

Of Cnut's many recorded acts of generosity to churches,

his placing of a crown on the head of a crucifix in the Old Minster, Winchester, is one of the most interesting. It is recorded that this happened when he had supremacy over four kingdoms—that is, probably after the conquest of Norway in 1028—and a drawing in the *Liber vitae* of the New Minster, Winchester, made in 1031, shows him with a crown which bears a distinct resemblance to that worn by the German emperors (BL, Stowe MS 944, fol. 6r). The drawing itself has parallels with German imperial portraits of the period, and it may be that after 1028 Cnut emphasized his position in the northern world by adopting a new crown consciously modelled on that of the court into which his daughter would eventually marry. By leaving his old crown on the head of a crucifix he further reminded onlookers of the links between kings and Christ.

The extravagance of Cnut's piety may have owed much to his own circumstances. Christianity had only been introduced to Denmark by his grandfather Harald Bluetooth, and his father, Swein Forkbeard, is alleged to have spent a period as a pagan before committing himself to Christ. Cnut was therefore almost certainly baptized as a child, probably, from his taking of the baptismal name Lambert, on 17 September, the feast day of St Lambert of Liège. Nevertheless, the Danish conquest of England was carried out by men who were either recent converts or still pagan, and had not only involved taxation of churches and the ravaging of their land, but also sometimes their destruction; and in 1012 the archbishop of Canterbury, Ælfheah, had been murdered at Greenwich by a Scandinavian army which had captured him the previous year. For all these reasons it would have been easy for Cnut's opponents to portray him as a semi-Christian barbarian. Thus, the rapid growth of a cult centred on Ælfheah's tomb in St Paul's may have been particularly embarrassing for him, and gratifying for the Londoners, who had withstood several Danish sieges in Æthelred's time and been taxed very heavily in 1018. If so, it was a situation that Cnut was able to defuse: in 1023 he made a great show of removing the relics to the wealthy and influential church at Canterbury, with which he seems to have wished to be on good terms; he kept troops on hand in case of trouble.

Increasing interest in the cult of St Edmund at Bury may have had similar overtones. East Anglia too had seen much fighting against the Scandinavians, and John of Worcester reports a story that St Edmund (d. 869), who was himself killed by Danes, was in some way responsible for the death of Cnut's father, after warning him not to levy tribute from his church's lands. When a new church was consecrated at Bury late in Cnut's reign, the date chosen (18 October) was the anniversary of the battle of 'Assandun' in 1016, a sure sign of a link with recent events. However, Cnut could again neutralize such problems by patronizing the saint himself: he may have been involved in the replacement of secular clerics by monks at Bury c.1020, and was generous to them in other ways. The wealthy abbey of Glastonbury, on the other hand, is not known to have received his patronage, but he made an important visit to the tomb of Edmund Ironside there on the anniversary of his death, and laid a cloak decorated with peacocks upon it. As the peacock symbolized the resurrection of the flesh, Cnut was no doubt expressing concern for the salvation of Edmund, whom William of Malmesbury says he was accustomed to call his brother. This may well be connected with John of Worcester's story that the treaty of 1016 established brotherhood between them (presumably, adoptive brotherhood), and with Cnut's awareness that it had not been unusual within the English royal family for brother to succeed brother. Favouring Edmund and stressing their treaty and brotherhood diminished the extent to which Cnut, who had set aside Edmund's male relatives to take the throne, looked a usurper. Religion and politics were closely connected.

It is therefore hardly surprising to find Cnut exercising close control over appointments to major churches. His relations with Archbishop Æthelnoth of Canterbury seem to have been good, and he went to some trouble to ensure his eventual replacement by the royal priest Eadsige. Other royal priests raised to the episcopate were Ælfwine, who received the wealthy see of Winchester, and Duduc, bishop of Wells; another, Stigand, was given the church built at 'Assandun', and eventually became a major figure under Edward the Confessor. A further king's man was probably Ælfweard, who became bishop of London in 1035 without relinquishing the abbacy of Evesham. The list of Cnut's known gifts to churches is very long. It includes lands and a reliquary for the remains of St Vincent given to Abingdon Abbey, the making of a new shrine for the relics of St Edith at Wilton, the gift of estates to St Cuthbert's Church at Durham, patronage of the great fenland monasteries of Ely and Ramsey, generosity to the archbishoprics of Canterbury and York, and the bestowal of relics on Westminster Abbey. A psalter and sacramentary, made in Peterborough and beautifully decorated, were sent to Cologne, and Bishop Fulbert of Chartres wrote to Cnut that when:

> we saw the gift that you sent us we were amazed at your knowledge as well as your faith … since you, whom we had heard to be a pagan prince, we now know to be not only a Christian, but also a most generous donor to churches and God's servants. (Lawson, 158)

This must have been the reaction that Cnut's policies to the church were intended to secure. His coronation, his lavish piety, his pilgrimage to Rome, all partly served the purpose of cloaking a bloody past and giving to his government a badly needed aura of legitimacy. They admitted him, in Sir Frank Stenton's words, into the 'civilized fraternity of Christian kings' (Stenton, 397). Nevertheless, he was quite prepared to defy ecclesiastics when it suited him, as his marital arrangements show. Despite his union with Emma in 1017, Ælfgifu of Northampton was retained in some sort of official position, and her sons' inheritance rights recognized when Swein was put in charge of Norway with his mother. In clear contravention of church teaching, Cnut maintained two consorts.

Last years, death, and burial, 1032–1035 Cnut's later years in England are difficult to piece together. He may have visited Glastonbury on 30 November 1032 and there are five royal land charters from 1033, the most to survive from any year of the reign. Perhaps he eventually suffered a lengthy period of illness, which encouraged the Norman hostility noted above. At least, in a charter in favour of Sherborne Abbey from 1035, Cnut expresses the hope that giving earthly riches will secure him redemption and absolution from his crimes and asks that the monks should intercede for him with God daily so that he may gain the heavenly kingdom. Probably already mortally ill when he made this grant, Cnut died at Shaftesbury on 12 November 1035 and was buried in the Old Minster, Winchester, perhaps near the relics of St Swithun. His bones, together with those of other pre-conquest monarchs, were later transferred into the new cathedral built by the Normans, and in 1642 were removed from the chest in which they lay and scattered by parliamentarian troops. In 1661 they are said to have been placed in two new receptacles, which are among the six mortuary chests still to be seen in the cathedral. However, it is hardly surprising that examination of all the chests has shown their contents to be thoroughly jumbled: there is now no way of knowing whether Cnut's bones survive in Winchester, and if so which they are.

Legacy and reputation Cnut left few identifiable political legacies. Norway was being lost to Olaf's son Magnus as he lay dying, and neither his empire nor his dynasty's position in England survived the early childless deaths of his sons Harold Harefoot, in 1040, and Harthacnut, in 1042. He has sometimes been accused of political irresponsibility in advancing the three great earls—Godwine of Wessex, Leofric of Mercia, and Siward of Northumbria—who dominated Edward the Confessor's reign, but too little is known of his patronage of them, and what motivated it, for this to be certain: Godwine, for example, may have acquired much of his considerable landed wealth after 1035. Although it did not have the sort of long-term effects on many aspects of English life that followed the Norman conquest, Cnut's reign illustrates the capacities of the pre-conquest English state better than any other. Its wealth and comprehensive administrative system were utilized by a conqueror to establish an extensive northern empire unparalleled before or since. Cnut's personality, like that of most early medieval kings, is ultimately elusive. He was probably ruthless and good at grasping political opportunities. He may have been genuinely pious; if not, he was shrewd enough to understand the importance of a king's religious role in a society where religion mattered. His achievements must to an extent have been based on oppression, often financial, of many of his subjects; but this had largely been forgotten within a century of his death. Archbishop Wulfstan's legal texts, the flattery lavished upon him by his wife's encomiast, and memories of his acts of piety secured for Cnut a favourable posthumous reputation which many of his contemporaries would hardly have recognized. M. K. LAWSON

Sources ASC, s.a. 1013–1035 • John of Worcester, Chron. • A. Campbell, ed. and trans., Encomium Emmae reginae, CS, 3rd ser., 72 (1949) • Die Chronik des Bischofs Thietmar von Merseburg, ed. R. Holtzmann,

2nd edn (Berlin, 1955) · *Magistri Adam Bremensis gesta Hammaburgensis ecclesiae pontificum*, ed. B. Schmeidler, 3rd edn, MGH Scriptores Rerum Germanicarum, [2] (Hanover, 1917) · *AS chart.*, S 949–992 · F. Liebermann, ed., *Die Gesetze der Angelsachsen*, 3 vols. in 4 (Halle, 1898–1916) · F. E. Harmer, ed., *Anglo-Saxon writs* (1952) · *English historical documents*, 1, ed. D. Whitelock (1955) · *Hemingi chartularium ecclesiæ Wigorniensis*, ed. T. Hearne, 2 vols. (1723) · *L'estoire des Engleis by Geffrei Gaimar*, ed. A. Bell, Anglo-Norman Texts, 14–16 (1960) · *Willelmi Malmesbiriensis monachi de gestis regum Anglorum*, ed. W. Stubbs, 2 vols., Rolls Series (1887–9) · Henry, archdeacon of Huntingdon, *Historia Anglorum*, ed. D. E. Greenway, OMT (1996) · M. Ashdown, *English and Norse documents relating to the reign of Ethelred the Unready* (1930) · M. K. Lawson, *Cnut: the Danes in England in the early eleventh century* (1993) · A. R. Rumble, ed., *The reign of Cnut* (1994) · R. Poole, 'Skaldic verse and Anglo-Saxon history: some aspects of the period 1009–1016', *Speculum*, 62 (1987), 265–98 · S. Keynes, 'The æthelings in Normandy', *Anglo-Norman Studies*, 13 (1990), 173–205 · F. Barlow, *The English church, 1000–1066: a constitutional history* (1963) · F. M. Stenton, *Anglo-Saxon England*, 3rd edn (1971) · E. A. Freeman, *The history of the Norman conquest of England*, 2nd edn, 6 vols. (1870–79) · B. T. Hudson, 'Cnut and the Scottish kings', *EngHR*, 107 (1992), 350–60 · A. Williams, '"Cockles amongst the wheat": Danes and English in the western midlands in the first half of the eleventh century', *Midland History*, 11 (1986), 1–22 · A. Farley, ed., *Domesday Book*, 2 vols. (1783) · *Knytlinga saga*, ed. H. Pálsson and P. Edwards (1986)
Likenesses drawing, BL, Stowe MS 944, fol. 6r [*see illus.*]

Coade, Eleanor (1733–1821), manufacturer of artificial stone, was born on 3 June 1733 in Exeter, the elder daughter (there were no sons) of George Coade, wool merchant, of Exeter, and his wife, Eleanor, daughter of Thomas Enchmarch, wool merchant, of Tiverton, Devon. She was brought up as a nonconformist. The family remained in Exeter until about 1760, when they moved to London. In the mid-1760s Eleanor was in business in the City on her own as a linen draper.

In 1769 George Coade died, bankrupt, and later in the year Eleanor joined Daniel Pincot, who was already established at Narrow Wall, Lambeth, making a form of artificial stone. They were there together until 1771, when Eleanor Coade sacked him for representing himself, instead of herself, as the proprietor of the factory. Shortly afterwards, she appointed John *Bacon (1740–1799) as supervisor, and his neo-classical models set a very high standard of design. He designed for the firm until the end of his life in 1799.

Soon Eleanor Coade was working for all the eminent Georgian architects, including Robert Adam, James and Samuel Wyatt, Sir William Chambers, John Nash, and John Soane. A talented modeller, she exhibited at the Society of Artists between 1773 and 1780. As her mother's name was the same as her own, it has been mistakenly assumed that Mrs Coade, the mother, ran the factory until her death in 1796, but 'Mrs' was a courtesy title for any unmarried woman in business at that time, and bills show that Eleanor Coade was in charge from 1771.

It was widely believed that Eleanor Coade had invented a new process for making artificial stone. Long thought to be a mystery, Coade stone is now known to be a ceramic material, and the British Museum research laboratory's analysis in 1985 showed that it was a form of stoneware so resistant to the weather that it is as precise today as when it was originally made. Its versatility allowed it to be used for all architectural details, commemorative and funerary monuments, fonts, statues, busts, coats of arms, chimney-pieces, garden ornaments, and furniture. Most is neo-classical, but there were also Gothic commissions such as Dalmeny House, Scotland, or Battle Abbey. Sizes range from the statue of Lord Hill in Shrewsbury (16 feet tall) to ornaments 1 inch long. Over six hundred and fifty examples have been traced, all over the British Isles, and in Canada, the United States, Brazil, and the Caribbean. Pieces were also sent to Russia, Poland, and South Africa.

In 1799 Eleanor Coade took as partner her cousin John Sealy, and the firm became Coade and Sealy. A showroom was opened at the east end of Westminster Bridge. Eleanor Coade had the royal appointment to George III, for whom she made the Gothic screen at St George's Chapel, Windsor, and to the prince of Wales, for whom, successively as prince regent and George IV, she did work at the first Royal Pavilion, Brighton, and Carlton House. Much work was done in the 1790s at the Royal Naval Hospital, Greenwich, and in 1810 work began on the pediment there, which was 40 feet long, designed by Benjamin West and Joseph Panzetta, and made in Coade stone. Sealy died in 1813, and Eleanor Coade appointed William Croggon as manager. The firm reverted to being Coade, and continued to flourish.

Eleanor Coade was unmarried. She died on 16 November 1821 in Camberwell, and rated an obituary notice in the *Gentleman's Magazine*. Croggon bought the factory and made many thousands of pounds' worth of Coade stone for Buckingham Palace, but in the late 1830s trade declined, and the firm came to an end about 1840.

ALISON KELLY, rev.

Sources I. C. Freestone, M. Bimson, and M. S. Tite, 'The constitution of Coade stone', *Ancient technology to modern science*, ed. W. T. Kingery (1985) · J. Havill, 'Eleanor Coade, artificial stone manufacturer', 1986, Devon and Exeter Institution, Exeter [copies also in Guildhall Library and Library of Congress] · A. Kelly, *Mrs. Coade's stone* (1990)

Coade, Thorold Francis (1896–1963), headmaster, was born in Dublin on 3 July 1896, the only son of the Revd Charles Edward Coade and his wife, Jessie Wilhelmine Spencer. He was educated at Glebe House School, Hunstanton, and at Harrow School (1910–15), where he became head of the headmaster's house. He then went to the Royal Military College, Sandhurst, and in 1916 to France with the Loyal North Lancashire regiment. There he was wounded on the Somme, losing an ear-drum when a bomb exploded in the trench; when he left hospital he was transferred to East Anglia.

On demobilization Coade went up to Christ Church, Oxford, on the shortened degree course in English. In 1921 he passed with distinction. Meanwhile, following in her father's line, his only sister, Eileen, went up to Oxford to read theology, in which she gained a first class in 1924. While at Oxford, Coade rekindled his youthful interest in drama, especially production, and also played golf for the university. In 1922, having been introduced to her by his sister, he married Kathleen Eleanor, daughter of Harold

Hugh Hardy, a businessman. They had two daughters. In 1922 he returned as an assistant master to Harrow, for which he always retained a romantic attachment. But his experience there gave insufficient scope for his widening vision.

In those ten years at Harrow, however, Coade's imagination was released through his wife's affection and rapport. They both loved poetry and the arts, and she was always to share deeply in his thoughts. In 1931 he began residential conferences for schoolmasters at Harrow.

By 1932 Coade was restive for change and looking for opportunity, and in that year he was appointed to the headship of Bryanston School. The school had been founded only four years before and its founding headmaster had resigned. It was a time of crisis when institutions of all kinds were at grave financial risk. Perhaps only the school's governors detected beneath Coade's shy unpretentious exterior his unswerving determination and purpose, supported by his Christian faith. With him at its centre, often almost hidden, the school passed from its troubled though exciting, seemingly eccentric, beginnings to its acceptance at large as an interesting experiment until, after about twenty years, it became recognized nationally as a remarkable creation.

Bryanston offered Coade an almost clear field. An appreciable number of ideas he inherited from his predecessor, and some he borrowed from others, but their management and interaction were his creative own. Private study was encouraged as a method of work, after a modified Dalton plan; the competitive spirit was reduced, there was no corporal punishment or private fagging, prefects were given responsibility not privilege. Relationships between masters and boys were less inhibited, more relaxed, than elsewhere. There was much opportunity for self-expression in the visual arts, in music, and for other creative uses of leisure. Estate work replaced the conventional training corps (except during the Second World War), and boys were deliberately given more free time than at other schools. When Coade was taunted as headmaster of a school where 'the boys do what they like', he replied that 'they like what they do'. A merry debunker, capable of witty asides that were often devastating, he could nevertheless be stern, even adamant. Compassion and tenderness were, however, his signal qualities.

Coade produced many school plays. One of his finest achievements was in the summer of 1954 when he produced the Chester mystery plays in the Greek theatre at Bryanston with over a hundred boys and girls from the sister school of Cranborne Chase taking part.

Coade shunned the limelight and was rarely prominent, for instance in the Headmasters' Conference. However, he was much in demand at conferences because of his wise and witty interventions. He could seldom meet strangers (or parents) half-way. His personality was complex, yet his presence gave reassurance, inspiring trust and confidence. He drew staff and others to him, leading them into strong partnership. For him wholeness, the balance and harmony of a boy's entire person, was the purpose of education, as is recognized so widely today. Over-specialization and narrowness of any kind was an intrusion into adolescence. Through creative encounters and relationships, a boy's imagination and talent can be captured for life itself. For Coade, therefore, the use of leisure, and through it self-discovery and realization, rang truer than the pursuit of outer objectives.

A man of ideas but still more of ideals, it was as if they came elusively to use Coade as their interpreter. His sight was more intuitive than observing, and his love of others was grounded in the faith that shaped his personality. The unifying thread was for him the awakening of mind, body, and spirit in each unique adolescent boy and their harnessing to the purposes of God, the Spirit moving where it will. 'You cannot teach boys to be religious', he said, 'for they are religious already.' *God with Us* by S. L. Frank, translated by N. Duddington (1946), was of central importance to him.

After twenty-six years the governors of Bryanston invited Coade to remain for a further five, but ill health compelled him to retire a year later, in 1959. Although one of the less well known, he was among the greatest headmasters of his time. He died at his home, Old Bell Cottage, at East Knoyle, Salisbury, not far from the school, on 1 February 1963.

Coade's published work included 'Education for leisure' in *Education of Today* (1935, ed. E. D. Laborde), and 'The new term' (*The Spectator*, 1937). He edited *Harrow Lectures in Education* (1931), and *Manhood in the Making* (1939), to which he contributed an essay entitled 'Maturity'. A posthumous selection of his papers forms *The Burning Bow* (1966), which includes an epilogue, 'Beneath his skin', contributed by Kathleen Coade.   A. R. DONALD WRIGHT, *rev.*

Sources M. C. Morgan, *Bryanston, 1928–78* (1978) · personal knowledge (1981) · *The Times* (4 Feb 1963)

Archives BL, corresp. with Albert Mansbridge, Add. MS 65257B

Likenesses T. Lesser, bronze head, 1958, Bryanston School, Blandford, Dorset · C. Rogers, portrait, 1958, Bryanston School, Blandford, Dorset · R. Tollast, portrait, 1978, Bryanston School, Blandford, Dorset · photograph, repro. in T. F. Coade, *The burning bow* (1966)

Wealth at death £6502 6s. 7d.: probate, 4 April 1963, *CGPLA Eng. & Wales*

Coan, John (1728–1764), sideshow performer, was born at Twisthall, Norfolk. Although he has been known as the Norfolk Dwarf, both accounts of his development and pictorial representations of him reveal that he was not a dwarf but a midget. Coan appeared to grow normally in his early years but by mid-adolescence was only 3 ft tall, and when he was first publicly exhibited in Norfolk in April 1750 he had reached his full height and weight of 3 ft 2 ins. and (with clothes) 34 lbs.

The first evidence of Coan's move to London is his presentation before Frederick, prince of Wales, at a party in Leicester House in January 1751, where he proved a highly popular guest. During this period dwarfs and midgets were very much in vogue with royalty in general and often lived in their patrons' homes. Much of Coan's appeal lay in the combined attraction of his very small but well-proportioned limbs (he was frequently referred to as the Man in Miniature) and his precocious personality. He was not simply a biological curiosity, therefore, but was distinguished from similar performers of the period by a sharp wit, intelligence, and capacity for entertainment through recitation, imitation, and singing.

Coan appeared at a number of London fairs and tavern venues. Thomas Frost describes an early appearance he made, aged twenty-three, at the Swan in Smithfield during the three days of Bartholomew fair in 1751. Although Frost reports that the 'principal show seems to have been one containing two dwarfs, a remarkable negro, a female one-horned rhinoceros, and a crocodile' (Frost, 167), a giant of 7 ft 4 ins. named Henry Blacker (b. 1724) from Cuckfield in Sussex was also included in the show. Coan is featured in an engraving by J. Roberts standing next to another giant named Edward Bamfield. Following this he featured much more as an individual performer. Although he was exhibited (for a payment of 2s. 6d.) as a curiosity to the public at a watchmaker's opposite the Cannon tavern, Charing Cross, Westminster, and for members of the Royal Society, it is clear that his twelve-hour-long daily exhibitions also included much active and interactive participation on his part. He appeared in taverns such as the Ship, the Anchor, and the Windmill near Temple Bar, and played an extravagant host in John Pinchbeck's Dwarf's tavern in Spring Gardens and at the Star and Garter tavern, both in Chelsea Fields, where Coan's humorous entertainments over dinner would be followed by Carlo Genovini's firework displays.

According to Highfill, not only does *Owens' Weekly Chronicle or Universal Museum* of 5–12 June 1762 print a prologue which explicitly invokes Coan and which is reported to have been spoken by the actor William Gibson (1713–1771) at a performance of Thomas Otway's *The Orphan* at the Haymarket Theatre on 31 May 1762 but, following Coan's death in London on either 24 or 28 March 1764, an effigy of him was displayed at Rackstraw's Museum of Anatomy and Curiosities in Chancery Lane (Highfill, Burnim & Langhans, *BDA*).   HELEN STODDART

Sources Highfill, Burnim & Langhans, *BDA* · T. Frost, *The old showmen and the London fairs* (1874) · W. Bodin and B. Hershey, *The world of midgets* (1935) · *Newcastle General Magazine* (Sept 1751) · *London Magazine*, 33 (1764) · *GM*, 1st ser., 34 (1764), 147
Archives Hunt. L.
Likenesses J. Roberts, engraving, repro. in Highfill, Burnim & Langhans, *BDA*, vol. 3

Coatalen, Louis Hervé (1879–1962), designer of cars and aero-engines, was born on 11 September 1879 at Concarneau, Finistère, the second son of a hotelier and wheelwright, François Marie Coatalen, and his wife, Louise Le Bris. From grammar school at Brest, he went to the École des Arts et Métiers at Cluny, then started as a draughtsman with De Dion-Bouton and afterwards with the Clement Company and Panhard and Levassor. Seeing greater opportunities in the motor industry in England, in 1900 he joined the Crowden Motor Car Company at Leamington Spa and then at the age of twenty-one became chief engineer with Humber at Coventry. For them he designed two models which restored the company's fortunes. The 10/12 hp model was so successful that the works had to be

expanded and profits attained figures that were not to be equalled for a quarter of a century. He drove a Coventry Humber in the 1906 Tourist Trophy race, finishing sixth.

In partnership with William Hillman of Coventry from 1907, Coatalen designed the 24 hp Hillman-Coatalen car with which he put up the fastest lap in the 1907 Tourist Trophy race before crashing at Quarter Bridge.

Thomas Cureton, managing director of the Sunbeam Motor Car Company, Wolverhampton, engaged Coatalen as chief engineer in February 1909 and his first product, the 16/20 hp Sunbeam, distinguished itself in the Scottish Six Days Trial in the same year. Encouraged by this, a smaller 12/16 hp model was produced which proved an even greater success. This model and its subsequent development established Coatalen's reputation as an automobile engineer and put Sunbeam in the forefront of motor manufacturers. During the next twenty-one years Coatalen produced a succession of touring cars, luxury cars, racing cars, record-breaking cars, and aero-engines which won international fame for Sunbeam and its associated marques, Talbot and Darracq. Coatalen was first married in 1902, in Birmingham, to Annie Davis; they had one son. The marriage ended in divorce, and on 3 September 1909 he married Olive Mary, daughter of Henry James Bath, one of Sunbeam's directors; they had two sons. Coatalen acquired British nationality during the First World War. He was divorced in 1922 and on 31 January 1923 married a divorcée, Iris Enid Florence van Raalte (*née* Graham); they had one daughter. This third marriage lasted until 1935, when he married Emily Bridson, who remained with him until his death.

Coatalen wrote in 1924: 'Racing car practice accelerates development. Racing stimulates designers and engineers and raises the morale of the factory workpeople.' He drove Sunbeams in races at Brooklands and entered them in the *voiturette* races run by *L'Auto* in France. They competed in international grand prix races and set up many world records. They held the Brooklands lap record five times and the land speed record in 1922 and 1924–7. Sunbeam cars won the *Coupe de L'Auto* in 1912, the Tourist Trophy in 1914 and 1922, the French grand prix in 1923, and the Spanish grand prix in 1924. The 1.5 litre Talbot-Darracqs were invincible in *voiturette* races from 1921 until 1925.

Coatalen was not only a competent engineer but also a skilled impresario, quick to spot and use the abilities of others. He engaged the design talents of Ernest Henry, Vincent Bertarione, Captain J. S. Irving, and others. The racing cars were handled by the leading drivers of their time: Sir Henry Segrave, K. Lee Guinness, Sir Algernon Guinness, Dario Resta, Jean Chassagne, Albert Divo, Réné Thomas, Sir Malcolm Campbell, André Boillot, J. Moriceau, George Duller, Count Masetti, and Kaye Don.

The Sunbeam company was among the first to standardize overhead valve engines and four-wheel brakes and in 1925 produced a twin overhead camshaft 3 litre sporting model. The company also played an important role in the development of aero-engines. The Crusader 150 hp V8 was already in production before the outbreak of war in 1914.

Lessons learned in racing were applied to meet the ever-increasing demands from the services for more power. Over twenty types of Sunbeam aero-engines were designed and produced and power output rose from 150 to 900 hp. Sunbeam-Coatalen engines were fitted to the British airship R34 which made the first out-and-home flight across the Atlantic in 1919. The French government nominated Coatalen chevalier of the Légion d'honneur for his work on aero-engines for the allies.

The development of a Sunbeam-Coatalen diesel aero-engine was undertaken in 1930 but economic conditions and Coatalen's ill health held it back. He was then living and working in Paris and Capri. With his stimulating influence removed, the fortunes of the Sunbeam Talbot Darracq Group declined and in 1935 it was taken over by the Rootes Group under W. E. Rootes. Meanwhile Coatalen became chairman and managing director of Lockheed Hydraulic Brakes in Paris and chairman of KLG Sparking Plugs (France). He continued his work on diesel aero-engines using a Hispano-Suiza engine which he converted using very high pressure injection. In 1953 the Société des Ingenieurs de l'Automobile elected him its president, and in 1954 he was made officier of the Légion d'honneur. He was actively engaged in his work until his death in Paris on 23 May 1962.   ANTHONY S. HEAL, rev.

Sources *The Times* (25 May 1962), 18d • *The Times* (1 June 1962), 21b • *Automotor Journal* (2 Dec 1911) • *Autocar* (1924) • *Autocar* (5 Sept 1979) • I. Nickols and K. Karslake, *Motoring entente* (1956) • *A souvenir of Sunbeam service, 1899–1919* (1919) • *The history and development of the Sunbeam car, 1899–1924* (1924) • *Motor Sport* (Sept 1979) • WWW • L. Pomeroy, *The evolution of the racing car* (1966) • m. certs.

Likenesses Lhoste, commemorative medal, 1974 (issued by French mint)

Coate, Winifred Annie (1893–1977), missionary teacher and relief organizer, was born on 25 April 1893 at 10 Alwyne Square, Islington, London, the younger daughter of Harry Coate, a Church of England clergyman, and his wife, Henrietta Mercy Nihill. She was educated at Westfield College, University of London, where she graduated BA in English in 1913. Her sister was the seventeenth-century historian Mary Coate. Winifred Coate trained for work overseas at the Church Missionary Society College (1918–19) and from 1920 to 1923 she taught English at the Jerusalem College. She was appointed a very young principal of the society's girls' high school in Cairo in 1924 and in 1928 she was asked to take over the principalship of the Jerusalem Girls' College.

Winifred Coate both spoke and read Arabic, essential qualifications in her work as a teacher in multi-faith, multi-ethnic schools and, later, as a relief organizer among the Palestinians. She piloted the Jerusalem Girls' College through the turbulent years from 1928 to 1943, always seeking to ensure a 'normalcy' of civilized tolerance and consideration for others within her school, whatever sectarian atrocities were being perpetrated outside its walls. On 6 September 1929 she reported to the Church Missionary Society in London:

> The Jews have undoubtedly suffered most and in some places, particularly Hebron, the Moslems have committed terrible atrocities, which will not soon be forgotten. I dare

say however that the Jews were in the first instance just as responsible as the Moslems for the ill-feeling which led to the outbreak.   (W. Coate correspondence, 6 Sept 1929, Jerusalem and the East mission archive, St Ant. Oxf., Middle East Centre)

Nevertheless Winifred Coate could also report her joy in 1929 at several girls qualifying to study at London University and at the University of Beirut—potentially the first Palestinian Arab women doctors. In 1933 she reported to London the immense bitterness she encountered among ordinary Arabs at the alienation of their land to Jewish immigrants. When violent rioting broke out in Jerusalem late in 1933 she opened the college as usual, although all the other schools were closed, being vindicated in that all the girls returned to the college 'perfectly friendly to us and to one another. I have seen no … unkindness of any kind. … I felt so relieved when I found that no one community was striking or boycotting us' (30 Oct 1933, Jerusalem and East mission archive). In 1940 the college pupils included 140 Christians, both Christian Arab and Russian Orthodox, seventy-five Muslims, and forty-five Jews. Shy, and with a tough exterior concealing her very warm heart, Winifred Coate was a hard worker who drove her staff hard also. By 1943 she was driving them harder than they could bear, and she was asked to resign as principal. She then went to the Anglican mission for Druse, Greek Orthodox, and Maronites at ʿAin Anub, Lebanon, as a teacher / supervisor, tackling adult as well as child illiteracy. The only European in the village, 'I listen more than I speak … and I feel that someone with a nurse's training could be much more effective' (*Bible Lands*, 12, October 1946).

The summer of 1948 found Winifred Coate back in Jerusalem, sheltering from bullets during the fighting after the creation of the state of Israel, in a corner of the garden of St George's Cathedral. She and the bishop and his wife discussed what they could do, even as a token, to show the church's desire to help the 700,000 destitute Palestinian Arab refugees. Winifred Coate decided to go to the pitiful tented camp at Zerka, east Jordan, and started up first a milk distribution centre, then supplementary feeding for mothers and babies, a girls' school, a sewing centre, and, eventually, a pottery and craft shop. In 1952 she was still there, by then organizing the building of brick houses instead of tents, establishing more and more cottage industries, and overseeing the training of Arab social workers. The Suez crisis led to the expulsion of all British missionaries in autumn 1956 but by April 1957 Winifred Coate was one of the first two missionaries invited back to Jordan.

Winifred Coate retired from the Church Missionary Society in 1960 and then, at the age of sixty-eight, she began perhaps her most important work—what she called her 'experiment'—the ʿAbdulliyyah agricultural co-operative. She based it on a tract of unwanted rocky desert which, using the archaeological evidence of nearby ancient hunting castles, she believed must have underground water. She drove an Arab water diviner around the area: 'We drilled where he indicated and there it was! It was such a good joke, finding water where the technical experts said there wasn't any' (*Daily Telegraph*, 26 Nov 1977). Winifred Coate established an irrigation project for landless peasants, Palestinian, Jordanian, and Bedouin; fifty fruit, vegetable, and chicken farms were started, followed by road building, tree planting, and the erection of a machine and transport repair workshop, schools, and a clinic. ʿAbdulliyyah became a significant pilot project for similar refugee settlements by Oxfam, Save the Children, and Christian Aid, recognizing that refugees need land and work, not mere relief.

Winifred Coate was shot in the thigh in crossfire during the Jordanian civil war of 1970; she was seventy-seven. She survived and continued to live and work at Zerka, having become a legend among the Arabs, until she collapsed seven years later. She was appointed MBE in 1951 and OBE in 1976, and awarded the Jordanian independence decoration of the second order in 1977. She died of old age and coronary thrombosis on 23 November 1977 at 3 Glebe Road, Cheam, Sutton—two months after being flown back from Jordan; her body was cremated on 1 December.

SYBIL OLDFIELD

Sources *Bible Lands*, 12 (Oct 1946) · *Outlook* (April 1955) · *Outlook* (April 1957) · *Outlook* (March 1958) · *Outlook* (July 1960) · W. Coate, 'Among Arab refugees in Jordan', 12 Nov 1950, U. Birm. L., special collections department, Church Missionary Society archive · *Daily Telegraph* (26 Nov 1977) · I. M. Okkenhaug, '"The quality of heroic living, of high endeavour and adventure": Anglican mission, women, and education in Palestine, 1888–1948', DPhil diss., University of Bergen, 1999 · W. A. Coate, *The years in the desert: Abdelliyeh, 1972* (1973) · *CGPLA Eng. & Wales* (1978) · b. cert. · d. cert. · W. A. Coate, *Abdelliyeh, 1961–1976: a pictorial record of progress in the Abdelliyeh village project, Jordan* (1977) · U. Birm. L., special collections department, Church Missionary Society archive
Archives St Ant. Oxf., corresp. · St Ant. Oxf., MSS on ʿAbdulliyyah co-op, Jordan · U. Birm. L., special collections department, Church Missionary Society MSS, report from Zerka, Jordan
Likenesses photograph, repro. in *Outlook* (April 1957)
Wealth at death £29,817: probate, 21 March 1978, *CGPLA Eng. & Wales*

Coates, Albert Henry (1882–1953), conductor and composer, was born on 23 April 1882 at St Petersburg, Russia, the youngest of seven sons of Charles Thomas Coates, businessman, and his wife, also born near St Petersburg, daughter of James Gibson and Mary Randall.

Coates was educated in England. After attending the Royal Naval College, Dartmouth, he read science at the Liverpool Institute and studied music informally with an elder brother. Later he returned to St Petersburg and joined his father's business. But music continued to attract him and he entered the Leipzig Conservatorium in 1902. There he studied the cello with Paul Klengel, the piano with Robert Teichmüller, and conducting with Arthur Nikisch. Coming from an affluent, bourgeois background, Coates was able to exploit his period at the institution fully. Envied by other students for his possession of two pianos, he used his financial security to further his knowledge. By buying and studying newly published works in four-hand arrangements for piano, he was able to experience new and progressive works at first hand.

Impressed by Coates's potential as an executant,

Nikisch offered him work at the Leipzig Opera. Having started as a volunteer répétiteur, Coates was promoted quickly, and in 1904 he made his conducting début with Offenbach's *The Tales of Hoffmann*. After a string of successful performances, Nikisch recommended Coates for the post of first conductor at the Elberfeld Stadttheater in 1905. But his tenure was short, and he moved to the prestigious Dresden Hofoper in 1907. Impulsive by nature, he soon came into conflict with his immediate superior, Ernst von Schuch, and decided to accept a post at Mannheim in 1909. Again his tenure was short and, after a performance of Wagner's *Siegfried* at St Petersburg, his appointment as principal conductor of the Russian Imperial Opera was announced in 1910. On 23 July that year he married Ella Lizzie Holland (*b.* 1881/2), daughter of Alfred Robert Holland.

Coates returned to Britain in 1919. Although his experience was gained mostly in the opera houses of continental Europe, he was familiar to London audiences: in 1910 he made his Queen's Hall début with the London Symphony Orchestra; in 1911 he performed for the Royal Philharmonic Society for the first time; and on 11 February 1914 he conducted Wagner's *Tristan und Isolde* at Covent Garden. But June 1919 was a watershed for the conductor: after returning successfully to Covent Garden, he was appointed principal conductor of the London Symphony Orchestra. Accepting the post at a time of financial uncertainty for the ensemble, Coates refused to accept a fee for their first six performances together. But the orchestra's fiscal problems did not inhibit his adventurous programming policy, and at his first concert on 27 October 1919 the inclusion of Skryabin's *Poème de l'extase* affirmed his commitment to both that composer and Russian music in general. But Coates was also a champion of British music, and as principal conductor he gave the first reading of the revised version of Vaughan Williams's *London Symphony* (1920), the first complete performance of Holst's *The Planets* (1920), and the première of Bax's symphony no. 1 (1922).

Successful in the theatre and the concert hall, Coates soon attracted the interest of the fast-growing gramophone industry. And it is unsurprising that the works he recorded first were by Russian composers. For Columbia he recorded Tchaikovsky's *Romeo and Juliet* on 6 August 1919, part of Rimsky-Korsakov's *Scheherazade* on 13 December 1919, and Skryabin's *Poème de l'extase* on 27 April and 7 May 1920. He continued to work for Columbia until 1935, and his recordings of Bach's mass in B minor, extensive excerpts from Wagner's stage works, and Stravinsky's *Petrouchka* and *Firebird* suite were important additions to that company's catalogue.

Coates made his American début in 1920, and three years later was appointed co-conductor of the Rochester Philharmonic. Sharing its 1923–4 season with Eugene Goossens, Coates conducted the ensemble between 16 January and 19 April 1924. His performances were successful, and he returned in 1925. Later that year he performed at the Leeds festival, conducting the first English performance of his tone poem *The Eagle* and the première of

Holst's *Choral Symphony*. But his career had begun to lack focus, and from the mid-1920s it began to decline slowly. For much of the next twenty years he toured as a guest conductor, directing performances with, among others, the Berlin State Opera and the Vienna Philharmonic.

Unfulfilled as an executant, Coates returned to composition: on 21 December 1929 his fourth opera, *Samuel Pepys*, was performed at Munich, and on 20 November 1936 his fifth opera, *Pickwick*, was staged at Covent Garden. *Pickwick* was the climax of the British Music-Drama Opera Company's first season. But both the organization, formed by Coates and the producer Vladimir Rosing, and the opera were moribund: the work fell from the repertory and the company disbanded after one season. Even so, *Pickwick* was important historically: it was the first opera shown on British television. Uncertain of his future in Britain, Coates spent most of the Second World War in the USA. He appeared as a guest conductor with the Los Angeles Philharmonic Orchestra and was involved in the films *Song of Russia* (1944) and *Two Girls and a Sailor* (1944). After the hostilities he returned to London and recorded for Decca. But his relationship with the company was short, and his six recordings of Russian music failed to impress either critically or financially. By 1946 it was clear that Coates's career had reached its nadir. That year he announced that he was moving to South Africa, and after a period with the Johannesburg Symphony Orchestra he settled in Cape Town. There he directed the local orchestra, taught at the university, and supervised the performance of his seventh opera, *Van Hunks and the Devil: the Legend of Table Mountain*, in 1952.

Coates was a talented musician whose inability to hold a tenured post for long periods harmed his career. Although he was important to the fortunes of the London Symphony Orchestra immediately after the First World War, his contribution to British musical life was ephemeral. As a composer he has lost his place in the repertory, and as an executant he is remembered generally by collectors with an interest in historic recordings. His second wife was Vera Joanna Nettlefold; little else is known about his personal life. Coates died at Milnerton, near Cape Town, South Africa, on 11 December 1953.

RAYMOND HOLDEN

Sources WWW, 1929–40 · WWW, 1971–80 · Grove, *Dict. mus.* (1954) · A. Buesst, 'Albert Coates: 1882–1953', *Music and Letters*, 35 (1954), 136–9 · Grove, *Dict. mus.* (1927) · C. Ehrlich, *First philharmonic: a history of the Royal Philharmonic Society* (1995) · R. Elkin, *Queen's Hall, 1893–1941* (1944) · R. Elkin, *Royal Philharmonic: the annals of the Royal Philharmonic Society* (1946) · H. Foss and N. Goodwin, *London Symphony Orchestra* (1954) · E. Goossens, *Overture and beginners: a musical autobiography* (1951) · M. Kennedy, *The Hallé tradition: a century of music* (1960) · P. Muck, *Einhundert Jahre Berliner Philharmonisches Orchester* (Tutzing, 1982) · *The Times* (12 Dec 1953) · *The Times* (17 Dec 1953) · *The Times* (19 Dec 1953) · *The Times* (31 Dec 1953) · *Who's who in music*, 3rd edn (1950) · S. Robinson, 'Albert Coates', *Recorded Sound: the Journal of the British Institute of Recorded Sound*, 57–8 (1975), 382–405 [with discography by C. Dyment] · H. Rosenthal, *Two centuries of opera at Covent Garden* (1958) · *Baker's biographical dictionary of musicians*, rev. N. Slonimsky, 8th edn (1992) · *New Grove* · B. Shore, *The orchestra speaks* (1938) · S. M. Stroff, 'Albert Coates', *Le grand baton*, 45/17/1 (March 1980), 3–27 · m. cert.

Archives SOUND BL NSA, performance recordings

Coates, Charles (*bap.* 1746, *d.* 1813), antiquary, was baptized in St Laurence's Church, Reading, on 27 March 1746, the son of John Coates, watchmaker in the City of London, and his wife, Elizabeth. He was educated at Reading School for a record nine years, under the Revd John Spicer, being admitted as a sizar at Gonville and Caius College, Cambridge, at the age of sixteen in May 1762; he became a scholar that same year. He obtained the degree of bachelor of medicine five years later.

Having chosen the church as his profession, Coates was ordained deacon at Salisbury in 1770 and priest a year later in London. After a curacy at Ealing, under the Revd Charles Sturges, in 1780 he was presented to the living of Preston, Dorset, with the help of John Spicer, then the prebendary there. In 1788 the bishop of Salisbury permitted him to take the nearby living of Osmington, and he received a Lambeth LLB.

In 1791 Coates issued proposals for a work on *The History and Antiquities of Reading*, and embarked on some intensive research. He studied the relevant manuscripts in the British Museum and the Bodleian Library and the records at the Tower of London, the rolls and augmentation offices, and those with the corporation of Reading. The 500-page quarto volume, handsomely illustrated, did not appear until 1802, when the *Gentleman's Magazine* commented ironically that 'those subscribers, who have been so lucky as to live long enough to reap the benefit of their subscription-money, have very sufficient reason to be satisfied with the work' (*GM*, 72/2, 1802, 620). In 1810 he published *A Supplement … with Corrections and Additions by the Author*. His history gives an unrivalled portrayal of the town, as well as its memorials and remains, at the beginning of the nineteenth century. Unfortunately it has no index. Coates was elected a fellow of the Society of Antiquaries in 1793. Having been appointed chaplain to the prince of Wales, he dedicated the history to him. In 1808 he was made prebendary of Wells.

Coates had many friendships in Reading. He was the benefactor of Mrs Ann Latournelle, the needy widow of a nonconformist minister, until her death in 1780. Although he would have welcomed preferment, or one of the Reading parishes that were in the gift of the crown, he never left Dorset. His later decades were clouded by his wife's chronic ill health, and it brought on a severe paralytic attack, which ended his literary career. He had been working on a new and enlarged edition of Elias Ashmole's *History of Berkshire*, which he did not complete. He had also collected documents for a continuation of John Le Neve's *Lives of the Protestant Archbishops*; these he presented to Alexander Chalmers for insertion in a new edition of the *General Biographical Dictionary*.

Mrs Coates died on 27 November 1812, leaving no children. The *Reading Mercury* published a tribute to her by him. However, it did not record Coates's own death at Osmington four months later, on 7 April 1813.

T. A. B. CORLEY

Sources DNB · *GM*, 1st ser., 61 (1791), 1088 · *GM*, 1st ser., 72 (1802), 620 · *GM*, 1st ser., 83/1 (1813), 813 · *GM*, 1st ser., 83/2 (1813), 88–9 ·

Venn, *Alum. Cant.* · C. Coates, preface, *The history and antiquities of Reading* (1802) · Nichols, *Lit. anecdotes*, 1.128 · T. Cooper, *A new biographical dictionary: containing concise notices of eminent persons of all ages and countries* (1873) · will, 1780, Berks. RO, MF 569 [Anne Latournelle] · *Reading Mercury* (7 Dec 1812) · parish register (baptism), Reading, St Laurence, 27 March 1746

Archives Bodl. Oxf., letters to John Nichols and John Bowyer Nichols and Richard Gough

Coates, Eric [*formerly* Frank Harrison Coates] (1886–1957), composer, was born on 27 August 1886 at Watnall Road, Hucknall, Nottinghamshire, the youngest of the three daughters and two sons of William Harrison Coates (*d.* 1935), a surgeon, and his wife, Mary Jane Gwynne, *née* Blower, of Usk, Monmouthshire. There was music in the family, for Mary Jane (known as Mi-Jane) was a fine pianist and Dr Coates a flautist and an admired amateur singer. Eric Coates (as he seems always to have been called) never went to school, but in his earliest years shared a governess with his siblings. His innate musicality was awakened on hearing a visiting friend of the family play the violin. He was then six years old, and promptly demanded an instrument for himself. His first lessons came from a local violin teacher, but at the age of thirteen he was sent to the respected Nottingham musician George Ellenberger. Violists were in short supply, so he changed instruments, and soon found himself in demand for chamber music. At the age of eighteen, in 1904, he heard his own *Ballad for Strings* performed at the Royal Albert Hall, Nottingham.

Coates's father proposed a banking career for him, but was persuaded to let him attend the Royal Academy of Music, where he studied composition with Frederick Corder and viola with Lionel Tertis. From the start, Coates insisted that he wished only to write light music. Corder's rigorous training laid the foundations for what was to be the most thorough of light music techniques. As a violist, Coates was soon to be in demand in the theatre orchestras, and he became a virtuoso second only to his teacher. In 1908 he toured South Africa as a member of the Hambourg String Quartet. Yet his prospects seemed insecure, which was why he encountered parental opposition when he wished to marry a sixteen-year-old fellow student. Phyllis Marguerite Black (*b.* 1895?) was an actress and the daughter of a former Corder student, Annie Black, and her husband, Francis, principal of the Camden School of Art. To earn a living, Coates concentrated on playing, first for Thomas Beecham and then, from 1911, for Sir Henry Wood's Queen's Hall Orchestra. This security enabled him to marry Phyllis, on 2 February 1913.

Despite the demands of orchestral playing, Coates had his successes as a composer. Wood's first wife, Olga, sang his *Four Old English Songs* at the Promenade Concerts in 1909, and Coates's association with the lawyer and poet Fred Weatherly produced in *Stonecracke John* (1909) the first of a number of huge ballad successes. Wood himself was the dedicatee of the *Miniature Suite*, the last movement of which was encored when he conducted its first performance, at the Proms, on 17 October 1911.

Coates never enjoyed robust health and suffered from

Eric Coates (1886–1957), by unknown photographer

neuritis in his left arm. Since sight-reading came effortlessly to him, he found it difficult to share Wood's dedication to relentless rehearsing. In 1919, after nine years as principal viola, his contract was not renewed. It was an affront but it was also a relief. He never played the instrument again, and thereafter earned his living entirely by composition. A not-too-onerous contract with his publisher required from him annually one orchestral piece of fifteen minutes' duration, one of five minutes, and three ballads. A founder member of the Performing Right Society, he was one of the first composers to derive the bulk of his income from radio and recording. To an extent, the playing time of a 78 r.p.m. record dictated the format of his work, which favoured the suite, the fantasy, the march, the valse, and the ballad. While he was at first influenced by Sullivan and German, Coates had an enviable ability to absorb new trends. Thus such works as *The Selfish Giant* (1925) and *The Three Bears* (1926, written to amuse his four-year-old son, Austin) made use of the syncopated and jazz styles of the period. His march *Knightsbridge* (1932, from the *London Suite*) was used as introductory music for the long-running radio programme *In Town Tonight* (from 1933), and from 1940 the march *Calling All Workers* set the pace for the *Music while you Work* broadcasts. In 1930 he had written a valse serenade, *By the Sleepy Lagoon*; after the Second World War it found its place as the theme tune for the radio programme *Desert Island Discs*, and it continued to be heard in that context at the end of the century.

Between the wars Coates's work dominated the repertory of the seaside and spa orchestras. He achieved a final triumph when the film *The Dambusters* (1954) employed a recently written march to which he gave the same name.

It illustrated all the characteristics of his music: strong melody, foot-tapping rhythm, brilliant counterpoints, and colourful orchestration. Coates was an effective conductor of his own work, which he tended to take at a brisk tempo. In 1936 he conducted his work in Scandinavia, making further visits abroad as a representative of the Performing Right Society to the USA (1946) and to South America (1948). He and his wife were enthusiastic dancers, and his rhythmic sense reflected this. Although his music sometimes described rural scenes, he was essentially a city man, happiest in London. Unassuming and quiet, he had a whimsical sense of humour. Modest to a fault, he showed no resentment that he never received the public honours that were surely his due. He died on 21 December 1957 in the Royal West Sussex Hospital, Chichester, having suffered a massive stroke a few days before. His wife survived him. GEOFFREY SELF

Sources E. Coates, *Suite in four movements* (1953) · G. Self, *In town tonight* (1986) · P. L. Scowcroft, *British light music: a personal gallery of 20th-century composers* (1997), 35–7 · E. Coates, personal scrapbook, priv. coll. · b. cert. · d. cert. · *CGPLA Eng. & Wales* (1958)
Archives BL NSA, documentary recording · BL NSA, oral history interview · priv. coll., MSS · priv. coll., scrapbook | SOUND BL NSA, documentary recording · BL NSA, oral history interview
Likenesses K. N. Collins, photograph, c.1935, Royal College of Music, London · W. Stoneman, photograph, 1947, NPG · photograph, c.1950, Hult. Arch. · photograph, priv. coll. · photograph, NPG [*see illus.*]
Wealth at death £53,124 0s. 3d.: probate, 3 March 1958, *CGPLA Eng. & Wales*

Coates, (Joseph) Gordon (1878–1943), prime minister of New Zealand, was born on 3 February 1878 at Ruatuna, just outside Matakohe in Northland, New Zealand, the son of an English father, Edward Coates (1843–1905), and his northern Irish wife, Eleanor Kathleen Aickin (1851–1935). His family gave qualified support to the New Zealand Liberal Party, which dominated politics in New Zealand between 1891 and 1912.

Coates grew to maturity on the 2420 acre farm at Ruatuna that was slowly being reclaimed from forest and scrub. The area was isolated and not connected to Auckland by road or rail until the 1920s. It was served by a daily steamer from Helensville across the Kaipara harbour. There were few roads in Northland; contact with neighbours was by horse or punt. Telephones were slow to arrive. Coates had several years' schooling at Matakohe School, but the gentlemanly polish that he displayed in later years came from a governess employed by his mother to help educate her two boys and four girls, and special tutoring. Edward Coates was a manic depressive. His land was owned by his brother-in-law, and money was short. In the 1890s Edward withdrew from the community in which he had been a leading citizen, leaving the farm to his wife and children. By the time he was twelve Gordon carried many responsibilities. He could handle a gun and shot wild pigs, ducks, and pheasants. He played rugby, rode horses at shows, and attended the small local Anglican church. Gordon grew to 6 feet, with broad shoulders and a head of auburn hair. By the time he was elected to the Otamatea county council in 1905 (he was chairman

(Joseph) Gordon Coates (1878–1943), by Lindsay Mitchell, c.1935 [detail]

between 1913 and 1916) Coates was a volunteer in the Otamatea mounted rifles and a vigorous supporter of the public works policies of the Liberal premier, Richard John Seddon, and his successor, Sir Joseph Ward.

In 1911 Coates stood for parliament for Kaipara as an independent Liberal, winning on the second ballot. He held the seat until his death. Believing that he had fulfilled his promise to his electors to support Sir Joseph Ward, he voted in July 1912 with W. F. Massey's Reform Party to topple the Liberal government, and became a Reform Party member before the 1914 election. Coates's early career in the house was undistinguished. He supported public works, particularly in the north, and championed kauri gum diggers who were exhausting their resource and who, after the outbreak of war in 1914, experienced reduced markets. Coates was no orator, but he possessed a genial informality that won him a wide circle of friends. He was best known as a handsome, eligible bachelor; nevertheless, there had been an earlier relationship with a Maori woman, with whom he was said to have had a son and a daughter. On 4 August 1914 he married a recent English immigrant, Marjorie Grace Coles (1891–1973). They had five daughters.

Coates had acquired a love of the empire at his father's knee. He left for France in November 1916 with the 19th reinforcements to the New Zealand expeditionary force, holding the rank of captain. On 31 July 1917 he won a Military Cross at La Basseville, and a bar to his MC at Mailly-Maillet on 26 March 1918. Promoted to major, and carrying a wound to his leg which in later years gave him a sometimes rolling gait that opponents put down to drink, Coates returned from the front and was soon promoted by W. F. Massey to his cabinet. On 2 September 1919 he became postmaster-general and minister of justice. After Massey's re-election in December 1919 Coates was minister of public works, then minister of railways after 1923. As the youngest minister in an ageing cabinet, and possessing a war record, Coates attracted attention. He prioritized road and rail construction programmes and edged the state into a monopoly position as the producer of hydroelectricity. He was the obvious successor to Prime Minister Massey when he died in May 1925.

Described as a 'tall, lithe man, erect and soldierly in figure, a stranger to fatigue' (*Evening Post*, 21 July 1925), Coates was sworn as prime minister on 30 May 1925. He was to become the first New Zealand born premier to win a general election. His breezy informality became the subject of an extravagant advertising campaign, and in the December election he was returned with the largest majority in Reform's career. However, a lacklustre cabinet, declining commodity prices, and rising unemployment proved beyond Coates's control. A botched effort to fix dairy prices on the London market in 1926 damaged his reputation, even though the idea was not his. Some Reform supporters accused Coates of socialist interventions both in welfare and commerce. After an election in November 1928, when Reform lost its majority, Coates's government was toppled from office on a confidence vote by a resurgent Sir Joseph Ward, now seventy-three, who briefly enjoyed the support of the growing Labour Party. Ironically, Coates had originally entered parliament as a supporter of Ward. Coates led the opposition for three years until a threatened economic collapse forced him into coalition with Ward's successor, George Forbes. Coates served as minister of public works and employment, then, from 1933 to 1935, as minister of finance.

Coates displayed a degree of unorthodoxy, supporting retrenchment, devaluation of the New Zealand currency, then the establishment of a reserve bank. He promoted legislation to allow farmers to refinance loans at lower interest rates, so as to bring their overheads into line with reduced incomes. This incurred the wrath of those with money, and led to the intervention at the 1935 election of a third party, the Democrats, who split the conservative vote. Nothing, it seemed, could lift Coates's standing with those who had lost jobs or farms as a result of the slump. The national coalition was defeated in November 1935 by the Labour Party. It proceeded to introduce state housing, guaranteed prices for dairy farmers, and social security for all. Coates's readjustments to the economy and better overseas prices made Labour's reforms easier to afford.

In opposition after 1935, Coates was not chosen to lead the newly formed National Party (formed out of the Reform and United parties in May 1936). He spent more time with his family on the farm at Ruatuna. When war broke out he offered his services to the Labour government. On 16 July 1940 he joined Prime Minister Peter Fraser's war cabinet, becoming minister of armed forces and war co-ordination. Coates became a trusted confidant of Fraser's and a strong advocate of a non-partisan approach to New Zealand's wartime effort, first in the Middle East, Greece, and Crete, then, after December 1941, also in the Pacific theatre of war. Coates's reputation as a depression skinflint was gradually transformed for the better. He got credit towards the end of his life for being a solid, sensible, patriotic New Zealander who put country ahead of party. He has been seen since as a reformer who vigorously pushed the state into public works and banking, and with

his rudimentary family allowances of 1926, nudged it into the area of income maintenance. After a lifetime of energetic activity and constant smoking Coates died suddenly on 27 May 1943 in his office in the parliament buildings in Wellington. He was buried at Matakohe church cemetery on 1 June. Appropriately, perhaps, it was Fraser's Labourites, more than his own colleagues, who mourned his passing. He was survived by his wife and daughters. Ownership of his farm subsequently passed to the New Zealand Historic Places Trust.

Coates moved with the ebbs and flows of New Zealand politics for more than thirty years. A vigorous proponent of state activity, he refused to accept that he was a socialist. Reviled by workers because of his depression policies, he was none the less friends with politicians of all stripes. MICHAEL BASSETT

Sources M. Bassett, *Coates of Kaipara* (1995) · M. Bassett, 'Coates, Joseph Gordon (1878–1943)', *DNZB*, 3.104–7
Archives NL NZ, Turnbull L., MSS | NL NZ, Turnbull L., R. M. Campbell MSS · NL NZ, Turnbull L., Montague MSS, 77/249 · University of Otago, Dunedin, Hocken Library, W. Downie Stewart MSS | FILM BFI NFTVA, news footage | SOUND Radio New Zealand, Christchurch, archives
Likenesses L. Mitchell, photograph, c.1935, NPG [*see illus.*]
Wealth at death possibly nil, owing to low government valuation of Ruatuna in which he had interest at the time of death

Coates, Robert [known as Romeo Coates] (1772–1848), actor, was born in Antigua, the only survivor of the nine children of Alexander Coates (1734–1807), a merchant and sugar planter, and his wife, Dorothy. When he was about eight Coates was brought to England, where he received a liberal classical education. After returning to Antigua he first showed his taste for the theatre by taking part in amateur theatricals. His father's death in 1807 left him in possession of a vast fortune and a large collection of diamonds, and he settled at Bath in England as a man of fashion. He soon became well known by the first of his series of nicknames—Diamond Coates. In consequence of his ostentatious manner of living, which included dressing in furs and diamonds, and driving in a curricle in the shape of a kettledrum with a large, brazen cock on its bar and the motto 'Whilst I live I'll crow', he was also called Cock-a-doodle-doo Coates.

Coates's habit of declaiming Shakespeare over breakfast attracted attention, and the Theatre Royal, Bath, was taken for 9 February 1810 for a production of *Romeo and Juliet*, with Coates in the part of Romeo and professional actors in all the other roles. He was laughed from the stage by the end of the fourth act, so the audience was on this occasion spared his death scene, in which, mindful of his clothes and desirous of presenting his best aspect to the audience at all times, he would take out his handkerchief, dust the stage, place his hat on the outspread handkerchief, and arrange himself into a becoming attitude for death. Inevitably, he became known as Romeo Coates.

On 9 December 1811 Coates presented himself before a London audience for the first time, in the part of Lothario in Nicholas Rowe's *The Fair Penitent* at the Haymarket. Again the performance did not pass the fourth act, as the crowing of the audience would not be quieted even by the direct plea of Coates from the stage. Despite public ridicule and critical panning, Romeo Coates continued to perform on the stage (including appearances at the Haymarket and at Drury Lane) until 1816. He always retained his amateur status, and his performances were invariably in aid of charitable causes: his own preferred sobriquet was 'the Celebrated Philanthropic Amateur'. Indeed, he was sufficiently celebrated to be the subject of an impersonation by Charles Mathews in his Covent Garden *At Home* in February 1813. His pretensions were the victim of a cruel hoax in 1813, when Theodore Hook sent him an invitation which purported to be to attend a ball at Carlton House; Coates was turned away from the door, but his face was saved by the angry prince regent, who invited him to view the decorations the following day.

By 1816 the public had tired even of laughing at Coates, and theatre managers refused him the use of their premises. He eventually fell into financial difficulties and retired to Boulogne. There he met his future wife, Emma Anne, the daughter of Lieutenant William McDowell Robinson RN. Having reached an arrangement with his creditors he returned to England, married Emma Robinson on 6 September 1823, and lived soberly and respectably on the wreck of his fortune. On 15 February 1848 he attended Allcroft's grand annual concert at Drury Lane, and, after the performance, was crossing Russell Street, when he was crushed between a hansom cab and a private carriage. He died from the effects of his injuries on 21 February 1848 at his residence, 28 Montagu Square; the coroner recorded a verdict of manslaughter by person or persons unknown. Later in the same year his widow remarried, her second husband being Mark *Boyd.

NILANJANA BANERJI and K. D. REYNOLDS

Sources J. R. Robinson and H. H. Robinson, *The life of Robert Coates* (1891) • *The Era* (27 Feb 1848) • Adams, *Drama* • P. Hartnoll, ed., *The Oxford companion to the theatre* (1951); 2nd edn (1957); 3rd edn (1967) • P. Hartnoll, ed., *The concise Oxford companion to the theatre* (1972) • N. Bentley, ed., *Selections from the reminiscences of Captain Grenow* (1977) • J. Scotney, 'Romeo Coates, the celebrated amateur of fashion', *The British eccentric*, ed. H. Bridgeman and E. Drury (1975), 149–60 • R. K. Dent, *Old and new Birmingham: a history of the town and its people*, 3 vols. (1879–80) • Hall, *Dramatic ports.*, 1.260–61 • 'Memoir of Robert Coates, Esq.', *European Magazine and London Review*, 63 (1813), 179–83 • *GM*, 1st ser., 78 (1808), 1188 • *GM*, 2nd ser., 29 (1848), 557–8 • *Morning Herald* [London] (11 Dec 1811) • Genest, *Eng. stage*

Likenesses etching, pubd 1811, NPG • T. Blood, engraving (after miniature by Newton), repro. in *European Magazine*, 63 (March 1813), 178 and frontispiece • S. De Wilde, watercolour drawing, Garr. Club • portraits, repro. in Scotney, 'Romeo Coates', 150–51, 153, 155–6, 160 • theatrical prints, BM, NPG

Coates, Wells Wintemute (1895–1958), architect and industrial designer, was born on 17 December 1895 in Tokyo, Japan, the eldest of the six children of the Revd Dr Harper Havelock Coates (1865–1934), Canadian-born Methodist medical missionary and professor of philosophy and comparative religion at the Aoyama Theological College in Tokyo, and his Canadian wife, Agnes Sarah Wintemute (1864–1945), co-founder of one of the first missionary girls' schools in Japan. Wells Coates lived in Tokyo until he was eighteen in an austere but intellectually stimulating atmosphere of proselytizing Methodism. He was educated informally by his mother, a strong-minded woman who, when young, had trained as an architect, reputedly in the office of Louis Sullivan. An English friend of the family, G. E. L. Gauntlett, whose wife was Japanese, was Coates's intermittent tutor both in academic subjects and in such manual skills as brush drawing, paper-making and printing, boat-building, cooking, and the domestic rituals of serving food. Coates later referred to Gauntlett as 'the most versatile teacher I have ever known' (Cantacuzino, 11). His years in Japan nurtured his deep appreciation of everyday arts and the belief in reduction to essentials that was to be central to his architecture.

In 1913 Coates set out on a world cruise, with his father and Gauntlett, on the SS *Cleveland*. Already an avid and observant traveller, he kept a diary of the four months' voyage to China, Egypt, England, and finally New York, where he went up the Woolworth Building. He then enrolled at McGill University College in Vancouver, reading mechanical and structural engineering. His studies were interrupted by the First World War. He fought in the trenches in France and Belgium with the 2nd division of Canadian gunners before applying to train as a pilot with the Royal Naval Air Service. He made his maiden flight over Orléans and Blois on 18 July 1918, shortly before the armistice. His passion for the aeroplane was to be lifelong.

Coates returned to the former McGill University College, now reincorporated as part of the University of British Columbia, and took the degrees of BA in 1919 and BSc in engineering in 1922. He went to England for postgraduate studies, achieving a PhD (engineering) degree at London University in 1924 with a thesis entitled 'The gases of the diesel engine'. His training in engineering brought particular intellectual rigour to his work in architecture and industrial design.

As an architect Wells Coates was a late developer. His first London job was as a journalist on the *Daily Express*, whose proprietor, Lord Beaverbrook, favoured applications from fellow Canadians. The image of the hard-boiled journalist pounding out his story on the typewriter appealed to the raffish side in Coates. He became official science correspondent on the paper. In 1925, on a journalistic assignation in Paris, his interest was aroused in the work of Le Corbusier. Coates's London milieu was that of burgeoning modernism. He became a close friend of the architect Maxwell Fry, and in 1925, in Elsa Lanchester's nightclub the Cave of Harmony, he met Marion Grove (1906–1983), then a student at the London School of Economics. They married on 5 August 1927, and in 1930 their only child, Laura, was born.

Coates had enormous confidence in his abilities. With no specific architectural training he took on, in 1928, the interior design of a shop in Cambridge for Crysede Silks, and then, in 1929, the internal planning of Cresta Silks' factory in Welwyn Garden City for the modernist textile entrepreneur Tom Heron, father of the painter Patrick

Heron. This led to a succession of Cresta shops in glass, plywood, and steel, in which the flair and coherence of design detailing set new standards of retail design.

By 1930 Coates was involved in discussions that led to his best-known and most influential project, Lawn Road Flats in Hampstead. He was fortunate in finding like-minded clients. The concept of a large-scale block of service flats for modern professional people was developed in collaboration with Jack Pritchard, one of Britain's few committed patrons of modernist architecture and design, and his wife, Molly, a psychotherapist. A new company, Isokon, was formed to build the flats, the name being derived from the term isometric unit construction. Each Isokon flat was equipped by Coates with purpose-designed minimal furniture and fittings; meals and laundry were to be provided centrally. The reinforced concrete Lawn Road Flats, completed in 1934, were socially experimental. As Coates wrote in an article in *The Listener* (24 May 1933), 'We cannot burden ourselves with permanent tangible possessions, as well as with our real new possessions of freedom, travel and experience.' Coates's flats became a gathering point for the Hampstead avant-garde. The Bauhaus émigrés Marcel Breuer, Walter Gropius, and László Moholy-Nagy were early residents. Nikolaus Pevsner looked back on Lawn Road Flats as 'giant's work of the 1930s' (Pritchard, 98). Their place in the history of the modern movement in Britain is significant.

In the early 1930s Coates had been emerging as a leader of the British modernists. He was a founder member of two important groups which stood for the 'contemporary spirit': Unit One, an association of painters, sculptors, and architects, and the more specifically architectural MARS Group. Coates invented the title, which stood for Modern Architectural Research Group. MARS was the British branch of the Congrès Internationaux d'Architecture Moderne (CIAM) and Coates attended CIAM's famous Athens Charter meeting in July 1933, where he conferred with Le Corbusier and other leading European architects.

While Lawn Road Flats was under construction, Coates was commissioned to design the interior of the new BBC studios in Portland Place in association with Raymond McGrath and Serge Chermayeff. His BBC news studios and special effects studios show his high skills of logical planning and technical inventiveness. His fascination with new forms and new materials made him a superlative product designer. A twelve-year association with Ecko, manufacturers of wireless sets and electric fires, began in 1932 with the AD 65, Coates's circular wireless in Bakelite which became a design icon of its time.

The interior in which Coates's vision of 'new habits of life' was most apparent was the studio flat at 18 Yeoman's Row in London, where he lived from 1935 to 1955. The oriental influence is obvious in this practical, serene, pared-down living–working space with its large, low cushions and Japanese matting spread over rubber flooring, in which Coates himself, dressed in his kaftan, dispensing hospitality, was integral to the *mise-en-scène*.

Most of Coates's realized buildings in the 1930s were for luxury living. Embassy Court Flats (1935), an eleven-storey block on the sea front at Hove, was designed with verandas and sun terraces to give its wealthy residents maximum exposure to sea air. The more structurally interesting Palace Gate Flats in Kensington (1939) put into practice Coates's ideas for 'planning in section'. Hampden Nursery School in Holland Park (1936) was a 'total design' concept, in the vanguard of progressive educational ideas.

But Coates's main ambitions lay in revolutionary mass housing. He pursued ingenious schemes for prefabricated structures, beginning with the two-storey Sunspan House first shown at the Daily Mail Ideal Home Exhibition in Olympia in 1934. During the Second World War he was transferred from the RAF to advise the Aircraft Industries Research Organization on Housing (AIROH), evolving the sectional unit AIROH aluminium house. The government put 75,000 into production, one complete house being produced every ten minutes in four transportable sections. After the war Coates remained a consultant to AIROH, designing a two-decker, three-unit, three-bedroom house for an associated company, and investigating needs for low-cost housing among the poorest populations of South America, proposing a series of experimental aluminium dwellings. Neither of these designs was ever manufactured. Simultaneously with the AIROH house, Coates developed his most potentially revolutionary scheme for standardized, prefabricated, lightweight, mobile room units, interchangeable from one site to another. He described them as 'Rooms in a Garden' and 'Rooms in a Frame'. His failure to find financial backing was a bitter disappointment to him.

In 1944 Wells Coates was appointed OBE (military class) for services to the RAF, and was elected a royal designer for industry. One might have expected his career to burgeon in post-war Britain. But apart from the Telekinema for the Festival of Britain, none of his many projects reached fruition at this period. His greatly admired boat designs—the Wingsail Catamaran cruising yacht (1948) and the 'Fey Loong' yawl (1954)—were finally abandoned. In the early 1950s his visionary plan for a mixed-development Canadian new town at Iroquois on the St Lawrence River was rejected in favour of a cheaper scheme.

Coates's life was in some ways a tragic one. He suffered from depressions, which appear to have intensified after the macabre death, in 1926, of his friend Alfred Borgeaud, who fell from the train in British Columbia on which they were both travelling. Coates retrieved and buried the mangled remains. After the early failure of his marriage, ending in divorce in 1937, his emotional life was in perpetual disarray. He was bad at managing finance, and his arrogance and tactlessness antagonized all but the most forgiving of his clients. But Wells Coates's extraordinary talent has never been in doubt. He left Britain a legacy of heroic modernism, of which his one-time assistant Denys Lasdun was main heir.

In 1955 he departed for Harvard University, where, from 1955 to 1956, he was visiting professor of architecture and urban design. In 1956 he returned to Vancouver, where he worked on abortive projects for the redevelopment of the downtown city and a mass rapid transit system of his own invention, the Monospan Twin-Ride. A heart attack in 1957 was followed by another on 17 June 1958, when he died on Vancouver beach at English Bay after bathing and picnicking with friends. He was cremated a week later in Vancouver.   FIONA MacCARTHY

Sources S. Cantacuzino, *Wells Coates: a monograph* (1978) · L. Cohn, ed., *Wells Coates, architect and designer* (1979) · L. Cohn, *The door to a secret room: a portrait of Wells Coates* (1999) · J. M. Richards, 'Wells Coates, 1893–1958', *ArchR*, 124 (1958), 357–60 · D. Dean, *The thirties: recalling the English architectural scene* (1983) · J. Pritchard, *View from a long chair* (1984) · personal knowledge (2004) · private information (2004) [family]
Archives NRA, corresp. and papers, incl. diaries · priv. coll., MSS · RIBA BAL, sketches, notes, and corresp. · RSA, Royal Designers for Industry archives, MSS · Tate collection, papers relating to Unit One | U. Newcastle, Pritchard archive · University of East Anglia Library, corresp. and papers · University of East Anglia Library, Isokon collection
Likenesses J. Banting, pencil and watercolour drawing, 1925, repro. in Cantacuzino, *Wells Coates* · photograph, 1926, RSA · P. Heron, pencil drawing, 1928–9, repro. in M. Gooding, *Patrick Heron* (1994) · H. Coster, photographs, 1930–54, NPG · H. Coster, photograph, 1937, repro. in Cohn, *Door to a secret room*
Wealth at death £4303 17s. 0d.: administration with will, 3 Oct 1958, *CGPLA Eng. & Wales*

Coates, William Albert (1919–1993), laboratory technician and lecture demonstrator, was born on 7 November 1919 at 56 Pearson Street, Shoreditch, one of seven children of Francis Thomas Coates (*c*.1878–1950), a police constable, and his wife, Lilian Martha, *née* Fenniman (*b. c*.1886) who had worked in a perfumery. He attended Shoreditch grammar school and in 1934 was apprenticed with the Exchange Telegraph Company; during his apprenticeship he appears to have attended physics and electrical engineering classes at a London polytechnic.

During this time Coates was a private in the London rifle regiment of the Territorial Army and with the outbreak of war in September 1939 he was called up. He saw action in Norway and volunteered to join the Parachute regiment when it was formed in 1941, based initially at the regiment's training school in Manchester. Commissioned as lieutenant in 1943, he took part in the D-day operations of June 1944, when he helped to capture the Pegasus Bridge. He was wounded later in the Normandy campaign (some shrapnel in his wrist was never removed) and invalided back to England. While training on Salisbury Plain after recovery he broke his ankle and so missed the attack on Arnhem. However, Coates was sufficiently fit to take part in the crossing of the Rhine in March 1945, in the course of which he jumped from a burning DC-3 and was mentioned in dispatches. With the end of the war in Europe he trained on the Isle of Wight for the continuing campaign in the East, but this proved unnecessary. Promoted captain in January 1946, he was demobilized the following autumn. Coates was always proud of his regiment and took part in the events marking the fortieth anniversary of D-day; he took any slight to the regiment as a personal insult.

While recovering from his wrist wound Coates met Daphne June Holdaway (*b*. 1923/4), a planning assistant at the Hawker Siddeley aircraft factory in Kingston, at a dance in a large tent erected near the Kingston gate of Richmond Park to entertain wounded service personnel. They married in August 1945 but although the marriage lasted and they had two daughters it was not especially happy and Coates was heard to remark that it was one of the casualties of war.

With demobilization Coates had to find work. Initially he applied to join the police, but to his incredulity he was rejected because of the state of his teeth. Using his prewar electrical skills he worked first as a fitter at Mullard Engineering and in 1947 became a technician at Charing Cross Hospital medical school. In November the following year he was appointed as laboratory assistant in the Davy–Faraday Research Laboratory of the Royal Institution, where in various capacities he spent the remainder of his career. The laboratory at this stage was being rejuvenated under the energetic direction of Eric Rideal. Coates first worked with the crystallographer D. P. Riley on a very large X-ray machine and then with Uli Arndt. He survived the upheavals caused by Edward Andrade, Rideal's successor as director of the laboratory, during the early 1950s and then worked very effectively with Lawrence Bragg, the next director.

It was Bragg who realized Coates's enormous potential for developing clear experimental demonstrations of sometimes quite complex scientific ideas. In 1957 Coates was appointed senior experimental officer in the Royal Institution. This position meant that he was in charge of the 'prep room' and was responsible for ensuring the successful demonstration of experiments at lectures delivered in the Royal Institution and elsewhere. Early in his period of office Bragg had founded the schools' lectures; their immense popularity increased the work-load of the prep room, in addition to the normal programme of Friday evening discourses and the Christmas lectures (first televised in 1966 when Eric Laithwaite delivered them). During the next two decades Coates became a household figure, as each Christmas he demonstrated the experiments that the lecturers wanted with hardly a failure (if an experiment did not work of its own accord, Coates ensured it did) and by the provision of witty interjections. He would regale the tea room of the Royal Institution with a large number of anecdotes about near disasters during the recording of the lectures. The reputation that Coates gained earned him the Bragg medal of the Institute of Physics (1975) and appointment as MBE (1980). His television skills also brought him other work, for example with Raymond Baxter, various Open University programmes, and the BBC series on Marie Curie.

Two days after his sixty-fifth birthday Coates gave a Friday evening discourse on his years at the Royal Institution. Reversing the normal roles, he was assisted by George Porter (director since 1966), although Coates drew the line at allowing Porter to handle a red hot cannon ball. This lecture drew a standing ovation from the audience (a rare event in the Royal Institution) as recognition of Coates's role and also a mark of affection. He retired from full-time work aged sixty-seven in 1986 and was employed part-time for the following three years. In 1989 he became a consultant to the schools liaison team at Imperial College. By this time, however, he was fighting ill health. He had a serious drink problem, attended rehabilitation centres on two occasions, and from 1991 did not drink. He was also an inveterate smoker and was never more frustrated than when a lecturer would not permit smoking near him as happened when Walter Bodmer, director of the Imperial Cancer Research Fund, delivered the Christmas lectures in 1984. From the late 1980s Coates suffered from lung cancer and although he eventually died of pneumonia, cancer was the main cause. He died in Kingston Hospital on 7 October 1993 and, as a man with no religious belief at all, was cremated at Kingston crematorium on 14 October.

FRANK A. J. L. JAMES

Sources Royal Institution of Great Britain, London, personnel file · *The Times* (16 Oct 1993), 19 · W. A. Coates, 'Sir William Bragg and his lecturer's assistant', *Selections and reflections: the legacy of Sir Lawrence Bragg*, ed. D. C. Phillips and J. M. Thomas (1990), 147–9 · personal knowledge (2004) · b. cert. · m. cert. · d. cert. · private information (2004)
Archives Royal Institution of Great Britain, London, administrative papers | FILM Royal Institution of Great Britain, London, film and video archive | SOUND Royal Institution of Great Britain, London, sound archive
Likenesses T. Cuneo, group portrait (at a 1961 Christmas lecture, Royal Institution), Royal Institution of Great Britain, London · photographs, Royal Institution of Great Britain, London

Coates, Sir William Henry (1882–1963), civil servant and businessman, was born on 31 May 1882 at Runcorn, Cheshire, the second son of T. Mallalieu Coates, a member of the Royal College of Veterinary Surgeons, and his wife, Esther, *née* Tough. Coates, who was known to his close colleagues as Billie, was educated at Loughborough grammar school. He entered the civil service in 1900, and worked in the War Office (1900–04), the tax inspectorate (1904–19), and the Inland Revenue department (1919–25), the last as director of statistics and intelligence. On 9 September 1909 he married Claire Annie (1884/5–1963), daughter of Edward Ferris, a clerk, at Canterbury. They had two daughters. During his time in the civil service Coates undertook part-time studies in law and economics at the London School of Economics, obtaining the degrees of LLB in 1916 and BSc in 1922. He received a PhD in economics in 1929.

Coates's most important work was his involvement with the origins and growth of Imperial Chemical Industries (ICI). In 1925, at the invitation of a former civil servant, Sir Josiah Stamp, he joined Nobel Industries, the explosives manufacturers, succeeding Stamp as company secretary. Nobel Industries was one of the four major firms which combined to form ICI in 1926, and Coates was active in the detailed organization of the merger. He was the first treasurer of ICI, in 1927–9, and a director on the main board of the company from 1929 until his retirement in 1950; from 1945 he was deputy chairman. He was the acknowledged expert in ICI on finance, taxation, and economic theory, a skilled administrator and the director with overall responsibility for financial affairs. Although he had neither the authority nor the force of personality of the chairman, Harry McGowan, Coates frequently

acted for the company in areas requiring detailed command of argument.

He gave evidence on behalf of ICI in the capital reconstruction case of 1935, when the company went to law to seek a reduction in its nominal issued capital; he was said to have been more than a match for Sir William Jowitt, a leading KC at the common law bar. He had extensive, though often informal, dealings with government. During the Second World War he drew up plans for transport nationalization, and in 1941 was appointed financial adviser to the high commissioner in Canada. Coates was a member of ICI's small post-war committee, which was set up in 1942 to identify needs and strategies for the future. He was the company's representative in antitrust legislation in the USA immediately after the war, and on the Federation of British Industry. He served in a variety of public roles, chairing, for example, the committee on excess profits tax refunds, from 1946 to 1956. Coates retired from ICI in 1950 and was appointed to a number of commercial positions, including that of deputy chairman of the Westminster Bank. He also served on the University of London senate from 1929 to 1933. He was knighted in 1947.

Coates possessed a clear and analytical mind, and was prone to writing donnish papers on economic and financial matters for his fellow directors. His views were not, however, always acted on within ICI, apparently being insufficiently pragmatic for some of his colleagues. He was of austere appearance and manner, and his meticulous habits are said to have included clipping his bus tickets to his expenses claims. (At that time ICI directors were not supplied with company cars.) Coates, a keen golfer, retired from his home in London to Eastbourne, where he lived at the Burlington Hotel. He died at the Esperance Nursing Home, Hartington Place, Eastbourne, on 7 February 1963.

JAMES DONNELLY

Sources *The Times* (8 Feb 1963) · *The Times* (9 Feb 1963) · WW · WWW · *ICI Magazine* (1950), 327–8 · *ICI Magazine*, 41 (1963), 57 · W. J. Reader, *Imperial Chemical Industries, a history*, 2 vols. (1970–75) · private information (2004) · d. cert. · m. cert.
Archives ICI Central Archive, Millbank, London
Likenesses photograph, ICI Central Archive, Millbank, London
Wealth at death £119,427 1s. 5d.: probate, 8 April 1963, CGPLA Eng. & Wales

Coats, Thomas (1809–1883), thread manufacturer and benefactor, was born at Ferguslie, Paisley, Renfrewshire, on 18 October 1809, the fourth of ten sons of James Coats (d. 1833), one of the founders of the Paisley thread industry, and Catherine Mitchell. He trained as a textile engineer at Johnstone, near Paisley, and after his father's death became a partner in the family firm with his brothers James (the managing partner) and Peter (in charge of finances); Thomas was production manager (also dealing with technical matters and training). Expansion was continuous, capacity doubling in the 1840s, and again in the 1850s, stimulated by demand from America. After James died in 1845 Thomas became managing partner, and during his tenure the firm became the most important in the world market. By 1860 Coats employed 1100 workers and sold annually over £200,000 worth of thread, 80 per cent and Peter Coats were presented with their portraits, painted by Sir Daniel Macnee, president of the Royal Scottish Academy.

At the time of Coats's death the assets of the firm were estimated at over £2 million; it employed about 6000 people, of whom 3000 worked in Paisley; the value of his estate in the UK was £1,308,734 17s. 6d. Coats was a great production manager, with outstanding technical knowledge; his management style was gentle and firm; he recognized the significance of quality control and was quick to adopt new ideas and new technology. He was also chairman of Clan Line Association Steamers and a director of the British and African Steam Navigation Company of Glasgow. Survived by his wife, Coats died on 15 October 1883 at Paisley and was buried there. The town square was presented with a statue in his memory, but the most substantial gift was the Thomas Coats Memorial Church, funded by his family in 1894.   JOHN BUTT

Sources A. K. Cairncross and J. B. K. Hunter, 'The early growth of Messrs J. & T. Coats, 1830–1883', *Business History*, 29 (1987), 157–77 · M. Blair, *The Paisley thread* (1907) · *Glasgow Herald* (17 Oct 1883) · *Glasgow News* (17 Oct 1883) · *The Scotsman* (17 Oct 1883) · *Paisley and Renfrewshire Gazette* (20 Oct 1883) · *Paisley Daily Express* (22 Oct 1883) · *Paisley Daily Express* (25 Oct 1883) · J. B. K. Hunter, 'Coats, Thomas', *DSBB* · W. W. Knox, *Hanging by a thread* (1995) · *DNB*
Likenesses D. Macnee, oils, 1881, Paisley Art Gallery [*see illus.*] · drawing, repro. in E. Burns, *Coinage of Scotland* (1887), vol. 1 · statue, town square, Paisley
Wealth at death £1,308,734 17s. 6d.—UK estate: will, NA Scot., SC/58/45/4; inventory, SC/58/42/51

Thomas Coats (1809–1883), by Sir Daniel Macnee, 1881

in America, where Andrew Coats, a younger brother, lived. To offset the effects of competition and increasing tariffs in the 1860s and 1870s, Coats bought an established company, Conants of Pawtucket (Rhode Island), and greatly expanded its American mills.

Coats's marriage to Margaret, daughter of Thomas Glen, a miller, was a stable and happy relationship; they had six sons and five daughters. In 1872 Coats bought Ferguslie House to accommodate his large family. An active Baptist in Paisley, he made many gifts to Baptist churches. A Liberal in politics, he was chairman of the town's school board (1872–83) and gave £1000 to each of the four local schools; the site for Ferguslie School and the sum of £1000 were also his donations. He made a number of gifts to Paisley: the fountain gardens (1868) and the observatory (1882) were the most significant. He served as chairman of the Philosophical Institution (1862–4) and on the committee of management of the free public library and museum which his brother, Sir Peter, had given to the town in the late 1860s. Thomas Coats was an enthusiastic numismatist, and his vast Scottish coin collection was the basis for Edward Burns's *The coinage of Scotland illustrated from the cabinet of Thomas Coats esquire of Ferguslie and other collections* (1887). At a municipal banquet in November 1881 Thomas

Cobb, Gerald (1900–1986), antiquary and architectural historian, was born on 8 June 1900 at Ivy Lodge, Hamilton Road, Reading, one of four sons of Joseph William Cobb, a banker's clerk, and his wife, Florence Kate Arnold.

Cobb studied art in Reading at the University Extension College (later Reading University). Inspired by finding an album of photographic images by Francis Frith in a local bookshop, he began to collect prints and photographs from markets, junk shops, and the book barrows in Farringdon Road, London. Introduced to the College of Arms in 1919, he became a heraldic artist who created designs and devices throughout his life and still had a room there in 1982. He collected illustrations for subjects as diverse as botany and ornithology in addition to his first love, ecclesiology, and was both artistic and accurate in all his visual creations. The proximity of his office to the City churches and the threats to them by commercial development and war inspired a lifetime of study and led to his writing in 1942 what long remained the single best survey—*Old London Churches*, which had become *London City Churches* by its third edition in 1977.

Cobb described to the Ecclesiological Society how he imagined in the churches of Wren and others 'a unique series of Baroque steeples—wonderfully varied and beautiful—arising above the resurgent City, and the splendid fittings with which they were originally furnished' (*Ecclesiological Society Newsletter*, 1982). His ability to bring text and illustrations together and his analysis of the history of demolitions before and after the great fire of 1666—some seventy churches were removed before 1939—highlighted the need to define and care for what remained. By 1945 only eighteen remained undamaged. Cobb became a fellow of the Society of Antiquaries in 1951 and was master of the Art Workers' Guild in 1952.

During the Second World War Cobb was a fire warden at St Paul's Cathedral, where he helped to preserve the fabric while compiling his files for every major ecclesiastical structure (and many minor ones) in Great Britain. The long study required to grasp such complex artefacts and designs bred catholic collecting habits which included ephemera if no other image was available. His extraordinarily rich visual inventories were complemented by many subsidiary files for towns, for specific architectural themes, and for comparison with European precedents. The systematic albums and files were continually expanded during his lifetime and present parallel views of exteriors and interiors at consecutive periods. At a time when photographs could be bought for very small sums he steadily accumulated an extensive archive.

In the 1940s only Cobb and the eminent photographic historian Helmut Gernsheim were actively collecting photographs in a society which had apparently forgotten the historic value of this medium in favour of finer or more established arts. Cobb's knowledge of the minutiae of each exterior and interior feature meant that he could unerringly comprehend the physical evolution of the entire corpus of British ecclesiastical heritage, and make this manifest with an invaluable body of record. His knowledge and collection were used and recognized by Nikolaus Pevsner in compiling *The Buildings of England* series, and remain vital for any restoration research. In 1980 Cobb wrote *English Cathedrals: the Forgotten Centuries*, which illustrated the development of ten cathedrals with material selected from his own collection. He never married, and lived for most of his life in a house in Streatham utterly packed with his finds. Until just before his death, on 9 June 1986 at Tooting Bec Hospital, he was still sorting, comparing, and interpreting what can now be seen as an objective picture library without equal.

Virtually the whole of Cobb's massive collection was deposited with or subsequently purchased by the National Monuments Record and the Guildhall Library. It is valuable not only for purely ecclesiastical or architectural reasons but also for its extraordinary range of commercial and amateur photographs, which for most of the twentieth century were deemed of minor interest by national collections. Only during the blitz was it belatedly recognized that such records were a vital adjunct to the traditional fine art and architectural forms which were the staple records of the past.

A pioneer in using photographs as a key tool in architectural records, Cobb became the foremost national authority on post-medieval cathedral fabrics and London City churches. Yet he should be seen as an antiquary in the English tradition begun by John Aubrey, one who was motivated by a deep love of the buildings he documented. When lecturing at the Art Workers' Guild and elsewhere, he

always commented on the *beauty* of things, or on how hideous something was. His remarkably sharp eye for comparative detail, combined with his collecting capacity, meant that as an individual he accomplished a greater visual synthesis than most national institutions.

IAN LEITH

Sources G. Cobb, 'Reminiscences of an ecclesiologist', *Ecclesiological Society Newsletter*, 7 (1982) · *Ecclesiological Society Newsletter*, 20 (1986) · private information (2004) [N. Redman, executor of estate] · private information (2004) [G. Stamp] · *The Times* (23 June 1986) · *Antiquaries Journal*, 67 (1987), 487 · G. Cobb, *London City churches*, 3rd edn (1977) · G. Cobb, *English cathedrals: the forgotten centuries* (1980) · G. Stamp, *The changing metropolis: earliest photographs of London, 1839–1879* (1984) · b. cert. · d. cert. · will, High Court of Justice, London, Family Division

Archives Coll. Arms, Cobb bequest · English Heritage, Swindon, National Monuments Record, cuttings, engravings, and photographs, relating chiefly to ecclesiastical architecture · GL, collection · priv. coll., diaries and papers

Likenesses G. Stamp, photograph, c.1984, Glasgow School of Art, Mackintosh School of Architecture

Wealth at death £96,352: probate, 13 Oct 1986, *CGPLA Eng. & Wales*

Cobb, Gerard Francis (1838–1904), composer and writer, was born at Nettlestead, Kent, on 15 October 1838, the younger son of William Francis Cobb, rector of Nettlestead, and his wife, Mary Blackburn. Educated at Marlborough College from 1849 to 1857, he matriculated in 1857 from Trinity College, Cambridge, where he won a scholarship in 1860. He graduated BA in 1861 with first-class honours in both the classical and the moral science tripos. Having been interested in music from an early age, Cobb then went to Dresden for a short time to study music. He was elected a fellow of Trinity in 1863, took his MA the next year, and in 1869 was appointed junior bursar, a post which he held with some success for twenty-five years.

In sympathy with the Tractarian movement, Cobb at one time contemplated, but finally declined, holy orders. He actively advocated reunion between the Roman and Anglican churches, and in 1867 published an elaborate treatise, *The Kiss of Peace, or, England and Rome at one on the Doctrine of the Holy Eucharist*. Two short tracts, *A Few Words on Reunion* and *Separation not Schism*, appeared in 1869.

Cobb was president of the Cambridge University Musical Society from 1874 to 1883, and as chairman of the University Board of Musical Studies from 1877 to 1892 gave Sir George Macfarren valuable help in the reform of that faculty. He married Elizabeth Lucy, daughter of John Welchman Whateley of Birmingham, and widow of Stephen Parkinson, tutor of St John's College, Cambridge, in 1893, and resigned his offices at Trinity College (although he continued to reside in Cambridge) to devote himself mainly to musical composition and the encouragement of musical study, which had already engaged much of his interest. He was a prolific composer of songs, and wrote much church music, including a setting of Psalm 42 for the festival of the North Eastern Choir Association at Ripon Cathedral in 1892, seven services (including the morning, communion, and evening service in C major for men's voices, commissioned by St George's Chapel, Windsor), and anthems. His most ambitious work was *A*

Song of Trafalgar, a ballad for chorus and orchestra, op. 41 (1900), though his most popular compositions were settings of twenty of Rudyard Kipling's *Barrack-Room Ballads* (1892–7), which were published collectively in 1904, and the songs 'The Last Salute' (1897), 'Love among the Roses', and 'A Spanish Lament' (1886). He also published a piano quintet in C, op. 22 (1892), and a piano quartet (1898).

Cobb was an enthusiastic cyclist, and was the first president of the National Cyclists' Union (originally the Bicycle Union) in 1878 and president of the Cambridge University cycling club. For the International Health Exhibition in 1884 he contributed a chapter on cycling to the handbook on athletics. He was active in the municipal life of Cambridge, and addressed to the district council in 1878 a pamphlet on road paving, in which he urged improvement of the roads.

Cobb died at his home, The Hermitage, Newnham, Cambridgeshire, on 31 March 1904, and was cremated at Woking. He was survived by his wife.

[Anon.], *rev.* David J. Golby

Sources Brown & Stratton, *Brit. mus.* · *The Times* (1 April 1904) · *Musical News* (9 April 1904) · *MT*, 45 (1904), 309 · Venn, *Alum. Cant.*
Archives King's Cam., letters to Oscar Browning
Wealth at death £6526 9s. 5d.: probate, 30 May 1904, *CGPLA Eng. & Wales*

Cobb, James (1756–1818), playwright, entered in 1771 the secretary's office of the East India Company, in which he rose to the post of secretary (1814). He sent anonymously, for the benefit of Jane Pope (Drury Lane, 30 March 1773), an occasional prologue, which was recited with some slight alteration by Garrick, to whom it was submitted. He also produced at Drury Lane, on 5 April 1779, his first dramatic piece, *The Contract, or, Female Captain*, for Pope's benefit. All the popularity of the actors could not galvanize the play into life, but under the second title it was acted at the Haymarket on 26 August 1780. This was followed by many operas, farces, preludes, and comedies, most of which served, more or less, a temporary purpose, and are now forgotten.

Such interest as any of Cobb's pieces possess arises generally from association with actors or composers. In *The Humourist* (Drury Lane, 27 April 1785), which owed its production to the application of Burke to Sheridan, John Bannister made a great hit as Dabble, a dentist. This piece was burned in the fire at Drury Lane in 1809. Genest, not too good-naturedly, says that if the whole of Cobb's pieces—about twenty-four in number—had shared the same fate, 'the loss would not have been very great'. In *Strangers at Home*, an opera (Drury Lane, 8 December 1785, published in 1786), with music by Linley, Dorothy Jordan is said to have made her first appearance as a singer, and to have played her first original character. *Doctor and Apothecary*, a two-act musical farce (Drury Lane, 25 October 1788), introduced to the London stage Stephen Storace, from whose 'Singspiel'—*Der Doctor und der Apotheker*—performed at Vienna on 11 July 1786, music and plot were taken. *The Haunted Tower* (Drury Lane, 24 November 1789), also with music by Storace, served for the début in English opera of his sister, Anna Selina Storace. It was very successful, and

frequently revived. On 28 December 1799 at St Mary's, Portsea, Hampshire, Cobb married Mary Starfell of Fratton, Hampshire.

Of the twenty-four works published by Cobb, some others include: *The First Floor*, a farce (Drury Lane, 13 January 1787); *Love in the East*, a comic opera (Drury Lane, 25 February 1788); *Ramah Droog, or, Wine does Wonders*, another comic opera (Covent Garden, 12 November 1798); and *A House to be Sold*, a musical piece in two acts (Drury Lane, 17 November 1802), which is a clumsy expansion of *Maison à vendre*, a one-act opera by Duval, with music by D'Aleyrac, first played in 1800. Other works include *The Wife of Two Husbands*, a musical drama (Drury Lane, 1 November 1803), a translation of *La femme à deux maris* by Guilbert de Pixérécourt (Paris, 1803); *Cherokee*, an opera (Drury Lane, 20 December 1796); and *Paul and Virginia*, a musical drama (Covent Garden, 1 May 1800). In addition to the composers previously named, Joseph Mazzinghi, Michael Kelly, and Samuel Arnold also supplied music to Cobb's pieces. In William Gifford's *Maeviad* 'Cobbe' (*sic*) is mentioned in contemptuous terms. Cobb died in 1818.

Joseph Knight, *rev.* Rebecca Mills

Sources *IGI* · will, PRO, PROB 11/1606, sig. 307 · [J. Watkins and F. Shoberl], *A biographical dictionary of the living authors of Great Britain and Ireland* (1816) · W. C. Oulton, *The history of the theatres of London*, 1 (1796), 143, 155, 165; 2 (1796), 30, 55 · T. Gilliland, *The dramatic mirror, containing the history of the stage from the earliest period, to the present time*, 1 (1808), 293–4 · [D. Rivers], *Literary memoirs of living authors of Great Britain*, 1 (1798), 103 · D. E. Baker, *Biographia dramatica, or, A companion to the playhouse*, rev. I. Reed, new edn, rev. S. Jones, 1 (1812), 131–2 · Watt, *Bibl. Brit.*, 1.241–2
Archives BL, plays, receipts, and accounts with Drury Lane Theatre, Add. MSS 24856, 25912–25915, 25951, 25977, 25987, 26017–26018, 38728, 38730 · BL OIOC, corresp. relating to East India Co., home misc. series · Herts. ALS, letters to Sir Harford Jones Brydges
Likenesses T. Blood, stipple, pubd 1809, BM · Chapman, stipple (after S. Drummond), BM, NPG; repro. in *European Magazine* (1796) · G. Dance, pencil drawing, NPG · W. Ridley, stipple (after Birch), BM, NPG; repro. in *Monthly Mirror* (1803)
Wealth at death approx. £5000: will, PRO, PROB 11/1606, sig. 307

Cobb, John (*c.*1715–1778), cabinet-maker and upholsterer, is presumably the person of that name put as apprentice in 1729 to Tim Money, a Norwich upholsterer (Boyd MSS). The Norfolk connection is feasible on account of Cobb's bequeathing in 1778 the interest realized on £20,000 (after his second wife's lifetime receiving of the same) to William Cobb, the grandson of William Cobb at Wallingford in Norfolk (PRO, PROB 11/1044, fols. 257r–258r). As apprentices were normally put to a trade at the age of fourteen, *c.*1715 seems a likely year for his birth, although nothing precise is known of his parentage or birth. Having come out of his apprenticeship about 1736 he may have continued to work for his master as a journeyman (that is, one who works in a business he does not own). Some chance then brought him in contact with William *Vile (1714/15–1767), his partner for the next fourteen years, until Vile's retirement in 1764.

The partnership between Cobb and Vile was set up in London in 1751, in the New Street ward of St Martin's-in-the-

Fields, and was, seemingly, capitalized by the successful cabinet-maker William Hallett (1707–1781). The rate books for 1751 show 'William Vile & Co.' with their patron, William Hallett, occupying the next-door premises (Westminster city archives, MS, fol. 527). By 1755 Hallett's name has been excised in favour of John Cobb. The bank accounts of Vile and Cobb show monthly payments to Hallett (who used the same bank), particularly in the years 1758–63 (Royal Bank of Scotland, Drummonds branch, London). On 31 March 1755 Cobb consolidated his position (although affection probably played a part) by marrying Sukey, daughter of Giles Grendey (1693–1780), a successful London furniture maker with an extensive export business. The newspaper account of the marriage described Cobb as 'an eminent Timber Merchant' (*General Evening Post*). Cobb, as his will makes clear, married twice; his second wife was called Mary. The date of Sukey's death, and the date of the second marriage, are unknown. There seems little reason for Cobb's adoption of a singularly haughty character, other than the fact that with his partner he had been a cabinet-maker to the crown since 1761 (PRO, LC 5/57). J. T. Smith records how, presumably in the 1760s, Cobb in full dress 'of the most superb and costly kind strutted through his workshops giving orders to his men' (Smith, 2.243). Smith also relates how George III placed Cobb's name second to that of Vile through annoyance at his pomposity and imperious delegation of duties to his foreman, John Jenkins. Cobb was in royal service from 1761 to 1764, and after the retirement of his partner turned to the provision of superb marquetry furniture in the neo-classical style.

After Vile's retirement Cobb continued in business for a further fourteen years: the full range of his commissions was listed by G. Beard and C. Gilbert in their *Dictionary of English Furniture Makers* (1986). Mindful of the upsurge of styling in the neo-classical taste, introduced from Italy, and particularly by the architect Robert Adam (1728–1792), Cobb worked in woods other than mahogany. In particular he used exotic veneers and floral marquetry. There was probably an urgent need to do so to counteract competition from other successful cabinet-makers working in this 'new' mode, such as Mayhew and Ince (active from 1758 to the end of the century), and by the insistence of patrons wanting such pieces. An early example of this styling came in 1765 when Cobb supplied Robert Adam and his patron, George William, sixth earl of Coventry, with furniture including '8 Mahogany Armd Chairs' at a cost of £30. They are after a drawing by Adam (Sir John Soane's Museum, London), and are thus an early essay in the revived 'antique' taste. The chairs are still in the possession of the estate trustees. Cobb continued to provide a wide range of furniture although he made no provisions for funerals—for many cabinet-makers undertaking was a profitable side-line. Seminal to the late work, however, is a series of commodes of superb quality which incorporate the elaborate veneering of curved surfaces and floral marquetry. A documented example is the inlaid commode and two satinwood vase stands supplied in 1772–4 to Paul Methuen (priv. coll.). The commode was charged in 1772 at

£63 5*s*. 3*d*.; the vase stands were supplied two years later at an unknown cost (Methuen archive, MS 1742, 8112, Wilts. & Swindon RO). The side panels incorporate Methuen's arms with those of his wife, Catherine Cobb (seemingly no relative to the maker), and the sinuous ormolu corner mounts enhance the form. They are among Cobb's finest achievements.

Cobb's work after Vile's retirement gave him an increasing fortune. At his death in London, which occurred between 26 and 31 August 1778, he had a dwelling house in St Martin's Lane, a house at Highgate, a chariot, horses, and the sum of £20,000 to 'support the name of Cobb' (PRO, PROB 11/1044, fols. 257*r*–258*r*). A notice in 1783 recorded that he was 'formerly partner with the late Mr Hallett of Cannons', a fact well attested by the earlier financial arrangement (*GM*). With his partner, William Vile, John Cobb was one of the most accomplished furniture makers active in the third quarter of the eighteenth century.   GEOFFREY BEARD

Sources P. Boyd, list of masters and apprentices, 18th century, GL, Perceval Boyd MSS · will, PRO, PROB 11/1044, sig. 314 · rate books, 1751, City Westm. AC, fol. 527 · bank accounts of Vile and Cobb, Royal Bank of Scotland, London, Drummonds branch · *General Evening Post* (1 April 1755) · J. T. Smith, *Nollekens and his times*, 2nd edn, 2 (1829), 243 · G. Beard and C. Gilbert, eds., *Dictionary of English furniture makers, 1660–1840* (1986) · A. Coleridge, 'English furniture supplied for Croome Court', *Apollo*, 151 (Feb 2000), 4–19 · L. Wood, *Catalogue of commodes: Lady Lever Art Gallery* (1994) · P. Methuen, daybook, Wilts. & Swindon RO, Methuen papers, MS 1742, 8112 · *GM*, 1st ser., 53 (1783), 692

Archives Wilts. & Swindon RO, archive of the Methuen family of Corsham, Wiltshire, ref. 1742, incl. daybook of Paul Methuen, MS 8112

Wealth at death £20,000; house in St Martin's Lane, London; house in Highgate, London: will, 1778, PRO, PROB 11/1044, sig. 314

Cobb, John Rhodes (1899–1952), holder of land and water speed records, was born at Hackbridge, Surrey, on 2 December 1899, the youngest son in the family of three sons and two daughters of Rhodes Cobb, a fur broker, and his wife, Florence Goad. Educated at Eton College and at Trinity Hall, Cambridge, he joined his father's business. Before the Second World War he was commissioned by the Soviet government to sell the annual Russian pelt stock. In addition to his fur business he was a joint managing director of Anning, Chadwick, and Kiver Ltd, and vice-chairman of the Falkland Islands Company Ltd.

From an early age Cobb loved to race on the Brooklands track which was near his family's home at Esher, and he became known as a courageous and skilled driver. He competed in his first race at the Brooklands Whitsun meeting of 1925. His early successes took place in the mid-1920s, driving a big 10 litre Fiat which had been made before the First World War. Nevertheless, it was still capable of lap speeds in excess of 110 miles per hour. Subsequently he raced an eight cylinder Leyland-Thomas car and then moved into the front rank of racing motorists with a number of victories driving a 10.5 litre Delage. Driving the Delage he broke the outer circuit lap record at Brooklands in 1929 with an average of 132 m.p.h.

By the beginning of the 1930s Cobb maintained Brooklands lap speeds of 135 m.p.h. To the design of Reid Railton, Thompson and Taylor manufactured for him the legendary Napier-Railton car, which became the fastest machine ever to race on the Brooklands circuit. Cobb's premier Brooklands record was a lap speed of 143.44 m.p.h., achieved in October 1935, a record that remained unbeaten. In that year he drove the Napier-Railton for the first time on the Bonneville Salt Flats, Utah. On this American visit he set new world land speed endurance records: for one hour at 152.7 m.p.h. and for twenty-four hours at 137.4 m.p.h. for the world's 24-hour record. Later in 1935 he won the 500 mile race at Brooklands, a feat which he repeated in 1937.

Cobb then set out to beat the world's land speed record, of 345 m.p.h., set at Bonneville by George Eyston in August 1938, and commissioned an entirely new car, built to an ingenious design by Railton. Once again the location was the Bonneville Salt Flats where, on 15 September 1938, Cobb set a new record of 350.2 m.p.h. On the following day, however, his rival Eyston exceeded this with a speed of 357.5. A year later, on 23 August 1939, Cobb returned and increased the world record to 369.74 m.p.h. The Second World War, during which Cobb served in the Royal Air Force and Air Transport Auxiliary, interrupted further attempts on the record. On 16 September 1947 Cobb made his final assault on the world land speed record at Bonneville, again driving the Railton. While his two-run average speed was 394.2 m.p.h., he reached 403.135 m.p.h. on one run, thus becoming the first person to exceed 400 m.p.h. His record, the last to be gained in a piston-engined vehicle, stood for sixteen years. In recognition of this feat he was awarded the 1947 Segrave trophy.

Other awards were gold stars from the British Racing Drivers' Club in 1935 and 1937, though he received no official honours. Throughout his racing career he was encouraged by his mother, with whom he lived until his marriage, in 1947, to Elizabeth Mitchell-Smith (d. 1948); following the death of his first wife he married Vera Henderson in 1950. There were no children of either marriage.

In September 1952 Cobb took on a new challenge in an unusual setting. He set out to break the world's water speed record at Loch Ness, Inverness-shire, driving a motor boat powered by a turbo-jet engine. Called *Crusader*, the boat was 31 feet long, weighed 3 tons, and was blasted through the water by a de Havilland Ghost engine, similar to those fitted to the pioneering British Comet airliner. The hull and sponsons were made of birch plywood reinforced with aluminium alloy. The boat, with its torpedo shell and ski-like floats, looked akin to a science fiction creation. Cobb said, 'It's like driving a London omnibus without tyres on' (Emery and Greenberg, 172). On a first run on Loch Ness he exceeded 200 m.p.h. On his second run, on 29 September 1952, when experts gauged his speed to be in excess of 240 m.p.h., *Crusader* took off, flipped over, and disintegrated. Cobb was killed instantly. His achievements, in terms of world or near world records on land and water, place him as one of the founding fathers of what are now classified as 'extreme' sports.

SCOTT A. G. M. CRAWFORD

Sources S. C. H. Davis, *The John Cobb story* (1953) · *DNB* · *The Times* (30 Sept 1952), 6, 8, 12 · *New York Times* (30 Sept 1952), 1, 6 · G. N. Georgano, ed., *The encyclopaedia of motor sport* (1971) · C. Posthumus, *Land speed record* (1971) · Diagram group, *Sports comparisons* (1982), 77 · D. Emery and S. Greenberg, *The world sports record atlas* (1986), 137; 172 · R. Hoffer, 'The great race', *Sports Illustrated*, 87/13 (29 Sept 1997), 60–66 · *CGPLA Eng. & Wales* (1952)

John Rhodes Cobb (1899–1952), by Harold Tomlin, 1934

Cobb, Richard Charles (1917–1996), historian and essayist, was born on 20 May 1917 at Hurstlyn, Fourth Avenue, Frinton-on-Sea, Essex, the only son of Francis Hills Cobb, a civil engineer in the Sudan civil service, and his wife, Dora, *née* Swindale. He was educated at Shrewsbury School and went to Merton College, Oxford, in 1935 with a postmastership to read modern history. He graduated in 1938 with a second-class degree. He immediately went to Paris to do research, but returned to England in September 1939 at the outbreak of war.

After failing the medical test, Cobb went into the Air Ministry in a civilian post until 1941. His ambition, however, was to work either in France or with the Free French. Unsuccessful in his attempts to achieve this, he became somewhat agitated and was only rescued from difficulty by the intervention of his mother through a military acquaintance. He was sent to work as liaison with the Czechoslovak independent brigade group, which he always saw as a compromise between himself and the government. Here he helped to prepare the assassination of Heydrich, the *gauleiter* of Bohemia. He was later attached to the Polish military authorities. Between 1944 and 1946 he served as an interpreter in France and Belgium.

Demobilized in France, he remained there until 1955 doing research in French national and local archives. He worked under Georges Lefebvre, the professor of the history of the French Revolution at the Sorbonne, with whom he began a monumental doctoral thesis, *Les armées révolutionnaires: instrument de la Terreur dans les départements, avril 1793–floréal an II* (2 vols., 1961–3). He did not in fact gain the doctoral degree in France since he did not write the *thèse supplémentaire* which was then a requirement.

Cobb's abiding passion for France and for the radical phase of the French Revolution was ignited during the year he spent in Paris, staying with a French family near the Porte Saint-Martin and working on a never-completed Oxford thesis on the Hébertiste faction. During his postwar years he became completely assimilated into the world of French, mostly communist historians in this field. Although not the only foreigner in the group, he was certainly the dominant one, both by the length of his stay and by the degree of his integration. Possessed of perfect French (*Les armées révolutionnaires* was written directly in French), he was sustained through years of real penury by a mixture of small jobs and free food brought to him by a network which was based on politically tinged camaraderie, admiration for his real gifts, and affection.

During these years, Cobb married for the first time, apparently the daughter of an official in the French national railways. He remained remarkably reticent about this marriage throughout his life and there is almost no available documentation. A son was born about

Richard Charles Cobb (1917–1996), by Deborah Elliott, 1984

1951 and it is likely that the marriage occurred near that time; it was dissolved in 1955. His second marriage took place at Tonbridge, Kent, on 6 March 1963 to Margaret Goggin, daughter of James Goggin, a quantity surveyor. She was then a student at Leeds University. Three sons and a daughter were born to the marriage, which lasted until his death.

Cobb had returned to the United Kingdom in 1955 in order to take up a lectureship at the University of Wales, Aberystwyth. By his own account, Georges Lefebvre, in receipt of a letter from the head of department there seeking advice on filling a post in the field, dispatched Cobb with words to the effect that he had been too long in France and needed a proper job. It is evident that the move to Aberystwyth was an enormous rupture for him. He later wrote some compelling sketches of the sense of isolation and claustrophobia in a small university town, where the most comforting event was a weekly walk to the railway station in order to check that it was still there and escape thus possible.

He spent the year 1959–60 as a Simon senior research fellow at Manchester University and moved to a lectureship at Leeds University in 1961. In 1962 he became a tutorial fellow at Balliol College, Oxford. It was during his ten years there that his historical writing developed a broad sweep and compelling maturity. At the same time his idiosyncratic character, unrestrained opinions, strong likes and dislikes, and fondness for liberal, noisy entertainment gave him something of a legendary reputation among students and colleagues. Many undergraduates and postgraduates found him inspirational; many people were attracted to him; few could be indifferent.

He was elected fellow of the British Academy in 1967. In 1969 he was appointed reader in French Revolutionary history at Oxford and then, in 1972, he took the chair of modern history, which was attached to a fellowship of Worcester College. He retired in 1984. He won the Wolfson prize for history in 1979. He was an honorary fellow of Balliol College (1977) and of Merton College (1980) and held honorary doctorates from Essex, Leeds, and Cambridge (1981, 1988, 1989). He was awarded the CBE in 1978 and created officier de l'ordre national du mérite (1977) and chevalier of the Légion d'honneur (1986). He died at his home, 18 Wintenbourne Road, Abingdon, on 15 January 1996.

The quality and the influence of Cobb's historical writing—principally *Les armées révolutionnaires* (1961–3), *Terreur et subsistances* (1965), *The Police and the People* (1970), *Reactions to the French Revolution* (1972), *Paris and its Provinces* (1975), *Death in Paris* (1978)—resided, first, in his exceptional and intimate knowledge of the French archives. The range of his experience in all types of national and local collections surpassed that of any contemporary French historian, let alone any foreigner. This was largely acquired during his long years in France and refreshed by visits at every opportunity subsequently. There was a long tradition of local erudition by local worthies in France; there had also been substantial scholarly monographs devoted to a department or particular region. It was Cobb who first brought this local perspective to underpin a broad sweep of national history across France.

The theme of Cobb's writing was popular history. He belonged to the group of historians at the time in Europe who were concerned with 'history from the bottom up'. However, he was clearly distinguished from them. He was a historian of the people by temperament and not by ideology. Indeed, it is extremely difficult to discover any theoretical basis to any of his writing. He was simply not interested in the debates about the social interpretation of the French Revolution or mentalities or political culture that divided historians in the 1960s, 1970s, and 1980s.

What shines through Cobb's historical writing is an intense intimacy with the individuals who form his subject matter. He had no particular historical method other than to listen to the voices of people through a great quantity of manuscript records, often police reports and interrogations, that he read assiduously. He had an exceptional empathy with the poor and the marginal in society; he had an exceptional ability to understand and capture their angers, their derision, their private concerns and rhythms of life, their personal joys and tragedies. Unlike others writing on this subject, he understood that the Revolution was not necessarily the most important event in their lives. Finally, he wrote with strong directness, full of the voices of his subjects who were given a vivid physical context. Cobb had a strong and detailed sense of place, a gift for atmosphere, and a talent for prose.

Cobb's greatest influence was upon a generation of postgraduate students from the United Kingdom and North America at Oxford. They learned the value of the provincial history of the period, the importance of large-scale reading of manuscript archives at all levels, and the necessity of a real enthusiasm for France. This was a new direction in the historiography of the French Revolution. It cannot be said that Cobb created a school of history. His

work was basically unrepeatable, given life by his own intimate relationship with it, too devoid of engagement with matters of interpretation.

Cobb's most formal scholarly work (*Les armées révolutionnaires*) was devoted to the most insubordinate and temporary of all the institutions of the French Revolution (the popular political armies of the interior). His work moved increasingly towards a concern with marginal individuals or groups and those outside society. Such figures are the least documented, only momentarily visible. This must have contributed to an apparently growing frustration with the contradiction between the essential unknowability of individuals in the past and his desire for intimacy with his subjects. These preoccupations are evident and unresolved in his last monograph, based on the inventories of Paris suicides in the 1790s (*Death in Paris*).

It is perhaps for this reason that Cobb turned to writing autobiographical essays and memoirs—principally *Still Life* (1983), *A Classical Education* (1985), *Something to Hold on to* (1988), and *The End of the Line* (1997). This genre allowed him to display to a high level all his talents for detail, sense of place and atmosphere, his quick sense of the absurd, and his capacity for compassion allied to derision in the face of pomposity and self-importance. These books brought him a considerable general readership. Certainly, *Still Life* is an enduring classic among middle-class memoirs.

Much of the power of Cobb's writing, whether historical or other, derived from the force and complexity of his personality. It is impossible to situate him in any political terms. He belonged essentially to the long tradition of English radical individualism. Temperamentally, he was insubordinate and had a quick dislike of authority, particularly that assumed with rank or office. Yet, at the same time, he had great respect for institutions, especially venerable ones, and enthusiasm for membership of them. He had also a liking for badges of rank. He delighted in the Légion d'honneur and was always disappointed when someone else wearing the distinctive red ribbon in the lapel did not give a sign of recognition of their mutual distinction.

Indeed, Cobb saw the world very much in terms of persons, not of hierarchies or social bonds or ideas. He was curious, inquisitive, and quick to judge. Dismissive of cant, pomposity, and moralizing (he was deeply antagonistic to Robespierre—and, hence, to dogs which Robespierre liked), he gave himself to numerous, diverse, and enduring friendships. His correspondence with friends was voluminous and a direct, vivid outpouring of opinions and narratives of the moment. He prized fidelity in friendship. Yet, he could on occasion rupture relationships irrevocably in one burst of passionate anger. Cobb lived an intensely sociable life, though it was never allowed to interfere with regular daily habits of research and writing. He loved rather schoolboy pranks and the company of students, as well as of like-minded colleagues. Lavish and prolonged evenings in common room and pub echoed similar releases of high spirits in Paris.

The French saw Cobb as a Jacobin. However, his very

English individualism did not translate into such institutionalized radicalism. He was not much concerned with the approval or disapproval of anyone. Indeed, this tension of cultures ran beneath his apparently complete absorption into France. France provided him with a second identity, as the title of one of his books put it. Revealed first perhaps by his choice of long-distance running as a means of securing a secret life at boarding-school, Cobb needed a separate world to step into. History certainly provided this for him. He lived with an imaginative landscape activated by memories, people, situations, history, and even place names. It was not the least of his complexities that such a sociable temperament should have co-existed with such a private other world of imagination.

COLIN LUCAS

Sources R. Cobb, *Still life: sketches from a Tunbridge Wells childhood* (1983) · R. Cobb, *A classical education* (1985) · R. Cobb, *Something to hold on to: autobiographical sketches* (1988) · R. Cobb, *The end of the line: a memoir* (1997) · *The Times* (17 Jan 1996) · *The Independent* (16 Jan 1996) · J. Jones and S. Viney, eds., *The Balliol College register, 1930–1980*, 5th edn (privately printed, Oxford, 1983?) · *WWW* · b. cert. · d. cert.
Likenesses D. Elliott, photograph, 1984, NPG [*see illus.*]
Wealth at death under £145,000: probate, 23 Feb 1996, *CGPLA Eng. & Wales*

Cobb, Samuel (*bap.* 1675, *d.* 1713), schoolmaster and author, was baptized on 17 October 1675. His father, Samuel Cobb, a cooper and citizen of London, died before April 1683, when the former lord mayor John Moore sponsored the boy, then of St Andrew's, Holborn, for admission to Christ's Hospital, London. Among the 'blue-coat boys' Cobb advanced to Grecian. Upon his discharge on 27 February 1694 Christ's Hospital sent him and one classmate for advanced education, providing £12 toward his BA (1698) and £15 toward his MA (1702) at Trinity College, Cambridge. Cobb gave his tripos speech on 19 February 1702; on 11 March he became 'under grammar master' of Christ's Hospital. He was granted residence in 1704, and although school records report him 'often disguised with strong liquors', he kept his place until his death.

Cobb's earliest experience with the London literary establishment was unpropitious. While still a pupil at Christ's Hospital he wrote *A Pindarique Ode … [in] Memory of … Queen Mary* (1694), only to see it printed as if 'written by J. D. Gent'. In his thoroughly entitled *Bersaba, or, The love of David … written by Samuel Cobb, student of Trinity College, Cambridge* (1695), he protested that 'the Ode was snatch'd from me … abruptly and unfortunately'. Readers acquiesced: 'J. D. Gent proves only Blue-Coat C[obb]' (H. MacDonald, *John Dryden: a Bibliography*, 1939, 183). Continuing to aim appropriate sentiments in the proper direction, without approaching Dryden's success, Cobb churned out *Pax redux … on the Return of His Majesty and the Happy Conclusion of the Peace* (1697), *The Portugal Expedition* (1704), *Honour Retriev'd … [re] Victories Obtain'd over the French and Bavarians* (1705), and the like. The same year that Dryden died, however, Cobb published a work with implications beyond the occasions of his truncated lifetime. *Poetae Britannici: a Poem, Satyrical and Panegyrical* (1700) surveys English literary history, emphasizing 'simplicity of style and beauty of content' in ways that anticipate mid-century developments of visual and sublime effects in poetry (E. Rothstein, *Restoration and Eighteenth-Century Poetry*, 1981, 183).

Cobb's work gained further respect with the publication in 1780–82 of John Nichols's *Select Collection of Poems*, which included seven poems by Cobb (7.238–66). Nichols further acclaimed *The female reign: an ode, alluding to Horace, B. 4. od. 14 … attempted in the style of Pindar, occasion'd by the wonderful successes of the arms of her majesty and her allies* (1709), recommending that Robert Dodsley republish it as adapted by Isaac Watts (*GM*, 23, 1753, 282–5) rather than as admired by Joseph Warton (Nichols, *Lit. anecdotes*, 1812–16, 6.170; R. Dodsley, ed., *A Collection of Poems*, 4 vols., 1748–9, 1.69–81).

Despite scholars' appreciation for that ode's Greek-derived verse form and Roman theme applied to current events, the book-buying public preferred two less scholarly items. In 1712 Cobb published both his modernization of Chaucer's *Miller's Tale* and his translation of Edward Holdsworth's *Muscipula* (1708), a Latin mock-heroic that inspired frequent reprints and ten other translations. Cobb's *Mouse-Trap* was separately published five times, and included in John Torbuck's *Collection of Welsh Travels* (1738). The only rival to Cobb's *Miller's Tale* was never reprinted, whereas Cobb's version reappeared at least eleven times in miscellanies and collections including *The Canterbury Tales of Chaucer, Modernis'd by Several Hands* (ed. G. Ogle, 3 vols., 1741). Only the equally bawdy *Reeve's Tale* modernized by Thomas Betterton (pseudonym for Alexander Pope) rivalled Cobb's *Miller's Tale* in frequency of republication. Thus, because few readers before 1775 overcame the barriers of Middle English editions, Cobb shares responsibility for the prevalent eighteenth-century impression of Chaucer as 'a comic poet chiefly remarkable for the scurrility of his verses' (C. Spurgeon, *Five Hundred Years of Chaucer Criticism*, 3 vols., 1925, 1.liii).

An anecdote and two published letters allow glimpses of Cobb's personality. His Cambridge professor Richard Bentley 'found his criticisms upon a Greek exercise, which Cobb had presented, refuted one after another by Pindar's authority, [whereupon Bentley] cried out at last, "Pindar was a bold fellow, but thou art an impudent one"' (S. Johnson, *Lives of the English Poets*, ed. G. B. Hill, 3 vols., 1905, 3.227). Audacity would seem to echo in Cobb's *Discourse on Criticism and the Liberty of Writing*, prefacing *Poems on Several Occasions* (1707) and addressed to his former classmate Richard Carter at his home in Barbados. With enthusiasm Cobb writes of 'secret Springs of the Soul, and those sudden Emotions, which excite illustrious Men, to act and speak out of the Common Road', and with cynicism of a war that has produced only 'What battles generally do; bad Poets, and worse Criticks'. Rushing for the mail ship, Cobb closes by promising Carter 'the rest on the Pindaric Style'. He published the rest with *The Female Reign*, addressing 'a gentleman in the University' and shrugging, 'Whether you will call the following lines a Pindaric ode, or irregular stanzas, gives me no disturbance'. Such comments accord with contemporary appreciation for Cobb's 'sound Learning, ready Wit, and good Humour', so described by Giles Jacob, who singles out *Clavis Virgiliana, or, New Observations upon the Works of Virgil* (1714).

Cobb's other posthumous publication likewise documents esteem both for his learning and wit. *News from both Universities* (1714) preserves his 1702 tripos speech, plus a Latin mock-heroic with English translation dated four months after his death. Perhaps its author was his friend from Barbados, for a Richard Carter was writing life insurance pamphlets in London between 1711 and 1715. Cobb, though, had many literary contacts. With John Ozell, Nicholas Rowe, and others he collaborated to translate from Greek *The Works of Lucian* (4 vols., 1710–11); from French *Boileau's Lutrin* (1708), and *The Works of Monsieur Boileau* (3 vols., 1711–13); and from seventeenth-century Latin the *Callipaedia* (1710) of Claude Quillet, whose writings on 'Eudoxus' and 'Gassendus' Cobb alone translated (both 1712).

School responsibilities motivated other works. For Christ's Hospital Cobb translated *A Synopsis of Algebra* (1709) from the Latin of Joannes Alexander of Bern. He composed lyrics to John Barrett's music for every extant Easter anthem during his years in residence. He also wrote 'The Oak and the Briar' published in *English Gratitude, or, The Whig Miscellany* (1713), and translated Robert Freind's Latin epitaph for the Westminster Abbey monument to Philip Carteret (J. Crull, *Antiquities of St Peter's*, 3rd edn, 2 vols., 1722, 2.101–2).

Cobb died, unmarried, at Christ's Hospital on 18 September 1713, and was buried in the cloisters.

BETSY BOWDEN

Sources *DNB* · [G. Jacob], *The poetical register, or, The lives and characters of all the English poets*, 2 (1723), 36 · D. F. Foxon, ed., *English verse, 1701–1750: a catalogue of separately printed poems with notes on contemporary collected editions*, 2 vols. (1975) · Venn, *Alum. Cant.* · *Samuel Cobb's Discourse on criticism*, ed. L. I. Bredvold (1946) · *National union catalog, pre-1956 imprints*, Library of Congress · *British Museum general catalogue of printed books … to 1955*, BM, 263 vols. (1959–66) · W. Trollope, *A history of the royal foundation of Christ's Hospital* (1834), 298, 334 · B. Bowden, ed., *Eighteenth-century modernizations from the 'Canterbury tales'* (1991) · S. Jeans, 'The Easter psalms of Christ's Hospital', *Proceedings of the Royal Musical Association*, 88 (1961–2), 45–60

Cobb, Thomas (*fl.* **1728–1736**). *See under* Dicey family (*per. c.*1710–*c.*1800).

Cobban, Alfred Bert Carter (1901–1968), historian, was born on 24 May 1901 at 40 Oakley Crescent, Chelsea, London, the only son of Robert Cobban, a furniture salesman employed by the Army and Navy Stores, and his wife, Edith Frances, *née* Carter. A quiet, studious boy, he won scholarships to Latymer Upper School, London, and then to Gonville and Caius College, Cambridge (1919). After gaining a first in both parts of the modern history tripos (1922) he became a graduate student and research fellow there until 1926, when, having completed his doctorate, he took up a lectureship in history at King's College, Newcastle. He married on 23 July 1929 (Kathleen) Muriel (1906/7–1988/9), daughter of James Hartshorn, a schoolmaster. She was a woman of immense energy and geniality who ran all aspects of his life outside the academic

allowing him to give a lifelong commitment to teaching and writing. They had two daughters: Ann (1930) and Lucinda (1939).

In 1937 Cobban became reader in modern French history at University College, London. He declined the offer of tenured professorship at the University of Chicago in 1947 and in 1953 was given the title professor of French history in the University of London.

Cobban was a prolific writer, with thirteen books and some fifty articles to his name. While a schoolboy he kept a remarkable commonplace book showing him from the age of sixteen to have devoured up to twenty books a month in three languages, English, French, and Latin. Political ideas (particularly the Enlightenment and its critics) and French history, especially the Revolution, preoccupied him throughout his academic career. He was opposed to two approaches: the first divorced ideas from their context and treated them as if they had a simple linear progression and evolved in ethereal space; the second was thought systems which sought to squeeze the historical record into an ideological corset. For this reason he was fundamentally at odds with Marxist historiography which dominated Revolutionary studies in France until the late 1970s, while retaining an enormous respect for Georges Lefebvre, who held the Sorbonne chair.

Cobban's first work, *Edmund Burke and the Revolt Against the Eighteenth Century* (1926) was a study of the arguments of the conservative tradition in British eighteenth-century politics and the events in France to which these arguments referred. In contrast *Rousseau and the Modern State* (1934) explores the development of ideas promoting state power. The approaching war prompted one of his most incisive analyses in *Dictatorship: its History and Theory* (1939). He held that the Enlightenment, in its remorseless opposition to despotism, and its belief in man's right to earthly fulfilment, represented a high-water mark in the history of political ideas, a view which found its fullest expression in *In Search of Humanity: the Role of the Enlightenment in Modern History* (1960), based on a series of lectures initially given in the United States, where his work was very highly valued.

Cobban did some archive-based work, for example, *Ambassadors and Secret Agents: the Diplomacy of the First Earl of Malmesbury at The Hague* (1954) on Anglo-French relations between 1784 and 1788. However, his outstanding talent lay in drawing upon the evidence contained in neglected volumes of printed documents and monographs in order to question received interpretation and offer a challenging alternative. His inaugural lecture at London, *The Myth of the French Revolution* (1954), which he subsequently enlarged into the Wiles lectures (1962) to form *The Social Interpretation of the French Revolution* (1964), disputed a Marxist interpretation of the Revolution—which represented it as the triumph of bourgeois capitalism over feudalism. Instead he demonstrated that the politically active bourgeois of 1789 were economically hard-pressed groups of professionals and office holders who were reluctantly pushed into the abolition of vestigial seigneurial dues by an insurgent peasantry and that the 'Revolution' left the distribution of propertied wealth and power largely unchanged. This work, now recognized as a historiographical landmark, initially generated much dissent in France but by the 1980s his interpretation was accepted. Indeed, his analysis of the vocabulary of social history anticipated some of the debates on discourse of the bicentennial. Cobban was the last major twentieth-century historian to posit a social rather than an 'ideas' interpretation of the Revolution.

Cobban's three-volume *History of Modern France* (1957–65), a lucid and compelling narrative, introduced more than three generations of Britons to French history. The communication of ideas to as broad an audience as possible, young and old, inside and outside the academy, and the importance of fostering balanced judgement based on evidence were for him the essence of his job, and made him a deeply committed editor of *History* (1956–67), who transformed the appeal of the journal. He was a brilliant teacher of undergraduates, generating confidence in the shy and diffident, and he attracted large numbers of graduate students from both sides of the Atlantic. He had a considerable impact upon the teaching of history in Canada and the USA as well as in Britain. A commemorative volume by his students (*French Government and Society, 1500–1850*, 1973) attests to the extent of his influence. His seminar at the Institute of Historical Research was rigorous, lively, and very democratic. He actually liked his students to prove him wrong, as this proved their development. Even when terminally ill he discussed ideas with them from his sickbed. His intellectual rigour endured to the end. He died in London, slowly and bravely, on 1 April 1968 at a Kensington nursing home which became, in the last weeks of his life, a place of pilgrimage for colleagues, former students, and international scholars.

OLWEN HUFTON

Sources UCL, personal file · priv. coll. · personal knowledge (2004) · private information (2004) [Prof. J. Burns, Prof. R. Davies, Prof. P. Pilbeam, Prof. C. Church; Lucinda Green (*née* Cobban), Ann Drummond (*née* Cobban), daughters] · b. cert. · m. cert.
Wealth at death £11,565: probate, 29 Aug 1968, *CGPLA Eng. & Wales*

Cobban, Sir James Macdonald (1910–1999), schoolteacher, was born on 14 September 1910 at Greenside in Scunthorpe, Lincolnshire, the second son and last of the five children of Alexander Macdonald Cobban (1864–1956), surveyor for Scunthorpe, and his wife, Kate Helen Rowbottom (1875–1958). His middle name, Macdonald, reflected the family's belief in their descent from one of Flora Macdonald's daughters. Cobban's grandfather was agent for the great house of Wentworth Woodhouse near Rotherham. His own childhood, lived in what he described in his privately printed memoir *One Small Head* as 'indigent gentility or genteel poverty' (Cobban, 4), was happy and unremarkable. In 1920 a scholarship of £50 a year enabled him to go as a boarder to Pocklington School, York, where he thrived under the guidance of Percy Sands, a headmaster whom he admired and who became a

lifelong friend. Already sure that he wanted to be a headmaster himself, he left Pocklington in 1929 with a scholarship to Jesus College, Cambridge. He took a first in the classical tripos in 1932 along with the Thirlwall medal, the Gladstone prize, and a Sandys studentship which financed him for six months at the University of Vienna and six months at the British School in Rome.

From 1933 Cobban taught for three years at King Edward VI School, Southampton, where he compiled his best-known book, the Latin reader *Civis romanus* (1936), which remained in print for fifty years and sold half a million copies. From 1936 until 1940, and again for a year after the end of the Second World War, he was classical sixth form master at Dulwich College. Nearly all his pupils won awards to Oxford or Cambridge, and on 10 January 1942 the sister of one, Lorna Mary Marlow (1913–1961), became his wife.

By then Cobban was serving in the intelligence corps. In 1944 he was deputy assistant quartermaster-general at Mountbatten's combined operations, but because of appendicitis it was six days after D-day before he reached France 'for a couple of days' hitch-hiking along the three British beaches', as he described his mission to report on conditions on the landing grounds (Cobban, 53). As a staff officer in the Allied Control Commission for Germany, first in London (where he escaped death in a V2 attack only because the bedroom door fell diagonally across his bed) and then from May 1945 in Frankfurt, he spent some weeks looking for documents and people who might be of interest to the allies before becoming involved in reorganizing local government in Germany. He ended the war as a lieutenant-colonel.

The move to Roysse's School, Abingdon, in April 1947 marked the real beginning of Cobban's life's work. His headmastership of nearly twenty-four years transformed Roysse's, an undistinguished grammar school of 250 boys, into Abingdon School, an academic direct-grant school drawing pupils from families associated with Oxford and the Atomic Energy Research Establishment at Harwell as well as the local area and numbering, when he retired in 1970, 630 boys. This was exactly—and intentionally—ten times the number for which John Roysse had founded it in 1563. Since ability to delegate was one headmasterly virtue which Cobban lacked, the school's remarkable rise was almost entirely his own doing.

Small of stature, with a bristling moustache, a piercing eye, a penetrating voice, enormous energy, an ability to walk as fast as most people can run, a delight in outrageous plays on words and in making public speeches, Cobban was a larger-than-life character to his pupils and a popular local figure. Although much involved in the life of the town and the church, he was a schoolmaster at heart, devoted to his boys, concerned for their manners and morals as well as their minds, and staying in touch afterwards with hundreds who wanted to keep in touch with him. His strong Christian faith helped him to come to terms with the untimely deaths of his two-year-old son, who fell from a window in 1947, and of his much loved wife, whose death in 1961 left him with four small daughters to bring up.

In retirement Cobban, who was appointed CBE in 1971, moved to Steventon, then to Sherborne, and finally to sheltered housing run by one of his daughters in Yeovil. From 1966 he was deputy lieutenant of Berkshire, and from 1974 of Oxfordshire. A JP from 1950, he chaired the Abingdon bench from 1964 to 1974. In 1971 he conducted an inquiry into the church in Bedford for Bishop Robert Runcie. From 1970 to 1985 he represented the Oxford diocese on the general synod (where he served from 1979 on the panel of chairmen), and from 1975 to 1982 he was vice-president of the diocesan synod. He wrote a regular column for his diocesan magazine. He governed numerous schools and colleges and from 1972 to 1982, the last six of those years as deputy chairman, was on the committee of the Governing Bodies Association. As a principal architect of the assisted places scheme, he was knighted in 1982. He died at Tyndale Nursing Home, 36 Preston Road, Yeovil, Somerset, on 19 April 1999, and his ashes were interred on 26 April in Trent churchyard, Somerset.

ERIC ANDERSON

Sources J. Cobban, *One small head* (Charlottesville, Virginia, 1998) • T. Hinde and M. St John Parker, *The martlet and the griffen* (1997) • *The Abingdonian* [magazine of Abingdon School] (1947–70) • E. Anderson, memorial address, *Abingdonian* (1999) • *Daily Telegraph* (20 May 1999) • *The Times* (26 April 1999) • *The Independent* (28 April 1999) • personal knowledge (2004) • private information (2004) [family]
Archives priv. coll., family papers | Abingdon School, Abingdon, Oxfordshire, archives
Likenesses E. Halliday, oils, Abingdon School, Abingdon, Oxfordshire • photograph, repro. in Cobban, *One small head*, cover • photograph, repro. in *The Times* (26 April 1999) • photograph, repro. in *The Independent* • photograph, repro. in *Daily Telegraph* • photographs, repro. in Hinde and Parker, *The martlet*, 142–75
Wealth at death under £200,000: probate, 24 June 1999, CGPLA Eng. & Wales

Cobbe, Sir Alexander Stanhope (1870–1931), army officer, was born at Naini Tal, Uttar Pradesh, India, on 5 June 1870, the second son of Lieutenant-General Sir Alexander Hugh Cobbe (1825–1899), 17th regiment, and his wife, Emily Barbara (d. 1886), daughter of Captain G. Stanhope Jones, 59th regiment. He was educated at Wellington College and at the Royal Military College, Sandhurst. Having been commissioned in the South Wales Borderers in 1889, he was promoted lieutenant in 1892 but transferred to the Indian Staff Corps that year, his appointment being confirmed in 1894. He was attached to the 32nd Sikh pioneers, with whom he saw active service in Chitral in 1895, taking part in Colonel F. H. Kelly's great march to the relief of the agency. He subsequently served in Nyasaland in 1898 and 1899 in various minor operations and with the West African regiment in the Asante kingdom in 1900, was wounded, and awarded the DSO. He was again on active service in 1902, in Somaliland, and won the VC at Erego on 6 October for good work with a Maxim gun when left alone in front of the line at a critical moment, while later he went out under heavy fire and brought in a wounded man. He had received his captaincy in 1900 and was promoted major and brevet lieutenant-colonel in

1907. Cobbe married on 1 October 1910 Winifred Ada (d. 1956), eldest daughter of Sir Albert Edward Bowen, first baronet, of Colworth Park, Bedfordshire; they had one son and two daughters.

Between 1902 and 1914 Cobbe held several staff appointments in India and at the War Office and was made aide-de-camp to the king and brevet colonel in 1911. He went to France in October 1914 as general staff officer of the Lahore division, was transferred to the staff of the Indian corps in June 1915, and was later brigadier-general, general staff, 1st corps. Cobbe returned to India in January 1916 as director of staff duties and military training; he took over the Meerut 7th Indian division in Mesopotamia in the following June, becoming major-general, and two months later succeeded General Sir Stanley Maude in the 3rd Indian corps, which he commanded in the operations of December 1916–February 1917 for the recapture of Kut al Amara, being particularly concerned with the clearance of the Khudhaira bend and the capture of the Sannaiyat position. He was later in charge of the operations which resulted in substantial success at Mashahida (March 1917) and Istabulat and the capture of Samarra (April) and also of the advance to Tikrit in October. In 1918 his corps carried out the advance upon Mosul which culminated after sharp fighting at Sharqat and on the Lesser Zab in the surrender of the main Turkish field force. Difficulties of supply and transport were great but Cobbe's plans resulted in an outstanding success.

Cobbe was appointed CB in 1915, KCB in 1917, CSI in 1918, and KCSI in 1919, the year in which he also became lieutenant-general. From October 1919 to June 1920 and from 1920 to 1926 he was military secretary at the India Office; he was general officer commanding-in-chief, northern command, in India from 1926 to 1930, and had returned to his old post at the India Office shortly before he died. He had been promoted full general in February 1924, being the youngest holder of that rank in the army, and was made aide-de-camp general to the king and appointed GCB in 1928. To the great pleasure of his old regiment he had been made colonel of the South Wales Borderers in 1922. An accomplished, as well as a gallant and popular, soldier, he had a fine record both as a staff officer and in command in the field and he inspired confidence as well as liking and respect. He died at 7 Portland Place, Marylebone, London, after an operation, on 29 June 1931. His son, an officer in the RAF, was killed in action during the battle of Britain in 1940. His younger daughter became a fellow and tutor in mathematics at Somerville College, Oxford.

C. T. ATKINSON, rev.

Sources *The Times* (1 July 1931) • J. W. B. Merewether and F. Smith, *The Indian corps in France* (1918) • J. M. Brereton, *A history of the royal regiment of Wales (24th and 41st foot)* (1989) • Burke, *Peerage* (1907) • Burke, *Gen. GB* (1958) • F. J. Moberly, ed., *The campaign in Mesopotamia, 1914–1918*, 4 vols. (1923–7), vols. 3–4 • CGPLA Eng. & Wales (1931)
Archives NRA, priv. coll., diary
Likenesses portrait, repro. in Brereton, *History of the royal regiment*, 261
Wealth at death £21,071 5s. 9d.: probate, 1 Aug 1931, CGPLA Eng. & Wales

Cobbe, Charles (1687–1765), Church of Ireland archbishop of Dublin, was born in Winchester, the youngest son of Thomas Cobbe, governor of the Isle of Man, and of his wife, Veriana, daughter of James Chaloner MP. He was first educated at Winchester College. He afterwards matriculated, on 12 November 1705, at Trinity College, Oxford, where he graduated BA in 1709 and MA in 1712. In August 1717 he went to Ireland as chaplain to the lord lieutenant, Charles, duke of Bolton. He married Dorothea, widow of Sir John Rawdon and daughter of Sir Richard Levinge, speaker of the Irish House of Commons and lord chief justice of the Irish court of common pleas.

Cobbe's first ecclesiastical preferment was the rectory of Skryne and Ballymagarvey in the diocese of Meath. Afterwards he was appointed dean of Ardagh (22 January 1719), whence he was promoted to the sees of Killala and Achonry by patent dated 30 May 1720. He was translated to the see of Dromore by patent dated 16 February 1727, and thence in March 1731 to Kildare, with which latter appointment he held, *in commendam*, the deanery of Christ Church, Dublin, and the preceptory of Tully, co. Kildare. On 19 July 1734 he was sworn of the privy council. He took the degrees of BD and DD at Dublin in 1735, and he was created DD at Oxford by diploma dated 9 July 1744. He was translated to the archiepiscopal see of Dublin by letters patent dated 4 March 1743.

Cobbe died at St Sepulchre's, Dublin, on 14 April 1765 and was buried at Donabate, co. Dublin, where he had a country seat. Historians have disagreed in their assessment of the vigour with which he performed his ecclesiastical duties. John Wesley met with him in 1747 to discuss Cobbe's opposition to lay preachers, but praised him for encouraging his clergy to distribute religious books to the poor (*Works of John Wesley*, 187–9).

THOMPSON COOPER, *rev.* R. G. INGRAM

Sources J. B. Leslie, 'Fasti of Christ Church Cathedral, Dublin', Representative Church Body Library, Dublin, MS 61/2/2, pp. 35–6 · H. B. Swanzy, ed., *Succession lists of the diocese of Dromore* (1933), 11–12 · *The works of John Wesley*, [another edn], 20, ed. F. Baker and others (1991), 187–9 · Foster, *Alum. Oxon.* · H. Cotton, *Fasti ecclesiae Hibernicae*, 6 vols. (1845–78) · R. Mant, *History of the Church of Ireland*, 2 vols. (1840) · C. R. Elrington, ed., *Records of the consecration of Irish bishops and archbishops from the year 1536* [suppl. to the *Irish Ecclesiastical Gazette*, June 1886]
Archives BL, corresp., Add. MS 32709, fols. 75, 294 · Newbridge House, Donabate, co. Dublin, journal
Likenesses A. Miller, mezzotint, pubd 1746 (after F. Bindon), BM, NG Ire. · A. Miller, mezzotint (after his mezzotint; after F. Bindon?), NG Ire.

Cobbe, Frances Power (1822–1904), writer and campaigner for women's rights, was born in Dublin on 4 December 1822. She was the fifth child and only daughter of Charles Cobbe (1781–1857), a landowner, of Newbridge House, co. Dublin, and his wife, Frances Conway (1777–1847). Cobbe was educated at home, except for two years (1836–8) at an expensive school in Brighton. Cobbe regarded her schooling, which cost £1000, as an interruption to her education and a complete waste of time. The

Frances Power Cobbe (1822–1904), by Florence Graham, 1897

noise, frivolity, pointless routine, and complete lack of intellectual stimulation contrasted strongly with her pleasurable life at home, spent in close contact with her accomplished and beloved mother. Cobbe was recalled from school when her mother's ill health made it necessary for her to take over the housekeeping.

Her mother's death in 1847 was a terrible loss to Cobbe and almost immediately brought her into conflict with her stern and forbidding father, whose housekeeper and domestic companion she now became. Their conflict centred on religion. The family was devoutly evangelical and engaged in regular prayers and Bible reading. Although subject to religious doubt before this, Cobbe had continued to participate in the family's religious observance. After her mother's death, however, she refused to do so, taking a certain pride in being the first heretic in a family which numbered five archbishops and a bishop among its members. As a result of this apostasy she was exiled to the home of a brother for ten months. She was recalled when her domestic services were again required, but remained always in a kind of moral quarantine. She accepted that it was her duty to care for her father, but refused ever to submit to his religious or moral views.

Although she was an agnostic for a short time in adolescence, Cobbe replaced the family religion with a form of deism heavily influenced by that of Theodore Parker, whose writings she subsequently edited in fourteen volumes (1863–71). Her religious beliefs were closely integrated with her feminism, as she replaced the heavily patriarchal Christianity of her father with Parker's idea of a God who was, 'not a king but a Father and Mother, infinite in power, wisdom and love' (T. Parker, 'Discourse on religion', *The Collected Works of Theodore Parker*, ed. F. P. Cobbe, 1863, 1.306). Cobbe later attended the ministry of James Martineau and occasionally conducted services in Unitarian chapels. She combined her domestic duties with private study and literary pursuits. Her reading of Kant's *Metaphysics of Ethics* suggested the theme for her first book, *The Theory of Intuitive Morals* (published in two parts, 1855 and 1857), which she wrote late at night and published anonymously to protect her father from annoyance. Throughout her life, Cobbe wrote extensively on religious and ethical subjects, fearing the spread of atheism and the impact of Darwinism on morality.

The death of her father in 1857 left Frances Cobbe free of familial duties but in drastically reduced financial circumstances. The £200 annuity with which she was left could not sustain the lifestyle to which she was accustomed. Moreover, the house which she had overseen for so many years now passed to her older brother, making it necessary for her to find a new home. Before doing so, she set out on an extended trip to Europe and the East, visiting Egypt, Lebanon, Palestine, and Syria, as well as France, Italy, and Greece. She was delighted to have visited the pyramids before the advent of Cook's tours, but found her greatest pleasure in Rome, where she got to know the large group of expatriate American and English women resident there, including Mary Somerville, Harriet Hosmer, and her subsequent life companion, Mary Lloyd. Cobbe discovered a great love of travel, returning to Italy six times in the next two decades.

On her return to England in 1858 Cobbe moved to Bristol, where for a short time she lived with Mary Carpenter, the Unitarian social reformer and philanthropist, assisting her with her ragged schools and reformatory work. This arrangement lasted only a few months. Cobbe desired a more intimate form of friendship than Carpenter was able to offer—and Carpenter's complete lack of interest in creature comforts was intolerable to Cobbe. Within a year, she had moved to Durdham Down, where she engaged in workhouse visiting and in societies devoted to the care and supervision of 'friendless' workhouse girls.

Shortly after this Cobbe moved to London, where she set up house with Mary Lloyd, a Welsh woman who had been studying sculpture with John Gibson in Italy. Lloyd apparently gave up sculpture, and became involved in a close domestic relationship with Cobbe. In London Cobbe expanded her range of journalism and became a feminist activist and the leading figure in the battle to outlaw vivisection. She contributed articles to most of the major periodicals. In 1867 she became a regular leader writer for *The Echo*, which earned her £300 per annum until she relinquished the position in 1875. She also wrote for *The Standard* and was for a time the Italian correspondent for the *Daily News*. In 1862 Cobbe published her articles 'Celibacy vs marriage' (*Fraser's Magazine*, vol. 65) and 'What shall we do with our old maids?' (ibid., vol. 66) and delivered a paper to the National Association for the Promotion of Social Science advocating the admission of women to university degrees (later published in her *Essays on the Pursuits of Women*, 1863). Through these activities she became known to the active feminist circle which had set up headquarters at Langham Place in London. She established a wide network of feminist friends, including Emily Davies, the founder of Girton College, John Stuart Mill and his stepdaughter, Helen Taylor, and the suffrage leaders Lydia Becker and Millicent Garrett Fawcett.

Cobbe was a member of the Married Women's Property Committee and, for a short time in 1867, of the London National Society for Woman's Suffrage. But the campaign to which she was most strongly committed was that for reform of the Matrimonial Causes Act of 1878. Cobbe was a somewhat difficult colleague. One of the few mid-Victorian feminists who came from the Anglo-Irish landed gentry, she carried from childhood a commitment to the Conservative Party, a belief that it was better to work through influential individuals rather than with popular support, and a particular sense of decorum. She was unhappy with committees which did not entirely endorse her views, and ended her association with a number of feminist colleagues when they refused to give wholehearted support to her anti-vivisection campaign.

Cobbe's greatest contribution to the women's movement came from her writing. She published in almost every major periodical, writing on the problems of marriage and the virtues of celibacy; the need for women to have independent activities; and on the persistent ill health of women, which resulted from fashions which constricted their bodies, from a medical profession which defined women as invalids, and from the fact that, unlike men, women lacked the services of a wife. Her powerful article 'Wife torture in England' (*Contemporary Review*, 32, 1878), which illustrated the extent of domestic violence and sought to make 'aggravated assaults' grounds for judicial separation, played a significant part in the passing of the Matrimonial Causes Act of that year.

The core of Cobbe's feminism lay in her belief in the moral autonomy of women on the one hand, and in her strong sense of sexual difference on the other. Women were rational beings with a primary duty to themselves and to their God, she argued, hence they could not submit themselves absolutely to the demands of either husband or parents. But Cobbe believed emphatically in the importance of sexual difference. She defined women as 'human beings of the mother sex' (F. P. Cobbe, *The Duties of Women*, 1881, 28) and insisted that innate maternal qualities would always determine what women did. Celibacy seemed preferable to marriage, in her view, but she assumed all celibate women would generally exercise their maternal qualities through some form of philanthropy.

For Cobbe, as for a number of other Victorian feminists, there was a close connection between feminism and the anti-vivisection campaign, in that both were fighting to protect defenceless creatures from the limitless powers of men. Her crusade against vivisection began in 1863. In 1875 she established the Victoria Street Society, and ran it alongside the National Anti-Vivisection Society as well as editing *The Zoopholist*. Cobbe's battles against vivisection soon encompassed a broader attack on the arrogance, brutality, and atheism of science and of the medical profession. For many, Cobbe personified the anti-vivisection movement, imbuing it with great energy but also with an intransigence that some saw as ultimately harmful to the cause.

In 1884, exhausted by the anti-vivisection campaign, Cobbe acceded to Lloyd's desire to return to her home, and they moved to Hengwrt, near Dolgellau. This did not mark the end of her interest in the anti-vivisection movement. Feeling that it had lost its force, she left the National Anti-Vivisection Society in 1898 to form a more thoroughgoing body, the British Union for the Abolition of Vivisection which, to her great regret, did not succeed in outlawing the practice completely. Nor did she end her active support of the women's movement, and she continued writing pamphlets and essays, and attending and addressing suffrage meetings. It was while she was in retirement that she wrote her autobiography, a work which celebrates the full and active life available to single women, and served as another vehicle for her to expound her feminist beliefs. It also highlighted her wide acquaintance among English literary and intellectual circles: there was, she insisted, scarcely a single notable woman whom she had not met, and only a few men.

Cobbe's final years were ones of material comfort. She had given up her most lucrative journalism in order to devote herself to the anti-vivisection movement in the 1870s and had consequently been forced to rely on her very small paternal legacy. Immediately after her retirement, however, her colleagues in the Victoria Street Society collected £1000 with which they purchased an annuity of £100 for her. In 1901 she inherited a quite considerable sum as the residuary legatee of the widow of Richard Vaughan Yates, a devoted anti-vivisectionist. Her greatest grief was to have outlived Mary Lloyd, who died in 1896. Cobbe survived her by eight years and died at Hengwrt on 5 April 1904. She was buried in Llanelltyd churchyard, alongside her beloved Mary Lloyd. Fearing premature burial, she left instructions that the arteries of the neck and windpipe be completely severed after her death.

Cobbe was a person of considerable energy and enthusiasm with a great enjoyment of life. Her concern for animals caused her to refuse to decorate her hats with feathers, but she had no sympathy for vegetarianism or teetotalism, seeing them as an indication of the diminution of the vitality and animal spirits which had characterized the world of her youth. She always relished social occasions, especially dinner parties, she insisted, because even if the company was lacklustre she could entertain herself with her knife and fork. She was a person of considerable charm, but one with a very forceful personality. Convinced of the rightness of all her own causes and beliefs, however, she often pursued her chosen path regardless of the beliefs or feelings of others. Thus, while her participation was welcome to the women's movement, her attempts to harness the suffrage movement to the Primrose League was a source of some embarrassment and difficulty to her colleagues. Ultimately Cobbe's most important contribution to nineteenth-century feminism lay in her attempts to set out a feminist ethic, developed most extensively in *The Duties of Women* (1881). One reviewer described her as the person who 'excepting John Stuart Mill, … has done more than anyone else to give the dignity of principle to the women's movement' ('Life of Frances Power Cobbe', *Academy*, 46, 1894).　　　BARBARA CAINE

Sources *Life of Frances Power Cobbe: by herself*, 2 vols. (1894); repr. with introduction by B. Atkinson as *Life of Frances Power Cobbe as told by herself* (1904) • B. Caine, *Victorian feminists* (1992) • F. A. Kemble, *Further records, 1848–1883: a series of letters*, 2 vols. (1890) • J. Manton, *Mary Carpenter and the children of the streets* (1976) • R. D. French, *Antivivisection and medical science in Victorian society* (1975) • A. J. Hammerton, *Cruelty and companionship: conflict in nineteenth-century married life* (1992) • M. L. Shanley, *Feminism, marriage and the law in Victorian England, 1850–1895* (1989) • P. Levine, *Feminist lives in Victorian England: private roles and public commitment* (1990) • autograph collection of letters, Women's Library, London • Bodl. Oxf., MSS Somerville • Hunt. L., Cobbe papers • Man. CL, National Union of Women's Suffrage Societies MSS • Girton Cam., Davies MSS

Archives Bodl. Oxf., corresp. • Hunt. L., corresp. and papers • Women's Library, London, autograph collection of letters | Bodl. Oxf., letters to Mary Somerville and Martha Somerville • Hist. Soc. Penn., letters to Sarah Wister • McMaster University Library, Hamilton, Ontario, letters to Lord and Lady Amberley • U. Nott. L., letters to Henry Septimus Sutton

Likenesses F. Graham, drawing, 1897, priv. coll. [*see illus.*] • photograph, repro. in Atkinson, ed., *Life of Frances Power Cobbe*, frontispiece

Wealth at death £18,711 4*s.*: probate, 15 Aug 1904, *CGPLA Eng. & Wales*

Cobbe, Marjory (*fl.* 1469–1475). *See under* Women medical practitioners in England (*act. c.*1200–*c.*1475).

Cobbett, John (*d.* 1657), parliamentarian army officer and Leveller, was son of Ralph Cobbett, a gentleman from Weston, Northamptonshire. John was a Londoner who probably served an apprenticeship during the 1630s, like his brothers Ralph and Robert. In 1642 all three brothers joined the parliamentarian army as officers of foot. Cobbett was initially lieutenant, and afterwards captain, in Colonel Holmstead's regiment under the earl of Essex. With the founding of the New Model Army in 1645 he transferred to Philip Skippon's foot regiment, in which he was promoted major during the political upheavals of June 1647. In that year he acted as one of the elected officer agitators for his regiment, which was then garrisoned at Newcastle. In this capacity he attended meetings of the general council of the army, where he expressed advanced views. According to a group of radical pamphleteers Commissary-General Henry Ireton scolded 'honest Major Cobbett of Snow Hill, [Holborn, London] … for joyning with the giddy headed Souldiers: and advised him not to run against the interest of himselfe and the Officers' (Ward and others, 13).

When some units mutinied at the army rendezvous at Ware, Cobbett must have either played a part, or questioned Sir Thomas Fairfax's right to try the arrested mutineers, for he himself was tried, and after a long debate in the council of war, was sentenced on 20 December 1647 to be cashiered at the head of his regiment. Pronouncing sentence, however, was left to the general council, which omitted to carry it out. Cobbett was evidently reinstated, since we find him active in the second civil war, assisting, for example, in the recapture of Tynemouth Castle in August 1648.

In the spring of 1649 Cobbett was embroiled again in seditious Leveller activity, for which he was cashiered a second time on 18 June. At the time he was stationed in Bristol as the commander of Major-General Philip Skippon's regiment. The Burford mutineers had expected him to bring two troops of horse to their rendezvous, but in the event the troops failed to materialize. Cobbett is most likely the author of *The Souldiers Demand* (1649), published anonymously in Bristol at the height of the Leveller agitation. The London bookseller George Thomason acquired his copy on 18 May. The pamphlet opens with a startling and sweeping confession of guilt for the misery and oppression that the army had inflicted on England: 'Oh! the ocean of bloud that we are guilty of. Oh! the intollerable oppression that we have laid upon our brethren of England'. Then, after chastising the officers for their enslavement of the rank and file, it unleashes a scathing indictment of the projected conquest of Ireland:

> What have we to doe with Ireland, to fight and murther a people and nation … which have done us no harme, only deeper to put our hands in bloud with [the officers'] own? We have waded too farre in that crimson streame (already) of innocent and Christian bloud.   (*The Souldiers Demand*, 12–13)

To characterize the Irish as both innocent and Christian was extraordinary for a protestant Englishman of the time.

Cobbett's military talents must have been highly valued, for he was forgiven once more, made adjutant-general of foot in the army which invaded Scotland in 1650, and fought at the battle of Worcester (3 September 1651), where he was credited with nearly capturing Charles II. Afterwards Cromwell wrote to the speaker of the House of Commons that Cobbett 'was equal in the performance of his duty, to most that served you that day' (*Writings and Speeches*, 2.463). He was honoured by Cromwell by being chosen to deliver the letter reporting the victory to the Commons. When summoned before the bar of the house he first told his own story of the battle, and then produced the king's gold chain and garter, which he had personally confiscated from the royal quarters at Worcester. Parliament rewarded him with a house and crown land in Scotland to the value of £100 a year.

Cobbett also participated in the army's purchases of English crown land. In 1652 he submitted an arrears debenture for £495 towards the purchase of Pevensey Manor, Sussex, which he acquired with his brother Robert and the radical pamphleteer and chaplain John Warr, for £1492. He died a lieutenant-colonel in January 1657 and was buried in Edmonton, Middlesex, where he had been living, on 8 January. Naming his 'trusty and well-beloved brother Ralph' his executor, he left a modest estate of lands and tenements in different parts of England worth £200 a year to his two daughters (PRO, PROB 11/274, sig. 147). His wife had evidently predeceased him.

IAN J. GENTLES

Sources The Clarke papers, ed. C. H. Firth, 1, CS, new ser., 49 (1891), 407 · I. Gentles, The New Model Army in England, Ireland, and Scotland, 1645–1653 (1992) · C. H. Firth and G. Davies, The regimental history of Cromwell's army, 2 vols. (1940) · The souldiers demand (1649) · PRO, PROB 11/274, sig. 147, fol. 329 · parish register, Edmonton, 1653–78, LMA, DRO 40/A1/2 [unfoliated] · R. Ward, T. Watson, S. Graunt, G. Jellis, and W. Sawyer, The hunting of the foxes from New-market and Triploe-heaths to White-hall by five small beagles (late of the armie) (1649), 13 · The Moderate (8–15 May 1649) · exchequer, certificates of sale of crown lands, PRO, E 121/4/9/95, 2/3/40, 4/5/64, 4/5/94 · The writings and speeches of Oliver Cromwell, ed. W. C. Abbott and C. D. Crane, 2 (1939), 463 · D. Massarella, 'The politics of the army, 1647–1660', PhD diss., University of York, 1978 · T. C. Dale, 'The members of the City companies in 1641 as set forth in the return of the poll tax', 1935, U. Lond., Institute of Historical Research · Drapers Company, London, index of apprentices, 1615–1750, Ralph Cobbett, 6 July 1636 · JHC, 7 (1651–9), 12–13, 191 · J. Rushworth, Historical collections, new edn, 7 (1721), 937, 940 · CSP dom., 1656–7 · B. Whitelocke, Memorials of English affairs, new edn, 4 vols. (1853), vol. 3, p. 55

Wealth at death £200 p.a.: will, PRO, PROB 11/274, sig. 147 · house and lands in Scotland valued at £100 p.a.

Cobbett, William (1763–1835), political writer and farmer, was born on 9 March 1763 in Farnham, Surrey, the third of four children of George Cobbett, publican and farmer, and his wife, Anne Vincent.

Early life and the army   As a youth Cobbett worked chiefly as a ploughboy and gardener: he frequently boasted in adult life that he was 'bred at the plough-tail' (*A Year's Residence in the United States of America*, 1818, general preface, paragraph 8). Although he vaguely recalled attending school for a brief period during his youth, Cobbett learned his letters at home, chiefly from his father. In 1783, longing for new horizons and adventure, he attempted to enlist in the Royal Navy, though by inadvertence he found himself in a marching regiment, the West Norfolk 54th foot. For the first year of his enlistment Cobbett was stationed at Chatham, where he worked at his military exercises and read voraciously: 'novels, plays, history, poetry, all were read', he later wrote, 'and nearly with equal avidity' (*Life and Adventures of Peter Porcupine*, ed. G. D. H. Cole, 1927, 33). Between 1785 and 1791, while stationed in New Brunswick, Cobbett put his knowledge of English grammar and letters to good effect, quickly becoming clerk to his regiment and rising from the rank of corporal to sergeant-major. In his office as clerk Cobbett believed that he encountered instances of peculation by the officers of his regiment, and upon returning to England and receiving his military discharge in 1791, wrote an anonymous pamphlet entitled *The Soldier's Friend* (1792), a passionate indictment of the harsh treatment and poor pay of the common soldier. At the same time Cobbett attempted to launch a court martial against the offending officers, and when this threatened to rebound on Cobbett himself, he and his new wife, Nancy Anne Reid (1774–1848)—an English woman whom he had first met in New Brunswick and married at Woolwich on 5 February 1792—fled to France

William Cobbett (1763–1835), by George Cooke?, *c.*1831

for six months and subsequently to the United States, where they remained from 1792 to 1800.

In America, 1792–1800 For the first eighteen months of his American residence Cobbett was employed tutoring French émigrés in the English language, but in the summer of 1794 he ventured into the American public press by authoring a pamphlet that vehemently denounced the scientist and democrat Dr Joseph Priestley, who had recently fled Britain and been jubilantly received by republican and democratic supporters at New York. For the next five years, usually under the pen-name of Peter Porcupine, Cobbett wrote numerous pamphlets and newspapers articles (he subsequently collected and reprinted his American writings in *Porcupine's Works*, 12 vols., 1801) which vigorously condemned the French Revolution as well as other expressions of democratic and republican thought—he characterized Thomas Paine, for example, as 'an unconscionable dog', 'a wretched traitor and apostate', and 'a man famous for nothing but his blasphemy and his hatred of England' (*Porcupine's Works*, 4.79, 4.87; 5.165; *Political Register*, 8 Jan 1803, 2). As an anti-Jacobin polemicist, Cobbett identified his politics most closely with the federalists—the pro-British and anti-French faction under the leadership of Alexander Hamilton—while taking angry aim at the pro-French, Jacobin-sympathizing democratic faction led by Thomas Jefferson. Yet despite his high profile in the United States, Cobbett always remained ambivalent towards American culture and society, and when pressed by a severe libel case in 1800, he and his family, which now included a

daughter, Anne, and a son, William, packed their belongings and set sail for England. Cobbett's farewell message to Americans observed that 'when people care not two straws for each other, ceremony at parting is mere grimace' (*Porcupine's Works*, 12.109–10).

The Porcupine* and the *Political Register The government of William Pitt, delighted with Cobbett's contributions to the anti-Jacobin cause, immediately offered him control over a government-owned newspaper, but Cobbett declined the offer, preferring to launch his own daily newspaper, and thus to maintain at least the appearance of independence. Cobbett's daily paper *The Porcupine*, bearing the motto 'Fear God, Honour the King', was duly launched on 30 October 1800, but circulation remained low, and late in 1801 he sold his interest in it. Within a few months, however, he began the *Political Register*, a periodical which was published, almost without exception, every week between January 1802 and Cobbett's death in 1835. Totalling eighty-nine volumes, or some 42,000 pages, the *Political Register* is the most important and detailed record of Cobbett's career. Most of his twenty books were serialized in the *Register* in whole or in part, and in almost each issue he set forth his political and social viewpoints in the leading article—an editorial innovation that Cobbett himself introduced to English journalism. Between 1809 and 1812 Cobbett was jointly involved in the editing and publishing of *Cobbett's Complete Collection of State Trials*, and between 1804 and 1812 he was active in collecting and printing parliamentary debates from the Norman conquest onward. Owing to financial difficulties he sold his shares in both projects in 1812 (as the purchaser of the latter was T. C. Hansard, it might be said that the official record of parliamentary proceedings that today is called 'Hansard' could justly be termed 'Cobbett').

Cobbett's political commentary in the early numbers of the *Register* was thoroughly anti-Jacobin, but by 1804 he began questioning the financial and political policies of the government. Under William Pitt's administration, Cobbett complained, the growing national debt and numerous awards of unmerited sinecures were beggaring the country and heightening animosity between those who paid taxes and those who lived off taxes. At first Cobbett's answer was to support the election of more independent country gentlemen to parliament, but by 1807 he was lending his support to Francis Burdett, John Cartwright, and other campaigners for parliamentary reform. At the same time Cobbett became increasingly obsessed with financial issues, especially the national debt and the government's increasing reliance upon paper money. He opposed these trends for the rest of his days, regularly decrying government debts and paper currencies in his writings, notably in his *Paper Against Gold* (1815). By the early 1820s Cobbett was convinced that the debt was too large ever to be paid off, and accordingly vowed to roast himself on a gridiron if the government could restore payment in specie without defaulting on the debt (henceforth Cobbett and his critics included sketches of gridirons in their writings and cartoons).

Cobbett and rural England During the early 1800s the *Register* focused chiefly on metropolitan politics but gradually from 1805 onwards Cobbett became increasingly concerned with rural England, particularly the economic hardship of farmworkers. In 1805 he purchased a farm at Botley in Hampshire, and it was here that Cobbett (save for the years 1810–12, which he spent imprisoned in Newgate after he was prosecuted by the government for publicly criticizing the flogging of several militiamen at Ely), together with his wife and four children, made his primary residence between 1805 and 1817. Life at Botley was happy for the Cobbetts. Political reformers were frequent guests and the Cobbett family became deeply involved in Hampshire rural society and in the daily routine of farming. As Mary Russell Mitford observed in 1806, Cobbett's ready hospitality, together with his ruddy complexion, red waistcoat, ample mid-section, and twinkling eye, gave him the appearance 'of a great English yeoman of the old time' (*Recollections of a Literary Life*, 1883 edn, 200–01). Similarly, William Hazlitt saw in Cobbett a Georgian gentleman farmer who 'speaks and thinks plain, broad, downright English' (*The Spirit of the Age*, ed. E. D. Mackerness, 1969, 244–56). Cobbett's countryman appearance came as a surprise to some observers, such as the tory adversary at a Hampshire county meeting in 1813 who nearly mistook Cobbett for 'one of the innocent bacon-eaters of the New forest'. Wisely, this same commentator went on to observe that 'when I knew that it was Cobbett, you may believe I did not allow his placid easy smile to take me in' (Letters of Timothy Tickler, esquire, *Blackwood's Edinburgh Magazine*, 14, 1823, 329).

Radicalism and its price The years 1816–17 were important but difficult ones for Cobbett. The massive demobilization which followed the end of the Napoleonic wars in 1815, together with the disastrous grain harvest of 1816, brought acute hunger and unemployment to the countryside. Cobbett's response was to launch a mass-circulation, broadsheet edition of the *Political Register* (priced at 2*d*. it was derisively labelled 'two-penny trash' by its detractors, a title that Cobbett gleefully adopted for the new venture), in which he urged English workers not to riot but to pursue parliamentary reform as the great answer to their economic plight. The election of radical reformers to parliament, he argued, would ensure lower taxes, fuller employment, and increased earnings for all working people. The first cheap *Register* alone sold 44,000 copies in the first month, and Home Office records for 1816–17 indicate that its distribution was sufficiently widespread to cause great concern to the government, particularly to the home secretary, Lord Sidmouth, who early in 1817 rushed several acts through parliament in an attempt to reverse the growth of public support for parliamentary reform. Fearing incarceration because of the new measures, Cobbett set sail for the United States, and arrived in New York on 5 May 1817. Having taken a lease on a Long Island farm, Cobbett lived a quieter life than during his first American sojourn, but he continued the *Political Register* from abroad as well as writing more books and tracts, most notably the agricultural treatise *A Year's Residence in the United States of America* (1818) and his widely selling *Grammar of the English Language* (1818). This latter work, which Cobbett saw as a testament to the intellectual capacity of himself and of the common people as a whole, was intended especially for the use of 'soldiers, sailors, apprentices, and ploughboys'; accordingly Cobbett cheekily drew his examples of faulty grammar from the writings and speeches of such renowned political leaders as the duke of Wellington, Lord Castlereagh, and George III himself. The English *Grammar* continued to be used in English schools into the 1920s and 1930s; Cobbett's *French Grammar*, first published in 1824, enjoyed rather less success, though even it had passed into fifteen editions by 1862.

When Cobbett returned from the United States in October 1819 his personal and political fortunes were at a low ebb. He was bankrupt and lost his farm at Botley as a result. The flight to America had damaged his relations with other leaders of the radical movement, most notably his erstwhile ally Henry Hunt, who had remained in Britain during Sidmouth's repressions and stoically endured a prison sentence. None the less, Cobbett believed that he brought with him—in the form of the bones of Thomas Paine—a powerful and emotive symbol around which all parliamentary reformers could rally. But it was not to be. After the Peterloo massacre of August 1819 a new cast of radical leaders began to emerge, and Cobbett himself proved uncomfortable on the hustings during his unsuccessful candidacy in a Coventry by-election in March 1820. During the latter half of 1820, however, Cobbett's fortunes began to improve, chiefly because of the increased circulation of the *Register* which resulted from his involvement with the Queen Caroline affair. Cobbett devoted numerous *Registers* to Queen Caroline's cause as well as writing some of her public statements, including the letter to the king which was published in prominent newspapers shortly before her trial in 1820. Happier times were also ushered in when Cobbett resumed his gardening and agricultural interests by beginning a 4 acre seed farm in Kensington. At the same time he wrote several 'sermons' (so-called to avoid the stamp tax), which were in part intended as answers to the conservative and moralizing tracts of Hannah More and the Cheap Repository Tract Society, and also his little manual *Cottage Economy* (1821), a delightful and highly readable book which instructs English workers in how to brew their own beer, keep bees, and fatten hogs.

Rural distress and *Rural Rides* The distressed state of English farming was Cobbett's single greatest concern throughout the 1820s. Sometimes to the irritation of local landlords and farmers, Cobbett would make uninvited appearances at county meetings, where he sought to convince landholders that the only solution to their post-war economic distress lay in a radical reform of parliament, which by 1820 he saw as entailing nothing less than universal manhood suffrage. It was partly to spread this message, and partly to strengthen his knowledge of rural England, that Cobbett now undertook his celebrated rural rides, most of them between 1821 and 1826. Describing his purpose as to hear 'what gentlemen, farmers, tradesmen, journeymen, labourers, women, girls, boys, and all have to say; reasoning with some, laughing with others, and observing all that passes' (*Political Register*, 14 Dec 1822, 686), Cobbett rode on horseback through most of the southern counties, attending county meetings, conversing with villagers, and then putting his observations into writing for the *Political Register*. A separate volume of his travel writings, entitled *Rural Rides*, first appeared in 1830 and the 'rides' have subsequently appeared in many different versions and editions on account of their accurate and colourful presentation of the English countryside and rural society of Cobbett's time. Late in the 1820s and early in the 1830s, Cobbett periodically ventured into the midlands, but owing to his frequently expressed disdain for 'northern' diets and Scottish 'feelosofers', he made only one trip to the north and only one to Scotland (he made his first and only trip to Ireland during the last year of his life). It was Cobbett's great boast that he was a 'South-of-England' countryman who disliked factories, industrial cities, and even the metropolis itself. He characterized London as the 'Great Wen' on account of its tendency to consume the lion's share of the produce of the countryside and, through its absorption of tax revenues, to deprive rural workers of their traditional fare of bread, bacon, and beer. Meanwhile, from 1827 Cobbett resumed large-scale farming upon leasing an 80 acre farm on the south side of the Thames at Barn Elms. Here he experimented with crops of maize (which he encouraged for human consumption) as well as growing a special straw, which he hoped would allow England to rebuild its straw-plait industry and thereby provide more winter employment for country workers. The results of his experiments are duly noted in his agricultural writing of these years, most notably *The Woodlands* (1825), *Treatise on Corn* (1828), and *The English Gardener* (1829).

Cobbett's rural involvements left him well placed to represent the interests of England's farmworkers, with whom he identified more and more closely during the last fifteen years of his life. It came to Cobbett's notice during his rural rides that the agricultural workers were barely subsisting, especially in the southern, south-eastern, and western counties. From 1828 until 1830 he frequently warned the government that a major rural revolt was in the making, and that steps should be taken to ensure that rural workers were amply provided with employment opportunities, a living wage, and the full protection of the poor law. True to Cobbett's predictions, the southern rural workers arose in rebellion during the Captain Swing disturbances of 1830–31. The new whig government of Lord Grey, suspecting that Cobbett had helped to foment the rising, put him on trial in 1831 for inciting rural workers to commit acts of violence and incendiarism. But Cobbett, conducting his own defence, received an acquittal when the twelve-person jury could not agree on a verdict. Cobbett's national reputation was now enhanced. Even some of his supposedly quirky opinions, such as his claim that the rural workers of southern England would rather be hanged than live on potatoes and tea, were now found to constitute part of the platform of the Swing rioters.

Immediately in the aftermath of the revolt Cobbett used his political momentum to agitate for the Reform Bill of 1832, though on this matter he enlarged his constituency to include anyone—whether landlord, farmer, banker, or merchant (he worked closely in 1831–2 with the Birmingham banker Thomas Attwood)—who was prepared to support the terms of the bill, even though the proposed enlargement of the suffrage fell far short of what Cobbett and other radical leaders had hoped for.

In the Commons The passage of the Reform Act in 1832 paved the way for Cobbett to realize his long-standing quest to be elected to the House of Commons. After unsuccessfully standing for Manchester in December 1832, he joined his friend and political ally John Fielden in a successful contest for the two seats representing the new parliamentary borough of Oldham. Cobbett had a short but distinguished career in parliament, frequently bringing on his head the ire of the house by such daring moves as his unsuccessful motion that the king be asked to dismiss Robert Peel from the privy council for gross mismanagement of the nation's finances. As he knew himself, he was more adept at representing the interests of southern agricultural workers than those of northern industrial labourers, a matter which brought praise from southern rural counties but complaints from some of Cobbett's Oldham electors. Opportunities to federate agricultural and industrial concerns were taken up by Cobbett from time to time, most notably in his support for the Tolpuddle Martyrs and in his unsuccessful but profound opposition to the Poor Law Amendment Act of 1834. The eventual passage of the Poor Law Amendment Act by the whig government demoralized Cobbett to the point where, for the first time in his public life, he called clearly and unequivocally for popular insurrection against the government. Two of his last books, *Legacy to Labourers* (1834) and *Legacy to Parsons* (1835), much like his earlier treatises *The Poor Man's Friend* (1826–7) and his best-selling *History of the Protestant Reformation* (1824–7), describe at length the means employed by the state to dispossess the English poor, beginning with the crown's appropriation of church lands during the Reformation.

Final years, death, and reputation Cobbett, though, was nearing the end of his long and varied career. Plagued by unhappy conflicts with his wife and the rest of his family during his final years, he continued to write and to farm until his death. In 1832 he agreed to rent a farm of 130 acres at Normandy, near Ash in Surrey, some 7 miles from his birthplace at Farnham. It was here, surrounded by family members, that he died on 18 June 1835. Nine days later, on 27 June 1835, he was buried in the graveyard of St Andrew's Church in Farnham. Leaving a bankrupt estate, Cobbett was survived by his wife, Nancy, three daughters (Anne, Eleanor, and Susan) and four sons (William, John, James, and Richard). There are no direct descendants remaining.

There are now a dozen biographies of Cobbett, and he has attracted interest and accolades from an enormous variety of thinkers and writers, including persons of such diverse political views as Karl Marx, Matthew Arnold, G. K. Chesterton, A. J. P. Taylor, Raymond Williams, Michael Foot, and E. P. Thompson. Cobbett's writings can appeal to both left- and right-wing thinkers on account of his populist style: he was conservative and backward-looking in many of his social and cultural ideals (one of his most resounding aims was to see a return to the rural England into which he was born in the 1760s) but at the same time he devised and fiercely promoted a thoroughly radical and democratic agenda in politics and economics. Unlike his mentor Thomas Paine, Cobbett was not interested in pursuing a republican programme for Britain; nor was he much interested in international politics. Cobbett was a 'Little Englander' who liked to boast that he was not a 'citizen of the world', for 'it is quite enough for me to think about what is best for England, Scotland and Ireland' (*Political Register*, 20 Aug 1831, 495). Never forgetting his origins as a self-taught ploughboy, Cobbett sought to rest his platform and writing upon popular English ideals, perhaps most notably in his enthusiasm for fair play, old-style hospitality, manly sports, and preference for a vigorous rural culture over the supposedly effeminate and degenerative environment of the towns. Cobbett retained to the last a strong sense of national identity, frequently chiding the United States and other rival powers that they had better not 'swagger about and be saucy to England' (*Political Register*, 2 June 1832, 545–6), and he stated that his attachment to the Church of England was partly motivated by the fact that it 'bears the name of my country' (*Life and Adventures of Peter Porcupine*, ed. G. D. H. Cole, 1927, 33). Altogether Cobbett wrote and published some 30 million words over the course of forty years (perhaps more than any other English writer), and while many of these words can be exposed as contradictory and self-serving, it can be said wholeheartedly with Karl Marx that Cobbett was 'a plebeian by instinct and sympathy' (K. Marx, letter to *New York Daily Tribune*, 22 July 1853).

For Cobbett the essence of England was its countryside, not the 'wen' of London or the industrial cities of the midlands and north. Although his agrarian and rural devotions sometimes drew criticism from even his fellow radicals, Cobbett's response was fair, simple, and personal: 'Born amongst husbandmen, bred to husbandry … it is natural that I should have a strong partiality for country life, and that I should enter more into the feelings of labourers of husbandry than into those of other labourers' (*Political Register*, 5 May 1821, 343). Non-agricultural workers were also of concern to Cobbett, but it became his great mission to articulate the wants and aspirations of the 'chopsticks' (as he fondly called the rural labourers) because they were in his estimation, 'the very best and most virtuous of all mankind' (*Political Register*, 29 Jan 1831, 288). Numerous commentators during the past century and a half have sought to measure or understand Cobbett in relation to urban and industrial models of politics, culture, and society. As a result Cobbett has too often been presented as anti-urban, anti-industrial, anti-modern. He was, in some ways, all of these things, but he was also a positive and original writer who sought to unite English

workers, whether of town or country, on a national reform platform that would bring about a new democratic order.   IAN DYCK

Sources G. D. H. Cole, *The life of William Cobbett*, 3rd edn (1947) · G. Spater, *William Cobbett: the poor man's friend*, 2 vols. (1982) · I. Dyck, *William Cobbett and rural popular culture* (1992) · J. Sambrook, *William Cobbett* (1973) · R. Williams, *Cobbett* (1983) · K. Schweizer and J. Osborne, *Cobbett in his times* (1990) · P. W. Gaines, *William Cobbett and the United States, 1792–1835* (1971) · M. L. Pearl, *William Cobbett: a bibliographical account of his life and times* (1953) · L. Melville [L. S. Benjamin], *The life and letters of William Cobbett in England and America*, 2 vols. (1913) · M. Wiener, 'The changing image of William Cobbett', *Journal of British Studies*, 13/2 (1973–4), 135–54 · L. Nattrass, *William Cobbett: the politics of style* (1995) · E. I. Carlyle, *William Cobbett: a study of his life as shown in his writings* (1904)
Archives Adelphi University, New York · BL, Add. MSS 31125–31127, 31857 · Boston PL · Farnham Museum · FM Cam. · Harvard U., Houghton L. · Hunt. L. · JRL · Nuffield Oxf. · NYPL · Rutgers University, Alexander Library · Trinity Cam. · University of Illinois | BL, letters to Akerman, Wright, Swann, Windham, Egerton MS 3808, Add. MSS 22906–22907, 37853 · Bodl. Oxf., correspondence with Wright, Swann · Hist. Soc. Penn., letters to James Mathieu · NL Wales, letters to William Williams · Som. ARS, correspondence with Daniel Badcock · Trinity Cam., Sraffa MSS · Yale U., Beinecke L., Osborn MSS
Likenesses J. R. Smith, portrait, 1800, priv. coll. · F. Bartolozzi, stipple, pubd 1801 (after J. R. Smith), BM, NPG · W. Ward, mezzotint, pubd 1812 (after J. R. Smith), BM · G. V. Palmer, line engraving, pubd 1817 (after miniature by G. M. Brighty), NPG · etching, c.1817 (after A. Buck), NPG · portrait, c.1830, priv. coll. · G. Cooke?, portrait, c.1831, Botley Market Hall [*see illus.*] · J. P. Dantan, caricature, plaster statue, 1834 (with Daniel O'Connell), Musée Carnavalet, Paris · G. Hayter, group portrait, oils (*The House of Commons, 1833*), NPG · bust, Farnham · monuments, Botley · oils, NPG · watercolour drawing, NPG
Wealth at death bankrupt

Cobbin, Ingram (1777–1851), Congregational minister, was born in London in December 1777, and educated at Hoxton Academy. He became minister at South Molton in 1802, and afterwards officiated at Banbury, Holloway, Putney, Crediton, Worcester, and Lymington. For some time he acted as secretary to the British and Foreign School Society, and in 1819 he was appointed the first secretary of the Home Missionary Society, which he had helped to form. Ill health compelled him to retire from the ministry in 1828, and from then on he devoted his energies at his residence in Camberwell to writing. His extensive publications included school textbooks on arithmetic and English grammar, both of which ran to many editions, and a number of commentaries on the Bible, including *The Bible Reader's Hand-Book* (1844) and *The Child's Commentator on the Holy Scriptures* (1846). He also dealt in three works with the subject of popery, concluding with *Scripture Light on Popish Darkness* (1851). He died at Denmark Cottage, Cold Arbour Lane, Kennington, London, on 10 March 1851.

THOMPSON COOPER, *rev.* DAVID HUDDLESTON

Sources *Congregational Year Book* (1851) · BL cat. · F. Boase, *Dictionary of biography* (1965)
Likenesses R. Woodman, stipple, pubd 1822, NPG · W. Finden, stipple (after E. B. Morris), NPG · engraving, repro. in E. Evans, *Catalogue of engraved British portraits*, 2 vols. (1836–53)

Cobbler of Gloucester, the. *See* Wallis, Ralph (*d.* 1669).

Cobbold, Cameron Fromanteel, first Baron Cobbold (1904–1987), banker, was born on 14 September 1904 at 23 Eaton Terrace, London, the only child of Lieutenant-Colonel Clement John Fromanteel Cobbold, barrister, of Belstead Manor, Ipswich, and his wife, Stella Willoughby Savile, daughter of Charles Cameron. He was educated at Eton College and went to King's College, Cambridge, in 1923. However, academic life did not offer the challenge he was seeking and he left after the first year.

After brief experience in accountancy, Cobbold worked in France and Italy, where, as manager in Milan of an insurance company, his skill in unravelling the tangled affairs of a failed Italian bank came to the notice of Montagu Norman, governor of the Bank of England. At Norman's invitation, he joined the bank in 1933, and rapid advancement followed. He became adviser to the governor in 1935 and, in 1938, one of four executive directors appointed to the court with the object of easing the load upon the governor. After the First World War and increasingly through the 1930s, problems of industrial reorganization and reconstruction had led the bank into areas that hitherto had been regarded as outside the concerns of a central bank. Norman's solution was to create a specialist team of advisers working outside the formal structures of the bank's staff. 'Kim' Cobbold occupied a special place in Norman's team.

Cobbold's bank apprenticeship was full and varied, both on the international and on the domestic fronts. Having joined shortly after the collapse of the gold standard, he immediately found himself closely involved in intricate international discussions, especially with the French, which led to the tripartite monetary agreement of 1936, designed to restore order in the troubled European foreign exchange markets. His domestic responsibilities were no less important and, increasingly, his time was taken up with the preparation of emergency plans for wartime operations in the bank and City. War finance itself, the transition from war to peace, problems of meeting the domestic financial needs of the country in the immediate post-war period, and, of special importance, negotiations which led to the creation of the International Monetary Fund and World Bank were matters of state that commanded the attention and honed the skills of the bank's young deputy governor, a post Cobbold attained in 1945.

As deputy governor Cobbold was closely involved in the negotiations with the government that preceded the nationalization of the bank in 1946 and, with the example of Norman to encourage him, he took on the governorship in 1949 determined to maintain the bank's integrity and independence of mind. Despite the pressures, crises, and uncertainties of his twelve years as governor, he succeeded in keeping the bank out of politics. Pressures there were—a sterling crisis and devaluation within months of his becoming governor, the bank rate tribunal of 1957, and the wide-ranging committee of inquiry into the operation of the monetary system chaired by Lord Radcliffe (1957–9)—but they were only episodes in what he saw as the proper role of the bank, dedicated to serving the national interest and providing sound practical advice to government. He was essentially a pragmatist and an able administrator, a 'markets' man and not an academic, happy to hear the arguments and to make up his own mind. To some around him he appeared reserved, even unfriendly, and he never succeeded in overcoming a dislike of public speaking. Some part at least of this was probably due to an inherent shyness, which others wrongly attributed to a lack of personal warmth. He set himself high standards and, by example and encouragement, succeeded in getting the best out of others. His public service did not end with his retirement as governor in 1961. He was a fellow of Eton (1951–67) and in 1962 he chaired the Malaysia commission of inquiry. A year later he was appointed lord chamberlain of the queen's household (1963–71), and brought to his new duties the same perceptive approach and professional expertise that had characterized his years at the bank. Tall and powerfully built, with a commanding presence, he was able to find genuine and satisfying relaxation in country pursuits. He had an honorary LLD from McGill University (1961), and an honorary DSc (Econ) from London (1963). He was sworn of the privy council in 1959, was appointed GCVO in 1963 and KG in 1970, and was created Baron Cobbold in 1960.

Cobbold met Lady (Margaret) Hermione Millicent Bulwer-Lytton in India in 1925 while staying with her father, Victor Alexander George Robert Bulwer-*Lytton, second earl of Lytton, governor of Bengal. They married in 1930 and Lady Hermione inherited the family seat at Knebworth on the death of her father in 1947. They had two daughters, one of whom died in 1937 at the age of five, and two sons, the elder of whom, David Antony Fromanteel Lytton-Cobbold (b. 1937), succeeded to the peerage. Cobbold, still active in mind and body, spent his last years in retirement happily surrounded by family and friends at Lake House, Knebworth. He died there on 1 November 1987.   PETER TAYLOR, rev.

Sources *The Times* (3 Nov 1987) · *The Times* (5 Nov 1987) · J. Fforde, *The Bank of England and public policy, 1941–1958* (1992) · personal knowledge (1996) · *CGPLA Eng. & Wales* (1988) · private information (1996)
Archives Bank of England Archive, London, letters and private file
Wealth at death £151,774: probate, 13 April 1988, *CGPLA Eng. & Wales*

Cobbold [née Knipe; other married name Clarke], **Elizabeth** (1764–1824), poet and artist in cut paper, was born on 25 February 1764 in Watling Street, London, and baptized at St Martin-in-the-Fields, on 11 March following. Her father was Robert Knipe (c.1731–1801), a Russia merchant and a director of the London Assurance Corporation, and her mother, his second wife, was Elizabeth Burchet. In 1783 the family was in Manchester and Elizabeth's first collection of poetry was published there. She met Sir Joshua Reynolds in a London bookshop and dedicated her third work, *Six Narrative Poems*, to him in 1787; four years later, when her fourth work appeared, the Knipes were at Liverpool and there Elizabeth married William Clarke (*bap.*

1731, *d.* 1791) at St Ann's Church on 16 November 1790. Clarke, an ailing sixty year old, was comptroller of customs at Ipswich, a portman who had been five times bailiff (joint mayor) there. Elizabeth was new to Ipswich and had only three months to taste the nonconformist and whig world that her husband inhabited before he died on 28 February 1791. She had less than six months to adapt to the idea of marrying again on 7 August 1791, but there was time that year for a two-volume novel, *The Sword* by Eliza Clarke, to be published in Liverpool. Her second husband, John Cobbold (1746–1835), was a prosperous Ipswich brewer and banker, a pillar of the established church and the blue party and only twenty years her senior. Elizabeth was the ideal person to take on his fifteen children aged under seventeen from a first marriage and they had six more sons and a daughter over the next ten years. Her hands were too full for much writing, but for Ann Candler's benefit, she did edit *Poetical Attempts*, with a memoir, in 1803. Recognizing a rare vocal talent, she encouraged the Ipswich girl Mary Ann Goward, later Mrs Robert Keeley, to a successful stage career. She corresponded with the Bonapartist Capel Lofft and with Sir J. E. Smith PLS over his *Flora Anglica*; George Sowerby the elder named a 'rare, and withal, elegant shell' (G. Sowerby, *Mineral Conchology*, 2.177, pl. 180) from the cragpits of the Suffolk coast *Nucula Cobboldiae*.

The Cobbolds moved from the Manor House on St Margaret's Green in Ipswich (where Margaret Catchpole served them) to Cliff House beside the brewery on the Orwell by 1798, then in 1814 to Holywells, newly built in the park whose healing springs fed the brewery below. At all their homes Elizabeth and the family entertained a wide circle of friends, generally including officers from the garrison—especially the King's German Legion commanded by her friend Count Linsingen—with genuine warmth and generosity. She wrote several dramatic pieces for the children (and even the officers) to perform, but none was published. An engaging speaker, Elizabeth founded, presided over, and raised funds for her Ipswich charities: the lying-in charity, the Society for Clothing the Infant Poor, and the annual charity bazaar.

From 1806 the highlight of each year at Cliff House was the valentine party for which Cobbold employed her greatest skill in advance: designing and making up to eighty scissors-cut valentines to present to each of the unmarried guests and mounting them with an appropriate poem on red or blue paper. By folding the paper first she could make two or three copies at once; one always went into albums for eventual presentation to her own children. There is a collection of thirty-six of her designs from 1811 in the Suffolk Record Office, and the recently discovered albums that she made for her sons Robert Knipe and Richard *Cobbold, each containing over a hundred examples, display great dexterity and originality.

The valentine parties ran until 1822 when Elizabeth Cobbold was prevented by illness from holding one as usual, and two years later she was struck down by 'an alarming illness' in July, which, returning in October, rendered her unconscious for the week before she died on 17 October 1824. She was interred six days later in the Cobbold vault in St Clement's Church, but subscribers paid for an imposing mural monument in the civic church, St Mary le Tower, as 'a public testimony of respect for exalted talents and unwearied exertion in the cause of benevolence and charity'. Her *Cliff Valentines* (poems only) for 1813 and 1814 were published in those years, and her 'Ode to Waterloo' in 1815. A memoir by Laetitia Jermyn (later the wife of James Ford) prefaces the posthumously collected *Poems* (1825), which includes many unpublished pieces, to which members of the family added poorly etched reproductions of some of her cuts. Her prolific writings, often witty and generally addressed to a friend on a particular occasion, illuminate the provincial social scene in which she was such a genial and romantic influence. Much of her verse stoops to doggerel, only inappropriate when she attempted epic subjects. Her son Richard, curate to his uncle Thomas Cobbold at the Tower church, continued to organize exhibitions of his mother's valentines as well as public dinners and balls to raise funds for her charities; his own illustrated *Valentine Verses* (1827) was published to promote the work further. Elizabeth's portrait conveys a comfortable, lovable personality; posthumous tributes praised her very diverse skills, but it is only the productions of her scissors that have enduring merit.

J. M. BLATCHLY

Sources L. Jermyn, 'Memoir', in E. Cobbold, *Poems* (1825) · E. Cobbold, correspondence, 1796–1824, Suffolk RO, Ipswich, HA 231/3 · E. Cobbold's valentines for 1811, Suffolk RO, Ipswich, HA 1027/1 · R. Cobbold, *Valentine verses* (1827) · J. J. Howard and F. A. Crisp, eds., *Visitation of England and Wales: notes*, 14 vols. (privately printed, London, 1896–1921), vol. 14, pp. 142–6 · parish register, London, St Martin-in-the-Fields, 25 Feb 1764 [birth] · parish register, London, St Martin-in-the-Fields, 11 March 1764 [baptism] · H. R. Lingwood, *EADT* (13 May 1933)

Archives BL, poems, and journal of a tour in the Lake District, Add. MS 19203 · Suffolk RO, Ipswich, corresp. and literary MSS · Suffolk RO, Ipswich, Valentine album 1811, HA 1027/1 | NL NZ, Turnbull L., letters to Gideon Algernon Mantell

Likenesses Gardiner, oils, *c.*1800, Christchurch Mansion, Ipswich · W. H. Worthington, line engraving (after Gardiner), BM, NPG; repro. in Cobbold, *Poems*

Cobbold, John Spencer (1768–1837), Church of England clergyman, son of the Revd Thomas Cobbold (1742–1831) and his wife, Anne, *née* Rust, was born at Occold, Suffolk, on 24 July 1768. He attended school in Ipswich and matriculated from Caius College, Cambridge, in 1786. He graduated BA as seventh wrangler in 1790, MA in 1793, and was a fellow of Caius, 1790–98. He taught at the Perse School, Cambridge, 1793–4, and at Nuneaton School from 1794. He was curate at Wilby, Suffolk, to his father, and followed him in 1805 to Woolpit, also as curate; on his father's death he became rector of Woolpit, where he spent the remainder of his life. He also held the vicarage of Shelland, Suffolk, to which he was instituted in 1793. In December 1798 he married Dorothy, daughter of Henry *Homer, rector of Birdingbury. Cobbold published several sermons, two essays—on immortality (1793) and on revelation (1797)—and discourses on predestination (1801), which reject both predestination and religious enthusiasm. He died at Woolpit, Suffolk, on 3 April 1837.

H. C. G. MATTHEW

Sources Venn, *Alum. Cant.* • *GM*, 2nd ser., 7 (1837), 665

Cobbold, Richard (1797–1877), novelist and Church of England clergyman, was born on 9 September 1797 at the manor house in St Margaret's parish, Ipswich, just opposite the church where he was baptized on 8 November. He was the twentieth of twenty-two children of John Cobbold (1746–1835), brewer and banker of Ipswich, and fifth of seven by his second wife, Elizabeth *Cobbold, née Knipe (1764–1824). Cobbold was educated at Bury St Edmunds under Charles Blomfield, father of the bishop, and went on to spend seven years at King Edward VI Grammar School. He then moved to the Paston School at North Walsham. Here for three years he studied under W. T. Spurdens, proceeding to Gonville and Caius College, Cambridge, as a pensioner in 1814. There two years later he won a scholarship and graduated BA in 1820, the year he was ordained deacon. He served as curate to his uncle Thomas Cobbold, resident rector at Woolpit, but absentee incumbent at St Mary-le-Tower, Ipswich.

At Hollesley on 27 November 1822 Cobbold married Mary Anne (*bap.* 1801, *d.* 1876), the only daughter of Jephtha and Mary Anne Waller. In 1824 John Cobbold purchased the right of presentation of the rich living of Wortham near Diss to provide for them, and Bishop Bathurst licensed Richard Cobbold's absence in Ipswich for the lifetime of the long-serving curate there. Cobbold was popular at the Tower church and enjoyed the social life of Ipswich, so that when in 1828 the time came to move his wife to the rectory he had built for them at Wortham they felt almost in exile. They were to spend the rest of their lives there; the last of their three sons, Thomas Spencer *Cobbold (1828–1886), was born there. He became a scientist, but the two elder sons followed their father into the church. From 1844 to 1869 Cobbold was rural dean of Hartismere.

Much influenced by his late mother's interests and charitable impulses, Cobbold published *Valentine Verses* illustrated with his own naïve lithographs in 1827 to benefit her favourite charities, but he came to be embarrassed by the critical reception of both poems and pictures. He is best known for his novel *The History of Margaret Catchpole* (1845), which romanticized and distorted the already adventurous life of a woman who had been a servant of his parents at about the time of his birth. It was a bestseller, and went into many editions, but Richard had parted with the copyright for only £1000. He wrote and published much else in poetry and prose, none of it great nor for him remunerative, but some in good causes. The novel *Mary Ann Wellington, the Soldier's Daughter, Wife and Widow* (1846) did benefit the real Mary Ann. *Freston Tower* (1850) is a shallow fictional account of the early days of the

Ipswich-born Thomas Wolsey. Cobbold edited *John H. Steggall: a Real History of a Suffolk Man* (1857), useful as social history.

Well into middle age, Cobbold indulged in the active pursuits popular with country clergymen. Fiercely partisan for his church, he would employ both inducements and sanctions to keep his flock loyal and his Sunday school full. Because he was nationally celebrated as an author, Cobbold attracted the interest locally of incognito sermon-tasters and journalists who wrote scathingly of his performance. Preaching in 1858, his voice was 'deep and very powerful; but his manner we could not help remarking is more pompous than impressive'. 'The exordium [of his sermon] was a trite collection of recurrences in Scripture of the words at the commencement of the text'. 'He grew verbose and proportionately feeble' (Gowing, 'Suffolk pulpit'). Despite the critics, he worked with devotion among his parishioners.

In 1977 the work likely to prove Cobbold's most enduring monument was published by Batsford in a copiously illustrated edition by Ronald Fletcher, *The Biography of a Victorian Village: Richard Cobbold's Account of Wortham, Suffolk, in 1860*. The original manuscripts, illustrated with Cobbold's charming amateur watercolour drawings, are preserved in the Suffolk Record Office. A sense of Cobbold's own isolation is combined with genuine understanding of and affection for all conditions of his parishioners. There is Old Soldier Smith who died in his wheelbarrow, sad Noah Fake, 'the Village carpenter—the Village politician—the Village factotum—performing almost all offices and knowing himself to be but a poor performer' (Fletcher, 131), and Mrs Balding, a 'very nice little woman who jumped out of her garrett window deranged and ran over the fields in a state of nudity' (ibid., 94).

The inspiration for Cobbold's record of his parish was a tragic one. In September 1860 his younger brother Edward, rector of Long Melford, burdened with personal problems, took his own life in a hotel room in Piccadilly. Reflecting on the many times he had walked from rectory to church on duty, Richard felt that as 'he was my youngest brother, so I must not expect to walk down many more times' (Fletcher, 69). It saddened him two years later when he felt bound to sell his right to the living of Wortham to King's College, Cambridge, to raise funds to help his sons to marry. He had another fifteen years to serve, and he left over £12,000 at his death, so ultimately the sale had been unnecessary. For the last year of their lives he and his wife suffered ill health, so that when on 26 December 1876 Mary Anne died aged seventy-five he was not told, and died himself on 5 January 1877. Each was buried after seven days in the churchyard at Wortham.

J. M. BLATCHLY

Sources Suffolk RO, Ipswich, Wortham albums • *The biography of a Victorian village: Richard Cobbold's account of Wortham, Suffolk, 1860*, ed. R. Fletcher (1977) • R. Gowing, *Public men of Ipswich and east Suffolk* (1875), 170–77 • R. Gowing, 'Suffolk pulpit, no. 22', *Suffolk Chronicle* (13 April 1858) • J. Glyde, 'Suffolk worthies, no. 12', *Suffolk Chronicle* (1858) • Richard Cobbold's own materials for *Margaret Catchpole* and *Mary Ann Wellington* · parish register (baptism), Ipswich, St Margaret, 8 Nov 1797

Archives Suffolk RO, Ipswich, corresp. and literary papers · Suffolk RO, Ipswich, notes relating to Wortham · Suffolk RO, Ipswich, further notes relating to Wortham · Suffolk RO, Ipswich, sermons and literary MSS · Suffolk RO, Ipswich, watercolours of Wortham and descriptions of villagers

Likenesses photograph (aged fifty), repro. in Fletcher, *Biography of a Victorian village*, 58

Wealth at death over £12,000: probate, 26 Feb 1877, *CGPLA Eng. & Wales*

Cobbold, Thomas Spencer (1828–1886), helminthologist, was born at Ipswich on 26 May 1828, the third son of the Revd Richard *Cobbold (1797–1877), novelist, and his wife, Mary Anne Waller (*bap.* 1801, *d.* 1876). He was educated at Charterhouse School, and in 1844 became a pupil of J. Green Crosse, surgeon to the Norfolk and Norwich Hospital. In 1847 he went to Edinburgh University, where he was assistant to professors Hughes Bennett and Goodsir; he graduated in medicine (as a gold medallist) in 1851.

After a short visit to Paris Cobbold returned to Edinburgh, where he became curator of the anatomical museum. While in post, in 1854 he attended the lectures of Edward Forbes, which further aroused his interest in natural history and geology. In 1857 he moved to London, where he was appointed lecturer on botany at St Mary's Hospital. In 1861 he obtained a similar post at the Middlesex Hospital, where for thirteen years he lectured on zoology and comparative anatomy. During this period Cobbold became devoted to helminthology, especially the study of parasitic worms. Many memoirs on the subject were contributed by him to the learned societies, and he was elected FRS in 1864.

The following year financial considerations pushed Cobbold into medical practice in London but by specializing as a consultant on cases where the presence of internal parasites was suspected he continued to build his reputation in helminthology. In 1868 he was, through Sir Roderick Murchison's influence, appointed Swiney lecturer on geology at the British Museum. His lectures proved popular and achieved a total cumulative audience of some 15,000 over the course of his five-year appointment. In 1873 he received an appointment as professor of botany at the Royal Veterinary College, which shortly afterwards instituted a special professorship of helminthology for him.

Cobbold's work, which was original and painstaking, successfully elucidated many obscure features in the history of animal parasites. His principal books included *Entozoa: an Introduction to the Study of Helminthology, with Reference more Particularly to the Internal Parasites of Man* (1864; supp. 1869), *The Internal Parasites of our Domesticated Animals* (1873), *Tapeworms* (1866; 4th edn, 1883), and *Parasites of Meat and Prepared Flesh Food* (1884). He was also a contributor to numerous encyclopaedias and dictionaries, and to journals including the *Annals of Natural History*, the *Journal* and *Transactions* of the Linnean Society (of which he was a fellow), the Zoological Society's *Proceedings* and *Transactions*, and the *Intellectual Observer*.

Cobbold died of heart disease on 20 March 1886 at his home, 74 Portsdown Road, Paddington, London. He was survived by his wife, about whom nothing is known, and at least one son. In 1887 they offered to institute a gold medal in his memory at the Linnean Society, but the conditions were too restrictive and the society declined.

G. T. BETTANY, *rev.* PETER OSBORNE

Sources *The Lancet* (27 March 1886) · W. T. Robertson, ed., *Photographs of eminent medical men of all countries, with brief analytical notices of their works* (1868), 77–81 · 'Illustration: T. Spencer Cobbold, MD, FRS', *Midland Medical Miscellany and Provincial Medical Journal*, 3 (1 March 1884), 65–8 · A. T. Gage and W. T. Stearn, *A bicentenary history of the Linnean Society of London* (1988) · Boase, *Mod. Eng. biog.* · J. B. S. [J. B. Sanderson], *PRS*, 67 (1889–90), iv–v

Wealth at death £12,600 1s. 2d.: probate, 19 April 1886, *CGPLA Eng. & Wales*

Cobden, Edward (1683–1764), Church of England clergyman and writer, the son of William Cobden, a gentleman, and his wife, Kathern, was born in July 1683 at Haslemere in Surrey and baptized there on 15 July. He was educated at Winchester College, and matriculated at Trinity College, Oxford, on 19 November 1702, graduating BA in 1706 and proceeding BD and DD in 1723. In 1713 he incorporated at Cambridge, taking the MA degree as a member of King's College. After entering holy orders he became chaplain to Edmund Gibson, bishop successively of Lincoln (1715–23) and London (1723–48). From 1711 to 1727 he was vicar of Sandon, Hertfordshire, a position which he held in plurality with that of Buckden, Huntingdonshire (1720–27). In 1721 he was advanced to the prebendal stall of Erpingham in the cathedral church of Lincoln, and he remained a canon of Lincoln until his death. Following the translation of Bishop Gibson to London Cobden acquired further preferments in rapid succession: the rectory of Acton, Middlesex, in 1726; a canonry of St Paul's Cathedral in 1727; and the rectory of St Augustine with St Faith, London, in 1730. He succeeded Dr Tyrwhitt as archdeacon of London in 1742, and became president of Sion College in 1751. He married a daughter of the Revd Thomas Jessop, of Tempsford, Bedfordshire; she died in 1762.

Cobden gained an early reputation as a poet. Several of his school compositions survive, among them *Duodecim scruporum lusus, Anglicè: a Game at Draughts* (1701), and in 1703 he published an encomium upon the recently completed chapel of Trinity College, Oxford. His tributes to 'Spot, a Favourite Cat' (1715) and to Joseph Addison (1720) were executed with feeling. However, he soon became better known as a fashionable preacher, who often addressed topical subjects, including the reformation of manners, hospital building, and the religious education of children. Cobden's pronounced high-churchmanship is evident in his first published theological work, *A Letter from a Minister to his Parishioner, upon his Building a Meeting-House* (1718), in which he warned sternly that 'separation from our Established Church is contrary to the Laws of God' (Cobden, *Discourses*, 1.305) and that wilful schism remained sinful, notwithstanding the legal indulgence provided by the Toleration Act. He was a friend of Dr Daniel Waterland, whom he described as 'alterum Athanasium' (ibid., 2.269), and in 1739 he published *The*

Instruction Afforded by the Church of England Considered, a sermon preached in St Mary-le-Bow at the Hutchins lecture, an annual high-church forum. Cobden maintained a high doctrine of episcopal ministry, pointed deliberately against the dissenters, in an address, *Sacerdotii delegatio, officium et dignitas*, delivered to the London clergy in 1752. Several of his later published poems celebrate the memory of King Charles I, the royal martyr, and Queen Anne, founder of the bounty to the clergy.

Despite these sympathies, and despite unwavering loyalty to his old schoolfellow Edward Holdsworth, whose open refusal to take the oath of allegiance to King George I was praised in *A Letter to the Author of the 'Muscipula'* (1718), Cobden was personally no Jacobite. He glorified the house of Hanover in verses of 1715 and 1727, and dismissed the Jacobite rising of 1745 as 'an insolent and dangerous rebellion' (Cobden, *Discourses*, 1.288). After his appointment as a chaplain-in-ordinary to King George II in 1730 Cobden became a noted court preacher. His sermon 'Of waiting for our change' was delivered in December 1737, only three weeks after the death of Queen Caroline, but in 1748 he forfeited royal favour by preaching 'A persuasive to chastity', a sermon on Genesis 39: 9, which many thought was intended to reflect on the king himself. Unmoved by fierce criticism Cobden duly published the text, contending that 'nothing in the sentiment or expression will be found unworthy of the sacred Function of a Preacher of the Gospel, or the serious attention of a Christian Assembly' (Cobden, *Persuasive*). He was never forgiven, and although he continued to preach at court, and gave one notable final sermon, *A Dissuasive Against Popery* (1751), advancing years and mounting resentment at the meagreness of his reward led him in 1752 to resign his place. In 1757 he printed *Discourses and Essays, in Prose and Verse*, dedicated to his parishioners at Acton and at St Augustine with St Faith: this included several previously unpublished sermons, including a group of nine on the beatitudes, and a large quantity of verse, previously collected as *Poems on Several Occasions* (1748). Cobden died on 22 April 1764.

RICHARD SHARP

Sources E. Cobden, *Discourses and essays, in prose and verse*, 2 vols. (1757) · *DNB* · Nichols, *Lit. anecdotes*, 1.555; 2.207–8 · Foster, *Alum. Oxon.* · Venn, *Alum. Cant.* · *IGI* · E. Cobden, *A persuasive to chastity* (1749)
Archives Hants. RO, probate and family papers

Cobden, Richard (1804–1865), manufacturer and politician, was born on 3 June 1804 in a small farmhouse at Dunford near the village of Heyshott in Sussex, the fourth of eleven children of William Cobden (1775–1833) and his wife, Millicent, *née* Amber (1775–1825).

Early life and business career The Cobdens had been small farmers in the Midhurst area of Sussex for several centuries. In 1809 William Cobden bought a small farm at Guillard's Oak, but it fared badly and in 1814 he was forced to sell and move to Hampshire, Surrey, and finally Barnet. He later established a shopkeeping business, but this too failed, in 1826. When the Guillard's Oak farm was sold relatives took charge of the eleven Cobden children, and

Richard Cobden (1804–1865), by Giuseppe Fagnani, 1865 [replica; original, 1860–61]

Richard was sent to school at Bowes Hall in Teesdale, Yorkshire. On finishing school at the age of fifteen, Cobden joined his uncle's warehousing business in Old Change, in the City of London, where he started out as a clerk, before becoming a commercial traveller, seeking muslin and calico orders in Ireland, Scotland, and the north of England. He was not particularly happy in this position. He tried to escape the firm by getting a job in the Southern Netherlands in 1823, and in 1826, following the collapse of his uncle's firm, he joined his uncle's partner's new firm, Partridge and Price.

In partnership with his friends Sheriff and Gillett, Cobden set up his own business in 1828 in Watling Street, not far from Partridge and Price, having raised £2000 to do so, some of it from John Lewis, the Regent Street retailer. The firm's initial business came from acting as London commission agents for Fort Brothers, the Manchester calico printers. In 1831 the duty on calico was repealed and Cobden and his partners leased a factory from Forts in Sabden, a small village near Burnley in Lancashire, and began printing their own calicoes. In January 1832 Cobden moved from London to Manchester, and bought a house there in Mosley Street shortly afterwards. Cobden's business thrived. By 1836 the firm had an annual turnover of £150,000, with profits of £23,000. It was not all plain sailing, however. In 1840 Cobden claimed the firm lost £20,000 in the 1837 trade crisis, and throughout the 1840s the firm's fortunes continued to fluctuate. However, in the mid-1830s the outlook was sufficiently stable to allow Cobden time to devote to other concerns, and in 1839 his elder brother Frederick (whose own business had failed in 1831) was put in charge of Cobden's interest in the firm.

Travels and early political writings Although Cobden's formal schooling ended at the age of fifteen, he read widely during his early adulthood, and broadened his horizons through travel in his early thirties. His diaries record acquaintance with Shakespeare, Burns, Washington Irving, and Cervantes among others, and from the library he left on his death it is clear that throughout his life he enjoyed works of history and political economy, especially those connected with France and America. But the earliest and most lasting impressions were made by the work of the Scottish rationalist writer and phrenologist George Combe (who became a friend) and of Adam Smith. Cobden's lifelong faith in individual improvement was derived initially from Combe's *Essay on the Constitution of Man* (1828), and his positive approach to economic development (often at odds with the political economy of the day) came from his reading of Smith's *The Wealth of Nations* (1776).

Cobden's first intervention in public affairs came as tensions worsened between whigs and radicals at Westminster. In September 1834, using the pseudonym Libra, he wrote a letter to the *Manchester Times* in which he defended Lord Brougham from the attacks of the London *Times*. Archibald Prentice, the manager of the *Manchester Times*, was clearly impressed by Libra's contribution, although the paper's editorial did wish that Libra's 'abilities had been occupied on some matter of more national importance' (27 Sept 1834, 3). Prentice later claimed that Cobden went on to write a series of letters for his paper in 1835. However, neither Cobden nor Libra reappeared in the paper in the ensuing months. Instead, Cobden did indeed turn his attention to national affairs, and using another pseudonym, this time A Manchester Manufacturer, wrote a pamphlet entitled *England, Ireland and America*, which was published by the London publisher Ridgway in the spring of 1835. In this pamphlet Cobden attacked David Urquhart, the secretary to the British embassy in Constantinople, who, along with some sections of radical opinion in the House of Commons, was calling for British intervention to prevent Russian encroachment on Turkey. Cobden argued that instead of costly intervention in the unstable affairs of the continent, Britain should look to her own problems, notably Ireland, and also strengthen the Atlantic economy.

In the summer of 1835 Cobden visited America for the first time, spending three months touring the eastern seaboard and travelling through Pennsylvania, upstate New York, and Massachusetts. The visit confirmed his earlier impressions of America's infinite capacity for the development of wealth and commerce, and made him realize that unless Britain changed its commercial policy America would soon outstrip all the old economies. In 1836 Cobden returned to his polemic with Urquhart, writing the pamphlet *Russia*, which was published in July, and which analysed the Russo-Turkish dispute in much more detail, attempting to play down the Turcophilia that was rife in Britain in the 1830s. In October Cobden embarked on a long tour, sailing via Lisbon, Gibraltar, and Malta to the eastern end of the Mediterranean, as far as Constantinople, meeting Mehmet Ali in Egypt, before returning via Greece in April 1837.

Municipal politics, 1836–1839 Despite the pamphlets, Cobden remained relatively unknown in national political circles. He did continue the polemic with Urquhart in *Tait's Edinburgh Magazine* during 1837–8 (Cobden probably came into contact with William Tait through Combe), but these contributions were not signed. In Manchester, however, Cobden became increasingly prominent in local affairs, and it was on the basis of this activity that he became more widely known in London. Cobden's initial involvement was in the field of education and social enquiry. He supported the founding of an infant school in Sabden, established a phrenological society in Manchester, joined the Manchester Literary Society (becoming vice-president in 1836) and the Manchester Statistical Society (in 1835), and helped found the Manchester Athenaeum (1836). Cobden played a leading role in the local Friends of Education, which in October 1837 organized a large public meeting in favour of national education. Through this particular organization Cobden first met John *Bright, when the latter invited him to speak on educational reform in Rochdale two months later. Cobden was also very active in municipal politics. He became a police commissioner, and in 1836 was elected to the board of the Manchester chamber of commerce. As a member of the chamber of commerce, he gave evidence to two important parliamentary select committees—on the postage in May 1838, and on banks of issue in April 1840, when he called for there to be only one bank of issue, though not necessarily the Bank of England.

In 1836 Cobden was called to serve as a juror on the court leet of the manor of Manchester, the main parochial body responsible for municipal administration in Manchester. The court leet had become increasingly ineffectual, and Cobden and other local Liberals (mainly dissenters) decided to avail themselves of the Municipal Corporations Act and gain incorporation for Manchester and for nearby Bolton as well. To do this meant not only defeating entrenched tory opinion in the city, but also winning the moderate and extreme wings of local radicalism, who were suspicious of what were seen as whig centralizing measures. With this in mind, at the end of 1837 Cobden wrote a pamphlet entitled *Incorporate your Borough*, in which he urged his fellow citizens to use incorporation to end landed dominion over the towns. Cobden's involvement in the campaign for incorporation took him to London, and there he met up with the leading radicals of the day, including Joseph Parkes (who knew of Cobden by reputation). Parkes masterminded many of the incorporation campaigns and became a lifelong friend. Through these metropolitan contacts, Cobden was put in touch with James Coppock, the prominent Stockport Liberal election agent, and he stood for that constituency in the general election of July 1837, appearing on a platform alongside Daniel O'Connell, but was unsuccessful. Manchester gained its charter of incorporation in September

1838, with Cobden promising that the flunkeyism of the old system—'the maces, cloaks, chains'—would be done away with. He became one of its first aldermen, although he rarely attended council meetings after 1839.

The Anti-Corn Law League, 1838–1846 Later in 1838 Cobden began his involvement with the campaign to repeal the corn laws, a campaign that was to occupy virtually all his time for the next eight years. Inspired largely by J. B. Smith, several Manchester merchants and manufacturers set up the Anti-Corn Law Association in October 1838. Cobden, who had left the country in August for a three-month tour of the German states, Austria, Switzerland, and Belgium, was not among the initial members, but did join later in the same month. Influenced by Smith, and also by G. R. Porter, the Board of Trade statistician, whom he had met at the British Association meeting in Manchester in 1837, Cobden had come round to believing the case for total repeal. However, as with the campaign for incorporation, Cobden and the other members of the Anti-Corn Law Association found that the rest of Manchester was reluctant to be dragged into an agitation for total repeal, and its sitting MPs were anxious not to do anything contrary to the whigs. In a move that anticipated the later tactics of the Anti-Corn Law League, Cobden, Smith, and others converted local opinion by acting on the electoral process. In December 1838 the anti-cornlaw advocates dominated the town council and mayoral elections, and in 1839 they purged the Manchester chamber of commerce of its moderate elements. The chamber of commerce then orchestrated the local petitioning campaign in support of C. P. Villiers's Commons motion for repeal in March 1839, and Cobden also sought to enlist Lord Brougham's support. When this motion was defeated, Cobden realized that more direct action would be required to convert parliament to repeal. MPs, he declared, needed to be 'made uncomfortable in their seats' (Edsall, 72). On 20 March 1839, the day after the defeat of Villiers's motion, the Anti-Corn Law League was formed at a meeting in Manchester.

Although still based in Manchester, the Anti-Corn Law League embarked on a national campaign, which had little impact initially. J. B. Smith gave up the league's leadership in 1841, owing to illness, and Cobden along with John Bright spearheaded the league's public agitation, especially during 1841–4, attending meetings in London and nationwide, in both rural and urban areas. Bright's first wife died in September 1841, and, encouraged by Cobden, he buried his grief by working flat out for the league, and the friendship between the two men intensified. They did hold different opinions on some subjects—notably education (they voted against one another over the Maynooth grant)—and had different priorities when it came to financial as opposed to parliamentary reform (a difference of view particularly evident after 1848). On several occasions Cobden also privately criticized Bright's direct, sometimes vituperative, style of public speaking. But such differences were seldom aired in public.

Cobden's contribution to the league was significant in several respects. Schooled in the municipal battles of the 1830s, Cobden understood the importance of organization, lecturing, and above all, election tactics, and his voice became one of the most influential when the council of the league determined strategy. The league's agitation changed constantly. The initial foray into the countryside, using paid lecturers, was a disaster, but the tactic, recommended by Cobden and adopted towards the end of 1840, of targeting electoral registers in the boroughs and fighting by-elections proved more successful, although it did alienate moderate whig supporters in the towns. In the latter stages of the league's campaign Cobden was the principal inspiration behind the move to create freehold votes in the large county electorates, which proved especially effective in south Lancashire and the West Riding of Yorkshire.

Cobden's rural background was also a great asset, particularly when the league devoted its resources to campaigning in the countryside from 1843 onwards. On many occasions Cobden styled himself as the friend of the farmer, telling the Commons in February 1843 that his

> ancestors were all yeomen of the class who have been suffering under this system … and I have therefore as good or a better right than any of you to stand up as the farmer's friend, and to represent his wrongs in this House. (*Speeches*, 1.32)

His knowledge of husbandry and the actual conditions of land tenure, both at home and on the continent, were vital in getting the league's message across in rural areas and, perhaps more importantly, in assuaging the fears of landowning Liberals in parliament.

However, perhaps the most important aspect of Cobden's contribution to the league came through his economic arguments. During the 1830s opposition to the corn laws had come mainly from those who wanted to reduce all indirect taxation, or from those who wanted to negotiate reciprocal commercial treaties with other European powers. Cobden gave the anti-cornlaw movement a more coherent ideology, by attacking the corn laws as a check on consumption, and, drawing on Adam Smith's ideas, as an obstacle to the balanced progress of both manufacturing and agriculture. Cobden argued that free admission of foreign corn would increase European demand for British manufactures, and the lifting of protection would make agriculture more competitive, leading to improvements in drainage and crop rotation, and increase investment in the land. Free trade would also enhance Britain's comparative advantage by discouraging the growth of manufacturing on the continent.

On 14 May 1840 Cobden married a Welsh woman, Catherine Anne Williams (1815–1877), who had attended school with several of Cobden's sisters before becoming a governess; among their six children were (Julia Sarah) Anne Cobden-*Sanderson, socialist and suffragette, and (Emma) Jane Catherine Cobden *Unwin. Cobden and Kate (as she was known in the family) made a ten-week honeymoon tour of Switzerland, taking in the French Alps and Savoy, before returning to London via Cologne and the Netherlands. Never one to miss an opportunity to proselytize, Cobden sent back accounts of the state of farming and industry in France, Switzerland, and along the Rhine which were published between June and December as a series of letters in the *Anti-Corn Law Circular*. In 1841 Kate Cobden moved into lodgings in Leamington Spa, and later in Tunbridge Wells, and Cobden kept in almost daily contact while on speaking tours, or from his own rented accommodation in London. In 1845 Cobden bought a new house in Victoria Park, Manchester, and the family, now including two children (another child had died in infancy), moved there and stayed for three years.

At the general election of 1841 Cobden stood again at Stockport and was this time successful. He had also been courted by the Bolton Liberals, and Prentice had tried to get him selected in Manchester. In parliament Cobden initially cut rather a lonely figure. Few of the other league leaders or orators were MPs at this time, and parliamentary radicals were less influential than they had been when the whigs were in office. Cobden was reluctant to stand forth in the Commons as the spokesman for the league. In his first speech, in August 1841, he couched much of his argument against the corn laws within a Christian framework, alluding to the concern at the distress in the manufacturing districts which had been expressed at a meeting of religious leaders in Manchester. Bright joined Cobden in parliament in 1843, and gradually from then on the two became more active there.

In 1842, as the economic distress spread and the league expanded its organization, the anti-cornlaw campaign gathered momentum. Headquarters were set up in London, a free-trade newspaper, *The Economist*, was established in the capital, and the league's *Anti-Bread Tax Circular* was renamed *The League* and it too began publication from London. The growing influence of the league brought with it more active opposition and notoriety, however. Many Chartists saw the repeal of the corn laws as a device to benefit those merchants and manufacturers involved in export industries, and suspected that wages might be driven down as a result. Some of this criticism fed into the question of factory legislation, with Cobden's opposition to statutory control of the length of the working day coming under attack. During the corn law debates in parliament in February 1842 Cobden's reputation as a factory master was attacked by W. B. Ferrand, the Knaresborough MP. The Anti-Corn Law League also came under fire as its opponents attributed violent language and tactics to the league's lecturers. Cobden did toy with the idea of a campaign of civil disobedience, involving refusal to pay taxes, and the closing down of factories, but such plans never left the drawing board. None the less, there was widespread suspicion that the league might have been involved in the 'plug' plots in Lancashire, and the Home Office authorized the opening of Cobden's personal mail. Leading whigs and Conservatives joined in as well. J. W. Croker published one such attack in the *Quarterly Review* in December 1842, and at the beginning of the parliamentary session that followed Lord Brougham denounced the methods of the league (although he was careful not to attack the league leaders in person). Matters came to a head on 17 February 1843, when Cobden stated in the Commons that he held Sir Robert Peel personally responsible, as head of the government, for the country's economic distress. This accusation, following a recent assassination attempt on Peel, touched a raw nerve and Peel charged Cobden with using language that might invite personal outrage.

During the remainder of 1843 and through the winter of 1843–4 the league turned its attention to the countryside, employing more effective rural lecturers and activists such as Alexander Somerville (the 'Whistler at the Plough') and Andrew Bisset. Along with Bright, Cobden travelled the length and breadth of the nation. In 1845 Cobden was more active in parliament, calling in a memorable and influential speech on 13 March for a select committee to inquire into the effects of the corn laws on the agricultural community. Cobden's reputation in parliament now reached a high point, but his business concerns plummeted. In June he contemplated retiring from public life and was dissuaded by Bright, who suggested he borrow money to prop up his firm.

By the following autumn, with the onset of the famine in Ireland, it was clear that corn law repeal or at least suspension of the corn duties was necessary. Cobden made sure the league maintained the pressure for total repeal. Peel's administration resigned in December, after defeat on the Irish Coercion Bill, but Lord John Russell was unable to form an administration (Cobden was offered the position of vice-president of the Board of Trade). Peel resumed office, proposing a phased total repeal (barring the retention of a duty of 1s.), a measure which Cobden supported, and which was passed before Peel resigned once more in June.

As repeal was enacted, Peel greatly offended his own supporters by praising the contribution of Cobden, and Cobden in turn privately urged Peel to now head a new party—a 'mixed progressive party'—based on further practical reforms. In July Russell formed his administration and wrote to Cobden leaving open the question of his joining the cabinet. Cobden's influence and role in the repeal of the corn laws were thus widely recognized, although he himself was more sanguine. In 1853 he told Prentice, who had completed writing the first history of the league, that 'it was but a blundering unsystematic series of campaigns, in which we were partly indebted for our triumph to the stupidity of our foes, and still more to the badness of their cause' (Prentice, 53).

The league campaign left Cobden almost ruined financially. As the agitation drew to a close a public subscription was organized on his behalf, which raised £76,759. The sum was used to pay off debts he had incurred; some was later invested in the shares of the Illinois Railway Company and in the Safety Life Assurance Company. A major part of the testimonial was used to purchase and renovate property at Dunford in Sussex, where he had been born. In 1848 Cobden sold his Manchester home, moved to Westbourne Terrace in London, and spent weekends at Dunford while extensive building and landscaping works were going on. The family moved permanently to Dunford in 1853, although the works were only finally completed in 1856. Between 1848 and 1861 Kate gave birth to four more daughters.

The struggle for repeal had also left Cobden physically exhausted, and at the beginning of August 1846 he and Kate embarked on a fourteen-month tour of the continent, travelling through France, Spain, the Italian and German states, Prussia, and Russia (Cobden completed the Russian portion of the trip on his own). Although the tour was intended to be recuperative, and Cobden did play the part of the tourist, he was overwhelmed by invitations to soirées, banquets, and lectures almost wherever he went (with the exception of Vienna). In France, free-traders led by Frédéric Bastiat provided the acclaim, as did the free-traders of the Hanseatic ports; in the Italian states he was hosted by agricultural reformers. He met with the monarchs of France, Spain, Sardinia, the Two Sicilies, and Prussia, and statesmen such as Thiers, Narvaez, Cavour, Metternich, Canitz, and Nesselrode. The tour impressed upon Cobden the extent to which the European states were undergoing what he called a 'social revolution', based on the subdivision of landownership, and convinced him that such was the growth of prosperity and social equality that governments would no longer have to resort to war or colonization in order to contain domestic strife. He welcomed the 1848 revolutions, for, although he distrusted the republicans, he believed that the 1848 uprisings would lead to greater civil freedom to accompany the social and economic progress he had witnessed.

The struggle for retrenchment, 1847–1853 Cobden returned from the continent in October 1847. In his absence, a general election had taken place, and he had been chosen for both Stockport and the West Riding of Yorkshire, where some of his Manchester friends had solicited support on his behalf. He chose to sit for the latter, at that time one of the largest constituencies in the country. Cobden occupied a pivotal place in Liberal Party politics in the late 1840s. Whig leaders were anxious lest he join forces with the Peelites, moderate London Chartists sought his backing, and radical MPs such as Sir Joshua Walmsley and Joseph Hume enlisted his co-operation in their parliamentary reform campaigns. Cobden was also by now a public celebrity: he made a cameo appearance in William Thackeray's *Pendennis* (1850), handkerchiefs bearing his portrait were sold, and he was made a commissioner for the Exhibition of All Nations, alongside Peel. (In fact, Cobden and Peel attended a meeting of the commission only hours before Peel's fatal accident.)

In the years after 1847 Cobden resumed many of the political campaigns with which he had been associated during the previous decade. Incurring the disapproval of his nonconformist constituents, Cobden became a leading supporter of the National Public Schools Association, believing that 'government interference is as necessary for *education* as its non-interference is essential to *trade*' (Cobden to James Coppock, 15 June 1847, Cobden MSS, W. Sussex RO). He continued his involvement in the freehold movement, helping to establish the National Freehold Land Society in 1850, and he pushed another organization, the National Parliamentary and Financial Reform

Association, into a campaign to create freehold votes in the large county electorates surrounding London. Cobden joined the committee of the Association for Promoting the Repeal of the Taxes on Knowledge, and he also took up the cause of colonial reform, in Ceylon, Borneo, and India, writing a pamphlet on the Second Anglo-Burmese War, *How Wars are Got up in India*, which was published in 1853.

But for all his stature in the late 1840s, Cobden's influence turned out to be limited. Joseph Parkes compared him to 'a whale on shore, alive'—magnitude without purpose (Parkes to Charles Wood, 31 Dec 1849, Hickleton MSS, University of York). Despite his commitment to a range of reform issues, Cobden became most associated in the late 1840s and 1850s with what proved to be an unpopular campaign for retrenchment in defence spending at home and non-intervention in European affairs. Cobden unveiled this new strategy in the new year of 1849, using his 'National Budget' to call for a return to the defence expenditure levels of the mid-1830s. In June he brought in a motion in parliament calling for international arbitration, and in October he set out his views on non-intervention in an article published in the *Westminster Review*. Cobden also became a leading supporter of the Peace Society. Its secretary, Henry Richard, became one of his main confidants, and he attended four international peace congresses between 1849 and 1853. In these years Cobden also sat on several parliamentary select committees—army expenditure (1848 and 1851) and official salaries (1850)—attempting to force reductions in the defence and diplomatic establishments.

After 1850 Cobden found little support in the Liberal Party for his campaign of peace and retrenchment. This was owing partly, as Cobden suspected, to the influence of Lord Palmerston as foreign secretary and later prime minister, against whose style of 'meddling' foreign policy Cobden spoke out in the Don Pacifico debate in the Commons in June 1850. But Palmerston was not the only factor. The Lancashire and Yorkshire merchants and manufacturers who had bankrolled the league were reluctant to throw their weight behind Cobden, although they responded rapidly to the return of the Conservatives in February 1852 by re-establishing the Anti-Corn Law League. Furthermore, the resurgence of fears of French invasion which followed Louis Napoleon's *coup d'état* of December 1851 increased calls for greater rather than less national defence, and Cobden was left arguing a lonely case for Anglo-French co-operation in his 'South Saxon' letters to *The Times* (January 1852) and later in his most controversial and hard-hitting pamphlet *1793 and 1853*, which was published in the new year of 1853.

The era of Palmerston The Crimean War delivered the final blow to Cobden's hopes for retrenchment and non-intervention. He was typically strident and outspoken in the months preceding Britain's intervention, arguing that British intervention on behalf of Turkey was a misguided policy, inasmuch as Turkey was a Muslim state in decline, while the interests of Russia, the perceived aggressor, lay in peaceful, commercial relations with the west. Once war was declared, Cobden fell relatively silent, reduced to 'let-[ting] the flood roll on' (Cobden to J. B. Smith, 12 Jan 1854, J. B. Smith MSS, Manchester Central Library). He appeared before his constituents at Leeds in January 1855 but he was generally disillusioned by the outbreak of popular support for the war, especially that kindled by his old sparring partner the Russophobe David Urquhart. Towards the end of the war Cobden returned to active politics, writing the pamphlet *What next? And next?* (1856)—an attack on those wanting to continue the war at all costs—and he was also involved in establishing the London-based newspaper the *Morning Star*.

In April 1856 Cobden's life was overtaken by domestic tragedy with the sudden death of his only son, Dick, aged fifteen, who was away studying at a school near Heidelberg. Kate Cobden was particularly struck by this heavy blow. Her hair blanched almost immediately, and she became over-dependent on opium to ease her bereavement. As a result Cobden was homebound at Dunford for long periods. About the same time John Bright suffered a physical breakdown.

Public humiliation was added to private grief in the general election of 1857, which followed the British bombardment of the Chinese port of Canton (Guangzhou). John Bowring, Cobden's former friend and parliamentary colleague (the two men had drifted apart in the 1850s), had ordered this action, after the Chinese had unlawfully boarded a ship alleged to be British. Initially, Cobden assumed that Bowring had been merely carrying out the instructions of the Foreign Office, but he later found out that this was not so. In parliament Cobden sought to criticize British policy without a direct motion of censure, which he knew would play straight into Palmerston's hands, as it had in the case of Don Pacifico. So, on 26 February he introduced a motion containing two resolutions. The first stated that the papers presented to the Commons failed to establish grounds for the bombardment of Canton; the second called for the appointment of a select committee to inquire into the state of commercial relations with China. However, only the first resolution was discussed and, although carried in Cobden's favour by a majority of sixteen (with the support of the Peelites, Disraeli, and Russell), it proved a pyrrhic victory, as Cobden had feared, for Palmerston dissolved parliament and called an election.

As the election got under way, Cobden's canvass of electors in the West Riding revealed that his chances of re-election there were slim, so he opted to stand in Huddersfield instead. At the same time he campaigned on behalf of the absent Bright in Manchester. Along with many other independent Liberal and radical MPs Cobden lost his seat in the 1857 election, and he remained absent from public life for the next two years. This respite was not altogether unwelcome. Cobden's faith in the body politic reached its nadir in 1857. He despaired at the once radical electorates of Lancashire and Yorkshire, and he told friends that he had no desire to enter a 'servile' parliament under Palmerston. There were private reasons too. Cobden's wife's grief continued unabated, and in the

spring of 1858 Fred, Cobden's elder brother, died after a long illness. Cobden's financial affairs were in a poor state by this time, too, mainly as a result of his speculative investment in the Illinois Railway Company. He was forced to borrow from friends in order to meet the company's further calls on shareholders, and in 1859 a further public subscription, totalling £40,531, was required to help him out. (Another subscription was mooted in 1861 but never undertaken.)

In February 1859 Cobden left Britain for his second visit to the United States, his main aim being to investigate the affairs of the Illinois Railway Company for himself. He spent four months there, criss-crossing between New York, Washington, and Chicago, impressed by the great progress the country had experienced since his first visit in the mid-1830s. On his return at the end of June Cobden found that Palmerston was forming a new government, and both he and Russell wanted Cobden to join the cabinet as president of the Board of Trade. From Liverpool, where he disembarked, Cobden travelled immediately to London to respond in person to Palmerston's offer. He declined the position, pointing out that to accept would be an act of inconsistency on his part as he had opposed Palmerston for so long.

The Cobden–Chevalier treaty In his absence Cobden had been returned as MP for Rochdale, partly through Bright's efforts. However, he took little part in parliament during the next two years, as he spent most of that time negotiating a treaty of commerce with France. In 1856, when Lord Clarendon, the British foreign secretary, visited Paris, Michel Chevalier had suggested to Cobden that the time was right for establishing free trade between the two countries, as a treaty did not have to be steered through the largely protectionist French legislature. Nothing came of this in 1856, but in the autumn of 1859 Chevalier renewed his suggestion, and Cobden contacted W. E. Gladstone, now chancellor of the exchequer, and visited him at Hawarden on 12 September 1859, when the issue was discussed at length. Both men were convinced that a commercial treaty would not only continue the reduction of indirect tax, but could also be the means of ensuring peaceful relations between the two countries. Gladstone backed Cobden's plan to undertake a voluntary mission to Paris in order to sound out the views of Napoleon III. Russell, the foreign secretary, and Palmerston were cooler, but they allowed the mission to go ahead.

Cobden left for Paris on 18 October, and despite ill health and the opposition of some of the emperor's ministers, he had two successful meetings with Napoleon III. It is doubtful whether the emperor was actually converted by Cobden's advocacy—he was not opposed to tariff reform, and Chevalier had already paved the way for Cobden through his own contacts with the emperor. Once committed to the idea of the treaty, however, the emperor sought its rapid completion. In the new year Cobden was given plenipotentiary powers by the British government and on 23 January 1860 the treaty was signed by Cobden and Lord Cowley, the British ambassador, on behalf of Britain. Duties were abolished on most French imports into Britain, although some duty was retained on French wines, while duties on British imports into France were gradually reduced.

The actual tariff schedules remained to be negotiated, and after a holiday in Cannes and a short visit to London, Cobden returned to Paris on 20 April, where he remained until November, in order to complete the task as chief commissioner. Apart from settling the details of the tariff, better postal facilities between the two countries were agreed, and passports were eliminated. Once the negotiations were over, Cobden headed south to Algiers with Kate and their eldest daughter and stayed there until the following April. The treaty was a major achievement, not so much for its actual provisions—which many felt benefited France more than Britain—as for the international harmony it symbolized. The treaty had been settled despite hostile protectionism in France, the emperor's vacillation, and a new invasion panic back in Britain. As in 1846, honours were now heaped upon Cobden—by chambers of commerce, manufacturers' associations, and various cities. In April 1861 Palmerston offered him a baronetcy or the rank of privy councillor, but Cobden declined. Throughout the negotiations Cobden felt he had not had sufficient backing from Palmerston. In the spring of 1860 Palmerston had announced new coastal fortifications, despite Cobden's plea that this be delayed until the completion of the treaty negotiations. Not surprisingly, on his return Cobden resumed his attack on the Palmerstonian system, producing in October 1861 a long memorandum on the Anglo-French naval build-up and, the following year, a pamphlet on *The Three Panics* of 1848, 1853, and 1862.

Final years Cobden's support for non-intervention intensified during the American Civil War, which broke out in 1861. He never doubted that morality was on the side of the Union, and that the future of America lay with the industrial and commercial supremacy of the north. However, Cobden remained suspicious of the protectionist tendencies of the Union, as manifested in the Morrill tariff of 1861, and he had a low opinion of the administrative abilities of the Republican Party: in March 1864 he commented to his friend Thomas Thomasson that 'if their [the North's] *cause* was not so good, I should certainly back the South whose men are much more capable whether as statesmen or generals' (R. Cobden to T. Thomasson, March 1864, Thomas Thomasson MSS, BLPES). Moreover, he opposed the blockade tactics used by the North, which had led to the drying up of the supply of southern cotton to Europe. But he thought throughout the war that Britain, along with the other European powers, should remain neutral. Cobden used his contacts with leading Americans such as Sumner and Adams, within the British and French governments, and also among the Lancashire cotton manufacturers to dampen calls for armed intervention to end the blockade. And he joined in attempts to relieve the distress of cotton workers during the Lancashire famine.

By the early 1860s it was clear that Cobden had aged considerably. He had lost much of his vigour and put on weight, and his hair was now greying rapidly. Although revered as an elder statesman within the Liberal Party, he lacked his usual fire and some of his judgement. In December 1863 he became embroiled in an acrimonious dispute with *The Times*, some thirty years after he had first stepped into public life in order to sound off against the paper. In November a *Times* editorial had accused Bright of wanting to divide the land of the rich among the poor, and had called on both Bright and Cobden to disavow any such schemes. Cobden leapt to Bright's defence, attacking J. T. Delane, the paper's editor, for making scandalous aspersions behind the screen of anonymous journalism. *The Times* refused to publish Cobden's reply to Delane, and a rather petty correspondence ensued. Cobden was by now an infrequent attender of parliament—in 1864 he spoke during the Schleswig-Holstein affair and on Chinese affairs—although he could at last draw some comfort from the waning of Palmerston's influence over foreign policy.

In November 1864 Cobden addressed a large meeting in his Rochdale constituency. It proved to be one public speech too many. For two months he was confined to Dunford, with asthma and bronchial and throat problems. When parliament reassembled the following year he was determined to take part in the debates on Canadian fortifications and on 21 March he travelled up to London, where he suffered another asthmatic attack on arrival. He died just under a fortnight later on 2 April 1865 in his lodgings at 23 Suffolk Street, Pall Mall. Palmerston, Disraeli, and Bright gave tributes in the Commons, and newspapers throughout Britain, America, and Europe provided fulsome obituaries, praising his achievements of 1846 and 1860, but passing over his political isolation during the 1850s. Cobden was buried on 6 April in the same grave as his son in the churchyard at West Lavington, a simple grave which looks out through the woods towards the gentle rolling hills of Sussex farmland.

As Cobden died, the principles of retrenchment and non-intervention for which he had campaigned so relentlessly in the last two decades of his life were becoming an integral part of the Gladstonian Liberal Party's philosophy. In the years after his death his reputation grew and his pamphlets and speeches were edited and expounded by the Cobden Club, and by Liberal Party luminaries such as J. E. T. Rogers, Louis Mallet, and Goldwin Smith. After 1900, when the Edwardian Liberal Party needed reminding of the first principles of free trade and anti-imperialism it looked to John Morley's *Life of Richard Cobden* (2 vols., 1881), a book that established new standards of biographical documentation and comment. But as internationalism and free trade have declined so too has Cobden's reputation, and his modern biographers have been rather disappointed by his commitment to the peace question, and generally been more interested in his role in early Victorian middle-class culture. Cobden's work as a land reformer has not featured so largely in his changing reputation. Yet his belief in the necessity of redistribution of land ownership was arguably the connecting arch in his whole political outlook, for he was convinced that individual proprietorship of the soil, both on the continent and in Britain, was the precondition for social stability, prosperity, and peace. As he told a journalist who visited him during his last illness, 'the decrease in the number of landowners has ever been the forerunner of decay in empires' (Edge, 26).   MILES TAYLOR

Sources BL, Cobden MSS · W. Sussex RO, Cobden papers · Man. CL, Cobden MSS · *The political writings of Richard Cobden*, 2 vols. (1867) · *Speeches on questions of public policy*, ed. J. Bright and J. E. T. Rogers, 2 vols. (1870) · *The American diaries of Richard Cobden*, ed. E. H. Cawley (1952) · *The European diaries of Richard Cobden*, ed. M. Taylor (1994) · *Mr Cobden and the Times, etc.* (1864) · *Mr Cobden on the land question* (1873) [first pubd in the *Morning Star*, 22 Jan 1864, signed R. S. T.] · A. Prentice, *History of the Anti-Corn-Law League*, 2 vols. (1853) · J. McGilchrist, *Richard Cobden: the apostle of free trade* (1865) · J. E. Ritchie, *The life of Richard Cobden* (1865) · [F. M. Edge], *Richard Cobden at home* (1868) · H. Ashworth, *Recollections of Richard Cobden … and the Anti-Corn-Law League*, new edn (1877) · J. Morley, *The life of Richard Cobden*, 2 vols. (1881) · A. Bisset, *Notes on the anti-corn law struggle* (1884) · E. W. Watkin, *Alderman Cobden of Manchester* (1891) · J. Schwabe, *Reminiscences of Richard Cobden* (1895) · J. A. Hobson, *Richard Cobden: the international man* (1918) · W. E. A. Axon, *Cobden as citizen: a chapter in Manchester history* (1907) · A. Dunham, *The Anglo-French treaty of commerce and the progress of the industrial revolution in France* (1938) · N. McCord, *The Anti-Corn Law League, 1838–1846* (1958) · D. Read, *Cobden and Bright: a Victorian political partnership* (1967) · N. C. Edsall, *Richard Cobden: independent radical* (1986) · W. Hinde, *Richard Cobden: Victorian outsider* (1987) · P. N. Farrar, 'Richard Cobden, educationist, economist and statesman', PhD diss., University of Sheffield, 1987 · J. S. Rogers, *Cobden and his Kate: the story of a marriage* (1990) · M. Taylor, *The decline of British radicalism, 1847–1860* (1995) · Gladstone, *Diaries*

Archives BL · Man. CL · W. Sussex RO | BL, Bright MSS · BL, Gladstone MSS · BL, A. Ireland MSS · BL, Russell MSS · BL, Charles Sturge MSS · BL, Joseph Sturge MSS · BLPES, Thomas Thomasson MSS · Bodl. Oxf., E. Alexander MSS, MS Don e 123 · Bodl. Oxf., Kimberley MSS · Bodl. Oxf., Thorold Rogers MSS · Co-operative Union, Holyoake MSS · CUL, Samuel Smiles MSS · Glos. RO, John Morton MSS · Herefs. RO, George Moffat MSS · Man. CL, George Wilson MSS · NL Scot., John Burton MSS · NL Wales, Hugh Williams MSS · PRO, Wellesley MSS · PRO, Russell MSS · U. Cal., Los Angeles, Schwabe MSS · UCL, Joseph Parkes MSS · W. Sussex RO, Joshua Walmsley MSS · W. Yorks. AS, E. Baines MSS · London, Peace Society MSS

Likenesses L. Saulini, chalk drawing, 1827?, Staatliche Kunstsammlungen, Dresden, Germany, Kupferstichkabinett · C. A. Duval, portrait, 1843, Man. CL · F. C. Lewis, stipple, pubd 1843 (after C. A. Duval), NPG · Cattier, portrait, 1849, Dunford House, near Midhurst, Sussex · S. Bellini, group portrait, mixed-method engraving, pubd 1850 (after *The Anti-Corn Law League* by J. R. Herbert, 1847), NPG · G. Fagnani, oils, 1860–61, New York Chamber of Commerce, New York · G. G. Adams, bronze statue, 1862, St Peter's Square, Stockport · G. Fagnani, oils, replica, 1865, NPG [*see illus.*] · C. G. Lewis, group portrait, mixed-method engraving, pubd 1865 (after *Intellect and valour of Great Britain* by T. J. Barker), NPG · M. Noble, marble bust, 1865, Dunford Museum, Midhurst, West Sussex · G. Scharf, pencil tracing drawing, 1865 (after L. C. Dickinson), NPG · M. Noble, marble bust, 1866, Reform Club, London · M. Noble, statue, 1867, Peel Park, Salford · M. Wood, bronze statue, c.1867, St Anne's Square, Manchester · C. Lucy, oils, 1868, V&A · W. and T. Wills, marble statue, 1868, Camden High Street, London · H. Daumier, cartoons, lithograph, NPG; repro. in *Le Charivari* (1856) · L. C. Dickinson, oils, NPG; version, Reform Club, London · S. Nixon, bronze statuette, U. Cam., Marshall Library of Economics · J. Philip, group portrait, oils (*The House of Commons, 1860*), Palace of Westminster, London · T. Woolner, marble bust, Brighton Art Gallery; replica, NPG · cartes-de-visite, NPG · photographs, NPG · portrait, repro. in W. C. Taylor, *National Portrait Gallery*, 3 (1847) · prints (some after photographs), BM, NPG · statue, Albert Square, Manchester

Wealth at death under £8000: double probate, July 1866, *CGPLA Eng. & Wales* (1865)

Cobham. For this title name *see* individual entries under Cobham; *see also* Oldcastle, John, Baron Cobham (d. 1417); Brooke, George, ninth Baron Cobham (c.1497–1558); Brooke, William, tenth Baron Cobham (1527–1597); Brooke, Henry, eleventh Baron Cobham (1564–1619); Temple, Richard, first Viscount Cobham (1675–1749).

Cobham family (*per. c.1250–c.1530*), gentry, was a prolific family which established itself in south-east England, from the late twelfth century, and dominated the administration of Kent and Surrey for much of the fourteenth century. Members of all three of its branches were summoned as peers to parliament, though only in one line did the title become hereditary for more than two generations. Those branches can be traced back to the marriages of **John** [i] **Cobham** (d. c.1251). From his first marriage, to Maud Fitzbenedict, descended the Cobhams of Cobham and the Cobhams of Rundale, both in Kent, while from his second marriage, to Joan, daughter of Hugh de *Neville (d. 1234), descended the Cobhams of Sterborough, also in Kent.

Cobham of Cobham The first of the Cobhams of Cobham was John [ii] Cobham (d. 1300), the eldest son of John [i] and Maud. All eight of his known children appear to have been born of the first of his two marriages, to Joan, daughter and coheir of Sir Robert Septvans. His eldest son and heir, **Henry Cobham**, first Lord Cobham of Cobham (1260–1339), married Maud, daughter of Eudes de Moreville and widow of Matthew de Columbers. He was constable of Rochester (a position previously held by his father) and Tonbridge castles. In 1300 and 1311–15 he fought in Scotland. In 1305 he became warden of the Cinque Ports and constable of Dover Castle, a position that had probably been held by his uncle, Reynold Cobham (d. 1258). He was summoned to parliament from 1313. He remained loyal to Edward II, and presided over the arraignment of the rebel Bartholomew, Lord Badlesmere, at Canterbury in 1322. He died at Hatch Beauchamp, Somerset, on 25 August 1339, and was buried in the Beauchamp chapel of his daughter-in-law Joan (fl. 1314–1343) at Stoke-sub-Hamdon in the same county. Henry Cobham's son and heir, **John** [iii] **Cobham**, second Lord Cobham of Cobham (d. 1355), was married first to Joan, daughter of John, Lord Beauchamp of Hatch, and second to Agnes, daughter of Richard Stone of Dartford. In 1320 he succeeded his father as warden of the Cinque Ports and constable of Dover Castle. He was knighted by 1327. He was associated with his father as constable of Rochester Castle for life in 1334, and the following year he became admiral from the Thames westwards. He was summoned to a royal council in 1342 and to parliament from 1350. In 1354 he was given the rank of banneret and a 100 mark annuity. He died on 25 February 1355, and was buried in Cobham church.

John *Cobham, third Baron Cobham of Cobham

John Cobham, second Lord Cobham of Cobham (d. 1355), memorial brass

daughter Joan, the only surviving child of his marriage to Margaret Courtenay, daughter of Hugh Courtenay, earl of Devon, married John Pole of Chrishall, Essex. Her daughter, Joan (d. 1433/4), married five times. With her second husband, Sir Reynold Braybrooke, she had a daughter, Joan, who took the Cobham title to the Brooke family of Somerset and Devon by her marriage to Sir Thomas. The elder Joan's fourth husband was Sir John *Oldcastle, the heretic and rebel executed in 1417.

Two of John [ii] Cobham's younger sons also enjoyed distinguished careers. Thomas *Cobham (d. 1327) obtained degrees in arts from Paris, in canon law from Oxford, and in theology from Cambridge, and was employed on diplomatic missions under Edward I and Edward II. In 1313, still only a subdeacon, he narrowly missed being created archbishop of Canterbury, when Edward II preferred Walter Reynolds, bishop of Worcester. Four years later he was consoled with Reynolds's former bishopric. He bequeathed his library to Oxford University, and after some vicissitudes his books were incorporated into Duke Humfrey's Library. **Ralph Cobham**, Lord Cobham (d. 1326), fought at Boroughbridge in 1322 and in France in 1325 and was summoned to parliament in 1324-5. With his wife, Mary Roos (d. 1362), he had a son, John [v] Cobham (1324-1378), who fought in France in 1359-60. John died without surviving issue, and shortly before his death, out of affection for Edward, the Black Prince, he named the crown as his heir.

Cobham of Rundale The Rundale branch originated with Sir Henry Cobham (d. c.1316), the younger brother of Sir John [ii] Cobham. He fought in France in 1297, and in Scotland in 1300 and 1314-16. His eldest surviving son, **Stephen Cobham**, Lord Cobham of Rundale (d. 1332), was summoned to parliament from 1326—the only Rundale Cobham to be so honoured. Stephen's son, Sir John [iv] Cobham (d. 1362), at his death held Allington Castle and the manors of Rundale and Hever, all in Kent. He fought in France and Scotland. His elder son and heir, **Sir Thomas Cobham** (c.1343-1394), had been knighted by 1372, and in the 1370s campaigned in Ireland and France. During the peasants' revolt of 1381 he was captured by rebels, but having regained his freedom took part in the revolt's suppression. With his first wife, Maud (d. 1380), daughter and heir of Thomas Morice, pleader and common sergeant of London, he had two sons, and was succeeded by the elder of these, Sir Reynold Cobham (1372-1405), who married Elizabeth (d. 1451), daughter of Sir Arnold *Savage of Bobbing, speaker of the Commons, and his wife, Joan. A more notable career was that of the uncle of Sir Reynold, **John** [vi] **Cobham** (d. 1399), the second son of Sir John [iv] Cobham (d. 1362). He received the manor of Hever from his elder brother in 1362, and also acquired property in Devon, possibly as a retainer of his cousins, the Courtenay earls of Devon, who may have introduced him to the court—he was a king's esquire by 1388. John was also on good terms with the lords Grey of Ruthin, and with his cousin, John, third Baron Cobham of Cobham (d. 1408), despite their political differences—unlike Lord Cobham, John never joined the opposition to Richard II. He was

(d. 1408), John [iii]'s son and heir from his first marriage, was probably the most distinguished member of the medieval family in any of its branches. Prominent both as a soldier and a politician, he fought in France between 1359 and 1376, being made a banneret in 1370, and was several times employed as an ambassador. A royal councillor at Richard II's accession, in 1386 he was appointed to the council set up to direct government in the king's name. For this he was never forgiven by Richard, and in 1397 he was impeached and exiled to Jersey, though he returned to favour under Henry IV. A friend of the poet John Gower, he was a notable builder at Cooling Castle and elsewhere in Kent, and refounded the parish church of Cobham as a chantry college. He is commemorated within it by an engraved brass, one of a magnificent collection which preserves the images of members of the family and their spouses from the fourteenth century to the sixteenth. His lieutenant to Thomas, duke of Gloucester, as constable of England before 1392, and he served in Ireland in 1394–5 and 1399: he died soon after returning with the king to face Henry Bolingbroke. Through his second wife, Joan (*d.* 1393), daughter of Sir John d'Oyley of Staffordshire and Margaret Tregoz of Sussex, he acquired substantial estates in Sussex and disputed property in the midlands. The last male of the Rundale line was Sir Thomas Cobham (1397–1424?), the son of Sir Reynold and Elizabeth, who left only a daughter, Elizabeth.

Cobham of Sterborough The Sterborough Cobhams originated with Sir Reynold [i] Cobham (*fl. c.*1285), half-brother of John [ii] Cobham of Cobham and Henry Cobham of Rundale. With his wife, Joan, daughter of William d'Evere, he had a son and heir, **Reynold** [ii] **Cobham**, first Lord Cobham of Sterborough (*c.*1295–1361). Reynold the younger had a distinguished military record in France and Flanders: admiral of the west in 1344 and 1348, he was part of the Black Prince's bodyguard at Crécy, and at Poitiers he was marshal of the prince's army and conducted the captured King John to the English lines. He was captain of Calais from 1353. In recognition of his service he was created a banneret in 1339, a knight of the Garter about 1353, and in 1347 he was given an annuity of £500. A diplomat as well as a soldier, he was employed on embassies to the papal curia and Brabant. He was summoned to a royal council in 1342 and to parliaments from 1347. His wife was Joan (*d.* 1369), daughter of Thomas, Lord Berkeley, and his wife, Margaret, daughter of Roger Mortimer, earl of March (*d.* 1330). He died of plague, and was buried in Lingfield church.

His son and heir, **Reynold** [iii] **Cobham**, second Baron Cobham of Sterborough (1348–1403), followed in his father's footsteps as soldier and diplomat, playing a prominent part in French and Gascon campaigns between 1369 and 1401, and participating in embassies in 1374 and 1377. He was summoned to parliaments from 1371. He married twice, first Elizabeth (*d.* 1376), widow of John, Lord Ferrers, and before him of Fulk, Lord Strange, and daughter of Ralph *Stafford, first earl of Stafford, and second, in 1380, Eleanor (1345–1405), granddaughter of John, first lord *Maltravers and widow of John, Lord Arundel. Reynold and Eleanor were related within the third degree (through Eleanor's Berkeley grandmother), and so after the birth of their son and heir, **Sir Reynold** [iv] **Cobham** (1381–1446), they obtained an annulment followed by a papal dispensation, and then remarried. After his father's death the inheritance of Reynold [iv] was seised by the king on the grounds that he was illegitimate, and in 1417/18 Reynold had to assert his right to inherit in the exchequer. Never summoned to parliament, he was knighted in 1426, and ten years later he received the custody of Charles, duke of Orléans, who had been captured at Agincourt. He married twice. His first wife was Eleanor (*d.* 1422), daughter of Sir Thomas *Culpeper (*d.* 1429) [*see under* Culpeper family]. With his second wife, Anne (1389–1453), daughter of Thomas *Bardolf, Lord Bardolf, and Amice, daughter of Ralph, Lord Cromwell, he founded

Lingfield collegiate church in 1431. Sir Reynold [iv] and both his wives were buried at Lingfield.

Reynold [iv] and Eleanor had four children. Sir Reynold [iv] was predeceased by his eldest son, Sir Reynold [v] Cobham, who died in 1441 or 1442. Sir Reynold [v] married twice. His only surviving child, Margaret (*d. c.*1460), born to his first wife, Thomasine, daughter of Sir Thomas Chideocke, married Ralph *Neville, second earl of Westmorland. At the time of Margaret's marriage, between 1441 and 1442, her grandfather settled the Sterborough inheritance on her and her children, with remainder to his second son, **Sir Thomas Cobham** (*d.* 1471). She died without surviving children, and was buried at Doncaster, and consequently Sir Thomas succeeded to the Sterborough inheritance. He married Anne (*d.* 1472), widow of Aubrey de Vere, son of the earl of Oxford, and daughter of Humphrey *Stafford, first duke of Buckingham, and his wife, Anne, daughter of Ralph *Neville, first earl of Westmorland. He had close links with Archbishop Thomas Bourchier, and was constable of Rochester Castle from 1415. He left an illegitimate son, Reynold [vi] Cobham, probably the child of a liaison with a sister of his friend Gervase Clifton, and a legitimate daughter, Anne (*d.* 1526), who as a child married Edward Blount, second Baron Mountjoy. Blount died aged only eight in 1475, and Anne then married Edward Burgh, Baron Burgh, who suffered from mental illness and died in 1528.

A startling comparison with the quiet lives of the other fifteenth-century Cobhams of Sterborough is provided by the spectacular rise and fall of the fourth child of Sir Reynold [iv], Eleanor Cobham (*c.*1400–1452), who married *Humphrey, duke of Gloucester, in 1428. She had been a lady-in-waiting to his former wife, Jacqueline of Hainault, and had probably begun an affair with the duke in 1424. In 1441 she was convicted of trying to predict the date of Henry VI's death through sorcery, and died a prisoner at Beaumaris Castle on 7 July 1452 [*see* Eleanor, duchess of Gloucester].   PETER FLEMING

Sources GEC, *Peerage*, 3.338, 343–55 · 'Cobham', HoP, *Commons* · T. May, 'The Cobham family in the administration of England, 1200–1400', *Archaeologia Cantiana*, 82 (1967), 1–31 · E. Hasted, *The history and topographical survey of the county of Kent*, 2nd edn, 12 vols. (1797–1801); facs. edn (1972) · J. C. Wedgwood and A. D. Holt, *History of parliament*, 1: *Biographies of the members of the Commons house, 1439–1509* (1936) · *Chancery records* · Calendars of ancient deeds, PRO · *CIPM, Henry VII*, 2 nos 884, 920, 921 · G. O. Bellewes, 'The Cobhams and Moresbys of Rundale and Allington', *Archaeologia Cantiana*, 29 (1911), 154–63 · R. A. Griffiths, 'The trial of Eleanor Cobham: an episode in the fall of Duke Humphrey of Gloucester', *Bulletin of the John Rylands Library*, 51 (1968–9), 381–99 · J. G. Waller, 'The lords of Cobham, their monuments, and the church', *Archaeologia Cantiana*, 11 (1877), 49–112 · P. Fleming, 'The character and private concerns of the gentry of Kent, 1422–1509', PhD diss., U. Wales, 1985

Archives PRO, ancient deeds

Likenesses funeral effigies, Cobham church, Kent · funeral effigies, Lingfield church, Surrey · memorial brass (John Cobham, second Lord Cobham), Cobham church, Kent [*see illus.*]

Cobham, Sir Alan John (1894–1973), aviator, was born on 6 May 1894 at Camberwell, London, the only child to survive of Frederick Cobham, a tailor, and his wife, Elizabeth

Sir Alan John Cobham (1894–1973), by Frank O. Salisbury, 1926

Burrows. He attended a local council school and Wilson's Grammar School and then started work in a clothes store. In 1912 he became a pupil farmhand. He was a warehouse employee when the First World War was declared. Promptly enlisting, he served as an artillery NCO veterinary assistant in France until 1917, before managing to transfer to the Royal Flying Corps, where he was eventually commissioned as a flying instructor.

Although he was of a lively temperament and had boundless energy, Cobham's only marketable asset, when he was demobilized in January 1919 at the age of twenty-four, was his piloting skill. But, after obtaining the requisite civil flying licence through the recommendation of his commanding officer, he found prospects were negligible in the post-war depression. He was lucky to find a job as a 'joy-riding' pilot, during which he carried 5000 passengers until the company over-extended itself and became bankrupt. Down to his last £3, Cobham became a photographic pilot with Airco Ltd, owned by Holt Thomas, who was helping Geoffrey De Havilland to form De Havilland Aircraft Ltd; Cobham joined the company in 1920 as a taxi pilot. He built up a ten-man team ready to 'fly anywhere anytime' using former war DH9s, and thanks to his great capacity for hard work and organization the business thrived. Cobham established himself as a public figure in 1921 by making a hitherto unimaginable 5000 mile air tour of Europe in which seventeen cities were visited in three weeks amid mystery and publicity caused by his American passenger withholding his name. Other trailblazing flights followed, extending from Europe to north

Africa. In 1924 he flew to Rangoon and back in the newly introduced DH50 taxi plane carrying Britain's director of civil aviation, Sir W. Sefton Brancker. Then with the same machine he went to the Cape of Good Hope and back in 1925–6 and also to Australia and back in 1926. That brought independence, and registration of Alan Cobham Aviation Ltd. In the following year he used a big twin-engined Short Singapore flying boat on behalf of Imperial Airways to make the first encirclement of Africa, and in 1931 he similarly surveyed the Nile route to the Belgian Congo using a triple-engined Short Valetta twin-float seaplane.

By then Cobham had become the self-appointed vigorous professional propagandist for British aviation, and in 1929, backed by C. C. Wakefield, had undertaken a municipal aerodrome campaign using a DH61 *Youth of Britain* for demonstrations at many key cities, during which 10,000 children were given educational flights. From that he developed the idea of a great 'barnstorming' business, in 1932–3 under the title of National Aviation Day Ltd and in 1934–6 as National Aviation Displays Ltd, during which 1250 payment admission displays were given by a skilled aircraft circus and 900,000 passengers were carried.

Cobham's ambition to set a new Australian record by refuelling in flight created a unique line of development. Initial experiments in 1933 were a failure, but nothing defeated Cobham for long, and in 1934 he was able to demonstrate to Air Marshal Sir Hugh Dowding a Handley Page tanker feeding 120 gallons of fuel to an Airspeed Courier. An official development contract followed, leading to the establishment of Flight Refuelling Ltd at Ford, Sussex, where several penurious years of experimentation produced a method of rocket-line ejection for the hose-coupling, which was successfully applied in 1939 to an Empire flying boat enabling 2.7 tons of fuel to be added after take-off at maximum weight and thus give transatlantic range. With the advent of the Second World War official interest waned, and Cobham devoted attention to such matters as thermal de-icing and methods of towing fighters by long-range bombers. After long advocacy he induced both the United States air force and the RAF late in the war to experiment with flight refuelling to give the range for raids on Japan.

Interest in refuelling airliners revived in 1947–8, when success was achieved with British South American Airways' flights to Bermuda, but the advent of the fast, long-range DH Comet stopped further Air Ministry support. Prospects for Cobham's business dropped to a low ebb until a new association with the USA brought contracts totalling over $7,500,000 to supply refuelling equipment for B29s and B50s. By then he had moved to Tarrant Rushton, Dorset, where a still more effective system was developed by which the receiver aircraft flew a self-locking probe into a cone-funnel on the tanker's hose. That led to the formation of an American company in 1951, after which all American fighters and bombers were equipped with this system. The RAF followed suit to a more limited extent.

Cobham was awarded the Britannia trophy for 1923 as

the first British pilot to cross the channel in an ultra-light plane; he also won the king's cup race in 1924. For his London–Rangoon flight he gained the Britannia trophy for 1925, and for his London–Cape Town flight of 1925–6 he was awarded the AFC (1926). In 1926 he received the Royal Aero Club gold medal, the Simms gold medal, and the aviation gold medal of the Institute of Transport, again won the Britannia trophy, and was appointed KBE in recognition of his Australian flight. In the following year he was made an honorary fellow of the Royal Aeronautical Society. He was a founder member of the Guild of Air Pilots and Air Navigators, of which he became master in 1964–5.

Since his early background emphasized the desirability of a good start in life, Cobham not only initiated his company's training school but endowed a scholarship at Southampton University. At Wimborne he provided a garden city factory for his employees and a river park for the community. He was chairman of the Bournemouth Symphony Orchestra (1956–67) and raised £25,000 to secure its future.

Cobham was author of *Skyways* (1925), *My Flight to the Cape and back* (1926), *Australia and back* (1926), *Twenty Thousand Miles in a Flying Boat* (1930), many articles, and an autobiography, *A Time to Fly* (1978). He also featured in a number of films on his travels and activities. He married in 1922 the actress Gladys Marie Lloyd (d. 1961), the daughter of William Lloyd, of Bristol. They had two sons. On retirement Cobham resided at Tortola, British Virgin Islands, where he died on 21 October 1973.   H. J. PENROSE, *rev.*

Sources A. J. Cobham, *A time to fly*, ed. C. Derrick (1978) · personal knowledge (1986) · private information (1986)
Archives NL Aus., logbook and papers relating to flight to Australia · NRA, papers |FILM BFI NFTVA, 'King's cup', Topical Budget, 4 Aug 1924 · BFI NFTVA, 'Mapping all red air route to India', Topical Budget, 24 Nov 1924 · BFI NFTVA, 'Back from world record tour', Topical Budget, 19 March 1925 · BFI NFTVA, 'Great welcome at end of record flight', Topical Budget, 4 Oct 1926 · BFI NFTVA, 'Sir Alan and Lady Cobham', Topical Budget, 7 Oct 1926 · BFI NFTVA, 'With Cobham to the Cape', 1926 · BFI NFTVA, performance footage |SOUND BL NSA, documentary recording · BL NSA, performance recordings · IWM SA, 'British civilian aviator recalls the early days of powered flight', BBC, 1959, 17784 · IWM SA, oral history interview
Likenesses photographs, 1922–53, Hult. Arch. · F. Roe, group portrait, pencil drawing, 1926, NPG · F. O. Salisbury, oils, 1926, NPG [*see illus.*] · H. Coster, photographs, 1927, NPG · group portrait, photograph, 1932 (*Banbury on Aviation Day*), NPG · W. Stoneman, photograph, 1952, NPG · H. Barron, oils, RAF Museum, Hendon; loan, Royal Aero Club · F. May, pen-and-ink caricature, RAF Museum, Hendon

Cobham, Eleanor. *See* Eleanor, duchess of Gloucester (c.1400–1452).

Cobham, Henry, **first Lord Cobham of Cobham** (1260–1339). *See under* Cobham family (*per. c.*1250–*c.*1530).

Cobham, Henry. *See* Brooke, Sir Henry (1537–1592).

Cobham, John (d. *c.*1251). *See under* Cobham family (*per. c.*1250–*c.*1530).

Cobham, John, **second Lord Cobham of Cobham** (d. 1355). *See under* Cobham family (*per. c.*1250–*c.*1530).

Cobham, John, **third Baron Cobham of Cobham** (*c.*1320–1408), administrator, was the son of John *Cobham, second Lord Cobham of Cobham (d. 1355) [*see under* Cobham family], and his first wife, Joan, daughter of John, first Lord Beauchamp of Somerset. He came from the senior branch of the family at Cobham, Kent, noted for public service since the days of Henry II. He was first summoned to parliament in September 1355 on his father's death. His wife, Margaret, the eldest child of Hugh Courtenay, earl of Devon, and Margaret de Bohun, was betrothed to him in 1333 (when he may have been thirteen and she six years of age) and the couple probably married in 1345: records show property was settled on them at these times. Margaret died in 1395, and their only child, Joan, predeceased them leaving a daughter, also Joan. One of Cobham's brothers-in-law was William Courtenay, archbishop of Canterbury (1381–96).

Cobham became a prominent national figure. He was frequently a judge in the court of chivalry, notably at the Scrope–Grosvenor trial in May 1389, and in 1392 in the Lovel–Morley dispute. He was regularly a trier of petitions for England from 1379 and for Gascony from 1382. In 1363 he was given safe conduct to Calais to take charge of hostages who had broken parole. Few records remain of his military career, but he served in France in 1359–60, 1366–7, and 1369 (perhaps frequently until 1377); he was probably made a banneret in 1353, and confirmed in 1370 with an annuity of 100 marks. In 1378 he was a member of the commission appointed to receive the castle of Brest from the duke of Brittany.

Cobham frequently went on embassies. He was ambassador to the curia in June 1367 to promote the marriage of Prince Lionel with Violante Visconti and William Wykeham's appointment as bishop of Winchester, and to question the pope's deprivation of the king's clerks' benefices. He was frequently appointed to treat for peace with France: he accompanied John of Gaunt, duke of Lancaster, to negotiate a year's truce in February and September 1375 (remaining in Bruges over the winter), and went on similar embassies in June 1376, and October 1377, April 1379, May and December 1381, and February and June 1392. He accompanied Gaunt to treat for peace with the count of Flanders in 1383; in September 1379 and in April 1380 he was engaged in negotiations for a royal marriage alliance with France.

Cobham's most important political involvement was as adviser to the young Richard II, to his own ultimate disadvantage. On 17 July 1377 he was elected by the lords to a continual council set up to advise the ten-year-old king and raise money for the French wars; Cobham advanced £100. He was paid £40 for his service and dropped from the council in October, but in April 1379, at the Commons' request, a committee of ten, including Cobham, was appointed, 'to examine the estate of the king' (Tout, *Admin hist.*, 3.347) and among other matters, the royal household expenses. From June 1379 to February 1380, moreover, Cobham was appointed 'to remain in the household for the safeguard of the king's person' (Tout, *Admin hist.*,

3.349). In 1385 and 1390 he was appointed to supervise payments by crown officials. His most significant appointment was to the commission of thirteen, deeply resented by Richard II, which was set up by parliament in November 1386 with powers that virtually gave it control of government for a year.

Parliament continued to place much confidence in Cobham's discretion. He was supervisor of the collection of the subsidy of 1385 and controller of the subsidy of 1390. In the crisis of 1387–8 he was first one of the intermediaries between the king and the lords, and then one of five lords spiritual and secular appointed in January 1388 for the king's continual guidance. The Westminster chronicle claims that during the Merciless Parliament of February 1388, it was Cobham and the duke of Gloucester who dragged Chief Justice Sir Robert Tresilian from a house within the sanctuary of Westminster Abbey to parliament, where he was condemned to execution. In March, at Richard's request, Cobham interceded unsuccessfully with the Commons for the life of Sir Simon Burley, the king's former tutor, because he was so ill; however, Burley was executed in May, and Cobham signed the order. In March Cobham was appointed to a committee of five who were to attend continually on the king until parliament met again in September: Richard was to do nothing without their consent, and Cobham was to oversee the king's personal affairs. In May 1388 Cobham was appointed by the king to sell manors and goods forfeited by those sentenced in parliament.

It has been suggested that Cobham sided with the lords appellant in 1388 because he resented Burley's growing power in Kent. But Cobham also had connections with the royal party: the father of one of his major feoffees, Arnald Savage, had been in the household of Richard's mother, Joan of Kent, and he himself had been one of her executors in 1385, while his cousin John Cobham of Hever was a king's esquire by August 1388. However, he had family associations with the appellants too; his wife's mother, like Bolingbroke's wife, was a Bohun, and in 1380 his cousin Reginald Cobham of Sterborough married into the family of the earl of Arundel. For over forty years from the 1350s Cobham was heavily engaged in local government in Kent, where he was a major landowner. He served regularly as a JP (in 1385 and 1386 alongside Geoffrey Chaucer), a commissioner of array, a commissioner of oyer and terminer, and a commissioner for the defence of the realm, responsible for protecting the Thames estuary marshes against French invasion. In 1367 he was granted an annual fair and weekly market at Cobham itself, and he financed and supervised much building work, both of his own property and elsewhere. In 1381, following the French and Spanish raid on the Thames estuary in 1379, he obtained licence to crenellate his manor house at Cooling, near Gravesend, for the realm's defence. It was completed in 1385. The architect Henry Yevele prepared plans and was quantity surveyor for the gatehouse (1381–4), on which an inscription in Kentish dialect survives:

Knouwyth that beth and schul be
That I am mad in help of the cuntre

In knowyng of whyche thyng
Thys is chartre and wytnessyng.
(Robertson, 134)

With Yevele, Cobham supervised the restoration of the walls of Canterbury in 1385, and used Yevele's designs for restorations in 1381 to the church of St Dunstan-in-the-East, near Cobham's town house in Tower Street.

In 1383 Cobham and Yevele were on the commission of inquiry for rebuilding the recently collapsed wooden bridge at Rochester, which was rebuilt between 1388 and 1391 in Kentish ragstone, supervised and financed by Cobham and Sir Robert Knolles. Knolles was with Cobham when Brest was taken under English control in 1378, and his London inn in Seething Lane was near Cobham's. Cobham formed a consortium including two relatives to acquire properties to endow the bridge, and at his own expense built a bridge chapel at the Rochester end in 1392, endowed as a chantry in 1395: his wife was among the deceased commemorated. In 1362 he refounded the parish church of Cobham, endowing it as a chantry college of priests; Cobham College was dissolved in 1535, but refounded on the same site in 1598 as an almshouse, still in use, by William Brooke, Lord Cobham, a descendant in the female line.

Cobham was still attending parliament in the 1390s, and was at a great council held at Eltham in 1395. In the Shrewsbury parliament on 28 January 1398 he was impeached and accused of membership of the commission of 1386, and of sending Sir Simon Burley and Sir James Berners to execution without the king's assent and in his absence. He defended himself on both counts: he was not guilty of making the commission of 1386 and had acted on it by the king's command—to which Richard responded that he had himself acted under constraint—and he had been told that the executions were the king's will. Gower commends his frankness; he says that Cobham was taking 'refuge' with the Carthusians when arrested in September 1397, but he was probably at the cell of Nutley Abbey in Maiden Bradley, where his chaplain was held during his imprisonment. He was sentenced to be drawn, hanged, beheaded, and quartered, forfeited and disinherited. Richard II, however, commuted the death sentence to banishment for life, with his cousin Reginald Cobham of Sterborough, to Jersey; if he escaped, the sentence would have full effect. By this date Cobham was about eighty, and responded that eternal life meant more to him than the reprieve. Cobham's banishment was one of the articles in Richard's indictment in 1399.

When Henry Bolingbroke returned from exile in June 1399 and claimed the throne, Cobham was recalled. The Monk of Evesham's statement that Cobham landed at Ravenspur with Henry may, however, refer to Reginald. By October John Cobham had returned, and he spoke at length in parliament of the need to punish those responsible for the evils of recent times, declaring that under Richard the English had sunk even lower than the heathens; the king had been rightly deposed and parliament should judiciously determine punishment for him and his counsellors. Disclaiming any desire for revenge for himself, according to Thomas Walsingham he observed: 'I stand for common justice and declare that if my own father who engendered me were guilty of crimes like these, I would without hesitation declare to you that he should be punished for them' ('Annales Henrici quarti', 307). He was present at Richard's abdication.

In 1403 Cobham was executor for Reginald Cobham of Sterborough, and attended parliament in 1406 to subscribe to the entailing of the crown on Henry IV's sons. He died in the severe winter of 1407–8, on 10 January in Maiden Bradley, Wiltshire, where he had lived very simply. He was buried in Cobham church, where his monumental brass shows him in armour and bearing a model of Cobham collegiate church, with an inscription recording his role as founder. The heir to Cobham's estate, consisting of lands, rents, and advowsons in Kent, Wiltshire, Surrey, and London, was his granddaughter, Joan, in her own right Lady Cobham. She married five times. The fourth of her husbands (whom she married in 1409), was Sir John *Oldcastle, the Lollard; he took the title Lord Cobham in his wife's right, and has sometimes been confused with the third baron. John Gower called Cobham 'noble, long-suffering, compassionate and kindly, efficient and fair-minded, firm in strength of character … a true friend of the realm' (Complete Works, 326), and for Walsingham he was 'straightforward and unaffected' (Ypodigma Neustriae, 379).   ROSAMUND ALLEN

Sources Chancery records · RotP, vol. 3 · L. C. Hector and B. F. Harvey, eds. and trans., The Westminster chronicle, 1381–1394, OMT (1982) · G. B. Stow, ed., Historia vitae et regni Ricardi Secundi (1977) [the Monk of Evesham] · The chronicle of Adam Usk, 1377–1421, ed. and trans. C. Given-Wilson, OMT (1997) · Ypodigma Neustriae, a Thoma Walsingham, ed. H. T. Riley, pt 7 of Chronica monasterii S. Albani, Rolls Series, 28 (1876), 320, 379, 439 · The complete works of John Gower, ed. G. C. Macaulay, 4 vols. (1899–1902), vol. 4 · Reports … touching the dignity of a peer of the realm, House of Lords, 4 (1829) · Rymer, Foedera, 3rd edn, vol. 3/2–4 · Rymer, Foedera, new edn, vol. 3/2 · Tout, Admin. hist., vol. 3 · E. Hasted, The history and topographical survey of the county of Kent, 4 vols. (1778–99) · J. G. Nichols, 'Memorials of the family of Cobham', Collectanea Topographica et Genealogica, 7 (1841), 320–54 · J. G. Waller, 'The lords of Cobham, their monuments, and the church [pt 1]', Archaeologia Cantiana, 11 (1877), 49–112 · W. A. Scott Robertson, 'Coulyng Castle', Archaeologia Cantiana, 11 (1877), 128–44 · A. A. Arnold, 'Cobham College', Archaeologia Cantiana, 27 (1905), 64–109 · H. C. M. Lyte, 'An account relating to Sir John Cobham, AD 1408', Antiquaries Journal, 2 (1922), 339–43 · J. Harvey, Henry Yevele (1944) · T. May, 'The Cobham family in the administration of England, 1200–1400', Archaeologia Cantiana, 82 (1967), 1–31 · B. Webster, 'The community of Kent in the reign of Richard II', Archaeologia Cantiana, 100 (1984), 217–29 · N. Saul, Richard II (1997) · N. Saul, Death, art, and memory in medieval England: the Cobham family and their monuments, 1300–1500 (2001) · 'Annales Ricardi secundi et Henrici quarti, regum Angliae', Johannis de Trokelowe et Henrici de Blaneforde … chronica et annales, ed. H. T. Riley, pt 3 of Chronica monasterii S. Albani, Rolls Series, 28 (1866), 155–420
Likenesses memorial brass, Cobham church; repro. in Waller, 'The lords of Cobham'

Cobham, John (d. 1399). See under Cobham family (per. c.1250–c.1530).

Cobham, Ralph, Lord Cobham (d. 1326). See under Cobham family (per. c.1250–c.1530).

Cobham, Reynold, first Lord Cobham of Sterborough (c.1295–1361). See under Cobham family (per. c.1250–c.1530).

Cobham, Reynold, second Baron Cobham of Sterborough (1348–1403). See under Cobham family (per. c.1250–c.1530).

Cobham, Sir Reynold (1381–1446). See under Cobham family (per. c.1250–c.1530).

Cobham, Stephen, Lord Cobham of Rundale (d. 1332). See under Cobham family (per. c.1250–c.1530).

Cobham, Thomas (c.1265–1327), bishop of Worcester, was the sixth son of John Cobham (d. 1300), of Cobham and Cooling, Kent, and his wife, daughter of Sir Robert Septvans [see Cobham family]. His early career is obscure, but from 1284 he was retained by the Canterbury chapter with a pension of 5 marks. The Pauline annalist wrote that he was regent in three universities: in arts at Paris (where an elder brother James also studied), in canon law at Oxford (regent in 1291), and in theology at Cambridge (DTh by 1314). Details of his ordination have yet to be traced—he was still a subdeacon in 1317—but Archbishop Pecham collated him in 1288 to his first benefice, Hollingbourne in Kent. He soon became a substantial pluralist. In 1306 he was dispensed to hold a benefice additional to his rectories of Hollingbourne, Boxley, Hackney, and Rotherfield, and his canonries of St Paul's London, Hereford, and Wells. He acquired the archdeaconry of Lewes in commendam by 1301, and secured the precentorship of York in 1312.

In the meantime Cobham had become a king's clerk, and more especially a diplomat, an expert versed in the intricacies of Gascon and French affairs. He was sent by Edward I to the papal curia in 1305–6, while following Edward II's accession he was deputed in December 1309 to examine the terms of the truce with France and on that account summoned to parliament the following February. Then in November 1310 he was appointed to join other envoys in Gascony, where he remained until the spring of 1311. In April he was one of the lawyers directed to examine articles concerning Guyenne (Gascony) and to report to the king's council. On 20 May he was instructed to travel to Paris and later associated with Gilbert Peche in assessing merchants' losses from breaches of the truce for consideration by the French king's arbitrators at Montreuil. February 1312 saw him with other councillors at York. He left London for France on 10 April, to return on 4 June. His mission was to excuse Edward II before his overlord, Philippe IV, from responding to a summons to enforce a citation of the count of Flanders. During the autumn he was given the task of preparing the English case vis-à-vis Guyenne so that response could be made in the parlement of Paris concerning the negotiations conducted at Périgueux in the previous year. He was in Paris in February 1313 as king's proctor with authority to deal with Gascon affairs.

On 11 May 1313 Archbishop Winchelsey died and on the

28th the Canterbury monks assembled to elect a successor. Proceeding by way of compromise, they chose Cobham—termed a local man born in Canterbury province—who was then with Edward II in Paris. The elect accepted on 8 June; the king prevaricated. When a delegation of monks and the elect reached the curia they found that Clement V had reserved the see on 27 April. Bulls of 1 October 1313 provided Walter Reynolds (d. 1327), the king's confidant. Contemporary chroniclers shrilly deplored Cobham's rejection, but some modern commentators, recalling Pecham and Winchelsey, regard the move as designed to promote harmony between church and king. By way of compensation Cobham was provided to Worcester on 31 March 1317 and consecrated at Avignon on 22 May. The temporalities were restored on 20 November, and he was enthroned in his cathedral on 28 October 1319.

The Canterbury election virtually terminated Cobham's diplomatic career, but with his colleagues he sought to mediate between Edward and his opponents in England. He is numbered among the nine bishops who endorsed the conciliatory Leicester agreement of June 1318, was a signatory of the treaty of Leake (9 August 1318), and a member of the standing council appointed to advise the king. After the Westminster parliament of October 1320 he reported his impressions in letters to the curia. His tone was avuncular, almost patronizing, as he recounted how the king had shown a promising—clearly unusual—attention to business. He was soon disillusioned by the threat of civil war—*bellum intestinum*. Disorder was rampant; the very shrine of St Oswald at Worcester was desecrated. Although he was in London in July 1321 he did not take any noticeable part in the mediation of his fellow bishops between Edward and the barons. When the king sought to persuade the episcopate to attend a December convocation at St Paul's to sanction the Despensers' recall, he wrote that he could not reach London in time and that the matter would be more appropriately dealt with in parliament. In 1324 he endeavoured to intervene on behalf of those bishops whose temporalities had been confiscated, and was one of the bishops who met the nuncios at London in November to discuss peace between England and France.

Following Queen Isabella's landing in 1326 the now-ailing bishop travelled to London to seek medical attention, to attend a convocation for papal business, to join his fellow bishops in reconciling Edward and Isabella, to press litigation in the royal court and that of Canterbury, and to fulfil a vow of pilgrimage to the shrine of St Thomas Becket. All proved vain; the king had fled; even pilgrimage was rendered impossible by the painfulness of travel. Cobham asked Bishop Adam Orleton of Hereford (d. 1345), with whom he seems to have been on good terms, to make his excuses to the queen and offered her the use of his houses and goods, with the hint that remedy could be found by summoning a parliament. He joined the rump of bishops that assembled fearfully at Lambeth on 26 October 1326. Illness prevented his contributing to the revolutionary changes that ensued, but one entry in his register has been dated 11 January (1327) from London.

As a diocesan, Cobham's performance was reasonably diligent, although political business prevented him from reaching his diocese until March 1319, two years after his provision. His protracted primary visitation was launched in November of that year. Commissaries performed most of it, but he visited many religious houses personally. It was still incomplete in 1321 when he travelled north to negotiate with Robert I of Scotland. He seldom used a suffragan for ordinations, and on the second occasion that he did so (December 1323) it was because of illness.

Cobham died on 27 August 1327, probably at Hartlebury, after a long and painful illness. It is fair to conclude that he did not respond to political crises in the robust manner that was expected of a man of his stature. Unlike Orleton or Stratford he was not a forceful politician, though undeniably a 'good clerk'. During his lifetime he provided money for the building of a house for the university congregation north of St Mary's Church in Oxford, but it was incomplete at his death. It should have received his library, but in the event, to defray their expenses, his executors sold his books to Adam Brome, the provost of Oriel College. He bequeathed plate and vestments to his cathedral, where he was buried. ROY MARTIN HAINES

Sources T. Cobham, register, Worcs. RO · *The register of Thomas de Cobham*, ed. E. H. Pearce, Worcestershire Historical Society, 40 (1930) · J. M. Wilson, ed., *The liber albus of the priory of Worcester*, Worcestershire Historical Society, 35 (1919) · Chancery records · Rymer, *Foedera* · H. G. Richardson and G. O. Sayles, eds., *Rotuli parliamentorum Anglie hactenus inediti, MCCLXXIX–MCCCLXXIII*, CS, 3rd ser., 51 (1935), 93, 158 · N. Denholm-Young, ed. and trans., *Vita Edwardi secundi* (1957), 45–6 · W. Stubbs, ed., *Chronicles of the reigns of Edward I and Edward II*, 2 vols., Rolls Series, 76 (1882–3) · E. H. Pearce, *Thomas de Cobham* (1923) · K. Edwards, 'The political importance of the English bishops during the reign of Edward II', *EngHR*, 59 (1944), 311–47 · W. E. L. Smith, *Episcopal appointments and patronage in the reign of Edward II*, SCH, 3 (1938) · J. R. Wright, *The church and the English crown, 1305–1334: a study based on the register of Archbishop Walter Reynolds* (1980) · R. M. Haines, *The church and politics in fourteenth-century England: the career of Adam Orleton, c. 1275–1345*, Cambridge Studies in Medieval Life and Thought, 3rd ser., 10 (1978) · R. M. Haines, *The administration of the diocese of Worcester in the first half of the fourteenth century* (1965) · R. M. Haines, *Ecclesia Anglicana: studies in the English church of the later middle ages* (1989), chap. 2B · *Fasti Angl., 1300–1541*, [Hereford] · *Fasti Angl., 1300–1541*, [Monastic cathedrals] · *Fasti Angl., 1300–1541*, [St Paul's, London] · *Fasti Angl., 1300–1541*, [York] · *Fasti Angl., 1300–1541*, [Chichester] · *Fasti Angl., 1300–1541*, [Bath and Wells] · *Fasti Angl., 1300–1541*, [Introduction] · Emden, *Oxf.* · Emden, *Cam.*
Archives Worcs. RO, register

Cobham, Sir Thomas (*c*.1343–1394). *See under* Cobham family (*per. c.*1250–*c.*1530).

Cobham, Sir Thomas (d. 1471). *See under* Cobham family (*per. c.*1250–*c.*1530).

Cobham, Thomas (1779/1786–1842), actor, was born in London. His father, who was 'distinguished as an algebraist, mathematician, and architectural draughtsman', died young, and Cobham was apprenticed by his mother to his cousin Joseph Aspin, an eminent printer. He rose to be reader and corrector for the press, and became acquainted with Edmund Malone, an edition of whose works of Shakespeare he read for the printers.

Cobham first appeared as an amateur in Lamb's Conduit Street as Shylock, a part in which George Frederick Cooke had greatly impressed him. His first professional performance was at Watford, Hertfordshire. Thereafter he played in various provincial towns, taking, like Edmund Kean, every part, from leading tragedian to harlequin. At Salisbury he married a Miss Drake, an actress at the city's theatre. When playing at Oxford, Cobham, with his wife, was engaged by William Penley for the theatre in Tottenham Street, London, where he appeared with much success as Marmion in a dramatization by William Oxberry of Scott's poem. He then went to the Surrey Theatre, and thence to the Royalty. About this time he became known as 'the Kemble of the minor theatres'.

On 16 April 1816 Cobham appeared as Richard III at Covent Garden. That the experiment was a failure was in part ascribed to the supporters of Kean, and especially to the club known as 'the Wolves'. Hazlitt, however, who was present on the occasion, declared his Richard to have been 'a vile one', a caricature of Kean, and continued:

He raved, whined, grinned, stared, stamped, and rolled his eyes with incredible velocity, and all in the right place according to his cue, but in so extravagant and disjointed a manner, and with such a total want of common sense, decorum, or conception of the character as to be perfectly ridiculous. (*A View of the English Stage*, 1818, 274)

The *Theatrical Inquisitor* (April 1816), on the other hand, said his portrayal was good and censured the audience for taking a cowardly advantage and condemning him before he was heard. The performance was repeated with some success on 22 April 1816, but Cobham then disappeared from the West End.

In 1817 Cobham appeared at the Crow Street Theatre, Dublin, as Sir Giles Overreach, and played afterwards Macbeth and Richard. He was again in Dublin in 1821–2 as a member of the Hawkins Street stock company, dividing with Warde the principal characters of tragedy. After Warde's disappearance he performed, in the memorable engagement of Kean in July 1822, Richmond, Iago, Edgar in *King Lear*, and the Ghost in *Hamlet*. Early in his career Cobham had played Glenalvon to the Young Norval of Kean at the Navy tavern, Woolwich. Later, at the Coburg Theatre, London, the two actors met once more, Kean playing Othello and Cobham Iago. The reception of Kean on this occasion by the transpontine audience, the faith of which in Cobham was never shaken, was unfavourable. (A full account of the scene of Kean's indignation and Cobham's speech to the audience appears in J. W. Cole's *Life of Charles Kean*, 1859, 1.161–3.)

Cobham had some resemblance in appearance and stature to Kean, being dark, with flexible features, and about 5 feet 5 inches in height. In spite of Hazlitt's unfavourable verdict, he was a fair actor, a little given to rant, and to so-called and not very defensible new readings. In his later life he rarely quitted the south London stage. He died on 3 January 1842, leaving a son and a daughter, both of whom worked in the theatrical profession. The latter acted under the name of Mrs Fitzgerald.

JOSEPH KNIGHT, rev. KATHARINE COCKIN

Sources Adams, *Drama* · *Oxberry's Dramatic Biography*, new ser., 1/1 (1827), 1–18 · Hall, *Dramatic ports.* · *N&Q*, 7th ser., 2 (1886), 318 · 'Theatrical scale of merit', *Dramatic Magazine*, 2 (1830), 209–10 · private information (1887)
Likenesses J. Rogers, engraving (*Mr Cobham as Marmion*), repro. in *Oxberry's Dramatic Biography* · portraits, Harvard TC · prints, NPG

Coborn, Charles [*real name* Colin Whitton McCallum] (1852–1945), music-hall entertainer and songwriter, was born Colin Whitton McCallum on 4 August 1852 at 25 Sydney Square, Mile End, London, the son of Colin McCallum (1799–1872), shipbroker and freeman of the City of London, and his wife, Frances, *née* Whitton, a district visitor, the daughter of a customs officer at Wapping. Educated privately, he had a series of clerical jobs in the City (1866–71) and was later a commercial traveller in briar pipes, artificial hair, and women's fur collars. An early talent for impersonating a drunken man led to his first salaried engagement as a twice-weekly music-hall artist (1872) at the Alhambra, north Greenwich. Originally appearing under the stage name Charles Laurie, he changed it to Coborn, after Coborn Road, Poplar. In 1875 came his first full week's engagement, at the Gilbert Music-Hall, Whitechapel (where Whitechapel underground station was later built), as well as his first performance outside London, at the Oxford, Gravesend, and his first pantomime, at Sandgate, Kent. He toured the midlands, the north of England, Scotland, and Ireland (1877–8), and first appeared on the regular West End variety stage (29 September 1879) at the Middlesex, Drury Lane, followed (20 October) by a six-month engagement at the Oxford, where the manager, J. H. Jennings, billed him as 'The Comic of the Day'. He married (26 January 1882) Ellen Stockley of Dublin; they had four sons and three daughters.

Coborn was an active campaigner for improved working conditions in music-halls, and he was largely instrumental in forming the Music-Hall Artistes' Association (1885) and later the Music-Hall Benevolent Fund. But such union activities eroded his popularity with managers, and he was often unemployed. He first sang 'Two Lovely Black Eyes' on 21 May 1886 at the Paragon Music-Hall, Mile End. It was a parody of a song successful in America, and Coborn plugged the chorus (in eight languages) so successfully that it became highly popular and the subject of political cartoons in *Punch*. The tune was even taken up by the Salvation Army, and was still being sung by the prince of Wales in Whitechapel in the 1920s. Its success secured Coborn a fourteen-month stint at the Trocadero and three years at the London Pavilion. In 1891 he bought Fred Gilbert's song 'The Man who Broke the Bank at Monte Carlo', which was based on the gambling exploits of a certain Charles Wells, and, donning evening dress, top hat, eyeglass, and buttonhole, Coborn portrayed a tough man about town. The song was again illustrated in *Punch*, and Coborn later acted in a film of the same name, made in Monte Carlo in 1919.

Charles Coborn (1852–1945), by unknown photographer [in costume for the Monte Carlo song]

In 1900–01 Coborn toured the United States and Canada, and on his return formed his own concert party. During the First World War he entertained the troops and produced a home-made periscope, which was fully tested by the army for use in the trenches. In the 1920s he did fourteen long-distance walks for charity. His autobiography, *The Man who Broke the Bank*, was published in 1928. A church sidesman and lay reader, he continued to make occasional appearances until shortly before his death at 27 Elgin Mansions, Paddington, London, on 23 November 1945.   BASIL MORGAN

Sources C. Coborn, *The man who broke the bank* (1928) • R. Busby, *British music hall: an illustrated who's who from 1850 to the present day* (1976) • *WWW* • M. W. Disher, *Winkles and champagne: comedies and tragedies of the music hall* (1938); repr. (1974) • R. Mander and J. Mitchenson, *British music hall: a story in pictures* (1965) • *Who was who in the theatre, 1912–1976*, 4 vols. (1978) • J. Parker, ed., *The green room book, or, Who's who on the stage* (1907) • E. Short, *50 years of vaudeville* (1946) • d. cert.

Likenesses photographs, *c*.1882–1928, repro. in Coborn, *The man who broke the bank*, 32, 88, 128, 192 • J. B. Partridge, cartoon, 16 Jan 1916 (of Coborn?) • G. Du Maurier, cartoon (of Coborn?; *Two lovely black eyes*), repro. in Coborn, *The man who broke the bank*, 182–3 • photograph (in costume for the Monte Carlo song), Mander and Mitchenson Theatre Collection, London [*see illus.*]

Coburn, Alvin Langdon (1882–1966), photographer and mystic, was born on 11 June 1882 at 134 East Springfield Street, Boston, Massachusetts, the only child of James

Alvin Coburn (1849–1891), manufacturer of Coburn and Whitman shirts, and his wife, Fannie E. Howe (*d*. 1928). In 1887 the family moved to Dorchester, Massachusetts, where Coburn attended the Chauncey Hall School (1891–5). His father having died, he moved with his mother in 1897 back to Boston, where they lived in Boylston Street, and the following year he met his distant cousin, Fred Holland Day, the American publisher of the *Yellow Book* and symbolist photographer of homoerotic orientation. In 1899 Coburn made the first of thirteen transatlantic crossings to London in the company of his devoted but domineering mother. He took rooms at 89 Guilford Street, Russell Square, and exhibited nine photographs at a Royal Photographic Society exhibition organized by Holland Day in 1900.

After touring in France, Switzerland, and Germany with his mother, Coburn opened a studio at 384 5th Avenue, New York, in 1902, and attended for two years running Arthur Wesley Dow's Summer School of Art in Ipswich, Massachusetts, where he mastered the principles of Japanese design. Arthur Symons's *Cities* (1903) provided a model for Coburn's own projected series, 'The adventures of cities', on London, Birmingham, Liverpool, Edinburgh, Paris, Pittsburgh, and New York. Coburn's symbolist aim was to draw confidences out of the very stones of the buildings and to transfigure such cities by means of his own special combination of Japanese composition, impressionist tone, and Thomas Dallmeyer's new telephoto lens. Between 1906 and 1913 he was informally tutored by Henry James in the typology of cities for the purpose of providing frontispieces for the collected New York edition of James's novels. Boyish but bearded, he appeared at the time of his most creative work like a young Whistler or William Morris, top-hatted but craftsman-like.

In 1909 Coburn and his mother moved from Guilford Street to 9 Lower Mall, Hammersmith, where he set up two printing presses to apply hard-won skills learned at the London County Council School of Photo-Engraving, Bolt Court. In the period 1909–14 he etched and steel-faced eighty-three plates, and oversaw the printing of some 40,000 hand-pulled gravures for his books *London* (1909) and *New York* (1910), his illustrations for H. G. Wells's *The Door in the Wall* (1911), and his portraits for *Men of Mark* (1913). His true medium was photogravure, though his gum-platinum exhibition photographs are among the finest produced in the history of photography.

In 1911 Coburn visited Yosemite and the Grand Canyon, and in 1912 he published in Los Angeles six photographs to illustrate Shelley's *The Cloud*. On 11 October 1912 in Trinity Church, 25th Street, New York, he married Edith Wightman Clement (*d*. 1957) of Boston, with his mother and the verger as the only witnesses; they then returned to England, and Coburn never visited the United States again. The couple had no children: it is possible that Coburn settled for an asexual but devoted marriage in response to a troubled sense of sexual identity. Closely attracted (and attractive) to Day, James, Edward Carpenter, and George

Alvin Langdon Coburn (1882–1966), self-portrait, 1908 [with a copper-plate printing press]

Bernard Shaw, he may have shared their less than clear sexual preferences.

Coburn attempted to modernize his symbolist sensibility in 1917 by making and exhibiting a series of prism-like images which he called vortographs, and devoted a great deal of time to the mechanical piano, the pianola. But he maintained his long-standing interest in the occult and derived deep satisfaction from becoming a freemason in 1919. He became a Mark mason and Royal Arch mason in 1921 and eventually achieved mastership in his two lodges. In 1922 he joined the Rosicrucian Society. But the definitive change in his life came in 1923 when he met a man who taught him the practice of quietist contemplation; in accordance with principles of anonymity and impersonality, this man's name remains unknown to those not of the hermetic society called the Universal Order. Coburn was an anonymous contributor to its journal, the *Shrine of Wisdom* (1919–47).

In 1930, after destroying 15,000 photographic negatives and giving a collection of photographs to the Royal Photographic Society, Coburn moved to Harlech in north Wales. On 24 May 1932 he was naturalized as a British subject. In 1935 he was appointed a lay reader in the Church in Wales, and in 1940 became honorary secretary of the joint county committee of Merioneth of the British Red Cross Society and the order of St John of Jerusalem. In 1945 the Coburns moved from Harlech to Colwyn Bay in Denbighshire. Edith died on 11 October 1957, on their forty-fifth wedding anniversary, and Coburn on 23 November 1966 at their home, Awen, 17 Ebberstone Road East, Rhos-on-Sea, Colwyn Bay. After a service at St George's Church, Rhos-on-Sea, he was buried in the churchyard of Llandudno-yn-Rhos with masonic prayers being said at the graveside.

MIKE WEAVER

Sources A. L. Coburn, *Alvin Langdon Coburn, photographer: an autobiography*, ed. H. Gernsheim and A. Gernsheim (1966); repr. (1978) · M. Weaver, *Alvin Langdon Coburn: symbolist photographer, 1882–1966* (1986) · d. cert. · *CGPLA Eng. & Wales* (1967)
Archives National Museum of Photography, Film and Television, Bradford, Royal Photographic Society collection · University of Rochester, New York, Eastman School of Music, archive

Likenesses photographs, 1907–15, Hult. Arch. · A. L. Coburn, self-portrait, photograph, 1908, repro. in *Alvin Langdon Coburn*, ed. Gernsheim and Gernsheim, frontispiece [*see illus.*] · A. L. Coburn, self-portrait, collotype, 1922, NPG · A. L. Coburn, self-portrait, photograph, repro. in Weaver, *Alvin Langdon Coburn*, 28
Wealth at death £19,385: probate, 24 Jan 1967, *CGPLA Eng. & Wales*

Cochran, Sir Charles Blake (1872–1951), impresario, was born on 25 September 1872 at 15 Prestonville Road, Brighton, Sussex, the fourth of the nine children of James Elphinstone Cochran (1840–1900), tea and cigar importer, and his wife, Matilda Arnold *née* Walton (1838–1929), daughter of a merchant navy officer and the widowed mother of a son by her first marriage. At the age of seven Charles saw the pantomime *Sindbad the Sailor*. This first unforgettable visit inspired a lifelong passion for the theatre. At Brighton grammar school (1883–8) his best friend was his contemporary Aubrey Beardsley; they shared an enthusiasm for acting and appeared at the Brighton Pavilion in a play written by Beardsley. Having left school and failed as a music-hall performer Cochran 'borrowed' some petty cash from the office where he worked as a reluctant clerk and sailed for America. There he lived precariously on menial jobs and occasional acting engagements, ending up as secretary to the actor–manager Richard Mansfield and gaining experience in running a theatrical company. After a brief disagreement with Mansfield he established an acting school in New York and launched his first theatrical production, Ibsen's *John Gabriel Borkman* (1897). Following a penniless interlude in London, he returned to Mansfield and organized his nationwide tour of *Cyrano de Bergerac*.

Back in London again in 1899 Cochran set up as manager to such figures as Houdini and the wrestler Hackenschmidt. The plays he produced were unsuccessful and resulted in 1903 in his first bankruptcy. Undeterred, he bounced back as a promoter of freak shows at Olympia, of roller-skating, of midgets, and of performing fleas, which, alas, failed to perform. Having paused briefly to elope with Evelyn Alice Dade (1885–1960) and to marry her in Covent Garden register office in 1905, he plunged back into his professional activities; these culminated in Max Reinhardt's spectacular production of *The Miracle* (1911) at Olympia, with a 200-strong orchestra and a chorus of 500. (Cochran revived it in 1935 with Lady Diana Cooper as the Madonna.) The next attraction he presented at Olympia was Carl Hagenbeck's giant zoo.

In 1914 at the Ambassador's Theatre Cochran took up the newly born genre of revue with *Odds and Ends*, starring his new discovery Alice Delysia. It set the standard of all his subsequent revues: beautiful dresses, taste, wit, elegance, brightness, and colour. This was followed by a series of glamorous entertainments, although he seasoned the mixture with 'problem' plays by Eugène Brieux. His greatest wartime success was *The Better 'Ole* (1917), based on the cartoonist Bruce Bairnsfather's anti-hero Old Bill. At the London Pavilion, which he had leased and renovated, he mounted *As you were* (1918), again with Alice Delysia, and the shows that followed confirmed his reputation

Sir Charles Blake Cochran (1872–1951), by Howard Coster, 1929 [left, with Beverley Nichols]

as a master of revue. He also promoted boxing matches featuring Wells, Beckett, and Carpentier. The murky underworld of boxing drove him into a nervous breakdown, and on recovery he took Suzanne Lenglen under his wing in an attempt to promote the gentler sport of lawn tennis. It failed, as did the sensational rodeo that he staged at Wembley in 1924. In 1925 he went bankrupt again. Such, however, was his persuasive charm that his creditors at the bankruptcy proceedings sang 'For he's a jolly good fellow' and wished him well. In business again, Cochran organized ballroom-dancing displays and midnight cabarets. His partnership with Noël Coward engendered *On with the Dance* (1925), *This Year of Grace* (1928), *Bitter Sweet* (1929), *Private Lives* (1930), *Cavalcade* (1931), *Words and Music* (1932), and *Conversation Piece* (1934). Eventually, believing he had been denied his fair share of profits, Coward ended the relationship, although his subsequent musical shows never prospered as had those which enjoyed Cochran's magic touch.

Cochran was a master of publicity, one of his cleverest ideas being Mr Cochran's Young Ladies, a troupe of hand-picked beauties who numbered among them Anna Neagle and Florence Desmond. One of his most talented discoveries was Jessie Matthews (*One Dam' Thing After Another* by Rodgers and Hart, 1927, and *Ever Green*, 1930); another was the German Elisabeth Bergner (*Escape me Never*, 1933, and Barrie's last play, *The Boy David*, 1936); yet another was Evelyn Laye, whom he starred in *Helen!*, a lavish reworking of Offenbach's operetta (1932). The Second World War reduced his fortunes, although in 1946 he found renewed prosperity with *Big Ben*, a happy collaboration between A. P. Herbert and the gifted Vivian Ellis. They followed it with the joyous *Bless the Bride* (1947), the longest run (886 shows) that Cochran ever achieved—although, quickly bored and ever keen on novelty, he took it off while it was still drawing full houses and replaced it with *Tough at the Top* (1949), which failed. After more than fifty years in the business he freely avowed that he was still unable to forecast public reaction to a new show. It was enough for him that it reached his own high standards. His optimism

remained unquenched to the end. At any given moment he was juggling a half-dozen new productions and running the same number of theatres. He had Diaghilev's rare gift for discerning new talent and for blending authors, artists, designers, composers, and performers in a perfectly harmonious ensemble.

Although Cochran gloried in the title of showman, he was irritated when critics dismissed him as a commercial producer. He prefigured Peter Daubeny with his remarkable international seasons that brought to London Sarah Bernhardt, Eleonora Duse, the Guitrys, Pitoëff, Pavlova, Chalyapin, the Diaghilev ballets, and the Chauve-Souris. The artists he commissioned included Augustus John, Bakst, Bérard, and Messel. His choreographers were Balanchine and Massine; his composers Walton, Sauguet, and Berners. He was also responsible for the London premières of O'Neill's *Anna Christie* (1923) and O'Casey's *The Silver Tassie* (1929). He was knighted in 1948 and elected to the Légion d'honneur in 1950.

Cochran was short and red-faced, a well-fed country squire in appearance. He wore a bowler hat, a monocle, and elegant double-breasted suits, and leant heavily on a walking stick made necessary by the crippling pain of an arthritic hip. His manner was staid, unlike that of his vivacious wife, who often exercised her notoriously sharp wit in revenge for his many infidelities and arcane sexual pursuits. She sought refuge in alcohol and in sentimental friendships with other, younger women. Cochran's art collection included impressionist paintings acquired long before they became fashionable, many of them gradually sold off to finance new productions. The library that he amassed contained numerous valuable items and first editions. He himself, when temporarily out of funds, wrote in total four volumes of readable memoirs. One day, on taking his bath—very hot water being the only thing that soothed his agonizing arthritis—infirmity prevented him from reaching to switch off the hot tap and he was horribly scalded. He died, almost unrecognizable, a week later on 31 January 1951, in Westminster Hospital, and was cremated at Golders Green on 3 February.

JAMES HARDING

Sources J. Harding, *Cochran* (1988) · C. B. Cochran, *I had almost forgotten* (1932) · C. B. Cochran, *Secrets of a showman* (1925) · C. B. Cochran, *Showman looks on* (1945) · C. B. Cochran, *Cock-a-doodle-doo* (1941) · V. Ellis, *I'm on a see-saw* (1953) · S. Heppner, *Cockie* (1969) · C. Graves, *The Cochran story* (1951) · private information (2004) **Archives** SOUND BBC WAC, recollections, 1925, DX 11911–5 · BBC WAC, reminiscences, 1930, MX 2169–31 · BBC WAC, *Cock-a-doodle-doo*, 1940, T 28058 · BBC WAC, dialogue with G. B. Shaw, 1947, 11312–3 · BL NSA, 'C. B. Cochran presents', 1CL00 47214 · BL NSA, Cochran in dialogue with G. Lawrence, L. Olivier, V. Leigh, 1941, M 4945W · BL NSA, performance recordings **Likenesses** H. Coster, photographs, 1928–9, NPG [*see illus.*] · Bassano, photographs, 1932, NPG · R. S. Sherriffs, caricature, ink-and-pencil drawing, 1934, NPG · P. Evans, pencil drawing, NPG · P. Lambda, bronze bust, Adelphi Theatre, London **Wealth at death** £22,921 10s. 7d.: probate, 8 May 1951, CGPLA Eng. & Wales

Cochran, William (1738–1785), portrait painter and history painter, was born at Strathaven, Lanark, and baptized on 12 December 1738 in the parish of Avondale, Lanarkshire, the son of John Cochran, barber. He began his artistic training in 1754 at the academy of painting in Glasgow newly founded by the well-known printers Robert and Andrew Foulis. As one of their most promising students, he was the first to be sent to Italy in 1761 to continue his education, the academy providing expenses for a two-year period. He became a pupil in Gavin Hamilton's studio in Rome, where he painted several historical and mythological pictures, of which the best-known were *Daedalus and Icarus* and *Diana and Endymion* (locs. unknown). He also studied at the Accademia del Nudo in that city and was at Naples in 1763. He returned to Glasgow *c*.1766, and devoted himself to portrait painting. He practised both in oil and in miniature, building up a thriving practice and supporting an elderly mother. Among his best-known portraits is that of William Cullen, professor at Edinburgh University, and first royal physician in Scotland (Scottish National Portrait Gallery, Edinburgh), engraved in mezzotint by Valentine Green. Cochran is often described as a modest and unambitious character, never exhibiting his works, and seldom putting his name to them. He continued to live in Glasgow, and died there on 23 October 1785. He was buried in the cathedral in that city, where a monument proclaimed, 'The works of his pencil, and this marble, bear record of an eminent artist, and a virtuous man' (McEwan, 134).   L. H. CUST, *rev.* KATE RETFORD

Sources P. J. M. McEwan, *Dictionary of Scottish art and architecture* (1994), 134 · *GM*, 1st ser., 56 (1786), 82 · Redgrave, *Artists*, 89 · J. C. Smith, *British mezzotint portraits*, 2 (1879), 546 · J. Ingamells, ed., *A dictionary of British and Irish travellers in Italy, 1701–1800* (1997), 222 · D. Murray, *Robert and Andrew Foulis and the Glasgow press* (1913), 85–6 · D. Irwin and F. Irwin, *Scottish painters at home and abroad, 1700–1900* (1975), 86–8 · Waterhouse, *18c painters*, 83 · B. Stewart and M. Cutten, *The dictionary of portrait painters in Britain up to 1920* (1997) · Bryan, *Painters* (1964), 1.307 · M. Pilkington, *A general dictionary of painters: containing memoirs of the lives and works*, ed. A. Cunningham and R. A. Davenport (1852), 124 · J. Halsby and P. Harris, *The dictionary of Scottish painters, 1600–1960* (1990), 34 · b. cert.

Cochrane, Sir Alexander Forrester Inglis (1758–1832), naval officer and politician, was born on 22 April 1758, the ninth of eleven children (all sons) of Thomas Cochrane, eighth earl of Dundonald (*bap.* 1691, *d.* 1778), and his second wife, Jean (1722/3–1808), eldest daughter of Archibald Stuart of Torrance, Lanarkshire. He joined the navy at an early age, and was made lieutenant on 19 May 1778 during the War of American Independence. On 17 April 1780, as a junior lieutenant in the *Montagu* under Captain John Houlton, he was wounded in action off Martinique. Made commander on 6 December that year, he continued on the West Indian station under Sir George Rodney and on 17 December 1782 achieved promotion to post captain.

When war ended in 1783 Cochrane returned to England; he remained unemployed on half pay until 1790, when he was appointed to the frigate *Hind*. On 26 April 1788 he married Maria, daughter of David Shaw and widow of Captain Sir Jacob Wheate, baronet; the Cochranes had three sons and two daughters. (The most notable of their offspring was their eldest son, Thomas John *Cochrane (1789–1872), who, in a naval career spanning more than sixty years,

Sir Alexander Forrester Inglis Cochrane (1758–1832), by Robert Field, 1809

was awarded three knighthoods, including a GCB and a KCB, and ended as admiral of the fleet.) Under Captain Cochrane's command his nephew midshipman Thomas *Cochrane (later tenth earl of Dundonald) began a colourful naval career in 1793. In that same year, when war began with revolutionary France, Cochrane cruised against enemy privateers off Norway during the spring and summer, then transferred to the *Thetis* (42 guns), commanding her on the North American station. Accompanied by the *Hussar*, on 17 May 1795 he fought a well-contested action against four large French storeships, capturing the *Prévoyante* and *La Raison*, two frigates armed *en flûte*.

In 1799 Cochrane was appointed to the *Ajax* (80 guns), and in the following year he served in the Channel Fleet under Lord St Vincent, being especially engaged in the detached squadrons under Sir Edward Pellew and Sir John Borlase Warren in the expeditions to Quiberon Bay and against Ferrol. He then joined Lord Keith in 'coasting along the shores of the Mediterranean in quest of adventures', which were found in Egypt. Superintending the landing of troops on the Egyptian coast in February–March 1801 and supporting them with a flotilla of armed boats on Lake Mareotis in August, he earned high praise from Keith and General Hutchinson. At the same time Cochrane proved troublesome to Keith, organizing an opposition clique within the fleet and accusing the admiral of dishonesty (C. Lloyd and W. G. Perrin, eds., *The Keith Papers*, 3 vols., 1927–55, 2.235, 285, 311–13).

After his ship was paid off following the peace of Amiens in 1802, Cochrane entered politics as MP for the Stirling burghs. The breakdown of the peace in 1803 reduced his effectiveness as a politician since, without relinquishing the seat, he returned to sea as captain of the *Northumberland* (74 guns), which he retained as his flagship when advanced to rear-admiral of the blue on 23 April 1804. Commanding a squadron off Ferrol, Cochrane sent home intelligence on Spanish armament and war preparations—information which led to the seizure on 5 October of Spanish treasure ships off Cape Santa Maria. In February 1805, still off Ferrol, he learned that Missiessy's squadron had sailed from La Rochelle for the West Indies, and simultaneously received orders to pursue. His chase was as fruitless as Nelson's later transatlantic chase of Villeneuve, but he was appointed commander-in-chief at the Leeward Islands and joined Nelson as a subordinate in the West Indies phase of the hunt for Villeneuve, continuing as commander-in-chief after Nelson left.

Cochrane became rear-admiral of the white on 9 November 1805. Following Trafalgar, the French maintained a *guerre de course* at sea, and in 1806 as second-in-command to Vice-Admiral Sir John Duckworth, he fought the battle of San Domingo (6 February), the second fight against survivors of Trafalgar. The British squadron included seven ships of the line and four frigates. Three of the five French ships of the line were captured and the other two destroyed; three frigates escaped. Cochrane was awarded a knighthood of the Bath (29 March 1806), a vote of thanks from both houses of parliament, the freedom of the City of London, and a sword of honour to the value of 100 guineas; however, having been an absentee MP for over three years, he was now defeated at the polls.

Still commander-in-chief at the Leewards, he became rear-admiral of the red on 28 April 1808. In 1809 he and Lieutenant-General George Beckwith began a joint campaign against the French in the West Indies, and on 24 February took the island of Martinique, Cochrane flying his flag in the *Neptune* (74 guns) and leading a fleet of 47 ships and other vessels. A naval general service medal was issued to mark the event, which the participant ships were also allowed to list as a battle honour. The French regimental eagles captured on this occasion were sent back to London and were the first seen in England. Cochrane became vice-admiral of the blue on 25 October 1809; Beckwith was knighted. In the *Pompée* on 5 February 1810, commanding a fleet of fifty assorted vessels, Cochrane captured Guadeloupe with Beckwith. This brought another naval general service medal for personnel and another battle honour for participant ships. Cochrane was appointed governor of the island, and advanced to vice-admiral of the white (31 July 1810) and of the red (4 December 1813).

War with America had begun in 1812, and in 1814 in the *Tonnant* (80 guns) Cochrane commanded the North American station, directing (but not actively participating in) coastal operations, including the failed attacks on Baltimore and New Orleans. With the peace he returned to England and was made GCB on 2 January 1815; though again unemployed he became admiral of the blue on 12 August 1819. Although keen to re-enter parliament Cochrane's alleged interest in standing in the Westminster

by-election for this year came to nothing. His last appointment was as commander-in-chief at Plymouth in 1821. He became admiral of the white on 27 May 1825, and on 26 January 1832 he died suddenly in Paris, where he is buried in the Père Lachaise cemetery.   STEPHEN HOWARTH

Sources DNB · Thomas, tenth earl of Dundonald [T. Cochrane], *The autobiography of a seaman*, ed. Douglas, twelfth earl of Dundonald [D. M. B. H. Cochrane], new edn (1890) · J. W. Fortesone, *Dundonald* (1906) · D. Syrett and R. L. DiNardo, *The commissioned sea officers of the Royal Navy, 1660–1815*, rev. edn, Occasional Publications of the Navy RS, 1 (1994) · A. B. Sainsbury, *The Royal Navy day by day*, 2nd edn [n.d., c.1991] · R. G. Thorne, 'Cochrane, Alexander Forrester Inglis', HoP, *Commons, 1790–1820* · GEC, *Peerage*

Archives New York Historical Society, papers · NL Scot., corresp. and papers | BL, letters to Lord Melville, Add. MS 41083 · Hunt. L., letters to Grenville family · NL Scot., letters to Lord Melville · U. Hull, Brynmor Jones L., letters to Sir Henry Hotham

Likenesses R. Field, oils, 1809, Scot. NPG [*see illus.*] · W. Beechey, oils, 1815–19, NMM · C. Turner, mezzotint, pubd 1824 (after W. Beechey), BM, NPG · mezzotints, NPG

Cochrane, Andrew (1692/3–1777), local politician and merchant, was born in Ayr, the son of David Cochrane, a local merchant there, and Janet Crawford. After gaining experience in commerce he moved in 1722 to Glasgow, where he became one of the city's most successful Virginia merchants or 'tobacco lords'. It was a tight-knit commercial community of a few large partnerships: Cochrane's entry on the scene was confirmed by his marriage in October 1723 to Janet (1699–1786), daughter of Peter Murdoch, head of one of Glasgow's prosperous trading families. With her brother John (who was, like Cochrane, a provost of Glasgow) he established the firm of Cochrane, Murdoch & Co. Both were also principals in William Cunninghame & Co., a tobacco trading enterprise which by the 1770s was part of the small élite of partnerships dominating the Clyde's highly successful and profitable trade in tobacco, and one of the largest commercial undertakings of any kind in Scotland. Cochrane's mercantile interests ran further afield: he was a partner in a range of industrial companies in the west of Scotland, including the King Street Sugarhouse, the Glasgow Tanwork Company, and the Greenland Fishing Company. In 1752 Cochrane and John Murdoch were also members of the Glasgow Ship Bank. Like many other successful merchants, Cochrane's position was reflected in the purchase of a country estate at Brighouse in Lanarkshire.

However, Cochrane is now best remembered for his local political services. Glasgow's 'greatest provost' was the verdict of J. O. Mitchell in 1905, and with some justice. Cochrane was six times the city's provost during the years 1744 to 1762. During his second term (1745–6) he was also preses of the convention of the royal burghs of Scotland, when the Jacobite rising provided his most serious political test. The city and its wealth constituted an obvious target for the highland army, but for all his urging the administration would provide no protection, nor even any arms, though the inhabitants, including Cochrane, were 'all hearty for the government'. Glasgow was duly occupied in mid-September, and a levy of £15,000 (later reduced to £5500) was demanded by Charles Edward Stuart's agents.

Under duress the city paid, and when the highland army revisited Glasgow in late December during its retreat north, it also provided coats, shirts, bonnets, and shoes. It was Cochrane's skill and judgement that steered the city through this difficult passage, making sufficient concessions to avert a pillage of the city, which many feared, while maintaining its loyalty to the crown even before the battle of Culloden. After that event Cochrane led a delegation in July 1746 to Holyrood to present a congratulatory address to the victor at Culloden, the duke of Cumberland. Late in 1748 he visited London to lobby for compensation to Glasgow for its losses during the rising: £10,000 was eventually secured. On further visits he lobbied on other Scottish matters, including the subsidies to whaling and the herring fishery, and (with the linen manufacturer William Tod) the renewal of the linen subsidy in 1754–5. After the completion of his last term of office as provost in 1761–2, Cochrane seems to have taken a lesser part in public life, except for his continuing interest in Hutcheson's Hospital, to which he left a modest bequest. He died, aged eighty-four, without children, at his country estate on 9 July 1777. He was survived by his wife, Janet, who died on 2 September 1786. There is a monument to Cochrane in Glasgow Cathedral.　ALASTAIR J. DURIE

Sources J. R. Anderson, ed., *The provosts of Glasgow from 1609 to 1832* (1942) · J. Dennistoun, ed., *The Cochrane correspondence regarding the affairs of Glasgow* (1836) · T. M. Devine, *The tobacco lords: a study of the tobacco merchants of Glasgow and their trading activities, c.1740–1790* (1975) · J. Mackie, *Records of the convention of royal burghs of Scotland, 1739–1759* (1915) · J. O. Mitchell, *Old Glasgow essays* (1905) · *Scots Magazine*, 39 (1777)

Cochrane, Archibald, **ninth earl of Dundonald** (1748–1831), chemical manufacturer, was born on 1 January 1748, the son of Thomas Cochrane, eighth earl of Dundonald (1691–1778), and Jean Stuart (1722/3–1808). His mother was keenly interested in technical matters. After brief service in both army and navy, he turned to scientific projects, applying chemical principles to manufacturing processes, though he never reaped financial rewards for his often brilliant ideas. He was married three times: on 17 October 1774 to Anne (1755–1784), daughter of Captain James *Gilchrist; on 12 April 1788 to Isabella (d. 1808), widow of John Mayne; and in April 1819 to Anna Maria (d. 1822), daughter of the writer Francis Peter *Plowden. The eldest son of his first marriage was Admiral Thomas *Cochrane, the tenth earl; there were no children of the second and third marriages.

Cochrane, styled Lord Cochrane from 1758 to 1778, succeeded to the title earl of Dundonald on the death of his father on 27 June 1778, but the family estates were severely impoverished and he had to borrow money in order to equip his son for the navy. Nevertheless, the estate of Culross Abbey in Perthshire was well supplied with timber and coal, and the Lamancha estate 12 miles south of Edinburgh contained iron ore. He also had a house in Hammersmith. His son complained that the unentailed estates were crippled by his father's extensive scientific pursuits. Contemporaries did not always appreciate Dundonald's efforts—he was sometimes known as

'daft Dundonald'—but the ninth earl was a man of active and enquiring mind who enjoyed the learned society afforded by Edinburgh and was on intimate terms with Joseph Black, the professor of chemistry. In literature on industrial history he is usually referred to as Lord Dundonald.

By the late eighteenth century a shortage of soda (commonly called alkali) was affecting all countries touched by the industrial revolution. In 1790 Dundonald joined the brothers John and William Losh in experiments on the production of synthetic soda from salt at Woodside near Carlisle. Three years later the results were sufficiently promising to justify setting up a works at Bells Close, west of Newcastle upon Tyne, where Dundonald had a tar distillery. In 1797 the Losh family inherited a share in a coalmine on the Tyne at Walker in which a brine spring had been discovered. This provided a private source of salt for making soda, though to avoid the heavy duty of £36 per ton the salt had to be mixed with soot or ashes, and an exciseman lived on the site to see that the law was obeyed. Several of Dundonald's patents were worked at Walker, but all depended on the successful sale of by-products.

Meanwhile an efficient process for converting salt to soda had been developed in France by Nicolas Leblanc, and William Losh visited Paris at Dundonald's suggestion to learn what he could. The Walker works was the first in England to work the Leblanc process, the partners being lords Dundas and Dundonald, the Losh brothers, and bankers John and Aubone Surtees. The original partnership soon dissolved and the Losh brothers, trading as Walker Alkali Works, were able to develop a profitable chemical business in which Dundonald no longer had a part. The alkali trade spread to Lancashire and Cheshire, and became the backbone of the heavy chemical industry.

Another area in which Dundonald was a significant catalyst was coal-tar technology. During his naval service he had observed the ravages made on ships' bottoms by worms. Believing correctly that coal tar might provide a remedy which could be produced more cheaply than Stockholm tar made from dwindling supplies of wood, he designed and built retorts for the distillation of tar from coal at Culross Abbey. He also superintended the working of his adjacent collieries. He did not invent the production of tar from coal; his innovation, embodied in his 1781 patent, was to avoid the use of an external fuel, allowing coal in the retort to smoulder slowly by controlling the air intake. He envisaged a complete industrial package in which the tar would be used to protect ships' bottoms, the 'cinders' (coke) would provide a clean fuel for salt boiling, malting, and brewing, and sal ammoniac from the ammonia liquors would be sold to calico printers and metal finishers. He also foresaw, but did not develop, the possibility of gas lighting. His vision of the tar industry is presented in his book *The Quality and Uses of Coal Tar and Coal Varnish* (1784).

Unfortunately, the Admiralty did not embrace the tar treatment, preferring to rely on copper sheathing. With one exception, Dundonald's creditors saw the potential of the tar process and were prepared to give him leeway to develop the concern. The dissident, named Cuthbert, pressed for foreclosure. Dundonald was thus forced to spread his risk (and reduce his hope of profit) by forming the British Tar Company, whose partners were Newcastle businessmen. The coal-tar industry was destined to become an important provider of dyes, perfumes, drugs, and explosives, but not within Dundonald's lifetime.

Dundonald was also active in a wide variety of other technological fields. He established a factory for the production of alum as a mordant for silk and calico printers. He published a *Treatise Showing the Intimate Connection between Agriculture and Chemistry* (1795), eighteen years before Sir Humphry Davy's famous work on that topic. He proposed the use of salt residues as manure, a new process for making white lead, the malting of grain for cattle feed, an improved method for preparing flax and hemp for sailcloth, and a scheme for purifying rock salt by washing out the impurities with brine.

Dundonald died at the rue Vaugirard, Paris, on 1 July 1831, in poverty. The Literary Fund Society had awarded him a pension in 1823 but it is not known how long this lasted. His son Thomas wrote: 'His discoveries, now of national utility, ruined him and deprived his posterity of their remaining paternal inheritance' (Cochrane, 1.39). Later biographers have cast doubts both on his science and his business sense. In fact he possessed a sound knowledge of the chemical properties of common substances, and was quick to see the industrial possibilities in simple chemical reactions. The impoverished condition of the family estates when he inherited meant that he was never able to command the capital to sustain his experiments through the difficult periods of development. The examples of alkali and coal tar show that his confidence and enthusiasm were justified, though too late to mend his fortunes.   ALEC CAMPBELL

Sources GEC, *Peerage* · Thomas, tenth earl of Dundonald [T. Cochrane], *The autobiography of a seaman*, 1 (1860) · A. Clow and N. L. Clow, *The chemical revolution* (1952) · *GM*, 1st ser., 101/2 (1831), 172 · *Transactions of the Newcastle Chemical Soc.*, 1 (1868), 32 · W. G. Armstrong, ed., *Industrial resources of Tyne, Wear and Tees* (1864), 158 · A. Clow and N. L. Clow, 'Dr James Hutton and the manufacture of sal ammoniac', *Nature*, 159 (1947), 425–7, esp. 426 · J. R. Partington, *A history of chemistry*, 3 (1962), 562 · *Abridgements of all specifications of patented inventions relating to Acids, alkalies etc., 1622–1866* · T. S. Ashton and J. Sykes, *The coal industry of the eighteenth century* (1929) · *Scots peerage*, 3.361
Archives NA Scot., papers relating to family and estate, incl. letters from his agent William Hamilton · NL Scot., accounts, corresp., and memoranda | BL, letters to the lords Liverpool, Add. MSS 38224, 38310, 38257–38260 · PRO NIre., corresp. with John Foster relating to machinery
Likenesses J. F. Skill, J. Gilbert, and W. and E. Walker, group portrait, pencil and wash (*Men of science living in 1807–8*), NPG

Cochrane, Archibald Leman (1909–1988), medical scientist and epidemiologist, was born in Galashiels on 12 January 1909, the second child in the family of a daughter and three sons of Walter Francis Cochrane, of Kirklands, manufacturer of Scottish tweed, and his wife, Mabel Purdom, daughter and granddaughter of lawyers from Hawick. His grandfather's family had become wealthy,

but the death of his father on active service in April 1917 led to his mother's relative impoverishment. He gained entry scholarships to Uppingham School and King's College, Cambridge, where he obtained first classes in both parts of the natural sciences tripos (1929 and 1931).

An inheritance gave Cochrane the means to continue study, and in 1931 he began research in tissue culture at the Strangeways Research Laboratory, Cambridge, hoping to become a university lecturer. The results of his experiments, however, seemed trivial and the concomitant development of what he believed (erroneously) to be a psychological symptom led him to abandon the project and seek medical advice. British doctors were unsympathetic, and he sought help at the Kaiser Wilhelm Institute in Berlin. He received sympathy there, but little else, and he turned to Theodor Reik, an early follower of Sigmund Freud, partly to obtain treatment and partly to learn enough about psychoanalysis to design ways of testing psychoanalytical hypotheses. The succeeding two and a half years did nothing for his complaint, but they provided an exceptional education, as he followed Dr Reik from Berlin to Vienna, and to The Hague, attending the clinical course in both the last cities.

Returning to Britain in 1934 with fluent German, a hatred of fascism, and a sceptical attitude to all theories not validated by experiment, Cochrane enrolled as a medical student at University College Hospital (UCH), London. The outbreak of the Spanish Civil War and the intervention of fascist Germany and Italy led him to abandon his studies for membership of a field ambulance unit supporting the International Brigades, in which he was probably the only member with neither party political nor religious affiliation. After a year's service on the Aragon and Madrid fronts, he returned to UCH with valuable experience of wartime triage and the realities of left-wing politics.

Cochrane qualified MB, BChir. (Cambridge, 1938) in time to complete a house physician's job at the West London Hospital and obtain a research appointment at UCH before war again intervened. He joined the Royal Army Medical Corps in 1940, and was posted to a general hospital in Egypt. He was then sent to Crete, where he was soon taken prisoner. There followed the darkest period of his life when, as medical officer for a prisoner-of-war camp in Salonika, he was confronted by major epidemics, severe malnutrition, and extreme Nazi brutality. During this time he undertook what he later described as his 'first, worst, and most successful controlled trial' in search of a cure for famine oedema, finding it in small amounts of yeast obtained on the black market. When he returned to Britain in 1945, a Rockefeller fellowship enabled him to take a course at the London School of Hygiene, where he became enthusiastic about the conduct of controlled trials by random allocation of treatments and obtained his diploma in public health (1947). He then went for a year (1947) to the Phipps Clinic in Philadelphia, where he developed a lifelong interest in the scientific study of diagnostic and prognostic error. In 1948 he accepted an appointment with the Medical Research Council's pneumoconiosis research unit in Cardiff. There

Cochrane designed and started an ambitious project to test the idea that tuberculosis played an important part in transforming the disease into its most disabling form.

In 1960 Cochrane was appointed David Davies professor of tuberculosis and diseases of the chest at the Welsh National School of Medicine, and transformed his team into a new epidemiology unit, of which he became director in 1969, under the Medical Research Council. With this support, he continued his studies of the progress of pneumoconiosis and conducted population surveys to study the natural history and aetiology of anaemia, glaucoma, and other common diseases. He showed the importance of building in checks on the reproducibility of any diagnostic procedure and demonstrated that it was regularly possible to get over 90 per cent of the public to participate in health surveys. The social importance of his trials was lucidly expressed in his short book, *Effectiveness and Efficiency* (1972), which won him international acclaim. He became fellow of the Royal College of Physicians in 1965.

In 1972 Cochrane became the first president of the new faculty of community (subsequently public health) medicine of the Royal College of Physicians. He had never been attracted by administration or ceremony and was relieved to hand over after two years. In this period, however, he succeeded in welding into a harmonious whole two mutually suspicious groups: academics in social medicine and practising medical officers of health. He was appointed MBE in 1945 and CBE in 1968, and had honorary doctorates from York (1973) and Rochester, USA (1977).

Archie, as Cochrane was generally known, combined concern for public welfare with that for the individual and discovered late in life, as a result of the trouble he took over an illness of his sister's, that they both suffered from hereditary porphyria, which may have been responsible for the sexual condition that so affected his early career. He created a garden included in the national garden scheme and collected with discrimination contemporary paintings and sculpture. A man of medium height and athletic build, he had reddish hair and a permanently quizzical expression. He never married, having resolved to have no more love affairs after an unfortunate experience in the USA in 1947. He died of cancer after a long illness on 18 June 1988, at his nephew's home in Holt, near Wimborne, Dorset. He is commemorated in Green College, Oxford, to which he left a substantial legacy, by a residence for students and a fellowship for the director of the Cochrane Centre, set up by the Department of Health to promote overviews of controlled trials.

RICHARD DOLL, *rev.*

Sources A. L. Cochrane and M. Blythe, *One man's medicine: an autobiography* (1989) • *The Times* (22 June 1988) • personal knowledge (1996) • *CGPLA Eng. & Wales* (1989) • A. Maynard and I. Chalmers, eds., *Non-random reflections on health services research* (1997)
Archives FILM RCP Lond., 'Medical sciences video-archive of the Royal College of Physicians and Oxford Brookes University', video, MSVA 024 [interview with M. Blythe]
Likenesses photograph (as a young man), Green College, Oxford • portrait, RCP Lond.

Wealth at death £681,456: probate, 8 Feb 1989, *CGPLA Eng. & Wales*

Cochrane, Douglas Mackinnon Baillie Hamilton, twelfth earl of Dundonald (1852–1935), army officer, was born at Auchentoul House, Banff, on 29 October 1852, the second son (his elder brother died a baby in 1851) of Thomas Barnes Cochrane, eleventh earl of Dundonald (1814–1885), army officer, and his wife, Louisa Harriet (1819/20–1902), daughter of William Alexander *Mackinnon (1784–1870) of Mackinnon, tory MP and 33rd chief of clan Mackinnon, who reportedly never wore a greatcoat or flannel. He was a grandson of Thomas *Cochrane, tenth earl of Dundonald (1775–1860), and inherited his secret chemical-warfare plans. A naval and military family, the Cochranes were within the peerage relatively poor, owning under 2000 acres in 1883.

Cochrane (styled Lord Cochrane 1860–85) was educated at a spartan and brutal private school at Walton-on-Thames, where he learned little, and at Eton College (1866–9). He had wanted to join the navy, but his parents dissuaded him as the family had suffered losses of property from Cochranes being so much away at sea. He purchased for £1260 a commission as cornet and sub-lieutenant (July 1870) in the 2nd Life Guards, which his cousin Sir Roger Palmer commanded. On his extensive leaves he visited Germany, to learn the language, and South America. He was promoted lieutenant in October 1871 and captain in April 1878. He studied for Staff College entrance but did not take it because, according to his memoirs, he had to go to Brazil on family business. On 18 September 1878 he married Winifred (1858/9–1924), only surviving child of Robert Bamford Hesketh, formerly 2nd Life Guards, of Gwyrch Castle, Abergele, Denbighshire, and an heiress; they had two sons and three daughters.

Cochrane wanted to go on the 1882 Egyptian campaign but was refused. In 1884, apparently through the influence of Angela Burdett-Coutts, Baroness Burdett-Coutts, a family connection, on Wolseley, he commanded the 2nd Life Guards contingent, which formed part of the heavy camel regiment, on the Gordon relief expedition. He was helping reload a camel when a heavy box of ammunition fell on him, causing internal injury which troubled him for years. With the desert column in January 1885, he was promoted major and fought at the battles of Abu Klea and Gubat. His desert rides with dispatches on the capture of Gakdul Wells and the death of Gordon brought him fame. He succeeded to the title in January 1885. He was mentioned in dispatches, and promoted lieutenant-colonel in June 1885. In 1889 he became brevet colonel. In 1890 he was captain of the queen's guard. Troops were then intermittently used in support of the civil power, and on 7 July during a police strike Dundonald, at the request of the chief commissioner of police and cheered on by the Drury Lane audience, led the guard in clearing a mob from Bow Street: a bird-cage was thrown at his helmet and dented it.

From January 1895 to January 1899 Dundonald commanded the 2nd Life Guards. A keen reformer, he concentrated on improving its shooting—establishing a shooting

Douglas Mackinnon Baillie Hamilton Cochrane, twelfth earl of Dundonald (1852–1935), by Robert Faulkner

club—fieldcraft, entrenching, and other dismounted action. Intelligent and innovative, he invented a light, one-horse machine-gun 'galloping carriage', demonstrated in 1897, for use with cavalry. The War Office rejected it but some, with Colt guns, were used by his brigade in the Second South African War. His other inventions included a waterproof bag for hauling men across rivers, a pneumatic-tyred light ambulance, the 'Instra' hand-warmer, an improved teapot, and—on his return from the Second South African War and responding to the high mortality from water-borne disease there—an improved military water cart. He inspected yeomanry regiments and became convinced they should train primarily as mounted riflemen. His ceremonial duties included command of the sovereign's escort at the 1897 jubilee procession, for which he was made an MVO.

Dundonald's only senior command in the field was in the Second South African War (1899–1902). Despite his aged mother's insistence that the war was unrighteous Dundonald, without an official appointment, on his own initiative went to South Africa, arriving on 14 November 1899. Sir Redvers Buller, whom he knew from the Sudan war, sent him to organize the mounted troops in south Natal. In Natal under Buller he commanded the mounted brigade, then, after reorganization at the end of January 1900, the 2nd cavalry brigade of irregular mounted infantry, and, after the relief of Ladysmith (28 February 1900)

and further reorganization, the 3rd mounted brigade. On 15 December 1899 at the battle of Colenso, on the right flank, his brigade attempted to capture Hlangwane Hill, a key position. Historians differ in their versions, but some agree with Dundonald's that they might well have succeeded if Major-General Geoffry Barton had not refused the infantry reinforcement he requested. On 18 January 1900, during Sir Charles Warren's disastrous offensive, Dundonald's brigade defeated a Boer force at Acton Homes and, in 'a situation … capable of being turned to great strategic advantage' (Amery, 3.222) if reinforced, might have turned the Boer flank, possibly resulting in the immediate relief of Ladysmith. However Warren angrily refused reinforcements, had a stormy interview with Dundonald, and detached two regiments from Dundonald's force, preventing him from exploiting the opening his initiative had created. In February Dundonald, whose brigade formed the advance guard, was cautious in his final move towards Ladysmith, arriving after Hubert Gough who had pushed on despite contrary orders. Dundonald continued to serve in Natal and the Transvaal and, like Buller, opposed farm-burning which he believed made inveterate enemies. In October 1900 the army of Natal was broken up and, the war apparently almost over, Buller, Dundonald, and others returned home. Dundonald was promoted major-general (March 1900) and mentioned in dispatches. He later offered to go back to the war but was not asked.

Nicknamed 'Dundoodle' by his colonial troops, Dundonald was, according to William Birdwood, who served on his staff, 'a curiously sensitive man, living largely on his nerves' (Birdwood, 100). Opinions varied on his military capacity. He was much praised by the British press, and dubbed 'the Stormy Petrel'. However Hubert Gough, who served on his staff, came to despise him. Gough wrote in his diary, 'Dundonald very pleasant. He means very well but has not anything like the steady nerves a soldier wants to do any good' (Farrar-Hockley, 57), and later wrote that he was 'another of Buller's weak subordinates … hesitating, vacillating and vain' (Gough, 70), lacking in dash, and gaining credit for the achievements of his capable subordinates. Historians have differed in their assessments. The marquess of Anglesey concluded that 'on the whole he seems to have done well enough, being quick-moving and clear-headed while not interfering unduly with his subordinates … who were … men of ability' (Anglesey, 4.75). According to his admiring friend Douglas Sladen he was 'a tall, upright man, with an elegant figure and a handsome and very aristocratic face' (Sladen, 204), and according to Basil Collier his 'merits would have been more apparent to his brother-officers if he had looked less like a matinée idol and been less of a favourite with the newspapers' (Collier, 65). The war was an important influence on his military thinking, especially on cavalry and firepower, and he long continued concerned with the war. Birdwood recalled that Dundonald when an old man 'devoured every book … on the South African campaign' (Birdwood, 415) and if he found any passage seeming to reflect on his own work, wanted it amended.

In the Second South African War and post-war controversy on the armament and role of cavalry Dundonald was a leading advocate of the 'firepower' school against the 'arme blanche' school, and was castigated by Haig. In December 1900 he became the only regular cavalryman on the War Office committee on the organization, arms, and equipment of the yeomanry. In his minority report he advocated they become rifle-armed mounted infantry and their name be changed from yeomanry cavalry to imperial yeomanry. His recommendations were essentially implemented—though more because they expressed the perceived lessons of the war and because Roberts favoured them than because Dundonald advocated them—but by 1914 they had been partly reversed in the cavalry traditionalist reaction: the sword was restored for war mobilization in 1913. Since before the 1884 Sudan war he had been much interested in machine-guns, and after the Second South African War he advocated their use in large numbers. In public speeches he advocated the auxiliary forces be reorganized into an effective second line of defence, and he privately urged Lord Roberts, the commander-in-chief, to do this.

In 1902 Dundonald was appointed general officer commanding (GOC) the Canadian militia. As an imperial officer with a statutory quasi-independent role, responsible to the dominion government, and so involved with Canadian politics and with Anglo-Canadian and Canadian–United States relations, Dundonald, like his predecessors, had a difficult task. Like them, and most notably Edward Hutton (GOC, 1898–1900), he aimed to make the militia an efficient fighting force for Canadian and imperial defence. Despite Hutton's efforts, political patronage and interference in the militia continued: an American critic had earlier described the militia as 'a kind of military Tammany' (Penlington, 161). Before Dundonald left, Chamberlain and others warned him of difficulties with politicians. However, he liked Canadians and he arrived in July 1902 determined to reform the militia. Energetic and enthusiastic, he planned reorganization and training, went on inspection tours, initiated affiliation of Canadian with British regiments, and encouraged the formation of cadet units and the adoption of Scottish characteristics by Canadian Scottish regiments. He re-equipped the artillery. He abolished the sword as a cavalry war weapon and wrote *Cavalry Training, Canada* (1904), stating that the rifle was 'the weapon for cavalry in the future' (Dundonald, 252). He advocated 'an economical Citizen Army', a large militia, compulsory cadet training, and preparation for possible war, and publicly stated his views in speeches at dinners and receptions. He warned Canadians on defence, that they were living in a fool's paradise, and criticized inadequate provision for the militia. There was friction with politicians, especially over their interference in officer appointments. His protests failed, so he decided to 'arouse the nation to the danger of practices which rendered organization useless and efficiency impossible'

(ibid., 260). On 4 June 1904, at an officers' banquet in Montreal, he denounced political interference in military appointments, naming the minister of agriculture (acting minister of militia), Sydney Fisher. The 'Dundonald incident' was much reported, and debated in the Canadian and—following Lloyd George's motion criticizing Dundonald—British parliaments. On 14 June he was dismissed by the Canadian government, then recalled by the British, leaving at the end of July. He was popular in Canada, and was supported by many Canadians and much applauded at farewell gatherings. He was the last imperial GOC: a new Militia Act stipulated a Canadian. After his departure his infantry and cavalry manuals were cancelled. He much resented Churchill, whom he had helped in South Africa, joining Lloyd George's attack.

In 1906 Dundonald was a member of the committee on the reorganization of the auxiliary forces appointed by Haldane. He was promoted lieutenant-general in December 1906 and was, to his 'astonishment and dismay' (Dundonald, 309), retired from the army in June 1907. From April 1907 to February 1919 he was colonel of the 2nd Life Guards. He helped the interests of former servicemen and particularly the new National Society of Ex-Naval and Military Men. From 1886 to 1922 Dundonald was, replacing his father, a Scottish representative peer: a Liberal Unionist who sometimes spoke on the Sudan and defence issues. In 1906 he advocated compulsory cadet training for youths. In January 1910 he spoke against Lloyd George's 'people's budget', alleging its land taxes would drive capital out of the country and decrease house building. However, he was not a 'diehard' peer. He lived at Wimbledon Park and, according to Sladen, was a 'lonely man who saw very little of his wife' (Sladen, 205).

At the outbreak of war in 1914 Dundonald offered his services, 'preferably for a command in the Field' (Dundonald, 326), and he hoped to command the Canadian contingent, but was unsuccessful. In 1915 he asked Kitchener for an appointment, but was told 'This is a young man's war' (ibid., 328). According to Sladen, 'Kitchener hated him' (Sladen, 208) and so excluded him. In 1914 he proposed the formation of a West Indian contingent, a proposal initially rejected. He decided to try to apply his grandfather's secret chemical-warfare plans to the war (unknown to Dundonald, and to his later chagrin, the plans had 'thoughtlessly' been published by Sir George Douglas and Sir George Ramsay in their 1908 edition of *The Panmure Papers*). In September 1914 he proposed to 'drive the enemy from their trenches by the use of asphyxiating vapour under cover of dense smoke clouds' (ibid., 331) but Kitchener rejected this. Dundonald contacted Churchill, first lord of the Admiralty, who had accompanied his brigade in South Africa. Churchill was keen (within the limits of international law), and in January 1915 advised him to confide the plans to Colonel Maurice Hankey, who had been experimenting with secret weapons. Dundonald did so 'under the seal of strictest secrecy' (Hankey, 1.230), and also made private experiments. In March Churchill appointed an Admiralty committee on smoke screens, chaired by Dundonald, which did useful work. Smoke screens were used by British sea and land forces, but Dundonald considered they were insufficiently used and could have changed the Gallipoli campaign.

Dundonald was appointed CB in May 1896, MVO in June 1897, CVO in June 1907, and KCB in 1913. In 1921 he was special ambassador at the Peruvian centenary. The countess of Dundonald took a great interest in the Anglican church in Wales, especially at the time of the disestablishment controversy. She died on 17 January 1924, and the archbishop of Wales officiated at her funeral (at Llanddulas parish church, north Wales, 19 January). She bequeathed £50,000 and a balance of her Gwyrch Castle estate to George V for establishing a royal residence in Wales. The king declined, so the bequests passed to the order of St John of Jerusalem, from which Dundonald bought the castle and estate.

Despite his earlier injury, Dundonald remained active into old age. In 1926 he published his memoirs, *My Army Life* (augmented edition, 1934), which included his criticism of government departments' abuse of the Official Secrets Act to conceal information about themselves unconnected with national security. In 1930, aged seventy-seven he, with a small crew, sailed his 14 ton yawl-rigged yacht, *Bonnie Joann*, to Brazil. He died at his residence, Fernwood, Victoria Road, Wimbledon Park, Surrey, on 12 April 1935; his funeral was at Achnaba church, Argyllshire, on 16 April. He was succeeded as thirteenth earl by his elder son, Thomas Hesketh Douglas Blair Cochrane (1886–1958). ROGER T. STEARN

Sources *The Times* (18 Jan 1924) · *The Times* (21 Jan 1924) · *The Times* (13 April 1935) · *The Times* (17 April 1935) · Earl of Dundonald [D. M. B. H. Cochrane], *My army life* (1934) · Marquess of Anglesey [G. C. H. V. Paget], *A history of the British cavalry, 1816 to 1919*, 4 (1986) · GEC, *Peerage* · N. Penlington, *Canada and imperialism, 1896–1899* (1965) · Lord Birdwood [W. R. Birdwood], *Khaki and gown: an autobiography* (1941) · H. Gough, *Soldiering on* (1954) · A. Farrar-Hockley, *Goughie: the life of General Sir Hubert Gough CGB, GCMG, KCVO* (1975) · T. Pakenham, *The Boer War* (1979) · Burke, *Peerage* · D. Sladen, *My long life* (1939) · I. F. W. Beckett, *The amateur military tradition, 1558–1945* (1991) · E. M. Spiers, *The late Victorian army, 1868–1902* (1992) · *The Panmure papers, being a selection from the correspondence of Fox Maule*, ed. G. Douglas and G. D. Ramsay, 2 vols. (1908), vol. 1 · A. Cochrane, *The fighting Cochranes* (1983) · J. Holland Rose and others, eds., *Canada and Newfoundland* (1930), vol. 6 of *The Cambridge history of the British empire* (1929–59) · W. S. Churchill, *The world crisis*, 3 (1927) · J. B. Brebner, *Canada: a modern history* [1960] · B. Collier, *Brasshat* (1961) · Local Studies Collection, Old Town Hall, Richmond, Surrey, Sladen MSS · *Annual Register* (1904) · Lord Hankey [M. Hankey], *The supreme command, 1914–1918*, 2 vols. (1961), vol. 1 · R. Kruger, *Good-bye Dolly Gray: the story of the Boer War* (1959) · H. W. Wilson, *With the flag to Pretoria: a history of the Boer War of 1899–1900*, 1 (1900) · H. W. Wilson, *With the flag to Pretoria: a history of the Boer War of 1899–1900*, 2 (1901) · L. S. Amery, ed., *The Times history of the war in South Africa*, 2–4 (1902–6) · H. E. Egerton, *British colonial policy in the XXth century* (1922) · Hart's Army List (1891) · Kelly, *Handbk* · m. cert. · d. cert.

Archives NA Scot., corresp. and papers | King's Lond., Liddell Hart C., corresp. with Sir B. H. Liddell Hart · NL Scot., letters to the fourth earl of Minto · Richmond Local Studies Library, London, corresp. with Douglas Sladen

Likenesses photograph, *c.*1895, repro. in Wilson, *With the flag to Pretoria*, 2 · portrait, *c.*1910, repro. in Cochrane, *The fighting Cochranes* · R. Faulkner, photograph, NPG [see illus.] · Faulkner & Co.,

photograph, repro. in Amery, ed., *The Times history of the war in South Africa*, 3 · Spy [L. Ward], chromolithograph cartoon, NPG; repro. in *VF* (29 Nov 1900) · Spy [L. Ward], chromolithograph cartoon, NPG; repro. in *VF* (8 May 1902) · photographs, repro. in Earl of Dundonald, *My army life*

Wealth at death £3628: administration, 19 Dec 1935, CGPLA Eng. & Wales

Cochrane, Sir James (1798–1883), judge in Gibraltar, the fourth son of Thomas Cochrane, speaker of the house of assembly of Nova Scotia, was born in Nova Scotia. He was admitted as a student in 1818, and was called to the bar at the Inner Temple on 6 February 1829. In the same year he married Theresa (*d.* 1873), the daughter of Colonel William Haly. They had at least one son, Thomas, who later became rector of Stapleford Abbotts, Essex.

In 1837 Cochrane was appointed attorney-general at Gibraltar, where he remained for the rest of his life. In 1841 he was made chief justice, a post he held for thirty-six years. He was knighted at St James's Palace on 12 March 1845. He resigned in 1877, four years after his wife's death. According to a speech made by General Lord Napier of Magdala, governor of the fortress, at the resignation, Cochrane had 'eminently maintained the high character of the bench'. His clarity of judgment, wisdom, and character had, according to Napier, 'commanded the respect of all classes of the community'. The general drew particular attention to Cochrane's 'firmness and perfect fairness', to his achievements with working-class people, and to his success in helping 'to dispel from the city of Gibraltar the crime of using the knife, which was unfortunately once so prevalent'. Cochrane died at Glenrocky, his home in Gibraltar, on 24 June 1883.

H. M. STEPHENS, *rev.* LYNN MILNE

Sources *The Times* (27 June 1883) · Boase, *Mod. Eng. biog.* · CGPLA Eng. & Wales (1883)

Wealth at death £7828 7*s.* 11*d.*: probate, 20 Aug 1883, CGPLA Eng. & Wales

Cochrane, Sir John (*b.* *c.*1604, *d.* in or after 1657), army officer and diplomat, was the eldest of the nine children of Alexander Blair (*d.* 1640/41), who assumed the name Cochrane on his marriage to Elizabeth, daughter of William Cochrane of Cochrane, Renfrewshire, and his wife, Elizabeth. Alexander Cochrane purchased the barony of Cowdown in 1623, but resigned it to his second son, William. Having been educated at Glasgow University, where he graduated MA in 1623, John Cochrane entered the army, and served in Ireland, acquiring land through his marriage to Lady Grace Butler, allegedly a cousin of the duke of Ormond.

On his return to Scotland he became an active covenanter and commanded a regiment at the sieges of Carlaverock and Threave (1639–40). He became a client of Montrose and was also linked to the Palatine–Bohemian connection. In 1640 the elector Palatine asked Cochrane to sound out Montrose about service abroad. In 1641 he was implicated in 'the incident', a plot for seizing Hamilton and Argyll, leaders of the parliamentary party; but, on his arrest, he was freed without bail on their petition (17

November). After resigning his Scottish estates (19 December 1642) to his next brother, William *Cochrane, later first earl of Dundonald, he joined the king at York. Recommended to Charles by his sister, Elizabeth of Bohemia, he was sent by the king to solicit help in men or money, first to the Netherlands and then to Denmark, Christian IV being the uncle of Charles I. On his return in company with the Danish ambassador, who aimed to mediate between the king and parliament, Cochrane was arrested and imprisoned in Hull and in Windsor Castle.

Having regained his liberty, he was put in command of Towcester, from where he complained to Prince Rupert (16 December 1643) that the town would fall unless the garrison was better supplied. After the royalists abandoned Towcester (18 January 1644), Cochrane appears at Oxford, the royalist headquarters; he soon headed north with Montrose to attempt a counter-invasion of Scotland (March). After another visit to the Netherlands Cochrane, now knighted, was sent as ambassador to Denmark (1644), but the Danish–Swedish War (1643–5) left Christian IV little opportunity to help his nephew. His estates were forfeited (1644) and parliament, in its peace negotiations with the king (1646) listed Cochrane among those to be excepted from pardon.

For almost a decade he was employed in raising money for the royal cause in Denmark, Hamburg, Danzig, and Poland, especially from the duke of Courland (1645–50). The wordiness of his letters and his account of negotiations at Hamburg confirm the estimation of Charles I that he was a man 'having many discourses, most of his own praises' (Simpson, 144). Although successful in raising supplies, he seems to have been dilatory in explaining his dealings, and in 1650 Charles II sent an apology to Scottish merchants in Poland for Cochrane's unauthorized exactions. In 1650 he was prohibited by the Scottish parliament from returning to his own country. On 26 February 1652 his wife, who was in prison in England (probably for aiding her husband's enterprises), secured a pass for him to return to England, which he did in 1653. Until 1657 his name occurs in various political negotiations, but he probably died before 1660.   BASIL MORGAN

Sources Scots peerage, 3.338–44 · CSP dom., 1639–57 · C. Russell, The fall of the British monarchies, 1637–1642 (1991) · H. F. Morland Simpson, ed., 'Civil war papers, … 1643–50', Miscellany … I, Scottish History Society, 15 (1893) · JHC, 2–3 (1640–44) · E. J. Cowan, Montrose—for covenant and king (1977) · Report on the Pepys manuscripts, HMC, 70 (1911) · The letters and journals of Robert Baillie, ed. D. Laing, 3 vols., Bannatyne Club, 73 (1841–2) · J. Spalding, Memorialls of the trubles in Scotland and in England, AD 1624 – AD 1645, ed. J. Stuart, 2 vols., Spalding Club, [21, 23] (1850–51) · Memoirs of Prince Rupert and the cavaliers including their private correspondence, ed. E. Warburton, 3 vols. (1849) · Correspondence of Sir Robert Kerr, first earl of Ancram, and his son William, third earl of Lothian, ed. D. Laing, 2 vols., Roxburghe Club, 100 (1875) · J. Maidment, ed., 'Sir John Cochrane's relations … since his coming to Hamburgh', Historical fragments relative to Scottish affairs from 1635 to 1664 (1833) · S. Reid, The campaigns of Montrose (1990)

Cochrane, Sir John (fl. 1662–1695), conspirator, born probably at Ochiltree, Ayrshire, was the second son of Sir William *Cochrane, later first earl of Dundonald (1605–1685), and his wife, Eupheme (d. after 1685), daughter of

Sir William Scott of Ardross, Fife. He was the brother of Lord William Cochrane (d. 1679) and of Lady Grizel, who married George, tenth Lord Ross. He and his wife, Margaret, second daughter of Sir William Strickland of Boynton, Yorkshire, had three children: William (d. 1728), John of Waterside (b. c.1663), and Grizel. The Scottish privy council appointed him a militia commissioner for Renfrew and Ayrshire in September 1668. For failing to protect the minister of Auchinleck, Ayrshire, he was fined by the council in March 1672, though it subsequently cancelled the penalty. He was close to the duke of Hamilton and the earl of Cassillis in the 1670s. A presbyterian, his chaplain for a time was William Carstares; in the autumn of 1677 Cochrane agreed to work with Sir Hugh Campbell of Cessnock and others to seek an indulgence for the presbyterians. Accused of attending conventicles, Cochrane was outlawed in February 1678 for refusing to take a bond making him responsible for his tenants' behaviour, including their attendance at illegal religious services. When he was elected a commissioner for Ayrshire, the Scottish council tried to void the appointment but was overruled by the convention of estates in June 1678. As commissioner Cochrane refused to levy rates to support the garrisoning of troops in Ayrshire to quash conventicles. Although he formally repudiated the Bothwell Bridge rebels in April 1679, his younger son joined the insurgents, and Cochrane himself helped some of them escape after their defeat.

During the spring of 1682 a group of Scots including Henry, Lord Cardross, invited Cochrane to participate in a scheme to establish a new colony, initially in New York, later in Carolina. By July that year Cochrane and Sir George Campbell were in London to purchase land from the Carolina proprietors, including the earl of Shaftesbury, agreeing to pay £36,000 per annum for eight years, with a renewal provision for a like amount. Charles II directed the Scottish council to support the plan. In the meantime, Cochrane was probably involved with the earl of Argyll's unsuccessful efforts to smuggle weapons from the Netherlands to his Scottish supporters; he was certainly raising money for Argyll. By early 1683 Monmouth's inner circle, including Lord William Russell and Algernon Sidney, had learned of the disaffection of Cochrane and his associates toward the government and dispatched the attorney Aaron Smith to invite Cochrane and others to London for discussions about co-ordinated insurrections in Scotland and England. By April, Cochrane and his younger son were in London with other Scots dissidents. Carstares came from the Netherlands to tell Cochrane that Argyll needed £30,000 to raise troops, a message Cochrane relayed to Russell. He also tried, unsuccessfully, to persuade Ford, Lord Grey, to provide horses from Northumberland for Argyll's recruits and conferred with Monmouth on at least one occasion.

On 4 June 1683 Cochrane and his younger son were cited to appear before the justiciary court in Edinburgh. According to Gilbert Burnet, with whom Cochrane associated in London, the latter fled to the Netherlands. On 16 August the Scottish council directed the king's advocate to bring charges of treason against Cochrane for having consorted with the Bothwell Bridge rebels. In late October the government was prepared to offer Cochrane a pardon if he confessed, but early the next month ambassador Thomas Chudleigh reported that he was 'hardend beyond all hopes of reclayming him, if it be not that he hopes by the means of his freinds to make his peace without acknowledging his guilt' (BL, Add. MS 41809, fol. 137r). Cochrane denied involvement in the conspiracy, refused to return to Scotland where he would have no right of habeas corpus, and professed his innocence in a letter to the earl of Middleton. He spent part of his exile in Cleves, in frequent contact with Grey, until he discovered that the woman with Grey was his mistress. In the autumn of 1683 Argyll and John Locke visited Cochrane in Cleves. Thereafter Cochrane and his son went to Hanover and Lüneburg in search of a place for dissident Scots to settle. Having ignored a council order of January 1684 to appear, the Cochranes were formally declared outlaws, while the younger John Cochrane was adjudged guilty of treason in April 1684 for his role in the Bothwell rebellion, and his estate at Waterside, a gift from Dundonald, was forfeited. On 3 December 1684 directions were again issued to prosecute the elder Cochrane for treason and in May 1685 he was found guilty of participation in the 1683 conspiracy and his lands were forfeited.

A member of the inner circle that planned Argyll's ill-fated rebellion, Cochrane attended the meeting that harmonized the manifestos of Monmouth and Argyll in April 1685. Before sailing with Argyll, he left letters to Scottish officers in German armies asking them to report to Amsterdam for service in the earl's cause. Argyll dispatched Cochrane and his troops to south-western Scotland, where they enjoyed some success before Cochrane dismissed them after learning of the earl's defeat. The government issued a proclamation for his arrest on 24 June, and by 1 July he was in custody; the wife of his uncle Gavin Cochrane had turned him in because Cochrane's troops had killed her brother during the rebellion. On 3 July the hangman led Cochrane and his son to Edinburgh's Tolbooth, bound and bare-headed. According to Burnet, Dundonald offered 'the priests' £5000 to save his son; a deal was struck whereby Cochrane would confess only to James, who had a yacht transport him to London in August. He reputedly told the king about meetings with the elector of Brandenburg and William of Orange, though the latter subsequently denied having met Cochrane. He also provided information against Sir Hugh and Sir George Campbell, Lord Stair, William Spence, and others. Both Cochranes were pardoned and released from the Tower in October 1685.

The government employed Cochrane in 1687 to negotiate with Scottish presbyterians about an indulgence for themselves and Catholics, but he did not recover his estates until 1689. Cochrane and the minister Robert Ferguson were imprisoned on 5 June 1690 for misprision of treason and treasonable activities because of their association with Sir James Montgomerie. Cochrane survived to become a farmer of the poll tax in 1693, but he failed to provide a satisfactory account of his receipts and, with three other offenders, was incarcerated by 3 September 1695. The date of his death is not known.

RICHARD L. GREAVES

Sources PRO, State papers, 29/397/146; 29/425/118, 122; 29/428/58; 29/429/189, 201, 206; 29/430/42, 51; 29/432/4; 29/435/55, 157; 29/436/90 · PRO, State papers, 31/2, 31 · PRO, State papers, 44/68, 345–6 · BL, Add. MS 41809, fols. 94r, 127r, 137r, 138r–146r, 153v, 158r · BL, Add. MS 41810, fols. 59r–60r, 168r · BL, Add. MS 41811, fol. 226r · BL, Add. MS 41812, fol. 26v–27r · BL, Add. MS 41817, fol. 65v · *Reg. PCS*, 3rd ser., vols. 2–3, 5, 10–11 · *CSP dom.*, 1677–91 · R. L. Greaves, *Secrets of the kingdom: British radicals from the Popish Plot to the revolution of 1688–89* (1992) · N. Luttrell, *A brief historical relation of state affairs from September 1678 to April 1714*, 1–3 (1857) · *State trials*, vol. 10 · *Historical notices of Scotish affairs, selected from the manuscripts of Sir John Lauder of Fountainhall*, ed. D. Laing, 2 vols., Bannatyne Club, 87 (1848) · *The manuscripts of his grace the duke of Portland*, 10 vols., HMC, 29 (1891–1931), vols. 1–2 · Bishop Burnet's History of his own time, new edn, 2 vols. (1838) · R. Douglas, *The peerage of Scotland*, 2nd edn, ed. J. P. Wood, 1 (1813), 472, 474 · [T. Sprat], *Copies of the informations and original papers relating to the proof of the horrid conspiracy against the late king, his present majesty and the government*, 3rd edn (1685) · *The manuscripts of the duke of Roxburghe*, HMC, 34 (1894), 113–15

Archives BL, Add. MSS 41809–41812, 41817 · PRO, State papers

Cochrane, John Dundas (1780–1825), traveller, was a nephew of Sir Alexander Cochrane and grandson of the eighth earl of Dundonald. Having entered the Royal Navy when ten years old, he served, chiefly in West and East Indian waters, until the peace of 1814. Captain Cochrane then made a tour on foot through France, Spain, and Portugal. He returned to England in January 1820 and offered his services to the Admiralty for the exploration of the Niger, but, being refused, decided to make a tour of the world by way of Russia, Siberia, and North America. He left England in February 1820 and travelled by Paris and Berlin to St Petersburg, most of the way on foot for the sake of economy (his prodigious journeys on foot earned him the nickname the Pedestrian Traveller). He was then helped by the Russian government, who supplied him with the means to hire horses, sledges, and canoes. He reached the coast at Okhotsk in June 1821. While in Kamchatka he married a local woman and abandoned the idea of travelling further. He returned to Europe with his wife, reaching St Petersburg in June 1823. In June 1824 he left England for South America, intending to take part in the mining industry, returned to England the following year, but after a brief stay sailed again for America. He died on 12 August 1825 of a fever at Valencia in Colombia, now Venezuela, having gone to South America with the intention of crossing it on foot. His *Narrative of a Pedestrian Journey through Russia and Siberian Tartary* (1820) passed through several editions. It is lively and contains much interesting incident, from help provided by a mysterious black stranger near St Petersburg, to robbery in Siberia. Of scientific value it is entirely destitute. The harsh judgement of his biographer, Knight, was that 'the eccentricities of this most hardy and indefatigable traveller sometimes approach to insanity', but Cochrane's courage still commands respect.

J. M. RIGG, rev. ELIZABETH BAIGENT

Sources *GM*, 1st ser., 95/2 (1825), 644 · J. Gorton, *A general biographical dictionary*, 3 vols. (1841) · H. J. Rose, *A new general biographical dictionary*, ed. H. J. Rose and T. Wright, 12 vols. (1853) · C. Knight, ed., *The English cyclopaedia: biography*, 6 vols. (1856–8)
Likenesses H. Meyer, stipple (after Harding), BM, NPG

Cochrane, John George (1781–1852), publisher and librarian, was born at Glasgow, where his father worked in the legal profession; little is known of his mother or of his early life. By the time he was twenty Cochrane worked in London, where he became a partner of John White. The publishing firm of White, Cochrane & Co. carried on an extensive business in Fleet Street, involved with the publication, for instance, of James Sowerby's *English Botany* (1790–1816) and Alymer B. Lambert's *Genus Pinus* (1803). Prosperity lasted until they became involved in the downturn in trade which followed the failure of Archibald Constable. Cochrane wrote anonymously a pamphlet, *The Case Stated between the Public Libraries and the Booksellers* (1813), calling attention to the hardship suffered by publishers, who were obliged, under the Copyright Act, to supply copies of their books, however expensive, to eleven public libraries. He and his partner were examined before the parliamentary committee of 1813. He also during this period published and edited in a limited edition of 250 copies *The English Works of Roger Ascham, Preceptor to Queen Elizabeth*, I (1815).

Cochrane subsequently became manager of the foreign bookselling house of Messrs Treuttel, Würtz, Treuttel jun. and Richter of Soho Square, London, which published in July 1827 the first number of the *Foreign Quarterly Review*. The editorship was accepted by Cochrane, who remained the sole editor until 1834, also contributing various reviews and articles. Cochrane was, in the words of the *Wellesley index*, a 'strong editor [who] gathered together an impressive, if seemingly disparate group of contributors' (Curran, 131). Richter became bankrupt on 9 December 1834, and Cochrane established *Cochrane's Foreign Quarterly Review* (1835), only two numbers of which appeared. Cochrane only an unsuccessful candidate for the librarianship of the Faculty of Advocates in Edinburgh, and for some time acted as the editor of the *Caledonian Mercury*. Friendship with Robert Cadell caused him to be chosen to assist George Huntly Gordon in cataloguing Sir Walter Scott's library at Abbotsford, and producing an index to the catalogue. It was necessary to print the catalogue, and extra copies were produced for members of the Maitland and Bannatyne clubs (1838). References to passages in Scott's writings connected with the books throw considerable light upon Scott's literary history.

Cochrane afterwards lived for some time at Hertford, where he was editor of a local newspaper. Owing to the strong support of his old friend Thomas Carlyle, on 17 February 1841 Cochrane became the first secretary and librarian of the London Library, founded in the previous year. This institution was opened on 3 May at 49 Pall Mall; in March 1842 the first catalogue was issued by Cochrane, who also issued two supplements to it in 1843 and 1844. In April 1845 the committee took a lease of the premises in St James's Square, and in 1847 an enlarged edition of the catalogue appeared, recording holdings after this move. A short time before Cochrane's death a supplementary volume was compiled, in which a general classified index was announced. Cochrane died at his apartments in the library, St James's Square, London, on 4 May 1852, in his seventy-second year. Sarah, his wife, who seems to have been older than her husband, predeceased him, dying on 20 August 1847. Thomas Carlyle and John Stuart Mill, among others, wrote in their letters sympathetically of Cochrane. Carlyle called him 'White Owl', and observed: 'Poor old Cochrane, our first librarian of London Library, and essentially the builder and architect there. The only real bibliographer I have ever met within Britain' (*Collected Letters*, 22.75, n. 8). H. R. TEDDER, *rev.* WILLIAM BAKER

Sources [E. Curran], 'The *Foreign Quarterly Review*, 1827–1846', *Wellesley index*, 2.131–8 · *The collected letters of Thomas and Jane Welsh Carlyle*, ed. C. R. Sanders, K. J. Fielding, and others, [30 vols.] (1970–) · W. Baker, *The early history of the London Library* (1992) · *The earlier letters of John Stuart Mill, 1812–1848*, ed. F. E. Mineka (1963), vol. 12 of *The Collected Works of John Stuart Mill*, ed. J. M. Robson (1963–91), 132–3 · S. Nowell-Smith, 'Carlyle and the London Library', in C. B. Oldman, W. A. Munford, and S. Nowell-Smith, *English libraries, 1800–1850: three lectures delivered at University College, London* (1958), 59–78 · J. Wells, *Rude words: a discursive history of the London Library* (1991) · W. Baker, 'J. G. Cochrane and the London Library at Pall Mall', *Library History*, 8/6 (1990), 171–9 · *GM*, 2nd ser., 37 (1852), 628 · Nichols, *Illustrations*, 8.467 · W. D. Christie, *An explanation of the scheme of the London Library* (1841) · *N&Q*, 5 (1852), 454 · R. Harrison, *Catalogue of the London Library*, 4th edn, 2 vols. (1875–80), vii–xi · d. cert. · J. Millgate, '"Litera scripta manet": George Huntly Gordon and the Abbotsford library catalogue', *The Library*, 6th ser., 20 (1998), 118–25
Archives NL Scot. | NL Scot., letters to Thomas Carlyle · NL Scot., corresp. with Archibald Constable
Wealth at death poor: *Collected letters*, ed. Sanders, Fielding, and others

Cochrane, Marion (*d.* 1559), tenant farmer, is first recorded in 1550 as the widow of John Stoddart of Lessudden (now St Boswell's), Roxburghshire. Having lost her husband when her children were young, she left on record her arrangements for the management of her family's affairs. It is the richness of the documentation, not the management, which is unusual. Although remarriage was common, many households in sixteenth-century Scotland were also headed by widows, who are found involved in all kinds of legal transactions. Lessudden had been cultivated since the fourteenth century by Melrose Abbey tenants, who had well-established rights of customary inheritance. In 1550 Marion and her unmarried son James added to the already substantial family holding. James died between then and January 1555 when Marion made arrangements for the future provision of her two daughters who were now joint heirs of their late brother. A marriage contract was drawn up by which Christian Stoddart, her elder daughter, would marry Robert, son of Ninian Bryden in Rutherford. Robert, so the contract laid down, would come to live with his wife in Marion's household and cultivate the family's farm, but under her direction. Full possession would pass to Christian and Robert only on Marion's death. The younger daughter, Catherine, was compensated for the loss of her rights as joint heir with £40 from her sister's future father-in-law, Ninian Bryden, and 40 merks from the annual profit of the farm until she also came to be married.

With the spread of feu-ferme tenure on church land in sixteenth-century Scotland many monastic tenants became owner–occupiers of their holdings, receiving heritable possession in return for large down payments and an annual fixed feu duty. Marion Cochrane was one of thirty-two Lessudden tenants to do so, but only after the land had been bought and then sold on to them at a profit by Henry Sinclair, dean of Glasgow, a piece of land speculation which took place elsewhere. The feu charter, granted by the abbot and convent of Melrose on 22 February 1557 conveyed one and three-quarters husbandlands (some 45 Scots acres) to Marion Cochrane for her lifetime and to her daughter Christian and her husband heritably after her.

Marion remained the practical head of the household until her death at Lessudden in November 1559. The family home at the centre of the farm appears to have been a peel house, a small fortified house within a palisade which was common in the English and Scottish border country at that time. Her net estate when she died was valued at only £16 Scots, about three times what she paid in feu duty and other dues annually. She left her family four plough oxen, two horses, three cows, and a few sheep, wheat in the barn ready to be sold at market, and peas and oats in the barnyard to be threshed. Among the witnesses of her will was John Turnbull, one of the monks of Melrose Abbey. Her family had some status in the settlement of Lessudden yet she left few worldly goods behind her. Towards the end of her life, however, she had seen her family achieve heritable possession of the land which they had held for generations by customary right. Her grandson John Bryden succeeded in 1614 and the family held on to their property until 1672 when, ironically, it was sold by two joint heiresses to Walter Scott of Raeburn. MARGARET H. B. SANDERSON

Sources NA Scot., Scott of Raeburn muniments, GD 104/2–147 · NA Scot., Lauder commissary court records, register of testaments, CC 15/5/1, fol. 22 · M. H. B. Sanderson, *Mary Stewart's people* (1987)
Archives NA Scot., Scott of Raeburn muniments, GD 104
Wealth at death £16 Scots: NA Scot., Lauder commissary court records, register of testaments, CC 15/5/1, fol. 22

Cochrane, Sir Ralph Alexander (1895–1977), air force officer, was born at Crawford Priory, near Cupar, Fife, on 24 February 1895, the second youngest of four sons (one of whom died in childhood) and four daughters (one of whom died in infancy) of Thomas Horatio Arthur Ernest Cochrane (1857–1951), who was created Baron Cochrane of Cults in 1919, and his wife, Gertrude Julia Georgina Boyle (1859–1950). His father, who was the third son of the eleventh earl of Dundonald, was an innovative large-scale dairy farmer and sat as Conservative MP for North Ayrshire from 1892 to 1910. His mother, who was appointed

OBE in 1920, was the elder daughter of the sixth earl of Glasgow. His brothers also made their mark: during the First World War Thomas (1883–1968) earned a DSO with the Black Watch, while Archibald (1885–1958) earned two DSOs with the Royal Navy and served as governor-general of Burma (1936–41).

Cochrane was educated in Crieff, Perthshire, and at the Royal Naval College at Osborne and Dartmouth. He was commissioned on graduation and two days later, on 17 March 1915, joined the Royal Naval Air Service as a flight sub-lieutenant in the newly created airship branch. He supervised airship erection during 1916, qualified as an airship pilot in February 1917, and from that July spent a year as a trial pilot at Kingsnorth, Kent. In April 1918 he transferred to the RAF as a major in 'dirigibles'. He was awarded an AFC in January 1919 and a permanent commission as a flight lieutenant in August. Cochrane remained in the Admiralty airship department until May 1920, when he moved to the Air Ministry directorate of research. The following month he was sent to Cairo to study fabric deterioration problems and assess the prospects for a proposed imperial airship route. He learned to fly aeroplanes in May 1921 and joined 45 squadron in Iraq in January 1922 as one of Arthur Harris's flight commanders. Harris, who made his name as head of Bomber Command (1942–5), became and remained an admirer of Cochrane's intelligent efficiency.

After returning to England in 1923 Cochrane spent over a year as administrative officer in the boys' wing at Cranwell, then in May 1925 attended the RAF Staff College, Andover. He was promoted squadron leader in July and from April 1926 was a staff officer at Wessex bombing area headquarters. He served in Aden for two years (1928–9), first at headquarters and then as commanding officer of 8 squadron.

Cochrane returned as an instructor to Andover (1930–31), where he became friends with the future Lord Tedder. On 22 December 1930 he married Hilda Frances Holme (d. 1982), the third daughter of Francis Holme Wiggin, a tea planter in Ceylon; they had two sons, one of whom was born in New Zealand, and a daughter. He spent two years, from January 1932, in the Air Ministry's directorate of operations and intelligence, working with the future Lord Portal: 'three of us', Cochrane recalled, 'in a small room on the sixth floor of Adastral House, with a window looking out on Aldwych. When the window was open the noise was intolerable and when it was closed the atmosphere soon became unbreathable' (Richards, 104). Promotion to wing commander in July 1933 doubtless consoled him. He spent 1934 studying at the Army Staff College, Camberley, and 1935 at the Imperial Defence College in London.

In 1936 the New Zealand government asked for the assistance of an RAF officer to advise on air defence matters and got Cochrane. He arrived by sea at Wellington on 4 November 1936 and submitted his report on the 20th, having written it during the voyage when not reading Margaret Mitchell's *Gone with the Wind* from cover to cover. His aristocratic manner, sound professional knowledge, and obvious delight in fishing, golf, gardens, and scenery appealed greatly to New Zealanders. He was promoted group captain and appointed the Royal New Zealand Air Force's first chief of air staff in April 1937. He began the transformation of a negligible adjunct of the army (seventeen officers, 120 men, two aerodromes, and a handful of obsolete aircraft) into an independent air force controlled by an air board under the minister of defence. Aerodromes were newly built or enlarged, training schemes were introduced for both air and ground crews, recruitment was actively encouraged, and a sensible plan was framed to cover both New Zealand's defence and her contribution to imperial defence in the event of war.

On his return to Britain in May 1939 Cochrane was appointed air aide-de-camp to the king and deputy director of intelligence, charged to monitor the strength and dispositions of the Luftwaffe. Between December 1939 and October 1940 he had his first experience of Bomber Command: as commanding officer of Abingdon, senior air staff officer at 6 group headquarters, and, on promotion to air commodore in July 1940, head of 7 group. During that time he introduced blindfold cockpit drill, later used widely in training units. He then spent almost two years in the Air Ministry as director of flying training. In December 1941 he was promoted air vice-marshal and helped to organize a massive production of aircrews in Britain and also (through the empire air training scheme) in Canada, Australia, and southern Africa.

Sir Arthur Harris had been head of Bomber Command since February 1942 and in September he secured Cochrane's return to that command, first as head of 3 group and then in February 1943 as head of 5 group. During the next two years Cochrane made of that group the command's sharpest weapon. He insisted that all pilots be commissioned and made responsible for briefing their own crews, he increased available flying hours by eliminating many purely formal aircraft inspections, and he devised a rapid landing system to reduce the strain on tired or wounded crews returning from operations. Under his efficient and determined leadership 5 group was responsible for many improvements in night bombing technique, and his squadrons carried out several spectacular raids—notably the breaching of some Ruhr dams in October 1943 by a specially trained squadron and the destruction of the battleship *Tirpitz* in Norwegian waters by attacks in September and November 1944.

Rivalry between Cochrane and Don Bennett, head of 8 (pathfinder) group, was intense throughout this period. Cochrane thought the pathfinders skilful at target marking for area bombing but not flexible enough to achieve similar success against small targets demanding precise marking. Harris usually favoured Cochrane's opinions, especially on the value of low-level target marking, using very fast Mosquitoes to improve accuracy, and on having the main force await orders from a master bomber (who had positioned himself over the target) before releasing its load. Cochrane's methods were best suited to 1944–5, when Luftwaffe opposition was weakened and relative accuracy, especially in raids on targets in occupied Europe, became politically essential. With hindsight, Sir Leonard Cheshire, who thought highly of Cochrane, reflected that the war might have finished earlier if Cochrane had replaced Harris as head of Bomber Command late in 1944; Cochrane would probably have co-operated more eagerly than Harris with his friend Tedder's plan to concentrate attacks on German transport links rather than on city centres.

As a reward for his efforts Cochrane was promoted air marshal and given a most demanding task in February 1945 as head of transport command—a task for which he had few experienced crews (ground or air): most of the suitable aircraft were American, supplies of which were cut as soon as the war against Japan ended. He moved troops and supplies out to the Far East until August, when Japan surrendered, and then began the even more daunting task of moving released prisoners and long-serving troops home as quickly as possible. Although these operations did not run smoothly, the fact remains that, in a period of twenty-one months ending in September 1946, transport command completed more passenger miles than had British civil aviation in the preceding twenty-one years.

In September 1947 Cochrane moved to Flying Training Command, a far less demanding task in a shrinking force before jets replaced pistons, but was promoted air chief marshal in March 1949. Tedder wished Cochrane to succeed him as chief of the air staff on his retirement in December 1949, but the position went instead to Sir John Slessor, who thought Cochrane 'the best group commander that Bomber Command ever had' (Slessor, 373) and appointed him vice-chief in March 1950, a position he held until his retirement in October 1952. He was a member of the Air Council and had special responsibility for the RAF's strength and fighting efficiency.

'But for the luck of the draw', wrote Harris after his death, 'he would have made an outstanding chief of the air staff and in my opinion an incomparable chief of the defence staff' (*The Times*, 20 Dec 1977). Perhaps, but Cochrane—unlike Slessor—had little inter-service experience and none at all with Americans, and a dour personality that would have dismayed them. All his life he had a lean and hungry look, a face not made for easy laughter, and a manner that was at best distant. On the other hand, intelligent men of every class and rank who valued efficiency and hard work as highly as Cochrane did never looked to him in vain for wholehearted support. On leaving the service he served as joint managing director of both the Atlantic Shipbuilding Company (1953–6) and Rolls-Royce (1956–61) and as chairman of an export company (1962). He was appointed CBE in 1939 and CB in 1943, knighted in January 1945 (KBE) and again in June 1948 (KCB), and became GBE in June 1950. He received a gold medal in 1935 from the Royal United Service Institution for an essay on imperial defence, the Edward Busk memorial prize from the Royal Aeronautical Society (of which he became a fellow) in 1948, and the Institute of Transport's triennial award of merit in 1958. A keen skier and climber, he was president of the RAF mountaineering association. He died on 17 December 1977 at Burford, Oxfordshire, and was buried on 22 December at Cults church, Cupar, Fife.

VINCENT ORANGE

Sources Wigram Air Historical Branch, London, RNZAF Museum, Cochrane MSS, mainly 1936–9 · *The Times* (19 Dec 1977) · *The Times* (20 Dec 1977) · *Daily Telegraph* (20 Dec 1977) · D. Richards, *Portal of Hungerford* (1978) · J. C. Slessor, *The central blue: recollections and reflections* (1956) · W. D. McIntyre, *New Zealand prepares for war* (1988) · M. Middlebrook and C. Everitt, *The bomber command war diaries: an operational reference book, 1939–1945* (1985) · M. Hastings, *Bomber command* (1979) · *WW* · *DNZB*, vol. 4 · 'Sir Ralph Cochrane: clearest mind in the Royal Air Force?', *Thanks for the memory: unforgettable characters in air warfare, 1939–45*, ed. L. Lucas (1989)
Archives Royal New Zealand Air Force Museum, Wigram, Christchurch, MSS | S O U N D IWM SA, oral history interview
Likenesses H. Lamb, oils, Scottish United Services Museum, Edinburgh
Wealth at death £65,698: probate, 5 June 1978, *CGPLA Eng. & Wales*

Cochrane, Thomas [Robert] (*d.* 1482), royal favourite, has left few traces in official records, and much of what is known about him is drawn from later chronicles, above all the histories of Lesley (1568–70), Pitscottie (*c.*1579), and Buchanan (1582). All these writers see Cochrane as the evil genius of *James III of Scotland, a low-born favourite who turned the king against his brothers Albany and Mar, became earl of Mar on Mar's death, and richly deserved his violent death, hanged over Lauder Bridge on 22 July 1482 by an incensed Scottish nobility. The Cochrane legend grew until by the early eighteenth century Cochrane, quaintly described as 'Prime Minister' of James III, became the subject of a short pamphlet war in London, conducted by individuals seeking to attack or defend the ministry of Sir Robert Walpole. In the nineteenth and twentieth centuries a reaction set in among historians who endeavoured to rehabilitate Cochrane, praising him as an important architect in the service of an unjustly maligned Renaissance monarch—all this on the strength of two isolated references in contemporary official records, a name on a notarial instrument, and the stories of chroniclers who, with one exception, are not contemporaries of the events which they describe and who cannot agree on Cochrane's forename, far less his occupation.

Nevertheless, it is impossible to ignore Cochrane, for there survives one striking piece of near contemporary evidence as to his existence and closeness to James III. In the first edition of his commentary on book 4 of Peter Lombard's *Sentences*, published in Paris in 1509, John Mair, who had grown up in Haddingtonshire during James III's reign, referred to a Robert Cochrane as the victor in a single combat with one William Tor, commenting that the fight, which was much talked about in its day, occurred in that king's reign. According to Mair, it was widely said at the time that Cochrane achieved his victory through witchcraft. The witchcraft theme is also to be found in a fragmentary, and probably contemporary, chronicle which attributes the death in 1480 of James III's brother John, earl of Mar, to his association with witches and warlocks. Thus a tentative link might be made between Cochrane and Mar's death, a connection greatly exaggerated in transmission by later writers.

The Cochrane of official record is Thomas rather than Mair's Robert, though probably the same individual. On 22 January 1480 the lords of council assigned the sum of £60 Scots to Thomas Cochrane; it had formerly been promised by four northern lords to Sir John Colquhoun, a royal usher who had been killed at the siege of Dunbar Castle in May 1479. Colquhoun's £60 Scots had been reassigned by the king to Cochrane, which suggests that he was a royal household servant who had recently come to James III's attention, perhaps through his victory over Tor.

Chronologically, Cochrane's next appearance in contemporary records is found in an otherwise unremarkable notarial instrument of 20 May 1482 appointing procurators in a land transfer; one of the named procurators is 'Thomas Cochrane, constable of the castle of Kildrummy'. There can be little doubt that this is the same Cochrane as in the council decision of January 1480, for the surname, though common enough in Renfrewshire and Lothian, is startlingly unfamiliar in Aberdeenshire. Two months before his demise at Lauder, then, Cochrane is to be found as keeper of the principal castle in Mar, which in turn suggests that, while James III may never have given him the title of earl, Cochrane could well have had possession of some or all of the revenues of Mar, amounting in total to £505 13s. 5d. Scots. Later local evidence points to his being responsible for building the formidable tower-house of Auchindoun, 20 miles from Kildrummy; if true, this might explain his later reputation as a stonemason.

Thus it would appear that Cochrane, a southerner, was active in the north-east as a royal agent, that he was very well rewarded by the crown for his pains, and that his presence in Mar was a snub to George Gordon, earl of Huntly, and to the earl's kinsman James Ogilvy of Deskford and Findlater. Huntly wanted Mar and the keepership of Kildrummy; Ogilvy, already in possession of Glenfiddich, near which Auchindoun stands, may have seen Cochrane as a threat. Both men were conspicuously present at the Lauder muster and hangings in 1482, and subsequently they duly acquired Kildrummy and Auchindoun.

Cochrane's third and last appearance in the records, on 2 May 1483, describes him as 'umquhile thomas of cochran', already dead and forfeited. The main event at Lauder had been not the hanging of Cochrane and other familiars, but the seizure of the king; and Cochrane was certainly never a primary target for the opposition, unlike, for example, Archbishop William Scheves (*d.* 1497). Cochrane's involvement in Mar's death cannot be proved. In the last analysis his real crime may have been his attempt to feather his own nest in Mar with James III's blessing, but in the teeth of implacable local hostility.

NORMAN MACDOUGALL

Sources [T. Thomson], ed., *The acts of the lords of council in civil causes, 1478–1495*, 1, RC, 41 (1839), 49, 82 · W. Fraser, ed., *The chiefs of Grant*, 3 (1883), 33 · I. Major [J. Mair], *Quartus sententiarum* (Paris,

1509), fol. xcviv, col. i · *The historie and cronicles of Scotland … by Robert Lindesay of Pitscottie*, ed. A. J. G. Mackay, 1, STS, 42 (1899), 165–70, 173–6 · G. Buchanan, *Rerum Scoticarum historia* (1582), bk 12 · J. Lesley, *The history of Scotland*, ed. T. Thomson, Bannatyne Club, 38 (1830), 48–9 · N. Macdougall, '"It is I, the earl of Mar": in search of Thomas Cochrane', *People and power in Scotland: essays in honour of T. C. Smout*, ed. R. Mason and N. Macdougall (1992), 28–49 · J. H. Burns, 'The Scotland of John Major', *Innes Review*, 2 (1951), 65–76 · BL, Royal MS 17 D.xx, fols. 299–308 · acts of the lords of council, NA Scot. · J. Gordon, *History of Scots affairs from 1637–1641*, ed. J. Robertson and G. Grub, 2, Spalding Club, 3 (1841), 216 · 'The testament and complaynt of our soverane Lordis Papyngo', *The poetical works of Sir David Lyndsay*, ed. D. Laing, 1 (1879), 77–8

Cochrane, Thomas, tenth earl of Dundonald (1775–1860), naval officer, born at Annesfield, Hamilton, Scotland, on 14 December 1775, was the eldest son of Archibald *Cochrane, ninth earl of Dundonald (1748–1831), and his first wife, Anne Gilchrist (1755–1784), second daughter of Captain James *Gilchrist RN. Destined for the army, his father obtained a commission in the 104th regiment for him, while he was still a child, through his uncle, Andrew Cochrane-Johnstone. However from 1790 another uncle, Captain Alexander Forrester Inglis Cochrane (1758–1832), placed his name on the books of the warships under his command, possibly securing him a small advantage in meeting the regulation requiring young officers to serve six years at sea before they could be commissioned. Despite six months at Chauvet's military academy in London in 1788 Cochrane expressed a strong desire to enter the navy. His father, after initial resistance, gave way. This decision may well have been hastened by his realization that, with his finances in ruins from attempts to develop a new chemical industry on the results of his scientific experiments, he could not afford to purchase military careers for all his sons. Having defied stern parental authority, Cochrane's confidence in his own judgement and lack of respect for mere authority were established. His father's financial ruin, leading to the sale of the family home, was an equally powerful stimulus. To the end of his life Cochrane was obsessed with money; it would be at the root of nearly all his problems.

Early career and war service, 1793–1812 Cochrane finally joined the Royal Navy, aged seventeen, on 27 June 1793, aboard HMS *Hind*, then commanded by his uncle. He was fortunate to receive his initial training in seamanship from the first lieutenant of the *Hind*, 'Jack' Larmour, a first-class seaman who had risen from the ranks. Cochrane, an able and enthusiastic pupil, quickly assimilated Larmour's teaching, and throughout his career he excelled in practical seamanship. The two men moved, with Captain Cochrane, into the *Thetis* destined for the North American station. Cochrane was appointed acting lieutenant in January 1795, a rank in which he was confirmed on 24 May 1796, by which time he had acquired the necessary six years of sea-time. After service in the station flagship *Resolution* he returned to England. He was appointed to the *Foudroyant* and then the *Barfleur*, successive flagships of Admiral Sir George Keith Elphinstone (Lord

Thomas Cochrane, tenth earl of Dundonald (1775–1860), by Peter Eduard Ströhling, exh. RA 1807

Keith), a fellow Scot. Having already given marked evidence of his ability and independence of thought he found the atmosphere on the flagship stifling; this led to a quarrel with the first lieutenant, Philip Beaver, which resulted in a court martial for 'disrespect'. It was an early indication of the pattern of his entire career. Anxious to get to sea, Keith acquitted Cochrane but admonished him to 'avoid flippancy'. Cochrane remained with Keith during the blockade of Cadiz and his cruise into the Mediterranean, following him into the *Queen Charlotte*.

When the French battleship *Généreux* was captured on 18 February 1800 Cochrane was appointed prize-master, taking the badly damaged and scratch-manned ship to Port Mahon in the Balearics, despite a gale that threatened to dismast the ship. Once given independent command his personal courage, seamanship, and leadership qualities were amply demonstrated. While on this service he missed the destruction of the *Queen Charlotte* by fire off Leghorn on 17 March. Evidently Keith recognized his weaknesses and his qualities, for he reported to the Admiralty that he was 'wrong-headed, violent and proud' (Thomas, 84); but on 28 March he appointed him commander and sent him to the brig *Speedy*, a 158 ton vessel with fourteen 4-pounder guns, a crew of ninety officers and men, and orders to cruise off the Spanish coast. Cochrane's success led the Spanish authorities to send a frigate out to capture the *Speedy*, but Cochrane had disguised her as a Danish merchant ship. When finally intercepted, on 21 December, he flew a plague flag to keep the frigate's boat from boarding. Putting into Malta on 1 February 1801, he caused a brawl at a fancy-dress party and fought a duel before returning to sea the following day.

Cochrane's operations on the Spanish coast continued to be successful and were crowned with an astonishing feat of arms. On 6 May he encountered the small Spanish frigate *Gamo*, a 600 ton ship of 32 guns and 319 men. Although he had only fifty-four men on the *Speedy*, Cochrane, aware that his earlier subterfuge had been criticized, decided to engage. He ran the brig alongside the larger ship, fired in several accurate broadsides from his pathetic little guns while the Spanish shot flew over his small ships, and then carried the Spaniard by boarding. The *Speedy* lost four killed and seventeen wounded, the Spaniards fourteen and forty-one respectively. To carry his prize to Port Mahon, Cochrane confined the Spanish crew to the hold, training cannon on them. The astonishing quality of the victory led many to consider it the result of a trick, and the rewards given were both tardy and inadequate.

In the interval Cochrane had been ordered to convoy a packet from Mahon to Gibraltar, and on 3 July fell in with a French squadron of three battleships. After a skilful defence he surrendered to overwhelming force. The French captain was so impressed that he insisted that Cochrane continue to wear his sword. The French squadron then anchored off Algeciras, where they were attacked by a squadron under Admiral Sir James Saumarez on 6 July. Cochrane witnessed the battle from the French battleship *Desaix*. The following day he was released on parole to Gibraltar, and exchanged after Saumarez's victory in the Strait of Gibraltar on the 12th. Cochrane was court-martialled for the loss of the *Speedy*, but honourably acquitted. Over the thirteen months under his command he claimed to have taken 50 vessels, 122 guns, and 534 prisoners. After his acquittal he was promoted captain, on 8 August 1801. His request for the promotion of his lieutenant was turned down by the first lord of the Admiralty, the earl of St Vincent, on the grounds that the casualties of the *Speedy* were too slight to warrant it. Typically Cochrane replied, and his reply was neither deferential nor polite. He observed that there were more casualties on the *Speedy* than there had been on the earl's flagship, the *Victory*, at the battle of Cape St Vincent, for which much greater rewards had been given.

With the peace he was not given another ship and in late 1802 became a student at the University of Edinburgh, where he attended lectures by Dugald Stewart on political economy and worked diligently at his studies. When war broke out again in 1803 he pestered St Vincent for a ship, but the earl, who had little time for any 'Scotchmen' and even less for those lacking a proper measure of respect for authority, gave him the *Arab*, a sixth-rate 20 gun French prize. The ship was in poor shape and was a poor performer at sea. Sent to join the command of Lord Keith, who was then blockading the French invasion shipping at Boulogne, Cochrane continued to complain about his ship and was 'rewarded' by being detached to cruise to the north-east of the Orkney Islands to protect the fisheries.

He remained here for fifteen months, no doubt as a mark of official displeasure at his insolent and hectoring correspondence. In 1804 the tory ministry returned. Lord Melville, the political manager of Scotland and a distant relative of Cochrane, became first lord and appointed Cochrane to the new 32 gun frigate *Pallas*. He had orders to cruise for a month off the Azores—a very rich station, as war had just broken out with Spain. This cruise, between February and April 1805, proved to be particularly fortunate, resulting in several rich Spanish prizes as well as another of Cochrane's brilliant ruses to escape a French squadron. He brought back the *Pallas* into Plymouth Sound, the frigate having gold candlesticks 5 feet high tied to each mast-head.

In May the *Pallas* escorted a convoy to the St Lawrence River in Canada, and on her return, in December, joined the squadron of Vice-Admiral Thornborough for operations in the Bay of Biscay. Between February and the end of May 1806 the *Pallas*, while generally on detached service, captured, drove ashore, and burnt a large number of merchant vessels. On 6 April her boats cut out a French sloop of war from the River Garonne, leaving the ship with only forty men on board; yet the *Pallas* pursued, drove ashore, and burnt three French corvettes, each of which was more heavily manned. This action was reported by Thornborough, but the new ministry of the talents, which relied on St Vincent for naval advice, took no notice of it, did not purchase the sloop, and did not pay any prize or head money for the ships destroyed. On 14 May, while reconnoitring the French fleet in the Aix Roads, she was engaged by the 40 gun frigate *Minerve*, which was accompanied by three brigs. Having effectively beaten the *Minerve* Cochrane was denied his prize by two other French frigates weighing anchor to support her, and having lost her fore-topmast and maintopsail yard the *Pallas* had to be towed out by the sloop *Kingfisher*. Four days later he was ordered back to Plymouth with a convoy, and he arrived home on 27 June.

In July 1806 Cochrane stood for election at the notoriously corrupt borough of Honiton in Devon, and he refused to pay the usual bribe. After his defeat he paid 10 guineas to all those who voted for him; as a result he was elected unopposed at the general election in October but refused to pay the 10 guineas a vote his previous conduct had led his supporters to expect. He also defaulted on bills for £1200 for the customary 'treats' to the electors. He was already imbued with a deep suspicion of corruption in government, particularly at the Admiralty, and he had formed a close connection with the radical journalist William Cobbett.

On 2 September the crew of the *Pallas* was turned over into the frigate *Imperieuse*, which put to sea on 17 November and joined the blockading squadron in the Basque Roads twelve days later. She returned to Plymouth in February 1807, and Cochrane took a month's sick-leave in April in order to stand for the large, popular constituency of Westminster in the general election of May 1807. With the support of Cobbett he was returned alongside Sir Francis Burdett. In his election campaign he accused St

Vincent of bartering naval commissions for borough influence, attacked abuses in naval administration, and called for the exclusion of government pensioners and placemen from the house. Ostentatiously refusing to adhere to any party, he launched an attack on a variety of abuses. On 7 July he called for an inquiry into places, pensions, and sinecures held by, or for, members, but it was defeated by the government. His call on the 10th for papers that would expose naval abuses did not even secure a division. It was thus hardly surprising that he was sent back to sea, on the Mediterranean station, shortly afterwards; he left Portsmouth on 12 September 1807. His constituents were so taken with his open and direct conduct that at a mass rally they gave him unlimited leave of absence.

Cochrane captured a Maltese pirate on 14 November and finally met up with the fleet of Admiral Lord Collingwood off Toulon on the 19th. Sent to act as senior officer at Corfu, he was soon recalled when his uncompromising attitude to trading with the enemy caused more problems than it solved. He rejoined the fleet on 2 January 1808 and at the end of the month was sent on a roving commission with instructions 'to harass the Spanish and French coast as opportunity served'. Collingwood had the good sense to know how to use the talents of this argumentative and opinionated officer to best advantage, and he sent him on detached service. On this cruise Cochrane brought the art of littoral warfare to a new level of intensity. In the absence of a serious naval challenge the Royal Navy was reconfiguring itself to exploit the command of the sea. The new targets were small coasting-vessels, isolated harbours, signal stations, batteries, and lighthouses. The intention was to cripple the enemy's power of movement, destroying the logistics that underpinned operations on land. It was a form of warfare for which Cochrane was almost uniquely gifted, and of which he remained for many years the exemplar. In June the Spanish rising changed the nature of his war, and he was now instructed to 'render every possible assistance to the Spaniards against the French'. The new circumstances redoubled the effectiveness of his campaign, providing local support, positions to hold, and intelligence. He ranged along the coasts of Catalonia and France, attacking roads, bridges, and stores. The object was to hamper the movement and operations of French armies, and this included the destruction of the semaphore system that was used to control the movement of coastal shipping. The manpower of a frigate, when deployed swiftly and skilfully, was invariably adequate to overwhelm the local defences of isolated posts and stations. In October Collingwood commented that:

Nothing can exceed the zeal and activity with which his lordship pursues the enemy. The success which attends his enterprises clearly indicates with what skill and ability they are conducted, besides keeping the coast in constant alarm, causing a general suspension of the trade and harassing a body of troops employed in opposing him.   (Lloyd, *Lord Cochrane*, 50)

In late November Cochrane, for a fortnight and against overwhelming odds, defended the castle of Trinidad, outside the besieged town of Rosas; he finally evacuated the garrison and destroyed the fort when the French secured the town.

Early in 1809 Cochrane received permission to return home. His health was suffering from the arduous service, he wished to attack the corruption of the prize court at Malta, and he wanted to command a small squadron on the west coast of France for a more extensive littoral warfare campaign aimed at denying the French the ability to keep their troops in Spain supplied. When the *Imperieuse* arrived at Plymouth in late March, he was immediately summoned to the Admiralty. A powerful French squadron had been assembled in the Aix Roads, and the Admiralty wanted to attack it there. As the leading practitioner of littoral warfare, and with considerable experience of the Aix Roads, Cochrane was an obvious adviser, and when Lord Mulgrave, the first lord, pressed for his opinion, he produced a plan of attack using explosion-vessels and fireships, supported by the fleet. Admiral Lord Gambier, who commanded the Channel Fleet, was less certain. He recognized the utility of fireships but considered them a 'horrible mode of warfare' (Thomas, 148). When Mulgrave invited Cochrane to carry out his plan, Cochrane expressed concern that his appointment would create jealousy and resentment. Mulgrave promised to settle such difficulties but, characteristically, did nothing. Consequently, when Cochrane joined the fleet he found that Gambier was unenthusiastic, while Admiral Sir Eliab Harvey had already volunteered for the service, and considered, along with many others, that in sending Cochrane the board had insulted the Channel Fleet. However, Cochrane pressed on, persuading Gambier to prepare fireships and explosion-vessels, the latter being filled with 1500 lb of gunpowder, packed under heavy logs to direct the blast, and loaded with hundreds of shells and William Congreve's rockets. The explosion-vessels were intended, along with the fireships, to create chaos in the French squadron, leading them to put their ships ashore, where they could be easily destroyed.

On the night of 11 April Cochrane led the attack, destroying the French boom with the leading explosion-vessel. Despite the failure of the other explosion-vessels to reach their proper positions, the French ships cut their cables and drifted ashore. However, with few fireships left and the main fleet 14 miles off, Cochrane was unable to complete the process. At daybreak he began to signal for assistance, drawing Gambier's attention to the exposed condition of the French ships and the ease with which they might be destroyed; but the admiral studiously refused to act. He moved the fleet to within 3 miles, but then anchored. Desperate to continue his action, Cochrane allowed the *Imperieuse* to drift into the roadstead until she was able to engage some of the French ships. Only then did Gambier send in some support, which led to the destruction of four enemy ships. Gambier then recalled his ships, leaving the French to refloat most of their fleet and withdraw under the batteries. Having left Gambier in no doubt of his opinions, Cochrane was sent back to England with dispatches; he sailed on the morning of the 12th.

Although Cochrane was made a GCB in 1809—only the second captain to be so rewarded, the first being his *bête noire* St Vincent—he was disgusted at the failure to exploit the success at the Aix Roads and to annihilate the enemy, as would have been expected of him by Horatio Nelson. He informed Mulgrave that if a vote of thanks was proposed for Gambier in the House of Commons he would oppose it, 'on the grounds that the commander in chief had not only done nothing to merit a vote of thanks, but had neglected to destroy the French fleet in Aix roads (the battle was known as Basque roads) when it was in his powers to do so'. Gambier applied for a court martial. On 29 May Cochrane was ordered to prefer his charges, but he declined, arguing that the logbooks and signal-logs of the fleet contained all the information required. This was a major tactical error, and it denied him the standing from which to direct the case for the prosecution. In consequence Gambier, tried by a friendly court, was 'most honourably acquitted' and then given the thanks of parliament for what was, under the most favourable interpretation, a gross error. The sentence of the court effectively convicted Cochrane of libelling a superior officer. Thus, his career in the Royal Navy could hardly survive. He submitted a plan to destroy the French ships and forts in the River Scheldt, but this was ignored. He was refused permission to rejoin his ship, then in the North Sea, but was ordered to do so a few months later when his speeches in parliament became embarrassing. Once again he was ordered to the Mediterranean, but he declined and went onto half pay, devoting his time to exposing abuses in the Admiralty. Although his efforts were ultimately successful, they did nothing to endear him to the government of the day, or to those officials who received all or part of their remuneration direct from those using their services rather than from the government. While this was normal practice in the eighteenth century, it had been swept away by the time Cochrane wrote his memoirs, helping to cement his 'liberal' reputation with progressivist historians.

Cochrane's performances in parliament were rarely effective, being too violent, uncompromising, and acrimonious to gather the support his cause required. One of the best, on 11 May 1810, drew a striking comparison between the pensions awarded to wounded naval officers and seamen and the sinecures held by ministers. The following year, after a visit to Malta, he was able to publicize the corrupt practices in the Malta prize court. He also criticized the use of large armies to prop up despotic Sicilian and Portuguese regimes when a maritime strategy would be more effective and far cheaper.

Cochrane's inventive and scientific mind led him to develop a plan to destroy the French fleets, which had long been skulking in defended harbours, beyond the reach of conventional attack, with a combination of massive bombardment from extemporized mortars, and poison gas created by burning sulphur. His plans were submitted to the prince regent, and though a committee headed by the duke of York and including Lord Keith, Lord Exmouth, and Sir William Congreve had little doubt they would succeed, they considered them inhumane and feared they might rebound to the disadvantage of Britain. When the plans were rejected Cochrane promised the prince regent that he would never allow them to fall into the hands of a foreign government.

On 8 August 1812, at Annan, Dumfriesshire, Scotland, Cochrane secretly married Katherine Corbett Barnes (1796–1865), a sixteen-year-old orphan, daughter of Thomas Barnes of Romford, Essex, despite the efforts of his uncle Basil to marry him to a rich heiress. The marriage, though ultimately held to be legal, was subject to considerable doubt, and the couple were married twice more, in Anglican and Scottish ceremonies in June 1818 and in 1825. Although their relationship was by no means smooth, which was hardly surprising in the circumstances, Katherine accompanied her husband on his South American visit during his career. While Cochrane was in service in Greece she had an affair with Lord Auckland, who was acting as his trustee. Thereafter she spent much of her life abroad. The couple had four sons and one daughter; their third son, Arthur Auckland Leopold Pedro Cochrane (1824–1905), had a successful naval career. Lady Dundonald died at Boulogne on 25 January 1865.

Scandal, politics, and South America, 1813–1825 In late 1813 Cochrane's naval uncle, now Admiral Sir Alexander Cochrane, was appointed to command the North American station, then at the heart of the Anglo-American War. He went out in a frigate, leaving his flagship the *Tonnant* to be fitted out by Cochrane, whom he had nominated as his flag captain. This was an ideal field for an expert in littoral warfare, the whole coastline of the United States lay open to sea-based attack, and Admiral Cochrane was only too anxious to carry the war to an American population he despised. However, fate once again intervened. Cochrane's uncle had agreed to take Captain De Berenger, a French exile officer, to instruct his marines in the use of rifles and explosives. However, De Berenger was also an undischarged bankrupt. On 20 February 1814, while at Dover, he sent word to the admiral at Deal that he was Lord Cathcart's aide-de-camp and was carrying news from France that Napoleon was dead and that the allied armies were advancing rapidly on Paris. This intelligence caused the value of government funds to rise rapidly, only to fall when the hoax was exposed. The opportunity was exploited by Andrew Cochrane-Johnstone, Cochrane's uncle, to net a large profit. De Berenger had posted up to London, taken a cab to Cochrane's home in Green Street after having changed out of the scarlet of a staff officer—which he was not entitled to wear—into his own green uniform, and persuaded Cochrane to lend him some plain clothes. He was traced to Cochrane's home, and when Cochrane learned of the swindle he informed the authorities. De Berenger, Cochrane-Johnstone, Cochrane, and others were arrested, tried before Lord Ellenborough, and found guilty. It appeared that Cochrane was ignorant of the whole affair, but the guilt of his uncle, his considerable stockholding, contact with De Berenger, and well-known interest in money, together with the evident bias of Ellenborough, were enough to convict him. He was condemned to pay a fine of £1000, to stand for one hour in the pillory, and to be imprisoned in the king's bench for one year. The pillory was remitted, probably because the government feared a riot. These penalties were as nothing compared to the indignity that was heaped upon him; he was struck off the navy list on 25 June, expelled from the House of Commons on 5 July, and from the chapel of the knight of the Bath. Within days he was returned to the House of Commons by the electors of Westminster, they having declared at a mass meeting their entire confidence that the charges were unfounded. Cochrane was imprisoned, and after escaping and being recaptured his conditions were made particularly severe. Finally, on 20 June 1815, he was entitled to be released, and after reluctantly paying the fine on 3 July, in the interests of his health, he still protested his innocence. He always blamed John Wilson Croker, the secretary of the Admiralty, for his disgrace, though there was never any proof, beyond a well-known political and personal hatred. More than thirty years later Admiral Sir Thomas Byam-Martin recalled his hearing the prince regent express his determination that Cochrane be degraded.

Cochrane returned to the House of Commons to vote against the increased pension for the duke of Cumberland, and for two years he was an energetic promoter of reform, and a committed opponent of the government. His opposition, though based on principle and well intentioned, was coloured by personal bitterness. In August 1816 he was charged with escaping from the king's bench—a charge which he believed was laid to punish him for his political opposition. Claiming that, as a member of parliament, his imprisonment had been illegal, he nevertheless admitted the charge and was found guilty. The sentence was deferred, but three months later, after he had spoken at another large public meeting, he was condemned to pay a fine of £100. He refused to do this, but after sixteen days' imprisonment he was released when the money was paid by a penny subscription that covered his earlier fine of £1000 and also much of his legal costs. Thereafter his radicalism shifted towards a liberal combination with the whigs.

After such evident signs of official hostility, which Cochrane believed included spies and well-founded fears that he was involved in a plot to liberate Napoleon from St Helena and take him to South America, it was scarcely surprising that he accepted the invitation of the Chilean government to organize and command their fleet in their war of liberation from Spain in May 1817. His political sympathies and financial ambitions intersected nicely in a well-paid mercenary role which also involved fighting for freedom. After the 1818 session of parliament, during which he organized the construction of the *Rising Star*, the first seagoing steam warship, he went to France in August and then sailed for Valparaiso on a merchant ship, arriving on 28 November to an enthusiastic welcome. His arrival was timely: a powerful Spanish squadron was preparing to attack Valparaiso, and the Chilean navy comprised only seven vessels, a captured Spanish 50 gun frigate renamed the *O'Higgins*, and a collection of old merchant ships and condemned vessels from the Royal Navy. Cochrane's real strength lay not in ships but in officers and men. His name ensured that he could recruit predominantly British and American crews for his flagship and could stiffen the resolve of his Chilean crews with these experienced men-of-wars-men. Against such an admiral as Cochrane, leading experienced crews, the inexperienced and ill-prepared Spaniards did not expect to win. They had recognized this even before he had left London, then trying to buy him into their own service. Putting to sea in the *O'Higgins* in January 1819, Cochrane blocked the Spaniards in the harbour and conducted a typical littoral campaign, scattering soldiers and capturing shipping and treasure to fund his activities. After an abortive attack on the Spaniards at Callao in Peru, he took his flagship to Valdivia; having reconnoitred the place and secured 250 soldiers from a nearby Chilean garrison, he landed and stormed the forts in his best style, which seemed impetuous but was in fact carefully planned. The garrison panicked and was driven out, leaving a hundred dead, while the Chileans lost no more than seven men. Cochrane then returned to Valparaiso and found his triumph ill-rewarded by jealous ministers. After tendering his resignation he was promised better treatment for himself and the seamen on which so much depended. The Valdivia prize money was never paid.

Having temporarily resolved his differences with the Chileans, Cochrane joined a large combined expedition to liberate Peru. General José de San Martín embarked almost 4000 men aboard the fleet and sailed from Valparaiso in late August 1820. Twice the army landed at a distance from the centres of Spanish power, despite Cochrane's call for an immediate strike at Callao and Lima. He knew that the Spanish position, while outwardly formidable, was brittle and would collapse much as Valdivia had, if attacked quickly. San Martín, encouraged by his army, was convinced that Peru had to secure its own independence if the nation were to be properly established. Unable to influence these operations, Cochrane resolved, without reference to San Martín, to cut out the frigate *Esmerelda*, the last major Spanish warship in the south Pacific, from under the batteries at Callao. On the night of 5 November the boats of the fleet were able to get into the harbour and board the ship at several places before the alarm was raised. Unable to escape, the Spaniards fought furiously but were finally overpowered, though not before eleven of the 'Chilean' force were killed and thirty wounded, including Cochrane, who sustained a severe injury. Once the fighting began the shore batteries fired on the ship without troubling to ascertain whether their own men were still aboard. Cochrane, having seen that the English and American warships in harbour were using a pattern of lights hoisted into the rigging, surmised that this had been pre-arranged with the shore batteries and therefore copied it, allowing the *Esmerelda* to escape relatively unharmed. His original intention, which was to capture or destroy the rest of the shipping in the harbour, was frustrated by his injury. This action reduced the Spanish to a hopeless position; unable to reinforce their navy on the station, and unable to operate on the coast, they could only wait to be overpowered by the forces of the new states. Cochrane, however, had other ideas. Once recovered, he persuaded San Martín to lend him 600 soldiers, with which he staged another littoral campaign of great audacity, virtually forcing the Spanish authorities at Lima to capitulate—which they did on 6 July 1821. San Martín proclaimed himself protector of Peru and demanded that Cochrane and the fleet swear loyalty to the new republic in return for their wages and prize money. Cochrane refused and sailed off to seize San Martín's treasury, out of which he paid the men and refitted the squadron. He returned to Valparaiso in June 1822, after an absence of twenty months, to receive a popular welcome—and the hostility of the ministers. When San Martín returned in October he was loaded with honours and rewards, despite Cochrane's denunciation of his treacherous conduct, while sums due to Cochrane and his men were unpaid. The Chilean republic was about to dissolve into anarchy, so Cochrane decided to leave rather than take sides; he took an extended leave of absence in November. He had done as much as any foreign national could.

Cochrane's services in Chile and Peru had increased the renown of his name, and other countries seeking independence desired to secure his services. Brazil, Mexico, and Greece were all anxious to hire him, but although Greece was his preference, he took service, temporarily, with the Brazilians when he reached Rio de Janeiro on 13 March 1823. He was appointed admiral by the new emperor, Pedro I, and spent eighteen months building up the Brazilian navy, securing British and American seamen, and defeating the attempts of Portugal to re-establish control. Once again his anxiety to secure the largest prize-fund, and his outspoken attacks on corruption, ensured that he had enemies in high places. He spent more time defending his position than he did serving the state. In early 1825, after Brazilian independence had been effectively secured, he took his flagship to sea and, finding her unequal to bad weather, ended up back in England at Spithead. When the Brazilian minister in London refused to fund a refit, Cochrane refused to take her to sea and remained ashore until the peace between Portugal and Brazil was settled, on 3 November, at which time he resigned the Brazilian admiralship.

Greek liberation, 1827–1828 The members of the London Greek Committee, notably his fellow radicals Burdett, Hobhouse, Bowring, and Hume, were certain that Cochrane was the only person who could secure the independence of Greece from Turkish rule. However, Cochrane was only too well aware of the petty jealousies and irresolution that had attended him in South America to enter into the project lightly. Consequently his acceptance was conditional on prior payment for his services, plus a heavy expenditure on six British-built war steamers, and two large American-built frigates. All were to be manned by British or American seamen, and he was to have complete

and uncontrolled command of the Greek fleet. This was agreed, but he spent the next eighteen months trying to advance the construction of the steamers, which he had long recognized as vital for littoral warfare, and which would be especially important in the Greek archipelago, giving him a priceless advantage over the larger Turkish fleet of sailing ships. In the event only two of the steamers actually reached Greece, and neither was particularly successful—a result of design failings, poor construction, corruption, and the intervention of Egyptian agents. Even so, the *Karteria*, under Captain Frank Abney Hastings, proved Cochrane's vision and made a valuable contribution to the war of independence.

When Cochrane arrived in Greece on a yacht in March 1827, he found that none of the new ships was ready; only one frigate and two steamers would be completed in time to serve. He found the Greek sailors singularly lacking in patriotism and, unable to pay them, had to watch them take their craft off to conduct their own piratical campaign. Without the British and American sailors he had demanded his fireship attack on Alexandria failed, and there was little he could do before Sir Edward Codrington destroyed the Turco-Egyptian fleets at Navarino on 20 October 1827. This victory ensured Greek independence. Cochrane's contribution lay largely in the prestige of his name, which was still the terror of the oceans, and the degree of urgency his presence impressed on the European powers to secure a settlement. His rewards were negligible: much of his pay was withheld and the rest locked up in depreciating Greek stock. Even so, he was once again accused of fraud, being connected with the committee that managed to make £200,000 disappear, without benefit for Greece. He returned to England to advance work on the steamships but in September 1828 went back to Greece, where he found that the imminence of peace made his presence most unwelcome. He left for the last time, on a Russian warship, in December. If the Greek war added nothing to his fame, it was only because there was precious little room for further lustre. He remained the greatest 'name' afloat, and his efforts in South America remained the outstanding example of enlightened mercenary service, in which maritime power was used to secure the independence of three countries.

Last years, 1828–1860 Fortunately for Cochrane the end of his mercenary career coincided with a major change in British politics. The end of more than twenty years of tory rule, combined with the accession in 1830 of a naval monarch, William IV, enabled him to return to the Royal Navy. He had first approached William in 1828 when, as duke of Clarence, he held the post of lord high admiral, but the tory cabinet had demurred. Finally, on 2 May 1832, he was given a 'free pardon' rather than the annulment of his conviction for fraud which he had sought. He was restored to his proper rank in the navy, now that of a rear-admiral, and was received at court. But he was not given back his GCB, and his banner was not replaced in St George's Chapel at Windsor Castle. His position remained anomalous: in effect he had been excused for something he had not done, in order that his name and reputation could be wielded by the British state as a deterrent. The first occasion on which this 'Cochrane rattling' occurred was the Russian scare of that year. For the next twenty years successive first lords of the Admiralty recognized that he would be given high command in war, even if they were generally reluctant to employ him in peace. In the interval he had succeeded his father, as tenth earl of Dundonald, on 1 July 1831. The popular naval fiction of his one-time midshipman Frederick Marryat helped pave the way for his return to favour, as Marryat publicized his remarkable exploits aboard the *Imperieuse*, giving them a strong liberal twist. If it was Marryat who created the genre of naval fiction, then it was Cochrane who inspired it. His career remains at the heart of the genre, notably in the work of Patrick O'Brien.

Once re-established in London, Cochrane turned his attention to the scientific and technical interests inherited from his father and reinforced by his experience of war at sea. The development of steam propulsion was his major interest, and he pursued several key technologies, often years in advance of the necessary metallurgical and engineering progress needed to make them practical. His work culminated in the steam warship HMS *Janus* of 1848, which combined his hull form, rotary engines, and boilers in a promising, if unsuccessful, package. Clearly he was indulged by the Admiralty, which was only too happy to see him occupied with engines rather than returning to his old line of attacks on naval administration.

After Cochrane had recovered his GCB from the new liberal ministry in 1847, his old friend Lord Auckland, the first lord of the Admiralty, re-examined his poison gas plans, for use against Cherbourg, and employed him afloat in 1848 as commander-in-chief in the West Indies. Auckland had long recognized Cochrane's value and considered it unwise to deny him the experience of command, if he was to be used in war. The three-year commission was interesting but uneventful. Cochrane sent in valuable reports on the colonies and their resources, and he brought back to England asphalt from Trinidad with which to pave the streets of Westminster—a premature stroke of genius that proved incompatible with horses. On 21 March 1851 he became a full admiral, and by the early 1850s he had become a national treasure, a reminder of past greatness to replace the recently deceased duke of Wellington. He was nominated rear-admiral of the United Kingdom on 23 October 1854 and was also elected an elder brother of Trinity House. He had no further sea service, though during the Crimean War of 1854–6 he offered to deploy a version of his poison gas plan of 1812 against Kronstadt and Sevastopol. This was initially rejected in 1854 by a committee of naval officers advised by Michael Faraday—largely, it would appear, because the plan gave a subordinate role to the battle fleet. It was taken up again in 1855, by a despairing Lord Palmerston, on the grounds that any failure would be attributed to Cochrane's age and eccentricity rather than to the government. However, Sevastopol fell before it could be put into effect.

During his last years Cochrane wrote several volumes of memoirs. These colourful, if imperfect, accounts helped to cement his place in the national pantheon. They were intended to support his financial claims against various governments, beginning with *Narrative of services in the liberation of Chili, Peru, and Brazil, from Spanish and Portuguese domination* (1859), followed by *Autobiography of a Seaman* (1860–61). The series was brought to an abrupt end by his sudden death at 12 Queen's Gate, Kensington, London, on 31 October 1860. He was buried in Westminster Abbey on 14 November.

After Cochrane's death the process of restoring his honours continued. A parliamentary committee of 1878 paid his son £5000 for his 'distinguished services'; in truth, this was the half pay he was owed for the period when he was struck off the navy list. The process went so far that Lord Ellenborough became the villain of the piece, and his side of the case had to be defended in print by the end of the century. The navies of Chile, Peru, and Brazil continued to celebrate his contribution for many years, and Chile named a succession of capital ships for him.

Cochrane was the most brilliant naval officer of the period that followed the death of Nelson in 1805, and he was the only one who achieved a world reputation. However, his true greatness has been much misunderstood. He never commanded a ship, let alone a squadron, against first-class opposition in good fighting order. (After 1805 such opportunities were rare.) His peculiar talents were honed in littoral warfare off the coasts of Spain and France, culminating in the assault on the Aix Roads, which, like much else that he did, relied on the enemy being already half beaten. In South America he deployed this system of warfare to the greatest effect, relying on his name, battle-hardened British and American sailors, and demoralized opponents to secure rapid and decisive results from apparently unpromising situations. To the end of his life his thoughts centred on the projection of maritime power ashore, not fleet-to-fleet encounters. As a result he was among the first to see the potential of steamships, at a time when they remained short-ranged, unreliable, and weakly armed. By contrast his political career lacked the tactical skill, insight, and cunning that made him so successful at sea; in this field his popularity was based on a straightforward, direct naval approach that was diametrically opposed to the usual conduct of business at Westminster. He made many enemies by incautious words, giving offence when he would have been better advised to be tactful; and by alienating St Vincent he missed the chance to co-operate with the other great naval reformer of the age. His disgrace in 1814 arose from a trusting nature and the obvious delight of those whom he had pilloried for so long to get their own back. That it kept him out of his uncle's major littoral warfare campaigns against the Americans helped his posthumous reputation more than it hindered the British war effort at the time. As a scientist and engineer he shared many of his father's eccentricities, but withal had a clear purpose and came close to success.

The key to Cochrane's complex character—the combination of ambition, genius, daring, and resource that made him great, the direct manner and rejection of authority where it did not meet his own high standards that set him apart, and the greed, pride, and vindictiveness that held him back—can be traced to his relationship with his father and, in all probability, a sense of rejection following the death of his mother and his removal to military academy on his father's second marriage. In private he was charming and had an honest and open character; his violent politics reflected an obsessive hatred of corruption and an inability to suffer slights. His qualities of leadership were beyond compare, securing the undying love of junior officers, seamen, and the unruly constituents of Westminster. In old age he tended to dwell on the political and financial wrongs of his career, pursuing the various governments he had served for moneys left unpaid, and passing on his claims to his son. Yet, like Nelson, his greatness rose above petty human failings. With his long life, full range of adventures, and variety of careers Cochrane remains one of the great, if unfulfilled, biographical subjects. He was, and remains, the romantic naval hero.

ANDREW LAMBERT

Sources HoP, *Commons, 1790–1820* · A. Prochaska, 'Cochrane, Thomas', *BDMBR*, vol. 1 · D. Thomas, *Cochrane* (1978) · I. Grimble, *The sea wolf* (1978) · C. Lloyd, *Lord Cochrane* (1947) · D. J. Cubitt, 'Manning the Chilean navy in the war of independence', *Mariner's Mirror*, 63 (1977), 115–28 · B. Vale, 'Lord Cochrane in Brazil: the naval war of independence, 1823 [pt 1]', *Mariner's Mirror*, 57 (1971), 415–42 · B. Vale, 'Lord Cochrane in Brazil: prize money, politics and rebellion, 1824–25 [pt 2]', *Mariner's Mirror*, 59 (1973), 135–70 · D. Dakin, 'Lord Cochrane's Greek steam fleet', *Mariner's Mirror*, 39 (1953), 211–24 · C. Lloyd, *Captain Marryatt and 'The Old Navy'* (1939) · C. J. Bartlett, *Great Britain and sea power, 1815–1853* (1963) · A. Cochrane, *The fighting Cochranes* (1983) · E. D. Law, Lord Ellenborough, *The guilt of Lord Cochrane in 1814* (1914) · GEC, *Peerage* · *Piracy in the Levant, 1827–8: selected from the papers of admiral Sir Edward Codrington*, ed. C. G. Pitcairn-Jones, Navy RS, 72 (1934) · DNB
Archives Archivo Nacional de Chile · BL, Add. MS 41370 · Duke U., Perkins L. · JRL · NA Scot. · New York Historical Society | Balliol Oxf., Urquhart MSS · BL, corresp. with J. C. Hobhouse, Sir F. Burdett, W. R. O'Byrne, letters to Lord Melville, Add. MSS 36461–36464, 36652, 41083 · British School of Athens, Finlay MSS · NA Scot., letters to Chilean ministers · NL Scot., letters to Sir Thomas Cochrane · NMM, letters to James Guthrie · PRO, corresp. with Henry Dean, etc., J90/531 · U. Lpool, letters to John Pascoe Grenfell
Likenesses P. E. Ströhling, painting, exh. RA 1807, priv. coll. [see illus.] · C. Turner, mezzotint, pubd 1809 (after P. E. Ströhling), BM · J. Ramsay, oils, 1811, Gov. Art Coll. · R. Cooper, stipple, pubd 1819 (after W. Walton), BM, NPG · Bonvier, lithograph, pubd 1827 (after J. Ramsay), BM · H. Meyer, mezzotint (after J. Ramsay), NPG · oils (posthumous; after photograph), NMM

Cochrane, Sir Thomas John (1789–1872), naval officer, eldest child of Admiral Sir Alexander Forrester Inglis *Cochrane (1758–1832) and his wife, Maria (d. 18 March 1856), daughter of David Shaw and widow of Captain Sir Jacob Wheate RN, fifth baronet, was born in Edinburgh on 5 February 1789. He was entered as a volunteer on board the *Thetis*, commanded by his father, in June 1796, and continued to serve under his father's pennant, or flag—including on the expeditions to Quiberon, Belleisle, Ferrol, and Egypt—until June 1805, when he was made lieutenant into the frigate *Jason* (32 guns). In September

1805 he was advanced to be commander of the sloop *Nimrod* (18 guns), on 23 January 1806 to be acting captain of the *Jason*, and his rank was confirmed on 23 April 1806, when only two months over seventeen. This rapid promotion, by the commander-in-chief, of a foreign station for his son was gross jobbery. There were few instances so flagrant of a practice then not uncommon. Off the coast of Surinam on 27 January 1807 Cochrane captured the French warship *La Favorite*, and in December served at the capture of the Danish West Indian islands. He continued in the West Indies until 1809, and after two years on half pay commanded the frigate *Surprise* (38 guns) on the coast of North America—capturing on 16 January 1813 the American privateer *Decatur*, and serving in the operations against Washington and Baltimore and on the Georgia coast—until the peace. From 1820 to 1824 he commanded the *Forte* (44 guns) on the same station, from 1825 to 1834 he was governor of Newfoundland, and on 23 November 1841 he became rear-admiral. He was knighted (29 May 1812) as proxy for his father at his installation as KB. He was himself made CB on 18 April 1839, KCB on 2 November 1847, and GCB on 18 May 1860. He was Conservative MP for Ipswich in 1839–41, and unsuccessfully contested Greenock in July 1841.

From 1842 to 1845 Cochrane was second in command in China, with his flag in the *Agincourt*, and he was commander-in-chief from 1844 to 1846. In August 1845 and July 1846 he punished Brunei pirates by destroying their forts and other buildings. He supported J. F. Davis's policy of conciliation at Canton (Guangzhou), with a minimal naval presence there so as not to inflame Chinese hostility. British merchants criticized him for ineffectiveness against Chinese pirates, but he was limited by government instructions. He was commander-in-chief at Portsmouth from December 1852 to January 1856. In due course of seniority he became vice-admiral on 14 January 1850, admiral on 31 January 1856, and admiral of the fleet on 12 September 1865.

Cochrane married on 6 January 1812 Matilda, eldest daughter of Lieutenant-General Sir Charles Ross, seventh baronet, and they had two sons and two daughters; she assumed the additional name of Wishart and died on 4 September 1819. He married on 8 January 1853 Rosetta (d. 27 May 1901), daughter of Sir J. D. Wheeler-Cuffe, first baronet, and they had children. He died at his residence, Quarr Abbey House, Ryde, Isle of Wight, on 19 October 1872, and was buried at Kensal Green cemetery, London, on 25 October. J. K. LAUGHTON, rev. ROGER T. STEARN

Sources O'Byrne, *Naval biog. dict.* · Burke, *Peerage* (1967) · W. L. Clowes, *The Royal Navy: a history from the earliest times to the present*, 7 vols. (1897–1903); repr. (1996–7), vol. 6 · G. S. Graham, *The China station: war and diplomacy, 1830–1860* (1978) · Boase, *Mod. Eng. biog.* · *WWBMP*, vol. 1 · *Annual Register* (1872) · CGPLA Eng. & Wales (1872)
Archives NL Scot., corresp. and papers, MSS 2264–2505; 2577–2607; 3022 · NMM, papers relating to HMS Forte, PLA/21 | NL Scot., corresp. with Charles Graham · priv. coll., corresp. with A. R. Drummond · PRO, 1844 corresp. with Henry Pottinger, F 0705
Likenesses W. C. Ross, oils, 1854, Admiralty, Portsmouth · R. Buckner, oils, NMM
Wealth at death under £200,000: probate, 29 Nov 1872, *CGPLA Eng. & Wales*

Cochrane, William, first earl of Dundonald (1605–1685), army officer and politician, was the second son of Alexander Blair (d. 1640/41) of Blair, Ayrshire, who assumed the name Cochrane on his marriage to Elizabeth, daughter of William Cochrane of Cochrane, Renfrewshire, and his wife, Elizabeth. He was educated first at Paisley grammar school, and then at Glasgow University, where he was laureated in 1626, and where he later founded the Dundonald bursaries. In 1632 he was appointed sheriff-depute of Renfrewshire. Some time before 1634 he married Euphame (Eupheme; d. after 1685), daughter of Sir William Scott of Ardross and Elie, Fife, director of the court of chancery. Cochrane acquired a substantial landed estate in the shire, including the lands of Dundonald, obtained in 1638. His father had purchased the barony of Cowdown in 1623, but resigned it to William in 1634. In 1641 he was granted particular privileges in the management of his father's patrimonial barony of Blair. The same year he was appointed chamberlain to the duke of Lennox and was elected to represent Ayrshire at the Edinburgh parliament which assembled in 1641. At its meeting Cochrane was knighted by Charles I, but despite misgivings about several clauses in the covenant, commented on by Baillie in 1638, he remained opposed to the king's disastrous attempt to entrench the Scottish episcopacy. As premier landlord in the west of Scotland he could hardly do any other.

During the civil war Cochrane was loyal to the committee of estates at Edinburgh, and assisted in the military campaigns against Montrose, bringing over 1400 men from the Scottish army in Ulster in 1645. He returned there again to fetch Major General Robert Monro when the covenanters failed to crush the royalists in the highlands, but the victory at Philiphaugh rendered his orders obsolete. In the aftermath of war Cochrane was closest to the Hamiltonian faction among the covenanters, and was granted the title Lord Cochrane of Dundonald by patent dated at Carisbrooke Castle on 26 December 1647, the very day on which the king entered into his ill-fated Engagement with the duke of Hamilton and his supporters in Scotland. Lord Cochrane raised forces in his native Ayrshire, and once more in Ireland, for the much delayed invasion, which eventually got off the ground in July 1648. His association with this malignant venture, and its disastrous conclusion, resulted in his proscription under the Act of Classes and his ostracism by the presbytery of Ayr in 1649. Like most fervent Scots loyalists he remained out in the cold until Charles II was installed on the throne at Scone in 1651.

Unlike his elder brother, Sir John *Cochrane, who undertook diplomatic duties in northern Germany, Lord Cochrane preferred to serve his royal master by remaining on his estate in Scotland. However, in the parliament which opened in 1651 he was once again to the fore, helping to organize the military venture on which the king pinned his hopes for the resumption of the English crown. Although he raised a regiment of horse of his own Cochrane was not optimistic about the king's chances in England—his misgivings possibly arising when Charles saw fit to deny Cochrane's brothers the command of his lordship's horse regiment, giving it instead to a Dutchman, Vandrosk. When Cochrane's worst fears transpired on the field before Worcester, he retired to private life in Scotland. He acquired the lordship of Paisley from Archibald, earl of Angus, for £160,000 Scots in 1653, and it is said that he lived there in great opulence. After the Cromwellian conquest Cochrane was fined £5000 sterling by the Act of Pardon and Grace, although in the end the pressure on him was eased and the mulct was reduced by the council at Whitehall to the more manageable sum of £1666 13s. 4d. In a sign of further attempts at some sort of reconciliation, promoted especially hard during the governorship of Lord Broghill, Cochrane was named to the commission of the peace for Ayrshire in 1656. Later in the year he was elected to sit at Westminster as the member for Ayrshire and Renfrewshire in Oliver Cromwell's second protectorate parliament.

It has been claimed that Cochrane supported General Monck financially to the tune of £20,000 in 1659, supposedly in order to promote the Stuart restoration, following which he was sworn of the privy council and appointed commissioner of the Treasury and excise in Scotland, which latter post he occupied from 1667 to 1682. He was created earl of Dundonald and Lord Cochrane of Paseley and Ochiltrie on 12 May 1669. He frequently acted on behalf of the duke of Monmouth, whose interests as duke of Buccleuch were not always well served by his absence at court. Later, the earl's second son, Sir John *Cochrane would also earn the duke's gratitude, his action in the 1685 rebellion almost costing him his life. In 1684, although Dundonald was under threat of prosecution for harbouring covenanter fugitives on his own land, his granddaughter Jean married John Graham of Claverhouse, scourge of the western rebels. Dundonald's tremulous signature appears attached to the marriage contract. The same year it was also alleged that his eldest son, William, Lord Cochrane, who had died five years earlier, had kept a chaplain who had prayed for God's blessing on the 1679 uprising. The story of this Cochrane connection with the covenanters was revived and exploited as a way of discrediting the powerful and influential Claverhouse. He himself was at pains to clear the family of any distasteful imputation, insisting that there were far fewer rebels on the earl's estates than there were on many other local lairds', but could not deny the religious sentiments of his mother-in-law, Lady Katherine, née Kennedy. The earl was, however, somewhat delayed in taking the oath of loyalty prescribed under the 1681 Test Act, although his procrastination was excused by his colleagues in the privy council by his age and infirmity. He died in November 1685, aged eighty, and was buried at Dundonald. Having been predeceased by his eldest son he was succeeded in the earldom by his grandson, John. His daughter, Grizel, married George, tenth Lord Ross.

SEAN KELSEY

Sources DNB · GEC, *Peerage*, 4. 526 · *Scots peerage*, 3.339–46 · A. I. Dunlop, 'Correspondence of the first earl of Dundonald', *Ayrshire Archaeological and Natural History Society Collections*, 2nd ser., 4 (1955–

7), 143–81 • F. D. Dow, *Cromwellian Scotland, 1651–1660* (1979) • D. Stevenson, *Scottish covenanters and Irish confederates: Scottish-Irish relations in the mid-seventeenth century* (1981) • A. Cochrane, *The fighting Cochranes: a Scottish clan over six hundred years of naval and military history* (1983)

Archives BL, letters to duke of Lauderdale, Charles II, etc., Add. MSS 23114–23138, 23242–23247, *passim*

Likenesses oils, *c.*1669, repro. in Cochrane, *Fighting Cochranes*

Cock, George (*bap.* 1615, *d.* 1679), merchant and friend of Samuel Pepys, was baptized at All Saints, Newcastle upon Tyne, on 25 April 1615, the son of Garrett Cocke. His family were deeply involved in trade and after his apprenticeship in 1631 to a corn merchant he became an influential and active member of the Newcastle Merchants Company, negotiating for them in their dispute with the Merchant Adventurers of London.

During the civil wars Cock was an early supporter of the king and was captured in 1643. He was released in exchange for a parliamentary prisoner but returned to Newcastle as a member of the marquess of Newcastle's army and was present at the siege when he was again captured, imprisoned, and eventually fined in 1646 as a delinquent. In one of several petitions after the Restoration he stated that he had been in exile for eleven years and was rewarded for his loyalty with the post of searcher in the port of Newcastle in 1660.

While abroad Cock was employed as an agent of the Eastland Company in Danzig. Here he may have met his first wife, Anna Marie Solomons, after whose death he married again. According to Pepys, Cock's second wife was 'a Germane lady, but a very great beauty' (Pepys, 22 Nov 1661). On his return to England he had houses in Greenwich and London. As a navy contractor and the 'greatest epicure in the world' (Pepys, 21 Aug 1665) he appears often in Samuel Pepys's diaries, usually with the prefix Captain. On 21 July 1662 Pepys records that 'I did take boat and down to Greenwich to Captain Cockes, who hath a most pleasant seat and neat'. Cock was one of the few merchants wealthy and experienced enough to deal in Baltic and Scandinavian timber, owned a tannery in Limerick, and dealt extensively in hemp and tar. Though frequently enjoying his company and hospitality Pepys and others were wary of him. When asked by Lord Sandwich how far he could be trusted in the rather shady affair of the prize ships which they had all invested in, Pepys replied 'not too far' (Pepys, 23 Sept 1665). He was suspected by Pepys of anonymously offering hemp at high price when supplies were low during 1665–6 but the risks for the merchants were considerable, given the Navy Board's frequent lack of money. Cock seems to have talked too much, particularly when drunk, a quality that would naturally make Pepys uneasy, especially on occasions such as that on 5 November 1665, when Cock interrupted a meeting 'as drunk as a dog, but could stand and talk and laugh … But very troublesome he is with his noise and talk and laughing, though very pleasant'. However he generously bestowed gifts on Pepys and other associates, sending them wine, sturgeon, plate, and money. Cock was treasurer of the Commission for Sick and Wounded Seamen (1665–7). He successfully petitioned for funds

towards this on several occasions but came under suspicion for irregular accounting in 1670. Cock was elected a fellow of the Royal Society on 21 March 1666 (proposed by Viscount Brouncker). A merchant to the bone Cock wrote after the fire 'the city will be rebuilt by trade' (*CSP dom.*, vol. 170, p. 105). His will, dated 19 February 1679 and proved on 3 April that year unravels many threads of his life while dealing with his considerable estate and includes £30 to repatriate a servant, 'Dutch Margaret'. His will also mentions four sons: John, George, Matthew, and William. He died in the parish of St Clement Danes, London, and, in accordance with his wishes, was buried at night near his first wife in the church of St Peter-le-Poer, London.   C. BATEY

Sources [J. R. Boyle and F. W. Dendy], eds., *Extracts from the records of the merchant adventurers of Newcastle-upon-Tyne*, 2 vols., SurtS, 93, 101 (1895–9) • Pepys, *Diary* • B. Pool, *Navy board contracts, 1660–1832* (1966) • M. Hunter, *The Royal Society and its fellows, 1660–1700: the morphology of an early scientific institution*, 2nd edn (1994) • will, PRO, PROB 11/359, fols. 349r–351r • *DNB* • *IGI*

Wealth at death extensive holdings in business and property: will, PRO, PROB 11/359, fols. 349r–351r

Cock, Gerald Alfred (1887–1973), television executive, was born on 23 July 1887 at The Cottage, Betchworth, Surrey, younger son of four children of Alfred Cock QC (1849–1898), barrister of the Middle Temple, and his wife, Eva Laura Bertha Liebreich. Cock, described as tall, lean, debonair, and dark-haired, was unmarried. He was educated at Tonbridge School. After an engineering training, he travelled in North America and Mexico where his experience included mining and explosives. He was commissioned in the Royal Engineers from 1915 to 1920, becoming a captain in 1917. Cock joined BBC radio outside broadcasts in 1925 and is credited with making important contributions to the range and style of events covered. He also organized broadcasts for George V, who appointed him a member in the Royal Victorian Order in 1935.

In February 1935 Cock became the BBC's director of television and was responsible for starting the world's first regular high-definition service. He held the post until transmissions ceased at the outbreak of the Second World War. His contribution must be seen in the context of an era when television's potential had not been grasped widely. Throughout its development attention focused on technology rather than on its application. Between 1929 and 1935 the BBC transmitted experimental programmes using John Logie Baird's 30-line picture mechanical system, but in 1932 research in Britain by Marconi-EMI concluded that television's future lay in electronics. In 1935 a government committee recommended that the BBC should run a public service for London.

Cock's appointment followed. He recalled in 1961:

I hadn't the slightest appreciation of what would be needed … and it wasn't for some little time that I got the feeling that … we've got the greatest medium of public communication the world has ever seen … When I said that in Broadcasting House … they just laughed at me as a sort of half-boiled enthusiast without any sense of proportion. ('Window on the world')

An interview published in December 1935 reflected the

general view: 'Their [the BBC's] job will be to sell the public something which nobody yet has ever tried to sell and it will take more than scientific machinery to do that' ('The BBC's plans', 692). In August 1936 radio manufacturers still advised, 'television cannot be regarded as an alternative to sound broadcasting; rather in the course of time, may it become a supplementary adjunct thereto' (Moss, *BBC TV Presents*, 11).

It was a slow start. When the service began on 2 November 1936 there were about 400 sets in use and 12 hours of programmes a week, which were available only within a radius of about 30 miles from the studios at Alexandra Palace, north London. The technology also presented difficulties for Cock and his team. The government committee had advised a trial between the Baird company's mechanical process, by then offering 240-line pictures, and Marconi-EMI's 405-line electronic system. Cock reported that the Baird system was 'being transmitted on a service basis in what are practically experimental conditions' (Moss, 'At the toss of a coin', 332). His view was supported and the Baird system was dropped early in 1937.

Cock believed that success depended on offering diversity and his approach laid the principles for modern television production. Applying his characteristic energy and enthusiasm he and programme organizer Cecil Madden devised a topical magazine programme, *Picture Page*, in which celebrities appeared. He appointed producers from outside broadcasting to make a wide range of material including drama, opera, ballet, variety, comedies, talks, and children's programmes. Coverage of major events, particularly sport, was popular. Their greatest triumph was the televising of the coronation procession of George VI and Queen Elizabeth in May 1937. Television cameras were not allowed into Westminster Abbey, so Cock found a point at Hyde Park Corner where the procession passed:

> I went to Buck House and asked the King if he'd be good enough to smile into the TV camera and damned if he didn't … His secretary told me he'd had a slip of paper inside the coach and he'd got on this, 'Look right outside the window at Hyde Park Corner and smile', and they both did. We got a beautiful close-up and it was really the making of that. ('Window on the world')

More than 100,000 viewers are thought to have watched.

Transmission hours expanded gradually, television sets became cheaper, and sales increased. Between 1937 and 1939 about 20,000 were sold with forecasts of 80,000 by Christmas 1939. Perhaps one key to its progress was Cock's commitment to keeping in touch with the audience. In December 1938 he invited viewers to question him by phone live on air and in June 1939 he invited 150 viewers to 'Television conference'.

In 1940, following television's wartime closure, Cock became the BBC's North American representative; he was its Pacific coast representative between 1942 and 1945 when he retired on health grounds. He died of heart disease on 10 November 1973 at the War Memorial Hospital, Crowborough, Sussex, and was cremated on 16 November at Tunbridge Wells.   NICHOLAS MOSS

Sources staff files, BBC WAC, L 2/40 · *The Times* (14 Nov 1973) · *The window on the world*, 7 Nov 1961, BBC WAC, LP 27065 [interview] ·

private information (2004) [The Librarian of the Honourable Society of the Middle Temple] · N. Moss, *BBC TV presents* (1986) · N. Moss, *This is BBC television* (1997) · N. Moss, 'At the toss of a coin', *Journal of the Royal Television Society* (Dec 1986), 327–32 · b. cert. · d. cert. · 'The BBC's plans for television', *Television and Short-wave World* (Dec 1935), 692–4 · *Law Times* (30 April 1898) · *Radio Times* (23 Oct 1936), 10 · *Evening News* (25 Feb 1946) · A. Briggs, *The history of broadcasting in the United Kingdom*, rev. edn, 2 (1995) · *CGPLA Eng. & Wales* (1974)

Archives BBC WAC | FILM BFI NFTVA, documentary footage | SOUND BBC WAC · BL NSA, current affairs recording

Wealth at death £50,114: probate, 6 June 1974, *CGPLA Eng. & Wales*

Cockayne, Dame **Elizabeth** (1894–1988), nursing administrator and teacher, was born on 29 October 1894 in Burton upon Trent, the youngest in the family of two daughters and three sons of William Cockayne, brewer's traveller and licensed victualler, and his wife, Alice Bailey. One of her brothers was killed in the First World War, the second died of tuberculosis, and the third died in 1943. Her father died when she was five. These distressing experiences sharpened Elizabeth Cockayne's deep commitment to Christianity and sense of duty to others. She went to Guild Street Girls' School in Burton upon Trent. After contracting smallpox as a child, she contemplated a career in nursing. In 1912 she embarked upon a two-year training in fever nursing at the Borough Hospital, Plymouth. Although asked by the matron to stay on the staff after her training was completed, she decided to leave Plymouth in 1915.

Cockayne had four years' training at Sheffield Royal Infirmary, which gave her a dual qualification. She was rapidly promoted to the post of ward sister in 1919 and then night sister, a post in which she oversaw the administration of the 500-bed hospital. While she was on night duty she undertook a course in hygiene and sanitary science offered by the local education authority. Much against the wishes of her employers, she left Sheffield to undertake midwifery training at Birmingham Maternity Hospital (1920–21). She impressed her supervisors with her intelligence and judgement, and took charge of caring for premature babies. Her mother died at this time. She left Birmingham to become a peripatetic nurse–tutor, travelling between the Gloucester and Cheltenham general hospitals. As her headmistress had noted earlier, she had a natural flair for teaching. Throughout her life she maintained a keen commitment to her own education as well as that of others. Although happy in Gloucester, she moved to London to be near her sister, a schoolmistress, who had fallen ill. She joined the West London Hospital as one of the first nurses to occupy a combined post as assistant matron and sister tutor. She excelled in her new position, and by the age of twenty-nine was appointed to a matron's post first at the West London, then at the St Charles, and finally at the Royal Free Hospital. She was at the Royal Free from 1936 to 1948, having succeeded the formidable Rachael Cox-Davies as matron. She displayed calmness and courage after the outbreak of the Second World War, when the hospital was bombed and she was buried in the rubble. At the same time she was invited by the matron-in-chief of the London county council to act as an examiner to training schools, and to review the policy on the length of the working week for nurses and domestics. She inspected work in training schools and factories, supervising the health of munitions workers during the Second World War. She had a continued interest in the effects of fatigue and strain on nurses' health and performance. She was honorary secretary of the Association of Hospital Matrons between 1937 and 1948, occupying one of the premier positions in nursing policy and politics. As a founding member of the sister–tutor section of the Royal College of Nursing, she recognized the prejudice faced by tutors, who were regarded as superfluous and a luxury in training schools.

In 1945 Elizabeth Cockayne was appointed a member of the working party (chaired by Sir Robert Wood) on the recruitment and training of nurses, which reported in 1947. It aimed to improve the intellectual calibre of nurse training by reducing the repetitive and routine nature of practical nursing experience and stripping the nursing role of its domestic functions. It reported (HMSO, 1947) that this could only be achieved by radically reducing the jurisdiction of the matron-dominated General Nursing Council over nurse training and substituting it with regional nursing boards. These recommendations made Elizabeth Cockayne unpopular with her fellow matrons. In 1948 she was appointed the first chief nursing officer in the National Health Service, where she remained until her retirement in 1958.

Elizabeth Cockayne was of slender build, with striking features, a kindly face, and keen intelligent eyes. An enlightened, energetic, and progressive leader, she had charisma, charm, a generous nature, humanitarian values, and an understanding of the various groups whose differences often clashed in the sectarian politics of health care. A shrewd but subtle strategist, she determined that the nursing voice should be heard at the highest levels of policy-making. She was gifted with the rare capacity to influence without alienating, and to assume multiple roles without undermining her integrity. She was committed to nurses' welfare and high standards of patient care. After her retirement she was a member of the South-West Metropolitan Regional Hospital Board (1959–65), and an adviser to the World Health Organization during the 1950s. In later life she cared for many old people near her home in Cobham, Surrey, some of whom were younger than herself. She lived alone in her cottage after the death of her sister in 1982. She received the jubilee medal (1935), the Coronation Medal (1953), and the Florence Nightingale medal of the International Red Cross committee in Geneva. She was appointed DBE in 1955. She was unmarried, and died on 4 July 1988 at her home, Rushett Cottage, Little Heath Lane, Cobham, Surrey. ANNE MARIE RAFFERTY, rev.

Sources interview with Dame Elizabeth Cockayne, 27 March 1987, Royal College of Nursing Archives, Edinburgh [in membership file] · K. Raven, memorial speech in honour of Dame Elizabeth Cockayne, Royal Free Hospital, 31 Oct 1988 · *The Times* (6 July 1988) · *CGPLA Eng. & Wales* (1988)

Archives Royal College of Nursing Archives, Edinburgh, archives, membership file · U. Leeds, Brotherton L., memoirs relating to nursing in First World War

Wealth at death £274,843: probate, 18 Oct 1988, *CGPLA Eng. & Wales*

Cockayne, Thomas Oswald (*bap.* 1809, *d.* 1873), philologist and teacher, was baptized on 20 January 1809 in Keynsham, Somerset, the eldest of nine children born to John Cockin, curate of Keynsham parish, and his wife, Louise. He was admitted into St John's College, Cambridge, as a sizar in 1824. Following a distinguished undergraduate career, Cockayne was awarded his BA degree as thirtieth wrangler in 1828, and proceeded MA in 1835. On 7 April 1833 Cockayne was ordained a deacon, and was immediately appointed as curate of Keynsham parish. Ordination to the priesthood followed on 10 October the following year. Four days later he married Janetta Edwards (1809–1894), daughter of a Keynsham Baptist surgeon. In 1835 their first daughter, Florence Louisa, was born.

By the time his other child, Alice Eden, was baptized on 25 March 1837, Cockayne had left his position as curate and schoolteacher, and had moved to London to take up the post of assistant master at King's College School. Among his future pupils were Walter Skeat (1835–1912) and Henry Sweet (1845–1912), leaders of the next generation of philologists. Cockayne and his wife supplemented the assistant master's modest salary by taking in as many as nine student boarders at their home at 17 Montague Street, Bloomsbury, and, later, at 13 Manor Park, Lee. He remained at this post until his abrupt dismissal, on 20 November 1869, amid charges of using unsuitable language in his classes and speaking on improper topics to his students. Cockayne vigorously denied the use of unsuitable language, but readily admitted to discussing matters usually avoided by the other masters when they appeared in Greek and Latin passages. Although the investigating committee acknowledged a complete absence of intent to corrupt the boys, it recommended the dismissal of Cockayne for acting 'in direct opposition to the feeling of the age … which will tolerate no such teaching in an English School' ('Report of a committee'). Cockayne promptly published a pamphlet in his own defence entitled *Mr. Cockayne's Narrative*.

It was during his long tenure at King's College School that Cockayne distinguished himself as one of the leading philologists of his day. He was an early and active member of the London Philological Society, where he presented several papers and served as a member of the society's council. During the course of his career he published more than twenty-five books and articles. While Cockayne's early philological works dealt primarily with Greek and Latin sources, he is principally noted for his work in Anglo-Saxon. Prominent among his contributions is a three-volume work published between 1864 and 1866, in English and Anglo-Saxon, entitled *Leechdoms, Wortcunning, and Starcraft of Early England*. Cockayne also edited several books for the Early English Text Society, including *Hali Meidenhad* (1866) and *The Liflade of St. Juliana*

(1872). He wrote an account of the Jews, histories of Ireland and of France, and a biography of Marshall Turenne. Between 1864 and 1870 Cockayne also published a wide-ranging series of critical and scholarly essays called *The Shrine: a Collection of Occasional Papers on Dry Subjects* (nos. 1–13). A number of Cockayne's unpublished philological manuscripts survive in the Houghton Library at Harvard University.

Although Cockayne was a gifted and productive philologist, his pugnacious personality and abrasive *ad hominem* attacks on influential critics closed the doors to higher academic positions. He was a well-intentioned but impolitic man whose life was driven by a love of language but whose life was ultimately ruined by the unbridled use of language.

In June 1873, at St Ives, Cornwall, Cockayne, unemployed and unemployable, and suffering increasingly from 'melancholia', died as the result of a self-inflicted gunshot wound to the head. He was buried in St Ives parish cemetery on 18 June 1873. DANIEL F. KENNEALLY

Sources council and committee minutes, 1837–70, King's Lond., archives · 'Report of a committee on a master in KCL School, 15 November 1869', King's Lond., archives, bundle C681 · in-correspondence, 1837–70, King's Lond., archives, bundle C · parish register, Keynsham; 14 Oct 1834 [marriage] · ordination papers, Som. ARS, records of the diocese of Bath and Wells · parish register, St Ives, Cornwall, 18 June 1873 [burial] · *Cornish Telegraph* (18 June 1873), (25 June 1873) · St John Cam., Archives · F. Miles and G. Cranch, *King's College School* (1979) · census returns, 1841, 1851, 1861, 1871 · Registers of Marriage, Birth and Death, Family Records Centre, London · Som. ARS, Keynsham and Saltford local history archives · King's College School, Wimbledon, archives · Crockford (1873)
Archives Harvard U., Houghton L., notes and extracts on Anglo-Saxon literature | BL, letters to Samuel Butler, MS 34,588, fols. 94 and 96 · King's Lond., corresp., C-bundles
Likenesses photograph, King's College School, Wimbledon

Cockayne, William (1717–1798), Church of England clergyman, the son of the Revd George Cockayne (*d.* 1746), vicar of Doveridge in Derbyshire, was born on 3 November 1717. After attending Merchant Taylors' School (1728–36), he went to St John's College, Oxford, and took degrees of BA, MA, and BD in 1740, 1744, and 1751 respectively. He was junior proctor of the university in 1750, and proceeded DD on 13 July 1754. When his uncle Francis Cockayne was elected lord mayor of London in 1750, he was appointed his chaplain, and preached before him the anniversary sermon of 5 November that year. In 1753 he was chaplain to the countess of Orkney and Inchiquin. From 1752 to 1795 he held the chair of astronomy in Gresham College, London, for which at that date no particular astronomical competence was required. On 20 September 1763 he was nominated rector of Kilkhampton in Cornwall, a post he occupied until his death in 1798. His only publications were religious in content. He left a widow, Mary, who died at Salisbury in 1807.

A. M. CLERKE, *rev.* ANITA MCCONNELL

Sources A. E. Cockayne, *Cockayne memoranda: collections towards a historical record of the family of Cockayne* (privately printed, Congleton, 1873), 182–5 · Mrs E. P. Hart, ed., *Merchant Taylors' School register,* *1561–1934*, 1 (1936) · *N&Q*, 7 (1853), 431 · *GM*, 1st ser., 20 (1750), 522 · *GM*, 1st ser., 65 (1795), 711

Cockburn, Adam, of Ormiston, Lord Ormiston (*c.*1656–1735), politician, was a younger son of John Cockburn of Ormiston (*d.* 1657), and his wife, Janet Hepburn, daughter of Sir Adam Hepburn of Humbie. He succeeded his elder brother, John, in the lands and barony of Ormiston on 28 December 1671. By the late 1670s he had married Lady Susanna Hamilton, third daughter of John Hamilton, fourth earl of Haddington; they had six children—John *Cockburn (1679–1758), Charles, Patrick, Adam, Christian, and Anne.

Ormiston first appears in the parliamentary record in June 1678, when he sat in the convention of estates as one of the two commissioners for Haddingtonshire. He was again elected in July 1681, his commission having been disputed but sustained. In May 1685 he was named as one of the commissioners of supply for the shire, a position he was to hold regularly prior to the union. However, Ormiston—described by the Jacobite commentator Colin Lindsay, third earl of Balcarres, as one of the leaders of the presbyterian and discontented party—had few opportunities in public life before the revolution of 1688, when he assumed a far more prominent role in national politics.

On 11 March 1689 Ormiston was again returned a commissioner for Haddingtonshire, and he took his seat in the convention on the 14th of that month. He subscribed both the act declaring the convention a lawful meeting of the estates and the letter of congratulation addressed to the prince of Orange. In April he was one of those appointed to discuss the prospect of a union with England, and elected a member of the committee of estates—a body charged with governing the country in the interval before the convention became a parliament on King William's instruction. The following month he was named a member of the privy council, an office he again occupied in 1696, 1698, and 1707. On 28 November 1692 he was appointed lord justice clerk in place of Sir George Campbell of Cessnock, consequently attending parliament in this capacity as one of the officers of state. In May 1695 Ormiston was part of the commission appointed to inquire into the massacre of Glencoe, the report of which was presented to parliament the following June. For his part in the commission and his conduct as lord justice clerk, Ormiston appears to have been subject to considerable criticism. One contemporary, Dr Houston, remarked:

> of all the party Lord Ormiston was the most busy, and very zealous in suppressing the rebellion and oppressing the rebels, so that he became universally hated in Scotland, and when ladies were at cards, playing the nine of diamonds, commonly called the curse of Scotland, they called it the Justice Clerk. (Brunton and Haig, 478–80)

Nevertheless, that month Ormiston was created a director of the ill-fated Company of Scotland trading to Africa and the Indies. Then on 6 February 1699 Ormiston was created lord treasurer-depute in place of the deceased Lord Raith. He took his new seat in parliament on 21 May 1700. At this point, consistent with his former conduct, he took the

Adam Cockburn of Ormiston, Lord Ormiston (*c.*1656–1735),
attrib. William Aikman

oath of allegiance, signed the same with the assurance
and association, and took the oath of parliament.

On the accession of Queen Anne, Ormiston was dismissed from office. However, his enforced retirement was
not to last long. On 8 January 1705 he obtained a commission restoring him to the office of lord justice clerk and
appointing him an ordinary lord of session, both in place
of Sir William Hamilton of Whitelaw. He assumed his seat
as justice clerk on 26 January, and as a lord of session on 31
January. Ormiston was superseded as justice clerk by
James Erskine of Grange in 1710, but retained his place as a
lord of session. Nevertheless, in 1714, on the accession of
George I, Ormiston had the office of justice clerk conferred on him for a third time; he retained it for the
remainder of his life.

Ormiston was one of the first Scottish landowners who
endeavoured to introduce long leases of farming land,
and as early as 1698 he attempted to break through the old
system of short leasing. Similarly it was on his own estate
of Ormiston that the fields were enclosed for the first time
in Scotland. He was evidently a capable man of considerable diversity, though his talents were matched by his
'hot, virulent, turbulent and domineering temper'
(Young, 131). He was described by one contemporary as a
gentleman who 'entered heartily into the measures of the
Revolution, and was zealous all King William's reign,
especially for Presbyterian church government'. He was
also 'too great a bigot in his principles, but in other
respects a very fine gentleman, both in person and manners, of strong good sense and great integrity' (*State Papers*

and Letters, 99). Following the death of his first wife Ormiston married Anne, daughter of Sir Patrick Houston of that
ilk and widow successively of Sir James Ingirs of Cramond
and Sir William Hamilton, Lord Whitelaw; they had one
daughter, Jean. Ormiston died at Edinburgh on 16 April
1735, aged about seventy-nine.   DEREK JOHN PATRICK

Sources M. D. Young, ed., *The parliaments of Scotland: burgh and
shire commissioners*, 1 (1992) • APS, 1670–1707 • Reg. PCS, 3rd ser.,
vol. 13 • G. Brunton and D. Haig, *An historical account of the senators of
the college of justice, from its institution in MDXXXII* (1832) • *State papers
and letters addressed to William Carstares*, ed. J. M'Cormick (1774) •
*Historical notices of Scotish affairs, selected from the manuscripts of Sir
John Lauder of Fountainhall*, ed. D. Laing, 2 vols., Bannatyne Club, 87
(1848) • W. H. L. Melville, ed., *Leven and Melville papers: letters and state
papers chiefly addressed to George, earl of Melville … 1689–1691*, Bannatyne Club, 77 (1843) • C. Lindsay [earl of Balcarres], *Memoirs touching
the revolution in Scotland*, ed. A. W. C. Lindsay [earl of Crawford and
Balcarres], Bannatyne Club (1841) • P. W. J. Riley, *King William and
the Scottish politicians* (1979)
Archives NA Scot., corresp. with Sir J. Clerk; letters to duke of
Montrose
Likenesses attrib. W. Aikman, portrait, Scot. NPG [*see illus.*]

Cockburn, Sir **Alexander James Edmund**, twelfth baronet (1802–1880), judge, was born on 24 December 1802,
the only son of Alexander Cockburn (1776–1852), later
envoy-extraordinary and minister-plenipotentiary to
Wurtemburg and then Colombia, and his wife, Yolande (*d.*
1810), daughter of the vicomte de Vignier of St Domingo.
Part of his early education took place on the continent,
leaving him fluent in French, and with some knowledge of
Spanish, German, and Italian. In September 1822 he was
admitted to Trinity Hall, Cambridge, where he was a
scholar and prizeman in 1823, and president of the Union
Society in 1824. He achieved first class in civil law in 1824–
5, and graduated LLB in 1829, and would remain a fellow of
his college until 1850. In November 1825 Cockburn was
admitted into the Middle Temple, and was called to the
bar in February 1829. After his call Cockburn joined the
western circuit. He acquired a large practice at the Devon
sessions, but was so doubtful of success in London that he
did not even keep his chambers open. He had an adventurous youth, observing in later years, 'Whatever happens, I
have had my whack' (*A Generation of Judges by their Reporter*,
10). On one occasion, he had to escape from bailiffs by
climbing out of the window of the robing rooms at Exeter
Castle. Ever keen on the company of women, he fathered
two illegitimate children, a girl and a boy, Alexander Dalton Cockburn, to whom he left the majority of his fortune.

Early practice at the bar and in politics After the Reform Act
of 1832, Cockburn began to practise in election cases and
published a set of election reports with William Rowe. He
was retained as counsel by the MPs for Coventry, Henry
Lytton Bulwer and Edward Ellice. It was thanks to the latter that he was appointed in 1834 to the municipal corporations commission, being assigned to the north midland
circuit. Some of his reports, written jointly with his fellow
commissioners Whitcombe and Rushton, were of high
quality; but those he undertook alone were less ample in
their detail, and appeared to have had less care bestowed

Sir Alexander James Edmund Cockburn, twelfth baronet
(1802–1880), by Hennah & Kent

on them. His election business introduced him to Joseph Parkes, the Liberal agent, and he would soon cultivate an interest in politics.

Cockburn's election and parliamentary practice was lucrative; but he was also very ambitious. In 1838 he turned down an Indian puisne judgeship worth £2000 a year, saying 'I am going in for something better than that' (Manson, 158). He soon began to reduce his election and parliamentary practice, to concentrate on higher profile cases, and in 1838 became recorder of Southampton. In 1841, the year in which he took silk, he argued successfully for his uncle Sir William Cockburn (1773–1858), the dean of York, in a proceeding against the archbishop of York for illegally depriving the dean on a charge of simony, which had been brought before Dr Phillimore. Two years later, he attracted much wider notice by his successful defence of McNaughten, who was acquitted of the murder of Peel's secretary, Edward Drummond, on the grounds of insanity. In a long and much publicized speech, Cockburn persuaded the jury to accept the view of the experts that the defendant could not tell right from wrong.

Cockburn's taste for high-profile cases continued. In 1844 he appeared for the owners in the celebrated case concerning the racehorse Running Rein. In 1852 he defended John Henry Newman in the libel action brought against him by Achilli, where his opponent was (as it would be in many cases at this time) Sir Frederick Thesiger. In the same year, he was engaged in the Hopwood will

case, in which the court of chancery referred to a Liverpool jury the question whether an elderly testator, with a fortune of £7000 a year, had been of sound mind when disinheriting his eldest son just prior to his death. Cockburn persuaded the jury that he had not. In 1856 he prosecuted William Palmer, a medical man with high gambling debts, in a case where all hinged on circumstantial evidence. Cockburn prepared by studying the effects of poisons day and night, and his mastery of the detail was so thorough that Palmer, who became known as the Rugeley poisoner, attributed his conviction to Cockburn's skill with a racing metaphor: 'It's the riding that has done it' (Yates, 2.131).

In 1847 Cockburn was elected Liberal member of parliament for Southampton. At first he spoke little, save on legal matters. However, in 1850 Palmerston required a cool, legalistic defence of his conduct of the Don Pacifico affair. After Crowder had turned down an invitation to supply this, Cockburn rose to the occasion, delivering the best speech of his life, and in effect saving the government from defeat. This performance secured for Cockburn the post of solicitor-general, which was accompanied in August 1850 by a knighthood. In March 1851 he was promoted to the attorney-generalship, which he retained until the fall of the government one year later. He was reappointed to the post at the beginning of 1853, and became recorder of Bristol in the following year. He was an active member of the government and not slow to assert himself politically: thus, in July 1855, he was one of the main leaders of the group of Liberal MPs who forced Russell to quit the government. However, he was cautious on law reform, as his opposition to J. G. Phillimore's bill in 1855 for a public prosecutor showed.

On the bench With the death of the chief justice of the common pleas, Sir John Jervis, in 1856, Cockburn, as attorney-general, was the obvious successor. However, he hesitated before accepting the post, for it entailed giving up an income at the bar of some £15,000 a year for a salary of £6000, as well as giving up his parliamentary career. At the same time, he did not relish the civil cases which filled the common pleas, not least because he was not a particularly distinguished technical lawyer. Three years later, on Palmerston's return to office, he was made chief justice of the queen's bench. He had in fact hoped to become lord chancellor, but Campbell was preferred. It would not be the only occasion when he would be disappointed at being overlooked for the great seal. On his promotion to the queen's bench, Palmerston offered him a peerage, but Cockburn turned it down, not desiring to hold a peerage as chief justice. The prime minister then promised him that he could have the peerage whenever he wanted it. In 1864 Cockburn asked for the promise to be made good; but the royal household informed the government that 'this peerage has been more than once previously refused upon the ground of the notoriously bad moral character of the Chief Justice' (*Letters of Queen Victoria*, 1.257). Given the queen's sincere disapproval, Cockburn did not press the matter. He had succeeded to the baronetcy held by his uncle in April 1858.

COCKBURN, ALEXANDER JAMES EDMUND

On the bench as at the bar Cockburn relished the lime-light offered by controversial cases. In April 1867 he delivered a six-hour charge to a grand jury at the Old Bailey in the case of Colonel Nelson and Lieutenant Brand, who had been charged with the murder of George William Gordon, executed under the martial law declared in Jamaica by Governor Eyre. Eyre regarded Cockburn's charge as 'violent and partisan', and claimed that the chief justice 'would do all in his power and beyond it to further the ends of the Jamaica Committee' (Heuston, 17). In a carefully reasoned address, Cockburn told the grand jury that the common law knew of no such thing as martial law. Though life might be protected and crime prevented by the immediate application of such force as was necessary under the circumstances, the crown had no power to go further, as Eyre had done. He declared that the seizure of Gordon had been illegal, and that his trial had been marred by improper proceedings. It was indeed an invitation to the grand jury to find the indictment; but in the heated atmosphere of the time, they found no true bill. Cockburn's charge, while lauded in the press for its liberal principles, had potentially disturbing implications for a government facing increasing Fenian hostilities in Ireland; and his views were attacked both by Eyre's supporters in the Lords and by Thomas Carlyle. Moreover, when in June 1868 Eyre himself faced a grand jury, Justice Blackburn took an entirely different view of the law, directing the jury to throw the bill out. Blackburn's assertion that all the judges—including the chief justice—agreed with him earned him a sharp rebuke in court from Cockburn.

Cockburn continued to choose to sit in controversial cases, for, as Bramwell put it, it was his great desire to have a page of *The Times* devoted to him every day. He presided over the case of *Saurin v. Starr* in 1869, when a sister of mercy expelled from her order sued for damages. Coleridge, who appeared in the case, commented that 'Cockburn enjoys the situation and goes on making things longer and longer' (Coleridge, 2.163). He also presided over the trial of the directors of the failed bank of Overend, Gurney & Co. The most controversial trial he handled, however, was the perjury case in 1874 of Arthur Orton, the Tichborne claimant, which followed the collapse of the civil suit where the claims were asserted. From the outset, the defence felt that the chief justice was biased against them—he had, after all, during the civil case, congratulated Coleridge for turning the tide of opinion against the 'monster', by accusing him of being a perjurer and a slanderer. The criminal trial proved long drawn out and difficult, thanks to the confrontational attitude of Orton's lawyer, Dr Edward Vaughan Kenealy, who ferociously attacked the character of many of the witnesses, and even appeared to cast aspersions on the bench. Though he was godfather to one of Kenealy's children, Cockburn was provoked by the barrister into making 'utterances to which a colder and less generous disposition would not have been tempted' (*Solicitors' Journal*, 18, 1874, 337). After many skirmishes during the trial, Cockburn exacted his revenge on Kenealy in his summing-up,

which lasted 18 days, and filled 800 pages in 2 volumes. He began by accusing Kenealy of mis-stating evidence, perverting facts, and attempting to make foul imputations against innocent people, and of abusing the liberty of the bar. Cockburn was playing to the crowd, and his speech was met with suppressed applause. His summing-up ended with a declaration that the jury's verdict would be received as sincere by all, except 'fanatics and fools'—a phrase seized on by the claimant's supporters in the popular press (*The Times*, 2 March 1874, 8).

Cockburn's handling of this case showed up some of his faults as a judge. It was generally agreed that his desire to play to the gallery had prolonged the case, and contributed to its highly charged atmosphere. Many in the profession regretted the overt antagonism shown towards the defence by the judge, and it was felt that too often he had over-ridden rather than over-ruled legal objections. It was not the only case in which it would be observed that Cockburn's 'cursed vanity led him into fireworks for ten minutes, which, to my thinking, spoiled the whole' (Coleridge, 2.167). Nevertheless, when Kenealy in 1874 sought a royal commission to look into the handling of this case, Cockburn's parliamentary friends rallied around him, Disraeli praising him as a 'man of transcendent abilities' (*Hansard 3*, 223, 1874, 1598).

Legal and political controversies In his later years, Cockburn never shied from entering into public controversies on legal matters. Although he professed to desire law reform, his attitude in practice was generally conservative and cautious. In 1870, for instance, he attacked the High Court of Justice Bill, which sought to effect a fusion of the courts of law and equity. While claiming to support the principle, he got the common-law judges to agree to a resolution that 'express provision shall be made as to what the law shall be in each particular instance'—a requirement which would have made fusion impossible. Equally damaging was the opposition of the judges to the government's proposal that the rules of the new court should be left to a committee of unnamed members to work out. The opposition organized by Cockburn—encapsulated in his letter to the Lord Chancellor Hatherley, entitled 'Our judicial system'—effectively delayed the reforms for three years. Cockburn abhorred any idea that the style and title of chief justice might be compromised by the reforms, and remained in office to become the first man to hold the legally recognized title of Lord Chief Justice of England.

In 1871 Cockburn clashed once more with Hatherley, over the appointment of Sir Robert Collier to the judicial committee of the privy council. To help reduce arrears in privy council cases, an act had been passed in 1871 to appoint four salaried members of the privy council, from men who had either been chief justices in India or superior court judges in England. However, since the salary was only £5000 a year, and since the judges would have to pay their own clerks, the government found great difficulty in filling the second common-law judgeship. After three had declined, and after Cockburn had let it be known that no judge would accept, Gladstone decided to offer it to the attorney-general. Collier was duly appointed to the common pleas for two weeks, in order to qualify under the statute for office on the judicial committee. Cockburn was furious, writing to Gladstone that such 'a colourable appointment to a judgeship for the purpose of evading the law appears to me most seriously to compromise the dignity of the judicial office'. The chief justice raised the stakes by publishing the letter in *The Times* (5 Dec 1871). He was especially irritated by the fact that he had only received a curt reply from Gladstone and an uncivil one from Hatherley. In turn, the lord chancellor, a man with a keen sense of decorum, felt mortified by an imputation of corruption coming from a man with Cockburn's reputation, and thought it inappropriate for the chief justice to launch a public attack without first being in full possession of the facts. He was also determined not to be accountable on a political matter to the chief justice, and to wait until the meeting of parliament to explain his actions. When the Lords met in February 1872, Cockburn ensured that his friends would attack Hatherley. However, the government fought back and, incensed by the attack on his conduct by the eighth duke of Argyll, the chief justice threatened to break all links with the government if he did not receive an apology.

In particular, Cockburn threatened to resign from his position as Britain's representative at the Geneva arbitration to settle the United States' claims arising from alleged breaches of neutrality during the American Civil War. The question of compensation had been referred to five arbitrators by the treaty of Washington of 1871, a treaty which Cockburn felt had been ineptly negotiated and badly drafted. He also formed a low opinion of the competence of the other arbitrators, and allowed his irritation to show through, even to the length of insulting them. His view was that they had determined to decide against Great Britain without first listening to the arguments, and without having a sufficiently detailed grasp of the principles of international law. In the end, £3.2 million damages was awarded against Great Britain, with Cockburn recording an elaborate dissent from the report in September 1872. While he admitted Britain's liability for the depredations of the ship the *Alabama* he dissented on the other matters. A peerage was once again made available to Cockburn at this stage. However, he again refused it, in part from his growing dislike of Gladstone, and in part because he did not want to resign as chief justice, and did not want a peerage while he held that office. Instead, in February 1873, he was awarded the grand cross of the Bath.

Cockburn's legal conservatism was seen again in 1874 and 1878 over proposals to codify criminal law. In 1874 he attacked a bill drawn by James Fitzjames Stephen to codify the law of homicide as partial and imperfect, with the result that the bill was withdrawn. Four years later, he sabotaged the codification bill of the criminal law commissioners by writing a letter to the attorney-general in protest. Cockburn took the view that codification was desirable, but that any partial measure which relied at all on common-law principles would merely create confusion. Stephen was furious, suspecting that Cockburn's hostility to the measure was connected to his resentment at having been omitted from the commission, and replied to his critic with an article in the *Nineteenth Century*.

In 1878 Cockburn issued another sharp letter to a judge, this time answering Lord Penzance's comments in *Combe v. Edwards*, which criticized Cockburn for issuing a writ of prohibition against his proceedings as an ecclesiastical judge in *Martin v. Mackonochie*. Though in form a private letter, it was once more an attempt at a public vindication of his own conduct, and was described by *The Times* as 'a singularly unedifying controversy' (22 Nov 1880).

Later life and reputation As a judge, Cockburn did not have the highest reputation. The quip in the legal profession was that he became a first-rate judge, but only by sitting alongside Justice Blackburn. For Selborne, he was 'splendid rather than learned or profound' (Palmer, 1.496), while Coleridge simply said 'I do *not* feel oppressed at having to succeed *him*' (2.300). He was not remembered as a deductive legal logician, but rather as a man of the world who knew how to master detail by hard work and present a rounded picture to the jury.

Nevertheless, Cockburn made a number of important judgments, notably in aspects of public law. In *R. v. Lords Commissioners of the Treasury* (1872), he ruled that the remedy of *mandamus* did not lie against the crown to compel those who held money as agents for the crown to hand it over to those legally entitled to it; and in *Rustomjee v. R.* (1876) he held that a petition of right could not be used to compel the crown to pay compensation acquired under a treaty to those who had suffered the damage to be compensated. In a leading case on the notion of fair comment in libel, *Campbell v. Spottiswoode* (1863), he ruled that it was actionable to say that the editor of a religious magazine who advocated a scheme for missions to the heathen was an impostor, and that his aim was merely a pretext for puffing his magazine, even if the libeller thought it was true. For Cockburn, the law should not sanction attacks on people's honour and character made without any foundation. However, in *Wason v. Walter* (1868), he ruled that fair reports of parliamentary proceedings should not be subjected to the law of libel, even if parts were defamatory. He was keen for the common law to continue to develop with society, and in cases like *Goodwin v. Robarts* (1875) sought to ensure that commercial law kept pace with commercial practice.

A short man, with a large head and an expansive brow, Cockburn had a warm charm, a distinguished air, and a melodious voice. He was highly courteous, witty and eloquent in company, and keen to share anecdotes with his friends, who included Charles Dickens. An enthusiastic follower of music, he generally entertained the prima donnas of the age, and hosted musical evenings for his friends, always retiring late, and rising only in time to rush to court. Cockburn was also a keen sailor, and enjoyed hunting, though more for the company than the shooting. He was the author of a pamphlet entitled *Nationality, or, The Law Relating to Subjects and Aliens* (1869), which discussed the report of the Naturalization Commission of

1868. At the time of his death, he had prepared a work on the authorship of Junius, and was writing a series of articles entitled 'The history of the chase' in the *Nineteenth Century*. An honorary fellow of his college, he was disappointed not to have been elected master of Trinity Hall in 1877, on the death of Dr Geldart. He was, however, chairman of the Cambridge University commission in 1877 and 1878. He continued to devote himself to his work, in spite of three heart attacks and repeated warnings from his doctors, and died suddenly at his home at 40 Hertford Street in Mayfair on 20 November 1880; he was buried six days later at Kensal Green.   MICHAEL LOBBAN

Sources Holdsworth, *Eng. law*, 15.429–43 · *The Times* (5 Dec 1871) · *The Times* (11 Dec 1871) · *The Times* (30 Jan 1874) · *The Times* (2 March 1874) · *The Times* (22 Nov 1880) · *The Times* (26 Nov 1880) · *Law Times* (27 Nov 1880), 68–9 · *Solicitors' Journal*, 18 (1873–4), 336 · *Solicitors' Journal*, 25 (1880–81), 76–7 · R. Palmer, first earl of Selborne, *Memorials. Part II: personal and political, 1865–1895*, ed. S. M. Palmer, 2 vols. (1898) · E. G. Petty-Fitzmaurice, *The life of Granville George Leveson Gower, second Earl Granville*, 2nd edn, 2 vols. (1905) · *The letters of Queen Victoria*, ed. G. E. Buckle, 3 vols., 2nd ser. (1926–8) · E. H. Coleridge, *Life and correspondence of John Duke, Lord Coleridge*, 2 vols. (1904) · T. A. Nash, *The life of Richard, Lord Westbury*, 2 vols. (1888) · W. R. W. Stephens, *A memoir of the Right Hon. William Page Wood, Baron Hatherley*, 2 vols. (1883) · J. B. Atlay, *The Victorian chancellors*, 2 vols. (1906–8) · E. Foss, *Biographia juridica: a biographical dictionary of the judges of England … 1066–1870* (1870) · E. Yates, *His recollections and experiences*, 2 vols. (1884), 2.129–38 · W. P. Lennox, *Celebrities I have known, with episodes political, social, sporting, and theatrical*, 2nd ser., 2 vols. (1877), 1.162–70 · [W. D. I. Foulkes], *A generation of judges* (1886) · 'Eminent members of the bar', *Law Magazine*, 46 (1851), 193–213 · B. Semmel, *The Governor Eyre controversy* (1962) · R. F. V. Heuston, *Lives of the lord chancellors, 1885–1940* (1964) · P. A. Howell, *The judicial committee of the privy council, 1833–1876* (1979) · K. J. M. Smith, *James Fitzjames Stephen: portrait of a Victorian rationalist* (1988) · E. Manson, *Builders of our law during the reign of Queen Victoria*, 2nd edn (1904), 157–66 · W. Ballantine, *Some experiences of a barrister's life*, 2nd–5th edns (1882) · M. E. Kenealy, *The Tichborne tragedy* (1913) · Gladstone, *Diaries* · A. Cook, *The Alabama claims: American politics and Anglo-American relations, 1865–1872* (1975) · Boase, *Mod. Eng. biog.* · Venn, *Alum. Cant.*
Archives Middle Temple, London, ledgers relating to legal practice and MS novel | BL, corresp. with W. E. Gladstone and others · Herts. ALS, letters to E. B. Lytton
Likenesses T. L. Atkinson, mezzotint, pubd 1871, NPG · Faustius, lithograph, *c.*1874, V&A · Ape [C. Pellegrini], chromolithograph caricature, repro. in *VF* (11 Dec 1869) · A. D. Cooper, oils, NPG · Hennah & Kent, photograph, NPG [*see illus.*] · London Stereoscopic Company, carte-de-visite, NPG · D. Maclise, drawing, V&A · G. F. Watts, oils, Trinity Hall, Cambridge; copy, 1895, Middle Temple, London and Trinity Cam. · woodcuts and prints, NPG
Wealth at death under £40,000: probate, 18 Dec 1880, *CGPLA Eng. & Wales* · £2868 15s.: probate, 31 Jan 1881, *CGPLA Ire.*

Cockburn [*née* Rutherford], **Alison** (1712–1794), writer and literary hostess, was born in the mansion house of her father, Robert Rutherford of Fairnalee, Selkirkshire, in the autumn of 1712. In 1731 she married Patrick Cockburn (*d.* 1753), the advocate son of Adam Cockburn of Ormiston, lord justice clerk. The marriage to Cockburn formally ended a romantic attachment to John Aikman, son of the painter William Aikman and a friend of Allan Ramsay. Alison's relationship with Aikman may have been the primary inspiration for her most famous lyrical lament

'Flowers of the Forest', although Sir Walter Scott attributed the occasion of its writing to a series of bankruptcies that devastated several ancient Selkirkshire families.

Although Alison Cockburn wrote poetry and songs throughout her life, only a few of her works were ever published. She seems to have regarded her poems as personal pieces or items to be shared with friends between dinner toasts. The enduring 'Flowers of the Forest', was only published in 1765 and initially not even under her name. When it first appeared many believed it to be an old ballad from the time of Flodden Field. Robert Burns, who recognized it as a more recent production, admired it nevertheless and imitated it in his own 'I dreamed I lay' in 1776.

Like her husband, Patrick, about whom little is known, Alison Cockburn was a whig Presbyterian with no time for the Jacobite inclinations of some of her tory friends and relations. This was a potentially dangerous position at a time of Jacobite activity. Returning by coach from Ravelston, where she visited relations during the Jacobite siege of Edinburgh Castle in 1745, Alison was accosted by the 'grim officer on guard' who proposed a search for 'Whig letters'. In her pocket she carried a squib that she had composed on Bonnie Prince Charlie entitled 'Clout the Caldron'; she was, however, spared the indignity of a search by the Ravelston arms on the coach (Tytler and Watson, 2.79–81).

Patrick Cockburn died on 29 April 1753 and was survived by his wife for another forty years. After her husband's death Alison transferred her residence to Edinburgh, where she helped to mould that city's dinner and drawing-room culture in the same way that a select set of French noblewomen ruled the salons of Paris. Her literary circle included David Hume, Henry Mackenzie, William Robertson, Lord Monboddo, David Dalrymple, John Home, and the young Walter Scott, her cousin on her mother's side. Cockburn lived long enough to act as 'a connecting-link between the Edinburgh of Allan Ramsay and Burns, and the Edinburgh of Scott—her house was the rallying-ground, while she was herself a queen, of the literati of Edinburgh' (Tytler and Watson, 2.179–80).

In the late twentieth century Alison Cockburn's reputation has owed much more to her effervescent correspondence, chronicling her role in the cultural and literary scenes of the day, than to her intermittent poems. Her correspondence is one of the finest sources of information on the changing social etiquette and Edinburgh season, visiting habits, balls and assemblies, and convivial dinners that characterized Edinburgh in the age of improvement and Enlightenment. This correspondence was only interrupted once, under the tragic circumstances of the death in 1780 of her son, Adam. Adam Cockburn had inherited the reserved character and fragile constitution of his father. His mother loved him deeply and one of the few times that her close friendship with David Hume was seriously tested was when her *bon David* failed to use an opportunity to promote her son's interest.

Alison Cockburn's relationship with Hume was one of intimate friendship. She constantly chided him for his atheism, encouraged him to make his famous visit to France, suggested that he bring her 'beloved' Jean-Jacques Rousseau to Scotland, and then took Hume's part against Rousseau when the latter proved a paranoid house guest. She even offered to find Hume a home and a wife when he settled down in Edinburgh. Their relationship was sufficiently close that she felt at ease to offer, whether in jest or in earnest, to 'play at quadrille and sleep with you. Will that do?' (Mossner, 533). Her connection with her cousin Walter Scott was more paternalistic. Their mutual admiration was firmly established when Walter was only six. While visiting Scott's father at his home in George Square, she pronounced the child prodigy 'the most extraordinary genius of a boy I ever saw'. Walter Scott returned the compliment by telling his aunt that Alison Cockburn was 'a *virtuoso* like myself' (Lockhart, 1.119).

As a young woman Alison Cockburn's beauty must have been remarkable. Dignified and charming, she had sufficient wit and vivaciousness to attract considerable attention and was ranked among Edinburgh's most beautiful women in a published piece by a visiting Frenchman. A portrait painted by Anne Forbes in Alison Cockburn's mature years depicts the woman that befriended David Hume—an open but clearly well-bred character with just a hint of sauciness. She died in 1794.   JOHN DWYER

Sources DNB · S. Tytler and J. L. Watson, 'Mrs Cockburn', *The songstresses of Scotland*, 1 (1871) · E. C. Mossner, *The life of David Hume* (1954); repr. (1970) · J. H. Burton, *Life and correspondence of David Hume*, 2 vols. (1846) · Chambers, *Scots.*, rev. T. Thomson (1875) · J. G. Lockhart, *Memoirs of the life of Sir Walter Scott*, [2nd edn], 10 vols. (1839) · W. Scott, *Minstrelsy of the Scottish border* (1839) · *The anecdotes and egotisms of Henry Mackenzie, 1745–1831*, ed. H. W. Thompson (1927); facs. edn (1996) [with introduction by J. Dwyer; incl. introduction by J. Dwyer] · *The Bee, or, Literary Weekly Intelligencer* (1791) · G. Eyre-Todd, ed., *Scottish poetry of the eighteenth century*, 2 vols. (1896); repr. (1997)
Wealth at death not much more than £300: Tytler and Watson, 'Mrs Cockburn'

Cockburn, Archibald (*fl.* 1722), Church of England clergyman and writer, is a figure about whom little is known. In his only published work he describes himself as being 'M.A., rector of the parishes of St Mary Cayon and Christ's Church, Nichola Town, in St. Christopher's' in the Caribbean. Cockburn recounts that at the request of the Hon. William Matthew, lieutenant-governor of the Leeward Islands, he wrote *A Philosophical Essay Concerning the Intermediate State of Blessed Souls* (1722). In this curious work Cockburn discussed the souls of the dead, and especially those which made a physical appearance to the living. As a later commentator noted, the author was very metaphysical, 'and firmly believed in ghosts and apparitions' (Noble, 3.141). It is not known when he died.
        GORDON GOODWIN, rev. ROBERT BROWN

Sources *A biographical history of England, from the revolution to the end of George I's reign: being a continuation of the Rev. J. Granger's work*, ed. M. Noble, 3 vols. (1806) · A. Cockburn, *A philosophical essay concerning the intermediate state of blessed souls* (1722)

Cockburn, Catharine. *See* Trotter, Catharine (1674?–1749).

Cockburn, (Francis) Claud (1904–1981), writer and journalist, was born at the British embassy in Peking (Beijing) on 12 April 1904, the younger child and only son of Henry Cockburn CB, Chinese secretary in the diplomatic service in Peking and later consul-general in Korea, and his wife, Elizabeth Gordon, daughter of Colonel Stevenson. He was the great-grandson of Henry, Lord Cockburn, the Scottish lawyer. At the age of four he was sent to Scotland with his Chinese nanny to be cared for by his grandmother. His father retired from the diplomatic service in 1909 and, after renting a number of houses, eventually settled near Tring, Hertfordshire. Cockburn was sent to Berkhamsted School where Charles Greene was headmaster. He became a close friend of Greene's son Graham, with whom he shared a liking for mischief-making and adventure stories, especially the yarns of John Buchan, in which brilliant but corrupted villains seek to overthrow the established order from within. Graham Greene's younger brother, Hugh Carleton Greene, was a pupil of Cockburn's when he briefly took over the classical sixth form during an Oxford vacation and remembered him as the most brilliant teacher he ever encountered.

Cockburn entered Keble College, Oxford, where he obtained second classes in classical honour moderations (1924) and *literae humaniores* (1926). At Oxford he joined the 'smart set' which included Robert Byron, Evelyn Waugh (a cousin), and Harold Acton. With Graham Greene he also joined the Communist Party, as a joke, in the vain hope of travelling to Russia. In 1926 he won a travelling scholarship from Queen's College, Oxford. He went to France and then Germany, where he attached himself to *The Times*'s correspondent Norman Ebbutt. His experiences in Germany kindled an interest in politics, and after reading the communist anthology *Against the Stream* he first felt attracted to Marxism. In 1929 he accepted a full-time post on *The Times*, the setting of many of his best stories. They featured a sub-editor who spent a whole day researching the correct spelling of Kuala Lumpur, and his own victory in a competition for the most boring headline with 'Small earthquake in Chile: not many dead' (although this became part of Fleet Street folklore, it has to be said that extensive research failed to locate it in *The Times*'s back numbers).

In 1929 Cockburn went to New York as the *Times* correspondent, occasionally reporting from Washington. There he stood in for the well-known reporter Willmott Lewis, who gave him what he always regarded as an essential piece of advice:

> I think it well to remember that when writing for the newspapers, we are writing for an elderly lady in Hastings who has two cats of which she is passionately fond. Unless our stuff can successfully compete for her interest with those cats, it is no good.

Meanwhile, influenced by the Wall Street crash and subsequent depression he became more and more drawn towards Marxism. In 1932 Cockburn married the left-wing American journalist Hope Hale, daughter of Hal Hale, high school principal and superintendent of schools, and his wife, Frances, *née* MacFarland. They had a daughter,

Claudia, who married the humorous songwriter Michael Henry Flanders (1922–1975). Cockburn also had a daughter, Sarah Caudwell *Cockburn (1939–2000), with Jean Iris *Ross (1911–1973), who inspired the character of Sally Bowles in Christopher Isherwood's *Goodbye to Berlin* (1939).

Shortly after his first marriage, however, Cockburn returned to England, gave up his employment on *The Times*, and joined the Communist Party—this time in earnest. He now embarked on his most successful venture, *The Week*, a cyclostyled news-sheet inspired by the French satirical paper *Le Canard Enchaîné*. Started on a capital of £50 provided by his Oxford friend Benvenuto Sheard, the paper, which was all his own work, was produced in a one-room office at 34 Victoria Street, and was obtainable only by subscription. Although he relied on information supplied by a number of foreign correspondents including Negley Farson (*Chicago Daily News*) and Paul Scheffer (*Berliner Tageblatt*), it was his own journalistic flair which gave the paper its unique influence. Cockburn was not an orthodox journalist. He pooh-poohed the notion of facts as if they were nuggets of gold waiting to be unearthed. It was, he believed, the inspiration of the journalist which supplied the story. Speculation, rumour, even guesswork, were all part of the process and an inspired phrase was worth reams of cautious analysis. (It was Cockburn who coined the expression 'the Cliveden set' to describe the pro-appeasement lobby.) In other hands it might have been a fatal approach, but Cockburn had great flair, and although many stories in *The Week* were fanciful, there was enough important information to win it an influence out of all proportion to its circulation. Cockburn boasted eventually among his subscribers the foreign ministers of eleven nations, all the embassies in London, King Edward VIII, Charles Chaplin, and the nizam of Hyderabad.

At the same time as producing *The Week* Cockburn joined the staff of the *Daily Worker* in 1935 as diplomatic correspondent, reporting the Spanish Civil War under the pseudonym of Frank Pitcairn. Following the declaration of war in 1939 the government suppressed the *Daily Worker* and *The Week*, although they were both later allowed to resume publication once the USSR became one of the allies. The new situation, which conferred respectability on the communists, was not to Cockburn's liking, and his Marxist fervour began to wane. He was further influenced by an interview with Charles de Gaulle in Algeria in 1943, in which the general suggested that his loyalty to the communist movement might perhaps be 'somewhat romantic'. Following the Labour victory in 1945 he became convinced that the communists were ineffective as a political force.

Cockburn's first marriage had ended in divorce in 1935, and in 1940 he married Patricia, the daughter of Major John Bernard Arbuthnot, of the Scots Guards, and his wife, Olive Blake. A highly resourceful and energetic woman, who had been an explorer in her youth, Patricia helped to support her husband, who was invariably short of money, first by selling ponies and then by making shell

pictures. They had three sons, all of whom became journalists.

In 1946 Cockburn decided to burn his boats, giving up his job on the *Daily Worker* and retiring with Patricia to her home town of Youghal in co. Cork. The move suited him well as, having spent so much of his life abroad, he had never felt part of the English scene. But despite resigning from the *Daily Worker* he never formally renounced communism. He wrote several novels including (as James Helvick) *Beat the Devil* (1953), which John Huston made into a film starring Humphrey Bogart. In 1953 Anthony Powell, an Oxford contemporary, introduced him to the then editor of *Punch*, Malcolm Muggeridge, who became a close friend. Cockburn contributed humorous articles for several years and later became a regular columnist on the *Sunday Telegraph*. In 1963 he was guest editor of *Private Eye* at the height of the scandal involving John Profumo, and continued to write for the magazine until his death.

Cockburn was a man of great charm, modest, unassuming, and possessed of a schoolboyish zest for life. His appearance was donnish and with his deep bass voice he spoke in staccato bursts in the manner of Mr Jingle in *The Pickwick Papers*. Both in conversation and in print he was an anecdotalist. His three volumes of highly diverting memoirs are full of very entertaining stories (many of them embellished over the years) as well as containing valuable and profound reflections on politics and journalism. During the final decade of his life he suffered from increasingly bad health. But his constitution was remarkably tough and he survived attacks of tuberculosis, cancer, duodenal ulcers, and emphysema before he died on 15 December 1981 in St Finbarr's Hospital, Cork. For one whose life had been so full of ironies, it was fitting that five priests celebrated a requiem mass for him in Youghal, although he had been a committed atheist.

RICHARD INGRAMS, *rev.*

Sources F. C. Cockburn, *In time of trouble* (1956) · F. C. Cockburn, *Crossing the line* (1958) · F. C. Cockburn, *Cockburn sums up* (1981) · P. Cockburn, *The years of the week* (1968) · P. Cockburn, *Figure of eight* (1985) · personal knowledge (1990) · private information (1990)

Cockburn, Sir George (1763–1847), army officer and writer, eldest son of George Cockburn, and his wife, the eldest daughter of Charles Caldwell and a sister of Admiral Sir Benjamin Caldwell GCB, was born in Dublin. He was commissioned ensign in the 1st, afterwards the Grenadier Guards, on 9 May 1781, and in 1782 went to Gibraltar, where he was aide-de-camp to General Eliott during the siege. For his services he was promoted captain-lieutenant in the 105th regiment in 1784, and transferred in 1785 to the 65th, then quartered in Dublin. His new colonel, the earl of Harrington, took a great fancy to the young man, and instead of letting him go to Canada with the rest of the regiment in June 1785, he kept him at home for recruiting duties, and sent him to study the Prussian autumn manoeuvres. In the following years he went to Austria, France, and in 1788 to Spain for the same reason, and in March 1790 was promoted captain in the 5th (Royal Irish) light dragoons. He married in 1790 the eldest daughter of Phineas Riall. In the same year he was made major of the royal Irish independent invalids, and in November 1793 was transferred to the 92nd, of which he purchased the lieutenant-colonelcy in the following month, and soon after went on half pay. In 1797 he was promoted colonel, in 1803 major-general, and from 1806 to 1810 held a command in the northern district.

In April 1810 Cockburn was appointed to the command of a division in the army of occupation in Sicily, and took charge of Messina, but his period of command was short, and in November, on his promotion to lieutenant-general, he had to resign. Previously, however, he had been present at the defeat of Cavaignac's division when it attempted to land in Sicily, but the chief credit for this action is due to the adjutant-general, James Campbell. Cockburn then travelled in Sicily, and on his return to England published two illustrated volumes called *A voyage to Cadiz and Gibraltar, up the Mediterranean to Sicily and Malta in 1810 and 1811, including a description of Sicily and the Lipari Islands, and an excursion in Portugal.*

On leaving Sicily, Cockburn settled down at Shanganah Castle, near Bray, co. Wicklow, which he had purchased, and began to devote himself to politics. He was initially a radical reformer and admirer of Cobbett, and erected a column in his grounds in memory of the Reform Bill, which he speedily demolished when the whigs ceased to please him. He became a supporter of Sir Robert Peel. In 1821 he was made a KCH by George IV, and in 1831 William IV made him a GCH, more for his activity as a magistrate than for his military services. In 1843 he published a pamphlet, praised at the time, *A Dissertation on the State of the British Finances*, in which he advocated banknotes be issued by government and not the Bank of England. In 1846 he issued another, in which he examined such historical puzzles as Hannibal's passage over the Alps, and the authorship of the *Letters of Junius*, which he ascribed, on the testimony of Dr Parr, to Charles Lloyd. In 1821 Cockburn was promoted general. When he died at Shanganah Castle, on 18 August 1847, he was fourth general in seniority in the British army.

H. M. STEPHENS, *rev.* STEWART M. FRASER

Sources *GM*, 2nd ser., 28 (1847), 539 · G. Cockburn, *A voyage to Cadiz and Gibraltar*, 2 vols. (1815) · R. Muir, *Britain and the defeat of Napoleon, 1807–1815* (1996)
Archives BL, journals and papers, Add. MSS 48316–48339 · NAM, papers relating to Chelmsford depot; legal corresp. | BL, letters to Sir Robert Peel, Add. MSS 40235–40549 · NA Scot., corresp. with Lord Melville · NL Scot., corresp. with Sir Thomas Cochrane

Cockburn, Sir George, eighth baronet (1772–1853), naval officer, second son of Sir James Cockburn, sixth baronet (*d.* 1804), and his second wife, Augusta Anne Ayscough, was born in Middlesex and brought up in a family of eight children and educated at schools in Marylebone and Margate. He also attended the Royal Navigational School in Old Burlington Street, London. At the age of nine he was entered as captain's servant on the books of the frigate *Resource* and afterwards of the yacht *William and Mary*, but he only went to sea in 1786. After serving in the channel and East Indies, he was confirmed in the rank of lieutenant on 2 January 1793. In June he was appointed as one of

Sir George Cockburn, eighth baronet (1772–1853), by John James Halls, 1817

the lieutenants of the *Victory*, Lord Hood's flagship off Toulon; in October he was promoted to the command of the sloop *Speedy*; and on 20 February 1794 he was posted to the frigate *Meleager*, which served in relaying signals in Hotham's two actions off Toulon, on 14 March and 13 July 1795. For the following twelve months the *Meleager* was employed in the Gulf of Genoa, under the orders of Captain Nelson, whose patronage Cockburn won by his 'zeal, ability and courage' (Nicolas, 2.176–7), for which in August 1796 he was moved into the *Minerve*, a large frigate lately captured from the French. That December, when Nelson was sent from Gibraltar to relieve the garrison of Elba, he hoisted his commodore's broad pennant in the *Minerve*, which, on 20 December, in company with the *Blanche* off Cartagena, captured the Spanish frigate *Sabina*. On her return, passing the straits of Gibraltar, the *Minerve* ran through the Spanish fleet and joined the fleet under Sir John Jervis the day before the battle of Cape St Vincent, at which the *Minerve* was present, though without any active participation. Cockburn remained in the Mediterranean until the peace, and the *Minerve* captured, or assisted in capturing, several of the enemy's privateers and smaller ships of war, more especially the frigates *Succès* and

Bravoure, which were driven ashore on the coast of Italy on 2 September 1801.

In July 1803 Cockburn was appointed to the *Phaeton*, which he commanded for the next two years in the East Indies. In July 1806 he was appointed to the *Captain*, and in March 1808 to the *Pompée*, in which in September he went out to the West Indies, where in the following February he assisted in the reduction of Martinique. In 1809 he commanded the flotilla of gunboats and bomb-vessels which co-operated with the army in the capture of Flushing, and which covered its retreat as it withdrew from the Scheldt. On his return he married his cousin Mary Cockburn on 28 November 1809; they had one surviving daughter, Augusta Harriot Mary. In February 1810 Cockburn was appointed to the *Indefatigable* and ordered to Quiberon Bay, where on 7 March he landed two agents who had undertaken to effect the escape of the king of Spain, then imprisoned in the castle of Valençay. However, these men were speedily arrested. The *Indefatigable* subsequently sailed for Cadiz, then besieged by the French, against whom in August 1812 Cockburn commanded the boats of the fleet in an amphibious attack on the town of Moguer. He was afterwards sent to Havana, Cuba, in charge of two Spanish three-deckers, and on his return was, in November 1811, appointed to act as a commissioner in the attempted mediation between Spain and its South American colonies. The attempt proved impracticable, and the commission was dissolved in August 1812.

Advanced to the rank of rear-admiral, with his flag in the *Marlborough*, Cockburn was ordered first to command the squadron off Cadiz, then in November, with the outbreak of war with the United States, to Bermuda, where Sir J. B. Warren, the commander-in-chief, sent him with a small squadron to attack the enemy in the Chesapeake. Here the war took the form of attacks by landing parties on selected economic and military targets. The squadron forced its way to the head of the Chesapeake and was in regular conflict with the American militia, especially at Havre de Grace, Georgetown, and Frederickstown.

In August 1814 Cockburn accompanied the joint naval and military force under Major-General Ross, which after the battle of Bladensburg seized the city of Washington for twenty-four hours. By then familiar with operations on shore, Cockburn provided support and guidance to the army throughout the campaign, for which, in reporting its success, Ross credited him with the idea of the attack on Washington. However, the idea had long been part of the strategy of Sir Alexander Cochrane, who succeeded Warren as commander-in-chief on the North American station early in 1814. Cockburn also accompanied Ross in the subsequent advance against Baltimore, and was with him in the skirmish on 12 September in which Ross was mortally wounded. Between January and March 1815, while Cochrane attempted to take New Orleans, Cockburn undertook diversionary attacks on the coast of Georgia from a base on Cumberland Island.

Cockburn was recalled to England following the conclusion of peace, only to find, on anchoring at Spithead on 4 May, that war with France had again broken out. He was

ordered to hoist his flag on board the *Northumberland* and to convey Napoleon to St Helena, which he reached on 15 October. He remained there as governor of the island and commander-in-chief of the Cape of Good Hope station until the summer of 1816, when he was relieved by Sir Hudson Lowe and Sir Pulteney Malcolm. Having been nominated a KCB in January 1815, he was made GCB on 20 February 1818, became vice-admiral on 12 August 1819, and was elected a fellow of the Royal Society in 1820. He was a junior lord of the Admiralty between April 1818 and May 1827, a member of the council of the lord high admiral between May 1827 and September 1828, and then first naval lord until November 1830. In 1828 it was principally Cockburn, as the leading council member and a privy councillor, who brought about the resignation of the duke of Clarence as lord high admiral for exceeding the terms of his patent.

Although a tory, Cockburn served under the whigs as commander-in-chief on the North America and West Indies station between March 1833 and May 1836. He became a full admiral on 10 January 1837, and, although aged sixty-nine, he returned to the Admiralty as first naval lord from September 1841 until July 1846. There, far from being the reactionary as which he was later depicted by Sir John Briggs, he ensured that the latest steam and screw technology adopted by the Royal Navy was appropriate to its requirements. He maintained the navy's traditional priority of professionalism over politics in appointments, and held as a prime criterion for professionalism the ability to manage seamen without the need to resort to physical punishment. He was, when there was no alternative, for long a champion of impressment, but he had, by the time of his retirement, contributed to the system of examining masters and mates of merchant ships for their competency, the registration of which later joined the register of seamen, transferred from the Admiralty to the Board of Trade, to permit the foundation of a naval reserve.

Cockburn's views were fluently expressed in the House of Commons, in which he became tory MP for Portsmouth in 1818, for Weobley in 1820, for Plymouth in 1828, and for Ripon in 1841. He became admiral of the fleet on 1 July 1851. On 26 February 1852, by the death of his brother James without a son, he succeeded to the family baronetcy, a dignity he enjoyed until his death on 19 August 1853. Cockburn was buried in Kensal Green cemetery. He was succeeded in the baronetcy by his brother William, dean of York. He was survived by his wife, Mary, who died in January 1859. His daughter, Augusta, married Commander J. C. Hoseason, his adviser on steam technology, in 1856.   J. K. LAUGHTON, *rev.* ROGER MORRISS

Sources R. Morriss, *Cockburn and the British navy in transition* (1997) · W. James, *The naval history of Great Britain, from the declaration of war by France in 1793, to the accession of George IV*, [4th edn], 6 vols. (1847), vol. 6 · J. Pack, *The man who burned the White House* (1987) · J. Drinkwater Bethune, *A narrative of the battle of St Vincent with anecdotes of Nelson*, 2nd edn (1840) · D. G. Shomette, *Flotilla: battle for the Patuxent* (1981) · L. de Evans, *Facts relating to the capture of Washington … by an officer serving as quarter-master general with the forces engaged* (1829) · O'Byrne, *Naval biog. dict.* · Burke, *Peerage* · C. J. Bartlett, *Great Britain and sea power, 1815–1853* (1963) · A. D. Lambert, *The last* *sailing battlefleet: maintaining naval mastery, 1815–1850* (1991) · *The dispatches and letters of Vice-Admiral Lord Viscount Nelson*, ed. N. H. Nicolas, 7 vols. (1844–6)

Archives L. Cong., corresp., logbooks, and papers · NMM, corresp. and journals; journal | BL, corresp. with Sir Robert Peel, Add. MSS 40342–40608 · BL, corresp. with Lord Wellesley, Add. MSS 37291–37310 · Lpool RO, letters to Lord Stanley · NA Scot., letters to Thomas, Lord Cochrane · NL Scot., corresp. with Sir David Milne · NMM, corresp. with John Wilson Croker; corresp. with Lord Minto; letters to Sir Watkin Pell · U. Mich., Clements L., letters to Sir Robert Barrie

Likenesses J. J. Halls, oils, 1817, NMM [*see illus.*] · W. Beechey, oils, 1820, NMM · T. W. Mackay, oils, 1851; formerly at United Service Club [c/o The Crown Commissioners] · J. Lucas, oils, Gov. Art Coll. · C. Turner, mezzotint, BM, NPG; repro. in E. P. Brenton, *The naval history of Great Britain* (1825)

Cockburn, Henry, Lord Cockburn (1779–1854)

Cockburn, Henry, **Lord Cockburn** (**1779–1854**), author and judge, was born in or near Edinburgh, on 26 October 1779, the son of Archibald Cockburn (*d.* 1820), and his wife, Janet Rannie. His father was one of the learned lairds who made up the country's *noblesse de robe*, a sheriff of Edinburghshire and a baron of Scotland's court of exchequer, a queller of riots, and a tory: Archibald Cockburn was the cousin and brother-in-law of Henry Dundas—minister of the younger Pitt and pro-consul of North Britain—and his marriage was witnessed by Dundas and by the ferocious judge Lord Braxfield, later arraigned in the writings of his son. Cockburn's principal vein was narrative history, the annals of his time, with reminiscence giving way eventually to the journal record of 'occurrences as they have arisen'. But he was a man of many parts, and his first fame was achieved as an advocate and politician who became a judge and a minister of the crown and who was a participant witness of two profoundly interesting public contentions: the passing of the Reform Bill in 1832 and the Disruption of 1843, when schism struck the Church of Scotland over the issue of patronage—decried as the intrusive appointment by landlords of ministers of the kirk.

Education and early influences Cockburn (nicknamed Cocky) attended Edinburgh high school and Edinburgh University, where he came under the influence of the moral philosopher Dugald Stewart, and shone as a debater in the university's Speculative and Academical societies. His experiences at what he remembered as a brutal, flogging school were to be reflected in the part he played in the foundation of an alternative institution, the Edinburgh Academy, in 1823 (he was also to serve as rector of Glasgow University and as a founder of the Commercial Bank, and was to have an Edinburgh street named after him). His education was summarized in one of his inspired exaggerations: he was 'kept about nine years at two dead languages which we did *not* learn' (*Memorials*, 19).

In 1796 Cockburn's father approached Dundas with a request that the small sinecure of presentership of signatures be bestowed on his son, in order to assist his legal studies. 'Your namesake Henry,' wrote Archibald Cockburn, 'in spite of every remonstrance and some degree of severity on my part, persists in being a limb of the Law'

Henry Cockburn, Lord Cockburn (**1779–1854**), by Sir John Watson-Gordon, exh. Royal Scottish Academy 1853

(Miller, 56). The post was denied him, but Cockburn persevered, and he passed advocate in 1800. He began to practise at the time when the *Edinburgh Review*, edited by Francis Jeffrey, began to appear. Jeffrey and John Richardson, a solicitor poet, were his closest friends, and Jeffrey's virtues are sung in his correspondence and in his *Life of Lord Jeffrey* (1852).

Cockburn testified that the 1790s were a time when the life of his community was steeped in a single event—the French Revolution. This event, and the sedition trials which were aimed at the punishment of Jacobin and reformist sympathies and which are discussed in a book of his published in 1888, helped to make a whig of him, to turn him, politically, against 'my kindred'. He shared Jeffrey's perception of a growing struggle between the aristocracy and democracy of Britain, and his wish for an accommodation, for the 'tranquillity' which the Reform Bill was later designed to secure. A decade after the presentership affair, the Dundases offered Cockburn a post as one of the lord advocate's deputes, which he accepted on the understanding that party loyalty would not be expected of him. His political opinions were deemed 'a mere youthful fervour' by his kin; his fear that they might think so 'only made the fervour warmer'. In 1810 he was sacked for insubordination. The following year, Dundas wrote of Cockburn's whiggery: 'Nobody can give me a reason how it began or why it continues' (Fry, 305).

A reforming advocate Cockburn's main purposes as a reformer were to bring about a wider parliamentary franchise, more and fairer juries, and an elected clergy. Parliamentary reform meant the enfranchisement of 'wealth and sense'. It also meant the prevention of revolution, and indeed of democracy. In his fervour, Cockburn foresaw a Scottish millennium over which flew the whig flag of 'sense and justice'. And yet his adult years can be considered those of a divided man. He was in love with the old feudal Scotland he was determined to change. His reason was with 'the modern world'; his dreams were with 'the old one'. His love for the old one is affirmed in the *Memorials*, which he started to prepare shortly after his father's death in 1820, at the point when northern politics awoke from the spell of Dundas-ship and 'our Scotch progress' started to accelerate; and his darkening view of the aftermath of reform is projected in the *Journal*. Cockburn's contradictions were an important aspect of his life. He was a patrician iconoclast, an Anglophile Scots patriot, and a classical romantic. He was both the enemy and the friend of Scotland's landlords.

In March 1811 Cockburn married Elizabeth MacDowall and set up his rural household gods at Bonaly in the lee of the Pentland hills, to the south-west of Edinburgh. Five daughters and six sons were born. His house in Charlotte Square stood at the heart of Edinburgh's new town, then under construction, from which he would sometimes recoil, thinking it unromantically commercial and mathematical. 'Nature and romance' were pursued at Bonaly, Cockburn's more modest Abbotsford, a farmhouse augmented by a peel tower. Bonaly was a convivial place, with its 'bouzes' and 'bowlifications'. But it was also a place where this public man could shed what he saw as the needful 'pugnacity' of his political and professional involvements, and be by himself. As did his recourse to the past, the Pentlands belonged in some measure to the category of dreams.

Cockburn's country pleasures are embodied in a series of youthful poems. These show none of that hostility to Romanticism for which the *Edinburgh Review* has been blamed, and can be credited with a feeling for Wordsworth. Extracts from 'Tintern Abbey' are the opening items in a commonplace book, a huge cento of favourite passages of verse, copied out by Cockburn and a circle of Pentlands friends and friends of the Pentlands, of whigs and of whig romantics.

Cockburn was an admired advocate, and was depicted as gaining the trust of juries by displays of homeliness, and by pleading in Scots and, at times, in tears. Two of his greatest occasions were his appearances for James Stuart of Dunearn, in 1821, and, seven years later, for Helen Mac-Dougal, the companion of body-snatching Burke, the

'resurrectionist' serial killer. Stuart had shot dead Boswell's son Alexander in a party-political duel, and Cockburn's defence was reckoned a masterpiece of forensic praise and pathos; at the time of the Burke and Hare trial, Stuart, once 'thought so pure and firm', as Cockburn observed, was revealed as a speculator who had run off to America in debt. Cockburn also spoke for western weavers accused of sedition. One of their number, Alexander Richmond, supported by Cockburn and Jeffrey, would appear to have served as a government spy.

With reference to Scotland's special backwardness in electoral matters, and to the crisis which overtook the Reform Bill in 1832, Cockburn wrote:

> The feeling of Scotland, whose *all*, as to representation, was at stake, was deep, intense and grave … It was an old covenanting business with them; who the Reform Bill brought literally out of the land of Egypt, out of the house of bondage.   (Miller, *Millennium*, 36)

This business was soon to succeed, and thus abolish the supremacy evoked in the best-known passage of the *Memorials*: 'Within this Pandemonium sat the town-council, omnipotent, corrupt, impenetrable. Nothing was beyond its grasp; no variety of opinion disturbed its unanimity, for the pleasure of Dundas was the sole rule for every one of them' (*Memorials*, 87–8). A Venetian cast is imparted here to Edinburgh's town council. In 1823, in the course of a continental tour, he had seen Venice for himself: by then, the 'impenetrable' mystery and secrecy which had enclosed the regime of the Doges, according to certain historians of the time, had been extinguished by Napoleon.

Church reform and law reform As Scotland's solicitor-general and lord advocate respectively, in the Grey administration of 1830–34, Cockburn and Jeffrey were charged with drafting the Scottish Reform Bill. For both men 'benchification' took place in 1834, and as lords of session they were caught up in a further momentous struggle. The evangelical (or 'wild') party had won an ascendancy in the general assembly of the Church of Scotland, and their opponents in the country, the moderates, were to challenge on civil grounds the Church legislation in favour of popular election in the kirks, which resulted from their ascendancy. This became a question of controverted parishes and disputed pastoral 'calls'. The battle of wills lasted until 1843, when the 'wild' (some 200 ministers and elders, almost half of the general assembly) broke away to form the Free Church.

For Cockburn, kirk was country, and his *Journal* accounts of the Disruption make this clear, as do the votes he cast in the course of the court's relevant adjudications. Patronage was the law of the land, and he could take the view that the court was asserting a rightful claim in respect of temporalities—manses and livings. But he could also see it as overreaching itself. The anti-intrusionist cause was, like parliamentary reform, a modern example of the old covenanting business of the seventeenth century. His was a patriotic piety. He was an opponent of religious intolerance, and was displeased by 'covenanting sublimities' and by the bletheraciousness of the cloth; but he was moved by the courage and idealism of the departing ministers and their flocks.

Among Cockburn's writings in the field of law reform is a discussion in the *Edinburgh Review* (April 1830) of the state of the Scottish legal system. The introduction of juries in civil causes, as in English law, was one of his foremost concerns. A civil jury court was formed in 1815 and was later merged with the court of session. Cockburn argued against the judiciary's power to pack juries, and against the exercise of its 'native vigour'—in effect, a law-making capacity, which had developed in reaction to a parliamentary neglect of Scotland. While harbouring mixed feelings on the subject, he welcomed the end of entails, seen as a constraint on capital investment.

Cockburn took a by no means progressive interest in the poor laws of his time, and questioned (in vain) the assessment of landowners in order to relieve distress, believing that compulsory provision on a regular basis tends 'to increase the very evil which it is meant to cure' (*Edinburgh Review*, October 1824). He was in sympathy with the position taken by one of his statesmanlike sages, the evangelical leader Thomas Chalmers, with regard to the virtues of self-help, as exemplified between 1819 and 1823 in the Glasgow parish of St John's. On the question of trade-union combination, he judicially upheld the innocence of strikes, while saying of one aspect of their coerciveness: 'It is *impossible* to defend a combination which is kept up by concussing me to join it' (Miller, 42).

The modern world, with the swiftness of its railroads and its mass migration to urban centres, reminded Cockburn of a well-known Scottish whirlpool: 'All things now are melted in one sea—with a strong Corryvreckan in it, sweeping everything towards the metropolis' (*Journal*, 2.91). There were improvements which he abhorred, such as 'furious communication', and he was an early environmentalist whose concern for his native city gave rise to the modest proposal set out in his 'Letter to the lord provost on the best ways of spoiling the beauty of Edinburgh' (1849). He was drawn to the new art of photography, and was portrayed not only in oils by Sir Henry Raeburn, in 1819, but in the calotypes of Octavius Hill and Robert Adamson.

Reputation and achievement A pugnacious and triumphant reformer like Cockburn was bound to arouse an answering pugnacity; lawyers in particular have sometimes been keen to put him on trial. A certain impatience on the bench, and an inaptitude for the intricacies of feudal law and the practicalities of Scottish life, have been laid at his door. Errors committed in the huddled circumstances which vexed the drafting of the Scottish Reform Bill have been thought to have subverted, and inverted, its designed effects. Among his critics was Patrick Fraser, who spoke of his indolence and love of enjoyment. The House of Lords, on appeal, sustained judgments of his which had been reversed by his colleagues at the court of session, and Fraser says of this: 'The utterly untechnical character of his mind made his judgements read in the eyes of a foreign lawyer with a force not due to their intrinsic merits' (Miller, 51, 248). But it was also said in

mitigation that no one by 'fits and starts' could make greater efforts. His alleged indolence might seem to be corroborated by a story which supposes him to have told a Pentlands shepherd, 'If I were a sheep, I would lie on the sunny side of the hill', and to have received the reply: 'Ah, my Lord, but if ye was a sheep, ye would hae mair sense.' The same reply was said by John Buchan, in 1940, to have been directed by a border shepherd at Gladstone.

Like other prominent Scotsmen of his generation, such as James Stuart and Walter Scott, Cockburn fell into debt, and late in life he was smitten with the need to retrench. A testament of 1847 states that 'there cannot be another shilling of debt', and that 'I can be plucked by sons no more'. The theme of an estranged kinship was one which stayed with him throughout his life. He died at Bonaly on 26 April 1854 and was buried in Dean cemetery. After his death, Bonaly and its contents were sold. Three years earlier Cockburn had written to a friend that he had had a very happy life.

For reasons of discretion Cockburn burnt many of his papers, and a son destroyed the original manuscripts for the *Memorials* and the *Journal*, derived from four 'red books' of his which have also gone. For similar reasons, the *Memorials* was pruned of some of Cockburn's outspokenness by its sheriff editors, Archibald Davidson and Thomas Cleghorn. Nevertheless, specimens of his writing which contain expurgated material have survived, as has a body of unpublished letters to friends. His portrait of the judge Lord Eskgrove, magnificent in its abbreviated form, is even more so as originally intended. In the passage that follows, deleted expressions that might have come from Cockburn's great-great-grandson Evelyn *Waugh are restored and shown in italics:

> His eyes were blue, and half cunning, half maudlin; the under lip enormous, and supported on a huge clumsy chin, which moved like the jaw of an exaggerated Dutch toy; his nose prodigious, *and absolutely purple with lust and liquor*. He walked with a slow, stealthy, sinister step, *as if conscious he was going to do what was wrong*—something between a walk and a hirple, and helped himself on by short movements of his elbows, backwards and forwards, like fins   (Bell, 176)

The power of Cockburn's calm and confident prose is evident here, together with its pungent idiosyncrasy, which is also evident in an epistolary passage on the removal of a public lavatory when his heavenly city of Edinburgh was undergoing its process of extension, a removal which coincided with the motion for reform in the Augean stables of the House of Commons: 'I must confess that walking out yesterday to the Foul Brig I saw the sun glittering three times on a large, distant, whitish object, which, being neared, turned out to be a bum.' This is the Cockburn who beheld George IV, at his Holyrood levee of 1822, 'in a *kilt* !!! … Bare or trousered, the knees were undoubtedly philabegged' (Bell, 14, 177).

Cockburn did something to bring about a more widely representative politics and a more responsible public life, and he took part in a struggle which embroiled the law of the land, the government of the day, and a national institution intent on its independence. He was a superb historian of these exemplary conflicts. No less valuable are his accounts of the manners of his day—of the regional Scotland described in his *Circuit Journeys* (1888), and of the seasonal Edinburgh life of his adult years. In summer, at Bonaly, 'we sauntered in the twilight of a mild, milky evening, amid a glorious profusion of breathing roses of every description' (Miller, 67). But winter had its glories too: 'Fall, thou snow—blacken, thou surly dark-souled night! Is it not Saturday? Have we not coals and claret, talk and time?' (Bell, 21).

Such raptures may occasionally be thought to smack of the 'withering self-sufficiency' ascribed by Sir Archibald Alison to these Scottish whigs. But Cockburn and Jeffrey were, as Scott in his toryism conceded, extraordinary men, and so were their friends, in whom, as in Cockburn and Jeffrey themselves, the likeness of a latter-day Scottish Enlightenment can be found. Cockburn was sombre and thoughtful, as well as happy, as well as supple and wiry and sparkling, and he was no crony. With new and enlarged editions of his annals, and with a collected edition of his letters, a wider recognition of his qualities might be hoped for. An attempt was made to contribute to this in publications of the mid-1970s, where he was praised as the Tacitus of Scotland. KARL MILLER

Sources *Memorials of his time*, by Henry Cockburn (1909); repr. with introduction by K. F. C. Miller (1974) · *Journal of Henry Cockburn: being a continuation of the 'Memorials of his time', 1831–1854*, 2 vols. (1874) · H. Cockburn, *Life of Lord Jeffrey, with a selection from his correspondence*, 2 vols. (1852) · H. Cockburn, *Circuit journeys* (1888) · H. Cockburn, *An examination of the trials for sedition ... in Scotland*, 2 vols. (1888) · *Letters chiefly connected with the affairs of Scotland between Henry Cockburn and Thomas Kennedy* (1874) · *Some letters of Lord Cockburn*, ed. H. Cockburn (1932) · K. Miller, *Cockburn's millennium* (1975) · A. Bell, ed., *Lord Cockburn: a bicentenary commemoration, 1779–1979* (1979) · J. Clive, *Scotch reviewers: the Edinburgh Review, 1802–1815* (1957) · L. J. Saunders, *Scottish democracy, 1815–1840* (1950) · H. W. Meikle, *Scotland and the French Revolution* (1912) · M. Fry, *The Dundas despotism* (1992) · R. Mitchison, *A history of Scotland* (1970)
Archives BL, critique on issue of *The Spectator*, Add. MS 47689 · NL Scot., corresp. and papers; letters | BL, letters to Macvey Napier, Add. MSS 34613–34629 · Mitchell L., Glas., Strathclyde Regional Archives, letters to John Strang · NL Scot., letters to Charles Anderson; letters to Leonard Horner; letters to John Archibald Murray · NL Scot., corresp. with John Richardson; corresp. with Andrew Rutherford · U. Edin. L., letters to David Laing · U. Edin., New Coll. L., letters to Thomas Chalmers
Likenesses H. Raeburn, oils, 1819, Faculty of Advocates, Parliament Hall, Edinburgh · A. Edouart, cut-paper silhouette, 1831, Scot. NPG · J. Syme, oils, exh. 1831, Parliament Hall, Edinburgh · A. H. Ritchie, marble bust, 1848, NPG · J. Watson-Gordon, oils, exh. Royal Scottish Academy 1853, Scot. NPG [*see illus.*] · J. G. Tunny, photograph, 1854 · W. Brodie, marble bust, 1855, Scot. NPG · W. Brodie, marble statue, 1862, Faculty of Advocates, Parliament Hall, Edinburgh · R. C. Bell, engraving (after portrait by H. Raeburn), probably Scot. NPG · B. W. Crombie, etching (after B. W. Crombie) · B. W. Crombie, pencil caricature, Scot. NPG · A. Edouart, group portrait, cut-paper silhouette (with his family), Scot. NPG · G. Harvey, group portrait, oils, Scot. NPG · D. O. Hill and R. Adamson, calotypes · Schenck and MacFarlane, lithograph (after H. F. Weisse), Scot. NPG · J. Steell, marble bust, Faculty of Advocates, Parliament Hall, Edinburgh · J. Steell, plaster bust, Scot. NPG · W. Walker, engraving (after H. Raeburn), probably Scot. NPG
Wealth at death £16,484 0s. 2d.: will, 1854

Cockburn, Sir James, **fifth baronet** (1723–1809), army officer, was the second son of John Cockburn (1675–1758), a surgeon of Kilkenny, and his wife, Martha Rich (*d.* 1756). In 1754 he married Laetitia Little (1732/3–1804), the daughter of Luke Little of co. Carlow. He entered the army about 1747, but, lacking funds, appears to have served as a volunteer before finally gaining an ensigncy in the 44th foot on 22 June 1755. The following year he transferred to a lieutenancy in the 35th foot and was appointed regimental adjutant; he subsequently saw action at Fort William Henry, was wounded at Louisbourg and Quebec, and in 1762 served at the capture of Martinique. With the onset of peace, Cockburn expressed resentment at the purchase of rank above him by richer but less well-qualified officers. Only on 13 April 1767 did he make captain, and only by exploiting in a presumptuous fashion the goodwill of his colonel, General Henry Fletcher, was he able, on 13 January 1776, to purchase his majority. The following October the lieutenant-colonel of the 35th was killed during the New York campaign at White Plains, and General Sir William Howe, in recognition of Cockburn's excellent conduct during the battle, promoted him to command the regiment. Cockburn, however, proved such a persecutor of his fellow officers that within a year three-quarters of them prepared a petition to General Howe complaining of their commanding officer's oppressive behaviour. Discord continued after the 35th moved to St Lucia and culminated in the court martial and cashiering of Major Edward Drewe, a rich dilettante whose rapid ascent to field rank particularly offended Cockburn.

In December 1780 Cockburn was appointed quartermaster-general of the army in the West Indies. Two months later he accompanied the expedition to capture the valuable Dutch island of St Eustatius. As agent for the captors and later military governor of the island he was a willing accomplice in the wholesale (and illegal) confiscation of goods by Admiral George Rodney and General Sir John Vaughan. Indeed, the contemplation of riches so blunted Cockburn's efficiency that in November 1781 he allowed St Eustatius to fall to a surprise attack. By subsequently asserting that £13,000 of confiscated money was his, and because the indulgent French commander actually let him keep it, Cockburn added a charge of scandalous and infamous behaviour (although many suspected treachery) to one of culpable neglect when, in May 1783, he came to be court-martialled for the loss of St Eustatius. The outcome was his dismissal from the army.

In January 1800 Cockburn inherited a baronetcy from his cousin. His wife, with whom he had four children, died in 1804 aged seventy-one. Cockburn, who was probably also the father of the traveller Claudius James *Rich (1786/7–1821), died on 9 June 1809, and his son William *Cockburn (1769–1835), also an army officer, succeeded to the baronetcy. ALASTAIR W. MASSIE

Sources W. Rogerson, *An authenticated copy of the proceedings on the trial of Lieut. Col. Cockburn, for the loss of the island of St Eustatius* (1783) · H. Fletcher, correspondence, W. Sussex RO, RSR MS 9/2 [copied from Fletcher of Saltoun MSS in NL Scot.] · E. Drewe, *The case of Edward Drewe, late major of the thirty-fifth regiment of foot* (1782) ·

R. Cockburn and H. A. Cockburn, *The records of the Cockburn family* (1913) · M. F. Odintz, 'The British officer corps, 1754–1783', PhD diss., U. Mich., 1988 · R. Hurst, *The golden rock: an episode of the American war of independence* (1996) · *Army List* · DNB

Cockburn, James Pattison (1779–1847), army officer and watercolour painter, was born on 18 March 1779 in New York, the son of Colonel John Cockburn and his wife, Mary, daughter of Colonel Sir James Cockburn. He entered the Royal Military Academy, Woolwich, as a cadet on 19 March 1793, and passed out, as a second lieutenant, Royal Artillery, on 2 March 1795; his promotions were: first lieutenant (1803), captain (1806), brevet major (1814), lieutenant-colonel (1825), brevet colonel (1837), and major-general (9 November 1846). He served at the capture of the Cape of Good Hope in 1795, in the expedition sent against Manila in 1798 but was recalled when on its passage owing to the threatening situation in the Carnatic, and also at the siege and capture of Copenhagen in 1807. In 1800 he married, at Cape Colony, Elizabeth Johanna Vansittart; they had five sons and two daughters. From November 1822 to June 1823 he visited Lower Canada. On 5 April 1826 he was given command of the Royal Artillery in the Canadas, to which he returned in August 1826; he left in August 1832. He was director of the Royal Laboratory, Woolwich, from 10 October 1838 to 15 November 1846, when he retired with the rank of major-general.

As a cadet Cockburn had been a pupil of Paul Sandby, Royal Academician (who was for many years professor of landscape drawing at the Royal Military Academy), and became an accomplished and prolific artist, whose work was exhibited and engraved. During leave from Malta and Woolwich, where he was stationed after 1815, he made many drawings of continental scenery, which were engraved and published as *Swiss Scenery* (1820) with sixty-two plates; *Views of the Valley of Aosta* (1822) with twenty-nine plates; *Views to Illustrate the Simplon Route* (1822) with fifty plates; and *Views to Illustrate the Mont Cenis Route* (1822). These drawings supplied the continental 'scenes' for illustrated editions, annuals, and similar works long afterwards. He also executed the landscapes in Professor T. L. Donaldson's *Pompeii Illustrated* (1829). He painted Canadian scenes (collections of his work are in Canadian galleries and museums), and in 1831 published anonymously a small 'picturesque guide' (with seven plates) to the town of Quebec and its environs. According to Ludwig Spohr, who met Cockburn when travelling, he 'made use of a machine, which transmitted the landscape on a reduced scale to the paper' (*N&Q*, 309)—presumably a camera lucida.

Cockburn, who had long been in feeble health, died at his residence, at Woolwich Common, Kent, on 18 March 1847.   H. M. CHICHESTER, rev. ROGER T. STEARN

Sources J. Kane, *List of officers of the royal regiment of artillery from 1716*, rev. edn (1869) · *GM*, 2nd ser., 27 (1847), 550 · *DCB*, vol. 7 · O. F. G. Hogg, *The Royal Arsenal: its background, origin, and subsequent history*, 2 vols. (1963) · A. J. Guy, ed., *The road to Waterloo: the British army and the struggle against revolutionary and Napoleonic France, 1793–1815* (1990) · Bryan, *Painters* (1886–9) · Bénézit, *Dict.*, 3rd edn · *N&Q*, 3rd ser., 8 (1865), 309

Cockburn, John (1652–1729), Church of Scotland minister and Church of England clergyman, was born on 20 April 1652, the son of John Cockburn (*c*.1620–1658), a tailor in the Canongate, Edinburgh, and his wife, Sarah Inglis (*d.* 1688). In 1666 he entered Edinburgh University, but in November 1668 was transferred to King's College, Aberdeen, by his uncle, Patrick *Scougal of Saltoun, bishop of Aberdeen, who oversaw his studies. After graduating MA on 20 June 1670 Cockburn probably continued to study under Scougal, until in 1673 he became tutor to Lord Keith, son of George, ninth Earl Marischal. He left his post in 1675 and was ordained by his uncle, who presented him to the parish of Udny, Aberdeenshire, on 14 February 1676. A public disturbance occurred at his institution in May, owing to the laird of Udny's claim to the patronal rights. In August Cockburn declined a presentation to the parish of Langton, Berwickshire, offered by his cousin, Cockburn of Langton. On 15 November 1677 he married Anna Garden (*d.* 1695), daughter of Alexander Garden, minister of Forgue, with whom he had at least four children, including Patrick *Cockburn (1678–1749).

Between 10 August and 7 September 1681 Cockburn was translated from Udny to Old Deer, Aberdeenshire, thanks to the patronage of the Earl Marischal. Baulking at the test oath, which from 31 August 1681 bound all civil and ecclesiastical office holders to adhere to the whole confession of faith of 1560 and to support the established government in church and state, Cockburn joined the strong opposition shown by Bishop Scougal and his clergy. However, in February 1682 he and eight 'loyall and learned' churchmen (*Reg. PCS, 1681–2*, 343), overcame their scruples concerning the confession and the royal supremacy, complied, and were allowed by the privy council of Scotland to return to their parishes. On 13 June 1683 he was translated to the parish of Ormiston, Haddingtonshire, in the gift of Sir Archibald Cockburn, filling a vacancy caused by John Sinclair's deprivation for refusing the test. Consequently Cockburn's assiduous ministry was fraught with difficulty, especially in persuading parishioners to act as elders in the kirk session, but it is unclear if he followed the common practice, alleged by Wodrow, of deliberately nominating presbyterians so they could be prosecuted for their refusal to serve.

Cockburn undertook the innovative publication of a monthly periodical in January 1688. The *Bibliotheca Universalis*, which was perhaps modelled on Pierre Bayle's *Nouvelles de la république des lettres*, contained translations of recent reviews of theological and other works from French periodicals. The duke of Perth construed some passages as anti-Catholic and the privy council quickly stopped further publication. That year Cockburn was made a doctor of divinity at Aberdeen. Following the revolution, like many other episcopal clergy, he was cited before the council for not reading the proclamation of 13 April 1689 which declared William and Mary as sovereigns, and instead of praying for them, praying for King James and confusion on his enemies. After one month in prison, until 7 August, he was deprived of his parish on 29

August. The privy council again gaoled him on 5 September 1690 for a period.

A sharp polemic against the presbyterian church settlement, *Historical Relation of the Pretended General Assembly*, and a second part (1691), are attributed to Cockburn during a stay in London, when he befriended the nonjuror Dr Thomas Smith. After returning to Edinburgh in December 1691, he occasionally preached in 1692–3. The council arrested and examined him in March 1693 on suspicion of practices against the government committed by nonjuring clergy. Although his papers contained nothing damning, he admitted managing charitable donations for the episcopal clergy. On 27 June 1693 he refused to take the oaths of allegiance and assurance, and was ordered to leave their majesties' dominions by August. His pass to travel to the Netherlands from England was dated 18 September 1693.

Next Cockburn lived at the court of the exiled James VII at St Germain, where he hoped to find sanctuary, if not reward. After a period he was represented as a dangerous man by priests who had failed to convert him to Rome and, like his cousin Cockburn of Langton the younger who also became *persona non grata* at St Germain, he was forced to quit France by the authorities. Cockburn returned to England about 1696, when he published *An Enquiry into the Nature, Necessity, and Evidence of Christian Faith*. In 1697 a second part appeared, followed by *Fifteen Sermons*. In early 1698, shortly after publishing his first narrative of *Bourignianism Detected*, against the Catholic mystic and prophet Antoinette Bourignon, his prolific output was interrupted briefly by his hurried departure from England following the act against corresponding with King James. An interim *Letter* on Bourignon was dated at Rotterdam on 11/21 April 1698, and his second narrative followed that year. He sought to demonstrate that she was a false prophet and saint, but his bitter denigration of her mystical piety reflected his own renunciation of the quietist spirituality which he had imbibed from his uncle and from his cousin, Henry Scougal. As his brother-in-law George Garden pointed out, Cockburn had once venerated Thomas à Kempis's *Imitation of Christ*. In 1708 Cockburn felt it necessary to clear himself of the imputation of unorthodoxy and Bourignonism in *Right Notions of God and Religion*.

At Rotterdam Cockburn lodged with the scholar Pierre Bayle, another enemy to Bourignonism, and forged a friendship with the bookseller Leers, who introduced him to the leading men of the place. He endeavoured to set up as chaplain to resident Anglicans, but his nonjuring principles and reluctance to pray for King William alienated the majority of the English merchants, as well as alarmed the English authorities, so he departed during 1699, leaving it to his successor to establish an official ministry. His first wife had died in July 1695. He married again apparently some two years later, while abroad; his new wife was Elizabeth Littlepage, daughter of Sir Joseph Littlepage of Buckinghamshire, with whom he had at least seven children. Settling next in Amsterdam, Cockburn began to hold prayer-book services in a private chapel on the first Sunday in January 1700. His persistent efforts were crowned with the success of a lasting congregation, and he enjoyed cordial relations with the burgomasters, who granted the Anglicans the right to worship. His political principles were perhaps not tested by the imposition of oaths applicable in England, but it was later claimed he prayed for King William and Queen Anne. Henry Compton, bishop of London, and John Sharp, archbishop of York, supported his ministry.

In March 1703, after returning from a brief visit to England in order to secure a royal grant of £60 for the chaplaincy, Cockburn began sending reports on public affairs to the earl of Nottingham, hoping for the gift of an English living to which he could retire. In January 1704, as financial hardship caused him to dispose of most of his library, he complained that Bishop Burnet's false allegations of his clashes with other clergy and the authorities had caused the Society for the Propagation of the Gospel to stop its grant. However, he persisted with his ministry, occasionally publishing sermons. In 1708 his crown grant was raised to £100.

That year Cockburn was granted the rectory of Beercrocombe, Somerset, where he hoped to employ his son Patrick as curate. He had left Amsterdam by 27 May 1709, when he was honoured with a doctorate in divinity by Oxford University in recognition of his successful chaplaincy. On 9 June he was instituted to the rectory of Curry Malet, Somerset, in the queen's gift, but resided in London. Taking the requisite oaths was an abandonment of his nonjurancy and an avowal of orthodox Anglican churchmanship. It was later claimed that Cockburn was so well thought of that, had the project for bishops for the American colonies been realized, the queen intended his appointment as one of them. It was at her instance that in 1714, as he was about to take up residence in one of his charges, he was somewhat reluctantly presented by John Robinson, bishop of London, to the vicarage of Northolt or Northall, Middlesex, one of the wealthiest in his diocese. Resigning his rectories, he devoted himself to his parochial duties at Northolt, and provided during his life for the education of ten boys and six girls of the parish. He wrote an account of Northolt's history and present state.

Cockburn continued to pen earnest works of a practical, moral cast, including *A Discourse of Self-Murder* (1716) and *The History and Examination of Duels*, written about 1717 and published in 1720 in support of the outlawing of duels. In 1717–18 he again displayed his conservative and orthodox credentials with two defences of the rights and authority of the church against the views of Benjamin Hoadly, bishop of Bangor. After the publication of Gilbert Burnet's *History of his Own Times*, about 1724 he was encouraged to write a pamphlet correcting, among other matters, Burnet's account of his Scottish career, in which he accused him of historical bias, indiscretion, and intemperate behaviour. However, he admitted having to rely on his memory of many papers, including some of Bishop Scougal's, which he had lost. In addition to about twenty-three published works, latterly Cockburn completed a history of the Scottish church from the Restoration to the revolution, which was probably one of several manuscripts left unpublished at his death aged seventy-seven, on 20 November 1729. He was described as 'true and sincere in his private friendships, kind and benevolent to all mankind' (Bodl. Oxf., MS Rawl. J.40.2). On 26 November he was buried in Northolt parish church; his wife survived him.

TRISTRAM CLARKE

Sources DNB · *Reg. PCS*, 3rd ser., vols. 7, 14–15 · *Fasti Scot.*, new edn, vols. 1, 8 · register of privy council, NA Scot., PC1/48 · letter, Cockburn to Archbishop Tenison, 1699, LPL, MS 1029 · vol. 9, letters and memorial from Cockburn, 1703–4, LPL, Society for Propagation of Gospel MSS · Bodl. Oxf., MS Rawl. J. 40.2 · R. Cockburn and H. A. Cockburn, *The records of the Cockburn family* (1913) · letters to earl of Nottingham, 1703–4, BL, Add. MS 29558 · letters to Archbishop Sharp, 1703, Glos. RO, Lloyd–Baker–Sharp MSS · J. Cockburn and T. Smith, correspondence, 1692–8, Bodl. Oxf., MSS Smith 48, 59 · F. W. Weaver, ed., *Somerset incumbents* (privately printed, Bristol, 1889) · Foster, *Alum. Oxon.* · *Remarks and collections of Thomas Hearne*, ed. C. E. Doble and others, 2, OHS, 7 (1886) · *A view of the court of St Germains from the year 1690, to 95* (1696) · account of vicars of Northolt, 1891, LMA, DRO 51/151/5 · H. Paton, ed., *Register of interments in the Greyfriars burying-ground, Edinburgh, 1658–1700*, Scottish RS, 26 (1902), 333, 132

Archives NL Scot., MS volume of sermons, Acc. 8938 | BL, letters to earl of Nottingham, Add. MS 29558 · Bodl. Oxf., corresp. with Dr Thomas Smith · Glos. RO, Lloyd–Baker–Sharp MSS, letters to Archbishop Sharp · LPL, Society for Propagation of Gospel MSS

Wealth at death see will, 1730, PRO; noted in LMA, MS account of vicars of Northolt, 1891, DRO 51/151/5

Cockburn, John (1679–1758), politician and agricultural improver, was born in Scotland, the second son of Adam *Cockburn (*c*.1656–1735) of Ormiston, lord justice clerk and lord of session with the judicial title Lord Ormiston, and his first wife, Lady Susanna Hamilton, daughter of the fourth earl of Haddington. He was educated at the University of Glasgow between 1691 and 1695. In 1700 he married Lady Beatrice Carmichael (*d*. 1702), daughter of the first earl of Hyndford; they had no children. His second wife was Arabella, third daughter of Anthony Rowe of Muswell Hill; they had one son, George, of the Navy Office.

Cockburn represented Haddingtonshire in the Scottish parliament from 1703 and voted for the parliamentary union of Scotland and England in 1707. He was a member of the parliament of Great Britain until 1741 and held minor office as a lord of trade, from 1714 to 1717, and then as a lord of the Admiralty until 1732. He gained a reputation for competence in office but was passed over for the position of first lord, after which he gave his political support to the opposition. Although Cockburn did not stand for re-election in 1741 he was reappointed to the Board of Admiralty from 1742 to 1744.

It is doubtful whether it was his failure to retain office that caused Cockburn to turn away from political life, because his main interests were already directed to agricultural improvement, particularly of his own estate of Ormiston in Haddingtonshire. His father had initiated improvements and these were greatly extended when John succeeded him, his elder brother having died young. Through much of the period when he was devoting his energies to improvement Cockburn was away in London, but he always directed and followed every aspect of his estate by correspondence. His improvements were those that others were to follow later in the century—enclosure, the planting of new crops such as barley and turnips, the use of artificial grasses and rotations, the planting of trees—but in Cockburn's case they formed part of two distinctive features of his work.

The first was his deliberate policy of granting long leases, usually of nineteen but sometimes even of thirty-eight years, to ensure that the tenants were encouraged to adopt the long-term outlook on improvements that Cockburn deemed essential. In this scheme he was fortunate in having among his tenantry succeeding generations of the Wight family, who made their own independent contribution to agricultural improvement and with whom he corresponded regularly when away. Cockburn's attitude to his tenantry, as well as his political philosophy, was expressed well in a letter he wrote to one of them:

> I hate tyranny in every shape, and shall always have greater pleasure in seeing my tenants making something under me, which they can call their own, than in getting a little more myself, by squeezing a hundred poor families, till their necessities make them my slaves. (*Farmer's Magazine*, 136)

Second, Cockburn extended his improvements to the entire reorganization of his estate. The village of Ormiston was rebuilt and used as the centre for a range of industrial activities, notably the manufacture and bleaching of linen. It became a place where others gained insights into the new ways and where Cockburn promoted them by launching a discussion group in 1736.

Posterity has accorded Cockburn his due recognition as an agriculturist but he himself did not reap a financial reward. Unable to finance the costly wait that (as he constantly reminded his tenants) had to be endured to gain the long-term benefits of improvement, he was forced to sell Ormiston to the earl of Hopetoun in 1747. As the family historian wryly commented, 'for the interests of his family, it would have been well had he been satisfied with a political life; but unfortunately he was an enthusiastic agriculturist' (Cockburn-Hood, 157). Cockburn died at his son's home in London on 12 November 1758.

R. H. CAMPBELL

Sources 'Memoir of John Cockburn', *Farmer's Magazine*, 5 (7 May 1804), 128–47 · *Letters of John Cockburn of Ormiston to his gardener, 1727–1744*, ed. J. Colville (1904) · J. Cockburn, letter to Alexander Wight, *Scots Magazine*, 20 (1758), 439–42 · T. H. Cockburn-Hood, *The house of Cockburn of that ilk* (1888) · M. D. Young, ed., *The parliaments of Scotland: burgh and shire commissioners*, 2 vols. (1992–3) · records, U. Glas., Archives and Business Records Centre · *Scots peerage*

Likenesses engraving, repro. in 'Memoir', *Farmer's Magazine*, 128

Cockburn, Patrick (*d*. 1568), Church of Scotland minister, was born at Choicelee, Berwickshire, in the early years of the sixteenth century, the second of the five sons of Christopher Cockburn (*d*. *c*.1520) and his wife, Margaret Hoppringle. The family was a cadet branch of the Cockburns of Langton. The head of the house, Cockburn's uncle Sir William Cockburn, was slain at Flodden in 1513. Cockburn matriculated at the University of St Andrews on 24 February 1526, and graduated BA in the same year (deferment of formal matriculation until graduation was not uncommon at the time). Afterwards he went to Paris to complete his education, and excelled in the study of Latin, Greek, and Hebrew. On his return to Scotland it seems likely that he was engaged to teach at his old university. He was also appointed prebendary of Pitcox in the collegiate church of Dunbar, Haddingtonshire, in which capacity he was present at the election of his kinswoman Janet Hoppringle as prioress of Coldstream, Berwickshire, on 23 February 1538.

In 1548 Cockburn was one of the attendants licensed to go to France with Lord James Stewart (afterwards earl of Moray), commendator of St Andrews Priory and probably a student of his. For most of the following decade Cockburn divided his time between St Andrews and Paris, where he became professor of oriental languages at the Sorbonne. While there he published two doctrinal works: *Oratio de utilitate et excellentia verbi Dei* (1551), with a dedicatory epistle to his friend John Hamilton, archbishop of St Andrews, in which he reflects, among other things, on the pleasure he derives from teaching; and *De vulgari sacrae scripturae phrasi* (1552), with a dedicatory epistle to Lord James Stewart, who in the same year granted him a pension of £50 per annum from the rents of the kirk of Leuchars in Fife. The latter work was popular enough to be translated into French by Jacques Vincent in 1553. At St Andrews Cockburn published *In Dominicam orationem pia meditatio* (1555), believed to be the first printed book to mention Mary, queen of Scots, by name. On 15 November 1557 Cockburn was one of several persons elected to an academic committee of his old college, St Mary's, at the University of St Andrews. He was in Paris in April 1558, once more in the company of his protégé Lord James Stewart, to attend the wedding of Queen Mary and the dauphin (afterwards François II). He remained there to see through the press a second and much enlarged edition of *De vulgari sacrae scripturae phrasi* in July.

Cockburn, who had always leaned towards the reformers, openly joined the protestant party at the advent of the Reformation in Scotland in the following year. In 1561 he published *In secundae partis catechismi (quae est de simbolo quod apostolicum vocant) enarrationem, de fide, et iustificatione, praefatio*, part of a much longer work which, in the foreword, Cockburn complains he has not money to publish. In 1562 he became first protestant minister of Haddington, a post he held until his death. It is inconceivable that he would not have known John Knox, a native of Haddington, who must have preached there many times. Along with Thomas Hepburn, David Lindsay, and John Craig, Cockburn was appointed in 1562 to preach in the unplanted kirks (that is, those lacking ministers) of the Merse in Berwickshire. In the same year his name was mentioned for the superintendency of Jedburgh; and in 1563 he was appointed chaplain of Trinity aisle in the parish of Haddington.

Cockburn died at Haddington in 1568 and was buried there. He was renowned in his lifetime for his learning and erudition, as also, in marked contrast to the tenor of the age, for his moderation and humanity.

ANTHONY ESPOSITO

Sources R. Cockburn and H. A. Cockburn, *The records of the Cockburn family* (1913) · *Fasti Scot.*, new edn · J. M. Anderson, ed., *Early records of the University of St Andrews*, Scottish History Society, 3rd ser., 8 (1926) · Bale, *Cat.* · J. Spottiswood, *The history of the Church of Scotland*, ed. M. Napier and M. Russell, 3 vols., Bannatyne Club, 93 (1850)

Cockburn, Patrick (1678–1749), Scottish Episcopal clergyman, was the eldest son of John *Cockburn (1652–1729), Church of Scotland minister, and his wife Anna (d. 1695), daughter of Alexander Garden, a leading cleric of the diocese of Aberdeen. Patrick was born at Udny, Aberdeenshire, during his father's incumbency of the parish. After the revolution in 1689 his father went abroad, though not apparently as a nonjuror as he prayed for King William and Queen Anne during his time as chaplain to the British congregations at Rotterdam and Amsterdam. It is not known whether Patrick accompanied his father, or where he was educated, but he was in Holland in 1705, for on 17 August of that year he received an MA from Edinburgh University and was described as being currently *in Batavia agens*. Early in 1708 he married the dramatist and philosopher Catharine *Trotter (1674?–1749), daughter of David Trotter and Sarah Ballenden. He is said to have shortly afterwards obtained the perpetual curacy of Nayland, Suffolk, but he was probably only a temporary curate-in-charge from June 1708. The sole reference to him in the Nayland registers is the entry of the baptism on 13 April 1712 of 'Mary, daughter of Patrick Cockburn, curate, and Catharine his wife'.

From Nayland Cockburn moved to London, where he was curate at St Dunstan-in-the-West, Fleet Street. Soon afterwards he had to give up his appointment owing to his refusal to take the oath of abjuration of the former Stuart royal line in 1714. For a time he made a scanty living by teaching Latin at a school in Chancery Lane, London. However, by 29 November 1726 he had reversed his former nonjuring position and, having taken the oath, was appointed at that date as the qualified, or Hanoverian, minister of St Paul's Episcopal Chapel, Aberdeen, which was built in 1722. Soon afterwards he was preferred to the parish of Long Horsley, Northumberland, but did not live there until 1737.

While in Aberdeen Cockburn published a number of apologetic works upholding the legitimacy of the Hanoverian regime, including a sermon, *On the Duty and Benefit of Praying for our Governors* (1728), and a pamphlet, *The Lawfulness and Duty of Praying for our Present King and Governor* (1735). These were probably engendered by a controversy with the predominantly nonjuring Scottish Episcopalians. Cockburn had a family connection to the eighteenth-century Scottish Episcopalian mystical tradition, which was influenced by French quietism through the works of Henry Scougall and George Garden. Garden was Cockburn's uncle, and Scougall his father's first cousin. Probably as a result of this connection he produced his edition of Scougall's *Life of God in the Soul of Man* (1726). The addition of Scougall's 'Nine Discourses' and Garden's funeral sermon for Scougall made this work an important contribution to Scougall's biography. Compelled to move to Long Horsley in 1737, Cockburn resigned his Aberdeen incumbency on 1 June 1739. He died on 4 January 1749 and was buried three days later at Long Horsley parish church cemetery. He was survived by his wife who, shocked by his death, died on 11 May of the same year.   ROWAN STRONG

Sources T. Birch, 'Life of Mrs Cockburn', in *The works of Mrs Catharine Cockburn*, ed. T. Birch, 2 vols. (1751) · G. Grub, *An ecclesiastical history of Scotland*, 4 vols. (1861), vol. 3 · *DNB*

Cockburn, Sarah Caudwell [*pseud.* Sarah Caudwell] (1939–2000), barrister and novelist, was born on 27 May 1939 at the Wandsworth maternity home, Weir Road, London, the daughter of (Francis) Claud *Cockburn (1904–1981), journalist, and Jean Iris *Ross (1911–1973), the daughter of Charles Ross, a cotton expert for the Bank of Egypt. Jean Ross, too, was a journalist, as well as a singer, actress, and political activist, and was the model for Sally Bowles in Christopher Isherwood's *Goodbye to Berlin* (1939). She was not married to Cockburn, who left the family home, 11 Trinity Close, London SW4, three months after Sarah was born, never to return.

Sarah Cockburn's childhood was peripatetic. During the Second World War, she lived with her mother and maternal grandmother in rented accommodation in Welwyn and Stevenage, Hertfordshire, before moving to Cheltenham in 1945. During the 1950s mother and daughter went to live in Scotland, where Sarah was educated at the Aberdeen High School for Girls, and subsequently read classics at Aberdeen University, obtaining an MA in 1960. She won a scholarship to visit Greece, where part of her second novel, *The Shortest Way to Hades* (1984), was set.

The family returned to London to share a house at 15 Clavering Avenue, Barnes, with one of Ross's sisters when Sarah went to Oxford University to study law at St Anne's College. Outraged that women were not allowed to join the Oxford Union, she persuaded two friends to enter the debating chamber dressed as men, and subsequently campaigned successfully for the rules to be changed. She became one of the first women to take part in a debate as a member rather than as a guest of the union. Having graduated BCL in 1962, she spent a short period in the following year lecturing in law at the University College of Wales at Aberystwyth, followed by a year at the Cité Universitaire des Jeunes Filles at Nancy, where she took a diploma in French law. She was called to the Chancery bar in 1965, working first in the Middle Temple, then at Lincoln's Inn, the principal setting of her four novels. Having been in practice for several years, she 'decided that the reward for being an overworked Chancery Junior was eventually to become an even more overworked Chancery Silk', and so in 1974 left the bar to work for the trust division of Lloyds Bank in London (dust jacket, *The Shortest Way to Hades*).

Sarah Caudwell, as she was known as a writer, had already started writing her first novel, *Thus was Adonis Murdered* (1981), the principal action of which is set in Venice. It is narrated by Professor Hilary Tamar of St George's College, Oxford, who becomes friends with a group of young barristers, all of whom Caudwell drew more or less from life, including Julia Larwood, whose disorganized life, physical clumsiness, expertise in tax planning, and weakness for slender young men with exquisite profiles were shared by her creator. There is also a great deal of Caudwell in Tamar, particularly in the professor's orotund mode of speech. Much of the narrative of Caudwell's novels is in the form of letters, although in real life Caudwell was a poor correspondent. The books were published as crime novels, but are highly sophisticated examples of the genre. Intricately plotted, highly mannered, witty, and allusive (particularly to the classics), they manage to make the complicated details of tax planning, investments, trusts, and legacies completely absorbing. Caudwell's greatest coup, however, is in never revealing whether Tamar is a man or a woman. Readers have argued strongly over this, but whenever Caudwell was asked, she said she did not know, and it is a measure of her skill that she carries off this ambiguity without the faintest hint of strain or contrivance.

Thus was Adonis Murdered was published in the United States in 1981 before it appeared in Britain, and Caudwell always had a devoted American readership. Part of the appeal may have been that the books are 'very English', in both style and setting (dust jacket of Penguin edition of *Thus was Adonis Murdered*). American editions were perfectly complemented by dust jackets designed by the Anglophile fantasist Edward Gorey. In 1991 Caudwell became the first recipient of the Wimsey award for superior achievement in comic mystery fiction. The trophy was a stuffed groundhog wearing a purple robe.

Caudwell did not share her mother's mannequin looks, but she was a striking figure, with bobbed brown hair, a straight nose, and brown eyes hidden behind tinted, thick-lensed spectacles. She tended to wear rather grubby mackintoshes (not always her own since she was inclined to grab whatever was hanging on a peg when she left an establishment), had long, tapering fingers, and was usually to be found with a glass of Sancerre at her elbow, smoking a pipe. She was genuinely eccentric, but also very generous. Keen on crosswords, she often reached the finals of competitions organized by *The Times*. She had affairs but never married (although she longed to have a child), and she kept her friends separate. Perhaps her closest ally was her mother's sister Billee, who inspired the character of Aunt Regina in the last, and arguably best, of her novels, *The Sibyl in her Grave*, which was published posthumously. Sarah Caudwell died of throat cancer at her flat, 149 Whitehall Court, Whitehall, London, on 28 January 2000, and was cremated at East Sheen, London, on 11 February.   PETER PARKER

Sources private information (2004) · *The Guardian* (8 Feb 2001) · *The Times* (4 Feb 2001) · *New York Times* (6 Feb 2000) · *Daily Telegraph* (4 Feb 2000)

Likenesses photographs, priv. coll.

Wealth at death £1,126,944: private information (2004)

Cockburn, William, of Henderland (*d.* 1530), criminal, enjoyed a laird's status in the Scottish borders, holding the twenty-pound land of Henderland and Sunderland in Peeblesshire and Selkirkshire, with tower and chapel. He preferred, however, to make his living from theft, blackmail, and collusion with Englishmen during the minority of James V. During 1518 and 1519 he was warded, and released only when information that his tenants were being attacked reached the government. He was to re-enter at three days' notice, with Malcolm, Lord Fleming, standing cautioner. Cockburn none the less continued his notorious thieving and evaded capture until his arrest in March 1530. On 16 May that year a convention of the nobility took place in Edinburgh. On the same day James V put many border surname chiefs into ward and ordered Cockburn, already imprisoned, to be executed by beheading. The king clearly wanted to make an example of border thieves as he executed the so-called 'king of thieves', Adam Scott of Tushielaw, on 18 May and also executed many Armstrongs in the following July.

A tombstone at Henderland commemorating Piers Cockburn and his wife, Marjory, has been associated with William Cockburn, but there is no evidence to suggest that he was brought back from Edinburgh for burial *sans tête*. On these and other grounds William Cockburn's link with the ballad 'The Lament of the Border Widow' remains highly questionable. One of the most eloquent of the border ballads, 'The Lament' depicts a widow's anguish at a king who 'brake my bower, and slew my knight'. The family's disgrace leaves her without servants, so she is forced to bury him alone.

> I digg'd a grave, and laid him in,
> And happ'd him with the sod sae green.
> (Scott)

This widow perhaps symbolizes the reality of life for well-born women in the Anglo-Scottish borders when their husbands fell foul of the law, but she cannot have been Mrs Cockburn. In 1532 James V granted Cockburn's estate to James Fleming, brother of the aforesaid Lord Fleming—a move that undoubtedly left Cockburn's family destitute.   T. F. HENDERSON, *rev.* MAUREEN M. MEIKLE

Sources J. M. Thomson and others, eds., *Registrum magni sigilli regum Scotorum / The register of the great seal of Scotland*, 11 vols. (1882–1914), vol. 3, p. 1155 · R. K. Hannay, ed., *Acts of the lords of council in public affairs, 1501–1554* (1932), 148, 328 · J. Cameron, *James V: the personal rule, 1528–1542*, ed. N. Macdougall (1998), 76–81 · G. Douglas, *A history of the border counties: Roxburgh, Selkirk and Peebles* (1899), 269 · F. H. Groome, ed., *Ordnance gazetteer of Scotland*, new edn, 3 (1903), 265 · G. M. Fraser, *The steel bonnets: the story of the Anglo-Scottish border reivers* (1971) · W. Scott, 'The lament of the border widow', *Minstrelsy of the Scottish border*, 2 vols. (1802)
Wealth at death lands forfeited: Thomson and others, eds., *Registrum*, vol. 3, p. 1155

Cockburn, William (1669–1739), physician, about whose early life nothing is known, proceeded MA at Edinburgh on 9 July 1688. The *Dictionary of National Biography* erroneously described him as a son of Sir William Cockburn of Ryslaw. His name occurs in the register of the University of Leiden as a student of medicine on 29 May 1691, he being then in his twenty-third year. While at Leiden he attended the lectures of his fellow Scot Archibald Pitcairne, and was strongly influenced by Pitcairne's combination of iatromechanism and Newtonian matter theory. Cockburn did not take a degree at Leiden, and returned to Britain about 1693. In that year he published his translation of Walter Harris's *De morbis acutis infantum* (1689), describing himself as 'W.C. M.S.', and in the preface praised the medicine of Thomas Sydenham. He dedicated the book to the countess of Roxburghe, alluding to his own 'particular ties' to her. The nature of these ties remains unknown, but Cockburn appears to have had a powerful patron, possibly Lady Roxburghe's father, the marquess of Tweeddale. On 2 April 1694 Cockburn became a licentiate of the Royal College of Physicians in London (he never got promotion in the college hierarchy), and about the same time he was appointed by the Admiralty board as physician to the Blue squadron. This was a sought-after position highly dependent upon patronage. His first book, *Oeconomia corporis animalis*, was published a year later, dedicated to Admiral Sir William Bridgeman. It was a sort of scheme of general pathology, or first principles of physic. Pitcairne's influence is evident in its mechanistic explanations, although his name is not mentioned.

In 1696 Cockburn brought out a small work entitled *An account of the nature, causes, symptoms and cure of the distempers that are incident to seafaring people*. This was a record of his two years' experience as ship's doctor on the home station. Among other things it points out that chills are due to the suppression of the perspiration, and it contains remarks on the cause of scurvy: the 'boatswain's favourites', he pointed out, suffered much more from scurvy than the men set to do the hard work, a diet of salt beef and pork requiring active exercise to carry it off. He had no notion, however, of the importance of citrus and other foods rich in vitamin C. Scurvy was not effectually banished from the fleet until Gilbert Blane's rules of victualling in 1795, and Cockburn was inclined to despise the ignorance of those who, 'at the name of scurvy, fly to scurvy-grass, water-cresses, and horse-radishes, but to what advantage may be easily understood by our foregoing theory'. He was sensible enough to see that land scurvy, which the dogmatists of the 'scorbutic constitution' discovered under many guises, 'is not so very frequent as it is commonly imagined, and that so-called cases of it are something else'.

Through his connection with the fleet Cockburn was able to introduce his secret remedy for dysentery, which made his fortune. The account given (pamphlet on a *Medicine Against Looseness*, by La Touche, 1757) is that in July 1696 he was dining on board one of the ships in the company of the Admiral Lord Berkeley of Stratton, and captains Meese and Beaumont when, after some compliments to him, it was remarked that 'there was nothing farther wanting but a better method of curing fluxes'. Cockburn replied that he thought he could be of use. The trial was made next day upon about a hundred patients on board Captain Meese's ship, the *Sandwich*, and proved brilliantly successful. The result was reported to the Admiralty board by Sir Cloudesley Shovell, who was directed to purchase a quantity of the electuary for the use of the Mediterranean squadron. Cockburn supplied the fleet with it for forty years, and it was probably in use also in the army on foreign service. William III conveyed his thanks to the inventor for a benefit of national importance, and Louis XIV tried to buy the secret for the French fleet through his ambassador in London, but war broke out in 1702 and put an end to the negotiations. Its fame brought Cockburn crowds of private patients suffering with fluxes of various kinds. During the spring of 1700 the admiral asked the Royal College of Physicians to comment on Cockburn's suggestion that all naval surgeons should record on a chart the exact symptoms of the dangerous fevers in the West Indies, and the effects of the remedies he proposed. After investigating, the eminent Walter Charleton reported that

> the Experientes and observations brought by the Dr. as the sole Ground, upon which he builds his new Method of treating the sick, seems to us neither authentick enough to engage our Belief, nor Consistent with those made by other physicians in the same countries.　(Cook, 24)

The college suggested that the Admiralty should find other cures.

Cockburn also sought fame as a natural philosopher. In 1699 he published an article in the *Philosophical Transactions of the Royal Society* which attempted to explain, in mechanical terms, the action of a blister in curing a fever. He had been elected a fellow of the Royal Society in 1696. On 26 March 1697 he was granted the degree of MD by King's College, Aberdeen. By about 1700 he had settled in London and begun building a successful career as a physician. He lived for many years on St James's Street, near Piccadilly. Cockburn seems to have kept his connection with the navy for many years, and in 1731 he became physician to Greenwich Hospital. When Swift went to London in September 1710 on the three years' visit chronicled in the *Journal to Stella*, the first of his many recorded dinners was with Cockburn. The latter is often mentioned in the *Journal*, once as 'honest Dr. Cockburn', and another time as having 'generally such a parcel of Scots with him'. Although Swift was more in the company of Drs Freind, Arbuthnot, and Garth, it was Cockburn whom he chose as his medical adviser. Cockburn possessed a large practice, some of it brought to him by his secret remedy for fluxes, and some of it doubtless by his other writings (in which the treatment was also vaguely given at first), on the *Virulente gonorrhoeae* (1717) and on the *Symptoms, Nature, and Cure of a Gonorrhoea* (2nd edn 1715). The latter was well thought of, went through four editions, and was translated abroad. In the same class of writings was his *Account of the Nature and Cure of Looseness* (2nd edn 1710). His other writings were pamphlets connected more or less directly with his secret remedy. One of these, *The Present Uncertainty in the Knowledge of Medicines* (1703), was a letter to the

physicians in the commission for sick and wounded seamen, in which he remonstrates with them for their dogmatic narrowness of view. Another, *The Danger of Improving Physick* (1730), is a well-written rejoinder to the cabal of academical physicians who opposed him on account of his secret remedy, and particularly to John Freind, who turned against him in his *History of Physick* (1725) after being on good terms with him for twenty years. 'The most learned physicians', Cockburn says, 'are always most subject to obloquy, on account of their superior knowledge and discoveries'.

Cockburn's first wife, whom he married in 1698, was Mary de Baudisson (1663/4–1728), a widow, who died on 5 July 1728, aged sixty-four. On 5 April 1729 he married Lady Mary Fielding, eldest daughter of Basil, fourth earl of Denbigh. According to the contemporary gossip he found the latter, who was his patient, in tears at the prospect of having to leave London owing to her reduced circumstances, whereupon the doctor said, 'Madam, if fifty thousand pounds and the heart of an old man will console you, they are at your service'. Cockburn is described as 'an old, very rich quack', and the lady as 'very ugly'. He died in November 1739, aged seventy, and was buried on 24 November in the middle aisle of Westminster Abbey. His will was written on 4 December 1738, probably after the death of his second wife, since she is not mentioned. It was proved on 12 December 1739. The executors were Richard Shelley and James Cockburn, secretary to the duke of Argyll. Cockburn left several small bequests to various relatives, revealing his role as a family benefactor: to his cousin Helen Cockburn, Lady Allenbank, he left 100 guineas and his wives' diamonds, and he left £200 to another cousin, Ann Cant, and her niece Amelia White. He forgave the debts of two other cousins. He left the bulk of his estate to Alexander Cockburn of Langtoun, whose relationship to the doctor was not specified. This included an estate at Stockton in co. Durham, which was leased for three lifetimes from the bishop of Durham. Cockburn died a wealthy man, although the exact extent of his wealth is not known.

CHARLES CREIGHTON, *rev.* ANITA GUERRINI

Sources A. Guerrini, 'Newtonian matter theory, chemistry, and medicine, 1690–1713', PhD diss., Indiana University, 1983 · T. M. Brown, 'The mechanical philosophy and the "Animal oeconomy"', PhD diss., Princeton University, 1968 · H. J. Cook, 'Practical medicine and the British armed forces after the "Glorious Revolution"', *Medical History*, 34 (1990), 1–26 · private information (2004) · Munk, *Roll*
Archives BL, Sloane MS 3198
Likenesses R. White, line engraving (after William Cockburn), Wellcome L. · line engraving, Wellcome L.
Wealth at death substantial; several bequests; main heir inherited estate in co. Durham: will, PRO, PROB 11/699, 253

Cockburn, Sir William, of that ilk, sixth baronet (1769–1835), army officer, was the only son of Colonel James *Cockburn, afterwards fifth baronet (1723–1809), and his wife, Laetitia Little (1732/3–1804), daughter of Luke Little of co. Carlow and heir of the Rossiter family in Ireland. According to the *Gentleman's Magazine*, Cockburn was born 'in a camp'. He became an ensign in the 37th regiment in

1778. He was promoted lieutenant in 1779, and after serving through the latter part of the American War of Independence became captain in the 92nd on 27 April 1783. His regiment was disbanded at the end of the war, and he went on half pay until 1790, when he received a company in the 73rd regiment, then in India. On 1 January 1791, in Madras, he married, as her third husband, Eliza Anne Davis (née Creutzer; first married name Clifton) (d. 1829) and they had a son and a daughter. He served through the last campaigns of the First Anglo-Mysore War in the western army, under Sir Robert Abercromby, and when the two armies met before Seringapatam he was appointed acting engineer, and made a valuable survey which was afterwards published.

Cockburn was promoted major in 1794 and lieutenant-colonel on 1 January 1798, and in 1802 he returned to Britain, and exchanged to the lieutenant-colonelcy of the 4th regiment. In 1804 he was appointed inspecting field officer of volunteers in Ireland, and was promoted colonel on 25 April 1808, and major-general on 4 June 1811. On his father's death in 1809 he succeeded as sixth baronet, but seems to have been confused as to which branch of the Cockburn family he was heir to, and often called himself 'of Ryslaw' as well as or instead of 'of Cockburn'. In 1813 he was appointed inspecting general officer for the Severn district, and on 19 July 1821 he was promoted lieutenant-general. His first wife died in 1829, and in July 1834 he married Martha Honora Georgina, née Jervis, widow of Osborne Markham and great-niece of John Jervis, earl of St Vincent. In his later years he was a prominent supporter of the local charities of Bath, and was particularly active in the Society for the Relief of Occasional Distress, founded by Lady Elizabeth King. Cockburn died on 19 March 1835 at his house in Lansdowne Crescent, Bath. He was survived by his second wife, who died in 1865, and by his children, Sir William Sarsfield Rossiter Cockburn of that ilk, seventh baronet (1796–1858), and Katherine, wife of Edward Cludde, of Orleton, Shropshire.

H. M. STEPHENS, rev. JAMES LUNT

Sources GM, 2nd ser., 3 (1835) • R. Warner, *Bath Chronicle* (March 1835) • J. Foster, *The peerage, baronetage, and knightage of the British empire* [1880–82] • C. E. Buckland, *Dictionary of Indian biography* (1906) • P. Moon, *The British conquest and dominion of India* (1989) • R. Muir, *Britain and the defeat of Napoleon, 1807–1815* (1996)
Likenesses J. Smart, miniature, 1791, Powis Castle, Montgomeryshire • T. Barker, oils, 1816, Victoria Art Gallery, Bath

Cockcroft, Sir John Douglas (1897–1967), physicist and engineer, was born on 27 May 1897 at 154 Halifax Road, Langfield, Yorkshire, the first of five sons. The Cockcrofts had been involved in the weaving industry for generations and Cockcroft's father, John Arthur Cockcroft, and mother, Annie Maude Fielden, moved from a mill at Todmorden to Birks Mill, Walsden, in 1899 where a water-wheel and steam engine were used as a source of power for spinning and weaving machinery. The training given by his father in the mill, and the machinery there, gave Cockcroft an interest in technology which affected his whole life.

Sir John Douglas Cockcroft (1897–1967), by Bassano, 1946

Education Cockcroft was educated at Todmorden secondary school from 1909 and he went with a scholarship to the University of Manchester in 1914 to study mathematics. He was taught by Horace Lamb, a decisive teacher, and attended the first-year lectures in physics by Rutherford, whose dedication to physics greatly impressed him. He volunteered for war service in 1915 and spent three years as a signaller in the Royal Field Artillery, and was twice mentioned in dispatches. This signalling experience prompted his return to Manchester in 1919, this time to the College of Technology, where he gained a first-class BScTechn. in 1920. On Professor Miles Walker's recommendation he was accepted as a college apprentice in engineering by the Metropolitan-Vickers Company. During the two years there he researched with Walker on the harmonic analysis of voltage and current wave forms at frequencies used for commercial power sources. This gained him the MScTech. in 1922, and was the subject of his first joint research paper (1925). Walker suggested that he should try to go to Cambridge and take the mathematical tripos; he won a scholarship at St John's College, and a Manchester College scholarship, and Vickers gave him a grant to encourage him 'to keep in touch' (autobiographical notes). In 1924 he gained a B* in part two of the tripos.

On 26 August 1925 Cockcroft married (Eunice) Elizabeth, daughter of Herbert Crabtree JP of Stansfield Hall. The Crabtrees were cotton manufacturers and John and Elizabeth had known each other from childhood. Their first child, a boy, died at two years. Subsequently they had four daughters and then a son.

Cavendish Laboratory Miles Walker and the director of research at Vickers recommended Cockcroft to Rutherford, by then at the Cavendish Laboratory, Cambridge, and he was accepted as a research student supported by a foundation scholarship of St John's College, a state scholarship, and a further grant from Vickers. For four years he studied the behaviour of metal atoms as they were deposited by condensation on surfaces cooled by liquid air, gaining his PhD in 1928 and experience of new vacuum techniques. It was during this period that Rutherford asked him to help the Russian scientist Peter Kapitza to produce very intense magnetic fields for use at very low temperatures. Cockcroft calculated the forces created in the solenoids used to create the fields, and helped in the design of the helium liquefiers. He also helped Vickers with calculations of the magnetic fields in the huge electric machines used to generate power.

In 1928 the Russian scientist G. Gamov developed a theory based on the new wave mechanics to explain why Rutherford had been able to disintegrate nitrogen atoms with alpha particles having an energy of only a few million electron volts. Cockcroft saw this calculation in December and calculated that protons of only 300 kV energy bombarding light elements such as lithium might result in disintegration. He spent 1929 building a discharge tube to accelerate protons; he energized this with the Tesla coil, and then with a transformer, but made little progress. E. T. S. Walton worked in the same room and Rutherford asked him to join Cockcroft in 1930. They constructed a higher voltage generator for 600 kV d. c., and a far higher vacuum tube in the new laboratory, and used M. Oliphant's design for the proton source. In April 1932 the proton beam was directed on to a lithium target and bright scintillations were observed. They were shown to be due to helium atoms:

$$Li + H = He + he$$
$$7 + 1 = 4 + 4$$

By developing a high voltage high energy beam, the atom had been disintegrated, transformed, and the whole scientific world realized that a new era of nuclear physics had arrived. A supply of heavy water from Berkeley in 1933 enabled Cockcroft to use deuterons instead of protons to create even more amazing disintegrations by 1935. Different accelerators had been built elsewhere, and in 1933 Cockcroft began to persuade a somewhat unwilling Rutherford that the Cavendish Laboratory should have a cyclotron. Work started in 1937, based on E. O. Lawrence's 36 inch machine at Berkeley.

Beyond the laboratory in 1933 he had been appointed junior bursar of St John's College responsible for the buildings, some of which had been neglected for years. The gatehouse of the college was partly taken down to replace roof damage and destruction by death-watch beetles; two new courts were built and rewiring done. In 1935 Kapitza was retained in Russia and Cockcroft took over direction of the Mond Laboratory; a new wing of the

Cavendish Laboratory was built with the aid of the great Austin bequest and in this project Cockcroft was indispensable. In 1936 Cockcroft was elected FRS, and in 1939 he was elected to the Jacksonian professorship in natural philosophy just as he was becoming increasingly involved with efforts being made in technical fields to prepare for war with Hitler's Germany.

Radar and atom bomb Sir H. T. Tizard spoke confidentially to Cockcroft early in 1938 about RDF, the highly secret radio technique for finding aircraft: 'These devices would be troublesome, and would require a team of nurses' (Cockcroft, 1948, in Oliphant and Penney, 155). Cockcroft played a major role in persuading about eighty physicists to spend a month at various coastal radar defence stations, and he also persuaded a number of leading physicists to participate. He personally took colleagues to set up radar stations in the far north, earning great respect from the admiral there who had previously been antagonistic. Some of these scientists made some of the major advances in radar and Cockcroft's part was one of his greatest contributions to the war effort. In August 1940 Cockcroft joined Tizard as his deputy on a mission to the United States to establish an exchange of defence science information. The disclosure to the Americans of the British microwave magnetron was to be of immense importance. Wherever he went in America or Canada he was welcomed by colleagues from the Cavendish Laboratory of old, and all the doors of military secrecy were opened to him.

Cockcroft became chief superintendent of the Air Defence Research and Development Establishment at Christchurch in late 1940. Radar was then being applied to direct anti-aircraft gunnery upon unseen targets. Coastal defence radar and radar for combat use by the army to detect moving vehicles and tanks in the darkness were other major projects. Attempts to produce a proximity fuse for use against aircraft was nearly successful. The failure was a frustrating experience for Cockcroft.

A special part of the history of the Second World War relates to a few men at the forefront of the worldwide nuclear physics community who perceived, at the beginning, the possibility of a nuclear explosive device of orders of magnitude greater than any military weapons using conventional high explosives. Cockcroft knew about these ideas and thought that Britain should make an effort to produce a nuclear explosive. However, for most of the war period he was so completely engaged in radar that his contributions were mainly advisory, until late in 1943 when his involvement sharply increased. Cockcroft's assignment was to go to Canada in 1944 and to take charge of the Montreal laboratory, and then to build the NRX heavy water reactor at Chalk River, together with associated facilities. His calm but energetic direction gave the laboratory, with its mixed British, Canadian, and French staff, a firm sense of purpose. The nuclear explosions at Hiroshima and Nagasaki brought the war to an abrupt end, but the nuclear work continued. The Canadians wanted Cockcroft to stay but he was wanted at home to direct the new establishment which was being built at Harwell for atomic energy research. Cockcroft commuted for a while and did both jobs but, as a result of high-level discussions, he moved full-time to Harwell in 1946. By this time the NRX reactor was almost complete, the laboratories were fully occupied, and the new township at Deep River was becoming a settled community.

Atomic energy Cockcroft's name and the excitement of atomic energy attracted many able people of all ages to work at Harwell, especially the young. Rapid progress was made, in spite of the shortages resulting from the war. The engineering side of atomic energy, under Christopher Hinton, and a little later the weapons side, under W. G. Penney, were also being developed at the greatest possible speed. Among many other activities a great deal of technology and design work on pressurized gas-cooled reactors made it possible in 1953 to base the production of additional plutonium on dual-purpose reactors to be built at Calder Hall. The justification was primarily military, but for the first time the vision of cheap nuclear power, so prominent in Cockcroft's mind, began to have a practical endorsement. The government decided in 1954 to take the responsibility for atomic energy from the Ministry of Supply and create the Atomic Energy Authority (AEA). Cockcroft became the first member for research, while also remaining director of Harwell. Cockcroft foresaw the need to improve British experimental facilities for high energy nuclear physics. His crucial decision and direction of construction at Harwell of the first post-war proton synchrotron by 1949 put Britain in a strong position. It secured Cockcroft and B. Lockspeiser important influence as the Conseil Européen de Recherches Nucléaires (CERN), the larger European project, was developed between 1954 and 1960.

Cockcroft always attached great importance to travel and to making personal contacts with scientists in other countries. When President Eisenhower addressed the general assembly of the United Nations in December 1953 he spoke about the 'atomic dilemma'. He suggested forming the International Atomic Energy Agency. The general assembly unanimously resolved in December 1954 to hold a technical conference under the auspices of the United Nations on the peaceful uses of atomic energy. An advisory committee from seven countries was formed to help the secretary-general, Dag Hammarskjöld, and Cockcroft was chosen as the British representative. This extraordinary conference, held at Geneva in August 1955, was a political event of outstanding importance which might have heralded the end of the cold war. Scientists from the communist countries fraternized so easily with those from the west, that, just as they shared science, they thought there must be a way to share political philosophies. Scientifically it was an enormous success. Cockcroft was able to invite I. Kurchatov, of the USSR, to give a lecture at Harwell on a subject (fusion research) which only a few months earlier was regarded as extremely secret. The second Geneva conference was held in 1958, and Cockcroft gave what was widely considered to be a masterly summary of the proceedings.

Meanwhile, at Harwell and elsewhere, ideas about possible new reactor systems were proliferating. Cockcroft persuaded the AEA to set up a site at Winfrith to test experimental or small prototype reactors. He obtained European support for a joint project on a high temperature reactor (HTR) and the Organization for Economic Co-operation and Development Dragon project was agreed and put at Winfrith. Technically the helium gas cooling and the coated particle fuel behaved well and internationally the project gained a good reputation. Ultimately, however, the project came to an end because of the great cost of engineering full-scale commercial nuclear power stations.

One of the special research projects in atomic energy was called CTR (controlled thermonuclear reactions) or, more briefly, fusion research. Cockcroft gathered much of the British work to Harwell and the major project was the toroidal discharge machine called ZETA. The work, and particularly the work with this machine, had its ups and downs but, in retrospect, ZETA was a major step forward in fusion research. Cockcroft was able to give a great deal of help and encouragement to the Medical Research Council in their work on radiological protection. Radio-isotopes for biological and industrial uses became an important and profitable part of the work of the research group. His influence led to the creation of the Rutherford High Energy Laboratory. He was also closely concerned with the early years of CERN.

Master of Churchill Cockcroft resigned as a full-time member of the AEA in 1959 but remained a part-time member and moved to Cambridge to become the first master of Churchill College, having been nominated by Sir Winston Churchill himself, who also insisted that the appointment of succeeding masters should be made by the crown. The concept of a new college grew from the concern of some prominent British industrialists that Britain was lagging behind the USA and the USSR in providing excellent technical education, and Lord Cherwell had pressed these views on Sir Winston. In due course Cambridge accepted the offer of finance for a college which would have nearly as many advanced scientists and fellows as undergraduates, all living in college. Churchill was gratified that this college would bear his name, and Cockcroft was about the most famous scientist or engineer in Britain at that time. Industry was completely satisfied with the choice. No better person could have been chosen. The Cockcrofts' hospitality, their international friendships among scientists, and Cockcroft's interests in all sides of industry exactly matched the purposes for which the college was formed.

Cockcroft was also busy with science policy and education, defence policy, university matters, and international science. He represented Britain in the conference which in due course led to the signing of the test ban treaty relating to atomic weapons; he supported the Pugwash conferences on science and world affairs, and was their president in 1967.

Cockcroft received many honorary degrees, awards, and honours, the three principal being the Order of Merit

(1957), the Nobel prize for physics, jointly with E. T. S. Walton (1951), and the atoms for peace award (1961). He was appointed CBE in 1944, knight bachelor in 1948, and KCB in 1953. Cockcroft wrote few scientific papers, but from 1935 devoted his outstanding ability to organizing and administering research in science and technology. He was always generous in acknowledging colleagues, and appreciating technicians. He was deeply interested in architecture and music. He was a man of few words and his writing was minute; he never lost his temper. He and his family enjoyed relaxing at their holiday home at Cley, walking and sailing in the crisp Norfolk air. Cockcroft died on 18 September 1967 at Churchill College. On 17 October, at noon, a service of memorial and thanksgiving was held in Westminster Abbey. He was survived by his wife.

T. E. ALLIBONE

Sources autobiographical notes, RS · M. L. E. Oliphant and W. G. Penney, *Memoirs FRS*, 14 (1968), 139–88 · personal knowledge (2004) · private information (2004) · G. Hartcup and T. E. Allibone, *Cockcroft and the atom* (1984) · M. Gowing, *Britain and atomic energy, 1939–1945* (1964) · M. Gowing and L. Arnold, *Independence and deterrence: Britain and atomic energy, 1945–1952*, 2 vols. (1974) · election certificate, RS · b. cert.
Archives CAC Cam., corresp. and papers · CUL, corresp. relating to Cavendish laboratory | Atomic Energy Research Establishment, Harwell, papers relating to Maud committee · Bodl. Oxf., corresp. with Sir Rudolf Peierls · CAC Cam., corresp. with Sir Edward Bullard · CAC Cam., corresp. with Sir James Chadwick · CAC Cam., corresp. with Thomas Haldane · CAC Cam., corresp. with A. V. Hill · CAC Cam., scientific notes by him and E. T. S. Walton · IWM, corresp. with Sir Henry Tizard · Nuffield Oxf., corresp. with Sir James Chadwick · Nuffield Oxf., corresp. with Lord Cherwell · PRO, papers relating to Harwell, AB27 · RS, corresp. with Lord Blackett · Trinity Cam., corresp. with Egon Bretscher · U. Leeds, Brotherton L., corresp. with Edmund Stoner · University of Copenhagen, Niels Bohr Institute for Astronomy, Physics, and Geophysics, corresp. with Niels Bohr | SOUND BL NSA, oral history interview
Likenesses Bassano, photograph, 1946, NPG [*see illus.*] · W. Stoneman, photograph, 1946, NPG · photograph, 1951, Hult. Arch. · H. A. Freeth, chalk drawing, 1957, NPG · R. Tollast, drawing, c.1964, CAC Cam.
Wealth at death £41,218: probate, 3 Jan 1968, *CGPLA Eng. & Wales*

Cocke, Charles George (d. 1682), parliamentarian legal writer, is said by Rye (*Norfolk Families*) to have been the eldest son of Francis Cocke (d. 1628), mayor of Norwich in 1627, and his wife, Sarah, daughter of Robert Mower of Norwich. By 1637 he was a member of the Inner Temple, though he was not called to the bar. On 16 May 1648 he was appointed by parliament to a committee to investigate the Norwich riot of April 1648, sparked off by parliament's response to the mayor's failure to declare void the election of a royalist alderman and to his permitting of celebrations on the anniversary of the king's accession. Later that month he was appointed deputy lieutenant for the city and county of Norwich, and in December of that year became a commissioner for the militia for Norwich. In 1649 Cocke was twice appointed to assessment commissions for Norwich and for Norwich and Norfolk, and in 1650 was elected steward of Norwich, holding the office until 1660. Also in 1650 came appointment both to a further assessment commission and as a commissioner of

the high court of justice for the eastern counties. Appointment to another high court of justice followed in 1653, and from at latest 1650 until 1655 he was active as a justice of the peace in Norfolk.

On 30 July 1651 Cocke was commissioned as a colonel in the volunteers raised upon the alarm of Charles II's invasion, and in the same year appeared his *English-law, or, A summary survey of the household of God on earth … together with an essay on Christian government*, which propounded 'a model of Christian government', and aimed to achieve 'the just reformation of all our laws' and 'the reduction of them to a rule and standard of Christian simplicity' (Cocke, *English-Law*, foreword). The chance to put law reform into practice came in 1652 with his appointment to the extra-parliamentary law reform committee chaired by Matthew Hale. One of the first four lawyers to be named for the commission by the Rump Parliament's selection committee, Cocke frequently took the chair at meetings and played a part in drafting bills. In common with the majority of the commissioners he was not a radical, and his moderate views were subsequently reflected in his pamphlet *England's Compleat Law-Judge and Lawyer*, dedicated to the lord protector, which appeared in March 1656. Cocke urged the need for all jurisdictions, common law, chancery, and ecclesiastical, to have their place, emphasizing the necessity for care in undertaking reform lest 'the laws be altered and the principles of property and privileges lost by degrees' (Cocke, *Compleat Law-Judge*, 'The epistle to the judges'). Cocke had been appointed a judge of the court of admiralty in 1653, the second non-civilian to be so appointed, and also a judge for the probate of wills and granting of administrations, and perhaps in consequence of these positions, while not advocating a replacement of the common law by the civil law, he urged a greater role for the civil law, recommending the establishment of an appeal court composed of civilian doctors and common-law judges which might aid the reconciliation of common law and civil law. Also in 1653 Cocke had been elected for the city of Norwich to the first protectorate parliament, only to be defeated by John Hobart in a second election rapidly engineered by the royalist sheriffs Roger Mingay and Christopher Jay. A petition against his defeat, as violating the 'Instrument of government' which had established the protectorate, attracted over 100 signatures but fell on deaf ears in London. Appointed a commissioner for ejecting scandalous ministers and schoolmasters in Norfolk in 1654, in the following year Cocke became recorder of Great Yarmouth, and represented the borough in the parliaments of both 1656, in the earlier part of which he was active as a committee member, and 1658. In 1656 he was appointed a commissioner to try cases of treason, and appointment as a militia commissioner followed in 1659, together with further appointments as an assessment commissioner in 1657 and 1660.

The Restoration diminished Cocke, and Samuel Pepys, encountering his father's former customer 'whom I have carried clothes to … a man of mighty height and authority in his time' in London in 1668, found that he 'now walks like a poor sorry sneake' and regretted being known by him (Pepys, 9.113). His marriage to Ann (*d.* 1654), daughter of Richard Bond, brought them two daughters, of whom one, Elizabeth, married Sir Isaac Preston of Beeston, Norfolk, and the other Sir Robert Nightingale and, subsequently, John Burkin of Burlingham, Suffolk. Cocke died in 1682.

N. G. Jones

Sources F. Blomefield, *The history of the city and county of Norwich* (1741) · C. H. Firth and R. S. Rait, eds., *Acts and ordinances of the interregnum, 1642–1660*, 1–2 (1911) · F. A. Inderwick and R. A. Roberts, eds., *A calendar of the Inner Temple records*, 2 (1898) · J. T. Evans, *Seventeenth-century Norwich* (1979) · *CSP dom.*, 1651; 1654; 1658–9 · M. Cotterell, 'Interregnum law reform: the Hale commission of 1652', *EngHR*, 83 (1968), 689–704 · D. Veall, *The popular movement for law reform, 1640–1660* (1970) · C. G. Cocke, *English-law, or, A summary survey of the household of God on earth … together with an essay on Christian government* (1651) · C. G. Cocke, *England's compleat law-judge and lawyer* (1656) · T. Hawes, ed., *An index to Norwich city officers, 1453–1835* (1989) · *JHC*, 7 (1651–9) · D. E. Howell James, ed., *Norfolk quarter sessions order book, 1650–1657* (1955) · B. Cozens-Hardy and E. A. Kent, eds., *The mayors of Norwich, 1403 to 1835* (1938) · B. Cozens-Hardy, 'Norfolk lawyers', *Norfolk Archaeology*, 33 (1962–5), 266–97 · W. Rye, *Norfolk families*, 1 (1911) · W. Senior, *Doctors' Commons and the old court of admiralty* (1922) · Pepys, *Diary*, vol. 9 · memorial inscription, St Stephen's Church, Norwich

Cockell, Donald John (1928–1983), boxer, was born on 22 September 1928 at 46 Ouseley Road, Balham, London, the son of Kate Cockell, a domestic servant, of 44 Havelock Terrace, Battersea. He never knew his father. Cockell was apprenticed to a blacksmith and developed a strong physique well suited to boxing. He showed promise as a footballer, but earned money from fighting in fairground booths on Saturday nights, and after rising through the amateur ranks he turned professional in 1946.

Don Cockell—he was known by the diminutive—won most of his early bouts inside the distance, defeating good second-class fighters, a number of them heavyweights. In 1950, though, he lost twice to the stylish American heavyweight Aaron Wilson, and after this he concentrated on the lower weight division. In October he knocked out Mark Hart to win the vacant British and empire light heavyweight titles. Cockell was 'exceptionally talented' in this division and defeated a number of ranking Americans (Gutteridge, 105). But he always had difficulty making the weight and in June 1952 he lost both titles to Randolph Turpin, who had moved up from middleweight. Although Cockell subsequently fought as a heavyweight, his weight continued to be an issue for the boxing press and public. A win over an out-of-condition Tommy Farr signified little, but in May 1953 Cockell answered his critics by defeating the quick-moving Welshman Johnny Williams to take the British and empire heavyweight titles. In February 1954 he defended the empire title against the South African Johnny Arthur. Later victories over the noted Americans Harry Matthews and Roland La Starza put Cockell's name before the American fight public. They also opened up a somewhat unlikely title bout against the world champion, Rocky Marciano. The Marciano camp sought an easy opponent after the gruelling title defence against Ezzard Charles, and Cockell's direct style seemed perfectly suited to the champion's needs.

This would be the first British world title bid since Tommy Farr fought Joe Louis in 1937, but it had considerably less significance in America. The press there gave Cockell no chance of winning and ridiculed his waistline, while Marciano himself seemed apathetic, and to take the outcome for granted. Cockell, however, travelled to San Francisco ready to fight and trained hard: he reduced his weight to 14 stone 10 lb against the champion's 13 stone 7 lb. Although Cockell had weight advantage, Marciano was stronger, quicker, and, at 5 feet 11 inches, an inch taller. The challenger thus entered the ring at the Kezar Football Stadium on 16 May 1955 with odds of ten to one, and much else besides, against him. Marciano dictated the terms of the contest, from the weight of the gloves to the size of the ring. He would also be allowed to use brawling methods that would have earned a disqualification had the fight been in Europe, and which drew protests from the British boxing board, though not from Cockell himself.

Before the fight Cockell told his manager: 'This is the biggest night and biggest chance of my life. No matter what happens out there you are not to stop the fight' (Carpenter, 39). And for the first three rounds he fought on level terms, even managing on occasion to look the better boxer. But in truth he lacked the power to hurt Marciano, or the skill to avoid 'as murderous a hail of blows as any champion has, perhaps, ever inflicted' (*The Times*, 18 May 1955). For nine rounds Cockell took punches 'from all angles, long and short, fair and foul' (ibid.). He was cut on the forehead in the fourth, took 'two wicked, low blows' after the bell had sounded for the sixth, and ended the eighth doubled over the middle rope (ibid.). Within the first minute of the ninth he had been floored twice, but gamely rose to his feet. On the second occasion he was still clearly dazed and the referee stopped the contest. Cockell's performance drew grudging appreciation from a hardened American audience and Marciano himself conceded: 'He could take a lot of punishment, I hit the guy with some of my best shots' (Skehan, 250). To the British public Cockell was a hero, a 'plucky loser'. Yet he was inconsolable in defeat: he had put up 'great fights' for years, he reflected, but had 'wanted to win this one' (*The Times*, 18 May 1955).

In the immediate aftermath there was the inevitable talk of a rematch, which mercifully failed to materialize. Just how much the Marciano fight had taken out of Cockell was subsequently revealed. In September 1955 he faced the Cuban Nino Valdes at White City. At 15 stone 6 lb Cockell was hardly in peak condition and he retired with a badly gashed eye after three savage rounds. And in April 1956 he was knocked out inside two rounds by Kitione Lave, the 'Tongan terror', in what was meant to be a warm-up bout for a title defence. Cockell's ring career was over, and the pressure of public opinion eased his decision to retire 'from the sport he had served so well' (Treharne, 117). In May 1956 he was stripped of his empire heavyweight title and in July he surrendered his British title and announced his retirement.

Cockell's distinguished career ended on a bitter note. After the Lave fight the *Daily Mail* published a front-page article accusing him of being unprepared for the bout and of not giving his all. The paper described him as being 'overweight and flabby' (*The Times*, 19 Feb 1958). He responded with a libel action which in February 1958 was resolved in his favour when he was awarded £7500 damages with costs. He sought various ways of making a living after this, including running a farm, a public house at Crawley Down in Sussex, and a haulage business. He also worked on an oil rig and as a bus driver, and at the time of his death was an emergency maintenance man.

Cockell died of cancer on 18 July 1983 at St George's Hospital, Tooting, London. He had attended a benefit dinner in his honour the month before. He left a widow, Patricia Mary Cockell.

MARK POTTLE

Sources *The Times* (18 May 1955) · *The Times* (21 May 1955) · *The Times* (2 May 1956) · *The Times* (9 July 1956) · *The Times* (9 Nov 1957) · *The Times* (19 Feb 1958) · *The Times* (20 Feb 1958) · *The Times* (19 July 1983) · E. R. Treharne, *British heavyweight champions* (1959) · J. Huntington-Whiteley, ed., *The book of British sporting heroes* (1998) [exhibition catalogue, NPG, 16 Oct 1998 – 24 Jan 1999] · E. M. Skehan, *Rocky Marciano* (1977) · H. Carpenter, *Masters of boxing* (1964) · R. Gutteridge, *The big punchers* (1983) · b. cert. · d. cert.
Archives FILM BFI NFTVA, sports footage
Likenesses D. Hill, oils, *c.*1950, priv. coll.
Wealth at death under £40,000: administration, 24 Feb 1984, *CGPLA Eng. & Wales*

Cocker, Edward (1631/2–1676), calligrapher and arithmetician, is sometimes said to have come from Northamptonshire but this is unsubstantiated. Nothing is known of his parentage and early life. He published five copybooks in 1657; one, *The Pen's Triumph*, mentions an earlier *Pen's Experience*, now untraced, as his first work. By 1657 he was married, and teaching writing and arithmetic in St Paul's Churchyard, London. He and his wife, Joanna (or Joane), had two sons—Edward (1658–1723), also a penman, and Charles (1661–1674).

Further books followed thick and fast, much to the consternation of rivals; in all, Cocker engraved more than two dozen. This proliferation was the output of a virtuoso performer with pen and burin. He 'delighted to embroider his copy-books with fantastic creatures, exotic birds … his knots and flourishes are wonderful pieces of exuberant penmanship' (Heal, 36). His originality extended to interspersing his instruction with rhyming couplets. Samuel Pepys, describing him as 'the famous writing-master' (10 Aug 1664), employed him to engrave his slide-rule, and admired his skill in executing such fine work.

Cocker engraved plates for other authors—about 1660 for his friend, James Hodder, and in 1664 at least sixty-seven plates for Richard Daniel, and four plates in *The Young Clerk's Tutor* by J. H. of Staple-Inne. His own *Tutor to Writing and Arithmetic* (1664) was part letterpress, part engraved, with arithmetic outlined as far as the rule of three.

In the autumn of 1664 Cocker removed about 100 yards from St Paul's Churchyard to start a school in Gutter Lane; in 1667 he was teaching in Northampton, perhaps as a consequence of the great fire of 1666. By 1674 he was back in the City, and shortly set up school again by the church of St George the Martyr, Southwark, a move probably forced on him by committal for debt to the king's bench

prison; he could have purchased the privilege of living outside but near the prison. He died in the poverty which seems to have dogged him all his life, due to the turbulent times, and possible losses in the fire. It may be assumed that he died at his schoolhouse, as he was buried at the church on 26 August 1676. The verse broadside of 1675, *Cocker's Farewel to Brandy*, ending in the death of a drunkard, must have been written by him, not about him, as sometimes suggested.

Although famous as writing-master and engraver during his lifetime, Cocker became more so in death. In 1678 his friend and successor in the Southwark school, John Hawkins (*fl.* 1676–1692), published *Cockers Arithmetick, being a Plain and Familiar Method*, which he claimed to have taken from Cocker's manuscripts. This textbook, originally of 334 pages, had reached its twentieth edition by 1700 and its fifty-fifth by 1758; there were others with repeat numbering or none, besides at least eight Dublin editions and some at Edinburgh and Glasgow up to 1787. Its popularity might have derived from its being adapted to the requirements of trade rather than those of the gentry and their tutors. In a popular play of 1756 Cocker's *Arithmetick* was dubbed 'best Book that ever was wrote' (Murphy, 10), with four more mentions, spawning the phrase (not Murphy's) 'according to Cocker'; both book and man became bywords for authority. It is for his arithmetic rather than his calligraphy that Cocker is remembered.

In 1685 Hawkins published *Cocker's Decimal Arithmetick*, including logarithms and algebra, with a sixth and final edition in 1729. Then J. Back, a bookseller involved with the *Arithmetick*, issued in 1696 *Cockers Accomplish'd School-Master*, 'The like never published', without explaining its origin, and A. Back in 1704 produced *Cocker's English Dictionary* 'from the Authors Correct copy, by John Hawkins'. Strange to say, Hawkins had died in 1692; the Backs were probably fraudulently capitalizing on Cocker's name.

In the nineteenth century Augustus De Morgan, who considered Hodder's *Arithmetick* superior to Cocker's, also cast doubt on the authenticity of the latter, claiming that it was largely, if not wholly, a forgery by Hawkins. His 'proofs' are, however, extremely weak. The style of the preface and typical concluding couplet appear to proclaim it as genuine Cocker. De Morgan himself rather undermined his own thesis in a textual analysis intended to ridicule the writer's verbosity, by not recognizing that this completely accorded with Cocker's character.

Equally, there is no doubt that Cocker in his lifetime intended to publish on arithmetic. Two publishers' advertisements, in 1661 and 1669, attest to this. The presumption therefore remains that *Cockers Arithmetick* and *Cocker's Decimal Arithmetick*, both undoubtedly edited by Hawkins, are the *Compleat Arithmetician* described in the advertisements, and are indeed 'according to Cocker'.

RUTH WALLIS

Sources R. Wallis, 'Edward Cocker … and his *Arithmetick*: De Morgan demolished', *Annals of Science*, 54 (1997), 507–22 · A. Heal, *The English writing-masters and their copy-books, 1570–1800* (1931), 33–7, 43, 58–9, 135–45 · W. A. Smith, *"According to Cocker"* (1887) · J. C. Witton,

'Cocker's *Arithmetic*', *N&Q*, 2nd ser., 3 (1857), 95–6 • [E. Hatton], *A new view of London*, 1 (1708), 247 • S. P. Rigaud and S. J. Rigaud, eds., *Correspondence of scientific men of the seventeenth century*, 2 (1841), 471 • A. Murphy, *The apprentice* (1756) • Pepys, *Diary*, 5.237–9, 289–92 [10–11 Aug 1664, 5 and 7 Oct 1664] • A. De Morgan, *Arithmetical books from the invention of printing to the present time* (1847), 46, 56–62

Archives Magd. Cam., Pepys "calligraphical collection"

Likenesses engraving, *c.*1657, repro. in E. Cocker, *Pen's triumph* (1657) • engraving, *c.*1660, repro. in E. Cocker, *Pen's transcendencie* (1660) • engraving, in or before 1670, repro. in E. Cocker, *Urania, or, The scholar's delight* (1670?) • E. Cocker?, self-portrait?, engraving, repro. in Heal, *English writing-masters*, pl. 7 • engraving (at older age), BL; repro. in E. Cocker, *Multum in parvo, or, The pen's gallantry* (1686) • oils (after R. Gaywood), NPG

Wealth at death in debt: Heal, *English writing-masters*, 33

Cockeram, Henry (*fl.* 1623–1658), lexicographer, is known only as the author of *The English Dictionarie, or, An Interpreter of Hard English Words* (1623). This was the third dictionary of English, and the first to bear the title of 'dictionary', following Robert Cawdrey's *A Table Alphabeticall* (1604) and John Bullokar's *An English Expositor* (1616).

In the dedication to Richard Boyle, earl of Cork, Cockeram claims to be 'tied in double bonds of bloud and friendship' to a Sir William Hull. That Cockeram had some connection with Ireland is also suggested by the existence of an issue of the fifth edition of his *English Dictionarie* (1637), for Andrew Crooke and Thomas Allot, 'to be sold at their shop neere the Castle-Bridge in Dublin'. The first edition is prefaced by dedicatory verses from six of Cockeram's friends, one of whom is the playwright John Webster. We also learn from these dedicatory verses that Cockeram was a citizen of Exeter. He may have been the Henrye Cockram who married Elizabethe Strashley at Holy Trinity, Exeter, on 2 February 1613.

The English Dictionarie is a small octavo volume, divided into three 'Bookes': the first contains 'the choicest words themselves now in use'; the second a list of 'vulgar' words with their more 'refined' synonyms; and the third an encyclopaedic section containing information about 'Gods and Goddesses, Giants and Devils, Monsters and Serpents, Birds and Beasts, Rivers, Fishes, Herbs, Stones, Trees, and the like'. It was a commercial success, going into eleven editions printed in 1623, 1626, 1631, 1632, 1637, 1639, 1642, 1647, 1650, 1651, and 1658, with a twelfth edition 'enlarged by SC' appearing in 1670. Until the publication of Thomas Blount's *Glossographia* in 1656, the only rival to Cockeram's dictionary was Bullokar's *English Expositor*.

The English Dictionarie is in the same 'hard words' tradition as the dictionaries of Cawdrey and Bullokar, intended not to provide a full account of the vocabulary of English, but, as Cockeram states on the title-page, to enable 'Ladies and Gentlewomen, young Schollers, Clarkes, Merchants, as also Strangers of any Nation, to the understanding of the more difficult Authors already printed in our Language'. The issue of *The English Dictionarie* printed and sold by Edmund Weaver in 1623 includes on the title-page an acknowledgement that it is 'a Collection of the choicest words contained in the *Table Alphabeticall* and the *English Expositor*, and of some thousand of words never published by any heretofore'. The

issue printed in the same year for Nathaniel Butter, and all subsequent editions, omits the reference to Cockeram's predecessors. Starnes and Noyes suggest that 'Weaver, as printer of the *Table Alphabeticall*, may have insisted on Cockeram's acknowledgment of his debt to Cawdrey' (Starnes and Noyes, 26).

The only contemporary criticism of *The English Dictionarie* comes from the anonymous author of the *Vindex Anglicus* (1644), who, while not mentioning Cockeram by name, 'chose his forty-nine examples of kinds of words to be expunged from the English language almost entirely from Henry Cockeram's *English Dictionarie*' (Riddell, 'Beginning', 117). Starnes and Noyes acknowledge that Cockeram extended the scope of the dictionary by including encyclopaedic information and anticipated 'the idea of a standard of good usage' in his section devoted to 'vulgar' words and their 'refined' equivalents (Starnes and Noyes, 35). However, they suggest that the majority of Cockeram's words and definitions were taken from either Cawdrey or Bullokar or from contemporary Latin–English dictionaries such as Thomas Thomas's *Dictionarium linguae Latinae et Anglicanae* (1st edn, 1587), and that the second part is essentially a plagiarism of Francis Holyoke's revisions (1606, 1612, 1617) of John Rider's *Bibliotheca scholastica*. They imply that Cockeram, by Anglicizing the Latin entries in Rider–Holyoke, invented words that had never been used in English. This impression is reinforced by the presence in the *Oxford English Dictionary* of some 600 words cited first from Cockeram and only from Cockeram and later dictionaries (Riddell, 'Reliability', 4). However, both Riddell ('Beginning') and Schäfer (*Early Modern* and 'Hard-word dictionaries') point out that Cockeram was a more careful compiler than Starnes and Noyes acknowledge: he took neologisms from contemporary texts, such as Thomas Nashe's *Christs Teares Over Jerusalem* (1593), and used Latin–English dictionaries to check the definition of a word found elsewhere rather than to augment the vocabulary artificially.   JOAN C. BEAL

Sources *Henry Cockeram: 'The English dictionarie'*, ed. R. C. Alston, English Linguistics, 1500–1800, 124 (1968) • De W. T. Starnes and G. E. Noyes, *The English dictionary from Cawdrey to Johnson, 1604–1755*, new edn, ed. G. Stein (1991) • J. Schäfer, *Early modern English lexicography*, 1 (1989) • R. C. Alston, *A bibliography of the English language from the invention of printing to the year 1800*, 5 [1966]; repr. with corrections (1974) • J. A. Riddell, 'The beginning: English dictionaries of the first half of the seventeenth century', *Leeds Studies in English*, 7 (1974), 117–53 • J. A. Riddell, 'The reliability of early English dictionaries', *The Yearbook of English Studies*, 4 (1974), 1–4 • J. Schäfer, 'The hard-word dictionaries: a reassessment', *Leeds Studies in English*, 4 (1970), 31–48 • T. Learmouth and S. McWilliam, *Historic English dictionaries, 1595–1899: a union catalogue of holdings in Exeter libraries* (1986) • IGI

Cockerell, Sir Charles, first baronet (1755–1837), banker, was born at Bishops Hull, Somerset, on 18 February 1755, the fifth son of John Cockerell (1714–1767), of Welsh descent, with interests in the West Indies, and of his wife, Frances (*d.* 1769), *née* Jackson, a descendant of Samuel Pepys, the diarist. Charles had four sisters; one of his brothers was the architect Samuel Pepys *Cockerell (1753–1827). After two years at Winchester College and a course of accounts and bookkeeping at a school in Bromley by Bow, Middlesex, in 1776 he followed his eldest brother, John (d. 1798), who had been commissioned into the East India Company's army, to Bengal as a writer in the company's civil service. With an interval of leave, Cockerell was to remain in India until 1801.

Nearly all Charles Cockerell's Indian service was spent in Calcutta, where his most important appointment was as the company's postmaster-general from 1784 until 1792. Thereafter he remained a servant of the company, but without official employment, while he devoted his time to transacting his own private business as a partner in what was called a 'house of agency'. Houses of agency were a relatively new development in British India. They handled the concerns of Europeans in India, acting as their agents for their business dealings, arranging remittances to Britain, and financing shipping, plantations, and other private enterprises.

In 1784 Cockerell became a partner in the agency house established by William Paxton (1744–1824). When Paxton went to London to extend their business there, Cockerell managed the Calcutta house, which as Paxton and Cockerell, later Paxton, Cockerell, and Trail, became the most successful agency concern of its time. Although one of his contemporaries doubted whether Cockerell had 'a heart that could raise a thermometer above the freezing point' (J. P. Wade to F. Fowke, 1 Feb 1789, BL OIOC, MS Eur. E 8, fols. 169–70), he seems to have been a popular as well as a conspicuous figure in Calcutta society. His brief first marriage, on 11 March 1789, was to Maria Tryphena Blunt (d. 1789), daughter of Sir Charles William Blunt, third baronet (1731–1802), of the East India Company's service. She died that October. Their marriage was commemorated by an opulent painting of the couple at a harpsichord by Francesco Renaldi (1755–c.1799). Cockerell was churchwarden of the new St John's Church in Calcutta.

In 1801 Cockerell moved to Britain. He became a partner in the London house of Paxton, Cockerell, and Trail (later Cockerell and Trail, and Cockerell & Co.), first in the Strand, then in Pall Mall and finally at Austin Friars in the City. The firm continued to transact Indian agency business, as well as banking for British clients. Cockerell's interests spread very widely beyond the bank. He became a director of the Globe Insurance Company, the Arkendale and Derwent Mining Company, and the Gas, Light, and Coke Company. No doubt a wealthy man when he left India, his fortune at his death was assessed at £140,000. Cockerell entered parliament as MP for Tregony in Cornwall in 1802 and, with an interval of two years, was to remain an MP, representing a number of constituencies, for the rest of his life. He identified himself politically with the former governor-general, Richard, Marquess Wellesley, to whom he appears to have advanced large sums of money. Through Wellesley's influence Cockerell was made a baronet in 1809.

Cockerell maintained a large London house at Hyde Park Corner, but he also set himself up as a landowner in Gloucestershire. He bought Sezincote from the estate of his late brother John and instructed his architect brother,

Samuel Pepys Cockerell, to convert it to a house in the Mughal taste. Samuel was aided by Humphry Repton and the artist Thomas Daniell, who had travelled in India, painted many buildings there, and could therefore check the designs for authenticity. Work was begun in 1806 or 1807 and continued into the 1820s: a pastiche of the Taj Mahal, and 'Hindoo' motifs were included in the house and its outbuildings. The result was probably the most ambitious attempt up to that time to reproduce Indian architecture in Britain.

On 13 February 1808 Cockerell married for the second time. His new wife, with whom he had a son and two daughters, was the Hon. Harriet Rushout (d. 1851), second daughter of John Rushout, first Baron Northwick (1738–1800). Through his brother-in-law's family interest Cockerell represented the borough of Evesham from 1819 until his death. Cockerell lived in London and at Sezincote in some state. He entertained lavishly. Warren Hastings, his near neighbour, was a frequent guest. The Indian traveller Mirza Abu Talib, who was once entertained by Cockerell with 700 other diners, paid tribute to his generosity: 'Had he been my brother, he could not have behaved with more kindness' (Head, 31). From 1835 to 1837 Cockerell was one of the commissioners of the Board of Control for India. He died at Sezincote on 6 January 1837, just before his eighty-second birthday. His title passed to his son, Charles Rushout Cockerell (1809–1869), who changed his name to Rushout in 1849. P. J. MARSHALL and WILLEM G. J. KUITERS

Sources W. G. J. Kuiters, 'William Paxton, 1744–1824: merchant and banker in Bengal and London', MA diss., 1992, Leiden, pp. 83–6 [appx 4, 'Charles Cockerell'] · R. G. Thorne, 'Cockerell, Charles', HoP, Commons, 1790–1820 · GM, 2nd ser., 7 (1837) · R. Head, The Indian style (1986), 31 · 'Rushout', J. Foster, The peerage, baronetage, and knightage of the British empire for 1882, 2 (1882) · I. Butler, The eldest brother: the Marquess Wellesley, 1760–1842 (1973) · BL OIOC, J/1/9, fols. 214–16 · Abu Taleb Khan, Travels of Mirza Abu Taleb Khan in Asia, Africa, and Europe during the years 1799, 1800, 1801, 1802, and 1803: written by himself, in the Persian language, trans. C. Stewart, 2 vols. (1810) · Bengal establishments, BL OIOC, L/F/10/4–6 · S. B. Singh, The European Agency houses in Bengal, 1783–1833 (1966) · BL OIOC, MS Eur. F 8, E 8, fols. 169–70
Archives BL OIOC, Bengal public consultations · BL OIOC, corresp. with Francis Fowke, MS Eur. D 12
Likenesses F. Renaldi, group portrait, oils, 1789 (with his first wife and sister-in-law), repro. in M. Archer, India and British portraiture, 1770–1825 (1979), 289 · engraving, pubd 1819 (after bust), BM
Wealth at death £140,000: probate, PRO, PROB 8/230

Cockerell, Charles Robert (1788–1863), architect, was born in London on 28 April 1788, the third of the eleven children of Samuel Pepys *Cockerell (1753–1827), architect and surveyor, and his wife, Anne, neé Whetham. He was educated at a private school near the City Road, Finsbury, and afterwards at Westminster School, where he remained from 1802 until the age of sixteen. He began his architectural training in his father's office, from which he moved after four or five years to the office of his father's friend Robert Smirke, then engaged in building the new Covent Garden Theatre (1808–9), a pioneering work in the Greek revival manner.

Charles Robert Cockerell (1788–1863), by Jean-Auguste-Dominique Ingres, 1817

Travels at home and abroad: the grand tour In the summer of 1808 Cockerell's father arranged for him to make a picturesque tour of the west country and Wales in the company of the distinguished watercolour painters Thomas and William Daniell. His perceptive journal of this tour, called *Memorandum*, survives. Two years later his father sent him on a continental grand tour from which he did not return until 1817, four years later than originally planned, having made many startling discoveries in the field of ancient Greek architecture and sculpture.

With Italy and France inaccessible to the British during the Napoleonic Wars, it was in the improbable role of a king's messenger, with dispatches for the fleet at Constantinople, that Cockerell set sail for Constantinople in April 1810. This plan had been arranged by his father's friend William Hamilton FRS, under-secretary of state for foreign affairs, and previously private secretary to Lord Elgin. A note of Byronic romance entered Cockerell's dramatic sea voyage, which involved passing within sight of Cadiz during its bombardment. It was therefore appropriate that in both Constantinople and Athens, where he arrived in June 1810, he moved in the circle of Byron. He also made friends with a group of international scholars, travellers, and architects, including Karl Haller von Hallerstein (with whom, so Cockerell wrote to his sister, he swore eternal friendship), the Liverpool architect John Foster, John Cam Hobhouse, later Lord Broughton (an old schoolfriend from Westminster), the landscape painter Jakob Linckh from Württemberg, the Hon. Frederick North (later Lord Guilford), Baron Otto von Stackelberg, and the Danish archaeologist Peter Brøndsted.

In April 1811 Cockerell, Hallerstein, Linckh, and Foster travelled to the island of Aegina, near Athens, after an evening drinking with Byron, to study the late Archaic temple of Aphaia, then known as the temple of Jupiter Panhellenius. In April 1811 Cockerell and his companions made the revolutionary discovery that the temple, of local limestone faced with cream-painted stucco, was richly painted in bright colours. Cockerell published his discovery that, contrary to the views of Winckelmann, polychromy was integral to Greek architecture from the start. They also excavated the pedimental sculpture, stylistically important as transitional between archaic and classical. Cockerell's hope that it might be purchased by the British government was thwarted when it was acquired for the Glyptothek in Munich by the crown prince of Bavaria (later Ludwig I).

In August 1811 Cockerell and his companions moved on to the temple of Apollo Epicurius at Bassae in the Peloponnese, a building ascribed by Pausanias to the architect of the Parthenon, Ictinus. Regarded today as one of the first Greek works with an aesthetically designed interior, this unique monument exhibited numerous divergencies from the supposedly rational Greek ideals: engaged columns, the first Corinthian capital, Ionic columns with uniquely flared bases and capitals, and a figured frieze in the interior, not on the exterior. In 1813, Cockerell arranged for the purchase of this 102 foot frieze by the British government for display in the British Museum. In his account of the temple, which he dedicated to the memory of William Hamilton, Cockerell evoked its almost proto-baroque quality by claiming that 'considerations of optics and perspective' were paramount in its design, and that its 'peculiarities … exhibit the perspective science of the architect, and show how freely and confidently he could deal with his material, regardless of the reproach of anomaly and caprice' (*The Temples of Jupiter Panhellenius at Aegina, and of Apollo Epicurius at Bassae*, 1860, 57, 48).

In November 1811 Cockerell and his friends founded a private club called the *Xeineion* ('token of friendship'), giving each other bronze rings which were inscribed *Xeineion* and bore images of the owl of Minerva. In 1811–12, together with Foster and Frederick North, Cockerell made a tour of Hellenistic sites in Asia Minor, meeting, in Smyrna, Captain Frederick Beaufort, who was in command of HMS *Fredericksteen*. Beaufort invited Cockerell to accompany him on a tour of investigation of the southern shores of Asia Minor. Cockerell left Beaufort in Malta to travel to Sicily, where he spent three months in 1812 measuring the problematical temple of Jupiter Olympius at Agrigento, the largest of all Greek Doric temples. The outer columns were, unusually, not free-standing, but were half-columns engaged against a continuous solid wall. The temple was also vigorously sculptural, incorporating male figures, or telamons, 25 feet high. Cockerell published his discoveries at this temple, which had a profound influence on his own buildings, in the supplementary volume of *The Antiquities of Athens* (1830) by J. Stuart and N. Revett.

In the summer of 1813 Cockerell fell seriously ill in Athens with a fever, but on recovery he returned via Albania to make a tour of the Peloponnese and the archipelago. With the abdication of Napoleon in April 1814, he was able to visit Italy, and spent the winter of 1815–16 in Rome. In the spring of 1816 he was in Florence, where he won further fame with a proposed restoration of the group of *Niobe and her Children* in the Uffizi as a pedimental sculpture. In the same year he made one of the first of his independent designs for a building, a palace for the duke of Wellington, an idea suggested by his father. He found the task so uncongenial that he wrote to his father from Milan in 1816 that:

> I am an artist & nothing but an artist. I am a good painter spoilt. The more I have seen of Italy the more persuaded I am that I was born to be a painter. If I must adopt architecture I must appear in this and this only, as professor of the beautiful in architecture.　(Watkin, *Life and Work*, xxi–xxii)

Establishment in architectural practice; early works; marriage and family　After returning to London in June 1817, Cockerell dutifully followed his father's advice, setting up as an architect in elegant premises in Old Burlington Street, Mayfair, provided for him by his ever generous father. In 1819 he was one of the founder members of the Travellers' Club, intended as a place where the British might entertain foreigners who had given them hospitality while on their grand tours. The Travellers' Club was an extension of Cockerell's *Xeineion* in that it was a late expression of the ideals of international fraternity, both social and intellectual, which were associated with the eighteenth-century Enlightenment. From 1819 Cockerell was a member of the committee of the Travellers' Club, together with Lord Auckland, Lord Lansdowne, Lord Palmerston, the Hon. Robert Clive, the diplomat and oriental scholar Sir Gore Ouseley, the classical topographer and numismatist Lieutenant-Colonel W. M. Leake, and the diplomat, antiquary, and Egyptologist W. R. Hamilton. The Travellers' Club was valuable to Cockerell as a source of patronage, for three of his fellow committee members, Lansdowne, Clive, and Ouseley, employed him to remodel their country seats, Bowood, Oakly, and Woolmers, respectively.

Cockerell's awareness of the richness and freedom of Greek architecture, and especially of its sculptural basis, made him recognize that the architecture of later periods from ancient Rome to baroque Italy retained many Grecian qualities. In this generosity and lack of pedantry he was very different from more pedestrian Greek revival architects such as William Wilkins and Sir Robert Smirke. He had been the first to note, and measure, the entasis on the columns of the Parthenon, sending the details in a letter to Smirke of 23 December 1814. In his early works he attempted to incorporate souvenirs of his Grecian discoveries, as in the dining-room at Grange Park, Hampshire (1823), a sumptuous interior inspired by the cella of the temple at Bassae, and in his dramatic staircase hall of the same year at Oakly Park, Shropshire, where he incorporated a top-lit cast of the Bassae frieze. In 1822 he was chosen by a Scottish committee to design the national monument on Calton Hill, Edinburgh, intended by its sponsors to be a full-scale replica of the Parthenon. Between 1824 and 1829 twelve columns were erected, after which work ceased.

Cockerell's most important early work was the Hanover Chapel (1823–5; dem. 1896), a twin-towered Grecian edifice with an iron and glass dome which was a striking feature of Nash's new Regent Street. We can follow the painstaking process by which his designs evolved in these years from his diaries which survive for the years 1821–30 and 1832. They reveal him as a fastidious perfectionist, concerned with self-improvement, both architectural and moral. Full of self-criticism, he was vigorously opposed to the dry manner of the Greek revival in which he had been trained by Smirke. In these years, too, he compiled a manuscript album, 'Ichnographica domestica', a fascinating illustrated record of his visits to English houses which reveals him as a remarkably early pioneer in the appreciation of the powerful and inventive work of Vanbrugh and Hawksmoor.

On 4 June 1828 Cockerell married Anna Rennie (1803–1872), daughter of the civil engineer John Rennie; they had ten children, of whom one, Frederick Pepys *Cockerell, followed him as an architect. Despite his early wish to be an artist, Cockerell became associated at the start of his career with the expanding world of banking and of life insurance. His first commercial building in London, the Westminster, Life and British Fire office, Strand (1831–2; dem. 1907), had a Greek Doric portico in antis combined with a rich surface texture embellished with figure sculpture, a form inspired by Palladio's Loggia del Capitaniato in Vicenza. He adopted this Grecian mannerism for his subsequent commercial buildings in London, notably the London and Westminster Bank, Lothbury (1837–9; dem. 1928), and the Sun Fire office, Threadneedle Street (1841–2; dem. 1971).

Major works　Cockerell created a more heroic language for his three major projects of the late 1830s, the University Library, Cambridge, the Ashmolean Museum and Taylor Institution, Oxford, and the unexecuted Royal Exchange. Of his Cambridge library, planned as a monumental courtyard, only the north range was executed, in 1837–40. Though with details of a Greek austerity of line, the entrance front is dominated by a Roman triumphal arch theme, developed from Alberti's S. Andrea, Mantua, where the arch similarly breaks through the entablature. Cockerell's library achieves much of its commanding visual effect by the contrasting colours of the two stones of which it is constructed, white Portland stone and a brownish Whitby stone from Yorkshire.

At the Ashmolean Museum and Taylor Institution, Oxford (1841–5), Cockerell similarly rejected the traditional local building stone, a brownish Oxford limestone, in favour of an inventive polychromy of three stones: a yellow Bath stone for the main walls, Portland stone for the columns and ornamental details, and Whitby stone for the basement. Conceived by Cockerell as a way of introducing Greek polychromy in a northern climate where external paint would not survive, this combination of materials had already been employed by one of his heroes, Inigo Jones, at the Banqueting House. At the Ashmolean Museum, Cockerell combined Greek elements with features derived from Vignola's Palazzo Farnese at Caprarola, a combination appropriate for a building intended to house the university's collection of antique sculpture, and of European paintings, mainly Italian.

The commission for the Ashmolean Museum also involved the provision of premises for the Taylor Institution, the university department of modern languages. Cockerell insisted that the columns of the Bassae Ionic order on the façade of his Taylor Institution should be crowned by four female figures, representing France, Italy, Spain, and Germany. The university authorities had wanted them to be statues of famous male authors, but Cockerell was an upholder of eighteenth-century generalization, not of Victorian nationalism. He was also aware that to surmount Ionic columns with female figures was an appropriate reflection of Vitruvius's claim that the Ionic order originated in the female form and dress.

Cockerell entered unsuccessfully a vast number of important competitions, including those for University College, London (1826), the Duke of York's column (1832), the National Gallery (1833), the Houses of Parliament (1835), the Reform Club (1837), the Royal Exchange (1839), and the Carlton Club (1844). In his highly individual design for the Houses of Parliament he largely ignored the requirement that the new building should be in either the 'Gothic or Elizabethan' style, producing a domed Renaissance building, incorporating echoes of Longleat and Hatfield. He also sensitively proposed preserving far more of the important remains of the medieval Palace of Westminster than his fellow competitors.

Cockerell's elliptical concert hall of 1851–6 at St George's Hall, Liverpool, where he took over from Harvey Lonsdale Elmes on his death in 1847, has a sensuous beauty which owes much to the undulating balcony of delicate cast-iron lattice-work carried on beautiful caryatids, inspired by those of the Erechtheion. With its golden-brown colouring, its richly decorated pilasters and friezes of papier mâché, its grained and varnished wooden surfaces, and its dramatic use of mirrors, it is one of the loveliest interiors of nineteenth-century England.

Academic life In his lectures as professor of architecture at the Royal Academy from 1841 to 1856, extensively reported in *The Athenaeum* and *The Builder*, Cockerell upheld a humanist view of classical architecture as an image of ideal beauty which would reprimand the modern world for its commercialism and lack of high ambitions. This was ultimately dependent on a Vitruvian view of architecture as a representation of the human body seen as an ideal type of beauty. Like his late eighteenth-century French predecessors such as Boullée and Ledoux, he believed that 'The universality of certain primordial forms in all styles favours the notion of innate ideas, the cube, the sphere, the ellypsoid … common to the art of all time and people' ('Lecture V', *The Athenaeum*, 18 Feb 1843, 159). He lectured in front of a large watercolour called 'The professor's dream': a symposium of the principal architectural monuments of modern and ancient times, drawn to the same scale, which he first exhibited at the Royal Academy in 1849. Its format echoed that of another painting for which he was also well known, *Tribute to the Memory of Sir Christopher Wren* (1838), in which he imaginatively assembled all of Wren's works in a single composition. He was one of the finest of all British architectural draughtsmen. Numerous drawings by him survive at the Victoria and Albert Museum, the British Architectural Library Drawings Collection, and Cambridge University Library.

Public offices Cockerell's numerous public offices included that of surveyor of St Paul's Cathedral, where he succeeded his father in 1819, and architect to the Bank of England, in succession to Soane in 1833; he was elected ARA in 1829, RA in 1836, and professor of architecture in 1840. In 1848 he was the first recipient of the royal gold medal of the Royal Institute of British Architects (RIBA), succeeding Earl de Grey in 1860 as the institute's first professional president. He was an honorary DCL of Oxford University, and a member of the Society of Dilettanti.

Cockerell's essentially European outlook was underlined by the numerous foreign honours lavished on him: in France, he was one of the eight *associés étrangers* of the Académie des Beaux-Arts, an associate member of the Institut de France, and a chevalier of the Légion d'honneur. He was one of the ten members of merit of the Accademia di San Luca in Rome, and a member of the royal academies of Bavaria, Belgium, and Denmark. He was also a member of the academies of Geneva and Genoa, of the Archaeological Society of Athens, and of the American Institute of Architects.

Later life After retiring from his professorship at the Royal Academy in 1857 and from practice in 1859, Cockerell died on 17 September 1863 at home at 13 Chester Terrace, Regent's Park. A week later, following his funeral in St Paul's Cathedral, he was buried in the crypt of the cathedral, where a monument was later erected to him and his wife from designs by their son Frederick Pepys Cockerell. Richly carved in low-relief sculpture, this tablet incorporates, appropriately, a capital of the Bassae Ionic order.

Cockerell was widely revered for his scholarship, his high professional and artistic ideals, and his dignified, even noble, bearing. Of strikingly handsome appearance, he was a perfect example of the Victorian Christian gentleman; his son claimed of him that 'Meanness, coarseness, or wrong-doing were abhorrent to him' (*Architectural Review*, 12, 1902, 146), and George Aitchison noted that he had 'the dignified and refined manner of the high-bred English gentleman' (*RIBA Transactions*, new ser., 6, 1890, 261).

Contemporary and later assessment Cockerell's subtle, learned, and allusive architectural language found no imitators in England, but it is in France that analogies can be found, in the néo-Grec work of Beaux-Arts architects such as Hittorff, Caristie, Labrouste, Duc, Nénot, Ginain, and Pascal. Cockerell's isolation from contemporary English trends is suggested by his portrayal in the carved frieze on the Albert Memorial in improbable association with A. W. N. Pugin and Sir Charles Barry. None the less, the merit of his work has been recognized from his own day to the present, with the exception of the fanatical Goth A. W. N. Pugin, for whom the Ashmolean Museum was an 'unsightly pile of pagan details … [which] if it pleases the admirers of gin-palace design … will draw down the indignation of every true disciple of Catholic and consistent architecture' (*An Apology for the Revival of Christian Architecture in England*, 1843, 3).

A more typical reaction to the Ashmolean was that of the influential architectural historian James Fergusson, who wrote of it, just thirty years later, that 'there is perhaps no building in England on which the refined student of architecture can dwell with so much pleasure' (*History of the Modern Styles of Architecture*, 2nd edn, 1873, 349). Of Cockerell's branch Bank of England, Liverpool, the critic Heathcote Statham wrote in 1912 that Cockerell 'produced two or three façades for the branch Banks of England—one especially in Liverpool—the study of the details of which is a liberal education' (*A Short Critical History of Architecture*, 1912, 527), while the architect H. S. Goodhart-Rendel went so far as to claim that, 'Never has there been a more accomplished English architect than he, nor one more originally creative' (*English Architecture since the Regency*, 1953, 74).   DAVID WATKIN

Sources *The Builder*, 21 (1863), 683–5 · *GM*, 3rd ser., 15 (1863), 785–91 · S. P. Cockerell, ed., *Travels in southern Europe and the Levant, 1810–1817: the journal of C. R. Cockerell, R.A.* (1903) · J. Harris, 'C. R. Cockerell's Ichnographica domestica', *Architectural History*, 14 (1971), 5–29 · D. Watkin, *The life and work of C. R. Cockerell* (1974) · D. Watkin, 'Newly discovered drawings by C. R. Cockerell for Cambridge University Library', *Architectural History*, 26 (1983), 87–91 · D. Watkin, 'C. R. Cockerell and the role of archaeology in modern classical architecture', *The Classicist*, 2 (1996), 16–24 · G. L. Carr, 'C. R. Cockerell's Hanover Chapel', *Journal of the Society of Architectural Historians*, 39 (1980), 265–85 · A. Forty, 'Thoughts on architecture and nationality … the Taylor Institution and the Martyrs' Memorial in Oxford', *A. A. Files: Annals of the Architectural Association School of Architecture*, 32 (autumn 1996), 26–37 · P. Broucke, ed., *The archaeology of architecture: C. R. Cockerell in southern Europe and the Levant, 1810–1817* (1993) · J. Olley, 'St George's Hall, Liverpool', *Architects' Journal* (18 June 1986), 36–57 · J. Olley, 'St George's Hall, Liverpool', *Architects' Journal* (25 June 1986), 36–61 · J. Olley, 'University Library [Cambridge]', *Architects' Journal* (8 Feb 1989), 34–63 · I. Jenkins, *Archaeologists and aesthetes in the sculpture galleries of the British Museum, 1800–1939* (1992) · S. Smirke, 'Some account of the professional life and character of the late professor C. R. Cockerell', *Transactions of the Royal Institute of British Architects* (1863–4), 17–28 · G. Aitchison, 'C. R. Cockerell', *Transactions of the Royal Institute of British Architects*, new ser., 6 (1899–1900), 349–68 · R. P. Cockerell, 'The life and works of C. R. Cockerell', *ArchR*, 12 (1902), 129–46 · R. P. Spiers, 'Cockerell's restorations of ancient Rome', *ArchR*, 29 (1911), 123–8 · C. A. Hutton, 'A collection of sketches by C. R. Cockerell, R.A.', *Journal of Hellenistic Studies*, 29 (1909), 53–9 · A. E. Richardson, *Monumental classic architecture in Great Britain and Ireland* (1914) · A. E. Richardson, 'Some early drawings by Professor C. R. Cockerell', *RIBA Journal*, 37 (1929–30), 725–7 · d. cert.
Archives NL Scot., corresp. and papers relating to the national monument, Edinburgh · RA, lecture drafts and notes · RIBA BAL, corresp., diaries, and papers; further corresp.; sketchbooks | BL, letters to Philip Bliss, Add. MSS 34573–34575 · Bodl. Oxf., letters relating to Taylor Institution and university galleries, Oxford · CUL, letters to Joseph Bonomi · U. Lpool L., drawings and papers relating to St George's Hall, Liverpool
Likenesses J.-A.-D. Ingres, drawing, 1817, priv. coll. · J.-A.-D. Ingres, pencil drawing, 1817, AM Oxf. [*see illus.*] · C. C. Vogel, drawing, 1817, Staatliche Kunstsammlungen, Dresden · F. P. Cockerell, medallion on monument, *c.*1863, St Paul's Cathedral, London · W. Boxall, oils, RIBA · attrib. A. E. Chalon, watercolour drawing, NPG
Wealth at death under £35,000: probate, 13 Nov 1863, *CGPLA Eng. & Wales*

Cockerell, Sir Christopher Sydney (1910–1999), electronic and mechanical engineer, was born at Wayside, Cavendish Avenue, Cambridge, on 4 June 1910, the only son in the family of one son and two daughters of Sir Sydney Carlyle *Cockerell (1867–1962), the distinguished director of the Fitzwilliam Museum in Cambridge, and his wife, Florence Kate (1872–1949), the daughter of Charles Tomson Kingsford of Canterbury. Sir Sydney's strong personality made a real relationship with his son very difficult. In contrast, his mother, a talented artist and a superb illuminator, lived by the interplay and subtle shades of things and was much loved by her children. Christopher was also influenced by the many distinguished visitors to their home, including George Bernard Shaw, Joseph Conrad, Freya Stark, Siegfried Sassoon, and T. E. Lawrence. However, the interest he showed in Lawrence's 1000 cc Brough Superior motor cycle led his father to categorize the boy as 'no better than a garage hand'.

Cockerell's earliest education was at home, where a succession of governesses found him very difficult, because all his interest was centred on science and engineering. He built his own crystal radio set and made a small steam engine to drive his mother's sewing machine. He was disappointed to find she much preferred to operate it by hand. His father could not understand the boy's interest in such devices or that he preferred a book entitled *The Boy Electrician* to *The Life of Rembrandt*. When Cockerell was eleven his parents sent him to Lydgate House preparatory school at Hunstanton in Norfolk. He was there for three years, during which time he built a complete wireless set for school use. His next school was Gresham's, at Holt, also in Norfolk, where he met W. H. Auden and Donald Maclean. While there he read all of Dickens's novels and again built a complete wireless set.

Although he found academic subjects difficult, with hard work and determination Cockerell obtained a place at Peterhouse, Cambridge, when he was eighteen. He spent much of his spare time overhauling motor bikes, which he raced, winning several cups. He spent many of his long vacations with Captain George Spencer-Churchill, who fostered his lifetime interest in antiquities and also allowed him to shoot pigeons. When Cockerell's father gave him £20 for his twenty-first birthday he bought a Mauser 0.22 rifle with telescopic sight and silencer. His father was disgusted, but it enabled him to reach a sufficient standard to shoot for the university.

Electronics engineering Following graduation with an engineering degree, Cockerell was employed for two years at W. H. Allen & Sons of Bedford, engineers, working as a pupil engineer. The company had a problem with pouring molten iron into moulds, which Cockerell solved by persuading them to build an additional 5 feet on the top of their furnaces. In 1934 he returned to Cambridge to research radio and electronics. He then joined the Marconi Wireless Telegraph Company at the Writtle site, near Chelmsford. At that time the only means of electrical amplification was the thermionic valve. Standard radio frequency (RF) connectors were unknown and instrumentation was primitive. Cockerell began work on the first BBC outside broadcast vehicle, due to begin service in 1936, and on the short-wave television beam aerials for Alexandra Palace. The technology involved had no precedent. Only seven months after he had joined Marconi, the company filed his first patent for this work. In 1937 he was promoted head of aircraft research and development. In the same year, on 4 September, he married Margaret Elinor Belsham (1913–1996). She really was the love of his life and a wonderful support to him throughout their married life. This support was of prime importance during the Second World War, when he worked exceedingly long hours. During this time they lived in Baddow Road, Chelmsford.

Cockerell's last design before the Second World War was a radio direction finder for the new Cunard liner *Mauretania*. In October 1939 he was visited by a wing commander of Bomber Command who required radically new radio communication and navigation equipment. During lunch Cockerell wrote a specification on the back of an envelope; he received an order the next day, a quick response possible only in wartime. Working seven days a week, Cockerell and his team produced a prototype for installation in a bomber in only eleven weeks, an incredible achievement. The device solved the homing problem by enabling the pilot to fly on the correct course with a special left–on track–right display soon known as the 'drunken men'. By June 1940 production equipment was being installed in bombers. The RAF required 1000 units per week, and the firm of E. K. Cole was contracted to assist Marconi with production. During the course of the war some 120,000 R1155 receiver units and 55,000 T1154

transmitters were produced, at a cost of £4000 per set. Cockerell regarded this equipment as the most important work of his career, providing bomber crews with highly effective navigation, communication, and homing devices. Marconi offered Cockerell promotion in 1940 but he refused to leave his team, whom he regarded as of equal importance.

This work was followed by the provision of a universal display unit for the Royal Navy, based on the Type 960 radar, enabling a single operator to keep control of the radar in very heavy seas and combine this data with other information, such as compass readings. The Fleet Air Arm was provided with a radio beacon and receiver to enable pilots to return safely to their aircraft-carriers. Shortly before the D-day landings Cockerell and his team were required to produce equipment to locate precisely the German radar stations on the coast of France. Again working very long hours, they succeeded in providing a special recording receiver for Pathfinder aircraft which swept all radar frequencies, marking a moving paper chart when the appropriate signal was detected. The equipment was code-named Bagful and was used successfully to identify German radar stations prior to the first landings.

After the war, Cockerell's team worked on a new range of airborne equipment, which secured the position of Marconi in this field. They also patented a hyperbolic navigation system for civil aircraft. This was followed by a patent solving the problem of positioning an aircraft on final approach. In 1948 Cockerell moved to the Marconi research laboratories at Great Baddow, near Chelmsford. Many other basic electronic ideas evolved, bringing the total number of patents in Cockerell's name to thirty-six, the last in November 1950, which concerned improvement in determining the height of an aircraft for traffic controllers using ground-to-air radar. He declined an offer of further promotion, which would have involved more administration; this was not to his liking and caused him to consider his whole future. He resigned on 8 August 1951

Sir Christopher Sydney **Cockerell** (1910–1999), by unknown photographer, 1979

as he wanted a life involving more imagination and initiative.

Invention of the hovercraft In 1947 Christopher and Margaret had decided to invest the inheritance she had received from her father in a boat-hiring and caravan-building business at Oulton Broad, near Lowestoft. When Cockerell left Marconi they sold their house and devoted all their time to this new business, called Ripplecraft Ltd. Initially he designed motor boats, all of which embodied new ideas. However, his restless mind soon caused him to think of bigger things, and he decided that the power required by motor boats could be significantly reduced.

Cockerell considered that the only way water drag could be reduced was by introducing air between the hull and the water, and he purchased a 20 foot long ex-navy launch for his experiments. These were not very successful, and so he decided to carry out a basic experiment with a small industrial electrical fan mounted above a Lyons coffee tin, with a Kit-e-Kat tin inside it to provide a downward circular jet of air directed at his kitchen scales. He found that the downward thrust with the inner tin in place was four times that without it. He had invented the amphibious hovercraft and patented the idea in December 1955. Tests with a special streamlined model 2½ feet long and 2 feet wide powered by a model aircraft engine showed a speed of 13 knots could be achieved, and Cockerell was delighted.

Cockerell could not get funding from leading industrial companies until his friend Lord Somerleyton enlisted the help of Lord Louis Mountbatten, who saw the potential of the idea and arranged a meeting of Admiralty representatives and the assistant director of aircraft research, R. A. Shaw, with Cockerell and his patent agent. The Admiralty were not impressed, but Shaw arranged for its potential to be examined at the Ministry of Supply and placed it on the secret list.

Shaw and Cockerell visited Saunders Roe on the Isle of Wight, who agreed to undertake the work, provided they were paid. Their detailed proposal was accepted by the Ministry of Supply in 1957. After carrying out comprehensive investigations and experiments Saunders Roe produced a favourable report in May 1958, supplemented in July by a proposal to build a manned model. Two months later a further report assessing the future potential included the suggestion that a 400 ton cross-channel passenger and car ferry was feasible.

Meanwhile, owing to an inadvertent disclosure, the invention had to be declassified, and the National Research Development Corporation (NRDC) agreed to provide financial support. Cockerell was advanced £1000 to defray patent fees, and Saunders Roe received a contract from the NRDC to construct their proposed manned model in October 1958. This was quickly followed by the NRDC forming a wholly owned subsidiary called Hovercraft Development Ltd (HDL) in January 1959. The chairman and managing director was Dennis Hennesey, one of NRDC's directors, and Cockerell was a director and technical consultant. Their first office was in Cockerell's house, White Cottage, in Victoria Grove, East Cowes,

within a few hundred yards of the Saunders Roe design team at Osborne. In 1960 the company moved to The Grove, at Hythe, on the west shore of Southampton Water. Later on Cockerell bought a house close by, and 16 Prospect Place remained his home for the rest of his life.

In eight months the Saunders Roe manned model, SRN1, was completed, and it was shown to the press on 11 June 1959. Trials were successful, and on 25 July the craft crossed the English Channel in celebration of the fiftieth anniversary of Blériot's first aircraft crossing. The craft's hover height of approximately 1 foot was soon found to limit its performance in wave heights of double the hover height, and it was fitted with peripheral flexible extensions, soon nicknamed skirts. These were made from rubber materials reinforced with nylon cloth. When a vertical height of 4 feet was reached it was found that overwave performance was very satisfactory.

Meanwhile the enthusiastic team at HDL were working on a variety of applications of the hovercraft principle. Several full-scale man-carrying craft were built, both amphibious and sidewall. A special team was set up to investigate hovercraft trains, and an experimental track was set up near Cambridge. The movement on cushions of air of very large loads such as redundant gasometers and smaller 1 ton loads was investigated. One team produced hospital beds for burns patients. The new company filed more than 200 patents, 59 in Cockerell's own name. (Cockerell filed a total of 98 patents in his lifetime.)

Commercial development The success of SRN1 led to the demand for HDL licences to build hovercraft, which were granted to Saunders Roe, Vickers, Folland, and Cushion Craft in the United Kingdom, Bell in the United States, and Mitsui and Mitsubishi in Japan. A licence was refused to Russia. The demand for financial support led the NRDC to encourage the United Kingdom companies to merge their hovercraft interests into a single company. Cockerell vehemently opposed the idea, as he considered it would significantly reduce development and remove competition. The NRDC persisted, and the British Hovercraft Corporation was formed from Saunders Roe—then a division of Westland Aircraft Ltd—and Vickers, with two NRDC directors on the board. Cockerell persisted in his opposition and decided to resign as director of HDL. In a letter dated 23 March 1966 from John Duckworth, the managing director of the NRDC, which wholly owned HDL, Cockerell was informed that the board had decided to accept his resignation. The letter also stated that 'it would not be appropriate' for him to continue in the executive position of chief engineer of HDL, and that this responsibility 'should come to an end', giving him just eight days' notice.

Cockerell was appointed CBE in 1966, elected a fellow of the Royal Society in 1967, and was knighted in 1969. He was delighted with the latter, regarding it as a 'very romantic' honour. It was not until 1972 that he received compensation of £150,000 for the loss of his shareholding in HDL. He was unhappy that he did not receive a pension.

In 1964 Cockerell, together with Edwin Gifford and Don

Robertson, a pilot, formed a company called Hover-transport Ltd to operate a large passenger/car ferry, designated the SRN4, across the Solent. This craft was conceived by Saunders Roe/British Hovercraft Corporation. British Rail decided to buy the first craft for operation across the English Channel, and Hovertransport withdrew their interest in the craft. Six craft were built, four were eventually widened, and two were both widened and lengthened. The last two, which could carry some sixty cars and more than 400 passengers, had operated successfully across the channel for over thirty years when they were withdrawn from service in October 2000. Cockerell was very proud that these craft carried many millions of passengers and cars across the channel and were the world's largest amphibious commercial hovercraft. British Hovercraft Ltd invested a great deal in research and development in the 1970s and employed Cockerell for seven years as a consultant.

From 1961 to 1974 the British government took a considerable interest in the military potential of hovercraft. An interservice hovercraft and trials unit, set up at Lee-on-Solent to evaluate their capabilities, found that the craft were very suitable for amphibious assault and mine counter-measures. The former role was taken up by the United States services, who built nearly a hundred tank landing craft, which were used in the Gulf War in the 1990s. In 1983 the Royal Navy ordered a craft for the mine counter-measures role, but the order was cancelled in a defence cut of 1985. Military and paramilitary craft continue to operate, and new craft are being designed in many countries throughout the world. The UK, the USA, Russia, Norway, Finland, Saudi Arabia, and China are among the nations using such craft.

In the mid-1970s Cockerell turned his attention to the provision of the world's energy when fossil fuels are exhausted. In 1974 he took out three provisional patents on the principle of extracting energy from waves. He and Gifford formed a company called Wavepower Ltd to exploit the invention. With some government support the idea was proved to work, but the cost of electricity production was greater than that of current methods. No further support was forthcoming, and the company was wound up in 1982. This did not stop Cockerell thinking of other means of solving the problem, and just before his death he had an idea for creating energy by electronic means.

Cockerell held very strong views on a variety of subjects and wrote many letters to the press and professional institutions. He was particularly concerned with the comparatively low status of engineers in society, and that the country's educational system produced half-educated people. He believed that education at all levels should concern itself with the formation of character; he opposed early specialization at schools and advocated broader courses at universities—science courses to include art subjects and vice versa, thereby producing 'whole men' instead of 'half-educated people'. His recreations included the visual arts, photography, gardening, fishing, sailing, shooting, tennis, motor cycling, chess, music, antiquities,

and antiques. In all these pursuits he was very knowledgeable. His upbringing served to make him very thoughtful and generous with his time and expertise to family, friends, and colleagues, with no tendency for self-aggrandizement. As a result, people who knew him became devoted to him for the rest of his life. He gave much of his time to encouraging engineering in schools, clubs, and colleges, particularly in the construction of small hovercraft.

Cockerell could not accept the concept of God and life after death in the accepted sense, believing that the good or bad effect we have on all our friends and relatives is the form in which we live after death. He believed that Christianity should be concerned with uplifting teachings rather than with established dogma. He died on 1 June 1999 in Sutton Manor Nursing Home, Sutton Scotney, Hampshire, a few days before his eighty-ninth birthday. He left behind not only a worldwide industry exploiting his basic inventions, but an example of how to live our lives. The private family funeral was followed by a memorial service on 12 July 1999 at the abbey church of the Blessed Virgin and Holy Child at Beaulieu. Edwin Gifford, a close friend, spoke for all who knew him when he said at the service, 'Sir Christopher was an original thinker of great humanity who will be remembered with admiration and deep affection.' He was survived by his two daughters, Anne and Frances.   R. L. WHEELER

Sources R. L. Wheeler, *Memoirs FRS*, 47 (2001) · *The Times* (3 June 1999) · *Daily Telegraph* (3 June 1999) · *The Guardian* (4 June 1999) · *The Independent* (4 June 1999) · *The Scotsman* (4 June 1999) · *WWW* · personal knowledge (2004) · private information (2004) [F. K. Airy, John Rapson, Hovercraft Society] · b. cert. · m. cert. · d. cert.
Archives priv. coll. | Hovercraft Museum Trust, Lee-on-Solent, Hampshire · Sci. Mus., corresp. and papers |FILM priv. coll. |SOUND priv. coll.
Likenesses J. Kingsford, pencil drawing, 1917/18, priv. coll. · E. Vulliamy, pencil drawing, c.1917, priv. coll. · D. W. Hawksley, watercolour drawing, c.1932, priv. coll. · photograph, 1959, repro. in *Daily Telegraph* · photograph, 1979, Hult. Arch. [*see illus.*] · photograph, 1983, repro. in *The Times* · E. Sargeant, oils, 1985, NPG · F. K. Kingsford, oils (as a boy), priv. coll. · F. K. Kingsford, pencil drawings (as a boy), priv. coll. · photograph, repro. in *The Guardian* · photograph, repro. in *The Independent* · photograph, repro. in *The Scotsman* · photographs, priv. coll.

Cockerell, Douglas Bennett (1870–1945), bookbinder, was born on 5 August 1870 at Clifton Cottage, Sydenham Hill, London, the fourth child of Sydney John Cockerell (1842–1877), coal merchant, and his wife, Alice Elizabeth (d. 1900), elder daughter of Sir John *Bennett, watchmaker and politician. He came from a middle-class family, but the death of his father threw them on hard times. Douglas was a failure at St Paul's School, Hammersmith— he could not read until he was twelve—so he was sent to Canada when he was fifteen, with £5 in his pocket. By the age of twenty he was managing a bank at Portage la Prairie, Manitoba, where 'he liked the cowboys very much indeed' (Rorke, 71).

After returning to London in 1891, Cockerell got a job as secretary of the Chiswick School of Arts and Crafts in west

London. In 1892 his older brother Sydney Carlyle *Cockerell began to work for William Morris, and through him Cockerell was drawn to the little workshops of the Arts and Crafts movement. In 1893 he was apprenticed to T. J. Cobden-Sanderson at the Doves Bindery in Hammersmith. Here he learned to bind books in a traditional way, sewing the sections onto cords whose ends were fixed securely to the boards; covering the book, usually in leather; and decorating the binding if required. Firms at the top end of the trade in London, such as Zaehnsdorf and Rivière, still worked in this way in the late nineteenth century, but most books were bound by partly mechanized methods, the sections sewn together, and cloth-covered boards simply glued around them.

In 1897 Cockerell set up his own bindery at 6 Denmark Street, off Charing Cross Road, London, moving to 29 Gilbert Street (later Gilbert Place), Bloomsbury, in 1899, and to Ewell, on the outskirts of London, in 1902. The bindery usually consisted of three employees, with some help from Florence Arundel (c.1870–1912), a craft jeweller whom Cockerell married on 5 August 1898. There were also a number of women pupils, who found opportunities in craft bookbinding denied them in the trade, where women were confined to sewing.

The construction of Cockerell's bindings followed the standards set by Cobden-Sanderson, but he had his own style of decoration. Whereas Cobden-Sanderson thought of the decoration of books as the embellishment of great literature, Cockerell thought of it more soberly, as the expression or flowering of the book's construction, arranging his simple vocabulary of flowers and leaves and scrolling lines into roundels, panels, and arabesques that echo the proportions and structure of the book.

If Cobden-Sanderson was the pioneer of craft bookbinding, Cockerell became its acknowledged teacher about 1900. He taught bookbinding at the London county council's new Central School of Arts and Crafts on two evenings a week from 1897 until 1905, and then again until 1935 from 1921. In 1899 his concern over the poor quality of bookbinding leather led to an enquiry by the Society of Arts and a report whose specifications for binding he wrote, or at least inspired. In 1901 he published *Bookbinding and the Care of Books*, in which he set out the principles and methods of craft bookbinding, dismissing ordinary trade bindings as 'casing' rather than binding. *Bookbinding and the Care of Books* remains the basic handbook of craft bookbinding today.

But in the early 1900s Cockerell began to build bridges between his high standards and the trade. In 1904 he was appointed 'controller' of a new trade bindery opened by W. H. Smith & Son in Goldsmith Street off Drury Lane. His Ewell bindery became a specialist annexe of W. H. Smith, whose output ranged from top-quality work, based on the specifications of the Society of Arts, to ordinary trade bindings. Between these two extremes stood an improved trade binding devised by Cockerell, with cloth covers and tapes inserted into split boards, which seems to reflect his belief that 'Binding can be, and is, produced that is sound in construction and pleasant to look at, and at the same time is reasonably cheap' (Cockerell, *Bookbinding: a Lecture*, 2). In 1907 the bindery moved to new, model premises in Letchworth Garden City, and Cockerell with it.

By that date the Cockerell family included two children, Catherine, known as Casty, and Sydney Morris *Cockerell, known as Sandy. A third child, Oliver, was born in 1908. Four years later Florence Cockerell died of tuberculosis. Published sources do not tell us much about Cockerell as a person, and we do not know what he felt at this time. He was a kindly, gentle man, who loved to grow flowers, 'to cut with a scythe and give away', as he put it (Rorke, 73). But he remains elusive behind the formal language of obituaries and memoirs. On 14 January 1914 he married (Bessie) Marion Gilford (c.1872–1956), a local doctor who had been guardian of his children since their mother's death.

During the First World War, Cockerell was involved in demanding work for the Ministry of Munitions, for which he was made MBE. Afterwards he was appointed adviser on printing to the Imperial War Graves Commission, and oversaw the massive task of printing and binding the registers of the dead which can be found in each cemetery.

The spirit of the Arts and Crafts movement lived on in the Cockerell family in the 1920s. Casty Cockerell became a jeweller and in 1924 Sandy went into partnership with his father as Douglas Cockerell & Son. The binding of manuscripts and early printed books with a view to their conservation was increasingly important in this phase of Douglas Cockerell's career. His approach, grounded in traditional structure and materials, lent itself to that kind of work, and in 1935 he rebound the celebrated fourth-century biblical text the Codex Sinaiticus for the British Museum. This approach came to be recognized as the 'Cockerell tradition' in British craft bookbinding. It was born of the romantic enthusiasms of the Arts and Crafts movement at the turn of the century, but it lasted beyond them because Cockerell's insistence on sound workmanship answered the conservation needs of university and cathedral libraries.

Douglas Cockerell died at his home, 298 Norton Way South, Letchworth, on 25 November 1945. After his death, the Cockerell tradition was carried on principally by Sandy Cockerell at the bindery, and by Roger Powell, who had worked there from 1935 to 1947. The bindery closed down with Sandy's death in 1987, after almost ninety years of work.

ALAN CRAWFORD

Sources N. Rorke, *Journal of the Royal Society of Arts*, 94 (1945–6), 71–3 • D. Cockerell, *Bookbinding and the care of books* (1901) • D. Cockerell, *Bookbinding: a lecture* (1905) • *Cockerell bindings, 1894–1980: an exhibition of bindings and conservation of manuscripts and printed books* (1981) [exhibition catalogue, FM Cam.] • *Art Journal*, new ser., 25 (1905), 161–4 • M. Tidcombe, *The Doves Bindery* (1991) • M. Tidcombe, *Women bookbinders, 1880–1920* (1996) • BL, Sir Sydney Cockerell MSS • W. Blunt, *Cockerell: Sydney Carlyle Cockerell, friend of Ruskin and William Morris, and director of the Fitzwilliam Museum, Cambridge* (1964) • *CGPLA Eng. & Wales* (1946)
Archives BL, archives of the bindery of Douglas Cockerell and Sandy Cockerell • BL, corresp. relating to binding of *Codex*

Sinaiticus • L. Cong., corresp. and papers | BL, Sir Sydney Cockerell MSS
Likenesses W. Strang, drawing, 1902, priv. coll. • O. Whiting, oils, 1928, priv. coll. • photograph, 1938, NPG • M. Osborne, etching, priv. coll. • photographs, priv. coll.
Wealth at death £9427 16s. 8d.: probate, 16 Feb 1946, CGPLA Eng. & Wales

Cockerell, Frederick Pepys (1833–1878), architect, was born in March 1833 at 87 Eaton Square, London, the second son of Charles Robert *Cockerell (1788–1863), architect, and his wife, Anna Rennie (1803–1872). He was educated at Winchester College from 1845 to 1848, and at King's College, London, where he remained for nearly two years from 1848 in the department of applied science. He was taught architecture and drawing by his father and by John E. Goodchild, his father's chief clerk and close friend. Powerfully influenced by his father's admiration for French architecture, he became, in an age of increasing nationalism, an essentially European figure in the cultural tradition of the eighteenth-century grand tour.

After a sketching tour in northern France in 1850, Cockerell travelled in France in 1851, spending two formative months in Paris in 1853 as a pupil of Caristie, who introduced him to Viollet-le-Duc, Visconti, and Douillard. In 1854 he became a pupil of Philip C. Hardwick RA, before leaving his office in 1855 for an extensive study tour of the chief cities of Italy. On returning in 1856, he began to work in his father's office on the Liverpool and London Insurance Office and on decorative details for St George's Hall, Liverpool. In 1856 he entered the competition for the government offices, in 1863 for the Albert memorial, and in 1866 for the National Gallery.

His father's belief that sculpture was the voice of architecture was reflected in Cockerell's own works, such as the memorial column at Castle Howard, surmounted by an inventive Ionic capital bearing a tripod of terracotta and wrought iron by Charles Kelsey, who also worked on St George's Hall, Liverpool. Of his London buildings, Cockerell's Freemasons' Hall (1861) had a heavy classical façade rich with symbolic sculpture by W. G. Nicholl, who carved the pedimental sculpture at St George's Hall, Liverpool. His gallery of the Society of Painters in Water Colours boasted much figure sculpture by Signor Fabbrucci, a Florentine sculptor settled in Chelsea.

After beginning his career as a country-house architect with houses such as Lythe Hill, Surrey (1868), in the still fashionable neo-Tudor style, Cockerell became in the 1870s a pioneer of the Queen Anne movement. This combined Gothic revival asymmetry in planning and composition with details from English and Dutch architecture of the seventeenth and eighteenth centuries. Examples of his work in this style include Crawley Court, Hampshire (1877; dem.), for A. S. Kennard, a London banker, and Woodcote Hall, Shropshire (1876), for C. C. Cotes MP. These houses were well related to their sites, as was Blessingbourne, Fivemiletown, co. Tyrone (1870–74), for Hugh de Fellenberg Montgomery, built of hard sandstone quarried on the hills of the estate, laid in random courses.

With its Jacobean flavour, turrets, and symmetrical garden front, it was furnished with wallpaper by William Morris and tiles by William De Morgan. Cockerell's most remarkable country house was the concrete-built Down Hall, Essex (1871–3), with Charles Drake, a pioneer in concrete construction, as his consultant. The decorative panels and friezes were ornamented with sgraffito by J. Wormleighton of South Kensington from cartoons by Cockerell. Inside, the 40-foot-square hall was inspired by a Pompeiian atrium.

In 1867 Cockerell married Mary Mulock, daughter of Thomas Homan Mulock of Bellair, King's county, with whom he had six children. He was elected an associate of the Royal Institute of British Architects (RIBA) in 1860, a fellow in 1864, and honorary secretary in 1871, and was a member of the Foreign Architectural Book Society, an exclusive private club within the RIBA. He was a trustee of Sir John Soane's Museum and a member of the Athenaeum. On the day of his sudden death, at 66 rue François, Paris, on 4 November 1878, he was due to attend a dinner party at the home of Duc, architect of the Palais de Justice. His funeral procession in Paris was followed by the distinguished French architects Duc, Lefuel, Hardy, Pelechet, Daumet, and Vaudremer. He was buried at Auteuil cemetery, Paris. At the time of his death he was living at 18 Manchester Square, London. A genial, charming, and handsome man, knowledgeable in literature and the arts, his premature death was widely regretted.

DAVID WATKIN

Sources *The Builder*, 36 (1878), 1183, 1194–5, 1230 • *Transactions of the Royal Institute of British Architects* (1879–80), 21–36 • RIBA BAL, Drawings collection • RIBA BAL, MSS collection • *Catalogue of the drawings collection of the Royal Institute of British Architects: C–F* (1972) • *Dir. Brit. archs.* • M. Girouard, *The Victorian country house*, rev. edn (1979) • M. Bence-Jones, *Ireland* (1978), vol. 1 of *Burke's guide to country houses* (1978–81) • CGPLA Eng. & Wales (1878)
Archives RIBA BAL, drawings collection, architectural sketchbooks
Likenesses photograph, RIBA BAL
Wealth at death under £14,000: probate, 7 Dec 1878, CGPLA Eng. & Wales

Cockerell, Samuel Pepys (1753–1827), architect, was born (according to the diary of his son C. R. Cockerell), on 6 January 1753, at Bishop's Hull, Somerset, the son of John Cockerell (1714–1767) and his wife, Frances Jackson (d. 1769). His mother was the daughter of John Jackson of Clapham, nephew and heir of Samuel Pepys, and from her Cockerell inherited many interesting relics of the great diarist. His brother was Charles *Cockerell MP (1755–1837) of Sezincote, Gloucestershire, who was created a baronet in 1809. Samuel Cockerell received his architectural training from Sir Robert Taylor, whom he later remembered in his will as 'the affectionate prop and support of my early steps and to whom … I was chiefly indebted for my first advancement in life'.

Cockerell, whose practice was in London, held a succession of public appointments through his career. In 1774 he was appointed district surveyor for the parish of St George's, Hanover Square. In 1775 he obtained the post of clerk of works at the Tower of London in the office of works, and in 1780 he was made clerk of works at New-market; both these office of works posts were lost when the department was reorganized in 1782. In 1785 he was appointed inspector of repairs to the Admiralty, and when Sir Robert Taylor died in 1788 Cockerell succeeded him as surveyor of the Foundling and Pulteney estates in London. In 1791 he became surveyor to the victualling office. He was diocesan surveyor for Canterbury and London, and surveyor of St Paul's Cathedral (1811–19). For the Found-ling Hospital, Cockerell prepared plans for the develop-ment of their Bloomsbury estate; building went on from 1790 to 1805. Some of the governors of the hospital were dissatisfied with Cockerell's supervision of the project and tried to have him dismissed. Though ultimately not held responsible, he resigned in 1808. Cockerell also pre-pared plans for the development of the bishop of Lon-don's Paddington estate, which were only partly imple-mented when he died in 1827; the scheme was eventually completed to a new design by his successor as surveyor, George Gutch. In addition, Cockerell had a fairly exten-sive private practice.

In his architecture Cockerell showed no consistent approach to design but produced work in several styles. Although it is not known whether he ever visited the con-tinent, some of his designs give hints of French influence: his church at St Martin Outwich, London (1796–8; dem. 1874), the façade of Gore Court, Kent, for G. Harper (1792–5; dem. c.1925), and the unusual tower of St Anne's, Soho (1802–3), were examples. Banbury church, Oxfordshire (rebuilt 1792–7), had an interior inspired by Sir Christo-pher Wren's St Stephen Walbrook and Sir Robert Taylor's Bank of England transfer office. At Tickencote in Rutland he made a 'serious if not very scholarly attempt' (Colvin, Archs., 262) to restore the twelfth-century church in Romanesque style. At Sezincote and Daylesford, both in Gloucestershire, he famously incorporated oriental archi-tectural forms in English houses for patrons who had made their fortunes in East Indian trade. The Indian style was popularized through the drawings of Thomas and William Daniell, whose volume *Oriental Scenery* was col-lected together and published in 1808. It provided useful source material for 'nabobs' and for Cockerell himself, who was surveyor to the East India Company from 1806 to 1824. Daylesford House, remodelled for Warren Hastings, from 1789 to 1793, had oriental hints only in the top of its dome; but Sezincote House, which he designed (c.1805–20) for his brother Sir Charles Cockerell, was in full-blown Indian style, and it is thought to have influenced the prince regent (later George IV), who visited it about 1807, in his remodelling of the Royal Pavilion, Brighton.

Cockerell first exhibited at the Royal Academy in 1785, sending some designs for ornamental structures in the park of White Knights in Berkshire. He did not exhibit again until 1792, from which year up to 1803 he was a fre-quent contributor, chiefly of designs for mansions and churches. Among other houses designed by him were Middleton Hall, Carmarthenshire, for Sir William Paxton (1793–5; dem. 1951), the austerely neo-classical Nutwell Court, near Exeter, for the second Baron Heathfield (1802),

and Toft Hall, Cheshire, where in 1810–13 he added a dining-room, library, and twin towers for Ralph Leyce-ster.

Cockerell lived at the house at the corner of Savile Row and Burlington Street; he designed a house for himself at 29 North Side, Clapham Common, but in 1800 he moved to Westbourne Lodge, Paddington (once the home of the architect Isaac Ware). He married Anne, daughter and coheir of John Whetham of St Ives, Huntingdonshire; they had six sons and five daughters; his second son was Charles Robert *Cockerell (1788–1863), also an architect. Cockerell's pupils, apart from his son Charles, were many, and included Joseph Kay, Benjamin Latrobe, Thomas Mar-tyr, James Noble, William Porden, Robert Sibley, and C. H. Tatham. He died at Westbourne Lodge on 12 July 1827.

PETER MEADOWS

Sources Colvin, *Archs.* · C. Hussey, 'Sezincote, Gloucestershire [pts 1–2]', *Country Life*, 85 (1939), 502–6, 528–32 · N. W. Kingsley, *The country houses of Gloucestershire*, 2: *1660–1830* (1992), 113–17 [Dayles-ford House] · *DNB* · J. Debrett, *Debrett's baronetage of England*, ed. W. Courthope, 7th edn (1835)
Archives RIBA, corresp. and papers
Likenesses T. Hodgetts, mezzotint, pubd 1824 (after oil painting by W. Beechey), BM · G. Dance, pencil drawing, BM · Daniell, engraving (after pencil drawing by G. Dance)

Cockerell, Sir Sydney Carlyle (1867–1962), museum dir-ector and book collector, was born at Brighton on 16 July 1867, the second child (and second son) of the family of four sons and two daughters of Sydney John Cockerell (1842–1877), coal merchant, of London, and his wife, Alice Elizabeth (d. 1900), the elder daughter of Sir John *Ben-nett, watchmaker and sheriff of London and Middlesex. His younger brother Douglas *Cockerell (1870–1945) became a distinguished bookbinder.

In May 1882 Cockerell entered St Paul's School, London, as a day-boy scholar but he remained there only until Christmas 1884, when he joined the family business, Geo. J. Cockerell & Co., of Cornhill, as a clerk. His father had died young, an event which had left his widow and six children badly off, and Sydney out of family duty there-fore decided against a university course and entered the coal business, which he found uncongenial. He joined his two uncles as a partner in May 1889 but stayed in the firm only until the end of 1891.

Church architecture in England and on the continent had already engaged his attention. So too had Octavia Hill, a family friend, who temporarily stimulated his involve-ment in social welfare work. Her friendship with John Ruskin, and Cockerell's absorption in Ruskin's political and artistic writings, emboldened him to begin a corres-pondence initiated by a gift of shells from his collection. In 1887 he visited Ruskin at Brantwood, his Lake District home, and a friendship developed rapidly, cemented by a chance meeting at Abbeville while on holiday in France in the summer of 1888. Nearly three weeks' exploring Abbe-ville and Beauvais in Ruskin's company was a formative experience for the young coal merchant. Ruskin was a powerful influence and Cockerell remained in touch throughout his hero's frail and secluded old age.

In 1886 Cockerell had met William Morris, his other great hero, initially through socialist interests but increasingly through the work of the Society for the Protection of Ancient Buildings: Cockerell joined its committee in 1890. Aesthetically stimulating contacts such as these unsettled him in his business career, and he decided to follow his own strong but still not fully formed inclinations. Morris offered him the educative task of cataloguing his library of manuscripts and early printed books, attractive (if unremunerative) employment to which in 1894 he added the duties of secretary to the Kelmscott Press.

Cockerell showed himself keen and knowledgeable and became *de facto* Morris's private secretary, zealously caring for him in his final illness in autumn 1896. Cockerell proved an efficient executor of Morris's will, winding up the press and seeing to the completion of various publishing projects. Literary executorship was a service he would confidently perform for many other literary and artistic friends. At Kelmscott House he had been introduced to the poet and traveller Wilfrid Scawen Blunt. For two years he became Blunt's part-time confidential secretary, working also for the wealthy connoisseur Henry Yates Thompson as adviser on his collection of medieval manuscripts. Seeking more permanent work, he went into partnership with Emery Walker, an agreeable colleague with whom he worked in his rather less congenial process engraving business from 1900 to 1904. In 1903 he found time to visit Tolstoy at Yasnaya Polyana.

On 4 November 1907, still without settled employment, Cockerell married (Florence) Kate (1872–1949), daughter of Charles Tomson Kingsford of Canterbury; she was a manuscript illuminator and artist. They had two daughters and a son, Sir Christopher Sydney *Cockerell, the inventor of the hovercraft. Soon after their marriage his wife developed disseminated sclerosis and eventually became bedridden (she died in 1949). Cockerell did not allow this grievous personal tragedy to interfere with his activities. Their marriage made it necessary for him to find regular work, and an ideal opportunity occurred in 1908, when Montague Rhodes James resigned the directorship of the Fitzwilliam Museum, Cambridge. Although he had no university education, Cockerell was appointed; he was director for twenty-nine years.

'I found it a pigsty; I turned it into a palace' (Blunt, 135), Cockerell opined in old age. Energetic and purposeful, he rehung its crowded walls and spaced out its jumbled exhibits, adding flowers and rugs and furniture, and by skilled use of light and space he gave the Fitzwilliam a cheerfulness and an accessibility that have been influential on museum display worldwide. The collections and buildings were not just rearranged but much augmented. Cockerell intrepidly pursued benefactors, and though he became notorious for his importunity he was usually successful. The Marlay (1922) and Courtauld (1931) galleries were added during his tenure. His determination made him some enemies in Cambridge, but his success was recognized by the award of an honorary LittD in 1930. He was a (short-term) fellow of Jesus College from 1910 to 1916, and after many years of deeply felt exclusion became a fellow of Downing from 1932 until his retirement in 1937 (when he was elected honorary fellow). He was knighted in 1934. For three years from 1936 Cockerell served as European adviser to the Felton trustees of the National Gallery of Victoria, Melbourne. He travelled to Australia to consult his employers, and visited American galleries and libraries on several occasions between the wars.

Cockerell was proud of his literary friendships and kept them in good repair by conversation and correspondence. Some (such as those with Wilfrid Scawen Blunt and Thomas Hardy) extended into literary executorships, in

Sir Sydney Carlyle Cockerell (1867–1962), by Dorothy Webster Hawksley, 1951

which his loyal but masterful manner led to difficulties with family representatives, but others were founded on exchanges of letters later anthologized for him by Viola Meynell in *Friends of a Lifetime* (1940) and *The Best of Friends* (1956). Unexpectedly for 'a man without any set creed' (Blunt, 226), he formed a close though mainly epistolary friendship with the scholarly Roman Catholic nun Dame Laurentia McLachlan (1866–1933) of Stanbrook Abbey, Worcestershire. He placed his connoisseurship and knowledge of fine book production at the disposal of this learned Benedictine house with its printing press, and his friendship with its abbess withstood even an imprudent introduction to another of his friends, George Bernard Shaw.

Since childhood Cockerell had been a dedicated collector, and by his early thirties he concentrated his efforts on medieval manuscripts. His means were small but his knowledge was wide and his connoisseur's eye and his instinct for a bargain were both very keen. He was prepared to resell to improve his collection, but the items he retained were closely studied and often carefully annotated on their flyleaves. He showed scholarly (and commercial) prescience in pursuing manuscripts of the humanist scribes of the Renaissance, and for other periods his collection included work by the first identifiable English scribe, the thirteenth-century Oxford artist W. de Brailes. By 1908 Cockerell's collection was strong enough to include no fewer than 17 of the 269 items displayed at the Burlington Fine Arts Club's loan exhibition of illuminated manuscripts, for which Cockerell was chief contributor to the large and important catalogue. The standard listing of his manuscripts shows that no fewer than 126 items had been in his possession during his lifetime, and in old age he shrewdly organized the sale of his remaining treasures both by private treaty and in the saleroom (Sothebys, 1956–9). He was a member of the Roxburghe Club from 1915, and published several fine editions under the aegis of its members. He bullied other collectors to improve their standards until they matched his own, and a characteristically English enthusiasm for the study of Italian humanistic manuscripts is very largely due to his initiative.

As a young man, Cockerell developed an idiosyncratic, squarely-formed humanist hand. It was fluent and graceful, tiny but (until his old age) easily legible, and consistent throughout the long period covered by his diaries (1886–1962), now in the British Library (Add. MSS 52623–52702). He was a friend of Edward Johnston, whom he encouraged in the revival of pen-formed lettering, and later did much to encourage the use of italic script in education and art work.

Cockerell settled in retirement at 21 Kew Gardens Road, Richmond, Surrey, where he remained—except for wartime exile to Gloucestershire and Old Windsor, Berkshire—virtually confined to his bedroom from 1951, until his death there from heart failure on 1 May 1962. He was an exigent invalid, supported by devoted volunteer attendants and to the end much visited by scholars, calligraphers, and biographers of Victorian eminences about

whom (in his tenth decade) he became the sole remaining—if rather proprietorial—living authority. Bald, and neatly bearded, he had a brusque manner but a not unkindly glint behind small gold-rimmed spectacles; his legendary astringency overlay a frequently attested genius for friendship. A settled agnostic in his opinions, he had no expectation of a future existence. His remains were cremated.

ALAN BELL

Sources W. Blunt, *Cockerell: Sydney Carlyle Cockerell, friend of Ruskin and William Morris, and director of the Fitzwilliam Museum, Cambridge* (1964) · V. Meynell, ed., *Friends of a lifetime* (1940) · V. Meynell, ed., *The best of friends: further letters to Sydney Carlyle Cockerell* (1956) · C. de Hamel, 'Medieval and Renaissance manuscripts from the library of Sir Sydney Cockerell (1867–1962)', *British Library Journal*, 13 (1987), 186–210 · D. F. Corrigan, *The nun, the infidel and the superman* (1985) · F. MacCarthy, *William Morris* (1994) · CGPLA Eng. & Wales (1962) · d. cert. · *DNB* · *The Times* (2 May 1962) · private information (2004) [F. K. Airy]

Archives BL, diaries and corresp., Add. MSS 45926–45927, 52623–52773 · Boston PL, corresp. · Harvard U., Houghton L., corresp. · Hunt. L., corresp. · Morgan L., corresp. · priv. coll. · U. Reading L., letters · V&A NAL, collections and corresp. | AM Oxf., letters to F. L. Griggs · BL, letters to Adelheid Heimann, Add. MS 60627 · BL, letters to E. G. Millar, Add. MS 58212 · BL, letters to George Bernard Shaw, Add. MS 50531 · Bodl. Oxf., letters to Alfred Fairbank · Bodl. Oxf., letters to J. Hely-Hutchinson · Bodl. Oxf., letters to J. Leighton and J. Leighton · Bodl. Oxf., corresp. with Lord and Lady Lovelace · Bodl. Oxf., corresp. with Graham Pollard · Castle Howard, North Yorkshire, letters to ninth earl of Carlisle · CUL, letters to M. R. James · CUL, letters to Lord and Lady Kennet · Dorset County Museum, Dorchester, letters to Bo Foster · Durham RO, letters to Virginia Surtees · FM Cam., letters to Wilfrid Scawen Blunt · FM Cam., letters to L. C. G. Clarke · FM Cam., letters to J. R. Halliday · Grolier Club, 47 East 60th Street, New York, letters to Harold Peirce · Harvard University, near Florence, Italy, Center for Italian Renaissance Studies, letters to Bernard Berenson · IWM, letters to Siegfried Sassoon · L. N. Tolstoy State Museum, Moscow, letters to Count L. N. Tolstoy · Princeton University Library, letters to Janet Camp Troxell · S. Antiquaries, Lond., letters to N. L. MacMinn · Society for the Protection of Ancient Buildings, London, letters · TCD, letters to Thomas Bodkin · U. Edin. L., letters to Catherine Borland · U. Glas. L., letters to D. S. MacColl · U. Reading L., letters to Nancy Astor · University of Colorado, Boulder, letters to Theodore Cockerell · University of Lancaster, Ruskin Library, letters to M. H. Spielmann · V&A NAL, corresp. with Dame Hildelith Cumming · V&A NAL, corresp. and papers, mainly relating to Edward Johnston · W. Sussex RO, corresp. with Oswald Barron

Likenesses photograph, 1891, NPG · W. Stoneman, photograph, 1917, NPG · F. Dodd, chalk drawing, 1937, FM Cam. · D. W. Hawksley, drawing, 1951, FM Cam. [*see illus.*] · D. W. Hawksley, pencil drawing, 1952, NPG · D. W. Hawksley, watercolour, 1957, BL, Add. MS 65280 · D. W. Hawksley, watercolour drawing, 1960, NPG · D. W. Hawksley, watercolour drawing, c.1960, priv. coll. · photographs, priv. coll.

Wealth at death £59,079 14s. 6d.: probate, 16 July 1962, CGPLA Eng. & Wales

Cockerell, Sydney Morris (1906–1987), bookbinder, was born on 6 June 1906 at 96 Earls Court Road, London, the second of three children and elder son of Douglas Bennett *Cockerell (1870–1945), bookbinder, and his wife, Florence Margaret Drew (c.1870–1912), daughter of Samuel Drew Arundel, box maker, of London. His mother died in 1912 and his father married again two years later. His father's training and background influenced much of Sandy's (as Cockerell was often known) own career. After

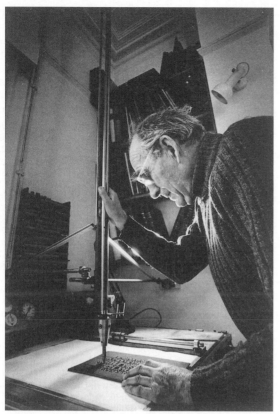

Sydney Morris Cockerell (1906–1987), by Philip Sayer, 1981
[using his ram to impress a design by Joan Rix Tebbutt on vellum]

St Christopher's School, Letchworth, in 1924 Cockerell joined his father as a partner in D. Cockerell & Son. Their workshop was in an extension to the family house at Letchworth and both there and, from 1963, in Grantchester, there was always an air of domesticity about Sydney Cockerell's surroundings. In 1932 Cockerell married Elizabeth Lucy (d. 1991), daughter of Harrison Cowlishaw, architect. She had been one of his father's students at the Central School of Art, and she brought her own contribution to the workshop. They had a son and two daughters. In partnership with his father, in 1935 Cockerell rebound the Codex Sinaiticus after its purchase for the nation. In the same year they were joined by Roger *Powell, who remained as a partner until 1947, when he established his own workshop, remaining in close and amicable contact. Douglas Cockerell died in 1945.

Cockerell's long association with university, national, and other libraries, as he repaired manuscripts and early printed books, began in the 1920s. Cambridge University Library was among the first such customers, and the most long-standing. Some of that library's greatest treasures, including the Codex Bezae, the Book of Cerne, the Book of Deer, and Sir Isaac Newton's papers, passed through his hands. For Trinity College, Cambridge, repairs included those for the twelfth-century Eadwine psalter and the autograph volume of John Milton's poetry. The extensive task of repairing papers for the Wordsworth Trust, at Dove Cottage, was spread over many years, while for the Fitzwilliam Museum, Cambridge, Cockerell repaired Handel's autographs and the Fitzwilliam virginal book, among others. In such work he was unsurpassed in his generation. He was also consulted widely from overseas, notably following the Florence floods in 1967.

As a binder of more recent books, the traditions shared with his father likewise led Cockerell to consider bookbinding as a process as much concerned with a book's structure and use as with its outward decoration. His many commissions included rolls of honour for both houses of parliament as well as for the armed services; he was regularly called on for lectern bibles in cathedrals. From 1948 collaboration with Joan Rix Tebbutt, of the Glasgow School of Art, led to a distinctive series of bindings in toned vellum, in which designer and binder co-operated in outstanding accord.

Adept with his hands, Cockerell was also of a highly practical turn of mind. Many of his tools he made himself, and the hydraulic ram (adapted from an aeroplane's wing flaps), with which he impressed gold leaf into his bindings, gave any visitor immediate notice of his ingenuity. Like his father, Cockerell insisted on the best materials appropriate to their purpose, paying special attention to leathers (especially goatskins) and to papers with a neutral pH value, and of the right weight and fibre structure. In the 1920s his experiments on marbling paper for bindings soon led to its regular production by his workshop. This continued until his death, principally in the hands of William Chapman. The necessary combs to create the repeatable and distinctive (yet always subtly different) patterns were made in the workshop.

Cockerell was an influential teacher, and succeeded his father at both the Central School of Arts and Crafts, London, and the Royal College of Art. At University College, London, he lectured to students of librarianship in 1945–76, and thus sought to demonstrate how his practical skill and knowledge could be applied to the proper care of books and manuscripts. In his workshop he trained a series of assistants, most of whom subsequently either joined major libraries, or established their own practices. His book, *The Repairing of Books* (1958), was offered as a further means of closing the gap between the librarian or collector and the craftsman.

Cockerell's appearance was dominated by prominent and luxuriant eyebrows, which formed an inseparable part of his conversation, helping by turn to orchestrate his dry sense of humour or forcefully express criticism, as necessary. He was scathing about poor workmanship, and formidable when he perceived incompetence in those charged with the care of the nation's collections of books and manuscripts. He was appointed OBE in 1980 and was awarded an honorary LittD by Cambridge in 1982. Cockerell died in Addenbrooke's Hospital, Cambridge, on 6 November 1987.   DAVID MCKITTERICK, *rev.*

Sources D. A. Harrop, 'Craft binders at work IV: Sydney Morris Cockerell', *Book Collector*, 23 (1974), 171–8 • *Cockerell bindings, 1894–1980: an exhibition of bindings and conservation of manuscripts and*

printed books (1981) [exhibition catalogue, FM Cam.] · *The Independent* (10 Nov 1987) · personal knowledge (1996) · *CGPLA Eng. & Wales* (1989)
Likenesses P. Sayer, photograph, 1981, priv. coll. [*see illus.*]
Wealth at death £69,072: probate, 31 Jan 1989, *CGPLA Eng. & Wales*

Cockerill, John (1790–1840). *See under* Cockerill, William (1759–1832).

Cockerill, William (1759–1832), inventor, was born in Lancashire, of unknown parentage, and began life by making 'roving billies', and flying shuttles. He was gifted, however, with an extraordinary mechanical genius, and could make with his own hands models of almost any machine. Although the identity of his wife remains unknown, he was probably married by the time he went to Russia in 1794, having been recommended as a skilful artisan to the Empress Catherine II. At St Petersburg he received every encouragement, but the death of the empress only two years later totally ruined his prospects. Her successor, the madman Paul, sent Cockerill to prison, merely because he failed to finish a model within a certain time. Cockerill, however, escaped to Sweden, where, joined by his sons Charles James and William, he was commissioned by the government to construct the locks of a public canal; but his attempts to introduce spinning and other machines of his own invention were not appreciated. He therefore proceeded in 1799 to Verviers in Belgium, where he entered into a contract with the firm of Simonis et Biolley, which enabled him to supply his machines. He was joined by a third son, John [*see below*], in 1802. On the expiry of the contract in 1807 Cockerill settled at Liège with his sons, and there established factories for the construction of spinning and weaving machines. His business increased rapidly. He had thus secured to Verviers supremacy in the woollen trade, and had introduced at Liège an industry of which England had hitherto possessed the monopoly. The merits of his inventions and workmanship were acknowledged by an industrial commission of 1810 and in the same year he took French nationality. Two years later Cockerill retired from business in favour of his two younger sons, Charles James and John. Of his eldest son, William, little is known. His daughter, Nancy, married James Hodson, a skilful mechanic, of Nottingham, who settled at Verviers in 1802, and realized a princely fortune. Cockerill died at the Château de Behrensberg, near Aix-la-Chapelle, the residence of his son Charles James, in 1832, aged seventy-three.

Cockerill's son **John Cockerill** (1790–1840), woollen manufacturer, born on 30 April 1790 at Haslingden, Lancashire, was consigned to the care of a relative in England until 1802, when he was apprenticed to his father in Verviers. In 1807, when only seventeen, he shared with his brother Charles James the management of the factory at Liège. Soon after the battle of Waterloo the brothers were permitted, through the kind offices of M. Beuth, the Prussian minister of finance, to set up a woollen factory at Berlin. Their success tempted John Cockerill to propose a still greater enterprise. On 25 January 1817 the brothers established at Seraing on the River Meuse what was to prove the most extensive iron foundry and machine manufactory on the continent. John Cockerill married Jannette Fédérique Pastor of Aix-la-Chapelle on the same day that his brother Charles married her sister. There were no children of the marriage.

The king of the Netherlands, William I, supported the Cockerill brothers' endeavours and was until 1835 a partner in the business, having invested in it the sum of £100,000. In that year (1835) John Cockerill became the sole proprietor. In February 1839 the firm was in liquidation, but the reverse proved only temporary. Shortly afterwards John Cockerill went to St Petersburg to submit to the tsar his plans for the construction of railways in Russia. On his return, he contracted typhoid fever in Warsaw, and after ten days' suffering he died in his wife's arms on 19 June 1840. In 1867 his remains were taken back to Seraing by his family, where their arrival was greeted by a popular demonstration on 9 June 1867. His statue was unveiled at Seraing on 29 October 1871.

GORDON GOODWIN, *rev.* ANITA McCONNELL

Sources *Bibliographie nationale de Belgique*, 4 (1872), cols. 229–39 · J. T., 'Cockerill, William', *The imperial dictionary of universal biography*, ed. J. F. Waller, new edn (1877–84) · *GM*, 2nd ser., 14 (1840), 550 · J. E. Tennant, *Belgium*, 2 (1841), 161–4, 174–85 · [J. C. F. Hoefer], ed., *Nouvelle biographie générale*, 11 (1855), cols. 12–15
Likenesses statue, *c.*1871; last known in Seraing, Belgium, 1872 · Vielvoye, portrait (John Cockerill); last known in Seraing, Belgium, 1872 · miniature, V&A

Cockie, James (d. 1573). *See under* Castilians in Edinburgh (act. 1570–1573).

Cockin, William (bap. 1736, d. 1801), schoolmaster and writer, was the son of Marmaduke Cockin (1712–1754), a schoolmaster, and his wife, Elizabeth (1716–1770), and was baptized at Burton in Kendal, Westmorland, on 6 September 1736. His father died when he was eighteen so he supported his family for several years. In 1764, following an unhappy period teaching in London boarding-schools, Cockin was appointed writing master and accountant at Lancaster grammar school. Here he influenced the broadening of the curriculum and originated a poetic tradition.

From 1784 Cockin taught at the Revd John Blanchard's Nottingham Academy, where one of his pupils was George Pryme, the economist. Cockin retired to Burton in 1792 to devote himself to literary pursuits. His friends included the artist George Romney, the physician John Dawson, Dr Thomas Wilson, of Clitheroe, and Dr John James, of Arthuret. Cockin successively became Romney's companion at Hampstead and his amanuensis at Kendal.

In the belief that no systematic school mathematical book existed, Cockin published *A Rational and Practical Treatise of Arithmetic* (1766). His important work on elocution dedicated to David Garrick, *The Art of Delivering Written Language* (1775), reflected his own 'mild and impressive' elocution and the 'fluency and judgement' of his wide-ranging conversation (Romney, 276).

Having assisted Thomas West in the compilation of his ground-breaking *Guide to the Lakes* (1778), Cockin enlarged two editions of this work which influenced Wordsworth's guide of 1810. Cockin's pride in great men of Lakeland led to his *Ode to the Genius of the Lakes* (1780) which was accompanied by short local biographies. Extraordinarily, he proposed here that inscribed pillars should be erected at Lakeland viewpoints in commemoration of significant visitors.

In 1777 Cockin corresponded with Joseph Banks regarding 'An extraordinary appearance in a mist', a description of a type of muted rainbow, which was published in the *Philosophical Transactions* (*PTRS*, 70, 1780, 157–62) and was considered important by Joseph Priestley. His only independent scientific publication, *The Theory of the Syphon* (1781), refers to an invention known by the ancient Egyptians. Cockin's philosophical and religious writing includes *The Freedom of Human Action Explained and Indicated* (1775), which considers the opinions of Joseph Priestley, and *The Fall of Scepticism and Infidelity Predicted* (1788), written as an epistle to James Beattie. *Occasional Attempts in Verse* (1776), demonstrating Cockin's wit and capacity for self-mockery, collects verses to both Romney and Sir Isaac Newton while the posthumous collection of verse entitled *The Rural Sabbath* (1805) includes his 'Stanzas on the Death of Dr Johnson', which praises that critic's possession of 'Albion's gift' (stanza 3). Cockin was not a brilliant poet himself but his verse is replete with mythological and spiritual references and hints at his disapproval of both industry and Sunday labour. He died at Romney's house at Milnthorpe Road, Kendal, on 30 May 1801 and was buried in the churchyard at Burton in Kendal on 2 June. Cockin's versatility militated against his prosperity but he was remembered for his generosity to the poor and for his shyness, modesty, and integrity.

DAVID A. CROSS

Sources J. Romney, *Memoirs of George Romney* (1830) · A. Murray, *The Royal Grammar School, Lancaster* (1952) · W. Cockin, *The rural sabbath* (1805), v–vii · *GM*, 1st ser., 71 (1801), 575 · W. Hayley, *The life of George Romney* (1809) · R. Bicknell, *The picturesque scenery of the Lake District (1752–1855): a bibliographic study* (1990) · D. A. Cross, *A striking likeness: a life of George Romney* (2000) · *Miscellanies of the Revd Thomas Wilson*, ed. F. R. Raines (1857) · W. Cockin, *The art of delivering written language*, ed. R. C. Alston (1969) · *DNB* · parish register, Burton in Kendal, 6 Sept 1736, Cumbria AS, Kendal [baptism] · parish register, Burton in Kendal, 2 June 1801, Cumbria AS, Kendal [burial]
Archives RS, essay | Cumbria AS, Barrow, Romney MSS · V&A, letters to G. Romney and from Peter Romney
Wealth at death probably little capital; lived in Romney's house for several years; described by Revd Wilson as 'grovelling towards the evening of life'

Cockings, George (*d.* 1802), writer, had a small place under the British government at Boston, Massachusetts, but little else is known of his origins or early life. On his return to England he obtained the post of registrar of the Society of Arts, Manufactures, and Commerce in the Adelphi, a post which he held for thirty years. His experiences in North America led him to write poems and dramas, which his contemporaries generally judged as of the feeblest order, particularly in respect of construction and literary style. Some of these, however, nevertheless obtained a measure of success, and went through three or four editions in America and England.

Cockings's writings include *The Conquest of Canada, or, The Siege of Quebec* (1766), a historical tragedy in five acts, which was harshly judged as a contemptible production with neither form nor significance. A twentieth-century assessment has been kinder, making allowances for the adherence of Cockings's play to the demands of 'the form of heroic tragedy' (Thomas, 129), and finding a kind of epic sweep to Cockings's drama, a play that found a model and template in some of the dramatic works and poetry of John Dryden.

> Admittedly its versification is frequently slovenly, and its expression is riddled with clichés; but, once the genre is recognized—and the conventions that were expected to operate within it—then one can see that the concept is worthy, the structural design usually excellent, the characterization (necessarily typical) as good as that in most heroic tragedies being played then, the staging at times imaginative, and even the diction possessed of an occasional moment of felicity. (ibid., 158)

Cockings's other works included: *Benevolence and Gratitude* (1772); *War, an Heroic Poem, from the Taking of Minorca by the French to the Reduction of the Havannah* (1760); *Poems on Several Subjects* (1772); and *Arts, Manufactures, and Commerce*, a poem (1766). Cockings died on 6 February 1802.

JOSEPH KNIGHT, *rev.* M. CLARE LOUGHLIN-CHOW

Sources D. E. Baker, *Biographia dramatica, or, A companion to the playhouse*, rev. I. Reed, new edn, rev. S. Jones, 3 vols. in 4 (1812) · Watt, *Bibl. Brit.* · Allibone, *Dict.* · *GM*, 1st ser., 72 (1802), 274 · W. K. Thomas, 'The conquest of Canada: our own heroic tragedy', *Canadian Drama/Art dramatique canadien*, 3 (1977), 128–61
Likenesses W. Evans, stipple, BM, NPG

Cockle, James (1782–1854). *See under* Cockle, Sir James (1819–1895).

Cockle, Sir James (1819–1895), lawyer in Australia and mathematician, was born on 14 January 1819, the second son of **James Cockle** (1782–1854), doctor and manufacturer of patent medicines, and his wife, Elizabeth. The elder James Cockle was born on 17 July 1782 at Woodbridge, Suffolk, the son (there was a younger daughter) of Andrew Cockle, a vintner, and his wife, Anne. Having matriculated at the University of Edinburgh in 1801, about four years later he began practising as a doctor. He became the parochial surgeon at Great Oakley, Essex, and about 1814 married Elizabeth (probably Moss); they had five sons and a daughter.

After inventing his 'family antibilious pills', in the early 1820s Cockle moved to the capital and worked as an apothecary in Hackney. By 1829 he had moved to New Ormond Street, which was fashionable enough for him to begin cultivating custom on a heroic scale, both as an apothecary and as a vendor of pills. By 1837 a list of 200 of the 'nobility, MPs and families of high distinction' who had 'experienced the most beneficial effects from the use of his medicine' was enclosed in each of the pillboxes. More startlingly, in 1838 Cockle revealed that among the seven dukes, fifty-six lesser peers, one archbishop, and fourteen bishops in the list of his patrons were five current cabinet ministers, including the prime minister, William Lamb, second Viscount Melbourne, and the foreign secretary, Henry John Temple, third Viscount Palmerston. In an era of excessive guzzling by the affluent classes, he proclaimed the merits of his vegetable and mercury-free nostrums for relieving derangements of the stomach's functions and 'a torpid state of the liver and bowels'. He publicized the recommendation of the surgeon John Abernethy (1764–1831). Charles Dickens occasionally took the pills, which were mentioned several times in his letters.

Cockle was able to educate his sons well, and sent at least four to university. His eldest son, John (1814–1900), also became a doctor and took over the business; another son, Charles Moss-Cockle (d. 1904), made a fortune as a solicitor. James Cockle died at 18 New Ormond Street, Queen Square, London, on 8 December 1854, leaving £37,085. By 1917, when the business became a limited company, its customers were principally elderly and expatriate, and it closed about 1960.

The younger James Cockle was educated at Stormond House, Kensington, from 1825 to 1829, as a day pupil at Charterhouse from 1829 until 1831, then privately at Ramsgate by Christian Lenny, a 'ten-year man' of St John's College, Cambridge, who discovered his mathematical talent. After a year's sojourn in the West Indies, Cuba, and America, he entered Trinity College, Cambridge, on 18 October 1837 as a pensioner with Thomas Thorp as his tutor. He enrolled at the Middle Temple on 12 April 1838. In the mathematical tripos of 1841 Cockle was placed thirty-third in the order of merit, though he published a paper in the *Cambridge Mathematical Journal* in the same year. He proceeded BA in 1842 and MA in 1845. In 1845 he began practice as a special pleader and was called to the bar on 6 November 1846. In 1848 he joined the midland circuit, but maintained his enthusiasm for mathematics.

As a young barrister Cockle gained a solid reputation for hard work, yet his manner was that of a retiring scholar. On a suggestion he stand for a parliament, he replied: 'My address to the electors shall run thus—Gentlemen, I am in favour of making things agreeable all round—all round!' (Harley, 1895, 225). He joined the Royal Astronomical Society (1854), the Cambridge Philosophical Society (1856), and the London Mathematical Society (1870), and was a corresponding member of the Manchester Literary and Philosophical Society. He was elected a fellow of the Royal Society on 1 June 1865.

Cockle possessed wide intellectual interests. He was well versed in classical philosophy, wrote on Indian astronomical literature (on the Indian cycles and lunar calendar, on the date of the Vedas and Jyotish Sastra, and on the ages of Garga and Parasara), and valued the study of the history of science generally. He published four elaborate memoirs on the motion of fluids and some notes on light under the action of magnetism. It was in pure mathematics, however, that he was held in especially high regard. In the flood of work following the discovery of quaternions by Sir William Rowan Hamilton, Cockle investigated 'tessarines'. A more constant field of enquiry was the theory of equations. In later years his research was confined almost entirely to algebra and differential equations and

their interconnection. He pioneered differential invariants (his 'criticoids'), thus contributing to invariant theory, the modern algebra of the day. Initially he distrusted Abel's proof (1824) of the insolubility of the quintic equation, though he came to appreciate it. He determined the explicit form of the sextic 'resolvent' equation on which a specialized quintic depended, and his result was confirmed by the Congregationalist minister and his close collaborator Robert Harley. This work attracted the attention of Arthur Cayley, who was able to place it in a broader context, complete the work for the general quintic equation, and discover its historical antecedents.

On 22 August 1855 Cockle married Adelaide Catharine Wilkin (d. 1916), the eldest surviving daughter of Henry Wilkin of Walton, Suffolk. In his legal career, Cockle's chance came in 1863. He was instrumental in drafting the Jurisdiction in Homicides Act (1862), and his ability attracted the attention of Sir William Erle, then chief justice of the court of common pleas. Erle named Cockle as chief justice for Queensland. It was a critical time for Queensland, which had separated from New South Wales only in 1859.

On arrival in the colony, Cockle defused an awkward situation with the outspoken maverick judge A. J. P. Lutwyche, who had hoped to be appointed to the senior position. As senior commissioner (1866–7), Cockle consolidated no fewer than 130 colonial statutes and prepared thirty draft bills. Erle remarked: 'I have had much knowledge of judicial men, and I am sure the Queen has never had a servant who more thoroughly earned every farthing of the wages he hoped to receive' (Harley, 1985, 217). Cockle was knighted on 29 July 1869.

Cockle was every inch the colonial administrator. He was above local politics yet willing to fulfil civic duty. He was chairman of the trustees of Brisbane grammar school (1874–7)—which he endowed with a mathematics prize—and his wife gave an annual picnic for local schoolchildren. He was president of the Queensland Philosophical Society (1863–77), to which he initially gave leadership, though he rarely attended meetings in later years. His administration of the law was scrupulous and in court only two of his judgments were reversed on appeal. His impartiality and tolerance were influenced by his strong Christian principles.

Cockle left Brisbane on 26 June 1878 on a year's paid leave. The colonists regarded their chief justice 'in every way fitted to this high position' and wished him a speedy return (*Brisbane Courier* 26 June 1878). But from England, one year later, Cockle tendered his resignation. He began an active retirement within the social and scientific life of London, though the transition from an equatorial climate impaired his health. He was a member of the Garrick and Savile clubs, though his favourite was the Savage, for which he was treasurer from 1884 to 1889. He was commissioner for the Queensland section of the Indian and Colonial Exhibition held in London in 1886. His ambition to serve as president of the London Mathematical Society was fulfilled (1886–8) and he was a member of the council of the Royal Astronomical Society (1888–92). He became a freemason and was inducted as worshipful master of the Nine Muses lodge on 12 February 1889.

In early 1895 Cockle caught a chill, and two days later, on 27 January 1895, he died at his residence, 12 St Stephen's Road, Bayswater. He was survived by his wife and eight of his nine children. He was buried at Paddington cemetery on 2 February 1895.

Cockle contributed to English and Australian scientific journals more than one hundred papers, many in the form of notes with suggestions for future work, but his reputation has not survived. In the second half of the nineteenth century it was not possible to make an indelible mark in both law and mathematics.

T. A. B. Corley and A. J. Crilly

Sources R. Harley, 'James Cockle', *Memoirs of the Literary and Philosophical Society of Manchester*, 9 (1895), 215–28 · R. Harley, 'James Cockle', *PRS*, 59 (1895–6), xxx–xxxix · A. R. Forsyth, 'James Cockle', *Proc. London Mathematical Society*, 26 (1895), 551–4 · *Monthly Notices of the Royal Astronomical Society*, 55 (1894–5), 192 · A. Cayley, 'On the invariants of a linear differential equation', *Quarterly Journal of Pure and Applied Mathematics*, 21 (1886), 257–61 · A. R. Forsyth, 'Invariants, covariants, and quotient-derivatives associated with linear differential equations', *PTRS*, 179A (1888), 377–489 · E. N. Marks, 'Cockle, Sir James', *AusDB*, vol. 3 · E. N. Marks, 'A history of the Queensland Philosophical Society and the Royal Society of Queensland from 1859–1911', *Proceedings of the Royal Society of Queensland*, 71 (1959), 17–42 · *Brisbane Courier* (26 June 1878) · E. B. Elliott, 'Robert Harley', *Proceedings of the London Mathematical Society*, 2nd ser., 9 (1911), xii–xv · 'Lutwyche, Alfred James Peter (1810–1880)', *AusDB*, vol. 5 · 'Lilley, Sir Charles (1827–1897)', *AusDB*, vol. 5 · Charterhouse Register, 1769–1872, Middle Temple Records · *The Times* (19 Nov 1900) · m. cert. · d. cert. · *The Satirist* (7 Jan 1838) · *The Satirist* (21 April 1839) · *The Times* (22 Dec 1837) · *London Medical Directory* (1847) · *The letters of Charles Dickens*, ed. M. House, G. Storey, and others, 7–8 (1988–93) · V. G. Plarr, *Plarr's Lives of the fellows of the Royal College of Surgeons of England*, rev. D'A. Power, 2 vols. (1930) · d. cert. [James Cockle (1782–1854)]

Archives CUL, letters to Robert Harley

Likenesses photograph, repro. in Harley, 'James Cockle', *PRS*, facing p. xxxii

Wealth at death £32,169 11s. 7d.: resworn probate, Feb 1896, *CGPLA Eng. & Wales* (1895)

Cocks, Arthur Herbert (1819–1881), administrator in India, third son of the Hon. Lieutenant-Colonel Philip James Cocks MP (1774–1857), of the Grenadier Guards, and Frances (d. 1870), daughter of Arthur Herbert of Brewsterfield, Killarney, was born on 18 April 1819, probably in the parish of Colwall, Herefordshire. His father was the third son of Charles Somers-Cocks, first Baron Somers. Arthur was educated at the Revd Mortlock's school in Brighton and, following his nomination in 1836 to the Bengal civil service, at the East India Company's college at Haileybury.

Cocks arrived in Bengal in 1837 and initially filled a variety of subordinate revenue and judicial posts in the North-Western Provinces. In 1847, after the First Anglo-Sikh War, Cocks was appointed Henry Lawrence's chief assistant in the Lahore residency. Although technically a political posting, the job required Cocks to advise the Sikh durbar on internal revenue and judicial reforms, and he enthusiastically toured the countryside around Lahore, settling legal disputes, adjusting revenue settlements,

and abolishing iniquitous taxes. Like many of his colleagues he saw himself bringing justice and order to a grievously oppressed peasantry. In October 1847 he wrote in his tour diary: 'My present is a delightful occupation. I feel I am doing some tangible good in every order I give' (Rayner, 433). In the same year he married Anna Marion Jessie (d. 1914), daughter of Lieutenant-General John Eckford. They had four sons and three daughters.

During the Second Anglo-Sikh War in 1848 Cocks was political officer to the commander-in-chief, Lord Gough, and was present at the battles of Chilianwala and Gujrat, on which latter occasion he was wounded in close combat with a Sikh trooper. He received the Punjab war medal for his services during the campaign.

In 1850 Cocks was briefly a deputy commissioner of the Punjab before taking furlough. In 1854 he was appointed magistrate and collector of Mainpuri and in 1858 judge of Mainpuri. District-level work seems to have best accommodated his desire to do 'tangible good' and, but for short postings to Aligarh and the Central Provinces, he remained as judge of Mainpuri until his retirement. During the rebellion of 1857 he joined with a small force of mounted volunteers and engaged in some sturdy but insignificant fighting around Aligarh.

In 1860 Cocks was made a CB, and in 1863 he resigned the service and returned to England. In retirement he became a JP for Worcestershire and from 1865 to 1872 was a captain in the Worcestershire militia. He died at his home, 8 Ashburn Place, Cromwell Road, South Kensington, London, on 29 August 1881. The second of his four sons was father of the sixth Baron Somers.

H. M. Stephens, rev. Katherine Prior

Sources *East-India Register and Directory* (1842–64) · H. T. Prinsep and R. Doss, eds., *A general register of the Hon'ble East India Company's civil servants of the Bengal establishment from 1790 to 1842* (1844) · [A. Rayner], ed., *Political diaries, 1847–49* (1915) [from Punjab government records] · Burke, *Peerage* (1939) · *The Times* (2 Sept 1881) · BL OIOC, Haileybury MSS · F. C. Danvers and others, *Memorials of old Haileybury College* (1894) · J. W. Kaye, *Lives of Indian officers*, new edn, 2 (1904)

Archives BL OIOC, diaries, corresp., and papers

Wealth at death £13,133 15s.: probate, 14 Oct 1881, *CGPLA Eng. & Wales*

Cocks, Arthur Herbert Tennyson Somers-, sixth Baron Somers (1887–1944), chief scout for Great Britain and the British Commonwealth and empire, and colonial governor, was born at Freshwater, Isle of Wight, on 20 March 1887, the second child and only son of Herbert Haldane Somers-Cocks (1861–1894), late lieutenant of the Coldstream Guards, and his wife, Blanche Margaret Standish (d. 1895), daughter of Major Herbert Clogstoun VC. Orphaned with their mother's death in 1895, he and his sister were raised by a range of family members. Alfred, Lord Tennyson, was his godfather and Arthur throughout his childhood continued to be brought into contact with literary and artistic figures. He had a well-developed appreciation of music and art. He succeeded his great-uncle as Baron Somers in 1899 at the age of twelve.

Educated at Mulgrave Castle private school and at Charterhouse School (1901–5), Somers joined the 1st Life

Guards in 1906 after a year at New College, Oxford. Being tall (6 feet) and an all-round athlete, he played cricket for Charterhouse, making a century in his first match against Westminster; he helped to win the army rackets for his regiment in 1908, and played cricket for Worcestershire, occasionally captaining the side in 1923.

After an accident at polo in 1911 Somers left the regiment and went to farm in Canada with his sister and her husband, Lord Hyde. On the outbreak of the First World War he rejoined his regiment and served in France throughout the war, being promoted, on 8 September 1918, to the command of the 6th battalion of the newly formed tank corps. For his services he was mentioned in dispatches, appointed to the DSO in 1918, awarded the MC, and made a chevalier of the Légion d'honneur.

On 20 April 1921 Somers married Daisy Finola Meeking (1896–1981), younger daughter of Captain Bertram Meeking of the 10th hussars. They had one daughter. In 1922 he inherited the Eastnor estates in Ledbury, Herefordshire, from his cousin, Lady Henry Somerset, and in the same year retired from the army as a lieutenant-colonel. When the Malvern hills were threatened by industrial development he was one of the first landowners to offer to the National Trust certain permanent rights over his (Eastnor Castle) property in the hills, which ensured the preservation of their amenities and free public access to them in perpetuity. He was joint master of the Ledbury hounds in 1923–4; lord-in-waiting and one of the spokesmen of the government in the House of Lords, 1924–6; and president of the Marylebone Cricket Club in 1936. He was appointed lord lieutenant of Herefordshire in 1933 and a director of the Great Western Railway Company in 1941.

From 1920 to the end of his life Somers took an active part in the Boy Scout movement, for which his gift of leadership and youthful outlook eminently fitted him. In 1932 he became a chief's commissioner to Lord Baden-Powell, who nominated him acting chief scout during his absence on a tour of South Africa in 1935; and deputy chief scout in 1936. He was designated by Baden-Powell to succeed him, and was appointed chief scout for Great Britain in January 1941, and for the British Commonwealth and empire in March of the same year.

In 1926 Somers became governor of Victoria, and was appointed KCMG. He was a popular and successful governor. His ease of manner, versatility, and unfeigned interest in all the activities of the state won the liking of all. His sincerity and shrewdness made him an effective and influential governor in many respects. His years of office were especially notable for the interest that he and his wife took in the youth of the state. When the more formal duties of his office permitted him, he delighted to lead a party of local scouts for a week's hike and demonstrate his interest in natural history and especially in bird life. Inspired by the success of the duke of York's camps in England, Somers initiated in 1929 a similar camp on the coast in Victoria for a hundred boys between sixteen and eighteen years of age selected from schools and commercial and industrial undertakings. Within two years the camp was equipped on a permanent basis by generous friends

and its name was changed to Somers by the state of Victoria as a permanent memorial to the governor. He was acting governor-general of Australia for a few months before the appointment of Sir Isaac Isaacs and completed his term of office in Victoria in 1931.

In 1940 Somers went to Egypt as commissioner for the Red Cross and St John Ambulance in the Middle East. He returned home in the following year after being diagnosed with cancer of the throat. He continued his work as chief scout for a few months following his return. He died at the Garden Cottage, Eastnor Castle, on 14 July 1944 and was cremated at Cheltenham on 18 July. He was succeeded in his titles by his uncle, Arthur Percy (1864–1953).

ASTOR OF HEVER, rev. MARC BRODIE

Sources *AusDB* · Burke, *Peerage* · *The Times* (15 July 1944) · *The Times* (19 July 1944) · B. M. Coldrey, *Lord Somers camp and power house: the early years, 1929–1939* (1993) · H. Collis, F. Hurll, and R. Hazlewood, *B.–P.'s scouts: an official history of the Boy Scouts Association* (1961) · *WWW* · E. M. Jameson and others, eds., *Charterhouse register, 1872–1931*, 3rd edn, 2 vols. (1932) · personal knowledge (1959) · private information (1959)
Archives Eastnor Castle, Ledbury, Herefordshire, Eastnor MSS
Likenesses W. Stoneman, photographs, 1926–39, NPG · O. Birley, oils, 1944, Scout Association, London · O. Birley, oils, Eastnor Castle, Ledbury, Herefordshire · photograph, repro. in *The Times* (15 July 1944)
Wealth at death £301,741 16s. 5d.: probate, 12 Jan 1945, *CGPLA Eng. & Wales*

Cocks, (Harry Francis) Lovell (1894–1983), United Reformed church minister and theologian, was born on 28 February 1894 at 4 Wesley Villas, New Windsor Street, Uxbridge, the son of Henry Edwin Cocks (1866?–1950), manager of a rope factory, and his wife, Ada Emma Bryant (1866?–1935), music teacher. He was educated at Uxbridge county school (1899–1912). Under the guidance of F. L. Riches Lowe, minister of Providence Chapel, Uxbridge, from 1903 to 1933, he proceeded to Hackney (Congregational) college, London (1912–17), where his teachers included P. T. Forsyth and A. E. Garvie. Impressed by both, it was to the former, he said, that 'I owe my theological soul and my footing in the Gospel' ('New College', Lovell Cocks MSS, 12). Following his college course he gained first-class honours in both the London BD (1920) and BA (1923) and took his MA in metaphysics in 1926. He was awarded the DD of London University in 1943 for a dissertation published in abbreviated form under the title *By Faith Alone* (1943).

Meanwhile Cocks had been ordained at Winchester Congregational Church in 1917, where he quickly impressed the discerning as being 'a man with a message', and earned the loyalty and affection of many. On 9 November the following year he married Lottie Violet Mary (Dot) Bollen (1890–1966). They had three children: Doris Evelyn, Peter Stuart, and Michael Francis Lovell (Lord Cocks of Hartcliffe). On leaving Winchester, Cocks was minister at Hove, Sussex (1922–7), and Headingley Hill, Leeds (1927–32). He held the chair of systematic theology and Christian social philosophy at Yorkshire United Independent College, Bradford (1932–7), and in the latter year became principal of the Scottish Congregational college, Edinburgh, where he also lectured in the postgraduate school of theology of the university. In 1941 he moved to Bristol where, in succession to R. S. Franks, he served as principal of Western (Congregational) College until his retirement in 1960.

Cocks was chairman of the Congregational Union of England and Wales (1950–51); he addressed the united service of tribute to George VI in the Central Hall, Bristol, on 15 February 1952, and the seventh International Congregational Council at St Andrews in 1953. His Drew lecture on immortality was published as *The Hope of Glory* (1955), and in 1961 he preached the founder's day sermon at Bristol University. For two years (1958–60) he was a member of the commission which produced the Congregational church's *Declaration of Faith* (1967), and in 1962, the tercentenary year of the Great Ejection, he was moderator of the Free Church Federal Council. In this significant year for English and Welsh nonconformity Cocks's moderatorial address was entitled *1662–1962: Free Church Witness— Then—and Now?* On 5 April 1966 he broadcast an Easter talk in which, following a reference to the death of his wife a few weeks before, he went on to proclaim the Christian hope. In 1968 he returned to Bristol to deliver the sermon at the closing of Western College, which united with its sister institution in Manchester; and on 5 September of the same year he married Edith Ethel Mutlow, *née* Turner (1897–1981). Prior to the formation of the United Reformed church in 1972 he delivered the sermon at the last meeting of the council of the Congregational church in England and Wales.

In his major work, *By Faith Alone*, Cocks argued that since the psychological and epistemological starting points of Schleiermacher and Kant respectively have been shown to lead to a theological humanism roundly denounced by Karl Barth, we must construe saving faith as presupposing natural faith, but as discontinuous with it. It is God's gift to human beings through his word, Jesus Christ. In *The Faith of a Protestant Christian* (1931) he sketched what became for him familiar themes: salvation by grace through faith, the necessity of the church, and the importance of its social witness. In the midst of war he published his incisive tract *The Nonconformist Conscience* (1943), in which he declared that 'The Nonconformist Conscience is the mark of a spiritual aristocracy, a counterblast to coronets and mitres' (p. 17); and in *The Religious Life of Oliver Cromwell* (1960) he argued that the lord protector owed much to Independency's principle of the gathered church. While finding much to admire in Cromwell, he lamented his blindness to the fact that 'not the sword but the Cross is the guarantee of final victory' (p. 79). That the atonement is the work of the triune God is the theme of *The Wondrous Cross* (1957), and, as he urged in *The Church in the Atomic Age* (1948), from the victory of the cross believers derive their confidence that 'Whatever happens now— whether it be the worst we fear or the best we hope for— God will wrest it to His saving purpose and overrule it for our eternal good' (p. 11).

Cocks died on 15 January 1983 at his home, 32 Highland Road, Amersham, Buckinghamshire. Over 200 people attended the funeral service at Amersham, where he was buried on 24 January, and John Huxtable, at whose own service of induction as secretary of the Congregational Union of England and Wales Cocks had preached, delivered a memorial sermon in Redland Park church, Bristol. Lovell Cocks valued Congregationalism's gathered church polity, which he construed as catholic, and his sympathies were ecumenical. He was a scholarly, modest man, who endeared himself to his students, and who was as adept at communicating with children and with the 'plain man'—not least through broadcast talks of which eight series were published—as with his academic peers. He could be counted upon to find the right words on formal occasions, whether solemn or festive, and his integrity and pastoral care were greatly valued by all who knew him.   ALAN P. F. SELL

Sources DWL, Lovell Cocks MSS · *Yearbook* [United Reformed church in the UK] (1984), 258–9 · A. P. F. Sell, *Commemorations: studies in Christian thought and history* (1993) · private information (2004) [D. Caulfield] · F. Carpenter, *Winchester Congregational Church tercentenary, 1662–1962* (1962) · *CGPLA Eng. & Wales* (1983) · b. cert. · m. cert. · d. cert.
Archives DWL
Likenesses photograph, repro. in R. F. G. Calder, ed., *Proceedings of the Seventh International Congregational Council* (1953), 45
Wealth at death £79,426: probate, 6 April 1983, *CGPLA Eng. & Wales*

Cocks, Richard (*bap.* 1565, *d.* 1624), merchant and East India Company servant, was baptized on 20 January 1565 at St Chad's, Seighford, Staffordshire, the fifth of the seven children of Robert Cocks of Stallbrook, yeoman, and his wife, Helen (*d.* 1614). The family had held Stallbrook, close to the city of Stafford, since the reign of Edward IV. Richard's brother Walter (the sixth child) was in the service of Sir Thomas Hewett, an influential member of the Clothworkers' Company of London, who, like his father and grandfather before him, had connections to the Dorrington family of Staffordshire. It was doubtless through them that Richard was apprenticed in London to William Hewett, clothworker and elder brother of Sir Thomas, became a member of the Clothworkers' Company himself, and was eventually made free of the Merchant Adventurers of England.

Between 1603 and 1608 Cocks lived and traded at Bayonne in France, from where he also supplied intelligence to Thomas Wilson, secretary to Lord Salisbury. The circumstances of his employment by the East India Company are not known but his experience of the cloth trade and the Spanish language would have been sufficient recommendation. He sailed as a merchant in the *Clove* in the company's eighth voyage of 1611 under John Saris, whose instructions included a settlement at Japan. During previous service at Bantam in Java, Saris had gathered information on the Japan trade which helped to persuade the company that purchases, mainly silk, at Chinese junk-destination ports in south-east Asia, carried to Japan, would yield sufficient silver to finance return cargoes of Indonesian spices, and thus counter complaints in England about the 'drain of national wealth' caused by the company exporting bullion. It was also known that the English pilot William Adams was living in Japan in great favour with the shogun Ieyasu.

Cocks remained in Japan in December 1613 as head of the new 'factory' at Hirado, a small island off the west coast of Kyushu, which had a flourishing overseas Chinese community and a Dutch Company settlement dating from 1609. He spent just over ten years there in an unsuccessful struggle for profit. Cargoes brought from England varied from unsuitable for such a sophisticated market to absolute rubbish, and silk, which would have been the key to profitability, was never available to the English in any significant quantities.

The diary which Cocks kept between June 1615 and March 1622 is an invaluable source of information not only for English and other European activities in Japan but also for Japanese economic, political, and social conditions in the early Tokugawa period. In addition more than a hundred of his letters home to London or to his fellow servants in Asia are extant, helping to make the Japan factory one of the best-documented episodes in the early history of the company.

Cocks's first years at Hirado were spent in organizing the factory and its sub-agencies at Kyoto, Sakai, and Edo, and in fitting out local junks for English voyages to mainland south-east Asia. He was subsequently forced to make five journeys to court, spending a great deal of his time on the Inland Sea or hurrying up and down the Tokaido highway: August–December 1616 to Edo, in an attempt to obtain a renewal of the English trading privileges after the death of the shogun Ieyasu; August–November 1617 to Edo, to appeal against the restriction of English trade to Hirado only; August 1618–January 1619 to Edo, to protest against Dutch aggression; August–September 1619 to Kyoto, to protest again about the Dutch; and November 1621–April 1622 to Edo, to smooth over the activities of the temporary Anglo-Dutch alliance in east Asian waters.

Cocks showed a distinct lack of judgement in his close involvement with Li Tan (or Andrea Dittis), head of the overseas Chinese community at Hirado, who fanned his dreams of direct English trade to China while pocketing the bribes intended for influential mandarins on the mainland, and he was undoubtedly a poor manager. The period of Anglo-Dutch hostility between 1618 and 1620 made life at Hirado dangerous as well as difficult, while subsequent co-operation with the Dutch Company between 1620 and 1622 in blockading Manila and plundering junk traffic in the South China Sea brought the problems of numerous ships and hundreds of seamen to the small port of Hirado. However, despite all the grumbling in his correspondence, Cocks was reluctant to leave Japan when the time came. As early as 1621 he was strongly advised to wind up affairs in Japan, but he ignored the order, perhaps realizing that he would be blamed for their unprofitability. In March 1623 the East India Company's council in Java was forced to send the ship *Bull* on a special voyage to close the Hirado factory. Cocks, with his colleagues William Eaton and Edmund Sayers, was ordered to London to face examination by the company. He

embarked on the *Anne Royal* from Batavia on 22 February 1624, but died and was buried at sea on 27 March 1624 in the southern Indian Ocean.

Measured against the outstanding pioneers of early European expansion in Asia, Cocks's career was a disaster. However, his diary presents a remarkable personal history of a residence he shared with his Japanese mistress Matinga. From the diary Cocks emerges as an unusually vivid and gentle figure—tending his garden at the English house at Hirado, caring for his goldfish, entertaining his Japanese neighbours with invitations to dinner and a hot bath, or carrying presents to them at new year.

ANTHONY FARRINGTON

Sources R. Cocks, diary, 1615–22, BL, Add. MSS 31300–31301 · R. Cocks, correspondence, 1613–23, BL OIOC, IOR, E/3/1–11 (*infra*) · R. Cocks, will and probate 1611/1627, PRO, PROB 11/151, fols. 458–9 · *Diary of Richard Cocks … 1615–1622*, ed. E. M. Thompson, 2 vols., Hakluyt Society (1883) · *Diary of Richard Cocks, 1615–1622*, ed. Institute of Historical Research (Shiryō Hensan-jō), University of Tokyo, 7 vols. (1978–81) [includes Japanese trans.] · A. Farrington, *The English factory in Japan, 1613–1623*, 2 vols. (1991) · parish register, Seighford, Staffordshire, St Chad, 25 Jan 1565, Staffs. RO [baptism]

Archives BL, diary, Add. MSS 31300–31301 · BL OIOC, corresp., IOR, E/3/1–11

Wealth at death 100 marks; plus £300: will, PRO, PROB 11/151, fols. 458–9 · very little, or none; wasted £40,000: Court minutes of the East India Company, 24 Nov 1626, BL OIOC, IOR B/11, pp. 202–3

Cocks, Sir Richard, second baronet (*c.*1659–1726), parliamentary diarist and religious controversialist, was the eldest son of Richard Cocks (1633–1669) of the Middle Temple and his wife, Mary (*d.* 1669), daughter of Sir Robert Cooke of Highnam, Gloucestershire. Cocks was only ten years old when his father and mother both died, leaving him heir to his paternal grandfather's baronetcy and estate at Dumbleton, Gloucestershire, and the remainder of his upbringing seems to have been entrusted to the strict guidance of his elder sister, Dorothy, who regulated the family to her own pattern of godliness. Cocks was admitted to the Middle Temple in 1667, while still a child, but he does not appear ever to have taken up residence. In 1677 he matriculated at Oriel College, Oxford, where he spent at least a year, and where he later claimed to have suffered a worthless and drunken tutor. Cocks married Frances (1663–1724), daughter of Richard Neville of Billingbear, Berkshire, in October 1688, the godly daughter of a family with strong puritan traditions. On his grandmother's death in 1690, he came to reside at Dumbleton and inaugurated an extensive programme of improvement, involving the construction of an entirely new manor house and the creation of fashionable gardens in the Dutch style.

Cocks's taste for public speaking was frequently indulged as chairman of the Gloucestershire quarter sessions, and in 1698, after several unsuccessful attempts to enter parliament, he secured election as knight of the shire. Various family connections, including his father's friendship with the lord chancellor, John, Baron Somers, drew him to the whig side in politics, despite his grandfather's support for the royalist side in the civil war. But he was no slavish follower of a party. Indeed, his stern morality and adherence to the ideals of classical republicanism, as mediated through such writers as Algernon Sidney and his own uncle by marriage, Henry Neville, made him into an archetypal 'country' member, and he was quickly to the forefront in the agitations against a standing army, the presence of placemen in the Commons, and political corruption in general. At the same time his pathological detestation of 'popery' guaranteed that he would vote with the whigs over other great questions of policy, such as the settlement of the Hanoverian succession and the resumption of war with France. So deep-rooted were his political principles and prejudices, and so pronounced his self-importance in pursuing them, that he came to be regarded in some quarters as not merely an individualist but something of a crank.

Cocks was not re-elected in the general election of 1702, nor thereafter, despite trying again more than once. Out of parliament he retired to his study and began to write—fragments of history, religious meditations, political satires, in prose, verse, and even in dramatic form—none of which were published, though some circulated in manuscript among his friends. From notes and other materials he was also able to construct in retrospect a diary of his parliamentary career, covering in particular detail the sessions of 1701–2, which, surviving in manuscript form, now constitutes his chief claim to fame. Not until 1717 did he appear in print, with a grand jury charge denouncing Jacobites. Then in 1721–2 he waded into the paper war over the so-called 'Bangorian controversy' initiated by the sermon on church government by Benjamin Hoadly, bishop of Bangor.

In rapid succession Cocks produced four pamphlets promoting an Erastian view of ecclesiastical authority and a comprehensive religious settlement designed to include presbyterians: *A Perfect Discovery of Longitude* (1721), *The Church of England Secured* (1722), *Over Shoes, Over Boots* (1722), and his *Farewel Sermon* (1722). Their violently anti-clerical tone, occasionally stooping to scurrilous abuse, provoked sharp replies from churchmen, some of whom themselves descended to the level of personal insults, mostly on the score of Cocks's diminutive size and renowned eccentricity. To Thomas Hearne, for example, he was 'a whimsical, crazed man'; to another high tory he was a 'peevish elf' (*Parliamentary Diary*, xiii). Undaunted, Cocks hit back with yet another tract, *A True and Impartial Inquiry … into the Late Bloody Execution at Thorn* (1727), though this was no more than a stale reprise of past polemic, and was published only posthumously.

Within a few months of the death of his first wife, in 1724, Cocks took as his second wife Mary Bethell (d. 1765), daughter of William Bethell of Swindon in Yorkshire and sister of Hugh Bethell MP. There were no children of either marriage, so that on his death, about 21 October 1726 at Dumbleton, where he was buried at St Peter's Church, the baronetcy passed to his brother Robert, rector of Bladon, in Oxfordshire. The estate at Dumbleton was, however, willed directly to his nephew, Robert's second surviving son and namesake. In characteristic style,

Cocks's will included a political valediction which gave expression to his resolute whiggism. He adjured his 'friends and relations' to

serve God in a manner worthy of Him, and not to disturb the peace of their country with party and idle distinctions, which in weak persons is only the effect of their folly in cunning of private interest and ambition. I desire them to love one the other, to be kind to their neighbours, and be faithful and loyal to King George and to have more regard to the Protestant interest than to any private views whatever. (*Parliamentary Diary*, lix)

D. W. HAYTON

Sources Bodl. Oxf., MSS Eng. hist. b. 209–10 · Bodl. Oxf., MS facs. b. 18, fols. 119–30 · *The parliamentary diary of Sir Richard Cocks, 1698–1702*, ed. D. W. Hayton (1996) · J. V. Somers Cocks, *A history of the Cocks family* (1966–7) · HoP, *Commons* [draft] · private information (1993) [J. V. Somers Cocks] · LPL, MS 640, nos. 501–23 · Boston PL, Somerset MSS, K.5.5 · Glos. RO, Ducie MSS, D 340a/C22/10, 12 · *Letter-books of John Hervey, first earl of Bristol*, ed. S. H. A. H. [S. H. A. Hervey], 3 vols. (1894)
Archives Bodl. Oxf., copybooks, parliamentary diaries, MSS Eng. hist. b. 209–10, MS Eng. misc., fols. 30–35 [damage to corners], photocopies of some loose leaves, MS facs. b. 18, fols. 119–30 | Boston PL, Somerset MSS · Glos. RO, Ducie MSS · LPL, Tenison MSS
Likenesses oils, priv. coll.
Wealth at death estate at Dumbleton, Gloucestershire, to nephew: Somers Cocks, *History*

Cocks, Roger (*fl.* 1611–1642), Church of England clergyman and poet, was a scholar of Trinity College, Cambridge, in 1611 and graduated BA in 1611/12. He contributed a set of Latin hexameter verses to the university's memorial volume for the death of Prince Henry in 1612. He later became a curate and lecturer at Acton in Suffolk, and in 1630 published *Hebdomada sacra: a weeke's devotion*. Cocks's text is a set of seven meditations, in rhyming couplets, on Matthew 2, the birth of Christ, and is dedicated to James, Lord Strange. Although the prefatory verse declares 'No profest Poet, but a Preacher wrote it' the work is not without merit. Cocks sets the story firmly in its political context, opening with a brief history of the Roman empire; the description of Herod's court in Tuesday's meditation, when news reaches it of the birth, is a lively portrait of political intrigue and paranoia. A poem 'Written in commendation of Mr Coxe [the lecturer of Acton] his booke of the birth of Christ' survives in the commonplace book of Anne Southwell (1573–1636).

In 1642 Cocks published *An Answer to a Book Set Forth by Sir Edward Peyton*. Peyton, a baronet who was MP for Cambridgeshire from 1620 to 1627, had been refused the sacrament by Cocks because he insisted on receiving it standing up, and had published a vindication of his refusal to kneel at communion, based chiefly on scriptural grounds. Cocks's answer to this was a closely argued little pamphlet on the importance of kneeling.

ALSAGER VIAN, *rev.* JOANNA MOODY

Sources BL cat. · S. E. Brydges, *Restitua*, 4 vols. (1814–16), 2.505 · *STC, 1475–1640* · Venn, *Alum. Cant.* · J. Carmel, 'New light on Robert Johnson, the king's musician', *Shakespeare Quarterly*, 16 (1965), 233–5

Cocks, William Alfred (1892–1971), clockmaker and bag-pipe scholar, was born on 8 October 1892 at St Mary's Terrace, Ryton, co. Durham, the son of John Cocks, banker's clerk, and his wife, Elizabeth Cummings, *née* Dunlop. As a small boy he conceived what proved to be a lifelong interest in the pipes after being given a toy set as a present. He worked as a master watch- and clockmaker but in his leisure became an expert craftsman and skilled player of the bagpipes. Over the years he made many fine sets of Northumbrian small pipes, taking pride in doing everything himself, down to sewing the bags and bellows. From the time of the First World War onwards, he travelled the country in search of instruments made by others. The important collection which he gradually acquired is now held at the Chantry Bagpipe Museum, Morpeth, Northumberland, on loan from the Society of Antiquaries of Newcastle upon Tyne.

As a pioneer member of the Northumbrian Pipers' Society, Will Cocks provided a set of pipes as a trophy in the annual Newcastle Musical Tournament. As a leading expert on the instrument he was a member (later fellow) of the Society of Antiquaries (Scotland) and an honorary member of the Gilpin Society. He contributed bagpipe articles to *Grove's Dictionary of Music and Musicians* (1954 edn) and wrote for Oxford University Press a *Tutor for the Northumberland Half-Long Bagpipe* (1925). In 1931 he produced, with Gilbert Askew, a revised edition of J. W. Fenwick's *Instruction Book for the Northumbrian Small-Pipes*, which had originally appeared in 1896. In his later years he renovated many old sets of pipes and also conducted extensive experiments in the use of new materials and methods of working. His book *The Northumbrian Bagpipes* (1967) is the definitive work on the construction of the instrument.

Cocks died at Hexham General Hospital on 31 March 1971 as a result of an accidental overdose of barbiturates; the inquest recorded a verdict of misadventure. Photographs show him as tall, slim, dark-haired, and moustached, yet he remained a bachelor throughout his long life, which he single-mindedly devoted to a passion for the sweet-sounding pipes of his native region. In *Bagpipes* Anthony Baines paid tribute to Cocks's 'vast store of knowledge and material', and assessed him as being 'one of the bagpipe's leading historians' (Baines, 14).

ROY PALMER

Sources Chantry Bagpipe Museum, Morpeth, Northumberland, instrument collection · *William Alfred Cocks, FSA (Scot)*, Society of Antiquaries of Newcastle upon Tyne [n.d.] · A. Baines, *Bagpipes*, rev. edn (1973) [orig. no date] · S. Sterck, 'Pipes thay can lure the tourists north', Local Biography Newspaper Cuttings, vol. 8, p. 338, Newcastle City Library · 'Tablets killed watchmaker', *Journal* (2 April 1971) [in Newcastle City Library, Local Obituaries Newspaper Cuttings, vol. 5, p. 135] · Northumbrian Pipers Society · Vaughan Williams Memorial Library, Cecil Sharp House, London · b. cert. · d. cert. · *CGPLA Eng. & Wales* (1971)
Archives Chantry Bagpipe Museum, Morpeth, Northumberland, instrument collection
Likenesses photograph, repro. in Baines, *Bagpipes* · photographs, Chantry Bagpipe Museum, Morpeth, Northumberland
Wealth at death £17,955: probate, 30 July 1971, *CGPLA Eng. & Wales*

Cockshut, John (1837–1912), wallpaper manufacturer, was born on 4 November 1837 at Tong with Haulgh, near Bolton, Lancashire, the eldest son of John Cockshut, plumber and glazier, and his wife, Alice (*née* Bromiley).

Cockshut is known largely for his contribution to the British wallpaper industry. His involvement began when, aged eight, he went to work for C. H. and E. Potter of Darwen, where mechanization was pioneered. Details of any formal education and of the nature of his work at Potters remain unknown but he was probably employed initially in the production of handblock-printed wallpapers. Apart from a short break at a cotton mill, Cockshut, joined later by his brother, James, remained there until he was about twenty, when they joined their uncle (formerly cashier at Potters) in his own firm, Lightbown, Aspinall & Co., at Pendleton, near Manchester.

Under Lightbown's direction, John Cockshut's commercial acumen and genial but shrewd salesmanship, and his brother's talents as a designer and colourist made them a formidable team. The firm grew dramatically, warehouses were opened in Manchester, Leeds, Glasgow, London, and Leipzig, and Cockshut became Lightbown's first manager at the Cannon Street warehouse in London, although he continued to collaborate with his brother on special machine-printed collections for overseas markets and new ranges for the home trade. Under his regime, a large export trade was established, particularly with Australia and other colonies. Subsequently he was joined by his son, Harry.

In 1888 the Cockshuts left Lightbowns, having acquired John Allan & Sons, an established wallpaper firm with a factory at Old Ford, east London. It became Allan, Cockshut & Co. and, determined to expand, Cockshut extended the premises substantially, subsuming the original mill in a new factory 400 feet long. Under his direction, the business flourished: within a few years the workforce had increased from 140 to 600, turnover had quadrupled, and output rivalled that of major manufacturers. In 1896 Cockshut embarked on the development of a range of raised decorations for walls and ceilings, a venture which proved highly successful despite intense competition.

In 1899 Cockshut played a major role in the amalgamation of thirty-one firms into the Wall Paper Manufacturers Ltd, which controlled more than 98 per cent of the UK wallpaper trade and rapidly became one of the largest firms in the British economy, with capital of £14.14 million and, by 1903, 3400 employees. John, James, and Harry Cockshut joined the board and John served as chairman from 1901 to 1903.

By 1904 Allan, Cockshut & Co. was producing 10 million rolls of wallpaper annually, largely as a result of the entrepreneurial flair and vigour of John Cockshut. He had a talent for selecting staff and maintaining good relations with the workforce, and emphasized the importance of establishing good relationships with customers, which paid off when his son returned from Australia with the biggest single order for wallpaper recorded. But it was his ability to make use of new technology and ideas, and his experience both of manufacturing and worldwide distribution, which enabled him to increase his firm's share when market conditions became difficult. However, his brother's death in 1905, followed by that of Harry, his only son, in 1909, were severe personal blows and, although he continued to direct the business, aided by his two nephews, he never fully recovered from Harry's death.

Both brothers were dedicated to wallpaper manufacture, regarding it as their hobby as well as their business, but they were also avid collectors of pictures, *objets d'art*, and, in particular, Sèvres, Chelsea, and Worcester porcelain. John Cockshut's was considered to be one of the finest private collections in existence and parts of it were displayed in several international exhibitions, including the Louisiana Purchase Exposition (1904)—for which the items in his display were valued at £30,000—and the Franco-British Exhibition (1908). Four watercolours were presented by him to the Atkinson Art Gallery, Southport, which he visited frequently, and his reputation as a generous benefactor extended to his local Presbyterian church in Willesden, which he helped to found and where he was an elder and deacon. He donated the organ and a house in Craven Park, which he presented as a manse. He was made a JP in 1895.

John Cockshut married his first wife, Alice Cheetham, before 1865 and was survived by his second, Leah. In addition to Harry, there were five daughters. Cockshut died at Glenmore, 243 Willesden Lane, London, on 11 November 1912. His funeral took place at Willesden on 14 November 1912.   CHRISTINE WOODS

Sources C. Shaw, 'Cockshut, John', *DBB* · A. V. Sugden and J. L. Edmondson, *A history of English wallpaper, 1509–1914* (1926) · 'The Wall Paper Manufacturers Ltd', *Journal of Decorative Art* (Sept 1905), 12–14, 22–3 [special supplement] · 'Tatler', 'Wall papers in the making', *African Commerce* (Jan 1904) · *Journal of Decorative Art* (Dec 1912) · *Willesden Citizen* (15 Nov 1912) · d. cert.
Likenesses photograph, repro. in *Journal of Decorative Art* (Dec 1912), 32.427 · photograph (after photograph, repro. in *Journal of Decorative Art*, Dec 1912), repro. in Sugden and Edmondson, *History of English wallpaper*, 194
Wealth at death £143,256 13s.: probate, 23 Dec 1912, CGPLA Eng. & Wales

Cockson [Coxon], **Thomas** (*bap.* 1569, *d.* before 1641?), engraver, the son of Ninian Cockson, was baptized on 3 April 1569 at Christ Church Greyfriars, London. He was apprenticed in the Worshipful Company of Goldsmiths to the celebrated William Rogers on 29 September 1584, and became a freeman of his father's livery company, the Merchant Taylors, on 21 February 1598.

Cockson's known work, comprising fewer than forty extant examples dated between 1591 and 1630, consists mainly of engraved portraits, the most impressive of which are equestrian studies of the earls of Cumberland, Essex, Nottingham, and Devonshire, dating from around 1600 and with cartographic backgrounds showing details of naval actions. Also of note are a 1596 chart of the operations at Cadiz, a satirical plate, *The Revells of Christendome* (1609), a large plate exhibiting the drill postures of musketeers and pikemen (1619), and a number of engraved title-pages. Cockson's work is justly characterized by

Joseph Strutt as being executed 'entirely with the graver, in a neat, stiff style, which seem to prove, that he had much more industry than genius' (Strutt, 1.208). He was none the less an important figure in establishing a London-based school of engraving, and numbered both Robert Vaughan and Thomas Fullwood among his apprentices. His premises in Foster Lane were in the heart of the gold-working district, and it is likely that, as with other engravers at this early period, he had a parallel career in the decorative engraving of gold and silver plate. His name, which appears in several variant forms, was often appended to his prints in the form of a monogram of his initials, a device apt to cause confusion with Thomas Cecill and Thomas Cross. The record of a 'Widow Cockson' on a poll-tax return of 1641 for the parish of St Sepulchre almost certainly indicates his death before that date.   LAURENCE WORMS

Sources A. M. Hind, *Engraving in England in the sixteenth and seventeenth centuries*, 1 (1952), 239–57 · GL, Worshipful Company of Merchant Taylors MSS · Worshipful Company of Goldsmiths archives, Goldsmiths' Hall, Foster Lane, London · private information (2004) · J. Strutt, *A biographical dictionary, containing an historical account of all the engravers, from the earliest period of the art of engraving to the present time*, 1 (1785), 208–9 · IGI
Archives BM, department of prints and drawings

Cockton, Henry [*pseud.* Sherry] (1807–1853), novelist, was born in George Yard, Shoreditch, London, on 7 December 1807, one of the eight children of William Cockton, a weaver, and his wife, Mary. Nothing is known of his life before 9 May 1837 when Cockton married Ann, daughter of Abraham and Eleanor Howes, in St James's Church, Bury St Edmunds, Suffolk. Her family owned the Seven Stars inn in Long Brackland in that town. Henry Cockton and his wife rented accommodation at 165 Blackfriars Road, Southwark, London. They had two children, Eleanor and Edward, born in 1839 and 1841 respectively.

Cockton's fame rests on his first novel, *Valentine Vox the Ventriloquist*, which he wrote in monthly numbers over 1839 and 1840, under the pseudonym Sherry. This was a comic story about a gifted ventriloquist who used his skills to play practical jokes. A sub-plot describing how Valentine's uncle, Grimwood Goodman, was confined in a private lunatic asylum by unscrupulous relatives was an important literary study of a person unjustly classified insane. Illustrations by Thomas Onwhyn were a feature of this and most of Henry Cockton's later works. *The Age* described *Valentine Vox* as the best novel of the day and predicted fame for the author. Thomas Prest, a hack writer, produced a plagiarized serial, *Valentine Vaux*, under the pseudonym Timothy Portwine. Yet Henry Cockton made little money from *Valentine Vox*, and his other works failed to equal his first success.

The popularity of *Valentine Vox* prompted Richard Bentley to commission Henry Cockton to write *Stanley Thorn*. This story about upper-class society (based on an unpublished novel started by Richard Harris Barham) appeared in *Bentley's Miscellany* between 1840 and 1841. A third serial, *George St George Julian*, appeared during 1841 and dealt with frauds and swindles (including Gregor MacGregor's

Poyais emigration scheme of 1821). But the publishers went bankrupt, causing Henry Cockton to be declared an insolvent debtor.

Between 1843 and 1845 Cockton wrote three more novels. The second of these, *Sylvester Sound the Somnambulist* (1844), the broadly comic story of a sleepwalker, enjoyed some popularity. These works seem to have brought him little financial profit. He then abandoned writing to run the Seven Stars inn at Bury St Edmunds for his wife's family, but was ruined by an unsuccessful malting speculation. This, combined with the debt which he incurred when his brother Edward, for whom he had provided surety, fled to Australia, caused Cockton to resume writing in 1850. He produced a further three novels before dying of consumption at his mother-in-law's house, adjoining the Seven Stars inn, on 26 June 1853. He was buried in the town churchyard in Bury St Edmunds. Tradition held that he died poor and friendless. In 1854 the Royal Literary Fund granted Ann Cockton £25. In 1856 a public appeal was made for his wife and family. Cockton was commemorated in Bury St Edmunds by a memorial erected in the town churchyard in 1884, and a plaque placed on his house in Long Brackland in 1907.

Valentine Vox and *Sylvester Sound* remained in print until 1920. (Routledge published 400,000 and 80,000 copies of these, respectively, between 1860 and 1902). Some of his other works were re-issued in the nineteenth and early twentieth centuries.   ROBERT HALLIDAY

Sources R. Halliday, 'New light on Henry Cockton', *N&Q*, 239 (1994), 349–51 · J. Sutherland, *The Longman companion to Victorian fiction* (1988) · D. MacAndrew, 'The author of Valentine Vox', *East Anglian Magazine*, 38 (1979), 440–42 · *Bury and Norwich Post* (25 June 1856) [appeal for his family] · *Bury and Norwich Post* (15 Jan 1884); (19 Feb 1884); (18 March 1884); (1 April 1884); (3 June 1884) [erection of a memorial to him in Bury St Edmunds town churchyard] · *Bury and Norwich Post* (19 Feb 1907); (11 June 1907); (9 July 1907) [placing of commemorative plaque on his house] · *BL cat.* · *The life and letters of … Richard Harris Barham*, ed. R. H. D. Barham, 2 vols. (1870) · BL, Royal Literary Fund archives, microfilm M1077/50, file 1335 · UCL, Routledge and Kegan Paul archives · W. L. Parry-Jones, *The trade in lunacy: a study of private madhouses in England in the eighteenth and nineteenth centuries* (1972) [useful information on the lunatic asylum episodes in *Valentine Vox*] · *DNB*

Archives BL, letters to and agreements with Richard Bentley, Add. MSS 46613–46614, 46650

Likenesses portrait (after J. W. Childe), repro. in H. Cockton, *George St George Julian the prince* (1841), frontispiece

Wealth at death died in poverty; left family in reduced circumstances: *Bury and Norwich Post*, 25 June 1856, 18 March 1884, 1 April 1884

Codd, Clara Margaret (1876–1971), suffragette and theosophist, was born on 10 October 1876 at Pill House, Bishops Taunton, Barnstaple, north Devon, the eldest of ten children of Henry Frederick Codd (d. 1899) and his wife, Clara Virginia. She was educated at home by governesses, and at fifteen rejected Christianity and declared herself an atheist. When she was twenty-three her father, a school inspector, died and the family moved to Geneva, Switzerland, where Codd financed her sisters' education by herself working as a governess. In addition to teaching English and music, she worked as a costume model and travelled across France and Switzerland playing the violin and piano in orchestras. She later wrote of how her experiences in Geneva marked

> the first time in life I came into contact with all sorts and conditions of men, and learned to be free and a friend of all that lives, instead of the proper, little caste-ridden Victorian that I was in the beginning.   (Codd, 24)

It was in Geneva that Codd first came into contact with the movement to which she dedicated her life. A friend took her to hear Colonel Henry Olcott speak on theosophy; she later wrote of how 'Life changed miraculously for me from that moment onwards' (Codd, 29). The family soon returned to England and settled in Bath, where Codd, and later her mother, began to attend the local Theosophical Society lodge.

Codd officially joined the Theosophical Society in 1903, at about the same time that she joined the socialist Social Democratic Federation. In 1907 she joined the militant, Pankhurst-led Women's Social and Political Union (WSPU), principally inspired by the work of one of the national organizers, Annie Kenney. Codd became close friends with Kenney and was active in arranging and speaking at street meetings in Bristol, often experiencing physical violence. In 1908 she participated in a 'rush' on the House of Commons, managing to enter the building despite a heavy police presence. She was discovered and arrested, and went on to serve a one-month sentence in Holloway gaol.

On her release Codd returned to Bristol, only to face increased violence in the local campaign. She was offered a paid position as a WSPU organizer but turned it down in order to dedicate herself fully to theosophy. After a short period of employment as a teacher, she was offered work as a lecturer by the Theosophical Society, and soon spent two years at the society's headquarters in Adyar, India, as the result of a private bequest. She continued to lecture for the society throughout the 1910s, her wages being raised by the head of the movement, Annie Besant. Codd spent the remainder of her life as a travelling lecturer for the Theosophical Society, spending several years in the United States, New Zealand, Australia, where she was general secretary from 1935 to 1936, and in South Africa, where she lived during the Second World War.

Codd was both unassuming and sincere; her ability to communicate directly across class and cultural barriers undoubtedly contributed to her international success as a lecturer. Her history of addressing working men and women in the socialist and suffrage movements had developed her skills as a public speaker, while her experiences as a young woman in the cosmopolitan circles of Geneva had encouraged her to be accomplished, informed, and, importantly, self-reliant.

There is little secondary work on Codd: the most detailed sources remain her own writings. Her autobiography, *So Rich a Life*, published in 1951, records details of her travels and remains the fullest published account of her life. She wrote several books on theosophy, including

Trust your Self to Life (1968), *The Way of the Disciple* (1964), *The Mystery of Life* (1963), and *On Lecturing* (1921), which featured a foreword by Annie Besant. Many of her works have remained in print and in use by members of the movement decades after her death. Codd died at Heatherwood Hospital, Ascot, Sunninghill, Berkshire, of heart failure on 3 April 1971. HELOISE BROWN

Sources C. M. Codd, *So rich a life* (1951) · L. Kreeger, 'A tribute to Clara Codd', *Theosophical Reflections*, 90 (Aug 1999), 6 · E. Crawford, *The women's suffrage movement: a reference guide, 1866–1928* (1999) · B. M. W. Dobbie, *A nest of suffragettes in Somerset* (1979) · Dyrham Park (NT), Gloucestershire, Blathwayt diaries · private information (2004) · b. cert. · d. cert.
Archives Dyrham Park (NT), Gloucestershire, Blathwayt diaries
Likenesses L. Blathwayt, photograph, *c.*1908, repro. in Dobbie, *A nest of suffragettes* · photograph, *c.*1910–1919, repro. in Codd, *So rich a life* · photograph, *c.*1920–1929, repro. in Codd, *So rich a life* · photograph, *c.*1960–1969, repro. in L. Kreeger, 'A focus on Clara Codd', *Theosophy: the Synthesis of Science, Religion and Philosophy*, 2 (Jan–Feb 2000)
Wealth at death £4913: probate, 29 Dec 1971, *CGPLA Eng. & Wales*

Coddington, Henry (1798/9–1845), natural philosopher and Church of England clergyman, was born at Oldbridge, co. Meath, Ireland, the son of the Revd Latham Coddington, rector of Tinolin, co. Kildare, and his wife, Anne Bellingham. He matriculated at Trinity College, Cambridge, in 1816 and graduated in 1820 as senior wrangler and first Smith's prizeman, being elected a fellow of his college the same year. He proceeded MA in 1823 and was tutor from 1822 to 1833. He was ordained priest in 1826 and he retired to the college living of Ware in Hertfordshire in 1832. Before 1839 he married a daughter of Joseph Hallet Batten, principal of East India College, Haileybury; they had a son, Henry Hallet Coddington (1839–1883), a clergyman.

Coddington was regarded as a good modern linguist, an excellent musician and draughtsman, and a skilled botanist. His scientific works, with the exception of an anonymous tract, *The Principles of the Differential Calculus*, were devoted to optics. *An Elementary Treatise on Optics* (1823; 2nd edn, 1825) was based on Whewell's lectures and displayed the prevailing Cambridge interest in 'geometrical' optics, de-emphasizing 'physical' questions about the nature of light itself. The book nevertheless hinted at an early acceptance of the new wave theory of light at Cambridge. *A System of Optics*, published in two parts, raised higher his claims as an independent enquirer in geometrical optics. The first part, *A Treatise on the Reflexion and Refraction of Light* (1829), contained a very complete investigation of the paths of reflected and refracted rays, while in the second, *A Treatise on the Eye and on Optical Instruments* (1830), were explained the theory and construction of the various kinds of telescope and microscope. His texts became standard material for Cambridge undergraduate studies. On 22 March 1830 he read a paper on the improvement of the microscope before the Cambridge Philosophical Society; his strong recommendation of the grooved sphere lens, first described by David Brewster in 1820, brought it into general use under the designation of the 'Coddington

lens'. He also wrote *A Few Remarks on the New Library Question, by a Member of neither Syndicate* (1831) and *The Church Catechism Explained, Enlarged, and Confirmed by Quotations from Holy Scripture* (1840).

Coddington was elected fellow of the Royal Society of London in 1829 and was in the first published list of members of the British Association for the Advancement of Science in 1832. He was a founding member of the Royal Astronomical Society and was a fellow of the Geological and Cambridge Philosophical societies. The stress of dealing with dissension within his parish evidently led to a burst blood vessel, and while travelling abroad for his health he died at Rome on 3 March 1845, leaving seven children. A. M. CLERKE, *rev.* DAVID B. WILSON

Sources *GM*, 2nd ser., 24 (1845), 90–91 · Venn, *Alum. Cant.* · D. B. Wilson, 'The reception of the wave theory of light by Cambridge physicists, 1820–1850', PhD diss., The Johns Hopkins University, 1968 · G. G. Stokes, 'Optics I' and 'Optics no. II', undergraduate reading notes, *c.*1840, CUL, Stokes Collection, Add. MS 7656, PA15 and PA16 · *Monthly Notices of the Astronomical Society of London*, 7 (1845–7), 48–9 · W. B. Carpenter, 'Microscope', *Encyclopaedia Britannica*, 9th edn (1875–89), vol. 16, pp. 258–78 · *Memoirs of the Royal Astronomical Society*, 16 (1847), 484 · *Report of the British Association for the Advancement of Science*, 1 (1831–2), 610 · H. W. Becher, 'Voluntary science in nineteenth century Cambridge University to the 1850s', *British Journal for the History of Science*, 19 (1986), 57–87 · *Annual Register* (1845), 257 · O. Henker, 'Microscope', *Encyclopaedia Britannica*, 11th edn (1910–11), vol. 18, pp. 392–407 · J. Morrell and A. Thackray, *Gentlemen of science: early years of the British Association for the Advancement of Science* (1981), 54, 431–3 · Burke, *Gen. GB*
Archives Trinity Cam., letters to W. Whewell, Add. MSS a.20260–20262

Coddington, William (1601?–1678), merchant and official in America, was born in Lincolnshire and may have been the son of Robert Coddington (*d.* 1615) of Marston, Lincolnshire. At the tender age of twenty-nine, while still in England, he was elected an assistant or magistrate of Massachusetts Bay Colony. He arrived in Salem in June 1630 with Governor John Winthrop and the first company of settlers, including his first wife, Mary, who died that winter. He married Mary Moseley (*d.* 1647) on 2 September 1631. During the next six years he was elected to numerous town and colony offices, including colony treasurer (1634–6). The upward trajectory of his Massachusetts political career was halted in 1637 when he supported Anne Hutchinson during the antinomian controversy. After her trial and banishment he moved in 1638, along with other religious dissenters, to Rhode Island, where, with Roger Williams's help, he purchased the island of Aquidneck from the Narragansett Indians. Accustomed to exercising political authority, he expected once again to occupy high office. Rhode Islanders, however, were far more fractious than Massachusetts settlers, and his path to power was not smooth. At Portsmouth, a town he founded on the northern end of Aquidneck, inhabitants organized the community according to a biblical model and selected him as judge, a powerful position based on an ancient Hebrew office. But just a year later, in 1639, he was ousted because of political and theological disputes with a faction led by Anne and William Hutchinson. Fed up with such contentiousness, he moved in 1640 with his supporters to the southern end of the island, where he established Newport. That same year, after Portsmouth and Newport united under a common administration, he served as governor. When those towns joined with Warwick and Providence in 1647, he was chosen the second president of the new political entity, serving from May 1648 to May 1649. While in office he attempted, unsuccessfully, to have Rhode Island included in the New England confederation, created by the other New England colonies for defence against the American Indians. He also evidently failed to establish his authority within Rhode Island with as much force as he would have liked. In January 1649 he departed for England; he returned two years later with a new spouse, Ann Brinley (c.1628–1708), an infant son, and a commission from the council of state naming him governor of Aquidneck for life, with complete judicial power. Other officials in Rhode Island were scarcely pleased, and years of political turmoil ensued. Finally, in 1654, Roger Williams negotiated an uneasy peace among the various factions, and Coddington abandoned his independent rule of Aquidneck, agreeing to serve as Newport's representative in the court of commissioners. His political career subsequently waned, in part perhaps because of his growing interest in spiritual matters. He eventually embraced Quakerism, and even entertained George Fox in his home in 1672. Towards the end of his life he was called again to public service, elected deputy governor in 1674 and governor in 1678.

Politics and government dominated Coddington's life, but family matters and economic interests likewise engaged him. He had thirteen children, six of whom survived to adulthood. A wealthy merchant and self-styled gentleman, he prospered in Rhode Island, despite losing property worth £400 in a fire in 1644. He was one of Rhode Island's most prominent stockmen, raising sheep on offshore islands and horses for sale to West Indies sugar planters; he also experimented with tobacco production. He owned one of the grandest mansion houses in Newport. It was in that town that he died in November 1678, in the middle of his term as governor. He was buried in Newport on 6 November 1678.   VIRGINIA DEJOHN ANDERSON

Sources R. C. Anderson, ed., *The great migration begins: immigrants to New England, 1620–1633*, 1 (Boston, MA, 1995) · *The journal of John Winthrop, 1630–1649*, ed. R. S. Dunn, J. Savage, and L. Yeandle (1996) · S. V. James, *Colonial Rhode Island: a history* (1975) · C. Bridenbaugh, *Fat mutton and liberty of conscience* (1974) · P. F. Gura, *A glimpse of Sion's glory* (1984) · J. O. Austin, *The genealogical dictionary of Rhode Island: comprising three generations of settlers who came before 1690* (1887) · *The correspondence of Roger Williams*, ed. G. W. LaFantasie and others, 2 vols. (1988)

Coddington, Sir William, baronet (1830–1918), cotton spinner and manufacturer, was born on 12 December 1830 at Salford, Lancashire, the eldest son of William Dudley Coddington (1799–1867), a Manchester merchant, and his wife, Elizabeth, daughter of Robert Hopwood, a Blackburn cotton spinner and manufacturer.

In 1842 the Coddington family removed to Blackburn, William Dudley Coddington entering into partnership with his father-in-law. William Coddington, then aged twelve, spent a few terms at Blackburn grammar school, before attending commercial courses at Bruch Hall, Warrington. On returning to Blackburn he joined his father in the family cotton business and, when Robert Hopwood died in 1860, three of the four mills that the firm operated in Blackburn, namely Crossfield, Wellington, and Ordnance, passed to the Coddingtons, who now styled themselves W. D. Coddington & Sons. When his father died in 1867 William Coddington assumed control of the business, and during the trade boom of the early 1870s he added considerably to both spinning and weaving capacity with the erection of Wellington new mill.

Having established his business career, Coddington sought to further his political ambitions. A strong Conservative, he failed to gain election to Blackburn borough council in 1869, but succeeded during the following year, and was installed as mayor in 1874. Six years later he was returned as one of Blackburn's two MPs, retaining his seat until 1906. Though he rarely spoke in the house, he gained a reputation as a useful committee man, seeking especially to further the interests of the cotton industry, not least with regard to tariff reform. This was most apparent over the reimposition of the Indian tariff on British cottons in 1894, Coddington leading a deputation to the secretary of state for India which was instrumental in securing a countervailing excise duty on the production of Indian cotton goods. He is remembered, too, for his work as chairman of the parliamentary committee for widening London streets, which led to the demolition of such historical edifices as Temple Bar at the junction of the Strand and Fleet Street.

In recognition of his political service, Coddington was created a baronet in 1896. He was also honoured for his public service to Blackburn, being granted the freedom of the town in 1912. He was then one of only five people to whom that accolade had been given. Coddington's public service extended beyond politics, however. In 1867, he became a magistrate and subsequently a deputy lieutenant of Lancashire. From 1868 to 1870 he also held a major's commission in the 3rd Lancashire artillery volunteers and aspired to high rank in freemasonry. His Anglicanism and love of music prompted him to give £2500 to purchase an organ for Blackburn parish church.

Coddington was twice married. On 16 September 1864 he married his first wife, Sarah Catherine Hall (d. 1911), third daughter of William Hall of Wakefield; they had one daughter, Beatrice. They lived in the fashionable suburbs of Blackburn along Preston New Road, first at Spring Mount and subsequently at Wycollar, further away from the town centre. Here they entertained distinguished guests, none more so than Princess Louise, and the duke of Argyll. They also leased property in London, including a mansion in Piccadilly formerly occupied by Baron Ferdinand de Rothschild. Family holidays were taken at Menton and other places on the Riviera.

The first Lady Coddington died on 31 December 1911, and on 13 January 1913 Coddington married his second wife, Aimée Josephine, daughter of W. J. S. Barber-Starkey of Aldenham Park, Shropshire. The marriage aroused particular interest because she was fifty-three years his junior. It took place at the Chapel Royal, Savoy, London, and was followed by a honeymoon on the continent. To celebrate the event, 1300 of Coddington's employees were treated to a Blackpool outing, travelling on two special trains.

Coddington died at his home, Wycollar, Preston New Road, Blackburn, on 15 February 1918, aged eighty-seven, after being ill for some time. He was buried in Blackburn cemetery.   J. GEOFFREY TIMMINS

Sources G. C. Miller, *Blackburn: the evolution of a cotton town* (1951), 391–3 · *Blackburn Times* (16 Feb 1918) · M. Rothwell, *A guide to the industrial archaeology of Blackburn*, 1: *The textile industry* (1985), 19, 21, 32, 38 · 'Blackburn's new freeman', *Blackburn Times* (20 July 1912) · 'Blackburn studies, XI—Sir William Coddington, MP', *Blackburn Weekly Telegraph* (16 Dec 1899) · *Blackburn Weekly Telegraph* (6 Jan 1912) · *Blackburn Weekly Telegraph* (10 Feb 1912) · *Blackburn Times* (18 Jan 1913) · *WWW* · *CGPLA Eng. & Wales* (1918) · Boase, *Mod. Eng. biog.* · d. cert.
Likenesses H. von Herkomer, portrait, repro. in *Blackburn Weekly Telegraph* (10 Feb 1912) · L. Shawcross, photograph (with Lady Coddington), repro. in *Blackburn Weekly Telegraph* (6 Jan 1912) · group portrait, photograph, repro. in *Blackburn Times* (10 May 1913) · photograph, repro. in *Blackburn Times* (16 Feb 1918) · photographs, repro. in *Blackburn Times* (27 July 1912)
Wealth at death £293,097 1s. 3d.: probate, 30 April 1918, *CGPLA Eng. & Wales*

Codner, Maurice Frederick (1888–1958), portrait painter, was born in Stoke Newington, London, on 27 September 1888, the third son of William Squires Codner, iron merchant, of Abbotskerswell, Devon, and his wife, Ada Mary Payne. Codner was educated at the Stationers' Company School, but the details of his early career are not recorded. In 1913 he married Eleanor Marion, daughter of Thomas Fairfield, a captain in the mercantile marine, and during the First World War he served in France in the Royal Devon hussars. His parents owned property at Dedham, Essex, where in 1919 he was befriended by Alfred Munnings while out hunting. At some point Codner attended the Colchester School of Art, but is recorded by Munnings as working part-time as assistant curator three days a week at the Iveagh Bequest, Kenwood, London, in the late 1920s. Encouraged by Munnings, he abandoned his employment and soon became widely known for his portraits in oils of distinguished men and women. These were exhibited principally from 1929 at the Royal Society of Portrait Painters, of which he became a member in 1937, and in 1945 the honorary secretary, but also from 1928 at the Royal Academy and in many galleries in Great Britain and elsewhere. His work was always notable for its sincerity. He was singularly modest about its merits and in occasional moods of depression would regard his portraits merely as a way of making a living.

Codner had several public successes. His portrait of George VI in field marshal's uniform and Garter robes as captain-general of the Honourable Artillery Company (Armoury House, London), executed in 1951, was admired at the time and was the last portrait painted of the king. His portrait of Queen Elizabeth the queen mother (1952),

painted for the twenty-fifth birthday number of *Woman's Journal*, won the silver medal in 1954 at the Paris Salon, where in 1938 his portrait of Sir George Broadbridge, lord mayor of London, in his coronation robes (Guildhall, London) had received an honourable mention. Many of his portraits, however, were pre-eminently what are called good likenesses rather than a penetrating analysis of character. In this he was extremely successful and at his peak in the 1940s and early 1950s was producing ten to fifteen such routine portraits a year, his work being especially in demand for the board-rooms of businessmen and company directors. For these he was often assisted by his only son, John Whitlock Orby Squires Codner, whose own work (under the pseudonym John Whitlock) is virtually indistinguishable from his father's.

Among Codner's well-known sitters were Field Marshal Lord Alexander of Tunis (1946), Gwilym Lloyd-George (later Viscount Tenby; 1955), and the architect Sir Albert Richardson (1956; Art Workers' Guild, London), but it was perhaps only with theatrical personalities that his portraits achieved anything like distinction. For the Theatre Royal, Drury Lane, London, he painted Sir George Robey in the role of Falstaff (1935), followed by a further version in the comedian's familiar make-up of bowler hat and red nose. Other portraits of actors and actresses included Athene Seyler, Evelyn Laye (1933), and Leslie Henson (1952). His portrait of the contralto Kathleen Ferrier (1946; National Portrait Gallery, London), with its theatrical lighting, lurid colours, and coarse brushwork, encapsulates both the best and the worst facets of his portrait style. With his occasional landscapes Codner felt that he had more freedom and in this was influenced by the example of Munnings, whose portrait of Codner, *Sketching at Wiston Bridge* (1935), is a striking tribute to their friendship. Open-air sketching was his great relaxation, as was the pleasure he shared with Munnings in riding and a love of horses.

In appearance Codner was extremely well groomed; tall, slim, with a neatly trimmed beard and moustache, closely cut hair, and a rather pronounced nose, he had the distinguished and rather theatrical air of the prosperous and successful artist. His studio, which adjoined his small house at 26 Temple Fortune Hill in Hampstead Garden Suburb, Middlesex, where he lived for his entire career, was a comfortable and workmanlike place, well adapted to his various sitters. This and his little garden full of roses and trees were his pride and joy. Maurice Frederick Codner died at Beaumont House, Beaumont Street, London, on 10 March 1958 and was buried at Dedham, Essex, in his much beloved Constable country.

ERNEST BLAIKLEY, rev. ROBIN GIBSON

Sources *Daily Telegraph* (11 March 1958) · *The Times* (11 March 1958) · M. Ross, 'The king's latest portrait and its painter' (1951), 16 [unidentified magazine article] · A. Jarman and others, eds., *Royal Academy exhibitors, 1905–1970: a dictionary of artists and their work in the summer exhibitions of the Royal Academy of Arts*, 6 vols. (1973–82) · A. Munnings, *The second burst* (1951), 352–7 · *Who's who in art* (1956), 151 · *Catalogue*, Royal Society of Portrait Painters (1929–58) [annual exhibition catalogues, London] · *CGPLA Eng. & Wales* (1958) · personal knowledge (1971) · private information (1971)

Archives NRA, priv. coll., sketchbooks and corresp.

Likenesses R. Eves, oils, 1932; Christies, 9 June 1988, lot 55 · A. Munnings, oils, 1935 · M. F. Codner, self-portrait, oils, 1947, Russell-Cotes Art Gallery, Bournemouth, *Self Portraits of Living Artists*, 1947, m. 828

Wealth at death £59,078 10s. 2d.: probate, 30 June 1958, *CGPLA Eng. & Wales*

Codrington, Christopher (1639/40–1698), planter and colonial official, was born in Barbados, the son of Christopher Codrington (d. 1656), a planter and land speculator in Barbados, and Frances Drax, the sister of the prominent planter Sir James Drax. Nothing is known of his wife, Gertrude, except that they had two sons, Christopher *Codrington and John. He was educated on the island, probably by a local clergyman, but did not attend university.

Codrington's career resembled the rise of the planter class in the English Caribbean. He became one of the wealthiest planters in Barbados, where his pioneering father had emigrated in the first year of English settlement in 1627. He had inherited considerable property from his father at the age of sixteen. He increased his fortune, owning some 618 acres of land in Barbados by 1680 and, together with his brother John, some 380 acres in Antigua as well as a fifty-year lease in the adjoining island of Barbuda. He lost land in St Kitts when part of the island was returned to the French at the treaty of Ryswick in 1697.

Codrington was among the earliest planters to cultivate sugar in Barbados, the island which pioneered the sugar revolution in the Caribbean in the 1640s. He also became one of the most prominent and influential colonial officials. His first known public office was trustee for the sale of the island of St Lucia at the age of twenty-three. He was appointed a member of the council of Barbados in 1666, and was acting governor of the island between 1669 and 1672. He thereafter sat in the assembly for the parish of St John and was elected speaker nine times between 1674 and 1682. He led the opposition in the assembly to Governor Sir Richard Dutton.

Codrington's ambitions were extended to the Leeward Islands, where he became acting governor following the fall of the Jacobite governor Sir Nathaniel Johnson in July 1683. He was officially appointed governor in 1689, assuming the difficult task of administering this dispersed colony of several islands, which included Antigua, Montserrat, Nevis, and St Kitts. Furthermore, his governorship coincided with King William's War when the Leeward Islands were a major object of the French, who, within a month of his appointment, captured St Kitts. The enemy were supported by rebellious white indentured servants, especially the Irish in St Kitts and Montserrat. The army garrisons were inadequate and the pay of the soldiers in arrears. The colony was also subject to periodic raids by the indigenous peoples of the region, the Caribs. The Leeward Islands were jealously antagonistic towards one another and unwilling to co-operate in their mutual defence. Few merchants or planters were willing to invest because of the vulnerability of the colony. Codrington

mounted expeditions, often at his own expense, to give the appearance of strength. Following the arrival of a fleet and army regiment from England, he recaptured St Kitts in March 1690. He later failed to take Guadeloupe and Martinique.

Codrington combined imperial ambition with private greed. In common with many other planters, he engaged in illicit trade, sometimes even with the enemy, and his last years were marred by complaints of his tyrannical behaviour. Nevertheless, he was a political survivor in a difficult colony where two governors were murdered by local planters before 1710. His military skills were well attested by contemporaries. He was a leader with vision, proposing, for example, to reserve land for small planters and to build schools in St Kitts. He foresaw that large planters like himself were displacing small planters, with disastrous future implications for the defence of English settlements in the Caribbean. As his opponents prepared to bring accusations against him before the House of Commons, he died on 20 July 1698 at the age of fifty-eight.

ANDREW J. O'SHAUGHNESSY

Sources V. Harlow, *Christopher Codrington, 1668–1710* (1928) · *CSP col.*, vols. 1, 5, 7, 9–45 · R. S. Dunn, *Sugar and slaves: the rise of the planter class in the English West Indies, 1624–1713* (1973) · V. T. Harlow, *A history of Barbados, 1625–1685* (1926) · C. S. S. Higham, *The development of the Leeward Islands under the Restoration, 1660–1688: a study of the foundations of the old colonial system* (1921) · G. A. Puckerein, *Little England: plantation society and Anglo-Barbadian politics, 1627–1700* (1984) · A. P. Thornton, *West India policy under the Restoration* (1956)

Codrington, Christopher (1668–1710), colonial governor and benefactor, was born in the parish of St John, Barbados, the elder son of Christopher *Codrington (1639/40–1698), member of the council and later deputy governor of Barbados and governor-general of the Leeward Islands, and his wife, Gertrude. The family's wealth derived principally from sugar plantations at Betty's Hope, Antigua, and Consett Bay, Barbados, and from the lease of the island of Barbuda, where both cattle and slaves were bred. From about 1680 Codrington was educated in England, where he attended Dr Wedale's school in Enfield until 1685; on 4 July that year, he matriculated as a gentleman commoner at Christ Church, Oxford. On 13 July 1687 he was admitted a member of the Middle Temple in London while keeping terms at Oxford. In 1690 he was elected a fellow of All Souls, Oxford; he graduated BA in 1691.

Codrington was a friend of many of the most prominent Oxford wits, including Joseph Addison, Charles Boyle, and Thomas Creech. As a pupil of George Smalridge at Christ Church he took the part of the auctioneer, Edward Millington, in a satire on the book trade, *Auctio Davisiana*. In January 1693, as a volunteer soldier, he sailed for the West Indies and fought in the attack on Martinique. When he returned to Oxford that autumn he was promoted to a captaincy, and he proceeded MA on 29 January 1694. He soon joined William III's army in Flanders, taking part in the capture of Huy in September 1694. In the summer of 1695 Codrington distinguished himself at the siege of Namur, where on 1 August he was promoted lieutenant-colonel and captain of the guards. He was briefly a candidate for the university seat in the election of 1695 and delivered the oration when William III visited Oxford on 5 November, but rejoined his company in April 1696. With the conclusion of hostilities Codrington travelled to Paris in 1698, where he made the acquaintance of Nicolas Malebranche and cemented his friendship with Matthew Prior.

Soon after his return to London in July 1698 Codrington learned of the death of his father. The ensuing two years were marked by frantic activity. Codrington secured his own appointment, confirmed in May 1699, as governor-general of the Leeward Islands and deployed his inheritance to purchase the family estate at Dodington, Gloucestershire, from his cousin Samuel in 1700. He composed laudatory verses for his friend Samuel Garth's poem *The Dispensary* (1699) and organized the publication of *Commendatory Verses* (1700), which defended Garth and others of his friends from the attacks of Sir Richard Blackmore. In 1700 he also wrote an epilogue for John Dennis's classical tragedy, *Iphigenia*. His widening circle of acquaintance now included John Locke, who presented him with a copy of the fourth edition of *An Essay Concerning Human Understanding* (1700). He also engaged the services of Alexander Cunningham to build a library which would eventually number more than 10,000 books, many purchased in continental Europe, but which its owner would never properly see. On 17 August 1700, having made a will, Codrington sailed for the West Indies, leaving Oxford gossips to speculate whether the Bodleian Library might be the intended beneficiary of his bibliomania.

Under the shadow of war Codrington worked to strengthen gubernatorial authority, fortify the islands, enforce the Navigation Acts, and discipline corrupt officials. Exploiting his friendship with several members of the council for trade and plantations, he also sought appointment as governor of Barbados. His ambitions were frustrated, however, by the scandal that engulfed him following his personal intervention in the case between William Mead and Thomas Herbert at the Nevis court house in spring 1701. Mead and his associate William Freeman brought a suit against Codrington before the council and later before the House of Commons, alleging that he had abused his power as governor, mismanaged their appeals, and forcibly evicted them from their property. Codrington's friends, notably Charles Boyle, came to his defence and he was exonerated in October 1702, by which time war had broken out again. After initial successes, however, his reputation as a soldier was damaged by his inability to co-ordinate army and naval activities and by the failure of the attack on Guadeloupe in 1703. From April to August of that year Codrington was gravely ill with dysentery and he eventually applied for leave only to be removed from office by the commissioners for trade and plantations.

After the death of his immediate successor, in December 1704, Codrington tried (unsuccessfully) to be reinstated as governor. His remaining political actions were devoted to preserving his reputation and his estates. He was never able to implement his plans for reform, in which officials were to be properly salaried and the law

rigorously applied by one who knew the ways of the Caribbean colonies. Although he had claimed: 'I have acted with the sincerity of a majestrate in a Platonick Commonwealth' (PRO, CO/152/4, no. 36), Codrington himself recognized the extent of his failure in public life, remarking that 'the vote has sunk too deep in my heart ever to be removed, and I act now very uncomfortably without pleasure and without ambition—If I live to see England, I will pass my life in my Library and be buryed in my garden' (*CSP col.*, 21.125). Exhausted by political struggles, Codrington left Antigua in August 1707. In 1708 he mediated in a dispute between the governor, Mitford Crowe, and the Barbados council. He died in the house where he had been born on 7 April 1710 and was buried on the following day in St Michael's Church, Bridgetown.

Codrington's death made public the charitable intentions set out in the will that he had written 'in his boots when he was going to Command the Expedition to Guardaloup' on 22 February 1703 (SPG Archives, A6, no. 111). He left £6000 to All Souls to pay for the building of a new library, with a further gift of £4000 to be laid out on books. His own collection was also bequeathed to the college. His Barbados plantations, valued at £30,000, and a share of the island of Barbuda, were to be given to the newly founded Society for the Propagation of the Gospel (SPG):

> My desier is to have the Plantations Continued Intire and three hundred negros at Least Kept always thereon, and A Convenient number of Professors and Scholars Maintained there, all of them to be under the vows of Poverty Chastity and obedience, who shall be oblidged to Studdy and Practice Physick and Chyrurgery as well as divinity. (MS Rawl. C. 983, fols. 157–8)

Codrington's will and the sentiments expressed in a sermon preached at his funeral by William Gordon revealed a deep and practical piety, tied to a desire to improve the moral and physical health of both the white and black inhabitants of the Caribbean colonies. Under the direction of the SPG, Codrington College opened in 1745, though its activities were initially limited to the schooling of white settlers. On 19 June 1716 Codrington's body was reinterred in the ante-chapel at All Souls, of which his generosity had made him a 'second founder' (Cotes and Young, 18).

SCOTT MANDELBROTE

Sources T. Harlow, *Christopher Codrington, 1668–1710* (1928) · *CSP col.*, 1699–1710 · Bodl. RH, United Society for the Propagation of the Gospel archives · Bodl. Oxf., MS Rawl. C. 983, fols. 157–8 · D. Cotes and E. Young, *Orationes duae* (1716) · W. Gordon, *A sermon preach'd at the funeral of the Honourable Colonel Christopher Codringon* (1710) · R. H. Codrington, *Memoir of the family of Codrington* (1910), 126–30

Archives BL, films of MSS sold at Sothebys, London, 15–16 Dec 1980, RP 2616 · BL, letters, Add. MS 34348 · Bodl. Oxf., letters, MS Ballard 20 · Glos. RO, estate and other papers, D 1610 | All Souls Oxf., archives and Add. MS. 429 · Bodl. RH, SPG Archives · LPL, SPG Archives · PRO, state papers, colonial

Likenesses oils, c.1700, Dodington Park, Gloucestershire · J. Thornhill, oils, 1702, All Souls Oxf. · oils, c.1730, All Souls Oxf. · H. Cheere, marble statue, 1734, All Souls Oxf. · Harding, engraving, 1796 (after J. Thornhill) · engraving, 1796 (after J. Thornhill) · bust (after H. Cheere), Codrington College, Barbados · oils, All Souls Oxf.

Wealth at death over £80,000–£100,000: Bodl. Oxf., Rawlinson MS, J 4to II, fol. 77

Codrington, Sir Edward (1770–1851), naval officer, of the old family of Codrington of Dodington in Gloucestershire, third son of Edward Codrington (1732–1775) of London and his wife, Anne, *née* Sturgeon, and grandson of Sir Edward Codrington, first baronet, was born on 27 April 1770. He entered the navy in July 1783; after serving continuously on the Halifax, Mediterranean, and home stations, he was confirmed lieutenant on 28 May 1793 and, by Lord Howe's desire, appointed to the frigate *Pegasus*. He was afterwards transferred to the *Queen Charlotte*, Howe's flagship, on board which he acted as signal officer during the anxious days preceding 1 June 1794. In the battle of that day he had command of the foremost lower-deck guns and, on the arrival of the fleet and prizes off the Isle of Wight, was sent up to London with Howe's dispatches. He was promoted on 7 October 1794 to be commander of the fireship *Comet* from which, on 6 April 1795, he was posted captain of the frigate *Babet* (22 guns). In her he was present in the action off Lorient on 23 June 1795; in July 1796 he was moved to the *Druid* (32 guns) on the Lisbon station, which ship he brought home and paid off early in 1797.

In May 1805 Codrington commissioned the *Orion* (74 guns). In August he joined the fleet off Cadiz, and on 21 October took part in the battle of Trafalgar; he afterwards continued in command of the *Orion*, attached to the fleet under Lord Collingwood until December 1806. In November 1808 he was appointed to the *Blake* (74 guns), which was employed during the next summer in the North Sea under Sir Richard Strachan, bore Lord Gardner's flag in the Walcheren expedition, and was hotly engaged in forcing the passage of the Scheldt on 14 August. In the early summer of 1810 Codrington, still in the *Blake*, was sent to co-operate with the Spaniards at Cadiz, and in August was charged with the difficult duty of convoying to Minorca four old Spanish line-of-battle ships, crowded with refugees, a task which was safely accomplished after a passage of thirty-eight days. During 1811 and 1812 he commanded a detached squadron on the east coast of Spain, co-operating with the Spaniards wherever opportunity offered and waging a harassing war against the French invaders. Early in 1813 he returned to England, and at the beginning of 1814 was sent out to the North American station with a broad pennant in the frigate *Forth*. On 4 June 1814 he was advanced to flag rank and appointed captain of the fleet to Sir Alexander Cochrane, under whom he conducted operations in the Chesapeake, and afterwards at New Orleans, with his flag in the *Havannah* (36 guns). On 2 January 1815 he was made a KCB, and in 1825 he became a vice-admiral.

In December 1826 Codrington was appointed commander-in-chief in the Mediterranean, and sailed for his station on 1 February 1827, with his flag in the *Asia* (84 guns). After some months at Malta he was induced by the great proliferation of piracy and the urgent appeals of Stratford Canning, the ambassador at Constantinople, to attempt to reduce the horrors of the war of Greek independence. He left Malta on 19 June and arrived on the coast of Greece in the early days of July. There the position

Sir Edward Codrington (1770–1851), by Charles Turner, pubd 1830 (after Sir Thomas Lawrence, 1826)

was one of extreme difficulty, for, while a large section of the British public was enthusiastic in the cause of the Greeks, the British government was suspicious of the aims of the Russians. George Canning, the prime minister, was anxious that any interference with the war should be made in concert; and in July he succeeded in concluding a treaty between Britain, France, and Russia, by which it was provided that each of the three powers should instruct its admiral in the Mediterranean to 'obtain the immediate effect of the desired armistice, by preventing, as far as should be in his power, all collision between the contending parties'. Codrington was further ordered to receive directions from Stratford Canning, who on 19 August interpreted the instructions of the British government to mean that the allies intended 'to enforce, by cannon-shot if necessary, the armistice which was the object of the treaty; the object being to interpose the allied forces and to keep the peace by the speaking-trumpet if possible, but in case of necessity by force'. This interpretation he repeated in even stronger language on 1 September, and it must be held as a sufficient warrant to Codrington to employ force if he should deem it necessary. Codrington himself favoured the Greeks and maintained friendly relations with the British officers in the Greek service—Thomas Cochrane, Frank Hastings, and Sir Richard Church—and unofficially permitted and even encouraged them to continue the war though this was forbidden by the treaty.

On 25 September, Codrington and the French admiral, De Rigny, had an interview at Navarino with Ibrahim Pasha, the commander-in-chief of the Turkish sea and land forces; they explained to him their instructions, and, through the interpreter, obtained from him a verbal assent to the proposed armistice. But a few days later, on receiving news of the attack on the Turkish ships and batteries in Salona Bay made on 29 September by Frank Hastings acting with the Greek forces, Ibrahim Pasha considered himself absolved from his engagement and sent a strong squadron from Navarino with orders to attack Hastings in the Gulf of Corinth. On 3 October this squadron was met off the mouth of the gulf by Codrington, and, yielding to his protests, returned to Navarino. Ibrahim, however, then landed in force in the Morea and devastated the country, committing various atrocities. Codrington gathered his whole available force, together with the French and Russian squadrons, numbering in all eleven ships of the line, eight large frigates, and eight smaller vessels; on 14 October they arrived off Navarino, where the Turkish fleet was still anchored. It consisted of three ships of the line, fifteen large frigates, and many smaller vessels, bringing up the total to eighty-nine—a force strong in number, but in its composition far inferior to that of the combined fleet of which Codrington was the commander-in-chief. As the Turks had shown that they intended to leave Navarino, and hostilities had already resumed, the allied admirals were of the opinion that the blockade of the bay was a necessary precaution. A very few days were sufficient to convince Codrington of the difficulty and danger of blockading Navarino so late in the autumn; he therefore determined to go inside and anchor. The dangers of doing so in the middle of the bay, exposed to the fire of the entire Turkish fleet, led him to order the ships under his command to anchor close in and alongside of the Turks.

Accordingly, on 20 October, with a fair wind, they stood into the bay, the guns loaded and the men at quarters. The Turks were equally prepared. It is impossible to suppose that Codrington had any real expectation of peace being preserved between two fleets so situated. The frigate *Dartmouth* found herself anchored dead to leeward of a Turkish fireship, and sent a boat to move her, or order her to move; and the Turk, assuming that the boat was coming on a hostile mission, fired a volley of musketry into it. The *Dartmouth* replied, other ships took it up, and within a few minutes the action became general. Although the real disparity of force was very great, the battle lasted nearly four hours; the Turks' loss in killed and wounded, never accurately known, was said to amount to 4000, while that of the allies was 650. The victory assured Greece's survival.

The news of the bloody battle and the destruction of the Turkish fleet was variously received in England. At the urgent request of the duke of Clarence, then lord high admiral, rewards were bestowed with unprecedented liberality; Codrington received the GCB, as well as the grand cross of St Louis from France, the second class of the order of St George from Russia, and, later, the gold cross of the Redeemer of Greece. As a matter of policy, however, the battle was very differently considered. Canning, the prime minister, had died the previous August, and his successors were as aware of the danger of Russian aggression

as of the advantage of Greek liberation. On the opening of parliament on 29 January 1828, the king accordingly lamented the conflict as an 'untoward event', an expression which conflicted with the strong philhellenic feeling in Britain, leading the ministry to state that 'they did not make the slightest charge, nor cast the least imputation upon the gallant officer who commanded at Navarino'. Nevertheless controversy ensued, the difficulty of resolving which contributed to Codrington's somewhat summary recall, the news of which reached him at Corfu on 21 June 1828. He arrived in England on 7 October and spent the winter in London, endeavouring in vain to arrive at some understanding of his recall. The duke of Wellington in a personal interview assured him of his esteem, but would give no explicit statement or explanation. Codrington consequently drew up and printed for private circulation a narrative of his proceedings in the Mediterranean, which was later published in the *Memoir* of his life.

In June 1831 Codrington was appointed to the command of the channel squadron for the summer experimental cruise, and hoisted his flag in the *Caledonia* until the end of the season, on 24 October. He was made GCMG in April 1827, and was Liberal MP for Devonport from 1832 to 1839. On 10 January 1837 he became admiral of the blue, and on 22 November 1839 commander-in-chief at Portsmouth. His active career ended with the termination of that command on 31 December 1842. He died at 110 Eaton Square, London, on 28 April 1851, after a few months' illness, and was buried on 2 May in the family vault at St Peter's Church, Eaton Square, London, where a tablet was erected to his memory.

On 27 December 1802 Codrington married Jane (*d.* 22 Jan 1837), daughter of Jasper Hall of Kingston, Jamaica; they had three sons and two daughters. One of the sons died young, drowned in a boating accident; the other two, William John *Codrington and Henry John *Codrington, both had distinguished careers. The eldest daughter, Jane Barbara, married Captain Sir Thomas Bourchier (who died superintendent of Chatham Dockyard in 1849) and in 1873 published a two-volume biography of her father.

J. K. LAUGHTON, *rev.* ROGER MORRISS

Sources *Memoir of the life of Admiral Sir Edward Codrington: with selections from his public and private correspondence*, ed. J. B. Bourchier, 2 vols. (1873) · *The dispatches and letters of Vice-Admiral Lord Viscount Nelson*, ed. N. H. Nicolas, 7 vols. (1844–6), vol. 7 · G. Finlay, *History of the Greek revolution*, 2 (1861) · D. Dakin, *The unification of Greece, 1770–1923* (1972) · A. D. Lambert, *The last sailing battlefleet: maintaining naval mastery, 1815–1850* (1991) · GM, 2nd ser., 36 (1851), 194–5 · Boase, *Mod. Eng. biog.* · W. St Clair, *That Greece might still be free: the philhellenes in the war of independence* (1972)

Archives NMM, corresp. and papers · PRO, papers relating to his conduct of naval affairs in Mediterranean, PRO 30/12 | Bodl. Oxf., corresp. with Sir Charles Doyle and Sir John Doyle · Inst. CE, corresp. and papers relating to Thames Tunnel · NMM, corresp. with Sir Benjamin Carew · NMM, corresp. with Parker · PRO, corresp. with Stratford Canning, FO 352 · PRO, letters and dispatches to Granville, PRO 30/29 · W. Sussex RO, letters to duke of Richmond

Likenesses F. Chantrey, drawing, 1819, NPG · C. Turner, mezzotint, pubd 1830 (after T. Lawrence, 1826), BM, NPG [*see illus.*] · H. Patterson, oils, exh. RA 1840, Town Hall, Devonport, Devon · H. P. Briggs, oils, 1843, NPG · F. Chantrey, plaster bust, AM Oxf. ·

J. Doyle, drawings, BM · G. Hayter, group portrait, oils (*The House of Commons, 1833*), NPG · B. Holl, stipple (after G. Hayter), BM, NPG · mezzotints (after T. Lawrence), BM, NPG · portraits, repro. in Bourchier, ed., *Memoir of the life of Admiral Sir Edward Codrington*

Codrington, Sir Henry John (1808–1877), naval officer, third son of Admiral Sir Edward *Codrington (1770–1851), and his wife, Jane, *née* Hall (*d*. 1837), was born in October 1808 and entered the navy in 1823 on board the frigate *Naiad*, Captain the Hon. Robert Cavendish Spencer, to whose early training he owed much. During 1824 the *Naiad* was active during the Algerian war, blockading the coast and burning corsairs. She was then nearly two years on the Greek coast observing the war of independence, and returned to England towards the end of 1826. Codrington then joined the *Asia*, flagship of Sir Edward Codrington, in the Mediterranean. He remained in the *Asia* during his father's command, and acted as signal midshipman at the battle of Navarino, where he was wounded in the leg. As a compliment to his father, he was decorated by the tsar and the kings of France and Greece.

On 12 June 1829 Codrington was made lieutenant, and, after serving through the summer of 1831 as his father's flag-lieutenant with the Squadron of Evolution, he was promoted commander on 20 October. Three years later he was appointed to command the sloop *Orestes* in the Mediterranean, and was promoted captain on 20 January 1836. During the following two years he was on half pay, and devoted himself to scientific study. In March 1838 he was appointed to command the *Talbot*, a small, old-fashioned sloop armed mostly with outdated short-range carronades, yet she was so handled by Codrington as to be an effective addition to the Mediterranean fleet, and to take a useful part in the bombardment of Acre on 4 November 1840, for which he received the CB. The preliminary survey of Acre was made by Codrington himself, taking the soundings by night close in under the walls of the town. In private letters afterwards he criticized Commodore Sir Charles Napier, since he was entirely ignorant of Napier's political correspondence with Lord Palmerston, and his central role in the rapid prosecution of the campaign. His complaint had more to do with Napier's manners than his abilities, which better men than Codrington never doubted. It was a mark of Codrington's limited intellect that he never appreciated Napier's leadership, decision, and energy, for these were the very qualities that he himself so signally lacked. Codrington described Napier as 'excellent at irregular shore work, and a most enterprising partisan warrior, but not what I call a good officer'.

Early in 1841 Codrington was recalled to England to command the *St Vincent* as flag-captain to his father, then commander-in-chief at Portsmouth. He held this appointment only until the end of 1842. Four years later, having quarrelled with Captain Sir Thomas Hastings of HMS *Excellent*, he was appointed to the frigate *Thetis*, which went to the Mediterranean in September 1847. In the following years the *Thetis* was employed on the coast of Italy, protecting British interests and British subjects, and acting as a refuge for displaced native rulers. Thanks to the first lieutenant, John McNeill Boyd, the *Thetis* was kept

Sir Henry John Codrington (1808–1877), by Lowes Cato Dickinson, 1857–63

fully up to the mark, and was praised by the commander-in-chief at Plymouth when she was paid off in May 1850. However, she gained a bad reputation, and Codrington and Boyd became unpopular in the service, because of the strict discipline over the midshipmen: possibly tact was occasionally wanting. While on station, in 1849, Codrington married Helen Jane Webb Smith of Lyndhurst. They had several children.

In October 1853, in anticipation of the war with Russia, Codrington was appointed to command the *Royal George*, an old three-decker with an auxiliary screw. She formed part of the Baltic fleet during the two seasons of 1854 and 1855. Controversy afterwards arose as to the conduct of the fleet in 1854. Between Sir Charles Napier, the commander-in-chief, and Codrington, the senior captain in the fleet, there was little love lost. There were faults on both sides; but Codrington's conduct bordered on mutiny, and could not be excused by any provocation. Codrington had an interest in steam tactics, but his views were impractical and over-complex, and in consequence were ignored by Napier, a far more experienced and practical officer. In February 1856 Codrington moved to the *Algiers* (90 guns), as commodore of a flotilla of gunboats; but the peace deprived him of any opportunity of using them, and his sea service ended with the St George's day review and a passage to the Crimea, where he embarked elements of the army, then commanded by his elder brother William John *Codrington (1804–1884).

On 19 March 1857 Codrington became a rear-admiral, and from 1858 to 1863 he was admiral superintendent at Malta. On 24 September 1863 he was advanced to be vice-admiral, on 18 October 1867 to be admiral, and on 22 January 1877 to be admiral of the fleet. He was appointed KCB on 13 March 1867 and, following the death of his first wife, married Catherine Compton of Lyndhurst in 1869. He was commander-in-chief at Plymouth 1869–72, but his flag was never hoisted on board a seagoing ship; he never had command of a squadron at sea or took a seat at the Board of Admiralty. This was a reflection of his abilities for, although a fine seaman and a strict disciplinarian, Codrington lacked the leadership and intellect required for a senior command, or the collaboration of the board. His career was made by his father, whom he hero-worshipped. His quarrels with senior officers suggest that he was an arrogant and fastidious snob. In 1854 Napier, a far greater man, was so incensed by Codrington's conduct that he wished to court-martial him, along with captains George Elliot and Alfred Ryder. All three deserved censure, but the board and the government would not back him, undermining his authority and his faith in the Admiralty. Codrington died at his home, 112 Eaton Square, London, on 4 August 1877.

J. K. LAUGHTON, rev. ANDREW LAMBERT

Sources *Selections from the letters … of Sir H. Codrington*, ed. Lady Bourchier (1880) · *Memoir of the life of Admiral Sir Edward Codrington: with selections from his public and private correspondence*, ed. J. B. Bourchier, 2 vols. (1873) · A. D. Lambert, *The Crimean War: British grand strategy, 1853–56* (1990) · C. J. Bartlett, *Great Britain and sea power, 1815–1853* (1963) · G. B. Earp, *Sir Charles Napier's Baltic campaign* (1856) · personal knowledge (1887) · *The Times* (6 Aug 1877)
Archives NMM, letterbooks, log books, and papers | BL, Napier MSS · BL, Wood MSS · Cumbria AS, Carlisle, Graham MSS · NMM, Edward Codrington MSS
Likenesses L. C. Dickinson, oils, 1857–63, NMM [*see illus.*] · photograph, repro. in Bourchier, ed., *Correspondence*, frontispiece
Wealth at death £60,000: probate, 21 Aug 1877, *CGPLA Eng. & Wales*

Codrington, Robert (1601/2–1665?), translator and writer, was the second son of Robert Codrington (*b.* 1573/4?) of Coddrington, Gloucestershire. Elected a demy or scholar of Magdalen College, Oxford, on 29 July 1619, he matriculated on 26 June 1621, aged nineteen, graduated BA on 18 February 1623, and proceeded MA on 27 June 1626. According to Anthony Wood he then travelled before settling in Norfolk, where he lived as a gentleman for several years and married; his wife's name is unknown. Later he moved to London, and may have been the Robert Coddrington who, with his wife, 'Haveningam' (*née* Heveningham?), presented their son Robert for baptism at St Andrew's, Holborn, on 9 November 1635.

The previous year Codrington began what was to be a thirty-year career of publishing translations from French, Latin, and Spanish, and occasional works of his own. Historical biography was a notable feature, but the context of and motivation for publication is unclear: all his works contained hopeful dedications, but usually to people with whom he claimed no prior acquaintance, and in which he revealed no personal details. The anti-Catholic *The Elegant Combat* (1634), describing the confrontation between leading Huguenot minister and Anglophile Pierre du Moulin and Jean-Louis Guez de Balzac, and dedicated to Sir

Anthony Mildmay, was complemented by a translation from du Moulin, *A Treatise of the Knowledge of God* (1634), addressed to the countess of Derby, as a well-known patron of learning. The following year he issued *L. A. Seneca the Philosopher, his Booke of Consolation to Marcia … in an English Poem*. He seems to have had at least a tenuous connection with the royal court, for the subject of his *An Elegie to the Immortall Memory … of Margaret Lady Smith* (1637) was one of the queen's gentlewomen; the dedicatee, her last husband, Edward Savage, was a gentleman of the king's privy chamber. By 1641 Codrington claimed to have written 'many hundred' poems. That spring he was imprisoned by parliament because of one interpreted as overly sympathetic to the earl of Strafford. Writing on 24 May to Sir Edward Dering, MP for Kent, with a plea for mercy for the unintentional offence, Codrington, lame and consumptive, made much of the suffering of his wife and children and of the 'many noble familyes, to whom I neerely am allyed' who 'bleed in my wounds', and protested that 'there was never a more hopefull parliament than this, never an assembly of more able and more excellent men in a more needfull time, for establishing of the kingdome' (Larking, 50–51). His release seems to have soon followed.

Wood thought Codrington a puritan and a parliamentarian. His writings reveal a commitment to protestantism, but it is difficult to discern a more precise religious or political stance. His *The Memorialls of Margaret de Valoys*, the first edition of which was published in 1641 with a dedication to Surrey gentleman Sir Anthony Vincent, was presented as the queen of Navarre's own account of courtly intrigue during the French wars of religion; new editions with almost identically worded dedications to (respectively) John Cecil, earl of Exeter, and George Meryfield appeared in 1647 and 1650. However, *The History of the most Illustrious Lady Queen Margaret* (1649), based on the same text and dedicated to Sir Horatio Townshend of Raynham, Norfolk, pointedly referred in the subtitle to its representation of 'the Bloody Massacre [of St Bartholomew's day] and the growth and fury of the Civill War in that Kingdome, occasioned by the policy and ambition of the Catholic Nobility, and by the pernicious Counsell of some Bishops'. If this had been his conscious theme all along then his translation of a manifesto published in Paris on 24 April 1642, issued as *A Declaration Sent to the King of France and Spayne from the Catholiques or Rebells in Ireland* (1642), was clearly meant to draw parallels between the conflicts in late sixteenth-century France and contemporary Britain: in this work the Irish Catholics who sought to subvert and convert susceptible protestants and to obtain foreign support emerged as latter-day equivalents of the Guise-led leaguers. *The Life and Death of the Illustrious Robert, Earl of Essex* (1646), a derivative work dedicated to Walter Devereux, Viscount Hereford, portrayed a protestant general (and son of another), following his death on 24 September 1646.

Codrington's subsequent output was more varied. *The Troublesome and Hard Adventures in Love* (1652), derived from Miguel de Cervantes and dedicated to James Compton, earl of Northampton, himself a translator, was followed by *The Ten Books of Quintus Curtius Rufus: Containing, the Life and Death of Alexander the Great* (1652), dedicated to Baptist Hicks, Viscount Campden; verses, *The Dimension of the Hollow Tree on Hampstead* (1653) and a 'corrected and revived' edition of Ludovick Lloyd's *The Marrow of History, or, The Pilgrimage of Kings and Princes* (1653), were dedicated to Charles Dimmock. There were further translations: from Marguerite de Valois, *Heptameron, or, The History of the Fortunate Lovers* (1654, dedicated to Thomas Stanley) and *The Grand Cabinet-Counsels Unlocked* (1658, dedicated to William Basset of Claverton, Somerset); from Justinus's Roman history, dedicated fulsomely to Oliver Cromwell (1654); and from Savoy Chapel minister Jean d'Espagne, *Shibboleth, Observations of Severall Errors in the Last Translations of the English & French Bibles* (1655).

After the Restoration, Codrington published *Ten Sermons* (1660), originally delivered in Latin at Oxford in 1647 by Robert Sanderson, one of the few Calvinists among the newly appointed bishops. In contrast was his 1662 English version of George Ruggles's Latin play, *Ignoramus*. In *The Prophecies of Christopher Kotterus* (1664), dedicated to Prince Rupert, Codrington revived predictions of 'the sudden destruction of the Popish Religion in the year 1666, presaging the uniting of all Religions into one visible Church, and how that Church shall be Governed by Bishops', while in *His Majesties Propriety and Dominion on the Brittish Seas Asserted* (1665), dedicated to the earl of Albemarle, he made a timely patriotic attack on the 'insupportable insolencies' of the Dutch. He also contributed the French and Latin sections of Francis Barlow's *Aesops Fables with his Life* (1666), collaborated on an edition of Thomas Hawkins's *The Holy Court*, and added to some editions of Francis Hawkins's *Youths Behaviour* a complementary *Youths Behaviour, or, Decency in Conversation amongst Women* (1664), which dealt with issues as diverse as preserving, obedience to parents, and sleep, and *A Collection of Select Proverbs … out of Several Languages* (1664).

According to Wood, Codrington died of the plague in London in 1665. That is the year of first appearance of his final publication, although many of his works were reissued. The 'second addition' of *Youths Behaviour … amongst Women*, with a title-page dated 1672 but with the imprimatur of 12 November 1663 and reference to addition 'this Year 1663', has a dedication by Codrington to Ellinor Pargiter and her daughter Elizabeth Washington dated 'Feb. 10. 66', but this may be a misprint.

VIVIENNE LARMINIE

Sources Foster, *Alum. Oxon.* · Wood, *Ath. Oxon.*, new edn · L. B. Larking, ed., *Proceedings principally in the county of Kent in connection with the parliaments called in 1640, and especially with the committee of religion appointed in that year*, CS, old ser., 80 (1862), 49–51 · IGI [register of St Andrew's, Holborn, London] · ESTC

Codrington [*alias* Mainwaring], **Thomas** (*c.*1640–1694), Roman Catholic priest, was the son of Edward Codrington of Sutton Mandeville, Wiltshire, and his wife, Frances, daughter of Francis Perkins of Ufton Court, Berkshire. He had several siblings, among whom his brother Bonaventure was also a priest. He was educated at the English College at Douai, where he used the alias Mainwaring. He was ordained priest in 1676, after only two years' study of theology, because he had been invited to Rome by Cardinal Howard; there he acted for some time as his chaplain and secretary. In July 1684 he returned to England, and was in 1686 appointed one of the chaplains and preachers-in-ordinary to James II. While at Rome he had joined the Institute of Secular Priests living in community (founded in Bavaria by Bartolomäus Holzhauser), and on his return to England he and his companion, John Morgan, were appointed procurators with a view to the introduction of the institute there. This design was cordially approved by Cardinal Howard. The rule of the institute was for two or more priests to live in common in the same house, without female attendance, and in subjection to the ordinary of the diocese. In 1697 the rules of the institute were published in England, under the title of *Constitutiones clericorum saecularium in communi viventium*. But the scheme encountered much opposition, especially from the secular clergy chapter, on whose behalf John Sergeant wrote 'A letter to our worthy brethren of the new institute'. This letter gave the death blow to the institute, which was subsequently, in 1703, suppressed by Bishop Giffard, vicar apostolic of the London district. Its funds were incorporated into the Secular Clergy Common Fund.

Codrington made his will in 1688, which he left with his sister on following James II into exile at St Germain-en-Laye. There he continued to officiate as his chaplain. He made another will in 1693, which was contested by his sister on the grounds that he was blind and *non compos mentis* as a result of smallpox, from which he died, at St Germain, on 4 or 14 February 1694. His only publications were two sermons preached at court in 1686 and 1687.

THOMPSON COOPER, rev. JEROME BERTRAM

Sources G. Anstruther, *The seminary priests*, 3 (1976), 37–8 · C. G. Herbermann and others, eds., *The Catholic encyclopedia*, 17 vols. (1907–18), vol. 4, p. 88 · *New Catholic encyclopedia*, 18 vols. (1967–89), vol. 3, p. 977a · J. Kirk, *Biographies of English Catholics in the eighteenth century*, ed. J. H. Pollen and E. Burton (1909), 50–51 · J. A. Williams, *Catholic recusancy in Wiltshire, 1660–1791* (1968), 109 · C. Dodd [H. Tootell], *The church history of England, from the year 1500, to the year 1688*, 3 (1742), 484 · Gillow, *Lit. biog. hist.*, 1.520 · W. T. Lowndes, *The bibliographer's manual of English literature*, ed. H. G. Bohn, [new edn], 6 vols. (1864) · BL cat. · T. A. Birrell, 'Holzhauser and England: three episodes', *Grenzgänge: Literatur und Kultur im Kontext*, ed. G. van Gemert and H. Ester (Amsterdam, 1990), 453–62

Archives BL, MS sermons, Add. MS 114, fol. 36 · Westminster Abbey, wills, corresp., 35:73; 36:28, 47, 70; 37:134

Codrington, Sir William John (1804–1884), army officer, second son of Admiral Sir Edward *Codrington (1770–1851), commander of the British fleet at the battle of Navarino Bay in 1827, and his wife, Jane (*d.* 22 Jan 1837), daughter of Jasper Hall of Kingston, Jamaica, and Otterburn, Hexham, was born on 26 November 1804. He had two brothers, both of whom joined the Royal Navy—Edward (1803–1819), a midshipman, and admiral of the fleet Sir Henry John *Codrington (1808–1877)—and three sisters, Jane-Barbara (*d.* 1884), Maria-Elizabeth (*d.* 1865), and Emma-Charlotte (*d.* 1863). Codrington purchased an

Sir William John Codrington (1804–1884), by Roger Fenton, 1855

ensigncy in the 88th foot on 22 February 1821, going on half pay on 25 October. Again by purchase, he became successively an ensign in the 43rd foot on 24 October 1822 and ensign and lieutenant in the Coldstream Guards on 24 April 1823. Similarly, he advanced in the Coldstreams to lieutenant and captain on 20 June 1826, and to captain and lieutenant-colonel on 8 July 1836. Codrington married Mary, bedchamber lady to Queen Adelaide and daughter of Levi Aymes of Hyde, Hertfordshire, on 7 May 1836. They had two sons and two daughters: Edward Bethell (1845–1853), Lieutenant-General Sir Alfred Edward (1854–1945), Jane-Emily, and Mary.

Codrington served with the 2nd battalion in Canada from 1838 to 1842, arriving back at Spithead on 31 October. Having become a brevet colonel on 9 November 1846, Codrington embarked with the 1st battalion Coldstream Guards at Southampton for Malta on 22 February 1854 as part of the British expeditionary force under Lord Raglan. After a brief stay on Malta the battalion reached Scutari on 29 April, and, as an acting regimental major, Codrington subsequently landed with it at Varna on 13 June. Seven days later, promoted major-general, he left the Coldstreams but remained in Bulgaria. When Brigadier-General Richard Airey succeeded Lord de Ros as Raglan's quartermaster-general, on 1 September Codrington took over the 1st brigade of the light division, comprising the 7th, 23rd, and 33rd regiments.

The combined British, French, and Turkish force landed on the Crimean peninsula on 14 September. Short-sighted, but not too vain to wear glasses, six days later Codrington led his brigade into battle at the Alma, where the Russians occupied high ground on the far bank astride the post road to Sevastopol. On the left of the allied line, the light division faced the dominant Kurgan Hill with two prominent redoubts, supported by infantry and field artillery. Having forded the river under heavy fire, on Codrington's order, 'Fix bayonets! Get up the bank and attack' (Glover, 71), the brigade advanced uphill to capture the Great Redoubt and two of its fourteen guns left by the defeated enemy. A Russian counter-attack was then wrongly identified as French by an unknown staff officer and, overwhelmed, Codrington's three battalions fell back towards the river to reform and advance once more, as the brigade of guards from the 1st division passed through them to retake the redoubt. *The Times*'s correspondent William Howard Russell wrote: 'The brunt of the action was borne by a brigade of the Light Division … they advanced against the strongest point of the enemy's works and over the most difficult ground' (Thomas, 164).

Raglan commended Codrington's initiative and courage at the Alma and noted, too, his 'admirable behaviour' (Cary and McCance, 84) during the battle of Inkerman on 5 November. Visiting outlying pickets in the pre-dawn mist, Codrington realized that an enemy attack was developing and spurred back to warn divisional headquarters. He remained with his brigade on Victoria Ridge throughout the ensuing action, engaging Russian troops in and across the critical Careenage Ravine. When Lieutenant-General Sir George Brown was wounded, as senior brigade commander Codrington took over the light division and retained its command until Brown returned to duty on 22 February 1855. He received a vote of thanks from both houses of parliament and, on 19 January 1855, an award of £100 per annum 'for distinguished service', backdated to 15 September 1854. Codrington attended the St David's day dinner of the 23rd (Royal Welch Fusiliers) on 1 March 1855, during which Lieutenant-Colonel David Lysons toasted his health: 'There was a grey horse … at the Battle of Alma … [which] carried an officer [Codrington] who, by his example and cheery voice, encouraged the men of the regiment in the moment of extreme danger' (ibid., 90). On 5 July 1855 Codrington was made KCB, being presented with the award in the field by Lord Stratford de Redcliffe. On 30 July he became local lieutenant-general.

Preceded by a three-day bombardment, on 8 September a major assault was launched against Sevastopol, with the French attacking the Malakhov on the far right and the British the Redan to their immediate left, which meant crossing almost 300 yards of open ground. The plan, drawn up by Codrington and Major-General Frederick Markham commanding the 2nd division, envisaged the first columns being quickly supported, but cross-fire from undamaged enemy batteries prevented this, and the attack failed. However, as the French decisively took the Malakhov, that night the Russians evacuated the southern part of Sevastopol in front of the allied lines. After Raglan's death in June, General Sir James Simpson assumed command of the army, but resigned four months later. Codrington took his place as commander-in-chief on 11 November 1855, still only a substantive major-general but promoted local general on 29 October 1855. Captain Temple Godman of the 5th dragoon guards wrote: 'Most people speak well of him, I have heard he is very active' and that he had been 'not to blame … for the unfortunate affair at the Redan' (Warner, 189). Shortly after taking command, Codrington ruled that all war correspondents thought likely to aid the enemy by publishing sensitive military information should leave the Crimea. An armistice at the end of February effectively ended the fighting, and on 24 March Codrington invited Russian officers to a celebratory race meeting near the Chernaya River. He left the Peninsula on 12 July 1856, having received another parliamentary vote of thanks and been promoted lieutenant-general on 6 June 1856. Before he sailed, he also received the thanks of the Tartars of the Baidar valley for the protection given to them by the British troops. Despite serving throughout the war and being frequently in action, Codrington had neither been wounded nor suffered serious illness.

On his return to England, Codrington became colonel of the 54th foot on 11 August 1856 and Liberal MP for Greenwich in 1857. He supported Palmerston's foreign policy, moderate reform, and civil and religious liberty, but opposed the secret ballot. He was governor and commander-in-chief at Gibraltar from May 1859 until November 1865, promoted general on 27 July 1863, and made GCB on 28 March 1865. He became colonel of the 23rd foot on 27 December 1860 and of the Coldstream Guards on 16 March 1875. He reputedly twice refused the rank of field marshal.

Codrington unsuccessfully contested parliamentary elections at Westminster in 1874 and Lewes in 1880, and for many years he was an active member of the Metropolitan Board of Works. He was a commander (third class) of the Légion d'honneur, knight grand cross of the military order of Savoy, and a member of the order (first class) of the Mejidiye. As a former governor of Gibraltar, he was twice drawn into controversy over its future. Writing to *The Times* on 3 February 1869, he deplored a proposal to exchange Gibraltar for Spanish-held Ceuta. To surrender it in this way would imperil other isolated parts of the empire such as Malta, Singapore, and Hong Kong, as well as the Channel Islands. Resurrection of the idea in 1882 caused re-publication of the letter, with a covering note from Codrington, as the article 'Gibraltar and Ceuta' in an anonymously edited collection of papers, *Egypt, Tunis etc, 1881–1883*. He died at Danmore Cottage, Heckfield, near Winchfield, in Hampshire, during the afternoon of 6 August 1884. Of his children, only Arthur Edward, then a brevet major in the Coldstream Guards, and Mary, widow of Major-General William Earle, survived him. Codrington was buried with full military honours at Woking on 9 August. JOHN SWEETMAN

Sources *Army List* · Burke, *Peerage* (1887) · J. Wyatt, *History of the 1st battalion Coldstream guards during the Eastern campaign, 1854–1856* (1858) · J. F. G. Ross-of-Bladensburg, *A history of the Coldstream guards* (1896) · A. D. L. Cary, S. McCance, and others, eds., *Regimental records of the Royal Welch Fusiliers (late the 23rd foot)*, 7 vols. (1921–), vol. 2 · H. A. Tipping, *The story of the Royal Welsh Fusiliers* [1915] · P. A. Warner, ed., *The fields of war* (1977) · C. T. Wilson, *Our veterans of 1854, in camp before the enemy* (1859) · J. Sweetman, *Raglan: from the Peninsula to the Crimea* (1993) · D. Thomas, *Cardigan: the hero of Balaclava* (1987) · A. Lambert and S. Badsey, *The war correspondents of the Crimean War* (1997) · WWBMP, vol. 1 · M. Glover, *That astonishing infantry: three hundred years of the history of the Royal Welch Fusiliers* (1989) · *Egypt, Tunis etc, 1881–1883* (1884) · *The Times* (8 Aug 1884) · Burke, *Peerage* (1879) · Boase, *Mod. Eng. biog.*

Archives NAM, military papers relating to Crimea, 6807/375–81, 7808/90 · PRO, corresp. and papers, PRO 30/31 | Bodl. Oxf., letters to Benjamin Disraeli · Bodl. Oxf., corresp. with Doyle · NA Scot., corresp. with Lord Panmure · PRO, corresp. with Lord John Russell, PRO 30/22 · Wellcome L., corresp. with Sir John Hall

Likenesses G. Hayter, study for a pencil, pen, ink, and wash drawing, *c.*1812, NPG · R. Fenton, photograph, 1855, NPG [*see illus.*] · lithograph, pubd 1856, NPG · W. Boxall, oils, The Convent, Gibraltar · L. Dickinson, lithograph (after F. Cruikshank), NPG · oils?, Harrow School, Middlesex · print (after photograph by Mayall), NPG; repro. in *ILN* (16 May 1857) · woodcut, NPG; repro. in *Illustrated Times* (9 Aug 1856)

Wealth at death £159,460 2s.: probate, 18 Sept 1884, CGPLA Eng. & Wales

Cody [*formerly* Cowdery], **Samuel Franklin** (1861–1913), showman and aeronautical designer, was born on 6 March 1861 in Davenport, Iowa, USA, the fourth of five children of Samuel Franklin Cowdery (1833–1902), a former Union soldier and jobbing carpenter, and his wife, Phoebe Jane (1834–1900). After education in local schools, he left home at the age of about fifteen to join a circus, and he adopted the name S. F. Cody, Jr, in emulation of the well-known showman Colonel W. F. 'Buffalo Bill' Cody, leader of a famous 'Wild West' touring company. On 8 April 1889 he married Maud Maria Lee, the daughter of Joseph Lee of Norristown, Pennsylvania, who assisted in his trick shooting act.

Cody left the USA late in 1890 for England; he was followed a few weeks later by his wife, and they performed a cowboy act in English music halls before moving to the continent in 1892. Soon afterwards Cody and his wife separated, and Cody began living with Lela Marie King (1853–1939), along with two of her younger sons from her previous marriage to Edward King, a licensed victualler. Lela, born Elizabeth Mary Davis, was the daughter of John Blackburn Davis, a horse dealer, and she and her sons took part in Cody's act. Cody's wife appears to have returned home to Norristown in 1892, apparently destitute and feeble-minded; she was later incarcerated in a local psychiatric hospital.

While touring with the company in Europe, Cody and Lela had a son, born in Basel in 1895. During this period Cody constructed an elaborate account of his life, in which he claimed to have been born in Birdville, Texas, in 1861, and to have spent several years as a cowboy and trail-rider, with a spell of gold mining in the Yukon in 1883–4. He claimed that he had then met Lela in Texas, and that their two sons were born there, before embarking on his career as a 'Wild West' performer. Such a fictive biography was perhaps not unusual in the theatre, but it undoubtedly added to the authenticity of Cody's show. By the time Cody returned to England in 1896 the original trick shooting and horse-riding acts had expanded to a full 'Wild West' show in which his 'wife and sons' took part. Cody's

Samuel Franklin Cody (1861–1913), by unknown photographer, 1912 [at the controls of his aeroplane *Cathedral*]

most famous melodrama was *The Klondyke Nugget*, first staged in 1898.

From 1900 Cody became actively interested in kite flying, and patented a man-carrying kite system in 1901. In 1903 he sold four sets of kites to the Admiralty; in 1905 the army ordered kites and engaged Cody to instruct the Royal Engineers in their operation. He thus became involved with the balloon factory at Farnborough, under Colonel J. E. Capper, and gave up his theatrical activities. Capper wished to develop both airships and aeroplanes for military use, and he took advantage of Cody's mechanical and practical skills to promote this work. Cody was largely responsible for the engine installation of the airship that flew in 1907, and he designed and constructed the machine on which he made the first powered aeroplane flight in Great Britain on 16 October 1908.

The War Office decided in 1909 to stop work on aeroplanes, but Cody was allowed to keep the machine. By July 1909 he was making successful flights of several miles, and in August he was awarded the Aeronautical Society's silver medal. In October he flew at the first British flying meeting at Doncaster, and there he became a naturalized British subject.

In the next four years Cody built some half-dozen aeroplanes, which he flew competitively with considerable success, winning four British empire Michelin trophies as well as other prizes. He won the military trials in 1912; the consequent War Office order for two machines was his only commercial sale. Cody was a tall, flamboyant character, and an exceptional pilot. He was widely admired by fellow pilots and show-business colleagues, as well as the general public.

On 7 August 1913, flying his latest machine, Cody crashed at Ball Hill, Cove Common, Farnborough; he and his passenger, W. H. B. Evans, were thrown out of the aircraft and killed. Cody was subsequently given a funeral on 11 August with full military honours by the Aldershot garrison, and he was buried in the military cemetery there. Following Cody's death, his legal wife's stepmother started a civil action for a share of the estate; settled in

1922, the proceeds were split between Cody's wife, Maud Maria, and his three sisters and brother. His archives were auctioned at Sothebys in 1996.   JOHN A. BAGLEY

Sources G. A. Broomfield, *Pioneer of the air* (1953) • A. S. G. Lee, *The flying Cathedral: the story of Samuel Franklin Cody* (1965) • P. B. Walker, *Early aviation at Farnborough: the history of the Royal Aircraft Establishment*, 2 vols. (1971–4); repr. (1974) • private information (1993) • Record of Green v. Cody, Chancery Division, PRO, XC5175/J48743 • *CGPLA Eng. & Wales* (1914) • d. cert. • b. cert. [Lela Marie King]
Likenesses photograph, 1912, Hult. Arch. [*see illus.*]
Wealth at death £6105 8*s.* 2*d.*: administration, 22 May 1914, *CGPLA Eng. & Wales*

Coelson [Colson], **Lancelot** (1627–1687?), astrologer and medical practitioner, was born on 25 March 1627 at Colchester. His astrological 'accidents' record that he married in 1645 (at the age of eighteen), but his wife's name is unknown. He was wounded fighting in Cromwell's Scottish campaign in 1650. By the mid-1650s he had settled in London, close to the Tower, where he remained for the rest of his life; from 1671 to 1685 he was at the Royal Oak, Still Yard, on Great Tower Hill. On 23 March 1656 he visited a Fifth Monarchist conventicle in Swan Alley, Coleman Street, apparently out of curiosity, and was so alarmed by the bloodthirsty rhetoric urging Cromwell's assassination that he gave a full account to Sir John Barkstead, lieutenant of the Tower. It was a glimpse of the disaffection that was to lead to Venner's attempted rising in April 1657.

From about 1655 Coelson practised astrology and medicine, specializing in venereal disease, deafness, and scrofula. He received patients in the morning and visited the sick in the afternoon. In 1656 he published *The Poor-Mans Physician and Chyrurgian*, dedicated to Barkstead. Based on traditional galenical principles, it provided sensible guidelines and details of 300 medical recipes. By 1668, when he published his alchemical work *Philosophia maturata*, he had come to adopt Paracelsian principles; the tract described the preparation of *aurum potabile* (drinkable gold), and gave details of chemical medicines taken from *L'or potable* (1611) by the Italian physician Angelo Sala. He also published a series of almanacs for the years 1671–87, passing them off as the products of a few weeks' recreation. They include copious historical notes on the 1640s and 1650s, which reveal some traces of his old parliamentary loyalties, and fiercely protestant comments on the Popish Plot. Several editions carry dedications to influential friends: Sir William Warren the shipowner, Sir John Friend MP, with whom Coelson served for twenty years in the Tower trained bands, Sir Richard Howe MP, sheriff of London and a major in the Surrey trained bands, William Coulson, gentleman, of Jesmond near Newcastle (possibly a kinsman), and Robert Seaman, surgeon and alderman of Harwich.

Coelson used the almanacs to advertise his medical services, cosmetic products, and proprietary medicines, which were supplied through several outlets in London and by a shopkeeper in Wiltshire. In his deposition in 1656 he described himself as 'gentleman', and the almanac dedications sought to convey a sense of respectability. In

1666, as 'Lan. Coleson M. D.', he signed a testimonial recommending another physician to be licensed by the bishop of London (Guildhall Library London, MS10, 116/4), which underlines the position he had achieved. His friends included many of the leading astrologers of the day, including Lilly, Richard Saunders, Richard Edlin, John Gadbury, and Henry Coley. Despite his 'incomparable' medicines Coelson suffered prolonged poor health. Noting serious recent illnesses in his almanacs for 1680, 1682, 1684, and 1685, he took the opportunity each time to correct reports that he was dead, reassuring readers that his professional services were still available. The almanac for 1687 was his last work, and he probably died in that year. It is possible that Coelson was related to John Colson the mathematician and Nathaniel Colson, who published a nautical almanac in 1675 which went through several editions. BERNARD CAPP

Sources B. S. Capp, *Astrology and the popular press: English almanacs, 1500–1800* (1979) • Bodl. Oxf., MS Ashmole 426, fol. 295*v* • Thurloe, *State papers*, 4.650–51

Cóemgen (*fl.* **7th cent.**). *See under* Leinster, saints of (*act. c.*550–*c.*800).

Coenred (*d.* after **709**), king of the Mercians, succeeded his uncle *Æthelred as king in 704, when the latter retired to the monastery at Bardney. He was the son of the previous Mercian king, *Wulfhere (*d.* 675), but may have been too young to have been his father's immediate successor. Æthelred seems to have remained an influential figure in the life of the new king: in 705 he summoned Coenred to Bardney and persuaded him to support and protect the exiled Bishop Wilfrid. According to the life of St Guthlac, there were serious Welsh raids into Mercia during Coenred's reign and he may have been recognized as overlord by the rulers of the kingdom of the Hwicce, for he attests the record of a grant of land in Warwickshire by Æthelheard and Æthelweard to an Abbess Cuthswith (*AS chart.*, S 1177).

At some point in 704 or afterwards Coenred confirmed a grant of land at Twickenham to Waldhere, bishop of London, which shows that his power, like that of his predecessor Æthelred, extended into Middlesex. In a letter which Bishop Waldhere wrote to Berhtwald, archbishop of Canterbury, in 704 or 705, he mentions that he had been summoned by Coenred to a meeting of bishops and noblemen who were to address the 'reconciliation' of a certain woman named Ælfthryth; he had declined to go, because he was uncertain of the archbishop's views on the issue (which was evidently a major controversy, although its details are now entirely unknown). St Paul's Church in London claimed that it had received a grant of privileges from Coenred, confirming an earlier grant by Æthelberht of Kent; but the charter preserved in the archive (*AS chart.*, S 1786) is clearly spurious, as are a series of diplomas in Coenred's name in favour of the abbey at Evesham (*AS chart.*, S 78, 79, 80). More convincing is a fragmentary record of a grant by Coenred to a nun named Feleburg of land in Herefordshire, which apparently passed into the possession of the minster at Much Wenlock in Shropshire (*AS chart.*, S 1801).

Coenred is likely to have been a significant patron of the church, for he would appear to have been a deeply religious man; Bede tells the story of his fervent attempts to reform one of his noble companions, who fell ill and died after experiencing a vision of hell. William of Malmesbury claims that it was this episode which prompted Coenred in 709 to resign his kingdom and travel to Rome, but that is probably no more than an inference from Bede's narrative. Coenred had before him the example of his uncle Æthelred, and that of an earlier West Saxon ruler, Cædwalla, who had abdicated in order to go as a pilgrim to Rome; moreover, other Anglo-Saxon rulers had been, and were to be, attracted by the idea of such pious rejection of their worldly status. Coenred was accompanied on his pilgrimage by Offa, the son of Sigeberht, king of the East Saxons; their arrival in Rome with a large following was significant enough to be recorded in the *Liber pontificalis*. Coenred was tonsured by Pope Constantine and spent the remainder of his life as a monk in Rome. The date of his death is unknown. He was succeeded as king by his cousin *Ceolred. S. E. KELLY

Sources Bede, *Hist. eccl.*, 5.13, 19, 24 • E. Stephanus, *The life of Bishop Wilfrid*, ed. and trans. B. Colgrave (1927), 124 • *Felix's life of Saint Guthlac*, ed. and trans. B. Colgrave (1956), 108 • *AS chart.*, S 78, 79, 80, 1177, 1786, 1801 • *English historical documents*, 1, ed. D. Whitelock (1955), 792–3 • *Willelmi Malmesbiriensis monachi de gestis regum Anglorum*, ed. W. Stubbs, 2 vols., Rolls Series (1887–9), vol. 1, p. 79 • L. Duchesne and C. Vogel, eds., *Le Liber pontificalis*, 3 vols. (Paris, 1886–1957), vol. 1, p. 391 • C. Stancliffe, 'Kings who opted out', *Ideal and reality in Frankish and Anglo-Saxon society*, ed. P. Wormald, D. Bullough, and R. Collins (1983), 154–76 • P. Sims-Williams, *Religion and literature in western England, 600–800* (1990)

Coetlogon, Charles Edward de (*bap.* **1747**, *d.* **1820**), Church of England clergyman, was the son of Dennis de Coetlogon, physician, and author of *An Universal Dictionary of Arts and Sciences* (1740). As his father died when his son was still very young, Coetlogon was admitted to Christ's Hospital in April 1755, where the entry records his date of baptism as 13 March 1747. He proceeded on a university exhibition to Pembroke College, Cambridge, where he was registered as a sizar on 28 June 1766 and thereafter graduated BA in 1770, proceeding MA in 1773. At university he was a member of a small religious club which was led by Rowland Hill and included among its other members David Simpson (later of Macclesfield), like Hill a student at St John's College, and Coetlogon's former school contemporary Thomas Pentycross (later of Wallingford). They engaged in the study of the Greek New Testament, prison visiting, and preaching in the town in Cambridge.

On graduation Coetlogon was briefly curate of Marden, Kent, in 1770, but he quickly came to the notice and secured the patronage of the influential evangelical earl of Dartmouth, as a result of which he was appointed assistant chaplain to Martin Madan at the Lock Hospital for reformed prostitutes in London. It was here that he established his considerable reputation as a popular and eloquent preacher, thereby securing further patronage in the person of Sir Sidney Stafford Smythe, lord chief baron of the exchequer, whose funeral sermon, *The Death of the Righteous a Public Loss*, he delivered in 1778 (it was published in the same year). He acted as chaplain to Alderman Pickett during his mayoralty in 1789–90, at the conclusion of which he published *Ten Discourses Delivered in the Mayoralty of 1790*. He also preached on the deaths of the evangelicals William Romaine (*The Life of the Just*, 1795) and William Bromley Cadogan (*The True Greatness and Excellency of the Ministerial Character*, 1797). Coetlogon's protestantism and patriotism were celebrated in other sermons such as *A Seasonable Caution Against the Abominations of the Church of Rome* (1779), *The Protestant Reformation of the Sixteenth Century* (1818), and *The king, or, Faint sketches for a true portrait of the venerable sovereign of the British empire* (1820), while his Calvinistic predilections no doubt inspired his decision to edit Jonathan Edwards's *The Justice of God in the Damnation of Sinners* (1774) and *The Eternity of Hell Torments* (1788). He also published an edition of Edward Young's *Night Thoughts* (1793), wrote a preface to Francis Quarles's *Emblems* (1788), and edited the *Theological Miscellany* which ran from January 1784 to December 1789. His *Miscellaneous Works* appeared in three volumes in 1807. He is there described as vicar of Godalming, Surrey, a mistake for Godstone, Surrey, to which he had been preferred in 1794.

Coetlogon enjoyed a considerable reputation as an extempore preacher. His imposing presence was reinforced by an impressive manner and use of gestures. These qualities of delivery were matched, in the eyes of the veteran evangelical Henry Venn, by the quality of content. He wrote of the young Coetlogon in February 1775, 'His discourses are all I want to hear—judicious, doctrinal in a proper degree, very experimental, and faithfully applied' (Venn, *Life … of the … Rev. H. Venn*, 224). A different view, however, was expressed by William Wilberforce, who was a regular attender at the Lock Hospital chapel. On Christmas day 1790, for example, he declared that he 'much disliked De Coetlogon' (Wilberforce, 1.286). In his last years Coetlogon became too ill to carry out his pastoral duties. He died at Stamford Street, Blackfriars Road, London, on 16 September 1820 and was buried nine days later in Godstone churchyard, where there is a memorial inscription to him. Charles Frederick de Coetlogon (*d.* 1836), who also has a memorial inscription there, was probably his son.   ARTHUR POLLARD

Sources *GM*, 1st ser., 90/2 (1820), 371–2 • *The Pulpit*, 2 (1812), 57–63 • L. E. Elliott-Binns, *The early evangelicals: a religious and social study* (1953), 243, 253–4, 360 • Venn, *Alum. Cant.*, 2/2.268 • *DNB* • J. Venn, *The life and a selection from the letters of the … Rev. H. Venn* (1834) • R. I. Wilberforce and S. Wilberforce, *Life of William Wilberforce*, 5 vols. (1838)
Likenesses J. Watson, mezzotint, pubd 1774 (with Martin Madan; after G. James), BM • W. Grainger, stipple, pubd 1791 (after T. Peat), BM • line print, BM, NPG; repro. in *Gospel Magazine* (1744) • line print, NPG; repro. in E. Young, *Night thoughts*

Coffey, Aeneas (*c.*1780–1852), exciseman and inventor of a still, was born probably in Dublin (though one source gives his birthplace as Calais), the son of Andrew Coffey, the city engineer of Dublin, who was employed in the Dublin city waterworks from 1774 to 1832. He is thought to have attended classes at Trinity College, Dublin, but there is no record of his having graduated from there.

Coffey entered the service of the excise in 1800 as a waiter, gauger, and searcher. In 1808 he married Sussana Logie. They had four sons. Coffey was appointed surveyor of excise for the city of Dublin in 1809, and in the following year was transferred to co. Donegal, where he was put in charge of operations against illicit distilling. The excise laws were widely regarded by the Irish as unnecessarily strict, and they resulted in harsh repressive measures being taken by excise officers, often in conjunction with military forces, although there is ample evidence that both sides resorted to violence at times. The Revd Edward Chichester published a pamphlet in 1818 entitled *Oppressions and Cruelties of Irish Revenue Officers*, in which he described how, in 1810, a detachment of the army led by Coffey was set upon and disarmed by the country people near Culdaff in Inishowen. Coffey was beaten 'until he was supposed to be dead'. That same year Coffey, by then acting inspector-general of excise, published his *Observations*, on Chichester's pamphlet, in which he restated the official policy but did not produce any very convincing arguments or evidence in its justification.

In 1821 Coffey began a series of experiments at Carrickfergus distillery on the design of a new type of still, which allowed the distiller to check the strength of the spirit without requiring access to it, while securing the still against any abstraction of the contents. Coffey's objective was to reduce illicit distilling, but his apparatus had obvious commercial advantages over the traditional pot still; it produced whisky more quickly and cheaply, in larger quantities, and in a continuous process. In 1824 he resigned from the excise and four years later established the firm of Aeneas Coffey & Co. at the Dock Distillery, South King Street, Dublin. The patent for his 'apparatus for brewing and distilling' (no. 5974) was granted (for Ireland only) for fourteen years from 1831.

Initial production problems and the conservatism of Irish distillers meant that Coffey had little success in introducing his apparatus in Ireland, and in 1835 he moved his business to St Leonard's Street, Bromley by Bow, Middlesex. From the 1840s his patent still gained in popularity, notably in Scotland. During his tour of 1887 Alfred Barnard found Coffey stills in all the major Scottish distilleries. Improved versions are widely used in the manufacture of grain whisky, gin, and other potable and industrial spirits.

Coffey's four sons all entered their father's business, three of them after studying at Trinity College, Dublin. Coffey died at St Leonard's Street, Bromley by Bow, on 26 November 1852, his eldest son, Aeneas Coffey, having died a few months earlier.

RONALD M. BIRSE, *rev.* CHRISTINE CLARK

Sources E. J. Rothery, 'Aeneas Coffey (1780–1852)', *Annals of Science*, 24 (1968), 53–71 • D. Daiches, *Whisky* (1970) • A. Barnard, *The whisky distilleries of the United Kingdom* (1887) • d. cert.

Coffey, Charles (*d.* 1745), writer, was born and educated in Ireland but no more details of his early years are known. His play *A Wife and No Wife*, published in London in 1732, but never acted there, appears in a Dublin imprint of 1724 entitled *Poems and songs upon several occasions, with love letters, and a novel, nam'd Loviso, to which is added a diverting farce, call'd 'Wife and No Wife'*. If all of these works are Coffey's, he was active for the greater part of a decade as a writer in Ireland before moving to England in 1729. Foxon attributes to him several poems on new spa- and pleasure-garden constructions from as early as 1723.

By October 1728, picking up on the success in London of *The Beggar's Opera* the previous season, Coffey created his own ballad opera, *The Beggar's Wedding*. However, the Smock Alley management's indifference in producing it, as shown by the delay to a bad Lenten date for audiences (24 March 1729), and poor acting, caused it to fail. Coffey must then have moved to London, for *The Beggar's Wedding* opened at the Haymarket on 29 May. There it became the hit of the season and a continuing repertory standard, especially as a one-act afterpiece (sometimes entitled *Phebe*). That same summer Coffey had a further short ballad opera, *Southwark Fair, or, The Sheep-Shearing*, at Reynold's Booth at the fair. His next ballad opera, the full-length *Female Parson, or, Beau in the Sudds* (Haymarket, 27 April 1730), failed.

In 1731 Coffey joined with John Mottley to transform into another ballad opera Jevon's old play *The Devil of a Wife*; this became *The Devil to Pay, or, The Wives Metamorphos'd* (Drury Lane, 6 August 1731). After it had been cut down to one act by Theophilus Cibber its success was sensational, becoming the most performed afterpiece of the century—in 1731–2 alone there were more than ninety-five performances in London. Kitty Clive rose to stardom as the original Nell. It was popular also on the continent. Translated into German by a recent ambassador, Count Caspar Wilhelm von Borcke, and subsequently retranslated and set to a composed score, it became the ancestor of the German *Singspiel*. Mottley and others allowed Coffey to have the public credit for *The Devil to Pay*, but as well as those who have been mentioned, words and ideas came from Rochester and Colley Cibber, and perhaps also Sidney and Shadwell. The writer of Coffey's entry in *A Compleat List of All the English Dramatic Poets* (1747), almost certainly Mottley himself, says that because it was an adaptation the two were not allowed the usual third-night author's benefit, but were none the less richly rewarded with £70 after waiting until the thirty-third.

After this came two more ballad opera disappointments, *The Boarding-School, or, The Sham Captain* (Drury Lane, 29 January 1733), based on D'Urfey's *Love for Money, or, The Boarding-School*, and Coffey's attempt to capitalize as full author on the previous success, *The Merry Cobler, or, The Second Part of the Devil to Pay* (Drury Lane, 6 May 1735). Coffey now had the idea of financing himself by getting up a subscription for a folio edition of the poet Michael Drayton, but he died before it was published in 1748. Mottley, writing while it was in press, believed that the benefit would go to Coffey's widow, but Joseph Knight in the *Dictionary of National Biography* says this was not the case.

Coffey was a hunchback, who chose to cope with public mockery by joining in with it: he played the part of Aesop in Dublin for one of his own benefits. Baker's verdict is that 'he had no very great share of original genius; his turn was humour', and Charles Dibdin, a full half century after his death, is withering in his scorn for Coffey (D. E. Baker, *The Companion to the Play House*, 2, 1764; C. Dibdin, *A Complete History of the English Stage*, 1797–1800, 5.73), but it has been noticed that managers treated him with some consideration and often gave him a benefit. As can be seen, he was usually unsuccessful writing by himself, but gifted, or lucky, in collaboration; Allardyce Nicoll feels that the ballad opera genre was itself difficult to work in (A. Nicoll, *Early Eighteenth-Century Drama*, 3rd edn, 1961, vol. 2 of *A History of English Drama*, 244). Coffey died on 13 May 1745 and was buried in the parish of St Clement Danes, London.   JOSEPH KNIGHT, rev. YVONNE NOBLE

Sources C. Coffey, *Poems and songs upon several occasions* (1724) [incl. dedications and other prefatory material] · C. Coffey, *The beggar's wedding: a new opera, as it is acted at the theatre in Dublin* (1729) [dedications and other prefatory material] · C. Coffey, *The female parson, or, Beau in the sudds: an opera* (1730) [esp. prefatory material] · C. Coffey, *The devil to pay, or, The wives metamorphos'd: an opera* (1731) [dedications and other prefatory material] · BL, MS letters, Add. MS 32692, fol. 453 · BL, MS letters, Sloane MS 4058, fol. 40 · [J. Mottley], *A compleat list of all the English dramatic poets*, pubd with T. Whincop, *Scanderbeg* (1747) · E. L. Avery, ed., *The London stage, 1660–1800*, pt 2: *1700–1729* (1960) · A. H. Scouten, ed., *The London stage, 1660–1800*, pt 3: *1729–1747* (1961) · S. Rosenfeld, *The theatre of the London fairs in the 18th century* (1960) · L. Hughes and A. H. Scouten, eds., *The devil to pay, ten English farces* (1948), 171–99 · B. Van Boer, 'Coffey's *The devil to pay*, the comic war, and the emergence of the German *Singspiel*', *Journal of Musicological Research*, 8 (1988), 119–39 · W. H. Rubsamen, 'Mr Seedo, ballad opera, and the *Singspiel*', *Miscelánea en homenaje a Monseñor Higinio Anglés*, 2 (1961), 775–809 · W. R. Chetwood, *The British theatre* (1752) · D. F. Foxon, ed., *English verse, 1701–1750: a catalogue of separately printed poems with notes on contemporary collected editions*, 2 vols. (1975) · W. J. Lawrence, 'Early Irish ballad opera and comic opera', *Musical Quarterly*, 8 (1922), 397–412 · T. J. Walsh, *Opera in Dublin, 1705–1797: the social scene* (1973) · F. L. Harrison, 'Charles Coffey and Swift's "Description of an Irish Feast"', *Swift Studies*, 1 (1986), 32–8

Coffin, Albert Isaiah (1790/91–1866), medical botanist, claimed to have been born in Ohio, USA, in 1798, but his death certificate suggests 1790 or 1791. Coffin's early life is obscure. According to his own account he received some formal medical instruction at an early age but had to withdraw from study because of an illness which orthodox physicians failed to cure. He recovered after being treated by a Native American woman who had called at his home. Coffin claimed to have been so impressed that he spent time among the Native American people learning about the herbs they used. Such 'foundation myths' were common among practitioners of unorthodox medicine, especially in the United States. Coffin was in practice in Troy, New York, by 1829, but he left the United States for France in 1832 after a court case. In 1838 he came to Britain, advocating a system of medical botany similar to that popularized by Samuel Thomson in the USA. Coffin's key remedies were lobelia (an emetic) and cayenne pepper (for warmth).

Albert Isaiah Coffin (1790/91–1866), by Henry Bryan Hall (after Charpentier)

Coffin began to be successful from the mid-1840s, especially in the north of England, where his medico-botanical societies attracted plebeian supporters also interested in temperance and Methodism. Adherents bought copies of his *Botanic Guide to Health* (1845) and purchased his recommended remedies, which he supplied from his headquarters in Manchester. Coffin attracted official attention in 1847 when one of his agents, Ellis Flitcroft of Bolton, was jailed for one month for manslaughter and then released to popular rejoicing. From 1848 Coffin was also active in London, though until 1853 he was described as practising in Manchester, in partnership with Thomas Harle.

Coffin was said to be a large man, weighing 14 stone (196 pounds). He seems to have been a brash American salesman with a simple message that appealed to working people. He argued against 'medical mysteries' and opposed the Medical Act of 1858 which increased the status of orthodox medicine. His many books and periodicals, some of which were regularly reprinted, included *Medical Botany* (1851), *A Treatise on Midwifery, and the Diseases of Women and Children* (1849), and his *Botanical Journal and Medical Reformer*, price 1d., which was issued in ten volumes between 1847 and 1861. In these works he advocated self-help and herbal remedies. According to Coffin, bodies, like steam engines, required heat, and women should not be corsetted, nor attended in childbirth by male doctors.

It was Coffin's custom to appoint assistants, with some of whom he later quarrelled. One of the best-known was John Skelton, a radical politician turned healer. John Boot, father of Jesse Boot, the founder of the pharmaceutical company, was a follower of Skelton. Some of Coffin's followers, and ex-followers, including Skelton, gained orthodox medical qualifications and, as in the USA, styled themselves 'eclectics'—taking the best from all medical systems. The later institutions of British herbalism, notably the National Institute of Medical Herbalists, can be traced back to Coffin.

Coffin died of cancer of the stomach on 1 August 1866 at 24 Montague Place, Russell Square, London, the address he shared with the patent medicine dealer John Morris Brooks. He was buried at Kensal Green cemetery. Coffin's obituary in John Skelton's *Eclectic Journal and Medical Free Press* claims that his 'name will be ever remembered wheresoever Medical Botany is known … and although he may have had some failings it is the duty of everyone to draw the veil of charity over them' (1.149).

JOHN V. PICKSTONE

Sources U. Miley, 'Herbalists and herbal medicine in the nineteenth and early twentieth centuries, with particular reference to north west England', MSc diss., University of Manchester Institute of Science and Technology, 1988 · J. V. Pickstone and U. Miley, 'Medical botany around 1850: American medicine in industrial Britain', *Studies in the history of alternative medicine*, ed. R. J. Cooter (1988), 140–54 · J. V. Pickstone, 'Medical botany (self-help medicine in Victorian England)', *Memoirs of the Literary and Philosophical Society of Manchester*, 119 (1976–7), 85–95 · *Eclectic Journal and Medical Free Press*, 1 (Sept 1866), 149 · P. S. Brown, 'Herbalists and medical botanists in mid-nineteenth-century Britain, with special reference to Bristol', *Medical History*, 26 (1982), 405–20 · E. Gaskell, 'The Coffinites', *Society for the Social History of Medicine Bulletin*, 8 (1972), 12 · J. V. Pickstone, 'Establishment and dissent in nineteenth-century medicine: an exploration of some correspondence and connections between religious and medical belief-systems in early industrial England', *The church and healing*, ed. W. J. Sheils, SCH, 19 (1982), 165–89 · W. F. Bynum and R. Porter, eds., *Medical fringe and medical orthodoxy* (1987) · L. Barrow, *Independent spirits: Spiritualism and English plebeians, 1850–1910* (1986) · J. F. C. Harrison, 'Early Victorian radicals and the medical fringe', *Medical fringe and medical orthodoxy*, ed. W. F. Bynum and R. Porter (1987) · d. cert. · CGPLA Eng. & Wales (1866)

Likenesses H. B. Hall, mezzotint (after Charpentier), Wellcome L. [*see illus.*] · H. B. Hall, stipple (after Charpentier), Wellcome L. · portrait, repro. in A. I. Coffin, *A botanic guide to health and the natural pathology of disease* (1845)

Wealth at death under £6000: resworn probate, May 1867, CGPLA Eng. & Wales (1866)

Coffin [*alias* Hatton], **Edward** (c.1570/71–1626), Jesuit, was the son of John Coffin (d. c.1583) of Cornwall, and was born in the diocese of Exeter, probably in Cornwall, about 1570–71. Educated at Liskeard, Cornwall, he travelled to London with Christopher Turner, a relative of his father, in 1584 after the second marriage of his mother. Concealed there for a month, he eventually crossed into France from Essex. Dangerously ill after the journey, Coffin remained in Rouen to recuperate and eventually followed Turner to Rheims, arriving on 19 July 1585. On 7 November 1586 he departed for Ingolstadt with Dr Robert Turner, who helped defray the cost of his education. Coffin received additional support from the bishop of Eichstätt first at a college in Eichstätt and then at Ingolstadt. He moved to the English College, Rome, on 26 July 1588 where he studied philosophy and theology. He was ordained on 13 March 1593 in either Ingolstadt or Eichstätt contrary to Anstruther's claim that Coffin was ordained in the Lateran. Upon his capture in 1598 Coffin admitted that he left Rome before ordination: 'butt before I ended my studyes, falling sicke, my bodye nott agreeing with the heats, I retourned into Germany, where by the successor of the other Bishop [of Eichstätt] I was made priest' (*De L'Isle and Dudley MSS*, 2.352). In March of 1594 he was sent to England. Entering the Jesuits on 13 January 1598 he and Thomas Lister were seized by Dutch soldiers at Lillo near Antwerp as Coffin was travelling to the noviciate. Sent back to England, Coffin was imprisoned in Newgate and Framlingham. There he remained until he was exiled in 1603 upon the accession of James I. After a year at the English College in St Omer, Coffin moved to Rome in 1604. Between 1604 and the spring of 1625 he worked at the English College, Rome, as consultor, confessor, spiritual prefect, and prefect of the church. He was professed of the four vows in Rome on 1 January 1615.

From Rome, Coffin's long preface to Robert Parsons's *A Discussion of the Answere of M. William Barlow* (1612—completed by Thomas Fitzherbert upon the author's death in 1610) contributed to the controversy surrounding the Jacobean oath of allegiance. Coffin interwove defences both of the Society of Jesus and of Robert Parsons in his explanation why 'so idle a worke as M. Barlowes Answere is knowne, and taken to be, should be answered at all by so grave and learned a man as F. Persons was' (preface, b). In his other major controversial work, *A refutation of M. Ioseph Hall his apologeticall discourse, for the marriage of ecclesiasticall persons* (1619), he defended clerical celibacy against protestant attacks. A translation under the title of *M. Antonius de Dominis archbishop of Spalato, declares the cause of his returne, out of England* (1623) publicized the return of the controversial archbishop to the Roman Catholic church. More important perhaps were his translation of Robert Bellarmine's work into English as *The Art of Dying Well* (1621) and his own account of the cardinal's final days, *A True Relation of the Last Sicknes and Death of Cardinall Bellarmine* (1622). Coffin petitioned to work once more on the English mission and returned to St Omer in May 1625. Illness prevented his crossing and he died in St Omer on 17 April 1626. Philip Alegambe described Coffin as 'a pious and learned man, of primitive simplicity' (P. Alegambe, *Bibliotheca scriptorum Societatis Iesu*, 1643, 98).

THOMAS M. McCOOG

Sources G. Anstruther, *The seminary priests*, 1 (1969), 81 · T. F. Knox and others, eds., *The first and second diaries of the English College, Douay* (1878), 207, 213 · T. M. McCoog, ed., *Monumenta Angliae*, 2: *English and Welsh Jesuits, catalogues, 1630–1640* (1992), 266 · W. Kelly, ed., *Liber ruber venerabilis collegii Anglorum de urbe*, 1, Catholic RS, 37 (1940), 67 · H. Foley, ed., *Records of the English province of the Society of Jesus*, 7/1 (1882), 145 · T. M. McCoog, *English and Welsh Jesuits, 1555–1650*, 2 vols., Catholic RS, 74–5 (1994–5) · A. F. Allison and D. M. Rogers, eds., *The contemporary printed literature of the English Counter-Reformation between 1558 and 1640*, 2 vols. (1989–94) · *Report on the manuscripts of Lord De L'Isle and Dudley*, 2, HMC, 77 (1933), 352
Archives Archivum Romanum Societatis Iesu, Rome · Stonyhurst College, Lancashire

Coffin, Sir Edward Pine (1784–1862), commissary officer, youngest son of the Revd John Pine (1736–1824) [*see* Coffin, John Pine], was born at Eastdown, Devon, on 20 October 1784. He entered the commissariat as clerk on 25 July 1805, and was made acting assistant in 1806, assistant commissary-general in 1809, deputy commissary-general in 1814, and commissary-general on 1 July 1840. He served at the Cape from 1805 to October 1808, in Spain in 1808–9 (including the Corunna retreat), and in the Peninsula from April 1809 to August 1810, from October 1810 to June 1811, and from July 1812 to September 1814. He was also in the Netherlands and France in 1815–16, on special service at Brussels in 1819, and in Canada from June 1819 to December 1822.

During the next ten years Coffin was on half pay in China, and afterwards on service in Canada from September 1833 to August 1835. From then until April 1841 he was in Mexico procuring silver dollars for the commissariat chests, after which he served from April 1843 to July 1845 in China. From January 1846 to March 1848 he was in Ireland and Scotland, and had charge of the relief operations at Limerick and in the west of Ireland during the famine up to August 1846, at the end of which he was knighted by patent. He was employed and paid from 1 April 1848 as one of the commissioners of inquiry into the working of the Royal Mint; their report was published in 1849 (*Parl. papers*, 1849, 28). Coffin, who was unmarried, died at his residence, 13 Gay Street, Bath, on 31 July 1862.

H. M. CHICHESTER, rev. JAMES LUNT

Sources Commissariat records, Ministry of Defence, London, army department · *GM*, 3rd ser., 13 (1862), 372 · 'Correspondence relating to … distress in Ireland and Scotland', *Parl. papers* (1847), vol. 51, no. 761 · *Accounts and papers, 1847*, Commissariat Series, 2 (1849) [Ireland, distress] · C. B. F. Woodham-Smith, *The great hunger: Ireland, 1845–1849* (1962) · Boase, *Mod. Eng. biog.* · CGPLA Eng. & Wales (1862)
Archives Oxf. U. Mus. NH, notebooks relating to the habitats of his collection of Mexican insects
Wealth at death under £16,000: resworn probate, March 1863, CGPLA Eng. & Wales (1862)

Coffin, Sir Isaac, baronet (1759–1839), naval officer, was the fourth son of Nathaniel Coffin, an officer of the customs at Boston, Massachusetts, where Isaac was born on 16 May 1759. His mother was Elizabeth, daughter of Henry Barnes, a Boston merchant. He entered the navy as a volunteer in 1773 under the patronage of Rear-Admiral John Montagu, then commander-in-chief on the North American station, and was promoted lieutenant five years later. He was then appointed to the command of the schooner *Placentia*, and afterwards the armed ship *Pinson*, the latter being wrecked on the coast of Labrador in 1779. Two years later he was one of the lieutenants of the *Royal Oak* with Vice-Admiral Marriot Arbuthnot, and acted as signal-lieutenant in the action off Cape Henry. On 3 July 1781 he was made commander, and towards the winter, when Sir Samuel Hood was returning to the West Indies, he obtained permission to serve as a volunteer on the *Barfleur*, Sir Samuel's flagship. He was thus present in the brilliant action at St Kitt's, and by Hood's interest was promoted captain of the *Shrewsbury* (74 guns) on 13 June 1782.

Coffin had scarcely taken up his commission before he was involved in a difficulty which an older officer might well have feared. Three youths of respectively five, four, and two years' service at sea were appointed by Sir George Rodney as lieutenants of the *Shrewsbury*. Coffin, in the first instance, refused to receive them, judging them unfit to hold this rank. Afterwards, understanding that it was Rodney's positive order, he did receive them; he was nevertheless tried by court martial for disobedience and contempt. The trial was held at Port Royal on 29 July, when his own commission was scarcely more than six weeks old. He was acquitted of contempt and also of the charge of disobedience. However, the three lieutenants remained on the *Shrewsbury* and it was not until Coffin wrote (20 September 1782), begging their lordships to have them suspended, that the Admiralty issued an order (14 December) cancelling their commissions. Before the order came out Coffin had been removed into the *Hydra* (20 guns), which he took to England and paid off.

Coffin then spent some time in France, and in 1786 was appointed to command the frigate *Thisbe*, which was ordered to carry Lord Dorchester and his family to Quebec. In 1787 he alerted the Quebec council to the New England exploitation of the fisheries in the Gulf of St Lawrence and to their illicit trade with the Magdalen Islands. In 1798 Coffin received letters patent to the seigneury of these islands. He failed to settle a single family there, and in 1806 he tried unsuccessfully to remove twenty-two families, who had relocated from St Pierre and Miquelon. While still on the North American station he was, in 1788, accused by the master of knowingly signing a false muster. When the case was brought before a court martial it was shown that four young gentlemen were borne on the ship's books as captain's servants, but had not been present on board. This was in fact a common custom and the charge was undoubtedly brought out of malice. The court was compelled to find Coffin guilty, and sentenced him to be dismissed his ship. When the sentence came home Lord Howe, then first lord of the Admiralty, at once saw that it was a blunder, and by way of correcting it ordered Coffin's name to be struck off the list (the punishment required by law). Coffin petitioned against Howe's decision, and by the king's command the case was submitted to the judges, who pronounced the court's sentence illegal, that it could not be enforced by another authority. Coffin was therefore reinstated in the service. The case continued to be quoted throughout the nineteenth century as a precedent, establishing the limits of Admiralty interference with the sentence of a court martial.

Coffin, who had retired to the continent, now returned to England, and in 1790 he was appointed to the *Alligator* (20 guns). In the following year the *Alligator* was sent to America to bring back Lord Dorchester and was paid off. Coffin subsequently made a lengthy visit to Denmark, Sweden, and Russia, possibly with the idea of entering the service of one of those states. On the outbreak of the war with France he returned to England, and was appointed to the *Melampus* (36 guns) in the channel. While serving in her towards the end of 1794 he suffered a recurrence of an injury he had sustained while in the *Alligator*. Coffin was

never again fit for active service. He was appointed regulating captain at Leith, but in October 1795 he was sent to Corsica as commissioner of the navy. When that island was evacuated in October 1796 he was sent to Lisbon in the same capacity. In 1798 he was removed to Minorca and in the following year he was appointed commissioner of Sheerness Dockyard. When instead this responsibility was given to Henry Duncan, then on leave in England, Coffin replaced Duncan at the Halifax yard.

Coffin's six months in Halifax from mid-October 1799, before he was newly appointed to Sheerness, were memorable principally for a reign of terror he initiated. He was the only Halifax commissioner ever regularly to issue orders. He told his yard officers to ignore the naval captains' orders, which frequently strayed from Navy Board rules. He countermanded the vice-admiral's order to the naval storekeeper to issue fuel to yard lodges for officers, occupied when ships were refitting. He accused all ships' warrant officers of embezzlement (a charge which he never investigated) and captains of twice storing their ships without ever proceeding to sea, which 'unprecedented insult' they denied (PRO, ADM 1/2139). He forbade the yard officers to offer, as had been their habit, immediate assistance to merchant vessels in grave difficulty when entering harbour. He suspected everyone in the yard of fraud and embezzlement, and suspended the master shipwright and foreman of the yard, both of whom were reinstated when Coffin departed. That he was able to act with such brashness undoubtedly owed much to the protection he received from his patron, the earl of St Vincent, then first lord of the Admiralty. As commissioner at Sheerness (1801–5) Coffin 'imposed a vigorous reorganization', with 'little regard for artificers' interests' (Morriss, 123). In April 1801, when he impressed a yard worker for insolence and disobedience, a large number of artificers, riggers, and labourers threatened his life, forcing him to revoke his order (Coffin to Admiralty, 13 April 1801, PRO, ADM 106/1844).

If often aggressive in his manner, Coffin was warmly praised by St Vincent for his skills of naval administration. Never losing the Admiralty's or Navy Board's support, he reached flag-rank in April 1804, and a month later was created a baronet. He became admiral-superintendent at Portsmouth, a post he held until promoted vice-admiral in April 1808. Although pensioned and on half pay he continued to be advanced in rank, and became admiral of the blue in June 1814. On 3 April 1811 he had married Elizabeth Browne (*d.* 1839), daughter and heir of William Greenly of Titley Court, Herefordshire. In February of that year he took the name Greenly in anticipation of his marriage, but he dropped it after March 1813. Coffin had expressed interest in becoming an MP for a number of years before he was finally elected for Ilchester in 1818. He sat until 1826 and spoke often on naval issues. In 1832 he was made governor of Greenwich Hospital, where he died on 23 July 1839, six months after his wife's death. Because he died without an heir Coffin's baronetcy became extinct.   J. K. LAUGHTON, *rev.* JULIAN GWYN

Sources W. A. B. Douglas, 'Coffin, Sir Isaac', *DCB*, vol. 7 · J. Gwyn, *Ashore and afloat: the British navy and the Halifax naval yard before 1820* (Montreal, [forthcoming]) · J. E. Candow, 'Sir Isaac Coffin and the Halifax dockyard "scandal"', *Nova Scotia Historical Review*, 1 (1981), 50–63 · R. Morriss, *The royal dockyards during the revolutionary and Napoleonic wars* (1983) · J. Gwyn, 'The culture of work: in the Halifax naval yard before 1820', *Nova Scotia Historical Society*, Journal 2 (1999) · T. C. Amory, *The life of Admiral Sir Isaac Coffin* (1886) · R. G. Thorne, 'Coffin, Isaac', *HoP, Commons, 1790–1820*
Archives Nantucket Historical Association, corresp. and papers | BL, letters to Lord Nelson, Add. MSS 34905–34930 · PRO, ADM106/2027; ADM106/1844; ADM1/2139; ADM1/3364 · Public Archives of Nova Scotia, Halifax, MG13/6
Likenesses W. Behnes, bust, 1826, Boston Athenaeum, Massachusetts · W. Ridley, stipple (after miniature), BM, NPG; repro. in *Naval Chronicle* (1804)

Coffin, Sir Isaac Campbell (*bap.* 1801, *d.* 1872), army officer in the East India Company, son of Admiral Francis Holmes Coffin RN, was baptized on 24 August 1801 at St Mary the Virgin, Dover, Kent. He was educated partly in France, and entered the military service of the East India Company on 3 June 1818. He arrived in India on 12 January 1819, and was posted as lieutenant to the 21st Madras pioneers in 1821. He was appointed adjutant to the 12th Madras native infantry from 4 June 1824, and served with them in Burma, being present in the attack on the enemy's lines before Rangoon on 9 and 15 December 1824. He was appointed quartermaster, interpreter, and paymaster to the 12th Madras native infantry on 27 October 1826, and then, successively, captain (26 July 1828), paymaster to the Nagpur subsidiary force (30 June 1829), paymaster in Mysore (7 January 1834), major (24 July 1840), and lieutenant-colonel (15 September 1845). He became lieutenant-colonel of the 3rd (Palamcottai) regiment, Madras native light infantry, on 7 October 1845, and attained the rank of colonel on 20 June 1854, of major-general on 29 May 1857, and of lieutenant-general on 18 July 1869. As colonel, with the rank of first-class brigadier, he commanded the Hyderabad subsidiary force from 6 November 1855, a post he held during the Indian mutiny. As major-general he commanded a division of the Madras army from 28 March 1859 to 28 March 1864. He was made a KCSI in 1866.

Coffin was twice married: first, on 12 February 1824, to Marianne, daughter of Captain Thomas Harrington. She died at Ootacamund on 13 February 1864, and he married, second, Catharine Eliza, the eldest daughter of Major John Shepherd. Coffin left several children and died suddenly at his home, 9 St John's Park South, Blackheath, London, on 1 October 1872, survived by his second wife.

H. M. CHICHESTER, *rev.* JAMES LUNT

Sources ILN (12 Oct 1872), 359 · ILN (9 Nov 1872), 454 · Hart's Army List · E. G. Phythian-Adams, *The Madras regiment, 1758–1958* (1958) · C. E. Buckland, *Dictionary of Indian biography* (1906) · P. Moon, *The British conquest and dominion of India* (1989) · T. A. Heathcote, *The military in British India: the development of British land forces in south Asia, 1600–1947* (1995) · Boase, *Mod. Eng. biog.* · *CGPLA Eng. & Wales* (1872) · records, BL OIOC
Wealth at death under £14,000: probate, 25 Oct 1872, *CGPLA Eng. & Wales*

Coffin, John Pine (1778–1830), army officer and colonial governor, fourth son of the Revd John Pine (1736–1824), of East Down, Devon, who took the additional name of Coffin by royal licence in 1797, and his wife, Grace, the daughter of James Rowe of Alverdiscot, Devon, was born on 16 March 1778. In 1795 he obtained a cornetcy in the 4th dragoons, in which James Dalbiac and George Scovell were also subalterns, and became lieutenant therein in 1799. He was attached to the quartermaster-general's staff of the army in Egypt in 1801, and was present at the surrender of Cairo, and the attack on Alexandria from the westward. On the formation of the Royal Staff Corps (for engineer and other departmental duties under the quartermaster-general), he was appointed to a company, but the year after was promoted major, and removed to the permanent staff of the quartermaster-general's department, in which capacity he was in Dublin at the time of Emmet's insurrection, and continued to serve in Ireland until 1806, afterwards accompanying Lord Cathcart to the Isle of Rugen and in the expedition against Copenhagen in 1807. In 1808 he was sent to the Mediterranean as deputy quartermaster-general with the rank of lieutenant-colonel, and was employed with the expedition to the Bay of Naples, which ended in the capture of Ischia and Procida.

In 1810 Coffin organized the flotilla of gunboats equipped for the defence of the Strait of Messina, when Murat's army was encamped on the opposite shore; and in 1813 he commanded the troops—a battalion of the 10th foot—on the *Thames* (32 guns, Captain Charles Napier), and the *Furieuse* (36 18-pounders, Captain William Mounsey), sent to attack the Isle of Ponza, which was captured by the frigates sailing right into the harbour, under a heavy cross-fire from the shore batteries, and landing the troops without losing a man. He was afterwards employed by Lord William Bentinck on staff duties at Tarragona, and at Genoa, and attained the rank of brevet colonel in 1814. After the renewal of hostilities in 1815, when the Austrian and Piedmontese armies of occupation, 100,000 strong, entered France, Coffin was attached, as British military commissioner with the rank of brigadier-general, to the Austro-Sardinians, who crossed Mont Cenis, and remained with them until they quitted French territory, in accordance with the treaty of Paris.

In 1817 Coffin was appointed regimental major of the Royal Staff Corps, at headquarters, Hythe, Kent, and in 1819 was nominated lieutenant-governor and second in command under Sir Hudson Lowe at St Helena, replacing Sir George Bingham. When Lowe left in July 1821, after Bonaparte's death, Coffin succeeded to the command, which he held until, the last of the king's troops having been removed, he was replaced in March 1823 by Brigadier-General Walker HEICS, when government of the island reverted to the East India Company. The council of the island was at first disposed to question Coffin's authority. He was promoted major-general in 1825.

Coffin married, on 13 April 1820, Maria, only daughter of George Monkland, late of Belmont, Bath; they had no children. He published *Account of the Battle of Austerlitz* (1806), translated from the German of Stutterheim. He died at Bath on 10 February 1830.

H. M. CHICHESTER, rev. ROGER T. STEARN

Sources Burke, *Gen. GB* · *GM*, 1st ser., 100/1 (1830), 369 · J. W. Gordon, *Military transactions* (1809) · H. Bunbury, *Narratives of some passages in the great war with France, from 1799 to 1810* (1854) · W. Henry, *Events of a military life*, 2 vols. (1843) · Fortescue, *Brit. army*, vol. 9 · R. Muir, *Britain and the defeat of Napoleon, 1807–1815* (1996) · A. J. Guy, ed., *The road to Waterloo: the British army and the struggle against revolutionary and Napoleonic France, 1793–1815* (1990) · Foster, *Alum. Oxon.* · Venn, *Alum. Cant.*
Archives Royal Military Academy Library, Sandhurst, Camberley, letters to General Le Marchant · U. Nott. L., corresp. with Lord William Bentinck

Coffin, Margaret, Lady Coffin (1490?–1550). *See under* Coffin, Sir William (*b.* in or before 1492, *d.* 1538).

Coffin, Richard (1622–1699), book collector and antiquary, was the son of John Coffin (1593–1622) of Portledge, Alwington, north Devon, and Elizabeth, the daughter of Henry Hurding of Dorset. As he was born after his father's death, Coffin immediately succeeded to the house and manor of Alwington, which had been the family's home since the time of Henry II. The extent of his education is unknown.

Coffin remained in Devon throughout the civil wars. He married first, by licence dated 28 June 1644, Mary Dennis of Orley, and second, on 3 February 1648, Dorothy Rowe (*d.* 1666), with whom he had two sons and nine daughters. Although he had royalist sympathies, Coffin took up Cromwell's invitation in the late 1650s to county gentlemen to sit on the commission of the peace and there was a suggestion in a letter from a J. Hanmer dated 23 March 1659 that he stand for parliament.

At the Restoration, Coffin was a JP and a commissioner for money for disbanding and paying off. He married, for a third time, by licence dated 29 July 1674, Anne, daughter of Edmund Prideaux of Padstow, Cornwall, and with her he had two more sons and two more daughters. His chief public office was to act as sheriff for Devon during the year 1684–5, when he was required to participate in the bloody assize. Correspondence with his under-sheriff, Thomas Northmore, survives concerning the disposal of the heads and quarters of those executed for their part in the Monmouth rebellion.

Coffin rarely left Alwington, his chief interests being antiquarian pursuits and book collecting. The historian John Prince (*d.* 1723) wrote of him: 'He hath a noble library and knows well to make use of it' (Prince, 181). Prince was aware of his extensive collections of local genealogical information and, when sending him a manuscript of John Hooker's 'Synopsis chorographical of Devonshire' on 20 March 1686, he suggested that Coffin was 'excellently qualefyed, both with learning judgment, manuscripts leisure and estate' to prepare a historical collection for the press (*Portledge Papers*, 6–7). None of his compilations was printed although a manuscript entitled 'Genealogical survey of gentlemen entitled to coat armour in the south-

west of England' survives among the Pine Coffin manuscripts in the Devon Record Office. To build up his extensive library, which was especially strong in historical and topographical writings, he used as his London agent the bookdealer Richard Lapthorne, some 400 of whose letters, written between 1683 and 1697, survive in the Pine Coffin manuscripts.

Coffin died on 25 December 1699 at Portledge, and was buried at Alwington on 4 January 1700. He was survived by his wife, Anne, who died on 10 August 1705, and succeeded by his eldest son, John. Later generations added little to the library, which was sold by the Exeter bookseller Shirley Woolmer in 1801 with a catalogue listing 4515 items.

IAN MAXTED

Sources M. Treadwell and I. Maxted, eds., 'Book trade references in the Lapthorne–Coffin correspondence, 1683–1697', www.devon.gov.uk/library/locstudy/bookhist/lapthorn.html · *The Portledge papers: being extracts from the letters of Richard Lapthorne ... to Richard Coffin*, ed. R. J. Kerr and I. C. Duncan (1928) · *Fifth report*, HMC, 4 (1876), 370–86 · *Fourth report*, HMC, 3 (1874), 374–8 · J. L. Vivian, ed., *The visitations of the county of Devon, comprising the herald's visitations of 1531, 1564, and 1620* (privately printed, Exeter, [1895]), 210 · J. Prince, *Danmonii orientales illustres, or, The worthies of Devon* (1701), 181 · M. Treadwell, 'Richard Lapthorne and the London retail book trade, 1683–1697', *The book trade and its customers, 1450–1900: historical essays for Robin Myers*, ed. A. Hunt, G. Mandelbrote, and A. Shell (1997), 205–22 · S. K. Roberts, *Recovery and restoration in an English county: Devon local administration, 1646–1670* (1985), 59
Archives Devon RO, letter-books, armory, historical miscellany

Coffin, Robert Aston (1819–1885), Roman Catholic bishop of Southwark, was born at Brighton on 19 July 1819. He was the son of Robert and Elizabeth Coffin. His father was a gentleman of great wealth who followed no particular profession. Coffin was sent to Harrow School in 1834. In 1837 he matriculated at Christ Church, Oxford, as a commoner, becoming a student in the following year. He read classics and graduated in 1840 with a third degree, graduating MA in 1843. In the same year he was ordained as an Anglican priest by Bishop Richard Bagot, and presented to the living of St Mary Magdalen, Oxford. The Tractarian movement had attracted him for some time, as he had been introduced to John Henry Newman on entering the university. He related later how, at that time, their relationship was like that of 'Father and Son' (Lubienski).

In 1845 Coffin resigned his preferment and was received into the Roman Catholic church at Prior Park College, Bath, on 3 December. He then became tutor to the family of Ambrose Phillipps De Lisle at Grace Dieu Manor near Leicester in the summer of 1846, on a one-year contract, travelling with them to Boulogne. In February 1847 he accompanied John Henry Newman and five other converts to Rome, where he went through the novitiate of the Oratory of St Philip Neri. He was ordained priest on 31 October 1847. From 1848 until 1849 he was superior of St Wilfrid's House, Cotton Hall, in Staffordshire, but became increasingly drawn to the Congregation of the Most Holy Redeemer following a visit to St Wilfrid's by their superior, Father Lans. Coffin left St Wilfrid's in late 1849, much to the annoyance of Newman, and in 1850 entered the novitiate of the Redemptorists at Trond in Belgium. He

Robert Aston Coffin (1819–1885), by unknown artist

179–84 · J. Sharp, *Reapers of the harvest—the Redemptorists in Gt. Britain and Ireland, 1843–1898* (1989) · R. P. Lubienski, 'Mémoires sur la vie de Mgr. Robert Coffin CSSR', Provincial Archives of the Redemptorists, Clapham

Archives NRA, corresp., papers, and notebook · Provincial Archives of the Redemptorists, Clapham, London · Southwark Roman Catholic Diocesan Archives, London, corresp., papers, and diaries | Birmingham Oratory, letters to J. H. Newman · Pusey Oxf., letters to T. Henderson · W. Sussex RO, letters to Lady Caroline Maxse

Likenesses portrait, Archbishop's House, Southwark, London [*see illus.*]

Wealth at death £510 9s. 2d.: probate, 21 May 1885, *CGPLA Eng. & Wales*

was professed on 2 February 1852 and returned to England to the Redemptorist house at Clapham, Surrey. He became rector of this house in 1855 and provincial superior in 1865. He was almost constantly employed for more than twenty years in attending retreats and missions throughout England, Wales, and Scotland.

In 1865 Coffin was in Rome and used his influence with Cardinal Reisach to secure the appointment of Henry Edward Manning as archbishop of Westminster in succession to Nicholas Wiseman. Following the death of Bishop James Danell in 1881 Coffin was chosen by Pius IX as the third bishop of Southwark. This appointment owed much to the influence of Manning, as Coffin was not one of the candidates chosen by the Southwark chapter. He tried to resist his appointment on grounds of age and infirmity, but was instructed to submit. He was consecrated bishop by Cardinal Henry Howard in Rome on 11 June 1882, and enthroned in Southwark Cathedral on 27 July of that year. However, his health was failing and after only two years he was forced to retire to the Redemptorist house of St Joseph at Teignmouth, Devon, where he died on 6 April 1885.

Coffin did not produce any original work of note but provided excellent English translations of the works of St Alphonsus Liguori. He was well known for his grand voice and persuasive preaching. His main achievement was to found several houses of the Redemptorist order in England, Scotland, and Ireland. Many of his brethren found him autocratic and domineering in manner. He hardly shone as a bishop but the ill health which he suffered for much of his episcopate disarms the critic.

MICHAEL CLIFTON

Sources *The Tablet* (8 April 1882), 520 · *The Tablet* (15 April 1882), 564–5 · *The Tablet* (11 April 1885), 583 · Gillow, *Lit. biog. hist.* · B. Guldner, 'Coffin, Robert Aston', *The Catholic encyclopedia*, ed. C. G. Herbermann and others, 4 (1908) · G. Albion, 'Bishops of Southwark: Robert Aston Coffin, 1882–1885', *Southwark Record*, 18 (1939),

Coffin, Sir William (*b.* in or before 1492, *d.* 1538), courtier, was probably born at Porthledge, Devon, the son of Richard Coffin (*d.* 1523). His mother, variously recorded as Jacoba, Jaquetta, and Alice, was the daughter of John Gambon of Merton. He seems to have begun his public career as a petty captain in Henry VIII's French campaign of 1513, when he was probably at least twenty-one, in the company of Sir Edward Neville. By 12 May 1515, when he was granted an annuity of £20, he had become a member of the royal household, while in September he was paid £40 for going on embassy to Flanders with other gentlemen of the privy chamber. In 1517 he persuaded Sir Nicholas Carew to obtain royal letters advancing his suit to marry Margaret Vernon [*see below*], a recently widowed heiress, despite the displeasure of Wolsey, who wanted her for Sir William Tyrwhit, one of his own servants. The dispute may have had repercussions for the standing of the privy chamber, but does not seem to have harmed Coffin, who was one of three gentlemen ushers by 1519, attended Henry VIII at the Field of Cloth of Gold and at his meeting with the emperor at Gravelines in 1520, and was probably the 'Mr Coffin' frequently mentioned in the Revels accounts. He was given the keepership of Combe Martin Park, Devon, in 1520, and was sewer of the chamber by 1526.

Coffin became master of the horse to Anne Boleyn, and followed immediately after her in her coronation procession on 31 May 1533, leading the queen's horse with a side-saddle. He also became master of the horse to Jane Seymour. Details of his life at court are few, but he gave the king a new year gift at the beginning of 1534, while in 1535 he is recorded as hunting with other gentlemen of the privy chamber in Waltham Forest, where they killed sixteen deer. He was cultivated by Honor, Lady Lisle, who was Cornish by birth and whose first husband was a Devonshire landowner, in order to find a suitable place in an aristocratic household for her daughter Katherine—he suggested that of the duchess of Suffolk. He may have been an MP in 1523. In 1529 he was elected knight of the shire for Derbyshire, where his marriage had brought him substantial property, and is recorded as discussing the staffing of his department in the royal household with John Peshall, MP for Newcastle under Lyme, as they travelled south for one of the sessions. He was sworn a knight of the privy chamber in May 1537, but was not formally dubbed until

18 October, during celebrations following the birth of Prince Edward.

Outside the court, Coffin was frequently active in local government in the north midlands. A JP for Derbyshire from 1524 until his death, and regularly appointed to commissions, he was sheriff of that county and of Nottinghamshire in 1531–2. In 1522 he was required to raise a force of 100 of his Derbyshire tenants for that year's French campaign. He may have attended the brief parliament of 1536 which attainted Anne Boleyn, and later that year acted as an agent for the fourth earl of Shrewsbury in his dealings with the Pilgrimage of Grace; his services included interrogating captured rebels.

Coffin died at Standon, Hertfordshire, where he had recently been appointed bailiff of the manor, on 8 December 1538, probably of plague—his wife immediately wrote to Thomas Cromwell, asking him to inform the king that Coffin had 'died of the great sickness, full of God's marks all over his body' (*LP Henry VIII*, vol. 14/2, no. 650). In his will, drawn up on the day he died, Coffin left all his hawks and his best horses to the king, his Devon estates to his nephew Richard Coffin, and all his goods and leases to his wife, whom he named sole executor. He was buried in Standon church, where his memorial records his offices, the date of his death, and his coat of arms.

Coffin's wife, **Margaret Coffin** (1490?–1550), had been born Margaret Dymoke. She was the daughter of Sir Robert *Dymoke (c.1461–1545) [*see under* Dymoke family] of Scrivelsby, Lincolnshire, and his wife, Anne Sparrow. Her first husband was Richard, son and heir of Sir Henry Vernon of Haddon, whom she married in 1507. When her father-in-law died in 1515 he left her eighty ewes 'to move my son hyr husband that he breke no parte of this my wyll, and also a paier of beds of Corale gawdet with sylver and gylt to pray for my Soule' (Carrington, 90). Richard Vernon died in 1517, leaving Margaret a wealthy widow with a young son, George, whose wardship was in the hands of Cardinal Wolsey. She rapidly married William Coffin, and the attraction of her estates seems to have been such as to bring her new husband north from Devon to Derbyshire, with which he became increasingly associated.

The wife of a courtier and a wealthy woman in her own right, Margaret Coffin also served at court. She was one of Queen Katherine's gentlewomen at the Field of Cloth of Gold and later served Anne Boleyn, accompanying her to the Tower, where she lay 'on the Quenes palet', following Anne's arrest in 1536 (*LP Henry VIII*, vol. 10, no. 793). The queen had earlier made it clear that she did not like Margaret Coffin, and would have preferred to have ladies about her of her own choosing, but in the desperation of her imprisonment Anne confided in her, as she attempted to unravel the details of the charges against her. This may not have been wise, for Lady Coffin seems to have been in close contact with Anne's gaoler, Sir William Kingston, and thus with Thomas Cromwell. Margaret was also a lady of the bedchamber to Jane Seymour, and rode in the third carriage at her funeral in 1537, bearing Princess Mary's train at the requiem mass. Her position at court made her

known to the Lisles, and Lady Lisle sent her a token in 1537, but by 1539 the two women's families looked likely to become embroiled in an inheritance dispute.

Widowed again in 1538, Margaret Coffin in 1539 married Sir Richard Manners (*d.* 1551), of Garendon, Leicestershire. Her wealth forwarded the career of her third husband as it had done that of her second, and she continued to live at Haddon. She does not appear to have had children from her two latter marriages. Sir George Vernon, the child of her first, was the last member of his family to reside at Haddon; he was known as 'the king of the peak' from his magnificence and generous hospitality. His mother died in 1550. An effigy had been prepared for her at Tong, Staffordshire, in 1517, alongside that of Richard Vernon, but the unfilled blanks left on it for her dates suggest that in the end she was buried in Derbyshire.

CATHARINE DAVIES

Sources HoP, *Commons, 1509–58*, 1.666–7 · *LP Henry VIII*, vols. 1–14/2 · M. St C. Byrne, ed., *The Lisle letters*, 6 vols. (1981) · D. Starkey, *The reign of Henry VIII: personalities and politics* (1985) · P. Gwyn, *The king's cardinal* (1990) · *VCH Hertfordshire*, vol. 3 · W. A. Carrington, 'Will of Sir Henry Vernon of Haddon', *Journal of the Derbyshire Archaeological and Natural History Society*, 18 (1896), 81–83 · W. Jerdan, ed., *Rutland papers: original documents illustrative of the courts and times of Henry VII and Henry VIII*, CS, 21 (1842) · E. W. Ives, *Anne Boleyn* (1986) **Archives** PRO, state papers, domestic and foreign, papers relating to Henry VIII **Likenesses** memorial, Standon church, Hertfordshire

Cogan, Alma Angela Cohen (1932–1966), singer, was born on 19 May 1932 in Whitechapel, east London, the second of the three children of Mark Cohen Cogan (formerly Kogin; 1902–1952), a costumier, and Fanny Cogan (*née* Carp). Mark Cogan had been born in Vinitza, Russia, into a Jewish family, whence his own parents had emigrated in the 1890s to Whitechapel. The Carp family were also Jewish immigrants. Alma's siblings were Ivor (*b.* 1930) and Sandra, an actress who took the stage name Sandra Caron.

Fanny Cogan was a gifted pianist who had played in cinemas in south London from the age of ten. Alma first sang at family gatherings at the age of four. The family moved from London in the late 1930s, living in Slough, Reading—where Alma was educated at St Joseph's Convent—and Worthing. She made her public début at a charity concert in Reading aged ten. In Worthing she studied dress design and sang with a local dance band.

In 1946 Alma Cogan won the Sussex Queen of Song contest and was given an audition by the bandleader Ted Heath. He told her to 'come back in six years'. Her first professional stage appearance was at the Grand Theatre, Brighton, in 1947 when she appeared in a variety show starring comedian Max Miller. She next had a minor role in the London production of the American musical show *High Button Shoes*, written by Jule Styne and Sammy Cahn. After work in cabaret and as a film extra she successfully auditioned for a recording career with Walter (Wally) Ridley at His Master's Voice (HMV) in 1950. Her first recording was *To be Worthy of You* (1952). While rehearsing with Wally Ridley, Alma developed her trademark vocal embellishment when she giggled and sang simultaneously. This led

Alma Angela Cohen Cogan (1932–1966), by Derek Allen, 1956

to her being known as 'the girl with the laugh in her voice'.

During the 1950s Alma Cogan appeared frequently on the BBC Light Programme after passing an audition which reported 'a Judy Garland type voice with very good diction'. She was a cast member of the comedy series *Gently Bentley* and *Take It From Here* and of the variety programme *The Forces Show*. Her television début came in 1954 in garrison theatre, where she sang her first hit song, 'Bell Bottom Blues', which sold more than 100,000 copies. Alma became the resident singer on the Morecambe and Wise television series *Running Wild*. She was adept at using the new medium, and by the 1960s she had her own BBC series.

In 1955 she appeared at the royal variety performance and had a number one hit with 'Dreamboat'. She had more hits than any other female singer of the era; her other successes included 'Twenty Tiny Fingers', 'Sugartime', and 'Cowboy Jimmy Joe'. She also appeared in summer season in Blackpool and in the pantomime *Aladdin* at the Chiswick Empire, London. She was renowned for her extravagant stage costumes. A dress created for an appearance at the London Palladium contained over 12,000 rhinestones and diamond beads and 250 yards of nylon tulle.

Alma made her first visit to the United States in 1957, where she appeared in cabaret at the Persian Rooms, New York. During the 1960s she made many overseas tours within Europe and to Australia, Japan, South Africa, and Kenya. The musical director of her concert cabaret shows was her regular pianist, Stan Foster.

However, her British record sales went into decline in the 1960s, and she attempted to change her musical direction from the novelty songs that had been her trademark to more substantial romantic numbers. She ended her partnership with Ridley and chose Norman Newell as her new recording manager. She also composed the songs 'It's You' and 'Now that I've Found You' with Stan Foster.

From the late 1950s the Kensington flat shared by Alma Cogan with her mother and sister was the scene of numerous parties attended by the show business élite of the era, including the musical writer Lionel Bart, the actor Stanley Baker, and members of the Beatles. She was known to John Lennon as 'Sara Sequin', and Paul McCartney wrote the melody of 'Yesterday' at the Cogan apartment. Alma was romantically linked with Cary Grant, Lionel Blair, and others but the companion of her final years was club owner Brian Morris.

In 1965 Cogan was admitted to hospital with appendicitis but doctors discovered she had cancer. An operation caused a remission, allowing her to make a final tour of Sweden. She returned to hospital early in October 1966, and died three weeks later, on 25 October, at the Middlesex Hospital, Marylebone, London. A posthumously released album included her recording of Lennon and McCartney's 'Yesterday'.　　　DAVE LAING

Sources S. Caron, *Alma Cogan* (1989) · B. Henson and C. Morgan, *First hits: the book of sheet music* (1981) · D. McAleer, *Hit parade heroes: British beat before the Beatles* (1993) · C. White, 'Alma Cogan', *Record Collector*, 81 (May 1986), 35–9 · b. cert. · d. cert. · *Jukebox heroes*, 30 July 2001 [television series] · *The Times* (27 Oct 1966)
Archives FILM BFI NFTVA, 'Girl with the giggle in her voice: Alma Cogan', 26 Aug 1991 · BFI NFTVA, *Jukebox heroes*, 17 July 2001 · BFI NFTVA, documentary footage · BFI NFTVA, performance footage | SOUND BL NSA, performance recording
Likenesses photographs, c.1955–1965, Hult. Arch. · D. Allen, photograph, 1956, NPG [*see illus.*] · photographs, repro. in www.bridges.freeuk.com/alma.html
Wealth at death £7268: administration, 4 April 1967, *CGPLA Eng. & Wales*

Cogan, Eliezer (1762–1855), Presbyterian minister, schoolmaster, and classical scholar, was born at Rothwell, Northamptonshire, the son of John Cogan (1698–1784), surgeon and author of *An Essay on the Epistle to the Romans*, and his second wife. There had been one son from his first marriage, Thomas *Cogan, later one of the founders of the Royal Humane Society. Cogan mastered Latin grammar before he was six years old. For six months he went to Stephen Addington's school in Market Harborough, but after that he studied at home and taught himself elementary Greek. During 1780–83 he was at Daventry Academy, studying under Thomas Belsham, and he remained there as assistant tutor until 1786. Most of his fellow pupils went on to become distinguished Unitarians. In 1787 Cogan was elected as minister of the Presbyterian congregation at Cirencester, and remained there until 1789. On 21 September 1790 he married Mary, the daughter of David Atchison of Weedon, Northamptonshire. She died in 1850 at the age of eighty-one, after sixty years of marriage. They had at least one son and one daughter.

In 1791 Cogan moved to Ware in Hertfordshire, but after a few months moved again to Enfield and then to Cheshunt, where he started a school in 1792. He was elected minister of the chapel in Crossbrook Street, Cheshunt, in 1800, and from 1801 to 1816 he was minister of the Old Presbyterian Chapel at Marsh Street, Walthamstow, Essex, where he taught the theology of Joseph Priestley. At the end of 1801 he moved his school from Cheshunt to Essex Hall, Higham Hill, Walthamstow. The school, which was open to pupils of all denominations, became very popular, and at one time he had seventy pupils, with a waiting list of twenty. His pupils included Samuel Sharpe, the Egyptologist and translator of the Bible; Benjamin Disraeli, afterwards earl of Beaconsfield (of whom he used to say, 'I don't like Disraeli; I never could get him to understand the subjunctive'); Russell Gurney, the recorder of London; and W. E. Nightingale, father of Florence Nightingale. He preached his farewell sermon at Walthamstow at the end of 1816, and in 1828 gave up his school. On his retirement Cogan's pupils presented him with his portrait, painted by Thomas Phillips RA, and exhibited at the Royal Academy in 1828. In retirement he continued to study Greek, and to play the violin and sing: he was still singing at the age of ninety.

Cogan was highly regarded as a Greek scholar, and had the reputation of having read more Greek than anyone else alive. His many publications included *An Address to the Dissenters on Classical Literature* (1789), *Moschi idyllia tria, Graece* (1795), and *Sermons Chiefly on Practical Subjects* (1817). His son, Richard, collected and published some of his contributions to periodicals in 1856. Cogan died at Essex Hall, Higham Hill, Walthamstow, on 21 January 1855, and was buried on 27 January in the cemetery at the Gravel Pit Chapel, Hackney.

W. P. COURTNEY, rev. ANNE PIMLOTT BAKER

Sources G. F. Bosworth, *Essex Hall, Walthamstow and the Cogan Associations* (1918) · W. D. Jeremy, *The Presbyterian Fund and Dr Daniel Williams's Trust* (1885), 183–4 · J. Murch, *A history of the Presbyterian and General Baptist churches in the west of England* (1835), 26 · N&Q, 6th ser., 11 (1885), 16 · 'Memoir of the late Rev. Eliezer Cogan', *Christian Reformer, or, Unitarian Magazine and Review*, new ser., 11 (1855), 237–59
Likenesses T. Phillips, oils, 1828 · S. Cousins, mezzotint (after T. Phillips), BM; repro. in Bosworth, *Essex Hall*, following p. 8 · lithograph, BM, NPG · portrait, repro. in Bosworth, *Essex Hall*, facing p. 10

Cogan, Thomas (*c*.1545–1607), physician, was born at Chard, Somerset. He was educated at Oxford, and graduated BA in 1563, MA in 1566, and MB in 1574. He became a fellow of Oriel College in 1563. He resigned his fellowship in 1575, and was appointed chief master of the Manchester grammar school. He practised as a physician at Manchester, and was canon of Exeter in 1567. Before 1586 he married Ellen (*d*. 1611), daughter of Sir Edmund Trafford, and widow of Thomas Willott, who had property in Manchester. Between 1591 and 1593 he was the family physician of Sir Richard Shuttleworth. In 1595 he presented Galen's works and other medical books to the library of

Oriel, where they were preserved. He resigned the school mastership before 1602, died in June 1607, and was buried on 10 June at St Anne's Church in Manchester. His will mentions property in Somerset and Manchester, and bequeaths books to all the fellows and other officers of the college, and 4*d*. to each boy in the school.

Cogan wrote *The well of wisedome, conteining chiefe and chosen sayinges … gathered out of the five bookes of the Olde Testament* (1577), and *The Haven of Health, Made for the Comfort of Students* (1584). This was published with 'A preservative from the pestilence, with a short censure of the late sickness at Oxford', and *Epistolarum familiarium M. T. Ciceronis epitome*, which contains an 'Epistle to all schoolmasters'; the book was intended as an introduction to Latin.

[ANON.], rev. RACHEL E. DAVIES

Sources Wood, *Ath. Oxon.* · W. Whatton, *History of Manchester School* (1833) · J. E. Bailey, 'Thomas Cogan, the student's physician', *Palatine Note-Book*, 3 (1883), 77–84 · *Reg. Oxf.*, vol. 1
Wealth at death land in Manchester and Somerset

Cogan, Thomas (1736–1818), physician, was born on 8 February 1736 at Rowell (Rothwell), Northamptonshire, the second of the four children of John Cogan, surgeon and apothecary (1698–1784), who came from a Somerset family, and his first wife, Martha Morrice, of Lukenham, Leicestershire. Thomas's half-brother, Eliezer *Cogan, was the son of John Cogan and his second wife. Raised as a Congregationalist, Thomas attended John Aikin's dissenting school at Kibworth Beauchamp, Leicestershire, for two or three years, before returning home at fourteen. Two years later, intending to become a minister, he joined the dissenting academy at Mile End, Middlesex, where Dr John Conder was divinity tutor; dissatisfied with the conduct of the institution, he left for the dissenting academy at Hoxton. In 1759, while in Harwich, he visited Rotterdam, where he obtained a preacher's post at the Presbyterian church, deputizing for the Revd Benjamin Sowden, and acting in conjunction with his colleague, the Revd Thomas Pierson, until 1760. In 1762 and 1763 Cogan walked the hospitals in London and exercised his ministry in Southampton, but alienated his congregation by his open rejection of the strict Calvinist beliefs currently maintained by orthodox Congregationalists: predestination and eternal damnation were incompatible with his belief in a God whose leading attribute was love, not power. Cogan adopted doctrines associated with Unitarianism, but although for most of his life he passed, and wished to pass, as a Unitarian, his love of truth for its own sake prevented his total acceptance of any human doctrine.

Cogan returned to the Netherlands as junior minister in the English church at The Hague. He married Johanna Maria Groen (*d*. 1810), a wealthy Amsterdam merchant's beautiful young daughter, who brought him a fortune of £8000 or £10,000. It was a condition of the marriage that Cogan was to take up the profession of medicine, and after a short visit to England, where he delivered a few well-received sermons, he matriculated at the University of Leiden on 16 October 1765, graduating MD on 20 February 1767 with his thesis, 'Specimen medicum inaugurale

Thomas Cogan (1736–1818), by James Basire, pubd 1814 (after François Pascal Simon, Baron Gérard)

de animi pathematum vi et modo agendi in inducendis vel curandis morbis'. His fundamentally optimistic view of the universe found congenial matter in his translation, from the French of John Bruckner, of *A philosophical survey of the animal creation, an essay, wherein the general devastation and carnage that reign among the different classes of animals are considered in a new point of view; and the vast increase of life and enjoyment derived to the whole from this institution of nature is clearly demonstrated* (1768).

In 1769 Cogan bought Cowleys and Sanders Down, Middlesex. He practised medicine successively at Amsterdam, Leiden, and Rotterdam, specializing in midwifery, before moving to Paternoster Row, London, where he had an extensive and lucrative midwifery practice. On 29 June 1772 he and his wife went through a marriage service at the church of St Laurence Pountney, London, presumably to conform with contemporary English law, which would not have recognized a marriage in a dissenting church.

In 1773 Cogan published the *Memoirs of the Society Instituted at Amsterdam in Favour of Drowned Persons*, adapted from the original Dutch, in which he encouraged the English to follow Amsterdam's example. He supplemented this work with observations, drawn from his own experience, on the successful mouth-to-mouth resuscitation of stillborn babies. Just as it was ready for the press, a more wide-ranging work on resuscitation, making similar proposals, was published by Alexander Johnson (1716–1799). Cogan acknowledged Johnson's priority in a prefatory 'Advertisement', but justified his own publication on the grounds that 'the Memoirs of the Society, intermixed with the cases, will not only be amusing, but will excite us

to imitate their example more effectually than the mere narration of facts, however extraordinary they may be'.

In 1774 Cogan joined William Hawes to form the institution destined to become the Royal Humane Society. He wrote the first six years' reports, and relieved the solemnly sentimental atmosphere of the society's annual fund-raising festivals by singing a song of his own composition, with the old and popular chorus of

And a begging we will go, will go, and a begging we will go.

His lighter literary talents also appeared in the anonymously published and underrated *John Buncle, Junior, Gentleman* (1775–6), the purported memoir of the youngest son of the hero of Thomas Amory's eccentric Unitarian romance, *The History of John Buncle* (1755). It contains telling parodies of the fashionable sentimental style, and Letter 18, 'An Invitation to Town, in Pastoral Verse', vividly describes the joys and inconveniences of London life.

In 1780, satisfied with the wealth he had acquired, and suffering from a suspected liver complaint, Cogan returned to the Netherlands with his wife, resigning his practice to John Simms. Cogan was able to enjoy more than three years of philosophical study and pastoral tranquillity in the splendid mansion of Zuylestein, near Utrecht. He visited Germany, his tour forming the basis of *The Rhine, or, A journey from Utrecht to Francfort, described in a series of letters in 1791 and 1792* (1793). He utilized his linguistic and medical knowledge in his translation, *The works of the late Professor Camper, on the connexion between the science of anatomy and the arts of drawing, painting, statuary, …* (1794).

The French revolutionary army's invasion of the Netherlands drove Cogan and his wife back to England in 1795; they landed at Harwich and spent some time in Colchester, ready to return to the Netherlands. Eventually, realizing that Dutch liberation was not imminent, they settled in Bath, accompanied by Mrs Cogan's niece, Mary Elizabeth Gurnault. They lived in Argyle Street, opposite William Jay's Independent chapel, which Cogan attended in the evening, after mornings at the Unitarian church. They subsequently moved to Widcombe Crescent. Cogan founded the Bath Humane Society in 1805. He devoted much energy to religious and philosophical writings, arguing that relationships between God, man, mind, body, the individual, and the universe were harmonious, beneficent, and susceptible to rational analysis. His most widely circulated work was *Letters to William Wilberforce on the Doctrine of Hereditary Depravity, by a Layman* (1799), defending human virtue and divine benevolence. Characteristically, he retained his personal admiration for Wilberforce, who deemed Cogan a fair and able disputant.

Cogan's main work was a series of treatises on the passions. These were *A Philosophical Treatise on the Passions* (1800), *An Ethical Treatise on the Passions* (part 1, 1807; part 2, 1810), and *Theological Disquisitions on Religion as Affecting the Passions and on the Characteristic Excellencies of Christianity* (2 vols., 1812–13). All five treatises were published as a set entitled *A Treatise on the Passions and Affections of the Mind* in 1813. Cogan's remorseless application of human reason to subjects often regarded as divine mysteries, his denial of the devil's existence, and his use of humour caused offence to more orthodox friends. To protect their sensibilities, Cogan restrained himself at first, but his expressions became more uncompromising, culminating in his assertion that, if any human being were condemned to eternal torment, 'then is the propagation of the human species to be placed among the most atrocious of crimes' (1813, 5.406). His last publication was *Ethical Questions* (1817); he bequeathed his manuscripts, including unpublished works, to his half-brother, Eliezer.

Cogan's lifelong interests were travel, literature, and agriculture. This last prompted him to take a farm at South Wraxall, Wiltshire; he joined the West of England Agricultural Society, winning several of its prizes for experimental farming. Cogan continued this pursuit in subsequent moves to Clapton, Somerset, and Woodford, Devon, and at his death held a small farm near Southampton. He said farming was 'never profitable, except the farmer drive the plough, his wife be dairy-maid and his children scarecrows'. Nevertheless, he took a continuing interest in the subject, bequeathing to John Dowley his 'large and small drill dibbling Machines', with advice to 'persevere in my plan of Husbandry until in the eyes of the judicious it shall be confuted or established'. Johanna Cogan died in 1810 and was buried at the church of St Thomas à Becket, Widcombe, Somerset, on 29 May. Cogan left for London with Miss Gurnault, who died shortly afterwards. He passed the rest of his life migrating between London, Bath, and Southampton.

On 31 December 1817 Cogan walked out from his lodgings at Henrietta Street, Covent Garden, London, into a very thick fog; this brought on an unusually troublesome cough, with complications. Believing he would not recover, he went to Eliezer's house at Higham Hill, Walthamstow, where he died on 2 February 1818. At his own request, he was buried on 9 February in the vault of the New Gravel Pit Unitarian Chapel burial-ground, Hackney, beside Miss Gurnault.

Cogan's estate was worth £14,000; he left £100 to the Royal Humane Society, one of whose gold medals is inscribed to his memory. He was of short stature, and stout in middle age. Despite a lifelong tendency to pulmonary complaints, he was very strong; at eighty he could make children admire his agile backward skipping with a rope. Although habitually neat, he dressed less formally than was customary for English physicians, looking more like a gentleman, or a Dutchman. Though his vivacity and terse, epigrammatic conversation enlivened all who enjoyed his society, he invariably claimed that through life he had been grave for himself, and cheerful for his friends; to most contemporaries, his outstanding characteristic was benevolence.   CAROLYN D. WILLIAMS

Sources *Annual Biography and Obituary*, 3 (1819), 73–99 · *Monthly Repository*, 14 (1819), 1–5, 74–6, 105 · *Old age in Bath: recollections of two retired physicians, Dr. John Sherwen and Dr. Thomas Cogan; to which are added … unpublished remains of William Wordsworth … and Joseph Hunter*, ed. H. J. Hunter (1873) · G. T. Streather, *Memorials of the Independent chapel at Rothwell* (1994) · *The autobiography of the Rev. William Jay*, ed. G. Redford and J. A. James, 2nd edn (1855) · *GM*, 1st ser., 88/1 (1818), 177–8, 648 · will, 1818, PRO, PROB 11/1602, fols. 64–6 · death duty records, PRO, IR26/736, fols. 169–174 · F. W. Bull, 'The Cogans, Rothwell's 18th century apothecaries', *Kettering Leader and Guardian* (10 Sept 1909) · P. J. Wallis and R. V. Wallis, *Eighteenth century medics*, 2nd edn (1988) · P. J. Bishop, *A short history of the Royal Humane Society* (1974) · J. Sparks, *Collection of essays and tracts in theology* (1824) · Bath and North East Somerset Council Archives and Record Office, Bath and N E Somerset Council

Likenesses J. Sharples sen., pastels, 1803, City Museum and Art Gallery, Bristol · J. Basire, line engraving, pubd 1814 (after F. Gérard), BM, NPG, Wellcome L. [*see illus.*] · F. P. S. Gérard, ink miniature, Royal Humane Society, London · J. Thomson, engraving (after F. Gérard), Wellcome L. · aquatint and stipple silhouette, BM, NPG · aquatint silhouette, Wellcome L.

Wealth at death £14,000: PRO, death duty registers, IR 26/736, fols. 169–74

Cogan, William (1676/7–1774), apothecary and philanthropist, was probably born in Kingston upon Hull, the son of John Cogan (*d.* in or before 1694), a merchant, and his wife, Elizabeth, the daughter of John Battie, of Warmsworth, and Mary Pierrepoint, of Wadworth. His parents were married on 3 June 1662 at Wroot, Lincolnshire, where Cogan's paternal grandfather, John Coggan, was rector from 1641 to 1684. On 4 September 1694 he was bound as an apprentice to a London apothecary named either John or Isaac Garnier, and in December 1706 he was admitted to the freedom of Hull by right of patrimony. He quickly became involved in town politics and was elected chamberlain in 1712, sheriff in 1714, and alderman in March 1717. In July he sat for the first time on the bench, and on 30 September 1717 he was chosen mayor.

Cogan did not make his mark in Hull until his second mayoralty, in 1736–7, when he addressed the problem of the poor. A governor of the town workhouse since 1726, he ordered inspections of the hospitals and invested corporation funds in apprenticeships. He also sought to improve the streets and reduce shipping congestion on the Humber. Cogan's most significant legacy to the town was his foundation, in July 1753, of a charity school for girls, to be administered by three trustees: aldermen William Wilberforce and Samuel Watson and the recorder Cornelius Cayley. He endowed the charity with £2000 stock in consols and his own house in Bowlalley to establish a school 'for teaching and cloathing twenty poor female children and fitting them for household servants' (Attwood, 319). Twenty girls of ten years and above would be admitted for three years and taught reading and the church catechism as well as domestic skills such as sewing, knitting, and washing. Uniforms of brown wool dresses, blue cloaks, and white straw bonnets, all with an orange trim, were provided for the girls. On leaving the school they would be given a Bible and 20s. to buy clothes to fit them out for service. Several years later Cogan invested a further £500 in a trust that would give £6 to each girl on her marriage; the interest would be used to buy religious books. The school opened in a newly built house in Salthouse Lane in 1755 under its first mistress, Anna Stevens, who was paid a salary of £14. Cogan's school flourished into the nineteenth century and moved to larger premises in Park Street in 1889.

In his final years Cogan made provision for the town's boys: in a codicil to his will, dated 1 October 1772, he set aside £2000 as a trust to fund apprenticeships for boys at the age of twelve. Cogan was a widower when he drew up his will, but nothing is known of his wife or whether they had any children. He died in the town in 1774 and was buried in the Quire Yard of Holy Trinity Church on 22 July; the burial register records that he was ninety-seven. His lasting contribution to educational provision is commemorated in the name of one of the town's schools, the Alderman Cogan Church of England primary school.

S. J. SKEDD

Sources G. M. Attwood, 'Alderman William Cogan and the establishment of his charity school for girls, Hull', *Studies in Education*, 3 (1962), 314–30 • J. Tickell, *The history of the town and county of Kingston-upon-Hull* (1796), 834–6 • G. Hadley, *A new history of Kingston-upon-Hull* (1788), 874 • *GM*, 2nd ser., 45 (1856), 151 • P. Railton, *Hull schools in Victorian times* (1995) • *DNB*

Likenesses engraving (after painting by unknown artist), repro. in J. Symons, *Hullinia* (1872), facing p. 82 • oils, Wilberforce House, Hull • oils, Guildhall, Hull

Coggan, (Frederick) Donald, Baron Coggan (1909–2000), archbishop of Canterbury, was born on 9 October 1909 at 32 Croftdown Road, Highgate, Middlesex, the youngest child of Cornish Arthur Coggan, at one time national president of the Federation of Meat Traders and mayor of St Pancras, and his wife, Fanny Sarah Chubb. Frail as a child, he was sent to the Merchant Taylors' School in Northwood, and it was at the time of his confirmation in 1924 that he felt the call to the Anglican ministry. His sisters had encouraged him by introducing him to an evangelical church, and these early influences never left him. Coggan proved to be studious and won an exhibition, soon to be turned into a scholarship, at St John's College, Cambridge. He was outstanding in oriental languages, Hebrew, Aramaic, and Syriac, and won a first in both parts of the tripos examinations in 1930 and 1931. While still harbouring a vocation, strengthened by his prominent involvement in the Cambridge Inter-Collegiate Christian Union, he chose to stay in academia for three years as assistant lecturer in Semitic languages and literature at Manchester University.

Curacy and Canada Donald Coggan trained for the ministry at Wycliffe Hall, Oxford, a theological college with which he kept in touch for the rest of his life and of which he was a generous benefactor. He was ordained in St Paul's Cathedral on St Paul's day (25 January) 1934. He served his only parochial appointment as curate at St Mary's, Islington, from 1934 to 1937. They were formative years which drew on Coggan's natural pastoral gifts. At the time of his move to Canterbury he said, 'What I liked to do in York I should very much like to continue at Canterbury—to mix as much as possible with the ordinary people, for there, I think, you learn so much' (Connell). His experience as a curate in the poorest parts of north London gave him both a compassion for the people and a thirst to relate the truth of his faith to their needs. Somewhat against the convention of the time, Donald Coggan married during his curacy, on 17 October 1935. His wife, Jean Braithwaite Strain (*b*. 1907/8), was the daughter of a surgeon, and her

(Frederick) Donald Coggan, Baron Coggan (1909–2000), by Eve Arnold, 1963

strength of character, personal faith, and loving care provided the stability for the rest of Donald's life.

It was inevitable that Coggan's intellectual gifts would be in demand, and in 1937 he accepted an invitation to become professor of Wycliffe College in the University of Toronto (later he also served as dean). The theological college's reputation had declined, and Coggan vigorously set about restoring it. Soon he was in much demand as a teacher and preacher, and he made a strong impact in radio broadcasting. It was in Canada that he developed an interest in the theology and teaching of preaching. He travelled widely in North America, setting up schools of preaching and forging links with other teachers, many of whom became lifelong friends. During this period his doctrinal theology began to broaden. He was always content to be styled an evangelical, for that meant a love of the Bible and a missionary dynamic. But he gradually shed the more fundamentalist attitudes, which meant that while he lost the confidence of extremists, he accepted invitations to platforms which expected a broader view of scripture and a higher emphasis on tradition. In other words, he was becoming even more appreciative of the Anglican position of 'catholic and reformed'. In Canada, too, his family grew. His daughters, Ann, who became a schoolteacher, and Ruth, a lifelong medical missionary in Pakistan, brought enormous enjoyment and pride to both Donald and Jean.

London College of Divinity These intellectual and personal developments, together with a growing international reputation, fitted well when Coggan moved back to England in 1944 to become principal of the London College of Divinity. This theological college hardly existed, for its buildings in Highbury had been destroyed by bombs and its staff and students dispersed. For the first year Donald left Jean and their daughters in Canada while he set about gathering together a college in Lingfield in Sussex and then supervising the building of a new college in Northwood, Middlesex. (Some years later it was to move again and become St John's College, Nottingham.) Coggan was in his element, overseeing the formation of priests and teaching them the basics of a devout and evangelistic life. He led, by stricture and personal example, an energetic and disciplined regime. Always given to a simple, some might say austere, lifestyle, he expected high standards from staff and students alike. An example of this was that he always advocated reading the newspaper standing up so that the essentials were digested and the tittle-tattle ignored. His discipline enabled him to use his time to the full. He attracted to the staff some prominent people in the liberal evangelical world, such as Max Warren and Douglas Webster. The result was that not only was he able to inspire and preside over the reconstruction of the personnel and buildings of a college, but he was ready to accept many invitations to preach and to teach. His reputation blossomed across a wide spectrum of church life, and it was during this period that he attracted the admiration of Geoffrey Fisher, archbishop of Canterbury. Fisher described Coggan as 'like a man with a wheelbarrow; however much you pile on him, he goes on pushing' (*Daily Telegraph*). It was not surprising, therefore, when after eleven years at the London College of Divinity, the new buildings completed and inhabited, Donald Coggan was appointed bishop of Bradford in 1956.

Bishop of Bradford For a Londoner, Coggan took remarkably well to the north of England, and during his eighteen years there his admiration for Yorkshire people was matched by their affection for him. He was particularly drawn to their straightforwardness, lack of sophistication, and 'tribal' allegiances. The diocese of Bradford is banana-shaped, with the city of Bradford at one extreme. From it there stretched out the old textile and market towns of Bingley, Keighley, and Otley and, beyond them, the splendour of upper Airedale and Wharfedale. In the city itself the fortunes of the textile industry were beginning to decline, and there were the first signs of mass immigration, particularly from the Indian subcontinent, a movement which was to change the city's whole character and present new challenges to the churches.

The diocese itself showed signs of the overlong incumbency of Bishop Alfred Blunt, and Coggan showed his genius for assembling strong teams around him. Hubert Higgs (whom Coggan later attracted to York as bishop of Hull) was his able lieutenant in rebuilding the confidence of the diocese, overseeing the construction of five new churches, and teaching and encouraging the clergy.

Near the village of Kettlewell in upper Wharfedale,

Coggan was the prime mover in buying a manor house and setting up a largely lay community for the purposes of teaching, evangelism, and reflection. It strongly influenced church life in the north of England and became the venue for many of Coggan's subsequent initiatives. Bishopscroft, on the edge of the city and overlooking a spectacular Yorkshire landscape, became a place where the Coggan family offered relaxed hospitality, the bishop himself often entertaining his guests at the piano. Coggan was an accomplished pianist, and although in later years he had less time for music, his playing became a feature of the Lambeth conference in 1978.

During his time at Bradford, Coggan became increasingly active in national church life. For a time he was chairman of the liturgical commission (1960–64), and during these years he supervised the revision of the catechism and the psalter. He became a world vice-president of the United Bible Societies in 1957, an office which took him on strenuous world tours and kept him in touch with the arena of biblical scholarship for nearly twenty years. It was widely known that as Fisher was approaching his retirement at Canterbury, he favoured Coggan as his successor. He saw in him someone who could continue the considerable reforms to church law and administration which he himself had achieved. Coggan was invited to breakfast by the prime minister, Harold Macmillan, though no mention of appointments was made. However, the outcome was that Michael Ramsey moved to Canterbury from York and Coggan became archbishop of York in 1961.

Archbishop of York In many ways the moves were ideal, certainly for Donald Coggan and probably for the Church of England. In York he was able to build on his social and ecumenical contacts in the north. The position gave him a wider platform in which to exercise his national leadership without the huge complexities of Canterbury's role. Though Ramsey and Coggan never had an easy working relationship (Coggan was frustrated by Ramsey's lack of incisiveness and woolly chairmanship; Ramsey thought Coggan was too simplistic), the combination worked well for the church. They brought together the best of the breadth of the Church of England. Ramsey's undoubted depth and transparent spirituality were matched by Coggan's scholarly clarity and goodness.

Coggan used York as a platform for his increasing international activities. He took a leading part in the Anglican congress in Toronto in 1963, in the Lambeth conference of 1968, and in the Canadian congress on evangelism in 1970. He visited four continents at least twice while at York. In 1967 he undertook a gruelling tour which included major events in all the state capitals of Australia and the cities of New Zealand on behalf of the United Bible Societies, filling public halls and cathedrals with his lectures on the place of the Bible in modern society. On the same tour he visited the British armed forces bases in Singapore and Borneo, where as well as meeting the most senior officers he led retreats and teaching schools for service chaplains throughout the Far East.

York also provided the setting in which Coggan could

bring together two of his burning enthusiasms—for the unity of churches and their combined mission to the world. He exchanged fruitful visits with Cardinal Suenens of Brussels, who had been influenced by the charismatic movement and was keen to build on the Malines conversations between Roman Catholics and Anglicans. Coggan also drew together all the ecumenical leaders in the north of England and launched an evangelistic programme which became known as 'Call to the north'. Though it perhaps never achieved Coggan's highest hopes in terms of church growth, it did break new ground, and the successors of Coggan and other church leaders continued the movement, in various forms, into the twenty-first century.

Never content with initiating things solely through established structures, Coggan founded, and energetically promoted, Feed the Minds, an ecumenical programme for providing Christian literature to the third world, and also the English College of Preachers, in which he built on his experience of a similar organization in the USA. In each of these new ventures he was, again, adept at finding assistants of real calibre. John Hunter, Alec Gilmore, and Douglas Cleverley Ford became national figures in their own right, and David Blunt, Coggan's lay chaplain at York and the son of his predecessor at Bradford, was a genial general to Coggan's field marshal in all these activities.

Nationally, one of Coggan's greatest achievements during these years was presiding over the scholars who produced the *New English Bible* (1970). In the diocese itself, another initiative, Opportunity Unlimited, served to encourage the parishes in prayer, teaching, and visiting, the three planks on which Coggan believed the parochial ministry to be based. His early appointments of three suffragan bishops were highly successful. George Snow, a former headmaster of Ardingly, at Whitby; Douglas Sargent, a former missionary in China, at Selby; and Hubert Higgs, his former archdeacon in Bradford, at Hull—all provided thoughtful loyalty and stimulating companionship. The theologian Alan Richardson was dean of York and became a close friend and confidant.

Nevertheless, it was the energy, compassion, and integrity of Coggan himself that made him such a success at York. His preaching was unforgettable to clergy and laity alike. At confirmations and institutions he would often take a single Greek word and open up its meaning, leaving laity enlightened and encouraged and clergy thirsting for more study.

As was to prove the case at Canterbury, he was often described as the laymen's archbishop. He made friends easily with business leaders and workers alike. He was perhaps less at ease with the landed gentry of the Yorkshire farms and wolds, but they warmed to him for his active support of the York Civic Trust, led by John Shannon, and the rebuilding of the foundations of York Minster, and for his deep appreciation of the countryside.

Archbishop of Canterbury Canterbury was an altogether different prospect. Succeeding to the chair of St Augustine in 1974 at the age of sixty-five, Coggan had only five years

before he must retire, but he refused to be called a caretaker, except in the most literal meaning of the word. Certainly, his energy seemed undiminished. His attempts to translate 'Call to the north' into 'Call to the nation' and the national initiative in evangelism did not have the wholehearted support of the bishops. They perceived such initiatives as naïve in the face of the complexities of English society in the 1970s. They also felt insufficiently consulted—an indication, perhaps, that Coggan saw his time was limited.

Among the structures of church life, Coggan made an impact in his appeal for more ordinands and in fearless, yet dignified, speeches in general synod, where he was often critical of party spirit and sought to draw the church back to its fundamental mission. Coggan was particularly passionate in his promotion of women's ministry in the church (his wife was among the first women readers, and he lived to see the first women ordained to the priesthood in 1994) and in the field of Christian unity. Like Michael Ramsey, he was bitterly disappointed to witness the failure of several schemes for visible unity of the Anglican and Methodist churches. Coggan was an impatient ecumenist, and his call for intercommunion during his visit to the pope in 1977 was seen by some as prophetic, by others as theologically naïve, and by the Roman Catholic church as embarrassing. Nevertheless, he made a great personal impression by his sanctity, clarity, and warmth in Rome, Geneva, and Istanbul.

Coggan's speeches were seldom drafted for him. The positive side of this was that everything he said came from the heart and he was a powerful communicator. The downside was that he sometimes seemed out of his depth in dealing with the ethical and political matters of the day. By his own admission, he was never at home in the House of Lords, where his call for a minister for the family was regarded as politically impractical. In 1979 he condemned strikes as 'selfish', and with Stuart Blanch, another evangelical, at York, many in the church wanted to see him take a more robust and radical political stance.

Coggan saved his radicalism for what he believed to be the root-and-branch changes in personal life which followed an acceptance of the Christian faith. Changes in society would be the result. This was closer to Conservative ideology than to socialism, and it is significant that he struck chords with large numbers of ordinary men and women who brought Margaret Thatcher to power in 1979. In these respects Coggan caught the mood of the nation and the deep respect, if not always the agreement, of the church.

Retirement and writing Coggan retired in 1980, moving first to Sissinghurst and then to Winchester. For all but the final few months, the next twenty years were as full and productive as the previous forty. He was honoured with the Royal Victorian Chain, no doubt a recognition of his close pastoral relationship with some members of the royal family. In 1980 he was created Baron Coggan, though he rarely appeared in the House of Lords. He became vice-president of the Council of Christians and Jews and spent much time travelling and speaking on its behalf. He was much in demand as a lecturer and expositor of scripture. He became a close friend of David Scott, his vicar at St Swithun's, Winchester, and built up a large following of people who went to hear his Lenten addresses. Above all he continued writing. Some of his most notable books were practical theological teaching: *Stewards of Grace* (1958), *Convictions—Sermons and Addresses at York* (1975), *On Preaching* (1978), *Cuthbert Bardsley* (1989), and *Psalms—2 Volumes* (1999), completed just months before his death. Perhaps his most important book, written at York, was *Prayers of the New Testament* (1967), which combined his biblical scholarship with his deeply prayerful and pastoral heart.

Donald Coggan died at the Old Parsonage Nursing Home, Main Road, Otterbourne, near Winchester, on 17 May 2000, survived by his wife. His funeral service, followed by cremation, was held at St Swithun's, Winchester, on 26 May 2000. A memorial service was held in Winchester Cathedral on 30 June 2000.

To those who knew him, Donald Coggan will be remembered for the countless notes of sympathy, encouragement, and humour which he wrote even in his busiest times. They will remember his impish sense of humour, his gift of mimicry, and his ability to play a mischievous game of Scrabble. To writers of church history, who know that no man is perfect for all the demands which this world makes, Donald Coggan will, perhaps, be seen as a teacher of the faith who, by his energy and personal integrity, helped the Church of England to jettison its institutional nostalgia and face an increasingly secularized world with greater simplicity and clarity.

MICHAEL TURNBULL

Sources M. Pawley, *Donald Coggan: servant of Christ* (1987) • B. Connell, *The Times* (20 Jan 1975) • *The Times* (19 May 2000) • A. Arnott, *Wife to the archbishop* (1976) [biography of Jean Coggan] • *The Guardian* (19 May 2000) • *Daily Telegraph* (19 May 2000) • *The Independent* (19 May 2000) • Burke, *Peerage* (1999) • b. cert. • m. cert. • d. cert. • *CGPLA Eng. & Wales* (2000)

Archives Borth. Inst., papers as archbishop of York • Church of England Record Centre, London, corresp. and papers • LPL, corresp. and sermons | Borth. Inst., papers and photographs, incl. minutes of joint committee, convocations of York and Canterbury

Likenesses E. Arnold, photograph, 1963, NPG [*see illus.*] • photograph, repro. in *Daily Telegraph* • photograph, repro. in *The Times* (19 May 2000) • photograph, repro. in *The Guardian* • photograph, repro. in *The Independent*

Wealth at death £390,084—net: probate, 28 Sept 2000, *CGPLA Eng. & Wales*

Coggenhoe, Joan (*fl.* 1423). See under Women traders and artisans in London (*act. c.*1200–*c.*1500).

Coggeshall, Henry (*bap.* 1623, *d.* 1691), mathematician, was the third son of John Coggeshall of Orford in Suffolk, where he was baptized on 23 November 1623. He married, and left one son, William Coggeshall of Diss, Norfolk. He invented a sliding rule which was named after him and was first described by him in 1677 in a pamphlet entitled *Timber-measure by a line of more ease, dispatch, and exactness than any other way now in use, by a double scale. As also stone-measure and gauging of vessels by the same near and exact way. Likewise a diagonal scale of 100 parts in a quarter of an inch, very*

easie both to make and use. He soon after improved the rule, and revised the little work in which the mode of using it was explained, republishing it in 1682, with the heading *A Treatise of Measures by a Two-Foot Rule which Slides to a Foot*. A third, considerably modified, edition appeared in 1722. It was entitled *The Art of Practical Measuring Easily Performed by a Two-Foot Rule which Slides to a Foot*, and also contained 'Some useful instructions in decimal arithmetick', and 'Some useful directions in dialling not hitherto published'.

The Coggeshall rule was most often used in measuring areas and solids of timber masonry, brickwork, and the like. There were several further editions of his book and the instrument itself was popular in England as late as the beginning of the nineteenth century, remaining in use until the 1870s. Coggeshall was buried in Orford on 19 February 1691.   A. M. CLERKE, *rev.* H. K. HIGTON

Sources E. G. R. Taylor, *The mathematical practitioners of Tudor and Stuart England* (1954) • F. Cajori, *A history of the logarithmic slide rule* (1909) • C. Hutton, *A mathematical and philosophical dictionary*, 2 vols. (1795–6) • D. E. Davy, 'Athenae Suffolcienses, or, A catalogue of Suffolk authors with some account of their lives, and lists of their writings', 1847, BL, Add. MSS 19165–19168 [4 vols.] • parish register (baptisms), 23/11/1623, Orford, Suffolk • parish register (burials), 19/2/1691, Orford, Suffolk

Coggeshall, Ralph of (*fl.* 1207–1226), historian and abbot of Coggeshall, was a monk of the Cistercian abbey of Coggeshall, Essex. Abbot from 1207 until his resignation, because of illness, in 1218, he was the major contributor to, and may have been the sole author of, the Coggeshall chronicle known as the *Chronicon Anglicanum*. The precise extent of Ralph of Coggeshall's role in compiling the *Chronicon* is difficult to determine because the text's earliest surviving manuscript, BL, Cotton MS Vespasian D.x, contains several changes of hand and ink, which may indicate that Ralph of Coggeshall was only one of several annalists who worked on the *Chronicon*, but may alternatively be evidence that Ralph of Coggeshall merely employed a number of scribes to copy an autograph for which he was entirely responsible.

Certain significant conclusions in relation to the nature of Coggeshall's contribution to the writing of the *Chronicon* can, however, be reached despite such ambiguous indications. Pronounced stylistic parallels between the annals from 1187 to 1206 and those from 1213 to 1224, do, for instance, strongly suggest that these two sections of the text, which are, in fact, the major parts of the *Chronicon*, are the work of Ralph of Coggeshall who, as the text itself relates, 'wrote his chronicle from the capture of the Holy Cross' (*Chronicon Anglicanum*, 162–3). The existence of such robust evidence more than compensates for the impossibility of determining the extent of Ralph of Coggeshall's involvement in the compilation of two other, more skeletal, sections of the *Chronicon*, of which the first covers the period from 1066 to 1186 with annals which have presumably been inserted, *en bloc*, in order to preface Ralph of Coggeshall's coverage of later events, while the second covers the period from 1206 to 1212 with annals which seem to have been added, shortly after 1212, in order to make up for the loss of an earlier text. In the thirty or forty years to 1226, therefore, Ralph of Coggeshall was responsible for at least two sets of highly detailed annals which were compiled more or less contemporaneously with the events that they describe, and which may, since there is some evidence of an earlier recension of the *Chronicon*'s annals to 1195, have been subject to subsequent revision by their author.

Ralph of Coggeshall was not an innovative historian, since his *Chronicon* is, in terms of its structure, no more than a traditional set of monastic annals, in which he is content to refer to a standard cyclical view of history to treat the unexpected demise of a king as God's punishment for uncorrected sins, and the death of an archbishop as an *exemplum* of the transitory nature of earthly achievement. The annalist's writing is, however, remarkable because of the way in which he deploys his considerable narrative skills to enliven his *Chronicon* with striking descriptions, based usually on oral rather than written evidence, of such exotic Suffolk phenomena as the two green children of Woolpit and the merman of Orford, and of such dramatic incidents as the capture of Richard I by Leopold, duke of Austria, in 1192, and the hurricane at Newark which marked the death of John on the night of 18 October 1216.

Three early texts of the *Chronicon* are extant. That in Cotton MS Vespasian D.x may be, in part, an autograph. The nearly contemporary copies in the Bibliothèque Nationale, Paris (MS Lat. 15076), and the College of Arms, London (MS 11), are closely related to this earliest surviving version of the text. Certain commentators have argued that Ralph of Coggeshall was the author not only of the *Chronicon*, but also of the *Libellus de expugnatione Sanctae Terrae* and of a set of annals from 1162 to 1178 which were added to the work of Ralph Niger. It is evident, however, that neither text can be ascribed to him.

DAVID CORNER

Sources *Radulphi de Coggeshall chronicon Anglicanum*, ed. J. Stevenson, Rolls Series, 66 (1875) · A. Gransden, *Historical writing in England*, 1 (1974) · G. Morin, 'Le Cistercien Ralph de Coggeshall et l'auteur des *Distinctiones monasticae*', *Revue Bénédictine*, 47 (1935), 348–55 · F. M. Powicke, 'Roger of Wendover and the Coggeshall Chronicle', *EngHR*, 21 (1906), 286–96 · F. Wormald, 'The rood of Bromholm', *Journal of the Warburg Institute*, 1 (1937–8), 31–45
Archives Bibliothèque Nationale, Paris, MS Lat. 15076 [copy] · BL, Cotton MS Vespasian D.x · Coll. Arms, MS 11 [copy]

Coghill, Marmaduke (1673–1739), judge and politician, was born in co. Dublin on 28 December 1673, the eldest son of Sir John Coghill (d. 1699?), formerly of Coghill Hall in Yorkshire, and of Hester Cramer, a descendant of Colonel Tobias von Cramer, of Swabian origin, who had settled in Ireland earlier in the century. Having entered Trinity College, Dublin, Coghill graduated BA and LLB in 1691 and was made LLD in 1695. Elected first, in 1692, to sit in the Irish House of Commons for co. Armagh he continued to sit in the house from 1713 onwards as a member for Trinity. In the Commons, following the accession of George I, Coghill was to align himself with like-minded individuals in Speaker Conolly's group. In 1699 Coghill succeeded his

father as judge of the Irish prerogative court, an elevation that began his close involvement with the affairs of the established Church of Ireland.

The post involved Coghill in deciding on grants of faculties but weightier business soon supervened. Under English legislation of 1701 Coghill was named one of six trustees for forfeited Irish impropriations, the income from which was to be used to build churches and to augment small vicarages. The restoration by Queen Anne's government in 1711 of the first fruits added to Coghill's administrative tasks. An original commissioner of the resultant board he was to earn plaudits as 'the great, and indeed principal cause of the numerous benefits' that accrued to the established church from the restoration (Taylor, 419). Coghill was also associated with the administration of the complementary augmentation scheme devised by Archbishop Hugh Boulter.

At the outset, the relationship between Coghill and Boulter was prickly enough. Coghill made no secret of his disenchantment over the choice of Boulter for the prelacy in 1727 but a *modus vivendi* soon emerged, despite Boulter's suspicion (which he never shrugged off) that Coghill was more sympathetic to the 'Irish interest' than was appropriate or the situation demanded. Boulter supported Coghill's appointment in 1729 as a commissioner of the revenue (which earned him a seat in the privy council), and six years later no objection was raised to his promotion to fill the largely honorific role of chancellor of the Irish exchequer.

Coghill's correspondence with the two Edward Southwells, father and son, successive Irish secretaries of state, reveals considerable political acumen, and nowhere is this clearer than in his blow-by-blow account (which elements in the London administration must surely have welcomed) of the crisis that unfolded over the attempt, initiated in 1722, to foist Wood's halfpence on a recalcitrant country.

As judge of the prerogative Coghill dealt with matters of testate and intestate succession, but questions of marriage law could equally come before him, and one celebrated decision of his in the latter area was destined to enter local folklore; it also explains why he never married. According to Deane Swift, Marmaduke:

> courted a lady, and was soon to have been married to her; but unfortunately a cause was brought to trial before him, wherein a man was sued for beating his wife. When the matter was agitated, the doctor gave his opinion, 'That, although a man had no right to beat his wife unmercifully, yet that with such a little cane or switch as he then held in his hand, a husband was at liberty, and was invested with a power to give his wife moderate correction'; which opinion determined the lady against the doctor.   (Swift, 1.304)

Gravely ill from gout and attendant complications Coghill resigned his judgeship in January 1739. He proposed a kinsman, Nathaniel Bland, as his successor, but Boulter, who had control of the appointment, refused Bland a permanency. Coghill witnessed only the first instalment of the ensuing crisis (resolved finally by a chancery decree in 1741) for he died on 9 March 1739. He was buried in the family vault in St Andrew's Church, Dublin. A handsome marble monument to him, by Peter Scheemakers, was erected by his sister Mary in Drumcondra Church of Ireland church. A lengthy inscription pays tribute to his virtues, which were also recalled in an anonymous tribute, 'The Wonderful Man', penned in the 1720s:

His Favours never yet were bought,
And often come, tho' never sought.

A portrait of Coghill hangs in All Hallows College in Dublin, which incorporates Drumcondra House, the fine Georgian mansion Coghill built for himself about 1725.

W. N. Osborough

Sources B. C. A. Windle, 'A genealogical note on the family of Cramer or Coghill', *Journal of the Cork Historical and Archaeological Society*, 2nd ser., 16 (1910), 66–81 · J. Swift, *Journal to Stella*, ed. H. Williams, 1 (1948), 304–5 · J. P. Campbell, 'Two memorable Dublin houses', *Dublin Historical Record*, 2/4 (1939–40), 141–55 · F. E. Ball, *The judges in Ireland, 1221–1921*, 2 (1926), 103–4 · *Letters written by … Hugh Boulter … to several ministers of state*, ed. [A. Philips and G. Faulkner], 2 vols. (1769–70); repr. (1770) · W. B. S. Taylor, *History of the University of Dublin* (1845) · *Boulter v. Bland*, Col. U., Singleton MS, 45 · correspondence between Coghill and Edward Southwell, 1735–8, NL Ire., MSS 875–876 · correspondence between Coghill and Edward Southwell, 1722–35, BL, Add. MSS 21122–21123 · Burtchaell & Sadleir, *Alum. Dubl.* · *Journal of the Association for the Preservation of the Memorials of the Dead, Ireland*, 2 (1892–4), 78; 7 (1907–9), 542 · 'The wonderful man', TCD, A.7.4, no. 130 · R. Mant, *History of the Church of Ireland*, 2 vols. (1840) · W. A. Phillips, ed., *History of the Church of Ireland*, 3 (1933) · monumental inscription, Drumcondra Church of Ireland parish church, co. Dublin · 'Coghill, Marmaduke', E. Johnston-Liik, *History of the Irish parliament, 1692–1800*, 6 vols. (2002), vol. 3, pp. 442–5

Archives NL Ire., MSS, MS 875; MS 876 | BL, letters to Edward Southwell, Add. MSS 21122–21123 · TCD, corresp. with William King

Likenesses P. Scheemakers, effigy on monument, Church of Ireland parish church, Drumcondra, Dublin · oils, All Hallows College, Dublin

Coghill, Nevill Henry Kendal Aylmer (1899–1980), university teacher and theatre producer, was born on 19 April 1899 at Castle Townshend, Skibbereen, co. Cork, the second of the three sons (the youngest child was a daughter) of Sir Egerton Bushe Coghill, fifth baronet, a noted amateur landscape painter, of Glen Barrahane, Castle Townshend, and his wife, (Elizabeth) Hildegarde Augusta, the younger daughter of Colonel (Thomas) Henry Somerville and sister of the writer Edith Anna Oenone Somerville. He was educated at Bilton Grange, a preparatory school on the edge of Rugby, Warwickshire, and at Haileybury, Hertfordshire, and served as second lieutenant in the trench mortar division of the Royal Artillery in Salonika and Bulgaria during the last few months of the First World War. In 1919 he went up as a scholar to Exeter College, Oxford, to read history, being placed in the second class in 1922. He then spent part of a recent legacy on an additional year at Oxford reading English under the tuition of F. P. Wilson, later Merton professor, and gaining a first class in 1923. After a short period of teaching at the Royal Naval College, Dartmouth, he was elected a research fellow of Exeter in 1924 and became an official fellow and librarian in 1925. In 1927 he married Elspeth Nora, daughter of Richard James Harley, a medical practitioner, of Inchture, Perthshire. The couple had one daughter; they divorced in 1933.

Nevill Henry Kendal Aylmer Coghill (1899–1980), by Ramsey & Muspratt, 1944

In Oxford Coghill led an in-college bachelor existence, extending warm and generous hospitality to students and younger colleagues. In the dedication to *Letters from Iceland* (1937) his pupil W. H. Auden wrote:

To Neville [sic] Coghill, fellow of Exeter, my tutor
I leave Das Lebendigste with which to form alliance.

This alludes to a line in the German poet Friedrich Hölderlin's *Sokrates und Alkibiades* (translated as 'He who has pondered the deepest things loves what is most alive') and expresses Auden's hope that Coghill might find a satisfying sexual love.

Coghill's dramatic productions began with Milton's *Samson Agonistes* in Exeter College garden in 1930, and he went on to produce many plays and some operas for the Oxford University Dramatic Society, the Oxford University Opera Club, and various college societies, mostly in the open air. These spectacles, which became something of a legend at Oxford, included Shakespeare's *Troilus and Cressida* in 1937, *The Winter's Tale* in 1946, and *Hamlet* in 1940 (on an apron stage). *The Masque of Hope*, which he organized and wrote with Glynne Wickham, was presented at University College, Oxford, to Princess Elizabeth in 1948. *The Tempest*, staged in 1949 in Worcester College gardens, was remembered for one of Coghill's most magical effects: Ariel appeared to run across the surface of the lake (supported, in fact, by a gangway hidden just beneath water-level).

Coghill's translations from Middle English began as a series of broadcasts of selections from *The Canterbury Tales* (first series, 1946–7; second series, 1949) for BBC radio. His complete translation of the *Tales* (Penguin Classics, 1951) was extremely popular, creating for the first time since the middle ages a nationwide audience for Chaucer. On the retirement of F. P. Wilson from the Merton chair of English literature in 1957, Coghill was elected his successor—much to his surprise, according to Lord David Cecil, and much to the chagrin of Helen Gardner, whom some regarded as a more eligible candidate, and who succeeded him in the chair. In 1959 he gave the Clark lectures, published as *Shakespeare's Professional Skills* (1964).

Coghill remained an inspiration to generations of undergraduates in Oxford theatre and in 1966, the year of his retirement, directed Richard Burton (a former pupil) and Elizabeth Taylor in Marlowe's *Doctor Faustus* at the Oxford Playhouse. The film of *Doctor Faustus*, with almost the same cast, was shot in Rome the following year, with Coghill and Burton co-directing. This was followed, in 1968, by his highly successful musical stage version (with Martin Starkie) of *The Canterbury Tales*, which ran for five years at the Phoenix Theatre, London, was also shown for a period on Broadway, and toured Europe and Australia. Coghill was elected a fellow of the Royal Society of Literature in 1950 and had honorary doctorates from Williams College, Massachusetts (1966), and the University of St Andrews (1971). He died in a nursing home in Cheltenham, on 6 November 1980.

Brought up in the old-world atmosphere of the south of Ireland, where sailing, fishing, hunting, shooting, and the painting of pictures provided gentlemanly pleasures, Coghill had the easy grace of the consummate amateur. A tall, handsome figure with rather leonine features, he was known in Oxford for the charm and vivacity of his conversation and the fineness of his taste.   JOHN CAREY

Sources *The Times* (10 Nov 1980) · D. Cecil, *Postmaster* [magazine of Merton College, Oxford University] (1981) · personal knowledge (2004) · private information (2004) · *Prose and travel books in prose and verse*, ed. E. Mendelson, 1 (1996), 370, 795 · *CGPLA Eng. & Wales* (1980)
Archives Bodl. Oxf. · Merton Oxf., letters concerning Rossetti and drawing of Marie Spartali Stillman | SOUND Merton Oxf., tape of Coghill reading
Likenesses Ramsey & Muspratt, photograph, bromide print, 1944, NPG [*see illus.*]
Wealth at death £94,800: probate, 22 Dec 1980, *CGPLA Eng. & Wales*

Coghlan, Charles Francis (*c.*1842–1899). *See under* Coghlan, Rose (1851–1932).

Coghlan, Sir Charles Patrick John (1863–1927), premier of Southern Rhodesia, was born at King William's Town, Cape Colony, on 24 June 1863, the third son of James Coghlan JP of Cypherfontein and later of Clocolan, Orange Free State, soldier, civil servant, and farmer, and his wife, Isabella Mary MacLaren, of Alice, Cape Colony. His early education was supervised by a 'resident schoolmaster', a rifleman named Broomhall. Subsequently he was educated at the Jesuit-run St Aidan's College, Grahamstown (1875–81), and the South African College, Cape Town. In 1882 he was articled to his brother James, a solicitor in Kimberley,

where he remained until 1900, when he moved to Bulawayo in Southern Rhodesia. He was widely regarded as an outstanding lawyer.

Coghlan's political development was crucially influenced by his Catholicism, inherited from his Irish father and Scottish highland mother, his legal training, and eastern Cape upbringing. In 1891 a St Patrick's day dinner in Kimberley provided him with his first public platform, when he called for vengeance on British politicians for their coercive Irish policy. This fiery and persuasive brand of oratory, together with personal innuendo that was often unscrupulous, proved to be enduring characteristics of his political style. He combined Irish home rule and Gladstonian Liberal sympathies with a deep attachment to the crown and a Burkean reverence for the British constitution. In 1897 he joined the pro-imperial South African League and strengthened his imperial and eastern Cape connections with his marriage in 1899 to Gertrude Mary Schermbrücker, daughter of Colonel Frederick Xavier Schermbrücker, ex-German legionary, MP for King William's Town, sometime eastern Cape separatist, and an avowed imperialist.

After arriving in Bulawayo he became legal adviser to the municipality and to the Chamber of Mines and junior partner to P. D. Frames, a prominent settler leader. By this time Coghlan's political outlook, based on his experience of the eastern Cape and Kimberley, had become rooted in a deep antipathy to the parliament at Cape Town, and a conviction that no settler community should depend on a monopoly capitalist company. He regarded the western Cape as remote and unsympathetic to the economic, racial, and security anxieties of the 'frontier'. These beliefs were greatly strengthened in Bulawayo. He soon developed a strong provincial loyalty to Matabeleland, regarding Salisbury as neglectful and dominated by civil servants, capitalists, and farmers. Rhodesian politics at this time were highly localized, based on a handful of elected members of the legislative council who were subject to pressure from various interest groups, including miners, farmers, merchants, and artisans. Political debate concentrated on the form of government which might succeed the British South Africa Company. The options included amending or abrogating the company's charter, representative or responsible government, amalgamating with Northern Rhodesia or the Transvaal, and, after 1910, integrating as a fifth province with the Union of South Africa. Coghlan never believed it was his role to guide public opinion. He distrusted grand geopolitical schemes such as those which motivated Cecil Rhodes and, later, General Jan Christian Smuts. Coghlan remained a follower, rather than a leader, of public opinion, reacting quickly to settler anxieties which transcended sectional interests, including the fear of African uprising and of sexual attack by black men on white women—the so-called 'black peril'. On several occasions he championed the settlers' right to resort to lynch law in such cases, if the government did not make attempted and actual rape capital offences.

Coghlan entered politics in 1901 in support of the movement for abrogation of the company's charter, and, as an acknowledged settler leader, he attended a conference in Salisbury in 1904 to discuss proposals for a financial settlement with the company. Sensing the public mood, he rejected the scheme, excusing himself from further discussions in London on the pretext of unavoidable professional duties. He also refused offers of the Matabeleland Political Association vice-presidency and nomination as candidate for the legislative council. In 1907, however, he represented Southern Rhodesia in negotiations with the company. A year later he was elected to the legislative council for the western division. His legal expertise and argumentative parliamentary style became highly valued in attacking the company's claim to own all unalienated land.

Coghlan was one of the Southern Rhodesian delegates to the South African National Convention of 1908–9, where he helped to draw up the clause of the union constitution which provided for the future accession of Southern Rhodesia, but he reluctantly accepted the union's unitary constitution, with Cape Town as its legislative capital. The erosion of provincial powers at the convention's committee stage further weakened his early enthusiasm for union. In 1912 he resisted the campaign of the Rhodesian League for a crown colony form of government as a preliminary to full responsible government. He also strongly opposed amalgamation with Northern Rhodesia as an alternative to the union, proposed by the company in 1916, on the ground that this would frustrate Southern Rhodesian ambitions to remain a 'white man's country'. He soon sensed a change in public opinion after the establishment in 1917 of the Responsible Government Association (RGA) by Mrs Ethel Tawse Jollie and John (Jock) McChlery. Essentially a representative of townsmen and small miners, Coghlan accepted the RGA presidency in 1919, by which time it had become clear that it had outgrown its farming connections. He echoed a widespread settler fear that union might bring a large influx of poor white Afrikaners and thus dilute and destroy the territory's Britishness. Strengthened by the privy council judgment against the company on the question of unalienated land, the RGA was victorious in the 1920 general election, but it still faced a powerful coalition of Rhodesian unionists, including the company and leading mining corporations. The British and South African governments regarded Southern Rhodesian accession as essential to bolster the pro-Commonwealth interest led by Smuts against General Hertzog's nationalists and the emerging power of labour. Coghlan rejected these appeals to a wider patriotism, along with Smuts's offer of cabinet rank in the union, and in 1922, in a campaign marked by widespread anti-Afrikaner xenophobia, the responsible government cause was carried by a majority of three to two. The victory owed much to Coghlan's oratory and the votes of artisans, merchants, and minor civil servants who felt threatened by union. Also crucial was the efficient running of the RGA by Mrs Tawse Jollie, for Coghlan preferred the convivial political atmosphere of the hotel lounge and the clubhouse to the tedium of party organization.

In 1923 Coghlan became premier, and his Rhodesia Party, formerly the RGA, proved in government to be more conservative and deferential to the administrative and economic inheritance of the British South Africa Company than its earlier populist and anti-capitalist character had suggested. He came to regret his earlier statements on native affairs and sought, in inter-racial cases, to preserve judicial independence against settler prejudice. He neglected his legal career and remained financially, in his own words, a 'poor man'. He had lived all his adult life in hotels, and never owned a house of his own. His political achievements were widely recognized. In 1910 he was created knight bachelor for his services in the South African convention, and in 1925 he was made a KCMG. Trinity College, Dublin, honoured him with an LLD in 1926, by which time he had become disillusioned with Ireland's separatist course. He died suddenly at home in Salisbury on 28 August 1927 and was buried two days later in the Roman Catholic section of the Bulawayo cemetery. In a written request, opened after his death, he asked the legislative assembly to provide for his widow and daughter. In 1930 the legislative assembly decided that he was one who had, in terms of Rhodes's will, 'deserved well of his country', and his remains were reinterred at World's View, in the Matopo Hills, near to the graves of Rhodes and Jameson. He was survived by his wife and daughter.

DONAL LOWRY

Sources J. P. R. Wallis, *One man's hand: the story of Sir Charles Coghlan and the liberation of Southern Rhodesia* (1950) · L. Hastings, review of *One man's hand*, *African Affairs*, 50 (1951), 167–8 · H. C. Hummel, 'A political biography of Sir Charles Coghlan', PhD diss., U. Lond., 1975 · H. C. Hummel, 'Sir Charles Coghlan: some reflections on his political attitudes and style', *South African Historical Journal*, 9 (1977), 59–79 · M. E. Lee, 'Politics and pressure groups in Southern Rhodesia, 1898–1923', PhD diss., U. Lond., 1974 · M. E. Lee, 'The origins of the Responsible Government movement', *Rhodesian History*, 6 (1975), 33–52 · M. E. Lee, 'An analysis of the Rhodesian referendum, 1922', *Rhodesian History*, 8 (1977), 71–98 · D. Lowry, '"White woman's country": Ethel Tawse Jollie and the making of white Rhodesia', *Journal of Southern African Studies*, 23 (1997), 259–82 · W. J. de Kock, ed., 'F. X. Schermbrücker', *DSAB*, 1.690 · Letter from Petal Coghlan to Sir Francis Newton, 26 Sept 1927, priv. coll., Newton MSS [in the hands of Mrs Susan Hummel, Grahamstown, South Africa] · drafts of letters sent 1925–6 (bequeathed to the National Archives by Mrs Joyce Baxter, *née* Webb, former personal secretary to Coghlan), and misc. Coghlan family MSS (bequeathed to the National Archives by Mrs Coghlan-Chennells, Coghlan's daughter), National Archives of Zimbabwe, CO unclassified
Archives National Archives of Zimbabwe, Harare, corresp. and papers | National Archives of Zimbabwe, Harare, Sir Francis Percy Drummond Chaplin MSS, general corresp. · National Archives of Zimbabwe, Harare, British South Africa Company records · PRO, Colonial Office records; original corresp. · PRO, Commonwealth Relations (formerly Dominions) Office records, original corresp.
Likenesses J. Tweed, statue; formerly in the gardens of the City Hall, Bulawayo, 1980
Wealth at death claimed he was poor, leaving family poorly provided for; seemingly never owned house: letter, 10 Dec 1926, to be opened on death, cited Wallis, *One man's hand*, 243–4

Coghlan, James Peter (1731?–1800), Roman Catholic printer and publisher, probably born on 22 October 1731 in Preston, Lancashire, was the son of James Coghlan (d. 1776), stonecutter, and Elizabeth Coghlan (d. 1760). In 1754, after an apprenticeship with Samuel Cope, book-binder of the parish of St James, Westminster, Coghlan established his own business as a bookbinder and sta-tioner. Coghlan's own 'Memorandum book', in which he noted down detailed technical information about the material and the tools purchased when he started his busi-ness, gives a unique insight into the practical background of the bookbinding trade in the 1750s. At least two of Coghlan's early bindings have been preserved and they are admired for their outstanding quality: Charles Barbandt's *Sacred Hymns, Anthems etc.* (1766) and Thomas Meighan's *The Office of the Holy Week* (1766).

On 6 February 1760 Coghlan married Elizabeth Brown (1728–1799) of Clifton-cum-Salwick, near Preston. There were six children of this marriage, four of whom, Peter, Elizabeth, Ann, and William, entered the religious life, William becoming a secular priest. Coghlan soon added printing to his business. Certainly as early as 1764 he brought out his own edition of the *Laity's Directory* as a rival publication to the one published by James Marmaduke. This *Directory*, published on Marmaduke's own authority from 1758 onwards, was a simple religious calendar to which were added some small features such as lives of saints and martyrs. Coghlan's rival edition, published 'by permission and with approbation' of the Roman Catholic episcopate, easily eclipsed Marmaduke's edition. Grow-ing steadily from thirty pages to more than ninety by the end of the century, Coghlan's *Directory* came to contain all the elements of a Catholic newsletter: pastoral letters, instructions for the observation of Lent and other direct-ives, obituaries, and advertisements for Catholic educa-tional institutes, besides Coghlan's own book catalogues.

After Coghlan had taken over the stock of Thomas Meighan's declining firm in 1774, he was the most import-ant printer, publisher, and bookseller for the English Catholic community. In the 1780s Coghlan published a large number of documents relating to the Catholic strug-gle for emancipation that were issued by the Catholic Committee. He played an important part as an intermedi-ary in the Catholic community of his time. He had con-tacts with a great many prominent Catholics, notably George Hay, who was the leading prelate of the Catholic church in Scotland. For many years he took care of young students who went by ship from London to the continent to be trained at one of the Catholic colleges abroad. From 1790 onwards Coghlan was closely involved in the relief operations for the benefit of English Catholic religious orders when the revolution forced them to abandon their monasteries and houses in northern France and Belgium. Coghlan used his influence with members of parliament and customs officials to obtain passports, collect funds, and find accommodation for the refugees.

Coghlan's correspondence gives a very good picture of the life of English Catholics during the final quarter of the eighteenth century. Coghlan was a devout and deeply reli-gious person and a confirmed Catholic. He died at 37 Duke Street, Grosvenor Square, London, on 20 February 1800, and the *Laity's Directory* for the year 1801 had the following obituary: 'Mr. J. P. Coghlan … upwards of 40 years Catholic Printer and bookseller, No 37 Duke Street, Grosvenor Square, age 68'. His last will and testament, signed 18 Feb-ruary 1800, was proved 15 March 1800 by the oath of his son William. Coghlan's business was taken over by his nephew Richard Brown, who, soon acting under the name of Keating, Brown, and Keating, continued to use Cogh-lan's name in the imprints of his publications for some time.

J. L. C. STEENBRINK

Sources B. C. Foley, *Some people of the penal times (chiefly 1688–1791)* (1991) · H. M. Nixon, 'The memorandum book of James Coghlan: the stock of an 18th-century printer and binder', *Journal of the Print-ing Historical Society*, 6 (1970), 33–52 · G. Anstruther, 'Catholic mid-dle class in the London of 1800', *London Recusant*, 6 (1976), 37–57, 81–94 · J. P. Coghlan, 'Memorandum book', BL, Add. MS 70932 · Lancs. RO, Coghlan papers, RCBu · Scottish Catholic Archives, Edin-burgh, Bishop Hay MSS · Gillow, *Lit. biog. hist.* · F. Blom and others, *English Catholic books, 1701–1800: a bibliography* (1996) · J. M. Blom, *The post-Tridentine English primer* (1982) · *The Mawhood diary: selections from the diary note-books of William Mawhood, woollen-draper of London, for the years 1764–1770*, ed. E. E. Reynolds, Catholic RS, 50 (1956) · Dublin Roman Catholic archdiocese, Archbishop Troy MSS · PRO, PROB 8/193 [will of J. P. Coghlan]
Archives BL, Add. MS 70932 · Lancs. RO, RCBu-14 | Dublin Roman Catholic archdiocese, Archbishop Troy MSS · Scottish Catholic Archives, Edinburgh, Bishop Hay MSS
Wealth at death £2000: will, PRO, PROB 8/193

Coghlan, Jeremiah (1774/5–1844), naval officer, was in January 1796 mate of a merchant ship at Plymouth, and on the occasion of the wreck of the East Indiaman *Dutton* dis-played such energy and courage that Pellew offered to put him on the *Indefatigable*'s quarter-deck. He continued for three years in the *Indefatigable* and in March 1799 followed Pellew to the *Impétueux*.

In June 1800 Coghlan was put by Pellew in command of the cutter *Viper*, and while watching Port Louis proposed to cut out a French gun-vessel at the entrance of the har-bour. Pellew lent him a ten-oared cutter, and in this, with eighteen men and a midshipman—Silas Hiscutt Paddon—on the night of 29 July, he boarded the gun-brig *Cerbère* and after a hard fight captured her 'within pistol-shot of three batteries, surrounded by several armed craft, and not a mile from a 74 bearing an admiral's flag, and two frigates' (E. Pellew, *Despatch*). Both Coghlan and Paddon received several severe wounds, six of Coghlan's men were wounded, and one was killed; but the *Cerbère* was taken and towed out under heavy fire from the batteries. The squadron, to mark their admiration, gave up the prize to the immediate captors; and Pellew, in his official letter to Lord St Vincent, emphasized the courage and skill 'which … effected so daring an enterprise' (ibid.). St Vin-cent, in forwarding Pellew's letter to the Admiralty, praised the achievement and in a letter to Pellew privately asked him to present to Coghlan a sword of 100 guineas' value.

On St Vincent's representation, Coghlan, though he had

served in the navy for only four and a half years, was promoted lieutenant on 22 September 1800 and continued in command of the *Viper* until she was paid off in October 1801. In spring 1802 he was appointed to the cutter *Nimble*, and on 1 May 1804 was promoted to command the sloop *Renard* on the Jamaica station. On 20 March 1805 he brought to action the French privateer *Général Ernouf*, which, after an action of thirty-five minutes, was set on fire and blew up with the loss of upwards of a hundred men. In August 1807 Coghlan was moved into the brig *Elk* on the same station, and for nearly four years was senior officer of a light squadron for the protection of the Bahamas. He was promoted captain on 27 November 1810 but continued in the *Elk* until the following summer.

In September 1812 Coghlan was appointed to the *Caledonia* as flag captain of Pellew, then commander-in-chief in the Mediterranean. At the end of 1813 he exchanged into the frigate *Alcmène* and continued in her until the end of the Napoleonic wars. On 4 June 1815 he was nominated a CB, and from 1826 to 1830 commanded the frigate *Forte* on the South American station.

Coghlan married a daughter of Charles Hay of Jamaica, widow of Captain John Marshall RN; they had no surviving children. He died at Ryde, Isle of Wight, on 4 March 1844, aged sixty-nine.

J. K. LAUGHTON, *rev.* ROGER MORRISS

Sources J. Marshall, *Royal naval biography*, suppl. 2 (1828), 298 · O'Byrne, *Naval biog. dict.* · W. James, *The naval history of Great Britain, from the declaration of war by France in 1793, to the accession of George IV*, [4th edn], 6 vols. (1847), vol. 3, pp. 20–21; vol. 4, p. 26 · J. C. Dalrymple Hay, *Lines from my log book* (1898), 20 · E. P. Brenton, *The naval history of Great Britain, from the year 1783 to 1836*, 2 (1837), 510–11

Coghlan, Rose (1851–1932), actress, was born in Peterborough, Lincolnshire, on 18 March 1851, the daughter of Francis Coghlan, the author and publisher of *Coghlan's Continental Guides*, and his wife, Anna Marie, *née* Kirby. Her elder brother **Charles Francis Coghlan** (*c.*1842–1899), who was born in Paris, and to whom she was very close, studied law and later decided on a career in the theatre; Rose followed him on to the stage. Rose Coghlan made her first appearance at the Theatre Royal in Greenock, Renfrewshire, in 1865, playing one of the witches in *Macbeth*, and made her London début as Pippo in *Linda of Chamouni* (Old Gaiety, September 1869). In the early 1870s she met the actor–manager Charles Calvert, who cast her as Nerissa in a production of *The Merchant of Venice*.

Coghlan went to the United States in 1872 to work with Lydia Thompson's burlesque company, and it was there that she built a solid reputation as a leading actress, performing major roles until the early 1920s. She acquired American citizenship in 1902. In the 1880s she became a leading lady with Lester Wallack's stock company, and in such roles as Rosalind in *As You Like It* (1880), Stephanie in *Forget-me-Not* (1880), and Lady Teazle in *The School for Scandal* (1882) she was a considerable critical and popular success. J. Rankin Towse termed her Lady Teazle 'one of the best witnessed by this generation' (Towse, 409). Frederic Edward McKay wrote of her as Rosalind: 'Miss Coghlan has conceived the character as it existed in the mind of the master, and represents it with a fidelity to truth almost marvelous in its near approach to perfection' (*New York Star*, 1 Oct 1880).

Many critics commented on the quality of Coghlan's voice. McKay praised her 'mellifluous vocalism': 'it seemed to me the Aeolian harp had been revivified' (McKay and Wingate, 250); another added, 'what a resonant, silvery, mellow voice it is'. Rose, a buxom, golden-haired woman of medium height, with large blue eyes, was a natural for comic roles, and critics praised once and again her 'romping spirits' and 'sportive gaiety' in such parts as Rosalind and Lady Gay Spanker (in *London Assurance*). During her years with Wallack's company she married the lawyer Clinton J. Edgerly (in April 1885), but the marriage soon failed and Edgerly sued her for divorce on grounds of desertion in September 1890. In the 1880s she also adopted a daughter, Rosalind Agnes Coghlan (*b.* 1881).

Charles Coghlan, meanwhile, was building his reputation in England, where he became known as a perfect type of the modern gentleman. With his dark-haired good looks, he perfected an urbane and easy manner, what critics termed his 'reserve force', and established his theatrical reputation during the Bancrofts' management of the Prince of Wales's Theatre in the 1870–76 seasons. He was a natural for the toned-down realism of Tom Robertson's plays. The critic Clement Scott was a naysayer, however, writing in Coghlan's obituary that his '"reserve force" was merely loss of memory and the inability to make the brain act as quickly as it should'. His style was described as 'so easy, so natural'—a quality that worked well in such plays as Bulwer-Lytton's *Money* (1872) but proved disastrous in the production of *The Merchant of Venice* (1875), in which Coghlan played Shylock: 'In light comedy he had often held his forces in reserve with great effect. Here he did it to such bad purpose that his performance nearly ruined the Bancrofts.' His subdued characterization, dubbed the 'Drawing-Room Shylock', went counter to the tradition of fierce and emotional acting of the part. Clement Scott termed his Shylock 'an absolute inanimate being, without force, without movement, without love, without hate, without expression' (*The Drama of Yesterday and Today*, 1899, 1.585).

Soon afterwards Coghlan went to the USA and played at Daly's and Palmer's Union Square Theatre in New York, where he assumed such roles as Lovelace in *Clarissa Harlowe* and Jean Renaud in *A Celebrated Case* (1878). He continued to work in England as well, playing Antony to Lillie Langtry's Cleopatra in 1890, at the Princess's Theatre. Some critics still could not bear his style in a Shakespearian context; G. B. Shaw summed up his Mercutio at the Lyceum in 1895, noting that 'he lounges' (*Dramatic Opinions and Essays*, 1901, 1.188); Shaw did approve, however, of his performance as the seducer in *A Woman's Reason* (Shaftsbury, 1895): 'Mr. Coghlan created the part, like a true actor, by the simple but very unusual method of playing it from his own point of view' (*Our Theatres in the Nineties*, 1932, 2.5). Coghlan also continued to try his hand as a playwright. His first play, *Good as Gold*, had been produced at the Lyceum in 1868; *Enemies* was produced at the Princess's in 1886.

In 1885 Rose Coghlan had set up her own company in New York, a short-lived venture; she continued to work with Wallack until his retirement in 1888. In 1893 she staged the first American production of Oscar Wilde's *A Woman of No Importance*, and with Charles she revived *Diplomacy* in 1892–3. Her reputation for high-spiritedness remained, and extended into her personal life. She had a second, rather tempestuous marriage to the actor John Taylor Sullivan, beginning on 7 June 1893 (the couple divorced on 11 June 1904); the newspapers followed the ups and downs of her private life, even reporting with horror in 1893 that she rode astride, 'like a dragoon', in Central Park. Her brother caused a scandal of his own in October 1893 when he married the heiress Kuhne Beveridge; it was generally assumed that he was already married to Blanche Wilson, whom he had presented as his wife for many years and with whom he had a daughter, Gertrude (*b.* 1878). The marriage to Beveridge incited much press coverage and led to a rift with his sister; it was annulled in September 1894, and Charles was reconciled with his first wife. In the late 1890s he toured the USA in a repertory that included his own play *Lady Barter*; it was during this tour that he became ill with acute gastritis, and he died in Galveston, Texas, on 27 November 1899. His coffin, along with many others, was washed away in the Galveston flood of 1900 (it was recovered four years later), an incident that led to persistent reports in later years that he had died during the flood itself.

After the turn of the century Rose Coghlan met increasing difficulty finding work. Since the mid-1890s she had been plagued by financial problems, and in 1898 she began to work on the vaudeville circuit, where she was employed over the next twenty years. Opportunities to appear in plays became less frequent, though, when she did find roles, she excelled. As Penelope in the ill-fated 1903 New York production of Stephen Phillips's *Ulysses*, she 'almost single-handedly' saved the show 'from instant and ignominious collapse' (*New York Evening Post*, 15 April 1922).

Other notable appearances from Rose's later years included a tour in Shaw's *Mrs Warren's Profession* in 1907 and roles in *The Winter's Tale* and *The Merry Wives of Windsor* at Winthrop Ames's New Theatre in 1910. She acquired some work in films, notably in *The Sporting Duchess* (1915) and *Beyond the Rainbow* (1922). Her last stage success came at the age of seventy, when she played Madame Rabouin in Harley Granville Barker's adaptation of Sacha Guitry's *Deburau* (Belasco, 1920). The *New York Post*, in a largely dismissive review, called her small performance 'one of the chief artistic features of the evening'; 'she vivified the whole picture—even the dialogue, poor stuff that it was, assumed significance as uttered in her clear, crisp, and deeply suggestive delivery' (24 Dec 1920).

Two years later Coghlan was destitute. A benefit was held for her in New York at the Apollo Theatre (set up by the Producing Managers' Association), which raised $10,000. She then retired to St Vincent's Retreat, Harrison, New York, a sanatorium run by Catholic nuns. According to some reports she was under the care of the Actors' Fund of America and the National Vaudeville Artists' Association. In November 1924 she offered at auction her collection of autographed photographs. She died of a cerebral haemorrhage on 2 April 1932 at St Vincent's Retreat, and was cremated on the 4th at Fresh Pond crematorium, Middle Village, Queens, New York. HEIDI J. HOLDER

Sources F. E. McKay and C. E. L. Wingate, *Famous American actors of today*, 2 (1896) • J. R. Towse, *Sixty years of the theatre* (1916) • A. M. Robinson, V. M. Roberts, and M. Barranger, *Notable women in the American theatre* (1989) • G. C. D. Odell, *Annals of the New York stage*, 15 vols. (1927–49), vols. 9–15 • C. E. Pascoe, ed., *The dramatic list*, 2nd edn (1880) • J. B. Clapp and E. F. Edgett, *Players of the present*, 1 (1899) • Boase, *Mod. Eng. biog.* • *Daily Argus* [Mount Vernon, NY] (11 April 1932) • *Chicago Tribune* (5 April 1932) • *New York Tribune* (6 April 1932) • *New York Times* (5 April 1932) • *Philadelphia Ledger* (5 April 1932) • *New York Sun* (4 April 1932) • *The American* (5 April 1932) • *Daily News* (5 April 1932) • *New York Star* (1 Oct 1880) • *New York Herald* (2 Aug 1891) • d. cert.

Archives Harvard TC • NYPL, Billy Rose Theatre Collection • Players Club, New York, Hampden-Booth Library • Ransom HRC, Hoblitzelle Theatre Arts Library

Likenesses photograph, *c.*1880, NYPL, Billy Rose Theatre Collection • photograph, *c.*1888, Ransom HRC, Hoblitzelle Theatre Arts Library • Forbes, poster, lithograph, Harvard TC • S. Hollyer, engraving (after Sarony), Harvard TC • K, woodcut (after photograph by Mora), Harvard TC • C. Mathesius, lithograph, Harvard TC • photograph, Harvard TC

Cogidubnus [Cogidumnus, Tiberius Claudius Cogidubnus, Togidubnus] (*fl. c.*AD 47–70), king in Britain, is mentioned only once in Roman literature, in the *Agricola* of Tacitus, when he is reported to have been assigned certain tribes and to have remained loyal to Rome down to the memory of the historian. The date at which the king was given these responsibilities in the newly emergent province of Britain is not closely defined, but it probably fell within the governorship of Ostorius Scapula (AD 47–52). The location of Cogidubnus's kingdom is also uncertain, but a vital clue was provided by an inscription found at Chichester (Noviomagus) in 1723. This is a dedication for a temple to the gods Neptune and Minerva, set up on the authority of Cogidubnus. Noviomagus was thus a major centre in his realm, though not necessarily the only one. The area to the north was occupied by the tribe of the Atrebates, the heart of the kingdom of Verica who fled to the Roman empire early in the reign of Claudius (*c.*AD 41–2). It is a plausible suggestion that Verica's kingdom was handed over to the pro-Roman Cogidubnus after the Roman conquest, along with the territories of other neighbouring peoples. The (translated) title of Cogidubnus on the Chichester inscription accords well with his honoured status: 'great king in Britain'. The text also indicates that the king had been invested with full Roman citizenship by Claudius and had taken the emperor's praenomen and nomen, Tiberius Claudius. The precise legal position of Cogidubnus has been much discussed. The only evidence is contained in the wording of the Chichester stone, the text of which is incomplete. The king's status was earlier interpreted as *rex et legatus Augusti in Britannia* ('king and imperial legate in Britain'). Such a combination of roles is without parallel and long seemed anomalous. A revised reading of the text gives the title *rex magnus in Britannia* ('great king in Britain') and this is to be preferred.

The origins of Cogidubnus are unknown. His name is not certainly established: the first two letters of his cognomen on the Chichester inscription are lost, and Togidubnus appears to have as strong a claim as any other. Tacitus called him Cogidumnus. He may have been a prince of the Atrebatic house who fled to the Roman world before the invasion of AD 43 and been subsequently given enhanced powers in the early years of occupation. Equally, he may never have left the island, but provided useful services to the occupying power, including bases for westward campaigns. The length of his reign is also undefined. Tacitus's comment that he continued his loyalty to Rome 'down to our memory' should mean that he remained in power until the 70s, Tacitus having been born *c*.AD 56. This would allow Cogidubnus a reign of twenty to twenty-five years. But this raises a problem. The employment of allied native rulers was favoured by Claudius but phased out by his successor Nero. The survival of a British king from the reign of Claudius to that of Vespasian would be an extreme exception, though not wholly beyond possibility.

The archaeological setting of the realm of Cogidubnus provides some evidence for the influence of the king on the early Romanization of southern Britain. Aside from the temple of Neptune and Minerva mentioned on the Chichester stone, Chichester has produced the base of a statue to Nero, an unusually early monument for the British province. The town of Calleva (Silchester) among the Atrebates also reveals early urban development along Roman lines, with an early forum and amphitheatre. Most impressive of all is the luxurious residence erected at Fishbourne, about a mile west of Chichester. The first phase of this palatial dwelling dates to the reign of Nero, *c*.AD 55–60. The building was never completed and its demolished remains were later covered by an immense palace arranged around a series of courtyards and light-wells, the whole complex covering some 6 acres. This went up about AD 75. Although the Neronian residence could have been planned for Cogidubnus, the later palace seems rather too late for him. It might have been built for his unknown successor, grown rich on the revenues and tolls amassed by the native kingdom.

Native rulers contributed much to the growth and stability of the Roman provinces. Relatively few such kings are attested in the western provinces. Although little is known about him for certain, Cogidubnus was one of the more successful and effective kings in Roman service. The rapid Roman conquest and occupation of southern Britain owed a great deal to his steadfast loyalty.

MALCOLM TODD

Sources Tacitus, *Agricola*, ed. and trans. M. Mutton (1914), xiv.1 · R. G. Collingwood and R. P. Wright, eds., *The Roman inscriptions of Britain*, 2 vols. (1965), RIB 91 · A. A. Barrett, 'The career of Tiberius Claudius Cogidubnus', *Britannia*, 10 (1979), 227–42 · J. E. Bogaers, 'King Cogidubnus in Chichester: another reading of RIB 91', *Britannia*, 10 (1979), 243–54 · E. Birley, 'The adherence of Britain to Vespasian', *Britannia*, 9 (1978), 243–5

Cohen, Sir Andrew Benjamin (1909–1968), civil servant and colonial governor, was born on 7 October 1909 at Berkhamsted, Hertfordshire, the twin son of Walter Samuel Cohen (1870–1960), financier and company director, and his wife, Lucy Margaret Cobb (1877–1942). On his father's side he stemmed from a wealthy Jewish business family, and on his mother's, from a radical Unitarian family; the two strains combined in the son to produce an elitist with a social conscience. His elder sister Ruth Louisa was principal of Newnham College, Cambridge, from 1954 to 1972. He won a scholarship to Malvern College, and another to Trinity College, Cambridge, where, although his spiritual home was King's, he obtained a double first in the classical tripos (1930–31). In 1932 he entered the civil service, where he spent a year as an assistant principal at the Board of Inland Revenue, before transferring to the Colonial Office to join the other classical scholars under Charles Jeffries.

For the next few years Cohen inhaled trusteeship with the dust on the African files; and he came to sympathize with the black African rather than the white settler. Contemptuous of colour bars, he was shocked by how little the colonial trustees seemed to him to have done for Africans in Rhodesia. For a time he was private secretary to Sir John Maffey, the permanent under-secretary; and he also visited central Africa as secretary to a financial commission. As an acting principal in 1939, he was chosen for a Commonwealth Fund fellowship to visit America, but his schedule was cut short by the outbreak of the Second World War. In 1940 he was sent to organize supplies during the siege of Malta, deputizing at times for the lieutenant-governor. It was his first taste of power (for which he was voracious), in an embattled government organizing a society to meet an emergency; the experience left him with a Fabian socialist's view of the state's duty to reorganize the social order. In 1943 he returned to the Colonial Office as an assistant secretary, to take part in post-war African planning.

By 1947, when he was appointed assistant under-secretary of state for the Colonial Office's African division, Cohen's vision for Africa was sharply defined. It seemed to him vital, in the interests of both Britain and Africa, to turn the colonies into self-governing nations within 'the next generation'. As head of the division and *alter ego* of his minister, Arthur Creech Jones, he helped to prepare a report for tropical Africa, in which he was able to give this meaning to the colonial shibboleths of the Labour Party. There were many in the euphoria of peace who wished to make colonies into modern welfare states and bring them into production to repair the ravaged United Kingdom economy. Cohen was one of the few who realized that colonial rule would have to be nationalized if those aims were to be fulfilled. Alien officials could never do so, he insisted, through petty chiefs; to achieve them, the excluded but educated African who understood modern ideas must be brought into partnership, and his price would be the most rapid possible transfer of power. As a realist, Cohen discerned that the age of empire was ended; as a moralist, he resolved to end it constructively.

African nationalists seemed a derisory band at the time, and some governors objected bitterly to the new course; to educate the colonial civil service there, Creech Jones and Cohen began the *Journal of African Administration*, and the annual conferences at Cambridge. They were prepared to concede power to progressive nationalist movements, but as a result of the Accra riots of 1948, the ballot box and a quasi-ministerial system were introduced in the Gold Coast earlier than intended; the extreme nationalists won the election and Kwame Nkrumah left gaol to become leader of government. What had been conceded in Ghana could not then be denied to Nigeria, and a 'domino effect' spread throughout British west Africa. Thus Cohen's plan, designed to educate the national movements gradually into responsibility, provoked them into swift action. By 1951 west Africa at least was set on course to self-government, although fifteen years later, contemplating the one-party states and military coups, Cohen was depressed by the outcome. Like many of Africa's friends, he had overestimated the power of the nationalists to transcend ethnic divisions and behave democratically in the Westminster tradition.

For central Africa, Cohen's construct in 1948–51 was more realistic if the outcome was less fortunate. Fearful of a white unilateral declaration of independence, and of apartheid spreading from South Africa, he advocated a confederation of the Rhodesias and Nyasaland: power was to be transferred to the white minority on condition that it was shared with the African majority. A version of the plan was carried out in 1953 after he had left the Colonial Office; but the offer of 'half a loaf' so angered Africans that Kenneth Kaunda and Hastings Banda could organize nationalist movements strong enough to break the association ten years later and achieve majority rule, save in Southern Rhodesia.

In September 1951, after James Griffiths had replaced Creech Jones as colonial secretary following the general election of 1950, Cohen was appointed governor of Uganda and sworn in early in 1952. Although he disliked the ceremonial, he gladly practised in the field what he had preached in Whitehall; Africans and Asians were invited to Government House and advanced in central government; Makerere was developed into a university to strengthen the educated cadre; local authorities were made more democratic, which encouraged political parties and national consciousness. But in underestimating the strength of traditional loyalty and deporting the *kabaka* of Buganda in 1953, only to restore him later on constitutional conditions, Cohen was strongly criticized on all sides, although when he finally left Uganda early in 1957 the foundations for independence were securely laid, and indeed the Ugandans themselves petitioned for his term of office to be extended.

Disappointed in his hope of a Labour seat in parliament, and despite being an unlikely choice as a diplomat, Cohen was appointed permanent representative (1957–60) on the Trusteeship Council at the United Nations. But he seemed to have been put on the shelf, and he did not always find it easy to square the representations which the Foreign Office instructed him to make with his personal convictions. In 1959 he published *British Policy in Changing Africa*, and, given his natural affinity with liberal Americans and his candid and widespread working relations with African and Asian leaders, he discovered another way to serve African independence: the idea of international and Commonwealth co-operation in aid of modernizing Africa captured his mind. In helping to link American aid to British schemes for developing east Africa, especially in university education, he took up the concepts of the United Nations 'development decade'. It was fitting, therefore, that he was recalled to Whitehall in 1961 to set up a department of technical co-operation, which took over most of the old Colonial Office's non-political functions. In 1964 the department was transformed into a Ministry of Overseas Development, with Cohen as its permanent secretary; he carried out the organization of first one establishment and then the other with his usual dynamic enthusiasm.

In 1949 Cohen married Mrs Helen Phoebe Donington (*d.* 1978) JP, commander of the order of St John of Jerusalem, only daughter of George Hope Stevenson, praelector in ancient history at University College, Oxford (1907–49); Cohen was as affectionate towards his three stepchildren as towards their own son (born in 1950). His marriage brought him closer to Bloomsbury and the political left. He was appointed OBE in 1942, CMG in 1948, and was advanced to KCMG in 1952; he was also appointed KCVO (1954), and received the honorary degree of LLD from the Queen's University, Belfast, in 1960.

Cohen was cut out to be a planner, even a philosopher king, and if reading lyric verse on an antique Mediterranean island may have been his private Elysium, he admired intellect most; arrogantly intellectual, and avid for original ideas, if they were to engage his excellent mind they had to be practical in shaping better things to come. With a heroic image of himself as idea in action—compounded of Carlyle and Euripides—Cambridge and Malta combined to make him unflinchingly realistic in finding means to achieve a passionately speculative vision of ultimate ends. Of giant stature, appetite, and energy, boyish in charm and enthusiasm, the intellectual dreamer of the Colonial Office was one of the most anti-colonial and unofficial of the imperial officials who finally dismantled the tropical African empire. In one way or another his measures helped to awaken the slumbering genius of African nationalism and, wittingly or unwittingly, he did more to bring about the fall of empire and the rise of the nationalists than most African politicians were able to achieve between them. Not for nothing did his biographer dub him 'The proconsul of African nationalism' (Robinson, 'Sir Andrew Cohen').

Cohen died suddenly at his home, 44 Blomfield Road, Maida Vale, London, on 17 June 1968.

R. E. ROBINSON, *rev.*

Sources *The Times* (19 June 1968) · R. E. Robinson, 'Andrew Cohen and the transfer of power in tropical Africa, 1940–1951', *Decolonisation and after*, ed. W. H. Morris-Jones and G. Fischer (1980), 50–72 · R. E. Robinson, 'Sir Andrew Cohen: proconsul of African nationalism', *African proconsuls: European governors in Africa*, ed. L. H. Gann and P. Duignan (1978), 353–64 · D. A. Low, *Buganda in modern history* (1971) · R. D. Pearce, *The turning point in Africa: British colonial policy, 1938–1948* (1982) · *WWW* · personal knowledge (1981) · private information (1981) · D. A. Low and A. Smith, eds., *History of East Africa*, 3 (1976) · *CGPLA Eng. & Wales* (1968)

Archives Bodl. RH, corresp. with Margery Perham · Bodl. RH, corresp. with E. B. Worthington · ICL, corresp. with W. Jackson · U. Lond., Institute of Commonwealth Studies, corresp. with Sir Keith Hancock | FILM BFI NFTVA, documentary footage

Likenesses R. Buhler, oils, 1957

Wealth at death £85,956: probate, 16 Oct 1968, *CGPLA Eng. & Wales*

Cohen, Arthur (1829–1914), lawyer, was born in Wyndham Place, Bryanston Square, London, on 18 November 1829, the youngest son of Benjamin Cohen (1789–1867), a prosperous bill broker. His grandfather, Levy Barent Cohen (1740–1808), moved to London from Holland about 1770. Through his mother, Justina (1800–1873), the youngest daughter of Joseph Eliahu Montefiore and sister of Sir Moses *Montefiore, he was connected with the great Jewish families of Montefiore and Mocatta. At an early age he was reading Newton's *Principia*; when he was about twelve years old, he was sent to Frankfurt, where he was educated by a tutor and at the *Gymnasium*. At the age of seventeen he became a student at University College, London. His family wished to send him to Cambridge, but entrance to Trinity and Christ's colleges was found to be impossible for a Jew. His uncle, Sir Moses Montefiore, with the support of the prince consort as chancellor of the university, secured his admission to Magdalene, where he read mathematics, in 1849. Even then he had to undergo an entrance examination on William Paley's *View of the Evidences of Christianity*.

Cohen had not had much opportunity to mix with his contemporaries and, supported by a large allowance, he participated enthusiastically in undergraduate life. He was secretary of the Union Society in 1852 and its president in 1853, and he rowed for at least one year in the Magdalene boat. It was probably due to these diversions that his name appeared only as fifth wrangler in 1853, to the disappointment of his family. As a Jew he could not take his degree until after the passing of the Cambridge Reform Act of 1856, which abolished the obligatory Christian oath which had formerly preceded graduation. In 1858 Cohen became the first professing Jew to graduate at Cambridge, taking his MA in 1860. Later on the university made him further amends: from 1879 to 1914 he was counsel to the university, and from 1883 an honorary fellow of Magdalene College.

In November 1853 Cohen became a member of the Inner Temple. In May 1857 he won the studentship of the inns of court, and in November of the same year he was called to the bar. He practised on the home and, later, the south-east circuits. In his early years he was helped by his uncle, Sir Moses Montefiore, who bought a law library for his nephew and, as chairman of the Alliance Assurance

Arthur Cohen (1829–1914), by Sir Frank Short, 1917 (after John Singer Sargent, 1906)

Company, put work his way. But Cohen, able and ambitious enough to succeed without backing, was soon busy, especially with commercial insurance and Admiralty cases. Commercial law was being adapted to meet the problems of increasing trade, and for many years Cohen appeared in nearly every important case. In 1872 he was selected by the attorney-general, Sir Roundell Palmer (Lord Selborne from October of that year), to be junior counsel for Great Britain in the *Alabama* arbitration at Geneva. In 1873 he was appointed by Chief Baron Kelly to the ancient post of 'tubman' in the court of exchequer, having previously been 'postman'. In the same year he was a member of the royal commission on unseaworthy ships, the result of the agitation of Samuel Plimsoll. In 1874 he became a queen's counsel, being the junior but one in a batch of fourteen. Thereafter, Cohen appeared frequently before the privy council and in the House of Lords. In 1875 he was appointed judge of the Admiralty court of Cinque Ports, a sinecure which he only resigned in the year of his death. In 1876 he became a bencher of the Inner Temple, and he held the office of treasurer in 1894. He became a member of the senate of the University of London in 1905, as a representative of the Inner Temple; he was reappointed in 1909 and 1913.

On 23 August 1860 Cohen married Emmeline Micholls (1843–1888) of Manchester, to whom he had become engaged when she was only fifteen. It was a happy marriage which produced three sons and five daughters. One of the sons, Benjamin, became a distinguished barrister.

In February 1874 Cohen stood unsuccessfully for the borough of Lewes as a Liberal. In April 1880 he headed the poll at Southwark, his fellow member being the political economist J. E. Thorold Rogers. In February 1881 Lord Selborne offered him the senior of two judgeships then vacant. At the request of W. E. Gladstone, who feared a by-election in the borough, Cohen declined. There was, apparently, an understanding that Cohen should be offered a judgeship subsequently, but he never had another chance: and for many years new judges, answering letters of congratulation from Cohen, uniformly assured him that he ought long ago to have been on the bench himself. Cohen sat for Southwark from 1880 to 1888, being re-elected twice, in November 1885 and July 1886. Described in *Dod's Parliamentary Companion* as a 'sincere and earnest' Liberal he favoured home rule, reform of bankruptcy law, and the establishment of a mercantile code. He was opposed to a hereditary House of Lords. He was not a successful Commons man, but though he spoke seldom, he was heard with respect and he exerted considerable influence behind the scenes. Even in court, Cohen's manner of speaking was somewhat artificial, and it was probably too drily analytical for the House of Commons, despite his employment of an elocution coach. A contemporary described his speech as 'smooth and persuasive', though with a tendency to 'drawl' (*The Times*, 4 Nov 1914). In 1888 Cohen resigned his seat, chiefly because of the serious illness of his wife. In the June of that year he suffered a severe blow by her death.

Between 1893 and 1914 Cohen was standing counsel to the India Office. In 1903 he was counsel for Great Britain in the Venezuela arbitration at The Hague. In the same year he was made a fellow of the British Academy, chairman of the bar council, and a member of the royal commission on trade disputes and trade combinations, which reported in 1906—not a bad record for a man of seventy-four. In 1905 he was made a privy councillor by the Conservative government. In 1906 he was appointed chairman of the royal commission on shipping rings. In 1911 he wrote the article on insurance in Lord Halsbury's *Laws of England*. This was his only published work of any length, and being upon a subject of which he had been long the acknowledged master it was one of the most valuable sections of that encyclopaedia. His lecture entitled *The Declaration of London* was also published in 1911.

Cohen continued his practice at the bar until about 1911, appearing at times with a junior who was born after his leader had taken silk. When he died, Halsbury alone was his senior among the benchers of his inn.

Cohen was a great lawyer, intelligent, industrious, and with a passion for legal principles. In dedicating to Cohen his *Conflict of Laws* (1896), A. V. Dicey said that his 'mastery of legal principles is surpassed only by the kindness with which his learning and experience are placed at the service of his friends'. He was not a great advocate in open court, but for the argument of a question of law before an appellate tribunal he had few equals. In all probability, up to the time of his death, no advocate had so often addressed the House of Lords and the judicial committee.

Tall and handsome, with brown eyes and a mass of dark hair which kept its colour until he was well past seventy,

Cohen was a kindly man, with the courteous and rather stately manners of a 'grand seigneur'. Although reserved, he had many friends, and was universally esteemed by the members of the bar. His interests included literature and the theatre. Although he gave up playing the cello when he left Cambridge, he maintained his university passion for mathematics: within a few months of his death he was reading works on the differential calculus. Although he had a fine physique, Cohen was not athletic. He did, however, enjoy walking while on holiday in the Alps. He was a heavy smoker of cigars, and had a tendency to gout. He was a slow and conscientious worker; although his income—even as a junior counsel—was up to £8000 p.a., he was never a rich man. About the acquisition of money he was as careless as he was lavish in spending it. His daughter recorded that he only once tried the experiment of riding in an omnibus; his brother, who died a millionaire, was never known to ride in anything else. Although Cohen ceased to be an 'observing' Jew when he left his childhood home, he was always a professing Jew, and proud of the traditions of the race. Throughout his life he took an active part in Jewish affairs, especially in the fields of education and charity. For many years president of the Borough Jewish schools, he was vice-president of the Jews' College (1892–1901) and president of the Meshibat Neplish Society (1873–80). He also served on the council of the United Synagogue and the committee of the Jews' Free School. He was for fifteen years (1800–1895) president of the Jewish board of deputies, resigning when the first of his children married outside the Jewish community. He died on 3 November 1914, at his home at 26 Great Cumberland Place, Hyde Park, London, and was buried by the side of his wife in the Jewish cemetery at Willesden.

F. D. MACKINNON, rev. P. W. J. BARTRIP

Sources [L. Cohen], *Arthur Cohen: a memoir by his daughter for his descendants* (1919) · I. Finestein, *Jewish society in Victorian England* (1993), chap. 11 · P. H. Emden, *Jews of Britain: a series of biographies* (1944), 178–84 · *Jewish Chronicle* (6 Nov 1914) · *The Times* (4 Nov 1914) · A. V. Dicey, 'The Right Hon. Arthur Cohen', *Law Quarterly Review*, 31 (1915), 96–105 · *WWW* · *WW* · *Law Journal* (7 Nov 1914), 609, 616 · *Law Times* (7 Nov 1914), 23 · *The Spectator* (14 Nov 1914), 669 · L. L. Cohen, 'Levi Barent Cohen and some of his descendants', *Transactions of the Jewish Historical Society of England*, 16 (1945–51), 11–23
Likenesses J. S. Sargent, portrait, 1897 · F. Short, mezzotint, 1917 (after J. S. Sargent, 1906), NPG [*see illus.*]
Wealth at death £83,949 18*s*. 11*d*.: probate, 19 Dec 1914, *CGPLA Eng. & Wales*

Cohen, Sir Benjamin Louis, first baronet (1844–1909),

politician and Jewish communal leader, was born on 18 November 1844 at South Street, Finsbury, London, the eighth of nine surviving children of Louis Cohen (1799–1882), founder of the City firm of Louis Cohen & Sons, and his wife, Rebecca Floretta Keyser (1807–1859). Benny was born a twin, but his brother Isaac died at the early age of sixteen in 1860. A further eight siblings had died at birth or in early infancy.

Cohen lost his mother while still in his early teens and was thus under the influence of his father, Louis, whom his daughter described as 'stern and very orthodox' (Cohen, 85). He was educated at home by James Wigan, father of the actors Alfred and Horace Wigan. He went into the family firm, becoming a member of the London stock exchange.

In 1870 Cohen married his third cousin, Louisa Emily Merton (1850–1931), the only daughter of Benjamin Merton (the family name was changed from Moses) and Hannah Cohen. The couple were both great-grandchildren of the Dutchman Levi Barent Cohen (1747–1808), the progenitor of the Cohen banking family in Britain. According to Bermant the marriage was not entirely happy. The liberal-minded Louisa was a cultivated woman, who had been partly brought up in France. They had four children, three sons and one daughter, all of whom went to Cambridge. Hannah *Cohen, the eldest, wrote an engaging, if not always factually accurate, memoir of her family. From 1883 they lived at 30 Hyde Park Gardens, London, and in 1897 Benjamin acquired a country house at Highfield, Shoreham, near Sevenoaks in Kent, that had originally been built by the architect Spencer Chadwick as his personal residence.

Cohen's tastes were those of the English country gentleman: he was a keen horseman and a member of the Carlton Club and his politics were Conservative. In July 1892 he was elected tory MP for East Islington, one of only a handful of Jewish tories in an era when English-born Jews were overwhelmingly supporters of the Liberal Party. In addition Cohen was elected to the newly formed London county council as a 'moderate' (that is Conservative) member for the City between 1889 and 1901, and was chiefly concerned to protect the privileges of the City against reforming tendencies in the new council. He served as a governor of several City hospitals and orphanages. He was a JP for London and Kent and a deputy lieutenant of the City of London. He was created baronet in 1905 but lost his parliamentary seat in the Liberal landslide of 1906.

The Cohen family were instrumental in the foundation and running of two major Anglo-Jewish communal institutions: the Board of Guardians for the Relief of the Jewish Poor (1859) and the United Synagogue (1870). Benjamin Cohen became a vice-president and later life president of the United Synagogue. He succeeded his older brother Lionel Louis Cohen (1832–1887) as president of the board of guardians from 1887 to 1900, turning the institution into virtually a Cohen fiefdom. One of his last acts before retirement was to alter the board's constitution in order to make women eligible to serve. This was a surprisingly progressive act for a Conservative gentleman, but was no doubt motivated by conviction; it eventually allowed his spinster daughter Hannah, educated at Roedean and Newnham, to serve as president from 1930 to 1940.

Benjamin Cohen's leadership was characterized by careful but unimaginative financial management at a time when the board's resources were under strain on account of the mass immigration of poor Jews from eastern Europe. In 1882 Louis Cohen & Sons played an important part in setting up the Russo-Jewish Committee (as it was later styled), following the Mansion House meeting called to protest against persecution of Jews in Russia in the wake of the assassination of Tsar Alexander II. Cohen

became treasurer. He was, according to his daughter, the author of the committee's report Persecution of the Jews in Russia (1882), which was first published in The Times. In 1884, together with his brother-in-law Samuel Montagu and Asher Asher, Benjamin went to North America to report on the fortunes of two agricultural colonies set up to aid Russian Jewish refugees. In 1886 he attended a conference in Vienna called to deal with the evacuation of Jewish refugees from the Galician border town of Brody. In 1890 Benjamin became a patron of the Hovevei Tsion ('lovers of Zion'), a proto-Zionist organization formed to encourage Jewish agricultural settlement in Palestine.

In contrast, Cohen became convinced that Jewish immigration to Britain must be on a selective basis only, and that restriction was necessary so long as the right of asylum was upheld. Under his management the board of guardians encouraged re-emigration and repatriation, and he justified this position on humanitarian grounds. He voted in favour of the Aliens Act in 1905, one of only four Jewish MPs—all tory or Unionist—to do so. Politically, both in general and Jewish affairs, Benjamin became an opponent of his brother-in-law Samuel Montagu, who was Liberal MP for the heavily Jewish immigrant neighbourhood of Whitechapel and founder of the Federation of Synagogues, East End rival of the establishment United Synagogue.

Benjamin Cohen died at his home in Hyde Park Gardens after 'a protracted illness' on 8 November 1909. He was buried three days later at Willesden Jewish cemetery.

SHARMAN KADISH

Sources The Times (17 March 1882) • The Times (9 Dec 1909) • The Times (21 Nov 1931) • The Times (24 Nov 1931) • Jewish Chronicle (17 March 1882) • Jewish Chronicle (12 Nov 1909) • Jewish Year Book (1897) • Jewish Year Book (1908) • C. Bermant, The cousinhood: the Anglo-Jewish gentry (1971) • H. Cohen, Changing faces: a memoir of Louisa, Lady Cohen (1937) • G. Alderman, London Jewry and London politics, 1889–1986 (1989) • G. Alderman, Modern British Jewry (1992) • E. C. Black, The social politics of Anglo-Jewry, 1880–1920 (1988) • V. D. Lipman, A century of social service, 1859–1959: the Jewish Board of Guardians (1959) • L. Magnus, The Jewish Board of Guardians and the men who made it, 1859–1909 (1909) • CGPLA Eng. & Wales (1909)

Archives King's Cam., letter from Cohen, his wife, and his sons to Oscar Browning

Likenesses caricature, 1870–1879?, priv. coll.; repro. in Lipman, A century of social service • photograph, c.1890–1899, priv. coll.; repro. in Magnus, Jewish Board of Guardians • S. J. Solomon, oils, 1899, United Synagogue, London; repro. in Cohen, Changing faces • oils (after painting by S. J. Solomon), priv. coll.

Wealth at death £385,146 3s.: probate, 17 Dec 1909, CGPLA Eng. & Wales

Cohen, Sir Bernard Nathaniel Waley-, first baronet

(1914–1991), public servant and businessman, was born on 29 May 1914 in London, the first son (and twin brother of Hetty) of the three children of Sir Robert Waley *Cohen (1877–1952), businessman and government adviser, and his wife, Alice Violet (1882–1935), daughter of Henry Edward Beddington, of Bayswater in London, and Heathside, Newmarket, and his wife, Floretta Marianne. The son of a man who was large in frame and large in personality, a

Sir Bernard Nathaniel Waley-Cohen, first baronet (1914–1991), by Miles & Kaye, 1961

pioneer of industry, and a leading figure in the Anglo-Jewish community, Waley-Cohen (the hyphen was introduced by deed poll in 1950) was groomed from an early age to be of service both to his country and to his co-religionists. His lifetime's achievements were proof that he more than fulfilled his father's expectations and his family's traditional role as a leader of Anglo-Jewry and a prime actor on the financial stage of the City of London.

Although his life was subsequently marked by achievement, the young Waley-Cohen had first to overcome the disappointment of having to give up all thoughts of a career at sea when he was forced to leave the Royal Naval College, Dartmouth, in 1930, after only three years, owing to a defect in his eyesight. His sight was to suffer still further when, in 1938, he lost the sight of one eye in a riding accident. A rugged, broad-shouldered young man, Waley-Cohen enjoyed horse-riding, rugby, and mountaineering—he climbed Mont Blanc in 1934. His schooling from 1930 to 1933 was at Clifton College, Bristol, where he was a boarder in Polack's, the Jewish house founded by his great-uncle Lionel Cohen. He then went to Magdalene College, Cambridge, to read modern history. Immediately after leaving Cambridge in 1936, he began his business career for, though 'born to a considerable fortune ... he had to make his own way in the City' (Bermant, 416); he began by joining Lloyds and within three years was appointed an underwriter.

Commercial activity was disrupted by the outbreak of the Second World War and, unable to serve his country in the armed forces owing to his eye injury, which had also caused him to be discharged by the Honourable Artillery Company, Waley-Cohen turned instead to public service. He became an executive officer attached to the Port of London Emergency Service, a recruiting officer and commander of the Exmoor patrol of the Home Guard, and, between 1940 and 1947, a principal at the Ministry of Fuel and Power alongside Harold Wilson. The end of the war enabled him to combine his commercial, financial, and public-service activities with his love of life in Somerset, where he could supervise his farm on the edge of Exmoor and ride to hounds. From 1953 to 1985 he was chairman of the Devon and Somerset staghounds, subsequently acting as president until his death. His love of hunting led to a number of confrontations with those who opposed blood sports, as well as some acrimonious correspondence in the press.

It was in the post-war years that, still young, Waley-Cohen made his greatest contribution to the City of London, both in his career as a banker—between 1947 and 1954 one of his major roles was as vice-chairman of the Palestine Corporation and the Union Bank of Israel—and as a public servant. At the age of only thirty-five he was appointed a lieutenant for the City of London and alderman for the Portsoken ward. Six years later he was elected to the shrievalty, and in his electoral speech he looked back to his forebear Sir David Salomons, in whose footsteps he was following some 120 years on. Salomons's example was further followed when Waley-Cohen was created KBE in 1957, and in 1960, when he became the seventh Jew and the second youngest individual to be elected lord mayor of the City of London.

It was as lord mayor that Waley-Cohen was truly fulfilled, able to serve the City and his country as best he could, and able to demonstrate, as had members of the cousinhood before him, that he was 'a proud Englishman of the Jewish faith' (*The Times*, 4 July 1991). On 21 December 1943 he had married Joyce Constance Ina (*b.* 1920), only daughter and older of the two children of Harry Louis *Nathan, first Baron Nathan, and his wife, Eleanor Joan Clara. Waley-Cohen and his vivacious wife made their presence felt at the Mansion House, which was enlivened by the four young Waley-Cohens, Rosalind Alice (*b.* 1945), Stephen Harry (*b.* 1946), Robert Bernard (*b.* 1948), and (Eleanor) Joanna (*b.* 1952). The charming, articulate lord mayor—Harold Macmillan considered his speech at the traditional Guildhall dinner one of the best he had heard—used his period of office to promote goodwill far beyond the normal lord-mayoral boundaries. During the summer of 1961—a period chosen so as to coincide with the civic recess—he travelled over 30,000 miles to Australia, New Zealand, and the Far East, in order to promote better relations between the City of London and distant lands. An indication of his respect for the ceremony of his position was demonstrated by his taking with him his lord mayor's chain of office and robes of ermine. He was also an active advocate of interfaith relations between Muslims, Christians, and Jews and, when possible, endeavoured to demonstrate his support in his civic capacity.

Following his period of office as lord mayor, in 1961 Waley-Cohen was made a baronet. Still a young man, he determined to devote himself to good causes and public service. He was appointed commissioner and deputy chairman of the Public Works Loan Commission in 1971 and, in that same year, became chairman of University College, London, of which he had been appointed an honorary fellow in 1963; it was a position he held for nine years. During 1975 he was master of the Clothworkers' Company; among the other causes with which he was closely involved were those of his alma mater, Clifton College, as well as the St Paul's Cathedral Appeal, the College of Arms, and the Marshall Aid Commemorative Commission. The more rural passions were not ignored, however, and Waley-Cohen devoted as much time as was possible to his herds of prize-winning pedigree Devon cattle.

Waley-Cohen was a thickset, bespectacled, physically strong, cigar-loving man, whose looks somewhat belied his affable and compassionate nature. He was a figure in the old-fashioned Anglo-Jewish establishment mould who, though little concerned with religious practice, was dedicated to communal loyalty: loyalty to the section of the Jewish faith which his family had served for well over a century. The nature of the man was revealed by the instructions that appeared in his will regarding his burial. It was to be simple and private, 'without any published date, time or place', and attended only by members of his family and specifically invited friends and colleagues. His modesty and *joie de vivre* were further underlined by his request that no memorial service be conducted for him, but that two parties be held, one in London and one in Somerset, both on a 'generous scale' in order that his friends could be brought together 'to remember me and speak of me not in any mournful sense but more in the sense that they have enjoyed my friendship as much as I have enjoyed theirs' (Waley-Cohen, will, 20 Jan 1980, proved at Bristol).

Waley-Cohen died on 3 July 1991 at his home, Honeymead, Simonsbath, near Minehead, Somerset, of a cerebrovascular accident. He was buried on 5 July 1991 at Willesden Jewish cemetery, Beaconsfield Road, London. He was survived by his wife and four children, and succeeded as baronet by his elder son.   ANNE J. KERSHEN

Sources C. Bermant, *The cousinhood: the Anglo-Jewish gentry* (1971), 357–76, 395–422 · R. D. Q. Henriques, *Sir Robert Waley Cohen* (1966) · *The Times* (4 July 1991) · *The Independent* (4 July 1991) · *Jewish Chronicle* (12 July 1991) · will of Sir Bernard Waley-Cohen, 20 Jan 1980, Principal Registry of the Family Division · d. cert. · *Clifton College register, 1862–1962* (1962) · *Jewish Year Book* (1975) · Burke, *Peerage* (1998) · *WWW, 1991–5*
Likenesses Popperfoto, photograph, 1960, repro. in *The Independent* · photograph, 1960, repro. in *The Times* · Miles & Kaye, photograph, 1961, NPG [see illus.]
Wealth at death £106,047: probate, 1991, *CGPLA Eng. & Wales*

Cohen, Chapman (1868–1954), freethought writer and lecturer, was born in Leicester on 1 September 1868, the elder son of Enoch Cohen, a Jewish confectioner, and his wife, Deborah Barnett. His upbringing was more noted for the absence of Christianity than for any positive Jewish features. He attended a local elementary school but was otherwise self-educated. Although an avid reader, versed in Spinoza, Locke, Hume, Berkeley, and Plato by the time he was eighteen, he was scarcely aware of the freethought movement in which he was to spend his life when he moved to London in 1889. A chance encounter with a Christian Evidence lecturer in Victoria Park in 1890 led him to respond to the speaker, and this brought an invitation to lecture from the local Secular Society. Some months later he joined the National Secular Society and was soon in demand as a lecturer, delivering over 200 lectures a year. He was elected a vice-president in 1895. The following year he was appointed temporary editor of the Bradford *Truthseeker* and in 1898 became assistant editor of G. W. Foote's *Freethinker*. He was clearly Foote's ablest young lieutenant, and in 1915 on Foote's death he was appointed both editor of the *Freethinker* and president of the National Secular Society.

Cohen was a witty, courteous, and effective public speaker and debater, and a prolific writer with over fifty titles to his credit. Typical of his writings are *A Grammar of Freethought* (1921), *Theism or Atheism* (1921), *Materialism Restated* (1927), and four series of *Essays in Freethinking* (1923–38), culled from occasional pieces in the *Freethinker*. His achievement was to transform Victorian freethought from an emphasis on anti-biblical argument to the positive advocacy of materialism, and his views were put before a wider public when he debated 'Materialism: has it been exploded?' with C. E. M. Joad at the Caxton Hall, Westminster, in 1928. In 1940 he published *Almost an Autobiography*, which provides a charming insight into his character and ideas but is frustratingly thin on biographical fact. As an organizer Cohen did much to build up the resources of secularism in the inter-war years, but by 1949, when he was persuaded to resign as president, many members felt he had stayed on too long. He remained editor of the *Freethinker* until 1951.

Cohen was married on 31 August 1897 to Cecilia Alice (1874–1966), the daughter of Walter James Holyfield, a customs officer. They had two children, Raymond Chapman (*b.* 1908), who survived his father, and Daisy, who died shortly after her marriage in 1928 or 1929, aged twenty-nine. Cohen himself died on 4 February 1954 at Warley Hospital in Brentwood. He was cremated at Golders Green on 11 February.   EDWARD ROYLE

Sources C. Cohen, *Almost an autobiography: the confessions of a freethinker* (1940) · *The Freethinker* (19 Feb 1954) · *The Freethinker* (26 Feb 1954) · *The Freethinker* (6 March 1954) · *The Truthseeker* (March 1895), 1–2 · E. Royle, *Radicals, secularists and republicans: popular freethought in Britain, 1866–1915* (1980) · D. Tribe, *100 years of freethought* (1967) · J. Herrick, *Vision and realism: a hundred years of the 'Freethinker'* (1982) · b. cert. · m. cert. · d. cert.
Archives SOUND National Secular Society, Bradlaugh House, 47 Theobald's Road, London, Cohen reading his own lecture 'The meaning and value of freethought', 1932 [Eddison Bell recording on a 10-inch double-sided record (commercial recording)]

Likenesses W. V. Amey, photographs, 1893–1917, repro. in Cohen, *Almost an autobiography*, 49, III · J. H. Amshewitz, oils, 1933, National Secular Society, London · H. Cutner, ink sketch, 1938, National Secular Society, London · H. Coster, photograph, 1940, repro. in Cohen, *Almost an autobiography*, frontispiece

Wealth at death £3724 5s. 5d.: probate, 6 May 1954, *CGPLA Eng. & Wales*

Cohen [*married name* Kellner], **Elsie** (*d.* 1972), cinema owner, is a figure whose origins are totally unknown. She entered the cinema industry in 1915 as a junior sub-editor on the trade paper *Kinematograph Weekly*, beating numerous male applicants who were liable to be called up in the war. She became deeply interested in films, particularly after conducting a long interview in 1916 with the director D. W. Griffith when he went to London for the opening of his epic *Intolerance* (1916). In 1919 she accepted the post of publicity manager for the Hollandia film-making company in Holland, becoming the studio manager and its travelling sales executive until the owner died and it closed down. She then worked in Germany before becoming floor manager on a British film, *His House in Order*, starring Tallulah Bankhead, made in 1927.

In 1929 Elsie Cohen discovered that an old cinema, the Palais de Luxe, in the West End of London was vacant for a short while prior to its reconstruction as the Windmill Theatre. She decided to use the building to show important foreign films which were not being seen in the centre of London, and achieved a great success. This became the first art cinema in the country.

It was not until 1931 that Elsie Cohen found a new base for showing foreign films—the Academy Cinema in Oxford Street, where she gained the support of cinema owner Eric Hakim. She started with one-week revivals of famous silent films from the continent and scored a huge success with the Russian *Earth* (1930), followed by *Turksib* (1929), *The End of St Petersburg* (1927), and others, also reviving the British documentary *Drifters* (1929). She then went abroad, acquiring new sound films from France, Germany, and Sweden, the Netherlands, and Russia to show at the Academy, supported by worthwhile shorts. Among her major successes were *Kameradschaft* (1931) and *Mädchen in Uniform* (1931), of which *Close-up* magazine in its June 1932 issue noted: 'Actually, we are becoming so accustomed to assisting at the best Cosmopolitan talkies at the Academy that we are apt to forget the initial miracle of having a specialised theatre in sleepy London'.

Elsie Cohen was soon launching films with lavish premières that attracted royalty and leading society figures, even persuading director René Clair to grace with his presence the opening in 1935 of *Le dernier milliardaire*—but she made a policy of providing a section of low-price seats within the reach of students and other impecunious film enthusiasts. Part of her marketing skill lay in building up a mailing list which was used to send detailed information about each new choice of film.

The Academy was so successful that it encouraged other cinemas like the Boltons at Kensington to show foreign pictures, widening the market for quality subtitled releases. Elsie Cohen herself expanded operations to run foreign films at Cinema House in Oxford Circus for several years, and later at the Berkeley Cinema in Mayfair.

After 1937 Cohen dropped German films and concentrated on French productions, introducing British audiences to such master-works as Jean Renoir's *La grande illusion* in 1938 and *Quai des Brumes* in 1939. She was managing director of Unity Films, which imported many of the productions.

Occasionally there were censorship problems. Showing the documentary *Spanish Earth* in the late 1930s, Elsie Cohen was forced to eliminate almost all the footage revealing German support for General Franco but alerted the press to the glimpse that remained, creating headlines. When she was refused a censor's certificate to show the Russian anti-Nazi film *Professor Mamlock* (1938), she gained a special licence from the London county council and was playing the film at the declaration of war in September 1939.

Elsie Cohen had planned to open a chain of Academy cinemas in the provinces until war intervened. The Academy itself was forced to close in October 1940 because of bomb damage and passed into the hands of a receiver. George Hoellering, an Austrian who had impressed Elsie Cohen with his film *Hortobagy* and settled in England, becoming a director of the Academy before the war, was able to re-open the cinema in 1944. It was soon re-established as London's leading art house but Elsie Cohen, to her regret, was no longer involved. During the war and until 1947, she organized the recording of entertainment broadcasts for the troops and their distribution overseas.

Married to a Dr Kellner, Elsie Cohen resided in Brighton where she died, following a long illness, on 26 January 1972.
ALLEN EYLES

Sources A. Slide, 'Elsie Cohen', *Silent Picture*, 10 (1971), [16]–[20] · E. Coxhead, 'Towards a co-operative cinema', *Close Up*, 10/2 (1933) · *The Times* (5 Feb 1972) · *Close-Up Magazine* (June 1932)

Likenesses photographs, BFI

Cohen, Hannah Floretta (1875–1946), philanthropist and civil servant, was born at 63 Queen's Gardens, Kensington, London, on 25 May 1875, the only daughter of Sir Benjamin Louis *Cohen, baronet (1844–1909). Her father was a great-grandson of Levi Barent Cohen, an Amsterdam merchant who had settled in London in the late eighteenth century, and whose twelve children formed the backbone of 'the cousinhood'—the network of wealthy families which provided the lay leadership of Anglo-Jewry until the mid-twentieth century. Her mother, Louisa Emily Merton (1850–1931), was also a great-grandchild of Levi Barent Cohen. Benjamin Cohen, besides being a stockbroker, was active both in party politics (he sat as Conservative MP for East Islington from 1892 to 1906) and in Anglo-Jewish affairs, serving as president of the Board of Guardians for the Relief of the Jewish Poor from 1887 to 1900. Hannah Cohen thus grew up in an opulent Anglo-Jewish milieu in which it was accepted that members of the dominant families would assume the burdens of communal leadership. In *Changing Faces*, a memoir of her mother which she published in 1937, she offered a sympathetic insight into this world in which affluence and leisure existed naturally alongside persistent philanthropy and public service.

Hannah Cohen was educated at Roedean School and Newnham College, Cambridge (1894–7), where she read for the classical tripos. Though of independent means, during the First World War she accepted employment in the factory department of the Home Office (1916–17), from where she moved to the Treasury (1917–20), becoming one of the first women to be entrusted with senior employment in the civil service; her work at the Treasury earned her an OBE. At that time the presidency of the Jewish Board of Guardians was held by her cousin, Sir Lionel Cohen, who had succeeded her father in that office. Established in 1859, the board of guardians had been regarded as a model of good practice in relation to voluntary poor relief, which in time extended also to financing schemes of apprenticeship and to providing loans and grants to enable impoverished Jewish immigrants to learn suitable trades. But the large-scale influx of Russian-Jewish refugees in the 1880s and 1890s had led it to adopt, under the influence of Sir Benjamin Cohen and other members of the Anglo-Jewish establishment, a series of highly unpopular panic-induced policies, including repatriation; Sir Benjamin himself had incurred considerable communal opprobrium by offering parliamentary support for the 1905 Aliens Act.

In 1900 Hannah Cohen had become the first woman to be elected a member of the board of guardians; over the next twenty years she familiarized herself with every aspect of its work. In 1921 she became the guardians' honorary secretary, succeeding to the vice-presidency in 1926; she held the presidency itself from 1930 to 1940. In the case of each of these offices, she was the first female incumbent. The revival of the reputation of the guardians was due in no small measure to Hannah Cohen's exertions. A brilliant administrator, she brought the guardians back to an appreciation of their original philosophy, arguing that the prevention of poverty was better than its cure, and emphasizing the importance of health and the value of convalescence. In the nineteenth century the Anglo-Jewish leadership had vigorously opposed any reliance on financial assistance from the state to help cope with the problems of the Jewish poor. Hannah Cohen had no such inhibitions: in 1929 she made, on behalf of the guardians, its first radio broadcast appeal for funds. Under her leadership the guardians took full advantage of the financial benefits of the rudimentary welfare state then in existence, covering sickness, unemployment, and old-age benefits. These were supplemented as necessary, but the major focus of the guardians was readjusted to concentrate on housing schemes, the provision of health services, and the expansion of convalescent facilities, especially for women and children.

Hannah Cohen served on the governing bodies of Roedean and Newnham, the Working Women's College, London, Swanley Horticultural College, and the Jewish Orphanage, Norwood. She never married. She died of gangrene in Stoneycrest Nursing Home in Hindhead, Surrey, on 21 November 1946. GEOFFREY ALDERMAN

Sources V. D. Lipman, *A century of social service, 1859–1959: the Jewish Board of Guardians* (1959) • L. L. Cohen, 'Levi Barent Cohen and some of his descendants', *Transactions of the Jewish Historical Society of England*, 16 (1945–51), 11–23 • C. Bermant, *The cousinhood: the Anglo-Jewish gentry* (1971) • H. Cohen, *Changing faces: a memoir of Louisa, Lady Cohen* (1937) • J. P. Strachey, 'Hannah Floretta Cohen', *Newnham College Roll Letter* (1947), 50–52 • *Jewish Chronicle* (29 Nov 1946), 15 • b. cert. • *Jewish Year Book* (1845–6), 3 • d. cert.

Archives Jewish Care, London

Likenesses photograph, Jewish Care, London • photograph, repro. in *Jewish Chronicle*, 15

Wealth at death £153,970 10s. 11d.: probate, 25 March 1947, CGPLA Eng. & Wales

Cohen, Harriet Pearl Alice (1895–1967), pianist, was born on 2 December 1895 at 58 Angell Road, Brixton, London, the daughter of Joseph Woolf Cohen, company secretary, and his wife, Florence White. An amateur cellist and composer, her father was of Lithuanian extraction. Her mother, a gifted pianist herself, taught Harriet the piano until the child was thirteen.

Harriet Cohen entered the Royal Academy of Music in 1909, the youngest student to win the Ada Lewis scholarship. She studied with Felix Swinstead and Tobias Matthay for the piano and Frederick Corder for theory and composition. She remained at the academy, and also at the Matthay School, until 1915; during that time she became associated with her piano professor, Tobias Matthay, as a teacher of other students. While at the academy her string of awards included the Sterndale Bennett, Edward Nicholls, and Hine prizes. She was part of a group based on current and former students of the academy—which included the composer Arnold Edward Trevor *Bax (1883–1953)—who responded to the craze for things Russian when the Diaghilev ballet visited London between 1911 and 1914, and she became known as Tania to her friends.

During the First World War, Cohen and Bax carried on a love affair. In March 1918, in consequence of the developing relationship, Bax left his wife and children, though he and Cohen never lived together, and she never married. Harriet Cohen's London début was in a joint recital with the soprano Raymonde Collignon at the Aeolian Hall in June 1919, *The Times* writing: '… lightest of light sopranos—delicate and rarified perfection. Miss Harriet Cohen is a pianist something after the same style' (*The Times*, 7 June 1919). However, Cohen's pianism was constrained by her small hands and the webbing of her fingers. She was launched on the concert scene in 1920, appearing in the repertory that coloured her career: a combination of the revival of Bach and the keyboard music of the Elizabethans played on the piano, as well as the new music of the day. In Arthur Bliss's 'Storm' for Shakespeare's *The Tempest*, scored for piano, percussion, trumpet, and trombone, in 1921, her part proved so vigorous that she smashed a thumbnail.

Harriet Cohen appeared at the Queen's Hall, London, in a solo recital in June 1920 with Bax's newly revised piano sonata no. 2, and in November that year reappeared with

Harriet Pearl Alice Cohen (1895–1967), by Fred Daniels, 1918

his enormous *Symphonic Variations* for piano and orchestra. Arnold Bennett, one of many admirers, noted in his diary, 'Such an ovation I have never before seen at a Prom' (*Journals*, 2). She was soon associated with other similar modern works, notably Manuel de Falla's *Noches en los jardines de España* ('Nights in the Gardens of Spain'), and later music by Shostakovich and Kabalevsky.

Her striking good looks also contributed to Cohen's early success, which placed her at the focus of the London artistic life of the early 1920s. She proved a celebrated organizer of musical parties. Here she integrated the literary and musical worlds, her guests including Bennett and George Bernard Shaw. She promoted the revival of Tudor church music and integrated the world of the Russian ballet into the London scene, particularly being associated with the ballerina Tamara Karsavina, for whom she first played in 1920. In 1924 Harriet Cohen appeared at the Salzburg chamber music festival of the International Society for Contemporary Music.

Harriet Cohen's early success was interrupted by illness, and in 1925 she spent some time at a TB clinic in Switzerland. By the time of her return to England in 1926 the relationship between her and Bax had somewhat cooled, though they appeared in public together until his death. She toured extensively and tended to be the chosen artist when new British works were played, appearing for example in Germany in July 1930 in an all-British programme playing William Walton's *Sinfonia concertante*, conducted by Constant Lambert.

Harriet Cohen recorded for Columbia and became well known in the 1930s for her pioneering recordings of Bach's preludes and fugues. Her other recordings included Mozart, Brahms, and Chopin. However, many of the surviving recordings of her playing, including the Bach keyboard concerto in D minor for which she was celebrated in her day, were made in the years immediately after the Second World War and possibly do not find her at

her peak. In 1931 a dozen British composers were persuaded to contribute arrangements of various works of Bach for *A Bach Book for Harriet Cohen*, which was published in 1932; the pieces were first heard at the Queen's Hall in October 1932.

In 1932 Harriet Cohen gave the first performance of Bax's second major work for piano and orchestra, *Winter Legends*, though it was seldom played thereafter. In February 1933 she gave the first performance of the Vaughan Williams piano concerto. This work, too, was little played, and in 1942 Sir Adrian Boult noted in a BBC internal memo:

> It is surely common knowledge that Harriet Cohen's performance of the … Concerto caused it to be completely dropped … the work … was laid out for a pianist of the Busoni calibre, and although she made a very valiant effort, she could get nowhere near the spirit of it, or even the notes in many passages.   (facsimile in Foreman, pl. 7)

Harriet Cohen had been associated with Sir Edward Elgar from the time when they both had lived in Hampstead; and in May 1933 she organized a Wigmore Hall concert in which all three of his mature chamber works (the violin sonata, the string quartet, and the piano quintet) were presented. This resulted in her recording the quintet with the Stratton Quartet. In 1936 Cohen published *Music's Handmaid*, in which she discussed the performance of the repertory with which she was principally associated. Two years later she was appointed CBE 'for services to British music'. This was one of many awards from countries as varied as Finland, Belgium, and Brazil.

At the beginning of the Second World War Harriet Cohen was on tour in the USA, and she did not return until the summer of 1940. She was untiring in what she felt to be positive artistic diplomacy, though the authorities did not always take her at her own valuation. A major shock came with the blitz when her house was bombed and burnt out, causing the loss of not only her piano but also her music. In the UK she undertook extensive provincial tours, but was no longer well thought of by the BBC music staff. Despite extensive lobbying, a succession of accidents and illnesses frustrated her success when dates were offered. In 1944 Bax bought her the flat in Gloucester Place Mews, Portman Square, London, where she lived until her death.

In 1946 Bax wrote *Morning Song*, a short piece for piano and orchestra to mark the twenty-first birthday of Princess Elizabeth in 1947. Cohen recorded it in February 1947, and it was first performed at a Promenade Concert in August and in the princess's presence in October.

In 1946 Bax's wife died, but Harriet learned of this only when the will was published in 1948. She imagined Bax would marry her, but on being pressed, he had to disclose the existence of another mistress, Mary Gleaves, whom he had known since 1926. This was in May 1948, when Bax's music for the film *Oliver Twist* was being recorded.

Subsequently Harriet suffered a serious accident and cut her right wrist, which stopped her from playing, an incident later marked in a BBC radio feature. Bax wrote a left-hand concerto (he called it *Concertante*) for her, in which she reappeared at Cheltenham in July 1950 and at the Promenade Concerts three weeks later. Her wrist made such a good recovery that in 1954 she was able to broadcast Bax's *Winter Legends* and also championed Peter Racine Fricker's piano concerto, op. 19, which was written for her. She gave the first performance in March 1954.

Harriet Cohen formally retired in 1960 and thereafter devoted her time to the Harriet Cohen international awards, which she had started in the early 1950s. She wrote her autobiography, *A Bundle of Time*, though it was unpublished at her unexpected death in the University College Hospital, London, from pneumonia on 13 November 1967.   LEWIS FOREMAN

Sources H. Cohen, *A bundle of time: the memoirs of Harriet Cohen* (1969) · H. Cohen, *Music's handmaid* (1936) · *The journals of Arnold Bennett*, ed. N. Flower, 2: *1911–1921* (1932); 3: *1921–1928* (1933) · *Letters of Arnold Bennett*, ed. J. Hepburn, 3 (1970) · L. Foreman, ed., *Vaughan Williams in perspective: studies of an English composer* (1998) · *DNB* · *The Times* (7 June 1919) · *The Times* (14 Nov 1967) · *The Guardian* (14 Nov 1967) · *Daily Telegraph* (14 Nov 1967) · *Irish News* (14 Nov 1967) · *Jewish Chronicle* (17 Nov 1967) · H. Cohen, letters to Arthur Alexander, priv. coll. · press cuttings, programmes, priv. coll. · H. Cohen, papers, BL, deposit 1999/10 [formerly reserved MSS 134/1–4] · personal knowledge (2004) · *CGPLA Eng. & Wales* (1968) · b. cert.
Archives BL, corresp. and papers, deposit 1999/10 · Royal Academy of Music, London, papers | CUL, letters to W. A. Gerhardie · UCL, corresp. with Arnold Bennett's solicitors
Likenesses F. Daniels, photograph, 1918, NPG [*see illus.*] · E. Kapp, drawing, 1930, Barber Institute of Fine Arts, Birmingham · E. Kapp, drawing, 1938, Barber Institute of Fine Arts, Birmingham · double portrait, photograph (with G. B. Shaw), NPG
Wealth at death £24,491: probate, 19 June 1968, *CGPLA Eng. & Wales*

Cohen, Henry, **Baron Cohen of Birkenhead** (1900–1977), physician, was born in Birkenhead on 21 February 1900, the youngest of the five children (four boys and one girl) of Isaac Cohen (*d.* 1939), a draper and a considerable Jewish scholar, of Liverpool, and his wife, Dora Mendelson (1862/3–1955), the dominant personality in the family. Her son was devoted to her to the end of her long life. Both parents were of Russian origin, and the family was very poor. Cohen was educated locally at the church school of St John, from which he won a scholarship to Birkenhead Institute. There he captained the rugby fifteen and the cricket eleven, was champion gymnast, and gained some experience in theatricals. From the institute he won a scholarship to Oxford, but on grounds of expense transferred it to Liverpool.

Cohen's original intention had been to study medicine in order to become a criminal lawyer, but as his work continued he realized that medicine alone had enough to offer him. He graduated MB, ChB, in 1922, with first-class honours and a distinction in every subject in the curriculum, and obtained his MD with special merit in 1924. He became a member of the Royal College of Physicians in 1926. His first appointment was as assistant physician (1924–31) to the Liverpool Royal Infirmary; he was physician to outpatients (1931–4) and was appointed honorary physician in 1934. He remained on the staff of the infirmary until his retirement after forty-one years, later becoming senior physician. He was also consultant to Hoylake

Henry Cohen, Baron Cohen of Birkenhead (1900–1977), by Edward Irvine Halliday, 1970

Hospital, the West Lancashire Mental Association, and the Liverpool Psychotherapeutic Clinic.

For Cohen to obtain his initial post within two years of qualifying showed exceptional brilliance, and in 1934 he was appointed to the chair of medicine at Liverpool University. This, as usual in those days, was a part-time position, enabling him to follow up the results of his teaching by keeping in contact with the practitioners in the area who asked him for a second opinion. However, there was an administrative problem which he never really solved. The four general teaching hospitals considered themselves autonomous units, and even when they were nominally incorporated into the United Liverpool Hospitals in 1936 there was little love lost between them. Welding a teaching and research unit together under such circumstances presented insuperable difficulties to a young man of whom many people were jealous. It was perhaps this background in his early years which determined Cohen's individualistic approach to his career. In later years (1947–71) he served as a member of the board of governors of the Liverpool teaching hospitals and of the regional hospital board.

From the time when he was appointed to the chair to the end of the war Cohen rose to eminence in the conventional way. He was elected FRCP in 1934 and later became an examiner to the college; he was a member of council in 1943–6. During this time he was also increasingly in demand as an orator: one of his outstanding accomplishments was his ability to speak in public, and his lectures and orations were brilliant performances, showing originality, breadth of vision, erudition, and wit. A prime example was the Harveian oration at the Royal College of Physicians in 1970, 'On the motion of blood in the veins'.

Of the same standard as Cohen's great clinical ability and his oratory was his grasp of administration, particularly his chairmanship of committees, and it was in this capacity that he was to be of special use after the introduction of the National Health Service, when he became one of the principal outside expert and voluntary advisers to the Ministry of Health. He chaired the standing advisory committee of the Ministry of Health from 1948 to 1963 and was the first vice-chairman of the Central Health Services Council (CHSC) when it was formed in 1949; he became chairman in 1957. His great contribution was that he brought to the ministry the professional knowledge of the active clinician, so that the administration was kept closely in touch with the outside medical world. 'His remarkable memory and powers of exposition made him a formidable figure in the councils of the ministry of health, and the debt owed to him by successive ministers and departmental heads was immense' (Munk, *Roll*).

In 1952 Cohen was seriously ill with a coronary thrombosis. Unlike most doctors, he strictly adhered to the medical advice he was given, and on recovery gave up his vast private practice and dedicated himself to the national work of the organization and advancement of British medicine. He presided over countless committees and was a household name to general practitioners, who had good reason to bless the Cohen categories which evolved from the work of a CHSC committee, presided over by Cohen, on drug classification in the National Health Service. One of his most important scientific contributions arose by virtue of his chairmanship of the Ministry of Health committee dealing with the organization of poliomyelitis vaccination in Britain. He also played a large part in the preparation of the reports on the medical care of epileptics and on staphylococcal infections in hospital, and served on Medical Research Council committees on deafness and on other subjects. He served on the British Medical Association (BMA) committees on the training of a doctor, and on general practice.

Cohen was proud of his Jewish heritage, though he was concerned more with its ethical, cultural, and historical aspects than with religious detail. However, throughout his public life if there was anything to be done in the Jewish fashion he did it; for example, when he entered the House of Lords he took the oath on the Old Testament and with his head covered. His contributions to Jewish causes and charities were very considerable.

Outside medicine Cohen's first love was the theatre and he took a very active part in the running of the Liverpool Playhouse. He helped to select the plays, and as he was a shrewd businessman the Liverpool Repertory Company was one of the few in the country to make money. His favourite theatre story was that, when a small boy, he had taken the part of the first watchman in *Much Ado about Nothing*, and it had been reported in the local press that 'the first watchman had two lines to speak and both were inaudible'. His later distinction as an orator showed that the words of the theatre critic had not fallen on stony ground. His other great love was the collection of old silver, and when he was president of the Liverpool Medical Institution in 1954 his inaugural lecture on the subject delighted his medical and lay audience. As a leisure occupation, he said, it satisfied the intellect as well as the aesthetic senses.

Cohen obtained numerous prizes, medals, and honorary fellowships, and was awarded honorary degrees at Oxford, Cambridge, London, Liverpool, Manchester, Hull, Dublin, and Sussex. He was chancellor of Hull University from 1970. He was knighted in 1949, and in 1956 accepted a barony. He was elected president of the BMA in 1951, of the General Medical Council from 1961 to 1970, and of the Royal Society of Medicine in 1964.

Cohen died unexpectedly after a short illness on 7 August 1977, at Bath. He was unmarried and the barony became extinct.   CYRIL CLARKE

Sources *The Times* (9 Aug 1977) · personal knowledge (2004) · Munk, *Roll* · *BMJ* (20 Aug 1977), 525 · *BMJ* (3 Sept 1977), 647 · *BMJ* (22 Oct 1977), 1094 · *The Lancet* (20 Aug 1977) · *WWW* · C. Webster, *The health services since the war*, 1 (1988) · private information (2004) · *CGPLA Eng. & Wales* (1977)

Archives U. Lpool L., corresp. and papers | Wellcome L., corresp. with Sir Ernst Chain

Likenesses E. I. Halliday, drawing, 1970, Royal Society of Medicine, London [*see illus.*] · H. Knight, portrait, Liverpool Medical Institution

Wealth at death £406,534: probate, 18 Aug 1977, *CGPLA Eng. & Wales*

Cohen, Israel (1879–1961), Zionist and author, was born at 9 Park Street, Red Bank, Cheatham, Manchester, on 24 April 1879, the son of Morris Cohen, tailor, and his wife, Fanny, *née* Levy. Both his parents were immigrants from Poland. He was educated at Manchester Jews' School (1884–92) and Manchester grammar school (1892–5); and then simultaneously at Jews' College and University College, London (where he studied for a BA). Actively involved in the Zionist movement from 1895, he played a noteworthy role in its achievements, being particularly concerned with maintaining good relations between the Zionist pioneers and the press. He was one of a group that included Harry Sacher, Herbert Bentwich, and Leopold Greenberg, the second and third generation of early east European immigration from which English Zionism drew its political and intellectual leadership.

Cohen's interest in Jewish affairs and political matters was first aroused in 1891 by an article in the *Jewish Chronicle* about pogroms in Russia. Theodor Herzl published his epoch-making pamphlet *The Jewish State* in February 1896, and on 12 July of that year Cohen was in the audience when Herzl spoke at the Jewish Working Men's Club in Great Alie Street in the East End of London, a speech that fired Cohen's imagination. The Zionist movement was officially established at the First Zionist Congress in Basel at the end of August 1897, and Cohen became a lifelong supporter. After a short spell as secretary of the English Zionist Federation, from 1909 to the outbreak of the First World War he directed the English department of the Zionist Central Office in Cologne and later in Berlin. Stranded in Germany at the outbreak of the First World War, he was interned in Ruhleben prison for sixteen months from November 1914, and wrote of his experiences in *Ruhleben Prison Camp*, published in London in 1917.

In 1918 Cohen rejoined the secretariat of the World Zionist Organization in London. It was on 29 July of that year that he married Theresa (Tessie; *b.* 1893/4), a school-mistress, daughter of Louis Jacobs, a hairdresser; she shared and supported his Zionist enthusiasm. They had two sons, and bought a house on the borders of Hampstead Heath in London, where they remained throughout the marriage.

Cohen described the years 1918–21 as the zenith of the Zionist movement in England, 'in which hopes soared highest concerning the fulfilment of Zionist ideals, and when it was comparatively easy to raise large sums towards their realisations' (Weisgal, 230–31). He wrote this in a contribution to a British memorial volume to Herzl published in 1929. During this period he made a number of important diplomatic and fund-raising missions on behalf of the Zionist leadership that took him to Poland to investigate and report on the pogroms there; to Hungary, to inquire into anti-Jewish outrages; and to Jewish communities in Australia, Hong Kong, India, China, Japan, and Manchuria to seek support for the Palestine Restoration Fund. On these tours, which he described in *The Journey of a Jewish Traveller* (1925) and in his autobiography, *A Jewish Pilgrimage* (1956), he raised nearly £120,000. Shortly after the Zionist Congress met in Karlsbad in September 1921, Cohen was appointed general secretary of the Zionist organization in London, a position he held until the end of 1939. For many years he was a member of the Board of Deputies of British Jews, being particularly active on its foreign affairs committee, and in 1946 was appointed head of its delegation to the peace conference in Paris.

Cohen was a prolific author and journalist. His first effort, an article on the Jewish new year that appeared in the *Manchester Evening Chronicle* in September 1897, was followed in January 1898 by a short sketch of a ghetto character that was accepted by *Jewish World*. Because he was still at Jews' College, and officially students were not allowed to have outside interests, it appeared under the pseudonym Enoch Scribe, Enoch being an anagram of his surname. He subsequently wrote hundreds of newspaper articles and pamphlets, and for Jewish and non-Jewish journals, on Zionism, antisemitism, and other Jewish subjects. When working in Germany he became the Berlin correspondent for *The Times* and *Manchester Guardian*, and continued to represent the latter at every Zionist Congress to 1946. His many books, including *Jewish Life in Modern Times* (1914) and *History of the Jews of Vilna* (1943), were well

received by critics. Israel Cohen died at his home, 29 Pattison Road, Child's Hill, London, on 26 November 1961, and was survived by his wife. GERRY BLACK

Sources I. Cohen, *A Jewish pilgrimage* (1956) · *Jewish Chronicle* (1 Dec 1961) · L. P. Gartner, *The Jewish immigrant in England, 1870–1914* (1960) · D. Cesarani, *The Jewish Chronicle and Anglo-Jewry, 1841–1991* (1994) · V. Lipman, *A history of the Jews in Britain since 1858* (1990) · P. Goodman, *Zionism in England: the English Zionist Federation, 1899–1929* (1929) · *CGPLA Eng. & Wales* (1962) · M. W. Weisgal, 'Theodore Herzl: a memorial', *The rise of Jewish nationalism in the Middle East* (1929), 230–31 · b. cert. · m. cert. · d. cert.
Archives JRL, letters to *Manchester Guardian*
Likenesses photograph, repro. in Cohen, *A Jewish pilgrimage*
Wealth at death £1771 15s. 10d.: probate, 1962, *CGPLA Eng. & Wales*

Cohen, Sir John Edward [Jack; *formerly* Jacob Edward Kohen] (**1898–1979**), grocer and creator of Tesco stores, was born in the City of London on 6 October 1898, the fifth of six children and the second of three sons of Avroam Kohen, an immigrant Polish-Jewish tailor, and his first wife, Sime Zamremba (*d.* 1915). Jack, as he was known from childhood, was educated at Rutland Street London county council elementary school until the age of fourteen, after which he joined his father as an apprentice tailor. After his mother's death his father remarried and the rising tensions between stepmother and children encouraged Jack to volunteer in 1917 at the age of eighteen for the Royal Flying Corps, where his tailoring skills were in demand for the making of balloon and aircraft canvas. He served in France, Egypt, and Palestine, narrowly escaping death in December 1917, when his troop carrier was sunk by a mine outside Alexandria. Demobilized early on account of a malarial infection which he had contracted, he returned to London in March 1919. As he was unwilling to resume tailoring and unable to obtain an office job in the City, he used his £30 demobilization gratuity to buy surplus NAAFI foodstuffs and established a stall in a street market in Hackney. Within a short time he was trading in a different market in the London area on each day of the week.

In 1924 Cohen married Sarah (Cissie), daughter of Benjamin Fox, master tailor and immigrant Russian Jew; they had two daughters. His wife encouraged his business endeavours, and Cohen extended his interests to wholesaling. Street trading remained, however, his main activity in the 1920s. One of his most successful lines was tea. He established the brand name Tesco by joining the first two letters of his surname to the initials of T. E. Stockwell, of Messrs Torring and Stockwell of Mincing Lane, his tea suppliers. Around 1930 he changed his given name by deed poll to John Edward in response to a plea from his bank manager at Mare Street, Hackney, whose staff could not distinguish the several Jacob Cohens among their customers.

The rapid expansion of London's suburbs in the house-building boom of the 1930s brought new retailing opportunities. The first two Tesco shops were opened at Becontree and Burnt Oak in 1931. Cohen's formula was to seek maximum turnover through low profit margins and prices. By 1939 there were 100 Tesco grocery shops in London and the home counties. During the Second World War, which precluded further shop development, Cohen acquired Goldhanger Fruit Farms in Essex and set up a fruit canning business, besides marketing their produce in Tesco shops. After the war, and a visit to the United States in 1947, Cohen became a pioneer in Britain of American-style retailing, based on self-service and payment at turnstile exits in place of traditional over-the-counter service. The new pattern made rapid strides, once the last elements of wartime consumer rationing were abolished in 1953. By 1959 the Tesco group comprised 185 stores, of which 140 were self-service, and net profits had increased from £78,000 in 1952 to almost £1 million.

Cohen had a colostomy operation in 1958, but returned promptly to resume his direction of the company. Takeovers and mergers brought faster growth in the 1960s. By 1968, when Tesco had acquired the Victor Value chain, it owned a total of 834 self-service shops, including many supermarkets, making it the fourth largest chain in the United Kingdom (after the Co-op, Fine Fare, and Allied Suppliers). Its net profits were nearly £6.7 million on a turnover of £240 million. By his trading policies during this period Cohen also played a major role in the campaign against resale price maintenance (RPM), the system whereby manufacturers of many products controlled the prices at which distributors sold them to the public. Tesco followed Fine Fare and other supermarket chains in introducing trading stamps, agreeing a deal in October 1963 with the Green Shield Trading Stamp Company. The use of stamps was widely seen as a roundabout way of cutting prices, and its opponents, who included both suppliers (such as the Distillers Company and Imperial Tobacco) and retailers (who formed the Distributive Trades Alliance under the leadership of Lord Sainsbury), took action to prevent the use of stamps in connection with items subject to RPM. The issue was settled with the help of government legislation: the Resale Prices Act was passed in 1964 and implemented gradually over the rest of the decade, eliminating RPM on all goods except books and pharmaceuticals.

Cohen was knighted in 1969. He relinquished the chairmanship of Tesco later that year, but remained active in the company's affairs. He was a freemason and a member of the Worshipful Company of Carmen, of which he served as master in 1976–7. He was a generous benefactor to charities, notably hospitals and old peoples' homes, in Britain and Israel. His distinctive features—broad nose and mouth, high cheekbones, and prominent ears—made him easily recognizable in public. He was an outgoing, restless, sociable man, deeply attached to his family and valuing the accomplishment of a task rather than its material rewards. He died at the London Clinic on 24 March 1979.   P. M. OPPENHEIMER, *rev.*

Sources M. Corina, *Pile it high, sell it cheap: the authorised biography of Sir J. Cohen, founder of Tesco* (1971) · private information (1986, 2004) · *Daily Telegraph* (26 March 1979), 3a–d · *CGPLA Eng. & Wales* (1979)

Likenesses photograph, repro. in Corina, *Pile it high, sell it cheap* · photograph, repro. in *Daily Telegraph*, 3 · photographs, Hult. Arch.
Wealth at death £1,957,640: probate, 14 June 1979, *CGPLA Eng. & Wales*

Cohen [*née* Waley], **Julia Matilda** (1853–1917), community worker and educationist, was born on 6 September 1853 at 20 Wimpole Street, Marylebone, Middlesex, the daughter of Professor Jacob *Waley (1818–1873), conveyancing counsel to the court of chancery and the first holder of the chair of political economy at University College, London, and his wife, Matilda Salomons (1828–1873), who was a niece both of Sir David Salomons and of Sir Moses Montefiore. Waley's father, Solomon Jacob Levi, had adopted the surname of Waley in 1834 from the maternal side. In 1873 Julia, who was familiarly known as Sissy, married Nathaniel (Natty) Louis Cohen (1846–1913), the youngest surviving son of the banker and stockbroker Louis Cohen. The Waley surname was added to that of the six surviving children of the marriage, four girls and three boys. The most prominent of these was Sir Robert Waley*Cohen (1877–1952), who became a director of Royal Dutch Shell, and also served as president of the United Synagogue.

The family lived at 11 Hyde Park Terrace, London, and had a country home at Round Oak, Englefield Green, Surrey, not far from Windsor Great Park, where Julia, 'a small wiry woman', could indulge her passion for 'horses and horsemanship' (Bermant, 358). Their day-to-day life had little to do with the organized Jewish community, but the dietary laws were observed to some extent and prayers were recited morning and evening.

Julia Cohen had been educated at Queen's College, Harley Street, and had received religious instruction from Professor D. W. Marks, minister of the West London Synagogue, the foremost synagogue of the Reform movement in Britain. As an adult, family membership of the Central Synagogue notwithstanding, Julia conducted the children's services at the West London Synagogue and wrote and edited several textbooks for children on Jewish themes: *The Children's Psalm Book* (1907), *Infants Bible Reader* (1913), and *Addresses to Children* (1922). Her educational work extended to the promotion of vocational training for women, and she was instrumental in establishing a domestic science course at Queen's College for the benefit of teenage girls. Subsequently, she became vice-president of the Domestic Training Home, based in Regent's Park, which specialized in the recruitment and training of Jewish girls from the poorer classes to prepare them for entry into domestic service with their better-off sisters. Julia Cohen was also a member of the council of College Hall, a hall of residence established for women medical students. In addition, she served on the committee of the Society for the Training of Jewish Teachers, set up in association with Claude Montefiore in order to provide opportunities for Jewish girls without means to qualify as teachers.

Julia Cohen, who was known as Mrs Nathaniel Cohen, is chiefly remembered for her part in the foundation of the Union of Jewish Women. From its inception in 1902 until her death she was president of the union, the first umbrella national women's organization in the Anglo-

Jewish community. It was founded following a conference of Jewish women attended by some 800 in the Portman Rooms, Baker Street, London, on 13 May 1902. The guest of honour was Millicent Garrett Fawcett, president of the National Union of Women's Suffrage Societies. Julia was typical of the women who staffed the union, who were mainly the wives of the well-to-do philanthropists who financed and ran the Jewish institutions of the day. Like their husbands, these women had a high-minded but basically paternalistic attitude to voluntary social service, and endorsed the self-help philosophy of the Jewish Board of Guardians. Moreover, they accepted without question the traditional gender-based division of roles, buttressed both by the Jewish religion and Victorian middle-class morality.

After her husband's death in 1913 Julia Cohen moved to 10 Sussex Square, London. She died of a heart attack at Courtlands, West Hoathly, East Grinstead, Sussex, on 17 December 1917. She was buried on 20 December at Willesden Jewish cemetery. In a memorial sermon Julia Cohen was eulogized by the chief rabbi, J. H. Hertz, for her quiet contribution to the educational advancement of women in Britain. SHARMAN KADISH

Sources Jewish Chronicle (7 March 1902) · Jewish Chronicle (16 May 1902) · Jewish Chronicle (21 Dec 1917) · Jewish Year Book (1897) · Jewish Year Book (1908) · C. Bermant, The cousinhood: the Anglo-Jewish gentry (1971) · J. H. Hertz, 'A noble life: a sermon in memory of the late Mrs N. L. Cohen', 1918, UCL, Mocatta collection [pamphlets] · E. C. Black, The social politics of Anglo-Jewry, 1880–1920 (1988) · L. G. Kuzmack, Woman's cause: the Jewish woman's movement in England and the United States, 1881–1933 (1990) · The Times (21 June 1873) [Jacob Waley] · The Times (23 June 1873) [Jacob Waley] · Jewish Chronicle (27 June 1873) [Jacob Waley] · B. B. Benas, 'Jacob Waley', Transactions of the Jewish Historical Society of England, 18 (1953–5), 41–52 · A. M. Hyamson, David Salomons (1939) · CGPLA Eng. & Wales (1918) · b. cert. · The Times (15 Jan 1913) [Nathaniel Cohen] · Jewish Chronicle (17 Jan 1913) [N. L. Cohen]

Likenesses photograph, repro. in Jewish Chronicle (7 March 1902)
Wealth at death £58,437 7s. 1d.: probate, 29 Jan 1918, CGPLA Eng. & Wales

Cohen, Kenneth Herman Salaman

Cohen, Kenneth Herman Salaman (1900–1984), intelligence officer, was born on 15 March 1900 at 1 Lower Terrace, Branch Hill, Hampstead, London, the son of Jewish parents, Herman Cohen (d. in or after 1932), a barrister, and his wife, Bessie Salaman (d. in or after 1932). He was educated at Elstree School and then at Eastbourne College before joining the Royal Navy as a 'special entry' cadet in 1918. He subsequently served on HMS Iron Duke, and later became an expert on torpedos. In 1935, as an interpreter in French and Russian, he transferred to the Secret Intelligence Service (SIS). On 22 July 1932 he married Mary Sarah, daughter of Ernest Martin Joseph, architect, with whom he had a son and a daughter.

Soon after joining SIS Cohen was placed in charge of the London headquarters of a European network known simply as Z, which operated under commercial cover in parallel to the more overt SIS organization that depended upon a string of passport control offices attached to diplomatic premises abroad. Masquerading as Kenneth Crane and designated Z-3, Cohen worked through a front company, Menoline Ltd, in Maple Street, and an office in Bush House, to recruit sources, including several distinguished foreign correspondents of British newspapers in France, the Netherlands, Switzerland, Czechoslovakia, and Italy.

Upon the outbreak of war Z's assets were amalgamated into SIS's main organization and Cohen was attached to the French country section known as A5, becoming head of the Vichy section, designated P1 in May 1940. His task was to recruit sources from within the unoccupied zone of France, and one of his successes was Jacques Bridou, who was parachuted into France in March 1941 to establish the Alliance network, based in Pau and Marseilles and later to be headed by the formidable Marie-Madeleine Meric.

In summer 1943, in anticipation of an invasion of Europe, Cohen was selected to take charge of Brissex, the British component of a large scheme, codenamed Sussex, to parachute sixty two-man allied intelligence teams behind enemy lines. This huge paramilitary enterprise was intended to disrupt Nazi communications and logistics immediately after D-day and then liaise with local resistance organizations until overrun by the allies. The role played by Cohen required considerable tact and diplomacy because the American volunteers were inexperienced and the French intransigent.

Cohen was appointed CMG in 1946, and in the aftermath of the war he held senior posts in SIS (chief controller of Europe and director of production). He retired in 1953 and was created CB. With his 'sensitivity, astringent mind and understanding of international problems' (The Times) he served as European adviser to United Steel Companies from 1953 to 1966. During the last twenty years of his life his main interest was in promoting cross-channel friendship, and he served as chairman of the Franco-British Society from 1967 to 1972. He died in the Westminster Hospital, London, on 19 September 1984, survived by his wife. NIGEL WEST

Sources The Times (27 Sept 1984) · WWW · N. West, MI6: British secret intelligence service operations, 1909–45 (1983) · b. cert. · m. cert. · d. cert.
Wealth at death £541,491: probate, 1985, CGPLA Eng. & Wales

Cohen, Lionel Leonard, Baron Cohen

Cohen, Lionel Leonard, Baron Cohen (1888–1973), judge, was born on 1 March 1888 in London, the only child of Sir Leonard Lionel Cohen KCVO (1858–1938), banker, and his wife, Eliza Henrietta (d. 1935), daughter of Sigismund Schloss, of Bowden, Cheshire. His paternal grandfather sat as MP for Paddington jointly with Lord Randolph Churchill.

Lionel Cohen was educated at Eton College and New College, Oxford, where he obtained a first class in history (1909) and in law (1910). He was called to the bar by the Inner Temple in 1913, but later joined Lincoln's Inn, of which he was appointed a bencher in 1934 and treasurer in 1954. During the First World War he served with the 13th Princess Louise's Kensington battalion of the London regiment, was wounded in France, and on recovery held a staff appointment. On 9 April 1918 he married Adelaide (d. 1961), daughter of Sir Isidore Spielmann CMG, director of art exhibitions; they had two sons and a daughter.

On demobilization Cohen joined the chambers of Alfred Topham, a leading practitioner in company law, and acquired a big practice in this field. He took silk in 1929. He became recognized in commercial circles as the leading expert in his subject. In court he was a sound and successful advocate whose integrity and industry always gained him an attentive hearing, though he lacked the forensic brilliance of some of his contemporaries. In chambers and on paper his advice, shrewd, practical, and authoritative, and his excellent judgement put him in the first rank.

After a period of service in the Ministry of Economic Warfare (1939–43) Cohen was appointed a judge of the Chancery Division and knighted in 1943; he was quickly promoted to the Court of Appeal in 1946 and to the House of Lords as a life peer in 1951. He was a popular judge, courteous and sensible, and a good colleague. Though, as at the bar, he was perhaps outshone by some of his more flamboyant contemporaries, his judgments display balance, conciseness, and avoidance of dogmatism and rhetoric.

Cohen's contribution to the law would certainly have been more ample if he had not been so often diverted to the wide field of public affairs; there his performance was remarkable. As chairman of the company law amendment committee he was largely responsible for the contents of the Companies Act of 1948, the first major reconstruction since 1908. In 1946 he was a member, together with Lord Greene, of the tribunal established to assess compensation for the assets vested in the National Coal Board on nationalization. In this demanding task, involving very large sums of money, his industry and acumen were invaluable. From 1946 to 1956 he chaired the Royal Commission on Awards to Inventors for the use of their inventions during the Second World War—these included radar and the jet engine. In 1951 he was made chairman of another royal commission, that on taxation of profits and income, but retired from this on appointment as a lord of appeal. His most conspicuous and somewhat controversial assignment was as one of the 'three wise men' (the other two were Sir Harold Howitt and Sir Dennis Robertson) whom Harold Macmillan appointed in 1957, in effect to devise an incomes policy. This Council on Prices, Productivity and Incomes produced three reports which aroused a great deal of interest after which Cohen resigned in 1959. In 1960 he retired as a lord of appeal in ordinary, but continued to sit in the House of Lords on invitation. His last case was *Phipps* v. *Boardman* (1966); his four colleagues being equally divided, it fell to him, much to his anxiety, to give the casting decision.

Another area to which Cohen gave time and devotion was that of Jewish culture and charity. He had been brought up in the Orthodox tradition, and came to take the Reformed and Liberal positions. He was not a Zionist but interested himself in many Jewish causes. He was president for seven years of the Jewish Board of Guardians; he did much for the Hebrew University of Jerusalem as chairman of its English friends, a Lionel Cohen Foundation being created there in his honour. He served as vice-president of the Jewish Board of Deputies from 1934 to 1939.

Cohen's personality at once inspired confidence. For a lawyer his appearance was unusual. He had a remarkably shaped cranium, warm brown eyes which conveyed essential kindliness, a moustache and a wide smile, and a rather husky voice which produced quick and effective utterance. He totally lacked arrogance and pomposity, but expressed his views confidently and firmly. He had an effective penetrating mind without any claim to be considered 'intellectual'. He was a man of many friends, gregarious and clubbable. He was an excellent golfer, handicap 3 at his best: a member of nine golf clubs. He won the bar tournament twice—once at the age of sixty—and achieved the crowning glory of captaincy of the Royal and Ancient. He was a brilliant card player—of bridge, bézique, and piquet—and a member of White's, St James's, and the Garrick Club, the epitome of a successful and popular barrister.

Cohen's other appointments included fellowship of Eton College (1950–60), honorary fellowship of New College (1946), membership of the council of St Mary's Hospital medical school, of which he was president from 1961 to 1966, and chairmanship of the college committee of University College, London (1953–63). He was a prominent freemason. He died on 9 May 1973.

RICHARD WILBERFORCE, *rev.*

Sources personal knowledge (1986) · private information (1986) [incl. family] · *The Times* (10 May 1973) · *The Times* (15 May 1973) · Burke, *Peerage* (1967)
Archives Bodl. Oxf., corresp. with A. L. Goodhart
Likenesses W. Stoneman, photograph, 1944, NPG · Lenare, photographs, 1953, NPG · D. Low, pencil drawing, NPG
Wealth at death £77,271: probate, 1 Aug 1973, *CGPLA Eng. & Wales*

Cohen, Sir Robert Waley (1877–1952), oil industrialist, was born in London on 8 September 1877, the second son of Nathaniel Louis Cohen, a leading figure in the City, and his wife, Julia Matilda *Cohen (1853–1917), daughter of Jacob *Waley (1818–1873). A sister of Robert, Dorothea [see Singer, Dorothea Waley], married Charles Singer, the historian of medicine and science. The family, who had long been leaders of the Anglo-Jewish community with connections extending from Sir Moses Montefiore to the Rothschilds, traced its origins back to the Netherlands in the seventeenth century. Educated at Clifton College, in the Jewish house, Waley Cohen early showed an interest in chemistry and mathematics. With a science scholarship he proceeded to Emmanuel College, Cambridge, where he obtained second classes in both parts of the natural sciences tripos in 1898 and 1900, with an interlude of a year for a trip round the world. A period in Berlin, between school and university, confirmed his attachment to music and science. One of the leading amateur cellists in the country, he played in the same quartet for forty years.

Although wealthy, the family believed that everyone should be profitably engaged. After Cambridge, Waley Cohen worked unpaid on research in the Meteorological Office, working under W. N. Shaw, his former tutor and secretary to the Meteorological Office. Aroused by family reproaches and helped by his future wife, he then drafted

Sir Robert Waley Cohen (1877–1952), by Bassano, 1946

an advertisement seeking industrial employment. Henri Deterding of the Royal Dutch oil company sent the sole reply, but meanwhile his father had spoken to Sir Marcus Samuel (later Viscount Bearsted), chairman of the Shell Transport and Trading Company. In July 1901 Waley Cohen began work for Shell, reporting directly to Marcus Samuel, and within three months he was given permission to sign company documents. In 1902 Shell and Royal Dutch joined forces against their rival, the Standard Oil Company. While maintaining their autonomy as separate companies, in 1903 they formed a new concern, the Asiatic Petroleum Company, to market oil produced by both parent companies. Deterding of Royal Dutch became managing director of Asiatic, with Waley Cohen as assistant manager at an annual salary of £1000.

In 1904 Waley Cohen married his kinswoman, Alice Violet (1882–1935), daughter of Henry Edward Beddington, and in the same year he was sent on his first overseas assignment with the Asiatic to examine marketing strategy in India. In 1905 he returned to London and in 1906 was appointed to the boards of Shell Transport and Trading Company and the Asiatic. By this time Shell was in such a weak position that it was forced to discuss amalgamation with Royal Dutch. Waley Cohen negotiated on Shell's behalf with the three Royal Dutch directors. Under the amalgamation two new companies were established: the Anglo-Saxon Petroleum Company and the Baatafsche Petroleum Maatschappij. Royal Dutch owned 60 per cent of the shares and Shell Transport and Trading owned 40 per cent. The Royal Dutch directors had been so impressed by Waley Cohen that it was they and not Shell who nominated him to the Anglo-Saxon board. He also served on the Baatafsche board until he was forced to resign in 1909 owing to changes in Dutch law.

Waley Cohen's early career proved his ability and integrity as a negotiator—a talent which he was to put to considerable use for the rest of his career. In 1908 he began negotiations with the Egyptian government concerning exploration rights, leases for concessions, and the building of a refinery at Suez. When oil was discovered in commercial volumes there, he became a director of Anglo-Egyptian Oilfields (a Shell company). In 1910 he negotiated to purchase the Shanghai-Langkat oil company in the Far East, greatly expanding Shell's influence in that area of the world.

Also of great benefit to his management of Shell's interests was Waley Cohen's scientific background. In dealing with oil from Borneo, for the first time in the oil industry he had petroleum subjected to scientific analysis, and discovered that what was considered an inferior product had 350 chemical compounds in a single distillate, including toluol, the essential element in TNT. The Admiralty rejected the idea of making use of this process, but a factory was consequently erected in Rotterdam. When the explosives position presented perilous shortages during the First World War, Waley Cohen organized the transport of the complete factory to the United Kingdom. Samuel had made an early attempt to persuade conservative naval experts to transfer from coal to oil. When war came Shell's management ensured that, notwithstanding damage to the company's prosperity, its great and widely distributed oil resources were at the country's disposal. Waley Cohen negotiated with the Admiralty for the chartering of Shell vessels and the supply of oil. The arrangement included a plan by Zulver, Shell's marine superintendent, to carry oil in the double bottoms of vessels. Waley Cohen was also appointed petroleum adviser to the army council; he went to the USA in 1917 to talk to the government and Standard Oil and made numerous journeys to France to examine petroleum supplies. He was appointed KBE in 1920, in recognition of his work during the war.

In 1924 it was decided that Waley Cohen should visit Shell's marketing organizations around the world, taking in the Middle East, the Far East, and the USA. He concluded that the company's greatest strength was its staff, most of whom he had originally selected to work for Shell. Throughout recruitment, he had interviewed graduate scientists, for whom he saw a great need in the developing oil industry. Many came to Shell through the Cambridge University appointments board, with which Waley Cohen had been involved since 1910. In 1928 he retired from day-to-day management at Shell, but not before realizing his ambition to open a Shell research laboratory, at Emeryville in California, and thus provide for proper scientific research in the oil industry.

In 1928 Waley Cohen purchased the Exmoor estate of Honeymead, and seemed to be moving towards semi-retirement. However in 1929 he accepted the chairmanship of African and Eastern, an independent concern operating in west Africa with heavy losses. The rival Niger Company, bought by Lord Leverhulme in 1920 and reorganized by D'Arcy Cooper, was also operating at a huge loss. Waley Cohen worked for amalgamation from the first, and the United Africa Company was formed in 1929. In the event, he failed to achieve the success which he had attained in the oil world, and he resigned in 1931.

Voluntary and charitable activities played a major role in Waley Cohen's life. He was the acknowledged head of Anglo-Jewry and played a leading role in the affairs of the Jewish community in Britain. For nearly forty years he was the chief figure of the United Synagogue and died in office as its president. He helped to found the Council for Christians and Jews, and played a prominent part in its activities. Opposed to Zionism, he nevertheless helped to create the Palestine Corporation (which contributed greatly to the establishment of the state of Israel). Waley Cohen continued to support the educational institutions which he had attended, and he was involved in the Sir William Ramsay centenary appeal at University College, London.

Of great stature and strong features, Waley Cohen was a formidable person. He and his wife had two sons and one daughter, but their marriage ended tragically when his wife died as a result of a motor accident in Palestine in 1935, in which Waley Cohen himself was seriously injured. Their elder son, Bernard Waley-*Cohen, followed the tradition of social service and at an early age became lord mayor of London. Sir Robert Waley Cohen died of heart disease at his London home, Southampton Lodge, Fitzroy Park, on 27 November 1952.

[ANON.], rev. ANGELA KENNY

Sources R. D. Q. Henriques, *Sir Robert Waley Cohen* (1966) • P. Jones, *Britain and Palestine, 1914–1948* (1979) • Shell International Petroleum, Shell Centre, Waley Cohen MSS • private information (1971) • D. K. Fieldhouse, *Unilever overseas: the anatomy of a multinational, 1895–1965* (1978) • S. S. Levin, ed., *A century of Anglo-Jewish life, 1870–1970* (1970) • C. Bermant, *The cousinhood: the Anglo-Jewish gentry* (1971)
Archives Shell International Petroleum, Shell Centre, London, MSS | U. Southampton L., corresp. with J. H. Hertz
Likenesses W. Stoneman, photograph, 1927, NPG • Bassano, photograph, 1946, NPG [*see illus.*] • J. Oppenheimer, portrait, priv. coll.
Wealth at death £58,138 6s. 11d.: probate, 21 Feb 1953, *CGPLA Eng. & Wales*

Cohen, Ruth Louisa (1906–1991), economist and college head, was born on 10 November 1906 in Bushey Heath, Hertfordshire, the second child and elder daughter of the two daughters and three sons of Walter Samuel Cohen (1870–1960), barrister and financier, and his wife, Lucy Margaret, *née* Cobb (1877–1942). The family background combined the *haute juiverie* of business with radical Unitarianism, free-thinking yet with a marked sense of public duty. After schooling with a governess and at Hayes Court in Kent, in 1926 Ruth Cohen followed her mother to Newnham College, Cambridge, to read for the economics tripos. Cambridge economics was at its most exciting and innovative and provided an atmosphere in which she thrived, being placed in the first class in part 2 in 1929 and winning an Adam Smith prize in 1930. In that year too she was awarded a Commonwealth fellowship and went off to spend two years in the United States, at Stanford and Cornell universities. On her return she became a research officer in the Agricultural Economics Research Institute in Oxford, where she remained until returning to Newnham as fellow and director of studies in economics in 1939. In 1930 she published *Factors Affecting the Price and Production of Potatoes*; in 1933 *Milk Marketing Schemes and Policies*; in 1934, with K. A. H. Murray, *The Planning of Britain's Food Imports*; in 1936 *The History of Milk Prices*; and in 1940 *The Economics of Agriculture*.

War service almost immediately took Cohen away from Cambridge again and she served first in the Ministry of Food (1939–42) and then in the Board of Trade (1942–5). She returned to teaching and research in Cambridge in 1945 when she was appointed university lecturer in economics. In 1954 she was enormously gratified to be elected principal of Newnham College. She led the college until 1972, a term of eighteen years which she afterwards characterized as too long both for an institution and for an individual. It was, however, a period in which Newnham followed her lead in wholehearted engagement with the affairs of the university (full membership of which had only been granted to women in 1948) and of the wider world, making its own modest contribution to the post-Robbins expansion of higher education with a new building.

In these decades Cohen served on the economics faculty board, on the university syndicates on education and on the relationship between the university and the colleges, as a university member of the county education committee, on the academic planning board for the new University of Essex, as a governor of the Hebrew University in Jerusalem, as a lay member of the General Medical Council, and as chairman of the Ministry of Agriculture committee for the provincial agriculture advisory service. She was appointed CBE in 1969.

Cohen approached administrative matters with the same immense energy, ruthless economy, grasp of detail, and directness, sometimes to the point of bluntness, with which she approached everything, including her beloved and beautiful garden. It made for brisk meetings and clear, if parsimonious, outcomes. She did not suffer fools gladly; but she took a broad and generous interest in all her students and her colleagues, often knowing and understanding far more about them than they realized. Her clarity of vision and unswerving sense of principle supported many of them in difficult and delicate situations.

External commitments, and the detailed grip on college affairs and finances which Cohen maintained, precluded much new research in these years, though in 1953 she had surveyed farm price controls in western Europe and in 1958 she published *Effects of Mergers* with P. L. Cook. However, she continued to keep abreast of new work, to teach, and to advise in her specialist field of agricultural economics. Her brother Sir Andrew *Cohen's term as governor of Uganda (1952–7) fostered a considerable interest in and knowledge of east African affairs.

On retirement from the principalship in 1972 Cohen

characteristically took herself off to France for six months, to give her successor a clear run and to learn to cook. Then with gusto she embarked on a new career as a Cambridge city councillor, holding Newnham ward for the Labour Party from 1973 to 1987. She tackled council business and fought for her constituents with the same attention to detail, economy, and pugnacity with which she had led her college, visiting the site of every planning application and proving a very tough and effective chairman of the finance committee when Labour took control of the council in 1980.

Peripheral neuropathy increasingly limited her mobility in her last years. With clear-eyed practicality she sold her house, found a ground-floor flat, and learned to use a Batricar. Instead of leading the canvassing on foot she organized it from her sitting room for everyone else. Cohen died suddenly, but peacefully, at her home, 2 Croft Lodge, Barton Road, Cambridge, on 27 July 1991, watching the test match on television, just as the progress of her illness was beginning to threaten her cherished independence. She never married. Her body was cremated at Cambridge crematorium. GILLIAN SUTHERLAND

Sources Newnham College Roll Letter (1992) · The Times (12 Aug 1991) · personal knowledge (2004) · private information (2004) · [A. B. White and others], eds., Newnham College register, 1871–1971, 2nd edn, 1 (1979) · WWW, 1991–5 · DNB
Archives Newnham College, Cambridge
Likenesses R. Spear, oils, c.1958, Newnham College, Cambridge · D. Hahn, photograph, c.1969, Newnham College, Cambridge
Wealth at death £587,474: probate, 1991, CGPLA Eng. & Wales

Coia, Emilio (1911–1997), caricaturist, was born at 244 Castle Street, Glasgow, on 13 April 1911, the son of Giovanni Coia, an ice-cream dealer, and his wife, Maria Salvatore. His parents, who had married in Govan in 1897, were part of that large émigré community of Italians who moved to Scotland in the late nineteenth and early twentieth centuries. Emilio was educated at St Mungo's Academy and was admitted to Glasgow School of Art at the age of sixteen, at a time when Maurice Greiffenhagen was director. Greiffenhagen was an accomplished graphic artist and spotted a similar talent in the young Coia, allied to a brilliant gift for caricature, which he encouraged. At the end of his art school days, and despite his parents' disapproval, Coia eloped to London with a fellow student, Marie Neale (1907/8–1978), whom he married in London on 11 November 1932. The couple lived in considerable hardship in Hampstead, particularly after the birth of their only child, Gino. They received much help, however, from their neighbours, particularly from fellow Scots such as the writers Catherine Carswell and Edwin and Willa Muir. Coia's energetic personality was unbowed, and things looked up when James Drawbell took him on as resident caricaturist of the *Sunday Chronicle*. He also drew for *The Bookman*, the *Daily Express*, the *News Chronicle*, and a number of other journals.

This work, during the early and mid-1930s, put Coia in touch with an enormous range of literary and artistic figures who were becoming some of the century's most notable figures: Rebecca West, Bernard Shaw, D. H. Lawrence,

Aldous Huxley, Herbert Read, Henry Moore, Wyndham Lewis, and many others. Their likenesses were recorded, more or less realistically, in a series of sketchbooks; these sometimes also illustrate the process of paring down and transformation which led to the final, often startling, caricature. Seven of these sketchbooks survive in the Scottish National Portrait Gallery.

The finished caricatures of these years (his first exhibition was held at Reid and Lefevre's in 1932) are Coia's finest and most original works, a rich amalgam of observation and inventive abstraction. Coia has been described as the 'first Cubist caricaturist' (*The Scotsman*, 18 June 1997), but the work of the English vorticists was perhaps a closer parallel. Their humanity may derive from Max Beerbohm, who was Coia's greatest hero (and whom he finally met at Rapallo in 1956). Two classic examples are the drawings of the 'red Clydesider' member of parliament, James Maxton (the sitting in the House of Commons was interrupted by a fascinated Winston Churchill), and the classical, later comedy, actor John Laurie (both Scot. NPG).

This period of Coia's life came to an end because of an unacceptably astringent image of the novelist Ethel Mannin; this led to a quarrel with her friend Beverley Nichols, principal columnist on the *Chronicle*, and Coia's dismissal from the paper. Economic necessity now drove him in a surprising direction. With help from the industrialist George Dickson, he was employed as assistant advertising manager with an engineering company in Rochester, Kent. Later he became the firm's personnel manager, a position he held throughout the Second World War.

After the war Coia returned to Scotland, where he worked in the shoe manufacturing industry, first in the advertising department of Dolcis and then in an advertising and design role with Saxone in Kilmarnock. The homecoming was prompted in part by his wife's homesickness. She, an artist in her own right, died in 1978, to his intense and lasting sense of loss.

In the early 1950s Coia returned to drawing for the press, a career he followed for the rest of his life. At the same time he was employed as art adviser to Scottish Television, and on occasion he demonstrated his skills live on camera. He drew regularly for the Glasgow *Evening Times*, and then for *The Scotsman*, under the editorship of Alastair Dunnett. From 1956 and for the next forty years he caricatured for *The Scotsman*, in black and witty line, an enormous range of performers at the Edinburgh international festival—including Yehudi Menuhin (who described him as 'every musician's favourite caricaturist'; *The Scotsman*, 18 June 1997), Shostakovich, Margot Fonteyn, Peter Ustinov, and Rudolf Nureyev. The last named, drawn at rehearsal, was one of the few subjects with whom Coia ever clashed, Nureyev snatching his proffered sketching pad away from him and scattering the pages. More upset than he liked to admit, Coia later described him as the rudest man he had ever met—yet there was no venom in the published caricature.

A considerable part of Coia's work in these latter years was of a rather different genre from the swift, linear type of drawing with which his press work is usually associated. These drawings were closer to straight portraiture, though with the caricaturist's disdain for conventional proportion. They were mostly small full-lengths in coloured chalks with the head set on a rapidly tapering body, whose characteristics were as keenly observed as the face. A number of these were published in the *Scottish Field* but many more were done to commission, or from love. They covered an amazing range of Scottish artistic and political society in the second half of the twentieth century: Sir Robin Philipson, Lord Wheatley, Eric Linklater, and James Robertson Justice, to name only a few.

Coia was a small man, with a contrastingly powerful head that might be described as Romano-Egyptian and large, dark eyes that usually glittered with pleasure at the spectacle of life. He was nicely vain (with a colossal collection of garish ties), and his charm and generosity were genuine. His voice was surprisingly soft. There is no doubt that he enjoyed his fame and the honours that came towards the end of his life—a fellowship of the Royal Society of Edinburgh, an honorary doctorate from the University of Strathclyde, and, perhaps best of all, an honorary fellowship of the Glasgow School of Art in 1996. He died from cancer on 17 June 1997, in St Margaret's Hospice, Clydebank.   DUNCAN THOMSON

Giacomo Antonio Coia (1898–1981), by Benno Schotz, 1969

Sources personal knowledge (2004) · L. Duncan, *The Herald* [Glasgow] (18 June 1997) · H. Reid, 'Profile', *Glasgow Herald* (22 April 1985) · M. Bryant, *Dictionary of twentieth-century British cartoonists and caricaturists* (2000) · *The Scotsman* (18 June 1997) · A. Taylor, *The Guardian* (27 June 1997) · *The Times* (18 June 1997) · b. cert. · m. cert. · d. cert.

Archives Scot. NPG, sketchbooks | *The Scotsman*, Edinburgh | FILM probably STV, Glasgow

Likenesses A. Forrest, bronze bust, *c.*1985, Glasgow Art Club, Bath Street · M. Coia (*née* Neale), oils · photograph, repro. in Duncan, *The Herald* · photograph, repro. in Reid, 'Profile' · photograph, repro. in *The Scotsman* · self-portrait, caricature, repro. in Taylor, *The Guardian*

Coia, Giacomo Antonio [Jack] (**1898–1981**), architect, was born on 17 July 1898 at 24 Salop Street, Wolverhampton, the eldest of the nine children of Giovanni Coia, a farmer's son, craftsman, and later a street pianist and accordionist, born at Filignano, near Naples, and Maria Ernesta Vanini, a dancer from Florence who had assisted in her stepfather's circus dog act. When his son, baptized Giacomo, was a year old, Coia's father bought a barrel organ and with his family continued moving north, performing musical and dancing acts, until he arrived in Glasgow, where he opened an Italian restaurant near Parkhead Cross. Coia attended St Aloysius's College in Glasgow while working in his father's restaurant.

Tired of making and serving ice-cream and exempted from military service owing to poor eyesight, Coia worked in 1915–19 as an apprentice for the Glasgow architect J. Gaff Gillespie, the former partner of James Salmon junior, while also attending Whitehill School evening continuation classes in architecture and then, after 1917, studying part-time at the Glasgow School of Architecture, where he obtained his diploma in 1923 and where he later

taught. The following year he spent four months in Italy under a travelling scholarship and then worked in London in the office of Herbert A. Welch. In 1927 Coia returned to Glasgow following the death of Gillespie at the invitation of his partner, William A. Kidd. Kidd's death shortly afterwards in 1928 left Coia the sole partner in what was now the firm of Gillespie, Kidd, and Coia.

Coia completed the extension of the Ca'd'Oro restaurant in John Honeyman's building in Union Street, but his first independent work was the elegant, exotic shop-front for the Léon salon in St Vincent Street (des.). Short of work, an approach to the archbishop of Glasgow resulted in a series of commissions for Roman Catholic churches which made Coia's reputation. All were faced in brick, then an unusual building material in Glasgow, and used an Italian Romanesque manner while exhibiting knowledge of progressive church design on the continent, and particularly the work of Dudok in the Netherlands. Coia later described them as 'essentially transitional structures. I was anxious to break with the red-sandstone neo-Gothic' (MacCallum and Baxter, 18). St Anne's, Dennistoun (1931–3), which was 'the first flower of my impetuous and exuberant youth' (ibid.), has a vaulted, cruciform interior; St Columbkille's, Rutherglen (1934–40), St Patrick's, Greenock (1935), and St Columba's, Maryhill (1937), the latter two with internal transverse arches, were more expressionist in style. In 1937 Coia was joined as partner by T. Warnett Kennedy, who later claimed responsibility for the church of St Peter in Chains at Ardrossan (1938) and the Roman Catholic pavilion at the 1938 Glasgow Empire Exhibition. In the latter, Coia followed the lead set by the architect-in-chief, Thomas S. Tait, in using a simplified modern style and prefabricated construction methods. Coia was then asked to execute the Palace of Industries North for the exhibition in Bellahouston Park in collaboration with Tait and his son Gordon Tait; with its glazed semicircular staircase bay and extensive glass walls, this represented a new direction in his architecture.

On 21 November 1939 Coia married Edith Marx (b. 1909/10), who called herself Eden Bernard, after her divorce from Harry Levingstone; she and Coia had two daughters. As Coia was the son of an enemy alien, he was left vulnerable by the outbreak of war with fascist Italy the following year and he closed his office, despite the fact that he was elected a fellow of the Royal Institute of British Architects in 1941. He was rescued from financial difficulty by the architect Sam Bunton, who asked him to assist in preparing reconstruction plans for Clydebank. Coia reopened his office in 1945 and resumed designing churches for the archdiocese of Glasgow. Most of these post-war buildings, however, were severely constrained by limited budgets and only St Laurence's, Greenock (1951–4), is comparable with Coia's pre-war work. He also designed the Hall of Shipbuilding and Railways in the Kelvin Hall, Glasgow, as part of the Festival of Britain in 1951.

During the 1950s Coia's office expanded and he found himself running an atelier. Argumentative, loquacious, and informal, he was surprisingly successful in finding and retaining clients but, as he himself remarked,

> gone was the peace of my pre-war days. The one-man architect could no longer survive. ... The strength of our office lies in the fact that we have built up an unusually co-operative team that is free to contribute what are sometimes regarded as daring ideas. ... With a team such as this it is possible, surely, to evolve a tradition, and with it form a collective personality.   (Fry and Carrick, 282)

This team radically changed the character of the work of the firm. This was first evident at St Paul's, Glenrothes, Fife (1956–7), which exhibited the strong influence of Le Corbusier as well as the ideas of the liturgical movement. This church was followed by a large number of innovative new buildings generated by the expansion of Glasgow and the building of new towns which established Gillespie, Kidd, and Coia as the leading exponent of the modern movement in Scotland. These included St Charles's, Kelvinside (1959–60), St Patrick's, Kilsyth (1961–5), St Bride's, East Kilbride (1963–4; campanile dem.), Our Lady of Good Counsel, Dennistoun (1964–6), St Benedict's, Drumchapel (1964–9; dem.), and St Peter's College, Cardross (1958–66; now abandoned), as well as schools and public housing in Cumbernauld and schools in Glasgow.

The post-war success of the practice made Coia a public figure in Scotland and he performed the role with relish, although after the mid-1950s the design work was largely directed by the two assistants who became partners in 1966: Isi Metzstein (born in Berlin in 1928), who joined the office in 1945, and Andrew MacMillan (born in Glasgow in 1928) who arrived from the East Kilbride Development Corporation in 1954. It was much to Coia's credit that he both encouraged and recognized this collective responsibility and, in his speech at the Royal Institute of British Architects in 1969 on receiving the royal gold medal for architecture, disowned 'genius' and asked that his two partners be associated with the honour (*Architects' Journal*,

1733). During the 1960s the work of the firm won many awards and in 1967 Coia was appointed CBE.

Jack Coia was short in stature and wore thick pebble glasses; Patrick Nuttgens described him as 'small, intense, unkempt, angry and bloody minded. ... He radiated conviction and total commitment' (Rogerson, preface). He died at 12 Winton Drive, Glasgow, on 14 August 1981. The funeral was held four days later at St Aloysius's, Glasgow. His wife survived him.   GAVIN STAMP

Sources R. W. K. C. Rogerson, *Jack Coia* (privately printed, Bearsden, 1986) • E. M. Fry and J. A. Carrick, 'Jack Coia: royal gold medallist 1969', *RIBA Journal*, 76 (1969), 281–2 • private information (2004) • 'Jack Coia joins roll of honour', *Architects' Journal* (25 June 1969), 1733 • C. MacCallum and N. Baxter, 'Gillespie, Kidd and Coia', *Mac Journal*, 1 (1994) [whole issue] • fellowship nomination form, RIBA BAL • K. Rogerson, 'Jack Coia', *RIBA Journal*, 88 (Nov 1981), 23 • *Glasgow Herald* (2 Nov 1994) • *Glasgow Herald* (12 Nov 1994) • *Glasgow Herald* (19 Nov 1994) • *Glasgow Herald* (3 Dec 1994) • *Glasgow Herald* (9 Dec 1994) • *Glasgow Herald* (19 Dec 1994) • b. cert. • m. cert. • d. cert.
Archives Glasgow School of Art, drawings and papers
Likenesses B. Schotz, bust, 1969, RIBA [*see illus.*] • A. Dawson, bronze bust (in youth), Royal Incorporation of Architects • A. Goudie, oils, Royal Incorporation of Architects • B. Schotz, plaster bust, Scot. NPG
Wealth at death £66,505.76: confirmation, 5 Oct 1981, *CCI*

Coiley, John Arthur (1932–1998), museum curator, was born on 29 March 1932 at 3 Pilgrim Hill, West Norwood, London, the only son of Arthur Henry George Coiley (1896–1993), a share transfer clerk and later a company registrar, and his wife, Stella, *née* Chinnock (1901–1985), a secretary. He was educated at Beckenham and Penge county grammar school and Selwyn College, Cambridge (1951–7), where he graduated BA (1954) in metallurgy and PhD (1959) with a thesis on the application of electron microscopy to metallurgical analysis. His marriage to Patricia Anne Dixon (b. 1932), a grammar school teacher, was solemnized at the Unitarian Memorial Church in Cambridge on 30 June 1956; they had a daughter and two sons.

Coiley is known principally for his role in establishing the National Railway Museum in York, the first national collection to be located outside London. His interest in railways started with a schoolboy enthusiasm which matured at university into a deep and abiding knowledge. The photographic skills acquired as part of his doctoral work sparked a lifelong hobby photographing railways in Britain and abroad. His early career was not, however, connected with railways. He worked as a research scientist, initially at the UK Atomic Energy Authority at Harwell (1957–60); a move to private industry, at first in a research capacity at Aeon Laboratories, Egham (1960–65), led to a post as development manager at Fulmer Research Laboratories (1965–73). Throughout this entire period Coiley's amateur interest in the history and contemporary practice of railways continued to grow, some of his photographic work being included in a compilation shared with four fellow graduates, *Images of Steam* (1968, 2nd edn, 1974). A love of mechanical things was also apparent in the interest he shared with the rest of his family in motor

John Arthur Coiley (1932–1998), by unknown photographer, 1992

rallying. His experience, mostly in the 1960s, as a navigator in competitive events left him with a taste for fast driving in ordinary traffic which often surprised those who had previously known only the unfailingly polite and seemingly mild-mannered man.

In 1973 Coiley was appointed an assistant keeper at the Science Museum, bringing together in what was to prove a gloriously successful combination his interest in railways and the managerial skills he had acquired in professional life. The controversial decision to locate the National Railway Museum outside London had just been taken, and Coiley was at the heart of preparations to move the greater part of the Science Museum's railway collection to York. There it was to join in a newly converted engine shed the collection of historic railway locomotives, rolling stock, and other items large and small built up by the private railway companies and their nationalized successor.

Appointment as the first keeper of the National Railway Museum in 1974 at the age of forty-one opened the most important and productive phase of Coiley's career. His unflappable manner, quiet diplomatic charm, and enormous drive disarmed critics of the move out of London and ensured that the museum opened on schedule on 27 September 1975, the 150th anniversary of the opening of the Stockton and Darlington Railway. The museum was an instant and outstanding success, attracting more than a million visitors a year. Its innovative coverage of the history, technology, and contemporary practice of Britain's railways rapidly gained it an international reputation,

which was further enhanced by Coiley's long-standing involvement in the International Association of Transport Museums, of which he was president from 1983 to 1986.

Coiley remained in charge of the National Railway Museum until his retirement in 1992. Acquisition of adjacent land and buildings in the 1970s provided space for storing much of the collection, which was judiciously expanded as the modernization of the railways continued to displace equipment. Although the general public perhaps most readily appreciated the static and working displays of large, beautifully restored locomotives and rolling stock, less spectacular history found a place among the many smaller items on show. Out of the public gaze, a reference library and archive, a huge photographic collection, and a more modest one of railway art and graphic posters provided for the needs of scholars and enthusiasts alike. In the last years of Coiley's leadership the museum expanded and renewed many of its exhibitions, in the process giving a greater emphasis to the railways' social and human side.

In retirement Coiley continued to live in Farnham, near Knaresborough, West Riding of Yorkshire, and maintained a close and supportive relationship with the museum through the organization of friends and volunteers he had helped to establish shortly after his arrival in York. He died, aged sixty-six, from a heart attack at Chur railway station in Switzerland on 22 May 1998, while leading a group exploring the delights of the Swiss railway system. Cremation on 1 June 1998 was followed by the burial of his remains at St Oswald's Church, Farnham.

COLIN DIVALL

Sources The Independent (28 May 1998) · The Times (6 June 1998) · The Guardian (5 June 1998) · Newsletter, 84 (1998) [Friends of the National Railway Museum] · private information (2004) [Mrs Patsy Coiley] · b. cert. · m. cert. · WW (1987)
Likenesses photographs, 1974–92, National Railway Museum, York · photograph, 1992, repro. in The Times [see illus.]

Coillard, François (1834–1904), missionary in Africa, was born at Asnières-les-Bourges, Cher, France, on 17 July 1834, the youngest of the seven children of François Coillard (d. 1836), at one time a prosperous yeoman, who also had a considerable dowry from his wife, Madeleine, née Dautry (d. 1875); both parents were of Huguenot descent. He was baptized in the temple at Asnières on 5 October 1834. Two years later his mother was left a widow, and nearly destitute.

Coillard worked briefly as a château gardener before enrolling in the protestant school at Asnières at the age of fifteen and later attending Strasbourg University. Inspired by revivalist preaching he offered himself in 1854 to the Société des Missions Évangéliques de Paris and became one of the first students at the recently opened Maison des Missions in Paris. After training under the veteran southern African missionary Eugène Casalis, he was ordained at the Oratoire in Paris in 1857 and assigned to the independent kingdom of Lesotho (Basutoland), where the society had been established since 1833. Coillard reached Cape Town on 6 November 1857 on the eve of a war between the kingdom and the Orange Free State which left the French stations in ruins. After the war he was assigned the task of opening a new station at Leribé in territory governed by the king's son, Malapo. From the time of his arrival on 12 February 1859 Coillard struggled fruitlessly to reclaim the chief for the Christian religion he had abandoned as a boy. The task was not made any easier by Coillard's intolerant attitude towards deeply rooted local customs and mores.

Coillard's activities are graphically described in his journal and in letters which he wrote in large characters to his elderly mother, until her death in 1875. In Union Church, Cape Town, on 26 February 1861, he married Christina Mackintosh, whom he had first encountered in 1858 in Paris where she worked as governess to the children of a French protestant family. Five years his senior, she was the daughter of Lachlan Mackintosh, a Scottish Baptist minister, who was a friend and colleague of James Alexander Haldane and of Robert Haldane. At the age of fourteen Christina had become an enthusiast for missions after hearing the southern African missionary Robert Moffat preach in company with a young African girl. She became her husband's co-worker and shared the hardships of his travels throughout their marriage, which was childless.

By 1865 Basutoland was again embroiled in disputes with Boer farmers, not just in the Orange Free State, but also in Natal. In July Coillard assisted in successful negotiations between local chiefs and Natal's secretary for native affairs, Theophilus Shepstone. When invading forces from the Orange Free State forced the evacuation of the mission in April of the following year, Coillard moved to Natal, where he assisted the American missionaries by occupying one of their vacant stations until the proclamation of the British protectorate over Basutoland in 1868 permitted his return to Leribé. In the same year he was commissioned to assess prospects for reoccupying a station near the headwaters of the Marico River which the French had abandoned twenty years before. He was warmly welcomed by Robert Moffat at Kuruman, who strongly encouraged a move to the north. An impulse in the same direction came from the Basutoland churches: by the mid-1870s they proposed to support a mission by their own evangelists to peoples across the Limpopo River who spoke closely related languages. After two of their expeditions were turned back by the government of the Transvaal Republic, Coillard was chosen to lead the third attempt.

The new party, which included Christina Coillard, four Sotho evangelists, and a niece, Elise Coillard, arrived in Pretoria in May 1877 to find the Transvaal annexed to the British crown under the governorship of Coillard's old acquaintance Theophilus Shepstone. After a hostile reception by the Shona chiefs in the south central region the party was forcibly conducted to Bulawayo, headquarters of Lobengula, king of the Ndebele (Matabele), who claimed suzerainty over the entire region. Prohibited absolutely from preaching in his domains, Coillard turned south-west to the territory of the Christian Tswana ruler, Khama, who suggested they might try their luck across the Zambezi with the Lozi kingdom, where the seSotho language of Basutoland was understood and

spoken. Although they failed in their attempts to arrange a meeting with the recently elected Lozi king, prospects were encouraging enough for Coillard to convince the Paris Missionary Society to support him in an attempt to plant stations in that country.

Delayed by a trip to Europe (1880–82) and complications in Basutoland, Coillard finally mounted his pioneering expedition to the Lozi kingdom (Barotseland) in 1884. He found the country in turmoil, the former king exiled, and a usurper on the throne. No sooner had he established friendly relations with the ruling party than another revolution brought the former king, Lewanika, back to power. Compromised by his initial diplomacy, it was not until March 1886 that Coillard was received by Lewanika at Lealui; from that time until 1891 he was engaged in establishing strong mission stations at Sesheke, Lealui, and Sefula. Lewanika enlisted the missionary's reluctant assistance in a plan to strengthen his shaky hold on the kingship by negotiating a British protectorate similar to the one which had recently been extended over neighbouring Bechuanaland. Misunderstanding the connections between the British crown and Cecil Rhodes's British South Africa Company, the king and Coillard were gradually entangled in a web of intrigue which resulted in assignment of all the Lozi kingdom to the company's domains on 27 June 1890. For a man of Coillard's limited political abilities the burden of serving as a diplomatic intermediary was severely trying, especially during the first seven years, during which the company failed to make any of its promised annual payments of £2000 or to provide any of the educational assistance which it had pledged to Lewanika. Added to these worries were Christina Coillard's death on 28 October 1891, and a persistent high mortality rate among his staff, due primarily to tropical fevers. However, the lively and moving letters he directed to his society's offices in Paris made him a heroic figure to mission supporters in many countries. A great many of these were published in 1889 as *Sur le Haut-Zambèze: voyages et travaux de mission*. Updated to 1895 in a second edition of 1898, his letters also appeared in an English translation by his niece, Catherine Winkworth Mackintosh (*On the Threshold of Central Africa*, 1897).

After a serious illness in 1895, Coillard spent 1896–8 in Europe; but by 21 February 1899 he was again at Leribé on his way back to the Zambezi. However, a large number of fatalities ensued among the missionary recruits of 1897 and onwards, eight out of twenty-four dying and eleven returning home. Coillard was further shaken in 1903 by a breakaway movement of his converts, led by Willie Mokalapa. Coillard was still preaching at the upper Zambezi stations when he suffered a fatal attack of haematuric fever, at Lealui, in Rhodesia, on 27 May 1904; he was buried near his wife under 'the great tree' at Sefula.

Coillard's right to recognition rests not so much on the number of his converts as on his pioneering work and diplomatic activity at crucial junctures in the history of Basutoland and modern Zambia. A short, keen-eyed, white-bearded man, his religious position was not strongly denominational. He acknowledged affinities with many strands of British evangelical nonconformity. As a result he found firm friends among the Congregational, Baptist, Calvinistic, and Methodist missionaries of southern Africa. He attempted in his own work to promote the aims enunciated by his idol, David Livingstone, as 'commerce and civilization'. He pinned his hopes for the future on economic development and education, which he believed would provide the most secure foundation for African Christianity.   NORMAN ETHERINGTON

Sources C. W. Mackintosh, *Coillard of the Zambesi* (1907) · E. Favre, *François Coillard: enfance et jeunesse* (1908) · F. Coillard, 'Preface', in H. Dieterlen, *Adolphe Mabille, missionnaire* (1898) · *Journal des Missions Evangéliques* (1865–1904) · M. Wilson and L. Thompson, eds., *The Oxford history of South Africa*, 2 vols. (1971), vol. 2 · J. Du Plessis, *A history of Christian missions in South Africa* (1965) · R. C. Germond, *Chronicles of Basutoland* (1967) · L. H. Gann, *A history of Southern Rhodesia: early days to 1934* (1965) · A. Hastings, *The church in Africa, 1450–1950* (1994); repr. (1996) · *DNB*

Archives CUL, Royal Commonwealth Society collection, MSS · National Archives of Zimbabwe, Harare, corresp. and papers, CO 5

Wealth at death £152 1s.: administration with will, 22 March 1905, *CGPLA Eng. & Wales*

Coirpre Crom mac Feradaig (d. 904). *See under* Meath, saints of (*act. c.*400–*c.*900).

Coirpre mac Néill (*supp. fl.* 485–494), high-king of Ireland, was one of the many sons of *Níall Noígíallach (d. c.*452), ancestor of the Uí Néill dynasties. He was the supposed progenitor of the medieval dynastic kingdoms of Cenél Coirpri ('kindred of Coirpre'), which ran in a broken band from what is now co. Sligo to northern co. Kildare. The early medieval dynasties claiming descent from his brothers Éogan, Conall Gulban, and Conall Cremthainne became more powerful than Cenél Coirpri, and much of what the sources say about him was written with this in mind. In his father's 'testament' (written long after Coirpre's time) he was willed only Níall's territories, while various of his brothers received sovereignty, rank, and valour: this suggests that his descendants were viewed as widespread but not powerful, as indeed seems to have been the case.

However, there are strong indications in early sources that Coirpre himself was a force to be reckoned with, for the chronicles show him in regular conflict with the Leinstermen, whose decline was mirrored by the rise of the Uí Néill. He may well have held the high-kingship of Ireland, and therefore supremacy among his kindred. With one exception, lists of the kings of Tara exclude him, but the exception is the earliest such list, *Baile Chuinn Chétchathaig*, which places him between Lóegaire mac Néill and Ailill Molt. The annals of Ulster show him defeating the Leinstermen both in the battle of 'Granairet' in 485 (though the chronicler was in some doubt as to Coirpre's involvement) and the battle of Tailtiu in 494 (most likely a late addition to the chronicle). There is other information, probably independent, which indicates that these annal entries are based on fact, for Coirpre is associated with both sites. Granairet seems to be Granard in modern co. Longford, which is said in the tripartite life of St Patrick to have been in the possession of Coirpre's sons;

one of the divisions of the kindred, Cenél Coirpri Gabra, was centred on this site. Tailtiu is connected with Coirpre in a late seventh-century account of Patrick, which says that Patrick encountered Coirpre in that place. Coirpre behaved offensively, and Patrick cursed him, saying 'Your seed shall serve the seed of your brothers, and of your seed there will never be a king' (Bieler, 133). This indicates both the state of the descendants of Coirpre in the late seventh century and the concept that they had formerly enjoyed greater significance (which is suggested by Coirpre's apparent possession of Tailtiu, the site of the royal fair of the Uí Néill). There is also a hint of their ancestor's importance in an early life of St Brigit.

References in other chronicles bear further testimony to the picture of Coirpre as the primary battler against the Leinstermen, showing him victorious in two more conflicts between 497 and 501. However, the absence of these entries from the most trustworthy chronicle means that they are open to particular doubt. Indeed, Coirpre may have been dead by this time, for in 495 there took place a second battle at 'Granairet', but on this occasion the victor was Coirpre's son, Eochu, and the main hand of the annals of Ulster never again refers to Coirpre.

Coirpre's mother was said to be Rígnach ingen Meadaib. There is no record of his wife, but three sons, Eochu, Cormac Cáech, and Cal, are attributed to him—the last certainly falsely.   PHILIP IRWIN

Sources *Ann. Ulster* · A. P. Smyth, 'The Húi Néill and the Leinstermen in the Annals of Ulster, 431–516', *Études Celtiques*, 14 (1974–5), 121–43 · L. Bieler, ed. and trans., *The Patrician texts in the Book of Armagh*, Scriptores Latini Hiberniae, 10 (1979), 133 · W. Stokes, ed. and trans., *The tripartite life of Patrick, with other documents relating to that saint*, 1, Rolls Series, 89 (1887), 91 · M. A. O'Brien, ed., *Corpus genealogiarum Hiberniae* (Dublin, 1962), 131 · G. Murphy, 'On the dates of two sources used in Thurneysen's *Heldensage*: 1. *Baile Chuind* and the date of *Cin Dromma Snechtai*', *Ériu*, 16 (1952), 145–56 · F. J. Byrne, 'Tribes and tribalism in early Ireland', *Ériu*, 22 (1971), 128–66, esp. 147

Coit, Stanton George (1857–1944), ethical reformer, was born on 11 August 1857 in Columbus, Ohio, the fourth of the eight children of Harvey Coit and Elizabeth Greer. He was educated at Amherst College, Massachusetts, where he graduated in 1879. Rejecting both his mother's spiritualism and conventional theocratic Christianity, he joined the Society for Ethical Culture, New York city, of Felix Adler, who offered a heady mixture of Kantian idealism, Emersonian transcendentalism, and traditional Jewish emphasis on conduct. Coit committed himself to faith in ethical value unsupported by theological sanctions. After courses at Columbia College, New York, in 1881–2, he took his doctorate at Berlin University (1885), where, shocked by the militarism of Heinrich von Treitschke, he became a socialist. The theme of Coit's dissertation, 'The inner sanction as final purpose for moral action', became the guiding principle of his life. In London, which he visited in 1885, he learned of social work settlements at Toynbee Hall, where educated young people lived with and worked for slum dwellers. Coit introduced the concept to Adler's working men's school in New York, and worked for the New York University Settlement.

On returning to London, Coit opened a neighbourhood guild in Kentish Town, the practice of which he explained in *Neighbourhood Guilds: an Instrument of Social Reform* (1891). In 1888 he was invited to become 'minister' at an old established freethinking community, South Place Religious Society, at its chapel in Finsbury. Coit's appointment was due to enthusiastic support from the outgoing minister, Moncure Daniel Conway, an American author, journalist, and humanist. The society agreed to Coit's demand that the chapel be known as South Place Ethical Society. Coit was minister from 1888 to 1891 but he was forced to resign because the independent and largely non-socialist members believed he was coercing them into the new British ethical movement. Coit founded in 1894 the West London Ethical Society, the Moral Instruction League, and a socialist journal, *The Ethical World* (later *Democracy*). J. Ramsay MacDonald and J. A. Hobson were prolific contributors. It kept up a high standard of commentary, especially on ethical issues in politics. Coit also inspired the formation of several ethical societies, which proliferated into a modest but none the less national network. The Union of Ethical Societies (formed in 1896) was the germ of the British Humanist Association. On 21 December 1898 Coit married Fanny Adela Wetzlar, daughter of a Frankfurt industrialist, who helped her husband fund the radiation (as he called it) of ethical societies. They had three daughters.

In 1903 Coit received naturalization as a British subject, joined the Independent Labour Party, and was adopted as parliamentary candidate for Wakefield. He participated in local affairs, and purchased the *Wakefield Echo*. He fought a vigorous campaign at the general election of 1906, but was defeated by the Conservative candidate by 217 votes. He was again defeated at Wakefield in January 1910. Coit's politics had a religious complexion: he was impressed by the ideas of J. R. Seeley on the social and psychological function of religion, expressed in *Natural Religion* (1882). The West London Ethical Society experimented with ethical worship. In 1909 Coit purchased a Methodist church in Bayswater, London, which he named the 'Ethical church'; the society itself was also given this name in 1914. Stained-glass windows showed Elizabeth Fry, Bernard Shaw, and Saint Joan; from 1923 there was a white column inscribed 'An Altar to the Ideal, the True, the Beautiful and the Good'. Coit prepared an elaborate service book, *Social Worship: for Use in Families, Schools and Churches* (1913), with musical arrangements by Charles Kennedy Scott. Coit's principles were expressed in *National Idealism and a State Church: a Constructive Essay in Religion* (1907), revised for American publication as *The Soul of America: a Constructive Essay in the Sociology of Religion* (1914), and *National Idealism: and the Book of Common Prayer: an Essay in Re-Interpretation and Revision* (1908). He hoped the Church of England would adopt some of his practices. Coit's ideas of the social, as opposed to supernatural, nature of religion were invigorated from 1923 by a study of Emile Durkheim's work and from 1930 by the *Ethics* of the German phenomenologist Nicolai von Hartmann, of which Coit, in his seventies, produced an esteemed English translation. Following Hartmann, he considered himself to be a Platonist. After the death of his wife he retired to Birling Gap, near Eastbourne, in 1933, and died there on 15 February 1944. In youth Coit was red-headed and of fiery temperament, which he retained in later years. He is vividly described in a novel, *The Prophet's Wife* (1929) by R. O. Prowse, a member of the Ethical church. IAN MACKILLOP

Sources G. Spiller, *The ethical movement in Great Britain* (1934) · H. J. Blackham, *Stanton Coit, 1857–1944: selections from his writings with a prefatory memoir* (1948) · I. MacKillop, *The British ethical societies* (1986) · S. Coit, 'My ventures on the highway to truth', priv. coll. [unpublished autobiography] · R. N. Bérard, 'Coit, Stanton', *BDMBR*, vol. 3, pt 1 · *CGPLA Eng. & Wales* (1944) · *WWW*

Archives British Humanist Association, Conway Hall, Red Lion Square, London · JRL, Labour History Archive and Study Centre, papers · People's History Museum, Manchester

Likenesses bust, Conway Hall · photograph, repro. in Blackham, *Stanton Coit* · portrait, priv. coll.

Wealth at death £19,082 1s. 6d.: probate, 17 June 1944, *CGPLA Eng. & Wales*

Cojamaul, Gregore (*fl.* 1768–1770). *See under* Indian visitors (*act. c.*1720–*c.*1810).

Cok [Coke], **John** (*c.*1393–*c.*1468), Augustinian canon and compiler of the cartulary of St Bartholomew's Hospital, London, came of unknown parentage. Autobiographical interjections in his writings provide most information on his life and work, the main source being the cartulary, in which he states that it was 'Compiled and written by brother John Cok … at Easter 1456 or 36 Henry VI [1457–8] … in the 37th year of the profession of John Cok aged 64' (cartulary, fol. 7r). Cok's reckonings are inconsistent but suggest he was born about 1393. The register of Richard Clifford, bishop of London (d. 1421), records that John Cok became a subdeacon at St Bartholomew's Hospital on 8 March, and a deacon on 22 March 1421. His earliest reminiscence is inserted in an entry in the cartulary concerning property in Wood Street, London: '… inhabited by Thomas Lamporte, goldsmith, in whose tenement and in whose time I John Cok … was apprenticed there' (ibid., fol. 25r). He refers to his presence at the coronation of Henry V in 1413 on 'a very rainy day' (ibid., fol. 647v); and another marginal note adds 'Written by John Cok in the two years before his profession who was serving with Master Robert Newton [master of the hospital 1413–15] AD 1418' (ibid., fol. 382r). Cok's life in the hospital was contemporaneous with John Wakeryng, who was master from 1423 to 1466 and under whom Cok was for some time the renter.

Entries in the cartulary draw attention to their effective estate management. Cok's association with other transcribers of books in the secular world is indicated by the request in the will of Sir John Shirley (d. 1456), translator and transcriber of Chaucer: 'To my which wife Margrete Shirley … I beseche … Sir John Wakering … Sir John Cok, prest and his brother professed, … will vouchsafe to assist, comfort and counsell all ways and times …' (London, Guildhall Library, MS 9171/5, fol. 213). There is no evidence in the London bishops' registers to confirm the description of Cok as a priest. Other compositions by Cok included an account of the works of John Wakeryng, two volumes of copies of theological tracts, and 'the fairest bible that I have seen, written in large vellam by a brother named John Coke at the age of sixty-eight' (Stow, 1.232). The whereabouts of the Bible and Wakeryng's biography are unknown but the treatises survive. In one volume (BL, Add. MS 10392) Cok used several styles of script, coloured initials and rubrics, and drew eight hands annotated with the names of virtues and vices. The second volume (Cambridge, Gonville and Caius College, MS 669*/646) is annotated on four pages with 'q.J Cok' or 'qd John Cok' as well as the cipher 'Qd ix and iii' on page 209. Ciphers interested Cok; Trinity College, Cambridge, holds an early fifteenth-century Flemish-made book of hours (MS B.11.14) containing on its flyleaf a Pentecostal hymn written in cipher, signed 'quod Johnes Cok', and a table of numbers in his handwriting. It has been suggested that the illuminated initial on folio 94r of the cartulary of St Bartholomew's Hospital was drawn by Cok himself, but it is now considered probable that it was the work of the limner William Abel (d. 1474). A further suggestion that the unidentified arms beneath the cross in this illustration belonged to Cok does not seem capable of proof. Several times Cok makes reference in the cartulary to his encroaching old age and unsteady hand. The note to which he attached the latest personal date reads 'Written by brother John Cok in the evening of his life AD 1468' (Cartulary, fol. 73v), and from this it is assumed that he died shortly afterwards. He would have been about seventy-five.

JUDITH ETHERTON

Sources cartulary, GL, St Bartholomew's Hospital MSS, HC 2/1 · N. J. M. Kerling, ed., *Cartulary of St Bartholomew's Hospital, founded 1123* (1973) · A. I. Doyle, 'More light on John Shirley', *Medium Aevum*, 30 (1961), 93–101 · M. R. James, *The western manuscripts in the library of Trinity College, Cambridge: a descriptive catalogue*, 4 vols. (1900–04), vol. 1, nos. 253, 354–5 · M. R. James, *A descriptive catalogue of the manuscripts in the library of Gonville and Caius College*, 2 (1908), 666–7 · J. Stow, *A survey of the cities of London and Westminster and the borough of Southwark*, new edn, ed. J. Strype, 1/3 (1720), 232 · J. J. G. Alexander, 'William Abell "lymnour" and 15th-century English illumination', *Kunsthistorische Forschungen: Otto Pächt zu seinem 70. Geburtstag*, ed. A. Rosenauer and G. Weber (1972), 166–70 · A. G. Watson, *Catalogue of dated and datable manuscripts, c.700–1600, in the department of manuscripts, the British Library*, 1 (1979), no. 29, p. 2 · diocese of London bishops' registers, Richard Clifford (1407–21), GL, MS 9531/4, fols. 95r, 96v · commissary court register of wills, GL, MS 9171/5, fol. 213

Archives BL, Add. MS 10392 · Gon. & Caius Cam., MS 669*/646, pp. 1, 209–10 · Trinity Cam., MS B.11.14

Cokayn [Cokayne], **George** (*bap.* 1620, *d.* 1691), Independent minister, eldest son of John and Elizabeth Cokayn, was born at Cotton End, Bedfordshire, and baptized on 16 January 1620 at Cople, Bedfordshire. Bulstrode Whitelocke placed Cokayn's father firmly (and admiringly) in 'the mediocrity & middle estate & condition … of a smalle Estate, yett having sufficient to live comfortably & conveniently, not riotously, yett plentifully' (Spalding, 56). George was admitted pensioner, on 25 February 1636, at Sidney Sussex College, Cambridge, where he graduated BA in 1640. On 2 December 1642 he was appointed lecturer at All Hallows Barking, London. During the civil war he served as chaplain to the regiment of Colonel Charles Fleetwood. In 1646 he wrote an epistle of commendation for Tobias Crisp's *Christ Alone Exalted* (1643). In this he stated:

> You shall find the sum of this Work, to be the sole exaltation of the Lord Jesus in Saints and Duties. … Now, if the world shall baptize this Doctrine *Antinomianism*, the Lord grant that all the Doctrine preached throughout the world, may deservedly be called by that name.

This early piece of Cokayn's writing also reveals his radical views on ecclesiastical polity:

> I know nothing you have that is long-lived but Jesus Christ … even the Kingdom of Heaven, so far as it is made up of forms and administrations, shall wither and die, but the Kingdom of God within you shall never be shaken.

In 1647–8 he lectured at St Michael, Crooked Lane, London. Some time during these years he became pastor to an Independent church which had been gathered by Nicholas Lockyer, and in 1647 he married Abigail, *née* Plott (d. 1697). In 1648 he obtained the ministry at St Pancras, Soper Lane. His Independent congregation followed him there.

Cokayn's church comprised prominent civic leaders of London during the revolutionary era such as Alderman Robert Tichborne, Alderman John Ireton, and Colonel Rowland Wilson. It was probably upon the recommendation of Wilson (MP for Calne) that he was invited to preach before the House of Commons on 29 November 1648. The sermon, later published under the title *Flesh Expiring, and Spirit Inspiring* (1649), was blatantly political in nature. Barely a week before the purge of the House of Commons by Colonel Thomas Pride, Cokayn boldly hinted what was soon to take place. 'God mingles with nothing', he told the Commons, and went on to quote Isaiah, 1: 25: '"And I will turn my hand upon thee, and purely purge away thy dross, and take away all thy Tin"' (Cokayn, *Flesh Expiring*, 4). He urged that 'you delay not to do Justice' and 'think not to save yourselves by an unrighteous saving of them, who are the Lords and the Peoples known Enemies' (ibid., 25). And he unmistakably enunciated his millenarian aspiration: 'The Saints that walk with God in Union with Holiness and Righteousness are the men by whom God at last will judg all the causes of the sons of men' (ibid., 17).

In 1649–50 Cokayn was chaplain in the household of Wilson, then one of the sheriffs of London; and when Wilson died in early 1650 he was wholly trusted by Wilson's widow, and consequently played an important part in her marriage to Sir Bulstrode Whitelocke later in the year. On 15 August 1651 he was again appointed chaplain to Fleetwood in a northern campaign against Scottish forces. In 1652–3 he was involved in the millenarian agitation in London and publicly associated himself with Christopher Feake, John Simpson, and Vavasor Powell, all of whom were leading Fifth Monarchy Men. He was also said to have held meetings with dissatisfied republicans such as Colonel Edward Sexby and Major John Wildman after the proclamation of Cromwell as protector. In the meantime, however, on behalf of Whitelocke, now ambassador to Sweden, he frequently met the Cromwellian government, especially John Thurloe, secretary to the council of state. In later years he was to provide Thurloe with intelligence.

In late December 1658 he was invited to preach before the City magistrates on a day of humiliation for the calling of Richard Cromwell's parliament. When the army took power and chose Fleetwood as commander-in-chief in October 1659, he was 'very great with Fleetwood and the officers of that party' (*Diary of Bulstrode Whitelocke*, 536).

Upon the Restoration, Cokayn either resigned or was ejected from the ministry of St Pancras. In 1661 he joined other Independent ministers in repudiating a Fifth Monarchist insurrection led by Thomas Venner. His activities, however, continued to give cause for suspicion on the part of the government. He co-authored with Henry Jessey *Mirabilis annus* (1661) and was probably responsible for *Mirabilis annus secundus* (2 vols., 1662). These collections of 'prodigies' were meant to show 'the more visibly', as it is clearly stated in the preface to *Mirabilis annus secundus*, that 'God doth from Heaven testifie against the Prophane, Superstitious, Apostatizing, and Persecuting Spirit of this day'. During the years 1661–4 he preached at various conventicles in London as well as in the country, sometimes joining his church with those of Nathaniel Holmes, Joseph Caryl, Matthew Barker, and George Griffith. It was also reported that his house in Soper Lane was frequented by Fifth Monarchy Men. He was arrested in 1664 but was released on bail. His house was searched in 1671. In spite of all these difficulties, he visited Whitelocke at Chilton Lodge in Wiltshire freely and frequently during the years 1666–75, and preached there in the hall. In 1672 he was licensed as an Independent teacher in his house at Red Cross Street, outside Cripplegate, London. Warrants were again issued in 1678 for his appearance and for the search of his house, and he was convicted for unlawful preaching at the Old Bailey in 1682 and 1683.

Cokayn continued his ministry at Red Cross Street until 1690, and there was a close intercommunion between his congregation and the church of John Bunyan in Bedford. In 1688 he wrote a preface for Bunyan's *Acceptable Sacrifice*, and may have been the author of *A Continuation of Mr. Bunyan's Life*. He was also instrumental in the creation of the Presbyterian–Independent Common Fund, to which he contributed £100 in 1690. Cokayn died at Red Cross Street on 21 November 1691, and was buried on 27 November at Bunhill Fields. He was survived by his wife, two sons (John and William), and a daughter (Elizabeth). He had land, a mansion house, and a number of messuages in Cardington, Bedfordshire.   TAI LIU

Sources St Pancras, Soper Lane, Churchwardens' accounts, GL, MS 5018(1) · St Pancras, Soper Lane, Vestry Minutes, GL, MS 5019(1) · St Michael, Crooked Lane, Churchwardens' accounts, GL, MS 1188(1) · cash accounts, 1647–9, CLRO · cash accounts, 1656–9, CLRO · G. Cokayn, *Flesh expiring, and spirit inspiring* (1649) [BL, E437(37)] · G. Cokayn, 'To all that live Godly in Christ Jesus', in T. Crisp, *Christ alone exalted*, new edn (1690) [1646] · *The diary of Bulstrode Whitelocke, 1605–1675*, ed. R. Spalding, British Academy, Records of Social and Economic History, new ser., 13 (1990) · *CSP dom.*, 1651; 1653–4; 1659–67; 1671 · A. Gordon, ed., *Freedom after ejection: a review (1690–1692) of presbyterian and congregational nonconformity in England and Wales* (1917) · *Calamy rev.* · J. B. Marsh, *The story of Harecourt: being the story of an Independent church* (1871) · J. Brown, *John Bunyan (1628–1688): his life, times, and work*, rev. F. M. Harrison, rev. edn (1928) · R. L. Greaves, *John Bunyan and English nonconformity* (1992) · M. Tolmie, *The triumph of the saints: the separate churches of London, 1616–1649* (1977) · P. Aubrey, *Mr Secretary Thurloe: Cromwell's secretary of state, 1652–1660* (1990) · Tai Liu, *Puritan London: a study of religion and society in the City parishes* (1986) · R. Spalding, *Contemporaries of Bulstrode Whitelocke, 1605–1675*, British Academy, Records of Social and Economic History, new ser., 14 (1990) · PRO, PROB 11/425 · Venn, *Alum. Cant.*, 1/1

Likenesses oils, Harecourt United Reformed Church, London; repro. in Spalding, *Contemporaries*, pl. 6

Wealth at death land; mansion house; messuages: will, PRO, PROB 11/425, fols. 225r–226r

Cokayne. *See also* Cokayne.

Cokayne, Sir Aston, baronet (1608–1684), poet and playwright, was born at Elvaston in Derbyshire in December 1608 and baptized at Ashbourne on 20 December, the eldest of the seven children of Thomas *Cokayne (1587–1638) and his wife, Anne Stanhope (*c.*1592–1664), daughter of Sir John Stanhope of Elvaston and half-sister of Philip Stanhope, first earl of Chesterfield. Cokayne's parents belonged to an extended network of interrelated midlands gentry and aristocracy, many of whose members—Cokaynes, Stanhopes, Hastings, Knyvetons, Reppingtons, Trenthams—are addressed or commemorated in his poems. Cokayne lived for much of his life on the family properties at Ashbourne in Derbyshire and at Pooley Hall at Polesworth in Warwickshire.

Cokayne was educated at Chenies in Buckinghamshire under the rector there, Peter Allibond, before matriculating at Trinity College, Cambridge, about 1624. In 1628 he moved, without having taken a degree, to one of the inns of court, possibly the Inner Temple. He knew his fellow Trinity man Thomas Randolph well when '*Cambridge* (for his wit) extol'd him so' (*Small Poems*, 'Epigrams', 2.89) and made many other literary contacts in London, claiming later that

Donne, Suckling, Randolph, Drayton, Massinger,
Habbington, Sandys, May, my acquaintance were.
(ibid., 2.99)

(Some friendships, however, he owed to his family background: he met Drayton through Warwickshire connections and he was a cousin of the poet Charles Cotton.) He frequented the theatre and contributed commendatory verses for Massinger's *The Emperor of the East* and *The Maid of Honour* in 1632; he also wrote his own comedy, *The Obstinate Lady*, about 1629–31. (There is no record of a performance of this or Cokayne's other plays.) His detailed knowledge of the theatre of this time is attested to later by his 'Praeludium' to Brome's *Five New Playes* of 1653 and by poems in which he complains that the editors of the Beaumont and Fletcher folio of 1647 have failed to give due credit to the shares of the different contributors, including his 'good friend Old *Philip Massinger*' (*Small Poems*, 'Letters to divers persons', 7; 'Epigrams', 2.53).

On 9 July 1632 Cokayne took an oath of allegiance, presumably in order to remove suspicion of recusancy on the eve of his tour of Catholic Europe; he was a particular friend of the Catholics Andrew Knyveton and Francis Lenton and was probably a Catholic himself, although perhaps not openly so until the 1670s. Having set off on 16

July 1632 Cokayne proceeded via Paris, with only brief halts, to Venice. There he remained for about six months, during which time he enrolled as a student at the University of Padua on 11 October. In Venice he twice saw the company of the Affezionati improvise a production on the scenario 'Il creduto principe'; on this he based his play *Trappolin creduto principe, or, Trappolin Supposed a Prince*. Although *commedia dell'arte* elements are evident the playwright 'has accommodated the plot-lines and figures of the improvised piece to a distinctively English dramatic style' (Richards, 246) and it seems likely enough—especially given his theatrical connections—to have achieved performance.

Trappolin was, according to its epilogue:

at Rome begun, half made
At Naples, at Paris the conclusion had.

Cokayne was in Rome for three weeks, including Easter 1633, in Naples for another three weeks, and in Paris for two months before returning to England in July 1633. After this, as far as is known, he lived mostly in Warwickshire (he inherited Pooley Hall from his father in 1639) and in Derbyshire. In 1634 he married Knyveton's sister Mary (d. 1683), daughter of Sir Gilbert Knyveton of Mercaston in Derbyshire. Their three children were Thomas (1636–1679); Mary (b. 1640), who married first Thomas Henslow and then William Lacy; and Isabella (b. 1654), who married William Turville. It is likely that Cokayne paid a second visit to Venice since his translation (published, probably without his involvement, in 1654) of Giovanni Francesco Loredano's *La Dianea* (1627) is dated 'from Venice, 25 Oct. 1635' ('The Author's Epistle'). Conceivably, however, the date is an error for 1632.

On twelfth night 1639 Cokayne's *A Masque* was performed at Bretby in Derbyshire, home of his uncle the earl of Chesterfield. Like many of the 'great Company' addressed by 'the *Lar Familiaris* of the house', Cokayne was evidently loyal to the royalist cause. He was created a baronet, probably either in January 1641 or after the outbreak of civil war in August 1642. (Probably also in 1642 he received an Oxford MA.) Few details of his war service are known except that he was serving under his kinsman Henry Hastings, Lord Loughborough, when Ashby-de-la-Zouch capitulated on 28 February 1646. He compounded as a delinquent on 1 March and was listed in May among those allowed to leave the country on any ship departing from Dover or Rye. In May 1648 he was in the Marshalsea prison. His fines were paid by a relative, William Cokayne, but he appears to have remained in prison until 1651, when he returned to Pooley.

Many of Cokayne's poems were written in the 1640s and early 1650s. They include references to puritan 'grumblings' about drinking and to the silencing of plays in London by 'the Presbyter', as well as epitaphs on such royalist kinsfolk as Colonel Michael Stanhope, who 'fought, and dy'd/When prosp'rous fortune left the Regal side' (*Small Poems*, 'Epigrams', 2.24, 1.107, 1.89). He claims, however, that 'such troubles disagree/Both with my Genius as well as me' (ibid., 1.87), and the poems take up relatively little space in the extensive collection of epigrams, translations, funeral elegies, verse letters, encomia, and other pieces that became *Small Poems of Divers Sorts* (1658; also issued, with cancel title-page, as *A Chain of Golden Poems*). His elegy on Henry, Lord Hastings, was first published in the memorial collection *Lachrymae musarum* (1649).

Possibly Cokayne had always intended to publish his works but the immediate impetus to do so seems to have come from the unauthorized printing of *The Obstinate Lady* in 1657. Much of the verse was set as prose and someone else's conclusion substituted for Cokayne's missing last leaf; fearing that 'my *Trappolin*, and other Poems should have run the like misfortune', he arranged publication of *Small Poems*, he explains in the 'Apology to the reader', including *A Masque, Trappolin*, and the corrected *Obstinate Lady*. *The Tragedy of Ovid*, described as in progress in 1658, was added in *Poems* of 1662 (reissued in 1669 as *Choice Poems of Several Sorts*).

Cokayne succeeded to the estate at Ashbourne on his mother's death in 1664 but debts forced its sale in 1671. Further fines were incurred for recusancy in November 1678, and Pooley Hall was sold in 1683. Cokayne died in lodgings at Derby 'upon the breaking of the great frost' in February 1684 (Wood, *Ath. Oxon.*, 130) and was buried on 13 February in the chancel of Polesworth church. By his will of 6 February 1684 (proved at Lichfield) he left £79 to be divided between his daughters Mary and Isabella, and Mary's children.

The only known representation of Cokayne—a somewhat unflattering laurelled bust—appears in the later editions of the poems; 'no genteel face', observes Wood (Wood, *Ath. Oxon.*, 129). According to Wood, Cokayne 'was esteemed by many an ingenious gent. a good poet and a great lover of learning, yet by others a perfect boon fellow, by which means he wasted all he had' (ibid., 130). Subsequent readers have found the poetry less 'good' than of biographical and historical value. The plays, especially *Trappolin*, have attracted more interest. *A Duke and No Duke*, a farce based on *Trappolin* by Nahum Tate, was first performed in 1684; in one version or another it remained popular throughout the eighteenth century.

MARTIN GARRETT

Sources A. Cokain [A. Cokayne], *Small poems of divers sorts* (1658) · *The poems of Sir Aston Cokayne*, ed. R. Morton (1977) · A. Cokayne, *The obstinate lady*, ed. C. M. Shaw (1986) · *DNB* · Wood, *Ath. Oxon.*, new edn, vol. 4 · G. E. Bentley, *The Jacobean and Caroline stage*, 7 vols. (1941–68), vol. 3 · K. Richards, 'The "Commedia dell'arte" and the Caroline stage', *Italy and the English Renaissance*, ed. S. Rossi and D. Savoia (1989), 241–51

Archives BL, MS corrections in a copy of *Small poems of divers sorts*, King's 238 b. 32

Likenesses engraving, repro. in *Poems* (1669); modern copy, stipple, BM

Wealth at death £79: will · impoverished by delinquency and recusancy fines; also allegedly 'boon-fellow', who 'wasted all he had': Wood, *Ath. Oxon.*

Cokayne, George. See Cokayn, George (*bap.* 1620, *d.* 1691).

Cokayne [*formerly* Adams], **George Edward** (1825–1911), genealogist, born at 64 Russell Square, London, on 29 April 1825, was the fourth son and youngest child (in a

George Edward Cokayne (1825–1911), by Kay Robertson, 1900

family of eight) of William *Adams (1772–1851), LLD, of Thorpe, Surrey, advocate in Doctors' Commons, and his wife, the Hon. Mary Anne (d. 1873), daughter of William Cockayne and niece and coheir of Borlase Cockayne, sixth and last Viscount Cullen. His mother belonged to the well-known family of Cokayne—the name was variously spelt Cockayne and Cokayne—of Rushton Hall, Northamptonshire. On 15 August 1873 Adams assumed the name and arms of Cokayne by royal warrant in accordance with his mother's testamentary directions. After private education owing to delicate health, he went to Oxford, matriculating from Exeter College on 6 June 1844. He graduated BA in 1848 and proceeded MA in 1852. He was admitted a student of Lincoln's Inn on 16 January 1850, and was called to the bar on 30 April 1853. On 2 December 1856 he married Mary Dorothea, third and youngest daughter of George Henry Gibbs of Aldenham Park, Hertfordshire, and sister of Henry Hucks Gibbs (afterwards Lord Aldenham). She predeceased him on 11 March 1906. They had eight children, of whom two sons and two daughters survived them. Entering the College of Arms in 1859, he held successively the offices of Rouge Dragon pursuivant-of-arms (1859–70) and Lancaster herald (1870–82). In his heraldic capacity Cokayne was attached to the Garter missions to Portugal (1865), Russia (1867), Italy (1868), Spain (1881), and Saxony (1882). Appointed Norroy king of arms in 1882, he succeeded to the post of Clarenceux king of arms in 1894. He was an active member of the Society of Antiquaries, being

elected fellow on 22 February 1866. He died of a heart attack at his residence, Exeter House, Roehampton, on 6 August 1911, and was buried at Putney Vale.

Cokayne was modest, industrious, and scholarly, with a great kindness and courtesy of manner. He published much on genealogy and the last part of his life was devoted to his major works, *The Complete Peerage* (8 vols., 1887–98; 2nd edn, rev. and enlarged by V. Gibbs and others, 13 vols., 1910–59), and *The Complete Baronetage* (5 vols., 1900–06; index vol., 1909). *The Complete Peerage* was (and is) unique in that it gave a full historical and genealogical account of all peerages created in the whole of the British Isles (including Ireland) from the conquest to the date of publication. This was unlike earlier peerages, which covered only those titles extant or extinct at the time of writing or dealt only with one country—England or Ireland, for example—or both. And whereas earlier works usually gave full (and often inaccurate) accounts of the whole family, 'G.E.C.' described the public life of the holders of the title and their direct heirs only, and, so far as he could, used original sources for his information. *The Complete Peerage* therefore quickly won the author general recognition as a genealogist of the first authority, and both it and the *Baronetage* (written on similar principles) have taken their place as primary authorities on their subjects.   G. S. WOODS, *rev.* P. W. HAMMOND

Sources G. A. Lee, 'The late Clarenceux king of arms', *The Genealogist*, new ser., 28 (1911–12), 150–51 · *The Times* (8 Aug 1911) · *The Times* (9 Aug 1911) · GEC, *Peerage* · J. Foster, *Men-at-the-bar: a biographical hand-list of the members of the various inns of court*, 2nd edn (1885), 92 · d. cert.
Archives Coll. Arms, abstracts of wills · Northants. RO, corresp. and papers · Shakespeare Birthplace Trust RO, Stratford upon Avon, extracts from Warwickshire parish registers and inscriptions · U. Birm. L., corresp. and papers | LUL, letters to J. H. Round · U. Glas. L., letters to J. R. Anderson
Likenesses K. Robertson, oils, 1900, Coll. Arms [*see illus.*]
Wealth at death £79,004 6s. 7d.: resworn probate, 1 Sept 1911, CGPLA Eng. & Wales

Cokayne, John (d. 1429), justice, is frequently confused with his nephew, Sir John Cokayne (d. 1438) of Ashbourne in Derbyshire. Contemporary sources distinguish the two by referring to the justice as 'the elder' or 'the uncle'. He was the younger son of John Cokayne (d. 1372), chief steward of the northern parts of the duchy of Lancaster, and Cecilia Ireton. His marriage, probably in the early 1380s—the marriage had produced grandchildren by 1400—to Ida (d. 1426), daughter of Reynold, Lord Grey of Ruthin (d. 1388), reflected the quality of his family's connections. He must already have been well established in the legal profession when, in April 1383, the king granted him a life annuity of £15. In the following decade he was appointed to his first major legal offices: by October 1394 he was serving as recorder of London—an office he surrendered in 1398—and in October 1396 he became a serjeant-at-law. By this time he had already followed the family tradition of service to the house of Lancaster, holding, as his father had done before him, the chief stewardship of the northern parts of the duchy (1398–1400). In his will of February 1398, John of Gaunt, duke of Lancaster, nominated

Cokayne as one of his executors. Such impeccable Lancastrian connections ensured further promotion on the accession of Henry IV. In November 1400 he was appointed chief baron of the exchequer, and in May 1405 he was elevated to the bench of the common pleas. He continued to hold both offices until Henry V's accession in 1413, when he surrendered his exchequer office.

The profits of office and royal patronage—while a justice he enjoyed the grant of several royal wardships—enabled Cokayne to lay the landed foundations of a gentry family that was to endure for more than 300 years. By 1394 he had acquired lands at Bearwardcote in his native Derbyshire, and in 1398 he secured a life interest in the Hertfordshire manors of Almshoe, in Ippollitts, and Radwell. His major purchase, that of the Bedfordshire manor of Bury (now Cockayne) Hatley, was made in 1417; when he drew up his will on 10 February 1428 he expressed his wish to be buried in the parish church there (his altar tomb is now lost). His bequests looked back to the patrons who had made his worldly success possible: he endowed prayers for the souls of John of Gaunt, the first two Lancastrian kings, and, most interestingly, Richard II. He died on 22 May 1429, probably at Bury Hatley.   S. J. PAYLING

Sources A. E. Cockayne, *Cockayne memoranda: collections towards a historical record of the family of Cockayne* (privately printed, Congleton, 1873) · *Chancery records* · R. Somerville, *History of the duchy of Lancaster, 1265–1603* (1953) · *VCH Hertfordshire* · *VCH Bedfordshire* · HoP, Commons
Likenesses engraving (in death; after monument), repro. in W. Dugdale, *Origines juridiciales, or, Historical memorials of the English laws ...* (1666), 100

Cokayne, Sir Thomas (1519–1592), soldier and huntsman, was the son of Francis Cokayne of the family of Cockaine, which for generations had owned estates at Ashbourne, Derbyshire, and his wife, Dorothy Marrow. Brought up in the household of Francis Talbot, fifth earl of Shrewsbury, Thomas came into his inheritance at the death of his father on 5 August 1538. The following year he was admitted to Gray's Inn. About 1540 he married Dorothy (d. 1595), daughter of Sir Humphrey Ferrers of Tamworth, who was his stepfather. Sir Humphrey's eldest son, John Ferrers, married Barbara Cokayne, Thomas's sister. Thomas and Dorothy Cokayne are known to have had seven daughters and three sons.

In 1544 Cokayne accompanied Edward Seymour, earl of Hertford, in the expedition to Scotland and was knighted at Leith on 11 May after the taking of Edinburgh. On 26 May 1547 his name appears for the first time on the commission of the peace for Derbyshire. He was with the forces sent to the relief of Haddington under George Talbot, sixth earl of Shrewsbury, named on a muster of 13 August 1548 as one of the captains selected 'For the Battaile'. The following year he was pricked for sheriff of Derbyshire, a position he filled also in 1559, 1569, 1579, and 1585. In 1587 he was one of the attendants on Mary, queen of Scots, on her journey 'with but a small trayne' as far as Derby, as she travelled towards her final imprisonment at Fotheringhay.

From 1583 Cokayne helped found the grammar school at Ashbourne, donating £18 and granting to it a yearly charge of £4 out of his estate, though it is clear that one Thomas Carter of the Middle Temple was the main mover and financier of the foundation. Raphael Holinshed, author of the famous chronicles, was a steward on an estate neighbouring Cokayne's manor of Pooley in Polesworth, Warwickshire, and is reported to have been a frequent visitor at Pooley. Though 'a professed hunter, and not a scholler', as he himself remarked, Cokayne was enough of the latter to write a manual on his passion: *A Short Treatise of Hunting* (1591), dedicated to Gilbert Talbot, earl of Shrewsbury. The book contains illustrations of the fox, the hare, and the stag and deals with the practical arrangements for hunting. Its preface to 'gentlemen-readers', dated from Ashbourne, 31 December 1590, argues that 'hunters by their continual travail, painful labour, often watching, and enduring of hunger, of heat, and of cold, are much enabled above others to the service of their prince and country to the wars'. It draws attention to the role of hunting in protecting the countryside 'from the hurt of foxes and other ravenous vermine' despite 'the carping speeches of the enemies thereof'.

Cokayne was buried on the night of 15 November 1592; his widow died at Derby on 21 December 1595. Both were interred at Ashbourne church in a tomb once described as 'a stately mural monument of marble, in the Renaissance style' (Cox, 2.386). Pevsner is more prosaic: 'Thomas Cokayne buried 1592, standing wall monument; rusticated pillars below, the figures lifesize and kneeling, facing each other across a prayer-desk; pilasters left and right with much strapwork; arch above the figures; the children in the predella below' (Pevsner, 44).

STEPHEN WRIGHT

Sources *A short treatise of hunting presented by G. E. Cokayne* (1897) · E. A. Sadler, 'The ancient family of Cokayne and their monuments in Ashbourne church', *Journal of the Derbyshire Archaeological and Natural History Society*, 55 (1934), 14–39 · E. A. Sadler, 'The earliest records of Ashbourne grammar school', *Journal of the Derbyshire Archaeological and Natural History Society*, 52 (1931), 80–98 · *CSP Scot., 1547–63* · A. E. Cokayne, *Cokayne memoranda* (1873) · patent rolls, Edward VI, Elizabeth · J. C. Cox, *Notes on the churches of Derbyshire*, 4 vols. (1875–9) · *Derbyshire*, Pevsner (1953) · J. Foster, *The record of admissions to Gray's Inn, 1521–1889* (1889)
Likenesses group portrait, monument (with his wife and children), Ashbourne church, Derbyshire
Wealth at death substantial landed property at Ashbourne, Derbyshire, and Pooley, Warwickshire

Cokayne [alias Browne], **Thomas** [pseud. T. C.] (**1587–1638**), lexicographer, was born on 21 January 1587 at Mapleton, near Ashbourne, Derbyshire, the son of Sir Edward Cokayne of Ashbourne (d. 1606), sheriff of the county, and his wife, Jane (d. 1647), daughter of Sir Nicholas Ashby of Willoughby in the Wolds, Nottinghamshire. He was the grandson of Sir Thomas *Cokayne of Ashbourne (1519–1592), sheriff of Nottinghamshire and Derbyshire, and author of *A Short Treatise of Hunting* (1591).

Thomas Cokayne entered Corpus Christi College, Oxford, but left without taking a degree, probably upon his inheritance of Ashbourne Hall and other family properties at his father's death. Shortly afterwards he married

Anne (or Ann) Stanhope (c.1592–1664), who was the daughter of Sir John Stanhope, of Elvaston, Derbyshire, and his wife, Dorothy Trentham, and half-sister of Philip Stanhope, first earl of Chesterfield. The eldest of their seven children was the poet Sir Aston *Cokayne, baronet.

Neither the grapes of Ashbourne's vineyards, however, nor the asparagus, apricots, and peaches of her gardens that Aston would write about in his poem to his mother in 1658 sufficed to keep Thomas Cokayne from leaving his wife, two sons, and five daughters shortly after 1616 to go to London, where he took lodgings in Gray's Inn Lane and lived under the assumed name of Browne (or Brown). A letter from John Donne to Anne Cokayne, who 'warmly engaged Donne's affections' (Bald, 501) in the late 1620s, suggests that Thomas Cokayne's 'perversnesse' put her to the 'necessity of hiding' her sons (A Collection of Letters, 345) to prevent his discovering their whereabouts. Presumably Donne visited Ashbourne more than once, for a room there was long known as 'Dr Donne's chamber'. In 'An Epitaph on my Father Mr. Tho. Cokain' (Poems, 128 [i.e. 228]), Aston Cokayne expresses no bitterness but praises his father's 'great worth' and implies that Thomas Cokayne experienced a spiritual awakening, choosing to sacrifice 'all terrene wealth'.

Details of Thomas Cokayne's life in London are not recorded, but it appears that he devoted his energies to lexicography. Anthony Wood claimed that he wrote, in collaboration with unnamed assistants, A Greek English lexicon, containing the derivations and various significations of all the words in the New Testament ('By T. C. late of C. C. C. in Oxford'), published posthumously in 1658, in which the etymologies, denotations, and connotations of biblical Greek words are expounded, with extensive references to New Testament chapters and verses. The lexicon is supplemented by Greek and English indexes (evidently prepared by Henry Jessey); an explication, verse by verse, word by word, of the book of Romans, chapter two; and an essay on Greek and Hebrew dialects. It is, according to the author, 'fitted for [those of] the meanest capacity', ignorant of Latin, who through diligent use of the lexicon may comprehend Greek more quickly and more fully than 'many who have spent many years time in Cambridg or Oxford to their friends no small expence and charges'—all for the 'bare price of this book' (T. C., A Greek English Lexicon, 1658, foreword). The work was reissued in 1661 with the title An English-Greek Lexicon, 'published, and recommended to all' by eight nonconformist London ministers, including Joseph Caryl, who had 'a prime hand' in the work (Wood, Ath. Oxon., 3.982), and George Cokayne (possibly a relation of Thomas Cokayne). The 1658 work has variously been attributed to each of them.

Having just passed his fifty-first birthday, Thomas Cokayne died at London and was buried on 27 January 1638 in the church of St Giles-in-the-Fields. On 6 December 1638 administration of his personal effects was granted in London; and in 1640 an inquisition post mortem was held concerning his estates at Ashbourne and Pooley, Warwickshire. His widow retired to Ashbourne Hall where she died on 29 August 1664, aged about

seventy-two. She was 'an honourable person … a royalist, of highest elevation, yet a woman of sense' (History … of Ashbourn, 24). Her nephew, the poet Charles Cotton, called her 'Mrs. Cokain in the Peake', an allusion to her eccentric headdress (N&Q, 3rd ser., 4, 1963, 415–16).   PAGE LIFE

Sources Wood, *Ath. Oxon.*, new edn, 3.470, 982 · *The history and topography of Ashbourn, the valley of the Dove, and the adjacent villages* (1839) · *A collection of letters, made by Sᵣ Tobie Mathews, Kᵗ* (1660), 338–56 · A. Cokayn, *A chain of golden poems embellished with wit, mirth, and eloquence* (1658) · *Dugdale's Nottinghamshire and Derbyshire visitation papers*, ed. G. D. Squibb, Harleian Society, new ser., 6 (1987), 17–19 · A. E. Cockayne, *Cockayne memoranda: collections towards a historical record of the family of Cockayne*, 2nd edn (1873), 222–37 · GL, MS 9050/7, fol. 29v · R. C. Bald, *John Donne: a life*, ed. W. Milgate (1970) · W. Wilson, *The history and antiquities of the dissenting churches and meeting houses in London, Westminster and Southwark*, 4 vols. (1808–14) · E. F. Rimbault, 'Mrs Cokayne of Ashbourne', *N&Q*, 3rd ser., 4 (1863), 415; reply by CPL, 3rd ser., 5 (1864), 20–21 · H. J. H., *N&Q*, 3rd ser., 4 (1863), 415–16 · *IGI* · *DNB* · E. Gosse, *The life and letters of John Donne, dean of St Paul's*, 2 vols. (1899), vol. 2 · S. Glover, *The history and gazetteer of the county of Derby*, ed. T. Noble, 2 (1833) · W. Dugdale, 'Cokaine of Ashbourne', *The visitation of Derbyshire begun in 1662 and finished in 1664*, ed. G. D. Squibb, Harleian Society, new ser., 8 (1989), 47–8 · J. J. Howard, ed., *Miscellanea genealogica et heraldica*, 3rd ser., 3 (1900), 221 · *GM*, 1st ser., 67 (1797), 554–9

Cokayne, Sir William (1559/60–1626), merchant, was the second of the seven sons of William Cokayne (d. 18 Nov 1599) of Baddesley Ensor, Warwickshire, a freeman of the Skinners' Company of London and sometime governor of the Eastland Company, and his first wife, Elizabeth (d. 2 April 1589), the daughter of Roger Medcalfe of Wensleydale, Yorkshire, and of Alspade and Meriden, Warwickshire, also a freeman of the Skinners' Company of London. His family had been established near Ashbourne, Derbyshire, since the middle of the twelfth century, and included the judge Sir John Cokayne (d. 1438); Thomas Cockayne, recorder of London in 1439, was probably a member of the same family. William was apprenticed to his father at Christmas 1582, and became free of the Skinners' Company by patrimony on 28 March 1590. He was admitted to Gray's Inn on 10 August 1600. On his father's death he succeeded to the latter's business, and quickly achieved prominence among London merchants. Like his father, he was a leading member of the Eastland Company, which at that time was the chief rival trading company of the Company of Merchant Adventurers (of which neither Cokayne nor his father were members). He was also an active member of the East India Company committee (1606–9), and was master of the Skinners' Company in 1609, 1611, and 1625.

Cokayne exported cloth to the Baltic on a considerable scale, becoming enormously wealthy, and he lent money to James I. By 1603, if not earlier, he was purveyor to the English force sent to quell the Irish rising, and for many years he employed William Cradock as his resident factor respecting the purveyorship in Hamburg (through which port most munitions used to be bought or transported at that time). Cokayne served as a sheriff of London (1609–10) and alderman for the wards of Farringdon Without (1609–13), Castle Baynard (1613–18), Lime Street (1618–25), and Broad Street (1625–6). He was lord mayor of London in

1619–20, and first governor of the Irish Society, from 1610 to 1614, when he took in hand the defences of Londonderry (1613). He was auditor (1606–7), colonel of the trained bands (1618–26), and president of St Thomas's Hospital (1622–6), as well as a benefactor and governor of Christ's Hospital.

Cokayne married, on 22 June 1596, at St Leonard Eastcheap, London, Mary (*bap.* 10 May 1573, *d.* 1648/9), the fifth and youngest daughter of Richard Morris of Suffolk, a freeman of the Ironmongers' Company of London, and his wife, Maud, formerly the wife of John Barlow, also a freeman of the Ironmongers' Company of London, and the daughter of John Daborne or Dawborne of Guildford, Surrey. After Cokayne's death Mary married Henry Carey, first earl of Dover, the father of her future son-in-law. Mary was buried on 8 January 1649 with Cokayne in St Paul's Cathedral.

Cokayne became an influential adviser to James I, who frequently consulted with him both in council and privately, speaking highly of his business methods and his 'language, accent and manner of delivering himself' (G. E. Cokayne). As early as 1606 Cokayne was concerned with what he considered to be the great project of his life: the dyeing and dressing of all cloths made in England before their exportation. His chance came in 1612, with the death of Salisbury: James was increasing his power, and the treasury was trying to improve the state revenues. Cokayne used his influence with the king to override privy council concerns and promote his own, and the Eastland Company's, project to transform the Merchant Adventurers' sole privilege of the exportation of undyed and undressed cloths into an exportation of the finished product. The Company of Merchant Adventurers considered the project doomed, refused to co-operate, and was suppressed. The New Company of Merchant Adventurers was established in its place and received its letters patent on 29 August 1615; Cokayne became its first governor. The nucleus of this company consisted of Eastland merchants, and included William Cradock, Cokayne's old factor from Hamburg, which became the King's Merchant Adventurers' staple town in Germany. All licences for the exportation of undyed and undressed cloth were withdrawn, which annoyed the Dutch, the principal buyers. The project, and the new company, failed, and gave rise to one of the most severe trade crises ever to devastate England.

During the brief term of the new company, on 8 June 1616 Cokayne entertained the king in his own home, Cokayne House, directly opposite the church of St Peter-le-Poer in Broad Street. The cost of the entertainment came to over £3000, and was paid for by the new company, although Cokayne took the credit; he was knighted with the City's sword at the end of the festivities on that day. A gold basin and £1000 was given to the king, and £500 to Prince Charles. However, by the autumn of 1616 the king had lost faith in the New Merchant Adventurers', and Cokayne was out of favour. By 1 January 1617 the king had restored the old Merchant Adventurers' company, and the New Company of Merchant Adventurers was dissolved.

Cokayne managed to avoid falling into disfavour for long, however, and by 1618 his reconciliation with the king was complete.

During his mayoralty, on 26 March 1620, Cokayne received in great state the king and the prince of Wales, who visited St Paul's Cathedral with a view to raising money to complete the spire, which had blown down in 1561. The title of his mayoral pageant, which was paid for by the Skinners' Company, was *The Triumphs of Love and Antiquity*; it was written by Thomas Middleton, who also wrote *The First Entertainment*, held at Cokayne House on Monday and Tuesday in Easter week 1620. On the Saturday following, 22 April, the latter entertainment was reworked for the privy council, and on the same day Cokayne's eldest daughter, Mary, married Charles Howard, third baron Howard of Effingham.

Cokayne was one of the financiers who equipped William Baffin for his voyage in search of a north-west passage in 1612, and in his honour Baffin named a harbour in Greenland Cockin's Sound.

As well as Cokayne House in Broad Street, which was destroyed by fire on 12 November 1623 and had to be totally rebuilt, Cokayne purchased large estates in several counties, including (in 1619) Elmesthorpe, Leicestershire, and Rushton, Northamptonshire, the latter of which was the home of his descendants until 1828. He also possessed a manor house, Coombe Nevill (once owned by the earls of Warwick), at Kingston, Surrey, where he died, after two days' illness, on 20 October 1626, aged sixty-six. He was buried on 12 December in St Paul's Cathedral, where a stately monument, including effigies of him and his wife and a lengthy Latin inscription, was erected to him. Of this monument, only part of his effigy, comprising his figure down to the knees, still survives in the crypt of the cathedral. The monument and epitaph are illustrated in Sir William Dugdale's *History of St Paul's Cathedral* (1658). His funeral sermon was preached by John Donne, dean of St Paul's. Letters of administration were granted on his estate on 20 December 1626, and his nuncupative will was proved on 20 June 1627. He left his son Charles estates worth £12,000 per annum and £10,000 for each of his six daughters, and he bequeathed to the Skinners' Company five silver-gilt loving cups, which they still possess, in the form of cocks standing on turtles.

Cokayne was the ancestor of a number of English aristocratic families. His only surviving son, Charles (1602–1661), was created Baron and Viscount Cullen of co. Tipperary in the peerage of Ireland in 1642 and married Lady Mary O'Brien, the first daughter and coheir of Henry, fifth earl of Thomond in Ireland. His eldest daughter, Mary (1598–1650/51), married Charles Howard, third Baron Howard of Effingham, later second earl of Nottingham. Anne (1604–1668) married Sir Hatton Fermor, of Easton Neston, Northamptonshire, and was the ancestor of the earls of Pomfret. Martha (1605–1641) married firstly John Ramsay, earl of Holdernesse, and secondly Montagu Bertie, Lord Willoughby de Eresby, who succeeded as second earl of Lindsey in 1642; by the latter marriage she was ancestor of the earls of Lindsey, the dukes of Ancaster, and the earls of Ancaster. Elizabeth (1609–1667/8) married Thomas Fanshawe, created Viscount Fanshawe of Dromore in Ireland in 1661, remembrancer of the exchequer. Abigail (1610–1687/8) married John Carey, Viscount Rochford, later second earl of Dover, whose father, the first earl, had married her mother some six months earlier. Jane (1611/12–1683), Cokayne's youngest daughter, married the Hon. James Sheffield, the son of the earl of Mulgrave.   VIVIENNE ALDOUS

Sources G. E. Cokayne, *Some account of the lord mayors and sheriffs of the city of London during the first quarter of the seventeenth century, 1601–1625* (1897) · A. Friis, *Alderman Cockayne's project and the cloth trade: the commercial policy of England in its main aspects, 1603–1625*, trans. [A. Fausbøll] (1927) · A. E. Cockayne, *Cockayne memoranda: collections towards a historical record of the family of Cockayne* (privately printed, Congleton, 1873) · A. B. Beaven, ed., *The aldermen of the City of London, temp. Henry III–[1912]*, 2 vols. (1908–13) · J. Nichols, *The progresses, processions, and magnificent festivities of King James I, his royal consort, family and court*, 3 (1828) · C. T. Carr, ed., *Select charters of trading companies, AD 1530–1707*, SeldS, 28 (1913) · J. F. Wadmore, 'Some account of the history and antiquities of the Worshipful Company of Skinners, London', *Transactions of the London and Middlesex Archaeological Society*, 5 (1876–80), 92–182 · W. Dugdale, *The history of St Paul's Cathedral in London* (1658) · *The sermons of John Donne*, ed. G. R. Potter and E. M. Simpson, 10 vols. (*c*.1953–1962), vol. 7 · C. R. Markham, ed., *The voyages of William Baffin, 1612–1622*, Hakluyt Society, 63 (1881) · will, PRO, PROB 11/152, sig. 61

Archives Northants. RO, corresp. and papers

Likenesses portrait; last known at Christ's Hospital, 1881 · portrait (of Cokayne?), priv. coll. · portrait; in possession of the Revd Cecil Henry Maunsell, Thorpe Maloor Hall, Northants., in 1897

Wealth at death over £72,000—estates worth £12,000 (and £1500 p.a.) to son; £10,000 to each of his six daughters: Cockayne, *Some account* (1897)

Coke. For this title name *see* Hatton, Elizabeth, Lady Hatton [Elizabeth Coke, Lady Coke] (1578–1646).

Coke, Daniel Parker (1745–1825), barrister and politician, was born on 17 July 1745, the only son of Thomas Coke (1700–1776), barrister, and his wife, Matilda (1706–1777), daughter and heir of Thomas Goodwin of Derby. He belonged to an old Derbyshire family, the Cokes of Trusley, of which he became in time the chief representative, though without an inheritance, the patrimonial estate descending in the female line. After being educated by the Revd Thomas Marlove at Derby School, he matriculated at Queen's College, Oxford, in 1762, and migrated to All Souls, graduating BA in 1769 and MA in 1772. He was called to the bar in 1768, at Lincoln's Inn, and practised for many years on the midland circuit. In 1776 he was elected to parliament as member for Derby, which he represented until 1780. At the general election in that year he visited neighbouring Nottingham, to assist the corporation candidate Sir Edward Every, but was himself persuaded to stand. He was elected with the whig Robert Smith, and represented the town until 1812, when he retired from parliament.

Coke built a solid base of personal support in Nottingham by assiduously promoting the interests of his constituents. On their behalf he urged the abolition of the receipt tax in parliament in December 1783. He suggested instead a tax on the stalls of deans and prebendaries, 'the most useless order of ecclesiastics in existence … he should be happy when the day arrived, on which they were to be abolished' (Cobbett, *Parl. hist.*, 101). This was a bold statement, given his strong Anglican ties, but one that was likely to be well received among Nottingham's politically powerful nonconformist community. In May 1784 he defended Nottingham trade by opposing the government's Irish commercial proposals on protectionist grounds. And in May 1788 he promoted the interests of Nottingham hosiers, with a bill to make frame-breaking punishable by death. It was rejected by the Commons as an unnecessary addition to the long list of existing capital crimes.

In 1791 Coke held a brief for the crown in the prosecution of the ringleaders of the Church and King mob which sacked the Birmingham house of the prominent dissenter Dr Joseph Priestley. He opened the second day of the trial with a personal declaration:

> [He] did not profess to agree with Dr Priestley either in his religious or his political opinions; but if he had been at Birmingham when the riots took place, he should have risked his life in the protection of Dr Priestley's house; and the more so, because he had differed in opinion from him. (*A Full and Accurate Report*, 39)

The following year, in 1792, he opposed a motion for an inquiry into the culpability of the magistrates at Birmingham. By then the effects of the French Revolution were beginning to be widely felt in Britain, and even liberal-minded independent politicians such as Coke turned instinctively to the defence of the established order.

Coke gave consistent support to the government during the war with France, which began in 1793, and in Nottingham this left him politically exposed. At the 1796 election in the town both he and Robert Smith faced opposition from Dr Peter Crompton, 'an opposer of the war, and all its train of ruinous consequences' (*Nottingham Journal*, 4 June 1796). Though they were both comfortably re-elected a new dimension had been added to the debate: 'Loyalists' had clashed with 'Democrats', and the French Revolution had become 'an object of admiration to one part of the people, and of terror to the other' (Blackner, 300).

By the time of the 1802 general election Coke was deeply unpopular in Nottingham because of his support for the war, 'to which was attributed the excessive high price of provisions' (Blackner, 301). Political radicalism and popular discontent now converged to produce a specially turbulent poll. Coke and his supporters were subjected to constant intimidation and abuse, and on one occasion Coke himself was stoned and bloodied by a crowd as he crossed the market place. He eventually withdrew from the contest 'from the just apprehension of hazard to his life' (Cobbett, *Parl. hist.*, 36, 1801–3, 1230). Victory went to his radical opponent, Dr Joseph Birch of Preston, described by one source as 'a whig, and something more' (Bailey, 222). Birch hailed his success, which came aptly on 14 July, as a triumph for civil liberty, and he alluded to the fall of the Bastille. Coke however saw at work 'Jacobinical' principles, which aimed ultimately at placing 'the Tenant above his Landlord, the Servant above his Master, and the Subject above his Prince' (*Coke and Birch*, 298–300).

Coke successfully petitioned parliament against Birch's election and in May 1803 they contested the seat again. To ensure freedom of election parliament had controversially extended to the town the jurisdiction of the county magistrates, who were predominantly conservative and in opposition to the corporation. In this changed setting Coke made a triumphant return to Nottingham, on 26 May, at the head of 1600 horsemen wearing his colours. It was a powerful display of strength and he won a resounding victory. At the nomination he and Birch had respectfully disputed the right of property to exercise influence at elections. Coke took a traditional view on this, and there is no doubt that such influence played its part in his success. He fought off another challenge from Birch in 1806, and from Crompton in 1807, before retiring in 1812. That year, significantly, both Nottingham seats were won by radicals. Coke continued as chairman of the Derbyshire quarter sessions until 1818. A lifelong bachelor, he died at his house, The College, in Derby, on 6 December 1825, aged eighty, and was buried in the local church of All Saints. A memorial stone there pays tribute to his record of public service, lauding him as 'high-minded, and in its true and just sense liberal'. MARK POTTLE

Sources Burke, *Gen. GB* (1838) · Foster, *Alum. Oxon.* · Cobbett, *Parl. hist.*, vol. 24 · J. Blackner, *The history of Nottingham* (1815) · T. Bailey, *Annals of Nottinghamshire*, 4 vols. (1852–5), vol. 4 · *Coke and Birch: the paper war, carried on at the Nottingham election, 1803* (1803) · J. F. Sutton, *The date-book of remarkable and memorable events connected with Nottingham and its neighbourhood, 1750–1850* (1852) · *Nottingham Journal* (1792–1816) · corporation archives, Notts. Arch., 4082a · *A full and accurate report of the trials of the Birmingham rioters at the late assizes for the county of Warwick* (1791) · *DNB* · HoP, *Commons*
Archives NRA, priv. coll., family corresp.
Likenesses J. Wright of Derby, group portrait, oils, *c.*1780–1782, Derby Museum Art Gallery · T. Gaugain, stipple, pubd 1809 (after T. Barber), BM, NPG

Coke, Sir Edward (1552–1634), lawyer, legal writer, and politician, was born on 1 February 1552 at Mileham, Norfolk, the only surviving son of Robert Coke (1513–1561), lawyer and landowner of Mileham, and his wife, Winifred (*d.* 1569), daughter of William Knightley of Norwich. The families whose arms Coke quartered bore names long known in Norfolk and the Conisford ward of Norwich—Coke, Pawe, Folcard, and Woodhouse—while the Knightleys were prominent in Northamptonshire. Coke's family were minor gentry. Estimates of the family's income vary from £40 per annum to £300 per annum. Robert Coke was a rising man, a member of Lincoln's Inn and an attorney and servant to the Townshend family. He obtained a coat of arms during Mary Tudor's reign and served as JP during the reign of Elizabeth. The fact that Winifred Coke owned law books suggests something remarkable. Her connections aided her son. Her sister Elizabeth married Sir Thomas *Gawdy, providing a useful link to that clan of lawyers and judges. Winifred's second husband, Robert Bozoun, of Whissonsett, Norfolk, was a man who drove hard bargains, even when dealing with Sir Nicholas Bacon, lord keeper, and probably taught his stepson some of his hard-headedness.

Sir Edward Coke (1552–1634), by unknown artist

Early years and education Coke was probably a middle child, the only boy among seven sisters. After attending the grammar school in Norwich, he enrolled in 1567 as a pensioner at Trinity College, Cambridge; he left at the end of 1570 without taking a degree. His years at Cambridge, significantly, were also the years of the vestiarian controversy—protests by puritan dons and students which culminated in an attack by Thomas Cartwright on the governing structure of the Church of England. During Coke's last term the protests ended with a crackdown by John Whitgift, master of Trinity College, presaging decades of conflict between the church establishment and puritan dissidents. Coke was enmeshed in these stirs both professionally and personally. Whitgift, Coke's college tutor, later sent his old student a Bible, urging that he study the law of God. Cartwright was linked to Coke by marriage, being brother-in-law to one of his sisters.

When Coke set off for London, it is said that he left with the horse on which he rode, £10 in his pocket, a rapier, and a diamond ring inscribed 'O prepare'. He reached the capital on 21 January 1571 and that same day enrolled at Clifford's Inn, an inn of chancery. In 1572 he moved on from this minor institution to the more prominent Inner Temple. In a Temple moot Coke reportedly won acclaim for arguing 'the cook's case'. This may be a stale pun on Coke's name, or, possibly, raised issues of parliamentary privilege: in 1532 the Inner Temple's cook had avoided arrest for debt because he also served Thomas Audley, speaker of the House of Commons. By early 1572 Coke was attending the courts in Westminster Hall. At some point during his student days he began keeping a commonplace book; in 1579, possibly in connection with his taking up a readership at Lyon's Inn, Coke began keeping detailed records of cases.

Early career Coke was called to the bar on 20 April 1578. In 1579 he argued his first case in the court of king's bench, and won because he presented it well and it was thoroughly researched. Edward Cromwell, third Baron Cromwell, had sued a parson for defamation, and construing the governing statute Coke showed that opposing counsel had cited a badly translated and recent law French abridgement rather than the original Latin text. Soon afterwards Coke's role in arguing *Shelley's case* (1581) brought him wider acclaim. The case featured anomalous facts, an ingenious new reading of standard conveyancing terms, and a prominent family bitterly divided over religion. Likely selected by William Cecil, first Baron Burghley and lord treasurer, to protect royal interests, Coke pulled off an energetic, brilliant defensive action. He commemorated the victory by circulating manuscript copies of his arguments.

During the 1580s and 1590s Coke became one of the most prominent lawyers in England. His fame grew. In 1579–80 he gave readings on the statute of 27 Edward I, *Finibus levatis*, and in 1592, at the Inner Temple, on the statute of uses. The readings in 1592 were cut short when plague broke out in London. To browse through any volume of Elizabethan law cases—the reports ascribed to Sir George Croke, William Leonard, John Godbolt, or Sir Francis Moore—is to find Coke representing a broad range of clients: country gentlemen, acquisitive parsons, Roman Catholic exiles, puritan dissidents, cockney publicans and City haberdashers, duellists, forgers, and burglars. He represented the Drapers' Company and other London guilds. The Howard family, struggling after the attainder of Thomas Howard, fourth duke of Norfolk, were important clients; others included the family of the financier Sir Thomas Gresham and the sons of Sir Nicholas Bacon (1509–1579)—Sir Nathaniel (d. 1624) and Sir Nicholas Bacon (d. 1624).

Coke argued successfully many of the great cases to come before the bar during the reigns of Elizabeth and James I and these helped to refine legal doctrine. In *Chudleigh's case* (1594) he argued that the statute of uses categorically made all transfers 'to use' subject to the rules on similar transfers made at law. In *Slade's case* (1602) he argued successfully that a plaintiff seeking payment for an unkept promise to pay money should be allowed to sue in assumpsit, rather than be required to bring an action for debt. Coke owed something of his success to his growing status. He married Bridget (1565–1598), daughter of John Paston of Suffolk, on 13 August 1582. It was rumoured that this connection brought a dowry of £30,000 and substantial amounts of property. Bridget Coke was a beautiful young woman and the couple set up house together at Huntingfield, Suffolk. They had seven sons and three daughters, including Anne (1585–1671/2)

[*see* Sadleir, Anne]. Coke became a notable figure in Norfolk's emerging county community—though local politics became more volatile in the wake of the collapse of the Howard family and the growing conflict among the gentry leaders. He was appointed JP for Norfolk in 1586 and for Suffolk and Middlesex by 1593. As his practice grew and he travelled to cities and towns throughout England, including Coventry and London, his expertise was sought by various municipal governments: he was appointed recorder of Coventry in 1585, Norwich in 1586, London in 1591–2, Orford in 1593, and Harwich by 1604.

Political conflict and state office In the closing years of Elizabeth's reign, Norfolk displayed the political fracture lines that later divided the nation under the Stuarts. Ambitious gentlemen allied with the episcopal hierarchy, and armed with royal patents and militia commissions, challenged the traditional system of county government. They were resisted by country magistrates and puritans, on whose side Coke generally stood. When the authorities cracked down on puritan ministers at Bury St Edmunds, Coke represented pastor William Fleming and won his acquittal. In 1591, from a Norfolk quarter-sessions bench, Coke and Francis Wyndham, justice of the common pleas, charged the grand jury that church courts could not force defendants to incriminate themselves. The statement resonates in Coke's later jurisprudence. In his native Launditch hundred, where his purchases made him a landowner to be reckoned with, he allied himself with puritan partisans—squires who feuded over grazing rights and brought lawsuits over rectories. During the parliamentary election of 1592 Coke stood as MP in partnership with the austere religious Sir Nathaniel Bacon; a hard-fought campaign saw them elected as knights of the shire.

Coke's partnership with the Cecil family was close. It was to Burghley that he owed his appointments as solicitor-general on 16 June 1592 and attorney-general on 10 April 1594 over the claims of his rival Francis Bacon, who had been supported by Robert Devereux, second earl of Essex. That conflict was part of the ongoing faction between Essex and the Cecils during the 1590s, being one of the biggest flashpoints. Coke was among the courtiers who profited from the wardships in which Burghley trafficked. He served as speaker of the House of Commons in 1593, the first parliament in which Sir Robert Cecil played a prominent part. Over the rest of the decade, as Norfolk politics became more volatile and popular, with mob violence and local rivalries (between supporters of the Cecils and Essex), Coke proved a shrewd electoral manager. As East Anglian boroughs put themselves into his pocket, allowing him to name the MPs that they returned, he dealt out seats to other Cecil partisans.

Coke as attorney-general In the early 1590s Coke advanced rapidly. In 1596 he became treasurer of the Inner Temple, and for years thereafter he had a strong influence on the inn, especially regarding admissions. As attorney-general he took part in the treason trials of Roderigo Lopez, Edward Squire, the Jesuits John Gerard and Henry Walpole, and Sir John Smyth. He badgered Essex after the earl's disastrous return from Ireland, and early in 1601, after Essex's frustrated *coup d'état*, Coke presented the case which sent the one-time favourite to the scaffold. He also helped to orchestrate the government's running battle against Catholic infiltrators. On 15 November 1602, with Sir John Popham, chief justice of the queen's bench, and 'such men as we could trust', he staked out a corner of Gray's Inn Fields and personally arrested couriers from an Italian cardinal (*CSP dom., 1601–3*, 261–2). He questioned suspects in the Tower of London, and Gerard, who later escaped, provided a unique account of one such interrogation from the prisoner's point of view. Coke served the crown in this position for twelve years, prosecuting Sir Walter Ralegh and Henry Brooke, eleventh Baron Cobham, in 1603. There were mundane, lawyerly duties as well—drafting pardons and engrossing commissions. However, if the treason prosecutions earned Coke prominence, the routine legal work finally brought him wealth. As attorney-general he collected fees for processing certain transactions, and the growing popularity of recourse to law made life particularly lucrative. During the 1590s, by Thomas Wilson's jaundiced but well-informed estimate, Coke's income rose from £100 per annum to £12,000 per annum, a figure comparable with those of the wealthiest men in the kingdom. In 1603, when James VI of Scotland succeeded Elizabeth, a coronation windfall came Coke's way. John Aubrey had the story: Coke advised 'every man of estate (right or wrong) to sue-out a pardon' from the incoming monarch. With a fee of £5 for processing each pardon, Coke was said to have gained £100,000 that year (*Brief Lives*, 162). However, this practice was rare and Aubrey may have exaggerated. In the heady days of James's arrival at Westminster, a knighthood followed, on 22 May.

In prosecuting Ralegh, the bitterest proceeding of his career, Coke was brutally vituperative. 'Thou viper', he called him, 'thou hast an English face, but a Spanish heart … thou art the most vile and execrable traitor that ever lived' (*State trials*, 2.7, 10, 25). Coke's language was so overwrought that Ralegh turned its force against the attorney-general, like a swordsman sidestepping the clumsy sweep of a halberd, and with fearless calm and quiet rejoinders redeemed his own reputation. Yet despite his eloquence and the lack of any real connection between the 'Main plot', with which he was charged, and the 'Bye plot', which Coke attributed to him, the fact remains that Ralegh could not explain why he had known so much and yet kept silent about Cobham's dubious political designs; and while proof of his guilt was weak, much stronger was the evidence that he had tried to conceal his own uncertain role. It was this part of the case that Coke hammered home, and, however inflammatory his rhetoric, he used language no more abusive than that with which Sir Thomas More had berated heretics. In other courtrooms, moreover—notably in *Lord Paget's case* (1591)—Coke argued just as forcefully on behalf of other enemies of the state.

By 1600 Coke was a very wealthy man with many possessions; he eventually owned at least 105 properties (manors, farms, rectories, advowsons, mills, and two mansions), most dotting the landscape in north-western Norfolk around Tittleshall and Holkham, with another cluster in Suffolk near Huntingfield. He was extremely acquisitive. A suit brought by Sir Francis Hubert, a hapless courtier and poet who blundered across his path, records the guile and audacity which the great lawyer could show. Coke acknowledged his tight-fistedness with a hint of self-mockery: when someone suggested that his high-living sons would spend his wealth faster than he had earned it, he replied, 'They cannot take more delight in the spending of it than I did in the getting of it' (*Brief Lives*, 162). Yet very often he showed a neighbourly generosity. Bridget Coke's household account book, preserved at Holkham, records regular payment for favours and the exchange of presents—salmon and venison traded back and forth between courtiers and her husband, 4d. was given to a boy who brought strawberries, and £1 was provided for Coke's superannuated nurse.

Bridget Coke died on 27 June 1598. On 6 November Coke married Elizabeth, Lady Hatton (1578–1646), daughter of Thomas Cecil, second Baron Burghley and first earl of Exeter, and his first wife, Dorothy, and widow of Sir William Hatton. By worldly standards it was a brilliant marriage. Elizabeth was a young widow, an heiress, a society beauty, and a niece of Sir Robert Cecil, principal secretary. Held at night without banns or licence, the wedding gave rise to considerable speculation. The incredulity of the letter writer John Chamberlain was typical:

> the quenes atturney married the Lady Hatton, to the great admiration of all men, that after so many large and likely offers she sholde decline to a man of his qualitie, and the[y] will not beleve it was without a misterie. (*Letters of John Chamberlain*, 29, 63)

Certainly Lady Hatton had her own motives. She was twenty-six years younger than Coke, kept her former title, and sparred with her new husband over her jointure property. Gossips questioned her faithfulness. Yet if Coke and she were not wholly compatible, at least they were well matched. They had two daughters and over the years, as she herself matured from a society beauty into a royal confidante, she stalwartly supported her husband's standing at court.

Coke's judicial career Coke was appointed chief justice of the court of common pleas on 30 June 1606, being created serjeant-at-law for the occasion, and chief justice of the king's bench on 25 October 1613. His tenure in these courts proved turbulent, being marked by friction with James and with two archbishops of Canterbury, Richard Bancroft and George Abbot. Early in James's reign, after the Hampton Court conference of 1604 had failed to resolve the tensions within the Church of England, the puritan leadership revived a strategy that had served them well in the 1590s. Facing prosecution by church courts and by the court of high commission—tribunals which were perennially criticized, not unjustly, for handling sectaries more harshly than Roman Catholic recusants—the puritans sued in common-law courts for writs of prohibition, orders enjoining prosecutions in such ecclesiastical tribunals. To enforce religious conformity, the commission compelled self-incrimination. Commissioners put defendants under oath in order to interrogate them about their religious principles as well as any plans further to reform the English church. (This was the notorious *ex officio* oath, so called because it was used in proceedings initiated directly by the commission.) The commission also meted out fines and prison terms. Critically, none of these powers was spelled out in the Act of Supremacy (1559), which authorized the commission. The commissioners claimed the powers because they were authorized by letters patent, as the statute had stipulated rather vaguely, commissions issued by crown officials. On the other side puritan lawyers argued that the commission's powers to interrogate, fine, and imprison were invalid, simply because these powers were not set forth in the statute. This set the common-law judges against the Church of England. To say that the commission's powers were limited by the statute was to say that the commission was subject to parliament and to the common-law judges who interpreted the law. More broadly, such arguments aligned judges and parliament against the crown. As a matter of constitutional logic, if the statute limited the powers which the king's commissions could grant, then parliament's authority on religious matters outweighed the king's.

In 1591, in *Cawdrey's case*, the judges ruled broadly in the high commission's favour—so broadly that the case settled little. By the first years of James's reign, many prohibitions had issued from the common-law courts. Coke was only the most prominent of the many common lawyers who favoured such limitations on ecclesiastical tribunals. In 1604 he sought to restrict the commission's use of the oath *ex officio*. In October 1605 Bancroft presented to the king a list of complaints against the judges, the so-called 'articuli cleri'. Over the next four years an indecisive series of conferences between the churchmen and the judges was held. In the meantime Coke and the judges continued to issue prohibitions, barring church-court prosecutions for churchyard altercations and vandalism, simony, and irregular sexual conduct. Coke was not opposed to the commission's existence, nor even categorically opposed to the use of the oath *ex officio*. Rather, he emphasized the need to limit the commission to serious, 'enormous' cases, and to prevent misuse of the power to compel self-incrimination. None the less, compared to other judges, Coke circumscribed the commission's jurisdiction more closely, and ruled more frequently against self-incrimination. He argued, with transparent naïvety, that the oath *ex officio* so strongly tempted men to perjury (at the risk of their souls) that only the common law or statute should require its administration.

Two years after Coke's appointment to the bench the controversy deepened. One milestone was *Fuller's case* (1607). Nicholas Fuller, a lawyer, tried and failed to obtain a ruling in a test case that the high commission lacked the power to fine and imprison. Until the end, he was supported by the judges of both common pleas and king's bench. Even though he went to prison, he retained Coke's

support. It had been determined in this litigation, Coke wrote, that 'when there is any question concerning what power or jurisdiction belongs to ecclesiastical judges … the determination of this belongs to the judges of the common law' (E. Coke, *Reports*, 1600–1659, 12.41). In November 1608, when James tried personally to resolve the feuds among his various courts of law, the controversy intensified. The king summoned the common-law judges to the council chamber in Whitehall Palace to explain their obstruction of the high commission. He informed the judges that he planned to decide the dispute among his courts; the judges were all his servants, he explained, and accordingly he could withdraw cases from their consideration and decide them himself. He questioned the decision. As Coke recalled the incident, he had told the king:

> God had endowed His Majesty with excellent science, and great endowments of nature; but his Majesty was not learned in the laws of his realm of England … which law is an act which requires long study and experience, before that a man can attain to the cognizance of it.   (ibid., 12.63, 65)

Other sources say that Coke denounced church-court jurisdiction as 'foreign', and asserted that James was 'defended by his laws'—which triggered an angry reaction from the monarch, who was already furious about Coke's assertion that he could not participate in judicial proceedings:

> [the king] fell into that high indignation as the like was never known in him, looking and speaking fiercely with bended fist, offering to strike him, etc., which the Lord Coke perceiving fell flat on all four; humbly beseeching his majesty to take compassion on him and to pardon him. (Usher, 'James I', 669–70)

James continued to rage, until Cecil (now first earl of Salisbury), also knelt and asked pardon for his niece's husband.

As tempers cooled James, rather than issuing further prohibitions, instructed his judges to refer jurisdictional conflicts to him. They ignored this. In May 1609 the churchmen asked for a declaration regarding the high commission's powers. The judges responded by denying that the commission could rule on 'any thing concerning meum and tuum [such] as legacies, tithes, and pensions', and that it was restricted to heresy and 'enormous' offences (Usher, 'James I', 191). The May conference ended inconclusively and the skirmishing continued. William Crashawe, an Inner Temple preacher and protégé of Coke's, was apprehended by the church authorities during the summer. In 1610 the Commons attacked one of Bancroft's closest allies, the civil lawyer John Cowell, an action traditionally ascribed to Coke. In May 1611 the judges were summoned before the privy council—'the first time', Coke told the privy councillors, 'that ever any judges of the realm have been questioned for delivering their opinion in matter of law according to their consciences in public and solemn arguments' (Usher, *High Commission*, 213). Coke reaffirmed the judges' stand that the commission could punish only 'enormous' crimes, and that it could fine and imprison only heretics, schismatics, and incontinent priests. Then he flung out a final barb: that the commission's penalties had to be reasonable, which would have allowed the judges to test the reasonableness of every fine or gaol term. He later turned against the churchmen even this concession. When heresy proceedings were opened against Bartholomew Legate, Coke's argument that heresy could be investigated only by the high commission, and not by any bishop, threatened briefly to derail the prosecution.

Comparing two decisions which Coke wrote or published about this time, *Mackalley's case* (1611) and *Allan Ball's case* (1609), shows how opinions had hardened. It should be adjudged murder if a debtor killed a bailiff arresting him for debt, Coke affirmed, but only manslaughter if a householder killed a high-commission pursuivant trying to make an arrest for adultery. In autumn 1611 Abbot offered a final compromise by allowing eight judges (including Coke) to sit as commissioners. The new body convened with an odd interlude of legal pantomime. The judges, after entering the conference room, refused to take their oaths as commissioners, asserting that they had not seen the oath's terms. To show that they did not sit officially, the judges physically remained standing, and on this singular discordant note the controversy faded away.

In these same years the high commission was not the only court whose jurisdiction the common-law judges sought to circumscribe. Prohibitions were issued against the court of admiralty, the king's council of the north, the council in the marches of Wales, and virtually all prerogative courts. (All of these, like the church tribunals, were courts with which the common-law courts had long-standing rivalries.) In 1608 Coke and the judges ruled that commissions of inquiry held only limited powers. In 1610, while affirming the king's right to issue proclamations, Coke and the judges implied that such royal action needed validation by their own decision. In *Bagg's case* (1615), Coke announced that the king's bench had the authority 'to correct all lesser authorities in the realm', a claim which could be stretched to cover even the court of chancery (E. Coke, *Reports*, 1600–1659, 11.93b, 98a).

However confrontational the course Coke steered as chief justice, the confrontations are not the entire story. He was not constantly at odds with the crown and with chancery; nor was he the only judge to infuriate James, or whom James bullied or suspended. Coke was frequently willing to favour the crown. *The prince's case* (1606) flattered royal finances, allowing James to recover many properties hastily sold off under Elizabeth. In *Calvin's case* (1608), Coke and the judges finessed a delicate political compromise over whether James's Scottish subjects, through his accession, had acquired the rights of English subjects. Coke threw James yet another favour in a lawsuit between the crown and the bishop of Bristol, ruling that benefices should pay taxes on their actual current values, not according to values discounted by decades of inflation—a decision which enriched the crown at the church's expense.

In the long pauses between the explosive confrontations, Coke prospered. The period 1603–25 saw Coke's children married into wealthy families. Coke himself bought up manors and profited every year in reputation and fortune, as volume after volume of his case reports was published. In 1614 Coke was named vice-chancellor of Cambridge University. He and his sons invested in the Virginia Company of London, profiting from the growth of English foreign trade. The storms of legend, so to speak, may also be considered the tempests of a balmy summer.

King's bench and chancery In 1613, against his own will, Coke was advanced to chief justice of the king's bench. Bacon had proposed his promotion: the lower fees of this office, he argued, 'will be thought abroad a kind of discipline to him for opposing himself in the king's causes'. Bacon also thought, however, that Coke would 'think himself near a privy councillor's place, and thereupon turn obsequious' (*Works*, 4.381). On 25 October Coke was sworn in as chief justice and on 4 November he was sworn in as a member of the privy council. This elevation did not make him obsequious.

For more than a century a quarrel had intermittently flared up between king's bench and chancery. King's bench judges asserted that lord chancellors could not interfere with the finality of their judgments, while lord chancellors just as often asserted their power to mitigate after a judgment had been made. Sir Thomas Fleming, chief justice, breathed new life into the dispute, and Coke, on his transfer to king's bench, inflamed the controversy. In *Heath v. Ridley* (1614) Coke announced that no court of equity could interfere with judgments given by common-law courts, and that any litigant who sought this would violate the statutes against *praemunire* (originally enacted to keep English litigants from appealing to papal courts, but which had more recently been used to rein in church tribunals). In *Glanvill v. Courtney* (1614), Coke and Thomas Egerton, first Baron Ellesmere and lord chancellor, clashed again. Richard Glanvill, a jeweller of dubious reputation, had won a king's bench judgment allowing him to collect on a transparently usurious contract. The debtor counter-sued in equity, alleging fraud; Ellesmere gaoled Glanvill when he failed to appear, prompting Coke to issue a writ of *habeas corpus*. Another conflict, with more exalted parties, was the *Case of Magdalene College* (1614). This pitted Magdalene College, Cambridge (which was suing to reclaim a property in London), against Henry de Vere, eighteenth earl of Oxford, who had erected buildings worth more than £10,000 on the site. When Coke ruled in the college's favour, the earl applied for relief to Ellesmere and won the appeal.

Within two years of his elevation, Coke stirred up the enmities which eventually brought him down. In 1614, during the Addled Parliament, he reversed precedent, and kept the judges from advising the House of Lords on points of law. He prevented the crown from appropriating the estate of Sir Thomas Sutton, ensuring that these went to endow Charterhouse School. A puritan parson in Somerset, Edward Peacham, was gaoled for writing a sermon which stressed God's judgments on wicked kings; Bacon polled the judges *seriatim* before the trial, asking each whether this were treason, but Coke growled at this 'auricular taking of opinions' (*Works*, 5.100). Coke would readily give out-of-court opinions to the crown—he did so, in these same months, in another treason prosecution, *Owen's case*—provided that the judges collectively considered the issues. What he resisted in *Peacham's case* was the king's attempt to exert pressure on individual judges. It is very likely (Coke thought so, among others) that Bacon's enmity ensured that the king remembered this resistance.

Coke's fall was postponed by the greatest scandal of James's reign, the prosecution of Robert and Frances Carr, earl and countess of Somerset, for the murder of Sir Thomas Overbury. During autumn 1615 this played out on the rostrum of Westminster Hall. Every motif of Jacobean melodrama was present: intrigue, adultery, love potions, poisons, the hint of witchcraft, and the suggestion of regicide. This was the last great investigation Coke directed and possibly the most intense, and he personally took more than 300 depositions. He had lost none of his prosecutor's harshness and sent several conspirators to the gallows while other defendants were still awaiting trial. Closely involved with the case, he is said to have voiced a suspicion he could not prove: that Somerset had procured the death of James's son Henry, prince of Wales, in 1612. Such overzealousness may have persuaded James to replace Coke with Bacon for the last phase of the proceedings. In spring 1616 hostilities resumed. Arrayed against Coke were the Church of England, chancery, and the crown—and now, perhaps most fatally, the rising George Villiers, duke of Buckingham, to whom Coke had denied a choice patronage appointment. Glanvill, who also acted as a moneylender, returned to king's bench, seeking a *praemunire* indictment against the chancery officials who had hindered his earlier lawsuit. A grand jury was convened; Coke tried futilely to browbeat the jurors into issuing charges.

Meanwhile a new case arose which pitted common-law rights against episcopal privilege. James supplemented the income of John Overall, bishop of Coventry and Lichfield, with the profits of an additional rectory, granted *in commendam*, only to see a landowner challenge his action. Coke's pivotal role in *Colt v. Glover*, also known as *The case of commendams* (1616), finally brought matters to a head. James wrote to the judges that the case concerned his power to govern the church, and asked that they stay proceedings until he decided whether further consultation between judges and churchmen was required. His position was strengthened by a writ which Bacon produced, *non procedendo rege inconsulto*, allowing the king to intervene in cases close to royal interests, which the attorney-general had tested in other cases. The judges countered unanimously, in a reply drafted probably by Coke, that the king's letter was 'contrary to law' and that 'our oath in express words is that in case any letter comes to use contrary to law that we do nothing by such letters, but certify your Majesty thereof, and go forth to do the law' (*Ninth Report*, HMC, 372). Responding forcefully, James summoned the judges before the privy council, tore up their letter, and demanded of each judge whether he would obey any future royal order. All the judges save Coke backed down. Asked what he would do, Coke answered, 'when that case should be, he would do that should be fit for a judge to do' (*Works of Francis Bacon*, 5.367).

Armed with memoranda from Bacon and Ellesmere, both strong critics of Coke's objectionable rulings, James offered his chief justice one further chance to conform. Late in June Coke was suspended from the privy council—charged, *inter alia*, with showing contempt for chancery and the crown. Meanwhile James ordered that Coke was not to ride on the summer assize circuit. Instead he was to censor his own law reports, 'wherein (as his majesty is informed) there be many exorbitant and extravagant opinions set down and published for positive and good law' (*Letters of John Chamberlain*, 2.14). Coke complied, albeit superficially. He acceded to James's views on the commendams lawsuit; more than that he would not do. On 2 October 1616, after perusing his *Reports*, Coke reported that he had found only five trifling errors. This was defiance, and James took up the gauntlet. He demanded that his obstinate chief justice explain five of his most dangerous conceits. When Coke refused this final opportunity to recant, yielding nothing, the king acted. On 16 November Coke was removed from the bench. It was said, Chamberlain wrote, that 'four p's' had overthrown the chief justice: 'that is, pride, prohibitions, praemunire, and prerogative' (ibid., 2.34).

Within six weeks Coke had bought back royal favour. He arranged a match between his fourteen-year-old daughter, Frances, and Sir John Villiers, Buckingham's older brother (apparently a gentle lunatic). Lady Hatton opposed the marriage. In July 1617 she carried the girl out of her husband's reach, and he pursued her. Both sides obtained warrants and exchanged charges in the court of Star Chamber, but the struggle was lawless: troops of bully-boys were hired, pistols issued to servants, and two doors smashed in with a heavy piece of timber. As his servants moved forward with their makeshift battering ram, Coke is said to have dispersed his wife's men by shouting that it would be justifiable homicide if his men killed any of them, but murder if he or his own people were killed. Little evidence supports this or the darker allegation that he tied Frances to the bedposts and whipped her until she agreed to the marriage. In September 1617, after final haggling—Coke refused to buy favour too dearly—the wedding was celebrated. The marriage was not happy, providing twenty years of scandal and doing nothing to improve Coke's reputation. Lady Hatton, who briefly suffered confinement at her husband's instigation, never willingly suffered his presence again. Coke returned to the privy council on 28 September, the day before Frances's wedding, though he was not restored to the judiciary. In winter 1619–20, when chronic illness kept Bacon from sitting in the Star Chamber, other privy councillors treated Coke as the senior member. Coke chaired the committee which ran the treasury. He sat in judgment on Thomas and Catherine Howard, earl and countess of Suffolk, and on Sir Henry Yelverton. Although he seems never to have returned to the courtroom, let alone to the bench, he proved too useful to be ignored.

Personality and cultural interests Coke showed an unusual blend of energy, obstinacy, bookishness, and vanity. 'He would play with his case as a cat would with a mouse, and be so fulsomely pedantic that a schoolboy would nauseate at it', John Aubrey wrote. 'But when he comes to matter of law, all acknowledge him to be admirable … He was of wonderful painstaking, as appears by his writings. He was short-sighted but never used spectacles to his dying day' (*Brief Lives*, 163). An anonymous puritan, who knew Coke well (possibly the young Joseph Hall), warned him in *An Expostulation to the Lord Coke* against loving his own words, preferring books to men, and patronizing sycophants. The other side of Coke's vanity was a ferocious energy. Not only did he regularly rise at three o'clock in the morning; he posted letters from the Tower of London at three in the morning. At the Northampton assizes in 1606 he spoke for two and a half hours. With this energy went a hard-edged inverse snobbery. Near the end of the great lawyer's career, after his prosecutions of Essex, Ralegh, Somerset, Bacon, and Lionel Cranfield, first earl of Middlesex, Sir Edward Conway quipped that Coke would die if he could not help ruin a great man at least once every seven years. 'Succedo arduus Eduardus cucus', runs an anagram penned in one of Coke's early law books: 'I Edward Coke succeed through hard work', or, 'To be Edward Coke is to work hard' (Hassall, 33). This was the most fitting motto Coke ever chose for himself. Neither of his two official mottos, *Prudens qui patiens* ('It is prudent to be patient'), which he copied from Burghley, or *Lex est tutissima cassis* ('Law is the surest protection'), which he took when created serjeant-at-law, offer as sharply drawn a self-portrait.

Coke was a handsome man, with something of the lawyer's vanity and pomposity. 'The jewel of his mind was put into a fair case, a beautiful body, with a comely countenance', Thomas Fuller flatteringly wrote, 'a case which he did wipe and keep clean, delighting in good clothes well worn, and being wont to say "that the outward neatness of our bodies might be a monitor of purity to our souls"' (Fuller, 415). A jibe from Bacon suggests that Coke gained weight as he prospered (neither the judge nor the philosopher took a lofty tone in comments about each other). Coke's portraits show that he had brown hair and a well-kept beard, with dark, penetrating eyes. They suggest a good deal of self-assurance and calculation.

Coke lived his life on the cusp between the international aspirations of Renaissance learning—extensive in its breadth, Latin in its ancestry—and the insular, assertive traditions of the English common law. When he quoted the Bible he generally quoted the Vulgate. It was in Latin that he composed serious verses—to commemorate his son's wedding, or to while away confinement in the Tower. He knew his classical authors well: Virgil, Cicero, Tacitus, Ovid, Sallust, Seneca. But while Coke knew Justinian's codes, he resisted the codification of the judges' wisdom. He challenged the civil law of the continent by reporting cases in the peculiar professional dialect, law French, of the English bar, and by using English for his institutional writings. He wrote:

> Our English language is as copious and significant, and as able to express any thing in as few and as apt words, as any other native language … And (to speak what we think) we would derive from the Conqueror as little as we could. (E. Coke, *Third Institute*, 'Proeme', 1642–4)

Deriving little from William the Conqueror—that is, finding the source of law in popular custom and judicial wisdom rather than in royal command—Coke gave mythic dimensions to the common law by tracing legal doctrines into dim antiquity. Following Sir John Fortescue he claimed that the unwritten law of England had operated unchanged since the days of the druids. He traced parliament to Anglo-Saxon days, possibly back to the *conventus* described by Tacitus, and he held that the rule against distraining beasts of the plough had been established by the mythical Celtic lawgiver Dunwallo Molmutius. This penchant for anachronism, common among Tudor lawyers, has been derided as a pathology of 'the common-law mind'. Yet Coke's myth-making was rooted less in mentality than in ideology. Like the Tudor divines who unearthed proofs that the Church of England was as ancient as the Church of Rome and preceded the establishment of papal authority, the lawyers' efforts to trace their discipline to a glorious British past reflected nationalist sentiment; the venerability of the common law reflected the heroic character of the English people. It was also a useful weapon against the encroachment of civil law. Fittingly, it was from Geoffrey Chaucer that Coke took his favourite judicial saying: 'out of the old fields, as men saith, cometh at this new corne fro yere to yere'.

Despite his reckless conclusions, Coke was a diligent searcher of the historical record. He collected manuscripts, trying to obtain the best possible versions and exchanging them with Sir Robert Cotton. Some of his historical manuscripts had been among those collected by Matthew Parker, archbishop of Canterbury, and Coke drew on the knowledge of prominent members of the Elizabethan Society of Antiquaries, Joseph Holland, Francis Tate, and Arthur Agard. Coke never questioned how the *feodum* of English law might relate to the *feodum* of the continent; but Sir Henry Spelman, who did make this connection—and so, as the legal historian Frederic Maitland put it, introduced the feudal system to England—was a neighbour and friend. Another member of Coke's circle was Sir John Davies, one of the shrewdest historians of his day. In this intellectual milieu Coke may have been something of a savant.

Coke's relationship with literature has been double-edged. He denigrated players and rhyming poets. In 1606 he advised a Norfolk grand jury that they might properly drive out of the shire 'stage players, wherewith I find the country much troubled'—but in the same speech borrowed from *The Summoning of Everyman* and stole from Shakespeare the famous patriotic speech of John of Gaunt in *Richard II* (E. Coke, *The Lord Coke his Speech and Charge*, 1607, sig. H2). Coke even alluded, very specifically, to *The Poetaster* by Ben Jonson, who returned the compliment with verses suggesting that Coke's rise owed everything to talent and industry. To James's great merriment the Cambridge production of *Ignoramus* (1615) broadly ridiculed both the common law and the chief justice. Coke's conflict with Ellesmere and the king found its way into the satirical twists of Jacobean drama (*The Widow's Tears*, by George Chapman, and *The Old Law*, by Thomas Middleton). For a flattering literary portrait, the chief justice had to wait three centuries, for the later cantos of Ezra Pound (particularly the 'Rock-drill' and 'Thrones' sections, published in the 1950s). In Pound's verses, which recite snippets of the *Institutes* to denounce usury and extol the people's ancient liberties, Coke appears alongside John Adams and classical Chinese mandarins, as a statesman and jurisprudent.

Puritan connections Across fifty years Coke befriended the puritans of England. The connections began with his own family. His cousin and ally in the Commons, Sir Richard Knightley of Fawsley, Northamptonshire, sheltered the Marprelate press. Even more important was Coke's sister Anne. She married into the Stubbe family, becoming sister-in-law to both Thomas Cartwright and John Stubbe. She was prominent among the sectaries of Norfolk, and criticized Cartwright vigorously for arguing that churches should be led by learned preachers rather than steered by the voice of the congregation.

Coke's religious beliefs were conventional. His household met for daily prayer, but he obtained a licence to eat meat himself on fast days. A deathbed prayer ascribed to him recites blocks of the Church of England liturgy. In churches under his influence (Weasenham in Norfolk, and Huntingfield and Bramfield in Suffolk), medieval decorations and rood screens survived intact. He could parrot the official line that Brownists were nearly as dangerous as papists. Nevertheless, inconspicuously but consistently, he favoured puritans. He was among the Inner Temple lawyers who took notes of the sermons preached by Walter Travers. He gave livings to ministers who avoided wearing surplices, omitted ceremonies, and taught in unlicensed schools: Robert Gold at Cokely in Suffolk, Edmund Stubbe at Huntingfield, and Coke's brother-in-law George Leedes at Holt. In 1600 he endorsed William Playfair as master of Clare College, Cambridge.

Coke attracted sermon dedications from godly divines such as Richard Rogers, Miles Mosse, and the literary executors of Thomas Perkins. The author of *A Godly Sermon Preached at Tittleshall* (1600), who dedicated this work to Coke, showed a puritan's concern with politics and disdain for chivalric romances. Coke's library at Holkham was filled with similar works: books by Hugh Broughton, William Crashawe, Samuel Hieron, Andrew Willet, and Thomas Brightman. Among his trusted servants in Norfolk were the Skippon family of Weasenham. Philip Skippon, Christian apologist and ramrod of the New Model Army, grew up on the edge of Coke's household. Coke's daughter Bridget chose John Milton to tutor her son Cyriack, and is said to have paid for the schooling of Andrew Marvell. Perhaps the most vital connection came late in Coke's career, between the elderly privy councillor and the young Roger Williams, who, long before he argued against religious persecution in England and made religious toleration a political reality in Rhode Island, took shorthand notes for Coke in the Star Chamber.

Coke as judge and jurisprudent Coke defined law as the 'artificial reason' of the judges, a professional consensus based on training and experience. Paying lip service to the view that the common law was custom, he was in fact a great believer in judicial action, who viewed the practice of law as an art: 'Reason is the life of the law', he wrote, 'nay the common law itself is nothing else but reason; which is to be understood of an artificial perfection of reason, gotten by long study, observation and experience, and not of every man's natural reason.' The common law of England, he continued, had 'been fined and refined by an infinite succession of grave and learned men, and by long experience grown to such a perfection, for the government of this realm' (E. Coke, *The First Part of the Institutes*, 1628, 97b). This view of law was grounded in the traditions of classical rhetoric, learning drilled into Coke and every other lawyer of his generation, in the grammar schools of Tudor England. It equated the good and the true with the persuasive and the public-spirited. Coke maintained (following Cicero and Quintilian) that, 'I never saw any man of excellent judgment in these laws, but was withall … honest, faithful, and virtuous' (E. Coke, *Reports*, 1600–1659, 2, preface). He asserted that the common law was inerrantly 'certain', in other words, reliable (ibid., 4, preface).

Part of this vision was conservative. Coke asserted that judges found law and did not make it. He felt that legal traditions were rich enough to solve any question facing a court. He felt that legal rules were best exemplified in individual cases and set great store by precedent, which he saw as the unique quality of common law. In *Calvin's case* he argued that medieval precedents on the rights of Edward III's Gascon subjects defined the rights of James's Scottish subjects. By contrast Ellesmere suggested frankly that, when new issues arose, courts made new law in resolving them. Rather than asking whether legal fictions, in order to ensure precedent, might be a cancer on the legal system, Coke unhesitatingly approved their use. In cases such as *Rockwood v. Feasar* (1591), he proved his magisterial ability, as George Croke admiringly put it, to devise a plea to alter the trial. His faith in the professional wisdom of bench and bar did not go unchallenged. Thomas Hobbes, most notably, argued that the law should be rooted in common reason rather than legal arcana. None the less, Coke's focus on the craft of lawyering—the etiquette of beheading a peer, the details of executing a will—emphasized the careful practice and broad learning necessary to put law into action.

Coke consistently held to the Tudor vision of the realm as a commonwealth, distinguishing public good from private gain. As a lawyer and judge—in cases such as *Davenant v. Hurdis* (1598), *Tooley's case* (1613), and the notable *Taylors of Ipswich* (1614)—he supported artisans seeking to follow their trades over opposition from craft guilds. In 1607, in the Star Chamber, Coke ruled in favour of a west country apothecary who faced hostility from the medical establishment. He mocked purveyance and wanted to abolish certain feudal tenures. He opposed the sale of office; the positions which he had held, he boasted, had all been acquired *sine prece et pretio*, without begging or bribery (*Ninth Report*, HMC, 374). In tithe litigation he led the judges who broke with medieval practice, forbidding the tithes on products of the earth (stone, brick, lead, coal, peat) and profits earned on sales of real estate and beer. He denounced torture, though he had signed warrants for torture in the past, including authorizing its use on Bartholomew Steer. He brooded over the number of felons who every year were sent to the gallows, and hoped that 'justice severé puniens' might be replaced with 'preventing justice', instruction in trade, and religion (E. Coke, *Institutes*, 1642–4, 3.243).

Coke and judicial review 'Nothing that is contrary to reason, is consonant to law', Coke wrote (E. Coke, *The First Part of the Institutes*, 1628, 56b). While such assertions dated back to Henry of Bratton, Coke and his colleagues pursued the principle with new-found energy. Defining law as the judges' reason allowed Tudor courts to review manorial customs, medieval precedents, municipal ordinances, and even acts of parliament. What they found reasonable, the judges approved; whatever failed to satisfy them, they struck down. Coke was willing to extract principles from yearbook jurisprudence, supplying new rules which the common law found indispensable. He preferred such reform by judicial action to reform by legislation. He looked down on statutes 'overladen with provisoes and additions', or 'penned or corrected by men of none or very little judgment in law' (E. Coke, *Reports*, 1600–1659, 2, preface; 4, preface). Despite his reputation as a master of the unwritten law, Coke worked routinely and comfortably with statutes. The law had three parts, he wrote—common law, statute, and custom—and he chose to report cases which elucidated important statutes.

In 1610, in *Bonham's case*, Coke laid the foundations for judicial review of legislation, allowing judges to strike down statutes. Thomas Bonham was a doctor practising in London, who, denied admission by the College of Physicians, was gaoled and fined when he continued to work. The court of common pleas, led by Coke, freed Bonham and fined the college. The relevant statute, Coke explained, improperly made the college a judge of cases in which it held an interest:

> And it appears in our books, that in many cases, the common law will control acts of Parliament, and sometimes adjudge them to be utterly void; for when an act of Parliament is against common right and reason, or repugnant, or impossible to be performed, the common law will control it, and adjudge such act to be void. (E. Coke, *Reports*, 1600–1659, 8.107a, 117b)

With this sentence Coke broke new ground: in the scattered medieval precedents which supported his ruling, judges might have ignored the effect of a statute, but 'to this fact Coke [had] really added an explanation and a theory all his own' (T. F. Plucknett, '*Bonham's case* and judicial review', *Harvard Law Review*, 40, 1927, 36). Pressed to recant

this ruling, Coke never explicitly did so; neither did he expressly reaffirm it, nor did he ever clearly state which he held to be the highest constitutional authority—the court of king's bench or the high court of parliament. However, in his *Fourth Institutes* he may have backed down somewhat. English courts soon abandoned the theory of judicial review, but in colonial Massachusetts and Virginia *Bonham's case* was cited as precedent for striking down unjust laws, and lawyers in the United States have not hesitated to see Coke's decision as a forerunner of *Marbury v. Madison* (1803), which asserted it for American federal courts.

Coke's service in parliament Coke's experience as a lawyer and judge was matched by his record as a parliamentarian. He sat in the parliaments of 1589 and 1593 as MP for Aldeburgh, Suffolk, and for Norfolk respectively, serving as speaker of the Commons during the latter session. He markedly tightened procedure. Absent from the Commons for nearly thirty years, he was returned for four parliaments in the 1620s: for Liskeard, Cornwall, in 1621, Coventry in 1624, Norfolk in 1625, and Buckinghamshire in 1628. In these assemblies he figured as one of the Commons' most prominent leaders. Always an oracle, Coke ended as something of a statesman, moving into opposition to the crown—ambivalently and intermittently, but ineluctably. Against the background of a trade depression Coke attacked bills of conformity (chancery orders which settled debts at a discount) and abuses within the legal system, seeking to define the courts' jurisdiction and to streamline proceedings in the exchequer and the court of wards. On trade and commerce, another area in which he hammered on grievances, his outlook was quintessentially mercantilist. He sought to keep wool prices high, rather than promote free trade; he attacked monopolies and trading companies' privileges, but intimated that trade was an area in which government policy had a role.

His fondness for denouncing abuses and attacking scapegoats made it easy for Coke to lead the Commons in its new-found vogue for impeaching state officers. He supported this effort by supplying medieval precedents and conducting crucial hearings himself—gradually distancing himself from royal interests. This zealousness drew from the king a pointed criticism, made in a speech to the Lords:

> For though Sir Edward Coke be very busy and be called the Father of the Law and the Commons house have divers young lawyers in it, yet all is not law that they say, and I could wish, nay I have told Sir Edward Coke, that he [should] bring precedents [from] good kings' times … [and not from the reigns of] silly weak kings [such as Henry VI].
> (Zaller, 69)

James concluded ominously, 'I hope in his vouching precedents to compare my actions to usurpers or tyrants' times you will punish him' (ibid.). This warning put at risk Coke's liberty and fortune, and possibly more. Yet within weeks he had snatched a great deal of gratification from the jaws of his own potential ruin. From corrupt patentees like Sir Giles Mompesson, the Commons turned relentlessly upon the man who had approved their patents—Francis Bacon, first Baron Verulam and Viscount St Albans, the lord chancellor—bringing well-founded charges of bribery. Coke headed the committee which investigated Bacon and fended off compromises which might have saved his rival. He must also have been active behind the scenes: some unknown individual had painstakingly gathered the evidence which the Commons now so quickly and devastatingly threw into public view, and the thoroughness of the inquiry betrayed a master's hand. Coke remained vulnerable himself to the rough powerplays of impeachment politics, even after Bacon resigned his office and was sent to the Tower. James long retained hopes that the Commons would vote him what he sought, and he continued to draw on Coke's legal knowledge. In autumn 1621, while the Commons continued to sit, James relied on Coke in a case involving Archbishop Abbot. Abbot had accidentally killed a gamekeeper while hunting, and, under scrutiny for shedding guiltless blood, was cleared by Coke's opinion that it was lawful for a bishop to hunt—implicit, Coke explained, in the old rule that a bishop's pack of hunting dogs escheated to the crown. Yet over the course of the autumn James's exasperation with the Commons and with his uncompliant privy councillor continued to grow. In November, with royal support, two patentees, John Lepton and Henry Goldsmith, prepared their own attack on Coke: a long list of alleged misconduct from his days as a judge. Coke parried this initiative, but James was ready to take stronger measures himself. At the end of the year, after Coke and the Commons had asserted the right to debate and legislate on all matters concerning the commonwealth, James struck. On 27 December, eight halberdiers marched Coke off to the Tower, and shortly thereafter the king dissolved parliament. Coke spent most of 1622 in confinement, first in the Tower and later under house arrest at his mansion in Stoke Poges, Buckinghamshire. He consoled himself by writing Latin verses which mentioned the lions roaring in the Tower precincts and wishing himself back at his house in Godwick, Norfolk.

In the parliament of 1624 Coke was returned for Coventry. The king planned to keep him out of the way by sending him on a commission to Ireland, but last-minute lobbying by Charles, prince of Wales, changed James's mind. Shifts in foreign policy had reduced frictions between crown and Commons and also contributed to the king's decision. Complaints were once more aired, but this time hopefully, and Coke chaired the committee on grievances. Two bills he had sponsored but seen voted down in 1621, on monopolies and bankruptcy reform, were now enacted. Some tensions remained in one bill that he sponsored, a limitations measure which would have protected against 'concealers' (and the crown) all land already held for more than sixty years. Concealers were typically vilified as minions of a corrupt and venal court; Coke played the country gentleman memorably in denouncing them as 'viperous vermin' and 'caterpillars of the commonwealth' (White, 72–6). Yet he worked well in this parliament with Buckingham. When the duke spoke of war with Spain, Coke seconded him—perhaps outdid

him. When the duke moved to bring down Cranfield, it was Coke who marshalled the evidence and managed proceedings in the Commons.

The parliament of 1625, the first convened by Charles I, saw a sea change in Coke's role. No longer was he the energetic committee-man who argued the details of countless bills. Instead, linked with Sir John Eliot and Sir Edwin Sandys in a loose opposition group, he pressed a series of initiatives uncongenial to the new king, criticizing Charles's foreign policy, challenging his decisions on religion, and hesitating to grant financial support. Coke clearly thought that the king's expenses could be trimmed. In a major speech on 4 August 1625 he analysed the income and expenses of the crown, making recommendations on both sides. He argued that the king should ordinarily live of his own, seeking taxes only for extraordinary ventures, and that the king could do this if he would only improve the management of crown lands and cut expenses by reducing the size of the royal household, limiting pensions, and eliminating prerogative courts. Amid the debate over tonnage and poundage, Coke seems to have intended an attractive compromise. He clearly meant to establish that tonnage and poundage was revenue which the king enjoyed only by parliamentary grant. However, he also proposed that parliament establish a new scale of customs tariffs, which would likely have adjusted duties to account for inflation, thus offering Charles a larger, more predictable income. On matters of religion Coke also joined vigorously in the Commons' attack on Richard Montague, whose Arminian beliefs were portrayed as crypto-Catholic. Beneath discussions of religious doctrine lay power politics. The crown had begun to pack the bench with its supporters among the Laudian clergy, and the wealth of the Church of England had become a reservoir upon which the king might draw without parliamentary approval.

As well as exploring fiscal concerns, debating crown finances, and defending the Church of England, parliament took the opportunity to review foreign policy. It found little to praise. Coke was among the veteran legislators who found putting royal finances in order more important than funding a fleet. As the parliament ended he obliquely criticized Buckingham with obscure historical references, approving the medieval practice of not creating dukes (Buckingham had reached this title with unseemly speed) and questioning whether one lord admiral (Buckingham's title) could meet the duties traditionally allotted to two. Charles fathomed Coke's historical allusions and prevented him from sitting in the parliament of 1626. Coke was among six former parliamentarians pricked by the crown that year to serve as sheriffs, a duty requiring that they remain in their home counties (in Coke's case, Buckinghamshire) rather than join the Commons at Westminster. Coke fought this. With a typical blend of antiquarian learning, protestant sympathy, and canny legalism, he insisted that he could not in good faith take the sheriff's oath because it required him to persecute Lollards. The government riposted, graciously and effectively; it struck the clause on Lollards, and required Coke to take the oath and serve.

The parliament of 1628 and the petition of right In 1628 Coke returned for what proved to be his most memorable parliament. Buckingham's wars with France and Spain led to new crises at home: soldiers quartered in citizens' homes, martial law (imposed on soldiers, threatened for civilians), and the king's penchant for demanding funds under colour of prerogative claims and then gaoling gentlemen who objected to paying the taxes that he demanded. Coke was perhaps the king's most prominent critic, speaking out against taxation without parliamentary consent, the creeping spread of martial law, and the royal power to imprison without cause shown, a prerogative claim which he sought to ban absolutely. Coke was now seventy-six. Some of his oratory was needlessly baroque, and gaps appeared in his vaunted memory. The king's lawyers nettled him with proof that he himself had long supported a royal power to gaol men without showing cause. Yet ultimately Coke proved invaluable. According to Conrad Russell, 'Other Parliaments had been concerned with particular liberties', purveyance and customs duties, and monopolies, but it was this parliament 'which first saw these liberties as collectively threatened by a threat to the ideal which held them all together, the rule of law' (Russell, 343). The metaphors on which Coke relied—his claim that no man was a tenant-at-will for his liberties, or that if a lord could not imprison a villein without cause then no king could imprison a freeman without cause—essentially provided an ideology which closely linked liberty and property, an ideal at the heart of the English psyche.

Coke led the Commons in rejecting compromise. With John Selden he carefully picked apart the ambiguities and omissions which made Charles's proposals meaningless. In conference with the Lords he proved an effective spokesman. He refused to trust the king's personal word. 'I know that prerogative is part of the law', he cautioned, 'but sovereign power is no parliamentary word: in my opinion, it weakens Magna Carta … Magna Carta is such a fellow that he will have no sovereign' (Russell, 352).

When Charles warned the Commons that he would veto any bill that did more than reconfirm Magna Carta, Coke must have scented a rare opportunity; the king's demand offered the old judge the chance to make new law out of the greatest medieval statute. The result was the petition of right, something more than a list of grievances, if less than an actual bill of rights. It was Coke who suggested the petition. The king answered the petition evasively, and on 4 June did so a second time announcing his intention to prorogue parliament. Coke now played a final, pivotal role. On 6 June, in highly dramatic circumstances, he spoke up, telling his colleagues that there were no abuses that the Commons could not debate or act on, and that medieval parliaments had not hesitated to name and condemn ministers of state. In this tradition Coke then pointed to Buckingham, finally, by name, as 'the grievance of grievances' and 'the cause of all our miseries'. This speech, wrote one Yorkshire MP, was 'answered with a cheerful acclamation of the House, as when one good

hound recovers the scent, the rest come in with a full cry' (Bowen, 502). Coke spoke in the afternoon; by evening work on impeachment was well advanced. With the favourite under attack, Charles backed down. On 7 June the king came to Westminster and assented to the petition, 'soit droit fait comme est desiré'—words acceptable to show royal assent, as Coke assertively told the Commons (E. Foster, 'Petitions and the petition of right', *Journal of British Studies*, 13, 1973, 22).

This was Coke's last venture into public life. He retired to his mansion at Stoke Poges. In 1628 he published *The First Part of the Institutes of the Lawes of England, or, A Commentarie upon Littleton*, and for the remaining six years of his life he seems to have worked to complete his *Institutes*. He was seriously ill in 1631. Friends sent him doctors, Lady Hatton set out for Stoke to claim what she could find there, and the government pondered seizing his papers. Coke recovered. He was still hale in many respects and could ride at eighty, worry over his sons' debts, and hunt ready money for orphaned granddaughters' marriage portions. He played out, too, an endgame with Charles. In April 1632 the king's men raided Stoke; newswriter John Pory reported that Coke wept as his papers were removed. In 1633 Charles sealed Coke's rooms at the Inner Temple. Finally, in the last days of August 1634, while the old man lay dying, the king's men ransacked both Coke's study at Stoke and his files at the Inner Temple. Roger Coke, the judge's grandson, wrote that they seized more than fifty manuscripts and other papers.

Coke died at Stoke House shortly before midnight on 3 September 1634, 'in his bed quietly like a lamb, without any groans or outward signs of sickness, but only spent by age', his friend Sir Julius Caesar noted (Inderwick and Roberts, 2.lxix). His body was interred in St Mary's Church at Tittleshall, Norfolk, exactly one month later. His papers vanished for seven years, until the Long Parliament voted that they be returned to his heir, Robert Coke, and published. The vote was taken, perhaps not coincidentally, on the same day on which Thomas Wentworth, earl of Strafford, was beheaded.

Roger *Coke (*c.*1628–1704x7) claimed that his grandfather's will was removed by Charles's servants and never seen again. However, a will and a codicil, signed by Coke in November 1623, were proved in early 1635. Throughout his career Coke had put in trust the lands he acquired, and his will added the briefest coda to these dispositions, directing simply that his executors dispose of his estate as directed by the trustees. This masterfully opaque directive left Coke's property in hands he trusted, revealed nothing to outsiders, and skirted the church courts' probate jurisdiction. The codicil added only one detail, his request that his library be preserved. Coke's executors, Sir Thomas Coventry and Sir Randolph Crewe, carried out the testator's intentions. Coke had amassed great wealth—all his sons had eldest sons' portions, it was said—and his heirs and their trustees kept firm hands on it. Indeed, in the reign of Elizabeth II his descendants retained much of the wealth that the family had acquired during the reign of Elizabeth I.

Coke's publications Coke's first well-known work was a manuscript report of *Shelley's case*, circulated soon after the decision in 1581. In 1600, afraid that unauthorized versions of his case reports might be printed—and probably following the example of Edmund Plowden, with whom he had worked and whom he revered—Coke issued the *First Part* of his *Reports*. He put out eleven volumes by 1615. Making available more than 467 cases, carrying the *imprimatur* and the authority of the lord chief justice, these case reports provided a critical mass of material for the rapidly developing modern common law. Reversing medieval jurisprudence, which had often relied on general learning and reason, Coke preferred to amass precedents. 'The reporting of particular cases or examples', he asserted, was 'the most perspicuous course of teaching the right rule and reason of the law' (E. Coke, *Reports*, 1600–1659, 4, preface).

Coke began by printing great cases. With the *Fourth Part* and *Fifth Part* (1604–5) he shifted to shorter cases, grouped by topics. The *Fifth Part* featured *Cawdrey's case*, with Coke's treatise on the crown's ecclesiastical supremacy. Beginning with the *Sixth Part* (1607), Coke emphasized recent decisions. For his massive *Book of Entries* (1614) he collected pleadings for his fellow lawyers' better guidance.

In reporting cases Coke could be robustly egocentric, trimming or omitting other lawyers' arguments. His accuracy could vary. Yet the value of these collections, as a working reference for the bar, has never been gainsaid. Bacon himself wrote:

> Had it not been for Sir Edward Coke's reports (which, though they may have errors, and some peremptory and extrajudicial resolutions more than are warranted, yet they contain infinite good decisions and rulings over of cases), the law, by this time, had been almost like a ship without ballast. (*Works*, 6.65)

In prefaces to each *Part*, very often free-standing essays, Coke found opportunity to expound his understanding of the law. It was in these pages, *inter alia*, that he praised the common law, honoured parliament, and attacked the Huguenot jurist François Hotman for his irreverence toward Littleton. In the prefaces to the *Fifth* and *Sixth* parts, Coke quarrelled with the exiled Jesuit Robert Persons, unwisely drawing return fire from a deadlier wit.

In 1628 Coke published his masterwork, the *Commentarie upon Littleton*, known ever thereafter as *Coke on Littleton*. The book ostensibly presents Coke's glosses on the text of Littleton's *Tenures*, an outline of the law of real property. In fact, however, his glosses overwhelm Littleton's language, ranging broadly across the law of his day. To Littleton's short first paragraph, defining tenancy in fee simple, Coke devoted eighteen folio pages of annotations. He is described as writing:

> like a helpful old wizard … anxious to pass on all his secrets, but not quite sure where to begin or end … [T]he commentary wanders through such disparate topics as etymology, alien status, misnomer in grants, interest rates and usury … the Domesday Book, the eight parts of a deed, the styles and titles of the kings of England, the ownership of the Isle of Man, and the legal status of monsters and hermaphrodites. (Baker, *Introduction*, 218)

The book long absorbed and exasperated lawyers. 'A mind more disorderly than Coke's', carped Sir James Fitzjames Stephen, 'it would be difficult to find' (Holdsworth, *Eng. law*, 5.482). The height of idiosyncrasy may be the section in which Coke collects the 119 places where Littleton uses the abbreviation '&c.'

Coke on Littleton was the first volume of Coke's four *Institutes of the Laws of England*. He probably chose the title to assert that his work, in epitomizing the law of England, ranked equally with Justinian's codification of Roman law. The *Second Institute* covers thirty-nine statutes of significance, glossing them on a clause-by-clause basis. It begins with Magna Carta, continues through Plantagenet and Tudor legislation, and ultimately ends with the Jacobean statutes on houses of correction. Coke heaped honorifics on Magna Carta, which he asserted merely declared the rights all English people enjoyed under common law. The *Third Institute* covers the criminal law. Coke's background as attorney-general shaped it: more pages are devoted to treason, misprision of treason, and heresy than to homicide, rape, robbery, burglary, larceny, and theft, because the first three crimes were more serious. The *Fourth Institute*, concerning the jurisdiction of courts, was a treatise on structural constitutional law and organs of government. Coke reviewed the powers of the various government bodies existing in England—legislative, administrative, fiscal, mercantile, ecclesiastical, collegiate, metropolitan, and baronial.

After Coke died some of his other works found their way into print, including his *Treatise on Bail and Mainprise* (1634) and *The Complete Copyholder* (1650). Publishers, working from manuscript collections of his opinions and memoranda, brought out books denominated the *Twelfth* and *Thirteenth* parts of the *Reports* in 1658 and 1659 respectively. Their uncertain provenance and varying quality long cast doubts on these reports' authority, but their connection with Coke now appears established. *The Complete Copyholder* explored a narrow topic in a rigorously structured manner, in sharp contrast to the sprawl of *Coke on Littleton*.

Coke's reputation Thomas Fuller wrote that Coke would be admired 'whilst Fame hath a trumpet left her, and any breath to blow therein' (Fuller, 416). Wherever the common law has been applied, Coke's influence has been monumental. Between the medieval era and the modern, Maitland wrote, 'Coke's books are the great dividing line, and we are hardly out of the Middle Ages till he has dogmatized its results' (Holdsworth, *Eng. law*, 5.489). Coke is the earliest judge whose decisions are still routinely cited by practising lawyers, and to whose writings one turns for a statement of what the common law held on any given topic.

As Sir William Holdsworth noted, Coke's works have been to the common law what Shakespeare has been to literature and the King James Bible to religion. No master of the common law bears more responsibility than Coke for creating the legal regime which Sir William Blackstone rationalized, and Jeremy Bentham attacked, the idea of law as a *forest sauvage* of archaicism and legal fictions. At the same time—and with no less fairness—Coke has always been honoured as a champion of progress and justice. His commentary on the phrase *nisi legem terrae*, in a discussion of Magna Carta, is one of the earliest judicial commentaries to give a truly constitutional resonance to the phrase 'due process of law'. John Lilburne and other Levellers cited his writings, and Thomas Jefferson considered that 'a sounder Whig never wrote, nor of profounder learning' (Bowen, 514). From Coke's stenographer and protégé Roger Williams derives a tradition of religious toleration and political independence which contrasts sharply with the intellectual legacy of Bacon's stenographer and protégé Thomas Hobbes.

The nineteenth century honoured Coke as an exponent of personal liberty and representative government. The twentieth century honoured him as the prototype of the activist judge—able to draw broadly on social and economic knowledge, and not afraid to strike down laws. For the learning he amassed, for the reports he published, for pioneering judicial review, and for asserting judicial independence, Coke deserves to retain this respect.

ALLEN D. BOYER

Sources C. Hill, *Intellectual origins of the English revolution revisited* (1997) · Holdsworth, *Eng. law*, 5.423–80 · C. W. James, *Chief Justice Coke: his family and his descendants at Holkham* (1929) · A. Boyer, *Sir Edward Coke and the Elizabethan age* (2003) · J. Bruce, 'Sir Edward Coke's "Vade Mecum"', *Collectanea Topographica et Genealogica*, 6 (1840), 208–22 · *CSP dom.*, 1547–1625, with *addenda, 1566–79* · *Calendar of the manuscripts of the most hon. the marquis of Salisbury*, 24 vols., HMC, 9 (1883–1976) · *The works of Francis Bacon*, ed. J. Spedding, R. L. Ellis, and D. D. Heath, 14 vols. (1857–74) · R. G. Usher, *The rise and fall of the high commission* (1913) · C. Russell, *Parliaments and English politics, 1621–1629* (1979) · *State trials* · L. A. Knafla, *Law and politics in Jacobean England: the tracts of Lord Chancellor Ellesmere* (1972) · *The letters of John Chamberlain*, ed. N. E. McClure, 2 vols. (1939) · W. O. Hassall, ed., *A catalogue of the library of Sir Edward Coke* (New Haven, Conn., 1950) · C. M. Gest, 'The writings of Sir Edward Coke', *Yale Law Journal*, 18 (1909), 504–32 · J. H. Baker, 'Coke's notebooks and the sources of his reports', *The legal profession and the common law: a historical essay*, ed. J. H. Baker (1986), 177–204 · A. Boyer, 'Understanding, authority, and law: Sir Edward Coke and the Elizabethan origins of judicial review', *Boston College Law Review*, 39 (1997), 43–93 · C. D. Bowen, *The lion and the throne: the life and times of Sir Edward Coke (1552–1634)* (1957) · A. H. Smith, *County and court: government and politics in Norfolk, 1558–1603* (1974) · D. MacCulloch, *Suffolk and the Tudors: politics and religion in an English county, 1500–1600* (1986) · J. H. Baker, *An introduction to English legal history* (1971); 3rd edn (1990) · R. Helgerson, 'Writing the law', in R. Helgerson, *Forms of nationhood: the Elizabethan writing of England* (1992), 63–104 · G. Burgess, *The politics of the ancient constitution: an introduction to English political thought, 1603–1642* (1993) · F. S. Fussner, *The historical revolution: English historical thought and writing, 1580–1642* (1962) · B. Malament, 'The "Economic Liberalism" of Sir Edward Coke', *Yale Law Journal*, 76 (1967), 1321–58 · S. White, *Sir Edward Coke and 'The grievances of the commonwealth', 1621–1628* (1979) · R. Zaller, *The parliament of 1621: a study in constitutional conflict* (1971) · HoP, *Commons, 1558–1603* · J. E. Neale, *The Elizabethan House of Commons* (1949); rev. edn (1963) · C. M. Gray, *The writ of prohibition: jurisdiction in early modern English law*, 2 vols. (New York, 1994) · L. Jardine and A. Stewart, *Hostage to fortune: the troubled life of Francis Bacon* (1999) · R. G. Usher, 'James I and Sir Edward Coke', *EngHR*, 18 (1903), 664–75 · G. A. Carthew, *The hundred of Launditch and deanery of Brisley, in the county of Norfolk*, 3 vols. (1877–9) · F. Blomefield and C. Parkin, *An essay towards a topographical history of the county of Norfolk*, [2nd edn], 11 vols. (1805–10) · *Ninth report*, 3 vols., HMC, 8 (1883–4) · *The papers of Nathaniel Bacon of Stiffkey*, ed. A. H. Smith, G. M. Baker, and R. W. Kenny, 1–3, Norfolk RS, 46, 49, 53 (1979–90) · J. F. Williams, ed., *Diocese of Norwich, Bishop Redman's visitation, 1597*, Norfolk RS, 18 (1946) · F. A. Inderwick and R. A. Roberts, eds., *A calendar of the Inner Temple records*, 5 vols. (1896–1936) · T. Fuller, *The worthies of England*, ed. J. Freeman, abridged edn (1952) · *Aubrey's Brief lives*, ed. O. L. Dick (1987)

Archives BL, corresp. and papers, Harley MSS 6686–6687 · BL, treatises, Add. MSS 48986, 58218 · CUL · Hatfield House, Hertfordshire, letters and papers · Holkham Hall, Norfolk, Holkham estate papers · Holkham Hall, Norfolk, family papers · Inner Temple, London, material, incl. unpublished notes · JRL, papers relating to family and estates · Norfolk RO · PRO · Yale U., Beinecke L., legal papers | BL, letters to Sir Julius Caesar, Add. MSS 12504–12507

Likenesses oils, 1593, Holkham Hall, Norfolk; repro. in James, *Chief Justice Coke* · oils, *c*.1606–1613, Holkham Hall, Norfolk · S. de Passe, line engraving, *c*.1606–1616? · N. Stone, relief effigy on monument, 1638, St Mary's Church, Tittleshall, Norfolk · L. F. Roubiliac, marble bust, 1757, Trinity Cam. · D. Loggan, line engraving, BM, NPG; repro. in *Juridiciales* (1666) · J. Payne, line engraving, BM, NPG; repro. in E. Coke, *Institutes*, 2nd edn (1629) · attrib. P. van Somer, oils, Inner Temple, London · oils, Palace of Westminster, London · oils, Holkham Hall, Norfolk [*see illus.*]

Wealth at death possibly one of the wealthiest private subjects, below the peers and barons, at the time of death; 105 holdings (manors, houses, wills, etc.) listed in inquisition post mortem, 21 Jan 1635; 'Advanced a fair estate, so that all his sons might seem elder brethren, by the fair possessions left unto them': Carthew, *Hundred of Launditch*, vol. 3, pp. 114–20 (inquest); Fuller, *Worthies of England*

Coke, Elizabeth, Lady Coke. *See* Hatton, Elizabeth, Lady Hatton (1578–1646).

Coke, George (1570–1646), bishop of Hereford, was born on 3 October 1570, the fifth son of Richard Coke (d. 1582) of Trusley, Derbyshire, and his wife, Mary (d. 1580), daughter of Thomas Sacheverell of Kirby, Nottinghamshire. He matriculated at St John's College, Cambridge, in 1588, graduating BA in 1593 and proceeding MA in 1596. He was made a fellow of Pembroke College in 1597, rhetoric lecturer in 1602, and was junior taxor of the university in the year 1605/6. In 1608 he was presented to the rectory of Bygrave in Hertfordshire, worth nearly £300 p.a., where, Fuller quaintly observed, 'a lean village (consisting of but three houses) maketh a fat living' (Fuller, *Worthies*, 115). About the end of 1609 he resigned his fellowship and between 18 November that year and 9 January 1610 he married Jane Heigham. He moved to Bygrave, where he remained for the next twenty-three years. Fuller called him 'a meek, grave and quiet man' (ibid.). Only after Sir John *Coke (1563–1644), one of his older brothers, was advanced to be secretary of state in autumn 1625 was this essentially mediocre yet personable cleric plucked from the obscurity of his country living and preferred beyond his abilities, a minnow in a world of sharks.

On 19 January 1626 Coke was collated to the prebend of Finsbury in St Paul's Cathedral, and, having received a DD degree in 1630, on 10 February 1633 he was consecrated bishop of Bristol. In June 1635 he was instituted as rector of Maiden Newton, Dorset, despite the opposition of Sir John Strangeways who believed that the advowson was his. Coke was translated to Hereford in July 1636, apparently, as in his elevation to Bristol, with the support of

William Laud. At the same time he resigned both Bygrave and his prebend at St Paul's.

Coke had an unhappy time at Hereford, which he described in February 1640 as 'this place of tryal, under so much variety of business and among such men, as are … too strong and cunning for me' (BL, Add. MS 69868, fol. 142r); two years earlier he had said that of all the justices in Herefordshire, no more than four were his defenders in a county where local juries were habitually against the church and the bishop. By the end of 1637, to add to his troubles, his eyesight was failing and in dim light he was forced to wear spectacles. In October 1638 he was censured by Archbishop Laud for presenting one who was insufficiently learned to cathedral office: one of Coke's sons had deserted his apprenticeship and run away to sea but, seeing in the storms that beset his vessel a providential sign, had turned back and sought ordination, and his father had made him precentor of Hereford Cathedral. On Laud's protest Coke replaced his son with his nephew Francis Coke (d. 1682), son of his eldest brother Sir Francis Coke, but he was soon complaining that Francis was unthankful and unfriendly to him.

In December 1641 Coke was one of the twelve bishops who petitioned parliament, for which he was impeached and imprisoned for seventeen weeks. Retiring to his see, he was in Hereford in April 1643 when it fell to the parliament but, under the articles of surrender of the town, escaped molestation. However, when Hereford fell for the second time, in December 1645, he was captured and taken to Gloucester, and on 3 January 1646 the Commons ordered that he and the other prisoners be sent to London. His estate at Queest Moor in the parish of Eardisley in Herefordshire was sequestrated on 13 August 1646 and, although thrifty, he was reduced to living on the charity of his relations. He died on 10 December 1646 at Queest Moor and was buried in Eardisley church five days later. After the Restoration an elaborate monument, with recumbent effigy, was erected in Hereford Cathedral; it was much altered in the mid-nineteenth century.

IAN ATHERTON

Sources Coke's letters to Sir John Coke, BL, Add. MS 69868 · *The manuscripts of the Earl Cowper*, 3 vols., HMC, 23 (1888–9) · T. Fuller, *The worthies of England*, ed. J. Freeman, abridged edn (1952) · Venn, *Alum. Cant.* · *Fasti Angl.* (Hardy), 1.216, 471; 3.635 · F. T. Havergal, *Monumental inscriptions in the cathedral church of Hereford* (1881), 11 · *Fasti Angl., 1541–1857*, [St Paul's, London], 34; [Bristol], 10 · *Walker rev.*, 8, 322 · J. Hunter, *Familiae minorum gentium*, ed. J. W. Clay, 2, Harleian Society, 38 (1895), 570–75 · parish register, Eardisley, 1630–62, Herefs. RO, AR 46/1 · *The works of the most reverend father in God, William Laud*, 4, ed. J. Bliss (1854), 297 · P. Heylyn, *Cyprianus Anglicus* (1671), 214 · Bodl. Oxf., MS Tanner 303, fol. 117r · Folger, MS Vb 2(3) · *A diary, or, An exact journall*, 18–24 Dec 1645, 8

Archives BL, corresp. with Sir John Coke, Add. MSS 64870–64924, 69868–69935

Likenesses oils, c.1632, repro. in J. Ingamells, *The English episcopal portrait, 1559–1835: a catalogue* (1981), 151; known to be in possession of R. S. Coke in 1932 · effigy on monument, c.1660, Hereford Cathedral; repro. in T. Dingley, *History from marble*, ed. T. E. Winnington, 2 vols., Camden Soc., 1st ser., 94, 97 (1867–8), vol. 1, p. cxli [original form] · portrait (after portrait, c.1632), bishop's palace, Hereford

Wealth at death 'The times trod so heavily upon him that (though he ever was a thrifty person) they not only bruised the

foot, but brake the body of his estate; so that he had felt want, if not relieved by his rich relations': Fuller, *Worthies*, 115

Coke, Gerald Edward (1907–1990), merchant banker and patron of the arts, was born on 25 October 1907 at Bruton Street, London, the only son and eldest of three children of Sir John Spencer Coke, major in the Scots Guards and royal equerry (seventh son of Thomas William *Coke, second earl of Leicester, of Holkham Hall, Norfolk), and his wife, Dorothy Olive, only child of Sir Harry Lawson Webster Levy-*Lawson, Lord Burnham (1862–1933). Coke was educated at Eton College and at New College, Oxford, where he obtained a third class in modern history (1929).

During the 1930s Coke worked at Barrow in Furness in a firm connected with haematite iron-ore mining. He served throughout the Second World War in the Scots Guards and attained the rank of lieutenant-colonel. From 1945 to 1975 he was a director of the merchant bank S. G. Warburg & Co., and rose to be vice-chairman. He also served as a director of the Rio Tinto-Zinc Corporation (1947–75), and as chairman (1956–62). His success in these enterprises owed as much to his charm, patent sincerity, and integrity as it did to his commercial acumen. He was a JP from 1952, and deputy lieutenant of Hampshire from 1974. He was appointed CBE in 1967 and became an honorary fellow of the Royal Academy of Music in 1968. The financial success of his work in commerce and banking allowed him to acquire his home, Jenkyn Place, Bentley, Hampshire, which he and his wife transformed into a residence of great beauty and refined taste, filled with libraries, precious porcelain, the great Handel collection, and many *objets d'art*. Both partners devoted long hours almost daily to the creation of the large and choice gardens surrounding their property, which were intermittently open, chiefly to connoisseurs and garden societies, and formed the subject of television programmes.

Coke's character obliged him to share the fruits of his wealth and accomplishments with many in the fields of music, scholarship, and similar concerns. His influence contributed much to the success of Glyndebourne, run by John Christie and Sir George Christie, of whose arts trust he was chairman (1955–75). He also served as a director of the Royal Opera House, Covent Garden (1958–64), and of the Royal Academy of Music (1957–74). He was a governor of the BBC (1961–6). Particularly close to his heart was his long association, as treasurer and benefactor, with Bridewell Royal Hospital, and King Edward's School, Witley, where there is a portrait of him by Sir William Coldstream. When Coke took over as treasurer, King Edward's School was a relatively small boys' school, which he made into a co-educational boarding-school of some importance.

The *pièce de résistance* of his life as a scholar and collector was the Coke Handel collection, which embraced important musical manuscripts, librettos, and autographs. Coke also enabled Handel scholars, such as O. E. Deutsch and W. C. Smith, to persevere with and complete their studies. Towards the end of his life he was instrumental in arranging for the publication of a Handel iconography, and for the creation of the Gerald Coke Handel Foundation, to manage the Coke Handel collection both before and after its transfer to the Foundling Museum, London. His *In Search of James Giles* (1983) was the culmination of his other great enthusiasm, his porcelain collection.

If Coke was an amateur, then this term can only be understood in the sense that music, opera, porcelain, or the art of garden cultivation were not the source of his income but the objects of his expenditure. His knowledge and expertise in so many disparate fields were prodigious, but they were always imparted to others with that modesty and self-effacement which characterized him, and which perhaps led to his failure to receive higher official honours.

In appearance Coke was tall and slender, with an upright bearing. On 2 September 1939 Coke married Patricia (*d.* 1995), daughter of Sir Alexander George Montagu *Cadogan, the diplomatist. The marriage was one of exceptional happiness and harmony, and of shared interests in gardening, music, and collecting. They had a daughter and three sons, the third of whom died of meningitis suddenly in 1972, a day after his successful final degree examination at London University. Coke died at Jenkyn Place, Bentley, of heart failure, on 9 January 1990. A concert in his memory was given at Glyndebourne on 5 August 1990, at which it was disclosed that Coke had persuaded his shipping heiress friend, the countess of Munster, to sell one of her ships, and with the proceeds endow a trust for education in music.

EDWARD ULLENDORFF, *rev.*

Sources D. Burrows, *The Guardian* (18 Jan 1990) · G. Coke, *The Gerald Coke Handel collection* (1985) · *Annual Reports* [Countess of Munster Musical Trust] · private information (1996) [H. Gronfeld, Sir G. Christie, L. Rothschild] · personal knowledge (1996)
Likenesses W. Coldstream, oils, King Edward's School, Witley
Wealth at death £2,629,665: probate, 1 May 1990, *CGPLA Eng. & Wales*

Coke, Sir John (1563–1644), politician, was born on 5 March 1563 in London, the fourth of eleven children born to Richard Coke (*d.* 1582) of Trusley, near Derby, and his wife, Mary Sacheverell (*d.* 1580), daughter and heir of Thomas Sacheverell of Nottinghamshire.

Education and early life As a youth Coke may have attended Westminster School. He matriculated from Trinity College, Cambridge, in 1576, received a scholarship there beginning in 1580, and earned his BA in 1581 and MA in 1584. He remained at Cambridge as a fellow of Trinity until 1591. During this time he apparently was a lecturer in rhetoric. Thomas Fuller wrote that Coke 'being chosen rhetoric lecturer in the university, grew eminent for his ingenious and critical readings' (Fuller, *Worthies*, 1.371). These years at Cambridge left an indelible impression on Coke. 'I was not bred in servile or illiberal trades; the university was my nurse', he later wrote (Coke to the marquess of Buckingham, 12 Oct 1622, Coke MSS). In particular he acquired a passion for order and a civic humanist's sense of duty to the public good. He also became loosely acquainted with the earl of Essex's circle, especially the literary figure and courtier named Sir Fulke Greville, who proved a lasting friend and patron. Coke needed a patron

Sir John Coke (1563–1644), by unknown artist, *c.*1665

because his older brother Richard had inherited the family lands, leaving him only a small annuity of less than £7. When he left Cambridge, he worked as an auditor or accountant for Greville's estate, and from 1593 to 1597 he travelled on the continent.

Early naval career and forced retirement Coke's first major employment by the crown lasted from 1599 to 1604 as deputy treasurer of the navy, working under Greville who was treasurer during those years. Together the two men battled against the gross corruption, thievery, and disorder that flourished in the navy under Lord Admiral Nottingham. In this effort, Greville told Coke, 'we will perish or prosper together' (Greville to Coke, *c.*1600, Coke MSS). They did not prosper for long. They had the misfortune of advocating an ambitious plan for naval reform at precisely the time Queen Elizabeth, Greville's sole patron, died. This left them perilously exposed to their enemies when James VI and I came to the throne. Nottingham succeeded in removing Greville from office, replacing him with the more compliant Sir Robert Mansell.

Forced into early retirement and exiled from the court, Coke spent the years 1604 to 1618 continuing to help manage Greville's personal estate and to build one of his own. Some time during 1604 he married Marie Powell (*d.* 1624), daughter of John Powell of Preston, Herefordshire, another one of Greville's employees. During the first years of their marriage they lived with Marie's parents while Coke continued to travel in connection with Greville's business affairs. The letters Coke and his wife exchanged reveal that they were very much in love, although he was torn between continuing to hope for a revival of his career or settling down in the countryside. About 1607 he chose the latter course; in 1608 he and Marie built a new home for themselves near her parents in Herefordshire. They named it Hall Court and lived there happily for a decade. In the course of time they had six children who survived infancy (Joseph, John junior, Thomas, Mary, Elizabeth, and Anne). Coke monitored events at court from a distance, looking for signs of change in his favour. In 1614 Greville made a surprising return to office as chancellor of the exchequer, and in 1618 another old friend, Sir Robert Naunton, was appointed secretary of state. At first Coke resisted their invitations, but eventually they succeeded in luring him back to court. 'I pray God from my heart', he wrote, 'I may not move from my retreat except it be for a better account of my life' (Coke to Naunton, early 1618, Coke MSS).

Naval commissioner and master of requests Coke returned to royal service in June 1618 when Lionel Cranfield, supported by the marquess of Buckingham, was reforming various departments of government, and was appointed to a commission responsible for investigating the state of the navy. This gave him a remarkable opportunity to pick up where he had left off fourteen years earlier, and he certainly made the most of it. Owing to his prior experience, knowledge of the navy, organizational ability, and zeal for reform, he quickly became the leading member of the commission and authored its report. Nottingham and Mansell were persuaded to step aside and Buckingham took the office of lord admiral, although he quickly delegated the actual daily administration of the navy to the commissioners. On 12 February 1619 the naval commission was converted from an investigative body into a board of governors with authority to implement their own proposals for reform. In less than a year Coke had managed a remarkable political comeback and turned the tables on his old enemies. By virtue of the trust that Buckingham put in him and his dominance of the commission, he was now the chief administrator of the English navy. He has justly been called 'the Samuel Pepys of his day' (Lockyer, 76).

Coke aimed higher, however. On 8 November 1621 he received a royal grant of £300 per annum for his services in the navy, but this did not wholly satisfy him. What he really wanted was the security of an office at court, and he continued to press Buckingham to find one for him. Buckingham eventually arranged for him to be appointed a master of requests and he took his oath on 20 November 1622. The following July he triumphantly moved his family to London. Triumph soon turned to tragedy, however. At the beginning of 1624 his oldest son, Joseph, died of spotted fever. A few months later his wife, Marie, died, shortly after giving birth to twins who barely outlived her. In late 1624 Coke, left with the responsibility of five children to care for, married again. His second wife was Joan Gore (née Lee), daughter of a former lord mayor of London, Sir Robert Lee, and widow of a former alderman, William Gore. Coke and his second wife had an amicable relationship, but it was essentially a marriage of convenience.

Parliaments and war in the 1620s Coke sat in all the parliaments of the 1620s. In 1621, when he sat for the borough of Warwick, presumably through Greville's influence, there is little evidence of his participation. In 1624, owing to the influence of his brother-in-law, Valentine Carey, bishop of Exeter, he sat for the borough of St Germans; he was knighted on 9 September that year. He was still a minor figure but enthusiastically supported the call for war. Like many others who came of age at the time of the Spanish Armada, he hated Roman Catholicism and wanted to resume the Elizabethan war against Spain. Unfortunately the harsh realities of renewed warfare made life infinitely more difficult for Coke. To him fell the task of preparing the war fleets, explaining their failures, and imploring parliament for money. He was involved in numerous employments: he oversaw preparation of the fleet that sailed to Cadiz; he was instrumental in extorting money from the East India Company; and he was involved in frantic efforts to ensure that English ships lent to the French government would not be used against the French protestants then in rebellion.

In 1625, in the first parliament of King Charles I's reign, Coke, again sitting for St Germans, was a much more visible participant. Both Buckingham and Charles employed him to make the case for further supply. He laid out the financial needs of the government in painstaking detail, but his pleas met with a hostile reception, especially from two personal enemies in the Commons, Sir Robert Mansell and Sir John Eliot. Eliot's animus towards Coke is evident in his account of these years entitled *Negotium posterorum*. Coke's speech on 4 August 1625 was especially controversial. The king chose him at the very last minute to address both houses of parliament and instructed him to ask again for money. Some objected simply to the fact that, as a mere commoner, he had been employed to deliver the king's pleasure to both houses. Coke had not coveted this dubious honour: 'For my part', he wrote to Greville, 'I neither had ambition nor thought of speaking in that place' (Coke to Greville, 4 Aug 1625, Coke MSS).

In September 1625 Buckingham arranged for Coke to be appointed one of the king's two principal secretaries of state. The senior secretary, Sir Edward Conway, retained fairly exclusive control over foreign affairs, but Coke had a great many additional responsibilities in the domestic realm now added to his continuing burden in the navy. He was particularly zealous in using prize goods or contraband to finance the war effort.

In the parliament of 1626 Coke, sitting now for Cambridge University, was again prominent in trying to defend the lord admiral and rally support for the war. He was very much on the defensive because he was deeply involved in many of the affairs complained of in this parliament, some of which became articles of impeachment against Buckingham. Coke and his old nemesis, Mansell, sparred over the role of the council of war, the controversial ships lent to the French, and the failure to protect the seas and coastlines from pirates. Coke was also employed again to ask for further supply. He now estimated that the war effort required £1,067,221.

When Charles dissolved parliament, resorted to a forced loan to raise money, and imprisoned resisters, there is reason to believe that Coke was one of the more moderate members of the privy council who was uncomfortable with this approach. This suspicion is reinforced by his performance in the parliament of 1628–9, where he again sat for Cambridge University. There were only three privy councillors in the Commons in 1628, and he was by far the most active. Though his performance has sometimes been judged harshly, his position as an intermediary between the king and Commons was a difficult one, especially given the constant sniping by Eliot. Coke took painstaking care not to offend. 'My desire', he declared, 'is not to stir but to quiet, not to provoke but to appease' (Johnson and others, 2.65). He admitted that illegal courses had been taken, and he actually encouraged passage of the petition of right. His performance was not flawless but generally speaking his conciliatory approach made the best of a bad situation.

Coke's participation in the parliament of 1628 was cut short when he was dispatched to Portsmouth to prepare another fleet in mid-May. He kept a detailed journal of his work at Portsmouth which illuminates the reasons why the navy performed so badly in these years. He had to contend with a chaotic situation, inexperienced commanders, rotten victuals, mutinous seamen, a chronic shortage of money, and resurgent corruption. One night someone even tried to shoot him. Of course Buckingham fared worse. When he was stabbed to death at Portsmouth on 25 August 1628, Coke interrogated the assassin.

The personal rule of the 1630s During Charles I's personal rule of the 1630s Coke undertook an enormous amount of work, as indicated by the many state papers, both foreign and domestic, which are in his hand: he was a member of all the standing committees of the privy council; he served on commissions to reform the wardrobe and ordnance office, though both reforms were thwarted; he played a major role in the successful reform of the postal system; and he continued to take great interest in the navy, though he had less authority over it than before. His passion for administrative efficiency made him a natural ally of Archbishop Laud and Thomas Wentworth, later earl of Strafford. Wentworth praised Coke for his integrity, arranged for him to receive a grant of Irish land, and vowed, 'I shall honour you all the Days of my Life' (*Earl of Strafforde's Letters and Dispatches*, 1.494).

As one of two principal secretaries of state Coke had worked harmoniously with two partners (Conway and Sir Dudley Carleton), but the appointment of Sir Francis Windebank in June 1632 initiated a debilitating rivalry that lasted throughout the decade. This rivalry is particularly evident in the conduct of foreign affairs where there was an unhealthy competition between the secretaries, for which King Charles must bear part of the blame.

On 22 June 1636 Coke gave a speech at Oxford University which is the best expression of his political views (*Works of*

… *Laud*, 5.1.126–32). Not surprisingly he took a hierarchical view of society and an absolutist view of the monarchy, yet these were tempered by his lifelong devotion to the public good and the rule of law. His views on matters such as swearing and drinking could be described as puritanical. His religious views were presumably similar to those of his brother George *Coke (1570–1646), bishop of Bristol and of Hereford: he was a firm anti-Catholic protestant and a prudent conformist, uneasy with all forms of separation and zealotry.

As Coke grew older others enviously eyed his office, particularly Robert Sidney, earl of Leicester, and Sir Henry Vane, who enlisted the support of Queen Henrietta Maria. By 1638 age was also taking its toll on Coke; he managed to accompany King Charles to Berwick in 1639 during the first bishops' war, but on 10 January 1640 Charles requested his resignation. He resisted, and Strafford strenuously supported him, but to no avail. On 31 January Coke surrendered the seals of office. Charles acted under pressure from the queen, but it was equally clear that Coke, at the age of seventy-six, was no longer able to discharge the duties of his office, especially given the prospect of renewed fighting in Scotland and the meeting of a new parliament.

Coke could well afford to retire. In 1628 he had sold Hall Court for £3000, and between 1626 and 1634 he purchased land in Derbyshire and Leicestershire costing at least £20,000. By the mid-1630s his annual income was approximately £3500 (£2000 from the secretaryship and £1500 from rents). Edward Hyde, earl of Clarendon, wrote of him: 'His cardinal perfection was industry, and his most eminent infirmity covetousness' (Clarendon, *Hist. rebellion*, 1.81). The centrepiece of his estate was Melbourne Hall, a manor in Derbyshire not far from his ancestral home of Trusley and it was to Melbourne that he retired in 1640.

Retirement and death Coke's retirement was far from peaceful. Following the outbreak of civil war in 1642 his property was destroyed, his home was invaded, and he was repeatedly harassed. His own family was divided because his oldest son, John, an MP for Derbyshire, sided with parliament, and his younger son, Thomas, an MP for Leicester, took the king's side. His own position is ambiguous; it has been described as neutralist or parliamentarian. It is true that he grew estranged from his royalist son, and he twice wrote expressions of support for parliament, declaring that 'my heart is faithful and my prayers assiduous for the prosperity of the Parliament, wherein consisteth the welfare of this church and state' (Coke to the earl of Essex, 20 Sept 1642, Coke MSS), but these poses could have been dictated more by expediency than conviction. Perhaps more revealing was a letter he wrote recounting his lifetime of tireless efforts at administrative reform under three different monarchs. 'Now by all these and such other employments', he concluded, 'I have been taught that which the Archbishop of Canterbury said often: that kings cannot be served against their wills' (Coke to John Coke, late 1640, Coke MSS).

Coke was eventually forced to leave Melbourne and take

refuge in his wife's home at Tottenham. There he died on 8 September 1644. Perhaps owing to the confusion of the civil war, his will could not be found after his death, and his place of burial is unknown. His wife survived him.

Historical appraisal Coke has sometimes been considered terribly hardworking but mediocre, being described as one of Charles I's 'more humdrum' ministers (Aylmer, 234). He was certainly exceptionally industrious but it is possible to regard the quality of his work, especially in the navy, more favourably. The embittered opinion of Sir John Eliot should not be accepted at face value. Compared to a man like Eliot, Coke lacked charisma and passion, but he had his own solid qualities of character. A dedicated and honourable man, he was an unusually able administrator, and if he had not possessed finer qualities of mind, he would not have enjoyed the friendship and admiration of Sir Fulke Greville.

Coke achieved high office, played a major role in the political life of the nation, and grew rich. Yet measured by other standards, his life was a failure. He professed to believe that a public office was 'a stage to do good', and he vowed not to 'dispose of my life for wages'. But in the end, what good had he achieved and what did he have to show for his work except wages? (Young, 62, 98, 275). There was no lasting achievement. Even reform of the navy, his chief accomplishment, was wrecked by the very war that he himself had eagerly advocated.

Coke has been criticized most severely for his apparent toadyism. To the modern eye his deferential demeanour may look like crass servility, but it was a function of his conservative nature and an absolute necessity for survival at court. Moreover, his final evaluation of his own career is hardly servile. As noted above, he himself concluded that the lesson of his whole life's work amounted to this: 'that kings cannot be served against their wills'.

MICHAEL B. YOUNG

Sources M. B. Young, *Servility and service: the life and work of Sir John Coke* (1986) · BL, Coke MSS · R. C. Johnson and others, eds., *Proceedings in parliament, 1628*, 6 vols. (1977–83) · R. Lockyer, *Buckingham: the life and political career of George Villiers, first duke of Buckingham, 1592–1628* (1981) · R. P. Cust, *The forced loan and English politics, 1626–1628* (1987) · C. Russell, *Parliaments and English politics, 1621–1629* (1979) · G. E. Aylmer, *The king's servants: the civil service of Charles I, 1625–1642*, rev. edn (1974) · Clarendon, *Hist. rebellion* · G. Radcliffe, *The earl of Strafforde's letters and dispatches, with an essay towards his life*, ed. W. Knowler, 2 vols. (1739) · J. Eliot, *An apology for Socrates and Negotium posteriorum*, ed. A. B. Grosart, 2 vols. (1881) · *The works of the most reverend father in God, William Laud*, ed. J. Bliss and W. Scott, 7 vols. (1847–60) · Fuller, *Worthies* · F. M. G. Evans, *The principal secretary of state: a survey of the office from 1558 to 1680* (1923) · D. Coke, *The last Elizabethan: Sir John Coke, 1563–1644* (1937) · J. T. Coke, *Coke of Trusley, in the county of Derby, and branches therefrom: a family history* (1880) · letters of admin., PRO, PROB 6/20, fol. 1; PROB 6/25, fol. 133; PROB 6/38, fol. 69; PROB 6/51, fol. 51 · Venn, *Alum. Cant.*
Archives BL, corresp. and papers, Add. MSS 64870–64924, 69868–69935 | Arundel Castle, corresp. with earl of Arundel · PRO, state papers, domestic, SP 14 and 16 · PRO, state papers, foreign, various countries · Sheff. Arch., letters to Lord Wentworth
Likenesses C. Janssens, oils, c.1622, Melbourne Hall, Derbyshire · portrait, c.1665, Melbourne Hall, Derbyshire [*see illus.*] · G. White, mezzotint, 1724, BM, NPG · R. Dunkarton, mezzotint, pubd 1813, NPG, BM · portrait, NMM
Wealth at death £20,000—in land: Young, *Servility and service*, 226; administration, PRO, PROB 6/20, fol. 1; PROB 6/25, fol. 133; PROB 6/38, fol. 69; PROB 6/51, fol. 51

Coke [*née* Campbell], **Lady Mary** (1727–1811), letter writer and noblewoman, was born on 6 February 1727, either at Sudbrook, Surrey, or at 27 Bruton Street, London, the fifth and youngest daughter of the soldier and politician John *Campbell, second duke of Argyll and duke of Greenwich (1680–1743), and his second wife, Jane (c.1683–1767), maid of honour to Queen Anne and Caroline, princess of Wales, daughter of Thomas Warburton of Winnington, Cheshire, and his wife, Anne. She grew up in Sudbrook or in London, at least once visiting her father's ancestral estate at Inveraray in Argyll.

After a courtship during which she relished the role of the disdainful maiden, Lady Mary married on 1 April 1747 the dissolute and disreputable Edward, Viscount Coke (1719–1753), son of Thomas Coke, earl of Leicester. He took his revenge by leaving her in solitary splendour on the wedding night and thereafter virtually imprisoning her. She responded by denying conjugal relations and plunging their two families into litigation. Following a period of practical imprisonment on the Coke estate at Holkham, Norfolk, a settlement in 1750 allowed Lady Mary (she never used the title Viscountess Coke) henceforth to live with her mother at Sudbrook. When Viscount Coke died in 1753, the 26-year-old Lady Mary, in possession of a generous legacy from her father, embarked upon an independent social life marked by gossip, travel, devotion to royalty, and self-imposed misadventure.

Lady Mary's aristocratic background and political connections gave her access to the highest circles of society; but her temper alienated many people, and her temperament rendered her the object of ridicule and contempt. Entertaining a very high opinion of her prerogatives and merits, she dramatized the ordinary events of life and magnified her own importance, particularly in the eyes of royalty. These pretensions, and the lamentable and sometimes comic consequences which ensued, satisfied her passion for the sensational.

Lady Mary never remarried but conducted a long and, on her part, intensely emotional flirtation with Edward Augustus, duke of York and Albany, who was twelve years her junior. Most accounts suggest that York regarded both Lady Mary and the supposed attachment as a joke, but she behaved as if it were a profound mutual passion, thus eliciting widespread ridicule. After the duke's death in 1767 her pompous demonstrations of grief and veiled hints that they had been secretly married provoked lasting derision.

Most of what is known of Lady Mary Coke stems from her journal, which she wrote to amuse herself and her sisters and never intended for publication. It was addressed mainly to her sister Anne (1719/20–1785), who had married William Wentworth, second earl of Strafford, in 1741. The manuscript version extends from August 1766 to January 1791, when Lord Strafford died; however, the printed edition, edited by her great-great-great-nephew James Archibald Home (1837–1909), includes entries only up to

Lady Mary Coke (1727–1811), by Allan Ramsay, 1762

December 1774. The journal ranges from banal descriptions of card games and weather to perceptive social observation and expressions of sincere affection, often closely and unselfconsciously juxtaposed. The personality which emerges from the whole combines elements of the mundane and the preposterous with the deeply sympathetic.

Lady Mary travelled frequently in Europe, and in Vienna became rapturously devoted to the court of Empress Maria Theresa, where on her first trip in 1770–71 she was warmly received. On a third visit, however, in 1773, she meddled in court intrigue and incurred the disapproval of the empress. Thereafter she fancied herself the victim of Maria Theresa's unremitting and far-reaching persecution. This pleasing delusion permeated all aspects of her life and transformed the most ordinary occurrences—the work of an incompetent servant, an unsuccessful bid at an auction, an attack of rheumatism—into what she regarded as evidence of a vast conspiracy.

For many years Lady Mary enjoyed a close friendship with Horace Walpole. He catered to her whims through flattery, devotion, and mock gallantry (she was the dedicatee of *The Castle of Otranto* in 1765), while his letters express continual bemusement at her total want of a sense of humour. Walpole several times exerted himself

to extricate her from scrapes attendant upon 'the height and violence of her temper' and repeatedly endeavoured to make her recognize the ludicrousness of her conduct. He referred to Lady Mary and her two sisters, Caroline *Townshend, Baroness Greenwich, and Lady Betty Mackenzie, as the three furies, but his exasperation was mingled with real affection, as shown in an excerpt from a letter to Horace Mann of 28 November 1773:

> She was much a friend of mine, but a later marriage [of the duke of Gloucester to Lady Waldegrave, Walpole's niece], which she particularly disapproved, having flattered herself with the hopes of one just a step higher, has a little cooled our friendship. In short, though she is so greatly born, she has a frenzy for royalty, and will fall in love with and at the feet of the Great Duke and Duchess, especially the former, for next to being an empress herself, she adores the Empress Queen, or did—for perhaps that passion not being quite reciprocal, may have waned. However … Lady Mary has a thousand virtues and good qualities: she is noble, generous, high-spirited, undauntable, is most friendly, sincere, affectionate, and above any mean action. She loves attention, and I wish you to pay it even for my sake, for I would do anything to serve her. I have often tried to laugh her out of her weakness, but as she is very serious, she is so in that, and if all the sovereigns in Europe combined to slight her, she still would put her trust in the next generation of princes. Her heart is excellent, and deserves and would become a crown, and that is the best of all excuses for desiring one. (Walpole, *Corr.*, 23.530)

Unfortunately, the two quarrelled in 1775 in Paris when Walpole declined to interfere in Lady Mary's altercation with Emily Barry (*née* Stanhope), countess of Barrymore, whom she accused of luring away her previously faithful servant so that Marie Antoinette's minions might assassinate her on the road to Calais. To Lady Mary, the queen of France seemed to have planned the murder as an agent for her mother, the empress. Although in 1780 Lady Mary accepted as suitable tribute Walpole's gift of volume 4 of his *Anecdotes of Painting*, their friendship never fully recovered.

Lady Mary was also an enthusiastic observer of the political scene. She was an avid collector of political information and deployed it to protect her own interests and those of her relatives where it was possible or necessary. She often visited the Commons and the Lords to witness political controversies such as the debate over the Cumberland election petition in 1768, where she supported Sir James Lowther, and the trial of Warren Hastings. Her journals acted as means of passing the gossip she had picked up to her sisters. Her comments were sometimes appropriate, as for example her praise of the political acumen shown by Georgiana, duchess of Devonshire, in 1787: 'As soon as ever any young man comes from abroad he is immediately invited to Devonshire House and to Chatsworth—and by that means he is to be of the opposition' (Chalus, 88). Among her wilder deductions was that Margaret Nicholson's attempt to assassinate George III in 1786 and Maria Fitzherbert's rumoured marriage to George, prince of Wales, were evidence of a Catholic conspiracy against the protestant succession.

Although Lady Mary ceased keeping a regular journal after Lord Strafford's death, she continued to make her opinions known to her friends and relatives, including her niece Lady Frances Scott, daughter of Lady Greenwich from her first marriage to Francis, earl of Dalkeith, and her first cousin once removed Lady Louisa *Stuart, who in 1827 wrote an acerbic memoir of Lady Mary. She died at Morton House, Chiswick, Middlesex, on 30 September 1811; she had bought the house four years before, characteristically, for the antiquarian reason that it had been built in the late seventeenth century by Sir Stephen Fox, and little had been altered. She was buried in the Argyll vault in Westminster Abbey on 11 October 1811.

JILL RUBENSTEIN

Sources *The letters and journals of Lady Mary Coke*, ed. J. A. Home, 4 vols. (1889–96) · L. Stuart, 'Some account of John, duke of Argyll, and his family', *Lady Louisa Stuart: selections from her manuscripts*, ed. J. A. Home (1899), 4–150 · Walpole, *Corr.*, vols. 4–7, 9–10, 23, 31–33, 35, 38 · E. H. Chalus, 'Women in English political life, 1754–1790', DPhil diss., U. Oxf., 1997 · H. A. Dobson, *Eighteenth century studies* (1914) · H. Swinburne, *The courts of Europe at the close of the last century*, ed. C. White, 2 vols. (1841); repr. (1895) · R. Whitworth, *Field Marshal Lord Ligonier: a story of the British army, 1702–1770* (1958), 175–9, 390–92

Archives priv. coll., journal and letters | BL, corresp. with Lady Suffolk, etc., Add. MS 22629

Likenesses T. Bardwell, oils, 1749, priv. coll. · I. Gasset, wax medallion, 1762, priv. coll. · A. Ramsay, oils, 1762, Mount Stuart House, Rothesay, Isle of Bute [*see illus.*]

Coke, Roger (*c.*1628–1704x7), political writer and economist, was the third son of Henry Coke (1591–1661), of Thorington, Suffolk, and his wife, Margaret, daughter and heir of Sir Richard Lovelace of Kingsdown, Kent. He was educated at Queens' College, Cambridge, where he 'became well vers'd in several Parts of Learning' though 'Mathematicks, for some time, seem'd to be his principal Study' (Coke, xiii). However, he was to leave Cambridge, for reasons unknown, without ever having completed his degree. By 1648 he was married to Frances (maiden name unknown) and on 6 February 1649 their daughter—and only child—was baptized at Mileham, Norfolk.

Coke appears to have welcomed the Restoration and in 1660 published *Justice Vindicated*, which attacked the 'false' theories of Thomas White, Thomas Hobbes, and Hugo Grotius, while supporting the monarchical system and the Church of England. Shortly after 1661 Coke was granted a pension of £100 per annum out of the 'grand estates' left to his nephew Robert Coke (1650–1679) of Holkham. In April 1672 he was charged with administering the property and finances of his family at Thorington and successfully renegotiated the lease of the manor at Farnham Royal, Buckinghamshire, in favour of his nephew's future heirs. However, his subsequent business ventures in the City of London failed and he was imprisoned for several years in the Fleet prison, as the result of the non-payment of his accumulated debts.

It was Coke's personal tragedy that his practical application of the principles of trade did not measure up to the entirely original and radical economic theories that he

was developing and expounding throughout the 1670s. Though he retained conventional mercantilist views on many subjects—such as the desirability of government control and supervision of the retail trades, the need for a council of trade to direct national policy, and the need to reserve colonial markets and the home waters purely for the benefit of English carriers—there is much in his thought that bridges the gap between the schools of mercantilist and *laissez-faire* economics (*A Treatise Concerning the Regulation of the Coyn of England*, 1696, 15, 69, 129–37; Coke, 2.486). In contrast to the vast majority of his contemporaries, he attempted to analyse economic criteria mathematically and with a greater degree of objectivity than before. As a result, he came to criticize the Navigation Acts which debarred 'the greatest part of the World from Trading with us', attacked the special privileges of the joint-stock companies which allowed them to monopolize the conditions and operation of trade, and argued for the free importation of goods into England as a stimulus to economic endeavour (*A Treatise*, 36, 59, 69; Coke, 1.xliii–xlvi, 16–17; *England's Improvements*, 1675, 114).

Coke's later years were spent in the production of more conventional historical and political studies. As a visceral opponent of King James II, the dispensing power, and the 'barefac'd design of introducing Popery to the Subversion' of both church and state, he enthusiastically supported the revolution of 1688, and wrote a withering attack—based jointly on political and economic critiques—of coin clipping and monopoly capitalism, as practised respectively by Jacobite sympathizers and by the tory grandees of the East India Company (*A Treatise*, 13, 17, 20–29, 42–3). This perspective had also informed his more popularist study, *A Detection of the Court and State of England* (2 vols., 1694) in which he presented an idealized portrait of England's 'ancient' constitutions and liberties, while radically reassessing his opinion of Charles II and concluding that though his actions 'were little and dark' he had corrupted the nation and squandered its wealth to an unprecedented level (Coke, 1.vi, 2. 390–91).

Following the publication of his two assaults on the abuses of the East India Company (*Reflections upon the East Indy and Royal African Companies*, 1695, and *A Treatise*), Coke quickly faded from the notice of the public. The anonymous editor of the fourth edition of his *Detection*, published in 1719, mistakenly thought that he had always been a bachelor and it may be concluded from this that by the turn of the eighteenth century Coke had already outlived both his wife and child by many years. He died in 'about the seventy-seventh year of his age', between 1704 and 1707, and was consigned to an unknown grave, probably within the bounds of the City of London.

JOHN CALLOW

Sources R. Coke, *A detection of the court and state of England*, 4th edn, 3 vols. (1719) · E. Lipson, *The economic history of England*, 3 vols. (1947), vols. 2 and 3 · P. W. Buck, *The politics of mercantilism* (1942) · E. F. Heckscher, *Mercantilism* (1931), repub. as new edn (1994) · P. J. Thomas, *Mercantilism and the East India trade: an early phase of the protection v. free trade controversy* (1926) · L. Magnusson, *Mercantilism: the* *shaping of an economic language* (1994) • S. S. M. Desai, *History of economic thought*, 2nd edn (1967) • G. A. Carthew, *The hundred of Launditch and deanery of Brisley, in the county of Norfolk*, 3 (1879)

Coke, Thomas (*bap.* 1674, *d.* 1727), politician and court official, was baptized on 19 February 1674 at Melbourne, Derbyshire, the great-grandson of Sir John Coke (1563–1644), politician, and the eldest son of John Coke (*c.*1653–1692) of Melbourne Hall and his wife, Mary (*d.* 1680), the daughter and heir of Sir Thomas Leventhorpe of Shingehall, Sawbridgeworth, Hertfordshire. He had a younger brother, John, a barrister, who died in 1736, and three sisters who lived to adulthood: Elizabeth, Mary, and Alice. Their father, MP for Derbyshire (1685–7, 1689–90) and gentleman usher of the privy chamber to Catherine of Braganza, was a critic of the policies of James II and an active supporter of the revolution of 1688. After his death at Geneva in 1692, the Coke children were placed in the care of Walter Burdett of Knowle Hills. From 1687 probably until 1689 Thomas had pursued his education in Rotterdam with the family of Monsieur Chauvois, a French protestant minister. He matriculated at New College, Oxford, on 17 June 1693 but left in 1696, having taken no degree. There followed trips to the Netherlands in the late summers of 1696 and 1697.

As a young man in the 1690s and early 1700s, Coke was part of a circle of rakes of literary and sporting bent which included James Brydges, Charles Davenant, George Granville, Robert Jennings, and Henry St John. Under William III some of these men came to be associated with Robert Harley's 'country'—and increasingly tory—party. Classed as a staunch churchman, Coke was elected knight of the shire for Derbyshire in 1698. His friend Robert Jennings characterized him at the time as:

> as proper a man to serve the nation in the House of Commons as any that will be there; for by your travelling and conversation in the world I believe you know the circumstances of Europe as it now stands as well as anybody. (*Cowper MSS*, 2.377)

Indeed, Coke's correspondence and papers reveal a keen interest in continental affairs, especially military and diplomatic. In his first year in the Commons he also involved himself in local navigation legislation and reform of the poor law and the land tax. In 1700, upon Harley's retreat on attacks of grants to courtiers, he stormed out of the house, 'cursing all house meeting dogs, meaning Robert Harley' (Horwitz, 266). Defeated in the winter of 1700–01, he was re-elected knight of the shire on his own and Lord Chesterfield's interest in December 1701, and again in 1702, 1705, and 1708. In January 1702 he proposed the address of thanks on the king's request for preparations for war, but also seconded the motion that 'the House of Commons had not right done them in the matter of the impeachments in the last parliament' (ibid., 300, 302). In the spring of 1702 he was named a commissioner of accounts.

Coke married, first, Lady Mary Stanhope (1664–1704), the daughter of Philip, earl of Chesterfield, in June 1698. The match produced two daughters, Mary and Elizabeth, and cemented a firm friendship and political alliance with the Stanhopes. Following a period of mourning after his wife's death on 11 January 1704, there is evidence of Thomas's return to an active and rakish social life. During the interval between his two marriages, his sister Elizabeth acted as mother to his children, as well as keeper of his house, overseer of his estates, and, in 1710, agent for his electoral concerns. Coke's daughter Mary eventually married Thomas, Viscount Southwell; Elizabeth married Bache Thornhill of Stenton, Derbyshire.

Under Queen Anne, Coke made the transition to the court characteristic of many Harleyites. In April 1704 he was named a commissioner of plantations, and there was talk of finding a more substantial post for him. In the following month he became a teller of the exchequer at the suggestion of Lord Treasurer Godolphin as part of a deal whereby the incumbent, Francis Godolphin, became cofferer of the household. In December 1706 Coke was sworn of the privy council, and on the 3rd of that month he was sworn in as vice-chamberlain of the household, in an exchange with the previous 'vice', Peregrine Bertie. He held this position until his death, signalling his complete identification with the court by refusing to resign with Harley in 1708 and by managing to weather the change of reign in 1714. His remuneration as vice-chamberlain consisted of wages of £66 13s. 4d. and board wages of £492 15s. The position also came with a pension of £600 per annum. Because the lord chamberlains under whom Coke served were either relatively inactive (Kent, 1704–10; Bolton, 1715–17) or frequently preoccupied with high politics (Shrewsbury, 1710–15; Newcastle, 1717–24), Coke took on many of the duties nominally associated with the lord chamberlain's office, including the outfitting and staffing of royal palaces, travel arrangements for royal progresses, security, and the routine business associated with the chamberlain's regulation of the London theatres. Indeed, Coke's theatre papers are a major source for understanding the sometimes bewildering shifts in the management of the London theatre and opera companies during the reign of Queen Anne. He gives every evidence of having worked assiduously and smoothly with the lord chamberlain's secretary, Sir John Stanley, and the office clerk, John Evans.

Coke became so indispensable to the queen that, despite the urgings of his sister Elizabeth, he was unable to leave the court in order to campaign for the 1710 election. His refusal to campaign and, in particular, to defend his vote against Sacheverell, led to his being thrown out as knight of the shire in the tory landslide. He only managed to return to parliament on the Lansdowne (Granville) interest as member for Grampound, Cornwall, which he represented until 1715. Anne rewarded 'his constant waiting and attendance on her person and the extraordinary expense occasioned to him thereby' (*Calendar of Treasury Books*, 30.290–91) with an additional pension of £1000 out of the privy purse, which was continued on the regular pension list by George I. Under that monarch he was made surveyor-general of the customs along with his son, George Lewis, and John Fanshaw, the place to revert to the longest lived.

As an MP, Coke was never particularly active in the business of the house, averaging about seven and a half committee assignments per session during Anne's reign. This went down to just a little over five such assignments per session once he assumed household office. He was characterized as a tory and a high-churchman early in his career, as a Harleyite in the middle, and as one of the 'leech-like placemen' (Holmes, 50) towards its end. In keeping with this pattern of development, he voted or was forecast to vote against keeping a standing army in 1699 and for the impeachment of the king's ministers in 1701, against the tack in 1704 and for the whig John Smith to be speaker in 1705, for the naturalization of protestants in 1709, against Sacheverell in 1710, and for the commercial treaty in 1713. However, Coke was capable of exerting some independence: for example, he deserted the court on 'no peace without Spain' in December 1711. Quixotically, while he spoke against the duke of Marlborough in February 1710, he is not listed among those tories who wanted to examine the mismanagements of the late ministry in the following year. It is possible to see in this record some remnant of the unpredictability characteristically associated with the country member; or, equally, a form of moderate toryism of the sort associated with Anne herself. On at least one occasion the queen used Coke to canvass for votes. Both before and after his appointment as vice-chamberlain he kept up a considerable correspondence with electors, who frequently lobbied him for a wide variety of favours, such as positions at court and in the government and military, support of local legislation (or the local point of view on great national questions), royal pardons for capital crimes, and exemptions from the lists of sheriffs.

It was presumably while performing his duties as vice-chamberlain that Coke met the noted beauty and maid of honour Mary Hales (d. 1724). Mary was the daughter of Richard Hales of King's Walden, Hertfordshire, and his wife, Elizabeth, the daughter of Isaac Meynell of Langley Meynell, Derbyshire. She served at court from 1 July 1708 to 15 October 1709. Thomas and Mary were married in October 1709. Their son, George Lewis Coke, was born in 1715 and became a barrister at Gray's Inn. Their first daughter, Charlotte, married Matthew Lamb of Brocket Hall, Hertfordshire, in 1740; she succeeded to the Melbourne estate at the death of her brother in 1750 and was the mother of Peniston Lamb, Viscount Melbourne. A second daughter, Anna Maria, born in 1713, died in childhood.

Melbourne Hall had been held by the Coke family from 1628 as a leasehold of the bishop of Carlisle. In 1704 Thomas Coke secured an act of parliament converting his interest in the rectory and estate into fee simple. At this point he began renovation of the magnificent gardens there, as well as conversion of the rectory into a muniment room. From 1696 he also rented a house in St James's Place, London, and, following his appointment as vice-chamberlain, had lodgings in St James's and Hampton Court palaces.

According to J. J. Briggs, Coke 'was tall in stature, of a handsome person and address, was reckoned extremely agreeable, and had a charm of manner that disarmed enmity, however, [sic] bitterly expressed' (Briggs, 110). Certainly, his correspondence suggests a man given to conviviality and friendship, in command of the respect and affection of numerous contemporaries. Coke was, moreover, a highly cultured man who demonstrated an avid interest in the theatre and world of letters from the time of his youth. His correspondence is full of witty banter, the exchange of manuscript poetry and pamphlets, and the transactions necessary to purchase and circulate books, paintings, statuary, and prints. He eventually amassed a library of more than 1000 volumes, on a wide variety of subjects (history, voyages, astronomy, architecture, painting, lexicography, classics, mathematics, French and Italian books of various sorts, numismatics, modern travel, antiquarian subjects, and, especially, English literature from Chaucer to Swift and Pope). A sale catalogue for the auction of his goods in 1728 also lists 127 paintings (including pictures attributed to Holbein, Michelangelo, and Lely) and 443 prints. Vanbrugh called him 'a great Lover of Musique And promoter of Operas' (Milhous and Hume, xxix), and indeed he sometimes hosted concerts and recitals featuring the leading visiting musicians at his own house in London. Colley Cibber had nothing good to say about his dealings with the lord chamberlain's office, as opposed to his flattery for individual lord chamberlains, charging that 'the several officers under them, who had not the hearts of noblemen, often treated us (to use Shakespear's expression) with all the insolence of office that narrow minds are apt to be elated with' (Cibber, 259) and that 'mere will and pleasure at that time, was the only law that dispos'd of all theatrical rights' (ibid., 223). However, whatever the general verdict on the crown's interference in the financial arrangements of the London theatre world, Coke's theatrical papers demonstrate a discriminating knowledge in artistic matters.

Mary Coke died in January 1724; Thomas died at Melbourne Hall on 17 May 1727 and was buried in the chancel of Melbourne church on 25 May. R. O. BUCHOLZ

Sources *The manuscripts of the Earl Cowper*, 3 vols., HMC, 23 (1888–9), vols. 2–3 · BL, Melbourne Hall MSS, Add. MSS 69936–69998 · J. J. Briggs, *The history of Melbourne in the county of Derby*, 2nd edn (1852) · J. Milhous and R. D. Hume, eds., *Vice Chamberlain Coke's theatrical papers, 1706–1715* (1982) · R. O. Bucholz, *The Augustan court: Queen Anne and the decline of court culture* (1993) · G. S. Holmes, *British politics in the age of Anne* (1967) · HoP, *Commons* · H. Horwitz, *Parliament, policy and politics in the reign of William III* (1977) · C. Cibber, *An apology for the life of Colley Cibber*, [new edn] (1914) · W. A. Shaw, ed., *Calendar of treasury books*, 30, PRO (1957), 290–91

Archives BL, corresp. and papers, Add. MSS 69936–69942, 69944–69952, 69954–69972, 69974–69994, 69996–69998 · Harvard TC, 'Vice Chamberlain Coke's theatrical papers', FMS Thr 348 · Melbourne Hall, Melbourne, corresp. and papers | NYPL, Drexel MSS, 'Coke, "English operas", 1725' [nineteenth-century transcripts of theatre papers] · PRO, LC

Likenesses portrait; known to be at Melbourne Hall, Derbyshire, c.1852

Coke, Thomas (1747–1814), Church of England clergyman and founder of Methodist missions, was born at Brecon on

Thomas Coke (1747–1814), by Henry Edridge, 1799

28 September 1747, the third but only surviving son of Bartholomew Coke (1701/2–1773) and Ann(e) Phillips (1712/13–1783), and was baptized on 5 October at St Mary's Church, Brecon. His father, the eldest son of Edward Cooke of Llanfrynach (d. 1730), prospered as an apothecary in Brecon, where he became a common councillor and alderman and was twice elected bailiff (or mayor), dying on 7 May 1773, aged seventy-one. His mother, the daughter of Thomas Phillips of Trostre, Cantref, a neighbouring parish of Llanfrynach, died on 17 May 1783, aged seventy. Following in his father's footsteps, Thomas was elected to the common council on 24 September 1769 and a year later became bailiff. He continued his association with the council *in absentia* at least until 1798.

Education and early ministry Thomas was educated at Christ College, Brecon (where he was a contemporary of Walter Churchey), and at Jesus College, Oxford, where he was enrolled as a gentleman commoner on 6 April 1764. He graduated BA in 1768 and MA in 1770, and in 1775 obtained his DCL with the support of the prime minister, Lord North. Meanwhile, he had been ordained deacon on Trinity Sunday 1770 and priest on 23 August 1772. No remaining evidence of a supposed curacy at Rode, Somerset, has been traced; but by 14 July 1771 he had taken up his duties as curate to the Revd Robert Twyford, vicar of South Petherton, and from the spring of 1773 seems to have been largely in charge of the parish, perhaps because of Twyford's ill health. Despite showing marked high-church tendencies at first, he came increasingly under Methodist influence, chiefly through reading the works of John Wesley and John Fletcher, and on 13 August 1776 rode

over to Kingston St Mary, north of Taunton, to meet Wesley. They talked at length and Coke appears to have been ready to leave his post to serve in Wesley's 'world parish'. But Wesley sent him back to South Petherton, advising him to do 'all the good he could, visiting from house to house, omitting no part of his clerical duty' and to avoid 'every reasonable ground of offence' (Moore, 2.9). Within a few months, however, Coke's Methodist 'enthusiasm', which included open-air preaching and cottage meetings, brought local opposition to a head, and a change of incumbent provided the opportunity his opponents sought to drive him from his curacy at Easter 1777. 'Dr Coke', wrote Wesley on 19 August 1777, 'has bid adieu to his honourable name and determined to cast in his lot with us' (*Journal of … John Wesley*, 6.169).

Wesley's right-hand man From this point on Coke was closely associated with the Methodist movement and quickly became a leading figure, enjoying the confidence of the ageing Wesley and entrusted by him with a variety of tasks and responsibilities. In London he acted as Wesley's amanuensis. As Wesley wrote to Mary Fletcher in 1782:

> It seems to have been the will of God for many years that I should have none to share *my proper labour*. My brother never did. Thomas Walsh began to do it; so did John Jones. But one died and one fainted. Dr. Coke promises fair; at present I have none like minded.   (J. Wesley to M. Fletcher, 12 July 1782, *Letters of … John Wesley*, 7.128)

Coke also found himself travelling more and more extensively through the British Isles as Wesley's representative and trouble-shooter. In 1782 he presided for the first time in place of Wesley over the Irish conference. His education and social background singled him out among the Methodist itinerants and was one cause of the misgivings and suspicions that surfaced from time to time. Charles Wesley was particularly unhappy, suspecting Coke of usurping his place in his brother's affections and confidence and of wielding too much influence on him. But Coke's usefulness was demonstrated in a variety of ways and situations, from the disputes that broke out in Birstall and Dewsbury over the legal settlement of the preaching-houses to the drafting of the Deed of Declaration, which gave official status to the conference as heir to Wesley's authority after his death. (Wesley, however, firmly denied that Coke had any say in the choice of preachers named as the legal hundred.)

In America These administrative and diplomatic roles, which earned Coke more criticism than approval, were no more than a prelude to the major tasks which later occupied his time and energies and for which he has chiefly been remembered. The year 1784 in which the deed was drafted proved to be a watershed in his life. His involvement from then on in the establishment of an American Methodist church independent of Wesley and the British conference, and also of the first Methodist overseas missions, placed him at the centre of developments in Methodism on both sides of the Atlantic in the two decades after Wesley's death in 1791. There had been Methodists in the American colonies since the 1760s and Wesley had sent over several of his itinerant preachers, notably Francis Asbury, to foster the work there. The War of American Independence had left the colonial Methodists 'as sheep without a shepherd' and bereft of the sacraments, since many of the Anglican clergy and the British itinerants had left the colonies. Legal and constitutional difficulties delayed any effective action by the bishop of London; and in August 1784 Wesley responded to repeated pleas for help from his American followers by ordaining two of his preachers and dispatching them to the newly independent United States. At the same time Coke was 'set apart' as superintendent of the American work. Presiding over the hastily convened Christmas conference in Baltimore, he in turn 'ordained' Asbury as deacon, elder, and fellow superintendent (a title soon changed to the more scriptural but controversial bishop) and an autonomous Methodist Episcopal church was formed, despite a last-minute attempt by two local clergymen to avert a formal separation.

Coke's role in this sequence of events has been much debated and the evidence is inconclusive at several points. Charles Wesley, when news of the ordinations belatedly reached him, was horrified, and in a series of sarcastic verses had no hesitation in blaming Coke for leading his ageing brother into such serious irregularities, identifying self-aggrandizement as his motive:

So easily are Bishops made
By man's or woman's whim?
W— his hands on C— hath laid,
But who laid hands on him?

Hands on himself he laid, and took
An Apostolic Chair;
And then ordain'd his creature C—
His Heir and Successor.
(*Representative Verse of Charles Wesley*, 367–8)

The questions remain: did the idea of his giving authority to Coke by setting him apart originate from Wesley himself or from the younger man? Was Coke responsible for encouraging the American Methodists to go further in the direction of independence from the Church of England (and the British Methodists) than Wesley ever intended? In particular, was he motivated by an unalloyed desire to serve the evangelical cause or by the self-seeking ambition of which his detractors accused him; or was it, more plausibly, a case of mixed (and at least partially unconscious) motives? On these matters the jury is still out, but it can at least be said that neither his contemporary critics nor subsequent scholarship have in general been willing to give him the benefit of any doubt.

Coke's visit to the United States in 1784–5 was the first of nine in the next twenty years. In spite of his growing commitments at home and the upheaval in the British connexion caused by Wesley's death in 1791, he continued to fulfil his episcopal responsibilities as fully as the American Methodists' allegiance to Asbury and Asbury's own reluctance to share his authority permitted. In particular, although Cokesbury College, the educational venture which he initiated in spite of Asbury's misgivings, proved abortive, it set a precedent which American Methodism

was to follow in later years. But the fact that he remained a British citizen, though sympathetic to the American cause, coupled with his frequent absences, restricted Coke's influence and usefulness there. Eventually it was his marriage in 1805 that brought his trans-Atlantic commuting to an end; and though he made one last offer to settle in America, his usefulness had passed its zenith and his offer was not taken up.

Coke was in America when news of Wesley's death reached him and he hurried back to England in time for the conference, no doubt expecting to step into Wesley's shoes. But this was not to be. Wesley's benevolent autocracy had left the itinerant preachers in no doubt that they would have 'no king in Israel' and they determined on an annual presidency, with one of their own number, William Thompson, as Wesley's first successor. It was not until 1797 that Coke was elected to the presidential chair. But whenever he was in England he served as secretary, and he was chosen as president a second time in 1805, when there was some fear that he might settle in America. But there was never any question of there being a second Wesley.

World parish In the course of his trans-Atlantic voyages, Coke also paid four visits to the West Indies, where he was instrumental in establishing Methodism in a number of islands; and it is as the pioneer of British Methodist overseas missions that he has chiefly been remembered in England. Methodism was transplanted to the Caribbean in the 1760s by lay persons who had come under its influence back home. Early appeals for spiritual nurture and leadership went unheeded, primarily because Wesley's limited resources were over-stretched by the rapid expansion of British Methodism. It was the enthusiasm of Thomas Coke which persuaded Wesley and the conference to appoint the first missionaries to overseas stations. At the end of 1783 (and eight years before William Carey's better known *Enquiry*), in conjunction with Thomas Parker, a Methodist layman from York, he issued a *Plan of the Society for the Establishment of Missions among the Heathens*. This first venture was abortive, largely because he failed to enlist Wesley's support in advance. It was, in any case, overtaken by the events of 1784, culminating in the Christmas conference at Baltimore. Two years later, however, Coke returned to the fray with an *Address to the Pious and Benevolent*, in which he proposed missions both to the Scottish highlands and islands and the Channel Islands, and to the West Indies and British North America. This time he had taken the precaution of obtaining Wesley's approbation and support; the proposals were given conference approval and Coke sailed for the New World with three of the itinerant preachers who had volunteered for the mission. The party landed in Antigua early on Christmas morning and Coke began a tour of the islands, in the course of which he left missionaries in Antigua, St Vincent, and St Kitts, despite the fact that two of them had been allocated to Newfoundland. This was the first of four visits, as a result of which by 1793, despite strong disapproval in some islands from slave-owning planters and government officials, Caribbean Methodism grew from a single society of 2000 in Antigua to a membership of 6570, with twelve missionaries working in ten of the islands. British Methodism's earliest mission field was firmly established.

During these years Coke was also involved in launching missions to Sierra Leone and India, as well as home missions in Ireland, north Wales, and parts of rural England untouched by Methodism. These ventures placed a considerable financial burden on a movement just emerging into denominationalism, and the Methodist preachers, meeting in their annual conference, gave only hesitant and qualified approval to them. Coke's enthusiasm and vision outran his organizing ability, but it is to his credit that he not only initiated and administered the missions, virtually single-handed, but also undertook their funding by a series of published appeals, by begging tours, and, in the last resort, from his own personal resources. The first effective missionary committee was not appointed until 1804. Its purpose was to contain and regularize what Coke had initiated, and a difficult period of adjustment between him and the new committee followed. But it was not until 1813, on the eve of his departure for India, that effective steps were taken to finance the missions adequately through district missionary societies. By then Coke's right to be considered 'father of the missions' was universally, if sometimes grudgingly, recognized.

Despite the peripatetic lifestyle to which he committed himself from 1777 onwards, Coke published a considerable amount, ranging from sermons and missionary reports to extracts from the journal he kept while travelling abroad (published in a collected edition in 1816). His most substantial works were a *Commentary on the Bible* in six large volumes (1801–7) and a three-volume *History of the West Indies* (1808–11). Both were heavily derivative. He also lent his name to the official life of John Wesley, largely written by Henry Moore and rushed into print in 1792.

Personal details Coke was short and in later years increasingly stout, with pleasant, boyish features described by Wilberforce as 'such a smooth apple face, and little round mouth, that if it had been forgotten you might have made as good a one by thrusting in your thumb' (Wilberforce and Wilberforce, 3.389–90). He was of a warm-hearted and friendly disposition, but impulsive sometimes to the point of indiscretion and offensiveness. His attitude towards the established church vacillated between outspoken criticism and attempts to repair the bridges between Methodism and the church on both sides of the Atlantic. John Wesley commented wryly that he and Coke were like a louse and a flea. 'I creep like a louse, and what I have I keep. Dr. Coke leaps like a flea and is often obliged to leap back again' (Vickers, *Thomas Coke*, 46). His enthusiastic good intentions often led him into naïvety, as when he made a bid for the proposed new Indian bishopric in 1813. But his faults were the defects of his merits, and his mistakes and errors of judgement may be deemed the price he paid for his considerable achievements. He remained a bachelor until 1805, when he met, fell in love with, and married (1 April) Penelope Goulding Smith (1762–1811), a spinster from Bradford-on-Avon, who was

among his more generous missionary subscribers. Her fortune, like his own, was devoted to keeping the missions solvent, but she died after about five years of sharing in his itinerant and hyperactive existence. Within a year (16 December 1811) Coke married Ann Loxdale (c.1755–1812), a well-known Methodist from Shrewsbury. He was devastated by her death on 5 December 1812, declared himself 'dead to Europe' (T. Coke to S. Drew, 28 June 1813, Drew, 350), and flung himself into preparations for a mission to Ceylon and India.

Mission to the East As early as 1784 Coke had had India in his sights and had corresponded with Charles Grant about the possibilities of a mission. But other commitments took priority without ever entirely obliterating the vision. Now, with the renewal of the East India Company's charter, the circumstances seemed right at last. For the last time Coke persuaded a hesitant conference to back his proposals, and six missionaries were recruited to accompany him. They sailed from Portsmouth at the end of 1813 on what was to prove a slow and stormy voyage, Coke devoting much of his time to a study of the Portuguese Bible. On the morning of 3 May 1814, as they were crossing the Indian Ocean, he was found dead on the floor of his cabin, apparently as the result of a stroke, and was buried at sea that afternoon. JOHN A. VICKERS

Sources J. A. Vickers, *Thomas Coke, apostle of Methodism* (1969) · J. A. Vickers, 'Thomas Coke of Brecon', *Brycheiniog*, 10 (1964), 1–13 · J. A. Vickers, 'The churchmanship of Thomas Coke', *Methodist History*, 7/4 (July 1969), 15–28 · J. A. Vickers, 'Coke and Asbury: a comparison of bishops', *Methodist History*, 11/1 (Oct 1972), 42–51 · J. Crowther, *The life of Thomas Coke* (1815) · S. Drew, *The life of the Rev. Thomas Coke* (1817) · J. W. Etheridge, *The life of the Rev. Thomas Coke* (1860) · W. A. Candler, *The life of Thomas Coke* (1923) · *Extracts of the journals of the late Rev. Thomas Coke, L.L.D.; comprising several visits to North-America and the West-Indies ... to which is prefixed a life of the doctor* (1816) [Life by J. Sutcliffe] · *The letters of the Rev. John Wesley*, ed. J. Telford, 8 vols. (1931) · *The journal of the Rev. John Wesley*, ed. N. Curnock and others, 8 vols. (1909–16) · R. I. Wilberforce and S. Wilberforce, *Life of William Wilberforce*, 5 vols. (1838) · *Representative verse of Charles Wesley*, ed. F. Baker (1962) · H. Moore, *The life of the Rev. John Wesley*, 2 vols. (1824–5)

Archives Drew University, Madison, New Jersey, United Methodist Archives and History Center, corresp. · Duke U., corresp. · Emory University, Atlanta, Georgia, corresp. · JRL, Methodist Archives and Research Centre, corresp. and papers · SOAS, Methodist Missionary Society Archives · Southern Methodist University, Dallas, corresp. · Wesley's Chapel, London, corresp.

Likenesses H. Edridge, pencil drawing, 1799, NPG [*see illus.*] · engravings; copies, SOAS · engravings; copies, Westminster Institute of Education, Oxford

Coke, Thomas William, first earl of Leicester of Holkham (1754–1842), politician and agriculturist, was born in London on 6 May 1754 and baptized at St James's, Piccadilly, on 22 May, the eldest son of Wenham Roberts Coke (1717–1776), a landowner, and his second wife, Elizabeth Chamberlayne-Denton (d. 1810), the daughter of George Chamberlayne-Denton of Hillesden, Buckinghamshire.

Education and early parliamentary career Coke was educated at Eton College (1765–71), after which he travelled abroad (between 1771 and 1774), spending lengthy periods in Turin and Rome, and visiting Naples, Florence, Vienna, and Paris. A strikingly handsome man, he was the subject

Thomas William Coke, first earl of Leicester of Holkham (1754–1842), by Thomas Gainsborough, 1778

of a flamboyant portrait by Pompeo Batoni (1774). Following his return to England he married, on 5 October 1775, his cousin Jane Lennox Dutton (1753–1800), the daughter of James Lennox Dutton of Loughcrew, co. Meath, and his second wife, Jane Bond. On the death of his father Coke succeeded to the family estates in Norfolk, and in May 1776 was returned as MP for the county. An archetypal whig country gentleman, he was a staunch supporter of Charles James Fox but an irregular speaker in the house. He was most likely to be found addressing his fellow MPs on agricultural matters, partly because he believed the landed interest to be neglected by the government. He claimed to be an unwilling politician, and recalled at the close of his political career in 1833: 'when I first offered myself for this county, I did so with great reluctance, for I had no wish to come into Parliament. I was no orator, no politician' (GM, 316). He stood because he was convinced by a number of local gentlemen that unless he did so a tory would take the seat: 'at the mention of a Tory coming in … my blood chilled all over me from head to foot, and I came forward' (ibid., 316). Be that as it may, he entered parliament as the youngest member elected that year and sat for fifty-six years with only one major interruption, from 1784 to 1790.

At the 1784 general election Coke was one of Fox's so-called martyrs when he did not present himself for

re-election. He temporarily retired to Norfolk, where in 1776 he had inherited a 30,000 acre estate with a rental income in 1780 of £13,118. Although the estate was well managed, with a substantial house, Holkham, completed by Matthew Brettingham in 1765, it also carried considerable debts as a result of building and of unwise speculation by his predecessors in the South Sea Company in 1720. Coke set about improving the estate. He bought up additional properties to round out his landholdings, he promoted enclosure acts in parishes where open fields still survived, and he encouraged his farmers to adopt new rotations designed to improve the output and productivity of the soil. The Park (or Home) Farm was cultivated to the highest technical standards, and the continuous experimentation was brought to the attention of a wider audience through the annual sheep shearings he instituted in 1800. This development followed the death of the acknowledged champion of improved farming, the fifth duke of Bedford. The shearings were for many years a highlight of the farming calendar until they were discontinued in 1821.

In 1790, after a careful canvass, Coke was returned unopposed as MP for Norfolk, and he subsequently became a frequent if not always regular attendant at the house, particularly when agricultural issues were discussed. He represented Norfolk, with one short break (1806–7), until 1832. Although he never held government office, he was a member of the board of agriculture from 1793. He opposed the war with France, and met regularly with other whig leaders at Holkham. On 8 April 1794 he complained in the house that Norfolk was 'very dissatisfied with the war' (Thorne). It was again Norfolk interests which he had in mind when supporting a motion for peace early in January 1795: 'the county of Norfolk felt the danger to which the coast was exposed by the French getting possession of Holland, and wished for peace' (ibid.). A month later he defended the Norwich petition for peace. Early in 1796 he was associated with a bill designed to amend the game laws to fix a later start to the game-shooting season.

From 1797 Coke was able to control the return of the second Norfolk MP, and in the longer term this led to animosity against him on the grounds that his political control appeared to be turning the county into the equivalent of a pocket borough. The issue came to a head in 1815. Although Coke, as a whig, supported the parliamentary reform cause, he always voted for the protection of agricultural interests, and this caused problems when he supported the corn law proposals in 1815. He addressed a meeting in Norwich in March, after which he was threatened with physical injury by an anti-corn law mob, and he was apparently saved only when a butcher by the name of Kett let loose a bull which hastily dispersed the crowd. Undaunted, on 6 June he presented a county petition in favour of the corn law.

In the aftermath of this incident, it was alleged in Norfolk that Coke's agricultural improvements were detrimental rather than beneficial to the local countryside. The 'reputed injury', Dr Edward Rigby told the Norwich

Philosophical Society in December 1816 during a spirited defence of Coke, 'was charged with producing various ill consequences, and depriving the poor of employment, and rendering corn dear'. Rigby argued that this was a misunderstanding: 'what before was, probably, principally a meagre sheep walk here and there only, exhibiting patches of ordinary rye, oats, barley and badly cultivated turnips, with not a single ear of wheat being seen … has become most productive land' (Rigby, 3.45). Rigby's was the first of a series of defences, most of which depended on Coke's own account of events at Holkham. In Earl Spencer's words in 1842, Coke was 'the only person now living who is able to recollect the former state of this district, and to tell the means by which it has been improved into its present flourishing condition' (Spencer, 2). This, however, was in the future.

Reputation as an agricultural improver In 1816 Coke had a political agenda because he was anxious to show that the new husbandry he was promoting, although requiring farm consolidation, increased rather than diminished employment opportunities by bringing into cultivation previously unused land. What Coke helped to foster from 1816 onwards was little less than a mythical view of his own achievements, and the older he grew the fewer were the number of contemporaries who could question his interpretation. He claimed, in Spencer's words, that when he inherited the estate in 1776:

> the whole district round Holkham was unenclosed, and the cultivation was of the most miserable character … no manure was purchased, and very little, and that of no value, was produced on the farm. The sheep were of the old Norfolk breed, and, with the exception of a few milch cows, there were no cattle kept upon any of the farms. (Spencer, 2)

His interest in agricultural improvement was sparked when in 1778 one of the tenants on his property refused a renewal of his lease at 5s. an acre. Coke decided to work the land himself, and since he knew little about farming he gathered around him a number of practical men, and each year invited farmers from neighbouring districts to examine his farm and discuss its management. These meetings gradually developed by 1800 into the famous sheep shearings. Coke also claimed that, by adopting an improved course of husbandry, including the regular application of marl and an increase in livestock, the land was rapidly improved, and in 1787 wheat was cultivated for the first time. Gradually, as a result of his initiative, the old farming systems fell into disrepute and he converted west Norfolk from a rye-growing into a wheat-producing district. The only help he acknowledged was from the tenant farmers, who were carefully restricted by their lease covenants to ensure good farming. Coke also claimed to have improved the breeds of sheep, cattle, and pigs on his estate, and as a result to have raised the rent from £2200 in 1776 to more than £20,000 forty years later—at the same time spending more than £100,000 on farm houses and outbuildings.

Coke's version of events was widely accepted in the nineteenth century, and he came to enjoy the reputation of being a pioneer of the English agricultural revolution. Obituarists went into raptures: Coke had 'raised forests where there was scarcely a blade of grass; from which, should it be required, the British navy may be hereafter amply supplied'. A vessel had been launched in 1832 'built of oak produced from acorns planted by Mr Coke himself' (*GM*, 316–17). More recently a reappraisal has taken place, and it is now accepted that much of what passed for fact was a carefully controlled exercise in public relations designed primarily to enhance his own reputation. Agriculture in north-west Norfolk was already well advanced when Coke inherited the Holkham estate from his father in 1776: Arthur Young had commented several years earlier on the great quantities of wheat already being grown, and in 1784 he was to single out Coke for praise because he had done so well 'in the midst of the best husbandry in Norfolk' (Young, 353). Many of the innovations Coke claimed to have pioneered were known and practised long before 1776; the farm which, according to his account, he had taken in hand in 1778 had actually been the home farm since 1721 (although he did extend it), and rents on the estate doubled between 1776 and 1816 (much as they did on similar land elsewhere in this period). Unfortunately Coke's response to the accusations levelled against him in 1816 led him into serious exaggeration, and the image had then to be maintained. At the 1819 sheep shearing Coke proposed a toast to Dr Rigby, who in turn took the opportunity of his response to re-emphasize the poverty of Norfolk before Coke inherited his family estates.

Much of the improvement which came to be attributed to Coke predated his inheritance of the estate and, equally, much of it was the work of tenant farmers upon whom Coke depended, and whose progress impressed visitors as much as the Park Farm. However, the myth became greater than the reality, particularly after Coke no longer needed it to serve a political purpose. By the time Spencer wrote in 1842 the drift of Coke's argument was to emphasize his own role in more or less transforming English agriculture. These views were later adopted by other writers, notably Lord Ernle, who wrote that between 1778 and 1842 Coke 'stood at the head of the new agricultural movement' (Prothero, 217), and that he had turned a landscape without wheat, with only scanty crops of rye and undernourished animals, into a thriving and progressive agricultural estate. At a later date he had helped to disseminate such knowledge more widely through the activities of his tenants, and through agricultural meetings convened at Holkham.

Coke's smokescreen all too easily obscured the undoubtedly important innovations he promoted. His farmers were on twenty-one-year leases, and from 1815 they were expected to follow the Norfolk four-course rotation of turnips, barley, grass, and corn. Although some were less conscientious than others, there is little reason to doubt that they largely worked their land in accordance with the terms of their leases, and Coke was himself of the view that his leases were the main reason for the improvements which took place on his estates. He was undoubtedly a pioneer of agricultural change, but he is no longer considered to have played the key role he attributed to himself over the period 1816–42.

In February 1816 Coke vouched in parliament for the agricultural distress, and he spoke against the renewal of the property tax and wartime malt taxes. He continued to speak on agricultural issues for the rest of his parliamentary career, and in February 1822 he introduced the Norfolk agricultural petition into the house in which it was argued that the present misery suffered by farmers was a result of high taxation causing distress.

Remarriage and retrenchment Coke and his first wife, who died on 2 June 1800, had three daughters, to each of whom he gave a portion of £30,000. On 26 February 1822, at the age of sixty-seven, and after twenty-two years as a widower, he married for the second time. His bride was his goddaughter, Lady Anne Amelia Keppel (1803–1844), the daughter of William Charles Keppel, fourth earl of Albemarle, and his first wife, Elizabeth Southwell; she was fifty years his junior, and seven years younger than his granddaughter. Coke was supposed to have married 'in consequence of dissatisfaction with his nephew and heir presumptive' (*GM*, 317), although other accounts suggest that he had originally intended her to marry his nephew and heir but the young people refused to marry. The difference in their ages led to considerable speculation in the newspaper gossip columns. The couple had five sons and a daughter, of whom the eldest son, Thomas William *Coke, agriculturist and landowner, was born on 26 December 1822.

Coke's remarriage led to an investigation of his financial position. In addition to extensive land purchases he spent perhaps £40,000 on elections, and he claimed to have invested £500,000 on estate improvements. As a result, between 1776 and 1822 his debts increased by £133,000, by which time he was facing something of a crisis. His spending, or predicted spending, exceeded his income by about £10,000, while debts and other charges on the estate amounted to nearly £300,000. At the same time, as a result of the post-war agricultural depression, considerable rent arrears had developed, rent abatements had to be granted, and new tenants were needed. To tackle this crisis Coke's estate at Hillesden in Buckinghamshire was sold for £127,000, and expenditure at Holkham was severely cut. Over the next twenty years, partly because Coke now had a son to succeed him, the burden of debt was gradually reduced—in 1828, for example, a mortgage of £10,000 outstanding since 1759 was finally redeemed. The total stood at only £8000 when he died.

Coke, despite his claims about providing agricultural work, was happy to break up labourers' protests in 1831, and in 1834 he welcomed the new poor law. It seems unlikely that farm labourers on his estate shared the respect, admiration, and gratitude that his tenants felt for him. He retired from the Commons at the end of the last unreformed parliament, having been for many years 'father of the house'. To celebrate his retirement a public dinner was given at St Andrew's Hall, Norwich, on 12 April

1833, with the duke of Sussex in the chair and more than 500 people sitting down to eat.

Peerage and final years Coke claimed to have rejected a peerage on six separate occasions. The offers were made in 1776 by the duke of Portland as a bribe to desert Fox, in 1778 by Lord North, in 1783 by Portland and again when he joined Pitt, in 1794, in 1806 by Charles James Fox, in 1831 by Earl Grey, and in 1837 by Lord Melbourne. He turned down the 1806 offer because 'he felt he could serve his country better as a commoner than as a peer' (Thorne). He accepted the offer in 1831 on the grounds that 'every measure for which I was most eager will be completed upon the Reform being carried; I have now sons, and feel, as a father, I should not be justified in refusing your offer' (Stirling, 556). Unfortunately the proposal was rejected by the king, apparently on the grounds that Coke had insulted George III. However, after enjoying for many years the unofficial title of 'the first commoner of England', he was eventually created earl of Leicester of Holkham and Viscount Coke on 12 August 1837, following Queen Victoria's accession. He had wanted to revive the title which had become extinct on the death in 1759 of his great-uncle, despite the fact that the Townshend family at that time had an earldom of Leicester. His ambition was achieved by taking the title earl of Leicester of Holkham, although he seems not to have intended to use the last two words.

Coke was the archetypal country gentleman. At Holkham he was a delightful host who loved hunting, shooting, and gambling as well as—by repute—cock fighting and bull baiting. He was a master of fox hounds, and numerous stories were told of his prowess in field sports. The Revd W. B. Daniel wrote in 1813 that 'Mr Coke is so capital a marksman that as he inflicts death whenever he pulls the trigger, he should in mercy forbear such terrible examples of his skill' (Stirling, 208). He was also a keen game preserver. He was active in the Norfolk yeomanry during the French wars, as major commandant of the Holkham yeomanry (1798), and captain (1803) and lieutenant-colonel in the West Norfolk yeomanry cavalry (1804).

Coke died at Longford Hall, Derbyshire, on 30 June 1842, aged eighty-eight, after a short illness during which—according to his doctor—'now and then in his sleep he talked about his farms' (Stirling, 596). On 11 July he was buried in the family mausoleum attached to Tittleshall church, Norfolk. A memorial column depicting agricultural scenes commemorating his work in Norfolk was erected at Holkham by public subscription. Coke was succeeded by his eldest son, Thomas William, Viscount Coke. His widow married the Right Hon. Edward Ellice MP, in June 1843, and died in childbirth on 22 July 1844.

J. V. BECKETT

Sources R. A. C. Parker, *Coke of Norfolk* (1975) · A. M. W. Stirling, *Coke of Norfolk and his friends*, new edn (1912) · R. A. C. Parker, 'Coke of Norfolk and the agrarian revolution', *Economic History Review*, 2nd ser., 8 (1955–6), 156–66 · S. Wade Martins, *A great estate at work: the Holkham estate and its inhabitants in the nineteenth century* (1980) · R. E. Prothero, *English farming past and present*, ed. D. Hall, 6th edn (1961) · A. Young, ed., *Annals of agriculture and other useful arts*, 2

(1784) • E. Rigby, *Holkham: its agriculture*, 2nd edn (1817) • Earl Spencer, 'On the improvements which have taken place in west Norfolk', *Journal of the Royal Agricultural Society of England*, 3 (1842), 1–9 • R. G. Thorne, 'Coke, Thomas William', HoP, *Commons, 1790–1820* • M. M. Drummond, 'Coke, Thomas William', HoP, *Commons, 1754–90* • GEC, *Peerage* • *GM*, 2nd ser., 18 (1842), 316–18

Archives Holkham estate office, Holkham Hall, Norfolk, corresp. and papers | BL, corresp. with Lord Holland, Add. MS 51593 • BL, letters to second Earl Spencer • BL, letters to Arthur Young, Add. MSS 35127–35131 • Linn. Soc., corresp. with Sir James Smith • NL Scot., letters to John Horseman • U. Durham L., corresp. with second Earl Grey

Likenesses P. Batoni, oils, 1774, Holkham Hall, Norfolk • T. Gainsborough, oils, 1778, Holkham Hall, Norfolk [*see illus.*] • G. Garrard, etching, 1806, NPG • G. Garrard, marble bust, 1806, Shugborough, Staffordshire • T. Lawrence, oils, 1807, Shire Hall, Norwich • R. R. Reinagle, oils, 1815, Shugborough, Staffordshire • T. Lawrence, oils, *c.*1818, Walker Art Gallery, Liverpool • F. Chantrey, marble bust, 1829, Holkham Hall, Norfolk • F. Chantrey, pencil drawing, NPG • G. Hayter, oils, Holkham Hall, Norfolk • J. Opie, oils, Holkham Hall, Norfolk • W. Ward, engraving, repro. in Parker, *Coke of Norfolk*, frontispiece • T. Weaver, group portrait, oils, Holkham Hall, Norfolk • oils (after R. R. Reinagle), Holkham Hall, Norfolk • portraits, repro. in Stirling, *Coke of Norfolk*

Wealth at death under £60,000: will

Coke, Thomas William, second earl of Leicester of Holkham (1822–1909), agriculturist and landowner, was born at Holkham Hall, the family seat in Norfolk, on 26 December 1822, the eldest son of Thomas William *Coke, 'Coke of Norfolk', afterwards first earl of Leicester (1754–1842), and his second wife, Lady Anne Amelia (1803–1844), third daughter of William Charles Keppel, fourth earl of Albemarle, whom he married when sixty-eight years old. Educated at Eton College and Winchester College, Coke received the courtesy title of Viscount Coke when his father became earl of Leicester at the accession of Queen Victoria in 1837. He was a minor when his father died on 30 June 1842, when he succeeded to the earldom.

Leicester did not take a prominent part in politics or public affairs, but followed in his father's footsteps in his interest in agriculture and forestry. He devoted himself to the management and improvement of his vast estate. He continued to improve farm buildings and he rebuilt the estate workshops at Longlands. Model Farm was built to house his prize herd of Devon cattle. Between 1857 and 1859 the sea bank at Wells was constructed, completing the reclamation of the marshes between Wells and Holkham. Leicester was also a major investor in the Wells and Fakenham Railway between 1853 and 1857. A table appended to R. H. Rew's report on the agriculture of Norfolk, made to the second royal commission on agriculture of 1893, gave some instructive details as to the expenditure of money by the earl and his father in keeping up and improving the Holkham agricultural estate of 39,612 acres. The first earl spent in buildings and repairs £536,992, and the second earl spent £575,048 up to 1894—in buildings, drainage, and cottages, £377,771, and in the purchase of land for the improvement of the estate, £197,277—giving a total by both owners of £1,112,040. The gross rents of the farms, which in 1878 were £52,682, were only £28,701 in 1894: a shrinkage of £23,981 (45.5 per cent).

In the year ending Michaelmas 1894 the disbursements on the estate were £12,311, despite the earl's personal supervision over all the details.

Leicester married twice. First, on 20 April 1843, before he was of age, at Cardington, Bedfordshire, he married Juliana (d. 1870), eldest daughter of Samuel Charles Whitbread (1796–1879), brewer and astronomer, of Southill, Bedfordshire. They had four sons and seven daughters. Then on 26 August 1875, at Latimer, Buckinghamshire, he married Georgiana Caroline (1852–1937), eldest daughter of William George Cavendish, second Baron Chesham, with whom he had six sons and one daughter. In his later years Leicester was thought of as a rather reserved, distant person of simple tastes, living quietly at Holkham. He must have been a striking figure with his flowing beard and wearing a wide-brimmed hat.

Leicester was a patron of agricultural causes and a member of the Royal Agricultural Society of England. He was responsible for building more than 200 new cottages on the estate from the 1860s onwards, and he was not prepared to join with other landowners against trade unions. Although many were singled out for abuse from union platforms, Lord Leicester escaped.

In his younger days, Leicester made Holkham a social centre, hosting huge shooting parties at which the prince of Wales was a regular guest after 1865. He was responsible for rebuilding the coach house and stables and for laying out elaborate parterres and terraces around the hall.

Following a national trend, Leicester was one of a number of great agricultural landowners who began diversifying their assets. Beginning with local investments in the 1850s, by the 1870s he held shares in railways in Britain, Canada, Australia, and Argentina, and also in British companies producing agricultural products such as manure and farm implements. He also invested in companies using the products of British agriculture, such as those involved in brewing (Wade Martins, 62–3). He took little interest in politics, which he left to his younger brother, Edward, who was MP for West Norfolk from 1847 until 1852. At a public meeting in Norwich in 1886, he said, 'I have never been in the habit of taking part in political matters of an entirely party description' (*Norfolk Chronicle*, 30 Jan 1909).

The earl was nevertheless appointed on 1 August 1846 lord lieutenant of the county of Norfolk, and he held this appointment for sixty years, retiring in 1906, when he was succeeded by his eldest son. In 1866 he was made a member of the council of the prince of Wales, and in 1870 he became keeper of the privy seal of the duchy of Cornwall; he retired in 1901 on the accession of King Edward VII. On 30 June 1873 he was made KG on the recommendation of Gladstone. He was in politics a whig of the old school, but rarely attended the House of Lords.

Leicester maintained his health until 1905. He died at Holkham of heart failure on 24 January 1909, and was buried there on 28 January. His second wife survived him, dying in 1937. The earl was represented as a young man on one of the bas-reliefs ('Granting a lease') of the monument erected in the park by public subscription in 1845–50 as a memorial to his father.

ERNEST CLARKE, rev. SUSANNA WADE MARTINS

Sources S. Wade Martins, *A great estate at work: the Holkham estate and its inhabitants in the nineteenth century* (1980), 52–66, 268–9 · A. M. W. Stirling, *Coke of Norfolk and his friends*, 2 (1908), 506 · A. M. W. Stirling, *The letter-bag of Lady Elizabeth Spencer-Stanhope*, 2 vols. (1913) · *Eastern Daily Press* (25 Jan 1909) · *The Times* (25 Jan 1909) · H. Rider Haggard, *Rural England* (1902), 2.449 · 'Royal commission on agriculture', *Parl. papers* (1895), 17.425–8, C. 7915 [report on the county of Norfolk] · Boase, *Mod. Eng. biog.* · *Norfolk Chronicle* (30 Jan 1909) · parish register, Norfolk RO · *Eastern Daily Press* (28 Jan 1909)

Archives Holkham Hall, Norfolk, Holkham MS, list of investments of Thomas William Coke, 1811–

Likenesses S. Lane, double portrait, oils, exh. RA 1832 (with Edward Keppel Coke), Shugborough, Staffordshire · bas-relief on monument, 1845–50, Holkham, Norfolk · G. Richmond, oils, exh. RA 1858, Holkham Hall, Norfolk · G. Bohme, terracotta bust, 1871, Holkham Hall, Norfolk · J. Collier, oils, 1905, Weasonham Hall, Norfolk · F. Joubert, mixed-method engraving (after oil painting by G. Richmond, exh. RA 1858), BM, NPG · Spy [L. Ward], chromolithograph caricature, NPG; repro. in *VF* (4 Aug 1883) · photographs, Holkham Hall, Norfolk

Wealth at death £880,894 18s. 9d.: resworn probate, 25 Feb 1909, CGPLA Eng. & Wales

Coke, Zachary (*bap.* 1618?), logician and lawyer, was the son of Thomas Coke, of Cornwall; he may have been the Zachary Cocke baptized at St Andrew's, Plymouth, on 27 December 1618. Coke was admitted to Gray's Inn on 28 December 1649. Nothing further is known of his life. His book, *The Art of Logick, or, The Entire Body of Logick in English*, published in 1654, had a second edition in 1657. There was a facsimile reprint in 1969. It is one of the earliest books on logic in English, the first being Sir Thomas Wilson's in 1552, and has received virtually no attention, not being mentioned even in Wilhelm Risse's vast *Logik der Neuzeit* (2 vols., 1964–70), or in other histories of logic. It comprises three books (1, categories; 2, propositions; 3, syllogism) and further sections on method. Coke is interested in applying logic to theology, giving his examples in religious terms wherever possible. This marks him off from his predecessors in English, to whom he owes an obvious debt, for example Thomas Blundevil (1599) and Alexander Richardson (1629), having in common with them some rare logical words, such as 'contradicent', 'polyzetesis', 'privatively', and with Blundevil in particular the expression 'first intention', and also new senses, for instance, the 'foundation' (of a relation), a use not discovered earlier than in Blundevil, and 'simply' (of conversion). Some influence of the translation (1574) of Ramus's logic is to be found in Blundevil and Coke, for instance, the categorial sense of the noun 'inferior', and (just in Coke) the unusual logic terms 'affirmant' and 'negant'. But it has to be remembered that the authors of logic books in English were writing against a background of logics in Latin, which were continuing to appear and were perhaps the major textbooks. These will have given rise to some of the terms and content of the books in English. Coke himself was a learned author, using some expressions in Greek, indicating direct knowledge of some Aristotle. He also appears to have coined (or at least translated) some terms, as they are not found in previous English logics, for example, 'conominative', 'consignificative', 'counterplacing' (that is, contraposition), 'coupler' (in the logical sense), 'disjoiner', 'distinctness', 'distributable', 'monstrative', 'paronymical', and 'pure' (that is, assertoric).

ROLAND HALL

Sources R. Hall, 'Antedatings in logic', *N&Q*, 215 (1970), 322–32 · R. Hall, 'Unnoticed terms in logic', *N&Q*, 217 (1972), 131–7, 165–71, 203–9 · *IGI* · J. Foster, *The register of admissions to Gray's Inn, 1521–1889, together with the register of marriages in Gray's Inn chapel, 1695–1754* (privately printed, London, 1889)

Coker, Ernest George (1869–1946), civil and mechanical engineer, was born at Wolverton, Buckinghamshire, on 26 April 1869, the son of George Coker, an engine fitter, and his wife, Sarah Tompkins. Educated at a private school from 1883 until 1887, he was an apprentice and then draughtsman in the London and North Western Railway carriage works at Wolverton. Evening study enabled him to enter the Normal School of Science, London, where he gained a first-class associateship in mechanics. A Whitworth scholarship in 1890 took him to Edinburgh University where he graduated BSc in engineering in 1892. The following year he entered Peterhouse, Cambridge, where he graduated BA in 1896 with a first class in part one of the mechanical sciences tripos. In 1897 he took part two with a double distinction in the first class.

During college vacations Coker spent periods in the railway works at Wolverton and at Crewe where, in the testing house, he carried out experiments which probably aroused his interest in the stress and strain in materials in which he was later to specialize. In 1892 he became an assistant examiner in the Patent Office and retained this post while he was at Cambridge, but in 1898 he resigned to enter upon his career as an engineering educationist. He married in 1899 Alice Mary (d. 1941), daughter of Robert King, an engineer, of Wolverton. They then moved to Canada where Coker became assistant professor in civil engineering at McGill University, Montreal. Later he became an associate professor, and during the whole of the period worked as principal assistant to Henry Taylor Bovey, both at the university and in his private practice, testing materials of various kinds and doing experimental work on Canadian water power schemes.

In 1905 Coker returned to England to become professor of mechanical engineering and head of the department of civil engineering at Finsbury Technical College, London, where he built a new engineering laboratory described in his paper before the British Association for the Advancement of Science in 1907. Here he began the experiments for which his name became known on the use of photoelastic methods for the determination of stress distribution in metals, machines, and structures, devising apparatus and models for this work, publishing in the technical literature, and, from 1910, giving public demonstrations. All this work continued, including consulting engineering, when in 1914 he became professor of civil and mechanical engineering at University College, London. He later became dean of the faculty of engineering and director of the engineering laboratories; he retired in 1934 as professor emeritus.

Coker's chief work, *A Treatise on Photo-Elasticity* (1931), was written jointly with L. N. G. Filon. He delivered the thirteenth Thomas Hawksley lecture to the Institution of Mechanical Engineers in 1926 ('Elasticity and plasticity'), and a lecture given to the Junior Institution of Engineers in 1935, 'The design and equipment of photo-elastic laboratories', summed up much of his life's work, which had an international reputation in its rather limited field. He was elected FRS in 1915, was also FRSE, and a member of the leading engineering societies, from which he received many medals, including the Thomas Hawksley medal (1922) from the Institution of Mechanical Engineers, the Telford medal (1921) from the Institution of Civil Engineers, and the gold medal of the Institution of Naval Architects (1911). The Royal Society awarded him the Rumford medal in 1936, and from the Franklin Institute, Philadelphia, he received the Howard N. Potts (1922) and Louis E. Levy (1926) medals. He was also an honorary DSc of the universities of Sydney and Louvain.

In person Coker was rather modest and retiring, and he was happiest when in his laboratory. Coker was living at 3 Farnley Road, Chingford, Essex, at the time of his death, which took place at 13 Miller Road, Ayr, on 9 April 1946.

A. R. STOCK, rev. JOHN BOSNELL

Sources H. T. Jessop, *Obits. FRS*, 8 (1952–3), 389–93 · G. T. R. Hill, *Nature*, 157 (1946), 722 · personal knowledge (1959) · *The Engineer* (19 April 1946) · *Engineering* (19 April 1946) · *Institution of Mechanical Engineers: Proceedings*, 156 (1947) · d. cert. · *CGPLA Eng. & Wales* (1946)
Likenesses W. Stoneman, photograph, 1917, NPG
Wealth at death £50,649 3s. 11d.: probate, 9 Sept 1946, *CGPLA Eng. & Wales*

Coker, Frances [Fanny] (1767–1820), freed slave and domestic servant, was born on 26 August 1767 on Mountravers plantation, Nevis, in the West Indies, the first of five children of Black Polly (b. c.1752, d. in or after 1823). Her mother was probably enslaved in Nigeria, aged about twelve, and was the only girl in the first group of nine child slaves purchased by the merchant and planter John *Pinney in January 1765 on St Kitts. He earmarked Black Polly as a seamstress and for house service. Fanny was described as a 'mulatto', and her father is believed to have been Pinney's married plantation manager, William Coker (bap. 1729, d. 1804). Between 1775 and 1780 Fanny was first trained as a seamstress by Mary Frances, then schooled by Mary Keep with two of Pinney's children. Mary Keep was probably a mason's wife who may have also instructed Fanny in domestic duties and those of a maidservant.

Fanny Coker was manumitted by John Pinney on 15 September 1778, one of the very few slaves whom he freed for reasons other than old age or illness. She remained in service as the maid of Pinney's wife, Jane, and sailed to England in July 1783 with the family and their slave manservant *Pero. Fanny left behind her mother, her ten-year-old half-brother Billey Jones (claimed by Black Polly to have been Pinney's son), and her half-sister Hetty, aged two.

After staying a few months in London and at William Coker's family home, Woodcuts in Dorset, the Pinneys moved to Bristol and from 1791 lived at 7 Great George Street. Fanny was one of several servants in the household and when Jane Pinney became pregnant she also undertook duties as a nursemaid. Baptized as a three-year-old on Nevis in the Anglican church, Fanny became a member of the Broadmead Baptist Church, Bristol. On 10 March 1789 'Frances Coker the descd.t of African ancestors, gave a most intelligent and pleasing acc.t of the work of God upon her soul, and was accepted as a candidate for Baptism' (Bristol RO, BD M1/3). She was probably re-baptized on 4 August 1789.

In the same year Fanny initially refused to accompany Jane Pinney on a short trip to Nevis but, threatened with dismissal, she sailed with her mistress from Bristol in November. Although John Pinney railed against Fanny's 'ungrateful conduct', 'unaccountable behaviour and cruelty' (letter to Elizabeth Pinney, letterbook 8, 27 Oct 1789), four months later she and Pero were the only servants retained when Pinney, with Pero, also left for Nevis. On her visit Fanny saw for the first time her five-year-old half-brother Cubbenna, and her two-year-old half-sister Molly. In the 1790s they, and Hetty, became field slaves but Hetty later progressed to house slave. Billey was apprenticed to a cooper. Throughout her life Fanny retained her contacts with Nevis. She wrote letters, and sent presents and trading goods to her mother, and cooper's equipment to Billey. Presumably she had friends among the many black Nevisians brought to England as servants, and enjoyed the company of the freed slaves Kate Coker and Polly Weekes on their visits to Bristol in 1785 and 1810–11 respectively.

Fanny frequently accompanied Jane Pinney on her visits to London, Weymouth, Sherborne, and Exeter. She received a regular wage (£3 per quarter with washing, £2 10s. without about 1800), and paid a tithe to the Baptist church. As early as 1802 John Pinney invested money on her behalf, and on his death left her an annuity, provided she remained in his widow's service. After a short illness, Fanny Coker died childless and unmarried on 12 April 1820. According to the Baptist records she had 'lived honourably and died comfortably' (Bristol RO, BD M1/3). She was buried five days later in the Baptist burial-ground, Redcross Street, Bristol. In 1926 its graves were moved to Greenbank cemetery, Bristol, where a memorial marks the reinterment. In her will she left £80, a metal watch, clothes, and other goods to her immediate family on Nevis. Her best tea chest was bequeathed to her fellow servant Ann Seymour and she provided £5 for the Baptist Missionary Society. Although her brother Billey Jones died before she did, Fanny was survived by her mother, her other siblings, and fourteen nephews and nieces.

CHRISTINE EICKELMANN

Sources D. Small and C. Eickelmann, 'Pinney and slavery', University of Bristol Library, Pinney MSS, DM 1867 · J. Pinney, letterbook 3 (5 Oct 1761–9 July 1775); letterbook 8 (11 March 1787–16 March 1790); letterbook 10 (12 Sept 1790–26 Oct 1793); letterbook 17 (6 Oct 1801–23 July 1803), University of Bristol Library, Pinney

MSS • account book 17 (12 Nov 1762–5 July 1783); account book 20 (1 March 1767–31 Dec 1777); account book 34 (15 Aug 1783–31 March 1802), University of Bristol Library, Pinney MSS • University of Bristol Library, Pinney MSS, Pinney domestic III, vol. 2, box 1814–1845 • Broadmead records, 1779–1817, Bristol RO, BD M1/3 • nonconformist registers, 1758–1808, Bristol RO, BD R1/4a–f • nonconformist registers, Baptist, Broadmead, Bristol RO, F 97, RG4 • common records, 1778–83, Nevis Court House, Charlestown, Nevis, West Indies • will, PRO, PROB 11/1645, fol. 266 • S. C. Hall and H. Mowrley, *Tradition and challenge: the story of Broadmead Baptist Church, Bristol, from 1685–1991* (1991) • christenings and burials, 1725–1812, Dorset RO, MIC/R/560

Archives FILM *Time team*, Channel 4, 21, 28 March 1999

Wealth at death £43 10s.5d. cash; about £100 in annuities; metal watch valued at £3 3s.; clothes and bed linen valued at £15; tea chest 10s.: will, PRO, PROB, 11/1645, fol. 266; Pinney, domestic III, vol. 2, box 1814–1845, University of Bristol Library, Pinney MSS

Coker, John (*d.* 1631/1635), Church of England clergyman and supposed antiquary, was the third son of Robert Coker (*d.* 1571/2) of Mappowder, Dorset, and Elizabeth, daughter and heir of Henry Beaumont of Giddesham, Devon. He appears never to have married. He was rector of Tincleton, Dorset, from 1576 until 1579, or perhaps 1582 when a new rector's name was noted. On his resignation of Tincleton, Coker perhaps retired to Mappowder, the parish register of which records the burial of a John Coker in 1631 and of another in 1635.

Coker was long known as the author of *A Survey of Dorsetshire … to which is Prefix'd a Map of the County* (1732). The map is by Richard Seale William, cartographer and engraver. The work is in fact by **Thomas Gerard** (1592–1634), who married Anne, daughter of Robert Coker of Mappowder. Through his own and his wife's family he was connected to many of the leading gentry families of Dorset. He wrote his 'General description' of the county in the 1620s, and it was the first systematic description of the history and topography of the county and the genealogy of its prominent families. On Gerard's death the manuscript passed into the hands of the Coker family and was published in 1732 as John Coker's work. A facsimile version of the survey was published in 1980, and the authoritative afterword by Rodney Legg established its true authorship.

ELIZABETH BAIGENT

Sources T. Gerard, *Coker's survey of Dorsetshire*, 2nd edn (1980) • C. R. J. Currie and C. P. Lewis, eds., *English county histories: a guide* (1994) • *DNB*

Cokkys, John (*d.* 1475), medical practitioner, is one of the few men whose name can be linked to the teaching and practice of medicine at Oxford in the fifteenth century. It is all the more frustrating that so few facts about his life can be established with any certainty. Emden lists a number of benefices held by a John Cokkys from 1435 onwards, but it seems unlikely that a man who was granted licence to study at an English university for three years on 21 January 1448, and was admitted BCnL at Oxford in June 1449, should already have held three benefices. His most significant qualification was the degree of bachelor of medicine to which he was admitted on 30 June 1450, and which seems to have given him entry to medical practice and teaching in Oxford for the rest of his career.

Three medical manuscripts in which his name appears testify to his medical learning and teaching, and one of these, Bodl. Oxf., MS e Museo 155, a collection of Roger Bacon's writings, is in the hand of Cokkys. He seems to have had the knack of getting his name attached to other people's writings. Thus he is credited (as Johannes de Gallicantu) with a commentary on the *Isagoge* of Johannitius, the fundamental introduction to medicine at Oxford, which in fact is the work of a thirteenth-century commentator known as Johannes Anglicus. A sentence in Cambridge, King's College, MS 16, part 2, folio 7, has led to the attribution of another text to him—first by Simon Forman, the owner of this manuscript from 1574—but in fact this text is the commentary of Bernardus Provincialis on the *Tabula Salerni*. While Cokkys seems to be claiming in this sentence that he is revealing the secrets of his practice to his pupils, his name has been interpolated into a commentary on medicinal simples. What these manuscripts do bear out is that Cokkys did teach medicine in Oxford, using the standard elementary texts and commentaries of the day as lecture materials. The Oxford medical curriculum seems in most respects to have been deeply conservative, though the interest in alchemical matters, and in Roger Bacon's work, taken by Cokkys was one also shared by another prominent Oxford doctor, Gilbert Kymer.

Cokkys also practised medicine, as is revealed in a chancery writ (PRO, early chanc. proc., C 1/45/175), dated 1467/73, in which he was summoned to answer for having withheld evidence relating to the death of John Walweyn, who had been his patient. John Clerk, mayor of Oxford, and the surgeon John Barbour were also co-defendants. A number of recipes given to Cokkys are quoted in Bodl. Oxf., MS Ashmole 1432: a drink for the stone 'proved upon hymselff', another for dropsy, others for palsy, bad sight, 'fleuma', and various aches. These are typical practical remedies of the sort found in commonplace and recipe books of this period. Cokkys appears to have remained in Oxford for the rest of his life. He was a benefactor of Canterbury College, as recognized by letters of confraternity from Christ Church Cathedral priory, Canterbury, on 5 May 1463. Emden, who identifies Cokkys with the rector of Mixbury, Witney, and Hardwick, parishes in Oxfordshire, estimates that he was dead by April 1475.

PETER MURRAY JONES

Sources Emden, *Oxf.*, 1.457 • C. H. Talbot and E. A. Hammond, *The medical practitioners in medieval England: a biographical register* (1965), 134–6 • Bodl. Oxf., MS e Museo 155 • Bodl. Oxf., MS Ashmole 1432 • Bodl. Oxf., MS Ashmole 1475, item 1 • King's Cam., MS 16, pt 2 • early chancery proceedings, PRO, C 1/45/175 • F. M. Getz, 'The faculty of medicine before 1500', *Hist. U. Oxf.* 2: *Late med. Oxf.*, 373–405 • F. Getz, 'Medical practitioners in medieval England', *Social History of Medicine*, 3 (1990), 265

Archives Bodl. Oxf., MSS Ashmole 1432; 1475, item 1 | Bodl. Oxf., MS e Museo 155

Colam, John (1826/7–1910), campaigner for animal welfare, was born in Louth, Lincolnshire. He was probably the 'John Coulam' who was born there on 1 September 1826 to John Coulam and Sarah Cordon (*IGI*). His early life is surprisingly obscure, given his importance. No precise date is known for his marriage to his first wife, Elizabeth, with whom he had eleven children. She died of pyaemia on 15 March 1871, and he remarried in 1874. His second wife, Frieda (born in Germany), survived him. No certificate of their marriage has been found, and it may have taken place abroad.

Colam's arrival in 1861 to succeed the recently deceased secretary of the Royal Society for the Prevention of Cruelty to Animals (RSPCA), Mr Middleton, was recalled by a member of the society's executive committee a quarter of a century later as 'like the waving of a Magician's wand' (RSPCA minute book, 19 July 1886, fol. 374). Not hitherto known to the committee, and chosen from twenty-four candidates, Colam was soon being praised at the society's annual meetings for his unusual combination of qualities. He was no mere office clerk: his personal intervention on 28 March 1870 at the Agricultural Hall, Islington, to prevent a bull-fight, incurring bruises in the confrontation that confined him to his bed for several days, became one of the society's oft-recalled epic events. Punctual, business-like, courteous, working long hours and never missing an executive committee meeting, Colam told the annual meeting in 1886 that he always considered 'that I am married to the cause' (RSPCA, *75th Annual Report*, 1898, 139). Strict but humane in handling the society's officers, he was quick to complement the society's prosecutions by educational effort, to build up the humanitarian case with improved annual reports and bulky evidence to public inquiries, and periodically to rejuvenate the office arrangements. Even-tempered and judicious, he kept a close grasp on detail and courageously conducted the society's own case in the lawcourts; he took pride in the fact that it was not until 1893 that he received a writ for malicious prosecution (RSPCA minute book, 12 June 1893, fol. 48). 'If he had selected the Bar as his profession', said the president of the Royal College of Veterinary Surgeons, Dr Fleming, in 1886, 'he would have risen to the top of the tree' (RSPCA minute book, 19 July 1886, fol. 378).

Colam was a shrewd strategist. Far from discouraging specialist offshoots from the society, he saw these as the best way to realize two desirable objectives: channelling off potentially distracting concern about what for him were side-issues into dogs' homes, bird and child-protection societies, beekeepers' associations, and homes of rest for horses; and protecting the society's reputation with governments, rich subscribers, and religious groupings by encouraging a distanced but nonsectarian and friendly rivalry from anti-vivisectionist and anti-hunting zealots operating on their own. Ever pursuing the practicable in a world beset by fanaticism and sentimentality, Colam maximized the support for edging forward year by year the state's commitment to humane objectives. He told an international conference in Paris in 1900 that he knew of no method so likely to benefit animals as 'a sensible attempt to convince mankind ... that we are not dreamers, but reasonable men and women ... trusting to a gradual development of our principles to accomplish that which at present cannot be attained' (*Animal World*, 1 Sept 1900, 132). Such a standpoint was not always welcome. He

was among the prime targets of the anti-vivisectionist Frances Power Cobbe when she grumbled about the RSPCA's timidity; the anti-hunting vegetarian H. S. Salt saw him as 'a veritable Proteus in the skill with which he gave the slip to any one who tried to commit him to any course but the safest' (Salt, 161).

Yet the society's executive committee was happy enough. Pay rises for Colam were frequent: up to £300 a year in 1862, £400 in 1866, £500 in 1872, with further annual rises of £100 in 1880 and 1886, and after his retirement in 1905 an annual pension of £1000 (RSPCA minute books). By 1867 the solicitor John Curling, who had regularly been making scenes at annual meetings, was publicly praising the new regime (*Annual Report*, 1867, 51), and by the 1880s the annual meeting had become a forum for eulogy. 'Without Mr. Colam I do not know what we should do', Dr Fleming told it in 1886 (RSPCA minute book, 19 July 1886, fol. 378). By 1888 there were three Colams at the society's headquarters: Frank Colam had by then been appointed to assist his father, and Robert Colam helped with pressing business when his father was absent.

On retirement Colam carried off many documents with which to write the society's history, but seems never to have delivered. The 1901 census found him living at 21 South Park Hill Road, Croydon, with his wife, cook, and housemaid. He died after a brief illness at Ingeborg, South Park Hill Road, Croydon, on 25 May 1910, aged eighty-three, and at the funeral in Norwood cemetery three days later his third son, R. F. Colam (recorder of Croydon, 1900–39), was among the principal mourners.

This major lifetime's achievement leaves a puzzle behind, for the RSPCA scarcely noticed Colam's death, *The Times*'s obituary was thin, and the *Dictionary of National Biography* and *Who's Who* ignored him. For this there may be two reasons. First, Colam saw his role as resembling that of a civil servant, tactfully and shrewdly leaving publicity to others. But second, his retirement was marred by an unfortunate incident. So concerned was he for the society's welfare that he mistakenly tried in a confidential letter to influence members of its executive committee on who should succeed him. He recommended an inside candidate trained as a solicitor, whereas the successful candidate was Captain G. L. Derriman, a disabled Grenadier Guards officer whom Colam saw as 'a martinet' (RSPCA minute book, 13 Feb 1905, 356), and who occupied the post from 1905 to 1908. It was an unfortunate lapse on Colam's part, for the society, after growing only slowly in the 1850s and being plagued by public disputes, had made remarkable advances from the 1860s onwards, and for these Colam deserves much of the credit. During his time as secretary the society's annual income rose fortyfold, and the number of its prosecutions fourteenfold. He is a voluntarist equivalent of the unobtrusively effective professional civil servant who was concurrently advancing in the public sphere. Whatever may have happened at the end of his career, Colam's influence as exemplar to other British and even overseas humanitarian bodies was considerable, and deserves acknowledgement.   BRIAN HARRISON

Sources H. S. Salt, *Seventy years among savages* (1921) · annual reports, executive committee minute books, Royal Society for the Prevention of Cruelty to Animals archive · Royal Society for the Prevention of Cruelty to Animals, *Animal World* (1 Sept 1900) · *The Times* (30 May 1910) · *Animal World* (July 1910), 136–7 · *Croydon Chronicle* (4 June 1910) · *Croydon Advertiser* (4 June 1910) · IGI
Archives Royal Society for the Prevention of Cruelty to Animals, Horsham, West Sussex, archive, executive committee minute books, annual reports
Wealth at death £15,580 5s. 11d.: administration with will, 5 July 1910, CGPLA Eng. & Wales

Colbatch, John (1665–1748), Church of England clergyman and university teacher, was the son of John Colbatch of Ludlow, Shropshire. He was educated at Westminster School, where he was made scholar in 1680, and at Trinity College, Cambridge, where he was admitted as a pensioner in 1683. He graduated BA (1687), MA (1690), BD (1701), and DD (1706). He became a fellow of his college in 1689 and was ordained priest in 1691. In 1693 he was appointed chaplain to the British factory at Lisbon, with a salary of £200 a year. At the request of Bishop Gilbert Burnet he wrote an *Account of the Court of Portugal* (1700), which attracted promises of preferment from Burnet and from Queen Mary, and which was quickly translated into French. In 1700 he returned to England to prepare Burnet's eldest son for Trinity College, at a salary of £40. In 1701, on the recommendation of Richard Bentley, Colbatch was appointed tutor to Lord Hertford, eldest son of the duke of Somerset, chancellor of Cambridge University. In 1703 Colbatch was persuaded by the duke to travel for a further two years with his pupil on the continent, at a salary of £100. But at the end of the tour the duke quarrelled with Colbatch and dismissed him from his post, refusing to pay his expenses. The duke was persuaded by Bentley to retract his slurs on Colbatch but he refused to pay additional salary or to fulfil his promises of preferment. Through Burnet's patronage Colbatch held the prebend of Yatminster, at Salisbury, worth just £20, from 1702 to 1720. In 1705 he returned to Cambridge, at the age of forty, impoverished and disappointed. From 1707 to 1748 he was professor of moral philosophy and his lectures brought him a great reputation; they represented the heyday of the professorship, which by 1769 held no duties. He formed friendships with many scholars, including Daniel Waterland, Ralph Thoresby, and William Whiston. He was also a donor of books to Edward Harley's collection.

Colbatch's residence at Trinity involved him in the feud between Richard Bentley and the fellows of the college. Initially Colbatch was a counsellor of moderation, and he published a pamphlet in defence of Bentley's contention that a BD or DD gave an MA seniority within the fellowship. He also refused to join Miller's attack on Bentley, and in 1717 he preached a sermon in the college, appealing to the religious feelings of his colleagues. He found it increasingly difficult to remain neutral in the quarrel, however. While in 1714 he refused Bentley's offer of the vice-mastership because of his lack of seniority, it sparked a long contest with him. Colbatch led the fellows in their

efforts to persuade Bishop Fleetwood to prosecute Bentley. In 1719 Colbatch petitioned Archbishop Wake, Lord Sunderland, and Lord Parker and persuaded them to bring the fellows' action against Bentley before the privy council. In 1720 Colbatch sought nomination to the college living of Orwell, and Bentley hoped to force him to surrender his fellowship. But Colbatch 'fairly threw Bentley on his back' (Monk, 2.98) and won the dispute when the fellows supported his claim.

In 1720 Bentley published a pamphlet attacking Colbatch, to whom he erroneously attributed an attack upon his proposals for a new edition of the Greek Testament. Colbatch endeavoured to get damages in the courts for this libel but it was litigation that lasted for more than a decade and was said to have cost Colbatch over £1000. In 1722 he issued a tract entitled *Jus academicum*, which attacked the failure of the vice-chancellor's court to bring Bentley to justice and sought the authority of the court of the king's bench over the university. In response Bentley brought an action against Colbatch in 1723. The judge imagined that Colbatch's attacks on Bentley were aspersions upon the king's bench and, owing partly to his own want of tact at the trial, Colbatch was fined £50 and imprisoned for a week. In 1727 Bentley generously presented him with the old college clock for his church at Orwell. But Colbatch had committed himself to the battle. In 1727 he wrote to Bishop Gibson of London, denouncing the unfitness of a candidate for orders, and in doing so drew his attention to the state of Trinity College. In 1729 he published a tract entitled *A defence of the lord bishop of Ely's visitatorial jurisdiction over Trinity College in general, and over the master thereof in particular*. In 1738 his fifteen-year refusal to pay Bentley, who was also archdeacon of Ely, his fees for the living of Orwell led to a prosecution. Colbatch was defeated in the courts but denounced Bentley for failing to visit his archdeaconry, in *The Case of Proxies Payable to Ecclesiastical Visitors*.

Colbatch died in Cambridge on 11 February 1748. He left £30 a year to a charity school at Orwell, and during his lifetime had been a considerable benefactor to the church.

WILLIAM GIBSON

Sources Venn, *Alum. Cant.* · T. E. S. Clarke and H. C. Foxcroft, *A life of Gilbert Burnet, bishop of Salisbury* (1907) · *A supplement to Burnet's History of my own time*, ed. H. C. Foxcroft (1902) · G. Burnet, autobiography, Bodl. Oxf., MS Add. D. 24 · J. H. Monk, *The life of Richard Bentley, DD*, 2nd edn, 2 vols. (1833) · D. A. Winstanley, *Unreformed Cambridge: a study of certain aspects of the university in the eighteenth century* (1935) · *The diary of Humfrey Wanley, 1715–1726*, ed. C. E. Wright and R. C. Wright, 2 vols. (1966) · R. T. Holtby, *Daniel Waterland, 1683–1740: a study in eighteenth century orthodoxy* (1966) · *Fasti Angl.* (Hardy) · *DNB*
Archives BL, corresp., Add. MS 22908

Colbatch, Sir John (bap. 1666?, d. 1729), physician, was probably the son of William Colbatch baptized at St Swithin's, Worcester, on 1 August 1666. John Colbatch began as an apothecary's apprentice in Worcester, gradually rising to the rank of master in the Mercers' Company (to which the apothecaries belonged); he moved from Worcester to London some time in the early 1690s. By the autumn of 1693 Colbatch was beginning to be known for his proprietary Vulnery Powder and Tincture of the Sulphur of Venus, which he claimed to have found empirically through his own studies, chemical experiments, and other experiments on dogs and other animals. The first remedy he promoted as being able to stop bleeding quickly even in very bad wounds, the second as restoring wounded flesh. The London surgical establishment evinced sceptical interest, and a public trial of his medicines was carried out on a dog; as reported by William Cowper (*PTRS*, 18, 1694, 42–4), the experiment performed on the dog was successful, but the subsequent trial on two patients of St Bartholomew's Hospital failed. In response to Colbatch's counter-claim that his envious rivals were lying about the results on the humans, Charles Bernard arranged for yet another experiment on patients at St Bartholomew's, but again it failed: Colbatch explained that the associate of his who had been present had not been allowed to use his remedy properly. Early in 1694, with the help of a patron among the army officers, Colbatch was allowed to try his wound remedies on soldiers, claiming to have performed a hundred experiments with only five miscarrying, for which failures he blamed his opponents. He obtained a pass from the government in May 1694 to go to the summer campaign in Flanders. There Major-General Sir Henry Bellasis arranged for wounded men to be treated by Colbatch; despite continued harassment from the surgeons, only one of them died. Colbatch published *Novum lumen chirurgicum, or, A New Light of Chirurgery* (1695), a book about his successes, shortly after his return from campaign, and claimed to have survived a surgeon's attempt to poison him. The surgeons replied with a pamphlet of their own (W. W., *Novum lumen chirurgicum extinctum*, 1695), lambasting Colbatch and claiming his powder to be nothing more than dried 'Vitriol of Copper … which hath a small Mixture of Iron', and his tincture to be 'a Mixture of Oil of Vitriol, and Spirit of Wine'. Colbatch defended himself with yet another pamphlet (*Novum lumen chirurgicum vindicatum*, 1695), and by returning to Flanders in the summer of 1695, where he may even have gained the position of local surgeon-general during the siege of Namur.

Colbatch moved to gain further legitimacy in 1696 by selling off his secrets to his publisher, Daniel Brown, who made and marketed the medicines. During the summer he began the process of gaining the licence of the Royal College of Physicians, and on 14 and 23 August, and 11 September 1696, he underwent the formal examinations in physiology, pathology, and therapeutics. He was admitted as a licentiate on 22 December 1696. Colbatch now sought to publish books setting out a rationale for why his medicines worked. His *Physico-Medical Essay Concerning Alkaly and Acid* (1696), and *Some Farther Considerations Concerning Alkaly and Acid* (1696), explained physiology and therapeutics in the light of the doctrine of acids and alkalis, which was more widely accepted on the continent than in England. But Colbatch's views, in arguing that acids rather than alkalis cured disease, were even more unorthodox, placing him among the few other advocates of acids, such as Edward Baynard and William Cole. He presented his claims in the language of the new and experimental philosophy, praising Robert Boyle especially, and argued for the usefulness of 'ocular demonstrations' over university learning. In elaborating this doctrine in a book on gout, and in writing of the blindness of orthodox medical opinion, he came under censure from the physicians. Samuel Garth's mock-epic poem, the *Dispensary* (May 1699), mentioned Colbatch as a target of abuse. But Colbatch, who apparently enjoyed the patronage of at least one person of influence, brushed aside these assaults and continued to produce more books. Colbatch's publisher, Brown, brought out collections and editions of Colbatch's works in response to the publicity.

In the end Colbatch gained a social reputation as a good physician, and published only a few books more. In his *Dissertation Concerning Misletoe* (1719) he not only mentions the continued friendship of Dr Cole, and his own continued preference for the theory of acids, but describes himself as driving through the countryside in a carriage, thereby letting it be known that he had become well-to-do. Colbatch received a knighthood from George I on 26 June 1716. During the threatened plague epidemic of 1720–21, Colbatch submitted an unexceptional scheme for its prevention to the king and parliament. In 1723 he could afford to give £50 to his manservant to set him up in business. Colbatch died on 15 January 1729. His will, witnessed by Sir Philip Boteler and Elizabeth Boteler of Teston, Kent, was probated in mid-March; he left all his estate to his wife, Elizabeth. After his death a manual of family medicine was published under his name.   HAROLD J. COOK

Sources annals, RCP Lond. · BL, Sloane MS 1783, fols. 80–81 · H. J. Cook, 'Sir John Colbatch and Augustan medicine: experimentalism, character and entrepreneurialism', *Annals of Science*, 47 (1990), 475–505 · PRO, PROB 11/628/67, fols. 162–3 · IGI

Colbeck, William (1871–1930), Antarctic explorer, was born at 8 Myton Place, Hull, on 8 August 1871, the second son and second child in the family of three sons and three daughters of Christopher Colbeck, baker, and his wife, Martha Ann Haggitt. He followed a seagoing career against his father's wishes, apparently influenced by the maritime traditions of his mother's family, and after attending Hull grammar school was apprenticed from 1886 to 1890 aboard the square-rigger *Loch Torridon*, sailing between Britain and Calcutta. He passed his master's ticket in 1894 with the aid of private tuition from Zebedee Scaping, headmaster of the Hull Trinity House Navigation School.

In 1894 Colbeck joined the Wilson Line in Hull as second mate of the SS *Draco* and three years later a chance meeting with the Norwegian explorer Borchgrevink, a passenger in his vessel, the *Montebello*, led to Colbeck joining the *Southern Cross* expedition (1898–1900) as magnetic observer, following an intensive course of instruction at Kew observatory. The party was the first to winter in Antarctica. With Ole Larsen, a Finn, Colbeck reached the furthest south (78° 50′) thus far achieved and made the first accurate map of the Ross ice shelf. These explorations convinced him of the best route to the south pole, later followed by Roald Amundsen, who in 1912 after his triumph sent Colbeck a letter of thanks. Friction between the Royal Geographical Society and Borchgrevink prevented their efforts from receiving due recognition, though Colbeck received the Murchison grant from the society. However, he impressed Sir Clements Markham, who selected him to command the SY *Morning* (formerly the Norwegian whaler *Morgen*), sent in 1902 to the relief of the *Discovery* expedition of Robert Falcon Scott. The crew consisted of Wilson Line men and hand-picked officers, including E. R. G. R. Evans as second mate.

In December 1902 new land was discovered which Colbeck called Scott Island and its prominent feature, a stone column, Haggitt's Pillar, was given his mother's maiden name. *Discovery* was found, ice-bound, on Christmas day. Unable to penetrate this obstacle Colbeck left 14 tons of provisions and 20 tons of coal for the marooned expedition. Leaving Hobart in December 1903 the *Morning* (now transferred to the command of the Admiralty) and *Terra Nova* reached *Discovery* early the next year and she was blasted free from the enclosing ice. Outstripped by the *Discovery*, the *Morning* reached Plymouth too late for the welcome celebrations but arriving back in Hull on 9 October Colbeck and ten of his crew were mobbed at Paragon station. In appreciation of his efforts he received a magnificent loving cup from the Royal Geographical Society, engraved with the course of the *Morning*, and was also given the Back grant. Scott named Cape Colbeck and Colbeck Bay after him. Colbeck remained as master in the Wilson Line until 1912, when he was appointed marine superintendent in the London office. He received the Polar medal in 1914 and in 1926 was a founder member of the Honourable Company of Master Mariners.

On 7 December 1904 Colbeck married Edith, daughter of John Robinson, a cotton manufacturer. They had four sons, the eldest of whom, Captain W. R. Colbeck RNR, was surveyor with the British, Australian, and New Zealand Antarctic research expedition of 1929–31, for which he received the Polar medal; Sir Douglas Mawson named the Colbeck archipelago after him. Colbeck died at his home, 51 Inchmery Road, Catford, London, on 18 October 1930, his exertions in the Antarctic having taken a considerable toll. He was buried at Hither Green, Lewisham.

ARTHUR G. CREDLAND

Sources private information (1993) [C. Markham Colbeck, son] · A. G. E. Jones, 'Captain William Colbeck', *Fram*, 1/1 (winter 1984), 177–85 · L. B. Quatermain, *Antarctica's forgotten men* (1981), 63–84 · G. S. Doorly, *The voyages of the Morning* (1916) · *The Times* (20 Oct 1930) · *The Times* (23 Oct 1930) · *The Times* (28 Nov 1930) · *Hull News* (1 Oct 1904) · A. Savours, *The voyages of the Discovery* (1992) · *GJ*, 76 (1930), 570–71 · J. Crawford, *That first Antarctic winter* (1998) · *CGPLA Eng. & Wales* (1930) · C. E. Borchgrevink, *First on the Antarctic continent* (1901) · b. cert. · m. cert.
Archives Canterbury Museum, New Zealand, collection · Norsk Polarinstitutt, Oslo, log kept on *Southern Cross* expedition · PRO, Antarctic relief expedition, Adm. 116/944 Case 310 · RGS, report, 16/1/1 · Scott Polar RI, log of the *Morning*, MS 366/9
Likenesses photograph, Scott Polar RI · photographs, Hull Maritime Museum
Wealth at death £6754 16s. 1d.: probate, 22 Nov 1930, *CGPLA Eng. & Wales*

Colborne, Sir Francis (1817–1895). *See under* Colborne, John, first Baron Seaton (1778–1863).

Colborne, John, first Baron Seaton (1778–1863), army officer and colonial governor, younger child of Samuel Colborne (d. 1785), a landowner of Lyndhurst, Hampshire, and his wife, Cordelia Ann (d. 1791), only daughter of John Garstin of Leragh Castle and Ballykerrin, co. Westmeath, was born at Lyndhurst on 16 February 1778. His father had lost money through unsuccessful speculations and left his widow and two children in straitened circumstances. Having been educated at Christ's Hospital, London (1785–9), and Winchester College (1789–94), where he took part in the great school rebellion of 1793, Colborne entered the army as an ensign in the 20th foot on 10 July 1794 by the interest of the earl of Warwick, and was to gain all subsequent rank without purchase. He served in the Helder campaign (1799) and, following his promotion to captain (January 1800), on the Belle Île expedition and in Minorca, Egypt, Malta, and Sicily. After distinguishing himself at Maida (4 July 1806) he was appointed military secretary to General the Hon. Henry Edward Fox, and later to General Sir John Moore.

The Peninsula War Gazetted major in January 1808, Colborne accompanied Moore to Sweden and Portugal, and was with him on the retreat to Corunna; in accordance with Moore's dying wish he was promoted lieutenant-colonel (5th garrison battalion) in February 1809. Colborne returned to the Peninsula in August, and spent some months liaising with the Spanish army of La Mancha; he witnessed its defeat by Soult at Ocaña (19 November), before assuming command of the 2nd battalion of the 66th foot. He was present at Busaco in temporary command of a brigade, and in the autumn of 1810 was appointed to the arduous charge of the advance guard at Alhambra outside the lines of Torres Vedras. In the following March he took part in the recovery of Campo Mayor and was then employed on detached duty, commanding a brigade of the 2nd division, in disrupting French communications south-east of Badajoz. He joined Beresford at Albuera, where, on 16 May his brigade, its visibility obscured by a hailstorm, was badly mauled by French lancers and chasseurs.

In July 1811 Colborne exchanged into the élite 52nd regiment, forming part of the famous light division, and at the siege of Ciudad Rodrigo he commanded the assault (8 January 1812) on Fort San Francisco and was wounded in the right shoulder and arm during the storming of the city (19/20 January). Partially disabled in his right arm, Colborne was invalided home. He married on 21 June 1814 Elizabeth (d. 28 November 1872, aged eighty-two), eldest daughter of the Revd James Yonge of Puslinch, Devon, rector of Newton Ferrers, Devon. Called 'the beauty of Devonshire' (Moore Smith, *Life of John Colborne*, 125) and by her niece Charlotte M. Yonge 'the brightest, most playful and lively of creatures' (ibid., 253), she was charming and gracious and a devout Anglican.

Colborne rejoined Wellington's army in July 1813. Taking temporary command of the 2nd brigade of the light

John Colborne, first Baron Seaton (1778–1863), by Jan Willem Pieneman, 1821

division, he led the attack at the storming of the pass of Vera (7 October) and commanded it at the battles of the Nivelle (10 November)—when Colborne, though his own force was outnumbered, bluffed the strong French garrison of the Star Redoubt to surrender—and the Nive (9–12 December). He returned to the 52nd and handled it brilliantly at the battle of Orthez in the following February and afterwards at the siege of Toulouse. With the coming of peace Colborne was promoted brevet colonel and aide-de-camp to the prince regent, receiving at the same time the peninsular gold cross with three clasps and, on 2 January 1815, following the reconstitution of the Order of the Bath, being appointed KCB.

Waterloo and after Colborne was appointed military secretary to the prince of Orange, then commanding the British forces in the Netherlands, and on Bonaparte's escape from Elba he resumed command of the 52nd, brigaded with the 71st and the 2nd battalion of the 95th under Sir Frederick Adam in the division of Sir Henry Clinton. At Waterloo the brigade was initially posted on the extreme right of the allied position, before advancing to the right centre of the front line soon after 3 p.m. Although the brigade was only partially protected by the lie of the ground from the unremitting French cannonade, thanks to Colborne's skilful handling of his regiment casualties were comparatively light. As the crisis of the battle approached (about 6.30 p.m.) the 52nd and 71st fell back to the crossroad on the ridge to the immediate left of Hougoumont. In the melée that ensued as the imperial guard attacked the English centre Colborne, anticipating

Wellington's orders, threw his regiment forward, wheeled it to the left of an advancing column to the west, fired volley after devastating volley into its flank, and drove it back in disorder. Although he deserved every credit for this bold initiative, it is absurd to speak of it as having assured a decisive victory. And while no slight was intended, the omission of Colborne's name from Wellington's Waterloo dispatch gave rise to a controversy which he correctly refused to enter.

Colborne remained with his regiment in Paris as part of the army of occupation until January 1816, when he obtained leave of absence. After an extensive tour through Europe he rejoined the 52nd in May 1818, being employed in garrison duty largely in the northern command to deal with the threat of disturbances in the manufacturing areas. In July 1821 he was appointed lieutenant-governor of Guernsey, the first of several civil postings in which he was to serve with distinction. A devout Anglican, of spartan habits and studious disposition, blue-eyed and curly-haired, tall and spare of person, he was very much the beau idéal of a soldier; contemporaries frequently remarked his striking similarity to the duke of Wellington in his simplicity of manner, integrity, and devotion to duty. Yet there the resemblance ended. He once described himself as a reasonable conservative, anxious to preserve institutions worth maintaining, but fully alive to the necessity of reforming those that were not (Moore Smith, *Life of John Colborne*, 341); and his administrative career revealed him as anything but a tory in the mould of his old commander. In Guernsey he was instrumental in restoring confidence in government by improving communications, agriculture, public works, and education. He reformed the decayed Elizabeth College (founded 1563), which reopened in 1824. Having been promoted major-general in May 1825, Colborne was offered the military secretaryship under a proposed reorganization of the War Office in July 1827. That project failing in consequence of Canning's death, Colborne was gazetted lieutenant-governor of Upper Canada in August 1828. Earlier he had refused the governorship of Trinidad.

Governor of Upper Canada, 1828–1836 Colborne arrived at York (Toronto) shortly after an election which had returned a sizeable 'reforming' majority to the provincial assembly, and in the wake of the publication of the proceedings of a parliamentary select committee (*Parl. papers*, 1828, 7.569) animadverting on administrative arrangements. While regarding the crude parochialism of local politics and the frequently unconstitutional proceedings of the assembly with distaste, his administration was conspicuous for its tact and conciliation, and strict impartiality towards the amorphous groups that constituted political life in the colony. Although, in what was still virtually a backwoods settlement, the province was unready for responsible government, he effected changes in the composition of the legislative council and was sparing in his use of patronage; in conjunction with the Colonial Office, steps were taken towards a greater fiscal autonomy and to render the judiciary more independent. Determined to promote English influence in a dependency which had been overly exposed to American settlement, he encouraged immigration from the United Kingdom and spared no effort or expense to ensure its success; and during his administration the population of the province increased by some 70 per cent. His Indian policy, in his efforts to persuade the tribes to come to terms with European settlement through education and agriculture, was distinguished by humanity and enlightenment. Elsewhere he initiated extensive public works, extended communications and education, and in 1830 instituted Upper Canada College. Despite his dislike of sectaries his attitude towards religious problems was generally pragmatic and clear-headed, though his policy in regard to the clergy reserves and the endowment of Anglican rectories was censured. An outstanding governor, Colborne had the misfortune to administer Upper Canada at a time of intense political animosities, exacerbated by the poisonous nature of the provincial press and colonial demagogues, most notably William Lyon Mackenzie who poured forth a constant stream of vituperation. His overt and prescient contempt for this vociferous, if unrepresentative, minority was to prove his undoing. On a visit to London in 1832 Mackenzie had acquired a fortuitous and wholly undeserved reputation in official circles as the mouthpiece of colonial opinion, and on Mackenzie's persuading a half-empty chamber to accept his *Seventh Report on Grievances* in April 1835, the new secretary of state, Lord Glenelg, reacted with alarm. Colborne was severely rebuked for the infrequency and meagreness of his public dispatches, his full and dispassionate analysis of events in his private correspondence with the Colonial Office being dismissed as partisan statements. Stung, he forestalled recall by resigning in high dudgeon.

Commander-in-chief, Canada, 1836–1839 Amid widespread regret Colborne left the province in January 1836, and was on the point of returning to England when he was offered the command of the forces in the Canadas. Accepting with reluctance, he moved to Montreal. He arrived at a critical juncture in the affairs of Lower Canada, where the long-running fiscal dispute between the French-dominated assembly and the executive had made government all but impossible. This volatile situation, aggravated by widespread economic distress, was scarcely eased by the announcement of coercive measures by the imperial government in April 1837, and Colborne began preparing to meet a possible uprising. When the highly localized outbreak did come, in mid-November, martial law was declared and he quickly isolated the insurgent areas and personally led 2000 regulars and volunteers against the rebel centres at St Eustache and St Benoît. Within barely a month the Lower Canadian 'rebellion' was over, and on the resignation of the governor-in-chief, Lord Gosford, Colborne assumed the administration of the government. With the arrival of Lord Durham as high commissioner to enquire into the affairs of the Canadas in May 1838, Colborne, though anxious to resign his command, was persuaded to remain at Glenelg's urgent insistence. Possessing little confidence in the home government and uneasy about the administrative innovations,

particularly the union of the two Canadas, proposed by Durham and his numerous suite, he meantime prepared to meet a further recrudescence of violence in the province. Viewing Durham's hasty resignation and departure (1 November) with evident relief, because it avoided possible friction between the civil and military commands, he moved swiftly to deal with the further insurrection. By 17 November the small groups of rebels in various locations had been dispersed and order restored, though the behaviour of some of his irregular forces was to earn him the name 'le Vieux Brulôt', and, after his elevation to the peerage, 'Baron Saton'. Gazetted governor-in-chief of British North America on 12 December, Colborne now eschewed the mildness with which he had dealt with the previous outbreak and determined, for the future peace of Lower Canada, that the rule of law had to be vindicated. Following a series of courts martial, twelve rebels were hanged and fifty-eight transported to the Australian colonies. Damned by 'loyalists' for his leniency and execrated by 'Patriotes' for his bloodthirsty tyranny (Moore Smith, *Life of John Colborne*, 307), he nevertheless hoped that a period of firm, but enlightened, administration would restore tranquillity and some much-needed realism to the political affairs of the Canadas. Yet such was not to be under his dispensation: with an astonishing insouciance, Melbourne's government now proposed to send out yet another whig civilian as governor-in-chief, but in the hope that Colborne would consent to remain commander-in-chief. Not surprisingly he reacted with indignation and refused to countenance the proposal. Having already been made GCH (October 1836) and promoted lieutenant-general (June 1838), he was invested GCB a few days before he left Montreal, on 23 October, after the arrival of his successor, Charles Poulett Thomson (afterwards Lord Sydenham).

The Ionian Islands, 1843–1849 On his arrival in England Colborne was raised to the peerage (14 December 1839) as Baron Seaton, with a pension of £2000 for three lives for his services, an honour generously made at the instance of Lord Melbourne, with whose administration he had so often been at odds. Rumours of an Irish command coming to nothing, he remained unemployed until January 1843 when he was offered, and eagerly accepted, the long-sought position of lord high commissioner of the Ionian Islands (GCMG, July). He arrived in April, following the enforced resignation of J. A. Stewart Mackenzie, and found the political and administrative affairs of the protectorate in some disarray. His predecessor, of whom much had been expected by proponents of liberalization, had not displayed any marked administrative talents and had been little trusted by the Colonial Office, while his acerbity of manner had antagonized many prominent Ionians. Initially unwilling to propose constitutional concessions Seaton, much impressed by the justice of Ionian demands, as also by the 'revolution' in Greece in the autumn of 1843, began preparing the ground for such concessions by cultivating the liberal intelligentsia in Corfu and associating the people more closely with the administration. Municipal authorities were encouraged and granted greater responsibility, the reform of the judiciary and the police establishment was extended, and the press laws were relaxed; and at a time of increasing economic prosperity he embarked on extensive projects of social amelioration and public works. Meantime he used his powers to promote his views: liberal politicians were advanced in both senate and assembly, and senior administrative positions hitherto held by Englishmen were thrown open to Ionians. He then, in a series of breathless dispatches between January and July 1848, advocated the freedom of the press, financial autonomy, and free elections to both the municipalities and assembly; in January of the following year he proposed an extension of the franchise, and in May the introduction of the secret ballot. Earl Grey, the secretary of state, then in the process of furthering colonial self-government throughout the empire, was generally sympathetic, though informed opinion within the Colonial Office, already alarmed at Colborne's taste for deficit financing and distrustful of his impulsiveness and assumption of Ionian willingness to actually work his reforms, was more cautious. As it was, a revolt in Cephalonia in September 1848 notwithstanding, his projects were blithely adopted in principle, but left to his successor, Sir Henry Ward, to implement (June 1849) (cf. *Parl. papers*, 1850, 36, 1276). When it became apparent that reform, far from proving a panacea for legitimate grievances, had provided Ionians with the means for loudly expressing discontent and agitation for union with Greece, Colborne's proceedings were attacked (most notably, and with considerable personal animus, by G. F. Bowen, in *The Ionian Islands under British Protection*, 1851, and *Quarterly Review*, 91, 1852, 315–52). Warmly defended by Ionian supporters (for example George Dracatos Papanicolas (d. 1862), in *The Ionian Islands: what they have Lost and Suffered*, 1851, and Antonios Dandolo (1783–1872), in *Des Îles Joniennes*, 1851), he published his own *Apologia* (*Edinburgh Review*, 97, 1853, 41–86).

Later career Although in his seventies and suffering from intermittent ill health, Colborne, long associated with the peacetime reform of the armed forces (for example 'Our defensive armament', *Edinburgh Review*, 96, 1852), and combining immense practical experience, an open mind, and a thorough theoretical knowledge, made an ideal choice for the command of the experimental manoeuvres at Chobham camp in June–August 1853. Promoted general in June 1854—age and infirmity precluded his appointment as Lord Raglan's successor in the Crimea and as commander-in-chief following the resignation of his friend, Lord Hardinge—he was still sufficiently robust to accept the command of the forces in Ireland in January 1855. There, at a time of relative tranquillity, he occupied himself with the reform of the Royal Hospital at Kilmainham, in training the regular troops and militia, and instituting a series of annual reviews at Curragh. His term of office having expired in March 1860, he was raised to the rank of field marshal in April and appointed an Irish privy councillor. Having purchased the house and grounds of Beechwood, by Sparkwell in Devon in 1856, Seaton spent his remaining years in improving his estate and promoting the welfare of the parish. Still consulted by government ministers—Colborne advised Sir George Cornewall Lewis on the defence of Canada when aged eighty-three in December 1861—he was gazetted colonel of the rifle brigade in February 1862, in succession to the prince consort at the express wish of the queen (having previously been colonel of the 94th foot, December 1834; 26th foot, March 1839; 2nd Life Guards, and bearer of the gold stick, March 1854). Following a lengthy illness he died at Valetta House, Torquay, Devon, on 17 April 1863, and was buried in the churchyard of Newton Ferrers on 24 April. He was succeeded by his eldest son, James (1815–1888), army officer.

Character and assessment Seaton was a man of many parts and wide sympathies, a Christian gentleman, and an inspiration and example to those with whom he served. 'J'ai grande confiance dans Colborne', said General Alava:

> officier du premier ordre, tres aimé tant de Sir J. Moore comme du Duc de Wellington, et quel bel éloge! Il est non seulement excellent militaire, mais qualifié pour tout espèce de commandement, et d'une moralité et probité dignes d'autres temps.

He was a soldier of singular abilities and a colonial governor of note, a man whose influence was decisive in the Canadas and whose Ionian administration determined, for good or ill, the ultimate fate of the protectorate; John Colborne, Field Marshal Lord Seaton, was, in fine, a most distinguished man in a most distinguished age.

In addition to his many English honours Colborne was appointed to the order of the Tower and the Sword of Portugal in March 1813, and was made knight of the Habsburg order of Maria Theresia and the Russian order of St George in August 1815. A bronze statue, by George Adams, raised by public subscription, was unveiled at Mount Wise, Devonport (November 1866), a cairn having already been erected in 1844 by the Glengarry Highlanders on an island in Lake St Francis, Ontario, with the inscription 'To the Saviour of Canada'.

Sir Francis Colborne (1817–1895), army officer, Colborne's second son, was born at Florence on 23 April 1817. He was educated at Elizabeth College, Guernsey (1824–9), became an infantry officer (ensign 15th foot, October 1836), served in the Crimea, commanded the troops at Hong Kong (1874–8), commanded the Perak expedition (1875–6), was promoted general in April 1882, and retired in April 1883 (CB July 1855, KCB March 1876). He died unmarried at Hembury fort, Buckerell, near Honiton, on 26 November 1895.

John Colborne (1830–1890), army officer, Colborne's fifth son, was educated at Eton College, became an infantry officer (ensign 30th foot, August 1848), served in the Crimea, and sold out in June 1872. He became a colonel in the Egyptian army, served on Hicks Pasha's staff in the Sudan in 1883, published *With Hicks Pasha in the Soudan* (1884), and died unmarried at Cairo on 13 February 1890.

A. A. D. SEYMOUR

Sources G. C. Moore Smith, *The life of John Colborne, Field-Marshal Lord Seaton* (1903) • G. C. Moore Smith, ed., 'Letters from Colonel William Napier to Sir John Colborne, chiefly in connexion with his

History of the war in the Peninsula', EngHR, 18 (1903), 725–53 · W. C. Yonge, *Memoir of Lord Seaton's services* (1853) · W. Leeke, *The history of Lord Seaton's regiment at the battle of Waterloo* (1866) [suppl. 1871] · [C. M. Yonge], 'Lord Seaton and his regiment', *Christian Remembrancer*, new ser., 54 (1867), 239–85 · W. S. Moorsom, ed., *Historical record of the fifty-second regiment (Oxfordshire light infantry), from the year 1755 to the year 1858* (1860) · E. A. Carey, ed., *Actes des États de l'île de Guernsey*, iv and v (1925–32) · *Addresses, presented to His Excellency Major General Sir John Colborne, Lieutenant-Governor of Upper Canada, on the occasion of his leaving the province* (1836) · D. B. Read, *The lieutenant-governors of Upper Canada and Ontario, 1792–1899* (1900) · M. Francis, *Governors and settlers: images of authority in the British colonies, 1820–60* (1992) · F. Ouellet, *Lower Canada, 1791–1840: social changes and nationalism*, ed. and trans. P. Claxon (Toronto, 1980) · J. J. Tumelty and A. A. D. Seymour, *The British protectorate of the Ionian Islands, 1815–1864* [forthcoming] · H. Strachan, *Wellington's legacy: the reform of the British army, 1830–54* (1984) · *The Times* (18 April 1863) · *The Times* (2 May 1863) · *Annual Register* (1863) · GEC, *Peerage* · Burke, *Peerage* (1924) · *CGPLA Eng. & Wales* (1863) · Boase, *Mod. Eng. biog.*

Archives NRA, priv. coll., corresp. and papers | BL, letters to Sir Henry Bunbury and others · Lpool RO, letters to fourteenth earl of Derby · NA Canada, corresp. with Lord Durham · NL Wales, Harpton Court MSS, corresp. with Sir George Cornewall Lewis concerning the Ionian Islands and imperial defence · NMM, Parker MSS, letters to Sir William Parker · PRO, Colonial Office MSS, dispatches, private letters, and memoranda in CO 42, 136 · PRO NIre., letters to Lord Gosford · W. Sussex RO, letters to Lord Edmund Lyons

Likenesses miniature, 1813, repro. in Smith, *Life of John Colborne*, facing p. 196 · J. W. Pieneman, oils, 1821, Wellington Museum, Apsley House, London [*see illus.*] · portrait, *c.*1840, NA Canada · G. Richmond, drawing, *c.*1852, repro. in Smith, *Life of John Colborne*, facing p. 364 · G. Richmond, sketch, 1853, repro. in Smith, *Life of John Colborne*, facing p. 352 · W. J. Edwards, stipple, pubd 1855 (after C. Richmond), BM · G. Jones, oils, 1860–63, NPG · W. Fisher, oils, 1861; formerly at United Service Club, London · G. Adams, marble bust, 1863; formerly at United Service Club, London · W. J. Edwards, stipple, pubd 1866, NPG · medallion, Winchester School Museum · oils, Regimental Museum of the Oxford and Berkshire Light Infantry, Oxford · plaster cast (after bust by G. Adams, 1863), NPG · portrait (as a child), repro. in Smith, *Life of John Colborne*, facing p. 2

Wealth at death £5000: probate, 23 July 1863, *CGPLA Eng. & Wales*

Colborne, John (1830–1890). *See under* Colborne, John, first Baron Seaton (1778–1863).

Colburn, Henry (*d.* 1855), publisher, began his career as an assistant in the circulating library of William Earle, a bookseller at 47 Albemarle Street, London. Colburn's origins are uncertain; rumour had it that he was an illegitimate son of 'old Lord Lansdowne' (Hall, 1.316) or of the duke of York (W. C. Hazlitt, *Four Generations of a Literary Family*, 2 vols., 1897, 1.168). An input of capital by a secret sponsor would help explain his establishment, probably in 1806, as the proprietor of the English and Foreign Circulating Library at 48–50 Conduit Street, off New Bond Street, London, from where his publishing operations shortly began. Between 1807 and 1815 Colburn published more than 100 works, of which almost half were of French origin or on French topics, a common procedure being the co-publishing of French and English versions. Fiction at this time represented virtually half his output, much of it in translation, with the other main components being memoirs and travel literature. From 1810 lists feature

more works by indigenous novelists, notable titles including Charles Robert Maturin's *The Milesian Chief* (1812), commissioned for £80, Eaton Stannard Barrett's *The Heroine* (1813), a parody of the Gothic, and Lady Caroline Lamb's *Glenarvon* (1816), with scandalous matter relating to Lord Byron. Colburn's first 'big-name' author, however, was Sydney, Lady Morgan, to whom he paid £550 for the copyright of *O'Donnel: a National Tale* (1814), which sold rapidly. The same author's *France* (1817), for which Colburn offered £1000, was well calculated to satisfy public interest in the wake of the Napoleonic war, and subsequent high payments helped retain Lady Morgan's services well into the next decade.

In 1814 Colburn joined Frederic Shoberl to found the *New Monthly Magazine and Universal Register*, originally projected as a counter to the alleged Jacobin tendencies of Richard Phillips's *Monthly Magazine*. Among its early editors were Dr John Watkins and Alaric Watts. A new series was begun on 1 January 1821, as the *New Monthly Magazine and Literary Journal*, under the editorship of Thomas Campbell, the poet, whose contract stipulated a salary of £500, though much of the practical work was carried out by Cyrus Redding, who resigned shortly before Campbell himself late in 1830. With the journal's literary and critical emphasis now established, other high-profile editors brought in were Edward Bulwer-Lytton (1831–3), Theodore Hook (1837–41), and Thomas Hood (1841–3), though ultimate control over the magazine rested with Colburn and his closest associates. The proprietorship was eventually sold to William Harrison Ainsworth in 1845 for £2500. In 1817 Colburn also set up the *Literary Gazette*, an innovatory weekly literary review, which enjoyed a rapid success. After six months a third share was bought by William Jerdan, who became editor, and another third was taken by the publishers Longmans. Colburn's barely disguised manipulation of these journals, and others, for his own purposes soon helped gain him an adverse reputation for 'puffing' his own books. When Jerdan proved resistant, Colburn's response was to purchase a half-share in *The Athenaeum*, which gingerly acknowledged his involvement in its first issue in 1828. Other Colburn journals included the satirical *John Bull* (founded in 1820) and the *Court Journal* and *United Service Journal*, both from 1829.

Colburn disposed of his circulating library to Saunders and Otley in 1824, moving to New Burlington Street, from where he concentrated on his publishing activities. His pioneering issue of *Memoirs of John Evelyn* (1818) was followed in 1825 by a similar publication based on the newly deciphered diary of Samuel Pepys. Colburn was also the publisher of Burke's *Peerage* and its various issues from 1826. Most common among his expanding lists between 1825 and 1829, however, were works of fiction. Colburn deliberately cultivated authors of social note, especially those claiming aristocratic credentials. Theodore Hook was initially offered £600 for his novel *Sayings and Doings* (1824), the success of which led to a bonus of £350 and two further series (1825, 1828). At the time of the financial 'crash' in the book trade of 1826, Colburn unlike most rivals continued to expand, more than doubling his output of fiction in that year. During the later 1820s works issued from New Burlington Street set the mould for several new modes. Three new-style fashionable novels—Robert Plumer Ward's *Tremaine* (1825), *Matilda* (1825) by Constantine Henry Phipps, later marquess of Normanby, and Thomas Henry Lister's *Granby* (1826)—triggered a craze for 'silver fork' fiction, which also involved female authors published by Colburn, such as Lady Charlotte Bury. Other modes developed through Colburn were the military-nautical novel, with titles such as Frederick Marryat's *The Naval Officer* (1829), and a new brand of historical fiction by authors such as Horace Smith and G. P. R. James. Colburn published nearly half the total of new novels bearing 1829 imprints, the large majority being in three volumes and set at the premium price of 31*s.* 6*d.*

In September 1829 Colburn entered into partnership with Richard *Bentley (1794–1871), the printer, the terms of the agreement stating that Colburn should receive three-fifths of profits, with Bentley undertaking the day-to-day running of the concern. One noteworthy product of the enterprise was the series Colburn and Bentley's Standard Novels, which offered single-volume copies of recent fiction at 6*s.*, commencing with James Fenimore Cooper's *The Pilot* in February 1831. This inaugurated the later, Victorian, practice of following expensive first editions with cheap reprints, and the first nineteen monthly issues of the series carried Colburn's and Bentley's joint imprint until the breakdown of the partnership in 1832. In an atmosphere of financial confusion and personal distrust, Bentley agreed to pay £4000 for his release, with Colburn pledging not to publish new books himself within 20 miles of London. Colburn nevertheless proved congenitally unfitted for semi-retirement: his series Colburn's Modern Novelists, consisting of unsold sheets of earlier novels, was promoted as if new, and in 1835 he set up as a publisher from Windsor, just outside the statutory limit. By an agreement with Bentley in June 1836, Colburn paid £3500 to be released from his pledge, setting up at new premises in central London at Great Marlborough Street. Often vying directly with Bentley, he published in this later period novels by Benjamin Disraeli, Catherine Gore, and Frances Trollope, as well as some profitable non-fiction, such as Agnes and Elizabeth Strickland's *Lives of the Queens of England* (1840–48) and Eliot Warburton's travel book *The Crescent and the Cross* (1845).

Colburn's first marriage, reportedly to the keeper of a small circulating library near Oxford Street who later died through drink, remained obscure to contemporary observers. On 2 March 1841 he married Eliza Anne, only daughter of Captain Crosbie RN. They had no children. Colburn retired in 1853, handing over his business to Hurst and Blackett, though retaining some of his key copyrights, which were later (May 1857) auctioned for 'about £14,000' (*N&Q*, 2nd ser., 75.458–9). He died at his home at 14 Bryanston Square, London, on 16 August 1855, his wife surviving him.

Notwithstanding his invasiveness in the publishing world, no single clear image of Colburn has survived. Contemporary accounts mention his shortness in stature as well as his bustling manner and indecisiveness, though Bentley for one felt this last attribute was calculated. While his promotion methods brought protests from rival publishers, and provoked numerous satirical attacks, Colburn's practice anticipated aspects of modern high-pressure advertising. His output alone makes him one of the most significant publishers of his period, and his sponsorship of publications such as the Evelyn and Pepys diaries points to more than just a mercenary literary concern.

PETER GARSIDE

Sources *GM*, 2nd ser., 44 (1855), 547–8 · J. Sutherland, 'Henry Colburn, publisher', *Publishing History*, 19 (1986), 59–84 · M. W. Rosa, *The silver-fork school: novels of fashion preceding Vanity Fair* (1936), 178–206 · 'The *New Monthly Magazine*, 1821–1854', *Wellesley index*, 3.161–71 · M. Sadleir, *XIX fiction: a bibliographical record*, 2 vols. (1951), vol. 2, pp. 91–122 · R. A. Gettmann, *A Victorian publisher: a study of the Bentley papers* (1960) · H. Curwen, *A history of booksellers, the old and the new* (1873) · *Lady Morgan's memoirs*, 2 vols. (1862) · S. C. Hall, *Retrospect of a long life*, 2 vols. (1883), vol. 1, p. 316 · A. A. Watts, *Alaric Watts*, 2 vols. (1884), vol. 1 · *Life and letters of Thomas Campbell*, ed. W. Beattie, 2 (1849) · C. Redding, *Fifty years' recollections, literary and personal*, 2nd edn, 2 (1858) · m. cert. · d. cert.

Archives BL, letters and memorandum · Bodl. Oxf., letters and memoranda · Harvard U., letters and memoranda | BL, corresp. with Richard Bentley and papers relating to partnership, Add. MSS 46611–46614, 46632, Add. Ch. 74760–74763 · Herts. ALS, corresp. with E. B. Lytton · Suffolk RO, Ipswich, corresp. with Richard Cobbold · U. Cal., Richard Bentley papers · University of Illinois, Richard Bentley papers

Wealth at death 'sworn to be under £35,000': *GM*

Colby, Thomas Frederick (1784–1852), surveyor and army officer, was the eldest child of Major Thomas Colby (d. 1813), Royal Marines, and his wife, Cornelia Hadden, sister of Major-General John Murray Hadden, Royal Artillery, surveyor-general of the ordnance. He was born in the parish of St Margaret, Rochester, on 1 September 1784, brought up by his father's sisters at the family home, Rhos-y-gilwen, near Newcastle Emlyn, Carmarthenshire, and educated at school in Northfleet, Kent, and at the Royal Military Academy, Woolwich. At sixteen he was commissioned into the Royal Engineers, in which he was to serve for the rest of his life. As a cadet Colby attracted the notice of William Mudge, superintendent of the Ordnance Survey, who in 1802 asked that Colby be attached permanently to the survey. This granted, Mudge came increasingly to rely on Colby, whose work he admired and whom he found sympathetic.

Colby's first duties were to help Mudge measure an arc of the meridian between Dunnose, Isle of Wight, and Clifton, south Yorkshire. In December 1803, when on duty at Liskeard, Colby was badly wounded when an overloaded pistol accidentally went off. His left hand had to be amputated at the wrist, his face was very badly scarred, and fragments lodged in his skull. Helped by youth, the care of friends, and the surgeons' reluctance to attempt further operations, Colby recovered and was able to return to active duties. As was normal, he divided his time between fieldwork in the summer and computing results and superintending the construction and engraving of

Thomas Frederick Colby (1784–1852), by William Brockedon, 1837

maps in the Tower of London in the winter. He and Mudge published an account of their progress in *An Account of the Trigonometrical Survey ... 1800–1809* (1811). In July 1809 Mudge was appointed lieutenant-governor of the Woolwich Academy and Colby became chief executive officer of the survey.

From 1813 to 1817 Colby was engaged in extending the measurement of the meridional line between Dunnose and Clifton into Scotland, in combination with a geological survey under John McCulloch. Colby was helped by James Gardner, but carried out much work himself. Because of Mudge's ill health Colby took charge of a visit to Shetland by Jean-Baptiste Biot who had been deputed by the Bureau des Longitudes to make pendulum and other observations there in connection with the extension of the arc of the meridian from the Balearic Islands, through France, and thence through England to Shetland. However, Biot's and Colby's intense mutual dislike resulted in British observations being made on Balta and French on Unst; this defeated the political and scientific objectives of the enterprise which were to demonstrate Anglo-French co-operation and compare results obtained using the Ramsden zenith sector with those obtained using the French repeating circle. Colby, however, afterwards accompanied Mudge and his son to Dunkirk and took part in the observations made, in conjunction with Biot and J. F. D. Arago, with Ramsden's sector, which was set up in Dunkirk arsenal. Colby was again in Scotland in 1819, when his extraordinary activity is evident from his

having covered on foot more than 1000 miles in mountainous terrain in forty-five days.

In 1820 Mudge died and Colby took the unusual step of writing to the duke of Wellington, then master-general of the ordnance, to press his case for appointment as superintendent of the survey. He was successful and was appointed that year. He immediately set about addressing problems: he instituted changes that led to an increase in sales of previously very slow-selling maps and, by ruthlessly rejecting sub-standard work and that done by unauthorized assistants, raised standards appreciably. In 1820 he was appointed to the board of longitude, on which he served until its dissolution in 1828. In 1821 he was again employed in Scotland and in 1821–3 was deputed by the Royal Society, with Captain Henry Kater, to work with the astronomers Arago and Matthieu of the Académie des Sciences to verify observations made forty years earlier connecting the triangulations of England and France. For cross-channel observations, Fresnel lamps with compound lenses 3 feet in diameter were used, and Colby's description of them influenced Robert Stevenson to adopt them in British lighthouses.

In 1824 a survey of Ireland at a scale of 6 inches to the mile was ordered, to allow the valuation of property so that the inequitable system of land taxation could be reformed. Colby was put in charge of the survey while continuing to be responsible for work on the British mainland. A comprehensive system of primary, secondary, and minor triangulation was necessary for the precise fixing of property boundaries. Colby determined to put the work under direct official supervision, instead of contracting the work out to civil surveyors as was often done in England. He obtained approval for raising three companies of sappers and miners to be trained in survey duties. The Irish survey was begun with a small party of sappers on Divis Mountain near Belfast in 1825. As the work progressed Colby perfected a system of checks which allowed the employment of Irish labourers on routine tasks. Dissatisfied with previously used instruments, Colby designed and perfected through experiment his compensation bar, using which a base-line 8 miles long was measured under his supervision in 1827–8 and later described in *An Account of the Measurement of the Lough Foyle Base* (1847). Colby was helped by Thomas Drummond, whose family claimed that the invention was his. Two of Colby's 3 foot compensation bars were used by the parliamentary committee to redefine the yard after the original was destroyed by fire in 1834. Colby held the view (later widely accepted) that national survey research could be extended to produce memoirs on the place names, geology, natural history, antiquities, and other features of the country. Sadly his ideas were overruled by financial considerations after the publication of one Irish memoir. Lack of trained men slowed progress in Ireland but Colby managed to resist attempts to make him adopt quicker but less accurate methods.

In 1828 Colby married Elizabeth Hester Boyd, second daughter of Archibald Boyd of Londonderry, treasurer of that county; they had four sons and three daughters. After their marriage Colby and his wife moved from London to Dublin, but the family returned to London in 1838 and then went to Southampton when the Ordnance Survey moved there in 1842.

Under Colby's superintendence in May 1833 the first Irish county map—Londonderry, in fifty sheets—was published. Other maps were published in quick succession with 2 or 3 million acres being published annually, until by completion in 1847 nearly 2000 sheets had been published of maps whose detail, accuracy, and pleasing appearance represented a cartographic achievement of world importance. The work had employed thousands of people and cost £720,000. Colby consistently and considerably exceeded his annual budget so as to maintain progress, for some time forgoing his salary, which he was unable later to recover. His insistence on rigorous if expensive methods meant that the resultant maps could be used to draw boundaries for poor-law assessment and valuation as well as for general valuation, the compilation of annual agricultural returns, the census, the sale of property, land improvement, and general engineering works. In addition a full series of tidal observations, later commended by the astronomer royal, were made under Colby's direction at stations around Ireland. In Ireland Colby built up from virtually nothing an unrivalled topographical corpus. He and Thomas Larcom also introduced electrotyping (whereby maps can be reproduced from duplicate plates without wearing out the original) and contour lines.

In 1833, while the Irish survey was still in progress, Colby was ordered to work with Henry De la Beche to prepare a geological map of the west of England. The Ordnance Survey was to finance the project and engrave the maps and De la Beche to supply geological information—an arrangement which continued until 1845. Colby moved to the mainland in 1838, leaving the Irish survey in the hands of Thomas Larcom, and became involved in the 'battle of the scales'. In 1840, after various scientific bodies in England and Scotland had pointed to the advantages of a 6 inch survey on the Irish pattern, the government agreed that the six unsurveyed counties in the north of England and the whole of Scotland should be surveyed and mapped at the scale of 6 inches to the mile, while the 1 inch map was published for the rest of England. As men involved on the Irish survey completed their work, they were transferred to England and some thence to Scotland. The work was moving very slowly when, in November 1846, Colby was promoted major-general; in accordance with the rules of the service he retired from his survey post the following April.

In retirement Colby devoted himself to the education of his sons, living for some time in Bonn. He died unexpectedly at New Brighton, near Birkenhead, on 9 October 1852. His widow was awarded a life pension by the government. Colby was a knight of Denmark (a distinction conferred in recognition of help given by the Ordnance Survey to Danish geodesists under Heinrich Schumacher), a fellow of the Royal societies of Edinburgh and London, LLD of the University of Aberdeen, and a member of various learned societies. Living in London and having some private means he took a keen interest in science. In appearance Colby was short and the best likeness of him is said to be the bust in the Ordnance Survey office in Southampton. He was extremely dexterous in using instruments, despite having lost one hand. He could be difficult to work with and fell out with several colleagues, one of whom, his biographer, Portlock, none the less described him as 'gentle and kind as a father'. He was an energetic and active participant in all the work he supervised and the high standards on which he insisted make his superintendence of the survey a noteworthy period in its history.

ELIZABETH BAIGENT

Sources J. H. Andrews, *A paper landscape: the ordnance survey in nineteenth-century Ireland* (1975) · W. A. Seymour, ed., *A history of the Ordnance Survey* (1980) · J. E. Portlock, *Memoir of the life of Major-General Colby* (1869) · *The old series ordnance survey maps of England and Wales*, Ordnance Survey, 8 vols. (1975–92) [introductions to each vol. by J. B. Harley and others] · T. Owen and E. Pilbeam, *Ordnance Survey: map makers to Britain since 1791* (1992) · Y. Hodson, *Map making in the Tower of London* (1991) · *DNB*
Archives Ordnance Survey, Southampton | BL, corresp. with Charles Babbage, Add. MSS 37182–37194
Likenesses W. Brockedon, chalk drawing, 1837, NPG [*see illus.*] · bust, Ordnance Survey, Southampton · portrait, repro. in Owen and Pilbeam, *Ordnance survey*, 26

Colchester. For this title name *see* Abbot, Charles, first Baron Colchester (1757–1829).

Colchester, William (*d.* 1420), abbot of Westminster, took his name from his place of origin. His parents, for whom he founded anniversaries at St Botulph's Priory, Colchester, and Hurley Priory, a cell of Westminster Abbey, were named Reginald and Alice and lived in the parish of St Nicholas, Colchester. William, though not mentioned at Westminster until 1361–2, when he said his first mass (at which, unless dispensed, he must have been at least twenty-four), may have entered the monastery several years earlier. He was, it appears, a well-educated recruit, who may have begun the study of theology as a very junior monk. He entered Gloucester College at Oxford in 1366 and incepted as BTh in 1370. After his return from Oxford in that year he held a variety of sometimes demanding offices, but was able, even so, to participate in the external relations of the monastery. Between 1377 and 1386, a period when the abbey's protracted dispute with the dean and canons of St Stephen's Chapel in the palace of Westminster proceeded vigorously, Colchester visited the papal curia on at least four occasions. No doubt some of the credit for the four papal judgments given in favour of the abbey in this dispute in these years belongs to him.

Colchester's active role in the dispute with St Stephen's may help to explain why Richard II strenuously opposed his election as abbot in succession to Nicholas Litlyngton in 1386 and urged the monks to elect John Lakyngheth, an experienced obedientiary, instead. The monks, however, preferred the diplomat and university graduate to the administrator and elected Colchester on 10 December. The king demonstrated his displeasure by withholding his assent for six weeks. Despite this inauspicious beginning, Colchester became one of Richard II's trusted counsellors. In December 1391 he was sent to the papal curia on confidential business for the king. In May 1399 he accompanied Richard to Ireland. After the king's capture at Flint in August of that year, Colchester, it appears, returned to Westminster. On the way, his baggage, including his private chapel, was plundered by the Welsh. When recovered later by his servants, the missing items were at Ludlow, in the custody of the Lancastrian adherent Sir Edmund (IV) Mortimer (d. 1409).

Though probably not a member of the delegation that obtained Richard II's renunciation of the crown in the Tower of London after dinner on 29 September 1399, Colchester, with other prelates, was present on the occasion, presumably to see fair play. A timely word from him may explain why, as recorded in *The Manner of King Richard's Renunciation*, Richard II expressed concern at this juncture lest arrangements in hand for the endowment of his and Anne of Bohemia's anniversary in Westminster Abbey be affected by the renunciation. Colchester attended the first parliament of Henry IV's reign, which convened a week later, but contrary to the precedent of the parliaments of January 1395 and June and September 1397, he was not appointed a trier of petitions. His sympathies at this time may be betrayed by his offer of security for the earls of Huntingdon, Kent, and Rutland on their degradation from ducal rank in November. The story that the conspiracy, which issued in the 'Epiphany rising' early in 1400, was planned at a dinner party in the abbot's house at Westminster on 17 December was first related in the unreliable *Chronicque de la traïson et mort de Richart Deux, roy Dengleterre*, later embellished by Holinshed, and underlies Shakespeare's perception of the abbot of Westminster as 'the grand conspirator' (*Richard II*, v.vi, l. 19). Colchester may not have known of the plot, but Henry IV's suspicion that he did so, fortified perhaps by Colchester's friendship with the politically unreliable Thomas Merk, explains his brief imprisonment, first in Reigate Castle and then in the Tower of London, and the confiscation of his temporalities; these, however, were soon committed to the prior and convent of Westminster.

After these events Colchester's public life took a few years to gather momentum again. He took part, first at Lucca and then at Pisa itself, in the events leading to the Council of Pisa (1409) and in 1414 was a member of the English delegation to the Council of Constance. He was president of the provincial chapter in 1411 and active in raising money for the expenses of monks attending the Council of Constance. In background and temperament a very different man from his aristocratic predecessor, Nicholas Litlyngton, Colchester achieved a position of some eminence, and at times discomfort, in church and state through innate ability, education, and a humane personality that was found congenial by many with whom he came into contact, including Richard II. He was unusually generous to the poor, and gave regular weekly alms to a considerable number of the deserving poor of his own manors. He must have approved, if he did not initiate, the

great increase in the number of maintained pupils in the almonry school at Westminster that occurred during his abbacy. He died in October 1420, and may have been a victim of the epidemic—very likely plague—that carried off a number of monks of Westminster in the summer and autumn of this year. He was buried in the abbey church, in the chapel of St John the Baptist.

BARBARA F. HARVEY

Sources Westminster Abbey Muniment Room, London, WAM 24536–24546; 24410–24419 • private information (2004) [N. Saul] • E. H. Pearce, *The monks of Westminster* (1916), 103–5 • E. H. Pearce, *William de Colchester, abbot of Westminster* (1915) • G. O. Sayles, 'The deposition of Richard II: three Lancastrian narratives', *BIHR*, 54 (1981), 257–70 • C. Given-Wilson, 'The manner of King Richard's renunciation: a "Lancastrian narrative"?', *EngHR*, 108 (1993), 365–70 • B. Williams, ed., *Chronicque de la traïson et mort de Richart Deux, roy Dengleterre*, EHS, 9 (1846) • J. J. N. Palmer, 'The authorship, date and historical value of the French chronicles on the Lancastrian revolution', *Bulletin of the John Rylands University Library*, 61 (1978–9), 145–81; 398–421 • Emden, *Oxf.*, 1.459–60 • Rymer, *Foedera*, 3rd edn, 4/2.91, 95 • *CClR, 1413–19*, 169 • E. F. Jacob, *Essays in the conciliar epoch*, 2nd edn (1953), 73 • R. Holinshed and others, eds., *The chronicles of England, Scotland and Ireland*, 2nd edn, ed. J. Hooker, 3 vols. in 2 (1586–7), 3.514/2/10 • R. Bowers, 'The almonry schools of the English monasteries, c.1265–1540', *Monasteries and society in medieval Britain*, ed. B. Thompson, Harlaxton Medieval Studies, 6 (1999), 177–222

Likenesses C. A. Stothard, etching, pubd 1812, NPG

Colclough, John Henry (1769/70–1798), Irish nationalist, was the son of Thomas Francis Colclough, a successful merchant at Wexford, of Ballyteigue Castle, near Kilmore Quay, co. Wexford. Though collateral to the Colcloughs of Tintern Abbey, the details of his immediate family are so obscure that his mother eludes identification. Arising out of his Roman Catholicism, he went abroad to train as a doctor, following which he married Elizabeth Berry.

On his return to co. Wexford, Colclough joined the United Irishmen, and though his precise involvement remains obscure he was, in his own words, one of 'the principal' activists (Madden, 4.496). His prominence is affirmed by the suggestion that he should become secretary to a proposed county committee in 1797. The committee was never established, but Colclough's public profile and Jonah Barrington's prophecy, arising out of a sequence of social encounters in April 1798, that he would die on the gallows has given the impression that he was more hardline than was in fact the case. Significantly, Colclough did not hold a military office in the United Irish organization. At the same time, his arrest, along with Bagenal Harvey and Edward Fitzgerald of Newpark, on 27 May, and his imprisonment in Wexford, impeded the rising in the south of the county. The success of the insurgent armies elsewhere ensured Wexford town soon came under threat, arising out of which the garrison directed Fitzgerald and Colclough on 29 May to go to the rebel camp at Vinegar Hill to request them to disperse. The fact that Colclough undertook this unusual request, that he did not follow the example of Edward Fitzgerald and stay with the insurgents once he had delivered the message, and that he sought, following his return to Wexford with the insurgents' reply calling upon the town garrison to surrender, to persuade United Irish units in the areas of Bargy and Forth not to join the rising, is consonant with his later claim that he was not persuaded of the wisdom of rebellion.

The capture of Wexford town on 30 May, however, left Colclough with little option but to join in military activity and he took his place with the leaders of the insurgent army that marched westward out of the town on 31 May. Control of New Ross was a key strategic object if the insurgents were not to be hemmed in by the gathering forces of the crown, but the units commanded by Colclough performed badly under fire and their abandonment of their position on 5 June contributed to the costly failure to take the town. Colclough's preference at this point was to sue for peace but the authorities were uninterested. He redeemed his military reputation by commanding the insurgents who almost broke through the lines of General Sir John Moore at Goff's Bridge on 20 June; realizing that military defeat was only a matter of time once the main insurgent army was defeated at Vinegar Hill a day later, he fled Wexford and took refuge on the Saltee Islands. Captured and taken to Wexford town a few days later, Colclough was tried by court martial, found guilty of involvement in the battle of New Ross, and hanged on Wexford Bridge on 28 June. He was in his twenty-ninth year, and he was buried in St Patrick's churchyard in Wexford. His wife survived him. It has been stated that he did not expect the sentence to be imposed. Certainly, his salute to 'king and constitution' (Madden, 4.496) at the gallows sustains the impression that he was never entirely committed to the rebellion.   JAMES KELLY

Sources R. R. Madden, *The United Irishmen: their lives and times*, 2nd edn, 4 vols. (1857–60) · E. Hay, *History of the insurrection in Wexford in 1798* (1803) · L. M. Cullen, 'The 1798 rebellion in Wexford: United Irishman organisation, membership, leadership', *Wexford: history and society*, ed. K. Whelan (1987), 248–95 · D. Gahan, *The people's rising: Wexford, 1798* (1995) · J. Barrington, *Personal sketches of his own times*, 1 (1827), 267–70 · S. Cloney, 'The Colcloughs', *Tintern Abbey, county Wexford: Cistercians and Colcloughs*, ed. K. Whelan (1993), 31–3 · C. Dickson, *The Wexford rising in 1798* (1955) · Burke, *Gen. Ire.*
Likenesses engraving, *c.*1798 (after death mask?), repro. in Whelan, ed., *Wexford* (1987), 257

Colcu ua Duinechda (d. 796). *See under* Meath, saints of (*act. c.*400–*c.*900).

Colden, Cadwallader (1689–1776), historian and colonial official, was born on 7 February 1689 in Enniscorthy, co. Wexford, Ireland, the eldest child of the Revd Alexander Colden (1654–1738), Presbyterian minister, and Janet Hughes (1662?–1731). His parents were Scottish and the family returned to Scotland the following year. Cadwallader was groomed for the Church of Scotland ministry by his father and studied at Edinburgh University, from where he graduated MA in April 1705. He decided not to follow the family clerical tradition, however, and went on to pursue medical training in London. He lacked the financial resources to establish his own medical practice in the capital and chose to move to the American colonies in 1710. Colden was assisted by his aunt Elizabeth Hill in Philadelphia, where he established himself as a merchant

and physician. He returned briefly to Scotland in 1715 and married Alice Chrystie (d. 1762) of Kelso on 11 November.

Colden returned to Philadelphia after his marriage and then moved to New York in 1718 at the invitation of its Scottish governor, Robert Hunter, and settled there for the remainder of his long life. He was appointed surveyor-general of New York in 1720 and was appointed also to the province's council in 1722. Colden demonstrated an intense commitment to his belief in the importance of sound government in the colonies from the very beginning of his public career, and he shared these political principles with fellow Scots in America, such as Archibald Kennedy and James Alexander in New York and William Douglass in Massachusetts. Colden's writings, both private and public, reveal his acquaintance with a wide range of classical and contemporary thinkers. He sought to apply this learning to his analysis of the nature and function of imperial and colonial constitutional relations. Colden's thought and deeds were shaped by his provincial experience on the fringes of the first British empire. He became a defender of metropolitan and executive authority in the colonies because he felt that this was the only solution for the problems of local factionalism and narrow economic self-interest, which in his view jeopardized the public good. A clear line can be traced in Colden's political philosophy from his examination of the strategic position of New York in the 1720s—which he believed to be endangered by the fur trade between merchants in his province and those in French Canada, which resulted in the alienation of the American Indian allies of the British—to his staunch upholding of royal authority in the political crises of the 1760s and 1770s. Colden maintained, on the basis of his interpretation of the history of North America, and the performance of other empires that the real interests of the colonists could be guaranteed only by an impartial government in London.

Colden has come to be acknowledged by historians as one of the leading intellectuals of colonial British America. His interests ranged widely across the sciences and the humanities, and this is reflected in his correspondence with such luminaries as Benjamin Franklin and Linnaeus (who named the plant *Coldenia* after him). Colden published a number of works in the British Isles, the European continent, and North America, which ranged from an attempt to modify Newtonian natural philosophy in *The Principles of Action in Matter* (1751) to *The History of the Five Indian Nations* (first published in New York in 1727, then expanded in subsequent editions in London and New York from 1747). His history of the Iroquois, or Five Nations, which built upon the earlier accounts of French analysts, is perhaps his most interesting achievement for later readers in that it demonstrated that his imperialism was the product of a deep engagement with the colonial situation. He displayed a genuine admiration for the patriotism of the Iroquois, which he extolled in the language of civic humanism and which he contrasted with the corruption of both colonial and metropolitan Britons. This fascination with Amerindian liberty and customs appears to have influenced other Scots such as Adam Ferguson and

Tobias Smollett, who both drew on Colden's history in their own works.

Colden's forceful opinions and personality meant that he was the target of a great deal of hostility in New York. He alienated leading figures in New York political society during his long participation in the bitter and rumbustious politics of the colony. He also attracted popular opprobrium during the Stamp Act crisis and the agitation that accompanied the American War of Independence, due to his position as lieutenant-governor of the province and his stout defence of the imperial government. Colden first led the government of New York as senior councillor in 1760 and was lieutenant-governor in 1761, 1763–5, 1769–70, and 1774–5. Colden died at Spring Hill, his estate in Flushing, Long Island, New York, on 20 September 1776.

PAUL TONKS

Sources *The letters and papers of Cadwallader Colden*, 9 vols. (1918–37) • *Fasti Scot.*, new edn • D. Laing, ed., *A catalogue of the graduates … of the University of Edinburgh*, Bannatyne Club, 106 (1858)
Archives Linn. Soc., botanical papers • New York Historical Society, corresp. and papers • NYPL, papers [transcripts] • U. Edin., special collections, lecture notes and papers | PRO, Colonial Office papers, 5 • U. Mich., Clements L., corresp. with Thomas Gage
Likenesses S. P. Graham, oils, New York chamber of commerce • M. Pratt, engraving (after S. P. Graham), repro. in *Letters* • M. Pratt, oils, Metropolitan Museum of Art, New York • J. Wollaston, oils, Metropolitan Museum of Art, New York
Wealth at death £952 14*s.* 7*d.* in cash; £19,097 19*s.* 1*d.* in bonds and notes owed to Colden: *Letters and papers*, 7.374

Coldingham, Geoffrey of (*d. c.*1215), Benedictine monk, chronicler, and probably hagiographer, is described as sacrist of Coldingham Priory, Berwickshire, one of Durham Cathedral priory's dependent cells, in the rubric that heads three of the four fourteenth-century copies of the portion of the Durham chronicle attributed to him. In this he followed a tradition established during the twelfth century, of adding to the work of Symeon of Durham, whose *Libellus de exordio Dunelmensis ecclesiae* provides an account of the see from its origins on Lindisfarne down to 1096. Geoffrey maintained the pattern set in the previous anonymous continuations, which were mainly structured as accounts of successive bishops of Durham, and so in his work, which begins at the death of Bishop William de Ste Barbe in 1152, the latter's successor, Hugh du Puiset (*d.* 1195), and his dealings with Durham's monastic community figure very prominently. As a writer of limited ambitions his significance derives essentially from Durham's importance as a major centre of power in the far north of England. His chronicle continues to the abortive election of Morgan as bishop in 1215, a strange point at which to break off, given that the royal chancellor, Richard Marsh (*d.* 1226), was successfully elected in 1217. In the only older copy (Durham Cathedral Library, MS A.IV.36), which dates from the early thirteenth century, the opening was rehandled to graft it onto the previous portion of the chronicle, so excluding any rubric; this copy ends abruptly with the coronation of King John in 1199. It is noticeable that the portion thus omitted is less exclusively devoted to purely local affairs than the earlier part.

Among the monks who joined the Durham community

during the last quarter of the twelfth century there were four called Geoffrey. None the less it is very likely that two works of local hagiography written by Geoffrey at the same time as the chronicle were the work of the chronicler. The prefatory letter to the life of Bartholomew of Farne (*d.* 1193), addressed to Prior Bertram of Durham (1189–1213) and the Durham monks, identifies the author as Geoffrey, a fellow servant; this work is the sole source of concrete information about Bartholomew. It is significant that it records Bartholomew's special affection for certain monks from Coldingham who attended his deathbed in 1192; Geoffrey may well have been among them. Similarly the prefatory letter to a life of Godric of Finchale, addressed to Prior Thomas and the brethren of Durham's cell at Finchale, just outside the city, identifies the author as Geoffrey, a fellow servant of the Lord. Thomas was prior at Finchale from 1196, according to Geoffrey's chronicle; a successor occurs by 1212. The author records that as a boy he had encountered the aged Godric, who died in 1170. The work is primarily an abbreviation of the much longer work by Reginald, but also includes some of the materials collected by Prior Germanus (*d. c.*1189).

A. J. PIPER

Sources [H. Wharton], ed., *Anglia sacra*, 1 (1691), 718–31 • Gaufridus de Coldingham [Geoffrey of Coldingham], 'De statu ecclesiae Dunhelmensis', in *Historiae Dunelmensis scriptores tres: Gaufridus de Coldingham, Robertus de Graystanes, et Willielmus de Chambre*, ed. J. Raine, SurtS, 9 (1839), 3–31 • Geoffrey, 'Vita S. Bartholomei', Symeon of Durham, *Opera*, 1.295–325 • Geoffrey, 'Vita S. Godrici', *Acta sanctorum: Maius*, 5 (Antwerp, 1685), 70–85 • [A. H. Thompson], ed., *Liber vitae ecclesiae Dunelmensis*, SurtS, 136 (1923), fol. 58 • [J. Raine], ed., *The priory of Finchale*, SurtS, 6 (1837), 62–3
Archives Durham Cath. CL, MS A.IV.36

Coldingham [Durham], **Reginald of** (*d. c.*1190), Benedictine monk and hagiographer, was a member of the northern monastery of Durham. A fourteenth-century source associates him with Coldingham in Berwickshire, perhaps because this was his birthplace or, more likely, because he lived for a time at Durham's daughter house there. Apparently of English descent, he was a member of the Durham community by about 1153. During the 1160s and 1170s a great deal of his time seems to have been spent at Finchale, near Durham, with the elderly hermit, *Godric, who may have been a relative of his. If the monk did live for a time at Coldingham, this may have been towards the end of his life, in the years after 1188. In addition to his literary skills, there is evidence to suggest he had received some training in medicine.

Three hagiographical works should definitely be ascribed to Reginald. That devoted to Godric, a life followed by a collection of posthumous miracles, was begun in the early 1160s and was probably completed after 1177. Ailred, abbot of Rievaulx (*d.* 1167), was one of those who urged the author to embark on this composition, and he also contributed material. The work survives in one twelfth-century manuscript, which formed the basis of the printed edition, while the text in the British Library (Harley MS 153) represents an earlier draft of the same composition. The short form of the life found in such manuscripts as CUL, Add. MS 3037, and BL, Harley MS 322, is an abbreviation of Reginald's work by an otherwise unknown writer called Walter.

The composition devoted to Cuthbert, on the other hand, is not a life of the saint but a collection of posthumous miracles, which date from 875 to the 1170s. Reginald began work on it no later than 1165 and it was completed in or after 1174. Ailred again played an important part in the initiation of this composition and supplied his friend with appropriate stories. Both the works on Godric and Cuthbert are long, colourful, and lively, largely because of the inclusion of much contemporary material. By contrast the life of St Oswald of Northumbria, to which Ailred also contributed, is relatively short and contains only minimal information from Reginald's own day. It is also very disorderly and owes a significant debt to Bede.

A fourth hagiographical composition has been associated with Reginald. A work by him may well underlie a sermon on St Æbbe of Coldingham (*Sermo de vita et miraculis sancte Ebbe virginis*) now found in Bodl. Oxf., MS Fairfax 6, fols. 164–173v. The sermon as it exists is not, however, written in Reginald's characteristic style. That style is all too often dauntingly verbose and diffuse, and can degenerate into almost incomprehensible turgidity. Nevertheless Reginald possessed the capacity to observe his world closely, and this, combined with a desire to reproduce what he saw and heard in detail in his narratives, frequently results in an extremely vivid evocation of contemporary conditions.   Victoria Tudor

Sources Reginald of Durham, *Libellus de vita et miraculis S. Godrici, heremitae de Finchale*, ed. J. Stevenson, SurtS, 20 (1847) • *Reginaldi monachi Dunelmensis libellus de admirandis beati Cuthberti virtutibus*, ed. [J. Raine], SurtS, 1 (1835) • Reginald of Durham, 'Vita sancti Oswaldi regis et martyris', Symeon of Durham, *Opera* [in pt], 1.326–85 • 'Sermo de vita et miraculis sancte Ebbe virginis', Bodl. Oxf., MS Fairfax 6, fols. 164–173v • C. Horstman, ed., *Nova legenda Anglie, as collected by John of Tynemouth, J. Capgrave, and others*, 1 (1901), 303–7 [summary of 'Sermo de vita …'] • V. M. Tudor, 'Reginald of Durham and St Godric of Finchale: a study of a twelfth-century hagiographer and his major subject', PhD diss., U. Reading, 1979 • V. M. Tudor, 'Reginald of Durham and St Godric of Finchale: learning and religion on a personal level', *Religion and humanism*, ed. K. Robbins, SCH, 17 (1981), 37–48 • V. M. Tudor, 'Reginald's life of St Oswald', *Oswald, Northumbrian king to European saint*, ed. C. Stancliffe and E. Cambridge (1995), 178–94 • V. M. Tudor, 'The cult of St Cuthbert in the twelfth century: the evidence of Reginald of Durham', *St Cuthbert, his cult and his community*, ed. G. Bonner, D. Rollason, and C. Stancliffe (1989), 447–67
Archives BL, Harley MS 153 • Bodl. Oxf., MS Fairfax 6, fols. 164–173v

Coldingham, Thomas (*d.* 1316), merchant, was possibly the son of the Gregory of Coldingham mentioned among the Berwick burgesses in 1291, and himself became a burgess of that town. Thomas was active in Berwick in the wool and hides trades possibly from 1293, certainly from 1303, while his transactions with Durham Priory are well documented from 1309, when boom conditions were experienced until 1315. The wool was presumably sold on to Flanders or Italy. He traded in wool futures, and made loans to the monks, and there is evidence that behind him was 'my company' (*societas mea*); some of his partners can be identified as his executors after his death. He dabbled in the land market, leasing the fishings of Paxton, and buying the wardships and marriages of tenants of Coldingham Priory, in order to make a profit on their estates during a minority. He is the earliest Scottish merchant of whose business there are any details. He died in 1316, between 9 February and 12 May, when the economy of his town was collapsing; his wife and children, if any, are unknown, unless the Thomas Coldingham, reputedly ejected from Berwick by Robert I, was a son.

A. A. M. Duncan

Sources J. Donnelly, 'Thomas of Coldingham, merchant and burgess of Berwick upon Tweed', *SHR*, 59 (1980), 105–25
Archives Durham Cath. CL

Coldock, Francis (1530/31–1603), bookseller, 'by birth a gentleman' (so runs his widow's monument), was apprenticed to William Bonham on 13 October 1556, but may have already served some years before then. He was made free of the Stationers' Company on 2 December 1557 and began to take apprentices on 6 July 1558. He served as under-warden in 1580 and 1582 and as upper warden in 1587 and 1588, and was twice master, in 1591 and 1595.

The first reference to Coldock in the Stationers' register is for Bishop Bale's *Declaration of E. Bonner's Articles* in 1561, which was printed for him by J. Tisdall. In the same year Coldock was fined 2s. 'for that he ded revyle Thomas Hackett with unsemely wordes' (Arber, *Regs. Stationers*, 183), as well as on other occasions for keeping open on St Luke's day and during sermon time. He was taken into the Stationers' Company livery on 29 June 1570, and became one of the largest dealers in books in London. In 1577 he was one of those who signed the petition setting forth their grievances from the various book monopolies, presented by the stationers and printers to Queen Elizabeth. He first had a shop in Lombard Street, 'over agaynste the Cardinalles hatte', and afterwards in St Paul's Churchyard at the sign of the Green Dragon. He was a benefactor to the Stationers' Company, presenting on 4 August 1589 'a spoone gilt poiz. 3 oz. 3s. or thereaboutes with his name on it', on being made warden, and in 1591 'a silver college pot' on being made master. He died on 13 January 1603 aged seventy-two, and was buried in the vault of St Faith, in the crypt of St Paul's. His will, dated 3 September 1602, left equal portions of his estate to his wife and his daughter Joan, who had married the bookseller William Ponsonby.

On Coldock's widow's monument in the church of St Andrew Undershaft is this inscription:

> Near … lieth Alice Byng, in a vault with her father, Simon Burton. She had three husbands, all bachelors and stationers. Her first was Richard Waterson, by him she had a son. Next him was Francis Coldock, by birth a gentleman; he bare all the offices in the company, and had issue two daughters, Joane and Anne, with whom she lived forty years. Lastly, Isaac Byng, gent., who died master of his company. She died the 21st day of May A.D. 1616, aged 73 yrs. 5 months and 25 days. (J. Stow, *A Survey of London*, ed. J. Strype, 1754, 1.400)

H. R. Tedder, *rev.* Eleri Larkum

Sources J. Ames, *Typographical antiquities, or, An historical account of the origin and progress of printing in Great Britain and Ireland*, ed.

W. Herbert, 3 vols. (1785–90), 2.918–22 • H. G. Aldis and others, *A dictionary of printers and booksellers in England, Scotland and Ireland, and of foreign printers of English books, 1557–1640*, ed. R. B. McKerrow (1910) • will, PRO, PROB 11/101/20, fols. 155v–156v • private information (2004) [M. Turner and M. Treadwell] • *STC, 1475–1640* • Arber, *Regs. Stationers*, 1.70, 183

Coldstream, John (1806–1863), physician, only son of Robert Coldstream, merchant, and his wife, Elizabeth Phillips, daughter of John Phillips of Stobcross, Glasgow, was born at Leith on 19 March 1806. After attending Edinburgh high school, he continued his studies at the University of Edinburgh, where he graduated MD in 1827. That year he also took his diploma at the Royal College of Surgeons of Edinburgh and proceeded to Paris to continue his medical education. In 1829 he settled down as a practitioner in Leith with Dr Charles Anderson, to whom he had been apprenticed when he began his medical studies. Anderson was an eminent practitioner in Leith and one of the founders of the Wernerian Society, of which Coldstream became a member on 9 January 1830.

Coldstream was considered to have been so 'devoted to both Christianity and natural science' that 'these subjects seem to have engaged his energies more than did medicine' (Boyd, 522). He took an early interest in Bible and missionary societies, and in 1822 he wrote the report of the Leith Juvenile Bible Society. For the rest of his life he remained a deeply religious man.

Coldstream also gained a great love of natural history early in his life. On 18 March 1823 he was elected as a member of the Plinian Society, and he acted as secretary and treasurer that same year. He was chosen as one of the society's presidents in 1824 and 1825. In 1828, having become so well known in the field of natural history, he was offered the post of assistant in the Natural History Institution at Portsmouth, which he declined. On 7 May 1835 Coldstream married Margaret Menzies, the youngest daughter of the Revd William Menzies of Lanark. They were to have ten children.

About 1840 the subject of medical missions began to occupy Coldstream's attention. With his friend Benjamin Bell he became associate secretary of the Medical Missionary Society. He was elected a fellow of the Royal College of Physicians in 1845, but scarcely took any part in its proceedings. In October 1846 he helped to establish at Leith a hospital for the sick poor; however, the following year he moved to York Place, Edinburgh, his weak health making him unable to cope with the workload of his practice at Leith. He was instrumental in the establishment in 1855 of the Home and School for Invalid and Imbecile Children, in Grayfield Square, Edinburgh. He was almost a daily visitor at this home for nearly five years. In September 1857 he went to Berlin to attend the meeting of the Evangelical Alliance in order to bring to its notice the cause of medical missions. During the winter of 1858–9 Coldstream first became ill with an organic disease of the stomach which eventually proved fatal. However, he was well enough to deliver a course of lectures on ethnography in the winter of 1859–60. After this the state of his health obliged him to move about from place to place.

Coldstream was a 'complex man with a high intellect and enquiring mind' (Boyd, 524). He wrote widely on a variety of medical, scientific, and religious subjects, presenting many papers to scholarly meetings and contributing to the transactions of the Plinian Society, the Wernerian Society, the Royal Medical Society, and the Edinburgh Medical and Surgical Society, among others. Of his works, 'On the periodicity of disease as connected with sol-lunar influences' (1827) and 'On a case of catalepsy' (1854), both in the *Edinburgh Medical and Surgical Journal*, are of particular interest. Coldstream died at his home, Irthing House, near Carlisle, on 17 September 1863.

G. C. BOASE, rev. JEFFREY S. REZNICK

Sources D. Boyd, 'The first four consulting physicians of Leith Hospital', *Proceedings of the Royal College of Physicians of Edinburgh*, 23 (1993), 518–29 • J. H. Balfour, *Biography of the late John Coldstream* (1865) • J. P. Coldstream, *Sketch of the life of John Coldstream* (1877) • Religious Tract Society, *Dr. J. Coldstream, the Christian physician* (1877)
Likenesses E. Edwards, photograph, repro. in Balfour, *Biography* • E. Edwards, photograph, repro. in Boyd, 'The first four consulting physicians of Leith Hospital'

Coldstream, Sir William Menzies (1908–1987), artist and arts administrator, was born on 28 February 1908 at the Doctor's House, West Street, Belford, Northumberland, the youngest in the family of two sons and three daughters of George Probyn Coldstream, general medical practitioner, and his wife, (Susan Jane) Lilian Mercer, elder daughter of Major Robert Mercer Tod (43rd light infantry), of Edinburgh.

Coldstream was two years old when the family moved to West Hampstead, London. Early interest in the natural sciences made him want to become a doctor but, at the age of twelve, with a suspected heart condition following rheumatic fever, he was removed from school and tutored at home. Although he went at sixteen to the University Tutorial Centre, Red Lion Square, to prepare for entry to medical school, by his eighteenth birthday he had failed matriculation, met W. H. Auden, and started to draw and paint seriously. In April 1926, with his father's support, he enrolled at the Slade School of Fine Art.

While there Coldstream was awarded the Slade certificate for drawing (1926), a Slade scholarship, the figure and summer composition prizes (1927), the summer landscape prize, and the second Melville Nettleship prize for figure composition (1928). Meanwhile, he had become greatly impressed by the work of nineteenth-century French masters, especially Cézanne, Braque, and Matisse, and by artists such as Walter Sickert, Duncan Grant, and Picasso; had attended outside lectures by Sickert on 'The technique of drawing and painting'; and, to increase his manual graphic control, had taken extra drawing instruction from a signwriter in Horseferry Road. By the time he left the Slade (1929) he was working wholly from nature, with intense interest in the appearance of things.

In 1930 Coldstream got his first commission, met Victor Pasmore, and was elected to the London Artists' Association. Over the next two years he became increasingly

Sir William Menzies Coldstream (1908–1987), by Jorge Lewinski, 1963

concerned at the conflict between his real interest in visual facts and his appreciation that abstraction was gaining ground, in response to current aesthetic theories and the support for subjective painting then centred on Paris. On 22 July 1931 Coldstream married Nancy, a student with him at the Slade, and daughter of Hugh Culliford Sharp, doctor of medicine, of Truro. They had two daughters. The marriage was dissolved in 1942. In 1932 he became temporary art master at Wellington College, and in 1933 briefly attempted 'objective abstraction', which Geoffrey Tibble and Rodrigo Moynihan were then moving towards. When elected that year to the London Group, he already felt convinced that abstract art appealed only to an élitist minority, and that broken communications between artist and public needed rebuilding.

Spurred by contemporary political and social problems and believing in film as a communicator, Coldstream got a job with the pioneering General Post Office film unit run by John Grierson. In 1935 he directed *The King's Stamp* and edited *Coal Face*, with lyrics by Auden and music by Benjamin Britten; but, after directing *Fairy of the Phone* (1936) and *Roadways* (1937), he decided to return to painting. The experience had convinced him that film was no answer to the current crisis in painting, that many of the approved preconceptions about art were for him unimportant, and that he had to start painting again—but now only in the way that interested him: directly from nature, as a pure transcription of what he saw.

To encourage an objective process in visual representation, in 1937 Coldstream joined with Claude Rogers and

Victor Pasmore in starting a school of drawing and painting at 12 Fitzroy Street (later 316 Euston Road) [*see* Euston Road School]. Although it closed on the outbreak of the Second World War (1939), it had much impact and created a 'new look' in English art. In 1940 Coldstream enlisted in the Royal Artillery but was soon transferred to the Royal Engineers and commissioned as a camouflage officer (1940). He served in England until appointed an official war artist (1943). He then went first to Egypt, painting mostly portraits at no. 11 Indian transit camp, between the pyramids and Cairo. From 1944 he was in Italy, doing outstanding war landscapes in Capua, Pisa, Rimini, and Florence. On demobilization (1945) he joined Victor Pasmore in teaching at Camberwell School of Arts and Crafts, later (1948) becoming its inspiring head of painting. In June the following year he was appointed Slade professor at University College, London, returning to the school he had always loved. During twenty-six dynamic years there he greatly strengthened its work, introduced postgraduate courses, and, for the first time, made film studies available at university level. Taking always a leading role in the life of University College, he was elected a fellow in 1953. On 30 March 1961 he married Monica Mary, daughter of Alfred Eric Monrad Hoyer, journalist, of London. They had a son and two daughters. During those years and after his retirement (1975), his paintings included a succession of outstanding nudes, a series of views of Westminster painted from the Department of the Environment in Marsham Street, and a number of commissioned portraits which rank among his most remarkable works. Among these are: *Dr Bell, Bishop of Chichester* (1954; Tate collection), *Sir Ifor Evans* (1958–60; University College, London), *Westminster Abbey I* (1973–4; Arts Council Collection, South Bank Centre, London), and *Reclining Nude* (1974–6; Tate collection).

An exceptional chairman, Coldstream discharged a formidable range of public duties. He was chairman of the National Advisory Council on Art Education (1958–71), and largely responsible for the liberalizing transformation of art education in Britain; a trustee of the National Gallery (1948–55, 1956–63) and of the Tate Gallery (1949–55, 1956–63); a member of the Arts Council (1952–62), vice-chairman of the council (1962–70), and chairman of its art panel (1953–62); a director of the Royal Opera House (1957–62); chairman of the British Film Institute (1964–71); and vice-president of Morley College (1977–83). In 1977 he was elected to the Society of Dilettanti, and became painter to the society. Appointed CBE in 1952, he was knighted in 1956 and received honorary degrees from the universities of Nottingham (1961), Birmingham (1962), and London (1984), and from the Council for National Academic Awards (1975).

First and foremost a painter, laden with self-doubt and ever diffident about his remarkable achievements, Coldstream was a good friend and immensely stimulating companion, whose outstanding work is a lasting tribute to his self-imposed discipline and the integrity of his painterly qualities. Small, wiry, grey-suited, and unobtrusive, he was highly intelligent and greatly respected, with an irrepressible wit which, in Rodrigo Moynihan's words, was 'an inspired sustained hilarity, directed towards the absurdities of art, the pretensions of artists, the short-comings of friends'.

By 1982 his health had begun to decline, and by 1984 he could no longer paint. Although he attended the private view of his last solo exhibition (June 1984) at the Anthony D'Offay Gallery, he was by then unable to work. After a long illness, he died at the Homoeopathic Hospital in Camden on 18 February 1987.

IAN TREGARTHEN JENKIN, *rev.*

Sources *The Times* (19 Feb 1987) · *Daily Telegraph* (19 Feb 1987) · *The Independent* (21 Feb 1987) · L. Gowing and D. Sylvester, *The paintings of William Coldstream* (1990) [exhibition catalogue, Tate Gallery, London] · *William Coldstream memorial meeting, 24 April 1987* (UCL booklet, 1988) · private information (1996) · personal knowledge (1996) · *CGPLA Eng. & Wales* (1987) · B. Laughton, biography [forth-coming]

Archives Tate collection, corresp., journals, and papers · UCL, corresp. relating to Arts Council | Tate collection, corresp. with Lord Clark; letters to C. G. H. Dicker; letters to John Rake · U. Birm. L., corresp. with Lord Avon |SOUND BBC, interviews by D. Sylvester, 13 April 1962, 4 Oct 1976 · BL NSA, National Life Story Collection, interview by E. Lucie-Smith and J. Bumpus, 3 Nov 1982

Likenesses J. Lewinski, photograph, 1963, NPG [*see illus.*] · photograph, repro. in *The Times* · photographs, repro. in Gowing and Sylvester, *Paintings of William Coldstream*

Wealth at death £104,483: probate, 15 April 1987, *CGPLA Eng. & Wales*

Coldwell, John (*c*.1535–1596), bishop of Salisbury, was born in Faversham, the elder son of Robert Coldwell, gentleman of that town, and his wife, Rycharden Thurston of Eastling, Kent. In 1560 John Coldwell became the lessee of the ancient hospital of the Maison Dieu in Ospringe, on the outskirts of Faversham. It was owned by St John's College, Cambridge, where he had matriculated in 1551, when he was probably in his middle to late teens, and graduated BA in 1555. He proceeded MA in 1558 and was admitted to the fellowship in the same year. In 1564 he became a doctor of medicine, practising for some years in Kent (he corresponded with a well-known local surgeon, John Hall of Maidstone). Coldwell was ordained deacon in London in 1569 and became chaplain to Archbishop Matthew Parker, and perhaps also his personal physician. He held two livings, both in Kent: he was instituted rector of Tunstall on 13 June 1572, and rector of Saltwood with Hythe in November 1582. In July 1571 he was collated to the archdeaconry of Chichester, but had resigned by 14 May 1575. On the recommendation of Archbishop Grindal he was installed dean of Rochester on 26 September 1581, a position he held for ten years.

When John Piers, bishop of Salisbury, was translated to York early in 1589, Coldwell was promised the vacant see by Lord Burghley. He was not consecrated, however, until 26 December 1591. The delay was caused by manoeuvres at court, centring on a rival candidate (John Thornborough, who had the support of Sir Francis Walsingham) and, still more, on Sir Walter Ralegh's determination to secure the manor of Sherborne, the most valuable property of the see. At the end of August 1590 Coldwell wrote to Burghley expressing anxiety, but the hold-up continued, and he

only secured his elevation by promising Ralegh a ninety-nine-year lease. The temporalities were restored on 14 January 1592, and within a week the dean and chapter were being required by the crown to confirm Coldwell's lease to Ralegh of the Sherborne estate.

Coldwell was enthroned, and installed as prebendary of Potterne, on 3 January 1592. He subsequently faced further demands from Ralegh for leases of episcopal manors, and to add to his difficulties he also inherited a running battle with the citizens of Salisbury arising from the bishop's lordship over the city, laid out on episcopal land by Bishop Poor in the early thirteenth century. The bishop reserved to himself the profits of fairs and markets and significant legal powers. Particularly resented was the fact that the mayor had to take his oath of office before the bishop or one of his officials, emphasizing the city's sub-servience and frustrating the citizens' ambitions for the freedom implicit in a charter of incorporation. The bishop's overlordship had been confirmed by letters patent in 1472, and again by a charter granted to Bishop Jewel in 1561. Nevertheless by 1591 the citizens were once more agitating for a charter, and although Coldwell seems to have been conciliatory at first, in 1593 they obtained writs of *quo warranto* against him, accompanied by a list of complaints against the bishop and his officers. Allegations of assault on mayoral officials and citizens suggest that the bishop's men could indeed be brutal and arbitrary. However, their differences remained unresolved during Coldwell's lifetime, and it was only under his successor, Henry Cotton, that a more conciliatory relationship was established, with the city obtaining its charter in 1612.

Coldwell's difficulties with the city administration did not prevent his being an active and effective bishop, carrying out diocesan business to within a month of his death. On 13 June 1593 he held a visitation of his cathedral, walking there through his private garden because of an outbreak of plague which had forced many people to flee the city. Its record, preserved in his register, reveals considerable slackness. Ministers and others did not come to church as diligently as they ought; there was some default in keeping the preaching turns; vicars-choral had been admitted with a test of 'their ability and sufficiency in voices and knowledge'; holy communion was satisfactory 'saving for the provision of bread and wine, there is default in the treasurer, which doth not supply it as he ought to do'. The cathedral fabric showed 'some decays, which are yearly amended as we may', and 'the church and choir is not decently kept for lack of sweeping, nor the clock duly kept, neither the bells rung to service as they should be' (Salisbury Cathedral Library, chapter act book 16, fols. 24–30). It is not known whether matters improved subsequently.

Coldwell was the first bishop of Salisbury to be married. With his first wife, Jane, daughter of Walter Henley of Lancashire, gentleman, he had five sons and a daughter. There were no children of his second marriage, to Clare, daughter of John Toke of Great Chart, Kent, esquire, and widow of Nicholas Moore of Elham, Kent, gentleman. He left no writings except a few letters. He died, at Salisbury, on 14 October 1596, in such poverty, according to Sir John Harington, that he had to be buried 'suddenly and secretly' in the grave that had once been Bishop Wyvil's in Salisbury Cathedral (Cassan, 82). No will survives. Administration of his goods was granted to his son Charles.

PENELOPE RUNDLE

Sources J. Coldwell, bishop's register, Wilts. & Swindon RO, D1/2/18 · bishop's archives, Wilts. & Swindon RO, D1/30/3 and 4 · Salisbury city archives, Wilts. & Swindon RO, G23/1/226 · chapter act book 16, Salisbury Cathedral Library · W. B. Bannerman, ed., *Visitations of Kent, 1574 and 1592*, Harleian Society, 75 (1924) · C. H. Drake, 'The hospital of St Mary of Ospringe, commonly called Maison Dieu', *Archaeologia Cantiana*, 30 (1914), 35–78 · *VCH Wiltshire*, vol. 6 · Venn, *Alum. Cant.*, 1/1.366 · W. H. Jones, *Fasti ecclesiae Sarisberiensis, or, A calendar … of the cathedral body at Salisbury* (1879) · S. H. Cassan, *Lives and memoirs of the bishops of Sherborne and Salisbury* (1824) · *Registrum Matthei Parker, diocesis Cantuariensis, AD 1559–1575*, ed. W. H. Frere and E. M. Thompson, 3, CYS, 39 (1933) · G. H. Smith, 'The excavation of the hospital of St Mary of Ospringe, commonly called Maison Dieu', *Archaeologia Cantiana*, 95 (1979), 81–184 · *Fasti Angl., 1541–1857*, [Chichester] · *Fasti Angl., 1541–1857*, [Salisbury] · admon, PRO, PROB 6/5, fol. 183v · F. O. White, *Lives of the Elizabethan bishops* (1898)
Archives Bodl. Oxf., medical prescriptions · Wilts. & Swindon RO, archives, D1/30/3, 4 · Wilts. & Swindon RO, register, D1/2/18
Wealth at death very little: administration, 1596, PRO, PROB 6/5, fol. 183v; Jones, *Fasti ecclesiae*

Cole, Abdiah (*fl.* 1602–1664), physician, was a prolific translator of medical books, of whose career little is known. He must have been born late in the sixteenth century, and is probably the Abdiah Cole of Yorkshire admitted as a scholar at Trinity College, Cambridge, in 1602, who graduated BA in 1604 and MA in 1607, was a fellow of Queens' College, Cambridge, from 1611 to 1618, and graduated BD in 1616. He was incorporated at Oxford in 1611 and was instituted as rector of Ashington with Buncton, Sussex, in 1615 but was deprived for simony in 1619. He apparently took up medicine about 1612, since he is described on the title page of his revised edition of Nicholas Culpeper's *Pharmacopoeia Londinensis* (1661) as having 'practised physick forty-nine years'. He appears to have passed the middle part of his life abroad, since he is said on the same title page to have 'lived above thirty years out of his own country', and to have 'seen the practice of France, Italy, Germany, Turkey and the Indies'. In the preface to his translation of Lazare Rivière's *The Practice of Physick* (1655) he is said to have spent 'twenty-nine years in the service of three of the greatest princes in Europe'. He describes himself as 'doctor of physick and the liberal arts', but where he obtained this degree is unknown. He did not belong to the College of Physicians. In addition to the above-mentioned edition of Culpeper's *Pharmacopoeia Londinensis*, his name is associated with Culpeper's in numerous translations of standard continental medical works published between 1655 and 1664 purporting to have been originally written by Culpeper and left unpublished at his death in 1654. Cole's role was, therefore, presumably largely editorial. The fact that all the works were printed and sold by Peter Cole suggests a possible relationship, but as he was a native of Suffolk this seems doubtful, if the identification of Abdiah Cole as a Yorkshireman is correct.

To complicate matters further several of the title pages also carry the name or initials of William Rowland who, in his translation of Johann Schröder's *The Compleat Chymical Dispensatory* (1669), claimed to have translated all the authors ascribed jointly to Culpeper and Cole. The works formed part of a series entitled The Rationall Physitian's Library or The Physitian's Library, which eventually extended to some thirty titles, though Cole was not involved in all of them. The authors in whose work he had—or was alleged to have had—a hand were Thomas Bartholin, Jean Fernel, Jan Jonston, Felix Platter, Lazare Rivière, Martin Ruland, and Daniel Sennert. The only translation in which his name appears unaccompanied is Santorio Santorio's *A New Art of Physick* (1663). A portrait showing Cole in advanced age and with a furred doctor's gown appears with portraits of Rivière, Culpeper, and Rowland on the frontispiece (engraved by Thomas Cross) to Rivière's *The Practice of Physick* (1655).

JOHN SYMONS

Sources Venn, *Alum. Cant.* · *VCH Sussex*, 6/2.71 · N. Culpeper, *Pharmacopoeia Londinensis*, ed. A. Cole (1661) · L. Rivière, *The practice of physick*, trans. A. Cole (1655)
Likenesses T. Cross, line engraving, 1655 (after portrait), V&A; repro. in Rivière, *Practice of physick*, frontispiece

Cole, Cecil Jackson- (1901–1979), businessman and charity founder, was born on 1 November 1901 at 27 Knox Road, Forest Gate, London, the elder child and only son (there was another son from a later marriage) of Albert Edward Cole, a dealer in new and secondhand furniture, and his wife (who was also his cousin), Nellie Catherine Jackson. Baptized Albert Cecil Cole, he changed his name by deed poll on 11 December 1927 to Cecil Jackson-Cole, in memory of his mother, who died that year. His boyhood, which was difficult, was spent primarily at 44 Whitehall Road, Grays Thurrock, Essex, but as his father moved house fairly frequently he lived also at various times in Barking, Walthamstow, Stratford, Walworth, Deptford, and Holborn. His father died in 1934.

Jackson-Cole attended several council schools, averaging only nine months in any one. He started full-time work at the age of thirteen, as an office boy at the Tooley Street branch of George and John Nickson, importers and general provision merchants. He left Nicksons in 1919 to become owner and manager of Andrews Furnishers, Highbury Corner, Islington. Andrews later had branches in Hammersmith, at The Angel, and in Oxford. In 1928 he enrolled as an external student for one year at Balliol College, Oxford, studying economics under G. D. H. Cole. In 1930 he developed a kidney complaint which kept him bedridden for almost three years. Later in life he was to suffer from indigestion. In 1937 Jackson-Cole married his cousin Phyllis Emily (*d.* 1956), daughter of Sidney and Florence Cole.

Jackson-Cole first became involved in charitable work through the Soldiers' and Sailors' Home, Watford. A pacifist, he was attracted towards the Quakers, who had the same beliefs. In May 1942 a group of concerned Oxford Quakers gathered in their meeting-house in Oxford to consider how to further opposition to the blockade of

Greece, where thousands were dying of starvation. Encouraged by Jackson-Cole and Canon Richard Milford, a broadly based public meeting was convened in Oxford the following October. It included not only the Quakers, but also representatives from the other main churches, the university, and local businessmen. The Oxford Committee for Famine Relief (subsequently Oxfam) was formed with Jackson-Cole as first honorary secretary. He became the business brain and dynamic driving force behind this relief and development agency. In 1948 the question arose of whether Oxfam should terminate its activities because Europe was felt to be on the road to recovery. The committee decided unanimously against this, and Jackson-Cole spearheaded the growth and expansion of the charity. For five years he virtually ran it himself. As a member of Oxfam's council of management he retained his interest and involvement until 1979, serving as secretary emeritus in later years. His vision led to the setting up of autonomous Oxfams in Canada, Quebec, the USA, and Belgium.

In 1945 Jackson-Cole created a business, Andrews & Partners, the staff for which were recruited from young men and women of Christian conviction or public-spirited ideals. His philosophy was that businessmen and -women were essential to the development of charities. He was willing that some of his senior staff's time should be given to charitable works. By this means he set up a number of charitable trusts and charities, the first of which was the Phyllis Trust, named after his first wife. Its objectives were broadly to give practical expression to the Christian injunctions. There followed the Voluntary and Christian Service Trust (VCS) and the Christian Initiative Trust. To all these trusts he gifted some of the equity shares of his businesses. VCS set up Help the Aged in 1961 and Help the Aged established the Help the Aged Housing Association in 1968. This later became independent as the Anchor Housing Association. VCS likewise set up Action in Distress in 1973, later known as Action Aid.

A successful entrepreneur, Jackson-Cole aimed to introduce business methods to fund-raising and charitable work and in this he was immensely successful. He believed, too, in seeking out new constituencies for charitable giving and increasingly saw charitable work on a global scale—for both giving and spending. He was a man of great integrity, believing passionately in doing good for its own sake. This allowed him space to work anonymously and with relative peace of mind. He refused the civic and national honours he was offered. His creative energy was paralleled by unpredictability, quick temper, and a single-mindedness of purpose, buttressed by an almost childlike enthusiasm for the cause in hand. He was endowed with vitality and energy. He woke mid-morning but would work through to the small hours, often seven days a week. He valued friends greatly and had little time for hobbies and recreations, other than walking. Although he was brought up an Anglican, he was ecumenical in outlook. A strong believer in divine healing, he was also convinced he had contact after their death with both his mother and his first wife. It was his religious motivation which gave rise to his worldwide concern for the

plight of the poor and underprivileged, both at home and overseas.

In 1973 Jackson-Cole remarried, his second wife being Mary Theodora (Theo) Handley, a teacher and college lecturer and a lifelong friend, daughter of the Revd Thomas Handley of Keighley, Yorkshire. There were no children from either marriage. Jackson-Cole died on 9 August 1979 at Burrswood, Groombridge, near Tunbridge Wells.

B. W. WALKER, *rev.*

Sources L. Martin, *Cecil Jackson-Cole* (1983) · private information (1986) · personal knowledge (1986) · *CGPLA Eng. & Wales* (1980)
Archives Oxfam archive, papers · W. Sussex RO, corresp. and papers | W. Sussex RO, memoirs of Raymond Andrews
Wealth at death £88,217: probate, 26 Feb 1980, *CGPLA Eng. & Wales*

Cole, Charles Nalson (1722/3–1804), lawyer, was the son of Charles Cole, rector of North Crowley, Buckinghamshire, and grandson of an apothecary of Ely. He was educated at St John's College, Cambridge, which he left after taking his BA in 1743, and became a student of the Inner Temple, where he was called to the bar.

Although not a practising barrister, Cole became registrar of the Bedford Level corporation and published *A collection of laws which form the constitution of the Bedford Level corporation, with an introductory history thereof* (1761). He also prepared the second edition of Sir William Dugdale's *History of imbanking and drayning of divers fenns and marshes, both in foreign parts and in this kingdom* (1772). Cole was a long-standing friend of the writer Soame Jenyns and became his literary executor after his death. Three years later Cole's edition of the *Works of Soame Jenyns* appeared, with a sketch of his life. He died in Edward Street, Cavendish Square, London, on 18 December 1804, aged eighty-one.

THOMPSON COOPER, *rev.* ROBERT BROWN

Sources A. Chalmers, ed., *The general biographical dictionary*, new edn, 32 vols. (1812–17) · *GM*, 1st ser., 74 (1804), 124–5 · Nichols, *Illustrations* · W. Hustler, ed., *Graduati Cantabrigienses* (1823), 107 [for the years 1659–1823]
Archives BL, letters to Lord Hardwicke and others, Add. MSS 35607–35693, 35126–35127, *passim*

Cole, Sir Christopher (1770–1836), naval officer and politician, born at Marazion in Cornwall on 10 June 1770, was the sixth and youngest son of Humphrey Cole of Marazion and his wife, Phillis, daughter of Francis Maugham. He entered the navy in 1780 as midshipman on the *Royal Oak* (Sir Digby Dent), where his second brother, John Cole (afterwards rector of Exeter College, Oxford), was chaplain. In the same year he was moved to the *Raisonnable* and he later served in the *Russell* and the *Princessa*, flagship of Sir Francis Samuel Drake. The *Princessa* formed part of Sir Samuel Hood's fleet in the actions off Martinique and the Chesapeake on 29 April and 5 September 1781. She was also present at Hood's manoeuvres off St Kitts in January and February 1782, and in Admiral Sir George Rodney's battles of 9 and 12 April.

At the peace of 1783 Cole joined the *Trepassey* (12 guns), commanded by his brother Captain Francis Cole, and accompanied him from the West Indies to Halifax, where he moved into the sloop *Atalante*, under Captain Thomas

Foley, where he remained until 1785. In the following year he proceeded to Newfoundland in the *Winchelsea* (32 guns), under his idol and fellow Cornishman Edward Pellew. In this vessel he remained until 1789, when, in consequence of the recommendation of Sir Francis Samuel Drake, he was placed on the *Crown* (64 guns), under Commodore William Cornwallis, with whom he proceeded to the East Indies.

On 18 September 1793 Cole was promoted lieutenant, and in October 1794 he was appointed first lieutenant of the *Cerberus*, a new 32-gun frigate, at the particular request of the captain, John Drew. In the following year he joined the *Sanspareil* (80 guns), bearing the flag of Lord Hugh Seymour. In 1799 he accompanied Seymour to the West Indies as his flag-lieutenant. Having been promoted to commander on 30 January 1800, Cole was, on the surrender of Surinam in August 1800, appointed commander of one of the prizes, the *Hussar*, a corvette of 20 guns, which was renamed the *Surinam*. In this command he distinguished himself by his activity in pursuing privateers and by his care for his men's health, which Seymour made the subject of an official recommendation to the Admiralty. He gained the good opinion of Seymour's successor, Sir John Thomas Duckworth, who promoted him into his flagship, the *Leviathan* (74 guns), and afterwards to command the frigate *Southampton*. His post commission was confirmed by the Admiralty on 20 April 1802.

After the treaty of Amiens in 1802, the *Southampton* was ordered home and paid off in September. In June 1804 Cole was appointed to the *Culloden* (74 guns), the flagship of his old friend and commander Sir Edward Pellew, who had been appointed commander-in-chief in the East Indies. On 25 September 1806 he captured the French corvette the *Émilien*, and on 27 November assisted the destruction of thirty Dutch vessels in the Batavia Roads. However, during this period, relations with Pellew suffered a complete breakdown. In March 1807 Cole was transferred from the flagship to the temporary command of the frigate HMS *Salsette*, subsequently renamed the *Doris*. There followed a long and tortuous correspondence in which Cole pressed his claims both with Pellew and directly with the Admiralty for a permanent appointment in a vessel of equal or superior rate. In April 1808, in command of the *Doris* and two other frigates, he escorted Colonel John Malcolm to Bushehr on his mission to the Persian court, and remained at Bushehr to protect the embassy. On his return he received the thanks of the governor-general in council and a present of £500. Yet such was the state of relations with Pellew that Cole found himself facing a letter of censure for quitting his post in the Persian Gulf without orders. During 1808 and 1809 he cruised in the straits of Malacca and the China seas. On the arrival of the news of the political changes in Spain, he was dispatched by Pellew's successor, Rear-Admiral Drury, to conciliate the governor of the Philippines, in which he was successful.

In 1810 Cole was moved at his own request into the *Caroline* (36 guns), and was soon after dispatched to relieve the garrison at Amboyna in command of a small squadron:

the *Caroline*, the *Piémontaise* (38 guns), the 18-gun brig sloop *Barracouta*, and the transport brig *Mandarin*. He left Madras on 10 May and arrived on 30 May at Prince of Wales Island, where he decided to make a daring raid to capture Neira, the chief of the Banda Islands. With less than 200 men he captured the island and its garrison of nearly 700 Dutch troops on 10 August. On his return to India, Cole received the thanks of the governor-general in council, the commander-in-chief, and the lords of the Admiralty. He was awarded a medal by the Admiralty, and his action was the subject of a public order from the governor-general to the three presidencies. In the House of Commons Spencer Perceval described the enterprise as 'an exploit to be classed with the boldest darings in the days of chivalry'.

In 1811 Cole joined Drury on the Malabar coast, where an expedition against Java was being prepared. On the death of Drury, Cole was left in command for some months until the arrival of Captain William Robert Broughton. The expedition sailed in June and, on its arrival at Java, Cole again distinguished himself by promptly landing troops on his own responsibility before the enemy was prepared, thus avoiding considerable loss. In 1812 the *Caroline* was paid off, and on 29 May Cole was knighted and presented with a sword by his crew. On 10 June he received an honorary DCL from Oxford University, and subsequently was presented with a piece of plate of the value of 300 guineas by the East India Company.

Early in 1813 Cole was appointed to the *Rippon*, a new vessel of 74 guns. He continued cruising in the channel until the end of 1814, when he was put out of commission. On 2 January 1815 he was nominated KCB. He also received Austrian and Russian orders. On 28 April 1815 he married Lady Mary Lucy Talbot (*d.* 3 Feb 1855), to whom he had long been attached; she was the daughter of Henry Thomas Fox-Strangways, second earl of Ilchester, and widow of Thomas Mansel Talbot (*d.* 1813) of Margam Park, Glamorgan; they had no children. Talbot had had a considerable interest in Glamorgan (the estate was held in trust for his young heir, Christopher Talbot) and this was the cause of Cole's entry into parliament. Invited by leading county interests, on 6 December 1817 'the conqueror of Banda' was elected, unopposed, MP for Glamorgan. He did not sit in the parliament that met in 1818, but he was again elected on 16 March 1820, and retained the seat until 1830. An independent, he made no mark in the Commons. In 1830 he made way for his stepson Christopher Talbot. In July 1821 he was elected deputy grand master of the freemasons of south Wales. In 1828 he was appointed to command the yacht *Royal Sovereign*, and in 1830 he was nominated colonel of marines. Cole lived at Killay, and died there on 24 August 1836.

E. I. CARLYLE, *rev.* ANDREW LAMBERT

Sources C. N. Parkinson, *War in the eastern seas, 1793–1815* (1954) • C. N. Parkinson, *Edward Pellew, Viscount Exmouth, admiral of the red* (1934) • S. M. Eardley-Wilmot, *Life of Vice-Admiral Edmund, Lord Lyons* (1898) • D. Syrett and R. L. DiNardo, *The commissioned sea officers of the Royal Navy, 1660–1815*, rev. edn, Occasional Publications of the Navy RS, 1 (1994) • HoP, *Commons* • *GM*, 1st ser., 81/2 (1811) • *GM*, 2nd ser., 6 (1836) • J. Marshall, *Royal naval biography*, 2/2 (1825)

Archives CUL, Sir Christopher Cole, naval letter-book, Indian Ocean, Persian Gulf, East Indies, and Philippines, 1802–09, Add. 9492 · NL Wales, papers · NL Wales, naval log book · Royal Naval Museum, Portsmouth, memoirs of the capture of the Banda Islands | West Glamorgan County Archive, naval log books and poll books
Likenesses G. H. Phillips, mezzotint (after W. Owen), BM · portrait, repro. in Eardley-Wilmot, *Life of Lord Lyons*, 30

Cole, Eric Kirkham (1901–1966), radio engineer, was born at 14 Windsor Road, Prittlewell, Southend-on-Sea, Essex, on 4 July 1901, the only child of Henry Cole, a dairyman, and his wife, Alice Laura, *née* Kirkham. He was educated at Southend Day Technical School and, after serving a three-year apprenticeship, went into partnership with his father as an electrical engineer. He set up his own business in 1922, making radio receivers to take advantage of the demand following the foundation of the BBC. His first premises were a single rented room in Westcliff-on-Sea, where, assisted by Muriel Bradshaw (1904/5–1965), he made on average six sets a week. These were conventional sets for the period, using headphones for the output and powered from batteries.

However, Cole was soon engaged in the production of less conventional apparatus. This was the result of reading an article written by William Verrels, a war casualty and semi-invalid, in a local newspaper. Verrels wrote of his dependence on his radio set for entertainment and of the inconvenience and expense of getting batteries recharged. Cole contacted Verrels, and eventually went into partnership with him to design and manufacture a 'battery eliminator', which would enable sets to be operated from the mains supply. This was still only a small-scale local operation: Cole, Bradshaw, and Verrels made their initial sales by calling at every house in Westcliff and Southend which displayed an external radio aerial. Their energy and commitment was such that their company expanded during a minor slump in 1924, when many small radio firms went out of business. Cole married Muriel Bradshaw on 15 July 1925; they had two children, a son, Derek, and a daughter, Anne.

In October 1926 Cole reorganized his business as a private company, E. K. Cole Ltd (Ekco), with an authorized capital of £2500. Verrels became chairman, Cole was vice-chairman, and three local businessmen joined them on the board. A new factory was built at Leigh-on-Sea in 1927, employing about fifty people. This business was converted into a public limited company on 25 April 1930.

By this time technical developments had made Cole's battery eliminators obsolete; the public now wanted all-mains radio receivers. Anticipating a substantial increase in business, Cole and Verrels decided that they needed additional technical expertise and more manufacturing capacity. They recruited John Wyborn (then twenty-six years old) from Marconiphone as their chief engineer and Michael Lipman as production engineer, they built a new factory at Southend-on-Sea—the first large factory in Britain intended specifically for manufacturing radio receivers—and they introduced Bakelite (an early plastic) in place of the wooden cabinets preferred by all other British manufacturers. This was something of a gamble in 1930: Bakelite moulding required considerable capital investment in machinery that could be used economically only for very large production runs. In the event, the gamble paid off. Ekco suffered a severe financial crisis after a factory fire in 1932; the firm survived by introducing a new range of receivers in attractive cabinets that could not have been made in more traditional materials. These new cabinets became a pattern for the rest of the industry and helped increase Ekco's turnover to more than a million pounds in 1934.

By the late 1930s Ekco had established an enviable reputation for the reliability of its products. This reputation must, obviously, be credited mainly to the quality control practices introduced by Wyborn and his staff. However, some acknowledgement is due to Cole's own standards and to the example which he set to his employees. During the Second World War Ekco was engaged in the production of portable radios, airborne radar sets, plastic practice bombs, and the T1154/R1155 radio sets for bombers. In 1943 Sir Stafford Cripps, then minister of aircraft production, described Ekco as 'one of the best, if not the best, units in the country producing wireless apparatus' (Geddes and Bussey, 263).

The post-war years brought a boom in demand for domestic television receivers, followed after a few years by a severe slump—very like the changes in the market for radio receivers after the First World War. Cole now controlled a large company. Profiting from his experiences three decades earlier, he appeared for a time to strengthen his own position within the radio industry. Ekco took over the television interests of Dynatron in 1955 and Ferranti in 1957, and also invested in overseas manufacturers. Cole was appointed CBE in 1958. But in fact all was not well with Ekco; its senior management generally was described as being 'woefully weak' (Lipman, 173). The company faced serious financial problems, and its overseas ventures, on the whole, were failures. In 1960 Ekco merged with Pye to form British Electronic Industries Ltd. Cole himself was appointed vice-chairman of the new organization, but retired in 1961 following a boardroom disagreement.

Cole could spare little time for hobbies while working, but was able in retirement to develop his interests in shooting and photography. His wife died in 1965, and he did not survive her for long. He died in a bathing accident at Fitts Village, St James, Barbados, on 18 November 1966.

ROWLAND F. POCOCK

Sources G. Bussey, 'Cole, Eric Kirkham', *DBB* · K. Geddes and G. Bussey, *The setmakers: a history of the radio and television industry* (1991) · M. I. Lipman, *Memoirs of a socialist business man* (1980) · *The Times* (21 Nov 1966), 12d · b. cert. · m. cert. · *CGPLA Eng. & Wales* (1967)
Archives priv. coll., business documents
Likenesses photographs, priv. coll.
Wealth at death £100,885: probate, 10 April 1967, *CGPLA Eng. & Wales*

Cole, George (1810–1883), landscape and animal painter, was born on 15 January 1810 in London, the second child and only son of James Cole (1772–1847) and Elizabeth

George Cole (1810–1883), by unknown engraver, pubd 1883 (after Henry van der Weyde)

Parker (d. 1819). Information about his early life is scanty: according to his grandson, Rex Vicat Cole, George Cole's father dissipated a fortune, and the boy began his life with no formal education as a ship's painter at Portsmouth. In another much repeated anecdote, recorded in the *Dictionary of National Biography*, he is at Wombwell's menagerie executing a canvas, measuring 20 feet by 20, of a tiger hunt in the jungle.

Cole's marriage in 1831 to Eliza Vicat (d. 1883), daughter of George and Catherine Vicat of Cosham, who were a Portsmouth Huguenot family, may have provided a starting point for his social and professional ascent. He was self-taught in art, and his surviving work from the 1840s includes portraits of individuals and, especially, of horses and dogs. He began to exhibit in London in 1838 and during the following decade experimented with a variety of genres, including animal painting, in which he gained considerable expertise, aiming to emulate Edwin Landseer and Thomas Sidney Cooper. He also produced a skilful *Still Life with Pheasant* (1847, City Art Gallery, Southampton) and a history painting, *Don Quixote and Sancho Panza* (exh. British Institution, 1840; photograph Courtauld Inst., Witt Library), which was much, though not always favourably, noticed.

By 1850 Cole had begun to concentrate on landscape, drawing on Dutch precedents for compositions such as *London Road, Portsdown* (1847, Portsmouth City Museum and Art Gallery). Working alongside him in the early 1850s was George Vicat *Cole (1833–1893), the eldest of Cole's five children, who later became a more eminent artist than his father. In search of sketching grounds they visited the river valleys of the Wye, Teign, and Dart and, in 1851 or 1852, the Moselle. While the father undoubtedly instructed the son, it seems likely that the influence of Pre-Raphaelitism, absorbed more fully by the younger artist, was transmitted through his work to the father. After a temporary estrangement in 1855 the two never worked together again. George Cole's landscapes of the later 1850s are, however, less formulaic than his early works and are often a combination of rustic genre subjects with carefully observed landscape, as in *Landscape and Cattle*

(1858, Russell-Cotes Art Gallery and Museum, Bournemouth).

By 1852 Cole was confident enough to sell up and move to London. After three years at 2 Lewes Place, Fulham, he made his home and studio at 2 Kensington Crescent. Subsequently, after a decade of conspicuous financial success, he purchased the larger house next door, no. 1, in 1863, as well as a country residence, Coombe Lodge, near Liss in Hampshire. In a series of richly coloured and detailed landscapes on large canvases executed during the 1860s and 1870s, Cole created an idealized version of the Hampshire moorlands and agricultural landscape; examples include *Fern Carting, Harting Coombe* (1873, Russell-Cotes Art Gallery and Museum, Bournemouth). Cattle continued to play an important role in his compositions, and he specialized in the depiction of river scenery with cows watering, including, for example, *Windsor Castle* (1876, exh. RA, 1878; Anglesey Abbey). Reassuring in their presentation of a seemingly timeless Englishness, these images were eagerly purchased by Victorian collectors.

Although he exhibited sixteen works at the Royal Academy, Cole's work formed a mainstay of the exhibitions of the Society of British Artists at Suffolk Street, where he exhibited 209 paintings from 1838 until his death in 1883. He was elected a member in 1850, became auditor in 1856, and vice-president in 1867. He was also awarded a medal for a harvesting scene in 1864 by the Society for the Encouragement of the Fine Arts. While, at his best, he was capable of sophisticated effects, the sheer volume of his production of smaller works, sold directly to dealers such as Thomas McLean and Arthur Tooth, inevitably led to a lowering of standards. His annual income rose from £842 in 1858 to £2580 in 1873.

A collector of topographical literature and an autodidact, Cole was reputed to know the works of Shakespeare by heart. Robert Chignell, the biographer of George Vicat Cole, saw the older painter as an exemplar of self-help: 'one who began with nothing', he had achieved success through 'great capabilities and force of character' (Chignell, 40). George Cole died on 7 September 1883 at his home at 1 Kensington Crescent and was buried in Kensal Green cemetery, London. Of his other children, Alfred Benjamin Cole was also an artist.   TIM BARRINGER

Sources T. J. Barringer, *The Cole family: painters of the English landscape, 1838–1975* (1988) [exhibition catalogue, Portsmouth and Bradford, 1 April – 30 Aug 1988] · R. Chignell, *The life and paintings of Vicat Cole, RA*, 1 (1896) · *Art Journal*, new ser., 3 (1883), 343 · *The Athenaeum* (15 Sept 1883), 345 · 'Four generations of landscape painters', *Hampshire Telegraph* (11 Feb 1938) · priv. coll., Cole MSS · *DNB* · census returns for London, 1871, 1881 · CGPLA Eng. & Wales (1883)
Archives priv. coll.
Likenesses G. Cole, self-portrait, oils, c.1850, repro. in Barringer, *The Cole Family*; priv. coll. · photographs, repro. in T. Barringer, *The Cole family*, 51, 59 · wood-engraving (after Henry van der Weyde), NPG; repro. in *ILN* (29 Sept 1883) [see illus.]
Wealth at death £20,999 12s. 5d.: probate, 26 Oct 1883, CGPLA Eng. & Wales

Cole, George Douglas Howard (1889–1959), university teacher and political theorist, was born in Cambridge on 25 September 1889, the son of George Cole, a jeweller who

George Douglas Howard Cole (1889–1959), by Howard Coster, 1938 [with his wife, Margaret Cole]

later moved to Ealing in west London and became a surveyor, and his wife, Jessie Knowles. He was educated at St Paul's School, London, and Balliol College, Oxford (1908–12), where he studied classical history and philosophy. As a student Cole became heavily involved in political and literary activities, joining both the Fabian Society and the Independent Labour Party, contributing to the Oxford *Blue Book*, agitating for the Workers' Educational Association, and editing the *Oxford Reformer*. Despite his tutors' concern, his education was unaffected by the extent of this political engagement. He completed his degree with firsts in both classical moderations (1910) and the final honour school of *literae humaniores* (1912) and was elected to a prize fellowship at Magdalen College, Oxford, in 1912.

Guild socialism On arriving at Magdalen, Cole abandoned the classics and began formally to study economics and political thought. In his initial research he endeavoured to construct a comparative account of the development of trade unionism across the western world. The result, *The World of Labour* (1913), published when he was still only twenty-four, received astonishing critical acclaim. Although a survey of existing trade unionism, *The World of Labour* also contained an uncompromising prescriptive message. He insisted that the tendency of the British left to expect that central governmental agencies would play the leading role in constructing a socialist future was essentially misplaced, in terms both of strategy and of principle. British socialists, Cole insisted, should abandon

their obsession with parliamentary elections and look instead to the direct action of trade unions. Social, economic, and political improvement could realistically be attained only by a policy of 'encroaching control', whereby trade unions would use strike action to gain an increasing amount of direct responsibility for the conduct of industry. Similarly, he contended, British socialists should strive to create an ideal society that would not require an overbearing state but which would rather ensure that power was radically decentralized and invested in a series of loosely federated industrial and social groups to be known as guilds.

The decentralizing element of Cole's agenda was widely popular in the first fifteen years of the twentieth century and Cole was one of an exceptionally broad alliance of thinkers advancing it. The argument was particularly closely associated with the London-based weekly newspaper the *New Age*, which drew on the work of a series of iconoclastic literary, cultural, and political figures, including Hilaire Belloc and G. K. Chesterton, consistently to outperform and outsell its more renowned counterparts. On publication of *The World of Labour* Cole rapidly became one of the most prominent figures of the *New Age* set, publishing an extensive article almost every week and frequently setting the paper's political agenda. Despite the prestige the paper allowed him, however, he was never entirely satisfied with a publication that presented attacks on the state from anarchists, *laissez-faire* liberals, disgruntled churchmen, medieval revivalists, and arch-conservatives. Such breadth had its limitations even for someone ideologically committed to diversity. Cole thus quickly developed a longing for an organization within which to develop and propagate his own unique message.

For a period during 1913–14, when he was living in Newcastle upon Tyne, Cole worked closely with the Social Democratic Federation, but the Fabian Society soon became the main focus of his efforts. Elected to the Fabian Society's executive committee in April 1914, he made an audacious attempt to take control of the society. Although he found a number of supporters among the younger members of the Fabian research department, his efforts to persuade the society at large to abandon their founding commitments and accept the guild ideal failed to attract widespread support. On learning of his defeat at the annual Fabian summer school at Keswick in June 1914, he heckled the speakers, organized a walkout, and then led a protest in the village square. His unruly behaviour was widely condemned, and few Fabians mourned his resignation from the society a year later.

Immediately after the failure of the Fabian take-over, Cole led a breakaway from the society, although he remained a member of the Fabian research department, and became its honorary secretary in 1916. Together with his fellow *New Age* contributors Ivor Brown, S. G. Hobson, William Mellor, and Maurice Reckitt, Cole formed an alternative political grouping, the National Guilds League (NGL). The NGL adopted its own constitution for the ideal society, known as the Storrington Document after the Sussex village in which it was written, and began to produce a series of journals, all of which were dedicated to shaping and propagating the anti-statist philosophy increasingly known as 'guild socialism'. The NGL also worked tirelessly to forge connections between leading guild socialist intellectuals and the larger trade union movement, managing as it did so to secure Cole appointment in 1915 as an unpaid research officer at the Amalgamated Society of Engineers. Cole advised the union on how to respond to wartime legislation including the Munitions Act. Although the job was relatively undemanding, it none the less enabled him to escape conscription on the grounds that he was conducting work of 'national importance'.

With exemption from military service secured, Cole spent the war years developing a fully fledged political theory of guild socialism. His work was shaped by a number of influences, including such ever-present socialist founding fathers as Robert Owen, William Morris, Jean-Jacques Rousseau (whose *Contrat Social* he translated in 1913), and John Ruskin. The most notable and unlikely source of inspiration, however, was the Anglican clergyman John Neville Figgis, the leading light in the English pluralist movement. Figgis had adopted the nineteenth-century idealist philosophy of Thomas Hill Green and transformed it into a plea for extensive decentralization of political, social, and economic power and especially for the effective independence of the church from governmental oversight. Figgis argued that the forms of communal attachment desired by Green could be developed only within small, localized units, and that the late nineteenth-century trend towards increasing the powers of the nation state ran counter to such requirements. In the early war years Cole used Figgis's arguments to attack the statist theories of the Fabian Society and other socialist groups, suggesting that a political system which guaranteed independence to trade unions and other voluntary organizations would realize a socialistic ideal of communal harmony more effectively than any efforts to impose communal attachments from above.

As the war progressed, however, Cole began to abandon this position and to replace it with a much more individualistic philosophy. By 1917 he had firmly rejected the communitarian assumptions which had underpinned Figgis's arguments. Instead he began to insist that socialists, English pluralists, and other reformers had failed to give enough emphasis to the uniqueness of each and every individual. It was 'of the essence' of each human being, Cole argued, 'that he is individual and cannot be absorbed into anything else'. The result was a political theory which emphasized the priority of individual liberty over all other commitments and which suggested that the only legitimate social, political, and economic obligations were those that the individual chose himself. Despite the far-reaching philosophical transformation, though, the political recommendations which this new theory generated remained very similar to his earlier ideas. The power of the state would have to be limited, if not abolished altogether, and a wide series of guilds should be established to govern each area of life independently. Cole also

insisted that such associations should all be radically democratized to ensure that the rules which governed people's lives were subject to the influence of the people themselves. These views were expounded throughout Cole's most accomplished theoretical works, including *Chaos and Order in Industry*, *Guild Socialism Restated*, and *Social Theory*, all of which were published in 1920.

The zeal and skill with which Cole presented these arguments made him a popular figure on the left. The libertarian underpinnings of his guild socialist message also seemed particularly attractive to reformers still reeling from the authoritarianism of wartime government. Thus in the immediate post-war world even old Fabian adversaries began to respond to his demands. Sidney and Beatrice Webb incorporated a number of guild socialist ideas into their post-war masterpiece *A Constitution for the Socialist Commonwealth of Great Britain*, and even nominated Cole, although unsuccessfully, for membership of Lloyd George's royal commission on the coal industry in 1919. Cole's work also found a considerable following overseas. In the United States many progressive and socialist reformers believed that the guild message was the perfect riposte to the centralizing powers adopted by Woodrow Wilson's wartime administration, and a few enthusiasts even opened a bookshop in New York's Greenwich Village dedicated to the guild socialist project.

Beyond the esteem of intellectuals, there was also a brief moment soon after the war when Cole had reason to believe that concrete political success was beckoning. Many British trade unionists, including Robert Smillie and Frank Hodges of the Miners' Federation, and some leading political figures, including Arthur Henderson, lent the guild socialist movement their explicit support. Cole, who had become the first honorary secretary for research in the Labour Research Department (successor to the Fabian research department), was appointed to represent the Labour interest alongside Henderson at the National Industrial Conference in 1919. The NGL even supported efforts to form guilds for piano workers and clerical officers, and to many people's surprise a short-lived guild was actually established in the building industry. Respected political and economic commentators, from both Britain and abroad, such as the *New Republic*'s Arthur Gleason urged 'industrial leaders' to 'study guild socialism' for 'soon they will be forced to accept it' (*The Survey*, 19 May 1917, 159).

Despite the excitement, however, efforts to build a long-lasting political movement failed. As the parliamentary prospects of the British Labour Party rapidly improved after the adoption of a new party constitution in 1918, the newly elected Labour élite became unwilling to risk the public suspicion that many feared would accompany association with radical movements such as the guild socialists. Nor did many trade unionists remain committed beyond the early 1920s. The sharp rise in unemployment in 1921 combined with the failure of many trade union activities leading to the collapse of the general strike in 1926 rendered most unions either too weak or too preoccupied to direct their energies in the direction of 'encroaching control'. As the guild socialists' political strategy faltered, so too did the apparatus of intellectual support. Although the quality of much of the argument and analysis in the journals Cole edited was high, incorporating contributions from the likes of Bertrand Russell and R. H. Tawney, most of the long list of guild periodicals, including the NGL's *The Guildsman* and *Guild Socialist*, had collapsed by 1922. All efforts at resurrecting them failed. The last guild journal, *New Standards*, ceased publication in 1924.

University teacher Dismayed by the failure of the guild socialist movement, Cole began in 1924 to reassess both his career and his fundamental theoretical and political commitments. After much deliberation he applied for the newly established position of reader in economics at the University of Oxford, and was appointed in 1925, resigning his position at the Labour Research Department. He also took up a teaching fellowship in University College, Oxford, to supplement his university lecturing duties. He initially found the intensive Oxford tutorial system exceptionally onerous and, although he completed a biography of Robert Owen in 1925, he produced no major theoretical or political works during his first three years as reader.

Early in 1929, however, Cole finally published a new substantial monograph, *The Next Ten Years in British Social and Economic Policy*, which was intended to produce both ideological principles and concrete guidelines for an incoming Labour government. Cole used this opportunity formally to retract many of his guild socialist commitments, including his dedication to the democratization of industrial associations, which had been at the heart of his earlier political vision. Such ideas, Cole now announced, were the result not of serious research into the demands and requirements of the working population but rather the naïve products of a 'politically minded person's utopia'. In their place, he outlined plans which bore more than a passing resemblance to the authoritarian, bureaucratic socialism against which he had previously railed, including an acceptance of planning and of nationalization. He even called for a national labour corps to offer unemployed workmen a place in a 'disciplined force' which would be directed by appointed government officials who would have 'the full power, subject to reasonable provision of appeal, of dismissing any member of it who fails to do satisfactory work' (*The Next Ten Years*, 52). It was a far cry from the individualistic, worker-centred programme of the guild age. Although the book was not a great success, Cole was welcomed back into the Fabian Society in 1929, and was rewarded a year later with a place alongside John Maynard Keynes in Ramsay MacDonald's Economic Advisory Council, established at the beginning of the second Labour government.

The reconciliation did not survive the collapse of MacDonald's government in 1931, after deep splits in the parliamentary Labour Party over the unemployment crisis, and Cole drifted back to the left of the party. In the next ten years he worked hard once again to produce a radically socialist alternative to mainstream labourism. He was convinced that the government's lack of clear principle had been the fundamental cause of its failure. Cole thus became a leading light in a variety of organizations designed to prompt a radical renewal in Labour thinking, including the Society for Socialist Inquiry and Propaganda (SSIP), founded in 1930, the New Fabian Research Bureau (1931), and the Socialist League (1932). As tensions in Europe increased, Cole also made sustained efforts to construct a British popular front against fascism, identifying the nature of the military threat long before many of his colleagues had abandoned their pacifism, and lending strong support to the republican cause in Spain.

Despite these radicalizing ambitions, though, Cole did not lose touch with more moderate influences in the labour movement; indeed in these years he developed a reputation for tolerance of the diverse forces operating in British left-wing politics. On accepting his readership in Oxford in 1925, he had formed an informal discussion circle known as the 'Cole group', which flourished throughout the 1930s and acted paradoxically as a seedbed for a more revisionist agenda for the party. In addition, he also concentrated throughout the 1930s on writing books about themes of general interest which he hoped would reach a broader audience than either academic texts or socialist polemics. His huge *History of Socialist Thought* was predated by *The Intelligent Man's Review of Europe Today* (1933), *The Condition of Britain* (1937) written with his wife, Margaret Cole, and, most notably of all, *The Common People* (1938), written with his brother-in-law Raymond William Postgate. All were outstanding successes. For several decades they remained classics in the emerging discipline of labour history, a field of study whose post-war prominence in British universities owed much to his inter-war endeavours.

In 1940 Cole returned to a position of political prominence when he was asked to assist Sir William Beveridge at the Ministry of Labour in drawing up a plan for the effective use of manpower during war. Early in 1941 he was appointed sub-warden of the newly founded Nuffield College, Oxford, and he combined these two roles in creating the Nuffield College Social Reconstruction Survey, which collated an enormous range of demographic, economic, and social data and employed it, much to government disapproval, to argue for an extensive programme of social reform. Cole's time at Nuffield was, though, cut short both by illness and by the government's withdrawal of funds for the survey. He resigned as sub-warden in September 1943, as director of the survey in January 1944, and as fellow in March. A few months later, however, he was appointed Chichele professor of social and political theory, and took up a fellowship at All Souls College. Claiming to be the only leading academic expert in all three branches of Oxford's final honour school of philosophy, politics, and economics, he continually encouraged the new college's fellowship to broaden their interests and maintain an interdisciplinary approach to a subject matter increasingly prone to narrow academic specialization.

He also returned to discuss some of the central philosophical themes that he had touched upon in his youth, including the legitimacy of state power and the place of democratic mechanisms in modern industry.

During his years at All Souls, and in common with others of his generation, Cole actively returned also to the commitments of earlier days, developing a renewed scepticism of state authority. He accepted the need for economic planning and some form of central control but insisted once again that it 'must be based on a recognition of diversity'. In trying to forward these ideas he stood unsuccessfully for one of the university's two parliamentary seats at the general election of 1945, his candidacy being endorsed by the university constituency Labour Party but not by the national party. He also refused to welcome the social policy reforms of the Attlee administration as warmly as might have been expected, demanding instead that the government take more seriously the need to involve welfare recipients, workers, and consumers directly in decision making at a local level.

Socialist intellectual Such continual changes of direction have led some critics to reject Cole as a permanent oppositionist, never able to settle on a conviction for more than a few years, especially if it was to become popular. Such a charge, however, overlooks both the merits of Cole's essential open-mindedness and the many aspects of his professional career which remained constant throughout his life. From his undergraduate days until his death Cole worked for the Workers' Educational Association and was celebrated widely as one of the association's finest tutors and administrators. Although not all the association's students appreciated his lecturing style—one reported that Cole would uncontrollably stroll up and down the raised dais as he spoke, often appearing as if he was going to fall off the other side—most praised his energy and his intellectual acumen, and many became active disciples. The association's administration certainly appreciated the continual efforts which he invested in the organization, stretching from his directorship of the association's early classes in London to long-term membership of its general purposes committee. Throughout the turmoil of the inter-war years Cole remained unstintingly committed to offering a broad-based, non-vocational, liberal education to those who had missed out on formal educational opportunities.

Cole also contributed to an enormous number of learned and popular periodicals throughout his long career, even at times of illness and personal distress. He found writing easy, was confident in his abilities, and rarely, if ever, agreed to alter his text on the basis of editorial advice or peer review. In choosing where to place his work, however, he displayed little intellectual arrogance, believing that he had a duty to promote socialist ideas as broadly as possible. He was thus always willing to write for an exceptionally wide range of audiences. The major outlet for most of his career was the *New Statesman*, for which he often acted as industrial correspondent, and he was considered for the editorship in 1930, but he also contributed regularly to minor professional journals, including

the *Library Assistant*, and even to eccentric publications such as the *Aryan Path*, a theosophical journal dedicated to the promotion of Eastern spirituality, a project for which Cole had little but disdain. His articles were almost always lucid, accessible, and engaging, and exhibited neither the self-conscious intellectual complexity that dogged the contributions of many of his colleagues on the left nor the obsession with scientific method and quantification that increasingly characterized the work of his academic colleagues. Cole preserved his articles and pamphlets throughout his life, and they are now in Nuffield College library, Oxford, stretching over eight large volumes, a testament both to his productivity and to his breadth of interest.

Cole's private life was less fulfilling than his public endeavours. In August 1918 Cole married Margaret Isabel Postgate (1893–1980) [see Cole, Dame Margaret Isabel], daughter of the classical scholar John Percival *Postgate and an active volunteer in socialist circles. The couple had one son and two daughters in a marriage that lasted forty-one years. They also jointly wrote a number of books and articles, including twenty-nine detective novels, which although not successful at the time have since become collectors' items. The marriage does not seem, however, to have been particularly happy. Despite his tendency to project a romantic, even sentimental, image in much of his writing, Cole had little interest in actual romantic attachment and even less in sexual relations, admitting openly to a lack of interest in 'passions of the flesh'. Friends also recalled that his emotional attachments, such as they were, tended to be with men rather than women. He was openly fond of some of his male students, including the future leader of the Labour Party Hugh Gaitskell, although there is no evidence of any homosexual encounters either before or during his marriage. After her husband's death Margaret Cole commented on his sexual proclivities and inadequacies, both unkindly and comprehensively, in her popular biography *The Life of G. D. H. Cole*.

Marital difficulties were not the only example of Cole's strained personal interactions. Margaret Cole described him as a most 'Unsocial Socialist' who got 'very little out of personal association with outside people except definite pieces of information', while others also dismissed his 'aloof' and 'aristocratic' manner (Cole, *Growing up into Revolution*, 78–9). He was widely accused of holding conservative views on issues stretching from cinemas and the wireless to women's clothes and American phrases, and later in the twentieth century some on the left even dismissed him as more of an old-fashioned tory radical than a real libertarian socialist. At least partly as a result, he appears to have been actively disliked by many of his most natural intellectual allies. Harold J. Laski, who shared many ideas with Cole in his guild socialist years, found him insufferable and rarely associated personally with him. Nor did Cole mellow with years. Indeed, blighted continually with ill health—diabetes was diagnosed in 1931—he exhibited an increasing degree of eccentricity. When he was elected to a research fellowship at Nuffield College after his retirement in 1957, many colleagues found him already surprisingly disconnected from everyday academic life; he reportedly told one research student that he believed he was already dead.

Despite the lack of close friendships and attachments, Cole was widely celebrated in left-wing intellectual circles throughout his life, and a collection of essays was prepared in his honour, some of which contained warm personal reminiscences, to be presented to him on his seventieth birthday. His death, in the North Western Hospital, Hampstead, London, on 14 January 1959, occurred before either the anniversary or the appearance of the book. At the time he was remembered most frequently for his major contribution to university teaching, to labour history, and to economic research. In subsequent years, however, labour history has declined as a subject of academic enquiry and Cole's own reputation as an economist has seriously diminished. Few, if any, scholars active in the late twentieth century believed that Cole fully understood either socialist economics or the importance of the Keynesian revolution. At the same time, on the other hand, his contributions to political theory increasingly attracted praise and attention. By the mid-1990s a number of political theorists had returned to *Social Theory* and *Guild Socialism Restated* to examine Cole's libertarian ideals and democratizing agenda in search of a pluralistic philosophy with which to replace an increasingly discredited statist socialism and social democracy. In this respect Cole's own judgement appears to have been sound, for he often suggested that of all his work it would be his contribution to guild socialism that posterity would treat most favourably.   MARC STEARS

Sources M. Cole, *The life of G. D. H. Cole* (1979) · M. Cole, *Growing up into revolution* (1949) · A. Wright, *G. D. H. Cole and socialist democracy* (1979) · M. Stears, *Progressives, pluralists and the problems of the state* (2002) · A. Briggs and J. Saville, eds., *Essays in labour history* (1960) · *DNB* · *CGPLA Eng. & Wales* (1959)
Archives Internationaal Instituut voor Sociale Geschiedenis, Amsterdam, corresp. and literary papers · Nuffield Oxf., corresp. and papers · People's History Museum, Manchester, papers · Ruskin College, Oxford, corresp., literary papers, biographical memoranda | BL, corresp. with Society of Authors, Add. MS 63219 · BLPES, Fabian Society papers · BLPES, corresp. with J. E. Meade · Bodl. Oxf., corresp. with Gilbert Murray · Glamorgan RO, Cardiff, letters relating to south Wales manpower survey · Internationaal Instituut voor Sociale Geschiedenis, Amsterdam, corresp. with Max Beer · JRL, letters to the *Manchester Guardian* · Nuffield Oxf., Bedford papers · People's History Museum, Manchester, corresp. with J. S. Middleton · Temple House, London, Workers' Educational Association papers · U. Leeds, Brotherton L., corresp. relating to Nuffield social reconstruction survey · Welwyn Garden City Central Library, corresp. with Frederic Osborn
Likenesses photograph, c.1905, Hult. Arch. · H. Coster, photograph, 1938, NPG [*see illus.*] · W. Rothenstein, chalk drawing, c.1940, Nuffield Oxf. · S. Bowen, oils, 1944–5, NPG · H. Coster, photographs, NPG
Wealth at death £46,617 9s. 9d.: probate, 26 Aug 1959, *CGPLA Eng. & Wales*

Cole, George James, Baron Cole (1906–1979), industrialist, was born in Singapore on 3 February 1906, the second of the three children and only son of James Francis Cole, who was on the staff of the Eastern Telegraph Company, and his wife, Alice Edith Wheeler. He was educated at the Raffles Institution, Singapore (1909–21) and Herne Bay College, Kent (1921–3). Thereafter his education was in what his later employer, the first Viscount Leverhulme, once called 'the University of Hard Knocks'—and he graduated with distinction. In 1923 he joined the Niger Company then recently acquired by Leverhulme, as a junior clerk; a year later he was put in charge of a newly created statistical department. In 1926 Cole made his first visit to west Africa; he came to know the area well and developed a lifetime admiration, affection, and understanding for its people. In 1929 Leverhulme's extensive interests in African commerce, the Niger Company, and the African and Eastern Trading Company, were merged under the name of the United Africa Company. Cole's employers represented a powerful influence in African affairs as well as in Europe and elsewhere, particularly after the merger in 1929 of Leverhulme's interests and the Dutch Margarine Union to create Unilever. Cole rose steadily in the United Africa Company, taking on responsibility for provisions buying and, later, transport.

When war broke out in 1939 Cole returned from Nigeria to London to manage all the United Africa Company's affairs in British west Africa. On 18 May 1940 he married Ruth Abercor, *née* Harpham (1904/5–1978), a divorcee. There were two children of the marriage, a son born in 1945, and a daughter in 1951. Cole was seconded to the staff of Lord Swinton, British resident minister in west Africa in 1941. He was, *inter alia*, responsible for handling materials through these territories for the allied campaign in north Africa. When the war ended, he was appointed to the board of the United Africa Company, becoming joint managing director from 1952 to 1955 and simultaneously chairman of the shipping subsidiary, Palm Line Ltd. In 1948 he was elected to the boards of the British and Dutch parent companies. His appointment was initially as the expert on African and overseas trade, but his talents were increasingly employed in the affairs of Unilever worldwide. In 1956 he was appointed vice-chairman of Unilever Ltd and became a member of the special committee, Unilever's ruling triumvirate from 1930 until the 1990s. When its redoubtable chairman, Lord Heyworth, retired in 1960 after a reign of eighteen years George Cole succeeded him: it was a formidable task, for under Heyworth and his Dutch colleague, Rykens, Unilever had itself expanded considerably in Europe, India, Africa, and North and South America.

As chairman, Cole worked to strengthen not only the organizational basis of Unilever to meet the growing competitive challenge of the 1960s but also the personal ties with his Dutch colleagues. By nature, and in his professional dealings, he was warm, friendly, and wholly without affectation or pomposity. His philosophy of business was basically simple but applied with shrewd acumen. He understood 'business' to mean 'profitable trade'. (He gleefully adopted the title of the African trader, invented for him by a colleague.) He fully accepted the current need to adopt scientific and technological methods for managing industry, always provided they did not obscure the fundamental end and purpose of profitable trade. Thus he stoutly defended Unilever's advertising budget against the Monopolies Commission which criticized it as excessive. In international affairs he believed that trade was a better means of bringing welfare to the 'third world' than 'aid' loosely administered.

Mercurial flashes of temperament were characteristic of Cole, and so too were 'excitable flashes of insight mingled with occasional rather wild flights of fancy' (*The Times*, 30 Nov 1979). An outstanding example of this was the scheme he produced late in 1968, with Sir Derek Pritchard, chairman of Allied Breweries, for a merger of Unilever and Allied; it was a scheme 'of staggering size and complexity' (Reader, 81). The proposal was referred to the Monopolies Commission, which raised no objection to the merger when it reported some six months later. However stock market valuations of the two corporations had changed so much that it could not go ahead. All this did nothing to blunt Cole's warm relations with his colleagues and staff. They knew him as a generous and inspiring business leader whose secret was his belief in mutual confidence between man and man.

Physically Cole was generously built, with strong features, a fresh complexion, and bright eyes that smiled readily. He occasionally betrayed an attractive diffidence, perhaps deriving from a consciousness that his formal education had ended early in life.

Cole was created a life peer in 1965, choosing Baron Cole of Blackfriars (home of Unilever House) as his title. An enthusiastic advocate of merger, his maiden speech in the House of Lords offered a realistic appraisal of the problems of the aircraft industry. In 1970 he retired from Unilever after forty-seven years. Six months later he accepted the invitation of the government to be chairman of Rolls-Royce at a time when the company's future in the aerospace industry was in jeopardy because of losses on the Tri-star engine. The appointment of Cole, a trader, to bring order to engineers in their own industry was a brave stroke, but he met the challenge with his customary brisk efficiency and was rewarded with a knighthood in 1973. He was a commander of the order of Orange Nassau (1963) and a member of the governing bodies of a large number of societies concerned with Dutch, African, South American, and international affairs, a trustee of the Leverhulme Trust (1970–75), and a director of Shell Transport and Trading (1971–5). He died at St Stephen's Hospital, Chelsea, London, on 29 November 1979.

CHARLES WILSON, *rev.* JUDY SLINN

Sources *The Times* (30 Nov 1979) · *The Times* (20 Feb 1980) · W. J. Reader, *Fifty years of Unilever* (1980) · Unilever company records, Unilever plc, London · *The Times* (2 March 1966) · *The Times* (12 Nov 1970) · m. cert. · d. cert.

Likenesses E. Halliday, oils, 1965, Unilever plc, London

Wealth at death £404,906: probate, 27 March 1980, *CGPLA Eng. & Wales*

Cole, George Vicat (1833–1893), landscape painter, was born in Portsmouth on 17 April 1833, eldest of five children of the landscape painter George *Cole (1810–1883) and Eliza Vicat (*d.* 1883). Initially exhibiting as 'George Cole, junior', from the mid-1850s he adopted his mother's French Huguenot maiden name to distinguish his name from that of his father. Later in life the younger Cole dropped 'George' altogether, using 'Vicat' (pronounced with a long *i*) as his first name. As a boy Cole was taught by his father and accompanied the older painter on journeys round country houses, where they would paint portraits of the owners, their horses, and dogs. He also made copies of prints after works of Turner and David Cox. Father and son took sketching tours together, in England, Wales, and also to the Moselle. In 1852 George Cole sold up in Portsmouth and moved to Fulham; among the auction lots were twenty-seven works by the younger artist. 1852 saw Cole's work exhibited in London for the first time: *View from Ranmore Common* was favourably hung at the British Institution galleries and sold for £21. At the time of his twentieth birthday, in 1853, two of his works were accepted for exhibition at the Royal Academy.

After a quarrel with his father in 1855, Cole rented rooms in Torriano Villas, Camden, and, on 7 November 1856, married Mary Ann Chignell (*d.* 1915), daughter of a wealthy Hampshire tradesman. The years 1857–9 were spent at the picturesque village of Albury in Surrey, where Cole, his wife, and the first of three daughters (Mary Blanche, born in 1858) were joined by the painter Benjamin Williams Leader. Cole's breakthrough came with *Harvest Time, Painted at Hombury Hill, Surrey* (1860; Bristol City Art Gallery), a large canvas completed in the open air, strongly influenced by the Pre-Raphaelites. The Society of Arts awarded Cole a silver medal for the work. In 1861 Cole moved to 19 Gloucester Road, Kensington, travelling annually in search of subject matter. In 1863 he resigned from the Society of British Artists in order to seek election as a royal academician. His works from this period, such as *Springtime* (1865; Manchester City Art Galleries), espouse a brilliantly detailed and highly coloured Pre-Raphaelite realism. His work increasingly concentrated on Surrey landscapes: *Summer's Golden Crown* returned to a harvest subject with conspicuous success at the Royal Academy in 1866 and the Paris Universal Exhibition of 1867. Cole's style broadened in the late 1860s: the dramatic *A Pause in the Storm at Sunset* (exh. RA, 1869) impressed public and critics alike. In January 1870 he was elected an associate of the Royal Academy, and from that time rarely exhibited his work in any other forum.

Assured of financial, if not always critical, success, Cole moved in 1874 to Little Campden House, an elegant early eighteenth-century mansion in Kensington. In the large studio he pursued his interest in science, also fitting automatic gates and an early telephone. His biographer, Robert Chignell, describes Cole's 'fine head, with handsome clearly-marked features … set on a well-knit form of about 5 feet 7 inches in height' (Chignell, 1.3). His character was quiet and reserved, though he was described by the landscape painter B. W. Leader as 'most good-tempered, liberal and hospitable, fond of a joke' (ibid., 3.141). Both at his home and on his Thames steam launch, *The Blanche*, he entertained a circle of friends which included Frederic Leighton, John Everett Millais, and many other leading artists, notably Edward Linley Sambourne who referred to the group as 'the Calithrumpkins' (Cole papers).

Cole continued to produce a series of large exhibition landscapes of Surrey and Sussex subjects through the 1870s, but expanded his range with *Richmond Hill* (exh. RA, 1875) and *The Alps at Rosenlaui* (exh. RA, 1878). After his election to the status of full academician, in 1880, he worked exclusively on a series of major paintings of the Thames from its source to the sea, commissioned by the dealer William Agnew. During these years he became a well-known figure on the river, often painting from his steam launch. After a series of rural scenes, he surprised his public in 1888 with a grandiose canvas, *The Pool of London* (exh. RA, 1888; Tate collection), in which smoke and cloud at sunset part to reveal the dome of St Paul's Cathedral. Dramatic and painterly, it betrays none of the precise naturalism that had distinguished his earliest work. *The Pool of London* was purchased for £2000 under the terms of the Chantrey Bequest. W. E. Gladstone later wrote to Cole's biographer, Robert Chignell, expressing his admiration for the work.

Vicat Cole's work, like that of his father, George Cole, is variable in quality, but he was able at his best to produce landscapes exactly suited to the demands of the mid-Victorian public. Despite the lavish tributes paid by Leighton and others after he died at his home in Kensington on 6 April 1893, his work soon came to seem outmoded. He was buried at Kensal Green cemetery, London. Robert Chignell's lavish three-volume biography, published in 1896, provides reproductions of a large number of his works. His son, Reginald George Vicat *Cole (1870–1940), who assisted his father in the early 1890s, became a landscape painter, author, and teacher. TIM BARRINGER

Sources R. Chignell, *The life and paintings of Vicat Cole, RA* (1896) · T. J. Barringer, *The Cole family: painters of the English landscape, 1838–1975* (1988) [exhibition catalogue, Portsmouth and Bradford, 1 April – 30 Aug 1988] · J. Dafforne, 'British artists, their style and character: no. CXII, Vicat Cole', *Art Journal*, 32 (1870), 177–9 · H. Schutz Wilson, 'Our living artists: Vicat Cole RA', *Magazine of Art*, 1 (1877–8) · 'Celebrities at home, no. CCCXCIX: Mr Vicat Cole at Little Campden House, Kensington', *The World* (6 May 1885) · *The Times* (29 April 1893) · R. V. Cole, *The artistic anatomy of trees* (1916) · C. Payne, *Toil and plenty: images of the agricultural landscape in England, 1780–1890* (1993), 120–22 [exhibition catalogue, U. Nott. Art Gallery, 7 Oct – 14 Nov 1993; Yale U. CBA, 15 Jan – 13 March 1994] · priv. coll., Cole papers · m. cert. · d. cert.

Archives priv. coll., papers

Likenesses photographs, c.1850–1885, repro. in Barringer, *Cole family* · A. S. Cope, oils, 1886, Aberdeen Art Gallery; repro. in Barringer, *Cole family*, 69 · photograph, woodburytype, NPG · woodcuts (after photographs), NPG

Wealth at death £10,371 5s. 5d.: resworn probate, May 1895, *CGPLA Eng. & Wales* (1893)

Cole, Henry (1504/5–1579/80), dean of St Paul's and religious controversialist, was born at Godshill, Isle of Wight. He entered Winchester College in 1519 at the age of fourteen, and was admitted to New College, Oxford, on 26 October 1521, becoming a fellow exactly two years later, and retaining his fellowship until 1540. Cole took his BCL on 3 March 1530 and was incepted as DCL in July 1540. In the interval he studied law in Padua and perhaps Greek. Although Cole's formal patron was Dr William Knight he became close enough to Reginald Pole to have known about the latter's *Pro ecclesiasticae unitatis defensione*, a fierce attack on Henry VIII which was completed in 1536, and told Thomas Starkey that Pole had changed his mind about papal authority while writing it. Cole accompanied Pole on his first (abortive) legation towards England in 1537 before they parted company in Paris. Returning to England, Cole became sub-warden of New College in March 1538, and, more importantly, by April had written a treatise on general councils defending Henry VIII's attack on the council of Mantua–Vicenza of 1537–8. Cole argued that the pope was not head of the council, that not even a council could determine things indifferent, and concluded that it would be easier 'to make a new head than to reform the old' (BL, Hatfield MS 46, fol. 75r).

Cole's first major benefice was Pole's old prebend of Yetminster secunda in Salisbury Cathedral (installed 30 September 1539), and he was collated to the rectory of Chelmsford, Essex, on 11 September 1540 (vacated by March 1548). Three prebends of St Paul's in succession followed: Holborn (1540–41); Sneating (1541 to before 22 March 1542); and Wenlocksbarn (1542 to 29 May 1559). Also in 1540 Cole was admitted to the College of Advocates. On 25 March 1542 he was ordained priest and on 4 October was elected warden of New College. He was the bishop of London's chancellor by 1543 at the time of the prebendaries' plot against Archbishop Cranmer, who suspected Cole of involvement in it. In early December Cole was arrested on the grounds of his association with Reginald Pole, now a cardinal, who had been attainted with other members of his family in 1539, but was pardoned on 24 April 1544 for all dealings with Pole and with the latter's agent, Michael Throckmorton. The pardon granted to one John Bekinsaw on 6 May following stated that Cole had sent Pole medicine and arranged a secret signal with Bekinsaw to let him know what happened to Pole following his departure from Flanders, presumably in 1537. Stephen Vaughan's report in January 1545 that Cole had been seen in Italy on his way to Rome cannot be accurate, since on 4 July following he personally surrendered a property of his college to the king, but it is of a piece with the attack on Cole as a popish traitor, 'one of Poolys ryght scolars', made by Vaughan's colleague Henry Brinklow in his *Complaynt of Roderyck Mors* (*Brinklow's Complaynt*, 61).

New College presented Cole to the rectory of Newton Longville on 16 May 1545 (vacated 1552), although he was not installed until three days after he had been dispensed on 11 September to hold an additional benefice. In 1550 the sub-warden and fellows tried to oust Cole, and were ordered in October not to proceed without royal licence. It may be that Cole had been imprisoned in the interval, for in August 1551 the sheriff of London was paid for keeping Cole and two of his servants for fifteen months. In January 1551 the privy council committed Cole's case to trial, and on 16 April he was forced to resign his wardenship. He was replaced by Ralph Skinner, a sound evangelical. Yet three days later Cole was allowed to proceed BTh and DTh 'without any exercise done for it' (Emden, *Oxf.*, 4.128). These episodes leave Cole's religious opinions under Edward VI unclear. According to John Jewel, Cole came 'to the church ... and heard the common prayers ... ministered, and received the communion' (*Works*, 1.61), assertions Cole did not dispute. Lawrence Humphrey later embroidered them in his *Joannis Juelli ... vita* (1573), emphasizing that Cole had preached obedience to Edward during the western rebellion of 1549. Nicholas Sander, by contrast, claimed that Cole had confessed his faith through resigning his benefices. On 25 October 1553 Cole became archdeacon of Ely, suggesting that Mary found him a reliable Catholic, and giving weight to Sander's interpretation. In 1553–4 he served on commissions to restore bishops Bonner and Tunstall, and at about the time of his participation in the disputation with Latimer and Ridley at Oxford on 17–18 April 1554, became canon and ninth prebendary of Westminster (presented 10 April, installed 21 April, held to 26 September 1556). On 13 July 1554 he was appointed provost of Eton (vacated by 5 July 1559), and was prolocutor of convocation in that year. On 17 March 1555 he brought word to Cranmer that there was no further hope for him.

Cole played a central role in the events immediately before Cranmer's execution on 21 March, above all by preaching a legally inventive sermon in the university church. In it Cole gave three reasons why Cranmer, although a repentant sinner, nevertheless had to die: the nullification of Henry's first marriage; heresy, 'of which he had been a most carnal defender' (Foxe, 1885); and in order to balance John Fisher's death. In summer 1556 Cole was one of Pole's visitors of Oxford, and he probably took a hand in revising the university's statutes. On 11 December 1556 he was elected dean of St Paul's, and then on the 29th was appointed to a commission to recover ex-monastic documents. Two days later he was entrusted with another important case, when Pole assigned him to investigate how the Drapers' Company of London was handling a bequest. On 1 January 1558 Cole received yet another appointment, becoming a member of a commission charged to survey the state of the church's finances, and was also ordered to help collect the clerical subsidy. On 8 February he received a commission to act against heresy and seditious books (he had already received a licence to read heretical works on 13 July 1555), which he immediately put to use in the visitation of Cambridge, where he was incorporated DTh on 16 February 1557. On 28 August Pole made him his archiepiscopal vicar-general, and on 1 October dean of arches, at which time he was apparently also acting as commissary of the prerogative court of Canterbury. On 16 November he and Dr Thomas Martin (a lawyer who had been Bishop Gardiner's chancellor) received a commission to burn anti-papal writings, and on 1 December Cole witnessed the installation of Sir Thomas Tresham as prior of the knights of St John of Jerusalem.

Cole figured prominently in the convocation of 1558, submitting to it a plan for the redistribution of ecclesiastical revenues. Pole collated him to the rectory of Wrotham, Kent, on 6 July 1558. Two weeks later he received orders to visit All Souls. Either the difficulties were too great, or he proved unexpectedly incompetent, for Nicholas Harpsfield, who had by then replaced Cole as dean of arches, revisited the college in November, perhaps simply because Cole failed to turn over the records of his visitation. Cole's replacement by Harpsfield reflected a realignment of Canterbury administration, since Cole moved by 4 November to be commissary of the prerogative court there. Robert Ware, writing in the second half of the seventeenth century, but citing the manuscripts of Richard Boyle, earl of Cork, and Sir James Ware, as well as the authority of Archbishop James Usher and others, and giving substantial amounts of circumstantial evidence, claimed that Mary, in October 1558, had sent Cole on a mission against heresy in Ireland. While waiting to embark from Chester his landlady, concerned for her brother in Dublin, substituted for Cole's commission a pack of cards, knave of clubs uppermost. When Cole arrived in Dublin and presented his 'commission', the deputy, the earl of Sussex, sent him back for a new one, remarking that 'we will shuffle the cards in the meanwhile' (Ware, 22–3). The episode was retold in doggerel verse by one Peregrine Wilton in *Blackwood's Magazine*, 25 (1829), 153–8. Queen Mary's death soon afterwards ended Cole's concern with Ireland. Cole was one of the supervisors of Pole's will, however, and continued to be commissary of the prerogative court of Canterbury until some time in 1559.

After Elizabeth's accession Cole took the leading role for the Catholic side at the Westminster conference in March 1559. Sander reported at length Cole's speech defending the use of Latin in worship and admitted that he was surprised by Cole's holiness. Sander described his new hero as 'most learned in both laws, philosophy and theology' and 'so abstemious in food, drink and sleep that no one would be thought to have lived in private life more happily' (Archivio Segreto Vaticano, armaria 64:28, fol. 266*v*). A version of Cole's text in English survives (Corpus Christi College, Cambridge, MS 121, fols. 183–91), and his major point concerned the necessity of unity with the whole church which vernacular worship would destroy. Cole put forward the subsidiary argument that English changed too much to be the language of divine service. Jewel contemptuously dismissed Cole's behaviour and remarks, writing to Peter Martyr that Cole, 'stamping his feet, throwing out his arms, bending sideways, snapping his fingers and raising and lowering his eyebrows by turns', had called the protestants the authors of sedition. Jewel concluded that 'I never heard anyone rave after a more solemn and school-masterly fashion' (*Works*, 4.1201–2). He also accused Cole of having wrecked the meeting by refusing to abide by the agreed rules, and Cole was supposedly fined 500 marks for contempt.

Between 29 May and 5 July 1559 Cole lost all his benefices. Perhaps seeing the end coming, probably about this time he gave sixty-three books to St John's College,

Oxford. They are primarily works of theology, philosophy, and biblical commentary, and include no legal texts. In early 1560 he engaged Jewel in a controversy which set the terms of Catholic–protestant debate for most of Elizabeth's reign. Among the substantive points raised were the role of custom, the importance of argument from history, the pope's status, and the nature of the eucharist. Summoned before Elizabeth's visitors at Lambeth, Cole was committed to the Tower on 20 May 1560—two days after Jewel's most detailed refutation of his arguments—and was transferred to the Fleet on 10 June. About July 1561 he was proposed as bishop of London by an English exile. By the time of his death Cole had been moved to the Wood Street compter, where he died between 4 December 1579 and 1 January 1580. Cole left his unspecified property to his executor, Humphrey Moseley, a lawyer who was also secondary of the prison, and a man whom Cole called 'my trusty and well-beloved friend' (PRO, PROB 11/62, fol. 24*v*).

T. F. MAYER

Sources Emden, *Oxf.*, 4.128–9, 717–18 · Wood, *Ath. Oxon.*, new edn, 1.450–54 · *LP Henry VIII*, vols. 9–10, 12/2–13/1, 18/2–19/1, 20/1–2 · BL, Cotton MS Nero B.vi, fol. 175*r* (*LP Henry VIII*, 10, no. 961); Add. MS 32091, fol. 149*r*–149*v* · PRO, SP 1/197, fol. 53*r* (*LP Henry VIII*, 20/1, no. 40) · PRO, SP 15/7/58 · PRO, PROB 11/42A, fols. 107*r*–108*r* · PRO, PROB 11/62, fol. 24*v* · PRO, PROB 29/10, fols. 121*r*, 134*v*, 141*v* · BL, Hatfield MS 46, fols. 40*r*–75*v* · LPL, MS 1135, fols. 1*v*–10*r* · Pole's register, LPL, fols. 27*v*, 28*r*–28*v*, 35*v*, 36*r*, 78*v* · *Fasti Angl., 1300–1541*, [Salisbury], 103 · *Fasti Angl., 1300–1541*, [St Paul's, London], 41, 62 · *Fasti Angl., 1541–1857*, [Salisbury], 92 · *Fasti Angl., 1541–1857*, [St Paul's, London], 57, 63 · *Fasti Angl., 1541–1857*, [Ely], 79 · GL, MS 9531/12, fol. 99*v* · bishop's register, Lincs. Arch., Lincoln diocesan archives, register 27, fol. 228 · Bibliothèque Municipale, Douai, MS 922, vol. 3, fol. 75*r*; vol. 5, fols. 7*v*–9*r*, 12*r*–12*v*, 98*r*–99*r*, 106*r*–106*v* · Biblioteca Apostolica Vaticana, Vatican City, Vat. lat. 5967, fols. 469*r*–471*r* · G. Burnet, *The history of the Reformation of the Church of England*, rev. N. Pocock, new edn, 5 (1865), 514–23 · Archivio Segreto Vaticano, armaria 64:28, fols. 252*r*–274*r* · *APC*, 1550–52, 139, 204, 334 · P. Heylin, *Ecclesia restaurata, or, The history of the Reformation of the Church of England*, 2 (1661); repr. J. C. Robinson, ed. (1849), 138 · *Henry Brinklow's Complaynt of Roderyck Mors*, ed. J. W. Cowper, EETS, extra ser., 22 (1874) · *CPR, 1553–4*, 75, 76, 121, 377; *1555–7*, 281; *1557–8*, 14 · *The works of John Jewel*, ed. J. Ayre, 4 vols., Parker Society, 24 (1845–50), vol. 1, pp. 26–80; vol. 4, pp. 1201–2 · L. Humphrey, *Joannis Juelli Angli, episcopi Sarisburiensis vita et mors* (1573) · J. Foxe, *Actes and monuments*, 4th edn, 2 vols. (1583) · C. Kitching, 'The prerogative court of Canterbury from Warham to Whitgift', *Continuity and change: personnel and administration of the Church of England, 1500–1642*, ed. R. O'Day and F. Heal (1976), 191–214, esp. 200–01 · R. Ware, *The reformation of the Church of Ireland in the life and death of George Browne, sometime archbishop of Dublin* (1681), 22–3

Cole, Sir Henry (1808–1882), civil servant, was born in Bath on 15 July 1808, the son of an army officer, Captain Henry Robert Cole, and his wife, Laetitia Dormer. He attended Christ's Hospital school from 1817 to 1823, and on leaving found employment as a clerk to Sir Francis Palgrave, one of the sub-commissioners at the record commission. Three years later he obtained rooms in the home of the writer, Thomas Love Peacock, whose son worked with Cole at the record commission. While living there Cole's circle of friends grew to include writers and artists, as well as young men such as John Stuart Mill and Charles Buller, who were to become known as the philosophical radicals. Cole's utilitarian connections and his employment as a

Sir Henry Cole (1808–1882), by Samuel Laurence, 1865

civil servant were the basis for what was to be a very influential career in public service.

Reforming the record commission The first indication that Cole was a man to be reckoned with was his successful campaign to reform the record commission. After a disagreement with his employer about his salary Cole decided that the time had come to expose the record commission as a hotbed of jobbery and corruption. He wrote articles, including two in *The Examiner*, describing the corruption and the lack of progress in achieving the aims of the commission, which had been set up to investigate the state of the public records which were housed in a number of more or less unsatisfactory buildings around London. Cole was removed from his post in 1835, and suffered a number of attacks on his honesty and character, but at the end of the resulting inquiry by a parliamentary committee he was reinstated, in 1837, and was made one of four senior assistant keepers at the re-formed record office of 1838. His career as a public servant was now at a higher level, but the rumblings about his motivation and honesty were never silenced.

Cole was a first-rate administrator with energy and commitment and an ability to pursue his aims undeterred by opposition and criticism. His superiors at the record commission gave him leave in 1838 to assist Rowland Hill (another utilitarian) in his campaign to introduce a national prepaid postage system. Cole devised a scheme by which the Post Office circulated the reform propaganda free of charge. At that time the Post Office carried newspapers free of charge. Cole edited a weekly newspaper giving news about postal reform, the *Post Circular*, which was printed and then, because it was presented as a newspaper, distributed free of charge by the Post Office. It may be that the cheap penny post was Cole's inspiration in commissioning and publishing the first Christmas card in 1843. The card depicted a family at table making a toast. Designed by J. C. Horsley RA, it was lithographed and hand coloured, selling at the considerable price of 1s.

In 1845 Cole, by now an accomplished journalist, began to contribute to the *Railway Chronicle*, producing a series of railway charts and articles on railway excursions. He joined in the campaigns for the uniform narrow gauge and for separation of freight from passenger traffic. His involvement in the commercial world paid well, and Cole earned more from his journalistic activities than he did as a keeper at the record office. With his salary of £500 and his additional earnings of about £750 he was a man in comfortable circumstances.

Cole's family life was very full. He married his cousin Marian Fairman Bond, a governess, on 28 December 1833. They had three sons and five daughters. He wrote a series of children's illustrated story books, published from 1841 as the *Home Treasury*, under the pseudonym of Felix Summerly, a name he continued to use when he began to sell 'art manufactures' in the late 1840s. His diary records time spent with his children. He was concerned that the girls as well as the boys should have an adequate education and find suitable occupations.

The Great Exhibition of 1851 It was through John Scott Russell, editor of the *Railway Chronicle*, that Cole was introduced into membership of the Society for the Encouragement of Arts, Manufactures, and Commerce in 1845. In this society Cole found the like-minded people with whom he could work to achieve reforms and improvements in almost any aspect of life, from sewage to education, industrial design to army reform. It was Cole's involvement with the society which placed him at the centre of the group which organized the Great Exhibition in 1851, where his roles were promoter, publicist, and administrator. As a council member of the Society of Arts he worked directly for its president, Prince Albert, travelling the country to promote the exhibition, and using the press to communicate as widely as possible. Once the commission for the exhibition was established Cole was seconded from the record office and appointed to a salaried position on the executive committee. He was chairman of council of the Society of Arts in 1850 and again in 1852 and continued to be a very influential member of the society throughout his life. Although he involved himself in all aspects of the management of the exhibition his primary responsibility was for the allocation of space for the 14,000 exhibitors from Britain, eleven colonies, and thirteen foreign countries. Cole was among those who fought to prevent the dismantling of the building at the end of the exhibition; the building was eventually re-erected at Sydenham. He was party to the discussions about the possible uses of the surplus funds which seemed likely to be available at the close of the exhibition. The surplus was used, together with a sum provided by the government, for the purchase of land at Brompton, just south of the exhibition site in Hyde Park. Prince Albert, as president of the commission for the exhibition, hoped that the site could be used to promote the same aims as the exhibition—the promotion of industry and the arts. Cole was to spend the next twenty years working to make 'South Kensington' a national centre for the arts and sciences.

Schools of art and design From 1848 Cole had been involving himself in the schools of design which had been established under the Board of Trade in 1836. His interest in industrial design had been stimulated by the offer of prizes by the Society of Arts in 1846. Cole had designed a tea service which won a Society of Arts prize. The tea service went into mass production at the Minton factory with great success. Cole was offered the chance to lecture at the Central School of Design, declined the offer, but began to campaign for reform of the schools and to discuss with Lord Granville, president of the Board of Trade, his concerns about copyright, patent law, and the schools of design. A select committee on the schools of design was established in 1849. After the close of the Great Exhibition, Cole, who had worked closely with Granville on the executive committee, was invited to be secretary of a new government department to control the schools, the department of practical art. He provided training for women as well as men at the schools at South Kensington, and after his retirement set up the National Training School for Music and the National Training School for Cookery.

In 1856 Cole's fledgeling department moved to the site purchased with the profits of the Great Exhibition. The first new building on the site was a temporary modular building, known as the 'Brompton Boilers', which housed the museum collections of the Central School of Design together with the collection of exhibits from the Great Exhibition which had been purchased by the Treasury at Cole's suggestion and loaned to the schools. By the time of Cole's retirement in 1873 the site housed the South Kensington Museum (later to divide into the Victoria and Albert and Science museums), the various schools of the department now called the Department of Science and Art, the Albert Hall, and the gardens of the Royal Horticultural Society. Cole, whose official responsibility was for the relatively small portion of the land which housed his department and its museums, had made himself responsible for the whole site and for making it the national centre for the arts and sciences which had been envisaged by Prince Albert. He used the device of public exhibitions which he promoted in order to justify the erection of buildings, notably that for the second Great Exhibition in 1862. He was involved in planning the Horticultural Society gardens at South Kensington and in fund-raising for the project. His determination that a large public hall suitable for exhibitions and concerts should be built at South Kensington resulted in the Albert Hall, a building opened in 1871 and used in its first few years for a series of themed international exhibitions, subsequently for a very wide variety of events, being affectionately known as 'the nation's village hall'. Cole's power within the small kingdom of South Kensington was recognized by his popular title of 'King Cole'.

Cole cared little for his personal appearance and his untidy, portly figure was ridiculed and caricatured, notably in *Vanity Fair* in 1871. His manner could be rather abrasive and his methods authoritarian. His civil service career ended under a cloud, when he was found to have inadequately supervised his department's less than honest accountant. Between 1876 and 1879 Cole lived in Birmingham and Manchester, and was involved with a company set up to promote a process developed by General Scott (a royal engineer employed at South Kensington in various capacities) for treating sewage. The company failed and Cole returned to London. He was created CB at the end of the Great Exhibition and was knighted in 1875. He died at his home, 96 Philbeach Gardens, Kensington, London, on 18 April 1882 and was buried in Brompton cemetery. He was survived by his wife.   ANN COOPER

Sources *Fifty years of public work of Sir Henry Cole*, ed. A. S. Cole and H. Cole, 2 vols. (1884) • E. Bonython, *King Cole: a picture portrait of Sir Henry Cole, KCB, 1808–1882* (1982) • A. Cooper, 'For the public good: Henry Cole, his circle and the development of the South Kensington estate', PhD diss., Open University, 1992 • d. cert. • *DNB* • *ILN* (29 April 1882), 416–17 • *CGPLA Eng. & Wales* (1882) • S. M. Avery-Quash, '"Creating a taste for beauty": Henry Cole's book ventures', PhD diss., U. Cam., 1997

Archives Col. U., architectural notes and sketches • ICL, Windsor Archives, royal commission for the Exhibition of 1851 • PRO, Department of Science and Art, corresp. and memoranda, ED23, ED24 • Royal College of Art, London, diary • RSA, minutes of council • V&A NAL, travel journals and papers • V&A NAL, corresp. and papers, 55.AA, 55.BB | BL, letters to Sir. A. H. Layard, Add. MSS 38991–39117, *passim* • Durham RO, letters to Lady Londonderry relating to alterations to Seaham Hall • PRO, letters to Granville, PRO 30/29 • UCL, corresp. with Edwin Chadwick • W. Sussex RO, corresp. with Richard Cobden

Likenesses S. Laurence, chalk drawing, 1865, NPG [*see illus.*] • Melluish, photograph, *c.*1870, V&A • J. E. Boehm, bust, 1875, V&A • J. E. Boehm, plaster cast of bust, 1875, NPG • engraving, 1882, repro. in *ILN* (29 April 1882), 417 • R. Doyle, pen-and-ink drawing, BM • Lock & Whitfield, woodburytype, NPG; repro. in T. Cooper, *Men of mark: a gallery of contemporary portraits* (1877) • H. W. Phillips, group portrait, oils (*The royal commissioners for the Exhibition of 1851*), V&A • attrib. J. Tissot, chromolithograph caricature, NPG; repro. in *VF* (1871) • wood-engraving, NPG; repro. in *ILN* (1851) • wood-engraving, NPG; repro. in *ILN* (1873)

Wealth at death £7689 13s. 8d.: probate, 27 May 1882, *CGPLA Eng. & Wales*

Cole, (William) Horace De Vere (1881–1936),

practical joker, was born on 5 May 1881, reputedly at Blarney, co. Cork, elder son of William Utting Cole (1851–1892), army officer, and his wife, Mary De Vere (1859–1930), niece and heiress of the scholars Aubrey and Sir Stephen De *Vere. His only sister married Neville Chamberlain; one of his two younger half-sisters married Sir Michael Palairet. He was educated at Eton College (1894–1900). While serving as lieutenant in the Duke of Cambridge's imperial yeomanry in South Africa (1900–02) he was severely wounded. As an undergraduate at Trinity College, Cambridge, he disguised himself as uncle of the sultan of Zanzibar and was elaborately received by the mayor of Cambridge. An elderly lady missionary who wished to address him in his native language was deterred by his mock interpreter explaining that his master could not meet her unless she contemplated entering his harem. After Cambridge he worked as a gondolier in Venice.

Cole's most famous hoax (10 February 1910) was perpetrated in concert with Duncan Grant, Adrian Stephen and his sister Virginia Woolf, and others. Together they impersonated the emperor of Abyssinia and his suite on a stately visit to HMS *Dreadnought* commanded by Admiral Sir William May at Weymouth. Afterwards he leaked this hilarity to journalists. Henceforth, for over fifteen years, he enjoyed high notoriety as a practical joker.

> Perhaps his greatest triumphs were simplicities like donning corduroy, providing a few poles for red lamps, and pulling up a stretch of Piccadilly, while policemen diverted traffic; or challenging conceited athletes to midnight races in the streets, and shouting 'stop thief' when they were well ahead …

Lord Vansittart reflected: 'our Chief Jester achieved a standard higher than the increasing imbecility of students' rags' (Vansittart, 122). Some of his pranks were gloriously absurd. Once he was driving in a taxi with Shane Leslie and a dummy of a nude woman; as the taxi passed a policeman at Piccadilly he opened its door, banged the dummy's head on the road shouting 'ungrateful hussy!' and drove off at high speed. He would walk with a cow's udder protruding from his flies and then cut it off with scissors before aghast bystanders. Police officers were often his targets. While strolling with Lord Aberdeen outside the viceregal lodge in Dublin, he transfixed the viceroy's coat-tails with a rapier to show the deficiencies of Irish detectives. Mistaken for Ramsay MacDonald he harangued a gang of navvies on the evils of socialism. Though he claimed to be puncturing pomposity (he had the tory MP Oliver Locker-Lampson arrested in St James's as a pickpocket) his most ambitious stunts humiliated his victims. He gave theatre tickets to a large number of bald men whose pates seen from the dress circle spelt out an expletive: characteristically he even remembered to dot the 'i'. He held a party for a group of men who introducing themselves in the absence of their host discovered that they all bore such surnames as Ramsbottom, Winterbottom, and Boddam-Whetham.

Horace De Vere Cole was a striking man with piercing blue eyes, bristling white hair, and stiff moustaches. His advanced deafness prevented him from realizing that his carefully timed coughing was inadequate to cover his explosive breaking of wind. Potentially a generous friend (when visiting someone ill he brought neither flowers nor books but the loan of a picture by Augustus John), in low moods he was pugnacious, abusive, or malicious. Always he was both conceited and lustful: *Who's Who* excluded him after he filled in his recreation as 'f—g'. In 1911 when involved in a 'sordid, gas-lit Piccadilly circus affair' with a disreputable woman he was described by Virginia Woolf as 'upon the downward path, sampling human nature and spitting it out' (*Letters of Virginia Woolf*, 1.453–4). His preference was for young girls. On 30 September (or possibly 30 October) 1918 Cole married a farouche heiress, Denise

Ann Marie José Lynch (*b.* 1900), posthumous only surviving child of Denis Andrew Malachy Daly (1865–1899), Galway landowner. They had one daughter. This marriage was dissolved (1928) after Cole had lost his money in Canadian land speculations, and in 1948 she married Anthony Radley Drew. Cole became a remittance man in France, where his pranks were much resented. Rashly he married Mabel Winifred Mary (Mavis; 1908–1970), formerly a scullery maid and Soho waitress, daughter of Samuel Charter Wright, grocer's assistant, on 31 January 1931. Her son (*b.* 1935) was fathered by Augustus John. Cuckoldry and poverty together broke Cole. He died after a heart attack on 26 February 1936 in Honfleur, France, and was buried (4 March) at West Woodhay churchyard, Newbury, Berkshire. His widow married Mortimer Wheeler (1939) and shot Lord Vivian (1954).   RICHARD DAVENPORT-HINES

Sources *The Times* (29 Feb 1936) · *The Times* (5 March 1936) · R. Owen and T. de Vere Cole, *Beautiful and beloved* (1974) · A. John, *Chiaroscuro* (1952) · *The letters of Virginia Woolf*, ed. N. Nicolson, 1 (1975) · Q. Bell, *Virginia Woolf: a biography*, 1 (1972), 157–60, 213–16 · Lord Vansittart, *The mist procession* (1958) · S. Leslie, *The film of memory* (1938), 262–3 · S. Leslie, *Long shadows* (1966), 110–12 · *Lady Gregory's diaries, 1892–1902*, ed. J. Pethica (1996) · *Carrington: letters and extracts from her diaries*, ed. D. Garnett (1970) · Burke, *Gen. Ire.* (1976), 258 · register, Eton

Likenesses A. John, pen-and-ink sketch, 1926, repro. in Owen and de Vere Cole, *Beautiful and beloved*, following p. 40

Cole, Humfrey (*d.* 1591), mathematical instrument maker and die sinker, described himself as 'a English man born in yᵉ north' (on a map of Palestine engraved in 1572), but neither the date or place of his birth nor his parents are known. Although the form of his name varies on his signed works, 'Humfrey Cole' is the most commonly used. The circumstances of his education are unclear, but he claimed on the map to be a goldsmith, and was referred to as such on 6 September 1577 in the Goldsmiths' court minutes, when a William Sysyswithe, formerly apprentice of Robert Fyllischurche, was turned over to him in order to complete his apprenticeship. For about fifteen years Cole was active as a die sinker at the mint in the Tower, where he first appears in 1563 as the established successor to John Lawrence. Throughout his tenure his salary was £20 per annum, an amount which he claimed in 1578 to be 'lacking sufficiente maintenance for me and my family' (Ackermann, 21), although it was in addition to lodgings in the Tower and a further £3 per annum 'diett' allowance.

This is the last evidence of Cole's employment in the mint, and he seems to have continued to sell 'Geometricall instruments in metall' at his house 'neere unto the North dore of Paules' (Worsop). Twenty-six spectacular mathematical instruments by Cole are known to have survived, all but one in public collections in the British Isles and on the continent. His work, which dates from 1568 to 1590, covered a wide time-span, including the period when he was still employed at the mint, where he paid a deputy for at least two years to do his work for half his salary. Cole was mentioned by name in the original account books of the first Frobisher voyage in 1576; he is the only one named among the makers who provided instruments for the expedition. He was also called upon when the instruments needed repair after the first journey, and again in 1578, to take part in the assay of the ore returned from Frobisher Bay, which was claimed to contain gold and silver.

Cole's 1572 map of Palestine was for Richard Jugge's Bishops' Bible. The only surviving map by Cole, it is based on an earlier map by Abraham Ortelius and appears to have served mainly as an advertisement of his engraving skills; it was probably intended to impress Elizabeth I's leading minister, Lord Burghley, who had expressed a strong interest in the mapping of England and Wales for administrative purposes. Nothing is known about Cole's family except for the name of his wife, Elizabeth, who was named as the beneficiary of an administration of 6 July 1591, issued one day after his burial, at St Gregory by Paul's, on 5 July.   SILKE ACKERMANN

Sources S. Ackermann, ed., *Humphrey Cole: mint, measurement and maps in Elizabethan England* (1998) · Goldsmiths' Company court minute book, Goldsmiths' Hall, Foster Lane, London, L, 333, 6 Sept 1577 · E. Worsop, *A discoverie of sundrie errours* (1582) · PRO, PROB 6/4, 183 · burial register of St Gregory by Paul's, GL, MS 10231 · R. T. Gunther, 'The great astrolabe and other scientific instruments by Humphrey Cole', *Archaeologia*, 76 (1927), 273–317, esp. 278–80 · E. G. R. Taylor, *The mathematical practitioners of Tudor and Stuart England* (1954), 171–2 · S. Tyacke, ed., *English map-making, 1500–1650: historical essays* (1983), 93–106 · J. Turner, 'An examination of the engraved lettering on English mathematical instruments, 1550–1800', BA diss., U. Reading, 1982, 27–97

Archives BM, mathematical instruments · Horniman Museum, mathematical instruments · Kunstgewerbemuseum, Berlin, mathematical instruments · MHS Oxf., mathematical instruments · Musée de la Vie Wallonne, Liège, mathematical instruments · Museo della Storia della Scienza, Florence, mathematical instruments · Museum of Scotland, Edinburgh, mathematical instruments · NMM, mathematical instruments · Royal Artillery Historical Trust, mathematical instruments · Sci. Mus., mathematical instruments · U. St Andr., mathematical instruments · Whipple Museum, Cambridge, mathematical instruments

Cole, John (1792–1848), bookseller and antiquary, was born on 3 October 1792 in Weston Favell, Northamptonshire. He was of unknown parentage, and was apprenticed to W. Birdsall, a bookseller in Northampton. He started his publishing career with books on the history and antiquities of Ecton in 1814, followed by Northampton and its vicinity in 1815. In 1817 he purchased the stock and goodwill of a bookseller in Lincoln and produced his first catalogue. He married Susannah Marshall (*d.* 1832), fourth daughter of James Marshall of Northampton, on 25 August 1817. *The History of Lincoln and Guide to its Curiosities and Antiquities* appeared in 1818.

After leaving Lincoln, Cole settled in Hull, before moving in 1820 to Scarborough, where he opened a bookshop and circulating library. Cole's most successful publishing activity was in Scarborough. He published over 100 small books on topographical and antiquarian subjects, especially on Northamptonshire and the area surrounding Scarborough. Most of the books were slender, in limited editions of between twenty-five and sixty copies. J. B. Barker in *The History of Scarborough from the Earliest Date* (1882) recalled his versatility as a lecturer

> on astronomy, the anatomy of costume, architecture and natural history. These several subjects are discussed in a

scientific and pleasing manner. The drawings are well executed, elegant and appropriate and the specimens in natural history are interesting and costly. Mr Cole's lectures always afforded me the highest gratification.

In 1825 Cole won a share of a lottery prize and travelled to London to receive it, and while there he was able to acquire some scarce views of Scarborough by Francis Place. In 1828 he was encouraged to edit a book on household cookery as a result of purchasing a library. 'Thus have I quite unexpectedly become the editor of a cookery book, an honour to which I had not thought to aspire' (J. Cole, preface to *The Oldfieldian Cookery Book*, 1828). His one attempt at a periodical in 1824, the *Scarborough Repository*, survived for only eight issues. His wife returned to the home of her parents in Northampton, where she died on 30 July 1832. Shortly afterwards, Cole returned to Northampton with his six children. He continued publishing, writing, and lecturing on philosophy and natural history, and in June 1833 organized a commemoration in honour of the Revd James Hervey at Weston Favell, at which he lectured. Following the failure of his business, he moved to Wellingborough in 1835 where he opened

a small school, and placed geological specimens, &c. [as well as such incongruous wares as apples, bacon, and ham] in his window for sale. He was a quiet man and regarded as very eccentric because he and his sons would go out all day and return laden with wild plants, &c. ... His industrious curiosity was never appreciated in Northamptonshire, where he dragged out a miserable existence. From Wellingborough he removed to Ringstead, or some village in its vicinity, where he ransacked every nook for relics of antiquity and natural curiosities. (*N&Q*)

His *History and Antiquities of Higham Ferrars* and his *Annals of Rushden, Irthlingborough and Knuston* were published in 1838. He tried his luck as a schoolmaster in Rushden in 1837, after which he probably lived in Polestead, and Huntingdon.

Cole spent his final years in the village of Woodford, near Thrapston in Northamptonshire, in greatly reduced circumstances. 'I was informed that he was in great want and distress in the retreat I alluded to' (*N&Q*). A few titles appeared in his remaining years, including a *Calendar of Every Day Reference for the County of Huntingdon* in 1845, but to all intents and purposes his publishing days were over. He moved to The Academy, Club Lane, where he lived until his death on 12 April 1848. He was buried in an unmarked grave in Woodford.

Cole's main achievement is in over 100 publications which contain carefully observed descriptions of village life and houses in both Scarborough and Northamptonshire. His detailed observations are often the only description of buildings which have been demolished, and his accounts of everyday village life provide excellent source material for local historians. His tireless pertinacity in searching out the minutiae of antiquarian detail was recognized, although his publications were criticized for not being very scholarly. His topographical works are collectors' items and much sought after because of their limited editions. However, his work was repetitive, and varied in quality. He was clearly industrious and enthusiastic in his antiquarian research but he lacked business acumen and was unsuited to running a bookshop.   DIANA DIXON

Sources DNB · J. B. Nichols, *Historical and genealogical notes relating to Northamptonshire* (1879) · 'The diary of John Cole', *Northampton Notes & Queries*, 2 (1888), 245–6 · J. B. Barker, *The history of Scarborough from the earliest date* (1882) · E. Humphries and M. Humphries, *Woodford juxta Thrapston, Rushden, Buscott* (1985), 16–18 · *N&Q*, 3rd ser., 1 (1862), 509 · IGI · *Northampton Mercury* (15 April 1848), 2
Archives Bodl. Oxf., autograph collection; corresp. · York Minster Library, York Minster archives, diaries and papers
Likenesses silhouette, repro. in W. Boyne, *The Yorkshire Library* (1869), 206

Cole, (Reginald) John Vicat (1903–1975). *See under* Cole, Reginald George Vicat (1870–1940).

Cole, Joseph Windle (*b.* 1808x10, *d.* in or after 1858), swindler, was a shipping clerk during the 1830s with the London merchant house of Forbes, Forbes & Co., and in 1840–44 represented them in Bombay. He was summarily dismissed as their Liverpool agent in 1845, and in the following year became a partner with John Johnson as East India merchants in Great Winchester Street, City of London. This firm went bankrupt in 1847. Within months he set up as an East India merchant under the title of Cole Brothers in Birchin Lane; he had no partners, but employed his two brothers as clerks. His business was weak, and in 1850 he resolved upon a novel experiment in credit fraud. He knew that discount houses, when making advances on dock warrants (the title to merchandise stored in warehouses), only cursorily examined the documents tendered, and that the loans advanced on them were always punctually met or renewed. He enlisted two bankrupt metal brokers, Daniel Mitchell Davidson and Cosmo William Gordon, who had been shadily associated with his 1847 bankruptcy, in a criminal conspiracy to borrow upon warrants representing non-existent goods (chiefly spelter, tin, steel, copper, iron, and lead). They leased a small Thames-side wharf (Hagen's Sufferance wharf) in St Saviour's Dock, Bermondsey. There were large and impressive warehouses abutting, and the goods stored in these warehouses were represented to visitors as those in the warrants. Cole also duplicated warrants to increase his ability to borrow. He constantly intermixed genuine and fictitious warrants to confuse the issue, and juggled the loans falling due. Cole's cash account as later supplied to the court of bankruptcy showed transactions worth £1,531,709 in 1852, £2,000,744 in 1853, and £770,751 for the first half of 1854.

The fraud was discovered in the spring of 1853 by the discounting house of Overend and Gurney, which kept it quiet in the hope of recovering some £400,000 which it had advanced to Cole and his accomplices. In October 1853 Overend and Gurney began selling its Hagen wharf warrants. Discrepancies in some warrants were noticed by others. This led to a slow unravelling of the fraud, and gradual revelation of Cole's complicity. When Cole finally stopped payment on 27 June 1854, the simulated warrants circulating on the part of Cole Brothers had a nominal value of £367,800; similar documents credited to David-son and Gordon were estimated at £150,800. Cole was arrested on 20 July and tried at the central criminal court on 25 October. He was only with difficulty convicted, being sentenced to four years' penal servitude; he was a co-defendant with Davidson and Gordon in further trials in August and December 1855. Following his release from prison in the autumn of 1858, a letter from him promising to refute the 'gross calumnies' directed at him was published in *The Times* on 21 December 1858. Nothing more is known of him. Though astute, bold, and calculating, Cole was too reckless or vain to realize that the discovery of his crimes was inevitable.   RICHARD DAVENPORT-HINES

Sources S. Laing, *The great City frauds of Cole, Davidson and Gordon fully exposed* (1856) · D. M. Evans, *Facts, failures, and frauds: revelations financial, mercantile, criminal* (1859) · *The Times* (1 Jan 1848) · *The Times* (9 March 1848) · *The Times* (21 July 1854) · *The Times* (22 July 1854) · *The Times* (29 July 1854) · *The Times* (26 Oct 1854) · *The Times* (3 Nov 1855) · *The Times* (21 Dec 1858)

Cole, Sir **(Galbraith) Lowry** (1772–1842), army officer and colonial governor, the second son of William Willoughby Cole, first earl of Enniskillen (1736–1803), and his wife, Anne (1742–1802), the daughter of Galbraith Lowry Corry, of Ahenis, co. Tipperary, and the sister of the first earl of Belmore, was born in Dublin on 1 May 1772. He entered the army as a cornet in the 12th light dragoons on 31 March 1787. While he was at the University of Stuttgart furthering his military studies, a lieutenancy in the 5th dragoon guards was purchased for him on 31 May 1791. He became successively captain in the 70th regiment in 1792 and major in the 86th in 1793.

On his way to his new regiment Cole joined Sir John Jervis and Sir Charles Grey as a volunteer for the attack on Martinique on 24 March 1794. He was then attached to Sir Charles Grey's personal staff as aide-de-camp and was present at the reduction of Guadeloupe and St Lucia. On 26 November 1794 he was promoted lieutenant-colonel. Cole then again went on staff service, and acted as deputy adjutant-general in Ireland, as aide-de-camp to Lord Carhampton, the commander-in-chief in Ireland in 1797, and as military secretary to General Lord Hutchinson in Egypt. In 1797 he was returned to the Irish House of Commons for Enniskillen, and sat until January 1800—retiring before the Anglo-Irish union. On 1 January 1801 he was promoted colonel and appointed to command the regiment with which his family was associated, the 27th Inniskillings; he assumed the command at Malta in 1805. From Malta he proceeded to Sicily and commanded his own regiment and a battalion of grenadiers as brigadier-general. He was second in command at the battle of Maida on 4 July 1806. It is true that the chief credit of that victory rests with Brigadier-General Kempt and with Colonel Ross but a mistake on Cole's part would have imperilled the success they had gained. He was promoted major-general on 25 April 1808, but left Sicily in the summer of 1809 on account of differences with Sir John Stuart, the commander-in-chief.

Cole asked to be sent to the Peninsula, and on arriving there was posted to command the 4th division in 1809.

This famous 4th division was always coupled with the 3rd and the light divisions by Wellington as his three best divisions. Cole had every qualification for a good general of division, especially obedience to the commander-in-chief. At the battle of Busaco the 4th division did not come into action at all, but in the following year it showed its strength at Albuera. After Marshal Masséna had been driven out of Portugal the 2nd and 4th divisions were detached to the south of the Tagus under Marshal Beresford to make an attack on Badajoz. On the way Cole was left to reduce the small fortress of Olivença, which surrendered to him on 15 April 1811. He then assisted at the first siege of Badajoz, and when Beresford advanced to form a junction with Blake's Spanish army and prepared to fight Marshal Soult, who was coming up from Andalusia to relieve Badajoz, Cole was left behind to cover the advance and destroy the siege material. There is some dispute whether Cole of his own volition ordered the advance of his fusilier brigade at Albuera to counter the commanding position that Soult had won on Beresford's right, owing to the confusion in the 2nd division. But Cole's decision to send forward the fusiliers saved the day, though at a fearful loss: one of the three colonels of the brigade, Sir W. Myers, was killed; the other two, Blakeney and Ellis, and Cole himself, were wounded. Cole, however, rejoined his division in July 1811, but left it again the following December to take his seat in the House of Commons, to which he had been elected in 1803 as MP for County Fermanagh. He thus missed the sieges of Ciudad Rodrigo and Badajoz, where Sir Charles Colville commanded the 4th division, but rejoined the army in June 1812 in time to be present at the great battle of Salamanca in the following month. In that battle Cole's division was posted on the extreme left of the position opposite to the French hill of the two known as the Arapiles, and for a moment the defeat of his Portuguese brigade under Pack made the day doubtful until the hill was carried by the 6th division under Major-General Henry Clinton. In the attack Cole was shot through the body. However, he soon rejoined his division at Madrid, and later covered the retreat from there.

In winter quarters Cole made himself very popular, especially for the excellence of his dinners. On 5 March 1813 Wellington invested Cole with the Order of the Bath. At the battle of Vitoria the 4th division acted on the right centre and did not bear any special part, though Cole was mentioned in dispatches. But in the series of battles known as the battles of the Pyrenees the 4th division played a very great part indeed, especially in the combat at Roncesvalles, when its hard fighting gave time for Wellington to concentrate on Sorauren. At the battle of the Nivelle the 4th division, under Cole, together with the 7th, carried the Sarre redoubt, at the Nive it was in reserve, at Orthes it carried the village of St Boës, the key of the enemy's position, and at Toulouse it was the 4th and 6th divisions, under the command of Beresford, which carried the height of Calvinet and repaired the mischief done by the flight of the Spaniards. On the conclusion of peace

Cole received the order of the Tower and Sword of Portugal and a gold cross with four clasps. He had also been promoted lieutenant-general on 4 June 1813.

When Napoleon escaped from Elba, the duke of Wellington at once asked for Cole as one of his generals of division in Belgium. But on 15 June 1815 Cole married Lady Frances Harris (d. 1847), the second daughter of the first earl of Malmesbury, and so missed the final victory of Wellington at Waterloo. On 15 August, however, Cole joined the army of occupation in France, and commanded the 2nd division until the final evacuation of France in November 1818.

In 1823 Cole resigned his seat in the House of Commons, which he had held for twenty years, on being appointed governor of Mauritius. Here he solidly managed the challenges of a conquered colony where the population was stratified into the French plantocracy, 'free persons of colour', and slaves. Not without difficulty, he presided over the amelioration of slave conditions, the institution of a council of advice, and the improvement of educational opportunities. It proved a suitable apprenticeship for his transfer in September 1828 to the Cape of Good Hope.

Cole was one of the few successful Cape governors. Although he did not solve the frontier problem, he firmly enforced meliorative slave measures, improved communications by building the 'Sir Lowry's Pass' into the interior, and promoted the municipal boards, which were successfully established shortly after his retirement. When he left in August 1833 the *South African Commercial Advertiser* praised his qualities of 'simple honesty of heart and sterling integrity of purpose'.

Cole then returned to England, and settled at Highfield Park, near Hartford Bridge, Hampshire, where he died suddenly on 4 October 1842. He had been promoted full general in 1830 and was governor of Gravesend and Tilbury from 1818 until his death. He was buried in the family vault at Enniskillen, and a column more than 100 feet high with his statue on it was erected on the Fort Hill near that city. The eldest of Cole's three sons and four daughters, Colonel Arthur Lowry Cole CB commanded the 17th regiment throughout the Crimean War.

H. M. STEPHENS, rev. JOHN BENYON

Sources M. L. Cole and S. Gwynn, *The memoirs of Sir Lowry Cole* (1934) · K. S. Hunt, *Sir Lowry Cole: a study in colonial administration* (1974) · C. W. C. Oman, *A history of the Peninsular War*, 1–5 (1902–14) · J. W. Cole, *Memoirs of British generals distinguished during the Peninsular War*, 2 vols. (1856) · C. B. Vere, 'Marches and movements of the 4th division', *United Service Magazine* (Jan 1821) · P. J. Barnwell and A. Toussaint, *A short history of Mauritius* (1949) · M. K. Jones, 'The slave trade at Mauritius', BLitt diss., U. Oxf., 1936 · A. K. Fryer, 'The government of the Cape of Good Hope, 1825–54: the age of imperial reform', *Archives Year Book for South African History* (1961) · B. J. T. Leverton, 'Government finance and political development in the Cape: 1806–1834', *Archives Year Book for South African History* (1964) · J. L. Dracopoli, *Sir Andries Stockenström: the origins of racial conflict in South Africa* (1969) · D. Rivett-Carnac, *Hawk's eye: a biography of Sir Henry Somerset* (1966) · T. J. Stapleton, *Magoma: Xhosa resistance to colonial advance* (1994)

Archives NAM, papers · NRA, priv. coll., corresp. and papers · PRO, corresp. and papers, PRO30/43 · Cape Town, South Africa, Cape Archives | BL, Bathurst MSS · Derbys. RO, letters to Sir R. J. Wilmot-Horton · PRO, Colonial Office MSS

Likenesses W. Dyce, oils, NPG · T. Farrell, statue on column, Fort Hill, Enniskillen, co. Fermanagh, Northern Ireland · C. Picart, stipple (after T. Lawrence), BM, NPG; repro. in *Contemporary portraits* (1816) · bust, Government House, Réduit, Mauritius · bust, Royal Military Academy, Surrey · portrait, Florence Court, Enniskillen, co. Fermanagh, N. Ireland · portrait, Government House, Cape Town, South Africa · portrait, South African Library, Cape Town, South Africa

Cole [*née* Postgate], **Dame Margaret Isabel** (1893–1980), political activist and author, was born in Cambridge on 6 May 1893, the eldest in the family of two daughters and four sons of John Percival *Postgate (1853–1926), fellow of Trinity College, Cambridge, and later professor of Latin at the University of Liverpool, and his wife, Edith Allen (1863–1962). After a generally happy early childhood in Cambridge she was sent to Roedean in September of 1907. She despised her schooling there, partly because she found the disciplinary regime excessively restrictive and also because of the lack of any significant intellectual challenge; in her popular autobiography, *Growing up into Revolution* (1949), she remembered being excluded from the school library for reading Macaulay's *Essays* after she had completed her set French preparation. She experienced liberation, both social and intellectual, at Girton College, Cambridge, which she entered in October 1911 to read classics. Almost every aspect of life in Girton delighted her. She formed lasting friendships with a large number of like-minded scholars and revelled in the study of the works of the leading classical scholars of the age, including Alfred Zimmern and Gilbert Murray.

During her time at Girton, Margaret Postgate became intellectually committed to a moderate form of British socialism, largely as a result of her voracious reading of J. A. Hobson, George Bernard Shaw, Sidney and Beatrice Webb, and H. G. Wells. She did not, however, join any of the progressive political clubs then proliferating in Cambridge and made few connections with the broader socialist movement. After taking a first in part one of the classical tripos in 1914, she left Cambridge a year earlier than her father desired to take up a position teaching classics in St Paul's Girls' School, London. Her active political engagement grew quickly during the First World War as she attempted to help her brother Raymond William *Postgate secure exemption from conscription on the grounds of conscientious objection. This campaign introduced her to many leading figures in the Independent Labour Party, the National Council for Civil Liberties, and, most importantly, the Fabian research department. Towards the end of 1915 she began working part-time for the research department, where she came into contact with the guild socialist thinkers George Douglas Howard *Cole (1889–1959) and William Mellor. In January 1917 they persuaded her to resign her teaching position and to join the research department full time as assistant secretary, a position she held until 1925.

During her time in the research department Margaret and G. D. H. Cole slowly became attached to one another, often taking weekend walks in the Chilterns, in the Cotswolds, or along the Thames in Oxfordshire. It was not a particularly romantic courtship; Margaret later recalled that G. D. H. Cole proposed with the words 'I suppose this has got to happen' (Cole, *Life of G. D. H. Cole*, 91). Nevertheless, she accepted the offer, and the couple were married in a slapdash ceremony in a register office behind King's Cross railway station in August 1918. After a honeymoon cut short by her husband's efforts to secure continued exemption from conscription, the couple moved to a large town house in Chelsea, furnished for them by his parents. Shortly afterwards they settled in Hampstead, where she enjoyed the intellectual milieu. She continued to conduct quantitative and qualitative research for the guild socialists and, although she and her husband never rivalled Sidney and Beatrice Webb as the leading domestic partnership of the progressive intelligentsia, the couple played host to a series of leading figures of the left. Not even the birth of their first child, Janet Elizabeth Margaret, in February 1921 or that of their second, Anne Rachel, in October 1922, appeared significantly to interrupt Margaret's dedication to a wide range of political causes.

New challenges emerged, however, in 1924 as the guild socialist movement collapsed, forcing both Margaret and her husband to seek a new direction for their careers. After some deliberation G. D. H. Cole accepted a university readership in economics at Oxford in 1925 and the couple relocated to a smaller house in Holywell Street, Oxford, overlooked by the buildings of New College. Margaret hated Oxford. She felt excluded from the academic community, which she felt exhibited a 'deep-rooted arrogance' and misogyny, and she 'profoundly disliked' the provincialism of the town itself (Cole, *Growing up into Revolution*, 110). Her only connection with politics and academia at this time came through Gilbert and Mary Murray, who invited her to join their social circle, and through the Workers' Educational Association, for which she toured the local region teaching politics and economics to large classes of working adults. Although she enjoyed both opportunities, she yearned for a return to the more socially liberated environment of London, and in 1928, shortly after the birth of the couple's third child, Humphry John Douglas, she persuaded her husband to return there. Although G. D. H. Cole did not resign his Oxford readership as planned, the couple bought a house in Hampstead in 1929, and Margaret immediately returned to playing a leading part in the intellectual life of the London left.

Reintroduced to the mainstream of political life, Margaret Cole was involved with her husband in founding the Society for Socialist Inquiry and Propaganda in 1930 and the New Fabian Research Bureau in 1931. She began to publish an increasing amount of her own scholarship, beginning to rival her husband's prolific output and even surpassed him in literary style and skill. Successful works included *The New Economic Revolution* (1938) and *Marriage Past and Present* (1938), which outlined a modest form of socialist feminism. She also began to collaborate with her husband, producing a series of statistical collections and general introductions to politics, including the popular *Intelligent Man's Review of Europe Today* (1933) and *The Condition of Britain* (1937), and even twenty-nine detective novels. She campaigned for republican Spain, opposed appeasement, and supported the popular front. After the Second World War she widened her participation in politics by becoming a member of the London county council's education committee and an alderman; she later drew on these experiences to write one of the most thorough accounts of the workings of post-war local government, *Servant of the County* (1956).

Towards the end of her husband's life Margaret Cole increasingly turned to historical studies as she attempted to document the considerable contribution that the couple and their friends had made to the British left. Her own autobiography, *Growing up into Revolution*, was beautifully and wittily written, and remains a classic of the genre. Her editions (1952, 1956) of the diaries of Beatrice Webb were a very significant source for a generation of historians. Some of her other work, however, courted controversy, even among friends. She broke an informal agreement with R. H. Tawney by producing the first edited collection of articles on the work of Beatrice Webb, generating ill feeling which she perpetuated after his death. In 1971 she published a frank biography of her husband, who had died in 1959, which included an unusually detailed critique of his personal inadequacies.

Despite these controversies, and a reputation for being personally abrasive, Margaret Cole was still generally respected on the left in the post-war world. Harold Wilson's Labour governments ensured that her contributions did not go unrecognized, appointing her OBE in 1965 and a DBE in 1970. In 1977 she became an honorary fellow of the London School of Economics. In her autobiography she recalled her joy at learning that her grandfather John Postgate had been included in the *Dictionary of National Biography* for his part in campaigning against adulterated food. She would have been delighted to know that posterity remembers her contribution to a wider series of social campaigns in the same manner. She continued to discuss her work with researchers right up until her death in a nursing home at Goring-on-Thames, Oxfordshire, on 7 May 1980, the day after her eighty-seventh birthday.

MARC STEARS

Sources M. Cole, *Growing up into revolution* (1949) · M. Cole, *The life of G. D. H. Cole* (1979) · M. Cole, *Servant of the county* (1956) · E. Vernon, *Margaret Cole, 1893–1980* (1986) · *DNB* · *CGPLA Eng. & Wales* (1980)

Archives Nuffield Oxf., corresp. and papers · Ruskin College, Oxford, corresp. relating to publications | BLPES, Fabian Society papers · BLPES, R. H. Tawney papers · Bodl. Oxf., letters to Gilbert Murray · JRL, letters to *Manchester Guardian* · U. Hull, Brynmor Jones L., corresp. with R. Page Arnot · U. Hull, Brynmor Jones L., corresp. with Betty Vernon · U. Sussex Library, corresp. with Leonard Woolf · Welwyn Garden City Central Library, corresp. with Sir Frederic Osborn

Likenesses H. Coster, photograph, 1938, NPG; *see illus. in* Cole, George Douglas Howard (1889–1959) · S. Bowen, oils, NPG · H. Coster, photograph, NPG

Wealth at death £137,957: probate, 29 Sept 1980, *CGPLA Eng. & Wales*

Cole, Monica Mary (1922–1994), geographer, was born on 5 May 1922 at 70 North Side, Clapham Common, London, the elder daughter of William Henry Parnall Cole (1887–1969), bank clerk, and his wife, Dorothy Mary Thomas (1887–1965). She was educated at Wimbledon county grammar school (1934–40) and Bedford College, University of London (1940–43), where she gained a first-class BSc honours degree in geography, with geology as her subsidiary subject. In 1944–5 she worked for the Ministry of Town and Country Planning as a research assistant. Meanwhile she registered for a PhD degree of the University of London with a thesis on 'the major geographic factors affecting the production and utilization of building materials' in the south midlands. It was approved in 1947.

In that year Monica Cole was appointed lecturer in geography at the University of Cape Town. Her skill and stamina as a fieldworker quickly became apparent. She accomplished in the Elgin district 'one of the most thorough and useful land utilisation surveys carried out anywhere in South Africa' (Jackson, 244). By the time she moved to the University of the Witwatersrand in 1948, she had developed a strong interest in the African savanna lands, especially the environmental constraints on land-use choice and management. She began an investigation of the Transvaal lowveld and her report, *Land Use Studies in the Transvaal Lowveld*, was published as occasional paper 1 by the World Land Use Survey (1956). She also began to study the use of vegetation anomalies as indicators in studies of mineralization.

Monica Cole's wide interest in South Africa continued after she took up a lectureship at the University of Keele in 1951. *South Africa*, a major study in regional geography, appeared in 1961. The book was strongest on the physical and economic geography of the country, far less firmly argued on the social and political aspects. It was widely used and a second edition appeared in 1966.

By the mid-1950s Cole had begun to identify and classify vegetation types within savannas and to apply the results to agriculture and settlement, especially in sparsely peopled African areas. After extensive fieldwork in Brazil in 1956, she made a new contribution in explaining the distribution of grassy savanna, caatinga, and mata in terms of the ages of their respective flora and the geomorphological evolution of the landscape. Her field experience was strengthened by a visit to Australia in 1960, as she worked towards a worldwide study of the distribution, form, and composition of savanna vegetation with special reference to the interplay between vegetation and environmental factors. She put forward suggestions in 1963 for standardizing nomenclature and classification (M. M. Cole, *South African Geographical Journal*, 45, 1963, 1–14).

Cole's fieldwork took her to savannas in southern, central, and eastern Africa, South America, and Australia. Her inaugural lecture, published as *Biogeography in the Service of Man* (1965), following her appointment in 1964 to the chair of geography at Bedford College, focused on this work and on its application to problems of human welfare. Thirty

years of work were brought together in *The Savannas: Biogeography and Geobotany* (1986). This was a major achievement, praised for its comparative approach and breadth of coverage although criticized for underestimating the roles of past and present human and faunal activities in savanna ecology (P. A. Furley, *Geographical Journal*, 155, 1989, 122–3).

Meanwhile Cole continued her work on biogeography and geobotany as prospecting tools and to extend the work on plant indicators of base metal mineralization begun in South Africa. She was associated with work in the Dugald River area, Cloncurry, Australia, published in 1965, which clearly demonstrated the value of plant indicators in the discovery and delimitation of copper, lead, and zinc mineralization. This led to further work in South-West Africa and Botswana. Investigations of the Empress nickel–copper deposit in Southern Rhodesia showed the significance of plant sampling studies in a savanna woodland environment. Between 1965 and 1969 she worked in the Kalgoorlie–Coolgardie area of Western Australia. She worked in the north of Finland in the 1970s.

Monica Cole was quick to recognize the importance of remote-sensing techniques, coupled with ground control, in the identification and distribution of plant cover and also the importance of differences in vegetation to mineral discovery and exploitation (*Proceedings of the Royal Society*, series A, 1968, 173–82). For Bougainville Island, in the Solomon Islands, she tested the value of air photographs under tropical forest conditions. She carried out significant studies on the ground truth of Landsat 1 imagery of the savanna of north-west Queensland in 1971. In 1979 she took part in a National Aeronautics and Space Administration (NASA) project to estimate possible uses of data from the Heat Capacity Mapping Mission for geological mapping. Her last main project, using Landsat and the detail of SPOT imagery, in 1990–91, was on the Thalanga zinc–lead–copper deposit near Charters Towers in Queensland. Her investigations attracted the confidence and financial support of research organizations, national governments, international bodies, and mining and industrial companies.

This success coupled with Cole's own determination, personal drive, and total conviction of the importance of her own research contributed to difficulties in the department at Bedford College. During her time as head (1964–75) the department became bitterly divided. At a time of student unrest she felt under threat because of her links with South Africa. Some colleagues argued that her personal research, including the development of a substantial research laboratory, had been achieved at the expense of other aspects of the department's life and work. She, in turn, was strongly protective of her work and of those who assisted her. Irreconcilable views led to considerable personal distress for Monica Cole and others involved. Following an official inquiry by the college she was replaced as head of department in 1975 to become director of research in geobotany, terrain analysis, and related resource use. She retired in 1987, becoming a professor emeritus, and in 1988 a Leverhulme professorial research fellow.

Monica Cole was president of the South African Geographical Society in 1963. She was made an honorary life member just before she died. She received the Murchison award of the Royal Geographical Society in 1987 for her contributions to the geography of South Africa and to the understanding of savannas. From 1972 until her death she was a keen member of the Department of Transport's landscape advisory committee which advised ministers on the alignment and landscape treatment of new major roads. Her camera was an essential part of her field equipment. She enjoyed painting and her love of landscape shines out from her work, of which some examples may be found in the geography department at Royal Holloway College, University of London. In her early days she had been an accomplished tennis player. She was elected to membership of the Geographical Club in 1990.

In her last years Cole suffered from cancer. She fought bravely and recovered for a time but died in the Royal Marsden Hospital, Sutton, Surrey, on 8 January 1994. After a service on 25 January at St Mary's Church, Wimbledon, her remains were cremated. She left £10,000 to the Royal Geographical Society, of which she had been a fellow since 1942, for a research travel grant for young women physical geographers. She never married.   M. J. WISE

Sources R. Potter and P. Catt, 'Monica Mary Cole, 1922–1994', *Transactions of the Institute of British Geographers*, new ser., 19 (1994), 372–7 • S. Jackson, 'Monica Mary Cole, 1922–1994', *GJ*, 160 (1994), 244–5 • private information (2004) [J. Osborne, C. Board, R. U. Cooke, D. Harris, D. Hilling, W. R. Mead, R. Potter] • personal knowledge (2004) • *The Times* (7 Feb 1994) • *The Independent* (22 Jan 1994) • *WWW* [forthcoming] • b. cert. • d. cert.
Likenesses photograph, repro. in Potter and Catt, 'Monica Mary Cole', 373
Wealth at death £66,244 8s.: probate, 15 July 1994, *CGPLA Eng. & Wales*

Cole, Peter (d. 1665), printer and bookseller, was the son of clothier Edward Cole, of Barfold, Suffolk. He was apprenticed to the London bookseller John Bellamy in October 1629, and on 11 January 1638 took his freedom, for which the minimum age was twenty-four. Initially a bookseller, Cole established a business in the same year at the sign of the Glove (later Glove and Lion) in Cornhill near the Royal Exchange, London, which he maintained for five years. He opened a new enterprise, reflecting his added speciality, at the sign of the Printing Press near the Royal Exchange in 1643. He sold books from there for the next twenty-two years, but printed and lived at another property in Leadenhall, also marked by the sign of a printing press. An active participant in the city's political life during the civil war, Cole published many of the petitions circulated by puritan leaders, such as Isaac Penington. Another early focus of Cole's was the scaffold confessional.

Cole was, however, in frequent trouble for his printing activities. On 20 June 1643 he had to post a £1000 bond in order to recover his printing materials which had been seized by the Stationers' Company a few days earlier, and the following February he asked for the pardon of the company's court for resisting a company search. On 19 November 1649 a warrant was issued by the council of state for apprehending Cole and two other London stationers for printing an account of King Charles's trial, but by the following year he was conducting searches for illegal books on behalf of the council. In 1651 he was examined by the council on two occasions, once for printing an inappropriate sermon. However, by the mid-1650s he was again in enough favour to be the authorized printer of Edward Hayward's *The Sizes and Lengths of Riggings for All the States Ships and Frigats* provided that he strictly restricted distribution of the copies to Cromwell, the council, and certain leading naval officers. Cole also made an extraordinary petition in 1656 requesting that he be allowed to license his own printing output as he had been unable to get a number of sermons licensed because the relevant manuscripts were insufficiently legible.

Many of Cole's titles during the Cromwellian era were of a theological nature, but he is principally remembered as the publisher of medical treatises by the radical herbalist Nicholas Culpeper who penned books in the 1650s making healthcare information accessible to the lay reader. Cole generally embraced the same iatric views and paid liberally to publish them, sometimes in collaboration with his brother, Edward. Cole printed seventeen Culpeper titles while the herbalist was alive, all of which enjoyed enormous sales. After Culpeper's death in 1654, his widow invited Cole to produce seventy-nine more, such as multiple editions of the pharmacopoeia, anatomies, herbals, and *The Art of Chirurgery*. Writing anonymously in a pamphlet entitled *Mr. Culpeper's Ghost*, Cole refuted the idea that Culpeper had been exclusively Paracelsian, reporting that he had mellowed toward Galenism during his final illness. The name of Abdiah Cole, a physician who translated, edited, and revised Culpeper's texts, appears on the title-pages of Culpeper's posthumous publications; he was probably a relative of the Coles. However, Nathaniel Brooks (occasionally Brookes), a nearby bookseller in Cornhill, expropriated some of the manuscripts Culpeper's widow intended for Peter Cole; Mrs Culpeper denounced Brooks, calling the manuscripts that he printed forgeries.

The Restoration brought fresh attention from the government. In 1660 Cole's apprentice went so far as to seek the help of the privy council; Cole, he alleged, was mistreating him upon suspicion that he had informed against Cole for printing treasonable and seditious books. The following year the privy council issued a warrant for Cole's arrest and for a search of his house for illegal books and pamphlets.

On 4 December 1665 Cole hanged himself from the rafters of his warehouse in Leadenhall, probably suffering from a painful illness and 'reported to be distracted' (Ellis, 70). Whether his contemporaries saw his death as suicide is unclear. Cole was accorded a Christian burial in the east yard of the parish of St Peter Cornhill on 11 December but the following day a warrant for a grant for Cole's estate, forfeit because of his suicide, was issued to John, Lord Berkeley, and Sir Hugh Pollard. However, as Cole's will was proved on 22 December it seems that the estate was never formally forfeited. He left lands and tenements in his native Suffolk to his nephew James Cole and bequeathed 'leases money goods and Chattels', including the two London printing shops, to three children of his brother, Edward. He gave Elizabeth Ridley, the youngest daughter of a deceased friend and comrade in bookselling, £200 to be paid in full within a year after Cole's demise, and to Ursula Parry and her children he left £250 'to be soe secured that her husband may not spend it' (PRO, PROB 11/318, fol. 358r). Cole bestowed £50 on haberdasher William Marsh and forgave fellow stationer Samuel Thompson a debt he owed and willed him £10 in the bargain.

ELIZABETH LANE FURDELL

Sources will, PRO, PROB 11/318, sig. 153 · H. R. Plomer and others, *A dictionary of the booksellers and printers who were at work in England, Scotland, and Ireland, from 1641 to 1667* (1907); repr. (1968) · D. F. McKenzie, ed., *Stationers' Company apprentices*, 3 vols. (1961–78), vols. 1–2 · F. N. L. Poynter, 'Culpeper and the Paracelsians', *Science, medicine and society in the Renaissance*, ed. A. G. Debus (New York, 1972) · STC, 1475–1640 · *A register of all the christninges burialles and weddinges within the parish of Saint Peeters upon Cornhill*, Harleian Society, 1 (1877), 219 · H. Ellis, ed., *The obituary of Richard Smyth* (1849) · D. Freist, *Governed by opinion: politics, religion and the dynamics of communication in Stuart London, 1637–45* (1997) · CSP dom., 1643–65
Wealth at death land; left £500 to friends and family: will, PRO, PROB 11/318, sig. 153

Cole, Sir Ralph, second baronet (*bap.* 1629, *d.* 1704), painter and patron of the arts, was baptized on 3 November 1629. Of his six sons, Ralph was the first surviving son and heir of Sir Nicholas Cole, first baronet (*d.* 1669), of Brancepeth Castle, co. Durham. The founders of this family were Nicholas and Thomas Cole, sons of James Cole, smith, of Gateshead. Thomas amassed a large fortune and died in 1620; Nicholas was the father of Ralph Cole, sheriff of Newcastle upon Tyne in 1625 and mayor in 1633, who bought Brancepeth Castle. The Brancepeth estates of Charles Neville, sixth earl of Westmorland, had been sequestrated by the crown for his support of Mary, queen of Scots, during the rising of the northern earls in 1569. In 1613 James I gave Brancepeth Castle to Robert Carr, earl of Somerset, who later forfeited it by attainder, and Ralph Cole bought it in 1636. Ralph Cole was the father of Nicholas Cole of Kepier, near Durham, who was created a baronet on 15 February 1641; Sir Nicholas Cole was sheriff of Newcastle in 1633, and mayor in 1640, 1641, and 1643. He defended the town against the Scots in the civil war, and for his loyalty to the royal cause he was imprisoned and fined. He married his first wife, Mary, second daughter of Sir Thomas Liddell, bt, of Ravensworth, on 28 September 1626 and left two sons, the eldest of whom was Sir Ralph Cole.

Sir Ralph Cole thus inherited the vast fortune of his ancestors, and spent the greater part of it on art and the patronage of artists. He reportedly took lessons in painting from Van Dyck, and is said to have retained several Italian painters in his service. He is described in a letter of 1677 as a 'very worthy ingeniouse gent: hee has furnished his house with incomparable Pictures of his drawing, and is very ingeniouse in making knives, guns, Pistols &c: & of

a very courteouse behaviour' (Hake, 64). He painted portraits, subject pictures, and miniatures. A portrait of Thomas Wyndham is preserved at Petworth House, Sussex, and was engraved in mezzotint by Richard Tompson, *c.*1677, though the mezzotint more closely resembles a painting that was sold through Christies in 1948 and might be a self-portrait. Sir Ralph Cole also engraved a portrait of Charles II in mezzotint. His own portrait was painted by Sir Peter Lely, *c.*1675, and used to hang in Brancepeth Castle; it was engraved in mezzotint by his friend and brother dilettante Francis Place, *c.*1677. He was twice married: first, by 1651, to Margaret (*d.* 1657), daughter of Thomas Windham of Felbrigg, Norfolk, and widow of one Shouldham, and second to Catherine (*b.* 1637), daughter of Sir Henry Foulis, second baronet, of Ingleby Manor, Yorkshire; she died on 29 September 1704 and was buried at Brancepeth. He represented Durham city in parliament in 1675–6 and 1678, and in 1685 commanded the Durham regiment of militia. In 1674 he sold Kepier, and in 1701 he sold Brancepeth to his friend Sir Henry Bellasyse. He died on 9 August 1704 and was buried at Brancepeth. Brancepeth Castle was still furnished with his paintings when John Loveday visited it in 1732; he mentioned in particular a portrait of Dean Sudbury by Sir Ralph Cole.

Cole had three sons, but he was succeeded by his grandson, Sir Nicholas Cole, third baronet. The family fortune having been considerably reduced, the fourth and last baronet, Sir Mark Cole, grandson of Sir Ralph, was buried at the expense of his cousin, Sir Ralph Milbanke, in 1720.

ARIANNE BURNETTE

Sources C. Surtees, *The history of the castle of Brancepeth at Brancepeth, co. Durham* (1920) · J. C. Smith, *British mezzotinto portraits*, 4 vols. in 5 (1878–84) · H. M. Hake, 'Some contemporary records relating to Francis Place, engraver and draughtsman, with a catalogue of his engraved work', *Walpole Society*, 10 (1921–2), 39–69 · HoP, *Commons, 1660–90*, 2 (1983) · C. Surtees, *The history of the parish of Brancepeth* (1930) · J. Loveday, *Diary of a tour in 1732 through parts of England, Wales, Ireland and Scotland*, ed. J. E. T. Loveday, Roxburghe Club, 121 (privately printed, Edinburgh, 1890) · GEC, *Baronetage*, vol. 2 · J. Brand, *The history and antiquities of the town and county of the town of Newcastle upon Tyne*, 1 (1789) · W. Hutchinson, *The history and antiquities of the county palatine of Durham*, 3 (1794) · J. Burke and J. B. Burke, *A genealogical and heraldic history of the extinct and dormant baronetcies of England, Ireland, and Scotland*, 2nd edn (1841) · E. K. Waterhouse, *The dictionary of British 16th and 17th century painters* (1988) · R. Surtees, *The history and antiquities of the county palatine of Durham*, 4 vols. (1816–40) · H. Walpole, *Anecdotes of painting in England: with some account of the principal artists*, ed. R. N. Wornum, new edn, 3 vols. (1849); repr. (1862) · Redgrave, *Artists* · J. Granger, *A biographical history of England from Egbert the Great to the revolution*, 5th edn, 6 vols. (1824) [copy annotated by Sir George Scharf, NPG] · C. H. Collins Baker, *Catalogue of the Petworth collection of pictures in the possession of Lord Leconfield* (1920) · J. B. Burke, *Vicissitudes of families*, 2 (1869) · R. B. Beckett, *Lely* (1951) · DNB
Archives NPG muniments, Lionel Cust's notes for DNB article · Gateshead register · Newcastle, St Nicholas's register · Brancepeth register
Likenesses P. Lely, oils, *c.*1675; formerly at Brancepeth Castle · F. Place, mezzotint, *c.*1677 (after P. Lely, *c.*1675), BM · R. Cole, self-portrait?; Christies, 9 July 1948, lot 32, Wombwell sale
Wealth at death sold Brancepeth estates in 1701 for £16,800, with life annuity of £500 and £200 for his wife if she survived him; bequests of £2600: GEC, *Baronetage*; Hutchinson, *History and antiquities*; will, Surtees, *History of the parish of Brancepeth*, appx, 55

Cole, Reginald George Vicat [Rex] (1870–1940), land-scape painter and art teacher, was born on 22 February 1870 in Kensington, London, the only son and youngest of the four children of George Vicat *Cole (1833–1893) and Mary Ann Chignell (d. 1915), daughter of a Hampshire tradesman. His paternal grandfather, George *Cole (1810–1883), was also a landscape painter. The birth of Reginald (always known as Rex) coincided with the election of his father, a successful landscape painter, to associate membership of the Royal Academy of Arts. Vicat Cole moved in 1874 to Little Campden House, Kensington, where Rex Vicat Cole spent his formative years at the heart of the Victorian art world. At Eton College (c.1878–1888), where he claimed to have learned little, he was encouraged by the art master Samuel T. G. Evans. His artistic education continued at the St John's Wood Schools of Art, London, from 1888 to 1890. He had already decided to follow the family tradition of landscape painting, and for two years from 1890 studied with his father, drawing in the buildings in the latter's *Westminster* (exh. RA, 1892; Guildhall Art Gallery, London).

From 1891 Cole journeyed regularly to Yorkshire in search of subject matter. At Bolton Abbey he executed a number of large landscapes, destined for the Royal Academy, and an exhibition of his smaller works, 'A year in Wharfedale', was held at the Dowdeswell Galleries, London, in 1901. In 1900 he married Hannah Gill (d. 1940), daughter of John Gill, of New Hall Farm, Bolton Abbey, where Cole had erected a temporary studio. Of their two sons, George Vicat Cole (1902–1986) and (Reginald) John Vicat Cole [see below], the former took over New Hall Farm, while the latter became a landscape painter, the fourth generation in an unbroken line. Between 1900 and 1914 Rex Vicat Cole concentrated on landscapes of woodland scenery, often including images of his wife and sons, which were exhibited annually at the exhibitions of the Royal Academy and the Royal Society of British Artists. In his lavish two-volume publication, *British Trees* (1906), closely observed, scientific drawings appear alongside photogravure reproductions of the romantic landscapes he exhibited, with a descriptive letterpress by the artist. Although 9 New Road, Campden Hill, Kensington, was his principal residence from 1900 until his death in 1940, in 1906 he took the lease of Brinkwells, a cottage in the countryside near Fittleworth, Sussex. The area was to provide subject matter for the majority of his landscapes until the 1920s, such as *Brinkwells Garden* (1916, priv. coll.; reproduced Barringer, 20). During the First World War he served in the West Sussex civil guard and, from November 1916, in the united arts rifles on east coast duty.

A dedicated teacher throughout his career, Cole had joined the staff of the women's department of King's College, London, in 1894, and his friend John Byam Liston Shaw joined him on the staff in 1904. The two left to found the Byam Shaw and Vicat Cole School of Art in 1910. Primarily intended to prepare students for entry to the Royal Academy Schools, the school was highly successful. On his retirement in 1926, Cole withdrew his name as a tribute to

Reginald George Vicat [Rex] Cole (1870–1940), by John Byam Shaw, 1898

his friend, who had died in 1919: the institution still survives as the Byam Shaw School of Art. In 1932 Cole published a biography of Byam Shaw. Examples of Cole's pedagogy can be found in his technical publications *The Artistic Anatomy of Trees* (1916) and *Perspective* (1921).

Cole was resolutely traditional in his aesthetic outlook, and modernism made no impact on his artistic production, teaching, or writing. During the 1920s, however, he abandoned the opulent romanticism of his earlier works in favour of a sparser style in which a single motif dominates the composition, as in *The Tow Path Bridge* (exh. RA, 1923; Art Gallery and Museum, Brighton). In some of his later landscapes, such as *Storiths in Wharfedale* (exh. RA, 1929; Chatsworth, Derbyshire), a new formality of composition suggests a revival of interest in the work of Claude Lorrain and Nicolas Poussin. A series of large, stylized paintings of the London parks continued this trend (for example, *Kensington Gardens*, exh. RA, 1934; Royal Borough of Kensington and Chelsea) and marked Cole's increasing fascination with the landscape and architecture of the capital. *The Destruction of St Olave's, Tooley Street, 1927* (exh. RA, 1928; Guildhall Art Gallery, London), urging the conservation of London monuments, was accompanied by the production of hundreds of smaller oil paintings, including images of every church in the City. These were exhibited at Dunthorne's Gallery, Vigo Street, London, as 'London, Old and New' in 1935. Throughout the 1930s Cole worked on the manuscript of a historical and descriptive account of 'The streets of London', to be published in a lavish volume illustrated by several hundred paintings, drawings, and maps. Although the manuscript was completed, his sudden death in Upwaltham, Sussex, on 4 February 1940 prevented its publication. He was buried in Upwaltham church.

A distinguished, bearded figure, as seen in Byam Shaw's portrait of him in 1898 (priv. coll.; reproduced Barringer, 111), Cole was held in great affection by students and friends; the manuscript of 'The streets of London' reveals a lively sense of humour. He was denied the financial success achieved by his father and membership of the Royal Academy also eluded him. Yet his work across a range of fields—as painter, teacher, and author—has been underestimated and demands reconsideration.

Cole's son **(Reginald) John Vicat Cole** (1903–1975), landscape painter, was born on 2 November 1903 in Kensington, London. He trained at the Byam Shaw and Vicat Cole School of Art in Campden Hill (c.1921–c.1924) and, like his father, developed a distinctive personal idiom through an extended period painting from nature in the Yorkshire dales, near Bolton Abbey. John Cole's painterly and atmospheric oils from this period, often dark in tone, evince a greater expressive freedom than his father's works; early influences on him included that of Philip H. Padwick and Oliver Hall, family friends and neighbours during his boyhood in Sussex. His early work, exhibited at the New English Art Club, the Royal Academy, and other London galleries from 1923, included flower pieces and during the late 1920s and 1930s he also experimented with stained-glass designs. From the early 1930s Cole found his most characteristic subjects in the shop-fronts and street scenes of the West End of London, many of them within walking distance of the converted Georgian public house, the Duke of Sussex, at 44 Uxbridge Street, Kensington, where he made his studio from 1923 and, from 1940, his home. Among the most impressive examples are In Church Street, Kensington (1936, Manchester City Galleries) and Knightsbridge from Wilton Place (1952, priv. coll.), the latter of which was awarded a gold medal at the Salon des Artistes Français in Paris in 1954. Although he continued to exhibit at the Royal Academy until his death, his later work took on a nostalgic and elegiac quality. After inheriting a house, L'Abri, at 1 Prince's Road in St Leonards, near Hastings, Sussex, in 1955, he concentrated increasingly on Sussex landscapes and shop-fronts—subjects which continued to fascinate him until the end of his life. He died, unmarried, on 5 September 1975 and was buried in St Mary's, Fittleworth, Sussex. An active member of the Royal Society of British Artists and the Royal Institute of Painters in Oils, John Cole also served on the committees of the Artists' General Benevolent Institution, the St James's Art Society for the Deaf, and the Byam Shaw School of Art.   TIM BARRINGER

Sources T. J. Barringer, The Cole family: painters of the English landscape, 1838–1975 (1988) [exhibition catalogue, Portsmouth and Bradford, 1 April – 30 Aug 1988] · A. Chester, 'The art of Mr Rex Vicat Cole', Windsor Magazine, 189 (July 1910), 396–82 · R. V. Cole, The art and life of Byam Shaw (1932) · R. V. Cole, British trees, 2 vols. (1906) · R. V. Cole, The artistic anatomy of trees (1916) · R. V. Cole, Perspective (1921) · R. Chignell, The life and paintings of Vicat Cole, RA (1896) · priv. coll., Cole MSS · CGPLA Eng. & Wales (1940) · private information (2004) · WW · Sussex Daily News (Feb 1940)
Archives priv. coll.

Likenesses eight photographs, c.1878–1940, repro. in Barringer, The Cole family · J. Byam Shaw, oils, 1898, repro. in R. V. Cole, The art and life of Byam Shaw (1932) [see illus.]
Wealth at death £8871 11s. 1d.: administration with will, 2 June 940 · £54,564—Reginald John Vicat Cole: probate, 5 April 1976, CGPLA Eng. & Wales

Cole, Thomas (c.1520–1571), archdeacon of Essex, is said to have hailed from Lincolnshire. He may have been brother of both Robert and William *Cole, whose early careers were inextricably confounded by earlier authorities. From the welter of conflicting data it is at least clear that Thomas studied at Oxford, where he commenced MA about 1550.

Headmaster of Maidstone School from 1546, Cole took to preaching against the doctrine of original sin and in January 1551 was one of a group of Kent and Essex 'freewillers' arrested by the privy council. Interrogated on 3 February and apparently detained or imprisoned, he thereafter renounced his errors. On 19 February 1553 he preached before Thomas Cranmer a 'ringing defence of predestination' (MacCulloch, 531). The archbishop arranged for its publication as A godly and frutefull sermon, made at Maydestone the fyrste sonday in Lent, against opinions of the anabaptistes and others. Two extended modern analyses have been published (Martin, 58–60; Penny, 69–73).

One of those specifically exempted from the general pardon issued at Mary's coronation, Cole departed for Frankfurt. A supporter of John Knox and William Whittingham, he sat on the committee that drew up Frankfurt's 'new discipline', later used as the basis of the order of Geneva.

Cole's career is partially explained by a hyperactive streak in his make-up, and his movements abroad, evidently multifarious, cannot be plotted with certainty. It remains unclear whether, like many who supported Knox, he finally abandoned Frankfurt for Geneva, although he certainly berated Robert Wisdom for dealing 'uncharitably' with those who chose to do so (Arber, 95). He was known to Heinrich Bullinger of Zürich and was befriended by Wolfgang Weidner of Worms. It is, however, generally accepted that it was William Cole and not Thomas who helped to prepare the Geneva Bible, and it has been persuasively argued (Collinson, 191–211) that he can have had no part in writing A Brieff Discourse off the Troubles Begonne at Franckford.

On Thomas Cole's return to England after Mary's death he was at once absorbed into the hierarchy of London diocese. Instituted rector of High Ongar, Essex, on 9 November 1559 at the presentation of Richard, first Lord Rich, he was collated by Edmund Grindal, bishop of London, both to the archdeaconry of Essex in early 1560 and to the prebend of Rugmere in St Paul's on the following 7 December. Meanwhile, between 20 February and 7 May he acted temporarily as Grindal's commissary in Essex and Hertfordshire. Whilst no commission survives in Matthew Parker's register he was also at this time appointed dean of Bocking, Canterbury's peculiar jurisdiction within Essex and Suffolk. Here was hyperactivity indeed.

Cole's surviving act books indicate that his self-imposed

task as archdeacon was to keep a sharp eye out for surviving Catholic sentiments and habits of worship in the parishes under his control. It was probably his vigilance in this respect which prompted the privy council in May 1564 to order an examination of a case of 'misdemeanour and contempt' against his authority (*APC, 1558–70*, 145).

Although Parker clearly contemplated some modest reform of the 1559 settlement as he prepared for the convocation of 1562–3, nothing was in the event achieved, perhaps because the lower house proved more radical than anticipated. Cole was one of thirty-four members, most of them former exiles, who proposed seven articles which, if passed and implemented, would have obviated the vestiarian controversy which divided the church during the following five years. Six more moderate articles were debated instead, failing by a single vote. From this debate Cole and others who had supported the seven articles abstained, possibly on the principle that if they subscribed to half-measures all hope of reopening the debate in the future would be lost.

Cole's radical views did not count against him in high places, probably because he had obtained the patronage of Robert Dudley, earl of Leicester. If the diarist Henry Machyn is to be believed Cole was in 1563 considered for the deanery of Norwich and in 1564 he proceeded DTh at Cambridge as an Oxford MA of fourteen years' standing. At about the same time he preached at Windsor. *A Godly and Learned Sermon, Made this Laste Lent before the Queenes Majestie* (1564) was an astonishingly bold performance in which he told the supreme governor to her face that princes should maintain true religion 'without any mingle mangle of their own inventions'.

Within weeks he had incurred Parker's wrath. It came to the archbishop's attention that as dean of Bocking Cole was flouting his orders with regard to clerical vestments. Parker evidently withdrew his commission for the deanery and on 10 November transferred it to John Puysant, rector of Latchingdon. Yet meanwhile, on 13 July, Cole had been instituted to the valuable rectory of Stanford Rivers, Essex, on the crown's presentation.

When after January 1565 Parker, ostensibly at Elizabeth's behest, intensified his drive against nonconformity, Cole was among those who orchestrated the opposition. On 20 March twenty leading nonconformists, headed by Miles Coverdale, Whittingham, Thomas Sampson, Laurence Humphrey, and Cole himself, requested the ecclesiastical commissioners to excuse them from the necessity of wearing the canonical habits. According to the endorsement they received a favourable response from Grindal, Robert Horne, bishop of Winchester, and (more surprisingly) Richard Cox, bishop of Ely, only Parker and Edmund Guest, bishop of Rochester, not being listed as 'assenting'.

Parker noted on 7 April that, among other signs of resistance, 'Mr Cole is now at the Court in his hat and short cloak, which will overthrow all this attempt' (Bruce and Perowne, 237). Although this was to omit reference to his Cambridge doctorate 'Mr Cole' is more likely to have been

Thomas than Robert or William. Always accounted an eloquent preacher, Cole appeared at Paul's Cross on 11 November 1565, delivering a diatribe against popish attire, and in March 1566 was chosen by the lord mayor and aldermen, along with Thomas Penny, to preach the city's Spital sermons. Parker was quick to veto the proposal, commenting predictably that he 'dare not adventure to commend them for comfortable' (ibid., 264). A fortnight later he summarily suspended thirty-seven city ministers who refused the prescribed vestments.

It is presumably a measure of the influence that Cole was able to wield that Parker had nevertheless restored him as dean of Bocking. At the end of March the archbishop officially instructed Cole to enforce conformity in the Essex and Suffolk peculiars. He cannot have done so in any spirit of facile optimism. Indeed, Cole merely carried the war into the countryside. On May day he preached at Chelmsford as archdeacon and shortly afterwards at Hadleigh, Suffolk, as dean of Bocking. Both sermons were inflammatory and Leicester, probably judging that he was providing Parker with too much ammunition, brought Cole to heel. Cole defended his Chelmsford sermon on the grounds that it was intended to rebut the 'impudent conceit' of Catholics (*Pepys MSS*, 90).

The vestiarian controversy in London ceased with more or less abruptness after the autumn of 1566. Cole remained dean of Bocking and archdeacon of Essex and in 1570 he was nominated dean of Salisbury. In the very act of packing up his household and travelling to Salisbury he fell ill and, as Richard Hilles later told Bullinger, died of quinsy after two days' illness. John Parkhurst, bishop of Norwich, also reporting his death, reminded Bullinger that Wolfgang Weidner had been 'fond' of Cole (Robinson, 1.256). Cole's widow, Susan (her maiden name is unknown), was granted letters of administration for his estate on 20 July 1571. Cole was probably buried in High Ongar or Stanford Rivers, Essex.   BRETT USHER

Sources Venn, *Alum. Cant.*, 1/1.368 · *APC, 1550–52*, 199, 206–7; *1588–70*, 145 · D. MacCulloch, *Thomas Cranmer: a life* (1996) · C. H. Garrett, *The Marian exiles: a study in the origins of Elizabethan puritanism* (1938) · J. W. Martin, *Religious radicals in Tudor England* (1989) · A. Penny, *Freewill or predestination* (1989) · [W. Whittingham?], *A brief discourse of the troubles at Frankfort*, ed. E. Arber (1908) · P. Collinson, *Godly people: essays on English protestantism and puritanism* (1983) [Troubles at Frankfort] · Essex RO, D/AEA 1–6 [Essex archdeaconry act bks, 1560–71] · LPL, Petyt MS 538, vol. 47 [convocation of 1562–3] · *The diary of Henry Machyn, citizen and merchant-taylor of London, from AD 1550 to AD 1563*, ed. J. G. Nichols, CS, 42 (1848) · B. Usher, 'The deanery of Bocking: a case study in the demise of the vestiarian controversy', *Journal of Ecclesiastical History* [forthcoming] · *Correspondence of Matthew Parker*, ed. J. Bruce and T. T. Perowne, Parker Society, 42 (1853) · *Report on the Pepys manuscripts*, HMC, 70 (1911) [Papers of state] · M. Byford, 'The price of protestantism: assessing the impact of religious change on Elizabethan Essex: the cases of Heydon and Colchester, 1558–1594', DPhil diss., U. Oxf., 1988 · D. J. Crankshaw, 'Preparations for the Canterbury provincial convocation of 1562–63: a question of attribution', *Belief and practice in Reformation England: a tribute to Patrick Collinson from his students*, ed. S. Wabuda and C. Litzenberger (1998), 60–93 · A. Macfarlane, *Witchcraft in Tudor and Stuart England* (1970) · H. Robinson, ed. and trans., *The Zurich letters, comprising the correspondence of several English* *bishops and others with some of the Helvetian reformers, during the early part of the reign of Queen Elizabeth*, 1, Parker Society, 7 (1842)

Cole, Thomas (1628–1697), clergyman and Independent minister, was baptized on 27 April 1628 at St Giles Cripplegate, London, the son of William Cole, gentleman. A pupil of Westminster School, he was a king's scholar in 1644 and was elected to Christ Church, Oxford, but remained at the school 'through the exigencies of war' (*Old Westminsters*, 268), matriculating only on 1 February 1647, aged eighteen. He graduated BA from Christ Church on 6 November 1649, and MA on 8 July 1651, the latter degree being incorporated in Cambridge in 1653. On 15 October 1656 Cole was admitted principal of St Mary Hall, Oxford, where he acted as tutor to John Locke, but from which position he was removed in 1660. In 1659 he compounded for the first fruits of the rectory of Ewelme, Oxfordshire, but was ejected the following year. On 2 August 1660, however, he was ordained a deacon and priest, and became minister at Brampton Bryan, Herefordshire; in November 1660 Thomas Harley wrote that he had preached there, and 'the whole parish are well satisfied with him' (Cliffe, 99). Cole refused the tests laid down by the Act of Uniformity of 1662, but 'appears to have deferred his resignation in order to allow his patron sufficient time to find a successor' (ibid.).

Cole may have retained a connection with his former benefice, for in April 1666 Philip Henry was 'at Aulam, where preaches one Mr Cole affectionately and to edification' (*Diaries and Letters*, 186). In that year he opened his academy at Nettlebed, Oxfordshire. The claim that Samuel Wesley, father of John Wesley, was a student there is incorrect; his later attack on Cole, and his generalizations about the poor moral tone of dissenting academies, drew chiefly on the remarks of James Bonnell, who attended as a student. Yet although Bonnell learned much 'Debauchery' from his fellow students and claimed Cole 'was too Remiss in matters of Morality and Religion', he refused to 'accuse him of anything that was ill' (*Calamy rev.*, 125). In 1672 Cole tried but failed to secure a licence to preach at Henley town hall, but was licensed for other premises in the town: on 22 April as a congregational teacher at John Tyler's house and Alexander Bernard's barn, and on 16 May at his own house.

Unfavourable political circumstances probably contributed to Cole's decision to close the academy at Nettlebed in 1674, and to move to London. There he succeeded Philip Nye as minister of the Independent congregation which at that time met at Cutlers' Hall, Cloak Lane, and was later at Tallow Chandlers' Hall, Dowgate Hill. He was also one of the ministers of the merchants' lecture at Pinners' Hall. Despite his nonconformity Cole appears to have prospered, investing substantial sums in the East India Company and purchasing landed property in Oxfordshire which formed the basis of substantial legacies to his wife, Hannah (whose surname may have been Partridge), and to a daughter-in-law, nephews, and grandchildren.

In his last years Cole lived in Lime Street, London. He did not join the 'happy union' between presbyterians and congregationalists, and was one of three London ministers who baulked at union with those who advocated sacramental communion with the Church of England. Though elected on 13 April 1691 as a manager of the ministers' Common Fund, he attended no meetings and refused to help in the enterprise. But in 1695, after the union fell apart, he became an original manager of the Congregational Fund board. Cole also took part in the renewed theological controversy which preoccupied his wing of dissent in the early nineties; his was an unbending high Calvinism: 'a secret conversing with a covenant of works … will worm out the covenant of grace, by turning it before you are aware, into a covenant of works'. Cole regretted only that 'I have been no more vigorous and active in defending those truths' against his neonomian opponents: 'God hath made me a man of contention; but I would have all the world know, that the doctrine I have been preaching, I can comfortably die in' (Wilson, 82–3). Cole preached his last sermon before his congregation, which now met at Pinners' Hall, on 22 August 1697. He died in London on Thursday 16 September 1697, aged sixty-nine, and was buried in the upper ground of Bunhill Fields. W. E. A. AXON, *rev.* STEPHEN WRIGHT

Sources *Calamy rev.* · W. Wilson, *The history and antiquities of the dissenting churches and meeting houses in London, Westminster and Southwark*, 4 vols. (1808–14), vol. 3, pp. 79–88 · E. Calamy, ed., *An abridgement of Mr. Baxter's history of his life and times, with an account of the ministers, &c., who were ejected after the Restauration of King Charles II*, 2nd edn, 2 vols. (1713) · A. Gordon, ed., *Freedom after ejection: a review (1690–1692) of presbyterian and congregational nonconformity in England and Wales* (1917) · 'Early nonconformist academies', *Transactions of the Congregational Historical Society*, 4 (1909–10), 233–53 · *Old Westminsters* · J. T. Cliffe, *The puritan gentry besieged, 1650–1700* (1993) · will, PRO, PROB 11/440, fols. 159v–161r · C. Whiting, *Studies in English puritanism* (1931) · G. F. Nuttall, *Visible saints: the congregational way, 1640–1660* (1957) · *Diaries and letters of Philip Henry*, ed. M. H. Lee (1882) · Wood, *Ath. Oxon.*, new edn · A. Wood, *The history and antiquities of the colleges and halls in the University of Oxford*, ed. J. Gutch (1786); appx (1790) · *IGI*

Wealth at death wealth chiefly in East India Company stock; also bequests: will, PRO, PROB 11/440, fols. 159v–161r

Cole, William (c.1530–1600), dean of Lincoln and college head, was born in Grantham, Lincolnshire. He was possibly the younger brother of Thomas *Cole, archdeacon of Essex. Admitted at Corpus Christi College, Oxford, on 28 July 1545, William Cole graduated BA in March 1548 and is credited with a fellowship from the time of his matriculation. He proceeded MA in 1552.

After Mary's accession Cole was among the distinguished group of Oxford scholars who sought refuge in Zürich. Early in 1554, with Robert Horne and his wife, James Pilkington, Thomas Lever, Thomas Bentham, Thomas Spencer, and Laurence Humphrey, among others, Cole petitioned the Zürich magistrates for permission to reside there and enjoy their protection 'against the violence of those … who would oppose and molest us' (Robinson, *Original Letters*, 1.752). Thereafter, with Humphrey and John Parkhurst, future bishop of Norwich, Cole was one of many who were welcomed into the household of the printer Christopher Froschover, who had been a pupil of Peter Martyr in Oxford in 1551–2. Here they lived together 'happily, like brothers', paying their way as if they were still undergraduates wherever they went ('simul fraterne & iucunde viximus, & ordinaria pensa quasi in Gymnasio quopiam persoluimus'; Humphrey, 89).

Although also kindly received by Rudolph Gualter, Heinrich Bullinger's eventual successor as Zürich's chief pastor, Cole migrated to Frankfurt, where in the tax list of October 1556 he was rated as worth 100 florins. With John Foxe he seems to have moved on to Basel during the winter of 1556–7, but on 5 June 1557 was accepted into John Knox's congregation in Geneva, on the same day as Alice Agar, widow of Colchester, Essex, and her children Thomas, Jane, and Priscilla. On 29 November Cole became a resident of the city. Before the end of 1557 Alice Agar married Thomas Spencer (who had arrived in November 1556), while Cole married Jane Agar. No child is recorded as being baptized in Geneva before the couple's departure.

During 1558 Cole assisted in the translation of the Geneva Bible. He perhaps continued to do so for several months after Elizabeth I's accession, since his Knoxian views on church discipline and the fact that his marriage prevented him from resuming his fellowship will have given him no immediate incentive to return to England. By May 1564 he was serving as chaplain to the Merchant Adventurers in Antwerp, where Edmund Grindal, bishop of London, permitted him to follow local protestant usage. Accordingly he ignored the prayer book ceremonies and was assisted in his ministry by six elders.

Yet his family connections finally drew Cole to Colchester, where on 20 November 1564 he was admitted burgess, without fine, as the town's common preacher. As such he was not obliged to observe the prayer book ceremonies, and perhaps for that reason did not, like Colchester's archdeacon, James Calfhill, publicly oppose Archbishop Matthew Parker's attempts to impose ritual conformity during the vestiarian controversy of 1564–6.

In 1568, at the recommendation of Robert Horne, now bishop of Winchester and the college's visitor, Elizabeth nominated Cole to the presidency of Corpus Christi College, Oxford. The senior fellows, still conservative in their approach to Elizabeth's settlement, had no wish to have a married president imposed upon them, and when Cole arrived to take formal possession the doors were closed against him. It was necessary to obtain a royal commission, dated 21 July 1568, to secure his admittance. He was granted the degree of BD on 18 November following.

Thereafter Cole appears to have shed much of his Knoxian austerity, becoming a modest pluralist in the process. Rector of Buscot, Berkshire, from 1571 to 1573, he resigned after institution to the college living of Lower Heyford, Oxfordshire, in 1572. On 21 September 1571 he had been collated by the dying John Jewel to the prebend of Durnford in Salisbury Cathedral, and on 10 May 1572 Horne collated him canon of the fifth prebend in Winchester Cathedral. He proceeded DTh in January 1574, and on the following 4 December was installed as prebendary of Bedford Major in Lincoln Cathedral.

Perhaps more than most of his generation Cole's Elizabethan career was conditioned by the Marian years. He had owed his preachership in Colchester to his marriage, and his presidency to Horne, while two Genevan fellow exiles, the London merchants Edward Caunt and John Bodley, were among those who stood surety for his first fruits, for Lower Heyford and his Salisbury prebend respectively. He also remained a friend of Foxe, Parkhurst, and John Aylmer. When Gualter's son visited England in 1573 as Parkhurst's protégé, Cole went out of his way to remind Gualter of the kindness he had received from him 'beyond all others', declaring that 'in mind and inclination I shall always be a Zuricher' (Robinson, *Zurich Letters*, 2.222). Given his subsequent removal to Geneva this smacks of special pleading, as does his letter the following year regretting that because young Gualter's stay in Oxford had been brief he had 'not treated him according to his merit' (ibid., 2.256). For his part young Gualter praised Cole and Laurence Humphrey, under whose tutelage at Magdalen he had placed himself, for their 'singular regard' and 'especial kindness' towards him (ibid., 2.218).

Although he was accounted an excellent teacher, Cole's presidency was undistinguished. The college estates were incompetently administered during his tenure, and complaints reached Horne that he had defrauded the college and allowed it to fall into debt. One of Horne's informants was Simon Tripp, who wrote in April 1572 of the contention and strife among the fellowship. Tradition asserts that when Horne decreed that 'he and the college must part without more ado', Cole 'fetched a deep sigh and said, "What, my lord, must I then eat mice at Zurich again?"' Touched, Horne bade him 'be at rest and deal honestly with the college' (Wood, 2.166). Since the story scarcely accords with the generous reception both men had received from Froschover, Bullinger, and Gualter, it should probably be discounted. Cole's later career, moreover, suggests that reports of his inefficiency were exaggerated and/or that he heeded Horne's advice. During 1577 he served as vice-chancellor, and by letters patent dated 17 May 1577 he succeeded John Aylmer, elevated to the bishopric of London, as archdeacon of Lincoln.

From this time, if no earlier, Cole appears to have been entirely reconciled to Elizabeth's settlement of religion and showed no sympathy for the aspirations of younger nonconformists. On 28 February 1579, condoling with Gualter on the death of his son, he observed laconically of the settlement that there had been 'no change whatever' since 1559 (Robinson, *Zurich Letters*, 2.306). In September that year he became a canon residentiary at Lincoln, and perhaps for that reason resigned his stall at Winchester. In June 1580 he was excused further residence in Lincoln on the grounds that he had been summoned to attend the earls of Warwick and Leicester. By March 1581 he had also resigned his archdeaconry but retained his Lincoln and Salisbury prebends, along with Lower Heyford, until his death.

Cole evidently approved of the three articles which John Whitgift, archbishop of Canterbury, introduced as his yardstick of conformity in late 1583. He served on a committee which on 5 February 1584 promulgated new and restrictive regulations with regard to university preaching licences. Later that year the bailiffs (joint mayors) of Colchester asked Cole to intercede with Aylmer following the suspension of their present town preacher, George Northey. Finding Aylmer inflexible, and informed that similar efforts by Walsingham, Leicester, and Warwick had all failed in council, he advised the bailiffs to abandon their suit unless Northey would subscribe Whitgift's articles 'for that opinion is very dangerous to the estate of the whole realm as I am verily persuaded' (Essex RO, Morant MS D/Y 2/5, p. 107). In March 1589 Cole expelled the radical William Hubbock from his fellowship following his imprisonment by the high commission and subsequent refusal to enter into bonds for his good behaviour.

Aylmer unsuccessfully recommended Cole for some promotion in 1591 or 1592, and, describing him as his 'coexile' and Burghley's 'countryman and faithful wellwisher' suggested on 1 June 1592 that he might succeed John Underhill as bishop of Oxford (BL, Lansdowne MS 72, fol. 103r). In the event the see remained vacant until 1604.

In 1598, when Whitgift wished to encourage John Reynolds, dean of Lincoln, to continue his writings against the Jesuits by returning him to the more congenial atmosphere of Oxford, Cole agreed to resign his presidency in exchange for the deanery. Whitgift successfully petitioned Sir Robert Cecil in September, describing Cole as 'an ancient Doctor of Divinity and an honest, learned and grave man' and the exchange as 'greatly for the benefit of the church, and for God's' (*Salisbury MSS*, 8, 332).

Elected on 28 October 1598 and installed as dean on 2 June 1599, Cole left no record in the chapter acts beyond his signature to receipts in a clear, well-formed hand. He made a brief nuncupative will on 31 August 1600, leaving a personal bequest to his daughter-in-law Elizabeth, wife of his eldest son, William, and the rest of his property to the disposal of his wife and executor, 'Joane'. He died before 14 September and was buried under the high altar of the cathedral. A monument, now destroyed, was erected in 1632 by his eldest daughter, Abigail, wife of Henry Stratford of Hawling, Gloucestershire. The epitaph was transcribed in full by Browne Willis.

It has been assumed that Thomas Cole, fellow of Corpus from 1576 and Cole's successor at Lower Heyford, must have been his son, but Thomas gave his birthplace as Stanley, Gloucestershire, and his age as twenty-six when ordained by Aylmer in 1578. Born, therefore, while Cole was still an Edwardian fellow of Corpus, he was probably a nephew.   BRETT USHER

Sources Foster, *Alum. Oxon.* • A. Wood, *The history and antiquities of the University of Oxford*, ed. J. Gutch, 2 vols. in 3 pts (1792–6) • *Fasti Angl., 1541–1857*, [Canterbury; Salisbury; Lincoln] • C. H. Garrett, *The Marian exiles: a study in the origins of Elizabethan puritanism* (1938) • C. Martin, *Les protestants anglais réfugiés à Genève au temps de Calvin, 1555–1560* (Geneva, 1915) • C. M. Dent, *Protestant reformers in Elizabethan Oxford* (1983) • P. Collinson, *Archbishop Grindal, 1519–1583: the struggle for a reformed church* (1979) • M. Byford, 'The price of protestantism: assessing the impact of religious change on Elizabethan Essex: the cases of Heydon and Colchester, 1558–1594', DPhil diss., U. Oxf., 1988 • H. Robinson, ed. and trans., *Original letters relative to the English Reformation*, 1 vol. in 2, Parker Society, [26] (1846–7) • H. Robinson, ed. and trans., *The Zurich letters, comprising the correspondence of several English bishops and others with some of the Helvetian reformers, during the early part of the reign of Queen Elizabeth*, 2 vols., Parker Society, 7–8 (1842–5) • L. Humphrey, *Joannis Juelli Angli, episcopi Sarisburiensis vita et mors* (1573) • will, PRO, PROB 11/97, fol. 238v • B. Willis, *A survey of the cathedrals of Lincoln, Ely, Oxford and Peterborough* (1730) • BL, Add. MS 6251, fol. 29r [letter bk of Simon Tripp] • Essex RO, Morant MS D/Y 2/5, 107 • *Calendar of the manuscripts of the most hon. the marquis of Salisbury*, 8, HMC, 9 (1899) • BL, Lansdowne MS 72, fol. 103r • J. S. Burn, *Livre des Anglois, à Genève* (1831)

Archives Archives of Zürich, Zurich letters | Essex RO, Colchester, Morant MSS

Wealth at death everything to wife: will, PRO, PROB 11/97, fol. 238v

Cole, Sir William (*bap.* 1576, *d.* 1653), army officer and landowner in Ulster, was baptized on 7 October 1576 at St Mary Woolnoth, London, the only son of Emmanuel Cole (*c.*1542–1592?), a member of the Goldsmiths' Company, of St Botolph, Aldersgate, and his first wife, Margaret Ingram (*d.* 1578), aunt of Sir Arthur Ingram. He was born into a London business family with derivation, as certified by heralds, from the gentry family of Cole of Slade in Devon. His early years and education are obscure and he did not attend either university or an inn of court.

Cole saw military service in the Netherlands before the turn of the century and then fought in Ireland during the Nine Years' War. Present at the siege of Kinsale in 1601 and having served as a lieutenant under Captain Richard Hansard for two years, Cole was selected to carry letters to Sir Robert Cecil and the privy council in England on 13 December, with a recommendation from Sir George Carew, president of Munster, for a command of his own. From October 1603 he was in Ulster as captain of boats and barges at Ballyshannon and on Lough Erne, but with peace and then a somewhat conciliatory policy towards Ulster he sought through former lord deputy Sir George Cary, in January 1607, a recommendation from principal secretary Salisbury for a foot company in the Low Countries. However on 15 May 1607 he secured royal instructions to lord deputy Chichester to confirm this office to him, and it was granted by patent, on a reduced stipend, on 10 September following. He became constable of Enniskillen, formerly Maguire's stronghold, in April 1609 and received substantial payments for building works on the fort and castle there (which may have included the watergate) over the next few years. When the plantation in Ulster was implemented from 1610 he was well positioned to acquire a servitor's estate nearby, and shortly thereafter he purchased another estate in the neighbourhood, Portora, which had been granted to a Scottish undertaker. He subsequently acquired some additional portions of land which had been granted to restored Irish owners.

Cole was the founder of the modern plantation town of Enniskillen, co. Fermanagh (which had over fifty new male inhabitants, English and Scottish, by 1630 and a new church), built on an island in Lough Erne and incorporated in 1613, and was granted the land designated to promote urbanization there in 1612. The town consisted of two zones or sectors, military and civil, and Cole received a grant of the fort zone in a cost cutting exercise in 1623, which integrated both under his ownership. He thus occupied a prominent position in the plantation in co. Fermanagh, and was on a number of occasions sheriff of the county and involved in the contentions of early plantation society there. Cole was knighted by lord deputy Sir Oliver St John in 1617. He married in Ireland Susanna, or Susan (*d.* in or before 1653?), widow of Stephen Seagar, lieutenant of Dublin Castle, and daughter of John Croft of Lancashire. Cole also maintained contact with relatives in London, one of them a lawyer of the Inner Temple and official of the court of wards. In 1633 he was briefly imprisoned for his refusal to pay contributions after the end of subsidies.

Sir William was a member of parliament for County Fermanagh both in 1634 and in 1640, and sat on various parliamentary committees, the most important that concerning the Commons' petition of remonstrance of 7 November 1640, and was on the committee sent to the king in England to present the grievances of the house. With the outbreak of the rising in 1641 (of which he had received some forewarning, passed on to the authorities in Dublin), Enniskillen was not captured, and Cole was one of those granted a commission by the king in November to raise troops to combat the rebellion. He received payments from the English parliament for the supply of his forces in 1642 and 1643. In December 1644 he was, however, accused before the committee of both kingdoms in London of partiality towards some of the Irish of co. Fermanagh, but responded that this had saved the lives of many protestants. He insisted too that he had been one of the first colonels of the British regiments in Ulster to take the oath of the solemn league and covenant, and he was in London for the trial of Connor, Lord Maguire, in February 1645. He sought substantial supplies from the committee of both houses for Irish affairs (after the battle of Benburb) in July 1646, and received a lesser amount in that and the following year. Cole's military actions during the 1640s are in some cases known: for example men of Enniskillen took part in the battle of Clones in June 1643. He also regained Crevenish Castle in co. Fermanagh after the cessation in September that year. In October 1645 Enniskilleners with others took part in a successful engagement in co. Sligo, but in November a detachment of Owen Roe O'Neill's army carried out an attack on his winter quarters on Boa Island in Lower Lough Erne, which, though this force was afterwards pursued by Cole's men, may have deterred him from taking part in a second intended intervention in Connaught. Eventually Enniskillen was seized from him by some of his own officers in March 1649 for the royalist cause, but it reverted to Commonwealth control in 1650.

Sir William was in London again, apparently, in 1651, but died in October 1653 in Dublin, where he had relations among its growing New English population; he was buried there in the same month in St Michan's Church. He may have been predeceased by his wife, who was not mentioned in his will. His eldest son, Michael, who predeceased him, having died during the confederate wars, had about 1640 married Katherine, daughter of Sir Laurence Parsons of King's county, while his second son, John, who acquired property in co. Dublin, married Elizabeth, daughter of John Chichester of Dungannon. His daughter Mary married the Revd Robert Barclay, the Scottish born dean of Clogher (Cole's agent in London in 1643), and his elder daughter, Margaret, married Sir James Montgomery, son of the Scottish settler Sir Hugh Montgomery. Cole's descendants became earls of Enniskillen and built the mansion house Florence Court in the eighteenth century, where what is taken to be a portrait of him hangs.

R. J. HUNTER

Sources *CSP Ire.*, 1601–3; 1633–47, esp. 1642–59 • PRO, AOI/289/1085; /290/1090 • *Calendar of the Irish patent rolls of James I* (before 1830) • *Calendar of the manuscripts of the most hon. the marquess of Salisbury*, 19, HMC, 9 (1965) • *The genealogie or pedigree of the right worshipfull and worthie captaine Sir William Cole* (privately printed, 1870) • *The information of Sir Frederick Hamilton … concerning Sir William Cole* (1645) • W. Cole, *The answere and vindication of Sir William Cole* (1645) • *A true and fuller relation from Ireland of the service performed by the men of Iniskillin, of Sir William Cole's regiment and troop at Lowtherstown, upon Thursday Novemb. 27, 1645* (1645?) • B. O'Ferrall and D. O'Connell, *Commentarius Rinuccinianus de sedis apostolicae legatione ad foederatos Hiberniae Catholicos per annos 1645–1649*, ed. J. Kavanagh, IMC, 1 (1932) • W. C. Trimble, *History of Enniskillen*, 1 (1919) • J. Edwin-Cole, *The genealogy of the family of Cole of the county of Devon* (1867) • B. McGrath, 'A biographical dictionary of the membership of the Irish House of Commons, 1640–1641', PhD diss., University of Dublin, 1997, 107–8 • J. M. S. Brooke and A. W. C. Hallen, eds., *The transcript of the registers of the united parishes of St Mary Woolnoth and St Mary Woolchurch Haw, in the city of London … 1538 to 1760* (1886), 16 • funeral entries, NL Ire., department of manuscripts, vol. 4, p. 7 • W. A. Shaw, *The knights of England*, 2 (1906), 166 • will, PRO, PROB 11/270, fols. 288v–291v • *DNB*

Archives PRO NIre., earl of Enniskillen MSS, D1702

Likenesses portrait (of Cole?), Florence Court, co. Fermanagh; repro. in Trimble, *History of Enniskillen*, facing p. 176

Cole, William (*c.*1622–1701), naturalist, was born in Dorset, from where his family moved to Salisbury about 1639 and thence to Southsea in 1644. Cole seems to have remained there until at least the mid-1660s; about 1668 he moved to Bristol where he obtained the post of surveyor of the customs (1671), which he retained until 1691. At Bristol, and at the small estate in Bradfield, Wiltshire, which he held in right of his wife, Anne James, he built up substantial collections of natural rarities, local and foreign, carried out experimental fieldwork, and corresponded with fellow natural philosophers. Sir Robert Southwell was an active and helpful patron, and he was also well known to Robert Hooke. He corresponded regularly with Robert Plot, John Ray, Martin Lister, John Woodward, and Edward Lhwyd.

Cole's early researches mainly centred on botany—particularly lichens and fungi. A letter of 30 September 1669 from him to Hooke (published in Hooke's *Lampas*, 1677) made important advances in explaining the reproduction of ferns. Thereafter Cole devoted many years to an (unsuccessful) attempt to find an experimental proof of the spontaneous generation of insects. He collected shells and fossils intensively, as well as investigating disparate subjects such as the crystalline structure of snowflakes, oysters, and the *Murex lapillus*. He published a detailed account of specimens of the last, gathered from near Minehead, to show that they belonged to the family that produced Tyrian purple in the Roman world.

Cole was a strong supporter of the natural history movement organized at Oxford by Robert Plot, and he presented many specimens to the new Ashmolean Museum there. From the early 1690s he engaged in protracted discussions with the university about donating to it his whole collection if the university would undertake publication of his *Generall Natural History*. Edward Lhwyd, Plot's successor at the Ashmolean, was eager to acquire Cole's collection because it consisted only of natural things, and because Cole had been careful to record the provenance of his specimens. These numbered well over a thousand with very few duplicates. Despite dragging on for some ten years the negotiations came to no conclusion. Cole died intestate in early October 1701, and the collection was sold elsewhere. He was buried on 12 October at Bradfield.

Although from his letters Cole emerges as a somewhat pompous, rather self-opinionated, person who could easily become tedious, he was also a very seriously committed naturalist who combined his passion for natural things with a deeply felt providentialist view of the world. His life exemplifies that interpenetration of natural theology with natural philosophy which his activities helped to establish.   A. J. TURNER

Sources correspondence with Robert and Edward Southwell, BL, Add. MSS 18598–18599 · correspondence with Robert Plot and Edward Lhwyd, Bodl. Oxf., MSS Ashmole 1814, 1817a, 1820a, 1829, 1830 · RS, early letters, C · RS, MS B.L.VII, nos. xlvi–xlvii · RS, CP VII, 60 · RS, CP IX, 43 · W. A. Shaw, ed., *Calendar of treasury books*, 3, PRO (1908) · V. A. Eyles, 'Scientific activity in the Bristol region in the past', *Bristol and its adjoining counties*, ed. C. M. MacInnes and W. F. Whittard (1955), 123–43 · A. J. Turner, '*Purpura anglicana*: a bibliographical note', *Journal of the Society of the Bibliography of Natural History*, 5 (1968–71), 361 · R. T. Gunther, *Early science in Oxford*, 4: *The Philosophical Society* (1925) · R. T. Gunther, *Early science in Oxford*, 12: *Dr Plot and the correspondence of the Philosophical Society of Oxford* (1939) · *Further correspondence of John Ray*, ed. R. W. T. Gunther, Ray Society, 114 (1928) · parish register (burial), Hullavington parish, Bradfield church, 12 Oct 1701 · A. J. Turner, 'A forgotten naturalist of the seventeenth century: William Cole of Bristol and his collections', *Archives of Natural History*, 11 (1982–4), 27–41

Archives AM Oxf. · Bodl. Oxf. · RS · Wellcome L., notebook | BL, corresp. with Robert Southwell and Edward Southwell, Add. MSS 18598–18599

Cole, William. *See* Coles, William (1626–1662).

Cole, William (*fl.* 1659), jurist, whose origins are unknown, was one of the most significant voices calling for legal, economic, and political reform at the end of the Cromwellian period. Cole stood with those who denounced the protectorate as a tyranny, and he demanded a restoration of the Commonwealth purged of all who had served Cromwell's regime. His vision of reform embraced a radical simplification and codification of the legal system and the removal of restraints on commerce. In his view justice, economic freedom, and political liberty were inseparably entwined, and their achievement depended on removing the entrenched élites who impeded equity and trade.

Cole's principal work was a 20-page pamphlet, *A Rod for the Lawyers*, which George Thomason catalogued on 12 July 1659. Its tone is summed up in the charge that:

> The major part of the laws made in this nation are founded on principles of tyranny, fallacy and oppression for the benefit of those that made them. The law in the generality is unjust and irrational, the execution desperately dangerous and chargeable; it is easier to find a thousand evils in it than one true principle in matter and form.   (Cole, *Rod*, 5)

To account for this condition Cole employed the theory of the Norman yoke made popular by John Lilburne and employed by other law reformers such as James Frese and John Warr, according to which the liberties of the free and equal citizens of Anglo-Saxon England had been extinguished by the Norman conquest and a regime of oppression imposed that had endured ever since.

As with the Levellers, Cole's politics were strongly populist, and he shared their perception that crime was fostered by social inequity. If thieves were to be hanged, he said, the 'great ones'—those who preyed on the poor—should be first on the scaffold. (Cole's point was rhetorical; with Hugh Peter, Peter Chamberlen, Samuel Chidley, and William Tomlinson, he categorically opposed the death penalty for theft.) The 'Poor Commons', he contended, had more to fear from those that had taken their liberties away than from cutpurses and highwaymen.

Cole laid out a sweeping programme of reform, though he was equivocal about how it was to be effected. Legal precedents were useless because founded on unjust laws and tainted by bribery. Parliament, dominated as it was by the 'insatiable cannibals' of the legal profession, was incapable of promoting change. Yet Cole did suggest that a parliament—presumably one suitably purged—might become a fit instrument, replacing the existing system of central courts and appointing in their stead 'a certain number of knowing men, the most conscientious they can think of, in several cities and counties' (Cole, *Rod*, 12) to clear all arrears of cases. After completing this task these overseers would yield authority to local judicial bodies whose officers would rotate annually. Trade based courts could also be established to resolve disputes in particular lines of occupation, such as cloth making. Cole further proposed that a land registry be established to enrol property titles, thus minimizing litigation. Without lawyers to plead specious causes or delay justice by 'lying sophistry and quibbles', litigants would speak for themselves or, if necessary, be represented by friends. The result would be speedy, efficient, and popular justice, and the elimination of frivolous suits. In another tract published in 1659, *Severall Proposals Modestly Tendered*, Cole called for the laws to be codified in a single-volume digest and presented in language accessible to the laity.

Cole's proposals for economic reform followed a similar pattern. He was hostile to monopolies and to the great trading companies that had so conspicuously profited under Cromwell, and called for the abolition of the custom and excise farm. Cole echoed and in many ways summarized a generation of popular reformers who sought to streamline, systematize, and democratize the law, and to remove restraints on enterprise and commerce. His work has affinities with the circle around Samuel Hartlib and the Baconian tradition from which it derived, while at the same time it shares the Levellers' rejection of received tradition and their staunch antipathy toward élites. It was a striking contribution in what stands as perhaps the most active year of political and social debate in English history. No other details of his life are known.

ROBERT ZALLER

Sources B. W. Painter, 'Cole, William', Greaves & Zaller, *BDBR*, 1.159–60 · M. James, *Social problems and policy during the puritan revolution, 1640–1660* (1930) · G. B. Nourse, 'Law reform under the protectorate and Commonwealth', *Law Quarterly Review*, 75 (1959), 512–29 · S. E. Prall, *The agitation for law reform during the puritan revolution, 1640–1660* (1966) · D. Veall, *The popular movement for law reform* (1970) · R. Zaller, 'The debate on capital punishment during the English revolution', *American Journal of Legal History*, 31 (1987), 126–44

Cole, William (1635–1716), physician, was the son of a Church of England clergyman. He matriculated at Balliol College, Oxford, on 9 December 1653, and by the late 1650s had become involved with the circle of researchers around Robert Boyle. Cole remained at Oxford until 1666, graduating BM from Gloucester Hall on 7 August 1660 and DM on 9 July 1666. While still at Oxford, about 1660, he married Jane (1638/9–1724), whose maiden name is not known; their eldest surviving daughter, also named Jane, was born about 1662. A son, William, was born in 1667 or 1668; he matriculated at Oriel College, Oxford, on 12 March 1686, aged eighteen, but nothing more is known about him. A second surviving daughter, Ann, was born about 1670.

Upon graduation Cole moved to Worcester, where he practised as a physician. There he composed his first medical work, *De secretione animali cogitata*, published in Oxford in 1674. Secretion was a favourite topic among mechanically inclined physicians, and Cole's work reflected his training with Boyle and Thomas Willis. In his book he employed Willis's concepts of chemical fermentation and took for granted Boyle's notions of the weight and 'spring' of the air. He also cited the work of Richard Lower, another Oxford mechanical philosopher.

Cole corresponded with Thomas Sydenham around 1680, agreeing with Sydenham's cooling regimen for smallpox. Cole did not know Sydenham personally, but both physicians were friends of John Locke. Cole's additional letter to Sydenham about hysteria elicited the latter's important essay on hypochondria and hysteria, the *Dissertatio epistolaris ad spectatissimum doctissimumq[ue] virum Gulielmum Cole, M.D.* (1682). After a brief discussion of smallpox Sydenham offered an interpretation of hypochondria in men and hysteria in women which defined them as essentially equivalent disorders.

In 1685 Cole published a few descriptions of clinical cases in the *Philosophical Transactions of the Royal Society*, but he was never made a fellow. His next major work (and his only medical work in English) was his *Physico-Medical Essay Concerning the Late Frequency of Apoplexies*, published in 1689, in which he attributed the apparent increase in apoplexy to the severely cold winter of 1683, explaining the effects of cold on this disorder. Cole also produced a work on natural history: *Purpura Anglicana, being a Discovery of a Shell-Fish Found on the Shores of the Severn* (1684).

Cole moved to London in the early 1690s. He was admitted a candidate of the Royal College of Physicians on 26 June 1693 and a fellow on 25 June 1694. In 1693 he was fined £4 by the college (later remitted) for reading an anatomy lecture at Surgeons' Hall without leave. He published three works between 1693 and 1702, comprising a mechanistic explanation of the digestion, a treatise on fevers (in which he advocated the use of cinchona bark), and a description of a case of epilepsy. The latter, addressed to Dr Thomas Hobart of Cambridge, also included a discussion of insensible perspiration.

Cole was one of a number of physicians who embraced the mechanical philosophy in the 1650s and 1660s, and his published works are in the iatromechanical vein of other authors in the group around Boyle and Willis. His works enjoyed a certain amount of popularity, and his book on secretion was reprinted several times, including an Amsterdam edition in 1698. Cole was apparently a well-liked and successful practitioner, described as 'learned without ostentation, and polite without affectation' (Munk, *Roll*, 1.510).

Cole was named an elect of the Royal College of Physicians on 9 October 1712, but some time after that he appears to have retired to the country. He died on 12 June 1716, aged eighty-one, and was buried at the church of Allesley, near Coventry. His grave in the church includes a memorial inscription. His widow, who died in 1724 aged eighty-five, is buried beside him, as are two daughters.

ANITA GUERRINI

Sources DNB · Munk, *Roll* · R. G. Frank, *Harvey and the Oxford physiologists* (1980) · K. Dewhurst, ed., *Dr Thomas Sydenham (1624–1689)* (1966)
Likenesses R. White, line engraving, 1689, BM, NPG, Wellcome L.; repro. in W. Cole, *Physico-medical essay concerning the late frequency of apoplexies* (1689)

Cole, William (1714–1782), antiquary, was born at the King's Arms, Bourn Bridge, in the parish of Little Abington, Cambridgeshire, on 3 August 1714 and baptized on 15 August 1714, the only son of William Cole (1671/2–1735), a prosperous gentleman farmer, and his third wife, Catherine (1682/3–1725), widow of Charles Apthorp and daughter of Theophilus Tuer of Cambridge. His father married four times: besides two daughters by his first marriage, he had by his third marriage four children, of whom William was the eldest and only boy.

William Cole (1714–1782), by Thomas Kerrich

Education and early life Cole was sent to live with his maternal grandmother in Cambridge at a very early age and began his schooling at a dame-school there before attending a school at Linton kept by a nonconformist minister. Sundays were passed with a relative who belonged to the Church of England so that he was spared from attending dissenting services. After a short time with the Revd Robert Butts of Saffron Walden grammar school, he was entered at Eton College in 1726 and stayed there for six years; by his own account he was idle and unhappy, was often beaten, and once ran away, yet he formed a lifelong friendship with Horace Walpole. He was admitted as a sizar at Clare College, Cambridge, on 25 January 1733, but after inheriting a comfortable income and property on his father's death he became a fellow commoner. He developed a close attachment to Thomas Western of the same college and when Western left and married, Cole migrated to King's College, the natural home of old Etonians in the university, in June 1736. He took the degrees of BA in 1737 and MA in 1740.

Cole learned French at Cambridge from a Monsieur Herebert; in April 1736 he accompanied his elder half-brother Stephen Apthorp on a tour of Flanders, and in the following year while suffering from a bout of low spirits he travelled on his doctor's advice to Lisbon where he remained for six months, returning in May 1738. He made other visits to Normandy and again to Flanders, and in

1749 undertook a long tour to Scotland with friends and was made a freeman of the city of Glasgow. Thanks to his distant relative Lord Montfort of Horseheath he was made a deputy lieutenant of the county and justice of the peace. He kept rooms at King's until 1753 without holding a fellowship and had also a small country retreat at Haddenham in the Isle of Ely. His time during all these years was devoted to collecting historical information, especially concerning Cambridgeshire; he visited parish churches and libraries, transcribed inscriptions and registers, copied heraldic arms, and made abstracts from voluminous reading in both printed books and manuscripts. This vocation never deserted him. He was elected a fellow of the Society of Antiquaries in November 1747.

The church and a scholarly retreat On 25 December 1744 Cole was ordained deacon and acted for a short while as curate to Abraham Stokes, rector of Withersfield in Suffolk. He was admitted to priest's orders in April 1745 and was made chaplain to George, earl of Kinnoul, through the kindness of his son who was MP and recorder of Cambridge. He was collated to the rectory of Hornsey in Middlesex by Bishop Thomas Sherlock in 1749 and inducted on 25 November of that year. Cole was not comfortable with the living and when he found that he was expected to reside and to pay towards work on the rectory, he at once tried to resign, although he was not able to do so until 1751. He resided little if at all and employed a curate. At about this time he had the idea of living among the English Benedictines at Paris, without converting to Catholicism, since his only ambition was 'to live retiredly and quietly, and pretty much to myself, after the monkish manner' (Cole, *Journal*, 142). The plan came to nothing when after strange negotiations in 1753 Cole was presented to the rectory of Bletchley in Buckinghamshire by Browne Willis, the eccentric antiquary. He remained there for fourteen years.

Cole did make another trip to France to meet Walpole in Paris from October to December 1765 and began to keep a full and characteristic diary that he continued until August 1770. He again wished to retire abroad, despite Walpole's warning that if he did so his goods, including his collections, might be seized for the crown if he died in France. Such a prospect was daunting. His volumes were, he wrote to Walpole (17 March 1765):

> my only delight—they are my wife and children—they have been in short, my whole employ and amusement for these twenty or thirty years; and though I really and sincerely think the greatest part of them stuff and trash, and deserve no other treatment than the fire, yet the collections which I have made towards an 'History of Cambridgeshire', the chief points in view of them, with an oblique or transient view of an 'Athenae Cantabrigienses', will be of singular use to any one who will have more patience and perseverance than I am master of to put the materials together. (Walpole, *Corr.*, 1.92)

The trip to Paris did not tempt Cole to move; too many aspects of French life from the habits of the people to what he considered irreligious thinking offended him. He had, however, many close Catholic friends such as Alban Butler and time after time in his writings he insisted robustly that the Church of England had more to fear from its own temporizing and the influence of dissent, to which he had a rooted aversion, than from Roman Catholicism, to which he was as strongly attracted. He believed he had little of a priestly calling, and yet performed his duties conscientiously according to his lights and the standards of the times, was hospitable and charitable, and did not forget the dignity of his office and the respect due to it. Although a high tory by principle he took little part in politics lest they should estrange him from his friends, claiming that 'I have all my life lived and acted with the Whigs, who were my friends, though perhaps might not always wish them success' (Walpole, *Corr.*, 2.86). His inherited means allowed a measure of independence and aloofness from preferment-hunting, though he sometimes worried about his income and was not rich when he died.

Cole did not approve of a married clergy and his relations with women were those of a confirmed bachelor, sociable enough and occasionally mildly flirtatious within safe limits, for although he could appraise a good-looking woman, there is no trace of his desiring a close or physical intimacy with any. His deep friendships were with men, and his domestic comfort and routine were attended to by several servants of whom the chief was Tom Wood, the general factotum of the household, who entered his service as a boy about 1760 and remained with his master until he died. Cole's affection for and care of him are plain in his diary. Tom was kept busy and was occasionally scolded, but his health and education were not neglected. He was one of Cole's executors and was remembered in his will.

Cole resigned the living at Bletchley as a point of honour in 1767 in favour of Willis's grandson, and after weighing several alternatives accepted the curacy of Waterbeach and a meagre income of £20 a year from his friend and fellow antiquary Robert Masters. Both had strong characters and were soon at loggerheads so that, using the excuse of the wetness of the place, Cole moved in 1770 to Milton 3 miles from Cambridge where he remained until his death, declining other offers of a church living until he was presented by Eton College to the vicarage of Burnham in Buckinghamshire. He was instituted there on 10 June 1774 but continued to live at Milton.

Antiquarian studies Cole's return to Cambridgeshire in 1767 and his hasty resignation from the curacy at Waterbeach allowed him to resume his studies with increased zeal. He possessed over fifty large volumes of his collections when he settled at Milton and compiled as many more before the end of his life. He continued to add to his own stores and to annotate and cross-reference what he had written earlier, and make the contents of his books accessible through a series of indexes. Besides armorial bearings his collections contain many sketches of churches and other buildings, crudely but faithfully drawn. He was entrusted with unique manuscripts to study at home, as, for example, Thomas Baker's history of St John's College which he transcribed and annotated in only six weeks during 1777. His correspondence was vast and, since he

kept copies of letters sent and received, his importance in supplying information and corrections for works published or in progress is evident and considerable. There was little that did not interest him, but Roman Britain did not. Except when prevented by illness he also regularly met resident Cambridge scholars such as Richard Farmer, master of Emmanuel College, and James Essex, the preferred architect of Georgian Cambridge. He was at the centre of a web of scholarly communication and in his own line was one of the most learned men of the eighteenth century and the most industrious historian that Cambridgeshire had before William Mortlock Palmer in the twentieth century. There can have been few days when he did not put pen to paper and his speed, accuracy, and legibility are remarkable. Among those with whom he corresponded and exchanged intelligence and favours were Horace Walpole, Thomas Gray, Michael Lort, Richard Gough, Thomas Pennant, Thomas Phillips, James Granger, and John Nichols. He was a member of the Benedictines, a group of antiquaries connected with Corpus Christi College, which included James Nasmith and Robert Masters.

A disinclination to publish was one of Cole's marked idiosyncrasies. He defended it on the ground that in future others would benefit 'who have not had the drudgery to collect, but have all ready to their hands' (Cooper, *Ath. Cantab.*, 1.vi). His materials have been routinely consulted and used (not always with acknowledgement) by historians, and they remain of value especially as a witness to lost records and buildings and as a repository of genealogical facts. He revised Browne Willis's manuscript history of two Buckinghamshire hundreds, as their author had asked, but seems to have made no attempt to print it, and shortly before his own death intended to give it to John Nichols. He wrote three short pieces in volume 47 of the *Gentleman's Magazine* (1777)—on corrections to Hawkins's *History of Music*, 'Origin of "Old Nick"', and 'Saint whose emblems are naked boys in a tub'—and 'Some observations on the horns given by Henry I to the cathedral of Carlisle' (*Archaeologia*, 5, 1779, 340–45). Cole often aided others in their researches. His earliest contribution appears to have been notes for Zachary Grey's edition of *Hudibras* in the 1740s; he gave A. C. Ducarel suggestions for his *Tour through Normandy* (1754) and a large amount of material for his unpublished 'Account of Doctors' Commons'. The principal authors whom he helped were James Bentham, for his *History of Ely Cathedral* (1771), James Granger, for his *Biographical History of England* (1775), Richard Gough, for his *British Topography* (1780) and other works, and John Nichols, for many of his works. He supplied an account of the school of Pythagoras at Cambridge to Francis Grose for his *Antiquities of England and Wales* and materials for several of Walpole's books, especially the second edition of his *Anecdotes of Paintings in England*. A list of works to which Cole contributed may be found in the Yale edition of his letters to Walpole (Walpole, *Corr.*, 2.376–7), to which should be added his notes on Wood's *Athenae Oxonienses* which were used by Philip Bliss for his edition of 1813.

While free in sharing his knowledge Cole was anxious

that few should examine his manuscripts; an exception was Walpole, to whom he lent the four volumes of his 'History of King's College' in 1777 with a warning that 'through life, I have never disguised artfully my opinions, and as my books were my trusty friends who had engaged never to speak till twenty years after my departure, I always without guile entrusted them with my most secret thoughts' (Walpole, *Corr.*, 2.42). He was troubled to know where to leave his manuscripts and changed his mind more than once. To give them to King's College would be like throwing them in a horse-pond since its members had only contempt for non-classical studies. In the end, in his will written four days before his death, he bequeathed them all to the British Museum with the stipulation that they were not to be looked into for twenty years after his death. His loose papers and letters were also to be gathered up, for:

> such papers are valuable when time has impressed his fingers on them. It is also my wish that no persons except my executors may be admitted into my study until all the letters and loose papers are sorted and locked up with my manuscripts. (Palmer, *William Cole*, 29)

Cole's manuscripts form a discontinuous series of 115 large volumes among the additional manuscripts of the British Library. An official catalogue was printed in 1849, and an alphabetical index of their contents, with curious juxtapositions, was published in 1912 by G. J. Gray. Volume 17, thought to contain a history of Queens' College, Cambridge, is missing, and there are other strays, such as a history of the parish of Fen Ditton now in Cambridge University Library, and a ten-page index to the life compiled by Gray in a fit of the gout on 16 May 1775 is now at Yale. Three catalogues of his library exist. He parted with about six hundred printed books, mostly classics and divinity, to a London bookseller, Benjamin White, when he left Bletchley in 1767; the remainder were dispersed by White after Cole's death intermixed with those of another collector, Charles Hedges. The sale catalogue of their combined libraries and other materials, dated February 1784, records almost 9000 volumes. Some of Cole's books were annotated by him and survive in the British Library and elsewhere. His prints, of which there were more than three thousand, were also dispersed together with the collection of stained glass which he built up to be one of the largest in private hands.

Death and reputation From 1769 Cole was increasingly a martyr to gout and other ailments, badly overweight for his medium height, and lame. At the end of 1782 he became seriously ill and died on 16 December in Milton. He was buried on 22 December in St Clement's Church in Cambridge, his grandmother's place of worship, and left money towards the building of the spire. When it was done almost forty years later the words 'Deum Cole' were displayed on it; they were wrongly said to have been his motto.

Cole's reputation has undergone several changes. Among many of his contemporaries he was well regarded for his learning, though they were alive to his singularities and prejudices which he took no trouble to disguise.

'With all his oddities', Michael Lort wrote just after his death, 'he was a worthy and valuable man' (Walpole, *Corr.*, 16.201). The terms of his will naturally caused alarm and defensiveness. Robert Masters, who did not live to see the manuscripts opened, supposed that the blending of personal scandal with his other collections would probably cause his work to sink into oblivion. Egerton Brydges, who printed extracts from Cole in his *Restituta*, described him as a known 'gossip' many of whose biographical notes 'consist of scarcely any thing but tattle' (Brydges, 4.242). Access to his original manuscripts after 1802 and the publication of parts of his correspondence, especially by John Nichols in *Literary Anecdotes* and *Illustrations*, revealed Cole's foibles and inconsistencies plainly and made him at once a figure of fun and morally reprehensible by the severer standards and increasing delicacies of the nineteenth century. Isaac D'Israeli patronized him; J. J. Smith observed that 'his style is rude and free to licentiousness' (Smith, 1.153); to C. H. Cooper he had the industry of Anthony Wood 'without his common sense' and his prejudices 'are simply ridiculous' (Cooper, *Ath. Cantab.*, 1.vi). A later generation observed more favourably how 'he took a lively interest in all that was passing around him' and left 'an invaluable storehouse of information' (Willis and Clark, 1.xcvi). The publication of two volumes of his diaries in 1931, edited by F. G. Stokes and with introductions by Helen Waddell, brought Cole before a much wider public who found their vivid and immediate manner attractive. They exemplify and justify Cole's own view that 'anecdotes of men of learning and character, notices of customs and manners, are not only amusing, but instructive of the usages of early ages, and of our country and ancestors' (Brydges, 3.39). W. M. Palmer's *William Cole of Milton* (1935), which includes an edition of Cole's parochial notes and church drawings for Cambridgeshire, and two elaborate volumes of Walpole's correspondence with Cole issued by the University of Yale in 1937 were well received, and Virginia Woolf took Cole and Walpole as the subject of an essay which has been reprinted several times. Cole became not simply of interest to academic scholarship and historiography: because of his individual qualities and distinctive expression he is numbered among the more entertaining and informative English letter writers and diarists. Indeed in a series of pastiche letters in *Notes and Queries* between 1946 and 1948 he was reborn as a fictional character.

JOHN D. PICKLES

Sources W. M. Palmer, *William Cole of Milton* (1935) · BL, Cole MSS · Walpole, *Corr.*, vols. 1–2 · Nichols, *Lit. anecdotes*, 7.87–9 · *The Bletchley diary of the Rev. William Cole, 1765–67*, ed. F. G. Stokes (1931) · *A journal of my journey to Paris in the year 1765, by the Rev. William Cole*, ed. F. G. Stokes (1931) · R. Willis, *The architectural history of the University of Cambridge, and of the colleges of Cambridge and Eton*, ed. J. W. Clark, 4 vols. (1886) · E. Brydges, *Restituta, or, Titles, extracts, and characters of old books in English literature*, 4 vols. (1814–16) · T. Baker, *History of the college of St John the Evangelist, Cambridge*, ed. J. E. B. Mayor, 2 vols. (1869) · J. G. Jenkins, *The dragon of Whaddon* (1953) · F. Madden, *Index to the additional manuscripts … 1783–1835* (1849) · G. J. Gray, *Index to the contents of the Cole manuscripts* (1912) · *Correspondence of Thomas Gray*, ed. P. Toynbee and L. Whibley, 3 (1935), 1324 · W. M. Palmer, *Monumental inscriptions and coats of arms from Cambridgeshire* (1932) · Cooper, *Ath. Cantab.*, 1.v–vi · J. J. Smith,

Cambridge portfolio, 1 (1840), 153 • Nichols, *Illustrations*, vol. 8 • V. Woolf, 'Two antiquaries: Walpole and Cole', *Yale Review*, 28 (1939), 530–39 • 'Letters and notes from the Cole manuscripts', *Records of Buckinghamshire*, 9 (1904–9), 60–70, esp. 67–70 • J. E. M., 'The Rev. William Cole revisits Strawberry Hill', *N&Q*, 190 (1946), 255–6 • J. E. M., 'Mr Cole repeats a visit, and rebuts an accusation', *N&Q*, 192 (1947), 98–9 • J. E. M., 'Mr Cole celebrates a bicentenary', *N&Q*, 192 (1947), 321–2 • J. E. M., 'The Rev. William Cole is baffled by a quotation', *N&Q*, 193 (1948), 552 • *DNB* • memorial inscription, January 1735, Babraham, Cambridgeshire [William Cole]

Archives BL, corresp. and papers, Add. MS 33498 • BL, notes relating to Cambridgeshire parishes and corresp., Add. MSS 5798–5887, 5952–5962, 5992–5994, 6034–6035, 6057, 6151, 6396–6402 • BL, printed works with MS notes and additions • CUL, Cambridgeshire and Ely collections, incl. biographies of bishops of Ely; letters and papers • Suffolk RO, Ipswich, copy of Thomas Gardner's *Account of Dulwich, Blithburgh, etc.*, with MS additions | BL, corresp. with Horace Walpole. Add. MSS 5952–5953, 5824–5874 • V&A NAL, letters to Horace Walpole

Likenesses line engraving, 1768 (after M. Tyson), BM, NPG; repro. in Nichols, *Lit. anecdotes*, 1 (1812) • J. Gooch, watercolour, 1771, BM • J. and G. Facius, stipple, 1809 (after chalk drawing by T. Kerrich), repro. in Walpole, *Corr.*, vol. 2, facing p. 83 • T. Kerrich, chalk drawing, BM [*see illus.*]

Wealth at death see will, Palmer, *William Cole*, 26–30

Cole, William (1753–1806), Church of England clergyman, was born at Mersham, Kent, on 8 December 1753. The names of his parents are not recorded, but his education was much assisted by a friend of his mother's, John *Chapman (*bap.* 1705, *d.* 1784), archdeacon of Sudbury and rector of Mersham. Cole's obituary in the *Gentleman's Magazine* may suggest that he was Chapman's son. He was sent to Ashford School, then to a private school at Bierton, near Aylesbury, Buckinghamshire. He was admitted as a king's scholar at Eton College in 1766, and he was there a favourite of the headmaster, Dr John Foster. On 11 August 1773 he was made scholar of King's College, Cambridge, where he was a fellow from 1776 to 1781. He graduated BA in 1778 and proceeded MA in 1781.

In 1777 Cole returned to Eton as an assistant master but was dogged by ill health, having ruptured a blood vessel in his lungs as an undergraduate. On 14 March 1779 he was ordained priest by Edmund Keene, bishop of Ely. He resigned from Eton for health reasons in 1780 and became tutor to George Spencer, marquess of Blandford, and Lord Henry Spencer, the sons of George Spencer, fourth duke of Marlborough, to whom he became chaplain. He dedicated his 'Oratio de ridiculo' to the duke—the work won the first of Sir William Browne's medals at Cambridge University. This was printed along with some Latin verse in 1780. Cole later published several sermons, and wrote the Latin preface to *Gemmarum antiquarum delectus*, an account of Marlborough's collection of antiquities published in two volumes in 1780 and 1791. In 1781 he was inducted to the rectory of Waddesdon (first portion), Buckinghamshire, on the presentation of the duke of Marlborough, but resigned it in 1788 when collated to the rectory of his birthplace, Mersham, by John Moore, archbishop of Canterbury. He held the rectory until his death. In 1792 he was appointed prebendary of Westminster and in 1795 received the degree of DD by the archbishop's diploma

during the visitation of the diocese of Canterbury. In 1795 he married Mary, second daughter of the legal authority Sir William *Blackstone; they had no children. In 1796 he was presented to the vicarage of Shoreham, Kent, by the dean and chapter of Westminster. Following several years of ill health, Cole died on 25 September 1806, and was buried in the north aisle of Westminster Abbey on 4 October.

RONALD BAYNE, rev. ANDREW ROBINSON

Sources *GM*, 1st ser., 76 (1806), 1072 • G. Lipscomb, *The history and antiquities of the county of Buckingham*, 4 vols. (1831–47), vol. 1, p. 497 • E. Hasted, *The history and topographical survey of the county of Kent*, 2nd edn, 12 vols. (1797–1801), vol. 3, p.13; vol. 7, p. 602 • R. A. Austen-Leigh, ed., *The Eton College register, 1753–1790* (1921)

Cole, William (*bap.* 1757, *d.* 1812), Church of England clergyman and writer, was baptized at Attleborough, Norfolk, on 17 March 1757, the eldest son of the Revd Denny Cole (*d.* 1790) of Sudbury, and afterwards of Wickham Market, Suffolk, and his wife, Anne. He was educated at Eton College and went up to King's College, Cambridge, in 1775; he graduated BA in 1780, and proceeded MA in 1783. He was elected to a fellowship of King's, which he held until 1788. Cole was ordained deacon on 6 June 1784, and priest on 12 March 1786. He was subsequently instituted to the vicarage of Broad Chalke in Wiltshire, on the presentation of his college, which he held from 1788 to 1812. For several years he resided at Yoxford, Suffolk, and had the curacy of Theberton in that neighbourhood. Cole subsequently moved to London, where he officiated at a chapel near his residence in Baker Street, Portman Square, where he died in December 1812.

Cole wrote a number of literary works. *A Key to the Psalms* (1788) provided an easy introduction to the language and allusions of the Psalms. A poem entitled 'To the Feeling Heart: Exalted Affection, or, Sophia Pringle' appeared in 1789. His novel *The Contradiction* was published in 1796.

THOMPSON COOPER, rev. ROBERT BROWN

Sources Venn, *Alum. Cant.* • *GM*, 1st ser., 82/2 (1812), 675 • R. A. Austen-Leigh, ed., *The Eton College register, 1753–1790* (1921)

Colebrook, Leonard (1883–1967), bacteriologist, was born in Guildford, Surrey, on 2 March 1883, the fifth child and third son of six children born to May Colebrook, a prosperous farmer and nonconformist preacher, and his second wife, Mary Gower. He was educated from 1891 to 1896 at Guildford grammar school, from 1896 to 1899 at Westbourne high school, Bournemouth, and from then for one year at Christ's College, Blackheath, London. In 1900 he began premedical studies at the London Hospital Medical College, from which he won an entrance scholarship at St Mary's Hospital, London, where he graduated MB, BS in 1906.

Colebrook's decision to go into medicine was apparently prompted by the nonconformist social conscience of the Colebrook family. Indeed, he first intended to become a medical missionary. But he was much impressed by the lectures in pathology and bacteriology of Sir Almroth E. Wright, and one year after graduation he accepted an appointment as assistant in the inoculation department of St Mary's Hospital medical school. There he worked partly on the vaccine therapy pursued by Wright; however, his second publication, in 1911, with Alexander Fleming, was on the treatment of syphilis with Paul Erlich's arsenical, salvarsan. On the outbreak of war in 1914 Colebrook became a captain in the Royal Army Medical Corps and worked on wound infections, first at St Mary's Hospital and later in Almroth Wright's laboratory at no. 13 general hospital in Boulogne.

Also in 1914 Colebrook married Dorothy Scarlett, daughter of John Scarlett Campbell, of the Indian Civil Service and judge of the high court at Lahore. She died in 1941, and in 1946 he married Vera Scovell, daughter of Thomas James Locke, a civil servant. She was a war widow working as a freelance broadcaster. There were no children of either marriage.

In 1919 Colebrook was appointed a member of the scientific staff of the Medical Research Council and worked on dental caries, but early in 1922 he was seconded to work again with Wright at St Mary's. It was under Wright that he developed his skill as a bacteriologist. Despite the contrast in their personalities and beliefs, the two men became close friends and Colebrook's loyalty and admiration for his old teacher lasted throughout his life. He published a biography of Wright in 1954.

In the mid 1920s Colebrook began the study of puerperal fever for which he is probably best known. Vera Colebrook has written that he was set on this course by the death of the wife of a close friend from a streptococcal infection in childbirth and by the suffering which followed. Wright's vaccine therapy was ineffective against these dangerous infections, which at that time contributed to many cases of maternal mortality, and treatment with arsenicals was of relatively little value. When, in 1930, Colebrook became honorary director of the research laboratories of Queen Charlotte's Maternity Hospital, he undertook a thorough investigation of the origins of infection in the labour wards and became a vigorous proponent of an aseptic regimen by which it might be reduced. In 1935 his attention was drawn to a German paper by Gerhard Domagk, reporting that a red dye, prontosil, could cure infection with virulent haemolytic streptococci. By the following year Colebrook and his colleagues had confirmed these findings and shown that the drug was effective in a number of cases of puerperal fever. With the subsequent use of sulphanilamide, the active fragment of prontosil which was produced from it *in vivo*, and then of other sulphonamides, the death rate in the isolation block of the hospital fell from 30 to 4 per cent. The life-saving power of the sulphonamides in human medicine was thus established.

In 1939 Colebrook went to France as a colonel in the Royal Army Medical Corps and bacteriological consultant to the British expeditionary force. There he became aware of the distressing prevalence of infected burns in mechanized warfare. After his return to England in 1940 he began work on the infection and treatment of burns, and

showed that infection could be controlled by sulphonamides and, in a later study, by penicillin. He renewed a much earlier interest in skin-grafting and consulted Peter Medawar in Oxford, to whom he introduced the problems of tissue rejection. From 1942 to 1948 he was director of the Burns Investigation Unit of the Medical Research Council, and was first based at Glasgow Royal Infirmary, and then at the Birmingham Accident Hospital. He developed ideas on the airborne transfer of infection and on procedures for asepsis during dressing, and from the start fought doggedly for changes in handling the problems of sepsis and for other causes in which he believed. Many of his patients with burns were young children. For more than ten years after 1946, with the support of his wife Vera, he was a persistent propagandist of measures to prevent burns to both children and old people in the home. His unit had acquired an outstanding reputation when he retired in 1948.

Colebrook was elected an honorary fellow of the Royal College of Obstetricians and Gynaecologists in 1944 and a fellow of the Royal Society in 1945. He received an honorary degree of DSc from the University of Birmingham in 1950 and became an honorary fellow of the Royal College of Surgeons of England in the same year. A variety of other honours came to him, including the Blair Bell medal of the Royal Society of Medicine (1954) and the Jenner medal (1962). Nevertheless, he was a man of true modesty. He insisted that he deserved no special recognition and that what had been achieved had come from the work of a team of people, and he made special mention of the contributions of his younger sister, Dora, herself a bacteriologist, and of Ronald Hare.

Colebrook, known as Coli to his friends and colleagues, was impelled by compassion for the sick. During his working life there were major discoveries in chemotherapy and he dedicated himself to their application in the treatment of life-threatening bacterial infections for which no effective remedy previously had been known. In the last phase of his life he was a supporter of the Euthanasia Society. He felt that there were situations in which people had the right to end their own lives, and also that the first duty of a doctor was to relieve suffering, even if life were thereby curtailed.

Colebrook was a small slim man, whose outdoor recreations included skiing and gardening. He could sometimes give the impression of severity, but the enduring memories of his friends were of his transparent honesty, his sense of humour, his humanity, and his generosity. He was not outstanding as a scientist or an originator, and certainly never thought of himself in this light, but he was a man who unremittingly used his energy and ability to confer great medical benefits on those of his generation. He died at Farnham Common, Buckinghamshire, on 29 September 1967, survived by his wife.

E. P. ABRAHAM, *rev.*

Sources C. L. Oakley, *Memoirs FRS*, 17 (1971), 91–138 · V. Colebrook, 'Leonard Colebrook: reminiscences on the occasion of the 25th anniversary of the Birmingham burns unit', *Injury: British Journal of Accident Surgery*, 2 (1971), 182–4 · R. Hare, *The birth of penicillin and the* *disarming of microbes* (1970) · W. Noble, *Coli: great healer of men* (1974)

Likenesses W. Stoneman, photograph, 1946, RS · W. Bird, photograph, 1960, RS

Wealth at death £14,148: probate, 30 April 1968, *CGPLA Eng. & Wales*

Colebrooke, Sir George, second baronet (1729–1809), banker, was born on 14 June 1729 in Chilham, Kent, the youngest in the family of three sons and seven daughters of James Colebrooke, a London banker, and his wife, Mary Hudson. He was educated at the University of Leiden between 1747 and 1749, and then entered the family's banking business, where he was left in sole control after the deaths of his father and brother James. He inherited a large fortune from them and succeeded his brother James as second baronet in 1761. In 1754 he married Mary, daughter of Patrick Gaynor of Antigua. They had three sons and three daughters, the youngest son being Henry Thomas *Colebrooke, who became a noted Sanskrit scholar. George Colebrook gained election as a fellow of the Society of Antiquaries, and was appointed as chirographer to the court of common pleas in 1766.

A key figure in the world of high finance, Colebrooke sat in the Commons as MP for Arundel between 1754 and 1774, and close links with Thomas Pelham-Holles, first duke of Newcastle, secured him a number of lucrative government contracts. This led to involvement in a wide range of speculative projects throughout Europe, North America, and the West Indies, and the huge resources at his disposal enabled him to embark on a vigorous attempt to secure control over the affairs of the East India Company. He was elected a director of the rapidly expanding company in 1767, and was appointed deputy chairman the following year. He served as chairman in 1769, 1770, and 1772, and was thus at the centre of public attention at a crucial stage in Anglo-Asian relations. His decisions and negotiations with the government shaped the manner in which the British crown extended its control over both the company and its Indian possessions, a process which culminated in the passing of the Regulating Act of 1773. But this success was tempered by the fact that Colebrooke's period in office coincided with the company's financial collapse, and for this he was heavily criticized. At the same time his own business affairs fell into disarray. He became financially involved on his own account in lead and alum mines and speculated heavily and unwisely in raw materials, principally hemp, flax, and logwood. In 1771 he lost £190,000 on a speculation in hemp and then failed in an attempt to corner the world market in alum. His bank closed its doors on 31 March 1773, much of his property was sold in 1774, to be followed by his extensive library and print collection. In 1777 he was declared bankrupt and he departed to live in Boulogne, where his poverty was charitably relieved by a small East India Company pension.

By 1789 Colebrooke was back in England, living in Bath, with some of his property having been restored. He died on 5 August 1809 in Batheaston. Much lampooned in the press, Colebrooke was a rather pompous, self-important man who considered himself to be the second most influential politician in England. He was succeeded in the baronetcy by his second son, James Edward (*b.* 1761), his eldest son having died in April 1809.

H. V. BOWEN, *rev.* ANITA MCCONNELL

Sources G. Colebrooke, *Retrospection* (1898) · *GM*, 1st ser., 79 (1809), 786–8 · HoP, *Commons* · *Bibliotheca Colebrookiana: a catalogue of the library of … Sir George Colebrooke* (1777) [sale catalogue, Christie and Ansell, London, 20 Feb 1777] · will, PRO, PROB 11/1503, sig. 679 · parish register, London, St Peter-le-Poer, 30 July 1729 [baptism]

Archives BL, corresp. with duke of Newcastle, Add. MSS 32874–32891, *passim* · BL, letters to C. Whitefoord, Add. MSS 36594–36595 · BL OIOC, Clive collection, corresp., MSS Eur. G. 37 · BL OIOC, Sutton Court collection, corresp., MSS Eur. F. 128 · BL OIOC, corresp., MSS Eur. D. 822 · Bodl. Oxf., corresp., MS Eng. hist. b. 237 · Bodl. Oxf., corresp., MS Eng. lett., d. 350 · U. Nott. L., letters to third duke of Portland

Colebrooke, Henry Thomas (1765–1837), administrator in India and scholar, was born in London on 15 June 1765, youngest son of Sir George *Colebrooke, second baronet (1729–1809), banker and for four years chairman of the East India Company (1769–73), and his wife, Mary, daughter of Patrick Gaynor of Antigua. When Henry was twelve, his father was ruined and went to live in France for several years. Nevertheless, he used his connections to gain employment for his two youngest sons with the East India Company, and Henry was appointed a writer. Henry was educated by a tutor at home in London but only until he was fifteen. He evidently excelled both in languages and in mathematics, but appears to have been largely self-taught. A sister remembered that as a boy he showed interest in joining the church, but no such inclination is discernible in what is known of his adult life.

Administrative career Colebrooke set sail for India in 1782 and reached Calcutta in 1783. On arrival in India he had to wait three years for a post. In 1786 he was appointed assistant collector in Tirhut; in 1789 he was transferred to the same post in Purnea; in 1793 he was transferred to Nator. In 1794, on the death of Sir William Jones, he took over the responsibility for making a digest of Hindu law, and this led to his transfer to the judicial branch of the company's service. In 1795 he was appointed magistrate in Mirzapur, near Benares. In 1798 he was temporarily moved to the diplomatic service and appointed resident at Nagpur; he arrived there in March 1799. His mission was to talk the raja of Berar into concluding a treaty with the British. He stayed two years but political shifts elsewhere in India rendered his mission hopeless; nevertheless, Lord Wellesley, the governor-general, congratulated him on his efforts. Soon after his return to Mirzapur in 1801 he was transferred to Calcutta as one of the first members of the superior court of appeal; in 1805 he headed it as chief justice.

In 1807 Colebrooke was at last promoted to a seat on the supreme council. He held this position for the usual five years under Lord Minto's administration, but left it in disfavour with the company's directors in London. He

Henry Thomas Colebrooke (1765–1837), by Sir Francis Legatt Chantrey, 1820

returned for six months to the superior court of appeal and was then appointed a member of the board of revenue. He left India for England in December 1814.

In 1810 in Calcutta he met and married Elizabeth Wilkinson (1784/5–1814). He intended to retire with her to England as soon as possible, but was delayed by litigation. The couple had three sons, of whom one died in infancy; then, in October 1814, his wife died at the age of twenty-nine, and he returned to England alone. He also had a daughter and a son before he married; who their mother was is not recorded. The only son to survive him, and to marry, was Sir Thomas Edward Colebrooke, who became his biographer. Quotations below are from that biography, *The Life of H. T. Colebrooke* (1873); its bibliography lists Colebrooke's publications.

Scholarly range His son justly remarks that Colebrooke's life 'was noted for the pursuit of severe and abstract studies, rarely exceeded by the resident at an University or the inmate of a cloister' (Colebrooke, 12). The learning Colebrooke acquired and the publications he produced in the interstices of an extremely busy career, pursued under the rigours of the Indian climate, seem quite beyond the scope of what a comfortable professional academic might achieve in the late twentieth century. What the son's assessment omits, however, is the sheer breadth of Colebrooke's interests and knowledge. With his pre-eminence in 'abstract studies' he combined expertise on many practical topics; indeed, perhaps only the visual arts were missing from his repertoire. Though it is his contributions to the humanities which have been the most

enduring, he probably devoted as much attention to science, technology, and realia.

A historian is bound to see Colebrooke as a kind of successor to the orientalist Sir William Jones. He arrived in Calcutta the year before Jones and others founded the Asiatic Society of Bengal. He published twenty papers in *Asiatic Researches*, the journal of that society, and became its president in 1807. Back in Britain he took the lead in founding the parallel society in London. Like Jones, he became involved in studying, and trying to codify, Hindu (Brahmanical) law because he had to apply it in court. Also like Jones, his political opinions were strongly liberal. Both men purchased property in America with the idea of retiring to a freer political climate than that of Britain—though neither achieved that goal. Equally impressive in their intellectual range, both are now remembered primarily for their Indology. Max Müller called Colebrooke 'founder and father of the Sanskrit scholarship in Europe'. Colebrooke's son has admirably summarized both how they complement each other and why his father remained the less well known. Jones was 'imaginative and inventive, powerful in illustration, always eager to trace analogies', so that his writings are 'attractive as well as instructive'. Colebrooke aimed, by contrast,

> to examine and record facts with the rigour of a student of physical science, and to lay down the results of [his] inquiries with a method necessarily dry, but affording a storehouse of important observations for future students. Mr. Colebrooke's comments, or general remarks, are few but weighty, and put forward with a caution that may be regarded as excessive, and render his writings unattractive to the general reader. (Colebrooke, 235)

The torch which Colebrooke received from Jones he passed on to Horace Hayman Wilson. In 1827 Colebrooke wrote to Wilson (who was still in India):

> Careless and indifferent as our countrymen are, I think, nevertheless, you and I may derive more complacent feelings from the reflection that, following the footsteps of Sir W. Jones, we have, with so little aid of collaborators, and so little encouragement, opened nearly every avenue, and left it to foreigners, who are taking up the clue we have furnished, to complete the outline of what we have sketched. It is some gratification to natural pride that the opportunity which the English have enjoyed has not been wholly unemployed.

On Colebrooke's death Wilson succeeded him as director of the Royal Asiatic Society of Great Britain and Ireland.

Natural history The first book Colebrooke wrote (though not alone) was privately printed in 1795 as *Remarks on the Present State of Husbandry and Commerce in Bengal*. Because of his support for free trade it could not then be published in London; when William Pitt had read it, Colebrooke was told he was lucky not to be dismissed from the service. But his part of the book was later recognized as a mine of information and republished. Another early publication was an article 'On Indian weights and measures'. 'Every branch of natural history attracted him, and he would say that the wonders revealed by the microscope were far more interesting than those of the telescope' (Colebrooke, 266). To see this remark in perspective one must be aware that Colebrooke became the second president of the Astronomical Society in 1824, succeeding Sir William Herschel. After retirement he even had his own chemical laboratory. In India he published articles on the gayal and 'On olibanum, or frankincense', and collected minerals and botanical specimens. In botany, 'an especially favourite study', he annotated Jones's posthumously published treatise on Indian plants, and a genus of Didynamia Gymnospermia was named *Colebrookia* in his honour.

Colebrooke took a keen interest in the exploration and surveying of the Himalayas, which he liked to call 'my mountains'. Jones had already written that they were the highest mountains in the world; Colebrooke estimated their height at 26,000 feet and asked for this to be checked. He corresponded with Lieutenant Webb, who had established that the Ganges rose in India (not, as previously thought, in Tibet), and in 1810 communicated this discovery to the Asiatic Society of Bengal. After leaving India he also published a paper on the height of the snow line, as well as papers on topics in oceanography, geology, and climatology.

His son wrote:

> Nothing came amiss to him; he amassed a large store of miscellaneous information, so that those who, in later life, sought for works to amuse him, were often impressed with the extent of his reading in lighter literature. On two occasions in India ... he applied himself to the surgeon's library, and acquired a very creditable knowledge of the general principles of surgery and medicine. (Colebrooke, 265)

Studies of Sanskrit It was Colebrooke's interest in mathematics and astronomy, his son claims, that gave him the initial impetus to learn Sanskrit. In a letter to his father in 1786 he writes, 'What leisure I find for study shall be given to Arabic, by which alone an accurate knowledge of Persian can be obtained', but in another letter shortly afterwards he reveals detailed knowledge of not only Arabic but also Sanskrit modes of time-reckoning. In 1807 he published *On the Indian and Arabic Divisions of the Zodiac*; in 1816 *On the notions of the Hindu astronomers concerning the precession of the equinoxes and motions of the planets*. Most of his knowledge of Sanskrit astronomy (*jyotihshastra*), however, remained unpublished, and has to be gleaned from his annotations on the Sanskrit manuscripts in the field which are now in the British Library. Colebrooke's study of Indian mathematics is his most enduring achievement; his editions and translations of Sanskrit mathematical works remain fundamental for any student of the subject.

In 1801 he was appointed honorary professor of Hindu law and Sanskrit at Fort William College, recently established in Calcutta. He did not teach, but examined in Sanskrit, Persian, Hindi, and Bengali. The author of an Arabic grammar, Lieutenant Baillie, repeatedly thanked Colebrooke for advice and assistance. Colebrooke initiated an imaginative but unsuccessful project to assemble vocabularies of all the languages spoken between Persia and China. His most impressive linguistic enterprise, however, was his *Grammar of the Sanscrit Language*, vol. 1 (1805, though a rare shorter version appeared in 1804), the first

European work to be based on the indigenous linguistic tradition. William Jones had said that Panini's grammar, the root of that tradition, was 'so abstruse as to require the lucubration of many years before it can be perfectly understood' (Colebrooke, 193). Colebrooke supplied that lucubration. His preface showed that he appreciated the unique importance of Panini for the study of Sanskrit and its culture. Unfortunately he never finished the second volume, being discouraged by the greater popularity of the simpler grammars which were being published on the Latin model familiar to Europeans. Nevertheless, Colebrooke's volume stands as a monument marking the beginning of the study of traditional Sanskrit linguistics (*vyakarana*) by non-Indians, and in due course that study was to bring *vyakarana* into the global development of linguistics.

Colebrooke had published for the first time two Sanskrit lexicons, Hemacandra's *Abhidhana cintamani* and the *Amarakosa*. In *On the Sanscrit and Pracrit Languages* he traced the history of what are nowadays known as the Indo-Aryan languages. His long article 'On Sanscrit and Pracrit poetry', with its 'Synoptical tables of Indian prosody', is a compilation of information on metrics from Vedic to medieval literature which has yet to be surpassed. This article alone contains, albeit with Colebrooke's typical condensation, as much material as one would hope to find in a modern doctoral dissertation. He took considerable interest in Indian history, and five published papers concern inscriptions.

Law, religion, and philosophy Jones had proposed to compile a digest of both Hindu and Muslim law, but when he died in 1794 all that existed of this enterprise was a voluminous compilation in Sanskrit by a pandit, Jagannatha, of Brahman law on inheritance and contract. Colebrooke undertook to translate this into English and hoped to do so in six months, working part-time; in fact it took him two years and was published (in 1798) in four volumes. In 1801, when he joined the superior court of appeal, he had the court's decisions embodied in reports. He published further books on inheritance in 1810 and on contracts in 1818. He wrote in 1822 that he had prepared a 'Supplementary Digest' in Sanskrit and English, but found it 'very little called for'. The only publication to result from this work was his essay 'On Hindu courts of justice' (1828), the last Indological work published during his lifetime. He corresponded often and at length with Sir Thomas Strange, chief justice at Madras, about the latter's book on Hindu law, and many of his remarks are included in it.

Colebrooke did great pioneer work on ancient Indian religion and philosophy. He wrote on all the major classical schools of Indian philosophy, though his translation of the Samkhya karika was published after his death. He published an article (long enough to be called a monograph) on the Vedas (1805), and a series of three articles (1798–1801) entitled 'On the religious ceremonies of the Hindus, and of the brahmins especially'. Astonishingly, in the same period he published 'On the origin and peculiar tenets of certain Mohammedan sects' (1801). His earliest published article (1795) was 'On the duties of a faithful

Hindu widow'. It quotes Sanskrit texts on a widow's duty to be burnt with her husband's body, adding that this was rarely done. When he was on the supreme council the government considered for the first time whether to suppress the custom: Colebrooke advised that to forbid it would be counter-productive and favoured regulation to ensure that the widow acted voluntarily.

His 'Observation on the sect of Jains' (1807) was the first significant contribution ever made by a non-Indian to knowledge of that religion; it is based on original Prakrit texts. Unlike his predecessors, he clearly distinguished Jainism from Buddhism, and speculated intelligently, albeit incorrectly, on the relation between them. Though he never devoted a publication to Buddhism, he was planning to do so in 1804, when he wrote to his father: 'I have lately obtained a considerable addition of authentic and important information on the religion and mythology of the Buddhists. Everything relative to a religion, which has spread even more widely than the Christian or the Mahomedan faiths, is particularly interesting' (Colebrooke, 217). He later refuted the theory that Buddhism had preceded Brahmanism, showing that Vedic literature was pre-Buddhist.

Benefactor Colebrooke was the individual who played the greatest part in founding and establishing the (later Royal) Asiatic Society of Great Britain and Ireland. He took the chair at all the preliminary meetings; the first, on 9 January 1823, was held at his house. It was evidently felt that the president should be someone of higher rank and greater influence; but it was unanimously decided to appoint, immediately below the president, a director, 'under whose particular care and protection Asiatic literature should be placed'. In this capacity Colebrooke was 'called to the chair' at the society's first general meeting on 15 March 1823. In his address he said that England had a special mission to repay a debt of gratitude to India. For the next three years he presided at most meetings both of the society and of its governing council; evidently it was he who really ran the society. His failing eyesight then limited his activity, but he remained director until his death. In 1824 he presented the society with drawings of Indian objects ranging from musical instruments to agricultural implements.

He had already presented, in 1819, his collection of 2749 Indian manuscripts to the library of the East India Company (later the India Office Library, now part of the British Library). This must at the time have been the largest collection of Indian manuscripts outside India. The vast majority of the manuscripts were in Sanskrit, but Prakrit, Hindi, Gujarati, Marathi, Punjabi, and Bengali were also represented. In recognition of this generosity the directors of the company commissioned from F. L. Chantrey a bust of Colebrooke which still stands in the library. The India Office Library was also indirectly benefited by Colebrooke when it inherited the library of Fort William College, Calcutta, which he had done much to form.

Colebrooke was 'small and spare in person' (Colebrooke, 383). Before his retirement he seems to have enjoyed good health. He was a strong walker, and when young was fond of hunting and other outdoor pursuits. To his son he appeared kind and yet rather formidable, perhaps with more intelligence than common sense. He enjoyed poetry and imaginative literature, but 'Tragic tales affected him so painfully that he generally shunned them' (ibid., 265). Though he had no small talk, he had an attractive dry wit: 'The Brahmins not inelegantly remarked of the occultation yesterday, that it was the emblem of the meeting between the Raja and his mother, which was, by the bye, to have taken place yesterday, but it did not; so that, it should seem, the planets were not informed of the postponement early enough' (ibid., 166).

Colebrooke's life was perhaps not very happy. In his early years in India he longed to leave; a free-trader employed by the East India Company was a misfit. On the supreme council he lost favour because he was associated with a decision to postpone remittances to London, after the heavy costs of a campaign against Java, and because he had favoured the unsuccessful attempt to institute a house tax in large towns. Never decorated, he felt unjustly treated. Anxious about money, he lost much of what he had made in India through unwise speculation; he bought land in the Cape of Good Hope and spent nearly a year there (1821–2) but lost his investment. His health declined with his finances. His eyesight worsened and in 1829 he went completely blind. He then had terrible back pains. Between 1822 and 1834 he keenly suffered the deaths of two nieces to whom he was guardian and two sons, all as young adults. For the last three years he was bedridden. He died in London of influenza, or its after-effects, on 10 March 1837.   RICHARD F. GOMBRICH

Sources T. E. Colebrooke, *The life of H. T. Colebrooke* (1873) · **Archives** BL OIOC, MS collection | NL Scot., Elliot-Murray-Kynynmound MSS, letters to first earl of Minto · **Likenesses** F. L. Chantrey, marble bust, 1820, BL OIOC [*see illus.*] · F. L. Chantrey, pencil drawing, *c*.1820, NPG · H. Weekes, bust (after F. L. Chantrey), Asiatic Society, Calcutta · H. Weekes, bust (after F. L. Chantrey), Royal Asiatic Society, London

Colebrooke, Sir William Macbean George (1787–1870), army officer and colonial governor, was the son of Colonel Paulet Welbore Colebrooke RA (*d.* 28 Sept 1816) and his wife, Mary, the daughter of Major-General Grant. He was educated at the Royal Military Academy, Woolwich, and entered the Royal Artillery as a second lieutenant on 17 August 1803.

In 1805 Colebrooke was ordered to the East Indies—first to Ceylon, then in 1806 to Malabar, then in 1807 back to Ceylon. He went to India in 1809, served with the field army, and became a captain on 27 September 1810. He next served in Java, and was wounded in the operations against the Dutch in 1811; he stayed on under the British occupation, became deputy quartermaster-general in 1813, and was promoted major on 1 June 1813. He was sent as political agent and commissioner to Palembong in Sumatra, and to Bengal in 1814. He resumed his old duties in Java in 1815, and was ordered to India on the conclusion of peace and the restoration of Java to the Dutch on 19 August 1816. He served through the Anglo-Maratha War of 1817–18, and accompanied the expedition to the Persian

Gulf in 1818. In 1820 he married Emma Sophia (d. 1851), the daughter of Lieutenant-Colonel Robert Colebrooke (d. 1808), surveyor-general of Bengal.

Colebrooke returned to England in 1821. From 1822 to 1832 he was a commissioner of the long and elaborate 'Eastern inquiry' into the administration and revenues of Ceylon, and he resided there from 1829 to 1831. His fellow commissioner Charles Hay Cameron investigated the judicial system. Following his return to England Colebrooke submitted four reports recommending major reforms in Ceylon, which were largely implemented. In 1834 he became KH and on 9 September of that year was appointed lieutenant-governor of the Bahamas. He arrived at Nassau via Jamaica on 26 February 1835 and made his first speech to the assembly on 7 April. During his administration slavery gave way to the apprenticeship system prior to its final abolition, and Colebrooke was well informed of the problems which confronted him.

On 13 February 1837, while on leave in England, Colebrooke was gazetted as governor of the Leeward Islands. He was knighted on 31 March 1837. He assumed the government of Antigua and the other islands on 11 May 1837; one of his earliest official acts was the proclamation of Queen Victoria. In this government, as in the Bahamas, he was anxious to improve education and reform prison discipline; he also urged the restoration of the old general council of the Leewards, which had last met in 1798. On 25 July 1840 he left Antigua for Liverpool, and after an extended leave was on 26 March 1841 made lieutenant-governor of New Brunswick. His attempts to reform the political system and create municipal institutions were thwarted by the provincial oligarchy. The question of the Maine boundary was then the chief public matter affecting the colony; Colebrooke's suggestion of a special scheme for colonization had no practical results. On 9 November 1846 he became colonel in the army, and on 27 November 1847 he was gazetted to British Guiana. However, he never took up the appointment, but proceeded instead on 11 August 1848 as governor to Barbados, where he also administered the Windward Islands. He continued his special interest in the suppression of crime and the improvement of the prisons, and his suggestions for a federation of all the Windward Islands foreshadowed much later proposals. In 1854 imperial troops were withdrawn from the smaller islands, but the island group remained peaceful and Colebrooke was well regarded by the people of Barbados. He became major-general on 20 June 1854.

In January 1856 Colebrooke relinquished his office and returned to England. He was promoted lieutenant-general on 16 January 1859 and general on 26 December 1865, and he was colonel commanding the Royal Artillery from 25 September 1859 until his death. He lived at Iver House, Salt Hill, near Slough, Buckinghamshire, where he died on 6 February 1870.   C. A. HARRIS, rev. LYNN MILNE

Sources Colonial Office List (1864) · The Times (10 Feb 1870) · G. C. Mendis, ed., The Colebrooke-Cameron papers, 2 vols. (1956) · Boase, Mod. Eng. biog. · M. Francis, Governors and settlers: images of authority in the British colonies, 1820–60 (1992) · Walford, County families · D. P.

Henige, Colonial governors from the fifteenth century to the present (1970) · CGPLA Eng. & Wales (1870)
Archives BL OIOC, description of Arab tribes · CKS, corresp. and accounts · NA Canada, corresp. and papers | Lpool RO, letters to Lord Stanley · U. Durham L., corresp. with third Earl Grey
Wealth at death under £12,000: probate, 18 March 1870, CGPLA Eng. & Wales

Colechurch, Peter of (d. 1205), organizer of the rebuilding of London Bridge, was priest of the London parish of St Mary Colechurch (probably named after a local market for charcoal), where St Thomas of Canterbury had been born. Peter is recorded as having in 1176 begun 'the stone bridge of London', and in later centuries was identified as its architect. His true role, however, was that of fund-raiser (with a group of collectors), warden (custos) of the work, and steward (procurator) of the fraternity responsible for the estate, existing by c.1190, which was devoted to the upkeep of the bridge. He is the chief witness to what are virtually identical documents drawn up for separate members of the powerful Blunt family, for whom he may regularly have performed legal services. He perhaps had a wide reputation as a man of affairs. His association with St Thomas was important, for the bridge was the most powerful symbol of the connection between London and Canterbury, and the work was in progress at a time when the citizens of London were adopting the martyr as their patron. In 1179/80 at least five guilds in the city were devoted to the bridge. The earlier bridge appears to have been built partly in stone, but under Peter there began the programme, probably completed soon after 1212, of reconstructing it entirely as a series of stone arches. His powers may have been failing by 1202, when Isenbert of Saintes was recommended to have care of the project and it was intended to erect houses for rent on the bridge. After his death in 1205, Peter's body was buried in the chapel on the bridge dedicated to St Thomas. Bones reputed to be his were removed from the undercroft of the chapel in 1832, and are now in the Museum of London. His seal (engraved Sigillum Petri Sacerdotis Pontis Londoniarum) shows a priest celebrating mass at a small altar.   DEREK KEENE

Sources Ann. mon., 2.240, 256–7, 268; 3.451; 4.400 · N. Moore, The history of St Bartholomew's Hospital, 1 (1918), 208–9 · W. O. Hassall, ed., Cartulary of St Mary Clerkenwell, CS, 3rd ser., 71 (1949), no. 247 · E. Mason, J. Bray, and D. J. Murphy, eds., Westminster Abbey charters, 1066–c.1214, London RS, 25 (1988), no. 385 · D. Keene and V. Harding, eds., Historical gazetteer of London before the great fire (1987) [microfiche, nos. 105/0, 18] · C. N. L. Brooke and G. Keir, London, 800–1216: the shaping of a city (1975) · G. Home, Old London Bridge (1931) · T. D. Hardy, ed., Rotuli litterarum patentium, RC (1835), 9, 58 · Pipe rolls, 26 Henry II · Pipe rolls, 31 Henry II · C. Welsh, History of the Tower Bridge (1894)
Archives CLRO, Bridge House deeds · St Bartholomew's Hospital, London, deeds · Westminster Abbey, deed witnessed by him
Likenesses seal, repro. in Moore, History of St Bartholomew's Hospital

Colefax [née Halsey], **Sibyl Sophie Julia**, Lady Colefax (1874–1950), hostess and interior decorator, was born on 4 December 1874, at The Poplars, Wimbledon Common, Surrey (the house of her uncle, Walter Bagehot). She was the third but only surviving daughter (and fifth and last child) of William Stirling Halsey (1831–1902), and his unhappily married wife, Sophie Victoria (1840–1926), daughter of James Wilson. Living mainly at Cawnpore until her father's retirement from the Bengal civil service in 1883, she was bright and imaginative but felt excluded and neglected. After schooling in Putney and Wimbledon she lived in genteel indigence as her mother's travelling companion, 'running after old ladies with their knitting' (Woolf, *Diary*, 3.116). Conversations about books and art with John Lockwood Kipling initially showed this receptive, lonely young woman how her life might be enhanced and enriched. A visit in 1894 to Italy, where she befriended Bernard Berenson, gave further intellectual and emotional nourishment.

In July 1901 Sibyl married (Henry) Arthur Colefax (1866–1936), barrister, the son of Joseph Samuel Colefax, a chartered accountant. They had two sons. Her husband, who was Unionist MP for South-West Manchester (January to December 1910) and took silk in 1912, specialized in Anglo-German patent and trade-mark law. He suffered a serious and permanent diminution of his practice in 1914, but was consoled with legal offices and was created KBE in 1920. A tolerant and good-humoured husband, he was described by Kenneth Clark as 'a heavy man with a very large face, who was thought by those who had never visited the provinces to be the biggest bore in England' (Clark, 212).

The Colefaxes had many political and legal friends, but were also connoisseurs of literature, music, drama, and the fine arts. Living first at 85 Onslow Square and later Old Buckhurst in Sussex, but famously from 1921 at Argyll House in Chelsea, Sibyl Colefax fulfilled her appetite for life and curiosity about people by creating a salon which represented the height of intelligent, discriminating pleasures. 'The Coalbox', as she was nicknamed, first won wider fame in London society by organizing a poetry reading in aid of charity (12 December 1917). 'Mrs. Colefax's star-climbing wagon', as her fellow organizer Robert Ross called it (Ross, 318), was chaired by Edmund Gosse; T. S. Eliot, three Sitwells, and Aldous Huxley recited (Siegfried Sassoon and Robert Graves declined).

Sibyl Colefax was not one of those brittle society women who are no more than a smart address, or present a surface as hard and varnished as a front door. Her memory of books, pictures, and people was keen. She was kind, loyal, practical, and unmalicious. Though she could be devious or insincere, her charms and stratagems were enticing. She never competed with the wit of her guests or domineered. In drawing out the merits of her friends—the clever young as well as veteran celebrities—she gave apt praise rather than flattery. She had a hunter's instinct for capturing lions and a brave's ruthlessness in collecting scalps. The term 'colefaxismus' was coined to describe those claiming special acquaintanceship with celebrities or inside knowledge of great events: she was notorious for exaggerating her intimacy with the famous dead like Henry James. Yet she loathed publicity. Her energy was formidable. While London still slept, she would write and address some sixty postcards and the telephone would

start shrilling before the postman dared call. Her illegible letters were littered with relentlessly dropped names, and could be irresistible. 'Do dine Tuesday', she scrawled to J. C. Squire. 'Just ourselves and Pirandello' (Pryce-Jones, 66). Virginia Woolf described her in 1923 as 'painted and emphatic … broadcheeked, a little coarse, kindly, glass-eyed, affectionate to me almost, capable, apparently disinterested' (Woolf, *Diary*, 2.275); later she likened her 'to a bunch of red cherries on a hard black straw hat' (Woolf, *Moments of Being*, 189). Lady Plunder in Edith Wharton's *The Gods Arrive* (1932) is modelled on her.

Sibyl Colefax was a well-informed and energetic traveller with cosmopolitan cultural interests: Valéry made his London début under her auspices. Her son Peter went to work on Wall Street in 1926, and she lost her investments there (estimated at £50,000) in 1929. To recuperate her finances, she began on a fee-paying basis to advise her friends on the interior arrangements of their houses. After several commissions, she inaugurated Sibyl Colefax Ltd in 1933. The reception rooms at Argyll House were compact, immaculate, and varnished: pale almond greens, greys, and opaque yellows provided discreet colouring. Her work for paying clients was, however, more theatrical and derivative. It was influenced by Edward Knoblock, an American dramatist who had cultivated an English taste for Regency Revival decorations and furnishings during the 1920s. Cecil Beaton pictured a typical room arranged by Lady Colefax: 'somewhat sparsely furnished, with a couple of delicate black and gold chairs, a settee, striped curtains, and a colour scheme of yellow and grey' (Beaton, 210). She worked initially in collaboration with the Bruton Street antique dealers Stair and Andrew, but in 1938 recruited a gifted young decorator, John *Fowler, and the Mayfair interior decorating firm of Colefax and Fowler was formed. The combination of her contacts and his flair brought prosperity until the war. Sibyl Colefax was industrious, but an inefficient manager and inconsiderate employer. The enforcement, during the post-war period, of official austerity measures limited the firm's opportunities for profitable work, as did its senior partner's failing health. The Anglo-American millionaire Ronald Tree was consequently able to buy Colefax and Fowler as a gift for his wife, afterwards known as Nancy Lancaster, at the time of their divorce in 1947. The subsequent Colefax and Fowler style—richly coloured chintzes, fringed and tasselled curtains, braided upholstery, bright colours, floral patterns—was the antithesis of the earlier Colefax interiors.

After Arthur Colefax's sudden death of pneumonia in February 1936, Sibyl Colefax left Argyll House. Her last dinner party there, on 11 June 1936, was perhaps her finest. King Edward VIII attended with Wallis Simpson. Artur Rubinstein played three Chopin piano pieces; Noël Coward sang. Guests included Lord Brownlow, Winston Churchill, Duff Cooper, Robert Vansittart, and Kenneth Clark with their wives, as well as Lord Berners and Robert Bruce Lockhart. She resumed entertaining at a small house in Westminster in May 1937. During the Second

World War, she ran a canteen in Belgrave Square, and, despite dangerous operations and broken limbs, held regular dinners called 'ordinaries' at the Dorchester Hotel, at which her guests paid their own expenses. Latterly some of her attractions waned but her dinner parties continued to draw guests. One of her last, on 21 February 1950, brought together Vivien Leigh, Lord Esher, Terence Rattigan, Beverley Nichols, Robert Lutyens, Osbert Lancaster, Edward Sackville-West, Viscountess Waverley, and Lady Jebb (there were no politicians in election week). Sibyl Colefax died of cancer of the lungs and left breast on 22 September 1950 at 19 Lord North Street, London. Her ashes are presumed to have been buried, as she had intended, in a wood near Old Buckhurst, Sussex. On the hall table her visitors' book lay open at the last dinner she had given. RICHARD DAVENPORT-HINES

Sources The Times (26 Sept 1950) · The Times (28 Sept 1950) · The Spectator (13 Oct 1950) · K. McLeod, A passion for friendship: Sibyl Colefax and her circle (1991) · The diary of Virginia Woolf, ed. A. O. Bell and A. McNeillie, 2–5 (1978–84) · V. Woolf, Moments of being: unpublished autobiographical writings, ed. J. Schulkind (1976) · K. Clark, Another part of the wood (1974) · M. Ross, ed., Robert Ross, friend of friends (1952) · A. Pryce-Jones, The bonus of laughter (1987) · H. Nicolson, Diaries and letters, ed. N. Nicolson, 3 vols. (1966–8) · J. Lees-Milne, Ancestral voices (1975) · J. Lees-Milne, Prophesying peace (1977) · J. Lees-Milne, Caves of ice (1983) · J. Lees-Milne, Midway on the waves (1985) · M. I. Curzon, Baronness Ravensdale, In many rhythms: an autobiography (1953), 84–7 · The diaries of Cynthia Gladwyn, ed. M. Jebb (1995) · C. Beaton, The glass of fashion (1954) · C. Jones, Colefax & Fowler (1989); pbk edn (2000) · A. Bennett, Journals, 1921–28 (1933) · d. cert. · m. cert. · CGPLA Eng. & Wales (1950)
Archives Bodl. Oxf., corresp.; corresp. and papers, photo albums, and scrapbooks | Harvard University, near Florence, Italy, Center for Italian Renaissance Studies, letters to Bernard Berenson · U. Sussex, letters to Virginia Woolf · Yale U., Beinecke L., Thornton Wilder MSS
Likenesses P. de Laszlo, pen-and-ink drawing, 1916, repro. in McLeod, Passion for friendship, frontispiece · P. Burne-Jones, pen-and-ink drawing, 1923, repro. in McLeod, Passion for friendship · photographs (in infancy, in childhood, as a schoolgirl, and as a young and middle-aged woman), repro. in McLeod, Passion for friendship
Wealth at death £14,770 8s. 11d.: probate, 30 Nov 1950, CGPLA Eng. & Wales

Coleman, Charles (d. 1664), musician and composer, was possibly the son of Clare Coleman (d. 1641), described at her burial in 1641 as 'an ancient widow gentlewoman' (Ashbee and Lasocki, 273). He first appears singing the part of Hymen in Cupid's Banishment, a masque by Robert White put on at Greenwich on 4 May 1617. By 27 February 1620, when the registers of St Andrew's, Holborn, London, record the baptism of his eldest son, Charles (d. 1645), 'in Churchyard Alley in Fetter Lane', he had married. Two further children, Edward *Coleman and Alice (d. 1627), were baptized in 1622 and 1624.

Exactly when Coleman became one of the king's musicians is not known, but he was listed among the lutes and voices at the funeral of James I in 1625. He took part in James Shirley's inns of court masque The Triumph of Peace (1634) as both singer and instrumentalist, and wrote the music for The King and Queen's Entertainment at Richmond, presented by Prince Charles on 12 September 1636.

According to Lucy Hutchinson (wife of the regicide John Hutchinson, whose music master he was) Coleman had a house in Richmond-on-Thames. She relates how

the man being a skilful composer in music, the King's musicians often met at his house to practise new airs and prepare them for the king; and divers of the gentlemen and ladies that were affected with music, came thither to hear; others that were not took that pretense to entertain themselves with the company. (Ashbee and Lasocki, 271)

It was probably through Colonel Hutchinson's influence that Cambridge University awarded Coleman the MusD degree on 2 July 1651. John Playford lists him among London teachers 'For the Voyce or Viole' (A Musicall Banquet, 1651), and he was sufficiently well known for Lodewijck Huygens—who calls him 'a famous musician'—to pay him a visit on 12 March 1652 while in London. Not finding him at home, he saw instead his wife, pronounced 'a pretty woman'; this must have been Grace, almost certainly his second wife, mother of his younger children Charles (d. 1694), Regina (bap. 1650), and Grace.

Coleman was one of the leading composers of his time. Though not a prolific songwriter, a number of his songs were published in John Playford's Select Musical Ayres and Dialogues (1652, 1653, 1659, etc.) and survive in manuscript, notably in Lambeth Palace Library, MS 1041, which once belonged to Lady Anne Blount, daughter of the earl of Newport, and whose music master he may thus have been in the early 1650s. They are musically more advanced than those of his most famous contemporary Henry Lawes; among the best are 'Wake, my Adonis, do not cry' from Cartwright's The Lady Errant (thought to have been performed at Oxford early in the civil war) and the dialogue 'Did you not once Lucinda vow' from The King and Queen's Entertainment. A half-dozen viol fantasias of five and six parts are extant (the latter dating from before 1625), as are more than 250 consort airs, mostly arranged in suites. These show him as a close runner-up to John Jenkins and William Lawes, both as to quantity and quality. Many were published in Playford's A Musicall Banquet (1651), Court Ayres (1655), and Courtly Masquing Ayres (1662), but many more remain in manuscript (BL, London; Bodl. Oxf. and Christ Church library, Oxford; also Dublin, New York, etc.). At least twenty-six airs for lyra viol are known from editions of Playford's Musick's Recreation on the Lyra-Viol (1652, 1661, etc.) and various manuscripts. Coleman also wrote instrumental music for Davenant's First Dayes Entertainment at Rutland-House (1656) and The Siege of Rhodes (1656).

Despite his anti-royalist connections Coleman set Shirley's Ode upon the Happy Return of King Charles to his Languishing Nation at the Restoration, though the music does not survive. In due course he was reappointed to his place in the King's Musick 'for the viall, among the lutes and voices' at a salary of £40 per annum with £20 for strings and livery of £16. 2s. 6d. In November 1662, on the death of Henry Lawes, he was appointed composer to the king, with a further £40 per annum.

Coleman died at his house in Churchyard Alley, Fetter Lane, and was buried in St Andrew's, Holborn, on 8 July 1664. His will, dated 2 July, was proved by his wife Grace on

16 July; in it he refers to himself as 'an Antient man' and mentions his children Charles (who succeeded to his place in the 'lutes and voices'), Regina, and Grace.

IAN SPINK

Sources A. Ashbee, ed., *Records of English court music*, 9 vols. (1986–96) · A. Ashbee and D. Lasocki, eds., *A biographical dictionary of English court musicians, 1485–1714*, 1 (1998), 271–5

Coleman, Donald Cuthbert (1920–1995), economic historian, was born on 21 January 1920 at Martlesham, Long Lane, Finchley, Middlesex, the son of Hugh Augustus Coleman, civil servant, and his wife, Marian Stella Agnes, *née* Cuthbert. Educated at Haberdashers' Aske's School, he left in 1939 to enter the London insurance industry. He served in the Royal Artillery from 1941 to 1946, seeing service in the Mediterranean and rising to the rank of major. He then entered the London School of Economics (LSE) and was awarded his PhD for a thesis on seventeenth-century Kent. This research served as a bridgehead for other studies and for his first book, *The British Paper Industry, 1495–1860* (1958). It also set the pattern of work, using primary sources (helped here by excise and customs records) and following the evolution of an industry over the long run, marking transformations of materials, technology, and markets. His next book, *Sir John Banks, Baronet and Businessman: a Study of Business, Politics and Society in Later Stuart England* (1963), closed in to focus on the importance of kinship in business. The relations between industry and the state, and between merchants and government in policy matters, were always central to his interests.

Recognition of Coleman's scholarship led to his appointment in 1951 to a new lectureship in industrial history at LSE, and after spending the academic year 1957–8 in the USA, at Yale, he rose to a readership in 1958. He married on 5 February 1954 Jessie Annie Matilda (Ann) Child, *née* Stevens, a divorcée ten years his senior. His appointment as historian of Courtaulds brought links with the Pasold fund for textile history and in 1969, with the publication of the first two volumes of *Courtaulds: an Economic and Social History*, came a personal chair at LSE. His academic standing was considerably enhanced by his joint editorship of the *Economic History Review* from 1967 to 1973. He was a notably firm, even authoritarian, editor, whose judgements markedly increased the status of the *Economic History Review* as it expanded from three to four issues annually.

The concept of proto-industrialization which gathered momentum during the 1970s was being proposed by some scholars as a universal stage in the historical process. This was not to Coleman's liking; he profoundly distrusted such all-embracing methodologies, whether from the left or the right of the political spectrum, and preferred 'middle-order' theorizing from an empirical foundation. He challenged its claims on the grounds of chronology and universality in an article whose title, 'Proto-industrialisation: a concept too many', characteristically did not end in a question mark (*Economic History Review*, 2nd ser., 36, 1983, 435–48). He was concerned with the origins of the industrial revolution in England; in *The Economy of England, 1450–1750* (1977) he examined the ways in which political, social, intellectual, agrarian, commercial, and industrial change in England had diverged from the situation in other European countries, so that industrialization began in England in the eighteenth century, rather than elsewhere. Many of his numerous papers examined aspects of this process in greater depth.

With his long view of industry Coleman also entered the debate over failings in the British economy after 1850. His principal contribution was 'Gentlemen and players' (*Economic History Review*, 2nd ser., 26, 1973, 92–116). The industrial revolution had been driven by 'those who were not gentlemen' but subsequently business and industrial leaders succumbed to the values of the older élite and 'too many of the revolutionaries became too busy becoming gentlemen'. Thus a fatal link was forged between the 'educated amateur' and the 'practical man' which excluded professionalization for the élite with dire consequences.

Coleman was intensely interested in the practical and financial world of his day and sympathetic in principle to those who made it work. He admired achievement and success attained through hard work, commitment, intelligence, and insight. That he was able to overcome the potential conflicts of interest between his role as adviser to firms about their history, and that of the independent and objective academic, and to win the respect, if not always the affection, of both parties, testifies to his strength of character.

The qualities Coleman admired in others were also his own; he disliked privilege and pomposity—whether social, political, or academic—and was liable to speak out against pretentiousness, with a lack of reticence that any friends had to accept. His own beliefs were sometimes less prominent than his castigations of false nostrums offered by others. He opposed any lowering of professional standards, and this opposition, coupled with a long memory, made his views forthright and often acerbic. Yet the standards he expected of others were also those he applied to himself, and he earned the unremitting affection and loyalty of his research students.

With work at LSE and life in London losing their attractions in difficult years, Coleman's move in 1971 to a chair in Cambridge and a professorial fellowship at Pembroke College brought him new personal and professional satisfaction. He was elected FBA in 1972. Life at Over Hall, Cavendish, Suffolk, in his spacious old vicarage and handsome garden, became increasingly congenial. He mellowed, became more relaxed with his visitors, devoted in caring for his wife as she became more frail, and generous even in his judgement of the failings of others.

With undergraduate teaching becoming more tedious and lecturing a painful duty which he saw no need to endure further, Coleman retired from the chair in 1981, keeping his fellowship. His great delight now was to work in his upstairs study at Cavendish, encompassed by his library. His academic priority was to write, while responding to invitations to help and advise. His own commitment to the Pasold fund continued until two years before his death: he was its governor from 1977 and chairman from 1985 to 1993. He died at the Evelyn Hospital, Cambridge, after a long and painful illness, the result of cancer, on 3 September 1995. His wife survived him, dying several years later.   PETER MATHIAS

Sources F. M. L. Thompson and P. Mathias, *PBA*, 115 (2002), 169–91 · N. Harte, *The Independent* (9 Sept 1995) · N. Harte, *Textile History*, 27/2 (1996), 127–31 · *The Times* (6 Sept 1995), 19 · preface, *Business life and public policy: essays in honour of D. C. Coleman* (1986) · D. C. Coleman, 'Dons: a memoir of LSE and Cambridge' (typescript), 1994, CUL · *WWW* · b. cert. · d. cert.
Likenesses photograph, repro. in *PBA* · photograph, repro. in *The Times* · photograph, repro. in *The Independent*
Wealth at death £208,852: probate, 5 Jan 1995, *CGPLA Eng. & Wales*

Coleman, Edward (*bap.* 1622, *d.* 1669), singer and composer, was baptized on 27 April 1622 at St Andrew's, Holborn, London. He was the second of seven children born to the viol player and composer Charles *Coleman (*d.* 1664) and his wife, Grace. He first comes to notice in John Playford's list in *A Musicall Banquet* (1651) of teachers 'for the Voyce or Viole'. He is, in fact, praised as Susanna Perwich's singing teacher in John Batchiler's *The Virgins Pattern* (1661), where he is described as having 'rare abilities in *singing*'. He sang in *The First Dayes Entertainment at Rutland House* in May 1656. An anonymous report on the *Entertainment* noted that 'the Singers were Capt. Cooke, Ned Coleman and his wife, another wooman and other inconsiderable voyces'. Coleman was to have taken the role of Alphonso in *The Siege of Rhodes* the following September. That production appears to have been thwarted at the last minute by an order from Cromwell for all those who had fought on the royalist side in the civil war (thus including William Davenant, who was both author and impresario) to leave London by 6 September. *The Siege of Rhodes* was eventually performed at the Cockpit in April–May 1659, but with a double cast; Coleman shared his role with Roger Hill. This first English opera was something of a family affair: Edward's father composed the instrumental music (with George Hudson), while his wife, Catherine Ferrabosco (*bap.* 1623), sang the part of Ianthe.

Edward Coleman's earliest known composition is the song 'The Glories of our Birth and State', which was written for James Shirley's *Contention of Ajax and Ulysses*, performed at Shirley's school at some time before its publication in 1659. (Coleman's song did not appear in print until 1667, in Playford's *The Musical Companion*, but was then reprinted in various anthologies up to 1680.) A number of his songs are included in the first volume of Playford's *Select Musicall Ayres and Dialogues* (1653).

At the Restoration, Coleman took up two positions in the court musical establishment. He became a gentleman of the Chapel Royal and was appointed to the 'private musick in ordinary … in the place of John Lanier for a voyce'. Since Coleman's place was taken after his death by the countertenor William Turner, we may assume that he too was a countertenor. He was listed among the gentlemen of the Chapel Royal who sang at the coronation of Charles II on St George's day (23 April) 1661. Like so many of the court musicians, Coleman seems to have got into financial difficulties as a consequence of the late payment of salaries. There were two instances, in 1662 and 1663, of

his assigning sums due to him from the exchequer to creditors, and the administration of his will was granted to another.

The only description of Coleman's singing comes from Pepys, and it is not particularly flattering. In the last few months of 1665 Catherine and Edward Coleman were frequent visitors at Pepys's house at Greenwich (where he had gone to escape the plague). Pepys noted in his diary on 8 November 'the best company for Musique I ever was in in my life … I have never lived so merrily … as I have done this plague-time, by … the acquaintance of … Coleman and her husband.' But his entry ten days earlier had been less enthusiastic about Coleman's voice—and his manners:

> By and by, I back again home, and there find him [Thomas Hill] return[ed] with Mr. Coleman (his wife being ill) and Mr. [Nicholas] Laneare—with whom, with their Lute, we had excellent company and good singing till midnight, and a good supper I did give them. But Coleman's voice is quite spoiled; and when he begins to be drunk, he is excellent company, but afterward troublesome and impertinent.

The Chapel Royal's book of remembrance records that Coleman died at Greenwich on 29 August 1669.

PETER WALLS

Sources A. Ashbee, ed., *Records of English court music*, 9 vols. (1986–96) · A. Ashbee and D. Lasocki, eds., *A biographical dictionary of English court musicians, 1485–1714*, 2 vols. (1998) · A. Ashbee and J. Harley, eds., *The cheque books of the Chapel Royal*, 2 vols. (2000) · J. Batchiler, *The virgins pattern in the exemplary life, and lamented death of Mrs Susanna Perwich* (1661) · J. Buttery, 'The evolution of English opera between 1656 and 1695: a reinvestigation', PhD diss., U. Cam., 1967 · *The dramatic works of Sir William D'Avenant*, ed. J. Maidment and W. H. Logan, 5 vols. (1872–4) · W. Davenant, *The siege of Rhodes: a critical edition*, ed. A.-M. Hedbäck (1973) · C. L. Day and E. B. Murrie, *English song-books, 1651–1702: a bibliography with a first-line index of songs* (1940) · A. Harbage, *Annals of English drama, 975–1700*, rev. S. Schoenbaum, 3rd edn, rev. S. S. Wagonheim (1989) · Highfill, Burnim & Langhans, *BDA* · Pepys, *Diary* · E. F. Rimbault, ed., *The old cheque-book, or book of remembrance, of the Chapel Royal, from 1561 to 1744*, CS, new ser., 3 (1872) · *The dramatic works and poems of James Shirley*, ed. W. Gifford, 6 vols. (1833); repr. (New York, 1966) · I. Spink, *Henry Lawes: cavalier songwriter* (2000) · I. Spink, ed., *The seventeenth century* (1992)

Coleman, Edward. *See* Colman, Edward (1636–1678).

Coleman, Helen Cordelia. *See* Angell, Helen Cordelia (1847–1884).

Coleman, Thomas (1597/8–1646), Church of England clergyman, was born in Oxford. On 28 April 1615, aged seventeen, he matriculated from Magdalen Hall, Oxford, from where he graduated BA on 10 June 1618 and proceeded MA on 6 July 1621. Appointed rector of Blyton, Lincolnshire, in 1623 by Sir John Wray, at an unknown date he married Elizabeth, whose surname was quite probably Burton and who almost certainly came from a local family. Nothing is known of Coleman's ministry there.

In 1642 Coleman left for London, claiming that he had been persecuted by royalists. On 7 March 1642 the House of Commons voted not to make him lecturer of St Giles-in-the-Fields, London, though it named him to the Westminster assembly on 23 April and appointed him rector of St Peter Cornhill, after William Fairfax had been sequestrated in 1643. In August that year the committee for plundered ministers had explicitly requested that he be appointed to a living in London or Hertfordshire. His fast sermon to the House of Commons on 30 August was published as *The Christians Course and Complaint* (1643), with an epistle that urged MPs to maintain the purity of religion and denounced burdensome impositions, illegal monopolies, inordinate delays between parliaments, and infringements on liberty. He preached on 29 September at St Margaret's, Westminster, when those present took the covenant; published as *The Hearts Ingagement* (1643), his address responded to objections to the oath. After the royalists failed to capture Hull, Coleman described the siege in *Huls Pillar of Providence Erected* (1644), attributing the city's deliverance to divine providence. On 12 September 1644 he preached another fast sermon to both houses of parliament, encouraging them to persevere in the war despite the terrible things that God's corrective rod might inflict on them; the sermon was published as *Gods Unusuall Answer to a Solemne Fast* (1644).

Coleman ignited a controversy by his fast sermon *Hopes Deferred and Dashed* (1645) to the House of Commons on 30 July 1645 in which he called for unity in the church by establishing as few things as possible on a *jure divino* basis, requiring clear scriptural support for all precepts espoused as divine, limiting the burden of government on ministers to what Christ designated, and recognizing that a Christian magistrate is a governor in the church. Prelacy, in his judgement, was 'the Grand-causer' of the civil war (p. 33), and he favoured presbyterian polity, although of an Erastian rather than a Scottish form. Although his views of independency were mixed he opposed gathered churches because of their inability to provide adequate support to clergy and their willingness to permit the unlearned to become ministers. His assertion that Scottish commissioners and Independents hindered unity so offended the former that he had to apologize on 1 August. Unsatisfied, George Gillespie attacked him in an appendix to *A Sermon* (1645) in which he averred that Coleman's proposed cure for disunity was worse than the disease and struck at the root of ecclesiastical government. Other Scottish ministers joined Gillespie in defending the church's unimpeded power to excommunicate against Coleman's Erastian position, and Adoniram Byfield, another member of the assembly, charged Coleman with slighting that body and 'our Sister churches' in *A Brief View of Mr. Coleman his New-Modell of Church Government* (1645).

In *A Brotherly Examination Re-Examined* (1646) Coleman responded to Gillespie, reiterating his preference for presbyterian polity but insisting on parliament's right to establish the church government it considers best. Replying in *Nihil respondes* ('1645'), Gillespie accused Coleman of propagating doctrine repugnant to the solemn league and covenant and treating parliament and the assembly derogatorily. Coleman defended himself against Gillespie and Byfield in *Male dicis maledicis* (1646), in part by insisting

that his views essentially accorded with Byfield's. Gillespie retorted, accusing Coleman in *Male audis* (1646) of having wronged the Church of Scotland and opposed the word of God, the solemn league and covenant, and parliamentary ordinances.

Coleman was not without supporters. A skilled Hebraist, he was known as Rabbi Coleman. The most prominent Erastian pamphleteer, he enjoyed the respect of Thomas Case, Thomas Edwards, Thomas Fuller, Lewis du Moulin, and Richard Baxter despite their differences of opinion. On 2 October 1645 he preached a thanksgiving sermon to the House of Commons, later that year he was invited to become the minister at St Bride's, Fleet Street (though he declined), and in March 1646 Robert Baillie complained about his influence with attorneys in the House of Commons. At that time Coleman was translating the writings of Erastus on excommunication, but on 18 March he was stricken with a fever, and four or five days later, according to Baillie, Coleman died in London as a consequence of divine judgment; he was buried in the chancel at St Peter Cornhill on 30 March. His widow retired to Blyton, where, on 7 February 1652, she made a will leaving property to her nephews and nieces in the Burton family; it was proved on 26 September 1653. RICHARD L. GREAVES

Sources Wood, *Ath. Oxon.*, new edn, 3.211–12 • Wood, *Ath. Oxon.: Fasti* (1815), 379, 398 • *The letters and journals of Robert Baillie*, ed. D. Laing, 2 (1841), 360, 364 • R. S. Paul, *The assembly of the Lord: politics and religion in the Westminster assembly and the 'Grand debate'* (1985) • W. M. Lamont, *Godly rule: politics and religion, 1603–1660* (1969) • *JHC*, 2 (1640–42), 543 • W. H. Coates, A. Steele Young, and V. F. Snow, eds., *The private journals of the Long Parliament*, 3 vols. (1982–92) • A. F. Mitchell and J. Struthers, eds., *Minutes of the sessions of the Westminster assembly of divines* (1874) • *CSP dom.*, 1645–7, 127 • Tai Liu, *Puritan London: a study of religion and society in the City parishes* (1986) • J. T. Cliffe, *The puritan gentry: the great puritan families of early Stuart England* (1984) • *Walker rev.*, 46–7 • will, PRO, PROB 11/228, sig. 207 [Elizabeth Coleman] • admin., PRO, PROB 6/21 [Thomas Coleman], fol. 58v • G. W. G. Leveson-Gower, ed., *A register of the christninges, burialles & weddings within the parish of St Peters upon Cornhill*, Harleian Society, 1 (1877)

Archives DWL, minutes of the sessions of the Assembly of Divines, 4 Aug 1643–25 March 1652, 3 vols.

Coleman [Colman], **Walter** (1600–1645), Franciscan friar, missionary, and writer, was born in 1600 in Cannock, Staffordshire, the son of Walter Coleman (d. c.1620) and his second wife, Elizabeth (d. 1618), daughter of Humphrey Whitgreave; his mother's family later sheltered Charles II at Mosley Hall near Wolverhampton in 1651. He had a brother named John and a sister, Dorothy. In September 1616 he was sent to the English College at Douai, where he was known as Walter Whitgreave; it seems that the boys there often used their mothers' names. A companion of his was Christopher Davenport, who joined the Franciscans the following year, and would later welcome Walter into the order. In 1617 Walter was said to have been sent to Louvain to escape the plague. He returned to England, but was later back on the continent to continue his education, and after the deaths of his parents he became a Franciscan at Douai in 1625, taking the name Christopher.

After his religious profession, probably in 1626, and his ordination to the priesthood he was sent back to England

Walter Coleman (1600–1645), by unknown engraver, pubd 1649

about 1630. On landing he was stopped and searched. His unusual clothing aroused suspicion, and his refusal to take the oath of allegiance got him thrown into prison; but he was bailed out by friends and was able to proceed to London. During his ministry there he took up again the writing of verse and, completing a work he had already begun, he published about 1632 *La dance machabre, or, Death's Duel*, which he dedicated to Queen Henrietta Maria. In it he was concerned with the need to prepare well for death and descanted on vices and virtues, as St Francis had told his friars to do. He prefixed the poem with the commendations of James Shirley and others.

After labouring as a missioner for some years Coleman returned to Douai for rest and recollection, and while there he prepared for the press a book in verse on the religious controversies of the time and also translated into English a life of St Angela; however, copies of these works were not found by Richard Mason, his contemporary biographer. Having spent some more years at Douai, Coleman went back to England about 1640 in disguise. An affable man, he mingled easily with others. However, he was eventually picked up by the priest hunters, and on 8 December 1641, on trial with six other priests, he was condemned on the testimony of one Wadsworth to be hanged, drawn, and quartered on 13 December. The French ambassador intervened on their behalf, and King Charles I asked parliament to pardon them; parliament wanted them condemned, but the king put the responsibility for this on parliament's shoulders, and nothing was

done. One of the priests died that December. The civil war was disastrous for the others in prison. Coleman remained in Newgate, where he died in 1645.

IGNATIUS FENNESSY

Sources Angelus à Sancto Francisco [R. Mason], *Certamen seraphicum provinciae Angliae pro sancta Dei ecclesia*, 2nd edn (Quaracchi, 1885), 211–18 · E. Hyde, earl of Clarendon, *The history of the rebellion and civil wars in England*, 3 vols. (1702–4), vol. 1 · R. Challoner, *Memoirs of missionary priests*, 2 vols. (1741–2), vol. 2 · C. Talbot, ed., *Miscellanea: recusant records*, Catholic RS, 53 (1961) · R. Trappes-Lomax, ed., *The English Franciscan nuns, 1619–1821, and the Friars Minor of the same province, 1618–1761*, Catholic RS, 24 (1922) · O. Shipley, 'Extracts from *La dance machabre, or, Death's duel*, by Walter Colman: *c*.1632', *Irish Ecclesiastical Record*, 4th ser., 22 (1907), 193–9 · E. H. Burton and T. L. Williams, eds., *The Douay College diaries, third, fourth and fifth, 1598–1654*, 1–2, Catholic RS, 10–11 (1911) · A. Hope, *Franciscan martyrs in England* (1878) · Gillow, *Lit. biog. hist.*, vol. 1 · J. M. Stone, *Faithful unto death: an account of the sufferings of the English Franciscans … contemporary records* (1892) · Father Thaddeus [F. Hermans], *The Franciscans in England, 1600–1850* (1898) · H. S. Reinmuth, 'Coleman, Walter', *New Catholic encyclopedia* (1967–89) · C. G. Herbermann and others, eds., *The Catholic encyclopedia* (1907–22) · *DNB* · C. H. Poole and R. Markland, eds., *Staffordshire poets* (1928) · B. Camm, *Nine martyr monks* (1931)

Likenesses line engraving, BM, NPG; repro. in Angelus à Sancto Francisco, *Certamen seraphicum* (1649) [*see illus.*] · portrait, repro. in Father Thaddeus, *Franciscans in England*

Coleman, William Higgins (*c*.1816–1863), botanist, was born in Middlesex, the son of John Coleman and his wife, Constance. Following early education at the Blue Coat School, Hertford, he went in February 1832 to St John's College, Cambridge, where he graduated BA in 1836 and MA in 1838. He was ordained deacon and priest at Lincoln in 1840. During his sojourn at Cambridge Coleman became a compulsive compiler of floristic lists, and in 1839 discovered the great pignut, *Bunium bulbocastanum* L., a species new to the British Isles. In the summer of 1836 he obtained a scholastic post near East Grinstead, Sussex, where he remained for six months. There he produced his best-known plant list, the manuscript of which was edited by T. C. G. Rich and published in 1994 under the title *W. H. Coleman's Flora of East Grinstead (1836)*. During 1837 Coleman moved to Essex, where he taught at Dedham grammar school, returning to Hertford in the following year and possibly becoming a master at Christ's Hospital, Hertford.

In 1841, in association with the Revd Richard Holden Webb (1806–1880), the compilation of a flora of Hertfordshire was announced. In the survey that followed Coleman recognized the specific status of the river waterdropwort *Oenanthe fluviatilis*, and identified the hybrid sedge *Carex boenninghauseniana* Weihe as new to the British flora. During 1847 he was teaching in Ashby-de-la-Zouch, Leicestershire, and in 1849 moved to Dunster, Somerset. Meanwhile, Webb had published the first part of *Flora Hertfordiensis*, citing Coleman as the senior co-author. The book contained innovations which were utilized by later local flora writers and set a new standard for the geographical study of British plants.

Back in Leicestershire and with the aid of the Revd Andrew Bloxam (1801–1878) Coleman studied the critical genus *Rubus* (which includes blackberries and raspberries) as well as the floristics of the county. Coleman remained unmarried and died at Burton upon Trent, Staffordshire, on 12 September 1863. His manuscript (with Bloxam) 'Flora Leicestrensis' passed to his friend Edwin Brown (1818–1876), and thence to the Leicester Museum.

D. H. KENT

Sources W. H. Coleman's flora of East Grinstead (1836), ed. T. C. G. Rich (1994), 1–3 · A. R. Horwood and C. W. F. Noel, The flora of Leicestershire and Rutland … with biographies of former botanists (1620–1933) (1933), 211–12 · H. C. Watson, Topographical botany, revised 2nd edn (1883), 540–41 · A. R. Pryor, A flora of Hertfordshire, ed. B. D. Jackson (1887) · CGPLA Eng. & Wales (1863)
Archives Bolton Museum, Lancashire, botanical notes · Hitchin Museum, Hertfordshire, notes for Hertfordshire flora · Leicester Museum · Linn. Soc., botanical catalogue · NHM, botanical catalogue · RBG Kew, botanical catalogues · U. Cam., department of plant sciences
Wealth at death under £800: administration, 25 Nov 1863, CGPLA Eng. & Wales

Coleman, William Stephen (1829–1904), book illustrator and painter, was born at Horsham, Sussex, and baptized there on 28 August 1836, one of the twelve children of William Thomas Coleman, a surgeon, and his wife, Henrietta Dendy. His sister Helen *Angell (1847–1884) became well known as a flower painter. Coleman trained as a surgeon, but never practised. Instead he became interested in natural history and published Our Woodlands, Heaths, and Hedges (1859) and British Butterflies (1860), illustrated by himself. He also helped to illustrate other books, mainly on natural history, assisted by his sister Rebecca Coleman. He provided the illustrations for some of J. G. Wood's natural history books including Common Objects of the Country (1858), Our Garden Friends (1864), and Common British Moths (1870), all published by Routledge in a series of shilling handbooks on natural history which were frequently reprinted. Among other books illustrated by Coleman were J. C. Atkinson's Sketches in Natural History (1861) and British Birds' Eggs and Nests (1861) and T. Moore's British Ferns (1861). He also designed the heading for The Field newspaper.

Coleman painted many watercolour landscapes, which proved very popular. In the 1860s he began to depict young girls. Two of his paintings are in the Victoria and Albert Museum: Girl, with a Basket of Coral, Seated Near the Shore and Girl with Shell. He also designed Christmas cards. A member of the management committee of the Dudley Gallery from the beginning, he contributed to the first exhibition there in 1865. He continued to exhibit until 1879, and remained on the committee until 1881. In addition he exhibited at the Royal Society of Painters in Water Colours from 1866 to 1899.

In 1869 Coleman entered on a third artistic career: he joined the Copeland factory in the Potteries, and painted china plaques. Later that year he moved to Minton's, in order to work with their famous turquoise colour. Inspired by Japanese prints, his tableware designs included the 'Game Plate' and the 'Naturalist' set of herbs, shellfish, butterflies, birds, and vegetables, and dessert services with maidens in oriental settings. In 1871 he became head of the new Minton's Art Pottery Studio in Kensington Gore, close to the South Kensington Museum, set up by Herbert Minton to enable eminent artists to paint on porcelain and earthenware. This grew out of the South Kensington Museum porcelain-painting class, where from 1867 to 1870 women students painted Minton tile blanks for the decoration of the grill room at the museum. Among Coleman's most successful designs during his two years at the studio were porcelain plaques decorated with scantily clad or nude young girls, women, and children, a fish bowl decorated with fish and aquatic plants, and circular bottles decorated with plants and birds in turquoise and blue. He also attracted designers such as Christopher Dresser. Although he gave up his position as art director in 1873, he continued to paint on Minton blanks and use the studio kilns until it burnt down in 1875, and he exhibited his Minton designs at the Vienna Exhibition in 1873 and the Paris Exhibition of 1878. Examples of his ceramic works are in the Victoria and Albert Museum. After 1873 he worked as a freelance designer, painter, and illustrator.

Coleman died after a long illness at his home, 11 Hamilton Gardens, St John's Wood, on 22 March 1904, survived by his widow. ANNE PIMLOTT BAKER

Sources The Times (28 March 1904) · J. L. Roget, A history of the 'Old Water-Colour' Society, 2 vols. (1891) · Lloyds Weekly Newspaper (9 Oct 1904) · The Queen (22 Oct 1904) · Wood, Vic. painters, 3rd edn · S. Houfe, The dictionary of British book illustrators and caricaturists, 1800–1914 (1978) · Mallalieu, Watercolour artists · J. Jones, Minton: the first two hundred years of design and production (1993), chap. 8 · E. Aslin and P. Atterbury, Minton, 1798–1910 (1976), 67–71 · L. Lambourne and J. Hamilton, eds., British watercolours in the Victoria and Albert Museum (1980) · IGI
Likenesses F. C. King, portrait

Colenso, Frances Ellen (1849–1887). See under Colenso, Harriette Emily (1847–1932).

Colenso, Harriette Emily (1847–1932), missionary and political activist, was born on 30 June 1847 at Tharston, Norfolk, the eldest daughter of John William *Colenso (1814–1883), first bishop of Natal, and his wife, (Sarah) Frances Bunyon (1816–1893). She had two sisters and three brothers. Her sister **Frances Ellen Colenso** (1849–1887) was born on 30 May 1849 at Forncett, also in Norfolk. The youngest child of the family, Agnes Mary (1855–1932), became Harriette's lifelong stalwart supporter; her brothers Robert John (1850–1926) and Francis Ernest (1852–1910) became a doctor and an actuary respectively. Both settled in England, but Francis continued to give unstinting support to his sisters in their controversies.

Harriette Colenso's appearance was pleasing, and she could be charming and humorous as well as strident and cutting. Her youth was spent at Forncett and Bishopstowe (Ekukanyeni), the estate granted to her father about 5 miles outside Pietermaritzburg, Natal. She became a fluent Zulu linguist. With her sisters, she was a pupil at Winnington Hall, Cheshire, during the early 1860s, when

Bishop Colenso—then at the centre of theological controversy—returned with his family to Britain.

Frances Ellen Colenso probably responded more warmly than her sisters to the literary and cultural impulses that the young Colensos experienced in these years. She also attended Winnington Hall (c.1862–1864) and subsequently studied at the Slade School of Art in London. She enjoyed the friendship of Georgiana Burne-Jones, wife of the painter. Although an aspiring artist, she was also the author of works of fiction and literary sketches. Her best-known works, however, were *My Chief and I* (published in 1880, but—apart from a sequel—written earlier) and the *History of the Zulu Wars* (1880), which were intended to support her father's criticism of official policy and to defend the reputation of Colonel Anthony Durnford, the man whom she could not marry because he was already caught in an unhappy marriage. Durnford was blamed by Natal colonists for the death of colonial volunteers in the skirmish at the Bushman's River pass in 1873; later, Chelmsford made him the scapegoat for the British disaster at Isandlwana.

Harriette Colenso remained uninterruptedly in Natal between 1864 and 1890, although all her siblings either visited Britain again or were educated there. In addition to her responsibilities on the mission station, she accompanied her father on his diocesan visits in Natal and when he went to Grahamstown and Cape Town in 1880. She served a vigorous apprenticeship in political controversy when she assisted her father over the Langalibalele affair.

On the death of Bishop Colenso in June 1883, Harriette Colenso became the acknowledged family leader: when fire destroyed their home in September 1884, it was she who decided the Colenso women would remain at Bishopstowe, living in a farm cottage. She also took over her father's role of advising Frances Ellen in her political writings, helping in the production of the massive and ill-digested two volumes of *The Ruin of Zululand* (1884–5), and supervising the family collaboration with 'Sir' George Cox over the *Life of Bishop Colenso* (1888–9). Neither work was well received. After suffering for several years from consumption, Frances Ellen died on 28 April 1887 in lodgings at Ventnor in the Isle of Wight, perhaps of a heart attack. The family grieved, but emphasized the causes she had championed.

Like her father after 1873, Harriette Colenso was bitterly opposed to arbitrary white authority over the black population of Natal, and she undertook decades of controversy on behalf of the Zulu people. During this period Zulu land was partitioned (1886), and part was annexed to Britain as a crown colony. In 1897 the white-dominated colony of Natal incorporated this previously separate colony of Zululand.

Harriette Colenso condemned policies hostile to Zulu cohesion. She supported Dinuzulu ka Cetshwayo, as the son of the man her father befriended, and hoped that Britain (later Natal) would acknowledge and guide his leadership of a cohesive Zulu nation. During many Zulu crises, Harriette's voluminous letters, *inter alia* to the Aborigines Protection Society, her use of the Bishopstowe press, and

her political pamphlets (some far from models of clarity) were evidence of her commitment. She twice visited Britain in the 1890s to appeal to the Colonial Office, address varied audiences, and lobby parliamentarians. She later gave evidence to important government commissions of inquiry and was well known to some of the early leaders of the African National Congress. She was the lifelong friend of Alice Werner, whose interest in African languages Harriette confirmed.

Nevertheless, the Zulu people lost more and more land. Dinuzulu was twice arraigned before special—and suspect—courts in 1888–9 and 1908–9. After conviction at Eshowe in 1889, Dinuzulu and two uncles were sent to St Helena, where Harriette Colenso twice visited them. When they were repatriated in 1898, she accompanied them. Dinuzulu was arrested again in 1907 after the Bambatha uprising and sentenced to imprisonment for harbouring dependants of a rebel leader. At both trials Harriette devoted money, energy, intellect, and legal acumen to the defence, attended the court proceedings assiduously, and encouraged appeals to Britain. In 1910 Louis Botha, first prime minister of the Union of South Africa, freed Dinuzulu shortly after the Union of South Africa was constituted. Dinuzulu was not allowed to return to Zululand but located near Middelburg in the Transvaal, where Harriette Colenso visited him.

Harriette Colenso believed she had the support of the 'better part' of the Natal colonists. Influenced by Harry Escombe, future prime minister of Natal, she supported responsible government for Natal and in January 1895 she telegraphed to London her view that the annexation of Zululand to Natal should precede the exiles' return. Harriette was later disappointed by Escombe but did not quarrel with him. When he died in 1899, she sought the goodwill of other Natal politicians. In 1908 a white audience in Pietermaritzburg listened to her ideas on 'native policy' with respect, but most white Natalians were hostile and contemptuous.

For most of their lives Harriette and Agnes Colenso lived at Bishopstowe, where they continued the mission. They held services, conducted a school, and republished some of their father's works of special value to missions. In 1899 they rebuilt a house (now a national monument) on the ruins of the old home and were living there when their brother Frank visited them in 1900.

Through decades of bitter ecclesiastical controversy between rival Anglican groups, Harriette Colenso fought hard to secure the survival of the Church of England in Natal. In 1886 she persuaded leading laymen to select 'Sir' George Cox as Colenso's successor, but Cox was denied consecration. William Ayerst was then chosen, but he, too, was not consecrated. Harriette Colenso had nothing to do with the selection of Ayerst, but she had much to do with the opposition to Arthur Hamilton Baynes, chosen by the archbishop of Canterbury to reconcile the divided Anglicans of Natal. Harriette argued that, because Baynes had signed the constitution of the Church of the Province of South Africa, he should not be accepted as bishop of the

Church of England. The church council of the Church of England agreed with her, but Baynes and his successor won over the separate vestries of individual congregations. In October 1897 even St Peter's, Colenso's own cathedral, reached an agreement with the Church of the Province of South Africa. Harriette subsequently interrupted a service to make a public protest and then withdrew.

Until 1910 judicial decisions of the 1880s denied the Church of the Province control of church property. Legislation was necessary, but attempts to have laws enacted failed in 1898 and—after vigorous contention—in 1903. When, in 1909, yet another bill was brought before the Natal parliament, Harriette Colenso urged and organized resistance. She attended the sessions of the Natal parliament and would have addressed the upper house if given timely opportunity. Nevertheless, the bill was passed in Natal and accepted by the British government as the Church Properties Act of 1910. In terms of this law each Colenso sister was allowed an annual pension of £150. Harriette thought this a politically motivated sop to conscience. She applied unsuccessfully to the courts to compel the Church of the Province of South Africa to pay a pension to Moses Sibisi, the catechist of St Mary's, the 'native' church in Pietermaritzburg where the Colensos worshipped. When the Colenso women and the Bishopstowe tenants were evicted, the Church of the Province sold off the land in individual plots to German settlers.

Harriette Colenso thought of moving near the exiled Dinuzulu but instead lived first in central Pietermaritzburg and then at Sweetwaters. Dinuzulu died in 1913. Harriette attended the obsequies and helped influence the choice of his heir. Though disquieted by the possible direction of Union policy, she realized that she could no longer undertake what she might previously have attempted. The Colensos' own household of retainers and black children absorbed much attention. Harriette and Agnes Colenso occasionally visited Durban to keep in touch with Christ Church, Addington, which had not joined the Church of the Province of South Africa. Harriette was always concerned for the black congregations that maintained the Colenso connection and was in touch with other black pastors. When the prince of Wales visited Pietermaritzburg in 1925, the sisters attended the racecourse gathering of black people. The only whites present, they were greeted affectionately by sons of men they had befriended. As they grew older and more frail, they withdrew more and more from white society. They both died in 1932 at Sweetwaters, Harriette on 2 June and Agnes a few weeks later on 23 July. They were buried alongside their mother in the cemetery in Pietermaritzburg.

There are many difficulties in assessing the role of the Colenso sisters. Radical historians are impatient of white missionaries, and it is disconcerting for the Church of the Province of South Africa, so vigorously critical of twentieth-century apartheid, to recall what was shabby in the way the Colensos were treated earlier. In addition, current political perspectives blur the image of the Colensos,

especially Harriette: Zulu loyalists appear reluctant to recognize the role of a white woman in fostering Zulu nationality. On the other hand, opponents of political movements based on ethnicity are uneasy about the way the Colensos praised Zulu national identity. In their own view the Colensos were simply loyal to their father's memory and his commitment 'to love righteousness and deal justly'. Harriette's best-known Zulu name, uDhledhlwe ('walking stick'), marked her devoted support of all her father stood for.   B. M. NICHOLLS

Sources S. Marks, 'Harriette Colenso and the Zulus, 1874–1913', *Journal of African History*, 4 (1963), 403–11 · S. Marks, *Reluctant rebellion: the 1906–1908 disturbances in Natal* (1970) · L. Swart, 'The work of Harriette Emily Colenso in relationship to Dinuzulu ka Cetshwayo culminating in the treason trial of 1908–1909', MA diss., University of Natal, 1968 · W. Rees, *Colenso letters from Natal* (1958) · H. C. Swaisland, 'The Aborigines Protection Society and British southern and west Africa', DPhil diss., U. Oxf., 1968 · D. R. Edgecombe, 'The influence of the Aborigines Protection Society on British policy towards black Africans and Cape Coloureds in South Africa', PhD diss., U. Cam., 1976 · N. Cope, *To bind the nation: Solomon ka Dinuzulu* (1993) · B. Burnett, *Anglicans in Natal* (1956) · S. Spencer, *British settlers in Natal: a biographical register*, 4 (1987) · B. M. Nicholls, 'Harriette Colenso and the Irish connection', *Southern African Irish Studies*, 1 (1991), 44–55 · B. M. Nicholls, 'Colenso letters', *Natalia*, 21 (1991), 17–30 · B. M. Nicholls, 'The Colenso endeavour in its context, 1887–1897', PhD diss., University of Natal, 1997 · F. E. Colenso, *My chief and I*, ed. M. J. Daymond (1994) · P. L. Merrett, 'Frances Ellen Colenso, 1849–1887: her life and times in relation to the Victorian stereotype', diss., University of Cape Town, 1980

Archives Bodl. RH, Aborigines Protection Society MSS · Bodl. RH · University of Natal, Durban, Killie Campbell Africana Library | Natal Diocesan Archives, Pietermaritzburg, Tatham MSS · National Library of South Africa, Cape Town, Schreiner MSS

Likenesses photographs, Natal Government Archives, Pietermaritzburg · photographs, Natal Diocesan Archives, Pietermaritzburg · photographs, University of Natal, Durban, Killie Campbell Africana Library · photographs, Bodl. RH, Colenso MSS (F. E. Colenso)

Colenso, John William (1814–1883), bishop of Natal, was born at St Austell, Cornwall, on 24 January 1814, the eldest child of John William Colenso, mineral agent for part of the duchy of Cornwall. Originally dissenters, his parents and their four children became members of the Church of England in his adolescence. For four years he attended the mathematical and classical school in St Austell. His mother, whose maiden name was Blackmore, died when he was fifteen and at about the same time a tin mine in which his father had an interest was flooded by the sea. This appears to have ended his formal schooling for he was obliged, in order to help the family finances, to accept employment as an usher at a Dartmouth school. He seems already to have made up his mind that he wished to be ordained and he was also showing a marked talent for mathematics. He was able, after private preparation, to enter St John's College, Cambridge, as a sizar on 22 May 1832, at the age of eighteen. Supporting himself by private teaching and what he could earn in the way of prizes and exhibitions, and with some small financial assistance from his mother's family, his life at Cambridge was hard and lonely but academically successful. He was second wrangler and Smith's prizeman in 1836, and was elected to a fellowship in the college in March 1837.

John William Colenso (1814–1883), by Samuel Sidley, 1866

Early career and South Africa Colenso was appointed mathematics tutor at Harrow School in 1838 and was ordained in 1839. In material terms this, too, was a period of hardship and financial stringency. The school was in a less than buoyant state and, though Colenso ran a boarding-house, usually a source of additional income for an assistant master, his house was destroyed by fire and he was soon several thousand pounds in debt, which hung over him for years. He returned to St John's College from 1842 to 1846 and from Cambridge published two textbooks, one on algebra in 1841 and one on arithmetic in 1843. Colenso's *Arithmetic*, in particular, was a considerable success and earned him substantial royalties. He married on 8 January 1846 (Sarah) Frances (1816–1893), daughter of Robert Bunyon of Highgate, head of the London office of the Norwich Union insurance company. Marriage necessitated resigning his fellowship, but his wife's family obtained for him the living of Forncett St Mary in Norfolk in the same year. The conscientious performance of his parochial duties in this quite small parish still left him time to coach pupils in mathematics and to edit the journal of the Society for the Propagation of the Gospel.

Colenso had been brought up an earnest evangelical, but had begun to question some of the doctrines usually associated with that tradition. Before his marriage, his future wife had introduced him to Frederick Denison Maurice, whose ideas were to influence him profoundly. A belief in the universal fatherhood of God and the unity of all humanity, together with doubts about 'the endlessness of future punishment', began to characterize his preaching. He does not appear, however, at this stage in his life,

to have regarded the Bible as other than literally true. In 1853, just as he was planning the publication of a volume of sermons to be dedicated to Maurice (which was to earn the sharp disapproval of the evangelical *Record*), his interest in missions brought him to the notice of Bishop Robert Gray of Cape Town, whose diocese was being divided and who was looking for potential bishops for two new sees. In April 1853 Colenso accepted the offer of the bishopric of Natal. Having been issued with royal letters patent, he was consecrated on 30 November, St Andrew's day, of that year and sailed for Natal almost immediately. His plan was to acquire as much information as possible so that he could return to England to raise money and recruit workers. On his return he published *Ten Weeks in Natal* (1855), setting out his impressions and his plans for the future, and also dealing with certain fundamental missionary principles on which he began to earn a reputation for unorthodoxy. He argued, for instance, that polygamy (which he disliked) was not incompatible with Christian morality.

In May 1855 Colenso arrived in Natal with his wife and children and a number of workers for the new diocese. His first task was to establish his headquarters at Bishopstowe, 6 miles east of Pietermaritzburg. Unfailingly energetic, by 1857 he had completed the cathedral in Pietermaritzburg and churches in Durban and Richmond, and within seven years of his arrival he had opened four mission stations in Natal and one in Zululand. And he had soon learned enough of the Zulu language to be able to teach and confirm.

Colenso from the first regarded the indigenous people, who called him Sobantu ('father of the people'), as his chief responsibility. He chose to live outside the capital of the colony so that his home at Bishopstowe could also be his chief mission station, Ekukanyeni. With white colonists he was less patient and less popular. Because he tried to do away with pew rents and to insist on strict observance of the provisions of the Book of Common Prayer, he was attacked as a ritualist and his effigy was burnt in the market square in Durban. The leading clergyman in Natal before the bishop's arrival was James Green, dean of Pietermaritzburg, who was an advanced Tractarian and, from the first, bitterly critical of Colenso's broad-church opinions.

The bishop was able, as early as 1855, to publish an elementary Zulu grammar and, four years later, an abridgement entitled *First Steps in Zulu*. His linguistic ability was also put to work in translating the whole of the New Testament, several books of the Old Testament, and much of the Book of Common Prayer, while his *Three Native Accounts of a Visit of the Bishop of Natal* (1860) made available Zulu texts, with grammatical notes and an English translation. His *Zulu–English Dictionary* (1861) was a substantial volume with more than 10,000 entries. Most of these works were printed, under his direction, on his own press at Ekukanyeni.

Old Testament scholarship In presenting Christianity to the indigenous people Colenso was not prepared to deny or ignore the findings of natural scientists. When questioned by Zulu converts, he admitted that much of the Old Testament was not factually true. Even more important, he came increasingly to feel that he could not present Old Testament accounts of massacres as if these were in accordance with the will of God, while telling his African hearers that battle and murder were immoral. He began to believe that the supposed acts of God as presented by some Old Testament texts were little better than the savageries committed during the Indian mutiny of 1857–8. It was this moral difficulty that first kindled his interest in biblical criticism. Because the questions of his converts played some part in the process, too, his opponents joked that, having gone to convert the heathen, the bishop had in fact been converted by them. However, 'conversion', as understood by most missionaries, played a small part in Colenso's vocation. He desired to Christianize Zulu culture rather than to remove individuals from their traditional 'heathen' way of life. He maintained his attitude on polygamy, agreeing with Theophilus Shepstone (1817–1893), secretary for native affairs in the colonial administration, that to insist on monogamy for Christian converts would, by putting aside other wives and calling the status of their children in question, entail the worse evil of destabilizing traditional society.

Colenso published a commentary on Romans in 1861 which stressed God's love for all mankind and insisted that his purpose was to destroy sin rather than punish it. This tendency to universalism was thought to contradict the Thirty-Nine Articles, and its implications for his sacramental theology were particularly unacceptable to the Tractarian clergy. The first volume of the bishop's *Pentateuch and the Book of Joshua Critically Examined* was published in 1862. It was typical of his immense and disciplined energy that he produced it, after reading all the works of German biblical scholarship on which he could lay his hands, in a matter of a few months. Kurtz and Hengstenberg seemed to him dishonest; Ewald's erudition impressed him; but Bleek and De Wette he thought nearest the truth. The technique he employed in applying critical methods to the first six books of the Bible was one which he would later use to great effect in attacking colonial government publications: if one could demonstrate that allegedly factual statements were untrue, one need not be bound by any principles said to be founded on them. If, for example, one could show that the Israelites could not possibly have camped in one place in the desert, as described in Exodus, without being buried under a mound of dung produced by their flocks and herds, then the text (since it was mistaken) could not be the product of divine direction and therefore one need not believe that God had commended some cruel atrocity. Unfortunately the first volume was chiefly concerned with the negative and destructive part of this programme. In comparison with some of the German critics, Colenso was moderate. He made no great contribution to the advance of scholarship, though it is possible that he influenced Abraham Kuenen (1828–1891) in his identification of P as the latest of the Pentateuchal sources and played some part in the growing consensus that Deuteronomy was Josiah's law book. Modern scholars inevitably regard Colenso's work as outdated and, while some some historians have treated him as little more than a figure of fun, others regard his critical writings as not insignificant. At the time this work gave great offence, alienating even F. D. Maurice and E. H. Browne, who had both previously been his friends. (The later volumes were a constructive reassessment of the Hexateuch in the light of developing scholarship, but were largely unread and unremembered. The seventh and final volume did not appear until 1879.)

Prosecution for heresy: the 'Colenso case' Bishop Gray, who had been created metropolitan by royal letters patent when his diocese was divided, was in the process of developing a synodical structure for the Anglican church in South Africa, including ecclesiastical courts for the new province. In this process Colenso had played a full part, but he was now delated for heresy before the metropolitan's court for teaching contained in his commentary on Romans and in *Pentateuch and … Joshua*. Gray sat, with two other bishops as assessors, found Colenso guilty, and deposed him from office on 16 December 1863. Colenso appeared by proxy, but only to protest against the court's jurisdiction. When he ignored its sentence, he was formally excommunicated. Gray had already been involved in an attempt to exercise ecclesiastical discipline over a clergyman in his diocese, and it rapidly became clear that his letters patent conferred on him no coercive jurisdiction. On Colenso's seeking redress from the civil courts by means of a petition to the crown, the sentence was set aside in 1865 by the judicial committee of the privy council, which held that the letters patent of both bishops were void since the Cape and Natal each possessed its own legislature. Nor did Colenso's oath of canonical obedience give the metropolitan any authority to depose him, since the letters patent were held, despite their invalidity, to have created ecclesiastical persons who could not be unmade except by the crown. In addition, because the letters patent could not confer jurisdiction, Colenso ought not to have taken an oath of obedience to a metropolitan who had no legal authority to demand it.

Gray and his supporters believed passionately that the church must be free from interference by the civil courts and achieved the passage of a constitution for the 'Church of the Province of South Africa' which enshrined this. In Natal it was regarded by many as an attempt to create a church different from the Church of England. However a new bishop, W. K. Macrorie, was appointed under this constitution and consecrated in Cape Town, without royal mandate, as 'bishop of Maritzburg' on 25 January 1869. Schism in Natal was inevitable and was to continue until after Colenso's death. A majority of the English bishops agreed to inhibit Colenso from officiating in their dioceses, but more liberal opinion supported him, and Dean Stanley was to invite him to preach in Westminster Abbey. In Pietermaritzburg, Green and his supporters used every device possible to exclude Colenso from the churches, but the bishop's preaching—and his notoriety—drew crowds to his services and the courts supported his right to use the buildings.

The master of the rolls, Lord Romilly, in a judgment of November 1866, pronounced Colenso to be entitled to all the property of the see. The case is cited as *Bishop of Natal v. Gladstone and others*, W. E. Gladstone being the treasurer of the Colonial Bishoprics Fund which was threatening to withhold from Colenso the income from the endowment of the diocese. In the eyes of the law he was bishop of Natal, and some two-thirds of the laity forgot their earlier suspicions of his 'popery' and supported him. The supreme court of the colony confirmed him in the possession of all land and buildings granted, donated, or bought for 'the Church of England', including all save one mission station. Macrorie and his adherents were obliged to build a new cathedral and churches, but had the support of almost all the original clergy and of the English missionary societies. Colenso's greatest difficulty lay in finding suitable clergymen: most of those who went to join him turned out to be misfits, indolent, or undesirable.

Colenso's position was weakened by hostility arising from his active championship of the Hlubi chief Langalibalele, and subsequently of the Zulu king Cetewayo. The bishop had always taken more than a passing interest in, and through his friendship with Shepstone had involved himself with, the colony's policies regarding the indigenous people. Langalibalele's offence was that in 1873 he ignored a summons to account for the failure of many of his Hlubi tribesmen to register firearms procured at the diamond fields. He had subsequently withdrawn to Basutoland, after a skirmish in which half a dozen colonial auxiliaries were killed. He was handed over to the authorities and tried, in accordance with the principles of indirect rule, under what purported to be 'native custom', in a court presided over by Lieutenant-Governor Pine as 'supreme chief'. Colenso was appalled by the procedures of this court, under which the tribal assessors gave their verdict on the first day, evidence was heard on the second, and the accused was permitted counsel on the third. The sentence was transportation to the Cape. Not only the rebel Hlubi but the neighbouring Ngwe (Putili) people suffered confiscation of land and cattle or were compelled to work on colonists' farms. Colenso at once denounced the injustice of these harshly punitive measures, offending Shepstone (who claimed to be 'the humane ruler of these natives'; Uys, 104), and campaigned in England for the imperial government to intervene. The breach with Shepstone was further widened by accusations of earlier treachery against a tribal chief made by the bishop against Shepstone's brother. In London, Lord Carnarvon, the new colonial secretary, heard the bishop, recalled Pine, and insisted on mitigation of the sentences. Many colonists in Natal turned against Colenso once more, and he became the target for much abuse.

When the Anglo-Zulu War broke out in 1879 Colenso contended that it had been precipitated by Sir Bartle Frere, the high commissioner, and that Cetewayo's strategy, when the British troops had first entered Zululand, had been purely defensive. He published a series of pamphlets sharply critical of Frere's Zulu policy and after the conclusion of the war did everything he could to put the deposed and exiled Zulu king's case in Britain. It was partly through his intervention that Cetewayo was invited to London in 1882 and received by Queen Victoria. The bishop had been made a member of the Natal native affairs commission in the previous year but, because he encouraged the Zulu people to resist government pressure, he was suspected by the Colonial Office as well as local officials of fomenting rebellion and riot. He was vilified in the Natal newspapers and became a very lonely and isolated figure. He died at Bishopstowe on 20 July 1883 and was buried in his cathedral.

Perhaps because of their isolation, Colenso's family was a very united one. Of the bishop's five children, one son (Frank) and his three unmarried daughters (Harriette Emily *Colenso, Frances, and Agnes) were committed to continuing their father's struggle for the rights of the indigenous people. His wife, who died on 23 December 1893, was an intelligent and gifted woman and an accomplished amateur water-colourist. She seems to have chosen deliberately to avoid Natal society, preferring to worship in the mission church rather than in the cathedral. She was well educated and was a friend of F. D. Maurice even before her marriage to Colenso; she maintained a regular correspondence for more than a decade with Lady Lyell, the wife of the eminent geologist Sir Charles Lyell. She supported her husband unreservedly, though quietly and from behind the scenes, and was responsible for seeing that G. W. Cox, the bishop's biographer, received such material as would put Colenso in the best possible light.

PETER HINCHLIFF

Sources G. W. Cox, *The life of John William Colenso, Bishop of Natal*, 2 vols. (1888) · P. B. Hinchliff, *John William Colenso* (1964) · J. Guy, *The heretic: a study of the life of John William Colenso* (1983) · J. Rogerson, *Old Testament criticism in the nineteenth century: England and Germany* (1984), 220–37 · W. Rees, *Colenso letters from Natal* (1958) · P. B. Hinchliff, *The Anglican church in South Africa* (1963), 64–8, 82–105 · A. O. J. Cockshut, *Anglican attitudes: a study of Victorian controversies* (1959), 88–120 · C. Lewis and G. E. Edwards, *Historical records of the Church of the Province of South Africa* (1934), 159–74, 310–39 · O. Chadwick, *The Victorian church*, 1 (1966), 550–51; 2 (1970), 90–97 · *DSAB* · C. J. Uys, *In the era of Shepstone* (1933) · *Gladstone, Diaries*

Archives Bodl. RH, family corresp. · Natal Provincial Archives, Pietermaritzburg · University of Natal, Durban, Campbell collections | Co-operative Union, Holyoake House, Manchester, letters to G. S. Holyoake · Hunt. L., letters to Frances Cobbe · Leics. RO, letters to R. Blunt · LPL, corresp. with A. C. Tait · Natal Provincial Archives, Pietermaritzburg, Carl Faye collection · National Library of South Africa, Cape Town, letters to Sir George Grey · Suffolk RO, Bury St Edmunds, copy of corresp. with Sir Bartle Frere · University of Witwatersrand, Johannesburg, Cullen Library, Church of the Province of South Africa archives

Likenesses S. Sidley, oils, 1866, NPG [*see illus.*] · Ape [C. Pellegrini], chromolithograph caricature, NPG; repro. in *VF* (28 Nov 1874) · E. Edwards, photograph, NPG · H. N. King, carte-de-visite, NPG · London Stereoscopic Company, carte-de-visite, NPG · Maull & Co., carte-de-visite, NPG · T. C. Wageman, watercolour drawing, Trinity Cam. · carte-de-visite, NPG · portrait, St John Cam.

Wealth at death £5454 1s. 7d.: administration with will, 23 Oct 1883, *CGPLA Eng. & Wales*

Colepeper, John, first Baron Colepeper (*bap.* **1600**, *d.* **1660**), politician, was born at Wigsell Manor in Salehurst, Sussex, and baptized at Salehurst on 17 August 1600. He was the second but eldest surviving son of Thomas Colepeper (*d.* 1613) and Anne Slaney (*d.* 1602). He may have studied at Peterhouse, Cambridge (1611), and at Hart Hall, Oxford (1616), as well as at the Middle Temple (1617). It seems that he then saw military service abroad; he was knighted on 14 January 1621. After his first marriage, to Philippa Snelling (*d.* 1630) on 29 October 1628, he settled at Hollingbourne in Kent and was a justice of the peace in Kent by 1638. After Philippa's death in the autumn of 1630 he married his cousin, Judith Colepeper (*bap.* 1606, *d.* 1691?), on 12 January 1631.

The Long Parliament Colepeper represented Rye, Sussex, in the Short Parliament and Kent in the Long Parliament. On 9 November 1640 he presented a petition from Kent and made a lengthy statement of the 'grievances of the Church and Common-wealth'. The most important of these he listed as 'the greater increase of papists', 'the obtruding and countenancing of many divers new ceremonies in matters of religion', 'the new canons', 'military charges', 'the heavy Tax of ship-mony', and lastly the monopolists, 'the leeches that have suck'd the Commonwealth' (*Sir John Culpeper his Speech in Parliament Concerning the Grievances of the Church and Common-Wealth*, 1641, 1–4). On 1 December he urged 'that an act may bee drawen against the growth of poperie' (*Journal*, ed. Notestein, 91). On 8 February 1641 he strongly opposed the committing of the London root-and-branch petition, and the previous week had referred to bishops as 'maine columnes of the realme' (ibid., 315). He supported the attainder of Strafford and when, on 3 May, the first army plot was revealed to the Commons, he immediately moved 'for the remonstrance and peticon of rights to be forthwith read, and then to goe to the lordes and by that we may try the effeccon of the kinge' (diary of Sir Simonds D'Ewes, BL, Harleian MS 477, fol. 28r).

Colepeper's desire to preserve episcopacy was again evident on 11 June when he moved that the statement in the preamble to the root-and-branch bill that 'the present government of the Church had been by long experience an hinderance to the full reformation of religion and to the civill state' be rephrased 'by late experience'. He believed that 'the grievances had growne from the abuse of the goverment and not from the goverment it selfe' (diary of Sir Simonds D'Ewes, BL, Harleian MS 164, fol. 217r). He was appalled at the growing threat of popular violence against the church during the summer of 1641, and on 1 September brought forward a resolution in defence of the prayer book. Throughout the summer and autumn he gradually drew closer to Charles I, whom he regarded as less of a danger to existing constitutional and ecclesiastical structures than his leading opponents. Colepeper advocated a grant to the king of tonnage and poundage for three years and worked intensively to get this passed before the debate on episcopacy was concluded, in the belief that this might enable Charles to dissolve the parliament. His strategy was linked to a proposal for a new book of rates, but this was abandoned as financially unworkable.

In November Colepeper protested against the grand remonstrance, arguing that 'all remonstrances should bee addressed to the king and not to the people, because hee only can redresse our greevances' (H. Verney, ed., *Notes of Proceedings in the Long Parliament … by Sir Ralph Verney*, CS, 1st ser., 31, 1845, 122). He similarly opposed the militia ordinance on the grounds that it would 'take the King's lawfull power from him' (*Journal*, ed. Coates, 303). On 2 January 1642 Charles appointed Colepeper a privy councillor and chancellor of the exchequer. Colepeper remained deeply committed to constitutional propriety and was embarrassed when the king, without his knowledge, attempted to arrest five members of the Commons and one member of the Lords on 4 January 1642. A desire to prove the king's integrity probably explains why he advised Charles to assent to the Bishops Exclusion Bill and the Impressment Bill. When, on 1 April, Sir Peter Wentworth queried whether Charles could be trusted any longer, Colepeper 'wondered that any man should dare to speak such language within these walls' (Coates, Young, and Snow, 2.115). On 19 May he acted as a teller against a clause that the king's oath bound him to accept bills passed by both houses for the good of the kingdom. Later that month Colepeper, who had earlier advised Charles to remove to the north of England, joined the king at York.

The civil war During the months immediately preceding the outbreak of the civil war Colepeper regularly collaborated with Falkland and Hyde in drafting the king's responses to the houses' messages and declarations. This polemical activity proved highly effective and culminated in the king's *Answer to the XIX Propositions*, which he and Falkland composed in June 1642. This presented a classic defence of royal government within the law, and asserted that the houses' terms formed 'a great chain … by which our just, antient, regal power is endeavour'd to be fetch'd down to the ground'; they thus directly threatened 'the antient, equal, happy, well-poised, and never enough commended constitution of the government of this kingdom'. The *Answer* argued that a 'regulated monarchy' was essential to 'preserve the laws in their force, and the subjects in their liberties and properties' and this commitment extended to preserving the existing features of the church 'as they are here established by law' (J. Rushworth, *Historical Collections of Private Passages of State*, 8 vols., 1680–1701, 4.725–35).

Three days after the king raised his standard at Nottingham he reluctantly agreed to send Colepeper, together with the earls of Southampton and Dorset and Sir William Uvedale, to inform the houses of his 'constant and earnest care to preserve the public peace' (Clarendon, *Hist. rebellion*, 2.304). However, although the four were permitted to deliver this message, the houses ordered them to withdraw from London immediately. Colepeper charged with Prince Rupert at the battle of Edgehill and was among those who urged the king to stand his ground. He was installed as master of the rolls on 28 January 1643, and his reluctance to surrender the chancellorship of the exchequer until 22 February caused a rift with Hyde, who had been promised the office. Colepeper sat in the Oxford parliament and soon found himself at odds with more hardline royalists over whether to pursue further talks with the houses. In the king's council he likewise urged that propositions be sent to Westminster. This did not endear him to more hawkish figures such as Digby and Prince Rupert, and there was considerable resentment at his creation as Baron Colepeper of Thoresway on 21 October 1644.

Colepeper served as one of the king's commissioners at the treaty of Uxbridge (January–February 1645). The following March, Charles appointed him to the prince of Wales's council, together with Hyde, and sent them to the west of England. Hyde, Colepeper, and the rest of the prince's council moved to Jersey in mid-April 1646, but when the prince set sail for France on 26 June Colepeper alone accompanied him. Throughout the mid-1640s Colepeper hoped to secure aid from Scotland, and to this end was prepared to make greater religious concessions than Hyde, and many other royalists, could accept. In September 1646, writing jointly with Henry Jermyn, he denied that episcopacy was 'jure divino exclusive', and together they told the king that 'the question in short is whether you will chuse to be a King of Presbitery or no King' (Bodl. Oxf., MS Clarendon 91, fols. 35v–36r). Such views prompted Hyde to beg him not to let 'the landmarkes bee removed, nor pillars upon which the fabrique relyes bee taken away' (Bodl. Oxf., MS Clarendon 29, fol. 55v), while the king 'never … much esteemed' Colepeper 'in religion' (Bruce, 30), and even told Sir William Davenant that he thought 'Culperad had no religion' (Clarendon, *Hist. rebellion*, 4.206). Equally, in another letter written jointly with Jermyn, Colepeper urged the king not to sacrifice his military powers, arguing that 'if you part with the militia, and place [it] in the Parlament as is desyred you will thereby consent to change monarchy into aristocracy' (Bodl. Oxf., MS Clarendon 91, fol. 36r). By this time Colepeper had suffered considerably for his royalist allegiance. On 22 January 1644 he was formally disabled, as a royalist, from sitting in parliament, and on 9 February the Commons ordered that Colepeper's estate was to be sequestrated and his goods sold. On 28 July 1644 the committee of the advance of money assessed him at £2000.

During the summer and autumn of 1647 Colepeper encouraged Sir John Berkeley's mission to England to promote negotiations between the king and the army. The following year, when part of the parliamentarian fleet revolted, Colepeper accompanied the prince to sea and was widely blamed for the failure of the expedition to achieve anything. After the prince and Colepeper returned to The Hague the latter's long-standing animosity with Prince Rupert flared up again. He vehemently opposed Rupert's nomination of Sir Robert Walsh as an agent for the sale of prize goods, and during one council meeting even threatened to fight Rupert. A few days later, on 23 October 1648, Walsh violently attacked Colepeper in the streets and was banished from court.

Career, 1649–1660, and relations with Edward Hyde After the execution of Charles I, royal counsels were for a while dominated by the 'Louvre' group, of which Colepeper, Jermyn, and Henrietta Maria were the most prominent members. Colepeper remained particularly keen to promote a rapprochement with the Scots, although he was anxious to secure alliances with other powers as well. He was deeply offended not to be chosen as ambassador to Spain in the spring of 1649, and the following year he was dispatched to Moscow to borrow money from the tsar. This mission proved highly successful. He was fêted in Moscow—one meal consisted of a hundred dishes of meat—and returned triumphantly in July 1650 with a loan of 20,000 roubles in corn and furs. However, with the king's defeat at Worcester the pro-Scottish activism of the Louvre group was discredited and thereafter its influence began to decline.

In the summer of 1652 Colepeper was sent to the Netherlands, then at war with the English Commonwealth, in the hope of securing armed assistance but by this time much of his influence as a royal counsellor had been eroded. An attempt to resurrect links with Scotland in May 1654 proved abortive, and a further symptom of his dwindling power came the following October when he urged Lord Percy 'to come to the King's Court for he needs helpe' (Warner, 2.113). From the mid-1650s onwards Colepeper was a much more marginal figure, and in April 1655 he professed himself 'a great stranger to all busines, especially designes in England, and was very seldom' at court (ibid., 2.252). The treaty of August 1654 between Cromwell and Mazarin required Colepeper's expulsion from French territory, and he apparently spent the rest of his exile in Flanders.

A few days after Cromwell's death Colepeper advised Hyde 'not [to] be over hasty in doing any thing in England' and warned him against a premature move which would 'only serve to unite our ennemyes'. Then followed this remarkably prescient passage:

> The person that my eye is cheefly on, as able alone to restore the King, and not absolutely avers to it, neither in his principles nor in his affections … is Monke, who commandeth absolutely at his devotion a better army … then that in England is, and in the King's quarrell can bringe with him the strength of Scotland, and soe protect the northerne countyes that he cannot faile of them in his march, the reputation whereof (if he declare) will as much give the will to the appearing of the King's party in the rest of England, as the drawing the army from the southerne, westerne and easterne countyes will give them the meanes to appeare in armes. Thus the worke will be certainly donne in spight of all opposition that can be apprehended, and the gaining of one man will alone make sure worke of the whole. (Bodl. Oxf., MS Clarendon 58, fols. 345v–346v)

Colepeper thus predicted with astonishing accuracy the chain of events which would lead to Charles II's restoration nearly two years later, and it was arguably the shrewdest insight of his political career.

Throughout the 1650s Colepeper's relationship with Hyde remained distinctly uneven. After the Restoration, Hyde claimed that although they were 'not thought to have the greatest kindness for each other, yet he knew he could agree with no other man so well in business, and was very unwilling [Colepeper] should be from the person of the King' (Clarendon, *Hist. rebellion*, 5.37). Hyde described him as 'a man of great parts, a very sharp and present wit, and an universal understanding' (*Life of … Clarendon*, 1.319). However, contemporaries frequently remarked on Hyde's poor relations with Colepeper; Lord Hatton for example thought Colepeper 'a sworne enemy to Sir E[dward] H[yde] even to death' (*Nicholas Papers*, 2.101). Yet by the later 1650s they appear to have been on increasingly friendly terms and in January 1658 Colepeper warmly congratulated Hyde on his appointment as lord chancellor. Both were agreed in opposing any plans for premature royalist insurrections within England. This did not, however, preclude negotiations with the French and Spanish monarchs, and in the autumn of 1659 Colepeper journeyed to Spain in a bid to gain some advantage for Charles from the treaty of the Pyrenees: he kept Hyde closely briefed throughout that trip. This growing closeness was reflected in Colepeper's appointment as chancellor of the exchequer in June 1660. However, he died only weeks later on 11 July, probably in London, and was buried at Hollingbourne. His estates were subsequently restored by a private act of parliament.

Hyde left a colourful portrait of Colepeper as of 'a rough nature, a hot head, and of great courage; which had engaged him in many quarrels and duels … a man of sharpness of parts, and volubility of language' (*Life of … Clarendon*, 1.106). This accords with Sir Philip Warwick's statement that Colepeper 'had an eagerness or ferocity, that made him less sociable than his other collegues' (Warwick, 195). In matters of religion, Clarendon thought Colepeper:

very indifferent; but more inclined to what was established, to avoid the accidents which commonly attend a change, without any motives from his conscience; which yet he kept to himself; and was well content to have it believed that the activity proceeded from thence. (*Life of … Clarendon*, 1.107)

This subtly nuanced account catches both the lack of an unshakeable conscientious commitment to the Church of England that both Hyde and the king had lamented in Colepeper during the later 1640s, and also the visceral attachment to established institutions that was characteristic of so many royalists. DAVID L. SMITH

Sources Clarendon, *Hist. rebellion* · *The life of Edward, earl of Clarendon … written by himself*, new edn, 3 vols. (1827) · F. W. T. Attree and J. H. L. Booker, 'The Sussex Colepepers', *Sussex Archaeological Collections*, 47 (1904), 47–81 · Keeler, *Long Parliament* · Bodl. Oxf., Clarendon MSS · GEC, *Peerage*, new edn, 3.363–4 · *The journal of Sir Simonds D'Ewes from the beginning of the Long Parliament to the opening of the trial of the earl of Strafford*, ed. W. Notestein (1923) · *The journal of Sir Simonds D'Ewes from the first recess of the Long Parliament to the withdrawal of King Charles from London*, ed. W. H. Coates (1942) · W. H. Coates, A. Steele Young, and V. F. Snow, eds., *The private journals of the Long Parliament*, 3 vols. (1982–92) · P. Warwick, *Memoires of the reigne of King Charles I* (1701) · *The Nicholas papers*, ed. G. F. Warner, 1, CS, new ser., 40 (1886) · *The Nicholas papers*, ed. G. F. Warner, 2, CS, new ser., 50 (1892) · *The Nicholas papers*, ed. G. F. Warner, 3, CS, new ser., 57 (1897) · *The Nicholas papers*, ed. G. F. Warner, 4, CS, 3rd ser., 31 (1920) · *Charles I in 1646: letters of King Charles the first to Queen Henrietta Maria*, ed. J. Bruce, CS, 63 (1856) · D. L. Smith, *Constitutional royalism and the search for settlement, c. 1640–1649* (1994)

Colepeper, Thomas (1637–1708), soldier and engineer, was born on Christmas day 1637 in Kent, possibly in either Dover or Hackington, the son of Sir Thomas Colepeper (1598–1643), governor of Dover Castle, and his wife, Barbara (1599–1643), daughter of Robert Sidney, first earl of Leicester. Sir Thomas was Lady Colepeper's second husband; her first was Thomas Smythe, first Viscount Strangford, with whom she had other children. It was to the Smythe household that Thomas went when in 1643 he was orphaned. What formal education he received seems to have been at home, where he was trained as a steward for his family estate at Stanford. Whatever the actual nature of his education, Colepeper possessed a formidable intellectual curiosity, and in later life he displayed remarkable energy in scientific pursuits.

With his half-brother Philip, second Viscount Strangford, the young Colepeper joined the royalist underground. From 1658 he claimed to be a colonel in the royal service, though he may never have actually been commissioned. Nevertheless, the council of state knew of his royalist connections, and in July 1659 ordered his appearance. He was arrested at Canterbury and sent as a prisoner to the Gatehouse in Westminster in early August. The council granted him bail of £3000 on 26 September 1659.

Like so many who devoted themselves to the Restoration, Colepeper received meagre rewards. In 1663 he claimed a grant from the Loyal and Indigent Officer's Fund, but whether he ever received one is unknown. By this time he was much in need of assistance, for his attempt to ally himself with a noble family had gone awry. About 1662 he eloped and married Frances (1638–1698), the youngest daughter of Lord Frescheville, who then refused to make her a settlement. Father and son-in-law were ultimately reconciled, but Frescheville never gave his daughter a fortune. The £300 annuity he granted her after his death in 1682 would have done little to rescue the struggling Colepeper, who had, by 1675, already sold the family estate. In any event Lord Frescheville's own estate was so heavily encumbered that it is doubtful that the annuity was regularly paid.

Colepeper's embarrassed circumstances compelled him to live by his wits and the exercise of his scientific imagination. In February 1665 he and several others petitioned the crown for a grant of marshland they planned to drain on the Lancashire coast. By September 1665 he had gained a foothold in the royal service as a gun-founder. His scientific interests led to his election to the Royal Society on 28 May 1668, not long after the crown granted him a patent for an iron hearth. In 1675 he was appointed engineer in the Ordnance office at an annual salary of £100; his work in the Ordnance office led to the invention of a grenade launcher in 1681.

Colepeper's fertile mind was, unfortunately, joined with a hot temper, and he wrecked his career as a military engineer by a rash act in the summer of 1685. On 9 July, standing near James II's bedchamber door, he met William Cavendish, fourth earl of Devonshire. The two men had a troubled relationship, inspired primarily by Colepeper's unreasonable belief that his wife should have inherited lands that Lord Frescheville sold to Devonshire's family shortly before his death. Bitter lawsuits ensued. Added to this was political animosity: Colepeper rudely demanded to know what 'an excluder' was doing at court. Devonshire, while whiggishly inclined, had in fact not been an avowed exclusionist, and gave Colepeper the lie. The result was a brawl conducted in full view of the king. Colepeper was not only bested by Devonshire, who knocked him to the floor, but also imprisoned by the king's command. On 20 July he was tried in the court of the verge of the palace, and received a savage sentence: the loss of his right hand, a fine of £1000, and life imprisonment. Under the circumstances, the royal order to sack him from the Ordnance office nine days later was no more than a minor inconvenience. Luckily, he did not suffer the full rigour of the law. His wife threw herself into his cause, and, with the help of the earl of Danby, secured his pardon. In December 1686 he petitioned James for the restoration of his place, though without success. In April the following year he had another altercation with Devonshire, who challenged him in the king's presence. Colepeper had learned his lesson, and refused the challenge; Devonshire was arrested and ultimately fined £30,000, which he never paid, and was in his turn pardoned by William III. The choleric earl assaulted Colepeper yet again in 1697, though in this case neither man was prosecuted. Colepeper, now in his sixtieth year, was, however, badly beaten.

By the time of Devonshire's last attack, Colepeper was declining into a destitute, if frenetic, old age. His penchant for invention never left him, but it never rewarded him with anything like the fame and riches he thought his due. In May 1688 he received a patent for a 'new water engine'. During William III's reign he proposed a comprehensive scheme which he guaranteed would make the king Europe's most powerful sovereign by, among other things, allowing royal naval vessels to be used as fire ships without actually burning, making all of the king's fortresses impregnable, and raising, at his own expense, a force of 12,000 men for the crown. None of these boons was taken up. Following his wife's death in December 1698 and the loss of her annuity—if it was paid at all—he sank further into poverty.

But Colepeper was fundamentally an optimist, and he never ceased hoping for better things. He compiled many volumes of evidence to prove his right to the Frescheville title, which availed him nothing, but reveal his quarrelsome and petulant nature. Only two months before his death he was writing to the king of Prussia, offering his services and claiming to have 'discovered' longitude. He died in his rented lodgings in Westminster in December 1708, and was buried at St Margaret's Church there on 28 December. VICTOR STATER

Sources BL, Harley MS 7005 · CSP dom., 1659–67; 1675–6; 1680–81; 1685; 1687–9 · Evelyn, Diary, 4.453–4 · N. Luttrell, A brief historical relation of state affairs from September 1678 to April 1714, 6 vols. (1857) · GEC, Peerage · parish register, St Margaret's, Westminster [burial] · www.gen.culpepper.com, 15 June 2001

Archives BL, memorandum book, Add. MSS 11, 265 · BL, papers, commonplace book, collections, Harley MSS 7005, 7587–7605, 6817–6818

Colepeper, William (d. 1726), poet and local politician, was the eldest son of Sir Thomas Colepeper, third baronet (1656?–1723), of Prevton Hall, near Maidstone, Kent, an MP. Nothing is known of his education and early life. He was involved in a trial in February 1701 before Lord Justice Holt in which certain people were fined for attempting to injure him. Colepeper claimed that an attempt had been made on his life on the instruction of Sir George Rook, with whom he had quarrelled. On 8 May of the same year he was one of five gentlemen who delivered a petition to the House of Commons from the deputy lieutenants, justices, and grand jurors of Kent. Colepeper, who was chairman of the quarter sessions at Maidstone, had been responsible for drawing up the petition, which requested that the house turned their loyal addresses into bills of supply. It was voted insolent and seditious and the five were ordered into the custody of the serjeant-at-arms and kept prisoners at the gatehouse until the end of the session.

Colepeper also wrote poetry, and was the author of 'A Heroick Poem upon the King' (1694), 'A Poem to the Lady Duty', and 'Poem to the Revd John Brandreth', included in *Miscellaneous Poems and Translations by Several Hands* (1726), published by Richard Savage. He was married to Elizabeth Gill, with whom he had three sons and three daughters.

PHILIP CARTER

Sources *Hasted's history of Kent: corrected, enlarged, and continued to the present time*, ed. H. H. Drake (1886) · Cobbett, Parl. hist., 5.1247–57 · D. Defoe, The history of the Kentish petition (1701)

Likenesses R. White, group portrait, line engraving, 1701 (The Kentish petitioners), BM

Coleraine. For this title name *see* Hare, Hugh, first Baron Coleraine (1605/6–1667); Hare, Henry, second Baron Coleraine (bap. 1636, d. 1708); Hare, Henry, third Baron Coleraine (1693–1749); Hanger, George, fourth Baron Coleraine (1751–1824); Law, Richard Kidston, first Baron Coleraine (1901–1980).

Coleridge, Alice Mary (1846–1907), promoter of girls' schools, was born on 27 March 1846 at the Manor House, Ottery St Mary, Devon, the youngest daughter by thirteen years of Francis George Coleridge (1794–1854), a solicitor and kinsman of S. T. Coleridge, and his wife, Harriet Thwaites, formerly Norris. After her birth, her mother suffered a protracted mental illness and she was reared by her sister Harriet, wife of Edward Clarke Lowe, curate of Ottery St Mary and later headmaster of Denstone College in Staffordshire, founded by Nathaniel Woodard. Miss Coleridge was educated privately within this Tractarian environment. A retiring, fair-haired woman, she showed a lively interest in art, architecture, and antiquities, learning Latin and Italian so that she could enjoy Dante. She was a notable needlewoman and examples of her work survive in churches. The influence of her godmother,

Charlotte Yonge, and Anna Sewell led her to the cause of female education on Church of England principles.

Alice Coleridge supported the foundation of St Anne's School, Abbots Bromley, Staffordshire, in 1874. It was designed by her brother-in-law Canon Lowe to extend education on the Woodard plan to middle-class girls. From 1875 she was lady-in-charge, and in 1878 she became lady warden when a headmistress was appointed. Her regime was spartan, religious, and notable for an emphasis on character and moral values. However, as numbers grew the school was divided into classes, more staff were recruited, and as well as reading, writing, and arithmetic the pupils were taught divinity, English history, literature, French, science, geometry, and book-keeping. Practical subjects included music, needlework, and games. By 1894 the school had success in higher local certificates; sports, notably cricket, were enjoyed, and there were dramatic and light opera performances which helped to raise money from the county for the building of an impressive school chapel, purchase of playing fields, and improvements in the security and convenience of buildings. Pupils were drawn from the middle and upper ranks of society, but, in keeping with the missionary interests of the founders, there was no distinction as to race.

Alice Coleridge had a vision of extending education to working-class girls. After the demise of the national school in Abbots Bromley during the later 1870s she began Little St Mary's in the coach house for village girls. Fees were minimal, and warmth and food as well as tuition in basic literacy were provided. After the age of twelve some girls stayed on as 'industrials', who did domestic work for the school but attended lessons when they were able. Following the extension of board school education in the area, this experiment faded out about 1880. Miss Coleridge tactfully continued plans to counter secularism and ignorance among the lower classes with Woodard's blessing, though he had doubts about the wisdom of female education. In 1882 St Mary's reopened to cater for pupils of the lower middle classes; they were drawn from the daughters of poor clergy and others of limited means in agriculture and commerce. Alice Coleridge's opinion of Woodard was high (she published a short, adulatory memoir of him in 1897), and she assisted in the foundation of St Winifred's Bangor (1887) and St Margaret's Scarborough (1901) on his principles. In 1884 the Guild of St Anne became the Guild of St Mary and St Anne, and Miss Coleridge presided as lady warden of the whole division, still teaching art, art history, and needlework.

A stroke cut short Alice Coleridge's career in 1898, and she lived as an invalid in Canon Lowe's home, Martyn Lodge, at Henfield, Sussex. She kept in touch with St Anne's and St Mary's, Abbots Bromley, developing her poetic and religious gifts in adversity until her death at Martyn Lodge on 12 February 1907. She was buried in Henfield churchyard.   V. E. CHANCELLOR

Sources V. M. Macpherson, *The story of St Anne's, Abbots Bromley, 1874–1924* (1924) • M. A. Rice, *Story of St Mary's (School), Abbots Bromley* (1947) • A. Wells and S. Meads, *S. Mary and S. Anne: the second fifty years* (1974) • M. E. Hall and V. M. Macpherson, *Marcia Alice Rice: the story of a great headmistress* (1961) • K. E. Kirk, *The story of the Woodard schools* (1937) • L. Cowie and E. Cowie, *That one idea: Nathaniel Woodard and his schools* (1991) • *St Mary's Magazine* (1903–8) • *S. Anne's Guild Magazine* (1907) • B. Heeney, *Mission to the middle classes: the Woodard schools, 1848–1891* (1969) • *Prospectus of St Anne's School* (1896?) • Foster Watson, ed., *The encyclopedia and dictionary of education: 1848–1891* (1922) • b. cert. • d. cert.
Archives Woodard School, Lancing, Sussex
Likenesses photograph, School of St Mary and St Anne, Abbots Bromley, Staffordshire • photograph, repro. in Rice, *Story of St Mary's*, 86 • photograph, repro. in Macpherson, *Story of St Anne's*, 49
Wealth at death £4930 11s.: probate, 11 March 1907, CGPLA Eng. & Wales

Coleridge, Bernard John Seymour, second Baron Coleridge (1851–1927), judge, of the distinguished Devon family, was born at the family seat at Ottery St Mary, Devon, on 19 August 1851, the eldest son of John Duke (afterwards first Baron) *Coleridge (1820–1894), lord chief justice of England, grandson of Sir John Taylor *Coleridge, judge, and great-grand-nephew of Samuel Taylor *Coleridge, the poet and philosopher. His mother was Jane Fortescue, daughter of the Revd George Turner Seymour, of Farringford, Isle of Wight. Coleridge was educated at Eton College and at Trinity College, Oxford, where he graduated BA in 1875 with a second class in history and was captain of the college boat club. He was made an honorary fellow of Trinity in 1909. In 1876 Coleridge married Mary Alethea, eldest daughter of John Fielder *Mackarness, bishop of Oxford; they had one son, Geoffrey Duke (b. 1877), who succeeded his father as third baron, and two daughters.

Coleridge read in chambers with the well-known special pleader, Baugh Allen, and was called to the bar in 1877 by the Middle Temple, of which he was bencher in 1894 and treasurer in 1919. He joined the western circuit where he acquired a large local practice, mainly in criminal cases. He was counsel for the defence in the Winford (1883) and Newton St Cyres (1888) murder cases. He shared his father's Liberal political outlook and was elected member of parliament for the Attercliffe division of Sheffield in 1885, holding the seat as a Gladstonian Liberal for nine years. In 1892 he became queen's counsel.

Coleridge succeeded to the peerage in 1894 but continued to practise at the bar, the first peer of the realm to pursue a regular forensic career. He also spoke in debates in the House of Lords: he strongly attacked Lord Milner's colonial policy and the employment of Chinese indentured labour in the Transvaal, and he supported the Trades Disputes Bill of 1906. The Liberal landslide at the general election of 1906 gave him the opportunity for early promotion, and in 1907 Lord Loreburn appointed him a High Court judge in the King's Bench Division. The Coleridge family was the first to see father, son, and grandson successively appointed judge.

Coleridge was neither a brilliant nor an erudite judge, but he had bearing, was careful and fair-minded, and his decisions were seldom reversed on appeal. He was at his best in jury cases, both civil and criminal. The prosecution of the famous murderer J. A. Dickman at Newcastle upon Tyne assizes in 1910 was one of his more famous cases (a full report of the proceedings, edited by S. O. Rowan-Hamilton, was published in 1914). Coleridge also presided at the trials of the suffragettes, Mrs Emmeline Pankhurst in 1912 and the Pethick-Lawrences in 1913. In 1917 he and the archbishop of Canterbury together heard the first appeal under the Benefices Act of 1898 (*Rice* v. *Bishop of Oxford*).

Coleridge had many outside interests. He was chairman of Devon quarter sessions and served regularly even while he was a judge. From 1912 to 1918 he was chairman of the coal conciliation board of the federated districts. He was a zealous humanitarian, a strong anti-vivisectionist, and an opponent of flogging, although he favoured retention of the death sentence for the most serious crimes. He was founder and first president of the Old Ottregian Society (so called after his family home at Ottery St Mary) and wrote 'The Ottery Song', which was sung at its gatherings. He also published *Ottery St Mary and its Memories* (1904), *The Story of a Devonshire House* (1905), and *This for Remembrance* (1925).

Coleridge retired from the bench because of illness in 1923. He lived out his retirement at his Devon home, the Chanter's House, Ottery St Mary, where he died on 4 September 1927.　　P. A. LANDON, *rev.* HUGH MOONEY

Sources *The Times* (4 Sept 1927) · private information (1937) · *CGPLA Eng. & Wales* (1927)

Likenesses D. May, oils, 1914, Trinity College, Oxford · W. Stoneman, photograph, 1922, NPG · G. Anzino, portrait, Chanter's House, Ottery St Mary, Devon · Spy [L. Ward], cartoon, watercolour study, NPG; repro. in *VF* (13 Jan 1909)

Wealth at death £33,560 12*s*. 8*d*.: probate, 16 Dec 1927, *CGPLA Eng. & Wales*

Coleridge, Christabel Rose (1843–1921). *See under* Coleridge, Derwent (1800–1883).

Coleridge, Derwent (1800–1883), writer and educationist, was born on 14 September 1800 at Greta Hall, Keswick, Cumberland, the second of the three surviving children of the poet Samuel Taylor *Coleridge (1772–1834) and his wife, Sara (1770–1845), daughter of Stephen Fricker of Bristol. From early childhood he showed the sturdy independence and dogged determination which characterized his life. After attending Keswick day school he was educated at the Revd John Dawes's school at Ambleside and spent his weekends with the Wordsworth family. For three years he was a private tutor in Lancashire and then in 1820 went to St John's College, Cambridge. Through the friendship of his cousin Henry Nelson *Coleridge (1798–1843) he was drawn into a brilliant circle which included Thomas Babington Macaulay, the poets Chauncey Hare Townsend and Sidney Walker, Winthrop Praed, and John Moultrie, the future vicar of Rugby who became his lifelong friend. (Much later, in 1864 and 1876, Derwent Coleridge edited the poems of Praed and Moultrie and wrote memoirs of them.) He joined his contemporaries in writing for *Knight's Quarterly*, contributing under the pseudonym Davenant Cecil mostly rather second-rate love poems. He was never happy as a creative writer, but his incisive intellect and organizational skills made him a natural critic and editor, as the lucid approachability of

Derwent Coleridge (1800–1883), by unknown photographer, 1856

his later work testifies. He was also an accomplished linguist: in addition to the usual European languages he also knew Zulu, Arabic, Hawaiian, Hungarian, and Welsh.

Derwent Coleridge's eventual pass degree at Cambridge does not deny his brilliance but reflects the misery of his final year, which began with a bout of typhus fever and continued with debt and confusion. Both he and Moultrie had lost their orthodox faith, but that autumn Moultrie regained his, leaving Coleridge feeling spiritually betrayed. Debt, caused by moving in wealthy circles on a frugal allowance, seemed about to be alleviated by two exhibitions, but he did not receive the money for months. He resented his father's failure to provide for him financially, while at the same time criticizing his debts. Throughout his life he was publicly loyal to his father. In private, however, he was angered by his hypocrisy and weakness, and the inherent dependence of his children on others. Sensitive and independent, he found intolerable the constant need to be overtly grateful. In 1823 he deliberately cast himself off from his family, until he could return from a new position of strength and identity. He moved to the west country, becoming third master at the proprietary school at Plymouth.

Derwent Coleridge became involved in the intellectual life of the city, including lecturing at the Athenaeum. His talk on Wordsworth was published by the *Metropolitan Quarterly* in 1826. In Plymouth he met Mary Simpson Pridham (1807–1887), whom he married on 6 December 1827.

His love for her gave purpose to his life again and made him receptive to a profound reaffirmation of faith. In January 1826 he returned to Cambridge to read for an MA in divinity. He was fully ordained on 15 July 1827, and accepted the living of Helston in Cornwall, which had a school attached. He transformed the school into a thriving concern which produced excellent examination results. He designed a new school building and had it erected. Architecture was a lifelong fascination. He believed that a suitable environment was essential for successful work. In each of his subsequent positions he was to instigate a major rebuilding programme.

In 1839 Derwent Coleridge's book *The Scriptural Character of the English Church* was published. It was a way of trying to clarify his beliefs in the light of his own reconversion and also in the climate of religious debate fuelled by the Oxford Movement and the dissident low churches. He writes of the threat of these divisions and appeals for a broad approach, stressing the impossibility of applying earthly theories and systems to the universal, timeless nature of God.

On 3 February 1841 Derwent Coleridge was appointed principal of St Mark's College, newly established in Chelsea, London, as the very first teacher training college. Over the next twenty years he did much to shape the course of education. His annual reports reveal the all-encompassing nature of the community he headed. The students were given a thorough education ranging from academic subjects to music, carpentry, and bookkeeping. They also worked on the college farm and in the house, which encouraged a sense of duty and humility and made them practically acquainted with the work and conditions of the poor among whom many of them would be placed. The theory of teaching was constantly reinforced by work in a real school within the college, which also benefited the poor children of the local community. Coleridge was convinced that the church should be on the front line of social change and the way was through education. He saw the daily choral service in the college chapel as the moral foundation of the college, but this too, like the education of the very poor, was attacked as excessive. In 1861 there was a public outcry against the government's revised education code. Among the many pamphlets published were Derwent Coleridge's *The Education of the People* and *The Teachers of the People*. The revised code overturned everything he had worked for in its plans for private rather than public funding, 'payment by results', and the reduction of grants for teacher training.

On the death of his brother Hartley *Coleridge (1796–1849) Derwent Coleridge collected, edited, and published his work, adding a moving and perceptive memoir (1851). After the death of his sister Sara *Coleridge (1802–1852) he carried on her editorship of their father's works. In 1864 he became rector of Hanwell, Middlesex, where his last great project was the building of a new church. At the age of eighty he retired to Torquay, where he died on 28 March 1883; he was survived by his wife. During his last years he enjoyed the companionship of his children. The eldest, Derwent Moultrie, had been sent to Australia and had died

there in 1881, but Ernest and Christabel Rose Coleridge remained close to him.

Christabel Rose Coleridge (1843–1921), writer, was born on 25 May 1843 at St Mark's College, Chelsea, London, the second of Derwent Coleridge's three surviving children. As a young woman she helped in her brother Ernest's school, but she wished to be a writer and subsequently had at least fifteen novels published, including *Lady Betty* (1869), *An English Squire* (1881), *A Near Relation* (1886), and *The Prophet's Mantle* (1897). Many of her works were published by the Society for Promoting Christian Knowledge. From 1890 she helped to edit the magazines the *Monthly Packet* and *Friendly Leaves*. Christabel held conservative views on 'the woman question' and produced *The Daughters who have not Revolted*, a collection of essays, in 1894. She was a close friend of her distant cousin, the novelist Charlotte Mary Yonge, and they collaborated in the writing of *Strolling Players* (1893). After Charlotte's death in 1901 Christabel published *Charlotte Mary Yonge: her Life and Letters* (1903), an authoritative arrangement of autobiographical and bibliographical material, interleaved with letters and comment. She died, unmarried, on 14 November 1921 at Cheyne, Bridge Road, Torquay, Devon.

CHERRY DURRANT

Sources Ransom HRC, Derwent Coleridge MSS · Ransom HRC, Christabel Rose Coleridge MSS · archives, College of St Mark and St John, Plymouth, Devon · *Collected letters of Samuel Taylor Coleridge*, ed. E. L. Griggs, 6 vols. (1956–71) · J. Moultrie, *The dream of life*, 1 (1876) · J. Sutherland, *The Longman companion to Victorian fiction* (1988), 137 [C. R. Coleridge] · R. Hainton and G. Hainton, *The unknown Coleridge: the life and times of Derwent Coleridge, 1800–1883* (1997) · *CGPLA Eng. & Wales* (1883) · d. cert. [C. R. Coleridge]
Archives College of St Mark and St John, Plymouth, archives · Ransom HRC, MSS · Wordsworth Trust, Dove Cottage, Grasmere, MSS | DWL, letters to Henry Crabb Robinson · Ransom HRC, Christabel Rose Coleridge MSS · Wordsworth Trust, Dove Cottage, Grasmere, letters to the Stanger family
Likenesses E. Nash, pencil drawing, 1820, Ransom HRC · ambrotype photograph, 1840–49, NPG · ambrotype photograph, 1856, NPG [*see illus.*] · oils, College of St Mark and St John, Plymouth
Wealth at death £9063 12s. 2d.: administration with will, 10 May 1883, *CGPLA Eng. & Wales* · £4615 10s. 2d.—Christabel Rose Coleridge: probate, 10 Jan 1922, *CGPLA Eng. & Wales*

Coleridge, (David) Hartley (1796–1849), writer, was born on 19 September 1796 in Oxford Street, Kingsdown, Bristol, the eldest of the three surviving children of the poet Samuel Taylor *Coleridge (1772–1834) and his wife, Sara (1770–1845), daughter of Stephen Fricker of Bristol. He was a remarkably precocious child, but Coleridge actively encouraged his inherent strangeness and powerful imagination. He watched and questioned him, trying to find in the behaviour of his child confirmation of his own theories of language and the imagination. Such overwhelming attention alternating with the bleakness of his father's frequent departures began to damage Hartley's ability to function in the real world and caused him increasingly to retreat into the security of his imaginary world, Ejuxria, a world which he could control. He knew

(**David**) **Hartley Coleridge** (**1796–1849**), by unknown engraver, *c*.1845

the boundary between the two worlds was there but he constantly strove to dissolve it.

After four unsettled years in Somerset and London the family moved to Greta Hall, Keswick, Cumberland, in July 1800. The house was shared with the landlord William Jackson and his housekeeper, Mrs Wilson, who became figures of stability in Hartley's young life, as did Robert Southey who came to visit and stayed for forty years. After attending Keswick day school, in 1808 Hartley went with his brother Derwent *Coleridge (1800–1883) to school at Ambleside, and weekends were spent with the Wordsworth family. The school was run by the Revd John Dawes, under whose enlightened guidance Hartley progressed well; in May 1815 he matriculated at Merton College, Oxford. In 1818 he was awarded a second-class degree and the following year became a junior fellow at Oriel College. In the early nineteenth century Oriel was characterized by austerity, sobriety, and adherence to regulations, and it quickly became apparent that Hartley Coleridge could not fit into it. He was expelled on charges of 'sottishness, a love of low company and general inattention to college rules' (Griggs, 306). It was eventually conceded that the reports of drunkenness were exaggerated. He did suffer from a degree of alcoholism for much of his life, but it was only just beginning at this point. It seems probable that lack of respect for college traditions and attitude was the real cause for the expulsion. He had quietly ignored those regulations he found petty or hypocritical, knowing that this would not be overlooked by the college authorities but unable to compromise.

Hartley Coleridge moved to London in 1820 and tried to establish himself as a writer. His first essays were published in the *London Magazine* at this time. But, having no money and no home, he had to rely on the charity of his parents' friends and in the autumn of 1822 had to submit to his father's insistence that he should return to Ambleside to work for the Revd Dawes. Initially all went well, but after Dawes's retirement Hartley Coleridge and a Mr Suard tried to expand the school and in 1826 it folded. This left him without a regular income but gave him time to return to writing. Over the next few years he was to publish mainly in *Blackwood's Edinburgh Magazine* and the *Winter's Wreath*, but also in *The Gem*, the *Literary Souvenir*, the *Christian Mother's Magazine*, and the *Academic Correspondent*, and then later in his life in the *Penny Magazine* and the *Englishwomen's Magazine*. His essays and letters reveal a persona, the Old Bachelor, behind which he could hide his feelings of guilt and failure and his sense of having been abandoned by his family. He came to view himself as a man of adverse destiny, out of step with nature and with time. His despair was hidden under the mask of whimsical drollery and chivalrous, gentle eccentricity. From 1822 until his death his essays changed very little in style, tone, or concerns. They mirror the quaint, digressive, learned Old Bachelor but they also throw out glimpses of the man behind the mask, illuminating his erudition about literature, art, and theology and revealing his social concern, especially his hatred of injustice and oppression. One volume of his poetry was published in 1833 and was well received. It was reissued as part of the two-volume collection published posthumously in 1851 with an introductory memoir by Derwent Coleridge. The poems are a curious mixture, sometimes narrated by the persona of the Old Bachelor, sometimes in specific genres, and sometimes very personal sonnets of extreme pathos which reveal the anguish he tried to suppress. Of the latter the most poignant are 'Long Time a Child' and 'Let me not Deem'.

In 1832 Hartley Coleridge moved to Leeds to the home of the publisher Bingley, to whom he was contracted to write short biographies for a series, *Lives of Distinguished Northerns*. The thirteen *Lives* he completed before Bingley went bankrupt in 1833 transcend the confines of word length and lack of source material, giving not only a sense of the subject but the added delight of Hartley Coleridge's intimate style. He returned to the Lake District, remaining in Grasmere until February 1837 when his friend Isaac Green, assistant master at Sedbergh School in Yorkshire, became ill and he offered to take his place. He stayed for two terms and was happy and successful. The following year he repeated his success, this time standing in for the headmaster. During his first stay at Sedbergh his landlady in Grasmere, Mrs Fleming, died, and on his return he lived with William and Eleanor Richardson. He returned to them after his second spell at Sedbergh, and when they moved to a larger house, Nab Cottage, on the road between Grasmere and Rydal, he moved with them and remained there until his death.

Hartley Coleridge did not marry or have children. His morbidly low sense of self-worth conspired with his need for the safety of self-containment to make sexual relationships almost impossible. But as the Old Bachelor he was loved and cared for by many people in the area. His papers are full of invitations to attend family gatherings. In his turn he tried to give help and consolation to all who needed it, regardless of their social status. And many friends understood the underlying desolation which led to occasional bouts of self-abandon and wandering. In 1839 the publisher Moxon asked him to write an introduction for a new edition of the plays of Massinger and Ford. Again he suffered from limitations of length and materials but eventually produced a useful and approachable piece of work, published in 1840, and with further editions appearing in 1848 and 1851. The work was well paid and he was also earning a small amount of money at this time from lecturing on poetry at the museum of the Natural History Society at Kendal. In early December 1848 he dined out, and walked home in the pouring rain. Afterwards he became ill, developed bronchitis, and became worse throughout December. By Boxing day the Richardsons were sufficiently concerned to send for his brother Derwent. Hartley Coleridge died on 6 January 1849 at Nab Cottage and was buried on 11 January in Grasmere churchyard. CHERRY DURRANT

Sources Ransom HRC, Hartley Coleridge MSS · Ransom HRC, Derwent Coleridge MSS · [H. Coleridge], *Letters of Hartley Coleridge*, ed. G. E. Griggs and E. L. Griggs (1937) · D. Coleridge, *Poems by Hartley Coleridge with a memoir of his life by his brother*, 2 vols. (1851) · E. L. Griggs, *Hartley Coleridge: his life and work* (1929) [incl. bibliography] · *Collected letters of Samuel Taylor Coleridge*, ed. E. L. Griggs, 6 vols. (1956–71) · *Further extracts from the letters of Robert Southey*, ed. M. Fitzgerald (1912) · H. Coleridge, *Essays and marginalia*, ed. [D. Coleridge], 2 vols. (1851) · M. Lefebure, *The bondage of love: a life of Mrs Samuel Taylor Coleridge* (1986)
Archives Ransom HRC, papers, incl. notebooks, corresp., essays, etc. · Wordsworth Trust, Dove Cottage, Grasmere, poems and corresp. | Bodl. Oxf., letters to Lord Lovelace
Likenesses D. Wilkie, portrait, 1807 (as a child; after unknown artist), repro. in Griggs and Griggs, eds., *Letters of Hartley Coleridge* · engraving, c.1845, Highgate Literary and Scientific Institution [*see illus.*] · lithograph, repro. in Coleridge, *Essays and marginalia*, frontispiece

Coleridge, Henry James (1822–1893), Jesuit, born in London on 20 September 1822, was the second son of Sir John Taylor *Coleridge (1790–1876), and his wife, Mary (1788–1874), the second daughter of the Revd Gilbert Buchanan. Henry was a great-nephew of the poet Samuel Taylor Coleridge and the younger brother of John Duke *Coleridge, Baron Coleridge. His only sister, Alethea, married the Revd J. Mackarness, later bishop of Oxford. Henry Coleridge was educated at Eton College and then Trinity College, Oxford, where he matriculated in 1840, graduating BA in 1845 and MA in 1847. From 1845 until 1852 he was a fellow of Oriel College. He came under the influence of the Tractarian movement and, after receiving Anglican orders, accepted the cure of Ottery St Mary and then that of Alphington in Devon, a part of the country with which

Henry James Coleridge (1822–1893), by unknown photographer

his family had long been associated. In 1852 he became a Roman Catholic and went to Rome to make a further study of theology at the Pontifical Jesuit University. Ordained priest in 1855, he received his doctor's degree in 1857, and in September of that year entered the Jesuit noviciate at Beaumont Lodge near Windsor. Two years later he joined the staff of St Beuno's, the Jesuit Theological College in north Wales, to lecture in holy scripture; he held this post for six years.

Throughout his life, Coleridge was a prolific writer; his many publications included *Vita vitae nostrae meditantibus proposita* (1869), *The Life and Letters of St Francis Xavier* (2 vols., 1872), *The Life of our Life* (18 vols., 1876–92), *The Prisoners of the King: Thoughts on the Catholic Doctrine of Purgatory* (1878), and *The Works and Words of our Saviour Gathered from the Four Gospels* (1882, 1897).

In April 1865 Coleridge was appointed the first Jesuit editor of *The Month*, a periodical begun by Fanny Margaret Taylor in 1864, which she sold to the Jesuits. Living in Hill Street, at the residence of the Jesuit fathers of Farm Street Church in west London, he remained editor until 1881 and was responsible for the successful launching of *The Month* as a Jesuit publication. John Henry Newman, whom he had known at Oxford and who had asked for his help with the Catholic University in Dublin, was one with whom he corresponded on the journal's affairs; Coleridge may be considered to have been Newman's closest friend among the Jesuits. A number of articles by Newman were published in *The Month* in the 1860s, both before and after the

Jesuits acquired ownership; Newman's 'The Dream of Gerontius' appeared in the May and June numbers of 1865. The last article Coleridge wrote for *The Month* (October 1890), entitled 'A father of souls', was about Newman. After the issue of the 'Syllabus of errors' (condemning certain liberal ideas) by Pius IX in 1864 and the promulgation of the definition of papal infallibility as a dogma by the First Vatican Council of 1870, W. E. Gladstone published his pamphlets *The Vatican Decrees in their Bearing on Civil Allegiance: a Political Expostulation* and *Vaticanism*. In reply Coleridge preached a sermon, 'The abomination of desolation', in Farm Street Church in November 1874 and sent Gladstone a copy; there followed a correspondence.

From 1881, when Coleridge retired from the editorship of *The Month*, he spent the rest of his active life writing and editing the Quarterly Series. Throughout his years in London he gave himself to the pastoral work of Farm Street Church. In June 1891 he suffered a paralytic stroke and, after two years as an invalid, died at Manresa House, Roehampton, on 13 April 1893. His remains were, at Lord Coleridge's special request, interred in the family vault at Ottery St Mary. Photographs show a handsome man of distinguished appearance.   GEOFFREY HOLT

Sources Foster, *Alum. Oxon.* · 'Father Coleridge', *The Month*, 78 (1893), 1–3 · 'Recollections of Henry James Coleridge', *The Month*, 78 (1893), 153–81 · *The Month*, new ser., 31 (1964), 223 · *The Tablet* (22 April 1893), 624 · E. F. Sutcliffe, *Bibliography of the English province of the Society of Jesus, 1773–1953* (1957) · *Letters and Notices* [Society of Jesus], 22/112, 214–18 · Burke, *Peerage*
Archives Archives of the British Province of the Society of Jesus, London, corresp., papers, and notebooks · Indiana University, Bloomington, Lilly Library, corresp. · U. Birm. L., special collections department, journal, incl. theological notes | Birmingham Oratory, letters to J. H. Newman · BL, corresp. with W. E. Gladstone, Add. MSS 44445–44504 · Bodl. Oxf., letters to Lord Lovelace · Westm. DA, corresp. mainly with E. H. Thompson
Likenesses photographs, Archives of British Province of the Society of Jesus [*see illus.*]
Wealth at death £144 5s. 5d.: probate, 6 May 1893, *CGPLA Eng. & Wales*

Coleridge, Henry Nelson (1798–1843), barrister and writer, was born on 25 October 1798 at Ottery St Mary, Devon, the fifth of the six surviving sons of Colonel James Coleridge (1759–1836) and his wife, Frances Duke Taylor, daughter of John Taylor. James Duke *Coleridge (1789–1857) and Sir John Taylor *Coleridge (1790–1876) were his brothers. He was educated at Eton College, where he became part of the brilliant academic circle, led by W. M. Praed, which produced *The Etonian* magazine. This evolved into *Knight's Quarterly* when the contributors went up to Cambridge, and Henry Coleridge contributed to it under the pseudonym Gerard Montgomery. He achieved great success at King's College, Cambridge, standing second for the university scholarship in 1819, winning both the Latin and Greek Ode prizes in 1820 and the Greek Ode prize in 1821, and eventually becoming a fellow.

At Christmas 1822 Henry Coleridge met his cousin Sara *Coleridge (1802–1852), the daughter of Samuel Taylor *Coleridge (1772–1834), and by March 1823 they were engaged. His only sister Fanny, the only person to know of this, anticipated family disapproval and cautioned that it

should be kept secret, but a year later Henry Coleridge told his father and shortly afterwards was sent to the West Indies to accompany his cousin, William Hart Coleridge, who was to become bishop of Barbados. The reason for his trip was ostensibly to improve his health, which was indeed poor throughout his life, but it is likely that the real reason was his family's attempt to break off the engagement. However, in 1826, Henry Coleridge's account of his excursion, *Six Months in the West Indies*, was published anonymously and not only upset some members of his family by its flippant tone and lively anecdotes but also included a thinly disguised reference to his love for Sara.

In 1826 Henry Coleridge was called to the bar, but both his salary and health remained precarious. In 1828 he became secretary to the committee of the newly opened King's College, London University, but after nine months had to leave because the college faced financial restraints. Throughout his life apparent success disguised financial insecurity, often caused by generous loans which were never repaid to him. He eventually married Sara, on 3 September 1829, with the family blessing. Their first home was in Hampstead, and Samuel Taylor Coleridge lived near by in Highgate. From 1830 until his father-in-law's death in 1834 he made regular visits and began to record Coleridge's conversation, a labour of love which became *Table Talk*, published in 1835. Coleridge's conversation was famously expansive, and Sara praised her husband's ability in this publication to 'narrow' him. Some critics disagreed, however, feeling that Henry had not so much 'narrowed' Coleridge as distorted him, twisting him into a reflection of his own conservative vision. Opinion on *Table Talk* remains divided. As Coleridge's literary executor, Henry Coleridge then began the huge task of collecting and editing his work. He was helped by Sara and she continued the work after his death. He published four volumes of *Literary Remains*; new editions of other work including *The Friend*, and *Aids to Reflection*; and began assembling material for another edition of *Biographia literaria*.

In addition to this and his work as a chancery barrister, Coleridge also lectured on equity to the Incorporated Law Society and contributed reviews to the *Quarterly Review* and the *British Critic*. In 1830 he had written the first volume of *An Introduction to the Study of Greek Classic Poets*. It was well received and went into several editions, but his legal career began to flourish at that time and he never found the time to write the proposed second volume.

Contemporary accounts suggest that Henry Coleridge was a man of great wit, irresistible charm, and sociability, adored by children and fond of flying kites. For much of his life he had suffered from rheumatic and spinal complaints and in May 1842 he lost the use of his legs from spinal paralysis. He died on 26 January 1843 at 10 Chester Place, Regent's Park, London, where the family had moved in 1837. He was survived by his wife and two children, Herbert *Coleridge, philologist, and Edith. On 3 February he was buried in Highgate cemetery, Middlesex, in the same grave as Samuel Taylor Coleridge, a grave which would later be shared with his wife, his mother-in-law, and his son.   CHERRY DURRANT

Sources B. J. S. Coleridge, *The story of a Devonshire house* (1905) • Ransom HRC, Coleridge Archives, Sara Coleridge MSS • H. N. Coleridge, *Six months in the West Indies* (1826) • *Memoir and letters of Sara Coleridge*, ed. E. Coleridge, 2 vols. (1873) • E. Coleridge, *Some recollections of Henry Nelson Coleridge and his family* (1910) • B. K. Mudge, *Sara Coleridge: a Victorian daughter* (1989)
Archives BL, corresp. and papers, Add. MSS 47557–47558 • CUL, MSS | BL, corresp. with Thomas Poole, Add. MS 35344 • Ransom HRC, Coleridge Archives, Sara Coleridge MSS

Coleridge, Herbert (1830–1861), philologist, was born at Hampstead, Middlesex, on 7 October 1830, the only son of Henry Nelson *Coleridge (1798–1843) and his wife, Sara *Coleridge (1802–1852). Having been educated at Eton College by his uncle, the Revd Edward Coleridge, he obtained the Newcastle medal and the Balliol scholarship in 1847, and in 1848 was declared Newcastle scholar. While at school he acquired an interest in Icelandic. His university career at Oxford, which began in 1848, led in 1852 to a double first-class in classics and mathematics, which gave 'high hopes of future eminence' (*GM*, 706).

On 31 March 1853 Coleridge married Ellen Persehouse, daughter of T. M. Phillips, and on 17 November 1854 he was called to the bar, and began practising as a chancery barrister at his chambers in Lincoln's Inn, specializing in conveyancing. As his private means were adequate to his needs he was free to devote his leisure hours to philology—Sanskrit, the northern tongues, and particularly the language and literature of Iceland. In February 1857 he was elected a member of the Philological Society (founded in 1842), and contributed two papers on diminutives in 'let' and the Latin words 'ploro' and 'exploro', which were read at their March and May meetings. The society was then engaged, following a paper by Chevenix Trench, 'On the deficiencies in our English dictionaries', on a proposal for supplementing the two standard dictionaries of Johnson and Richardson, but in late 1857 Trench made proposals for a complete new English dictionary. Coleridge threw himself into this project with his characteristic enthusiasm, became its chief workman, and was appointed honorary secretary of a special committee 'formed for the purpose of collecting words and idioms hitherto unregistered', a post for which he was well fitted by his learning, literary facility, and methodical habits. His new duties, amounting to a general editorship of the work, involved a large correspondence with the numerous volunteer helpers. The results of his researches are embodied in his *Glossarial Index to the Printed English Literature of the Thirteenth Century* (1859), which he describes as 'the foundation-stone' of the proposed English dictionary. The scheme developed into the momentous *New English Dictionary* (later the *Oxford English Dictionary*).

Coleridge's efforts were necessarily relaxed, though never entirely relinquished, in consequence of a decline in health, which ended in consumption. He had a bad haemorrhage in 1858 yet, in spite of increasing weakness, he continued to write papers on various philological

topics, as well as reports of the progress of work; and during the last fortnight of his life, while confined to bed, he still sometimes dictated notes for the dictionary. An essay on King Arthur was printed by the Philological Society after his death, which took place on 23 April 1861 at his home, 10 Chester Place, Regent's Park, London.

EDITH COLERIDGE, rev. JOHN D. HAIGH

Sources personal knowledge (1887) • J. D. Coleridge, *Macmillan's Magazine*, 5 (1861–2), 56–60 • R. M. Hogg, ed., *The Cambridge history of the English language*, 4: 1776–1997, ed. S. Romaine (1998), 559–61 • *GM*, 3rd ser., 10 (1861), 706 • 'Coleridge, Henry Nelson', *DNB* • 'Coleridge, Sara', *DNB* • m. cert. • d. cert.
Wealth at death £7000: probate, 25 May 1861, *CGPLA Eng. & Wales*

Coleridge, James Duke (1789–1857), Church of England clergyman, was born on 13 June 1789, the eldest son of James Coleridge of Heath's Court, Ottery St Mary, Devon, and Frances Duke Taylor, daughter of Bernard Frederick Taylor and one of the coheirs of Robert Duke of Otterton; he was the elder brother of Sir John Taylor *Coleridge and of Henry Nelson *Coleridge. He went to Balliol College, Oxford, where he matriculated on 21 May 1808. Initially he took no degree, and was improvident. On 9 June 1814 he married Sophia, daughter of Colonel Stanhope Badcock. It was intended that he should have a military career, but desiring to take orders, he gained a degree by taking a BCL on 27 January 1821 (he proceeded DCL on 5 March 1835).

Coleridge then began the life of a clergyman, his whole time as such being served in the diocese of Exeter. In 1817 he was curate of the small parish of Whimple, near Exeter, and a year or two later he was working energetically as curate in the city benefice of St Sidwell's, Exeter. William Carey, his diocesan bishop, promoted him in 1823 to the vicarage of the then united parishes of Kenwyn and Kea, Cornwall, where he worked until 1828. During this period the church of Chacewater, with seating for 1500 persons, and the smaller church of St John, Kenwyn, were built in the parish, and became the centres of separate work. One of Coleridge's published sermons was *On the Funeral of the Late Mr William Gill of Chacewater* (1827), Gill being his most active assistant in the building of that church. From 1826 to 1839 he held the rectory of Lawhitton, and from 1831 to 1841 he was vicar of Lewannick, both livings situated in Cornwall. In 1839 he was appointed vicar of Thorverton, Devon. He held the post of official to the archdeacon of Cornwall, and in August 1825 became a prebend of Exeter Cathedral.

Coleridge was an old-fashioned high-churchman, his views being quite similar to those of Henry Phillpotts, his diocesan bishop from 1830. He was an energetic propagandist, writing numerous sermons and pamphlets. He emphasized the importance of family religion in *Joshua's Choice* (1819), which was several times reprinted, wrote interestingly on sickness in several pamphlets (1825 and 1832), and warned his parishioners about errors of doctrine (1834) and regeneration (1836). His *Practical Advice to the Young Parish Priest* (1834) was a work of some substance.

James Duke Coleridge (1789–1857), by Charles Holl (after Jane Fortescue Coleridge)

His *Companion to First Lessons* (1838) has a touching dedication to his brother, John Taylor Coleridge. Coleridge died at the vicarage, Thorverton, on 26 December 1857, survived by two daughters. H. C. G. MATTHEW

Sources B. J. S. Coleridge, *The story of a Devonshire house* (1905) · *GM*, 3rd ser., 4 (1858), 224 · Burke, *Peerage* · *Clergy List* (1847–57) **Likenesses** C. Holl, engraving (after J. F. Coleridge), AM Oxf., Hope collection [*see illus.*] · portrait, repro. in Coleridge, *Story of a Devonshire house*

Coleridge, John (*bap.* 1719, *d.* 1781), Church of England clergyman and schoolmaster, was baptized on 21 January 1719 at Crediton, Devon, the son of John Coleridge (1697–1739), a weaver, and his wife, Mary Wills (1698–1776). Having become a respectable draper in Crediton, John Coleridge senior went bankrupt when his son John was fifteen. According to family legend the boy, a promising scholar at the grammar school at Crediton, left school and walked off to seek his fortune; he was found weeping by the roadside by a gentleman who got him a job as an usher at a nearby school.

On 24 May 1743 Coleridge married Mary Lendon (*d.* 1751?), of Crediton; they had four daughters, three of whom survived infancy. From 1745 to 1748 he was a schoolmaster at Clysthydon, Devon. In 1747, at the age of twenty-eight, he took the unusual step for a married man of matriculating at Sidney Sussex College, Cambridge. He became a distinguished classical and Hebrew scholar, and might have had a fellowship if he had been single. He returned to Devon in 1749, before becoming a teacher at

Squire's Grammar School in South Molton and a curate at Mariansleigh.

Mary Coleridge having died, probably in 1751, John Coleridge married, on 18 December 1753, Ann Bowden (1727–1809), daughter of Roger Bowden and Mary Zeatherd, in St Mary Arches Church in Exeter. Ann's background was as humble as her husband's. 'The Bowdens inherited a house-stye & a pig-stye in the Exmore County, in the reign of Elizabeth', according to their son Samuel, and 'they have inherited nothing better since that time' (*Collected Letters*, 1.302). This second marriage produced ten children, nine of whom survived infancy. The eight sons took up a variety of professions, mostly with great success; one joined the army, one the navy, three the church, and another became a doctor. The last, the child of his father's old age, was Samuel Taylor *Coleridge (1772–1834), poet, who was born on 21 October 1772.

In 1760 Coleridge was appointed headmaster of the King's School at Ottery St Mary and vicar of Ottery St Mary church, the largest and most important parish church in Devon. He published articles on biblical scholarship in the *Gentleman's Magazine* and helped Dr Benjamin Kennicott with his edition of the Hebrew Bible. He also printed some idiosyncratic scholarly works, mainly by subscription raised among local worthies and admirers: *Miscellaneous dissertations, arising from the XVIIth and XVIIIth chapters of the book of Judges* (1768), *A critical Latin grammar: containing clear and distinct rules for boys just initiated, and notes explanatory of almost every antiquity and obscurity in the language, for youth somewhat advanced in Latin learning* (1772), and a sermon declaring that America's success in the American War of Independence was God's punishment of British sinfulness, *Government not originally proceeding from human agency, but divine institution, shewn in a sermon preached at Ottery St Mary, Devon, December 13th 1776, on the fast-day, appointed by reason of our much to be lamented American War* (1777). Samuel Taylor Coleridge declared that his father's works went largely unnoticed and unread. His reputation seems not to have spread much beyond Devon, where he was admired for his scholarship—his *Miscellaneous Dissertations* lists over 300 subscribers—and his Sunday sermons.

Coleridge died suddenly, probably of apoplexy, at the age of sixty-two, in the early morning of 6 October 1781, only hours after returning home to the School House at Ottery from Plymouth, where he had enlisted his second youngest son, Francis, as a midshipman. He was buried on 10 October in the chancel of Ottery St Mary church. His death had severe consequences for his precocious youngest son, who on losing his father also lost his home and was sent the following year, aged nine, to London as a boarder at Christ's Hospital school.

Coleridge was, by all accounts, including that of Samuel, who relished comparisons between himself and his beloved father, an original—an absent-minded scholar, bookish, enthusiastic, careless of his appearance, 'an Israelite without guile', 'a perfect Parson Adams' (*Collected Letters*, 1.310, 355), of whom it was told that he once mistook the apron of his female neighbour at dinner for his own shirt, stuffing it into his trousers, and on another occasion appeared before his bishop with a shaven head, having forgotten to put on his wig (Gillman, 3–4, 5).

ROSEMARY ASHTON

Sources B. J. S. Coleridge, *The story of a Devonshire house* (1905) • *Collected letters of Samuel Taylor Coleridge*, ed. E. L. Griggs, 6 vols. (1956–71) • J. Gillman, *The life of Samuel Taylor Coleridge* (1838) • *Coleridge: the early family letters*, ed. J. Engell (1994) • E. K. Chambers, *Samuel Taylor Coleridge: a biographical study* (1938) • parish register, Ottery St Mary, 10 Oct 1781 [burial] • parish register, Crediton, 21 Jan 1719 [baptism] • parish register, Exeter, St Mary Arches, 18 Dec 1753 [marriage] • Venn, *Alum. Cant.*
Likenesses watercolour drawing, priv. coll.; repro. in Coleridge, *Story of a Devonshire house*

Coleridge, John Duke, first Baron Coleridge (1820–1894), judge, was born at 7 Hadlow Street, London, on 3 December 1820, the eldest son of Sir John Taylor *Coleridge (1790–1876), barrister and judge, and his wife, Mary (1788–1874), the daughter of the Revd Gilbert Buchanan DD, vicar of Northfleet and rector of Woodmansterne. Reporting his birth in a letter to John May (Bodl. Oxf., MS Eng. lett. c. 289), his father observed 'The Lord Chancellor for 1865 made his appearance this morning about 6'. Henry James *Coleridge was his younger brother. Coleridge was educated at Eton College (from which he was very nearly expelled for an unspeakable offence in May 1833) and at Balliol College, Oxford, where he was elected a scholar in 1838. He was a frequent speaker at the Oxford Union, of which he was president in Michaelmas term 1843. On 27 February 1840 he moved a motion highly critical of the way in which the House of Commons was handling the issue of parliamentary privilege. His speech impressed the *Morning Post*, and the motion was carried by fifty votes to nine. He was also a member of the Decade, a select debating society in Balliol, whose other members included Jowett, Clough, and Matthew Arnold. He took a keen interest in the Tractarian movement and was profoundly influenced by John Henry Newman. Severe and prolonged illness in 1842 interrupted his studies and he graduated with an ordinary pass degree. Ill health was a recurrent feature of his life, assailing him in 1855, when he became recorder of Portsmouth; in the form of typhus in October 1859; most dramatically in March 1863, when he was taken suddenly ill in the middle of a case at Exeter assizes; and in the long vacation in 1871 in the middle of the Tichborne trial. He took his MA in 1846, however, and was elected to a fellowship at Exeter College, which he held from 1843 until his marriage on 11 August 1846 to Jane Fortescue Seymour, third daughter of the Revd George Turner Seymour of Farringford Hill on the Isle of Wight, and sister of his Balliol contemporary, J. B. Seymour.

Coleridge was called to the bar by the Middle Temple on 6 November 1846, and practised from chambers in 3 King's Bench Walk until 1864. It was a difficult time for a young barrister with a family and with uncertain health. In 1847 there were nearly twice as many barristers on the western circuit as there had been thirty years earlier; the County Courts Act 1846 had removed the small cases, and there was a general lack of civil business. The turning point in Coleridge's career came at Exeter assizes in March 1853 with his defence of George Sparkes, the Clayhidon murderer. He made a brilliant speech, ending with a quotation from *Othello* and the words of the communion collect, which 'produced an immense sensation' (*The Times*). As his seniors, Montague Smith, Robert Collier, and Thomas Phinn, took silk, he built up a large junior practice. In 1855 he resisted the temptation to become clerk of the assize on the midland circuit, and was appointed recorder of Portsmouth, a position he held until 1866. By the summer of 1860 he had the largest junior practice on the western circuit. In that year his fees reached £4000.

Coleridge was reluctant to apply for silk because of the risks involved, but in February 1861 Lord Chancellor Campbell offered a silk gown both to him and to his fellow Devonian, personal friend, and professional rival, John Karslake. They took silk together on 25 February 1861 and were elected together as benchers of the Middle Temple. The western circuit had never been stronger than it was in those years. The leader was Montague Smith, a future judge of the common pleas and the privy council, and there were three future attorneys-general, Collier, Karslake, and Coleridge. Those four completely dominated the circuit, and when Karslake became solicitor-general in 1866 Coleridge became leader of the circuit until 1868. He relied heavily on his juniors, Montague Bere and, especially, Charles Bowen, who first appeared before him at Portsmouth sessions in October 1861. In 1867, the last full year before he became solicitor-general, his fees amounted to £12,200.

Coleridge was always politically ambitious. In August 1847, when Gladstone was elected for Oxford University, Coleridge was joint secretary of his London committee. For many years he was tempted to enter parliament himself. By education and family background he was a high-church tory, and he was approached several times as a candidate in the Conservative interest. But over the years his churchmanship became broader and his politics more liberal. 'Democratic feeling and convictions only strengthen with me every year I live … *Delenda est aristocratia*' (letter to Sir William Heathcote, 19 August 1860, Coleridge, *Life and Correspondence*, 1.259–60). He was finally adopted as Liberal candidate to contest Exeter at a by-election in 1864 and though defeated after a short and rough campaign, which convinced him of the necessity for the ballot, he won the seat at the general election in the following year. He made his maiden speech on 21 March 1866 to propose the second reading of the Tests Abolition (Oxford) Bill, and he was actively involved in the campaign to abolish religious tests in the universities until it finally succeeded in 1871. Oxford University made him a DCL in 1877, and Exeter College elected him to an honorary fellowship in 1882. In the same parliament he made major speeches against marriage with a deceased wife's sister, which he opposed firmly throughout his life, and, at Gladstone's request, moved the instruction at the committee stage of the 1867 Reform Bill to impose a £5 annual rating limit on the franchise.

Re-elected for Exeter after a tight contest at the general

election in November 1868, Coleridge was asked by Gladstone to be solicitor-general. He refused, apparently because of friction between himself and Collier, the attorney-general, on circuit many years before. When his refusal became public and Gladstone insisted, he agreed to accept the office, and was knighted (12 December 1868).

In the new parliament Coleridge spoke again on university tests and in favour of Irish church disestablishment and also on law reform; but much of his time was occupied with private practice. He was leading counsel for the plaintiff in *Saurin* v. *Starr*, the convent case, which lasted most of February 1869. He obtained a verdict of £500 damages, and finally established his professional reputation in London. He successfully defended Overend and Gurney against a charge of fraudulent conspiracy in a nine-day trial in December in the same year. His income in 1869 was over £19,000. From May 1871 to March 1872 he spent an enormous amount of his time on the Tichborne case, with the able and devoted assistance of Charles Bowen, to the detriment of both men's health. His cross-examination of the plaintiff lasted three weeks, and his opening speech for the defendants lasted twenty-three days. By painstaking attention to detail he was able to overcome the widespread public bias in favour of the claimant, and the jury stopped the case on 6 March 1872. His attention to the case was hardly distracted in November 1871 when Collier was appointed to the court of common pleas and then immediately to the privy council, and Coleridge became attorney-general. On 3 May 1872 the practice of allowing the law officers to devote so much time to their private practice was attacked in the House of Commons, and Coleridge made a characteristically eloquent and successful defence.

In November 1873 Chief Justice Bovill died suddenly, worn out, it is said, by the Tichborne case, and Gladstone appointed Coleridge as chief justice of the common pleas and gave him a peerage (the only chief justice of the common pleas since 1688 to receive a peerage, apart from Lord Gifford in 1824). When Sir Alexander Cockburn died on 20 November 1880, Gladstone, who had returned to power that year, appointed Coleridge as lord chief justice of England in his place, and the offices of chief justice of the common pleas and chief baron of the exchequer (vacant by the death of Sir Fitzroy Kelly) were abolished. 'He [Gladstone] did nothing for me till I entered Parliament, but he did everything for me afterwards', Coleridge commented in a letter to Grant Duff, on 16 November 1886 (Coleridge, *Life and Correspondence* 2.354).

Soon after Coleridge's appointment to the bench his mother, father, and wife (a distinguished portrait painter whose sitters included J. H. Newman) died in quick succession (1874, 1876, and 6 February 1878 respectively). He was devastated and for a while withdrew from society, and rifts began to appear in his family. Particular difficulties arose over his daughter, Mildred, who met Charles Warren Adams, secretary of the Anti-Vivisection Society, of which Coleridge was a keen supporter. The rest of her family thought that he was thoroughly undesirable, and when she left home to live with him, Bernard John Seymour *Coleridge (later second Baron Coleridge) wrote her a long letter to say so. This led to two libel actions in the Queen's Bench Division, for two days in November 1884 and for eight days in November 1886, when the chief justice was sued in his own court and all the family linen was washed in public. Mildred married Charles Adams on 24 June 1885. Stephen William Buchanan *Coleridge, the third of Coleridge's four children, also became a prominent anti-vivisectionist.

In August 1883 Coleridge went to America as a guest of the New York Bar Association and visited New York, Boston, Chicago, and Washington. He had always been interested in America and had a number of American friends, like Ellis Yarnall, with whom he corresponded for forty years. On his way home he met Amy Augusta Jackson, daughter of Henry Baring Lawford, of the Bengal civil service. They were married on 13 August 1885. With her he found happiness again. He died at his London home, 1 Sussex Square, on 14 June 1894 and was buried at Ottery St Mary on 22 June. His second wife died on 24 May 1933.

Coleridge presided over the trial of many *causes célèbres*: *Lonsdale* v. *Yates*, the *World* libel case in 1884; *R.* v. *Dudley & Stephens*, who had killed and eaten the cabin-boy, the only case in which a sentence of death has been passed in the Royal Courts of Justice (1884); *Wood* v. *Cox*, the racing libel case (1888); *O'Donnell* v. *Walter* (1888); and the great Baccarat case, *Gordon-Cumming* v. *Wilson* in which the prince of Wales gave evidence in court (1891). But he did not leave his mark on English law. He rarely sat on appeal, and, since cases tried on circuit were no longer reported, his decisions in civil and criminal cases on circuit have not been preserved. He was not a great lawyer: indeed his close friend Jowett went so far as to say: 'I don't think him a first rate intellect' (Quinn and Prest, 93). And his administration of the Queen's Bench Division left much to be desired. But he will be remembered for his silver-tongued eloquence and as a trial lawyer, both at the bar and on the bench.

Coleridge was tall and handsome, and had an extremely beautiful voice. His language was refined and forcible, and no one could, on occasion, produce a greater sense of solemnity with less effort. He had an abrasive manner, which not infrequently caused friction with his colleagues, but no one could have been more loyal to his friends. He had a great love and wide knowledge of English literature, especially of the poetry and drama of the Elizabethan period. During his early years at the bar he wrote for *The Guardian*, the *Quarterly Review*, and the *Edinburgh Review*; and there were frequent literary quotations in his speeches at the bar and in parliament, and in his judgments and summings-up on the bench. William Butterfield designed an enormous and splendid library for him at his Devonshire seat, Heath's Court, Ottery St Mary, to contain 12,000 volumes, including a substantial collection of Elizabethan literature.   DAVID PUGSLEY

Sources E. H. Coleridge, *Life and correspondence of John Duke, Lord Coleridge*, 2 vols. (1904) · C. Yarnall, ed., *Forty years of friendship: Coleridge/Ellis Yarnall letters, 1856–1894* (1911) · E. Yarnall, *Wordsworth and*

the Coleridges (1899) · S. Coleridge, *Memories of the Hon. Stephen Coleridge* (1913) · T. J. Toohey, *Piety and the professions: Sir John Coleridge and his sons* (1987) · *A Victorian diarist: extracts from the journals of Mary, Lady Monkswell*, ed. E. C. F. Collier, 1: *1873–1895* (1944), 142–4 · Russell of Killowen, *North American Law Review* (1894), 257–67 · *Dear Miss Nightingale: a selection of Benjamin Jowett's letters to Florence Nightingale, 1860–1893*, ed. V. Quinn and J. Prest (1987) · C. Hollis, *The Oxford Union* (1965) · R. F. V. Heuston, *Lives of the lord chancellors, 1885–1940* (1964) · *Wellesley index* · GEC, *Peerage*

Archives Chanter's House, Ottery St Mary, Devon · Devon RO, letters · Indiana University, Bloomington, Lilly Library, corresp. | BL, corresp. with W. E. Gladstone, Add. MS 44138 · Bodl. Oxf., letters to Sir William Harcourt; corresp. with Lord Kimberley · CUL, letters to Lord Acton · Keble College, Oxford, letters to John Keble · LPL, letters to Lord Selborne; letters to A. C. Tait · NL Wales, letters to George Cornewall Lewis · PRO, letters to Lord Cairns, PRO 30/51

Likenesses F. J. Williamson, marble bust, 1892, Gov. Art Coll. · Aτη [A. Thompson], chromolithograph caricature, NPG; repro. in *VF* (30 April 1870) · Ape [C. Pellegrini], watercolour study, NPG; repro. in *VF* (5 March 1887) · M. Carpenter, oils, Eton · J. Coleridge, oils, Chanter's House, Ottery St Mary, Devon · C. Holl, stipple (after J. T. Coleridge; Grillion's Club series), BM · Shee, oils (after E. U. Eddis, 1878), Middle Temple, London · carte-de-visite (in robes), NPG · group portrait, repro. in *Green Bag*, 5 (1893), 345 · pencil drawing, Balliol Oxf. · photographs, repro. in Coleridge, *Life and correspondence* · portrait, repro. in *Punch* (16 March 1872) · portrait, repro. in *Green Bag*, 3 (1891), 129 · portrait, repro. in *Harper's Weekly*, 35 (1891), 452 · portrait, repro. in *ILN*, 98 (1891), 736 · portrait, repro. in *ILN*, 104 (1894), 787 · portrait, repro. in *Pall Mall*, 29 (1903), 521 · portraits, repro. in *Green Bag*, 6–7 (1894–5), 67, 305

Wealth at death £15,445 4s. 8d.: probate, 4 July 1894, CGPLA Eng. & Wales

Sir John Taylor Coleridge (1790–1876), by Herbert Watkins, 1858

Coleridge, Sir John Taylor (1790–1876), judge, was the second son of Colonel James Coleridge and his wife, Frances Duke, daughter of Bernard Frederick Taylor and descended from the wealthy Duke family of Otterton. A nephew of the poet Samuel Taylor *Coleridge, he was born on 9 July 1790 in St Peter's Street, Tiverton, where his parents lived after their marriage until 1796, when the colonel bought Heath's Court, Ottery St Mary, from the Heath family.

Coleridge was educated from 1796 until 1803 under his uncle, George Coleridge, at the King's School, Ottery St Mary, and then at Eton (1803–9) and Corpus Christi College, Oxford, where he was elected a scholar in 1809. At Corpus he was a friend of Keble and Arnold. His university career was one unbroken triumph. He won the chancellor's prize for Latin verse, the prizes for English and Latin essays, and the Vinerian scholarship. He was placed alone in the first class in classics in 1812 and was elected to a fellowship at Exeter College.

In 1814 a loan from John May, a wealthy Richmond wine merchant and a friend of the family, enabled Coleridge to make a tour of the continent. Between July and December he visited Paris, Lyons, Geneva, and the north of Italy as far as Venice, Bologna, and Florence. On 7 August 1818 he married Mary (1788–1874), second daughter of the Revd Gilbert Buchanan, rector of Woodmansterne, Surrey.

After a period as a special pleader, Coleridge was called to the bar by the Middle Temple on 26 June 1819, helped by a further loan of £1000 from John May. He practised from chambers in 2 Pump Court, Temple, and joined the western circuit and the Exeter sessions.

The early years were financially difficult; on one occasion Coleridge was unable to pay his ironmonger and upholsterer. For the first three years he frequently walked long distances on the western circuit. He supplemented his income from other sources: by taking pupils, including Francis Baring, the future Lord Northbrook, and John Boileau; by writing articles for the *Quarterly Review* and the *British Critic*; by editing Blackstone's *Commentaries*; and by being the editor of the *Quarterly Review* in 1825. In that year he made £962 at the bar, £1000 from the *Quarterly Review*, and £500 for his edition of Blackstone.

From 1826 Coleridge concentrated on his profession. He was leader of the Exeter sessions from 1826, and county counsel from 1827 to 1829. At his best sessions in 1827 he made more than £103. On the western circuit his progress was uneven: Serjeant Wilde was undisputed leader of the circuit from 1826 to 1834; Follett quickly overtook everyone else, but Coleridge established his position immediately after them. On 27 January 1832 he was elected recorder of Exeter by ten votes to seven against Follett. In London he had little business. He was appointed a commissioner in bankruptcy on 12 December 1827. He was counsel in the great case of *Rowe v. Brenton* in November 1828 which brought him into contact with the leading barristers of the time and with the king's advisers. He was appointed serjeant on 14 February 1832, but his practice suffered when the court of common pleas was opened in 1834. In 1834 his income was just under £4000. By 1839 he was in a position to purchase Heath's Court from his elder brother, James Duke Coleridge.

On 27 January 1835 Coleridge was appointed a justice of the court of king's bench by Lord Lyndhurst in the place of Mr Justice Taunton. In civil cases his judgments were learned and elegant: for example, *Stockdale* v. *Hansard* (1839) in constitutional law; the *Bishop of Hereford's case* (1848) in ecclesiastical law; and *Lumley* v. *Gye* (1853) in the law of contract, a dissenting judgment which was praised by Holdsworth. He was involved in unfortunate controversy arising out of *Pooley's case* at Bodmin assizes in 1857. Pooley was convicted of a very offensive blasphemy and sentenced by Coleridge to twenty-one months in prison, but subsequently received a free pardon on grounds of insanity. The case was used in J. S. Mill's *On Liberty* to show that penalties for opinion still existed, and the controversy dragged on in *Fraser's Magazine* and elsewhere. Coleridge retired from the court of queen's bench on 12 June 1858. He had been made a privy councillor on 5 June and served on the judicial committee in ecclesiastical cases for several years. He was offered a peerage by Gladstone in 1869 but refused because of the potential effect on his son's career: if he had become a peer and then died, his son, John Duke *Coleridge, would have lost his position as MP and solicitor-general and, under the accepted rule at that time, the right to practise at the bar.

Coleridge served on a number of commissions, including those on the assize circuits in 1845, on the inns of court in 1854, and on the law courts and popular education in 1858. In 1852 he received the degree of DCL at Oxford, and in 1854 he was appointed a commissioner under the Oxford University Act, in spite of a motion in the House of Commons to exclude him on the grounds that he was an extreme high-churchman. His published lecture entitled *On Public School Education* (1860) contributed to the appointment of a royal commission on the public schools in 1861.

A prolific writer, Coleridge left a manuscript journal covering the period from 1820 to 1876, of which a few extracts have been published in books about the Coleridge family. He corresponded with Arnold, Southey, Newman, Pusey, and Keble, and his *Life of Keble* (1869) is heavily based on that correspondence. He was a close friend and admirer of the Tractarians, though never in entire agreement with them, as he made clear in his *Life of Keble*.

Coleridge had six children: Mary Dorothy Frances Coleridge (1819–1820); John Duke (1820–1894), the future lord chief justice; Henry James *Coleridge (1822–1893), an Anglican priest who entered the Roman Catholic church in 1852; Mary Frances Keble Coleridge (1824–1898), who rejected a proposal of marriage in 1845 from Roundell Palmer, the future Lord Chancellor Selborne, to her father's deep regret; Alethea Buchanan Coleridge (1826–1909), who married J. F. Mackarness, the future bishop of Oxford; and Frederick William Coleridge (1828–1843). Coleridge's wife died on 8 March 1874; he died at Heath's Court, Ottery St Mary, on 11 February 1876 and was buried in the family vault there on 17 February.

DAVID PUGSLEY

Sources J. Coleridge, journal, 1820–76 · T. Toohey, *Piety and the professions: Sir John Coleridge and his sons* (1987) · E. H. Coleridge, *Life of Lord Coleridge*, 2 vols. (1904) · B. J. S. Coleridge, *The story of a Devonshire house* (1905)
Archives BL, corresp. and family papers, Add. MS 47553 · Bodl. Oxf., corresp., MSS Eng. Lett. d. 126–31 · Chanter's House, Ottery St Mary, Devon, Coleridge family MSS · Devon RO, letters · Glamorgan RO, Cardiff, opinion relating to Criminal Law Consolidations Bill · Indiana University, Bloomington, Lilly Library, corresp. · Notts. Arch., opinion relating to mining rights of Mundy and Charlton | BL, corresp. with W. E. Gladstone, Add. MS 444138 · Bodl. Oxf., letters to John May · Devon RO, letters to Sir Thomas Dyke Acland · Keble College, Oxford, letters to Keble family · LPL, letters to Lord Selborne · NL Scot., letters to J. G. Lockhart
Likenesses M. Carpenter, oils, 1829, Chanter's House, Ottery St Mary, Devon · H. W. Pickersgill, oils, 1835, Exeter College, Oxford · H. Watkins, photograph, 1858, NPG [*see illus.*] · J. Fortescue, portrait, 1872, Chanter's House, Ottery St Mary, Devon · M. Carpenter, oils, Eton · S. Cousins, mezzotint (after M. Carpenter), BM, NPG; repro. in *Art Journal*, 56 (1904), 29 · wood-engraving (after photograph), repro. in *ILN*, 68 (1876), 213
Wealth at death under £35,000: probate, 8 March 1876, *CGPLA Eng. & Wales*

Coleridge, Mary Elizabeth [*pseud.* Anodos] (**1861–1907**), poet and writer, was born on 23 September 1861 at Hyde Park Square, London, the elder of the two daughters of Arthur Duke Coleridge and Mary Ann Jameson (*d.* 1898). Her father, the great-nephew of the poet Samuel Taylor *Coleridge (1772–1834), was clerk of the assize on the midland circuit; her mother's family came from Dublin.

Mary's parents were both keen amateur musicians. Her father held musical evenings at their home attended by singers such as Jenny Lind, and also entertained poets and painters. Tennyson, Browning (one of Mary's heroes), and Millais were all frequent visitors to their house at 12 Cromwell Place, London, though shyness often prevented Mary from speaking to them. She was educated largely at home, and at the age of twelve, intrigued by the strange shapes of Hebrew letters, asked her father to teach her the language. By nineteen she had also mastered German, French, and Italian, and had begun to teach herself Greek. Throughout her childhood she wrote verse and stories, revealing early the signs of the unique imagination which shaped her later novels and poetry.

Mary was tutored by her father's friend William Cory, a scholar and schoolmaster of some repute, whose career at Eton had been cut short after a scandal arose over a letter written to a favourite pupil. Cory moved to Hampstead when Mary was in her early twenties and she began to attend lessons in Greek and Latin at his home, along with a group of friends. He fondly referred to them as his 'Grecian Ladies' (Mackenzie, 129). A poet himself, Cory had a profound influence upon Mary.

By her early twenties Mary had established a close circle of female friends made up of five women from similarly sheltered backgrounds. She once declared that she found the Elizabethan idea of friendship 'much stronger and more sensitive, and closer to the Victorian, than anything in between' (*Gathered Leaves*, 255). When she visited Italy in 1893 she found it to be the 'Motherland … [she] had always longed for and never known' (ibid., 35). Poems such as 'The White Women' and 'A Day-Dream' echo this need for female space, mapping out imaginary or mythic territories inhabited by communities of women. On the smaller scale, other poems ('Gone', 'Friends', 'Mortal Combat') chart the pleasures and pains of friendship.

At the age of twenty Mary had begun to write articles for periodicals such as the *Monthly Packet* and *Merry England*. In 1893 her first novel, *The Seven Sleepers of Ephesus*, a fantastical romance, was published. Although the work earned praise from Robert Louis Stevenson for the 'devilish' ingenuity (*Gathered Leaves*, 56) of its plot, it was not a commercial success. Henry Newbolt, the young barrister with literary aspirations whom she had met when he married one of her circle, Margaret Duckworth, had become a close friend by this time. The Newbolts met regularly with Mary and another friend, Ella Coltman, to discuss work in progress. This group, facetiously nicknamed 'The Settee' by excluded friends, witnessed the publication, in 1897, of Mary's second novel, *The King with Two Faces*. This historical romance, set in eighteenth-century Sweden, ran to several editions, firmly establishing her reputation as a novelist.

When the poet Robert Bridges came across the manuscript of Mary's poems, which had been purposely left lying on a hall table at his home by Mary's friend (and his wife's cousin) Violet Hodgkin, he expressed a desire to see them published. With his help, her first volume of poems, *Fancy's Following* (1896), was published, semi-privately, by the Daniel Press in Oxford. Ever aware of the long shadow cast by Samuel Taylor Coleridge, her 'fairy great-great-uncle' (*Gathered Leaves*, 11), she refused to publish the poems in her own name, and took her pseudonym, Anodos ('on no road'), from George MacDonald's fairy romance *Phantastes*. Throughout her life she was to feel the mixed blessings of such a famous ancestor, and some of her best poems, such as 'The Witch' and 'Wilderspin', are haunted by his presence.

In 1897 another volume, *Fancy's Guerdon*, was published by Elkin Matthews, and throughout the last eight years of Mary's life poems appeared in *The Spectator* and *The Pilot*. During the 1890s, influenced by Tolstoy, she began teaching literature to a group of working women, first at her home and later at the Working Women's College in Fitzroy Street, London. However, she remained steadfastly opposed to the condescending attitude behind many Victorian 'good works' and once declared her hatred of philanthropy (*Collected Poems*, 71). She continued to contribute articles to the *Monthly Review* and *The Guardian* and in 1902 began to write for the *Times Literary Supplement*. She also published three more novels: *The Fiery Dawn* (1901), *The Shadow on the Wall* (1904), and *The Lady on the Drawing Room Floor* (1906).

In 1907, on the family's annual visit to Harrogate in Yorkshire, Mary suffered an attack of acute appendicitis. She died a few days later, on 25 August. During her last weeks she had been working on a biography of the Pre-Raphaelite painter Holman Hunt, which was published in 1908. Her best poems include brief, intense lyrics such as 'L'oiseau bleu' and 'The Lady of Trees' which seem effortlessly to convey a mood or spirit of place. Others, such as 'An Insincere Wish Addressed to a Beggar', offer an ironic comment on contemporary society. The late twentieth century witnessed something of a revival of critical interest in her work.   KATHARINE McGOWRAN

Sources E. Sichel, 'Memoir', in *Gathered leaves from the prose of Mary E. Coleridge*, ed. E. Sichel (1910) · T. Whistler, ed., *The collected poems of Mary Coleridge* (1954) · R. Bridges, 'The poems of Mary Coleridge', *Cornhill Magazine*, [3rd] ser., 23 (1907), 594–605 · F. C. Mackenzie, *William Cory: a biography* (1950) · T. Whistler, *Imagination of the heart: the life of Walter de la Mare* (1993) · *The Times* (28 Aug 1907) · R. Russell, 'Mary Elizabeth Coleridge and her poetry', BLitt diss., U. Oxf., 1951 · M. E. Coleridge, *Non sequitur* (1900) · 'Mary E. Coleridge', *Victorian women poets: an anthology*, ed. A. Leighton and M. Reynolds (1995), 610–26 · *DNB* · *CGPLA Eng. & Wales* (1907)

Archives Bodl. Oxf., letters and MSS relating to Robert Bridges · Worcester College, Oxford, letters to C. H. O. Daniel

Wealth at death £147 16s. 3d.: administration, 18 Oct 1907, *CGPLA Eng. & Wales*

Coleridge, Samuel Taylor (1772–1834), poet, critic, and philosopher, was born on 21 October 1772 at Ottery St Mary, Devon, and baptized there on 30 December, the youngest of ten children born to John *Coleridge (*bap.* 1719, *d.* 1781), vicar of the town and master of the grammar school, and his second wife, Ann, *née* Bowden (1727–1809). There were also three surviving half-sisters by John Coleridge's first wife, who died in 1751.

Childhood and schooling From earliest years Coleridge was singularly precocious and imaginative. 'I never thought as a Child', he said, 'never had the language of a Child' (*Notebooks*, 5.6675). He early showed a devotion to books, claiming to have been able to read a book of the Bible by the time he was three, and the *Arabian Nights* when he was five. His nurse's preference for his brother Frank caused him, he said, to read at his mother's side and to play only by himself. His precociousness led to flattery from old women and to a growing unpopularity among fellow children: soon he was far more accustomed to the conversation of adults. A quarrel on one occasion in which Frank baited him as their mother's favourite led to his running away from home and staying out all night by the River Otter; he was rescued eventually by a neighbour, Sir Stafford Northcote, though not before he had suffered exposure to which he partly attributed his later rheumatic ill health. He continued to be absorbed in books, notably romances and tales of magic—so much so that his father became alarmed and burnt some of them.

The most traumatic experience of Coleridge's early years, in 1781 when he was nearly nine, was the sudden death of his father in the middle of an October night. Immediately before, John Coleridge had travelled to Plymouth with his son Frank, who was enlisting as a midshipman, a typical move for the Coleridge family, their mother being strongly ambitious for them—even though her husband would have been content for them to become blacksmiths so long as they were happy. The sudden bereavement left Ann Coleridge with the difficult task of planning at short notice for the future of her precocious youngest, and she must have felt that his promise called for a course of action commensurate with his potential.

Samuel Taylor Coleridge (1772–1834), by Peter Vandyke, 1795

According to Henry Crabb Robinson, Judge Buller, a former pupil of John Coleridge's, said he would take him to London and send him to Charterhouse, an offer which was gratefully accepted; but in the event he arranged a presentation to Christ's Hospital, a school for orphans. Despite its strong academic reputation, Coleridge claimed, the ambitious members of the family felt degraded by this eventuality and his brothers later refused to receive him in his bluecoat uniform. His mother signed the application, nevertheless, and he was accepted. Coleridge departed for London and for a time was looked after by his mother's brother, who treated him kindly and took him round coffee houses to be admired as a young prodigy; in July he was given his uniform and taken to the junior school at Hertford, where again he was treated well before being transferred in the autumn to the great school itself.

Plucked from Devon surroundings where he was looked up to locally while enjoying the intense emotions of family life, and set down in the impersonal surroundings of a late eighteenth-century London school, Coleridge evidently found it hard to forgive his mother for countenancing the dramatic change; it probably accounts for a coldness in their subsequent relationship. Life at Christ's Hospital, as described both by his friend Charles Lamb in 'Christ's Hospital thirty-five years ago', and by himself in poems such as 'Frost at Midnight' and his verse 'Letter to Sara Hutchinson', was harsh. Food was poor and meagre, the dormitories Spartan; the reaction of the young Coleridge was apparently one of depression and recalcitrance. Despite his omnivorous reading, he acquired in the lower school a reputation for dullness and ineptitude marked by a general unwillingness to learn simple rules of syntax;

his older friend Thomas Middleton found him reading Virgil for pleasure, however, and reported the fact admiringly to the headmaster. Boyer, a man of brusque Johnsonian common sense, took notice and ensured that he was put in the way of becoming a Grecian; being addicted also to the infliction of corporal punishment after the pedagogic practices of the time, however, he in no way relaxed his discipline, and Coleridge, while respecting his teaching abilities, maintained that his severities haunted the nightmares of his later life.

The rigours of the school were by no means unremitting. Coleridge was initially received at Buller's house, but imagining himself slighted by being put at the lower table he soon stayed proudly away. Although feeling lonely and neglected as a result, he continued to be entertained occasionally at his uncle's house. His bookishness was meanwhile assisted by a strange incident. A passer-by in the street against whom he struck a glancing blow mistook him for a pickpocket, and relented only on being told that his sweeping gesture had been that of Leander swimming the Hellespont; he was then sufficiently impressed to make Coleridge free of Thomas Boosey's lending library in Cheapside, where he proceeded to devour his way through the whole catalogue. Coleridge describes the effects of this mixture of physical deprivation and imaginative richness on him at fourteen vividly: how he would find himself in Robinson Crusoe's island, 'finding a Mountain of Plum Cake, and eating out a room for myself, and then eating it into the shapes of Chairs & Tables—Hunger and Fancy—' (*Notebooks*, 5.6675). His brothers George and Luke both went to London, and Coleridge, walking the wards of the London Hospital with Luke and delighted if he could hold a plaster or attend the dressings, became for a time eager to pursue medicine as his career. At another time, not relishing the prospect of proceeding to university, he decided to become apprenticed to a neighbouring friendly shoemaker (possibly hoping to follow in the footsteps of his hero the shoemaker mystic Jacob Boehme). The man accordingly approached Boyer for permission, to be met with such a storm of anger that he retreated forthwith.

Coleridge went on to 'bewilder' himself—a term suggesting Milton's argumentative devils—in metaphysics and theological controversy (Coleridge, *Biographia literaria*, *Collected Works*, 7/1.15). A declaration of allegiance to the principles of Voltaire occasioned a flogging of particular severity—the only just flogging, he later claimed, that he ever received at Boyer's hands. A different fruit of his reading was an enthusiasm for the Neoplatonists, whose writings were being translated by Thomas Taylor; Middleton meanwhile introduced him to the poetry of William Lisle Bowles. Nor can he have been unaware of religious developments in London such as the advent of Swedenborgianism, or of the events abroad that were changing human thought—the making of a new sovereign state in America, the stirrings that were shortly to produce the French Revolution.

Other diversions of Coleridge's schooldays included swimming: a dip in the New River with all his clothes on was followed by an attack of jaundice and rheumatic fever that exacted a long period in the school sick ward. He also formed another attachment. Mrs Evans, mother of one of his schoolfellows, he came to regard as a mother more adequate than his own, while Mary, one of her daughters, was the object of his first intense love: they soon agreed that they 'thought in all things alike' (*Collected Letters*, 1.113). In summer 1789 he revisited Ottery for the first time in many years.

Cambridge Coleridge left Christ's Hospital on 7 September 1790 and was appointed by his school to an exhibition of £40 a year in the following January, being admitted in his absence as a sizar at Jesus College, Cambridge, on 5 February 1791. He entered into residence the following October, was made a pensioner on 5 November 1791, and matriculated on 31 March 1792. At Jesus he also held a Rustat scholarship, restricted to the sons of clergymen and worth about £25 a year, and was subsequently made chapel clerk; on 5 June 1793 he was elected a foundation scholar. In his first year he seems to have worked hard, encouraged by Middleton (then in his last year at Pembroke College) and won the Browne medal for classical poetry with a Greek Sapphic ode on the slave trade which he read at Commencement. The summer was spent in Ottery, where among other things he helped a friend prepare a paper on recent poetry, probably for the Society of Gentlemen at Exeter.

The following academic year was more eventful. With events in France building up towards the terror, politics were under intense discussion. Charles Le Grice later recalled how the group he belonged to would meet in the evening to discuss the latest pamphlet: 'There was no need of having the book before us. Coleridge had read it in the morning, and in the evening he would repeat whole pages verbatim' (Chambers, 20). In the university, meanwhile, attention became focused on the trial of William Frend, fellow of Jesus College, for publishing a tract, *Peace and Union Recommended ...*, in which he attacked the liturgy of the church, expressing views which the authorities, apprehensive, like many in the country at that time, of possibly seditious activities, regarded as dangerous to church and king. At Frend's trial in the Senate House in May 1793 Coleridge was prominent among the undergraduates who thronged the gallery, and narrowly escaped punishment for vociferous applause. After Frend was banished from the university (though without losing the benefit of his college fellowship) Coleridge continued to see him through shared acquaintances in London such as Lamb and George Dyer.

After another visit to his Devon relatives in the long vacation Coleridge returned to college where he participated in a literary group convened by Christopher Wordsworth, expressing his enthusiasm for Neoplatonic philosophy and the poetry of Bowles and reporting to them that his west country associates had rated highly the recently published poems of Christopher's older brother William. By now, problems were accruing. Debts had mounted for Coleridge, beginning with his rashness in ordering furniture thoughtlessly for his college room. He had hoped to

meet them first by winning the Craven studentship (for which he was in the final four, the award being made, however, to the youngest) and then by winning the Browne medal again with his Greek 'Ode to Astronomy', but was this time unsuccessful. Earlier in the year, in February, he was addressing Mary Evans 'with the ardour of fraternal friendship' (*Collected Letters*, 1.52) while being, by his later account, desperately in love with her and knowing that she reciprocated his feelings, yet not daring to declare his love, given his lack of means to support her. Instead, he plunged into a course of life which included associations which he was privately to term his 'Unchastities' (ibid., 2.734). His description in 1803 of a dream in which Sal Hall, a Cambridge prostitute, was importuning him and his account in 1799 to Godwin of waking up in a house of ill fame in London in December that year offer clues to this part of his life.

Enlistment and Pantisocracy In December, at his wits' end, Coleridge fled to London. There, after spending his last money on a lottery ticket which failed to win, writing a poem on the event, and contemplating suicide, he presented himself as a volunteer for the 15th light dragoons under the assumed name Silas Tomkyn Comberbache. Despite the family tradition of military service, it is a measure of his desperation that he was willing to put himself at the service of an army already engaged in a war so unpopular with him and his friends; it is an indication of the army's current need for men that it was willing to enlist so unpromising a recruit. Coleridge described himself as 'a very indocile Equestrian' (*Collected Letters*, 1.66) and means were soon found by which he could serve without training directly for battle. Meanwhile he took no great steps to guard his anonymity, if accounts are to be believed of how he startled officers by casual interventions betraying his conversancy with the classical languages; eventually his identity was unmasked through a chance meeting in the street with some college friends. Penitent letters to his brothers at the beginning of February were followed by the purchase of his discharge, and he returned to Cambridge, where, it is recorded, he was 'admonished by the Master in the presence of the Fellows' on 12 April 1794.

In spite of this reprieve and his acceptance of the penalties that accompanied it, Coleridge had been unsettled by his military experience and found it hard to resume a normal academic life. By mid-June he was setting off with a companion, Joseph Hucks, for a walking tour to north Wales. On the way they stopped in Oxford, hoping to find subscribers for Coleridge's projected 'Imitations from the Modern Latin Poets', and called on his fellow Grecian Bob Allen, who introduced him to a Balliol undergraduate, Robert Southey (1774–1843). The two young men got on so well that the Welsh tour was delayed for three weeks while they discussed the parlous state of current civilization and brooded on a democratic alternative. Then Coleridge set off on the tour to the Snowdon region, which was marked by an unexpected event: attending church at Wrexham, he saw Mary Evans's sister Anne, and afterwards Mary herself passing his inn. The effect of seeing her again was so overwhelming that social and political questions were momentarily driven from his mind.

On returning to Bristol these questions again assumed full prominence, as the scheme which Southey and Coleridge came to call Pantisocracy (from the Greek, 'government by all equally') took shape—strongly influenced no doubt by the departure earlier that year of Joseph Priestley for America with a plan (never fully carried out) to found a settlement in Pennsylvania on the banks of the Susquehannah. The young men's version was for a community in the same area of North America, consisting of twelve young men and twelve young women who would marry and bring up their children in innocence of the corrupt traditions and conventions of the Europe they had left behind, educating them in principles of wisdom and benevolence that would ensure a better new generation. Opportunely, they came to know the family of Mrs Fricker, a widow whose daughters seemed likely and willing to provide the desired female companionship; Southey was attached to Edith, while Coleridge interested himself in her sister Sara. An important addition to their circle of acquaintance came with a visit to Thomas Poole, an independent-minded tanner at Nether Stowey, who combined social concern with strong common sense, and who listened sympathetically to their ideas. There would be no private property; according to Poole the men expected to labour for two or three hours each morning to support the colony (basing their figure on Adam Smith's calculation that only one-twentieth of working time in Britain was spent on productive labour), while their leisure hours would be devoted to study, discussion, and the education of the children.

As time passed, the planning was dogged by difficulties: the problem of raising sufficient money for the passage, questions such as whether further relatives should accompany them, or servants should have equal status. Coleridge returned for the Michaelmas term to Cambridge, where Pantisocracy became a central topic of interest and controversy. He defended the scheme against all comers but met strong criticisms, including a friend's sharp comment that 'the women' would spoil it (*Collected Letters*, 1.122). Women were indeed proving to be a problem in another manner. Coleridge had promised to write to Sara but was failing to do so, and his allegiance to the scheme received a sharp set-back when he unexpectedly received a thoughtful and finely phrased letter from Mary Evans, recalling the closeness of their intellectual companionship and exercising all her rational powers in an attempt to dissuade him from the Pantisocratic venture. His feelings for her swept back. Hearing that she was engaged to be married, he wrote shortly after to ask if the story was true, at last declaring his love. Her reply, which has not survived, was evidently a death blow to his hopes. Having left Cambridge during the term to pay a visit to London he lingered, drinking egg-hot, smoking Oronooko, and exchanging condolences with the recently jilted Lamb, while delighting all by his conversation. Southey, increasingly disquieted, wrote pointing out that he must make his intentions clear to Sara, who was being

pursued by other men. Eventually he went to London and Coleridge, still mourning the loss of Mary Evans ('my ideal standard of female excellence rises not above that woman'; ibid., 1.145), was reclaimed for Pantisocracy and Sara Fricker.

Lecturing and *The Watchman* The two young men now set up as lecturers in Bristol, with Coleridge speaking on political issues of the day such as the slave trade and then undertaking a series entitled 'On revealed religion, its corruptions and its political views'. Politically, he was sailing near the wind, given the recent actions of the government against persons supposed guilty of seditious statements, but the collapse of the London treason trials at the end of 1794 had acted as a safeguard for free speech. His views, attacking the government and the war against France but also condemning the violence of the French Revolution, with a call for wider education and strong criticisms concerning current political abuses of language, were tolerated or ignored.

In October, still acting on the sense of duty instilled by Southey, Coleridge married Sara Fricker (1770–1845). The apprehension he felt was increased by the fact that the church, St Mary Redcliffe in Bristol, was closely associated with the poet Thomas Chatterton. The couple spent their honeymoon in nearby Clevedon, where Coleridge showed his growing poetic and speculative capabilities in 'The Eolian Harp', written there probably just before their marriage. He was surprised at his contentment, writing to Southey in November, 'I love and I am beloved, and I am happy!' (*Collected Letters*, 1.164). Another poem soon followed, 'Reflections on Having Left a Place of Retirement', when he left Sara for a time while he returned to Bristol, intent on finding a way of meeting his growing responsibilities. In the poem's last line, voicing his future commitment to 'Science, Freedom and the Truth in Christ', Coleridge summarized succinctly the guiding principles of his reformist views, based on those of the admired Priestley and his enthusiasm for scientific investigation, libertarian politics, and Unitarian religion. The Pantisocratic scheme, meanwhile, quietly collapsed, a chief factor being Southey's unwillingness to proceed.

As an important gateway to America and a central outlet of the sugar trade, Bristol was at this time an important centre for new movements and ideas, creating new wealth in the district and not only stimulating a spirit of enterprise, enquiry, and libertarianism but raising political issues such as the employment of slaves in the West Indian plantations. After considering various alternatives, Coleridge decided to start a journal of his own devoted primarily to such matters, to be called *The Watchman*. A tour to the midlands and north canvassing potential support produced enough subscriptions to make the project a practical one while enabling him to meet leading figures of the day such as Erasmus Darwin and Joseph Wright at Derby. The first number appeared on 1 March 1796, bearing the 'seditious'—yet biblical—motto, 'That all may know the Truth; and that the Truth may make us free!' Publishing every eighth day to avoid the weekly stamp tax, Coleridge relied heavily on extraneous sources, but could also use much writing, including verse, of his own. The magazine lasted for ten issues. In April he also published his first verse collection, *Poems on Various Subjects*, beginning with his 'Monody on the Death of Chatterton' and ending with the long 'Religious Musings', where he eulogized both Priestley and a new hero, David Hartley, related to his growing psychological interests. 'Metaphysics, & Poetry, & "Facts of Mind"', he wrote to Thelwall in November, 'are my darling studies' (*Collected Letters*, 1.260). The evidence of his reading is that he was constantly trying to bring together esoteric psychological insights—especially from the Neoplatonists and from modern investigators—to throw more light on the human mind.

Subventions from his friends and a grant of £10 from the Royal Society of Literature helped cover Coleridge's losses but the need to find a means of support was now urgent. An offer of a tutorship fell through, that of a London co-editorship was turned down. An important new association was with William Wordsworth (1770–1850), met the previous year in Bristol and currently living with his sister Dorothy (1771–1855) at Racedown in Dorset: in May Coleridge referred to him as 'a very dear friend … in my opinion the best poet of the age' (*Collected Letters*, 1.215). Awareness of the Wordsworths' frugal way of life may have prompted a new plan, following the birth of his first child—named (David) Hartley *Coleridge (1796–1849) in honour of his new hero—to find a cottage at Stowey near Tom Poole where he might bring up his children 'in the simplicity of peasants, their food, dress and habits completely rustic' (ibid., 1.240). Early in December he wrote to Poole asking him to buy a cottage available there in Lime Street, which Poole (reluctant on grounds of its smallness and dampness) was eventually persuaded by his entreaties to do. The little family moved there at the end of the year.

Collaboration with the Wordsworths At the invitation of Sheridan, Coleridge began writing a play, *Osorio*, for production at Drury Lane, hoping for recognition and some financial reward; he also prepared a new edition of his poems for publication by Cottle. A visit from Wordsworth in March prompted a visit to both William and Dorothy at Racedown, where Dorothy responded enthusiastically to his intelligence. Both poets had now finished tragedies, which they read to one another. After a fortnight William returned with Coleridge to Stowey, where he was joined by his sister at the beginning of July; a neighbouring mansion, Alfoxden, being temporarily vacant, Poole negotiated a lease and they moved in shortly afterwards. This initiated an intensively productive period for the three, in which writing was coupled with frequent walks in the Quantocks and beyond, Dorothy's acute sensibility acting as a powerful stimulus to both men. Coleridge entered on the most brilliant period of his career: although oppressed by severe doubts about his ultimate religious beliefs, he was excited by the world of speculation opened out by scientific discoveries concerning oxygen and the vital powers of the human body.

In July Coleridge was visited by Lamb, who joined the walk described in the poem 'This Lime-Tree Bower my

Prison', and John Thelwall, whose theories of vitality had recently intrigued him. Having recently been tried and narrowly escaped being found guilty of treason as a result of his progressive political views, Thelwall wished for a quiet place of retirement and hoped to find a house in the neighbourhood. By this time however alarm had been aroused locally by the abortive invasion at Fishguard and the Wordsworths were suspected of being French spies: a government agent was sent down to investigate. His report from Stowey, which has survived in the Home Office papers (domestic, vol. 137, Geo. III, 1797), stated that 'a sett of violent Democrats' had taken possession of Alfoxden; they were not French but a mischievous group of disaffected Englishmen, known to be in contact with Thelwall and with the Tom Poole who had established a 'Poor Man's Club' in the town. Coleridge advised Thelwall that it would not be easy to find a house for him nor politic for him to settle so close.

A few weeks later a new and important figure made his presence felt. Thomas Wedgwood, who knew Wordsworth through the Pinney family and who was, with his brother Josiah, devoted to advanced thinking, had come to Bristol to be under the care of Thomas Beddoes at Clifton, being in poor health. He had recently conceived a plan for educating a genius according to the latest theories by rigidly controlling the sense impressions it received from birth onwards, with hard objects hung around it in the nursery to irritate and no time spent outdoors: 'How astonishingly the powers and produce of the mind would be increased by a fixed habit of earnest thought' (Cornwell, 177–8). The scheme was to be governed by a committee of philosophers, the only likely superintendents he knew being Wordsworth and Coleridge. In September he came over to Alfoxden and spent several days there. The details of the proposed scheme no doubt prompted both poets to reflect on what they considered the proper way of educating genius in children—not by exerting an iron control over all their sense impressions, but by encouraging cultivation of their imagination, even—in Wordsworth's view at least—a freedom to run wild.

Collaboration between them flourished. Early in November the three set out on an excursion to Linton and the Valley of Stones in the course of which a poem was planned, to be called 'The Wanderings of Cain'. In the event Coleridge produced only a draft—and then mostly in prose—while Wordsworth found himself powerless, but different possibilities arose. It may well have been during this same walking tour (in one account, Coleridge, *Poems*, 232, Coleridge refers to 'the fall of the year') that the 'retirement between Lynton & Porlock' (*Notebooks*, 3.4006) took place, during which Coleridge, having taken 'two grains of Opium … to check a dysentery', composed in 'a sort of Reverie' (Coleridge, *Poems*, 232) his poem 'Kubla Khan', to be recited in company on several subsequent occasions and published nearly twenty years later as a 'psychological curiosity' (ibid., 228). (The 'Cain' scheme may help to explain some of the imagery of the poem, as well as the significance of the name 'Can', spelt thus in the manuscript version.) Coleridge's account in the 1816 preface of being interrupted by 'a person on business from Porlock' whose visit blocked completion of the poem, though in all probability a fiction, has found a permanent place in subsequent literary tradition. In mid-November Dorothy Wordsworth reported that the three had undertaken another, shorter expedition, during which the two poets had laid the plan for a ballad, to be published with some pieces by her brother. This was the first conception of 'The Rime of the Ancient Mariner' and of *Lyrical Ballads*, the volume in which it was published. Although the work was planned jointly, Wordsworth recorded that Coleridge's invention soon took over the ballad as a whole. Just as the content of 'Kubla Khan' had been determined by Coleridge's previous readings in poetry and mythology, he was able to draw for this new poem on his reading in travel literature, supplemented by these same sources. Recognizing it also as a contribution to the growing literature of the supernatural, he planned a further poem, 'Christabel', where he hoped to be even more successful in casting a spell of imagination over a story realistically narrated.

These were not the only poetic fruits of 1797. In the autumn an enlarged version of Coleridge's *Poems* appeared, freshly entitled *Poems, to which are now Added, Poems by Charles Lamb and Charles Lloyd*. Any gratification his two friends might have felt at being included in the same collection seeped away, however, when he sent to the *Monthly Magazine* under the pseudonym of Nehemiah Higginbottom three 'Sonnets attempted in the manner of contemporary poets', in which, according to his own account, he satirized the defects of all three authors, including himself—notably an 'affectation of unaffectedness' and a cult of 'simplicity'. Lamb and Lloyd were not amused by what they took to be directed primarily against themselves. Lloyd, meanwhile, was producing his novel *Edmund Oliver*. Coleridge, thinking the hero's 'love-fit, debaucheries, leaving college & going into the army' were clearly based on his own (*Collected Letters*, 1.404), was resentful in his turn at the breach of confidence.

The Wedgwood annuity In December Coleridge was invited to stay at Cote House, near Bristol, where the Wedgwoods' brother-in-law James Mackintosh, a gifted philosopher, was impressed by his capabilities and recommended him to his late wife's brother Daniel Stuart, now editor of the *Morning Post*. The introduction produced helpful offers of work but Coleridge still faced the need to find a settled income to support his growing family. Tom Wedgwood wrote with his brother Josiah shortly after to express concern at his having to look for an inevitably time-consuming profession when he might be developing his talents through further study, and enclosing a draft for £100. Coleridge first wrote, with Poole's encouragement, to accept then decided to return it, on the grounds that he needed a more permanent source of income.

Coleridge had recently been preaching by invitation in Unitarian chapels in his neighbourhood and, according to his own later account, was coming to be thought of by some as the 'rising star' of the movement. His friend J. P. Estlin, the minister in Bristol, had heard that John Rowe, the current minister at Shrewsbury, was planning to join him in Bristol and arranged for him to be considered for the vacant post. Accordingly, Coleridge travelled to the Shropshire town, though he thought it unlikely he would be appointed, to meet and preach to the congregation there. Among those present was the young William Hazlitt (1778–1830), who had walked 10 miles from Wem and who described the occasion in his essay 'My first acquaintance with poets':

> Coleridge rose and gave out his text 'And he went up into the mountain to pray, HIMSELF ALONE' … and when he came to the two last words, which he pronounced loud, deep and distinct, it seemed to me who was then young, as if the words had echoed from the bottom of the human heart, and as if that prayer might have floated in solemn silence through the universe. (*Complete Works*, 17.108–9)

Coleridge, he recalled, discoursed on the necessary separation between the spirit of the world and that of Christianity, describing vividly the evils of militarism: aware that Shrewsbury was home to many aristocrats he was no doubt anxious to put all his cards on the table straight away. He told Hazlitt, similarly, that before accepting the post at Shrewsbury he would have preached two sermons, one on infant baptism, the other on the Lord's Supper, showing that he could not administer either. He was attracted by the Shrewsbury post, particularly since its doctrinal requirements would have been minimal: 'it will be necessary for me, in order to my continuance, to believe that Jesus Christ was the Messiah—in all other points I may play off my intellect *ad libitum*' (*Collected Letters*, 1.366). While he was considering the position, however, he received a further letter from the Wedgwoods containing the unconditional offer of an annuity of £150 per annum, which after no more than a little thought he accepted, withdrawing his candidacy, looking after Mr Rowe's duty for two weeks, and then returning to Stowey. Hazlitt, who had been enchanted by the visit, was invited to visit Nether Stowey in the spring and did so.

Coleridge was now faced with the need to organize his life in accordance with his newly found independence. The judgement of a later biographer that 'perhaps the worst thing possible had happened to him' since 'it was time for him … to take up his share of the economic burden which is … the common lot of humanity' (Chambers, 90) is hard to support, given the flowering of his genius during the period that immediately followed. In these months he wrote 'Frost at Midnight', completed the 'Ancient Mariner', and produced one or two more contributions for the *Lyrical Ballads* volume. Considering how he might best spend his time in accordance with the hopes of the Wedgwoods, he concluded that he should fulfil a plan he had been nursing for some time by spending a period in Germany and following the current intellectual developments there, in fields ranging from nervous physiology to biblical criticism. William and Dorothy Wordsworth, whose lease of Alfoxden had not been renewed, agreed to join him. All three no doubt looked forward to seeing life under a political system differing significantly from that in their own country and in the disappointing France, where suppression of the Swiss cantons had led Coleridge to write a poem, called first 'Recantation' and then 'France: an Ode', to mourn the eclipse of liberty signalled by that event, and publish it with 'Frost at Midnight' and 'Fears in Solitude'. (The two men may also have been apprehensive at the possibility of being called on for military service, but there is no direct evidence to support this.)

Germany, 1798–1799 On 16 September the three friends set sail from Yarmouth, accompanied by John Chester, a neighbour and admirer in Stowey. Having arrived in Hamburg, then a centre of political intrigue owing to the international tensions of the war, they called on the poet Klopstock and made their way south, the Wordsworths to Goslar, where they hoped to live cheaply, and Coleridge first to learn the German language at Ratzeburg, then to the university town of Göttingen, at this time one of the most stimulating centres of learning in Europe. Coleridge benefited from his stay in various ways. He was instructed in the language by Tychsen and Benecke and studied the origins of German poetry, particularly the Minnesinger; acquainted himself with Eichhorn's biblical criticism (considerably in advance of similar studies in England); talked with the Kantian philosophers, acquiring a knowledge of the rich Spinozist tradition; and heard the physiological lectures of Blumenbach, to whom he had an introduction. Only in the last case did he suffer a set-back; if he was hoping to hear about the latest work on hypnotism (which had made brief appearances in the original 'Ancient Mariner') it must have been dispiriting to discover that Blumenbach did not even believe in the existence of the phenomenon.

In February Coleridge's second son Berkeley, born the previous May, died of convulsions, but he did not hear the news until April. He was discouraged by Poole from returning home immediately and in the event did not arrive until late July, having in the meantime undertaken walking tours to the Brocken and elsewhere. It is likely that his failure to be with his wife during this time contributed to the subsequent rift between them.

West country and London, 1799–1800 The situation had changed in other ways. Whether or not Coleridge recognized the fact at the time, the German stay had proved to be a turning point in his career. He could not simply return to the provincial English society he had left and take up the threads as he had left them. Although he did not formally acknowledge the fact at the time, his enthusiasm for Unitarianism, also, was dying. Instead he was working out the implications of Spinozism as encountered in Germany. A new and exciting acquaintance was with Humphry Davy, Spinozist poet and experimenter with nitrous oxide, Beddoes's young assistant in Bristol, who was shortly to move to London, where Coleridge would attend his lectures 'to increase his stock of metaphors' (Paris, 1.138). Much as he might strive for a continuity with his earlier west country life, talking to Poole and planning a joint poem on Muhammad with Southey, his true magnetism was to the Wordsworths, now in the

north. At Sockburn in co. Durham in October he found them visiting their childhood friends Mary Hutchinson (later William's wife) and her sister Sara, and set off with William and his brother John on a walking tour of the Lake District. At the end he returned to Sockburn, where he fell in love with Sara Hutchinson as they stood together by the fire one evening.

Next Coleridge travelled south to London, where Daniel Stuart had recently offered him a post as staff writer on the *Morning Post*, enabling him to comment directly on current political events. Exactly how much influence he wielded is hard to determine, and after his death Stuart claimed that his subsequent estimates had been exaggerated. Yet it was a time when the public was especially in need of informed commentary, and the contemporary format of newspapers, consisting mainly of news and advertisements, made contributions such as Coleridge's more prominent. He and Stuart discussed politics constantly, following his changing views during the previous decade: while his dislike of Pitt remained constant, his attitude towards France wavered between a warmth engendered by his earlier radicalism and a forceful patriotism prompted by current French aggression and the fears of invasion. The rise of Napoleon presented the greatest challenge. Coleridge perceived at once that he was a man of 'commanding genius' (*His Times, Collected Works*, 3/1.208–10) but at first cast him as a French version of General Washington, saving the republic by adherence to strong principles; when it became clear that Napoleon was embarking on a career of conquest, he warned his fellow countrymen not to underestimate his powers. Since some of his articles made a considerable impact, Coleridge's belief that he became a marked man later in Italy need not be lightly discounted.

In London Coleridge worked intensively for a few months, not only reporting on the parliamentary debates and writing political commentaries but translating Schiller's *Wallenstein*. He also enjoyed the company of William Godwin, seen for a time as a potential ally in developing the radical potentialities of the new age: 'Let me tell you, Godwin!' he wrote in May, 'four such men as you, I, Davy, & Wordsworth, do not meet together in one house every day of the year—I mean four men so distinct with so many sympathies' (*Collected Letters*, 1.588). He was also moving a good deal in literary society more generally: he cultivated some fashionable women writers, among them Mary 'Perdita' Robinson, who addressed poems to him and to his new baby son, Derwent *Coleridge (1800–1883), and to whom he wrote a poem of his own, 'A Stranger Minstrel'.

Political feelings were currently running high, particularly with the publication of *The Anti-Jacobin*, in which, along with his poetic associates, Coleridge found himself lampooned. He turned against James Mackintosh, who had recently abjured the principles of support for the French Revolution set forth in his *Vindiciae Gallicae* (1791) and had attacked Godwin in the 'Introductory discourse' to a series of planned lectures. Taking Godwin's part, Coleridge wrote a scurrilous poem, 'Two Round Spaces on the

Tombstone', published anonymously in the *Morning Post*, and satirized Mackintosh in some lines which Stuart found too personal to include. In April he visited the Wordsworths in Grasmere, collaborating on a second edition of *Lyrical Ballads*; resolving to settle his family locally, he negotiated successfully to acquire Greta Hall in Keswick. On the way to take up residence, in July 1800, they stayed in Liverpool, where he met several of the local literati, including James Currie, William Roscoe, and William Rathbone. He was impressed by the wealth displayed in such institutions as their Athenaeum, but not unmindful of its source. 'The slave-merchants of Liverpool', he wrote to Poole, 'fly over the head of the slave-merchants of Bristol, as Vultures over carrion crows' (*Collected Letters*, 1.608).

Keswick, the Scottish tour, and opium The move to Keswick signalled a further shift in Coleridge's plans for himself. Instead of a London based group which might have rallied the talents of Davy, Godwin, and Wordsworth to a radical new thinking, he had now committed himself more specifically to the Wordsworth circle (including of course Sara Hutchinson) and to William's dream of writing great poetry from the vantage point of retirement in his native countryside. Coleridge's activities in the subsequent period varied between writing articles and poems for London, mostly for the *Morning Post*, and work toward a more important achievement, largely to be carried out away from the metropolis. (De Quincey, in June 1803, heard to his surprise that Coleridge intended to 'astonish the world with a *Metaphysical* work … on which he intends to found his fame' (De Quincey, *Diary*, 191).) He set to work on studies of thinkers ranging from the ancients, through scholastic writers such as Aquinas to the volumes of Kant he had acquired from Germany—all with the aim of undermining the suppositions of eighteenth-century philosophy. His attitude to Kant was ambiguous. On the one hand he was deeply impressed, naming several works, the 'clearness and evidence' of which 'took possession of me as with a giant's hand' (Coleridge, *Biographia literaria*, *Collected Works*, 7/1.153); but when he found Kant identifying the Will with the practical Reason, he questioned his authority: 'Again & again he is a wretched Psychologist' (*Notebooks*, 1.1717). Nevertheless he was to absorb and use Kant's terms so thoroughly as to be accused of plagiarism; it has even been suggested that he did not properly understand Kant's thinking—though it would be truer to say that he could not always believe Kant had meant exactly what he said and so sometimes imposed his own construction. In the course of these studies Coleridge's health suffered, partly from overwork, partly from rheumatic disorders associated with the dampness of his new surroundings. Increasingly he took laudanum, at this time the common remedy for such disorders, gradually realizing that he had become addicted. His own account threw some of the blame on the 'Kendal black drop', a notorious local concoction, which he probably took during the first winter at Greta Hall, and on his discovering in an old medical journal a case similar to his

own in which a patient had been cured by rubbing laudanum into the swollen joints while taking it internally, trying it with results that seemed at first miraculous but afterwards proved enslaving.

These accounts should be examined with care, given the known tendency of opium addicts to distort facts concerning their condition. Coleridge clearly found the effects of laudanum pleasant from an early stage, writing to his brother George in 1798, 'you, I believe, know how divine that repose is, what a spot of enchantment, a green spot of fountain and flowers and trees in the very heart of a waste of sands!' The 'Kubla Khan'-like imagery causes one to wonder whether he may have sometimes turned to opium in the hope of repeating the miracle that had produced that poem. Some of his accounts of experiences of heightened sensibility—especially in states of convalescence—may also owe something to opium. He distinguished between sensibility and sensuality, however, denying that he had ever taken opium purely for pleasure: 'My sole sensuality was *not* to be in pain' (*Notebooks*, 2.2368). It is possible to accept his claim without supposing that either his intellectual curiosity or his liking of comfortable sensations was ever suppressed. Before the penalties of his addiction became apparent, he could regard such fruits simply as a pleasant bonus.

Meanwhile Coleridge's domestic life deteriorated. Despite her devotion to their children, Sara's lack of warm sensibility and hastiness of temper rendered his existence with her, as he put it a few years later, 'incompatible with even an endurable Life' (*Collected Letters*, 3.7). For sympathy he turned increasingly to Sara Hutchinson, who spent periods both in Grasmere and Keswick. She in turn felt the strain of the relationship, particularly since he insisted that his marriage was indissoluble. After a visit to London at Christmas 1801 he wrote more newspaper articles and in late February went to Gallow Hill in Yorkshire, where he found Sara ill and helped nurse her in her new home; after his return to Keswick he wrote a verse letter expressing his despair which was later pared to less than half its length, readdressed to Wordsworth, given the title 'Dejection: an Ode', and published on the Wordsworths' wedding day, 4 October 1802. A final child, Sara *Coleridge (1802–1852), was born in December.

In the following summer, while Mary Wordsworth recovered from the premature birth of her first child, Coleridge, Dorothy, and William decided to renew their threefold companionship on a trip with a jaunting car into Scotland. After a time Coleridge separated from them, setting off to Fort Augustus (where he was briefly arrested as a suspected spy) and then to Fort William and Perth. During this period Southey and his wife, Sara Coleridge's sister, took up residence at Greta Hall. There they stayed for the rest of their lives as Southey assumed control of the house and became increasingly responsible for bringing up Coleridge's family as well as his own. Coleridge, meanwhile, nursed plans to create an '*Instrument* of practical Reasoning in the business of real Life' (*Collected Letters*, 2.947). He had spent time in close discussion of such matters with Thomas Wedgwood (whose health was declining and who was to die, probably of cancer, in 1805).

At first sight, Coleridge's output during this period looks disappointing: the translation of *Wallenstein* (1800), a handful of poems—few of unimpeachable quality—and some pieces of political journalism. Yet when his letters, full of seminal thoughts, and his notebooks, with their enquiring and intelligent observations—some made in the quiet night watches when he was ill—are also included, the picture is transformed.

Malta and Italy, 1804–1806 With his intermittent illnesses (not to mention the continuing effects of opium) Coleridge came to feel that his best hope was to spend time in a warmer, drier climate. After considering Madeira and other destinations he opted for Malta (a patriotic gesture, given the island's precarious status in the current war with France) and set sail from Portsmouth on 9 April 1804, arriving some six weeks later. Once there, he was taken up by the high commissioner, Sir Alexander Ball, whom he was to eulogize later in *The Friend*. Asked to perform secretarial duties for a small salary he gained insights into administration, enhanced when he was made acting public secretary the following January; he was not, however, liked by his clerk, who, like Poole and De Quincey, noticed a practice of reproducing the same impressive information for the benefit of successive people. During the autumn he travelled in Sicily and ascended Etna.

Early in February John Wordsworth was drowned when the *Earl of Abergavenny*, of which he was captain, sank off Portland Bill. Coleridge, receiving the news at the end of March, was deeply distressed, all the more since he had believed that Sara Hutchinson, still the subject of yearning notebook entries, might have found married happiness with John on his return. From now on he made plans to travel back to England (overland, since he dreaded another sea voyage). The stay in Malta had not improved his health and he was increasingly dependent on opium and spirits; he was also oppressed by the noise there.

During this period Coleridge was continuing the long reappraisal of his religious position that had begun during his period of doubt at Stowey. Having been drawn first to Spinozism and then to a combination of the thinking of Plato and St John, he had for a time put his previous allegiances on hold, expressing in 1802 to Estlin, his chief Unitarian friend, a wish that religious deism could flourish in France, being closer to true religion than the '*gross* Idolatry of Popery', together with his belief that Quakers and Unitarians were the only Christians pure from idolatry (*Collected Letters*, 2.893). By 1805 he had come to believe in the centrality of the Trinity: not 'the inanity of Jehovah, Christ and the Dove' but 'the adorable Tri-unity of Being, Intellect, and Spiritual Action' (*Notebooks*, 2.2444). On 12 February he summed up his new position in the phrase 'no Trinity, no God' (ibid., 2.2446).

For some months Coleridge could not leave Malta owing to the absence of the new public secretary, E. T. Chapman, who was away buying grain for the beleaguered island. When on 23 September 1805 he finally found himself free to leave, he visited Sicily again and then proceeded to Naples, probably with a British troopship. Despite Napoleon's victory at Austerlitz, which left him free to attack Italy, Coleridge set off for Rome in December and decided to stay, disregarding rumours of imminent invasion. He met Ludwig Tieck, and translated one of his love lyrics, and made contact with a number of artists under the patronage of Wilhelm von Humboldt, the Prussian minister. The beginning of a long, admiring friendship with the painter Washington Allston may have been a chief inducement to his prolonged stay. When Napoleon ordered all British travellers out of Rome he moved through the 'heavenly country' (*Notebooks*, 2.2856) of the Arno valley to Pisa, making notes there in the Campo Santo, and Livorno, from which (an overland journey being now debarred by Napoleon's ascendancy) he finally sailed on 23 June 1806.

Restless wanderings, lectures, and *The Friend*, 1806–1810 On 11 August, after a journey dogged by opium-related medical troubles and a period of quarantine, Coleridge landed at Stangate Creek in Kent and offered a prayer of thanksgiving at a 'curious little chapel' (*Collected Letters*, 2.1176). Finding it difficult to meet his wife he moved between various addresses in the south, taking up residence in September at the offices of Daniel Stuart's *Courier* in the Strand. A month later he was writing on religious questions, including his renewed Trinitarianism, and negotiating to give lectures at the Royal and London institutions. Resolved on separation from his wife, he renewed contact with the Wordsworths, who were dismayed at his changed appearance, and spent a period with them and Sara Hutchinson at a farmhouse at Coleorton in Leicestershire which had been offered them by Sir George Beaumont.

This stay was marked by extremes of emotion: on the one hand a growing jealousy of the relationship between Sara Hutchinson and Wordsworth culminated in an incident on 27 December when Coleridge imagined that he saw them in bed together; on the other a reading by Wordsworth on 7 January of the 'Poem to Coleridge' (later *The Prelude*), which had been enlarged to full length during his absence, prompted the composition of a long poem of his own entitled 'To W. Wordsworth' (published ten years later as 'To a Gentleman', *Poems*, 436–43) in which, regaining his best poetic style, he expressed his admiration for Wordsworth's achievement and mourned his own predicament.

Part of the separation agreed with his wife was an understanding that Coleridge should take charge of his sons. Feeling the need to reconcile his family at Ottery to the changed circumstances of his domestic life, he arranged a trip with his wife and children to the west country in the summer. Although the family visit was not achieved, illness at Ottery intervening, there was a profitable reunion with Poole; the trip also resulted in his first meeting with De Quincey, who subsequently escorted Sara Coleridge twice to Keswick and made Coleridge an anonymous gift of £300, which he agreed to accept as a loan.

After illness during the autumn of 1807 and renewed

contact with an old Bristol friend, John Morgan, whose wife and sister nursed him, Coleridge moved to London to prepare for lectures on 'Poetry and the principles of taste' at the Royal Institution. These were delayed first by Humphry Davy's indisposition and then by illnesses of his own which also prevented him from arriving at all on some occasions, to the irritation of his fashionable audiences. Later, as the lectures became regular, they gained in popularity. A double lecture on education, given at the end on 4 May to compensate for those missed, proved controversial in its advocacy of the principles of his friend Andrew Bell as against those of Joseph Lancaster and offended the proprietors of the institution. He concluded the lectures after giving eighteen.

During the summer Coleridge spent some time with the Clarkson family at Bury St Edmunds, and reviewed Thomas Clarkson's *History of the Slave Trade* for the *Edinburgh Review*. A letter to his brother George reproaching him for not having received them the previous summer was answered by one in which his brother said that he considered the separation from his wife 'an irreligious act' (*Collected Letters*, 3.705). By now Coleridge was making plans for a new journal, *The Friend*, again to be produced mainly by himself, which would deal not with the events of the day but with the questions of principle raised by them. In September he settled with the Wordsworth family at their recently acquired house in Grasmere, Allan Bank, where he planned to look after his children and work on his new venture, with Sara Hutchinson as amanuensis: it was to be printed at Penrith, calling for a journey on foot over the fells from Grasmere every time a fresh number was ready. Despite the apprehension of some of his friends that it would never appear, and Wordsworth's feeling that this might be as well since Coleridge was unfitted by temperament for any course of action demanding application, a week with Wordsworth's friend Thomas Wilkinson during which he was kept without stimulants helped him to produce the first number on 1 June. From then on, although dogged by problems concerning the supply of stamped paper for its printing, *The Friend* appeared steadily if irregularly until the twenty-eight issue in March 1810, assisted by contributions from Wordsworth (the first of his 'Essays upon epitaphs' and a fragment of the 'Poem to Coleridge') and Christopher North (John Wilson). Coleridge drew on a variety of sources and subjects, including letters he had sent home from Germany and recollections of Sir Alexander Ball in Malta, but his prime object was to attack the French revolutionary thinkers and their forerunners, comparing Voltaire unfavourably with Erasmus and Rousseau with Luther, and work towards the establishment of better principles in public life. His arguments, which he shared with Wordsworth, helped to establish a principled conservatism in the England of the time.

Quarrel with Wordsworth and despair, 1810–1814 Eventually *The Friend* lapsed, its demise hastened by the departure of Sara Hutchinson; she left Grasmere, tired, to join her brothers in their recently acquired Welsh farm; Coleridge

moved to Keswick for a time, teaching his wife and daughter Italian. He thought that Sara's withdrawal had been secretly encouraged by the Wordsworths, and his suspicions were supported when Montagu, accompanying him on a visit to London, where he hoped to gain help in overcoming his continuing opium problem, told him that Wordsworth had warned him against entertaining Coleridge in his house, and had 'commissioned' him to say that he had been an absolute nuisance in his own and that he had no hope of him. The Wordsworths had privately used the expression 'no hope' about him, and Dorothy had described the difficulties of having him as an inmate (*Letters of William and Dorothy Wordsworth*, 2.397–9), but it is unlikely that Wordsworth had intended to convey their sentiments so directly, however great the provocation. Coleridge was shattered not only by the information but by the means which, as he thought, had been chosen to convey it; he moved to Hudson's Hotel in Covent Garden and nursed his wounds, recalling his constant support for his friend. Meanwhile he kept up outward appearances, powdering his hair, and presenting himself sleek and conversational in company; Lamb described with relish the fate and supposed sentiments of 'goblet after goblet' as he downed them (C. Lamb and M. Lamb, *Letters*, 3.62). The Wordsworths, hearing such reports, failed to grasp the extent of his grievance and did nothing; only private notebook entries fully expressed his despair: 'Whirled about without a center—as in a nightmair—no gravity—a vortex without a center', and 'No hope of me! absolute nuisance! God's mercy is it a Dream!' (*Notebooks*, 3.3999, 3997). He turned to the Morgans again and lived with them for a time in Hammersmith. At the same time he wrote long notes about the foundations of his Christian faith, mingling them with remonstrances concerning the Wordsworths' behaviour.

Coleridge was helped at this time by the restored presence of Washington Allston, who had taken up residence in London. Coleridge seems to have found in him an acceptable substitute for Wordsworth and was delighted by the 'spiritual' element in his painting, expressed often through images of illumination; he promoted his interests in both London and Bristol, and showed notable perseverance in looking after him when he fell ill a little later. In the autumn he planned a new series of lectures, on the English poets, which began at Scot's Corporation Room, Fleet Street, in November 1811. Byron and Samuel Rogers were among those who attended one or more; 'incomparably the best' of them, according to Henry Crabb Robinson, was in December, on love in *Romeo and Juliet* (Robinson, 1.54). In the later lectures, at least, Coleridge drew on Schlegel, whose lectures had been published in 1809–10, after his previous series; his own view of the organic was much more subtly developed than Schlegel's, however, and, like his view of Hamlet's introspectiveness, seminal for future criticism. His sense that he had 'a smack of Hamlet' himself (Coleridge, *Table Talk*, *Collected Works*, 14/2.61) struck a chord with his listeners: when he dwelt on the harmful effects of Hamlet's procrastination, one of them remarked 'this is a satire on himself', to which

Crabb Robinson replied, 'No, it is an Elegy' (Coleridge, *Lectures*, *Collected Works*, 5/1.391).

New work for *The Courier* during 1811 was not so successful as previous contributions had been; the regularity of his contributions gradually lapsed into more occasional writing, which however continued until 1818. Interest in *The Friend* was growing, on the other hand, and Coleridge went to the Lakes early in 1812 to organize materials for a reprint. This was his last visit to the area; passing through Grasmere he did not call on the Wordsworths, to the distress of his children. Wordsworth himself left for London in April, hoping to effect a reconciliation; this, after some correspondence on both sides and largely through the good offices of Crabb Robinson, was achieved in May. On 11 May national attention was arrested by the assassination of the prime minister, Spencer Perceval, in the House of Commons; Coleridge hurried to *The Courier* office to offer his services. His new course of lectures at Willis's Rooms, due to begin next day and postponed for a week as a result of the news, was largely devoted to the drama; by now he seems to have evolved a method of lecturing extempore, while still having a copy of Schlegel to which he could refer. Wordsworth attended some of these lectures and walked with Coleridge, but the relationship was no longer the same.

In the autumn Coleridge's drama *Osorio*, now renamed *Remorse*, was accepted for early production at Drury Lane and he published with Southey a joint collection of their notes and observations under the title *Omniana*. At this point Josiah Wedgwood wrote to say that in his present financial state he could no longer afford to continue paying his half of the annuity unless it should appear that he was 'bound in honour to do so' (*Collected Letters*, 3.420). Coleridge accepted the position gracefully, while stating in his reply that he had been much calumniated by others—a claim which Wedgwood resisted (ibid., 421 and n.). The remaining half of the Wedgwood annuity, left in trust by Tom, had been made over to Mrs Coleridge; Coleridge had also taken out an insurance policy on his own life, the payments being kept up until his death. During the winter he gave lectures at the Surrey Institute and in January 1813 *Remorse* was produced with considerable success, to be published later in the year.

A new crisis arose when John Morgan, in whose household Coleridge had been living, first fell ill and then was made bankrupt; while he took refuge in Ireland, Coleridge showed considerable business acumen in devising rescue plans. He also devoted himself to the welfare of Morgan's wife and sister-in-law; there are signs that he found in them substitutes for the lost Hutchinson sisters, with Charlotte at least vestigially a surrogate Sara. During the autumn he met Madame de Staël, who described his conversation as '*tout à fait un monologue*' (Southey, 2.332n.), and delivered a further series of lectures on Shakespeare and on education. In December he settled Mrs Morgan and Charlotte Brent for the time being at Ashley, near Box in Wiltshire, and stayed there from time to time. Subsequently he was taken ill at the Greyhound Hotel in Bath

and remained in the area for several months in a state of crisis, including guilt about opium. When he felt well enough to deliver a set of lectures on Milton at Bristol in April he alienated his old friend Estlin by his description of Milton's Satan as a scoffing Socinian, while Cottle, grasping for the first time the extent of his addiction, urged him to efforts of will power—eliciting the reproach, 'You bid me rouse myself—go, bid a man paralytic in both arms rub them briskly together, & that will cure him' (*Collected Letters*, 3.477). Simultaneously, discovering the saintly Archbishop Leighton and his commentary on 1 Peter (later a nucleus for his *Aids to Reflection*) he wrote repentant notes in its margins. He also called on Hannah More, who told Wilberforce how delighted she was to hear strong evangelical doctrines from this erstwhile Unitarian.

Renewed literary activities, 1814–1820 This was the nadir of Coleridge's career. From the summer of 1814, with the help of his Bristol friend Josiah Wade, he began to plan new work. He outlined his scheme for a work on 'the communicative intelligence in nature and in man' (*Collected Works*, 11/1.369–70) in which he adumbrated his later writing on the Logos and gave further substance to his longstanding plan for a great work offering a new Christian philosophy for the age. In December he moved with the Morgans to the house of a Mr Page, a surgeon at Calne in Wiltshire, where in the course of the next year he moved a good deal in local society and delivered a speech against the Corn Bill in the market place. A plan to bring together his poems in a new collection led him to ask Wordsworth for a copy of the poem addressed to him and to offer a few criticisms of the recently published *Excursion*—prompting in turn an attempt to elaborate his critical ideas further in the context of his own life and thought. What was first thought of as a preface to the new collection became his *Biographia literaria*: not a straightforward or full autobiography, but a more digressive account of his life in the course of which he both explained his objections to the associationist theories of Hartley and offered searching criticisms of Wordsworth's poems—while still asserting him to be the greatest poet of the age. Much more was embraced, however. His ideas of literary growth produced the theory of 'desynonymization', by which words, like twigs and leaves on a tree, gradually diverged and differentiated their meanings. His prime example was the distinction between 'fancy' and 'imagination', expressing the difference between a mechanical making and a creative artistic power linked to the divine. Towards the end of what was to be the first volume (uneasy, perhaps, at the pantheistic implications of such ideas) he drew increasingly on the ideas, and even the phrasing, of Schelling, in a manner condemned by later writers. In the second he mounted a detailed criticism of the social theory of the preface to *Lyrical Ballads* (to which he himself had contributed) arguing against the idea of a 'natural' language existing among the lower classes and in favour of the one cultivated by living in a Christian civilization. Much of the discourse was written down by John Morgan at his dicta-tion, a mode of composition he increasingly favoured. He thought of writing a tragedy, but in the end settled on a 'Dramatic Entertainment', which he entitled *Zapolya: a Christmas Tale* (published 1817). This was in due course offered to both Covent Garden and Drury Lane but was rejected by both; it was eventually performed for ten nights at the Surrey Theatre in February 1818.

1816 was a notable year. In April Coleridge met Byron, who had been urging John Murray to publish 'Christabel', and read 'Kubla Khan' to him a few days before he left Eng-land for good. One result was the publication of both poems, together with 'The Pains of Sleep', a poem which Coleridge no doubt felt ought to appear alongside 'Kubla Khan' as a corrective to any temptation to laudanum tak-ing that might be encouraged by its preface. The little vol-ume appeared in May, and despite unfavourable reviews was reprinted twice during the year. In April Coleridge also took the momentous step of appearing (with the proof sheets of 'Christabel' in his hand) at the door of the house of James Gillman, a Highgate surgeon, and asking to be taken in as an inmate to help cure his addiction; in the event he was to stay for the rest of his life. Continuing to dictate to Morgan there he also wrote for *The Courier* and began preparing two *Lay Sermons*, the first of which, *The Statesman's Manual, or, the Bible the Best Guide to Political Skill and Foresight* (particularly notable for its distinction between 'symbol' and 'allegory', pp. 30–31), appeared in December. This and the 'Christabel' volume were both bit-terly attacked in the *Edinburgh Review* by Hazlitt, who resented the accounts of an earlier lakeland escapade of his that he believed Coleridge to have circulated in Lon-don and denounced him as a renegade from his earlier political principles. Coleridge poured out his own bitter-ness to a new acquaintance and admirer of *The Friend*, Hugh J. Rose.

After the second *Lay Sermon*, 'Addressed to the Higher and Middle Classes, on the Existing Distresses and Discon-tents', a response to contemporary post-war unrest, appeared in April 1817, *Biographia literaria* finally saw the light of day, along with the new collection of Coleridge's poems now entitled *Sibylline Leaves*, in July. During the spring Coleridge had negotiated with their publisher, Rest Fenner, towards publishing an encyclopaedia, the *Encyclo-paedia metropolitana*, which would attempt to present the sum of contemporary knowledge in an ordered form. The negotiations fell through, since the publisher required him to live in Camberwell where his work could be more closely monitored, but Coleridge did produce a 'Prelimin-ary treatise on method' which appeared as a 'General introduction' to the finished work and was a basis for the essays on method in the revised *Friend*. (The *Encyclopaedia metropolitana* became an important forerunner of other modern encyclopaedic enterprises.) During the summer he renewed acquaintance with Ludwig Tieck, first encountered in Rome, a welcome harbinger of contacts with Germany which were now being renewed following the conclusion of the Napoleonic wars. Coleridge learned among other things that Blumenbach had abandoned his

doubts concerning hypnotic phenomena, prompting him both to revive his own interest and to follow the current wave of interest in *Naturphilosophie*. For some years he explored such possibilities with his new friend and dis-ciple the surgeon Joseph Henry Green. After a holiday at Littlehampton, in the course of which he met H. F. Cary, the translator of Dante, he lectured in December to the London Philosophical Society on the principles of experi-mental philosophy and met Wordsworth again. Just as Byron had taken exception to Coleridge's attack on Maturin in *Biographia literaria*, however, Wordsworth had evidently been offended by some criticisms of his own poetry there and appeared cold and scornful.

1818 began with the delivery of fourteen lectures on the history of philosophy—a familiar method for Coleridge to adopt when wishing to prime the pump of his intellect for work on a difficult subject—to the London Philosophical Society, where he met a new friend and disciple, Thomas Allsop. He also became disillusioned by the behaviour of Rest Fenner (shortly to become bankrupt) and negotiated with the more respectable publishers Taylor and Hessey, who took over until the mid-1820s. In the spring he cham-pioned the cause of the child labourers in the cotton mills and wrote a pamphlet in support of Sir Robert Peel's bill to regulate their employment. He also undertook a major revision of *The Friend*, adding the essays on method, where his ideas of growth were set out more fully, and reorder-ing the whole more coherently. At the turn of the year he began delivering his lectures on philosophy again, along with six on Shakespeare, at the Crown and Anchor in the Strand, continuing until March. On 11 April 1819, while walking with Green in Highgate, he encountered a 'loose, not well-dressed youth' (Coleridge, *Table Talk*, *Collected Works*, 14/1.325), a former student at Guy's Hospital who had known Green as his demonstrator, and who after seeking permission walked with the pair for about 2 miles. This was John Keats, who set down a list of the things covered as Coleridge 'broached a thousand things' (Keats, 2.88) including nightingales and dreams: to the untutored eye a rich gallimaufry of unrelated topics, but to someone more familiar with his thought an interlinked disquisition concerning the imaginative consciousness. Coleridge later recalled an impression of feverishness in Keats's farewell handshake which had, he claimed, made him think he had not long to live.

A few days later Hartley Coleridge, whose university education at Oxford had been supported largely by Cole-ridge's relations and friends, was elected, to his father's delight, to a probationary fellowship at Oriel College. Coleridge exerted himself further on the question of child labour as Peel's bill passed the Lords, and began writing from time to time for *Blackwood's Magazine*. His summer holiday was spent with the Gillmans at Ramsgate, which became their favourite resort in the years following. At this time, also, it was felt by Coleridge's admirers that some records of his extraordinary conversation ought to be kept; Allsop was an early recorder, to be followed from 1822 onwards by Coleridge's nephew, Henry Nelson

*Coleridge (1798–1843), whose notes from then until Coleridge's death formed the basis of the posthumous volumes of *Table Talk* (1835, 1836).

Towards the great work The conclusion of Coleridge's lectures in March 1820 left him with the desire to concentrate on his great work, for which he continued to make plans. In May, however, there was a severe set-back in his private life when the fellows of Oriel College refused to renew Hartley's probationary fellowship on the ground of irregular behaviour, including drunkenness. Coleridge, anxiously aware of the implications of his own addiction, wrote a heartfelt and eloquent plea to the provost of the college, Edward Copleston, without success. His own work was becoming more religious in character, with Green acting as the amanuensis for his work on the Old and New Testaments. Early in 1821 he reported good progress on a treatise on logic; he also gave some writing on Prometheus to Hartley, hoping that he might be stimulated to work of his own on the subject. Sundays in that year were devoted to work with Green on his larger work, the *Assertion of Religion*. Feeling once again meanwhile the need to produce some work of more immediate benefit he turned back to the works of Archbishop Leighton, which had so impressed him at the time of his spiritual crisis in 1814 and proposed to John Murray a selection of his 'Beauties', with comments of his own. At the same time he continued to prepare for his larger work by dictating his 'Logic' to two young men, C. B. Stutfield and John Watson.

Although no further poems on the scale of the unfinished 'Christabel' had been forthcoming, Coleridge never stopped writing verse. He contented himself often with light contributions that could be entered in private albums or included in letters but he also contributed to the increasingly fashionable annuals, keepsakes, and general drawing-room literature, sometimes using such occasions for heartfelt meditations on lost love. By constantly experimenting with new forms and metres he demonstrated yet again his extraordinary versatility. From the 1820s, moreover, the critical climate changed. The adverse criticism that had greeted his poetry in the previous decade, when a stance of incomprehension often masked political hostility, gave way to more sympathetic accounts, pioneered by J. G. Lockhart's article in *Blackwood's Magazine* in 1820. Such eulogies often dwelt on the new kind of music to be heard in his lines.

The voice of criticism was still raised occasionally, directed now toward Coleridge's prose, with thinly veiled insinuations of plagiarism, as with the '*Noctes ambrosianae*' dialogue, attributed to John Wilson, in the October 1823 issue of *Blackwood's*, in which the 'Opium-eater' is made to characterize him as 'a thief', albeit 'a man of surpassing talents'. 'Strip him of his stolen goods, and you will find good clothes of his own below' (p. 500). The best comment on this and related aspects of his personality was Wordsworth's: 'The activity of his imagination, which I must call morbid, disturbs his sense & recollection of facts' (Coleridge, *Table Talk*, *Collected Works*, 14/1.546): his occasional

cavalier way with the truth ought, in other words, to be regarded as the defect of his distinctive excellences. It also enabled an expansiveness in conversation. From November 1823, when the Gillmans moved to The Grove in Highgate, with an extended bookroom upstairs where Coleridge could entertain guests for his 'Attic nights' (*Collected Letters*, 5.368), it became common to call on Thursdays and hear the greatest talker of his time holding forth by the hour in what he admitted were all too often his '*oneversazioni*' (ibid., 6.790). Earlier that autumn at Ramsgate he enjoyed the renewal of another old intimacy when he re-encountered Sara Hutchinson, who reported his comment that kissing a baby was 'the next best thing to Bathing in the Sea' (Hutchinson, 263). Their paths had already crossed in London through common acquaintance with the Monkhouse family and they met socially on subsequent occasions, her kindly behaviour to him possibly prompting the bitter poem 'The Pang more Sharp than All'.

Aids to Reflection and later work The 'Beauties of Leighton' scheme having been declined, along with a proposal that Murray should publish the 'Logic', Coleridge offered the Leighton volume to the publishers Taylor and Hessey in August 1823 under the title 'Aids to reflection' and they accepted, agreeing to include a life of Leighton (afterwards dropped from the scheme), and also to publish his 'Logic' manuscript (the 'Elements of discourse'), followed by the ambitious 'Assertion of religion'. The main body of the Leighton volume, meanwhile, which had begun by following the original scheme fairly closely, began to change shape as Coleridge completed his groupings of 'Prudential' and 'Moral and Religious' aphorisms and moved into the final one, devoted to the 'Spiritual'. The task of defining this for his culture brought to a head many of his most difficult problems. How far could the spiritual be aligned with the natural? Despite the fact that the earlier pages were already in proof, the scope of the work spread as Coleridge drew on passages from other early Anglican writers. Some of his comments were affected by anxieties about Derwent and his association with sceptical friends at Cambridge, including the young T. B. Macaulay (about which after a time he was able to report more reassuring news). In February 1824 he reported that the volume had been 'growing and new-forming itself' (*Collected Letters*, 5.333) under his hand.

Early in 1824, when Coleridge was visited by his wife and daughter, he was delighted to discover how marvellously the intellectual and imaginative powers of the young Sara had developed: she was, he said, 'every thing (save that her Health is delicate) that the fondest & most ambitious Parent could pray for' (*Collected Letters*, 5.336). During her visit Henry Nelson Coleridge's diary recorded that he had become secretly engaged to her—an attachment which was to cause Coleridge anxiety in view of the dangers associated with marriage between first cousins.

Work towards completion of Coleridge's volume was affected by other events. In March he was elected a 'royal associate' of the Royal Society of Literature, with an annuity of £100 in return for a yearly essay. A misunderstanding of some sort with the Gillmans arose shortly afterwards, and he withdrew from their house for a few weeks, before a reconciliation brought him back. In June he was visited by Carlyle, whose acid, not altogether unappreciative, account in his *Life of John Sterling* (1851) became famous, and in January 1825 Gioacchino de' Prati introduced him to the work of Giambattista Vico, which delighted him. March saw him delivering his first (and, as it proved, only) essay to the Royal Society of Literature, on the Prometheus of Aeschylus.

Aids to reflection in the formation of a manly character on the several grounds of prudence, morality, and religion was finally published in June. The bishop of London (prompted by the Beaumonts) expressed his approval and favourable opinions came not only from previous well-wishers but from some who, like Joseph Blanco White—a refugee priest from Spain who found its arguments a powerful support for the Anglicanism which he had since espoused—were discovering him for the first time. Among enthusiasts for the volume was James Marsh, president of the University of Vermont, who liked it for encouraging its readers to think for themselves and more particularly for opposing 'pseudo-Calvinism'. Although Coleridge the poet had long had his admirers in North America, Marsh's American edition of *Aids to Reflection* initiated a new wave of praise for him there as a religious thinker. Following the first crossing of the Atlantic under steam in 1826 a number of prominent Americans such as James Fenimore Cooper and Emma Willard visited him in succeeding years.

Encouraged by the appearance of *Aids to Reflection*, Coleridge proposed six new disquisitions to Taylor and Hessey: on faith; on the eucharist; on the philosophy of prayer; on the Hebrew prophets; on the church; and on the use of the scriptures. Of these the last already existed, to be published only after his death as *Confessions of an Inquiring Spirit* (1840). His delay may have been partly due to diffidence about presenting for general publication a view of books of the Bible challenging uncritical and total acceptance of their inspiration while in his notebooks extensive work on the interpretation of others such as Genesis was more or less taking for granted their divine status. He was also attracted for a time to the eloquent preaching of Edward Irving, the current focus of fashionable religious attention in London through his interpretations of biblical prophecy; soon, however, he became disturbed by Irving's lack of intellectual discipline.

The great work or 'Logosophia' (referred to also as his 'Opus maximum') was again resumed, though the 'Logic' (thought of by some twentieth-century writers as the most coherent among Coleridge's achieved philosophical works) found no publisher and remained in manuscript. The major effort of his writing, meanwhile, went increasingly into marginal annotations on other writers and into the notebooks he had kept since youth—fragmentary observations and critical comments which would not find full reproduction and commentary until more than a hundred years later. He was also generous with his time to those who visited him in a spirit of discipleship and free enquiry, including John Sterling, A. H. Hallam, and Richard Monckton Milnes, early members of the Cambridge Apostles.

Former coolnesses were forgotten when Coleridge agreed at short notice to accompany Wordsworth and his daughter Dora on a tour of the Rhineland and the Netherlands from late June to early August 1828. He was in particularly good spirits that summer. His poetical works, which had gradually been growing over the years, were published in three volumes by Pickering—not the last edition in his lifetime but the last to be produced fully under his supervision. During these years he could also be gay. In 1824 Robinson met him at a 'dance and rout' at the house of Joseph Henry Green, and heard him declaim on his favourite topics in the dancing-room (Robinson, 1.307). On 18 August 1828 he participated in a bachelor dinner party during which he and Theodore Hook threw glasses through the window panes and then participated in a sport of throwing forks at wineglasses. Lockhart described his 'roseate face … lit up with animation, his large gray eye beaming, his white hair flowing, and his whole frame, as it were, radiating with intense interest' as he joined in (Chambers, 308).

The later history of Coleridge's opium taking, meanwhile, is obscure. He reports no further struggles to free himself from overwhelming addiction, and it is clear that in some sense the battle was over. Indeed, one might think that he had left off the drug entirely were it not for the existence of letters, including some to the Highgate chemist T. H. Dunn between 1824 and 1833, which make it clear that he had obtained supplies privately for some time before and was continuing to do so. It is possible that the short rupture between himself and the Gillmans in the spring of 1824 was connected with a discovery that he had been obtaining amounts surreptitiously; what is not clear is how far Gillman himself succeeded in regularizing his supply so as to contain the addiction. Two things can be established: that in 1832, when in letters of April he wrote to Green that it was '5 weeks' since he had taken laudanum, and to H. F. Cary of the 'miracle of grace' that had worked 'a sudden emancipation from a 33 years' fearful Slavery' (*Collected Letters*, 6.899, 901), and when his wife could write in August that he had 'intirely left off the use of Laudanum' but had 'suffered greatly by the effort' (Potter, 165), he ordered supplies from Dunn both in January and December, suggesting that the 'emancipation' was at best short-lived. When he was on his deathbed two years later, also, his medical attendants gave him injections of laudanum to ease his pain.

Continued orders for opium did nothing to assist Coleridge's financial state. Having received nothing from the 1828 edition of his poetical works, he participated in a reissue of 1829 and received £30 as an advance; £20 of this was sent to Mary Morgan, who, with Charlotte Brent, was now living in poverty following John Morgan's death in 1820 and had already been helped the previous December. He also made further publishing plans. In January 1829 he negotiated with Taylor (whose partnership with Hessey had been dissolved in 1826) terms for a second edition of *Aids to Reflection*, along with two volumes of his philosophical system and one on the use of words. A month later he was forced to give up further work on the first of these projects: a revised edition of *Aids to Reflection* did appear later in the year but from the firm of Hurst, Chance & Co., substantial alterations being found only in the early pages.

Final writing and death, 1829–1834 Religion had in the meantime come to the fore among national issues, as the position of Roman Catholics was debated and George IV agreed to a discussion in cabinet in January 1829. Coleridge, who had refused in that month to sign a petition against Catholic emancipation, felt that he must clarify his own position and turned back to his former plan for a disquisition on the church, producing—with unexpected speed considering his state of health—his pamphlet *On the Constitution of the Church and State*. The work, remembered particularly for advocating the establishment of a 'clerisy', an educated class between the laity and the ordained clergy that should further the purposes of the church in a Christian society, confutes the supposition that in later life his work was invariably digressive and inconclusive. Drawing on the images of vine and olive, respectively, and recalling the benefits accruing from their cultivation side by side, he argued for preserving an intimate relationship between church and state. The argument, with its relevance to current concerns, was presented clearly and cogently; only the last pages left a ragged effect. A promised appendix entitled 'What is to be done now?', which may have been intended to provide a rounded conclusion, was never in the event added. A second edition was swiftly called for, nevertheless, and although published too late to affect the issue of Catholic emancipation, the legislation for which had been passed during the year, was seen by some readers as a powerful defence of the Anglican establishment. Others such as Keble and Pusey found that dealing with its arguments led them to assert the church's independent authority and the need to avoid state interference; the meeting in 1833 which launched the resulting Tractarian movement was held at Hadleigh rectory, home of Coleridge's friend Hugh J. Rose. When Newman read the pamphlet some years later, his rejection of Coleridge's presentation of Christianity as a religion of symbols was important in driving him to find authority in the Roman Catholic church.

In the spring of 1831 Coleridge was irritated to find a poem on which he and Southey had earlier collaborated, 'The Devil's Walk', being republished as 'by Professor Porson' and took steps to ensure its reissue with the true authorship asserted. Parliamentary reform was very much in the air; while not committing himself to print on the subject he repeatedly voiced his opposition, and, when the legislation was eventually passed, his despair. A legacy of £300 from Adam Steinmetz and an annuity by a Mrs Dashwood in the last month of his life came too late to help establish financial independence, and in his will he could bequeath to his children little more than his affection and gratitude to the Gillmans.

Although increasingly ill, and frequently confined to his room for long periods, Coleridge found it possible in 1833 to attend the meeting of the British Association in Cambridge, where he met Michael Faraday, who, he thought, had 'the true temperament of Genius' (Coleridge, *Table Talk, Collected Works*, 14/1.392–3), acquired at least one new follower, William Rowan Hamilton, and complained about the hardness of the beds: 'Truly I lay down at night a man, and arose in the morning a Bruise' (ibid., 392). He was visited in London by Emerson, who was disturbed to find him by now so rigid in his religious opinions, once again found himself much restored by bathing in salt water at the sea, and composed his epitaph, in which he prayed that he might be granted forgiveness rather than fame, and after his long death-in-life attain life in death.

In the following spring the appearance of a red erysipelas streak on his cheek, associated by him with his night on the Brocken in 1799, convinced him that his end was imminent. He lingered for four months more, but with an increasing desire for liberation from the body. His mind, he said, remained unclouded: 'I could even be witty' (*Collected Letters*, 6.992). In his last years 'by-gone images, and scenes of early life' would steal into his mind 'like breezes blown from the spice-islands of Youth and Hope'—which, he went on, were the 'two realities of this Phantom World' (ibid., 705; Coleridge, *Table Talk, Collected Works*, 14/2.296).

In July Coleridge became severely ill, though still without organic disfunction, and said farewell to his friends and relatives one by one. Green was called in to hear some final words for the 'Opus maximum', a declaration of the need to reaffirm God as the absolute good who is also the eternal 'I am' and yet to preserve a distinctity, allowing for the operation of the Logos. Finally he asked to be left alone 'to meditate on his Redeemer' (*Collected Letters*, 6.991). On 24 July Gillman saw him fall into a sleep which became comatose and he died at 6.30 the following morning. At his request an autopsy was carried out, revealing an unusual enlargement of his heart, apparently of thirty years' standing.

On 2 August Coleridge's body, followed in due time by those of other members of his family, was buried in a vault in Highgate churchyard, with a number of his young followers in attendance, including Charles Stutfield and John Sterling. When a new chapel was built for Highgate School in 1866 the vault became part of the building; there was some dispute as to responsibility for its maintenance, and it fell into disrepair. Eventually, in 1961, the remains of the Coleridges were reinterred in St Michael's Church, close to the Gillmans' house in The Grove.

Appearance and personality Observers differed about Coleridge's physical appearance, disagreeing even about the colour of his eyes. Most agreed, however, that their first impression changed once he opened his mouth. 'He is a wonderful man', wrote Dorothy Wordsworth in June 1797.

> At first I thought him plain, that is for about three minutes: he is pale and thin, has a wide mouth, thick lips and not very good teeth, longish loose-growing half-curling rough black hair. But if you hear him speak five minutes you think no

> more of them. His eye is large and full, not dark but grey; such an eye as would receive from a heavy soul the dullest expression; but it speaks every emotion of his animated mind.   (*Letters of William and Dorothy Wordsworth*, 1.189)

Coleridge's own self-description, written a few months before, had been equally unsparing, with not dissimilar positive touches:

> my face, unless when animated by immediate eloquence, expresses great Sloth, & great, indeed almost ideotic, good nature. 'Tis a mere carcase of a face: fat, flabby, & expressive chiefly of inexpression.—Yet I am told, that my eyes, eyebrows, & forehead are physiognomically good—: but of this the Deponent knoweth not. As to my shape, 'tis a good shape enough if measured—but my gait is awkward, & the walk, & the *Whole man* indicates *indolence capable of energies* … I cannot breathe thro' my nose—so my mouth, with sensual thick lips, is almost always open.   (*Collected Letters*, 1.259–60)

In middle life he became more corpulent; Keats's account of his 'alderman-after dinner pace' (Keats, 2.88) and Carlyle's evocation of his snuffling voice as he discoursed on 'om-m-mject' and 'sum-m-mject' (Carlyle, chap. 5) develop features of his former self-description. But although his early brilliance was sapped by disappointment and illness—to the extent that even by 1806 the Wordsworths could hardly recognize him when he returned from Malta—his physical resilience was almost as remarkable as his mental. Lamb's comment of 1816 has become famous: 'I think his essentials not touched, he is very bad, but then he wonderfully picks up another day, and his face when he repeats his verses hath its ancient glory, an Arch angel a little damaged' (C. Lamb and M. Lamb, *Letters*, 3.215). Lamb recalled *Paradise Lost* (1.742–3) again in another eulogy: 'He would talk from morn to dewy eve, nor cease till far midnight; yet who ever would interrupt him,—who would obstruct that continuous flow of converse, fetched from Helicon or Zion?' (*Works of Charles and Mary Lamb*, 1.351–2). In 1829 John Wheeler's account of their first meeting added a touch of the elfin:

> … soon saw an elderly man come peeping out from the shrubbery … an elderly man scarcely of medium stature, of full habit. white & long hair with a full face, full forhead, prominent orbits of eyes … His respiration rather hurried & oppressive from taking *snuff* in great quantities.   (Coleridge, *Table Talk, Collected Works*, 14/2.429)

All would have agreed that such itemized descriptions had little to do with their central sense of the man: 'The only man I ever met', wrote Hazlitt, 'who corresponded to the idea of a man of genius' (*Complete Works*, 5.167).

From the beginning of his career Coleridge was a polarized man—divided between attraction to what his own powerful imagination favoured, and a sense of the demands imposed by his original clerical background. The disjunction is already present in his poem of 1795 'The Eolian Harp', where he first indulges in the delights of near-pantheist speculation on a pleasant autumn evening and then reproves himself (in the person of Sara) for indulging unhallowed thoughts. It haunted his attraction to the sympathetic temperament of Sara Hutchinson, as against his belief in the indissolubility of marriage. It also played a key part in his opium addiction, where, not understanding the nature of withdrawal symptoms, he

made repeated will-driven attempts to break free of the habit, only to collapse into resumption when the painful effects of deprivation overwhelmed him. In view of his post-mortem examination it is in any case likely that his physical debilities made the need for palliatives irresistible.

The positive benefit of Coleridge's divided nature was an ability to think and work in more than one psychic dimension. At his best he could do this brilliantly as in 'The Rime of the Ancient Mariner', where the effect of dramatizing the conflicts in his own psyche was a lack of direct consistency assisting the sense of mystery. In the case of 'Christabel' and 'Kubla Khan', where the effect was also achieved, the conflicts ran too deep to allow full completion. Yet it is not in his poems that the effects of his self-division are experienced most sharply: there and in his more poetic prose descriptions he is always capable of a sensuous brilliance and delicacy which possess a virtue all their own. It is in his more philosophical works that the reader becomes conscious again and again that by trying to reconcile the moral and the natural, the ancient and the new, Coleridge is attempting a task beyond his powers and most probably beyond the powers of any human being. Yet the same developments have served to clarify his intellectual stature, showing how far he was caught in contradictions that in time became steadily more evident to his successors. In that sense he was a great allegorical figure.

Posthumous reputation Commentators always had difficulty in characterizing the special nature of Coleridge's achievement: indeed, his true legacy lay, perhaps, in the creativity he awakened in those he met. Lamb, Wordsworth, Hazlitt, De Quincey, Byron, and Keats, touched by him in turn, each manifested the effects in the quality of their writing. According to Thomas Arnold 'I think with all his faults old Sam was more of a great man than anyone who has lived within the four seas in my memory' (A. Stanley, *Life and Correspondence of Thomas Arnold, D.D.*, 1844, 2.56). De Quincey, in an access of extreme enthusiasm after his death, termed him 'the largest and most spacious intellect, … the subtlest and most comprehensive, that has yet existed among men' (De Quincey, 'Coleridge', *Tait's Edinburgh Magazine*, new ser., 1, 1834, 509).

Since the early 1820s it had been in Cambridge that his standing was strongest. Julius Hare, tutor of Trinity College, recalled how under the influence of Coleridge's conversation one felt one's soul teeming and bursting 'as beneath the breath of spring' (J. C. Hare, *Memorials of a Quiet Life*, 1873, 2.87); a number of students, including John Sterling and Frederick Denison Maurice, members of the Cambridge club which came to be known as the Apostles, agreed. 'To Coleridge', said Sterling:

> I owe education. He taught me to believe that an empirical philosophy is none, that Faith is the highest Reason, that all criticism, whether of literature, laws, or manners, is blind, without the power of discerning the organic unity of the object.   (J. Sterling, *Essays and Tales*, 1848, xv)

Arthur Henry Hallam, another Apostle, called him 'the

good old man, most eloquent' (A. H. Hallam, *Writings*, ed. V. Motter, 1943, 42–3, 160–71).

Thinkers such as these produced what came to be known as the broad-church movement, and in some cases the beginnings of Christian socialism. Across the Atlantic, in the same years, Coleridge's influence, while affecting writers such as Emerson and Poe, was most strongly felt in religious and theological fields, particularly in New England and Vermont. It would in time extend to a few philosophers such as John Dewey, who maintained that he had shown how one might be 'both liberal and pious' (C. Lamont, *Dialogue on John Dewey*, 1952, 15–16). It is sometimes suggested in addition that Coleridge's influence was manifested in Tractarianism, though it should be noted that Newman and his associates, despite their respect, were concerned to combat the Coleridgean idea that the church could be rescued by treating its doctrines as symbolic. Coleridge's exhortation to concentrate on the statements in the Bible that *find* the reader, and his attempt to introduce into Britain critical modes of reading the Bible that had become well known in Germany, proved similarly controversial, the eventual publication of his major statement under the concessive title *Confessions of an Inquiring Spirit* being delayed until 1840.

More secularly minded readers who found themselves beset by the growing doubts of the time found that the account in his 'Dejection' ode of the ills induced by over-developed habits of analysis rendered with unexpected exactitude a drabness of feeling they recognized from experience: indeed, such writers might recognize in his often fragmentary and divided thinking some self-contradictions of their own. The arguments in which he urged the reader to adopt an empirical approach to Christianity on the ground that only if one did so would the truth of the doctrines be revealed had a strong appeal for minds that wished to move from such questioning to action. Meanwhile, however, in his *Life of John Sterling*, Carlyle, a great proponent of the need for action, was stirred to write a chapter which disparaged Coleridge's reputation as a sage, blaming his influence for the propagation of 'strange Centaurs, spectral Puseyisms, monstrous illusory Hybrids, and ecclesiastical Chimeras,—which now roam the Earth in a very lamentable manner!' (pp. 69–80).

The divided response that can be discerned even within Carlyle's account when read in full was displayed more equitably by Matthew Arnold. While censuring Coleridge's moral weaknesses he believed his view that Christianity was identical with the highest philosophy to be one of the crucial ideas for his time: 'it is true, it is deeply important, and by virtue of it Coleridge takes rank, so far as English thought is concerned, as an initiator and founder'. It was, he thought, 'henceforth the key to the whole defence of Christianity' (M. Arnold, *Prose Works*, ed. R. H. Super, 11 vols., 1960–77, 10.226–7). Arthur Hugh Clough, Thomas Arnold's star pupil and a close friend of Matthew's, was less happy with such a view, on the other hand, writing in 1841 that he kept 'wavering between admiration of his exceedingly great perceptive and analytical power and other wonderful points and inclination

to turn away altogether from a man who has so great a lack of all reality and actuality' (A. Clough, *Correspondence*, ed. F. L. Mulhausser, 2 vols., 1957, 1.106). Such modified attitudes were reinforced from 1859 onwards by the impact of Darwin's *Origin of Species*, as the forcefulness of earlier arguments concerning religion and morality declined and a new intellectual and moral stringency was demanded. The possibility of defending Christianity by retreating to permanent elements that would survive the assaults currently being mounted—a hope which Coleridge's work had seemed to support—faded as religious significance drained from the post-Darwinian universe.

In these circumstances Coleridge's more permanent gifts came to be found less in his religious teaching than in his poetry, his criticism, and his psychological insights, including his capacity for viewing the mind at more than one level. As his ideas were rediscovered by aesthetes of the late nineteenth century, beginning with Walter Pater, he reached a new generation through the first full collection of his *Letters* and the selection from his notebooks entitled *Anima poetae*, both of which were edited by his grandson and published in 1895. In the twentieth century such production of his writings turned into a flood, as the letters and notebooks were both edited in full and a collected edition of his entire works, including his marginal annotations, was set in process. Running, with their notes, to about fifty volumes, they dispelled for ever the legend (which he himself had sometimes helped to propagate) that he had been unproductive.

During the twentieth century Coleridge's reputation was sometimes affected by new movements in literary fashion. The rise of Imagism at the time of the First World War prompted one study of considerable power: John Livingston Lowes's *The Road to Xanadu* (1929), in which the remarkable visual effects in the poetry were traced to remembered images he had discovered in his reading, particularly in travel books. Unfortunately, however, Lowes disparaged Coleridge's intellectual pursuits, encouraging a view of the poetry that concentrated simply on its vividness and its associative qualities. If the other concerns were in danger of being neglected, however, other studies showed that they could not be ignored. I. A. Richards's *Coleridge on Imagination* (1934) renewed the sense of his critical theories and their importance, while studies towards the end of the century discussed the impact of contemporary political events and the extent of his own involvement. In other work Coleridge's relevance to religious thinking continued to figure strongly, while his psychological insights, contributing to what might be termed a 'psycho-synthetic' view of the mind, received constant attention, often in the form of sidelong references rather than extended discussion. The possibilities of thinking in such a way were explored further by writers such as Virginia Woolf, whose novels and literary criticism rested on a dual mode of perception similar to his, and Ted Hughes, with his belief that every poet must, like him, create his own mythology. With the growing interest in popular culture towards the end of the century Coleridge became iconic to a larger public, his problems with opium being reinterpreted by proponents of the drug culture while his supernatural poems provided a frequent quarry for new works in art and music; such matters as the nature of his relationship with the Wordsworths and even of the 'person from Porlock' who interrupted composition of 'Kubla Khan' were explored not only in biographical studies but also in poems and dramatizations.

This tendency towards universal approbation has not gone unchallenged. From the middle of the nineteenth century negative views included accusations of plagiarism in which the note of moral reprobation often sounded. A century later the theme was resumed in Norman Fruman's *Coleridge: the Damaged Archangel* (1961), which surveyed extensively the range of his unacknowledged borrowings. Other writers, by contrast, stressed his originality, which the fuller publication of his writings served only to emphasize. The countless writers whose writings betray the existence of their debts would no doubt endorse the tribute of Wordsworth, whose chosen word in 1834 was the same as his sister's had been in 1797 (*Letters of William and Dorothy Wordsworth*, 1.188): Coleridge was 'the most *wonderful* man he had ever known' (*Prose Works*, 3.469).

In spite of such admiration, nevertheless, commentators have always had difficulty in characterizing the distinctive nature of Coleridge's achievement, some of the best attempts recalling John Stuart Mill's description of Coleridge's and Jeremy Bentham's as 'the two great seminal minds of England in their age':

> By Bentham … men have been led to ask themselves, in regard to any ancient or received opinion, Is it true? and by Coleridge, What is the meaning of it? … With Coleridge … the very fact that any doctrine had been believed by thoughtful men, and received by whole nations or generations of mankind, was part of the problem to be solved, was one of the phenomena to be accounted for. (Mill, 40, 99–100)

In that formulation Coleridge the 'inquiring spirit', the bridge-builder between ancient truths and modern growings, receives a portion of his due that has increasingly supplemented his reputation as poet and critic.

JOHN BEER

Sources *The collected works of Samuel Taylor Coleridge*, ed. K. Coburn and B. Winer (1969–) · *Collected letters of Samuel Taylor Coleridge*, ed. E. L. Griggs, 6 vols. (1956–71) · *The notebooks of Samuel Taylor Coleridge*, ed. K. Coburn, 4 vols. (1959–) [5 vols. projected] · S. T. Coleridge, *Poems*, ed. J. Beer, new edn (1999) · S. Hutchinson, *The letters of Sara Hutchinson*, ed. K. Coburn (1954) · *The letters of William and Dorothy Wordsworth, 1787–1853*, ed. E. de Selincourt, 2nd edn, rev. A. G. Hill and others, 7 vols. (1967–88) · W. Wordsworth, *The prose works of William Wordsworth*, ed. A. B. Grosart, 3 vols. (1876) · *The complete works of William Hazlitt*, ed. P. P. Howe, 21 vols. (1930–34) · T. De Quincey, *A diary of Thomas De Quincey, 1803*, ed. H. A. Eaton (1926) · T. De Quincey, *The collected writings of Thomas De Quincey*, ed. D. Masson, 14 vols. (1889–90) · H. C. Robinson, *Henry Crabb Robinson on books and their writers*, ed. E. J. Morley, 3 vols. (1938) · J. Keats, *Letters of John Keats, 1814–1821*, ed. H. E. Rollins, 2 vols. (1958) · C. Lamb and M. Lamb, *The works of Charles and Mary Lamb*, ed. E. V. Lucas, 7 vols. (1903–5) · *The letters of Charles and Mary Lamb*, ed. E. V. Marrs, 3 vols. (1975–8) · *Selections from the letters of Robert Southey*, ed. J. W. Warter, 4 vols. (1856) · *Byron's letters and journals*, ed. L. A. Marchand, 12 vols. (1973–82) · R. W. Emerson, *The journals and miscellaneous notebooks of*

Ralph Waldo Emerson, ed. W. H. Gilman and others (1960–) · T. Carlyle, *The life of John Sterling* (1851) · J. S. Mill, *Mill on Bentham and Coleridge* (1950) [with an introduction by F. R. Leavis] · D. Stuart, 'Anecdotes of the poet Coleridge', *GM*, 2nd ser., 10 (1838) · J. Gillman, *The life of Samuel Taylor Coleridge* (1838) · E. K. Chambers, *Coleridge* (1938) · J. Cornwell, *Coleridge, poet and revolutionary, 1772–1804: a critical biography* (1973) · R. Ashton, *The life of Samuel Taylor Coleridge: a critical biography* (1996) · R. Holmes, *Coleridge: early visions* (1989) · R. Holmes, *Coleridge: darker reflections* (1998) · V. Purton, *A Coleridge chronology* (1993) · E. S. Shaffer, *'Kubla Khan' and The fall of Jerusalem* (1975) · T. McFarland, *Coleridge and the pantheist tradition* (1969) · E. P. Thompson, 'Disenchantment or default?: a lay sermon', *Power and consciousness*, ed. C. C. O'Brien and W. D. Vanech (1969) · S. Potter, *Minnow among Tritons: Mrs S. T. Coleridge's letters to Thomas Poole, 1799–1834* (1934) · C. W. Dilke, *Papers of a critic*, 2 vols. (1875) · C. Carlyon, *Early years and late reflections*, 4 vols. (1836–58) · T. C. Grattan, *Beaten paths and those who trod them*, 2 vols. (1862) · J. Beer, 'Coleridge's "great circulating library"', *N&Q*, 201 (1956), 264 · H. W. Piper, *The active universe: pantheism and the concept of the imagination in the English romantic poets* (1962) · J. A. Paris, *Life of Sir Humphry Davy* (1831)

Archives BL, lecture notes, Egerton MS 3057 · BL, letters, notebooks, and literary papers, Add. MSS 47496–47554 · BL, memorandum book, Add. MS 27901 · BL, notes, treatises, and papers, Egerton MSS 2800–2801, 2825–2826 · BL, transcribed prose, letters, and marginalia, Add. MS 63785 · BL, various printed works with his MS notes and additions · Boston PL, letters and papers · Bristol Reference Library, MS poems, letters, and a commonplace book · Duke U., Perkins L., notebook · Eton, letters · FM Cam., corrections to 'Poetical Works'; letters · Harvard U., Houghton L., corresp. and literary MSS · Harvard U., Houghton L., letters and papers · Highgate Literary and Scientific Institution, papers · Hunt. L., letters and literary MSS · Indiana University, Bloomington, Lilly Library, corresp. · Jesus College, Cambridge, papers and corresp. · Morgan L., corresp. and papers · NYPL, MSS and notebook · Ransom HRC, family papers · Royal Institution of Great Britain, London, letters · St John Cam., annotated 'Christabel' · Swedenborg Society, London, letters · University of Toronto, Victoria University, corresp., notebooks, and papers · V&A NAL, MS of 'The Friend' and letters and instructions to Brown the printer and Joseph Cottle · Wordsworth Trust, Dove Cottage, Grasmere, letters · Wordsworth Trust, Dove Cottage, Grasmere, literary MSS and corresp. · Yale U., papers | BL, corresp. with Thomas Poole, Add. MSS 35343–35345 · BL, letters to Daniel Stuart, Add. MS 34046 · BL, corresp. with Josiah Wedgwood and Thomas Wedgwood, Add. MSS 35343–35344 · Bodl. Oxf., letters to Josiah Wedgwood and Sons · County Reference Library, Bristol, letters to John Prior Estin · CUL, letters to W. Kinglake · DWL, letters to Henry Crabb Robinson · Keele University, Wedgwood papers, corresp. with Josiah Wedgwood II and Tom Wedgwood · NL Scot., corresp. with Blackwoods · Royal Institution of Great Britain, London, corresp. with Sir Humphry Davy

Likenesses P. Vandyke, oils, 1795, NPG [*see illus.*] · R. Hancock, drawing (pencil and wash on paper), 1796, NPG · W. Shuter, oils, 1798, repro. in Coleridge, *Collected letters*, frontispiece · pastel drawing, 1799, repro. in Holmes, *Coleridge: early visions*, jacket · W. Hazlitt, portrait, 1803 · G. Dance, black chalk drawing, 1804, Dove Cottage, Grasmere, Cumbria · J. Northcote, oils, 1804, Jesus College, Cambridge · W. Allston, oils, 1806, Harvard U., Fogg Art Museum · W. Allston, oils, 1806, Harvard U. · M. Betham, miniature, 1808, Bristol City Museum and Art Gallery · G. Dawe, bust, 1812 · G. Dawe, chalk drawing, 1812, Chanter's House, Ottery St Mary, Devon · W. Allston, oils, 1814, NPG · C. R. Leslie, pencil drawing, 1816, repro. in A. W. Gillman, *The Gillmans of Highgate* [1895] · C. R. Leslie, pencil drawing, 1818, repro. in Coleridge, *Collected letters*, vol. 5 · T. Phillips, oils, 1818–21, repro. in Coleridge, *Collected letters*, vol. 4, p. 912 · Cooper, oils, c.1830, Highgate Literary and Scientific Institution, London · M. Haughton, oils, 1832, Christ's Hospital, Horsham, West Sussex · J. Kayser, pencil drawing, 1833, repro. in Coleridge, *Collected letters*, vol. 6 · A. Wivell, drawing,

1833 · J. Gillman, death mask, 1834, repro. in A. W. Gillman, *The Gillmans of Highgate* (1895), facing p. 13 · L. Haghe, lithograph, pubd 1835 (after T. Phillips), BM, NPG · T. Woolner, bronze memorial, 1875 (the Bluecoat Group), Christ's Hospital, Horsham, West Sussex · W. H. Thornycroft, marble bust, 1885, Westminster Abbey · G. Coleridge, bronze bas-relief plaque, 1932 (after Thornycroft), Ottery St Mary churchyard, Devon; copy, Jesus College, Cambridge, in 1933 · D. Maclise, drawing, V&A; repro. in *Fraser's Magazine*, 8 (1833), 64 · C. de Predl, chalk drawing; copy, oils, 1826, Highgate Literary and Scientific Institution, London · R. Stone, Westmorland green slate memorial, St Michael's Church, Highgate, London · W. Wagstaff, stipple (after A. Wivell), BM, NPG; repro. in *The works of Lord Byron*, ed. Moore, 17 vols. (1832–3)

Wealth at death approx. £2560—insurance policy: E. Coleridge, *Memoir … of Sara Coleridge by her daughter* (1873)

Coleridge, Sara (1802–1852), writer and literary editor, was born on 23 December 1802 at Greta Hall, Keswick, the youngest of the three children of Samuel Taylor *Coleridge (1772–1834), poet and philosopher, and his wife, Sara Fricker Coleridge (1770–1845). Although she spent little time in the company of her father, who, estranged from his wife, preferred London to the Lake District, young Sara and her two brothers, Derwent *Coleridge (1800–1883) and (David) Hartley *Coleridge (1796–1849), grew up with all the benefits of living in a well-known literary household. Sharing Greta Hall with their aunt and uncle, Edith and Robert *Southey (1774–1843), the Coleridges were also close friends of William Wordsworth and his family. The ongoing literary labours of Wordsworth and Southey thus ensured an almost constant stream of visitors at Greta Hall, and by the age of twenty Sara had met many of the most famous writers of her day. This stimulating environment, the excellent tutelage of her mother and uncle, her own intellectual prowess, and the impecunious state of the Coleridge family all contributed to Sara's first literary efforts.

When in 1818 Derwent found himself unable to afford study at Cambridge, Sara and Derwent, at Southey's suggestion, together began a translation of Martin Dobrizhoffer's book on Paraguay, *Historia de Abiponibus* (1784). Derwent soon lost interest, but Sara persisted, and in January 1822 John Murray published *An Account of the Abiphones, an Equestrian People of Paraguay*. Three years later she published a second translation, *The right joyous and pleasant history of the facts, tests, and prowesses of the Chevalier Bayard* (1825). By 1825 Sara had visited her father in London and had become secretly engaged to her first cousin, Henry Nelson *Coleridge (1798–1843). Their engagement was long and difficult. Each suffered from ill health, and Sara had already begun to depend on opium, a dependence which, like that of her father, was to continue throughout her life. After Sara and Henry finally married on 3 September 1829, they moved to London, where Henry practised law and where it was assumed that Sara would renounce her literary labours for the more dutiful roles of wife and mother.

Sara and Henry lived at 21 Downshire Hill, Downshire Place, Hampstead, not far from her father's house in Highgate. Sara's first child, Herbert [see Coleridge, Herbert (1830–1861)], was born on 7 October 1830; her second, Edith, followed in July 1831. Although she continued to

Sara Coleridge (1802–1852), by Richard James Lane, 1852 (after Samuel Laurence, 1848)

read widely and to maintain an impressive correspondence, Sara became an invalid soon after the birth of her children. She suffered from a variety of physical and mental ailments, all of which were exacerbated by her increasing dependence on opium. In January 1834 she gave birth to twins, Florence and Berkeley, who lived only a few days and whose deaths plunged her into depression. Her illness notwithstanding, she worked hard educating her children, and later in 1834 J. W. Parker published a collection of poems, *Pretty Lessons in Verse for Small Children*. Although the book went through five editions in almost as many years, Sara never considered it anything more than a family project. *Pretty Lessons* was followed in 1837 by *Phantasmion*, a long prose fairy tale with numerous poems interspersed.

The crucial event of this period was the death of Sara's father on 25 July 1834. His *Poetical Works* had appeared the previous January, and his death was followed by a critical reassessment of his poetical and philosophical career, the most notorious of which was Thomas De Quincey's damning four-part serial in *Tait's Edinburgh Magazine*. Although irate about De Quincey's discussion of her father's opium addiction and his failed marriage, Sara was more upset by the charges of plagiarism, and rather than sink to the level of undignified journalism, she and her husband began an editorial campaign that was designed to protect and preserve Coleridge's reputation. Aided by Sara, Henry Nelson Coleridge published *Table Talk* in 1835 and four volumes of *Literary Remains* between 1836 and 1839. In addition to assisting Henry, Sara began a systematic rereading of her father's works, an exercise that required analysis of his theological and philosophical predecessors. Plagued by ill health (she had three miscarriages between 1836 and 1839) and by a move to 10 Chester Place, Regent's Park, Sara nevertheless began work on a new edition of *Aids to Reflection* (1825).

Henry Nelson Coleridge never lived to see that edition. In May 1842 he collapsed with degenerative nerve disease. When he died the following January, Sara, after the appropriate period of mourning, assumed control of the editorial campaign, and although she took advice from her brother Derwent and from her cousin John Taylor *Coleridge, it was her vision, her labour, and her scrupulous research that kept her father's works before the public eye. After seeing the 1843 edition of *Aids to Reflection* through the press, the second volume of which included her own long essay 'On rationalism', Sara published *Biographia literaria* (1847), *Notes and Lectures upon Shakespeare* (1849), *Essays on his Own Times* (1850), and *The Poems of Samuel Taylor Coleridge* (1852). Each new edition was accompanied by a lengthy introduction or appendix in which Coleridge's theories were explicated, defended, or qualified. Her finest achievement was her edition of the *Biographia*, which took her four years and which continues to be acknowledged by modern scholars. Her introduction to that edition itself occupies almost an entire volume.

In addition to her editorial labours, Sara wrote two reviews for the *Quarterly Review*, the first on Tennyson's *The Princess* for the March 1848 number, and the second on a new edition of Beaumont and Fletcher the following September. By this time an entrenched member of the London literati, Sara counted among her correspondents Joanna Baillie, Elizabeth Barrett Browning, Anna Jameson, F. D. Maurice, Henry Crabb Robinson, William Gladstone, Henry Taylor, and Aubrey de Vere. She continued to read voraciously and offered opinions on everything from the inconsistencies of the Oxford Movement to architectural excesses of the Great Exhibition. When she died at her home at 10 Chester Place, on 3 May 1852, after a long and horrific battle with breast cancer, Sara Coleridge left hundreds of pages of unpublished manuscripts—essays, letters, journals, poems, and theological dialogues in the style of Landor's *Imaginary Conversations*. Many were fragments. For a woman who spent the greater part of her intellectual life putting her father's literary house in order, it is the last irony that she, arguably the most Coleridgean of Coleridge's offspring, was unable to order her own.   BRADFORD K. MUDGE

Sources B. Mudge, *Sara Coleridge: a Victorian daughter* (1989) · E. L. Griggs, *Coleridge fille* (1940) · *Memoir and letters of Sara Coleridge*, ed. E. Coleridge, 2 vols. (1873) · M. Lefebure, *The bondage of love: a life of Mrs Samuel Taylor Coleridge* (1986) · *Minnow among tritons: Mrs S. T. Coleridge's letters to Thomas Poole, 1799–1834*, ed. S. Potter (1934) · E. Towle, *A poet's children: Hartley and Sara Coleridge* (1912)

Archives Ransom HRC, papers · Wordsworth Trust, Dove Cottage, Grasmere, letters | BL, corresp. with Sir John Taylor Coleridge, Add. MS 47557 · Bodl. Oxf., letters to Lady Taylor · DWL, letters to Henry Crabb Robinson and others · Wordsworth Trust, Dove Cottage, Grasmere, letters, mainly to Mary Stanger

Likenesses E. Nash, miniature, 1820 (with her cousin Edith Southey), NPG · C. Jones, engraving, 1827, repro. in Coleridge, ed., *Memoir and letters of Sara Coleridge* · G. Richmond, drawing, 1845, Ransom HRC · S. Laurence, engraving, 1850, repro. in Coleridge, ed., *Memoir and letters of Sara Coleridge* · R. J. Lane, lithograph, 1852 (after S. Laurence, 1848), NPG [*see illus.*] · M. Carpenter, charcoal and chalk drawing, BM

Coleridge, Stephen William Buchanan (1854–1936), author and anti-vivisectionist, was born in London on 31 May 1854, the second son of John Duke *Coleridge, first Baron Coleridge (1820–1894), lord chief justice of England, and his first wife, Jane Fortescue, daughter of the Revd George Turner Seymour, of Farringford, Isle of Wight. He was brother of the judge Bernard John Seymour *Coleridge, second Baron Coleridge, and of Gilbert Coleridge, assistant master of the crown office from 1892 to 1921.

Stephen Coleridge was sent to school in Brighton and then, aged eleven, 'to a horrible school at Honiton, conducted by a monster of cruelty named Izod' (Coleridge, 4). He then went to Bradfield School, Berkshire, and, in 1874, to Trinity College, Cambridge, graduating in 1877. After a year (1879–80) spent in travel in Latin America, he became private secretary to his father (1884–90). In 1886 he was called to the bar by the Middle Temple. In 1890 the lord chief justice appointed him clerk of assize for the South Wales circuit. His natural kindness and courtesy made him popular with the members of the circuit.

An inherited rhetorical faculty characterized Coleridge's writings both in prose and in verse. He appreciated good literature, and was an acceptable lecturer. His large output includes *A Morning in my Library* (1914), *An Evening in my Library among the English Poets* (1916), and other books of the same kind. He also published four volumes entitled *Letters to my Grandson* (1921–3), telling him of the world about him, the happy life, and the glory of English prose and poetry. He was a competent amateur artist, especially of landscape, and showed at various exhibitions.

Coleridge hated cruelty in all its forms and believed in action to reduce it. He was one of the founders, in 1884, of the London Society for the Prevention of Cruelty to Children, renamed in 1889 as the National Society for the Prevention of Cruelty to Children. Although fond of games and outdoor pursuits, he hated any sport that involved the death of animals, and became president of the League for the Prohibition of Cruel Sports. His chief energy, however, was devoted to the ending of experiments on animals. On this subject he had uncompromising views and was opposed not only to vivisection but to exhibitions of stuffed animals and to posters illustrating vivisection, though intended to demonstrate its cruelty. He was active in the Victoria Street Society for the Protection of Animals Liable to Vivisection and was the protégé of Frances Power Cobbe, its leader. The society came to support total abolition. In 1898 Coleridge ousted Cobbe from the society's executive committee; the society was renamed the National Vivisection Society and pursued a step-by-step policy, of which total abolition would be the final achievement rather than the only goal (Cobbe in fury founded a rigidly abolitionist counter-organization). Coleridge attempted to set anti-vivisection in a wider context, as part of a resistance to the onset of science, which he saw as causing moral decline and economic slavery (French, 412).

Coleridge was twice married: first, in 1879, to Geraldine Beatrix (d. 1910), daughter and coheir of Charles Manners Lushington, of Norton Court, Kent, and niece of Stafford *Northcote, first earl of Iddesleigh; and second, in 1911, to Susan, second daughter of Allan Duncan Stewart, of Bun Rannoch and Inverhadden, Perthshire, an area that became the subject of many of his paintings. With his first wife he had three sons, the eldest of whom predeceased him. Coleridge died at his home, The Ford, Chobham, Surrey, on 10 April 1936.

ALFRED COCHRANE, rev. H. C. G. MATTHEW

Sources The Times (11 April 1936) · S. Coleridge, Memories (1913) · R. D. French, Antivivisection and medical science in Victorian society (1975) · private information (2004) **Archives** Bodl. Oxf., corresp. with Sir Henry Burdett · U. Reading L., letters to the Bodley Head Ltd **Likenesses** Elf, caricature, NPG; repro. in VF (27 July 1910) · photograph, repro. in Coleridge, Memories **Wealth at death** £7853 3s. 9d.: probate, 1 July 1936, CGPLA Eng. & Wales

Coleridge, William Hart (1789–1849), bishop of Barbados and the Leeward Islands, was the only son of Luke Herman Coleridge (brother of Samuel Taylor Coleridge) of Thorverton, Devon, and Sarah, his wife, third daughter of Richard Hart of Exeter. His father died during his infancy, and he was educated by his uncle, the Revd George Coleridge, master of the grammar school of Ottery St Mary. He entered as a commoner at Christ Church, Oxford, and graduated BA (on 21 November 1811), MA (on 1 June 1814), BD (on 17 June 1824), and DD (on 18 June 1824).

Soon after leaving Oxford (in 1811), Coleridge became a curate at St Andrew's, Holborn, in London, and afterwards he was secretary to the Society for Promoting Christian Knowledge; he was also preacher at the National Society's chapel in Ely Place. On 25 July 1824 he was consecrated bishop of Barbados and the Leeward Islands at Lambeth. In 1825, he married Sarah Elizabeth, eldest daughter of Dr Thomas *Rennell, dean of Winchester and master of the Temple; she was also a granddaughter of Sir William Blackstone, the judge. They had one son and one daughter, both of whom outlived him.

The diocese of Barbados was made up of the islands of the British West Indies with, in 1826, the addition of British Guiana. Coleridge arrived in Barbados in January 1825 and almost immediately set out on his first visit, travelling to Trinidad, Grenada, St Vincent, and St Lucia. He found the diocese in an unsatisfactory condition, judging that the number of clergymen and churches was insufficient, and that there were too few daily schools and Sunday schools. In his first charge (delivered in 1830) he felt able to congratulate the congregation on the improved spiritual condition of the black population who, he noted, had almost entirely abandoned traditional grieving customs such as lamenting the dead with loud cries and leaving food at burial sites.

During his episcopate Coleridge worked closely with the Society for the Propagation of the Gospel. The society provided all the diocese's clergy and managed the slave-worked Codrington estates and Codrington College on Barbados itself. It had attracted some odium from British abolitionists for not being strenuously engaged in the abolition movement, though from 1830 it was proceeding towards gradual emancipation in the belief that

> as Trustees of the Codrington Estates [they] are able not only to suggest a course, but to make the trial themselves, for the satisfaction of others; and to shew the planters how they may gradually enfranchise their Slaves without destruction to their property. (Pascoe, 202)

Coleridge seems to have been in full agreement with this course of action, for as he himself wrote:

> To prepare the minds of a mass of persons, so peculiarly situated, for a change such as this, was a work requiring the exercise of great patience and altogether of a most arduous nature. And it was chiefly owing to the Society of the Propagation of the Gospel that that day not only passed in peace, but was distinguished for the proper feeling that prevailed and its perfect order. (Pascoe, 203)

In a charge delivered in July 1838, just before the legal emancipation of slaves in the West Indian colonies, he stated that the native population flocked to the churches and chapels, and were civil in their behaviour and decent in their appearance.

By the time of emancipation the number of communicants was unusually large, the number of diocescan clergy had risen to ninety-nine, and there were fifty-three parish churches and forty-two school houses. Of the many churches which had been damaged in the great hurricane which devastated Barbados on 11 August 1831, seven had been rebuilt, thanks partly to a parliamentary grant and partly to a grant of £2000 from the Society for the Propagation of the Gospel. Other institutions established or remodelled during Coleridge's episcopate included a diocesan committee of the Society for Promoting Christian Knowledge, a clerical library, a branch association of the Negro Conversion Society, a 'daily meal' society, a medical dispensary society, four friendly societies, an asylum for the 'coloured poor', and three societies for the education of the 'coloured poor'. Soon after his arrival in the diocese Coleridge had also been engaged, together with the trustees, in the reorganization of Codrington College, Barbados.

In 1842, after about eighteen years' zealous labour, Coleridge was compelled to resign his see through the failure of his health. The large diocese was then divided, the three archdeaconries of Barbados, Antigua, and Guiana being erected into separate sees. On the establishment of St Augustine's Missionary College at Canterbury, Coleridge became the first warden. He held the office until his sudden death, caused by a rupture of a vessel of the heart on 21 December 1849, at his home, Salston, in Ottery St Mary.

W. W. WROTH, rev. CLARE BROWN

Sources S. Goodridge, Facing the challenge of emancipation: a study of the ministry of William Hart Coleridge, first bishop of Barbados, 1824–1842 (1981) · C. F. Pascoe, Two hundred years of the SPG, rev. edn, 2 vols. (1901) · GM, 2nd ser., 33 (1850), 207 · Annual Register (1849) · d. cert.
Archives Bodl. RH, Society for the Propagation of the Gospel archives · U. Birm. L., letters to the Church Missionary Society

Likenesses T. Phillips, oils, exh. RA 1825, Christ Church Oxf.

Coles, Charles Edward

Coles, Charles Edward [*called* Coles Pasha] (1853–1926), prison administrator in Egypt, was born at Buge, India, on 17 November 1853, the only son of Major-General Thomas Gordon Coles of the Indian army, and his wife, Maria, daughter of Colonel Charles D'Oyle Straker, also of the Indian army. After being educated privately at Bath, Coles entered the Indian police department in 1873, serving in the Bombay residency. In 1881 he married Mary Emma Isabella (*née* Alston) of Odell, Bedfordshire. They had four sons (two of whom died in the First World War) and two daughters. In 1883 his services were lent to the Egyptian government, which in 1884 appointed him deputy inspector-general of police. From 1894 to 1897 he held the post of commandant of the Cairo city police. Upon his promotion in 1897 to the office of director-general of Egyptian prisons, Coles began the most important phase of his career.

During the sixteen years (1897–1913) of his administration of the prison department Coles transformed the Egyptian prisons, once a source of reproach to the government, into a source of pride. In the period before he began work Egyptian finances had been limited and the prison budget insufficient. Prisoners were lodged in disused barracks, factories, and other inadequate and insanitary buildings, and no regular provision was made either for feeding or for clothing the inmates. Coles took up his duties with energy and enthusiasm, and with plans for large-scale reform. Egypt had recently become more prosperous, and Coles approached the financial authorities with determination, informing them that he should require £E500,000 for the rebuilding of all the prisons, and probably an additional £E150,000 a year for their maintenance. Sixteen years later he was able to boast that he had spent £E473,738 on building, and that the budgetary provision for maintenance in the preceding year had been £E160,000.

Among other reforms achieved during Coles's administration, arrangements were made for trades to be taught and practised in prisons, and for short-term inmates to work off their sentences in supervised work outside the prison walls. Boys' and girls' reformatories, conducted on contemporary English principles of character training, were established; and a reformatory was created for adults under 'indeterminate sentences', which appears to have been the first institution of its kind in the world. In the course of his service Coles had to deal with two or three serious convict riots and he made a point of relying largely on his personal influence with the prisoners to restore order. When shooting prisoners seemed unavoidable, he shot them himself.

The development of the Egyptian prison system under Coles's administration was his most important achievement, but he did not spend all his time in official duties. He was a keen sportsman who became a leading figure in Egyptian racing, and was the founder of the Alexandrian Sporting Club and of the Egyptian Jockey Club. In 1900 Coles was created CMG for his services abroad and retired

in 1913 to Somerset where he wrote *Recollections and Reflections*, which was published in 1918. In 1921 he moved to Biarritz, France, publishing *Occupational Franchise* in 1922. He died at his home, the Villa Sans Atout, Biarritz, on 12 November 1926. M. S. AMOS, *rev.* LYNN MILNE

Sources *The Times* (16 Nov 1926) · Coles Pasha [C. E. Coles], *Recollections and reflections* [1918] · *WWW*, 1991–5 · *CGPLA Eng. & Wales* (1927) · private information (1937)

Wealth at death £1088 17s. 9d.: probate, 22 Feb 1927, *CGPLA Eng. & Wales*

Coles, Cowper Phipps

Coles, Cowper Phipps (1819–1870), naval officer and inventor of a gun turret, third son of the Revd John Coles of Ditcham Park, Hampshire, passed his examination for a commission in 1838, and in January 1846 was promoted lieutenant. In October 1853 he was chosen by Sir Edmund Lyons, his uncle by marriage, as his flag-lieutenant on the *Agamemnon* in the Mediterranean, and served in the fleet's attack on the Sevastopol forts on 17 October 1854. On 13 November he was made commander, and during 1855 commanded the paddle steamer *Stromboli* in the Black Sea and Sea of Azov. On 27 February 1856 he was promoted captain.

While in the Sea of Azov, Coles designed and constructed a shallow-draft gun-raft, which was capable of carrying a heavy gun protected by an iron shield 4 inches thick. He was ordered home to superintend the construction of similar rafts for the projected attack on Kronstadt, a work that was prevented by the end of the war in May 1856. But from then he devoted himself to the study of defensive armour for ships and forts. The early idea of a raft and shield gradually transformed itself into a conical shield on a revolving turntable, suggested by Isambard Kingdom Brunel, for shore fortification, and finally into the simple cylindrical section for shipboard mounting. The system was attractive because it coincided with a sudden increase in the size and weight of naval artillery, making a broadside of four heavy guns appear to be an adequate replacement for fifty or sixty smaller weapons. Similar ideas were developed in the USA by John Ericsson, and the claims of the two men to the original conception have often been discussed. Probably the crude idea occurred independently to each, but their further progress reacted on each other. As finally developed, Coles's turret was far more sophisticated than Ericsson's, and the two men's ideas on the ideal ship to mount the turret were radically different. Both men were forced by the turret's weight to build low freeboard vessels: Ericsson created the monitor, while Coles wanted to combine the turret with a full ship rig to create a first-class battleship. By securing the support of Prince Albert, after whom the first purpose-built British turret ship was named, and of Lord Palmerston, *The Times*, and large sections of the daily and service press, Coles secured the conversion of the steam battleship *Royal Sovereign* into a mastless turret ship. After offering his patent rights to the Admiralty for £20,000, Coles was left to settle for £5000 in recognition of his efforts, and £100 for every turret installed during the term of his patent. This was in addition to being kept on full pay for most of the decade as an adviser. Despite successful

Cowper Phipps Coles (1819–1870), by J. Harris

trials in 1864, he was not satisfied with this limited application, and through his brother-in-law Captain G. T. P. Hornby used the Conservative Party to press for a fully rigged first-class ship to be built. The Admiralty ordered the chief constructor, Sir Edward Reed, to design this ship, ordered in 1866 as HMS *Monarch*, but Coles remained dissatisfied. Eventually the duke of Somerset allowed him to call on private industry to design his own ship. Coles selected Laird Brothers of Birkenhead, who had already built several turret ships for foreign governments, and their design was authorized on 23 July 1866, notwithstanding the submission of the controller of the navy, that it was doubtful whether the proposed freeboard, 8 feet, would be satisfactory for a seagoing cruising ship. The ship was named the *Captain*. Coles intended that she should function as a seagoing cruising ship, and he was supported by public opinion. The Admiralty, which included many of his supporters, of whom the first lord and first sea lord were the most notable, laid the responsibility on Coles and the Lairds, and sanctioned her being commissioned, although it was found that the freeboard was nearly 2 feet less than had been designed. Apparently

they did not realize that this was a source of great danger; and the responsibility they had mentioned referred to the cost of any necessary material alterations. The *Captain* was commissioned early in 1870; after an experimental cruise she joined the Channel Fleet, accompanied it to Gibraltar, and on the way home, in a fresh gale off Cape Finisterre on the night of 7 September, capsized and sank. Almost all aboard her were drowned, including Coles, who was travelling as the guest of Captain H. T. *Burgoyne.

Coles left a widow, Emily, *née* Pearson, and ten children, among them Sherard Osborn Cowper-*Coles, electro-metallurgist and inventor. He was a significant figure in the mid-nineteenth century naval technical revolution. His turret transformed the design of modern warships in the space of a decade, reflecting great credit on his abilities as a publicist and lobbyist. His single-minded determination, however, left him unable to see the other side of the debate, and this led to a decade of controversy with Reed and Admiral Sir Spencer Robinson. The duke of Somerset blamed his 'obstinate conceit' (Mallock and Ramsden, 388) and the support of *The Times* for the *Captain* disaster. Unfortunately, Coles combined a heavy system of protected gun mounting with outdated views on the necessity of a full sailing rig for first-class battleships. Lacking the scientific skill to assess the results of his efforts, he designed the *Captain* with a heavier rig than the Admiralty-designed *Monarch*, which he was anxious to outperform, and so she capsized. The real line of development for the turret ship lay not in the masted type, but through the coastal designs to the mastless seagoing battleship *Devastation*, designed by Coles's arch rival Edward Reed and launched in 1871.

J. K. LAUGHTON, rev. ANDREW LAMBERT

Sources S. Sandler, *The emergence of the modern capital ship* (1979) · J. P. Baxter, *The introduction of the ironclad warship* (1933) · Mrs F. Egerton, *Admiral of the fleet: Sir Geoffrey Phipps Hornby, a biography* (1896) · private information (1887) · CGPLA Eng. & Wales (1870) · W. D. Mallock and G. Ramsden, *Edward Adolphus Seymour, twelfth duke of Somerset* (1898)

Archives NMM, pamphlets and newspaper cuttings | Bucks. RLSS, Somerset MSS · PRO, Admiralty Archive · W. Sussex RO, letters to Richard Cobden

Likenesses J. Harris, carte-de-visite (in uniform), NPG [see illus.] · engraving, repro. in Sandler, *Emergence of the modern capital ship*, 178 · wood-engraving, NPG; repro. in ILN (19 April 1862) · wood-engraving (after photograph by J. Harris), NPG; repro. in ILN (24 Sept 1870)

Wealth at death under £4000: probate, 24 Sept 1870, CGPLA Eng. & Wales

Coles, Elisha (*b.* in or before **1608**, *d.* **1688**), writer on religion, was a native of Northamptonshire. Originally a trader in London, he had settled in Oxford by 1651, for on 23 May of that year he was appointed deputy registrar to the parliamentary visitors there in the absence of Ralph Austen, the registrar. In 1657 Dr Thomas Goodwin, president of Magdalen College, named him the college's steward.

As a commissioner for the ejection of scandalous ministers in Oxfordshire, Coles served with such colleagues as Dr Joshua Cross and Dr John Palmer. Their ejection of Henry Beesley from the living at Swerford in 1658 was upheld by the council of state. On 11 August 1660 the commissioners responsible for the visitation of the university and its colleges ordered Coles's removal from his stewardship on the grounds that he had been improperly admitted. Coles then became a clerk in the East India Company. An Independent, he wrote *A Practical Discourse of God's Sovereignty: with other Material Points, Deriving Thence* (1673), a work claiming to be grounded solely on scripture. According to his preface Coles had received some training in Calvinist tenets in his youth, but he was motivated to compose this 275-page treatise after discussions with some Arminians. Originally intended as a legacy for his children, the treatise was published after Coles received requests to do so from 'Antient and Sober Christians' (Coles, A4r). The third edition, issued by Nathaniel Ponder (who published John Bunyan's *Pilgrim's Progress*) and others in 1678, included commendatory epistles by Thomas Goodwin and (jointly) by John Owen and Samuel Annesley. The latter two praised Coles for his practical application of such doctrines as election, effectual calling, the atonement, and perseverance.

Coles and his wife, Elizabeth (d. 1715x20), had a son, also **Elisha Coles** (fl. 1688), whom he apprenticed to a trade, and who should not be confused with his cousin Elisha *Coles (c.1640–1680), the lexicographer. Coles died in his house in Scalding Alley, London, about 28 October 1688, 'aged eighty years or more' (Wood, *Ath. Oxon.* 3.1274–6). He was interred in a nonconformist burial-ground, probably Bunhill Fields. He was survived by his wife and son, but the latter seems to have died before 1715, as he is not mentioned in his mother's will signed on 27 August in that year, and proved on 21 March 1720.

RICHARD L. GREAVES

Sources E. Coles, *A practical discourse of God's sovereignty: with other material points, deriving thence* (1673) • Wood, *Ath. Oxon.*, new edn, 3.1274–6 • M. Burrows, ed., *The register of the visitors of the University of Oxford, from AD 1647 to AD 1658*, CS, new ser., 29 (1881) • CSP dom., 1658–9 • F. J. Varley, ed., 'The Restoration visitation of the University of Oxford and its colleges', *Camden miscellany, XVIII*, CS, 3rd ser., 79 (1948) • D. D. Wallace, *Puritans and predestination: grace in English protestant theology, 1525–1695* (1982) • DNB • will, PRO, PROB 11/393, sig. 147 • will, PRO, PROB 11/373, sig. 57 [Elizabeth Coles]

Coles, Elisha (c.1640–1680), lexicographer and stenographer, the son of John *Coles (1623/4–1678), schoolmaster of Wolverhampton grammar school, and his wife, Joyce, was probably born about 1640 in Northamptonshire. He was the nephew of Elisha *Coles the Calvinist, and has been often confused with his uncle's son, also Elisha *Coles [see under Coles, Elisha]. A schoolmaster like his father, Coles evidently possessed a playful sense of humour: 'I was born and bred [for a dozen years] in the very heart of *England*, I spent almost as many in her very eye, and after that as many more in [or about] the very head of the Kingdom' (*The Compleat English Schoolmaster*, 103). (England's 'very eye' alludes to Oxford, and her 'very head' to London.)

Coles entered Magdalen College, Oxford, towards the end of 1658, matriculated on 26 March 1659, and

remained a chorister until 1661 when he left without taking a degree. Shortly afterwards, he set up as a schoolmaster in London (he was at Russell Street, near Covent Garden, by 1674), teaching Latin to English youths, and English to foreigners. Coles considered himself a perennial pupil, for 'Learning and Teaching are so nearly Related, that we cannot possibly suppose the one without the other' (*Syncrisis*, 1675, preface). More than a decade passed before he submitted his efforts to the public: then from 1674 to 1677 works on shorthand, language instruction, and lexicography rolled regularly from the London presses.

In *The Newest, Plainest and the Shortest Short-Hand* (1674), a copy of which was in the library of Samuel Pepys, Coles presented the first historical survey of English shorthand, citing thirty shorthand authors and comparing fourteen alphabets. His own alphabet was apparently based on that of Thomas Shelton's second system (*Zeiglographia*, 1650). Believing monosyllables to be the great stumbling block in English shorthand, Coles advanced the innovative notion of positioning characters on, above, and below a line for great versatility, a method not adopted until 1692 in Abraham Nicholas's *Thoographia*. Coles's book was 'deservedly well received' (Kippis, 1.538).

Also published in 1674 was *The Compleat English Schoolmaster*, a spelling-book that offers valuable information about seventeenth-century pronunciation and orthographic conventions. In 1675 two Latin textbooks appeared: *Nolens volens, or, You shall make Latin whether you will or no*; and *Syncrisis*, a precursor of the Loeb Classical Library series in its juxtaposition of Latin text and facing English translation. The popularity of *Nolens volens*, with its 'delightfully uncompromising title' (Mander, *History*, 289), quaint illustrations, and amusing frontispiece of a teacher lecturing his youthful charge, may be suggested by the fact that its title was parodied in *Nolens volens, or, You shall learn to play on the violin whether you will or no* (1694).

Coles was best-known as a lexicographer. *An English Dictionary Explaining the Difficult Terms* (1676; 13 edns to 1732) was the first general dictionary to include both a wide range of dialect (from John Ray, *Collection of English Words not Generally used*, 1674), and 'canting terms', or criminal slang or flash talk (from Richard Head's *The Canting Academy*, 1673). ''Tis no disparagement to understand the Canting Terms: It may chance to save your throat from being cut, or (at least) your Pocket from being pickt' (foreword). Coles was granted a licence (27 February 1678) for the exclusive right to print for fourteen years *A Dictionary, English-Latin and Latin-English* (1677; 27 edns to 1772), a work still in vogue after the publication of Robert Ainsworth's *Thesaurus linguae Latinae compendiarius* (1736).

Coles became second under-master at Merchant Taylors' School on 3 August 1677. In February 1678 he applied unsuccessfully for the mastership of Wolverhampton grammar school, a post left vacant by his father's recent death. It has been stated that he left Merchant Taylors' School 'upon some default, not now to be named' (Wood, *Ath. Oxon.*, 3.1275), but on 14 December 1678 Coles wrote from Dublin to resign and to inform the school that he had accepted the mastership of the free school of Galway, Ireland, at the behest of its founder, Erasmus Smith, saying that 'I aime at nothing more then [*sic*] to serve God comfortably & faithfully in my generation' (Mander, *History*, 156n.). His tenure there was brief, for he died at Galway on 20 December 1680 and was buried in the south aisle of the collegiate church of St Nicholas:

> He was a curious and critical person in the English and Latin tongues, did much good in his calling, and wrote several useful and necessary books for the instruction of beginners, and therefore 'twas pitied by many that he was unhappily taken off from his prosperous proceedings. (Wood, *Ath. Oxon.*, 3.1275)

Coles may have written other works. An E. Coles penned an enthusiastic commendatory poem for William Hopkins's *The Flying Pen-Man* (1674). The poem *Christologia* (1671; published under different titles, 1679, 1680), with preface signed 'Elisha Coles, junior', has been attributed both to him and to his cousin Elisha. While there might be a wish to assign this pedestrian verse to the cousin, it is arguable that Elisha Coles lexicographer is the author. In addition, a work on penmanship by the 'Author of *Nolens volens*' was advertised in November 1687 but was evidently never published.   PAGE LIFE

Sources Wood, *Ath. Oxon.*, new edn, 3.1274–6 · J. Hardiman, *The history of the town and county of the town of Galway* (1820); repr. (1926), 260 · W. J. Carlton, *Bibliotheca Pepysiana*, 4: *Shorthand books* (1940) · H. B. Wilson, *The history of Merchant-Taylors' School*, 2 vols. (1814) · G. P. Mander, *The history of the Wolverhampton grammar school* (1913) · G. P. Mander, 'The identity of Elisha Coles', *The Library*, 3rd ser., 10 (1919), 34–44 · W. J. Carlton, 'The identity of Elisha Coles', *N&Q*, 165 (1933), 11 · E. Bensley, 'The identity of Elisha Coles: Oxford, "the eye of England"', *N&Q*, 165 (1933), 49 · J. H. Lewis, *An historical account of the rise and progress of short hand* (privately printed, London, c.1825) · De W. T. Starnes and G. E. Noyes, *The English dictionary from Cawdrey to Johnson, 1604–1755* (1946), 58–63 · E. Arber, ed., *The term catalogues, 1668–1709*, 3 vols. (privately printed, London, 1903–6) · A. Heal, *The English writing-masters and their copy-books, 1570–1800* (1931) [repr. 1962] · A. Kippis and others, eds., *Biographia Britannica, or, The lives of the most eminent persons who have flourished in Great Britain and Ireland*, 2nd edn, 5 vols. (1778–93); repr. (1974), vol. 1, pp. 538–9; vol. 4, pp. 2–3 · *CSP dom.*, 1677–8, 681, 683 · M. F. Wakelin, 'The treatment of dialect in English dictionaries', *Studies in lexicography*, ed. R. Burchfield (1987), 156–77 · T. Hayashi, *The theory of English lexicography, 1530–1791* (1978) · A. Gabrielson, 'Elisha Coles's *Syncrisis* (1675) as a source of information on 17th century English', *Englische Studien*, 70 (1935–6), 149–52 · J. A. G., 'Elisha Coles's Dictionary', *N&Q*, 4th ser., 2 (1868), 590 · S. H. Harlowe, '"Caught napping": Elisha Coles's Dictionary', *N&Q*, 4th ser., 2 (1868), 471–2 · E. Coles, *The compleat English schoolmaster* (1674)
Likenesses E. Coles?, line engraving, 1707, repro. in E. Coles, *The newest, plainest and best short-hand extant*, 10th edn (1707) · oils; formerly in possession of Edward F. Rimbault, in 1875

Coles, Elisha (*fl.* 1688). *See under* Coles, Elisha (*b.* in or before 1608, *d.* 1688).

Coles, George (1884–1963), architect, was born on 2 April 1884 at 38 Shrubland Grove, Dalston, London, the son of Walter James Coles, a commercial clerk, and his wife, Mary Haines Sharp. He was educated at Newport School, Leyton, London. He was one of the first students at the local technical institute, and then studied architecture at the Regent Street Polytechnic. He subsequently worked as an assistant to the architect Percy Adams, and became a member of the Society of Architects in 1909.

In Coles's childhood films were seen as a novelty and many cinemas were makeshift conversions of shops and small halls. When it became clear that the cinema would remain a popular attraction and a new Cinematograph Act came into effect in 1910 setting safety standards, promoters began engaging architects to design purpose-built cinemas. George Coles became not only one of the first architects to specialize in this field but also one of the most versatile, accomplished, and long-lasting. Seven of his cinemas have been listed, although most have become bingo halls.

By 1912 Coles had become Adams's partner; their first known cinema work was the small Popular at Stepney, north-east London, for the Hyams family, in 1912, and it was followed by the Empire at Dalston in 1915. The firm's first major achievement after the First World War was the huge Rivoli at Whitechapel, east London, which opened in 1921 and was bombed during the Second World War. All this early work was in the theatrical style of the period. Practising on his own from 1922, Coles was recruited by the Hyams brothers, Phil and Sid, to turn an old tramshed at Stratford, north-east London, into the vast Broadway Super cinema. The brothers persuaded the prince of Wales to attend the opening in 1927, guaranteeing national press coverage.

The major influence on British architects and cinema owners was the work being done in America, where the movie palace evolved as a new type of building with many distinctive and colourful variations. Coles would have been aware of Grauman's Egyptian (1922) and Grauman's Chinese (1927) in Hollywood when, between 1928 and 1930, he designed three London cinemas with notably exotic front elevations: in Egyptian style for the Carlton, Upton Park (bombed), and the Carlton, Islington, and in Chinese style for the Palace, Southall. Their auditoria were less interesting, but Coles demonstrated a flair for interior design with the huge, neo-classical drum-shaped auditorium of the Elephant and Castle Trocadero in south-east London, opened in 1930 and now demolished.

The Trocadero was the first of three major picture palaces which Coles designed for the Hyamses and their partner, Major Arthur J. Gale, in the London suburbs. In 1933 came the Troxy, Stepney, with many art deco details, followed in 1938 by the State, Kilburn; the State was the largest cinema ever built in England, with 4004 seats and, in its overall site area, probably the biggest in Britain. Respecting his clients' wishes, Coles provided a sleek, skyscraper-style tower that is still a landmark, but audiences stepped into a main entrance hall and auditorium in Italian Renaissance style of astounding opulence for such a poor area.

George Coles became the leading independent cinema designer of the 1930s working on tight budgets and even tighter deadlines for many of the promoters and syndicates of the period, delivering large buildings of a high standard of luxury and decoration with the maximum number of seats. His major clients included Goide and

Glassman (for whom he built the Savoys at Acton, Enfield, Burnt Oak, and Hayes, Middlesex) and Kessex cinemas in Essex (the Savoy, Ilford, and the Rio, Barking). His practice was further kept busy thoroughly modernizing and enlarging early cinemas, including Coles's own Popular, Stepney, as well as adapting theatres and building a modern auditorium inside the old Borough Theatre at Stratford. Coles was also highly influential in the film trade as architectural editor from 1932 of the *Ideal Kinema*, a supplement to the *Kinematograph Weekly*, to which he contributed many articles on the fundamentals of cinema design.

Most of Coles's own design work was concentrated in inner London and Essex, but he also became one of the principal architects working for the new and fast expanding Odeon circuit. With his characteristic versatility, he provided some outstanding cinemas in the streamlined, art deco style favoured by circuit head Oscar Deutsch and perfected by the Birmingham architectural practice of Harry Weedon. Coles's contributions included the Odeons at Muswell Hill, Woolwich, and Bury St Edmunds, as well as the Odeons at Bournemouth, Halifax, and in Horsham, where he lived. In much of his Odeon and other work between 1927 and 1939, Coles was assisted by Arthur H. Roberts (1903–1990).

There were many other architects besides Coles who specialized in cinema work. The talents of W. E. Trent and W. R. Glen were fully engaged as chief architects for, respectively, the major Gaumont and ABC circuits. Coles competed in the independent field with such figures as Leslie H. Kemp and Robert Cromie, while other notable architects found a niche in particular regions, including Sidney Colwyn Foulkes (north Wales and Liverpool), Reginald Cooper (Nottingham), W. H. Watkins (the west country), William T. Benslyn (northern England), and Frederick E. Bromige (west London). A few architects, such as the town hall designer T. Cecil Howitt, made cinemas a small but notable part of a wider output.

The Second World War brought an end to a boom decade in cinema construction. From 1949 onwards Coles worked frequently for the Granada circuit, modernizing its older properties and adapting its acquisitions to the house style. There was one further opportunity to design a major new auditorium—in the balcony area of the Empire, Leicester Square. This opened as the new Empire in 1962—a modern palace with cove lighting in changing colours which has become one of the key West End cinemas. This was Coles's swansong, as he died on 30 April 1963 at his home, Buck's Head, Mannings Heath, Lower Beeding, near Horsham. The practice continued for many years, carrying out the subdivision of cinemas and their conversion to bingo halls, and even designing the first purpose-built bingo hall at Mansfield, Nottinghamshire, but its founder's creative spirit was lacking.

ALLEN EYLES

Sources A. Moss, 'George Coles, FRIBA', *Picture House*, 17 (1992), 3–4 · R. Gray, *Cinemas in Britain* (1996) · *Daily Telegraph* (31 Jan 1990) · *The Builder*, 204 (1963), 915 · b. cert. · d. cert. · *CGPLA Eng. & Wales* (1963) · opening programme, Savoy, Leyton, 1928

Wealth at death £79,416 13s. 0d.: probate, 26 July 1963, *CGPLA Eng. & Wales*

Coles, Gilbert (1617?–1676), Church of England clergyman, was born at Burfield in Berkshire, the son of Edmund Coles, then or later of Winchester, a clergyman. In 1626 Coles was admitted to Winchester College and on 6 November 1635, aged eighteen, he matriculated from New College, Oxford, where he obtained a full fellowship in 1637; he graduated BA on 13 June 1639 and proceeded MA on 12 April 1643. On 8 May 1648 he was one of those members of New College who formally refused to recognize the authority of the parliamentary visitors at Oxford. Coles was expelled by them from the university a week later, but was admitted a week after that as a fellow of Winchester. By this time he had acquired the rectory of East Meon in Hampshire; later he became rector of two other Hampshire livings, Easton, near Winchester, and Ashe. He was created DD at Oxford on 2 July 1667.

Coles had married his first wife, Ann, by January 1654, when their son Gilbert was baptized at Lockerley, Hampshire, the first of two sons and six daughters baptized there in the period up to September 1660. After her death he married again, by a licence dated 26 June 1669, and when he made his will in July 1672 there were living: his second wife, Mary (*née* Henderson); four daughters, Anne, Cicely, Martha, and Mary; and three sons, Gilbert, Edward, and Robert, the last an infant when his father died. On Gilbert, then eighteen, Coles, as he ruefully recalled in his will made in 1672, had spent £100 on two apprenticeships and on paying off his debts 'unworthily Contracted' (PRO, PROB 11/352, 91v).

Coles's *Theophilus and Orthodoxus, or, Several conferences between two friends, the one a true son of the Church of England, the other fallen off to the church of Rome* was published in 1674. The author thought that Anglicanism had lacked effective champions ever 'since a puritan faction made the schism, disturbing the peace of the church and state; approving themselves better skilled at their weapons than their arguments; instead of writing against their adversaries, writing against their friends'. But 'since his majesty's miraculous and happy return, the church hath had time to breathe, and all things move in their own sphere' (sig. A2). In the following year, 1675, Coles resigned his Winchester fellowship, and on 4 August his son Edward, then of Mottisfont, near Romsey in Hampshire, was admitted as a fellow of the college.

Gilbert Coles died on 19 June 1676, aged fifty-eight, and was buried in the church at Easton. He was wealthy enough to leave £1200 to his children, and property for the use and financial support of his wife, who survived him.

STEPHEN WRIGHT

Sources T. F. Kirby, *Winchester scholars: a list of the wardens, fellows, and scholars of … Winchester College* (1888) · will, PRO, PROB 11/352, sig. 120, fols. 91–2 · Wood, *Ath. Oxon.*, new edn, 3.1047 · M. Burrows, ed., *The register of the visitors of the University of Oxford, from AD 1647 to AD 1658*, CS, new ser., 29 (1881) · IGI · J. L. Chester and G. J. Armytage, eds., *Allegations for marriage licences issued from the faculty office of the archbishop of Canterbury at London, 1543 to 1869*, Harleian Society, 24 (1886), 108

Wealth at death over £1200 (probably more than £2000): will, PRO, PROB 11/352, sig. 120, fols. 91–2

Coles, John (1623/4–1678), translator, was born in Adderbury, Oxfordshire, the son of John Coles, a clergyman. Having been educated at Winchester College, which he entered in 1638, he was admitted as a scholar of New College, Oxford, on 19 August 1643 and matriculated there on 27 October aged nineteen, by which time he appears to have been also teaching at the grammar school in the college's cloister. He was made a full fellow of the college on 19 August 1645. Coles was ejected from the university by the parliamentary visitors in May 1648, before he had taken a degree. In 1652 he became first undermaster at the Merchant Taylors' School in London but resigned in 1658 when he was appointed master of Wolverhampton grammar school, of which the Merchant Taylors' Company were also trustees. With his wife, Joyce, who Coles married when he was still in Oxford ('but not to his content', according to Wood, *Ath. Oxon.*, 4.540), he had ten children, of whom the eldest, Elisha *Coles (c.1640–1680), published books of lexicography. The maintenance of his family brought Coles into debt, from which the Merchant Taylors' Company extracted him on more than one occasion.

Coles translated several parts of the romance *Cléopatre* by Gauthier de Costes de la Calprenède, which describes the adventures of the daughter of Antony and Cleopatra. Although the translation was begun by Robert *Loveday, Coles's collaboration, according to his address to the reader in the 1656 edition, led to the completion of part 4: 'It was committed to my hands, and finished in his lifetime, but whether he would have laid it by, or have sweetened it with some live-touches of his own, and permitted it to have been publick, I know not' (Calprenède, pt 4, sig. A1r).

Coles deprecated this first offering, declaring a preference for 'sence before sound', and likened his subsequent efforts in translating parts 5 and 6 (both published 1656) to those of a candle that 'may be sometimes serviceable, when the Sun affords not his rayes' (Calprenède, pt 4, sig. A1r; pt 6, sig. A4v). His translations, however, have not always been correctly attributed and in the complete version of the romance (1665) Loveday is erroneously credited with parts 4, 5, and 6. This edition also contains Coles's version of part 7 (first published in 1658 under the title *Hymen's praeludia, or, Love's Master-Piece,* by which name the entire translation later became known). To all his publications are prefixed laudatory verses by, among others, Kenelm Digby and Thomas Manley. Taken together Coles's translations form a hefty work and, on completing part 7, he 'willingly quit[s] the employment' (ibid., pt 7, sig. A2v). Nevertheless, for all the romance's rambling, cumbersome narrative, his rendering is lucid and coherent and even allows of some elegant touches. It stands well alongside the earlier sections by Loveday and the later ones by James Webb and John Davies, and often exceeds them in terms of readability.

In 1666 Coles published his thoughts on education in

Apotheca scholastica. Alongside the schoolmaster's unorthodox means of increasing his pupils' Latin vocabulary via rhyming English equivalents—for example, '*Lepidus*, pretty; *Ingeniosus*, witty; *Lendosus*, nitty' (Coles, 11)—the book contains some verses in Latin and English and a Latin speech on Charles II's coronation. Coles was buried in Wolverhampton, Staffordshire, on 3 February 1678. He was survived by his wife.   ROSS KENNEDY

Sources Foster, *Alum. Oxon.* · T. F. Kirby, *Winchester scholars: a list of the wardens, fellows, and scholars of … Winchester College* (1888), 178 · Wood, *Ath. Oxon.*, new edn, 4.540 · G. P. Mander, *The history of the Wolverhampton grammar school* (1913), 143–56 · H. B. Wilson, *The history of Merchant-Taylors' School*, 2 vols. (1814), 1179 · J. C. [J. Coles], *Apotheca scholastica* (1666) · [G. de Costes de la Calprenède], *Hymen's praeludia*, trans. J. Coles, pts 4–7 (1656–8) · private information (2004) [C. Dalton, New College, Oxford]

Coles, Sherard Osborn Cowper- (1866–1936), electro-metallurgist and inventor, was born Sherard Osborn Cowper Coles on 8 October 1866 in Ventnor, Isle of Wight, the fourth son of Captain Cowper Phipps *Coles RN CB (1819–1870) and his wife, Emily (*née* Pearson). Cowper-Coles was educated privately and at King's College, London, later studying at the Crystal Palace School of Engineering (1883–4) followed by research work at laboratories in London. He entered business as a mechanical engineer in 1888 but in late 1890 became manager of the London Metallurgical Company. He soon began work on electrodeposition, being awarded a silver medal, for the electrodeposition of silver-cadmium alloys, at the 1892 Crystal Palace Exhibition. That year he made electrogalvanizing a commercial possibility, its being adopted by the Admiralty and numerous dockyards.

In 1893 Cowper-Coles again set up in business. In 1898 he won the Bessemer premium for research on protective metallic coatings for iron and steel, and gave a paper to the Institution of Electrical Engineers (IEE) on an electrolytic process for making parabolic reflectors; for this process he was awarded a silver medal at the Paris Exhibition of 1900. Another paper to the IEE on his electrolytic centrifugal process for making copper tubes won him a gold medal at the St Louis Exhibition of 1904. At the 1908 Franco-British Exhibition he was awarded a grand prix for electrochemistry. He received the John Scott medal from the Philadelphia Society in 1912. Cowper-Coles invented the sherardizing process, which electrolytically produced a zinc coating on iron and steel rendering them rustproof. It was a chance discovery, made when annealing iron and steel packed in zinc dust to exclude air. The metal was found to be coated with a thin layer of zinc with some surface penetration. Many other electrolytic inventions followed. He also worked on the deposition of non-metallic surfaces, including rubber, recovering gold from cyanide solutions, and the treatment of complex sulphide ores.

The sherardizing (or dry galvanizing) patent was taken out in 1900, numerous experiments leading to trial apparatus being established in a workshop in Danvers Street, Chelsea. This was so successful that a small company was formed and plant built at Willesden. The American rights were sold and a company formed to control them. As the process evolved many extravagant claims were made for it in the technical press, but they were often not borne out in practice and thus commercial development was slow until the process, and its limitations, were better understood. Cowper-Coles, with limited scientific training, was perhaps unable to solve such problems. By the 1930s, when companies had adequately qualified staff and better facilities, he had lost the patent rights.

In 1912, adjacent to his home, Rossall House in Sunbury-on-Thames, a cottage had been converted into an office and laboratories where eventually a team of fifteen researchers worked. There was no planned research programme: staff worked on a subject at the forefront of Cowper-Coles's interest until it was superseded by another. Promising ideas could be abandoned when they ran into difficulties and new ones taken up. Work was often sponsored by firms such as Westinghouse, or by the government when, for example, investigating processes potentially injurious to health. There was little actual contact between Cowper-Coles and his workers, and he rarely involved himself in real experimentation. However, 'he did bring to a practical issue a number of valuable inventions ... and many of his uncompleted ventures started other, more plodding, experimenters on fruitful lines of development' (Tait, 219). On 2 August 1919 Cowper-Coles married, at the parish church of St James, Piccadilly, Constance Hamilton Watts (b. 1887/8), of Sunbury-on-Thames, one of his research workers, and daughter of the late Henry Hamilton Watts. They had three sons.

Not only were his technical articles numerous (and his letters to *The Times* on a large variety of topics), but more than 900 British patents were taken out by Cowper-Coles, the first in 1885. During the First World War he invented a sound-recording instrument for detecting the position of aircraft, and worked on one-man tanks and on wooden and fabric aircraft wings. In later years he developed a process for recording sound directly onto metal records (and experimented with recording on electro-formed tape), special types of window glass, a means of fireproofing and preserving timber, and mowing machines. He was also an experimenter in television. He was interested in psychic research, working with Oliver Lodge in this area. But in not concentrating on a few potentially valuable projects his undoubted genius was to a certain extent wasted. Too often time and money were spent on seeking solutions to problems of no importance. 'Despite his enthusiasm, fertility of mind and practical ingenuity ... he never had much commercial success ... [dying] ... with his affairs in a muddle' (Sutton and Davies, 18–19).

Cowper-Coles became a member of the Institution of Mechanical Engineers in 1892, the Society of Chemical Industry in 1895, the IEE in 1897 and the Iron and Steel Institute in 1900. He was an associate member of the Institution of Civil Engineers. He was also a member of the American Institute of Electrical Engineers and the American Electrochemical Society. He became a fellow of the Royal Institution in 1898 and was a founder of the Faraday Society but soon fell out with the latter. In 1901 he

had established the periodical *Electrochemist and Metallurgist* and was its editor. He co-founded the society in 1903 and gave his own periodical the subtitle 'Organ of the Faraday Society', but it was virtually killed off when the society began to publish its own transactions in 1905. Cowper-Coles resigned from the society in a huff the following year. He rejoined in 1911 but without the same influence, and his membership lapsed. In 1935 he wanted to publish a paper on some practical applications of Faraday's discoveries. Rejoining the society, he was to give the paper as the F. S. Spiers memorial lecture but died before he could do so. In compensation and in tribute his widow was paid an honorarium.

Cowper-Coles died on 9 September 1936 at his home, Rossall House, of cancer of the oesophagus. His wife and sons survived him. He was buried at Sunbury cemetery. A memorial plaque to his memory was erected at South Harting parish church in Sussex.   ROBERT SHARP

Sources W. H. Tait, 'Sherard Cowper-Coles: an inventor of the old school', *The Metallurgist*, 2 (1962–3), 219–24 · C. A. Smith, 'Sherard Cowper-Coles: a review of the inception of sherardizing', *Transactions* [Newcomen Society], 49 (1977–8), 1–4 · *Institution of Mechanical Engineers: Proceedings*, 133 (1936), 546–7 · *Journal of the Institution of Electrical Engineers*, 79 (1936), 692 · *Journal of the Iron and Steel Institute*, 134 (1936), 644–5 · *Journal of the Society of Chemical Industry*, 55 (1936), 747 · L. Day and I. McNeil, eds., *Biographical dictionary of the history of technology* (1996) · *WWW* · L. Sutton and M. Davies, *The history of the Faraday Society* (1996) · b. cert. · m. cert. · d. cert.
Archives Sci. Mus., design drawings, offprints, trade literature
Likenesses photograph, repro. in Tait, 'Sherard Cowper-Coles', 220
Wealth at death £103 12s. 0d.: probate, 23 Nov 1936, *CGPLA Eng. & Wales*

Coles, Vincent Stuckey Stratton (1845–1929), Church of England clergyman and hymn writer, was born on 27 March 1845 at the rectory, Shepton Beauchamp, Somerset, the only son of the Revd James Stratton Coles (1810–1872), rector of Shepton Beauchamp from 1836 and later rural dean and a prebendary of Wells Cathedral. His mother, from whom Coles imbibed the high-church principles which inspired him throughout his life, was Eliza, daughter of Vincent *Stuckey [see under Stuckey family] of Langport, banker and shipowner, who had been private secretary at the Treasury to Pitt and Huskisson. The Stuckey and Bagehot families had long dominated Langport; Walter Bagehot, the economist, was Coles's cousin. George Anthony Denison, archdeacon of Taunton, was a neighbour and family friend, and the attack on Denison's exposition of eucharistic doctrine in 1856 made a strong impression on Coles.

In 1858 Coles went to Eton College, where he boarded with the Revd C. C. James. His closest friends were Digby Mackworth Dolben, Robert Bridges, and Archibald Primrose, Lord Dalmeny (afterwards earl of Rosebery). In 1864 he entered Balliol College, Oxford. His Eton contemporary W. R. Anson urged him to enter for an exhibition, which he won, but resigned from conscientious scruples on gaining only a third class in classical moderations in 1866. He obtained a third class in *literae humaniores* in 1868, and proceeded to Cuddesdon Theological College, of which

Edward King (afterwards bishop of Lincoln) was principal. Gerard Manley Hopkins was a close associate, and Coles also came to know Henry Parry Liddon, who heard his first confession and became his greatest friend.

Coles was ordained deacon at Winchester by Bishop Samuel Wilberforce at Advent 1869, and licensed to a curacy at Wantage under the Revd William John Butler, later dean of Lincoln. He was ordained priest by Bishop Mackarness of Oxford in 1870. On his father's sudden death in 1872 he succeeded him as rector of Shepton Beauchamp. He resigned the living in October 1884 in order to become one of the librarians of Pusey House, Oxford, together with Charles Gore and Frank Edward Brightman. Coles was widely known as a preacher, missioner, and spiritual guide; he had taken part in the second London Mission in 1874, made a preaching tour in the United States in 1876, and had been appointed frequently by Dean Church and Liddon to preach in St Paul's Cathedral. During his incumbency Shepton Beauchamp became a model parish of the Anglo-Catholic revival.

After King left Oxford for Lincoln in 1885 Coles carried on his apostolate to young men at the university. His keen sense of fun, his discerning sympathy, and his charismatic holiness attracted undergraduates of every type and class, and his great energies were devoted to helping them appreciate the Catholic revival in Anglicanism. He was appointed principal of Pusey House in 1897 and held the position until 1909, when he resigned due to ill health. In 1903, at the request of Bishop Wilkinson of St Andrews, he undertook a missionary tour through South Africa in preparation for the later 'mission of help'. From 1910 to 1920 Coles was warden of the Community of the Epiphany at Truro, and in 1912 Bishop Gore made him honorary canon of Christ Church and his diocesan chaplain, in which capacity Coles worked indefatigably in the Oxford diocese until Gore resigned in 1919. He lived thereafter with one of his sisters at Shepton Beauchamp, where he died on 9 June 1929 and is buried.

Coles published little: his major works were *Pastoral Work in Country Districts* (1906, being lectures delivered at Cambridge in Lent 1905), which was full of practical experience, *Lenten Meditations* (1899), and *Advent Meditations* (1899). Some of his best hymns, notably 'We pray thee, Heavenly Father', first appeared in *Hymns Ancient and Modern* and the *English Hymnal*. Possessed of considerable private means, he distributed them generously, living himself in severe simplicity.

S. L. Ollard, *rev.* Leon Litvack

Sources V. S. S. Coles, *Letters, papers, addresses, hymns and verses*, ed. J. F. Briscoe (1930) [Memoir by G. W. Borlase] • J. Julian, ed., *A dictionary of hymnology*, rev. edn (1907); repr. in 2 vols. (1915) • E. Routley, *An English-speaking hymnal guide* (1979)
Archives Pusey Oxf., corresp. | Bodl. Oxf., corresp. with Robert Bridges
Wealth at death £15,124 6s. 9d.: probate, 9 Aug 1929, *CGPLA Eng. & Wales*

Coles [Cole], **William** (1626–1662), botanist, was born at Adderbury, Oxfordshire, one of at least three sons and five daughters of John Coles. He entered New College, Oxford,

in 1642, and was soon after made a postmaster of Merton College by his mother's brother, John French, senior fellow and registrar of the university. He graduated BA on 18 February 1650, having become a public notary, with the intention of following his uncle. His enthusiasm for botany developed while he was at Oxford; he afterwards resided at Putney, Surrey, where he was a friend of Dr William How, founder of the Westminster botanic garden, and 'where he became the most famous simpler or herbalist of his time' (Wood). His principal work was *The Art of Simpling, or, An Introduction to the Knowledge and Gathering of Plants* (1656), with which was bound *Perspicillum microcosmologicum, or, A prospective for the discovery of the lesser world, wherein man is in a compendium, theologically, philosophically, and anatomically described, and compared with the universe.* His *Adam in Eden, or, Nature's Paradise* (1657) classified plants by the antiquated Galenic system by relating them to parts of the body, according to their supposed 'signatures'.

At the restoration in 1660 Coles became secretary to Brian Duppa, bishop of Winchester, in whose service he died, probably at New Sarum, in 1662.

G. S. Boulger, *rev.* Anita McConnell

Sources C. E. Raven, *English naturalists from Neckam to Ray: a study of the making of the modern world* (1947) • Wood, *Ath. Oxon.* • will, PRO, PROB 11/309 sig. 114 • A. Chalmers, ed., *The general biographical dictionary*, new edn, 32 vols. (1812–17)

Colet, Sir Henry (*c*.1430–1505), merchant and mayor of London, was a younger son of Robert Colet of The Hale, Wendover, Buckinghamshire. He was apprenticed in 1446 to John Colet, mercer of London, his own elder brother. His marriage, *c*.1465, to Christian, daughter of Sir John Knyvet of Buckenham Castle, Norfolk, and Alice Lynn of a London merchant family, gained him important contacts at court. Highly praised by Erasmus and Polydore Vergil, Christian was to survive her husband and children—ten girls and ten boys, according to a window in St Antholin's Church—and die in 1523. The only son to survive his father was John *Colet, scholar and dean of St Paul's, London.

Details of Colet's trade are few: trade with the clothiers of Essex, Suffolk, and Coventry may have supplied him with his main exports as a merchant adventurer; he also exported wool as a merchant of the Calais staple, and served as mayor of the staple of Westminster in 1499, 1500, and 1504. An alderman from 1476, Colet moved to Cornhill ward in 1487 where he stayed until his death. He served five times as master of the Mercers' Company, as MP for London in 1487 and 1489, and was twice mayor of the city. He was knighted during his first mayoralty of 1486–7, a period which included the battle of Stoke. His second mayoralty of 1495–6 coincided with war with Scotland and the Intercursus Magnus with the Netherlands, a treaty he facilitated by his personal bond when the city of London declined to proceed without further negotiations. He benefited from the Tudor accession and assisted the new king financially: he had a close relationship from 1480 at least with Reginald Bray (*d.* 1503), long-time servant of the king's mother and then of Henry VII himself; a book of hours of Bray's wife appears to have passed to John Colet, the dean; he sold an estate at Ditesworth, Leicestershire, to Lady Margaret Beaufort, which went to endow Christ's College, Cambridge; and he is reputed to have escaped the impositions associated with Empson and Dudley.

Colet was a parishioner of St Antonin's, London, when he died, and also of St Dunstan and All Saints, Stepney, where his son John held the living and where he and his wife enjoyed a country retreat. He made his will on 27 September 1505 and died on 1 October at Stepney, where he and his widow were buried. He had bought lands in twelve counties (worth over £170 p.a.) and in London, perhaps originally to provide for his large family. The death of his son Richard, aged about twenty-three in 1503, ended any hopes of a landed dynasty. The plans of his heir, John, to endow a school using the Buckinghamshire and Stepney lands in particular, may have met with Henry's approval, as he left £100 for university exhibitions. His executors were his widow and son.   ANNE F. SUTTON

John Colet (1467–1519), after Pietro Torrigiano, c.1520

Sources J. H. Lupton, *A life of John Colet, DD, dean of St Paul's and founder of St Paul's School*, new edn (1909), 311–12 [pedigree] · M. Albertson, 'London merchants and their landed property during the reign of the Yorkists', Bryn Mawr [printed 1932], 47, 54, 58, 61, 66, 90–1 · L. Lyell and F. D. Watney, eds., *Acts of court of the Mercers' Company, 1453–1527* (1936) · *Chancery records* · *CIPM, Henry VII*, 3 vols. · will, 27 Sept 1505, PRO, PROB 11/14, sig. 41 [proved 20 Oct 1505] · cartulary of John Colet, Mercers' Hall, London · R. Virgoe, 'The earlier Knyvetts: the rise of a Norfolk gentry family [2 pts]', *Norfolk Archaeology*, 41 (1990–93), 1–14, 249–78 · J. J. G. Alexander, 'Katherine Bray's Flemish book of hours', *The Ricardian*, 8 (1988–90), 308–17 · C. E. Collett, 'The family of Dean Colet. Summary of facts obtained from the records of the Mercers' Company', *Genealogists' Magazine*, 7 (1936), 242–3 · S. Knight, *The life of Dr John Colet* (1724), 1–6, app. 4, no. 1 · M. K. Jones and M. G. Underwood, *The king's mother: Lady Margaret Beaufort, countess of Richmond and Derby* (1992), 221

Wealth at death over £171 9s. 4d. p.a.: Albertson, 'London merchants', 58

Colet, John (1467–1519), dean of St Paul's and founder of St Paul's School, was born in January 1467, as attested by a contemporary document; Erasmus, always vague as to chronology, believed him to have been about thirty, two or three months younger than himself, when they first met in 1499. Colet's birthplace was almost certainly the London residence of his father, Sir Henry *Colet (c.1430–1505), Mercer and twice mayor of London, and mother, Christian Knyvet (d. 1523), in the parish of St Antholin, Watling Street. Both parents were from well-to-do stock, Henry Colet's relations being connected with the Mercers' Company and he a younger son of Robert Colet of The Hale, Wendover, Buckinghamshire; his wife was the eldest daughter of John Knyvet of Homerton, Huntingdonshire, and Buckenham Castle, Norfolk, and Alice (née Lynn), of a London merchant family. Henry Colet and Christian Knyvet married about 1465–6, he to become wealthy and she to bear at least twenty children. Only John survived past 1503, when a brother, Richard, of Lincoln's Inn, was living; another brother, Thomas, died in infancy in 1479. According to Erasmus John was the eldest son and sole survivor of eleven sons and eleven daughters;

he is followed by Polydore Vergil of Urbino, who arrived in England in 1502, and George Lily, son of the first high master of Colet's St Paul's School, William Lily. John Stow's *Survey of London* (1598) records a stained-glass window in the former church of St Antholin, Watling Street, showing Sir Henry and Dame Christian with ten sons and ten daughters.

Colet was survived by his mother by some four years; in her will, dated 13 January 1523 and proved on 2 November, she asks to be buried near her husband in St Dunstan and All Saints, Stepney. In letters of 1512 and 1516 Colet tells Erasmus that she is spending a healthy and contented old age in the country—that is, in Sir Henry's house, Great Place, Stepney, which passed to the Mercers at her death—and that she speaks often with pleasure of Erasmus; Erasmus wrote admiringly of her in 1521 and in 1532 recommended her stoical example to Bonifacius Amerbach. In 1510 the German theologian, physician, and magus Henricus Cornelius Agrippa was her guest, no doubt in connection with a visit to her son. On 1 December of that year Dame Christian was granted letters of fraternity by Christ Church, Canterbury. Co-executor of her husband and of her sons Richard and John, she was left well provided for and presented the Mercers with two silver-gilt standing cups and covers.

Education and church preferments Colet was taught the rudiments of Christian belief, good conduct, and Latin either at the school of St Antholin's Hospital in Threadneedle Street or the hospital school of St Thomas of Acon. His holy and religious nature, according to Polydore Vergil, impelled him towards divine studies, with St Paul as his preceptor, at both Oxford and Cambridge. The

Oxford registers of congregation for 1464–1504 being lost, Anthony Wood's assertion in 1691–2 that Colet was a student at Magdalen College, Oxford, graduated BTh in 1501, and was incorporated DTh in 1504 lacks confirmation; the doctorate is mentioned in a letter from Erasmus; and at his election as dean he was styled 'sacre theologie professor', that is DTh. A John Colet is recorded at Cambridge University as questionist in Lent term 1485, when he would normally have spent four years in study, and in Lent term 1489 incepting as MA. Given family connections and holdings in the east midlands and Sir Henry's name among those few appealed to by the university in 1503–4 for funds to rebuild Great St Mary's, these entries almost certainly relate to his eldest son. At Cambridge Colet would have completed his necessary regency in 1490; later, he glossed the word *philopompi* ('lovers of display') as *Cantabrigienses* ('Cambridge men').

Before being ordained deacon on 17 December 1497 and priest on 25 March 1498 Colet had been admitted on 6 August 1485 to the rectorship of Dennington in Suffolk (which was in the gift of his mother's family and which he held until his death) and of the free chapel of Hilberworth, Norfolk, in 1486. Rector of Thurning, Huntingdonshire, a living in his father's gift, from 1490 to 1494 and canon of York and prebendary of Botevant from 1496 to 1519, he was also canon of St Martin's-le-Grand and prebendary of Goodeaster by 1497 until 1504. He held the living of Stepney—in the 1530s the richest in England—from 1499 to 1505, was canon of Salisbury and prebendary of Durnford from 1502 to 1519, rector of Lambourn, Berkshire, in 1505, and treasurer of Chichester, Sussex, from after 1508 to 1519. In a letter usually dated December 1504 but perhaps of mid-1505 Erasmus congratulates him on his deanship of St Paul's. Collated prebendary of Mora on 5 May 1505 and elected dean at the instance of the king on 2 June, he held both deanship and prebend until his death.

European travel Colet passed an indeterminate portion of the 1490s in France and Italy, visiting France first according to Erasmus. Though he is not mentioned in the extant university records of either Orléans or Paris, he spent time in both cities. Towards the end of 1516 the jurist François Deloynes wrote to Erasmus that he had been impressed with Colet's learning and holiness when they studied together at Orléans. In Paris Colet may have frequented the circle of conservative theologians with an interest in the Florentine Neoplatonist philosopher Marsilio Ficino; he did not then meet Erasmus, however, who arrived in the city in the late summer of 1495.

Encouragement for a European journey must have come from the example of William Grocyn, Thomas Linacre, and William Lily, Grocyn's godson, who had improved their Latin and Greek in Italy and elsewhere, but precise dates for Colet's departure and return are lacking. By September 1492 he was in Rome, quartered in the English Hospice; on 13 March 1493 he inscribed himself, his parents, and his brother Richard in the Fraternitas Sancti Spiritus et Sanctae Mariae de Urbe, giving all four a

share in the spiritual benefits of the fraternity's charitable works; and on 3 May was enrolled as *confrater* of the English Hospice also. He may not have stayed in the city beyond that year. In Rome he was in contact with Christopher Urswick who, leaving in the late summer or early autumn of 1492, asked Colet to secure for him a manuscript of the *Historia Bohemica* of Aeneas Sylvius Piccolomini (Pius II); Colet sent him a printed edition, with an apologetic letter, dated from Rome 1 April 1493. Urswick's annotations show an interest in the Hussite movement; Erasmus's report that Colet valued the stimulus of heretical writings suggests that he read Pius's book before passing it on, though his letter is merely complimentary to Urswick and to history, in stock humanist mode. It is likely that Colet followed Grocyn's, Linacre's and Lily's example in spending time in Florence. There were intellectual attractions for him in the city, Ficino was at Careggi nearby, and the distance along the land route to and from Rome was not great.

Oxford and Erasmus The date of Colet's return to England is unknown: probably some time in or after 1495, and more certainly to Oxford, where he remained continuously until 1504 or 1505. Thereafter his only documented Oxford contacts are two dinners at Exeter College in 1516. From Oxford he had written to Erasmus, greeting him on his first arrival in England during late summer or autumn 1499; in Oxford that year they debated at least twice. When they met in 1499 (according to Erasmus in 1521), Colet had been giving successful free public lectures on the Pauline epistles in Oxford for some years. Polydore Vergil says that he lectured on St Paul in London. How far the manuscripts of one commentary on 1 Corinthians and two on Romans by Colet that survive preserve the text or even the substance of the lectures is unclear. The most satisfactory witness to Colet's approach to St Paul in the 1490s may be his letter of 1498–9 to Richard Kidderminster, abbot of Winchcombe, containing a series of precepts extracted from Romans 1.

Of letters between Colet and Erasmus some twenty-three survive; seven—dating from 1499 to 1517—are from Colet. In a letter to Johannes Sixtinus of November 1499 Erasmus gives an animated account of Colet's heated after-dinner disquisition on the sacrifices of Cain and Abel (Genesis 4), putting his unmediated Pauline view that Abel's offering had been more acceptable 'by faith' (Hebrews 11: 4). His reaction to Erasmus's attempt to lower the temperature with a facetious Old Testament fable is not recorded. Two letters to Colet of 1499, which Erasmus worked up and published (*Lucubratiunculae*, 1503), give access to an earlier debate in the Augustinian College of St Mary, Oxford, on the agony in the Garden. Erasmus's arguments from reason and authority that Christ's human nature was expressed in his plea that the cup should pass from him were met by Colet's contention that this implied derogation of Christ's divinity; rather, he was prescient of Jewish guilt.

At the end of the letters in 1503 Erasmus alludes to Pauline questions too delicate for public discussion, which might be aired on their walks together. That he does this in Greek is probably an adroit enhancement of his complimentary reference a few lines before to learning in both ancient languages acquired in Italy by Colet, who never, in fact, had more than a few words of Greek, as he acknowledged regretfully to Erasmus in 1516. The same year Erasmus reports Colet so conscious of his handicap that, stimulated by Erasmus's publication of the Greek New Testament in his *Novum instrumentum*, he was working at it with John Clement, Thomas More's pupil-servant and alumnus of St Paul's School. In 1519 an anonymous contemporary stated that Colet knew no Greek.

In the letter sent with his *Lucubratiunculae* from Paris (1504?–5) Erasmus is delighted at Colet's doctorate and deanship, expresses surprise that Colet's Pauline and gospel commentaries have not been printed, enquires about money for copies of his own *Adagia*, and asks for help. His London stay (late 1505 – early June 1506) followed the death of Sir Henry Colet on 1 October 1505, which had made his son rich; in his father's memory, a little later, Colet commissioned from the Brabantine scribe Pieter Meghen imposing codices with Ghent–Bruges illustrations of the Vulgate epistles and gospels (BL, Royal MS 1 E.v; CUL, MS Dd.7.3).

Dean of St Paul's   Royal favour had secured Colet's translation from the academy to the important deanship of St Paul's. The prominence he achieved before being possibly robbed of a bishopric by death resulted partly from zealous performance of ecclesiastical duty, including his preaching and his insistence that his chapter mend their ways, partly from his refoundation of St Paul's School, and partly from his involvement in affairs of state. In London he continued his association with the Christian humanist circle to which Erasmus became a constant mentor, whether by intermittent physical presence or *in absentia*. Thomas More, Erasmus's host during his third visit, was also a leading constituent of a group that included Grocyn, Lily, Linacre, Cuthbert Tunstall, William Latimer, Richard Fox, Urswick, John Clerk, Thomas Lupset, and Richard Pace, Colet's successor as dean of St Paul's, Latin secretary to Henry VIII, and diplomat, who in 1517 dedicated to Colet *De fructu qui ex doctrina percipitur*, addressed to the pupils of St Paul's School. Most of these, together with John Yonge and the Italians Polydore Vergil and Andreas Ammonius, belonged to Doctors' Commons, the loose association of civilians and clergy concerned with matters in the jurisdiction of the ecclesiastical courts. Colet was probably admitted in 1505. His closest English friend was More, his junior by ten years, to whom he was 'vitae meae magister' ('my life's overseer') and who, thinking him more learned and holy than anyone in England for centuries past, praised the bishop of Lincoln as a second Colet. Colet in turn thought More 'Britanniae unicum ingenium' ('the ablest man in Britain'), though he was out of sympathy with *Utopia*.

Of Colet's early activities as dean there are a few minor traces, some autograph, among papers from St Paul's (London, Guildhall Library, MSS 25121/1804, 25187); they include his visitation, using thirteen horses, of cathedral properties outside London in May and July 1506; new furniture and a cross; and armorial glass for his summer parlour at Stepney. More importantly, he framed statutes for the chapter, accepted by them after 20 June 1506 (a fair copy made by Meghen is lost), and exhibited to Wolsey in 1518. Conventional in their nature, they do not in themselves justify reports of the chapter's resentment, which is more likely to have resulted from Colet's authoritarian and high-minded expectations. On 28 April 1507 he added statutes for the Guild of Jesus associated with the cathedral. In 1510–11 the dean of St Paul's may have been involved in the campaign against Lollards of the bishop of London, Richard Fitzjames, on whose behalf he acted in other ecclesiastical matters, including censorship. He certainly took part in the drives of William Warham, archbishop of Canterbury, in 1511–12, being one of the formidable bench of examiners in two Kentish cases (8–19 May, 8 May – 3 October 1511).

To Colet's seriousness and dramatic power as a preacher both Erasmus, comparing his name to Coheleth, and More bear witness. The substance of many sermons given in Oxford and in London must be represented in his Latin commentaries on St Paul and Pseudo-Dionysius the Areopagite; he also preached, according to Erasmus, on the creed and Pater noster as well as the gospels. That some of his homilies were in English is implied in Erasmus's statement that Colet had studied the English poets to prepare for preaching the gospel. From 1510 to 1517, with perhaps an interval in 1514, Colet regularly received 20s. for the Good Friday sermon at court, although evidence of his preaching does not survive in quantity; his homily to the first assembly since 1504 of the convocation of Canterbury is the only one of which the text is extant. For the others, there remain only brief summaries, by Erasmus and an unknown reporter. Colet's surviving sermon was delivered in Latin on 6 February; internal evidence suggests the year was 1510, though the version printed in London by Richard Pynson gives 1511 and the printing has been assigned to probably 1512. The sermon has been an important element in Colet's later reputation as a precursor of the Reformation; an anonymous English translation, perhaps made in the Reformation interest, was printed in London by Thomas Berthelet probably in 1530–31. Taking as its text Romans 12: 2—'Be ye not conformed to this world: but be ye transformed in the renewing of your mind'—the sermon was a strongly worded example of the critical and hortatory discourse usual on such occasions, without doctrinal emphasis but pressing on the clergy the need for an absolute purity of life and a restraint in temporal matters such as would justify the church in its claims to liberty from state interference and obedience from the people at large.

Erasmus's account of sermons for which he is the sole witness as to content places Colet's candour in a context of difficulties, triumphantly resolved in his favour, first with the episcopate and then with Henry VIII. According to Erasmus, Colet had quoted in a sermon the Ciceronian maxim that an unjust peace was preferable to the most just of wars, at the very time that war with France was imminent. His clerical enemies attempted to make capital of this, and Colet was summoned to an interview with the king, who promised him protection. Then in a Good Friday sermon, which Erasmus briefly summarizes, Colet compounded his offence by declaring that war and Christianity could not accord. At this his enemies renewed their efforts and he was again summoned by the king, who required the easing of his conscience as to certain scruples and an undertaking from Colet to preach again in a way that would not sow doubt in the minds of the rough soldiery. That conversation over, Henry publicly embraced and commended Colet, so that his opponents, whose attempts to bring Colet down had included delation to Archbishop Warham for heresy, were discomfited. A laconic reference by Colet to Erasmus of October 1514 to unspecified problems with his bishop, Fitzjames, may refer to this situation. It is clear in any case, despite any distortion due to the vague chronology, antipathy to worldly and conventional ecclesiastics, and a generally admiring tone in Erasmus's narrative, that the Pauline Christianity of Colet's preaching had aroused resentment among his fellow clergy.

In the same brief letter of October 1514 in which he complains of his bishop's harassment, Colet tells Erasmus of Thomas Wolsey's translation to the archbishopric of York. Just over a year later he was chosen to preach, in Westminster Abbey on 18 November 1515, in honour of Wolsey's elevation to the cardinalate. The sermon survives only in notes taken by a listener, from which it appears to have begun with Wolsey's praises before passing to a discourse on the secular authority and nobility of the cardinalate, and dilating upon its spiritual significance and its correspondence in the ecclesiastical hierarchy to the burning red seraphim in the celestial.

St Paul's School The first surviving indications of Colet's intention to apply his patrimony to education by the reconstitution of St Paul's Cathedral school in new premises, reflecting a preoccupation with education as prerequisite for spiritual regeneration, belong to 1508. Precedents for his preference for laymen as trustees had existed for more than a century. According to Erasmus he believed reputable married men to be least corrupt; he may also have thought them more trustworthy than the chapter and more businesslike than churchmen in general, as well as less vulnerable in the clutching times that were already threatening the church. In his selection of the Mercers, there may also be a hint at preservation of his father's memory. Admitted a freeman of the company without payment in 1508, in April 1510 he opened and concluded negotiations with them for the school's endowment, and on 27 June obtained the chapter's consent to the school's ordinances. In March 1511 the site at the east end of the churchyard was formally transferred to the Mercers, with whom Colet was in constant consultation; on 17 June 1512 he 'shewed forth and read' the school statutes to their court of assistants, petitioning the pope in the same year for a bull to confirm the statutes and annul the power over schools of the chancellor of St Paul's. The statutes describe the school buildings as finished in 1512;

it is doubtful whether any extant manuscript of them dates from before 1517–18; that inscribed by Tunstall or another as having been deposited in the hands of the high master on 18 June 1518 gives both 1512 and 1517 as completion date.

On 4 November 1511 Colet had devised property, in what was perhaps a draft will intended for the court of husting in the city of London, to the Mercers for the school's benefit. A longer and fuller will for that court, dated 10 June 1514, may be connected with the intention announced by Colet to retire from active life. In that year he built himself a *nidus* (nest)—Erasmus calls it a very splendid house—in the precincts of the Charterhouse at Sheen; his will of 1519 requires that all 'boardwork' and 'painted images upon the walls' remain there.

Dedicating his school to the Virgin and the Christ Child, Colet retained power over the appointment of its teachers. Lily was high master by 27 July 1510, when he was granted a stall in the cathedral choir; though he was a good Graecist, it is uncertain how much Greek was taught before 1516. No record of John Ritwise, Lily's son-in-law and first surmaster (second master), is extant from before 18 December 1517, when Colet petitioned Wolsey on his behalf; a chaplain was envisaged by 1513 and a chantry established in 1514. Colet's intention, avowed in his statutes, 'specially to incresse knowledge, and worshipping of god and oure lorde Christ Jesu, and good Cristen lyff and maners in the Children' is clear in his close definition of the required moral, intellectual, and physical conditions for pupils and teachers. Acceptance of Erasmian humanist ideas about the need for Greek and of how Latin should be taught, with brief lip-service to pagan Latin, are overwhelmed by a rigidly literal and passionately expressed insistence on Christian morality. The authors prescribed are the fathers of the church and other early Christian writers (with two late ones, Baptista Mantuanus and Erasmus himself), pure in doctrine as in expression, to the utter exclusion of the language of scholasticism, 'adulterate, of the later blind world … rather … blotterature than literature'. In this, boys 'of all nations and countries indifferently' to the number of 153, large by contemporary standards and referring to the miraculous draft of fishes, were to be instructed without fee. The masters, who might be (married) laymen or in orders (but without benefice), were allotted good salaries and perquisites. Knowledge of reading and writing, and of the catechism, qualified for entry; the creed, in Erasmus's Latin verse (*Institutum Christiani hominis*), was required reading, along with Colet's own Latin accidence in English adapted to young needs, preceded by prayers and precepts for living (*Aeditio*, 1509?; first extant edition 1527). Colet probably commissioned from Lily *Rudimenta*, a Latin syntax in English, later frequently reprinted with the *Aeditio*, and certainly *De constructione*, a more advanced syntax in Latin. Erasmus, on request, revised this so thoroughly that neither man would thereafter acknowledge it as his: it was first printed as an anonymous work in 1513. Though Colet's conservative curriculum seems later to have been abandoned in practice, the method of Latin teaching used at St Paul's was influential, and modifications of the grammatical works for the school enjoyed a long life as the Paul's, Royal, and Eton grammars. Erasmus, less inflexible than Colet in attitude to classical learning, though refusing to teach in the school, defended it against criticism, helped with appointments, and advised on how to deal with Linacre, whose Latin grammar Colet had rejected as too advanced for his purposes. He also wrote for it *Concio de puero Jesu*, and suggested an inscription for the schoolroom. His *De copia* (1512), aimed at improving rhetorical fluency and dialectical invention and hugely influential throughout Europe, was prescribed for the school by Colet, to whom it had been dedicated; *De ratione studii* (1512), a blueprint for Christian humanist aims and methods in education, has special reference to St Paul's.

The original stone schoolhouse at the east end of old St Paul's, rebuilt on the same site in 1670, after the great fire, was again replaced in 1822. In 1884 the school moved to Hammersmith, where a new and larger building had been erected for it, and in 1968 to new premises across the Thames in Barnes.

Last years The selection of Colet to preach on 18 November 1515 at Wolsey's receipt of the red hat makes clear his alliance with the rising power of the new cardinal. This is confirmed by his appointment by convocation in December that year to the five-man committee that was to inquire into the dispute about ecclesiastical revenues that led to Warham's being forced out of the chancellorship of England and replaced by Wolsey. To the cardinal's favour he must have owed his place in the king's council. His entry date is not documented and he was never one of the small number that constituted its core, though on 18 June 1517 he was made a member of its committee to hear poor men's causes, an appointment renewed on 18 June 1518. His attendance is recorded at three at least of a minimum of eight meetings between 25 June and 6 November 1518.

In 1517 Colet's health had begun to deteriorate; he suffered the first of three attacks of the sweating sickness which, weakening him and exacerbating a liver condition revealed by his autopsy, led to his death on 16 September 1519. His last will, dated 22 August 1519 and proved in the prerogative court of Canterbury on 5 October, required that he be buried in St Paul's Cathedral near the image of St Wilgefortis, where he had made 'a little monument'. Erasmus writes of an unassuming grave identified by the letters 'Joan. Col.'. In 1548 George Lily recorded the existence of a more elaborate tomb and the Latin verses by his father hung up beside it (there was also a prose epitaph); and in 1575–6 the Mercers laid out a large sum for marble for it. A coloured miniature attributed to Sir William Segar and thought to be of 1585–6, on the cover of the Mercers' Hall copy of the school statutes, shows a *transi* tomb, with a bust of Colet; there is an engraving in William Dugdale's *History of St Paul's Cathedral* (1658). Refurbished in 1618, the tomb survived the great fire and in 1667–8 was taken down and laid, with the effigy, in Convocation House Yard. In 1680 what was believed to be Colet's coffin was found and investigated by members of the Royal Society.

Portraits and personality Colet was a grave and impressive presence, tall and handsome. Several representations survive. The kneeling, tonsured figures in the miniatures at the opening of Colet's New Testament manuscripts (1506–9) are conventional representations of a cleric. Two closely contemporary portraits only have a claim to authenticity. Of one, attributed to Pietro Torrigiano and probably made from a death mask about 1520, there is a plaster version of uncertain date in Mercers' Hall. The portrait drawing made before 1535 by Hans Holbein the younger during his second visit to England is most likely based on this image. An engraving by Willem or Magdalena van de Passe is in Henry Holland's *Herōologia Anglica* (1620); there are eighteenth-century portrait engravings by George Vertue and Francesco Bartolozzi. Colet invariably wears clerical robe and bonnet; Segar's miniature of the tomb shows him pen and book in hand. The head of the full-length statue by Sir Hamo Thornycroft (1901) in the grounds of St Paul's School is of the Torrigiano–Holbein type.

Erasmus saw in Colet a quick-tempered but pure Christian with a fertile, powerful, profoundly serious mind, always bent on seeking the moral. As aids to self-control he used prayer and fasting; as guides to goodness of life scripture, especially St Paul, the early fathers and the Pseudo-Dionysius. His views, impatiently expressed, were individual, definite, and strongly held. Benevolent towards children, he loved chastity (by his own testimony he deprecated marriage); and he delighted in sacred reading and holy conversation, particularly with friends, with whom he would relax his severity. Sometimes tight-fisted with money and needing reminders of a patron's duty, intolerant both of undue pomp and of slovenliness, he did not follow certain English habits, dressing habitually in plain black woollen, being frugal with food and drink, and not celebrating mass daily. Mistrusting religious and collegiate institutions, conventional piety, and over-scrupulosity in confession, he was intolerant of pilgrimage and particularly of the cult of images and relics as vulgarly practised—as is recollected by Erasmus in *Modus orandi Deum* (1524), where Colet is named, and taken up more fully in 'Peregrinatio religionis ergo' ('A pilgrimage for religion's sake'), which records their experiences and reactions at Canterbury about 1512–14 (*Colloquies*, 1526). There Colet is thinly disguised as Gratianus Pullus ('Gratiane colte' in the English version printed in probably 1540). In 'Pia confabulatio' (1522) Colet's trust in faith and prayer is commemorated.

Erasmus, paying Colet's eloquence the stock humanist compliment of comparison with Plato's, also recounts how Colet was taken in by the feigned arguments against rhetoric of *Antibarbari*. Colet also amused him by reporting that a bishop had denounced St Paul's School as idolatrous because poets were part of its curriculum, and by passing on another English cleric's foolish Latin etymology. Erasmus, judging Colet's written Latin to be fluent rather than pedantically correct, surmises that he failed to publish for this reason; he remarks also that Colet had not been entirely persuaded to adopt the 'new' humanist mode in speaking that language and retained his childhood habit of pronouncing *ie* as *ii* (*De pronuntiatione*).

Learning and library What Colet read is more easily characterized than precisely when, where, and in what form, manuscript or print, he read it, let alone when he used it. Besides his own works, his will mentions a manuscript New Testament and St Jerome.

Among his English contemporaries Colet was unique in his firsthand knowledge and use of Florentine Neoplatonism, with its combination of esoteric philosophy and Christian piety; he was also familiar with the work of some of those who had felt its impact. His heavily annotated copy of Marsilio Ficino's *Epistolae*, in the edition of Venice, 11 March 1495, is now in All Souls College, Oxford; he must at least have had in his hands a copy of Ficino's *Theologia platonica* (1482), from which he quotes; and he probably knew Ficino's translations of Plato (a copy of the edition of 1491 was in England then), Plotinus, and the *Corpus hermeticum*. Colet also read and used such writings by Giovanni Pico della Mirandola as the *Heptaplus* (printed 1490?), *Apologia* (printed 1482), and *Oratio*, as well as perhaps *Adversus astrologiam divinatricem*, all included in Pico's *Opera omnia* of 1496 and 1498. It was probably from Pico that he derived his interest in the Hebrew cabbala, which was strengthened by his reading of Johann Reuchlin's *De verbo mirifico* (1494); and that interest was augmented by Cornelius Agrippa, with whom in 1510 he toiled over St Paul and who made acknowledgement to Colet's teaching. In a letter of 1517 to Erasmus, who the year before had assured Reuchlin of Colet's good opinion of him, however, Colet professed to prefer the 'love and imitation of Christ' to Reuchlin's recent speculations in his *De arte cabbalistica*. The meditations, commentaries, and denunciatory preaching of Girolamo Savonarola (1452–1498), which might have been expected to appeal to Colet, have left no explicit trace in his extant works; nor have other Savonarolan writings circulating in the England of his time. He may have known Pseudo-Dionysius the Areopagite in Ficino's Latin versions (1496) and certainly used Ambrogio Traversari's (1436), in the second edition of Pseudo-Dionysius's *Works* overseen by Jacques Lefèvre d'Étaples (Paris, 1499), for his responses to the *Celestial* and *Ecclesiastical Hierarchies*. Like Lefèvre, he remained unmoved by Erasmus's publication in 1505 of Lorenzo Valla's treatise showing that their author was not the convert of St Paul (Acts 17: 34; the belief that he invited Grocyn to lecture on Pseudo-Dionysius at St Paul's is erroneous). He cites the fifteenth-century Christian Virgil, Baptista Mantuanus; and uses the etymologies in Nicolò Perotti's standard *Cornucopiae*.

Other modern works included Erasmus's *Novum instrumentum* of 1516; he interested himself in progress towards *Novum Testamentum*, its second edition (1519), and joined in opposition to Edward Lee's strictures. Among Colet's books would also have been Erasmus's *Lucubratiunculae* (1503), which included the *Enchiridion militis Christiani* whose 'philosophia Christi' so chimed with his own; *Copia* (1512), dedicated to him, and other educational works; *The Praise of Folly* (1511); *Institutio principis*

Christiani (1516); and the commentary on Romans (1517), of which he was critical. He would also have had a copy of Pace's *De fructu* (1517). In the British Library are two transcripts by Meghen, perhaps for Colet: an incomplete, undated glossed psalter and Lefèvre's translation of the Pauline epistles, printed in 1512 (BL, Royal MSS 1 E.iii, 1 D.xi–xv).

In Colet's library would have figured the early Christian writers he read, according to Erasmus, while he was in Europe. St Augustine, to whom Erasmus reports Colet as *iniquior* ('more prejudiced', probably in favour), is most often cited and has left other traces. Colet himself refers to St Jerome; St John Chrysostom; St Ignatius of Antioch; Lactantius, the Christian Cicero (also commended to St Paul's School); and Polycarp of Smyrna. He quotes the Pseudo-Clementine *Recognitions* and Origen (whom he seems to have known both directly and indirectly), and cites Philo Judaeus and Pseudo-Aristeas (probably indirectly). Erasmus adds St Ambrose and More's favourite St Cyprian; he arranged to have his edition of Jerome sent to Colet on 2 October 1516.

Among the transmitters of the pagan wisdom so suspect to Colet as a means to scriptural exegesis, he refers to Cicero (whom he devoured, according to Erasmus), Ovid, Suetonius (whose life of Claudius he invokes in connection with Romans 13), Terence, Varro, and Virgil. Of late antique writers he knew Macrobius; and of medieval, Thomas Aquinas's *Summa theologica* and *Catena aurea*; St Anselm (perhaps indirectly); Durandus; Gratian; Pseudo-Ivo of Chartres; and Leo I (the Great), whom he cites explicitly in relation to the extra-scriptural verities entrusted to the church by the Holy Spirit. Though his own theology was biblical and Neoplatonic, he had received and retained a training in scholasticism discernible in his preference, reported by Erasmus, of Scotus to the defining, presumptuous, and worldly Aquinas. His mass books and books of devotion included an illuminated Flemish book of hours (now at Stonyhurst College), once owned by Dame Katherine Bray (d. 1507), widow of Sir Reginald Bray, which bears a petition in his hand for prayers for her soul and Colet's.

Colet's Jerome, with unspecified printed books and his bed and bedding from his house in the grounds of the Sheen Charterhouse, he left to one John Bambrughe. Thomas Lupset, 'my scholer', was to have such printed books as he needed; those remaining went to poor students and others 'who have been scholars with me'. Some of the manuscripts of Colet's own works went to St Paul's School. Other codices reached the royal library. In the three volumes containing the epistles (1506) and gospels (1509), Erasmus's new version was transcribed by Meghen from the edition of 1522 into the space originally left for commentary; pages were added and the set completed with a separate volume containing both versions of Acts and Apocalypse. The three may have been augmented for Henry VIII and the fourth, written for him and Katherine of Aragon (Hatfield House, Cecil papers, MS 324), appropriated by Lord Burghley to add to his other Meghen manuscripts, including the fair copy of Colet on Pseudo-Dionysius (BL, Add. MS 63853).

Colet's writings and their dissemination Colet's surviving writings are almost exclusively in Latin. Some, listed by sixteenth-century authorities such as John Bale (1548, 1557–9) and John Pits (1619), are not extant; others remained in manuscript, often singly. Works in English, chiefly sermons perhaps, are also lost, the few printed English versions all dating from after his death. The English of his convocation sermon may be Lupset's; and the English in which Latin accidence is presented in his printed *Aeditio* and the few miscellaneous texts preceding it, most likely Colet's, is just possibly that of a translator. Editions of his grammatical work from before 1527 are not extant, and no printing is known of his *Right Fruitful Monition* from before 1534. An English paraphrase of the Lord's prayer attributed to him was not printed until 1534. Of his extant manuscripts only the school statutes and a prayer to the Virgin (almost Colet's only surviving reference to Mary) among the annotations in the All Souls Ficino are in the vernacular.

The only Latin work by Colet to have been printed in his lifetime is his convocation sermon. Some codices of the Latin works, according to a note in one of them, probably by Tunstall, were lost 'incuria puerorum' ('through the carelessness of the boys' [or 'of his servants']). The rest, remaining in manuscript until the nineteenth century, present severe chronological problems; assigned by some to his Oxford period, they have also been seen as belonging to the second decade of the sixteenth century. Colet's chief Latin works are: two commentaries on St Paul's epistle to the Romans, one on the whole epistle, the other, unfinished, on the first five chapters; a commentary on 1 Corinthians; a commentary on 1 Peter, with maxims from other Pauline epistles; a commentary on, or rather a series of responses to, the *Celestial* and *Ecclesiastical Hierarchies* of the Pseudo-Dionysius; two brief tractates, *De sacramentis* and *De corpore Christi mystico*; an unfinished commentary on the account of creation in the opening chapter of Genesis; and annotations of the *Epistolae* in which Ficino briefly explained his doctrines. None of the manuscripts bears a date; the make-up of one, in particular, may confirm Bale's report that works were discovered 'unbound' ('divaricatis pagellis') after Colet's death.

Colet's copy of Ficino's *Epistolae* could have been acquired in England or France, but is more likely to have been an Italian purchase. His annotations of it must post-date its publication on 11 March 1495, though they, still less the transcripts and notes in his hand on its flyleaves, need not belong to a single period. The transcripts consist of two polished letters from Ficino to Colet, one brief, playing self-deprecatingly with light and sun imagery; the other longer and dealing with the currently important questions of intellect and will, on which Colet's position remained voluntarist. They are accompanied by two awkwardly expressed drafts, again in Colet's hand, of a short letter to Ficino. That these indicate a Florentine visit and a meeting with Ficino (1433–1499) at Careggi is at least likely; Pico della Mirandola (1463–1494) Colet seems to

have known only through his writings. Exactly how long after his return Colet jotted down that he would do his best, 'next Monday, at the usual time and place', to expound 1 Corinthians is unsure.

One of the manuscripts of Colet on 1 Corinthians (CUL, Gg.4.26, which contains more than one work and may consist of loose papers gathered together by a later hand) is autograph, on paper, the script sometimes careful, sometimes hurried, with Colet's diagrams, corrections, and insertions and an occasional single word in Greek. The other manuscript (Cambridge, Emmanuel College, MS III.3.12) is a fair copy on vellum by Meghen, with no Greek or diagrams and only minimal signs of later intervention. The unique manuscript of the commentary on the whole of Romans, a scribal transcript with corrections and insertions by Colet, begins the Cambridge University Library codex: it concludes with the word 'Oxoniae'. Colet's commentary on the first five chapters of Romans, addressed to a young man named Edmund and ending imperfectly, in Meghen's transcript, with additions and corrections by Colet, begins Cambridge, Corpus Christi College, MS 355: it too is unique. The maxims extracted from the Pauline epistles and the brief commentary on 1 Peter exist only in Trinity College, Cambridge, MS O.4.44. The hand of this is more Italianate than any of those in other Colet manuscripts; its old royal library pressmark is of *c*.1548.

Colet's commentary on Genesis is addressed to an unidentified Ralph and breaks off, unfinished, at 1: 14; it exists uniquely in a fair copy, probably not by Meghen, which occupies the second part of Corpus Christi College, MS 355. The treatise on Christ's mystical body, like the unique surviving copy of the letter to Kidderminster, is preserved in Colet's autograph in the Cambridge University Library manuscript; which also contains a perhaps scribal transcript, with Colet's additions and corrections, of his responses to the texts he selected from the *Celestial Hierarchy* of the Pseudo-Dionysius. Meghen's transcript of Colet on both *Hierarchies* and *De sacramentis* constitute BL, Add. MS 63853, where the text of the *Celestial Hierarchy* is a fair copy of the Cambridge University Library manuscript, incorporating Colet's changes. A copy made from the British Library manuscript later in the sixteenth century is now in St Paul's School Library.

Meghen's copies, with the second part of the Corpus Christi codex, apparently constitute a sort of collected edition intended to preserve the views of its author, for his private use. That three of its constituents are unfinished and at least two addressed to specific persons suggests that, if they record Colet's Oxford lectures, they do so in a modified form. When the collected edition was put together is uncertain; it may have been soon after Colet left Oxford and came into his inheritance, about the time when he was employing Meghen on his New Testament manuscripts. Meghen had been working for English patrons from about 1503 at latest; no date later than 1509 appears in any undoubted surviving work of his for Colet, and the hand of the transcripts is stylistically related to his work of about that time. Some at least of Colet's emendations and annotations on some of the copies may have been made at any time before September 1519; a few headings and annotations were added after his death, probably by Tunstall.

In responding to Pseudo-Dionysius's *Ecclesiastical Hierarchy* Colet quotes at length from Pico's *Apologia* or *Oratio*, repeating the substance of the quotation in both his commentaries on Romans. Pico's mode of regarding the creation in the *Heptaplus* is simplified and moralized in Colet's commentary on Genesis, and the *Heptaplus* quoted both in his commentaries on 1 Corinthians and the whole of Romans. To Pico he is indebted for at least one quotation from the commentary on Romans by Origen, whom Erasmus names as Colet's favourite. *Contra Celsum*, available through Cristoforo Persona's Latin version in manuscript or print (1482), he cites once, to emphasize the allegorical character of the writings attributed to Moses; he also knew Origen on Romans in Rufinus's Latin, first printed in 1506. Colet's awareness of the Greek father of allegorical exegesis, regarded by Erasmus as first after St Paul among the interpreters of scripture who go beyond the literal meaning, may belong to the same time as his preoccupation with what he could know through Pico and Reuchlin of the Hebrew cabbala as a guide to hidden biblical significance.

The chronological and interpretative problems of Colet's surviving works are not diminished by the constancy both of his exegetical method—which is homiletic, individual, idiosyncratic, and, by the end of his life, old-fashioned, especially in its failure to take account of Greek—and of the attitude to humanity and divinity at its root. His tendency to respond unsystematically to those sections of a given text that support him in his search for what he called 'living wisdom', visible most clearly in his annotations of Ficino and in his encounter with Pseudo-Dionysius, is also apparent in his Pauline commentaries. These do not attempt to treat every biblical verse, nor are they preoccupied with theology, philology, or history. Colet's single-minded purpose is to move men to holiness by instructing them in the relevance to it of selected propositions. Insisting on the primacy and inexhaustible meaningfulness of scripture, he applies everything in it, in the Pauline manner, to Christ, the great exemplar. Spiritual significance being both pervasive and paramount can be truly grasped and imparted, not through knowledge but through grace, only by the spiritual man, who is not necessarily a priest. All but dualistic in his estimate of diabolic power, troubled by the world's depravity, Colet is continually severe against the flesh. Only by asceticism and prayer can the grace be sought that will lead through purgation and illumination to perfection and the soul's union with God.

Attachment to the Neoplatonism he knew from the Pseudo-Dionysius, from Ficino's original works, and Ficino's translations of Plato and Plotinus must have strengthened Colet's mistrust of scholasticism and partiality to St Paul. Mistrust would have been augmented by his association with Erasmus, whose influence on him

was plainly immense; the importance of Colet in the formation of Erasmus's thought, long regarded as proven, less so. Always capable of opposing or rejecting the positions to which the more learned and acute Erasmus sought to steer him, however, Colet remained profoundly his own man as he attempted to arrive at holiness through a true perception of scripture.

Influence and reputation Colet's posthumous influence, limited by his reluctance to publish and exerted indirectly through St Paul's School, is entirely English. The same may almost be said of his reputation. Though, as the Basel reformer Johannes Oecolampadius noted, Colet's name echoes through the writings of Erasmus, only two other continental scholars, Marquardt von Hattstein and Martin Bucer, are recorded as catching its resonance. The long retrospective assessment of his friend and patron that Erasmus addressed, almost two years after Colet's death, to Justus Jonas in the hope of dissuading him from conversion to Lutheranism, failed in that attempt, though its publication in the year of its composition (it is dated 13 June 1521) must have attracted attention.

This biographical memorial letter, an extended comparison of the well-to-do dean of St Paul's with the poor Franciscan, Jean Vitrier, as exemplars of true piety, was intended also to demonstrate to Jonas how far criticism of the church of the time could go without apostasy. It was early converted to their use by English reformers. On 2 July 1533 an English translation by Matthew Tyndall was sent by Tyndall to Thomas Cromwell, and Erasmus's letter itself was drawn on by John Foxe in *Actes and Monuments* (1563). Foxe added the testimony of two Lollards that they had gone to London to hear Colet preach, but also rightly names Colet as among persecutors of their sect. By then Colet had disappeared from English Catholic consciousness and his transformation from a firmly faithful member of the pre-Reformation Catholic church, unorthodox in opinion and less than discreet in expression, to a reformer *avant la lettre* was well under way. In 1529 William Tyndale had reported him as in trouble with his bishop for rendering the Pater noster in English; in 1552 Hugh Latimer had him in danger of burning as a heretic; and in 1562 John Jewel, bishop of Salisbury, attempted to enlist him among the forerunners of protestantism—to which the Catholic Thomas Harding in 1566 retorted: 'as for John Colet, he hath never a word to show, for he wrote no works'.

If Colet's protestant reputation depends to an extent on the protestant interpretation of the testimony of Erasmus in this letter and elsewhere, the same is true, in a sense, about Colet's reputation at large, at least until the later twentieth century, when Erasmus's accounts came to be treated with greater caution. There are ways in which Colet's situation *vis-à-vis* Erasmus parallels that of Thomas More, of whom Erasmus also gave an account in a Latin letter, addressed to a Lutheran sympathizer, Ulrich von Hutten, in 1519, and with whom he corresponded more copiously than with Colet. The letters are alike in presenting their subjects as they were before the convulsions of the Reformation, in which More was deeply involved and which Colet was spared by death. More, however, was already famous in the European humanist community for his *Utopia* and his poems (which Erasmus had helped him to publish), and for his involvement in the controversies that followed the *Praise of Folly* and Erasmus's new New Testament. From both before and after Erasmus's letter, firsthand evidence from More's own writings has long been available in quantity. For Colet, that was lacking until the later nineteenth century. Erasmus, with his discreetly flattering accounts of his and Colet's debates and other dealings, sometimes affected in recollection and by a tendency to favour his own part, is often the only witness to important aspects of Colet's life and character. Like Erasmus's estimates of others, More included, the portrait of Colet in the letter to Jonas of 1521 has elements in it of a self-portrait.

Colet's protestant reputation is discernible in Samuel Knight's biography (1724, reprinted 1823), which was based on the seventeenth-century collections of White Kennett, bishop of Peterborough (BL, Lansdowne MS 1030); it is still visible in the work of the nineteenth-century pioneer in Colet studies, J. H. Lupton, surmaster of St Paul's School. Much is owed to Lupton who, in a series of volumes published between 1867 and 1876, made available for the first time Colet's Latin writings with, for the most part, accompanying English translations, to which he added a translation of Erasmus's letter to Jonas and a *Life* of his hero. Lupton's imperfect texts and versions were for well over a century, with the important exception of Jayne's edition and translation of Colet's marginalia to the *Epistolae* of Marsilio Ficino, virtually the only published means of access to Colet's writings; they have been superseded only partially by O'Kelly and Jarrott (1 Corinthians, 1985) and Gleason (*De sacramentis*, 1989). Lupton was much influenced by his friend Frederic Seebohm's *Oxford Reformers of 1499*, particularly in his ideas about Colet's originality and his importance for the English church. Their Colet gave place only in the second half of the twentieth century, especially in the study of Gleason (1989), to a Colet made more credible by a fuller appreciation of the religious and intellectual context of his time.   J. B. TRAPP

Sources STC, 1475–1640, nos. 5542–5550.5, 15610ff. · *John Colet's commentary on first Corinthians*, ed. and trans. B. O'Kelly and C. A. L. Jarrott (Binghampton, NY, 1985) · S. Jayne, *John Colet and Marsilio Ficino* (1963) · J. B. Gleason, *John Colet* (Berkeley, Los Angeles, and London, 1989) · *Opus epistolarum Des. Erasmi Roterodami*, ed. P. S. Allen and others, 12 vols. (1906–58), nos. 106–11, 113, 115–16, 118, 120, 123, 159, 164–5, 180–81, 195, 218, 225, 227, 230–31, 237, 244–5, 248, 258, 260, 270, 278, 291, 296, 298, 300, 314, 341, 373, 414, 423, 455, 457, 467–8, 471, 474, 480, 491, 494, 535, 543, 563, 593, 653, 707, 713, 786, 825, 855, 891, 966, 976, 999, 1023, 1025–30, 1053, 1064, 1075, 1103, 1110, 1211, 1227, 1229, 1347, 1523, 2209, 2684 · *Collected works of Erasmus*, ed. W. K. Ferguson and others, [86 vols.] (1974–), vols. 1–11, 23–6, 28, 39–40, 56, 70 · D. Erasmus, *Vies de Jean Vitrier et de John Colet*, trans. A. Godin (Angers, 1982) · J. Colet, *Works*, ed. and trans. J. H. Lupton (1867–76) · J. H. Lupton, *Life of Dean Colet ... with an appendix of some of his English writings* (1887) · *Opera omnia Desiderii Erasmi Roterodami*, ed. J. H. Waszink and others, 1 (Amsterdam, 1969), 1–4, 6, 7; 4 (1973), 1; 5 (1975), 1 · Emden, *Cam.*, 148 · Emden, *Oxf.*, 1.462–4 · *Fasti Angl., 1300–1541*, [Salisbury], 48 · *Fasti Angl., 1300–1541*, [St Paul's, London], 7, 49 · *Fasti Angl., 1300–1541*, [York], 38 · *Fasti Angl., 1300–1541*, [Chichester], 11 · L. Lyell and F. D. Watney, eds., *Acts of court of the Mercers' Company, 1453–1527* (1936) · W. Sparrow Simpson, ed., *Registrum statutorum et consuetudinum ecclesiae cathedralis S. Pauli Londinensis* (1873), 418–19 · W. Sparrow Simpson, ed., 'A newly discovered manuscript containing statutes compiled by Dean Colet for the government of chantry priests and other clergy of St Paul's', *Archaeologia*, 52 (1890), 144–74 · M. F. J. McDonnell, *A history of St Paul's School* (1909) · M. McDonnell, *The annals of St Paul's School* (privately printed, Cambridge, 1959) · E. W. Hunt, *Dean Colet and his theology* (1956) · F. Grossmann, 'Holbein, Torrigiano and some portraits of Dean Colet: a study of Holbein's work in relation to sculpture', *Journal of the Warburg and Courtauld Institutes*, 13 (1950), 202–36 · P. G. Bietenholz and T. B. Deutscher, eds., *Contemporaries of Erasmus: a biographical register*, 3 vols. (1985–7) · J. B. Trapp, *Erasmus, Colet and More: the early Tudor humanists and their books* (1991) · J. B. Trapp, 'Pieter Meghen van 's-Hertogenbosch', *Essays on the Renaissance and the classical tradition* (1990), item XIV (and cf. XI–XIII) · J. J. G. Alexander, 'Katherine Bray's Flemish book of hours', *The Ricardian*, 8 (1988–90), 308–17 · LP Henry VIII · will, PRO, PROB 11/19 [John Colet] · will, PRO, PROB 11/14 [Sir Henry Colet] · will, PRO, PROB 11/21 [Christian Colet]
Archives CCC Cam. · CUL · Emmanuel College, Cambridge · GL · Mercers' Hall, London · St Paul's School, London · Trinity Cam. | BL, Lansdowne MSS; Royal MSS, Add. MSS, and charters
Likenesses manuscript, 1506, BL, Royal MS E I. V, vol. 2, frontispiece · P. Meghen, manuscript, 1506–9 (kneeling before St Matthew and St Paul), CUL, MS Dd 7.3 · P. Torrigiano, marble or bronze bust, c.1520; now lost · H. Holbein the younger, drawing, before 1535 (after P. Torrigiano, c.1520), Royal Collection · W. Segar, coloured representation of tomb, 1585–6, Mercers' Hall, London · W. or M. van de Passe, engraving, repro. in H. Holland, *Herōologia Anglica* (1620) · line engraving (after monument at St Paul's Cathedral, London), BM; repro. in Dugdale, *St Paul* (1658) · plaster bust (after P. Torrigiano, c.1520), St Paul's School, London [see illus.] · plaster bust (after P. Torrigiano, c.1520), NPG · plaster bust (after P. Torrigiano, c.1520), Mercers' Hall, London

Coley, Henry (1633–1704), astrologer and mathematician, was born on 18 October 1633 in the parish of St Mary Magdalen, Oxford, the son of a joiner. His birth was said to have occurred at 32 seconds after 2.14 p.m., 'a sufficiently exact Estimate' for astrological analysis, according to his friend John Kendal (Kendal, 30). He was probably related to Thomas Coley, an Oxford tailor who served as a common councillor from 1603 to 1630. His astrological 'accidents' record that he had smallpox at nine, almost died from plague at ten, and suffered a severe attack of ague at fourteen. In the spring of 1648 he became clerk to 'a Person of Military Command' in the parliamentary army. In 1652 he settled in a 'better' employment, before moving to London on 1 April 1654, where he worked as a ladies' tailor in Gray's Inn Lane. He married in May 1656 and had a child the following year, though the match proved short-lived and unhappy. After his wife's death he married again in April 1660, and this time was 'reasonably happy' (Kendal, 30–31). A son born in September 1661 survived only six days.

In his spare time Coley taught himself mathematics, astrology, Latin, and French, and in 1669 he published the fruits of his astrological studies as *Clavis astrologiae, or, A Key to the Whole Art of Astrology*. Its second part, *Genethliaca*, has a separate title-page and carries the date 1668. Though described as merely an introduction, the work is a thorough and systematic account of nativities and the practice of horary astrology, explaining for the first time, for English readers, the innovations of Kepler in this branch of astrology. It was very well received. A massively expanded second edition followed in 1676, with 750 pages of text and a further hundred pages of astronomical data drawn from Kepler and Jean-Baptiste Morin. It was dedicated to Elias Ashmole and carried a glowing tribute by William Lilly, who hailed it as complementing and completing his own *Christian Astrology* (1st edn, 1647).

The success of the *Clavis* encouraged Coley to launch an annual almanac in 1672, which he continued, under various titles, until his death. Coley's admiration for William Lilly—'that great Luminary of Astrology'—and Lilly's reciprocal respect led to the older man's 'adopting' the younger as his son. After Lilly's serious illness in November 1675 Coley helped him with his celebrated annual *Merlini Anglici Ephemeris*, staying at Lilly's house at Hersham, Surrey, each summer to complete the task. Coley himself, unable to get away from London, composed the edition for 1679 but assured Lilly that he had followed his methods and that he would be able to amend the proofs. After Lilly's death in 1681 Coley continued the title himself. He became one of the linchpins of the almanac business of the Company of Stationers, compiling several titles besides his own, and investing some of his savings in the company. Aspiring authors often sent him their manuscripts for approval, including ten in 1683 alone.

In 1663 Coley moved to a house in Baldwin's Gardens, Baldwin's Court, off Gray's Inn Road, where he taught astrology and mathematics, boarded some of his pupils, and received clients. By the 1670s he had a very flourishing practice. Writing to Lilly in July 1677, he complained that he was visited all day long by 'Scholars and Querents, little can be don 'till night, and by Candle light I do most of my work' (Bodl. Oxf., MS Ashmole 240, fol. 213). In his almanacs he advertised tuition in arithmetic, logarithms, geometry, trigonometry, geography, astronomy, navigation, dialling, surveying, and music, besides astrology. He was a respected mathematician, consulted by Edmond Halley to help him calculate the moon's parallax. Joseph Moxon was a close friend and acknowledged Coley's substantial contribution to his mathematical dictionary, *Mathematics Made Easy* (1679). In 1686 Coley published a revised edition of William Forster's textbook *Arithmetic, or, That Useful Art Made Easie*, designed for 'Merchants, Factors, Accomptants'. His almanac for 1687 contained mathematical calculations by Sir Jonas Moore, and the 1691 edition featured a brief discussion of gravitation, referring readers to Isaac Newton for further information. An enthusiast for the new science in general, Coley declared that the telescope and microscope had revealed wonders unknown to any earlier age, and that Europe now far outstripped all previous civilizations. He had a wide circle of friends, among them the virtuosi Elias Ashmole, John Aubrey, and Sir John Hoskins, astrologers such as John Gadbury (for a time), George Parker, William Salmon, and Charles Bernard, and the whig journalist Henry Care, and counted numerous country gentlemen and lawyers among his clients and patrons. John Brown, surgeon to

Charles II and senior surgeon at St Thomas's Hospital, Southwark, was also a patron.

Coley took a warm interest in the reform of astrology, a lively issue in the second half of the century, arguing that it must be founded on experiments like other sciences. His own interests lay mainly in the refinement of nativities and of horary astrology. On judicial astrology, especially concerning politics, he was more cautious than many of the other leading practitioners of his time. His almanacs offered mostly vague and innocuous prophecies for England and western Europe, though he was happy to promise 'vast slaughter' of Turks and Tartars in 1684 (*Merlini Anglici Ephemeris*, 1684, sig. A5). More typically he remarked that whig astrologers were rash to predict the death of Louis XIV, 'for Kings and Princes have long Arms, and can reach a person when he least expects it' (ibid., sig. B3). At home his almanacs preached obedience to the government of the day, with varying degrees of enthusiasm. The 1685 edition gave full details of the Popish Plot, but he had no difficulty in hailing 'Great James' the following year and remained obedient to the very end of James's reign. The edition for 1690, however, took a strongly protestant, patriotic line, and by 1692 he was hailing William III as 'Our King by Miracle, as well as Right' (*Merlinus Anglicus Junior*, 1692, sig. A3), and predicting that he would lead his victorious armies to the very heart of popish France. In the late 1690s Coley drew attention to the still bolder predictions of his former pupil John Holwell and others that a millennial age was at hand: a messianic emperor arising in the north would crush France and bring about the ruin of Rome and conversion of the Turks and Jews. Characteristically Coley remained noncommittal, observing cautiously, 'let our own Experience confirm or contradict' (*Merlinus Anglicus Junior*, 1698, sig. C7v).

Coley is best known as William Lilly's successor. George Parker described him in 1699 as a 'Person of a quiet and peaceful Disposition' (Parker, *Ephemeris*, 1699, sig. A3v). Aubrey agreed that he was 'as good a natured man as can be' (*Brief Lives*, 1.181). Coley did not avoid controversy altogether, however. John Gadbury, whose *Ephemerides* he had criticized as inaccurate, hit back in 1684 by accusing Coley of plagiarizing his work in *Clavis astrologiae*. Some years later, in 1698, John Partridge mocked Coley's almanac *Nuncius Syderius* as 'Duncius Syderius', and attacked him for selling astrological sigils and charms. Claiming that Coley was selling bogus charms to prevent unwanted pregnancies or retain a lover, charging 4 and 6 guineas respectively, Partridge urged dissatisfied customers to indict him for fraud under the statute of 1604. Despite these attacks, Coley's learning and modesty secured him an unusually wide range of friends, from radical whigs to neo-Jacobites. The portrait attached to the first edition of *Clavis astrologiae* shows a soberly dressed young man, wearing his hair long. Coley died in London on 30 April 1704.   BERNARD CAPP

Sources B. S. Capp, *Astrology and the popular press: English almanacs, 1500–1800* (1979) • W. Lilly, *Mr William Lilly's history of his life and times: from the year 1602, to 1681*, 2nd edn (1715); repr. with introduction by K. M. Briggs (1974) • *Brief lives, chiefly of contemporaries, set down by*

John Aubrey, between the years 1669 and 1696, ed. A. Clark, 2 vols. (1898) · J. Kendal, *Chronometria, or, The measure of time by directions … practically illustrated in the geniture of Mr Henry Coley* (1684) · E. G. R. Taylor, *The mathematical practitioners of Tudor and Stuart England* (1954) · *Mercurius Anglicanus* (1699) · G. Parker, *Royal Speculum* (1705) · Bodl. Oxf., MS Ashmole 240 · Bodl. Oxf., MS Add. B8 · BL, Sloane MSS 2281–2285 · J. Merrifield, *Catastasis mundi, or, The true state, vigor, and growing greatness of Christendom, under the influences of the last triple conjunction of Saturn and Jupiter in Leo* (1684) · J. Partridge, *Merlinus Liberatus* (1698) · H. E. Salter, ed., *Oxford council acts, 1583–1626*, OHS, 87 (1928) · M. G. Hobson and H. E. Salter, eds., *Oxford council acts, 1626–1665*, OHS, 95 (1933)

Archives BL, astrological and mathematical papers, Sloane MSS 1405, 2279–2285, 2328, 3880 · Bodl. Oxf., notebook, Add. MS B8 | Bodl. Oxf., Ashmolean MSS

Likenesses R. White, line engraving, BM, NPG · engraving, repro. in H. Coley, *Clavis astrologiae* (1669) · engraving, repro. in H. Coley, *Merlinus Anglicus junior* (1686) · line engravings, BM, NPG

Colfe, Abraham (1580–1657), Church of England clergyman and benefactor, was born in Canterbury on 7 August 1580, the eldest son of Richard Colfe (*d.* 1613), a Church of England clergyman, and his first wife, whose maiden name was Thorneton; he was a nephew of Isaac *Colfe. After early education at Canterbury Cathedral grammar school, Abraham Colfe matriculated at Oxford from Christ Church in November 1594 and graduated BA in October 1599.

Colfe was still in residence at Christ Church when, in April 1601, 'publicly in hall' he made what the vice-chancellor, George Abbot, and the dean, Thomas Ravis, described as a 'very offensive' outburst, passionately commending the earl of Essex as a great general, 'Veri Dux', and 'Pater Patriae', whose very virtue had been the cause of his overthrow (*CSP dom.*, 1601–3, 35). A month later he wrote a supplicatory letter to Secretary Robert Cecil from Newgate prison, offering an eloquent if disingenuous explanation of his conduct. Likening himself to Icarus, 'indiscreetly' flying too near Essex, who 'shine[d] like the sun in his height', he had intended to praise his virtues, 'and darkly to point at his death under the history of Cicero', but not, as a loyal subject, to challenge his condemnation (ibid., 44).

Shortly afterwards Colfe must have transferred to Cambridge to resume his studies for he obtained his MA from Trinity College there in 1603, the year in which he was ordained. Although there is no university record of further degrees, he was later described as having a DD. He was curate of Lewisham, Kent, from 1604 to May 1610, when he succeeded Hadrian Saravia in the vicarage. Three months earlier, having obtained a dispensation for pluralism, he had also become rector of St Leonard Eastcheap, London, but he continued to live in Lewisham; about this time he married Margaret Valentine, *née* Hollard (*c.*1566–1644), the widow of a local tanner, whose family connections, especially with the Leathersellers' Company, were to become important to him.

Identifying himself with the interests of his Lewisham parishioners, whom in 1614 and 1615 he helped to a successful defence of their rights over Westwood Common, Colfe only occasionally officiated in person in his London parish, but his preaching was apparently well received by the pious in that congregation. Feeling that 'a minister should labour earnestly … to stir up all professed Christians' (*Hasted's History*, 1.258n.), Colfe, on the evidence of his will, took preaching very seriously, usually delivering two sermons on Sundays and, for the last twenty years of his life, expounding the Bible on Wednesdays, Fridays, and holy days. He was one of the earliest members of Sion College, and was a benefactor of the library. As early as 1626 he determined to buy land to found and endow charitable institutions, and in 1634 proposed to convey land from the manor of Sydenham to the Leathersellers' Company for pious uses.

Relations with some inhabitants of Lewisham were soured during 1642 and 1643 when Colfe and others resisted parliamentary orders to admit John Batchelor, soon to be notorious for licensing sectarian books, as a weekly lecturer at Lewisham. Colfe complained that 'at the instigation of their impudent lecturer' (Black, xxiv) the parishioners tried to turn him out of the living by proceeding against him before the committee of plundered ministers, but in the event he remained in place until his death, although he lost his London living to Henry Roborough in 1647.

Continuing the charitable impulses shared by his wife, whose funeral monument erected in Lewisham church after her death in 1644 celebrates her 'having bene above 40 yeares a willing nurse, midwife, surgeon and in part physition to all both rich and poor, without excepting reward', in 1652 Colfe founded and opened a free grammar school in the town. As his will of 7 September 1656 explained, it was intended for thirty-one boys drawn from the Blackheath hundred; the trustee was not, 'as he shall answer for it at the Judgement seat of Jesus Christ', to admit the sons of the wealthy, and there were very strict limits on the extent of corporal punishment (*Hasted's History*, 1.258n.). He died on 5 December 1657 in Lewisham, leaving no children of his own but having had a good relationship with his stepsons, whom he had assisted during his life. He was buried in Lewisham church. Charitable bequests dominated his will, with money left for '30 or 40' chained bibles for the use of strangers and parishioners, and a library of books left to the school. In 1662 his trustees built almshouses in Lewisham in accordance with his instructions, and in 1664 the ownership and governorship of his various charitable institutions were vested by act of parliament in the Leathersellers' Company.

WILLIAM HUNT, *rev.* VIVIENNE LARMINIE

Sources *Hasted's history of Kent: corrected, enlarged, and continued to the present time*, ed. H. H. Drake (1886), 255–68 · W. H. Black, *Bibliothecae Colfanae catalogus: catalogue of the library in the free grammar-school at Lewisham* (1831) · *CSP dom.*, 1601–3, 35, 44 · Foster, *Alum. Oxon.* · Venn, *Alum. Cant.* · *Walker rev.*, 45 · *Calamy rev.*, 34

Archives BL, material on his grammar school, Add. MS 10602 · Leathersellers' Company, London, letters and papers apparently relating to his benefactions

Wealth at death entire estate donated for charitable purposes: *Hasted's history of Kent*, ed. Drake; Black, *Bibliothecae*

Colfe, Isaac (1558/9–1597), Church of England clergyman, was born at Canterbury, the fourth son of Almundus or Amandus Colphe and his wife, Katherine Bradfield. He was the brother of Joseph (a future mayor of Canterbury) and Richard; the latter was the father of Abraham *Colfe. His parents were probably Huguenot refugees who arrived in England having left their estate at Guînes, near Calais, after the reconquest of the town by the French in 1558. The family took up residence at the West Gate in Canterbury. Isaac entered Broadgates Hall, Oxford, as a commoner in 1576; he is recorded as matriculating on 23 July 1579, aged twenty, and graduated BA on 17 February 1580, proceeding MA on 4 July 1582. On 20 June 1583 he married Alice Caxston, a widow of Lydd; their sons Isaac and Jacob were educated at Oxford, at Christ Church and All Souls (perhaps as an unofficial poor scholar) respectively. Colfe was presented to the vicarage of Stone in Oxney, Kent, on 25 February 1585 but resigned on his appointment as vicar of Brookland near Lydd. He seems to have been in good standing with the town's authorities, to whom he dedicated a sermon preached there in 1587 on the anniversary of Elizabeth's accession. On 18 June 1596 he was inducted to the mastership of Kingsbridge Hospital, Canterbury, and on 5 August the same year was collated one of the six preachers of the cathedral. Colfe died on 15 July 1597 and was buried in the chapter house of Canterbury Cathedral.   STEPHEN WRIGHT

Sources Foster, *Alum. Oxon.* · Wood, *Ath. Oxon.*: *Fasti* (1815), 212, 221 · I. Colfe, *A sermon preached on the queene's day* (1588) · *Fasti Angl., 1541–1857,* [Canterbury] · D. I. Hill, *The six preachers of Canterbury Cathedral, 1541–1982* (1982) · E. Hasted, *The history and topographical survey of the county of Kent*, 2nd edn, 11 (1801) · W. K. Jordan, 'Social institutions in Kent, 1480–1660: a study of the changing patterns of social aspirations', *Archaeologia Cantiana*, 75 (1961) [whole issue]

Colgan, John (1592?–1658), hagiographer, was born in the parish of Donagh, co. Donegal. Little is known of his background and early years: it is not clear whether a reference in a 1607 letter of George Montgomery, Church of Ireland bishop of Derry, to John MacColgan, son of the rector of Donagh, and a skilled student of law at Glasgow and speaker of both Irish and Latin, is to the same man. By 1615 at the latest he had left Ireland for the continent and, having been ordained about 1618, entered the Franciscan order at St Anthony's College, Louvain, on 26 April 1620. He continued his theological studies there under Father Robert Chamberlain and Father Thomas Fleming. It is very likely he subsequently taught scholastic philosophy at Aachen before being appointed lector of theology at Mainz in 1628. He returned to Louvain some time before June 1634, when he was stated to have been novice master at St Anthony's. Already in the early 1620s when he had just entered Louvain, Father Hugh Ward, Brother Michael O Cleirigh, and Father Patrick Fleming were engaged in collecting and editing Irish historical and, in particular, hagiographical materials and Colgan's correspondence in the 1620s suggests interests in this work, although his activities in the field are only vaguely known before 1635. In November that year Father Ward died and Colgan succeeded him as professor of theology at Louvain and as director of this work.

Under Colgan the project crystallized into a plan for a seven- or eight-volume work. The first volume from this proposed scheme went to the press on 24 November 1643, and appeared in 1645 as *Acta sanctorum veteris et maioris Scotiae, seu, Hiberniae sanctorum insulae*. It comprised 270 lives, containing the lives of all saints whose feast days fell in the first three months of the year, with the exception of Brigid and Patrick. It is in the preface to *Acta sanctorum* that Colgan uses the title annals of the four masters for the annalistic compilation of Michael O Cleirigh and collaborators, *Annála Ríoghachta Éreann*, and it is by this title that this illustrious work has since been known. *Acta sanctorum* was actually the third volume of the projected scheme. The first was to have consisted of the 'sacred and profane history of the country, its kings, the Irish apostolate abroad etc' and never appeared. The second projected volume was published two years after *Acta sanctorum*, and was the occasion for the casting of a new set of Irish type: *Triadis thaumaturgae* was a collection of sources for the lives of Patrick, Brigid, and Columcille. According to Father Luke Wadding, the fourth projected volume, containing the lives of the saints for the next three months of the year, was in the press soon after. However, it never appeared. The cost of publishing seems to have been the crucial issue. The two published volumes owed their appearance to, respectively, Hugh O'Reilly, archbishop of Armagh, and Thomas Fleming, Colgan's former tutor and then archbishop of Dublin. Various appeals were made but it is likely that a lack of patrons for the remaining volumes proved a fatal stumbling block.

In June 1651 Colgan was appointed commissary of the three Irish Franciscan colleges of Louvain, Prague, and Vielan. However, complaining of severe ill health, he asked to be relieved of the position the following February. He also declined a request from his order to write a reply to Father Zacharius Borenius's stricture of the Franciscan observants. In 1655 he published a short work on John Duns Scotus which revolved around the hotly disputed question of his nationality and that of all those to whom the term *scotus* had been applied.

Colgan died at St Anthony's College, Louvain, on 15 January 1658. A printed obituary notice survives in the Franciscan Library, Killiney. At his death Colgan is believed to have left several volumes of the hagiographical project completed in manuscript. Father Thomas Sheeran took charge of the work but in the years before his own death in 1673 he managed to see only Thomas Sheeran's *Vita S. Rumoldi* and Patrick Fleming's *Collectanea sacra* through the press. Colgan's unpublished work appears to have been extant in the mid-eighteenth century but does not seem to have survived the dispersal of the Louvain archives after the French Revolution.

A contemporary assessment of Colgan may be taken from the comments of Nicholas Verunlaeus, historiographer to the king of Spain and a professor at Louvain, in the preface to *Acta sanctorum*:

> Well have you merited, O most learned Colgan, of heaven and earth, of your country and the whole world. Others of your fellow countrymen have arisen in these times to vindicate in arms the Catholic religion. … You vindicate the saints of your country with your pen. … Your glory will be

that you restore her saints to the Island of Saints, that the church accepts them, and that the world acknowledges them. … With infinite labour you have brought their lives to light, with incredible industry, you have described them, now with immense study and work you make them available. (O'Donnell, 26)

Three centuries later it was evident that 'no writer on this subject during the last three hundred years, however eminent, has or could have dealt with the subject without continual reference to him' (Jennings, 'Introduction', iv). Ludwig Bieler's 1958 assessment was that, while *Acta sanctorum Hiberniae* had been succeeded by the work of Charles Plummer, *Triadis thaumaturgae* had yet to be superseded, despite the faults modern scholars might find with it. With regard to the Patrician materials Bieler's 1971 *Four Latin Lives of St Patrick: Colgan's 'Vita secunda, quarta, tertia and quinta'* now provides such a successor, although the *Triadis* sections on Brigid and Columcille remained unchallenged at the end of the twentieth century.

MIHAIL DAFYDD EVANS

Sources T. O'Donnell, ed., *Father John Colgan, O.F.M., 1592–1658: essays in commemoration of the third centenary of his death* (1959) · B. Jennings, introduction, in *The Acta sanctorum Hiberniae of John Colgan* (1948) · B. Jennings and C. Giblin, eds., *Louvain papers, 1606–1827*, IMC (1968) · W. Reeves, 'Colgan's works', *Ulster Journal of Archaeology*, 1 (1853), 295–302 · *Four Latin lives of St Patrick: Colgan's 'Vita secunda, quarta, tertia and quinta'*, ed. L. Bieler (1971) · B. Jennings, *Michael O Cleirigh, chief of the four masters, and his associates* (1936) · C. P. MacDonnell, 'Notice of some of the lives which seem to have been ready, or in preparation, for the continuation of the *Actae sanctorum Hiberniae* at the death of Colgan', *Proceedings of the Royal Irish Academy*, 7 (1857–61), 371 · C. Graves, 'Manuscripts of the celebrated John Colgan, preserved at St Isidore's Rome: with a note by C. P. MacDonnell on a lost work of Colgan', *Proceedings of the Royal Irish Academy*, 6 (1853–7), 95 · B. Cunningham, 'The culture and ideology of Irish Franciscan historians at Louvain, 1607–1650', *Ideology and the historians*, ed. C. Brady (1991), 11–30 · Pádraig Ó Súilleabháin, 'Litir ó Bhonarentúr Ó Conchoblair, OFM, cluig Seán Mac Colgáin, OFM', *Catholic Survey*, 1 (1951–3), 130–32 · obituary notice, Franciscan Library, Killiney, co. Dublin

Archives Biblioteca Apostolica Vaticana, Vatican City, Biroiani Lat 96 · Bodl. Oxf., Rawl. MS B. 487 · Franciscan Library, Killiney, co. Dublin, MS F. 2; Gaelic MS A 16; MS Section F; Gaelic MS A 34 · St Isidore's College, Rome

Likenesses E. di Como, fresco, *c.*1670, St Isidore's College, Rome; repro. in Jennings, *Introduction*, frontispiece · pencil and watercolour drawing (after Fra Emmanuello da Como), NG Ire.

Colins, Alice (*fl.* 1521). *See under* Lollard women (*act. c.*1390–*c.*1520).

Colinton. For this title name *see* Foulis, Sir James, of Colinton, second baronet, Lord Colinton (*d.* 1688).

Collace, Katherine. *See* Ross, Katherine (*c.*1635–1697).

Collar, (Arthur) Roderick (1908–1986), mathematician and aeronautical engineer, was born on 22 February 1908 in West Ealing, London, the second of three children and elder son of Arthur Collar, of Whitstable, Kent, who had a successful ironmonger's and builder's business, and his wife, Louie Gann, who also came from a Kent family. He was educated at the local board school in Whitstable, from where he gained a scholarship to Simon Langton School in Canterbury. Here he developed his mathematical and scientific ability, and became good at games and

an accomplished piano-player and violinist. It was in a football match that, at the age of fifteen, he was struck a blow that led to the permanent loss of sight in his right eye. In 1926 he entered Emmanuel College, Cambridge, as an open scholar. He obtained a first in part one of the mathematical tripos in 1927, and a second in part two of the natural sciences tripos in 1929.

Collar sought an appointment in 1929 in the National Physical Laboratory (NPL) at Teddington, and soon found working there, in the aerodynamics department under E. F. Relf, so congenial that he stayed from 1929 until the beginning of the Second World War in 1939. In 1930 the airship R101 crashed in France on its maiden voyage to India, and Collar's ability came to the fore when he made skilful step-by-step calculations on the airship's motion prior to the disaster. It was, however, for his work on the application of matrices to aeroplane flutter that Collar was best known at the NPL. Initiated by R. A. Frazer, this work had been fostered by the Aeronautical Research Committee, which later brought Frazer, W. J. Duncan, and Collar together to produce in 1938 the first textbook on the subject—*Elementary Matrices*, which proved a bestseller in Britain and the USA, and was later translated into Russian and Czech. This basic work on flutter was developed at the Royal Aeronautical Establishment (RAE) into a design tool in time to ensure that the new fighter aircraft being built prior to the Second World War—the Hurricane and Spitfire—were flutter-free. With the onset of war, in 1941 Collar was transferred to the RAE, to help with this design work.

After the war several universities considered introducing aeronautical engineering into their engineering faculties. One of the first to do so was Bristol University, which in 1945 invited Collar to be the first holder of the Sir George White chair in aeronautics. After he took up the post in 1946 his new department prospered in new accommodation. From 1954 to 1957 he was dean of the faculty, and in 1968, after the sudden death of the vice-chancellor, he was persuaded to hold this position for seventeen months, pending the appointment of a successor. Collar's personality made all this seem natural; a sincere Christian and a born raconteur, with a slim athletic build, who enjoyed cricket and music, he was an attractive colleague.

Collar always took an active part in the Royal Aeronautical Society (he was president in 1963–4, and became an honorary fellow in 1973), and won a number of its principal prizes, including the society's gold medal in 1966. He was appointed CBE in 1964, and elected a fellow of the Royal Society in 1965. His outstanding aeronautical work led to his appointment as chairman of the Aeronautical Research Council (1964–8). He also served on the councils of the Rolls-Royce Technical College, the Royal Military College of Science, Clifton College, the Cranfield Institute of Technology, and the Royal Society. He had honorary degrees from Bristol (1969), Bath (1971), and Cranfield (1976).

In 1934 Collar married Winifred Margaret Charlotte, of

East Molesey, Surrey, daughter of Ernest George Whittington Earl Moorman, a clerk in the office of works at Hampton Court Palace. They had two sons. After his retirement in 1973 from Bristol University, Collar began to suffer from rheumatoid arthritis in his hands and feet. Following a fall in a friend's garden in 1983, he developed leukaemia. This left him severely ill for the last years of his life, and led to his death at his home, 12 Rockcleaze, Sneyd Park, Bristol, on 12 February 1986.   A. G. PUGSLEY, rev.

Sources R. E. D. Bishop, *Memoirs FRS*, 33 (1987), 163–85 • personal knowledge (1996) • *CGPLA Eng. & Wales* (1986)
Archives University of Bristol Library, corresp. and papers
Wealth at death under £40,000: probate, 16 Oct 1986, *CGPLA Eng. & Wales*

Collard, Frederick William (*bap.* 1772, *d.* 1860), piano manufacturer, son of William and Thamosin Collard, was baptized at Wiveliscombe, Somerset, on 21 June 1772. At the age of fourteen he went to London and worked for Longman, Lukey, and Broderip, music publishers and piano makers, at 26 Cheapside. In 1799 Longman & Co. fell into commercial difficulties, and a new company, consisting of John Longman, Muzio Clementi, Frederick Augustus Hyde, F. W. Collard, Josiah Banger, and David Davis, took over the business, but on 28 June 1800 Longman and Hyde retired, and the firm henceforth was known as Muzio Clementi & Co. After some time Collard's brother William Frederick became a partner, and on 24 June 1817 Banger left the company. On 24 June 1831 the partnership between F. W. Collard, W. F. Collard, and Clementi expired, and the two brothers continued the business until 24 June 1842, when W. F. Collard retired, and F. W. Collard, then sole proprietor, took into partnership his two nephews, Frederick William Collard jun., and Charles Lukey Collard. After 1832 the pianos which had long borne the name of Clementi began to be called Collard and Collard, and many patents were taken out for improvements in both the action and the frame of the instruments; Clementi's serial numbers were continued in Collard and Collard's square pianos. The firm soon gave up the business of music publishing, and confined themselves to piano making, except that they had also the contract for supplying bugles, fifes, and drums to the regiments of the East India Company until 1858. To the Great Exhibition of 1851 Collard sent a square semi-grand, which was awarded the council medal by the musical jury (the award was not confirmed, owing to some feeling of jealousy), and two small cottage pianos, which subsequently sold well.

The firm suffered twice from large fires; on 20 March 1807 the factory in Tottenham Court Road was burnt to the ground, and on 10 December 1851 a new factory, in Oval Road, Camden Town, was entirely destroyed. F. W. Collard died at his home at 26 Cheapside on 31 January 1860, aged eighty-eight, having lived in the same house since his arrival in London in 1786. **William Frederick Collard** (*bap.* 1776, *d.* 1866), his brother and partner, was baptized at Wiveliscombe on 25 August 1776, and, in addition to an inventive genius respecting improvements in pianos, also developed a taste for lyric poetry. He retired from business in 1842, and died at Folkestone on 11 October 1866.

In 1929 the Chappell Piano Company took over Collard, whose business had already run down, and production stopped in 1971. A fire destroyed all Collard records in 1964.   G. C. BOASE, rev. H. C. G. MATTHEW

Sources *GM*, 1st ser., 102/1 (1832), 466–8 • private information (1887) • *A short history of a great house* (1938) • C. Ehrlich, *The piano: a history* (1976) • *New Grove*
Likenesses C. Turner, mezzotint, pubd 1829 (after J. Lonsdale), BM, NPG
Wealth at death under £140,000: probate, 28 March 1860, *CGPLA Eng. & Wales* • under £70,000—William Frederick Collard: probate, 5 Feb 1867, *CGPLA Eng. & Wales*

Collard, William Frederick (*bap.* 1776, *d.* 1866). *See under* Collard, Frederick William (*bap.* 1772, *d.* 1860).

Collcutt, Thomas Edward (1840–1924), architect, was born on 16 March 1840 in Jericho, Oxford, the son of James Collcutt, servant at St John's College, Oxford, and his wife, Emma, *née* Blake. He was educated at the Oxford diocesan school, Cowley, Oxford. Articled to R. W. Armstrong of London in 1856, he later worked in the office of Mills and Murgatroyd of Manchester, in G. E. Street's office, and in the Brighton town surveyor's office (1867–9), before establishing his own practice in the City of London, initially with H. Woodzell. In 1871 the partnership was placed first in the Blackburn Free Library and Museum competition, a 'mildly Gothic' building with 'touches in the direction of the Arts and Crafts' (Pevsner, *North Lancashire*, 1969, 64), indicative of Collcutt's way ahead. Exhibiting at the Royal Academy in 1873 from 12 Finsbury Place South, by 1875 Collcutt had moved his office to 17 Essex Street, Strand, and was engaged on houses at Mill Hill. He built a house for himself and another for a doctor at Ravenscourt Park, Hammersmith: 'inexpensive domestic work marked by intuitive taste and a cultured individuality' (Adams, 24). Other houses followed, at Sheen and elsewhere. About 1878 he moved to a large, red brick house, again of his own design, at 36 Bloomsbury Square (dem.). The sanitary engineer George Jennings introduced him to terracotta, which he first used in houses for Jennings in Nightingale Lane, Clapham. Collcutt's reputation as a house architect caused him to be invited to design one for the 1878 Paris Exhibition's street of houses. Picturesque and half-timbered, his houses were found comfortable to live in and easy to work. In the 1890s and 1900s he designed additional buildings for Mill Hill School and boarding-houses for Eton College.

It was, however, the success of his powerfully original design in local stone in the Wakefield town hall competition (1877) that put Collcutt in the first rank of English architects. An assiduous competitor, so keen was Collcutt to win at Wakefield that he put in two designs, one in Gothic, the other in the Queen Anne style. Street, the assessor, recognizing that they were by the same hand, placed the Queen Anne design first, and told the promoters 'that if they liked to have the other that was first also' (*RIBA Journal*, 3rd ser., 15, 1907–8, 10). In 1887 Collcutt was successful in a competition of six architects invited to

Thomas Edward Collcutt (1840–1924), by Sir Arthur Stockdale Cope, 1909

design the Imperial Institute in South Kensington, commemorating Queen Victoria's jubilee. Important commissions multiplied, and in 1890 he was engaged on the English Opera House exterior (1889–93; later the Palace Theatre) at Cambridge Circus for D'Oyly Carte, the Bechstein (later Wigmore) Hall, and the City Bank, Ludgate Hill. Characteristic in all these buildings was his employment of a pale buff terracotta of larger size and more complex modelling than that which Waterhouse made fashionable: Phillips's China and Glass Emporium (later Waring's), 175–181 Oxford Street, was the precursor. Walter Smith was Collcutt's modeller, Doulton his manufacturer. The 1890s were the outstanding period of his work, comprising 'the delicacy and minuteness of detail and ornament combined with the largeness and simplicity of form which are the outstanding features of his designs' (RIBA Journal, 3rd ser., 31, 1923–4, 667). In the lavish Lloyd's Registry of Shipping, Fenchurch Street (1900), his use of Portland stone produced broader, bolder features in a baroque version of arts and crafts.

Soon after the erection of the Savoy Hotel, D'Oyly Carte had employed Collcutt on some interiors, followed in 1905 by an extension to the Strand, faced in Doulton's Carrara blocks of creamy matt-glazed terracotta designed to cope with London's sooty climate, an example of Collcutt's care for the practical; he employed him again for the extension on the river front (1910). Collcutt designed furniture as a hobby, and interior design and furniture became an important side of his practice. A notable interior in 1894 was the opulent King's Hall in the Holborn Restaurant (dem.). He also worked for the Peninsular and Oriental Line, designing music saloons for several liners in 1896–7, suites in liners subsequently, pavilions at international exhibitions, and hotels at Algeciras and Colombo (1912). In 1904 Gloucester House, a gabled block of flats in green and white striped faience, broke the skyline on Piccadilly and Park Lane; the John Lewis store, Oxford Street, however, was reckoned a failure.

Collcutt, like his sometime master Street, was ferociously energetic in his daily office work. 'Always the most practical of constructors' (RIBA Journal, 3rd ser., 31, 1923–4, 667), he employed an instructor two or three times a week to expound construction to his staff, which included L. Stokes and J. S. Gibson. From 1908 he was in partnership with Stanley Hinge Hamp. 'Singularly simple and direct in the statement of his views', Collcutt 'gave a lead and developed a rendering of the movement of the day, characteristic of his own genius … it was a thoroughly English rendering of the Renaissance' (ibid., 668). He had, said Beresford Pite, the capacity to design charming buildings 'which displayed extraordinary vigour and grip, and that peculiar power to design Gothic works as they really were supposed to be' (RIBA Journal, 3rd ser., 15, 1907–8, 11), work that evoked enthusiasm among the younger generation of architects. Marked by successful composition and grouping, his elevations were ruled by contrasting lines of subdivision and by carefully considered ornamentation. Collcutt received the RIBA gold medal in 1902. He was much concerned with professional questions, such as the proper management of competitions (he organized a petition in 1876 in favour of boycotting them unless there were a professional assessor), and he was intensely interested in architectural education. A man of innate modesty, though of strong opinions, he was reluctant to become president of the RIBA in 1906, but he was seen as 'a model of integrity' (ibid., 14, 1906–7, 10), his 'wisdom of judgment and sympathy with earnest effort … [endearing] him to all who knew him' (ibid., 31, 1923–4, 667). He was re-elected for a second term in 1907. Among the issues he brought forward was the idea of moving the Charing Cross railway terminus to the south bank of the Thames, and constructing a street bridge with arcaded buildings. In 1906 he was one of eight architects invited by the London county council to design façades for Kingsway, but finding the conditions unacceptable he withdrew. Anxious to improve London, particularly in terms of housing for the working classes, he urged replacing slums by towers of flats eight or ten storeys high, and published a small book on this theme in 1923.

Collcutt was an impressive figure, bearded, with high forehead and aquiline nose, genial in personality, with many friends. He formed a notable collection of clocks. On 30 April 1868 he married a Londoner, Emily Green or Tagg (b. 1844), and they had two sons and four daughters. At the time of the 1881 census they were supported in Bloomsbury Square by a governess, a cook, and three other young women servants. Later they also lived at West Lodge, Totteridge, Hertfordshire (with stables and coachman's lodge), where Collcutt had built several houses, but his wife was dead by 1917 and he died a widower at Grosvenor House Nursing Home, Southampton, on 7 October 1924. After a funeral service four days later he was buried at Totteridge parish church. M. H. PORT

Sources The Builder, 127 (1924), 587 · J. S. Gibson, 'Thomas Edward Collcutt, past president, royal gold medallist', RIBA Journal, 31 (1923–4), 666–8 · Building News (3 Jan 1890), 51 · M. B. Adams, 'The late Thomas Edward Collcutt', RIBA Journal, 32 (1924–5), 24 · RIBA Journal, 15 (1907–8), 10–11, 502 · T. E. Collcutt, 'The opening address delivered by the president', RIBA Journal, 14 (1906–7), 1–10 · The Times (9 Oct 1924), 17 · census returns, 1881, PRO, RG 11/321, fols. 25–6 · will, Principal Registry of the Family Division, London · T. E. Collcutt, London of the future (1923) · A. S. Gray, Edwardian architecture: a biographical dictionary (1985); repr. (1988) · biographical file, RIBA BAL · Graves, RA exhibitors · b. cert. · m. cert. · CGPLA Eng. & Wales (1924)
Archives RIBA, drawings collection, MSS
Likenesses A. S. Cope, oils, 1909, RIBA [see illus.] · Barraud, photograph, repro. in Building News · photograph, repro. in Building News (1906), 46 · photograph (after A. S. Cope), repro. in Architects' and Builders' Journal (30 Dec 1913) · photograph, repro. in The Builder, 594 · photograph, repro. in RIBA Journal, 3rd ser., 31 (1923–4), 666
Wealth at death £19,074 1s. 1d.: probate, 15 Nov 1924, CGPLA Eng. & Wales

Colledge, Thomas Richardson (1796–1879), surgeon and missionary in China, received his medical education in London under Sir Astley Cooper. He practised in Canton (Guangzhou) and Macao and some other Chinese ports, first under the East India Company, and then under the crown, and was superintending surgeon of the hospitals for British seamen. During his residence in Canton and Macao he founded the first infirmary for indigent Chinese—Colledge's Ophthalmic Hospital. He was also the founder, in 1837, of the Medical Missionary Society in China, having published in 1836 two pamphlets on medical missions, and continued as president of the society to the time of his death. On the abolition of the office of surgeon to the consulate at Canton in May 1841, and his consequent return to England, regret was expressed by the whole community, and a memorial of his services was addressed to the queen by Portuguese residents of Macao, which caused Palmerston to grant him an annuity from the civil list.

Colledge took the degree of MD at King's College, Aberdeen, in 1839. He became a fellow of the Royal College of Physicians, Edinburgh, in 1840, a fellow of the Royal Society of Edinburgh in 1844, and a fellow of the Royal College of Surgeons, England, in 1853. The last thirty-eight years of his life were spent in Cheltenham, Gloucestershire, where his courtesy and skill won him regard. He died at his home, Lauriston House, Cheltenham, on 28 October 1879. His widow, Caroline Matilda, died on 6 January 1880. G. C. BOASE, rev. ELIZABETH BAIGENT

Sources Medical Times and Gazette (15 Nov 1879), 568 · The Times (5 Nov 1879) · Proceedings of the Royal Society of Edinburgh, 10 (1878–80), 339 · T. R. Colledge, The Medical Missionary Society in China (1838)
Likenesses W. Daniell, aquatint, 1834 (after G. Chinnery), Wellcome L. · G. Chinnery, double portrait, oils (with his wife), Hong Kong and Shanghai Banking Corporation, Hong Kong
Wealth at death under £30,000: probate, 19 Nov 1879, CGPLA Eng. & Wales

College [Colledge], **Stephen** (c.1635–1681), poet and political activist, was born in Watford, Hertfordshire, where he married and began a family. Neither the names of his parents, nor that of his wife (who probably predeceased him), are as yet known. He saw military service during the Second Anglo-Dutch War (1665–7), when he also became acquainted with another antic poet of the Restoration, John Wilmot, earl of Rochester. College (or Colledge, the spelling he may have preferred himself) relocated to London thereafter, becoming a freeman and pursuing his trade as a joiner. In 1680 he was living in Water Street in St Ann Blackfriars parish.

The Protestant Joiner College was a reformed protestant who had exchanged presbyterianism for the restored Church of England in 1660, but he returned to his presbyterian roots in reaction to the coercive practices of Restoration Anglicanism. Remaining an occasional conformist, he respected Anglican divines like John Tillotson; and he hoped for union between a reformed establishment and those dissenters who were prepared to embrace a more comprehensive church. He was friendly with Titus Oates, Israel Tonge (who died in his house), and several other Popish Plot witnesses. He appeared at the trial of Lord Stafford to support the credibility of a chief witness for the prosecution. He constructed several of the effigies for the London pope-burning processions of 1679–80. Bishop Gilbert Burnet described him as 'an active and hot man', and he was known to his contemporaries as the Protestant Joiner (Burnet's History, 2.296).

College became notorious as the author and reciter of satirical poems and ballads that translated the religious and political concerns of the parliamentary opposition into the language of ordinary people. At the centre of the flourishing popular print culture of 1679–81, he is known to have read his work in London coffee houses and public houses, where he was observed 'bawling against the government' (State trials, 8.610). He was also a defender of the Long Parliament, which he believed had 'stood up for the rights of the people' (ibid., 691). The satires of 1679–80 that have been attributed to him vary in quality; but they consistently turn anti-popish language against the court and against James, duke of York, the Catholic successor to Charles II.

Another particular target of College's pen was Lord Chief Justice Sir William Scroggs, who was blamed by the whigs for the acquittal of suspected Catholic conspirators. College depicted Scroggs as a bloated persecutor of protestants who followed in the sanguinary footsteps of his father, falsely identified in whig rumour as a butcher. Indeed, College invested Scroggs with all the attributes of the loathed Thomas Wolsey (another supposed butcher's son), including the papal rewards of a cardinal's cap and legatine authority. College further directed his poetic attacks against Catholic nobles, courtiers, and royal favourites, 'who would convert us by a sea of blood, and turn the laws of England out of doors by standing army, pensioners and whores' (S. College, 'Truth brought to light', Lord and others, 2.15).

College's ultimate target, however, was Charles II himself. 'Alas! poor nation,' he wrote in 1679, 'how art thou undone by a bad father, and now a worse, his son!' (Lord, 2.16). An advocate of parliamentary solutions to the nation's crisis, College also endorsed popular action: 'We'll die at our doors ere in Smithfield we'll burn' (S. College, 'A lampoon on Lord Scroggs', Lord, 2.289). He has been credited, accurately or not, with the invention of 'the protestant flail', a weapon with which ordinary people could defend themselves against menacing Catholics who sought to 'enthrall' and to 'enslave' the nation (S. College, 'Justice in masquerade', Lord, 2.284).

College's success as a popular spokesman brought him to the attention of London whig leaders like Sir Robert Clayton and Sir Thomas Player, and of such whig grandees as the earl of Shaftesbury and William, Lord Russell. In his capacity as a joiner College was asked by them to search the Westminster cellars on the eve of the 1680–81 parliament for incendiary devices that might have been planted by Catholics. In March 1681 College attended the brief third Exclusion Parliament in Oxford, which was dissolved within days of its opening, when the Commons proceeded again with a bill to exclude the duke of York from the throne. College came to Oxford with arms and in the company of William, Lord Howard; William, Lord Paget; and the earls of Clare and Huntington, who were also armed. He was seen about town engaging in political conversation, and he distributed blue ribbons with the slogan 'No Popery, No Slavery'. He was involved in an altercation outside the meeting place of the House of Lords, and he returned to London in the company of the City MPs.

A Ra-Ree Show College was also armed at Oxford with the satirical ballad *A Ra-Ree Show* (1681). The poem depicted Charles II as a deceptive showman, as a master of political puppetry who held 'freeborn fools' in contempt, and who intended to substitute 'brave strong government' for the rule of king in parliament (S. College, 'A raree show', Lord, 2.427, 429). The ballad also criticized the bishops and the clergy of the Anglican church as inclined to popery, and it recalled the punishment of Charles I 'for fleecing England's flocks' (ibid., 429). It concluded with a call 'to pull down raree show' (Charles's duplicitous political game), to preserve parliament, and to 'free … the nation', for 'the hunt's begun … like father, like son' (ibid., 430, 431). According to hostile sources, the ballad was sung in Oxford and at Lord Lovelace's country house, 'where some Aldermen, and choice Lads of *London*', reportedly including Clayton and Player, 'got drunk, and trolloll'd it bravely' (North, *Examen*, 101–2). A companion piece to the ballad was a cartoon in which Charles II was shown being knocked over by agents of parliament, while bishops and courtiers were stuffed into the king's bag of political tricks. A second cartoon that circulated at Oxford was also associated with College: *A Prospect of a Popish Successor* [1681] depicted the duke of York in the guise of a devil and the Anglican bishops as papal minions.

College was seen at the April 1681 treason trial of Edward Fitzharris, the Irish informant, from whom the whigs had hoped to secure further revelations about Catholic plotting, and from whom the court hoped to secure revelations damaging to the whigs. Fitzharris's ultimate tale about a whig conspiracy at Oxford did not save him from the scaffold. But Fitzharris's story did provide the government with a pretext for arresting College, his fellow London whig activist John Rouse, and lords Shaftesbury and Howard.

College was now caught up in the loyalist counter-offensive of 1681–2, which was designed to rally the nation around Charles II as the near victim of violence supposedly intended by the whigs. The court's real target was Shaftesbury, but the prosecution of College—for his alleged involvement in a design to raise a rebellion and to seize the king—provided a dress rehearsal for the case against Shaftesbury. On 8 July 1681 College was tried before a Middlesex grand jury who returned a verdict of *ignoramus* to the charge. Impanelled by the whig sheriffs Slingsby Bethel and Henry Cornish, the jury was truly made up of College's peers: most of the jurors were nonconformists and tradesmen. With Shaftesbury's fate much in mind, the whigs celebrated this outcome, but loyalists protested that justice could not be found in London.

The trial for treason The ministry responded by arguing that since College's alleged treason had occurred in two places, London and Oxford, he could be tried in either locality. The Joiner was accordingly indicted again in Oxford. The government carefully planned a second case against him, hoping even to turn College's anti-papal rhetoric against him by finding evidence that he was secretly a Catholic.

From the Tower, Shaftesbury assisted College in his Oxford defence, providing him with the hired legal assistance of Aaron Smith and Robert West. The duke of Buckingham's lawyer, Edward Whitaker, also sought to aid him. Recognizing the importance of the trial, the 'buisy factious partymen' of London flocked to Oxford to show their support for the Protestant Joiner (North, *Life of the Lord Keeper*, 74). The home of the mathematician John Wallis, who was a friend of John Locke, became a meeting place for those hoping to assist College. The result of his Oxford trial on 17 August was a foregone conclusion, however, given that a jury of dutiful loyalists had been as carefully assembled as the whig jury of London had been. Sir George Jeffreys, the former recorder of London, who had been a target of whig reprisals in parliament, was a chief counsel for the prosecution.

A variety of political witnesses, many of them once useful to the whigs, claimed that College was at the heart of a design against the king. They cited *A Ra-Ree Show* to demonstrate College's treasonable intentions. College's defence, which he claimed he 'took out of the [law] books myself', was a spirited one (*State trials*, 8.585). The proceedings, which began at 9 a.m., did not conclude until 3 a.m. the following morning. Deprived of legal papers provided by Aaron Smith, which the judges claimed were libellous,

College presented himself as a victim of judicial miscarriage: 'My Lord Coke says, it is the birth-right of every Englishman to have counsel in matters of law, and [John] Lilburne had it … in his Trial' (ibid., 573). College denied that he was the author of the verses in question or of the cartoon they inspired. He called Titus Oates and others to discredit the witnesses against him, and he sought to turn the political tables on the court. According to him, the charges really emanated from the papists, who sought to undermine those who had uncovered their disloyalty by false reports of whig plotting: 'This is a most horrid conspiracy to take away my life; and it will not stop here, for it is against all the Protestants in England' (ibid., 575).

Found guilty, College was executed in the Oxford Castle yard two weeks later, on 31 August, after declining to offer information against whig leaders. He protested his innocence to the end, but he acknowledged that in 'heat of talk' he had sometimes 'uttered some words of indecency … concerning the King' (*True Copy of the Dying Words*, verso). Gilbert Burnet was particularly outraged by the behaviour of Chief Justice Sir Francis North at the trial, and other whig observers also alleged numerous legal irregularities in the proceedings against College. In a final letter to his son Stephen, College urged him to forgo 'that folly of Riming, for … it will do you hurt' (Clark, 2.553n.). Charles II permitted his remains to be buried (at St Gregory by Paul in London) rather than exposed.

The whig martyr College continued to be a critical public figure after his death. Loyalist lampoons celebrated his demise as a sign of the nation's recovery from the political courses of 1641. Aphra Behn included an outspoken London joiner in *The Roundheads* (1682), and John Crowne presented College in the character of the Bricklayer, 'a bold, saucy, factious fellow', in *City Politiques* (1683). Loyalists were also determined to employ College's story as a warning to articulate 'mechanicks' to observe their proper places. Even Lord Macaulay, writing a century and a half later, judged College from an aristocrat perspective, dismissing him as 'a noisy and violent demagogue of mean birth and education' (Macaulay, 1.252).

For contemporary whigs, however, College became the most important victim of Catholic intrigue since Sir Edmundberry Godfrey. His apotheosis as an image of the virtuous protestant citizen was instantaneous, and his picture was hawked in the London streets. The tory propagandist Sir Roger L'Estrange sought unsuccessfully to prevent this popular canonization of College. By 1683 the Protestant Joiner was revered in London as 'good Stephen College' and as a 'martyr for the people's privileges' (*CSP dom., July–Sept 1683*, 309). Indeed, the government's treatment of College was an important factor in drawing some of his political acquaintances into the conspiracies of 1682–3. Among those involved in conspiracy were the attorneys who had aided College in his Oxford trial, Robert West and Aaron Smith; his fellow joiner William Hone, who may have worked with College; and College's sister, who remained in touch with West after College's death. According to West, the Rye House conspirators intended to try Lord Keeper North at Oxford for his part in College's

case and to 'hang him upon the same post on which Colledge was hanged' (*State trials*, 9.422). One version of the manifesto for the duke of Monmouth's 1685 rebellion also stressed the 'barbarous murder of Stephen Colledge under pretence of law' as a rationale for resistance (Harley MS 6845, fol. 257).

College's story was prominently recounted in the whig martyrologies published after the revolution of 1688. Historians have generally followed whig observers in believing that College was the victim of judicial murder. His poetry and his political behaviour were indiscreet; but the evidence for the treasonable actions attributed to him was largely contrived.   GARY S. DE KREY

Sources G. de F. Lord and others, eds., *Poems on affairs of state: Augustan satirical verse, 1660–1714*, 7 vols. (1963–75), vol. 2, pp. 12–16, 280–91, 425–31 · *Poems on affairs of state … by the greatest wits of the age*, 3 (1704), 178–91, 193–96 [contemporary attributions of poems to College] · [J. Tutchin], *A new martyrology, or, The bloody assizes*, 4th edn (1693), 27–40 [additional attribution] · *State trials*, 7.1465–6; 8.549–746, 809; 9.422 · *The arraignment, tryal and condemnation of Stephen Colledge for high-treason* (1681) · *CSP dom.*, 1680–81; 1683–4 · B. J. Rahn, 'A Ra-ree show—a rare cartoon: revolutionary propaganda in the treason trial of Stephen College', *Studies in change and revolution: aspects of English intellectual history, 1640–1800*, ed. P. J. Korshin (1972), 77–98 · R. L. Greaves, *Secrets of the kingdom: British radicals from the Popish Plot to the revolution of 1688–89* (1992), 27–32, 35, 42, 118, 335, 364n., 383n. · K. H. D. Haley, *The first earl of Shaftesbury* (1968), 461, 593, 632, 653, 657–60, 663–5, 669, 676, 680, 684, 687 · 'College, Stephen', Greaves & Zaller, *BDBR*, 1.161–2 · T. Harris, *London crowds in the reign of Charles II* (1987), 101, 106, 118, 121–2, 149, 185, 225 · M. S. Zook, *Radical whigs and conspiratorial politics in late Stuart England* (1999), 89–91, 107, 122, 134 · P. Harth, *Pen for a party: Dryden's tory propaganda in its contexts* (1993), 89, 90, 91–7, 220, 301n. · N. Luttrell, *A brief historical relation of state affairs from September 1678 to April 1714*, 1 (1857), 104, 108–10, 117, 120–21 · *The life and times of Anthony Wood*, ed. A. Clark, 2, OHS, 21 (1892), 544–5, 551–4; 3, OHS, 26 (1894), 133 · *Burnet's History of my own time*, ed. O. Airy, new edn, 2 (1900), 296–7 · R. L'Estrange, *Notes upon Stephen College* (1681) · R. North, *The life of the Lord Keeper North*, ed. M. Chan (1995), 74–5, 171–3 · R. North, *Examen, or, An enquiry into the credit and veracity of a pretended complete history* (1740), 101–2, 585–92 · BL, Harley MS 6845, fol. 257 · T. B. Macaulay, *The history of England from the accession of James II*, new edn, ed. C. H. Firth, 6 vols. (1913–15), vol. 1, p. 252 · *A prospect of a popish successor* [1681] · *The speech and carriage of Stephen Colledge at Oxford* (1681) · *The last speech and confession of Mr Stephen Colledge* (1681) · *A true copy of the dying words of Mr. Stephen Colledge* (1681) · *DNB*
Likenesses engraving, repro. in Macaulay, *History of England*, ed. Firth, vol. 1 · line print, BM, NPG · mezzotint (after unknown artist), BM, NPG · pen, ink, and wash drawing, NPG

College of justice, procurators of the (*act.* 1532), lawyers, were the eight men admitted by the lords of session to act as procurators and advocates in all actions coming before the college of justice when that court was established in Edinburgh in 1532. The precise significance of this event has been a matter of historical debate, and emphasis has been placed on preceding institutional developments and on the regular and increasingly specialized judicial 'sessions' which were held to deal with civil matters, leading in turn to the foundation of a central civil court. This view has led to a downgrading of the events of 1532. The college was founded using money diverted from papal revenues with the consent of Pope Clement VII, and has been seen as merely an example of James V's opportunism in appropriating church funds to his own use. Legal historians, however, have pointed to jurisdictional issues which suggest that the foundation marked, if not a new departure, then at least an important milestone in the development of Scots law.

All eight advocates were well educated (most of them attended continental as well as Scottish universities) and forensically skilled.

Robert Galbraith (*d*. 1544) was the son of David Galbraith (*fl. c*.1480), of Kimmerghame in Berwickshire. Having graduated MA from the University of Paris in 1503 he lectured in logic at the Collège de Coqueret. In 1510 he published a book on logic, *Quadrupertitum*, which was reprinted in 1516. He also wrote works of poetry, though none appears to have survived. Before the end of 1515 Galbraith had returned to Scotland and was appearing as an advocate before the lords of council. He represented Margaret Tudor as queen's advocate, from her return to Scotland in June 1517 probably until her death in 1541. Designated as a chaplain in 1526, Galbraith became treasurer of the Chapel Royal in Stirling in 1528. Before 1526 Galbraith had been made a burgess of Edinburgh and as early as 1516 he had been one of a number of people asked to convene in the Tolbooth to advise the burgh council. During his career as an advocate Galbraith acted for more than 250 clients before taking office as a lord of session on 7 November 1537. By that time he had also become parson of Spott in Haddingtonshire. As well as holding lands in the vicinity of the Tolbooth in Edinburgh, from 1523 he began acquiring property in Haddingtonshire and Berwickshire, particularly the estate of East Windshiel. Galbraith was murdered by John Carkettle of Finglen and others in Greyfriars kirkyard, Edinburgh, on 27 January 1544; the motive for the killing remains unknown. The murderers were granted a remission on payment of assythment to Galbraith's kin; part of the money was spent employing a chaplain at St Giles's, Edinburgh, to say prayers for his soul. Galbraith left behind a manuscript of legal sources which was later used by James Balfour of Pittendreich in compiling his *Practicks* and referred to by him as the 'Liber Galbraith'.

William Johnston (*fl*. 1516–1550) was the son of the Edinburgh burgess James Johnston (*fl. c*.1500–1516). He graduated in arts from St Andrews in 1516 and then studied law at the University of Orléans, where in 1518 he was elected procurator of the Scots nation. The following year he received David Beaton (the future cardinal) there as a novice. In 1524, along with Henry Lauder, he was appointed sheriff of Linlithgowshire *in hac parte* (to hear a specific case only). Johnston's legal career as an advocate was reasonably busy by the late 1520s and he acted as commissary of Lothian in 1531. In 1534 he was appointed to an embassy to England, where he appears to have had numerous protestant contacts. Later that year he was accused of heresy and fled abroad, later being escheated. Johnston subsequently recanted but his goods were again escheated in 1550 after sentence of relapse was pronounced against

him. He survived the Reformation but his later career remains obscure.

Thomas Kincraigie (*d*. 1564) was the legitimated natural son of James Kincraigie (*fl. c*.1500), dean of Aberdeen. A student of arts at St Andrews, Kincraigie's legal career leaned heavily towards the church courts, though he also had a steady practice in the secular courts from the late 1520s. He may also have worked briefly in the royal chancery, since in 1532 he received a payment from the fees of the privy seal. In 1528 he acted as commissary in that part for James Beaton, archbishop of St Andrews, and later he acted as his procurator fiscal, an office he subsequently retained under Cardinal David Beaton. In 1548 Kincraigie was appointed advocate for the poor—an office which he probably held, sometimes in conjunction with other advocates, until his death in 1564.

Henry Lauder of St Germains (*d*. 1561) was the son of the Edinburgh burgess Gilbert Lauder (*fl. c*.1490) and Margaret McCalzeane (*fl. c*.1490). He married Agnes Stewart and they had a son, Gilbert, and possibly other children. A graduate by November 1513, Lauder may have studied abroad. He was certainly admitted burgess of Edinburgh before the end of 1517. In that year he also began appearing as an advocate before the lords of council and by the late 1520s his legal services were very heavily in demand. This continued until 1538, when he replaced Adam Otterburn as king's advocate. Earlier that year he had made a speech of welcome in French to Mary of Guise on her entry into Edinburgh and had also acted as deputy to the marischal in parliament. In January 1539 the king directed that Lauder be permitted to remain in the council chamber so that he could intervene in any case where the king's interest was affected. This was a temporary measure until Lauder could fill a vacancy on the bench, which he had done by March 1540. Lauder remained king's advocate, holding the office jointly from 1555 with John Spens of Condie, until he died on 19 July 1561.

Robert Leslie of Inverpeffer (*d*. 1536) was the son of Walter Leslie (*fl. c*.1480), parson of Menmuir and commissary of Dunkeld. His mother is unknown. Leslie married Christine Wardlaw and they had six children: Andrew, John, George, Gilbert, Elizabeth, and Janet. He also had a sister, Euphemia, who with his help became the last prioress of the Cistercian convent at Elcho in Perthshire. In return for his assistance Leslie received in feu-farm from the convent the lands of Kinnaird in Fife. Little is known of his education, though he may have been a determinant at the University of St Andrews in 1508. By 1518 he had become a burgess of Edinburgh, but it was in Fife and the north-east that his legal career took root. His major client in the area was, for over two decades, George Leslie, fourth earl of Rothes, to whom he may have been related through his father. By 1525 Leslie had acquired the estate of Inverpeffer in the sheriffdom of Forfar. A year later he was described as keeper of the signet, and in 1529 as custodian of the privy seal. Leslie last appeared before the lords of council on 31 July 1536. He was dead by 1 December that year. In 1540 James V had the corpse exhumed so that it could be tried for *lèse majesté*, alleging Leslie's involvement in a 1529 plot to kill the king. There is no evidence of any such involvement.

John Lethame (d. c.1549) was of unknown origins. He had obtained an arts degree, possibly by studying abroad, before October 1507, when he is described as a cleric of Glasgow diocese, and recorded in Edinburgh acting as a notary by apostolic authority. In April 1511 he was evidently studying at the University of Orléans, being then elected procurator of the Scots nation there. Lethame's career as an advocate began around 1514 and reached the peak of its success in the years immediately after 1532. In 1521 he acted as commissary of Lothian and may have retained that office throughout the 1520s. By 1527 he had become subdean of Trinity collegiate church near Edinburgh and he later became parson of Kirkchrist. In 1530 he is referred to as commissary of the Chapel Royal at Stirling and from that date there are references to him as commissary south of the Forth. Lethame became a lord of session, apparently sitting for the first time in that capacity on 10 December 1538, though there is no record of him taking the oath *de fideli administratione*. He resigned the parsonage of Kirkchrist on 17 April 1542 and died before 13 February 1549.

Thomas Marjoribankis of Ratho (d. c.1561) was originally from the diocese of Glasgow (or possibly from Dumfries), and was educated at the University of Orléans where he was procurator of the Scottish nation in 1517. He married Janet Purves before 1523 and they had four sons, John, Thomas, Robert, and James; Marjoribankis also had a natural daughter, Janet. His name does not appear in the Edinburgh burgess roll until 1538, even though he obtained the status of burgess by right of his wife. The timing may be explained by the fact that in 1538 he also acted as a burgh assessor. Marjoribankis's career as an advocate progressed during the 1520s and reached its peak in the 1530s. In 1535 he and John Gladstanes were appointed advocates for the poor; the following year he acted as clerk to the king's treasurer. Two years later he produced a letter from the king before the lords which granted actions involving advocates the same privileged status in court procedure as those concerning judges. A creditor to Cardinal Beaton and his relatives, Marjoribankis had trading connections with France; in 1545 he was 'custumar' of Inverness and in the following year he was granted the privilege of exempting his merchandise from royal customs. In 1549 he was appointed lord clerk register and also purchased a share in a three-year lease of the mint. Marjoribankis purchased part of the estate of Ratho in Lothian in 1538. He became secured creditor in the rest of the estate in 1540 and eventually became infeft as owner, his title surviving legal challenge in 1547. Although dismissed as clerk register in 1554 and replaced by James MacGill, Thomas Marjoribankis does not appear to have died until about 1561, when he was succeeded by his grandson, Thomas.

Henry Spittall (d. 1536) appears to have been the son of James Spittall (fl. c.1490), of Blairlogy in Perthshire; his mother is unknown. Hector Boece describes him as a relative of William Elphinstone, bishop of Aberdeen, but the degree of relationship is not known. Spittall is first recorded attending the commissary court in Aberdeen in January 1508, several months before he became a student at the University of Orléans. He returned to Aberdeen, becoming canonist at the university in 1512 and rector of Snow Kirk. Spittall married Margaret Bothwell, an event which in February 1517 allowed him to be admitted as a burgess of Edinburgh, and in 1525 he became a bailie of the burgh. Spittall later married, as his second wife, Elizabeth Forbes. Following his first marriage he maintained links with Aberdeen, becoming in 1518 clerk of the coquet of that burgh. By then he was also a notary by apostolic authority. From 1516 until his death he remained one of the busiest advocates in the realm, with numerous clients particularly in Fife and the north-east. He died without legitimate children in 1536, when he was succeeded by his nephew, Alexander Spittall. A natural son, James, was legitimated in 1558.

The surviving evidence for the careers of these eight advocates indicates that the highest rank of the nascent legal profession in Scotland was comparable in standard to similar professions elsewhere. At the foundation of the college of justice, the judges made a restatement of the ethical and professional standards expected of advocates, and there is some evidence during the following decade of the development of corporate identity among the leading advocates. It is also apparent that their practice could be a source of considerable personal profit. Although there is much that remains obscure about the origin of the Faculty of Advocates, there can be no doubt that its early development was greatly advanced by the events of 1532, and by the distinguished careers of nearly all the men appointed in that year.

JOHN FINLAY

Sources MS acts of the lords of council, NA Scot., C.S. 5, C.S. 6, C.S. 7 · register of deeds, NA Scot., RD 1 · R. K. Hannay, ed., *Acts of the lords of council in public affairs, 1501–1554* (1932) · J. M. Thomson and others, eds., *Registrum magni sigilli regum Scotorum / The register of the great seal of Scotland*, 11 vols. (1882–1914), vols. 2–4 · M. Livingstone, D. Hay Fleming, and others, eds., *Registrum secreti sigilli regum Scotorum / The register of the privy seal of Scotland*, 8 vols. (1908–82) · C. B. B. Watson, ed., *Roll of Edinburgh burgesses and guild-brethren, 1406–1700*, Scottish RS, 59 (1929) · J. Finlay, 'Professional men of law before the lords of council, c.1500–c.1550', PhD diss., U. Edin., 1997 · J. Kirkpatrick, 'The Scottish nation in the University of Orleans, 1336–1538', *Miscellany … II*, 44 (1904), 45–102 · A. I. Dunlop, ed., *Acta facultatis artium universitatis Sanctiandree, 1413–1588*, 2, Scottish History Society, 3rd ser., 55 (1964) · J. M. Anderson, ed., *Early records of the University of St Andrews*, Scottish History Society, 3rd ser., 44 (1904) · C. Samaran and A. A. van Moe, eds., *Auctarium chartularii universitatis Parisiensis*, 3 (Paris, 1935) · G. Brunton and D. Haig, *An historical account of the senators of the college of justice, from its institution in MDXXXII* (1832) · F. J. Grant, ed., *The Faculty of Advocates in Scotland, 1532–1943*, Scottish RS, 145 (1944) · R. K. Hannay, *The college of justice* (1933); repr. Stair Society, suppl. ser., 1 (1990)

Collen, Sir Edwin Henry Hayter (1843–1911), army officer, was born on 17 June 1843 at Somerset Street, London, the son of Henry Collen (b. 1798), miniature painter, of Holywell Hill, St Albans, and his wife, Helen Dyson. Educated at University College School, London, Collen passed to the Royal Military Academy, Woolwich, and became lieutenant, Royal Artillery, on 1 July 1863. He first served in the Abyssinian expedition (1867–8). After passing through the Staff College at Camberley in 1871–2, with honours, he was transferred to the Indian army in 1873. In the same year he married Blanche Marie Frederika, daughter of Charles Rigby JP, of Soldiers' Point, Anglesey.

Collen was promoted captain on 1 July 1875. His efficiency as secretary of the Indian ordnance commission of 1874 led to his entering in 1876 the military department of the government of India as assistant secretary. Newly appointed, in June 1876 he submitted at Simla a memorandum proposing the formation of an intelligence branch in the quartermaster-general's department, modelled on that in Britain. Both the Indian commander-in-chief, Sir Frederick Haines, and his quartermaster-general, Roberts—who wrote that Collen's memorandum was 'singularly able' (Fergusson, 73)—generally agreed with Collen's proposal, and so for a year (1877–8) he was attached to the intelligence branch at the War Office to study and report on it. His lengthy report (October 1878) described the British branch, and asserted the benefits of an Indian intelligence branch, based on the British model but adapted to Indian requirements. Collen's memorandum and report were instrumental in the establishment of the Indian military intelligence branch. Moreover his report later became an important historical source—'a detailed and invaluable inside view of the Intelligence Branch at the War Office during the late 1870s' (Fergusson, 59).

Collen acted as deputy assistant quartermaster-general at the Delhi durbar of 1 January 1877. In 1878 he was appointed secretary of the Indian army organization commission. His administrative talents were recognized in 1800, in the later phases of the Second Anglo-Afghan War, when as assistant controller-general he was mainly responsible for the relatively smooth and efficient working of the supply and transport system.

Collen's routine work was interrupted by a short spell of active service. Promoted major on 1 July 1883, he joined the eastern Sudan expedition of 1885, and served with distinction in the intelligence department and as assistant military secretary to Major-General Sir Gerald Graham VC. He served at Tamai (2 April 1885) and Thukul (5 May), was mentioned in dispatches, and received the brevet of lieutenant-colonel (15 June 1885).

On his return to India, Collen was appointed in 1886 accountant-general, and in 1887 military secretary to the government of India, serving an exceptional nine years in the post. On 15 June 1889 he became full colonel, and in April 1896 military member of the executive council. During his administration many improvements were made in the composition of commands and regiments, in military equipment, and in mobilization. The defects in army administration revealed by the Second South African War (1899–1902) gave fresh impetus to Collen's activities, but desirable reforms had to be postponed due to financial constraints. In the debate on the budget in the legislative council on 27 March 1901 Collen summarized the army improvements. The Indian army was being rearmed with the latest weapons, the building of factories for the manufacture of war material had already been begun at Wellington, Kirkee, and Jubbulpore, a scheme for decentralization had been drawn up, and a remount commission had been established. Fresh drafts of officers were added to the Indian army and staff corps, and the supply and transport corps were reorganized. Lord Curzon, viceroy from 1899 to 1905, considered Collen inadequate as military member—'mentally composed of India-rubber' (Gilmour, 192)—and his department inefficient. Nevertheless publicly he stated that Collen 'had left an enduring mark on the personnel, the organisation and the equipment of the Indian army' (Curzon, 2.265). Like other Indian army officers, Collen opposed the appointment of Kitchener as commander-in-chief in India, claiming he lacked Indian experience, and would offend people and turn everything upside down. However, reforms inaugurated by Collen were continued by Kitchener.

Collen was promoted major-general on 18 January 1900 and lieutenant-general on 3 April 1905. He was made CIE in 1889, CB in 1897, and KCIE in 1893. He was made GCIE on his retirement in April 1901, and in May of that year represented India at the opening of the first parliament of the Australian commonwealth. He served on the War Office regulations committee from 1901 to 1904, and as chairman of the Staff College committee of 1904. When the controversy between Curzon and Kitchener on army administration broke out in 1905, Collen actively supported Curzon's views on keeping a military member on the council. A zealous member of the British Empire League, the National Service League, and the Essex Territorial Association, he was a frequent speaker and contributor to the press on military subjects, and published books on the British and Indian armies. He died on 10 July 1911, at his residence, The Cedars, Kelvedon, Essex. He was survived by his wife, three sons, and a daughter.

G. S. WOODS, rev. JAMES LUNT

Sources *The Times* (12 July 1911) • L. Fraser, *India under Curzon and after* (1911) • T. G. Fergusson, *British military intelligence, 1870–1914* (1984) • G. N. Curzon, *Speeches of Lord Curzon*, 2 vols. (1900–02) • D. Dilks, *Curzon in India*, 2 (1970) • Lord Roberts [F. S. Roberts], *Forty-one years in India*, 2 (1897) • P. Magnus, *Kitchener: portrait of an imperialist* (1958) • B. Robson, *The road to Kabul: the Second Afghan War, 1878–1881* (1986) • B. Robson, *Fuzzy-wuzzy: the campaigns in the eastern Sudan, 1884–85* (1993) • T. A. Heathcote, *The military in British India: the development of British land forces in south Asia, 1600–1947* (1995) • D. Gilmour, *Curzon* (1994) • Boase, *Mod. Eng. biog.* • Burke, *Peerage* (1907) • D. Foskett, *Miniatures: dictionary and guide* (1987) • *WWW, 1897–1915* • *CGPLA Eng. & Wales* (1911)

Wealth at death £6422 17s. 5d.: probate, 2 Dec 1911, *CGPLA Eng. & Wales*

Colles, Abraham (1773–1843), surgeon, was born on 23 August 1773 at Milmount, near Kilkenny, Ireland, the second son of William Colles (1745–1779), a quarry owner, and Mary Anne (d. 1840), daughter of Abraham Bates, of co. Wexford. At some point during the time of his education, in Kilkenny grammar school, a flood swept away part of the house of a local physician, Dr Butler, and carried a work on anatomy into a field near Colles's home. The boy picked it up and returned it to the doctor, who then gave him the book, and this, it is said, led to Colles's choice of medicine as a profession. He entered Trinity College, Dublin, in September 1790, and eleven days later was apprenticed to Philip Woodroffe, resident surgeon in Dr Steevens' Hospital. In spite of showing early literary promise he refused to give up medicine, even though Edmund Burke, a family acquaintance, recommended that Colles publish his writings entitled 'Remarks on the condition of political satire'. When Colles's uncle talked of the name he was sacrificing, the youth replied: 'A name, sir! Yes, as an author, and then not a dowager in Dublin would call me in to cure a sore throat' (Fallon, 30).

Having graduated BA in February 1795, and obtained the diploma of the Royal College of Surgeons in Ireland in the same year, Colles studied at Edinburgh for two sessions, and graduated MD in 1797 with a thesis, 'De venaesectione'. He next went to London, where he stayed for some time, assisting Astley Cooper in the dissections for his work on hernia, and attending the London hospitals. In 1797 Colles returned to Dublin with little means and no connections to assist him. At first he practised medicine and was appointed visiting physician to the Meath Dispensary. He also became an active district visitor for the Sick and Indigent Roomkeepers' Society, a charitable gesture that brought him to the attention of a number of members of his profession. In 1799 he gave up being a physician on receiving the appointment of resident surgeon to Dr Steevens' Hospital. This he held until 1813, when he became visiting surgeon to the same hospital.

Colles quickly became a masterly surgeon, being cool, dexterous, and resourceful. A number of his operations were significant advances. When he first tied the subclavian artery for aneurysm, the operation had been attempted only twice in England, and never in Ireland. He was the first man in Europe successfully to tie the innominate artery. In his *Treatise on Surgical Anatomy* (1811) he discussed the forms of hernia and various important surgical operations in a manner which showed his deep and accurate study developed over many years of daily dissections. His name is, however, best-known in connection with the Colles fracture of the radius, a common fracture just above the wrist and usually the result of a fall on the palm of the hand; despite its frequency this had escaped the notice of previous surgeons. His paper on the subject appeared in the *Edinburgh Medical and Surgical Journal*, in 1814.

Colles was also influential in introducing new principles for the use of mercury in the cure of syphilis, replacing the high dosages, which practitioners following John Hunter's example used, with a more cautious approach that helped to revive the flagging reputation of the treatment among surgeons. Through this Colles came into a long conflict with Richard Carmichael, a fellow Irish surgeon, whose experience in the Peninsular War had made him cynical about the effectiveness of mercury.

As surgeon of Dr Steevens' Hospital, Colles had quickly begun clinical and surgical teaching. In 1802 he failed to win the chair of anatomy and surgery at Trinity College.

He then unsuccessfully challenged the election in law, and never after had anything to do with that institution. He immediately became active in the Medico-Chirurgical Society, and was soon its president, and in the following year he was appointed surgeon to Cork Street Fever Hospital. In 1804, however, he became professor of anatomy and surgery in the Royal College of Surgeons in Ireland, an office he held for thirty-two years.

Colles's ability as a lecturer greatly extended the reputation of the college and of the Dublin medical school, with the number of students rising from 60 on his arrival to about 1000 by 1836. On his retirement the Royal College of Surgeons in Ireland voted on an address stating that he 'had been the principal cause of the success and consequent high character of the school of surgery in this country' (McDonnell, 2). In his lectures Colles was always careful to prevent the influence of preconceived theories on his own and his pupils' judgement. His lectures were published in 1844 in the *Dublin Medical Press*, and separately in two volumes, from notes by Simon McCoy; for many years they were among the most easily comprehended and practical extant.

Colles's practice, both as physician and surgeon, was very remunerative, for many years exceeding £5000 per annum. He remained surgeon to Dr Steevens' Hospital until 1841. He was twice president of the Royal College of Surgeons in Ireland, in 1802 at only twenty-eight years old, and again in 1830, and he was offered a baronetcy in 1839, but declined it. In 1807 he married Sophia, daughter of the Revd Jonathan Cope, rector of Ahascragh; they had a large family. In the same year he took a house in St Stephen's Green, Dublin, and he lived in the same square for the rest of his life. Colles died on 16 November 1843 and was buried in Mount Jerome cemetery. A son, William Colles, became regius professor of surgery in Dublin University and was also president of the Royal College of Surgeons in Ireland in 1863–4.

Though somewhat lacking in imagination, Colles had great perspicuity and possessed the skill of recognizing the salient points of any matter. Cautious in criticism, he expressed simple ideas in clear language. He was cheerful, generous, and modest, a liberal in politics, and a protestant in religion, despising fanaticism and charlatanism. He was never shy of frankly admitting his mistakes. On one occasion at a post-mortem examination of a patient on whom he had operated for stricture of the rectum, he turned to the class and said, 'Gentlemen, it is no use mincing the matter; I caused the patient's death' (McDonnell, 15). Colles was of medium build, well-proportioned, and of dignified manner, with a shrewd, clear eye, a fine forehead, and a decided mouth.

G. T. BETTANY, rev. PATRICK WALLIS

Sources R. McDonnell, 'Memoir of Abraham Colles', *Selection from the works of Abraham Colles*, ed. R. McDonnell (1881) · T. P. C. Kirkpatrick, *The history of Doctor Steevens' Hospital, Dublin, 1720–1920* (1924) · M. Fallon, *Abraham Colles, 1773–1843: surgeon of Ireland* (1972) · W. Stokes, *Work done in surgery by its professors in the Royal College of Surgeons in Ireland* (1887) · C. A. Cameron, *History of the Royal College of Surgeons in Ireland* (1886) · *Nomina eorum, qui gradum medicinae doctoris in academia Jacobi sexti Scotorum regis, quae Edinburgi est,* *adepti sunt, ab anno 1705 ad annum 1845*, University of Edinburgh (1846)

Likenesses T. Kirk, sculpture, exh. 1837, Royal College of Surgeons, Dublin · M. Cregan, oils, 1838, Steevens' Hospital, Dublin · D. Lucas, line, stipple and mezzotint, pubd 1850 (after M. Cregan, 1838), NG Ire.

Colles, Henry Cope (1879–1943), music historian and critic, was born at Bridgnorth, Shropshire, on 20 April 1879, the third child and elder son of Abraham Colles MD FRCS (and thus the great-grandson of Abraham *Colles), and his wife, Emily Agnes Georgina, daughter of Major Alexander R. Dallas, and granddaughter of A. R. C. Dallas. He was educated privately and at the Royal College of Music (1895–9) where he studied music history under Sir Hubert Parry, the organ under Walter Alcock, and counterpoint under Walford Davies. In 1899 he became organ scholar at Worcester College, Oxford, where he attracted the attention of Henry Hadow, then dean of the college, whose lectures and writings were to have an important influence in shaping Colles's future career and critical thought.

At Oxford, Colles obtained the degree of BA in 1903 and the additional degree of BMus in 1904, and in 1932 the university awarded him an honorary degree of DMus; he was elected honorary fellow of Worcester in 1936. After leaving Oxford he studied at the Temple Church, London, with Walford Davies, a lifelong friend whose biography he wrote in 1942. As a writer he often stressed the value and importance of English church music and as a practical musician he gave strong support to the School of English Church Music founded by his friend Sir Sydney Nicholson, to the Church Music Society, and to St Michael's College, Tenbury, Worcestershire.

In 1905, at the instigation of Hadow, Colles began his career as a writer, contributing a weekly article on music to *The Academy* at the request of H. H. Child. These articles were dominated by discussion of Brahms and Richard Strauss. Colles took Hadow's view that Brahms, in restoring the classical traditions, pointed a way forward that had been eclipsed through the huge expansion of orchestral resources in the late Romantic period. His articles in the more specialist music press were primarily of musicological interest, and many of them dealt with English music from Byrd to Elgar. In 1906 he married Hester Janet (*d.* 1952), daughter of Thomas Matheson, a member of Lloyds. Also in 1906 he began work at *The Times*, becoming assistant to J. A. Fuller-Maitland, whom he succeeded as musical editor in 1911; he retained this post until his death. On his appointment as musical editor he at once inaugurated and maintained the weekly articles on music—for the most part written by himself, although necessarily anonymous—which attracted wide attention both in Britain and abroad. In appraising contemporary music Colles continued along similarly conservative lines as his predecessor, dismissing the work of many leading composers including Stravinsky and Schoenberg.

During the First World War Colles served in Macedonia as a captain in the Royal Artillery, receiving the Greek cross in 1918. On his return he was invited, in 1919, by Hugh Allen to join the staff of the Royal College of Music as lecturer in music history and analysis. In 1923 he accepted an invitation from the *New York Times* to act as guest music critic, remaining in America for some months. In 1927 he was Cramb lecturer at Glasgow University, taking for his subject the interdependence of the English language and English musical genius, especially as exemplified in Purcell. The substance of these lectures was reproduced in his *Voice and Verse* (1928). He lectured also at Liverpool University, the Royal Institution, and elsewhere.

In 1927 appeared the third and revised edition of *Grove's Dictionary of Music and Musicians*, the editorship of which had been entrusted to Colles some years before. It was an extensive revision for which his scholarship eminently qualified him. He was also responsible for a further revision and a supplementary volume in 1940 and this, along with the seventh volume of the *Oxford History of Music*, entitled *Symphony and Drama, 1850–1900* (1934), must be counted as his most substantial and enduring work. His most popular work, *The Growth of Music* (1912–16), a study of music history designed for use in schools, continued the evolutionary method of documenting music history that characterized the work of Parry. His other works include *The Chamber Music of Brahms* (1933) and *On Learning Music, and other Essays* (1940). A collection of his shorter writings was edited by his wife, with a short memoir, and published as *Essays and Lectures* (1945). Colles died at his home in London, 91 Swan Court, Chelsea, on 4 March 1943.

IVOR ATKINS, rev. NIGEL SCAIFE

Sources *New Grove* · H. J. Colles, 'H. C. C.: a memoir', in H. C. Colles, *Essays and lectures* (1945) · *The Times* (6 March 1943) · *TLS* (13 March 1943) · *Music Review*, 4 (1943) · F. Howes, 'Henry Cope Colles—a tribute', *MT*, 84 (1943), 109–10 · A. Fox-Strangways, 'H. C. Colles', *Music and Letters*, 24 (1943), 131–2 · *CGPLA Eng. & Wales* (1943)

Archives BL, corresp. with Macmillans, Add. MSS 55237–55238

Likenesses C. Dodgson, chalk drawing; formerly priv. coll. · photograph in music score, Royal College of Music, London

Wealth at death £2771 1s. 2d.: probate, 24 Dec 1943, *CGPLA Eng. & Wales*

Collet, Clara Elizabeth (1860–1948), civil servant and promoter of women's education and employment, was born at Sunny Bank, Hornsey Lane, Islington, London, on 10 September 1860, the second daughter and fourth child of Collet Dobson *Collet (1812–1898), a prominent champion of press freedom and editor of *The Free Press* (later the *Diplomatic Review*), and his wife, Jane, *née* Sloan, who ran a laundry in north London. The surname Collet was one which Clara's father and her aunt, Sophia Dobson *Collet, an authority on Brahmo Samaj, had added to their given surname Dobson, as an inheritance from their grandmothers. The family tradition was unitarian and radical, and Clara's father was closely associated with Karl Marx; in childhood Clara was very friendly with the Marx family (especially Eleanor Marx), though in adult life she was unimpressed by Marx's philosophy.

Clara Collet was educated at the North London Collegiate School for Girls from 1873 to 1878, when she was persuaded by the headmistress, Frances Buss, to take up a teaching post at Wyggeston Girls' School, Leicester, where she worked from 1878 to 1885. While there she read for her first degree, and followed this by enrolling at University College, London, where she took an MA in mental and moral science (possibly the first woman to do so); she won the Joseph Hume scholarship in political economy in 1886, and completed her course in 1888. Her tutor was the economist H. S. Foxwell, whose friend and partisan she quickly became. She also acquired a deserved reputation as a statistician and an economist.

In 1891 Collet began a long and distinguished career in government service, with her appointment as assistant commissioner to the royal commission on labour. From 1888 to 1892 she also collaborated with Charles Booth on his classic sociological study, *The Life and Labour of the People of London*. This fitted in well with her statistical and sociological background and inclinations. Her published contributions to the text were her essays on women's work in the East End of London, and on secondary education for girls, reflecting her lifelong concerns with women's education and employment. In 1893 she was appointed labour correspondent to the Board of Trade. She made reports to the royal commission on secondary education in 1894, and to parliament on the wages of domestic servants in 1899. In 1903 she became senior investigator (for women's industries) at the Board of Trade, and from 1909 she attended meetings chaired by the president of the Board of Trade (then Winston Churchill). Her initial enthusiasm for working in close contact with leading politicians rapidly led to frustration, to the extent that she threatened resignation in 1910 over the treatment of women in labour exchanges. Despite this she remained at the Board of Trade and in 1920 was appointed a member of the trade boards, a position which she held until 1932.

In addition to her government employments, Collet held various posts concerned with women's education, most notably as president of the Association of Assistant Mistresses in Secondary Schools, in 1891, and as a governor of Bedford College, London, from 1902 until her death in 1948. She was also a member of the council of the Royal Statistical Society from 1919 to 1935, and a member of the council of the Royal Economic Society from 1920 to 1941, as well as being an active member of the Fabian Society, and of the Charity Organization Society.

Collet published a number of articles on the situation of working women, some of which she collected and published together in three highly influential books: *The Economic Position of Educated Working Women* (1890), *Educated Working Women* (1902), and *Women in Industry* (1911). In addition she provided statistics for the inquiries of the British Association for the Advancement of Science into women's employment in 1900. She was probably the first British promoter of women's employment to base her arguments on a foundation of statistical evidence and systematic interviewing. In this she found herself able to challenge the pronouncements of such established economists as Alfred Marshall and, ironically, she appears to have influenced his wife, the equally eminent economist Mary Paley Marshall.

In 1893 Collet became a friend of the novelist George Gissing, on whose works she had already lectured publicly. A long and vigorous correspondence with him rapidly developed into a close friendship, in which she acted as his confidante as well as helping him financially when she was able. After his death in 1903, as a trustee of his estate she continued to take an active interest in his sons and remained a friend of Gabrielle Fleury, his common-law wife at the time of his death.

Collet had a considerable interest in her family history, and in her later years she devoted considerable time to this, lecturing in India on Joseph Collet, a former governor of the Madras presidency, whose notebooks she finally prevailed upon Longmans to publish (with her annotations), in 1933.

Collet was short and dark-haired. Although not from a poor background, she had to work to support herself, and her earnings and consequent savings were her only guarantee of financial security and independence. Her manner appears to have been decisive and authoritative; and her nephew Robert Collet recalled that she always had to be right about everything, and she usually was (Tindall, 171). She appears to have dominated her family in her latter years, and after a mastectomy in 1936 she moved them all from Hampstead in London to Sidmouth, Devon. Clara Collet died at her home, Clifton, Cliff Road, Salcombe Regis, Sidmouth, Devon, on 3 August 1948.

DAVID DOUGHAN

Sources *The Times* (5 Aug 1948) · *WWW* · J. Miller, 'An odd woman', *Seductions: studies in reading and culture* (1990), 70–107 · G. Tindall, *The born exile: George Gissing* (1974) · M. A. Dimand, R. W. Dimand, and E. L. Forget, *Women of value: feminist essays on the history of women in economics* (1995) · private information (2004) · C. Barwell, 'Collet, Clara (Elizabeth)', *The Europa biographical dictionary of British women*, ed. A. Crawford and others (1983) · *CGPLA Eng. & Wales* (1949) · b. cert. · d. cert.
Archives U. Warwick Mod. RC, corresp. and papers | BLPES, letters to James Bonar relating to the formation of the British Economic Association
Likenesses photograph, repro. in Tindall, *Born exile*; priv. coll. · photographs, priv. coll.
Wealth at death £7768 3s. 3d.: administration, 24 Jan 1949, *CGPLA Eng. & Wales*

Collet, Collet Dobson (1812–1898), radical and tax reformer, was born on 31 December 1812 in London. He was the eldest son of John Dobson (1778–1827), a London merchant, and his wife (and first cousin), Elizabeth Barker (1787–1875). Collet assumed the name of his maternal grandparents, as did his sister, Sophia Dobson *Collet. He was educated at Bruce Castle School, north London, and then studied law at University College, London, where he took third prize in the subject in 1833. Lacking the independent means that would have enabled him to study at the bar, Collet instead pursued musical studies at the Royal Academy of Music, and was a member of the choir at Drury Lane, under William Macready, and then at the Royal Opera House in Covent Garden. In 1841 he was appointed director of the choir at South Place Chapel, Finsbury Square, then under the ministry of W. J. Fox.

At South Place, Collet began his lifelong association

Collet Dobson
Collet (1812–1898),
by unknown
photographer

with the milieu of Finsbury radicalism. In February 1848 he went to Paris with W. J. Linton and other members of the Democratic Committee of Observation of the French Revolution in order to congratulate the French on the overthrow of Louis-Philippe and the declaration of the republic. Back in London in April 1848, Collet joined with other Finsbury radicals in the People's Charter Union (PCU), the main purpose of which was to oppose Feargus O'Connor's leadership of the Chartist movement. In February 1851 the PCU evolved into the Association for Promoting the Repeal of the Taxes on Knowledge (APRTK), and Collet became its secretary.

Supported in parliament by Thomas Milner Gibson and Richard Cobden, the association spearheaded the campaign to repeal those remaining indirect taxes which affected the newspapers—not only the newspaper stamp itself, but also the advertisement and paper duties. The association also campaigned against the security system, which in order to discourage libel and blasphemy required that newspapers be registered so as to make proof of liability easier. Collet and, to a lesser extent, Richard Moore, undertook virtually all of the organization of the association themselves. Collet gave evidence to the select committee on the newspaper stamp in 1851, and during 1853–4 deliberately tested the limits of the law by publishing (along with G. J. Holyoake) unstamped papers that carried news. The duty on advertisements in newspapers was abolished in 1853 and the stamp duty in 1855. In 1854 Collet married Mrs Jane Marshall, née Sloan, widow of a Dunfermline newspaper proprietor.

During the Crimean War, much to his colleagues' surprise, Collet became associated with David Urquhart, the Russophobe and vehement enemy of Lord Palmerston. Collet joined with Urquhart in the Turkish Association, and then in August 1855, when the Urquhartite *Free Press* moved from Sheffield to London, he became its editor (and, when it became the *Diplomatic Review*, its publisher as well), a connection he retained for over twenty years. Collet also became Urquhart's unofficial secretary, dealing with the correspondence and the organization of the self-styled working men's foreign affairs committees which were established between the mid-1850s and early 1860s. Collet's work with the *Diplomatic Review* brought him into contact with Karl Marx, and during the 1860s and 1870s the two men's families became friendly with one another.

When the *Diplomatic Review* folded in 1877, Collet found another outlet for his considerable propagandist energies. In October 1877 he became secretary of the Travelling Tax Abolition Committee, which was set up to press for the repeal of the railway (and tramway) passenger duty—a repeal which had been recommended by a parliamentary select committee in 1876. The publicity that the committee gave to the issue undoubtedly contributed to the partial repeal of the duty in 1883.

Collet's journalism spanned some forty years, and a handful of newspapers and reviews. As well as publishing the *Potteries Free Press*, and editing the *Diplomatic Review* and the APRTK's *Gazette*, and the Travelling Tax Abolition Committee's *Gazette*, he also contributed to G. J. Holyoake's *The Reasoner*, the *Industrial Review* (formerly *The Beehive*), the *Anglo-American Times*, and *Vanity Fair* (as Diplomaticus). He was a well-known music critic, and wrote for the *Musical World*. (He also sang in the annual Handel festival at the Crystal Palace until well into his eighties.) Collet wrote a number of pamphlets connected with the campaign to repeal the passenger duty, and towards the end of his life he wrote what remains a worthy account of the repeal of the newspaper taxes: *History of the Taxes on Knowledge* (2 vols., 1899).

Collet died three days short of his eighty-sixth birthday at 7 Coleridge Road, his home in Finsbury, on 28 December 1898; he was survived by his wife. Among their five children were Clara Elizabeth *Collet (1860–1948), the educationist, and Wilfred Collet (1856–1929), the colonial administrator, who was created KCMG in 1915.

MILES TAYLOR

Sources G. J. Holyoake, *Daily News* (30 Dec 1898), 3 · G. J. Holyoake, *History of the travelling tax* (1900) · C. E. Collett and H. H. Collett, eds., *The family of Collett*, 4 vols. (1935) · Boase, *Mod. Eng. biog.* · d. cert.
Archives Balliol Oxf., Urquhart bequest · Co-operative Union, Holyoake House, Manchester, Holyoake MSS, corresp. with Richard Cobden; corresp. with Karl Marx
Likenesses photograph, NPG [*see illus.*] · portrait, repro. in C. D. Collet, *History of the taxes on knowledge* (1899), frontispiece
Wealth at death £2181 12s. 11d.: probate, 24 March 1899, CGPLA Eng. & Wales

Collet, John (*c.*1725–1780), painter, was born in London, the son of a public office holder. He was a pupil of the landscape artist George Lambert, and also attended the St Martin's Lane Academy. His work was first exhibited in 1761 at the exhibition of the Free Society of Artists held in the Strand, in the form of three landscapes; in total forty-seven paintings by Collet would hang at the society's exhibitions between 1761 and 1783. The following year *A Gypsy Telling some Country Girls their Fortune* was submitted to the society, its title suggesting the direction in which Collet's style was developing, away from conventional landscapes towards humorous genre pieces. Frequent, if not always flattering, comparisons were drawn by contemporaries between Collet's work and that of William Hogarth, often citing a lack of moral guidance and instruction in the former's œuvre: in his *Anecdotes of Painters* Edward Edwards notes 'pieces of humour … less satirical than narrative, more ludicrous than witty, and oftentimes displeasing' (Edwards, 67). Similarly an anonymous critic at the Free Society's exhibition of 1767 surmises that

> The colouring of Hogarth is here greatly excelled, his humour agreeably kept up, and was this painter not to follow him in his debauched scenes, but to keep to innocence only, he would be surpassed by none of his contemporaries. (GM, 1767)

Despite the lack of moral instruction, Collet's work appears to have acquired an increasing popularity with the public and a number of publishers, including Robert Sayer and Carington Bowles, sold engravings after many of his paintings. A substantial selection of these prints can be found in the British Museum's collection of political and personal satires.

The habits and pretensions of the professional and middle classes were a popular subject for Collet's brush. Typical of this focus is *The Ladies' Disaster* (c.1771), engraved by James Caldwell, where the hat, cap, and wig of a fashionable young lady are blown into the arms of an amused onlooker. The often absurd intricacies of social etiquette were equally mocked by Collet in popular paintings such as *Grown Ladies Taught to Dance* and its companion piece *Grown Gentlemen Taught to Dance* (c.1768), both reproduced in mezzotint for Robert Sayer. The latter composition even found its way onto the stage, introduced as a sequence in a pantomime. Conversely the stage itself could prove a source of inspiration: in 1775 Collet produced a series of paintings based on several scenes, including *The Drinking Scene in the Convent*, from Richard Brinsley Sheridan's comedy *The Duenna*.

Collet's interest in social behaviour embraced not only the manners of the middle and upper classes; many of his paintings focus upon scenes of low life and debauchery set against London's urban sprawl. While producing paintings which illustrated the pleasures and pursuits of the capital's bourgeoisie, such as *Promenaders in St James's Park* (V&A), Collet appears to have been equally adept at picturing less refined activities. In *Covent Garden Piazza and Market* (c.1775; Museum of London) the elegant and imposing façades of the piazza contrast sharply with a bustling mélange of pickpockets, street musicians, hawkers, and traders. Finely drawn social distinctions, however, were often blurred to comic effect: in *May Morning* (c.1760; Museum of London) Collet presents a milkmaid sporting a silver-draped garland and a chimney-sweep parading in a gentleman's wig, such festivities and street customs temporarily challenging and reinterpreting the usual class structure.

In contrast to many of the personae within his paintings, Collet himself was considered to be 'a man of grave manners and conversation … [who] maintained a very respectable character', a respectability furthered by the inheritance of what contemporaries termed a 'fortune' from a relative (Edwards, 67). He appears to have remained a bachelor throughout his life. Formerly of Millman Street, Chelsea, London, he resided at Cheyne Row, Chelsea, where he died on 6 August 1780. His considerable estate was divided between the families of his two sisters, Philippa and Mary, and several close friends. He was buried at Chelsea on 11 August 1780.   HELEN PIERCE

Sources E. Edwards, *Anecdotes of painters* (1808); facs. edn (1970) · G. Paston, *Social caricature in the eighteenth century* (1905) · Redgrave, *Artists* · T. Wright, *A history of caricature and grotesque in literature and art* (1864) · *Somerset House gazette and literary museum*, 2 vols. (1824) · C. Fox, *Londoners* (1987) · M. D. George, *Hogarth to Cruickshank: social change in graphic satire* (1967) · Graves, *Artists* · *GM*, 1st ser., 37 (1767), 239 · *GM*, 1st ser., 50 (1780), 395 · F. G. Stephens and M. D. George, eds., *Catalogue of prints and drawings in the British Museum, division 1: political and personal satires*, 11 vols. in 12 (1870–1954) · will, PROB 11/1068, sig. 388

Wealth at death approx. £850; plus £100 p.a. for thirty years from Jan 1776 in annuities; also bequeathed furniture, jewellery, books, paintings, and prints: will, proved 11 Aug 1780, PRO, PROB 11/1068, sig. 388

Collet, Sir Mark Wilks, first baronet (1816–1905), merchant and banker, was born at Highbury Grove, Highbury, Middlesex, the second of three sons of James Collet, a native of the Isle of Man, and his wife, Wendelina Elizabeth van Brienen, of Dutch origin. His father died when Mark was young, and his mother initially moved to Douglas, Isle of Man, and subsequently to Archangel, Russia, where her family were merchants. Mark was educated in Archangel, where he learned both Russian and French; his first language, which he used with his mother, was German. In 1832 Wendelina returned to London, where she ran a boarding-house, and Mark became a clerk in Liverpool with Henry Patry & Co., a firm associated with the leading London merchant house of Thomas Wilson & Co. Collet was henceforth to devote his career to trade with the United States.

Collet claimed in 1833 that his main recreation was listening to sermons, and he was a deeply religious man throughout his life, who believed that subordination to an all-powerful and all-wise God gave strength to bear any problems. Certainly, he had his share of family responsibilities, for he supported both his mother and his two feckless and incompetent brothers. The consolations of religion also helped him in his own difficulties, for Thomas Wilson & Co. failed in the crash of 1837, when a number of merchant houses specializing in the Anglo-American trade failed. The business was taken over by Purton, Parker & Co., with whom Collet continued as a clerk, making two trips to the United States in 1840–42. The firm was not successful, and was dissolved in 1842. Although Collet would have preferred to remain with a merchant house, he reluctantly accepted a position as sub-manager of the Bank of Liverpool, at a salary of £500. He returned to his mercantile career in 1846 as a partner of J. W. Cater and Thomas Arnott, whose partnership in the existing Liverpool merchant house of J. W. Cater & Co. was dissolved and reconstituted as J. W. Cater, Collet & Co. in London and J. W. Cater & Co. in Liverpool. The capital of

£30,000 was supplied by Cater, who took a minimal role in the business, drawing interest and a small share of the profits. Arnott ran the business in Liverpool in return for a quarter of the profits and £750 a year; Collet was responsible for the business in London, for which he received a third of the profits and a salary of £1000 a year. Collet followed the pattern of many able men without capital, providing the expertise which allowed firms to continue despite the absence of capable family members in the next generation. The initial term of partnership was seven years, with the right to give notice after three or five years, an option which Collet used in 1851 when he was approached by another, more prestigious, American merchant house which urgently needed a new partner: Brown, Shipley & Co.

The business of Brown Shipley had been developed by the family of Alexander Brown (1764–1834), a Belfast linen merchant, who had emigrated to Baltimore in 1800, where he became a successful general merchant. One son, John, was sent to Philadelphia in 1818 to establish John A. Brown; another son, James, went to New York in 1825 to form Brown Brothers; and Alexander Brown & Sons continued in Baltimore. The eldest son, William (1784–1864), left for Liverpool in 1808, where he became a major merchant, above all in raw cotton, which was ordered from his father's agents in the American south. In 1825 William was joined by Joseph Shipley, an American who was agent in Liverpool for a Philadelphian merchant. He was crucial to the survival of the firm in the crisis of 1837, and the name of the firm was subsequently changed to Brown Shipley when he became a partner in Liverpool and the firms in the United States.

Increasingly, the focus of the business shifted from trade to finance, and away from Baltimore and Philadelphia to Brown Brothers in New York, and William devoted more time to politics. Shipley was responsible for most of the business, with the assistance of F. A. Hamilton, who had been the Browns' agent in New Orleans before he was offered a partnership in 1845. When Shipley retired and returned to America in 1850 it was crucial to recruit a new junior partner, and the choice fell on Collet, whose expertise in American trade finance was invaluable. With some hesitation, he accepted the offer of 26,000 shares to become a partner.

Collet was, like other major figures in the City of London, a meritocrat whose technical skills and business competence were crucial to the success of a family firm. Such men were sometimes kept in salaried positions and denied partnerships; in other cases, they became junior partners with a share in the profits, who were accorded less status. The relationship between family and non-family members was prone to tensions, and a careful negotiation of the competing dictates of a competitive market and dynastic ambitions was crucial for continued success. In the case of Collet and the Brown family, the relationship was threatened on two occasions in the 1860s, when Collet complained that he was exploited and slighted by the family.

William Brown died in 1864, and left his shares to his brother James in New York, who failed to increase the holdings of Collet and Hamilton, much to their annoyance. It was, Collet informed Hamilton, unreasonable that James 'should appropriate to his family the shares which have been held out to the Juniors for years as their future reward' (Collet to Hamilton, 15 Aug 1865, Collet MS U1287, C79/5). When Collet was offered additional shares, he angrily complained that they were inadequate recompense for his work, and was even more outraged by the demand that he cede power to James to dispose of shares and appoint his successors as senior partners by will. Collet was horrified that his and Hamilton's judgement should be ignored and their property controlled by an unknown nominee. 'If Mr Brown suspects you or me of any design in the event of his death to oust his family and to appropriate to ourselves the goodwill and style of the house, he grievously misjudges the men who have placed a confidence in him, which should have called forth some response of a similar feeling towards ourselves' (Collet to Hamilton, 8 April 1865, ibid.).

Brown responded by simply handing all the shares to his son. James Brown, it seemed to the aggrieved junior partners, 'wishes to legislate for eternity' with the result that he was threatening the survival of the firm through his 'foolish attempt to obtain advantages to the detriment of others in which he is not likely to succeed' (Hamilton to Collet, 7 and 10 April 1865, Collet MS U1287, C79/6). The tension resurfaced in 1868, when two issues collided. Collet was weary of his 'severe and incessant labour' and wished for some relief through the appointment of another partner, provided that it did not mean the renewal of a 'claim to an absolute hereditary proprietorship in the House' and the appointment of a senior partner over his head (Collet to Hamilton, 3 and 7 March 1868, ibid., C79/9). At the same time, James Brown was contemplating retirement and the withdrawal of his capital, or at most leaving it in the firm without bearing risks. Collet feared that the firm would decline to second-class status, and that the junior partners would be left to bear the risks and the work. 'If the family wish to maintain the House', he pointed out to Hamilton, 'they must assume the risks incident to doing so; certainly, it would not be fair nor just to ourselves if we tied ourselves to stay and keep our property in and liable, while they seriously reduced theirs' (Collet to Hamilton, 19 March 1868, ibid.). Although the immediate crisis passed, the problems of the 1860s exposed in a stark way the difficulties of reconciling the hereditary principle with the maintenance of a successful firm. The attempt to entrench family control alienated the junior partners, who were often the more competent members of the firm; the withdrawal of capital left non-family members to carry risks to an unacceptable extent.

Despite the slight to Collet's self-esteem, he became a leading figure in the establishment of the City after the main operation of Brown Shipley moved from Liverpool to London in 1863. He became a director of the Bank of England in 1866, and served until his death; he was governor in 1887–9 and was created baronet in 1888. He amassed a fortune of £248,500 by the end of 1876, with his house at 2 Sussex Square, London, and personal investments valued at £88,500; the balance was presumably in the firm. In 1878 he bought a small estate of 399 acres, St Clere, Kemsing, in Kent, for £50,000, and subsequently invested in a wide portfolio of English and American shares. Meanwhile, the firm was trapped in conservative ways, largely dependent on supplying credit to customers of Brown Brothers in New York, and the aged Collet was not the man to revive the firm. He pointed out, rather defensively, to Brown Brothers in 1899 that even J. P. Morgan had difficulties in finding a suitable partner in London and it was scarcely surprising that he had no more success (Kynaston, 190–91).

Eventually, the answer was found through dynastic ambitions which the Browns no doubt appreciated. On 23 July 1850 Collet had married, in Bury St Edmunds, Suffolk, Susanna Gertrude, the daughter of James Eyre, a Church of England priest. She died in 1851, leaving a daughter, Linda Susan Penelope, who married in 1870 Frederick William Norman, the son of Collet's fellow director of the Bank of England, Geoffrey Warde Norman. Frederick Norman was a director of Martin's Bank, and their son, Montagu Collet *Norman (Collet's grandson), spent some time at Martin's before joining Brown Shipley in 1894. He gained experience in the United States before he became a partner in 1900. Only in 1903, after service in the Second South African War, did he take an active role in the firm. Montagu Norman proved to be Collet's successor in business; Collet's heir to the landed estate was his son by his second marriage, on 8 May 1862, to Antonia Frederica, the daughter of Joseph Edlmann, merchant, of Chislehurst in Kent. Their only child, Mark Edlmann Collet, was born in 1864, but he took no interest in the City, and settled in the south of France with his invalid wife before moving to the Isle of Man. Collet died on 25 April 1905 at his London house, 2 Sussex Square, of bronchial pneumonia.

MARTIN DAUNTON

Sources CKS, Collet papers, U1287 · A. Ellis, *Heir of adventure: the story of Brown, Shipley & Co., merchant bankers* (privately printed, London, 1960) · J. R. Killick, 'Risk, specialization and profit in the mercantile sector of the nineteenth century cotton trade: Alexander Brown & Sons, 1820–80', *Business History*, 16 (1974), 1–16 · D. Kynaston, *The City of London*, 2 (1995) · J. C. Brown, *A hundred years of merchant banking: a history of Brown Brothers and Company, Brown Shipley and Company and the allied firms* (privately printed, New York, 1909) · R. C. K. Ensor, *England, 1870–1914* (1936) · d. cert.
Archives CKS, papers | Guildhall, London, Brown, Shipley & Co. MSS
Wealth at death £448,052 1s. 1d.: probate, 20 May 1905, CGPLA Eng. & Wales

Collet, Sophia Dobson (1822–1894), writer and campaigner for women's rights, was born Sophia Dobson on 1 February 1822 at Judd Place East in the parish of St Pancras, London, the fifth of the seven children of John Dobson (1778–1827), a merchant, and his wife (and first cousin), Elizabeth Barker (1787–1875), a teacher prior to her marriage. John and Elizabeth Dobson came from intellectually orientated dissenting families who moved within leading literary and political circles. At some point, probably in the early 1840s, Sophia and her brother Collet

[see Collet, Collet Dobson], to whom she was very close, changed their surnames to Collet. Their reasons for so doing remain unclear, but it was possibly connected to a wish to revive the family name of their Unitarian grandmothers. Certainly, Unitarianism remained an important guiding force in Sophia Collet's life. By the 1840s she had become intimate with the leading figures in the radical, feminist Unitarian set who revolved around the ministry of William Johnson Fox at South Place Chapel in Finsbury, London. Many of her transcriptions of Fox's sermons were later published in reforming journals, providing a vital record of his thought and work. She developed particularly close relationships with the musical composer Eliza Flower and her sister, the poet Sarah Flower Adams. In common with her brother Collet, she was a gifted musician who had a particular talent for composition. Her work (some of which was published by her friends the Novello family) included several hymns for South Place Chapel. Much of her musical work was indicative of the progressive tenor of her political beliefs, including as it did 'A Song for the People's Charter Union' and 'A Welcome for Elihu Burritt' (the American peace campaigner). A committed radical, Sophia Collet also contributed articles and reviews to many of the reforming publications of the day. She wrote frequently (often under the pseudonym Panthea) for journals such as *The Reasoner* and *The Movement* which were conducted by her close associate the secularist radical George Jacob Holyoake, whose political views she shared, though she differed with him on religious matters. She published, at her own expense, a well-received analysis of his life and work in 1855 entitled *George Jacob Holyoake and Modern Atheism*. During the 1840s she also moved in the literary reforming circles which were heavily influenced by the transcendentalism of Ralph Waldo Emerson, whom she met. Her association with transcendentalist circles continued throughout her life; she later published articles in the Boston journal *The Dial*, and she was a house guest of the novelist Louisa May Alcott and her family.

During the late 1860s Sophia Collet, whose family had connections with India, developed an enduring interest in the Brahmo Samaj, the Hindu reform movement. She published extensively on this subject, including the 1876 *Brahmo Year Book* (which Gladstone read annually at Christmas) and *Outlines and Episodes of Brahmic History* (1884). She was the author of the entry on the religious and social reformer Rammohun Roy in the *Encyclopaedia Britannica*. Her biography of Roy was completed anonymously by F. H. Stead and published posthumously in 1900.

During the 1880s Sophia Collet's views on the 'woman question', which had long been the subject of her journalism, began to develop into a more sustained contribution to the women's rights movement. She became closely involved in the campaign for social purity and was an active member of the Moral Reform Union. She was extremely close to the journalist William T. Stead, whose revelations concerning the extent of child prostitution so shocked Britain in 1885, and she provided considerable support to Stead and his family when he was imprisoned in Holloway later that year. Sophia Collet was also able to draw upon her Indian connections to help Josephine Butler in her campaign to repeal the Contagious Diseases Acts in India. Her positions on these issues severely strained her close relationship with her friend Richard Holt Hutton of *The Spectator* (to which paper she was also a frequent contributor).

In 1889 the *Fortnightly Review* published extensive lists of public figures who supported the petition for female suffrage—Sophia Dobson Collet's signature appeared prominently in the literature section. She proved to be an important inspiration to her niece Clara Elizabeth Collet (1860–1948), who achieved recognition as a civil servant and advocate for women's rights at the turn of the century. Throughout her life Sophia Collet maintained lively correspondences with many of the leading reformers of the day, including such figures as Francis Newman and Frances Power Cobbe (whose work to end vivisection she strongly supported). Despite her lifelong radicalism on social and political issues, her religious views became increasingly conformist as she grew older. She became closer to the Christian socialism of F. D. Maurice, probably from the late 1860s, and following pressure from her sister, appears finally to have been baptized in 1870. Personal associates remembered her for her sheer energy and her 'utmost amiability of disposition' (Garnett, 223). This vitality was in spite of a physical deformity and disabling illness against which she battled all her life. The extent of this disability is not easy to gauge. While some of her acquaintances perceived her to be severely constricted, this often appears to be more the result of a rather patronizing attitude than an accurate reflection of her physical capabilities. The evidence largely indicates that throughout her life, though often incapacitated, she attended such events as Chartist meetings and women's rights functions with little fuss or hesitation.

Sophia Dobson Collet died at her home, 135 Avenell Road, Highbury, London, on 27 March 1894 and was buried in Highgate cemetery. Her death prompted numerous (but ultimately unsuccessful) calls from both the Brahmo Samaj community in India and the British literary and reforming world for her biography to be written.

KATHRYN GLEADLE

Sources private information (2004) · R. Garnett and E. Garnett, *The life of W. J. Fox, public teacher and social reformer, 1786–1864* (1910) · M. D. Conway, *Autobiography: memories and experiences*, 2 (1904) · J. Miller, 'An odd woman', *Seductions: studies in reading and culture* (1990), 70–107 · letters to George Jacob Holyoake, National Co-operative Archive, Rochdale · D. Killingley, *Rammohun Royin Hindu and Christian tradition: the Teape lectures, 1990* (1993) · b. cert. · d. cert. · register, London, Mornington Church, 12 March 1870 [baptism]
Archives Co-operation Union, Holyoake House, Manchester, Co-operative Union archive, letters to and material relating to the life of G. J. Holyoake
Wealth at death £3665 4s. 11d.: probate, 28 April 1894, *CGPLA Eng. & Wales*

Colleton, John (1548–1635), Roman Catholic priest, was the son of Edmund Colleton or Collington (d. c.1576), gentleman, of Milverton, Somerset. In 1565 John Colleton entered Lincoln College, Oxford, but took no degree. He had grown up a protestant but converted to Catholicism about 1568 before leaving for the continent in the early 1570s. His family converted to Catholicism on Colleton's return to England. His father was arrested as a recusant soon afterwards and died in Gloucester prison about 1576.

In 1572 Colleton joined the Carthusian order at Louvain at the age of twenty-three or twenty-four. A speech impediment made him think that he wished to live a contemplative rather than an active religious life. However, after about a year he left the order because of his deteriorating health. The fact that he was a bad singer also seems to have influenced his decision to leave. The last of his six music teachers

> delivered my unaptness to the Prior in these tearmes, That he could teach a Cow to bellow in tune, as soone as me to sing in tune. Further, my state of body, and unaptness to sing was such, that two of the Senior Monks of the house, advised me to content my selfe with an other state of life, namely, to take Priesthood and go into *England*. (Colleton, *Just Defence*, 300)

Colleton arrived at the English College in Douai on 14 January 1576. He was ordained at Binche on 16 June and was sent to England on 19 July the same year, using the alias of Peters. In England he finally recovered his health. He worked as a missionary priest in several places until the arrival in England of the first Jesuits, Edmund Campion and Robert Persons. Colleton was arrested in the company of Campion at Lyford, Berkshire, on 17 July 1581. A few days later he was a prisoner in the Tower of London. On 31 July he was moved to the Marshalsea, thus escaping torture. On 20 November Colleton was tried together with nineteen other priests on the charge of having plotted, at Rome and Rheims, the murder of the queen and an invasion of England. As Colleton could prove that he had not been out of the country he was acquitted, but remained in prison until he was exiled on 15 January 1585, together with other leading missionary priests such as William Bishop and Thomas Worthington. Colleton then visited the English College, Rheims, and spent some time in Rome. At Rouen he met Persons, who apparently tried to dissuade him from entering the religious life because of his inclination to melancholy. Colleton lived abroad until 1587, when he returned to England, settling first in London and later in Kent.

From about 1600 Colleton became involved in the appellant or archpriest controversy (1598–1602), the virulent and bitter controversy between a group of Catholic secular priests, the appellants, and the English Jesuits, about the organization and control of the Catholic mission in England. Colleton sided with appellants such as John Mush, opposing the appointment in 1598 of Archpriest George Blackwell and the political influence of the Jesuits, especially Robert Persons. In their attempts to organize the English clergy Colleton and Mush became known as the more moderate or responsible appellants, though their opinions did not differ fundamentally from those of their party who chose to express themselves in an extremist manner. Though Colleton was never a prisoner at Wisbech Castle, he signed the appeal at Wisbech on 17 November 1600. In 1601 he was suspended by Blackwell, who deemed him and the appellant movement schismatic. In order to defend himself Colleton at this time published a learned contribution to the archpriest controversy, *A Just Defence of the Slandered Priestes* (1602), a theological work which was also intended to answer Persons's *A Just Apologie, or Defence of the Catholike Ecclesiastical Hierarchie* (1601). In 1603 Colleton signed the declaration of allegiance to Queen Elizabeth and the appeal to the pope. In 1604 he wrote *A Supplication to the King's most Excellent Majestie*, an anonymous petition to James I for the toleration of Catholics.

In 1608 Colleton was appointed archdeacon of London by Archpriest George Birket. Despite his protestations of political submission to the English sovereign and his repudiation of the pope's deposing power, Colleton refused to take the oath of allegiance. He was once more arrested, about 10 December 1609, and sent to the Clink prison. Apparently he was free to work in Sussex for a brief span in 1610 but subsequently spent several years in prison. From 1613 to 1618 he was in the Clink, Southwark, and from 1621 in the New prison. Although he was ordered to be banished he remained in prison until 5 April 1622 when he was released. When in 1623 William Bishop was consecrated the Roman Catholic bishop of Chalcedon and created the chapter Colleton was constituted the first dean and vicar-general for the eastern district. Because of his great age and declining health Colleton was assisted by George Fisher, alias Musket, the archdeacon of Surrey and Middlesex.

During the latter part of his life Colleton lived and worked as chaplain in the household of the recusant Sir William Roper of Well Hall in Eltham, Kent. He died at Eltham on 19 October 1635, the cause of his death unknown. He was buried the following day in the churchyard of Eltham parish. THEODOR HARMSEN

Sources G. Anstruther, *The seminary priests*, 1 (1969), 82–5 · T. F. Knox and others, eds., *The first and second diaries of the English College, Douay* (1878), 100, 105, 108, 204, 206 · J. Colleton, *A just defence of the slandered priestes* (1602); repr. (1976), 217 · [J. Colleton], *A supplication to the king's … majestie, wherein, severall reasons of state and religion are briefely touched* (1604); repr. (1975), 247 · PRO, SP 14/97 no. 95, 14/128 no. 100, 15/32 II, i; KB 9/656 pt. 1 no. 41 · Westm. DA, Old Brotherhood papers, MSS OB 1.26, OB 1.114 · Westm. DA, MSS AAW, A Series, vol. 9, no. 78 · parish register (burial), Eltham, Kent, 20 October 1635 · A. F. Allison and D. M. Rogers, eds., *The contemporary printed literature of the English Counter-Reformation between 1558 and 1640*, 2 (1994) · T. G. Law, ed., *A historical sketch of the conflicts between Jesuits and seculars in the reign of Queen Elizabeth* (1889), lvi–lvii, cxii, cxli–cxliii · *Dodd's Church history of England*, ed. M. A. Tierney, 5 vols. (1839–43), vol. 3, pp. 133, 144–5 · *APC*, 1581–2, 147, 184, 349 · J. Sergeant, *An account of the chapter erected by William, titular bishop of Chalcedon*, ed. W. Turnbull (1853) · *The memoirs of Gregorio Panzani*, ed. and trans. J. Berington (1793); repr. (1970), 53, 59, 72, 92, 104 · T. H. B. M. Harmsen, *John Gee's Foot out of the snare* (1624) (1992) · G. McGregor, 'The Roman Catholic church of St. Mary', *The story of royal Eltham*, ed. R. R. C. Gregory (1909), chap. 73 · A. Pritchard, *Catholic loyalism in Elizabethan England* (1979), 141–2, 156–7 · P. Milward, *Religious controversies of the Elizabethan age* (1977), 116–24 · Wood, *Ath. Oxon.*, new edn, 2.596 · Gillow, *Lit. biog. hist.*, 1.538 · Foster, *Alum. Oxon.* · C. Dodd [H. Tootell], *The church history of England, from the year 1500, to the year 1688*, 3 vols. (1737–42), vol. 2, p. 507; vol. 3, p. 83 · R. Simpson, *Edmund Campion* (1867)

Archives BL, MSS, Add. MS 22052, fol. 30 | Archivio Vaticano, Vatican City, Borghese Archives, appeal to the pope, MS Borghese I, 594, fol. 184; MS Borghese II, 448, fol. 388 · BL, corresp. with pope, Add. MSS 15389, fol. 90; 24204, fol. 25 · Bodl. Oxf., Wood MS, D. 7 (2), fol. 22

Collett, Sir Henry (1836–1901), army officer in the East India Company and botanist, was born on 6 March 1836 at Thetford, Norfolk, the fourth son of the Revd William Collett (1796–1865), perpetual curate of St Mary's, Thetford, and his second wife, Ellen Clarke, daughter of Leonard Shelford Bidwell of Thetford. Educated at Tonbridge School and at Addiscombe College (1853–5), he entered the Bengal army on 8 June 1855, and joined the 51st Bengal native infantry on 6 August 1855 at Peshawar.

Collett served with the expeditions under Sir Sydney Cotton on the Yusufzai frontier in 1858, being present at the actions at Chingli and Sitana. He served in Oudh during the mutiny campaign of 1858–9, and was at the storm and capture of the fort of Rampur Kussia by Sir Edward Robert Wetherall on 3 November 1858. During the uprising of 1862–3 in the Khasi and Jaintia Hills, Assam, he was present at the capture of Oomkoi, Nungarai, and at Oomkrong, where he was wounded in the ankle. He was mentioned in dispatches. Promoted captain in 1867, he served in the Abyssinian expedition, and was again mentioned in dispatches. He became major in 1875 and lieutenant-colonel in 1879. In the Second Anglo-Afghan War (1878–80) he acted as quartermaster-general on the staff of Sir Frederick (afterwards Lord) Roberts, and was present at the capture of the Paiwar Pass, and in the operations in Khost valley and round Kabul in December 1879. He accompanied Roberts on the march from Kabul to Kandahar (August 1880) and commanded the 23rd pioneers at the battle of Kandahar on 1 September 1880. He was mentioned in dispatches, and was made CB on 22 February 1881. He was promoted colonel in 1884. During 1886–8 he commanded the 3rd brigade in the expedition to Burma. He took part in the Karenni expedition in 1888 and commanded the eastern frontier district during the Chin Lushai expedition in 1889–90, receiving the thanks of the government of India.

In 1891 Collett was prominent in the expedition to Manipur, and was left in command when the uprising of the Manipuris was suppressed, acting there temporarily but resolutely as chief commissioner of Assam. He received the thanks of the government of India, and was made KCB on 19 November 1891. From 1892 to 1893 he commanded the Peshawar district with the rank of major-general. He was given the reward for distinguished service and was placed by his own wish on the unemployed list on 8 June 1893. His military reputation was high, but increasing deafness unfitted him in his opinion for active duty.

Collett was a keen student of botany, in which he first became interested in 1878 during the Kurram valley expedition. He collected plants in Afghanistan, Algeria, Burma, the Canaries, Corsica, India, Java, and Spain. He was made a fellow of the Linnean Society in 1879, and published the results of his botanical work in the southern Shan States, Burma, in the society's journal. He was an original member of the Simla Naturalists' Society. In retirement he worked assiduously at the Royal Botanic Gardens herbarium, Kew, and at his death was preparing a handbook of the flora of Simla, which appeared posthumously, edited by W. B. Hemsley FRS, as *Flora Simlensis* (1902). He died, unmarried, at his residence, 21 Cranley Gardens, South Kensington, London, on 21 December 1901, and was buried in Charlton cemetery, Blackheath. His herbarium was presented by his family to the Royal Botanic Gardens, Kew.   H. M. VIBART, *rev.* JAMES LUNT

Sources *The Times* (24 Dec 1901) · *Hart's Army List* · Lord Roberts [F. S. Roberts], *Forty-one years in India*, 2 vols. (1897) · J. Willcocks, *From Kabul to Kumassi* (1904) · 'Correspondence relating to Manipur', *Parl. papers* (1890–91), 59.261, C. 6353; 59.405, no. 392 · W. T. Thiselton-Dyer, 'Memoir', in H. Collett, *Flora Simlensis* (1902) · D. G. J. Ryan, G. C. Stahan, and J. K. Jones, *Historical record of the 6th Gurkha rifles, 1817–1919* (1925), vol. 1 of *Historical record of the 6th Gurkha rifles* [for Manipur] · E. St C. Grimwood, *My three years in Manipur and escape from the recent mutiny* (1891) · H. M. Vibart, *Addiscombe: its heroes and men of note* (1894) · private information (1912) · B. Robson, *The road to Kabul: the Second Afghan War, 1878–1881* (1986) · B. Bond, ed., *Victorian military campaigns* (1967) · Burke, *Peerage* (1894) · Desmond, *Botanists*, rev. edn · Venn, *Alum. Cant.*, 2/2
Wealth at death £10,912 12s.: resworn probate, March 1902, CGPLA Eng. & Wales

Colley, Eleanor Davies- (1874–1934), surgeon and a founder of the South London Hospital for Women and Children, was born on 21 August 1874, at Hilliers, Petworth, Sussex, the second daughter of John Neville Colley Davies-Colley, a surgeon on the staff of Guy's Hospital, London, for many years, and Sophia Margaret, daughter of Thomas Turner, treasurer to Guy's Hospital. As a child Eleanor lived in Sussex and in Harley Street, London. She attended Baker Street High School for Girls and then spent a year at Queen's College, London. Despite coming from a medical dynasty and having a private income, she chose, on leaving school, to study the lives of the poor, especially children, in the East End of London for some years, living for part of the time in a cheap flat on a very low income.

In her mid-twenties Miss Davies-Colley decided to enter medicine, which required studying in the evenings at Regent Street Polytechnic for matriculation and the preliminary science examination for London University. She enrolled at the London School of Medicine for Women in 1902 and following an outstanding student career graduated MB BS in 1907. She was immediately appointed house surgeon at the New Hospital for Women (a hospital staffed only by medical women, later renamed the Elizabeth Garret Anderson Hospital after its founder). There she worked under surgeon Maud Chadburn MD (1868–1957), who was to recall her as 'one of the best house surgeons ever' (*The Lancet*). Positions as demonstrator in anatomy at the London school of medicine and surgical registrar at its associated teaching hospital, the Royal Free, followed, both stepping stones to a career as a surgeon. In 1910 she was awarded the degree of MD by the University of London. In

1911 she was the first woman to obtain by examination the fellowship of the Royal College of Surgeons of London when, after many years of obduracy, the college finally rescinded its prohibition on women members and fellows.

Opportunities for women to pursue careers in surgery in England were, at this time, largely confined to the small number of hospitals established and staffed solely by women doctors. Indeed, providing career opportunities for medical women while simultaneously providing improved access to hospital care for respectable women was a prime reason for the founding of such hospitals. In 1911 Miss Davies-Colley and Miss Chadburn began to raise funds for such a hospital for women and children in south London. Aided by some active suffrage campaigners, including Harriet Weaver (who was both publisher of the feminist journal, *The Freewoman*, and Miss Davies-Colley's cousin), by publicity for the appeal occasioned by a hostile medical man's letter to the press, and by a large anonymous donation, the out-patients' department opened in 1912 in Newington Causeway.

Despite the war, the first in-patient beds in purpose-built premises on Clapham Common opened in 1916. Miss Davies-Colley was on the honorary staff of the South London Hospital for twenty-two years from its inception, and was senior surgeon at the time of her death. She was also surgeon to the Marie Curie Cancer Hospital in north London, another medical women's hospital, and for many years senior obstetrician at the Elizabeth Garret Anderson Hospital. She was a founder member of the Medical Women's Federation in 1917. Tall, striking looking, 'impatient of bombast' and self-importance (*The Lancet*), transparently honest, and 'intolerant of anything but the best' (*BMJ*, 1198), Miss Davies-Colley lived and worked with Miss Chadburn for twenty-five years. Although not a prominent feminist campaigner in public Miss Davies-Colley was active in the network of professional, mainly single women that developed in London from the years immediately preceding the First World War to the 1930s. She enjoyed gardening at her country cottage in Essex, travel, and good literature. She died unexpectedly of thyroid toxaemia at her home, 16 Harley Street, London, on 10 December 1934.   M. A. ELSTON

Sources *Medical Women's Federation Newsletter* (Jan 1935), 66–7 · *BMJ* (22 Dec 1934), 1181 · *The Lancet* (15 Dec 1934), 1371–2 · M. A. Elston, '"Run by women, (mainly) for women": medical women's hospitals in Britain, 1866–1948', *Clio Medica*, 61 (2001) · Wellcome L., Medical Women's Federation archives · b. cert. · d. cert. · CGPLA Eng. & Wales (1935)
Archives Royal Free Hospital, London, medical school, archives
Likenesses photograph, repro. in *BMJ* · photograph, repro. in *Medical Women's Federation Newsletter*
Wealth at death £11,345 8s. 0d.: resworn probate, 14 Feb 1935, CGPLA Eng. & Wales

Colley, Sir George Pomeroy Pomeroy- (1835–1881), army officer, was born in Dublin on 1 November 1835, the third and youngest son of the Hon. George Francis Colley, formerly Pomeroy (1797–1879), commander in the Royal Navy, of Rathnangan, co. Kildare, and his wife, Frances (*d.* 1 March 1871), third daughter of the Very Revd Thomas

Sir George Pomeroy Pomeroy-Colley (1835–1881), by unknown photographer

Trench, dean of Kildare, and niece of first Baron Ashtown. George Francis, third son of Revd John Pomeroy, fourth Viscount Harberton (1758–1833), assumed the surname Colley in 1830. George junior (who was to assume the additional prefix surname Pomeroy on 8 May 1880), after touring Europe with his parents and receiving his early education at Cheam School (1841–7), entered the Royal Military College, Sandhurst, in 1849, and passed out first in 1852. He was appointed to an ensigncy without purchase in the 2nd foot on 28 May 1852. After service in Ireland and promotion to lieutenant without purchase, Colley was posted to the Cape Frontier with his regiment in August 1854, where he was employed in building a settlement for military colonists, surveying the Transkei, and as a border magistrate. He rejoined his regiment when it was ordered to China in February 1860 and, after receiving promotion to captain on 12 June 1860, saw action at the capture of the Taku (Dagu) forts and in the advance on Peking (Beijing). He returned briefly to the Cape and then entered the Staff College, Camberley, in February 1862. Finding the teaching undemanding, he worked on his own and passed out first in only ten months instead of the usual two years, with the largest aggregate of marks ever obtained. Colley acquired the habit of spending the early hours in the study of subjects, including economics, apart from his chosen profession; he spent his leave on sketching tours and became an accomplished watercolourist. He also played the flautina and, later, became an authority on South African birds. Evelyn Wood believed him the 'best

instructed soldier I ever met' (Wood, *From Midshipman to Field Marshal*, 2.112), while Garnet Wolseley thought him 'one of the very ablest men I ever knew' (Wolseley, *Story of a Soldier's Life*, 2.317).

Colley was slight in build but well-proportioned, and his receding hairline gave greater prominence to a strong brow, taken to be a mark of his intellect, though his eyes were said to be soft. In the last three years of his life he was bearded. Despite his accomplishments Colley often appeared shy and modest, and was given on occasion to self-doubt. None the less, as Frederick Roberts wrote, Colley was 'the kind of Englishman who feels one is equal to three foreigners' (Royal Archives, Ponsonby MSS, Add MS A36/20, Ponsonby to wife, 3 March 1881).

Having been promoted to a brevet majority on 6 March 1863 (major on 12 May 1875), Colley served as brigade major at Devonport. In 1867 he became an examiner for the Staff College at the Royal Military College, Sandhurst, and the Royal Military Academy, Woolwich. In 1869, however, his appointment to head garrison instruction in England was vetoed on the grounds that he was too junior, and Colley himself turned down the post of military secretary in Bombay. He worked on a number of papers for the War Office, and was then professor of military administration and law at the Staff College from July 1871 to November 1873. During this period he wrote a long article, 'Army', for the ninth edition of the *Encyclopaedia Britannica*, completing it a few days before being summoned to join Wolseley's Asante expedition in November 1873. Colley, now lieutenant-colonel, demonstrated considerable administrative skills in reorganizing the expedition's carrier transport. He was a member of the *Wolseley ring, those talented officers favoured by and associated with Wolseley.

After receiving his colonelcy and being appointed CB (March 1874) as a result of his services, Colley joined Wolseley's special mission to Natal in February 1875, designed to reform the administration and persuade the colonists to accept a southern Africa federation. Colley acted as colonial treasurer, but unaccountably succumbed to nerves and lapsed into silence in a major speech to the legislative assembly on 20 May, to Wolseley's surprise and consternation. Colley then undertook an extensive tour of the Transvaal, Swaziland, and Mozambique. Having expected to take up a post at Aldershot, Colley found himself instead in April 1876 military secretary to the new viceroy of India, Lord Lytton, and in April 1878 he became the latter's private secretary, a position he held until February 1880. Colley exercised considerable influence, Sir Neville Chamberlain noting on one occasion that, while Colley 'is always present but sits away and says nothing' he 'has given the Viceroy the key to the discourse and is his real military mentor' (Forrest, 153). A strong advocate of a 'forward policy', Colley played a significant role in formulating British political and military policy, leading to the Second Anglo-Afghan War in November 1878.

Colley, who was appointed CMG in 1878 and created KCSI on 29 July 1879, chose to remain with Lytton rather than become commandant at Camberley in 1877, and in 1878 he was considered too junior for the Cape command. The duke of Cambridge, the commander-in-chief, regarded Colley as one of those intriguing to get Wolseley the Indian command. Accordingly Wolseley had to fight hard to secure Colley as chief of staff in Zululand in May 1879, and Colley received only the rank of brigadier-general, rather than major-general as Wolseley had wished. With the renewal of the Second Anglo-Afghan War in September 1879 Colley was immediately recalled to India.

Wolseley, however, succeeded in having Colley appointed his successor as governor of Natal, high commissioner for south-eastern Africa, and commander-in-chief in Natal and the Transvaal with the rank of major-general on 24 April 1880. Colley arrived back in South Africa in June at a critical moment with the Boers in the Transvaal, which Britain had annexed in 1877, becoming increasingly restive. The political settlement of Zululand, however, seemed a more pressing problem and Colley was misled as to Boer attitudes by the faulty judgement of Sir Owen Lanyon [see Lanyon, Sir (William) Owen], the British administrator in the Transvaal. On 17 December 1880 a Boer republic was proclaimed and on 20 December a British column, moving from Lydenburg to Pretoria, was fired upon at Bronkhorstspruit. Colley's small force was widely dispersed, though he had initiated a consolidation prior to the outbreak of hostilities by abandoning three posts in the Transvaal. The six remaining imperial garrisons there were all besieged by the Boers. Because he had declined to employ colonial volunteers in the belief that to do so would lead to unacceptable escalation, Colley's field force totalled only twelve infantry companies, with a handful of mounted troops and some seamen landed from HMS *Boadicea*.

Colley had never exercised independent field command and underestimated the Boers' military capability. His decision to advance before reinforcements reached him and despite wet summer weather, which made all movement difficult, was partly governed by the urgent need to relieve the besieged garrisons. In north Natal, finding his route into the Transvaal blocked by some 2000 Boers at Laing's Nek, Colley attempted a frontal assault on 28 January 1881. On this the last occasion regimental colours were carried into action Colley was repulsed with 197 casualties, including several of his own staff. At Ingogo on 8 February he moved to reopen the line of communications between Newcastle and his base at Mount Prospect, which had been cut by the Boers. He drove them back, but suffered another 150 casualties and was forced to retire to his base. Having been reinforced by a column under Wood and fearing the damage done to British prestige by his reverses, Colley and his acting chief of staff and fellow Wolseley protégé, Colonel Herbert Stewart, resolved to turn the Boer position at Laing's Nek by seizing the commanding heights of Majuba, some 2000 feet above it. Gladstone's government, newly in office following the 1880 general election, had begun negotiations with the Boers,

but Colley regarded the seizure of Majuba as a legitimate move to strengthen the British bargaining position.

It was also said that Colley was urged to further action by his wife. Colley's marriage, on 14 March 1878, to Edith Althea Hamilton, daughter of Major-General Henry Meade 'Tiger' Hamilton and sister to a future general, Bruce Hamilton, had taken many by surprise. Edith Colley was regarded as highly intelligent, but also extremely ambitious to the extent that, according to Wood, she 'obliterates apparently every thought of the personal danger which [Colley] has undergone' (Royal Archives, 038/276, Wood to Queen Victoria, 27 Feb 1881). Indeed it was remarked that, when the first train arrived at Pietermaritzburg in October 1880, while Colley stood on the footplate, Lady Colley was at the engine's throttle and, thus, symbolically in control of her husband's destiny. It is clear from Colley's own touching last letter to her, in which he lamented that he could not believe in a hereafter, that he loved her deeply.

Colley chose to take a mixed force from the 58th and 92nd foot and the naval contingent, in all a total of just 365 men, conceivably to allow all to share in the anticipated victory, though some suggested it was intended to give as much prominence to the short-service recruits of the 58th as to the long-service veterans of the 92nd. Colley's aide-de-camp and brother-in-law, Bruce Hamilton, was too ill to accompany the force, but two other future generals were present with the 92nd, Ian Hamilton and Hector MacDonald. After an eight-hour climb to Majuba's summit on the night of 26 February 1881 Colley considered his men too tired to entrench and, in any case, both he and Stewart believed the position impregnable, Colley remarking, 'We could stay here for ever' (Lehmann, *First Boer War*, 239). On the following morning (27 February), the Boers began to ascend the mountain, making skilful use of dead ground and pinning down the defenders with accurate rifle fire. Indeed, while the defenders suffered 285 casualties including 92 killed, it is estimated that the Boers lost only two dead and four wounded. Panic overtook the British as the Boers reached the summit, and Colley was shot through the head at about 1.30 p.m. while trying to rally his men.

Some 17,000 troops were now on their way to South Africa, but Wood was directed to conclude an armistice; agreement restoring the Transvaal self government was reached on 21 March 1881. Colley's body was brought down from Majuba and buried at Mount Prospect cemetery, Natal, on 1 March 1881. Majuba came to be seen as a national humiliation such that 'Remember Majuba' was to become a rallying cry at the time of the Second South African War in 1899.

After Colley's death Lady Colley played the widow's role to the full. She married on 17 February 1891 Wentworth Blackett Beaumont (1829–1907), MP, from 1906 first Baron Allendale. In the light of this her second marriage and swift and lucrative separation in 1891, Wolseley eventually believed she had married Colley as a matter of convenience. She died on 19 May 1927.

IAN F. W. BECKETT

Sources W. Butler, *The life of Sir George Pomeroy-Colley* (1899) • B. Bond, 'The South African War, 1880–81', *Victorian military campaigns*, ed. B. Bond (1967), 199–240 • I. Beckett, 'Women and patronage in the late Victorian army', *History*, new ser., 85 (2000), 463–80 • I. Beckett, 'Cavagnari's *coup de main*: the projected attack on Ali Masjid, October 1878', *Soldiers of the Queen*, 82 (1995), 24–8 • I. Beckett, 'Command in the late Victorian army', *Leadership and command: the Anglo-American experience since 1861*, ed. G. Sheffield (1997), 37–56 • J. H. Lehmann, *The First Boer War* (1972) • Boase, *Mod. Eng. biog.* • Burke, *Peerage* • GEC, *Peerage* • *The South African diaries of Sir Garnet Wolseley, 1875*, ed. A. Preston (1971) • *The South African journal of Sir Garnet Wolseley, 1879–1880*, ed. A. Preston (1973) • B. Robson, *The road to Kabul: the second Afghan War, 1878–1881* (1986) • I. Beckett, 'Military high command in South Africa, 1854–1914', *Ashes and blood: the British army in South Africa, 1795–1914*, ed. P. Boyden, A. Guy, and M. Harding (1999), 60–71 • J. H. Breytenbach, ed., *Majuba Gedenbock* (1980) • G. W. Forrest, *Life of Field-Marshal Sir Neville Chamberlain* (1909) • I. Hamilton, *Listening for the drums* (1944) • E. Wood, *From midshipman to field marshal*, 2 vols. (1906) • Viscount Wolseley [G. Wolseley], *The story of a soldier's life*, 2 vols. (1903) • *CGPLA Eng. & Wales* (1881)
Archives Royal Artillery Institution, Woolwich, London, notebook | BL OIOC, letters to Sir Owen Burne, MSS Eur. D951/11 • BL OIOC, corresp. with Lyall, MSS Eur. F132/14 • Bodl. Oxf., letters to Lord Kimberley, MSS Eng. a2013–2014, b2047–2049, c3933–4514, d2439–2492, e2790–2797 • Glos. RO, letters to Sir Michael Hicks Beach • Hove Reference Library, Wolseley collections, autobiographical collection, corresp. with Wolseley • ING Barings, London, corresp. with earl of Northbrook • University of Natal, Durban, South Africa, Killie Campbell Africana Library, Wood MSS, letters
Likenesses W. H. Dugan, portrait, exh. 1881; now probably lost • W. G. S., lithograph (*How Colley died!*), NPG; repro. in *The Whitehall Review* (10 March 1881) • group portrait, print (with the 3/60 at Ingogo), Royal Greenjackets Museum, Winchester, Hampshire • photograph, NAM; repro. in Butler, *Life of Sir George Pomeroy-Colley* • photograph, NPG [*see illus.*] • sketch (on Majuba), repro. in Lehmann, *The First Boer War* • wood-engraving (after photograph by Maull & Fox), NPG; repro. in *ILN* (21 June 1879)
Wealth at death £2336 13s. 2d.: administration with will, 27 Oct 1881, *CGPLA Eng. & Wales*

Colley, John (*fl.* 1440), Carmelite friar and theologian, joined the order in Doncaster, the town in or near which he may have been born. He studied at Oxford University, where he reached the level of *lector*, and John Bale claims that only an early death prevented him from incepting as a doctor. He is said to have been an elegant Latin writer, and an eloquent preacher who had a unique ability to adapt his words to his audience. Bale preserves the titles of four of his works: *De laudibus apostolorum*, *De passione Christi*, and collections of letters and of sermons; none of them survives.   RICHARD COPSEY

Sources J. Bale, BL, Harley MS, 3838, fols. 98v–99, 208 • J. Bale, *Illustrium Maioris Britannie scriptorum … summarium* (1548), fol. 251v • Bale, *Cat.*, 2.91–2 • Emden, *Oxf.*, 3.2164

Colliber, Samuel (*fl.* 1718–1737), author, published in 1727 *Columna rostrata, or, A Critical History of English Sea Affairs*, a naval history largely concerned with the Dutch wars of the seventeenth century. The work was once thought to derive some value from the fact that Colliber had been familiar with Dutch and French, and had examined the works of writers in those languages, but it is now entirely superseded. A second edition was published in 1742.

Colliber wrote also a number of semi-religious or rather pantheistic tracts, including *An Impartial Enquiry into the Existence and Nature of God* (1718), which ran through several editions; *The Christian Religion Founded on Reason* (1729); *Free Thoughts Concerning Souls* (1734); and *The Known God, or, The Author of Nature Revealed* (1737). They display considerable ingenuity of argument, the style of which, as well as occasional illustrations, shows him to have had some knowledge of mathematics, Latin, and Greek, as well as Locke's *Essay on Human Understanding* (1690) and Samuel Clarke's Boyle Lectures, *A Demonstration of the Being and Attributes of God* (1704). Central to all of Colliber's work is the nature of God, souls, and matter which leads to related fields concerning human perception and the characteristics of space, time, and the relationship of man to animals.

Nothing is known of Colliber except what little is gathered from his writings. Although he wrote on religious subjects, he was not a clergyman; and though he wrote on naval subjects he was not a seaman: in his own words he was a 'layman' discussing subjects best left for 'Divines'. He may possibly have served for some little time in the navy as a volunteer, or more probably as a schoolmaster.

J. K. LAUGHTON, *rev.* RANDOLPH COCK

Sources S. Colliber, *Free thoughts concerning souls* (1734); facs. edn with new introduction by J. W. Yolton (1990)

Collie, John Norman (1859–1942), organic chemist and mountaineer, was born at Ferns Cottage, Alderley Edge, Cheshire, on 10 September 1859, the second son of John Collie, a businessman, and his wife, Selina Mary (*d.* 1883), daughter of Henry Winkworth, a silk merchant, and sister of Catherine Winkworth and Susanna Winkworth. Collie was educated at Charterhouse (1873–5) and Clifton College (1875–7). He studied chemistry under Edmund Albert Letts (1852–1918) at University College, Bristol (1877–9), where he obtained a chemical scholarship, and at Queen's College, Belfast (1879–83). He decided to pursue a career of teaching and research in chemistry, and became assistant to Letts at Queen's College from 1880 to 1883. In 1883 he went to work with Johannes Wislicenus at Würzburg University, obtaining the degree of PhD the following year. On his return he became science lecturer at the Ladies' College, Cheltenham (1885–7), and then went on to be: assistant to William Ramsay at University College, London (1887–96); professor of chemistry at the College of the Pharmaceutical Society, London (1896–1902); and professor of organic chemistry in the University of London at University College (1902–28). After his retirement he was elected an honorary fellow and continued scientific work at University College until 1933.

Collie was a skilful experimenter who could construct his own apparatus, including 'vacuum' tubes in which gases could be exposed to electrical discharges. He collaborated with Ramsay in much work on argon and helium, and he constructed the first neon lamp. Independently of each other, Collie and Hubert Sutton Patterson detected the presence of neon in hydrogen after the passage of an electrical discharge through the latter at low pressure. This apparent 'transmutation' could not be repeated by other skilled investigators, and must have been due to the leakage of minute quantities of air. Collie was responsible in 1896 for the first photograph taken by means of X-rays of a metal object in the human body. His principal scientific activity was in the field of organic chemistry, where he worked, *inter alia*, on phosphonium compounds and phosphines, and on dehydracetic acid, its constitution, reactions, salts, and derivatives. Also of interest was his work on the derivation in practice and theory of many natural systems from the polyacetic acids, and the construction of a possible general relation between all these systems and the carbohydrates. This work was published mainly in the *Journal of the Chemical Society* and the *Proceedings of the Royal Society* over a period of nearly fifty years.

Collie was elected FRS in 1896 and received the honorary degrees of LLD from the universities of Glasgow and St Andrews, and DSc from Belfast and Liverpool. Besides his eminence as a scientist, he acquired great fame as a climber and explorer of mountains. Beginning with the Cuillin peaks in Skye, where he discovered many new climbs, he climbed with notable success in the Alps, and went in 1895 with A. F. Mummery to the Himalayas, where they attempted the ascent of Nanga Parbat; during this expedition Mummery was killed, an episode which deeply affected Collie. The latter also climbed in the Lofoten islands off the Norwegian coast, but his greatest work was done in his pioneering climbing, mapping, and surveying in the Canadian Rockies. His books, *Climbing on the Himalaya and other Mountain Ranges* (1902) and (with Hugh E. M. Stutfield) *Climbs and Exploration in the Canadian Rockies* (1903), are famous records. In Britain, Collie climbed particularly in Skye, Snowdon, and the Lake District. He was elected president of the Alpine Club in 1920 and was an honorary member of many other climbing clubs.

Collie was also a connoisseur of many fine things, including cigars and French wines, and a great collector, of minerals, books, and pictures, and particularly of antique objects of Japanese and Chinese art. He made an investigation of certain coloured glazes on Chinese porcelain, published in the *Transactions of the Oriental Ceramic Society* (1921–2).

Glen Brittle House and the Sligachan Inn became Collie's summer homes on Skye, where he spent his time fishing, shooting, and climbing. He died, unmarried, at Sligachan on 1 November 1942, having suffered complications from neuritis, lumbago, and sciatica. He was buried beside his close friend and climbing companion, John Mackenzie, in the churchyard at Struan on the shore of Loch Harport. To those who knew him he was a great host and a faithful friend.

F. G. DONNAN, rev. K. D. WATSON

Sources E. C. C. Baly, *Obits. FRS*, 4 (1942–4), 329–56 · C. Mill, *Norman Collie, a life in two worlds: mountain explorer and scientist, 1859–1942* (1987) · J. E. C. Eaton, E. L. Strutt, and G. W. Young, 'In memoriam: John Norman Collie, 1859–1942', *Alpine Journal*, 54 (1943–4), 59–65 · *DSB* · *Nature*, 150 (1942), 655–6
Archives Archives of the Canadian Rockies, Banff, Alberta, corresp. and papers · RS · UCL, corresp. | ICL, Armstrong MSS · Music Library, Edinburgh, Scottish Mountaineering Club archives
Likenesses A. T. Nowell, oils, before 1927, repro. in Eaton, Strutt, and Young, 'In memoriam: John Norman Collie'; formerly in possession of Collie's niece, Mrs Holmes, Featherston, Wellington, New Zealand, 1959 · photograph, repro. in Baly, *Obits. FRS*, facing p. 329 · photographs, repro. in Mill, *Norman Collie*
Wealth at death £3193 1s. 10d.: probate, 24 Dec 1942, CGPLA Eng. & Wales

Collier, Arthur (1680–1732), metaphysician, was born on 12 October 1680 at the rectory, Langford Magna, Wiltshire, the third and eldest surviving son of Arthur Collier (d. 1697), the rector of Langford Magna, and his wife, Anne, daughter of Thomas and Joan Currey of Misleton, Somerset. The rectory of Langford Magna had been presented to Joseph Collier, Collier's great-grandfather, in 1608; he owned the advowson, and the benefice continued to be enjoyed by his descendants: it was held in trust by Francis Eyre between the death of Arthur Collier sen. in 1697 and the succession of Arthur Collier jun. in 1704. Collier's grandfather, Henry Collier, had been ejected from the living during the Commonwealth; two of his sons, Henry and Joseph, had taken part in Penruddocke's rising at Salisbury, and were transported into slavery in Jamaica for their pains. Henry Collier was restored to his living in 1660, dying in 1672, when it was inherited by his son, Arthur Collier sen. Collier attended school in Salisbury, and was entered at Pembroke College, Oxford, in June 1697, migrating thence to Balliol College in October 1698, along with his younger brother, William.

Their father having died on 10 December 1697, Arthur Collier inherited the living, and, having taken priest's orders, was instituted to it in 1704. He held it until his death in 1732, having previously sold the advowson for 1600 guineas to Corpus Christi College, Oxford. Arthur and William were deeply interested in metaphysics, and both read Descartes and Malebranche. By the age of twenty-three Arthur had come to believe that there was no such thing as an external world, a proposition he defended in a series of writings. He lived close to John Norris of Bemerton, whose *Theory of the Ideal World* (1701–4) was praised by Collier; Norris was another English follower of Malebranche, and a defender of Platonist immaterialism. Collier reached his position independently of Bishop Berkeley; a manuscript version of his tract *Clavis universalis, or, A new inquiry after truth, being a demonstration of the non-existence or impossibility of an external world* (1713) dates from January 1708, a year before the appearance of Berkeley's *Theory of Vision*, and he claims to have waited 'ten years' before publishing the work (A. Collier, *Clavis universalis*, 1713, 1). Whatever the true relationship between their work, their similarities can largely be attributed to their common indebtedness to Malebranche. Collier's work was dry and scholastic, and it remained unpurchased and unread when Berkeley's more stylish work was beginning to be taken up. The *Clavis universalis* was later highly commended by both Sir James Mackintosh and Dugald Stewart, who thought him unduly neglected; a German translation was made by J. C. Eschenbach in 1756. The *Clavis* was reprinted in Samuel

Parr's *Metaphysical Tracts by some English Philosophers of the Eighteenth Century* (1837). Collier corresponded about the work with Samuel Clarke, to whom he had sent a copy, in 1714. He remained unknown, however, though he took a keen interest in the controversies of the time and wrote letters to Daniel Waterland, Francis Hare, Benjamin Hoadly, and William Whiston. He was intimate with Bishop Burnet; he occasionally preached at Salisbury Cathedral. His sermons, most of which were prepared for his own parishioners, were unaffected by his metaphysical opinions.

Collier was an unorthodox high-churchman, and an opponent of occasional conformity; he opposed Henry Sacheverell, and acted as a mediator in the Bangorian controversy, about which he wrote in the Jacobite *Mist's Journal* in 1719. He was a mystic, believing that all things were comprehended through God, and his greatest interest lay in understanding the opening verse of Genesis; he was also inclined to Arianism, and was an Apollinarian on the subject of the incarnation. These questions are addressed in *A Specimen of True Philosophy … not Improper to be Bound up with the 'Clavis universalis'* (1730), and in his very rare tract, *Logology: a treatise on the logos or word of God in seven sermons on St. John's gospel, chap. i. verses 1, 2, 3, and 14* (1732). Such speculations led him to correspond with William Whiston, whom he invited to Salisbury, but they left him some way from his neighbour, the Salisbury deist Thomas Chubb, whom he made it his business to oppose.

Collier married in 1707 Margaret (*d.* 1749), the daughter of Nicholas Johnson, paymaster of the army, and his wife, a sister of Sir Stephen Fox. Fox was an executor of Johnson's will and guardian of his children, in which capacity Collier brought an action against him in 1710: the case was heard in a chancery suit, the issue of which does not appear. Mrs Collier is said to have been extravagant, and he also lived beyond his means: hence the sale of the advowson of Langford Magna. He died at Langford Magna in 1732, and was buried on 9 September 1732 in Langford church. His brother William, who became rector of Baverstock in 1713, took a keen interest in metaphysics and horseracing, and also died in 1732. Arthur Collier's wife and four children survived him. One son, Arthur, a civilian, died in 1777; Charles became a colonel; Jane *Collier was the author of *An Essay on the Art of Ingeniously Tormenting* (1753); Margaret *Collier accompanied Henry Fielding on his voyage to Lisbon. Collier's papers were rediscovered in a house in the close at Salisbury; many had been burnt earlier by servants. Many of these papers were published, along with a memoir, by Robert Benson, in 1837, at the behest of Dr Fowler of Salisbury, a pupil of Dugald Stewart. B. W. YOUNG

Sources C. J. McCracken, *Malebranche and British philosophy* (1983) · R. Benson, *Memoirs of the life and writings of the Revd. Arthur Collier, M.A.* (1837) · *DNB* · Foster, *Alum. Oxon.*

Collier, Sir Francis Augustus (1783?–1849), naval officer, was the son of Vice-Admiral Sir George *Collier (1738–1795) and his second wife, Elizabeth, *née* Fryer. He entered the navy in 1794, and after a few years' service in the channel was, early in 1798, at the wish of Nelson, appointed to

the *Vanguard*, Nelson's flagship in the Mediterranean and at the battle of the Nile. He was afterwards moved into the *Foudroyant*, with Nelson and Sir Edward Berry, and continued serving in the Mediterranean until the peace of Amiens in 1802. He was promoted lieutenant on 11 April 1803, commander on 25 January 1805, and captain on 13 December 1808. In those years he was on routine active service in the West Indies. On 8 December 1815 he was made a CB, and in February 1818 was appointed to the *Liverpool* (50 guns), going out to the East Indies. In December 1819 he was sent to the Persian Gulf, in naval command of a joint expedition against the 'Joasmi pirates'. Recent reinterpretation has suggested that the supposed piracy was a pretext for the destruction of rival traders by the East India Company. The pirates' chief fortress, Ras al-Khaimah, was captured, their fortifications all round the coast were blown up, and their shipping was destroyed; on 8 January 1820 a formal treaty of peace was signed, and piracy, on the part of the Arabs, was declared to be at an end for ever. The treaty was fairly well kept and put an end to national piracy in the area, although other piracy continued.

Collier returned to England in October 1822. From 1826 to 1830 he was commodore on the west coast of Africa. His services in the Persian Gulf had been rewarded by the Persian order of the Lion and Sun; he was knighted on 28 July 1830, and made KCH on 1 January 1833. On 14 March 1831, following the death of his first wife, of whom no details are known, he married Catherine, daughter of Thomas Thistlethwaite of Southwick Park, Hampshire; he had at least one child.

From 1841 to 1846 Collier was superintendent of Woolwich Dockyard, and in 1846 commanded a squadron in the channel. On 9 November 1846 he became a rear-admiral, and in April 1848 was appointed to the command of the China station; he died suddenly of apoplexy at Hong Kong on 28 October 1849.

J. K. LAUGHTON, *rev.* ANDREW LAMBERT

Sources M. Al-Qasimi, *The myth of Arab piracy in the Gulf* (1986) · G. S. Graham, *Great Britain in the Indian Ocean: a study of maritime enterprise, 1810–1850* (1967) · K. Breen and R. L. DiNardo, 'Commissioned sea-officers of the Royal Navy', *Mariner's Mirror*, 81 (1995), 485 · O'Byrne, *Naval biog. dict.* · *Annual Register* (1849), 279 · C. R. Low, *History of the Indian navy, 1613–1863*, 2 vols. (1877)
Archives NMM, letters and papers

Collier, Sir George (1738–1795), naval officer, was born in London on 11 May 1738, the son of George Collier. He was promoted lieutenant on 3 July 1754 and served on the home station, and under Sir George Pocock in the East Indies. Having been made commander on 6 August 1761, he was posted to the *Boulogne* frigate on 12 July 1762, and commanded her until the peace in the following year. On 3 September 1763 he married Christiana, daughter of Richard Gwyn of Middleton Hall, Carmarthen; they had one son. He was then appointed to the *Edgar*, guardship at Plymouth, which he commanded for three years; and afterwards to the frigates *Tweed*, *Levant*, and *Flora*. During his stay on shore prior to the American War of Independence he adapted for the stage a version of 'Beauty and the Beast' under the title *Selima and Azor*. Collier's production was the work of a man of refined taste with a passion for literature, and it was well-received at the Drury Lane Theatre in 1776.

In the previous year Collier seems to have been sent to North America on some special service, the circumstances of which are not known, but for which he received a knighthood on 27 January 1775. He was then appointed to the *Rainbow* (44 guns), in which he sailed for America on 20 May 1776. Shortly after his arrival on the station he was charged by Lord Howe with the duties of senior officer at Halifax, and on 17 June 1777 he received the thanks of the assembly of Nova Scotia for his defence of the province. On 8 July 1777, after a long chase, he captured the *Hancock*, a large frigate which the American revolutionaries had recently built and commissioned, and which was added to the British navy as the *Iris*. In the following month, on intelligence of an imminent invasion of Nova Scotia, Collier burnt the magazines and stores at Machias, where the American invasion force was gathering and, proceeding along the coast, destroyed some thirty assembled vessels. For this well-timed service he was again officially thanked by the governor and council of the colony on 24 August 1777.

Collier continued in this command until February 1779, when, by the recall of Rear-Admiral James Gambier, the command of the station temporarily devolved on him. He was summoned to New York, and hoisted his broad pennant in the *Raisonnable* (64 guns). The strength of the squadron was then severely depleted by the redeployment of all the ships of force in the West Indies. Nevertheless Collier immediately proposed to Sir Henry Clinton, military commander-in-chief, a joint expedition to the Chesapeake, which accordingly got under way, Clinton supplying 2000 men under the command of General Matthews. On 9 May the squadron anchored in Hampton Roads, and over the next fortnight it destroyed or captured 137 vessels (including ships of war built or building, privateers, and merchant ships). Within twenty-four days the squadron was back at New York, having destroyed stores valued at an estimated £1 million or more. Collier later co-operated with Clinton in expeditions up North River and along the coast of Connecticut, and burnt a great number of boats and small vessels.

In early July 1779 Collier received news that a settlement lately established in Penobscot Bay was under attack by sea and land. He immediately proceeded there, with a force of four frigates and the 64-gun ship, but Collier's ships were obliged to anchor for the night at the mouth of the bay, and the Americans used the delay to re-embark their troops and the greater part of their stores. The next day, as the British squadron advanced, the American forces fled up the river, and, being closely pursued, set fire to and destroyed four of their own ships; four more armed vessels fell into Collier's hands. On his return to New York, Collier found that Vice-Admiral Marriot Arbuthnot had come out to assume the command. Collier could not have expected to retain his position but his correspondence indicates he was aggrieved at being superseded by the less

able Arbuthnot after his own brilliant defence of Penobscot. Collier returned home in the *Daphne* frigate, arriving at Portsmouth on 27 November 1779. He kept a journal of his part in the American War of Independence, which he subsequently prepared for publication as 'A detail of some particular services' (NMM, JOD/9 and BGR/28) and later printed in the *Naval Chronicle* (32, 267–96, 353–83). This followed a similar record of his visit to Paris and Brussels in 1773, later published as *France on the Eve of the Revolution* (1865).

Early in 1780 Collier was appointed to the *Canada* (74 guns), which he commanded in the channel during the summer of 1780, and at the relief of Gibraltar by Vice-Admiral George Darby in the spring of 1781. On the homeward voyage he chased and came up with the Spanish frigate *Leocadia* (44 guns), which he took after a short though spirited resistance. Collier had been divorced from his first wife, Christiana, in March 1772, and on 19 July 1781 he married Elizabeth, daughter of William Fryer, an Exeter merchant; they had four sons and two daughters.

Owing, it is said, to some discontent with the government, or dissatisfaction with Lord Sandwich, then first lord of the Admiralty, Collier resigned his command on his return to England. There is nothing to suggest that Collier was personally at odds with Sandwich, and his decision may have been prompted by a failed bid for patronage. In 1784 he was returned to parliament as member for Honiton. After his return from America in 1779 he had incurred displeasure in the Commons by expressing the belief that the war could not be won by the means and men employed. During Pitt's ministry he similarly earned no favours for his opposition to the government's attempt to limit the powers of the regent in 1786. It was Collier's belief that his defence of the prince of Wales cost him his flag. He had no further naval employment until 1790, by which time he had ceased to represent Honiton. In the crisis following the Spanish action at Nootka Sound he was appointed to the *St George*, but he considered himself insulted by an order to prepare her to receive a flag officer, in light of his previous service as an independent commander. With the approval of his brother officers he wrote to the Admiralty, and the order was revoked. The *St George* was paid off when the threat of war receded, but after its return he was promoted rear-admiral of the white on 1 February 1793, and advanced to vice-admiral of the blue on 4 July 1794. In the following January he was appointed to the command-in-chief at the Nore, but by then his health would no longer support the burden, and he was compelled to resign the position a few weeks later. 'In person', it was noted in the *Naval Chronicle*, 'Sir George was of a middle stature; active, and well made. His countenance was open and manly—his eye blue, and beaming with intelligence; his hair light, and complexion fair' (*Naval Chronicle*, 32, 265). Collier:

> was an enemy to the mode of manning the navy by impressment. He conceived it perfectly practicable to attract all the youthful mariners on our coasts, by a wise and liberal system of reward and promotion; in which case he thought

the use of the lash might safely be abolished—cases of theft only excepted. (ibid.)

His life during the last fifteen years was embittered by a feeling that his really distinguished service in America, during the few months of his independent command, had not received due recognition. He died in Manchester Square, London, on 6 April 1795.

All four sons from Collier's second marriage served in the armed forces. George, the eldest, reached the rank of lieutenant-colonel in the Coldstream Guards, and died of wounds received at Bayonne on 10 May 1814. The second son, Francis Augustus *Collier, entered the navy and served under Schomberg, and Nelson, and died a rear-admiral in 1849. Henry Browne Collier passed through all the ranks of the navy, latterly as a 'yellowed' flag officer, and died in 1872. The fourth son, Charles, had an army career, serving in the cavalry in Bengal. His two daughters were Louisa and Georgina.

J. K. LAUGHTON, rev. NICHOLAS TRACY

Sources J. Ralfe, *The naval biography of Great Britain*, 4 vols. (1828) · 'Biographical memoir of Sir George Collier', *Naval Chronicle*, 32 (1814), 265–96, 353–400 · M. M. Drummond, 'Collier, George', HoP, *Commons, 1754–90* · NMM, JOD 9; BGR/28

Archives NMM, journal · NMM, memorial | NMM, letters to Lord Sandwich · priv. coll., letters to Lord Shelburne · U. Nott. L., letters to duke of Portland

Collier, Sir George Ralph, baronet (1774–1824), naval officer, was born in London, the second son of Ralph Collier, chief clerk of the victualling office. Educated at the Chelsea Maritime Academy, he went to sea in HMS *Carysfort* in 1787 already a capable navigator, astronomer, surveyor, and linguist. Commissioned lieutenant on 22 January 1796, he was first lieutenant of the flagship of Admiral Mitchell at the capture of the Dutch fleet at The Helder in 1799. He brought home Mitchell's dispatches, and was promoted commander on 3 September; he was then appointed to command the 18 gun *Victor*. After escorting a troop convoy to the Red Sea coast of Egypt, Collier engaged the French 18 gun *Flèche* off the Seychelles on 2 September 1801 until heavy damage to his rigging allowed it to escape. Collier followed, after completing his repairs. On 5 September, the *Flèche* was sighted entering Mahe, and after surveying the entrance at night Collier sailed into the harbour, anchored, and reduced the French ship to a beached wreck. Only two of his men were wounded. The first lord of the Admiralty, Earl St Vincent, highly approving his conduct, promoted him captain on 20 April 1802, to ensure his precedence over a large block promotion given at the peace. In addition to his well-earned naval support Collier was also a protégé of Prince William of Gloucester. On 18 May 1805 Collier married Maria Lyon of Liverpool; there were no children. While on shore he proposed an operation to block the Texel, where he had been active in 1799.

From February 1806 Collier commanded the frigate *Minerva* on the north coast of Spain, conducting cutting-out attacks on Spanish privateers and forts. In April 1807 he moved into HMS *Surveillante*. In the same year he brought home Admiral Gambier's dispatches from the Copenhagen expedition, and was knighted. Collier returned to the Bay of Biscay, capturing a French corvette and four privateers, and harassing French coastal shipping. In 1812 Collier operated on the north coast of Spain, under Admiral Sir Home Popham, supporting the Spanish guerrillas. On 1 August he captured the castle at Santander, but was wounded and forced to withdraw. Two days later the French evacuated the vital position. In 1813 Collier was a commodore with twelve vessels, supporting the Spanish along the coast. He also co-operated with General Sir Thomas Graham at the capture of San Sebastian in August.

In November 1813 Collier was moved into the new 50 gun *Leander*, specially built to counter successful American heavy frigates like the *Constitution*. After arriving on the American coast he captured the brig USS *Rattlesnake*, on 22 June 1814, and blockaded the *Constitution* in Boston. While Collier was taking on stores at Halifax his quarry escaped, and he pursued her across the Atlantic, taking a large privateer on passage and picking up intelligence. On 11 March 1815, two months after the peace of Ghent had ended the Anglo-American War of 1812–14, Collier—who did not know this—with the *Newcastle*, another new 50 gun frigate, and the 40 gun *Acasta*, encountered the *Constitution* beating out of Porto Praya in the Cape Verde Islands, with the prize sloops *Cyane* and *Levant* in company. In the fog the captains of the other two ships mistook the two smaller ships for frigates, while Collier never obtained clear sight of them. When a signal directing *Acasta* to pursue *Levant* fouled on hoisting, it was followed by *Newcastle* as well. The squadron finally pursued *Levant* back to Porto Praya, where she was recaptured. The *Constitution* escaped, but Collier quickly moved to a position off Cayenne, where he expected to intercept her. He abandoned this position when he heard of the peace; two days later the Americans passed, as he had expected. Collier's distinguished services earned him a baronetcy on 20 September 1814, and he was created KCB on 2 January 1815.

Between 1818 and 1821 Collier commanded the six-ship coast of Africa squadron, to suppress the slave trade. He carried out this task with the vigour of a convinced abolitionist, significantly reducing the large-scale shipment of slaves. His reports, produced for the House of Commons, were widely consulted. In 1820 his work was recognized by election to honorary life membership of the African Institution. Mortified by William James's account of his action with *Constitution* in the *Naval Occurrences of the War of 1812*, which implied incompetence at the least, Collier requested an Admiralty rebuttal. When this was denied, 'in a fit of insanity', he cut his throat, on 24 March 1824 (*GM*, 284). After his death his conduct was stoutly defended by the naval biographer John Marshall. American accounts agree with Marshall that the weather was too thick for a positive identification of the ships.

A brave, resourceful, and effective sea officer, Collier was denied by early death the opportunity to distinguish himself in peacetime commands, and the service was deprived of one of its brightest ornaments. His baronetcy became extinct on his death, and his suicide may account for his omission from the *Dictionary of National Biography*.

ANDREW LAMBERT

Sources J. Marshall, *Royal naval biography*, 2/2 (1825) · J. C. Bradford, L. R. DiNardo, and D. Syrett, 'The commissioned sea officers of the Royal Navy, 1660–1815', *American Neptune*, 57 (1997), 172 · T. Roosevelt, *The naval war of 1812* (1882) · W. James, *The naval history of Great Britain, from the declaration of war by France, in February 1793, to the accession of George IV in January 1820*, 5 vols. (1822–4) · W. E. F. Ward, *The Royal Navy and the slavers* (1969) · *Letters of … the earl of St Vincent, whilst the first lord of the admiralty, 1801–1804*, ed. D. B. Smith, 2, Navy RS, 61 (1927) · *The Keith papers*, 3, ed. C. Lloyd, Navy RS, 96 (1955) · *Letters and papers of Charles, Lord Barham*, ed. J. K. Laughton, 3, Navy RS, 39 (1911) · H. Thomas, *The slave trade: the history of the Atlantic slave trade, 1440–1870* (1997) · C. Lloyd, *The navy and the slave trade* (1949) · *GM*, 1st ser., 94/1 (1824), 284 · C. J. Parry, *Index of baronetage creations* (1967)
Archives NMM, material | NMM, reports on Gold Coast; letters to Lord Keith; letters to Lord Melville

Collier, Giles (*bap.* 1622, *d.* 1678), Church of England clergyman, was born at Norton, near Evesham, Worcestershire, and baptized there on 13 October 1622, the son of Giles Collier. In 1637 he entered New Inn Hall, Oxford, as a battler or servitor and graduated BA in 1641. Having left Oxford he proceeded MA in 1648 at the time of the parliamentary visitation. At the end of the first civil war of 1642–6 Collier 'clos[ed] then with the Presbyterians' (Wood, *Ath. Oxon.*, 3.1171). He took the covenant in 1648. In May 1646 he became rector of Aston Somerville, Worcestershire, and in 1647 he became vicar of Blockley, Gloucestershire. He also kept a school in his vicarage at Blockley.

When the Worcestershire association of ministers was formed in 1652 Collier was one of the earliest members. He was also one of the leading members of the Evesham branch of the association. He became an assistant to the Worcestershire ejectors in 1654.

On 1 January 1655 Collier wrote to Richard Baxter, then in London, asking Baxter to stay with him on his way back to Kidderminster. He also remarked on the 'inconvenience' of 'idle profane ignorant curates' being allowed 'to creepe into our Parishes and baptize etc with the Common praier booke'. Next Collier stressed 'how expedient 'tis that a law be made against the observation of Christmas, hereby Episcopal men their keeping it up will be at an end, whereby our ignorant and superstitious people are much hard'ned against us' (*Reliquiae Baxterianae*, 162–3). In an appendix of 1656 to his *Vindiciae thesium de sabato* (1653) Collier argued, against his clerical neighbour Edward Fisher of Mickleton, Gloucestershire, that there was no valid reason for the keeping of Christmas.

At the Restoration Collier, to the surprise and chagrin of neighbouring 'episcopal men', conformed and so kept the living of Blockley. The years before his death in 1678 were marked by a feud with his parishioner Thomas Childe of Northwick and by attempts to prosecute other parishioners for working on the sabbath. In a letter of 27 June 1678 to the Oxford mathematician John Wallis he wrote that two of his daughters had died of smallpox. His own death occurred in July 1678 and he was buried on 31 July in the chancel of Blockley church.

In his will of 27 July 1678 Collier mentioned his wife, Mary (*d.* 1695), possibly the daughter of William Stephens of Broadway who was baptized in 1621, and his sons Stephen and Nathaniel, both clerks in holy orders. To Nathaniel he left Matthew Poole's *Synopsis criticorum*; to his 'daughter Hering' he left 'the Reversion at Littleton [near Evesham] purchased of my Father Stephens'. There was also an unspecified bequest of money to 'the honest Poore of Blockley, such who being able do ordinarily come to Church' (PRO, PROB 11/358).

C. D. GILBERT

Sources H. E. M. Icely, *Blockley through twelve centuries* (1974) · *Reliquiae Baxterianae, or, Mr Richard Baxter's narrative of the most memorable passages of his life and times*, ed. M. Sylvester, 1 vol. in 3 pts (1696) · *Calendar of the correspondence of Richard Baxter*, ed. N. H. Keeble and G. F. Nuttall, 2 vols. (1991) · A. J. Soden, *The history of Blockley* (1875) · will, PRO, PROB 11/358, sig. 122 · D. Gilbert, 'Richard Baxter, Giles Collier and the festival of Christmas', *Baxter Notes and Studies*, 3/1 (1995), 3–5 · Wood, *Ath. Oxon.*, new edn · D. Gilbert, 'The Worcestershire association of ministers', *Baxter Notes and Studies*, 4/2 (1996) · parish register (burial), Blockley, 31 July 1678 · parish register, Norton-with-Lenchwick, Worcestershire, 13 Oct 1622 [baptism] · W. A. Shaw, *A history of the English church during the civil wars and under the Commonwealth, 1640–1660*, 2 vols. (1900) · G. F. Nuttall, 'The Worcestershire Association: its membership', *Journal of Ecclesiastical History*, 1 (1950), 197–206, esp. 198–9
Archives DWL, Baxter letters
Wealth at death see will, PRO, PROB 11/358, sig. 122

Collier, Jane (*bap.* 1715, *d.* 1755), novelist, was born at Steeple Langford, near Salisbury, and baptized there on 16 January 1715, one of four children of the Revd Arthur *Collier (1680–1732) and Margaret (*d.* 1749), daughter of Nicholas Johnson and niece of Sir Stephen Fox. Her father was rector of Langford Magna, Wiltshire, from 1704, a friend of Bishop Gilbert Burnet, and a theological controversialist. In 1716 money troubles (which Benson blames on his wife) made the family move to lodgings in Salisbury. Jane and her sister, Margaret *Collier (1719–1794?), learned Greek and Latin from their father. He died in 1732 'in embarrassed circumstances'; their brother Charles became a soldier, their brother Arthur a lawyer who caused their family friend Henry Fielding to be gaoled in 1746 after standing surety for a sum of £400. Their lives were shaped by poverty and literary friendships. In 1748 or 1749 Jane had left Salisbury and was living with her mother and brother Arthur in lodgings in London, in Doctors' Commons. Either she or her sister had been living with Samuel Richardson's family in 1750, and by late 1751 she was living in Beauford Buildings with Sarah Fielding (whose example as a published author she must have found an encouragement).

Jane Collier has been undervalued as a writer. On 4 October 1748 she wrote to Richardson to argue against his proposed alterations to Sarah Fielding's *The Governess, or, Little Female Academy*. The reasons she advances for maintaining the book's integrity are based on modesty of intention: it is better not to divulge the precise methods of punishment used by its Mrs Teachum, since anything said might antagonize readers of one persuasion or another. Richardson duly published it (1749) in its original form. Whereas her critique of his *Clarissa*, written for the *Gentleman's*

Magazine, never appeared there, Sarah Fielding's reached print, anonymously, in 1749.

Jane Collier's first known appearance in print is *An Essay on the Art of Ingeniously Tormenting* (1753). The daughter of Collier's old Salisbury friend James Harris later claimed that 'great part' of it was written by him, but she offered no evidence. Its frontispiece shows a cat and mouse with the motto 'Celebrare Domestica Facta'. Quoted by Samuel Johnson in volume two of his *Dictionary* (in spirit, if not literally, this was one of his few infringements on his principle of excluding living authors), it is couched in the Scriblerian tradition of ironic instruction in undesirable skills, like Pope on poetic bathos, Swift on malpractices of servants, or Henry Fielding on the writing of inspirational biography. Under this guise it probes the 'labyrinths and inward turns of the mind' in abuse of power in human relationships, especially that of mistress to servants or 'humble companion', with acute psychological insight no doubt won while living as a dependant. Its closing fable relates how an account of 'the misery that is endured, from the entrance of teeth and claws into living flesh' was adjudged after much debate to have been written from experience not of preying but of being preyed upon. A reprint of 1804, edited by 'J. S. C.', signs its dedication 'The Invisible Girl'; it notes that Jane Collier's brother Arthur regretted that his sister's abilities should be known only from 'a satirical work'. Jane Collier, however, in ironically claiming kinship with Addison, Swift, Richardson, and (Henry) Fielding, does so as moralist, not satirist.

Collier probably produced a second work, *The Cry: a New Dramatic Fable* (1754), jointly with Sarah Fielding, who was apparently thought by Richardson and other readers to be sole or chief author. Its authorship continues to be argued over. It is both experimental and learned, aiming 'to strike a little out of the beaten track of novels and essays', with scenes and dialogue borrowed from the drama, an allegorical framework explicitly borrowed from Edmund Spenser, scholarly footnotes, and invented words like 'turba' for a legion of evil passions, 'trouble, bustle and confusion' (1.194–5). Una personifies Truth; the 'Cry' is the name of 'ERROR and her NUMEROUS TRAIN … when cloathed in mortal forms' (1.20). The central story, of good characters attaining happiness against odds, is unremarkable; the picture of societal forces constricting women's lives (Portia compelled constantly to defend her behaviour to the Cry) recalls that drawn in Sarah Fielding's work. The inventive, non-narrative means of composing this picture was disliked by, for instance, Elizabeth Carter, Lady Mary Wortley Montagu, and the *Monthly Review*; but it seems to bear Collier's distinctive mark, a natural development from the *Art of Tormenting*. Jane Collier died in 1755, unmarried, and was buried at Saint Benet's Church, London, on 28 March 1755.   ISOBEL GRUNDY

Sources *The correspondence of Samuel Richardson*, ed. A. L. Barbauld, 6 vols. (1804) · R. Benson, *Memoirs of the life and writings of the Rev. Arthur Collier … with some account of his family* (1837) · T. C. D. Eaves and B. D. Kimpel, *Samuel Richardson: a biography* (1971) · M. Battestin, *Henry Fielding* (1989) · *Correspondence*, ed. M. Battestin and O. T. Probyn (1993) · T. Keymer, 'Jane Collier, reader of Richardson, and the fire scene in *Clarissa*', *New essays on Richardson*, ed. A. J. Rivero (1996), 145–55 · C. T. Probyn, *The sociable humanist: the life and works of James Harris, 1709–1780* (1991) · B. Rizzo, *Companions without vows: relationships among eighteenth-century British women* (1994) · [J. Collier and S. Fielding], *The cry*, ed. C. Woodward (2002)

Archives V&A, Forster collection, Richardson corresp.

Likenesses J. Faber jun., mezzotint, NPG

Collier, Jeremy (1650–1726), anti-theatrical polemicist and bishop of the nonjuring Church of England, was born on 23 September 1650 at Stow-cum-Quy, Cambridgeshire, son of Jeremy Collier, a fellow of St John's College, Cambridge, under the Commonwealth, and at the time of Collier's birth master of Aldenham School, Hertfordshire, and his wife, Elizabeth, *née* Smith, of Stow-cum-Quy. He was educated at the free school at Ipswich, where his father became master in 1663. He was admitted sizar at Gonville and Caius College, Cambridge, on 6 June 1666 and again on 10 April 1669, where he graduated BA in 1673 and MA in 1676. He was ordained deacon on 24 September 1676 and priest on 24 February 1678. He was chaplain to Mary Sackville, *née* Bagot, countess of Dorset, at Knole House in Kent from 1677 to 1679 and rector of Ampton, in Suffolk, from 1679 to 1685. In 1685 he resigned his benefice and moved to London. There, according to the entry in the *Biographia Britannica*, believed to be based on notes by Collier, he obtained a lecturer's appointment at Gray's Inn, but there is no record at the inn of his having held the post. If he did he was displaced in 1689 when he failed to swear allegiance to William III and Mary II on the ground that his oaths to James II were still valid.

A nonjuring controversialist Collier had already published two of his sermons in 1686 and 1687 and he now began to publish pamphlets and tracts on political issues, especially on the question of the validity of the succession of William and Mary to the throne. In his *The Desertion Discussed. In a Letter to a Country Gentleman* he controverted arguments published by Gilbert Burnet in *An Enquiry into the Present State of Affairs*. Collier's pamphlet advanced a favourite argument of the supporters of James II in 1689, that since the king had left London under duress and in fear of his life his departure should not be construed as an abdication and that, therefore, though the king was temporarily absent, the throne was not vacant. William was consequently, in Collier's view, a usurper and his landing at Torbay constituted an armed rebellion against the civil power, which violated the Restoration Anglican doctrine of non-resistance. Collier was seized by the government and committed to several months' imprisonment in Newgate. He was, however, finally released without trial and during the next three years wrote several further pamphlets opposing the revolution settlement in church and state, including *Vindiciae juris regii*, published in 1689, where he argued that security in the kingdom could come only from divine hereditary right, and *Dr Sherlock's 'Case of Allegiance' Considered with some Remarks on his Vindication*, in 1691, replying to William Sherlock's justification of his decision to abandon the nonjuror position and take the oaths to William and Mary in 1690. Other pamphlets discussed the nature of a *de facto* monarch and the duties of

Jeremy Collier (1650–1726), by William Faithorne the younger (after Edmond Lilly)

clergy towards bishops who occupied the sees of non-jurors. Collier's writings argued that the Church of England was in schism from the true church, represented by the nonjurors, who in Collier's view came as close as possible to the practices of the early church and maintained the independence of the spiritual order and its representatives from the state. The civil order was an expression of the divine will; in collaborating with the revolution of 1688 and concurring in the removal of James II churchmen were rejecting the structure of Christian society and opening the doors to moral as well as political disorder.

In 1692 Collier was again briefly imprisoned on allegations that he and another nonjuring clergyman, George Newton, had visited Romney Marsh with the intention of opening communications with James II. They were interrogated by Daniel Finch, second earl of Nottingham, secretary of state, but no solid evidence could be produced and the two clergymen were released on bail. Collier then surrendered to the authorities, as giving bail implied his acceptance of the authority of William and Mary's courts. During his brief imprisonment in the king's bench that ensued, he wrote another pamphlet justifying his position, entitled *The Case of Giving Bail to a Pretended Authority*. Collier was released from the king's bench on the application of his friends. His early pamphlets had been written on the assumption that the revolution, as a rebellion against divine authority, would lead to the collapse of civil order, which would swiftly lead to the restoration of James II as the only means of guaranteeing social stability, but *A Perswasive to Consideration*, published in 1693, accepted that William's rule was probably permanent and

called on James's supporters to 'glory in Persecutions and despise Contempt' (Hopes, 161). In 1694 and 1695 he published his *Miscellanies*, which in later editions from 1697 was called *Essays upon Several Moral Subjects*. One of the essays, 'Upon the office of a chaplain', demonstrated Collier's pugnacious sense of his own independence and of the proper independence of the church. The essay was probably influenced by Collier's experience as a chaplain at Knole. In it he inveighs against the attitude of members of the aristocracy who treated their chaplains as domestic servants. He intended to enhance the self-respect of chaplains as well as remind their employers that churchmen should not be expected to be servile.

On 3 April 1696, when Sir John Friend and Sir William Parkyns were to be executed for their parts in the assassination plot against William III, Collier, with two other non-juring clergymen, Shadrach Cook and William Snatt, accompanied them to Tyburn and gave them absolution by laying on of hands, as Collier argued was the practice of the early church. Since neither Friend nor Parkyns had publicly repented of their roles in the plan to murder the king, the clear implication of the absolution ceremony was that the two prisoners were being absolved of the general human sins of a lifetime, of which their plot against the king was not part. Collier and his colleagues thereby gave their tacit approval to the plot by demonstrating that they did not consider it sinful. Collier, to avoid possible arrest, was compelled to go into hiding. His house in London was raided by the authorities on 6 April and papers and documents were seized. This did not, however, prevent him from publishing *Defence of the Absolution* on 9 April. On 25 April he published a second pamphlet replying to a published declaration signed by Thomas Tenison, archbishop of Canterbury, and John Sharp, archbishop of York, and twelve bishops, that Collier and his two colleagues offered 'an open affront to the Laws both of Church and State' (*A Declaration*, 11). Cook and Snatt were tried on a charge of absolving traitors on 2 July, were found guilty, and released. Collier evaded arrest and was outlawed. For six or seven months he remained in hiding, but gradually during 1697 he drifted back into normal life without any further punitive measures being taken against him, although he remained an outlaw for the rest of his life.

Collier's attacks on the theatre Collier's concern for the threat posed to the moral order of society was widely shared by churchmen influenced like Collier by late seventeenth-century study of the primitive church. The religious societies, the first initiated by Anthony Horneck in London in 1678, and the societies for the reformation of manners, which sprang up in London during the 1690s, sought to provide the moral discipline which many high-churchmen felt the church should be empowered to enforce upon the laity. The involvement of dissenters in the societies for the reformation of manners showed that concern about the decline of moral standards was not limited to churchmen anxious to demonstrate the Church of England's proximity to the ideals of the primitive church. However, the movement was a divided one, as high-churchmen remained suspicious of the involvement of dissenters in the societies for the reformation of manners, and disagreed about whether the societies existed to thank God for his mercy in delivering England from Catholicism in 1688, or (as would have been consistent with Collier's point of view) to combat the collapse of the moral order consequent upon William's invasion. Outside the clergy and the religious societies there was widespread anxiety about profane speech and scandalous behaviour, which included criticism of the stage for providing examples of immoral conduct. The government of William III indicated that it accepted this argument when in 1697 the lord chamberlain issued orders against the 'Prophaneness and Immorality' of the theatre.

For Collier the condition of the stage provided the most telling example of the moral anarchy that he had predicted would follow the rejection of James II and the establishment of a government that, as it was founded upon rebellion against the civil and moral order, was constitutionally incapable of guaranteeing such order. Collier must have been aware that his campaign against the stage was one with which a larger number of readers would identify compared to his intellectual advocacy of the restoration of James II. In his anti-theatre writings there is a vigour, a verbal resilience, a clarity and directness of invective which is absent from his other moralizing, solemn pieces. This is clearest in his justly famous first contribution on the subject, *A Short View of the Immorality and Profaneness of the English Stage, together with the Sense of Antiquity upon this Argument*, which appeared in 1698. Its thunderous periods ring with a sense of the joy of battle. Altogether, between 1698 and 1708 Collier published six pieces of writing on this theme: some of them (such as *A Letter to a Lady Concerning the New Playhouse*, 1708) are only a few pages long, whereas the original *Short View* ran to 268 pages and his *A Second Defence of the 'Short View'* (1700) is 142 pages long.

Collier claimed in *A Short View* that his objections were not to the theatre itself, but to particular practical matters of behaviour, such as obscene language, oaths, blasphemy, and sexual innuendo. He regarded these as corrupting, whether or not they were actually intended to corrupt, although he implied that there was malicious intent in many cases. Each chapter dealt with a particular concern: the first was headed 'The immodesty of the stage', the second, 'The profaneness of the stage', the third 'The clergy abused by the stage', and the fourth 'The stage-poets make their principal persons vicious and reward them at the end of the play'. About all these matters of social and religious observance he went into great detail, quoting multiple examples from many contemporary plays to illustrate the various offences about which he complained, and here and there excusing himself from giving chapter and verse because of the 'smuttiness' of the language used in that particular passage. At the opening of the book he proposed:

> The business of Plays is to recommend Virtue and
> discountenance Vice; to shew the Uncertainty of humane

greatness, the suddain Turns of Fate, and the Unhappy Conclusions of Violence and Injustice: 'Tis to expose the Singularities of Pride and Fancy, to make Folly and Falsehood contemptible and to bring every thing that is Ill Under Infamy and Neglect.   (Collier, *A Short View*, 1)

The playwrights, Collier argued, were setting out to turn this purpose against itself. God had intended women for modesty but instead female characters were frequently depicted as aggressive and lewd, particularly those of high social status. Noblemen were presented as competing in debauchery when their place in the civil order demanded that they be presented as virtuous and responsible. Collier found that deceitful characters often triumphed, being rewarded with material prosperity and promotion in the social hierarchy, when drama that reflected moral truth should have cast them low. He thought the language of the stage was lewd and blasphemous, alluding to sexual acts and casually invoking heaven and hell, reducing people to the level of ignorant beasts. He was also aggrieved by dramatic portrayals of the clergy, who too frequently appeared as fools when they should be worthy of respect as the maintainers of religion and virtue. To Collier it was essential that the stage should portray a society that respected the alliance between social rank and virtue in both the civil and religious spheres. If it could not then it was questionable whether the theatre should continue.

Collier versus Dryden   Although there were several contemporary dramatists whose works presented Collier with examples of immorality John Dryden in particular articulated a creed that called all Collier's principles into question. Collier's opposition to Dryden underlies his general dislike of the theatre. Dryden had, thirty years before Collier wrote *A Short View*, expressed in its most perfect form in *An Essay of Dramatick Poesie* and *A Defence of an Essay*, both published in 1668, the essence of the aesthetic dilemma which the single-minded Collier resolved by overlooking. Including but not confining his definition to stage poetry, Dryden, in the 'Defence', wrote: 'I am satisfied if it cause delight: for delight is the chief, if not the only end of Poesie: instruction can be admitted but in the second place, for Poesie only instructs as it delights' (Dryden, 'A Defence', 5–6). Collier argued of Dryden's work:

> The strength of his Defence lies in this choice maxim, that
> the Chief End of Comedy is Delight. He Questions whether
> Instruction has any thing to do in Comedy; If it has, he is
> sure 'tis no more than its secondary end; For the business of
> the Poet is to make you laugh.   (Collier, *A Short View*, 156)

Collier was paraphrasing from Dryden's preface to 'An Evening's Love', published in 1671, where Dryden argued that 'Comedy is not so much oblig'd to the punishment of the faults which it represents, as Tragedy' (Dryden, preface to 'An Evening's Love', 209) on the ground that 'the faults and vices are but the sallies of youth, and the frailties of human nature, and not premeditated crimes' (ibid.). For Collier youthful folly was not an excuse, and theatre existed to correct, not indulge, human weakness. Dryden, introducing the concept of delight as aesthetic appreciation in the 'Defence' was concerned with the particular kind of writing best suited to tragedy, and not comedy. Collier conflated the argument taken from the 'Defence' with that from the preface to 'An Evening's Love' and equated delight with laughter (a connection Dryden never made) and therefore in Collier's estimation with frivolity and triviality. Nevertheless, though he misunderstands—or pretends to—Collier, reading Dryden's *A Defence of an Essay*, recognizes a most dangerous opponent—a man whose life is guided by a God who is to Collier a total stranger. For Dryden:

> The employment of a Poet, is like that of a curious
> Gunsmith, or Watchmaker: the Iron or Silver is not his own;
> but they are the least part of that which gives the value: the
> price lyes wholly in the workmanship.   (Dryden, preface to
> 'An Evening's Love', 212)

The extent to which the workmanship matches, measures up to, and enhances the intrinsic beauty of the iron or the silver is the gauge by which aesthetic delight is judged, said Dryden. But Collier regarded words, however or wherever deployed, as instruments by which to tell people what they should believe and how they should behave.

Critics of Collier's Short View Dryden never published a pamphlet of rebuttal or recrimination against Collier, but did occasionally refer ironically to him in other places. In an epilogue that Dryden wrote for a revival of John Vanbrugh's adaptation of Francis Beaumont's and John Fletcher's *The Pilgrim*, in 1700, Dryden managed to get in a sly comment on Collier's allegiance to the cause of divine right monarchy and his assumption that the restoration of James II would improve society's morals:

> Perhaps the Parson stretch'd a point too far
> When with our Theatres he wag'd a war.
> He tells you, That this very Moral Age
> Receiv'd the first Infection from the Stage.
> But sure, a banisht Court, with Lewdness fraught,
> The Seeds of open Vice returning brought.
> (Dryden, epilogue to *The Pilgrim*, 265)

And in the opening passage of 'Cymon and Iphigenia' Dryden wrote:

> The World will think that what we loosely write,
> Tho' now arraign'd, he read with some delight;
> Because he seems to chew the Cud again
> When his broad comment makes the Text too plain
> And teaches more in one explaining page
> Than all the double Meanings of the Stage.
>
> What needs he Paraphrase on what we mean?
> We were at worst but Wanton; he's Obscene.
> (Dryden, 'Cymon and Iphigenia', 513)

The *Short View* provoked immediate replies from four of the playwrights whom Collier had attacked: William Congreve, John Vanbrugh, Thomas D'Urfey, and John Dennis, all of whom published pamphlets before the end of 1698 defending their own plays and ridiculing Collier's arguments. Of these the first three tended to be petulant and to rely on scorn and a tone of broad mockery. Dennis,

however, in *The Usefulness of the Stage to the Happiness of Mankind, to Government, and to Religion*, took Collier's statements one by one and suggested that their passionate pronouncements often failed to take historical and social fact into account. Dennis argued that it was not the theatre that had corrupted society but, as Dryden would imply in his epilogue to *The Pilgrim*, the licentious court of Charles II. Theatre educated the public against superstition and the pretensions of priests.

Another critic, the journalist George Ridpath, took an opposite path, extending Collier's argument to suggest that the stage was wholly evil and had always been so. Ridpath's *The Stage Condemn'd*, which also appeared in 1698, gave a complete history of the stage from earliest times, purporting to show that the most responsible opinion in every age was always against all theatrical representations. He also included the entire text of Inigo Jones's and William Davenant's court masque *Britannia triumphans*, performed before Charles I on twelfth night, 1637, which fell on a Sunday, so the reader 'might see what sort of Religion or Evening Sermons, it was that the Court and Laud's Faction of the Church then aimed at' (Ridpath, 30) and question the reputed piety of Charles I. Ridpath both articulated a wider objection to and condemnation of the stage than Collier, and implicated Collier, a nonjuror and Jacobite, as part of the movement that encouraged the immorality of the stage in the first place.

Collier replied to his critics with *A Defence of the 'Short View of the Profaneness and Immorality of the English Stage'*, which appeared in 1699. In the following year Collier published *A Second Defence of the 'Short View of the Profaneness and Immorality of the English Stage'*, in reply to James Drake's *Antient and Modern Stages Survey'd* (1699). The *Second Defence* introduced no new arguments against the stage, but sought to discredit Drake by finding flaws in Drake's history and his translations from Latin and Greek authors.

Perhaps the most reasonable, logical, and best argued refutation of Collier was Edward Filmer's *A Defence of Plays, or, The Stage Vindicated*, published in 1707 but written at some point before Filmer's death in 1703. Filmer's book refutes Collier chapter by chapter; his concluding statements condemn Collier's methods and intentions, alleging that he had manipulated the controversy to keep it alive, and always intended to destroy, not reform, the theatre. Apparently unaware that Filmer was dead, Collier replied in 1708 with *A Further Vindication of the 'Short View' … in which the Objections of 'A Defence of Plays' are Considered*, which offered no new ideas but forcefully reiterated his original case.

Influence of A Short View *A Short View of the Immorality and Profaneness of the English Stage* was widely approved and immensely influential in and beyond Collier's lifetime. Even Filmer conceded that it was 'A Piece! That has been receiv'd by the World with a general Applause, and stood the Shock of some of the greatest Wits of the Age' (Filmer, 1–2). A presbyterian alderman of London and MP for Reading, Sir Owen Buckingham, gave Collier 20 guineas as a reward for the book. Collier was aware that he had found an audience, and his defences of *A Short View* were usually shorter and more pointed summaries of his arguments that could be easily digested by his readership. Collier's warnings seemed confirmed when new productions of *Macbeth* and *The Tempest* in 1703 were followed by the great storm of 26–7 November that year. Collier published *Mr Collier's Dissuasive from the Playhouse, in a Letter to a Person of Quality*, in the wake of the storm. The Society for the Promotion of Christian Knowledge established a committee to supervise the regulation of the playhouses and draw up reasons to recommend their suspension. They also bought 200 copies of the *Dissuasive* for distribution outside churches.

Before the end of the first decade of the eighteenth century both Richard Steele and Colley Cibber had publicly declared that they approved of Collier's attack and both of them claimed that their own plays were influenced by Collier's views. Steele went so far as to say of *The Lying Lover*, of 1703,

> Mr. Collier had, about the time Wherein this was published, written against the Immorality of the Stage. I was (as far as I durst for fear of witty Men, upon whom he had been too severe) a great Admirer of his Work and took it into my head to write a Comedy in the Severity he required. (Steele, 'Mr Steele's apology for himself and his writings', 311)

There can be no doubt that Collier's expressed views influenced the emergence of the sentimental or genteel comedy which, with a few exceptions, dominated English theatre writing until well into the nineteenth century.

Collier clinches his argument, from his point of view, by making it clear that he intends to be no respecter of persons: 'As for Shakespear, he is too guilty to make an Evidence: But I think he gains not much by his Misbehaviour; He has commonly Plautus's Fate, where there is most Smut there is least Sense' (Collier, *A Short View*, 50). Here again Collier's fingerprints can be discerned on the eighteenth-century adaptations of Shakespeare by Colley Cibber, Nahum Tate, and others.

Later works Collier's publications subsequent to *A Short View* that were not part of his campaign against the stage were designed both to furnish him with income and to further his case for the independence of the church's authority from that of the civil power, as well as to emphasize the perfection of the early church as an ideal. *The Great Historical, Geographical, Genealogical and Poetical Dictionary* appeared in 1701; a supplement followed in 1705 and an appendix in 1721. The *Dictionary* was translated largely from Louis Moréri's *Grand dictionnaire historique*, first published in Lyons in 1674 and revised in Amsterdam by Jean Le Clerc in 1691, but it contained new material on English and church history from Collier. He did not write entries dealing with events after 1688, presumably because his Jacobite sympathies would conflict with the interest of the publisher. Thomas Hearne dismissed the work as inaccurate, but it sold well. Meanwhile Collier also published *An Ecclesiastical History of Great Britain* in two volumes published in 1708 and 1714. This was better regarded by Hearne and by other scholars and was still thought of as a valuable church history by William Hunt in his entry on Collier for the *Dictionary of National Biography* in 1887. The

Ecclesiastical History derived its constitutional history from the work of Robert Brady, who had been master of Gonville and Caius when Collier was an undergraduate, and who had argued that the English constitution was not handed down from the Anglo-Saxon period or earlier, but instead rested on the conquest of William I. Collier sought to demonstrate, in contrast to the comparatively recent origins of the civil power, 'the continued existence in England of the bearers of the divine commission, free both from papal and royal interference' (Hopes, 171). The nonjurors were presented as the representatives of an unchanging ecclesiastical tradition handed down from the early church. The *Ecclesiastical History* brought accusations that Collier was a Roman Catholic sympathizer from Gilbert Burnet and others, but Collier never sought union with the Church of Rome, and continued to reject its doctrine and claim to supremacy.

Nonjuring bishop By the second decade of the eighteenth century Collier seems to have become established officiating to a small congregation in an upper room in Broad Street, London, perhaps assisted by Samuel Carte, brother of the historian Thomas Carte. He rejected approaches during Anne's reign that encouraged him to take the oaths and rejoin the established church, and supported the continuation of the nonjuring episcopate. On 14 May 1713 he was consecrated a bishop of the nonjuring Church of England, alongside Nathaniel Spinckes and Samuel Hawes, by George Hickes, nonjuring bishop of Thetford, and the Scottish episcopalian bishops James Gadderar and Archibald Campbell. Collier and his colleagues were 'catholic bishops', ministering to nonjurors without regard to diocesan borders. Hickes died in December 1715, and on 23 July 1716 Collier was elected his successor as primus of the nonjuring communion. By this time he had probably married Cecelia Deacon (*fl.* 1697–1733), widow of William Deacon (*d.* 1706), a mariner, sometime housekeeper to Hickes, and mother of the nonjuring churchman Thomas *Deacon (1697–1753), whom Collier had ordained in March. A letter from Archibald Campbell on Collier's death reveals that Collier had been married before, but no details of his first wife are known.

A project of the nonjurors that Collier took forward from 1716 was the scheme for union with the Eastern Orthodox churches in the hope that this would further perfect the nonjuring Church of England as the descendant of the primitive church. A concordat was prepared in consultation with Arsenius, archbishop of Thebais, a representative of the Egyptian church. The Russian emperor, Peter the Great, acted as an intermediary between the English nonjurors and the Greek, Russian, and Egyptian Orthodox churches. The nonjurors were willing to accept patriarchal authority, with Jerusalem as their mother see, thereby avoiding recognition of Rome as the patriarchate of the West, but were reluctant to accept transubstantiation and the invocation of the saints. Following the death of Peter the Great in 1725, negotiations ceased. By this time the nonjurors were themselves divided by an internal schism.

Collier had shared with Hickes a preference for the

eucharist as prescribed by the 1549 prayer book over that of 1662. Collier sought to introduce a revised form of this service influenced by his study of early Christian writers. The new liturgy would have introduced four usages not known in the 1662 prayer book; water was to be mixed with communion wine, prayers for the church were to encompass the faithful departed as well as the church militant on earth, a prayer was to be said for the descent of the holy ghost on the consecrated elements, and a further prayer would offer the consecrated elements to God as symbols of Christ's body and blood. Despite opposition from most of the nonjuring clergy, who were supported in exile by James Stuart, the Old Pretender, whom most non-jurors regarded as the rightful King James III, Collier imposed what he referred to as 'Primitive and Catholic Usages' (Overton, 294) on 20 December 1717, and from then on he regarded those nonjurors who adhered to the prayer book of 1662, the non-usagers, as schismatic. Collier led a pamphlet war with his critics: *Reasons for Restoring Some Prayers and Directions as they Stood in the First English Reformed Liturgy* appeared in 1717 and reached its fourth edition the next year, when Collier also published a new service book for the use of his division of the nonjurors. The usagers came to predominate among the nonjurors, helped by respect for Collier and his scholarship, which was superior to that of the leader of the non-usagers, Nathaniel Spinckes.

Collier continued to publish despite declining health, and from about 1718 the nonjuring scholar Samuel Jebb served as his librarian. *Several Discourses upon Practical Subjects* appeared in 1725 and *God not the Author of Evil* in 1726. He was reported in 1725 to be 'very poor in his old age' (Self, 11), a condition blamed on the demands of Mrs Collier, who was alleged to aspire to govern the nonjuring church. Collier remained passionately sincere and unwaveringly true to his principles. Dogma and doctrine he held, but, in the last analysis, not wisdom. Worn down by gall-bladder disease, he died in London on 26 April 1726 and was buried in the churchyard of St Pancras, London, on 29 April; he was survived by his widow and stepson.

ERIC SALMON

Sources DNB · T. B. Macaulay, *The history of England from the accession of James II*, 2nd edn, 5 vols. (1849–61) · J. A. Winn, *John Dryden and his world* (1987) · J. Collier, *A short view of the immorality and profaneness of the English stage* (1698) · J. Collier, *A defence of the 'Short view of the profaneness and immorality of the English stage'* (1699) · G. Ridpath, *The stage condemn'd* (1698) · *The stage acquitted* (1699) · J. Drake, *Antient and modern stages survey'd* (1700) · E. Filmer, *A defence of plays, or, The stage vindicated* (1707) · J. Collier, *A further vindication of the 'Short view of the profaneness and immorality of the English stage'* (1708) · C. Leech, T. W. Craik, L. Potter, and others, eds., *The Revels history of drama in English*, 8 vols. (1975–83), vol. 4 · B. Dukore, ed., *Dramatic theory and criticism* (1974) · J. Hopes, 'Politics and morality in the writings of Jeremy Collier', *Literature and History*, 8 (1978), 159–74 · D. Self, *The single source of all filth* (2000) · R. Anthony, *The Jeremy Collier stage controversy, 1698–1726* (Milwaukee, 1937) · M. Goldie, 'The nonjurors, episcopacy, and the origins of the convocation controversy', *Ideology and conspiracy: aspects of Jacobitism, 1689–1759*, ed. E. Cruickshanks (1982), 15–35 · J. H. Overton, *The nonjurors: their lives, principles, and writings* (1902) · H. Broxap, *The later non-jurors* (1924) · R. D. Cornwall, *Visible and apostolic: the constitution of the church in high church Anglican and non-juror thought* (1993) · E. Duffy,

'Primitive Christianity revived: religious renewal in Augustan England', *Renaissance and renewal in Christian history*, ed. D. Baker, SCH, 14 (1977), 287–300 · A. J. Turner, 'The Jeremy Collier stage controversy again', *N&Q*, 218 (1973), 409–12 · J. C. Findon, 'The nonjurors and the Church of England, 1689–1716', DPhil diss., U. Oxf., 1978 · I. Rivers, 'Biographical dictionaries and their uses from Bayle to Chalmers', *Books and their readers in eighteenth-century England*, ed. I. Rivers (2001), 135–69 · J. Dryden, 'An essay of dramatick poesie', in *The works of John Dryden*, 17: *Prose: 1668–1691*, ed. S. H. Monk and A. E. Wallace Maurer (1972), 3–81 · J. Dryden, 'A defence of an essay of dramatique poesie, being an Answer to the preface of *The great favourite, or, The duke of Lerma*', in *The works of John Dryden*, 9: *Plays: The Indian emperour, Secret love, Sir Martin Mar-all*, ed. J. Loftis and V. A. Dearing (1967), 3–22 · J. Dryden, 'Cymon and Iphigenia, from Bocace', in *The works of John Dryden*, 7: *Poems, 1697–1700*, ed. V. A. Dearing (2000), 513–32 · J. Dryden, preface to 'Fables: ancient and modern', in *The works of John Dryden*, 7: *Poems, 1697–1700*, ed. V. A. Dearing (2000), 24–47 · J. Dryden, preface to 'An evening's love', in *The works of John Dryden*, 10: *Plays: The tempest, Tyrannick love, An evening's love*, ed. M. A. Novak and G. R. Guffey (1970), 202–13 · J. Dryden, epilogue to 'The pilgrim', in *The works of John Dryden*, 16: *Plays: King Arthur …*, ed. V. A. Dearing (1996), 265–6 · R. Steele, 'Mr Steele's apology for himself and his writings', in *Tracts and pamphlets by Richard Steele*, ed. R. Blanchard (1944), 275–346 · *A declaration of the sense of the archbishops and bishops; now in and about London, upon the occasion of their attendance in parliament; concerning the irregular and scandalous proceedings of certain clergy-men at the execution of Sir John Freind and Sir William Parkins* (1696)
Likenesses R. White, line engraving, pubd 1701, BM, NPG; repro. in Anthony, *Jeremy Collier*, frontispiece · W. Faithorne the younger, mezzotint (after E. Lilly), NPG [*see illus.*] · J. Hopwood, engraving, Hult. Arch.; repro. in Self, *Single source*, xii · oils, repro. in Collier, *Short view*, 5th edn (1730)

Collier, Joel. See Veale, George (*b.* 1757, *d.* in or before 1833).

Collier, John [*pseud.* Tim Bobbin] (**1708–1786**), satirist and caricaturist, was born at Church Lane, Urmston, Lancashire, on 16 December 1708. He was the third of nine children of John Collier, Church of England clergyman (*c.*1676–1739) and his wife, Mary Cook (*d. c.*1726). John initially attended Urmston School, but plans for his education were abandoned when his father's sight failed. In 1722 he was apprenticed to a dutch-loom weaver at Newton Moor, near Mottram, where his father had family links. 'Hating slavery in all shapes', as he later put it (Corry, iii), he left after a year and spent the next few years as an itinerant schoolmaster in the region of Manchester. In 1729 he became assistant schoolmaster to Robert Pearson, the decrepit curate of Milnrow, near Rochdale, formally taking over the post of schoolmaster in 1742 after Pearson's death. Richard Townley of Belfield, a local mercer and landowner, became his patron. Collier supplemented his meagre income by private teaching and by acting as hedge lawyer, composing letters, wills, indentures, and other documents. He acquired notoriety through squibs, satires, poetry, and practical jokes, on one occasion blasting the 'Prickshaw witch' (a local conjuror) with fire and water.

On 1 April 1744 Collier married Mary Clay (*c.*1726–1786), a young Huddersfield midwife with a family connection in Milnrow, brought up in London. Notwithstanding the early exhaustion of her fortune the marriage seems to

John Collier (1708–1786), self-portrait, c.1750

have been a success and produced nine children, seven of whom survived into adulthood.

In 1746 there appeared under the name Tim Bobbin, Collier's first and most famous work, *A View of the Lancashire Dialect, or, Tummus and Mary*, the earliest significant piece of Lancashire dialect to be published. Subsequently expanded to include a glossary, illustrations, and other material, it went through seven editions in his own lifetime and was prolifically pirated both before and after his death. Running short of money Collier in 1750 reluctantly accepted an offer from an admirer, Richard Hill, of the well-paid post of clerk at his woollen clothworks at Kebroyd, near Halifax. Finding himself 'metamorphosed from a petty monarch, to a species of slave' (*Works*, 214) he soon rebelled against the discipline of work and jubilantly returned to Milnrow at Christmas 1751 to take up his old post of schoolmaster, later declaring: 'Liberty in rags, is preferable to dependance in gorgeous trappings' (*Works*, 247).

Collier now developed his trade as a painter, increasingly with the help of his sons, producing inn signs, painted panels, and grotesque caricatures which were widely distributed, reaching the American colonies via a Liverpool merchant. He promoted and distributed his own work, travelling all over northern England collecting and delivering orders and commissions for books and pictures and consuming the proceeds as he went. Publicans were among his best customers, and they his. In 1773 was published his *Human Passions Delineated*, an upmarket edition of his caricatures which acted as a catalogue, in

which he described himself as the 'Lancashire Hogarth'. His writings occasionally brought him into conflict with authority. His 1757 intervention in Manchester's food riots, *Truth in a Mask*, and his 1760 'Remarks on the reign of George II' both had to be printed clandestinely, bearing the imprint 'Amsterdam'. During the American War of Independence he openly sided with the colonists and was reportedly indicted for producing a picture libellous on the king. His politics, however, were those of the court jester: when he signed himself 'reforming John', it was as a drunkard rather than as a radical (*Works*, 244). His targets were the standard butts of eighteenth-century satire: old wives, 'Oliverian dotards', Methodists, Scots, tax-eaters, fops, courtiers, lawyers, and swindling printers. He reserved his fiercest hostility for wealthy clergy and pluralists, thick on the ground thereabouts, best expressed in the epitaph:

Full three feet deep beneath this stone
Lies our late vicar Forster
Who clipp'd his sheep to the very bone
But said no Pater Noster.

In his declining years Collier was conveyed around Milnrow in an armchair equipped with wheels, while his wife's was adapted as a sedan chair. He died there, unreformed and contented, on 14 July 1786, having lived heartily up to his own motto, 'Laugh and be fat'. His wife had died the previous month, and they were buried close together in Rochdale churchyard. His three eldest sons were apprenticed to coachmakers and subsequently had notable careers, Charles as portrait painter, Thomas as persecuted radical, and John successively as artist, historian of Newcastle upon Tyne, and lunatic, his insanity recognizable as a bizarre caricature of his father.

Commentators in all ages have had trouble in allocating a cultural level to Tim Bobbin. Two local radicals, Robert Walker (writing as Tim Bobbin the Second in 1796) and James Butterworth (as Paul Bobbin in 1819), later attempted to appropriate his reputation to the radical cause. Walter Scott visited his grave in 1818, and he was revered by later generations of dialect writers. Metropolitan contemporaries were prone to view him with condescension as a naïve rustic, a product of the culture he portrayed. The 1810 London edition of *Human Passions* systematically softened his caricatures, while an 1828 edition of the *Lancashire Dialect* was supplied with more conventionally crafted pictures by George Cruikshank. The Victorian antiquary W. E. Axon thought his pictures 'execrable … gross and cruel', while the *Dictionary of National Biography* found them 'grotesque' and 'absolutely devoid of artistic merit'. Collier himself referred to 'my old trade of boggart-painting' (*Works*, 242). He drew, however, not only on traditions of inn sign and carriage painting but on the work of Hogarth and on Flemish low-life art, and encountered Flemish and London artists in Lancashire.

Similarly, while Corry regarded Collier's poetry as 'incorrect, coarse and vulgar' (Corry, xxvi), he was in fact well educated, familiar with Chaucer, the classics, and contemporary literature of all kinds, and pursued antiquarian interests. In 1771, 'having a natural antipathy to tyranny in writing, as well as politics' (*Works*, 105), he launched a learned and devastating satirical assault on the Revd John Whitaker's overblown *History of Manchester*, claiming (for example) that a find identified by Whitaker as a Saxon lachrymatory was in fact a witch bottle, filled with piss, and comparing the whole to 'the towering smoke of Ossian' (*Works*, 108). His *Lancashire Dialect* similarly was serious but not solemn, based on careful collection and glossing of the language he heard, and influential in defining the comic figure of the impoverished Lancastrian, downtrodden, ridiculous, and obtusely irrepressible. Samuel Bamford, author of a fine poem, 'Tim Bobbin's Grave', spoke the dialect but thought Collier's orthoepy betrayed his Mersey region origins and issued his own edition in 1850. Later scholars of dialect agreed that Collier's version of south-east Lancashire dialect was the closest surviving English relative of Anglo-Saxon. The unorthodox vigour of Collier's etchings, the informal directness of his prose, and the eloquent vulgarity of his verse appeal directly from the eighteenth century to the present.   ROBERT POOLE

Sources *The works of John Collier*, ed. H. Fishwick (1894) • R. Townley, 'Account of Tim Bobbin', in J. Aikin, *A description of the country from thirty to forty miles round Manchester* (1795), 250–59 • J. Corry, 'Memoir of Tim Bobbin', in *The works of Tim Bobbin* (1819); [another edn] (1862) • S. Bamford, *The dialect of south Lancashire* (1850) • E. Waugh, *The village of Milnrow* (1850) • E. Waugh, *The birthplace of Tim Bobbin* (1858) • J. Heywood, 'On the south Lancashire dialect', *Mamecestre: being chapters from the early recorded history of the barony*, ed. J. Harland, 3, Chetham Society, 58 (1862), 1–84 [copy in Chetham's Library annotated by F. R. Raines] • *Enter Tim Bobbin* (1980) [exhibition catalogue, Rochdale Art Gallery, 23 Feb – 23 March 1980] • D. Donald and B. Maidment, *Human passions delineated: an exploration of the work of Tim Bobbin* (1990) • J. Bond and P. Bond, *Tim Bobbin lives! The life and times of a Lancashire legend* (1980) • J. A. Hilton, 'Tim Bobbin and the origins of provincial consciousness in Lancashire', *Journal of the Lancashire Dialect Society*, 19 (1970), 2–7 • H. Fishwick, 'Tim Bobbin versus John Whitaker', *Transactions of the Lancashire and Cheshire Antiquarian Society*, 13 (1895), 19–26 • J. Lee, 'Memoir of John Collier', Man. CL, Lee MSS • Collier family Bible, Chetham's Library, Manchester • Chetham's Library, Manchester, Collier MSS • gravestone, parish churchyard, Rochdale [H. Fishwick] • E. Axon, 'The children of Tim Bobbin', *Bygone Lancashire*, ed. E. Axon (1892), 116–31

Archives Chetham's Library, Manchester, literary MSS, sketchbooks, and accounts • Man. CL, MSS, notebooks, accounts, and unpublished proofs • NRA, letters and poems • Rochdale Museum, artefacts | Man. CL, Jesse Lee MSS

Likenesses J. Collier, self-portrait, caricature, *c*.1750, Rochdale Art Gallery [*see illus.*] • J. Sanders, line engraving, 1773, BM, NPG; repro. in Fishwick, ed., *Works* • C. Collier, oil sketch, Rochdale Art Gallery • stipple, NPG

Wealth at death approx. £50: inventory, Collier MSS, Chetham's Library, Manchester, E 3.6/9.3

Collier, John (1850–1934), portrait painter, was born at 18 Gloucester Road, Paddington, Middlesex, on 27 January 1850, the second son of Robert Porrett *Collier, first Baron Monkswell (1817–1886), a distinguished lawyer and judge, and Isabella Rose (1815–1886), daughter of William Rose Rose of Wolston Heath near Rugby and Daventry. Collier was educated at Eton College (1862–5) and then at Heidelberg. Deciding against his intended career in the diplomatic service, he returned to England, where he worked,

temporarily, in the city office of Sir John Pender of the Telegraph Construction and Maintenance Company. With the encouragement of his father, who himself was a capable amateur artist, Collier then studied at the Slade School of Fine Art, London, under Edward John Poynter. He remained there for three years after which he went to study in Munich and then in Paris under Jean Paul Laurens. His father also introduced him to Lawrence Alma-Tadema and John Everett Millais, from whom he received guidance and encouragement.

Collier first exhibited at the Royal Academy in 1874, sending a study of a head. His portraits of Major and Mrs Forster, exhibited in 1877, attracted attention and helped establish him as a society portrait painter. Thereafter he exhibited annually—sending a total of 140 pictures—until his death (though he was never elected a member). He also exhibited 165 works at the Royal Society of Portrait Painters of which he later became vice-president. His output was prolific; over 1100 pictures are recorded in his sitter book and of these over eight hundred are portraits. His sitters included Anthony Ashley-Cooper, seventh earl of Shaftesbury, George Bernard Shaw, Sir Oswald Mosley, Henry Irving, Rudyard Kipling, first Earl Kitchener, and Ellen Terry.

Collier's methodical and faithful rendering of his subjects has led to comparisons with the work of Frank Holl, but some of his more imposing portraits are clearly reminiscent of Millais's statesmen. Collier's portraits of the naturalist Charles Robert Darwin (1881; Linnean Society, 1883 replica; NPG) and of the biologist Thomas Henry Huxley, whom he painted twice (1883; NPG; and 1890; Royal Society, London), are notable works. Collier also produced dramatic depictions of classical and historical scenes such as *Priestess of Delphi* (1891; Art Gallery of South Australia, Adelaide) and *A Glass of Wine with Caesar Borgia* (1893; Ipswich Art Gallery). During his own lifetime Collier's reputation also rested, in part, on his so-called 'problem pictures'. Intended simply to be depictions of moments of domestic tragedy, contrary to his efforts, their interpretation was felt by many to be unclear; conundrums to be unravelled by the viewer. Of these, two examples are *The Prodigal Daughter* (1903; Usher Gallery, Lincoln) and *A Confession* (1902).

Collier married on 30 June 1879 Marian (1859–1887), daughter of Professor Thomas Henry Huxley. She too had studied at the Slade and exhibited three works at the Royal Academy between 1839 and 1841. Having suffered from mental illness since the birth of their daughter Joyce in 1884, she was taken by Collier to Paris in 1887 in the hope of finding a cure. Tragically she died of pneumonia on 18 November 1887. In 1889 Collier married, with Huxley's blessing, Marian's youngest sister, Ethel Gladys. Owing to the rejection of the Deceased Wife's Sister Bill (finally passed in 1907) the marriage took place in Christiania, Norway. Their marriage was not warmly accepted by everyone; Collier's sister-in-law, Lady Monkswell, broke off all contact. With Ethel, Collier moved to North House, Eton Avenue—a building he had commissioned from his brother-in-law, Frederick Waller. They had two children, Laurence *Collier and Joan.

Collier had various one-man exhibitions during his lifetime: an exhibition of landscapes at the Leicester Galleries in 1915; a retrospective show at the Sunderland Art Gallery in 1922; another at the Museum Galleries, Haymarket, in 1931. He published various treatises on painting: *A Primer of Art* (1882), *A Manual of Oil Painting* (1886), and *The Art of Portrait Painting* (1905). His writings encouraged a strict, practical, accurate approach, thoroughness and attention to detail being rated above artistic flair.

The obituary in *The Times* described him as 'a thin, bearded man, he gave the impression of polite independence—a sort of quiet ruthlessness—in personal intercourse, a character which was undoubtedly reflected in his painting' (*The Times*, 12 April 1934). Collier was one of the few rationalists of the Victorian establishment. He published his views on religion, morality, and citizenship in *The Religion of an Artist* (1926). During the First World War he was employed by the Foreign Office as a clerk in the deciphering department. He was appointed OBE for his services.

Collier died on 11 April 1934 at his home, North House, in Eton Avenue. He had suffered from paralysis for years but worked right up until his death installing a lift in North House so that he could get to his studio, from where he worked from his wheelchair using brushes tied to bamboo staves. His second wife survived him.

Collier, who has no fewer than thirteen works in the National Portrait Gallery, London, is also represented in numerous other collections including the National Gallery of Ireland, Dublin, Brighton Art Gallery, Southampton City Art Gallery, the Tate collection, and the Guildhall Art Gallery, London.　　　　　　　　　　JILL SPRINGALL

Sources Graves, *RA exhibitors*, vol. 1 · A. Jarman and others, eds., *Royal Academy exhibitors, 1905–1970: a dictionary of artists and their work in the summer exhibitions of the Royal Academy of Arts*, 6 vols. (1973–82), vol. 2 · W. H. Pollock, 'The art of the Hon. John Collier', *Art Annual* (1914) · W. H. Pollock, 'John Collier', *Art Journal*, new ser., 14 (1894), 65–9 · R. W. Clark, *The Huxleys* (1968) · *The Times* (12 April 1934) · *Ceylon Observer* (12 April 1934) · *Daily Mail* (12 April 1934) · *Nottingham Guardian* (12 April 1934) · *The Observer* (15 April 1934) · *Manchester Guardian* (12 April 1934) · *Hampstead Advertiser* (19 April 1934) · *Morning Post* (12 April 1934) · K. K. Yung, *National Portrait Gallery: complete illustrated catalogue, 1856–1979*, ed. M. Pettman (1981) · R. Treble, ed., *Great Victorian pictures: their paths to fame* (1978) [exhibition catalogue, Leeds, Leicester, Bristol, and London, 28 Jan – Sept 1978] · J. Turner, ed., *The dictionary of art*, 34 vols. (1996) · Wood, *Vic. painters*, 3rd edn · B. Stewart and M. Cutten, *The dictionary of portrait painters in Britain up to 1920* (1997) · J. Collier, sitter book, 1874–1934, NPG, Heinz Archive and Library · GEC, *Peerage* · b. cert. · m. cert.
Archives NPG, sitter book, 1874–1934
Likenesses S. P. Hall, pencil drawing, c.1895, NPG · J. Collier, self-portrait, oils, 1907, Uffizi Gallery, Florence, Italy · E. X. Kapp, drawings, 1930–31, Barber Institute of Fine Arts, Birmingham · S. P. Hall, group portrait, chalk and wash drawing (*The St John's Wood Arts Club*, 1895), NPG · London News Agency, photograph, NPG · J. Russell & Sons, photograph, NPG
Wealth at death £12,500 12s. 4d.: probate, 15 June 1934, CGPLA Eng. & Wales

Collier, John Gordon (1935–1995), chemical engineer, was born on 22 January 1935 at 84 Thrale Road, Streatham, London, the only child of John (Jack) Collier, a professional double bass player, and his wife, Edith Georgina de Ville (d. 1948). The Second World War disrupted Collier's education and family life; he moved many times, and the family was reunited only after the war. He gained his O levels at St Paul's School in 1951 and then joined the Atomic Energy Research Establishment at Harwell, a part of the UK Atomic Energy Authority (UKAEA), as a student apprentice. He achieved his A levels by part-time study at Oxford Technical College and gained an award to study at University College, London. There he obtained a first-class honours degree in chemical engineering in 1956, before returning to Harwell. This apprenticeship among the 'other ranks' served Collier well and resulted in his easy relationships with people at all levels. On 18 August 1956 he married Ellen Alice Mary (1935–1998), a secretary at Harwell and daughter of David Frank Mitchell, a laboratory assistant. They were a happy couple; Ellen was highly supportive and an able aide. Collier was proud of his family and the achievements of their children, Clare and John Douglas, who both enjoyed successful careers.

Collier's service with UKAEA was broken by several periods elsewhere, which were formative in his development and gave him a breadth of experience that greatly contributed to his later success. From 1962 to 1964 he worked with Atomic Energy of Canada at Chalk River, and then returned to Britain to join Atomic Power Constructions Ltd in 1966. Back with UKAEA, he became head of its chemical engineering division in 1975, and director of its safety and reliability division (1982–3). After three years as director-general of the Central Electricity Generating Board, he returned to UKAEA as deputy chairman in 1986 and chairman the following year.

There was a marked transition in Collier's work from the early 1970s, when he collaborated with Walter Marshall, former director at Harwell. Their projects included the two Marshall study group reports on the structural integrity of the light water reactor pressure vessel, which challenged a current view on the safety of pressure vessels and largely contributed to the eventual acceptance of the pressurized water reactor design in the United Kingdom. Collier and Marshall also worked on the International Atomic Energy Agency's international nuclear fuel cycle evaluation programme and on the pressurized water reactor task force, chaired by Marshall, a body that integrated the efforts of a large number of relevant UK organizations to introduce the pressurized water reactor into the UK. Collier became a member, then head, of the atomic energy technical unit, known familiarly as 'Walter's think-tank'.

Collier was the first chairman of Nuclear Electric plc, set up in 1990 to operate the nuclear power stations in England and Wales. He was at this time chairman of UKAEA and relinquished this post with some reluctance because he felt able to cope with both jobs. The achievement of the key targets he set for the new company caused a turnaround in performance and established the base for the eventual privatization of its nuclear power stations. Success in meeting these targets, and in setting nuclear power in the United Kingdom on its new path, was Collier's great lifetime achievement.

Collier was a giant of a man, both physically and intellectually. Unpretentious in manner, he was capable of intense concentration and had a memory to match, backed up by a large filing system. He could digest a large amount of information and then reorganize it in simpler but understandable form. He wrote many books and papers and was an excellent reviewer. His *Convective Boiling and Condensation* (1972) became a standard reference work for engineers. As a natural communicator he was in demand as a speaker and made many presentations to various audiences. He was elected a fellow of the Royal Academy of Engineering in 1988, and a fellow of the Royal Society in 1990, was made an honorary DS of Cranfield University in 1988, and an honorary DEng of Bristol University in 1993, the year in which he was also president of the Institution of Chemical Engineers.

In addition to his great love of cricket—his exuberant youthful bowling having struck terror into the batsmen who faced him—Collier was an enthusiastic supporter of most sports, and had a deep appreciation of music and painting. These interests were reflected in the wide range of support given by Nuclear Electric plc to many individuals, organizations, and events in these fields. He was particularly pleased when the derelict Bankside power station, which Nuclear Electric had inherited from the former Central Electricity Generating Board, was taken over by the Tate Gallery. He died at his home, Field House, Longridge, Sheepscombe, Gloucestershire, on 18 November 1995.   L. Myrddin Davies

Sources G. F. Hewitt, *Memoirs FRS*, 45 (1999), 67–75 · *The Independent* (23 Nov 1995) · b. cert. · d. cert.

Wealth at death £102,544: probate, 16 Feb 1996, *CGPLA Eng. & Wales*

Collier, John Henry Noyes (1901–1980), writer, was born on 3 May 1901 at 23 St Lawrence Road, Brixton, London, to John George Collier (1852–1939), a commercial clerk, and Emily Mary, *née* Noyes (1865–1939), a kindergarten teacher. He had no formal schooling besides a brief spell at preparatory school; his mother and his paternal uncle, Vincent Collier, a writer, were his chief tutors.

In 1921 Collier moved to Pimlico, London, with the intention of becoming a writer. He supplemented an allowance from his father by writing a regular column for the *Osaka Mainichi*, an English-language Japanese broadsheet. He was a great frequenter of parties and a satellite of the literary scene, counting the Sitwells, E. M. Forster, and Wyndham Lewis among his acquaintances. A selection of the poetry he wrote during this time was published as *Gemini* (1931). It carried an 'Apology' in which Collier rejected his muse and extolled the virtues of prose. The volume won *This Quarter*'s poetry prize in the year of its publication.

Collier's reputation as a young and daring writer of prose was secured by the publication of *His Monkey Wife* in December 1930, a wicked and witty satire about a man seduced by a chimpanzee. Its range of literary reference reflects the author's wide reading. A novella, *No Traveller Returns*, a Wellsian pastiche about a cannibalistic future, was issued in a limited edition in 1931. He left London for rural retreat in this year, settling at Crux Easton, near Newbury. Here he wrote two further novels, the post-apocalyptic *Tom's a-Cold* (1933) and *Defy the Foul Fiend* (1934), loosely based on Collier's experiences of the London scene. Collier worked on a fourth novel, 'Easy Go Grange', from 1937 to 1939. It is cited by Edwin Muir in his *Introduction to English Literature: the Present Age* (1939) but it was never completed. Collier edited *The Scandal and Credulities of John Aubrey*, a popular edition of Aubrey's *Brief Lives* and, with Iain Lang, co-wrote a history of Britain between the wars, *Just the Other Day* (1932).

In 1935 Collier spent time in Cassis in the south of France; from here he travelled to Hollywood under contract to RKO to work on *Sylvia Scarlett* (1935), the first of a number of screenplays. The following year he was commissioned to write a screenplay for MGM at the request of the actor Charles Laughton ('Policeman', never produced). He returned to England in summer 1936 with his wife, the actress Shirley Lee Palmer, whom he had married in January; the novelist Hugh Walpole was best man. Collier had plans to set up home with the artist Eric Boston and his family at Wilcote, near Finstock, Oxfordshire. Here he worked on 'Easy Go Grange' and travelled to the Denham film studios, employed by the director Robert Flaherty to create a coherent narrative from reels of footage he had shot in India without a script (*Elephant Boy*, 1937). In 1938 the Colliers left for France and travelled across Europe, concluding their grand tour by taking a boat from Ireland to New York in October 1939. Collier's agent, A. D. Peters, had secured a contract with the *New Yorker*, giving the magazine first refusal on the short stories the author was to write. This was the beginning of a period of great—if enforced—productivity for Collier. Work not taken by the *New Yorker* appeared in a wide range of publications, including *Argosy*, *Bystander*, *Harper's Bazaar*, *Lilliput*, and *Tatler*. The most comprehensive anthology of Collier's stories, *Fancies and Goodnights* (1951), was awarded the first International Fantasy award in 1952. Collier wrote over 125 macabre miniatures: 107 have survived, of which fourteen remain unpublished and twenty-eight remain uncollected.

Collier took American citizenship in December 1941. From 1941 to 1953 he lived in Hollywood and earned a living as a screenwriter. He divorced Shirley in December 1943, marrying Margaret Elizabeth Eke, a film studio reader, in 1945; they divorced in 1952. Collier's film work from this time includes *Her Cardboard Lover* (1942); *Holy Matrimony* (uncredited, 1943); *Deception* (1946); and *Roseanna McCoy* (1949). Collier was said to have approached Jack Warner with the idea of turning C. S. Forrester's novel *African Queen* into a film, with Bette Davis and Cary Grant in the leading roles. His screenplay differs from the film that was eventually produced. The author received no on-screen credit, though he claimed to have received a good percentage of the royalties.

This new-found financial security enabled Collier to retreat to a ramshackle mansion in Grasse in the south of

France. He lived here with his third wife, Harriet Hess Pollack (d. 1992), a film studio employee, whom he married in Mexico on 25 May 1954. A son, John George Stafford, was born in Nice on 18 May 1958. In Grasse he continued to write short stories and collaborated on screenplays (*I am a Camera*, 1955; *The War Lord*, 1965). He worked on what he considered his most important work, a screenplay for Milton's *Paradise Lost* (1973), which came close to being filmed. In 1975 the *John Collier Reader* was published with material selected by Collier himself and an introduction by Anthony Burgess. The volume reproduces the Hart-Davis text (1957) of *His Monkey Wife*, two chapters of *Defy the Foul Fiend*, and forty-seven short stories. Collier refused to allow the republication of his poetry and forbade mention of *Tom's a-Cold* which he considered juvenilia.

In 1979 Collier returned to California. He died of a cerebral thrombosis at his home in Pacific Palisades on 6 April 1980. His widow reported that Collier had started work on a novel that very morning. He was cremated in Los Angeles on 13 April.

Frances Partridge, who met Collier in 1933, remembered him as a 'dapper little man with a wicked smile' (private information). Photographs from the time bear this memory out: dressed in tweeds or plus fours and sporting a moustache, Collier was every inch the country squire. Collier continued to project a quaint and formal image throughout his life, always offset by wit and grin. At his funeral service on 13 April 1980 the writer Paul Jarrico observed that it was 'difficult to decide sometimes whether John Collier was a mischievous devil posing as an English gentleman, or an English gentleman posing as a mischievous devil'. MATTHEW McFALL

Sources M. McFall, 'John Collier (1901–1980): life and works', DPhil diss., U. Oxf., 1998 · B. Richardson, *John Collier* (Boston, MA, 1983) · T. Milne, 'The elusive John Collier', *Sight and Sound*, 45 (1975–6), 104–8 · P. Theroux, introduction, in J. Collier, *His monkey wife* (1983), v–xviii · J. Kessel, 'John Collier', *Supernatural fantasy writers*, ed. E. F. Bleiler (1985), 577–83 · *The Times* (23 May 1980) · E. Muir, *The present age from 1914* (1939), vol. 5 of *Introductions to English literature*, ed. B. Dobrée · private information (2004) [Harriet Collier, wife; son; F. Partridge] · b. cert.

Archives LUL · U. Texas, corresp. and MSS · University of Iowa, Iowa City, corresp. and MSS | Col. U., Harold Matson Co. Archives

Likenesses J. Jones, oils, c.1926, priv. coll. · E. X. Kapp, pencil drawing, c.1930, priv. coll.

Collier, John Payne (1789–1883), literary editor and forger, was born on 11 January 1789 in New Broad Street in the City of London, the second of five children of John Dyer Collier (1762–1825) and his wife, Jane Payne (1768–1833), the spirited and artistic daughter of a London sugar refiner.

Family background, early career, and marriage, 1789–1828
John Dyer Collier, talented, headstrong, and luckless, was the son of a prosperous London apothecary, whose capital stake of £10,000, given him at his majority, he dissipated in the Spanish merino wool trade. Subsequently he tried farming in Essex, but was bankrupted in 1802; he studied law briefly and in extremes turned to journalism. He edited the *Monthly Register* for Charles and John Wyatt

John Payne Collier (1789–1883), by unknown engraver, pubd 1883 (after Sydney and Ernest White, 1873)

(1802–3), translated fiction, and published an *Essay on the Law of Patents* (1803) and a *Life of Abraham Newland* (1808); in 1804 he joined the staff of *The Times* as a law and parliamentary reporter, and later moved on to the *Morning Chronicle* (1808–15). In 1816 he embarked on his final literary venture with the purchase of the moribund *Critical Review*, which he converted from tory to liberal in its politics, and from post-Augustan to Romantic in its literary predilections. This he edited, with the assistance of his son, until its final collapse eighteen months later. John Payne, educated at home and taught shorthand by his father, had himself joined *The Times* by 1806, and also participated largely in the family enterprise of supplying, by subscription, handwritten newsletters to provincial papers.

Many details of Collier's early life are recorded in the diaries and correspondence of Henry Crabb Robinson, who lodged with the family from 1806 to 1813 and remained devoted to most of them—but especially to Jane—thereafter. A religious nonconformist and a liberal idealist, John Dyer Collier numbered among his acquaintances William Godwin, Thomas Holcroft, William Hazlitt, and Leigh Hunt, and through Robinson the Colliers became intimate with Charles and Mary Lamb and friendly with the Wordsworths and S. T. Coleridge. When in 1811–12 Coleridge gave a series of lectures on Shakespeare and Milton, John Payne Collier took down several in his professional shorthand, to which alone they owe their preservation. Encouraged by Robinson, Collier took up the study of law and was admitted to the Middle Temple on 31 July 1811, but journalism continued to dominate his working hours. In 1812 he left *The Times* for the rival *Morning Chronicle*, but was back at *The Times* in 1815 for a second stint as parliamentary reporter; after being dismissed in mid-1823 by his old comrade Thomas Barnes (1785–1841), Collier returned to the *Chronicle*, where he remained until 1847. In the 1830s and 1840s he also served as theatre critic for *The Observer* and wrote, anonymously, for other periodicals.

On 20 August 1816 Collier married a cousin of his mother, Mary Louisa Pycroft (1787–1857), the daughter of William Pycroft, a Whitechapel sugar refiner; their first child, a daughter, born in 1817, was followed over the next ten years by two sons and three further daughters. By the time of his marriage Collier had begun to collect early English literature on a modest scale but with considerable discrimination, and to publish both verse and antiquarian essays, first in the *British Lady's Magazine* (1815). He was responsible for more than forty literary reviews in his father's *Critical Review*, for which he also wrote a series of sixteen essays on pre-Restoration literature, under the heading 'Bibliotheca antiqua' (1816–17). In 1818–19 Collier temporarily succeeded Frederic Shoberl (1775–1853), a family friend, as editor of Ackermann's *Repository*, to which he also contributed numerous articles and poems under a variety of pseudonyms; nine essays 'On the English dramatic writers who preceded Shakespeare' appeared in the *Edinburgh Magazine* (1818–21). A series of mildly indiscreet sketches of leading barristers and magistrates, signed 'Amicus Curiae' and first published in Leigh Hunt's *Examiner*, were collected by Collier as *Criticisms on the Bar* (1819), and proved an embarrassment to his legal career—'foolish, flippant, and fatal to my prospects, if ever I had any', he remarked of it later (*DNB*). Almost simultaneously he suffered a 'scrape' with the House of Commons over an episode improperly reported in the *Morning Chronicle*, and while he was pardoned, and even praised for his candour and courage in response, the long-term professional effect was again negative. He was not called to the bar until 6 February 1829, and never seriously practised.

Collier's two-volume *Poetical Decameron*, a series of informative but arcane dialogues on early English popular literature, appeared in 1820, and in 1822 he brought out, privately and anonymously, *The Poet's Pilgrimage*, a laboured Spenserian allegory, which in old age he believed his own best claim to remembrance; it was reissued under his name in 1825, and drew tempered praise from Charles Lamb, its dedicatee. His first editorial work (1825–7) was the completion of a new edition of Robert Dodsley's *Select Collection of Old Plays*, begun by Octavius Gilchrist; Collier's notes, signed 'C.', appear throughout the twelve volumes, and he added six plays previously unedited. Five further plays edited by Collier were separately published by Septimus Prowett in 1828–9 and reissued as *Five Old Plays* in 1833. The same publisher in 1828 engaged Collier to provide the text for a series of engravings by George Cruikshank illustrating the popular Punch and Judy puppet show. By 1881 at least eight English editions of the resulting *Punch and Judy* had appeared; Collier's play-text, based loosely on a performance by Piccini, remains standard, and his introductory history of puppet theatre is still often cited.

Literary achievement and literary forgery, 1828–1837 By the late 1820s Collier was at work on his most important, if flawed, work of scholarship, a *History of English Dramatic Poetry and Annals of the Stage* (to about 1660), which John Murray published in three volumes in 1831 (*HEDP*). Although some whimsical fictions and slight literary impostures had found their way into Collier's earlier works—from the *Critical Review* in 1819 to verse by 'Lord Byron' in *Punch and Judy*—here, for the first time *in extenso*, fabrications of historical evidence and documentary text are interspersed in an otherwise meticulous and original scholarly work. Some twenty instances of fakery have by now been identified in *HEDP*, mostly involving text for which no source has ever come to light, but several are based upon physical forgeries in the British Museum manuscript collections, the State Paper Office, and among the Alleyn and Henslowe papers at Dulwich College. Collier's personal responsibility both for the unsubstantiated reports and for the forged handwritten material in public repositories was long disputed, not least by himself, but the accumulation of subsequent evidence seems to rule out the agency of any other mischievous perpetrator. Why he should thus have marred a work of great merit, and blighted a literary career already successfully advanced, has always vexed his biographers, but whatever the reason or reasons, once indulged, his propensity for invention never subsided. For decades, however, no one suspected *HEDP* of corruption, and it served most Victorians as a blameless authority and the principal guide to its subjects.

Collier dedicated *HEDP* to William Spencer Cavendish (1790–1858), sixth duke of Devonshire, the leading private collector of old English drama, who had befriended him and commissioned him at £100 a year to be his part-time librarian in London. For a time Devonshire's patronage made the lucrative appointment of Examiner of Plays, in succession to George Colman the younger, seem a possibility, but this came to nothing. Collier oversaw for the duke a fine facsimile of an Inigo Jones sketchbook in 1831, organized his old plays, and procured for him many significant additions, including quartos from the Richard Heber dispersal of 1834–6; he also contributed valuable catalogue notes to part IV of that sale, the richest portion of Heber's early poetry and popular prose (1834), and on the day bought what he could for himself, as well as for Devonshire.

Under Devonshire's sponsorship Collier became in 1832 the twelfth member of the new Garrick Club, long to be a favourite haunt, although he was later passed over for the Athenaeum. In December 1830 he was elected a fellow of the Society of Antiquaries, put forward by Francis Douce and Thomas Amyot; he later served as treasurer (1847–9) and vice-president (1849–56), and recycled at least one youthful invention, originally aired in the *Critical Review*, in the society's *Archaeologia*. Following the publication of *HEDP* he gained access to the largely uninvestigated collection of books and manuscripts kept at Bridgewater House by Lord Francis Leveson Gower, afterwards Lord Egerton (1833) and earl of Ellesmere (1846). Collier produced an elaborate printed catalogue of the rarer English books in the Bridgewater collection (1837), and in 1840 edited a selection of *Egerton Papers* for the Camden Society. The family muniments, particularly those relating to James I's chancellor, Sir Thomas Egerton, yielded material for three Shakespearian tracts, published by Collier through the learned bookseller Thomas Rodd: *New Facts Relating to the*

Life of Shakespeare (1835), *New Particulars etc.* (1836), and *Farther Particulars etc.* (1839). Alongside genuine material, however, Collier again printed a number of forgeries and fabrications, including 'antique' ballads of his own composition, as well as several 'contemporary' letters and documents referring to Shakespeare that he claimed to have found among Egerton's uncatalogued papers.

Shakespeare and other studies, 1837–1851 In 1837 Collier became a sub-editor at the *Morning Chronicle*, and for the next two or three years was responsible for many of the paper's political columns and leading articles. By 1841, however, he was displaced and his salary cut, and he returned to the tedious routine of the parliamentary gallery. He now projected and advertised (in *Reasons for a New Edition of Shakespeare*, 1841) an elaborate eight-volume edition of Shakespeare, which was published by Whittaker in 1842–4 and embodies some spurious 'contemporary' annotations from a First Folio at Bridgewater House. A few new details in the life of Shakespeare included there are also spurious, and many old impostures are repeated. In 1838 Collier participated in founding the Camden Society, devoted to reprinting 'materials for the Civil, Ecclesiastical, or Literary History of the United Kingdom', and, in 1840, the Percy and Shakespeare societies (ballads and popular literature; drama and theatrical history). For the Camden Society he produced four volumes, including the first edition of John Bale's *Kynge Johan* (1838), prepared from the manuscript he had purchased on Devonshire's behalf, and for the Percy Society he was responsible for ten more little volumes over the years 1840–44. In addition to serving as director of the Shakespeare Society and editing four volumes of its papers, Collier wrote or edited a further twenty-two volumes under its imprint (1841–51). These included a life of Edward Alleyn (1841) and an edition of Philip Henslowe's diary (1845), both based upon manuscripts at Dulwich College, and both valuable in part, but again riddled with fabricated material, some of it based on forged interpolations in the Dulwich originals. Two volumes of extracts from the registers of the Stationers' Company (Shakespeare Society, 1848–9), and a continuation in *Notes and Queries* (1861–3), are likewise contaminated: several forged additions to the original registers, especially those attributing authorship, have been blamed upon Collier, as well as a large number of otherwise unknown 'contemporary' ballads published as illustrative matter in the extracts.

In 1847 a royal commission was appointed to inquire into the management of the British Museum, and through the influence of its chairman, Lord Ellesmere, Collier was named secretary at a stipend of £300 a year for the limited duration of the inquiry; he thereupon resigned from the *Morning Chronicle*, which paid him less for more work. In two privately printed tracts addressed to his patron, and in appearances before the commission as an expert witness, Collier determinedly opposed Sir Anthony Panizzi (1797–1879), then keeper of printed books, by advocating a printed rather than a manuscript catalogue of the library. His views were publicly ridiculed by Panizzi, and the final report of the commission (1850)

endorsed Panizzi's original plan. Collier was unsuccessful in an attempt to rejoin *The Times*, but was granted a civillist pension of £100. He left London for good in the spring of 1850, taking his wife and four daughters to Holyport, Berkshire; at the end of 1853, following the death from consumption of the two eldest daughters, the family moved for the last time, to Riverside, Maidenhead.

The 'Perkins folio' and Collier's exposure, 1852–1862 In *The Athenaeum* for 31 January 1852 Collier announced his discovery of a Shakespeare Second Folio (1632) extensively 'corrected' in a mid-seventeenth-century hand. In 1853 he published the annotations, mostly providing plausible new readings, as a volume of notes and emendations to his 1842–4 Shakespeare, and gave in the preface an account (later somewhat adjusted) of his purchase of the volume from the bookseller Thomas Rodd the younger (*d.* 1849). This was followed in the same year by a one-volume edition of Shakespeare incorporating the emendations, and in 1858 by a new six-volume critical edition; the folio itself, usually called the 'Perkins folio' from an ownership inscription on its cover, was presented by Collier to the duke of Devonshire in 1853.

Over the next years the emendations of Collier's anonymous 'Old Corrector' were attacked on textual grounds by a wide range of commentators, including his young friend J. O. Halliwell, later Halliwell-Phillipps (1820–1889), his former friend Alexander Dyce (1798–1869), and his professed adversaries S. W. Singer (1783–1858), Howard Staunton (1810–1874), C. M. Ingleby (1823–1886), and A. E. Brae (1800/01–1881). Brae alone, in newspaper articles and in *Literary Cookery* (1855), suggested the possibility of forgery, and simultaneously cast doubt on the shorthand transcripts of Coleridge's 1811–12 lectures, which Collier had announced in 1854; this provoked Collier to an unsuccessful libel action against the publisher of the pamphlet, John Russell Smith. Other of Collier's 'discoveries' were questioned in the 1850s, chiefly by Halliwell, who condemned some of the Bridgewater papers in 1853, never suggesting, however, that Collier had forged them. Collier himself continued his editorial labours, preparing a volume of Michael Drayton's poems for the Roxburghe Club (1856) and beginning an elaborate new edition of Spenser, which finally appeared, in five handsome volumes, in 1862. His patrons Ellesmere and Devonshire died in 1857 and 1858, and on 10 December 1857 his wife, Mary Louisa, of cancer.

Continued speculation about the 'Perkins folio' led Sir Frederic Madden, keeper of manuscripts at the British Museum, to request a sight of the book, and in May 1859 the seventh duke of Devonshire placed it on loan there, where Madden, his assistant N. E. S. A. Hamilton, and Nevil Maskelyne, keeper of the mineral department, examined it carefully. Hamilton and Maskelyne published their findings in three letters to *The Times* (2 and 16 July), asserting that the annotations in ink were recent forgeries in a mock seventeenth-century hand, frequently corresponding (in content) to pencilled notes in an undisguised modern hand, found elsewhere in the margins; furthermore, microscopic analysis by Maskelyne showed that in some cases 'old' ink notes had been penned over similar pencillings, likewise undeniably modern. Collier replied on 7 and 20 July, again testifying that all the ink notes had been present when he purchased the book, and declaring—although he had not yet been accused of it—that he had inserted none of the suspect pencil or ink annotations. Hamilton, aided and encouraged by Staunton, Ingleby, and Madden, continued to pursue the matter, and to work up a case against Collier himself. Early in 1860 Hamilton published an inquiry into the Perkins affair that also questioned some of the Bridgewater and Dulwich papers, as well as a petition in the State Paper Office, naming Shakespeare, which had first surfaced in *HEDP*. Collier immediately published a reply in *The Athenaeum* (6 Feb 1860), expanding it to a pamphlet in the following weeks, but Hamilton's attack was soon followed by others, including a review of the controversy by T. D. Hardy of the State Paper Office (1860) and a lengthy *Complete View* by Ingleby (1861).

Rare books, revisions, and death, 1862–1883 Collier's steadfast refusal to comment further on the various accusations—of forgery in person, of complicity in deceit, or even of sustained carelessness—convinced many of his guilt, but by 1862, when he published his long-delayed Spenser to critical approval, public interest in the Perkins controversy was all but extinct. Unwilling to remain idle, in May 1862 Collier projected a scheme of reprinting rare English works of the sixteenth and seventeenth centuries in limited editions offered only by subscription. Through 1871 no fewer than eighty-one volumes appeared, ranging from pamphlets of a few pages to substantial texts such as *England's Parnassus* and *Tottell's Miscellany*. At the age of seventy-four Collier began work on his *Bibliographical and Critical Account of the Rarest Books in the English Language*, a compilation of old and new notes on minor Tudor and Stuart literature, published in two stout volumes by Joseph Lilly in 1865; it was immediately reprinted in New York and remains valuable for the out-of-the-way material it describes, despite its perpetuation of fabricated report. In the 1860s and 1870s Collier privately published several other books, including a romanticized autobiography for the years 1832–3 (*An Old Man's Diary*, 1871–2) and selections of ballads both from the seventeenth century (*Broadside Black-Letter Ballads*, 1868) and of his own composition (*A Few Odds and Ends*, 1871); he described his *Twenty-Five Old Ballads* (1869) as 'taken' from a seventeenth-century manuscript, but all the ballads were in fact written by Collier himself.

Between 1875 and 1878 Collier published his final edition of Shakespeare, issued to subscribers in forty-three parts, purporting to offer 'the purest text and the briefest notes'. On its completion he revised, very lightly, his *History of English Dramatic Poetry* for George Bell (1879), modifying only a few of the suspect entries of 1831. Now aged ninety, increasingly frail and nearly blind, Collier seldom left his home at Maidenhead, where an unmarried daughter kept house for him. He died there on 17 September 1883, and was buried in Bray churchyard three days later, survived by two sons and two daughters. Many of his rare English books had earlier been sold to J. O. Halliwell or to Frederic Ouvry (1814–1881), Collier's nephew by marriage, and the bulk of his remaining books and papers were offered by Sothebys on 7–9 August 1884, when they made £2105 16s. 6d. At that sale the British Museum acquired one of Collier's forged volumes of ballads (lot 214, now Add. MS 32380) and Dulwich College purchased a transcript in Collier's hand of Edward Alleyn's diary (lot 200), examination of which confirmed the case for his having forged interpolations in the original manuscript. Other papers remained in the family, but most, including Collier's late diary (1872–82), his 1811 shorthand notes of Coleridge's lectures, an incomplete autobiography, and the so-called Hall commonplace book, containing ballads in a faked seventeenth-century hand, have now found institutional homes, principally at the Folger Shakespeare Library, Washington, DC.

Personal life and reputation Collier's personal life, although dogged by overwork and ill health, was not overall an unhappy one. Despite the falling away of old friends such as Frederic Madden and Alexander Dyce in the mid-century, he was cherished in old age as 'the Nestor of all living Restorers of our Old Literature' by Edward Arber (*Transcript of the Registers of the Stationers' Company*, 1875, 30), flattered by Swinburne, and courted by such new friends as J. W. Ebsworth (1824–1908) in England and H. H. Furness (among many others) in America, where his following remained loyal. His critical and editorial achievement over seventy years would ensure him a high place between Edmond Malone and the moderns, had not much of it been tainted by fraud or caprice, or by the contagion of doubt that exposures have fostered. Countless genuine and acute scholarly observations—many of them still held in suspicion, unjustly—will always be overshadowed by a minority of impostures. Even his 1862 Spenser, regarded by G. F. Warner as 'an excellent edition' (*DNB*) and widely employed by Collier's editorial successors, incorporates fabricated emendations by Michael Drayton—forged in Collier's own copy of the 1612–13 folio—and the task of sorting out Collier's true from false scholarship, in literally hundreds of questioned or questionable instances, has continued for a century and more. ARTHUR FREEMAN and JANET ING FREEMAN

Sources A. Freeman and J. I. Freeman, *John Payne Collier: scholarship and forgery in the nineteenth century* (2004) · D. Ganzel, *Fortune and men's eyes: the career of John Payne Collier* (1982) · H. B. Wheatley, *Notes on the life of John Payne Collier; with a complete list of his works* (1884) · S. Schoenbaum, *Shakespeare's lives*, new edn (1991) · A. Freeman, 'A new victim for the Old Corrector', *TLS* (22 April 1983) · O. Wellens, 'The Colliers of London: early advocates of Wordsworth, Lamb, Coleridge, and other Romantics', *Bulletin of Research in the Humanities*, 86 (1983), 105–27 · A. Freeman and J. I. Freeman, 'Scholarship, forgery, and fictive invention: John Payne Collier before 1831', *The Library*, 6th ser., 15 (1993), 1–23 · J. W. Velz, 'The Collier controversy redivivus', *Shakespeare Quarterly*, 36 (1985), 106–15 · G. Dawson, 'John Payne Collier's great forgery', *Studies in Bibliography*, 24 (1971), 1–26 · S. S. Wagonheim, *John Payne Collier and the Shakespeare Society*, PhD diss., 1980, University of Maryland · C. M. Ingleby, *A complete view of the Shakspere controversy* (1861) · G. F. Warner, ed., *Catalogue of the manuscripts and muniments of Alleyn's College of God's Gift at Dulwich* (1881) · F. Dickey, 'The old man at work: forgeries in the Stationers' registers', *Shakespeare Quarterly*, 11 (1960), 39–47 · A. W. Ashby, incomplete biography and bibliography of John Payne Collier, *c*.1950, Bodl. Oxf., MSS Eng. misc. d.1455–1456/1–2 · H. C. Robinson, manuscript diaries, letters and reminiscences, 1798–1866, Dr William's Library, London · G. Ziegler, 'A Victorian reputation: John Payne Collier and his contemporaries', *Shakespeare Studies*, 17 (1985), 209–34 · S. Schoenbaum, *William Shakespeare: records and images* (1981) · R. A. Foakes, ed., *Coleridge on Shakespeare: the text of the lectures of 1811–12* (1971) · M. Spevack, 'James Orchard Halliwell and friends: I. John Payne Collier', *The Library*, 6th ser., 18 (1996), 124–53

Archives BL, papers, Add. MSS 32379–32382; Egerton 2623 · Bodl. Oxf., corresp. and collections for actors' biographies · Boston PL, letters and papers · Folger · Hunt. L., letters · Shakespeare Birthplace Trust RO, Stratford upon Avon, letters | BL, corresp. with Thomas Amyot, Add. MS 33963 · BL, letters to W. Hazlitt and W. C. Hazlitt, Add. MSS 38898–38913 · BL, letters to Sir Frederick Madden, Egerton MSS 2838–2846 · BL, letters as sponsor to the Royal Literary Fund, loan no. 96 · Bodl. Oxf., letters to Thomas Amyot; letters to H. S. Harper · Bodl. Oxf., corresp. with Sir Thomas Phillips · Chatsworth House, Derbyshire, letters to sixth duke of Devonshire · DWL, letters to Henry Crabb Robinson · U. Edin. L., corresp. with J. O. Halliwell-Phillipps; letters to David Laing · U. Newcastle, Robinson L., corresp. with Walter Trevelyan · V&A NAL, letters to Alexander Dyce

Likenesses T. C. Wageman, miniature, *c*.1820, priv. coll. · photograph, 1873, priv. coll.; repro. in Ganzel, *Fortune and men's eyes* · wood-engraving (after photograph by S. and E. White, 1873), repro. in *ILN* (29 Sept 1883) [*see illus.*]

Wealth at death £5101 0s. 3d.: resworn probate, 1883/4

Collier, Sir Laurence (1890–1976), diplomatist, was born at 4 Marlborough Place, Marylebone, London, on 13 June 1890, the only son and elder of the two children of the Hon. John *Collier (1850–1934), portrait painter, and his second wife, Ethel Gladys (1866–1941), the youngest daughter of Thomas Henry *Huxley, president of the Royal Society. His father's first marriage had been to Marian (1859–1887), second daughter of T. H. Huxley, and Collier had an older half-sister, Joyce, as well as a younger sister, Joan. His paternal grandfather was Robert Porrett *Collier, first Baron Monkswell, politician and judge. Collier was educated at Bedales School, then an ultra-modern institution. His experience there made it difficult for him to understand colleagues from more traditional schools. At Balliol College, Oxford, where his tutors were A. L. Smith and H. W. C. Davis, he was a Brackenbury scholar, won the college history prize, and graduated with a first-class degree in modern history in 1912. Although tempted to become a historian, he chose a career in the Foreign Office.

Collier entered the Foreign Office in October 1913 and after a brief apprenticeship in the ciphering room he was assigned to the eastern department. In 1914, upon the outbreak of war, his department was merged into the new war department, in which he served throughout the conflict. On 31 May 1917 he married Eleanor Antoinette Watson (*d*. 1975), only daughter of William Luther Watson. They had one son, William Oswald (*b*. 1919).

In May 1919 Collier was posted as second secretary at Tokyo. He returned to the Foreign Office in January 1921. He was initially assigned to the treaty department (1922–3), where he was promoted first secretary in September 1923, and then the far eastern department (1924–5), before

being employed in the northern department (1926–41). It was for his connection with the northern department remit that his career was especially notable. He was promoted to counsellor in November 1932 and appointed CMG in June 1934, and was head of the northern section from 1933 to 1941. His assignment reflected not only his ability but the fact that some of his colleagues preferred him to be in a section away from the mainstream of affairs.

Despite serving in a marginal department, Collier was nevertheless able to make the force of his views felt. He was one of the strongest opponents of appeasement before the Second World War, having concluded that while communism's aims and goals had gone wrong it did at least possess an ideology, while fascism was merely brute force. His views estranged him from many of his colleagues. A notable rift occurred in 1935 with Sir Orme Sargent, over the Franco-Soviet pact, with Collier arguing that the pact would help check Germany, while Sargent was concerned that it would help to drive Germany and Japan together. With the coming of the Spanish Civil War in 1936 Collier accurately predicted that Germany and Italy would be drawn together and would ultimately be joined by a militant Japan.

While Collier did not admire Anthony Eden, some of his memoranda occasionally influenced the foreign secretary. In a paper for the committee of imperial defence in November 1937 Eden presented the view, initially expounded by Collier, that attempting to drive a wedge between Germany and Italy by acquiescing in their plans for expansion was doomed to failure: their interests were inimical to those of Britain. The alternative that Eden and Collier proposed was a policy of 'cunctation' (that is, playing for time), which although perhaps unheroic would bring security. This would be achieved by a return to the armed truce based on the balance of power which had existed during 1870–1914. In 1939 a notable exchange occurred between Collier and D'Arcy Godolphin Osborne (minister to the Holy See) on the merits of fascism as opposed to communism. Collier argued with great verve that fascism was the greater immediate threat, and in the process swayed Sir Alexander Cadogan, the permanent under-secretary. Collier's opposition to appeasement was comprehensive, and he found himself isolated even from Sir Robert Vansittart, who was willing to see some accommodation with Italy in the interests of isolating Germany. Collier was one of the first to envisage what Churchill would later call the grand alliance, pushing for some form of agreement as early as 1935.

Because Collier gave greater weight to the threat posed by the fascist states than that posed by communism, some colleagues viewed him as sympathetic to the Soviet Union. Incidents such as his strong backing in 1935 for a loan to the latter country seemed to support this conclusion. This was not the case; rather, he preferred to focus on the immediate danger posed by Germany. When the Soviet Union seized the three Baltic republics, Collier advised a policy of non-recognition. This policy was adopted and as a result, when those republics regained their independence in 1990, Britain was able simply to resume normal diplomatic relations. Collier felt a strong aversion to the depredations of both fascist and communist regimes. He was much involved in attempts to rescue the British Metro-Vickers engineers, who were the objects of one of Stalin's show trials. He was also involved, in a semi-official capacity, in the rescue of Max Salvadori, a dual national, from imprisonment in Italy for involvement in the Giustizia e Libertà movement against Mussolini.

By 1939 Collier had been earmarked as the next minister to Norway, in part to move him out of the Foreign Office, where his conclusions conflicted with the prevailing wisdom. Following the outbreak of the Second World War, and the German invasion of Norway, Collier found himself appointed in May 1941 envoy-extraordinary and minister-plenipotentiary to the Norwegian government-in-exile in London; he was raised to ambassador in May 1942. On the liberation of the country in May 1945 he travelled to Oslo, and remained there as ambassador until the end of 1950. He was promoted KCMG in 1944. In his last months at the northern department he had worked to obtain an assurance of defence for Norway in the event of an attack by Germany, and as ambassador he played a major role in bringing Norway into NATO. He retired in January 1951.

In retirement Collier was active in the affairs of the Royal Geographical Society, and served on its council. He also wrote an unpublished memoir, 'North House' (named after his parents' house in Hampstead), which described the family's social circle in the years before the First World War. A rationalist, he did not agree with the work of his cousin Aldous Huxley and he published a sharp attack on his ideas, *The Flight from Conflict* (1944). In common with his father he had a stammer, which none the less did nothing to impair his ability and effectiveness as a diplomatist. He was good at anecdotes, often about past characters in British diplomacy, with which he often regaled his juniors.

During his career in what was predominantly a conservative service, Collier was one of the few who could be viewed as left-of-centre politically. He was unusual during his time at the Foreign Office for his intellectual and analytical approach. He did not see the issues confronting Britain in terms of a choice between pro- and anti-fascism, but rather as necessitating a realist approach. It was Collier who kept the debate going in an office where there was little inclination for abstract thought. He enjoyed debate, and believed it was important to discuss key issues thoroughly. In some ways his approach was reminiscent of the intellectual approach of Sir Eyre Crowe. He died at the Kings Ride Nursing Home, 289 Sheen Road, Richmond upon Thames, on 20 October 1976, and was survived by his son; his wife had predeceased him.   ERIK GOLDSTEIN

Sources L. Collier, 'The old foreign office', *Blackwood*, 312 (1972), 256–61 · *GJ*, 143 (1977), 162–3 · R. W. Clark, *The Huxleys* (New York, 1968) · *The war diaries of Oliver Harvey*, ed. J. Harvey (1978) · M. Roi, *Alternative to appeasement* (Westport, Connecticut, 1997) · *Documents on British Foreign Policy*, 2nd ser., 19 (1982), docs. 311 and 348 · *FO List* ·

WWW · Burke, *Peerage* · college register, Balliol Oxf. · private information [William Collier, son; Dr Zara Steiner, Dr Keith Neilson] · b. cert. · d. cert.
Archives BLPES · priv. coll., unpublished MS, 'North House'
Wealth at death £46,315: probate, 14 Jan 1977, *CGPLA Eng. & Wales*

Collier, Margaret (1719–1794?), correspondent of Samuel Richardson, was born in Salisbury, the youngest of four children of Margaret Johnson (d. 1749) and Arthur *Collier (1680–1732), the metaphysician. Her sister, Jane *Collier (bap. 1715, d. 1755), collaborated with Sarah Fielding on *The Cry* and independently wrote *An Essay on the Art of Ingeniously Tormenting* (1753). Until 1716 Arthur Collier had been rector of Langford Magna, Wiltshire, but at that point debts incurred by his wife forced him to take less extravagant lodgings in Salisbury. Just before his death he was forced to sell the advowson of Langford. Margaret Collier was left to find her way without any inheritance, and Henry Fielding, Sarah's brother, welcomed her (in spite of a debt owed him by her brother Arthur) to his house at Ealing as a companion, first to his daughter and, later, to his second wife. She accompanied Fielding on his final journey to Lisbon and she is rumoured to have cut out a paper profile of him that Hogarth used as a guide for his portrait. She also witnessed his will.

After her sister's death in 1755 Collier retired to Ryde, where she lived with an elderly couple to whom she read Richardson's *Clarissa* and *Sir Charles Grandison*. During this time she corresponded sporadically with Richardson, describing her surroundings and discussing the plight of intellectual women. Her letters led to her reputation as Richardson's devotee; she described him as the 'only champion and protector' of women (3 Oct 1755, Barbauld, 78); their entire correspondence is included in this edition, 58–112). The letters also indicate a pride in helping the couple in Ryde, whom she claimed she could not leave:

> without expressing my happiness in them, and gratitude to all my kind friends, who put it in my power, by the help my little pittance is to them, to afford them more of the necessaries and comforts of life than they enjoyed before I came. (11 Feb 1756, ibid., 100)

She complained somewhat disingenuously that Fielding's *Voyage to Lisbon* had been ascribed to her and worried that:

> the reason which was given for supposing it mine, was to the last degree mortifying, viz. That it was so bad a performance, and fell so short of his other works, it must needs be the person *with him* who wrote it. (3 Oct 1755, ibid., 77)

In spite of the few pleasures that Collier experienced toward the end of her life Anna Laetitia Barbauld is probably correct in assuming that 'her resignation was mixed with the pang inflicted by solitariness and neglect' (ibid., cxcv). She died, unmarried, at Ryde in 1794.

ANNA LOTT

Sources T. C. D. Eaves and B. D. Kimpel, *Samuel Richardson: a biography* (1971) · *The correspondence of Samuel Richardson*, ed. A. L. Barbauld, 6 vols. (1804) · T. Keymer, 'Jane Collier, reader of Richardson, and the fire scene in *Clarissa*', *New essays on Samuel Richardson*, ed. A. J. Rivero (New York, 1996) · M. C. Battestin and R. R. Battestin,

Henry Fielding: a life (1989) · J. Todd, ed., *A dictionary of British and American women writers, 1660–1800* (1985) · P. Rogers, *Henry Fielding: a biography* (New York, 1979) · A. D. McKillop, *Samuel Richardson: printer and novelist* (1936) · *DNB* · Allibone, *Dict.*, suppl. · *IGI* · B. Rizzo, *Companions without vows: relationships among eighteenth-century British women* (1994)
Wealth at death see will, PRO, PROB 11/1250/492

Collier, Mary (1688?–1762?), poet, was born near Midhurst, Sussex. There is disagreement about her parents and her date of birth: 'She is probably the Mary Collier baptized in Lodsworth, Sussex, October 1688, the daughter of William Collier' (*DNB*).

Information about Collier's life is mostly drawn from 'Some remarks on the author's life drawn by herself', prefaced to her *Poems on Several Occasions* (1762). She describes the education she received from her parents, 'by whom I was taught to read when very Young'. On the early death of her mother she did not attend school but was 'set to such labour as the country afforded' (Collier, iii).

Collier lived with her father, 'who was long sickly and infirm' until his death in the 1720s, when she moved to Petersfield, earning a modest living by washing, brewing, and other manual labour. Nevertheless she kept up her reading, and at some time after 1730 she came to know the work of the thresher-poet Stephen Duck. His poem *The Thresher's Labour*, which Mary Collier read and 'soon got by heart', provoked her by his charge that rural women had an easier life than men. Her riposte, entitled *The Woman's Labour: an Epistle to Mr Stephen Duck*, was intended 'to call an Army of Amazons to vindicate the injured sex' (Collier, iv).

Collier did not originally intend publication, but after she repeated her verses to a local family news of her 'soon became a Town Talk'. *The Woman's Labour* was published at her own expense in 1739, the *Advertisement* stating 'Her Friends are of Opinion that the Novelty of a *Washerwoman*'s turning Poetess, will procure her some Readers'. The novelty was too much for some: the 1740 edition includes a testimony by Petersfield citizens to the authenticity of authorship. Her later comment on this venture was: 'I lost nothing, neither did I gain much, others run away with the profit' (Collier, iv).

Mary Collier's reputation rests on *The Woman's Labour*: a spirited polemic, sharply descriptive of female labour. Witty and energetic, the poem displays a real quality of mind and technical ability in its depiction of the long hours of toil of both the agricultural labourer's wife and of the domestic servant.

Collier continued as a washerwoman until she was sixty-three, when she moved to Alton, Hampshire, to take care of a farmhouse. At the age of seventy, in poor health, she retired to a garret in Alton 'to pass the Relict of my days in Piety, Purity, Peace and an Old Maid' (Collier, v). At this time she prepared for publication her *Poems on Several Occasions*, which was well supported by local subscribers. She died soon after, probably in 1762.

WILLIAM R. JONES

Sources M. Collier, 'Some remarks on the author's life', *Poems on several occasions* (1762), iii–v · *DNB* · R. Lonsdale, ed., *Eighteenth-*century women poets: an Oxford anthology (1989) · M. Ferguson, introduction, in S. Duck and M. Collier, 'The thresher's labour' (1736) ... and 'The woman's labour' (1739) (1985), iii–xii · E. P. Thompson and M. Sugden, eds., 'The thresher's labour' by Stephen Duck, 'The woman's labour' by Mary Collier: two eighteenth century poems [1989] · M. Ferguson, *Eighteenth-century women poets: nation, class, and gender* (1995) · M. Ferguson, *First feminists: British women writers, 1578–1799* (1985) · J. Todd, ed., *A dictionary of British and American women writers, 1660–1800* (1984)

Collier [*née* Hardcastle], **Mary Josephine**, Lady Monkswell (1849–1930), diarist, was born at Hintlesham Hall, Suffolk, on 2 November 1849, the third surviving daughter and fourth of five children of Joseph Alfred Hardcastle (1815–1899), Liberal MP, and his first wife, Frances, *née* Lambirth (d. 1865). She was educated by governesses, and studied drawing and painting at the Slade School of Art. Her father remarried in 1869; his new wife was Mary Scarlett Campbell (d. 1916), the daughter of Lord Campbell, the lord chancellor. She was welcomed by her stepchildren, and it was she who introduced the Collier family to Mary Hardcastle. On 5 July 1873 Mary became engaged to Robert Collier (1845–1909), elder son of Robert Porrett *Collier (later first Baron Monkswell). Collier was a lawyer, increasingly involved in radical political circles. They were married on 21 August 1873 at St Mary Abbots, Kensington, and went on to have three sons. Mary Collier's interest in art was enhanced by her new family connections: the artist John *Collier was her brother-in-law.

Mary Collier (who became Lady Monkswell in 1886 on the death of her father-in-law) is of interest chiefly for her diary, selections from which were published in two volumes, edited by her youngest son: *A Victorian Diarist: Extracts from the Journals of Mary, Lady Monkswell, 1873–1895* (1944) and *A Victorian Diarist: Later Extracts from the Journals of Mary, Lady Monkswell, 1895–1909* (1946). It was initially written without any intention of publication, although Blodgett argues that a change of style from around 1907 to include more explanatory matter suggests that in later years at least she expected other readers. Although far from literary, the diary is full of lively observations on the social and political scene of late Victorian London, from the perspective of a woman who, despite her title, seems always to have remained on the fringes of aristocratic and political circles.

Lady Monkswell gives a vivid account of her husband's several unsuccessful electoral attempts and of his appearances in the House of Lords, but her interest in his career waned rapidly after 1885. Monkswell, who was an associate of Sir Charles Dilke and a member of the Radical Club, remained a committed Gladstonian and a supporter of home rule throughout his life. Lady Monkswell, by contrast, was a firm unionist and regarded Parnell as 'a man upon whose head rest at least a *hundred murders*' (9 July 1889; *Victorian Diarist: Extracts*, 152). She commented that 'I am quite unable to take any interest in politics since Mr Gladstone turned round & went in for Home Rule for Ireland' (17 Oct 1887; ibid., 144), and her opinion of Gladstone veered from considering him 'the greatest man in England' (7 March 1884; ibid., 112) to finding him 'awful and almost repulsive' (3 May 1893; ibid., 224). The account of

Gladstone's funeral—he had in retirement returned to Lady Monkswell's pantheon—is one of the big set pieces of the diary, alongside the accounts of Queen Victoria's jubilees and funeral. Disagreement with her husband over politics must have soured their relationship somewhat, but she was equivocally delighted by his appointment as a lord-in-waiting in 1892—'if it were not for this beastly hateful government to which he belongs' (16 May 1892; ibid., 224), and as under-secretary for war in 1895—'this miserable mischievous Government' (1 Jan 1895; ibid., 262). Such differences could be socially awkward, as for example when talking to John Dillon's father-in-law: 'I had some difficulty in restraining my feelings when he, thinking I must be a Home Ruler because Bob is, began talking to me very intimately about Dillon whom I consider a murderer' (4 March 1896; *Victorian Diarist: Later Extracts*, 8). Despite the relative failure of Monkswell's political career, politics provided a framework for Lady Monkswell's life and diary. She identified strongly with the national interest (it was always 'we' who were fighting wars, promoting peace, or proving superior to foreigners), and was plunged into despair by British failures and exulted in British triumphs: 'It is impossible to say what I have suffered since Magersfontein on 15 Dec.', she wrote on 2 March 1900, '& now the relief [of Ladysmith] has come and it is another world' (ibid., 66).

Lady Monkswell was a frequent traveller, and the diary has many accounts of visits to Switzerland, but more interestingly charts the Monkswells' tour of the United States in 1881, taking in New York, Chicago, Salt Lake City—where she was horrified by the practice of polygamy: 'I could not believe my ears—that women should be such arrant fools as to marry a man on the understanding that he may discard them when he pleases & leave them unprovided for' (22 Sept 1881; *Victorian Diarist: Extracts*, 67)—California, and Boston (where she met Oliver Wendell Holmes). But it is the comments on now forgotten events—the Maybrick poisoning trial (1889), the Martinique volcano (1902), on personalities, and on novelties (from vegetarianism to the wireless, from radium to motoring)—that bring the diary to life and single it out from many similar productions.

Lady Monkswell stopped keeping her journal after the death of her husband from cancer on 22 December 1909. His spirit had been broken by his exclusion from the Liberal government of 1906 and the loss of the seat on the London county council that he had held as a Progressive since its formation in 1889. Lady Monkswell lived for another twenty years, dying on 14 May 1930 at the Stone House in Beaminster, Dorset, where she had settled in 1912.   K. D. REYNOLDS

Sources *A Victorian diarist: extracts from the journals of Mary, Lady Monkswell*, ed. E. C. F. Collier, 1: *1873–1895* (1944) · *A Victorian diarist: later extracts from the journals of Mary, Lady Monkswell*, ed. E. C. F. Collier, 2: *1895–1909* (1946) · Burke, *Peerage* · H. Blodgett, *Centuries of female days: Englishwomen's private diaries* (1989)
Likenesses W. & D. Downey, photograph, c.1894, repro. in Collier, ed., *A Victorian diarist: extracts* (1944) · photograph, 1902, repro. in Collier, ed., *A Victorian diarist: later extracts* (1946)

Wealth at death £9695 7s. 1d.: probate, 21 July 1930, *CGPLA Eng. & Wales*

Collier, Robert Porrett, first Baron Monkswell (1817–1886), judge, was born at Mount Tamar, near Plymouth, on 21 June 1817, the eldest son of John Collier (1769–1849), a merchant, and his wife, Emma, fourth daughter of Robert Porrett, of North Hill House, Plymouth. The firm of Collier & Co., corn and timber merchants, had been established in Southside Street, Plymouth, in 1676. Collier's father, who ran the business, was agent for Lloyds for nearly fifty years, and vice-consul for Norway, Sweden, and Portugal. Formerly a member of the Society of Friends, he was an alderman for Plymouth, a justice of the peace, a deputy lieutenant of Devon, and Liberal MP for Plymouth from 1832 to 1841. With such a family background it is not surprising that Robert Collier should have developed an interest in commercial, maritime, and international law. He was educated at Plymouth grammar school and then received private tuition from Revd John Kempe, curate of Tavistock, before entering Trinity College, Cambridge, in 1836. Poor health forced him to give up reading for honours and he left the university for a period, returning to take an ordinary BA degree in 1843. He had already developed political ambitions, making speeches at Launceston in 1841 with a view to contesting the seat, though he did not go to the poll, and later becoming an active member of the Anti-Corn Law League, addressing league meetings in Covent Garden Theatre. On 14 April 1844 he married Isabella Rose (1815–1886), daughter of William Rose Rose of Wolston Heath, Warwickshire.

Collier joined the Inner Temple on 4 June 1838 and was called to the bar on 27 January 1843. He practised from 1 Mitre Court Buildings, Temple, and joined the western circuit and the Devonshire, Plymouth, and Devonport sessions. His first case to attract public attention was *R. v. Serva* at Exeter assizes in July 1845. Some Brazilian slave traders had killed an English naval officer on board the Brazilian vessel the *Felicidade*, and they were tried for murder in this country. Serjeant Manning defended some of the prisoners, Collier the others. Collier made a very vigorous speech at the trial in Exeter and, after successfully laying the matter before the home secretary (Sir James Graham) and Sir Robert Peel, a very learned speech on the question of jurisdiction when the point was reserved for all the judges in November. On his next visit to Exeter he had nineteen briefs. In 1845 he published a treatise on the Railway Clauses Acts, followed in 1849 by an account of the law relating to mines, and in 1851 by a letter to Lord John Russell on reform of the superior courts (2nd edn, 1852).

Local influence and wide practical knowledge gave Collier a good practice; he was an excellent jurist and an eloquent, sharp, and witty advocate. He was recorder of Penzance from July 1848 to March 1856. On 8 July 1854 Lord Cranworth granted him a patent of precedence (QC) at the age of thirty-seven and after only eleven years at the bar; and he was elected a bencher of the Inner Temple. From

1854 to 1863 he was one of that brilliant quartet, Montague Smith, Collier, Karslake, and Coleridge, who dominated the western circuit during its golden age. In the earlier part of that period there was friction on the circuit between him and Coleridge which permanently affected the relations between them.

In July 1852 Collier was elected Liberal MP for Plymouth, holding the seat until October 1871. He made his maiden speech in the House of Commons on 29 November 1852 on the Courts of Common Law (Ireland) Bill, supporting the fusion of common law and equity in England and their administration in one common court. After that he spoke frequently and with good effect, especially on the Russian blockade on 20 February 1855, but chiefly on questions of law reform. In 1859 he was appointed counsel to the Admiralty and judge-advocate of the fleet. In 1862 the American minister, Adams, consulted him about vessel 'no. 290' being built at Liverpool for the Confederate navy. In his opinion (23 July 1862) he said that he thought it was the duty of the port authorities to detain her, but before the government could take action she had escaped to a destructive career on the high seas as the *Alabama*. On 2 October 1863, when Sir William Atherton retired and Sir Roundell Palmer was promoted to be attorney-general, Collier was appointed solicitor-general and knighted, and filled the office with success until the Liberal government resigned in 1866. One of his first duties as solicitor-general was to defend the government's record on the Confederate cruisers, including the *Alabama*, in the House of Commons on 4 March 1864. In December 1868 Collier became attorney-general with Coleridge, after an initial refusal, as solicitor-general. In 1869 he was responsible for the Bankruptcy Bill in the House of Commons.

In August 1870 Collier was appointed recorder of Bristol on the death of Serjeant Kinglake, thereby causing a by-election in his constituency. Plymouth Dockyard was suffering badly from cuts in government expenditure, and at his adoption meeting an amendment was passed that he should resign the recordership. Although there were good precedents for the attorney-general holding the recordership of Bristol, which was one of the most valuable in the country, he decided to resign the position, amid widespread criticism in *The Times*, the *Law Journal*, and elsewhere, and was duly re-elected as MP for Plymouth without opposition.

Collier ran into another storm in 1871. On 5 August he moved the second reading of the Judicial Committee of the Privy Council Bill in the House of Commons, providing for the appointment of four salaried judges on the judicial committee. The appointments were limited to persons of high judicial authority: the new judges had at the date of their appointment to be or have been English superior court judges or Indian chief justices. Two Indian chief justices were found, and Sir Montague Smith was promoted from the court of common pleas. The fourth vacancy was refused by three English judges and likely to be refused by more, because the act made no provision for the clerks of the new judges. To solve the problem the lord chancellor, Hatherley, appointed Collier to the vacant seat

in the court of Common Pleas, which he held for a few days (7 to 22 November) only before Gladstone appointed him to the judicial committee. The 'Collier Juggle' was technically legal, but in blatant conflict with the spirit of the act, and a long and bitter controversy ensued, notably captured in a *Punch* cartoon (16 Dec 1871). There were letters from both chief justices, Cockburn and Bovill, published in *The Times*, and motions of censure in both houses of parliament. The government won by only a single vote in the House of Lords, and by twenty-seven in the House of Commons thanks to a brilliant speech by Sir Roundell Palmer. Collier held this post until his death, and he was frequently responsible for giving literary shape to the judgments of the privy council. On 1 July 1885 he was created Baron Monkswell, of Monkswell, Devon.

Collier was highly versatile and accomplished. At Cambridge he wrote some clever parodies, and published a satirical poem called *Granta*; and he also wrote some very pretty verses both in Latin and English. He was an excellent scholar, publishing a translation of Demosthenes' *De corona* (1875), and a good billiard player. But it was chiefly in painting, of which he was passionately fond, that he was distinguished. As a young man he drew very clever caricatures in the H. B. manner. When solicitor-general he painted in St James's Park, and he exhibited frequently at the Royal Academy and Grosvenor Gallery, especially pictures of the neighbourhood of Rosenlui, Switzerland, where he spent many vacations. He was president of the Devonshire Association in 1879, and his presidential address at the annual meeting at Ilfracombe dealt mainly with the progress and development of the art of painting. His wife died suddenly on 10 April 1886. In failing health he went to the Riviera, and died at Grasse, near Cannes, on 27 October 1886. He was buried at Brompton cemetery on 3 November. He had three children: Robert, second Baron Monkswell (1845–1909); John *Collier (1850–1934), a well-known artist who painted the portraits of a number of eminent lawyers, including Lord Chancellor Halsbury; and Margaret Isabella, who married Count Arturo Galletti di Cadilhac. Mary Josephine *Collier, Lady Monkswell, the diarist, was his daughter-in-law.   DAVID PUGSLEY

Sources *The Times* (28 Oct 1886) · *Report and Transactions of the Devonshire Association*, 19 (1887), 44–6 · C. Robinson, *Victorian Plymouth* (1991) · E. H. Coleridge, *Life and correspondence of John Duke, Lord Coleridge*, 2 vols. (1904) · J. B. Atlay, *The Victorian chancellors*, 2 vols. (1906–8) · R. Palmer, first earl of Selborne, *Memorials. Part I: family and personal, 1766–1865*, ed. S. M. Palmer, 2 vols. (1889) · A. Harwood, *Circuit ghosts: a western circuit miscellany*, rev. edn (1997) · GEC, *Peerage* · DNB · Boase, *Mod. Eng. biog.* · Venn, *Alum. Cant.* · Burke, *Peerage*
Archives BL, corresp. with W. E. Gladstone, Add. MSS 44412–44491
Likenesses Aτη [A. Thompson], caricature, watercolour study, NPG; repro. in *VF*, 2 (19 Feb 1870), pl. 41 · W. Boxall, oils, Inner Temple, London · Lock & Whitfield, woodburytype photograph, NPG; repro. in T. Cooper, *Men of mark: a gallery of contemporary portraits* (1880) · J. and C. Watkins, cartes-de-visite, NPG · portrait, repro. in *ILN*, 54 (1869), 446 · portrait, repro. in T. Cooper, *Men of mark: a gallery of contemporary portraits*, 4 (1880), pl. 33 · wood-engraving, NPG; repro. in *ILN*, 43 (17 Oct 1863), 393
Wealth at death £82,999 16s. 10d.: probate, 10 Dec 1886, CGPLA Eng. & Wales

Collier, Samuel Francis (1855–1921), Wesleyan Methodist minister, was born on 3 October 1855 in Runcorn, Cheshire, the eldest child of Samuel Collier (d. 1883), grocer, and his second wife, Mary Littler. Collier was educated at Mill House Academy, Runcorn, and Bickerton House, Southport, a Wesleyan school where he was tutor from 1874 to 1876. He was a competent student and keen cricketer. Converted in 1871, in 1874 he preached his first sermon as a local preacher. From 1877 to 1881 he trained at Didsbury College, Manchester, for the Wesleyan ministry. His interest in evangelism developed through frequent preaching which resulted in conversions.

In 1881–2 Collier was district missioner in Kent, followed by three years in Brentford circuit, Middlesex, where he experimented with systematic visitation aided by a body of voluntary lay workers. In 1883 the city-centre Oldham Street Chapel in Manchester was closed because it had lost its congregation to the suburbs, but under pressure from H. J. Pope, the secretary of the connexional chapel committee, it was replaced by a mission hall (rather than a church), the construction of which began in May 1885. Meanwhile, Collier was appointed for one year only to serve the surviving congregation. He had hopes of completing his external London degree at Owens College but soon abandoned this in favour of a successful policy of expansive evangelism. Through Pope's influence he was unexpectedly appointed to run the new Central Hall from 1886. Wesleyan ministers had at one time been limited to three-year postings to groups of churches, but multi-purpose halls, combining evangelistic, social, and recreational work under long-serving ministers, were becoming the Wesleyan policy for city centres.

Collier quickly developed an expanding and varied programme. In 1887 the crowds at the Central Hall provoked him to hire the St James's Theatre for additional services; and from 1889 to 1910 he ran an evening service in the Free Trade Hall, claimed to be the largest Methodist congregation in the world. In 1910 this was replaced by the purpose-built Albert Hall as a regular mission centre, while several run-down churches were taken over and rejuvenated. By 1904 it was claimed that Sunday attendances throughout the mission amounted to 16,000.

Collier's initial programme included free seats, advertising, a popular Sunday afternoon service, a Saturday night concert, and brass band; and in early annual reports evangelistic work clearly predominated. But from the first he found that need and compassion compelled him to offer material aid to the poor. This rapidly became systematized into an extensive network of social agencies such as a men's home and labour yard, women's home, maternity home, and hospital, and rescue work among prostitutes. Saturday night concerts featured professional singers to provide 'pure' entertainment to counter public houses and music-halls. Earlier missions had commonly hoped to feed converts into ordinary churches, but Collier's hall unexpectedly acquired a large church membership with the conventional range of Wesleyan meetings. In 1895 the regular membership reached 1484, most of it apparently new, though some was absorbed from older chapels. It has been claimed that the halls largely attracted regular churchgoers and had only a limited impact on the unchurched working classes, but descriptions in the 1890s suggest that along with respectable artisan families there were many 'from the ranks of unskilled and unsettled labour, nay, probably from the criminal classes' in shabby clothes (Jackson, 68). The social work, sometimes dismissed as a mere palliative, was, as Collier asserted, essential for the poor's survival when state provision was lacking. His work was much praised locally.

Collier saw his work primarily as evangelistic, social work and evangelism being different aspects of the same enterprise. Unlike his more famous contemporary Hugh Price Hughes (in his *Social Christianity*, 1889) Collier did not indulge in Christian social theory, though his methods were much the same. He was also happy to support men with talents different from his own. He sponsored lectures on Christian apologetics, and was on the boards of Samuel Edward Keeble's *Methodist Weekly* (1900–03), which was far more left wing than Hughes, and of Keeble's Wesleyan Methodist Union for Social Service (1905).

Robust and gregarious, Collier readily befriended strangers and, aided by his practical business sense, was able to lead an incessantly busy life without obvious worry. Though always 'the chief', he readily delegated to colleagues and trusted them. As a preacher his effectiveness was due to a homely, practical style and personal rapport with his congregation. Though no scholar, he read mainly during the night (for he needed little sleep), having a special interest in spirituality and hymns. He edited *The Free Church Council Hymnal* (1911). Collier married Henrietta Emma (Ettie) Collin of Manchester on 23 April 1889. They had five sons, of whom one died in infancy and two were killed in the First World War.

In 1913–14 Collier was president of the Wesleyan conference and conducted a campaign with Rodney ('Gypsy') Smith to revive evangelism in Wesleyanism. In 1920–21 he made an exhausting preaching tour in Australia, which weakened his health. He died in Manchester at his home, The Olives, Anson Road, Victoria Park, on 2 June 1921 from influenza complicated by pleurisy and pneumonia, and was buried in the city's southern cemetery on 6 June; his wife survived him, dying after 1923.　HENRY D. RACK

Sources G. Jackson, *Collier of Manchester* (1923) · *Annual Report of the Manchester and Salford Wesleyan Mission* (1888–92) · *Rescue, relief, preventive work of the Manchester and Salford Mission* (c.1894) · 'The man of the moment: Rev. S. F. Collier', *Manchester Illustrated Weekly* (16 Oct 1903), 35 · 'The head of the Central Hall: Rev. S. F. Collier's twenty-five years' service', *Manchester City News* (3 Sept 1910), 3 · I. Sellers, 'Nonconformist attitudes in later nineteenth century Liverpool', *Transactions of the Historic Society of Lancashire and Cheshire*, 114 (1962), 215–39, esp. 230–33 · I. Sellers, 'Charles Garrett and the Liverpool Mission', *Journal of Lancashire and Cheshire Branch of the Wesley Historical Society*, 4 (1980), 5–11 · M. L. Edwards, *S. E. Keeble: pioneer and prophet* (1949), 53, 65–6 · M. S. Edwards, 'The Methodist Weekly', *Journal of Lancashire and Cheshire Branch of the Wesley Historical Society*, 2 (1973), 144–6 · letters, JRL, Methodist Archives and Research Centre, S. F. Collier MSS, PLP 27.34.7–17 · J. Banks, *Samuel Francis Collier* (1996) · *CGPLA Eng. & Wales* (1921)

Archives JRL, Methodist Archives and Research Centre, corresp. relating to preaching appointments, PLP 27.34.7–17

Collier, Thomas (d. 1691), Baptist preacher, may have been the yeoman farmer of that name from Witney, in Surrey, prosecuted in 1634 for withholding tithes. Nothing is certainly known of his birth or early life.

'A master sectary' Collier was reported to have acted as a teacher of a church at York, whose origins are obscure, though elements of the earl of Manchester's army, arriving before the city in June 1644 at the onset of the famous siege, were already said to have been infected by 'either Anabaptisme or Antinomianisme, or both' (*Letters and Journals of Robert Baillie*, 2.185). During that winter, or perhaps the next, several were rebaptized by immersion in the River Ouse, and when the future Quakers William and Anne Dewsberry were married at York, probably in 1646, Anne was already a member of a Baptist congregation there. This church may very well have been that taught by Collier.

But Collier had left before then and was far from York, active as a travelling lay preacher. Though proof is lacking, the pattern of Collier's itinerary is consistent with attachment to the army. He was in correspondence with John Sims, arrested in May 1646 at Middlezoy, a village near Taunton where the army had camped after the battle of Langport on 10 July 1645. And he was reported to have been expelled from Guernsey for 'turbulent behaviour', possibly among the troops besieging Castle Cornet. Released from prison in Portsmouth, he toured through Dorset, Hampshire, and Sussex, and, having preached at Guildford at the end of May 1646, made his way to London. Letters passed between him, local adherents, and other evangelists. To Thomas Edwards he appeared as 'a master sectarie, a man of great power among them, and hath Emissaries under him, whom he sends abroad' (Edwards, 3.41). At least at Taunton, Collier seems to have been able to found, or at least help sustain, a functioning organization, though it is not known how long this or other possible fruits of his early evangelism survived. But as orthodox ministers grimly surveyed the trail of theological destruction in the wake of the preacher—'the first that sowed the seeds of Anabaptism, Anti-sabbatarianism and some Arminianism … in these parts'—they were forced to concede that 'doubtless it was strong poison he gave them that wrought so strongly at first' (ibid., 3.29).

The hostility of the presbyterians was wholly reciprocated. In *Certaine Queries, or, Points now in Controversy*, which George Thomason picked up on 24 July 1645, Collier called upon parliament to 'dismiss that assembly of learned men who are now called together for to consult about matters of religion', since he knew 'no rule in the Book of God for such an assembly' (Collier, *Certaine Queries*, 27). Also during 1645, in his *Three Great Quaeries*, Collier took issue with the Arminianism later attributed to him. In terms of predestination, he opposed the Arminians, while

defending a heavily qualified doctrine of general redemption. In most points, he remained a high-Calvinist, but one whose theology of free grace tended, in the early years, to undermine the role in salvation of obedience to the law. This strongly spiritualistic and antinomian tendency was widespread among the radical army chaplains, and it alarmed the orthodox at least as much as did Arminianism itself. Men such as Robert Baillie felt justified in lumping the two together because of the licence they seemed to offer to saints who jibbed at church discipline. In works of the later 1640s, indeed, Collier stressed the spiritual aspects of religion to the point of denying significance to formal ordinances. Later, he acknowledged having held these views, now seen as errors, in order to repudiate them decisively.

Political preacher The earliest definite evidence of Collier's formal employment in the army is the payment to him of £31 13s. 9d. in May 1650, for duties undertaken not earlier than August 1647, as chaplain to Colonel Twistleton's New Model regiment of horse. In the autumn of 1647 he was accustomed to speak with 'both opportunity and freeness' at the army headquarters at Putney, and there delivered, on 29 September, the sermon later published as *A Discovery of the New Creation*. This address incorporated much of the Leveller programme, and breathed reforming zeal and millenarian expectancy. Christ's kingdom would soon be established: 'nations shall become the nations of Christ and the government shall be in the hands of the saints'; 'tyrannical and oppressing laws and courts of justice' and other grievances would be taken away (Collier, *Discovery*, 32, 35). At the Whitehall debates in December 1648, he opposed Ireton's defence of magistratical powers to punish in religious matters, because this was to claim for the state 'power from God, and not from the Agreement of the people' (Firth, 2.125). Collier, however, did not join the Levellers in protesting against the political solution imposed by the army generals in the winter of 1648–9. He issued a pamphlet which defended the execution of the king and attacked the corruption and betrayals of parliament, but urged that in settling a peace, 'those who are saved spiritually know best what is good for the nations temporal well being' (Collier, *Vindication*, 6). The army generals were identified and defended as having set about the necessary task of destroying enemies whom readers would have understood to include the Levellers.

In the early 1650s, Collier was active in Somerset and also seems to have retained some relation with the army. Accounts of a sermon at Axbridge in 1651 reported him to be living at Westbury. At a dispute at Wiveliscombe on 4 May 1652, he appeared, according to a hostile witness, 'guarded as it were with some soldiers, and a great company of his furious disciples', engaging an army captain as a moderator in the debate (Fullwood, sig. C2r). Collier continued to demand a radical separation between the spheres of religion and the state. In 1652 he asked rhetorically of the commissioners for the propagation of the gospel 'whether a State-maintenance for the Ministery of

Christ, be agreeable to any Rule in the Gospel?' (Collier, *Font-Guard*, sig. P1v).

West country leader But there was also pressure upon Collier and other Baptist leaders to deal with disorderly practices in their churches and with the influence upon them of seeking, ranting, and now quaking, which tended towards the subversion of external authorities, of church, and scripture. Baptist associations were founded partly in order to help establish and police 'orderly walking' in the face of these challenges. Collier helped build one such organization, aligned with the Particular Baptist churches of London, in the west country. He reported to the several churches from its first general meeting at Wells on 8–9 November 1653, and from many subsequent gatherings. This body was welcomed by the Baptists it sought to organize. But the proposal to ordain Collier as a 'messenger' empowered to spread the word outside the already constituted congregations of the association aroused dissension, and even after the ceremony, at Bridgwater in May 1654, a minority remained unhappy. Ordination merely legitimated Collier's existing practice, and he acquired through it no new powers or any titles, such as general superintendent. But the absence for many years of any such formal qualification may indicate the attachment of local Baptists to informal practices favouring lay initiative. The new concern for order was reflected in other ways. Collier attacked the Quakers as Levellers, writing angrily against those who undermined the gospel 'under pretence of holiness and light within' and 'their pernicious ways in stirring up to despise dominion and to speak evil of dignities and government' (White, *Association Records of Particular Baptists*, 90).

Yet Collier did not play the unambiguously restraining role of men such as William Kiffin: more than other Calvinistic leaders, he continued to stress the active role of ordinary church members, and especially the development of their gifts in prophesying. This originated in the mid-1640s, and drew from the millenarian mood among the saints of the new model, which Collier had both shared and helped to strengthen. Dampened for a time, perhaps, by the more prosaic routines of rural life, his hopes were never quite extinguished. In 1652 he asked 'Whether it be not the duty of the Magistrate to permit the *Jews*, whose Conversion is promised, and we pretend to expect it, to live peaceably amongst us?' (Collier, *Font-Guard*, sig. P2r). During the rule of the first Rump Parliament and the early protectorate, the saints experienced as a double affront to their great expectations the fortune hunters who clustered round the centres of power. Febrile high politics helped rekindle the flames of millennial anticipation, both in organized circles of the Fifth Monarchists and among others, such as Thomas Collier, who did not adopt that name.

Collier and they, however, confronted a widening gap between the prospect of Christ's imminent rule on earth and the apathy of so many, even among the churches, to the message of its prophets. And thus, letters signed by Collier, Captain Nathaniel Strange, and others strained to urge upon the congregated saints of the western counties the need for fervent prayer, so that God would

> guide those who wait for Zion's redemption … searching after and hastening unto the fulfilling of all the glorious promises and prophesies which relate to the downfall of all that rise up against the work of Christ in both themselves and in the earth. (White, *Association Records of Particular Baptists*, 81)

It may not be thought surprising that some interpreted such injunctions as a call to arms. In 1658 at Dorchester, a meeting was held between Baptist representatives (millenarian and moderate) and others who expected, and hoped to hasten by military force, the coming of the fifth monarchy. Government spies reported the presence of Kiffin, who sought to restrain the participants from uniting in violent activism. Thomas Collier presided over at least one of the sessions. His political role is not certainly known, but his opposition in 1657 to the open insurrectionism of Tillinghast may suggest that he sided with the moderates.

Later years After the Restoration, Collier continued his activities in the Baptist cause in at least two counties. He was reported to be teaching at Axbridge, Somerset, in 1669, and was licensed there in 1672 as a Baptist preacher, at the house of Edward Woollcot, an associate in the town in 1651. In 1672 he was also licensed as a teacher at North Bradley, Wiltshire, where there was soon a clash with the London leaders. Collier's dogmatics continued to arouse their hostility. During the 1650s he had moved towards a more orthodox Calvinism, though his 'Somerset confession' still differed in points of detail from that issued in 1646 by the seven London Particular Baptist churches and expounded by Benjamin Cox. Thirty years later Collier published a synopsis of his views on election, general redemption, and Christology, which ranged him against Cox's son Nehemiah. Finding Collier's views heterodox, the London leaders persuaded the young Cox to write a refutation, *Vindiciae veritatis* (1677), and in October 1676 themselves descended on North Bradley 'to settle some disorder' arising from his 'unsound doctrine or new notions' (Hayden, 185).

But in response to all this, and to a new and very orthodox Calvinist second London confession of faith (1677), the unrepentant Collier published his own, appending to it a critique of the official version, which was endorsed by the Western Association in 1691: it seems his personal prestige in Somerset was undiminished by the Londoners' campaign. Certainly his antipathy to official positions deepened. Collier's last work, *A Doctrinal Discourse of Self Denial* (1691), attacked those who 'teach the people, a justifying, saving faith without works' (Collier, *Doctrinal Discourse*, 70–71). In its strict demands upon the saints, the book stood opposed to the incipient libertarianism of its author's youth. But these were sides of a single coin: his continuing rejection of outright determinism as a source of self-satisfaction and falsity in faith. And thus, in a reignited radicalism of almost half a century's vintage, Collier raged against the ethos of Williamite England:

self it is that rules, in city and country, self profit and advantage it is, that manageth all callings … self honour, self pride and self will it is that is the cause of most of the wars and blood in the world;

and this spirit ruled 'not only in the profane but in professors too' (ibid., 36). Thomas Collier died before the publication of his last book. John Collier, who was perhaps a relation, informs us in his preface that the author delivered his manuscript 'but a day or two before he died'.

STEPHEN WRIGHT

Sources T. Collier, *Certaine queries, or, Points now in controvercy examined, and answered by scripture* (1645) · [T. Collier], ed., *A confession of faith of several churches of Christ in the county of Somerset* (1656) · T. Collier, *A discovery of the new creation … preached at the headquarters at Putney Sept 29 1647* (1647) [extracts in A. S. P. Woodhouse, *Puritanism and liberty*, 1938, 390–96] · T. Collier, *A doctrinal discourse of self denial* (1691) · T. Collier, *The exhaltation of Christ in the days of the gospel* [1646] · T. Collier, *A looking-glasse for the Quakers* (1657) [Thomason tract E896(11)] · T. Collier, *The pulpit guard routed* [1651] · T. Collier, *The font-guard routed* (1652) · T. Collier, *The right constitution and true subjects of the visible church of Christ* (1654) · T. Collier, *A vindication of the army remonstrance*, Thomason tracts (1640–61), E477(6) (1649) · T. E. Dowley, 'A London congregation during the great persecution: Petty France Particular Baptist Church 1641–88', *Baptist Quarterly*, 27 (1977–8), 233–9 · T. Edwards, *Gangraena, or, A catalogue and discovery of many of the errours, heresies, blasphemies and pernicious practices of the sectaries of this time*, 3 vols. in 1 (1646) · F. Fullwood, *The churches and ministery of England* (1652) [Thomason tract E671(2)] · R. Hayden, ed., *The records of a church in Christ in Bristol, 1640–1687*, Bristol RS, 27 (1974) · G. F. Nuttall, 'The Baptist western association', *Journal of Ecclesiastical History*, 11 (1960), 213–18 · G. F. Nuttall, 'Thomas Collier: an unrecorded tract', *Baptist Quarterly*, 28 (1979–80), 40–41 · B. R. White, ed., *Association records of the Particular Baptists of England, Wales, and Ireland to 1660*, 4 vols. (1971–7), vol. 2 · B. R. White, 'Thomas Collier and Gangraena Edwards', *Baptist Quarterly*, 24 (1971–2), 99–110 · *The Clarke papers*, ed. C. H. Firth, 4 vols., CS, new ser., 49, 54, 61–2 (1891–1901) · *The letters and journals of Robert Baillie*, ed. D. Laing, 3 vols. (1841–2)

Collier, Thomas (1840–1891), landscape painter, was born on 12 November 1840 at Howardtown, Glossop, Derbyshire, one of four children of Thomas Collier (1796/7–1859), clockmaker and tea dealer, and of Martha Siddall (1800/01–1857). Nothing is known of his childhood or schooling but he attended Manchester School of Art in the early 1860s. By 1864, following in the footsteps of David Cox, he had established himself in one of his favourite milieux, Betws-y-coed in north Wales. In 1863 he exhibited his first watercolour at the Society of British Artists, from a Manchester address, the home of his future wife, Hermione Beatrice Holdstock (1839–1879), whom he married on 28 December 1865.

Until about 1869 Collier painted in north Wales and occasionally in the Lake District; three Cumbrian subjects were hung at the Royal Academy in 1870. He then moved to London and began to explore the Sussex downs and the byways of rural Surrey. Having been rejected in his efforts to join the Society of Painters in Water Colours, he was elected associate of the Institute of Painters in Water Colours in 1870 and a full member in 1872, the year of a single trip to Scotland. In 1876 he began to work in East Anglia, a favoured sketching ground, and in 1878 he was made chevalier of the Légion d'honneur for a watercolour of Arundel Park, which was shown at the Paris Universal Exhibition. A year later, on 20 December 1879, his wife, tragically, died, just before the completion of their permanent Hampstead home, a residence of substance and good taste, where Collier lived for the rest of his life.

Inspired by the naturalist tradition of Constable, Cox, and DeWint, Collier eschewed the contemporary Victorian taste for highly finished pictures. He was much the most distinguished of a group of landscape painters in the institute who admired the rougher, wilder, freer late work of Cox and the breadth of early English watercolours. In Collier's case this inspiration sprang not from nostalgia but from conviction, a passionate response to nature. Working in pure watercolour with a restricted palette, and *en plein air* in all weathers, his work always had the freshness and breadth of a great sketcher. The brooding, overpowering skies of his early work were later, like Constable's, suffused with light. Even in those early years occasional landscapes and beach scenes anticipate this development. His rare figures merge seamlessly with their surroundings as do uncommon and often lonely buildings; almost always these are seen as mere punctuation marks in the vast harmony of nature. Above all his sky painting and feeling for space characterize his work, from tiny sketches to large studio pieces. His few, small-scale, oil paintings earned him election to the Institute of Painters in Oil Colours in 1883.

Collier's means enabled him to paint how he pleased, without dependence on pupil or public, although his work sold readily enough. The only known photographs of him suggest a sensitive, shy, even melancholy man. He entertained a small circle of artist friends but preferred not to involve himself in art politics. After his wife's death, on 2 July 1881 he married her friend Jessie Ida Tawell (1856–1937), who brought up the two children of his first marriage. Never robust in health Collier struggled with consumption throughout his later years. He died at his home, Etherow, 9 Hampstead Hill Gardens, London, on 14 May 1891 and was buried in the family grave in Highgate cemetery, as were his first wife, his son, his daughter, and eventually his second wife. Substantial collections of his work can be found in the British Museum and the Victoria and Albert Museum, London, and in the Fitzwilliam Museum, Cambridge.

JOHN DARLINGTON

Sources A. Bury, *The life and art of Thomas Collier R.I.* (1944) · M. Hardie, *Water-colour painting in Britain*, ed. D. Snelgrove, J. Mayne, and B. Taylor, 3: *The Victorian period* (1968) · T. J. Barratt, *The annals of Hampstead*, 3 vols. (1912) · F. Wedmore, *Painters and painting* (1913) · A. Wilton and A. Lyles, *The great age of British watercolours, 1750–1880* (1993) [exhibition catalogue, RA, 15 Jan – 12 April 1993, and National Gallery of Art, Washington, DC, 9 May – 25 July 1993] · S. Wilcox and C. Newall, *Victorian landscape watercolors* (1992) [exhibition catalogue, New Haven, CT, Cleveland, OH, and Birmingham, 9 Sept 1992 – 12 April 1993] · b. cert. · b. cert. [Hermione Beatrice Holdstock] · b. cert. [Jessie Ida Tawell] · m. cert., 1865 · m. cert., 1881 · d. cert. [Hermione Beatrice Holdstock] · d. cert. [Jessie Ida Tawell] · d. cert. [Thomas Collier] · d. cert. [Martha Collier] · *CGPLA Eng. & Wales* (1891)

Likenesses photograph, repro. in Bury, *Life and art of Thomas Collier*, pl. 84 · photograph, repro. in Barratt, *Annals of Hampstead*
Wealth at death £6550 7s. 1d.: resworn probate, May 1892, *CGPLA Eng. & Wales* (1891)

Collignon, Catherine (*bap.* 1754, *d.* 1832), translator, was the daughter of Dr Charles *Collignon (1725–1785), physician and professor of anatomy at Cambridge, and his wife, Elizabeth, *née* Vandactselver, and was baptized on 29 November 1754 at Holy Sepulchre, Cambridge. Two elder sisters had died in infancy. At the suggestion and with the encouragement of senior members of the university and others she undertook in middle age a full, uncorrected, and literal translation from the French of the *Dictionnaire historique* compiled by the Abbé Jean-Baptiste Ladvocat (*d.* 1765) of the Sorbonne. The original had become scarce in England. Her translation, of which 750 sets were printed, was issued in four volumes by the Cambridge University printer between 1799 and 1801 as *An Historical and Biographical Dictionary*.

In later life Catherine Collignon lived at Bromley, near Bow, in Middlesex where she died, a wealthy woman, on 4 February 1832. She was buried in her cousin's vault at St Mary Aldermary, London. Most of her fortune was willed to relatives, but she made a number of charitable bequests, for example to the London Hospital, and to societies for the indigent blind and for deaf mute people. Doubtless in recognition of her father's long association with it, she left £1000 in stock to Addenbrooke's Hospital, Cambridge. JOHN D. PICKLES

Sources parish register, St Sepulchre, Cambridge, Cambs. AS [baptism] · will and codicils, 1830–31, PRO, prerogative court of Canterbury · death duty registers, 1832, PRO · J.-B. Ladvocat, *An historical and biographical dictionary*, trans. C. Collignon, 4 vols. (1799–1801) [preface] · *GM*, 1st ser., 102/1 (1832), 187 · CUL, Cambridge University Press archives
Wealth at death under £80,000: will, 1830–31, PRO; PRO, death duty registers, 1832

Collignon, Charles (1725–1785), anatomist and physician, born in London on 30 January 1725, was the son of Paul Collignon, a minister of the Dutch church in Austin Friars, London, who was a native of Hesse-Cassel, Germany. He died when his son was still young. After attending school in Bury St Edmunds, Suffolk, Collignon was admitted a pensioner of Trinity College, Cambridge, in 1743, where he graduated MB in 1748 and MD in 1754. While still a student Collignon visited France, London, Edinburgh, and Leiden, before returning to Cambridge in 1750; in 1751 the university granted him a licence to practise. During the same year he married Elizabeth Vandactselver in Colchester. The marriage produced four children; only Catherine *Collignon (*bap.* 1754, *d.* 1832) survived her father. She translated from the French the Abbé Ladvocat's *Historical and Biographical Dictionary*.

Collignon settled in St Sepulchre's parish, Cambridge, and established himself in practice in the town. He began lecturing in the university in 1754 and was 'much esteemed by all his pupils' (Rook, 341). Collignon emphasized the importance of a knowledge of anatomy for physicians, the desirability of a better legal supply of bodies for dissection, and the importance of post-mortems to improve knowledge of disease. It is said that in March 1768 Laurence Sterne's body turned up in Collignon's dissecting room a few days after it had been buried in London. Collignon's *Compendium anatomico-medicum* (1756) provided a general introduction to students of anatomy. This was followed in 1763 by *Tyrocinium anatomicum* in which he stated that 'the first and principle end of the study of the human body should be to awaken in us an aweful sense of the amazing power of the creator' (Rook, 342). Collignon's next book, *Enquiry into the structure of the human body relative to its supposed influence on the morals of mankind*, was a more philosophical work that intended 'to remove the objections that have been made against Providence by some, as if he had formed men of such materials as almost necessarily impelled them to illicit actions' (Rook, 343).

Collignon became a governor of Addenbrooke's Hospital, Cambridge, in 1766 and in September that year he was appointed physician, a post he held until his resignation in 1775. A year after his resignation he published *Explanatory Remarks on the Great Utility of Hospitals for the Sick and Poor*, which was unusual in that it argued that those suffering from incurable illnesses, epilepsy, and venereal diseases should not be denied admission into hospitals. Collignon's other works were *Medicinia politica, or, Reflections on the art of physic as inseparably connected with the prosperity of the state* (1765) and *Moral and Medical Dialogues* (1769); according to Rook, the latter are 'so pretentiously elaborated that they are almost unreadable' (Rook, 343). Collignon was elected a fellow of the Royal Society in 1770.

The Revd Cole, who knew Collignon well, says of him:

> He is an ingenious, honest man, and if they had picked the three kingdoms for a proper person to represent an anatomical professor, they could not have pitched upon a more proper one, for he is a perfect skeleton himself, absolutely a walking shadow, nothing but skin and bones; indeed, I never saw so meagre a figure, such as one can conceive a figure to be after the flesh and substance is all dried away and wasted, and nothing left to cover the bones but a shrivelled dry leather; such is the figure of our present professor of anatomy, 19 June 1770. (Rook, 339)

Collignon died on 1 October 1785 in Cambridge. A collection of his writings, *The Medical Works of Charles Collignon MD*, was published the next year. MICHAEL BEVAN

Sources A. Rook, 'Charles Collignon (1725–1785): Cambridge physician, anatomist, and moralist', *Medical History*, 23 (1979), 339–45 · *DNB* · Venn, *Alum. Cant.* · *GM*, 1st ser., 55 (1785), 835

Collin, Mary (1860–1955), headmistress, was born in Cambridge on 1 April 1860, the daughter of William Collin. Educated at a private school in Cambridge and at Notting Hill High School for Girls, London, she graduated in honours French and German at Bedford College, London. She taught for a time on the staff of her former school and of Jersey Ladies' College, and in 1884 went as second mistress to Nottingham high school, another of the schools founded by the Girls' Public Day School Company. In 1892 she became principal of St Catherine's School in Park Place, Cardiff.

Miss Collin's experience both as a pupil and as a teacher had been until that point within the private sector of girls' education. When, under the far-reaching and visionary Welsh Intermediate Education Act of 1889, it was decided to set up a municipal secondary school for girls in Cardiff, Miss Collin was appointed as its first head in 1895.

Miss Collin was a dignified figure, a fine-looking, attractive woman with sparkling blue eyes, which twinkled with merriment or bore down on wrongdoers as the occasion demanded. Contemporaries invariably commented on her sharp intellect, her integrity, and delightful sense of humour. The girls of Cardiff high school regarded her with awe, respect, and affection. Her achievement as headmistress is impressive. Drawing her inspiration from the public and high schools of England, she turned what had originally been designated as Cardiff Intermediate and Technical School for Girls into a first class girls' high school. She promoted high standards and an academic ethos within the school. She extended the curriculum to include the sciences, not then usually considered appropriate for girls, and she devoted much time to encouraging extra-curricular activities. Although criticized by some contemporaries as élitist because she was reluctant to accept girls from elementary schools, under her autocratic but benign regime the numbers rose from ninety-four girls in 1895 to more than 400 on her retirement in 1924, making Cardiff high the largest girls' school in Wales.

Influenced by Harriet Morant Jones, headmistress at Notting Hill, an early pioneer of girls' secondary education and third president of the Association of Headmistresses, following Miss Buss and Miss Beale, Mary Collin was a committed feminist. The education of girls in Wales profited from the wealth of experience she brought with her and which she had gained in the formative years of its development in England. She assisted many Welsh educational organizations, always promoting the cause of girls and women, including the Association of Welsh Head Teachers, the University of Wales, and the Central Welsh Board. The University of Wales awarded her the degree of MA for services to Welsh education in 1925.

A 'new woman' in the 1890s, who shocked the Cardiff tradespeople by riding a bicycle, and a dedicated and tireless suffrage campaigner, Mary Collin worked throughout her life to promote the cause of women. An admirer of Mrs Fawcett, whom she recalled from her Cambridge childhood, she aligned herself with the moderate wing of the suffrage campaign and became the acknowledged leader of the women's suffrage movement in Cardiff. She was for many years the 'chairman [sic] of executive' of Cardiff and District Women's Suffrage Society. During the First World War the Cardiff society, under her guidance, suspended its activities and threw itself into the war effort and into helping the local community to cope with the difficulties created by the war. She played an active part in assisting unemployed women and women war workers, and enthusiastically engaged in the recruitment of women to the women's auxiliary services: she held recruiting meetings at the school and, to set an example to others, released her own two domestic servants to join the Women's Army Auxiliary Corps. At the end of the war, she resumed her suffrage activities and continued to play a leading role in the newly reconstituted Cardiff Women's Citizens' Association, which in 1921 replaced the suffrage society. In the inter-war years she campaigned vigorously on such issues as widows' pensions and women police, and throughout her life pressed for the involvement of more women on public bodies.

Mary Collin died on 22 July 1955 at St David's Hospital, Cardiff. She retained close contacts with the school until the end and, mindful of the continuity of Cardiff high, bequeathed in her will the treasured album bearing the names of old girls which she had received on her retirement in 1924. She died in the school's diamond jubilee year.

DEIRDRE BEDDOE

Sources C. Carr, *The spinning wheel: City of Cardiff High School for Girls, 1895–1955* (1955) · *Welsh Secondary Schools Review* (Dec 1955) · *Western Mail* [Cardiff] (17 July 1924) · minutes, cuttings, and annual reports of Cardiff and District Women's Suffrage Socciety (later Cardiff Women's Citizens' Association), Glamorgan RO, D/DX/158 · *Western Mail* [Cardiff] (25 July 1955) · W. G. Evans, *Education and female emancipation: the Welsh experience, 1847–1914* (1990) · B. Leech, *Full circle: City of Cardiff High School for Girls, 1950–1970* (1986) · d. cert.

Archives Cardiff High School, Cardiff, album of names of old girls · Cardiff High School, Cardiff, cabinet 'bearing names'

Likenesses group portrait, photograph, 1897 (with her staff), Cardiff High School, Cardiff · B. Ward, pastel drawing, 1920–24, Cardiff High School, Cardiff

Wealth at death £4177 15s. 11d.: probate, 10 Nov 1955, CGPLA Eng. & Wales

Colling, Charles (1751–1836), stockbreeder, was the second son in the family of two sons and two or three daughters of Charles Colling (1721–1785), farmer, and Dorothy Robson (d. 1779). He succeeded his father in the occupancy of a farm at Ketton, near Darlington, in 1782, shortly after a visit he paid to Robert Bakewell (1725–1795), the well-known breeder at Dishley, Leicestershire.

> It is generally supposed that the great lesson that Charles Colling learnt during the three weeks he spent at Dishley was the expediency of concentrating good blood by a system of in-and-in breeding ... What he really learnt at Dishley was the all-importance of 'quality' in cattle, and he resolved to devote himself to the preservation and amelioration of the local cattle on the Tees and Skerne. (Bates, 'The brothers Colling', 5–6)

On 23 July 1783 Colling married Mary Colpitts (1763–1850), who was almost as interested as her husband in the breeding of improved shorthorns and who helped him a great deal.

Colling bought his first good bull from his elder brother, Robert *Colling, and it was later known as Hubback. This bull was mated while at Ketton with cows—afterwards famous—called Duchess, Daisy, Cherry, and Lady Maynard. In 1795 one of Hubback's female offspring produced, by another celebrated bull called Favourite, a roan calf, which grew to be the famous Durham Ox. By the time it was five and a half years old it weighed 3024 lb, and it was sold as a show animal for £140. After five months' exhibition, its then owner refused £2000 for it, and for the next six years he took it around the country. A portrait of the Ox, painted by John Boultbee and engraved by John Whessell, was published in March 1802. At ten years old the Ox weighed about 3800 lb, but after dislocating its hipbone it was killed at Oxford in April 1807. A still more famous animal was Comet, born in the autumn of 1804, which 'Charles Colling declared to be the best bull he ever bred or saw, and nearly every judge of shorthorns agreed with him' (Bates, 'The brothers Colling', 16).

On 11 October 1810 Colling sold off his entire herd at a public auction, which was very well attended. Comet sold for 1000 guineas, and the forty-seven lots went in all for £7116 18s., or an average of £151 8s. 5d. A testimonial was presented to Colling by forty-nine subscribers in the shape of an inscribed silver-gilt cup.

Charles and Robert Colling, in making the shorthorn into a good beef animal, applied the principles developed by Robert Bakewell in breeding longhorn cattle. They were regarded as next in importance to Bakewell in improving the cattle of the United Kingdom. Thomas *Bates and Thomas Booth built on their work, and Amos Cruikshank of Sittyton (1808–1895) produced Scottish shorthorns based on Colling stock. Robert Colling died in 1820, but Charles lived on in retirement until his death on 16 January 1836. He had no descendants.

ERNEST CLARKE, rev. ANNE PIMLOTT BAKER

Sources C. J. Bates, 'The brothers Colling', *Journal of the Royal Agricultural Society of England*, 3rd ser., 10 (1899), 1–30 · C. J. Bates, *Thomas Bates and the Kirklevington shorthorns* (1897) · T. Bell, *The history of improved shorthorn or Durham cattle and of the Kirklevington herd from the notes of the late Thomas Bates* (1871) · The Druid [H. H. Dixon], *Saddle and sirloin, or, English farm and sporting worthies* (1870), 146–8

Likenesses T. Weaver, double portrait, c.1811 (Charles and Robert Colling) · W. Ward, engraving, 1825 (after T. Weaver), repro. in Bates, 'The brothers Colling', frontispiece · G. Cook, line engraving (after J. M. Wright), BM, NPG; repro. in *The Farmer's Magazine* (Feb 1844)

Colling, Mary Maria (*b.* 1804), poet and domestic servant, was born on 20 August 1804 (although she later claimed to have been born a year later), in Tavistock, Devon, and was baptized there on 2 September 1804, the daughter of Edmund Colling, husbandman and assistant to the surveyor of the highways, and Anne Domville. At the age of ten she was sent to a dame-school to be taught needlework, and it was there that she learned to read and write. At the age of fourteen she was hired as a lady's maid. In 1831 Anna Eliza Bray, historical novelist, discovered Colling's poetic abilities and assisted her in publishing her work. Bray also interested Robert Southey, poet laureate, in Colling as a 'poet of nature' (Bray, 12), with 'the eye, and the ear, and the feeling of the poet' though 'the art may be wanting' (ibid., 78). Colling published *Fables and other Pieces in Verse* by subscription in 1831. The volume contains thirty-nine verse fables that teach values such as the acceptance of one's social position and the equality of all stations before God, as well as forty poems on miscellaneous subjects, including several poems to her various sponsors, several non-controversial poems describing the effects of war on rural life, and several poems describing rural life in general. The volume opens with three letters

from Bray to Southey, detailing Colling's familial background and 'unblemished character' (ibid., 19). Little is known about Colling after 1831. SUSAN J. LEVASSEUR

Sources A. Bray, 'Letters to Robert Southey', in M. M. Colling, *Fables and other pieces in verse … with some account of the author*, ed. A. Bray (1831) · 'Fables and other pieces in verse by Mary Maria Colling', *Monthly Review*, 127 (Dec 1831), 552–66 · [R. Southey], review of *Fables and other pieces in verse*, QR, 47 (1832), 80–103

Colling, Robert (1749–1820), stockbreeder, was born in December 1749, the eldest son in the family of two sons and two or three daughters of Charles Colling (1721–1785), farmer, of Ketton, near Darlington, and his wife, Dorothy Robson (*d.* 1779); his brother was Charles *Colling. After receiving some education, he was apprenticed to a grocer in Shields, but because of poor health he came home to his father's farm and embarked on an agricultural career.

After spending some time at Hurworth, co. Durham, Colling took a farm nearby at Barmpton, under the Lambton family. At first he kept only dairy cows, and had no plans to breed shorthorns. The foundation of his pedigree herd was a yellow-red and white bull (known in shorthorn history as Hubback), originally bought on the advice of his brother Charles for 8 guineas, and afterwards sold to his brother for the Ketton herd. A 'shyness' sprang up between the brothers, which became accentuated in March 1793, and the Barmpton and Ketton herds for some time lived apart, though later more amicable relations were restored. When in October 1810 Charles Colling sold off his Ketton herd of shorthorns, Robert's herd at Barmpton became the centre of interest to the breeders of shorthorns, which had then become fashionable.

A famous white heifer (daughter of the bull Favourite), which at four years old weighed 1820 lb, was painted by Thomas Weaver; an engraving of the picture was made by William Ward, and published on 13 December 1811, with a dedication to Robert Colling. The heifer was purchased by two butchers and exhibited at Christmas 1811 at the stables of the Three Kings, Piccadilly, as 'the greatest wonder of the world of the kind', and then weighed 2448 lb. 'The same system of in-and-in breeding that had been in vogue at Ketton was pursued without interruption at Barmpton, and that without any admixture of fresh alloy' (Bates, 'Brothers Colling', 22). Robert carried on his herd until Michaelmas day 1810, when it was sold by auction; sixty-one lots fetched £7852 19s. Colling died unmarried at Barmpton on 7 March 1820, leaving his property to his brother Charles, and a final sale was held on 3 October 1820.

Colling was considered a model all-round farmer—good cattle, good sheep, good crops, neat hedges, neat farm-buildings—but, not being so much of a specialist, he was less known than his more businesslike and versatile brother, Charles.

ERNEST CLARKE, rev. ANNE PIMLOTT BAKER

Sources C. J. Bates, 'The brothers Colling', *Journal of the Royal Agricultural Society of England*, 3rd ser., 10 (1899), 1–30 · C. J. Bates, *Thomas Bates and the Kirklevington shorthorns* (1897) · T. Bell, *The history of improved shorthorn or Durham cattle and of the Kirklevington herd from*

the notes of the late Thomas Bates (1871) • The Druid [H. H. Dixon], *Saddle and sirloin, or, English farm and sporting worthies* (1870), 146–8
Likenesses T. Weaver, double portrait, *c*.1811 (Robert and Charles Colling) • W. Ward, engraving, 1825 (after T. Weaver), repro. in Bates, 'The brothers Colling', frontispiece

Collinges, John (1623/4–1691), clergyman and ejected minister, was born at Boxted, Essex, the son of Edward Collinges, a minister. Educated at the neighbouring grammar school of Dedham, he was influenced by the puritan clergyman John Rogers and his successor, Matthew Newcomen. His father died when he was fifteen, leaving 'little above £50 a year to maintain my Mother, and self and two sisters young and sickly' (Collinges, *New Lesson*, 9), but John was allowed to complete his schooling. On 9 April 1639 he was admitted as a sizar at Emmanuel College, Cambridge, 'where I lived, though in no height, yet in no want, by the favour of my learned tutor'. Collinges was a diligent student, graduating BA in 1643, but fell 'into the temptations of those sinful times' and acquired 'a hatred of holiness' (ibid., 10). The sharp disapproval of Newcomen helped him towards a different path. He proceeded BD in 1653 and DD in 1658.

Before 18 October 1645 Collinges became a chaplain to the family of Isaac Wyncoll of Bures, Essex, whose eldest daughter, Elizabeth (*d*. 1692), he later married. They had at least one son and two daughters. In 1645 he was also installed as rector of Alphamstone, Essex, in the place of Rowland Steward, accused in March 1644 of gambling, drunkenness, and adultery. The living, according to a terrier of 1637, comprised a parsonage house, barn, stable, and more than 20 acres. In 1646 Collinges moved to Norwich and became vicar of St Saviour's and also of St Augustine. The sequestered minister of the latter, Joseph Reading, returned in an effort to unseat him but on 1 December 1646 the committee for plundered ministers ordered Collinges to continue in both parishes. Already in September 1646 Collinges had been invited by Sir John Hobart of Chapelfield House, Blickling, 'to take my chamber in his house whilst I discharged my ministerial office in the county, and to take some oversight of his family as to the things of God' (Collinges, *Par nobile*, 21). Soon after her husband's death in 1647 Frances, Lady Hobart:

> converted some less useful lower rooms of her house into a chapel which was conveniently capacious of more than 200 persons. Here she obliged me at first to preach a lecture every week, and to repeat one or both of my sermons every Lords Day at night, after the more publick sermons were finished in the Town. (ibid.)

Collinges was a signatory of the attestation of Norfolk ministers in 1648, and was selected by Norwich corporation to read the afternoon sermon on the day of thanksgiving appointed after the royalist riot in the city in May 1648. On 2 February 1650 he was named by the committee of plundered ministers to serve the parish of St Stephen, Norwich, where on 21 June 1654 he was formally admitted as vicar; also in 1654, he was appointed assistant to the Norfolk commission into the ministry. Collinges was a prolific controversialist. His opponents included Theophilus Brabourne, and those such as William Sheppard who

advocated lay preaching. On church organization he had firm views: 'I believe Presbyterian Government will be in credit at the great day (when Christ shall have trod all his enemies under his feet) yet from my soul I wish that all God's people had one heart and one way' (Collinges, *New Lesson*, 11). And, 'if the Devil were aske a courtesie of a state, he should aske no more than 1) An universall toleration, and 2) an uncontrouled liberty for every one to preach and expound scriptures' (Collinges, *Responsoria ad erratica pastoris*, 1652, 37). On 28 November 1660 the Commons rejected a bill which would have curtailed episcopal power and allowed some latitude in the forms of worship; Collinges later recalled this as disastrous:

> Whether the wisdom of his Majesty, or that party of the House of Commons who then opposed the passing of it into an Act, were greater let the experience now of twenty years more determine, which for the most part have been years of confusion and disorder as to matters of religion. (Cliffe, 42)

On 26 April 1661 Collinges was licensed to continue preaching at St Stephen's, and he served in that year as a commissioner at the Savoy conference, which sought to amend the prayer book in a direction acceptable to moderate dissent. In 1661–2 he was involved in a law suit against the dean and chapter of Norwich, patrons of St Stephen's, for recovery of a yearly pension of 53*s*. 4*d*. Collinges was ejected with the other dissenting ministers in August 1662. Shortly afterwards Chapelfield House was searched by the authorities. The lord lieutenant, Horatio, Lord Townshend, felt obliged to apologize for the intrusion, but warned against allowing 'any scandalous number to meet' (Cliffe, 111); after the death of Lady Hobart in November 1664 Collinges wrote an affectionate account of her life and virtues. He maintained close links with the family and was described in 1688 as chaplain to Sir Henry Hobart, Sir John Hobart's son. In 1669 Collinges was reported to be preaching, with Benjamin Snowden, to 'about 300 Presbyterians and Independents at the house of John Barnham, hosier' in the parish of St John Maddermarket, Norwich. On 30 April 1672 he was licensed as a presbyterian teacher at John Wilson's house in St Stephen's, and on 14 May Norwich corporation leased to his congregation the East Granary behind St Andrew's Hall. At Easter 1674 Collinges was presented by churchwardens of St Laurence for not receiving the sacrament.

Collinges played a notable role in the civic struggle of 1678–81 in Norwich, when local and national politics collided. Robert Paston (Viscount Yarmouth), lord lieutenant of Norfolk, was determined to make the city an Anglican royalist stronghold and had obtained Bishop Sparrow's assurance that proceedings against Collinges would follow a by-election of February 1678. No action was taken, however, until in July 1678 rumours circulated of a plot on Bishop Sparrow's life; on the orders of Yarmouth the mayor arrested the suspects, who included Collinges. They were obliged to give security of £500 each for good behaviour, and appear at the next quarter sessions. In a letter of 22 July 1678 Yarmouth reported that 'Dr. Collinges, a man long famous in that country for his ill-affections to the Crown' was 'under a process for non-conformity and preaching in conventicles'. But the chancellor of the diocese of Norwich was sent 'a minatory letter from an unknown hand to desist in the prosecution' (*CSP dom.*, *March–December 1678*, 306) and the justices summoned to the quarter sessions conspicuously failed to attend. The tories won all three general elections of 1679–81 and controlled the court of aldermen and the Norwich assembly; but the recorder of Norwich, Francis Bacon, 'refused to assist Mayor Davey in investigating the case against John Collins' (Evans, 271). Collinges continued in his ministry. One tory described him in 1682 as 'a man of some learning, which he employs in promoting Presbytery, and, were he removed, tis probable many of that sect would fall off' (*CSP dom.*, *1682*, 54). His survival probably owed something to Sir John Hobart, the cousin and heir of his former patron, now a leader of the anti-court party in Norwich.

In 1685 Collinges was twice arrested as a 'non juring suspect' (*Lothian MSS*, xii), but then seems to have lived quietly until James II issued his declaration of indulgence of which Collinges took full advantage. On 14 April 1687 the bishop of Norwich wrote scathingly:

> Dr. Collins who not long since sent me wonderfull submissive letters is now grown very pert and pragmatical, and tells some of the Clergy of this City, that now he stands upon a levell with them, and well remembers the horrid persecutions of the saints, and that he had rather owne the kindness of the indulgence then submitt to the unreasonable Terms of the Church of England.

He concluded dismissively that Collinges was 'made up of spleene and choler and is not much to be regarded' (*Calamy rev.*). In 1689 a new meeting-place, certified on 19 July, was built for Collinges and his congregation in the parish of St John Colegate, and in the winter of 1689–90 his salary was given as £56 a year. His last days were spent in implementing the union of presbyterians and congregationalists. He died at Walcott, Norfolk, on 17 January 1691, aged sixty-seven, and was buried there on 20 January; his funeral sermon was preached by Martin Fynch. His wife, Elizabeth, died the following year.

STEPHEN WRIGHT

Sources *Calamy rev.* · A. Gordon, ed., *Freedom after ejection: a review (1690–1692) of presbyterian and congregational nonconformity in England and Wales* (1917), 240 · J. Collinges, *A new lesson for the eductus doctor* (1654) · J. Collinges, *Par nobile: two treatises* (1669) · J. T. Evans, *Seventeenth century Norwich, politics, religion and government* (1980) · R. W. Ketton-Cremer, *Norfolk in the civil war: a portrait of a society in conflict* (1969) · J. T. Cliffe, *The puritan gentry besieged, 1650–1700* (1993) · J. Browne, *A history of Congregationalism and memorials of the churches in Norfolk and Suffolk* (1877) · Venn, *Alum. Cant.* · *Walker rev.* · F. Blomefield and C. Parkin, *An essay towards a topographical history of the county of Norfolk*, [2nd edn], 11 vols. (1805–10) · A. E. R., 'Account books of St Stephen's church and parish, Norwich', *East Anglian*, new ser., 8 (1899–1900), 378–82 · R. Newcourt, *Repertorium ecclesiasticum parochiale Londinense*, 1 (1708) · *CSP dom.*, 1678; 1682 · *Sixth report*, HMC, 5 (1877–8) · *Report on the manuscripts of the marquess of Lothian*, HMC, 62 (1905) · E. Calamy, ed., *An abridgement of Mr. Baxter's history of his life and times, with an account of the ministers, &c., who were ejected after the Restauration of King Charles II*, 2nd edn, 2 vols. (1713)

Likenesses R. White, line engraving, BM, NPG; repro. in J. Collinges, *Several discourses concerning the actual providence of God* (1678)

Collingridge, Peter [*name in religion* Bernardine] (1757–1829), vicar apostolic of the western district, was born on 10 March 1757 at Fritwell, Oxfordshire, the son of Peter Collingridge and his wife, Mary. He may have received his early education in England. What is certain is that he entered the Franciscan friary of St Bonaventure, Douai, where he received the habit on 26 June 1773. Record of his ordination was probably destroyed by the revolutionaries, although it is known that he was lecturing in both philosophy and theology even before he was ordained. In 1788 he was elected guardian of the friary.

After some twenty years in Douai, Collingridge returned to England to work at St George's Fields, Southwark. After a short spell in Coventry he was appointed to the Sardinian embassy chapel, Lincoln's Inn Fields, London. On 2 January 1807 he was named titular bishop of Thespiae and coadjutor to Bishop G. W. Sharrock, vicar apostolic of the western district, but his consecration did not take place until 11 October. Bishop Poynter performed the ceremony at St Edmund's College, Ware. Collingridge succeeded Sharrock on 17 October 1809 and moved the episcopal residence from Bath to the Benedictine convent at Cannington, near Taunton.

Emancipation was the major issue which divided the Catholic community and its leaders. The matter was urgent, and Collingridge felt that 'by not accepting even an imperfect emancipation, numbers of non-Catholics were being prevented from entering the Church' (Dockery, 89). Although a regular himself who had already welcomed the Benedictines to Downside, near Bath, and who had been the first of the vicars apostolic to allow the Jesuits to resume their work after their reinstatement in 1814, Collingridge was nevertheless said to be 'prepared to accept legislation for Emancipation which, as a condition, would have sacrificed the regular clergy' (Norman, 82). Popular suspicions were based on the perception that, unlike the seculars, their endeavours were under the direction of superiors who lived abroad. Collingridge aligned himself with Bishop W. Poynter of the London district against Bishop John Milner (midland district) in being prepared to accept the guarantees then on offer from the government. However, he was not prepared to accept emancipation at any price.

Bishop Collingridge was given the help of a coadjutor in 1823. Peter Augustine Baines, a former Benedictine and now titular bishop of Siga, was of an entirely different mould, whose ambition it was to put the Catholic community in the region 'on the map' and to provide a supply of secular clergy for the growing industrial areas of the vicariate. Because he judged the religious orders to be ill-equipped for such a task, he approached Downside with a view to turning it into a seminary for seculars. In this serious error of judgement Collingridge acquiesced, and therefore some of the ensuing acrimony must be laid at his door.

Collingridge was a devout, forgiving man. Franciscan simplicity remained his way of life, even as far as begging

Peter Collingridge (1757–1829), by unknown artist

hay for his horse. Such traits endeared him to his impoverished flock of some 5500 souls scattered throughout Wales and the west country. (At that time the chief centres of Catholic population were at Bristol, Bath, and Plymouth, with a strong enclave in and around the estate of Lord Arundell at Wardour in Wiltshire.)

Collingridge died on 3 March 1829 at the Benedictine convent at Cannington, Somerset, where he had lived, and was buried in the bishop's garden there. When the body was exhumed in 1914 prior to its reinterment at Downside, the curious formation of his skull as shown in a contemporary drawing was confirmed. The simplicity of his tomb in the north choir of the abbey church is in sharp contrast to the adjacent, more ornate, monument to his successor. J. A. HARDING

Sources J. B. Dockery, *Collingridge: a Franciscan contribution to Catholic emancipation* [1954] · Gillow, *Lit. biog. hist.*, vol. 1 · E. R. Norman, *The English Catholic church in the nineteenth century* (1984) · G. Oliver, *Collections illustrating the history of the Catholic religion in the counties of Cornwall, Devon, Dorset, Somerset, Wilts, and Gloucester* (1857)

Archives Birmingham Roman Catholic diocesan archives, Archbishop's House, St Chad's, Queensway, Birmingham · Bristol RO, corresp., papers, and personal accounts · Clifton Roman Catholic diocese, Bristol, diary · Downside Abbey, near Bath · Sacra Congregazione di Propaganda Fide, Rome, Propaganda Fide archives · Westminster Roman Catholic diocesan archives, 16A Abingdon Road, London

Likenesses oils, Franciscan friary, Clevedon, Somerset · oils, St Ambrose, Leigh Woods, Bristol [*see illus.*]

Collings, Jesse (1831–1920), politician, youngest son of Thomas Collings, of Littleham, Exmouth, Devon, and his wife, Anne Palmer, was born at Littleham on 9 January 1831. His father was a bricklayer, afterwards proprietor of a small building business; but in later life Jesse Collings was fond of tracing his descent from the Palmers because they had, he believed, been yeoman farmers. He was educated at a dame-school 'for tradesmen's sons', and also spent a year at Church House School, Stoke, Plymouth, which was kept by a cousin. At the age of fifteen he became a shop assistant, later a clerk and commercial traveller in the ironmongery trade. In 1850 he entered, as a clerk, the firm of Booth & Co. of Birmingham, which was renamed Collings and Wallis when he became a partner fourteen years later; he retired in 1879. He married, in 1858, Emily, daughter of Edward Oxenbould, a master at King Edward VI's Grammar School, Birmingham. They had one daughter.

While living at Exeter and representing his firm, Collings obtained much knowledge of rural conditions by his travels through the west of England. His first public work was done when he helped to establish the Devon and Exeter Boys' Industrial School in 1862. Influenced by study of American education, his interest in education developed when he went to live in Birmingham in 1864, and in 1868 he published *An Outline of the American School System*, which was the immediate cause of the formation of the National Education League for the advocacy of free and non-sectarian elementary education. He was elected a town councillor for the Edgbaston division of Birmingham in that year, and thereafter became prominently associated with the programme of municipal reform in the city carried out by Joseph Chamberlain, with whom he developed a close personal and political friendship. He was mayor from 1878 to 1880.

Outside municipal affairs Collings was becoming widely known as an advocate of free education and of land reform. In the latter connection he, with a number of other radicals, was closely associated with Joseph Arch and the National Agricultural Labourers' Union, and with the Highland Land Law Reform Association. In 1880 he was returned for Ipswich as a Liberal, and in 1882 he secured the passing of the Allotments Extension Act. In January 1886 his small-holdings' amendment to the queen's speech united Liberals and home-rulers and felled Salisbury's government. Gladstone made Collings parliamentary secretary to the Local Government Board, while controversially reducing his salary. Collings was unseated on petition in April 1886, thus missing the home-rule debates; but he followed his friend Chamberlain into Liberal Unionism. In July 1886 he was elected for Bordesley, Birmingham, as a Liberal Unionist, holding the seat until 1918. In the Salisbury administration of 1895 he was under-secretary to the Home department, retaining office until 1902. In 1892 he had been made a privy councillor. A loyal colleague and good party servant, his work in office was mainly administrative, and unconnected with his life interests. He died at Southfield, Church Road, Edgbaston (once Chamberlain's home), on 20 November 1920.

From the days when he appeared on the platforms of the National Agricultural Labourers' Union until he retired from public life, Collings was an enthusiastic advocate of land reform. It was he who, in 1885, began to

Jesse Collings (1831–1920), by Bassano, c.1908

Sources J. Collings and J. L. Green, *The life of Jesse Collings*, 2 vols. (1920) · J. L. Garvin and J. Amery, *The life of Joseph Chamberlain*, 6 vols. (1932–69) · M. C. Hurst, *Joseph Chamberlain and west midland politics, 1886–95* (1962) · *The Times* (24 Nov 1920) · R. Douglas, 'Collings, Jesse', *BDMBR*, vol. 3, pt 1

Archives BL, Indian travel journal, Add. MS 58773 | BL, Gladstone MSS · HLRO, Blumenfeld letters to R. D. · Plunkett Foundation, Oxford, corresp. with Sir Horace Plunkett · U. Birm. L., special collections department, corresp. with Joseph Chamberlain

Likenesses B. Stone, photographs, 1897, NPG · Bassano, photograph, c.1908, NPG [see illus.] · F. C. Gould, double portrait, ink and watercolour caricature (with Joseph Chamberlain), V&A · P. Jonathan, oils, Birmingham Museums and Art Gallery · Spy [L. Ward], chromolithograph caricature, NPG; repro. in *VF* (1 Dec 1888)

Wealth at death £34,979 16s. 6d.: probate, 8 Feb 1921, *CGPLA Eng. & Wales*

Collings, Samuel (d. 1793?), painter and caricaturist, exhibited regularly at the Royal Academy between 1784 and 1789. Paintings accepted were *Children in the Wood*, 1784; *The Chamber of Genius*, from which an engraving was made, 1785; *The Triumph of Sensibility*, 1786; *The Convict: a Portrait*, 1787; *Chalk Pit Near Lewisham*, 1788, and *Frost on the Thames, Sketched on the Spot*, 1789. The last was sold at Christies on 11 March 1960, and is now at Yale University, as is the self-portrait offered in the same sale. These are the only known oil paintings by the caricaturist. A signed watercolour titled *Elijah Going up to Heaven* is in the British Museum (1881–11–12–174). Other paintings that formed the subject of engravings are a pair in the style of William Hogarth's *The Rake's Progress*, titled *The Heir Disinherited* and *The Disinherited Heir*, aquatinted by F. Jukes, and portraits of George III and Lord Thurlow.

Collings appears to have abandoned painting to concentrate on his work as a caricaturist during the last few years of his life. His earliest dated pieces in this vein appear to be the folding plates published in the *Wit's Magazine* in 1784. Of the seven signed plates, four were engraved by William Blake. Another engraved by Smith, *Gilpin Going Farther than he Intended*, is probably the earliest illustration of Cowper's famous character. Collings's best-known caricatures are the twenty designs reproduced as etchings by his friend Thomas Rowlandson, published anonymously in two parts under the title *Picturesque Beauties of Boswell, Designed and Etched by Two Capital Artists* (1786), reprinted in the mid-nineteenth century as the work of Rowlandson. Six of Collings's drawings for the series are in the Victoria and Albert Museum (Dyce bequest, 754–9), including two unused designs. The figures portrayed are similar to those by Rowlandson himself, but in Collings's other work his style is closer to that of Hogarth and the other early caricaturists. The two friends also collaborated to produce a similar satire on Goethe's *Sorrows of Werther*. Other periodicals in which Collings's caricatures appear are the *Carlton House Magazine*; *Attick Miscellany*; and *The Bon-Ton Magazine, or, Microscope of Fashion and Folly*. Caricatures published under the pseudonym Annibal Scratch have also been attributed to him. He is thought to have died at an early age. He was described by Henry Angelo as 'a great tavern goer … [whose] fate was lamented, he being found dead on the steps of an hotel' (Angelo, 1.133) in Soho.

MICHAEL HESELTINE

use the phrase 'three acres and a cow', which for many years was the war-cry of the land-reformers. The home-rule controversy of 1886 scattered the group of radical land-reformers that had gathered round the agricultural labourers' movement. They were henceforth in opposing political camps. Arch and his associates adhered to the Gladstonian party, Collings and his associates became unionists, and the effectiveness of both groups was destroyed. In 1883 Collings had formed the Allotments Extension Association; and in 1888 he became its president, but was deposed, partly as a result of differences on the question of home rule. He then formed the Rural Labourers' League (afterwards known as the Rural League) with which he was connected until 1919. He supported the tariff-reform campaign on agricultural grounds. He continued his interest in rural affairs, including education, allotments, small-holdings, and the administration of charitable trusts.

In education Collings was the advocate of a vocational system of elementary education in rural areas, and in land reform the advocate of a system of peasant proprietorship. His views on education were never embodied in legislation, though to a small extent they were adopted in teaching practice and administration. His ideas on land reform were partly embodied in the ineffective Small Holdings Act of 1882, and again in the Land Settlement Act of 1919. He published *Land Reform* (1906), *The Colonization of Rural Britain* (1914), and *The Great War: its Lessons and Warnings* (1915).   A. W. ASHBY, rev. H. C. G. MATTHEW

Sources *DNB* · Graves, *RA exhibitors* · Thieme & Becker, *Allgemeines Lexikon*, vol. 7 · Waterhouse, *18c painters* · M. Bryant and S. Heneage, eds., *Dictionary of British cartoonists and caricaturists, 1730–1980* (1994) · H. Hammelmann, *Book illustrators in eighteenth-century England*, ed. T. S. R. Boase (1975) · J. Riely, *Samuel Collings' designs for Rowlandson's 'Picturesque beauties of Boswell'* (1975) · M. D. George, *English political caricature: a study of opinion and propaganda*, 2 vols. (1959), vol. 1 · J. Grego, *Rowlandson the caricaturist*, 1 (1880) · *Catalogue of English pictures and drawings* (1960) [sale catalogue, Christies, 11 March 1960] · H. Angelo, *Reminiscences*, 1 (1828)
Likenesses S. Collings, self-portrait, oils, *c*.1790, Yale U. CBA

Cuthbert Collingwood, Baron Collingwood (1748–1810), by unknown artist, 1790–95

Collingwood, Cuthbert, Baron Collingwood (1748–1810)

Collingwood, Cuthbert, Baron Collingwood (1748–1810), naval officer, was born on 26 September 1748 on The Side, Newcastle upon Tyne, the eighth child and eldest son of Cuthbert Collingwood (1712–1775), a merchant in Newcastle, and Milcah (1713–1788), daughter of Reginald Dobson of Barwise near Appleby, Westmorland. Two more sons followed. His father was of an old but impoverished Northumberland family.

Long apprenticeship for command, 1761–1779 Collingwood attended Newcastle Free School under Hugh Moises, a renowned teacher, until he was twelve, when, on 28 August 1761, he and his next brother, Wilfred, joined the frigate *Shannon*, commanded by their mother's cousin, Captain Richard Brathwaite. The brothers were to serve together for the next twelve years. The *Shannon* was employed mostly off Norway and in the Channel Fleet until she paid off in February 1763 at the end of the Seven Years' War. After eighteen months at home the brothers rejoined the *Shannon* under Captain Boteler in October 1764, and spent most of the next year in Commodore Thomas Graves's expedition to west Africa. Brathwaite resumed command in October 1765 and the brothers followed him into the frigate *Gibraltar* the following February. In March 1767, after eight months off Newfoundland and Cadiz, Brathwaite and the Collingwoods transferred to the frigate *Liverpool*, in which they went back to Newfoundland for eighteen months and then served almost continuously in the western Mediterranean for three and a half years. As well as a return to Cadiz, it was Cuthbert's first experience of the waters off Minorca and Toulon, which he was to know so well forty years later. The *Liverpool* paid off in March 1772 and the brothers joined the *Lenox* (74 guns), guard-ship at Portsmouth, commanded by a fellow Northumbrian, Robert Roddam. In the following year Cuthbert spent six months in the West Indies in the *Portland* (50 guns) and the *Princess Amelia* (80 guns).

In February 1774, after another six months in the *Lenox*, Collingwood joined the *Preston* (50 guns), flagship of Vice-Admiral Samuel Graves, and sailed for Boston, Massachusetts, as war with the American colonists grew imminent. At the battle of Bunker Hill on 17 June 1775 he landed with what he described as 'a party of seamen, supplying the army with what was necessary for them' (*Naval Chronicle*, 23, 380). For his services Graves promoted him lieutenant from that date. It had been a long apprenticeship—he had been at sea for thirteen years as able seaman, midshipman, and master's mate, had passed the examination for lieutenant in 1772, but was without an influential patron. He joined the *Somerset* (74 guns) as fourth lieutenant immediately after Bunker Hill and returned home in February 1776.

Collingwood's next appointment, as first lieutenant of the sloop *Hornet*, which he joined in March 1776 and which sailed for the West Indies in December, was an unhappy experience under a brutal captain, Robert Haswell. During one period of six months Haswell ordered the flogging of a third of his ship's company. In September 1777 he brought against Collingwood charges of contempt, disobedience of orders, and breach of the captain's instructions. Collingwood was court-martialled and acquitted of all charges but advised by the court to conduct himself with more 'alacrity'.

With the arrival in Jamaica of Rear-Admiral Sir Peter Parker as commander-in-chief, Collingwood's fortunes were transformed. In July 1778 Parker appointed him to succeed Lieutenant Horatio Nelson, a friend since 1773, as second lieutenant of the *Lowestoffe* (32 guns, Captain William Locker). In December Parker took him into his flagship, the *Bristol* (50 guns), as second lieutenant and in June 1779, recognizing his qualities, gave him his first command, the brig *Badger*, again succeeding Nelson.

Early commands, 1779–1791 On 22 March 1780 Collingwood was made post captain, less than five years since his promotion to lieutenant, and sent to San Juan, Nicaragua, to take command of *Hinchinbroke* (28 guns) from Nelson, who had caught a dangerous fever during an expedition against the Spaniards. Collingwood found that four men, including the first lieutenant, had just died, seventy men were ill with fever, and the ship was 'very leaky'. Despite his erecting a hut ashore for the sick and regularly washing the ship with vinegar, another 154 men died on board during the next four months out of a ship's company of 200. More died in hospital after the ship's return to Jamaica in August. Deaths from fever in the army and the transport ships were on a similar scale.

After this harrowing experience Collingwood was given command of the *Pelican* (24 guns). In August 1781, after capturing a French frigate and five privateers, she was wrecked on the Morant keys near Jamaica in a hurricane.

After ten days of extreme privation the ship's company, her carronades, and most of her stores were saved and taken back in a frigate sent from Jamaica. Collingwood was honourably acquitted at the mandatory court martial, and he and his ship's company were commended for 'doing everything becoming good officers and men' (18 Aug 1781, PRO, ADM1/5318).

Collingwood returned to England in 1782 after four and a half years of active employment during the American War of Independence. The kindness he received from Sir Peter Parker was touchingly recalled twenty-five years later in a letter to Parker (by then admiral of the fleet) eleven days after Trafalgar:

> Had it not been for the fall of our noble friend … your pleasure would have been perfect—that two of your own pupils, raised under your eye, and cherished by your kindness, should render such service to their Country as I hope this battle will in its effect be. (1 Nov 1805, NMM, RUSI/NM/214(i))

After eighteen years' sea service, most of it abroad, Collingwood was ashore for a year before receiving his next command, the *Sampson* (64 guns); but with the war over she paid off in April 1783. However, he was immediately appointed to the frigate *Mediator* and sailed again for the West Indies, where he was joined the following year by Nelson in the *Boreas* as senior captain. Nelson, supported by Collingwood, saw it as his duty to uphold the navigation laws and prevent illegal trading in the islands by foreigners (now including Americans), which was considered harmful to the lawful trade of Canadians and Nova Scotians. The captains received no support, indeed opposition, from their commander-in-chief, Rear-Admiral Sir Richard Hughes, but their actions to suppress the trade were fully approved of by the government in London. 'This station has not been over pleasant', wrote Nelson to Captain Locker. 'Had it not been for Collingwood, it would have been the most disagreeable I ever saw' (5 March 1786, Nicolas, 1.156). They had recently drawn each other's portraits. In July 1786 the *Mediator* returned home and Collingwood spent four years in Northumberland, 'making my acquaintance with my own family, to whom I had hitherto been as it were a stranger' (*Naval Chronicle*, 23, 381).

In July 1790, on the threat of war with Spain after the Nootka Sound incident, Collingwood took command of the frigate *Mermaid* and sailed once more for the West Indies. With the end of the dispute *Mermaid* returned home in April 1791 and Collingwood to Northumberland. On 16 June he married in Newcastle, Sarah (*bap.* 1762, *d.* 1819), daughter of John Erasmus Blackett, a well-to-do merchant and four times mayor of Newcastle. Sarah was the granddaughter of Robert Roddam (1711–1744) of Hethpoole and Caldburne (not Admiral Robert Roddam, as is often stated). Later in the year they moved to Morpeth, where their daughter Sarah was born on 28 May 1792, followed by a second child, Mary Patience, on 13 August 1793.

War with France, 1793–1805 On 22 February 1793, three weeks after the outbreak of war with France, Collingwood took command of the *Prince* (90 guns) at Plymouth. In July she hoisted the flag of Rear-Admiral George Bowyer and

sailed with the Channel Fleet until the end of the year. Bowyer and Collingwood then transferred to the *Barfleur* (98 guns) and took part in the five-day engagement culminating in the battle of the Glorious First of June (1794). *Barfleur* was warmly engaged on 29 May and throughout the main battle three days later. Bowyer lost a leg early in that encounter and as he fell was caught by Collingwood, who then conducted Bowyer's subdivision as well as fighting his own ship. But, though Bowyer was created a baronet, Collingwood was not one of the captains specifically mentioned in Lord Howe's report and he was therefore not awarded the gold medal. He was deeply hurt.

In July 1794 Collingwood transferred to the *Hector* and in December to the *Excellent* (both 74 guns). After a few months off Ushant he sailed for the Mediterranean and joined the fleet guarding Corsica and blockading Toulon. In the defeat of the much larger Spanish fleet off Cape St Vincent on 14 February 1797 *Excellent*, famed for the rapidity of her gunfire, had a most distinguished share. She was quickly in action with the *Salvador del Mundo* (112 guns). 'Soon after, her colours being struck and her fire ceasing, I hailed her, and understanding she surrendered shot ahead under the lee of the next ship in succession (the San Ysidro) when the former ship rehoisted her colours' (14 Feb 1797, PRO, captain's log, *Excellent*). *Excellent* then engaged the *San Ysidro* (74 guns), which struck after a short but fierce engagement, the first to surrender to the British fleet. Collingwood immediately pressed on to assist Commodore Nelson in the *Captain* by engaging the *San Nicolas* (80 guns), 'giving her a most awful and tremendous fire' (Nicolas, 2.345). This caused her to 'run on board' the *San Josef* (112 guns) and enabled Nelson to capture both ships. *Excellent* with other ships then engaged the Spanish flagship, *Santissima Trinidada* (136 guns), for an hour and inflicted much damage, but she had to be abandoned when several Spaniards which had seen little action came to her assistance. Nelson wrote the next day to Collingwood: 'My dearest Friend. "A friend in need is a friend indeed" was never more truly verified than by your most noble and gallant conduct yesterday in sparing the *Captain* from further loss' (NMM, LBK/15). 'Nothing', wrote Vice-Admiral William Waldegrave, 'could exceed the spirit and true officership which you so happily displayed yesterday … May England long possess such men as yourself—'tis saying everything for her glory' (ibid.).

Gold medals were awarded to all flag officers and captains. When Collingwood was told this by John Jervis (now earl of St Vincent) he replied that he could not receive his while that for 'the First of June' was withheld. 'To receive such a distinction now would be to acknowledge the propriety of that injustice.' 'That is precisely the answer which I expected from you', replied St Vincent; in due course both medals were sent to him by Lord Spencer, the first lord, who wrote rather lamely: 'The former medal would have been transmitted to you some months ago if a proper and safe conveyance had been found for it' (3 April 1797, NMM, COL/14).

Excellent spent the next twenty-one months blockading

the Spanish fleet in Cadiz, and returned home in November 1798. For a few months from September 1797 Collingwood was appointed a commodore by St Vincent with command of the Cadiz blockade. *Excellent* paid off at Portsmouth in January 1799 and Collingwood was able to go to Morpeth to visit his family, whom he had last seen for eight days in December 1794. On 14 February 1799 he was promoted rear-admiral of the white and in May hoisted his flag in the *Triumph* (74 guns). His division sailed immediately to reinforce Lord Keith in the Mediterranean. After an unsuccessful search for a French fleet under Admiral Bruix, Keith and his fleet returned to Ushant in August to find that the French had entered Brest a week earlier.

Thereafter, until May 1802, Collingwood was almost continuously at sea blockading the French in Brest with occasional visits to Torbay and Cawsand Bay, usually for shelter from gales. In January 1800 he transferred his flag to the *Barfleur*. On 1 January 1801 he was advanced to rear-admiral of the red, and on the 27th his wife, their elder daughter, and her little dog arrived on a visit to Plymouth while he was dining with Nelson. But the same evening he had to sail for Brest, leaving them to wait six weeks for his return; they then had two weeks together before he returned to Ushant. It was not until May 1802, two months after the signing of the peace of Amiens, that Collingwood was able to strike his flag, go home to Morpeth, and have a rare opportunity for his legendary pastime of planting acorns to provide timber for ships of the line of the future.

With the resumption of war in May 1803 Collingwood left home and on 3 June hoisted his flag in the *Diamond* (38 guns). He never saw his wife or children again. He sailed at once, joining Admiral William Cornwallis off Ushant—'Here comes my old friend Coll, the last that left and the first to join me' (J. Ralfe, *Naval Biography of Great Britain*, 1828, 2.341). During the next two and a half years he was in command of a detached squadron blockading the enemy fleets on the Atlantic coasts of France and Spain except again for occasional brief visits to Cawsand Bay or Torbay for shelter. He changed his flagship frequently to avoid quitting his station for repairs or victualling. *Venerable* (twice), *Minotaur*, *Colossus*, *Culloden*, *Prince*, and *Dreadnought* all flew his flag in this unglamorous, testing, but essential task. On 23 April 1804 he was promoted vice-admiral of the blue, and on 21 May 1805, after ten days in Cawsand Bay, he sailed for Cadiz with eleven ships of the line, never to see England again.

Trafalgar, 1805 While Nelson was searching for Villeneuve's fleet in the West Indies, Collingwood blockaded Cadiz and Cartagena. On 20 August, when he was off Cadiz with only three ships and a frigate, Villeneuve's fleet sought refuge there after its return from the West Indies thinking, wrongly, that Nelson was on its tail. For his skill in deceiving the enemy as to the size of his force and for resuming the blockade the moment all thirty-six ships had entered Cadiz, Collingwood received high praise: 'Everybody in England admired your adroitness', wrote Nelson (Nicolas, 7.114). Ten days later Collingwood

had twenty-six ships of the line off Cadiz, on 29 September Nelson arrived to resume command of the fleet, and on 10 October Collingwood, as second in command, transferred his flag to the *Royal Sovereign* (100 guns).

At Trafalgar on 21 October, with thirty-three French and Spanish ships facing twenty-seven British, Collingwood led the weather column. His flagship was the first to engage the enemy—'See how that noble fellow, Collingwood, carries his ship into action!', exclaimed Nelson (J. Ralfe, *Naval Biography of Great Britain*, 1828, 2.342). The *Santa Ana* (112 guns), the Spanish vice-admiral's flagship, was his main target and after a two-hour duel, during which she was at times assisted by four other ships, she struck to the *Royal Sovereign*, which had lost two of her masts. Collingwood received a slight wound; indeed nearly all on the *Royal Sovereign*'s quarterdeck and poop were either killed or wounded.

At the end of the day, with the Franco-Spanish fleet defeated, Lord Nelson dead, and the *Royal Sovereign* unable to manoeuvre, Collingwood transferred to the frigate *Euryalus* (Captain Blackwood) and assumed the command-in-chief of the victorious though much damaged British fleet. He was faced with a formidable task. Seventeen enemy ships had been captured, one had sunk, four escaped south to be caught by Strachan two weeks later—'really a nice nick', as Collingwood told Admiral Duckworth (2 Dec 1805, priv. coll.)—and eleven fled towards Cadiz. But early the next day an onshore gale sprang up and blew with increasing severity for five days. Collingwood has been criticized for not following Nelson's intention to anchor the fleet at the end of the battle, but many ships had lost their anchors or had their cables shot and this, with the heavy swell preceding the gale, made anchoring impossible for most ships. The first priority was for disabled British ships and enemy prizes to be taken in tow. As the gale grew more violent many of the prizes were wrecked on the rocky coast; others had to be destroyed to prevent their recapture, which enemy survivors indeed attempted on the 23rd, losing two more ships in the process. Disabled British ships and four prizes were towed to Gibraltar; no British ship was lost. 'Collingwood's desire to preserve the prizes was as great as anyone in the fleet', wrote William Blackwood (although a devotee of Nelson) to his wife on the 25th. 'Could you witness his grief and anxiety (who has done all that an Admiral could do) you would be very deeply affected' (*Blackwood's Magazine*, July 1833, 13).

Wounded Spanish prisoners were sent ashore, an act of humanity by Collingwood which the Spaniards never forgot, and in return British wounded were given beds in Spanish hospitals. In *Euryalus* Collingwood was soon joined by Admiral Villeneuve and two other senior prisoners of war. His official dispatch, his letter of thanks to the fleet, and his call for a day of thanksgiving for the victory, written in his cramped and heaving quarters, are masterpieces of the English language.

On 9 November 1805 Collingwood was promoted vice-admiral of the red and created Baron Collingwood of Caldburne and Hethpoole, two small properties inherited by his wife. 'I hear considerable difficulty arose in finding where my estate lay, and what it was called. I thought all the world knew I was no Land-Lord' (Collingwood to Mrs Moutray, 9 Dec 1805, *Public and Private Correspondence*, 1.226). He was also awarded a pension of £2000 p.a. for life with, after his death, £1000 to his widow and £500 to each of his daughters. Not having a son he was anxious that his title should descend through his daughters but to his deep disappointment this was not allowed. Gold medals were awarded to all admirals and captains, making Collingwood one of only three officers (with Nelson and Sir Edward Berry) to win three gold medals throughout the twenty-two years of war.

Commander-in-chief, Mediterranean With the abandonment of his plans to invade England, Napoleon turned his attention to the domination of the eastern Mediterranean, the Ottoman empire, and the route to India. The Mediterranean thus assumed major strategic importance just as Collingwood took over as commander-in-chief. His fleet had to watch enemy fleets in Cadiz, Cartagena, and Toulon, secure the bases of Gibraltar, Malta, and Sicily, maintain squadrons in the Adriatic and the Levant, and protect British trade while denying it to the enemy. Collingwood was the only servant of the government in the Mediterranean who, with responsibilities from Cadiz to Constantinople, could survey the whole theatre; thus in many ways he became the originator and co-ordinator of British policy, diplomatic as well as naval.

Since communication with London was so slow and uncertain Collingwood had to make his own political judgements as changing circumstances required, conducting 'political correspondence with the Spaniards, the Turks, the Albanians, the Egyptians, and all the States of Barbary' (who supplied beef and water to the fleet) (Collingwood to his wife, 8 Nov 1808, *Public and Private Correspondence*, 2.286). To these he could have added the kingdoms of Sardinia and Sicily, the governor of Malta, and British ambassadors, generals, and consuls as well as ministers in London. At the same time he had to operate and administer a fleet of up to eighty ships, including thirty of the line. To assist him in these tasks Collingwood had the part-time services of his young flag captain (Richard Thomas), his flag lieutenant, and his competent but even younger secretary, W. R. Cosway. In his conduct of the fleet he was able to delegate business in the normal way to his subordinate flag officers and captains in the various regions of his command. But he was not by nature a delegator and in his political and diplomatic work there was nobody to whom he could delegate:

> I do everything for myself, and never distract my mind with other people's opinions. To the credit of any good which happens I may lay claim, and I will never shift upon another the discredit when the result is bad. (ibid., 2.286)

Collingwood lacked the charisma of a Nelson and did not have the opportunity to command a fleet in a major battle. He was a man of great rectitude and drove himself hard, though his seemingly cold professional exterior concealed a much softer heart and sensibility. This is revealed in his letters to his family and friends, by his dry sense of humour, and by the respect in which he was held in his ships. He was good at encouraging youngsters, and had a reputation for keeping his ship's company, even the troublesome, contented as well as proficient with a minimum of corporal punishment. He insisted they should be called by their name or 'sailor' rather than 'you there', and took particular care over their comfort and health. He experimented with treatments for scurvy and invented a ventilator to improve the flow of fresh air in the lower decks; on one occasion, after fifteen months at sea without letting go an anchor, there was not a sick man among the 750 in his ship. As a supreme commander, which he virtually was in the Mediterranean, Collingwood had intelligence and patience that were ideal for his strategic and diplomatic tasks, and he held throughout the confidence of the foreign secretary and the first lord. He has, perhaps justly, been criticized for spending so much of his time at his desk, but his administrative burdens were enormous and he had no chief of staff or first captain to help him. Some writers seem to have undervalued his diplomatic skills and the respect in which he was held by allies, foes, and neutrals. Probably none of his contemporaries, including Nelson, could have conducted the command so successfully.

The Mediterranean, 1805–1810 Ten days after Trafalgar, Collingwood transferred from *Euryalus* to the *Queen* (90 guns)—to be reunited with his devoted dog, Bounce—and in April 1806 to the *Ocean* (98 guns). His flagship took him to wherever at the time was the most danger from the French or he could best assist an ally. For his first nineteen months this meant blockading Cadiz or Cartagena. In July 1807 he led a squadron to the Dardanelles in support of an attempt by Sir Arthur Paget to coerce Turkey away from her alliance with France. They arrived just as news was received of the treaty of Tilsit between Russia and France. Paget was unable to persuade Turkey to break with France but Collingwood ensured that the Russian fleet did not fall into French hands.

The safety of Sicily, essential for the maintenance of the fleet and for its strategic position, was always an anxiety, and a strong squadron had to be maintained off the island to forestall a French invasion from Italy. In January 1808 five French ships of the line escaped from Rochefort, entered the Mediterranean, and joined Vice-Admiral Ganteaume's five ships at Toulon. The combined squadron sailed on 10 February. When Collingwood at Syracuse learned of this on the 22nd he was set the triple tasks of finding them, bringing them to battle with sufficient force, and guarding Sicily, which seemed their most likely objective. To his great chagrin they eluded him and retired to Toulon.

> My heart was bent on the destruction of that fleet, but I never got intelligence where they really were until they were out of reach … Their escape was by chance, for at one time we were very near them without knowing it. (Collingwood to Admiral Lord Radstock, 18 June 1808, *Public and Private Correspondence*, 2.162)

Shortage of frigates was, as ever, the drawback. Piers Mackesy's account of the incident refutes the *Dictionary of*

National Biography's criticism of Collingwood for failing to bring the French to battle (*Mariner's Mirror*, 41, 1955, 3–14 and 137–48). The *Dictionary of National Biography*'s criticism of Collingwood's 'general order' for battle of 23 March 1808 is similarly well answered in the *Naval Review* (24, 1936, 384).

In May 1808 Spain rose against Napoleon's invasion of its country. Collingwood sailed immediately to Cadiz to provide assistance:

> There was great joy amongst the Spaniards when I came here … My first business was to remove all those doubts of our good intentions which I succeeded in … When I went on shore the multitudes of people was immense that came to receive me. (Collingwood to W. Spencer-Stanhope, 20 Aug 1808, priv. coll.)

They had not forgotten his chivalry after Trafalgar. Now he gave them much valuable political guidance and sent his frigates to assist their army against the French invasion of Catalonia.

In April 1809 Collingwood shifted his flag from *Ocean* to the *Ville de Paris* (110 guns). Although the blockade of ships and troop convoys in Toulon was still essential, the weight of naval effort shifted eastwards. Turkey was no longer an enemy and Austria had once more become an ally. Frigates and brigs were sent to support Austria in the Adriatic, destroying trade and capturing forts, garrisons, and castles, 'scaling towers at midnight and storming redoubts at mid-day … Those youths [the captains] think that nothing is beyond their enterprise and they seldom fail of success' (Collingwood to Rear-Admiral Thomas Sotheby, 30 June 1809, *Public and Private Correspondence*, 2.376).

In October, on Collingwood's initiative and with the reluctant assent of the military commander, Sir John Stuart, the Ionian Islands of Zante, Cephalonia, Ithaca, and Cerigo were liberated from the French in order to provide a foothold in the Adriatic should the French attack Greece or Turkey. They remained under British protection until 1864. Later that month, having withdrawn his ships from a close blockade of Toulon, Collingwood was off Minorca hoping to lure the French fleet of seventeen of the line to sea. But only five men-of-war and a convoy of eighteen vessels for Barcelona sailed. Nevertheless two of the ships and seventeen of the much needed storeships were captured or sunk.

From 14 November 1809 to 7 January 1810 Collingwood's flagship lay in Port Mahon, Minorca—the longest period he had spent in harbour for over seven years. After a further period off Toulon he returned to Port Mahon on 25 February. His health was rapidly deteriorating and on 6 March, having turned over his command to Vice-Admiral Purvis, he sailed for England. Reassured to find his flagship underway, he rallied and said 'then I may yet live to meet the French once more' (*Public and Private Correspondence*, 2.427). But twenty-four hours later he died (probably from cancer of the stomach) on board the *Ville de Paris*, aged sixty-one. He had spent only one year ashore in seventeen years of war and was worn out in the service of his country.

As early as August 1808 Collingwood had written to Lord Mulgrave, the first lord, asking to be relieved because of his very weak state of health, which he attributed to the long time he had been at sea. To this Mulgrave wrote that he knew

> not how I should be able to supply all that would be lost to the service of the country and to the general interests of Europe by your absence from the Mediterranean … Through a variety of difficult and delicate arrangements, political as well as professional, your Lordship has in no instance failed to adopt the most judicious and best-concerted measures. (6 and 25 Sept 1808, NMM, LBK/40)

Collingwood's acceptance was characteristic of his overriding sense of duty and he had stayed on for another eighteen months. But by February 1810 his health had further deteriorated and he applied again to Mulgrave to be relieved. After his death, but before news of it reached London, Admiral Sir Charles Cotton was appointed as his successor. Collingwood's body was taken to England, landed at Greenwich on 26 April, and, after lying in state there, was buried on 11 May in the crypt of St Paul's Cathedral near his friend Nelson. There are monuments to him in the south transept of St Paul's and in Newcastle Cathedral, and a statue on a massive pedestal at Tynemouth, defended by four guns from his flagship at Trafalgar. Three battleships have been named after him, and the Royal Navy training establishment at Fareham has been called HMS *Collingwood* since 1940.   C. H. H. OWEN

Sources PRO, Admiralty MSS · Collingwood and other MSS, NMM · *A selection from the public and private correspondence of Vice-Admiral Lord Collingwood, interspersed with memoirs of his life*, ed. G. L. Newnham-Collingwood, 5th edn, 2 vols. (1837) · *The private correspondence of Admiral Lord Collingwood*, ed. E. Hughes, Navy RS, 98 (1957) · P. Mackesy, *The war in the Mediterranean, 1803–1810* (1957) · C. H. H. Owen, ed., 'Letters from Vice-Admiral Lord Collingwood, 1794–1809', *The naval miscellany*, Navy RS, 6 (2003) · BL, Add. MSS 14272–14280 and 40096–40098 · O. Warner, *The life and letters of Vice-Admiral Lord Collingwood* (1968) · W. C. Russell, *Collingwood* (1891) · *The dispatches and letters of Vice-Admiral Lord Viscount Nelson*, ed. N. H. Nicolas, 7 vols. (1844–6) · G. Murray, *The life of Admiral Collingwood* (1936) · W. Davies, *A fine old English gentleman … Lord Collingwood* (1875) · private information [family] · parish registers, St Nicholas's Church, Newcastle upon Tyne · *Naval Chronicle*, 23 (1810), 380–84 · *Annual Register* (1805)

Archives BL, corresp. and papers, Add. MSS 14272–14280, 23207, 40096–40098 · Hunt. L., corresp. · NMM, corresp., letter-books, and journals, COL AGC/17, 25, 35; LBK/15, 40 · Northumbd RO, corresp. and MSS, NRO 1147 · U. Durham L., journal [transcript] | BL, letters to Edward Collingwood, Add. MS 52780 · BL, corresp. with Arthur Paget, Add. MS 48397 · BL, letters to Horatio Nelson, Add. MSS 34903–34907, 34930–34931 · Edinburgh National War Museum of Scotland, letters to Sir Hew Dalrymple · Hunt. L., letters to Grenville family · NL Scot., letters to Carlyle family · NMM, corresp. with Lord Barham · NMM, corresp. with Edward Blackett; corresp. with Hugh Elliot; letters to Samuel Hood; Waldegrave MSS, letters to Lord Radstock · Northumbd RO, Newcastle upon Tyne, corresp. with Edward Blackett and J. E. Blackett · U. Durham L., Grey of Howick MSS, letters to second Earl Grey

Likenesses H. Nelson, silhouette, 1784, NMM · miniature, 1790–95, NMM [*see illus.*] · engraving, *c*.1802, repro. in Murray, *Life*, p. 90 · R. Bowyer, print, *c*.1803, repro. in R. Bowyer, *Commemoration of the four great naval victories obtained by the English during the late war* (1803) · Gaugain & Scriven, stipple, pubd 1806, BM · W. Say, mezzotint, pubd 1806, BM · G. Politi of Syracuse, oils, 1807, priv. coll. · C. Turner, mezzotint, 1807 (after G. Politi), NMM · C. Turner, mezzotint, 1811 (after G. Politi), NPG · J. Lonsdale?, oils, 1812, Laing Art Gallery, Newcastle upon Tyne; repro. in Murray, *Life*, frontispiece · J. C. F. Rossi, marble bust, 1819, Newcastle Cathedral · F. Howard, oils, 1827, NPG · H. Howard, oils, *c*.1827 (after G. Politi), NMM · J. G. Lough, effigy on monument, Portland stone, 1845, Tynemouth, Northumberland · attrib. J. G. Lough, marble bust, *c*.1845, NPG · H. R. Cook, stipple (after R. Bowyer), NPG · R. Westmacott, monument, St Paul's Cathedral, London

Wealth at death approx. £163,000: *Private correspondence*, ed. E. Hughes, 306, n. 2

Collingwood, Cuthbert (1826–1908), naturalist, was born on 25 December 1826, probably at Christchurch, Hampshire, the fifth of six sons of Samuel Collingwood, architect and contractor, of Wellington Grove, Greenwich, and his wife, Frances, daughter of Samuel Collingwood, printer to Oxford University. Educated at King's College School, London, he matriculated from Christ Church, Oxford, on 8 April 1845, graduating BA in 1849, MA in 1852, and MB in 1854. He subsequently studied at Edinburgh and Cambridge universities, and at Guy's Hospital, and spent some time in the medical schools of Paris and Vienna. From 1858 to 1866 he held the appointment of lecturer on botany to the Royal Infirmary medical school at Liverpool. Elected a fellow of the Linnean Society on 1 November 1853, he served on the council in 1868. He also lectured on biology at the Liverpool School of Science.

In 1866–7 Collingwood served as surgeon and naturalist on board HMS *Rifleman* and HMS *Serpent* on voyages of exploration in the China seas, doing research in marine zoology. *Rambles of a Naturalist on the Shores and Waters of the China Seas* (1868)—probably his best-known work—was the result of this. On his return to Liverpool he became senior physician of the Northern Hospital and took a leading part in the intellectual life of the city.

Collingwood was through life a prominent member of the Swedenborgian or 'New' Church. Besides some forty papers on natural history in scientific periodicals he published many expositions of his religious beliefs, of which the chief were: *A Vision of Creation* (1872), a poem with an introduction, critical and geological; *New Studies in Christian Theology* (published anonymously in 1883); and *The Bible and the Age, Principles of Consistent Interpretation* (1886).

Collingwood married Clara (*d*. 1871), daughter of Lieutenant-Colonel Sir Robert Mowbray of Cockavine; they had no children. In the later years of his life he lived in Paris, but returned to England in 1907. He died in Lewisham on 20 October 1908, aged eighty-two.

ROBERT STEELE, *rev.* GILES HUDSON

Sources *Proceedings of the Linnean Society of London*, 121st session (1908–9), 35 · *New Church Magazine*, 27 (1908), 575–6 · Venn, *Alum. Cant.* · Desmond, *Botanists*, rev. edn

Archives Linn. Soc., corresp., drawings, and papers

Likenesses Maull & Fox, photograph, Linn. Soc. [*see illus.*]

Collingwood, Sir Edward Foyle (1900–1970), mathematician and medical administrator, was born at Lilburn Tower, near Wooler, Northumberland, on 17 January 1900, the eldest of the four sons of Colonel Cuthbert George Collingwood (1848–1933), landowner, of Glanton Pyke, and his wife, Dorothy, daughter of the Revd William Fawcett of Somerford Keynes, Gloucestershire. Fawcett's wife was

Cuthbert Collingwood (1826–1908), by Maull & Fox

a coheir of the Foyle estate at Somerford Keynes. Collingwood and his brothers all enjoyed shooting and fishing and the social life of the country. Collingwood's mother, who survived him, was always a strong influence in the family.

Collingwood went to the Royal Naval College at Osborne in 1913 and Dartmouth in 1914. A year later he joined the Royal Navy as a midshipman in the *Collingwood* (by special arrangement). Before experiencing any action he fell down a hatchway, sustaining serious injuries, and was in a hospital ship which followed the battle of Jutland. He was invalided out of the navy. After passing twelfth for Woolwich he failed the medical examination, whereupon he went up to Trinity College, Cambridge, in 1918 to read mathematics. At Lilburn there were letters of Edward's great-grandfather Vice-Admiral Cuthbert Collingwood, showing his interest in the teaching of mathematics to the young; Collingwood was much interested in these and other papers, in the small observatory built by his grandfather, and in biology, bacteria, and photographic techniques.

At Cambridge Collingwood's director of studies, G. H. Hardy, inspired him to aim at mathematical research, to the dismay of his father and uncle. He obtained a third class in part one of the mathematical tripos in 1919 and in political specials one and two in the Michaelmas term of 1920, and then took his degree the following year. This

Sir Edward Foyle Collingwood (1900–1970), by Elliott & Fry, 1962

unorthodox course left him free to study those parts of mathematics which interested him at his own pace and omit large parts of the heavy course for part two of the mathematical tripos. As an undergraduate he kept somewhat aloof from his mathematical contemporaries, and had a full, but entirely separate, social life. He used his private means to entertain well, but never ostentatiously.

When Hardy went to Oxford in 1920, J. E. Littlewood advised Collingwood on research. He obtained a Rayleigh prize in 1923, but failed to obtain a Trinity research fellowship. At the invitation of W. H. Young he went to Aberystwyth in 1922. There Professor G. Valiron of Strasbourg was lecturing in French on integral functions, and Collingwood made translations which eventually formed a book. In 1924–5 he held a Rouse Ball travelling studentship, mainly at the Sorbonne, and thus became the only one of the Hardy–Littlewood school to have close relationships with French mathematicians.

Collingwood took his MA degree in 1925 and, returning to Cambridge, read for a PhD degree (which he obtained in 1929) for a dissertation which included material from some already published papers on integral and meromorphic functions. He was made a member of the high table at Trinity, and in 1930 steward. Most unusually for a non-fellow, he was elected to the council of Trinity College. He still entertained well. He also regularly gave two advanced courses for the mathematical faculty, but did no regular undergraduate teaching. The six mathematicians Littlewood, Collingwood, Macintyre, Clunie,

Rahman, and Joyal constituted a sequence, each the PhD student of the one before.

In the 1930s Collingwood became interested in pictures, and, when a family trust fell in on the death of an aunt, he bought some fine contemporary and eighteenth-century pictures through Geoffrey Agnew, one of his earlier Cambridge friends. He also made a collection of Chinese porcelain, becoming quite an expert on the subject.

Collingwood was lieutenant in the Northumberland hussars in 1923–7 and became a JP in 1935. He was chairman of the bench for many years and deputy lieutenant for Northumberland in 1959. He gave much time and thought to the management of the Lilburn estate. When in 1937 he became high sheriff of Northumberland he gave up his Cambridge obligations, but continued to visit, in particular for the college commemoration feast.

In the Second World War Collingwood joined the Admiralty minesweeping division as an officer of the Royal Naval Volunteer Reserve, reaching the rank of acting captain. He served as director of scientific research with the Admiralty delegation in Washington in 1942, as officer in charge of the sweeping division in 1943, chief scientist, Admiralty mine design department in 1943–5, and as one of a delegation to Moscow on a special scientific mission. His all-round ability and wide experience, backed by his determination, were effective in getting the money needed for the scientists' work; he also impressed the scientists as having a sound grasp of physical principles. In 1946 he was appointed CBE, and became an officer of the American Legion of Merit.

Collingwood's first paper in 1924 generalized Nevanlinna's second fundamental theorem from 2 to p exceptional values, a result which Littlewood had, independently, stated in a letter to Nevanlinna. Collingwood's second paper, also in 1924, developed the idea of deficient values, questioning whether they were asymptotic. During the war this was proved false. After a gap from 1932 to 1948 Collingwood returned to this subject and discussed the islands in which $|f(z)-a| < \sigma$ and $f(z)$ takes no value more than p times, where σ and p may tend to infinity with $|a|$. These later papers seem less effective than the first two but led to fruitful discussions with Weitsman in June 1970. Collingwood's wide knowledge of the literature of mathematics enabled him and the writer to develop the theory of cluster sets in a joint paper in *Acta Mathematica* (87, 1952) which W. K. Hayman described as the beginning of the modern subject. If $f(z)$ takes values on the Riemann sphere in $|z| < 1$, and there exists a sequence $z_n \rightarrow e^{i\theta}$ such that $f(z_n) \rightarrow w$, then w belongs to the cluster set $C(f, e^{i\theta})$ of $f(z)$ at $e^{i\theta}$. Their relationship to the range of values taken by $f(z)$ near $e^{i\theta}$, and to neighbouring Fatou points, $e^{i\theta_n}$, $\theta_n \rightarrow \theta$ at which $f(z)$ tends to a limit in any angle, and so on, formed the subject matter of the rest of Collingwood's mathematical papers. The standard textbook, written by Collingwood and A. J. Lohwater (1966) includes Collingwood's important applications to prime ends.

After 1945 Collingwood actively sought mathematical contacts. In particular he attended the new British Mathematical Colloquium, where he helped to organize special sessions on the theory of functions, and thus soon became a well-known figure. In 1959 he obtained a Cambridge ScD, in 1962 he was knighted, and in 1965 he was elected FRS and made an honorary LLD of Glasgow University where in 1961 he had given the seventh Gibson lecture. He joined the council of the London Mathematical Society (LMS) in April 1959 and was treasurer from 1960 to 1969, when he became its president. Collingwood made the fullest use of the benefaction of G. H. Hardy to strengthen and widen the activities of the society—including the founding of the Applied Probability Trust for the publication of the *Journal of Applied Probability*, edited by J. Gani, which began in 1964. Collingwood took a large part in drafting the petition, draft charter, and statutes for a royal charter (approved by the privy council in 1964) for the LMS to mark its centenary in 1965.

An interest in bacteria, as well as in local affairs, led Collingwood into medical fields. He was an active supporter of Newcastle hospitals, vice-chairman of the Central Health Services Council (1959–63), vice-president of the International Hospital Federation (1959–67), a member of the Medical Research Council (1960–68) and treasurer (1960–67), and a member of the royal commission on medical education (1965–8). He was made an officer of the French ordre de la Santé Publique, in 1963. He had a great effect on medicine by contributing to the technical development of the use of computers in that area. He spoke at the annual congress of the British Institute of Radiology in 1967 and at that of the British Dental Association in 1970. He also had a strong interest in history, and knowledge of it.

Collingwood was short and fair and walked with long strides. He early became very bald. He was made an honorary DSc of Durham in 1950, and was active in Durham University affairs until his death at home at Lilburn Tower on 25 October 1970. He never married. His large mathematical library and many manuscripts were left to the department of mathematics at Durham, and a college has been named after him.   M. L. CARTWRIGHT, *rev.*

Sources M. L. Cartwright and W. K. Hayman, *Memoirs FRS*, 17 (1971), 139–59 · *The Times* (27 Oct 1970), 10h · *The Times* (30 Oct 1970), 12h · *The Times* (3 Nov 1970), 14f · *The Times* (21 Nov 1970), 14e · *The Lancet* (31 Oct 1970) · private information (1981) · personal knowledge (1981)
Likenesses Elliott & Fry, photograph, 1962, NPG [*see illus.*] · photograph, repro. in Cartwright, *Memoirs FRS*
Wealth at death £892,034: probate, 8 Dec 1970, *CGPLA Eng. & Wales*

Collingwood, George (*c.*1679–1716), Jacobite insurgent, was born in Eslington, Northumberland, the eldest son of William Collingwood (*c.*1654–1715), gentleman, and Mary (*b.* 1659), daughter of Sir Richard Forster of Stokesley, second baronet. He held estates at Eslington worth approximately £900 per annum. The family were staunch Roman Catholics and maintained a Jesuit priest at Eslington. One contemporary described George as 'a very pious gentleman and well-beloved in his country' (Patten, 141); his brother Thomas became a Jesuit priest and served as chaplain to the Selby family of Biddlestone, Northumberland.

In 1710 George married the Hon. Catherine Browne (1684/5–1776), daughter of Henry Browne, fifth Viscount Montague (marriage bond 3 June 1710). Catherine was a fellow Roman Catholic, and her father had served as secretary of state to James II in exile. They had three daughters: Isabella (*b.* 1711), Barbara (*b.* 1712), and Catherine (*d.* 1761).

George Collingwood took part in the Jacobite rising of 1715, joining the Northumbrian forces raised by the earl of Derwentwater. It was said that he joined only at his wife's insistence; however it is known from his correspondence that he was in close social contact with other Catholic gentry of the north-east who also rallied to the Jacobite cause. He joined the march to Preston, where he was taken prisoner. He was among the gentry prisoners ordered to be taken to London for trial. Once in the capital he would probably have faced a couple of years in gaol before being released under the general pardon of 1717. Like the majority of the Northumbrian gentry Jacobite insurgents he would have forfeited his estates but not his life. However at Wigan he had an attack of gout and, unable to travel to London, was transferred instead to Liverpool. In the north-west the government wished to prevent any further disturbances and acted swiftly and uncompromisingly against the dissidents. George Collingwood was tried on 9 February 1716. According to Lady Cowper, his wife wrote to a friend in London for assistance but received the following reply: 'I think you are mad when you talk of saving your Husband's Life. Don't you know you will have five hundred Pounds a Year Jointure if he's hanged, and that you won't have a Groat if he's saved?' (*Diary*, 78). No reprieve was forthcoming, and on 25 February 1716, aged about thirty-seven, George Collingwood was hanged, drawn, and quartered at Liverpool. His estate at Eslington was forfeited and sold to the Liddell family of Ravensworth, co. Durham.   TAMSYN HADDEN

Sources R. Patten, *The history of the late rebellion*, 2nd edn (1717) · *Diary of Mary, Countess Cowper*, ed. [S. Cowper] (1864) · news of the 1715 rebellion, Northumbd RO, Allgood papers, NRO.ZAL 3/1/5, 8, 11 · M. H. Dodds, ed., *A history of Northumberland*, 14 (1935), 516, 524–6 · D. D. Dixon, *Whittingham Vale* (1979), 92–9 · [J. C. Hodgson], ed., *Northumbrian documents of the seventeenth and eighteenth centuries, comprising the register of the estates of Roman Catholics in Northumberland*, SurtS, 131 (1918) · J. O. Payne, ed., *Records of the English Catholics of 1715* (1889) · G. Collingwood, letters to Ralph Salvin of Tudhoe, Durham RO, Salvin papers, DRO. D/Sa/ C28 and C32 · parish registers, Whittingham, Northumbd RO · marriage bond, U. Durham L., archives and special collections, Durham bond books · papers relating to the rebellions of 1715 and 1745, Northumbd RO, QSB88 · *Newcastle Courant* (29 Feb 1716) · *IGI*
Likenesses line engraving, BM, NPG
Wealth at death £930 p.a.: Dixon, *Whittingham Vale*, 98–9

Collingwood, Harry. See Lancaster, William Joseph Cosens (1843–1922).

Collingwood, Robin George (1889–1943), philosopher and historian, was born on 22 February 1889 at Cartmel Fell, Lancashire, the only son and third of the four children of William Gershom *Collingwood (1854–1932) and his wife, Edith Mary (1857–1928), daughter of Thomas

Robin George Collingwood (1889–1943), by Walter Stoneman, 1934

Isaac, corn merchant, of Notting Hill, London. W. G. Collingwood, son of the landscape painter William Collingwood, was a writer, painter, and archaeologist, much influenced by John Ruskin, whose secretary (and eventually biographer) he became, while his wife was an accomplished pianist and watercolourist. The family was poor but highly cultivated, and Robin Collingwood was initially educated by his father at home, an education which combined formal instruction with many practical excursions to study and sketch the natural history and archaeology of the area around their home next to Coniston Water in the Lake District. The generosity of a family friend enabled Collingwood to attend preparatory school in Grange for a year when he was thirteen, from where he entered Rugby School in 1903. Collingwood was precocious, with highly developed scholarly and artistic interests and no great enthusiasm for organized games—not a recipe for happiness as a boarder at one of the leading public schools of the period. Thirty years later he recalled with undiminished aversion 'the pigsty conditions of our daily life' and the fact that team games 'constituted the real religion of the school'. Although by his own account he became 'a rebel, more or less declared, against the whole system of teaching' (Collingwood, *Autobiography*, 8–9), he none the less won a classical scholarship to University College, Oxford, in 1908. There he relished the freedom to pursue his reading without interruption; he seems

largely to have shunned the social and athletic life of the university, studying with such unchecked appetite that it may even have been during his undergraduate years that he laid the foundations for his later insomnia and ill health. Having obtained a first in classical moderations in 1910, he proceeded to read *literae humaniores* or Greats, though, unusually, he chose not to specialize but rather to cultivate both the philosophical and the historical sides of the school. None the less, he made a particular mark in the former, and it was to a fellowship and tutorship in philosophy at Pembroke College that he was elected in the summer of 1912, shortly before his first-class degree result was announced.

Early philosophical works During the First World War Collingwood worked in the intelligence department at the Admiralty; among other tasks, he wrote a study of the juridical problems of the navigation of the Scheldt up to Antwerp. In 1918 he married Ethel Winifred, third daughter of Robert Chelles Graham, landowner, of Skipness; they had a son and a daughter. In the decade after the end of the war, Collingwood bore an extremely heavy tutorial burden, for some years undertaking the philosophy teaching for Lincoln College as well as for Pembroke; this burden was somewhat alleviated by his appointment as university lecturer in philosophy and Roman history in 1927. But his always intense inner intellectual life managed to find expression in writing throughout this period. His earliest philosophical publications addressed questions of religion and aesthetics, including a short book entitled *Religion and Philosophy* (1916) which defended religion as a form of knowledge rather than as a mere expression of need or emotion (he remained a committed if unorthodox Anglican all his life), and an admiring centenary appraisal of Ruskin (published in 1922 as *Ruskin's Philosophy*) in which he endorsed the idea of art as an expression of 'the whole self'. His first substantial book was *Speculum mentis, or, The Map of Knowledge* (1924), an ambitious attempt, in the manner of philosophical idealism, to chart the 'forms of experience' as an ascending series, moving through art, religion, science, history, and philosophy. A broadly similar point of view informed *An Essay on Philosophical Method*, published in 1933, where the account of the relations between the forms of knowledge is still more emphatically dialectical and historical, so that philosophy becomes consciousness's never-ceasing striving for self-understanding. The work was a thoroughgoing repudiation of the sceptical and nominalist manner of philosophizing favoured among the 'realists' and other analytic schools. As one later commentator summarized the force of Collingwood's case, 'It follows that philosophy studies not an inert object capable of being split into the clean-cut divisions of a classificatory system, but an object which is living and developing, an object at least akin to, if not identical with, history' (Knox, *PBA*, 471). *An Essay on Philosophical Method* is, in addition, a notably stylish, indeed writerly, book; looking back in 1938, conscious perhaps that his last works would have to be written hurriedly, Collingwood described it as 'my best book in matter; in style, I may call it my only book' (Collingwood, *Autobiography*, 118). Its rather lordly deployment of idiosyncratic distinctions and assimilations is not very helpful, but it does contain a brilliant section on philosophical style itself.

Roman Britain Throughout his time as an Oxford philosophy tutor Collingwood continued to pursue his researches into the history and archaeology of Roman Britain. His master here had been F. J. Haverfield, professor of ancient history in Oxford, and following Haverfield's death in 1919 Collingwood determined to continue the work of describing and cataloguing all the Roman inscriptions in Britain, a subject upon which he became recognized in his lifetime as the leading authority. He was an active and enterprising archaeologist, directing excavations in northern England nearly every year; he published numerous articles and reports in the *Transactions of the Cumberland and Westmorland Antiquarian and Archaeological Society* (of which he was for some years joint editor), many of them illustrated by his own sketches. Collingwood insisted that his archaeological work was a practical application of what he was to term the 'logic of question and answer' (Collingwood, *Autobiography*, 37), and on occasion his bold hypotheses about the meaning of the archaeological evidence were spectacularly confirmed, as in his reasoning that if Hadrian's Wall comprised a series of signal-stations, then further signal-stations should have existed along the shores of Cumberland, which later excavations proved to be the case. His standing in the field was acknowledged by the invitation to write, with J. N. L. Myres, the opening volume in the Oxford History of England entitled *Roman Britain and the English Settlements*, which was published in 1936. The bibliography of Collingwood's writings in this area contains, in addition to two other more popular books on Roman Britain, more than 120 shorter items, and though his work was often controversial and sometimes overturned by subsequent findings, he made a remarkable contribution to a subject in which original work is necessarily somewhat technical and highly specialized.

Philosophy and history Collingwood identified the attempt 'to bring about a rapprochement between philosophy and history' as his life's work (Collingwood, *Autobiography*, 77), and in the course of the 1930s he thought his way ever more deeply into the problems of historical knowledge, often in courses of lectures which remained unpublished at his death. His most famous dictum, which has been taken as something of a motto for his whole approach, was the claim that 'all history is the history of thought … and therefore all history is the re-enactment of past thought in the historian's own mind' (Collingwood, *Idea of History*, 215). In this and many other remarks to the same effect Collingwood was identifying what was involved in understanding an intentional human action. It is important that this was intended not as a prescription for the method of historical enquiry, but a description of its success: only insofar as historians can 're-enact' in their own thought what an act meant to its agent can they explain that act. This insistence on the need for imaginative identification with historical agents can be separated from two other, more extreme, views which Collingwood also held: that only intentional actions provide the material of history, and that because history is concerned with the reasons for actions, it cannot have recourse to causal explanation. One of the characteristic and distinctive features of Collingwood's writing on the philosophy of history was the wide range of actual historical examples on which it drew for illustration, thereby bearing out his larger contention that philosophy was essentially a form of reflection on practice and that it always gained in power when the philosopher had firsthand experience of the relevant practice. He underwent fifty sessions of psychoanalysis before considering himself qualified to comment on it (Collingwood, *Essays in Political Philosophy*, 81).

By the late 1930s Collingwood had published sketches of these ideas only in a few essays and addresses, though he had devoted several of his Oxford lecture courses to them (further series of lectures on the history of cosmological and scientific thinking were to be published posthumously as *The Idea of Nature*, 1945). Collingwood's polished and provocative lectures won him a considerable local reputation at the time; some of his abler tutorial pupils also found him a stimulating, if somewhat intimidating, teacher. But he was always a rather removed figure, visibly absorbed in his own speculation and scholarship, an impression enhanced by his habit of spending weekends and vacations at his house in North Moreton some miles outside Oxford. He took relatively little part in college and university business, though he was a very active delegate of Oxford University Press between 1928 and 1941. He was elected to the British Academy in 1934, an honour all the more welcome for providing him with what he regarded as 'a more open-minded audience' than he was used to finding in Oxford (Collingwood, *Autobiography*, 116). In 1935 he was elected to the Waynflete professorship of metaphysics, in succession to his friend J. A. Smith; his election entailed a move to Magdalen College. Despite his own sense of isolation and neglect, it would seem that his distinction as a philosopher had been recognized even in Oxford. In 1938, the year in which he published *The Principles of Art*, his major work in aesthetics, he was also awarded the honorary degree of LLD by the University of St Andrews.

Autobiography and *Essay on Metaphysics* The year 1938 was a crisis and turning point in Collingwood's life. In February that year, a few days before his forty-ninth birthday, he suffered a stroke. There had been serious worries about his health for some time: as early as 1932 he had needed a period of recuperation after an earlier breakdown. Now his doctor ordered a complete change of scene. Oxford gave him an entire year's medical leave: Collingwood retired first to his beloved Lake District, where he wrote *An Autobiography* (1939); then he embarked on a long sea voyage to the East Indies, a journey which occupied the period from October 1938 to April 1939. After his return he resumed his duties at Oxford, but his health continued to deteriorate, and he finally resigned his chair in 1941. It was during these final years that he wrote some of his most important work, though parts of it had a rather complicated publication history.

Collingwood completed *An Essay on Metaphysics* (1940) during his voyage to the East Indies (its preface thanks the captain of the ship for providing 'ideal conditions' for the book's composition). After his return he devoted much of his energy to a large, and largely neglected, work of political theory, published in 1942 as *The New Leviathan*. But during these years he also began a work on the philosophy of history for which he clearly had high ambitions. For example, he wrote to his son on 14 February 1939 from the East Indies: 'I have begun writing "The Principles of History", which will go down to posterity as my masterpiece' (Dussen, 61), and to his friend Gerald Simpson, in late spring 1939, he described it as 'the book which my whole life has been spent in preparing to write' (Collingwood, *Principles*, lviii). But he was never to complete it; his former pupil, T. M. Knox, professor of moral philosophy (and later principal) at St Andrews, drew on one chapter for *The Idea of History*, but then the manuscript appeared to have been lost, and it was not published in its entirety (under the title *The Principles of History*) until 1999.

The books of this last period were more immediately controversial than Collingwood's earlier work had been. He had become acutely conscious of the threat posed by Hitler and Mussolini, and he deplored the apparent unawareness or even indifference to this threat manifested by so many of his countrymen, including the majority of professional philosophers. For this reason he enthusiastically supported A. D. Lindsay who stood, unsuccessfully, as an anti-appeasement candidate in the Oxford by-election of 1938; 'your candidature', he wrote to Lindsay, 'shows the spirit of English democracy is not dead' (D. Scott, *A. D. Lindsay: a Biography*, 1971, 251). These convictions were given forceful expression in some of his later writings. The autobiography, for example, contained not only a swingeing attack on the British government's response to the Spanish Civil War and its policy of appeasement towards Germany, but also a vigorous denunciation of the 'realists'—notably John Cook Wilson, and in Cambridge G. E. Moore—for what he saw as their pedantic and uncreative conception of philosophy, and their scepticism about its possible social role. 'The minute philosophers of my youth, for all their profession of a purely scientific detachment from practical affairs', were in fact, Collingwood asserted, 'the propagandists of a coming Fascism' (Collingwood, *Autobiography*, 167). The beard he sported on his return from the East Indies was taken by some of his colleagues as confirmation of a lurch to the left in his political views. *The New Leviathan* was in part Collingwood's attempt, by contrast, to put philosophy at the service of his sense of the gravity of the contemporary political situation and to diagnose the nature of the 'new barbarism' now threatening civilization.

But perhaps the philosophically most important and original aspect of Collingwood's later work was the elaboration, in *An Essay on Metaphysics*, of his radically historicist notion of metaphysics as the exploration of 'the absolute presuppositions' of different periods. Collingwood thought that any proposition or statement was (implicitly) an answer to a question, and that every question involved a presupposition of that question's being appropriate or, indeed, intelligible. There are some presuppositions that make questions intelligible without themselves being the answer to any question, and these are 'absolute'. It follows that they are not propositions or statements; they are implicit in practice, and not always amenable to being explicitly formulated by those engaged in the practice. It was part of the thorough-going historicism of this final phase of Collingwood's thought that he did not believe, in Kantian manner, that the preconditions of 'our' practices of enquiry were universal and timeless—absolute presuppositions are always changing.

Since metaphysics is identified as the study of absolute presuppositions, it seems to be assimilated to the history of ideas. Collingwood was prepared, in a sense, to accept this, both because the study of remoter systems of thought itself involved having those thoughts, and because he saw the present as in effect always 'the recent past'. Reflection on the presuppositions of inquiry in the past, and on our own in the present, equally involves the aim, which can never be completely realized, of making an inchoate set of presuppositions coherent. The questions of relativism that have been much discussed by Collingwood's commentators in this connection are perhaps best directed to the issue of how far criteria of coherence are themselves historically variable.

Death and legacy Collingwood's final years also saw significant changes in his hitherto settled way of life. He was always a keen sailor, and only a couple of months after returning from his East Indian voyage he set out with a group of Oxford undergraduates to spend the summer sailing round the Aegean; he published the journal of this voyage as *The First Mate's Log* in 1940. After resigning his chair in 1941, he moved first to Berkshire, and eventually to Lanehead, the family home he had inherited at Coniston. In 1942 his marriage was dissolved on his wife's petition, and in the same year he married Kathleen Frances, daughter of Francis Edgcumbe Edwardes, schoolmaster; they had one daughter. Collingwood died of pneumonia at Coniston on 9 January 1943; he was buried in the local churchyard three days later.

Though he always repudiated the label of idealist, Collingwood's work recognizably belonged to that style of philosophizing which, broadly speaking, took its inspiration from Hegel's critique of Kant. (He claimed that T. H. Green and his followers, though often labelled Hegelians, especially by their opponents, really represented 'a continuation and criticism of the indigenous English and Scottish philosophies of the middle nineteenth century' (Collingwood, *Autobiography*, 15). His work displays particularly close affinities with the philosophy of the Italians Croce and Gentile, though not with the latter's fascist politics; he translated several works by Croce and by his good friend Guido de Ruggiero (Collingwood was an exceptionally accomplished linguist, moving easily in several modern European languages as well as, of course, being proficient in Latin and ancient Greek). But philosophical idealism of any kind was out of favour in Oxford in the 1920s and 1930s, where first the 'realist' school led by Cook Wilson was dominant, until that in turn was challenged by the beginnings of logical positivism and 'ordinary language' philosophy. Collingwood, by nature an intellectual loner and something of a social recluse, resented what he felt to be his philosophical isolation in Oxford, indeed in Britain more generally, and his lack of engagement with the work of his contemporaries may have contributed to the neglect into which his work fell immediately after his death. Such reputation as he did continue to have rested largely on *The Idea of History*, published posthumously in 1946. This work drew on essays, lectures, and drafts mostly written during the 1930s, including some material from the manuscript left incomplete at the end of his East Indian voyage of 1938–9; Knox was responsible for the selection and arrangement of the material (as also of *The Idea of Nature*), making editorial decisions of which later scholars have not always approved.

The Idea of History has become something of a classic in a field not over-supplied with classics written in English. This standing was to some extent a by-product of a broader development, to which the book in turn contributed, namely, the rise of the philosophy of history as a reputable sub-field in the course of the 1950s and 1960s (more reputable among historians than among philosophers, perhaps). Collingwood's emphasis upon history as the interpretation of purposive action, and hence upon the primacy of the need to recover historical agents' own understanding of their situation, provided a valuable antidote to the aridities of the neo-positivist attempt to reduce historical explanation to the general operation of causal laws. 'If the philosophy of history is now in a flourishing state in English-speaking countries', observed one authority in 1995, 'this is due in no small measure to the stimulus provided by the writings of R. G. Collingwood' (Dray, 1).

With the revival of interest in Collingwood's work which began in the 1960s and 1970s, several of his other works, particularly *An Essay on Philosophical Method* and *The Principles of Art*, have won fresh admirers, not least for the elegance of their style. *An Essay on Metaphysics* contains interesting ideas, some of them related to questions about practice and its reflective description, that are also raised by the later work of Wittgenstein. For most readers, however, it seems likely that the two works by which Collingwood has been best-known since his death—*An Autobiography* and *The Idea of History*—will remain the most widely read, and with good reason. It was in these two books that he came nearest to realizing his ideal of persuading a wide readership to think seriously about the distinctiveness of history as a form of knowledge. Through these works he almost single-handed kept alive an anti-positivist understanding of history through a dark period largely dominated by the narrow sympathies of analytic philosophers and the brisk empiricism of political historians. Only in the closing decades of the twentieth century was his achievement fully recognized, installing him as the presiding spirit of a remarkable efflorescence in the English-speaking world of enquiries into the nature and scope of historical understanding.

STEFAN COLLINI and BERNARD WILLIAMS

Sources R. G. Collingwood, *An autobiography* (1939); with introduction by S. Toulmin (1978) · R. B. McCallum, *PBA*, 29 (1943) [incl. suppl. notices by T. M. Knox and I. A. Richmond] · W. J. van der Dussen, *History as a science: the philosophy of R. G. Collingwood* (1981) · R. G. Collingwood, *The principles of history*, ed. W. H. Dray and W. J. van der Dussen (1999) · D. Boucher, *The social and political thought of R. G. Collingwood* (1989) · R. G. Collingwood, *An essay on metaphysics*, ed. R. Martin (1998) · R. G. Collingwood, *The idea of history* (1940) · R. G. Collingwood, *The new leviathan* (1942); rev. edn with new introduction by D. Boucher (1992) · R. G. Collingwood, *Essays in political philosophy*, ed. D. Boucher (1989) · W. H. Dray, *History as re-enactment: R. G. Collingwood's idea of history* (1995) · D. S. Taylor, *R. G. Collingwood: a bibliography* (1988)

Archives AM Oxf., notebooks of sketches, inscription, tour notes, etc. · Bodl. Oxf., papers | Bodl. Oxf., corresp. with H. A. Prichard; corresp. with Gilbert Ryle

Likenesses W. Stoneman, photograph, 1934, NPG [*see illus.*] · photograph, Pembroke College, Oxford · photograph, Magd. Oxf.

Wealth at death £5037 15s. 5d.: probate, 17 Feb 1943, *CGPLA Eng. & Wales*

Collingwood, Roger (*fl.* 1495–1517), mathematician, originated in the diocese of Durham, of unknown parentage. He was admitted as a questionist in May 1495 to the University of Cambridge, probably to Queens' College, graduating BA in 1496 and MA in 1499. During his tenure of a fellowship at Queens' in 1497 to 1510, Collingwood resided partly at Cambridge, where he held the first known mathematics lectureship in 1501–2, 1504–7 (receiving a fee of £4 in 1506), and 1514–17, and partly on the continent, where he was permitted to study canon law. He was living away from Cambridge in 1502–3, in Paris, and in 1507–11.

Collingwood's lectureship had probably been instituted by his teacher, Bishop Richard Foxe, patron of humanism and founder of Corpus Christi College. He was dean of chapel at Queens' in 1503–4, was appointed rector of Albury in Surrey in 1509, and served his college as senior proctor in 1513. Collingwood was also a practising mathematician and under the name of Carbo-in-ligno left a treatise in manuscript, 'Arithmetica experimentalis', dedicated to Bishop Foxe, and preserved in the library of Corpus Christi College. Nothing is known of Collingwood's subsequent life nor of the circumstances of his death.   A. M. CLERKE, *rev.* ANITA MCCONNELL

Sources Cooper, *Ath. Cantab.*, 1.24, 526 · P. L. Rose, 'Erasmians and mathematicians at Cambridge in the early 16th century', *Sixteenth Century Journal*, 8 (1977), suppl. 2, pp. 47–9

Collingwood, William Gershom (1854–1932), author, artist, and antiquary, was born on 6 August 1854 at 87 Chatham Street, Liverpool, the eldest son of the artist William Collingwood RWS (1819–1903), and his wife, Marie Imhoff (*d.* 1873) of Arbon, Switzerland. At Liverpool College he acquired sound classical scholarship, but much of his early life was spent travelling and drawing with his father in the Alps. Meanwhile in England he spent long holidays in the cottage of a fisherman, William Alexander, at Gillhead, Windermere. In 1872 he went up to University College, Oxford, where in 1876 he won the Lothian prize and obtained a first in Greats. More importantly, at Oxford he met and fell under the spell of John *Ruskin. He attended Ruskin's lectures and breakfasts, and helped build Ruskin's road at Hinksey. In his introduction to Collingwood's *Limestone Alps of Savoy*, Ruskin was later to describe him as 'one of the best and dearest of those Oxford pupils', and during the summer of 1873 Collingwood, with his father, visited Ruskin at Brantwood, Coniston. Two years later Collingwood was staying at Brantwood with Alexander Wedderburn, translating Xenophon's *Economist* for Ruskin's *Bibliotheca pastorum*, and helping with the enlargement of the harbour there. Ruskin admired his draughtsmanship, and on leaving Oxford, Collingwood went to the Slade to study, between 1876 and 1878, under Alphonse Legros; he exhibited for the first time at the Royal Academy in 1880.

The succeeding years were dedicated to helping Ruskin. Collingwood stayed at Brantwood in 1881 as his assistant and travelled with him in the following year to Switzerland, where he filled his sketchbooks with details of French and Italian sculpture and collected material for his *Limestone Alps of Savoy*, published in 1884 as a supplement to Ruskin's *Deucalion*. Meanwhile, in 1883 he had already published his *Philosophy of Ornament*. That same year he married Edith Mary Isaac (1857–1928) and settled at Gillhead, though in 1891 he moved to Lanehead, Coniston, to be even nearer to Ruskin. In this decade he edited a number of Ruskin's texts: *Poems* (1891), *Studies in both Arts and Poetry of Architecture* (1893), *Verona and other Lectures* (1894), and *Lectures on Landscape* (1897). His biography of Ruskin, published in 1893 and rewritten in 1900, became a standard work, but after Ruskin's death in 1900 Collingwood declined to edit the Ruskin Library Edition because he saw it as a mere money-making venture by Ruskin's executors. However, he arranged Ruskin exhibitions in Coniston (1900 and 1919), London (1901), and Manchester (1904).

In 1896 Arthur Ransome first met the Collingwoods and their children, Dora (*b.* 1886, later Mrs Ernest Altounyan), Barbara (*b.* 1887, later Mrs Oscar Gnosspelius), Ursula (*b.* 1891, later Mrs Reginald Luard Selby), and Robin (Robin George *Collingwood, the historian and philosopher). An excursion in the Collingwoods' boat *Swallow* was followed by a firm friendship, and much later, after teaching Collingwood's grandchildren to sail in *Swallow II*, Ransome's *Swallows and Amazons* series resulted. Partly because of lack of income, Collingwood and his wife educated their children at home for their early years.

In the 1890s Collingwood found his vocation as a painter and also became drawn into the group of men studying Lake District history. He joined the Cumberland and Westmorland Antiquarian and Archaeological Society in 1887 and wrote a large number of papers for its *Transactions*; he became editor in 1900, a post which he nominally relinquished in 1920 on being nominated the society's president. Collingwood was particularly interested in Norse

lore and the Norsemen in Lakeland, and he wrote a series of novels, including *Thorstein of the Mere* (1895) and *The Bondwoman* (1896), against this background. In 1897 he visited Iceland for three months, and two years later published, with Jon Stefansson, his *Pilgrimage to the Sagasteads of Iceland*. He was a member of the Viking Club and served as its president. Adverse criticism of *The Bondwoman* directed Collingwood's interests to a more intensive study of Norse and Anglican archaeology in the north, particularly the artistic aspect of it, on which he became widely recognized as the leading authority. Following Ruskin's death Collingwood continued to help for a while with secretarial work at Brantwood, but in 1905 he went to University College, Reading, as master of drawing and painting, and served as professor of fine art from 1907 until 1911.

Collingwood was sixty at the outbreak of the war; he joined the Admiralty intelligence division, but life in London did not improve his health. He returned to Coniston in 1919. He was vice-president of the Lakes Artists Society from its formation in 1903, and he and his wife regularly exhibited at their shows. His writing continued with *Lake District History* (1925) and perhaps his most important work, *Northumbrian Crosses of the pre-Norman Age* (1927). The intense activity of Collingwood's life was taking its toll, and in 1927 he experienced the first of a series of strokes. His life was further saddened by the death of his wife in the following year. Collingwood's last task was the revision of his *Lake Counties*. Originally published in 1902, this highly regarded book had long been out of print and was reissued in 1932. Collingwood died on 1 October 1932 at Lanehead, Coniston, after a stroke and was buried four days later in Coniston churchyard, near to Ruskin whose monolithic memorial cross he had designed.

In stature Collingwood was short, broad-shouldered, and erect; his eyes, like Ruskin's, were bright and piercingly blue. He was great climber and swimmer, and a tireless walker into advanced age. A fellow of the Society of Antiquaries and an honorary member of the Yorkshire Archaeological Society, the Society of Antiquaries of Ireland, the Alpine Club, and the Carlisle Society of Arts and Crafts, Collingwood was an artist of no mean accomplishment, a scholar of great versatility, and an accomplished musician. Few English scholars have been better versed in Scandinavian languages. His books in various fields remain standard works at the end of the twentieth century and continue to be reprinted.

JAMES S. DEARDEN

Sources *The Times* (3 Oct 1932) · [R. G. Collingwood], *Transactions of the Cumberland and Westmorland Antiquarian and Archaeological Society*, new ser., 33 (1932–3), 308–12 · *Barrow News* (8 Oct 1932) · W. Rollinson, 'Introduction', in W. G. Collingwood, *Lake Counties* (1988) · H. G. Viljoen, *The Brantwood diary of John Ruskin* (1971) · R. G. Collingwood, *An autobiography* (1939)

Archives Abbot Hall Art Gallery, Kendal, watercolours, sketchbooks, and corresp. · AM Oxf., notes, drawings, photographs, etc., relating to pre-conquest crosses and tombstones; notes on Northumbrian crosses · Brantwood, Coniston, Cumbria · Cumbria AS, Kendal, letters relating to place names; personal and family corresp. · Millennium Gallery, Sheffield, Ruskin Gallery · Museum of Lakeland Life and Industry, Kendal, diaries, notebooks, drawings, etc. · University of Lancaster, Ruskin Library | Armitt Library, Ambleside, letters to the Armitt family · Bodl. Oxf., letters to E. J. Thompson · FM Cam., letters to Edith Crum, with MS notes on painting · NL Scot., letters to William Marwick

Likenesses W. G. Collingwood, self-portrait, 19 Dec 1893, Brantwood, Coniston, Cumbria, Brant. 719 A · B. Collingwood, bust, c.1915, Coniston Museum, Cumbria · H. S. Thompson, photograph, 14 Oct 1928, repro. in V. A. Burd, *John Ruskin and Rose La Touche* (1979), pl. 3

Wealth at death £323 9s. 8d.: probate, 28 Dec 1932, CGPLA Eng. & Wales

Collins family (*per. c.*1820–*c.*1980), publishers, came to prominence with **William Collins** (1789–1853), who was born at Pollokshaws, near Glasgow, on 12 October 1789. The identity of his parents is not known, although his father may have been Edward Collins, an Englishman who arrived in Glasgow in 1746 and is known to have founded the Collins paper mill at Dalmuir, near Glasgow. William Collins was educated at the local parish school, where he did well; he left about 1800, and went to work at the loom at Pollokshaws. Some six years later he became a clerk in John Monteith's cotton mill. By now an active, ambitious, and devout Christian, he offered on Sundays religious instruction and on weekday evenings lessons in English, writing, and arithmetic.

On 14 March 1807 Collins married Jean Barclay (*d.* 1846), the daughter of a Paisley engineer. He left the mill in 1813 to open a private school in Campbell Street, Glasgow, and within four years his income from the school had tripled. He founded a Sunday school in 1815 and over the next two years established a chain of Sunday schools throughout Glasgow. He became an elder of the kirk at the Tron Church in 1814, and a year later arranged for the translation to that church of Dr Thomas Chalmers. This inspirational preacher became the most influential figure in his life, his spiritual mentor who was not averse to combining religion with business.

In 1819 Collins closed his school and established himself in the Candleriggs as William Collins & Co., printers, and (in partnership with Chalmers's brother Charles) as Chalmers and Collins, booksellers and stationers. Their first book, Dr Chalmers's *The Christian and Civic Economy of Large Towns*, was published on 23 September 1819, and despite growing social unrest Collins managed to establish his business on a firm footing during 1820. In December that year he was caught up in a quarrel between Dr Chalmers and the Glasgow publisher John Smith over a booklet originally published by Lesslie of Dundee, a quarrel (outcome unknown) which lasted for over two years and revealed Chalmers's formidable pride, temper, and obstinacy.

The character of the early Collins list—a character which was to endure for well over a hundred years, particularly in the Glasgow publishing departments—was built on evangelical preaching and awareness of the next world: educational, instructive, edifying, above all Christian. It featured collections of sermons, schoolbooks, and a body of rather fearsome children's fiction written to

Sir William Collins (1817–1895), by unknown artist

glorify the covenanters. Collins was an outspoken opponent of slavery, and arranged meetings with William Wilberforce and Zachary Macaulay on his first journey south to sell his new books to the English book trade. In 1822 he started to publish his Select Library of Christian Authors, designed to make theological classics accessible to the rapidly growing reading public. By 1829 there were almost fifty volumes in print. The first of so many Collins bestsellers, *The Christian Philosopher* by Thomas Dick, appeared in 1823 and was regularly reprinted for over half a century.

Collins found another best-seller in 1825, *The Christian Psalmist*, an anthology edited by James Montgomery, which was to be reprinted four times within the next twelve months; but 1825 also saw a sudden recession in retail bookselling, which ruined Archibald Constable and threatened the survival of every under-capitalized publisher. Not only was Collins under-capitalized (even though he printed most of the books he published himself, as his successors continued to do for the next century and a half), but his energetic expansion of his list also left him particularly vulnerable to bad debts and dwindling orders. Collins solved the immediate problem by borrowing enough from his brothers-in-law to buy out the Chalmers family's interest in the retail business, which had been losing money, and close it down. Remarkably, he achieved this on terms which avoided any serious breach with his mentor, Thomas Chalmers, but the climate of their relationship remained changeable. Thunder and lightning could be expected whenever Chalmers felt himself taken for granted or otherwise ill-treated. Thus he placed more blame upon his publisher for the disappointing critical reception of his *Political Economy* (1832) than could reasonably have been expected.

By now Collins had thrown himself with characteristic fervour into the temperance movement. At the height of the cholera epidemic in 1829 he founded Britain's first temperance society, and wore himself out with journeys to other great cities and passionate speeches to packed meetings; in 1831 he founded the London Temperance Society. Temperance speeches, tracts, and magazines poured from the Collins printing works. In 1834 he took up yet another crusade and founded the Glasgow Church Building Society with the aim of constructing no fewer than twenty new churches in that city—a target which was reached within seven years, a direct result of Collins's relentless drive.

In 1835 Collins published Nathaniel Paterson's *The Manse Garden*, *Leitch's Practical and Economical Readers*—of which one and a half million copies were sold within fifteen years—and the first of the twenty-five volumes of the collected works of Thomas Chalmers. In the same year he joined with other evangelicals in urging state aid for church extension, appearing on platforms and printing lectures. In 1837 he was accompanied by his son William [see below] on a visit to London in pursuit of this aim. Returning to London in 1838, he met the archbishop of Canterbury, the duke of Wellington, Sir Robert Peel, and the young W. E. Gladstone.

Every publisher has on his list an author who feels that he is neglected and bitterly resents any attention paid to another author. Dr Chalmers played this part in the life of William Collins. Feeling entitled to greater sales and greater critical esteem, and yearning for a London publisher who might be expected to achieve this for him, he was quick to complain about trifles and tried from time to time to interfere with Collins's arrangements with the retail trade. The final storm arose as a consequence of the Disruption of the Church of Scotland and the establishment of the Free Church of Scotland in 1843: both men supported the new church, and Chalmers became its first moderator. In 1844 Collins undertook extensive printing work for the Free Church. In the same year the Free Church authorities determined to distribute many thousands of copies of the *History of the Reformation* by the Swiss historian Merle d'Aubigné among their flock. Three volumes of this work had already been published in Britain by three publishers including Collins. The right to publish the fourth volume was won by Oliver and Boyd of Edinburgh. Chaos ensued. In 1846 Chalmers suddenly transferred his literary interests to Oliver and Boyd. In 1847 'the

most illustrious Scottish churchman since John Knox' (said Lord Rosebery) died.

Growing pressure for the termination of the monopoly in Bible printing enjoyed by successive king's and queen's printers for Scotland since 1580 was rewarded in 1839, when all Scottish printers were given the right to print the scriptures 'under bond and caution' (to ensure that their work contained no errors). Collins printed his first New Testament in 1841. By the end of 1843 he had completed three bibles, thus establishing a tradition which continued as long as the company maintained its own printing works.

William Collins died in simple lodgings in Rothesay, Buteshire, on 2 January 1853, and was buried in the Necropolis, Glasgow. He left many memorials; the *Scottish Guardian* praised 'the strength and simplicity of his faith … his burning zeal … his liberality … his readiness for every good work'. To this we may add praise for his vision, drive, and Calvinistic rectitude in commercial matters. Jean Collins had died in 1846; his sole surviving son, William, inherited a well-established printing, publishing, and bookselling business.

Sir William Collins (1817–1895) was born in Glasgow on 12 October 1817. In 1829 he left Glasgow grammar school and was apprenticed to the business; in 1843 he became a partner; and on 24 June 1845 he married Annabella Proudfoot Glen (d. 1862). He inherited more than ambition and a prosperous business: like his father, he was a fervent supporter of many good causes, but in one respect he went even further by preaching total abstinence.

By 1853 the Scottish literary renaissance led by Sir Walter Scott and J. G. Lockhart had wound its course, but the publishers of such English authors as Dickens, Tennyson, and Thackeray kept book printers busy throughout the land, not least in Edinburgh. Scotland was now on the threshold of rapid commercial advance, and with it came an ever-increasing appetite for education and, therefore, schoolbooks. The appointment of Collins as publisher to the Scottish School Book Association swelled the tide in the early 1860s. His list was widening in scope, although it was still overwhelmingly educational in tone, and the installation of ten new steam-driven presses made it economically attractive to print and publish dictionaries and other reference books and standard editions of household classics.

The new presses also helped to establish Collins as one of the leading publishers of the Bible. In 1860 he stated in evidence to the select committee on the Bible printing patents that he had seventeen editions in print and was printing over 100,000 copies per year; the cheapest was priced at 1s. In 1861 the house of Collins moved into the fine new premises at Herriot Hill, later known as Cathedral Street, that they continued to occupy for over a hundred years. In 1862 Collins was appointed queen's printer for Scotland.

The Collins list continued to expand during the middle years of the century, the seminal period of modern science, and Collins recognized this with a Science Series comprising seventy-two titles at various levels, of which more than 2.5 million copies were sold. Trotter's *English Grammar* sold over half a million copies, and by 1868 the firm was selling more than a quarter of a million illustrated dictionaries per year.

On 26 September 1865, his first wife having died on 12 September 1862, Collins married Helen Jamieson, with whom he had two children (he had eleven in all). Outside business he devoted himself earnestly to temperance reform (earning himself the nickname Water Willie) and, as a Glasgow city councillor for the Liberal persuasion from December 1868, to close scrutiny of the city's expenditure of public money. In 1877 he became lord provost of Glasgow, and a year later led the corporation and his affluent fellow citizens in the prompt establishment of a relief fund to help the thousands of genteel investors left penniless by the collapse of the City of Glasgow Bank. He was knighted in 1881.

In 1871 Collins bought the copyright in the Popular Poets series from the fading London publishing firm of Edward Moxon; under the new title Grosvenor Poets they sold well for the next half-century. In the following year he published *Domestic Cookery* and *Domestic Medicine* to compete with Mrs Beeton's *Book of Household Management*. In 1875 he bought out the Scottish School Book Association, and the schoolbook list rose to 920 titles. Like so many other Scots, Collins and his sons William Collins [*see below*] and Alexander, now both partners in the firm, were drawn to explore the expanding world markets of the Victorian empire. They had already achieved substantial exports, particularly of schoolbooks, to Australia and New Zealand, where the name of Collins was respected and reassuringly familiar to the many Free Church families who had emigrated there after the Disruption of the Church of Scotland. The mid-1870s saw Collins representatives travelling all over Canada, India, and the Antipodes; within ten years new offices in Sydney and Cape Town had been added to those in Glasgow, Edinburgh, and London (Auckland followed in 1888). Editorially, too, the firm was quick to realize that it was imperative to create new educational books for these new markets and to adapt many of the books already on the list, originally written with British schools and schoolchildren in mind, for use abroad. By the end of the decade the gospels had been translated into African languages, printed in Glasgow, and exported to missionaries on the west coast of Africa.

In 1879 Collins bought a paper mill at Bowling, Dunbartonshire, for his third son, John. In the same year the publishing and printing business was converted to a limited company. It had grown very large, with nearly 2000 employees. Twenty-eight presses were producing about 2 million books per year, but still could not keep pace with the demands of the publishing departments. The stationery side was already flourishing (120 million envelopes were manufactured annually on machines invented by the third William Collins) when in 1881 the firm produced the first of the many millions of diaries that it was to print over the following 120 years. By the early 1890s the rate of progress had still not slackened: two more paper mills at Denny, Stirlingshire, had been acquired, more presses installed, and an innovatory process had been introduced to add colour by lithography to the monochrome letterpresses illustrations in school and children's books.

Although it was still open to any Scottish printer to apply for a licence to print the whole Bible or part of it, in practice Collins had by now secured a virtual monopoly through the economies of scale that could be achieved in their large, efficient plant—and hence a virtual monopoly also in publishing the Bible north of the border. A new enthusiasm had developed for the addition of maps, illustrations, and explanatory material ('helps') to the plain text of the Authorized Version, and Collins were quick to benefit while it lasted. In 1892 the firm opened the International Bible Agency in New York to act as its sole agents, and a new typeface (Clear-Type, from which the press took its name for the next eighty years) was introduced for use in dictionaries and bibles.

William Collins died on 20 February 1895 at Edinburgh, aged seventy-seven. As a boy and young man he had watched his father expand the firm he had started so humbly into an important employer in Glasgow and a considerable force in the book trade. His life, like his father's, was distinguished by hard work, driving ambition, strict financial rectitude, generous philanthropy, and exemplary care and consideration for his staff (not least in repeatedly taking the lead among Scottish printers in reducing the working week). The city fathers recognized his contribution to Glasgow by burying him high up on the Necropolis, near his father's grave and the John Knox memorial statue.

William Collins (1846–1906) was born at Glasgow on 6 September 1846. He developed his natural bent for science and technology through attending Glasgow University. On 2 December 1875 he married Annie D. Leisk, but the couple remained childless. Although he inherited a relentless drive to expand the family business, his character differed markedly from that of his father and grandfather. Everything was done at top speed. A partner before the age of thirty he was censured more than once by his fellow directors for impetuously exceeding his responsibilities.

William's brother Alexander Glen Collins, born on 25 June 1848, became a partner before the age of twenty-eight, and concentrated on increasing the sales of bibles and schoolbooks. He married Cornelia, the daughter of the late Godfrey Thomas Hope Pattison, an American merchant, on 18 June 1872; his first son, William, was born in 1873, and his second, Godfrey, in 1875. An art lover, he worked with his father on an exhibition designed to help the relief of hardship occasioned by the collapse of the City of Glasgow Bank. He is known to have shared his father's enthusiasm for yachting. A genial, well-liked figure—who must nevertheless have his share in any celebration of the success of Collins bibles—he lived for some years in semi-retirement before his death in 1911.

The third William Collins, as has been noted, lived and worked in the fast lane. A fashionable though often absent-minded dresser, he kept two fine carriages, a yacht, a flat in London, and a hunting-box in Northamptonshire (a taste later shared by his great-nephew William Alexander Roy Collins), yet found time also for old-master paintings, music, literature, and gambling on the Riviera. Above all, he was a hard worker and a thinker, and he soon saw clearly that the firm had been too reliant for too long on its staple lines of bibles, school and reference books, classics, and stationery. In adding to these a new and more adventurous list of original fiction and non-fiction books for children, and thus reviving memories of his grandfather's early publishing initiatives, he shaped the firm as it was to develop and thrive over the next century. This new list became known in the trade as Reward Books, as it was composed of wholesome and godly titles, intended as Sunday-school prizes, or birthday and Christmas presents. It featured such popular authors as Katherine Tynan, Andrew Lang, and the future Mrs Thomas Hardy, Florence Dugdale.

The turn of the century saw the inception within the space of seven years of five outstanding series of hardback pocket classics designed to sell at 1s. per copy: Nelson's, the World's Classics, Collins's, Routledge's, and Everyman's. These series inevitably shared a great many features, serving as they did the needs of the same classes and categories of reader as understood and anticipated by publishers and editors of similar commercial and scholarly standing. Collins, like Nelson, published mainly fiction; the other imprints cast their nets much wider, with a high-minded appeal, as J. M. Dent put it, 'to every kind of reader'. The new rotary presses brought over from Germany in 1900 proved well suited to the mass production of these little books, and Collins Handy Illustrated Pocket Classics (unlike the other series, embellished with newly commissioned illustrations) were launched three years later. The series eventually numbered almost 400 volumes, including twenty-one by Sir Walter Scott. In the next fifty years Collins sold some 29 million Classics: their best-sellers included *David Copperfield* and three other Dickens titles, *Wuthering Heights*, *Vanity Fair*, *Treasure Island*, *Pride and Prejudice*, and *Jane Eyre*. The Gem series, originating with an English dictionary in 1902, grew to over 100 titles and provided further business for the rotary presses for the whole twentieth century.

William Collins continued to develop and consolidate his firm at a brisk pace. But his life was tragically cut short on 15 July 1906, in an accident stemming from the combination of his mechanical ingenuity and his literally breakneck pace of life. He had fashioned his own gate-key to the lift in the block of flats at Westminster where he stayed when in London. This saved him seconds when the hall-porter was busy, but on this occasion it cost him his life: the electricity supply had failed, the porter was elsewhere mending the fuse, the hall was dark, and the lift-shaft was empty.

Again the family was lucky enough to have two brothers and their cousin ready to step up. **William Alexander Collins** (1873–1945), the nephew of the third William Collins, was born in Glasgow on 26 March 1873, the son of Alexander Glen Collins (1848–1911) and Cornelia Pattison

(*b.* 1854/5). He was educated at Harrow School. He married Grace Brander, and they had two sons: William Alexander Roy Collins [*see below*] and Ian Glen Collins (1903–1975). William Alexander Collins was elected to the board in 1897, and succeeded to the chairmanship in 1906 at thirty-three. He assumed particular responsibility for stationery and the overseas offices; his brother, Sir Godfrey Pattison *Collins (1875–1936), who had trained for the Royal Navy, was appointed a director in 1899 and took charge of publications; and his cousin William Collins Dickson, born on 12 October 1876 and educated at Fettes College and Glasgow University, also appointed a director in 1899, took charge of engineering and costing. Retrenchment soon became the first priority, when it was discovered that before his death in 1906 the impetuous William Collins had invested too optimistically in new equipment and branch offices in the empire.

May 1907 saw the simultaneous appearance of both the Collins and the Nelson Sevenpennies, cheap pocket hardback editions of copyright novels from their proprietors' and other publishers' lists. Many publishers declined to lease titles to them, but enough were available to feed the hungry rotary presses. Even these did not represent the cheapest line of fiction on the Collins list—there was a Penny Library for schools, and the Pocket Library of eighty full-length novels priced at 3½*d.*, of which several million copies were sold before the First World War. Business was now booming in the empire, and the workforce in Britain was producing nearly 90,000 books per week.

In 1910 Godfrey Collins embarked on his long second career of public service, winning Greenock for the Liberal Party at both general elections in that year. He quickly found political favour and was appointed parliamentary private secretary to the secretary of state for war, Jack Seely. He continued his editorial overview of the Collins lists, and in 1913 put his experience to the firm's service in launching a new series, the Nation's Library. For a shilling one could read *Socialism and Syndicalism* (by Philip Snowden), *Aviation*, *The Case for Railway Nationalisation*, *The Land Problem*, or *The Relations of Capital and Labour*.

Godfrey Collins, aged thirty-nine, and William Alexander Collins, aged forty-one, were not slow to join the Army Service Corps after the outbreak of the First World War. William won the DSO in France, and rose to the rank of lieutenant-colonel; Godfrey served in France, Egypt, India, Gallipoli, and Mesopotamia, and was appointed CMG in 1917. Collins sent nearly 300 other members of staff to the war, and struggled like so many other firms with the consequent scarcity of craftsmen and skilled workmen. Costs tend to rise in wartime, and supplies of materials dry up. The scarcity of paper dictated some pruning of the list to ensure that books needed for the national emergency (not to mention books which could be relied on to be profitable) were accorded priority over more marginal items. Thus it was that the Nation's Library and the Sevenpennies fell under Godfrey's rationalizing axe on his return to business in 1917, while the *Collins Children's Annual*, launched in 1914, survived the war (and stiff competition from other publishers' similar products) and well beyond. As the war progressed it was joined in the children's list by *Hunting the U-boats*, *With Beatty in the North Sea*, and *'Midst Shot and Shell in Flanders*.

Godfrey Collins seems to have inherited from his uncle William the ability to run headlong, without in his case falling down a lift-shaft. In that same year, 1917, realizing that there was simply not enough good fiction reliably available—from the Collins list and other publishers—to support the series of cheap reprints that had so flourished before the war, he decided to move general publishing to London and to broaden its base, found premises at 48 Pall Mall, recruited an editor, Gerald O'Donovan, and issued an autumn list of no fewer than fourteen titles. This would have been a considerable performance at the best of times. In 1917, with the Glasgow factory short of 132 craftsmen and already at full stretch producing bibles and school books, it was a miracle, which Godfrey achieved by employing outside printers and binders—crumbs from the table for them, of course, but 80,000 crumbs, and a very promising table.

That first list included works by Henry James (the firm bought four titles from his executors, including *The Ivory Tower*), Mrs Humphry Ward (*Missing*), and Edward Garnett (*Turgenev*). The list over the next few years included works by Sir Arthur Quiller-Couch, Victoria Sackville-West (her first three novels), J. Middleton Murry (*Aspects of Literature*), Rose Macaulay (Collins published all her novels from 1920 to 1956), Henry Williamson (*The Beautiful Years*), Walter de la Mare (*Memoirs of a Midget*), and Michael Arlen (*The Green Hat*, of which 70,000 copies were pre-ordered by booksellers in 1923, and of which 200,000 were sold within three years). New poetry began to appear on the list, with volumes by the Georgian poets Edward Shanks, Francis Brett Young, and Gerald Gould.

Godfrey Collins had been re-elected for Greenock in 1918 as a Coalition Liberal, and again in 1922, as a Liberal. Re-elected in the following year at Greenock, he became Liberal chief whip. He continued to represent Greenock throughout the 1920s. This increase in his workload, and the success of his new list, necessitated two new key appointments at Pall Mall: that of S. J. Goldsack, who became sales manager, and F. T. Smith, who transferred from Glasgow as chief editor. They held these positions, and much later directorships, until well after the Second World War.

By the early 1920s detective stories were in vogue. Collins had already published their first, *The Skeleton Key* by Bernard Capes: the floodgates opened, unsolicited manuscripts poured in, Freeman Wills Crofts, G. D. H. Cole and Margaret Cole, and Agatha Christie (with *The Murder of Roger Ackroyd*) joined the list, and in 1930 the Crime Club was born. Its members—20,000 within the first twelve months—received a monthly mailing giving details of the new books. Writers of the calibre of Rex Stout, Ngaio Marsh (creators respectively of Nero Wolfe and Roderick Alleyn), and Nicholas Blake (Cecil Day Lewis) joined what became a large stable of authors. Christie, promoted as the 'Queen of Crime', was always the most popular, particularly when she featured Miss Marple or Hercule Poirot.

Alongside pure whodunits, adventure stories or thrillers gained in popularity on the coat-tails of John Buchan; all were to feature on the Collins list for the next half-century.

Meanwhile the sale of bibles, testaments, and liturgical books continued to flourish: by 1931 sales exceeded 600,000 copies, helped no doubt by the sales jingle:

Satan trembles when he sees
Bibles sold as cheap as these.

Overseas markets, to which William Alexander Collins paid personal attention, were particularly successful, notably in the United States. The Collins brothers, sensing the post-war ferment of new ideas in education, realized that many of the schoolbooks which had remained in print since before the turn of the century were obsolescent if not obsolete. They set up four new series of reading and geography books, histories, and Shakespeares. A new educational manager was appointed at Cathedral Street, John Crossland, whose Laurel and Gold series included his own verse anthology, of which over half a million copies were sold. Other notably successful anthologies followed. Children's home reading was supplied by books on the open air and transport subjects.

Returned again for Greenock in 1931 as a National Liberal, Sir Godfrey Collins was appointed secretary of state for Scotland in 1932, and so could no longer be an active director of Collins. Re-elected in 1935, he was taken ill while on holiday in Switzerland, and died at Zürich on 13 October 1936. One of his authors, Rose Macaulay, said in tribute: 'Never did any publisher realize more fully than he the identity of interest of publisher and author'. By then William Alexander Collins's sons William Alexander Roy, always known as Billy, and Ian Glen (b. 23 April 1903) were hard at work in the firm—unless they were playing tennis in the men's doubles at Wimbledon or, in Ian's case, cricket for Scotland. Ian had immersed himself in Glasgow business: manufacturing technologies, bibles, schoolbooks, diaries and stationery, and the intricacies of the export trade. Billy Collins, who had been working at Pall Mall with his uncle, took charge when he died, ambitious to enhance the house's standing in the modern world of London publishing.

Winifred Holtby's *South Riding*, written in seven months in 1935 and completed just before she died, was published in early 1936 to critical applause, winning the James Tait Black memorial prize for the best novel of the year; it remained in print for many years. In 1936 also appeared *The Weather in the Streets* by Rosamond Lehmann. The same outstanding year saw débuts by T. H. White, Peter Cheyney, and Nigel Balchin. Other well-known authors published by Collins before the Second World War included Howard Spring (*My Son, my Son*), Margery Sharp, Leo Walmsley, and the poet laureate John Masefield (*The Country Scene* and *A Tribute to Ballet*, both illustrated by Edward Seago). Trips by Collins to the United States also secured British rights in novels by Mary Ellen Chase, Kenneth Roberts, Agnes Sligh Turnbull, and James Ramsey Ullman, among others.

To meet the manufacturing demands of this expansion

in their publishing, Collins extended their Cathedral Street empire in 1936 by acquiring the adjoining printing works of the publishing house of Blackie (premises which had been bought by Blackie in 1829 from A. and J. M. Duncan, then printers to the University of Glasgow). The 1920s and 1930s witnessed the typographic revolution led by Stanley Morison, when the Monotype Corporation revived the great type designs of the previous centuries in a form suited to single-character machine typesetting. The directors of Collins sought the advice of the distinguished printer and typographer Giovanni Mardersteig: when he asked to see the vaunted Clear Type, he was told that no such type now existed. The outcome in 1936 was Collins's Monotype Fontana (the name refers to the firm's device), modelled by Mardersteig on the Scottish roman types made about 1760 at Alexander Wilson's Glasgow foundry.

The Second World War brought back the problems of the First World War that were still familiar to many members of the staff, almost 500 of whom served in uniform, and the same number in munitions factories. Paper was soon in short supply and, before long, rationed. Bombed schools, bookshops, and wholesalers arose from the ashes and demanded replacement books. Imported materials and exported bibles, books, and stationery were lost in Atlantic raids on allied shipping. Collins was hardest hit in London: the warehouse at Bridewell Place and the office at Pall Mall were destroyed in air raids in, respectively, 1940 and 1944. The editorial offices under Billy Collins moved to 13–14 St James's Place, where they remained until 1983.

As had happened in the First World War, wartime difficulties coincided with enormous demand for bibles, classic fiction, and patriotic and escapist literature of all kinds. The boredom of the long hours of inactivity between battles and in air-raid shelters and hospitals intensified the value of the book as a never-failing friend to millions of readers and introduced the habit of reading to millions of newcomers. Indeed, to quote Desmond Flower, 'Anything printed, even if upside down and/or in Sanskrit, was saleable' (D. Flower, *The Paper-back*, 1959, 17). 'Cometh the hour, cometh the man', and Arthur Bryant, already the author of a three-volume biography of Samuel Pepys, joined the Collins list in 1940 with *English Saga, 1840–1940*. He published many more works of popular history with the firm until his death in 1985.

In 1941 Collins published Peter Quennell's *Byron in Italy* (sequel to *The Years of Fame*, 1935). In the same year appeared the first twenty of the Britain in Pictures series. These elegantly produced essays on all aspects of British life, work, history, and arts, each plentifully illustrated in full colour, represented only the second large-scale appearance in Britain of that phenomenon of post-war publishing, the 'packaged' book. The series was the brainwave of Hilda Matheson, then engaged on propaganda work for the Ministry of Information, and seems to have been designed to quicken patriotic feelings. W. J. Turner was appointed general editor. Publication was entrusted to Collins and design and production to Adprint, whose

directors Wolfgang Foges and Walter Neurath had previously sold the King Penguin series to Allen Lane. By 1951 nearly 3 million copies of 133 titles had been sold: the best-sellers were *The Birds of Britain* by James Fisher (84,218), *Life among the English* by Rose Macaulay (61,636), *Wild Flowers in Britain* by Geoffrey Grigson (60,574), and *The English Poets* by Lord David Cecil (60,247).

Succeeding years of the war brought work from Bernard Darwin, Noel Streatfeild, Thomas Armstrong, Hammond Innes, Norman Collins (no relation), Hesketh Pearson (*Bernard Shaw*, 1942), and Edmund Blunden (*Cricket Country*, 1943). Three months after the war ended came the first two volumes in the New Naturalist Library, which had been under discussion for three years between Billy Collins and a distinguished editorial board. Unlike Britain in Pictures, which saw a brief revival in 1951 to coincide with the Festival of Britain and was then remaindered, the New Naturalist Library, which grew to over eighty titles by 1976, remained in print.

William Alexander Collins, who had been appointed CBE in recognition of his work for servicemen in 1943, died on 3 September 1945 at a nursing home in Prestwick, Ayrshire. A caring and generous employer, a friendly, modest, yet lively man, he had been content to see his brother Godfrey succeed as a West End publisher and his sons take responsibility for important departments of the firm, while remaining firmly in charge at board level. The final key member of this generation of the Collinses, his cousin William Collins Dickson, who had been living in retirement since 1929, died nine days later. So **William Alexander Roy** [Billy] **Collins** (1900–1976) became chairman and presided at St James's Place. He was educated at Harrow School and Magdalen College, Oxford, where he distinguished himself more as a sportsman than as a *littérateur*, obtaining a third-class degree in modern history in 1922. His brother Ian, who for his war service was appointed OBE and chevalier of the Légion d'honneur, and received the Croix de Guerre, became vice-chairman, and made a speciality of bibles, prayer books, and stationery, while his cousin William Hope Collins (Godfrey's son, born on 5 September 1903) took charge of the printing works.

The return of peace saw a number of promising additions to the Collins list: H. J. Massingham (*The Wisdom of the Fields*) and John Moore (the Brensham trilogy)—evidence of people's longing to recapture the innocence of the pre-war countryside—Neville Cardus (*Autobiography*), Christopher Sykes (*Four Studies in Loyalty*), Ivor Brown (*Shakespeare*), and Milton Waldman, who published his *Elizabeth and Essex* and joined the firm as literary adviser. They flourished alongside war stories, for which an apparently insatiable public appetite was developing. Gerald Hanley's *Monsoon Victory* and Bernard Fergusson's *Beyond the Chindwin* had been published during the war, but they were eclipsed after 1945 by Roy Farran's *Winged Dagger*, Desmond Young's *Rommel*, Paul Brickhill's *Reach for the Sky*, and *The Great Escape*. *The Wooden Horse*, by Eric Williams, which outstripped them all and sold half a million copies, had been first published as *Goon on the Block* by another publisher, was acquired by Collins after it failed, and was substantially rewritten by Waldman.

On 14 December 1949 the directors floated the first public issue of shares in the company's history, oversubscribed four times within a few minutes (this led eventually to the acquisition of a controlling interest by News International and the cessation of family interest in the firm). By now Collins employed some 2500 people in Glasgow alone, and it was calculated that the printing presses could together produce at least 15,000 copies of a 256-page book per hour. Throughout the 1950s Collins was either first or second in the annual count of new books and new editions published; their total in 1960, when they again came first, was 576 titles.

In 1950 appeared the first of many beautifully illustrated books on the ballet, brought to Collins by the editor Mark Bonham Carter and printed away from Glasgow by photogravure. This was *Baron at the Ballet* (Baron was a celebrated photographer, and Arnold Haskell contributed an introduction); 60,000 copies were sold in twelve years. A new 'packager', Rainbird McLean, sought out Collins in 1951 for a sumptuous new edition of Robert Thornton's *Temple of Flora*; Sacheverell Sitwell's equally sumptuous *Fine Bird Books* (1953) and *Great Flower Books* (1956) followed from the same stable. Further, more modest Rainbird McLean titles were published from time to time.

Billy Collins took a particular interest in natural history and wildlife. The flourishing New Naturalist Library may have been largely his creation, and R. S. R. Fitter's *Collins Pocket Guide to British Birds*, published in 1953 (and followed a year later by *A Field Guide to the Birds of Britain and Europe*), sold 100,000 copies in the next ten years and presaged a long list of nature books and field guides to wildlife the world over.

In 1953 Collins bought the publishing house of Geoffrey Bles Ltd, which had been founded in 1923. With Vicki Baum's *Grand Hotel* (1930) and books of popular piety by C. S. Lewis and J. B. Phillips, the firm had enjoyed occasional success; ironically, it proved to be seriously undercapitalized when its best-sellers, Lewis's children's stories in the Narnia series, arrived in the early 1950s. Bles was allowed autonomy, but its list dwindled and stopped altogether in 1974.

Most significant of all in that hectic year of 1953 was the launch of Fontana Books, the firm's own paperback imprint. Collins had taken a one-quarter share in the Reprint Society book club on its foundation in 1939, and Pan Books (of which Collins owned a one-third share) was established as its independent paperback subsidiary in 1944. Until the early 1950s Collins had been content to lease paperback rights in their books to Pan and their only rivals, Penguin Books, but by 1953 the paperback market was expanding and it was clear that the house should take advantage of the riches of its backlist. The rights in many books were brought back to Collins as their leases expired, and the first batch of Fontana paperbacks included titles by Armstrong, Williams, Bryant, Christie, Cheyney, Spring, Balchin, and Hammond Innes, a very

successful writer who published all his thrillers with Collins.

In 1955 Collins bought another small publishing house, the Harvill Press, created in 1946 by two Catholics, Manya Harari and Marjorie Villiers. Their aim had been to rebuild the bridges, destroyed during the war, between peoples of different nationalities and religions. Their eclectic list included translations from the European languages, and through the critic and translator Max Hayward Harvill became particularly well known for Russian literature, usually by dissidents. They found an ally at St James's Place in Billy's wife Priscilla Marian, *née* Lloyd (1901–1990), whom he had married some twenty years earlier, on 14 October 1924. Known as Pierre to her friends, she had converted to Catholicism and was building one of the leading British religious lists. The Collins imprint on protestant works satisfied her adviser Ronald Gregor Smith and the shade of Dr Chalmers, and the Harvill imprint widened the ecumenical spectrum. Fontana enjoyed enormous success with its religious list, launched in 1957 with a range of authors from Phillips and Lewis to Georges Bernanos (*The Carmelites*) and the *Confessions* of St Augustine.

In 1955 Collins published *H.M.S. 'Ulysses'*, the first of many thrillers by Alastair MacLean. In 1956 came the firm's last substantial British acquisition, the fashionable Hatchards bookshop in Piccadilly, London; again its management enjoyed reasonable autonomy, though Billy Collins was always very keen to see his new books in the window. Rose Macaulay's last novel, *The Towers of Trebizond*, was published this year to critical acclaim, as were *Naught for your Comfort* by Father Trevor Huddleston, and *The Fortress*, an account of his wartime experiences by a Collins editor, Raleigh Trevelyan. But this was nothing beside the massive success of Boris Pasternak's *Doctor Zhivago*, published in 1958—an *annus mirabilis*—under a joint Collins–Harvill imprint: the first printing of 25,000 copies sold out in four days. In that same year came *The Memoirs of Field-Marshal Montgomery*, with a first printing of 135,000 copies; the *Collins Guide to English Parish Churches*, edited by John Betjeman with illustrations by John Piper; the *Autobiography* of St Theresa of Lisieux, translated by Ronald Knox; books by Sybille Bedford and Roy Jenkins, both new to the list; and *The King's War*, the second volume of C. V. Wedgwood's account of the English civil war (*The King's Peace* had been published in 1955).

The following year saw the publication of *The Phenomenon of Man* by the mystical Pierre Teilhard de Chardin. This was widely reviewed but perhaps less widely understood (although the author was a Catholic priest, his books appeared under the Collins imprint because, it was said, Harari and Villiers found them more obscure than transcendental). A prolonged strike in the printing trades during the summer severely curtailed output, yet Collins's profits rose by £100,000.

In 1960 came two new books under the Collins–Harvill imprint: Giuseppe di Lampedusa's *The Leopard*, one of the century's great novels, and *Born Free: a Lioness of Two Worlds* by Joy Adamson, the account of how an African game warden and his wife raised a motherless lion club, taught it to hunt for itself, and set it free. Sales of *Born Free* totalled 135,000 after six months, 230,000 after twelve months. This year also saw the completion of the highly important *Statistical Account of Scotland* and the launch of the Fontana Library, a remarkably ambitious and wide-ranging series of what were then called 'egg-head paperbacks', for which the rights in almost all the titles were acquired from other publishers, though a few such as Lord Acton's *Lectures on Modern History* were out of copyright. That the Fontana Library soon spawned a sub-series Theology and Philosophy was due to Pierre Collins's urge to publish, for example, Karl Barth, Paul Tillich, Father Martin D'Arcy, and Helen Waddell. No fewer than ten Fontana religious titles featured in the autumn 1961 list, together with *The Correspondence between Richard Strauss and Hugo von Hofmannsthal* and *The Non-Existent Knight*, the second book by Italo Calvino to be published by Collins. The children's department in London published the first six (including Dr Seuss's *The Cat in the Hat*) of a series initiated by Random House in New York, the Beginner Books, destined to print many million copies in hard covers and later in paperback. The profit on the year rose to £800,000.

In 1962, Collins and Macmillan bought Heinemann's share in Pan Books to become joint owners of Pan—a shrewd move, as Pan were larger than Fontana and second only to Penguin in British paperback publishing. Later in the year the book trade staged its successful defence of the net book agreement (to the great relief of booksellers around the country), and Collins opened a new million-pound six-storey warehouse capable of dispatching 100,000 books per day. Maurice Collis, Compton Mackenzie, Michael Frayn, Norman Lewis, and Philip Ziegler joined the list; Ross Macdonald joined the Crime Club; Jean Renoir wrote *Renoir, my Father*; and Harvill published a new translation of Pascal's *Pensées*. In November came an illustrated translation of Goethe's *Italian Journey* by W. H. Auden and Elizabeth Mayer, printed by Mardersteig at the Stamperia Valdonega.

The Companion Guides were launched in 1963 under the general editorship of Vincent Cronin: the first titles dealt with Paris, the south of France, and the Greek islands, and some twenty further titles followed. Sybille Bedford's second novel, *A Favourite of the Gods*, was published seven years after her first, the acclaimed *A Legacy*. Lord Beaverbrook joined the list with *The Decline and Fall of Lloyd George*, and the film-maker Elia Kazan with his first novel, *America America*. Fontana issued the first ever paperback Bible, the plain text of the Revised Standard Version. By now paperbacks were booming in Britain, with 10,000 titles in print. The same year saw the first title in a new series of paperback originals, the Fontana History of Europe: Geoffrey Elton's *Reformation Europe*.

The mid- to late 1960s saw the Collins list expanding to include important titles such as Roy Jenkins's *Asquith* (1964), Søren Kierkegaard's *Journals of his Last Years* (1964), and Max Mallowan's *Nimrud and its Remains* (1966), an account of his principal Mesopotamian excavation. Nigel

Nicolson also edited for Collins at this time the first of three volumes of his father Harold's *Diaries and Letters* (1966), covering the years 1930–39. Bryant launched his two-volume English social history with *The Medieval Foundation* (1966). Malcolm Muggeridge, Edward Crankshaw, and Gerald Durrell joined the ranks of Collins authors, and the Harvill Press continued to publish translations of writers such as Julio Cortàzar and Mikhail Bulgakov. Harvill's interest in Russian books in particular was to continue into the 1970s, with books by Sinyavsky and Sakharov, as well as Solzhenitsyn's *The Gulag Archipelago* (1974). Fontana also flourished, with the publication in 1967 of the *Fontana English Dictionary* ('including the new terminology of the space age'), Iris Murdoch's *Sartre* (1967), and the attainment of 6 million sales of religious titles.

William Hope Collins, Billy Collins's cousin in charge of the factory, died on 21 August 1967. After his death the printing operation moved to another former Blackie factory at Westerhill; warehousing and the Glasgow publishing offices followed over the next ten years, and the Cathedral Street premises were sold to the University of Strathclyde.

Despite these changes, the company continued to flourish. The first volume of William Barclay's new translation of the New Testament appeared in 1968. Carlos Baker's life of Ernest Hemingway was followed in 1970 by a major coup for Collins, the novelist's previously unpublished *Islands in the Stream*. The year 1970 also saw the appearance of *Master and Commander*, the first of the Jack Aubrey series of novels about the navy in Napoleonic times written by Patrick O'Brian. The book was at first largely unnoticed by the book trade on either side of the Atlantic, but Collins's faith in the writer resulted in a steadily growing readership as successive books in the series were published. At the same time, Fontana Modern Masters was launched under the general editorship of Frank Kermode, with lives of Camus, Fanon, Guevara, Lévi-Strauss, and Marcuse. Herman Wouk's *The Winds of War* was a popular success for Collins in 1971—its first printing of 100,000 copies sold well. The first volume of Malcolm Muggeridge's autobiography appeared in 1972, along with biographies of Sybil Thorndike and Rose Macaulay, and novels by Peter Levi, Julian Symons, and Catherine Gaskin.

In 1974 Collins acquired the American World Publishing Company, which proved a costly disappointment. Nevertheless, sales of such important titles as *The Common Bible* ('published with the blessing of the Protestant, Catholic, and Orthodox churches'), and *The Good News Bible* (1976), demonstrated the sound footing of the company. *The Good News Bible* was one of the best-sellers of the year—it had been co-published with the bible societies, and the first printing totalled 1 million copies. The autumn list of 1976 published from St James's Place alone included twelve other religious titles, thirty fiction, fifteen Crime Club, twenty-seven non-fiction titles, and fifty Fontanas (including an original title by Noam Chomsky, *Reflections on Language*). Collins, now printing 60 million books per year, had indeed come a long way since 1819.

Sir William Alexander Roy Collins died at his home, Hayle Farm House, Horsmonden, Kent, on 21 September 1976 and was buried at Horsmonden church. He had been appointed CBE in 1966 and knighted in 1970. He had two sons, William, known as Jan (*b.* 10 June 1929), and Mark (*b.* 3 June 1935), and two daughters, Deborah (*b.* 30 May 1926) and Sarah (1933–1967). All worked for the firm for a time, Jan in Glasgow (where he remained after succeeding his father as chairman) and the others at St James's Place. Sarah built up a highly successful foreign rights department. The secret of Billy Collins's success as one of the twentieth century's greatest publishers lay in three outstanding qualities, all of which were also evident in his predecessors. His larger-than-life enthusiasm was infectious, bringing in new authors (some of whom were irresistibly tempted away from their previous publishers), flattering booksellers across the Commonwealth, harrying literary editors into reviewing his books, above all selling his books to his own sales team and making sure that their saleability was fully appreciated by every representative within reach. Almost all Collins's geese were swans. He was obsessive over detail, and he drove his colleagues and himself very hard: for many years he started the day by opening the post, he approved every book jacket, Fontana cover design, and national media advertisement. Essential additional strength came from his wife, Pierre, whose eye for good writers and successful books confirmed his taste and extended his horizons. On Friday evenings Billy and Pierre rushed down to the country (first Northamptonshire, later Kent) where weekends were vigorously occupied in farming, hunting, gardening, and above all reading manuscripts. These strengths were offset, his critics maintained, by an impatient lack of purely intellectual or cultural concern, a mischievous but transparent interest in setting senior colleagues against each other, and an occasional insensitivity to others' feelings which a privileged upbringing and a powerful ambition would account for. He could be brisk, terminating discussion with a clinching 'isn't it' which was not to be interpreted as an invitation to further argument, but he was invariably courteous, and his was a kind heart.

Jan Collins became non-executive chairman in 1979 and sold his shares in the firm to Rupert Murdoch in 1981. The firm was sold to News Corporation in January 1989.

JOHN TREVITT

Sources D. Keir, *The house of Collins* (1952) · *DNB* · personal knowledge (2004) · private information (2004) · m. reg. Scot. [William Collins] · b. reg. Scot. [Sir William Collins] · *IGI* · m. reg. Scot. [Sir William Collins and Annabella Proudfoot Glen] · m. cert. [Alexander Glen Collins and Cornelia Pattison] · b. reg. Scot [Alexander Glen Collins] · b. cert. [Ian Glen Collins] · d. reg. Scot. [William Alexander Collins] · b. cert. [William Alexander Roy Collins] · d. cert. [William Alexander Roy Collins] · m. cert. [William Alexander Collins and Grace Brander]
Archives U. Glas., Archives and Business Records Centre, William Collins, Sons & Co. Ltd, cashbooks, ledgers, minutes, records | Sheff. Arch., letters to James Montgomery [William Collins] · U. Edin., New Coll. L., letters to Thomas Chalmers [William Collins]
Likenesses portrait (Sir William Collins), repro. in Keir, *The house of Collins* [see illus.]

Wealth at death £5661 4*s.* 11*d.*—William Collins: recording, 9 Feb 1854, NA Scot., SC 8/35/7 pp. 118–25

Collins, An (*fl.* 1653), poet, is known only as the author of *Divine Songs and Meditacions* (1653), the sole source of information about her. This volume is in part a spiritual autobiography, but specific details about her life are either lacking, only briefly or cryptically disclosed, or woven into a generic pattern that makes it difficult to separate person from persona.

Collins's poems describe afflictions in conventional though often moving fashion, as Job-like storms of anguish, and winters preceding spring-like recoveries, but there are also more personal references. She alludes to her external unattractiveness, bodily imperfections, and physical incapacity in metaphors that suggest that she may have been disfigured by an illness such as smallpox and immobilized by the loss or paralysis of a limb, perpetually housebound as a result of some early 'weakness'. That she was able to turn retirement into creative uses by practising her intellectual, spiritual, and poetic powers in 'morning exercise' apparently did not erase her lifelong sense of physical vulnerability, disability, and shame, recurrent themes in her lyrics.

Collins gives no information about her family: she offers her poems to 'some neare Kindred' (Collins, ed. Gottlieb), but her strongest ties are to a community of saints constituted by shared religious beliefs rather than blood relations. She never mentions a husband or intimate companion, roles abrogated by God, the one truly essential 'Sweet presence' in her life, who instigates and supports her 'calling' to poetry and accepts her poems as 'the offspring of my mind'.

Frequent references throughout Collins's volume to flowers, rocks, and caves, and 'the beauty of the Land' suggest a country rather than city life, but one filled with tension and strife. The typical struggle between the godly and the ungodly appears in her portraits of a community filled with dissension and slander, often aimed at her, and a countryside ravaged by civil war. Presumably with the parliamentarians in mind, Collins identifies those who ruin the land by forced oaths, confiscations, and innovations in religion and government as dangerous enemies of truth and liberty, but she also criticizes the kind of libertinism often associated with the court, comments favourably on the aims of the 'Good Old Cause', and supports what is often thought of as the radical challenge of continuing to reform the Reformation.

Collins's religious beliefs are difficult to pin down exactly. One of the poems in the volume, 'The Discourse', is a relatively unexceptional primer of traditional protestantism, and Collins's profound sense of sin has led some critics to call her a Calvinist, but her lack of emphasis on election and predestination and bracing descriptions of the human inclination to goodness make this doubtful. And although she is occasionally critical of 'Novelties' in religion, she displays affinities with some of the sects of the time that were attuned to a personal inner light, apocalyptic, aware of being shunned by respectable secular society, and ever ready to combat publicly the enemies of the godly.

Collins gives voice to the pains of her triple affliction—as a physically disabled person, one of the godly living 'where profanenesse did abound', and a woman traditionally constrained to silence and a limited range of activities—but challenges these pains and constraints in metrically inventive songs and meditations that are 'memorandums' of praise to God and powerful assertions of her own role in typological and contemporary history.

SIDNEY GOTTLIEB

Sources A. Collins, *Divine songs and meditacions*, ed. S. Gottlieb (1996) · S. Gottlieb, 'An Collins and the experience of defeat', *Representing women in Renaissance England*, ed. C. J. Summers and T. Pebworth (1997), 216–26 · A. Collins, *Divine songs and meditacions* (1653); facs. edn, ed. S. N. Stewart (1961) · E. Graham, H. Hinds, E. Hobby, and H. Wilcox, eds., *Her own life: autobiographical writings by seventeenth-century Englishwomen* (1989), 54–70 · E. Hobby, *Virtue of necessity: English women's writing, 1649–1688* (1988), 59–62 · G. Greer and others, eds., *Kissing the rod: an anthology of seventeenth-century women's verse* (1988), 148–54 · E. R. Cunnar, 'An Collins', *Seventeenth-century British nondramatic poets: third series*, ed. M. Thomas Hester, DLitB, 131 (1993), 49–53

Collins, Anthony (1676–1729), philosopher and freethinker, was born on 21 June 1676 at Isleworth, Middlesex, the eldest child of Henry Collins (1646/7–1705), lawyer, and Mary Dineley. He was educated at Eton College and then at King's College, Cambridge, from 1693 to 1696, but did not take a degree. At King's his tutor was Francis Hare, the future bishop of St Asaph and of Chichester. It was from Hare, Thomas Woolston wryly observed, that Collins 'imbibed his Notable notions about Religion and Liberty' (T. Woolston, *Fourth Discourse on the Miracles of our Saviour*, 1727, v). He was admitted to the Middle Temple on 24 November 1694, although a career in law, in the footsteps of his father and grandfather, did not attract him. On 8 July 1698 he married Martha Child (*bap.* 1676, *d.* 1703), a daughter of the prominent banker, lord mayor of London, and MP Sir Francis *Child (1641/2–1713) and his wife, Elizabeth Wheeler (1651/2–1720). Their marriage was governed by a settlement stipulating that the extensive properties accumulated by Collins's father and grandfather in Middlesex and Essex were to be held in trust. The couple had four children, two sons and two daughters; the elder son died in infancy, and the birth of the second daughter occasioned the death of her mother, in 1703.

Early on Collins came to know and be influenced by two other well-known freethinkers, John Toland and Matthew Tindal. Collins financially assisted Toland, who dedicated two books to him: *The Fables of Aesop* (1704) and *Adeisidaemon, sive, Titus Livius a superstitione vindicatus* (1709). Henry Dodwell, Thomas Hearne, and Thomas Burnet, among others, claimed that Collins helped Tindal to write a number of other works, especially *The Rights of the Christian Church*. Collins's intense friendship with John Locke, whom he came to know in 1703, was seminal to his intellectual and personal development. Locke treated him like a son and saw in him an intellectual successor, nurturing his philosophical talents. Collins later arranged for

Locke's letters to him to be published, together with other scarce materials and unpublished manuscripts shown to him by Locke, in *A Collection of Several Pieces of Mr John Locke* (1720), edited by his friend Pierre Des Maizeaux. The most significant compliment that Locke bestowed on him, in a letter of 29 October 1703, was that Collins's love of truth for its own sake was as great as that of anyone he had known. The theme of the love of truth, especially in religion, pervades Collins's writings.

Collins made his début as an author with *A Letter to the Learned Mr Henry Dodwell*, prompted by the controversy that the nonjuring Dodwell aroused with his *An epistolary discourse, proving, from the scriptures and the first fathers, that the soul is a principle naturally mortal* (1706). Newspaper advertisements show that it appeared in print in November 1706, well before the work commonly thought to have been Collins's first, *An Essay Concerning the Use of Reason in Propositions*, which was published in March 1707. Like all his writings it appeared anonymously. Dodwell had notoriously argued that though the soul was naturally mortal God had immortalized it with the Christian revelation to save the blessed or punish the wicked. In a reply to Dodwell, Samuel Clarke argued that the soul was naturally immortal by proving that it was immaterial. Furthermore Clarke maintained that consciousness could not be attributed to a material subject and accused Dodwell of thoughtlessly publishing views that encouraged sceptics in their attempts to undermine religion. Collins addressed his letter to Dodwell as a defence of his right to publish his opinions even if, as Collins made clear, he disagreed with most of them. Collins argued that Clarke's argument for the soul's immateriality was misguided because, like Locke, he held it to be neither in the power of unaided human reason to prove such a conclusion nor necessary for the defence of religion. Unlike Locke, however, Collins maintained that experience suggested a material subject of consciousness. In a series of exchanges with Clarke over the next two years Collins argued that Clarke had been mistaken to infer that if consciousness belonged to a material and divisible subject it would necessarily belong to all parts, which would be an absurd conclusion. He also defended the idea that human liberty, defined as the power of acting as one wills or pleases, is compatible with necessity. He developed this view in *A Philosophical Enquiry Concerning Human Liberty* (1717) and insisted that the endemic obscurity of such philosophical debates could be ended only by using clear and distinct ideas. His arguments were rebutted by Clarke, and their exchange was overshadowed in significance only by Clarke's correspondence with Leibniz. His philosophical duel with Clarke was regarded by the French philosopher Jacques-André Naigeon as having established Collins's place in eighteenth-century thought.

In *An Essay Concerning the Use of Reason in Propositions* (1707) Collins attacked the clergy for insisting that the mysteries of religion, such as the Trinity, are not only 'above reason' but also are required to be believed as a condition of Christian faith. Like Toland in *Christianity not Mysterious* (1696), he claimed that we cannot assent to what we do not understand; the proper response is suspension of belief. In *Priestcraft in Perfection* (1710) and *An Historical and Critical Essay, on the Thirty-Nine Articles of the Church of England* (1724) he challenged the power of the bishops to settle controversies of faith and their claim to possess a divinely sanctioned authority in religion akin to the divine right of kings. Such claims struck him as expressions of 'priestcraft' and assaults on the rights of individual reason. In *A Vindication of the Divine Attributes* (1710) he examined the views of the Huguenot philosopher Pierre Bayle on the intractable problem of evil for a Christian monotheistic theology and criticized Archbishop William King's attempt to evade this difficulty by claiming that God's attributes only bear an analogy to their human counterparts. Collins showed that King's solution removed the possibility of human beings emulating divine attributes and came dangerously close to an atheist's view. His handling of the controversy displayed his talent for sceptical modes of argument, asserting little in his own right while showing how proposed solutions to theological difficulties only exacerbated the problem that gave rise to them.

At the core of Collins's philosophy is his defence of 'freethinking'. He first used the term in *A Discourse of Free-Thinking* (1713), where he defined it as the impartial use of the understanding to determine the meaning of propositions, and to judge their truth or falsity, their probability or improbability on the strength or weakness of available evidence. He argued that freethinking, so defined, is a universal right and in religion a duty. In defending the latter he catalogued how the clergy differed on nearly every issue—so much so that some readers saw his real purpose as being to show that all these differing opinions were false. There were dozens of replies in Britain and on the continent, where a French translation soon appeared, including responses from Jonathan Swift, George Berkeley, Benjamin Hoadly, Richard Bentley, and Francis Hare. The theme common to the attacks was that freethinking was nothing more than a disguise for a covert, self-serving, sceptical, atheistic, and libertine agenda. The work was publicly burnt by the common hangman, and the controversy was said to have occasioned the second of two journeys that Collins made to the Netherlands, the first having occurred in 1710.

About 1716 Collins moved from London to rural Essex, where he assumed the responsibilities of a country gentleman. He served as JP, and as county treasurer restored the county's chaotic finances to good order. Whether in London or the country he was praised by those who knew him for his upright moral character, and as such his life was a standing reproof that freethinking was a licence for moral libertinism. In 1720 he collaborated with John Trenchard, a friend of his, and Thomas Gordon on a famous paper, the *Independent Whig*, in which they attacked clerical claims to authority and accused the high-church clergy of practical atheism. Among the closest of his friends who frequently visited him was Pierre Des Maizeaux, whose reviews of Collins's works drew them to the attention of continental readers. One of the many attractions of Collins's house to

Des Maizeaux was its splendid library. When it was auctioned after his death there were more than 7000 lots, including complete runs of continental periodicals and pamphlets. Collins boasted to Dodwell that his collection of works by Anglican divines could rival anyone's. He owned rare manuscripts of biblical criticism by Spanish Jews and a copy of the scandalously irreligious work *La vie et l'esprit de Spinosa*, better known as the *Treatise of the Three Imposters*. Collins remained a widower until the premature death of his son Anthony, in 1723, after which he married Elizabeth Wrottesley (*d.* 1737), fourth daughter of Sir Walter Wrottesley, third baronet (1659–1712), and his first wife, Eleanor Archer (*d.* 1694), in 1724. She was the sister of Hugh Wrottesley (*d.* 1725), a lawyer at Lincoln's Inn and a book collector, to whom Des Maizeaux dedicated *A Collection of Several Pieces of Mr John Locke*.

The period from 1723 until Collins's early death from the stone, from which he suffered throughout this time, was highly productive. Starting with *A Discourse of the Grounds and Reasons of the Christian Religion* (1724), he subjected the argument from prophecy, widely relied on to demonstrate the truth of Christianity, to painstaking scrutiny. The truth of Christianity would be demonstrated, he argued, only if Jesus Christ could be shown to be the Messiah prophesied by the Old Testament. But, he claimed, the Old Testament Messiah was a temporal not a spiritual figure; furthermore the Old Testament prophecies were not uniquely and literally fulfilled in Jesus. Although William Whiston had explained this mismatch between the Old and New Testaments by arguing that scriptural texts had been corrupted with the object of undermining Christianity, Collins masterfully set the rival accounts against each other. Following the Dutch scholar Grotius, he accepted that even the most defensible text supported only typical fulfilment of the prophecies by Jesus, and then only by extended analogy. Thus, working from premises granted by others in the classic sceptical manner, Collins accepted both that the text was suspect and that its most defensible interpretation fell short of the proof required.

Collins's fondness for such modes of argument makes it difficult to place him. He himself repeatedly claimed to be nothing more than a freethinker who was prepared to follow reason wherever it took him and ready to expose the weakness of conventional arguments. Some, like Voltaire, viewed him as a deist and a scourge of Christianity, whereas others, such as Berkeley, saw him rather as an atheist. Others still, like Clarke, maintained that in practice all these positions reduced to the same. The attacks on Collins's *Discourse of Free-Thinking* were skirmishes compared with the outpouring occasioned by his *Discourse of the Grounds and Reasons* and his subsequent works. Some such as Edward Chandler, bishop of Lichfield, and John Rogers, sometime chaplain to George II, urged the state to take action against him for questioning widely held and well-established views whose maintenance, they argued, was crucial to good order. In his last works Collins responded to his critics by arguing that it was in the interests of both the state and society to extend, not restrict, the rights of free expression and of religious toleration in worship as well as belief. These rights were necessary to give effect to the right of free examination and to promote rather than undermine the peace and well-being of communities. For him they were the real legacy of the protestant Reformation.

Collins died on 13 December 1729 at Cavendish Square, London, and was buried in the new burial-ground belonging to St George's, Hanover Square. He left his library to his widow, who sold it at auction, and his manuscripts to Des Maizeaux. Des Maizeaux, upset that Collins left him only £50, sold the manuscripts to Elizabeth Collins, an action that he quickly regretted but was powerless to undo. She took pains to ensure that they would not see the light of day. Collins is known to have drafted defences of his position on the liberty and necessity of human action, and referred in his published works to other manuscripts on subjects such as ecclesiastical history and miracles, but at the beginning of the twenty-first century all remained undiscovered. J. DYBIKOWSKI

Sources *The correspondence of John Locke*, ed. E. S. de Beer, 8 vols. (1976–89), vols. 7–8 • J. O'Higgins, *Anthony Collins: the man and his works* (1970) • D. Berman, 'Anthony Collins' essays in the *Independent Whig*', *Journal of the History of Philosophy*, 13 (1975), 463–9 • P. Russell, 'Hume's *Treatise* and the Clarke–Collins controversy', *Hume Studies*, 21 (1995), 95–115 • J. Dybikowski, 'Anthony Collins' defense of free-thinking', *Scepticisme, clandestinité et libres pensées* (2002), 299–326 • J. H. Broome, 'Une collaboration: Anthony Collins et Desmaizeaux', *Revue de Littérature Comparée*, 30 (1956), 161–79 • J. M. Robertson, *The dynamics of religion*, 2nd edn (1926) • J. I. Israel, *Radical enlightenment* (2001) • J.-A. Naigeon, *Encyclopédie méthodique: philosophie ancienne et moderne*, 3 vols. (1789–93) • N. L. Torrey, *Voltaire and the English deists* (1930) • T. Birch, 'Anthony Collins', in P. Bayle and others, *A general dictionary historical and critical*, 10 vols. (1734–41), vol. 4, pp. 395–405 • S. Lalor, 'Matthew Tindal', *The dictionary of eighteenth-century British philosophers*, ed. J. Yolton, J. V. Price, and J. Stevens, 2 vols. (1999), vol. 2, pp. 876–80 • *DNB* • G. Wrottesley, 'A history of the family of Wrottesley of Wrottesley, co. Stafford', *Collections for a history of Staffordshire*, William Salt Archaeological Society, new ser., 6/2 (1903), 342 • *Bibliothèque raisonnée*, 4 (1730), 34–5 • parish register, Isleworth, All Saints', 22 June 1676 [baptism] • J. L. Chester and J. Foster, eds., *London marriage licences, 1521–1869* (1887) • parish register, Heston, St Leonard's, 24 Feb 1705 [burial: H. Collins] • A. Collins, *A letter to the Rev. Dr. Rogers* (1727), 4 • register, King's Cam. • C. Freret, *Fulham old and new* (1900), vol. 2, p. 94 • will, PRO, PROB 11/685 • A. Collins, letters, BL, Add. MS 4282 • register and records, Lincoln's Inn, London • *British Journal* (20 Dec 1729)
Archives BL, Des Maizeaux papers, Add. MS 4282 • Bodl. Oxf., Locke MSS, St Edmund Hall MSS • King's Cam., Keynes MSS • University of Kansas, Lawrence, Kenneth Spencer Research Library, Simpson papers • University of Leiden, Leiden, Marchand MSS
Likenesses oils, Pascotts Farm, Haywards Heath, West Sussex; repro. in O'Higgins, *Anthony Collins*
Wealth at death approx. £60,000

Collins, Arthur (1681/2–1760), genealogist, was the son of William Collins, a gentleman usher to Charles II's consort, Queen Catherine of Braganza, and his wife, Elizabeth Blyth, daughter of Thomas Blyth. It seems likely that the family was Roman Catholic and that record of birth and marriage would have been found among the records of the Portuguese embassy chapel, which have not survived. Collins is said to have been given a liberal education and to have dissipated a large fortune in his youth. Certainly, he later spent much on his publishing ventures. He is first noticed as a bookseller at 'the Black Boy, opposite St Dunstan's Church in Fleet Street', in partnership with Abel Roper, a name which appears among those of the publishers of Dugdale's *Baronage* issued in 1675–6.

From most written letters of his forty-seven years in publishing peerages, Collins appears to have lived in Enfield and, towards the end of his life, in Holloway. He married in 1708, though the identity of his wife is unknown. Of several children, one son was a lieutenant in the Royal Navy who served in two campaigns in the Netherlands, at the battles of Fontenoy, Falkirk, and Culloden, and died in 1756. Another was Major-General Arthur Tooker Collins, whose name may give a clue to the identity of his mother.

In 1709 the first edition of Collins's *The peerage of England, or, An historical and genealogical account of the present nobility ... collected as well from our best historians, publick records, and other sufficient authorities, as from the personal information of most of the nobility*, was published anonymously, although it was described on the title-page as 'printed ... for Abel Roper and Arthur Collins'. An octavo volume of only 470 pages, it supplied a want by its meagre accounts of noble families and of peerages conferred after the publication of Dugdale's *Baronage*. In the preface to the larger second edition, again printed for A. Collins (2 vols. and supplement, 1712–16), Collins spoke of the extraordinary success of the first. In the text of the 1712 edition Collins inserted rather crude woodcuts of armorial bearings, 'as they may be serviceable to instruct young gentlemen in the terms of Heraldry', which would not be 'a sufficient excuse for their not being done in a more commendable manner, were it not known to be an almost impracticable work of printing them with these sheets to any manner of perfection' (A. Collins, *The Peerage of England*, 2nd edn, 1, pt 1, 1712, preface).

In 1716, in expectation of a situation in the custom house, Collins gave up his business in Fleet Street, but his *Baronetage of England, being an Historical Account of Baronets from their First Introduction* appeared in 1720 with a dedication to John Anstis, Garter king of arms. Collins's preface stressed the care he had taken with documentation and described great 'discouragements' in compiling the work caused by the failure of many families to let him see their pedigrees. The bibliographer Thomas Moule described the work as being 'as free of error as any of his successors in this laborious pursuit' (Moule, 308). In March 1723 Collins wrote to Sir Robert Walpole stating his continued poverty and expectations of some provision from the government; he explained that he did not intend to publish any more editions of the *Baronetage* but was instead preparing an enlarged peerage. A single-volume instalment was issued in 1727 as *The English baronage, or, An historical account of the lives and most memorable actions of our nobility, with their descent, marriages, and issue*. Dedicated with a flattering note on Sir Robert Walpole and an account of his family in the preliminary address to the reader, Collins commemorated the elevation to the peerage of Sir Robert's eldest son. He stated that 'with much labour, and at no small expense' he had made large collections of material for his *Baronage* and that he intended to publish the peerage in order of precedence. He admitted to having a manuscript of Dugdale's work with many additions by Gregory King, Lancaster herald, to which he had added his own researched notes.

Greatly benefiting from King's work, Collins published his *Proceedings, precedents and arguments, on claims and controversies concerning the baronies by writ and other honours* in 1734, dedicated to Spencer Compton, earl of Wilmington. In 1735 the first edition to be entitled Collins's *Peerage* appeared in three volumes, with engravings of the arms, crests, and supporters of the then existing peers. In a second edition of 1741 he added copious references to his authorities and dedicated the four volumes to the duke of Rutland, the earl of Halifax, and Walpole, which brought him some of the financial support he required. Thomas Wotton edited Collins's work for another edition, published as *The English Baronetage* (5 vols., 1741) but more accurately known as *Wotton's Baronetage*, in which the volume on marquesses and earls was dedicated to another benefactor, the earl of Shaftesbury. Acknowledging the assistance of Collins, Wotton admitted his obligations to the works of Peter Le Neve, which he had purchased in 1731.

In the preface to his two-volume supplement (1750) to the 1741 edition of the *Peerage* Collins complained that he had spent his fortune in researches and would be unable to publish the results without help. Pathetically, he contrasted the neglect of himself with the favour which had been shown to Dugdale and Ashmole. In a plaintive letter to the duke of Newcastle, dated 3 February 1752, he wrote that he was engaged on a new edition of the *Peerage* but did not have the funds to pay for a transcriber. At the same time he acknowledged kindness from Lord Granville. In a subsequent letter to the duke of Newcastle he blamed his poverty on the cost of printing his account of Newcastle's mother's family, the Holles family, and asked for a warranty for some money. Ultimately he received a pension of £400 a year from the king, which enabled him to complete the third of the enlarged editions of his *Peerage* (1756), dedicated to the king, the earls of Shaftesbury, Holdernesse, and Northumberland, and the marquess of Abergavenny. This was the last to be overseen by Collins himself. His confidence had been so enhanced that he could proudly write,

> I am not conscious of delivering the least untruth; my accounts of these, and other families I have published, being warranted by Records and Informations I cannot distrust … and my readers may be appraised by the authorities I have cited, and which prove the difficulties of the undertaking, and the expense that attends the performance.   (A. Collins, *The Peerage of England*, 3rd edn, 1756, preface)

He acknowledged the assistance of antiquaries such as Charles Townley, Clarenceux king of arms.

Three posthumous editions of Collins's *Peerage* were published: the fifth edition was edited by the engraver Barak Longmate, and brought the work up to date, and the final edition (1812), edited by Sir Egerton Brydges, became the standard work before the appearance of G. E. Cockayne's *Complete Peerage*. In his preface Brydges described the exceptional and indefatigable industry of Collins, and the general accuracy, which rivalled Dugdale, whose method Collins had, by and large, followed.

Collins exhibited modesty in describing himself as a printer or a bookseller. He did not presume to call himself an author for some ten years. His general disinterestedness must be set against what may often seem to be adulation of birth and rank. In his own words he stated that his only inducement to persevere was 'an innate desire to preserve the memory of famous men' (A. Collins, *Historical Collections of the Noble Families of Cavendish, Holles, Vere, and Harley, and Ogle*, 1752, preface). He was, none the less, self-assured as a scholarly researcher. Carlyle, in his rectorial address to the students of Edinburgh University, acknowledged that he 'got a great deal of help out of poor Collins', when writing his life of Oliver Cromwell, and he pronounced Collins's *Peerage* to be 'a very poor peerage as a work of genius, but an excellent book for diligence and fidelity' (*DNB*). In a letter of 9 February 1752 to the duke of Newcastle, Collins says: 'I have left, in manuscript, an account of my family, my life, and the cruel usage I have undeservedly undergone' (Nichols, *Lit. anecdotes*, 8.392), but no trace of its survival or of other papers has been discovered. He had expended not only a lifetime of labour but all that he possessed, as he observed with customary candour and innocence of courtly customs in his last preface:

> I could cite instances of other authors, that have been preferred, though it has been my hard fate to be soliciting the chief of power (his Majesty and the royal family excepted) for several years without effect, and have not been wanting in setting forth, by printed case, my pretensions to preferment, a Place having been resigned to me by a relation, and given from me to proceed on the work I have been engaged in, with a promise of being better provided for.   (A. Collins, *The Peerage of England*, 3rd edn, 1756, preface)

Collins was an assiduous researcher and a prolific compiler and editor. To several smaller and unpublished works, he added an ephemeral package of papers on peerage, families, and other matters published between 1732 and 1756. These works, which would challenge scholars of any era, included *The Life of William Cecil, Lord Burleigh* (1732), *The Life and Glorious Actions of Edward, Prince of Wales, Commonly called the Black Prince* (1740), which, with *The History of John of Gaunt* (1740), was written for the uncompleted *English Baronage* of 1727. Similarly, he published genealogical and historical accounts of the Harley, Sackville, Percy, Windsor, and Carteret families, and made extensive use of the papers owned by the Sydney family to publish *Letters and Memorials of State* from the reign of Queen Mary through to that of Charles II. He published a volume of papers belonging to the Cavendish, Holles, Vere, Harley, and Ogle families, with the financial help of the countess of Oxford.

Collins died on 16 March 1760 in Holloway, aged seventy-eight, and was buried in Battersea church. It is known that he was survived by his son Major-General Arthur Tooker

Collins, author of *The Account of the English Settlement in New South Wales*, who died on 4 January 1793, leaving a son, David Collins. David Collins was judge-advocate in New South Wales and died there on 24 March 1810.

CECIL R. HUMPHERY-SMITH

Sources *GM*, 1st ser., 53 (1783), 414 · *GM*, 1st ser., 69 (1799), 282, 474 · *DNB* · T. Moule, *Bibliotheca heraldica Magnae Britanniae* (privately printed, London, 1822) · Burke, *Peerage* · [J. Hunter], ed., *Letters of eminent men, addressed to Ralph Thoresby*, 2 vols. (1832) · G. W. Marshall, *The genealogist's guide* (1903) · J. B. Whitmore, *A genealogical guide* (1953) · Society of Genealogists, Collins MSS · *IGI* · Nichols, *Lit. anecdotes*, 8.392 · D. Lysons, *Supplement to the first edition of 'The environs of London'* (1811), 4

Archives BL, historical notes and papers, incl. genealogical account of the earls of Essex, Add. MSS 4127, 4188, 20706, 40730 · Bodl. Oxf., genealogical and heraldic papers | BL, letters to the duke of Newcastle, Add. MSS 32689–33055, *passim* · CKS, letters to William Perry · Essex RO, letters to William Holman · Northumbd RO, corresp. with Sir William Swinburne and Edward Swinburne

Collins, Benjamin (*bap.* 1715, *d.* 1785), newspaper proprietor and publisher, was baptized in the parish church at Faringdon, Berkshire, on 14 October 1715, the eighth of nine children of William Collins (1682–1729), a Faringdon tallow chandler, and his wife, Margaret Pierce (*d.* 1719) of Idstone in the nearby parish of Ashbury. On 1 June 1743 Benjamin married Edith Good (*d.* 1751) of Shaftesbury. They had two surviving children, William (1745–1810) and Elizabeth (*b.* 1749). After Edith's death he married Mary Cooper (1725?–1808); they had four children—Jane (1753–1823), Sarah (1754–1847), Benjamin Charles (1758–1808), and Charlotte (*b.* 1762). Collins's sons, who succeeded to his various businesses, died without issue; his daughter Sarah married Peter Bellinger Brodie (1742–1804) and one of their sons, Sir Benjamin Collins *Brodie (1783–1862), became Queen Victoria's sergeant-surgeon; Collins's daughter Jane married George Leonard *Staunton (1737–1801), the diplomat.

Benjamin Collins's career began early, when he assisted his elder brother William (1705–1740?), to whom he was probably apprenticed, in establishing Salisbury's second newspaper, the *Salisbury Journal*. Their first attempt in 1729 failed after about one year, but the second attempt in 1736 was successful; indeed the *Salisbury Journal* was still in existence more than 250 years later. Periodicals remained Collins's speciality. He managed the *Journal* single-handedly after his brother left the business in 1740, and retained his interest in the paper for the rest of his life. When he died he was able to bequeath the whole copyright to his favourite son, Benjamin Charles. Samuel Johnson's favourite paper, the *London Chronicle* (established 1757), was, Collins claimed, his 'own scheme at the setting out' (Welsh, 19). His pride in these two achievements is evident in his portrait, for Collins had both the *Chronicle* and the *Salisbury Journal* painted into the background. Along with a large partnership, in 1760 he established another London paper, the daily *Publick Ledger*, 'to serve the Purposes of Trade and Commerce in a better Manner than the other Daily Newspapers then in being' (articles of agreement, PRO). Collins was able to add a rival country paper to his repertory in 1778, when the bankruptcy of its

Benjamin Collins (*bap.* 1715, *d.* 1785), attrib. Thomas Burgess, *c.*1775

founder, James Linden (*d.* 1806), offered Collins the opportunity secretly to purchase the controlling interest in the *Hampshire Chronicle* (established 1772). Buying up the competition was an effective way of dealing with it, and is not untypical of the aggressive manner in which Collins conducted business. He owned shares in other important periodicals too: a one-sixteenth share in *The Rambler* (purchased for £22 2s. 6d. from William Strahan (1715–1785) in 1757), a one-twelfth share in the *Gentleman's Magazine* (purchased for £333 6s. 8d. in 1755), and a one-quarter share of Ralph Griffiths's *Monthly Review* (£755 12s. 6d. in 1761).

Periodicals provided Collins with a steady income, but more important, they provided the introduction to the London book-trade networks that established his success as a publisher. One of Collins's most important partnerships was with John Newbery (1713–1767), with whom he shared a shrewd sense of the book market. They published a number of children's books, including *A Set of Fifty* [later fifty-six] *Squares* (1743), and Collins's own *Royal Battledore* (*c.*1746), *Royal Primer* (1751), and *Pretty Book for Children* (1751), all of them extraordinarily successful: the *Squares* went through many editions, the *Battledore* is recorded as selling nearly 100,000 copies between 1771 and 1780, and the *Primer* about 20,000 copies in a single year. Benjamin Collins joined with the London booksellers to publish numerous other titles, most notably Samuel Richardson's *Pamela*, George Tobias Smollett's *Humphry Clinker*, and Oliver Goldsmith's *Vicar of Wakefield*. Although Collins seldom left Salisbury, his good economic and business sense ensured that he was accepted—to an unusual degree for a provincial bookseller—into the inner circles of the London trade. This may be demonstrated in an unresolved legal case of 1758, when Collins colluded with Jacob Tonson (d. 1767) and others in an attempt to settle the contentious issue of copyright. Collins, playing the part of defendant, was charged with illegally selling Scottish-printed copies of *The Spectator*. He was supposed to lose the suit and so confirm the London book trade's monopoly in certain lucrative copyrights, but the case was referred when the court realized that Collins, as much as his London colleagues, stood to gain from that decision.

Like many of his associates, Collins was always ready to supply his customers with medicines, along with the usual books and periodicals. He went beyond that to market his own invention, the Cordial Cephalic Snuff, a product successful enough that he found it useful to protect it by letters patent in 1773, by which time it had even appeared on stage, in the second act of *The Clandestine Marriage* (1766) by David Garrick and George Colman.

As early as the 1750s Collins was lending large sums of money; later, as his newspaper, book, and medical-supplies business generated a more reliable and larger income, he was able to turn more of his attention to banking. Although he maintained many of his interests in the book and newspaper trade, in the 1770s he began to style himself Benjamin Collins, esquire, banker of Salisbury. He died at Salisbury on 16 February 1785, leaving a large estate. He also left a number of enemies who were prepared to spend years fighting for shares in it. His younger son, Benjamin Charles Collins, with the help of a good lawyer, was able to preserve most of the estate, and Benjamin Collins's will was proved in 1810. He was buried at St Edmund's, Salisbury, on 23 February 1785, and was survived by his second wife.   C. Y. FERDINAND

Sources C. Y. Ferdinand, *Benjamin Collins and the provincial newspaper trade in the eighteenth century* (1997) · C. Welsh, 'Extracts from the account books of Benjamin Collins', *A bookseller of the last century: being some account of the life of John Newbery* (1885), appx 7 · parish register, Faringdon, Berks. RO, D/P53/1/2 · parish register, St Thomas, Salisbury, Wilts. & Swindon RO, 1900/7 · parish register, Holy Trinity, Shaftesbury, Dorset RO · Articles of agreement, *Collins* v. *Faden*(chancery suit), 3 Jan 1760, PRO, CH12/104/32 · will, proved, 1810, PRO, PROB 11/1127/120 · *Considerations of the nature and origin of literary property* (1767) · BL, Hardwicke MSS, Add. MS 36201, fol. 53 · B. Woodcroft, ed., *Alphabetical index of patentees of inventions from March 2, 1617 … to October 1, 1852* (1854) · *Salisbury Journal* (21 Feb 1785) · parish registers, St Edmunds, 1901–4, Wilts. & Swindon RO

Likenesses attrib. T. Burgess, portrait, c.1775, Salisbury Journal Office, Salisbury [*see illus.*]

Wealth at death under £85,000–£100,000: will, 1810, PRO, PROB 11/1127/120

Collins, Cecil James Henry (1908–1989), painter, was born in Plymouth on 23 March 1908, the only child of Henry Collins, an engineer in a Plymouth laundry, and his wife, Mary Bowie. He won scholarships to the Plymouth School of Art (1924–7) and the Royal College of Art (RCA) (1927–31), where he was a favourite pupil of William Rothenstein. At the RCA he met a fellow student, Elisabeth Ward Ramsden [*see below*], whom he married on 3 April 1931. There were no children of the marriage: according to

Elisabeth Collins, 'I could never have had children; Cecil was a child' (*The Independent*, 22 Feb 2000).

The chief contemporary artistic influences on Collins at this time were Picasso and Klee; other strong influences were Byzantine art, the music of Igor Stravinsky's classical period, and contemporary scientific illustrations, both of cell biology and of astronomy. His early love of Shelley and Shakespeare was now augmented by his studies of Coleridge and Milton. When he and his wife went to live in a lonely cottage near Speen, Buckinghamshire, these influences, together with readings in the English mystics and the silence of the place, inspired him to do his first visionary paintings, which were successfully shown at his first London exhibition, at the Bloomsbury Gallery in 1935. Herbert Read, much impressed, included his work in the London International Surrealist Exhibition in 1936. Collins's association with the surrealists was short-lived, for he was accused of religious sympathies and excluded from the movement.

In the late 1930s Collins and his wife went to live near Dartington Hall, Devon, where the American artist Mark Tobey was teaching. Tobey and Bernard Leach aroused his interest in Eastern thought and art. There he painted several great works, such as *The Voice*, *The Quest*, and the double portrait *The Artist and his Wife* (1939; Tate collection). The artistic and intellectual stimuli at Dartington, together with the threat of war, inspired Collins to paint his most famous series of works, based on the image of the Fool, which he began in late 1939. To him the Fool signified 'purity of consciousness', and he gave to his many depictions of the image qualities that were threatened by the Second World War: charm, fun, compassion, and insight. Rejected for war service at a time when the Dartington community was depleted by the internment of many of its teachers, who had taken refuge there from Germany, Collins was asked to teach, and it was then that he discovered his great gifts as a teacher.

Collins's exhibition at the Lefevre Gallery in 1944, even though cut short by a flying bomb, was an outstanding success. He and his wife had left Dartington by this time and lived variously in London, Yorkshire, Oxford, and Cambridge. In this period Collins produced his 'paradisal drawings' and experimented with print making. He also published in 1947 his essay *The Vision of the Fool*, a work that expresses his feelings about the role of the artist (the Fool) in the modern world of war and industrialization. This time of success was to be followed by a long period when some critics turned against him and others neglected him. He took up teaching again, at the Central School of Arts and Crafts from 1951 onwards, and leaned towards the traditional images of Christianity. He found a new freedom in painting large works, based on the principle of what he called the 'matrix': he would let the image come to him out of a preliminary working with his paints in a seemingly wild and chaotic manner. Thus he independently discovered something of what the American abstract expressionists had been doing for years. These new works were shown in a major retrospective of his work at the Whitechapel Gallery in 1959. The matrix period led him to explore in greater depth the three main images of his work: the Fool, the Lady or Anima, and the Angel. The matrix period was followed by a return to a calmer, more classical, style in which he continued to express the moods of the spiritual worlds these images conveyed to him. The Fool, the Lady, and the Angel all have access to the world of the Great Happiness, which is the true source of creativity. In his portrayals of the Lady, Collins gave new expression to the ancient tradition of Wisdom or Sapientia as a beautiful woman, and in his angels he showed creatures who are constantly and mysteriously always present and ready to give guidance.

When in 1975 the Central School of Art tried to end Collins's teaching contract, his students arose in rebellion on his behalf. His contract was extended for a year, but the battle had to be fought again with each new generation of students marching and demonstrating, and with correspondence in national newspapers supporting his cause. The conflict, which arose from objections to the originality of his teaching methods and the metaphysical ideas on which they were founded, often debilitated him and distracted him from painting. Nevertheless he received support from other quarters, notably from his association with the Anthony d'Offay Gallery from 1976 onwards, an Arts Council film of his work in 1978, and a Tate Gallery exhibition of his prints in 1981, the year in which his poems *In the Solitude of this Land* and a reprint of *The Vision of the Fool* were published. These were followed by two full-length television documentaries in 1984 and 1988.

In early manhood and into middle age Collins wore a beard. In later years the curvature of his spine, brought about by deprivations in his early life, became very pronounced, though it never affected his co-ordination. He had great physical calm, with long, fine, thin fingers with which he would seemingly shape his sentences in front of him as he spoke. He was very nervous of catching colds and would often be seen in the hottest weather wearing a tweed suit, a thick tweed greatcoat, and a hat. His eyes were expressive, witty, and sharply observant.

Collins was present at the opening of the retrospective exhibition of his work at the Tate Gallery in May 1989 and died shortly afterwards in the London Clinic on 4 June 1989. He was buried in Highgate cemetery. He had been appointed MBE in 1979 and elected RA in 1988. A man of deep metaphysical interests, and with a scholar's analytical mind, he was regarded by some as Britain's greatest visionary artist since William Blake.

Collins's wife, **Elisabeth Ward Collins** [*née* Ramsden] (1904–2000), painter and sculptor, was born on 31 October 1904 in Halifax, Yorkshire, the eldest child of Clifford Ramsden, editor and proprietor of the *Halifax Courier and Guardian*, and his wife, Nellie, *née* Ward, an amateur concert pianist from Charleston, West Virginia. Despite initial parental reluctance—she later said that she had 'had a terrible row with my family—they had expected me to stay at home and do the flowers!' (Collins, Hyman, and Lane)—she trained at Leeds School of Art and the Royal College of Art, London. After her marriage to Collins she devoted much of her life to encouraging and supporting

him, but she also continued to paint, initially exhibiting her gouache paintings under the name Belmont to keep her work independent of Collins's growing reputation. Radiant, friendly, spontaneous, and enthusiastic, Elisabeth Collins was tall, slender, latterly frail, and elegant in an old-fashioned quasi-Bohemian style with big hats and flowing dresses and scarves. Her art, influenced by Redon and Chagall, was magical, visionary, and charming, depicting a colourful dreamlike world described by one critic as from 'the Eastern European fairy-tale province of her imagination' (*Independent*, 8 Feb 2000). After Collins's death she used his studio and produced a substantial number of small gouache paintings. Her exhibition at England and Co. in 1996 led to the Tate's acquiring four of her paintings. Although she told interviewers in 1999 that she would never describe herself as a Christian, latterly she was drawn to the rites of the Russian Orthodox church. She died on 17 January 2000 in London, and her funeral was at the Orthodox church in Knightsbridge, London.

WILLIAM ANDERSON, *rev.*

Sources W. Anderson, *Cecil Collins: the quest for the Great Happiness* (1988) · C. Collins, *Paintings and drawings, 1935–45* (1946) · K. Raine, *Cecil Collins, painter of paradise* (1979) · J. Collins, *Cecil Collins: a retrospective exhibition* (1989) [exhibition catalogue, Tate Gallery, London, 10 May – 9 July 1989] · personal knowledge (1996) · private information (1996) · *CGPLA Eng. & Wales* (1989) · *The Independent* (8 Feb 2000) · *The Independent* (22 Feb 2000) · *The Guardian* (16 Feb 2000) · *Daily Telegraph* (6 March 2000) · E. Collins, T. Hyman, and J. Lane, 'A woman of radiance: Elizabeth Collins', *Resurgence*, 200 (2000); also online, resurgence.gn.apc.org, 1 June 2002

Archives Tate collection, corresp., papers, and sketchbooks | Tate collection, corresp. with Lord Clark | FILM Arts Council film, 1978

Wealth at death £140,741: administration, 1989

Collins, Charles (*c*.1680–1744), bird and mammal painter, of whose parents nothing is known, lived and worked in London. George Vertue noted that he 'painted all sorts of fowl and game. He drew a piece with a hare and birds and his own portrait in a hat' (*Anecdotes of Painting*, 2.122). He used watercolour when making records of single species of birds and mammals for patrons, and he painted still life and composite pictures in oil. A set of twelve oil paintings of landscapes with British birds was used as the basis for a set of twelve oblong folio etched prints, without text, published under the title *Icones avium cum nominibus anglicis: designed by Charles Collins, published by him and John Lee according to the act of parl. Sept 29th 1736*. Six were engraved by Henry Fletcher and six by James Mynde. Nine of the original oil paintings are at Anglesey Abbey, Cambridgeshire; the remaining three were sold at Sothebys, London, in July 1995 from the collection of the Gilby family. The set included 114 figures of birds flying, preening, and perching, in landscapes with cottages or river landscapes. Collins's bird figures are more lively and better drawn than those of his contemporaries Eleazar Albin, George Edwards, and Peter Paillou, though they are not as natural and convincing as those of the Flemish artist Pieter Casteels, who issued a similar set of twelve prints from his oil paintings under the title *Icones avium* (*c*.1726). Collins also painted several still lifes in oil of dead birds.

Many of Collins's watercolour studies were made from stuffed birds in the collection of Taylor White of Wallingwells, Nottinghamshire, a judge on the north Wales circuit and an enthusiastic, wealthy collector of curios and natural history specimens. He commissioned Collins, Peter Paillou, and others to paint records of the live and stuffed birds and mammals in his collection, resulting in a long series of 659 watercolours which included 201 signed bird paintings by Collins (including a dodo) and some unsigned mammal paintings. Each bird drawing had one figure subject in a conventional composition with a grassy mound or stump; but Collins attempted to make his models appear alive and active. They were very well coloured, with the addition of delicate highlights on the soft feathering. Most of the signed drawings are dated 1737-9, but many others in his style are neither signed nor dated. This, the largest collection of his work, is in the Blacker Wood Library at McGill University, Montreal, Quebec.

A preparatory watercolour study of a buzzard by Collins was used by Thomas Pennant for an illustration in his *British Zoology* (1766). The watercolour for the buzzard (*Buteo buteo*), signed and dated 1739 (Cecil Higgins Art Gallery, Bedford), is particularly fine. With their finely detailed plumage of dead birds, and their sombre colouring, Collins's still-life paintings were done in the style of the Dutch old masters, as seen, for example, in *Lobster on a Delft Dish* (1738, Tate collection). He frequently signed and dated his compositions. Charles Collins died in London in 1744. Examples of his work are in the collections of the British Museum, London; City of Birmingham Museum and Art Gallery; National Gallery of Ireland, Dublin; Leeds City Art Gallery; and the Minneapolis Institute of Arts.

CHRISTINE E. JACKSON

Sources I. O. Williams, *Early English watercolours and some cognate drawings by artists born not later than 1785* (1952), 27 · sale catalogues (*c.*1978-1998) [Christies] · C. A. Wood, *An introduction to the literature of vertebrate zoology* (1931) · C. E. Jackson, *Bird painting: the eighteenth century* (1994), 50-53 · H. Walpole, *Anecdotes of painting in England, collected by the late George Vertue, digested and published from his original MSS by Horace Walpole*, 3 vols. (1933-4)

Collins, Charles Allston (1828-1873), painter and writer, was born on 25 January 1828 at Pond Street, Hampstead, Middlesex, the second son of the landscape and genre painter William John Thomas *Collins RA (1788-1847) and his wife, Harriet Geddes (1790-1868), a teacher and writer, daughter of Lieutenant Alexander Geddes and his wife, Harriet Easton. Geddes's sister was the portrait painter Margaret *Carpenter. Born, according to Percy Fitzgerald's *Memoirs of an Author*, 'a blue-eyed red-haired bonny bairn' (Fitzgerald, 1.297), he was named after his godfather Washington Allston (1779-1843), the American history painter. Charles's eldest brother, to whom he was very close, was the novelist William Wilkie *Collins. Collins grew up in the Hampstead, Highgate, and Bayswater areas of London where his neighbours included the landscape painter John Linnell and his family. Collins was tutored at home by his mother. Like his father, subject to depression,

he too became exceedingly religious and adopted high-church practices.

In 1843 Charles Collins entered the Royal Academy Schools where he formed lasting friendships with William Holman Hunt and especially John Everett Millais, and met other members of what subsequently became the Pre-Raphaelite Brotherhood. However, in spite of Millais's nomination, the sculptor Thomas Woolner (1825-1892) later blocked Collins's election to the Pre-Raphaelite Brotherhood. Collins and Millais spent the summer of 1850 painting in Oxfordshire and between September and November stayed at the home of the printer Thomas Combe in Walton Street, Oxford. There Millais drew a portrait of his friend, whom he nicknamed Saint Carlo, depicting a nervous, anxious, chiselled face with high eyebrows and large eyes. Millais presented this portrait to Combe, and it later formed part of the Combe bequest to the Ashmolean Museum, Oxford. Collins's evident nervous temperament may have been aggravated by an accident five years earlier in which he nearly drowned. As a result Collins was petrified by water. Millais wrote, 'One could not induce him to commit his body (for fear of drowning) within a coffin bath of hot water' (Peters, 105). At Oxford, Collins painted a portrait of Mrs Combe's uncle, William Bennett, which, as Malcolm Warner has observed, was probably intended as a pendant to Millais's portrait of the printer (both Ashmolean Museum, Oxford); both works were presented by the artists to Combe. It was also probably during this time that Collins began his most famous work, *Convent Thoughts* (Ashmolean Museum, Oxford), which he exhibited at the Royal Academy in 1851. It was purchased by Combe and formed part of his growing collection of Pre-Raphaelite paintings. A powerful painting, it depicts a young nun, probably a novice, standing in an enclosed garden holding a passion flower, the symbol of the crucifixion. In her other hand is an illuminated medieval book. Part of her shadow is glimpsed in the lily pond before her. In common with other works by the Pre-Raphaelites, Collins's painting was attacked and parodied. *The Times*, on 7 May 1851, accused them of Catholic tendencies, an 'absolute contempt for perspective and the known laws of light and shade', and attacked their strangeness and use of form. Ruskin, in letters to *The Times* of 13 and 30 May 1851, vigorously defended the artists and praised Collins's painting for its meticulous attention to botanical detail.

Other works from the 1850s include *Berengaria's Alarm* (exh. 1850; Manchester City Galleries), the challenging and highly original *May in the Regent's Park* (1852; Tate collection), and *Good Harvest of '54* (1855; V&A). Collins's exceptional skills as a portrait painter are seen in *Georgina Hogarth as 'Lady Grace'* (1855) in his brother's drama *The Lighthouse* (1855). This portrait is noteworthy for the depiction of its subject's startling eyes and intense pupils. He was represented at the 1857 Pre-Raphaelite exhibition at Russell Place by *The Long Engagement* and *The Fuchsia*, both of which have disappeared from view. However, Millais and other contemporaries observed that Collins often failed to follow through his ideas, leaving drawings and paintings half-finished. William Holman Hunt noted in his *Pre-Raphaelitism* that the talented and idealistic Collins:

> could have held the field for us had he done himself justice in design and possessed courage to keep his purpose ... he continually lost heart when any painting had progressed half-way toward completion, abandoning it for a new subject, and this vacillation he indulged until he had a dozen or more unfinished canvases never to be completed. (Hunt, 2.314)

In a letter of 1855, Charles Collins confessed to Holman Hunt 'the extreme suffering and anxiety which painting causes me' (Hunt MSS, Hunt. L.). Whenever he tried to paint, he had acute stomach pains. In 1857 he gave up painting and attempted to make a living as a writer. Introduced by his elder brother to Charles Dickens and his circle, Collins contributed both fiction and non-fiction to *Household Words* (1858–9), the *Cornhill Magazine* (Dec 1867 – March 1868), and *Macmillan's Magazine* (1860–66). Most of his writing appears in Dickens's *All the Year Round*, including his first book, *The New Sentimental Journey* (1859), sketches of his Parisian visits, which was published in parts between 11 June and 9 July 1859. *The Eye Witness and his Evidence of many Wonderful Things* (1860) is an anthology of all twenty-one of his 'Our eye-witness' accounts. *A cruise upon wheels: the chronicle of some autumn wanderings among the deserted post-roads of France* was published in 1862. He wrote three novels: *The Bar Sinister: a Tale* (1864); *Strathcairn* (1864); and *At the Bar: a Tale* (1866). Wilkie Collins, writing his brother's entry in the *Dictionary of National Biography*, believed that Charles's prose writings showed 'rare ability in the presentation of character ... gave promise of achievement in the future, never destined to be fulfilled'.

Collins married Katherine Elizabeth (Kate) Macready (1839–1929), the youngest daughter of Charles Dickens, on 17 July 1860, at Gad's Hill. There were no children. The couple lived in France and London. Collins wrote to his mother that in London 'we are paupers—abroad we are rich' (Peters, 231). Increasingly he and Kate became estranged. Kate said after Collins's death that she had wished to obtain a legal separation but her father was opposed to it. G. H. Fleming, the biographer of Millais, bluntly describes the reason for the disintegration of the marriage: 'Charles Collins was incurably impotent' (Fleming, 190). His brother Wilkie wrote in the *Dictionary of National Biography*, 'The last years of [Charles's] life were years of broken health and acute suffering, borne with a patience and courage known only to those nearest and dearest to him.' Just before his own death, Charles Dickens encouraged Collins to illustrate *The Mystery of Edwin Drood* (1870).

On 9 April 1873 Charles died at 10 Thurloe Place, South Kensington, aged forty-five, from a cancerous tumour in the stomach. He was buried in Brompton cemetery on Monday 13 April 1873 in a grave covered by a flat granite slab without text or an inscription. His widow, Kate, observed an obligatory year of mourning before remarrying another painter, Charles Edward Perugini (1839–1918).

As Wilkie Collins remarked, 'it was in the modest and sensitive nature of the man to underrate his own success. His ideal was a high one; and he never succeeded in satisfying his own aspirations' (*DNB*).   WILLIAM BAKER

Sources C. Peters, *The king of inventors: a life of Wilkie Collins*, new edn (1993) · S. M. Ellis, 'Charles Allston Collins', *Wilkie Collins, Le Fanu, and others* (1931); repr. (1951), 54–73 · *The letters of Charles Dickens*, ed. M. House, G. Storey, and others, 12 vols. (1965–2002), esp. vols. 8–11 · *DNB* · A. Gasson, 'Collins, Charles Allston', *Wilkie Collins: an illustrated guide* (1998), 30–31 · W. M. Clarke, *The secret life of Wilkie Collins* (1996) · *The letters of Wilkie Collins*, ed. W. Baker and W. M. Clarke, 2 vols. (1999) · P. Funnell, ed., *Millais: portraits* (1999) [exhibition catalogue, NPG, 19 Feb – 6 June 1999] · T. Barringer, *Reading the Pre-Raphaelites* (1999) · J. A. Gere, 'Charles Allston Collins (1828–1873)', *Pre-Raphaelite drawings in the British Museum* (1994), 101–22 · W. H. Hunt, *Pre-Raphaelitism and the Pre-Raphaelite Brotherhood*, 2 vols. (1905) · P. Fitzgerald, *Memoirs of an author*, 2 vols. (1894) · G. H. Fleming, *John Everett Millais: a biography* (1998) · J. R. Cohen, 'Charles Collins', *Charles Dickens and his original illustrators* (1980), 210–20, 269–71 · P. Fuller, *Theoria: art and the absence of grace* (1988) · [L. Parris], ed., *The Pre-Raphaelites* (1984) [exhibition catalogue, Tate Gallery, London, 7 March – 28 May 1984] · m. cert. · d. cert.
Archives Morgan L. · priv. coll. · U. Cal., Los Angeles | Hunt. L., letters, mainly to William Holman Hunt · NYPL, Berg collection · Princeton University, New Jersey, Parrish collection
Likenesses J. E. Millais, pencil and wash drawing, 1850, AM Oxf. · Elliott & Fry, group portrait, photograph, c.1860 (with Dickens and family), NPG · photograph, c.1860, repro. in Baker and Clarke, eds., *Letters*, vol. 1, pl. 5 · Elliott & Fry, photograph, NPG · A. Geddes, group portrait (*Charles and Wilkie as children*), repro. in Baker and Clarke, eds., *Letters* · woodcut (after photograph by J. Watkins), NPG; repro. in *Illustrated Review* (24 April 1873)
Wealth at death under £10,000: probate, 15 May 1873, CGPLA Eng. & Wales

Collins, Charles James (1820–1864), writer, was connected with the London press for more than twenty years, during which time he was on the parliamentary staff of *The Sun*, *Daily Telegraph*, and *The Standard*. He edited the *Comic News* from 1847 and helped to found, and edited (from 1861), the *Racing Times*. He died at his home, 9 Manor Terrace, Brixton, on 31 December 1864, leaving a widow, Phoebe.

Collins was the author of *Kenilworth*, a burlesque, and other dramas of a similar character, and of novels such as *Dick Diminy, or, The Life and Adventures of a Jockey* (1855; 2nd edn, 1875), *Sackville Chase* (3 vols., 1863–5), *Matilda the Dane: a Romance of the Affections* (1863), *Singed Moths: a City Romance* (3 vols., 1864), and *The Man in Chains* (3 vols., 1864).

THOMPSON COOPER, *rev.* JULIAN LOCK

Sources GM, 3rd ser., 18 (1865), 258 · Boase, *Mod. Eng. biog.* · CGPLA Eng. & Wales (1865)
Wealth at death under £600: probate, 27 Jan 1865, CGPLA Eng. & Wales

Collins [*married names* Cooney, Tate], **Charlotte Louisa** [Lottie] (1865–1910), music-hall entertainer, was born on 16 August 1865 at 50 Richard Street, St George-in-the-East, London, the daughter of William Alfred Collins, wood-turner, and his wife, Charlotte, *née* Atkinson. Her father was also a 'blackface minstrel', and at the age of eleven Lottie began working as a skipping-rope dancer. She developed an act with her two younger sisters, Lizzie and Marie, and as the Three Sisters Collins they appeared in their

Charlotte Louisa Collins (1865–1910), by London Stereoscopic Co.

own sketch, 'Skiptomania', at the Oxford Theatre and at three subsequent pantomimes at the Pavilion, Whitechapel. Lottie Collins subsequently went solo with an act that included singing, comic sketches, and whistling. In 1886 she played Mariette in Richard Henry's Gaiety Theatre burlesque *Monte Cristo Junior*, and she went on tour, billing herself as the Kate Vaughan of the Halls. It was under this sobriquet that she toured the United States. Though the tour was a disaster, Collins drew on her early talent for developing novelty material that suited her, and she discovered the song that was to make her famous, 'Ta-ra-ra-boom-de-ay'.

The roots of the song are obscure, although they may lie in the black music of the southern United States. Henry J. Sayers of Thatcher's Minstrels made an arrangement of it for his musical *Tuxedo*. Angelo Asher and Richard Morton composed an English version, which Collins first sang at the Tivoli Music Hall in the Strand in October 1891. Bernard Shaw always maintained that it had been stolen from the opening allegro of Beethoven's seventh symphony, and that it had chord sequences from a Mozart piano sonata in F and from Mendelssohn's violin concerto; the very variety of treatments, he suggested, was an indication of the tune's relentless catchiness. Whatever its origins, 'Ta-ra-ra-boom-de-ay' turned Lottie Collins into a symbol of the 'naughty nineties'. In style and dress she exploited to the full the contrasts in the song, wearing an elegant Gainsborough hat, and the short frilly petticoats of a can-can girl. The verses suited her serene and wide-eyed

beauty, slow, demure, and with only the slightest *risqué* edge:

> A smart and stylish girl you see
> The belle of good society
> Fond of fun as fond could be
> When it's on the strict QT.

Then, in the chorus she launched into a kind of Apache can-can dance with an energy that often left her fainting with exhaustion. She liked to boast that in the 'mad rush and whirl of the thing … I got round a forty foot wide circle twice in eight measures'.

It was, however, a highly individual whirl, which others found hard to imitate. Shaw compared the 'screaming abandon' of another can-can performer, Violette, to Collins's 'perfect self-possession and economy of effort' (Green, 52). To achieve, as he remarked, the 'ringing brilliancy' of Collins, nothing could be left to chance: every kick was planned and rehearsed to come perfectly on the beat with three low kicks to set off the wild high kick that accented the 'boom' of the song. Although Collins, like many fellow performers, found herself attacked by the social purity movement, her enormous popularity with the audience suggests that her appeal was complex and not simply dependent on her sexuality. 'Ta-ra-ra-boom-de-ay' is charged with an energy that is reflected in her vigorous management of her own life; her dance certainly used the sexy attitudes of the chorus line at the Moulin Rouge and the acrobatic skill of a ballerina in a romantic *pas de deux*, but as a solo, with its boasted 40 foot space, it also offered an appealing image of a woman taking charge of the space around her and enjoying the power as well as the delicacy of her body.

Collins was employed by both Charles Morton and George Edwardes, the major music-hall entrepreneurs of the day. 'Ta-ra-ra-boom-de-ay' found its way into Edwardes's production *Cinder-Ellen up to Date* at the Gaiety in 1891 and into Collins's role as Alice Fitzwarren in *Dick Whittington* at the Grand Theatre in Islington in the same year. In 1893 she revisited the United States, this time with her own company, the Lottie Collins Troubadours; here she expanded her comic talents with a number of sketches, including 'The Coachman's Wife', 'The Little Widow', 'The Girl on the Run-dan-dan', and 'Gertie the Gaiety Girl'.

In 1887 Lottie Collins had an illegitimate daughter, Josephine (José) *Collins, with Joseph Van den Berg, a music teacher; José subsequently enjoyed considerable success as an actress and singer, notably as Teresa in *The Maid of the Mountains*. Lottie was married twice, first to Stephen Patrick Cooney, and then to comedian James William Tate (1875–1922), who was best-known as That in the double act Clarice and That, and as a composer of light music. Lottie Collins died at 134 Albany Street, London, on 1 May 1910, from heart disease and bronchitis.   FRANCES GRAY

Sources R. Busby, *British music hall: an illustrated who's who from 1850 to the present day* (1976) · B. Green, ed., *The last empires: a music hall companion* (1986) · L. Senelick, D. Cheshire, and U. Schneider, *British music-hall, 1840–1923: a bibliography and guide to sources, with a supplement on European music-hall* (1981) · *The Era* (7 May 1910) · *Boston Herald* (3 May 1910) · J. Collins, *The maid of the mountains: her story*

(1932) · W. Macqueen-Pope, *Gaiety: theatre of enchantment* (1949) · b. cert. · d. cert.

Likenesses London Stereoscopic Co., photograph, Hult. Arch. [*see illus.*] · photographs, repro. in R. Mander and J. Mitchenson, *British music hall* (1965) · photographs, repro. in Busby, *British music hall* · photographs, Trinity College of Music, London, Jerwood Library of the Performing Arts, Mander and Mitchenson Theatre Collection

Collins, David (1756–1810), judge and army officer, was born on 3 March 1756 at Cross Street, London, the third surviving of the eleven children of Arthur Tooker Collins (1718–1793) and his wife, Henrietta Caroline Fraser. His father was an officer of marines, while his mother came from a cultivated 'middling gentry family' of Park, King's county, Ireland. His paternal grandfather, Arthur Collins, a noted antiquarian and genealogist, published extensively on the British nobility.

Collins began his education in London, but studied at Exeter grammar school from 1765 until 1770 after his father went to Plymouth in command of a detachment of marines. He himself joined the marines as an ensign in 1770 and was gazetted second lieutenant on 20 February 1771. A year later he sailed aboard HMS *Southampton* for Denmark to take into safe keeping Queen Caroline Matilda, the wife of King Christian and a member of the British royal family. Having been arrested for a liaison with the king's physician, the queen was released following demands from England and brought home.

Three years later, in March 1775, Collins sailed to the American colonies, where he fought at Bunker Hill on 17 June 1775 and later rose to first lieutenant. After evacuating loyalists from Boston to Halifax, Nova Scotia, in 1776 he returned home and for three years was adjutant of marines at Chatham. His wife, whom he had married at St Paul's Church, Halifax, on 13 June 1777, travelled with him. She was Maria Stuart Proctor (*d.* 1830), the daughter of Captain Charles Proctor of Halifax. The couple had one daughter, who died young. Collins was promoted captain-lieutenant in August 1779 and captain in July 1780, and from February 1781 until January 1783 he served aboard the *Courageux* in the channel squadron. He took part in the relief of Gibraltar under Lord Howe, and two days before the declaration of peace, on 3 September 1783, he was placed on half pay. For the next three years he and his wife lived at Rochester in Kent. On 24 October 1786 Collins was appointed deputy judge-advocate to the detachment of marines destined for the penal settlement at Botany Bay and to a position with the same title for the settlement itself. However, his means were insufficient, obliging him to seek assistance from his father, who had helped him secure the appointment.

Collins served in New South Wales between January 1788 and August 1796. Experienced, level-headed, and reliable, he became Governor Arthur Phillip's confidential secretary. The departure of the marines in December 1791 reduced his responsibilities and salary, and he sought to return to England where his wife and father were ill (the latter died in 1793). Only a strong sense of duty kept him in the colony. His integrity prevented him succumbing to the corruption that arose following Phillip's departure in December 1792, when the officers of the New South Wales Corps gained power. He concentrated on his legal duties, and won praise from Phillip's eventual successor, John Hunter, for his ability and zeal.

Collins knew no more law than could be gained from laymen's texts and military service, and as judge-advocate he operated under difficulties; he lacked the assistance of clerks and presided over a criminal and civil court system that made no provision for trial by jury. Hampered by his lack of expertise, he followed governors' wishes too readily, doing too little to assert the independence of the judiciary. Some of his judgments were questionable, but he achieved a 'rough and ready' justice, demonstrating that humane treatment of convicts could achieve more than undue severity.

In August 1795, after serving longer in New South Wales than any other first fleet officer, Collins sailed home. Despite numerous applications for promotion he was given only the brevet rank of lieutenant-colonel of marines (1 January 1798), with the substantive rank of captain. While in England on half pay he successively published, in 1798 and 1802, the two volumes of *An Account of the English Colony in New South Wales* that made his name as a writer.

Collins's first volume drew on his extensive experiences *en route* from England and in the colony. It was a well-illustrated chronological account, with a wealth of information about events and people, much of it available nowhere else. A gregarious man, Collins had a keen eye for detail and a lively curiosity. He depicted the lives of the white settlers and devoted attention to the Aborigines, providing a description of their language and culture that was for long the best available. The second volume covered the years 1796 until 1800, the period following his departure from Sydney, but was based only on material available in England and possessed none of the detail and freshness of its predecessor. Volume 1 also had shortcomings: the writing lacked literary merit according to the conventions of the time, and revealed little of the inner workings of government or of the malpractices of the New South Wales Corps. Nevertheless, the two volumes formed one of the earliest pieces of historical writing in Australia and stand out as the most important of the journals by officers of the first fleet. Maria Collins, who wrote several novels, produced an abridgement in 1804, by which time her husband's career had taken a new turn.

On 4 January 1803 Collins was commissioned lieutenant-governor and sent in command of a party of troops and convicts to establish a settlement in Bass Strait designed to protect the region from French claims. He sailed aboard HMS *Calcutta*. Judging Port Phillip to be unsuitable, and with Governor P. G. King's approval, he moved to Van Diemen's Land, reaching the mouth of the Derwent River on 16 February 1804. For the next six years he controlled this penal outpost, founding a town at Hobart and a varied economy based on farming, grazing, sealing, and whaling. The region was isolated, some of the officers were corrupt, the convicts were unreliable, and supplies were uncertain. Accommodating 500 free settlers who had been sent from the former settlement at

Norfolk Island between 1806 and 1808 created further problems. So too did the presence between March 1809 and January 1810 of the intemperate Governor Bligh, nominally his governor-in-chief, who had been removed from office in Sydney by the New South Wales Corps. Bligh was unduly critical of Collins, as was the British government, which accused him of failing to curb waste and fraud.

Collins's sudden death at Government House, Hobart, on 24 March 1810, at the age of only fifty-four, apparently in good health, aroused suspicions of suicide, or even murder by corrupt officers. A more likely cause was a coronary attack brought on by isolation, financial worries, and overwork. Whatever the case, he had lived long enough to make a mark on Australian history. The personal cost had been considerable, involving exposure to hardship and long separation from his wife and friends. In Sydney he found consolation in the company of Ann Yeates, by whom he had a son and a daughter, and at Hobart successively with the convict Hannah Power and with the Norfolk Islander Margaret Eddington, who bore him a girl and a boy. He believed that nature had intended him 'for the tranquil rather than the bustling walk of life', perhaps as a scholar or priest (Collins to his father, 12 Sept 1791, Collins MSS, Mitchell L., NSW, 1.58). His career took him in other directions, but, besides his judicial work in Sydney and the settlement at Hobart, where he was buried, his enduring legacy was his book, which at least partly fulfilled his early aspirations.   BRIAN H. FLETCHER

Sources Mitchell L., NSW, Collins MSS · [F. Watson], ed., *Historical records of Australia*, 1st ser., 1–7 (1914–16) · [F. Watson], ed., *Historical records of Australia*, 3rd ser., 1–3 (1921) · F. M. Bladen, ed., *Historical records of New South Wales*, 1–4 (1892–6) · D. Collins, *An account of the English colony in New South Wales*, 2 vols. (1798–1802); repr., ed. B. H. Fletcher (1975) · L. Andel, 'David Collins: his early life and background', *Tasmanian Historical Research Association Papers and Proceedings*, 35 (1988), 23–36 · J. F. Nagle, *Collins, the courts and the colony: law and society in colonial New South Wales, 1788–1796* (1996) · C. R. Collins, *Saga of settlement* (1956) · M. Tipping, *Convicts unbound: the story of the Calcutta convicts and their settlement in Australia* (1988) · L. Robson, *A history of Tasmania, 1: Van Diemen's Land from the earliest times to 1855* (1983)
Archives Mitchell L., NSW, personal and family corresp. and papers · NL Aus., corresp. · State Library of New South Wales, Sydney, Dixson wing, corresp. · photoprints of Collins family and letters from the State Library of Tasmania
Likenesses A. Cardon, stipple, pubd 1804 (after miniature by I. T. Barber), NPG · portrait, 1804, Mitchell L., NSW

Collins, Dominic (c.1566–1602), Jesuit and martyr, was born in Youghal, co. Cork, Ireland. His father's name was John, his mother Felicity O'Dril or O'Duala. John Collins and one of his sons were mayors of Youghal. Dominic knew Latin, which suggests that he attended a school such as was briefly run by Jesuits in Youghal at the close of the 1570s.

Collins went to France in 1586, worked as a servant until he obtained sufficient money to commence a career in the cavalry, and then entered the army of Philip Emmanuel de Vaudemont, duke of Mercoeur, one of the Guise family, who was fighting against the Huguenots in Brittany. After some time Collins was made governor of the château and

territory of Lapena, Brittany, but when Mercoeur made submission to Henri of Navarre in 1598 Collins handed over Lapena to the Spanish general Juan del Aguila. He then went to Spain where, on 8 December 1598, he joined the Society of Jesus as a religious brother.

Collins made his noviceship at the Jesuit college in Santiago de Compostela, and at the end of it, in 1601, he was appointed, at the request of his fellow Jesuit James Archer, to the Spanish expedition to Ireland. In the catalogue of the college at the time he was described as of physical strength and good judgement, mature and prudent, naturally agreeable in disposition but irascible and stubborn at times. His ship was delayed by storm, and it arrived eventually at Castlehaven rather than Kinsale. Collins and Archer joined up with O'Sullivan Beare, who continued to hold out at Dunboy, near Castletownbere, after Aguila's surrender. Archer set out for Spain to hasten the expected aid. Collins stayed on. When Dunboy fell he was arrested, brought to Cork, intensively interrogated, tried by court martial, and sentenced to death as guilty of treason.

Unlike his fellow prisoners, Collins's execution was deferred. He was promised immunity and honourable rank in the crown forces, or alternatively, it seems, ecclesiastical preferment in the established church if he renounced his Roman Catholic religion. He refused, and was hanged, drawn, and quartered at Youghal on Sunday 31 October 1602. He was buried the same night. His refusal to renounce his religion and his consequent death provided, after detailed research, the grounds for his beatification at Rome on 27 September 1992. Collins was presented as a model to successive generations of the young ecclesiastical students being prepared in the Spanish territories for their return to Ireland. A portrait of him appeared in the Irish seminary college at Douai in the early 1620s, and a portrait in oils, which now hangs in St Patrick's College, Maynooth, was displayed at the Irish College, Salamanca, about the same time. It is unlikely that in either of these there is an accurate likeness. Collins epitomizes the dilemmas of the conflicts of loyalty in sixteenth-century Ireland, executed as a traitor by the English government, hailed as a martyr by Irish Catholics.   THOMAS J. MORRISSEY

Sources F. Finnegan [P. Ó Fionnagáin], in the detailed case presented by the archdiocese of Dublin for the beatification of 17 Irish people to the Congregation for the Cause of Saints, 1 (1988) · T. Morrissey, 'Among the Irish martyrs: Dominic Collins, S. J., in his times (1566–1602)', *Studies: an Irish Quarterly Review*, 81 (1992), 313–25 · D. Forristal, *Dominic Collins: Irish martyr, Jesuit brother, 1566–1602* (1992), 5–26 · letter of Richard Haries to James Archer, 19 Jan 1603, Jesuit Archives, Rome, MS Castil. 33, fol. 94
Likenesses oils, St Patrick's College, Maynooth, Ireland

Collins, Dorothy Ann [Dolly] (1933–1995), folk musician, was born on 6 March 1933 at Fernbank Nursing Home, Old London Road, Hastings, the elder of the two daughters of (Leonard) George Collins (1910–c.1970), a milk roundsman, and his wife, Dorothy Florence Ball (b. 1912). Her younger sister and frequent musical collaborator, the defining folk revival singer Shirley Elizabeth Collins, was born in 1935.

Dolly Collins first demonstrated a musical precocity at

Dorothy Ann Collins (1933–1995), by Brian Shuel, 1966 [right, with her sister Shirley Collins]

the age of three when, standing on top of a village pub table, burbling over lyrical gaps with vocal approximations, she sang a comic song; a charabanc party passed the hat, making it her first paid performance. As her musicality developed, she came much to prefer composing and arranging to public performance. Nevertheless, it was for her collaborative work with her sister that she is chiefly remembered, and, as the folk revival's foremost keyboardist and composer-arranger of the second half of the twentieth century, she occupied a vital place in a nexus of 'artistic types' that included Peter Bellamy, Alan Bush, Maureen Duffy, Christopher Hogwood, and David Munrow.

At home Collins soaked up the music of Byrd, Purcell, Paul Robeson, and Vaughan Williams, along with left-wing and folk music, music-hall, and country-dance tunes. By the age of ten she was taking piano lessons. In addition to literary evenings and social singing at home, she sang locally in choirs and at socialist socials. Her maternal uncle F. C. Ball (the novelist and biographer of Robert Tressell) moved in left-wing circles. About 1951 Ball mentioned his composer niece to Alan Bush of the Workers' Music Association. Bush, Collins explained, was 'greatly interested in working-class people coming up' (Hunt, part 1) and asked to see her work. Accepting her as a student for composition, he halved his fees, knowing that even the rail fares were cripplingly expensive. At Bush's recommendation she began formal piano lessons with Mabel Landers. In the long term, studying with Bush proved untenable, and she took local and seasonal work. Collins crystallized her musical approach in a general rule: 'Let the music be suited to the people (the audience) rather than the people be "trained" to the music' (D. Collins)—words which Bush himself could have uttered.

Folk music captivated both sisters. Increasingly their fortunes became linked to the folk revival. A tentative attempt by Collins to set folk-song using three french horns was superannuated when a replica of a

seventeenth-century instrument arrived in her life. Her sister's *Sweet Primeroses* (1967) introduced the folk world to the flute organ (sometimes misnamed a portative pipe organ); arrangements of 'All things are quite silent' and others demonstrated an approach to arranging for keyboards in a folk context that pensioned off decades of spineless parlour folk-song arrangements for piano. With joint recordings such as *The Power of the True Love Knot* (1968), *The Holly Bears the Crown* (1969; with the Young Tradition), *Love, Death and the Lady* (1970), and *For as Many as Will* (1978), and scores of concert performances with her sister, Collins redefined how high 'folk arrangement' could reach. Commissions followed to score and arrange for artists such as the Incredible String Band (1968), the Young Tradition (1968–9), and Christ Darrow (1973). Despite critical acclaim and commercial approbation, hers was often a precarious livelihood. At one point she lived in a field in an ex-Maidstone and district double-decker bus that her partner from about 1954 onwards, the literary agent Jonathan Clowes, had purchased 'with a piano installed on the lower deck' (S. Collins). She regularly needed alternative work to supplement her musical income. Part-time gardening proved a lifelong joy, reflecting her love of nature—as did growing her own food and home wine making. On 2 November 1968 she married David Charles Busby (*b.* 1944/5), a teacher, with whom she had a son, the musician and songwriter Tom David Collins (*b.* 1972), who changed his name by deed poll to Buz Collins after his parents' divorce.

In August 1968 BBC Radio 1 broadcast the sisters' most visionary project—with the Dolly Collins Harmonious Band and the Home Brew supporting—focusing on how the First World War had emasculated England's folk ways and on all those wars where 'young men [were] taken away to fight wars they didn't understand' (*Anthems in Eden*, 1969). Released as *Anthems in Eden* (1969), it ranks as the sisters' finest achievement. Nobody subsequently trumped the triumphant and distinctive marriage of folk and early music elements in its eponymous song suite. *Love, Death and the Lady* wisely avoided direct comparisons with its pared-down arrangements. Collins continued to record and work in concert with her sister (as the boxed retrospective set *Within Sound* issued in 2002 showed), yet her next major achievement was to create reconstructed wind-band arrangements for Peter Bellamy's ballad opera *The Transports* (1977). Bellamy's and Collins's *We have Fed the Seas* (1982), a semi-successful BBC radio project, never saw a commercial release. She worked on a mass with Maureen Duffy using Duffy's 'Missa humana' from *Lyrics for the Dog Hour* (1968) as a libretto. On 7 October 1989 she married Stuart Edwin Hollyer (*b.* 1943), a geologist. Among her last major works were a cycle of six poems by First World War poets and a full score of Gay's *The Beggar's Opera*.

Dolly Collins died of a heart attack at her home, Hooked Mead Cottage, Crawley Lane, Balcombe, Sussex, on 22 September 1995 and was cremated in Brighton; her second husband survived her. Although she was best-known for her compositional, arranging, and performance work with her sister, it is for her blurring of *Gebrauchsmusik*, art, and folk music in an utterly original English setting that she will be remembered.   KEN HUNT

Sources K. Hunt, 'Shirley & Dolly Collins: part 1', *Swing 51*, 1/1 (1979), 4–19 · K. Hunt, 'Shirley & Dolly Collins: part 2', *Swing 51*, 1/2 (1980), 6–29 · D. Collins, 'Albion's electric morris', *Folk Review* (May 1973), 14–15 · K. Dallas, 'Conversations with the Misses Collins', *Folk News*, 16 (1978), 12–14 · S. Collins, sleeve notes, in S. Collins and D. Collins, *The power of the true love knot* (1968) [Polydor Fledg'ling 583025FLED 3028] · [S. Collins and A. J. Marshall], sleeve notes, in S. Collins and D. Collins, *Anthems in Eden* (1969) [Harvest, CDEM51477] · R. Denselow, 'Dolly Collins: songs of the spirit', *The Guardian* (5 Oct 1995), 17 · D. Arthur, *The Independent* (19 Oct 1995), 18 · K. Hunt, *English Dance and Song*, 57/4 (winter 1995), 18–20 · personal knowledge (2004) · private information (2004) [family] · b. cert. · m. certs. · d. cert.
Archives English Folk Dance and Song Society, London · priv. coll.
Likenesses B. Shuel, photographs, 1966, priv. coll. [*see illus.*] · P. Boyce, photograph, repro. in Denselow, 'Dolly Collins' · B. Shuel, photograph, repro. in Arthur, *The Independent* · B. Shuel, photographs, priv. coll.

Collins, Edward Treacher (1862–1932), ophthalmologist, was born at 1 Albert Terrace, Regent's Park, London, on 28 May 1862, the second son of Dr William Job Collins (*b.* 1818), a London physician; his father was of an old Warwick family, one of whom, Francis Collins, wrote Shakespeare's will, and his mother, Mary Ann Francisca, was the daughter of Edouard Treacher, of Huguenot stock. He was educated in London at University College School and at the Middlesex Hospital, received his medical diploma at the age of twenty-one, and was a house surgeon at Moorfields Eye Hospital from 1884 to 1887. He was then appointed pathological curator of the museum, and librarian, and remained in that position until 1894; he became FRCS in 1890. He also held a large number of appointments at other London hospitals while building up a private practice. Thereafter he held the post of senior surgeon in Moorfields until his retirement.

It was during his tenure of the curatorship that Collins laid the foundations of his subsequent career. This was the period of reorganization of surgery and medicine on the basis of specialization in practice as it is known today. Collins improved and built up the specimen collection, and observations in clinical pathology and the scientific principles underlying them became his major interest. Of his many published papers, at least 150 refer to histology or pathology, indicative of his persistence in research in the subject, and of the immense energy and steady industry with which he worked. He was especially interested in the evolution of the eye and its congenital aberrations, one of which (mandibulo-facial dysostosis) was originally described by him and at first carried the name Treacher Collins syndrome, though it has since been renamed Franceschetti syndrome as its wider developmental significance has become known. Collins often attended and took part in scientific as well as clinical meetings, and it was said that very frequently his remarks in a discussion were of much greater value than the paper that gave rise to them.

In addition to a long list of publications on ocular pathology, Collins wrote a number of influential books. Most of these dealt with medical topics, though one, *In the Kingdom of the Shah* (1896), described his visit to Persia in 1894 to operate on the eldest son of the shah. This working holiday was also his honeymoon, as before his departure he married Hetty Emily (*b.* 1870/71), daughter of Lieutenant-Colonel J. L. Herrick of Hawkes Bay, New Zealand; they had a son and a daughter. An important later publication was Collins's *History and Traditions of the Moorfields Eye Hospital* (1929), covering the hundred years up to 1904. Biographical details given in this work of some senior members of the hospital staff, with their abilities described in the most generous terms, were suspected by others to have led to the reported excessive pride of subsequent Moorfields staff and alumni, and its perceived undesirable effects on ophthalmology in England.

This undeserved criticism only serves to emphasize the most striking and admirable of Collins's traits: despite his eminence, he was entirely free from any greed for wealth or honours. He was an excellent teacher and took great pains to help and advance his pupils and younger colleagues in any way possible. Obituary notices state that he was without any envious thought, always willing to do anything to help a colleague, and that he never had a mean thought. His modesty was such that, when required to retire from his hospital appointment in his sixtieth year, he completed his day's clinical work and left without a word, even ahead of the due date, rather than face the fuss of a more formal farewell. His lack of ambition contrasts with his elder brother, William Job, who also became an ophthalmic surgeon; in addition William served as chairman of the London county council and as vice-chancellor of the University of London, and he was for some years a Liberal MP (for St Pancras and for Derby) and was knighted.

In addition to many other honours Collins was awarded the Nettleship medal (1915) and was Bowman lecturer (1921) of the Ophthalmological Society of the UK (OSUK), of which he held all the offices in turn. After his death the triennial Treacher Collins prize was established in his memory. Collins served on many national and local ophthalmic teaching and registration bodies, and was active in helping to found the precursor of the Faculty of Ophthalmologists, later to become the Royal College of Ophthalmologists. He spent much time in administrative work, and was intimately involved in the organization of Moorfields Eye Hospital, including its removal to the City Road site.

During his retirement from hospital work (from 1922 onwards) Collins played an active part in re-establishing the international congresses of ophthalmology which had been interrupted by the First World War. In recognition of his efforts he was made honorary president of the International Council of Ophthalmology, which succeeded in organizing the Thirteenth International Congress in 1929. Collins died at 16 Fitzroy Square, London, on 13 December 1932, and was buried on 17 December. After his death a memorial fund, built up by voluntary donations, was established with the aim of rebuilding the pathology department at Moorfields, to be named the Treacher Collins Pathological Institute. Despite sponsorship by the OSUK, the fund never reached the required level, and the proceeds were eventually devoted to the promotion of original work by younger members of the society.

J. M. TIFFANY

Sources *American Journal of Ophthalmology*, 16 (1933), 256–62, 452–4 [by 'B. G.'] · L. P. [L. Paton], J. B. Lawford, and J. Rowan, *British Journal of Ophthalmology*, 17 (1933), 112–22 · E. T. Collins and F. W. Law, *The history and traditions of the Moorfields Eye Hospital*, 2: *Being a continuation of Treacher Collins's history of the first hundred years* (1975), 1–5, 60 · W. S. Duke-Elder, *Text-book of ophthalmology*, 2 (1938), 1236–7 · b. cert. · d. cert. · m. cert. · Ophthalmological Society of the UK, membership lists, 1885–1931
Archives Wellcome L., papers
Likenesses photograph, 1884–7 (aged between twenty-two and twenty-five), repro. in *American Journal of Ophthalmology* · photograph, 1888–93, Wellcome L. · photograph, 1929, repro. in *American Journal of Ophthalmology* · L. C. Smith, photograph, Wellcome L. · photograph (middle-aged), repro. in *American Journal of Ophthalmology* · photograph (in later life), repro. in Collins and Law, *History and traditions* · photograph (in later life), repro. in *British Journal of Ophthalmology* · photograph, repro. in Collins and Law, *History and traditions*
Wealth at death £47,624 17s. 6d.: resworn probate, 15 Feb 1933, CGPLA Eng. & Wales

Collins, Elisabeth Ward (1904–2000). *See under* Collins, Cecil James Henry (1908–1989).

Collins, Sir Godfrey Pattison (1875–1936), politician and publisher, was born on 26 June 1875 at 14 Park Grove Terrace, Glasgow, the second of three children of Alexander Glen Collins (1848–1910), printer and publisher, and his wife, Cornelia (1853–1938), daughter of Godfrey Pattison, merchant, of Glasgow. He was the great-grandson of the founder of the Collins publishing enterprise [*see* Collins family]. While other sons of the Collins dynasty had been educated at Harrow, Godfrey, intended for a career in the navy, was sent after preparatory school at Temple Grove, East Sheen, to HMS *Britannia* at the age of thirteen. After service in the East India station he retired from the navy in 1893 to join the expanding family firm, and married on 26 April 1900 (Margaret Jean) Faith, daughter of J. C. Aitken Henderson, with whom he had a son and a daughter.

Collins was first sent to London to train as a compositor and to learn the technicalities of printing. In 1899 he was dispatched to Germany to investigate state-of-the-art printing machinery. In Leipzig he found revolutionary rotary printing presses and supervised their installation in Glasgow. The Collins enterprise now had its own modern paper-making, printing, and publishing organizations. Cheap books were now possible. First came the Collins Illustrated Pocket Classics for 1s. each. Some 80,000 copies (ten titles from *David Copperfield* to *East Lynne*) were sold in the first six months. Then came even cheaper series, the Nation's Library and the Sevenpennies.

By 1910 the company, under the joint control of Godfrey Collins and his older brother, was highly successful and Godfrey felt able to follow the family tradition of public service. A known advocate of the social policies of the

'new Liberals' and Lloyd George, he was invited to stand as Liberal MP for Greenock. Elected in January 1910, he almost at once became parliamentary private secretary to the secretary of state for war, and was a member of the War Office supplies committee. During 1915–16 he was parliamentary private secretary to the chief Liberal whip.

At the outbreak of the First World War, Collins and his brother, together with 275 of their employees, volunteered for service in the army. He was first appointed to the War Office staff of the quartermaster-general. He then served in Egypt, Gallipoli, and Mesopotamia. There he reorganized the chaotic systems of supply and accounting, saving millions of pounds. In recognition he was made CMG in 1917.

Now Lieutenant-Colonel Collins, he returned to the House of Commons. His main interest was in the economy, particularly in the supervision of government expenditure, about which he had found abundant scope for criticism during his war service. His efforts in the Commons were responsible for the establishment of the select committee on public expenditure. In 1919 he was knighted and made a junior lord of the Treasury in Lloyd George's coalition government. But he quickly became disheartened by the squabbles within the divided Liberal Party and with the government's failure to secure the supervision of public expenditure that he saw to be necessary. Finally, unable to accept government policy over reprisals in Ireland, he resigned in February 1920 and crossed the floor of the house to join the Liberals under Asquith. In 1924 he was appointed Liberal chief whip in the House of Commons by Asquith, but was removed when Lloyd George became party leader in 1926.

Collins remained active in publishing. Because of the war, supply of paper and other materials had become difficult and costs had risen. Cheap book production from Glasgow was now impossible. He established an office at 48 Pall Mall, London, and began to publish 'new' authors. His first books were previously unpublished works by Henry James. His list soon included H. G. Wells, Rose Macaulay, and Walter de la Mare, among others. He then launched the Crime Club, publishing Agatha Christie, Dorothy Sayers, Ngaio Marsh, and other new authors. His final venture was into the 'westerns' so much enjoyed by his former colleague Lloyd George.

In 1931 Collins threw in his lot with the National Government, and retained his Greenock seat with an enlarged majority at the general election held in that year. He was appointed as secretary of state for Scotland in September 1932 and began the Indian summer for which he will be best remembered. He initiated the Calton Scheme to establish the centre of Scottish administration in Scotland rather than in London. Although he did not live to see the completion of St Andrew's House on Calton Hill in Edinburgh, before his death 96 per cent of the Scottish administrative apparatus had been moved north of the border. During his few years of office he brought in over thirty bills to improve conditions in Scotland. His finest performance in the house was on the Housing (Scotland) Bill of 1935, a measure to tackle Scotland's notorious housing conditions. Other bills related to education, land reform, and inshore fishing. He set up the economic development committee to consider ways of restoring Scotland's economy that had been devastated earlier in the century. He appointed the committee on Scottish medical services that produced the plan that led, in 1948, to the creation of a national health service in Scotland that was appropriate for Scottish conditions. He was made LLD of Glasgow University in 1935.

Collins was an enthusiastic stalker, an excellent tennis player, and an experienced yachtsman (he represented Britain in the British–American 6 metre cup in 1931). He died of septicaemia on 13 October 1936 following a minor nose operation in Zürich, Switzerland. He was buried three days later at the Glasgow necropolis. In a relatively short life he had been a successful publisher and an outstandingly effective secretary of state for Scotland who had never been a partisan politician.

MORRICE MCCRAE

Sources D. Keir, *The house of Collins* (1952) • G. Pottinger, *The secretaries of state for Scotland, 1926–1976* (1979) • *The Times* (14 Oct 1936) • *The Scotsman* (14 Oct 1936) • I. Levitt, ed., *The Scottish office: depression and reconstruction, 1919–59*, Scottish History Society, 5th ser., 5 (1992) • G. McLachlan, ed., *Improving the common weal* (1987) • J. W. R. Mitchell, 'The emergence of modern Scottish administration', DPhil diss., U. Oxf., 1987 • *WW* • R. Douglas, *History of the liberal party, 1895–1970* (1971) • b. cert. • m. cert. • d. cert.
Archives NA Scot. • U. Glas., Wm Collins & Sons records | HLRO, corresp. with David Lloyd George
Likenesses photograph (after portrait), repro. in Keir, *House of Collins* • photograph (after portrait), repro. in *The Scotsman*
Wealth at death £153,995 17s. 6d.: probate, 9 March 1937, CGPLA Eng. & Wales

Collins, Greenvile (d. 1694), naval officer and hydrographer, sailed between 1669 and 1671 with Sir John Narborough as master of the *Sweepstakes* on a voyage to the south seas. He was in sole charge of navigation on this voyage. In 1676 he was master of the *Speedwell* (Captain John Wood) on a voyage to try to discover a north-west passage to China and the East Indies. Wood had been on the *Sweepstakes* and, like Narborough, held Collins in high regard. The voyage ended with the wreck of the *Speedwell* off Novaya Zemlya, but the crew were rescued and brought home. Collins's journal was the most important surviving record of this voyage and its use brought him to the attention of the king. He was given the mastership of the *Charles* galley, in which he sailed in 1677 for Tangier, transferring to the *James*, the *Newcastle*, and finally the *Plymouth*, Narborough's flagship, as master in each case. In 1679 he was gazetted captain and made commander of the *Lark* (18 guns). His journal records his time in the Mediterranean and his encounters with the Algerines, and the maps drawn to accompany the text show Collins's hydrographic skill.

In 1681 Collins was made commander of the *Merlin* yacht (8 guns), in which he was to undertake the first comprehensive survey of the coasts of Britain. Yachts were small, handy boats which did not draw much water and this made them ideal for surveying. There was certainly a need for such a survey since the best existing charts, mainly

Dutch 'waggoners', were known to be defective, and there was no systematic way of collecting and disseminating the better sketch maps and information which experienced seamen made of areas and noted in their journals: the fact that the work was entrusted to Collins was a tribute to his skill and shows the extent to which he had won royal notice by this date. It also followed his own proposals of 1680 in which he both lamented the parlous state of the charts then available and outlined the methods by which he could conduct an improved survey. The work was supported financially and supervised by Trinity House, of which Samuel Pepys insisted that Collins be made a younger brother. (In 1693 he was made an elder brother.)

The survey took seven years and was undertaken from the *Merlin*, *Monmouth*, *Martin*, and the *Younge Spragge*. Collins probably used existing charts and seamen's sketches and notes, as well as his own observations in this remarkably ambitious undertaking. From 1683 Collins was allowed to style himself hydrographer in ordinary to the king. Charts were published as they were completed but in 1693 when the work was completed, and about one third of the charts were engraved—in itself a laborious task—they were privately published together as *Great Britain's Coasting Pilot* by Freeman Collins, who may have been Greenvile's brother, and sold by Richard Mount. The work was in two parts and covered England and Scotland: Greenvile Collins announced his intention of producing a third part devoted to Ireland, but nothing came of the plan. A bill of 1694 itemizes the cost of the survey and shows that Collins spent £40 on instruments, and charged £80 for the 120 manuscript maps he delivered, £200 per annum in expenses for the seven years of the survey, and his wages of £394 10s., making a total of £1914 10s., of which he had received a small proportion in advance. He finally received the rest in arrears. The huge cost of the work, more than three times Collins's original estimate, as well as Collins's death go to explain why the Irish section was not completed and why there was some criticism of the work when it appeared.

In 1694 Collins was made master of the *Fubbs* yacht but on about 25 March of that year he died. In 1695 his widow, of whom no more is known, received £500 from the treasurer of the navy. His charts were republished in 1753 by Mount and Page, a course of action which he would not have approved since he thought all masters' journals should be scrutinized by Trinity House and charts constantly updated from them. Had his plan been adopted then, although his own charts would have been more rapidly superseded, mariners would have benefited still more from his modern vision of hydrography.

ELIZABETH BAIGENT

Sources F. E. Dyer, 'The journal of Grenvill Collins', *Mariner's Mirror*, 14 (1928), 197–219 • G. P. B. Naish, 'Hydrographic surveys by officers of the navy under the later Stuarts', *Journal of the Institute of Navigation*, 9 (1956), 44–55 • J. Burney, *A chronological history of the discoveries in the South Sea or Pacific Ocean*, 3 (1813) • E. G. R. Taylor, *The mathematical practitioners of Tudor and Stuart England* (1954)
Archives GL, charts, MS 2745 • PRO, journal, ADM 7/688 • PRO, maps, MPI 17

Collins, Henry Michael (1844–1928), news agency manager, was born at Furze Coppice House, North Savernake, Wiltshire, on 22 January 1844, the fourth of the twelve children of Francis Michael Collins, land agent for the second marquess of Ailesbury, and his wife, Mary Ann, *née* Woods. He attended preparatory schools in Ealing and Cheltenham and grammar school in Marlborough, but at the age of sixteen was obliged to take a job teaching at a preparatory school in Streatham, London. Here he became personal tutor to the seven-year-old Herbert de Reuter. Herbert's father, Baron Julius de Reuter, had founded Reuters Telegram Company in 1851. Collins petitioned the baron for a job with the fledgeling news agency and was duly employed in the London head office, beginning a lifelong association with the company.

In February 1866 Collins was posted to Bombay to establish the first Reuters office in India. In 1871 he travelled to the Straits Settlements, China, and Japan on behalf of the company and set up a Reuters office in Shanghai. As general manager of the Eastern branches he was able to develop a knowledge of all aspects of Reuters activities, including the supply of political, commercial, and financial news services and the handling of private telegraphic traffic.

Returning to Britain in 1872 Collins was immediately sent to Persia, where the shah had granted Baron de Reuter an extensive, but ill-fated, concession covering irrigation, forestry, and mineral rights, customs administration, banking, and road- and railway-building. He spent six years in Persia, leaving only when the baron finally conceded defeat. On 2 October 1875 he married Isabella Maria Baker (*d.* 1917). They had four sons (one of whom was killed at Ypres in 1917) and four daughters.

Within days of his return to London, Collins was offered the job of Reuters general manager for Australasia, a post that he held until retiring from active company service in 1909. Here he worked alongside his brother Ernest and established close relations between the company and the colonial governments. By 1902 Reuters was sending back to Britain official news provided by the Australian state and commonwealth authorities. This provided prestige rather than profit, establishing the company as 'the channel for the publication of authoritative information relating to Australian public affairs' (Henry Collins to Edmund Barton, 20 Oct 1902, National Archives of Australia, ACT Division, A1/1, 1903/1833). From 1907 the New Zealand government also subsidized the transmission of an official service of news to London. The Collins brothers were less successful, however, in dealing with opposition to Reuters arising from powerful private newspapers' associations. By 1887 these groups had succeeded in preventing Reuters from selling its services directly to local newspapers in Australia and New Zealand.

Collins effectively acted as an imperial troubleshooter for Reuters, travelling around the British empire to deal with local problems. In the months preceding the outbreak of the Second South African War of 1899–1902, the company's Cape Town manager began to face damaging accusations of pro-Boer bias. Collins, travelling back to Britain from Australia on leave, was instructed to investigate the situation. After reporting on the extent of the problem he was appointed temporary manager until a permanent replacement, H. A. Gwynne, could arrive. During his time in South Africa, Collins again displayed his talent for currying official favour. He worked closely with Lord Milner's party at the Bloemfontein conference and suppressed reports hostile to British interests. After a short interlude in Britain, Collins returned to South Africa in November 1899 to run the agency while Gwynne covered the British military campaign. Collins cultivated further official support by supplying the full Reuters news service free of charge to British administrators and military commanders. He remained in South Africa until October 1900.

Collins also visited Canada in winter 1906–7 to investigate the possibility of expanding Reuters operations in the increasingly prosperous dominion. As in South Africa and Australia, while he succeeded in developing a closer relationship between Reuters and the government, he failed to secure a position for the company in the field of news distribution to Canadian papers.

Collins was lively, energetic, and observant. He was blessed with a keen sense of the historical significance of events witnessed and places visited during his long life. In his autobiography, *From Pigeon Post to Wireless* (1925), he recalled early memories of soldiers marching off to quell Chartist riots in 1848; images of a Japan in the early stages of cultural transformation; the emotions stirred by visiting Cawnpore, Lucknow, Agra, and Delhi only ten years after the Indian mutiny of 1857; and the experience of donning the improvised suit of armour worn by the recently captured Australian bushranger Ned Kelly.

Collins worked for Reuters during its rise to the position of premier news agency of the British empire. His strong sense of imperial patriotism and his willingness to work closely with the British and dominion governments both shaped and reflected company policy. He believed that the empire could be strengthened and held together through an improved internal flow of news. Reuters could help achieve this aim and make a profit to boot.

After his retirement from Reuters in 1909, Collins remained in Australia, where he played an active role on the board of Melbourne's Alfred Hospital. He died at Swanston Street in Melbourne on 11 June 1928.

SIMON J. POTTER

Sources H. M. Collins, *From pigeon post to wireless* (1925) · D. Read, *The power of news: the history of Reuters* (1992) · *AusDB*, vol. 8 · G. O. Fenwick, *The United Press Association* (1929) · National Archives of Australia, ACT Division, A1/1, 1903/1833 · Henry Collins to Baron Herbert de Reuter, 22 Nov 1906, Reuters Archive, London, Roderick Jones papers, section 1, box 1 · W. H. Atack to L. Mackinnon, 30 April 1908, manager's letter book, Oct 1907 to May 1908, NL NZ, Turnbull L., Press Association MSS, box 78 · b. cert. · *CGPLA Eng. & Wales* (1928)

Likenesses photograph, *c.*1925, repro. in Collins, *From pigeon post to wireless*, frontispiece

Wealth at death £800 9s. 3d.: probate, 27 Nov 1928, *CGPLA Eng. & Wales*

Collins, Hercules (d. 1702), Particular Baptist minister, appears to have received little formal education. A keen interest in Christianity showed itself at an early age, which may indicate religious parentage. Beyond this, though, nothing is known about his parents. By the mid-1670s he may have been a member of Petty France Particular Baptist Church, London. On 23 March 1677 he was appointed pastor of Wapping Particular Baptist Church, situated at that time between Broad Street and Old Gravel Lane, Wapping. Ten years later, in 1687, Collins led the congregation in a move to a location on James Street, Stepney, where a new building was erected for worship. Although this came after the declaration of indulgence issued by James II in April of that year, plans for the new building had been in the making before the declaration. The move is typical of the vigorous leadership that Collins exercised within his church and the larger Baptist community in London.

In 1684 Collins was imprisoned in Newgate under the provisions of the Five Mile Act. His earlier defence of nonconformity in *Some reasons for separation from the communion of the Church of England, and the unreasonableness of persecution upon that account* (1682) may have been a factor in his imprisonment. When toleration for nonconformists did come in 1689, Collins was involved in the national assembly of Particular Baptists that gave official sanction to the confessional document known as the second London confession of faith, the doctrinal standard for the British Particular Baptist community throughout the next century.

Although Collins had not had the advantage of a learned education, he was well versed in theology. This is evident in his publications. In 1680 he published a Baptist version of the *Heidelberg Catechism* (1562), which he entitled *An Orthodox Catechism*. A steady stream of books and tracts issued from his pen in the 1690s, dealing with such subjects as divine sovereignty (*Mountains of Brass, or, A Discourse upon the Decrees of God*, 1690), believers' baptism (*Believers Baptism from Heaven, and of Divine Institution*, 1691), and the death of infants (*Truth and Innocency Vindicated*, 1695). A final work, *The Temple Repair'd* (1702), is an eloquent plea for Baptist churches to serve as seminaries for aspiring ministers.

By the time of his death, in London, on 4 October 1702, Collins was probably preaching to an auditory of around 700 people. His funeral sermon was preached by fellow Baptist John Piggott and subsequently printed. It contains the scantiest of biographical particulars. He was buried in Bunhill Fields, London.   MICHAEL A. G. HAYKIN

Sources T. Crosby, *The history of the English Baptists, from the Reformation to the beginning of the reign of King George I*, 4 vols. (1738–40), vol. 3 • J. Ivimey, *A history of the English Baptists*, 4 vols. (1811–30), vols. 2–3 • M. D. MacDonald, 'London Calvinistic Baptists, 1689–1727: tensions within a dissenting community under toleration', DPhil diss., U. Oxf., 1982 • E. F. Kevan, *London's oldest Baptist church* (1933)
Archives Church Hill Strict Baptist Church, Walthamstow, London, Wapping Church Book, I

Collins, Hyman Henry (1832/3–1905), architect, was born in London, the only son of Henry Hirsch Collins. An only sister apparently died when he was ten. His paternal grandparents were Hyman Collins of Cockspur Street, a founder of the Western Synagogue, at St Alban's Place (1826), and his wife, Polly, daughter of Samuel ('Sam Irishman') Davis. He was a great-grandson of Zvi Hirsch Kalisch, *hazan* (cantor) of the Bristol Synagogue and secretary to the Ba'al Shem of London, Rabbi Samuel Falk (c.1710–1782). He was a great-great-grandson of Isaac Levi, a government agent from the town of Kalisch or Kalisz, in Poznan, which in the nineteenth century was under alternate German and Russian control. The family, it seems, emigrated to Britain from Frankfurt am Main, Germany, and were probably related to Marcus Kalisch, the Hebraist, whose wife was also from Frankfurt.

Hyman Henry Collins was educated at Neumegen's school, Highgate, and at Kew and was one of the earliest students in the Royal Academy Schools at Somerset House. He trained as an architect and surveyor, only the second professing Jew known to have taken up the profession in the nineteenth century (the first was David Mocatta). He was articled to Henry John Hammon, district surveyor of St Luke's, and commenced independent practice about 1854, before operating for much of his career from 61 (Old) Broad Street in the City of London. Although he worked occasionally with other architects, he never acquired a business partner outside his own family. He was nominated ARIBA on 7 March 1859 and elected FRIBA on 19 November 1877. He was also a fellow of the Surveyors' Institution, and became district surveyor for the eastern and southern divisions of the City of London.

Collins married Matilda Marcus (1838–1911) of Dublin in 1857 and they had eight children. The second son, Marcus Evelyn Collins (1861–1944), was taken into partnership about 1889, and the firm was renamed Messrs H. H. and M. E. Collins. While a grandson also went into the architectural profession, the Collins's family associations were mainly theatrical. One son, Arthur Collins, became manager of the Drury Lane Theatre; another was Frank Collins, theatrical manager to C. B. Cochran; and Horace Collins was secretary of the Theatrical Managers' Association. In 1863–4 Hyman Henry Collins had been joint architect of the Strand Music Hall: his female relatives included the vaudeville stars Marie, Lizzie, and Lottie Collins (1865–1910), whose most popular tune was 'Ta-ra-ra-boom-de-ay' (1891). Her daughter José Collins (1887–1958) became a star on Broadway and in the silent movies during the First World War. Later descendants of the family were the glamorous Collins sisters Joan (b. 1933) and Jackie (b. 1939).

For many years Hyman Collins served on Paddington vestry. In November 1900 he was elected an alderman of the new borough council of Paddington. He was on the executive of the Paddington Conservative Association and a master of the Globe lodge of freemasons, no. 12, but combined his politics with a marked interest in social reform, as chairman of the borough council's public health committee. Collins was a member of the council of the Sanitary Institute of Great Britain, of the National

Health Society, and of the British Fire Prevention Committee, and long-standing secretary of the Social Science Association. He was often called upon to give evidence in legal cases concerning light and ventilation, and published several pamphlets on the subject of hygiene and architecture. His architectural practice was responsible not only for numerous commercial developments, warehouses, shops, offices, upmarket villas, and apartments, but also for a number of large-scale projects of a public nature, including the Metropolitan Hospital in the Kingsland Road, Hackney, and the West London district schools. In addition, Collins designed model dwelling blocks near Golden Square, Soho (1886), and in the East End, in Commercial Street (1863) and Brady Buildings (1880s), both home to many Jewish immigrant families. He worked on extensive housing and town planning schemes in Stepney and Bethnal Green.

Collins was active in Jewish communal affairs, and served on the councils of both the Anglo-Jewish Association and the United Synagogue. He was a prolific synagogue architect. His earliest commission was the renovation of the Western Synagogue at St Alban's Place in 1857, no doubt owing to the family connection with that congregation, although he later joined the Bayswater Synagogue. In 1859 he won a limited competition for the Spanish and Portuguese branch synagogue, Upper Bryanston Street (1861–3). He designed a series of Italianate synagogues in London—Borough New Synagogue, Walworth (1867), North London Synagogue, Barnsbury (1868), St John's Wood, Abbey Road (1880–82), the only one in the capital to survive—as well as the Westminster Jews' Free School (1883) and the fashionably mock-Jacobean Jewish Home and Hospital, Tottenham (1901), the latter in conjunction with his son Marcus. He had unsuccessfully entered the competition for the London Jews' Hospital, Norwood, in 1859 and came second in that for Princes Road, Liverpool, in 1871. However, in 1867 the outcome of a limited competition for the West London Synagogue (Reform), in which Collins had lost to the rival firm of Davis and Emanuel [see Davis, Henry David], was the subject of an undignified dispute in the correspondence columns of The Builder.

In the regions Collins built Southampton Synagogue (1864–5; bombed in the Second World War), Bristol (1870–71; with S. C. Fripp of Bristol), both Italianate, and the Romanesque Chatham Memorial Synagogue, Rochester (1865–70), perhaps his finest synagogue. The bold octagonal ohel (chapel) at the Witton old cemetery in Birmingham (1870) was his only known experiment with Gothic in a Jewish context. His earlier buildings for the West Ham Jewish cemetery (1856–7) have been lost and their physical appearance was never recorded.

On 13 December 1905 Collins died suddenly at home at Frankfort House, Randolph Road, Maida Vale, London, of influenza that had turned to pneumonia. His competition-winning design for the rebuilding of the City of London Lying-in Hospital, City Road, was still on the drawing-board. He was buried on 15 December at Willesden Jewish cemetery. SHARMAN KADISH

Sources The Times (14 Dec 1905) · The Times (15 Dec 1905) · Jewish Chronicle (15 Dec 1905) · The Builder (23 Dec 1905) · RIBA Journal, 3rd ser., 13 (1905–6), 111 · biography file, RIBA BAL · Dir. Brit. archs. · Jewish Year Book (1901) · A. Barnett, The Western Synagogue through two centuries, 1761–1961 (1961) · R. H. Harper, Victorian architectural competitions: an index to British and Irish architectural competitions in The Builder, 1843–1900 (1983) · E. Jamilly, 'Hyman Henry Collins: a profile', Quest [New London Synagogue], 1 (Sept 1965), 41–5 · C. Welch, London at the opening of the twentieth century (1905), 240 · d. cert. [Matilda Collins]
Archives RIBA BAL, biography files
Likenesses photograph, repro. in Welch, London at the opening, 240
Wealth at death £38,537 1s. 1d.: resworn probate, 17 Jan 1906, CGPLA Eng. & Wales

Collins, John (c.1576–1634), physician, was born in Surrey, and matriculated as a sizar at St John's College, Cambridge, about 1591, where he gained a fellowship on Lady Margaret's foundation on 7 April 1598. He proceeded BA in 1596 and MA in 1599. From 1600 to 1604 he was Linacre lecturer at St John's while pursuing his MD. The college then gave him leave to 'travaile [three years] beyond the seas for his increase in learning' (Baker, 457). It is unclear where he studied, but he returned in 1608 and received his MD. On 8 November 1626 he succeeded John Gostlin as regius professor of physick.

Collins was the first regius professor who was also a fellow of the London College of Physicians, having been admitted a candidate 'the day after Palm Sunday' 1611 ('Annals', vol. 3, fol. 7). He became a fellow on 7 May 1613, censor in 1615, and anatomy lecturer in 1624. This last post was also held at times by William Harvey. Although they were contemporaries and colleagues Collins seems not to have been persuaded by Harvey's theory of circulation, thus affirming Harvey's famous statement that no one over forty years of age accepted his views. It would be incorrect, however, to dismiss Collins's medical thought as entirely traditional. There is evidence that he was influenced by Paracelsian chemical theory and prescribed mercury (Webster, 11). He was also responsible for establishing 'anatomies' (dissections) as a required part of the Cambridge medical curriculum in 1627. The original Grace and an eyewitness account of an anatomy during Collins's tenure survive (Heywood and Wright, 2.358–9, 364).

In 1630 Cambridge suffered a severe outbreak of plague. Collins and vice-chancellor Henry Butts were responsible for handling the crisis. They organized and administered the policy of isolation and had a pest-house built on Midsummer Common. Collins and Butts apparently enforced the quarantine strictly, since the fellow Joseph Mede complained, 'You see what it is to have a physician among the heads. We cannot have leave to scarce take the aire' (Birch, 1.47). It seems that degree requirements could be flexible at such times of emergency when students had to disperse on short notice. Collins would later acknowledge this when he differentiated between degrees 'pestilentae' and 'eminentae' ('of the plague' and 'of prominence'; Fuller, 166). In 1634 the registrar of the College of Physicians wrote to Collins complaining of the lax degree requirements at Cambridge. The main complaint of the college concerned the practice of granting degrees and licences to foreign trained practitioners who lacked, as the college saw it, proper training. Caught between his two professional affiliations Collins wrote an impassioned plea to his friend William Clement acknowledging the problem but confessing he was powerless to change such a long-standing practice ('Annals', vol. 3, fol. 147). On 7 August 1616 Collins was licensed to marry Judith Easton, a widow. Collins died at Cambridge in December 1634 and was buried in the chapel of St John's College on the 14th. By his will, dated 8 December and proved on 24 December, he bequeathed most of his 'phisick books' to St John's College, and £100 to buy more (PRO, PROB 11/166/108).

GORDON GOODWIN, rev. KEVIN P. SIENA

Sources *CSP dom.*, 1625–6 • Munk, *Roll* • annals, RCP Lond., 3.7–8, 13, 22, 60 • annals, RCP Lond., 4.147 • G. Clark and A. M. Cooke, *A history of the Royal College of Physicians of London*, 1 (1964) • T. Fuller, *The history of the University of Cambridge since the conquest* (1655) • F. Valadez, 'Anatomical studies at Oxford and Cambridge', *Medicine in seventeenth century England: a symposium held … in honor of C. D. O'Malley* [Berkeley 1974], ed. A. G. Debus (1974), 393–420, esp. 406–8 • J. Heywood and T. Wright, eds., *Cambridge University transactions during the puritan controversies of the 16th and 17th centuries*, 2 (1854) • T. Baker, *History of the college of St John the Evangelist, Cambridge*, ed. J. E. B. Mayor, 2 vols. (1869) • H. D. Rolleston, *The Cambridge medical school: a biographical history* (1932) • H. P. Bayon, 'William Harvey, physician and biologist: his precursors, opponents and successors', *Annals of Science*, 3 (1938), 59–118, esp. 83 • C. Webster, 'William Harvey and the crisis of medicine in Jacobean England', *William Harvey and his age*, ed. J. Bylebyl (1979) • W. Costello, *The scholastic curriculum at early seventeenth-century Cambridge* (1958) • Venn, *Alum. Cant.* • will, PRO, PROB 11/166, sig. 108 • [T. Birch and R. F. Williams], eds., *The court and times of Charles the First*, 1 (1848), 47
Wealth at death over £100: will, PRO, PROB 11/166, sig. 108

Collins, John (1626–1683), mathematician and scientific administrator, was born on 5 March 1626 at Wood Eaton near Oxford, the son of a poor nonconformist minister. Though not allowed to preach in church, Collins's father was permitted to do so in prisons, and he added to his small income by proof-reading for a publisher. Nevertheless, his financial situation did not allow him to provide for the higher education of his son.

Collins attended a grammar school in the Oxford area, but when orphaned at the age of thirteen he became an apprentice of the bookseller Thomas Allam, outside the Turl Gate, Oxford. After Allam's business failed, he worked for three years as a junior clerk under John Marr, clerk of the kitchen to the prince of Wales (afterwards Charles II). Marr, eminently skilled in mathematics, had constructed sundials for the king's garden. With him Collins began to learn accounting and several areas of applied mathematics, including dialling (the theory of the construction of sundials), and during this time he probably lived at court. About the time that the king removed to Oxford, Collins went to sea for seven years (1642–9) on board an English merchantman, engaged as man-of-war in the Venetian service. He became acquainted with all aspects of navigation and, in his leisure time, continued his education in accounting, mathematics, and Latin.

On his return to London, Collins earned his living as an accountant and teacher of writing (of which his clear hand is a proof) and mathematics. As accountant to the allom (alum) farmers he built up a network of correspondents that later helped him to procure books and mathematical news from overseas. About 1670 he married Bellona, laundress of the table linen to the queen, and the younger daughter of William Austen, head cook to Charles II; they had seven children.

After the Restoration, Collins was appointed accountant to the Excise Office, a post he held for about a decade. In March 1669 he declined a lucrative offer from the surveyor-general, Sir James Shaen, to go to Ireland. In 1671 he lived in a house 'next to the sign of the Three Crowns in Bloomsbury Market, London' (Rigaud, 1.140). For about three years he was secretary to the council of plantations, exchanging this post in 1672 for that of manager of the farthing office, when he moved to a 'fair dwelling-house' (1.201) in or near Fenchurch Street. This post, however, ceased to exist about five years later, when Collins failed with his arguments against the issue of tin farthings.

For lack of capital Collins was unable to realize his intention of setting up a stationer's shop and printing books (a pension of £50 a year from the Excise Office was not paid for several years). Thus in 1677 he accepted a small post as accountant to the Royal Fishery Company. In spite of good credentials and patronage (Sir Philip Warwick strongly recommended him to various offices), he was not able to obtain a well-paid permanent office. Among the various remunerative tasks he engaged in was the disentangling of intricate accounts, a facility for which he became well known.

In spite of his limited education, in October 1667 Collins was elected fellow of the Royal Society. It was here that he had the opportunity to render the services for which he is remembered. For about ten years he served the society as a kind of unofficial secretary for all kinds of mathematical business. (The official secretary, until his death in 1677, was Henry Oldenburg who, in mathematical questions, relied heavily upon Collins's advice and assistance.) Collins conducted an extensive correspondence with some of the leading mathematicians in Britain and abroad, and he also drafted the mathematical details for Oldenburg's correspondence with these mathematicians (who included Barrow, Gregory, Huygens, Leibniz, Newton, Pell, Sluse, Tschirnhaus, and Wallis among others); Isaac Barrow called him 'Mersennus Anglus'. Collins obtained current mathematical news and foreign books for the Royal Society and its fellows, often in exchange for British scientific publications.

Collins was extremely well acquainted with the publishing business, especially in London. In the difficult years after the great plague (1665) and the fire of London (1666) he saw through the press several important mathematical and scientific works: Thomas Salusbury's *Mathematical Collections* (1661–5); Isaac Barrow's *Lectiones opticae* (1669), *Lectiones geometricae* (1670), and *Archimedes* (1675); John Wallis's *Mechanica* (1669–71) and *Algebra* (1685); Jeremiah Horrocks's *Opera posthuma* (1672–8); and others. However, his attempts to have some of Newton's early mathematical works published had no success.

Collins's own published works reveal competence in

elementary applied mathematics but not a creative mind. His most important books are *An Introduction to Merchants' Accompts* (1652), *The Sector on a Quadrant* (1658), *Geometrical Dialling* (1659), and *The Mariners' Plain Scale* (1659). He also published *A Plea for the Bringing in of Irish Cattel, and Keeping out Fish Caught by Foreigners ...* (1680) and *Salt and Fishery* (1682). His main interest in the field of theoretical mathematics was the (numerical) solution of algebraic equations; for an understanding of the new infinitesimal methods he lacked the necessary background. He greatly underestimated the seminal force of the mathematical ideas of Descartes, while propagating the significance of the contributions of some of his countrymen, such as Oughtred or Harriot.

Collins was described as 'a man of good arts, and yet great simplicity; able, but no ways forward', and of great modesty. His skill in accounting seems to have been generally acknowledged, as well as his understanding of the intricacies of trade. Above all his acquaintances praised his disinterested love of science and willingness to serve it wherever he could. He was a lover of music and an able player of the viol da gamba.

In 1682 Collins was invited to advise on a proposed canal between the Isis and the Avon, and while engaged on the project became ill with asthma and consumption (which he was said to have contracted while riding on a hot day and drinking too much cider). He never recovered and died at his lodgings on Garlick Hill in London on 10 November 1683; he was buried in the parish church of St James Garlickhythe on 13 November.

Due to his extensive correspondence, Collins's papers are an important source for the study of Restoration science. Most of them, formerly in private hands, were rarely made available to historians, but are now in Cambridge University Library. Some of them were printed in Rigaud's *Correspondence of Scientific Men of the Seventeenth Century* (1841). Always eager to establish the priority of English mathematicians, Collins collected letters written by Newton in the 1670s on the subject of the infinitesimal calculus, partly with the intention of preparing a book on English mathematical achievements. After the outbreak of the priority dispute between Newton and Leibniz, well after Collins's death, this collection became an important source of evidence, and an edited selection of the letters was published on behalf of the Royal Society as *Commercium epistolicum* (1712).   CHRISTOPH J. SCRIBA

Sources 'biography', BL, 'Biographical anecdotes, A–C', Add. MS 4221, fols. 331r–339r · T. Birch, *The history of the Royal Society of London*, 4 vols. (1756–7), vol. 4, pp. 232–4 · S. P. Rigaud and S. J. Rigaud, eds., *Correspondence of scientific men of the seventeenth century*, 2 vols. (1841); repr. (1965) · Wood, *Ath. Oxon.: Fasti* (1820), 202–4 · D. T. Whiteside, 'Collins, John', *DSB* · H. W. Turnbull, ed., *James Gregory tercentenary memorial volume* (1939), 16–18 · *DNB* · private information (2004)

Archives BL, papers, Sloane MSS 2279, 2281 · CUL · RS, corresp. and papers | BL, corresp. with John Pell, Add. MSS 4278–4476 · CUL, corresp. with Sir Isaac Newton · U. St Andr. L., corresp. with James Gregory

Collins, John (1632?–1687), Independent minister, born in England but educated in America, was the son of Edward

Collins (*d.* 1689), a deacon of the Congregational church at Cambridge, Massachusetts. Collins graduated from Harvard College in 1649, proceeding MA in 1652, and was incorporated MA at the University of Cambridge in 1654. He was a fellow and tutor at Harvard for some eighteen months in 1651–3. In the latter year he returned to Britain and was appointed to preach in Scotland and was given £50 for his journey and an income of £200 for the first year. In 1659 he was acting as chaplain to General Monck, whom he accompanied from Scotland to London. Collins was present in a neutral capacity when Monck interviewed the Independent deputies from London, following which in March 1660 Monck dismissed his Independent chaplains and turned to the presbyterians.

Collins held no preferment at the time of the Act of Uniformity of 1662, but is included by Edmund Calamy among the silenced ministers. Subsequently he succeeded Thomas Mallory, who had been ejected from the lectureship of St Michael, Crooked Lane, as pastor of an Independent church in Paved Alley, Lime Street, London. In 1669 Collins is recorded as preaching in Bell Lane, Spitalfields, and on 29 May 1672 he was licensed as a congregational teacher at Duke's Place, Aldgate. He was also one of the six original Pinners' Hall lecturers appointed in 1672, and was obviously very popular among his congregation: Cotton Mather related how when Collins was on his deathbed Matthew Mead 'poured out before God for his recovery' and there 'was hardly one dry eye to be seen in the great congregation' (Mather, *Magnalia*, 4.200). Nathanael Mather wrote of him, 'Hee is one of the best preachers in or about London as most agree; some say the best' ('Letters', 68). Edmund Calamy described him as 'a man mighty in the scriptures, and one of a sweet temper, and very charitable to all good men, without confining himself to a party' (Calamy, *Abridgement*, 2.838).

Collins maintained strong links with Massachusetts. In 1672 he added a personal recommendation to the collective one of London Independents which he had signed in favour of Leonard Hoar's candidacy as president of Harvard, later having cause to draw attention to the caveats in the original endorsements when Hoar proved a less than successful choice. He also acted as an unofficial agent for the colony, receiving and disbursing funds on its behalf and relaying back to the governor news of court politicking around the New England colonies. He paid, and later stopped on his own authority, the retainer to John Rushworth to represent the colony at court. When plans were in train in early 1675 to purchase the propriety of Maine and New Hampshire for the duke of Monmouth, Collins acted vigorously in investigating the matter on behalf of Massachusetts. Collins informed Governor John Leverett

if my owne industry, with the help of Major Thomson [the East India merchant Maurice Thomson], had not sifted this busines, about which I have taken many a step, [Rushworth] had not the least crevise of light into this busines; all he hath and what now hee prosecutes is upon my information. (*Hutchinson Papers*, 2.206–7)

Collins himself had an interview with the earl of Anglesey, the lord privy seal, over the business. However, Collins continued, his own situation, especially as the renewal of the persecution of dissent loomed, limited the direct influence he could wield for the colony: he had 'not bin at Whitehall but twice in many years; and persecution is pretty hot, and if it goes on I may expect a prison for my living in the towne' (ibid.). In 1683 Collins was rewarded by the Massachusetts general court for his services for the colony when it lacked an official agent with the grant of 500 acres of land in Quenetusset in the Nipnuck country.

Collins apparently wrote very little. A sermon on Jude was published in 1663 in *A Compleat Collection of Farewell-Sermons* by silenced ministers, in which he discussed how to retain and manage faith. Another sermon, 'How the religious of a nation are the strength of it', was published anonymously in Samuel Annesley's *A Continuation of Morning-Exercise Questions and Cases of Conscience* (1683). He also wrote two prefatory epistles, one to Ralph Venning's *Venning's Remains, or, Christ's School* (1675) and the other to a work by the New England divine Jonathan Mitchel, *Discourse of the Glory to which God hath called Believers* (1677).

Collins was subject to recurring bouts of ill health. At the beginning of August 1687 Nathanael Mather reported that

> Mr Collins is in a weak & wasted condicon as to his bodily health (by a scorbuticall diarrhoea as the physicians agree which hath hung upon him these many years). He is now at Tunbridg, by which waters he hath formerly had reviving many times. ('Letters', 67–8)

On this occasion, however, the cure had little effect. Collins died less than four months later, of a dropsy, and was buried at Bunhill Fields on 22 November 1687. His will, made three weeks earlier, gave his residence as St Giles Cripplegate; his mother and father, as well as his wife (whose name we do not know), were all alive at that point. Collins's only daughter had died in 1674; of the four sons named who survived, two—Thomas and John—entered the ministry. Nathanael Mather, who provided a Latin epitaph for Collins, succeeded him as pastor of the Lime Street congregation, and was in turn succeeded by Collins's son Thomas, who was elected co-pastor in 1697.

CAROLINE L. LEACHMAN

Sources *Calamy rev.*, 127–8 · E. Calamy, ed., *An abridgement of Mr. Baxter's history of his life and times, with an account of the ministers, &c., who were ejected after the Restauration of King Charles II*, 2nd edn, 2 vols. (1713), vol. 2, pp. 837–8 · C. Mather, *Magnalia Christi Americana*, 7 bks in 1 vol. (1702) · A. Gordon, ed., *Freedom after ejection: a review (1690–1692) of presbyterian and congregational nonconformity in England and Wales* (1917), 241 · D. Neal, *The history of the puritans or protestant nonconformists*, 4 vols. (1759) · E. Calamy, *A continuation of the account of the ministers … who were ejected and silenced after the Restoration in 1660*, 2 vols. (1727), vol. 2, p. 962 · *Hutchinson papers*, 2 (1865), 206–7, 962 · W. Wilson, *The history and antiquities of the dissenting churches and meeting houses in London, Westminster and Southwark*, 4 vols. (1808–14), vol. 1, pp. 235–8 · 'Letters of Nathaniel Mather', *Collections of the Massachusetts Historical Society*, 4th ser., 8 (1868), 1–69, esp. 67–8 · will, PRO, PROB 11/389, sig. 149 · *Harvard College records: corporation records, 1636–1750*, 2 vols. (1925)

Archives DWL, sermons and notes

Wealth at death incl. 500 acres in New England and 1/64th share of the *Royal Ann*: will, PRO, PROB 11/389, sig. 149; *Calamy rev.*

Collins, John (*c*.1725–1758/9), landscape painter, was born in London; he is of unknown parentage. He was patronized by the aristocracy from an early age and studied art in Italy at the expense of the duke of Ancaster, the marquess of Exeter, and others. On his return to London he painted scenes for one of the principal theatres, probably Covent Garden, but was most highly regarded by contemporaries for his landscapes. Vertue says of his style: 'his pencil free and neat his composition rich his skyes and distance hills soft and delicate' (Vertue, 155). Comparing his landscapes with those of William Jackson, John Hayes reproduced his *Landscape with River and Hills*, signed and dated 1853, in 'William Jackson of Exeter' (*The Connoisseur*, 173, 1970, 20). Of these Gaspardesque landscapes, perhaps the best-known are a set of six landscape views with figures from Tasso's *Jerusalem Delivered*, etched by Paul Sandby, E. Rooker, P. C. Canot, and others, and published by his widow, Elizabeth Jane Collins. He caught an infectious fever and died at a silversmith's in Henrietta Street, Covent Garden, London, in 1758 or 1759, leaving her and two children.
L. H. CUST, rev. KATE RETFORD

Sources *GM*, 1st ser., 54 (1784), 741 · Redgrave, *Artists*, 91 · Thieme & Becker, *Allgemeines Lexikon*, 7.237 · M. H. Grant, *A chronological history of the old English landscape painters*, rev. edn, 2 (1958), 110 · J. Hayes, 'British patrons and landscape painting', *Apollo*, 85 (1967), 254–9, esp. 257 · Vertue, *Note books*, 3.155 · Waterhouse, *18c painters*, 85 · J. Ingamells, ed., *A dictionary of British and Irish travellers in Italy, 1701–1800* (1997), 230 · S. W. Fisher, *A dictionary of watercolour painters, 1750–1900* (1972), 51 · Bryan, *Painters* (1964), 1.315

Collins, John (1741–1797), literary scholar, was probably born at St Erth, Cornwall, on 28 September 1741, the only son of the Revd Edward Collins (1692–1755), vicar of St Erth, and Elizabeth (*d*. 1749), daughter of Nicholas Kendall, canon of Exeter and archdeacon of Totnes. John Collins was educated at Eton College and in the same class as George Hardinge, his friend at school and later his generous benefactor. From Eton, Collins matriculated at the Queen's College, Oxford, on 10 May 1759, and was awarded a BCL degree in 1766. Having taken holy orders, he was sent to Ledbury, Herefordshire, where he was rector. In 1769 he married his cousin Mary (*c*.1745–1781), only daughter of Walter Kendall of Pelyn, Lanlivery, Cornwall.

Edward Capell, the Shakespearian editor and scholar, was not known personally to Collins. Yet when George Steevens, in the preface to his 1773 edition of Shakespeare, published some characteristically cutting remarks on the labours of his rival Capell, an anonymous pamphlet refuting these criticisms, *A Letter to George Hardinge*, was published in 1777 by Collins. Capell was deeply grateful for this defence, and before his death in 1781 he appointed Collins, who visited him during his last illness, an executor, leaving him a large sum of money, together with books and manuscripts, as well as the copyright of his important *Notes and Various Readings to Shakespeare* (2 vols.). In return Capell obtained 'a promise … the discharge of which I leave to [Collins's] honour and (I am proud to say) his friendship' (Nichols, *Illustrations*, 8.593). Thereafter Collins oversaw the publication of the *Notes* and *The School of Shakespeare* which Capell had failed to get published in their entirety.

After his wife's death in 1781, Collins's health deteriorated, and for the rest of his life he struggled with mental anxieties and financial problems. Collins seems to have had a contradictory personality: he was scholarly, very personable, with a clear voice and a cheerful manner, but he also seems to have inherited the 'inflammable temperature' and 'strong prejudices' of his father (Polwhele, 157–8), which may have precluded higher office. His schoolfriend Hardinge, who had revived their friendship after a chance visit to Ledbury, together with other old friends helped him financially, though not everyone appealed to responded positively. Lord Camelford wrote briskly to Hardinge that there was 'no chance of any preferment … till [Collins] becomes a *citoyen actif* … a better recommendation than all your nonsense of suffering merit and genius' (Nichols, *Illustrations*, 6.133).

In the *European Magazine* (7, 1785, 52), Collins is dubbed 'a sleep-compelling divine'; his *Letter to George Hardinge* is styled 'a heavy half-crown Pamphlet', and Johnson is credited with some rough remarks on Collins's grief at the loss of his wife. These anecdotes are, however, attributed to George Steevens and therefore may be altogether fictitious, or at least coloured by Steevens's unprincipled streak. It is generally accepted that Steevens, possibly in revenge for the accusation of plagiarism levelled against him in *A Letter to George Hardinge*, fathered on Collins notes of a suggestive nature in the second Johnson–Steevens edition of Shakespeare (1778). However, Steevens had already attached the name Collins to questionable notes in his 1773 Shakespeare, before John Collins entered the Shakespearian fray in 1777, and again in the 1803 edition, six years after John Collins's death. It is therefore unclear exactly which notes the mischievous Steevens intended as an embarrassment to John Collins and which to some other hapless Collins, long since forgotten.

John Collins died at Penryn, Cornwall, on 20 March 1797. His name, along with those of his wife and four of their six children, is recorded on a monument in Lanlivery church.   W. P. COURTNEY, rev. PENELOPE HICKS

Sources Boase, *Mod. Eng. biog.*, vols. 1, 3 · Nichols, *Illustrations*, vols. 3, 6, 8 · Nichols, *Lit. anecdotes*, vol. 8 (1814) · R. Polwhele, *Reminiscences in prose and verse*, 2 (1836) · IGI · Foster, *Alum. Oxon.*

Collins, John [*called* Brush Collins] (1742–1808), actor and poet, was born in Bath and baptized at Bath Abbey on 24 September 1742, the son of William Collins, a tailor, and his wife, Elizabeth. After serving an apprenticeship to a staymaker Collins became an actor. His first appearance was at Bath. A number of other actors named Collins were active at the time, and it is not always clear from contemporary records which was which. For example, in his *Memoirs*, Charles Lee Lewes claimed that Collins had been in George Farquhar's *The Recruiting Officer* (as Captain Plume) at Covent Garden, but failed on account of a cold and returned to the provinces, but this is not borne out by the playbills. If it was John Collins who acted at Birmingham in 1762, it was the beginning of a long association with that city. When he appeared in Dublin in 1764 Collins was

announced as from Edinburgh, and proved 'a very respectable acquisition to the Irish stage' (Hitchcock, 2.133–8). There was a Collins in Roger Kemble's company in Coventry and Bath in 1766 and 1767–8, and Margaret Cavendish Bentinck, duchess of Portland, recommended a Collins to Garrick in 1767. Garrick was unimpressed, describing him as having 'the most unpromising aspect for an Actor I ever saw—a small pair of unmeaning Eyes stuck in a round unthinking face' (Highfill, Burnim & Langhans, *BDA*, 3.398), a physical description that could apply to John Collins.

Anthony Pasquin's suggestion that Collins worked as a miniature painter in Ireland appears, according to Strickland, to be based on a confusion between Collins and his wife, Ann Shellard or Shillards, whom he married at Walcot church in Bath on 24 January 1768. She was a portrait painter who died, at an unknown date, after surgery for breast cancer. They had no children.

Collins's main claim to theatrical fame lies in his development of a kind of cabaret performance that combined his own light verse with songs, imitations of popular actors, and dialect performances. Dr Thomas Campbell of Clogher, who saw Collins perform his show in London in 1775 as 'A Lecture upon Oratory', noted that 'the fellow displayed good enunciation and good sense' (Highfill, Burnim & Langhans, *BDA*, 3.399). Early in 1776 Collins was in Belfast, acting in *The West Indian* and performing his entertainment as 'The element of modern oratory'. He was apparently a member of the company at the King Street Theatre, Birmingham, for some seasons and, according to the *Carlisle Magazine* (5 Oct 1776), was the author of a tragedy, *King Charles I, or, The Royal Martyr*, staged in Birmingham in September of that year, which he followed with his 'satirical, mimical and analytical lecture on modern oratory'. He was also apparently co-owner of the Concert Booth, 'a small theatre in Moseley Road' (newspaper cutting, Birmingham Central Library) that burned down in 1778. Sylas Neville saw Collins in Norwich on 6 November 1784, and noted in his diary that 'he gives specimens of bad as well as good acting' (Highfill, Burnim & Langhans, *BDA*, 3.399) and that his best imitations were of Garrick, Barry, Macklin, and Powell, each in character.

In 1788 Collins was living at 7 Shorter Street, Wellclose Square, London. In 1790 he was a partner with King and Chapman in a bookseller's at 38 King Street, Covent Garden, where he performed in the evenings. In February that year the *Biographical and Imperial Magazine* praised his 'union … of classical wit with eccentric humour'. Collins performed his entertainment in many venues in London and in the provinces, bowing out in 1795 at York. The performance generally went under the title of *The Brush* or *The Evening Brush*, because, according to an advertisement of 1793, it was intended 'for rubbing off the rust of care'. Collins thus became popularly known as Brush Collins. *The Brush* was published in Newcastle about 1800, and a well-used partial manuscript is now in the Birmingham Central Library. According to James Winston, Collins may have been an innkeeper in Plymouth and an auctioneer in

Bath in the 1790s, but he was performing and living in Birmingham in 1793 and about 1798 became joint owner with Miles Swinney of a newspaper, the *Birmingham Chronicle*, for which he wrote many poems and essays on local events. Collins probably owed his inclusion in the *Dictionary of National Biography* to William Palgrave's decision to reprint one of these poems, 'Tomorrow', in *The Golden Treasury*. At that point only his surname was known, but further details soon emerged, mainly through *Notes and Queries*, to form the basis of his entry. In 1804 Collins and Swinney published a collection of his poems and songs under the title *Scripscrapologia, or, Collins's Doggerel Dish of All Sorts*. Miss Brent, a niece, lived with Collins in Birmingham, where he died on 2 May 1808.

TREVOR R. GRIFFITHS

Sources R. K. Dent, *Old and new Birmingham: a history of the town and its people*, 3 vols. (1879–80) · J. Collins, 'The brush', Birm. CL · Highfill, Burnim & Langhans, *BDA* · newspaper cutting, Birm. CL · *Biographical and Imperial Magazine* (Feb 1790) · *Carlisle Magazine* (5 Oct 1776) · A. Pasquin [J. Williams], *An authentic history of the professors of painting, sculpture, and architecture who have practiced in Ireland ... to which are added, Memoirs of the royal academicians* [1796] · W. G. Strickland, *A dictionary of Irish artists*, 2 vols. (1913) · *N&Q*, 3rd ser., 4 (1863) · *N&Q*, 3rd ser., 5 (1864) · *N&Q*, 3rd ser., 10 (1866) · *N&Q*, 4th ser., 2 (1868) · *N&Q*, 4th ser., 8 (1871) · C. L. Lewes, *Memoirs*, 4 vols. (1805) · R. Hitchcock, *An historical view of the Irish stage from the earliest period down to the close of the season 1788*, 2 vols. (1788–94) · *IGI*
Likenesses J. C. B., ink drawing, BM · engraving, repro. in J. Collins, *Scripscrapologia* (1804) · stipple, BM

Collins, (Lewis) John (1905–1982), Church of England clergyman and social reformer, was born on 23 March 1905 at Hawkhurst, Kent, the youngest of the four children (two daughters and two sons) of Arthur Collins, master builder, and his wife, Hannah Priscilla Edwards. He was brought up in a conservative, churchgoing home and at the age of six he felt called to the church's ordained ministry. This was reinforced during his time at Cranbrook School, and also at Sidney Sussex College, Cambridge, where he went as a scholar. He obtained a third class in part one of the mathematical tripos (1925), and a second in part one (1927) and a first in part two (1928) of the theological tripos. He was ordained in Canterbury Cathedral in 1928 and became curate of Whitstable (1928–9).

Within a year, however, he was invited to return to Cambridge as chaplain of his old college, where he remained until 1931. During this time he became interested in the work of Albert Loisy, a French Roman Catholic scholar who had been excommunicated because of his liberal interpretation of the Bible. The two men became friends and Collins began to question various elements in his own faith, as well as his conservative approach to politics and the ordering of society. In 1931 he became an assistant lecturer in theology at King's College, London, and minor canon of St Paul's, but three years later returned to Cambridge as vice-principal of Westcott House (1934–7). Soon after his appointment in 1938 as dean of Oriel College, Oxford, he joined the Labour Party, having noted the effects of the 1930s economic depression on the working class. In 1939 he married Diana Clavering Elliott (1917–2003), a gifted and dynamic woman who shared fully in

every aspect of his work and was appointed DBE in 1999; her father was Jan Elliot, a company director. They had four sons.

In 1940 Collins left Oxford in order to become a chaplain in the Royal Air Force. For most of the war he was at a training station in Wiltshire, where he conceived the idea of forming a fellowship of Christian airmen and airwomen who would meet regularly to study their faith and its practical implications. This experiment aroused considerable interest, though his choice of socialist speakers and his frequent challenges to authority brought him into serious conflict with his senior officers.

When the war ended Collins resumed his post at Oxford and in December 1946 convened a meeting in Oxford town hall which was addressed by several prominent speakers, all of whom urged a large audience to take their religious convictions into the social and political life of the nation. As a result of this meeting Christian Action came into being, and in 1948 the prime minister, Clement Attlee, appointed Collins to a canonry at St Paul's so that he might devote more time to the new movement and provide it with a London headquarters.

Before long Collins had become a national figure and for the next three decades was one of the world's leading Christian protagonists of action in the causes of justice, freedom, and peace. Christian Action itself never had a very large membership but it provided an organization to support his own highly controversial personal work and its influence was quite out of proportion to its size. In home affairs it gave strong support to a successful campaign for the abolition of capital punishment and undertook pioneering work among the homeless and persons displaced by war. But the emphasis was soon to change. In 1956, after Collins had visited South Africa, over £20,000 was raised on behalf of some 156 opponents of apartheid who had been arrested and imprisoned in Johannesburg. This was intended to pay for their legal defence and to provide support for their families. Two years later a separate organization known as the International Defence and Aid Fund was set up, with Collins as president and director, and this soon became an important instrument of British, and later international, opposition to apartheid. His work in this field was recognized in 1978 by the award of the gold medal of the United Nations Special Committee Against Apartheid.

The explosion of the first nuclear bomb at Hiroshima in 1945 disturbed Collins greatly and during the early part of 1958 he was one of the sponsors of the national Campaign for Nuclear Disarmament (CND), with the philosopher Bertrand Russell as its president and Collins as its chairman. The main public manifestation of the campaign's activities was a series of Easter marches to and from the nuclear research establishment at Aldermaston. The numbers taking part ranged from 7,000 to 20,000. Soon, however, there were serious disagreements. A breakaway committee of 100 was formed in 1960 to organize civil disobedience. This caused dissension, indiscipline, and violence in CND and Collins resigned from the chairmanship.

Collins continued to serve as a canon of St Paul's, where he held, successively, the offices of chancellor (from 1948), precentor (from 1953), and treasurer (from 1970). The cathedral pulpit was used by him to promote Christian Action causes and, although he did not himself attract large congregations, his controversial sermons received wide publicity. Collins would have been a disturbing member of any cathedral chapter, but he had a great affection for St Paul's and never lost his vision of this national cathedral as a centre of culture and of Christian faith and witness. It was therefore a great blow to him when, on the retirement of W. R. Matthews from the deanery in 1967, he was not chosen as his successor. He remained at St Paul's until his seventy-sixth birthday and after a brief retirement died in a London hospital on 31 December 1982. At the end of his life the British churches were more deeply aware than ever before of their social and political responsibilities, and the man who symbolized this change and helped to bring it about was John Collins of St Paul's. There is a memorial stone to him in the crypt of the cathedral he served for a total of thirty-six years.

TREVOR BEESON, *rev.*

Sources L. J. Collins, *Faith under fire* (1966) · I. Henderson, ed., *Man of Christian action* (1976) · private information (1990) · *CGPLA Eng. & Wales* (1983) · *The Times* (3 Jan 1983) · D. Collins, *Partners in protest: life with Canon Collins* (1992) · *The Guardian* (2 June 2003)
Archives LPL, travel diary and papers | Bodl. Oxf., corresp. with William Clark · LPL, corresp. with Alfred Loisy · PRO, corresp. with Sir Stafford Cripps, CAB 127/124 · U. Warwick Mod. RC, corresp. with Sir Victor Gollancz
Likenesses photographs, 1954–64, Hult. Arch. · J. Pannett, chalk drawing, 1976, NPG
Wealth at death £32,081: probate, 8 April 1983, *CGPLA Eng. & Wales*

Collins, John Churton (1848–1908), university extension teacher and advocate of the academic study of English literature, was born on 26 March 1848 at Bourton on the Water, Gloucestershire, the eldest of the three sons of Henry Ramsay Collins, physician, and his wife, Maria, *née* Churton (d. 1898), of Chester. His father died of consumption on 6 June 1858 at Melbourne, on a visit to Australia as a ship's doctor, and from this time John Churton (d. 1884), his mother's brother, paid for his education. He attended Ellesmere School, from which the headmaster, J. D. Day, wrote to his mother in 1862, suggesting that Collins was 'unfitted for the duties of a clerk in an office. ... His mind is, as you say, quite set on literary pursuits' (Collins, 11). He went on to recommend that she send him to a school where more classics were taught, and so Collins entered King Edward's School, Birmingham, in 1863, under the headmaster Charles Evans and, as a potential university candidate, was placed in the classics department. He was entirely self-taught in English literature, through wide and voracious independent reading, in the course of which he committed whole texts to memory.

Financed by his uncle, allegedly to become a clergyman, Collins entered Balliol College, Oxford, on 20 April 1868, where his fellow students included Andrew Lang, Herbert Asquith, and Alfred Milner. Perhaps Collins felt the need to impress in such company, and so affected the jaunty

John Churton Collins (1848–1908), by Thomas W. Holgate

mannerisms of a promising literary man, flaunting a velvet coat and being accompanied by a deerhound called Prince: an ironic pose for someone later renowned for his antipathy to the aesthetic movement. Collins had no great admiration for the then master of Balliol, Benjamin Jowett, and on Jowett's death in 1893, Collins wrote that although he was 'kind and good ... to others ... my experience [was] much otherwise' (Collins, 131). It was his tutor T. H. Green who had the major impact on his development. As Collins later put it: 'For two or three terms he was my College Tutor. No man had greater influence or was so deeply respected by the best men of my time' (ibid., 53).

Collins's notebooks from his Oxford years indicate that he emulated other self-respecting undergraduates of his day, and simply absorbed English literature as he went along. Thus he read histories of English and European literature, especially the volumes of Thomas Warton's *History of English Poetry* (1774–8) and Henry Hallam's *Introduction to the Literature of Europe* (1837–9). It was Collins's overriding interest in literature as a reflection of life that made him the knowledgeable critic and biographer he eventually became. By reading English literature side by side with the classics, he developed an 'obsessive concern with questions of literary influence ... [that] led him to insist that, wherever possible, ancient and modern literature must be studied together' (Kearney, 5). Andrew Lang recalled that Collins 'always reminded me outwardly of Will Ladislas [sic] in the then new novel "Middlemarch". He was slimly built and very active' (Collins, 17). However, in 1872, Collins was awarded only a second-class honours degree, with no chance of pursuing an academic career.

Since he no longer wished to enter the church, his uncle withdrew financial support and they never met again.

Like many before, and since, Collins found himself, in 1872, with an Oxford degree, expensive tastes, empty pockets, and no prospects. Yet he never really left Oxford, returning during most vacations to stay in lodgings. Lacking helpful friends to provide letters of introduction to prominent editors, Collins wrote his first 'turn-over' article, published in *The Globe* newspaper during December 1878. However, the income from his contributions to the daily press was hardly enough to live on and, at times, Collins was wholly dependent on non-literary pursuits, and chiefly the speed with which he could address envelopes (he received 2*s*. 6*d*. per thousand).

By 1873 Collins was employed by William Baptiste Scoones at his coaching school in Garrick Street as tutor in English literature and classics, preparing students for the civil service. Many of them were Oxford and Cambridge graduates who had never studied English literature formally, but needed it none the less for the Indian Civil Service examinations, originally set in 1855 by a committee which had included both Jowett and T. B. Macaulay. In later life Collins often referred to this when berating universities for neglecting the teaching of English literature. His fourteen years of tutoring for Scoones developed his great talent for teaching, and gave him time and opportunity to ponder educational issues in depth.

Following Trollope's advice, in *The Duke's Children*, that 'no young man should dare to neglect literature', Collins carried it further than most by his mania for facts and details about famous men, either where they lived or were buried. His curiosity and writing also extended to the criminal element, and led him to interview the claimant in the Tichborne case, and he also became a frequent visitor to police stations and mortuaries (Kearney, 18–19). He also sent flattering letters to literary men and, in this way, he met Thomas Carlyle after writing to him for advice and guidance in 1874. In later life, he followed Carlyle's recommendation to add a knowledge of German to his repertoire of French, Greek, Latin, and Italian. In 1874 Macmillan's commissioned and published Collins's first book, *Sir Joshua Reynolds as a Portrait Painter*, for which he wrote brief commentaries on twenty portraits.

Another well-known figure to whom Collins wrote was Algernon Swinburne, himself a Balliol man, who was impressed by Collins's plan to edit *The Plays and Poems of Cyril Tourneur*, the Jacobean dramatist, and on the book's publication in 1878 Collins dedicated it to Swinburne. Unfortunately, later editors found it a careless and inadequate edition, although T. S. Eliot was convinced that 'Collins' introduction is by far the most penetrating interpretation of Tourneur that has been written' (Eliot, *Selected Essays*, 1951, 189).

It was in 1878, however, that Collins truly arrived on the London literary scene. His first periodical article appeared in the March 1878 issue of the *Cornhill Magazine*, and it was followed by pieces in *Temple Bar* and the *Quarterly Review*. He also became better acquainted with literary figures,

associating with men such as William Rossetti and Mark Pattison, and establishing an extensive social circle that was later to include Arthur Conan Doyle, with whom he was to establish a dining club known as the Murder Club. His improving prospects enabled Collins to marry, on 11 April 1878, Pauline Mary Strangways, the only daughter of the solicitor Thomas Henry Strangways. They had been involved for some time; in the previous January she had given birth to the first of their seven children, Laurence Churton Collins, who was to become his father's first biographer.

From 1880 onwards Collins found a new outlet for his great energy, lecturing for the London Society for the Extension of University Teaching, one of the most influential creative educational forces in the last quarter of the nineteenth century. Collins and such friends as Henry Morley used their teaching as a power base for securing the admission of English literature as a subject for study in the curricula of British universities. Collins also lectured for the Oxford Extension Society and delivered more than 10,000 lectures (Collins, 231) throughout the midlands and southern England, until his last presentation in Kingston, in 1907. This lecturing and teaching (which also included a great deal of marking) provided Collins with his first regular income of £30 per course. In total, he taught at seventy different centres, delivering fifteen weekly lectures, six days a week, in places as far apart as Birmingham and Brighton. A train enthusiast, who often rode on the footplate, he used the railways extensively in the pursuit of this work. On top of all of this, Collins often worked until the early hours of the morning, writing articles for the literary journals—in total he produced more than fifty substantial articles, often more than fifty printed pages long. These often took him months of concentrated work, and he regularly collected and republished them in book form.

Between January 1880 and July 1881 Collins published three articles on Tennyson's poetry in the *Cornhill Magazine*, where he continued exploring his theme of the relationship between classical and modern literature and how the study of one must be allied with that of the other. So Collins illustrated 'how [Tennyson's] *In Memoriam* was suggested by Petrarch; his *Dream of Fair Women* by Chaucer; his *Dora* is the versification of a story by Miss Mitford' (J. C. Collins, *The Study of English Literature: a Plea for its Recognition and Organization at the Universities*, 1891, 7–8). Collins went on to state that 'as is usual with him in all cases where he borrows, the details of the work are his own; he has added grace, elaboration, and symmetry. A rough crayon draught has been metamorphosed into a perfect picture' (ibid., 58). Even so, by maintaining that Tennyson's poetry was so directly indebted to the work of earlier authors, Collins opened up the possibility of accusations of plagiarism, or at least of a distinct lack of originality. Tennyson, naturally, was less than pleased, and exercised his anger by referring to Collins as 'the louse on the locks of literature' (Charteris, 197), perhaps echoing Robert Burns's poem 'Ode to a Louse'. Yet, in later editions of his poetry, Tennyson quietly slipped in some of Collins's references (Pattison, 7) and Collins himself later edited selections of Tennyson's poetry, publishing his essays in expanded book form as *Illustrations of Tennyson* in 1891.

Collins's notoriety among the British literati increased with the publication of his review of John Addington Symonds's *Shakspere's Predecessors in English Drama* (1884). Collins began his review in April of that year, but took such care over it that it was not until October 1885 that his fifty-one pages appeared in the *Quarterly Review*. Collins wrote that:

> what we found was, we regret to say, every indication of precipitous haste, a style which where it differs from the style of extemporary journalism differs for the worse—florid, yet commonplace; full of impurities; a narrative clogged with endless repetitions, without symmetry, without proportion. (*Quarterly Review*, 161, October 1885, 330–31)

This was Collins's way of arguing the case for critical discipline and scholarly rigour in advocating that English literature be made a subject of serious critical study. It was also his way of distancing himself from those, like Swinburne and the aesthetic movement, whom he felt would reduce 'criticism to mere impression and personal caprice' (Kearney, 56). Collins's review helped to establish his credentials as the follower of Thomas Carlyle and Matthew Arnold.

After the failure of his candidature for the newly established Merton professorship of English literature at Oxford in 1885, Collins wrote an article in the *Quarterly Review* for October 1886 entitled 'English literature at the universities'. In it he denounced the first Clark lecturer appointed at Cambridge University, Edmund Gosse, whose book *From Shakespeare to Pope: an inquiry into the causes and phenomena of the rise of classical poetry in England* was based on his lecture series. The historian Joseph Baylen comments how Collins was 'motivated by a blend of envy and contempt for Gosse's pretentious and careless scholarship, [and] was quite right in his criticism of the book as "a mass of error and inaccuracy"' in which centuries and even poetry and prose were confused and garbled. Gosse, charged Collins, was guilty of 'ephemeral literal journalism' and 'an offence to sound scholarship' (Baylen, 127). As another modern scholar more succinctly observed: 'If Collins was a louse on the locks of literature, Gosse was something of a flea on the skirts of scholarship' (Sutherland, *Times Literary Supplement*, 26 Jan 1973, 75).

Collins collected the views of leading men on the proposal to include English literature in university curricula, and published them in the *Pall Mall Gazette* (December 1886). Several other articles followed, incorporated into *The Study of English Literature* (1891), and Collins's modern biographer comments on the volume's significance when he states that: 'when the English tripos was being set up at Cambridge [in 1919], Collins's book was still being used by the English propagandists' (Kearney, 154). Oxford University eventually established a final honours school in English in 1894 and in 1903 set up a chair in English literature.

Whatever the squabbles in the London literary world, Collins was viewed as an ideal spokesman for literary education, as well as a powerful propagandist for the extension movement. His audiences in Richmond had included members of the royal family, and, in London, Margot Tennant had attended his classes before marrying his old college friend H. H. Asquith. His reputation spread to the United States and, in 1894, he lectured for the American University Extension Society in New York and Philadelphia, as well as at Harvard and Yale universities. Also in 1894, Collins was appointed to the staff of the *Saturday Review*, alongside H. G. Wells and George Bernard Shaw, under Frank Harris's editorship, and Collins spent most of his 'free' Sundays writing his contributions for the following Saturday's issue of the *Review*.

Collins published more than twenty books, edited another twenty textbooks, and served as general editor for the publisher Edward Arnold's *Shakespeare and British Classics for Schools*. In 1904, after several attempts elsewhere, Collins was finally rewarded with a chair of English literature at the new University of Birmingham, and was awarded an honorary doctorate by Durham University in 1905. Never one to rest on his laurels, nor jealously to guard the provenance of English literature's place, once gained, within the curriculum, from June 1907 he was involved in negotiations with Birmingham journalists on the establishment of a school of journalism in the university, and wrote on the topic in the *Nineteenth Century* for February 1908. The debate inaugurated by these articles contributed to the decision, in 1910, between London University and the Institute of Journalists, to set up a university course for journalists, which started in 1919 (Hunter, 1982).

In July 1908 Collins made his usual vacation visit to Oxford and, on a visit to Lowestoft, Suffolk, died in mysterious circumstances on 12 September. His body was found in a shallow dyke at Carlton Colville, Oulton Broad, with a bottle of sedatives lying nearby. An inquest on 18 September 1908 returned a verdict of accidental death and he was buried in Oulton churchyard; his widow was subsequently awarded a civil-list pension of £100 in 1909.

FRED HUNTER

Sources A. Kearney, *John Churton Collins: The louse on the locks of literature* (1986) • L. C. Collins, *Life and memoirs of John Churton Collins* (1912) • D. J. Palmer, *The rise of English studies* (1965) • J. Gross, *The rise and fall of the man of letters: aspects of English literary life since 1800* (1973) • J. O. Baylen, 'Edmund Gosse, William Archer, and Ibsen in late Victorian Britain', *Tennessee Studies in Literature* (1975), 124–37 • P. Grosskurth, 'Churton Collins: scourge of the late Victorians', *University of Toronto Quarterly*, 34 (1964–5), 254–68 • D. Bennett, *Margot: a life of the countess of Oxford and Asquith* (1984), 31 • F. N. Hunter, 'Grub Street and Academia: the relationship between journalism and education, 1880–1940, with special reference to the London University diploma for journalism, 1919–39', PhD diss., City University, London, 1982/4, 59, 112–16, appx V, VI • E. Charteris, ed., *The life and letters of Sir Edmund Gosse* (1931) • R. Pattison, *Tennyson and tradition* (1979), 7 • d. cert. • m. cert.

Archives Bodl. Oxf., letters • London Society for the Extension of University Teaching, University of London library council and reports from lecturers • NL Scot., letters • U. Birm., calendar; report of the dean of the faculty of arts • U. Birm. L., commonplace books with some diary entries; notebooks and letters • U. Oxf.,

Bodleian Library and lecturers' and examiners' reports; minutes of the committee for university extension | BL, corresp. with Macmillans, Add. MS 35032 · U. Leeds, Brotherton L., corresp. with Sir Edmund Gosse · U. Reading L., letters to George Bell & Sons **Likenesses** T. W. Holgate, oils, Bodl. Oxf. [*see illus.*] · G. Phoenix, watercolour drawing, Balliol Oxf. **Wealth at death** £1544 10*s.* 6*d.*: probate, 14 Nov 1908, *CGPLA Eng. & Wales*

Collins, John Ulric (*c.*1750–1807), army officer in the East India Company and diplomatist, is of unknown parentage; although his name suggests Irish ancestry, there is evidence for an early connection with Devon. An East India Company cadet, Collins sailed for Asia on 2 December 1769 on board the *Vansittart* and arrived at Madras on 26 July 1770. As there were then limited vacancies in the commissioned ranks of the Bengal army, he joined the select picket of gentleman cadets, a separate company of young men waiting to be commissioned into a regiment which, in the field, formed part of the advance guard. With the select pickets he likely saw action in 1774 during the Rohilla War. Three years later the 19th native infantry regiment was created, and Collins obtained his commission. Initially known as Jack by his fellow officers, he was anyway regarded as vain. Later, as his style became increasingly pompous, he was called King Collins, or Little King Collins. In November 1780 Collins was made a captain, and in 1785 was appointed military storekeeper at Fort William, Calcutta. On 24 November 1790, in Calcutta, he married Charlotte (1772–1857), daughter of William and Elizabeth Wrangham of St Helena. The couple had two sons, George Theophilus (1792–1833) and Henry John (*b.* 1793).

By the early 1790s Collins was Calcutta's town major. From 1793 he was the private secretary to Governor-General Sir John Shore. Made a lieutenant-colonel on 27 July 1796, early in the next year he travelled with Shore to Lucknow to meet Asaf ud-Daula, nawab-vizier of Oudh. In January 1798, after Asaf ud-Daula's death, he was again in Lucknow, when Shore secured the succession of the late ruler's brother Saadat Ali against the claims of Wazir Ali, the late ruler's son. Days before relinquishing office in March 1798 Shore appointed Collins resident to the court of Sindhia, the Maratha leader based at Gwalior who, possessing a powerful army, dominated the Delhi–Agra tract. Taking charge of the residency in September 1799 while Sindhia was at Poona, Collins resided at Fatehgarh. In October 1799, while leading his lavishly clothed personal escort to Jaipur and carrying Rs 10,000 from Governor-General Mornington for the raja, he secured the surrender of Wazir Ali, who was accused of murdering the Benares resident George Cherry. On 29 May 1800 Collins became a colonel. He attended Sindhia's court on two occasions, between February and May 1802 and February and August 1803, and twice failed to negotiate Sindhia's peaceful accession to the governor-general's system of subsidiary alliances. The second mission's failure and his frustrated departure from Sindhia's camp on 3 August 1803 was the immediate cause of the Second Anglo-Maratha War.

In September 1803 Collins, en route to Hyderabad and suffering from gout, met General Arthur Wellesley and members of his staff. Captain John Blakiston later described the occasion:

> In front of a noble suite of tents, which might have served the great Mogul, we were received by an insignificant, little old-looking man, dressed in an old fashioned military coat, white breeches, sky-blue silk-stockings, and large glaring buckles on his shoes, having his highly powdered wig, from which depended a pig-tail of no ordinary dimensions, surmounted by a small, round black silk hat, ornamented with a single black ostrich feather, looking altogether not unlike a monkey dressed up for Bartholomew fair. There was, however, a fire in his small black eye, shooting out from beneath a large, shaggy, pent-house brow, which more than counter-balanced the ridicule that his first appearance naturally excited.

Blakiston notes how they laughed at 'the little man' and his warnings about Sindhia's deadly efficient artillery (Blakiston, 1.144–5). At this time Collins may also have kept a zenana.

In recognition of his efforts as resident with Sindhia, Wellesley made Collins his honorary aide-de-camp and in early 1804 appointed him resident to the nawab-vizier of Oudh. In 1805, a still gouty Collins described himself as infirm. He died at Lucknow on 11 June 1807 and, with sons of the nawab-vizier attending, was buried that day near the Aminabad bazaar with full civil and military honours. A Christian cemetery, the Kallan-ka-Lat, or Collins's monument, grew around his imposing tomb.

BRENDAN CARNDUFF

Sources J. Sarkar and others, eds., *English records of Maratha history: Poona residency correspondence*, 8–10 (1943–51), vols. 8–10 · J. Blakiston, *Twelve years military adventures in three quarters of the globe* (1829) · A. S. Bennell, *The Maratha War papers of Arthur Wellesley, January to December 1803* (1998) · V. C. P. Hodson, *List of officers of the Bengal army, 1758–1834*, 4 vols. (1927–47) · J. Philippart, *East India military calendar*, 1 (1823) · Devon RO, Kennaway papers · Dodwell [E. Dodwell] and Miles [J. S. Miles], eds., *Alphabetical list of the officers of the Indian army: with the dates of their respective promotion, retirement, resignation, or death … from the year 1760 to the year … 1837* (1838) · A. Fuhrer, *List of Christian tombs and monuments of archaeological or historical interest and their inscriptions in the North-Western Provinces and Oudh* (1896) · *Asiatic Annual Register* (1808) · F. G. Cardew, *A sketch of the services of the Bengal native army to the year 1895* (1903)

Archives BL, corresp. with Arthur Wellesley, Add. MSS 13526–13527, 13530, 13600, 37282 · BL OIOC, Barlow MSS, MS Eur. F 176/28 · BL OIOC, corresp. as resident at court of Sindhia, home misc. series · U. Southampton, Hartley Library, Wellington MSS

Collins, Josephine [José] (1887–1958), actress and singer, was born on 23 May 1887 in Whitechapel, London, the illegitimate daughter of Joseph Van den Berg, a professor of music, and Charlotte Louisa (Lottie) *Collins (1865–1910), an actress, singer, and dancer. Lottie Collins was a flamboyantly successful music-hall artist who popularized the song 'Ta-ra-ra-boom-de-ay', which she had heard first in America and then introduced to London at the Tivoli music-hall in the Strand during October 1891, accompanied by her own dance. One of José Collins's earliest memories was of imitating this at a tea party at home.

José had successively two stepfathers, the first Stephen Patrick Cooney, and the second James W. Tate (*d.* 1922), a composer of light music. In the haphazard early chapters of her autobiography, *The Maid of the Mountains: her Story*

Josephine Collins (1887–1958), by Guttenberg [as Dolores in *A Southern Maid* by Adrian Ross (Arthur Reed Ropes)]

(1932), she describes herself as having been born Josephine Charlotte Cooney in May 1893 in Salford.

The facts of Collins's life become clearer after her professional stage début. She appeared at a Glasgow music-hall with Harry Lauder, illustrating his song 'I Love a Lassie' by doing a toe-dance in a tartan frock and glengarry as the 'little Scottish bluebell'. Soon after this, at the age of seventeen, by then with a contralto voice and already a strikingly confident stage presence, she was engaged in a touring company performing George Dance's *A Chinese Honeymoon* (music by Howard Talbot) and later took the leading part of Mrs Pineapple: in her book she speaks of herself as 'fourteen and a half and the baby of the company' (Collins, 41). At Christmas 1905 she was back with Lauder in a Glasgow pantomime, *Aladdin*. She had a variety of work in the years that followed, in the music-halls, in touring companies, and in pantomime; and in 1911, not long after her first marriage, to the actor Leslie Chatfield, she confidently set off to the United States seeking work. There she established herself so well in New York as a singer in operetta and in revue (she was in the *Ziegfeld Follies* for some time) that she did not return to London until 1916. She returned to appear at Daly's Theatre in a musical comedy, *The Happy Day*, written by Seymour Hicks with music by Sidney Jones and Paul A. Rubens. Although she was not the lead in *The Happy Day*, within a year (1917) she

was Teresa in *The Maid of the Mountains*, an operetta with words by Frederick Lonsdale and music by Harold Fraser-Simson and her stepfather J. W. Tate which ran at Daly's for more than three years: 1352 performances in all. It grew quickly into one of the favourite London plays of the war. Soldiers on leave crowded to see José Collins, and her song 'Love will Find a Way' was heard everywhere. For nearly a decade Collins was hugely popular with lovers of musical comedy. Invariably an attacking actress, she took to the stage with the same spirit and confidence which her mother had shown in the music-halls. Her strong bravura performances, her looks, the quality of her voice, and her well-known 'forceful personality' (*The Times*, 15) were famous far beyond the circle of the West End theatres. She was described as 'the uncrowned queen of the musical comedy kingdom' (ibid.). But her success as Teresa typecast her in the same kind of good-hearted romantic roles, and such parts could not continue indefinitely.

She followed *The Maid of the Mountains* with a similar part, that of Dolores in *The Southern Maid* (1920). Still at Daly's, in 1921 she was Sybil Renaud in *Sybil*. She left Daly's after a quarrel with James White, the financier from Rochdale who had bought the theatre and who had entered her dressing-room uninvited with a party of friends. Always hot-tempered, she was quick to resent any slight or attempt to lessen her privileges. She moved across, under Robert Evett's management, to the Gaiety Theatre, where for a time she continued her success in such different parts as Vera in *The Last Waltz* (1922) by R. Evett and R. Arkell (music by Oskar Straus), the name-part in *Catherine* (1923) by R. Arkell and F. de Gresac, and Nell Gwynne in *Our Nell* (1924). Although a generous portrait, the last was an undistinguished piece by L. N. Parker and R. Arkell, to music by Harold Fraser-Simson and Ivor Novello.

In 1925 Collins invested and lost a good deal of her own money through the failure of a production of *Frasquita* at the Prince's Theatre. She had a nervous breakdown following this episode, and although she toured various variety theatres in Britain and the United States, and took part in a brief and stormy run of George W. Meyer's revue *Whitebirds* at His Majesty's Theatre in 1927, she 'never regained her commanding position in the theatre' (*The Times*, 15). Eventually her intermittent stage work ceased altogether.

Her first marriage ended in divorce in 1917. On 27 October 1920 she married Lord Robert Edward Innes-Ker (1885–1958), third son of the seventh duke of Roxburghe. They were divorced in 1935. That year she married Dr Gerald Baeyertz Kirkland, who survived her. She had no children. During the Second World War, when her husband served as a major in the Royal Army Medical Corps, she trained as a nurse in order to work voluntarily at the hospitals where he was stationed. During her later years she lived a quiet domestic life in suburban Essex. She died in an Epping hospital on 6 December 1958.   J. C. TREWIN, *rev.*

Sources *The Times* (8 Dec 1958) · J. Collins, *The maid of the mountains: her story* (1932) · B. P. Kanner, *Women in context: two hundred years of British women autobiographers* (1997) · Burke, *Peerage* · *Theatre*

World, 10 (1958–9), 32 · J. Parker, ed., *Who's who in the theatre*, 6th edn (1930) · K. Gänzl, *The encyclopedia of the musical theatre*, 1 (1994), 296
Archives FILM BFI NFTVA, news footage
Likenesses photograph, *c.*1920, Hult. Arch. · photograph, *c.*1930, Hult. Arch. · H. van Dusen and Hassall, lithograph, NPG · Guttenberg, photograph, repro. in J. Collins, *The maid of the mountains: her story* (1932) [*see illus.*]

Collins, Michael

Collins, Michael (1890–1922), Irish revolutionary and chairman of the provisional government of the Irish Free State, was born on 16 October 1890 at Woodfield, co. Cork, the third son and youngest of eight children of Michael John Collins (1815–1896) and Mary Anne O'Brien (1855–1907), on the farm Michael senior had inherited from his father. Their holding was a substantial one, and his was an established and active family.

Civil servant and Irish Volunteer Michael's father's death left his mother in charge of the family, and it was she who set for him the goal of a Post Office position, a common ambition in west co. Cork. Already enrolled at the local national school—under a determinedly nationalist teacher—he was dispatched to nearby Clonakilty to be tutored for the Post Office exams. He was duly awarded a temporary boy clerkship in the Savings Bank, which he took up in July 1906.

Collins spent the next nine and a half years living with his sister Hannie in west London. He was studiously ambitious, and acquired a knowledge of accounting, but failed on several occasions to gain a permanent civil service post. In 1910 he took a job with an accounting firm, moving later to a stockbroker's office. In 1914 he moved on again, to the bills department of an American bank.

Collins moved in largely Irish circles, first among his fellow employees at the Post Office and then within the patriotic clubs and societies to which many of them belonged. His was a self-educated radicalism, but his political instincts were rooted at home: local policemen described the Collinses of Woodfield as 'brainy', 'disloyal', and 'dangerous' (Stewart, 41–5). He joined the Gaelic League and studied Irish. He played hurling and football with a Gaelic Athletic Association club and became its secretary—and subsequently the treasurer of the London board. He was a member of Sinn Féin by 1908; in 1909 he was sworn into the clandestine Irish Republican Brotherhood (IRB); in 1914 he became an Irish Volunteer. In the same year, he was appointed treasurer of the IRB for southern England, and became privy to its plans for a rising in 1916. He also contemplated joining his brother Pat in Chicago. The introduction of conscription in Britain in January 1916 forced his hand. Although later accused of being merely a draft dodger, it was as a committed republican rebel that he relocated to Dublin in January 1916.

The Easter rising Collins's reputation was that of a 'wild' Corkman, fiercely attached to his native county and as high-spirited in all his other attachments and relations. Mick was quick-witted, humorous, gregarious, and tall and handsome—attractive to men and women alike. He formed good friendships easily but was equally liable to fights and fits of temper; he was easy to bait. His relationships with men often had a bantering, competitive edge to

Michael Collins (1890–1922), by Keogh Brothers, 1916

them. With women he could sometimes be awkward, but also charming and confiding. His physical exuberance made him a keen sportsman, and occasionally a bully. He was a frequent and serious theatregoer, and had an omnivorous appetite for Irish, English, and American novels and poetry. These he could quote and discuss with relish.

As he had been in London, Collins was soon an insider in Dublin. He met most of the leaders of the coming insurrection and joined the influential Keating branch of the Gaelic League, already well endowed with Cork people and up-and-coming revolutionaries. When the delayed and crippled Easter rising finally began on 24 April he was an aide to Joseph Plunkett, its chief planner.

Collins spent the following week in the General Post Office, the nerve-centre of the rebellion, attending the tubercular Plunkett and generally making himself useful. He was cool under fire, but did not take part in the fighting. After the general surrender he was not considered dangerous enough to be court-martialled, and was instead sent to Stafford detention barracks. In late June he was transferred, with hundreds of other rebels, to a makeshift camp at Fron-goch in Wales.

It was here that Michael Collins began to break out of his orbit as a clerk, secretary, treasurer, and aide. He became a commanding presence, and a key organizer in the wearying struggle to resist British control. He assumed the *de facto* leadership of his fellow 'refugees' from Britain and was elected head centre of the camp IRB. Other men were beginning to fall into orbit around him.

The Fron-goch prisoners were released on 23 December

1916 as a conciliatory gesture by the British government, one which they interpreted as a victory. They quickly began to make an enthusiastic impact on Irish politics in a series of successful by-elections, in which Collins took part. He had been dismayed by the 'much, much too careful' opinions prevalent in Cork (Coogan, 59). The 1917 canvasses in Roscommon and Longford showed the unprecedented electoral vulnerability of the dominant Irish party.

The rebellion had been arranged by IRB activists, prosecuted largely by a radical fraction of the Irish Volunteers, and officially and popularly identified with Sinn Féin. Only the IRB had been officially committed to revolutionary means and republican ends. Sinn Féin—a tiny party—was not involved at all, although some of its members were. British repression had dislocated all three organizations, but unexpected popularity now beckoned.

Republican activist and leader Collins was a central figure in the ensuing struggle to shape a new movement. He travelled widely, spoke frequently, and became an adept at the back-room arts of committee packing, delegate selection, and election rigging. His power base was his new position as secretary to the Irish National Aid Association, to which he was appointed in February. From here he funnelled American money to former prisoners and their dependants, and built up an unequalled network of contacts. In fact National Aid was an IRB front, and with his new job came a place on its supreme council. Harry Boland, another rising man and expert wire-puller, became his fast friend and partner in intrigue.

These young militants were working to create a truly revolutionary movement. At first they backed Count Plunkett as a radical alternative to Arthur Griffith's Sinn Féin. But Plunkett was eccentric and incompetent, and the name Sinn Féin now had extraordinary popular resonance, so the faction fighting shifted to the conditions of a proposed merger, culminating in the party's official relaunching at a national convention in October 1917. The brotherhood's preferred candidate, Eamon de Valera, was acclaimed as president but its machinery was overwhelmed by the sheer scale of the fast growing movement. In electoral combat with the forces of moderation Collins barely scraped onto the last available seat on the executive.

Collins was by this time a familiar figure among activists. He had shown his Fenian colours at the funeral of Thomas Ashe, the president of the IRB, who died on hunger strike in September. This was a paramilitary occasion with a huge public audience, climaxing with Collins's ominous declaration that 'Nothing additional remains to be said' after the graveside volleys (Beaslai, 1.166). His stage management helped make his name among the reorganizing volunteers. When their convention was held on the heels of Sinn Féin's, committed republicans were elected to key positions and Collins himself became director of organization.

In 1917 Collins was one of many previously unknown people to rise to prominence and responsibility. Although he was unique in being on the national executives of the IRB, the Irish Volunteers, and Sinn Féin, other men held a similar clutch of positions at lower levels. The events of 1918 allowed him to dominate all three.

The driving force behind Collins's ascendance (and that of his cause) was the threat of conscription, which was given legislative force in April 1918. This united the nationalist population behind Sinn Féin, with the volunteers as the first line of resistance. A headquarters staff had been set up in March, which added the job of adjutant-general to his portfolio. The British government compounded its mishandling of the Irish situation in May by deporting most of the Sinn Féin leadership, while leaving the military and radical wings of the movement intact. Collins had himself been arrested in early April. He was bailed out once the conscription crisis began, and managed to evade the May round-up. From then on he was on the run from the authorities.

Collins now assumed the role of organizer-in-chief, and quickly became known to militant volunteers as their man in Dublin: the man who could get things done. He covertly encouraged aspiring gunmen and took gun running in hand, using the British IRB as an arms pipeline. Harry Boland simultaneously took over much of the day-to-day control of Sinn Féin.

Collins also began his intelligence work at this time. Before the May arrests he was approached independently by two detectives—one a well-placed confidential clerk—who warned him of the impending round-up. Both continued to pass him information. Collins was able to recruit two more and eventually assembled a remarkable network of agents within Dublin Castle, the Post Office, prisons, and even military headquarters. For all its impressive apparatus of safe houses, codes, and operatives, however, the success of this 'secret service' depended on its opponents' incompetence and lack of resources. Secret policemen and spies rarely posed much threat to Collins or the revolution.

Minister for finance in the first Dáil Conscription was successfully deterred and, in the December 1918 general election, Sinn Féin won 73 of the 105 Irish seats. Collins was elected in South Cork, and he and Boland had personally chosen many of the other candidates. They would prove a reliable caucus for the coming revolution. Those not in prison assembled in Dublin in January 1919, declared themselves a sovereign parliament—Dáil Éireann—and then declared independence. Collins was in Britain, arranging de Valera's dramatic escape from Lincoln gaol. Before sailing to the United States in May to raise support for the new republic, de Valera was elected president of the Dáil and named a cabinet, including Collins as minister of finance.

It was as a minister that Collins achieved his greatest administrative triumph. The revolutionary government was to be financed by subscriptions to a Dáil loan. Collins devised the scheme in the summer of 1919, organized a staff, offices, collection system, and camouflaged bank accounts, and managed the project closely. The fund was heavily oversubscribed and closed in September 1920 at more than £370,000.

In 1919 Collins officially relinquished his previous volunteer responsibilities and assumed the title of director of intelligence, as well as that of president of the IRB. A group of gunmen under his personal control ('the squad') began to assassinate pursuing detectives in July, in a campaign later extended to include intelligence officers, agents, and miscellaneous enemies of the revolution. Its culminating blow came on 21 November 1920—bloody Sunday—with the massacre of twelve British officers. These killings were as important for their symbolic as their counter-intelligence value, reflecting Collins's role as godfather to the militant underground within the volunteers who sought direct action against the wishes of many senior officers and the moderate majority in Sinn Féin. The Irish Republican Army (IRA) which emerged in 1920—a fusion of the IRB and volunteers—was led by these men. Collins did not plan or direct the subsequent guerrilla warfare, but the creation of this truly revolutionary institution—for which he laboured so hard—was one of his chief accomplishments, and his most ambiguous legacy.

Collins's life on the run became the stuff of legend in 1920 and 1921. His days were filled with work, carried out in numerous smoke-filled offices (he smoked up to fifty cigarettes a day, but was able to quit) secreted in houses and shops around Dublin. He cycled to his endless rendezvous with couriers, agents, guerrillas, and friends without disguises, bodyguards, or a gun. His correspondence, notable for its precision, was vast. Many of his opponents became obsessed with his capture, and several men who shared his name suffered or died as a result. His friends and admirers, to whom he was known as the Big Fellow, came to regard him as indispensable. Numerous newspaper stories depicted him as a figure of glamour and mystery, and his name became internationally well known.

The Anglo-Irish treaty When the struggle between the IRA and British forces ended in a truce on 11 July 1921 Collins was one of the two most powerful men in republican Ireland. De Valera, who had returned to Dublin in December 1920, was the undisputed leader of the movement, but Collins was the hero of the revolution. He had a wide network of personal loyalists, and both he and de Valera maintained coteries of devoted followers. This court politics grew almost inevitably polarized as Collins's enemies—including Cathal Brugha, the minister of defence, and Austin Stack, the minister for home affairs— gravitated together, and de Valera himself became suspicious of Collins's intentions.

It was thus a matter of great surprise that de Valera chose to send Collins as a member of the Irish delegation to the decisive peace conference in London while staying at home himself. The negotiators were divided from the start. Collins, a reluctant participant, lodged apart from the others, and he and Griffith were at frequent loggerheads with their more intransigent fellow travellers, as well as with de Valera, Brugha, and Stack in Dublin. The weeks of talks that followed their October arrival were often bitterly tense, compounded by Collins's and Griffith's secrecy in meeting separately with their counterparts in the British cabinet.

The treaty they eventually signed on 6 December, under Lloyd George's threat of immediate war, gave dominion status to southern Ireland, with the promise of boundary revisions to partitioned and protestant-dominated Northern Ireland. It passed the cabinet by one vote, with de Valera opposed, and was accepted by the Dáil on 7 January 1922 by an almost equally slim margin. Having led the fight with considerable parliamentary skill, Collins became both chair and finance minister of the transitional provisional government. He would be its dominant personality and charismatic figurehead.

The treaty debate was also the occasion for Collins to announce his engagement. His fiancée was Kitty Kiernan, whom he had met at the 1917 Longford by-election. Collins in turn found himself pursued by London and Dublin socialites—most notably Lady Hazel Lavery—whose attentions he returned with varying degrees of ardour. Whether any were physically consummated is unclear, although his romantic and sexual accomplishments were as subject to rumour and exaggeration as the rest of his career.

Collins spent the next seven months trying to hold together his new government, its relationship with Britain, and the republican movement. He defended the treaty as a writ of real sovereignty, and was closely involved in the transfer of power to the nascent free state. As always with Collins, however, conspiracies and schemes flowed beneath his official pronouncements and policies, and often in contrary directions. Thus, while he worked those parts of the treaty he liked, he attempted to subvert those he found troublesome. Public co-operation with Sir James Craig, the unionist premier of the separatist northern province, was matched with a covert campaign to make it ungovernable. In this he had the help of his opponents in breakaway IRA units, who otherwise accused him of undermining their own position with a rival army and police force.

The ultimate sleight of hand would be to give the free state a quasi-republican constitution, thereby assuaging Collins's critics and reassuring his more doctrinaire supporters. His attempt to reunite the sundering movement relied on this promise, and on power sharing deals made with various factions of opponents in May. Under a pact signed with de Valera, Sinn Féin would put forward a single slate of pro- and anti-treaty candidates in the June general election, on a platform of coalition government. Parallel talks within the divided IRA concluded that it would remain independent, with an agreed executive made up largely of IRB men.

Civil war and martyrdom Everything fell apart in June 1922. Collins's northern policy was a failure on all fronts. The British government angrily rejected the draft constitution. All anti-treatyites rejected the revised version. The IRA executive and convention rejected the proposed terms for army unity. His favourite instrument, the IRB, had broken in his hands, and most of his cabinet were hostile to his deal making and intrigues. And finally, the voters rejected the Sinn Féin pact in the 16 June election, and chose an overwhelming pro-treaty majority. Collins had lost his room to manoeuvre, but nevertheless retained his popularity—'what's good enough for Mick is good enough for me' was a common refrain.

Collins played his last card when he agreed to a direct assault on the recalcitrant IRA executive in Dublin on 28 June. Urgency was required to pre-empt a threatened British intervention, and he hoped it would be an isolated action, leading to renewed negotiations. The Dublin fighting was soon over, but it proved to be only the beginning of civil war. Collins took charge as commander-in-chief in July. He sought a quick victory, and never lost hope of a quick peace by agreement. When Cork fell to the national army in August he sensed an opportunity for both, and returned home in triumph. On 22 August his convoy was ambushed as it travelled through Béal na mBláth in west co. Cork. Collins took part in the fighting and was shot dead; despite numerous conspiracy theories, it was just bad luck. He was buried in Glasnevin cemetery, Dublin, on 28 August, his funeral the occasion for mass grief.

Collins's reputation has been embalmed by youthful martyrdom. Many biographies and memoirs have been written; none has been seriously critical with the partial exception of Frank O'Connor's brilliant The Big Fellow (1937). Most embrace the theme of indispensability: his genius was necessary to the success of the revolution, and his loss permanently diminished Irish public life thereafter. After the IRA renewed its campaign in 1970 he was used by republicans as a symbol of revolution, and by their nationalist opponents as an exemplar of pragmatism over fanaticism. Neil Jordan's feature film Michael Collins (1996) ensured his status as a contemporary popular icon. PETER HART

Sources T. P. Coogan, Michael Collins: a biography (1990) · P. Beaslai, Michael Collins and the making of a new Ireland, 2 vols. (1926) · F. O'Connor, The Big Fellow: a life of Michael Collins (1937) · Irish Military Archives, Dublin, Michael Collins MSS · NL Ire., Michael Collins MSS · NL Ire., Art O'Brien MSS · University College, Dublin, Richard Mulcahy MSS · University College, Dublin, Ernie O'Malley MSS · PRO, war office and colonial office records · M. Forester, Michael Collins: the lost leader (1971) · T. R. Dwyer, Michael Collins: 'the man who won the war' (1990) · G. Doherty and D. Keogh, Michael Collins and the making of the Irish state (1998) · Official reports of Dáil debates, Dublin (1921–2) · Forth the banners go: reminiscences of William O'Brien, ed. E. MacLysaght (1969) · NA Ire., Dáil Éireann MSS · A. T. Q. Stewart, Michael Collins: the secret file (1997) · M. Hopkinson, Green against green: the Irish civil war (1988) · M. Ryan, Michael Collins and the women in his life (1996) · M. Ryan, The day Michael Collins was shot (1989) · M. Laffan, 'The unification of Sinn Féin in 1917', Irish Historical Studies, 17 (1970–71), 353–79 · CGPLA Éire (1922)

Archives Irish Military Archives, Dublin, MSS · NL Ire., corresp.; papers · PRO, war office and colonial office records · University College, Dublin, corresp. and papers | NL Ire., Art O'Brien MSS · TCD, corresp. with Erskine Childers · University College, Dublin, Richard Mulcahy MSS · University College, Dublin, Ernie O'Malley MSS | FILM BFI NFTVA, 'Hang up your brightest colours — the life and death of Michael Collins', BBC2, 13 August 1994 · BFI NFTVA, 'Let the Dublin guards bury me!', Topical Budget, 31 August 1922 · BFI NFTVA, news footage · Radio Telefis Eireann Archives, Dublin

Likenesses Keogh Brothers, photograph, 1916, Hult. Arch. [see illus.] · Lavery, portrait, 1921; now lost · J. Lavery, oils, 1922, Hugh Lane Municipal Gallery of Modern Art, Dublin · T. Spicer-Simson, bronze medallion, 1922 (after his plasticine medallion), NG Ire. · T. Spicer-Simson, plasticine medallion, 1922, NG Ire. · F. W. Doyle-Jones, bronze bust, 1923, NG Ire. · J. Lavery, oils, 1935, Hugh Lane Municipal Gallery of Modern Art, Dublin · A. Power, bronze bust?, 1936, NG Ire. · S. Murphy, marble bust?, Hugh Lane Municipal Gallery of Modern Art, Dublin · B. Partridge, double portrait, pen-and-ink caricature (with Viscount Craigavon), NPG; repro. in Punch (15 Feb 1922) · S. Trinseach, charcoal drawing (Michael Collins?), NG Ire. · L. Whelan, oils (posthumous), Dáil Éireann, Dublin · photographs, Hult. Arch. · photographs, repro. in Cork Examiner · photographs, Michael Collins Association, London · photographs, NL Ire. · photographs, Ulster Folk and Transport Museum, Cultra, co. Down · portrait (as commander-in-chief), Dáil Éireann, Dublin

Collins, (Edward James) Mortimer

Collins, (Edward James) Mortimer (1827–1876), novelist and journalist, was born on 29 June 1827 at Plymouth, Devon, the only child of Francis Collins, a solicitor and mathematician, and his wife, Maud Branscombe (d. 1873) of Devon. Francis Collins published a volume called Spiritual Songs (1824) and died in 1839.

Collins was educated at private schools, and while still a schoolboy contributed to papers. He was eager to become a journalist, but his mother encouraged him to accept a teaching post at Queen Elizabeth College, Guernsey, where he taught mathematics from 1849 until 1856. On 9 May 1850 he married Susan Crump (1807/8–1867), daughter of John Hubbard and widow of the Revd J. H. Crump; they had one daughter, Mabel Collins.

While at Guernsey, Collins started the Channel Islands Magazine in 1853, which folded after three issues, and published his first collection of poetry, Idyls and Rhymes, in 1855. In 1856 he left Guernsey to concentrate on literature. He became a well-known journalist, at first working on the Leamington Mercury from 1856, moving to the Plymouth Mail three years later, and editing the Nottingham Guardian in 1861. While he adopted a worldly pose and was known as the 'King of the Bohemians', in his early years he was essentially conservative and a lover of old fashions in books and in his principles. He had strong religious sentiments and an aversion to positivists and freethinkers. In 1862 he bought a cottage at Knowl Hill, Berkshire, which was to become his permanent home. He edited The Selected Works of Walter Scott for the popular Moxon Miniature Poets series in 1865.

Collins published one of his better known novels, Who is the Heir?, in 1865, which ran to several editions and was reissued posthumously. He was appointed joint editor of the London Globe in 1866, the paper with which he was to be especially associated, though he was to write for many journals, including Punch and the British Quarterly, throughout his life. His wife, Susan, died on 5 August 1867, and on 4 May 1868 he married Frances Dunn Cotton (1841–1886); the couple settled at Knowl Hill. In 1869 he suffered a debilitating attack of rheumatic fever, which weakened his heart. Two years later he produced a second collection of poems, The Inn of Strange Meetings and other Poems, which the Saturday Review described as 'full of rich and delicate humour' (Allibone, Dict.). In 1871 he also published The Marquis and the Merchant, considered his best novel, and a collection of essays, *The Secret of Long Life*, first issued anonymously. These essays went through five editions and became his most successful work.

Collins was a prolific writer, producing seventeen novels and several volumes of poetry as well as miscellaneous essays and articles during twenty years. His literary friendships included that of R. D. Blackmore, whose influence can be seen throughout his fiction, particularly in the melodramatic *Sweet Anne Page* (1868). Collins's novels were light romances, showing, in the words of the *Illustrated London News*, 'a tendency to display the more attractive side of life, but not to delve beneath the surface' (26 Aug 1876). It was also noted that 'his plots construct themselves, and his heroes run away with him' (*The Academy*, vol. 12, 182). His second wife, Frances, was not only his muse, as her brother gallantly suggests in his preface to the *Selected Works of Mortimer Collins* (1877): 'Those who know Mrs Collins will understand why Mortimer Collins' poetical faculties developed during the last decade of his life' (Cotton, Preface). Frances was also co-author of the novels *Frances* (1874), *Sweet and Twenty* (1875), and *The Village Comedy* (1876). Collins died of heart disease on 28 July 1876 at Nightingale Hall, Richmond, London, after a short illness. He was buried on 1 August at Petersham churchyard, Richmond. After his death his wife published several novels as well as a memoir of her husband.

Collins's daughter, Mabel (1851–1927), married Keningale Cook in 1871, but they were separated about 1880 when he became mentally ill. She was also a novelist and wrote on women's suffrage, occultism, and antivivisection. Her autobiographical novel, *In the Flower of her Youth* (1883), contains a description of her childhood and a portrait of her father in the figure of 'Brough Warrington, the King of Bohemia'. KATHERINE MULLIN

Sources *Men of the time* (1875) · W. D. Adams, *Dictionary of English literature*, rev. edn [1879–80] · L. C. Sanders, *Celebrities of the century: being a dictionary of men and women of the nineteenth century* (1887) · Allibone, *Dict.* · Boase, *Mod. Eng. biog.* · M. Collins, *Pen sketches by a vanished hand* (1879) · Mrs M. Collins, *Mortimer Collins: his letters and friendships with some account of his life*, ed. F. Collins (1877) · R. Cotton, 'Preface', in *Selected works of Mortimer Collins* (1877) · *ILN* (26 Aug 1876) · R. F. Littledale, *The Academy* (5 Aug 1876), 137 · E. C. Brewer, *The reader's handbook of famous names in fiction, allusions, references, proverbs, plots, stories, and poems …*, rev. E. M. E. C. Hayman, new edn (1898) · J. Sutherland, *The Longman companion to Victorian fiction* (1988) · *DNB*

Archives NL Scot. | Bodl. Oxf., letters to Benjamin Disraeli · DWL, letters to Henry Allon · NL Scot., letters to William Blackwood & Sons · Yale U., Beinecke L., corresp. with Frederick Locker-Lampson

Likenesses photograph, repro. in Collins, *Pen sketches*, frontispiece

Collins, Norman Richard (1907–1982), television company executive and author, was born in Beaconsfield, Buckinghamshire, on 3 October 1907, the only son and youngest of the three children of Oliver Norman Collins (*d.* 1917/18), a publisher's clerk and illustrator, and his wife, Lizzie Ethel Nicholls. One of his sisters died in childhood and the family was left hard up after the father's death when his son was ten. Being attracted towards the

Norman Richard Collins (1907–1982), by Howard Coster, 1939

written word from an early age, Collins joined the publicity department of the Oxford University Press on leaving the William Ellis School in Hampstead. In 1929 he moved to the *Daily News* as assistant to Robert Lynd, the paper's literary editor. On 26 December 1930 Collins married Sarah Helen, daughter of Arthur Francis Martin, mining engineer. They had a son and two daughters. In January 1933, when he was twenty-five, he became assistant managing director in the publishing house run by Victor Gollancz.

Gollancz and Collins made an effective if incompatible pair, each needing the other but without the bonds of mutual affection or unquestioning trust. The firm prospered on Gollancz's flair and drive, but it was as much Collins's managerial competence as deputy chairman from 1934 which kept the venture moving forward during the preoccupation of its mercurial governing director with the Left Book Club and socialist politics in the later 1930s. Delegation did not come easily to Gollancz, who tended to see his colleagues as rivals, and in 1941 after a business association lasting for eight years their partnership was terminated when Collins departed to join the BBC in the relatively lowly position of talks assistant (empire talks). The annual salary, he noted, was less than the amount of a tax demand just received in respect of income from his previous employment.

At the wartime BBC Collins was soon marked out as a coming man. He had a talent for administration and a feel for corporate life; his interests and contacts were wider than most; he had already made a name for himself as a popular novelist (published, although without enthusiasm, by Gollancz); and in a larger organization his urbanity and witticisms were more readily appreciated. Energetic and ambitious, Collins rose fast in the General Overseas Service and by the time the war ended he was its director. After nearly two years in charge of the Light Programme (1945–7), he was selected by the corporation's director-general, Sir William Haley, in November 1947 to head the BBC's television service.

Collins felt cramped by what he regarded as an unadventurous and hesitant attitude on the part of the hierarchy at Broadcasting House. In peace, as in war, radio was the BBC's *raison d'être*. When Collins took over, television licences stood at 31,243; three years later the total had risen to 656,649 and a new transmitting station at Sutton Coldfield had been opened to extend the service from the London area to the midlands. To reflect the growing significance of television Collins pressed for its interests to be represented on the BBC's board of management. In this contention, far-sightedness and personal advancement ran hand in hand, and in October 1950 he experienced the mortification of seeing his proposal accepted but an existing member of the board of management, George Barnes, appointed over his head as director of television. Faced with this rebuff, Collins resigned immediately. Insisting that the clash was one of principles rather than of personalities, he condemned the apathy and even open hostility towards television to be found in some parts of the corporation, protesting that television was being merged into the colossus of sound broadcasting. Prophetically, he added that the future of television did not rest solely with the BBC.

For the next three years Collins was at the heart of an organized campaign which co-ordinated a variety of political and commercial interests held together by a common dislike of monopoly. Eloquently and persistently he maintained that competition need not result in a diminution of standards and urged the hybrid concept of a public agency regulating private enterprise companies which would be licensed to produce the programmes. The dignified title he devised, the Independent Television Authority, ultimately found its way into the Television Act of 1954. The BBC monopoly was ended when parliament responded to demands from the Conservative back benches. It was ironic that shortly after the great prize had been secured, Collins's ascendancy went into decline. Although a company he formed with his backers in 1952 was successful in obtaining one of the earliest programme contracts to be awarded, it was compelled to merge with a rival group owing to a lack of adequate financial resources before going on the air in September 1955. Collins became (and remained) deputy chairman of Associated Television (ATV) but lacked management control.

Over the next quarter-century Collins was the elder statesman of independent television, serving his own company and the industry in numerous capacities, notably by a long and satisfying connection with Independent Television News, of which he was a director for many years, periodically acting as chairman. In the non-profit-making news company Collins may have seen a miniature BBC thriving in the more open and competitive structure of the commercial system. Collins was a wealthy man from his original investment in ATV, yet he retained the instincts of a public service broadcaster throughout his career. He retired from the board of Associated Communications Corporation (as ATV had become) only five months before his death.

An unmistakable mark of Collins's power of application and creative energy was that he continued to write fiction throughout such a busy life. Although never a full-time writer he was a fluent and prolific author with sixteen titles and two plays to his credit between 1934 and 1981. An autograph edition of twelve of his novels was published during the 1960s. His best-known book, *London Belongs to me*, was an instant success in 1945: 884,000 copies were sold and the novel was adapted both for a film and for a television series.

A sociable man, Collins enjoyed conversation and clubs, the political committee of the Carlton being a particular favourite in his later life. He relished political as well as literary friendships. Collins died in London on 6 September 1982.   LORD WINDLESHAM

Sources H. H. Wilson, *Pressure group: the campaign for commercial television* (1961) · A. Briggs, *The history of broadcasting in the United Kingdom*, 4 (1979) · B. Sendall, *Origin and foundation, 1946–62* (1982), vol. 1 of *Independent television in Britain* (1982–90) · *CGPLA Eng. & Wales* (1983) · *WWW* · b. cert. · m. cert.
Archives FILM BFI NFTVA, documentary footage | SOUND BL NSA, current affairs recordings · BL NSA, oral history interviews
Likenesses H. Coster, photograph, 1939, NPG [*see illus.*]
Wealth at death £229,015: probate, 5 Jan 1983, *CGPLA Eng. & Wales*

Collins, Patrick (1859–1943), showman and politician, was born on 12 May 1859 at 58 Broughton, Chester, the son of John Collins, agricultural labourer (later, general dealer), and his wife, Annoia McDermott. One of five children, he attended St Wedburgh's School in Chester, but left at the age of ten and travelled Lancashire, Cheshire, and Shropshire with his family. He married Flora (1861–1933), daughter of James Ross, watchmaker, on 20 July 1880 in Liverpool. Their only child, Patrick Ross, was born on 7 March 1886.

No details of Collins's early business activities are available until 1881, when he was listed in the census as a proprietor of travelling swings on the Beast Market, Wrexham Regis. He is known to have attended Bloxwich Wakes in 1882 with an unspecified roundabout from his base in Walsall. Collins subsequently leased the Old Pleck fairground in Aston for fifteen years. This was further consolidated by his acquiring sites to run fairs at Oldbury, Darlaston, and Walsall, and the famous Birmingham Onion Fair. In an interview with the *Newport Advertiser* in 1895 it is claimed he started with 'two doll stalls and a set of swings' (Allen and Williams). He leased the Gondola works in Walsall in 1889, but was already proprietor of several roundabouts, including a set of 'three-abreast galloping horses' from Savages of King's Lynn in 1886, 'A sea on land' in

Patrick Collins
(1859–1943), by
unknown
photographer

serving president in the guild's history. Co-opted as councillor for Birchills Ward in Walsall in 1918, he was elected Liberal member of parliament for the borough of Walsall in November 1922 with a majority of 325. Collins was re-elected in the 1923 general election with a majority of over 2000 votes, but defeated in the 1924 general election by the Conservative candidate, W. Preston. Pat Collins continued to serve as a councillor in the borough and became an alderman in 1930. His political career continued alongside his amusement concerns, in whose management his son Pat was taking a larger role.

Flora Collins died on 8 April 1933, and on 8 November 1934 he married Clara Mullett (b. 1880), who had acted as manager for Pat Collins Amusements Ltd and secretary from 1911 onwards. She was the daughter of William Mullett, amusement caterer. Elected mayor of Walsall in 1938, Collins reputedly declined a knighthood from Chamberlain on the grounds that he had been born plain Pat Collins and would die the same. Pat Collins died on 8 December 1943 at his home, Lime Tree House, High Street, Bloxwich, and was buried on 14 December in Bloxwich cemetery. The news of his death was reported in the *World's Fair* with the headline 'Showland loses its G. O. M.' (11 Dec 1943). Pat Collins's favourite saying was: 'We only pass this way once—Let us do what we can when we can' (Allen and Williams). Of all the showmen who bridged the gap from the nineteenth to the twentieth century, Pat Collins did more than any other to live up to that statement.

VANESSA TOULMIN

1887, a second set of 'three-abreast galloping horses', and a 'switchback roundabout' in partnership with his older brother John in 1888. Pat Collins Ltd was floated on 4 January 1899 with a capital of £40,000 in £1 shares, all of which were subscribed and allotted. Details of the firm's assets included a 'top motion galloping horse machine', 'mountain ponies', an 'ostrich Machine', two 'living wagons', and a menagerie. Collins also purchased five new steam road locomotives from Burrells of Leinster between 1894 and 1920, as well as fifteen second-hand ones.

By the late 1890s Pat Collins was the leading roundabout proprietor in the country and by 1900 was expanding his business concerns into the fledgeling film industry. At Bloxwich Wakes in 1900 he presented moving pictures in his cinematograph show. Collins went on to travel with at least five bioscope shows and to open thirteen cinemas. Of the five shows he travelled, the finest were the two 'Wonderland' shows custom-built by Orton and Spooner of Burton upon Trent in 1907. The second of these, with its mammoth 112-key Marenghi organ, was operated by his son, Patrick Ross Collins. Collins's firm ceased travelling both shows by 1914 and then expanded into the cinema business. By the mid-1920s the firm operated fourteen cinema or assorted variety establishments; these included three cinemas in the Black Country, the purpose-built Cinema De Luxe in Chester, the Waldorf Skating Ring in Birmingham, and many others throughout the midlands. The name of Pat Collins became synonymous with fairs in the midlands. So extensive did his business become that during the 1920s he was running as many as four fairs a week, as well as a chain of cinemas and skating rinks.

Collins was elected president of the Showmen's Guild of Great Britain after the retirement of Lord George Sanger in 1909, having been one of twelve vice-presidents since 1900. He held the position until 1929 and was the longest-

Sources PRO, BT/31/8287/60177 · census returns, 1881, PRO, RG 11/5520, fol. 83, p. 33 · F. Allen and N. Williams, *Pat Collins, king of showmen* (1991) · T. Murphy, *History of the Showmen's Guild of Great Britain*, 1 (1940) · T. Horne, ed., *Showmen's Guild of Great Britain yearbooks, 1900–04* · T. Horne, ed., *Showmen's Guild of Great Britain yearbooks, 1904–18* · W. Savage, ed., *Showmen's Guild of Great Britain yearbooks 1919–34* · M. Lane, *Burrell showmen's road locomotives* (1971) · K. Scrivens and S. Smith, *The circular steam switchback* (1995) · K. Scrivens and S. Smith, *The travelling cinematograph show* · uncatalogued correspondence, Pat Collins to Thomas Murphy, 9 Sept 1938, National Fairground Archive, Showmen's Guild of Great Britain Collection · photographic records of Pat Collins's fairground equipment, University of Sheffield, National Fairground Archive · *The Showman* (3 April 1903) · b. cert. · m. cert. · d. cert.
Archives University of Sheffield, National Fairground Archive | FILM Staffordshire Film Archive, Stoke-on-Trent
Likenesses photographs, University of Sheffield, National Fairground Archive [see illus.]
Wealth at death £72,419 4s. 4d.: probate, 23 Nov 1944, CGPLA Eng. & Wales

Collins, Richard (d. 1732), portrait painter and topographical draughtsman, was the son of the Peterborough artist Richard Collins. He trained under the painter Michael Dahl. Based in Peterborough, he painted in and around Lincolnshire and Leicestershire. He made a number of portraits of the Pochin family of Barkby Hall, as well as an early conversation piece of a family taking tea, now in the Victoria and Albert Museum, London. The Lincolnshire antiquary William Stukeley recorded in a list of his portraits 'my profile, by Collins' (Sewter, 73) and a copy of a half-length portrait after Collins.

Collins was a freemason and, together with another

painter, de la Fountain, 'initiated Several persons of this [Spalding] & other Towns as members in Masonary' (Sewter, 72). On 10 August 1727 he was elected an honorary member of the Spalding Gentlemen's Society. He offered to draw for the society 'Such Things as they should judge worthy whenever he was in these parts into wh his busyness leads him' (ibid., 71). Collins attended a few of the society's meetings and presented them with several drawings and a large print of the west front of Peterborough Cathedral, engraved after him by Gerard van der Gught. His views of Croyland Abbey and the triangular bridge at Croyland were engraved by Samuel Buck and published in his Lincolnshire views. Collins died in 1732.

DEBORAH GRAHAM-VERNON

Sources A. C. Sewter, 'A minor English painter of the XVIIIth century: Richard Collins', *Apollo*, 36 (1942), 71–3, 103–5 · *DNB*

Collins, Richard (1755–1831), miniature painter, was born and baptized at Gosport, Hampshire, on 30 January 1755, the son of James and Sarah Collins of Gosport. He travelled to London in April 1776 and on 4 October that year entered the Royal Academy Schools; he was trained in the arts of miniature painting and enamelling by Jeremiah Meyer from 1777 to 1778. He may also have been instructed by Ozias Humphry, with whom he shared lodgings in 1780. He became established in practice in London, producing miniatures on ivory and enamel, the brushstrokes so smoothly rendered in both media that his work is characterized by a rather waxy appearance as well as by the fine quality of his draughtsmanship. One of his best works, the undated *Portrait of a Lady* (Rijksmuseum, Amsterdam), shows him to have been capable of penetrating characterization and he was certainly superior in this respect to his master, Jeremiah Meyer. He tended, when working on ivory and enamel, to use rather warm and rich tones, which testify to 'an aspiration toward the glossy tones of oil painting' (Reynolds, 149). Collins rarely signed his work, only occasionally using the monogram R. C., or signing in full on the reverse, as on his miniature of Augustus, duke of Sussex (Victoria and Albert Museum, London): 'R^d Collins pinxit 1789, Portrait Painter in Enamel to His Majesty'.

Collins was married to Sarah, *née* Sales (d. 1788), the daughter of a London merchant, on 20 December 1783, with whom he had one daughter. He exhibited miniatures at the Royal Academy between 1777 and 1818. The royal family had already been introduced to Collins's work when the countess of Pembroke employed him to paint a copy of a picture of Queen Charlotte at Windsor in September 1783, and George III saw his miniatures again on a visit to the Royal Academy exhibition in 1787. Following Jeremiah Meyer's death in 1789 the post of enamel painter to the king fell vacant. Collins claimed to have been appointed to the post in preference to Robert Bowyer and Richard Crosse, who had already been assigned the position, at the personal discretion of the king, in sympathy for Collins's deep grief at the recent loss of his wife. Collins painted only members of the royal family between 1788 and 1791, turning to public practice again after that.

Several examples of his miniatures of George III and Queen Charlotte copied after Gainsborough and Beechey remain in the Royal Collection. Having worked successfully in London from 23 Pall Mall and later from 39 Devonshire Street, Portland Place, Collins was able to retire on his earnings to Pershore in Worcestershire in 1811. He missed the cultural life of London, however, and returned to live in Islington for three years before his death in Dorset Place, London, on 5 August 1831.   V. REMINGTON

Sources R. Collins, autobiographical memoir, [n.d.], V&A NAL, MSL 1981/52 · *GM*, 1st ser., 101/2 (1831), 473 · R. Collins, letter to Ozias Humphry, 18 May 1780, RA, Ozias Humphry MSS, HU 2/102 · G. Reynolds, *English portrait miniatures* (1952); rev. edn (1988), 149 · R. Walker, *The eighteenth and early nineteenth century miniatures in the collection of her majesty the queen* (1992), 83–6 [cites Ozias Humphry memoir, MS said to be in Royal Academy Library] · D. Foskett, *Miniatures: dictionary and guide* (1987), 306, 307, 374–5, 512 · B. S. Long, *British miniaturists* (1929), 75 · L. R. Schidlof, *The miniature in Europe in the 16th, 17th, 18th, and 19th centuries*, 1 (1964), 156–7 · Graves, *RA exhibitors* · S. C. Hutchison, 'The Royal Academy Schools, 1768–1830', *Walpole Society*, 38 (1960–62), 123–91, esp. 142 · parish register, Gosport, Holy Trinity, 30 Jan 1755, Hants. RO [birth and baptism] · parish register (marriage), 20 Dec 1783, London, St Martin-in-the-Fields · *DNB*

Archives BL, corresp. with G. Cumberland, Add. MSS 36493–36515, *passim*

Likenesses R. Collins, self-portrait, c.1818 · P. Sandby, group portrait (*Sketches taken at print sales*), Royal Collection

Collins, Richard Henn, Baron Collins (1842–1911), judge, was born in Dublin on 1 January 1842, the third son of Stephen Collins QC (d. 1843), of the Irish bar, and his wife, Frances (d. 1842), daughter of William Henn, a master in chancery. He was educated at Dungannon School, and entered Trinity College, Dublin, in 1860, was elected scholar in 1861, and passed his final examinations in 1863 with honours in classics and moral science, but left without graduating. He did, however, receive the honorary degree of LLD from the college in 1902. In 1863 he moved to Downing College, Cambridge, where he came fourth in the classical tripos of 1865, and was elected to a college fellowship the same year. He was made an honorary fellow of Downing College in 1885. He joined the Middle Temple on 8 May 1862, and was pupil in the chambers of John Welch and R. C. Williams. He was called to the bar on 18 November 1867. In September 1868 he married Jane Ogle (d. 1934), daughter of Ogle William Moore, dean of Clogher; they had three sons and two daughters.

Collins joined the northern circuit and made a slow start in practice. He was not showy, and was less successful with juries than some barristers of less ability. His strength lay rather in his industry and knowledge of the common law. In 1876 he was chosen, with G. Arbuthnot, to edit the seventh edition of John William Smith's *Leading Cases*, which had previously been edited by justices Willes and Keating; he was also jointly responsible for the eighth (1879) and ninth (1887) editions of Smith's *Leading Cases*. This experience helped his reputation as a case lawyer both at the bar and on the bench. He was made queen's counsel on 27 October 1883. Complicated business transactions and litigation between rival municipalities or railway companies were his speciality.

Collins did not possess the characteristic manner or voice of an advocate, but he excelled in presenting his case and framing his arguments. Lord Esher, master of the rolls, then the dominant force in the Court of Appeal, showed that he was impressed by Collins's arguments, and this enhanced his reputation among solicitors. He was regularly employed in the heaviest cases in the Court of Appeal and in the House of Lords, and he was one of the very few common-law counsel who argued in the chancery courts. He was appointed a judge of the Queen's Bench Division of the High Court of Justice on 11 April 1891, on the resignation of Sir James Fitzjames Stephen. His exceptional learning and acuteness were at once recognized. His judgments combined clear arrangement and logical accuracy with an unusual insight into commerce and business. Expertise in traffic laws led him to be chosen in 1894 to succeed Sir Alfred Wills as judicial member and chairman of the railway and canal commission.

Collins nevertheless continued with the ordinary routine of *nisi prius* and circuit work and was an able criminal judge. When the president was absent through ill health, he also sat for two or three months in the divorce court.

On Lord Esher's retirement in November 1897, Collins was appointed to the Court of Appeal and was sworn of the privy council. In 1901 he succeeded Sir Archibald Levin Smith as master of the rolls, and on the death of Horace, Lord Davey, in 1907 he was made a lord of appeal, and granted a life peerage with the title of Lord Collins of Kensington. In the Court of Appeal he showed no inclination to interpret liberally statutes of which he disapproved, such as the Workmen's Compensation Act of 1897, and his numerous judgments under the act were frequently reversed by the House of Lords. A tendency to undue subtlety and over-refinement brought him more than one rebuff from their lordships.

Collins took on much external public work. As master of the rolls he was chairman of the Historical Manuscripts Commission from 1901 to 1907. He played a leading part in the management of the Patriotic Fund. In 1899 he represented Great Britain on the tribunal to determine the boundaries between British Guiana and Venezuela. The inquiry, held at Paris, resulted in a unanimous decision in favour of Great Britain. In 1904 Collins was appointed chairman of a commission consisting of himself, Sir Spencer Walpole, and Sir John Edge, set up to investigate the case of Adolf Beck, a Swedish resident in London who had been twice (in 1896 and 1904) wrongfully convicted at the central criminal court on charges of defrauding and robbing prostitutes. Their report helped to bring about the Criminal Appeal Act of 1907.

Collins's health was already failing during his last years in the Court of Appeal, and he was seriously ill when promoted to the House of Lords. He resigned as lord of appeal on 7 October 1910, and was succeeded by the attorney-general, Sir William (afterwards Lord) Robson. He died at 24 First Avenue, Hove, on 3 January 1911 and was buried in Brompton cemetery on 9 January. He was survived by his wife and five children.

In private life Collins was unassuming and sympathetic in manner. His sense of humour made him a popular after-dinner speaker. The prose and verse contributions he made as a barrister on the northern circuit won him the honorary title of poet laureate. He was also the first president of the Classical Association (1903). Collins never stood for parliament.   J. B. ATLAY, rev. HUGH MOONEY

Sources *The Times* (4 Jan 1911) · *Annual Register* (1904) · *CGPLA Eng. & Wales* (1911) · GEC, *Peerage*
Likenesses Quiz, cartoon, chromolithograph, NPG; repro. in *VF* (14 Jan 1893)
Wealth at death £55,199 17s.: probate, 1 March 1911, *CGPLA Eng. & Wales*

Collins, Samuel (1576–1651), college head, was born at Eton College, Buckinghamshire, on 5 August 1576, the son of Baldwin Collins (1544–1616), vice-provost of Eton and formerly a fellow of King's College, Cambridge. His younger brother, Daniel, followed in their father's footsteps, first as a fellow of King's, then at Eton. Samuel Collins studied at Eton from 1583 to 1591. At his entrance interview for King's College the provost, Roger Goad, was so impressed with his translation of Horace as to acclaim 'This is my child, who if he lives shall be my heir and successor' (A. A. Leigh, *King's College*, 1899, 97). Collins entered the college on 26 August 1591, became a fellow in 1594, graduated BA in 1596, and proceeded MA in 1599 and BD in 1605.

Collins was ordained deacon on 26 May 1605 and, against recent canon law, was made priest in the diocese of London a fortnight later, on 9 June. Chaplain to Archbishop Bancroft and, from 1610, to his successor, Abbot, he preached at Paul's Cross on All Saints' day 1607 as part of the debate over subscription. In his sermon, dedicated to Bancroft, he defended ceremonies as a moderate Calvinist, without making any case for their religious worth, while attacking Catholics for:

> sacrificing for sinnes of quicke and dead with a Wafer-Cake, treading down Kings, the deputies of God, from their throne of Maiestie to set up a foxie Intruder in their roome … taking away Bibles, mangling of Sacraments … selling pardons for six pence, soule ease for money, heaven at pleasure. (S. Collins, *Sermon at Paules-Crosse*, 1610, 53)

For Abbot he undertook to support Lancelot Andrewes in his dispute with Cardinal Bellarmine, publishing his *Increpatio Andreae Eudaemono-Johannis Jesuitae* in 1612.

Collins defended three questions for his doctorate of divinity at the Cambridge commencement of 3 March 1613 against John Williams, later bishop of Lincoln. His performance prompted the comment that '[N]o flood can be compared to the Spring-tide of his Language and Eloquence … these things will be living in the memory of the longest survivor that ever heard him' (Hacket, 24). His scholarship and Latinate wit, of which a few verses survive in print, brought him due reward. Rector of Fen Ditton in Cambridgeshire in 1614, held with the sinecure rectory of Milton until 1643, he was elected provost of King's College in April 1615. By 1617, when he produced his second substantial tome supporting Bishop Andrewes against the Jesuit Thomas Fitzherbert, *Epphata to F. T.*, he could include 'chapleine to His Majestie' among his titles.

On 22 October 1617 Collins was elected regius professor of divinity at Cambridge, a chair he held until his death and for which he was able to draw a £40 stipend from the rectory of Somersham, which James VI and I had annexed to it. He was also collated to a prebend at Ely on 19 February 1618, which he held until at least 1646. By about 1621 he had married a Cambridge widow, Susan Robinson, with whom he had two sons, James and John, both later fellows of King's. By 1621 he was no longer a royal chaplain. In December 1622 unsuccessful attempts were made to have him surrender the provostship to Sir Henry Wootton's nephew Albertus (Albert) Morton, an unsuccessful suitor for the provostship of Eton the following year. Collins was denounced by the college fellows to their visitor, Bishop John Williams, in 1628, for bribery, simony, and partiality in appointing Eton fellows. Williams found in his favour, attributing the rancour within the fellowship to the provost's 'slings of wit' (Hacket, 24), but indignation continued. Further complaints were heard before the chancellor, the earl of Holland, and, in December 1633, before Archbishop Laud. Yet Collins was a popular university lecturer who 'constantly read his Lectures twice a week …, giving notice of the time to his Auditors in a ticket on the School-doores, wherein never any two alike; without some considerable difference in the critical language thereof' (Fuller, *Worthies*, 133).

Collins undertook much work beautifying the chapel at King's College, in association with Thomas Weaver, whom he encouraged to provide the coats of arms for the unfinished stalls and for a raised wooden screen and reredos at the east end, and who certified in May 1629 that he had assigned £100 in his will for the unfinished work. Queen Henrietta Maria was able to view 'the wondrous and stately structure' of the work being undertaken in 1632 (Cooper, 3.250). The screen was completed by Lady day 1634. Collins paid towards a purple velvet communion cloth and for altar linen. By 1637 this open espousal of the beauty of holiness included the provision of altar candlesticks, tapers, and crucifixes. At much the same time Sir Henry Wootton warned Daniel Collins that his brother was subject to a court rumour that, 'either in a Sermon or in a Lecture or in some open place, with compagnie', Collins was traduced to have said that 'he was hartily gladd He had never spoken agaynst Transubstantiation in his whole lyfe hetherto And that he hoped to live till he might speake of it' (King's Cam., provosts' letters, IV, 10). Wootton seems to have been warning a friend of likely censure, and the two remained on good terms after Wootton had become provost at Eton, the latter sending Collins a portrait of the historian Paolo Sarpi as well as the Lambinus edition of Horace once owned by Pietro Bembo. A similar interest in anti-Calvinism is suggested by his support of his long-standing childhood friend Richard Mountague or Montagu, to whom he wrote warmly to congratulate him on his controversial elevation to the episcopate in 1628.

By 1640 Collins had moved the college altar and placed it tablewise, removed some of the chapel furniture, and prohibited adoration to the east. Such alterations were, however, too little and came too late. He was removed from the rectory of Fen Ditton and on 19 March 1644 he was charged with thirteen articles by a dozen witnesses under the earl of Manchester's commission to 'regulate' the university and remove 'scandalous' clergy within the eastern association counties. Mostly the complaints concerned ceremonialism, including bowing three times before reading the second service and also after his sermons, his beautifying the chapel at King's as well as his alleged habit of supplying his absence in the parish with malignant clergy, of advocating Sunday games, and of entertaining parishioners so well after the Sunday morning service that they 'spewed most shamefully' at afternoon service (*Walker rev.*, 78).

In January 1645 Collins was deprived of the provostship at the parliamentary visitation. With his professorial stipend, augmented with a small discretionary grant from his successor, Benjamin Whichcote, he lived in a house in St Rhadegund's Lane, on the other side of Cambridge. Later prudence prevented his becoming the last Caroline bishop, Charles I having nominated him bishop of Bristol in 1646, and allowed him to live among his books until his death at home, aged seventy-five, on 16 September 1651. He was buried in the same grave as Provost Hacomblen, in King's College chapel. NICHOLAS W. S. CRANFIELD

Sources provosts' letters, MSS, King's Cam. · Fuller, *Worthies* (1662) · R. Willis, *The architectural history of the University of Cambridge, and of the colleges of Cambridge and Eton*, ed. J. W. Clark, 4 vols. (1886) · D. M. Hoyle, '"Near popery, yet no popery": theological debate in Cambridge, 1590–1644', PhD diss., U. Cam., 1991 · J. Hacket, *Scrinia reserata: a memorial offer'd to the great deservings of John Williams*, 2 pts (1693) · CCC Oxf., MS E 297 · C. H. Cooper and J. W. Cooper, *Annals of Cambridge*, 5 vols. (1842–1908) · BL, Harley MS 7019 · BL, Add. MS 5802 · *Walker rev.* · *The life and letters of Sir Henry Wotton*, ed. L. P. Smith, 2 vols. (1907) · Venn, *Alum. Cant.* · *DNB*
Archives King's Cam., provosts' letters
Likenesses oils, King's Cam.

Collins, Samuel (1617–1685), physician, was the son of Daniel Collins (c.1579–1648), vice-provost of Eton College and rector of Cowley, Middlesex. He was born at Tring, Hertfordshire, and educated at Eton. In 1634 he was elected to a scholarship at King's College, Cambridge, where his uncle Samuel Collins (1576–1651) was provost. He was elected a fellow in 1637, proceeded BA in 1638, and on 1 June 1639 was entered on the physic line at Leiden. He commenced MA at Cambridge in 1642, and was created MD in 1648. On 27 July 1649 he was admitted a candidate of the College of Physicians, London, and a fellow on 25 June 1651. He was married to Mary, daughter of Robert Brett. Collins was incorporated at Oxford in his doctor's degree in May 1650, and about that time was elected a fellow of New College, Oxford, by an ordinance of parliament. He settled in London; was appointed censor of the College of Physicians in 1659, 1669, and 1679; was Harveian orator in 1665, and again in 1682, Goulstonian lecturer in 1675, and registrar from 1682 to his death. He was buried at Cowley, Middlesex, on 11 June 1685. He should not be confused with Samuel Collins (1619–1670), the author of *The Present State of Russia* (1671).

THOMPSON COOPER, rev. MICHAEL BEVAN

Sources Munk, *Roll* · Venn, *Alum. Cant.* · Wood, *Ath. Oxon.* · *N&Q*, 2nd ser., 10 (1860), 42 · *Retrospective Review*, 14 (1826), 32 · B. Hutchinson, *Biographia medica*, 1 (1799), 213 · T. Harwood, *Alumni Etonenses, or, A catalogue of the provosts and fellows of Eton College and King's College, Cambridge, from the foundation in 1443 to the year 1797* (1797) · E. Peacock, *Index to English speaking students who have graduated at Leyden University* (1883)

Collins, Samuel (*bap.* 1618, *d.* 1710), anatomist and physician, was the only son of John Collins, rector of Rotherfield, Sussex, who was descended from a family long established in Somerset and Devon. He received his education at Trinity College, Cambridge, where he was elected to a scholarship, and afterwards to a fellowship. Collins graduated BA in 1639 and MA in 1642. Then he travelled on the continent and visited many universities in France, Italy, and the Low Countries, but found none to compare with those of his native land. He was created MD at Padua on 25 August 1654, and incorporated in that degree at Oxford on 24 June 1659, and at Cambridge in 1673. He was admitted a candidate of the College of Physicians of London in 1656, and a fellow in 1668. About the latter date Collins was appointed physician-in-ordinary to Charles II. Between 1671 and 1707 he was frequently elected to the office of censor in the College of Physicians; he was anatomy reader in 1684, and on 10 September 1694 was appointed Lumleian lecturer, an office which he retained to his death. He was constituted an elect in 1689, was several times appointed consiliarius, and in 1695 was elected president of the college.

Munk says that Collins, who is mentioned in Samuel Garth's *Dispensary*, was an accomplished anatomist, and stood foremost among his contemporaries, whether at home or abroad, in his knowledge of comparative anatomy. His most important work, which contains a full account of his investigations, is his *A systeme of anatomy, treating of the body of man, beasts, birds, fish, insects, and plants. Illustrated with many schemes* (2 vols., 1685). It is often referred to by Boerhaave and Haller.

Collins married, first, Ann, eldest daughter of John Bodenham, of Wiltshire, and second, Katherine, dowager countess of Carnwath in Scotland, daughter of John Abington, of Dowdeswell, Gloucestershire. Collins died on 11 April 1710 and was buried at St Martin-in-the-Fields. To his memory is inscribed the view of the interior of the nave of St Paul's in Sir William Dugdale's *History* of that church. (The date of 1658 refers to the plate, and not to Collins's death.)

THOMPSON COOPER, *rev.* MICHAEL BEVAN

Sources Venn, *Alum. Cant.* · Munk, *Roll* · BL, Add. MS 5865, fol. 65 · *Annals of Queen Anne*, 9, 414 · J. Guillim, *A display of heraldry*, 6th edn (1724), 431 · B. Hutchinson, *Biographia medica*, 1 (1799), 213 · W. T. Lowndes, *The bibliographer's manual of English literature*, 4 vols. (1834) · *N&Q*, 2nd ser., 10 (1860), 42 · Wood, *Ath. Oxon.: Fasti* (1820), 172, 221
Archives BL, Sloane MSS 1822–1824, papers
Likenesses W. Faithorne, line engraving, BM, NPG, Wellcome L.; repro. in S. Collins, *A systeme of anatomy* (1685)

Collins, Samuel (1619?–1670), physician, was the eldest son of Samuel Collins (*d.* 1667), vicar of Braintree, Essex.

From 1635 Collins was a pensioner at Corpus Christi College, Cambridge, which he left in 1637 without taking a degree. On 1 June 1639 he matriculated at Leiden University. He then travelled to Montpellier in the company of Thomas Bartholin. On 30 October 1641 Collins took his MD at Padua University; he incorporated it at Oxford in 1652. He travelled to Russia in 1660 as one of Tsar Alexis's physicians, after an invitation had been issued to him by John Hebdon, Alexis's agent abroad. However, on 12 March 1662 Collins petitioned to be allowed to return to England, to settle his affairs following the death of his brother. He returned to England with the embassy of Prince Prozorovsky, who had been sent to congratulate Charles II.

In August 1663 Collins was back in Russia, and in the autumn resumed his duties as a royal physician, a position he shared with a German doctor, Andreas Engelhardt. Despite Collins's prolonged stay in Moscow, there is little information about his professional activities there. His main patient was Tsar Alexis, who suffered from extreme obesity; Collins therefore presented a number of notes about the need for a regular diet and moderation in eating and drinking. On 31 May 1664 Collins submitted a paper on phlebotomy which contained a brief general discourse and gave detailed information about the dates suitable for the operation. In June of that year, he submitted a paper about the properties of tea and coffee, and on 20 January 1665 he gave a discourse on obesity, its consequences, and possible remedies. In April 1665 Collins discoursed on the properties of valerian; and in 1666 he issued several prescriptions for a pregnant woman, paying special attention to the changing needs of her frail physique.

During his time in Moscow, Collins, like all royal physicians, was treating large numbers of nobles, as well as the royal family and courtiers. Like every other physician at court, he had orders to write out his prescriptions for treatment; a considerable number of these have survived. Some are in Latin, although most survive (in the State Archive of Ancient Acts, Moscow) in contemporary Russian translations made by the interpreters of the apothecary chancery, the bureaucratic body that governed all aspects of life and work of every foreign medical practitioner in Russia. During most of Collins's time in Moscow, his personal interpreter was John Tewe, the son of Robert Tewe, an English apothecary in the tsar's employ.

In the autumn of 1665 Collins was placed under house arrest and his pay was suspended. The matter appears to have been resolved by December, when the order to continue his pay as usual was issued. His salary was the same as that of Engelhardt and any other senior royal physician in Moscow from the 1620s to the 1680s: 1114 roubles a year. It consisted of two parts: a lump sum of 250 roubles and monthly payments of 72 roubles. In Moscow Collins lived consecutively in three houses, the last of which was slightly further away from the Kremlin, the royal residence, than the previous two. Before his final leave Collins was allowed to sell this house to the treasury and received sables worth 2800 roubles.

On 3 June 1667 Collins petitioned for leave, explaining that his contract, renewed in 1664 after the negotiations with the English ambassador, the earl of Carlisle, was for only three years. As the contract had expired, Collins asked for transport to convey him to the border; he nevertheless offered to act as a procurer of royal medical supplies. Although the order releasing him from service was given on 1 July, the customary commendatory letter, a parting present, and the transport were provided only on 21 July 1667.

Through family connections, and the patronage given to his father by the countess of Warwick, sister of Robert Boyle, Collins became acquainted with Boyle himself. Whether they had met before Collins's departure to Russia is uncertain, but they maintained a long correspondence in which they debated medical matters and exchanged information on diseases and their treatment. Collins also assisted Boyle in his research into the effects of extreme cold on elements and on humans. In 1669 Collins was in England and in a letter to Boyle complained of ill health. He had diagnosed himself as having a 'catthar' and scurvy, describing, among other symptoms, the weakening of the gums on his left side. Collins hoped that the warmer climate of France would improve his health and he soon left for Paris, where he died on 26 October 1670. In accordance with his will, a memorial plaque was inserted in Braintree church, Essex, where he was buried.

Collins's only book, *The present state of Russia, in a letter to a friend, written by an eminent person residing at the great tzar's court at Mosco for the space of nine years*, was first published in London in 1671. It was published in French in 1679. This book provides an interesting and insightful account of Russian life, although it suffered in part from the improbable anecdotes inserted for the entertainment of the reader, probably by the editors of the book. It is illustrated with a number of copperplates. M. UNKOVSKAYA

Sources PRO, PROB 11/334, 160, fol. 249*v* · C. H. Cooper and T. Cooper, 'Dr Sam Collins, provost of King's College; Samuel Collins, vicar of Braintree, and three contemporary physicians of that name', *N&Q*, 2nd ser., 10 (1860), 42–3 · Foster, *Alum. Oxon.* · Venn, *Alum. Cant.* · Russian State Archive of Ancient Acts, Moscow, Dela aptekarskogo prikaza, 143/2/- · Russian State Archive of Ancient Acts, Moscow, Vyezdy inostrantsev v moskovskoe gosudarstvo, 150/69, 1667 · N. E. Mamonov, ed., *Materialy dlya istorii meditsiny v Rossii*, 4 vols. (1881–5) · N. Y. Novombergskii, *Materialy dlya istorii meditsiny v Rossii*, 1 (1905) · PRO, PROB 11/193, fols. 209*v*–210 · I. Gurland, *Ivan Hebdon, resident i commissarius* (1903) [collection of documents] · L. Loewenson, 'The works of Robert Boyle and *The present state of Russia*, by Samuel Collins', *Slavonic and East European Review*, 33 (1954–5), 470–85 · J. Appleby, 'British doctors in Russia, 1657–1807: their contribution to Anglo-Russian medical and national history', PhD diss., University of East Anglia, 1979 · *The works of the Honourable Robert Boyle*, ed. T. Birch, new edn, 6 vols. (1772)

Archives RGADA (Russian State Archive of Ancient Acts), Moscow, Dela aptekarskogo prikaza

Collins, Samuel (1735–1768), miniature painter, was born in Bristol, the son of a clergyman. He first studied law before turning to miniature portraiture, and little is known about his artistic background or training. By the mid-1750s, however, he had a well-established miniature portrait practice in Bath.

Collins painted portraits on enamel and on ivory. In scale his work is close to that of Luke Sullivan and Nathaniel Hone. Their work is usually grouped together, and as miniaturists they form a significant part of what Graham Reynolds has called a 'modest school' of miniaturists that worked in mainly provincial centres during the middle part of the eighteenth century (Reynolds, *English Portrait Miniatures*, 109). Collins's style in watercolour on ivory closely resembles the work of his contemporary Gervase Spencer; both shared an understanding of the qualities of the ivory base and the watercolour medium. Collins allowed a considerable amount of ivory to show through the watercolour, particularly in the painting of the face. The shaded areas are done in greyish-brown and pale blue hatched lines. He used the technique of scratching through or scraping away areas of the watercolour, especially in the painting of hair and shadows, thereby giving strength to a portrait which was always relatively small. An example of this technique may be seen in *Portrait of a Young Girl* (Yale U. CBA). In developing the technique of painting in watercolour on ivory Collins had a lasting influence on his pupils, most importantly on Ozias Humphry and the next generation of miniaturists. His work is extremely fine and delicate and he enjoyed a very good reputation among his fashionable Bath clientele. He painted portraits of *George III* (exh. South Kensington Museum Exhibition, 1865), *Princess Amelia* (Pierpont Morgan collection, New York), and *The Second Viscount Gage*. His own portrait was painted by Gainsborough, an indication of his status and popularity as an artist. He was described in *Nollekens and his Times* as 'a man of gay and expensive habits' (Smith, 2.357). His extravagant behaviour led to financial difficulties and in 1762 he had to leave Bath and abandon his pupil Ozias Humphry, who took over his practice.

Collins went to live in Ireland and continued to have a successful career in Dublin painting miniatures on ivory. A writer in *Walker's Hibernian Magazine* referred to 'the celebrated Mr. Collins, few if any, excelled him in miniature painting; his drawing, colouring and touch were as perfect as in an oil portrait' (1, June 1771, 230). Usually critical of artists' work, Anthony Pasquin described him as 'one of the most perfect miniature painters that ever existed in the realm' (Pasquin, 28). Collins died of a fever at his home in Summer Hill, Dublin, in October 1768 and, according to the *Dublin Mercury*, was 'not only regretted by every artist and admirer of the arts, but by a numerous acquaintance' (27–9 Oct 1768).

There is a certain amount of confusion in attributing work to Collins, as he had the same initials as Samuel Cotes (1734–1818). The only difference between the execution of the initials is that Collins's are made up of smooth brushstrokes and Cotes's initials are made up of several strokes. Miniatures by Collins are in the following collections: the National Gallery of Ireland, Dublin; Kenwood House (the Draper gift) and the Victoria and Albert Museum, London; the Metropolitan Museum of Art, New York; the New Orleans Museum of Art (the Latter-Schlesinger collection); and the Yale Center for British Art, New Haven, Connecticut. PAUL CAFFREY

Sources B. S. Long, *British miniaturists* (1923), 76 · J. T. Smith, *Nollekens and his times*, 2 (1828), 357 · A. Pasquin [J. Williams], *An authentic history of the professors of painting, sculpture, and architecture who have practiced in Ireland … to which are added, Memoirs of the royal academicians* [1796], 28 · W. G. Strickland, *A dictionary of Irish artists*, 1 (1913), 190–91 · D. Foskett, *Miniatures: dictionary and guide* (1987), 512 · G. Reynolds, *English portrait miniatures* (1952); rev. edn (1988), 109 · P. Caffrey, *John Comerford and the portrait miniature in Ireland, c.1620–1850* (1999), 23, 34–5 · P. J. Noon, *English portrait drawings and miniatures* (New Haven, CT, 1979) [exhibition catalogue, Yale U. CBA, 5 Dec 1979 – 17 Feb 1980] · J. Murdoch and others, *The English miniature* (1981) · G. Reynolds, *European miniatures in the Metropolitan Museum of Art* (1996) · P. P. Bardo, *English and continental portrait miniatures* (1978) · *Hibernian Magazine* (June 1771), 230 · *Dublin Mercury* (27–9 Oct 1768) · P. Caffrey, 'Irish portrait miniatures, c.1700–1830', PhD diss., Southampton Institute, 1995
Likenesses T. Gainsborough, portrait

Collins, Samuel (1802–1878), poet and radical, born on 1 December 1802 at Hollinwood, near Manchester, was the son of a hand-loom weaver. He began his working life while still very young and before he had any education beyond basic literacy. While still in his teens he became an ardent follower of Henry Hunt and Cobbett, and was present at the Peterloo massacre in 1819. During the 1830s and 1840s he was involved with the Chartist movement. He joined a local radical association, and deployed his pen and tongue on behalf of the reform movement. He suffered for a time some obloquy for his temerity in denouncing Feargus O'Connor's land scheme.

Collins wrote homely verses, some of them in the Lancashire dialect, which were collected in 1859 in a small volume entitled *Miscellaneous Poems and Songs*, with a biographical notice by Benjamin Brierley. Collins, who worked at his loom almost to the last, died at Hale Moss, Chadderton, near Manchester, on 8 July 1878, leaving a son, Joseph Collins.   C. W. SUTTON, *rev.* MATTHEW LEE

Sources B. Brierley, 'Biographical notice', in S. Collins, *Miscellaneous poems and songs* (1859) · B. Brierley, *Home memories* (1886) · *Manchester Examiner* (10 July 1878) · d. cert.

Collins, Thomas (*fl.* 1610–1615), poet, was the author of a religious poem entitled *The penitent publican, his confession of mouth, contrition of heart, unfained repentance, and fervent prayer unto God for mercie and forgivenesses* (1610). The dedicatory epistle, dated 6 July 1610, is addressed 'To the Right Honourable, Grave and Vertuous Lady, the Lady Katherine Hastings, Countesse of Huntington' and is signed with the author's name. The poem is written in rhyme royal. In 1615 Collins published a pastoral poem, *The teares of love, or, Cupid's progresse: together with the complaint of the sorrowfull shepheardesse; fayre (but unfortunate) Candida, deploring the death of her deare-lov'd Coravin … in a passionate pastorall elegie composed by Thomas Collins*. The poet Coravin, whose death Collins laments, has not been identified. The poem is full of conceits but at its close Sidney, Spenser, and Drayton are eulogized, and allusion is made to Lodge. 'Jo. B[eaumont?]' and Samuel Rowlands contributed prefatory verses. The former refers to a third poem by Collins entitled 'Newport's Bloudy Battell … with Yaxley's Death', which is not otherwise known. Nothing further is known of Collins's life.   SIDNEY LEE, *rev.* MATTHEW STEGGLE

Sources *STC, 1475–1640*

Collins, Thomas (1775–1806), actor, was born in Chichester, Sussex, the son of Thomas Court (professionally known as Thomas Collins), originally of Edinburgh, and his wife, the former Mrs King, an actress. Thomas Collins senior was co-manager with James Davies of the Salisbury Comedians, whose circuit of theatres was based in Salisbury, Winchester, Chichester, Southampton, Newport, and later Portsmouth. The young Collins was sent to Bath to study music under Brooks, the violinist and leader of the orchestra at the Theatre Royal, but when he returned to Chichester in 1793 he forsook instrumental music for a place as a light comedian in his father's company.

Over the next nine years Collins established himself on the performance-circuit as a romantic tenor, able to play dialect roles and to move nimbly about the stage, a trait he inherited from his father. He performed such characters as Gunnel, a young sailor, in *Netley Abbey* by William Pearce and Motley, the jester in M. G. Lewis's *The Castle Spectre*. James Davies's daughter Henrietta, who had appeared on the stage since her childhood, often performed with Collins, and in 1795 the two were married. Their child died at Southampton in 1797.

Collins was invited by Richard Brinsley Sheridan to join the company at the Theatre Royal, Drury Lane. Presumably Sheridan saw the young man at the theatre in Jewry Street during one of his visits to Winchester, where Sheridan was courting Esther Jane Ogle, the daughter of the dean. An actor named Sheridan, possibly a cousin of the London manager, was a member of the Collins–Davies company. In 1802 Collins transferred to London together with Andrew Cherry, the dialect comedian and playwright. Sheridan had employed both men to replace Thomas King, the retiring comic lead who had established the role of Sir Peter Teazle in *The School for Scandal*. For his opening role Collins took the part of Jabal, servant to Sheva in Richard Cumberland's sentimental play *The Jew*, gaining commendations. This was followed by *Fortune's Frolic* by John Till Allingham, in which the new member played Robin Roughhead. 'We have no doubt that Mr Collins will become a favourite with the public', wrote a London correspondent to the *Hampshire Chronicle*.

That same year Sheridan revived *The Merry Wives of Windsor*, in which Collins played Slender, a part, *The Times* noted (27 October 1802), he 'fooled … to the top of his bent; his simplicity was irresistibly laughable'. Samuel De Wilde painted the actor in this role, clad in brown and blue, looking out towards his audience from a background representing Windsor Forest.

In 1804 Collins established the role of Timothy Quaint in Cherry's popular comedy *The Soldier's Daughter*, surrounded by long-serving members of the company. Nevertheless, according to the *Gentleman's Magazine*, it was to Collins that Cherry presented a portrait of Quaint inscribed:

> Honest Tim, when this you view,
> Remember who created you,

Not man, nor mortal, sage or saint,
Hath made you Tim, but Nature, Quaint.
(*GM*, 484)

The painting is unidentified. Later De Wilde painted a full length of Collins in this role in 1805.

The young actor was summed up as a 'promising genius in his line of acting'. The *Thespian Dictionary* said his humour lay in a 'peculiarity in his voice and manner'. Collins realized his limitations and began to experiment with character parts, disguising himself in a brown wig to play Old Dubbs in *The Dash*. Little time was left to him, though. Frenetic performances and a predominating nasal twang were caused by vocal strain, tiredness, and illness. Collins's condition worsened when, in March 1806, Henrietta died. She had been childhood sweetheart, wife, and colleague to the actor. Two months later, on 4 May, Thomas Collins also died, at a lodging in Brompton Row, Chelsea.

PAUL RANGER

Sources A. Hare, *The Georgian theatre in Wessex* (1958) · P. Ranger, 'I let the curtain fall: the tragic story of a Wessex comedian on the London stage', *Hatcher Review*, 3 (1988), 273–83 · *The thespian dictionary, or, Dramatic biography of the present age*, 2nd edn (1805) · *Hampshire Chronicle* (6 July 1795) · *Hampshire Chronicle* (19 Aug 1799) · *Hampshire Chronicle* (16 Nov 1801) · *Hampshire Chronicle* (16 July 1804) · *Hampshire Chronicle* (17 March 1806) · *GM*, 1st ser., 76 (1806), 484 · *Monthly Mirror*, 17 (1804), 147 · R. Mander and J. Mitchenson, *Guide to the Maugham collection of theatrical paintings* (1980)
Archives *Hampshire Chronicle* office, Winchester, playbills · BL, Burney collection of playbills · BL, collection of provincial playbills · Central Library, Portsmouth, Reference Library, Madden collection of playbills · Hampshire County Library, Winchester, local history collection, playbills
Likenesses S. De Wilde, oils, 1802, Royal National Theatre, London · S. De Wilde, oils, exh. RA 1805, Garr. Club · W. Ridley, engraving (after De Wilde), repro. in *Monthly Mirror*

Collins, (William) Wilkie (1824–1889)

Collins, (William) Wilkie (1824–1889), writer, was born on 8 January 1824 at 11 New Cavendish Street, St Marylebone, Middlesex, the elder of the two children of the painter William John Thomas *Collins (1788–1847), and his wife, Harriet (1790–1868), daughter of Captain Alexander Geddes of Alderbury, near Salisbury. He was of mixed Irish, Scottish, and English descent but lived all his life in or near London, as an adult always in the Marylebone district. He was baptized William Wilkie, for his father and his godfather, the painter Sir David Wilkie, but dropped his first forename after childhood. His unconventional preference for being called Wilkie, rather than Collins or Mr Collins, by his friends—women and children as well as men—was typical of his dislike of formality. He was born with a prominent bulge on the right side of his forehead, and his head and shoulders were disproportionately large for his short body and very small hands and feet. He was short-sighted, clumsy, and unathletic, though otherwise healthy as a child, and he later wore glasses. Clean-shaven as a young man, he later grew a full beard and moustache.

Childhood and early career As a child Collins met the poets Coleridge and Wordsworth, as well as many of the painters of the day. His childhood was happy, though he rebelled against the evangelical Christianity imposed by his parents, particularly his father. He admired his father

(William) Wilkie Collins (1824–1889), by Sir John Everett Millais, 1850

for his hard-working dedication to his art, a trait he shared, but Collins came to dislike his snobbishness and conventionality. He was devoted to his lively mother who, he claimed, first awoke his interest in literature, and he was protective of his less robust younger brother, the painter Charles Allston *Collins (1828–1873).

From 1826 to 1830 the family lived in Hampstead. In 1830 they moved to 30 Porchester Terrace, in Bayswater, where Collins remembered seeing, in 1832, the mass demonstrations in Hyde Park in favour of the first Reform Bill. He was at first educated by his mother, who had worked as a governess before her marriage. From January 1835 to July 1836 he attended a day school, the Maida Hill Academy. His schooling was interrupted when William Collins took the entire family to France and Italy from September 1836 to August 1838. He later wrote that he had learned more in Italy 'among the scenery, the pictures, and the people, than I ever learned at school' (Morris L. Parrish collection, Princeton University Libraries). He also claimed, in conversations with Charles Dickens and others, to have fallen in love, aged twelve, with a married woman in Rome and to have seduced her. On the family's return to London they moved to 20 Avenue Road, in St John's Wood, and Collins attended a boarding-school at 39 Highbury Place, run by the Revd Henry Cole. Here he felt out of place and was often rebuked for laziness and inattention. But it was at this school that he first discovered his powers of story-telling, to appease the dormitory bully.

Although Collins showed some aptitude for painting, and had a painting hung in the Royal Academy summer exhibition of 1849, his gift was less marked than his brother's, and he had no particular inclination for any profession. He was first found employment as a clerk in the Strand offices of a tea merchant, Edward Antrobus, where he remained from 1841 to 1846. Bored by his work, he scribbled compulsively in office hours. His first signed publication was a short story, 'The Last Stage Coachman' (*Illuminated Magazine*, 1.209–11). He also wrote a lurid novel, *Iolani*, set in Tahiti before its discovery by Europeans; it was not published during his lifetime. In 1845 he began a historical novel, *Antonina*, set in ancient Rome. His father, impressed by his determination to write, allowed him to leave the firm of Antrobus and enrol as a student of Lincoln's Inn. Although he was called to the bar in 1852, Collins never practised law, but retained a fascination with legal processes which is reflected in his fiction.

First publications Early visits to France—Paris was to remain one of his favourite cities—confirmed Collins in his dislike of English bourgeois life. He developed a taste for French cooking and for flamboyant and unconventional clothes. His hatred of formality extended to evening dress, and he was known, in later life, to appear at evening engagements in a tweed suit, with a pink or blue striped shirt, and a red tie.

When William Collins died in 1847, leaving his widow and sons in reasonable financial circumstances, Collins suspended work on *Antonina* in order to write a life of his father, *Memoirs of the Life of William Collins, Esq., RA* (2 vols., 1848), his first published book. At home there was a more relaxed atmosphere. Harriet Collins welcomed her sons' friends to the house and gave informal dinner parties at which smoking was allowed. Amateur performances of plays by Oliver Goldsmith and Richard Brinsley Sheridan were staged in the back drawing-room. Collins also translated a French play, *A Court Duel*, which was given a charity performance by the Collins brothers and their friends on 26 February 1850. Two days later *Antonina* was published to excellent reviews. Its success was the deciding factor in Collins's determination to make a career as a writer, though he never wrote another historical novel. In the summer of 1850 he wrote a lively travel book, *Rambles beyond Railways* (1851), based on a journey through Cornwall on foot with a friend, Henry Brandling, who supplied the illustrations.

In 1851 Collins met Dickens, when he was recruited as an actor in one of Dickens's amateur productions; it was to prove one of the most important relationships of his life. Dickens took the younger writer under his wing, and from 1853 Collins became a regular contributor to Dickens's periodicals *Household Words* and *All the Year Round*, in addition to working for other journals, in particular *Bentley's Miscellany* and *The Leader*. Collins and Dickens also became close personal friends, as Dickens found Collins's enjoyment of life and disregard for the conventions refreshing. The association was close enough to arouse the jealousy of Dickens's friend and biographer John Forster, and was of great benefit to Collins, especially in his early years as a professional writer, though Dickens was sometimes alarmed at Collins's refusal to conform, either in his life or his writing, to nineteenth-century British prudery. But Collins was not confined exclusively to the Dickens circle: he had many other friends. Through his work for *The Leader* he knew G. H. Lewes and George Eliot; he was close to John Everett Millais, who illustrated his story *Mr Wray's Cash Box* (1852), and to William Holman Hunt. Charles Reade was a friend in his later years. Nevertheless Dickens's advice and encouragement were vital. He was the first to recognize the originality of *Basil* (1852), Collins's first novel of contemporary life, which drew hostile reviews for its outspoken depiction of sexual obsession.

Collins's next novel, *Hide and Seek* (1854), was dedicated to Dickens, and is the most Dickensian of his novels. In the early chapters he drew heavily on his own experiences as a child and young man. The novel has a deaf heroine, the first exploration in his work of the effects of physical handicap on perception and character. This, with the altered states of consciousness caused by mental disturbance, became a lifelong preoccupation, and a feature of his fiction. The novel was welcomed enthusiastically by reviewers, who found it more acceptable than *Basil*.

Health, the stage, and the novel About of illness in the summer of 1853 was the first intimation of the serious ill health which was to dog Collins for the rest of his life. By October he was well enough to join Dickens and the painter Augustus Egg for an extensive journey to Switzerland and Italy, described in amusing detail in the letters of both Dickens and Collins. Dickens began to treat Collins less as a disciple and more as a collaborator. Much of their free time was spent together, wandering by night in the less respectable areas of London and Paris, looking for material for their novels and journalism.

Collins's fascination with the stage, encouraged by his association with Dickens's amateur acting company, led him to write his first play, *The Lighthouse* (1855), given several performances at Tavistock House, Dickens's home, and professionally produced, with great success, at the Olympic Theatre in 1857. Collins's next book, *After Dark* (1856), a collection of his short stories with a framing and linking narrative, consolidated the success of *Hide and Seek*.

Collins spent six weeks in Paris in the spring of 1856, living next door to Dickens and his family. He was ill for most of his stay, with a serious attack of the rheumatic disorder described as 'rheumatic gout', which continued to afflict him for the rest of his life. Yet he managed to complete his novella *A Rogue's Life* (1879), serialized in *Household Words* in 1856, and work out the plot of his next novel, *The Dead Secret* (1857). He also visited the theatres and music-halls with Dickens, and he discovered on a bookstall the volumes of records of French trials which provided the basis of the plot of *The Woman in White*.

On his return to London, Collins took lodgings near Fitzroy Square, since his mother was about to move house. He wrote a powerful article for *Household Words* (13.517–23) on the unpleasantness of his landlady to her exploited maidservants. The plight of the disadvantaged and outcast, particularly if they were women, continued to be a theme of his writing. It was probably at this time that he met Caroline Elizabeth Graves, *née* Compton (1829–1895), with whom he was to live from January 1859. Mrs Graves (known as Carrie), a widow with a young daughter, Harriet, was keeping a shop in a nearby street.

Caroline Graves was popularly considered to be the inspiration for the principal female character in *The Woman in White*, Collins's best-known novel. However, there is no foundation for the sensational story, told by John Guille Millais in his biography of his father (1899), that Collins, his brother, and Millais met a distraught woman in white whom Collins later rescued from a villain who had been holding her captive in a villa in St John's Wood. Caroline Graves's past was perfectly respectable, though she went to some lengths to conceal her humble origins.

In September 1856 Collins became a member of the regular staff of *Household Words* and the Christmas number was, for the first time, a collaboration between Dickens and Collins. *The Dead Secret* was, at Collins's insistence, serialized under his own name in the magazine. When the volume edition appeared the critic Edmund Yates wrote an article on Collins's fiction, suggesting that it was exceeded only by that of Dickens, Thackeray, and Charlotte Brontë (*The Train*, 3.352–7).

Collins's ambition to succeed in the theatre was still strong and in 1857 he wrote *The Frozen Deep* (privately printed, 1857), his best-known play; a production of it was staged that year by Dickens's amateur company to great acclaim. After the original London run, the play was given three performances in the Free Trade Hall in Manchester, where the women's parts were played by professional actresses. It was on this occasion that Dickens, playing the lead, met and fell in love with one of them, the eighteen-year-old Ellen Ternan. The play's success led Collins to experiment further with drama, and a melodrama, *The Red Vial*, was given a professional production in 1858. The audience found it absurd, and it was taken off after one night. Collins then returned to journalism, and his many contributions to *Household Words* that year included 'The unknown public' (18, 1858, 217–22), a plea for better literature for the readers of penny dreadfuls.

Complex relations with Dickens, and *The Woman in White* Collins's relationship with Dickens became more intermittent in 1858, as each was preoccupied with new personal entanglements. Dickens parted from his wife; Collins set up house with Caroline Graves, first at 124 Albany Street, and from the spring of 1859 at 2A New Cavendish Street. Although he never married her, they lived together, with one break of about two years, until Collins's death in 1889, and he treated her daughter Harriet as an adopted child for whom he took complete responsibility. However, although he made no secret of his domestic arrangements, he was still a man of his time. He never attempted to make Caroline Graves a part of his social life, and

although she was introduced to his circle of male friends, she never met their wives or stayed in their houses, where Collins appeared as a bachelor.

A further collection of short stories, *The Queen of Hearts* (1859), was followed by Collins's greatest success, *The Woman in White* (1860). It began serialization in *All the Year Round* in November 1859, and by Christmas it was the talk of London. Collins thoroughly enjoyed the fame and fortune it brought him. He moved with Caroline Graves to rooms at 12 Harley Street, spending a considerable amount on redecoration and refurbishment, and employing two servants. He entertained generously, in a typically informal way, and indulged the appreciation of rich food and fine wines which was to contribute to the undermining of his health. His success was at its peak during the 1860s, when his four best-known novels, *The Woman in White*, *No Name* (1862), *Armadale* (1866), and *The Moonstone* (1868), were published. The term 'sensation novel' was coined by reviewers to describe them, and Collins was seen as the originator of this highly popular genre.

The marriage of his brother, Charles Collins, to Dickens's daughter Kate in 1860 increased the detachment of Dickens from Collins. Dickens disapproved of the marriage, and also of Collins's open liaison with Caroline Graves. Collins, now financially secure but increasingly unwell, resigned from the staff of *All the Year Round* to concentrate on writing *No Name*. As he was struggling to finish the novel he was alarmed by the development of new symptoms added to his now familiar 'rheumatic gout', caused by the laudanum prescribed by his doctor to ease the pain of his illness. Although he made several attempts to do without the drug he was to remain dependent on ever-increasing doses of laudanum for the rest of his life, eventually taking amounts large enough to kill anyone not habituated to opiates.

Collins was given the considerable sum of £5000 for *Armadale* by the publisher George Smith. However, the serialization in the *Cornhill Magazine* had to be postponed because of the increasing severity of his illness. He travelled widely with Caroline Graves while planning the book, visiting the spa towns of Aix-la-Chapelle and Wildbad and spending the winter of 1863–4 in Rome, where he celebrated his fortieth birthday. Although physically ageing, he wrote to his mother that he still had 'no regular habits, no respectable prejudices … none of the melancholy sobrieties of sentiment … which are supposed to be proper to middle-age' (Pierpont Morgan Library, MA 3150 80).

A complicated personal life A sailing holiday in Norfolk in August 1864 seems to have proved his point, for it was probably then that Collins met Martha Rudd (1845–1919); a Norfolk shepherd's daughter then working as a servant in the Great Yarmouth area, she was to become the mother of his three children. However, there is no definite record of their relationship until 1868. In 1867 Collins and Caroline Graves moved to 90 Gloucester Place, where he lived for over twenty years. In the same year he became the temporary editor of *All the Year Round* while Dickens was in the United States, and wrote, in collaboration with him, the play *No Thoroughfare* (privately printed, 1867), which was his first commercial success in the theatre.

The Moonstone has remained second only to *The Woman in White* in popularity among Collins's novels. Although not the first detective story, it is a classic of the genre, with many features repeatedly borrowed by later writers such as Arthur Conan Doyle, Agatha Christie, and Dorothy L. Sayers. Collins's accomplishment was remarkable, for the novel was written while he was under great stress. His mother, ill from the beginning of 1868, died in March. Collins, suffering the worst attack of illness he had ever had to endure, called her death the bitterest affliction of his life. He was too ill to attend her funeral, and for the first time dictated a short section of his novel to Harriet Graves, later to become his regular amanuensis. His suffering, and the effects of the laudanum which relieved it, are reflected in the experiences of the character Ezra Jennings in *The Moonstone*.

Collins's personal life was also in turmoil. Probably in response to his affair with Martha Rudd, Caroline Graves married Joseph Clow, a vintner's son eleven years her junior, in October 1868. Dickens believed that the marriage was the result of her failed attempt to force marriage on Collins. Collins was present at the wedding, and Harriet Graves continued to live with him, taking over the running of his household. Martha Rudd, under the name of Mrs Martha Dawson, was now installed in lodgings within walking distance of Collins's house, Collins adopting the alias of William Dawson whenever he visited her or stayed with her in lodgings at Ramsgate, Kent. Their first child, Marian, was born on 4 July 1869, and their second, Constance Harriet, on 14 May 1871. Their only son, William Charles Collins Dawson, was born on Christmas day 1874.

In spite of Collins's commitment to Martha, Caroline Graves abandoned her marriage to Clow and resumed her former name after about two years, returning to live with Collins. His failure to marry either woman was probably a reflection of his sense of responsibility to both. His will treated them equally, and Harriet Graves was given the same consideration as his own children. It is unlikely that Caroline and Martha ever met, but Martha's children often went to stay at Gloucester Place, and with Collins and Caroline Graves at Ramsgate.

Later writings, ill health, and decline During the 1870s Collins's attempts to establish himself as a playwright met with increased success. A dramatization of *The Woman in White* was staged in 1871, and he now planned a number of his novels with stage adaptation in mind from their inception. *Man and Wife* (1870), in which he attacked the state of the marriage laws and the cult of athleticism, was first conceived as a play and staged very successfully in 1873. Although *Poor Miss Finch* (1872) was not dramatized, *The New Magdalen* (1873), a plea for sympathy for 'fallen women', was equally successful as a novel and a play. Dramatizations of *Armadale* (entitled *Miss Gwilt*) and *The Moonstone* followed in 1876 and 1877. Many of the friends he made in the last twenty years of his life were connected with the theatre. In part because of his interest in the stage, and in an attempt to keep the public's favour,

driven by the need to make more money to support his two households, his later fiction became more melodramatic and didactic. Although his work remained popular, he never again matched his literary successes of the 1860s.

In 1873 Collins made his only visit to America, taking up an invitation to tour the United States and Canada giving readings from his works. He enjoyed the appreciative audiences, and the less formal manners, and made several new friends. But his health was increasingly precarious, and he found the constant travelling exhausting. He cut short his visit, and made only about £2500 from the tour, considerably less than Dickens had made with his American public readings in 1867.

The Law and the Lady (1875) was the first of Collins's novels to be published by Chatto and Windus, who thereafter became his main publishers and later issued collected editions of his novels. (Collins had always wanted his novels to be available to readers of all classes and incomes, and Chatto and Windus agreed to issue thirteen of his earlier titles in 6s. and 2s. editions. After his death Chatto and Windus editions in various formats continued to be issued, from a luxury 'Library' edition to a 6d. edition in paper wrappers.) *The Two Destinies* (1876) was followed by *The Haunted Hotel* (1879), *The Fallen Leaves* (1879), and *Jezebel's Daughter* (1880), a fictional version of his failed melodrama, *The Red Vial*. In 1881 Collins further relieved himself of the business side of authorship when he appointed A. P. Watt as his literary agent. His final play, *Rank and Riches*, produced in 1881, was a disastrous failure, and for the remaining eight years of his life he confined himself to writing novels and stories, producing *The Black Robe* (1881), *Heart and Science* (1883), *I Say No* (1884), *The Evil Genius* (1886), *The Guilty River* (1886), *Little Novels* (1887), a collection of short stories, and *The Legacy of Cain* (1889).

Collins's health continued to decline. In addition to his long-standing arthritis, he began to suffer from angina, which caused him intense pain. But he still felt deeply involved with his writing. The composition of the antivivisection novel *Heart and Science* so excited him that he wrote week after week without a break. He also continued to fight for better conditions for authors. He had been a lifelong campaigner for improvements in international copyright, and was one of the founder members of the Society of Authors in 1884.

In 1888 Collins moved to 82 Wimpole Street. He was by now an invalid, and although he continued to see his close friends he became something of a recluse, in contrast to his earlier conviviality, though he attended a dinner of the Society of Authors in July, 'dreadfully crippled', as his obituarist observed, 'but in fair spirits, and anxious for me to point out such celebrities as had risen since his time' (*The World*, 25 Sept 1889, 12). Six months later he survived a carriage accident when he was thrown from a cab in a collision. In June 1889 he suffered a stroke and, fearing that he would not live to complete his last novel, *Blind Love* (1890), arranged for Walter Besant to do so. An attack of bronchitis finally led to his death, on 23 September 1889, at his home in Wimpole Street. His funeral was attended by Caroline Graves but not by Martha Dawson or his children, and it is Caroline Graves who shares his grave in Kensal Green cemetery, London, where he was buried on 27 September.

The popularity of Collins's writing, with the exception of his two best-known novels, *The Woman in White* and *The Moonstone*, continued to fall after his death. However, this trend was halted in the last quarter of the twentieth century and has recently been reversed. At the end of the twentieth century all his fiction, with the exception of his first novel, *Antonina*, was in print, much of it in inexpensive editions. Television adaptations of the better-known novels, of varying quality, are being produced. As yet, his plays have not been reprinted or restaged. Collins's work is also being re-evaluated. Many of his novels have appeared in critical editions, and there has been a proliferation of studies of his work as the subject of serious critical enquiry.   CATHERINE PETERS

Sources C. Peters, *The king of inventors: a life of Wilkie Collins* (1992) · K. H. Beetz, *Wilkie Collins: an annotated bibliography, 1889–1976* (1978) · L. Nayder, 'Wilkie Collins studies 1938–1999', *Dickens Studies Annual*, 28 (1998) · W. M. Clarke, *The secret life of Wilkie Collins* (1988) · *The letters of Charles Dickens*, ed. M. House, G. Storey, and others, 6–9 (1988–97) · *The letters of Charles Dickens*, ed. W. Dexter, 3 (1938) · A. Gasson, *Wilkie Collins: an illustrated guide* (1998) · *The letters of Wilkie Collins*, ed. W. Baker and W. M. Clarke, 2 vols. (1999) · N. Page, ed., *Wilkie Collins: the critical heritage* (1985) · Princeton University Library, Morris L. Parrish collection · Morgan L., MA 3150 80 · parish records (baptism), Marylebone parish church, 7 Feb 1824 · d. cert.
Archives BL, literary drafts, Add. MS 41060 · Bodl. Oxf., letters, MS Autog. d. 21 · Bodl. Oxf., letters, MS Eng. Lett. · Boston PL, letters and papers · Folger · Harvard U., Houghton L., letters and literary MSS · Hunt. L., letters, Eng MS · Hunt. L., letters and literary MSS · Morgan L., family corresp. · priv. coll., MSS · Ransom HRC · University of Iowa, Iowa City · V&A, MSS · Yale U., Beinecke L. | BL, agreements, accompts, etc., with Richard Bentley and George Bentley, Add. MSS 46615–46619, 46652, *passim* · BL, letters and MSS · Hunt. L., Holman Hunt collection · Hunt. L., letters to Edward Smyth Piggott · Mitchell L., Glas., letters, mostly to W. F. Tindell, his solicitor · Morgan L., Harper MSS · New York University, Fales collection · NL Scot., letters to the *Cornhill Magazine* and George Smith · NYPL, Arents collection · NYPL, Berg collection · NYPL, Berg collection, A. P. Watt & Son files · Pembroke Cam. · Princeton University Library, Morris L. Parrish collection, letters · Princeton University Library, Robert H. Taylor collection · Ransom HRC, Dorothy L. Sayers MSS · Ransom HRC, Wolff collection · University of Illinois, Urbana-Champaign, Bentley MSS · University of Illinois, Urbana-Champaign, Mudie collection · V&A NAL, letters to W. P. Frith and Mrs Frith
Likenesses W. Collins, crayon drawing, *c*.1827, Princeton University, New Jersey · E. M. Ward, sketch, exh. RA 1846, Dickens House Museum, Doughty Street, London · J. E. Millais, oils, 1850, NPG [*see illus.*] · C. A. Collins, oils, 1855, FM Cam. · R. Lehmann, drawing, 1862, BM · L. Ward, pencil drawing, 1862, Ransom HRC · N. Sarony, photograph, *c*.1873–1874, NPG · R. Lehmann, oils, 1879, NPG · A. Cecioni, caricature, watercolour study, NPG; repro. in *VF* (3 Feb 1872) · Cundall, Downes & Co., carte-de-visite, NPG · Cundall, Downes & Co., photograph, NPG · Lock & Whitfield, woodburytype photograph, NPG; repro. in T. Cooper and others, *Men of mark: a gallery of contemporary portraits*, 2 vols. (1876–7) · R. and E. Taylor, woodcut, NPG; repro. in *Illustrated Review* (10 July 1873) · H. Watkins, cartes-de-visite, NPG · chromolithograph, BM · double portrait, photograph (with Martha Rudd), priv. coll.; repro. in Clarke, *Secret life* · photographs, NPG · photographs, Dickens House Museum, Doughty Street, London · woodburytype photograph, NPG · woodcut (after photograph by H. Watkins, 1858), NPG
Wealth at death £10,831 11s. 3d.: probate, 11 Nov 1889, *CGPLA Eng. & Wales*

Collins, William (1721–1759), poet, was born on 25 December 1721 at Chichester, Sussex, the third of three children of William Collins (1674–1733), a respectable vendor of hats and a haberdasher by trade who was twice mayor of Chichester, and Elizabeth Martin (1682–1744). Educated as a gentleman, he published two slim volumes of verse by the age of twenty-five and very few poems thereafter. It is remarkable that an author who published so little—some twenty poems in all—before his death at the age of thirty-seven should have early acquired (and still retain) the status of an important poet. Although little is known of his life, reports of his genius, his neglect, his poverty, and his madness have attracted readers since his own day.

From the age of four until the age of twelve Collins was probably sent to the local prebendal school, and in 1734 (shortly after his father died) was admitted as a scholar at Winchester College, where he began lifelong friendships with Joseph Warton and with lesser writers James Hampton, John Mulso, and William Whitehead. A contemporary portrait shows a bewigged young gentleman with prominent wide-set eyes and nose and a delicate mouth. A precocious poet—though no more precocious than many—he published a little eight-line poem in the *Gentleman's Magazine* in 1739 over the pseudonym Delicatulus, and while still at Winchester is said to have begun his *Persian Eclogues*.

In 1740 Collins left Winchester for Oxford. Though placed first on the list for a scholarship at New College, Collins was matriculated at Queen's College on 22 March, there being no vacancy at New College, and was on 29 July elected demy at Magdalen (where his cousin William Payne was a fellow). At Oxford he continued a friendship with Warton and Mulso, and developed one with Gilbert White of Selborne. Said by Langhorne to have been distinguished both 'for genius and indolence' (*Poetical Works*, vi), Collins like many young Oxford gentlemen wrote poems and contracted debts. But his poems—the revised *Persian Eclogues*—found a London publisher in January 1742. And he seems not wholly to have neglected his studies. Johnson, a serious scholar, thought Collins 'a man of extensive literature, and of vigorous faculties. He was acquainted not only with the learned tongues, but with the Italian, French, and Spanish languages' (Johnson, 337). Shortly after taking his BA on 18 November 1743 Collins published *Verses Humbly Address'd to Sir Thomas Hanmer* (a statesman with literary tastes) 'by a Gentleman of Oxford' and by early 1744 had arrived in London where he was soon regarded as 'entirely an author' (Holt-White, 1.38), circulating a subscription, republishing his poem to Hanmer in May (this time with his name attached), and projecting a 'History of the revival of learning'.

No penniless hack, Collins had a small income from freehold property inherited from a recently deceased uncle, and soon had an allowance from another uncle. After his mother's death (July 1744) and the settlement of her estate (August 1745) he had income from other inherited property. He dressed decently, and enjoyed the pleasures of the town, 'spending his time in all the dissipation of Ranelagh, Vauxhall, and the playhouses' (White, 11). In his London years he continued to see Mulso and Warton. He called on his cousin George Payne and apparently sought out John Hardham, a native of Chichester, now a London tobacconist and under-treasurer of Drury Lane Theatre. He made the acquaintance of writers (Samuel Johnson, John Gilbert Cooper, and John Armstrong) and actors (Garrick, Foote, Tom Davies, and James Quin). But a poet's income was uncertain: a 'literary adventurer' (Johnson, 335) puts himself in the hands of chance. Collins also managed his rental income imprudently, and was often in want and in debt to his landlady in King's Square Court, Soho. Despite his several ambitious literary projects (a translation of Aristotle's *Poetics*, verse tragedies, a new periodical to be called the 'Clarendon Review'), and humbler tasks such as engaging to write brief lives for the compiler of the *Biographia Britannica*, Collins had apparently not committed himself irrevocably to literature. Having been intended by his father for the church, and having successfully applied to the duke of Richmond in 1744, he was persuaded by Hardham to decline the offer of a curacy. But within a year he travelled to Flanders to seek advice and assistance from his uncle, Lieutenant-Colonel Edmund Martin, who was in a position (Collins hoped) to make him chaplain in a regiment. Martin found Collins 'too indolent, even for the army' (Hay, 527).

Meanwhile, by early 1746 Collins had written perhaps three or four odes, including at least two on recent fatalities at Fontenoy and (perhaps) Falkirk. In May, at the Guildford races, he and fellow poet Joseph Warton discussed a joint publication. Collins's 'Ode, to a Lady, on the Death of Col. Charles Ross, in the Action at Fontenoy on 11 May 1745' was published in Dodsley's *Museum* in June 1746. The collaboration was abandoned, but Collins continued to write through the summer and autumn, and on 20 December Andrew Millar published his collection of twelve *Odes on Several Descriptive and Allegoric Subjects* (Warton's odes were published by Dodsley on 4 December). Warton's odes were successful enough to go into a second edition almost immediately; Collins's sold poorly. Deeply disappointed, he later bought up unsold copies and burnt them (*Poetical Works*, xi).

But Collins continued to write, though at a slower pace. By 1747 he had moved to Richmond, where he met James Thomson (Millar was his publisher, too) and John Ragsdale, and perhaps several other Scotsmen, including John Home, through their mutual friend Thomas Barrow, native of Chichester and in 1749 a resident of Winchester. When Thomson died in August 1747 Collins wrote an *Ode Occasion'd by the Death of Mr. Thomson* (1749). When Home returned to Scotland, Collins wrote (January 1750?) an 'Ode on his Return &c', addressed to Home, published in 1788 as *An ode on the popular superstitions of the highlands of Scotland, considered as the subject of poetry*. In February and March 1750 two London journals advertised that a new poem by Collins, 'An Epistle to the Editor of Fairfax his Translation of Tasso's Jerusalem', was soon to be published. (It probably never appeared; no MS survives.) In

November 1750 he wrote to a friend about another new poem, 'An Ode on the Music of the Grecian Theatre'. It was perhaps never completed; only a fragment survives. He told friends he still intended to complete the 'History of the revival of learning' and to produce the 'Clarendon Review'.

Although Collins had published little new work since 1746, his odes were beginning to reach a wider audience. The 'Ode to a Lady' appeared in the *British Magazine* in July 1747. Dodsley included three of the 1746 odes in his 1748 *Collection*. (In his 1755 edition he would print the *Epistle to Hanmer* and a 'Song from Shakespeare's *Cymbeline*'.) The 'Song from *Cymbeline*' was reprinted in the *Gentleman's Magazine* in October 1749. In June 1750 Collins's *The Passions: an Ode for Music* (from the 1746 *Odes*) was performed at encaenia at Oxford, and republished as a pamphlet. His financial circumstances improved when he received a substantial inheritance (perhaps as much as £2000) from his uncle Colonel Martin, who died on 19 April 1749. But by Easter 1751 Thomas Warton thought him very ill. The nature of the illness is not known, but it may already have affected both body and mind. By June he had apparently recovered, but over the next three years he travelled to Bath and to France in 'hopes his health might be restored' (*The Reaper*, 484). When Johnson saw him in lodgings in Islington, on his return from France, Collins had 'withdrawn from study'. As he told Johnson, 'I have but one book [an English New Testament] but that is the best' (Johnson, 339).

What Johnson called 'depression of mind' (Johnson, 338) continued to afflict Collins intermittently, and he was for a time confined to McDonald's madhouse in Chelsea, from which his sister Anne removed him in 1754, to take him back to Chichester. His sister Elizabeth died there in June. The Wartons visited him in the cathedral cloisters, where he and his sister lived, in September 1754. There they saw the manuscript 'Ode to a Friend' and received from Collins a revised draft of the *Persian Eclogues* and a number of poetic fragments. Preserved in Thomas Warton's papers at Trinity College, Oxford, and not published until 1956, all but one fragment appear to date from 1744–6. In November Collins travelled to Oxford for a change of scene and perhaps to relieve his depression. He took lodgings across from Christ Church, where Thomas Warton saw him 'labouring under the most deplorable langour of body and dejection of mind' (Boswell, *Life*, 276n.) and Gilbert White saw him 'under Merton wall, … struggling and conveyed by force, in the arms of two or three men, towards the parish of St. Clement, in which was a house that took in such unhappy objects' (White, 11).

Of Collins's final years very little is known. He apparently remained at Chichester and may have continued revising his *Eclogues*. A second edition was called for— Joseph Warton reported that Collins was 'greatly mortified' that the *Eclogues* 'found more readers and admirers than his Odes' (*Works of Alexander Pope*, 1.115)—and the retitled *Oriental Eclogues* were published in 1757, perhaps under the supervision of Warton. Collins continued to speak to the Warton brothers of his unfinished 'History'. During his final illness, though 'accustomed to rave much' (*The Reaper*, 479) he was calmed by listening to a servant read from the Bible. Collins died in Chichester on 12 June 1759, and was buried on 15 June in St Andrew's Church in East Street. A tablet by Flaxman to his memory was erected in the cathedral in 1795.

In stature Collins was 'somewhat above the middle size' with 'keen, expressive eyes, and a fixed, sedate aspect, which from intense thinking, had contracted an habitual frown' (*Poetical Works*, xiv). He was 'very temperate in his eating and drinking', his grey eyes 'so weak at times as hardly to bear a candle in the room; and often raising within him apprehensions of blindness' (White, 11). He never married, though this is perhaps not remarkable; his two sisters remained unmarried until the ages of forty-six and fifty respectively. One contemporary reported that the 'Ode to a Lady' was addressed to Elizabeth Goddard of Harting, Sussex, with whom the poet had fallen in love (Wendorf and Ryskamp, 144). Langhorne thought it 'very remarkable' (*Poetical Works*, p. xv) that the passion of love should be omitted from Collins's *The Passions*.

About the symptoms of Collins's nervous disorder contemporary observers agree in referring both to a 'langour' (*Works of Alexander Pope*, 276n.) or 'depression of spirits' (*Poetical Works*, xiii), 'general laxity and feebleness, a deficiency rather of his vital than intellectual powers' (Johnson, 340), and (in his last years) to occasional 'great moanings' (*The Reaper*, 479). Its essential nature is impossible to identify, but this has not prevented biographers from attributing it variously to 'poetical disappointments' (D'Israeli, 200), poverty, the 'enthusiasm of poetry' itself (*Poetical Works*, ii), or from linking it with Collins's 'indolence' at Oxford, 'want of steadiness', and 'dissipation' in London. A modern medical expert suggests 'depressive psychosis' (Ober, 153). It now seems clear that his madness did not appear until about 1751, that it recurred, that it left him lucid intervals, and that none of his poems was written under its influence. Contemporary references to his poverty are not inconsistent with modern findings that Collins squandered his legacies. Contemporary references from Goldsmith, John Gilbert Cooper, and James Grainger to his neglect support the view that his work was often reprinted and was admired by fellow writers: Collins's ambitions were high, and both he and his early admirers thought he deserved more attention. Wider fame dates from Langhorne's 1765 edition.

Collins has long served literary historians as a representative of his mid-century poetic generation and an acute register of their sensibility. Critical accounts depend on how one views the age. Still regarded by some as a typical 'pre-Romantic' who reacted against the moralizing poetry of the 'Augustans', Collins took Pope for his own model in his early work. Said to have displayed acute anxiety about the overbearing influence of Milton, he displayed remarkable urbanity, originality, and lofty confidence in his abilities. Identified as a solipsistic bard of an age of graveyard poets, his back turned on the world of history, he is also the author of a set of patriotic odes that engage topics of contemporary war and peace, liberty, and mercy to the Jacobite rebels.   DUSTIN GRIFFIN

Sources S. Johnson, *Lives of the English poets*, ed. G. B. Hill, [new edn], 3 (1905) · *The poetical works of Mr William Collins*, ed. J. Langhorne (1765) · R. Lonsdale, ed., *The poems of Thomas Gray, William Collins, Oliver Goldsmith* (1969) · J. Hampton, 'Some account of the life and writings of Mr William Collins', *Poetical calendar*, ed. F. Fawkes and W. Woty, 12 (1763), 107–12 · *The Reaper*, no. 26; repr. in N. Drake, ed., *The Gleaner*, 4 (1811), 474–84 · R. Holt-White, *The life and letters of Gilbert White of Selborne*, 2 vols. (1901) · G. White, 'Memoirs of the life of William Collins, the poet', *GM*, 1st ser., 51 (1781), 11–12 · A. Hay, *The history of Chichester* (1804) · *The works of Alexander Pope*, ed. J. Warton, 9 vols. (1797) · [I. D'Israeli], *Calamities of authors*, 2 (1812) · Boswell, *Life* · W. B. Ober, 'Madness and poetry: a note on Collins, Cowper, and Smart', *Boswell's clap and other essays* (1979) · R. Wendorf and C. Ryskamp, eds., *The works of William Collins* (1979) · P. L. Carver, *The life of a poet: a biographical sketch of William Collins* (1967) · R. Wendorf, *William Collins and eighteenth-century English poetry* (1981) · parish register, Chichester, St Peter the Great [baptism], 1 Jan 1722 · T. F. Kirby, *Winchester scholars: a list of the wardens, fellows, and scholars of … Winchester College* (1888), 238 · J. R. Bloxam, *A register of the presidents, fellows … of Saint Mary Magdalen College*, 8 vols. (1853–85), vol. 6, pp. 254–5 · parish register, Chichester, St Andrew's [burial], 15 June 1759 · memorial tablet, St Andrew's, Chichester

Archives BL, letter to John Gilbert Cooper, Add. MS 41178, fols. 35–6

Likenesses J. Flaxman, medallion on monument, 1795, Chichester Cathedral · engraving, 1796 (after J. Flaxman), repro. in Wendorf, *William Collins*, 12 · stipple, BM, NPG; repro. in *European Magazine*, 59 (1811)

Collins, William (1721–1793), sculptor, served as a hand in the workshops of Henry and John Cheere until he was about thirty-eight years old. It is likely that he produced charming panels on light-hearted arcadian subjects for chimney-pieces. J. T. Smith recalled that he gained a reputation for carving 'pastoral scenes that were understood by the most common observer' (Gunnis, 111). About 1759–60 he opted to become independent of his main employer, Henry Cheere, who had begun to reduce the productivity of his Westminster workshops. Setting up a business in Channel Row, close to his master's former shop in St Margaret's Lane, Collins was immediately successful. By 1760 he had received a major commission to carve a series of relief medallions, allegories of Liberty, Britannia, Commerce, and Agriculture, for the adornment of Harewood House in Yorkshire. A year later he was working on medallions on the façade of Kedleston House, Derbyshire.

With a number of other sculptors Collins was associated with the St Martin's Lane Academy and was a subscriber to James Paine's *Plans, Elevations and Sections of Noblemen and Gentlemen's Houses* (1767–83). In this book Collins was fulsomely praised as 'the ingenious Mr William Collins' (1.14). Paine singled out for particular commendation the 'very fine alto relievo' carving on the pediment of Sandbeck Park, west Yorkshire (c.1763–1768), the country seat of the earl of Scarbrough (ibid.). It was at one of the architectural schemes where Paine was employed, the extension of Merly House, Dorset, where Collins executed his masterpiece, an ambitious cycle of stucco reliefs on themes including the history of the ancient religions of the world. This adorned the library, commissioned by

Ralph Willett and built and decorated in the mid-1760s, but subsequently destroyed. An indication of the excellent design and workmanship of Collins's stucco panels is evident in a set of privately printed engravings commissioned by Willett. These include an image of an allegory of *The Triumphs of Britannia* that contains a self-portrait of Collins.

Collins was among the artists at the St Martin's Lane Academy who supported the scheme to set up the Incorporated Society of Artists of Great Britain. Together with Paine he devoted considerable energy to the establishment of the society, and he became one of its first directors. As a means to further his career, at the society's annual exhibitions between 1760 and 1768 he showed works of relief carving and modelling in a range of materials, including freestone, marble, and stucco. His first exhibits, such as *A Clown and Country Girl* recorded in the catalogue of 1761, were of his early pastoral type. He abandoned the cheerful rocaille style of these reliefs when commissions demanded more gravitas. An example of his more sober style may be seen at Bath Abbey in the monument to Jacob Bousanquet (*d.* 1767), which includes a signed relief of *The Good Samaritan*. His fine plaster relief of *The Resurrection* (completed before 1764) formerly above the altar of Magdalene College chapel, Cambridge, and now in the college library, similarly reveals a greater profundity of theme. Here, as in the altarpiece of St Mary's Church, Warwick, he invested the rocaille Gothic design of the architect, Timothy Lightoler, with a dignified solemnity. Collins also adapted himself to work in the restrained classical style that became fashionable in Britain during the early 1760s. His mastery in this milieu recommended him to Robert Adam, who employed him in 1767 to make chimney-pieces at Nostell Priory, Yorkshire.

Like that of the Society of Artists, however, Collins's reputation did not long survive the foundation of the Royal Academy in 1768. He seems to have received no further large commissions after 1770 (when he was forty-nine), and the last twenty-three years of his life remain obscure. Collins died on 31 May 1793 at his home in Tothill Fields in the parish of St Margaret's, Westminster, where he had made his will on 23 May that year, and was buried in the old cemetery in King's Road, Chelsea. He left his freehold house to his only daughter, Elizabeth, and small sums of money to his four nieces, the daughters of his brother John. MATTHEW CRASKE

Sources J. Paine, *Plans, elevations, and sections of noblemen and gentlemen's houses*, 2 vols. (1767–83) · R. Willett, *A description of the library at Merly in the county of Dorset* (1785) · E. Hargrove, *The history of the castle and town of Knaresborough* (1767) · J. T. Smith, *Nollekens and his times*, 2 vols. (1828) · Colvin, *Archs.* · R. Gunnis, *Dictionary of British sculptors, 1660–1851* (1953); new edn (1968) · *DNB* · will, PRO, PROB 11/1233, fols. 144r–145r

Collins, William (1789–1853). *See under* Collins family (*per. c.*1820–*c.*1980).

Collins, Sir William (1817–1895). *See under* Collins family (*per. c.*1820–*c.*1980).

Collins, William (1846–1906). *See under* Collins family (*per. c.*1820–*c.*1980).

Collins, William Alexander (1873–1945). *See under* Collins family (*per. c.*1820–*c.*1980).

Collins, Sir William Alexander Roy (1900–1976). *See under* Collins family (*per. c.*1820–*c.*1980).

Collins, William Edward (1867–1911), bishop of Gibraltar, was born in London on 18 February 1867, the second son in a family of five sons and four daughters of Joseph Henry Collins, mining engineer and writer on geology, and his wife, Frances Miriam Denny (*d.* 1888), who was born in Ireland. Collins had his early education at Mr Nuttall's Collegiate School in Lemon Street, Truro, Cornwall, where his family had moved soon after his birth. The family in 1881 relocated to Spain, where his father had taken up a position with Rio Tinto Mines. Collins learned Spanish, of great use in his later career, and enjoyed his period in the country, but returned to England early and lodged with his eldest brother, who had remained there. After a short period as a lawyer's clerk, Collins decided to study with a view to holy orders. He spent some time at the Chancellor's School, Truro, and became reacquainted with Canon Arthur James Mason, whom the family had known earlier in Truro and who later became master of Pembroke College, Cambridge.

In 1884 Collins was able, through financial support organized by Canon Mason, to proceed to Selwyn College, Cambridge, and graduated BA as junior optime in the mathematical tripos of 1887, proceeding MA in 1891 and DD in 1903. His later studies concentrated upon church history. He was much influenced by the teaching of Mandell Creighton, then Dixie professor of ecclesiastical history. In 1889 Collins won the Lightfoot scholarship in ecclesiastical history, and in 1890 the prince consort's prize. In the same year he was ordained deacon, and priest in 1891, serving his first curacy under Canon Mason, who invited him to become a mission preacher at All Hallows Barking by the Tower. He continued to combine his historical study with the holding of missions and retreats, and in 1891 returned to Cambridge as lecturer at St John's College on international law and at Selwyn on divinity.

In 1893, at the age of twenty-six, Collins was appointed professor of ecclesiastical history at King's College, London. It was said of his teaching style that, like his method as a preacher, it 'was decidedly sympathetic, if not altogether virile' (*The Times*, 25 March 1911, 11). But Collins maintained a high level of publication of historical studies, including *The Authority of General Councils* (1896), *The English Reformation and its Consequences* (1898), and *Church and State in England before the Conquest* (1903). Along with Mandell Creighton he was one of the founders of the Church Historical Society. In 1894 he renewed his connection with All Hallows, where he took part in the celebration of the 250th anniversary of Archbishop Laud's execution (10 January 1895), subsequently editing a commemorative volume of lectures on Laud (published in the same year). His reputation as a student of historical documents steadily grew, and his advice on church questions was frequently sought. In May 1899, when the archbishops heard at Lambeth arguments for and against the liturgical use of incense, Collins was able to draw upon early and medieval authorities in his contribution, which largely settled the question on the side of those opposing its use.

On 26 January 1904 Collins married Mary Brewin Sterland (d. 1909), a governess many years his senior with whom he had had 'a very close and peculiar relation' since his youth (Mason, 65). They had no children.

His intellectual achievements, and his language skills, made Collins a suitable choice when a new bishop was required to be selected for Gibraltar in 1904. Collins accepted this appointment although his health was already delicate. His physical character was summed up by an early comment on his 'pale face, and his great eyes' (Mason, 9). His duties, which included not only the administration of the diocese of Gibraltar and Malta but also the supervision of the English chaplaincies and congregations in southern Europe, involved constant travelling. In 1907 he visited Persia and Asiatic Turkey for the archbishop of Canterbury's Assyrian Mission, and on his return published his journal, *Notes of a Journey to Kurdistan* (1908). At the same time he continued to contribute a good deal to the church at home. During the meetings in Britain of the Pan-Anglican Congress in June 1908 his encyclopaedic knowledge was frequently in evidence and much in demand, and he presided successfully over the debates on the Anglican communion. He also assisted Dr Randall Davidson, archbishop of Canterbury, in drafting an encyclical letter which was issued on behalf of the Lambeth conference in August that year. Davidson noted that in the most difficult aspects of that conference Collins 'bore a leading, sometimes even the foremost, part' (Mason, 186–7).

The strain of travel and work produced a serious health breakdown for Collins in 1909, when he developed lung and throat trouble. His health never fully recovered and he died at sea on 22 March 1911 on his way to Smyrna, Turkey, after falling ill at the British embassy, Constantinople, with pleurisy and congestion of the lungs. He was buried on 27 March at St John's Church, Smyrna. A posthumous collection of his sermons was published in 1912.

G. S. WOODS, rev. MARC BRODIE

Sources A. J. Mason, *Life of William Edward Collins* (1912) · *The Times* (25 Nov 1911) · Venn, *Alum. Cant.* · *WWW* · private information (1912) · *CGPLA Eng. & Wales* (1911) · *The Guardian* (31 March 1911) · *Truro Diocesan Magazine* (April 1911) · L. Creighton, *Life of Mandell Creighton*, 2 vols. (1904)
Archives Canterbury Cathedral, archives, reminiscences · LPL, sermons | LPL, letters to A. S. Green · LPL, letters to John Wordsworth · NL Ire., letters to A. S. Green
Likenesses J. Russell & Sons, photograph, repro. in Mason, *Life*, frontispiece
Wealth at death £3724 2s. 11d.: resworn administration with will, 20 April 1911, *CGPLA Eng. & Wales*

Collins, Sir William Job (1859–1946), ophthalmic surgeon and politician, was born on 9 May 1859 at 46 Gloucester

Sir William Job Collins (1859–1946), by James Russell & Sons, pubd 1907–9

Road, Regent's Park, London, the eldest of the four children of William Job Collins (1818–1884), surgeon and pharmacist, and his wife, Mary Anne Francisca Treacher (1824–1880), who belonged to the Huguenot family of Garnault. The family traced its descent directly from a Warwickshire branch which included Francis Collins, the lawyer who drafted, and was one of the witnesses to, Shakespeare's will. Suggestions of distant relationships with other Collins families are only speculative. Collins had a happy childhood. His father's strong character and involvement in public affairs in the St Pancras district and his consistent opposition to compulsory vaccination were both strong influences on his son. William and his brother Edward, his lifelong friend, were educated locally, at University College School, and William went to St Bartholomew's Hospital, London, in 1876, gaining the Jeaffreson entrance exhibition. He was a scholar, fellow, and gold medallist in sanitary science and in obstetrics at the University of London. He qualified BSc in 1880 and MD in 1881, and gained the University of London's certificate in sanitary science in 1887.

Collins seemed destined for a brilliant career on the surgical staff at St Bartholomew's, but his opposition to vaccination was said to have prevented his election. From 1885 onwards he specialized mainly in ophthalmology, becoming surgeon and later consulting surgeon to the Royal Eye Hospital and the Western Ophthalmic Hospital. He was also ophthalmic surgeon to the Hampstead and North West London Hospital and to the National Temperance Hospital. However, he published little on ophthalmology and his main interests lay increasingly elsewhere. His career, like that of his father, was in public life. This public career was an extraordinarily broad one. He was a senator of the University of London from 1893 to 1927. He strenuously opposed R. B. Haldane's scheme for its reconstitution, which he termed the Germanization of the university. He was vice-chancellor of the university twice, in 1907–9 and again in 1911–12.

In 1892 Collins was elected as the Progressive member for West St Pancras to the London county council (LCC). He was re-elected in 1895, 1898, 1901, and 1904. The Progressive political programme included municipal provision of services and rate equalization, together with the unification of the City of London with the county. These aims were opposed by the Moderates and Collins was a leader in these struggles. For two years he was chairman of the public control committee, and of the general purposes committee. He was vice-chairman of the council in 1896–7 and chairman in 1897–8. When the London Education Act transferred responsibility from the London school board to the county council in 1904, Collins was the first chairman of the education committee, which laid the foundation of the education service in London. He took an interest in the LCC hospitals and an inquiry he set up in 1895 led to the establishment of the Claybury Laboratory, with the eminent neuropathologist Sir Frederick Mott as superintendent. Collins was created a knight in 1902 and KCVO in 1913.

Collins entered parliament in 1906 as the Liberal member for West St Pancras, after earlier unsuccessful contests in West St Pancras in 1895 and for the University of London in 1900. He seemed destined for high office, but these prospects were not fulfilled. Henry Campbell-Bannerman offered him the under-secretaryship at the Local Government Board, but John Burns, president of the board, intervened with a candidate of his own, and Collins withdrew. Later Collins's hopes of becoming deputy speaker were also disappointed. Collins consistently refused to 'play for his own hand' (MacNalty, 21). He was never a strict party man, and would speak against the party line in a debate if he felt strongly on an issue. He lost his seat in the 1910 general election, and was returned as Liberal MP for Derby in 1917 at a by-election. He then lost the seat in Lloyd George's 'coupon election' in 1918, and thereafter gave up political ambitions. As an MP he was successful in obtaining the establishment of a motor ambulance service for London, from 1915, after several years of campaigning.

Collins was a member of the royal commission on vaccination (1889–96), where his opposition to vaccination led to his drafting a minority report. The commission unanimously conceded the right to refuse vaccination to those who believed it useless or dangerous, a right subsequently embodied in the 1898 Vaccination Act. Collins found satisfaction in the successful conclusion of a campaign in which his father had been a pioneer. In 1906 he was a member of the royal commission on vivisection, for which he jointly drafted the scientific section of the report and its moral and ethical sections. He and others also drafted a dissentient memorandum.

Collins was actively involved in the discussion of an alcohol and drug control policy. He sat as the British government plenipotentiary at the three international opium conferences at The Hague in 1911–12, 1913, and 1914. The Hague Convention, the result of these meetings, was the foundation of all subsequent international narcotics control. Collins, in his writings, saw alcohol and drug addiction as diseases of the will rather than having any physical causation, and favoured restriction rather than prohibition so far as alcohol was concerned. His *Ethics and Law of Drug and Alcohol Addiction* appeared in 1916.

Collins was also involved in a large number of charitable and medico-political organizations. He was president of the Medico-Legal Society (1902–6), of the Society for the Study of Inebriety (1916–19), and of the Sanitary Inspectors' Association (1922–7), among many others. He was a member of the council of the King Edward's Hospital Fund for London, where he secured a more equitable pension provision for hospital administrative staff. His writings were wide-ranging and prolific, covering philosophy, law, and social reform.

In the inter-war years, Collins's primary interests were in the field of district nursing in London, where he was chairman from 1914 to 1944 of the Central Council for District Nursing. He was chairman of the Chadwick Trust from 1924 to 1946. Despite the advent of bacteriology, Collins remained a believer in Edwin Chadwick's view of the importance of a sanitary environment and fresh air, and he published *The Life and Doctrines of Sir Edwin Chadwick* in 1924. Collins was vice-lieutenant of the county of London from 1924 until 1945.

On 2 August 1898 Collins had married Jane Stevenson Wilson (*b.* 1855/6), daughter of John Wilson, MP for Govan. Jane Collins was a sister at the National Temperance Hospital, and was already well known through her work in the League of Mercy. She died after a long illness in 1936. Thereafter Collins's 'zest and pleasure in life departed' (MacNalty, 33), though his mental faculties and involvement in public affairs remained undimmed until his death.

Collins was of striking physical appearance with a massive head, firm set lips, and a penetrating gaze. His career did not quite fulfil its early promise. His qualities were judged to be those of the chairman rather than of the front bench, and he was seen as a 'chairman sent from heaven' (*BMJ*, 967), firm, fair, and always urbane. He was also an individualist with a 'disdain for expediency at the expense of principle' (MacNalty, 34). He threw a copy of *Ann Veronica* signed by H. G. Wells, who had been his patient, into the fire because he disapproved of its content. Collins's career was by no means a failure, for, in London especially, he achieved much in the field of citizenship. Collins died at 1 Albert Terrace, Regent's Park, where he had lived since the age of two, on 12 December 1946. A school in Somers Town was named after him until its name was changed to the South Camden community school.   VIRGINIA BERRIDGE

Sources A. S. MacNalty, *Sir William Collins: surgeon and statesman* (1949) • *BMJ* (21 Dec 1946), 967 • *The Lancet* (28 Dec 1946), 963 • *The Times* (14 Dec 1946), 7 • V. Berridge, 'The Society for the Study of Addiction, 1884–1988', *British Journal of Addiction*, 85/5 (1990), whole issue • b. cert. • m. cert. • d. cert. • *WWW*

Archives LUL, corresp. and papers | Bodl. Oxf., corresp. with Sir Henry Burdett • NL Scot., corresp., incl. with Lord Rosebery

Likenesses J. Russell & Sons, photograph, pubd 1907–9, NPG [*see illus.*] • photograph (as young man), repro. in MacNalty, *Sir William Collins* • photograph (as old man), repro. in *The Lancet*, 963

Wealth at death £33,554 7s. 0d.: probate, 6 Feb 1947, CGPLA Eng. & Wales

Collins, William John Thomas (1788–1847), landscape and genre painter, was born on 18 September 1788 at Great Titchfield Street, London. He was one of three children; an elder sister died before his birth and his younger brother, Francis, predeceased him in 1833. His father, William Collins (d. 1812), was Irish but had settled in England. He was a picture dealer and writer and the author of a memoir of the painter George Morland (1763–1804), who had allowed the young artist to observe him at work in his studio. Although in later years Collins denied that he had gleaned any useful training from Morland, a comparison between their work demonstrates that Collins emulated Morland's work, both in its style and subject matter. Collins's mother (d. 1833) was from Edinburgh. Collins entered the Royal Academy Schools, London, in 1807 and thereafter began to exhibit small landscapes and genre subjects. He also produced a few portraits during these early years, presumably to supplement his income rather than from any real vocation in that direction. In 1813 he had his first popular success at the Royal Academy exhibition with *The Sale of the Pet Lamb* (Guildhall Art Gallery, London). The composition, combining a narrative incident of touching pathos with a carefully observed landscape setting, became the model for future subjects. The popularity of such pictures ensured Collins's election as an associate of the Royal Academy in 1814. *The Reluctant Departure* (1815; Birmingham City Art Gallery) was the first of many seashore compositions adopting a similar sentimental formula, as a mother takes leave of her child. It is typical of Collins's early highly finished and luminous style. Collins's choice of narrative genre subjects was not wholly original but formed part of a revival of interest in genre painting in Britain during the early decades of the nineteenth century. The taste for narrative scenes from everyday life was epitomized in the work of Sir David Wilkie (1785–1841), whose early popular success encouraged other artists, including Collins, William Mulready (1786–1863), and Thomas Webster (1800–1886), to experiment with similar themes. Collins and Wilkie became close friends and Wilkie's influence is clearly present in Collins's choice of subjects. Collins's most original contribution to genre painting was in the recurrent and popular theme of childhood and he was one of the most successful artists to deal consistently with this theme. His childhood genre subjects were predominately rural, set against a backdrop of a country cottage or village scene and focused on a trivial domestic incident, as in *The Kitten Deceived* (1816; Guildhall Art Gallery, London).

Following the death of his father in 1812, and subsequent financial concerns, Collins appears to have made a deliberate decision to widen the scope of his subject matter in the hope of increasing his commissions. In 1816 he made a prolonged stay at Hastings and thereafter began to paint coastal subjects which, however, still relied on the activities of shrimp boys and fishermen's children, working or playing by the seashore, for their main interest. A slight variation on the coastal subjects were those of children fishing or playing by rivers or woodland streams:

Young Anglers (1820; RA) was presented as his diploma picture following his election as a royal academician in 1820. In 1822 Collins married Harriet Geddes (1790–1868), a cousin of the painter Andrew Geddes ARA (1783–1844).

Collins was somewhat unusual as a painter of genre in habitually using a rural landscape setting for his compositions, particularly since he was born and permanently resided in London. Throughout his career, however, he made almost annual trips to stay at the houses and country seats of important patrons, among whom were Sir Robert Peel, Sir Thomas Baring, and Lord Liverpool. In addition to his short residences with patrons and friends, he also embarked on sketching tours solely with the aim of gathering material for his paintings. His earliest trips took him to the coast of Norfolk in 1815, Hastings in 1816, and the Lake District in 1818, where he became acquainted with the poets Wordsworth, Coleridge, and Southey. During the course of his career he continued to travel widely in Britain and in the 1820s took up summer residences in Hampstead or Hendon, in the countryside north of London, so that he could sketch directly from nature. It is in his approach to naturalism that Collins's work can be related to the landscape paintings of his contemporaries although, unlike John Constable (1776–1837) and the painters of the Norwich school, he seems to have built up his compositions by sketching the components directly from the motif and combining them in his studio to form imaginary landscapes. His aim was not simply to capture the beauties of an actual scene but to create a suitably idealized backdrop for his narrative events. During the 1830s the narrative element of Collins's genre scenes, particularly those involving children, took on a more vigorous role. The comparatively uneventful scenes of his earlier works gave way to compositions with a more actively dramatic element, as in *Rustic Civility* (1833; V&A), one of the artist's most original compositions. As his subjects became more lively, so did his brushwork, and he no longer painted with the high degree of finish that had made his earlier works so attractive.

Collins's foreign travels were few; his first journey abroad, in 1817, was to Paris in the company of the painters Washington Allston (1779–1843) and Charles Robert Leslie (1794–1859). He visited Holland and Belgium in 1828, Boulogne in 1829, and Germany in 1840. The only prolonged foreign journey was to Italy, between 1836 and 1838. The trip had an important impact in providing material for a new range of Italian subjects, including landscapes and genre. Soon after his return from Italy he began to produce a range of figure subjects such as *Poor Travellers at the Door of a Capuchin Convent, Near Vico, Bay of Naples* (1839; Sudley Art Gallery, Liverpool), as well as scenes illustrating events from biblical history. Collins continued to exhibit Italian and figure subjects until 1844 when, according to his son, his illness caused him to revert to more familiar subjects. However, his return to his more popular English landscapes may have been the result of the criticism which his new endeavours had received. His final works were mostly coastal views, which resulted from short trips to the Isle of Wight in 1844 and

Devon in 1845. His last important work was *Early Morning—Cromer* (1846; Tate collection), which, prior to its exhibition that year, was praised by John Ruskin in his *Modern Painters*.

Collins was an established figure in his profession and throughout his life was closely involved with Royal Academy affairs, serving as librarian in 1840–42. He died at his home, 1 Devonport Street, Hyde Park Gardens, London, on 17 February 1847 and was buried at St Mary's, Paddington. He had two sons, William Wilkie *Collins (1824–1889), the novelist, and Charles Allston *Collins (1828–1873), the Pre-Raphaelite painter.   DIANE PERKINS

Sources W. W. Collins, *Memoirs of the life of William Collins, esq. RA*, 2 vols. (1848) · W. Collins, 'List of pictures and patrons', 2 vols., 1808–46, V&A NAL · *DNB* · *The Athenaeum* (20 Feb 1847) · D. Perkins, 'William Collins: an examination of his work and reputation', MA diss., Birkbeck College, London, 1992 · M. Salvesen, 'William Collins and William Mulready: the increase of child genre', MA diss., Courtauld Inst., 1968 · C. Payne, *Rustic simplicity: scenes of cottage life in nineteenth-century British art* (1998) [exhibition catalogue, Djanogly Art Gallery, U. Nott. Arts Centre, 26 Sept – 8 Nov 1998, Penlee House Gallery and Museum, Penzance, 25 Nov 1998 – 9 Jan 1999] · W. M. Clarke, *The secret life of Wilkie Collins* (1988) · L. Lambourne, *Victoria and Albert Museum: 'Victorian' genre painting* (1982)
Archives V&A NAL, list of pictures painted and diaries of wife | BL, corresp. with R. Peel, Add. MSS 40403–40406, *passim*
Likenesses H. Robinson, engraving, 1848 (after J. Linnell), repro. in Collins, *Memoirs* · C. A. Collins, chalk drawing, NPG · J. Linnell, oils, NG Ire. · wood-engraving (after J. Landseer, 1844), NPG; repro. in *ILN* (10 May 1845)
Wealth at death £11,000: Clarke, *Secret life*, 52

Collins, William Lucas (1815–1887), Church of England clergyman and author, was born at Oxwich, Glamorgan, where he was baptized on 23 May 1815, the only son of Revd John Collins (*d*. 1854), rector of Ilston, Nicholaston, and Penrice, and his wife, Elizabeth. He was educated at Rugby School (1829–33), among the first generation of pupils under Thomas Arnold, and at Jesus College, Oxford, where he matriculated in 1833, gaining second-class honours in classics in 1838, and graduating BA in 1838 and MA in 1840. Ordained in 1840, he was presented in the same year to the crown living of Cheriton, Glamorgan, which he held until 1867. On 9 April 1840 he married Anna Frances, daughter of John Wood of Berth-lwyd, near Llandeilo, Carmarthenshire. Their eldest son, Clifton Wilbraham Collins, was born in 1844.

Collins served as curate at Great Houghton, Northamptonshire (1853–62), where he lived at the rectory and became a diocesan inspector of education. In 1867 he was presented by Francis Jeune, the low-church bishop of Peterborough, to the living of Kilsby, Northamptonshire. He exchanged this for the rectory of Lowick, near Thrapston, Northamptonshire, in 1873, which from 1876 he held in combination with the vicarage of Slipton. From 1870 he held an honorary canonry at Peterborough Cathedral.

As well as being a country parson Collins had a literary career, which began soon after his ordination when he became a regular contributor to *Blackwood's Magazine*. His early articles were on university life, but he came to make a speciality of articles on the ancient public schools, his *Etoniana* being published separately in 1865 followed by *The Public Schools* (1867). The latter, a self-conscious attempt to record the traditions and history of the 'Clarendon' schools on the eve of changes in their government and character, is notable for its revisionist account of Arnold's influence at Rugby, Collins taking issue with Arnold's liberal eulogists, whom he thought had unfairly denigrated the latter's predecessors. He also assigned importance to the example of Spencer Thornton, an evangelical schoolboy contemporary. John Blackwood encouraged him to take up reviewing; his perceptive reviews of George Eliot's novels were his most significant work. He also edited for Blackwoods a successful series, Ancient Classics for English Readers, to which he contributed several volumes, including those on Homer's *Iliad* (1870) and Thucydides (1878). Collins died at Lowick rectory on 24 March 1887 and was survived by his wife.   M. C. CURTHOYS

Sources [M. Oliphant], *Blackwood*, 141 (1887), 734–6 · Foster, *Alum. Oxon.* · *IGI* · Crockford · *Wellesley index* · E. Jay, *Mrs Oliphant: 'a fiction to herself'. A literary life* (1995) · J. Chandos, *Boys together: English public schools, 1800–1864* (1985) · A. T. Mitchell, ed., *Rugby School register*, 1: *From April 1675 to April 1842* (1901) · *The George Eliot letters*, ed. G. S. Haight, 9 vols. (1954–78) · m. cert.
Archives NL Scot., corresp. with Blackwoods
Wealth at death £4464 2s.: resworn probate, Sept 1887, CGPLA Eng. & Wales

Collinson, Francis James Montgomery (1898–1984), musical director and musicologist, was born on 20 January 1898 at Coates House, Manor Place, Edinburgh, the third of five children (three sons, two daughters) of Thomas Henry Collinson (1858–1928), organist at St Mary's Episcopal Cathedral, Edinburgh, and his wife, Annie Wyness Scott (*d*. 1939). His father was Northumbrian, his mother Scottish. He attended Daniel Stewart's College, Edinburgh, leaving in 1914 to serve an apprenticeship under his father at St Mary's, where Francis had been a chorister. During the First World War he served for three years in motor transport in the Army Service Corps (having first been a Red Cross volunteer). On demobilization in 1919 he matriculated in music studies at Edinburgh University, studying under Professor Sir Donald Tovey. He threw himself into university musical life, playing in and conducting the Reid Orchestra, conducting the student Yahoo Orchestra (which he developed into a large-scale theatre orchestra), and composing the annual musical show run by the student representative council, the S. R. Ceenium. In the orchestra was his future wife, the law student Elizabeth Grant (1898–1983), whose grandfather had established the well-known Banffshire whisky distilling firm. He was described in the student magazine as the pleasantest person to work with in the university, honest, hardworking, efficient, tactful, and accommodating, yet stubborn and principled when necessary. His remarkable ability to compose, orchestrate, and rehearse to tight schedules—while not neglecting his studies—was matched by a rapidly assimilated knowledge of stage management, and although it clearly ran against the grain of his musical upbringing it is perhaps not surprising that after gaining a MusBac in 1923 he sought his fortune in the sphere of musical entertainment in London, marrying Elizabeth there on 3 March 1925. Their only child, Margaret Anne, was born in 1936.

A quiet, gentle man, Collinson nevertheless managed to find a number of jobs as chorus master, including for the revival of John Gay's *The Beggar's Opera* at the Lyric, Hammersmith. He had the good fortune to be employed to copy out the band parts for Nigel Playfair's review *Riverside Night* when the musical director, Alfred Reynolds, fell ill at the first rehearsal; Playfair asked Collinson to take Reynolds's place. He was thus launched on a successful career as a conductor and director of musical comedy and revue (recalling in later life that he was strongly advised to keep quiet about actually possessing a degree in music), working eventually for many years with the famous impresario C. B. Cochran and his equally famous Cochran's Young Ladies. He was catholic and eclectic in his musical career, and was proud not only of having conducted for both Cole Porter and Richard Tauber, but also of having restored William Walton's *Ballet* from a single piano score when the original music was destroyed in the London blitz. In 1941 he published the acclaimed *Orchestration for the Theatre*, with an introduction by Cochran; it was reprinted in 1949.

Theatre and revue were badly hit by the advent of the Second World War and in 1941 Collinson took charge of the BBC's *Country Magazine* programmes, with their famous signature tune, 'The Painful Plough', of which he was to make many arrangements, including one for the bagpipe. The programmes, many of them outside broadcasts, involved Collinson in the study, collection, and arrangement of folk-songs (bringing the Copper family to public attention, for example) throughout Britain. He not only published these arrangements in a series with Francis Dillon from 1946 onwards but also issued three unique 78 r.p.m. recordings of folk-songs in the Gramophone Company's Plum Label series. Now collector's items, the songs were beautifully delivered by the baritone Robert Irwin, accompanied by an orchestra conducted by Collinson. He composed a wide range of music, mainly for broadcasting, from 'folk' orchestral suites to musical comedy, and won the Italia prize in 1950 for his *Rumpelstiltskin*.

In 1951 Edinburgh University established the School of Scottish Studies, and Collinson was invited back as the first musical research fellow, concentrating on the collection, study, and transcription of traditional song in both Scots and Gaelic. This he carried out in his customary scrupulous and meticulous manner, and in 1966 he made his name in the field of traditional music with his comprehensive and scholarly book *The Traditional and National Music of Scotland*. Thereafter, under the editorship of the great Gaelic folklorist John Lorne Campbell (1906–1996) he brought out three volumes of *Hebridean Folksongs* (1969, 1977, and 1981), presenting to the world genuine Gaelic traditional song, previously traduced and popularized by Marjory Kennedy-Fraser in her highly successful art-song arrangements, *Songs of the Hebrides* (1921–5). During this

period he even ventured into the ultra-conservative world of the highland bagpipers; *The Bagpipe: the History of a Musical Instrument* (1975) was very well received, but his piobaireachd 'The Lament for Calum Maclean', composed after the untimely death of a fellow worker in the school (brother to the great Gaelic poet Sorley Maclean), did not, unfortunately, enter the piping repertory.

Highly arranged folk-song, sung by classically trained professional singers to orchestral accompaniment, no matter how beautifully done, was looked at askance by later scholars and performers of traditional song. But in *Country Magazine* Collinson had been obliged to work to BBC practice, which was against 'untrained' singers marring the airwaves, and when such Scottish singers were eventually broadcast in the late 1950s, popular reaction was indeed remarkably hostile, even from fervent Scottish nationalists such as Hugh MacDiarmid. But Collinson more than compensated for such early 'transgressions' by the assiduity and accuracy of his later research and publication for the School of Scottish Studies. His writings, which cover in scholarly depth virtually the complete range of Scottish traditional music and song from both sides of the highland line, firmly remained classics in their field. It may well be regrettable that, as his *Scotsman* obituary commented, he attracted no honours, not even from his own university; that would in no way have concerned this thorough, kindly, generous, and gentle musician who valued most of all in life a capacity to enjoy whatever he was engaged upon. Collinson died on 21 December 1984 in Peel Hospital, Galashiels, and was buried in Mortlach churchyard, Dufftown, Banffshire, on the 28th.   IAN A. OLSON

Sources T. A. D. [T. A. Davis], 'Francis Collinson', *The Collegian* (Nov 1985), 103 · 'Francis M. Collinson', *The Student*, 22 (1924), 164–5 · *University of Edinburgh Journal*, 31 (1983–4), 62–3 · H. MacPherson, review, *University of Edinburgh Journal*, 27 (1975–6), 98–9 · A. B. [A. Bruford], 'Francis Collinson', *Tocher*, 40 (1986), 255 · *The Scotsman* (10 Jan 1985) · *University of Edinburgh Journal*, 32 (1985–6), 58 · b. cert. · d. cert.

Archives NL Scot., corresp., papers, and music · U. Edin., School of Scottish Studies | SOUND U. Edin., School of Scottish Studies

Likenesses line drawing, repro. in *The Student*, 159

Wealth at death £365,693.60: confirmation, 26 April 1985, *CCI*

Collinson, James (1825–1881), genre painter, was born in Mansfield, near Nottingham, on 9 May 1825, the youngest of the three children of Robert Collinson (*c*.1770–*c*.1830), a prosperous bookseller, and his wife, Mary (*c*.1785–*c*.1860). Little is known about Collinson's father, who died during his childhood, which was spent in Nottinghamshire. By the time James Collinson was twenty years old the bookselling business had long been taken over by his married elder brother, Charles; his sister, Mary, was living with their mother, then aged about sixty, in a small house at Pleasley Hill just outside Mansfield. James was more than ten years younger than either of his siblings.

In the mid-1840s Collinson was a meek-mannered, fair-haired young man of diminutive stature and boyish appearance with a habit of falling asleep indiscriminately. Enrolled at the Royal Academy Schools in London, he met there the slightly younger Dante Gabriel Rossetti and William Holman Hunt. They admired their fellow student's art, although Holman Hunt found him dull company, writing of Collinson in *Pre-Raphaelitism and the Pre-Raphaelite Brotherhood* (1905) that 'he could but rarely see the fun of anything, although he sometimes laughed in a lachrymose manner, and I fear our attempts to enliven him were but futile' (1.161–2). Drawn to the Oxford Movement which was reinvigorating high-church worship, Collinson was a devoted and pious worshipper at Christ Church, Albany Street. There he would have known, and been known by, if only by sight, Christina Rossetti and her mother, who attended the same church to listen to the fiery Puseyite sermons of the Revd William Dodsworth.

Collinson's painting *The Charity Boy's Debut* was exhibited in the Royal Academy exhibition in 1847 and much praised. A genre scene which showed a parish lad putting on his uniform, it was followed in 1848 by *The Rivals*, a sentimental depiction of a girl child with two boys. *The New Curate* and *The Noviciate to a Nunnery* followed: most of Collinson's early work, like these two paintings, was heavily devotional. At about the same time that Dante Gabriel Rossetti, his brother William Michael, and the four other founder members of the Pre-Raphaelite Brotherhood asked him to join them, Collinson took what must have seemed a logical step forward from Tractarianism and converted to Roman Catholicism. Although described by William Rossetti as 'hardly a writing man' (Rossetti, 20), in March 1850 Collinson contributed quite an imaginative, five-part narrative poem entitled 'The Child Jesus' to the second issue of *The Germ*, the short-lived Pre-Raphaelite journal. It was accompanied by an etching which showed a haloed, juvenile figure of Christ blessing other children; Collinson's reputation at the time was such that editor William Rossetti thought it worth flagging 'with an Etching by James Collinson' on the front cover of the issue.

Collinson lodged in Somers Town and became a frequent visitor to the Rossetti family home at 50 Charlotte Street, where, in his hesitant way, he got to know Christina Rossetti better. He painted portraits of her and her sister Maria, presenting Christina as a prim nervous figure in stark contrast to the full-featured voluptuous portraits of her by Dante Gabriel Rossetti. In 1848 he proposed marriage to Christina but was refused on the grounds of his Roman Catholicism. He reconverted to Anglicanism and was accepted, although Christina was only seventeen years old and Collinson was still financially dependent on his family. At the same time Collinson was working on his major Pre-Raphaelite painting *St Elizabeth of Hungary* (exhib. 1851; Johannesburg Art Gallery, South Africa) which shows the saint entering a convent, rather than remarrying after the death of her devout husband.

In 1850 Collinson finished, in time for exhibition at the Royal Academy that year, his oil painting *Answering the Emigrant's Letter*. Now in the City of Manchester Art Galleries, it is a genre scene depicting a working man in shirt sleeves with his wife and children around a table in a dark kitchen. The three eldest children are poring over a letter to their absent elder brother. With *The Emigration Scheme* which was exhibited at Liverpool Academy in 1852 (ex Sothebys, 15 March 1967) it demonstrates Collinson's interest in the topical subject of emigration during the early 1850s.

Early in 1850 Collinson reverted to his Catholic faith and renounced the Pre-Raphaelite Brotherhood and his connection with *The Germ*. He felt unable 'conscientiously as a Catholic to assist in parading the artistic opinions of those who are not' as he explained in his resignation letter to Dante Gabriel Rossetti (Thomas, 90). This left Christina with no choice but to release him from their engagement. A few months later he sold his painting materials and, in late 1852 or early 1853, entered the Jesuit community at Stonyhurst College at Clitheroe in Lancashire where he remained until some time before September 1854. By 1855 Collinson was once more exhibiting at the Royal Academy and two new pictures by him were shown at the British Institution in 1858, but he had no further contact with the Rossettis and their circle. On 9 February 1858 Collinson married Eliza Alvinia Henrietta Ann Wheeler at Brompton Oratory. She was a vigorous, plainly dressed Catholic aged forty, related by marriage to Collinson's friend J. R. Herbert. Collinson's only child, a son, Robert, was born in 1859.

Collinson exhibited regularly at the Royal Academy, the British Institution, and the Society of British Artists—of which he was a fellow—from 1855 until 1870, after which he lived quietly in retirement. Much of his post-Stonyhurst work was artistically unremarkable and concentrated on saleable domestic or humorous subjects. It is difficult to get an overview of Collinson's work as so much of it has been dispersed or is lost. One surviving work, *For Sale* (exh. RA, 1858), is now in the Tate collection: it depicts a girl opening her purse at a charity when the item really on sale is herself. It was a companion piece to a similar painting entitled *To Let* which showed a young woman offering lodgings in her house. Collinson died on 24 January 1881 at his home, 16 Paulet Road, Camberwell. He was survived by his wife.

SUSAN ELKIN

Sources J. Marsh, *Christina Rossetti: a literary biography* (1994) • F. Thomas, *Christina Rossetti* (1992) • K. Jones, *Learning not to be first: the life of Christina Rossetti* (1991) • W. M. Rossetti, ed., *The Germ: thoughts towards nature in poetry, literature and art* (1850); repr. (1901) • *DNB* • R. Parkinson, 'James Collinson', *Pre-Raphaelite papers*, ed. L. Parris (1984), 61–75 • m. cert. • d. cert.

Wealth at death under £2000: probate, 21 Feb 1881, *CGPLA Eng. & Wales*

Collinson, John (1757–1793), antiquary, the son of the Revd John Collinson of Bromham, Wiltshire, and his wife, Elizabeth, was born in Bromham on 19 July 1757. He matriculated at Brasenose College, Oxford, on 8 April 1775 but from July 1777 until June 1779 was intermittently resident at the Queen's College. He was made deacon by the bishop of Oxford on 21 November 1779 at the request of Thomas Meyler, to whom Collinson had offered his services. Meyler, who described him as 'an ingenious, sober and well-behaved youth' (Wilts. & Swindon RO, D1/14/17), employed Collinson as his curate at Preshute and Marlborough between January and August 1780.

Collinson did not proceed to a degree but in 1779, before ordination, published his first book, *The beauties of British antiquity: selected from the writings of esteemed antiquaries with notes and observations*. In June 1780 he issued proposals, never fulfilled, for a history of Wiltshire, for which he had been collecting material for three years.

Probably late in 1780 Collinson moved to Cirencester where, on 25 March 1781, he married Mary Hill (d. 1787). In the following December he was licensed as curate there, and was appointed vicar of Clanfield, Oxfordshire, in 1782. His antiquarian studies, probably undertaken in the library of the second Earl Bathurst at Cirencester Park, were evidently made in association with Samuel Rudder, the Gloucestershire historian, and with Joseph Kilner, collector of material on Cirencester. In June 1784 Collinson was admitted a fellow of the Society of Antiquaries of London with the support of Daines Barrington, William Boys, and Edward Hasted.

In August 1781 Collinson issued a prospectus for a history of Somerset, but the project was apparently abandoned a year later because he found that the papers of John Strachey, an earlier historian of the county, were not available to him. New proposals were issued in October 1784 under which Collinson's historical material, to be collected from a variety of sources, was to be combined with a contemporary survey to be made by Edmund Rack, then secretary of the Agricultural and Philosophical societies of Bath.

In August 1787 Collinson became vicar of Long Ashton and perpetual curate of Whitchurch, both on the Somerset side of Bristol. He moved to Long Ashton with his young son, John, some time after the death of his wife, Mary, in Cirencester in November 1787. *The History and Antiquities of the County of Somerset*, in three volumes, was published in 1791 and gave rise to much criticism. It was, however, based on much accurate unpublished work of earlier antiquaries, some now lost, though on only a limited use of Rack's survey, most of which survives, with evidence of Collinson's use, among the archives of the Smyth family of Long Ashton at Bristol Record Office.

Collinson died after a 'lingering illness' (*Notes and Queries for Somerset and Dorset*, 15, 1916, 84) at the Hotwells, Bristol, on 27 August 1793, and was buried at Long Ashton on 1 September.   ROBERT W. DUNNING

Sources R. Dunning, introduction, in J. Collinson, *The history and antiquities of the county of Somerset*, ed. R. Dunning (1983) · testimonials for ordination, 1779, Wilts. & Swindon RO, D1/14/17 · T. W. Bull, 'Rev. John Collinson', *Notes and Queries for Somerset and Dorset*, 15 (1916–17), 7–11, 84–5 · R. W. Dunning, 'Somerset', *English county histories: a guide*, ed. C. R. J. Currie and C. P. Lewis (1994), 348–54 · Foster, *Alum. Oxon.* · *DNB* · *IGI*

Collinson, Peter (1694–1768), botanist, was born at the sign of the Red Lion, Gracechurch Street, London, on 28 January 1694, the son of Peter Collinson, cloth merchant, and his wife, Elizabeth Hall. He was raised in a Quaker family of cloth merchants and became a partner in the family business, which had extensive trade with America. Through this connection he became acquainted with Benjamin Franklin, to whose experiments with electricity he contributed information about similar work in Germany. Franklin also informed him of the discovery of mastodon bones on the banks of the Ohio River in 1767, a subject on which Collinson gave two accounts to the Royal Society (*PTRS*, 57, 1767, 46–7). He also supported the foundation of a subscription library in Philadelphia and encouraged the colonists to experiment with a wider range of crops.

As a small boy Collinson had lived with relatives in Peckham, then a separate hamlet south of London. From the garden there, which he later inherited, he acquired a love of plants which was to last for the rest of his life. Probably his greatest contribution to horticulture was through his friendship with John Bartram, the father of American botany. In the early 1730s, Bartram wrote to Collinson soliciting the post of king's botanist in North America, a position that Collinson was able to obtain for him only in 1765. In the meantime, however, Collinson established a scheme whereby Bartram supplied seeds and seedlings to British patrons in return for an annual subscription.

This scheme eventually attracted at least sixty subscribers, including such eminent landscape planters as the dukes of Argyll, Bedford, and Richmond. Collinson cultivated a similar passion for planting in the duke of Newcastle's heir, Henry Fiennes Clinton, earl of Lincoln. Largely through botany, Collinson, who was a lifelong whig, knew at least two prime ministers—Lord Lincoln's uncle, Henry Pelham, and Lord Bute, the effective founder of the botanical garden at Kew. His greatest protégé and friend, however, was Lord Petre, who at his premature death in 1742 had planted 40,000 American trees on his estate at Thorndon in Essex.

Collinson was a fellow of the Society of Antiquaries and of the Royal Society (elected 1728), to which he submitted reports on a wide variety of natural history topics. He was acquainted with a wide range of natural historians. Through his connection with the Royal Society, he became a close enough friend of Sir Hans Sloane to expect that he might have been made curator of Sloane's collection after his death, an expectation in which he was frustrated. He was also close to John Fothergill (who wrote his first biography), and numbered among his acquaintance such eminent botanists as John Ellis, Stephen Hales, and J. J. Dillenius. He also knew Linnaeus, having been introduced to him by Hermann Boerhaave in 1736. The connection later led Linnaeus both to encourage Collinson to catalogue his plants and to name horse balm (*Collinsonia canadensis*) after him.

Collinson was equally interested in more ordinary plantsmen. He lent Mark Catesby the money to publish his *Natural History of Carolina*, and he corresponded with the American botanists Alexander Garden and Cadwallader Colden. He also passed on many of his seeds to James Gordon, the nurseryman who had been gardener to Lord Petre. Collinson owned and heavily annotated several editions of the *Gardeners Dictionary* by Philip Miller, the gardener of the Chelsea Physic Garden, who was another friend. He was fearful that such men would be excluded from botany by Linnaeus's new system of nomenclature and wrote to him in 1754 to object that only 'real professors' could now pretend to attain to the science.

Collinson's famous garden was at Mill Hill, an estate which he inherited (in 1749) through his marriage to Mary Russell in 1724. They had four children, of whom Michael (1727–1795) was also a distinguished botanist. Among Collinson's garden's curiosities was a rare collection of magnolias, one of them (*Magnolia acuminata*) introduced by him. One of his many contributions to the *Gentleman's Magazine* is a paper in 1751 listing forty-three plants imported in that year. He was responsible for introducing into Britain the American alder, three species of azalea, black birch, hemlock, sugar maple, mountain laurel, and many medicinal herbs. In 1843 Lewis Dillwyn published *Hortus Collinsonianus*, a reconstructed list of all the plants in this garden. Collinson died at Mill Hill in August 1768, having been taken ill at Thorndon. He was buried at the Quaker burial-ground, Long Lane, Bermondsey.

DOUGLAS D. C. CHAMBERS

Sources N. G. Brett-James, *The life of Peter Collinson* (1925) • W. Darlington, *Memorials of John Bartram and Humphry Marshall: with notices of their botanical contemporaries* (1849) • L. W. Dillwyn, *Hortus Collinsonianus* (1843) • *William Bartram: botanical and zoological drawings, 1756–1788*, ed. J. Ewan (1968) • J. Fothergill, *Some anecdotes of the late Peter Collinson* (1785) • B. Henrey, *British botanical and horticultural literature before 1800*, 3 vols. (1975) • J. C. Loudon, *Arboretum et fruticetum Britannicum, or, The trees and shrubs of Britain*, 8 vols. (1838) • *A selection of the correspondence of Linnaeus, and other naturalists, from the original manuscripts*, ed. J. E. Smith, 2 vols. (1821) • *Brothers of the spade: correspondence of Peter Collinson, of London, and of John Custis, of Williamsburg, 1734–1746*, ed. E. G. Swem (1949)
Archives American Philosophical Society, Philadelphia, corresp. and papers • BL, corresp. and papers, Add. MSS 4440, 28726–28727 • Essex RO, Chelmsford, horticulture papers • Linn. Soc., corresp. and commonplace books • NHM, account of introduction of American seeds into England | American Antiquarian Society, Worcester, Massachusetts, letters to J. Custis • BL, letters to Thomas Binch, Add. MSS 4303 • BL, corresp. with E. M. da Costa, Add. MS 28536 • BL, letters to Hans Sloane, Add. MSS 1968, 3322, 4025, 4053–4058, 4069 • Burgerbibliothek Bern, Bern, letters to A. von Haller • L. Cong., letters from J. Custis • Linn. Soc., letters to Carl Linnaeus • New York Historical Society, corresp. with Cadwallader Colden, etc. • RS Friends, Lond., letters to E. Robinson
Likenesses N. Hone, miniature on ivory, 1765, NPG • T. Gainsborough, oils, repro. in Brett-James, *Life* • Miller, engraving (after T. Gainsborough), repro. in J. Fothergill, *Some account of the late Peter Collinson* (1770) • Trotter, engraving, repro. in J. Fothergill, *Works* (1781) • oils, Mill Hill School, London

Collinson, Sir Richard (1811–1883), naval officer and explorer, was born on 7 November 1811 at Gateshead, co. Durham, where his father, the Revd John Collinson (c.1791–1857), was rector. His mother was Amelia, *née* King (b. 1783), daughter of the philanthropist Frances Elizabeth *King. He entered the navy in December 1823, and in 1828 served as a midshipman of the *Chanticleer* (Captain Forster) in a surveying voyage round South America. In 1834 he was a mate of the *Medea*, one of the first steamers in the navy; he was promoted lieutenant on 23 March 1835 and appointed on 28 September to the surveying vessel *Sulphur*. In June 1838 he was appointed to the *President*, the flagship of Rear-Admiral Ross in the Pacific; and in January 1840 to the *Wellesley*, on which Sir James John Gordon

Bremer subsequently hoisted his broad pennant as senior officer in China. During the First Opium War Collinson was employed as surveyor and pilot, and to his skill and ability was largely due the success of the operations both in the Canton River and especially in the Yangtze (Yangzi) River. After commanding for some time the brig *Bentinck* on this service, he was promoted commander on 19 February 1842, was advanced to post rank on 23 December 1842, and was nominated a CB the following day. However, he continued in command of the *Bentinck*, renamed the *Plover*, until 1846, during which time he was employed in the exact survey of the coast of China, from Chushan to Hong Kong, the results of which afterwards formed the basis of the navigational publication *China Pilot*.

In 1849 Collinson was appointed to command an expedition for the relief of Sir John Franklin, by way of the Bering Strait; he himself had command of the *Enterprise*, and with him was Commander Robert Le Mesurier McClure in the *Investigator*. The two ships sailed together from Plymouth on 20 January 1850 but unfortunately separated in the neighbourhood of Cape Horn and did not meet again. The *Enterprise* passed Point Barrow, Alaska, on 21 August, but the ice forced Collinson to return south and winter in Hong Kong. In 1851 he was again hampered by ice and in 1852 was frozen in at Cambridge Bay for the winter. In 1853 the *Enterprise* was caught in the ice at Camden Bay, and there passed a third winter. She reached Point Barrow on 8 August 1854, after being shut up in the Arctic, entirely on her own resources, for upwards of three years. Of the many who had searched for Franklin, Collinson came closest to the place where the expedition had ended. Collinson's addition to geographical knowledge on this Arctic trip was very considerable, and would have been tantamount to the discovery of the north-west passage, had this not been already actually achieved by the men of the *Investigator*. The Royal Geographical Society awarded him its gold medal in 1858, but he had expected some official reward and was mortified by the scanty acknowledgement his service received. He never again applied for employment under the Admiralty, though he acted on commissions on the naval defence of the Great Lakes, and of the United Kingdom generally.

Collinson attained his flag in 1862; became a vice-admiral (retired) in 1869; and admiral (retired) in 1875, in which year he was also made a KCB. In 1857 he had settled at Ealing, Middlesex, and there, with his mother and sisters, spent the remainder of his life. In 1862 he was elected an elder brother of Trinity House, and in 1875 to be deputy master, an appointment rarely conferred on an officer of the Royal Navy. He was an active fellow of the Royal Geographical Society, serving for many years on its council and in 1871 assisting in editing the *Hints to Travellers*. In 1862 he contributed 'Three weeks in Canada' to Francis Galton's *Vacation Tourists* and edited for the Hakluyt Society *The Three Voyages of Martin Frobisher in Search of a Passage to Cathaia* (1867). He was also active in local affairs, serving as churchwarden, on the local board, and in other offices of the parish and district. He died on 12 September 1883 at his home, The Haven, Ealing, Middlesex, and was buried at nearby Perivale, where a monument to his memory was erected by subscription.

J. K. LAUGHTON, *rev.* ANDREW LAMBERT

Sources G. S. Ritchie, *The Admiralty chart: British naval hydrography in the nineteenth century* (1967) · A. Friendly, *Beaufort of the Admiralty* (1977) · G. S. Graham, *The China station: war and diplomacy, 1830–1860* (1978) · O'Byrne, *Naval biog. dict.* · Foster, *Alum. Oxon.*
Archives NMM, corresp., journals, and papers · Scott Polar RI, letters | BL, letters to John Barrow, etc., Add. MSS 35308–35309 · NL Scot., letters to Sir Thomas Cochrane
Likenesses S. Pearce, oils, 1855, NPG; replica NPG · Lock & Whitfield, woodburytype photograph, NPG; repro. in T. Cooper, *Men of mark: a gallery of contemporary portraits* (1877) · memorial, Perivale, London · photograph, RGS · wood-engraving, NPG; repro. in *ILN*, 83 (29 Sept 1883), 309
Wealth at death £12,745 5s. 3d.: probate, 26 Oct 1883, *CGPLA Eng. & Wales*

Collinson, Septimus (1739–1827), college head, was born at Gotree, near Huntsonby, Cumberland, on 11 September 1739, the seventh son of Joseph and Agnes Collinson. He was brought up at Great Musgrave, Westmorland, where his parents had bought a small estate. He was educated at Appleby grammar school, and entered Queen's College, Oxford, in 1759; he graduated BA in 1763 and MA in 1767. In 1778 he became rector of Dowlish Wake and Dowlish West, near Ilminster, Somerset, a post he held until his death. He graduated BD in 1792 and DD in 1793. For some years he was one of the city lecturers at Oxford. In 1794 he received his college's living of Holwell, Dorset, but in 1796 was appointed provost of Queen's College. In 1798 he became Lady Margaret professor of divinity, which made him a prebendary of Worcester Cathedral. His lectures on the Thirty-Nine Articles, though admired at the time, were never printed. He was a frequent university preacher until an advanced age. His later sermons express alarm at moves towards Catholic emancipation. He died, unmarried, at Queen's College lodge on 24 January 1827 and was buried in the provost's vault. He was a generous benefactor, and left £1500 to found a school on the Madras or Bell system, which provided free schooling for children in the parish of Great Musgrave.

THOMPSON COOPER, *rev.* JOHN D. HAIGH

Sources J. Collinson, 'Memoir', *The duty and advantages of cultivating the understanding* (1829), v–vii · *GM*, 1st ser., 97/1 (1827), 178–9 · Foster, *Alum. Oxon.* · J. Foster, *Oxford men and their colleges* (1893) · Nichols, *Illustrations*, 1.785
Wealth at death 'great bulk of his fortune' went to relatives, 'but also £1500 stock in 3 per cent consolidated annuities, in trust, 'that the produce of interest of the said stock be applied to the foundation and support of a school, on the Madras system of education in the parish of Great Musgrave': Collinson, 'Memoir'

Collis, John Day (1816–1879), headmaster and educational writer, son of the Revd Robert Fitzgerald Collis (1790–1863), prebendary of Kilconnell, co. Galway, and his wife, Maria, daughter of Edward Bourke of Nun's Island, Galway, was born on 24 February 1816 at Rathcormack, co. Cork. He was educated at Rugby School from 1832 to 1834 under Thomas Arnold, and entered Merton College, Oxford, as a postmaster in 1834. In 1835 he became Eaton scholar of Worcester College, taking first-class honours in

classics in 1838 and proceeding BA in 1838, MA in 1841, and BD and DD in 1860. He gained the Kennicott, and Pusey and Ellerton Hebrew scholarships (1839–41), and was a fellow of his college from 1839 to 1847. On 18 June 1846 he married Josephine Martha (d. 16 Oct 1868), eldest daughter of John Chatfield Tyler, of Kingswood, Gloucestershire.

In December 1842 Collis was nominated headmaster of Bromsgrove School. Through his tireless energy Bromsgrove became one of the leading schools in England; the number of pupils rose from 17 in 1843 to 100 in 1865. A new chapel was built in 1856, and new classrooms were added and the old buildings enlarged and improved at a cost of £5000. He was less effective as a preacher and was an uninspiring teacher; his applications for the headships of Durham (1853) and Rugby (1857) were unsuccessful. By turning Bromsgrove into predominantly a boarding-school, Collis incurred local unpopularity for excluding boys from the town, and some of his policies were strongly criticized in 1865 by James Bryce, one of the assistant commissioners to the schools inquiry commission. He resigned from the headmastership in October 1867 on his appointment to the vicarage of Stratford upon Avon. But his qualities as an educational entrepreneur were again shown by the prosperity of Trinity College School at Stratford, a private venture of which he was both founder (27 January 1872) and first warden. He had earlier married, on 11 October 1871, Elizabeth, daughter of Edward Castleman of Chettle, Dorsetshire, and widow of Rear-Admiral Douglas Curry of Shottery Hall, Stratford upon Avon. A well-known figure in educational circles, he was vice-president of the College of Preceptors and of the Association for the Registration of Schoolmasters. He was a prolific author of classical school textbooks. His *Chief Tenses of Latin Irregular Verbs* (1854) and its Greek counterpart both went through thirty-four editions.

Collis was nominated an honorary canon of Worcester Cathedral in 1854, and in 1856 was offered, but declined, the colonial bishopric of Grafton and Armidale. At Bromsgrove he was chairman of the local board and of the poor-law guardians, and took a leading part in local controversies, promoting the restoration of Bromsgrove parish church, which was carried out in 1859 by G. G. Scott. During his incumbency Stratford church was restored and improved, and he completed the formation of the water terrace in the churchyard. Past master and grand chaplain in the Middlesex province of freemasons, Collis was a freeman of the City of London. He died at Shottery Hall, Stratford upon Avon, on 1 April 1879, and was buried at Bromsgrove cemetery on 4 April 1879.

G. C. BOASE, *rev.* M. C. CURTHOYS

Sources Boase, *Mod. Eng. biog.* · H. E. M. Icely, *Bromsgrove School through four centuries* (1953) · *Stratford on Avon Herald* (4 April 1879) · *Stratford on Avon Herald* (10 April 1879) · *The Times* (2 April 1879)
Archives U. Edin. L., letters to James Halliwell-Phillipps · Worcester College, Oxford, letters to T. P. Phelps
Wealth at death under £12,000: probate, 8 May 1879, *CGPLA Eng. & Wales*

Collishaw, Raymond (1893–1976), air force officer, was born in Nanaimo on the south-east coast of Vancouver

Raymond Collishaw (1893–1976), by unknown photographer, 1918 [in a Sopwith F1 Camel aircraft]

Island, British Columbia, Canada, on 22 November 1893, the son of John Edward Collishaw (*d.* 1923), of Wrexham, Denbighshire, 'a university man with a musical education' (Collishaw and Dodds, 1) who spent most of his life as an itinerant gold prospector and coalminer. He was educated in Nanaimo and in August 1908 joined the Canadian Fisheries Protection Service, which in 1910 became a civilian department of the Royal Canadian Navy. By 1914 he had advanced from cabin boy to first officer.

Collishaw was recruited by the Royal Naval Air Service in 1915 as a probationary flight sub-lieutenant and in January 1916 sailed to England, where that July he qualified as a pilot at Redcar, on the north Yorkshire coast. He joined 3 (naval) wing at Manston, Kent, on 1 August and flew the two-seat fighter version of a Sopwith single-seat bomber known as the 1½ Strutter (because of an unusual strut arrangement supporting the upper wings). This was the first British machine with synchronizing gear enabling a machine-gun to fire through the propeller arc, and 3 wing was the first British unit formed specifically for the purpose of long-range strategic bombing. Collishaw was sent to Luxeuil (45 miles west of Mulhouse in eastern France) on 21 September 1916. He escorted one raid from there on targets in the Saar, Germany's most important industrial region, and six from Ochey (south-west of Nancy). His courage and skill earned him the first of many decorations: the Croix de Guerre avec étoile.

Early in February 1917 Collishaw joined 3 (naval) squadron at Vert Galand, 10 miles north-west of Albert, on the Somme front. That squadron was equipped with the single-seat Sopwith Pup, a superb flying machine but too slow and lightly armed to match the latest German fighters. Even so Collishaw achieved several victories in aerial combat. On 26 April he was transferred to Furnes, near the Belgian coast, 10 miles east of Dunkirk, as flight commander in a newly formed unit made up almost entirely of Canadian pilots: 10 (naval) squadron, equipped with the Sopwith Triplane, a better single-seat fighter than the Pup, but still inferior to its opponents in speed and armament. Nevertheless, further victories underline

Collishaw's exceptional ability. He had the engine cowlings and wheel covers of the five Triplanes in his flight painted black and named appropriately: he flew *Black Maria*, and other pilots flew *Black Death*, *Black Sheep*, *Black Prince*, and *Black Roger*.

Collishaw received his first promotion, to flight lieutenant, on 3 June 1917; his first British decoration, the DSC, was awarded on 14 June that year and his second, the DSO, on 8 July. He left the squadron on 3 August, went home to Canada on leave, and returned in mid-November as flight commander in the seaplane defence squadron at St Pol, Dunkirk. There he flew one of the war's most agile single-seat fighters—the Sopwith Camel, armed with two machine-guns—on protective patrols over shipping and on close escort of bomber raids behind enemy lines. On 23 January 1918 he took command of his old squadron—3 (naval)—6 miles up the coast, at Bray Dunes. It flew the same aircraft on the same duties, but Collishaw himself was forbidden to fly on operations. The squadron moved 45 miles south to Mont-St Eloi, between Lens and Arras, on 1 March, just in time to help stem a massive German offensive, beginning on the 25th. Even so, Collishaw was not permitted to resume his active career until 9 June. He then eagerly made up for lost time, not only in aerial combat but also in low-level strafing and bomber escort duties. On 4 July he was awarded the DFC and on 1 August a bar to his DSO. He returned to England on 21 October 1918.

Collishaw went to southern Russia in May 1919, having recruited volunteers to serve with a re-formed 47 squadron, equipped with de Havilland DH 9 and DH 9a two-seat bombers and Camels. Until 30 March 1920, when it was obliged to withdraw, the squadron assisted White Russians fighting against Bolsheviks in a region between the north-east coast of the Black Sea and Volgograd, some 420 miles to the north-east. He was granted a permanent commission as a squadron leader in August 1919, was appointed OBE (military) in November, and received three tsarist decorations.

Like other successful fighter pilots, Collishaw attracted a great deal of public praise during and after the First World War, but he emphasized in his memoirs that artillery observation, reconnaissance, bombing, and convoy patrol 'represented the main reasons for maintaining an air force and the work of the fighters was completely subsidiary to their role' (Collishaw and Dodds, 104). As for the number of his victims, careful scrutiny of squadron records at the end of the twentieth century drastically reduced the scores of all aces. It seems that Collishaw certainly destroyed twenty-seven enemy aircraft and not the sixty or so claimed in his memoirs and elsewhere. Although some of those now disallowed may well have crashed, no conclusive evidence survives: 'in almost every case the accepted and published British Empire totals overstate the case. Only the British, and later the United States Air Service, accepted claims for victories made by pilots without independent verification from the ground' (Shores and others, 7, 114–16). Nevertheless, Collishaw remains a highly successful combat pilot on any reckoning.

Collishaw commanded 30 squadron in Iraq (1920–23) and 41 squadron at Northolt, west London (1923–4), attended the RAF Staff College in Andover, Hampshire (1924–5), commanded 23 squadron at Kenley, south London (1925–6), and in October 1927 went to Uxbridge, west London, as head of operations and intelligence at the headquarters of air defence of Great Britain. In July 1929 he was promoted wing commander and sent to Malta as senior RAF officer aboard an aircraft-carrier, HMS *Courageous*. Although he was placed in 'a delicate position', as he recalled (Collishaw and Dodds, 229), between the Admiralty rock and the Air Ministry hard place, his background of both sea and air service kept him safe from both hazards until September 1932, when he took command of two bomber squadrons at Bircham Newton in Norfolk.

Collishaw was promoted group captain in July 1935 and spent the next year in the Sudan. Between August 1936 and April 1939 he commanded a station at Heliopolis, near Cairo. He was promoted air commodore and took command in Cairo of a new formation, Egypt group, renamed 202 group in September (and renumbered 204 group in April 1941). Shortly before Italy declared war in June 1940 he moved his headquarters to Maaten Bagush, on the Egyptian coast, some 200 miles west of Cairo. In July 1941 Air Marshal Arthur Tedder, newly appointed head of Middle East air command, decided to replace him with Arthur Coningham. In Tedder's opinion, Collishaw was too anxious to attempt every task in daily operations himself and too often foolishly optimistic about what could be done with a handful of men and aircraft.

In Collishaw's defence, it must be said that he had identified and tried to solve the problems of combining the punch of fighter and bomber forces with each other, and with the efforts of ground forces. He had done his best to establish secure, reliable communications, fix realistic bomblines (between enemy and friendly forces), and rank targets in order of priority. Wherever possible, forward landing grounds had been laid out swiftly, kept clear, guarded vigilantly, and amply supplied with water, food, and fuel. Attempts had been made to provide squadrons with their own transport, and they tried to carry with them their own workshops. They exercised their own pilots regularly, knowing that training facilities outside the squadron were negligible.

Collishaw realized that strength must not be wasted on standing patrols, wearing out men and machines and consuming precious reserves of fuel and spares. Above all, he understood that air superiority was to be obtained—and constantly maintained—before any other task, even close support for troops in advance or retreat, could be attempted with any reasonable hope of success. He had no radar, a poor radio network, and much less signals intelligence than his successors enjoyed, and he commanded a motley force, made up largely of what the historian John Terraine rightly called 'assorted antiques' (Terraine, 304).

Nevertheless, under Collishaw's direction the RAF showed plenty of tactical ingenuity, forged excellent relations with the army commander (Lieutenant-General Sir Richard O'Connor), and concluded a triumphant campaign, despite depending on equipment that was at best obsolete against Italians who had an apparently overwhelming numerical superiority. Had it not been for the Greek diversion in March 1941, O'Connor and he might well have captured Tripoli, ending the desert war there and then. Collishaw was rightly proud of his north African command, 'when we had to outwit and outfight a numerically superior enemy by a combination of deception, superior tactics and fighting spirit' (Collishaw and Dodds, 255). He was made a CB in 1941.

Collishaw served at Fighter Command headquarters until March 1942, when he was promoted air vice-marshal and sent to Inverness in north-east Scotland as head of 14 group. On 14 July 1943 he was retired, and two years later he returned to Vancouver. He became OBE for a second time, this time in the civil list, in 1946.

Collishaw was a big man—always chubby and sometimes portly—with a round face made for smiling. He had large eyes, a prominent nose, and full lips. On 14 July 1923, having been engaged for six years, he married Juancita (Neita) Eliza Trapp, the daughter of Thomas John Trapp, a merchant, of New Westminster, British Columbia; they had two daughters. 'Perhaps, given another chance, I should not wait so long to get married' (Collishaw and Dodds, 256). He died in British Columbia on 29 September 1976.

VINCENT ORANGE

Sources R. Collishaw and R. V. Dodds, *Air command: a fighter pilot's story* (1973) · C. Shores and others, *Above the trenches: a complete record of the fighter aces and units of the British empire air forces, 1915–1920* (1990) · [Lord Tedder], *With prejudice: the war memoirs of marshal of the Royal Air Force, Lord Tedder* (1966) · R. Jackson, *At war with the Bolsheviks: the allied intervention into Russia, 1917–1920* (1974) · J. Terraine, *The right of the line: the Royal Air Force in the European war, 1939–1945* (1985) · D. Richards and H. St G. Saunders, *Royal Air Force, 1939–1945*, 1 (1953) · A. Longmore, *From sea to sky: 1910–1945* (1946) · J. H. Morrow, *The great war in the air: military aviation from 1909 to 1921* (1993)

Archives FILM IWM FVA, news footage

Likenesses photograph, 1918, NA Canada [*see illus.*] · photograph, repro. in Shores and others, *Above the trenches*, facing p. 241 · photograph, repro. in Tedder, *With prejudice*, following p. 224 · photographs, repro. in Collishaw and Dodds, *Air command*, facing p. 49, facing p. 129, following p. 224, facing p. 241

Collison, William (1865–1938), workers' leader, was born on 22 June 1865 at 22 Greenfield Street, Mile End, London, the eldest of twelve children of William Collison, policeman, and his wife, Leah (*née* Brett). Collison's formal education did not progress beyond elementary school; it must be presumed that his later fluency with the pen was the result of his own efforts at self-improvement. A long series of casual jobs, punctuated by a two-year period of service in the British army, took him into the world of London's dockland. His talents as an agitator and as an organizer soon became apparent. In 1886 he was elected as a delegate to the Mansion House Unemployed Relief Committee, where he was befriended by Cardinal Manning. Later he became a paid official of the Tramway and Omnibus Employees' Trade Union.

Collison's early enthusiasm for trade unions began to wane. In 1890 he declined to support a strike called by the

Tramway Union in protest against moves by the employers to counter dishonesty among their workers. He left the union, and attempted to obtain casual work again in the London docks, but was refused employment. This was because he was not a member of the dockers' trade union formed the previous year, when the great dock strike had marked the beginning of trade union organization (the so-called 'new unionism') among unskilled manual workers. Collison's anti-union views now took on a definite shape. He resented the manner in which (as he argued) professional socialists were exploiting the plight of the poor for their own political ends. The tactics of the closed shop, of which he now found himself a victim, were one of the hallmarks of new unionism; another was the use of the strike as a weapon of first rather than last resort. Collison regarded new unionism as a form of socialist tyranny, and he determined to fight it. He knew that there were many other like-minded members of the working classes who shared his views. On 16 May 1893, at Ye Olde Roebuck public house, Aldgate, he called a 'General Conference of men interested in Free Labour': this became the National Free Labour Association (NFLA).

Collison hoped that the NFLA would become the free labour equivalent of the Trades Union Congress. The NFLA held annual conferences, open to the press and lavishly advertised. It is clear from revelations subsequently made by some of Collison's former associates that these annual gatherings were heavily stage-managed. But the *Free Labour Gazette* (later *Free Labour Press*) which the NFLA published between 1894 and 1907 was professionally produced, its editor from 1896 being John Charles Manning, an experienced journalist. Collison himself branched out into journalism of a sort: it was he who supplied *The Times* with the material used in the sensational series of attacks on trade union practices which appeared anonymously in that paper between 18 November 1901 and 16 January 1902.

The ostensible purpose of the NFLA was to maintain a network of free labour exchanges, by means of which non-union labour might be supplied wherever it was needed. In practice, this network acted as the major supplier of blackleg labour to British industry in the period from the NFLA's foundation until the First World War. Most of Collison's interventions were small-scale; he could not hope to replace craftsmen, though the sight of his blacklegs, protected by the police, undoubtedly had an effect on the morale of strikers. In 1900, however, he scored a coup. Asked by the Taff Vale Railway Company to organize a supply of railwaymen to break a strike called by the Amalgamated Society of Railway Servants, Collison made certain that every free labourer had signed an agreement to enter into the service of the company, which was thus enabled to obtain damages from the railwaymen's union for inducing breaches of contract.

The Taff Vale dispute established the principle that trade unions were liable to pay damages in respect of industrial action. The case convinced many trade unions, hitherto lukewarm in their response to the Labour Representation Committee (forerunner of the Labour Party),

that they must now support it to obtain legislative reversal of the legal judgment. This was effected through the Trade Disputes Act of 1906, enacted by the incoming Liberal government. No less important was the reluctance of that Liberal administration to sanction the use of the police to protect blacklegs. More fundamentally, although it was the case that some groups of employers (most notoriously, the railway companies) undoubtedly shared Collison's anti-union sentiments, they were in a decided minority. Spurred by the Conciliation Act passed by the Unionist government in 1896, most large employers of labour had come to accept the reality of organized labour and to recognize the benefits and conveniences of collective bargaining. What most employers wanted, even in the 1890s, was conciliation, not the politics of confrontation which Collison offered them. Certainly after 1906 the political and industrial climates in which the NFLA had flourished rapidly disappeared. However, the organization continued to exist, certainly until 1929, operating from offices in the City of London.

It is easy to dismiss Collison as a tool of those employers whose counter-offensive against new unionism was at its height in the period from 1890 to 1906. But the surviving archival evidence suggests otherwise. Collison was paid by employers, but mainly for services rendered. It seems safer to regard him as a particularly vivid example of working-class hostility to new unionism and to socialism at this time.

An accomplished self-publicist, sporting curly hair, wide-brimmed hat, and bow-tie, Collison rubbed shoulders with the powerful but never forgot his proletarian origins. Practically nothing is known of his private life. He died at his home, 160 Eccleston Crescent, Ilford, on 8 March 1938, of heart disease, bronchitis, and emphysema; he was survived by a daughter, Emilie.

GEOFFREY ALDERMAN

Sources W. Collison, *The apostle of free labour* (1913) · J. C. M. [J. C. Manning], *The National Free Labour Association: its foundation, history, and work* (1898) · J. Saville, 'Trade unions and free labour: the background to the Taff Vale decision', *Essays in labour history in memory of G. D. H. Cole, 25 September 1889 – 14 January 1959*, ed. A. Briggs and J. Saville (1960), 317–50 · G. Alderman, 'The National Free Labour Association', *International Review of Social History*, 21 (1976), 309–36 · b. cert. · d. cert.
Archives NRA Scotland, Wemyss MSS
Likenesses photograph, repro. in Collison, *The apostle*, frontispiece

Collop, John (*bap.* 1625), poet, was baptized at Flitwick, Bedfordshire, on 4 July 1625, the son of John Collop, who was probably a mercer. Collop was educated at the Charterhouse and as an exhibitioner at Pembroke College, Cambridge, commencing studies in 1641 under the tutelage of William Quarles. Though it is difficult to be certain, it appears that Collop was licensed as a physician; at any rate he allowed himself the title of MD. Owing to the scarcity of marriage records during the Commonwealth period, it is difficult to establish when Collop's first marriage took place, though it can be said with greater certainty that he later moved to London, making a second marriage, to Anne Evington, about 1676.

Collop was the author of *Poesis rediviva, or, Poesie Reviv'd* (1656) (containing a lengthy dedication to Henry, marquess of Dorchester) and *Itur satyricum in Loyall Stanzas* (1660), a poem on the Restoration. His massive debt to Donne is evident throughout the corpus, though the imitation of Donne's verbal precision and intentional probing of the reader's habits of thought and moral complacency is not a match for Donne's incandescent intelligence or natural skill with language. Quite frequently Collop begins with an arresting, if syntactically awkward, couplet, yet is unable to develop the theme or build on the opening. His conciliatory attitude to the political and religious controversies of the day is found throughout most of his occasional verse. Basically a moderate royalist (he did not approve of cavalier excess) he also attempted to reconcile himself to Cromwell's power.

In religious matters Collop's conservatism was ill-matched to the 1650s and he took little pleasure in the sectarianism of the period, identifying the arguments of the rival parties as being based in attempts to gain temporal power and authority, unrelated to the divine. A popular tract, *Medici Catholicon* (1656, reprinted as *Charity Commended*, 1658 and 1667) pursues Collop's belief in toleration in religion. The opening of 'Sectaries' neatly encapsulates his views on this subject and is also telling in terms of its strength and poetic allegiance:

> See of phanatique fowlers a fresh shole,
> With baits of Liberty who decoy the Soul,
> *Copernicism* these by their whimsies prove;
> Where all are giddy, how can the Earth not move?

However unlike most of Collop's occasional verse, the poem ends strongly:

> All 'gainst Idolatry cry; yet all approve,
> While they the idols of their Fancies love.

This illustrates the difference between the Herbert-inspired religious lyrics, written from personal conviction, and the more awkward occasional verse.

Collop's range extended beyond the religious to include the less familiar genre of poems addressed to the physically hard-favoured mistress, including four poems to a yellow-skinned lady. 'On the Wearing of the Tag of her Blew Point' begins with the memorable couplet

> Though like a Liquorish stick you're thin,
> Yet all its sweetness is within.

Collop also wrote against quackery, including the common belief in the relation of the humours and elements to well-being, phlebotomy (bloodletting), purging, and the practising of non-licentiates:

> These like the Dogs in errors darker night,
> Bark at the Moon, but cannot reach the light.

'Chymistrie' is also criticized, as is the use of the occult ('On Sigils'), alchemy, astrology, and mysticism of all kinds. Occasionally Collop provides a lively metaphor such as in 'Man a Microcosm' in which 'Our flesh is earth, our blood is as a Sea'. Yet it is poems such as 'On Truth' that portray Collop at his best, able to identify the folly of religious controversy, but frustrated by his lack of ability to change the temperament of the times in which he found

himself, and cast adrift from the period when toleration was viable:

> See each Divine is but an advocate,
> As if Religion was a temporal state:
> They with illusion, forgeries, for it plead,
> And do't like Lawy'rs, onely to be fee'd.

Itur satyricum is an attempt to praise the Restoration, yet a combination of platitude and verbal awkwardness limits its effectiveness as poetry, if not as an apposite and well-timed welcome, written by a man who had argued that Charles I had bargained away his own life on the beheading of '*Wisdoms* Monopoly', the earl of Strafford.

NICHOLAS JAGGER

Sources *The poems of John Collop*, ed. C. Hilberry (1962) · Venn, *Alum. Cant.*
Archives BL · Bodl. Oxf. · CUL · Hunt. L. · Pembroke Cam. · Princeton University, New Jersey · Yale U.

Colls, (John) Howard (1846–1910), builder and employers' leader, was born on 30 August 1846 at Camberwell, Surrey, the second son of Benjamin Colls (1813–1878), housepainter and builder, and Elizabeth Jackson. Early in life he acquired practical skills in his father's joinery workshop. In 1867 he married Annie M. McMillan, daughter of shipbuilder Archibald McMillan; they had one son and at least seven daughters. Colls's father, who had been active in local government, ultimately becoming chairman of the City lands committee and thus 'first commoner' of the corporation of London, left an estate of less than £18,000 and a relatively small building business. The business passed to Colls and his elder brother William (1842–1893), and thereafter Colls & Sons specialized in building City offices, banks, and similar premises. It retained workshops at 240 Camberwell Road and established premises at Dorking in Surrey from which prepared joinery was brought to be fixed on jobs in the City. As wage costs in Dorking were lower than in London, this was one of the foundations of Colls's business success.

The bulk of Colls & Sons' building work after 1880 was undertaken in the City of London. Its finest City building was probably that for the Institute of Chartered Accountants, constructed in 1889–92. The firm did, however, execute other work, including projects at Stratfield Saye for the duke of Wellington.

Colls was also active in industrial politics. He was vice-president of the National Association of Master Builders of Great Britain, 1885–9, and its president in 1889–90. As president he served on the association's committee on the difficult matter of the form of contract between builder and architect. It has been suggested that he deserves much of the credit for the standard form of building contract agreed in 1903. He was also president of the Institute of Builders, 1887–8. He was president of the Central Association of Master Builders of London in 1890–91. His presidential term was dominated by the eight-hour-day dispute with the London United Trade Committee of Carpenters and Joiners. This dispute was particularly hard-fought and brought building in London to a virtual standstill between May and November 1891. In the main, the master builders were successful: the hours of work were reduced but the rate of payment remained unchanged. For Colls & Sons, however, the decision to increase overtime rates was a setback. Most of its business consisted of alterations and extensions to City offices and many of the contracts could only be carried on outside the working hours of City businesses.

William, Colls's elder brother and subordinate partner, died in 1893. That there was no ill feeling on the part of the elder man is demonstrated by his will, which ensured the continuance of the family firm under Colls's control. Following his brother's death Colls seems to have given up active involvement in the affairs of employers' associations.

Arguably Colls's greatest service to the building industry was in his conduct of the celebrated case of *Colls v. Home and Colonial Stores Ltd* which went to the House of Lords in 1904. The issue turned on the legal definition of 'ancient lights', the rights of the proprietor of an existing building over light and air and (by implication) against new buildings. The new building in question was erected in Worship Street, Finsbury, by Colls & Sons. The final ruling was that the Home and Colonial Stores was entitled to sufficient air and light for ordinary purposes, but did not have a perpetual right to the same amount as it had previously enjoyed. In effect the law was substantially modified, by means of a judicial review. Previously many of those who had lodged claims and sought injunctions had done so in order to extort compensation. Few of them were genuinely concerned about ventilation or daylight.

Colls became a member of Joseph Chamberlain's tariff commission of which his son-in-law, Francis Elgar, managing director of the Fairfield Engineering and Shipbuilding Company, was also a member. At the end of 1903 the firm of Colls & Sons ceased to exist and was incorporated in the new firm of Trollope and Colls. Colls became joint chairman with George Haward *Trollope. The merger of the two firms was probably facilitated by the shared experience of industrial strife which these two key figures had in common, and their complementary political opinions. Both held Conservative views, although neither sought public office in the Conservative cause. The agreement for the sale of the assets of Colls & Sons to Trollope and Colls, excluding freehold and leasehold property, stipulated a purchase price of £165,375 10s. By comparison the assets of George Trollope & Sons were valued at £234,624 10s., so clearly the Trollopes were the dominant partners in the new firm.

Colls died of a heart attack at or near Buenos Aires, Argentina, on 29 December 1910, while on a sea cruise for his health's sake.   ALISTAIR G. TOUGH

Sources J. H. Colls, letter, *The Times* (15 Oct 1879) · J. H. Colls, letter, *The Times* (8 Jan 1904) · J. H. Colls, letter, *The Times* (8 July 1909) · *City builders for 200 years, 1778–1978*, Trollope and Colls Ltd (1978) · National Federation of Building Trades Employers, *Outline history of NFBTE* (1978) · J. Newenham Summerson, *London building world of 1860s* (1973) · H. J. Dyos, *Victorian suburbs: study of growth of Camberwell* (1961) · C. G. Powell, *Economic history of British building industry, 1815–1979* (1982) · b. cert. · d. cert.

Archives BLPES, Building Employers' Confederation Tariff Commission papers
Wealth at death £419,797 1s. 10d.: probate, 3 March 1911, *CGPLA Eng. & Wales*

Collyer, Joseph, the elder (1714/15–1776), translator and bookseller, was probably the son of Joseph Collyer (d. 1724), a bookseller and treasurer of the Stationers' Company. He married Mary Mitchell [see Collyer, Mary (1716/17–1762)], who was also a translator and novelist; their son, Joseph *Collyer the younger [see under Boydell, John, engravers], became a well-known engraver. Collyer had a shop in Plough Court, London. Collyer the elder married a woman named Anne after the death of his first wife.

Collyer's translations include selections from Voltaire (1754), Plutarch (1762), and J. J. Bodmer (1767); and shortly before his death he completed a translation from the German of Sophie von La Roche's work, as *History of Lady Sophia Sternheim*. He also published *The Parent's and Guardian's Directory* (1761); *A History of England* (14 vols., 1774–5); and, with D. Fenning, *A New System of Geography* (2 folio vols., 1765–6).

According to a contemporary, Collyer was 'habituated to domestic life and studious retirement; he filled up the relations of husband and father with endearing affection; though an author by profession, he possessed no kind of petulance, self-sufficiency, or envy'. He suffered a 'lingering illness and want of employment', but 'his long course of severe application had afforded him no opportunity to make provision for the decline of life' (*New System*, 1.4). Collyer died on 20 February 1776, probably at his home in Islington, at the age of sixty-one. He left a widow, Anne.

THOMPSON COOPER, rev. JOYCE FULLARD

Sources *A new system of geography … by D. Fenning … and J. Collyer*, rev. T. Hervey, [rev. edn] (1785), preface to vol. 1 · *GM*, 1st ser., 98/1 (1828), 184 · *GM*, 1st ser., 46 (1776), 95 · S. von La Roche, *The history of Lady Sophia Sternheim*, ed. J. Lynn, trans. J. Collyer the elder (1992) · *BL cat.* · Nichols, *Illustrations*, 3.607, 8.723, 9.809 · Watt, *Bibl. Brit.* · W. T. Lowndes, *The bibliographers' manual of English literature*, ed. H. G. Bohn, [new edn], 2 (1864); repr. (1967), 501 · Graves, *Soc. Artists*
Wealth at death poor: *New system of geography*, preface

Collyer, Joseph, the younger (1748–1827). *See under* Boydell, John, engravers (act. 1760–1804).

Collyer [née Mitchell], **Mary** (1716/17–1762), translator and novelist, is of unknown parentage, nor has her birthplace been identified. Although her work demonstrates a good knowledge of languages and literature, there is no record of her early life or education, with the exception of one comment by Elizabeth Carter, saying she had been 'a little acquainted with her before she was married' (*Letters*, 1.151). She married Joseph *Collyer the elder (1714/15–1776), a writer and bookseller who had a shop in Plough Court and a house in Islington; their son, Joseph *Collyer the younger [see under Boydell, John, engravers], born in 1748, engraved illustrations for one edition of her extremely popular *Death of Abel* (1761), a translation from Salomon Gessner. In dedicating this work to the queen, Collyer states: 'It is in order to contribute to the support and education of my children, I have taken up the pen' (Gessner, sig. A2). There is evidence, however, for only the one child, Joseph.

Collyer published *The Virtuous Orphan*, her translation and completion of Marivaux's *La vie de Marianne*, in instalments in the *London Evening-Post* during 1742, and in a single volume in 1743. McBurney and Shugrue describe this as 'the most popular translation during the eighteenth century, the period of Marivaux's greatest influence upon the English novel' (*Virtuous Orphan*, vi). *Felicia to Charlotte* (2 vols., 1744–9), Collyer's original novel, in which she introduces a hero who is both a man of feeling and a man of reason, was also successful.

Collyer also published *Memoirs of the Countess de Bressol … from the French* (2 vols., 1743) and *The Christmas Box* (1748–9). Her husband completed her final work, a translation of Klopstock's *Messiah* (2 vols., 1763); and in a preface, he states that his wife's death followed 'a lingering illness occasion'd by the agitations of mind she suffer'd in writing' *Death of Abel* and the first part of *The Messiah*. She died on 31 December 1762 and was buried at St Mary's, Islington, on 5 January 1763.   JOYCE FULLARD

Sources *The virtuous orphan, or, The life of Marianne countess of xxxx: an eighteenth-century English translation by Mrs. Mary Mitchell Collyer of Marivaux's 'La vie de Marianne'*, ed. W. H. McBurney and M. F. Shugrue (1965) · H. S. Hughes, 'The life and works of Mary Mitchell Collyer', PhD diss., University of Chicago, 1917 · H. S. Hughes, 'An early Romantic novel', *Journal of English and Germanic Philology*, 15 (1916), 564–98 · H. S. Hughes, 'Translations of the *Vie de Marianne* and their relation to contemporary English fiction', *Modern Philology*, 15 (1917–18), 491–512 · S. Gessner, *The death of Abel*, trans. M. Collyer (Boston, 1761) · F. Klopstock, *The Messiah*, trans. M. Collyer and J. Collyer, 1 (1763) · *Letters from Mrs. Elizabeth Carter, to Mrs. Montagu, between the years 1755 and 1800*, 3 vols. (1817), vol. 1, pp. 151–2 · M. A. Schofield, 'Mary Collyer', *Masking and unmasking the female mind: disguising romances in feminine fiction, 1713–1799* (1990), 91–7 · *BL cat.* · *GM*, 1st ser., 14 (1744), 344, 669 · *GM*, 1st ser., 98/1 (1828), 184 · J. Todd, ed., *A dictionary of British and American women writers, 1660–1800* (1984) · J. Todd, ed., *Dictionary of British women writers* (1989) · J. C. Beasley, 'English fiction in the 1740s: some glances at the major and minor novels', *Studies in the Novel*, 5 (summer 1973), 155–75 · Graves, *Soc. Artists*

Collyer, William Bengo' (1782–1854), Congregational minister and religious writer, was the only surviving child of a builder, Thomas Collyer, and his wife, Ann. He was born in Deptford on 14 April 1782. After an education at the Leathersellers' Company School at Lewisham, he entered the Independent Homerton Academy as a scholar in 1798. In 1800 he began his ministry to a small congregation at Peckham, where he was ordained in December 1801. The congregation speedily increased, and, after the chapel had been enlarged several times, it was rebuilt in 1816 and reopened under the name of Hanover Chapel. In 1813 he was invited to succeed to the pulpit at Salters' Hall Chapel, which, with the agreement of his congregation at Peckham, he accepted in addition to his existing duties. On 20 October 1813 he married Mary (d. 1828?), the only daughter and coheir of Thomas Hawkes of Lutterworth; they had one daughter.

Collyer was a prolific author. His works included many sermons and hymns, and a series of popular lectures on scriptural subjects, including *Lectures on Scriptural Facts* (1807), *Scripture Prophecy* (1809), and *Scripture Duties* (1819). In 1823 he published, in seven volumes, *Lectures on the Evidences of Divine Revelation*. In 1808 he received a DD from Edinburgh University. In 1823 he was so greatly distressed by allegations of moral misconduct, which arose from his amateur interest in medicine and his practice of physically examining applicants for medical relief before sending them on to the relevant charity, that he published a letter in vindication of his conduct. He died on 9 January 1854 at 5 Rye Lane, Peckham, and was buried on 16 January.   [ANON.], rev. DAVID HUDDLESTON

Sources *GM*, 2nd ser., 41 (1854), 655–6 · *European Magazine and London Review*, 72 (1817), 407–11 · *Congregational Year Book* (1855) · J. Waddington, *Congregational history*, 4 (1878) · R. Tudur Jones, *Congregationalism in England, 1662–1962* (1962) · *The Reverend W. B. Collyer's interesting letter in vindication of his own conduct, from the calumnious reports circulated against him*, [2nd edn] (1823) · d. cert. · *IGI*
Archives DWL, corresp. and papers
Likenesses C. Picart, stipple, pubd 1806 (after J. H. Stevenson), BM, NPG · J. Young, mezzotint, pubd 1812 (after C. C. Coventry), BM · Fittler, line engraving, pubd 1816, NPG · Freeman, stipple, pubd 1818 (after Wivell), NPG · C. Penny, stipple and line engraving, pubd 1820, NPG · H. Meyer, engraving (after S. Drummond), repro. in *European Magazine* · oils, DWL
Wealth at death £5000: *GM*

Colmán [St Colmán] (d. 676), bishop of Lindisfarne, was an Irish monk from Iona. He may conceivably be the 'Colmanus abbas' recorded by the seventeenth-century scholar Patrick Young as the addressee of a charter, now lost, from Wulfhere, king of the Mercians (r. 657–74), preserved in the archive of Worcester Cathedral (*AS chart.*, S 1822). If so, he held ecclesiastical office in Mercia about the same time as the first two bishops of the Mercians, Diuma and Ceollach, both of whom were Irishmen. However, the charter reference is by no means reliable, and in any case Colmán is one of the most common early medieval Irish names.

On the death of Finán in 661, Colmán succeeded him as abbot of Lindisfarne and bishop of the Northumbrians. His appointment coincided with, and may have exacerbated, intensifying disagreements in the Northumbrian church between those who followed the customs of Iona and its dependencies (generally labelled, inaccurately, as the 'Irish' tradition), and those who followed practices current in northern Italy and Merovingian Francia (usually equally inaccurately termed the 'Roman' tradition). The fullest coverage of the dispute is given by Bede, whose *Historia ecclesiastica gentis Anglorum*, completed in 731, pays most attention to the conflict over the method of calculating the date of Easter, the central festival in the Christian calendar. The practice characterized as Roman was based on a system first devised at Alexandria centuries earlier, which placed Easter on a Sunday between the end of the fourteenth and the twenty-first days of the lunar month after the vernal equinox, avoiding the Jewish passover festival on the fourteenth of that month. The 'Irish' system put Easter between the fourteenth and the twentieth days: thus the 'Irish' Easter Sunday would sometimes fall earlier than the 'Roman' one. Further dislocation was caused by the use of different cycles of years designed to reconcile the lunar calendar with the solar months of the Roman calendar: the Alexandrian system was based on a ninety-five-year cycle, the Irish on one of eighty-four years, derived from a treatise attributed (wrongly, as it turns out) to a third-century bishop. Another point of contention was the method of tonsuring monks: Roman practice left a circle of hair around a shaven crown (in imitation of the crown of thorns), while the Irish shaved the hair at the front, leaving it long at the back.

Controversy between the two sides culminated at a synod convened at Streanaeshalch (Whitby) in 664. Bede's account of this event is likely to have been coloured by his own prejudices: adherence to the Roman practice, but also considerable respect for the asceticism of the monks of the Ionan tradition, and, perhaps, a dislike of the Roman side's spokesman Wilfrid. Bede includes a rose-tinted passage evoking the virtues of the Irish way of monasticism, its frugality and austerity, and the respect it elicited from the Northumbrians, both king and people, and implicitly contrasts it with the monasticism of his own time, which he saw as corrupted by secular influence. His report of the synod is animated by the distinction he draws between Colmán's measured exposition of his case and Wilfrid's learned but high-handed, if not insulting, responses (at one point he called the Irish adherents *stultus*—'stupid'). The synod began with the king of the Northumbrians, Oswiu, asking Colmán to describe the origins of his customs. Colmán said that 'all our fathers' had celebrated Easter in the way that he did, and he invoked the example of St John the Evangelist (Bede, *Hist. eccl.*, 3.25). Wilfrid explained that St John had followed Jewish law 'when the church was still Jewish in many respects' (ibid.), but that the example to be preferred was that of St Peter who, he wrongly claimed, had celebrated Easter at Rome on the Sunday following the fourteenth day of the lunar month. Colmán posited the counter-examples of the third-century bishop Anatolius, whose calculations his tradition followed, and of Iona's founder, St Columba. Wilfrid stated that the Irish had misinterpreted Anatolius, and that Columba had acted through ignorance. He again invoked the example of St Peter, to whom Christ had given the keys to the kingdom of heaven, and King Oswiu asked Colmán if there was anything to show that an equal authority had been granted to 'your Columba' (ibid.). When the bishop admitted that there was not, Oswiu declared that he intended to obey the commands of the door-keeper of heaven, and the matter was decided in favour of the 'Roman' usage.

While Bede relates that all those present at the synod gave their assent to Oswiu's ruling, it is evident that Colmán dissented, for he left Northumbria soon after. It is less clear that he rejected the decision 'for fear of his fellow-countrymen', as Wilfrid's biographer Stephen of Ripon asserts (*Life of Bishop Wilfrid*, 23): the implication that only threats from others prevented Colmán from accepting the rightness of Wilfrid's case looks like special pleading on the part of the hagiographer. Colmán took with him all those who could not accept the decision, together

with some of the relics of St Áedán. Before leaving he won from Oswiu—who admired Colmán's 'innate wisdom' (Bede, *Hist. eccl.*, 3.26)—the favour that Abbot Eata of Melrose should be appointed the new leader of the Lindisfarne community. Colmán's replacement as bishop of the Northumbrians was Tuda, a monk from the southern part of Ireland, where the Roman customs were followed. Tuda, however, lasted only a short time, and was succeeded as bishop by Eata.

Colmán travelled first to Iona, and thence to an island off the west coast of Ireland, Inishbofin ('the island of the white cow'), where he founded a new community of both Irish and English monks. Dissension soon arose, however:

> because the Irish, in summer time when the harvest had to be gathered in, left the monastery and wandered about, scattering into various places with which they were familiar; then when winter came, they returned and expected to have a share in the things which the English had provided. (Bede, *Hist. eccl.*, 4.4)

Colmán therefore moved the English monks to a new foundation on the Irish mainland at Mayo. By Bede's time this community was flourishing, and he reports that the monks had 'adopted a better Rule'—perhaps meaning that they had abandoned the Ionan method of Easter calculation and custom of tonsure, as well as that they were living more according to Benedictine precepts, under a canonically elected abbot.

Entries in the annals of Ulster and other Irish annals (in which he is given the title bishop of Inishbofin) date Colmán's death to 676. Irish martyrologies commemorate him on 8 August.   MARIOS COSTAMBEYS

Sources Bede, *Hist. eccl.*, 3–4 · E. Stephanus, *The life of Bishop Wilfrid*, ed. and trans. B. Colgrave (1927) · *AS chart.*, S 1822 · H. Mayr-Harting, *The coming of Christianity to Anglo-Saxon England* (1972) · P. Grosjean, 'La date du colloque de Whitby', *Analecta Bollandiana*, 78 (1960), 233–74 · *Ann. Ulster*, s.a. 675 · *Félire Óengusso Céli Dé | The martyrology of Oengus the Culdee*, ed. and trans. W. Stokes, HBS, 29 (1905) · R. I. Best and H. J. Lawlor, eds., *The martyrology of Tallaght*, HBS, 68 (1931) · *Félire húi Gormáin | The martyrology of Gorman*, ed. and trans. W. Stokes, HBS, 9 (1895)

Colman family (*per.* 1814–1898), mustard and starch manufacturers, traced its origins in that trade to **Jeremiah Colman** (1777–1851), originally a flour miller at Bawburgh, who in 1814 purchased the flour and mustard making concern of Edward Ames at Stoke Holy Cross, near Norwich, Norfolk. On 15 November 1802 Jeremiah married Ann, daughter of Thomas Theobold, textile manufacturer; their childless marriage led to their adoption, about 1806, of their nephew **James Colman** (1801–1854). Born on 18 November 1801, James was the eldest of fifteen children of Robert Colman (1775–1867), a dairy and turkey farmer of Rockland St Andrew, Norfolk, and his wife, Ann Mills. James was taken into partnership with Jeremiah in 1823. On 1 August 1826 James married Mary (1805–1898), daughter of John Burlingham, a Norfolk miller and seed merchant. They had two children, the eldest being **Jeremiah James Colman** (1830–1898), born on 14 June 1830 at Stoke Holy Cross. Little is known about the education of either the elder Jeremiah or James. They

Jeremiah James Colman (1830–1898), by Sir Hubert von Herkomer, 1899 [replica; original, 1890]

became part of the J. and J. Colman organization in 1844. James's death, however, left Jeremiah James as the sole manager of the Stoke business at the age of twenty-four. The most formative influences on Jeremiah James were the Colman family traditions of liberalism and non-conformity and the belief which his parents expressed in the importance of applying the principles of both to life and labour. His early education at the Poringland Mill School of Samuel Colman, an uncle, and then at a small dame-school was followed by private tuition in Norwich under John Doman, Samuel Colman's brother-in-law. Further education continued through membership of the Norwich Young Men's Mutual Improvement Society, a group whose members met to write, read, and discuss religious, moral, political, and social issues. He was a teaching member of St Mary's Baptist Chapel in Norwich from the 1850s, where he was deacon between 1861 and 1870.

Devout and serious in his approach to life, Jeremiah James was also a somewhat reluctant entrepreneur, requiring reassurance from his mother that the moral imperatives of a nonconformist conscience would not conflict with the demands and responsibilities of running the family business. Perhaps reflecting on the experience of his father he expressed a fear that a life dedicated to success and expansion of the company might leave insufficient time for service in the faith, self improvement, and earnest recreation and that selfishness, influence, and wealth so often associated with business would need to be resisted. On assuming control of J. and J. Colman when his father died he also acknowledged the 'perilous position' of being 'at so young an age, master absolutely and unreservedly of so many people, and sometimes to have to demand an implicit though be it reluctant obedience' (Colman, 80). On 25 September 1856 he married Caroline [**Caroline Colman** (1831–1895)], eldest daughter of William Hardy Cozens-Hardy of Letheringsett Hall, Norfolk. Caroline shared his religious and social views and was an active partner in his life while raising their family of six children at Carrow House, Carrow, Norwich.

Between 1856 and 1862 Jeremiah James organized the relocation of the factory from Stoke to a newly built, large integrated factory and workshops at Carrow in Norwich, producing mustard, starch, and laundry blue. Growth led to incorporation in 1896, capitalized at £1,350,000, though ownership remained entirely within the Colman family. In business Jeremiah James sought to be 'useful', in accordance with his mother's prescription for a fulfilling but reverential business life, in two ways. One was by increasing employment opportunities for Colman employees and their families in a town which had seen its staple industry destroyed: by 1869 the number of workers employed at the Carrow works was 1100 rising to 2500 by 1898. The second form which usefulness took was an attempt to promote their employees' general well-being. The first was achieved by successful innovation, partly in production and organization but principally through innovative marketing policies first introduced by the elder Jeremiah and James during the 1840s. From that time the sale of mustard, starch, and blue began to be

were committed Baptists, upheld liberal principles, and campaigned for civil and religious liberties and free trade. The elder Jeremiah was a founder member of the committee of a local Lancastrian school, was elected to the first board of guardians, and initiated the Stoke Holy Cross New Benefit Society and the politically progressive *Norfolk News* in 1846. He served as sheriff of Norwich in 1845–6 and became mayor the following year, filling the offices occupied later by James and his son, Jeremiah James. The elder Jeremiah's move to Norwich in 1841 in effect left James in charge of the mustard-making business of J. and J. Colman at Stoke. The death of Jeremiah at Newmarket Road, Heigham, Norwich, on 3 December 1851, led to the partnership's being extended to include Jeremiah James. Three years later James died, on 19 October 1854, at 8 Marine Parade, Lowestoft, from the cumulative effect of many wearisome years as a commercial traveller and his exertions in expanding the business. The workforce had grown from fewer than fifty workers in the 1830s to about 500 by the late 1850s.

As the business expanded the partnership was extended to include two of James's brothers, Henry Jeremiah (1814–1895) and Edward Colman (1808–1874), whose London agency, which they had established independently, made in small amounts packed in containers distinctive in size, shape, label, and colour.

The bull's head logo introduced in 1856, one of the first merchandise marks of its kind, heralded such a growth in brand advertising that in the 1870s a separate advertising department was formed at Carrow. In 1871 the partners appointed an outsider, Robert Haselwood, as manager (and later general manager) of the Carrow works. His responsibility was to implement the partners' policies. The appointment of accountants also marked the beginning of systematic accountability and control over the business.

Successful managerial delegation was accompanied by an informal arrangement whereby Caroline Colman took responsibility for supervising welfare provision in the company. When in 1857 the company school, started by the elder Jeremiah and James at Stoke, was transferred to Carrow, Caroline became responsible for its management and for planning the new purpose-built accommodation on Carrow Hill. She also originated several welfare initiatives. The Carrow works kitchen, forerunner of the works canteen, was opened in 1868 to serve commuting workers with early morning tea and coffee and hot midday meals at nominal cost. Basic, low cost lodging accommodation, including laundry, was available to young female workers under the immediate charge of a matron. To help women workers to save, Caroline organized a clothing club, to which she contributed a bonus added to their savings, and purchased drapery in bulk annually for sale at cost at Christmas. To help young women to sew and 'to become better women and wives' in 1874 the company engaged a dressmaking teacher.

The provision of medical and health care was exceptional, available within a context defined by the company's insistence that employees must be insured either through the company's accident, sickness, and provident schemes or through an independent friendly society. A dispensary was opened in 1864, staffed by a doctor and a nurse. In 1878 an assistant was appointed for the sole purpose of visiting sick employees with food from the works kitchen, probably the first example of industrial nursing in the country. Jeremiah James ensured that the charitable activities within the company designed to alleviate sickness and the consequences of infirmity and old age of Colman employees and families were continued after his death by inserting a clause in the 1896 articles of association. His will included the annual provision of £20,000 for twenty years to be used by trustees for this purpose.

As the Liberal MP for Norwich between 1871 and 1895 Jeremiah James voted as a Gladstonian Liberal until the Parnell sex scandal. He became a friend of the prime minister, who stayed with him at the Cliffe, Corton, Suffolk, on a number of occasions. Lacking oratorical skill Colman made little impact on an institution with which he quickly became disillusioned. However, as a Norwich town council representative between 1859 and 1871 (sheriff in 1862 and 1868 and mayor in 1869) he was the central figure in the movement to remove bribery and corruption for which Norwich was notorious. As the founder chairman of a committee of independent reformers set up in 1859 he campaigned for measures which advanced the liberty and interests of nonconformists and for franchise reform.

In February 1895 Jeremiah James's and Caroline's son Alan Cozens-Hardy Colman (b. 1867) died. In the early part of 1895 Caroline's health, too, declined and she died on 5 July at Corton. She was buried five days later at the Rosary burial-ground, Norwich. Depressed by the deaths of his wife and son, Jeremiah James took up again the burden of work. In February 1898 he started out for the Riviera but was detained in Paris by an attack of influenza. His penultimate visit to London was to attend Gladstone's funeral on 28 May. His final weeks were spent at Corton surrounded by the youngest members of his family. News of his mother's death, at the age of ninety-three, on 15 September further depressed him, and he died at the Cliffe, Corton, on 18 September 1898. Four days later he was buried alongside his wife at the Rosary. After his death, James *Stuart (1843–1913), who was married to his eldest daughter, Laura Elizabeth, ran the firm for some years.

Members of the nineteenth-century Colman family were responsible for three enduring achievements: the establishment of a business which, well before the merger with Reckitts in 1938 had become one of Britain's 100 largest manufacturing companies, and whose products, especially Colman's mustard, became part of national life; second, the success of the *Eastern Daily Press*, with which Jeremiah James was closely involved when it was launched in 1870; not least, the family had a significant impact on the physical and cultural environment of Norwich. This was largely the effect of 'Citizen Colman's' campaigning to promote the civic gospel, a cause to which he was a major contributor. He was a leader of the subscription campaign to ensure the use of all historic buildings for the public benefit, which by 1886 had seen both the castle and Blackfriars Hall pass into corporation ownership, and for the inclusion of the city walls and towers as part of the process of preservation. As a trustee of the Norwich Museum, in 1876 he bequeathed a large, varied collection which included paintings of the Norwich school. His library, relating to the history of Norwich and Norfolk, was donated posthumously by the Colman family to the city library, forming the unique Norfolk Studies Collection. Jeremiah James also purchased land for an extension to the children's hospital, the Jenny Lind Infirmary, in 1895, following the death of his son. Behind his conduct and achievements in business and public life lay his insistence that 'it is by taking our religion into everyday life, and by so acting that the world around us sees that in party strife, or commercial enterprise, we do that, and that only, which is consistent with our Christian profession' (Colman, 134).   ROY CHURCH

Sources Colman archives, Carrow works, Norwich · H. C. Colman, *Jeremiah James Colman: a memoir* (privately printed, London, 1905) · R. H. Mottram, 'A history of J. & J. Colman Ltd, of Carrow and Cannon Street', unpublished typescript, c.1950, priv. coll. · L. Stuart, *In memoriam, Caroline Colman* (privately printed,

Norwich, 1896) · E. Burgess and W. L. Burgess, *Men who have made Norwich* (1904) · Gladstone, *Diaries* · J. Stuart, *Reminiscences* (1911) · d. certs. [Jeremiah Colman, James Colman] · *CGPLA Eng. & Wales* (1895) [Caroline Colman] · *CGPLA Eng. & Wales* (1898) [Jeremiah James Colman]

Archives Carrow works, Norwich, archives · Norfolk RO, Colman Library, corresp. and papers

Likenesses H. von Herkomer, portrait, 1890 (Jeremiah James Colman) · group portrait, photograph, 1890 (with family and W. E. Gladstone), priv. coll. · H. von Herkomer, portrait, second version, 1899 (Jeremiah James Colman), Norwich Castle Museum and Art Gallery [*see illus.*]

Wealth at death £1587 7s.—Caroline Colman: administration, 29 Oct 1895, *CGPLA Eng. & Wales* · £687,024 5s. 10d.—Jeremiah James Colman: probate, 10 Nov 1898, *CGPLA Eng. & Wales*

Colmán Elo (d. 611). *See under* Meath, saints of (*act. c.*400–*c.*900).

Colmán mac Léníne (530–606). *See under* Munster, saints of (*act. c.*450–*c.*700).

Colman, Caroline (1831–1895). *See under* Colman family (*per.* 1814–1898).

Colman, Cecil (1878–1954), shoe manufacturer and retailer, was born on 30 May 1878 in Bournemouth, one of nine children of the Revd Robert Colman, Baptist minister, and his wife, Sophia (née Allen). His father was the son of a partner in the mustard firm of J. and J. Colman, and became involved in a number of civic and business enterprises. After an unexceptional school career at Christchurch School, Hampshire, Colman was educated privately before taking his first job at seventeen in a small Bournemouth shoe manufacturing and retailing company of which his father was a director. In 1897 the company failed and Colman set up a short-lived shoe factoring partnership with his brother, Robert. This widened his experience in the wholesaling and retailing of shoes.

In 1901, aged only twenty-two, Colman joined Howlett and White, a leading firm of shoe manufacturers, founded in Norwich in 1846. He became the London sales manager and export agent. In 1903 he married Florence Beatrice Laws; they had four sons and one daughter. In 1912 he was appointed to the board of Howlett and White and he played an increasingly important role in its affairs thereafter. Appointed deputy chairman and joint managing director of the expanded company in 1935, he served as chairman from 1947. By this stage the restructured company employed some 1700 employees in two Norwich factories, over 1000 in a Northampton subsidiary and several hundred more in its Mansfield subsidiary. Colman retired in June 1953.

Colman was the central figure in a managerial team responsible for the company's growth. His precise role is not always easy to distinguish from that of others in the team, but he was highly regarded by his colleagues for his innovative methods and organizational ability in finance and marketing. He was responsible for organizing the process of expansion by merger, which led to the acquisition of a number of important rivals: the Mansfield Shoe Co. in 1919, Oakeshott and Finnemore, a large Northampton

firm, in 1922, and S. L. Witton of Norwich, which specialized in children's shoes, in 1934. The company was restructured in 1935 as the Norvic Shoe Co. Ltd and in 1946 it further expanded by acquiring the old Northampton house of John Marlow & Son.

The development of new marketing strategies also owed a lot to Colman. In 1911 the Norvic trade mark was adopted, and an advertising department was created in order that national advertising campaigns could be organized. Impressed by American experience, Colman pioneered the Norvic concentration plan, an early form of franchising which involved over fifty shops. Colman was also involved in the development of a company pension scheme and the expansion of wider welfare provisions, building on a paternalistic tradition in Howlett and White, which had recognized relatively early the rights of its workforce to organize. At the end of the Second World War he supervised the shift of the firm's headquarters to London and its reorganization. The importance of the group in the British shoe industry meant that Colman's influence was able to extend more widely. He was a president of the Boot and Shoe Manufacturers' Association of Great Britain and chaired the Branded Retailers' Association.

After the First World War Colman made his home in Sutton and Cheam where he was first elected councillor in 1929, alderman in 1934, and mayor in 1935. He was also a magistrate and was involved in various local charitable activities as well as the chamber of trade and the Rotarians. A Liberal in politics he was for a long period the president of the Epsom division Liberal Association.

An important figure in the manufacturing and retailing of shoes, Colman played a vital role in the transformation of the industry in the inter-war period. Under his leadership, merger of a number of small businesses led to the emergence of the Norvic Shoe Co. Ltd as the largest manufacturer of shoes in Britain. Colman died at 32 The Avenue, Cheam, on 11 March 1954, and was buried at the South London crematorium on 15 March. He was survived by his wife.   MICHAEL HAYNES

Sources *The Times* (12 March 1954) · *Surrey Country Herald* (19 March 1954) · *Sutton Times and Cheam Mail* (18 March 1954) · *Sutton and Cheam Advertiser* (18 March 1954) · *Shoe and Leather News* (18 March 1954) · *Eastern Daily Press* (12 March 1954) · *Eastern Daily Press* (16 March 1954) · *Norfolk News* (19 March 1954) · K. B. Brooker, 'Colman, Cecil', *DBB* · F. W. Weldon, *A Norvic century and the men who made it* (1946) · W. L. Sparks, *Story of shoemaking in Norwich* (1944) · *CGPLA Eng. & Wales* (1954)

Likenesses portrait, c.1935 (in mayoral robes; after portrait [now mislaid]), Sutton Council, Heritage Department · photograph, repro. in Weldon, *A Norvic century*

Wealth at death £256,914 15s. 7d.: probate, 1954, *CGPLA Eng. & Wales* · £397,724: Brooker, 'Colman, Cecil'

Colman [Coleman], **Edward** (1636–1678), courtier, was born on 17 May 1636 at Brent Eleigh, Suffolk, the second of five children and only son of Thomas Colman (d. 1661), vicar of Brent Eleigh and later rector of Thorpe Morieux, and his wife, Margaret (d. 1680), daughter of Philip Wilson of Bocking, Essex. He matriculated at Trinity College, Cambridge, on 16 October 1651, and graduated BA in 1656 and MA in 1659. He entered royal service as a gentleman pensioner to the king on 28 June 1661. At some point between 1664 and 1667 he married his first cousin, Mary Orme (b. c.1640, d. after 1678), daughter of his late aunt, Jane Colman, and her husband, Simon Orme of Goldhanger, Essex. This marriage probably produced no children.

Colman converted to Roman Catholicism in the early 1660s, and few advocates of the Catholic cause in late seventeenth-century England were as charismatic as he. Several highly publicized conversions were credited to his influence, and it can even be speculated that he may have played some part in that of James, duke of York (later James II). York's belief that the Catholic church would make headway in England only by supporting a policy of religious toleration echoed Colman's own views. What is certain is that he was associated with York by the early 1670s (probably, in the first instance, because his cousin Richard Colman, MP for Salisbury, was related to the Hydes, York's kin by marriage), and in 1673 York appointed him as secretary to his second wife, Mary of Modena.

During the mid-1670s Colman conducted what was arguably an independent foreign policy on behalf of the duke of York. A visit by him to Cardinal Falconieri in Brussels in spring 1674 was an unsuccessful attempt to make indirect contact with the papal court. He was more persistent in cultivating several members of the French court, most notably the king's confessors, Jean Ferrier and François de la Chaise. However, it would appear that none of those in France with whom he corresponded thought the matter of sufficient importance to require the attention of Louis XIV. The exact extent of York's knowledge of these negotiations was never established: he knew a great deal about what Colman was up to and he was probably less than truthful when he later claimed that he had 'oft forwarn'd him [Colman] to be careful how he carryd himself, not to be so busy and meddlesome' (Life of James the Second, 1.533–4). Their principal aim throughout was to obtain subsidies to reduce Charles II's dependence on parliament at a time when further legislation against Catholics seemed likely. No money was forthcoming and, when a French subsidy was eventually secured, it was through the efforts of the king and his own advisers. The lord treasurer, Thomas Osborne, earl of Danby, and the bishop of London, Henry Compton, came to view Colman as a dangerous influence on York and so plotted to remove him. They succeeded in getting him dismissed as the duchess's secretary in late 1676 after he was caught leaking naval intelligence in a newsletter. His activities thereafter on behalf of York are more shadowy, but he did receive substantial sums of money from Barrillon, the French ambassador, which he may have disbursed as bribes to MPs.

As one of the most prominent lay Catholics in York's circle, it was unsurprising that Colman should figure in the elaborate fantasy plot dreamed up by Titus Oates and his associates in autumn 1678. According to Oates, Colman was to become secretary of state once the murder of Charles II had paved the way for York's accession. This detail may have been added by Oates only when he expanded on his original claims at his second meeting with Sir Edmund Berry Godfrey on 28 September. It later emerged that Godfrey got in touch with Colman immediately after that meeting, presumably so that York could be warned of the extent of Oates's new allegations. On 29 September 1678, the day after Oates was questioned by the privy council, officials raided Colman's house on the south side of Dean's Yard, Westminster. The search failed to find him, but did uncover a hidden cache of letters documenting his secret negotiations. The following day Colman, who may not have realized that the letters had been discovered, gave himself up and appeared before the privy council. His decision to come forward impressed the council and, at that stage, they were inclined to believe him. Their mood changed as soon as the decoding of the letters began. Taken out of context, much of what they contained could be interpreted as evidence of a Catholic plot, and there was a strong case for saying that the notorious letter of 29 September 1675 to de la Chaise did violate the anti-Catholic statutes then in force.

Colman stood trial for treason in king's bench on 27 November, by which time Godfrey's murder had reinforced Oates's apparent credibility. Colman's conduct in court was considered 'very temperate' (Ormonde MSS, 4.481), and he was sharp enough to expose several factual errors in Oates's evidence. The jury took less than a quarter of an hour to reach their guilty verdict. The death sentence was carried out at Tyburn on 3 December 1678, with Colman holding out to the very end the hope that York would obtain a last minute pardon for him. After he had been hanged, drawn, and quartered, his body was buried on unconsecrated ground next to St Giles-in-the-Fields. His wife, who survived him, is believed to have committed suicide several years later. Colman was beatified as one of the English martyrs by Pope Pius XI in 1929.

ANDREW BARCLAY

Sources A. Barclay, 'The rise of Edward Colman', HJ, 42 (1999), 109–31 · J. Miller, 'The correspondence of Edward Coleman, 1674–78', Recusant History, 14 (1977–8), 261–75 · J. Kenyon, The Popish Plot (1972) · Derbys. RO, Fitzherbert papers, D 239 M/O · G. Treby, ed., A collection of letters and other writings relating to the horrid popish plott (1681), pts 1 and 2 · Suffolk RO, Bury St Edmunds, Brent Eleigh Hall estate MSS, Acc. 1754 · State trials, vol. 7 · The life of James the Second, king of England, ed. J. S. Clarke, 2 vols. (1816) · The manuscripts of the earl of Westmorland, HMC, 13 (1885); repr. (1906) · The manuscripts of the House of Lords, 4 vols., HMC, 17 (1887–94), vol. 1 · The manuscripts of Sir William Fitzherbert … and others, HMC, 32 (1893) · Calendar of the manuscripts of the marquess of Ormonde, new ser., 8 vols., HMC, 36 (1902–20), vol. 4

Archives Suffolk RO, Brent Eleigh Hall estate papers | Derbys. RO, Fitzherbert MSS

Colman, Edward (1936–1958). See under Busby Babes (act. 1953–1958).

Colman, George, the elder (bap. 1732, d. 1794), playwright and theatre manager, was born in Florence and baptized there at the church of San Giovanni on 18 April 1732, the son of Francis Colman (bap. 1691, d. 1733), envoy to the court of the grand duke of Tuscany, and his wife, Mary, née Gumley (d. 1767). His father, who is credited with the

George Colman the elder (*bap.* 1732, *d.* 1794), by Thomas Gainsborough, *c*.1778

authorship of the *Opera Register*, adapted the libretto for Handel's *Arianna in Creta* (1734) and helped the composer re-engage the leading castrato Senesino for London. After her husband's death at Pisa on 20 April 1733 Mary Colman returned with her son to London, where a house was provided for her in St James's Park in which she lived until her death.

Education and early literary work George Colman's education was overseen by his shrewd and wealthy guardian William Pulteney, earl of Bath, who was the husband of Mary Colman's sister. George was sent to Westminster School, where Pulteney's son William was also a pupil. There he made many friends, including Charles Churchill, Robert Lloyd, Bonnell Thornton, and William Cowper, and had a successful academic career, entering Christ Church, Oxford, in 1751 as first among the Westminster king's scholars. In September 1753 his essay on literary criticism, 'A vision', was published anonymously in *The Adventurer* and January 1754 saw the first issue of *The Connoisseur*. This weekly publication, consisting largely of polished, lively, pleasantly satirical essays, was produced jointly by Colman and Bonnell Thornton and ran to 140 issues before it closed in September 1756. The editors personalized themselves jointly as 'Mr Town', and wrote most of the articles, although there were contributions by William Cowper, Robert Lloyd, and others. Colman and Thornton also collaborated on a two-volume edition of work by female poets, *Poems by Eminent Ladies* (1755). Pulteney was determined that his nephew should distinguish himself in the law and in May 1755 Colman entered Lincoln's Inn. He was called to the bar in January 1757 and between 1758 and 1761 he worked on the Oxford circuit.

His autobiographical poem 'The law student', written in 1757, depicts family pressures upon him, with his aunt insisting 'Turn Parson, Colman! That's the way to thrive' and his uncle crying 'stick close; close, Coley, to the Bar!'. However, 'the brisk heir to forty thousand pound' was disinclined to legal labours and attracted to the world of literature and the London theatre (Colman, *Prose*, 2.285–7).

David Garrick and Drury Lane In May 1757 Colman published and sent to David Garrick a pamphlet in the actor's praise, ironically entitled *A Letter of Abuse, to D—d G—k, Esq.* This led to his friendship with Garrick, who encouraged Colman and staged his comic afterpiece *Polly Honeycombe* at Drury Lane on 5 December 1760. The piece, which makes fun of sentimental novels and their female readers, had a shaky first night but recovered to achieve fifteen performances during the season and frequent later revivals. It appeared anonymously and was generally attributed to Garrick himself until on 12 December, at a performance specially requested by the king, the actor-manager added lines to the prologue declaring it was by 'a young Beginner' not 'a batter'd sinner' (Danchin, 771). Colman's pamphlet *Critical Reflections on the Old English Dramatick Writers*, addressed to Garrick, appeared in January 1761. Garrick helped Colman to prune his comedy *The Jealous Wife*, which was premièred at Drury Lane on 12 February with the leading roles played by Hannah Pritchard, Kitty Clive, and Garrick himself. Hopkins, the company's prompter, noted that it 'met with greater applause than anything since the *Suspicious Husband*' (Stone, 843) and the *Gentleman's Magazine* (1st ser., 31, 1761, 54) found it a comedy with 'few equals, and no superior'. It held the stage for the rest of the century and beyond.

Charles Churchill's satire *The Rosciad* (March 1761), which praised Garrick, Colman, and Thornton while attacking many theatrical personalities of the day, gave rise to vicious attacks on Colman and his associates by the playwright Arthur Murphy and others. As a result 'much good writing and much wit and humour were thrown away in this very acrimonious and disgraceful controversy' (Baker, 1.136). In April 1761 Colman and Thornton, with the support of Garrick, began publication of the *St James's Chronicle*. The paper appeared three times a week and contained literary and theatrical gossip, anecdotes, and entertaining articles. In addition to many smaller items, Colman contributed fifteen longer papers, signed 'Genius', between June 1761 and January 1762. The issue for 20 June consists of his 'Portrait of the author, and description of his person', a comic dissertation on his lack of height:

> As I walk along the street, I hear the men and women say to one another, *there goes a little man!*—In a word, it is my irreparable misfortune to be, without my shoes, little more than five feet in height. (Colman, *Prose*, 1.22–3)

Colman's comic afterpiece *The Musical Lady* was premièred on 6 March 1762. It ridiculed the fashion for Italian music and Jane Pope played the affected heroine, as she had done so successfully in *Polly Honeycombe*.

Colman had now abandoned the law and his identification with the world of the theatre was strengthened by his liaison with Sarah Ford (d. 1771), the mother of his son George *Colman, who was born on 21 October 1762. Sarah had been seduced by the actor Henry Mossop, who deserted her and their daughter Harriet when he moved to Ireland in autumn 1759. Colman became her protector, treating Harriet as his own child. In September 1763 Garrick, who was exhausted by the strain of acting and managing the Drury Lane company and depressed by the theatre riots that January, left England for an extended continental holiday. He did not return to London until April 1765 and in his absence the theatre was managed by his brother George, James Lacy, and Colman. William Powell, who had been coached by Garrick, made a successful stage début at Drury Lane in October 1763 in the title role of an adaptation by Colman of Beaumont's and Fletcher's *Philaster*. A month later came the première of Colman's comic afterpiece *The Deuce is in him*, which was received with cries of bravo. A version of Shakespeare's *A Midsummer Night's Dream* (23 November 1763), with the fifth act cut and many songs added, was Colman's first theatrical failure. Hopkins commented: 'The Performers first Sung the Audience to Sleep, & then went to Sleep themselves' (Stone, 1021). Colman, who had taken considerable trouble over the production, pruned it ruthlessly into an afterpiece, *The Fairy Tale*, which was performed only three nights later with considerable success. The fairies were played by children, with the nine-year-old Harriet Ford as Titania.

Colman's cousin William, the only surviving child of the earl of Bath, died in February 1763 and it was generally expected that Colman, who had been treated as 'his second son' (Colman, *Some Particulars*, 5), would inherit the earl's fortune. However, when Bath died in July 1764 he provided Colman with an annuity of 900 guineas but left his estate to his childless brother, General Henry Pulteney. Colman wrote no new plays or adaptations for Drury Lane during the second season of Garrick's absence but continued to be active in the management. *The Comedies of Terence*, his translation of six plays into blank verse, with an introductory essay and commentaries, was published in 1765 to critical acclaim.

Before Garrick's departure for the continent, he and Colman had begun writing a comedy together and work on this was resumed when Garrick returned to London in 1765. Letters and drafts of *The Clandestine Marriage* show that there were joint discussions on all parts of the play and that it was very carefully designed for the acting skills and personalities of the Drury Lane company. The friends quarrelled when Garrick, who wished to withdraw from the creation of new roles, refused to play the part of the elderly fop Ogleby which had been designed for him, and there were then arguments about their respective shares in the work. However, they were on friendly terms again by Christmas 1765. In the first edition of the play text (1766) the work was jointly acknowledged, and the 'Advertisement' to the play in Colman's *Dramatick Works* (1777) states: 'Some friends, and some enemies, have endeavoured to allot distinct portions of this play to each of the Authors. Each, however, considers himself as responsible

for the whole' (1.152). *The Clandestine Marriage* was premièred on 20 February 1766, with a superlative cast led by Thomas King as Ogleby and Kitty Clive as Mrs Heidelberg, and enjoyed an unbroken run of thirteen nights. The mixture of sentiment and satire, the humour of the situations, and the opportunities offered to its actors have kept the play in the theatrical repertory to the present day. It was soon translated into French and German and an operatic version, Cimarosa's *Il matrimonio segreto*, premièred in Vienna in 1792, has also enjoyed lasting success. Garrick wanted Colman to work with him on an adaptation of Wycherley's *The Country Wife*, but Colman was feeling unwell and went to Paris to recuperate, taking Sarah Ford and Harriet. Garrick wrote cheerfully to him about meetings with little George and the progress of Colman's villa, Bath House, which was being built at Richmond. A new piece by Colman, *The English Merchant*, a five-act comedy based on Voltaire's *L'Écossaise*, was produced at Drury Lane in February 1767. More sentimental and moral than Colman's earlier plays, it enjoyed some success, largely because of the character of the plain-spoken, benevolent English merchant, Freeport, created by Richard Yates.

Covent Garden patentee While Garrick ruled at Drury Lane, London's other patent theatre, Covent Garden, was managed by John Rich until his death in 1761 and then by his son-in-law, the tenor John Beard. By 1767 Beard's increasing deafness made him wish to retire from the theatre and the patent was made available for purchase at £60,000. Two wealthy young businessmen, Thomas Harris and John Rutherford, invited the actor William Powell and Colman to join them in running the theatre. With the help of a legacy of £6000 from his mother, who died in May 1767, Colman raised £15,000 for his share of the patent. He still had hopes that he would finally inherit the Bath fortune, but when General Pulteney died in October 1767 he bequeathed the bulk of the estate to a distant relative and left Colman an annuity of £400. Although Colman later claimed that Pulteney had accepted his acquisition of the share in the patent, it is almost certain that it was his involvement with the theatre and his refusal to give up Sarah Ford which alienated the general. Colman married Sarah on 12 July 1768 at St John, Horsleydown, Bermondsey.

The contract between the new Covent Garden patentees was carelessly drawn up, Colman's actions being subject to veto by Harris and Rutherford, who had no practical knowledge of the theatre. They soon had mistresses in the company and problems started when they demanded preferential treatment for their favourites. They accused Colman of assuming excessive powers, the quarrel became public, and a pamphlet war about the dispute was waged throughout 1768. Despite the disarray, Covent Garden had a successful and profitable first season under the new management, with the actors responding well to Colman's direction. Rutherford sold his share in the patent to Henry Dagge and James Leake in summer 1768, and they joined Harris in a lawsuit against Colman which reached chancery in July 1770, when judgment was given in Colman's favour. By this time passions were cooling, for Covent Garden under Colman was consistently profitable. In November 1771 the managers 'met together without the interposition of any other persons, shook hands, dined at Mr. Colman's, and put a final stop to all the proceedings at law' (*GM*, 1st ser., 41, 1771, 520). Harris matured into a very competent manager who was to remain at Covent Garden until his death in 1820.

The strength of Covent Garden under Rich and Beard had been in music and spectacle, so Colman set out to reinforce the acting company. He engaged Richard Yates and his wife, persuaded Charles Macklin to give his famous interpretation of Shylock, and gave William Powell six leading Shakespearian roles in the first season. He produced his own short farce *The Oxonian in Town* in November 1767, while February 1768 saw his adaptation of *King Lear*, which was nearer to Shakespeare than the version generally in use but retained a happy ending and omitted the Fool. Powell's sudden death at Bristol in July 1769 was a serious blow. Colman wrote a prologue for the benefit performance for Powell's family at the Bristol Theatre and an epitaph for Powell's tomb in Bristol Cathedral. The actor's widow took over his share in the patent and was co-defendant with Colman in the case brought by the other patentees. Colman's contribution to the theatre as a dramatist in the 1769–70 season was his comedy *Man and Wife, or, The Shakespeare Jubilee* (7 October 1769), which capitalized quickly on Garrick's rain-soaked celebrations at Stratford that September. The play incorporated a pageant of characters from seventeen of Shakespeare's plays, accompanied by appropriate music.

The following season Colman wrote two successful afterpieces, the burletta *The Portrait* (22 November 1770) and the pantomime *Mother Shipton* (26 December 1770), both with music by Samuel Arnold. Thomas Augustine Arne became musical director in 1771 and provided music for Colman's masque *The Fairy Prince* (12 November 1771), which was based on Ben Jonson's *Oberon*. Colman made a two-act version of *Comus* (17 October 1772) for which Arne had written music many years before and Arne provided new music for two other Colman adaptations, *Elfrida* (21 November 1772), from a 'dramatic poem' by William Mason, and *Achilles in Petticoats* (16 December 1773), from John Gay's ballad opera *Achilles*. However, the most important theatrical event of these years for English theatre was the première of Goldsmith's *She Stoops to Conquer* (15 March 1773), put on by Colman without any great hopes of success after Garrick had procrastinated over its production.

Sarah Colman died suddenly on 29 March 1771 after taking the wrong medicine for an illness from which she was recovering. Fanny Burney wrote in her diary:

> In point of understanding she was infinitely inferiour to Mr Colman, but she possessed an uncommon sweetness of Temper, much sensibility, & a generous & restless desire of obliging, & of making her friends happy. So amiable a Character must, I am sure, endear her infinitely to Mr Colman, of whom she, with the greatest reason, was beyond expression attached to. He is one of the best Tempered,

> (though I believe very passionate) of men, lively, agreeable, open Hearted, & clever. (*Early Journals and Letters*, 1.144)

Colman made the sixteen-year-old Harriet, whom Fanny Burney thought genteel and very well educated, the mistress of his household until she married in 1777. On 30 November 1771 Colman was 'suddenly seized with a fit' at the theatre (*London Chronicle*, 30 Nov–3 Dec 1771) and was forced to rest for several weeks. Personal tragedy and the strain of managing Covent Garden were taking their toll. The 1773–4 season was full of problems, particularly with the elderly and cantankerous actor Charles Macklin. Colman's sentimental comedy *The Man of Business* (29 January 1774) managed fourteen performances but was never revived. At the end of the season he sold his share in the patent to the actor Thomas Hull for £20,000.

Colman spent six months recuperating in Bath before returning to London. In the summer of 1775 he took his twelve-year-old son on an extended holiday tour, showing him his future Oxford college and travelling north to Yorkshire and Durham. Colman was soon writing again. He contributed a prologue to Garrick's farce *Bon Ton*, began a translation of Horace's *Ars poetica*, which he published eight years later, and contributed six essays entitled 'The gentleman' to the *London Packet*, a paper in which he had a share. Garrick staged Colman's adaptation of Ben Jonson's *Epicoene, or, The Silent Woman* in January 1776, and his satiric farce *The Spleen, or, Islington Spa* that March, but neither proved a success. At the end of the season Garrick retired from the stage. He had hopes that Colman would purchase his share of the Drury Lane patent, but his friend was unwilling to venture again into management where he could not have sole control. Colman wrote *New Brooms! An Occasional Prelude* for the first night under the new management, led by Richard Brinsley Sheridan, and the following May he wrote the epilogue for *The School for Scandal* while Garrick provided the prologue.

Management of the Haymarket Theatre In 1776 Samuel Foote, the comic actor and dramatist who had run the Little Theatre in the Haymarket for fifteen years, wished to retire. Foote had been granted a patent to run summer seasons at his theatre, and Colman agreed to make him a guaranteed payment of £1600 a year for life in return for the theatre and the use of the patent. He also paid £500 for the rights to Foote's plays. When Foote died, in October 1777, after receiving only one half-year payment of £800, the patent became invalid and Colman had to apply annually for a licence for his summer season. It was at the Haymarket that Colman's abilities as a manager had the greatest effect on the capital's theatrical life. For the first time London had theatrical performances on almost every night between late May and mid-September. Colman brought forward talented actors and singers, promoted new dramatists, including Mrs Inchbald and other women writers, and attracted a wider and more discriminating audience than had previously attended the theatre during the unfashionable summer months.

The new manager immediately extended the repertory at the Haymarket, strengthened the acting company, and improved production standards. He encouraged the comedian John Edwin, who had been in Foote's company for a year, and introduced the young Elizabeth Farren from Liverpool. John Henderson was brought from Bath to play Shylock, Hamlet, Falstaff, and Richard III in the first season. After a performance of *She Stoops to Conquer* followed by the musical afterpiece *Midas*, the *Morning Chronicle* (10 June 1777) noted 'All the business of the stage perfect, all the little parts smoothly given, and the whole rather superior than inferior to a performance at either of the Winter Theatres!' 1777 also saw the première of John Gay's ballad opera *Polly*, banned by the lord chamberlain in December 1728, and of *The Spanish Barber*, Colman's very popular adaptation of Beaumarchais's *Le barbier de Séville*. Samuel Arnold became the Haymarket's musical director and continued to work for the Colmans, father and son, until his death in 1802. Colman wrote two original plays for later seasons, an interesting satiric comedy, *The Suicide* (1778), for which Garrick provided the epilogue, and a comedy of modern manners, *The Separate Maintenance* (1779). In 1778 Colman brought out a ten-volume edition of the dramatic works of Beaumont and Fletcher with critical and explanatory notes and that summer he staged his adaptation of Fletcher's *Bonduca*, using Henry Purcell's music. Colman's adaptation of George Lillo's tragedy *The Fatal Curiosity* was surprisingly popular in 1782 and the following year he revived *The Fox*, his version of Jonson's *Volpone* made for Covent Garden in 1771.

Colman's lighter pieces included *The Manager in Distress* (30 May 1780), a short theatrical satire where he portrayed himself as the playhouse manager 'little Dapperwit'. In *The Election of the Managers* (2 June 1784), another one-act piece designed to open the evening's entertainment, the Haymarket's manager was 'little Bayes', but its amusing parallels with the recent Westminster election, where the duchess of Devonshire reputedly bought votes with kisses, led to trouble with the censor and a section of the audience. Colman's *The Genius of Nonsense* was advertised as 'An Original, Whimsical, Operatical, Pantomimical, Farcical, Electrical, Naval, Military, Temporary, Local Extravaganza. The Overture and new Musick by Dr. Arnold' (*Public Advertiser*, 4 Sept 1780). This exposé of the quack doctor James Graham and his Temple of Health starred the lovely and notorious Ann Cargill as the Goddess of Health and Genius of Nonsense. The following season she played the highwayman Macheath in Colman's travesty production, *The Beggar's Opera Reversed*, with Edwin as Lucy and Charles Bannister singing in his natural bass voice as an incomparable Polly. Colman framed it with *A Preludio* and *Medea and Jason*, satirizing Italian opera and the opera ballet. Charles Bannister was one of the Haymarket's most popular performers and Colman nurtured the careers of Bannister's son John and of the sopranos Elizabeth Harper and Georgina George. Colman's pantomime *Harlequin Teague, or, The Giant's Causeway*, written jointly with John O'Keeffe, was premièred in 1782. He commissioned a number of comic operas from O'Keeffe and Arnold including *The Son-in-Law* (1779), *The*

Agreeable Surprise (1781), and *Peeping Tom* (1784), which filled the theatre season after season.

In December 1784 Colman went to Bath to take the waters as a cure for his gout. The following September he chose Margate and sea-bathing after the exertions of the summer, but he had a stroke there in early October which left him partially paralysed. He recovered to some extent, but was increasingly prone to epileptic attacks. Nevertheless he continued with the Haymarket seasons supported by his son, who tried to 'assist him, without appearing to do so,—for he was extremely jealous of the least interference in his concerns' (*Random Records*, 2.304). *Tit for Tat*, Colman's adaptation of Joseph Atkinson's comedy *The Mutual Deception*, was produced in 1786. The next season saw the première of George Colman the younger's popular success *Inkle and Yarico* and his father's farce *The Village Lawyer*, based on De Brueys's *L'avocat patelin* and written for Edwin's benefit. In the same year Colman published *Prose on Several Occasions, Accompanied with some Pieces in Verse*, a three-volume collected edition of his essays, criticism, occasional verse, and theatrical prologues and epilogues. He also prepared the pamphlet *Some Particulars of the Life of the Late George Colman, Esq.* which he left for publication after his death, giving proof that he was not the illegitimate son of the earl of Bath, a rumour which had dogged him throughout his life, and denying that he had knowingly forfeited the Bath inheritance by purchasing a share in the Covent Garden patent.

Final years Colman made a new will in April 1789, ignoring the fact that he was seriously in debt. He left his theatre and literary property to his son but made very generous provision for Sophia Croker, the wife of an army officer, whom the younger George described as 'a kept Mistress or Common Prostitute' (Vincent, 39). By 1784 she was living with Colman at his house in Gower Street and in 1788 she persuaded him to give her the house and its furnishings. Colman's final stage work, *Ut pictura poesis!*, an afterpiece based on Hogarth's *The Enraged Musician*, opened the 1789 season, but by then he was incapable of the proper management of the theatre or his own finances. On 18 June he suffered a fit which left him mentally deranged and in November he was declared lunatic. His son arranged for him to be well cared for in the house of Mrs Ann Clarkson in 'a healthful and airy situation' in Paddington, and paid the wages of a keeper, a manservant, and a maid to look after him (Vincent, 47). Colman experienced some comparatively lucid intervals but 'his mind … was, in the last stages of his malady, fill'd, like a cabalistick book, with delusions, and crowded with the wildest flights of morbid fancy' (*Random Records*, 2.287). He died at Paddington on 14 August 1794, and was buried at St Mary Abbots, Kensington, ten days later.

George Colman the elder is chiefly remembered today as co-author of *The Clandestine Marriage*. His lesser dramatic works gave much pleasure in their day and frequently served a genuine satiric purpose. Despite his poor health he was a man of considerable energy, and the range and quality of his essays, journalism, translations, and criticism remain impressive. A member of the Beefsteak Club and Dr Johnson's 'Club', he enjoyed the friendship of the leading writers, artists, and wits of his day. Above all, he was one of the finest theatre managers of the century, the great little manager.

OLIVE BALDWIN and THELMA WILSON

Sources G. W. Stone, ed., *The London stage, 1660–1800,* pt 4: *1747–1776* (1962) · C. B. Hogan, ed., *The London stage, 1660–1800,* pt 5: *1776–1800* (1968) · E. R. Page, *George Colman the elder* (1935) · *The plays of George Colman the elder,* ed. K. A. Burnim (1983) · G. Colman the elder, *Dramatick works* (1777) · G. Colman the elder, *Prose on several occasions, accompanied with some pieces in verse* (1787) · G. Colman the elder, *Some particulars of the life of the late George Colman, esq.* (1795) · G. Colman the younger, *Posthumous letters from various celebrated men* (1820) · G. Colman the younger, *Random records* (1830) · *GM,* 1st ser., 31 (1761), 51–4 · *GM,* 1st ser., 41 (1771), 520 · *GM,* 1st ser., 59 (1789), 1084 · *GM,* 1st ser., 64 (1794), 772–3 · *London Chronicle* (27–9 Oct 1767) · *London Chronicle* (30 Nov–3 Dec 1771) · *Morning Chronicle* (10 June 1777) · *Public Advertiser* (7 Dec 1771) · *Public Advertiser* (4 Sept 1780) · *The letters of David Garrick,* ed. D. M. Little and G. M. Kahrl, 3 vols. (1963) · H. P. Vincent, 'Christopher George Colman, "lunatick"', *Review of English Studies,* 18 (1942), 38–48 · D. E. Baker, *Biographia dramatica, or, A companion to the playhouse,* rev. I. Reed, new edn, rev. S. Jones, 3 vols. in 4 (1812) · *The early journals and letters of Fanny Burney,* ed. L. E. Troide, 1: *1768–1773* (1988); 2: *1774–1777* (1990) · *The plays of David Garrick,* ed. H. W. Pedicord and F. L. Bergmann, 1 (1980) · Walpole, *Corr.,* vols. 22, 32–3, 41 · P. Danchin, *The prologues and epilogues of the eighteenth century,* 6 (1997) · K. Sasse, 'Opera register from 1712 to 1734 (Colman-register)', *Händel Jahr-Buch,* 5 (1959), 199–223 · J. Dunbar, *A prospect of Richmond* (1966) · copies of the wills of George Colman the elder, the earl of Bath, and General Henry Pulteney, Family Records Centre, London EC1R 1UW · *Old Westminsters* · *Scots Magazine,* 29 (1767), 279

Archives Liverpool Central Library, papers relating to a quarrel between Colman and Charles Macklin | Theatre Museum, London, corresp. with David Garrick

Likenesses J. Reynolds, oils, 1767 · studio of Reynolds, oils, 1767, NPG · G. Marchi, engraving, 1773 (after J. Reynolds, 1767), BM · T. Gainsborough, oils, *c.*1778, NPG [*see illus.*] · J. Jackson, drawing, 1810 (after J. Reynolds), BM · M. D[arly], caricature (*View Colman in the lap of Mother Shipton*), repro. in N. Nipclose [F. Gentleman], *The theatres* (1772) · S. Fisher, engraving (after J. Reynolds, 1767), repro. in R. B. Peake, *Memoirs of the Colman family* (1841), frontispiece · J. Hall, engraving (after T. Gainsborough, *c.*1778), repro. in Colman, *Prose on several occasions,* frontispiece · N. Schiavonetti, engraving (after J. Reynolds, 1767), Harvard TC · J. Scott, engraving (after T. Gainsborough, *c.*1778), BM · E. Scriven, engraving (after drawing by J. Jackson; after J. Reynolds, 1767), repro. in *Contemporary portraits* (1813) · A. Smith, engraving (after T. Gainsborough, *c.*1778), Harvard TC · E. Smith, line engraving (after J. Zoffany), BM; repro. in B. W. Procter, *Effigies poeticae,* 2 vols. (1824) · J. Zoffany, oils, priv. coll.; copy, Garr. Club · caricature, repro. in Rubrick [W. Kenrick], *The spleen, or, The offspring of folly* (1776), frontispiece · double portrait, engraving (*The rival managers;* with David Garrick), repro. in *The Lady's Magazine* · double portrait, engraving (*The manager in distress,* tête-à-tête portrait with 'The adorable Alicia'), repro. in *Town and Country Magazine* (June 1780) · engraving (after T. Gainsborough, *c.*1778), repro. in *European Magazine* (Aug 1785) · engraving (after T. Gainsborough, *c.*1778), BM · engraving, BM

Wealth at death £16,068 debts (incl. £2615 mortgage on house); income, incl. two Bath annuities and profit from the Haymarket Theatre, calculated at £3284 p.a.; son supposedly inherited nothing: Vincent, 'Christopher George Colman', 44

Colman, George, the younger (1762–1836), playwright and theatre manager, was born in London on 21 October

George Colman the younger (1762–1836), by Thomas Goff Lupton (after John Jackson)

1762, the son of George *Colman the elder (*bap.* 1732, d. 1794), playwright and theatre manager, and his mistress, later his wife, Sarah Ford (d. 1771). Little is known of his very early years, but Colman had all the advantages available to the son of a successful and well-connected father.

Childhood and education Until the age of eight Colman lived at his father's house in London and his country estate, Bath House, in Richmond, at which time he was enrolled in Marylebone Seminary, which was intended to provide the boy with the foundation for admittance to an élite public school. He had only a few months in school, however, before his mother died on 29 March 1771 from accidentally taking the wrong medication, and he was brought home. On 30 June 1772 Colman was admitted to Westminster School, which his father had attended. Colman records in his memoirs that during this period he first came to know many of the distinguished men of the age, including David Garrick, Edward Gibbon, and Samuel Johnson.

Colman was intended by his father for a career in law and was duly sent to Christ Church, Oxford, on 28 January 1780 on completing his studies at Westminster. By this time his father, already a prominent playwright and theatre manager, had purchased from Samuel Foote in 1777 the ownership of the summer company at the Little Theatre in the Haymarket, an event which had an enormous impact on the young man's life. Attracted by the glamour and excitement, Colman spent much time at the theatre to the detriment of his studies. Taking more extreme action, the father in autumn 1781 sent his over-stimulated son to King's College, Aberdeen, where he remained until he was called home early in 1784.

First writings and early success During this period Colman wrote his first play, *The Female Dramatist*, which was performed for the single night of 16 August 1782 at his father's theatre. In this conventional farce Mrs Metaphor, a widow whose life is dedicated to drama, is nearly tricked into marriage by a fortune-hunter, when at the last moment Beverly, a suitor for the hand of Mrs Metaphor's daughter, exposes the scam. While still at King's, Colman completed his second play, *Two to One*, late in 1783. It reached the boards at the Little Haymarket on 21 June 1784 and achieved a respectable run of nineteen evenings. This musical comedy anticipated many salient features of Colman's later successes, including witty dialogue, catchy songs, and broad-humoured stage action. Thus by the age of twenty-two Colman had joined an élite circle including Congreve, Fielding, and his contemporary Sheridan, all of whom had achieved success on the London stage by their early twenties.

After a short trip to Paris, at his father's insistence Colman was admitted to Lincoln's Inn on 9 August 1784, but he never seriously considered a career in law. While his father was away on holiday, he eloped to Gretna Green and on 3 October 1784 married Catharine Morris (*d. c.*1820), a young actress at the Little Haymarket, initiating a long and unhappy relationship which was kept secret from Colman the elder for several years. How they lived is a mystery, as details of the early years of the marriage were completely suppressed by Colman and in the many reminiscences and biographies of his gossipy contemporaries such as Thomas Dibdin, Charles Matthews, and Joseph Munden. Summer 1785, in addition to seeing the première on 9 July of his third play, *Turk and No Turk*, had, however, more serious implications. Colman the elder, while on holiday at Margate, suffered a serious illness which left him greatly weakened and which began a long period of decline in his health. The result was that the younger Colman began helping to run the theatrical company, a challenge for which he showed great capability. He was soon to excel in writing, as well. On 4 August 1787 Colman mounted his first great success, *Inkle and Yarico*, based on a tale from *The Spectator* (issue 11). Inkle's repentance and marriage to Yarico in the play's heavily sentimentalized finale, which completely reverses Steele's conclusion, no doubt was the deciding factor in the play's enormous initial and continuing popularity. This play convincingly demonstrated to the London theatrical community that the younger Colman had much in him of his father's dramatic abilities.

The death of George Colman the elder and financial burdens Hit after hit followed in subsequent summers until 1794, bringing much glory and financial gain to the family concern. *Ways and Means* (1788), a farce, did not fare well in its first season, but went on to become one of Colman's most enduring plays. With *The Battle of Hexham* (1789) Colman created a new genre, the historical musical drama, which audiences found original and intriguing. He continued in this genre with the highly successful *The Surrender of Calais* (1791) and *The Mountaineers* (1793). His father's health, however, steadily declined, with death coming at last on 14 August 1794, but the elder Colman's financial condition had also suffered an irreversible disaster. Though he had amassed a considerable fortune during the previous thirty years through his playwriting achievements and his managerial acumen both at Covent Garden and the Little Haymarket, he learned to his horror in 1787 (as legal documents unknown to previous biographers reveal) that nearly his entire savings had been embezzled from him by his banker. In short, the elder Colman died in debt. The upshot was that Colman the younger, on coming into his estate in 1795, inherited and chose to honour those debts, which were substantial, requiring him to place a heavy mortgage on the theatre's income and facilities. This indenture burdened the son for the next two decades, ultimately driving him into debtors' prison and forcing him out of the theatre business. Thus the received wisdom regarding the activities of Colman the younger, namely that after the death of his father he ruined the business through improvidence, turns out to be incorrect.

During the years 1795 to 1805 Colman carried on as sole owner and manager of the theatre, but he was forced in 1795 to mortgage the business to repay his father's creditors. This arrangement remained in force until 1800, by which time the theatre's profits were falling. A new and, for Colman, even more financially restrictive arrangement was negotiated, but these terms could not be met. By 1805 the situation had eroded to the point where Colman had no choice but to sell off half the business for £7000 to David Morris (his brother-in-law), Peter Tahourdin, and James Winston in order to raise most of the rather large sums demanded by the mortgagees. Thus while Colman certainly was not averse to the pleasures of gracious living, and later achieved some reputation for excessive drinking, he never had the resources after 1795 to waste on any but a modest scale.

A related misconception casts Colman as reckless in regard to the operations of the Haymarket Theatre and prone to disputes and litigation. Colman did spend large sums of money during 1803 and 1804 to finance two extravagant musical productions which never recovered their initial costs, and he certainly erred in thinking that this sort of play would be profitable. His wise choices of plays, however, greatly outnumbered his losers; had his fling with expensive musicals come ten years earlier, he would simply have moved on after licking his wounds. Unfortunately the timing was crucial, and the production debts were a factor forcing the sale of the shares in 1805.

As for the claim that Colman was unduly litigious, detractors note that he was involved in a protracted chancery dispute from 1809 to 1816 with his business partner and brother-in-law David Morris. The fault, however, was with Morris, not Colman. The extensive chancery records and newspaper accounts reveal that Morris, who had purchased Tahourdin's share in 1808, was a headstrong, uncompromising, quarrelsome, and often irrational partner, who in April 1809 sued not only Colman, but also an additional Haymarket partner, James Winston, who was himself aligned with Colman. This protracted and expensive litigation involved managerial control of the company and was so disputatious that the theatre was forced to remain closed during the summer of 1813. The court eventually found on behalf of the defendants, Colman and Winston, on every point, and Morris was ordered to pay all costs and to abide by the partnership guidelines set down by an arbitrator.

The sale of half the business in 1805 satisfied some of Colman's debtors, but S. J. Arnold, the son of Dr Samuel Arnold, the well-known composer, from whom Colman had borrowed significant sums, was not among them. After the elder Arnold's death, the son and widow had Colman arrested as of 28 February 1806. He was committed to the king's bench prison, but, as befitted those debtors with some assets, he was not required to remain within the prison proper but was restricted to residence within the rules until his discharge on 27 September 1817 resulting from the passage of an insolvency act by parliament. His first verified residence was on Lambeth Road as of August 1807, but he moved by March 1809 to 4 Melina Place on Westminster Road and then to 5 Melina Place by April 1816. From these locations he ran the Haymarket Theatre as best he could for over eleven years, wrote plays mainly for other theatres, and dealt with the legal challenges of his brother-in-law.

Later works and royal appointments Between 1795 and 1810 Colman wrote the lion's share of the plays on which his reputation is founded. The dozen or more hits include *The Iron Chest* (Drury Lane, 1795), *The Heir at Law* (Haymarket, 1797), *Bluebeard* (Drury Lane, 1798), *Feudal Times* (Drury Lane, 1799), *The Castle of Sorrento* (Haymarket, 1799), *The Review* (Haymarket, 1800), *The Poor Gentleman* (Covent Garden, 1801), *Love Laughs at Locksmiths* (Haymarket, 1803), *Who Wants a Guinea?* (Covent Garden, 1805), *We Fly by Night* (Covent Garden, 1806), *Forty Thieves* (Drury Lane, 1806), *The Africans* (Haymarket, 1809), *X.Y.Z.* (Covent Garden, 1810), *The Quadrapeds of Quedlinburgh* (Haymarket, 1811), *Doctor Hocus Pocus* (Haymarket, 1814), and *The Actor of All Work* (Haymarket, 1817). His greatest commercial success, *John Bull* (Drury Lane, 1803), earned him at least £1200 and achieved the singular reputation of being the play receiving the largest author's fee ever paid to that time. In *John Bull*'s heavily charged scenes of sentimentality, dogged honesty, and patriotism Colman gauged precisely the audience's interests and needs in the midst of the darkest years of the Napoleonic wars. By 1809, therefore, although he was living in the rules of the prison, his reputation was at its peak when he was asked to write the prologue spoken by J. P. Kemble which opened the new Covent Garden Theatre on 18 September 1809, and some years later, though by then past his zenith, he also wrote the address for the opening of the newly rebuilt Drury Lane Theatre on 16 October 1822.

At long last in 1817 the financial and legal difficulties began to diminish. Soon after his release from debtors'

prison, he negotiated the sale of the remainder of his interest in the Little Haymarket company. Cleared from his debts but now a considerably older and more subdued man, he thereafter wrote plays for the Covent Garden and Drury Lane theatres from time to time, but he never again matched his earlier successes. These later works include *The Gnome-King* (Covent Garden, 1819), *A Figure of Fun* (Covent Garden, 1821), *The Law of Java* (Covent Garden, 1822), *Stella and Leatherlungs* (Drury Lane, 1823), and *Five Minutes too Late* (Drury Lane, 1825).

On his ascent to the throne in 1821 Colman's old friend the prince regent did not forget him, and granted him the position of lieutenant of the yeomen of the guard, a sinecure which Colman kept for several years. An elegant watercolour portrait in the Victoria and Albert Museum depicts Colman in full regalia for the coronation. The royal appointment, however pleasing, was not lucrative, and Colman continued to live in the familiar confines of Melina Place until 1824, when he moved to the newly built Brompton Square. This relocation to the stylish Brompton area was made possible by yet another patronage appointment from the king in January 1824 to the position of examiner of plays, which Colman held until his death. He took the job seriously and performed his duties as examiner in a systematic and timely fashion, but his actions generated controversy, as his contemporaries claimed that he was censorious far beyond the range of his predecessors and hypocritically moralistic in his standards, since he now censored the very sort of material that appeared in his own successful plays. When questioned on these contradictions by the select committee on dramatic literature in 1832, Colman replied that he was careless in his younger days and that the examiner then ought to have required him to revise. Further, he asserted that he was earlier an author and was now an examiner, and sought to bring merit to the position.

In addition to plays, Colman also wrote several volumes of poetry, an autobiography, and songs, as well as prologues and epilogues for other playwrights. *My Nightgown and Slippers, or, Tales in Verse* appeared in 1797 and went through many editions, as did the ostensible sequel *Broad Grins* (1802). His *Poetical Vagaries* was published in 1813, no doubt necessitated by the financial problems due to the law proceedings then at their most strident point, and was followed three years later by *Eccentricities for Edinburgh* (1816). Late in life he brought forward a two-volume set of memoirs entitled *Random Records* (1830) which, sadly, covers only his childhood and very early adulthood. The decision to publish that segment only of his life suggests that he intended a continuation if sales were encouraging, but the project remained unfinished at his death. In addition Colman contributed extensively to the plays of his fellow dramatists. No complete census has been established, but scattered through the productions of the first thirty years of the nineteenth century one often may find his hand, as he contributed to the works of many dramatists, such as W. R. Rhodes's *Bombastes furioso* (August 1810) and Robert Jameson's *Love and Gout* (August 1814). His assistance was required so often that he complained to his partner James Winston in an unpublished letter that he was 'sickened by the ungrateful task of tinkering for Authors' (Burling, 297, n. 68).

Surprisingly little is known of Colman's personal life during his adult years. His autobiography ends with his early twenties, he did not keep a journal, and his surviving correspondence deals mainly with his professional activities. Such evidence as exists reveals that his marriage to Catharine Morris had completely collapsed by 1801, and she was provided with an income for life in the terms of the 1805 sales agreement. By 1801 Colman and Maria Gibbs (1770?–1844), an actress of some repute, had established a felicitous relationship which lasted for the duration of Colman's life. After some years of simple cohabitation, they apparently married in the early 1820s following the death of Colman's estranged first wife, though no record of their betrothal has been found.

Colman fathered two sons, of whom the first, George, was born to Catharine Morris. The date of birth is not known but is usually assigned to 1785. George, the son, entered the army and achieved the rank of captain, but further details are elusive because two captains bearing the name of George Colman flourished during the same period. Thus without further evidence it is impossible to differentiate their careers. Somewhat more is known concerning the second son. Edmund Craven Colman apparently was born in June 1802 to Maria Gibbs, and his relationship with his parents was close for many years. Through his father's influence he entered royal service in 1824, his career lasting at least until 1833 and possibly until 1840.

Though Colman lived to seventy-four he was in poor health for much of the last thirty years of his life from the ravages of gout, as his surviving correspondence reveals. At the time of his death at 22 Brompton Square on 26 October 1836, he had left instructions for a quiet burial in the family vault in Kensington church, where he was duly interred with the remains of his father and grandfather. On 3 November a small party, which included Mrs Colman, Thomas Harris (the son of Henry Harris, the manager of Covent Garden Theatre), Dr Chinnock (his physician), General Phipps, and, presumably, his son Edmund, laid him to rest. Mrs Colman apparently inherited some of his property and immediately retired to Brighton, where she lived until her death in 1844.

Colman was much beloved among the members of the theatrical community for his good humour and generosity, many times providing assistance for performers and other friends in need. He achieved a considerable reputation as a dramatist, being termed in the press of the 1790s as second only to Sheridan, and when the illustrious creator of *The School for Scandal* died in 1814, Colman then became recognized as the foremost playwright of his era. Many of his plays remained repertory standards well into the nineteenth century, throughout the British empire and the United States, though in the early twenty-first century they are virtually unknown except to specialists.

WILLIAM J. BURLING

Sources J. F. Bagster-Collins, *George Colman the younger, 1762–1836* (New York, 1946) · G. Colman the younger, *Random records* (1830) · R. B. Peake, *Memoirs of the Colman family* (1841) · W. J. Burling, *Summer theatre in London, 1661–1820, and the rise of the Haymarket Theatre* (2000) · M. J. Wood, 'George Colman the younger', *Restoration and eighteenth-century dramatists: third series*, ed. P. R. Backscheider, DLitB, 89 (1989)
Archives BL, corresp. · Bodl. Oxf. · Chatsworth House, Derbyshire · City Westm. AC · Folger · Hunt. L., letters · PRO · Theatre Museum, London, corresp. relating to opening of summer seasons · Theatre Museum, London, letters · V&A NAL, letters and papers | BL, letters as examiner of plays, RP852 [copies]
Likenesses Cosway, portrait · De Wilde, portrait · Drummond, portrait · T. G. Lupton, mezzotint (after J. Jackson), NPG [*see illus.*] · F. P. Stephenoff, portrait (in coronation regalia), V&A · F. E. Turner, portrait · engraving (after Drummond) · engraving (after Turner) · engraving (after De Wilde)

Colman, Grace Mary (1892–1971), educationist and politician, was born at 7 Dorlcote Road, Wandsworth, London, on 30 April 1892, the daughter of Frederick Selincourt Colman (1857–1917), vicar of Earlsfield and later a canon of Worcester Cathedral, and his wife, Constance Mary Hawkings. Grace's cousin was the actor Ronald Colman. Educated at home by governesses, in 1914 she gained a scholarship to Newnham College, Cambridge, where she rowed with the first women's eights on the Cam and gained firsts in history (1916) and economics (1917). Despite coming from a Conservative background she joined the Labour Party while at Cambridge and also converted her family.

After completing her studies in 1917 Colman had a short, unhappy stint as a civil servant in Whitehall before beginning a career in university adult education as a tutor in history and economics at Ruskin College, Oxford, from 1920 to 1925. She was staff tutor for tutorial classes at the University of London from 1925 until 1940, and was organizer of the women's committee of the Workers' Educational Association in London. During this period she also began teaching at Labour Party summer schools for women in the north of England, and published two books for the Workers' Educational Association, *Capitalist Combines* (1927) and *The Structure of Modern Industry* (1930). Her labour movement affiliations included membership of the National Union of General and Municipal Workers. During the general strike she was assistant secretary to a committee of Nottingham Trades Council.

Colman eventually sought election to parliament, seeing her political role as an extension of her background in adult education: as an MP she could continue her educational work in economics and social questions among a wider audience. Her great skill was in explaining complex economic systems in terms that could be easily understood, but like most women candidates during this time she was consistently nominated for seats held safely by the opposition. She was soundly defeated by the Conservative Sir Philip Sassoon in Hythe, Kent, in 1929 and 1931, and she was also unsuccessful contesting Sheffield Hallam in 1935. Obliged to concentrate on extra-parliamentary activity, she became chairman of the Standing Joint Committee of Industrial Women's Organizations in 1938, and was a magistrate in London. In 1939 she was adopted as

Grace Mary Colman (1892–1971), by Bassano

the Labour Party candidate for Tynemouth, though the war postponed the election, and in the following year she chaired the National Conference of Labour Women. During the war she returned to Whitehall to work for the Ministry of Labour and the Board of Trade. Despite charges of carpet-bagging, she was elected for Tynemouth as part of the Labour landslide of 1945, taking what had been a Conservative seat since 1918.

After her election Colman moved to North Shields and proved very devoted to her constituency. Rejecting the example set by her Conservative predecessor in Tynemouth, Sir Alexander West Russell, who was famous for never having spoken in parliament, she spoke on local issues such as coastline erosion, the future of the fishing industry, and fishermen's wages and conditions. Such was her overriding concern for her constituents that she declined Clement Attlee's invitation to join a parliamentary commission in India to help with preparations for independence, preferring to remain where she could work for her district. Appointed a member of the select committee to consider financial provision for the newly married Princess Elizabeth and Prince Philip in December 1947 she was a signatory to the minority report proposing a lower allowance than the majority recommended. She contended that the more generous allowance widened the gulf between the lives of the royal family and those of ordinary people, and that this was not in the interests of the monarchy.

Colman also declined to attend the first post-war Buckingham Palace garden party, as she did not own the hat which the invitation required. This reflected her disregard for fashion. Friends remembered her attending summer garden parties in a tweed skirt, wool stockings, and flat shoes, her round spectacles giving her the appearance of a schoolmistress. She lived austerely, maintaining a frugal diet and living alone with her dogs in a sparsely decorated home. It was for her dogs, with whom she went for long walks in the countryside, that the unmarried Grace reserved her affection. She supported the RSPCA and in parliament supported bills to ban hunting with dogs and improve the conditions under which pets were sold. As an MP she was described as difficult to approach and unsentimental, though compassionate towards her constituents, and she inspired devotion among her students.

Tynemouth's boundaries were redrawn and additional Conservative voters introduced so, despite her devotion to the constituency, Colman was defeated at the general election of 1950 by Irene Ward, the Conservative candidate who had lost her own nearby seat in 1945. Ward's defeat of Colman, as well as her earlier defeat of Labour's Margaret Bondfield, demonstrated that the political courtesies which women MPs had exchanged in the 1920s had given way to party considerations. After failing to regain her seat in 1951 Colman moved to London to edit educational publications for the Labour Party, but after retirement she returned to North Shields, an area she had grown to love as its MP. Despite failing to be adopted as a candidate once more, she remained active with the party and other organizations. She belonged to local branches of the United Nations Association, and the Co-operative Society, and in 1964 she co-wrote *Full Employment in the Northern Region*, a Labour alternative to the Hailsham plan for the north-east. Her greatest contribution to the party was her work for women's education, and her efforts were commemorated by the Northumberland Women's Advisory Council with a Grace Colman award, which provided free tuition to Labour summer schools. Colman died at her home, Lenaville, 48 Linskill Terrace, North Shields, Northumberland, on 7 July 1971, and her ashes were scattered over a moor near Wooler. DUNCAN SUTHERLAND

Sources J. Sleight, *Women on the march* (1986) · *DLB* · A. Lockwood, *A celebration of pioneering labour women* (1995) · *North Shields Evening News* [1945 and 1950 election coverage] · *Hansard 5C* · *The Vote* (20 Feb 1931) · private information (2004) · b. cert. · d. cert.
Likenesses Bassano, photograph, NPG [*see illus.*]
Wealth at death £7403: probate, 24 Aug 1971, *CGPLA Eng. & Wales*

Colman, James (1801–1854). *See under* Colman family (*per.* 1814–1898).

Colman, Jeremiah (1777–1851). *See under* Colman family (*per.* 1814–1898).

Colman, Jeremiah James (1830–1898). *See under* Colman family (*per.* 1814–1898).

Colman, Maria. *See* Gibbs, Maria (1770–1850).

Colman, Sir Nigel Claudian Dalziel, baronet (1886–1966), politician, was born at Carlyle House, Chelsea Embankment, London, on 4 May 1886, the second son of

Frederick Edward Colman, chairman of J. and J. Colman, and his wife, Helen, daughter of Davison Octavius Dalziel. He was thus born into a major industrial family, and was later a director both of Reckitt and Colman Holdings Ltd and of J. and J. Colman Ltd. He was brought up, though, in Surrey, and retained links with that county: he owned from 1950 a house near Reigate in addition to his main residence in Grosvenor Square, London. During the First World War he served initially in the Royal Navy: he started as an able seaman but was later commissioned, before transfer to the Royal Flying Corps, where he reached the rank of captain.

A lifelong Conservative where earlier members of the family had mainly been Liberals, Colman was politically active during the 1920s in London, and became Conservative member of the London county council for Brixton in 1925. Then a fortuitous by-election came up in Brixton when his uncle Sir Davison Dalziel, chairman of the International Sleeping Car Company, received a barony in the birthday honours of 1927. Following Dalziel's advice and no doubt anxious to continue with the family's generosity, the local party selected Colman, who proclaimed himself a staunch supporter of Baldwin and all his government's policies, including the unpopular Trades Disputes Bill. He was comfortably elected Brixton's MP, partly no doubt because the mere twenty-four days between Dalziel's peerage being announced and polling day left the other parties no time to establish any momentum. The *Evening Standard* recommended a candidate who was 'young, handsome and dapper', and photographs show a trim figure who carried his forty years well (20 June 1927).

Colman did not seek re-election to the London county council in 1928, but remained active in the Conservatives' London organization, serving on the area council from 1927 to 1965, and becoming at different times treasurer, chairman, and president. He remained Brixton's MP until the Labour landslide of 1945, but made little impact: in eighteen years he made few speeches and rarely asked questions, while outside election campaigns his activities were reported in *The Times* only half a dozen times. Loyalty and self-effacing support for his leaders and his party were the watchword. But lack of progress in parliament, where he achieved no ministerial appointment, was balanced by a steady increase in influence outside. He served on the party's national executive committee from 1934, and was chairman of the central council in 1939; he missed the chance to chair a party conference only because his turn came in 1943, when no conference was held. But he was elected to the chair of the national executive in 1945 and held that post until 1951, and so steered the party membership through the post-war Conservative recovery. He deserves to be seen, alongside Lord Woolton and David Maxwell-Fyfe, as an architect of that recovery, while his tenure of the chairman's office set a pattern by which unknown figures could exercise influence through continuity in office and the acquisition of expertise that came to match that of the paid officials.

After retirement from the national executive chair Colman received a baronetcy in January 1952, and on 30 July 1952 married Nona Ann, daughter of Edward Henry Miles Willan. They had no children, so the baronetcy became extinct when he died at their home, Flat 3, 49 Grosvenor Square, London, on 7 March 1966. His wife survived him.

Alongside but preceding his political career, Colman took a lifelong interest in horses and dogs. He was at various times president of the National Horse Association of Great Britain and of the Hackney Horse Society, chair of the British Horse Society, which awarded him its medal of honour in 1953, and a committee member for the Kennel Club. He devoted most of his spare time to breeding and exhibiting harness horses, and was a respected judge at horse shows.   JOHN RAMSDEN

Sources WW (1928) · WW (1940) · WW (1966) · *The Times* (8 March 1966) · *Daily Telegraph* (8 March 1966) · *Daily Telegraph* (June 1927) · *Morning Post* (3–28 June 1927) · *Evening Standard* (3–23 June 1927) · J. Ramsden, *The age of Churchill and Eden, 1940–1957* (1995) · WWBMP · b. cert. · m. cert. · d. cert.
Archives Bodl. Oxf., Conservative Party archive, minutes of national executive committee
Likenesses photographs, repro. in *Evening Standard* (20 June 1927)
Wealth at death £1,355,544: administration with will, 9 May 1966, CGPLA Eng. & Wales

Colman, Ronald Charles (1891–1958), actor, was born in Richmond, Surrey, on 9 February 1891, the second son and fourth child in the family of two sons and three daughters of Charles Colman, a silk merchant, and his wife, Marjory Read Fraser. He was educated at a boarding-school in Littlehampton, Sussex, but had to leave abruptly at the age of sixteen for financial reasons when his father died suddenly of pneumonia. He started work as a clerk in the British Steamship Company in the City, and he joined the London Scottish regiment as a territorial soldier in 1909. Colman's regiment was the first of the territorials to serve with the regular army in France after the outbreak of the First World War and he was severely wounded by shrapnel in the leg, acquiring the limp which he was to spend much of the remainder of his life and career attempting, often in considerable pain, to conceal from audiences and cameras alike. Invalided out of the army in 1915, Colman began to take up the acting career which had fascinated him since amateur dramatics in childhood. He made his début with Lena Ashwell at the London Coliseum in 1916, playing a black-faced herald in a short sketch called *The Maharani of Arakan* by Rabindranath Tagore; he was soon after that taken by Gladys Cooper into her Playhouse company for minor roles, which Miss Cooper considered he played 'with amiable but remarkable clumsiness'. Very soon, however, his natural good looks were recognized by a film producer and by 1919 he had appeared in three short silent dramas, despite a casting card that read 'does not screen well'.

From 1920 Colman made regular appearances on Broadway and on tour in America, finally achieving fame in 1921 as the temple priest in *The Green Goddess* with George Arliss. Colman started his American screen career in 1923 with Lillian Gish in *The White Sister*, and three years later played in one of the classics of the silent era, *Beau Geste*

(1926). But it was with the coming of sound in 1929 that Colman's Hollywood career really came into its own: the producer Sam Goldwyn was the first to realize the magic of Colman's infinitely poetic, English voice, and he put him under a long-term contract that was to last for virtually the rest of his life. Colman's film credits are a roll-call of Hollywood films at their pre-war and most Anglophile best—*Bulldog Drummond* (1929), *Raffles* (1930), *Cynara* (1932), *Clive of India* (1935), *A Tale of Two Cities* (1935), *Under Two Flags* (1936), *Lost Horizon* (1937), and *The Prisoner of Zenda* (1937)—all establishing him as one of the richest and most reliable of the Hollywood raj, the man on whom a whole later generation of expatriates, led by David Niven, modelled themselves and their officer-and-gentlemanly acting careers.

Colman's wartime and post-war work before the camera was less distinguished, though he did win an Oscar in 1947 for an uncharacteristically highly charged dramatic role in *A Double Life*; he then moved on to a lucrative second career in American radio and television, playing the professor in *Halls of Ivy* (1950–52), a series he also produced and owned. Colman's last screen appearances were a fleeting role in Michael Todd's all-star *Around the World in Eighty Days* (1956) and, finally, in *The Story of Mankind* (1957). These were the only two films he had made in seven years, and there could have been little doubt that his particular tradition of uniformed, clenched, period Englishmen had become unfashionable in America with the coming of the new realist cinema immediately after the war.

In 1919 Colman had married the actress Thelma Raye. This marriage was dissolved in 1933, and in 1938 he married Benita Hume, also an actress. There was one daughter from this second marriage. Ronald Colman died on 19 May 1958 in Santa Barbara, California, and was buried there. *The Times* called him 'the most complete gentleman of the cinema'.   SHERIDAN MORLEY, *rev.*

Sources J. B. Colman, *Ronald Colman: a very private person* (1975) · *The Times* (20 May 1958) · personal knowledge (1993) · J. Parker, ed., *Who's who in the theatre*, 6th edn (1930) · *CGPLA Eng. & Wales* (1958) **Likenesses** photographs, 1920–55, Hult. Arch. · T. Allan, bromide print, 1935, NPG **Wealth at death** £10,436 1s. 7d.—in England: administration with will, 24 Sept 1958, *CGPLA Eng. & Wales*

Colman, Walter. *See* Coleman, Walter (1600–1645).

Colmore, Gertrude. *See* Weaver, Gertrude Baillie- (1855–1926).

Colnaghi family (*per. c.*1785–1911), art dealers, were established in England by **Paul** [Paolo] **Colnaghi** (1751–1833), who was born in the Brianza region near Milan, the younger son of Martino Colnago (*d.* 1783), a distinguished Milanese lawyer, and his wife, Ippolita Raggi. Having settled his father's encumbered estate, Paul left Italy for France in 1783 and became the Paris agent of Antony Torre to sell English prints from a shop in the Palais Royal in 1784. Antony Torre was the son of Giovanni Battista Torre (*d.* 1780), who had established himself, first in London in 1753, then in Paris in 1760, as a maker of fireworks and

Paul Colnaghi (1751–1833), by Charles Turner

instruments (principally barometers and thermometers) and bookseller. Antony ran a London branch at 14 Market Lane, Pall Mall, from 1767. On his father's death, Antony entered briefly (1780–82) into partnership with an optician, Ciceri of Milan (who had employed Paul Colnaghi on his arrival in Paris), before asking Colnaghi, on Ciceri's recommendation, to open his Paris branch.

Torre and Colnaghi became partners in May 1785, when Colnaghi moved to London (and was naturalized English), and brothers-in-law when Paul married Maria Elizabetha (Elizabeth) Baker, sister to Antony's wife, on 21 March 1787. The Market Lane shop was abandoned in 1786 for grander premises at 132 Pall Mall, and two years later Torre handed the business over to Colnaghi. After a brief partnership with Anthony Molteno, printseller, Colnaghi assumed full control. Thus the firm, which began as instrument makers and booksellers in 1760, only later specializing in printselling, underwent a similar evolution to that of Agnews sixty years later.

Paul Colnaghi must have been an impressive man, erudite, fluent in several languages, and charming; he attracted Benjamin Franklin's notice in Paris and was almost persuaded by him to emigrate to America. Giovanni Battista Torre's shop in the rue St Honoré had become a meeting place for savants, and for collectors of English mezzotints (known as *manière anglaise*) by William Woollett, William Sharp, and Sir Robert Strange and coloured stipple-prints by Francesco Bartolozzi (1727–1815), a superb engraver with whom the firm dealt for forty years. The flourishing market for English prints collapsed with the outbreak of the French Revolution and the Napoleonic wars; but Colnaghi survived by shrewdly publishing such popular colour stipple engravings as *The Cries of London*, after Francis Wheatley, in 1792–7, and a portrait of Nelson, after Hoppner, which appeared on the day (7 November 1805) that news came of the battle of Trafalgar. He also supplied the British government with views of besieged towns on the continent, thus providing invaluable information for the attacking allied armies.

In 1799 Paul Colnaghi moved his London premises to 23 Cockspur Street, where he held monthly 3 o'clock levees attended by the aristocracy and landed gentry. From these sprang a series of engraved portraits entitled Royal and Noble Ladies; Lawrence was paid £700 for permission to engrave his painting of Princess Charlotte (1817; Belgian Royal Collection). Appointed printseller to the prince regent, Colnaghi received further royal warrants from him as George IV, and from William IV; other royal patrons included the duc d'Orléans and the duc d'Aumale.

Paul and Elizabeth Colnaghi had two sons and a daughter: the elder son, **Dominic Charles Colnaghi** (1790–1879), was born at 132 Pall Mall, London, on 15 July 1790; another son, Martin Henry Lewis Gaetano, followed, and there was a daughter, Caroline (*b. c.*1786). All three siblings worked in the firm, but Dominic was the most outstanding and joined his father about 1808–10. He travelled to Italy in 1816–17 and collected specimens of armour, thus opening up a new field of connoisseurship. He sold these to Sir Samuel Rush Meyrick (1783–1848) in 1818, and continued to act for this famous antiquarian; much of Sir Richard Wallace's collection (Wallace Collection, London) originally came from Meyrick.

Martin Colnaghi (*c.*1792–1851) was also active, but showed less judgement and diligence than his brother. In 1821 Paul Colnaghi wished to retire to Italy and settled the business, then worth some £25,000 in stock, on his two sons. Martin quarrelled with his father and brother, and in 1824 sued them in chancery. The suit was settled in April 1825, through the good offices of a family friend, by buying out Martin for £3000. Paul and Dominic Colnaghi then moved to 14 Pall Mall East and began trading as P. and D. Colnaghi & Co., the name by which the firm is still known. Martin remained at Cockspur Street, and the two brothers thereafter ruthlessly bid against each other, to Paul's chagrin. John Constable, with whom the family became intimate, as the correspondence between Dominic and Constable attests, recorded in his journal for 16 June 1824:

> I hear there is quite a bustle at Colnaghi's. … They are all brisking up. Martin seems to be clearing the house of the old man & Dominic—but he is not quite liked himself—he is said to make love to all the ladies who look over prints there. (*Constable's Correspondence*, 4.154)

Constable had reason to be grateful to Paul, who, vouching for the Paris-based dealer John Arrowsmith, enabled Constable to show *The Hay Wain* (1821; National Gallery, London) at the Paris Salon in 1824, where it created a sensation and won him a gold medal. Colnaghi's tried, with only moderate success, to sell prints after Constable's

work, and acted as his agents for the 1827 Paris Salon exhibition. In November 1829 Paul admitted his daughter, Caroline, into partnership until her son John Anthony Scott (*d.* 1864) came of age. On 30 September 1807 Caroline had married John *Scott (1784–1821), editor of *The Champion*, who had died after a duel defending the 'Cockney school' of poetry. A subscription for the widow raised £800, which enabled her to join the firm. After Constable's death in 1837 Dominic Colnaghi helped lead the subscription campaign to purchase *The Cornfield* (1826) for the National Gallery.

Dominic Colnaghi married Catherine Pontet (*d.* 1881) on 15 October 1831, and they had two sons, neither of whom entered the firm, but the elder, Sir Dominic Ellis Colnaghi (1834–1908), became a consular official; posted to Florence in 1865, he served as consul-general for northern Italy from 1881 to 1896, and wrote *A Dictionary of Florentine Painters from the Thirteenth to the Seventeenth Centuries*, which was edited by P. G. Konody and Selwyn Brinton and published posthumously in 1928 (reprinted 1986).

Dominic Colnaghi greatly admired the work of R. P. Bonington, and in 1827 commissioned from him a number of Italian scenes with Shakespearian characters. After the artist's death the following year Dominic organized the two-day sale of his work at Sothebys in July 1829, buying thirty-five lots for himself, and later that year issued thirteen lithographs after Bonington's Scottish views. Some insight into Dominic Colnaghi's activities for special clients such as Sir Robert Peel emerges from his correspondence with Peel in November and December 1842, when he informed him about the availability of a Lawrence portrait of Lord Brougham (presumably the one of *c.*1825 now in the National Portrait Gallery, London) that the owner was willing to sell; and in March 1844 Colnaghi explained that Lawrence painted two versions of a portrait of Antonio Canova, the sculptor. There is also a contract with Henry Graves & Co. for a joint venture of August 1836 for selling an engraving by James Bromley after Sir George Hayter's portrait of Lord John Russell, then home secretary, in an edition of 750 prints, the proceeds to be evenly divided between Graves and Colnaghi. This continued the tradition, begun by Paul Colnaghi, of selling engraved portraits of prominent personalities of the day. Paul Colnaghi died, after a short illness, at his London home in St George's Place, Hanover Square, on 26 August 1833, aged eighty-two. His son Dominic and his daughter, Caroline Scott, took over the business, with her son John Anthony Scott and his cousin Andrew McKay joining as clerks. Dominic, or Old Dom as he became affectionately known, continued with the firm until about 1865, when he retired. He died at his home, 62 Margaret Street, Cavendish Square, on 19 December 1879, and was buried in Brompton cemetery.

In 1858 Colnaghis joined with Agnews in publishing *The Gems of the Art Treasury*, two de luxe volumes of photographs by Leonida Caldesi and Montecchi of the exhibition held at Manchester in 1857. The possibilities of this new medium were speedily recognized, and in 1864 Julia Margaret Cameron contracted with Colnaghis for the sale of her photographs; in 1866 she held an exhibition there. Earlier, in 1854, John Anthony Scott had commissioned William Simpson to tour the Crimea to prepare material for an account of the war, illustrated with forty lithographs and published in two folios as *The Seat of the War in the East* (1855–6), which earned the firm £12,000. After John Anthony Scott's death in 1864, Andrew McKay became sole proprietor, to be joined by his son William as partner in 1879. After his father's retirement William took over, and introduced E. F. Deprez (retired 1907) and Otto Gutekunst (retired 1939) as partners in 1894; but the direct family link with P. and D. Colnaghi & Co. ended with William McKay's retirement in 1911.

Paul Colnaghi's younger son, Martin, married Fanny Boyce Clarke, and their eldest son, **Martin Henry Colnaghi** (1821–1908)—baptized Martino Enrico Luigi Gaetano—was born at 23 Cockspur Street, London, on 16 November 1821. Although he was educated for the army, his father's bankruptcy in August 1843 thwarted this ambition. The elder Martin Colnaghi traded first as Colnaghi & Co. (from 1825), and from 1840 as Colnaghi and Puckle, the business passing to Edward Puckle in 1845. Martin died in Piccadilly in May 1851. Martin Henry struggled to established himself, and for two or three years organized the system of railway advertising afterwards taken over by W. H. Smith.

About 1860 Martin Henry Colnaghi turned to art, and for some years travelled as an expert and buyer for his uncle Dominic's firm (although he was never a partner), then for Henry Graves, and then on his own account. He began to specialize in Dutch and Flemish seventeenth-century art, working from his house in Pimlico. He 'discovered' Jan van Goyen, and dealt in many works by Frans Hals, long before these masters became fashionable; among the first important collections he helped to form was that of Albert Levy, dispersed at Christies in March 1876. He took over Flatou's Gallery at 11 Haymarket in 1877, renaming it the Guardi Gallery and remaining there until 1888, when he acquired the galleries of the Royal Institute of Painters in Water Colours at 53 Pall Mall, which he named the Marlborough Gallery. He began buying at auction on a substantial scale from 1875, purchasing Frans van Mieris's *Enamoured Cavalier* for 4100 guineas (£4305), and from the Lucy sale a Jan Both classical subject for 4500 guineas (£4725). He negotiated several major private purchases, notably the Raphael altarpiece *Madonna and Child with Saints* (Metropolitan Museum, New York) from the Colonna collection, which he bought from the earl of Ashburnham for £17,000 in June 1896. After unsuccessfully offering it to the National Gallery for £40,000, he sold it to C. Sedelmeyer of Paris, who sold it to J. Pierpont Morgan for £80,000.

Martin Henry claimed that his wide connoisseurship—his 'eye'—was gained, not from academic study, but by practical experience and careful examination of the works of art themselves. He outlived all his brothers and sisters, and was thrice married: first to Sarah Nash, second to Elizabeth Maxwell Howard (d. 1888), and third, on 17 October 1889, to Amy Mary, daughter of George Smith,

the artist; he left no children. He died at the Marlborough Gallery on 27 June 1908, and after a funeral service at St James's, Piccadilly, on 1 July, was buried in the family grave at Highgate.

Martin Henry Colnaghi bequeathed four paintings to the National Gallery: Lorenzo Lotto's *Madonna and Child and Saints*, Philips Wouwermans's *The Gypsies*, Aert van der Neer's *Dawn*, and a small landscape by Thomas Gainsborough, *The Bridge* (c.1783). He left the residue of his estate (some £90,532) to his wife, and stipulated that £80,000 should go to the National Gallery, after her death, for the purchase of pictures, these to form the Martin Colnaghi bequest. Colnaghi's picture stock was sold in six groups from 22 October 1908 to 7 January 1909 at Robinson Fisher & Co., realizing some £15,000.

The firm of Colnaghi continued to flourish after the family's direct links with it ended, moving to sumptuous premises, designed by Lanchester and Rickards, at 144–6 New Bond Street, vacating them in 1940, eventually to settle at 14 Old Bond Street. Gustavus Mayer (and later his daughter Katerina) and James Byam Shaw became directors in 1937; after the war Byam Shaw, himself an outstanding scholar, established close links with the museum world, especially the British Museum and the Ashmolean Museum. While their collections benefited greatly from his expertise, Colnaghis gained pre-eminence as dealers in fine prints and drawings. In January 2002 P. and D. Colnaghi and Co. was acquired by Konrad O. Bernheimer and trades now as Bernheimer and Colnaghi.

DENNIS FARR

Sources DNB · E. Manning, *Colnaghi's, 1760–1960* (privately printed, 1960) · D. Garstang, 'Colnaghi, 1760–1984', *Art, commerce, scholarship, a window onto the art world: Colnaghi, 1760 to 1984* (1984) · *The Times* (27 Aug 1833) · *The Times* (22 Dec 1879) · *The Times* (24 Dec 1879) · *The Times* (29 June 1908) · *The Times* (2 July 1908) · *The Times* (5 Aug 1908) · *The Times* (23 Aug 1843) · BL, Add. MSS 40519, 40541, 46140 · *John Constable's correspondence*, ed. R. B. Beckett, 4, Suffolk RS, 10 (1966) · CGPLA Eng. & Wales (1908) · CGPLA Eng. & Wales (1880) · d. cert. [Dominic Charles Colnaghi] · m. cert. [Martin Henry Colnaghi and Amy Mary Smith] · will [Dominic Charles Colnaghi] · IGI

Archives BL, letters to Sir Austen Henry Layard, Add. MSS 38993–39120 [Dominic Ellis Colnaghi] · BL, letters to his parents, Add. MSS 59502–59505 [Dominic Ellis Colnaghi] · Royal Arch., corresp. with members of the royal family · U. Leeds, letters to William Gott [Dominic Paul Colnaghi] · W. Sussex RO, letters to duke of Richmond [Dominic Paul Colnaghi]

Likenesses H. Monnier, pen and watercolour drawing, 1831 (Dominic Charles Colnaghi) · R. L. Aldridge, oils, 1870 (Martin Henry Colnaghi), National Gallery, London · J. C. Horsley, oils, 1889 (Martin Henry Colnaghi), National Gallery, London · J. C. Horsley, portrait, 1889 (Martin Henry Colnaghi), Tate collection · J. Adams-Acton, marble bust (Martin Henry Colnaghi) · K. Brocky, double portrait, pastel drawing (Paul Colnaghi and Dominic Charles Colnaghi), BM? · R. Easton, stipple, medallion (Paul Colnaghi; aged eighty-two; after Danlan), BM, NPG · E. Morton, lithograph (Paul Colnaghi; after R. Smith, 1800), BM, NPG · C. Turner, brush and sepia drawing (Paul Colnaghi), P. & D. Colnaghi? [*see illus.*] · stipple (Dominic Charles Colnaghi; after K. Brocky), BM, NPG

Wealth at death £90,531 14s. 4d.—Martin Henry Colnaghi: probate, 31 July 1908, CGPLA Eng. & Wales · under £450—Dominic Charles Colnaghi: probate, 29 Jan 1880, CGPLA Eng. & Wales

Colnaghi, Dominic Charles (1790–1879). *See under* Colnaghi family (*per. c.*1785–1911).

Colnaghi, Martin Henry (1821–1908). *See under* Colnaghi family (*per. c.*1785–1911).

Colnaghi, Paul (1751–1833). *See under* Colnaghi family (*per. c.*1785–1911).

Colnbrook. For this title name *see* Atkins, Humphrey Edward Gregory, Baron Colnbrook (1922–1996).

Colnet, Nicholas (d. 1420), physician, was of obscure origins, and all that is known of his early career is that his first studies at Oxford were provided, as to a scholar of the founder's kin, by Merton College from 1391. He became fellow of Merton in 1398 (vacated 1411). He was second bursar in 1404–5 and 1406–7, subwarden in 1407–8, and one of three nominees for the wardenship of the college in 1416, after he had entered royal service. Evidence that he took degrees beyond the MA is lacking, but he must have studied and practised medicine while in Oxford. Certainly he had access at Merton to a fine library of medical and scientific books, especially from the gift (perhaps in 1374) of William Rede (d. 1385) and the bequest of Simon Bredon (d. 1372), a predecessor as a Merton-trained physician to the nobility.

Evidence of Colnet's practice of medicine in Oxford was documented by Thomas Fayreford, a peripatetic medical practitioner in Devon and Somerset in the first half of the fifteenth century. In an autograph manuscript (BL, Harley MS 2558) Fayreford copied out medical texts and compiled his own Latin–English medical commonplace book. In this he recorded (fol. 122v) a detailed case history of the treatment by Colnet of an Oxford apothecary named Hugh, whose symptoms (fever, jaundice, internal aposteme, and leg ailment) are described in the language of scholastic medicine. Colnet utilized uroscopy for his diagnosis and prescribed cold syrups in specific quantities, purgation with rhubarb, and fumigation. Whether other references to 'Nicholas' in Fayreford's commonplace book also refer to Colnet is not clear.

Colnet's education and experience may have commended him to royal service. He attended Henry V at least from Henry's accession in 1413, for, designated as a clerk, he received a royal appointment that year to the living of the hospital of St Bartholomew, Playden by Rye, Sussex, and was described in July as king's clerk, sergeant, and physician in a nomination for a pension from Bermondsey Priory, Surrey. In 1414 he received, at the petition of the king on behalf of his *medicus*, a seven-year papal dispensation from advancing to higher orders that allowed him to retain the income from his benefices—the parish church at Sutton Courtenay, Berkshire, and canonries and prebends at Sneating (St Paul's, London) and Wisborough (Chichester). The reference in the letter to 140 marks probably refers to the total revenue of the benefices rather than to Colnet's income.

An indenture of 29 April 1415 records Colnet's attendance on Henry V during the Agincourt campaign. It promises payment of 40 marks per annum for service in the duchy of Guyenne and 12 deniers per day should he enter the kingdom of France with Henry. He was to be provided with transport (horse, harness, and victuals), in addition to the company of three archers; in the event of an invasion of France, 100 marks would support thirty men-at-arms in his retinue. Colnet may well have treated Charles, duke of Orléans, after his capture by the English at Agincourt, for Colnet's will includes the bequest of a ewer which he had received as a gift from the duke.

Nicholas Colnet prepared his will before he again attended the king in France, in 1417, and died three years later, in November 1420. The will suggests that he was both prosperous and generous. Bequests total more than £115 in money, in addition to extensive gifts of plate, cloth, and jewellery. He was generous to his own benefices, and also to the hospital of Bethlehem outside Bishopsgate, London. He was likewise generous to his sister Edith and to an unnamed brother, and especially to his sister Johanna Mynikam and her daughter Johanna. His six bequests to Merton College are noteworthy: the largest was a gift of £20 for the main altar. He also left a copy of Bernard de Gordon's medical compendium, the *Lilium*, to John Mayhew, fellow of Merton.

Colnet's medical reputation survived him. In addition to the case history recorded by Thomas Fayreford, he was also cited by a later royal physician, Roger Marchall (d. 1477), who attended Edward IV (and perhaps Henry VI) and who owned and annotated some forty-five surviving manuscripts. Marchall seems, like Fayreford, to have compiled his own medical commonplace book, in the flyleaves of what is now Cambridge, Gonville and Caius College, MS 98/50. These notations cite ancient, Arabic, and continental medical authorities as well as the earlier English physicians Gilbert the Englishman (d. c.1250) and John Gaddesden (d. 1348/9). Somewhat unusual, however, are references to eight English physicians and surgeons from the late fourteenth and fifteenth centuries, including Nicholas Colnet, who is cited as the authority for a compound laxative remedy utilizing rose-sugar and rhubarb. These citations by Fayreford and Marchall, along with the records of royal service, and the evidence of his prosperity, suggest that Nicholas Colnet was a physician both respected and rewarded.

LINDA EHRSAM VOIGTS

Sources E. F. Jacob, ed., *The register of Henry Chichele, archbishop of Canterbury, 1414–1443*, 2, CYS, 42 (1937), 215–16 · *CEPR letters*, 6.507 · Rymer, *Foedera*, 3rd edn, 4/1.116–17 · *CClR, 1413–19*, 82 · Fayreford commonplace book, BL, Harley MS 2558 · medical notes (perhaps by Roger Marchall, MD), Gon. & Caius Cam., MS 98/50 · Emden, *Oxf.*, 1.469 · *CPR, 1413–1516*, 19 · P. M. Jones, 'Harley MS 2558: a fifteenth-century medical commonplace book', *Manuscript sources of medieval medicine*, ed. M. R. Schleissner (1995), 35–54 · G. Gask, 'The medical services of Henry the Fifth's campaign of the Somme in 1415', *Essays in the history of medicine* (1950) · C. H. Talbot and E. A. Hammond, *The medical practitioners in medieval England: a biographical register* (1965)

Wealth at death more than £115 in cash bequests; plus plate, cloth, and jewellery: will, 1417, Jacob, ed., *Register*

Colnett, James (*bap.* 1753, *d.* 1806), naval officer and fur trader, was baptized on 18 October 1753 at Stoke Damerel parish church, Plymouth, the son of James and Sarah Colnett. He went to sea in June 1770 as an able seaman in the *Hazard*, joined the *Scorpion* (Lieutenant James Cook) in September 1771 as a midshipman, and followed Cook in December of that year to the *Resolution*. In this ship Colnett served as midshipman throughout Cook's second voyage, in the course of which he was described as 'Clever and Sober' (Cook, 2.876). During the voyage Colnett was the first person to sight New Caledonia, with the result that Cook named the headland Cape Colnett. Colnett was appointed to the *Juno* as gunner on 1 January 1776, and during the American War of Independence he served as master of the *Adventure*. He passed for lieutenant on 4 February 1779 and ten days later he was appointed third lieutenant of the *Bienfaisant*, in which he served until 1783 when he joined the *Pégase* as first lieutenant. On 17 August he was placed on half pay.

About a month later, having obtained permission from the Admiralty, Colnett took command of the *Prince of Wales*, with the *Princess Royal* (Charles Duncan) as consort, in Richard Cadman Etches & Co.'s fur-trading expedition to the north-west coast of America under licences from the South Sea Company and the East India Company. The botanist Archibald Menzies, whose appointment had been specially obtained by Sir Joseph Banks, was surgeon on the *Prince of Wales*. After reaching the north-west coast the two ships spent the summer of 1787 trading in the Queen Charlotte Islands and the adjacent mainland and off-lying islands. After wintering in Hawaii, Colnett traded alone in Prince William Sound before rejoining the *Princess Royal* in the Queen Charlotte Islands. The two ships then sailed for Hawaii, and from there they went to Canton (Guangzhou) to sell the sea-otter pelts they had collected. They arrived on 12 November 1788, and Colnett met John Meares, who had been trading illegally on the north-west coast under Portuguese colours; together they formed a new company, known as the Associated Merchants Trading to the Northwest Coast. The *Prince of Wales* was sent back to England with a cargo of tea and the *Argonaut* was purchased to replace her.

Colnett sailed for the north-west coast in the *Argonaut* on 26 April 1789, taking with him twenty-nine Chinese artisans and material for building ships and establishing a permanent settlement in Nootka Sound. However, on his arrival in the sound Colnett discovered that he had been forestalled by the Spanish, who had set up their own establishment there under the command of Estéban José Martínez. At first relations between the two were reasonably polite, but following a violent drunken argument between the two on board Martínez's vessel, Colnett was placed under arrest and his vessel seized. According to a Spanish scientist who visited the sound three years later 'the churlish nature of each one precipitated things up to this point, since those who sailed with both complained of them equally and condemned their uncultivated boorishness' (Wilson, 74). The *Princess Royal* was also seized on her arrival in the sound on 12 July. The seizure of these two ships almost led to war between Great Britain and Spain. Following his arrest Colnett and the two ships were sent to the Spanish naval base of San Blas, in present day Mexico, where he and the *Argonaut* were released on 8 July 1790 under the terms of the Nootka convention, signed earlier in the year between Spain and Great Britain. The *Princess Royal*, being then engaged in the Spanish service, was released later.

Colnett then resumed his fur trading until 3 March 1791 when he sailed once more for China, where he found that Chinese ports were now closed to fur traders. After a mostly unsuccessful attempt to sell his furs in Japan Colnett sailed for England, where he sold the remainder of his skins to the East India Company for £9760. Colnett was next nominated by the Admiralty to command the sloop *Rattler*, which had been converted to a whaler, for a voyage to the Pacific to discover suitable anchorages for British whalers to refit and obtain refreshments. During the voyage (3 January 1793 – 2 November 1794) Colnett surveyed a number of islands and anchorages, and in 1798, after his return to England, a series of charts, engraved by Aaron Arrowsmith, were published. Colnett's account of his voyage, which appeared in the same year, was instrumental in opening up the south Pacific sperm whale fishery.

Colnett was promoted commander on 19 December 1794 on his return to England and was appointed to command the *Merlin*. The following March he was instructed to examine the coastal defences of the east coast of England from the River Thames to Boston in the galley *Hawk*, in co-operation with Captain Hay of the Royal Engineers. His report to the Admiralty was accompanied by a series of manuscript maps, mainly topographical in detail, which also contain the occasional soundings. On 4 October 1796 Colnett was appointed to command the *Hussar*, being promoted captain the following day. In late December 1796 the *Hussar* was wrecked off the coast of Brittany and Colnett was taken prisoner by the French. On being released six months later he was tried by court martial for the loss of his ship, but acquitted. He remained on half pay until 29 June 1802 when he was appointed to command the naval transport *Glatton*. On 23 September he sailed for Port Jackson with 399 convicts on board, only twelve of whom died during the voyage. Colnett returned to England with a cargo of timber for use in his majesty's dockyards. He remained in command of the *Glatton* until 7 March 1805 when he was placed on half pay.

Colnett does not appear to have married, but from the £5000 he left in his will he provided for 'the education, clothing and maintenance of my natural daughter Elizabeth Caroline Colnett, daughter of Catherine Aulte'. He died on 1 September 1806 at his lodgings in Great Ormond Street, London, and was buried on 6 September in St Dunstan and All Saints, Stepney. ANDREW C. F. DAVID

Sources *The journal of Captain James Colnett aboard the Argonaut*, ed. F. W. Howay (1940) • C. Bateson, *The convict ships* (1969), 381 • B. M. Gough, 'Colnett, James', *DCB*, vol. 5 • J. Colnett, *A voyage to the South Atlantic and round Cape Horn into the Pacific Ocean* (1798) • J. Colnett, various reports on his examination of the east coast of England, 1795–6, PRO, ADM 1/1621 and 1622, Cap letters C • W. L. Cook, *Flood tide of empire: Spain and the Pacific northwest, 1543–1819* (1973) • F. M. Bladen, ed., *Historical records of New South Wales*, 4–5 (1896–7) • I. H.

Wilson, ed., *Noticias de Nutka* (1970), 74 · parish register, Stoke Damerel parish church, 18 Oct 1793, Plymouth and West Devon Record Office, Plymouth [baptism] · parish register, St Dunstan and All Saints, Stepney, 6 Sept 1806, LMA [burial]
Archives BL, journal kept by Colnett on board *Rattler*, Add. MS 30369 · PRO, journal kept by Colnett on board *Prince of Wales*, ADM 55/146 · PRO, journal kept by Colnett on board *Argonaut*, ADM 55/142 | PRO, reports and maps relating to Colnett's examination of the east coast of England, ADM 1/1621 and 1622, Cap letters C · United Kingdom Hydrographic Office, Taunton, various charts relating to Colnett's Pacific voyages
Likenesses R. Dodd, engraving, 1791, repro. in Cook, *Flood tide of empire*
Wealth at death £5000: *Journal*, ed. Howay, p. xvi

Colomb, Sir John Charles Ready (1838–1909), defence strategist and advocate of imperial federation, second son of Lieutenant-General George Thomas Colomb (1788–1874), colonel of the 97th regiment, and his wife, Mary, daughter of Sir Abraham Bradley King, bt, of Corrard, co. Fermanagh, was born on the Isle of Man on 1 May 1838. Vice-Admiral Philip Howard *Colomb was his elder brother.

Colomb was educated privately and at the Royal Naval College, Portsmouth. He entered the Royal Marine Artillery in June 1854; he was promoted lieutenant in 1855 and captain on 3 August 1867, and retired on 20 October 1869. He was subsequently adjutant of the Cork artillery militia until May 1872 but, enjoying a comfortable private income, for the rest of his life devoted most of his energies to advocacy of the causes with which he became so closely associated: imperial federation and imperial defence.

The Royal Navy's nineteenth-century adoption of steam power necessitated the creation of a worldwide network of coal depots, which had to be defended. Colomb was the first to consider publicly the problems involved. In 1867 he published anonymously *The Protection of our Commerce and Distribution of our Naval Forces Considered*, generally regarded as the first systematic enunciation of imperial defence requirements in the machine age.

British defence planning was dominated by fears of invasion of the home islands. In 1859 the royal commission on the defence of the United Kingdom had concluded that the country could not depend on the navy alone, and advocated elaborate fortifications to defend major ports and arsenals. Colomb disagreed with this fortress mentality. National security was, he acknowledged, an issue of 'paramount importance'; also crucial was the protection of commerce, and commercial and imperial security required overseas bases from which naval forces could protect commerce, be established and defended. He emphasized the necessity of coal to the steam-powered navy, and advocated stockpiling supplies at the overseas bases and coaling stations.

So far from perceiving imperial defence to be solely a naval task, as did later and more extreme proponents of the 'blue water school' of strategy, Colomb envisaged two important roles for military forces. First, warships were too valuable as commerce protectors to be used to defend the bases from which they operated; such local defence, he maintained, was best provided by fixed fortifications

Sir John Charles Ready Colomb (1838–1909), by Bassano, *c.*1894

and either marines (his preference) or soldiers. Second, the bulk of the army should be held in readiness not for home defence but for amphibious operations. The navy, as he said, should be the 'shield' and the army the 'spear' of imperial defence (D'Egville, 15–16). He did not deviate significantly from these fundamental strategic premises for the rest of his life.

Colomb also devoted much time and energy to pressing two ancillary issues: the essential tasks of securing army–navy co-operation and fostering imperial–colonial defence co-operation. To these ends he frequently addressed the Royal United Service Institution and the Royal Colonial Institute, and his speeches were published as pamphlets. Other speeches were collected in *The Defence of Great and Greater Britain* (1880). He was one of the founding members of the Imperial Federation League (1884), the chief aims of which were collective security and a preferential imperial tariff policy. He was one of the league's delegation which pressed Lord Salisbury's government to call the first Colonial Conference (1887), the *raison d'être* of which was apportioning defence responsibilities between the British government and Canada, South Africa, New Zealand, and the Australian colonies. In recognition of his efforts he was made CMG in 1887 and KCMG in 1888.

Colomb unsuccessfully contested the Bow and Bromley division of Tower Hamlets, London, at the 1885 general election. He was Conservative MP for Bromley and Bow from 1886 to 1892, and for Great Yarmouth from 1895 until he retired in 1906. He spoke frequently on subjects related to imperial defence. His observations made in a 1901 speech on the navy estimates succinctly summed up his impelling ideology: 'Can we go on indefinitely paying for the defence of an Empire which covers all parts of the world out of the resources of an island in but a corner of it? I am a true imperialist—I always have been that; but I hate the Imperialism which perorates about the Empire and refuses to face the real question of making the arrangements for its common security a matter of practical and united action of all of its parts' (*Hansard 4*, 91, 21 March 1901, col. 783). His expertise prompted appointment to the royal commission on the supply of food and raw material in time of war (1905). After he left parliament he continued a tireless advocate of imperial federation, writing to *The Times*, making speeches, and using every opportunity to press for greater home–colonial co-operation.

Colomb lived to see one of his great aims achieved with the establishment of the committee of imperial defence to co-ordinate the activities of the services. Sir George Sydenham Clarke attributed much of the credit for Balfour's reconstituting the cabinet defence committee as an imperial defence body proper to Colomb, and Howard D'Egville—Colomb's parliamentary private secretary and biographer—claimed that he 'was in constant private communication with the Prime Minister, and was to a large extent responsible for the increasing interest which Mr. Balfour showed in the study of the higher policy of defence' (D'Egville, 59–60).

Colomb's other public interest—Ireland—doubtless resulted from the acquisition of the estate of Dromquinna, Kenmare, co. Kerry, by his marriage. As an Irish landlord he spoke frequently in parliamentary debates on Ireland, and he published numerous essays and letters on various aspects of the Irish situation. He was also active as an Irish JP, served as chairman of appeals under the Local Government Act (1898), became a privy councillor for Ireland (1903), and served on the royal commission on the congestion of Ireland (1906–7).

Colomb married Emily Anna (d. 1907), daughter of Robert Samuel and Anna Maria (*née* Spread) Palmer, and widow of Charles Augustus Francis Paget, lieutenant RN, on 1 January 1866. According to D'Egville, her 'active sympathy and co-operation with her husband throughout his life was to him a source of perpetual encouragement and inspiration' (D'Egville, xi). They had a son and two daughters. Colomb himself was remembered by his daughter Lady Snagge as a charming and cultivated man, known affectionately to his family as Uncle Johnny. He died on 27 May 1909 at his residence, 75 Belgrave Road, London, ten days after a serious operation.

Vice-Admiral Philip Howard Colomb credited his younger brother with the leading role 'in laying down and continually differentiating the governing principles of Imperial Defence', calling *The Protection of our Commerce* 'the key-note to all subsequent discussions', and this assessment captures contemporary perceptions of the man and his life's work (D'Egville, xiv). There can be no disputing his importance as a lobbyist and publicist for imperial defence and federation. How much impact his efforts had on official policy is less clear. Certainly the Admiralty was aware of the importance of stockpiling coal and defending depots by the late 1850s, several years before Colomb's first pamphlet, and the evolution of imperial defence policy during the 1860s, 1870s, and early 1880s owed little to him directly. His star rose with the growth of imperialist sentiment after 1880, and by the beginning of the twentieth century he was widely regarded as an imperial defence pioneer. 'As pioneers of British naval thought and history', Donald Schurman has concluded, the influence of the Colomb brothers 'is hard to exaggerate' (Schurman, *Education of a Navy*, 11).

JOHN F. BEELER

Sources D. M. Schurman, *The education of a navy: the development of British naval strategic thought, 1867–1914* (1965) · H. D'Egville, *Imperial defence and closer union: a short record of the life-work of the late Sir John Colomb* (1913) · *The Times* (25 March 1874) · *The Times* (6 July 1907) · *The Times* (28 May 1909) · *The Times* (2 June 1909) · *The Times* (14 July 1909) · D. M. Schurman, 'Imperial defence, 1868–1887: a study in the decisive impulses behind the change from "Colonial" to "Imperial" defence', PhD diss., U. Cam., 1955 · W. C. B. Tunstall, 'Imperial defence, 1815–1870', *The growth of the new empire, 1783–1870*, ed. J. Holland Rose and others (1940), vol. 2 of *The Cambridge history of the British empire* (1929–59), 807–41 · W. C. B. Tunstall, 'Imperial defence, 1870–1897', *The empire-commonwealth, 1870–1919*, ed. E. A. Benians, J. Butler, and C. E. Carrington (1959), vol. 3 of *The Cambridge history of the British empire* (1929–59), 230–54 · private information (2004)

Archives NMM · Queen's University, Belfast, corresp. and papers [copies] · Royal Military College of Canada, Kingston, Ontario

Likenesses Bassano, photograph, *c*.1894, NPG [*see illus.*] · B. Stone, photograph, 1898, NPG · Ape [C. Pellegrini], chromolithograph, caricature, NPG; repro. in *VF* (26 March 1887) · photograph, repro. in D'Egville, *Imperial defence*, frontispiece

Wealth at death £72,026 10s. 2d.: probate, 10 July 1909, *CGPLA Eng. & Wales*

Colomb, Philip Howard (1831–1899), naval officer, was born in Scotland on 29 May 1831, the third son of Lieutenant-General George Thomas Colomb (1788–1874), colonel of the 97th regiment, and his wife, Mary, daughter of Sir Abraham Bradley King, first baronet, of Corrard, co. Fermanagh, twice lord mayor of Dublin. He was the elder brother of Sir John Charles Ready *Colomb (1838–1909). Educated privately, he entered the navy in February 1846 on board the *Tartarus* on the Irish station, and from November 1846 to March 1849 was in the steam frigate *Sidon* in the Mediterranean. He was then appointed to the *Reynard* on the China station, and remained on the station as a supernumerary in various ships, until in September he was appointed to the 16-gun brig-sloop *Serpent* in which, from November until May 1852, he was engaged in the Second Anglo-Burmese War and was present at the capture of Rangoon. He passed his examination in seamanship in May 1852, and continued in the *Serpent* as acting mate and acting lieutenant until she was paid off in January 1854. In March he joined the screw-sloop *Phoenix* for a voyage to Smith Sound under the command of Captain (afterwards Admiral) Sir Edward Augustus Inglefield. On his return to England in October he was appointed to the guardship *Ajax* and on 3 February 1855 was promoted seconded to the Royal Engineers, to improve military signalling.

In July 1868 Colomb commissioned the wooden steam sloop *Dryad*, part of the British naval force which patrolled the Indian Ocean, capturing Arab slave dhows sailing from east Africa to Arabia. Colomb's *Dryad* captured seven slavers with 365 Africans on board. From his experiences Colomb wrote *Slave Catching in the Indian Ocean* (1873), a useful historical source and an expression of his opinions: he considered the Australian Aborigines the lowest race he ever saw and that, unlike Africans, they could not be improved by civilization. On 4 April 1870 he was advanced to post rank, and for approaching four years worked at the Admiralty preparing the *Manual of Fleet Evolutions*, officially issued in 1874. From 1874 to 1877 he commanded the battleship *Audacious* on the China station, as flag-captain to Vice-Admiral Alfred Phillipps Ryder; in 1880 he commanded the turret-ship *Thunderer* in the Mediterranean, and from 1881 to 1884 was captain of the steam reserve at Portsmouth, from which in September 1884 he was appointed to the shore establishment as flag-captain to Sir Geoffrey Thomas Phipps Hornby. On 20 May 1886 he was retired owing to age, still nearly a year from the top of the captains' list. In 1886 he published *Fifteen Years of Naval Retirement*, criticizing the 1870 naval officer retirement scheme and opposing compulsory retirement. He became rear-admiral on 6 April 1887 and vice-admiral on 1 August 1892 but received no official honours. From 1887, succeeding his friend John Knox Laughton, he lectured on naval strategy and tactics at the Royal Naval College, Greenwich. He resided at Botley, Hampshire.

The coming of steam and a perceived 'scientific age' had led many naval officers to reject as irrelevant the lessons of sailing warfare. Initially the work of neither Colomb nor his brother John was historically informed, but from the later 1880s, influenced by Laughton, Colomb developed the historical side of his work, and in turn influenced Laughton. He was also influenced by his brother, with whose ideas he agreed and on whose foundations he built. He acknowledged John's primacy on imperial defence, writing that John had 'the leading part in laying down and continually differentiating the governing principles of Imperial Defence' and claimed John's 1867 pamphlet *The Protection of our Commerce and Distribution of our Naval Forces Considered* gave 'the key-note to all subsequent discussions' (Colomb, *Essays*, 1).

In his retirement Colomb devoted himself to the study of naval history as a key to the problems of naval policy and strategy. Like Laughton and Alfred Thayer Mahan, he argued the continuities of sailing and steam warfare and the validity of lessons drawn from sailing warfare, notably on command of the sea, blockade, and defence against invasion. He asserted in 1887, 'it is impossible to form correct views of the present or future of naval warfare unless they are based on a pretty thorough investigation of its history in the past' (Colomb, *Essays*, 197). The science of naval evolutions he had, theoretically, a complete mastery of, though fate prevented him from combining practice with his theory, and his views did not always

Philip Howard Colomb (1831–1899), by Elliott & Fry, pubd 1899

lieutenant of the *Hastings*, going up the Baltic under James Crawford Caffin. In May 1856 he was appointed to the *Excellent* for the gunnery course and, having passed out in November 1857, was in December appointed flag-lieutenant to Rear-Admiral Sir Thomas Sabine Pasley, then admiral superintendent at Devonport, and later to Pasley's successor, Thomas Matthew Charles Symonds. In 1857 Colomb married Eleanor Bourne, daughter of Captain Hook, 34th regiment; they had two daughters and six sons, of whom five entered the public service.

Colomb in 1858 was ordered by the Admiralty to examine and report on a system of day signals which they had bought. On his showing its unsuitability for sea service, he was asked to improve night signals, then still made in the seventeenth-century manner. Colomb had already studied this problem, without success; he resumed his experiments, and after many months' work devised a system long used in the navy, known as Colomb's flashing signals, using Morse code with long and short flashes from a lamp by night, or blasts from the foghorn or steam whistle in fog. Their novelty has been disputed, and possibly the method had been more or less vaguely suggested before. After opposition, unfavourable reports, and much testing, it was adopted first by the Channel Fleet, under Sidney Colpoys Dacres, before being fully adopted in the navy in February 1867.

On 12 December 1863 Colomb was promoted commander, but continued attached nominally to the *Edgar* or the *Victory*, to perfect his signalling system. In 1867 he was meet, among naval men, with that ready acceptance many believed they were entitled to. Fisher and others criticized him as a 'theoretical' admiral. Laughton claimed in 1893 that some of the opposition to Colomb's theories reflected the 'imperfection' of his language. An untiring correspondent of *The Times*, Colomb had an opinion to express on many contemporary naval issues: for example, he condemned very heavy guns but advocated convoys. He was 'an ardent advocate for strengthening the Navy' (*Annual Register*, 171). He wrote voluminously and was generally known as 'Column and a Half'. At the meetings at the Royal United Service Institution (RUSI) he was a regular attender, a frequent speaker, and contributed several important papers, some of which were published in *Essays on Naval Defence* (1893). He claimed that the essays merited republication because up to then no single book existed on the whole subject of naval defence 'where the great principles of strategy and tactics are placed side by side with the material and personal conditions which either govern or are governed by them' (Colomb, *Essays*, iii). His major work was *Naval Warfare: its Ruling Principles and Practice Historically Treated* (1891; 2nd edn, 1893; 3rd edn, 1899), whose great merit was somewhat obscured by its length. This work attempted to make history a determining guide for the analysis of naval problems of that age. Contemporaneous with Mahan's classic *Influence of Sea Power upon History* (1890)—which overshadowed Colomb's work, and which he generously praised—Colomb's *Naval Warfare* attempted a scientific explanation of how history shaped international politics and British imperial defence.

In Britain Colomb was the precursor of other naval historian-strategists, notably Sir Julian Corbett, and later, Soviet naval theory embraced Colomb for a time. In contrast to Mahan's historical survey, Colomb's work followed a logical structure, working up from securing command of the sea to power projection operations. It was a more accurate reflection of British thinking, particularly in its emphasis on the offensive: for this reason Russian naval thinkers took his work to heart. Its most valuable contribution to naval thought was the concept of a fleet-in-being, which he developed from Herbert's rationalization of his defeat at Beachy Head in 1690. Colomb was a major intellectual influence on the late Victorian navy. His *Memoir of Sir Astley Cooper Key* (1898) as a biography was among the best of its kind and era. An advocate of the ascendant 'blue water' school, Colomb argued an extreme navalist case in the controversy over the relative roles of warships and fortifications, notably in his 1889 RUSI paper, 'The relations between local fortifications and a moving navy'.

During his last years Colomb worked at a memoir of Arthur Herbert, earl of Torrington, whose character and conduct of the battle of Beachy Head (30 June 1690) he considered misrepresented by popular historians. He published numerous pamphlets on naval matters. With J. F. Maurice, Archibald Forbes, and others, he wrote the future war fiction *The Great War of 189-*, published serially in *Black and White* (1892), then in book form (1893). He was one of the founders of the Navy Records Society (1893). A war games enthusiast, he wrote the influential *The Duel: a Naval War Game* (1879), used by the United States navy in the 1880s.

Colomb died at his home, Steeple Court, Botley, Hampshire, suddenly from an affection of the heart, on 13 October 1899. He was survived by his wife.

J. K. LAUGHTON, rev. BARRY M. GOUGH

Sources B. M. Gough, 'The influence of sea power upon history revisited: Vice-Admiral P. H. Colomb', *RUSI Journal*, 135/2 (1990), 55–63 · P. H. Colomb, *Naval warfare: its ruling principles and practice historically treated*, 3rd edn (1899); repr. 2 vols. (1990) · R. C. Howell, *The Royal Navy and the slave trade* (1987) · P. H. Colomb, *Essays on naval defence* (1893) · *WWW, 1897–1915* · *Annual Register* (1899), pt 2, p. 171 · *The Times* (16 Oct 1991), 11 · A. D. Lambert, *The foundations of naval history: John Knox Laughton, the Royal Navy, and the historical profession* (1998) · *United Service Magazine*, 3rd ser., 20 (1899–1900), 214, 305–12 · R. Higham, ed., *Consolidated author and subject index to Journal of the Royal United Services Institution* (1964), 31–2 · D. M. Schurman, *The education of a navy: the development of British naval strategic thought, 1867–1914* (1965), 52–3 · Boase, *Mod. Eng. biog.* · I. F. Clarke, *Voices prophesying war, 1763–1984* (1966) · *CGPLA Eng. & Wales* (1899)

Archives BL, corresp. with Charles Babbage, Add. MS 37204; corresp. with Dilke, Add. MS 43915; corresp. with Martin, Add. MS 41412

Likenesses Elliott & Fry, photograph, NPG; repro. in *ILN* (21 Oct 1899) [*see illus.*]

Wealth at death £4348 2s. 8d.: probate, 11 Dec 1899, *CGPLA Eng. & Wales*

Colomiès, Paul (1638–1692), writer and librarian, was born on 2 December 1638 at La Rochelle, France, the son of Jean Colomiès, a doctor at La Rochelle. His family came from Béarn, but his grandfather Jérome was a minister of the Reformed church at La Rochelle. Colomiès was sent to the academy of Saumur at the age of sixteen and was there taught Hebrew by Louis Cappel. He went to Paris in 1664, and became acquainted with Isaac Vossius, who took him to Holland. Colomiès's first and most useful work, *Gallia Orientalis*, an account of the lives and writings of French scholars in Hebrew and other oriental languages, was published at The Hague in 1665. He intended to follow this with accounts of such scholars from other nations, but only *Italia et Hispania orientalis* was sufficiently advanced for publication, long after Colomiès's death, at Hamburg in 1730. The rest of his output was prolific, and included *Rome protestante* (1677), an apology for the reformed faith, and *Theologorum presbyterianorum icon* (1682), in which his movement towards an episcopalian standpoint became clear.

Colomiès remained at La Rochelle until 1681, but then moved to England, perhaps to visit Vossius, who had been there since 1670 and had become a canon of Windsor. Vossius's influence may have lain behind an introduction to Archbishop William Sancroft; Colomiès was librarian at Lambeth Palace by 1684. As librarian he compiled a manuscript *Catalogus librorum bibliothecae Lambethanae a Paulo Colomesio Ecclesiae Anglicanae presbytero et bibliothecae curatore*. It is a list in shelf order of the more than 9000 books in the library. It also bears extensive corrections by Sancroft himself. He was thus, evidently, in Anglican orders, and became '*Lecteur*' in the new church established by Peter Allix in Jewin Street, Aldersgate, in 1686. He was licensed as a deacon by 9 October 1687. Some dissatisfaction with his advancement in the church (expressed in a letter to William Cave, Bodl. Oxf., MS Tanner 30, fol. 140) was remedied by his collation by the archbishop to the rectory of Eynesford in Kent on 15 November 1687. As Sancroft's librarian, he also compiled a catalogue of Isaac Vossius's manuscripts. This was published in the *Catalogus manuscriptorum Angliae et Hiberniae* (1697)—though Vossius's manuscripts were in fact sold to Leiden. Colomiès was naturalized in March 1688 (W. A. Shaw, ed. *Letters of Denization and Acts of Naturalization for Aliens in England and Ireland, 1603–1700*, 1911, 204).

With Archbishop Sancroft's deprivation as a nonjuror in 1690, Colomiès's appointment as Lambeth librarian came to an end. He had been ill for some time at the time of his death in London in January 1692. He made a will on 2 January 1692; it was proved on 8 January. The principal legatee was his cousin Peter Hamelot. The will does not mention the considerable library of books and papers which Colomiès must have owned. The bookseller Paul Vaillant was one of the witnesses to the will, and there is a possibility that the books were dispersed abroad, though some annotated volumes survive in the British Library. Paul Colomiès was buried in the churchyard of St Martin-in-the-Fields.

Colomiès's books, beyond those already mentioned, consisted largely of collections of annotations on topics humanistic and patristic. Pierre Bayle's judgement was that he was able to profit from his extensive reading and to draw attention to many matters of interest (Bayle, 904–6). This view is supported by the posthumous reprinting of his works in London, Paris, and Amsterdam, and in particular by the (partial) collection of his *Opera theologici, critici et historici argumenti*, edited by J. A. Fabricius (1709).

R. JULIAN ROBERTS

Sources L. E. Arcère, *Histoire de la ville de La Rochelle* (1756–7) · D. C. A. Agnew, *Protestant exiles from France, chiefly in the reign of Louis XIV, or, The Huguenot refugees and their descendants in Great Britain and Ireland*, 3rd edn, 2 vols. (1886) · J. P. Nicéron, *Memoires*, 7 (1729), 197 · J. A. Fabricius, preface, in P. Colomiès, *Opera theologici, critici et historici argumenti*, ed. J. A. Fabricius (Hamburg, 1709) · P. Bayle, *Dictionnaire historique et critique*, 1 (1720), 904–6 · C. R. L. Fletcher, 'Some troubles of Archbishop Sancroft', *Proceedings of the Huguenot Society*, 13 (1923–9), 209–61 · LPL, Records F10 · will, 2 Jan 1692, PRO, PROB 11/408, sig. 6
Archives Bodl. Oxf., catalogue of Vossius's MSS, MS 271, fols. 30–52 · LPL, catalogue of printed books, records F10 | Bodl. Oxf., letter to W. Cave, Tanner MS 30, fol. 140 · Bodl. Oxf., letter to Sancroft, Tanner MS 32, fol. 229
Wealth at death see will, PRO, PROB 11/408, sig. 6

Colone, Adam de (*fl.* 1595–1628), portrait painter, is likely to have been born shortly before 1595, the earliest year for which the Edinburgh baptismal registers survive. The first precise record of his life is a request for a protection (in effect, a passport) made to the Scots privy council in Edinburgh on 3 February 1625, so that he could travel to the Low Countries. In that document he is described as the son of the late 'Adriane de Coline … our paynter'—that is,

an office-holder under James VI and I. No such painter is known, but the king's principal painter at the court in Edinburgh between 1584 and 1602 was Adrian van *Son, whose wife was a Susanna 'Declony'. It is highly probable, therefore, that 'de Coline' is an error for van Son and that Adam de Colone is the son of these two. Van Son was certainly dead by 1610, when Susanna was described as his widow. It has to be assumed, therefore, that Adam grew up using the surname by which his mother would have been known.

There were at least four other children in the family: Adrian, Susanna, James, and Frederick, the eldest of these, Adrian, being baptized on 19 October 1595. Among the witnesses at this baptism was Sir Adrian van Damman, who had been a professor at Leiden and was now ambassador of the confederate provinces at the Scottish court. The family circle was distinctly Netherlandish and included merchants, clockmakers, and jewellers who were likely to have been fairly recent immigrants. Among the jewellers was Abraham Vanson, who was probably an uncle.

In these circumstances, it is not surprising that when de Colone set out to be a painter like his father he should seek his training in the Low Countries. Thereafter, he was employed at the court in London, where, on 4 July 1623, he was paid for two full-length portraits of the king (Hatfield House, Hertfordshire, and Newbattle Abbey, Midlothian). A notable patron was George Seton, third earl of Winton, whose commissions included a portrait of himself with his two sons, which is probably de Colone's finest surviving work (Scot. NPG). Most of his clients, like Winton, were Scots who were frequently in London, so that it is not always clear if his portraits were painted north or south of the border. His works, of which some thirty are known, are not usually documented but are easily distinguished. Their technique, which is robust in a distinctly Netherlandish way, and their style, which is firm and premeditated, set them apart from those of his Scottish contemporary George Jamesone (1589/90–1644), whom he must have rivalled during the 1620s. In addition, nearly all of his portraits bear inscriptions of date and age, which have such a distinctive form of calligraphy that their single authorship can hardly be doubted. All of these inscribed dates fall within the narrow range of 1622 to 1628.

It is not known what use de Colone made of the passport which he applied for in 1625, but he appears not to have gone abroad immediately. If he finally did travel to the continent in 1628, he did not fulfil his promise to return and 'sattle [settle] his aboad in the said kingdom of Scotland' (*Reg. PCS*, 698–9), for there are no further records of him.

DUNCAN THOMSON

Sources D. Thomson, *The life and art of George Jamesone* (1974) · D. Thomson, *Painting in Scotland, 1570–1650* (1975) [exhibition catalogue, Scot. NPG, 21 Aug – 21 Sept 1975] · *Reg. PCS*, 1st ser., 13.698–9 · *APC*, 1623–25 · Second report, HMC, 1/2 (1871); repr. (1874) · O. Millar, *The Tudor, Stuart and early Georgian pictures in the collection of her majesty the queen*, 2 vols. (1963) · E. Auerbach, *Painting and sculpture at Hatfield House* (1971) · NL Scot., Denmilne MSS, Adv. MS

33.1.1/40 · old parochial registers, General Register Office for Scotland, Edinburgh, vol. 1, fols. 9, 26*v*, 32, 59*v*, 101, 116

Archives General Register Office for Scotland, Edinburgh, old parochial registers, vol. 1 · NL Scot., Denmilne MSS, Adv MS, 33.1.1/40

Colonia, Adam Isaacszoon de (1634–1685), painter, was born in Rotterdam on 12 August 1634, the son of the painter Isaac Adamszoon de Colonia (1611–1663) and Machtelt Becx. De Colonia probably trained under his father, as well as his grandfather Adam Louiszoon de Colonia (1574–1651), also a painter. In his early career de Colonia was influenced by the importation of fully fledged Italianate styles into Utrecht, and possibly also by Dutch Italianate models such as Nicolaes Berchem (1620–1683).

De Colonia married Cornelia, daughter of Arendt Kerckhoven, in Rotterdam on 28 December 1661, and they had four children. He is recorded in Rotterdam in 1669. Some time after this they moved to London, and are listed as members of the Dutch Reformed church at Austin Friars in 1674. In Britain, de Colonia continued to produce the village genre scenes and biblical and Italianate landscapes, with lively figures, that had characterized his work in Rotterdam. He often painted night scenes, and pastoral images, following the development of these themes by Francesco Bassano (1549–1592) in Venice. De Colonia reportedly copied the Bassano paintings—presumably those by Jacopo—in the Royal Collection, and maintained a steady reputation in Britain throughout his career, with his imitations 'esteemed his best performances' (Buckeridge, 407). He occasionally etched. De Colonia was buried in St Martin-in-the-Fields, London, on 10 September 1685, after which his reputation lessened. Examples of his work are in museums in Holland; Lille, France; and Copenhagen, Denmark.

One of de Colonia's sons, **Hendrick Adriaen de Colonia** (1668–1701/2), often called Adrian de Colonia, also became a painter with some contemporary reputation. Born on 17 April 1668, Hendrick probably trained with his father, and the chief source of his fame is the figures he inserted into landscapes painted by Adriaen van Diest, a Dutch artist working in London, who was also Hendrick's brother-in-law through his sister Huberta. He also drew a number of 'academy pieces' (Buckeridge, 407), and some landscapes, rougher in style than those of his father. He is reputed to have died, and been buried with his father in St Martin-in-the-Fields, in 1701 or 1702, aged thirty-three, but there is no record of this.

L. H. CUST, *rev.* NICHOLAS GRINDLE

Sources [B. Buckeridge], 'An essay towards an English school of painters', in R. de Piles, *The art of painting, and the lives of the painters* (1706), 398–480 · G. Meissner, ed., *Allgemeines Künstlerlexikon: die bildenden Künstler aller Zeiten und Völker*, [new edn, 34 vols.] (Leipzig and Munich, 1983–) · C. Wright, *Images of a golden age: Dutch seventeenth-century paintings* (1989) [exhibition catalogue, Birmingham Museum and Art Gallery] · J. Briels, *Vlaamse schilders en de dageraad van Hollands gouden eeuw, 1585–1630* (Antwerp, 1997) · E. Croft-Murray and P. H. Hulton, eds., *Catalogue of British drawings*, 1 (1960) · parish register, St Martin-in-the-Fields, London, 10 Sept 1685, City Westm. AC [burial, microfilm vol. 7] · Bénézit, *Dict.*, 4th edn · E. K. Waterhouse, *The dictionary of British 16th and 17th century painters* (1988)

Colonia, Hendrick Adriaen de (1668–1701/2). *See under* Colonia, Adam Isaacszoon de (1634–1685).

Colonsay and Oronsay. For this title name *see* McNeill, Duncan, Baron Colonsay and Oronsay (1793–1874).

Coloribus, John de (*fl.* 1502–1538), Dominican friar, was Walloon in origin. He first appears as a member of the Dominican convent at Lille in 1502, when he was sent to study philosophy at Paris. In the nine years following he was recorded at a number of other houses in the Low Countries and northern France, and at the end of 1509 was appointed by the master-general to lecture at Lille on the *Sentences*. By 1511, however, he had left the continent under a cloud: he and a colleague had fled the Paris convent with a 'noteworthy' theft and were consequently condemned to severe punishment and imprisonment wherever they should be found. Instead he came to Oxford, where he preached the university sermon on Ash Wednesday 1511 and successfully supplicated for the degree of BTh on 15 October following, describing himself as having studied logic, philosophy, and theology for sixteen years. On 10 May 1516 he supplicated for the degree of DTh, and was dispensed on 11 November 1522. In 1521 he was one of the theologians reported by the university as available to support the king in attacking Luther; like the others he had already written unpublished *opuscula* in this cause. In 1525, according to Wood, he was one of the fellows of Wolsey's Cardinal College.

John de Coloribus remained a Dominican, and it was as such that he received letters of denization on 17 March 1527. By 1531 he had left Oxford and moved to Cornwall, where he entered the employment of the Arundell family of Lanherne. During that year his services were required by the bishop of Lincoln, perhaps in connection with Henry VIII's divorce, but he preferred to be in the southwest, and begged Sir Thomas Arundell to speak up for him, 'that I may obtain some good provision to return to Cornwall' (*LP Henry VIII*, 5, no. 214). He certainly did so return, but perhaps not to the 'provision' he hoped for, since on 22 September 1538 he was one of the black friars of Truro who surrendered their house to the king's commissioners. On 3 December following he was among the former Dominicans dispensed to hold a benefice, but it is not known if he obtained one, and he disappears from the record at this point. HENRY SUMMERSON

Sources Emden, *Oxf.*, 1.470 · Wood, *Ath. Oxon.*, new edn, 1.47 · A. de Meyer, *La congrégation de Hollande ou la réforme Dominicaine en territoire bourguignon, 1465–1515* (1949) · *LP Henry VIII*, vols. 4/2, 5, 13/2 · W. T. Mitchell, ed., *Epistolae academicae, 1508–1596*, OHS, new ser., 26 (1980) · D. S. Chambers, ed., *Faculty office registers, 1534–1549* (1966)

Colpoys, Sir John (*c.*1742–1821), naval officer, details of whose parents and upbringing are unknown, possibly entered the navy in 1756 at the beginning of the Seven Years' War. Colpoys served at the capture of Louisbourg in 1758 and Martinique in 1762 and was promoted lieutenant in October 1762. In 1770 he was sent to the East Indies in the sloop *Lynx* where he was promoted commander.

Raised to post captain in August 1773, he was given command of the *Northumberland* (70 guns). Between 1776 and 1778 he commanded the frigate *Seaford* and then in 1779 he became flag captain to Admiral Sir John Lockhart Ross on the *Royal George*. In the same year Colpoys sat as a member of the court martial on Vice-Admiral Sir Hugh Palliser, who was tried after the acquittal of Admiral Augustus Keppel for an indecisive action against the French fleet off Ushant in July 1778. Palliser, a supporter of the tory government and a lord of the Admiralty, was acquitted. Subsequently Colpoys was given command of the frigate *Orpheus* and sent to the North American station where, in 1781, in company with the *Roebuck*, he captured the American ship *Confederacy*, which was carrying stores for Washington's army. Colpoys commanded the frigate *Phaeton* in the Mediterranean for a short time in 1783 but was then not employed again until 1790, when he was given the *Hannibal*, guardship at Portsmouth.

In 1793, upon the outbreak of war with France, Colpoys was sent with a squadron to guard the Channel Islands and subsequently to the West Indies with Rear-Admiral Alan Gardner's squadron. He was raised to the rank of rear-admiral in April 1794 and, with his flag in the *London* (98 guns), was present in Lord Bridport's action off Lorient in July 1795. On 11 December 1796 a division of the French fleet evaded Colpoys's blockading squadron off Ushant and joined Admiral Richery's fleet in the port of Brest. On 16 December Captain Sir Edward Pellew, commanding the inshore frigate squadron, realized that the French fleet was putting to sea and sent a lugger to warn Colpoys. Colpoys's squadron, however, had either been blown off station or had withdrawn into the channel and it was left to Pellew in the frigate *Indefatigable* to harass the French fleet until he lost sight of it. Colpoys and his squadron returned to Plymouth while the French sailed in an abortive attempt to land an army on the coast of Ireland at Bantry Bay.

In April 1797 the first major mutiny broke out among the Channel Fleet at Spithead. Although the seamen's grievances were partly settled, the crews of four ships maintained their strike, and these were left at Spithead under the command of Colpoys in the *London*, while the remainder of the fleet moored at St Helens, off the Isle of Wight. On 1 May the Admiralty issued a general order instructing the officers in its ships vigorously to suppress any attempted mutiny and bring ringleaders to punishment. The order was met with dismay and was concealed by many officers in the Channel Fleet in an effort to keep it from the seamen. By 7 May, however, news of the order was out and the fleet at St Helens mutinied again. Colpoys, at Spithead, apparently realizing that a new mutiny had broken out, summoned his crew on deck and asked them if they had any remaining grievances. The crew said they had none and Colpoys ordered them below deck. In an attempt to prevent any communication between the crew and the mutineers' delegates, Colpoys tried to seal the ship by closing the gunports and confining the men below.

The crew of the *London* now held a meeting and demanded to be allowed on deck. When this was refused they attempted to force their way up, and Colpoys ordered the ship's officers and marines to open fire on them. Most of the marines dropped their weapons, but several seamen were mortally wounded before Colpoys ordered the officers to cease firing. Lieutenant Peter Bover, who had been responsible for wounding one of the seamen, was immediately seized and threatened with hanging. Colpoys intervened quickly by claiming responsibility for the actions of his officers, and both Bover and Colpoys, together with the ship's captain, Edward Griffith, were confined in their cabins. The crew of the *London* next moved the ship to St Helens, to join the other ships under mutiny. Once there they considered holding a trial for both Colpoys and Captain Griffith. However, three days later they sent the officers on shore.

Shortly afterwards the mutineers included Colpoys's name among the list of those they wanted removed from their commands, but in fact Colpoys had already asked to be relieved. On 14 May he was ordered to strike his flag, an order which reflected expediency rather than any form of reprimand. In 1798 he was made a knight of the Bath.

In January 1801 he was advanced to the rank of admiral of the Blue squadron, but he remained without employment until June 1803 when he was appointed commander-in-chief at Plymouth. In May 1804, apparently at the request of Lord Melville, first lord of the Admiralty, Colpoys gave up his command in order to take a seat at the Admiralty. It is possible that, shortly after, he was considered for the position of commander-in-chief in the Mediterranean but this came to nothing and in 1805 he was appointed treasurer of Greenwich Hospital. In January 1815 he was awarded the grand cross of the Bath and on 27 January 1816, following the death of Lord Hood, he became the governor of Greenwich Hospital, where he died, aged about seventy-nine, on 4 April 1821. It is possible that he was buried in the mausoleum at Greenwich.

J. K. LAUGHTON, *rev.* TOM WAREHAM

Sources J. Ralfe, *The naval biography of Great Britain*, 2 (1828), 3 · *Naval Chronicle*, 11 (1804), 269–72 · D. Syrett and R. L. DiNardo, *The commissioned sea officers of the Royal Navy, 1660–1815*, rev. edn, Occasional Publications of the Navy RS, 1 (1994) · C. N. Parkinson, *Edward Pellew, Viscount Exmouth, admiral of the red* (1934) · G. E. Manwaring and B. Dobrée, *The floating republic: an account of the mutinies at Spithead and the Nore in 1797* (1935); repr. (1966) · J. Dugan, *The great mutiny* (New York, 1965); repr. (1966)
Archives NA Scot., corresp. with Henry Dundas, Ref. GD51
Likenesses R. Earlom, mezzotint, pubd 1777 (after Pellegrini), BM, NPG · W. Ridley, stipple, pubd 1804 (after M. Brown), NPG · J. Young, mezzotint, pubd 1812, BM · M. Brown and W. Ridley, engraving, NMM · W. Savage, oils (with Bath star; after M. Brown), NMM

Colquhoun, Archibald Campbell- (*c.*1754–1820), lawyer and politician, was the only son of John Campbell (formerly Coates), a merchant of Clathick, Perthshire, and provost of Glasgow, and his wife, Agnes, the only child of Laurence Colquhoun of Killermont, Dunbartonshire. On succeeding to the estate of Killermont upon the death of his father in 1804 he assumed the additional surname and arms of Colquhoun. He was educated at Glasgow University and admitted an advocate in 1779. In 1796 he married Mary Ann, daughter of the Revd William Erskine, Episcopalian minister at Muthill, Perthshire, and sister of William Erskine (1769–1822). They had six daughters and two sons—John Campbell-*Colquhoun (1803–1870), a writer, and William Laurence Campbell-Colquhoun, who died on 16 January 1861. Their eldest child died within a year of her birth, prompting Carolina Oliphant, afterwards Lady Nairne, to write 'The Land of the Leal', which she sent to her old friend Mrs Colquhoun. Colquhoun himself was a good classical scholar, a sound lawyer, and an eloquent pleader. However, being wealthy and reserved, he did not seek to obtain a large practice.

On the downfall of the 'ministry of all the talents' Colquhoun was appointed lord advocate, on 28 March 1807. At this time most Scottish patronage was in the hands of the Dundas family, and William Erskine, Alexander Maconochie, and Henry Cockburn were actually chosen deputes by Lord Melville before Colquhoun had received the appointment. In May 1807 Colquhoun was elected MP for the Elgin district of burghs, but after three years he resigned his seat, in pursuit of a safer one. In July 1810 he was returned unopposed as member for Dunbartonshire, with the support of the duke of Montrose, and he held this seat securely until his death in 1820. In parliament he defended Lord Eldon's bill for the reform of the Scottish judicature. As the lord advocate he took part in reforming the constitution of the court of session, and he was appointed one of the thirteen commissioners who sat for the first time on 30 November 1808 for the purpose of inquiring into the administration of justice in Scotland. The correspondence between Colquhoun and Henry Erskine, the late lord advocate, on the subject of the respective merits of Lord Grenville's and Lord Eldon's bills for the reform of legal procedure was published in the 1808 edition of the *Scots Magazine*. Colquhoun was antagonized by the failure of the ministry to appoint him lord president in 1811, but he was made lord clerk register on 4 July 1816. Erskine's friends were much disappointed by the latter event; they had hoped that the post would have been offered to him. Other than in Scottish affairs Colquhoun was not a successful parliamentary speaker. He was shouted down in March 1809 when he attempted to defend the duke of York. He voted against Catholic relief in 1813.

Colquhoun was sheriff of Perth from 1793 to 1807 and rector of Glasgow University from 1807 to 1809. He died on 8 December 1820, after a short illness, at the house of his son-in-law, Walter Long, at Hartham, Wiltshire, and was buried in the parish churchyard of New Kilpatrick, near Glasgow. His wife survived him for many years, and died at Rothesay on 15 May 1833.

G. F. R. Barker, rev. Eric Metcalfe

Sources HoP, *Commons* · W. Fraser, *The chiefs of Colquhoun and their country*, 2 (1869), 253–8 · G. W. T. Omond, *The lord advocates of Scotland from the close of the fifteenth century to the passing of the Reform Bill*, 2 (1883), 224–9 · Anderson, *Scot. nat.* · J. Kay, *A series of original portraits and caricature etchings … with biographical sketches and illustrative anecdotes*, ed. [H. Paton and others], new edn [3rd edn], 2 (1877), 431 · *Memorials of his time, by Henry Cockburn* (1856), 228–9 · C. Nairne, *Life and songs*, ed. C. Rogers (1869), xxx, 3–4, 181–4 · *Hansard* 1 (1809), 8.577–8 · *Scots Magazine and Edinburgh Literary Miscellany*, 69 (1807), 134–5 · *Scots Magazine and Edinburgh Literary Miscellany*, 70 (1808), 69–70, 953 · *Scots Magazine and Edinburgh Literary Miscellany*, 78 (1816), 555 · Burke, *Gen. GB*

Archives LUL, draft letters and legal opinions · NL Scot., letter and account books | BL, corresp. with second earl of Liverpool, Add. MSS 38242–38257, 38320–38323 · NA Scot., corresp. with Lord Melville · NL Scot., corresp. with Lord Melville · NRA, priv. coll., corresp. with Rt Hon. Richard Ryder

Likenesses J. Kay, etching, 1813, NPG; repro. in Kay, *Series of original portraits* · Raeburn, portrait, priv. coll.

Colquhoun, Archibald Ross (1848–1914), explorer, colonial administrator, and author, was born at sea off the Cape of Good Hope in March 1848, the fifth of six children of Dr Archibald Colquhoun (c.1804–1890) of Edinburgh, an employee of the East India Company, and his wife, Felicia (c.1817–1855), née Anderson. Educated at Glasgow Academy, Helensburgh School, and the Moravian School at Neuwied in the Rhineland, he joined the Indian Public Works Department in 1871 as an assistant surveyor. In 1879 he was secretary and second in command of a government mission to Siam and the Shan States, and in 1881–2 he travelled from Canton (Guangzhou) to Bhamo to find the best railway route between China and Burma. Widely regarded as an explorer of the first rank, his Indian administrative obligations prevented him from accepting an offer from Henry Morton Stanley to act as second in command of his Congo expedition. In 1883 *The Times* appointed him its correspondent in the Franco-Chinese War and for the Far East, and in 1884 he was awarded the Royal Geographical Society founders' gold medal; his publications on the trade potential of Burma were welcomed by British chambers of commerce. In 1885 he became deputy commissioner in Upper Burma; his career came to an abrupt end, however, when a frank criticism he made of government policy fell accidentally into the hands of his superiors.

In 1889, through the offices of James Rochfort Maguire and Alfred Beit, Colquhoun accepted an offer from Cecil Rhodes of the post of first administrator of Mashonaland. In 1890 he secured the eastern frontiers of the territory through treaties with local chiefs. Subsequently, however, he complained to Rhodes that proper administrative procedures were not being followed. Leander Starr Jameson regarded Colquhoun as a pedantic bureaucrat, largely because the latter tried to exercise strict controls over land grants to avoid clashes with the African population. Colquhoun retired on grounds of ill health and was succeeded by Jameson.

In 1894 Colquhoun became the agent in Peking (Beijing) for the Hongkong and Shanghai Bank and in the following year he surveyed Nicaragua and Panama as possible routes for a Central American canal. From 1896 until 1913 he undertook several tours of Siberia, China, Japan, the Philippines, the Dutch East Indies, southern Africa, North and

South America, and the Habsburg empire. In 1900 he married Ethel Maude Cookson [see below], who shared Colquhoun's conviction that British public opinion should be informed about the perceived threat to British interests in Asia from other great powers, as well as his belief in the need for compulsory military service, naval preparedness, imperial federation, and 'national efficiency', concerns which he stressed at lectures to various learned and military societies. He was an active member of the Royal Colonial Institute and in 1908–9 took a leading role in a campaign to reform its constitution. He edited *United Empire* from 1910 until his death on 18 December 1914 at 26 Iverna Gardens, London.

Powerfully built, with a walrus moustache and a fondness for champagne, Colquhoun was a mercurial character whose life embodied several paradoxes. For all his experience of administration and exploration, he seems to have been unable to deal with South African frontiersmen because he lacked the common touch. He advised on economic development, yet his own business deals were a failure. Unfairly accused by Jameson's biographer, Ian Colvin, of being one of Rhodes's mistakes, he was in reality an accomplished writer of more than fourteen scholarly books and numerous articles on colonial administration, comparative ethnography, railway and canal construction, land settlement, trade prospects, and geopolitics and defence in the European colonial empires, Russia, China, east Asia, and the Americas. He was a regular contributor on these subjects to British, North American, and German journals and newspapers. He was one of the most widely respected travel authors of his time and he built up a series of influential friendships, counting sometime American presidents Theodore Roosevelt and William Taft, and the Canadian imperialist Sir George Parkin, among his friends.

Colquhoun's widow, known after her remarriage as **Ethel Maude Tawse Jollie** (1876–1950), founder of the Rhodesian Responsible Government Association, was born Ethel Maude Cookson, the eldest daughter of Dr Samuel Cookson of Foregate, Stafford. She studied art about 1894 under Anthony Ludovici at the Slade School of Art, where she first met Colquhoun, although their friendship did not develop until they met again in 1900; within a few weeks of this second encounter they were married. The couple shared political interests, and Ethel Colquhoun was a leading member of several organizations of particular interest to him, such as the National Service League, the Imperial Maritime League, the British Women's Emigration Society, and the Women's Unionist Association, of which she was an executive member. She also shared her husband's interest in the colonial empire and gave several scholarly papers to learned societies on colonial subjects. They remained married, apparently very happily, until his death in 1914. Given Colquhoun's disappointment with the slow development of Southern Rhodesia after his departure in 1891, it is perhaps ironic that it was his widow, by then remarried—her new husband was a Rhodesian farmer from Melsetter called John

Tawse Jollie—who in 1917 founded the Responsible Government Association there, which set the territory's course outside the Union of South Africa in 1922. She became a thorn in the side of the British South Africa Company, and was elected to the legislative assembly of Southern Rhodesia in 1923 as the first woman parliamentarian in the British overseas empire. She regarded the attainment of self-government as in no small way revenge for what she saw as the British South Africa Company's bad treatment of her first husband. She died in 1950.

DONAL LOWRY

Sources A. R. Colquhoun, *From Dan to Beersheba: reminiscences of public service* (1908) · E. Colquhoun, 'Archibald Colquhoun—a memoir', *United Empire*, 6 (1915), 99–109 · J. A. Edwards, 'Colquhoun in Mashonaland: a portrait of failure', *Rhodesiana*, 4 (1963), 1–17 · I. Colvin, *The life of Jameson*, 2 vols. (1922) · E. Tawse Jollie, 'The Pungwe route to Southern Rhodesia: a footnote to history', *United Empire*, 21 (1930), 432–5 · E. Colquhoun, *Two on their travels* (1902) · T. R. Reese, *The history of the Royal Commonwealth Society, 1868–1968* (1968) · A. R. Colquhoun, *Across Chrysê: from Canton to Mandalay*, 2 vols. (1883) · D. Lowry, '"White woman's country": Ethel Tawse Jollie and the making of white Rhodesia', *Journal of Southern African Studies*, 23/2 (1997), 259–81 · m. cert. · d. cert.
Archives National Archives of Zimbabwe, Historical MSS, Misc/CO 9 · National Archives of Zimbabwe, Public Archives, Administrator's Office (A) · RGS | Bodl. RH, Rhodes MSS · National Archives of Zimbabwe, Historical MSS, Sir Leander Starr Jameson MSS · National Archives of Zimbabwe, Public Archives, British South Africa Company · National Archives of Zimbabwe, Historical MSS, Rhodes MSS · NL Scot., letters to W. M. Colles
Likenesses H. G. Herkomer, portrait, *c.*1905, National Archives of Zimbabwe · photographs (as Administrator of Mashonaland), National Archives of Zimbabwe · portrait (aged about thirty-five), repro. in Colquhoun, *Across Chrysê*, vol. 1, frontispiece
Wealth at death £1807 13*s.* 3*d.*: probate, 10 Feb 1915, *CGPLA Eng. & Wales*

Colquhoun, (Margaret) Ithell (1906–1988), painter and poet, was born on 9 October 1906 at Shillong, Assam, India, the daughter of Henry Archibald Colebrooke Colquhoun (1870–1942), assistant to the political agent in Manipur, and Georgia Frances Ithell Manley (b. 1873). She was educated at Thornlow School in Rodwell, near Weymouth, Dorset, and afterwards at Cheltenham Ladies' College. While still at school her article 'The prose of alchemy' was published in *The Quest*. She joined the short-lived and occult Quest Society and read studies on the cabbala. Although she studied at the Slade School of Fine Art, London, under Henry Tonks and Randolph Schwabe, in many ways she was self-taught in art. During a visit to Paris with fellow students in 1931 Colquhoun discovered surrealism, especially the work of Salvador Dalí, under whose influence she painted quasi-photographically a series of enlarged views of plants and flowers which occupied the entire canvas. In 1936 she held her first one-woman exhibition, at Cheltenham Art Gallery, following which she exhibited regularly in London, in regional galleries, and abroad. In June 1936 she visited the International Surrealist Exhibition in London, and in 1939, just after showing at the 'Living Art in England' exhibition, she joined the English Surrealist Group. Two years earlier she had joined the Marxist-inspired Artists' International Association; after remaining a member for three years she rejoined in 1942 for a further two years. In June 1939 she exhibited with Roland Penrose at the Mayor Gallery; they asked a tramp to sit in the window, thus creating a scandal. In the same year she visited the French writer André Breton, who introduced Colquhoun to the psychomorphological work of the Chilean artist Roberto Matta, and Onslow Ford, who defined such work as an attempt to 'bind trees and stars into one unity by auras and lines of force' (O. Ford, 'The painter looks within himself', *London Bulletin*, 18–20 June 1940). Two of Colquhoun's major works date from this period: *Scylla* (1938; Tate collection) shows rocks joined at the top into whose feminine opening appears the sharp phallic point of a boat's prow, and *Rivières tièdes* (1939; Southampton Art Gallery) shows rivulets of strange liquid flowing from under the doors of a hermetically closed Mediterranean church, probably an allusion to the Spanish Civil War.

During the Second World War Colquhoun lived at 44 Fairfax Road, London, with the art critic and essayist Toni del Renzio (*b.* 1915), whom she married on 10 July 1943. The couple had no children and the marriage was later dissolved. In 1940 Colquhoun had been expelled from the English Surrealist Group by its leader, E. L. T. Mesens, for refusing to abandon her occult research. From this time onwards she used a wide range of artistic experiments to explore the subconscious and the roots of consciousness. These included various forms of automatism, those already used by the surrealists, such as decalcomania, fumage, frottage, and collage, especially Merz collages, and others which she invented herself, such as superautomatism, stillomanay, parsemage, and entoptic graphomania, which she defined in her article 'The mantic stain' (*Enquiry*, October–November 1949). From this period *The Pine Family* (1941; Jerusalem Museum), *A Visitation* (1941; priv. coll.), and *Dreaming Leaps* (1945; priv. coll., France) stand out as masterpieces. The first confronts the viewer with the monstrous facts of dismemberment and castration, the second shows a kind of heart laid flat and opening out to liberate luminous cells and astral beams of multicoloured light, while the third, based on the use of decalcomania, is a homage to Sonia Araquistain, whose suicide in September 1945 was attributed by the judge to her reading of Freud. In 1946 Colquhoun bought a studio hut called Vow Cave near Penzance, Cornwall, but continued to live at Windmill Hill, Hampstead, London, until 1957, when she moved to Paul, near Penzance.

During the same period Colquhoun wrote short topographical accounts, entitled 'experiments', which take the reader through a highly detailed description of places along a gradual descent into the secret life of land and water, pebbles, stones, plants, flowers, and insects. These texts are published together in *The Crying of the Wind: Ireland* (1955) and *The Living Stones: Cornwall* (1957). In them, the borderline between a precise, sensitive rendering of reality and a plunge into the fantastic becomes imperceptible. Similarly, her celebration of Celtic lore, her fascination for stone circles and druidic rituals, and her investigation into the occult coalesce in two quite different

works: *Goose of Hermogenes* (1961), a Gothic novel of initiation whose narrative follows the successive stages of alchemical processes in the refinement of matter, and *Sword of Wisdom* (1975), a study of MacGregor Mathers and the hermetic order of the Golden Dawn. Her poems, some of them collected in *Grimoire of the Entangled Thicket* (1973), aim at re-establishing contact with the primitive energy which links letters, numbers, and vegetal cycles of life and death. Colquhoun died on 11 April 1988 in Lamorna valley, Cornwall.

In her paintings, drawings, constructions, prose, and poetry, the organic and the inorganic, the masculine and the feminine, the earthly and the spiritual join in often strongly erotic, if not outspokenly sexual, encounters, in an attempt to fuse with the forces of the beyond. A member of the occult Druidic Order and the Order of the Stella Matutina, Colquhoun was a 'fantasmagiste'. This descriptor, used by the international movement in the 1950s, refers to unorthodox surrealists who were criticized by Breton for being so passionately attracted to the arcane and the occult that these were no longer seen as means but as ends in themselves. Colquhoun's visions, whether written down or visually expressed, nevertheless throw an interesting light on the process of condensation at the core of surrealism.

MICHEL REMY

Sources I. Colquhoun, *Surrealism, paintings, drawings, collages, 1936–1976* (1976) [exhibition catalogue, Newlyn Orion Galleries, Cornwall] · I. Colquhoun, *Paintings and drawings* (1977) [exhibition catalogue, Michael Parkin Gallery, London] · personal knowledge (2004) · Tate collection, Colquhoun Archive · Artists' International Association Archives, Tate collection · *Evening Herald* (24 Nov 1988) · *Daily Telegraph* (29 Nov 1988)

Archives Tate collection, elements for autobiography, letters, papers, short stories

Likenesses photograph, repro. in Colquhoun, *Paintings and drawings* · photographs, repro. in *London Bulletin* (15 June 1939), 13

Wealth at death £246,561: probate, 3 Nov 1988, CGPLA Eng. & Wales

Colquhoun [*née* Sinclair]**, Janet**, Lady Colquhoun (1781–1846), religious writer, was the second daughter of Sir John *Sinclair of Ulbster, first baronet (1754–1835), and his first wife, Sarah (*d.* 1785), the only child and heir of Alexander Maitland of Stoke Newington. She was born in London on 17 April 1781, but, together with her elder sister Hannah, passed her childhood at Thurso Castle with their grandmother Lady Janet Sinclair, daughter of William Sutherland, Lord Strathnaver. This lady took the sisters to live in the Canongate of Edinburgh, before they went to complete their education at a school at Stoke Newington. The younger of the two was about fifteen when they returned to be introduced into Edinburgh society.

On 11 June 1799 Janet Sinclair married Major James Colquhoun (1774–1836), eldest son of Sir James Colquhoun of Luss, second baronet, on whose death, in 1805, her husband succeeded to the title, and Rossdhu, on Loch Lomond, became her home. In this year Lady Colquhoun began to keep a diary, which she continued for forty years. She was the mother of five children, three sons, including John *Colquhoun, and two daughters, whom she helped

Colquhoun, John (1748–1827), theological writer, was born at Luss in Dunbartonshire in January 1748. His brother was the Revd James Colquhoun of Perth. He was originally a shepherd and weaver but, after attending a village school, he studied at Glasgow for the Scottish ministry. He was licensed in August 1780 and took up a charge in South Leith in March 1781. He was married; his wife's name was Euphemia. A supporter of the SPCK and the Edinburgh Continental Society, his publications include *A Treatise on Spiritual Comfort* (1831) and two treatises on the covenant of grace and of works. He died on 27 November 1827 at South Leith.   J. M. RIGG, *rev.* EMMA MAJOR

Sources will, PRO, PROB 11/1735, sig. 11 · Allibone, *Dict.* · *GM*, 1st ser., 97/2 (1827), 570–71 · Irving, *Scots.*
Likenesses J. Kay, caricature, etching, 1793, BM, NPG
Wealth at death approx. £6000: will, PRO, PROB 11/1735, sig. 11

Colquhoun, John (1805–1885), writer on sport, second son of Sir James Colquhoun, third baronet (1774–1836), of Luss and Janet, *née* Sinclair (1781–1846) [*see* Colquhoun, Janet], the religious author, was born in Charlotte Square, Edinburgh, on 6 March 1805. Together with his elder brother he was educated first at Edinburgh high school, subsequently at a private school in Lincolnshire run by the Revd Grainger of Winteringham, and finally at the University of Edinburgh. An ensign in the 33rd regiment from 1826, in 1828 he was in the wilds of Connaught as a lieutenant; there he had plenty of hard work and a full share of adventures in the way of protecting the excise, or 'still-hunting', as it was called. In 1829 he was gazetted into the 4th dragoon guards but sold out the following year.

On 29 January 1834 Colquhoun married Frances Sarah (1813–1877), fourth daughter of Ebenezer Fuller Maitland of Park Place, Henley-on-Thames; they had four sons and five daughters, among them Lucy Bethia *Walford. Frances herself, when fourteen years old, contributed to the *Hymns for Private Devotion, Selected and Original* (1827), a completion by her mother, Bertha Fuller Maitland, of Henry Kirke White's fragment beginning 'Much in sorrow, oft in woe', and this completion was widely accepted for church use. A small volume of her poems was published in 1876 under the title *Rhymes and Chimes*.

Colquhoun was always a keen sportsman and an accurate observer of nature; but in his sympathy for the Scottish highlands' wilder days and for the preservation of endangered fauna, he confessed to 'having sunk the sportsman in the "amateur naturalist"' (Colquhoun, *The Moor and the Loch*, preface to 3rd edn, 1851). During his life he visited nearly every district of Scotland, so that his opportunities for observation were especially favourable. In 1840 he embodied his experiences in *The Moor and the Loch*, which speedily took a high rank among books on Scottish sport. The fourth edition (1878) contained many additions, notably the most valuable portions of some other books written in the meantime: *Rocks and Rivers* (1849); *Salmon Casts and Stray Shots* (1858); and *Sporting Days* (1866). The fifth edition (1880) added an autobiographical preface; two more editions followed by 1888. Besides these works Colquhoun wrote two lectures, 'On the feræ naturæ of the British islands' (deploring the extinction of

Janet Colquhoun, Lady Colquhoun (1781–1846), by Henry Thomas Ryall (after Colvin Smith, 1834)

to educate. She visited the poor and sick among her tenants. In 1818 she turned her attention to female education and established a school of industry for girls, near Rossdhu; Lady Colquhoun taught at the Sunday school attached to this institution. She took a keen interest in other philanthropic and religious schemes, especially in the Luss and Arrochar Bible Society.

In 1820 Lady Colquhoun's health declined, and she was prevented from taking any active share in philanthropic schemes. She then devoted herself to the composition of religious works, the first of which was published anonymously in 1822 under the title of *Despair and Hope*. This was followed by *Thoughts on the Religious Profession* (1823), *Impressions of the Heart* (1825), *The Kingdom of God* (1836), and *The World's Religion* (1839). She allegedly converted her husband to evangelicalism; it was not until after his death, on 3 February 1836, that her name was appended to her books. James Hamilton remarked that her works were: 'like the conversation of their compiler, … genuine and inartificial, spontaneous and heartfelt'. At the time of the Disruption of the established church in 1843, she took great interest in religious politics, throwing herself heart and soul into the Free Church cause. She died at Helensburgh on 21 October 1846, and was buried on the 27th of that month at Luss.

J. A. F. MAITLAND, *rev.* ROSEMARY MITCHELL

Sources J. Hamilton, *Memoir of Lady Colquhoun* (1849) · W. Fraser, *The chiefs of Colquhoun and their country*, 2 vols. (1869) · H. G. Adams, ed., *A cyclopaedia of female biography* (1857) · Burke, *Peerage*
Likenesses H. T. Ryall, stipple (after C. Smith, 1834), BM, NPG [*see illus.*] · stipple and line engraving, NPG

Scottish species due to 'improvement'), and 'On instinct and reason', which were published in 1873 and 1874 respectively. Colquhoun died on 27 May 1885 at his home, 1 Royal Terrace, Edinburgh, after a short illness.

J. A. F. MAITLAND, rev. JULIAN LOCK

Sources J. Colquhoun, The moor and the loch, 5th edn (1880), with autobiographical preface · Boase, Mod. Eng. biog. · Burke, Peerage · W. Fraser, The chiefs of Colquhoun and their country, 2 vols. (1869) · J. Julian, ed., A dictionary of hymnology, rev. edn (1907) · GEC, Baronetage · Walford, County families · private information (1887) · Army List · CGPLA Eng. & Wales (1885)
Archives NL Scot., corresp. with Blackwoods
Wealth at death £7049 10s. 6d.: confirmation, 17 July 1885, CCI · £2042 15s. 4d.: additional estate, 16 Nov 1885, CCI

Colquhoun, John Campbell (1785–1854), writer on animal magnetism, was the third of five sons (there were four daughters) of Sir James Colquhoun of Luss, second baronet (1741–1805), sheriff of Dumbarton and principal clerk of session, and his wife, Mary, daughter of James Falconer. He was born at Edinburgh on 31 January 1785 and was educated mainly at home. In 1804–5 he attended law classes at Edinburgh University. He then studied Roman law at the University of Göttingen, where he acquired a lasting interest in German literature and philosophy. He was called to the Scottish bar in 1806, and in 1815 was appointed sheriff-depute of Dunbartonshire, a post which he held until a few months before his death. An obituary in the Dumbarton Herald spoke of his 'accurate discrimination, and strict and undeviating impartiality'.

Colquhoun's life, however, centred round Edinburgh, where he lived with his sister, Helen, at 10 Melville Street; he never married. His legal duties seem to have left him ample leisure for his literary and philosophical pursuits, and by 1820 he was a fellow of the Royal Society of Edinburgh (he resigned about twenty years later). His particular interest was in animal magnetism (mesmerism), which, though little known in Britain, had been a topic of keen debate in Germany during his student days. Subsequently a medical friend, who wished him to take it up, from time to time sent him the latest French and German publications. After some experimentation and a great deal of reading, Colquhoun undertook a translation, published in 1833, of a report on the subject recently presented to the French Royal Academy of Medicine. To this he added a long introduction. In 1836 he expanded his introduction into a two-volume treatise, Isis revelata, which displayed a knowledge unparalleled in Britain both of the continental mesmeric literature, and of relevant classical and medical texts. He regarded mesmeric 'somnambulism' as closely analogous to ordinary somnambulism. Colquhoun was particularly interested in cases of apparent clairvoyance, which he accepted somewhat uncritically and held to refute materialism.

The publication of Isis shortly preceded an upsurge of British interest in animal magnetism and Colquhoun was soon recognized as a leading authority. An enlarged second edition of Isis came out in 1844. Meanwhile he continued to pursue the subject. He vainly attempted to rouse

medical interest, and in 1839 started a short-lived Journal of Zoomagnetism; in 1843 he wrote a pamphlet attacking 'phrenomesmerism'; in 1845 he published a translation from the German of Arnold Wienholt's lectures on somnambulism, adding a long introduction discussing somnambulic clairvoyance; he had various controversies with James Braid, the pioneer of hypnotism, who disbelieved in a physical animal magnetism, and in 1851 he brought out a History of Magic, Witchcraft and Animal Magnetism, which treated the subject along lines foreshadowed in Isis revelata.

Though a man of great courtesy, Colquhoun was modest and rather reserved. But within his own intimate circle (which included Sir William Hamilton, the philosopher) he was regarded as an agreeable companion and a steady friend. He died at 10 Melville Street, in Edinburgh, on 21 August 1854 and was buried in Dean cemetery, Edinburgh.   ALAN GAULD

Sources W. Fraser, The chiefs of Colquhoun and their country, 1 (1869) · R. P. Gillies, Memoirs of a literary veteran, 3 vols. (1851), vol. 3 · W. Lang, Mesmerism: its history, phenomena, and practice, with reports of cases developed in Scotland (1843) · J. Braid, Magic, witchcraft, animal magnetism and electro-biology …, 3rd edn (1852) · J. Veitch, Memoir of Sir William Hamilton, Bart (1869) · Edinburgh Evening Courant (31 Aug 1854) · Dumbarton Herald (31 Aug 1854) · Burke, Peerage · DNB · parish register (death), 21 Aug 1854, Edinburgh
Archives NL Scot., letters
Wealth at death £8409 17s. 5d.: confirmation, 1854, Scotland

Colquhoun, John Campbell (1803–1870), politician and writer, was born at Killermont, Dunbartonshire, on 23 January 1803, the elder son of Archibald Campbell-*Colquhoun (c.1754–1820), lord clerk register, and his wife, Mary Anne (d. 1833), daughter of William Erskine, Episcopalian minister of Muthill. He was educated at Edinburgh high school and Oriel College, Oxford, where he matriculated in March 1820 and took his BA, with first-class honours, in 1823. On the death of his father in 1820 he inherited Killermont, and in 1821 he also inherited estates at Garscadden from his kinswoman Jean Colquhoun. On 10 September 1827 he married Henrietta Maria Powys (1799–1870), eldest daughter of Thomas Powys, second Baron Lilford. She was to be a strong influence on him, particularly in reinforcing his evangelical inclinations. They had two sons.

Colquhoun began his political career as an advocate of moderate reform. He was first returned to parliament in 1832, representing Dunbartonshire and sitting as a radical. Over the next few years, however, his evangelical convictions led him to join the growing rally in defence of the established churches and hence to change his political loyalties. Between 1834 and 1836 he played a major part in extra-parliamentary agitation in defence of the Church of Ireland, and subsequently campaigned in favour of the maintenance of church rates in England. He did not contest the 1835 general election, but in 1837 was returned for the Kilmarnock burghs, as a tory.

In the late 1830s Colquhoun was admitted to the inner counsels of the Conservative Party, where his staunch protestantism was found consistent with the mood of the moment. At the same time Thomas Chalmers saw him as the potential leader of 'a religious party in Parliament' (Colquhoun MSS, bundle 85, 26 June 1841). Although himself an Episcopalian, Colquhoun supported the causes of evangelicalism and non-intrusion in the Church of Scotland. In the 1841 general election campaign, however, he refused demands to make his support for Peel conditional on the latter agreeing to further the cause of the church's independence. He accordingly lost his seat and, subsequently, desiring above all to see the Church of Scotland strong and united, he was to regard the Disruption in 1843 as a calamity. Thereafter he distanced himself from his Scottish roots.

Although Colquhoun was shortly to be back in the Commons, returned for Newcastle under Lyme at a by-election in 1842, Peel failed to reward his loyalty and left him on the back benches at a juncture when his views were becoming politically less convenient. In 1845 the Maynooth question was the spark which ignited Colquhoun's feelings of personal betrayal and outraged principle. He moved to open revolt against the prime minister, not only opposing him in the house, but also publishing pamphlets denouncing the government's record. In addition he organized the National Club as a rallying point for those who sought a stronger protestant and Anglican basis for politics. Nevertheless, despite his evident ambition, he lacked a sufficiently credible and broad basis of support to become a major player in the post-Peel Conservative Party.

In 1847 Colquhoun, suffering from failing health and political disappointment, decided to take 'refuge in religious politics' and rule 'supreme in Exeter Hall' (Disraeli MSS, A/X/A/13). He retired from parliament and over the next two decades took a prominent role in the National Club and in other Anglican societies committed to the maintenance of protestant interests, notably the Irish Church Missions and, in the 1860s, the Church Association. He also developed his literary and historical interests. As well as several pamphlets on contemporary political and religious questions, he published a historical volume on France and Italy, and a number of biographical works.

Colquhoun was devastated by his wife's death in January 1870, and himself died at home at 8 Chesham Street, London, on 17 April 1870. He was buried at Crockham church, Kent. In his youth he had seemed to be a man with outstanding prospects, but he eventually showed himself lacking in the toughness and breadth of outlook requisite for a successful secular politician. His most significant role was as a key lay leader of Anglican evangelicalism in the generation after the death of William Wilberforce.

JOHN WOLFFE

Sources J. C. Colquhoun, *Memorials of H[enrietta] M[aria] C[olquhoun]* (1870) · J. Wolffe, *The protestant crusade in Great Britain, 1829–1860* (1991) · B. Disraeli, memorandum, Bodl. Oxf., Dep. Hughenden A/X/A/13 · Cultybraggan Estates Office, Comrie, Perthshire, Colquhoun MSS · letter, Colquhoun to Graham, 22 June 1841, BL, Graham MSS, Add. MS 40318, fol. 275 · Burke, *Gen. GB* · Burke, *Peerage* · NA Scot., GD 314/62 [undertaker's bill and legal papers] · *IGI*

Archives Cultybraggan Estates Office, Comrie, Perthshire · NA Scot., letters | Bodl. Oxf., National Club records · Bodl. Oxf., letters to Benjamin Disraeli · U. Southampton L., Shaftesbury diary

Wealth at death under £12,000: probate, 1870 · under £18,000—personalty: Scotland

Colquhoun, Patrick (1745–1820), magistrate and a founder of the Thames police, and his twin, Ann, were born on 14 March 1745 in Dumbarton. Their parents, Adam Colquhoun (1711–*c*.1755), sheriff-substitute and keeper of the register of sasines for Dunbartonshire, and Isabell, *née* Colquhoun, had at least three other children: David (*b*. 1743), Mary (*b*. 1748), and Adam (*b*. 1753). Colquhoun attended Dumbarton grammar school before travelling to Virginia, aged fifteen, to learn the tobacco trade. He returned to Scotland in 1766 and, despite his youth, became a leading Glasgow merchant. He married Janet (*d*. 1810), daughter of James Colquhoun (bailie, later provost of Dumbarton), on 22 July 1775. Six of their seven children were born in Glasgow: Frances (1776); Isabella (1777); James and Adam (1780); Janet Jane (1782); Margaret (1787). The seventh child has not been traced. The family lived in Argyle Street, Glasgow. In 1782, in a somewhat ostentatious display of wealth, Colquhoun built Kelvingrove House (possibly using James Adam as architect) for use as his country residence.

Colquhoun was a prominent and energetic member of Glasgow society. He held a number of offices in the city, served as lord provost from February 1782 to October 1784, and was a founding member and first chairman of Glasgow chamber of commerce. He was active in identifying and encouraging new commercial opportunities to help the city survive the economic dislocation of the American War of Independence. Colquhoun visited London several times to lobby on behalf of the city's businessmen. By 1785 he was acting for British cotton manufacturers in general. Although he found lobbying tedious, writing contemptuously of 'the supineness of the landed interest' and of the disagreeableness of having to deal with men unable to see beyond party politics, he was proud of his achievements, among which he included the creation of a Commons standing committee on trade (Glasgow chamber of commerce MSS, Colquhoun, 9, 14, 21 June 1783; 4, 5, 21 May 1785). Ironically, by 1788 it had become clear that his own business was unable to adapt to new trading conditions. He moved to London intending to create a specialized commercial information and lobbying service (Glasgow chamber of commerce MSS, 'Plan of a public agency in London for commercial affairs', October 1788) and with ambitions to become consul-general to the USA.

In 1792 Colquhoun was appointed, through the influence of Henry Dundas (later Viscount Melville), as a stipendiary magistrate at Worship Street police office, Shoreditch, in London. Anxious to prove his worth, he prepared an analysis of metropolitan crime and ways to prevent it. The basis of his preventive scheme was to introduce an extensive system of regulation of all those aspects of lower-class life that he deemed likely to lead to crime.

Patrick Colquhoun (1745–1820), by Robert Dunkarton, pubd 1802 (after Samuel Medley, exh. RA 1802)

This was a system of police in the eighteenth-century sense of the term: a series of regulations and regulatory agencies for the supervision of the manners, morals, and health of society rather than a body of officers in the way that the term would now be understood.

To Colquhoun, as to so many of his contemporaries, the liquidation of the national debt was a major priority; accordingly his scheme of police was an elaborate one designed not only to regulate social ills and to prevent crime but also to raise revenue. Successive home secretaries were advised that the scheme was poorly drafted, that it threatened civil liberties, that the proposed duties were too high, and that there were procedural difficulties in piloting a bill through parliament that aimed to tax as well as to regulate, but Colquhoun failed to understand any of these objections.

In January 1795 Colquhoun wrote to Dundas, outlining a number of posts that might be suitable for his talents, adding that although 'I am infinitely indebted to your goodness for the letter you did me the honour to write … it would be more consonant to my feelings to enjoy emolument as the price of labour applied usefully for the benefit of the state' (NA Scot., GD 51/6/1029/1). Frustrated by Dundas's refusal even to see him, Colquhoun seems to have concluded that the best way to secure implementation of his proposals (and hence his own advancement) was to make an appeal to public opinion. His paper to Dundas was revised and published anonymously early in

1796 as his *Treatise on the Police of the Metropolis*. Its novel use of statistics added authority to arguments already familiar from the works of earlier writers such as Beccaria and Henry Fielding, and helped it to become an immediate success. Public recognition brought him an honorary LLD from the University of Glasgow, the ability to command a personal interview with the home secretary, and a transfer to a much less demanding post in Westminster. His evidence to the select committee on finance (1798) kept his name before the public. He worked hard to keep up the momentum, producing a pamphlet on the subject of his proposed board of police revenue in 1799 and revising and expanding his *Treatise* through another six editions.

Colquhoun's reputation was bolstered still further by the recognition that he received for his part in creating the Thames police. The initial plan for the Thames police was drawn up by John Harriott, probably in close collaboration with his uncle, John Staples. Harriott was an expert on river crime and, like Colquhoun, a stipendiary magistrate. Colquhoun became involved when he was asked to advise on Harriott's plans by the West India merchants. Final details were settled at a meeting between Colquhoun, Harriott, and Staples in April 1798. Thereafter, it was Colquhoun's 'superior knowledge and clearer insight into the management of obtaining attention to things of this kind' (Harriott, 2.110–11) that secured sufficient private-sector finance for an experimental scheme in the summer of 1798. Colquhoun sought statutory backing for the new force, outlining his proposals in his *Treatise on the Commerce and Police of the River Thames* (1800), but the bill subsequently passed by parliament bore little relation to his suggestions.

Colquhoun craved recognition and bitterly resented what he interpreted as the government's failure to grant him appropriate reward for his services. He treasured several gifts of silver plate that were presented to him by organizations that did appreciate his efforts, instructing his children to keep them as perpetual family heirlooms (some of these are now owned by Glasgow chamber of commerce). Within his own circle of family and friends (who included Jeremy Bentham and John Lettsom) he inspired respect, admiration, and genuine affection, but even Colquhoun's admirers admitted that he was pompous and prone to 'hyperbolic notions' (Holloway, 182–6; BL, Add. MS 33107, Pelham MSS, fol. 308). He was convinced of his own expertise, once even arguing a point of law with the law officers (PRO, TS 11/931/3302). His famous (though possibly apocryphal) admission that 'Even I myself have made a mistake' was relished in Glasgow long after his departure from that city (*Glasgow Ancient and Modern*). He was so unpopular in Shoreditch that in 1794 he was targeted by rioters. Colquhoun claimed that the attack was aimed at the magistracy in general, but the circulation of handbills identifying 'Informers, spies and agents to Mr Justice Colquhoun' suggests otherwise (PRO, HO 42/22, Colquhoun, 26 Nov 1792; HO 42/26, Colquhoun, 25 Oct 1793; HO 42/33, Colquhoun to Nepean, 21 Aug 1794).

In 1802, in yet another attempt to secure preferment, he

prepared a lengthy account of his public services (PRO, HO 42/66, 'Statement of the public services of Patrick Colquhoun esq.', 1 Sept 1802), which became the basis of an adulatory memoir by his son-in-law, G. D. Yeats (Iatros). His posthumous reputation rested partly on this memoir and partly on a misunderstanding of his characteristically eighteenth-century use of the word 'police'. His reputation suffered in the later twentieth century as historians became more critical of the historiography of police reform and more aware of the untapped archival sources that can be used to enrich its study. It is now known that the Home Office had other sources of advice on issues of policing, that Colquhoun's reform proposals were considered unrealistic and unworkable, and that his criticisms not only exaggerated the faults of existing systems but also caused considerable resentment among his colleagues. The wider impact of his writings, however, and the extent to which they shaped long-term changes in public opinion still remain a matter for speculation.

The passing of the Thames Police Act marked the beginning of Colquhoun's disengagement from police reform. He continued to interest himself in measures to deal with the problems of the labouring poor, including the relief of indigence, the provision of a cheap system of elementary education, and emigration schemes, regularly producing promotional tracts to popularize his causes. He retired from office in 1818 and died in Westminster on 25 April 1820 of a 'schirrous stomach' and was buried at St Margaret's, Westminster.   RUTH PALEY

Sources Iatros [G. D. Yeats], *A biographical sketch of the life and writings of Patrick Colquhoun, esq.* (1818) · Mitchell L., Glas., Glasgow chamber of commerce MSS · NA Scot., Melville Castle muniments, GD 51 · U. Nott. L., Portland MSS · BL, Pelham MSS · PRO, HO 42, HO 65, TS 11 · R. Holloway, *Some strictures on the characters of the most prominent practising attornies* (1805) · J. Harriott, *Struggles through life* (1815) · *Glasgow ancient and modern* (1872) · W. Fraser, *The chiefs of Colquhoun and their country*, 2 vols. (1869) · Chambers, *Scots.* (1835) · bap. reg. Scot. · m. reg. Scot. · *IGI* · directories · monumental inscription, St Margaret's, Westminster
Archives LMA, corresp. and papers | BL, corresp. with Lord Grenville, Add. MS 58998 · Mitchell L., Glas., Glasgow chamber of commerce MSS · NA Scot., letters to Henry Dundas · NA Scot., Melville Castle muniments · U. Nott. L., Portland MSS
Likenesses R. Dunkarton, mezzotint, pubd 1802 (after S. Medley, exh. RA 1802), AM Oxf., BM [*see illus.*] · H. Meyer, stipple, 1818 (after S. Drummond), BM, NPG; repro. in *European Magazine* (1818) · J. Green, watercolour drawing, NPG · oils (in middle age), Glasgow chamber of commerce
Wealth at death £16,000: PRO, death duty registers, IR 26/817

Colquhoun, Sir Patrick Macchombaich (1815–1891), diplomatist and legal writer, was born on 13 April 1815, the eldest son of James Colquhoun (1780–1855) and grandson of Patrick *Colquhoun. His father was chargé d'affaires of the king of Saxony, the duke of Oldenburg, and of the Hanseatic republics, Lübeck, Bremen, and Hamburg; he was also political agent for many of the West Indian islands, a knight of the Ottoman empire, and commander of the Saxon order of merit. Patrick entered Westminster School on 25 May 1826, left in August 1832, and was admitted pensioner of St John's College, Cambridge, on 27 February 1833. He graduated BA in 1837, MA in 1844, and LLD

in 1851; he was also LLD of Heidelberg (1838). On 1 May 1834 he was admitted student of the Inner Temple, and on 4 May 1838 he was called to the bar; he became QC in 1868, bencher of his inn in 1869, and treasurer in 1888. In 1843 he married Katherine, daughter of M. de St Vitalis. They had at least one child, Eliza, who married the orientalist James William Redhouse in 1888.

Through his father's connection with the Hanse towns, Colquhoun was in 1840 appointed their plenipotentiary to conclude commercial treaties with Turkey, Persia, and Greece. These duties occupied him for four years, and on his return to England in 1844 he joined the home circuit. In 1845 he was elected a fellow of the Royal Society of Literature, during Hallam's presidency; he was placed on the council in 1846, was made librarian in 1852, vice-president in 1869, and president in succession to the duke of Albany in 1886. During his residence in England he wrote a substantial work in four large volumes on Roman civil law (1849–54). In 1857 he was appointed aulic councillor to the king of Saxony, and he was standing counsel to the Saxon legation until it was abolished by the war of 1866.

In 1858 Sir Edward Bulwer Lytton, then colonial secretary, appointed Colquhoun a member of the supreme court of justice in the Ionian Islands, and in 1861 he became chief justice of the court, and was knighted. In the following year the high commissioner, Sir Henry Knight Storks, dismissed two Ionian judges. Colquhoun took their part, and in 1864, after the cession of the islands to Greece, he published a bitter attack on Storks. Storks's action was, however, upheld by the Colonial Office.

Between 1875 and 1878 Colquhoun published two works on legal subjects and one on foreign affairs, provoked by events in Bulgaria. In 1886 he was elected honorary fellow of St John's College, Cambridge. He died at his chambers in King's Bench Walk, 41 the Temple, on 18 May 1891; he was survived by his wife.

Colquhoun was a man of remarkable linguistic attainments; he spoke most of the tongues and many of the dialects of Europe, was a thorough classical scholar and a jurist. He received orders of merit from the sultan of Turkey, the kings of Greece and of Saxony, and the duke of Oldenburg. He was also, like his brother, James du Colquhoun (d. 1891), who founded the Cercle Nautique at Cannes, a noted oarsman. In 1837 (one source says 1835) he won the Wingfield sculls, which made him amateur champion of England, and in the same year he founded the Colquhoun sculls for the benefit of the Lady Margaret Boat Club; in 1842 the prize was thrown open to the university. In 1837 he also rowed at Henley in a race between St John's College, Cambridge, and Queen's College, Oxford, the head boats of the respective universities, and for many years he was secretary of the Leander Boat Club.

A. F. POLLARD, rev. CATHERINE PEASE-WATKIN

Sources *The Eagle*, 16 (1891), 567–72 · P. Colquhoun, 'Sir Patrick Colquhoun on the "Sculls"', *The Eagle*, 14 (1887), 228–30 · *The Times* (19 May 1891) · H. R. Luard, ed., *Graduati Cantabrigienses*, 7th edn (1884) · J. Foster, *Men-at-the-bar: a biographical hand-list of the members of the various inns of court*, 2nd edn (1885) · J. Foster, *The peerage, baronetage, and knightage of the British empire for 1880*, [2 pts] [1880] ·

G. F. R. Barker and A. H. Stenning, eds., *The Westminster School register from 1764 to 1883* (1892) • W. B. Woodgate, *Boating* (1888) • *Men and women of the time* (1891) • private information (1901) • Venn, *Alum. Cant.*

Archives LMA, papers | Herts. ALS, letters to Lord Lytton
Wealth at death £8873 7s. 0d.: resworn probate, Nov 1892, *CGPLA Eng. & Wales* (1891)

Colquhoun, Robert (1914–1962), painter, was born on 20 December 1914 at Kilmarnock, Ayrshire, the eldest child of Robert Colquhoun, an engineering fitter, and his wife, Janet Candlish. He was educated at Loanhead primary school and then transferred to Kilmarnock Academy in 1926 where his artistic ability was soon observed by James Lyle, his determined and dedicated art teacher. Colquhoun's father, responding to the severe economic pressures of the time, arranged for Robert to leave school at the age of fourteen to begin an engineering apprenticeship. On learning of the boy's departure, Lyle was concerned enough to persuade two wealthy benefactors to fund his return to school and prepare, with eventual success, for a scholarship to the Glasgow School of Art, which he entered possibly in 1932 but most probably in 1933. Here he met Robert MacBryde [see below], with whom he formed a tender and ultimately inseparable relationship.

Robert MacBryde (1913–1966), painter, was born on 5 December 1913 at Weevers Vennel, Maybole, Ayrshire, the eldest child of John McBride and his wife, Agnes McKay. MacBryde's background was more humble than Colquhoun's. His father's meagre wage as an unskilled hide stripper in a tannery was supplemented by that of his mother, who sold reject fabric scraps from local mills. Having left school at fourteen, MacBryde found menial employment in a boot factory and a grocer's shop before entering the Glasgow School of Art at a similar time to Colquhoun.

While at art school Colquhoun and MacBryde were perceived as talented and conscientious students who, nevertheless—probably to obscure the intensity of their relationship—distanced themselves from the college's social life. Having taken studio accommodation opposite the school, they settled into a life of hard-working domesticity. Ian Fleming, their tutor and later a close friend, painted a large portrait of the two students in their Renfrew Street digs. He and Hugh Crawford, another influential teacher, directed their attention to French painting from the impressionists onwards. Both of the Roberts, as they became affectionately known, were especially influenced by Degas. Dedication to their work won them prizes for drawing and painting, enabling them to visit France on several college excursions. In 1938, having completed their studies, they were awarded post-diploma scholarships to study at the Patrick Allan Fraser School, near Arbroath, Angus, under the expert, but irritatingly dogmatic, tutelage of James Cowie.

Facing uncertain futures, both students had applied for Glasgow's much-coveted annual travelling scholarship. Colquhoun was the chosen recipient but, owing to concern that this might separate the unique working relationship, the chairman of the school's governors, Sir John

Robert Colquhoun (1914–1962), self-portrait, c.1940

Richmond, personally donated an equal sum to MacBryde, enabling the Roberts to tour Europe together for an indefinite period. They travelled through France, Italy, Belgium, and the Netherlands, visiting museums and galleries and continuing to paint and draw, occasionally under formal tuition such as at the Académie Julian in Paris, where, for a small fee, students attended life-drawing classes. Suddenly, it seemed, they could live together openly without the secrecy and restraint necessitated by Scottish puritanism. Shortly before war with Germany was declared in September 1939, the British government's call for all nationals in Europe to return to the United Kingdom prompted the Roberts' grudging return home.

Back in Kilmarnock, working from a shed in Colquhoun's grandparents' garden, the Roberts mounted an exhibition of works for sale, which gave them some much needed but short-lived income. Demoralized and in ill health, they maintained a penurious existence while anticipating the inevitable call up. Colquhoun reluctantly trained as an art teacher before being conscripted into the Royal Army Medical Corps in July 1940. MacBryde, however, was exempted from military service when diagnosed as tubercular.

Distraught at their separation, MacBryde followed Colquhoun to Edinburgh and Leeds, living in lodgings near the military camps and lobbying on Colquhoun's behalf to procure a war artist's commission with the ultimate hope of securing his release. A mutual friend introduced MacBryde to the author and editor Cyril Connolly, and to Peter Watson, the wealthy art patron with whom Connolly was planning to found the magazine *Horizon*. Proffering help, Watson offered MacBryde accommodation at his luxurious London apartment. Colquhoun, his mental and physical health deteriorating, suffered a collapse in February 1941 and was medically discharged from the army. Pausing only to collect a few belongings from Kilmarnock, he immediately set out to join MacBryde in London during the height of the blitz.

Initially Watson's influence was considerable. Not only were many established artists friends of his, including Ben Nicholson and Graham Sutherland (several of whose works adorned his walls), but he also introduced them to his younger painter–protégés John Craxton, Lucian Freud, and John Minton, soon to become friends of the Roberts. Following his arrival in London, Colquhoun suffered a creative block, while MacBryde relentlessly attempted to secure a foothold in London's art world. During an autumn sojourn in Worcestershire, a re-energized Colquhoun painted three landscapes influenced by Samuel Palmer, while MacBryde, affronted by English indifference to Scottish culture, began planning a show of work by Scottish artists, including their own.

The critically successful exhibition 'Six Scottish Artists' opened in May 1942 at the prestigious Lefevre Gallery, and this began a fertile association between the gallery and the two Roberts, who exhibited there together in 1943, 1944, and 1949, with Colquhoun showing separately in 1947 and 1950. In 1943 the critic Robert Melville described Colquhoun as 'the most promising young painter England [sic] has produced for a considerable time' (The Listener, 17 June 1943, 721). In 1947 Wyndham Lewis, reviewing Colquhoun's work, stated that he was 'recognised as one of the best—perhaps the best—of the young artists' while maintaining that Colquhoun's and MacBryde's work was 'almost identical' and 'one artistic organism' (The Listener, 13 Feb 1947).

After their arrival in London the Roberts' early success afforded them an introduction to a broad spectrum of the capital's artistic community. Both were seen as alluring, charismatic figures whose engaging personalities and physical appearances, though distinctly different, quickly charmed most of those with whom they came into contact. MacBryde, the shorter of the two, exhibited an extrovert, animated, and gregarious personality that perfectly complemented the withdrawn, and occasionally menacing, animus of the tall and saturnine Colquhoun. Their success facilitated a move to 77 Bedford Gardens in Kensington, a studio apartment which rapidly became a noisily boisterous venue for a bohemian coterie. Friends attending their regular weekend soirées included Francis Bacon, Dylan Thomas, and Michael Ayrton. The painter John Minton briefly lived with the Roberts for a time but growing emotional tension forced his departure.

In 1943 the Polish émigré artist Jankel Adler entered the Roberts' lives, having occupied the studio above theirs. A friend of Picasso and Georges Braque and a teaching colleague of Paul Klee, Adler was a living link with the European cosmopolitanism from which the war had isolated the Roberts. His profoundly metaphysical approach to art endowed him with a guru-like status. He encouraged both men to paint from imagination, not observation, advice heeded especially by Colquhoun. Prior to meeting Adler, their chosen subjects had been landscape and still life, but, in future, MacBryde would introduce figures into his increasingly formal still-life compositions while Colquhoun concentrated almost exclusively on the figure. Although the Roberts were perceived as pivotal to British neo-romanticism, European influences on their work, strengthened by seeing the large post-war Picasso exhibition in London, helped them to avoid some of the mawkish excesses of this style. Braque's growing influence on MacBryde's work can be clearly identified as he gradually moved away from the painterly still lifes of the early 1940s to the formally decorative compositions of later years.

Oil paint had been the Roberts' preferred medium since art school days and was to remain so throughout their artistic careers, though both drew extensively with pencil and pen. As their creative repertory developed, they began to use other media such as lithography and monoprinting. Colquhoun, always more artistically daring than MacBryde, also worked in watercolours, chalk, and crayon. Both were adept colourists. MacBryde, as befitted his subject matter of still lifes (mostly fruit and vegetables), employed an evocatively Mediterranean palette, counterposing Hellenic blues with terracottas, lemon yellows, and pimento reds. Colquhoun's colours, though never sombre, were more muted: acidic yellows were contrasted against bottle greens and burgundy reds—'the colours of tartan', as they were once described.

Colquhoun's work particularly, with its stylized figures frozen in hieratic gestures, personified and appealed to the pervasive angst engendered by the war. Wyndham Lewis, his admirer, described it as existential and seemingly to have 'a grave dug behind all … [the] canvasses' (The Listener, 23 Oct 1947, 736). Two paintings of 1946, Woman with a Bird Cage and The Fortune Teller, represent Colquhoun's creative zenith. His artistic influence can be seen in the work of several contemporary artists such as William Scott, Michael Rothenstein, Keith Vaughan, and, more specifically, John Minton. Although some of Colquhoun's subjects, such as The Beggar or Grieving Women, might imply sentimentalism, the dry passion and puritanical dignity of his subjects confounds any such criticism. His work was dominated by female figures which were often inspired by family memories, though paintings such as The Two Students and The Lovers are thinly disguised, imaginative portraits of the Roberts themselves. Following a visit to Ireland, Colquhoun experimented with monoprinting, a rarely used medium which he made very much his own. By 1948 successful exhibitions, appearances in fashionable magazines, and the purchase by the Museum of Modern Art in New York of a major work by each of them made the Roberts' success appear boundless. In reality, however, MacBryde's compulsive jealousy was endangering their relationship. Alcohol consumption, initially a convivial pursuit, was now a chronic necessity, and, more ominously, reviews of Colquhoun's work signalled a possible waning of the emotional infusion apparent in earlier, acclaimed works.

About this time the Roberts were evicted from their studio home. Two eccentric sisters, Frances Byng-Stamper and Caroline Lucas, offered them accommodation at Miller's Press, their print studio in Lewes, Sussex. This initiated for the two men a fruitful period of lithographic printmaking. Colquhoun was commissioned to illustrate a book on Italy to be written by their friend, the poet George Barker; however, the book was never published. While they were abroad, in 1949, Duncan MacDonald, their champion at the Lefevre Gallery, died. When Colquhoun returned he held an exhibition of work of Italian subjects. The show proved a failure and the gallery terminated the relationship. The Roberts never again established a similar partnership with a gallery, though the Redfern spasmodically exhibited their works throughout the 1950s.

Homeless again, the Roberts were housed by the writer Elizabeth Smart at Tilty Mill, her country home in Essex, where they acted as surrogate parents to her four children. Out of favour and alcoholic, their decline seemed inevitable. At Kenneth Clark's suggestion, however, they were commissioned to design sets and costumes for *Donald of the Burthens*, a ballet based on a Scottish myth and choreographed by Léonide Massine. Their designs were favourably reviewed, but Colquhoun's later attempt at theatrical work for a production of *King Lear*, starring Michael Redgrave, elicited a tepid response. Embittered by the lack of a public commission for the Festival of Britain in 1951, Colquhoun practically forsook painting in favour of works on paper. However, in 1953 he produced *Figures in a Farmyard* (Scottish National Gallery of Modern Art, Edinburgh), possibly his largest and most complex painting, and a work of powerful creativity and intense expressionism.

In 1954 Smart, unable to continue to fund the Roberts' inebriated lifestyle, abandoned Tilty, rendering the Roberts homeless once more. Adrift, they moved from one cheap lodging to another. An honourable attempt to revive Colquhoun's stagnating talent was made in 1958 by Bryan Robertson, director of the Whitechapel Art Gallery, when he offered to stage a large retrospective. Although the exhibition was respectfully reviewed, Colquhoun's attempt to produce several fashionably large canvases for it was ill received. In 1959 the Roberts again lived in East Anglia, at Kersey in Suffolk, where a short television film was made about them by Ken Russell. Ultimately, the lure of Soho pub life proved irresistible, and they relocated in London, where they were increasingly viewed as two tiresome and occasionally violent alcoholics whose moment of glory was long past. Their last joint exhibition was held in 1959 at the Kaplan Gallery, demonstrating that, given the opportunity, both of them were capable of working assiduously. Colquhoun's health had suffered from years of alcoholic excess and self-neglect, and in the early hours of the morning of 20 September 1962, while working in rooms above the Museum Street Gallery for an exhibition shortly to be held there, he suffered a heart attack and died in MacBryde's arms. MacBryde insisted that the exhibition should be held, and when it opened a fortnight

later the work, mostly monotypes, testified to Colquhoun's technical virtuosity and emotional profundity. He was buried in his home town of Kilmarnock.

Generously funded by Francis Bacon, a distraught MacBryde visited Spain before moving to Ireland, where, drifting aimlessly, he worked briefly as a barman and art teacher, latterly sharing an apartment with the poet Patrick Kavanagh. On the night of 6 May 1966, as he left a Dublin pub, he was knocked down in the street in a road accident and died as a result of his injuries. Like Colquhoun, his body was returned to Scotland and he was buried in his birthplace of Maybole. Their friend George Barker wrote a moving eulogy for MacBryde, as he had done earlier for Colquhoun.

Works by Colquhoun and MacBryde are included in many public collections throughout Great Britain. In addition to the Museum of Modern Art in New York, Colquhoun is represented in other American galleries, as well as in Canada and Australia. The National Portrait Gallery in London has a self-portrait in pencil of Colquhoun and a portrait of MacBryde. Other self-portraits, and portraits the artists did of each other, are in the Scottish National Gallery of Modern Art and the Scottish National Portrait Gallery in Edinburgh. Ian Fleming's large double portrait of the Roberts as art students is owned by the Glasgow School of Art.

ROGER BRISTOW

Sources J. Rothenstein, *Modern English painters*, [3rd edn], 3 vols. (1984) · R. Melville, 'June art exhibitions', *The Listener* (17 June 1943), 721 [review] · [W. Lewis], 'Round the art galleries', *The Listener* (13 Feb 1947) [review] · [W. Lewis], 'Round the art exhibitions', *The Listener* (23 Oct 1947), 736 [review] · *Robert Colquhoun* (1958) [exhibition catalogue, Whitechapel Gallery, London, March–May 1958] · private information (2004) · *Secretary and treasurer's correspondence, 1940*, Glasgow School of Art, Glasgow
Likenesses R. Colquhoun, pen and ink, 1938 (Robert MacBryde), NPG · J. Laurie, double portrait, pencil and chalk drawing, 1939 (with Robert MacBryde), Scot. NPG · R. MacBryde, black chalk drawing, 1939, Scot. NPG · R. Colquhoun, self-portrait, c.1940, Scot. NPG [*see illus.*] · R. Colquhoun, self-portrait, pencil, NPG · I. Fleming, double portrait, Glasgow School of Art

Colson, John (1680–1759), mathematician and translator, was born in Lichfield, the eldest of six children of Francis Coleson (or Colson), vicar-choral of Lichfield Cathedral, and his wife, Elizabeth. He was the nephew and godson of John Strype, the ecclesiastical historian. He attended Lichfield grammar school and on 26 May 1699 matriculated at Christ Church, Oxford, but left without taking a degree. His first publication, 'The universal resolution of cubic and biquadratic equations' (*PTRS*, 5, 1670), describes a method using geometric constructions of circles and parabolas to solve third and fourth degree polynomial equations. This monograph was appended to Newton's *Arithmeticae universalis* (1732). In 1709 Colson was appointed master of the new mathematical school founded by Joseph Williamson at Rochester in Kent, and he was elected fellow of the Royal Society on 11 June 1713. On 10 September 1724 he was appointed vicar of the parish church at Chalk near Gravesend.

In 1726 Colson published his 'Account of negativo-affirmative arithmetic' (*PTRS*, vol. 34), describing an innovative method for representing integers using positive and negative digits and how to add, subtract, multiply, and divide using his two-way numerical notation. He collaborated with the Revd Samuel D'Oyly, vicar of St Nicholas's in Rochester, in producing the *Chronological Dictionary of Rev. Father Dom Augustin Calmet* (3 vols., 1732), a translation from the original French. The work reveals Colson's interest in arithmetic, calculations, tables, and measurement. In 1736 he published 'The construction and use of spherical maps' (*PTRS*, vol. 39). The treatise dealt with a mapping problem and recommended the use of cylinders to project from spheres onto planar maps. His interest in geography led to the invention of the 'British hemisphere', a map of the habitable world confined to a hemisphere with London located at the top.

Most of his life Colson was employed as a translator by booksellers. *The Method of Fluxions and Infinite Series* (1736), the first complete English translation of Newton's 1671 untitled manuscript on fluxions, helped build Colson's reputation as a scholar. In order to temper the conciseness of Newton's style and make Newton's works more accessible to both mathematician and non-mathematician alike he added extensive explanatory notes.

On 23 April 1728 Colson was elected a member of Emmanuel College, Cambridge, and granted a master's degree by George II. In 1737 Gilbert Walmsley, registrar of the ecclesiastical court at Lichfield, wrote to Colson recommending Samuel Johnson and David Garrick to his care and encouragement, and subsequently Garrick studied for a few months at Rochester. Two years later Colson resigned his headmastership at the Rochester school. As a teacher and administrator his record was not impressive: he was characterized as too concerned with his own 'speculations to have much interest in the efforts of young pupils to master the first principles of mathematics' (Flower, 31).

After leaving the Rochester school Colson was admitted to Sidney Sussex College, Cambridge, where on 11 March 1739 he was appointed the college's first Taylor lecturer. Two months later, on the death of Nicholas Saunderson, he was elected fifth Lucasian professor in preference to the mathematician Abraham De Moivre. Colson used his influence and skills to help publish Saunderson's *Elements of Algebra* the following year, and appended an explanation of Saunderson's palpable arithmetic, a device with which Saunderson, who was blind, used to perform intricate arithmetic calculations. He also assisted in the publication of Saunderson's *Method of Fluxions* (1751) and an abridged edition of his *Elements of Algebra* (1756).

As Lucasian professor, Colson was a member of the board of longitude when it recommended financial assistance to John Harrison to complete a third chronometer. William Cole, the antiquary, wrote that Colson 'was a plain, honest man, of great industry and assiduity, but the University was much disappointed in its expectations of a professor that was to give credit to it by his lectures' (Cole MSS, BL, Add. MS 5866, 3).

In 1744 Colson published *Elements of Natural Philosophy*, translated from the Latin work of Pieter Musschenbroek,

and in 1752, *Lectures in Experimental Philosophy*, from Jean Antoine Nollet's original. He then became captivated by Maria Agnesi's *Instituzioni analitiche ad uso della gioventu italiana* (1748). He learned Italian in order to translate the work, prepared it for press, drew up a proposal to finance the project by subscription, and wrote an introduction and an outline entitled 'A plan of the lady's system of analytics', but the work was not published during his lifetime. A mistranslation by Colson of 'versed sine' gave rise to a curve bearing the name 'witch of Agnesi'. In 1801, at his own expense, Francis Maseres, with the editorial assistance of John Hellins, published Colson's translation. Colson died in Cambridge on 16 December 1759 and at the time of his death held the position of rector of Lockington in Yorkshire.   JAMES J. TATTERSALL

Sources DNB · D. E. L. Flower, *A short history of Sir John Williamson's mathematical school, Rochester, 1701–1951* (1951) · H. C. Kennedy, 'The witch of Agnesi—exorcised', *Mathematics Teacher*, 62 (1969), 480–82 · G. Borlase, ed., *Cantabrigienses graduati … usque ad annum 1787* (1787) · BL, Cole MSS, Add. MS 5866, 3 · Emmanuel College, Cambridge, admission records, col. 3.2 · Foster, *Alum. Oxon.* · E. Hasted, *The history and topographical survey of the county of Kent*, 1 (1778), 521 · Nichols, *Lit. anecdotes*, 8.467n. · Sidney Sussex College, Cambridge, register, 2.147 · N. Tildesley, *Lichfield Cathedral register* (1974), 146–7 · Venn, *Alum. Cant.* · E. Waring, BL, Newcastle, Hardwick and Cole MSS, Add. MS 3290, fol. 109 · E. Hillman, 'John Colson', *Colson News*, 2 (1985), 75–8

Likenesses J. Wollaston, oils, 1741, Old Schools, Cambridge · oils, 1741; formerly at Sidney Sussex College, Cambridge, 1951

Colson, Lancelot. *See* Coelson, Lancelot (1627–1687?).

Colston, Edward (1636–1721), merchant and philanthropist, was born on 2 November 1636 in Temple Street, Bristol, the eldest of probably eleven children (six boys and five girls are known) of William Colston (1608–1681), a merchant, and his wife, Sarah, *née* Batten (d. 1701). His father had served an apprenticeship with Richard Aldworth, one of the wealthiest Bristol merchants of the early Stuart period, and had prospered as a merchant. A royalist and an alderman, William Colston was removed from his office by order of parliament in 1645 after Prince Rupert surrendered the city to the roundhead forces. Until that point Edward Colston had been brought up in Bristol and probably at Winterbourne, south Gloucestershire, where his father had an estate.

The Colston family moved to London during the English civil war. Little is known about Edward Colston's education, though it is possible that he was a private pupil at Christ's Hospital. In 1654 he was apprenticed to the London Mercers' Company for eight years. By 1672 he was shipping goods from London, and the following year he was enrolled in the Mercers' Company. He soon built up a lucrative mercantile business, trading with Spain, Portugal, Italy, and Africa. Much of his wealth is thought to have been made in buying and selling slaves. In 1680 he became a member of the Royal African Company and subsequently sat on a number of their committees.

During the 1680s Colston began to take an active interest in his native city, where his parents had resettled. In 1682 he made a loan to the Bristol corporation. In 1683 he visited his fatally ill brother Thomas in the city; on this occasion he became a member of the Society of Merchant Venturers and a burgess. After Thomas's death in 1684 he inherited a mercantile business in Small Street and also became a partner in a sugar refinery at St Peter's Churchyard. He seems to have lived in Bristol for a while, but by 1689 he had taken up residence at Mortlake, Surrey, which was his base for the rest of his life. He continued to engage in overseas trade, mainly in London ventures, and made substantial business profits.

Though there is no record of a further visit by him to Bristol until 1700, Colston in middle age became one of the most famous philanthropic benefactors to his native city. In the 1690s he founded and endowed almshouses in King Street and on St Michael's Hill. He also endowed Queen Elizabeth's Hospital, a school for boys, and was instrumental in helping the Merchant Venturers to found Colston's Boys' School, which opened in 1710. Two years later he donated money for a school in Temple parish to educate and clothe forty poor boys. He gave money to other charity schools in Bristol and provided funds for the embellishment of several of the city's churches, including Temple, St Mary Redcliffe, St Werburgh, All Saints, and Bristol Cathedral. His munificence also extended to other parts of the country, and he gave benefactions to churches, hospitals, workhouses, and almshouses in London, Surrey, Devon, and Lancashire. But these did not match the extent of his charitable gifts to Bristol.

Colston was a strong tory and high-churchman who attended daily service at the cathedral when he was staying in Bristol. An opponent of Catholicism, dissent, and whiggism, he insisted that the boys at Colston's School should be Anglicans and that they be prepared for apprenticeships. He laid down strict conditions for his public charities, and founded a series of Lenten lectures in 1710 for which he chose the subjects. He was elected a member of the SPCK in 1709. In October 1710 he was returned as an MP for Bristol, but he took little active part in parliament and did not seek re-election after the dissolution that occurred with Queen Anne's death.

An obstinate man who set restrictions to his charitable donations, Colston remained a bachelor. He retired from business in 1708 and died on 11 October 1721 at his home in Mortlake. His public charities amounted to nearly £71,000 and he bequeathed £100,000 to his relatives. He left detailed instructions for his funeral: his body was carried in a hearse from London to Bristol, and then accompanied by people who had benefited from his Bristol charities to his burial on 27 October amid much pomp and ceremony at All Saints' Church. The effigy on his tomb was executed by Rysbrack from Richardson's portrait of him in the Council House, Bristol.

Colston has been remembered in Bristol since his death. His memory was celebrated for many years by the Colston or 'Parent' Society, founded in 1726; by the Dolphin Society, set up by the tories in 1749; by the Grateful Society, founded in 1758, which had no political affiliation; and by the Anchor Society, founded by the whigs in 1769. Celebrating Colston's memory was part of the civic ritual of Georgian Bristol, the anniversary of his birth becoming

virtually a public holiday after the 1720s. It still serves as a time for raising large donations, which are used for charitable purposes. Many of his foundations flourish today, notably the Bristol schools he established. A bronze statue of him stands in Colston Avenue, and the philanthropist is also honoured by the city's chief concert venue, the Colston Hall, and various streets that are named after him.

KENNETH MORGAN

Sources H. J. Wilkins, *Edward Colston (1636–1721 AD): a chronological account of his life and work together with an account of the Colston societies and memorials in Bristol* (1920) • T. Garrard, *Edward Colston, the philanthropist*, ed. S. G. Tovey (1852) • J. Latimer, *The annals of Bristol in the seventeenth century* (1900) • J. Latimer, *The annals of Bristol in the eighteenth century* (1893) • B. D. G. Little, *The city and county of Bristol: a study of Atlantic civilisation* (1954) • P. McGrath, *The merchant venturers of Bristol: a history of the Society of Merchant Venturers of the city of Bristol from its origin to the present day* (1975) • J. F. Nichols and J. Taylor, *Bristol past and present*, 4 vols. (1881), vol. 3 • J. Evans, *A chronological outline of the history of Bristol* (1824) • *DNB* • will, PRO, PROB 11/582, sig. 236; PROB 11/586, sig. 168 • K. Morgan, *Edward Colston and Bristol* (1999)

Likenesses G. Kneller, portrait, 1693, St Bartholomew's Hospital, London • J. Richardson, oils, 1722, Bristol council house • J. M. Rysbrack, marble tomb effigy, 1728, All Saints' Church, Bristol • G. Kneller, portrait, Society of Merchant Venturers, Bristol • G. Vertue, engraving (after J. Richardson), BM, NPG • bronze statue, Colston Avenue, Bristol • portrait, Colston Boys' School, Bristol

Wealth at death approx. £71,000 donated to public charities; £100,000 bequeathed to relatives: *DNB*; Evans, *Chronological outline*

Colt, Henry Shapland [Harry] (1869–1951), golf course architect, was born on 4 August 1869, in Bishopwood House, Highgate, when his first name was given as Henry (though he was always known as Harry), the son of George Nathaniel Colt, a barrister, and his wife Georgiana Ellen Bruce. He was educated at Monkton Combe School and at Clare College, Cambridge (1887–90), where he read law and graduated BA in 1890. He first began to play golf during the summer holiday of 1880 when, as 'a tall red-haired schoolboy', he hit a ball among the lamp-posts, ditches, and washing lines of the common at Malvern Wells, the original course of the Worcestershire Golf Club (Colt and Alison, ix). He played for Cambridge against Oxford in 1889 and captained the team the following year. With his great friend John Low he helped found the Oxford and Cambridge Golfing Society, and was a member of its convivial early touring sides. After leaving Cambridge he joined the Royal and Ancient club: he won the jubilee vase in 1891 and 1893, played four times in the amateur championships (he reached the semi-final at Hoylake in 1906), and made a single international appearance, for England against Scotland in 1908. From 1897 he was a member of the Royal and Ancient rules of golf committee.

Colt began his working life as a solicitor and in 1893 moved to Hastings, where he practised with the firm Sayer and Colt. In April 1894 he married Charlotte Laura Dewar (1864–1948), younger daughter of the Revd David E. Dewar. They afterwards lived at The Priory, St Margaret's Road, St Leonards. Colt began his architectural career as an amateur at Rye Golf Club, where, as captain, he laid out the course. He was honorary secretary at Rye (1896–9) and was still overseeing tee construction there when, in 1901, the Sunningdale club advertised for its first secretary. Colt was impressively qualified for the post, to which he was appointed in July, and he moved to Ascot. He proved a popular secretary at Sunningdale, though he was a hard taskmaster with an 'austere, authoritarian front': his maxim was 'the member is always right' (Hawtree, 37).

It was at Sunningdale that Colt began the transition to professional golf course designer. The burgeoning of golf clubs on the sandy heath lands around London at the end of the nineteenth century led to a corresponding growth in golf course design and, alongside Herbert Fowler and J. F. Abercromby, Colt became one of the leading architects of the day. He was painstaking in his approach to detail and saw his commissions through from pegging out to the opening day. He had a special reverence for the old course at St Andrews, the layout of which influenced his work. Without destroying the natural beauty of a site he aimed to create courses that were challenging and exciting to golfers of differing levels of skill. He gave advice about the maintenance of the old and new courses at St Andrews, where he built the Eden course (1914); he also created Stoke Poges (1908), Swinley Forest (1910), and St George's Hill (1913). Before the First World War he made two extended trips to North America, where he built the Toronto golf course (1912) and assisted George Crump in the construction of the famous Pine valley course at Clementon, New Jersey.

As a designer Colt was aware of the social tensions arising in England from the great expansion of golf as a middle-class game. In cases where objections from local residents were likely, he saw 'an instrumental value in encouraging some key artisans to play', and in some places working men's clubs were established under the auspices of parent bodies (Lowerson, 142). But this arrangement did nothing to challenge the social distinctions that were already entrenched in the game. And Colt's own paternalistic attitude was apparent in a series of articles that he contributed to *Golf Illustrated*, in July and August 1909, on the subject of 'The caddie evil'. The proliferation of middle-class golfers had met with a proliferation of working-class caddies, and Colt shared a general concern that the game was creating 'a rotten class of loafer unfit for any sort of occupation other than that of carrying a few golf clubs round a course for a few hours a day' (*Golf Illustrated*, 30 July 1909, 149). He wanted the work of caddies restricted to boys, since he believed that it was unsuitable for able-bodied men; in other respects he was advanced in his thinking, and advocated, for example, the proper regulation of caddies as a profession. At Sunningdale he even introduced evening classes of a vocational nature to help prepare them for future employment.

Colt's external activities multiplied after 1906, while his value to the Sunningdale committee in no way lessened, and a compromise was reached whereby he was given increasing time to pursue his own work. But the inevitable could not long be delayed and in 1913 he resigned as secretary. He entered into partnership with C. H. Alison

and Alister MacKenzie, both of whom undertook substantial work in North America. Business inevitably stagnated during the First World War and Colt, who was not wanted for military service, moved from Ascot to St Amand's House, East Hendred. There he bought an apple orchard, and became a justice of the peace and a deputy commissioner for the south-west area of the Ministry of Food. After the war he re-emerged at the height of his powers, initially in partnership with Alison and MacKenzie, but from 1928 with the more enduring combination of Alison and John S. F. Morrison. The firm of Colt, Alison, and Morrison Ltd remained a prominent force in British golf design for a decade after Colt's death.

Colt's list of courses after 1918 is an impressive one. He designed the new course at Sunningdale (1922), Moor Park West (1923), Burning Tree, Bethesda, Maryland (1924), Wentworth (1924), Milwaukee country club, Wisconsin (1929), and the sea course at Le Touquet (1930). He also created 'scores of others, not all so well-known, but every one attractive to the eye and to the golfer' (Colt and Alison, xi). His remodelling guaranteed the future pre-eminence of courses such as Muirfield, Lytham St Annes, Ganton, Porth-cawl, and Formby. Many would perhaps agree that 'his masterpiece' was Royal Portrush, co. Antrim, 'a magnificent natural course which he almost entirely reconstituted and lived to see chosen for the open championship' (*The Times*, 24 Nov 1951). Colt remained active after the Second World War but his powers waned as he grew increasingly deaf and concerned about his wife's health. He died at St Amand's House on 21 November 1951. Colt had an important influence on the post-war generation of golf course designers, having 'spanned the whole popular development of golf from rugged beginnings to modern refinement both in layout and construction' (Colt and Alison, xiii).   MARK POTTLE

Sources H. S. Colt and C. H. Alison, *Some essays on golf-course architecture* (1990) · F. W. Hawtree, *Colt & Co.: golf course architects* (1991) · D. Steel, *Daily Telegraph golf-course guide* (1996) · *The Times* (17 March 1913) · *The Times* (24 Nov 1951) · J. Lowerson, *Sport and the English middle classes, 1870–1914* (1993) · B. S. Klein, 'Harry S. Colt: golf course architect', portsillustrated.cnn.com/golfonline/travel/architects/colt.html · *Golf Illustrated* (23 July 1909), 125 · *Golf Illustrated* (30 July 1909), 149 · *Golf Illustrated* (6 Aug 1909), 173 · *Golf Illustrated* (13 Aug 1909), 197 · *Golf Illustrated* (20 Aug 1909), 221 · *Burke's Who's who in sport* (1922) · Venn, *Alum. Cant.* · b. cert. · d. cert. · *CGPLA Eng. & Wales* (1952)

Wealth at death £42,738 5s. 8d.: probate, 17 Jan 1952, *CGPLA Eng. & Wales*

Colt, John, the elder (d. 1637). *See under* Colt, Maximilian (*fl.* 1595–1645).

Colt, John, the younger (bap. 1606, d. 1665). *See under* Colt, Maximilian (*fl.* 1595–1645).

Colt [*formerly* Poultrain or Poutrain], **Maximilian** (*fl.* 1595–1645), sculptor, was born at Arras. After a stay in Utrecht he went to England, probably as a protestant refugee. He was in London by 1595 and Anglicized his surname (his former name, Poultrain or Poutrain, is taken from English sources and is possibly corrupt). In January 1607 he became an English citizen.

On 31 January 1604 Colt had married Susanna Gheeraerts (*d.* 1645), a niece of the king's deputy serjeant painter John De Critz the elder. The royal connection was to be of enormous value and must have helped him secure the most prestigious commission available to any sculptor in England at the time, that of the tomb of Elizabeth I in Westminster Abbey (1605–6). Traditional in form but upto-date in style, it was very competently executed and seems to have given satisfaction. In the year it was completed Colt was asked to make another royal memorial, this time commemorating Princess Sophia, the infant daughter of James I, who had died the previous June. This is a work of remarkable, indeed unprecedented naturalism and shows the child asleep in a cradle, lying at Queen Elizabeth's feet. It was complete by December 1607. In the same month Sophia's elder sister Mary died and Colt found himself making a third royal memorial (1608). The two girls are represented side by side, but Mary, who was only two years old at the time of her death, is portrayed as a miniature adult, dressed in her best clothes and reclining on a tomb chest in a stiff, awkward posture which was then becoming fashionable.

In July 1608 Colt was appointed to the specially created post of master sculptor or master carver to the king. In this capacity he was called upon to do a wide range of work; much of it was quite humble and routine, and it included carving in wood as well as marble and stone. Most notably, he supplied and installed three chimneypieces at Denmark House (old Somerset House) in 1610–11 and carved a 'great newe wyndowe' (probably a pierced wooden screen) for the chapel at Greenwich Palace in 1623–4. He also did decorative carving on the royal barges and supplied effigies for the funerals of Anne of Denmark (1619) and James I (1625). The effigies survive in part only at Westminster Abbey and the rest of the work has entirely perished.

Colt's greatest patron was not James himself but his lord treasurer, Robert Cecil, earl of Salisbury. A man of culture and artistic discernment, Cecil advanced Colt's career in the royal service and employed him privately. For the earl's country seat, Hatfield House in Hertfordshire, Colt executed at least three chimney-pieces, including, almost certainly, that in the King James drawing-room, which has a life-size statue of the king on the upper tier. This work was begun *c.*1609 and in the same year Colt submitted a model of Salisbury's own tomb which was eventually erected after his death in Hatfield parish church (*c.*1614–*c.*1618). The tomb must rank as Colt's masterpiece, though it probably owes much to Salisbury's own ideas and initiative. The earl is shown recumbent on a slab of black marble supported by kneeling figures of the cardinal virtues while below the slab is a symbolic skeleton on a rolled straw mat. The work was revolutionary for the England of its day in that it was not painted in bright colours or embellished with features borrowed from architecture; instead, it depends for its effect on the character and disposition of the figures and on a simple contrast of black and white marbles. The white marble was Carrara, supplied at great expense from Italy by Salisbury himself.

After the funeral of James I in 1625, Colt gained no further royal patronage. His career, which seems to have been already in decline by this time, apparently petered out by the end of the 1630s. Either he or his son of the same name (*bap.* 1609) was released from the Fleet debtors' gaol by 1641. He appears to have been still alive in 1644–5 and no replacement had been found for him in the royal service before the restoration of the monarchy in 1660, strongly suggesting that he had held office at least until the outbreak of the English civil war in 1642.

Colt's brother **John Colt** [*formerly* Poutrain] **the elder** (*d.* 1637) was born in Arras and arrived in England before him but did not achieve the same success and seems to have been dogged by poverty for much of his career. His only certain work is the effigy of Elizabeth I which he made for her funeral in Westminster Abbey. By 1602 he had married Ieudique (Judith) Breule; their son **John Colt the younger** (*bap.* 1606, *d.* 1665) was baptized on 13 April 1606 at the French church, Threadneedle Street, in the City of London. John Colt the elder was buried on 9 August 1637 at St Bartholomew-the-Great, Smithfield, in the City of London. The younger John was an assistant to Hubert Le Sueur, court sculptor to Charles I. One of the two Johns, probably the younger, made sculpture for the chapel of the London Charterhouse in the late 1630s. It consisted mainly of a commandment table flanked by statues of Moses and Aaron which probably served as an altar reredos; a wall tablet with figures of the twelve apostles, also supplied by the same sculptor, may have formed part of the same structure. The tablet is lost but parts of the commandment table have been rediscovered. The younger John married Elizabeth Woodham at St Bartholomew's Church on 21 May 1635 and died of plague thirty years later, being buried at St Bartholomew's on 20 August 1665.   ADAM WHITE

Sources A. White, 'A biographical dictionary of London tomb sculptors, *c.*1560–*c.*1660', *Walpole Society*, 61 (1999), 1–162 · A. White, 'Maximilian Colt: master sculptor to King James I', *Proceedings of the Huguenot Society*, 27/1 (1998), 36–49 · M. Edmond, 'Limners and picturemakers', *Walpole Society*, 47 (1978–80), 60–242, esp. 162–72 · H. M. Colvin and others, eds., *The history of the king's works*, 3–4 (1975–82) · E. Auerbach and C. Kingsley Adams, *Paintings and sculpture at Hatfield House* (1971), 109–12 · S. Porter and A. White, 'John Colt and the Charterhouse chapel', *Architectural History*, 44 (2001), 228–36 · parish register, London, St Bartholomew-the-Great, 21 May 1635 [marriage, John Colt the younger] · parish register, London, St Bartholomew-the-Great, 20 Aug 1665 [burial, John Colt the younger]

Colt, Sir William Dutton (*bap.* 1646, *d.* 1693), diplomat, was baptized at Sherborne, Gloucestershire, on 2 March 1646, the third son of George Colt (1614–1659) of Coltishall, Suffolk, and his wife, Elizabeth (*d.* 1674), daughter and coheir of John *Dutton of Sherborne [*see under* Dutton family of Sherborne]. Having been ruined financially by his support for the royal cause George Colt went into exile with Charles II and was accidentally drowned near Dordrecht in the Netherlands on 20 January 1659. Of William's brothers the eldest, John (1643–1722), became MP for Leominster and a prominent supporter of exclusion; another, Henry, was created a baronet; the youngest,

Edward, was a captain in the Anglo-Dutch brigade in 1688 and eventually became a colonel. William Dutton Colt's early career is obscure. Nothing is known of his education. By the early 1670s he had married Dorothy Sanderson, with whom he had a son, William Dutton Colt (*d.* 1698). Following Dorothy's death he married Lucy Webb, with whom he had at least three children, Elizabeth (*bap.* 1675), Henry (*b.* 1676/7), and Lucy (*bap.* 1680).

By 9 September 1680, when he was created DMed at Oxford University, Colt was master of the horse to Prince Rupert, and in a letter Colt received from Rupert's sister Princess, later Electress, Sophia, dated November 1681, she described herself as 'votre trés affectioneé aime' ('your very affectionate friend'; BL, Add. MS 38000, fol. 2). By 1684 he was a member of the retinue of one of Charles's illegitimate sons, the duke of Northumberland, and he assisted in the bizarre attempt by Northumberland in 1686 to install his wife in a Flemish nunnery. Colt was knighted at Whitehall on 26 November 1684, six days after he had married for the third time. His new bride, Mary Shipman, *née* Garneys (1656–1725), was the widow of a London merchant; they married on 20 November 1684 and had two sons, William and John, and at least two daughters, Sophia and Elizabeth.

Colt's formal diplomatic career began on 28 May 1689, when he kissed William III's hand on his appointment as envoy to Brunswick-Lüneburg, Wolfenbüttel, and Hesse-Cassel. He went out to Germany in July 1689 and was then usually resident at Celle or Hanover until the end of 1692. He was allowed £30 for a house at Hanover and for lodgings at Brunswick and Wolfenbüttel, 'there being no accommodation to be had in the inns but what is very miserable and mean' (*CSP dom.*, 1693, 176). Nevertheless there was entertainment galore: the annual Hanover carnival, for example, or else 'the finest operas and comedys that ever were seen' as Schweinfurt, Colt's secretary, described them (PRO, SP 105/84, Schweinfurt to Johnston, 8/18 Jan 1692). Accommodation and social life apart, Colt's main role was to cement the adherence of his assigned states to William III's grand alliance against France. In January 1693 Colt formally admitted the new elector of Hanover into the alliance, having managed to reconcile the other princes to whom he was accredited to this elevation of their neighbour.

Colt then went as envoy-extraordinary to Saxony, ostensibly to invest the elector, John George IV, with the Order of the Garter, but also to engineer Saxony's entry into the alliance (his instructions to this effect had been dated 25 November 1692). As usual in seventeenth-century diplomacy much depended on the relative abilities of the allies and the French to provide a big enough bribe: 'necessity has no law', Colt wrote in January 1693, 'and there is no time to be lost; our enemies are so vigilant and offer such large sums to thwart us' (PRO, SP 105/84, Colt to Stepney, 28 Jan/7 Feb 1693). The particular complication at the Saxon electoral court was the need to win over John George's mistress, Magdalene Sybilla von Neitschütz. In January 1693 Colt wrote that 'the Elector's inclinations lead him to the party of the allies, if he be not hindered by

others' but that the allies' hopes might be dashed by his choosing 'to stay at home, for he is lost in his love, and she being young with child he will hardly leave her'. The remedy was financial: 'there must be a yearly present on which they may depend, and that will be also our future security; besides there must be money given to three or four ministers who will be ordered to treat with us' (Kemble, 143–4). The price that the mistress was paid for exercising her persuasive talents on the elector almost certainly included her elevation in the following month to the dignity of countess of Rocklitz. Even so, Colt remained scathing about the situation:

> When we have done all we can, and … in appearance we have what we desire, then I doubt that we cannot be sure one day of this elector, but that he will have new things put into his head; for I never in my life have seen so fickle a man, which makes me long to see the end of this business, that I may return to my post; and all the intimacy I have gained with him hath been by the grossest flattery imaginable; and for giving money to the lady never fear me, before all things are concluded to his Majesty's satisfaction.   (ibid., 145–6)

Colt returned to Celle by May. He was then given a special mission to treat with the elector of Saxony over aspects of war policy, and arrived at Frankfurt on 24 June to attend the elector on campaign in the Rhineland—a campaign which was graced by the presence of the now heavily pregnant (but considerably richer, following a 'present' of £1500 from England), countess of Rocklitz. Colt had the debatable honour of being one of the godfathers when the infant daughter was baptized at Frankfurt am Main. In July Colt was additionally given powers by the Dutch states general of the United Provinces to treat with the elector on their behalf, there being then no Dutch minister at Leipzig. It was while fulfilling this role that Colt fell ill of a 'bloody flux' at Heilbronn, and died there on 11 September 1693. His secretary, Schweinfurt, reported that 'he dyed … between 1 and 2 a clock in the afternoon being the eleventh day of his sickness, he was very sensible all the time, but very much afraid of death'; the burial took place the following day 'in the great church at Heilbronn, before the altar, where I intend to have a fine tomb made for him' (PRO, SP 105/84, fols. 204, 211). The countess of Rocklitz survived him by only a few months, thereby thwarting any further attempts by the elector to persuade an incandescent Emperor Leopold to make her an imperial princess.

Leaving aside his role in bringing Hanover and Saxony into the grand alliance, the first element of Colt's particular importance as a diplomat was the close relationship that he struck up with the Hanoverian ruling house at a time when its place in the British succession was becoming increasingly prominent. This relationship clearly went beyond diplomatic niceties, and constituted a genuine personal friendship. It evidently long predated Colt's official appointment to Hanover and built on his relationship with Electress Sophia, 'our excellent duchess' as Colt described her (SP 105/84, Colt to Stepney, 7/17 Dec 1692). Sophia stood as godmother to Colt's youngest daughter, giving her own name to the child, and a correspondence was kept up between Sophia and Lady Mary Colt long after

Sir William's death. Indeed, the last letter from the princess was dated 15 May 1714, three weeks before her death, and thanked Lady Mary for her affection over the years. Colt's other claim to fame was his part in preserving the life of William III. The evidence is sketchy, but, according to Gilbert Burnet, shortly before his death in 1691 the marquis de Louvois had approved a plan to assassinate William. This was to be carried out by two agents, Grandval and Du Mont, the latter of whom spent the winter of 1692 in Celle, where his indiscreet behaviour drew him to Colt's attention. The envoy reported his suspicions, the authorities took action, Du Mont confessed and was executed, and the life of the architect of the grand alliance and victor of the Boyne was preserved.

Sir William Dutton Colt's death seemed to be a disaster for his family. His will, made on 4 May 1689 with a codicil at Heilbronn on 29 August 1693, declared that 'because I have been so unfortunate to live in troublesome times, I think fit to declare myself an unworthy member of the best church in the world, the church of England'. He went on to make bequests of £500 or £1000 to each of his children, but apologized for the smallness of the amounts, 'this being all my care and honest industry could attain to' (PRO, PROB 11/418, fols. 172–4). In the summer of 1694 Lady Colt petitioned to the effect that her husband had expended not only his allowance but also his own estate in his time in Germany, leaving her and her five (mainly infant) offspring 'in a most deplorable condition' (*Calendar of Treasury Books*, 1694, 375). William junior became a page to William III—perhaps a small recognition of the father's role in thwarting the Grandval plot—but the king's death again wrecked the family's hopes. The Colts turned once more to Hanover, 'the most sober court in Europe' according to Lady Colt (BL, Stowe MS 222, fol. 188), and in 1703 William entered the elector's service, subsequently undertaking diplomatic missions to Italy for the electoral court: in 1709 Sophia thanked Lady Colt for preferring her service for William to any others. As Sir William's brother noted when recommending his nephew in 1703, the Colt family had long been entirely devoted to the house of Hanover, and had been penalized by the then ministry because of that fact. The untimely deaths of Sir William in 1693, before he could capitalize on the successes of his diplomacy, and then of Sophia, barely two months before she would have become queen in 1714, probably prevented the Colts becoming more prominent figures in the history of Augustan England.   J. D. DAVIES

Sources D. B. Horn, ed., *British diplomatic representatives, 1689–1789*, CS, 3rd ser., 46 (1932) • PRO, SP 105, esp. SP 105/48, 58, 59, 82–4 • corresp. of Princess Sophia with Colt family, BL, Add. MS 38000 • *CSP dom.*, 1689–93 • W. A. Shaw, ed., *Calendar of treasury books*, 10, PRO (1935) • J. M. Kemble, ed., *State papers and correspondence illustrative of the social and political state of Europe from the revolution to the accession of the house of Hanover* (1857) • *Le Neve's Pedigrees of the knights*, ed. G. W. Marshall, Harleian Society, 8 (1873) • Colt pedigrees, Bodl. Oxf., MS Rawl. A. 497 • *Bishop Burnet's History* • will, PRO, PROB 11/418, fols. 178–9 [Sir William Dutton Colt] • will, PRO, PROB 11/610, fols. 32–4 [Dame Mary Colt] • will, PRO, PROB 11/346, fols. 301–2 [Elizabeth Colt, mother] • BL, Add. MS 34095–34096, 36662, 37513 [Colt's letterbooks] • BL, Stowe MS 222 • A. W. Ward, *The Electress Sophia and the Hanoverian succession* (1909) • Foster, *Alum.*

Oxon. • *Report on the manuscripts of Allan George Finch*, 5 vols., HMC, 71 (1913–2003), vol. 2 • *Report on the manuscripts of the marquis of Downshire*, 6 vols. in 7, HMC, 75 (1924–95), vol. 1 • W. A. Shaw, *The knights of England*, 2 vols. (1906), vol. 2, p. 260 • J. L. Chester, ed., *The marriage, baptismal, and burial registers of the collegiate church or abbey of St Peter, Westminster*, Harleian Society, 10 (1876) • IGI
Archives BL, corresp. and letterbook, Add. MSS 36662, 37513 | PRO, letters to James Johnston, SP 105/84 • PRO, letters to George Stepney, SP 105/58, 59, 84 • SOAS, corresp. with Lord Paget • Yale U., Beinecke L., letters to William Blathwayt
Wealth at death see will, PRO, PROB 11/418, fols. 178–9

Coltman [*née* Todd], **Constance Mary** (1889–1969), Congregational minister and the first woman to be ordained to the Christian ministry in Britain, was born in Putney, London, on 23 May 1889, the oldest of the four children of George Todd (1844–1912), headmaster and educational administrator, and Emily Ellerman, one of the first generation of women to study medicine and a member of the wealthy shipping family. She was educated at St Felix School, Southwold, from where she won an exhibition to read history at Somerville College, Oxford (1908–11). The family's love of travel helped to inculcate an early and strong international outlook.

The Todd family were members of the Presbyterian Church of England, and it was to that church that Constance Todd first turned when she became convinced of a vocation to ordained ministry. When that door was closed she visited the principal of Mansfield College, Oxford, W. B. Selbie, and convinced him that her vocation was genuine. She was admitted to Mansfield for preparation for the Congregational ministry in 1913 and completed the course with some distinction within three years. During these years she acquired her deep interest in Hebrew, took an active part in college life, and met and became engaged to a fellow student, Claud Marshall Coltman (1889–1971). She described herself as a 'suffragist', but took no active part in the suffrage movement. Her lifelong abhorrence of violence led her to take a pacifist stance and to active membership of the Fellowship of Reconciliation.

Drawn to the preaching of the Presbyterian pacifist William Edwin Orchard, she became a member of his (Congregational) church, the King's Weigh House, London, in 1917. In the summer of that year she and her fiancé received a call to take charge of the Weigh House's mission in the East End of London. On 17 September they were both 'solemnly ordained to the Holy Ministry by the laying on of hands and invocation of the Holy Ghost' (King's Weigh House Church meeting minute book). Orchard (who eighteen years later became a Roman Catholic priest) was the presiding minister, assisted by three Congregational ministers. The following day the two were married. Constance Coltman's ordination was officially recognized by the Congregational Union Council two months later, and her name subsequently appeared in the lists of accredited ministers of the Congregational Union of England and Wales. Other women began to follow her example, though very slowly at first.

After three years at Darby Street, east London, the Coltmans had a series of joint ministries at Kilburn; Cowley

Road, Oxford; Wolverton, Buckinghamshire; and Haverhill, Suffolk, before a return to the Weigh House in 1946. They shared the ministerial work according to the particular needs and wishes of the church. They also brought up their family of two daughters and a son.

Constance Coltman believed that women had a distinctive contribution to bring to the interpretation and commendation of Christian theology, and to the practice of Christian ministry, especially through the experience of motherhood. She was an active member of the Society of Free Catholics, an ecumenical society founded by J. M. Lloyd Thomas, and contributed to its journal.

In 1927 Coltman was elected president of the new Fellowship of Women Ministers, which arose out of a conference in the previous year, and three years later helped to found the interdenominational Society for the Ministry of Women, of which she was a vice-president, and in which she was active for many years. She offered valuable support to younger women who felt called to ministry not only in Britain but elsewhere in Europe. She was a close friend of the Anglican preacher Maude Royden, with whom she collaborated in writing *The Church and Woman* (1924).

Throughout her active life Coltman was involved in peace movements. She was a vice-president of the Women's International League for Peace and Freedom and one of the founders of the Christian Campaign for Nuclear Disarmament. She retired from active ministry in 1949, and after her husband's retirement in 1957 moved to Bexhill for her remaining years. She died on 26 March 1969. A memorial service was held on 26 April at Whitefield Memorial Church in London. ELAINE KAYE

Sources Congregational Year Book (1969–70), 429–30 · D. M. Northcroft, *Women Free Church ministers* (1929) · *Christian World* (20 Sept 1917) · *Christian World* (4 Oct 1917) · *British Weekly* (4 Oct 1917) · meeting minute book, King's Weigh House Church, 1916–26, DWL · JCR minute book, 1909–17, Mansfield College, Oxford · *Magazine* [Mansfield College] (1909–17) · newsletters of Society for the Ministry of Women, Women's Library, London · S. Fletcher, *Maude Royden: a life* (1989) · Wolverton Congregational Church records, Wolverton United Reformed Church, Buckinghamshire · minutes, Cowley Road Congregational Church, Oxon. RO · E. Kaye, 'Constance Coltman, a forgotten pioneer', *Journal of the United Reformed Church History Society*, 4 (1987–92), 134–46 · CGPLA Eng. & Wales (1969) · WWW, 1897–1915 · Congregational Year Book (1972) · Congregational Year Book (1917–69)
Archives Mansfield College, Oxford
Likenesses photograph, c.1917, Mansfield College, Oxford
Wealth at death £1953: probate, 2 July 1969, CGPLA Eng. & Wales

Colton, (Charles) Caleb (bap. 1777, d. 1832), writer and Church of England clergyman, was baptized at Shrivenham, Berkshire, on 11 December 1777, the son of Barfoot Colton (bap. 1736, d. 1803), who had been elected to King's College, Cambridge, in 1755, and was afterwards canon of Salisbury. Caleb Colton was educated at Eton College before being elected in 1796 to King's College, Cambridge, where he matriculated in 1799, and graduated BA in 1801 and MA in 1804. In 1801 he was presented by his college to the rectory of Prior's Portion, Tiverton, tenable with a fellowship. Here he published a sermon in 1809, a *Plain and*

Authentic Narrative of the Sampford Ghost in 1810, and *Hypocrisy: a Satire in Three Books* (only one book published) in 1812.

Colton's character, talents, and opinions were better suited to a literary than to a clerical career, and he was also better known for his skill as a sportsman and fisherman than for any work as a divine. In 1818 he was presented to the college living of Kew and Petersham, Surrey, but it was here that his eccentricities, such as precipitately ending a service to go partridge shooting, became marked. A writer in the *Literary Magnet* who first met him in company with 'Walking Stewart' (John Stewart) (1749–1822) found him wearing military dress, appropriate, Colton claimed, to 'an officer of the church *militant*' (*GM*, 565). Colton apparently maintained that it was cheaper to live in London than at his living, and the same writer described his lodgings, which were over a marine-store shop, as squalid and littered with books, fishing-rods, and manuscripts. Cyrus Redding, however, countered this with his own declaration that Colton was always temperate, and his living quarters were clean. For a time Colton carried on business as a wine merchant.

In 1816 Colton published a poem, initially entitled *Napoleon*, as *Lines on the Conflagration of Moscow* (4th edn, 1822), and his *Remarks Critical and Moral on the Talents of Lord Byron* appeared in 1819. The first volume of his best-known work, *Lacon, or, Many Things in Few Words Addressed to those who Think*, was published in 1820, and had run to six editions by 1821. A second volume was added in 1822, and it was frequently reprinted. It is a collection of moral aphorisms, often very forcibly expressed, and some contemporaries charged him with borrowing from Bacon's *Essays* and the *Materials for Thinking* of William Burdon.

Colton was addicted to gambling, and became financially embarrassed. He had associated with John Thurtell, who murdered William Weare in 1823. When Colton disappeared about the same time, Thurtell was at first thought to be involved. According to Redding, however, Colton had in fact retired to America, his debts having been caused by speculations in Spanish bonds. He went to Paris, and in 1827 returned to claim his living. In 1828, however, he was officially removed for non-residence, and a successor was appointed.

Colton again visited America, and finally settled in Paris. He gambled at the Palais Royal, and is said at one time to have gained £25,000, to have collected a picture gallery, and afterwards to have been ruined. Colton suffered from a painful disease, and falsified one of the remarks in *Lacon*, that no one ever committed suicide from bodily anguish, though thousands have done so from mental anguish, when, rather than submit to a surgical operation, he shot himself on 28 April 1832, while visiting Major Markham Sherwell at Fontainebleau. A volume called *Modern Antiquity, and other Poems* was edited by Sherwell in 1835. [ANON.], rev. JOHN D. HAIGH

Sources C. Redding, *Fifty years' recollections, literary and personal*, 2nd edn, 2 (1858), 303–11 · *GM*, 1st ser., 102/1 (1832), 564–6 · Venn, *Alum. Cant.* · *Literary Magnet*, new ser., 3 (1827), 218–23 · [Clarke], *The Georgian era: memoirs of the most eminent persons*, 3 (1834), 582 ·

M. Sherwill [M. Sherwell], introduction, in C. C. Colton, *Modern antiquity, and other poems* (1835)

Colton, John (*d.* 1404), archbishop of Armagh and justiciar of Ireland, was born at Terrington, Norfolk. Chaplain by 1343 to William Bateman, bishop of Norwich, Colton became doctor of canon law at Cambridge *c.*1348. In June 1349 he was made first warden of Gonville Hall, founded by Edmund Gonville, rector of Terrington. He succeeded his patron in Terrington from 1350 to 1351, retaining his post at Gonville until 1360. He was collated on 14 August 1377 to the prebend of Bugthorpe, York, exchanged (1380) for the prebend of Coton in St Mary's royal free chapel, Stafford. Colton's Irish connection dates from at least 1361, when, described as chamberlain to the late archbishop of Armagh (Richard Fitzralph), he was papally provided to the treasurership of St Patrick's Cathedral, Dublin. He was certainly in residence by the early 1370s, and described as dean of St Patrick's before October 1373. Other Irish preferments included the prebend of Clashmore in Lismore diocese.

Colton's appointment as treasurer of Ireland on 2 September 1372 is unlikely to have been his first administrative office. He gained considerable military experience in the lordship's defence, particularly in Leinster, and on occasion personally funded emergency troops. He subsequently accounted as treasurer, from 1372 until September 1375. In May 1378 Colton went to England where, in December, he undertook to answer charges laid by Nicholas Dagworth. Appointed chancellor on 8 May 1380, he remained in office until 15 February 1382, although his successor, William Tany, was named on 26 November 1381. He was with the lieutenant, Edmund (III) Mortimer, earl of March, when the earl's sudden death in Cork in December 1381 caused an emergency. Colton reluctantly and conditionally accepted the post of justiciar in January 1382 and successfully defended Cork. He resigned the office on 3 March 1382 and went immediately to England. After Archbishop Sweetman's death in August 1380, he initially had charge of the temporalities of Armagh, and was himself promoted to the archbishopric by papal provision in January 1381. He was consecrated in London on 8 March 1383.

As archbishop Colton did not again hold administrative office. He used his influence in the defence of the lordship, helping, for example, in negotiations to buy off the menace of the Ó Raghallaigh family in Meath in 1391–2. Richard II wrote to him (letter undated) thanking him for his service in the lordship. During the royal expedition to Ireland, 1394–5, Colton played a key role in the submission of the Ulster Irish, as evident in surviving letters from Ó Néill and Ó Catháin to him and from the Ulster Irish to Richard II. He was absent on the king's business in Rome from 12 August 1398 to 8 September 1399, including the period of Richard's second Irish expedition. In 1401 he accompanied the archbishop of Dublin as envoy to Henry IV with a plea from the Irish council for aid for the lordship. During this visit Irish letters patent of 1333 were exemplified, confirming the primacy of Armagh.

Colton succeeded in establishing Armagh's claim to the Blackpriory of St Andrew in the Ards in September 1392, a grant confirmed three times within the decade. A notarial copy of his metropolitan visitation of Derry in October 1397 provides a rare record of conditions within an Irish diocese in the late fourteenth century. In 1398, to augment the impoverished *mensa* of the archbishop, he was granted the patronage of St James's, Athboy, in the diocese of Meath. He participated in enquiries concerning the life and miracles of Archbishop Fitzralph. Colton died on 27 April 1404 in Drogheda, Meath, having shortly before resigned his see, and was buried in St Peter's, Drogheda. His episcopal register does not survive, although a few relevant documents are found in the register of his successor, Archbishop Swayne.

Colton had a reputation for learning and wrote two treatises, not extant, on the papal schism: *De causis schismatis* and *De remediis ejusdem.* D. B. JOHNSTON

Sources *The whole works of Sir James Ware concerning Ireland*, ed. and trans. W. Harris, rev. edn, 2 vols. in 3 (1764) · *Chancery records* · E. Tresham, ed., *Rotulorum patentium et clausorum cancellariae Hiberniae calendarium*, Irish Record Commission (1828) · W. Reeves, ed., *Acts of Archbishop Colton in his metropolitan visitation of the diocese of Derry, AD 1397*, Irish Archaeological Society (1850) · W. H. Bliss, ed., *Calendar of entries in the papal registers relating to Great Britain and Ireland: petitions to the pope* (1896) · H. G. Richardson and G. O. Sayles, eds., *Parliaments and councils of mediaeval Ireland*, IMC, 1 (1947) · E. Curtis, ed., *Richard II in Ireland, 1394–1395, and submissions of the Irish chiefs* (1927) · Exchequer, enrolled accounts, PRO, E364/17/7 · M. D. Legge, ed., *Anglo-Norman letters and petitions from All Souls MS 182*, Anglo-Norman Texts, 3 (1941) · J. Graves, ed., *A roll of the proceedings of the King's Council in Ireland… AD 1392–93*, Rolls Series, 69 (1877) · J. A. Watt, 'John Colton, justiciar of Ireland (1382) and archbishop of Armagh (1383–1404)', *England and Ireland in the later middle ages: essays in honour of Jocelyn Otway-Ruthven*, ed. J. Lydon (1981), 196–213 · *Emden, Cam.*

Colton, Sir John (1823–1902), businessman and politician in Australia, one of the five sons of William Colton (1795–1858), a Devon farmer, and his wife, Elizabeth, was born at Harbertonford, Devon, on 23 September 1823. When he was sixteen his family obtained free passage to Australia, and his father took up wine growing as a tenant farmer in McLaren Vale, South Australia. John was apprenticed to an Adelaide saddler. In 1842 he set up his own saddler's shop, which developed into a substantial manufacturing and retail business called Colton & Co. On 4 December 1844 he married Mary, the daughter of Samuel Cutting of London. Of their five children, two sons entered the family business, from which Colton himself retired in 1883.

Colton entered public life in 1859 as an alderman of the city of Adelaide, and was mayor in 1874–5. He was elected to the South Australian house of assembly in March 1862 as member for Noarlunga, which he represented, with short intervals, throughout his public life. A firm liberal, he served from November 1868 to May 1870 as commissioner of public works in the Strangways ministry. He was out of political life between 1870 and 1872, but was re-elected in the latter year and was briefly treasurer under Sir James Boucaut in 1875–6. As premier and commissioner of public works from June 1876 until October 1877 he had time to persuade parliament to pass a single consolidating Land Act to replace the existing thirty-three.

Colton resigned his seat for Noarlunga on 29 August 1878 on account of ill health, but re-entered parliament on 6 January 1880, when he sat with the opposition because of his antipathy to the property tax. In June 1884 he again became premier and chief secretary. His government carried a bill which settled the long-disputed details of land and income taxation and instituted progressive legislation on public health and land tenure, encouraging agriculture on the best lands, while giving pastoralists greater security of tenure elsewhere. Defeated in June 1885, Colton led the opposition for a time, but at the close of the parliament he again withdrew from public life owing to ill health, and visited England.

A staunch Wesleyan, Colton was benefactor and trustee to more than a hundred Wesleyan churches in the colony. He worked enthusiastically for temperance and himself shunned worldly pleasures such as dancing and theatre-going. Severe and rather humourless, he was none the less generous with his time and money in the causes of public health, religion, and education. He was long treasurer and benefactor of Prince Alfred College, Adelaide.

Colton was made a KCMG on 1 January 1891. His wife died in 1898, and he suffered a stroke shortly afterwards; he died at his home in Hackney, near Adelaide, on 6 February 1902, and was buried on 8 February in the West Terrace cemetery in that city.

CHEWTON ATCHLEY, rev. ELIZABETH BAIGENT

Sources *AusDB* · D. Pike, *Paradise of dissent: South Australia, 1829–1857*, 2nd edn [1967] · B. Burke, *A genealogical and heraldic history of the colonial gentry*, 2 vols. (1891–5) · *The Times* (7 Feb 1902) · *The Advertiser* [Adelaide] (7 Feb 1902) · *The Advertiser* [Adelaide] (10 Feb 1902) **Wealth at death** never exceptionally rich: *The Advertiser* [Adelaide] (7 Feb 1902)

Colum mac Crimthainn (d. 549). *See under* Munster, saints of (act. c.450–c.700).

Colum, Padraic [*formerly* Patrick Collumb] (1881–1972), writer, was born on 8 December 1881, in the parish of Collumbkille, co. Longford, in the midlands of Ireland, the eldest of the eight children of Patrick Collumb and his wife, Susan, *née* MacCormack, daughter of a gardener at Powerscourt, in co. Wicklow. His father was the last of an ancient line of peasant farmers, but a graduate of the national school and a teacher in the same institution, and later master of the Longford workhouse. Like his father he was christened Patrick, but after joining the Gaelic League and the Irish Republican Brotherhood in 1901, he began using the Irish Gaelic Padraic, and changed his family name to Colum.

Colum took pride in maintaining that of his generation of Irish writers he alone was peasant-born and Roman Catholic; he also enjoyed telling people that he was born in a workhouse, but neglected to mention that his father was in charge of the place at the time. Colum's finest play, *Thomas Muskerry* (1910), is set in a workhouse, and many of the characters that people his poetry and stories are derived from his early acquaintance with the residents of such an institution. He also drew inspiration for story-

Padraic Colum (1881–1972), by John Butler Yeats, 1906?

telling from an uncle, Mickey Burns, a yarn-spinning, travelling wholesale buyer of fowls, with whom the young Colum sometimes rode through co. Cavan. His uncle had an increased influence on Colum when his alcoholic father, having lost his position in Longford, spent time in America trying unsuccessfully to accumulate some money. On his return to Ireland, Patrick Collumb moved the family to Sandy Cove, near Dublin, where he was employed as a railway clerk. In time he became stationmaster and employed Padraic and his brother Fred, later a soldier in the British army, as delivery boys.

At seventeen, and having had only eight years of formal education, Padraic Colum passed an examination for a clerkship in the Irish Railway clearing house in Kildare Street in Dublin. He was now able to contribute money to the family and help support his younger siblings. Despite working a nine-hour day (six days per week), he wrote poetry and plays, and was soon discovered by Arthur Griffith, publisher and Sinn Féin leader, and later first president of the Irish Free State.

Griffith became Padraic Colum's patron, publishing his poems and short plays in the *United Irishman*. One of the latter, *The Saxon Shillin'*, won a prize for a drama written to discourage young Irishmen from enlisting in the British army. As a result, Colum was invited by Frank and W. G. Fay to join the newly formed Irish National Dramatic Company as both playwright and actor; soon the company merged with the Irish Literary Theatre founded by W. B. Yeats, Lady Gregory, George Moore, and Edward Martyn. Under the new name, the Irish National Theatre Company, what became the great Irish National Theatre, the Abbey, was established.

Colum's first full-length play was *Broken Soil*, later rewritten and published as *The Fiddler's House* (1907). In it a middle-aged peasant farmer chooses life as an itinerant musician over obligations to his children and the land he works. His choice of art over property and a comfortable life is forcibly contrasted with the priorities of his grasping, mercenary peers. The play's chief strength is its authentic depiction of Irish rural character in the early 1900s.

Colum's second drama, *The Land*, opened at the newly acquired Abbey Theatre on 9 June 1905, and promptly gave that theatre its first real triumph. *The Land* also established the 'peasant play' as a staple of the Irish National Theatre. Unfortunately the headstrong young playwright quarrelled with Yeats and the Fays, and despite Lady Gregory's attempt to reconcile the parties, Colum left the company. In 1910 the Abbey performed Colum's last commercially successful play, the tragedy *Thomas Muskerry*, which has been called the *King Lear* of Irish drama. Although Colum wrote plays for the rest of his life and always considered himself a playwright first, his continuing significance as a writer lay in poetry, folklore, and children's books.

Colum's first book of poetry, *Wild Earth* (1907), was well received for its sheer lyric beauty and simplicity, as well as for its strong characterizations of country folk, who lived according to the ancient ways with courage and nobility. *Wild Earth* is the foundation of Colum's poetic canon. It established his early reputation, and as long as he was emotionally, if not geographically, close to Ireland, his poetry was highly effective and well regarded. Yet from the time of its publication onward, Colum's stark, lucid, sympathetic vision of the Irish people slowly faded.

In 1912 Colum married Mary Gunning Maguire (1884–1957), a woman born into the Sligo middle class, and a graduate of University College, Dublin. She was also a gifted writer who became a major literary critic in America. They had no children. Unable to earn a satisfactory livelihood as writers in Dublin, the couple 'accidentally' emigrated to the United States in 1914, just before the outbreak of the First World War. Josephine Colum, an aunt in Pittsburgh, had sent them money for a honeymoon trip to the United States as a gift at the time of their marriage, and the war prevented their return. They decided to settle in New York city, perceiving that, as a writing couple, there were more opportunities for them in New York than in Dublin. Later they undertook part-time teaching careers at Columbia University and New York University. In New York, Colum continued to write poetry and plays but earned his primary living as a writer of folklore and books for children. He produced a series of stories at this time for the children's column of the *New York Sunday Tribune*, and his first children's book, *The King of Ireland's Son*, was published to great acclaim in the United States in 1916; it was republished in Britain in 1920. Colum was to support himself financially throughout the rest of his life with his popular children's books, which included accessible adaptations and translations of mythology and the classics.

In 1916 *Wild Earth and other Poems* was published in New York and it established Colum as an important voice on the American poetry scene. The collection was revised and added to in 1922, 1927, and 1950. Two subsequent collections continued Colum's early lyric portrayal of Irish country life with some success: *Dramatic Legends and other Poems* (1922) and *Old Pastures* (1930).

In 1922 the Colums made a triumphant return visit to Ireland, expecting to see, among other friends, Arthur Griffith (with whose biography Colum later struggled and finally published as *Ourselves Alone* in 1959), who was now the free state's president. But news of Griffith's unexpected death and the death of Michael Collins reached the Colums on their ship, and they found Ireland in mourning, although the new president, William Cosgrave, received them with great cordiality. Colum had earlier published an Irish travel book entitled *My Irish Year* (1912), and after this Irish visit he was to produce his finest work in this vein, *The Road Round Ireland* (1924), which was in turn followed by *Cross Roads in Ireland* (1930).

After their stay in Ireland, the Colums went on to visit James Joyce and his wife in Paris, the first of several such visits in the 1920s and 1930s. Colum even typed some of *Finnegans Wake* for Joyce. Padraic and Mary Colum later collaborated on the highly regarded biographical memoir, *Our Friend James Joyce* (1958), and after his death in 1941 they generously raised and personally contributed funds to assist Nora Joyce.

Meanwhile the Hawaiian legislature had invited Colum to codify the folklore of the islands. His in-country investigations and research at the Bishop Museum resulted in *At the Gateways of the Day* (1924) and *The Bright Islands* (1925), reissued together as *Legends of Hawaii* (1937). His work was the key to the foundation of Hawaiian folklore studies.

In his middle years Colum's reputation as a poet faded and he failed utterly as a playwright. *Creatures* (1927) indicated that Colum had lost interest, temporarily at least, in writing poems about people, and *Poems* (1932) is a collection of previously published material. *The Story of Lowry Maen* (1937), Colum's longest poem, was an attempt at epic narrative, composed of over 1800 lines of blank verse about the break-up of Bronze Age order with the advent of Iron Age invaders. The poem is, however, distinguished neither in narrative nor in language, and is too close to a children's fairy tale to serve as a national epic. *Flower Pieces* (1938) offered lovely little descriptions of hollyhocks, morning glories, hibiscus, marigolds, and other decorative plants. It testifies to Colum's gentle nature and descriptive powers, and in the next year *The Vegetable Kingdom* gave the edibles equal poetical time with creatures and flowers. But it must be said that as Colum settled fully into the New York scene and the international literary set his poetry suffered. None of this later work served to advance his reputation, and it appeared that he had written all of his memorable poetry by the age of fifty. His collection *Ten Poems* (1957) did little to refute this assessment, with the exception of one poem, 'The Book of Kells', depicting the work of a medieval manuscript illuminator, which is one of his finest pieces. It presaged the skill and profundity that Colum would display in his last work.

Colum's desire for production of his plays tormented him for some fifty years. He became an experimental playwright, abandoning the naturalism and colloquial but eloquent language that had been the hallmark of his early success. *Theodora* (1912), based on the life of the Byzantine empress, went through several revisions and changes of title (including *The Bear Keeper's Daughter*) but was never produced or published. *The Grasshopper*, a free translation of a Keyserling play, was produced at the Abbey on 24 October 1922, to no great success. Later, the script was burnt in an Abbey fire. He wrote at least four versions of the same play: *The Desert*, *Timbuktu*, *The Vizier*, and *Mogu the Wanderer*. It had one brief run as *Mogu the Wanderer*, at the Dublin Gate Theatre from 29 December 1931 to 7 January 1932, but proved a complete failure. The audience and even the actors laughed at its pretentiousness. The play is remembered today only because Orson Welles made his stage début in the production. Colum had hoped for a Broadway production of the impressionistic *Balloon*, set in and around the glamorous world of a first-class cosmopolitan hotel called the Hotel Daedalus (perhaps in homage to Joyce). It was published in 1929 after a two-week run in a summer theatre in Ogunquit, Maine, but it never went to New York.

Colum also tried his hand at fiction, but his two novels, *Castle Conquer* (1923), a romance, and *The Flying Swans* (1957), a moving story of an Irish peasant boyhood in the nineteenth century, were not commercially successful.

In his old age Colum returned to Irish themes and found renewed celebrity. After his wife died in 1957 and he took her body back to Ireland, Colum divided his time between New York, Woods Hole, Massachusetts, and Ireland. He renewed his bonds to his mother country, producing in a series of *Irish Elegies* (1958, 1961, 1963) powerful and poignant biographical poems centring on deceased friends who had contributed to the winning of Irish independence, or to the creation of Ireland's international reputation for art and literature. At the time of his death Colum was working on a cycle of Noh plays, influenced by Yeats's experimental dramas, and based on the classical Japanese performance form, Noh, which combines elements of dance, drama, music, and poetry into a highly stylized stage performance. His completed plays in this genre (*Moytura*, *Glendalough*, *Cloughoughter*, *Monasterboice*, and *Kilmore*, 1961–6) achieved some success both as written poetry and in small productions performed by dancers.

Colum's final poetry collection, *Images of Departure* (1969), is a subtly crafted and moving collection of poems of farewell to much loved people, such as his wife and mother, and nostalgic tributes to favoured spots in Dublin. It also represents a farewell to Ireland, his memories, and his life. A remarkable achievement for an eighty-seven-year-old poet, *Images of Departure* is one of the finest Irish poetry collections of the last half of the twentieth century.

Padraic Colum died at the Parkway Pavilion, a nursing home in Enfield, Connecticut, on 11 January 1972, one month after his ninetieth birthday. His body was viewed at the Abbey Funeral Home in Manhattan, and a high mass of the resurrection was conducted at St Patrick's Cathedral. His body was returned to Ireland and interred in St Fintan's cemetery, Sutton, co. Dublin, in the same grave as his beloved wife.

Padraic Colum has long been recognized as an early contributor towards developing the Irish National Theatre, and as one of the significant Irish poets of the twentieth century. It is as a lyric poet that Colum will be best remembered. The beauty and discipline of his early and very late verse, his surety in characterization, and his unquestioning belief in God are the foundations of his achievement. His real monument is the last full collection: *The Poet's Circuits: Collected Poems of Ireland* (1960).

Colum conceptualized the early modern Irish poet as a peasant bard, a preserver of the oral tradition, a storyteller with dramatic skill, a codifier of mores, and a conveyer of cultural values. Unlike Yeats, Colum never philosophized deeply, being content to respond emotively in his poetry to his country, his wife, his friends, and the poor hardworking people of the rural Ireland of his youth. Today Colum's lyrics are read and memorized by thousands of Irish school children yearly, although often they do not learn or remember the author's name. Thus Padraic Colum has become both a national poet and an anonymous bard, exactly as he would have wished.

SANFORD STERNLICHT

Sources S. Sternlicht, *Padraic Colum* (1985) · Z. Bowen, *Padraic Colum: a biographical-critical introduction* (1970) · Z. Bowen, 'Ninety years in retrospect: excerpts from and interviews with Padraic Colum', *Journal of Irish Literature*, 2 (Jan 1973), 14–34 · C. Burgess, 'A playwright and his work', *Journal of Irish Literature*, 2 (Jan 1973), 40–58 · A. Denson, 'Padraic Colum, 1881–1972', *Capuchin Annual* (1973), 43–54 · R. Fallis, *The Irish Renaissance* (1977) · R. Hogan and M. O'Neill, eds., *Joseph Holloway's Abbey Theatre* (1967) · P. Remo, *Mary Colum: woman of letters* (1982)

Archives Col. U., Rare Book and Manuscript Library, corresp. and literary MSS · NL Ire., corresp.; letters; notebooks and literary papers · State University of New York at Binghamton, corresp. and papers | BBC WAC, corresp. with BBC staff · BL, corresp. with Lytton and James Strachey, Add. MS 60662 · JRL, letters to *Manchester Guardian* · TCD, corresp. with Thomas Bodkin · TCD, corresp. with Nancy and Joseph Campbell · TCD, letters to Thomas MacGeevy · TCD, letters to Seumas O'Sullivan | SOUND BL NSA, recording of readings from his own works by Padraic Colum

Likenesses J. B. Yeats, portrait, 1906?, NG Ire. [*see illus.*] · T. Spicer-Simson, bronze medallion, 1923, NG Ire. · R. Gregory, charcoal drawing, NG Ire.; Coole, Lady Gregory sale, 1932 · E. T. Quinn, bronze bust, Hugh Lane Gallery of Modern Art, Dublin · L. Williams, pastel drawing, Abbey Theatre, Dublin · J. B. Yeats, pencil drawing, Abbey Theatre, Dublin · portrait (of Colum?), New York University, Birmingham, New York, archives

Columba. *See* Colum mac Crimthainn (*d.* 549) *under* Munster, saints of (*act. c.*450–*c.*700).

Columba [St Columba, Colum Cille] (*c.*521–597), monastic founder, was also known by the Old Irish name of Colum Cille, meaning, approximately, 'Church Dove'. He was the son of Fedelmid, of the royal lineage of Conall Gulban mac Néill, and of Ethne, daughter of Mac Naue. His immediate paternal relatives were rulers in the north-west of Ireland while his wider kin group, the Uí Néill ('descendants of Niall') were already emerging in the sixth century as Ireland's dominant royal dynasty. Columba thus was born into the highest rank of Irish nobility. Gartan, in Donegal, is traditionally claimed as his place of birth, but there is no documentary source earlier than the twelfth century to verify this. It may be assumed, however, that his homeland was in the north-west, among the Cenél Conaill ('the kindred of Conall'), the people whose designation commemorated Columba's great-grandfather.

Early life The date of Columba's birth, c.521, is based on the known fact that he died in the year 597, aged about seventy-six. The fifth century had seen Christianity established widely in Ireland, and while it cannot be assumed that the process was complete by Columba's time, nevertheless, there seems no good reason to doubt that his family was Christian. The seventh-century life of Columba (Adomnán's *Vita Columbae*), the main source of biographical information, makes brief mention of his foster father, a priest called Cruithnechán, and refers also to his teachers: a master called Gemmán in Leinster, with whom he studied as a young deacon, and a bishop called variously Findbarr, Finnio, or Uinniau. The implication is that Columba's commitment to religion began at an early age, but the life, which focuses primarily on the manifestations of sanctity in his monastic career, does not trace his progress towards this goal. In fact, while it may be inferred that he became a monk and priest, and that he may have founded monasteries in his native territory, Columba's career up to his forty-second year is unrecorded. The defining moment of his life came in that year, 563, when he left Ireland for the west coast of Scotland.

Departure to Britain The life of Columba states that he went to Britain in the second year following the battle of Cúl Dreimne, 'wishing to be a pilgrim for Christ' (*Adomnán's Life of Columba*, second preface). While the reference to the battle may have served merely as a chronological marker, the conjunction of battle and exile have long prompted speculation that they were connected. Irish sources from the tenth or eleventh century onward portrayed Columba's departure from Ireland as a penance, self-imposed or otherwise, for having instigated the battle. Annalistic accounts of the battle itself, while not contemporary, may retain a genuine record of the defeat of the king of Tara, from the southern Uí Néill, by a northern alliance which included two of Columba's relations. A reference in the life to the wrongful excommunication of Columba by an Irish synod in Tailtiu in southern Uí Néill territory has been viewed as a further significant factor in these events. Did the Tara king seek to avenge his defeat at the hands of Columba's kin by inducing clerics from his own kingdom to this act of censure? It is possible that Columba could have incurred the wrath of opponents of his royal relations. Yet there is no corroborating evidence to suggest a direct connection between battle, synod, and exile.

In broader terms, however, it may be supposed that Columba's membership of the Uí Néill royal dynasty was not a negligible factor in determining the course of his career. His family's involvement in secular politics may have made a life of monastic withdrawal in his homeland increasingly difficult. Therefore, having formerly renounced his secular position, Columba may have felt compelled to further renunciation, to distancing himself from familial territory for the sake of Christ. Indeed, as early Irish secular law equated exile from community with loss of status and rights, so Irish monasticism viewed voluntary separation from home and kin as self-abnegation meriting high heavenly reward.

How was the destination of Columba's exile chosen? The sources do not provide a direct answer. However, a list, dating from the early eighth century, of the twelve companions on the journey from Ireland includes an uncle, Ernán, and two first cousins, Baíthéne and Cobthach, suggesting that Columba's journey was planned with the support of his kin. Moreover, the life depicts Columba soon after arrival in Britain in the company of the ruler of Dál Riata, the area of south-west Scotland colonized by Irish settlers some decades previously. This suggests, not a random sea journey, but conscious choice of an Irish overseas community, whose ruler may have had some association with Columba's royal relatives. The assertion in the Irish annals that Iona was given to Columba by Conall mac Comgaill, king of Dál Riata, is not contemporary, but it seems to be confirmed by the available evidence.

The foundation of Iona Columba's Scottish career thus began in the Dál Riata kingdom, which retained ties of language, culture, and politics with Ireland. His decision to settle on the small, apparently unpopulated, island of Iona, off the south-western tip of Mull, indicates that the primary focus of his pilgrimage was ascetic. The sources suggest that Dál Riata was mainly Christian at this time. But if Columba had initially sought a pastoral role within the kingdom, or a missionary role beyond, he would surely have wished his chief foundation to be closer to a centre of power and population. The earliest surviving source about Columba, a vernacular praise poem known as *Amra Coluim Cille* ('The eulogy of Colum Cille'), written in Ireland at about the time of his death, provides independent support for the testimony of Adomnán's *Vita Columbae* that Columba's religious vocation was to the monastic life.

However, since the island community needed outside assistance to maintain itself, especially in its early stages, Iona's intended function cannot have been as an isolated hermitage, but rather as a monastery open to visitors. Whether or not Columba's fame as a churchman had preceded him from Ireland, his reputation in Dál Riata apparently became established within a short time. The life reveals that, as well as those bringing necessary supplies, there came to Iona a constant stream of pilgrims, penitents, and aspiring monks. Was the response to his foundation greater than Columba anticipated? It certainly seems to have led to the extension of the activities of his community beyond Iona, and to the establishment of monastic foundations on other islands and on mainland Dál Riata territory. Some outlying monasteries may have served Iona in a specific way, as in the case of Campus

Lunge, on the island of Tiree, where penitents who came to Iona were accommodated. Other foundations probably replicated the activity of Iona, maintaining a monastic community which served also as a focus of religious life for secular and ecclesiastical visitors.

Columba's monastic *familia* A telling vignette in the life depicts Columba setting off into the wilder parts of Iona to find a place secluded from other people where he could pray alone. It encapsulates a life dedicated to following the monastic vocation, while also energetically involved in overseeing a growing ecclesiastical organization. Although Columba may have relinquished the privileges accorded by his birth, nevertheless his royal background appears to have had a formative influence on the way he governed his churches. In the case of the additional monasteries founded from Iona, he nominated a prior to administer each of these communities under his own overall authority. He visited outlying churches and constantly maintained communication with his growing *familia*. This pattern of government, wherein Iona retained primacy over its dependent churches, seems to derive from the secular Irish model of royal overlordship. It is notable, moreover, that kinship played an important role in Columba's monastic organization. Members of his extended family who had accompanied him into exile were among his first appointees to govern Iona's dependencies. The life reveals that Ernán, Columba's uncle, was prior of the important foundation on the island of 'Hinba', while his cousin Baíthéne was in charge of Campus Lunge on Tiree. Ties of family as well as of religion thus consolidated the unity of the churches.

Moreover, the umbilical connection with Ireland was not cut. Columba's Iona monastery was visited by pilgrims and churchmen from his homeland, and he is depicted in his life as sending emissaries to Ireland, and as visiting the country himself on at least two occasions. It was probably envisaged that Columba's native territory should continue to provide members of his monastic community in Scotland, yet the contact went beyond the necessities of recruitment. In fact, about two decades after his initial departure, Columba returned to Ireland to found the new monastery of Durrow in the midland region of the country. Moreover, he placed another of his relatives, Laisrén, a monk of Iona, in charge there. It is possible that churches such as Derry and Drumhome in Columba's native northern Uí Néill territory had already been founded by him before his Iona mission but there is no evidence as to their status *vis-à-vis* Iona. It is the foundation of Durrow which emphatically links Ireland with Scotland within the monastic *familia* of Columba.

Columba and kings Columba's royal descent seems to have been as influential in the external relations of his monastic community as in its internal government. Family contacts may have facilitated his initial settlement in Dál Riata and the granting to him of Iona, yet his relationship with the ruling dynasty of Dál Riata is not the conventional relationship of beneficiary towards patrons. Rather, the Iona abbot is portrayed as actively monitoring the conduct of kingship in his adopted territory. The life of Columba tells of his prayers to ensure royal success in battle and of his concern regarding succession to the Dál Riata kingship. There may be scepticism about the historical accuracy of the Old Testament-influenced account of Columba's 'ordination' of Aedán mac Gabrán as king of Dál Riata about 574, but it does seem credible that it had become politic for the local king to associate himself with Columba's prestige, and to receive the holy man's blessing on his inauguration. Subsequently, moreover, Columba apparently instigated a 'conference of kings', which brought the Scottish ruler to Druim Cett in the north of Ireland to meet Áed mac Ainmerech, overking of the Uí Néill, who was Columba's cousin. The resulting alliance between the Scottish ruler and Columba's royal kinsman in Ireland can be attributed to the Iona abbot's status and to his unique position of influence on both sides of the Irish Sea. The meeting of kings not only formalized relations between Columba's native and adopted kingdoms, but also provided a secure environment in which his monastic endeavour might flourish.

While hagiography is not historical fact, it is notable that kings, both in Ireland and in Britain, are consistently depicted in the life of Columba as subjects of saintly intervention. That Columba held that a king of his Uí Néill kin had 'the prerogative of monarchy over the kingdom of all Ireland predestined … by God' (*Adomnán's Life of Columba*, bk 1, cap. 14) is literary representation, yet it finds some corroboration. For instance, historical evidence places the Iona abbot's return to Ireland to found the monastery of Durrow between the years 585 and 589. From about 587 Áed mac Ainmerech, as king of the northern Uí Néill, had extended his dominance over his southern Uí Néill kinsmen. Thus, the timing of Columba's return to Ireland to establish the monastery of Durrow among the southern Uí Néill may be seen both as the outcome of, and as a support for, the achievement of political overlordship by his royal relatives.

Columba and the Picts While Columba's closest royal contacts were in Dál Riata and in Ireland, nevertheless, his horizons extended beyond a world which was ethnically and linguistically Irish. The life states that the king of the neighbouring British kingdom of Strathclyde was Columba's friend. Moreover, Columba is represented as visiting the stronghold of the Pictish king, Brude son of Maelchon. While the life does not provide a chronological framework for narratives concerning Columba's activities in Pictland, it does indicate the likely catalyst of his first visit. He travelled beyond 'the Spine of Britain', the mountain boundary between Dál Riata and Pictland, after the monk Cormac had put to sea in search of a hermitage. Thus, concern to ensure the safety of monastic voyagers who might land in Pictish-dominated areas apparently impelled the Iona abbot to visit the king.

It is reasonable to assume that Columba and his brethren were made aware on their travels of a need to preach Christianity to the pagan Picts. *Amra Coluim Cille* may be interpreted as declaring that 'he preached to the tribes of

Tay' (Stokes, 164–5). There are references in the life to individual conversions, and to Columba's preaching the gospel through an interpreter. Yet there is little to indicate that a large-scale mission of conversion was initiated from Iona at that time. Certainly, conversion was a prized saintly attribute, and the life of Columba includes some stock hagiographical episodes describing his confrontation with a pagan Pictish *magus*. There is, however, no historical warrant for the view that missionary activity came to dominate Columba's life. Although Bede states that Columba converted the Picts and received Iona from them, it would appear, rather, that the abbot's diplomacy, and his negotiating status as a fellow nobleman, had won from the Pictish king toleration of travelling and preaching in his territory. This tenuous *modus vivendi* did gain access to Pictland for Christian teaching, and thus paved the way for the subsequent evangelization of the kingdom.

Columba, monk of Iona In a career of thirty-four years in Britain, Columba organized, travelled, and negotiated in the interests of his community. He used his influence with kings for the welfare of the church and of secular society. His activities spanned both Scotland and Ireland, as indeed did his federation of monasteries. Yet his base was Iona, and monasticism, with its daily round of prayer, work, writing, and study, remained at the core of his religious life. The Iona monastic regime of observance and work seems to have been guided, moreover, by the abbot's humanity and empathy rather than by his strict insistence on law. The life of Columba portrays his solicitude for monks who were hard-worked at the harvest and at building. It reveals his willingness to relax the fast when visitors came to the island, and his clemency toward those who came to Iona to expiate past sins. Attachment to his native land is linked with compassion, as in the story of his care for a crane from Ireland cast by buffeting winds onto the Iona shore. Certainly Columba castigated evil doing, as in the memorable portrayal of his striding out knee-deep into the water in pursuit of marauders. But his altruism is what predominates, to the extent that, having unwittingly blessed a knife, he is said to have at once prayed that it should hurt neither man nor beast.

It is notable that Columba's lack of awareness that he had blessed a potentially deadly implement is attributed to his concentration on his writing. That scholarship was as important as asceticism in Columba's community is attested by the evidence of the vernacular *Amra* and of the life. In stating of Columba that 'he could not pass even the space of a single hour without applying himself to prayer or to reading or to writing or some other kind of work' (*Adomnán's Life of Columba*, second preface), the life significantly adds writing to a list of activities otherwise similar to that found in the life of Martin of Tours by Sulpicius Severus (*d.* 410). The copying of books is mentioned throughout the life, and among works stated to have been copied by Columba were the Psalms and a book of the week's hymns.

The *Amra*, in praising Columba's learning, is more specific about what he read and studied. The Bible is cited, in particular the Psalms, the books of Solomon, and 'the books of the Law'. Moreover, Columba is said to have used the judgments of St Basil (*d.* 379) and to have studied Greek grammar, as well as the movement of the heavenly bodies and the course of the sea. While poetic eulogy may have idealized the range of his learned activity, nevertheless, the *Amra* testimony is sufficiently close to the period of his lifetime to reflect contemporary scholarship. Most telling among *Amra* citations is a reference to John Cassian (*d.* 435), leading interpreter of monasticism in western Christendom. That Columba's monasticism was guided by the principles of a recognized authority is consistent with other evidence that his vocation combined intellectual scrutiny with ascetic and humanitarian commitment.

It was fitting that Columba should end his days among his own Iona community, after a full life of about seventy-six years. Reflecting community recollections of his last days, Adomnán's life of Columba tells how he inspected the barn to see that his *familia* was well supplied with food, and how the monastery's horse came up to him and mourned, sensing that its master was to depart for ever. Columba's final work, the copying of a psalter, ceased at the words of the thirty-third psalm: 'But they that seek the Lord shall not want for anything that is good.' The abbot rose to attend the midnight office as usual with the brethren, on 9 June 597, but he collapsed and breathed his last in the church, surrounded by his monks. His wish that his funeral ceremonies should not be an occasion for large crowds in Iona was granted, as a storm prevented any boat from crossing to the island during the ritual three days of obsequies. Thus, his monastic community laid Columba in the Iona earth, in a simple grave marked only by the stone which he had used for a pillow in his spartan cell. The location of this grave cannot now be identified.

Columba's monastic legacy His gravestone was not, in any case, the sole remembrance of Columba's achievement. The organization which he had put in place ensured that his monastic *familia* continued to flourish under the leadership of Iona-based abbots of his own kin [*see* Iona, abbots of]. In the seventh century, as new churches in Ireland and in Pictland were added to the *familia*, an invitation from the Northumbrian ruler Oswald took Iona clerics to Lindisfarne, where a short-lived Columban presence made a substantial contribution to the Christianization of the north of England. In 697, the centenary year of Columba's death, about ninety of the most prominent ecclesiastical and secular leaders of Ireland and Scotland endorsed a law for the protection of non-combatants brought forward by Columba's Iona successor and biographer, Adomnán. In the eighth century, further Irish enactments of a church–state measure, termed *Lex Columbe Cille*, testify to the continuing influential role of Columba's community in alliance with powerful kings.

From the beginning of the ninth century, however, the transmarine unity of the Columban world was put in jeopardy by the appearance of viking raiders around the Irish and British coasts. Iona was among churches severely attacked, so that Kells in the Irish midlands was founded as a refuge for Iona monks and its precious relics. By the tenth century, under the impact of the vikings, Irish and Scottish Columban churches had begun to go their separate ways. The Irish churches continued in federation under the headship of Kells, and subsequently of Derry, retaining a prominent role in the country until the mid-twelfth century. In Scotland, while individual churches retained their dedications to Columba, organizational unity does not seem to have prevailed. But Iona, although no longer at the hub of a far-flung Columban world, still managed to survive as a monastic centre, as a hallowed place of pilgrimage, and as a burial-place of kings, in this last capacity perhaps down to the end of the eleventh century. The Columban monastery was replaced by a Benedictine abbey about 1203, while in modern times the foundation of the ecumenical Iona community in 1938 has underlined the island's continued standing as a holy place.

The cult of Columba The longevity of his monastic enterprise ensured that Columba's name remained prominent for centuries in the insular ecclesiastical world. Yet his reputation as a holy man was as important as his reputation as patron of influential churches. The composition by an Irish poet of the eulogy known as the *Amra* testifies to Columba's immediate post-mortem acclamation as a dweller of heaven. Moreover, the life of Columba compiled by Adomnán, ninth abbot of Iona, illuminates the record of Columba's sanctification within his own community in the century after his death. Reminiscences from contemporaries, collected as formal evidence in the abbacy of Ségéne (623–52), appear to have formed the content of Iona's first hagiographical work, the *Liber de virtutibus sancti Columbae* by Cumméne, abbot of Iona from 657 to 669.

These early reminiscences, now known only through the incorporation of Cumméne's work into the life of Columba, reveal the conviction that Columba's sanctity imbued all the deeds of his life. Thus, instead of spectacular miracles, mundane happenings were seen to take on the hue of the supernatural. Some decades later Adomnán's work presents a portrayal more in keeping with the norms of Latin hagiography. The text reveals its familiarity with, for instance, Sulpicius Severus's account of Martin of Tours and Evagrius's translation of the life of Antony. Its three books, detailing prophecies, miracles, and supernatural revelations, highlight manifestations which liken Columba to the great holy men of Christendom. It would appear that Adomnán, whose own career as churchman and royal intermediary extended through Dál Riata, Pictland, Northumbria, and Ireland, was concerned that his patron's sanctity should be acknowledged in ecclesiastical circles far beyond Iona.

The life of Columba documents practical realizations of devotion to him in the century after his death. Adomnán himself recalls the Iona community's liturgical use of the saint's tunic and books to invoke his intercession against drought and contrary winds. The hagiographer asserts also that prayers to Columba were instrumental in his own assistance. Moreover, the life provides evidence of popular, as well as of monastic, devotion to Columba, recounting how certain brigands were protected during enemy attack by songs sung in Irish in praise of the saint. The survival of two seventh-century vernacular poems of this sort reinforces the view that Columba's cult was widely established in his homeland at an early date.

The hagiography of Columba Indeed, literary evidence of Columba's posthumous reputation comes mainly from Ireland. There is continuity with his earliest memorials, in so far as books and writing figure prominently. Medieval Irish legend linked the saint's departure from Ireland with his having surreptitiously copied a book belonging to St Finnian, and thereafter roused his kinsmen to battle in defiance of the judgment of King Diarmait mac Cerbaill that 'to every cow belongs her calf and to every book its copy' (*Betha Colaim Chille*, 178). Having been commemorated by a vernacular poet in the *Amra*, Columba came to be viewed as a patron of poets and their defender against banishment from Ireland. Moreover, he was himself claimed as a poet. Not only were Latin hymns such as the Iona-composed *Altus prosator* fathered on him by the eleventh century, but from that time onward a considerable amount of verse in Irish became associated with his name. The themes of exile and of prophecy are prominent. As Ireland and Scotland had grown politically apart, so Columba's life in Iona was reinterpreted as a painful isolation from a homeland lovingly remembered and revisited only in imagination. The focus on prophecy in the life probably set the tone for the saint's prophetic role through which warnings of impending disaster were channelled down through the centuries.

After Adomnán's life of Columba the only significant conventional work of hagiography was an austere twelfth-century vernacular life, the product of an era of ecclesiastical reform, which drew on that earlier life and eschewed legend. In the sixteenth century, however, as an act of *pietas*, Manus O'Donnell, a Donegal chieftain of Columba's lineage, directed the production of *Betha Colaim Chille*, a vernacular life which encompassed every available earlier memorial of the saint from the seventh century. Its wealth of anecdote and verse provides the most eloquent testimony to the continuing vitality of Columba's legend and cult throughout the thousand years after his birth.

It is appropriate that Manus O'Donnell should have chosen to celebrate his patron in a book, since written works not only bear witness to Columba's reputation but also constitute his most famous memorial objects. The *Cathach*, now in the Royal Irish Academy in Dublin, is a late sixth-century copy of the Psalms, said to have been written by the saint himself. It had been enshrined and was venerated in Columba's native Cenél Conaill territory. Being identified with the illicit copy which provoked the battle of Cúl Dreimne, the manuscript used to be borne around the host of the saint's kinsmen as they went into battle. The Book of Kells, 'the great gospel of Colum Cille', now in Trinity College Library, Dublin, seems to have been begun in eighth-century Iona, perhaps in celebration of the bicentennial of Columba's death. It was brought to

Kells, Iona's daughter house, probably in the ninth century, and was venerated there until the seventeenth century. As the illumination of the gospel book combines motifs of Celtic, north British, and Christian design, it reflects and commemorates the Christian unity forged by Columba across the Irish Sea.

Modern perceptions of Columba While we have no formal hagiographical works about Columba after the seventeenth century, the saint remained the subject of legend and folklore both in Ireland and in Scotland. Modern folklore indicates that down to recent decades he featured in traditional tales and religious sayings as a hero-figure, protector, or divine intermediary. His memory is also preserved to this day in church dedications and place names on both sides of the Irish Sea. Yet such survivals do not, in themselves, testify to a living cult. It would seem that his native Donegal is the most significant remaining place of continuous preservation of his religious commemoration. In the valley which bears his name, Glencolumbkille, in the south-west of the country, Columba's feast day, 9 June, is still marked by the performance of the 'turas' (literally 'journey'), in which pilgrims process along a designated route, offering prayers and seeking the saint's intercession. Alongside rare survivals of age-old devotion are contemporary refashionings of the saint. The modern Iona community may be seen as articulating Christian ideals in accordance with contemporary needs, thereby linking the island's religious past with present exigencies. Columba has also been refigured as a romanticized prototype of a lost 'Celtic Christianity', and therefore as embodying ideals missing from mainstream Christianity. Yet the saint's legacy has not been confined to the sphere of religion. The symbolic significance of Columba's career has been acknowledged in the naming of the 'Columba Initiative', a transnational initiative for the promotion of closer cultural links between Ireland and Scotland, inaugurated in 1997, the year of the celebration of the 1400th anniversary of the saint's death. Indeed, the diverse manner of celebration of this anniversary witnessed to the plurality of modern appropriations of Columba. While there were traditional and innovative religious ceremonies, the commemoration was also encouraged by secular interests, promoting cultural co-operation, conferences, heritage centres, and travel. In the modern quest for Columba's legacy, sightseeing features alongside pilgrimage, and transinsular political and cultural links draw on the symbolism of the founder of a religious institution whose influence spanned the Irish Sea.

MÁIRE HERBERT

Sources Adomnán's Life of Columba, ed. and trans. A. O. Anderson and M. O. Anderson, rev. edn, rev. M. O. Anderson, OMT (1991) • The life of St. Columba, founder of Hy written by Adamnan, ed. W. Reeves (1857) • W. Stokes, ed. and trans., 'The Bodleian Amra Choluimb Chille', Revue Celtique, 20 (1899), 31–55, 132–83, 248–87, 400–37 • W. Stokes, 'The Bodleian Amra Choluimb Chille', Revue Celtique, 21 (1900), 133–6 [corrections and additions] • Betha Colaim Chille: life of Columcille compiled by Manus O'Donnell in 1532, ed. and trans. A. O'Kelleher and G. Schoepperle (1918); repr. (1994) • Adomnán of Iona, Life of St Columba, ed. and trans. R. Sharpe (1995) • M. Herbert, Iona, Kells, and Derry: the history and hagiography of the monastic familia of Columba (1988) • J. F. Kenney, The sources for the early history of Ireland (1929); repr. (1979) • A. O. Anderson, ed. and trans., Early sources of Scottish history, AD 500 to 1286, 2 vols. (1922) • Ann. Ulster • Argyll: an inventory of the ancient monuments, 4: Iona, Royal Commission of Ancient and Historical Monuments of Scotland (1982) • F. Kelly, 'A poem in praise of Columb Cille', Ériu, 24 (1973), 1–34 • F. Kelly, 'Tiughraind Bhécáin', Ériu, 26 (1975), 66–98 • 'Changing perceptions of Columba', D. E. Week, The quest for Celtic Christianity (2000) **Likenesses** manuscript illumination (large coloured representation of saint in episcopal robes), Bodl. Oxf., manuscript copy of Betha Colaim Chille, sixteenth century, MS Rawlinson B 514, fol. 2

Columbanus [St Columbanus, Columban] (d. 615), missionary and monastic founder, was born in the Irish province of Leinster.

Origins and education Traditionally Columbanus's date of birth has been assumed to be somewhere about the year 543, though the reliability of this is questionable, since it was established on the basis of a reference in a poem whose former attribution to the saint is now in serious doubt. The first date that can be established with some certainty is that of his arrival in Gaul. In a letter probably written in 603 he remarks that he has spent twelve years in Gaul, which would mean that he arrived in 590–91. According to his biographer Jonas, Columbanus was by then twenty years of age; in some manuscripts this was changed to thirty years, which seems closer to the mark. Columbanus might therefore have been born somewhere about 560–70, though an even earlier date cannot be excluded.

Thanks to Jonas, much is known of Columbanus's life. Jonas was from Susa, and entered the monastery of Bobbio three years after Columbanus had died there. Not only did he have access in Bobbio to people who had known his subject, he also travelled with Amandus to visit other monasteries founded by Columbanus, in order to gather information for his literary works. His life is the main source of information for Columbanus's youth; Columbanus's own extant works add to Jonas's tale only for his later life.

Although her name is unrecorded, Columbanus's mother plays a significant role in the life; his father is not mentioned once. As is customary in saints' lives, Jonas starts his story with a premonition of the child's future greatness. He records how Columbanus's mother while pregnant had a dream in which a radiant sun came out of her body to light the world that had been lying in the darkness of a silent night. It was explained to her that this signified that the child she was bearing would be a man of such great talents that he would be of much help, not only for his own salvation, but also for that of his fellow men. According to Jonas, Columbanus's mother took charge of her son's education, in the course of which he was instructed in grammar and the liberal arts. This suggests that she was of some social standing. It was also his mother who tried with all her might to prevent her son from leaving his parental home to take up the monastic life. She stood in the doorway to obstruct his departure, but broke down before her son's determination. With one big step he then leapt over his crying mother and over the threshold, never to return again.

Columbanus is said to have been an attractive young man. Lascivious girls fell in love with him, but he defended himself with the sword of the gospels, because he did not want his studies in grammar, rhetoric, geometry, and Holy Scripture to have been in vain (as Jonas explains with another hagiographical topos). An unnamed anchoress induced him to take up the monastic life. His first teacher was a certain Sinilis, maybe Mo Sinu (or Sillan), who at that time may have been a teacher in one of the daughter houses of Bangor (Down), of which monastery he later became abbot. Under his supervision Columbanus apparently wrote a commentary on the psalms, and 'several other works that were useful in chant and instruction' (Jonas, 69). Thereafter he entered the monastery of Bangor under its founder abbot, Comgall. After a number of years the characteristically Irish inclination towards pilgrimage (*peregrinatio*) made itself felt, and he asked the abbot for permission to leave the monastery. Comgall reluctantly gave his consent and let Columbanus go, together with twelve companions.

Foundations in Merovingian Gaul Columbanus and his followers arrived in Brittany about 591. From there they went to Frankish Gaul, where, according to Jonas—who certainly exaggerated in order to highlight his hero's achievements—Christian life had sunk to a very low level. The ascetic life of these foreign monks apparently so impressed the Merovingian king (of uncertain identity) and his entourage that they enabled Columbanus to found the monastery of Annegray, some 10 miles east of Luxeuil-les-Bains in Burgundy. This community grew steadily because of its attraction to members of Merovingian aristocratic families. In a few years it had become so overcrowded that it was necessary to found a new community in the neighbourhood: the monastery of Luxeuil. This foundation was sponsored by a grant from King Childebert II. Again this house attracted a great multitude of monks, so that yet another foundation, that of Fontaines, 5 miles north-west of Luxeuil, became necessary. Jonas tells that the community of Fontaines numbered some sixty monks, while the three houses together counted two hundred and twenty monks. The precariousness with which their inmates maintained a bare subsistence in these communities seems to be reflected in Jonas's concern with questions of food shortages and in his accounts of miracles which relieved the monks. Following the Irish custom, Columbanus ruled these three houses in person.

From the moment of their foundation Columbanus's monasteries appear to have enjoyed immunity from episcopal interference. Columbanus may even have brought a monastic bishop with him, for in one of his letters he refers to the altar in Luxeuil that was blessed by the holy Bishop Aid. Aid may have been one of his early companions, since the name is clearly a form of the Irish Áed, unless Columbanus is referring to a portable altar that he took from Ireland after Aid had blessed it. Foundation charters of these monasteries have not survived, but other monasteries in the Columbanian tradition received written monastic immunities. Nevertheless, Columbanus

came into conflict with the Frankish episcopacy over the Irish method of calculating the date of Easter. During this controversy he appealed to Pope Gregory the Great in a fascinating, self-conscious letter, probably dating from the year 600, in which he challenged the pope to abandon the fifth-century Victorine calculation in favour of the Irish one that he attributed to Anatolius. In a letter from 603 to the bishops assembled in Chalon-sur-Saône to discuss the case, his tone was much more yielding. The pressure on him, including a threat of banishment, had become so great that he now wanted to be left in peace to follow his own customs. Other differences of opinion may also have played a role, since Columbanus in this letter stressed the different vocations of secular clerics and monks. When the bishops remained hostile, Columbanus again appealed to the pope, this time probably to Gregory's successor Sabinian, whose name he did not yet know. Again he asked to be left in peace and for permission to observe the customs of his fatherland, especially since he still considered himself to be in his homeland (*in patria*), an expression which possibly refers to some sort of monastic immunity.

Notwithstanding these difficulties with local bishops, Columbanus remained in royal favour until 609–10. According to Jonas, King Theuderic II of Burgundy, the southernmost of the three kingdoms which comprised the Merovingian realm, was very pleased to have a man of such renown in his kingdom and invited him to court. On one such occasion Brunechildis, the king's grandmother, presented the king's sons to the holy man for a blessing. But the saint refused this, apparently because the children had not been born in lawful wedlock. Theuderic and Brunechildis urgently needed legitimate heirs, so Columbanus's staunch refusal posed a significant threat to their authority. Jonas particularly blames Brunechildis for the conflict, depicting her as a second Jezebel, while the king seems to have been more cautious. Columbanus broke off all contact with the royal court and Theuderic retaliated by banishing Columbanus from his kingdom and commanding him to return to his native country. The holy man, however, refused to leave his monastery, whereupon the king's men tried in vain to force him into exile. In the end Columbanus yielded, not to force, but out of compassion for the king's men, who would have been killed if they had not succeeded in their task. At least, that is how Jonas describes this episode, in which Columbanus's power and determination are highlighted.

Columbanus's banishment from Burgundy did not mean the end for his foundations. Some of his followers remained behind, while another group followed him. According to Jonas, only the foreigners were expelled, while the indigenous monks were allowed to stay. In a consolatory letter sent to the brethren he left behind, Columbanus hints at some disagreement among his followers, which may have caused some of his monks to flee to the Austrasian court.

Exile, wanderings, and death Columbanus was taken to Nantes in Brittany, where Bishop Soffronius and Count Theudald were to ensure he departed for Ireland. While

Jonas holds a miracle responsible for the fact that Columbanus did not, in the event, sail away, in his consolatory letter Columbanus suggests that he was urged to flee. He then turned to King Chlothar II of Neustria (the western Merovingian kingdom), who tried to persuade him to settle in his kingdom. For reasons which remain obscure, Columbanus declined this offer. The motives Jonas provides, namely that Columbanus foresaw trouble between Chlothar and the Austrasian king, Theudebert, on his account and wanted to continue his pilgrimage, do not seem very convincing. Travelling via Meaux and Ussy-sur-Marne (where he blessed the aristocratic children Burgundofara, Dado, and Ado, who would later found monasteries in the Columbanian tradition), Columbanus arrived at the court of Austrasia (the eastern Merovingian kingdom), where he met some of his former monks who had come there as refugees. Since King Theudebert II received him with due respect, Columbanus offered to settle down in the ancient city of Bregenz, on Lake Constance, to Christianize the neighbourhood. He miraculously interfered with an apparently pagan beer-offering, in which, however, Christians also seem to have participated; he condemned this practice in his penitential. But, according to Jonas, Bregenz did not appeal to Columbanus and he subsequently travelled to Italy, leaving his disciple Gall behind, probably after a quarrel, as Gall's biographies suggest.

In Italy, Columbanus was received honourably by the Lombard King Agilulf and in Milan he preached against the Arians and took sides in the Three Chapters controversy (a dispute arising from a condemnation of Nestorian heresy issued by the emperor Justinian) against Pope Boniface IV. Finally, he founded a new monastery at Bobbio, on the River Trebbia in north-west Italy, where he died on 23 November 615.

Letters and penitential writings While some of Columbanus's writings are still extant, some have been lost, and others attributed to him are of dubious authenticity. Among the first group, the letters are the most personal. Six letters have survived, three addressed to popes: one to Gregory the Great, one probably to his successor Sabinian, and one to Boniface IV. A fourth letter is addressed to the Frankish bishops who assembled at Chalon-sur-Saône to discuss the Easter question; another is written from Nantes to his disciples who had remained behind in Luxeuil; and the sixth is a letter of instruction addressed to an unknown pupil. The letters seem to have been collected at Bobbio, possibly by his biographer; a manuscript containing all six was available there in the seventeenth century, but has since been lost. Only the sixth letter, addressed to the anonymous disciple, has been preserved in manuscript form, since it was transmitted in combination with his sermons and penitential.

Columbanus's penitential, a handbook intended as a manual for hearing confession and assigning an appropriate penance for each sin, has also only been preserved in manuscripts from Bobbio. The work documents Columbanus's adherence to the Irish custom of secret penance, which in this form had previously been unknown on the continent. In Gaul up to that time penance had normally been a public affair, to be administered by the bishop only once in a lifetime. In Ireland, in contrast, the monastic custom of devotional confession had been extended to the clergy and laity; and this structure is nicely reflected in Columbanus's penitential, which is divided into three parts: one devoted to monks, one to secular clerics, and one to the laity. This Irish form of penance was repeatable and could be administered by a simple priest, and perhaps even by monks. Although Irish customs differed in this respect from continental ones, the introduction of this new form of penance does not seem to have aroused any controversy, not even at the Council of Mâcon of 626–7, where the former Columbanian monk Agrestius attacked Columbanus's teachings. From Jonas's life it seems that the medicine of penance (*penitentiae medicamenta*) was particularly attractive to the population in Gaul. Columbanus made extensive use of older insular works of this genre, such as the penitential of Finnian.

Columbanus's *Regula coenobialis* is a sort of monastic penitential prescribing penances for sinful behaviour by monks. It goes into considerable detail, providing the appropriate penance for scratching on the table with a knife, for not blessing the spoon, or for losing crumbs of food. Penances consist mainly of corporal punishment, psalm singing, and fasting. The ritualism of this rule was criticized by Agrestius, but apparently the bishops assembled at Mâcon saw nothing irregular in it. The *Regula coenobialis* shows striking similarities to early insular penitentials by Columbanus and others; it was even called a penitential in one ninth-century manuscript. Columbanus's *Regula monachorum*, on the other hand, is a totally different kind of text. It is a moral treatise concerned with an exposition of monastic virtues, among which those of obedience, silence, and fasting seem to be of paramount importance. Apart from some provisions regulating daily worship, the text contains no practical regulation whatsoever.

The textual history of these rules and of the penitential is rather complicated. They seem to have been freely abridged or enlarged as seemed appropriate, and it is not always clear which parts were originally written by Columbanus or reflect his actual teaching, and which were added later. Nevertheless, these texts can be said to stand in the tradition of Columbanian monasticism. This is not so clear with the thirteen sermons attributed to Columbanus.

Sermons and poems The authenticity of the sermons has been questioned on the basis of a passage in which the author speaks of Faustus, bishop of Riez in the fifth century, as his teacher. The two do not coincide chronologically, which would seem to rule out Columbanus as author of this text and therefore of the whole collection of sermons. However, early medieval rhetorical conventions appear to have permitted referring to a dead person as one's teacher. The collection seems to have been intended as a coherent series of sermons to be used for a monastic audience. Their emphasis on trinitarian matters suggests that they might have been written in Milan, where Columbanus condemned Arianism and took sides in the Three Chapters controversy. The strong moral content of the sermons is similar to the tenor of his *Regula monachorum*. The manuscript tradition strongly suggests a Columbanian origin, and parallels with the poem known as *Carmen de mundi transitu*, which is generally accepted as a genuine work by Columbanus, strengthen this supposition. Stylistically the sermons would fit nicely with what is known of Columbanus as an author, while the sources used in them point in the same direction. The fifth sermon, a short tract on the miseries of the human life, had a wider circulation than the rest, and was particularly associated in manuscripts with Columbanus's monastic rules.

The attribution of poems to Columbanus has been hotly disputed. The editor of his collected writings included five poems as written by him, but of these only the *Carmen de mundi transitu* is now regarded as being from his hand. A case has been made, however, for the three poems addressed to Seth, Hunaldus, and Fidolius; the first of these might be Columbanus's disciple Gall, who seems to have been known by this nickname. The hymn 'Precamur patrem' in the antiphonary of Bangor could also be the work of Columbanus, written before he left Ireland, as it seems to conform to the intricate stylistic features of which Columbanus made ample use.

Columbanus is also said to be the author of a commentary on the psalms, which has probably been lost. The same fate awaited his work against Arianism and on the Three Chapters controversy, written while in Milan. From his letters it is clear that parts of his correspondence, in particular with the papacy, have also been lost. Two short tracts *De homine misero* and *De VIII vitiis principalibus*, though usually counted among the dubious works of Columbanus, stand a good chance of being authentic.

Achievement and cult   Columbanus is regarded as the instigator of Hiberno-Frankish monasticism, in which Irish monastic vigour was soon taken up by Franks. His immediate successors in Luxeuil and Bobbio, for example, were Franks. Many monasteries in Gaul followed Columbanus's rule in combination with the rule of St Benedict, and possibly other monastic regulations, as exemplified, for example, by the rules of Donatus and Waldebert. Perhaps it was from such foundations that the rule of St Benedict reached England. Columbanus's penitential was also influential mainly in combination with other texts. His injunctions form the basis of the so-called 'simple' Frankish penitentials, in which they were combined with canons from Frankish councils. These texts were in turn incorporated in compilations that added material from the penitential of Theodore of Canterbury and that of the Irish abbot Cummene Fota. Columbanus's cult did not spread far beyond the monasteries he had founded, Luxeuil and Bobbio, and the foundation of his disciple Gall, the abbey of St Gallen in Switzerland. His literary remains, almost without exception, come from these places, where they were apparently well preserved. It was also in Bobbio that Jonas wrote his life to honour this vigorous monk, and to keep alive the legacy of a man who was, in his own words, a 'dissenter whenever necessary' (Walker, 56).   ROB MEENS

Sources   Jonas, 'Vita Columbani abbatis discipulorumque eius', *Passiones vitaeque sanctorum aevi Merovingici*, ed. B. Krusch, MGH Scriptores Rerum Merovingicarum, 4 (Hanover, 1902) · *Sancti Columbani opera*, ed. G. Walker and G. S. M. Walker, Scriptores Latini Hiberniae, 2 (1957); repr. (1970) · M. Lapidge, ed., *Columbanus: studies on the Latin writings* (1997) · H. B. Clarke and M. Brennan, eds., *Columbanus and Merovingian monasticism* (1981) · K. Schäferdiek, 'Columbans Wirken im Frankenreich (591–612)', *Die Iren und Europa im früheren Mittelalter*, ed. H. Löwe, 1 (Stuttgart, 1982), 171–201 · I. Wood, 'The *Vita Columbani* and Merovingian hagiography', *Peritia*, 1 (1982), 63–80 · J. Laporte, *Le pénitentiel de saint Colomban*, Monumenta Christiana Selecta, 4 (Tournai, 1958) · *Saint Colomban: règles et pénitentiels monastiques*, ed. and trans. A. de Vogüé, P. Sangiani, and J. B. Juglar, 2 (Bégrolles-en-Manges, 1989) · J. W. Smit, *Studies on the language and style of Columba the Younger (Columbanus)* (1971) · M. Lapidge, 'The authority of the Adonic verses *Ad Fidolium* attributed to Columbanus', *Studi Medievali*, 3rd ser., 18 (1977), 249–314 · P. C. Jacobsen, 'Carmina Columbani', *Die Iren und Europa im früheren Mittelalter*, ed. H. Löwe, 1 (Stuttgart, 1982), 434–67 · D. Schaller, 'Die Siebensilberstrophen "de mundi transitu"—eine Dichtung Columbans?', *Die Iren und Europa im früheren Mittelalter*, ed. H. Löwe, 1 (Stuttgart, 1982), 468–83 · M. Herren, 'A ninth-century poem for St Gall's feast day and the *Ad Sethum* of Columbanus', *Studi Medievali*, 3rd ser., 24 (1983), 487–520 · M. Lapidge, 'Columbanus and the "antiphonary of Bangor"', *Peritia*, 4 (1985), 104–16 · D. Howlett, 'The earliest Irish writers at home and abroad', *Peritia*, 8 (1994), 1–17 · D. Howlett, 'Two works of Saint Columban', *Mittellateinisches Jahrbuch*, 28 (1994), 27–46 · H. Löwe, 'Columban und Fidolius', *Deutsches Archiv*, 37 (1981), 1–19 · P. Wormald, 'Bede and Benedict Biscop', *Famulus Christi: essays in commemoration of the thirteenth centenary of the birth of the Venerable Bede*, ed. G. Bonner (1976), 141–69 · H. L. C. Tristram, *Early insular preaching: verbal artistry and method of composition* (Vienna, 1995) · *Acta sanctorum: November*, 2/2 (Brussels, 1931), 617

Columbine, Edward Henry (1762–1811), hydrographer and colonial governor, was born on 2 July 1762. Nothing is known about his parents or upbringing, but he had a sister, Sarah, who married into the Dorrington family, later of Lypiatt Park, Gloucestershire. He went to sea as a midshipman aged fifteen in 1778, and on 9 July of that year he was wounded and captured; he spent seventeen months as a French prisoner before being exchanged. As a junior officer he saw action in many of the engagements with the French in the West Indies and North America, and was promoted lieutenant following the battle of the Saints (1782). Columbine was an accomplished artist in pencil and watercolour and this may well have first attracted him to the skills of hydrographic surveying. Many beautifully drawn charts and landscapes produced by him are preserved in various archives although, due to the absence at the time of any organized system of chart publication, few found their way into print.

On 29 April 1802 Columbine was promoted captain and given command of the frigate *Ulysses* (44 guns), guardship for the island of Trinidad. He took with him a complete set of instruments in order to undertake a survey of the island in addition to his anti-privateer duties, but although the renewed outbreak of war with France prevented him from completing the survey, his work formed the basis of the chart of Trinidad published by the Admiralty in 1816. He returned to England in 1804, and soon afterwards married Anne Curry (*d.* 1810), with whom he had a son, Edward, and a daughter, Charlotte, neither of whom survived to adulthood. In 1808 he was selected, together with two other captains with hydrographic experience, to form a committee to advise the Board of Admiralty on the future organization of the hydrographic department of the navy. The recommendations put forward by this important body, known at the time as the Admiralty chart committee, were instrumental in making that department the foremost hydrographic organization in the world by the mid-nineteenth century. Probably because of experiences during his service in the West Indies, he developed strong sympathies with the anti-slavery movement and became a commissioner of the African Institution. Following the passing of the Abolition Act of 1807, in 1809 he was appointed governor of the newly established crown colony of Sierra Leone in the rank of commodore with the authority to establish an Admiralty prize court for the disposal of captured slaving vessels and the release and resettlement of their cargoes. To assist in enforcing the act he was given command of a frigate, the *Solebay* (32 guns), together with some smaller vessels. On the voyage to Sierra Leone the squadron attacked and captured Senegal, the sole remaining French colony in west Africa. However, while Columbine was onshore in command of the landing parties, the master of the *Solebay*, while endeavouring to engage the shore batteries, allowed the ship to get too close inshore and it was wrecked. Columbine was court-martialled for her loss but was acquitted of blame and provided with another frigate, the *Crocodile*.

It was not until February 1810 that Columbine finally reached Freetown for what was to prove an unfortunately brief period as governor. The notoriously unhealthy climate of west Africa proved disastrous for the Columbine family. Within seven months his wife and infant daughter died of fever, while his young son, although sent home, did not survive to his majority. Although himself debilitated by frequent bouts of sickness, Columbine struggled on and much was achieved. The finances of the colony were put on a sound footing, a printing press was established, and two Rhode Island slave ships were captured under false colours and their cargoes released. However, in May 1811 he felt unable to continue and embarked for home in the *Crocodile*. On 18 June 1811 he died of yellow fever on the ship and was buried at sea.

CHRISTOPHER TERRELL

Sources H. Columbine, journals and correspondence when governor of Sierra Leone, 1809–11, University of Illinois, Chicago, the Sierra Leone collection, 22949 · documents relating to the admiralty hydrographic office, 1795–1808, PRO, ADM 1/3522 and 1/3523 · H. Columbine, report on his survey of Trinidad, 1804, hydrographic department, Taunton, misc. papers AC 8/46 · C. Terrell, 'Captain Columbine, Alexander Dalrymple and the troubled birth of the British admiralty hydrographic service', *Journées franco-anglaises d'histoire de la Marine* (1986) · Notes on the naval career of E. H. Columbine, 1891, *Cheltenham Ladies College Magazine* (1891) · captain's log of HMS *Ulysses*, 1802–4, PRO, ADM 51/1485 · *GM*, 1st ser., 79 (1809), 866 · *GM*, 1st ser., 81/1 (1811), 285 · will of Edward Henry Columbine, 1811, PRO, PROB 11/1525 · private information (2004) [Dorrington family records]

Archives Bristol City Industrial Museum, model of a corvette, *Sea Horse* · Glos. RO, accounts · Library, Carlisle, volume of drawings of the Lake District · NL Scot., journal; letters relating to anti-smuggling duties in Ulster, western Scotland, Orkney, and Shetland · NMM, drawings, paintings, and charts · Tullie House Museum and Art Gallery, Carlisle, album of sketches · University of Illinois, Chicago, journals, corresp., and papers | U. Hull, Brynmor Jones L., letters to Thomas Perronet Thompson, and papers

Wealth at death bequeathed all property 'in the Public Funds' for education of son; also books, plate, drawings, papers, instruments, swords, and pistols to son; bureau and dispatch box to Samuel Currs: will, PRO, PROB 11/1525

Colvile [Coldewel], **George** (*fl.* 1556), translator, is said by Anthony Wood to have been a student at Oxford University, but his name appears in none of the university records. He may perhaps be identified with the physician George Coldwell of Northamptonshire. This Coldwell was granted conditional permission to graduate MB at Cambridge in 1542 after nine years' study and practice in London and elsewhere. He is next noticed on 29 January 1558, when he was licensed to practise by the College of Physicians. By 1596 he was living in Northampton, where he appears to have died about 1612.

Colvile was responsible for a translation of Boethius's *De consolatione philosophiae* into English prose. This translation was first printed in London by John Cawood in 1556. Wood and Thomas Tanner record editions of 1561, 1566, and a further undated edition, but if these editions were ever printed, it appears that they are no longer extant. Colvile's translation was not printed again until it was published by the Tudor Library at the end of the nineteenth century. His version was made directly from Boethius's Latin, from 'a very old prynt' according to the title-page. Cawood printed the translator's Latin text in his inner margin alongside the English, while the commentary runs in the outer margin. Colvile's translation is generally accurate and his prose clear. He sometimes resorts to parenthetical expansions of the text, some of which go beyond Boethius's meaning. This technique is most apparent in his prose renderings of Boethius's verse interludes, where he explains the poetic metaphors. The slight marginal commentary details mythological references, briefly points the moral, or simply indicates the subject treated. Colvile dedicated his 'rude' translation to Queen Mary (*Consolation*, ed. Bax, 4). His dedicatory letter takes as its theme *mens sana in corpore sano*, a factor which provides some slight support for the identification of the translator with the Northamptonshire physician.

P. BOTLEY

Sources *Boetius de consolationae* [sic] *philosophiae / the boke of Boecius: called 'The comforte of philosophye or wysedome'*, trans. G. Colvile (1556) · Wood, *Ath. Oxon.*, new edn, 1.48 · Venn, *Alum. Cant.*, 1/1.366 · Cooper, *Ath. Cantab.*, 2.208–9 · H. B. Lathrop, *Translations from the classics into English from Caxton to Chapman, 1477–1620* (1967), 54–6 · Tanner, *Bibl. Brit.-Hib.*, 192 · *Thomas Warton's history of English poetry*, ed. D. Fairer, 2 (1998), 35 · J. Ames, T. F. Dibdin, and W. Herbert, eds., *Typographical antiquities, or, The history of printing in England, Scotland and Ireland*, 4 vols. (1810–19), 4.397 · *Boethius' 'Consolation of* *philosophy', translated from the Latin by George Colville, 1556*, ed. E. B. Bax (1897)

Colvile, Sir Henry Edward (1852–1907), army officer, born at Kirkby Mallory, Leicestershire, on 10 July 1852, was the only son of Colonel Charles Robert Colvile (1815–1886) of Lullington Hall, near Burton upon Trent, Liberal-Conservative (later Liberal) MP for South Derbyshire 1841–9 and 1865–8, and his wife, the Hon. Katharine Sarah Georgina, eldest daughter of Captain John Russell RN, and Sophia, Baroness de Clifford. His mother's father was grandson of John Russell, fourth duke of Bedford. Educated at Eton College, he entered the army as lieutenant in the Grenadier Guards on 1 October 1870, and was promoted captain on 15 March 1872. From 1876 to 1880 he was regimental instructor of musketry, and from 1880 to 1883 aide-de-camp to the Hon. Leicester Smyth, the general commanding at the Cape of Good Hope.

In 1884 Colvile served in the intelligence department in the Sudan. He was at the battles of al-Teb and Tamai, and was mentioned in dispatches. Later in 1884 he served on the Gordon relief expedition, with the intelligence department, and was at the action of Abu Klea in January 1885. He was made CB on 25 August 1885. From 1885 to 1888 he was on the staff in Egypt, partly with the frontier field force, and was at the battle of Giniss on 30 December 1885.

Repeatedly mentioned in dispatches, Colvile achieved a reputation as one of the army's best intelligence officers, and was promoted lieutenant-colonel in November 1882 and colonel in January 1886. In 1893 he was sent to the Uganda protectorate as acting commissioner, and in 1894 he commanded the successful expedition against Kabarega, king of Bunyoro. He was awarded the brilliant star of Zanzibar, second class, and was made CMG in January 1895. Forced to retire from Uganda by ill health, he came home; in July 1895 he was promoted to KCMG, and in March 1898 he became major-general.

After briefly commanding a brigade at Gibraltar, Colvile in 1899 commanded the guards brigade in the Second South African War. He was with Methuen's force attempting to relieve Kimberley (besieged since 15 October 1899), and took part in the successful actions at Belmont (23 November) and Modder River (28 November), and the defeat of Magersfontein (10–11 December). When the South African field force was reorganized under Lord Roberts (in 1900) Colvile commanded the new 9th division, and marched with the main army to attack General Cronje's force. Colvile's and General Kelly-Kenny's division hemmed in Cronje at Paardeberg after desperate fighting (18 February). Colvile took part with Roberts in the occupation of Bloemfontein (13 March), after engagements at Poplar Grove (7 March) and Driefontein (10 March).

While at Bloemfontein Colvile became entangled in events which ruined his military career. He failed in his attempt to relieve General Broadwood's column after it had been ambushed by General C. R. De Wet at Sannah's Post (30–31 March 1900), and his failure was unfairly assigned by Roberts to a reprehensible lack of vigour.

Roberts had been slow in ordering Colvile to try to rescue Broadwood. A further disaster befell Colvile later. Roberts, on his advance from Bloemfontein to Pretoria in May, left Colvile, still nominally in command of the division, on the line of communication, with orders to press on to Heilbron. At the end of May, Colonel Spragge, in command of 500 men of the 13th battalion imperial yeomanry, which had been directed to join Colvile's division, allowed his force to be surrounded outside Lindley by General P. D. De Wet's force, which was not much larger. Appeals for help reached Colvile, who disregarded them, and arrived at Heilbron, after severe fighting, according to his orders, on 29 May. Spragge's force was captured by the Boers, with heavy casualties, on 31 May. Colvile's position was difficult: he had been led to believe that his presence at Heilbron by a certain date was essential to Robert's plans, but he had also received an appeal for help from a part of the force assigned to him.

After the Lindley disaster the 9th division was broken up; Colvile was sent home and reverted to the command of a brigade at Gibraltar. But when Roberts became commander-in-chief in November 1900 he insisted that Colvile be recalled. Colvile returned to England, and on landing at Dover on 31 December stated his case to a Reuter's reporter. On 19 January 1901 he was placed on retired pay as a lieutenant-general. He stated his defence and complained of his treatment by Roberts in *The Work of the Ninth Division* (1901). Colvile published several other books on his experiences as a soldier and traveller, and, for the War Office, *The History of the Soudan Campaign* (1889).

Colvile's first marriage was on 6 August 1878, to Alice Rose (d. 1882), eldest daughter of Robert Daly and granddaughter of John Daly, second Baron Dunsandle; they had one daughter, who died in 1882. In 1886 he married Zélie Isabelle, daughter of Pierre Richaud de Préville of Château des Mondrans, Basses Pyrénées, France. They had one son, and Zélie survived her husband.

Colvile settled at Bagshot. On 24 November 1907, while riding a motor cycle, he collided at Frimley with a car driven by Colonel Sir H. Rawlinson, and died almost immediately of his injuries at Brompton Sanatorium. He was buried at Lullington, near Burton upon Trent, where his ancestral estates lay.

H. M. VIBART, *rev.* M. G. M. JONES

Sources Army List · Hart's Army List · *The Times* (26 Nov 1907) · T. Pakenham, *The Boer War* (1979) · L. S. Amery, ed., *The Times history of the war in South Africa*, 3 (1905) · L. S. Amery, ed., *The Times history of the war in South Africa*, 4 (1906) · *WWBMP*, vol. 1 · C. N. Robinson, *Celebrities of the army*, 18 pts (1900) · J. F. Maurice and M. H. Grant, eds., *History of the war in South Africa, 1899–1902*, 4 vols. (1906–10), vols. 1–2 · *The Scapegoat: being a selection from a series of articles which have appeared in 'The review of the week', on the case of Sir Henry Colvile* (1901) · *GJ*, 31 (1908), 113 · Burke, *Gen. GB* · Burke, *Peerage* · *DSAB* · R. H. Vetch, *Life, letters and diaries of Lieut.-General Sir Gerald Graham* (1901)

Archives BL, letters to his mother, Add. MS 41658 · Derbys. RO, military corresp. and papers

Likenesses F. S. Baden-Powell, silhouette, NPG · Elliott & Fry, photograph, repro. in Robinson, *Celebrities of the army*

Wealth at death £58,996 8s. 9d.: probate, 28 Feb 1908, *CGPLA Eng. & Wales*

Colvile, Sir James William (1810–1880), judge in India, was born on 12 January 1810 in London, the eldest son of Andrew Wedderburn (*d.* 1856), of Craigflower and Ochiltree, Fife, and his wife, the Hon. Louisa Mary Eden (*d.* 1858), daughter of William, first Baron Auckland (1744–1814). His father, who assumed the surname of Colvile on 22 June 1814, was the founder of the Royal Mail Steam Packet Company. Eden Colvile (1819–1893), governor of Rupert's Land from 1849 to 1852, was his younger brother.

Colvile was educated at Eton College and at Trinity College, Cambridge, where he matriculated in 1827 and graduated BA in 1831, ranked third in the second class of mathematical honours, and MA in 1834. He was an intimate friend at Cambridge of Monckton Milnes, afterwards Lord Houghton. Admitted to Inner Temple in 1832, he was called to the bar in Hilary term 1835, and for ten years practised as an equity draftsman in chambers in Lincoln's Inn. He became a bencher of the Inner Temple in 1866.

In 1845 Colvile was appointed advocate general of Bengal. He was young for the post, but at least ten other nominees had turned it down in the wake of a discomforting row in the House of Lords over the unscrupulous readiness of the East India Company's directors to appoint their dependants to such lucrative situations. Colvile's own links with India were not insignificant; his uncle George Eden had been governor-general from 1835 until 1841. In 1848 he was raised to the bench as a puisne judge of the supreme court of Bengal and was knighted (9 December 1848) and in 1855, in succession to Sir Lawrence Peel, he was appointed chief justice. On 3 April 1857 in Calcutta Cathedral he married (Frances) Elinor (1838–1919), eldest daughter of John Peter Grant, of Rothiemurchus, a future lieutenant-governor of Bengal and governor of Jamaica.

Colvile acquired a reputation in Bengal as a learned and courteous man, helpful and friendly to his juniors. He was an active president of the Asiatic Society and opened relations between it and the Royal Society, of which he afterwards became a fellow. He retired from the chief justiceship and returned to Britain in 1859. With the youthful Lady Colvile's care, his London residence at 8 Rutland Gate, Hyde Park, was soon established as a small but select salon, patronized by Lawrence Alma-Tadema, Robert Browning, Mary Ann Evans (George Eliot), J. A. Froude, Mrs George Grote, Frederick Leighton, John Millais, Alfredo Piatti, and George Frederic Watts. In April 1875 he was elected FRS. Colvile, however, never retired from legal work. Soon after his return from India he was sworn a privy counsellor to act, with Sir Lawrence Peel, as an Indian assessor to the council's judicial committee. In November 1865 he was made a member of that committee, and in 1871, under the Judicial Committee Act, he was appointed one of its four paid judges (at an annual salary of £5000) who were charged with clearing the backlog of appeals to the privy council. He was the senior of these judges when he died suddenly, on 6 December 1880, at his house, 8 Rutland Gate, Hyde Park, London. He was buried on 11 December 1880 at his estate, Craigflower, near Dunfermline, Fife, of which county he had been a JP and deputy lieutenant. He was survived by his wife; their only child, Andrew John Wedderburn, born in 1859, had died in 1876. In recollection of Colvile, Alexander Kinglake wrote that, even in youth, he was thought of as 'the true model of the sterling, the wise, the highly-bred English Gentleman' (Kinglake to Lady Colvile, 7 Dec 1880, Strachey MSS, BL, Add. MS 60633, fol. 90).   KATHERINE PRIOR

Sources *The Times* (8 Dec 1880), 8 · *The Times* (9 Dec 1880), 1 · *The Times* (10 Dec 1880), 9 · *The Times* (11 March 1889), 5 · E. Cotton, *Memories of the supreme court at Fort William in Bengal, 1774–1862* (1925) · BL, Add. MSS 60632–60634 · J. E. Martin, ed., *Masters of the bench of the Hon. Society of the Inner Temple, 1450–1883, and masters of the Temple, 1540–1883* (1883) · Venn, *Alum. Cant.*, 2/2.106 · Burke, *Peerage* (1926) · W. W. Rouse Ball and J. A. Venn, eds., *Admissions to Trinity College, Cambridge*, 4 (1911), 276 · H. E. C. Stapylton, *The Eton school lists, from 1791 to 1850*, 2nd edn (1864) · H. E. A. Cotton, *Calcutta old and new: a historical and descriptive handbook to the city* (1907) · *GM*, 3rd ser., 3 (1857), 97 · Bengal ecclesiastical records, BL OIOC, N/1/50, fol. 117 · Boase, *Mod. Eng. biog.* · W. A. Shaw, *The knights of England*, 2 (1906), 247

Archives BL, corresp., Add. MSS 60632–60634 · BL OIOC, corresp. etc., MS Eur. F 127

Wealth at death under £80,000: probate, 1 March 1881, *CGPLA Eng. & Wales*

Colvill [Colville], **Alexander** (1699/1700–1777), nonsubscribing Presbyterian minister, was probably born at Newtownards, co. Down, where his father, Alexander Colville (*d.* 1719), was ordained minister on 26 July 1696. He originally spelt his name Colville but changed it to Colvill about 1715. He graduated MA from Edinburgh University in 1715 and studied medicine at Glasgow University; he graduated MD from Edinburgh in 1728. His father, who in 1700 became minister at Dromore, co. Down, was an early member of the Belfast Society and successfully introduced New Light ideas to the congregation. When he died, on 1 December 1719, the Dromore congregation wanted Colvill to succeed as minister and delayed filling the post until he was qualified. He duly studied theology at Edinburgh, under William Dunlop, and after briefly working as tutor in the family of Major Hay of Parbroath he was licensed by the Cupar-Fife presbytery on 19 June 1722. Called to Dromore, he was refused ordination in 1724 by the Armagh presbytery, because he refused to renew his subscription to the Westminster confession. He appealed to the sub-synod and then to the general synod but finally resorted to going to England, where in December 1724 he was ordained in Edmund Calamy's vestry by Joshua Oldfield, leader of the London non-subscribers.

On his return to Ireland the Armagh presbytery refused to receive Colvill. He appealed to general synod, which in June 1725 suspended him from ministerial duties for three months and sent a replacement minister to Dromore, despite threats from Calamy to withdraw the *regium donum*. Colvill had earlier, on 29 March 1725, applied for admission to the non-subscribing presbytery of Dublin and was duly installed at Dromore on 25 October 1725. The subscribers in the Dromore congregation immediately called a new minister, who was ordained in May 1726, but the majority (over 400 heads of families) adhered to Colvill. In

1730 he and his congregation transferred themselves to the non-subscribing presbytery of Antrim, which had been expelled from the synod in 1726. A new meeting-house was built for him on Pound Hill, Dromore. On the outbreak of the Jacobite rising of 1745 Colvill obtained from Lord Chesterfield a commission for raising a volunteer corps, which he himself commanded. He published only a few works; the first was the sermon that he preached at the funeral of fellow non-subscriber Thomas Nevin of Downpatrick, on 24 March 1745. In 1749 he attacked the seceding ministers from Scotland who were seeking to recruit new adherents from Ulster congregations in a pamphlet entitled *The Persecuting, Disloyal, and Absurd Tenets of those who Affect to Call themselves Seceders*, in which he accused them of antinomianism. He returned to the subscription controversy in his final work, *Some Important Queries* (1773), defending John Cameron against the criticisms of Benjamin McDowell. Some years earlier, in 1759, Colvill had led a delegation of non-subscribers to propose reconciliation to the general synod, and a dialogue between the two was resumed in 1768 when Cameron was moderator of the general synod.

According to his will (dated 3 October 1772) Colvill had a son, Maturin, and five daughters, two of whom married. He died, of apoplexy, at Dromore on 23 April 1777, aged seventy-seven, and was buried there on 4 May. His funeral sermon, 'On the immortality of the soul', was preached by James Bryson, who eulogized his 'rich, clear, and comprehensive understanding' (Bryson, 154). His congregation returned to the general synod after his death but left it with the remonstrants of 1829.

ALEXANDER GORDON, *rev.* S. J. SKEDD

Sources *Belfast News-Letter* (29 April 1777) · J. Bryson, *Sermon on several important subjects* (1778), esp. 152–7 · 'Progress of non-subscription to creeds', *Christian Moderator*, 2 (1827), 193–8 · J. S. Reid and W. D. Killen, *History of the Presbyterian church in Ireland*, new edn, 3 (1867), 191ff. · T. Witherow, *Historical and literary memorials of presbyterianism in Ireland, 1731–1800* (1880), 71–8 · J. S. Reid, *History of congregations of the Presbyterian church in Ireland*, ed. W. D. Killen (1886), 122 · W. I. Addison, *A roll of graduates of the University of Glasgow from 31st December 1727 to 31st December 1897* (1898), 117 · I. R. McBride, *Scripture politics: Ulster Presbyterians and Irish radicalism in the late eighteenth century* (1998) · J. McConnell and others, eds., *Fasti of the Irish Presbyterian church, 1613–1840*, rev. S. G. McConnell, 2 vols. in 12 pts (1935–51), 135–6

Colvill, Alexander, **seventh Lord Colville of Culross** (1717–1770), naval officer, was born in Scotland (probably at Dundee) on 28 February 1717, the eldest son of John Colvill, sixth Lord Colville (*d.* 1741), army officer, and Elizabeth Johnstone. His family was impoverished and lacked service connections, so Colvill entered the navy in 1732 as a volunteer per order. In 1733 he joined the *Lime* (20 guns). In 1737 he was in the *Phoenix* and in 1738 the *Rose* (both 20 guns). Having been promoted lieutenant on 31 August 1739, he was appointed to the bomb vessel *Alderney* and took part in the attacks on Portobello and Cartagena. In 1740 he saw his father, who was serving in his regiment in the West Indies, for the first time since 1732. Following his father's death a year later, Colvill succeeded to the title and at last acquired some standing in the navy. In 1742 he

became second lieutenant of the *Russell* (80 guns) which went out to Admiral Thomas Mathews in the Mediterranean. After serving in Mathews's flagship, the *Namur*, Colville commanded a fireship and a bomb vessel, and in April 1743 he was promoted commander in the *Dursley Galley* (20 guns). On 24 July 1744 he was posted to the *Leopard* (20 guns), and he soon made a reputation. Before the war ended in 1748 he captured or destroyed a large number of enemy vessels, his share of prize money amounting to about £5000.

From 1749 to 1752 Colville commanded the *Success* (20 guns) and convoyed the salt trade between the West Indies and Boston to the satisfaction of the Bostonian merchants. Having also pleased the Admiralty by markedly reducing the usual costs of careening, he was appointed in January 1753 to the *Northumberland* (70 guns) which he commanded for nine years. With a new French war looming Colville sailed in March 1755 and took part in Edward Boscawen's attempt to prevent the reinforcement of French North America. In 1757 he was with Francis Holburne off Louisbourg. After the hurricane of September the fleet retreated to Halifax. On 14 November Holburne ordered Colville to hoist a commodore's broad pennant and left him in the chief command. He spent that severe winter preparing for a fresh attempt on Louisbourg. Coming under Sir Charles Hardy in March 1758, Colville contributed materially to the blockade that preceded Boscawen's arrival. After Louisbourg fell in November the *Northumberland*, with scurvy rife on board, returned to England. In 1759 he participated in Charles Saunders's celebrated progress up the St Lawrence to Quebec. Saunders left Colville to winter for a second time as commander-in-chief at Halifax. By having five ships of the line ready by May to raise Lévis's siege of Quebec, and by using them thereabouts to good effect, Colville made an important contribution to the conquest of Canada.

Meanwhile in 1759 Colville had appointed James Cook, who had come to Saunders's notice, as master of the *Northumberland*. Cook was still with him in 1762 when Colville forced de Ternay's squadron to abandon St John's in Newfoundland. Colville ordered Cook, who had sharpened his relevant skills when wintering at Halifax, to survey the coastline. Cook, having thus made a name, later commemorated Colville in his charts of New Zealand's Hauraki Gulf by naming Cape Colville, the Colville Channel, and Colville Bay. In 1760–62 Colville busied himself at Halifax by regulating pilotage and assisting the army in and around Quebec. Although suffering from 'sore throats, swelled legs, innumerable pains all over me, sciatica, scurvy, rheumatism' (*DCB*), he also did much to improve the dockyard facilities at Halifax. Having been finally recalled to England, he arrived on 26 October 1762 to find that he had been promoted rear-admiral of the white five days earlier.

From January 1763 Colville served as port admiral at Plymouth until, several months later, he reluctantly accepted the new North American command. He reached Halifax on 13 October, believing that he would derive financial benefit from his assigned anti-smuggling role, but in this he was disappointed. However, he did mitigate the smuggling and he promoted further surveys of Newfoundland and the Gulf of St Lawrence. He also established Halifax as a peacetime naval base. In 1766 he returned to England, thus completing thirty-four years of meritorious naval service.

On 1 October 1768 Colville married Lady Elizabeth Macfarlane (*née* Erskine), widow of Walter Macfarlane, and daughter of the fifth earl of Kellie. Colville died on 21 May 1770 at Drumsheugh, near Edinburgh, and was survived by his wife. Although the couple had no children, outside marriage Colville had had various mistresses and three children: Charles, born near Boston in 1751 (commissioned in the navy, with Colville's backing, in 1765); James Alexander, born in England in 1760; and Sophia, born to Elizabeth Greene of Halifax in 1765. Colville made provision for his wife and for all his other surviving family members, guardians included. RUDDOCK MACKAY

Sources W. A. B. Douglas, 'Colvill, Alexander', *DCB*, vol. 3 · N. A. M. Rodger, *The wooden world: an anatomy of the Georgian navy* (1986) · W. L. Clowes, *The Royal Navy: a history from the earliest times to the present*, 7 vols. (1897–1903); repr. (1996–7), vol. 3 · D. Syrett and R. L. DiNardo, *The commissioned sea officers of the Royal Navy, 1660–1815*, rev. edn, Occasional Publications of the Navy RS, 1 (1994) · will, PRO, PROB 11/960, fol. 383
Archives NRA, priv. coll., corresp., journals, and notebooks | PRO, Admiralty records
Likenesses portrait, priv. coll.
Wealth at death see will, 1767, PRO, PROB 11/960, fol. 383; Douglas, 'Colvill, Alexander'

Colville. For this title name *see* individual entries under Colville; *see also* Colvill, Alexander, seventh Lord Colville of Culross (1717–1770).

Colville family (*per.* 1861–1916), iron- and steelmasters, came to prominence with **David** [i] **Colville** (1811/12–1898), who was baptized in Campbeltown, Argyll, on 17 February 1813, the eleventh and last child of Robert Colvill [*sic*] and his wife, Janet Mitchell. In early manhood he participated in the family business of owning and controlling a number of coasting vessels and managing several local enterprises, the most important of which was whisky distilling. In the late 1840s he decided to strike out on his own, most probably because his temperance convictions made the family interest in strong drink abhorrent to him. Provided with some capital by his father, he migrated to Glasgow and set up as a provisions merchant in the Trongate. In June 1845 he married Janet (known as Jessie), daughter of the Revd John Barr; they had a family of four sons and seven daughters.

Within a few years Colville had resolved to abandon dealing in tea and coffee, his principal activity, and to enter the buoyant iron trade. Being completely ignorant of iron making, he required a partner possessing the necessary expertise. Such a partner he found in Thomas Gray, the manager of a small malleable-iron works at Coatbridge. The firm of Colville and Gray was established in June 1861 with a capital of £6500, of which Colville provided £5000. Although the Clifton ironworks was successful, relations between the two men began to deteriorate

when Gray's drinking habits became intolerable to Colville. It was resolved to dissolve the partnership in 1870 and to sell the going concern to the partner submitting the higher bid. Colville put in a most generous offer and was mortified to lose out to Gray, who had gained the backing of a Mr Wylie, a licensed grocer and former provost of Hamilton, who saw the Clifton works as both a sound investment and a thriving business in which his sons could become interested.

It was a bitter disappointment to Colville but, unexpectedly provided with ample funds from the sale of his three-fourths share in the firm, he decided to set up another ironworks entirely under his own control, in the management of which he would be assisted by two of his sons, **John Colville** (1852–1901) and **Archibald Colville** (1853–1916). John Colville was born on 3 July 1852 at Glasgow, and acquired a knowledge of iron manufacture at the Clifton works. He married, first, Janet, daughter of Dr Joseph Brown of Glasgow, and then Christian, the daughter of Provost Downie of Kirkintilloch, with whom he had one son and one daughter. Archibald Colville was born in 1853 in Glasgow, and received a commercial training at the famous East India trading house of James Finlay & Co. He married Jeannie Miller, and they had two sons and five daughters. The search for a possible location led to David [i] Colville's accepting the offer of a suitable site on highly favourable terms by the agents of the Hamiltons of Dalzell, who were anxious to develop their estates around the small burgh. Construction began in February 1871 and in just over a year the first of the twenty furnaces was commissioned. Rolling began two weeks later in April 1872.

While Colville was laying down the Dalzell works, the Steel Company of Scotland was established. Within a few years it had become apparent that steel would displace malleable iron as the basic raw material in the heavy industries of the west of Scotland. Keenly aware of this possibility, David [i] Colville sent his youngest son to the Steel Company's Hallside works to be fully trained in the new technology. This was **David** [ii] **Colville** (1860–1916), who was born on 10 March 1860 at Coatbridge, Lanarkshire; and who married Katherine Harvey, daughter of Robert Greenlees, distiller, on 18 August 1887. They had one son and one daughter. The consequence of David [ii] Colville's training was that, having successfully established himself in iron making, his father, David [i] Colville, at an age when the majority of wealthy businessmen had retired to their country estates, decided to go into steel.

A licence was obtained from William Siemens, the firm's capital (already enhanced by the retention of the profits resulting from the supply of iron bars for the rebuilding of the Tay Bridge) being doubled by a loan of £33,000 from J. S. Napier, a Glasgow iron merchant. Under the direction of David [ii] Colville five 10 ton open-hearth furnaces, a rolling mill, and ancilliary plant were erected at Dalzell. The first melt of steel was made in 1881. On this occasion the timing could not have been more auspicious: it was during the 1880s, when mild steel drove wrought iron from the Clydeside shipyards. The works prospered and were further extended (again partially with Napier's help), and net profits, which fuelled the expansion, rose to reach £50,000 in the second half of 1889.

Not until the early 1890s did David [i] Colville allow control of his firm to pass to his sons; and not until the redemption of the loans from Napier and the election of his eldest son, John, to parliament as Liberal member for North-East Lanarkshire in 1895 would he countenance the conversion of the partnership into a private limited company. Three years later he died at Glasgow, on 29 October 1898, aged eighty-six. His wife predeceased him. A quiet, abstemious man, David [i] Colville devoted himself almost entirely to his business, taking little part in public life. A paternalistic figure, all the evidence confirms the accuracy of contemporary, eulogistic accounts of his high moral character. He was deeply religious, an ardent temperance reformer, and universally trusted. 'His manner', observed an anonymous obituarist in *Engineering*, 'was that of the old school—courteous and gentle, and guileless to a degree, nevertheless he possessed great strength of purpose' (*Engineering*, 4 Nov 1898, 581).

David [i] Colville left his sons a thriving business and they pushed it forward. David [ii] Colville was the driving force behind the policy of expansion and continuous modernization which by the eve of the First World War made the firm the largest in the Scottish steel industry and second only to Dorman Longs in Great Britain. While his older brother John—the first chairman of the limited company—became increasingly absorbed by public works, serving the community by promoting the causes of religion, temperance, and social reform, and Archibald grappled with the commercial and financial implications of his brother's plans, David [ii] scoured Europe and America to investigate and adopt the latest steel-making practices, dealt ruthlessly with the growing and increasingly well organized labour forces either personally or, with somewhat greater tact, through the Board of Conciliation and Arbitration of the Manufactured Steel Trade of the West of Scotland, and secured the loyalty of the senior managers by offering them shares in the company.

David [ii] captured the imagination by his flamboyance and his grand manner. He was the master of the firm. His ambitions were constrained only by his older brother Archibald, chairman of the company after John's sudden death at Cleland House, Motherwell, Lanarkshire, on 22 August 1901. John's wife survived him. Archibald was shrewd and calculating—reputed, as the labour leader John Hodge put it, 'to have an absolute knowledge of how many beans make five' (Hodge, 34). But the exigencies of the war gave David his chance to break free from the constraints imposed by his brother. He willingly agreed to meet the government's request for a massive increase of steel output and, with the backing of the Ministry of Munitions, took over the Clydebridge and Glengarnock works, gained control of Fullwood foundry, and purchased the ordinary shares of a major colliery company, Archibald Russell Ltd, in order to safeguard his fuel supplies. The physical and mental strain of such rapid growth proved too much. David Colville collapsed and died on 16

October 1916 at Jerviston House, Motherwell, Lanarkshire. His wife survived him. He was fifty-six. Two months later Archibald, utterly exhausted with the effort of implementing his brother's schemes, succumbed to a brief illness at the age of sixty-three and died on 11 December 1916 at The Moorings, Clyde Street, Motherwell. He also left a widow.

The third generation of Colvilles were all either serving in the army or too inexperienced to assume the leadership of the company and the task fell upon one of the very managers whom David had admitted to the firm, John Craig (1874–1957). Not until Ronald John Bilsland *Colville, second Baron Clydesmuir (1917–1996), John Colville's grandson, became a member of the board in 1958 was a member of the Colville family again to play a major role in running the concern, but within a decade Colvilles had passed into the hands of the state, becoming a major constituent of the British Steel Corporation.

PETER L. PAYNE

Sources British Steel records, NA Scot., GD464 · P. L. Payne, *Colvilles and the Scottish steel industry* (1979) · Souvenir booklet, jubilee of *David Colville & Sons, 1871–1921*, David Colville & Sons Ltd (privately printed, 1921) · *John Colville: an account of his life and work* (1901) [In memoriam pamphlet] · *Colvilles Magazine*, 1 (1920) · *Motherwell Times* (20 Oct 1916) · *Motherwell Times* (15 Dec 1916) · *Engineering* (4 Nov 1898) · *Engineering* (2 Dec 1898) · *Engineering* (20 Oct 1916) · *Engineering* (15 Dec 1916) · J. Hodge, *Workman's cottage to Windsor Castle* (1931) · R. Duncan, *Steelopolis: the making of Motherwell, c.1750–1939* (1991) · I. F. Gibson, 'The economic history of the Scottish iron and steel industry', PhD diss., U. Lond., 1955 · T. J. Byres, 'The Scottish economy … 1873–1896, with special reference to the heavy industries of the south-west', B.Litt diss., U. Glas., 1962 · A. Miller, *The rise and progress of Coatbridge and surrounding neighbourhood* (1864) · *CCI* (1898) [David [i] Colville] · *CCI* (1901) [John Colville] · *CCI* (1917) [Archibald Colville; David [ii] Colville] · d. cert. [John Colville] · d. cert. [Archibald Colville] · d. cert. [David [ii] Colville] · *DNB* [David [i] Colville]

Archives NA Scot., British Steel records, GD 464

Likenesses T. Johnstone, photograph (David [ii] Colville), repro. in *Motherwell Times* (20 Oct 1916) · J. T. Kirkwood, photograph (John Colville), repro. in *John Colville* · monument (John Colville), Motherwell cemetery, Lanarkshire · photograph (David [i] Colville), repro. in *Souvenir booklet* · photograph (Archibald Colville), repro. in *Souvenir booklet*

Wealth at death £85,229 12s. 3d.—David [i] Colville: confirmation, 9 Dec 1898, *CCI* · £314,328 3s. 5d.—David [ii] Colville: 28 Feb 1917, *CCI* · £83,676 17s.—John Colville: confirmation, 20 Dec 1901, *CCI* · £292,025 14s. 10d.—Archibald Colville: confirmation, 28 April 1917, *CCI*

Colville, Alexander (d. 1597), judge, was the second son of Sir James *Colville of Easter Wemyss (d. 1540) and his second wife, Margaret Forrester (d. in or before 1562). Under his parents' marriage contract of 21 May 1536 Colville received an annual allowance of £100, but in May 1562 he renounced this in return for payments totalling 1000 merks. In February 1567 he received a charter of the abbey of Culross, succeeding his uncle William Colville as commendator. On 12 May of that year he was present when Queen Mary announced before the court of session that she had not married Bothwell under duress. In December 1571 Colville became a lord of session, and about the same time he began collecting decisions of the court of session.

Between 1570 and 1572 he attended the national conventions which successively elected the earls of Lennox, Mar, and Morton as regent. On 20 January 1574 he was authorized to pay only 100 merks for the thirds of the benefice of Culross, a substantial reduction from the 500 merks which the kirk commissioners had originally required him to remit. From November 1575 he sat as a privy councillor. In November 1578 he was appointed to the parliamentary commission to review the laws of the realm, and at the same time he acted as an arbitrator in the Gordon–Forbes feud.

Colville subscribed to the 'Defence of the king of Scots' as a supporter of the Ruthven raid in August 1582, and when that regime collapsed in June 1583, to be followed by a royalist reaction, he became for a time less involved in government. He ceased to collect session decisions in 1584, and in May and June 1585 temporarily vacated the bench in favour of his nephew John Colville, the chanter of Glasgow. But with the return of the Ruthven exiles he again became active in public affairs, serving as one of the lords of the articles (4 December 1585)—as a privy councillor in at least sixty sessions from December 1585 to December 1596, and on four conventions of estates between 1588 and 1596. On 6 March 1590 he was made a commissioner to enforce anti-Jesuit legislation for the shires of Clackmannan and Kinross, and in 1592 he was named to a commission to reform hospitals. With his wife Nicholas [sic], daughter of Alexander Dundas of Fingask, he had nine children. Alexander Colville died in May 1597.   J. R. M. SIZER

Sources *Scots peerage*, 2.546–50 · *CSP Scot.*, 1563–83; 1585–97 · *Reg. PCS*, 1st ser., vols. 2–5, 8 · *Reg. PCS*, 2nd ser., vol. 14 · G. Brunton and D. Haig, *An historical account of the senators of the college of justice, from its institution in MDXXXII* (1832) · P. G. B. Macneill, *Senators of the college of justice, 1569–1578* [suppl.] · D. D. Hailes, *Catalogue of the lords of session, from the institution of the college of justice, in the year 1532* (1767)

Colville, Alexander, *de jure* third Lord Colville of Culross (1595/6–1666), college head, was born in St Andrews, Fife, the eldest son of John Colville (d. 1645x50) of Culross and later of Wester Cumbrae and his wife, Elizabeth *Melville (fl. 1599–1631), daughter of Sir James Melville of Halhill, and the grandson of Alexander *Colville (d. 1597) of Culross. He was educated for the ministry, but on 30 June 1619 left for France, where his family had connections with the Reformed church. He immediately obtained appointment as master in Hebrew and physics at the protestant academy in Sedan. Eight years later, on 31 May 1627, he also obtained the chair of philosophy, and the following December started teaching theology with a salary of 300 livres. He became a doctor in theology on 6 November 1628. His *Theses de natura logicae*, dated 24 July 1629, was published that year. On 27 September 1631 Colville married, in Sedan, Anne le Blanc de Beaulieu, daughter of Louis le Blanc de Beaulieu, minister, and Charlotte Cappel, whose brother was a minister and professor of theology at the academy of Sedan; they had at least three sons and two daughters.

In or before 1642 Colville received an invitation to take up a post at St Andrews. About the same time his father resigned Wester Cumbrae in his favour, and he was granted a crown charter of these and other lands on 8 March 1642. It is not clear when he returned to Scotland, but he was finally appointed to a chair of divinity at St Mary's College, St Andrews, in 1647. On 23 June 1648 he was appointed to a similar chair at Edinburgh but was not admitted; the general assembly finally refused his transfer in 1650. In 1654 he succeeded as third Lord Colville, following the death without legitimate heirs of his kinsman James Colville of Culross, but he never used the title, perhaps partly because of the competing claims of James's sons.

At an unknown date Colville almost certainly returned to France, as he was apparently teaching in Sedan in 1656, when Jacques de Vaux praised him as being a clever philosopher, a subtle logician, and a methodical master, whose expression was brilliant and accurate. While Colville's eldest son, John, was educated at St Andrews, and became a regent there, his son Abraham (b. 1638) read his thesis at Sedan under the presidence of his uncle Louis le Blanc de Beaulieu on 19 November 1657 and obtained the chair of theology at the academy from 1658. Colville himself was again in Scotland in 1662, when he became principal of St Mary's College, St Andrews. In 1663 he received parliamentary ratification of all his lands because 'he had remained a loyal and peaceful subject during the troublous times preceding the Restoration' (*Scots peerage*, 2.551). In 1665 he settled lands at Lurg and Kincardine on his son John, now a minister at Midcalder, in connection with the latter's marriage (contract 20 October and 4 November 1665) to Mary, daughter of Sir George Preston of Valleyfield. Colville died in January 1666, aged seventy. He was survived by his wife, Anne (d. in or after 1670), his sons John (d. 1670/71) and Abraham (who died in Sedan in March 1673, a few weeks after marrying Madeleine Desreumaux), and his daughter Sarah (alive in January 1681); a son and a daughter had died in St Andrews in June 1664. John's son Alexander (1666–1717) became *de jure* fifth Lord Colville.   MARIE-CLAUDE TUCKER

Sources [J. B. J. Boulliot], *Biographie ardennaise, ou, Histoire des Ardennais ... par m l'abbé Boulliot*, 1 (Paris, 1830), 270–72 · E. Henry, *Notes biographiques sur les membres de l'académie protestante et pasteurs de l'église réformée de Sedan* (1826), 52, 54, 56, 59 · Archives des Ardennes, Sedan, France, fonds Courjault, C126-14 · *Scots peerage* · GEC, *Peerage* · *Fasti Scot.*, new edn, 7.382, 420, 428

Colville, Archibald (1853–1916). *See under* Colville family (*per.* 1861–1916).

Colville, Sir Charles (1770–1843), army officer, second son of John Colville, eighth Lord Colville of Culross (1724/5–1811), and his wife, Amelia (d. 1788), *née* Webber, was born on 7 August 1770. He entered the army as an ensign in the 28th regiment on 26 December 1781, but did not join until 1787, the year he was promoted lieutenant. In May 1791 he was promoted captain into the 13th (Somersetshire) light infantry, with which he remained nineteen years, until he became a major-general. He joined it in December 1791 in the West Indies, and remained with it until its return to England in 1797, seeing much service in the interval, especially in San Domingo, and being promoted major on 1

Sir Charles Colville (1770–1843), by George T. Payne, pubd 1844 (after Sir Henry Raeburn)

September 1795, and lieutenant-colonel on 26 August 1796. He then commanded the 13th in the suppression of the Irish uprising of 1798, and in the expedition to Ferrol, and to Egypt in 1800 and 1801. In Egypt the 13th formed part of Major-General Cradock's brigade, and distinguished itself in the battles of 8, 13, and 21 March, and in the siege of Alexandria. On leaving Egypt, Colville, who had there established his reputation as a good regimental officer, took the 13th to Gibraltar, where he remained until 1805, the year he was promoted colonel. After a short period in England he went with the 13th to Bermuda in 1808, and in 1809 he was made a brigadier-general, and commanded the 2nd brigade of Prevost's division in the capture of Martinique in that year.

On 25 July 1810 Colville was promoted major-general, and at once applied for a command in the Peninsula. In October 1810 he took over the command of the 1st brigade of the 3rd division, which was under the command of Picton. It was now that he had his great opportunity, and he soon became not only Picton's trusted lieutenant, but one of Wellington's favourite brigadiers. He commanded his brigade in the pursuit after Masséna and in the battle of Fuentes d'Oñoro, shared the superintendence of the trenches with Major-General Hamilton at the second siege of Badajoz, commanded the infantry in the affair at El Bodon on 25 September 1811, and the 4th division in the place of Major-General Cole in the successful siege of Ciudad Rodrigo. He shared the superintendence of the trenches in the third and last siege of Badajoz with generals Bowes and Kempt, and commanded the 4th division in the storming of the Trinidad bastion, where he was shot through the left thigh, and lost a finger of his right hand.

He had to go to England for his cure, and thus missed the battle of Salamanca, but returned to the Peninsula in October 1812, and commanded the 3rd division in winter quarters until superseded by the arrival of General Picton. He commanded his brigade only at the battle of Vitoria, where he was slightly wounded, but was specially appointed by Wellington to the temporary command of the 6th division from August to November 1813, when he reverted to the 3rd division, which he commanded at the battles of the Nivelle and the Nive. He was again superseded by the arrival of Sir Thomas Picton, but in February 1814 Wellington appointed him permanently to the 5th division in the place of Sir James Leith. With it he served under Sir John Hope in the siege of Bayonne, and superintended the final embarkation at Passages of the last British troops left in France.

Colville's services were well rewarded: he received a cross with one clasp, and was made KCB in January, and GCB in March 1815; he was appointed colonel of the 94th regiment in April 1815; and following Bonaparte's return from Elba, he was made a local lieutenant-general in the Netherlands at Wellington's special request, and took command of the 4th division there. Colville's division was posted on the extreme right of the English division at Hal during the battle of Waterloo. To compensate him for not being more actively engaged there, Wellington gave him the duty of storming Cambray, the only French fortress which did not immediately surrender. He succeeded with the loss of only thirty men killed and wounded.

Colville married, on 16 February 1818, Jane, eldest daughter of William Mure of Caldwell, Ayrshire; they had six children. Colville did not again see active service. He was promoted lieutenant-general in 1819, and was commander-in-chief at Bombay from 1819 to 1825, and governor of Mauritius from 1828 to 1832. He was promoted general on 10 January 1837, and died on 27 March 1843 at Rosslyn House, Hampstead. His eldest son, Charles John Colville (1818–1903), who succeeded as eleventh Lord Colville of Culross, was created baron (1885) and Viscount Colville (1902) in the peerage of the United Kingdom.

H. M. STEPHENS, rev. ROGER T. STEARN

Sources J. Philippart, ed., *The royal military calendar*, 3 vols. (1815–16) · *GM*, 2nd ser., 19 (1843), 532 · W. F. P. Napier, *History of the war in the Peninsula and in the south of France*, 6 vols. (1828–40) · Fortescue, *Brit. army*, vols. 9–10 · A. J. Guy, ed., *The road to Waterloo: the British army and the struggle against revolutionary and Napoleonic France, 1793–1815* (1990) · R. Muir, *Britain and the defeat of Napoleon, 1807–1815* (1996) · T. Pakenham, *The year of liberty: the story of the great Irish rebellion of 1798* (1969)

Archives NRA, priv. coll., corresp. and papers | BL OIOC, letters to Mountstuart Elphinstone, MSS Eur. F87–89

Likenesses G. T. Payne, mezzotint, pubd 1844 (after H. Raeburn), AM Oxf., BM [*see illus.*] · A. Blaikley, chalk drawing, 1849, Scot. NPG

Colville [*née* Crewe-Milnes], **Lady** (**Helen**) **Cynthia** (1884–1968), courtier and social worker, was born on 20 May 1884, the third daughter of Robert Offley Ashburton Crewe-*Milnes (1858–1945), Liberal politician, who the year after her birth succeeded as second Baron Houghton and who subsequently became the first and last marquess of Crewe. Her mother was his first wife, Sybil Marcia (d. 1887), daughter of Sir Frederick Graham, third baronet, and his wife, Lady Jane St Maur. She had a twin sister, Celia Hermione; her only brother died in childhood. After their mother's death the children lived principally with their uncle, the third Baron Crewe, and had a spell in Dublin when their father was Gladstone's lord lieutenant of Ireland (1892–5). Cynthia was educated by governesses and studied piano at the Royal College of Music.

On 21 January 1908 Lady Cynthia married George (Geordie) Charles Colville (1867–1943), barrister, third son of Charles Colville, first Viscount Colville of Culross. They had three sons. Lady Cynthia shared her husband's enthusiasm for sailing, and they made the annual pilgrimage to Cowes. After her marriage she became very active in social work, joining the committee of the Charity Organization Society in Shoreditch, the district of London with the highest infant mortality rate in the city. She was for twenty years the honorary secretary of the pioneering infant welfare centre opened there and became involved in many other committees and organizations devoted to the welfare of the borough, including a school for mothers and the council's public health committee. In 1948 the metropolitan borough of Shoreditch renamed the Felton Street estate the Colville estate in the light of her long association with the borough. 'My sole "qualification" I think, is that I just love Shoreditch, and have done so for quite a long time' Lady Cynthia was minuted as writing to accept the honour (Hackney Archive Service, S/CE 48, p. 321). A strong Liberal, she was invited to stand for parliament for the party in Shoreditch in 1923. In 1929 she was appointed a magistrate and served in the east London juvenile court, becoming eventually a juvenile court chairman. She shared the conviction of her generation and class that there had been a slackening of morals, attributable to 'the over-indulgent parents, the absentee mother, the lack of any fixed standard of right and wrong, the silly sexy stories that constitute the bulk of light reading matter, [and] the dramatic presentation of violence' (C. Colville, 142). She believed that 'kindly deflation' was a more effective approach to take to young male delinquents and criminals than 'fear-inspired seriousness', while 'the quasi-prostitute girl of fourteen or fifteen can be made to feel ignorant and pathetic sooner than adult and romantic' (ibid., 143–4). In 1952 she was appointed a lay justice at Bow Street magistrates' court.

In 1923, following a royal visit to Shoreditch, Lady Cynthia was invited to become a woman of the bedchamber to Queen Mary, and retained the position until the queen's death in 1953. She was invaluable to the queen as a source of information on health and welfare issues, in which the queen was very interested. According to her son, Lady Cynthia lent Queen Mary a copy of *Lady Chatterley's Lover* in 1933, earning a rebuke from the king, who was subsequently found reading it himself as it was 'his duty to study the kind of temptations to which his subjects were exposed' (J. Colville, 41). She had also the unenviable task of breaking to Queen Mary the news of the deaths of two

of her sons: the duke of Kent and King George VI. The Colville family connections with the royal court were continued in the next generation: her youngest son, Sir John Rupert *Colville, served as a page of honour to King George V and later as private secretary to Princess Elizabeth.

Lady Cynthia Colville was appointed DCVO in 1937 and DBE in 1953. She was made an honorary LLD by Leeds University, and delivered the Clark Hall lecture ('Social progress and the individual') in 1954. She published her autobiography, entitled *Crowded Life*, in 1963 and died at her home, 4 Mulberry Walk, Chelsea, on 15 June 1968.

K. D. REYNOLDS

Sources C. Colville, *Crowded life* (1963) · *The Times* (17 July 1968) · *WWW* · Burke, *Peerage* (1999) · J. Colville, *Footprints in time* (1976) · K. Rose, *Kings, queens and courtiers* (1985) · S. Bradford, *George VI* (1989)
Likenesses double portrait, photograph (with Queen Mary), repro. in F. Prochaska, *Royal bounty: the making of a welfare monarchy* (1995) · photograph, repro. in Rose, *Kings, queens and courtiers*
Wealth at death £4558: probate, 6 Jan 1969, *CGPLA Eng. & Wales*

Colville, David (1811/12–1898). *See under* Colville family (*per.* 1861–1916).

Colville, David (1860–1916). *See under* Colville family (*per.* 1861–1916).

Colville, Elizabeth. *See* Melville, Elizabeth (*fl.* 1599–1631).

Colville, Sir James, of Easter Wemyss (d. 1540), administrator, was the eldest son of Robert Colville of Ochiltree (d. 1513) and his wife, Elizabeth Arnot (d. in or before 1528). Though associated with his parents in tenancies of crown lands in 1505, he was probably still a minor when his father died at Flodden. Two kinsmen then occupied the house of Ochiltree, claiming this was 'for the weile of the said Elizabeth and James, and that utheris thair ill willaris suld nocht have entres tharin' (Hannay, 3). Colville was appointed to his father's office of director of chancery before 31 October 1518. Having agreed to replace Robert Barton as comptroller, he tried to back out, but finally took up office on 13 August 1525. His comptrollership was marked by financial crises and threats of resignation; despite close association with the Douglas-dominated regime, he survived its fall in 1528 and was made custumar of Edinburgh. On 10 August that year he agreed with the treasurer to supply the royal household for the following year, but in February 1529 he petitioned to be released from office and was replaced by Barton.

On 10 March 1529 James V confirmed Colville as director of chancery for life and appointed him to the council, with a place in exchequer and session. On 13 December 1530 he exchanged his barony of Ochiltree with Sir James Finnart for the barony of Easter Wemyss in Fife. His judicial position as a lord of session was made permanent in May 1532 when he became a senator of the new college of justice. He was knighted between then and June 1533 and was one of the commissioners sent to Newcastle to negotiate the truce with England.

When Barton's second term as comptroller left him ruined financially, James V turned again to Colville, who took office on 9 September 1530. Under his management the crown revenues increased, though, as James reached adulthood, so did spending on the royal household. The position deteriorated after the king's marriages in 1537–8, and by September 1538 Colville's excess expenditure had reached £2667, which was to have been repaid from the tax for the king's expenses in France. Instead Colville was dismissed following the revelation that he had assisted Archibald Douglas of Kilspindie, charged with treason in 1528. Himself charged with treason, Colville fled to England, but he returned in July 1539 to submit to the king's will. On being threatened with imprisonment in August 1540 he again went to England, where he died before 4 December. On 14 March 1541 sentence of forfeiture was pronounced against him and his heirs. His barony of Easter Wemyss and other lands were annexed to the crown, along with lands owned by others who had fallen victim to James V's vengeance or greed. After the king's death the forfeiture was rescinded on 12 December 1543, and on 1 February 1545 his illegitimate brother William Colville, commendator of Culross, was appointed comptroller.

James Colville was twice married. His first wife, Alison Bruce (d. in or before 1536), is said to have been a daughter of Sir David Bruce of Clackmannan. He married second (by contract dated 21 May 1536) Margaret Forrester (d. in or before 1562), sister of David Forrester of Garden. He had a son and a daughter from each marriage. The elder son, James Colville, who succeeded to Easter Wemyss on reversal of the forfeiture, was the father of the first Lord Colville of Culross. The younger, Alexander *Colville, succeeded his uncle William as commendator of Culross in 1567. There were also two illegitimate sons, one of whom, Robert Colville of Cleish (d. 1560), was the ancestor of the lords Colvill of Ochiltree.   ATHOL MURRAY

Sources Scots peerage, 2.544–52 • A. L. Murray, 'Financing the royal household: James V and his comptrollers', The Renaissance and Reformation in Scotland: essays in honour of Gordon Donaldson, ed. I. B. Cowan and D. Shaw (1983), 41–59 • R. K. Hannay, ed., Acts of the lords of council in public affairs, 1501–1554 (1932) • M. Livingstone, D. Hay Fleming, and others, eds., Registrum secreti sigilli regum Scotorum / The register of the privy seal of Scotland, 1–2 (1908–21) • G. Burnett and others, eds., The exchequer rolls of Scotland, 13–17 (1891–7) • LP Henry VIII, vol. 16 • J. B. Paul, ed., Compota thesaurariorum regum Scotorum / Accounts of the lord high treasurer of Scotland, 5–7 (1903–7) • APS, 1424–1567

Colville, James, first Lord Colville of Culross (c.1551–1629), soldier and diplomat, was the first son of Sir James Colville, (b. 1532?, d. in or before 1562), laird of Easter Wemyss, and his wife, Janet, daughter of Sir Robert Douglas of Lochleven. He was the grandson of Sir James *Colville of Ochiltree and Easter Wemyss (d. 1540). Like many of the Fife gentry at this time Colville was a committed Calvinist and spent his younger years fighting for the Reformation in Scotland and France. In 1567 he reportedly accompanied the earl of Moray to France, where he attached himself to the Huguenot cause, subsequently becoming a lifelong friend of the future Henri IV. By 1569

he had returned to Scotland to fight as a staunch supporter of the king's men in the civil war. In 1570 he married Isabel, daughter of Patrick *Ruthven, third Lord Ruthven (c.1520–1566), and his first wife, Jean or Janet Douglas; they had two sons. In 1572 Colville participated in the Leith convention that conferred the regency on James Douglas, earl of Morton.

Colville spent time in both Scotland and France during the following years, returning from France on 27 July 1582 with letters from Henri and the prince de Condé which, among other things, apparently warned against Esmé Stewart and other crypto-Catholics who then dominated the young James VI and his government. A month later Colville participated in the Calvinist coup d'état that would subsequently be known as the Ruthven raid. The counter-revolution that followed in June 1583 prompted Colville to flee to France, but by September he had returned, made his peace with the king, and obtained pardon. By 1586 he had earned the king's confidence sufficiently to be sent on an embassy to France 'and other places beyond the sea' (Reg. PCS, 4.127). In 1589 he went as ambassador to England, and James's description of him as 'my trusty and familiar servant' was doubtless more than simply formulaic (Salisbury MSS, 13.408). Still, his efforts to achieve the grand promises made by Elizabeth at the height of the armada crisis, his prime charge, were unsuccessful, and the mission was generally regarded as having 'wrought little good'—a circumstance that caused him considerable political embarrassment in Scotland (CSP Scot., 10.72). Despite this failure Colville again served as Scottish ambassador to England and also to France in 1594, a mission successful at least in its French objectives. A further mission to France was mooted in 1597 and again in 1598 but probably did not take place. Colville was generally recognized as the key figure in Scottish-French relations, and the individual who restored Scotland's 'ancient' privileges there.

In spite of his abiding French connections Colville was rightly perceived by contemporaries as one of the most resolute members of the English party in Scotland. He was constantly in touch with the English court, especially with Francis Walsingham, at one point suggesting to Walsingham that he would 'be les suspectit' if he travelled from Paris directly to Scotland rather than via England (CSP Scot., 7.210). His strenuous opposition to James's Danish match actually placed him in physical danger from the Edinburgh merchants. On his return to Scotland in 1589 he began raising troops for Henri's service, and eventually joined the king with a force of some 1500 Scottish soldiers. He served briefly as the military governor of St Valéry. Yet in December 1595, with the prospect of a second armada invasion, he also offered to help Elizabeth defend England with 'a band of gentlemen his friends of good action' (ibid., 12.74). Immediately after the 1589 mission to England, Colville had written a memorandum in which he claimed, 'I shal insist withe his majestie for the ferm unioun of the realmes' (ibid., 10.72). Colville's commitment to both England and France (and to a French marriage for James) did not strike him or his contemporaries as in any way incompatible. Still less did they appear inconsistent with his Scottish identity. The Reformation gave coherence to all of these endeavours and Colville's ideological priorities are beyond doubt—steadily worsening his financial circumstances to a point verging on catastrophe by 1601. Meanwhile, his first wife having died, Colville had married some time before 1599 Helen Schaw, widow of Robert Mowbray of Barnbougle. His younger, but by 1595 only surviving son from his first marriage, Robert Colville (d. 1614), married after 24 September 1603 Christian Bruce; it was their son James Colville (1604–1654) who was to be Colville's eventual heir.

Colville's best opportunity to press for a 'ferm unioun' between England and Scotland came with the 1603 union of crowns. Made Lord Colville in 1604 and an occasional participant on the Scottish privy council, he played arguably his most important, if least documented, role as a promoter of King James's British vision. In 1607 and 1608 the government orchestrated a famous test case intended to establish the right of Scots born after the regnal union to inherit property in England. Such right of inheritance was claimed for Colville's three-year-old grandson James, and it is impossible that Colville was other than instrumental in the government's strategy. Raising the case had proved no easy matter, for the English approached the question only with great reluctance, and contemporaries at court spoke of 'all the difficulties in reducing [the issue] … to a public judgement'—'the judges misliked any fiction to be used in a case of such consequence' (Salisbury MSS, 19.275). The government faced a real problem, and Colville's part in its solution cannot have been incidental or trivial. The case—known in English legal records as Robert Calvin's case (Calvin being a corruption of Colvil or Colvin, and Robert a conflation of the child with his father)—assumed major importance for three reasons: it raised fundamental constitutional issues about the connection between the person of the king and the fabric of the law, and it defined British citizenship for the next two centuries; but, for the king and Colville, it was virtually the last direct effort to create a genuinely British polity.

Subsequently, Colville attended the parliaments of 1609 and 1612, the 1625 convention, and, it seems, the 1618 Perth assembly. He also sought to maintain the coherence and privileges of the Scots guards in France, making trips there for that purpose in 1611 and 1623. Colville is said to have died at his home in Tillicoultry, Clackmannanshire, from a fall, in September 1629. His widow was living in August 1630.   ARTHUR H. WILLIAMSON

Sources CSP Scot., 1571–97 · D. Calderwood, The history of the Kirk of Scotland, ed. T. Thomson and D. Laing, 8 vols., Wodrow Society, 7 (1842–9), vols. 3–7 · Reg. PCS, 1st ser., vols. 2–8 · Calendar of the manuscripts of the most hon. the marquess of Salisbury, 19–21, HMC, 9 (1965–70) · APS, 1124–1707 · R. Chambers, Domestic annals of Scotland, 3rd edn, 1 (1874) · W. Forbes-Leith, The Scots men-at-arms and life-guards in France, 1 (1882) · F. Michel, Les écossais en France, les français en Écosse, 2 vols. (1862), vol. 1 · L. A. Knafla, Law and politics in Jacobean England (1977) · J. M. Thomson and others, eds., Registrum magni sigilli regum Scotorum / The register of the great seal of Scotland, 11 vols. (1882–1914), vols. 4–8 · G. Burnett and others, eds., The exchequer rolls of Scotland, 20–21, 23 (1899–1908) · GEC, Peerage · Scots peerage, 2.552–7

Archives BL, Add. MS 23108 · PRO, state MSS concerning Scotland | Hatfield House, Hertfordshire, Salisbury MSS

Colville, John (1542?–1605), conspirator and Church of Scotland minister, was born in Scotland, the second son of Robert Colville of Cleish (d. 1560) and Francesca (d. 1591), daughter of Patrick Colquhoun of Drumskeath. He was educated at St Leonard's College, University of St Andrews, where he graduated MA, probably in 1561. He was probably then aged about nineteen. He entered the ministry and by 1567 held the parsonage and vicarage of Kilbride in Clydesdale. Two years later he was confirmed as chantor (precentor) of Glasgow, while in 1571, as representative of the archdeacon of Teviotdale, he took part in the election of a new archbishop there. In 1574 Colville was recorded as minister of the united parishes of Kilbride, Torrens, Carmunnock, and Eaglesham, where his stipend extended to £200 (from which he had to pay for readers in each of his parishes). Frequent complaints were made about him in general assembly, and from 1575 to 1579 he was periodically exhibited for non-residence and neglect of his parishes. In 1580 it was stated that 'he was presently at the point of excommunication' (Thomson, Acts and Proceedings, 451) and by 1584 he had been removed from the chantory of Glasgow.

Colville simultaneously developed interests outside the church: in 1572 he married Janet Russell, with whom he had at least three sons and two daughters; he maintained a household at Stirling and lands (held of his cousin James Colville of Easter Wemyss) at Strathrudie in Fife; in November 1578 he was appointed master of requests for life with an annual pension of £200 (his father had been master of the household for James Stewart, later Regent Moray); and in March 1581 he was described as 'pedagogue to the Earl of Mar' (CSP Scot., 5.649). Although he was frequently employed on royal business, he was one of the most consistent suppliers of information to Queen Elizabeth's government concerning the political affairs of Scotland during the last quarter of the sixteenth century.

Following the arrest of James Douglas, fourth earl of Morton, in December 1580, Colville attached himself to the discontented protestant faction. He was stripped of his office of requests in March 1581—it was claimed he had obtained it 'sinisterlie and surreptitiouslie' (Livingstone and others, 8.31)—and subsequently took part in the Ruthven raid in August 1582. A manifesto issued in vindication of that enterprise (published as Ane declaration of the just and necessar caussis moving us of the nobilities of Scotland, and utheris, the kings majesties faithful subjectis to repair to his hienes presence and to remane with his etc, directit from Striviling, anno 1582) is normally attributed to him. When James VI removed himself from the control of the Ruthven regime in July 1583, Colville obtained licence to pass overseas for three years (except to England or Ireland). Ignoring his licence, he retired to England and was consequently forfeited in parliament, whereupon his offices were again declared vacant. After the earl of Arran had been driven from court in November 1585, Colville returned to Scotland in the company of Lord John Hamilton and was pardoned. Restored to royal favour he resumed the style chantor of Glasgow, and instructions were issued for the payment of the arrears of his pension as master of requests; this was a relief to Colville, who constantly was short of funds (and was stated to have been owed 5400 merks by James and the state). On 2 June 1587 he was admitted as a senator of the college of justice in place of his uncle, Alexander Colville, commendator of Culross (fulfilling a royal promise made in November 1582). However, after less than three weeks he resigned his seat in Alexander's favour. Also in 1587 Colville attended parliament as commissioner for the burgh of Stirling and was employed as collector of the taxation granted to James for his forthcoming marriage. He also accepted a number of pension payments from England on behalf of James VI. Despite all these offices and responsibilities, Colville was still owed money by James in the early 1590s.

On 27 December 1591, in the company of Francis Stewart, first earl of Bothwell, Colville attacked Holyrood Palace with the intention of seizing Chancellor Maitland, whom he hated. Colville had been involved in the earl's affairs since at least 1584, and in June 1592 was forfeited in parliament for this association. Undeterred, he attended Bothwell on the latter's raid against Falkland Palace at the end of June, and at some point composed a sympathetic tract, De causa Comitis Bothwellii (now lost). On 24 July 1593, however, Colville accompanied Bothwell to Holyrood Palace where both fell on their knees and craved pardon for their offences before the king. Despite a brief return to favour, on 11 December in the same year the two men were declared outlaws. Colville led one of the earl's divisions of horse against royal forces at the so-called raid of Leith in early April 1594, but later in the year severed connections with the earl when Bothwell allied himself with the Catholic faction. On 13 September Mar purchased a pardon from the king for Colville, who by 4 December had 'laid open as much as he knows of the manner of the carriage of all matters with Bothwell' (CSP Scot., 11.492). Still trusted by his former allies, in February 1595 Colville assured Bothwell's natural brother, Hercules Stewart, of his life, but on meeting with him betrayed Hercules to the government authorities and to execution. This action secured him greater royal favour, but discredited him in the eyes of his countrymen, and he had to seek sanctuary in Holyrood Abbey after Bothwell threatened to kill him.

With his sponsor Mar, Colville looked to benefit from the death of Chancellor Maitland in 1595: it was hoped that he might become secretary (a position he had held briefly upon his recovery of favour in autumn 1593) or at least keeper of the great seal. These plans came to nothing, and in July 1597 Colville was in the Netherlands 'with his Majesties good liking, under his hand and Great Seall for his lawfull affairs' (CSP Scot., 13.54). James's pleasure cooled a year later, when he found out that Colville was still deep in correspondence with England and had even 'kissed hands' with Elizabeth. An angry king alleged that any licence Colville possessed had been stolen. Whether Colville ever revisited Scotland is uncertain. In 1599 he was in London in a state of destitution, offering his services in vain to Robert Cecil. Leaving his wife in England,

he withdrew to France and arrived at Paris in February 1600. During his continental exile to Colville was reconciled to Bothwell and like him renounced protestantism. With a view to inducing his countrymen to follow his example, he wrote his *Paraenesis ad ministros Scotos super sua conversione* (1602). He also made a pilgrimage to Rome. Two years earlier he had published his *Palinode*, which he represented as a refutation of a former work of his own attacking James's title to the English crown. His previous argument that James was a bastard had much offended the king. He now caused a copy of his recantation to be forwarded to King James, who received it with great satisfaction. It was reissued in 1604. Spottiswoode, however, asserts that Colville was not the author. Colville wrote several other political works and has traditionally been cited as the most likely author of the *Historie of King James the Sext*. This attribution is now considered uncertain and open to doubt. There has also been some doubt over his death: although it was formerly claimed that he died while on pilgrimage to Rome in 1607, it is now accepted that he died in Paris in November 1605.

ROB MACPHERSON

Sources *Original letters of Mr John Colville, 1582–1603*, ed. D. Laing, Bannatyne Club, 104 (1858) · [T. Thomson], ed., *The historie and life of King James the Sext*, Bannatyne Club, 13 (1825) · G. Brunton and D. Haig, *An historical account of the senators of the college of justice, from its institution in MDXXXII* (1832) · *CSP Scot., 1569–1603* · D. Calderwood, *The history of the Kirk of Scotland*, ed. T. Thomson and D. Laing, 8 vols., Wodrow Society, 7 (1842–9) · J. Spottiswood, *The history of the Church of Scotland*, ed. M. Napier and M. Russell, 3 vols., Bannatyne Club, 93 (1850) · R. G. Macpherson, 'Francis Stewart, fifth Earl Bothwell, 1562–1612: lordship and politics in Jacobean Scotland', PhD diss., U. Edin., 1998 · *Reg. PCS*, 1st ser., vols. 1–7 · D. Moysie, *Memoirs of the affairs of Scotland, 1577–1603*, ed. J. Dennistoun, Bannatyne Club, 39 (1830) · M. Livingstone, D. Hay Fleming, and others, eds., *Registrum secreti sigilli regum Scotorum / The register of the privy seal of Scotland*, 5–8 (1957–82) · J. Bain, ed., *The border papers: calendar of letters and papers relating to the affairs of the borders of England and Scotland*, 2 vols. (1894–6) · T. Thomson, ed., *Acts and proceedings of the general assemblies of the Kirk of Scotland*, 3 pts, Bannatyne Club, 81 (1839–45) · J. Kirk, ed., *The books of assumption of the thirds of benefices: Scottish ecclesiastical rentals at the Reformation* (1995) · G. Donaldson, ed., *Accounts of the collectors of thirds of benefices, 1561–1572*, Scottish History Society, 3rd ser., 42 (1949)
Archives NA Scot. | BL, corresp., Cotton MSS

Colville, John (1852–1901). *See under* Colville family (*per.* 1861–1916).

Colville, (David) John, first Baron Clydesmuir (1894–1954), politician and colonial administrator, was born on 13 February 1894 at Motherwell House, Lanarkshire, the only son and younger child of John *Colville (1852–1901) [*see under* Colville family], an industrialist, and his second wife, Christian Downie (*d.* 1936). His paternal grandfather, David *Colville (1811/12–1898) [*see under* Colville family], had pioneered Scottish steel making; his father was Liberal MP for North-East Lanarkshire (1895–1901).

Born to wealth (unlike his forebears), Colville attended Charterhouse School and Trinity College, Cambridge, where he obtained a third in part one of the historical tripos in 1914. He was already an officer in the Territorial Force of the 6th battalion, the Cameronians (Scottish

Rifles) and, during four years on the western front, he was three times wounded. Colville married Agnes Anne (1890–1970), the daughter of Sir William *Bilsland, first baronet, a Glasgow businessman, on 6 October 1915. Their children were Ronald, Mary, and Rosemary.

Major Colville served on Lanarkshire county council (1919–26) and the board of the family steel firm, David Colville & Sons (managed by Sir John Craig). As a Lloyd George Liberal, he came fourth at Motherwell at the general election of 1922. As a Unionist he narrowly failed to take Midlothian and Peebleshire North at a by-election in January 1929 before winning it at the general election five months later. He retained the seat until 1943.

In parliament Colville spoke mainly on economic matters, missing no chance to recommend protective tariffs. The best way to combat unemployment, he said, was to 'safeguard' British iron and steel. He knew a lot about industrial 'rationalization', as mergers and amalgamations gave Colvilles Ltd a near monopoly of steel making in Scotland after it became a public company in 1931. Following two months as parliamentary private secretary to Noël Skelton, under-secretary for Scotland, Colville stopped asking questions about imports and answered them instead, as parliamentary secretary to the overseas trade department from 10 November 1931. He was responsible for export credit guarantees and helped to negotiate reciprocal trading agreements with nineteen countries after Britain abandoned free trade. In 1932 his military rank advanced to lieutenant-colonel in the Territorial Army.

Colville became under-secretary for Scotland on 28 November 1935 and worked under Sir Godfrey Collins on agricultural initiatives, such as the Scottish raspberry marketing scheme. A privy councillor from June 1936, he impressed his superiors by always mastering his brief and never straying beyond it. His tone was businesslike yet courteous; narrow eyes and a military moustache gave him a determined appearance. Conservatives felt confidence in an officer and a gentleman who also had a head for figures. In London he lived at 56 Eaton Square; his country home was Braidwood House, Braidwood, near Carluke, in Lanarkshire. He enjoyed shooting and fishing, and touring the western isles aboard his yacht, *Iolanthe*.

Promotion to financial secretary to the Treasury on 29 October 1936 entailed Colville's working for Neville Chamberlain and Sir John Simon. He ably defended the national defence contribution, a tax on the growth of profits, and had the satisfaction of imposing a tariff on imported beef. In his view, the National Government had inherited the old Liberal motto of 'peace, retrenchment, reform'.

Chamberlain appointed John Colville to the cabinet as secretary of state for Scotland on 16 May 1938 in the reshuffle caused by the departure of Lord Swinton. In this office much of his time was devoted to developing policies initiated by his predecessor, Walter Elliot, such as larger subsidies for council housing and industrial estates in depressed 'special areas'. In the months preceding the Munich agreement Colville had to busy himself with aid to herring fishermen. He voiced no support in cabinet for Czechoslovakia.

The Reorganization of Offices (Scotland) Act 1939 was the most comprehensive reform of Scottish administration since 1885. It replaced the system of semi-autonomous boards with four new departments within the Scottish Office—agriculture, education, health, and home affairs—directly subject to the secretary of state and all located in Edinburgh at the newly built St Andrew's House on Calton Hill. However, because the legislation followed the recommendations of Sir John Gilmour's committee, published in September 1937, it sounded anticlimactic in Colville's lucid but mundane exposition.

Plans for air-raid precautions, evacuation, and increased food production were priorities at the Scottish Office in 1939, and civil servants marvelled at Colville's unremitting application. In March he found time to abolish 'irregular' marriages, thus ending the romantic tradition of Gretna Green. Thereafter, non-emergency measures were shelved, including proposals for a highland development commissioner. His expanded department mobilized Scottish civil authorities for war in the autumn.

When Churchill chose his coalition government in May 1940, there was no place for Colville (who is to be distinguished from Sir John Rupert Colville, later Churchill's principal private secretary); he became a full-time colonel on the staff of the lowland district, raising the Home Guard. In 1941 he warned the Scottish advisory council of ex-secretaries of state on post-war problems ('the council of state') that the policy of industrial concentration threatened to damage Scotland's economy by penalizing light industry in favour of war-producers bound to close down at the end of hostilities.

In November 1942 Colville replaced Sir John Dill as governor designate of the Bombay province. As his support for Churchill in the censure debate of July 1942 had been grudging, many saw this as the exile of another old Chamberlainite, though Amery, the Indian secretary, and Linlithgow, the viceroy, both judged that Sir John Colville (as he became in February 1943) would make an excellent pro-consul—and they were right. When he arrived in Bombay on 23 March 1943, the situation remained tense after the suppression of the 'quit India' campaign. With Congress Party leaders imprisoned in the province, the British ran it without cabinet or legislature under Section 93 of the Government of India Act (1935). Colville exercised his broad powers shrewdly in successive crises. In April 1944 the accidental explosion of an ammunition ship in Bombay docks made 20,000 people homeless. In February 1946 sailors of the Indian navy mutinied. Communal violence escalated after an elected provincial government took office in April 1946.

As the only former secretary of state to hold a governorship in India since crown rule began in 1858, Colville ranked above his colleagues and deputized several times for the viceroys, Wavell and then Mountbatten, during their absences in London (20 March–6 June and 24 August–16 September 1945, 1–23 December 1946, and 19–30 May 1947). He offered his resignation in February 1947, when the British government removed Wavell and set a terminal date for imperial rule that struck him as premature; the offer was not accepted.

Sir John Colville continued as governor of Bombay for five months after Indian independence and retired on 6 January 1948. As Baron Clydesmuir from March 1948, he addressed the House of Lords on Scottish, industrial, and army matters. A governor of the BBC from 1950 and lord lieutenant of Lanarkshire from 1952, Lord Clydesmuir died at home at Braidwood on 31 October 1954. He was buried on 4 November 1954.

Colville was a proficient executive politician, safe rather than showy. Historians paid him minimal attention, though he was occasionally mentioned as a representative type of Scottish tory: the Clydeside capitalist in politics.   JASON TOMES

Sources Hansard 5C · G. Pottinger, The secretaries of state for Scotland, 1926–76 (1979) · N. Mansergh, ed., The transfer of power, 1942–7, 12 vols. (1970–82) · The Times (2 Nov 1954) · M. Fry, Patronage and principle: a political history of modern Scotland (1987) · cabinet minutes, 1938–9, PRO, CAB 23/94–97 · Wavell: the viceroy's journal, ed. P. Moon (1973) · Parliament and politics in the age of Churchill and Attlee: the Headlam diaries, 1935–1951, ed. S. Ball, CS, 5th ser., 14 (1999) · R. H. Campbell, 'The committee of ex-secretaries of state for Scotland and industrial policy, 1941–45', Scottish Industrial History, 2/2 (1981), 3–10
Archives BL OIOC, for Bombay · NA Scot., Scottish Office files · PRO, Treasury files · PRO, Board of Trade files | FILM IWM FVA, actuality footage
Likenesses W. Stoneman, photographs, 1931–43, NPG · S. Cursiter, portrait, posthumous c.1955, priv. coll.
Wealth at death £371,243 11s. 3d.: confirmation, 21 Jan 1955, CCI · no value given: confirmation, 3 Feb 1955, CGPLA Eng. & Wales

Colville, Sir John Rupert (1915–1987), diplomatist and civil servant, was born in London on 28 January 1915, the youngest of three sons (there were no daughters) of the Hon. George Charles Colville (1867–1943), barrister, and his wife, Lady (Helen) Cynthia *Colville (1884–1968), daughter of Robert Offley Ashburton Crewe-*Milnes, marquess of Crewe. He was educated at West Downs School and Harrow School, and continued on a senior scholarship to Trinity College, Cambridge, where he obtained a first class in part one of the history tripos and a second class (division one) in part two (1936). In 1937 he joined the diplomatic service and after only two years was seconded to 10 Downing Street to act as assistant private secretary to Neville Chamberlain. He liked and admired Chamberlain and would have favoured Viscount Halifax to succeed him in May 1940—'I am afraid it must be Winston', he wrote regretfully in his diary—but even then he conceded the drive and determination of Winston *Churchill, and he was quickly converted into one of the most devoted of his supporters. Exciting and congenial though he found the work in no. 10, after the outbreak of the Second World War Colville resolved to enter the armed forces, and in October 1941 he overcame the opposition of the Foreign Office and the handicap of bad eyesight and joined the Royal Air Force volunteer reserve. After training in South Africa he was commissioned as a pilot officer and joined 268 squadron of the second Tactical Air Force, flying Mustang fighters. In spite of periodic efforts by Churchill to

recapture him, he remained with the air force until the end of 1943 and was allowed to rejoin his unit for the invasion of France; he returned to Whitehall for good in August 1944.

Although in spirit a Conservative, who had contemplated standing as such in 1945, Colville greatly admired C. R. Attlee's honesty, efficiency, and common sense, and found no difficulty in serving under him when Labour came to power. However, his career was still diplomacy and in October 1945 he returned to the Foreign Office to work in the southern department. After the dramas of no. 10 the work lacked savour, and within two years he had moved away again to become private secretary to the twenty-year-old Princess Elizabeth, a post he held until 1949. It was a natural appointment for a former page of honour to George V, whose mother was a woman of the bedchamber to Queen Mary. No one would have been surprised if he had remained in royal service, but after two years he returned to diplomacy and was posted to Lisbon (1947–51) as first secretary.

It was not for long; when Churchill became prime minister in October 1951, Colville was invited—commanded, almost—to rejoin him as principal private secretary. When Churchill suffered a severe stroke in June 1953 but refused to allow his powers to be delegated, Colville and the prime minister's son-in-law and parliamentary private secretary, Christopher Soames, found themselves called on to make decisions on matters about which they would normally never have been consulted. For almost a month, with the encouragement and support of the secretary of the cabinet, Sir Norman Brook, they dealt with government departments which had no conception of the gravity of the prime minister's condition, acting in his name and articulating what they believed would have been his views. They handled their duties with tact and discretion, but the experience fortified Colville's resolve not to return yet again to diplomacy after Churchill's resignation in April 1955.

Instead, Colville embarked on two new careers. He joined Hill Samuel and became a director of the National and Grindlay, Ottoman, and Coutts's banks, and chairman of Eucalyptus Pulp Mills. He also took to writing. His first book, a biography of the sixth Viscount Gort, Man of Valour (1972), was well received and encouraged him to follow it with, among others, a study of Churchill's entourage, The Churchillians (1981), and an autobiographical volume, Footprints in Time (1976). His best-known work, however, was his edition of the diaries that he had kept while at no. 10, The Fringes of Power (1985), a colourful, informative, and admirably honest account of the years he spent working for Churchill. He also served as treasurer of the National Association of Boys' Clubs, and president of the New Victoria Hospital in Kingston. Colville was appointed CVO (1949) and CB (1955), and was knighted in 1974. He was an officer of the Légion d'honneur, and an honorary fellow of Churchill College, Cambridge (1971), in whose foundation he played a role.

By birth, upbringing, and career, Colville seemed a quintessential establishment figure, but any tendency to pomposity or undue conventionality was curbed by his keen eye for the ridiculous. His tact, charm, good judgement, and readiness always to tell the truth when necessary, made him an ideal private secretary. He was stocky and of medium height, very dark, with a roundish face and slightly Latin appearance—'Who is that foreigner with an English wife?' people would sometimes ask when he was abroad. His hair went grey when he was in his forties, which gave him a more distinguished air: this concerned him little; he took no particular trouble over his appearance and, without being scruffy, was rarely smart. He married in 1948 Lady Margaret Egerton, lady-in-waiting to Princess Elizabeth and daughter of John Francis Granville Scrope Egerton, fourth earl of Ellesmere. They had two sons and a daughter. He was still leading and enjoying an active life when on 19 November 1987 he suffered a heart attack while at Winchester Station, and died almost immediately.   PHILIP ZIEGLER, *rev.*

Sources J. Colville, *The fringes of power* (1985) · J. Colville, *Footprints in time* (1976) · personal knowledge (1996) · private information (1996) · *CGPLA Eng. & Wales* (1988)
Archives CAC Cam., diaries and papers | CAC Cam., corresp. with Lady Spencer-Churchill · Nuffield Oxf., corresp. with Lord Cherwell
Wealth at death £954,485: probate, 12 May 1988, *CGPLA Eng. & Wales*

Colville, Ronald John Bilsland, **second Baron Clydesmuir** (1917–1996), businessman and banker, was born on 21 May 1917 at 28 Park Circus, Hillhead, Glasgow, the only son and eldest of the three children of (David) John *Colville, first Baron Clydesmuir (1894–1954), steel manufacturer, politician, and public servant, and his wife, Agnes Anne (1890–1970), elder daughter of Sir William *Bilsland, first baronet. He was educated at Charterhouse School and Trinity College, Cambridge, where he read economics. No sooner had he graduated in 1939 than he was drawn into the Second World War, joining the Cameronians (Scottish Rifles), in which his father had served in the First World War. He was in action with his regiment at Dunkirk, in Italy, and in the Normandy landings. He served throughout the war, during which he was mentioned in dispatches and awarded the MBE (1944). On 10 April 1946 he married Joan Marguerita Booth, elder daughter of Lieutenant-Colonel Ernest Brabazon Booth, of Darver Castle, co. Louth. They had two sons, David (*b.* 1949) and Andrew (*b.* 1953), and two daughters, Diana (*b.* 1947) and Anne (*b.* 1955).

On his return to civilian life after the war, Colville joined the company with which his family name would forever be associated: Colvilles, the dominant firm in the Scottish iron and steel industry. It had always been intended that he should play a major role within the company, but it was typical of Colvilles' management at that time that he first underwent an intensive eighteen months' training in various departments of most of the firms within the group. After two further years at the head office in Glasgow, he joined the Steel Company of Scotland, becoming managing director in 1953. Not until 1958 was Clydesmuir (he inherited the title in 1954) appointed to the main

board of Colvilles Ltd. In 1964 he became the director responsible for the group's public relations. Three years later Colvilles passed into public ownership and was absorbed by the British Steel Corporation. Although Clydesmuir remained with the nationalized concern for a further six years—first as a director of Colvilles Ltd and, after a convulsive reorganization designed to dissolve the multi-company system inherited under the Iron and Steel Act of 1967, as director of the Strip Mills division of BSC from 1970—his heart was not in it, and in 1973 he resigned.

A director of the British Linen Bank since 1955, Clydesmuir became governor in 1966, and almost immediately began informal discussions with Lord Polwarth, governor of the Bank of Scotland, to merge the two banks. A merger was effected in 1971 when Clydesmuir became deputy governor, succeeding Polwarth as governor of the Bank of Scotland in the following year, when the latter resigned to take up a political appointment. Clydesmuir remained governor for ten years, a decade which saw rapid and highly beneficial developments in the Scottish economy. But he was more than just a banker. In the post-war years a complex network of interlocking directorates held by financiers and members of dominant families had developed which welded Scottish business into a densely connected system. Clydesmuir was at the very heart of this system, holding directorships in Scotbits Securities, Scottish Save and Prosper, the Scottish Western Investment Company, Scottish Provident, the Caledonian Offshore Company, and Barclays. In these various capacities—not least his governorship of the Bank of Scotland—he played a significant role in developing the North Sea oil and gas industries and for seventeen years (1972–87) he was chairman of North Sea Assets, a company established to acquire substantial minority holdings in companies operating both on- and off-shore.

Nevertheless, Clydesmuir always realized that Scotland could not live by oil alone. As early as 1952 he had been a member of the Scottish Council (Development and Industry), becoming chairman of its executive committee in 1966 and president in 1978. The focus of the council was avowedly industrial. Believing that the principal need in Scotland was for new industries which would employ men, it was convinced that electronics—hitherto almost entirely absent from Scotland—was capable of constituting a vital sector in Scotland's economic structure. As early as 1948 the council had embarked on a pioneering campaign to attract companies possessing the necessary capital, expertise, and market connections from the United States. David Packard later told Tam Dalyell that one of the reasons why he and Bill Hewlett set up their huge plant at South Queensferry was because of the helpfulness of Clydesmuir and his chief executive, Dr Willie Robertson. Others said the same. Clydesmuir was indefatigable in staging industrial exhibitions of Scottish products and leading trade delegations to, among other places, China and the Soviet Union. An abiding memory of Dalyell was of an immaculately turned-out Clydesmuir striding through the paddy fields and pig compounds of the

Sino-Albanian Friendship Commune, near Beijing, and discussing labour deployment in a truck factory at Shanghai. His preparations for such ventures were meticulous. He had read Mao's *Little Red Book* and he could, moreover, 'recite Marx with the best of them' (Dalyell, 20), having been supervised at Trinity by the redoubtable Marxist economist Maurice Dobb, a fellow Carthusian.

Clydesmuir, the great-grandson of David Colville, the creator of the Scottish steel industry, realized more clearly than most the necessity of reducing Scotland's dependence on heavy industry by developing more diversified, technologically advanced products and exporting them widely. His efforts to effect such a transformation explain his devotion to the activities of the Scottish council and his seizure of the opportunities presented by the discovery of North Sea oil. In this he was motivated not simply by a desire to enhance the growth and profitability of the many industrial and financial institutions with which he was associated but because, as Viscount Weir once said, 'Ronnie Clydesmuir was ... a tremendous Scottish patriot. He really did care about Scotland and Scottish industry' (Dalyell).

Among the many honorary and voluntary activities which benefited from Clydesmuir's support were the Scottish Council of Physical Recreation, the Scottish branch of the National Playing Fields Association, and the Scottish Outward Bound Association, of all of which bodies he was president. He retained his connection with the army, being chairman of the Council of the Territorial, Auxiliary, and Volunteer Associations (1969–73), and later president (1974–81). He commanded the 6/7th (territorial) battalion of the Cameronians, and was later honorary colonel (1967–71); he was also honorary colonel of the 52nd Lowland reserve volunteers, Territorial Army and volunteer reserve (1970–75). Many honours were heaped on him. He was appointed CB in 1965 and knight of the Thistle in 1972. A lifelong member of the Church of Scotland, and an elder of St Michael's, Linlithgow, he was lord high commissioner to the general assembly in 1971 and 1972. He held office as lord lieutenant of Lanarkshire from 1963 to 1992, having been deputy lieutenant (1955–9) and vice-lieutenant (1959). A member of the Royal Company of Archers, queen's bodyguard for Scotland, he held the office of captain-general from 1986 until shortly before his death.

For all his distinctions, Clydesmuir was never remote or pompous. Beneath his erect military bearing, clipped white moustache, and superbly tailored suits, there lurked an irrepressible sense of fun. A wonderful raconteur, with a fund of amusing anecdotes, he possessed a natural charm which endeared him to all, high and low. Despite his punishing business and ceremonial commitments, he made time for shooting and fishing, and nowhere was he happier than with his family. He died of a stroke at Kello Hospital, Biggar, Lanarkshire, on 2 October 1996, and was buried in Biggar parish churchyard on 7 October. He was survived by his wife and their four children, and was succeeded as third baron by his son David. Of the many observations occasioned by his death, perhaps

the most apt was that by Sir Thomas Risk, a colleague for over thirty years and his successor as governor of the Bank of Scotland: 'He was a man of his time, born with outstanding gifts which he used unselfishly to the full' (Risk, 133).

PETER L. PAYNE

Sources T. Risk, *Yearbook of the Royal Society of Edinburgh* (1999), 131–3 · *Glasgow Herald* (5 Oct 1996) · *The Scotsman* (5 Oct 1996) · *The Times* (5 Oct 1996) · *Daily Telegraph* (9 Oct 1996) · T. Dalyell, *The Independent* (7 Oct 1996) · J. Scott and M. Hughes, *The anatomy of Scottish capital* (1980) · R. Saville, *Bank of Scotland: a history, 1695–1995* (1996) · *Colvilles Magazine*, various issues, esp. spring 1958, pp. 10–11 · P. L. Payne, *Colvilles and the Scottish steel industry* (1979) · P. L. Payne, 'Scottish council (development and industry)', *Oxford companion to Scottish history*, ed. M. Lynch (2001), 574–5 · C. Harvie, *Fool's gold: the story of North Sea oil* (1994) · WWW · Burke, *Peerage* · personal knowledge (2004) · b. cert. · d. cert.

Archives Bank of Scotland, Edinburgh, archives · NA Scot., British Steel records, GD 464

Likenesses A. Morrocco, oils, *c*.1980, Bank of Scotland, 38 St Andrew Square, Edinburgh · photograph, repro. in *The Times* · photograph, repro. in *The Independent* · photograph, repro. in *Daily Telegraph*

Wealth at death £577,759.87: confirmation, 13 Dec 1996, CCI

Colville, Sir Stanley Cecil James (1861–1939), naval officer, was born at 42 Eaton Place, London, on 21 February 1861. He was the second son of Charles John Colville, tenth Lord Colville of Culross, later first Viscount Colville of Culross (1818–1903), chamberlain to Queen Alexandra as princess of Wales and queen. His mother was Cecile Katherine Mary (*d*. 1907), daughter of Robert John Carrington, second Baron Carrington. After attending Marlborough College, Colville entered the Royal Naval College, Dartmouth, as a naval cadet in July 1874. In October 1876 he was appointed as midshipman to the battleship *Sultan* in the Mediterranean under its captain, Prince Alfred, duke of Edinburgh. He remained with the duke when he transferred to the ironclad *Black Prince*, Channel Fleet, in May 1878. In January 1879 he was appointed as midshipman to the corvette *Boedicea* commanded by Commodore F. W. Richards at the Cape station. Colville landed with the naval brigade during the Anglo-Zulu War, and took part in subsequent land operations. He was promoted sub-lieutenant in October 1880, and continued training and examinations at Portsmouth.

In July 1882 Colville joined the battleship *Alexandra*, Mediterranean Fleet, flagship of Admiral Sir F. B. P. Seymour, and was present at the bombardment of Alexandria (11 July) and subsequent land operations. He was promoted lieutenant in November 1882. In May 1883 he joined the corvette *Canada*, North America station, in which Prince George of Wales (the future George V) was midshipman. In September 1884 Colville rejoined the *Alexandra* in the Mediterranean, and served with the naval brigade attempting to relieve General Gordon at Khartoum. Colville served for three years again under the duke of Edinburgh, now commander-in-chief, Mediterranean Fleet, being appointed to his flagship *Alexandra* in February 1886. In October 1889 Colville joined the sloop *Buzzard* under Commander J. A. Baker on the North America and West Indies station.

In August 1890 Colville was appointed as first lieutenant

Sir Stanley Cecil James Colville (1861–1939), by Walter Stoneman, 1917

to the royal yacht *Victoria and Albert*. He served for two years and was promoted commander in August 1892. Colville joined the battleship *Trafalgar*, flagship of Admiral Sir Compton E. Domvile, commander-in-chief, Mediterranean Fleet, in May 1893, where he served for three years. In 1896 Colville was seconded to the Egyptian government at the request of the sirdar, General Sir Herbert Kitchener, to command gunboats of the Nile flotilla and support the British army's campaign against the khalifa. Colville was badly wounded but was mentioned in dispatches, promoted captain in October 1896, and appointed CB.

During 1897–8 Colville held a shore appointment as naval adviser to the inspector-general of fortifications at the War Office, London. In September 1898 he joined the battleship *Barfleur*, China station, as flag captain to Admiral Penrose Fitzgerald for eighteen months. In March 1900 Colville was appointed flag captain to Vice-Admiral Sir Frederick Bedford in the cruiser *Crescent* on the North America and West Indies station for two years. On 19 December 1902 Colville married Lady Adelaide Jane (*b.* 1876/7), youngest daughter of admiral of the fleet Richard J. Meade, fourth earl of Clanwilliam; they subsequently had four sons.

In May 1902 Colville was appointed as chief of staff to Admiral Sir Compton E. Domvile, commander-in-chief, Mediterranean Fleet, flying his flag in the battleship *Bulwark*, and served for three years. In December 1905 Colville was appointed captain of the battleship *Hindustan*, Atlantic Fleet, his only independent captain's command. He reached flag rank in November 1906 at the early age of

forty-five. In January 1908 Colville hoisted his rear-admiral's flag in the battleship *Bulwark*, Home Fleet, under Admiral Sir Francis Bridgeman. In February 1909 he was appointed rear-admiral, 1st cruiser squadron, Channel Fleet, flying his flag in *Drake*. In July 1909 he transferred his flag to *Indomitable*, one of the three new battle cruisers of the dreadnought era which now comprised the prestigious 1st cruiser squadron, Home Fleet. Colville was promoted vice-admiral in April 1911. He attended a senior officers' course at Portsmouth and in June 1912 hoisted his flag in the battleship *Collingwood*, 1st squadron, Home Fleet, spending two years in this command. At the outbreak of the First World War in August 1914 Colville was ashore on half-pay. In early September 1914 he accepted the shore command of vice-admiral, Orkneys and Shetlands, under Admiral Sir John Jellicoe, commander-in-chief, Grand Fleet. Colville was promoted admiral in September 1914.

Although Colville missed the sea war, this was a vital appointment. He was responsible for the naval establishments and defence of the islands, particularly Scapa Flow, the Grand Fleet's main anchorage. Jellicoe so approved of Colville's competence that in early 1916 the Admiralty officially expressed its appreciation. Colville was also Jellicoe's choice to succeed him and Vice-Admiral Sir Cecil Burney, second in command, Grand Fleet, in the event of any disaster. In February 1916 Colville was appointed as commander-in-chief, Portsmouth, the most important royal dockyard and another vital shore appointment. Colville hauled down his flag in March 1919, and in July was appointed principal aide-de-camp to George V. He was placed on the retired list in April 1922.

Colville was appointed rear-admiral of the United Kingdom in 1927 and vice-admiral of the United Kingdom and lieutenant of the Admiralty in 1929, ancient offices revived by Edward VII in 1901. Colville was appointed CVO in 1902, KCB in 1912, GCVO in 1915, GCMG in 1919, and GCB in 1921. His foreign decorations included appointment to the Japanese order of the Rising Sun and the Légion d'honneur. He died at his home, Larchwood, Crawley Down, Sussex, on 9 April 1939. Lady Colville survived him. Colville owed much to his royal connections in his fortunate sea and shore appointments. Yet he was a fine seaman and able administrator, who met the challenge of rapid technological change while embodying the virtues of his patrician class: courage, loyalty, honour, a deep responsibility for the men under his command, and complete devotion to the Royal Navy.   JOHN R. BULLEN

Sources *Navy List* (1875–1925) · *DNB* · A. J. Marder, *From the Dreadnought to Scapa Flow: the Royal Navy in the Fisher era, 1904–1919*, 5 vols. (1961–70), vol. 2 · S. W. Roskill, *Admiral of the fleet Earl Beatty: the last naval hero, an intimate biography* (1980) · J. Winton, *Jellicoe* (1981) · A. Gordon, *The rules of the game: Jutland and British naval command* (1996) · *WWW* · *CGPLA Eng. & Wales* (1939) · b. cert. · m. cert.
Likenesses F. Dodd, charcoal and watercolour drawing, 1917, IWM · W. Stoneman, photograph, 1917, NPG [*see illus.*] · W. Llewellyn, oils, 1927, priv. coll. · W. Stoneman, photograph, 1938, NPG
Wealth at death £11,326 13s. 4d.: probate, 28 June 1939, *CGPLA Eng. & Wales*

Colville, William (d. 1675), Church of Scotland minister and university principal, was from Cleish, Kinross-shire, and was the brother of Sir Robert Colville of Cleish. He appears to have graduated MA from St Andrews University in 1631 and was ordained to the ministry and appointed to his first charge at Cramond, near Edinburgh, in 1635. Shortly after the covenanting revolution he was translated to Trinity College, Edinburgh, to which he was presented by the town council of Edinburgh on 14 January 1639 and admitted soon after. Colville was chosen to act in the capacity of emissary from the covenanting regime to the United Provinces and to Louis XIII of France. In particular he was entrusted with soliciting Dutch and French backing against Charles I and his royalist followers. In 1641 he took part in church discussions designed to end the controversy over private meetings for worship. He was translated to and inducted as pastor of the Tron Kirk, Edinburgh, in December that same year.

Colville's defence of the engagement led to his suspension from the ministry by the general assembly in July 1648 and deposition on 26 July 1649. He left Scotland and was soon called to the ministry of an English congregation in Utrecht. Not bereft of admirers in the Scottish capital, in April 1652 he was chosen by the town council to be principal of Edinburgh University. However, his appointment was opposed by the ministry and was vetoed by the protectorate government in Scotland. On 8 November 1654 the synod of Lothian restored him to the ministry and the following year he was admitted to the charge of Perth.

Colville remained at Perth until, in 1662, he was appointed principal of Edinburgh University. As principal he is best remembered for initiating a series of administrative and legislative articles designed to improve student discipline and facilitate learning. He was the author of *Refreshing Streams* (1655), *Ethicam Christianam* (1670), and *The Righteous Branch* (1673). His pamphlet, 'Submission to the censures of suspension and deposition exemplified in the case of the Very Reverend Mr William Colvill, sometime one of the ministers of Edinburgh, and afterwards principal of the college there. From authentic and unquestionable vouchers', was published posthumously in 1734. Colville was married twice, first to Marion Brisbane, with whom he had four sons and a daughter, and second to Marion Fyfe, with whom he had a son. He probably died in Edinburgh in late May 1675, for he was buried there on 3 June.   A. S. WAYNE PEARCE

Sources *Fasti Scot.*, new edn, vols. 1, 4 · *The letters and journals of Robert Baillie*, ed. D. Laing, 3 vols., Bannatyne Club, 73 (1841–2) · J. Kirk, ed., *The records of the synod of Lothian and Tweeddale, 1589–1596, 1640–1649*, Stair Society, 30 (1977) · D. Stevenson, *The Scottish revolution, 1637–44: the triumph of the covenanters* (1973) · F. D. Dow, *Cromwellian Scotland, 1651–1660* (1979) · A. Grant, *The story of the University of Edinburgh during its first three hundred years*, 2 vols. (1884) · A. Morgan and R. K. Hannay, eds., *University of Edinburgh: charters, statutes, acts … 1583–1858* (1937)

Colvin, Sir Auckland (1838–1908), administrator in India and Egypt, was born at Calcutta on 8 March 1838, the third son of the ten children of John Russell *Colvin (1807–

Sir Auckland Colvin (1838–1908), by unknown photographer

1857), lieutenant-governor of the North-Western Provinces, and his wife, Emma Sophia, daughter of Wetenhall Sneyd, vicar of Newchurch, Isle of Wight. Three of his brothers, Bazett Wetenhall Colvin, Elliott Graham Colvin, and Sir Walter Mytton Colvin [*see below*], all had distinguished careers in India, and a fourth, Clement Sneyd CSI, was secretary of the public works department of the India Office in London. His grandfather John Colvin was a merchant in Calcutta.

Educated at Eton College from 1850, Colvin went to the East India College, Haileybury, in 1854, and returned to India to begin an administrative career on 17 January 1858. He married on 4 August 1859 Charlotte Elizabeth (d. 1865), daughter of Lieutenant-General Charles Herbert CB, and had a son, who died in infancy, and three daughters. Initially posted to the North-Western Provinces (later the United Provinces of Agra and Oudh), where his father had been governor, he held administrative posts in various districts until becoming under-secretary in the home department of the government of India in 1864–5. From 1866 to 1870 he was assistant settlement officer in Etawa and Allahabad districts, working on the revision of the land revenue assessment. In 1870 he was appointed secretary to the board of revenue of the government of the North-Western Provinces. From 1875 to 1878 he held various posts in the government of India as commissioner for excise and inland customs, although he was returned briefly to district work as a collector in 1877 following a disagreement with the lieutenant-governor of the North-Western Provinces, Sir George Couper.

Colvin's career began to take on a wider significance when he was transferred to Egypt in January 1878, initially as head of the cadastral survey. He resigned from this post the next year when Khedive Isma'il, the titular head of the Egyptian government, attempted to exclude all Europeans from his administration, but was appointed commissioner of the debt in May 1879 and succeeded Evelyn Baring (later Lord Cromer) as controller-general in June 1880. These posts gave him responsibility for the management of the Egyptian government's debts to its foreign creditors, payment of which absorbed about two-thirds of government revenues each year.

Colvin now became identified with the interests of British and French bondholders, and he used his influence through official channels, and through his access to the press as the Egyptian correspondent of the *Pall Mall Gazette*, to stress the responsibilities of the British government to the interests of private investors. In a perceptive memorandum written for the British government in December 1881, for example, Colvin argued that liberal nationalists should be encouraged to take over the internal administration of Egypt, but that the European powers must recognize openly their own material interests in financial administration. During the political upheavals of 1880 to 1882, as the nationalist movement led by Urabi Pasha and backed by the local military and landed élites gathered support for opposition to European financial control, Colvin and Sir Edward Malet, the British consul, saw their position under increasing threat. The reports of these men on the spot helped to fan fears (possibly exaggerated) of anarchy and an anti-European military revolt, which prompted the British occupation of Egypt following riots in Alexandria in June 1882. After the British occupation Colvin became financial adviser to the khedive. He was created KCMG in 1881.

Colvin returned to India as finance member of the viceroy's council in August 1883, again succeeding Evelyn Baring in office. Here he faced familiar financial problems, as the rising costs of the British military establishment and an unstable and weakening rupee rate of exchange put severe pressure on the revenues of British India. Colvin found that military demands, especially for the strengthening of the defences of the north-west frontier region against a possible invasion by Russia and the pacification of Burma, were hard to control, while the exchange costs of the depreciation of the silver rupee against gold meant that the government of India had to raise increased taxation to meet its fixed sterling expenditure in England on the home charges for military costs, pensions, and debt servicing. Colvin argued strongly for the British government to take action to stabilize the world price of silver, arguing that this posed a bigger threat to the raj than did the Russian army, but with no effect; instead, he was forced to impose politically sensitive new forms of taxation, including a reimposition of income tax and a 25 per cent increase in the salt excise.

As in Egypt, Colvin's political judgements in India were sophisticated. In 1883 he played a major role in diffusing the 'white mutiny' which broke out over the proposals of the Criminal Jurisdiction Bill (Ilbert Bill) to increase the powers of Indian judges to try European civilians, arranging a compromise that allowed such defendants the right to claim a jury, at least half of whom were to be Europeans. The opposition to the Ilbert Bill, often expressed in racist, anti-Indian language, was widely seen as an attack on the liberal policies of the viceroy, Lord Ripon, who was closely identified with political and administrative reforms that increased Indian participation in the machinery of government. On Ripon's retirement in December 1884 Colvin defended his reputation in an article in *The Pioneer* (an English-language newspaper published in Allahabad) that drew attention to the limited vision and small-mindedness of the bulk of the expatriate community.

Colvin was appointed lieutenant-governor of the North-Western Provinces in 1887. Here, as at Calcutta, he identified a clear link between the financial stability and political legitimacy of British rule in India. Increased taxation required increased representation, and Colvin urged that what he called 'leading native gentlemen' should be associated with government policy through municipal self-government and provincial legislatures. To this end, he built up links between his administration and the large landowners of Oudh, founding Colvin Talukdars College to educate the sons of landed aristocrats; he also lent his support to the emerging strand of loyalist Muslim opinion centred around Saiyid Ahmad Khan, whom he had first supported as a young district officer in the 1860s. By contrast, Colvin campaigned vigorously, in the press and elsewhere, against the liberal nationalism of the Indian National Congress, and published an open correspondence with one of its founders, A. O. Hume, in *The Pioneer*. He was particularly critical of the levelling effect of the new franchise rules for local self-government in 1883, which gave access to municipal councils to professional and commercial men whose elevation he thought threatened the position of the established social and political order.

Colvin was created a CIE in October 1883 and was gazetted a KCSI in May 1892, six months before retirement. In England he settled at Earl Soham Lodge, Framlingham, Suffolk. From 1896 onwards he was chairman of the Burma Railways, the Egyptian Delta Railway, and the Khedival Mail Steamship Company, and was on a number of other company boards. He wrote *John Russell Colvin* (1895), the life of his father, for the Rulers of India series, and an account of Egyptian affairs in *The Making of Modern Egypt* (1906), which is not revealing of his own part in events and was quickly overshadowed by the rival polemics of William Scawen Blunt's *The Secret History of the English Occupation of Egypt* (1907) and Lord Cromer's *Modern Egypt* (1908). Colvin died at Suffolk House, Maple Road, Surbiton, Surrey, the residence of his eldest daughter, on 24 March 1908, and was buried at Earl Soham.

Sir Walter Mytton Colvin (1847–1908), lawyer, Sir Auckland's youngest brother, was born at Moulmein, Burma, on 13 September 1847 and was educated at Rugby School and Trinity Hall, Cambridge. He was called to the bar at the Middle Temple in 1871, went out to Allahabad the following year, and there built up a large practice as a criminal lawyer. He married in 1873 Annie, daughter of Wigram E. Money, and had a family of three daughters. He served for several terms as a nominated member of the legislative council of the North-Western Provinces, and was a prominent member of the government of India police commission of 1902–3. He was knighted in 1904 and died at Allahabad on 16 December 1908, where he was buried.   B. R. Tomlinson

Sources earl of Cromer [E. Baring], *Modern Egypt*, 2 vols. (1908) · F. Robinson, *Separatism among Indian Muslims: the politics of the United Provinces' Muslims, 1860–1923* (1974) · S. R. Mehrotra, *The emergence of the Indian National Congress* (1971) · *The Times* (26 March 1908) · *Times of India* (28 March 1908) · A. Schölch, *Egypt for the Egyptians: the socio-political crisis in Egypt, 1878–1882* (1981); trans. of *Ägypten den Ägyptern! Die politische und gesellschaftliche Krise der Jahre 1878–1882 in Ägypten* (1972) · *CGPLA Eng. & Wales* (1908) · *CGPLA Eng. & Wales* (1909) [Walter Mytton Colvin] · *DNB* · *WWW*
Archives BL, letters to Lord Ripon, Add. MS 43600 · BL OIOC, letters to Arthur Godley, MS Eur. F 102
Likenesses photograph, BL OIOC [*see illus.*]
Wealth at death £27,029 12s. 8d.: probate, 7 May 1908, *CGPLA Eng. & Wales* · £69,531 4s. 2d.—Walter Mytton Colvin: probate, 10 Feb 1909, *CGPLA Eng. & Wales*

Brenda Colvin (1897–1981), by unknown photographer, 1962

Colvin, Brenda (1897–1981), landscape architect, was born on 8 June 1897 at Simla in India, where her father, Sir Elliot Graham Colvin (1861–1940), became resident in Kashmir (1902) and later agent to the governor-general in Rajputana (1905–17). Her mother, Ethel Bayley, was the elder daughter of Sir Stewart Colvin Bayley, who also served with distinction in India, as had previous generations of the Colvin family. She had a brother and a sister. Her earliest schooling was on a house boat on the River Jhelum, a childhood which she remembered for the wild flowers, almond blossom, orchards, and picnics on the banks of the lakes and in the gardens of the Shalimar. Formal education came later, when she lived with a family friend in a Hampton Court apartment and attended a variety of schools in England and France. She was fond of remarking that this background and upbringing classified her on the census as an illiterate immigrant.

In 1919 Colvin attended Swanley Horticultural College to study gardening and market work, preceding by a year Sylvia Crowe, her lifelong and sympathetic colleague. However, during the first year she became interested in the design course under Madeline Agar, a landscape architect trained in the United States then working on the rejuvenation of Wimbledon Common; she worked for two years as a pupil and foreman in Miss Agar's office. Then about 1922 Colvin founded her own practice, which remained at the centre of her endeavours throughout her long working life. For the next two decades she advised on the creation and improvement of gardens, both private and institutional, writing many articles on design with plants, a field in which she excelled. The few remaining black and white photographs of her early work show an architectural handling of texture and form in foliage design combined with a delicate overlay of flowers, sometimes like a short-lived mist over massy landforms. She

was conscious of the need to arrange gardens to provide interest throughout the year and to achieve coherence of colour in both foliage and flowers. By 1939 she had advised on about 300 gardens. Her largest work before that date was an extensive addition to the garden at Zywiec in Poland for Archduke Charles Albert Habsburg; it is a measure of her reputation during the 1930s that she should have received such a commission.

No account of Brenda Colvin is complete without reference to the two books she wrote in the late 1940s. *Trees for Town and Country*, written with Jacqueline Tyrwhitt and published in 1947, describes, with fine line illustrations by S. R. Badmin, the character, size, and requirements of selected common trees, and was long a standard reference work. *Land and Landscape*, published in 1948, was a book of tremendous vision, an inspiration to all land-based professionals, in which the benefits of landscape architecture were lucidly expounded. A revised edition, dedicated to Geoffrey and Susan Jellicoe, was published in 1970. It became a standard textbook and was translated into Japanese. This classic work reviewed the state of the British landscape and foreshadowed movements promoting applied ecology and countryside conservation as the backbone of a sophisticated design philosophy. Its opening lines sum up Brenda Colvin's views:

> The control which modern man is able to exert over his environment is so great that we easily overlook the power of the environment over man … We should think of this planet, Earth, as a single organism, in which humanity is involved. The sense of superior individuality which we enjoy is illusory. Man is a part of the whole through evolutionary processes, and is united to the rest of life through the chemistry of lungs and stomach; with air, food and water passing in constant exchange between the soil and the tissues of plant and animal bodies. (Colvin, *Land and Landscape*, 2)

Land and Landscape arose from a memorable series of lectures delivered to students at the Architectural Association which had a direct influence on many post-war architects, leading them to see buildings as part of the landscape at large.

Finally in 1977 Colvin published privately a collection of poems and short prose statements under the title *Wonder in a World*. This very personal work belies the dry pessimism which she sometimes expressed about the world. It reveals both her sparkling intellect and a great joy in life; for instance: 'Well may we count our blessings and be grateful for the conditions on this planet so amazingly adapted to the evolution of the creative spirit of man' (Colvin, *Wonder in a World*, 19).

Writing and serving her profession occupied only the smaller part of Brenda Colvin's energies from 1945. Always the first demand on her time was design. Until about 1965 she practised from an office in Gloucester Place, London, which she shared with Sylvia Crowe (though they never worked as partners). After reaching the age of fifty she designed at least another 300 landscapes, most of which were carried out; some were small, some very large. She still designed many gardens, sometimes within a flowing but never a random line, always effortlessly planted. However, she had come to believe that the design of the landscape at large is a more significant contribution to human and terrestrial well-being. Therefore it was with delight that she accepted commissions to design extensive urban and industrial landscapes. These commissions arose in response to strategies being promoted by the landscape profession, that all construction work should include assessment and design of the landscape, and that schemes to disturb land should include creative ideas for its subsequent restoration.

Colvin was early to design one of the new generation of reservoirs, at Trimpley in Worcestershire (from 1962), and studied with the engineers means of integrating the bunding into its setting by judicious adding of soil along the face and an elegant detail of rockwork at water level on the inner concrete face. She designed the landscape for the new University of East Anglia, but fell out with the architect, Sir Denys Lasdun, because she insisted upon providing paths for students to walk across grassland and remodelling the landform alongside the buildings to look undisturbed. She ensured a natural setting, incorporating native habitats, for the university, which later became a centre for environmental studies. She designed industrial landscapes around several of the new generation of power stations, including Stourport (from 1952), Drakelow (from 1963), Rugeley (from 1963), and Eggborough (from 1961), emphasizing the need to work on a large scale compatible with the undertaking. Colvin fearlessly opposed proposals of which she did not approve. For example, she represented the opponents of a proposed electricity power line along the Thames at Goring Gap. Her colleague representing the promoters at a public inquiry, Dame Sylvia Crowe, could only agree with the principles which she expounded.

In 1962 Colvin was appointed landscape consultant for the rebuilding of Aldershot military town, a project on which she worked for over fifteen years. The macadam atmosphere of the barracks was slowly converted into a community in a woodland setting. This was achieved by perceiving that on the thin Bagshot gravels two fundamentally different types of landscape were needed. Trim grass with well-spaced trees provided military precision as a foil to naturally regenerating woodland in fenced enclosures. So effectively was nature called in to assist design that the original budget was halved in the face of inflation without loss of content. Aldershot was also given a new park: by extracting gravel an ornamental lake was created; behind this a long hill was built of urban rubbish and covered with the gravel. The project cost less than removing the rubbish. However, Colvin's tetchy capacity for effective tactlessness was illustrated at Aldershot, when she criticized the brigadier in command, in front of aghast subordinates, for allowing her planting to be poorly maintained. A particularly long-term project was Gale Common in Yorkshire (begun in 1962), a hill of waste coal ash from power stations, about a square mile in size and 50 metres high, designed with tracks and woods spiralling up the carefully profiled sides. These unapologetically man-made silhouettes, derived from the patterns created by ancient lynchets on chalk downs, illustrate Brenda Colvin's ideas about the connection between past and future, about time as a dimension in the creation of landscapes, and about aftercare as an essential corollary to design.

Brenda Colvin's whole life was devoted to landscape architecture, both to its practice and to the promotion of the profession. In 1951 she was elected president of the Institute of Landscape Architects, and was the first woman to be president of any of the environmental or engineering professions; she had been a founder member of the institute in 1929, and from that date she was re-elected for forty-seven years without a break as a member of council of the institute, a mark of her standing among her peers. In 1948 she was a British representative at the foundation of the International Federation of Landscape Architects. She served tirelessly on professional committees, and her tall, thin frame and distinguished profile were to be seen at meetings and conferences; while she was shy on social occasions, she was concise and unhesitatingly to the point when her profession was under consideration.

In 1969, at the age of seventy-one, with several long-term commissions in hand, Colvin converted her practice into the partnership of Colvin and Moggridge. Having formerly always worked on her own with only a few assistants, she started afresh, handing work on to younger colleagues. On this basis she initiated a practice which could gradually expand beyond her own lifetime to suit changing circumstances, discussing partnership policy and landscape ethics over lunches of asparagus freshly cut from the garden. She was appointed CBE in 1973.

Brenda Colvin died on 27 January 1981, unmarried, at her home, Little Peacocks, Filkins, in west Oxfordshire, where she had created around her home and office an exquisite small garden. She was buried in Filkins cemetery. She pursued her long professional life, starting when both landscape and women were equally undervalued, into an era when both began to receive recognition. Part of that recognition was the result of her own intellectual force, applied with dry wit, idealism, and energy to the art of landscape design. HAL MOGGRIDGE

Sources S. Harvey, ed., *Reflections on landscape* (1987), 139–51 · M. Emanuel, ed., *Contemporary architects* (1980) · H. T. Moggridge, *The Garden*, 106 (1981), 447–53 · B. Colvin, *Land and landscape*, 2nd edn (1970) · B. Colvin, *Wonder in a world* (1977) · S. Harvey and S. Rettig, eds., *Fifty years of landscape design* (1985) · Brenda Colvin file, Landscape Institute Library · B. Colvin and J. Tyrwhitt, *Trees for town and country* (1947) · *WWW*, 1929–40 · personal knowledge (2004)
Likenesses photograph, 1962, Colvin and Moggridge, Lechlade and London [see illus.] · photograph, 1968, repro. in Harvey, ed., *Reflections*, 139
Wealth at death £118,615: probate, 16 April 1981, *CGPLA Eng. & Wales*

Colvin, Ian Duncan [*pseud.* Rip Van Winkle] (1877–1938), journalist, was born at Inverness on 29 September 1877, the second son of Duncan Colvin, Free Church minister, and his wife, Grace Macpherson Strother. He was educated at Crieff Academy and at Inverness College, and worked for a short time on the *Inverness Courier* before going in 1897 to Edinburgh University, where he studied under the professor of rhetoric and English literature, G. E. B. Saintsbury, and won the gold medal for history and literature.

Having left Edinburgh for London, where he served for a time in the London office of the Allahabad *Pioneer*, Colvin went to India in 1900 to join the staff of that journal. Three years later he moved to South Africa and the *Cape Times* under Maitland Park. Apart from his leading articles, he became famous there for his political verse and tales signed Rip van Winkle. He returned to London in 1907 and married, in 1909, Sophie, daughter of the Revd George Robson of Edinburgh. They had three sons and one daughter.

In 1909 Colvin became a leader writer on the *Morning Post*, then edited by Fabian Ware, and, from mid-1911, by H. A. Gwynne. He remained on this ultra right-wing daily for the rest of his, and its, career. He did so, despite approaches from other papers, because, in his words, 'Most newspapers are lost in the pursuit of Mammon, party, etc.' and because 'A paper without a cause is a paper without soul—and must rot'. Colvin spearheaded many of Gwynne's causes and political campaigns, and was the inspiration behind the one which, begun in 1915, led to the formation of the National Party in 1917, a party which Colvin wished had 'a good Aristocrat' to lead it. During the First World War Colvin was a member of the council and of the executive committee of the Anti-German Union. He saw the war, however, as

> really a spiritual struggle not with Germany only but with what is bad in ourselves. We had sunk into such a horrible slough of corruption, selfishness and false ideas before the war, that if the Germans had been wise enough to keep the peace, they might have conquered us in ten years time without a war. (Colvin to Lady Bathurst, 7 May 1914, 10 July 1915, Glenesk-Bathurst MSS 2948, 2948a)

Colvin espoused protectionism, excoriated free trade, and wished to eliminate all manifestations of socialism and radicalism from the British Isles. Having published

The Germans in England, 1066–1598 in 1915 and *The Unseen Hand in English History* in 1917, he went on, noting that Sir Francis Bacon had put 'strangers as foreigners' as one cause of revolutions, to contribute more (36 per cent) than any of the other contributors to *The Cause of World Unrest* (1920), Gwynne's exegesis of *The Protocols of the Elders of Zion*.

In the 1920s Colvin was active in the *Morning Post*'s denunciation of Lloyd George's attempt to settle the Irish question, and its championing of General Dyer's action at Amritsar in 1919, when he ordered British troops to fire into an unarmed crowd. Colvin went on to produce a typically hagiographical *Life of General Dyer* in 1929, to follow his *Life of Jameson* of 1922.

Throughout the 1930s Colvin and the *Morning Post* steadfastly opposed all moves in the direction of the independence of India, and made clear their sympathies with the cause of General Franco in Spain.

The satirical style of his political commentaries continued to have many admirers across the political spectrum, but fewer and fewer readers—if the circulation figures of the *Morning Post* are anything to go by—remained of that paper's, and Colvin's, die-hard persuasions.

Intermittent ill health did not prevent Colvin from publishing, in 1934 and 1936, volumes 2 and 3 of the *Life of Lord Carson* (Edward Marjoribanks had produced volume 1 in 1932). His satirical verse was collected in *Party Whips* (1912), *Intercepted Letters* (1913), and a *Wreath of Immortelles* (1924). On 10 May 1938 he died at Old Court Clinic, Hangar Lane, Ealing, London. KEITH WILSON

Sources *DNB* · *The Times* (12 May 1938) · K. M. Wilson, *A study in the history and politics of the Morning Post, 1905–1926* (1990) · U. Leeds, Brotherton L., Glenesk-Bathurst MSS · Bodl. Oxf., MSS H. A. Gwynne · *CGPLA Eng. & Wales* (1938)
Archives Bodl. Oxf., MSS H. A. Gwynne · U. Leeds, Brotherton L., Glenesk-Bathurst MSS
Wealth at death £2105 10s. 3d.: probate, 28 June 1938, *CGPLA Eng. & Wales*

Colvin, John Russell (1807–1857), administrator in India, second son and fourth child of James Colvin, of the mercantile house of Colvin, Bazett & Co. of London and Calcutta, and his wife, Maria, *née* Jackson, was born in Calcutta on 29 May 1807. He was educated at St Andrews University (1819–21), and, after a short time with a tutor in Hampstead, highly distinguished himself as a student at the East India College, Haileybury, where he won eleven prizes and was ranked first in the leaving class of 1825. In that year he went to Bengal as a writer, and spent a year studying the principal Indian languages at Fort William College, Calcutta.

Colvin's first appointment, in September 1826, was as an assistant in the *sadr* (chief) civil and criminal court in Calcutta. The following year he was appointed second assistant to the resident at Hyderabad; serving there essentially as a collector, he became conversant with land revenue questions. In January 1831 he became an assistant secretary to the judicial and revenue departments in Calcutta, and in March 1835 he became secretary of the *sadr* board of revenue, Lower Provinces. This post was something of a plum, and carried a significant salary. It also brought him to the attention of the governor-general, Lord Auckland, and in 1836 he became Auckland's private secretary, a post he held for six years. Colvin had Auckland's entire confidence, and in consequence has often been held responsible for leading Auckland into his disastrous involvement in Afghanistan; however, the driving force behind the policy to prop up Shah Shuja at Kabul in place of Dost Muhammad was actually Sir William Hay Macnaghten, Auckland's chief secretary for foreign affairs. When Auckland retired in 1841 Colvin took a three-year furlough. He had earlier married Emma Sophia, daughter of Wetenhall Sneyd, vicar of Newchurch, Isle of Wight; with her he had ten children, among them Sir Auckland *Colvin.

In 1845 Colvin was appointed resident at the court of Nepal, and in 1846 commissioner of the eastern Tenasserim provinces. In 1849 he was promoted to the *sadr* court, where he showed remarkable judicial acumen, despite his lack of formal legal training. He succeeded his friend James Thomason as lieutenant-governor of the North-Western Provinces in 1853. Considered an able and active administrator, his seniority assured his promotion. In this office he showed great mastery of the details of government, and learned much from his collectors on cold weather tours. All departments, including criminal justice and police, came under his purview, as well as the application of the revenue system to the previously unsettled Saugor and Nerbudda territories. He also promoted road building, and under his rule the Ganges Canal was completed. Colvin presided over the grand opening of the canal in 1854. He pursued the scheme of primary education introduced by Thomason until Charles Wood's education dispatch of 1854. It was sometimes said that he overgoverned, concerning himself with minute details and overburdening his secretaries.

When the Indian mutiny broke out in May 1857 Colvin appeared to be in a very perilous position. Unlike John Lawrence in the Punjab, Colvin had no warning of the insurrection; when he heard that the rebels had taken Delhi, he acted promptly and vigorously. He held a parade of the troops, at which he tried to calm their fears, and on 24 May he offered a pardon to all soldiers under his jurisdiction who had been involved in the disturbances, provided they had committed no serious crimes. This proclamation was disavowed by Lord Canning, the governor-general, and despite an able defence of his position, Colvin had to modify his terms. On 1 June he disarmed the two Indian regiments at Agra, and replaced them with volunteer forces to protect the city. He strengthened the fort and made arrangements for the reception within its walls of the entire Christian population of the cantonment and city (about 6000 people), including the Christian village of printers that had been organized by the Church Missionary Society at nearby Sikandra. An indecisive skirmish with the now mutinous regiments on 5 July ended with the retreat of the British forces into the fort just as their opponents had exhausted their ammunition and were on

the point of retiring. Much criticized for his handling of the affair, Colvin suffered his first collapse immediately before his entry into the fort. He was transferred to the cantonments, where he died on 9 September 1857; he was buried in the fort the next day. His collapse and eventual death appear to have been caused by physical and nervous exhaustion. Announcing Colvin's death, Canning described him as 'one of the most distinguished among the servants of the East India Company' and praised his 'ripe experience, his high ability, and his untiring energy'.   G. C. BOASE, *rev.* PETER PENNER

Sources F. C. Danvers and others, *Memorials of old Haileybury College* (1894) · A. Colvin, *John Russell Colvin: the last lieutenant-governor of the north-west under the company* (1895) · M. Edwards, 'North-west frontier', *The British empire* (1971–3), 505–14; repr. 2 (1981), 169–90 · P. Penner, *The patronage bureaucracy in north India* (1986) · P. Penner, *Robert Needham Cust: a personal biography* (1987) · *The Times* (25 Dec 1857), 10 · *GM*, 3rd ser., 4 (1858), 212–19
Archives BL OIOC, Home misc. series, corresp. · BL OIOC, diaries, MS Eur. E 359 | BL, Auckland MSS, Add. MSS 37689–37713 · BL OIOC, corresp. with Sir George Russell Clerk, MS Eur. D 538 · W. Yorks. AS, Leeds, letters when lieutenant-governor of north-west provinces, to Lord Canning, governor-general (later viceroy) of India
Likenesses portrait, repro. in Colvin, *John Russell Colvin*, frontispiece

Colvin, Dame Mary Katherine Rosamund (1907–1988),

army officer, was born on 25 October 1907 at Morleys, Shermanbury, Steyning, Sussex, the daughter of Lieutenant-Colonel (John) Forrester Farnell Colvin of the 9th Queen's Royal Lancers and his wife, Isabella Katherine McClintock Bunbury. Almost nothing is recorded of her early years except that she had the opportunity to travel widely in South Africa and India, perhaps as a result of her father's, and later her brother's, service with the lancers. In 1938, with the outbreak of war imminent, she joined the élite First Aid Nursing Yeomanry as a driver, before taking a commission in the Auxiliary Territorial Service (ATS) in September 1939, where she recalled sharing just four vehicles between 250 drivers at her first posting. She served with motor transport companies around the country for the next four years, and then in 1943 embarked on a tour of anti-aircraft command.

One month after the end of the war Colvin was posted to Germany, where she served for a very happy if intensely demanding two years in a first-grade appointment on the staff of the military government in Hamburg. Part of the military government's role was to help the population re-establish local democracy, and although Colvin described herself as very naturally appalled at the size and scope of her task in planning and forming a local council in an area which had seen 60 per cent of its housing destroyed, she set to work immediately to familiarize herself with the region, its traditions, and its history. An excellent leader who gained the admiration and co-operation of the men and women on her staff, she was appreciated by her commanding officers not only for her unparalleled capacity for hard work and her sense of duty, but for her abounding vitality, intelligence, and clear-headedness.

She was appointed OBE in 1947, but despite both her outstanding success in and her immense enjoyment of the post she was forced to return to Britain in order to be closer to her elderly and increasingly infirm mother and aunt.

On her return to the United Kingdom Colvin served for eight months in Northern Ireland before being appointed to command the ATS officer cadet training unit at Windsor in 1948. She oversaw the school's move to Hindhead, where the scope of her command increased to include the ATS non-commissioned officer school. That the ATS should become a permanent component of the armed forces in peacetime had never really been in doubt, but it was not until 1 February 1949 that the necessary legislation was passed and the ATS at last became the Women's Royal Army Corps (WRAC), a regular corps of the British army. It was under Colvin's instruction, then, that the first women cadets to be commissioned officers of the British army passed out on 9 August 1949. As a result of this change of status, WRAC officer training needed to be brought more closely into line with the male officer cadet training, and Colvin oversaw the expansion of the training courses and broadening of the syllabus.

From Hindhead Colvin was then posted to Scotland, where she spent three years as assistant director of the WRAC at Scottish command. On this posting she was able to indulge her love of horses, keeping her own horse at Kelso and riding whenever she could, as well as serving as the visiting commissioner of the Pony Club, where she helped with instructing and directing dressage competitions.

In spite of the regularization of women's service with the army, by 1954 recruitment was at a low ebb and Colvin's promotion to inspector of recruiting presented a new set of challenges. She worked hard, and with some success, to raise the profile of the WRAC as both a worthwhile and an attractive career for women. By this time she was a familiar and well-respected figure, hugely experienced in the ways of the British army, and after a short spell as deputy director of the WRAC in eastern command from 1956 to 1957 her appointment as WRAC director in 1957, at the young age of forty-nine, was universally welcomed. Under her direction the quality of the WRAC gained widespread recognition and through this (and perhaps also through her introduction of the glamorous and popular officers' mess kit) the service's prestige and public profile reached new heights. Her own public profile was also increased by the well-deserved appointment as DBE in 1959. A leader among her peers, both at home and internationally, Colvin led the British contingent at the first conference of the directors of the women's services of NATO countries in Copenhagen in 1961, and was by common consent elected spokeswoman for all.

Mary Colvin retired in 1961 after twenty-three distinguished years' service, but continued to serve as lady-in-waiting to the princess royal, the WRAC's controller commandant, whom she accompanied on a visit to Canada in 1962. Her return to civilian life enabled her once again to pursue wholeheartedly her interest in horses, not only by hunting regularly with the Blackmore Vale hounds, but also by using her experience and formidable organizing ability to the benefit of the British Horse Society, for whom over the next twenty-five years she served first as a senior dressage judge, then as chairman of the dressage group, and finally as president. While she was a formidable figure and forceful personality who did not suffer fools gladly, Mary Colvin was also great fun, and her kindness and generosity of spirit, particularly towards those in need of help and encouragement, were unstinting. She died, unmarried, at her home, Pasture House, 10 Glebe Road, North Luffenham, Oakham, Leicestershire, on 23 September 1988.   TESSA STONE

Sources Lioness [Women's Royal Army Corps Association], 1 (1989) · NAM, Colvin papers, ref. 9401-240 · The Times (27 Sept 1988) · WWW · CGPLA Eng. & Wales (1989) · b. cert. · d. cert.
Archives NAM, papers
Wealth at death £276,260: probate, 11 Jan 1989, CGPLA Eng. & Wales

Colvin, Sir Sidney (1845–1927), art and literary scholar and museum administrator, was born at Norwood, Surrey, on 18 June 1845, the youngest of the three children (all sons) who survived infancy of Bazett David Colvin (1805–1871), East India merchant, and his wife, Mary Steuart (1821–1902), eldest daughter of William Butterworth Bayley. Both sides of the family had long been connected with India, as either merchants or administrators. Colvin was privately educated at the family home, The Grove, Little Bealings, near Woodbridge, east Suffolk. He went to Trinity College, Cambridge, in 1863 and was third in the first class of the classical tripos in 1867; he became a fellow in 1868.

On leaving university Colvin moved to London and established a reputation as a critic, mainly of the fine arts; he wrote for the Pall Mall Gazette, the Fortnightly Review, The Portfolio, and other journals. In 1872 his Portfolio papers appeared in book form under the title Children in Italian and English Design; this was followed in 1873 by A Selection from Occasional Writings on Fine Art (privately printed). In 1873 Colvin was elected Slade professor of fine art at Cambridge and held the appointment until 1885. A special interest was the sculpture and archaeology of ancient Greece and in 1875 he visited the excavations in progress at Olympia.

In 1876 Colvin became director of the Fitzwilliam Museum, Cambridge, where he established a gallery of casts from antique sculpture. He left there in 1884 to become keeper of the department of prints and drawings in the British Museum, a post he held until his retirement in 1912. By his thorough scholarship and enthusiasm Colvin made the department more important than it had ever been before; he reorganized the arrangement and mounting of the collection and secured spacious accommodation where exhibitions could be held. A special feature was the excellent guides written by Colvin or under his supervision; the most important was the guide to the exhibition in 1899 of Rembrandt's etchings, arranged for the first time in chronological order. His greatest achievement was to persuade the government to purchase the

Sir Sidney Colvin (1845–1927), by Alphonse Legros, 1893

magnificent John Malcolm of Poltalloch collection of drawings and engravings (1895), which 'almost doubled the importance of the department' (Colvin, 207). Thanks to Colvin's influence many private collectors made important bequests to the museum. Among the most notable were William Mitchell's collection of early woodcuts (1895), Henry Vaughan's collection of drawings by John Flaxman, Thomas Stothard, and others (1900), the second Baron Cheylesmore's collection of mezzotints (1902), and George Salting's drawings and engravings by old masters (1910). An important purchase was James Reeve's collection of drawings by the Norwich school (1902). During the later years of his keepership Colvin took a great interest in Japanese and Chinese art and greatly enriched the museum's holdings by his purchases.

Colvin had a special interest in early Italian art. In *A Florentine Picture-Chronicle* (1898) he reproduced in facsimile, with detailed commentary, a book of drawings (purchased from John Ruskin) which he attributed to Maso Finiguerra (1424–1464), the reputed inventor of engraving. In the same field was the official *Catalogue of Early Italian Engravers* (1910), prepared in collaboration with Arthur Hind. Another major work, also in collaboration with Hind, was *Early Engraving and Engravers in England* (1905). In 1894 Colvin failed in his bid to become director of the National Gallery and in 1909 he was an unsuccessful candidate for the directorship of the British Museum. He was knighted in 1911.

Some time in the late 1860s Colvin met and fell in love with Frances Jane Sitwell, *née* Fetherstonhaugh (1839–

1924), a woman of great beauty, wit, and personality, unhappily married to the Revd Albert Hurt Sitwell. She finally parted from her unsatisfactory husband in 1874 and for the next thirty years she and Colvin lived apart but maintained a close friendship. She acted as visiting hostess at his official residence at the British Museum, and thanks to her influence it became a literary and artistic centre. Although the Revd Sitwell died in 1894 they did not marry until 7 July 1903; apparently Colvin did not feel able to support a wife in addition to his mother (who was financially dependent upon him) and he did not marry until after the latter's death.

In 1869 Colvin joined the New (soon to become the Savile) Club; he was also from 1879 a member of the Athenaeum and from 1893 of the Burlington Fine Arts Club. In 1871 he joined the Society of Dilettanti and was its honorary secretary from 1891 to 1896. He was elected to the Literary Society in 1886 and became in due course treasurer and then president.

Colvin was on friendly terms with most of the great literary figures of his day, from Matthew Arnold and Robert Browning to Meredith and Swinburne. As a boy he had worshipped Ruskin, who was a family friend; his next great admiration was for the work of Edward Burne-Jones, who became a close friend. Burne-Jones introduced him to Rossetti and Colvin was a member of his circle from 1868 to 1872. Basil Champneys the architect was his oldest friend and there were close friendships too with Henry James and Joseph Conrad.

Colvin's most celebrated friendship, shared by his future wife, was with Robert Louis Stevenson. Colvin and Mrs Sitwell met the young Scot in the summer of 1873 at Cockfield rectory in Suffolk, the home of Professor Churchill Babington, whose wife, Maud, was Stevenson's cousin. It was a turning point in Stevenson's life; they helped to steady him through the emotional problems caused by disagreements with his father over religion and by uncertainties about his future as a writer. Colvin recognized Stevenson's genius and helped and encouraged him by introducing him to editors and publishers and tirelessly promoting his interests. Stevenson fell in love with Frances Sitwell and for the next two years poured out letters of love and adoration to her; after the intensity of these feelings had passed the friendship remained. For the rest of his life Stevenson regarded Colvin as his literary mentor and his dearest friend. In a letter from the south seas he made it clear that when he thought of 'home' it was Colvin and his house in the British Museum (jokingly called 'The Monument') that he had in mind. Colvin's own unselfish devotion, both to Stevenson himself and later to his memory, never faltered. To maintain the intimacy of their friendship Stevenson wrote to him the journal-letters from Samoa which Colvin published as *Vailima Letters* (1895). Colvin edited the Edinburgh edition of Stevenson's works (1894–8). After acrimonious rows with Stevenson's widow and stepson he was forced to relinquish the project of writing the official biography, which he called 'the great hope and interest of my life' (Mehew, 1.53). Instead, he edited Stevenson's *Letters* (1899, enlarged 1911, and in final form 1924); the texts are now known to be flawed by bowdlerization and expurgation.

Although art had provided him with his livelihood, Colvin's chief interest was in literature. He had a special regard for Landor and Keats, and wrote short biographies of both for the English Men of Letters series: *Landor* (1881) and *Keats* (1887). He edited *Selections from Landor* (1882), and published editions of the letters of Keats in 1891 (characteristically omitting the letters to Fanny Brawne) and of his poems in 1915. He devoted the early years of his retirement to the completion of his major biography, *John Keats, his Life and Poetry, his Friends, Critics and after-Fame* (1917). It was followed in 1921 by *Memories and Notes of Persons and Places*, a volume of reminiscences.

In appearance Colvin was tall and thin with a pointed beard; in 1903 he broke a leg in an accident and thereafter walked with a slight limp. Stevenson described him as having 'the air of a man accustomed to obedience' (Mehew, 1.49) and Laurence Binyon, a museum colleague, recalled that 'under a manner that often seemed stiff and shy he concealed an emotional and excitable temperament, capable of occasional explosions' (Lucas, 182).

Lady Colvin's death, on 1 August 1924, was a great blow to Colvin; his last years were also marred by deafness and loss of memory. He died on 11 May 1927 at his home, 35 Palace Gardens Terrace, Kensington (to which he had moved on leaving the British Museum). After cremation his ashes were buried in his wife's grave in the cemetery at Church Row, Hampstead.   ERNEST MEHEW

Sources E. V. Lucas, *The Colvins and their friends* (1928) • *The Times* (12 May 1927) • *DNB* • E. Mehew, 'The main correspondents: Stevenson's family and friends', in *The letters of Robert Louis Stevenson*, ed. B. A. Booth and E. Mehew, 1 (1994), 44–62 [esp. pp. 44–54] • S. Colvin, *Memories and notes of persons and places, 1852–1912* (1921) • d. cert.
Archives Camden Public Library, London, corresp. • FM Cam., corresp. • U. Reading L., letters | BL, letters to William Archer, Add. MS 45291 • BL, corresp. with Sir Sidney Cockerell, Add. MS 52710 • BL, corresp. with Macmillans, Add. MS 55018 • Castle Howard, letters to ninth earl and countess of Carlisle • CUL, letters to William Conway • Elgar Birthplace Museum, Worcester, letters to Sir Edward Elgar • Keats House, Hampstead, letters to W. E. Doubleday • King's Lond., letters to Oscar Browning • NL Scot., corresp., incl. with Lord Rosebery, Sir Graham Balfour, Sydney Lyttelton, and William Gladstone • U. Glas., letters to D. S. MacColl • U. Leeds, Brotherton L., letters mainly to Sir Edmund Gosse • U. Reading L., letters to George Bell & Sons • Yale U., Beinecke L., letters to Stevenson and others in Stevenson's circle
Likenesses A. Legros, pencil drawing, 1893, BM [*see illus.*] • E. Poynter, oils, 1896, Brooks's Club, London, Society of Dilettanti; copies, Courtauld Inst., NPG • W. Rothenstein, lithograph, 1897, NPG; repro. in W. Rothenstein, *English portraits* (1898) • T. Roussel, oils, 1908, Savile Club, London • M. Beerbohm, caricature, before 1911, Lilly Library, Indiana; repro. in *The Bookman*, 8 (1911) • photograph, 1911 (after drawing by D. Landau), NPG • photograph, 1921, repro. in Colvin, *Memories and notes*, frontispiece • photograph, 1921, repro. in E. V. Lucas, *The Colvins*, frontispiece • W. Stoneman, photograph, 1924, NPG • F. Hollyer, photograph, repro. in *Harper's Magazine* (May 1888) • E. O. Hoppé, photograph, repro. in *Stevenson Extra Number of The Bookman* (1913), 137 • E. O. Hoppé, photograph, repro. in J. Calder, *RLS: a life study* (1980), 67 • J. Russell & Sons, photograph, NPG • double portrait, photograph (Sir Sidney and Lady Colvin), repro. in E. V. Lucas, *Reading, writing and remembering* (1932), facing p. 100 • photograph, repro. in *The Year's Art* (1892) •

photograph, NPG • photograph, BM • photograph, photogravure, NPG
Wealth at death £3630 18s. 4d.: probate, 2 July 1927, CGPLA Eng. & Wales

Colvin, Sir Walter Mytton (1847–1908). *See under* Colvin, Sir Auckland (1838–1908).

Colwall, Daniel (*d.* 1690), merchant and philanthropist, has an obscure family background, and nothing is known about his early life. He was elected a fellow of the Royal Society on 16 January 1661, and was a council member (1663–86 and 1689) and treasurer from 1665 to 1679. He became a vice-president of the society in 1682.

During his long, influential period as treasurer, Colwall helped the society to survive its frequent financial difficulties. Fellows were reluctant to pay the weekly subscription of a shilling. In 1667 and 1673 the council instructed Colwall to require members to pay their subscriptions, but in vain. In 1667 the arrears approached £1000 and in 1674 £2000 when only 53 of the 146 fellows paid regularly.

In 1663 and 1666 Colwall presented the society with £50 on condition that he was not exempted from his weekly subscriptions; and the council decided that these sums should be expended to purchase 'the collection of rarities belonging to Mr Hubbard', which was the beginning of the society's museum. Colwall himself presented gifts including 'an Arabian stone to provoke wine' and 'a piece of wood good for green wounds' and spoke on such subjects as 'making vitriol' and 'ordering oysters at Colchester' (Birch, 1.20, 41; 4.178).

In 1681 Nehemiah Grew published *Musaeum regalis societatis*, dedicated to Colwall, who paid for the engravings. Grew hoped that the society 'may always wear this Catalogue, as the miniature of Mr. Colwall's abundant respects near their hearts' and added

> Besides the particular regard you had to the Royal Society itself, which seeming (in the opinion of some) to look a little pale, you intended, hereby, to put some fresh blood into their cheeks; pouring out your box of oyntment not in order to their burial, but their resurrection. (Weld, 1.278)

The other philanthropic cause Colwall supported was Christ's Hospital, the charitable school in London of which he was long a governor. As such he was a member of the court, the supreme body of the hospital, and regularly attended its meetings and served on the general committee hearing cases and petitions. He was present on 27 March 1683 for the visitation of the mathematical school, grammar school, and reading and writing school. In 1678 the court accepted his offer to give the hospital £1000 provided the court would pay him £50 a year in half-yearly instalments.

Samuel Pepys, who became secretary of the Admiralty in 1672, was worried by the inadequate supply of skilled sailors as navigators and encouraged Charles II to establish in the hospital the royal mathematical school. Colwall made a gift to it, though the hospital doubted whether the king would agree to any augmentation of his establishment, but the king's reply was 'so far was he from disliking this that he would be glad to see any gentleman graft upon his stock' (Trollope, 2.560). In 1676 Colwall took the charge, an admonition then given by the court to enable him to nominate a child for admission to the hospital, and in 1684 he presented a child to be admitted to the school.

In Colwall's will, proved on 20 November, he bequeathed to the hospital 'for ever one rent or yearly payment of sixty-two pounds and eight shillings issuing and payable out of the hereditary excise which was assigned to me by Sir Robert Viner, knt. and bart. deceased', and the sum of £4000; besides supplementing the salary of master of the grammar school by a life annuity of £20.

The court set up a committee to consider how Colwall would have wished the £4000 to be used. They decided, first, that it should assist the children sent to two places in Hertfordshire after the London fire of 1666 since 'he did generally approve of making such a kind of reception for the nurses and children at Hertford as has been lately made at Ware'; and, second, to make 'a new Writing School in the Hospital'. They asserted, 'We think ourselves bound both in gratitude and for transmitting the memory of so bountiful a benefactor as also for the great usefulness of the things themselves' (Christ's Hospital general committee minutes, 1687–98, fols. 224, 229, 243).

In 1670 and again in 1673 Colwall was recorded as living in a house with twelve hearths in Tower Hill East in the liberty of the Tower of London, the inhabitants of which, after being sworn and registered by the steward of the Tower court, became 'free men of the Tower'. This absolved them from jury service at assizes and county sessions and exempted them from the jurisdiction of the City of London and county of Middlesex. Its inhabitants were expected to support their own poor; and after Colwall's death in November 1690 in the liberty, his will made generous provision for the poor there.   EVELYN E. COWIE

Sources C. R. Weld, *A history of the Royal Society*, 2 vols. (1848) · W. Huggins, *The Royal Society*, 2 vols. (1906) · G. A. T. Allan, *Christ's Hospital*, ed. J. E. Morpurgo (1984) · W. Trollope, *A history of the royal foundation of Christ's Hospital* (1834) · J. P. Malcolm, *London redivivum*, 4 vols. (1802–7) · T. Birch, *The history of the Royal Society of London*, 4 vols. (1756–7) · H. G. Lyons, 'The society's finances, 1662–1830', *Notes and records of the Royal Society* (1938), 73–87 · G. W. Marshall, ed., *The Genealogist*, 3 (1879) · N. Grew, *Musaeum regalis societatis* (1681) · M. Hunter, *The Royal Society and its fellows, 1660–1700: the morphology of an early scientific institution*, 2nd edn (1994) · *DNB*

Archives GL, Christ's Hospital court minute book · GL, Christ's Hospital general committee minutes

Likenesses R. White, line engraving, 1681, BM, NPG; repro. in Grew, *Musaeum* · line engraving, Wellcome L. · oils, RS · portrait, Christ's Hospital, Horsham

Wealth at death approx. £10,000: will, PRO, PROB 11/407, sig. 232

Colyear, David, first earl of Portmore (c.1656–1730), army officer, born in Brabant, was the elder son of Sir Alexander Robertson, first baronet (d. 1680), apparently of the family of Strowan, Perthshire, who took the name Colyear and settled in the Netherlands, where he acquired considerable property, and his wife, Jean, the daughter of Lieutenant-Colonel Murray. The son entered the army of William of Orange as a volunteer in 1674 and served as an officer in his father's regiment in 1676. Later he was promoted major and in January 1683 lieutenant-colonel in Mackay's regiment. At the revolution he accompanied William to England and in late December 1688 was promoted colonel in command of Wauchope's regiment. Sir David Colyear (he succeeded to his father's baronetcy in 1680) served in William's Irish campaigns (1689–91) and in October 1691 was appointed governor of Limerick. He was promoted major-general in June 1696. For his distinguished service in Ireland and in Flanders he was created a peer of Scotland, as Lord Portmore and Blackness, on 1 June 1699.

About August 1696 Colyear married Catherine *Sedley (1657–1717), the daughter of Sir Charles *Sedley of Southfleet, Kent, and formerly the mistress of James II. She had been created countess of Dorchester for life in 1685, and received a substantial official pension. They had two sons. In 1702, at the commencement of the War of the Spanish Succession, Colyear was recommissioned major-general and served in the expedition to Cadiz and the attack on Vigo Bay. On 13 April 1703 he was raised in the peerage, as earl of Portmore. He was promoted lieutenant-general in February 1703, and the following year he held the command of the forces in Portugal for a short period. In 1710 he succeeded Lord Galway as commander-in-chief of the forces in Portugal, and in January 1711 was raised to the rank of general. In 1712 he served under the duke of Ormond in Flanders, was sworn of the privy council, and was made a knight of the Thistle. In August 1713 he was appointed governor of Gibraltar, and in October 1713 was chosen one of the sixteen representative peers of Scotland. In April 1714 he was appointed to the command of the Royal North British Dragoons (the Scots Greys), which he retained until February 1717.

However, disenchantment with the accession of George I led Portmore to dabble in Jacobite politics. Before the earl of Mar raised his standard at Braemar in September 1715 Bolingbroke attempted unsuccessfully to bring Portmore over to the Jacobite side. Further efforts were made by Mar during the rising to turn Portmore's regiment, the Scots Greys, but without success; the regiment, under the acting command of Lieutenant-Colonel Sir James Campbell, was to play a key role in the suppression of the rising down to its last remnants in 1719. However, Portmore maintained and increased his Jacobite connections, providing military advice for a possible landing in England in 1716 as well as financial support. He relinquished the colonelcy of the Scots Greys in February 1717 as part of a move towards further involvement in the Jacobite cause. Rumours began to circulate among Jacobite leaders that he was preparing to leave England for the continent. In late July 1718 he travelled to the Netherlands to meet Sir Henry Patterson, who reported to the earl of Mar that Portmore:

> was resolved, as soon as he returned to England, to disengage himself entirely of all engagements with the Elector of Hanover and the English ministry … for he says he has no satisfaction in England, where the discontents are general and particularly with the nobility and he spoke with great

contempt of both the Elector and his son and said he thought the Restoration could not fail was there the least foreign resistance. (*Stuart Papers*, 7.113)

However, Portmore did not sever his connections with the Hanoverians, and in the fullness of time he came to an accommodation with them.

When Gibraltar was besieged by Spain in 1727, Portmore embarked to assume command there, but the siege was raised before he arrived. He died at his family seat at Weybridge, Surrey, on 2 January 1730, and was buried there on 13 January. John Macky described him thus, at the age of about fifty:

> He is one of the best foot officers in the world; is very brave and bold; hath a great deal of wit; very much a man of honour and nice that way, yet married the Countess of Dorchester, and had by her a good estate; pretty well shaped; dresses clean; but one eye.

Portmore's eldest son predeceased him; the second, Charles Colyear (1700–1785), succeeded as second earl. A great patron of the turf and a conspicuous figure in London, in his youth the second earl was known as Beau Colyear. The peerage became extinct on the death of the fourth earl in 1835.

T. F. HENDERSON, *rev.* JONATHAN SPAIN

Sources GEC, *Peerage* · *Scots peerage* · *Calendar of the Stuart papers belonging to his majesty the king, preserved at Windsor Castle*, 7 vols., HMC, 56 (1902–23) · M. Haile, *James Francis Edward, the old cavalier* (1907) · E. Almack, *The history of the second dragoons, 'royal Scots greys'* (1908) · M. Blacklock, *The royal Scots greys (the 2nd dragoons)* (1971) · *Memoirs of the secret services of John Macky*, ed. A. R. (1733)
Archives BL, corresp., Add. MS 56079 | BL, corresp. with B. Keene and Count Montemar, etc., Add. MSS 32752–32754 · HMC, Stuart papers

Colyer, Sir (James) Frank (1866–1954), dental surgeon and museum curator, was born on 25 September 1866 at 2 Loughborough Villas, Loughborough Road, Lambeth, London, one of the sons of James Colyer, dentist, and his wife, Rebecca Hastings, *née* Farrow. There is no information about Colyer's early years, but by the time he became a student at the Royal Dental Hospital, London, it was clear that he had exceptional talents and a natural aptitude for dental surgery. He quickly gained a reputation for his skill and intellect, quick mind, and responsive hands, and at the age of just twenty, in November 1887, he qualified LDS. Following the advice of the then dean of the school, Morton A. Smale, that a dentist should also be a qualified surgeon, Colyer studied at Charing Cross Hospital, London, and became MRCS LRCP in 1889.

As well as developing his private practice Colyer held a number of hospital and other appointments: he became consultant dental surgeon at Charing Cross Hospital and at the Royal Dental Hospital, and he was honorary consultant dental surgeon to the Croydon War Hospital, the Ministry of Pensions, and the Queen's Hospital, Sidcup, Kent. Dental students who were fortunate enough to come under his wing found Colyer an inspired teacher, who was unceasingly fair and generous in his outlook. His dynamic personality and natural gift for public speaking were enhanced by his brilliant memory, so that he rarely relied upon notes. In his spare time Colyer enjoyed ball games

and took pleasure in a round of golf, but his particular passion was cricket, and he seldom missed a match at Lord's.

Colyer's marriage on 11 March 1896 to Lucy Olivia Margaret Anna Simpson (1871/2–1950), daughter of George Simpson, a wholesale bookbinder, was an enduring and supportive relationship, but was marred by the untimely death of their youngest daughter, Eileen, a talented lawn-tennis player. The couple had one other daughter and a son.

Colyer was the recipient of many prizes and honours, both in England and North America. Included among these was his admission to the fellowship of the Royal College of Surgeons in 1916, and the honour of being created a knight of the British empire in 1920, for services rendered during the war. The Royal Society of Medicine also paid him a great tribute when in 1926 they named a prize after him, a rare accolade to be made during a person's lifetime.

As well as the practice and teaching of dentistry, Colyer was a prolific journalist and author. He contributed many articles to professional journals and wrote numerous books on dental subjects. His earliest such work, *Diseases and Injuries of the Teeth* (first published in 1892, co-written with Morton A. Smale, and later revised with the help of Evelyn Sprawson and reissued as *Dental Surgery and Pathology*), was a textbook which filled a gap in the sphere of teaching. It ran to many editions and became widely accepted as the bible of dental students and practitioners alike. Other important works reflected Colyer's lifelong interest in the history of dentistry. He received wide acclaim for his book *John Hunter and Odontology* (1913), but was perhaps best-known for his work *Old Instruments used for Extracting Teeth* (1952), which came about largely as a result of his long-term involvement with the Odontological Society.

Colyer was already secretary and editor of *Transactions of the Odontological Society* when, in 1900, he accepted the post of honorary (unpaid) curator of the society's museum, then housed at the Royal Dental Hospital, and subsequently resited at the Royal College of Surgeons. The museum's collection, which was later described by Sir Arthur Keith as the most complete representation of the history and diseases of teeth in the world (Keith, 304–5), was Colyer's personal passion, and he became the presiding genius over it. For fifty years he devoted hours of his time and energy, and much of his own money, to arranging and cataloguing the specimens, and he was distraught when a massive bomb fell on the museum in May 1941, destroying thousands of irreplaceable specimens.

Colyer remained in London but his latter years, especially after his wife's death in 1950, were fraught with problems: his personal position as curator of the museum became somewhat difficult and he found it hard to accept the changing policy of the council of the Royal College of Surgeons, which seemed to him to value the social aspects and teaching policy of the college over that of the Hunterian Museum, of which he was trustee. Added to this, the collection of the Odontological Museum was dismantled, and only a few cases of specimens were transferred to the general museum. Ever mindful of the needs of students, and displaying extreme spirit, he continued cataloguing new specimens, even though this meant working in very difficult conditions in dingy premises in Lincoln's Inn Fields.

Colyer died at his home, Queenswood, 39 Palace Road, Streatham, London, on 30 March 1954. A memorial service was held at St Martin-in-the-Fields, London, on 12 April 1954.   SUSAN L. COHEN

Sources R. H. O. B. Robinson and W. R. Le Fanu, *Lives of the fellows of the Royal College of Surgeons of England, 1952–1964* (1970), 84–5 · *The Lancet* (10 April 1954), 786 · *Journal of the Canadian Dental Association*, 20 (June 1954), 351 · *The Times* (2 Feb 1920), 15 · *The Times* (1 April 1954), 8 · *British Dental Journal*, 96 (1954), 197–8 · *WWW*, 1951–60 · *Annals of the Royal College of Surgeons of England*, 14 (1954), 344–6 · E. Smith and B. D. Cottell, *A history of the Royal Dental Hospital of London and School of Dental Surgery, 1858–1985* (1997) · A. Keith, *An autobiography* (1950) · b. cert. · m. cert. · d. cert. · *CGPLA Eng. & Wales* (1954)

Archives RCS Eng., odontological collection, letters, MSS · RCS Eng., corresp. · Royal Society of Medicine, London, corresp.

Likenesses C. White, oils, RCS Eng.; repro. in *British Dental Journal*, 80 (1946), 245

Wealth at death £55,244 15s. 1d.: probate, 1954, *CGPLA Eng. & Wales*

Colyer, Kenneth (1928–1988), jazz musician, was born in Great Yarmouth, Norfolk, on 18 April 1928, the third son in a family of three sons and two daughters of Kenneth Edward Colyer, a chauffeur and butler, and his wife, Ruby Erhardt (d. c.1986), a housemaid. His father was a good pub pianist. Colyer grew up in Soho, and attended St Anne's School there, where he was in the choir and received his first payment of 6d. for performing. Then, during the Second World War, the family moved to 38 Eaton Road, Cranford, Middlesex, where he attended William Ellis School. After leaving school in 1942 he did various jobs, and was then in the merchant navy until 1948; during this period he taught himself to play the trumpet.

Back on shore Colyer practised with the Mick Mulligan band and in 1949 became a founder member of the Crane River Jazz Band, which included Monty Sunshine, the clarinettist, John R. T. Davies on trombone, and his brother Julian Davies on bass. They made several recordings. The band was the first of the many British bands to attempt to play in the ensemble style of traditional jazz generally known as the New Orleans revival, emulating the 1940s recordings of the elderly Louisiana musicians Bunk Johnson and George Lewis. In 1951 Colyer joined the Christie Brothers Stompers for several months and recorded with them for the Esquire label before returning to sea. This enabled him to visit New Orleans, where he lived for three months (1952–3); but he overstayed his visitor's visa, and was jailed for thirty-eight days in the New Orleans parish prison before being deported. From prison he wrote a series of letters which was published in *Melody Maker*. This escapade greatly enhanced his position as a martyr in the cause of jazz among his followers in Britain and confirmed his authenticity. While in New Orleans he played with George Lewis and recorded with other local musicians. When he returned home in 1953, Monty Sunshine organized a band for him which included Chris

Kenneth Colyer (1928–1988), by David Redfern

Barber on trombone and Lonnie Donegan on banjo. The band toured Denmark, where they recorded for Storyville. Back in London they made some important sides for Decca, including *The Isle of Capri*. The band also broadcast for the BBC.

In 1954, after policy disagreements, the band and Colyer parted, leaving him to build a new outfit with the help of his brother Bill, which included Acker Bilk on clarinet, Diz Disley on banjo and guitar, and Stan Greig on drums. This band too recorded for Decca. Colyer also led a New Orleans-style marching band, the Omega Brass Band, and he had a skiffle group, in which he sang and played the guitar. Further changes to his band in 1955 brought in Ian Wheeler on clarinet and Mac Duncan on trombone; this is thought by many to have been Colyer's best band. They made important recordings for Decca in 1955, including *Red Wing* and *Hiawatha Rag*. Another release came out as *Club Session with Colyer*, which Colyer himself believed was one of his best recordings. The band continued largely unchanged until 1960 and was the key band in the postwar British New Orleans jazz revival movement. It was widely copied by purists. Colyer often appeared with the band at the club which bore his name at Studio 51, Great Newport Street, London. In 1957 George Lewis toured Britain and recorded with the band; further recordings were made in Germany with Lewis in 1959. In 1963 Colyer appeared at the Australian Jazz Convention, and Lewis, on his 1966 British tour, again recorded with the band. Many musicians passed through the Colyer band, including clarinettist Sammy Rimmington, who joined in 1960.

Colyer was known to millions of followers as the Gov-'nor, and his contribution to the post-war European New Orleans jazz revival was very significant. A musician of modest skills but natural talent, he played a simple melodic ensemble lead without show, which suited perfectly the music he loved. His restrained but commanding presence meant that whichever band he appeared with immediately sounded like a Colyer outfit. Of medium height and upright stance he retained the manner of an old sea dog, and with his greying hair and beard he fitted perfectly the image of the patriarch to his tribe of followers. On 24 November 1954 he married a telephonist, Delphine Frecker (b. 1935), who, although seven years younger than Colyer, had known him since she was a little girl as she lived nearby at 54 Eaton Road. They had a son, Russell Lewis, but were divorced in 1981. They first lived at 66 Lilly Road, Earls Court, and subsequently at 99 The Drive, Hounslow, Middlesex.

In the 1970s Colyer continued to play despite periods of ill health, often appearing with bands led by other well-known musicians such as Chris Barber, Monty Sunshine, and Max Collie. In July 1987 illness finally forced him to stop playing, and he went to live at Le Dattier, plot E9. CD4, Route D, Bagnols-en-Forêt, 83600, Frejus, near Nice, France. Later he was befriended by Nicole Demain and went to live at Parc de Gorsaire, 83380, 61 Chemin de la Ronde, Les Issambres, Var. After leaving London he never played trumpet again, apart from a couple of numbers with Max Collie's band at a concert in Germany. He died from a heart attack at his home on 8 March 1988. He was cremated in Frejus and his ashes scattered by his son in the sea on the French side of the English Channel.

A. J. H. LATHAM

Sources K. Colyer, *When dreams are in the dust* (1989) · G. Bielderman, *Ken Colyer discography*, 8th edn (1998) · J. Chilton, *Who's who of British jazz*, 2nd edn (1998) · B. Kernfeld, ed., *The new Grove dictionary of jazz* (1994) · *Ken Colyer Trust Newsletter* · private information (2004) [B. Colyer; D. Frecker; Ken Colyer Trust] · *CGPLA Eng. & Wales* (1989)
Likenesses D. Redfern, photograph, Redferns Music Picture Library [see illus.]
Wealth at death £51,619: administration with will, 20 Jan 1989, *CGPLA Eng. & Wales*

Colyngham, Thomas (*fl.* 1387), Cistercian monk and theologian, is said by the early seventeenth-century Scottish antiquary Thomas Dempster to have attended the University of Paris about 1387, and to have gained a doctorate, presumably in theology, and then to have entered the Cistercian order. While at the university he is reported to have composed a treatise *De eucharistia*—a work described by Dempster as 'serious and weighty' (*opus serium et grave*)—which was published at Paris by Johannes Cheyneus (who is otherwise unknown) from a manuscript preserved in the library of the abbey of St Victor (though it does not appear in Claude de Grandrue's catalogue of the abbey library compiled in 1514). No copy of the book is known to survive. Since Dempster's sources cannot now be verified, and since his testimony is often unreliable, Colyngham's place among Scotland's *eruditi* cannot be regarded as certain.

DAVID N. BELL

Sources T. Dempster, *Historia ecclesiastica gentis Scotorum* (Bologna, 1627), 185 (3. 326) [all other sources are dependent on this]

Colyton. For this title name *see* Hopkinson, Henry Lennox D'Aubigné, first Baron Colyton (1902–1996).

Combe, Andrew (1797–1847), physician and phrenologist, the fifteenth child and seventh son of George Comb, a brewer, and his wife, Marion (*née* Newton), was born in Edinburgh on 27 October 1797. Among his siblings was George *Combe, the leading British proponent of phrenology. Although the family home was cramped and in an insalubrious location, George Comb was reasonably prosperous and able to employ servants. Family life was conducted according to strict Calvinistic principles. Andrew attended an elementary school on Frederick Street in Edinburgh, and then in October 1805 he entered the city's high school. In October 1810 he enrolled in 'the town's college', as Edinburgh University was at that time known, and spent two sessions studying Greek and Latin. While complimentary about the professor of Greek, Combe was later scathing about the quality of the Latin teaching he experienced at the university.

At this time Combe showed no clear inclination toward any occupation, but his father was determined that at least some of his sons would rise above the stigma of being in trade and apprenticed him to Henry Johnston, a surgeon who maintained premises on Princes Street; such an apprenticeship was a necessary first step to becoming a member of the Royal College of Surgeons of Edinburgh. According to his brother George, Andrew showed no enthusiasm for this arrangement and on his first day had to be manhandled at least part of the way to Johnston's shop. Thereafter, however, he appears to have pursued his medical studies with diligence and some success. After attending the requisite courses of lectures given by teachers in both the extramural and the university schools of medicine, he was admitted to the College of Surgeons in 1817. Later in that year he went to Paris for further professional studies, taking the opportunity also to visit Switzerland and Lombardy. Combe was obliged to spend two winters in Italy and the south of France, owing to the first onset of the symptoms of pulmonary disease. On his return to Edinburgh, Combe began in 1823 to cultivate a practice; in 1825 he enhanced his standing by taking the degree of MD at the university and he attracted a large number of patients. He obtained a number of honorary appointments, including in 1838 that of physician-extraordinary to the queen in Scotland.

Together with his brother George, Andrew Combe became one of the foremost proponents of phrenology in nineteenth-century Britain. Initially both brothers, guided by the scornful rebuttals of phrenology that appeared in the *Edinburgh Review*, were dismissive of the new system. George's conversion occurred when Johann Caspar Spurzheim, one of the founders of phrenology, visited Edinburgh in 1815. Andrew's scepticism took longer to dispel. By his own account, 'it was only after witnessing the examination of many brains in the extensive hospitals of Paris, that I became convinced that the skull really represents the configuration of its enclosed brain' (A. Combe, *Phrenology—its Nature and Uses*, 1846, 20). In 1820 George and Andrew Combe were among the founders of the Edinburgh Phrenological Society; and in 1823 Andrew helped to establish the *Phrenological Journal*, of which he remained a proprietor until 1837. Combe's first published article appeared in this periodical and many others were to follow. In addition, he produced a number of longer pieces expounding phrenological doctrines. Combe made ambitious claims regarding phrenology's potential for achieving social amelioration, and also maintained that it had enabled him to achieve greater self-understanding and mastery, and had helped him in his clinical practice. Moreover, according to Combe, patients themselves had come to appreciate the value of such knowledge in a physician: Combe maintained that he was much in demand as a practitioner precisely because of his phrenological expertise. Although in some quarters phrenology was associated with materialism and infidelity, Combe strenuously maintained that its precepts were altogether compatible with Christian doctrine; indeed, a phrenological understanding of human nature would enable society and the individual to practise religion more effectively.

From early in his career Combe showed a particular interest in mental diseases. During his time in Paris he attended the lectures of the noted alienist Jean-Étienne-Dominique Esquirol as well as observing patients in the Salpêtrière. In Edinburgh he was often consulted in cases of insanity or 'nervousness'. Combe maintained that mental disease was the medical field in which the applications of phrenology were most obvious. He was especially concerned about the disregard that judges and juries in Britain paid to medical evidence when deciding questions of mental competence in civil and criminal cases. In *Observations on Mental Derangement* (1831) Combe maintained that mental disorder was in fact a 'symptom of cerebral disease', and therefore to be regarded in the same way as the diseases of any other organ.

In 1834 Combe published *The principles of physiology applied to the preservation of health, and to the improvement of physical and mental education*. Several portions of the work had previously appeared in the *Phrenological Journal*; its underlying philosophy was in many ways an extension of phrenological precepts and it aimed to provide a more general understanding of health and illness. Combe emphasized the individual's responsibility for his or her own well-being and the importance of attention to corporeal needs. He dismissed the notion that Christian piety demanded a disdain for the body and an exclusive concern for spiritual edification. Instead he believed that God had created 'organic laws', which it was the duty of each person to obey; disease was the inevitable result of a neglect of these wise regulations and the great majority of human ills could be remedied if rational measures for the preservation of health were adopted both by the individual and by society. According to one contemporary, the promulgation of these ideas represented Combe's 'peculiar distinction among medical writers. He burns ... to bring back the bodily economy of man to its allegiance to the Supreme

Guide' (Brown, 134). *Principles* was immensely popular both in Great Britain and in the United States, and went through numerous editions.

Combe published two health texts for a popular audience: *The Physiology of Digestion Considered with Relation to the Principles of Dietetics* (1836) and *The Management of Infancy, Physiological and Moral* (1840). This was to be his last book. His chronic pulmonary complaint grew worse, and voyages to Madeira and the United States provided only temporary relief. Combe died at Gorgie, near Edinburgh, on 9 August 1847. He did not marry and had no known progeny.

L. S. JACYNA

Sources G. Combe, *The life and correspondence of Andrew Combe, M.D.* (1850) · J. Brown, *Locke and Sydenham* (1858) · R. Cooter, *The cultural meaning of popular science: phrenology and the organization of consent in nineteenth-century Britain* (1984)
Archives NA Scot., corresp. and papers · NL Scot. | Bodl. Oxf., letters to Lady Byron · NL Scot., corresp. with George Combe · W. Sussex RO, letters to Richard Cobden
Likenesses J. Hutchinson, marble bust, 1889, Scot. NPG · G. H. Garraway, oils (after D. Macnee, 1836), U. Edin. · photograph (after a painting?), Wellcome L.

Combe, Charles (1743–1817), physician and numismatist, was born on 23 September 1743 in Southampton Street, Bloomsbury, where his father, John Combe (*d.* 1768), carried on business as an apothecary. His mother was called Elizabeth. He was educated at Harrow School, and among his schoolfellows he remained on close terms with Sir William Jones, the father of comparative philology, and Samuel Parr. He rose to the sixth form but did not proceed as hoped to Oxford, on account of a brother's illness and death which compelled him to remain at home and assist his father. Having pursued medical courses in London, he took over his father's business in 1768. On 9 May 1769 he married Arthey, daughter of Henry Taylor, watchmaker, of Red Lion Street in Holborn.

In addition to his medical studies Combe maintained an active interest in classical studies, and especially numismatics. He was elected FSA on 10 January 1771 and FRS on 11 January 1776. In 1773 he published *Index nummorum omnium imperatorum, Augustorum et Caesarum*, a listing of imperial 'large brass', including provincial issues, down to Domitian. That year, or earlier, he made the acquaintance of William Hunter, the anatomist and founder of the great coin collection now held in Glasgow. Combe's knowledge of Greek, Roman, and Anglo-Saxon coins, his eye for authenticity, and his understanding of the market, were instrumental in creating this collection. Over the next ten years he was of the greatest assistance to Hunter, not merely in acquiring desirable single coins but in valuing entire cabinets and negotiating their purchase. Having initially collected in his own right, he ceased to do so and sold his better pieces to Hunter in 1777. He also played a vital part in Hunter's scheme for a large seven-volume catalogue of the entire collection, divided according to series, each volume to be entrusted to a specialist. Combe would undoubtedly have been responsible for several volumes had the scheme been carried through; in the event only one came out, and Combe was its author. The *Nummorum veterum populorum et urbium ... descriptio* (1782), a catalogue of Hunter's Greek pre-imperial issues, was the best work of its kind produced in the eighteenth century. It has been much corrected in detail, and the illustrations, contained in sixty-eight engraved plates, are poor as works of art, but Combe took care that they should be more faithful to the coins than the illustrations in previous numismatic works, and the volume as a whole earned praise from the eminent Austrian numismatist Joseph Eckhel. In many ways it set a standard for all later coin catalogues to emulate.

Combe was only one of several prominent antiquarians advising Hunter; his memoir of another, William Southgate, was prefaced to *Musaeum Southgatianum*, a reprint of the catalogues of the latter's library and coin collection in 1795. He was one of the three trustees appointed in Hunter's will to have care of his collection in London for thirty years, after which it was to pass to Glasgow University. Hunter died in 1783, and the trustees were happy to relinquish possession earlier than the prescribed term; in 1807 the coins travelled north under armed guard.

Combe was also associated professionally with Hunter, and this doubtless helped him to gain the degree of MD from Glasgow University in 1784. That year he went into practice as an obstetric physician, and he was admitted licentiate in midwifery by the College of Physicians on 5 April, and nominated governor of St Bartholomew's Hospital on 30 June. In 1789 he was chosen physician to the British Lying-in Hospital in Brownlow Street, and on resigning the post in 1810 was appointed consulting physician to the same institution. He also had a considerable private practice, and assembled a library of rare medical books (sold in 1808) and a collection of *materia medica* which was purchased by the College of Physicians shortly after his death. His collection of prints, an extensive array assembled on historical principles, with particular emphasis on mezzotints, had been auctioned in 850 lots in May 1803.

Combe's only other numismatic publication was a contribution to an appendix in the second edition of Vertue's *Medals … of Thomas Simon* (1780). After Hunter's death he turned his attention to classical literature, and in 1788 he began to work with Henry Homer, fellow of Emmanuel College, Cambridge, on an edition of Horace with variorum notes. Samuel Parr was also originally to have taken part in the work. Homer died before the first volume was completed, and Combe finished the work alone; it was published in 1792–3. Though the text was well edited and laid out, the copious notes were not free from errors, particularly when quoting in Greek. A severe criticism by Parr in the *British Critic*, however, went far beyond these faults by throwing doubt over Combe's judgement in selecting the notes and his faithfulness to the scheme as conceived by Homer. Combe responded with *A Statement of Facts Relative to the Behaviour of Dr Parr* (1793) and was answered by Parr in *Remarks on the Statement of Dr Charles Combe* (1795).

Combe died after a short illness at his house in Vernon Place, off Bloomsbury Square, on 18 March 1817, and was buried in the cemetery for St George's, Bloomsbury, in Brunswick Square, on 24 March. His wife had died in 1799,

and of their four children only two survived him; the elder was Taylor *Combe (1774–1826), keeper of antiquities in the British Museum.

W. W. WROTH, *rev.* C. E. A. CHEESMAN

Sources *GM*, 1st ser., 87/1 (1817), 467–8 • Munk, *Roll*, 2.337–8 • G. Macdonald, *Catalogue of Greek coins in the Hunterian collection, University of Glasgow*, 1 (1899), ix–lxvi • *A catalogue of a valuable and extensive collection of prints* (1803) [sale catalogue, Sothebys, London, 20–28 May 1803] • will of Henry Taylor, dated 18 Sept 1770 and proved, 20 Feb 1771, PRO, PROB 11/964, sig. 85 • Nichols, *Lit. anecdotes*, 3.162–3; 6.359; 8.75 • parish register, St George's, Bloomsbury, 20 Oct 1743 [baptism] • parish register, St Pancras, 9 May 1769 [marriage] • parish register, St George's, Bloomsbury, 24 March 1817 [burial]
Archives BM, department of coins and medals, MS handlist of English coinage from Saxon kings to the house of Hanover • BM, department of coins and medals, MS handlist to Hunterian coin collection
Likenesses N. Branwhite, group portrait, stipple, pubd 1801 (*Institutors of the Medical Society of London*; after S. Medley), BM
Wealth at death considerable medical practice; sold large collections of prints and books in 1803 and 1808

Combe [Comb], **George** (1788–1858), phrenologist, was born in Livingstone Yards, Edinburgh, on 21 October 1788, one of the seventeen children of George Comb (*d.* 1815), a brewer, and Marion Newton (*d.* 1819), who came from a family of tenant farmers. Combe recalled in his autobiography that the family home, at the foot of Edinburgh Castle, was attached to his father's brewery and surrounded by other manufacturing concerns: 'A more unhealthy residence can scarcely be conceived' (Gibbon, 1.2). These surroundings almost certainly account for Combe's poor health as a child and his later delicacy. Combe's parents imposed a strict Calvinist regime upon their children and, though Combe was later to reject his religious upbringing, certain aspects of the Calvinist outlook remained central to his thinking. Described as being hard, dry, cold, and as tall, puritanical, and 'dissenter-looking', 'he remained all his life within an ascetic mold, forever preoccupied with the virtues of thrift, industry, and order' (Cooter, 104).

Early years Combe was initially educated at the parish school of St Cuthbert's and then in 1797 he proceeded to Edinburgh high school. Here he was subjected to severe discipline which involved the liberal use of corporal punishment. While George Comb himself refrained from beating his children, he had no objection to schoolmasters' employing the tawse on them. From 1802 to 1804 Combe attended humanities classes at the University of Edinburgh. His father was anxious to see his sons achieve social advancement, and in the spring of 1804 Combe was articled to a firm of Edinburgh lawyers. After a period as a solicitor's clerk Combe was admitted as a writer to the signet, in January 1812, and began to practise as a lawyer. After the death of his father in 1815 Combe also took charge of the family brewing business for a time.

Combe's relations with his siblings were close. His elder sister, Jean, kept house for him until her death in 1831. His younger brother Andrew *Combe also shared a house with him. George and Andrew Combe became collaborators in what was to become the major enterprise of both

George Combe (1788–1858), by David Octavius Hill and Robert Adamson, 1843

men's lives: the promotion of the science of phrenology, with George Combe going on to play a pre-eminent role in 'phrenology's transformation from an arcane theory of brain and character to that of a socially respectable vehicle of "progressive" ideas on social life and organization' (Cooter, 101).

Introduction to phrenology By his own account Combe's first acquaintance with the doctrines of phrenology was derived from a reading of a damning critique of the system written by John Gordon in the June 1815 issue of the *Edinburgh Review*. Impressed by Gordon's arguments he 'regarded [the phrenologists'] doctrines as contemptibly absurd, and their authors as the most disingenuous of men' (Combe, *A System of Phrenology*, v). In 1816, however, Combe attended a dissection of the brain given in the house of a barrister friend by Caspar Spurzheim. He already had some background in the subject through following John Barclay's lectures on anatomy; such dabbling in scientific and medical subjects was not uncommon among early nineteenth-century Edinburgh lawyers. Most of Spurzheim's audience was convinced by his refutation of the criticisms that had been levelled by the *Edinburgh Review*. Combe subsequently followed Spurzheim's lectures on phrenology. He remained in some doubt, however, about the validity of phrenology's claims until he undertook his own researches; he 'appealed to Nature by

observation, and at last arrived at complete conviction of the truth of Phrenology' (ibid., vi).

Combe's researches took the form of both the collection of numerous skull casts supposed to show to advantage the various phrenological organs, and the observation of the heads of individuals whom he encountered. He found himself increasingly asked to demonstrate to others the truths of phrenology he had gleaned by these means, 'until at length the applications for an account of the casts became so numerous that I was forced to devote certain days and hours to gratify public curiosity' (Gibbon, 1.95). Combe thus took on the role of an exponent of the doctrines of phrenology. His early informal presentations to members of his circle eventually developed into courses of public lectures in Edinburgh, Bath, Newcastle, Glasgow, Birmingham, and Aberdeen.

For some time, however, Combe pursued this role as a teacher in parallel with his career as a lawyer, the occupation on which he still relied for the greater part of his income. Additionally, some of his best friends were alarmed 'lest I should ruin myself by espousing a cause which was the laughing-stock of all men of reputation' (Gibbon, 1.96). These fears were to prove unfounded, but such sentiments were an indication of the controversial character of the doctrine with which Combe now became associated. George Combe founded the Edinburgh Phrenological Society in 1820.

Combe's interest in social questions led him in 1820 to visit Robert Owen's model community at New Lanark, but he remained unconvinced about its success. His brother Abram (d. 1827) tried and failed with a similar experiment at Orbiston, Lanarkshire.

Writings and ideas Combe's status as the leading British champion of phrenology was enhanced by a series of publications. The first of these was an exposition of the 'physiognomical system' of Spurzheim and Franz Josef Gall, which appeared in April 1817. A year later Combe published in the *Literary and Statistical Magazine for Scotland* the first of a series of essays that in 1819 were collected into a book entitled *Essays in Phrenology*. In 1824 Combe published a further volume: *A System of Phrenology*. Both these books passed through several editions. He was also a contributor to, and sometime proprietor of, the *Phrenological Journal*.

Combe's most important work was, however, *The Constitution of Man* (1828), in which phrenology was placed in the context of a wider scheme for understanding human nature and ameliorating the human condition. The title suggested that it would be a descriptive work, providing an account of human nature. This is indeed what Combe attempted. But *The Constitution of Man* was at the same time a prescriptive text: Combe maintained that from a proper understanding of human beings it was possible to derive a comprehensive system of not only personal but also social and political morality.

Crucial to this transition from the factual to the normative was Combe's notion of natural law. He maintained that cause followed effect with the same inevitability in the human as in the physical realm, and that it was as futile and dangerous for an individual or a community to seek to defy the laws of human nature as it was to attempt to override the law of gravity. However, Combe claimed that until recently these laws had been imperfectly understood; it was only with the rise of phrenology that people could obtain an accurate account of human nature and thus a reliable guide to conduct: phrenology was no less than 'the greatest and most important discovery ever communicated to mankind' (Combe, *System of Phrenology*, vii). Phrenology revealed, for instance, that social inequality was part of the natural order of things. Different individuals had different aptitudes depending on the unequal development of the various cerebral organs. Individuals should therefore seek phrenological guidance when choosing a career, and employers should make use of cranioscopy when hiring workers. The phrenological doctrine of mind thus endorsed the division of labour by showing the natural basis of this economic arrangement.

Combe was nevertheless critical of certain aspects of the capitalist manufacturing system. He maintained that it encouraged a blind pursuit of short-term profit without regard to longer-term economic and social consequences. This was because capitalists were excessively influenced by their faculties of 'acquisitiveness' and 'self-esteem'. He defended the rights of workers to form combinations to protect themselves against such exploitation. Moreover, while phrenology might seem to encourage a deterministic attitude to human endowments, Combe denied that the brains of the lower classes were noticeably inferior in size or quality to those of the upper classes. What primarily determined the difference in ability between the two was the disparity in the education of the classes. Given proper training of their cerebral equipment, he believed, there was no reason for workers not to improve their lot and rise to join the middling orders of society.

Combe was also anxious to demonstrate the relevance of phrenology to the reform of the penal system. He opposed capital and corporal punishment and desired that prison discipline be adapted to the moral reform of the individual convict. He maintained that 'in dealing with criminals we are dealing with the *mind*' (Combe, *Remarks on the Principles of Criminal Legislation*, 35) and that penal policy should therefore be directed towards a reform of the offender's mind rather than to taking revenge on his body. Once a criminal's mental faculties were restored by means of education and discipline to a state of proper harmony he or she would no longer be inclined to offend against the law but would become a useful member of the community.

The Constitution of Man enjoyed remarkable success, going through numerous editions and selling hundreds of thousands of copies in Europe and the United States. Ironically, it was not the phrenological aspects of the work that proved most popular or had the most durable appeal. It was rather Combe's meliorist, humanitarian, and individualist message that found most resonance among nineteenth-century middle-class readers. These core ideals could be retained while jettisoning Combe's more particular doctrines.

The book also aroused opposition in some quarters. Theologians were quick to point out that Combe's constant insistence upon the centrality of nature and natural law left little room for divine providence. Although Combe denied that he advocated atheism or materialism, these critics touched on an important point. By making nature a virtually self-sufficient source of moral law, Combe rendered the deity at most a remote being with little direct influence on human affairs. The system of rewards and punishments Combe described was of this world and determined by natural forces. *The Constitution of Man* can therefore be seen as a precursor to later attempts to create a purely naturalistic understanding of the world and of humanity's place within it.

Marriage and foreign lecture tours On 25 September 1833 Combe married Cecilia Siddons (1794–1868), daughter of the actress Sarah *Siddons. He allegedly subjected both himself and his prospective wife to craniological examination before deciding on the match. With the help of Cecilia's fortune Combe was able to retire from legal practice and devote himself to his activities as a publicist for phrenology. The couple had no children.

Between 1838 and 1840 Combe toured Canada and the United States, seeking to propagate his views by lecturing and by establishing links with like-minded reformers. His impressions of this visit appeared in 1841 as *Notes on the United States*. In 1842 Combe travelled to Germany, where he lectured on phrenology in Heidelberg. Due to poor health he was, however, shortly afterwards obliged to give up lecturing. He then bought a house at 45 Melville Street, Edinburgh.

Combe continued to publish on various topics; he was, in particular, interested in questions of education policy. In a series of publications he advocated a system of national secular education. A school based on these doctrines was established in Edinburgh; its curriculum included lessons in physiology and phrenology.

Science and religion In 1847 Combe also published a pamphlet on the relations between science and religion; this was subsequently turned into a book. In this work Combe maintained that 'Science has banished from [people's] minds belief in the exercise, by the Deity, in our day, of special acts of supernatural power as a means of influencing human affairs, and it has presented a systematic order of nature, which man may study, comprehend, and obey, as a guide to his practical conduct' (Combe, *On the Relation between Religion and Science*, 6).

Towards the end of Combe's life the phrenological movement in Britain was increasingly disrupted by schism and controversy. One faction, of which William Engledue was the chief spokesman, insisted upon a materialistic interpretation of phrenology which was favoured by political radicals. More moderate phrenologists insisted that there was no incompatibility between their science and Christianity. The Combes favoured the latter position. However, George's religious views were sufficiently heterodox for him to be denounced in Edinburgh and elsewhere as an atheist and materialist. This reputation may well have contributed to the failure of his attempt in 1836 to be appointed to the chair of logic at Edinburgh University.

Combe suffered from ill health throughout his life. After a brief final illness, diagnosed as pleuro-pneumonia, he died at Moor Park, Surrey, on 14 August 1858, and was buried in the Dean cemetery, Edinburgh. He was survived by his wife.

L. S. JACYNA

Sources C. Gibbon, *The life of George Combe: author of 'The constitution of man'*, 2 vols. (1878) · R. Cooter, *The cultural meaning of popular science: phrenology and the organization of consent in nineteenth-century Britain* (1984) · G. Combe, *The constitution of man: considered in relation to external objects* (1828) · G. Combe, *A system of phrenology*, 2nd edn (1825) · G. Combe, *Remarks on the principles of criminal legislation, and the practice of prison discipline* (1844) · G. Combe, *On the relation between religion and science* (1847) · CGPLA Eng. & Wales (1859) · DNB **Archives** NL Scot., corresp. and papers | BL, corresp. with Richard Cobden, Add. MSS 43660–43661 · NL Scot., letters to Robert Dunn · U. Newcastle, Robinson L., letters to Sir Walter Trevelyan **Likenesses** D. Macnee, portrait, 1836 · D. O. Hill and R. Adamson, photograph, 1843, NPG [*see illus.*] · S. Wood, plaster medallion, 1849, Scot. NPG · Hähnisch, lithograph, 1855, BM · J. Watson-Gordon, portrait, 1857 · L. Macdonald, marble bust, 1895, Scot. NPG · W. Brodie, plaster medallion, Scot. NPG · L. Bump, lithograph (after J. Lump), Wellcome L. · B. W. Crombie, caricature etching, NPG; repro. in W. S. Douglas, *Modern Athenians* (1882) · G. H. Garraway, oils (after J. Watson-Gordon), U. Edin. · R. M. Hodges, mezzotint (after D. Macnee), Wellcome L. · C. H. Jeens, stipple (after D. Macnee), BM, Wellcome L.; repro. in Gibbon, *Life of George Combe* **Wealth at death** £5448 10s. 6d.: confirmation, 10 Jan 1859, NA Scot., SC 70/1/99, 682–92 · £3940 6s. 1d.—in USA

Combe, Harvey Christian (1752–1818), brewer, was born in Andover, Hampshire, the second but eldest surviving son of Harvey Combe, a prosperous Andover attorney, and his wife, Christian, *née* Jarman. His father was a third generation lawyer, while his mother's family, the Jarmans, were London based, with interests in the corn, sugar refining, and brewing trades. Having no liking for his early legal training in his father's office, Combe then served an apprenticeship with his uncle, Boyce Tree, a prosperous City corn and malt factor, who had married Christian Combe's sister. He became Tree's partner, and eventually his heir. On 9 May 1780 Combe married his first cousin, Tree's daughter Alice Christian (*d.* 1828); they had four sons and six daughters.

In 1787, enjoying an annual income variously stated at between £2000 and £3000 from his corn and malt business, Combe acquired a major share in the well-known Gyfford's Wood Yard brewery (in which a Jarman cousin had previously had an interest) which came on the market in that year. Founded in 1739 in the crowded Long Acre centre of the London coach making trade, it was a progressive brewery, the fifth or sixth largest of the capital's great porter breweries. The five partners in the new management, continuing to trade as Gyfford's brewery, raised £90,000 to carry on the business. The two largest stakeholders, Combe and his friend George Shum (1751?–1805), a founding director of the Pheonix Insurance Company and an immensely rich sugar refiner, each found £26,000. The brewery seems to have been largely run by two of the

Harvey Christian Combe (1752–1818), by Benjamin Burnell, 1800

other three partners, Joseph Delafield, one of Samuel Whitbread's brewers, and William Packer, long employed at the Wood Yard brewery. In the next thirty years the brewery prospered, although less spectacularly than those of Barclay Perkin, Whitbread, Truman, and Meux-Reid. Nevertheless, a stock account of 1796 reveals Gyfford's brewery to be valued at no less than £295,587 (Janes, 73), and the banker Sir William Curtis (1752–1829), fellow MP for London with Combe after 1796, told the diarist Joseph Farington that his great friend, Combe, was worth £100,000. With considerable social and political ambitions, Combe and Shum probably milked the profits of the brewery quite hard.

After 1795, like George Shum, Combe became closely involved in City and national politics. He also had a reputation as a gambler and socialite, and as an enthusiast for pugilism. First elected alderman for the City in 1790, he was returned as one of London's MPs in 1796, the same year Shum became MP for Honiton. Combe was a moderately radical whig who, like Sir William Curtis, spoke frequently in parliament as the joint representative of City interests. He joined the Whig Club in 1785 and was admitted to Brooks's Club on Charles James Fox's nomination in 1792. Immensely public spirited, he successfully balanced public duty with his business interests. He occupied the office of lord mayor of London with great ceremony in the difficult year 1799–1800, at the height of wartime inflation and shortage. He was a governor of the Irish Society, founded for the relief of poverty in Ireland, from 1793 to 1817 and served as lieutenant-colonel in various London militia regiments between 1794 and 1809. In the City's business community he was master of the Brewers' Company (1804–5) and warden of the Fishmongers' Company (1812–14); he was a director of the Globe Insurance Company after 1805 and the West India Dock Company after 1811; he was president of the Society for Prosecuting Felons in 1817.

Joseph Farington found Combe 'to possess a very warm heart and great kindness of disposition. He is always ready to do acts of service when applied to, and engages by his manner.' Farington also noted that:

> The connexion with the City has been attended with great expense to him, and he has the honour for it but not profit. In politics he is a party man, but the City have confidence in him when business is to be transacted. (*Farington Diary*, ed. Greig, 2.110)

No brewer, except perhaps Combe's contemporary, the second Samuel Whitbread, better demonstrates the social and political range of London's super-rich brewing fraternity in the late Georgian period. He was a close friend of Charles James Fox (after whom he named in full his youngest son), Richard Brinsley Sheridan, and the prince of Wales. His annual entertainment of royalty and his aristocratic whig friends at the brewery for traditional beefsteaks, before a more extended collation at his house in Great Russell Street, became legendary. In 1807 he acquired a country seat at Cobham Park, Surrey. He appears to have suffered a series of strokes after 1812 and resigned his aldermanic and parliamentary seats in 1817.

Combe died on 4 July 1818. His eldest son, Harvey (1782–1858), continued his father's interest in the brewery, and served as high sheriff of Surrey in 1831 as well as being a notable horse breeder and well-known master of the Old Berkeley foxhounds. The brewery later formed an important part of the brewing firm Watney Mann.

R. G. WILSON

Sources P. Mathias, *The brewing industry in England, 1700–1830* (1959) · H. H. Janes, *The red barrel: a history of Watney Mann* [1963] · *The Farington diary*, ed. J. Greig, 8 vols. (1922–8) · 'Combe, Harvey Christian', HoP, *Commons* · 'Curtis, Sir William', 'Shum, George', HoP, *Commons* · Burke, *Gen. GB* (1937) [Combe of Oaklands Park] · GM, 1st ser., 88/2 (1818), 83–4

Likenesses J. Opie, portrait, 1799–1800 (as lord mayor of London), repro. in Janes, *The red barrel*, 55 · B. Burnell, portrait, 1800, Guildhall Art Gallery [*see illus.*]

Wealth at death £140,000: GM

Combe, Martha Howell Bennett (1806–1893). *See under* Combe, Thomas (1796–1872).

Combe, Simon Harvey (1903–1965), brewer, was born at Frensham, Surrey, on 4 May 1903, the second son of Major Boyce Combe of Great Holt, near Farnham, Surrey, and his wife, Katherine Mabel, *née* Tombs. Educated at Eton College, he spent a year in France before joining the family brewery, Watney Combe Reid & Co., in 1922. During the Second World War he served as a captain in the Irish Guards, winning the Military Cross at Anzio in 1943.

Combe was an archetypal representative of British 'family capitalism'. He stayed with Watneys all his working life, being appointed an 'annual' director in 1926 and a full director in 1931. In 1950 he succeeded Major Arthur Bonsor as chairman, a position he retained until his death.

Combe's years at the top were crucial ones for both the company and the industry. The early 1950s saw the acquisition of Charles Hammerton & Co. of Stockwell (1951), Tamplin's of Brighton (1953), and Henty and Constable of Chichester (1955). In 1955 Watneys came close to effecting an ambitious merger with Bass before merging with Mann Crossman and Paulin three years later to form Watney Mann. The move was designed to give effect to a long contemplated strategy: to obtain additional brewing capacity in London so that the company's valuable Pimlico site, on which the Stag brewery stood, could be developed.

Elected chairman of the enlarged company, Combe helped it weather the storm created by the hostile takeover bid for the company by Charles Clore of Sears Holdings in 1959. Property development was something which Watneys, unlike many of its rivals, fully appreciated at an early stage. In May 1959, just before Clore's bid, it announced the formation of a separate property company to exploit the development potential of properties no longer required as licensed premises. However, exploitation of the company's development potential had to wait for Combe and his colleagues to beat off the biggest threat to Watneys' independent existence since the financial problems caused by the famous Watney Combe Reid merger of 1898.

The story of the Clore takeover bid for Watneys has been told many times. Suffice it to say that Combe proved every bit as stubborn a battler as his rival. This was no brewing lamb for the slaughter. Under Combe's direction the company had already shown considerable enterprise in all aspects of modern brewing—production, retailing, and property development. Unfortunately, as with many established breweries, the book value of its assets did not reflect their current market value, making it vulnerable to a bid. The share price rose during the contest to the point where Clore deemed it prudent to withdraw. Combe then led Watney Mann to national status through the acquisition of several more companies in the period from 1960 to 1965. This included substantial brewing concerns in Northampton (Phipps), Trowbridge (Ushers), Manchester (Wilson and Walker), Norwich (Steward and Patteson, and Bullard), and Edinburgh (Drybrough). The three acquisitions of 1960—Phipps, Wilsons, and Ushers—added 3200 public houses to Watneys' retail estate, making a total of just under 7000 pubs. The Norwich breweries taken over in 1963 added another 2000.

The 1960s were very much Watneys' golden age. Combe encouraged the establishment and consolidation of leading brands such as Draught Red Barrel and bottled Stingo, which were marketed on a national basis. The company also entered into important product exchange agreements with United and Allied (for lager) and Guinness (stout), and diversified into wines, spirits, and soft drinks (the company acquired the lucrative Coca Cola franchise for southern England in 1956, and a similar franchise for the eastern counties following the purchase of Morgan's brewery in Norwich in 1961). The company also made diversified investments in motels and garages through

Watney Lyon Motels and Swift Garages. Combe was also a director of South African Breweries, Rhodesian Breweries, and Wiley & Co.

Despite being a shrewd business leader, Combe played the part of traditional brewer with aristocratic pretensions. He was a keen farmer, gardener, and golfer. On 15 October 1932 he married Lady Silvia Beatrice Coke (b. 1909/10), elder daughter of the fourth earl of Leicester, and they lived at the Manor House, Burnham Thorpe, Norfolk. They had one son and one daughter.

Combe was a prominent figure in the brewing lobby. In 1945 he was elected a member of the Brewers' Society council, serving on its parliamentary committee for twenty years, and acting as chairman of its hop committee from 1947 to 1956, during which time he helped to develop the industry's hop marketing scheme. He became vice-chairman of the society in 1953 and chairman in 1955-6, and was subsequently a vice-president. He was also master of the Brewers' Company in 1954. Noted for his wide experience, leadership, firmness, and wise counsel, he turned Watneys into a major brewing company, but was also loyal to a tradition of family brewing. But this did not mean that he was either conservative or unadventurous. The scheme he drew up with Bass in 1954-5 was extremely bold. If it had succeeded it would have created a mega-brewery thirty years ahead of its time.

Combe died at Watney House, Stag Place, London, on 1 April 1965 aged sixty-one. He was survived by his wife.

TERRY GOURVISH

Sources T. Corran and C. Shaw, 'Combe, Simon Harvey', DBB · WWW · T. R. Gourvish and R. G. Wilson, The British brewing industry, 1830-1980 (1994) · H. H. Janes, The red barrel: a history of Watney Mann [1963] · The Times (2 April 1965) · Directory of Directors · Brewing Trade Review (April 1965) · m. cert. · d. cert.
Likenesses D. Hill, portrait, repro. in Gourvish and Wilson, British brewing industry, pl. 63 · portrait, Brewers' Society
Wealth at death £18,243: probate, 23 June 1965, CGPLA Eng. & Wales

Combe, Taylor (1774-1826), numismatist and archaeologist, was the eldest son of Dr Charles *Combe (1743-1817), the physician and numismatist, and his wife, Arthey Taylor (d. 1799). He was educated at Harrow School and at Oriel College, Oxford, where he matriculated on 18 October 1791, graduated BA on 5 June 1795, and proceeded MA on 10 July 1798. Combe joined the Society of Antiquaries in 1796 and in 1803 he obtained an appointment in the British Museum, as superintendent of the coins and medals collection. In 1807 he became keeper of the newly created department of antiquities, the coins still remaining in his charge. The following year he married Elizabeth Gray, the youngest daughter of Dr Edward Whitaker Gray. He was elected a fellow of the Royal Society in 1806, and was its secretary from 1812 to 1824, during which period he edited the Philosophical Transactions. He also became the director of the Society of Antiquaries in 1813 and superintended the publication of the latter portions of the Vetusta monumenta. His importance in the British Museum grew and in 1814 he was sent to Zante, to carry out the purchase of the Phigaleian marbles.

As a numismatist and archaeologist Combe did much useful and accurate work, best represented in A Description of the Collection of Ancient Terracottas in the British Museum (1810), A Description of the Collection of Ancient Marbles in the British Museum (1812-20), a Catalogue of Greek Coins in the British Museum (1814), and a Description of the Anglo-Gallic Coins in the British Museum (1826). He also contributed many articles to Archaeologia.

Combe died after a long illness, on 7 July 1826, at the British Museum, and was buried on 14 July 1826, in the family vault in the burial-ground of St George's, Bloomsbury. His extensive library of classical and numismatic books, together with a collection of prints and some of his manuscripts, was sold by auction at Sothebys in December 1826. His premature death deprived the department of antiquities of an able curator, who had successfully organized the Towneley galleries and superintended the arrival of the Elgin and Phigaleian marbles. The next keeper, Edward Hawkins (1780-1867), proved a worthy successor who built substantially on Combe's early work.

W. W. WROTH, rev. NILANJANA BANERJI

Sources GM, 1st ser., 96/2 (1826), 181 · GM, 1st ser., 87/1 (1817), 467-8 · Foster, Alum. Oxon. · E. Edwards, Lives of the founders of the British Museum (1870) · E. Miller, That noble cabinet: a history of the British Museum (1974)
Likenesses Archer, group portrait, oils, 1819 (The temporary Elgin Room), BM · B. Pistrucci, bronze medal, c.1826 (after W. J. Taylor), NPG · oils, RS

Combe, Thomas (1796-1872), printer and patron of the arts, was born on 21 July 1796 in Leicester, the second of six children of Thomas Combe, the town's leading bookseller, and his wife, Theodosia (née Dalby). He had an older sister, three younger sisters, and a younger brother. He was educated at Repton School, Derby, which he entered in August 1808.

After Repton, Combe worked in his father's bookshop, and then moved to Oxford about 1824 to assist Joseph Parker in his new bookshop in the Turl. He lived in St Mary Hall Lane with one of his sisters, who kept lodgings. Here Combe met John Henry Newman and Edward Pusey, who lodged, briefly, in the house. Two years later Combe went into partnership with Michael Angelo Nattali, in a bookselling business at 24 Tavistock Street, London, but within a year or so he left for Leicester to take a share in his father's bookselling and printing business at Gallowtree Gate.

In 1838 Combe joined the university press at Oxford, which was then made up of two quite separate businesses: the learned side, which printed classical texts; and the Bible side, which was a commercial enterprise exploiting the university's monopoly (shared with Cambridge and the queen's printer) in the printing of Bibles and prayer books. Combe began as superintendent of the learned side, a salaried post bringing a comfortable income of £450 a year. He lived in North House, one of two conjoined managers' houses in the quadrangle of the press buildings, in Walton Street, Oxford, where he remained for the rest of his life.

Thomas Combe (1796–1872), by Sir John Everett Millais, 1850

After returning to Oxford, Combe renewed his acquaintanceship with Newman and through him met Martha Edwards [**Martha Howell Bennett Combe** (1806–1893)], one of five daughters of John Edwards, an ironmonger with premises in the High Street. Combe married her on 3 September 1840, Newman officiating at the ceremony. They had no children. Throughout their married life they were strong supporters of the Tractarian movement.

In 1841 Combe bought shares in the Bible business at the university press and gradually increased his holding until, in 1851, he became senior partner. He relinquished his post on the learned side to take full control of the Bible business. Output and profits rose under his management; by 1853 he was receiving nearly £4000 a year in dividends, almost ten times what he had been paid for his services on the learned side. He was now a rich man. The university benefited immensely from the dividends and in 1859 conferred on Combe the honorary degree of MA in recognition of his business achievements and for furthering the interests of employees. 'Before his coming to Oxford the University chest had been … in a sick and dying condition', the public orator announced at the ceremony; 'by his honourable exertions and ceaseless labours [Combe] has revived, upheld, supported, and enlarged that chest' (OUP archives). This was not strictly true, as the press had been profitable before his arrival. Moreover, although Combe was a shrewd and energetic manager, the prosperity of the press in the 1850s was as much a product of a booming economy, and an unprecedented demand for Bibles, as it was of his own efforts. Combe relished the award: one observer recorded seeing him around the press in later life 'with his white beard and hair set off by a

Magdalen blazer, under his MA gown' (*Clarendonian*, 23, 1969, 39).

In 1850 Combe met the young Pre-Raphaelite painters John Everett Millais and Charles Allston Collins, who were painting near Oxford. Impressed by the boyish charm of Millais, the Combes invited them to stay at their house, where Millais painted a portrait of Thomas Combe, and Collins one of Mrs Combe's uncle, William Bennett. Thanks mainly to the persuasive powers of Millais, Combe began to acquire Pre-Raphaelite paintings: William Holman Hunt's *A Converted British Family* in 1850, and Millais's *The Return of the Dove to the Ark* and Collins's *Convent Thoughts* in 1851. These were acquired at a time when Pre-Raphaelite paintings were being savaged by the critics, and the survival of the movement owed much to Combe's patronage.

The Combes met Hunt in 1851 and invited him to Oxford. It was the first of many visits: 'Hunt saw little of his family now,' his granddaughter wrote later, 'the Combes had taken their place' (D. H. Hunt, *My Grandfather, his Wives and Loves*, 1987, 92). In 1853 Combe bought Hunt's *The Light of the World*, perhaps the most famous of all Victorian paintings, for 400 guineas. Other paintings bought from Hunt include *The School-Girl's Hymn* (1860) and a small version of *The Afterglow in Egypt* (1861). Combe bought just one painting by Rossetti: *Dante Drawing an Angel*, purchased in 1855.

Combe provided £3000 for a new chapel at the Radcliffe Infirmary. It was designed by Arthur Blomfield and completed in 1865. To meet the need of the growing population of Jericho, where the press was situated, Combe was also responsible for providing the church of St Barnabas. Again designed by Blomfield, this was completed in 1869 at a cost of £6500, and the church's Tractarian furnishings and rituals soon attracted huge congregations.

Working at the press until the last, Thomas Combe died suddenly of angina on 29 October 1872. A request, supported by the prime minister, Gladstone, that Combe should, exceptionally, be interred within the walls of St Barnabas, was turned down by the home secretary, and he was buried in St Sepulchre's cemetery in Walton Street on 6 November 1872.

Combe's wife, Martha, lived on at the press building until her death in 1893. With one or two exceptions, she bequeathed all the Pre-Raphaelite paintings—which had been augmented by acquisitions of her own (notably Hunt's *London Bridge by Night*)—to the university, which placed them in the Ashmolean Museum. The major exception was Hunt's *The Light of the World*, which she had already given to Keble College. The collection was one of the most comprehensive private collections of early Pre-Raphaelite art. Martha Combe died on 27 December 1893. She was buried at St Sepulchre's, beside her husband, on 2 January 1894.   COLIN HUGHES

Sources Orders of the delegates of the Clarendon Press, and record of the press school, concerts, etc, 1853–9, and other papers, Oxford University Press, archives · AM Oxf., Combe bequest MSS · A. H. T. R. Smith, *The Radcliffe chapel and the Combe benefactions* (1965) · J. Whiteley, *Oxford and the Pre-Raphaelites* (1989) · P. Bliss, notebook, 1821–c.1857, Bodl. Oxf., MS Top. Oxon e. 270 · P. Sutcliffe, *The Oxford University Press: an informal history* (1978) · J. Whiteley, 'The Combe bequest', *Apollo*, 117 (1983), 302–7 · M. Lutyens, 'Selling the missionary', *Apollo*, 86 (1967), 380–87 · A. T. Bassett, *S Barnabas' Oxford* (1919) · *The Clarendonian*, 23 (1969), 38–40 · Gladstone, *Diaries* · parish register, St Martin's, Leics. RO [baptism] · Repton School register · m. cert. · d. cert. · *Oxford Times* (6 Jan 1894)

Likenesses J. E. Millais, oils, 1850, AM Oxf. [*see illus.*] · W. H. Hunt, chalk drawing, 1860, AM Oxf.; repro. in W. H. Hunt, *Pre-Raphaelitism and the Pre-Raphaelite Brotherhood*, 2nd edn, 1 (1913), 140 · W. H. Hunt, chalk drawing, 1861 (Martha Combe), AM Oxf. · T. Woolner, marble bust, exh. RA 1864, AM Oxf. · group photograph, c.1871, Oxford University Press archives; repro. in H. Carter, *Wolvercote mill: a study in paper-making at Oxford* (1957) · group portrait, stained-glass window, St Paul's, Walton Street, Oxford · portrait (Martha Combe), repro. in Whiteley, 'The Combe bequest'

Wealth at death under £70,000: probate, 17 Dec 1872, CGPLA Eng. & Wales · £77,342 12s. 1d.—Martha Combe: probate, 8 Feb 1894, CGPLA Eng. & Wales

Combe [*formerly* Combes], **William** (1742–1823), writer and literary imitator, was born in London on 25 March 1742, the son of Robert Combes (*d.* 1756), a prosperous wholesale ironmonger, and his wife, Susanna Hill (*d.* 1748), daughter of a wealthy Quaker merchant with interests in the West Indies. William was baptized in St Alban's Church, Wood Street, London, on 16 April. He was named after his godfather William Alexander, his father's business partner.

A life of wandering William matriculated at Eton College in 1752, four years after his mother's death. On his father's death in October 1756, William was withdrawn from Eton by William Alexander, now his guardian and executor of his father's will. Very little is known about Combes's life during the three years after Eton. It has been suggested that he attended Oxford University, but there is no record of this. On 22 February 1760 Combes was admitted as a bencher of the Inner Temple, but he left his chamber soon after Alexander's death on 23 September 1762, and never qualified to be called to the bar. As residuary heir to his father's estate of approximately £2500 and legatee of £2000 from his guardian's estate when he turned twenty-four years old, William had ample money and credit to conduct himself as a fashionable man about town when he came of age in March 1763. Rejecting his mercantile origins later in life, he changed the spelling of his last name to Combe and habitually signed himself 'esquire', affecting the status of a gentleman.

Like many other young men, Combe took advantage of the end of restrictions on travel at the close of the Seven Years' War to travel to France, where the tall, handsome young man's extravagant dress and behaviour earned him the nicknames Duke Combe and Count Combe. Among those he befriended during his approximately six-month visit was Laurence Sterne, whom he also visited in England the following year. Combe seems to have exhausted his funds before 1770, spending his time from the end of 1769 to mid-1773 in France, the west midlands, and Wales, outside the fashionable circles in Paris and London. According to some accounts, he may have spent part of that time serving in the British army. He may also have

William Combe (1742–1823), by George Dance, 1793

spent some time at Douai, where English Roman Catholics maintained a seminary. Combe's wandering ended in 1773, when Robert Berkeley offered him the job of editing *A Description of Patagonia*, by Berkeley's chaplain, Thomas Falkner, a former Jesuit missionary. The assignment introduced Combe to his career as a writer and to the business of producing and distributing books (he saw the book through the press in Charles Pugh's Hereford printing office).

Sentiment, comedy, and imitation Early in spring 1775 the local newspapers reported Combe's re-entry into fashionable society in Bath and Bristol. During the summer Combe's comic afterpiece *The Flattering Milliner, or, A Modern Half Hour* was performed on the Bristol stage as part of a benefit for the actor John Henderson. His early friendship with Laurence Sterne also gave rise to an edition of *Sterne's Letters to his Friends on Various Occasions* (1775) and *Letters Supposed to have been Written by Yorick and Eliza* (1779), which were combinations of authentic and fabricated correspondence. The latter was a two-volume imitation of correspondence between the late Sterne and his recently deceased friend Eliza Draper (with whom Combe late in life claimed to have had an affair before she met Sterne). In these Sternian imitations (which included *Original Letters of the Late Reverend Mr. Laurence Sterne, Never before Published*, 1788) Combe established himself as a skilful literary imitator and prolific professional writer in various genres. He had embarked on a lifelong habit of conflating the factual and the fictional and misleading his contemporaries (as well as subsequent scholars and biographers).

Although he always published anonymously, his authorship was an open secret because he frequently acknowledged it in private conversation, and in later works often included his own name on the list of subscribers.

Combe also quickly established himself as a man of feeling and taste by publishing at his own expense a collection of sentiments in prose, *The Philosopher in Bristol* (1775), in two separately published parts, and a topographical poem, *Clifton, a Poem. In Imitation of Spenser* (1775). After unsuccessfully republishing his works in London, Combe attempted to recover financially by agreeing to marry Maria Foster (d. 1814), the discarded mistress of Francis Seymour-Conway, Viscount Beauchamp, Combe's schoolmate at Eton, who was about to marry for the second time. Combe may have entered into a financial agreement with Beauchamp in order to protect the latter from embarrassment. Combe married Foster (who was also known as Miss Harley) on 16 May 1776; the notice in the *Morning Post* describes Combe as 'a Gentleman who is universally known, from having distinguished himself in this, and other countries, in various shapes and characters'. Either Combe misunderstood his arrangement with Beauchamp or Beauchamp failed to pay, but by the end of the decade Combe was burdened with the expense of his wife's confinement in Stephen Casey's private madhouse in Plaistow, Essex, which may have cost him as much as £300 annually.

Early satires and other writing The man of feeling turned satirist in revenge, producing nine verse satires in 1777 alone, with more during 1784, aimed primarily at Simon Luttrell, Baron Irnham, a notorious reprobate of the day, but also targeting Beauchamp, Beauchamp's father, Lord Hertford, his younger brother, Henry Seymour Conway, and their politically anti-ministerial circle of friends, including Charles James Fox. The first satire, *The Diaboliad, a Poem. Dedicated to the Worst Man in his Majesty's Dominions*, was a great success, earning Combe recognition as the best satirist since Charles Churchill and prompting the publication the same year of *Additions to the Diaboliad* and *The Diaboliad, a Poem. Part the Second*. A spate of imitations by others followed. Other poems actually written 'By the author of the diaboliad', such as *A Poetical Epistle to Sir Joshua Reynolds*, mocked various social sinners. The duchess of Devonshire was the target of several satires, among them *The First of April, or, The Triumphs of Folly: a Poem. Dedicated to a Celebrated Duchess* (1777), *An Heroic Epistle to the Noble Author of the Duchess of Devonshire's Cow, a Poem* (1777), and *A Letter to her Grace the Duchess of Devonshire* (1777). The Revd William Dodd, the recently executed forger, was a subject of the prose pamphlet *A Dialogue in the Shades between an Unfortunate Divine, and a Welch Member of Parliament, Lately Deceased* (1777).

Between 1778 and 1785 Combe turned from poetry to prose, beginning in January 1778 with the first of a series of nine volumes over the next seven years of the pro-ministerial *R[oya]l Register*, which purported to be King George III's observations on eminent people recorded in his private notebook. That same year Combe ghost-wrote John Hunter's *A Practical Treatise on the Diseases of the Teeth*.

Combe and his publisher John Bew took advantage of the death of another Eton schoolmate, the notorious Thomas, 'the Wicked' Lord Lyttleton, in November 1779, to publish several volumes of Lyttleton's supposed letters and poems. Many contemporaneous reviewers, while noting the apparent spuriousness of these and other Combe publications, none the less praised his literary talents. Combe also published several sentimental epistolary novels: *Letters of an Italian Nun and an English Gentleman. Translated from the French of J. J. Rousseau* (1781), *Letters between Two Lovers and their Friends. By the Author of Letters Supposed to have been Written by Yorick and Eliza* (1781), and *Original Love-Letters between a Lady of Quality and a Person of Inferior Station* (1784). In addition, a verse satire on Benjamin Franklin, entitled *The Traitor*, and one on the prince of Wales called *The Royal Dream, or, The P[rince] in a Panic. An Eclogue, with Annotations* appeared, respectively, in 1781 and 1785.

Imprisonment and government patronage But frequent and even well received publications were not enough to keep Combe solvent. He was arrested on 18 October 1785 and imprisoned in the king's bench prison the following May for a £100 debt owed to John Palmer since 1775, when Palmer had been the manager of the Bath theatre. Palmer, now the comptroller-general of the Post Office under the prime minister, William Pitt, apparently used the outstanding debt to convince Combe to become a ministerial writer. Although Combe was not formally discharged from prison until 25 May 1787, with Palmer's help he was able to obtain his physical freedom from gaol by August 1786. Combe may also have been aided by John Walter, publisher of the *Daily Universal Register* (renamed *The Times* in 1788) and the Logographic Press. Either Palmer or Walter, or both, presumably paid the 10 or 12 guineas that bought Combe the privilege of living outside the prison, 'within the rules' technically restricting a debtor to the area of Southwark adjacent to the prison, so that he might come to terms with his creditors. In practice, the geographical restriction was very inconsistently enforced. Palmer and Walter were motivated by the desire to use Combe's proven writing and editing talents on behalf of their own patron, Pitt. Combe was soon contributing essays on various political and social subjects to Walter's logographic newspaper.

Combe also worked on more substantial works for Walter's press until its closure in 1792, including its most ambitious publication, a new edition, in 1789, of the work commonly referred to as Adam Anderson's *History of Commerce*, first published in 1764. Combe researched and wrote the more than 700 pages of volume 4, which brought the *History* up to the present, and he dedicated the work, 'by permission', to William Pitt. For the first time, Combe included his own name on the subscription list. By the end of 1788 Combe was on the Treasury payroll, earning £200 per year from Pitt for such pro-ministerial writings during the Regency crisis and in the aftermath of the French Revolution as his *Letter from a Country Gentleman to a Member of Parliament on the Present State of Public Affairs* (1789), *History of* the Late Important Period; from the Beginning of his Majesty's Illness (1789), and Word in Season to the Traders and Manufacturers of Great Britain (1792).

Combe was not financially dependent solely on government patronage, however. In March 1790 he published The Devil upon Two Sticks in England, an artistically and commercially successful satiric narrative in four volumes, with two more published the following year. Sections of this episodic novel, in which the devil Asmodeus introduces his pupil, Don Cleofas, to a survey of the full range of English society, had first appeared in Walter's Daily Universal Register in 1787.

Combe the historian Combe also capitalized on his success as a historian, receiving commissions to write, edit, translate, and ghost-write many other works, including his History of the Late Important Period (1789), John Meare's Voyages Made in the Years 1788 and 1789, from China to the North West Coast of America (1791), Aeneas Anderson's A Narrative of the British Embassy to China, in the Years 1792, 1793, and 1794 (1795), Charles Grant's History of Mauritius (1802), and Alexander Mackenzie's Voyages from Montreal … to the Frozen and Pacific Oceans; in the Years 1789 and 1793 (1802). Combe's modern biographer Harlan Hamilton estimates that between his government stipend and his private commissions Combe must have been earning annually at least £500 during the early 1790s. By the end of 1794 he was living on Craven Hill, Paddington, near Kensington Gardens, and had a horse and servant.

A major source of Combe's income came from a commission he was given in 1792, soon after Walter closed down the Logographic Press. The artists, engravers, and art dealers John Boydell and his nephew Josiah, proprietors of the Shakspeare Gallery in Pall Mall, hired Combe to write the text to accompany the illustrations engraved from the drawings by Joseph Farington, the artist and diarist, for a projected multi-volume The Picturesque Views and Scenery of the Thames and the Severn, the Forth and the Clyd, from their Sources to the Sea, illustrated with hand-coloured aquatints. The work progressed more slowly than the publishers had promised, with the first two (and ultimately only) volumes of the work, now renamed An History of the Principal Rivers of Great Britain, appearing in 1794 and 1796. Although the volumes display painstaking and time-consuming research in archival sources, Farington was probably correct in thinking that paying Combe by the week slowed the work's production: Combe received £364 for the first volume, and £200 for the second. But Combe's progress must also have been slowed by other projects he undertook at the same time. He edited Humphry Repton's Letter to Uvedale Price (1794) and Sketches and Hints on Landscape Gardening (1795) and Miss A. E. Booth's two-volume translation of C. B. E. Naubert's German novel Alf von Deulmen, or, The History of the Emperor Philip, and his Daughters (1794), and wrote the anonymous Letter to a Retired Officer (1796).

The Boydell commission brought Combe into contact with the leading artists of the day, their patrons, and other celebrities he met at the gallery, as well as on his tours throughout Britain to choose scenes for Farington to sketch. For example, on his visit to Nuneham Park, home of George Simon, second Earl Harcourt, he met the famous actress Sarah Siddons. Farington records that Combe dined at various times with the artists Benjamin West and Maria and Richard Cosway, the latter one of Combe's oldest friends. Combe's portrait was drawn by George Dance in 1793 and painted by James Northcote in 1798. When George III learned from Farington that Combe was the author of the texts of An History of the Principal Rivers and the Diaboliad, he pronounced him 'a clever man'.

Domestic and financial troubles At the height of his prosperity Combe startled his friends by eloping in early 1795 with Charlotte Hadfield, Maria Cosway's sister and twenty years his junior, who had been living with the Cosways. Despite their claim to have been married on 28 January 1795, no record has been found of the marriage, which would have been illegal anyway because Combe's first wife was still alive. She died in 1814 in Casey's madhouse, and Combe paid for her burial. After living briefly in Knightsbridge, Combe and Charlotte leased a house and garden near Harrow for £40 a year. A comment Combe made later in life indicates that he and Charlotte adopted a daughter at some time before he was again imprisoned for debt four years after their elopement. Charlotte moved to Ireland shortly thereafter. Although they never again lived together, they maintained a correspondence, and always identified themselves as husband and wife. They also maintained their friendships with the Cosways, especially Maria. At Combe's death, however, the biography of Richard Cosway he promised Maria he would write was barely begun.

Combe's financial situation declined even more rapidly than it had improved. Perhaps even at its height he had been living beyond his means. But about 1796, according to Farington, Combe's government stipend stopped, at a time of great economic stress in England because of the war with France. The Boydells were unable to continue publishing Rivers because all their capital was committed to the paintings and engravings for their 1802 edition of Shakespeare. Combe scrambled to cover costs, doing hack work such as writing sermons and assisting James Colnett in producing his privately printed Voyage to the South Atlantic and Round Cape Horn into the Pacific Ocean (1799). He even proposed himself as a candidate for the position of professor of history in the Royal Academy in 1798, but he failed to be nominated. Debts owed to his tailor, harpsichord makers, the painter George Romney, the madhouse keeper Stephen Casey, and others, led to Combe's arrest on 4 May 1799 for just over £350.

Hack work for both John Debrett and John Wright enabled Combe to gain permission to live again 'within the rules' by February 1800 and rent an apartment from a Mrs Ryves at 12 Lambeth Road, London. There he quickly published translations of several lengthy works to exploit popular interest in Napoleon's recent military activities: History of the Campaigns of Count Alexander Suworow Rymnikski (1799, from the original by Friedrich Anthing), Memoir of the Operations of the Army of the Danube (1799, Jean-Baptiste Jourdan), Travels in Upper and Lower Egypt (1800,

C. N. S. Sonnini de Manoncourt), *Official Correspondence* (1800, Congress of Rastadt), and *Report of the Commission of Arts … on the Antiquities of Upper Egypt* (1800, Louis-Medeleine Ripault).

During the same period Combe also published his *Brief Observations on a Late Letter Addressed to the Right Hon. W. Pitt* (1801), probably hoping to regain a political patron. When Pitt was succeeded as prime minister by Henry Addington, Viscount Sidmouth, in March 1801, Combe quickly applied to Addington for employment as a ministerial propagandist, but was politely rejected with a payment of £100. Combe was re-hired, however, when Pitt resumed office in 1804 and remained on the government payroll at £200 per year until Pitt's death in January 1806, though he was never able to collect the last £100 owed him.

'Old Combe' Combe resumed his career as a periodical editor when Colonel Henry Francis Greville employed him to produce the weekly newspaper *Pic Nic* in January 1803, and later that year its successor, *The Cabinet*. Greville started the papers in response to the opposition of Richard Brinsley Sheridan, manager of the licensed Drury Lane Theatre, to private, unlicensed, theatrical performances staged by Greville's Pic Nic Society. *Pic Nic* and *The Cabinet* introduced the practice of unbiased drama reviewing. Besides editing, Combe also contributed pro-ministerial essays, a sonnet on Samuel Johnson, and more forged Sterne letters. By the time *The Cabinet* folded in 1803, Combe had already been hired by John Walter's son, John Walter II, as supervising editor and sometime contributor to rescue the failing *Times*, a position he held until 1808. Combe wrote many of the leading articles, including the pro-government series of letters signed 'Valerius', subsequently collected and published as *The letters of Valerius, on the state of parties, the war, the volunteer system, and most of the political topics which have lately been under public discussion* (1804). Among the colleagues of 'Old Combe', as he was now commonly known, was Henry Crabb Robinson, who joined the newspaper in 1807.

Combe's duties at *The Times* and his desire for society necessitated his frequent breaking of the 'rules' of the prison, leading inevitably to his arrest on 28 June 1808 for their violation. Until mid-1812 he was restricted by the 'day rules', which required him to return to the prison by nightfall each day. His income enabled him to afford one of the best private rooms in the prison's state house. To maintain appearances he continued to use his Lambeth Road quarters as his mailing address.

Throughout his varying degrees of incarceration, Combe retained his wide circle of friends, including a number of much younger women. One relationship led to the somewhat embarrassing posthumous publication in 1823 of *Letters to Marianne. By William Combe, Esq.*, which contains a silhouette of Combe prefacing his sentimental and platonic correspondence between 1806 and 1809 with Marianne Brooke, a young seamstress.

Doctor Syntax and final years In Combe's last years most of his income came from his relationship with Rudolph Ackermann, an art dealer and publisher whose Repository

of Art, at 101 Strand, rivalled the Boydells' Shakspeare Gallery. In 1809 Ackermann hired Combe to write the letterpress to accompany the last volume of the very successful three-volume *Microcosm of London*. Thomas Rowlandson designed the figures, and Augustus Charles Pugin the architectural details. Working with Ackermann's staff of artists, Combe wrote the texts for illustrated histories, of varying degrees of reliability, entitled *Westminster Abbey* (1812), *York* (1813), *Oxford* (1814), *Cambridge* (1815), *Colleges of Winchester, Eton, and Westminster* (1816), and *Madeira* (1821). For other publishers he provided the letterpress for *The Thames, or, Graphic Illustrations* (1811), *Picturesque Views on the Southern Coast of England* (1826), and *Pompeii* (1827). In addition Combe wrote for Ackermann's *Poetical Magazine* (1809–11) and his *Repository of Arts, Literature, Commerce, Manufactures, Fashions, and Politics*.

But most importantly, Ackermann published Combe's letterpress for Rowlandson's illustrations that resulted in the series of comic poetry for which Combe is still most famous, and which earned him his best-known nickname, Doctor Syntax: *The Tour of Doctor Syntax, in Search of the Picturesque* and its two sequels (1812, 1820, 1821), *The English Dance of Death* (1815, 1816), *The Dance of Life* (1817), and *The History of Johnny Quae Genus, the Little Foundling of the Late Doctor Syntax* (1822). Combining light-hearted satire of William Gilpin's theory of the picturesque in art with a central character modelled on Cervantes' Don Quixote and Henry Fielding's Parson Adams, Combe created a lovable eccentric whose misadventures on the road structure the *Tour*. For over a century the many editions and numerous imitations of the *Tour* attested to the popularity of Combe's humorous hero.

No matter how much Combe earned from his various publications, however, he always spent more. He died, still in debt, at his Lambeth Road address on 19 June 1823. The obituary in *The Times* the next day stated that:

> [h]e was a gentleman who, in the course of this protracted life, had suffered many fortunes, and had become known … to so many people in every rank of society, that it hardly seems necessary to draw his character … There was hardly a person of any note in his time, with whose history he was not in some degree acquainted.

The Sun, edited by his friend John Taylor, observed that:

> The Life of Mr. Coombe [sic], if impartially written, would be pregnant with amusement and instruction; but those whose literary contributions might have provided interesting materials, are probably most of them with him in the grave; and he will hereafter be chiefly remembered as the Author of Doctor Syntax.

Less than two weeks before his death, at the request of Ackermann, Combe compiled a list of seventy-five titles of his works. The *Gentleman's Magazine* published the list in 1824 and 1852. Unfortunately, Combe, who always guarded his personal history, never wrote the autobiography he had repeatedly projected. An undischarged debtor, he was buried on 22 June 1823 at the church of St George the Martyr, Southwark, just south of the king's bench prison.   VINCENT CARRETTA

Sources W. Hamilton, *Doctor Syntax: silhouette of William Combe, esq. (1742–1823)* (1969) • *GM*, 1st ser., 94/2 (1824), 643 • R. Cole, 'William Coombe and his works', *GM*, 2nd ser., 37 (1852), 467–72 • Farington, *Diary* • Walpole, *Corr.* • *Diary, reminiscences, and correspondence of Henry Crabb Robinson*, ed. T. Sadler, 3 vols. (1869) • *The Times* (20 June 1823)
Archives BL, Add. MSS 29300; 44740, fol. 313; 30262, fols. 82, 84; 71584; 71585 • BL, notebooks compiled while in debtors' prison, deposit 9426 • Bodl. Oxf., MS Curzon b.5, fol. 182 • Bodl. Oxf., MS Montagu d.3, fols. 101–3 • CUL, Add. MS 8274 • Harvard U. • Hunt. L., MSS HM 3166, 7260, 59542–59543, Ms. JE 243 • Morgan L. • Wordsworth Trust, Dove Cottage, Grasmere, Stranger autographs, vol. 3 | Hunt. L., Ms. JE 245 • NYPL, Berg collection • PRO, 30/8/229, fol. 152 • PRO, Discharges, Pris. 7/7 • PRO, K.B. 122/518, no. 1291 • PRO, K.B. 122/790, no. 1057 • PRO, K.B. Commitment Book, no. 10 • PRO, King's Bench Commitment Book, no. 16, s.v. Combe • PRO, Plea Roll, K.B. 122/177, no. 1753 • PRO, Plea Roll, K.B. 122/723, no. 1064 • PRO, Pris. 5/1 • PRO, Pris. 10/201 • U. Newcastle, White papers, miscellaneous album
Likenesses G. Dance, pencil drawing, 1793, NPG [*see illus.*] • silhouette, *c.*1800, BM • portrait, Bodl. Oxf., MS Montagu d.3, fols. 101–3

Comber, Thomas (1575–1654), college head and dean of Carlisle, was born at Shermanbury, Sussex, on 1 January 1575, the twelfth child of John Comber (*d.* 1608), barrister, and his wife, Jane (formerly Dunstall). From a public school at Horsham he matriculated as a pensioner at Trinity College, Cambridge, in 1592 and was elected to a scholarship in the following year. He graduated BA in 1595, was elected to a fellowship in 1597, and took his MA in 1598. Subsequently he went abroad for three years and is known to have spent some time at the home of the French reformed theologian Pierre du Moulin, presumably in Charenton. His travels over, he returned to Trinity, to which he was to devote most of the rest of his life. He held office as both junior and senior dean and senior bursar; he proceeded BD in 1609 and DD in 1616.

An outstanding scholar, Comber was well versed in Hebrew, Arabic, Coptic, Samaritan, Syriac, Chaldee, Persian, Greek, and Latin, in addition to having a colloquial knowledge of French, Spanish, and Italian, and was the author of Greek and Latin verses on the death of William Whitaker, published in 1610. A dispute with some Jesuits appears to have confirmed his rising reputation and he was invited by James I to dispute publicly at St Andrews with some Scottish divines. On 26 June 1615 he was instituted to the rectory of Worplesdon, Surrey. Presented to the deanery of Carlisle on 28 August 1629, on 1 November that year he was admitted chaplain-in-extraordinary to Charles I. The same year he married Susan Cotton, a widow, at Kingston in Cambridgeshire; they had one child, Mary.

In October 1631, helped by the patronage of the earl of Portland, Comber became master of Trinity College, Cambridge, where he distinguished himself with a reputation for good scholarship and impartiality. He published some Latin letters in 1633, and is deservedly identified as one of the few who refused to side with either of the two factions which dominated the life of the university in the 1630s. None the less, the college chapel in Trinity was elaborately decorated and reordered during his mastership. He served as vice-chancellor in 1631 and again in 1636.

During the 1640s Comber was ejected from all his preferments and imprisoned for assisting in sending the university plate to the king, and for refusing the covenant. He died in Cambridge on 28 February 1654 and was buried on 3 March in St Botolph's Church, Cambridge, without a tombstone; his wife survived him. His funeral sermon, preached in Trinity College chapel by Robert Boreman, was later published under the title of *The Triumph of Faith over Death, or, The Just Man's Memoriall* (1654). A portrait in Trinity shows Comber with a beard and moustache, and what Trevelyan describes as kindly and jovial features.

DAVID HOYLE

Sources R. Boreman, *The triumph of faith over death* (1654) • D. Lloyd, *Memoires of the lives … of those … personages that suffered … for the protestant religion* (1668) • *Querula Cantabrigiensis* (1647) • J. Comber, *Sussex genealogies*, 3 vols. (1931–3), vol. 1 • W. W. Rouse Ball and J. A. Venn, eds., *Admissions to Trinity College, Cambridge*, 2 (1913) • *Walker rev.* • G. M. Trevelyan, *Trinity College: a historical sketch* (1943) • J. B. Mullinger, *The University of Cambridge*, 3 (1911) • J. Twigg, *The University of Cambridge and the English Revolution, 1625–1688* (1990) • J. Walker, *An attempt towards recovering an account of the numbers and sufferings of the clergy of the Church of England*, 2 pts in 1 (1714) • T. Comber, *Memoirs of Thomas Comber* (1799) • PRO, LC5/132, p. 146
Likenesses oils, Trinity Cam.

Comber, Thomas (1645–1699), dean of Durham and liturgist, was born on 19 March 1645 at Westerham, Kent, and baptized at the parish church on 23 March, the fourth of the five children of James Comber (*bap.* 1615, *d.* 1671), a member of the Cutlers' Company of London, and his wife, Mary (*bap.* 1617, *d.* 1672), daughter of Brian Burton, yeoman of Westerham. Apart from Thomas, only his older brother James survived to adulthood, although Mary, a daughter by their mother's first marriage, to Edward Hamden (*d.* 1639), also survived to maturity. Comber later made great play of the fact that he was the last child to be baptized at Westerham according to the prayer book rite before it was outlawed. His family were royalists: his maternal grandfather had had his property sequestered and his father found it necessary to flee to Flanders, only returning in 1649. These experiences no doubt cast a shadow over the life of the sickly Thomas as he grew up, lending a vividness to the many references to the horrors of the civil war which punctuate his later writings.

At four, when he could barely walk, Comber was sent to a local elementary school, before moving on at six to the Revd Thomas Walter's school in Westerham, where he learned Latin and Greek. From 1653 he alternated between attendance at Sevenoaks grammar school and a school kept by John Evans on Tower Hill, his life being threatened by bouts of severe illness. From 1656 Comber found himself back in the much more congenial care of Walter, with whom he remained until the latter's death in February 1658. He was by then ready to go to university but his admission, to Sidney Sussex College, Cambridge, was delayed by a year until 18 April 1659, on the advice of William Holland, vicar of Westerham. With the encouragement of his tutor, Edmund Matthews, the senior fellow of the college, Comber's studies at Sidney Sussex were wide ranging, covering scientific subjects as well as music, painting, and oriental languages. But his time at Cambridge was only sustained with the help of a variety of charitable benefactions and, perhaps prematurely discounting his chances of a fellowship, he left in 1663, having graduated BA in January that year.

Comber's academic career may have foundered but his clerical one took off shortly afterwards and continued at a precocious pace. He was ordained deacon on 18 August 1663, aged only eighteen, in order to help out William Holland, who had moved on from Westerham to be rector of All Hallows, Staining, but after barely six weeks, he was on his way to Stonegrave in the North Riding of Yorkshire to serve as curate there, at the behest of the absentee incumbent Gilbert Bennett. The archbishop of York, Richard Sterne, completed Comber's whirlwind induction to the ministry by ordaining him priest on 25 September 1664, an uncanonical move, given his youth, which Sterne, on his own account, never regretted. Even at this early age, Comber was a ready, almost extempore preacher, although his fame was to come from his formidable output as a liturgical writer and Church of England polemicist. Physically Comber was of medium stature, with light brown curly hair and blue eyes.

In March 1665 Comber moved to nearby East Newton Hall, the seat of the Thorntons, a local gentry family to whom he acted as chaplain alongside his parochial duties at Stonegrave. At the end of 1666 he became domestic chaplain to Lord Freschville, a relation of Mrs Thornton, who proved a loyal patron to Comber. He maintained his close relationship with the Thornton family, courting and marrying Alice Thornton (1654–1721) on 17 November 1668, in a secret ceremony at East Newton Hall, in the face of opposition from some members of her wider family; they had four sons and two daughters. In 1669, thanks to his recently acquired patrons, Comber succeeded to the living of Stonegrave on the king's presentation in place of the incumbent, who had been persuaded to resign.

From this secure base Comber now embarked upon his writing career. In the summer of 1672 he published the first part of what was undoubtedly his greatest work, *A Companion to the Temple and the Closet*, a detailed commentary on the Book of Common Prayer designed to promote its public and private devotional use. It was to prove a massive and enduring monument: the 1841 edition ran to seven volumes, the shortest of which is 366 pages long, and it had a wide readership and influence among clergy and laity within Comber's own lifetime. It was hardly a work of detached scholarship, beginning to appear as it did while Charles II's declaration of indulgence was in force and peppered as it was with polemical asides against both Rome and protestant dissent. Nevertheless, Comber felt it necessary to indulge in more directly polemical works against these twin threats. In 1674 he published anonymously the somewhat inaptly named *Friendly and Seasonable Advice to the Roman Catholics of England*, which had its origins in conversations with Lord Fauconberg, whom certain Roman Catholics had been seeking to convert. In 1677 Comber attacked the Quakers in *The Right of*

Tithes Asserted and Proved from Divine Institution (1677), following this up with a wider attack on Quaker views, as advocated by Thomas Ellwood in *Christianity No Enthusiasm* (1678); both were published anonymously.

Partly through his writings and partly through his family connections (Mrs Thornton was a cousin of Lord Treasurer Danby), Comber was looked on with growing favour at court, becoming a prebendary of York in 1677 and a doctor of divinity at Archbishop Sancroft's behest in June 1678. On 11 February 1679 the combined efforts of Danby and lords Freschville and Fauconberg finally secured for Comber the living of Thornton-le-Dale, some 10 miles from Stonegrave, which Sancroft granted him a dispensation to hold in plurality. In April Comber was elected proctor in convocation for the archdeaconry of Cleveland. Finally, in May 1679, he was received at court by Princess Anne, who had read the third part of his *A Companion to the Temple and the Closet* in preparation for her first communion (in 1682 she would make him one of her chaplains).

With his court connections and his polemical bent, it is not surprising that Comber should go into print for the tory cause in the exclusion crisis, publishing in the summer of 1681, again anonymously, *Religion and Loyalty Supporting each other*, a tract which defended the loyal addresses then flooding into Whitehall and bitterly attacked whig constitutional and historical arguments. Next Comber turned his attention to 'the enemy within'— those churchmen who failed to give the Church of England their full support—clashing angrily with Gilbert Burnet on the subject of tithes, both in print and in private correspondence. John Tillotson, a long-standing friend of Comber, was among those who sought to mediate and at least when Comber published the second part of his *Historical Vindication of the Divine Right of Tithes* in 1685 it contained no personal references to Burnet, though this owed as much to Dr George Hickes and Dr William Cave as to Tillotson.

In October 1683 Comber was made precentor of York at the behest of John Dolben, the new archbishop, and for the next two and a half years he worked hand in glove with him to reform the minster. According to Dr Henry Watkinson, the chancellor of York diocese, Comber was as good as an extra archdeacon in the place. Dolben's early death in April 1686 and the two-and-a-half year vacancy that followed were blows to Comber, compounding the crisis of James II's abandonment of the tories and promotion of Catholicism. He had a prominent role in the opposition to the king's policies in and around York, in 1688 being ejected from the commission of the peace for his pains. He rallied to the revolution, taking the opportunity to renew his connection with Danby, who acted as godfather to his second son, Thomas, while in York following the seizure of the city. If Comber would have preferred a different constitutional settlement from the one that emerged, he gave no hint of it and very soon set to work defending the new regime in print. Former friends such as Dean Granville of Durham became nonjurors but Comber showed no sign of following them. In fact, Granville's departure gave him a long-looked-for promotion when he succeeded him as dean in 1691, in part thanks to the patronage of Danby (now Carmarthen). Comber was also made chaplain-in-ordinary to William and Mary in 1692.

His twentieth-century editor, Whiting, designates Comber a whig on the basis of his post-1688 career (Whiting, 2.xii). In his writings Comber certainly moved a long way from his uncompromising toryism of the early 1680s. For example, although he probably did not write *A Letter to a Bishop Concerning the Present Settlement and the New Oaths* (1689), in subsequent correspondence he did defend the work, which stated that the crown was one of the three estates in England, a position Comber had roundly rejected in *Religion and Loyalty Supporting each other* as leading to rebellion. Nevertheless, many of his former attitudes—his extreme deference for Charles I, his bitter hatred of parliamentarianism, his regard for Charles II, and his suspicion of protestant dissent—survived his change of allegiance intact (as in *A Discourse on the Offices for the Vth November, XXXth January and XXIXth May*, 1696; Bodleian Library, MS Tanner 27, fol. 93). Whiting also notes Comber's 'diligent search for preferment' throughout his career (Whiting, 2.x). He was certainly a long-term pluralist (and a self-righteous one at that), who never seemed to be satisfied with what he had and whose cures were not necessarily well served in his absence. Whether he was untypical of the aspiring churchmen of his generation, however, seems open to doubt. Comber died of consumption on 25 November 1699 at East Newton and was buried at Stonegrave parish church, on 30 November.

ANDREW M. COLEBY

Sources *The autobiographies and letters of Thomas Comber, sometime precentor of York and dean of Durham*, ed. C. E. Whiting, 2 vols., SurtS, 156–7 (1946–7) · *Memoirs of the life and writings of Thomas Comber*, ed. T. Comber (1799) · T. Birch, *The life of the Most Reverend Dr John Tillotson, lord archbishop of Canterbury* (1752) · Sancroft papers, Bodl. Oxf., MSS Tanner · 'The remains of Denis Granville, DD, dean and archdeacon of Durham', ed. [G. Ornsby], *Miscellanea*, SurtS, 37 (1861) · *The remains of Denis Granville ... being a further selection from his correspondence, diaries, and other papers*, ed. [G. Ornsby], SurtS, 47 (1865) · *The autobiography of Mrs Alice Thornton*, ed. [C. Jackson], SurtS, 62 (1875) · Nichols, *Lit. anecdotes*; vols. 1–3 · *N&Q*, 2nd ser., 9 (1860), 307, 371
Archives Durham Cathedral, MSS · W. Sussex RO, papers · York Minster Library, York Minster archives, commonplace books, notes and papers | Bodl. Oxf., Tanner MSS, Sancroft MSS
Likenesses portrait, 1680, repro. in T. Comber, ed., *Memoirs of the life and writings* (1799) · G. Lumley, mezzotint, BM, NPG
Wealth at death see will, *Autobiographies ... of Thomas Comber*, ed. Whiting, vol. 1, pp. 70–75

Comber, Thomas James (1852–1887), Baptist minister and missionary to the Congo, was born on 7 November 1852 at 15 Clarendon Street, Camberwell, Surrey, the second of five children, the third of whom died in infancy, of Thomas James Comber, a manufacturing jeweller, and his first wife, Sarah Lemmett Youldon, formerly Tucker, who died in Comber's fourteenth year. Comber's parents were members of the Baptist chapel at Denmark Place, and they enrolled their son aged three in the Sunday school at Crawford Street. He subsequently attended the British School in the same building until aged twelve, when he began to work in his father's workshop. At fifteen he

enrolled in evening classes at Spurgeon's College, Stockwell, London, and after his baptism at Denmark Place Chapel in 1868 he became a Sunday school teacher. He aspired to be a missionary, and so studied at the Baptist college, Regent's Park, London, from 1871 to 1875. While a student he held weekly children's services at Camden Road Chapel, between 1874 and 1876, demonstrating a particular gift for working with the young. The Baptist Missionary Society (BMS) accepted him in April 1875 and assigned him to a year of medical training at University College, London, for service in Africa. After his medical studies he sailed from Liverpool on the SS *Ethiopia* on 4 November 1876 and arrived at the BMS station at Victoria in the Cameroons on 5 December. Comber served in the Cameroons until 1878, preaching, providing medical care, and exploring the interior as far as Bakundu.

Robert Arthington (1823–1900) of Headingley, Leeds, though not himself a Baptist, was a leading supporter of Baptist missions. Unmarried, miserly, reclusive, and eccentric, he had inherited from his father, a Quaker malster and brewer, a fortune which he increased by careful investment. He believed Christ's second advent awaited only the fulfilment of the command to evangelize all nations. In 1877, at the time of H. M. Stanley's much-publicized transcontinental expedition, he offered the BMS £1000 to pay for a mission on the Congo River. The BMS accepted and in January 1878 commissioned Comber and the Revd George Grenfell to survey the lower Congo. They travelled by trading steamer down the coast. Comber criticized the trade—in rum, gin, and gunpowder—and the traders: he wrote, 'Oh! it is awful the amount of corruption and filth introduced by Europeans' (Myers, *Comber*, 71). Comber and Grenfell made a preliminary, three-week visit to the lower Congo region. They returned to be received by the king of Kongo, Dom Pedro V, at San Salvador on 8 August 1878. They proceeded into Makuta territory as far as Tungwa, where the principal Makuta chief forbade their advance. They returned to San Salvador, from which Comber returned to England in November to make arrangements for further exploration. He read a paper before the Royal Geographical Society on 10 February 1879, and was elected FRGS on 24 March.

The BMS authorized Comber to return to the Congo to establish a mission station at San Salvador, in anticipation of further evangelical expansion, and before he left he married at Westbourne Park Baptist Chapel, Paddington, on 2 April 1879, Marianne Amy (Minnie; *b.* 1853/4), the daughter of his Sunday school teacher, Samuel David Rickards. The couple reached the Congo in June 1879 with a missionary party that included H. E. Crudgington, W. Holman Bentley, and John S. Hartland. Comber promptly established the BMS station at San Salvador and prepared to travel along the south bank of the Congo to Stanley Pool, the beginning of the navigable upper river. Tragically, Minnie Comber died on 24 August 1879, apparently of cerebral malaria, though Hartland wrote that 'she died of meningitis ... brought on by bad news from home' (Myers, *Comber*, 91). Comber and Hartland none the less set out a week later in the first of thirteen unsuccessful attempts to reach Stanley Pool. During one of these in late 1880, Comber was shot in the back at Mbanza Makuta while fleeing from attack by men of a local village. Comber's colleagues Bentley and Crudgington were the first to reach Stanley Pool, on 29 January 1881, via a route along the river's north bank.

Comber established a mission station at Isangila and a supply depot at Musuka in 1881. In the next year he established a BMS station at Stanley Pool. On 7 July 1884 he and Grenfell set out from Stanley Pool on the mission steamer *Peace* (her purchase and maintenance paid by Robert Arthington), and explored the Kwa, Kwango, and Kasai rivers. Comber returned to England between January and August 1885. He spoke at Exeter Hall, read another paper to the Royal Geographical Society, and wrote a manual for Congo missionaries. Following his return to the Congo, his Congolese servant, William Mantu Parkinson, was the first BMS convert to be baptized, on 29 March 1886.

Practical, hard-working, and energetic—his Kikongo name was Vianga Vianga ('Hurry Hurry')—Comber was not considered a particularly gifted theologian or preacher. He, like others, saw exploration as a crucial part of missionary activity. Like other missionaries he accepted a practical co-operation with the authorities of Leopold II's International Association and subsequent Congo Free State (CFS), in a period before the rubber atrocities made it notorious. However, in February 1886 he wrote to A. H. Baynes of the BMS opposing the CFS demand that the steamer *Peace* be required to carry its troops and munitions.

Comber suffered a fever and severe haematuria in June 1887, prompting his brethren to arrange his return home. He died aboard the German steamer *Lulu Bohlen* off the coast of Loango on 27 June 1887 and was buried that day on the shore of Mayumba Bay, some 200 miles north of the Congo River. Comber was survived by his father and his brother Percy, who also died a missionary to the Congo in 1892; their elder sister, Carrie, had died a missionary at Victoria, Cameroons, in 1884, and another brother, Sidney, had died a missionary to the Congo in 1885. Admired as a Christian hero, Comber was commemorated by a memorial tablet in the schoolroom of Denmark Place Baptist Chapel.   KEVIN GRANT

Sources J. B. Myers, *Thomas J. Comber: missionary pioneer to the Congo* (1888) · E. A. Payne, *The great succession: leaders of the Baptist Missionary Society during the nineteenth century* (1938) · B. Stanley, *The history of the Baptist Missionary Society, 1792–1992* (1992) · B. Stanley, 'Comber, Thomas James', *Biographical dictionary of Christian missions*, ed. G. H. Anderson (1998), 146 · R. M. Slade, *English-speaking missions in the Congo Independent State, 1878–1908* (1959) · J. B. Myers, *The century volume of the Baptist Missionary Society, 1792–1892* (1892) · 'The Congo mission: the decease of the Rev. T. J. Comber', *The Missionary Herald* (Sept 1887), 321–4 · A. Hastings, *The church in Africa, 1450–1950* (1994) · *Baptist Magazine*, 79 (1887), 481–3 · *Report of the committee of the Baptist College … at Regents Park* (1870–75) · R. E. Cooper, *From Stepney to St Giles: the story of Regent's Park College, 1810–1960* (1960) · b. cert. · m. cert.

Archives RGS, papers | Regent's Park College, Oxford, Baptist Missionary Society archive

Likenesses Debenham & Gould, photograph, repro. in Myers, *Thomas J. Comber*, frontispiece · photographs, repro. in H. Johnston, *George Grenfell and the Congo*, 1 (1908), 89, 223

Comberford, Nicholas. *See* Comerford, Nicholas (c.1540–c.1599).

Combermere. For this title name *see* Cotton, Stapleton, first Viscount Combermere (1773–1865).

Combridge, John Theodore (1897–1986), mathematician and university administrator, was born on 28 August 1897 at 5 Leopold Road, Brighton, the son of Daniel Thomas Combridge, a retired butcher, and his wife, Rhoda Rebecca Gardner. Educated at Brighton College (1912–17), he served in France as a lieutenant in the Royal Field Artillery before entering St John's College, Cambridge, in 1919. He gained a mathematics wranglership in 1921 and entered King's College, London, in 1922, gaining the MSc with distinction in 1924. By this time he had also started as a demonstrator in mathematics (1923–6) at the City Guilds Engineering College, Kensington. His lecturing career continued at King's College, London, where he served as assistant lecturer (1926–9) and lecturer (1929–37). On 30 December 1926 he married Norah Elizabeth Charlwood, a schoolteacher. They had three children in a happy marriage which was terminated by her sudden death in 1966.

Combridge's early scholarly interest in general relativity was stimulated by contact with Arthur Eddington at Cambridge and the link continued through correspondence until 1936. His own scholarly work in mathematics was largely confined to wide-ranging and meticulous bibliography. His card index, with annotation, of some 1700 papers in general relativity, was eventually published by King's College under the title *Bibliography of Relativity and Gravitation Theory, 1921–1937* (1965).

In 1937 Combridge's career took a different direction when he accepted the post of assistant secretary at King's College. He played a leading part in managing the college's wartime precautions, including the evacuation to Bristol (1939–43). In 1947 he was appointed registrar—a new position—alongside a new secretary. This division of labour, and his administrative skill, helped him also to pursue with vigour and growing influence his wider interests in the post-war development of mathematics education.

In 1930 Combridge had joined the Mathematical Association, an influential organization involving secondary school and university teachers. He was soon active in the association's committee work and major report production, becoming chairman of its teaching committee (1950–56). During his chairmanship the association published authoritative reports on the teaching of trigonometry (1950), calculus (1951), and higher geometry (1953), for which he acted as a writer. He later played a major part in the production of a report on the teaching of mechanics (1965). He served on the association's council, acted as a trustee, and became president (1961–2) in the year of his retirement from King's College.

During his early 'retirement' Combridge continued to

work tirelessly for both the association and the advancement of British mathematics education. He was an energetic chairman of the schools and industry committee (1963–72), which, with sponsorship from industry, organized industrial placements for mathematics teachers, and promoted the development of 'numeracy' in a broad sense, notably through a publication edited by Combridge, *Count me in: Numeracy in Education* (1968). He also played a significant part in the establishment of both the Joint Mathematical Council of the United Kingdom (1962) and the Institute of Mathematics and its Applications (1963).

Through his work for the Mathematical Association Combridge met his second wife, another schoolteacher, Winifred Adelaide Cooke. They both contributed strongly to the work for the association's centenary in 1971; he became the unofficial historian and archivist. They married on 22 April 1972 and shared their retirement in St Albans until Winifred's death in 1986.

Combridge was widely respected both at King's College and in the Mathematical Association, not only for his administrative skill but also for his unswerving loyalty, integrity, inspiring leadership, and sympathetic support for all sectors of the teaching profession. His very sharp but kind sense of humour helped to enliven many committee meetings and social gatherings. He died of old age, two months after his wife, on 10 December 1986 at 18 Alexandra Road, Watford, and was buried on 17 December at St Peter's Church, St Albans. MICHAEL H. PRICE

Sources *Bulletin of the London Mathematical Society*, 20 (1988), 156–9 · *Mathematical Gazette*, 71 (1987), 307–9 · biographical archive sheet, St John Cam. · G. Huelin, *King's College, London, 1828–1978* (1978) · M. H. Price, *Mathematics for the multitude? A history of the Mathematical Association* (1994) · personal knowledge (2004) · b. cert. · d. cert. · m. certs. · Mathematical Association membership lists, Mathematical Association archives, 259 London Road, Leicester
Archives 259 London Road, Leicester, Mathematical Association archives · King's Lond., research notes
Likenesses photograph, repro. in *Mathematical Gazette*, 46 (1962), 179 · photograph (after a photograph, repro. in *Mathematical Gazette* (1962)), repro. in *Bulletin of the London Mathematical Society*, 159
Wealth at death £293,411: probate, 1987, *CGPLA Eng. & Wales*

Combrune, Michael (*d.* 1773), brewer, was the fourth son among the six children of Peter de Vesis de Comberbrune (*d.* 1731) and his wife, Judith Elizabeth, daughter of Constantin de Coursy, both Huguenot refugees settled in the parish of St Anne, Westminster. Peter de Comberbrune had taken English nationality in 1701 and held the rank of major of dragoons. He left generous bequests to his sons, his wife having predeceased him; as the residuary legatee Michael Combrune inherited at least £5000 in property and stocks. Nothing is known of Combrune's education, but his father's will makes provision for the sons' being at sea, possibly in connection with the wine trade. He married, on 16 March 1742 in London, Mary Asselin, or Bayeux (*d.* 1778); they had two daughters.

Combrune was made free of the Brewers' Company by redemption on 13 May 1743. By 1746 he was the owner of a brewery and dwelling house in Pont Street, Hampstead,

near the banks of the Fleet River, and over the years he acquired many copyholds of public houses in the area. Gideon Combrune (*d.* 1787), son of his brother James, a wine merchant in Lisbon, was apprenticed to him in 1764; Gideon later became master of the Brewers' Company and owner of a brewery in Golden Lane in the City of London.

At this time, progressive brewers were beginning to adopt a more scientific approach to their art. The use of a thermometer to control the various stages in brewing and winemaking was first proposed by Combrune, in his *Essay on Brewing: some Account of the Rise, Progress and Present State of the Brewery* (1758). This book was condemned at some length for its vague and untechnical treatment in the *Gentleman's Magazine*. Perhaps in response to this attack Combrune expanded it as *The Theory and Practice of Brewing* (1762). With a commendatory preface written by his friend Peter Shaw, physician to the king and experimental scientist with an interest in chemistry, the book demonstrated a clear grasp of basic principles and how these could be profitably applied to the brewing trade. He described experiments carried out to determine the drying temperatures required to yield malts of different colours and recorded observations on mashing and fermentation temperatures, and those for each stage of winemaking.

Combrune's elder daughter, Ann Magdalen, married John Glen King FRS (1731/2–1787), chaplain to the English merchants at St Petersburg. Combrune subsequently moved to Honiton, Devon, where he died in 1773, leaving his Hampstead properties and other goods to his widow; she returned to live in Great Russell Street, Holborn, where she died in 1778. Their younger daughter, Wilhelmina, died unmarried in 1792. ANITA MCCONNELL

Sources VCH *Middlesex*, 9.125 · *GM*, 1st ser., 29 (1759), 58–61 · M. Combrune, *Essay on brewing: some account of the rise, progress and present state of the brewery* (1758) · PRO, PROB 11/984 · PRO, PROB 11/649 [P. de Vesis de Comberbrune] · H. Wagner, 'The Huguenot refugee family of Combrune', *The Genealogist*, new ser., 24 (1907–8), 194–5 · H. S. Corran, *A history of brewing* (1975), 131–2 · H. A. Monkton, *A history of English ale and beer* (1966), 138–9 · Brewers' Company admissions, GL, MS 5448 · Brewers' Company freemen, 1724–54, GL, MS 5449A

Comenius, Johannes Amos [Jan Amos Komenský] (1592–1670), theologian and educationist, was born on 28 March 1592, the only son of Martin Segeš Komenský (*d.* 1602), a burgher in Uherský Brod, and his wife, Anna (*d.* 1603). Comenius was born in Moravia, but the exact place of his birth is a matter of some debate. The village of Komna has some claims, and he would later describe himself as 'Niwniczensis', from Nivnice, as well as 'Hunnobrodensis', from Uherský Brod, where his father certainly owned a house and some land.

Early life and education Both Comenius's parents died when he was still a young child, and he was brought up by relatives at Strážnice. In May 1605, however, a marauding party of supporters of the Transylvanian insurgent, Stefan Bocskai, tried to carry the civil war into Moravia. Strážnice was burnt to the ground and a suburb of Uherský Brod was sacked. Comenius's early education was in

Loe, here an Exile who to serue his God,
Hath sharply tasted of proud Pashurs Rod,
Whose learning, Piety, & true worth beeing knowne
To all the world, makes all the world his owne,

Johannes Amos Comenius (1592–1670), by Wenceslaus Hollar, 1652

elementary schools run by the Unitas Fratrum, or Unity of Brethren, first at Uherský Brod, then at Strážnice, and finally, from 1608 to 1611, at the more eminent Gymnasium at Přerov. Whether he imbibed any distinctive intellectual attitudes from the brethren at this stage of his life may be doubted—his teachers included well-educated schoolmasters from Herborn. He himself later referred to his own uncertainties at school, which a Socinian Latin catechism circulating among his fellow students may have served only to fuel. He certainly acquired an excellent knowledge of Latin and the powerful protection of two of the leading benefactors of the brethren in Moravia—Jan Lanecius (Lánecký), senior of the brethren, and Charles (the elder) of Žerotín (Karel Starší z. Žerotín), who had himself studied in Strasbourg and Basel, and under Beza at Geneva. Destined for the ministry in the brethren, Comenius was given the biblical name Amos and dispatched to complete his education at Herborn in 1611. The Calvinist academy in the county of Nassau had already earned itself an impressive reputation as an eclectic and innovative Calvinist educational centre. The paedagogiarch (head teacher) of the first class in the Gymnasium and extraordinary professor of philosophy when Comenius arrived there was Johann Heinrich Alsted. His senior, the professor of theology in the academy, was the biblical exegete from Strasbourg Johannes Fischer (Piscator). During his two years at Herborn, Comenius soaked up Alsted's objectives and methods, and would integrate them into his own. Alsted had already published (in his *Panacea philosophica* of 1610) a brief encapsulation of his aim. He perceived this as a harmonizing of Aristotelian and Ramist principles with Lullian mnemonics, by which he aspired to structure a 'universal encyclopaedia'. Human nature before the fall, the *imago Dei,* had been perfect, and philosophical knowledge had been acquired effortlessly. With the fall, the image of God in man's mind had been destroyed and so had mankind's natural mental dexterity. But what nature could no longer provide might be restored by art. This art, or method, involved strengthening memory, logic, and language so that, when applied across the whole spectrum of knowledge in an educative framework, a universal reformation (or 'instauratio imaginis Dei') would be begun and the coming millennium advanced.

After a brief visit to Amsterdam in 1613, Comenius completed his formal studies at Heidelberg University. A letter of recommendation from Piscator enabled him to study for a year with David Wängler (Pareus). It is now thought that Pareus's earlier attempts to reconcile the confessional differences between protestant churches had no influence on Comenius. In the spring of 1614 Comenius returned by foot to Moravia to become a pastor and headmaster back in Přerov. Two years later he was ordained pastor to the Unity of Brethren, and in 1618 he was promoted head teacher of its school in the north Moravian town of Fulnek. There, on 19 June 1618, he married Magdalena Vizovská (*d.* 1622).

Exile and early works By 1618 the crisis in the Bohemia polity that conventionally marks the beginning of the Thirty Years' War had begun to unfold. Comenius reluctantly sided with the confederate estates and welcomed the arrival of the king that they had newly elected to the Bohemian throne, Frederick of the Palatinate. He came to regard the resulting unsuccessful insurrection as an ill-considered response to calculated provocation. But with the disastrous defeat of the confederate forces at the White Mountain near Prague on 8 November 1620, the cause was lost. Fulnek was burned in June 1621, and in December the pastorate of the Unity of the Brethren was expelled from Moravia. Comenius sheltered on the estates of Charles the elder in eastern Bohemia, while his wife and their two sons died of plague the following year in Přerov; his books were publicly burnt in the town square at Fulnek in May 1623. In September 1624 he married Marie Dorota (Dorothy) Cyrillová (*d.* 1648), the daughter of the brethren's senior, Jan Cyrill. The latter had placed the crown on Frederick's head and was at the heart of the network of Bohemian political outcasts and expatriates, such as the Sádovský of Sloupno. It was on the Sádovský estates at Bílá Třemešná that Comenius sheltered when he was not travelling to Poland, Brandenburg, and the exiled Palatinate court in the Netherlands in support of the brethren. In February 1628 he moved with some of the expatriate brethren to Leszno in Poland, a town close to

Bohemian lands and under the protection of the tolerant Leszczyński family. There he became a teacher at the local Gymnasium, and at their synod of October 1632 the brethren made him a senior and its secretary.

Comenius's early works have only partly survived; those that we know about reflect both the influence of Alsted and the turbulent environment in which they were written. An early textbook, *Grammaticae facilioris praecepta* ('Precepts for understanding grammar more easily'), printed in Prague in 1616, and other works, on the antiquities of Moravia and the history of the Žerotín family, have not survived. Ambitious projects to produce a dictionary of the Bohemian language (*Thesaurus linguae Bohemicae*) and a universal encyclopaedia (*Theatrum universitatis rerum* and *Theatrum divinum*) were interrupted. Only his *Labyrint světa a ráj srdce* ('The labyrinth of the world and the paradise of the heart'), a masterpiece of Czech literature (written in the early 1620s), and the *Truchlivý* ('Sorrowful') (written in 1623–4) adequately measure Comenius's potential to use late Renaissance humanist learning as a means to register the gulf between human follies and capacities for good.

In the late 1620s and early 1630s Comenius worked on and completed the Czech version of the *Didactics*, his first major statement on the objectives, scope, and organization of a universal educational system. He envisaged a progression in six-year stages from elementary schooling (in the vernacular and at the parish level) through secondary schools (in Latin and organized in urban centres) to higher education in academies (in provincial capitals). The process was to be based on discipline without force, and aimed to draw on the innate interest of the learner through games and interactive learning. New textbooks would be required at every level in order to support the far-reaching reform of learning that was envisaged. After 1632 Comenius abandoned any immediate hopes of returning to Czech lands, and turned to translating the *Didactics* into Latin—it would finally see the light of day in print only as part of his *Opera didactica omnia* (Amsterdam, 1657)—and producing the textbooks that would be required for his reformed pedagogy. The latter would turn out to be his greatest success and enduring legacy. That on the teaching of Latin, the *Janua linguarum reserata* ('The gateway of languages opened'; 1631), was Comenius's reaction to a traditional language textbook compiled by William Bathe in Salamanca in 1611 under the title *Janua linguarum*. Comenius abandoned elaborate memorization of texts in favour of a direct explanation and interpretation of vocabulary, drawing on the relevant experience of daily life and examples from the physical world. This was followed by an even more elementary textbook for the beginner, first published in Leszno in 1632, the *Vestibulum januae linguarum* ('The antechamber of languages'). These regularly reprinted works earned Comenius his wider reputation. He began corresponding with important figures in the precocious world of German schooling—Johann Mochinger in Danzig, Johan Docemius in Kassel and Hamburg, and Abraham Pöhmer in Nuremberg. Czech exiles and the millenarian Paul Felgenhauer also took a great interest in his work. However, Johann Valentin Andreae, whose utopian endeavours have often been compared with Comenius's, proved unresponsive to Comenius's attempts to engage in dialogue. And behind these publications lay a grander project for a *Janua rerum* ('Gateway of things'), an encyclopaedia of the physical world that would put into practice a method capable of uniting our understanding of the physical world with that of God. Borrowing a word already coined by Peter Lauremberg (Laurembergius), Comenius termed this *pansophia* ('pansophy').

Comenius and England Comenius's influence in England should not be overestimated. As in Germany, it began with republished editions of his textbooks and correspondence with particular individuals. As elsewhere in Europe, it was the printers and publishers that determined the success of these works. Following the initial translation of the *Porta linguarum* (the title was changed because the Stationers' Company would not allow a duplicate of one that already existed) by John Anchoran for the London printer Michael Sparke in 1631, there were thirty-one editions of the work to 1685, including a rival one in 1643 by James Young. When it came to the publication of a new translation and edition by the London printer Roger Daniel, he carefully included a letter from Comenius to validate it. Comenius's principal correspondent, Samuel Hartlib, became his most devoted agent and public promoter. How Hartlib came into initial contact with Comenius is unknown. Hartlib's brother Georg had been at the University of Heidelberg at the same time as Comenius, but it is unproven and perhaps unlikely that they were put in contact via that route. The two men were in correspondence as early as 1633, and it is perhaps significant that these transactions involved Hartlib's acting as an agent for Comenius in the acquisition of copies of unpublished Baconian materials. Given Hartlib's charitable endeavours on behalf of other exiled continental protestants, it is not surprising that this extended to collecting money towards providing Comenius with secretarial assistance as early as 1634. In 1636 an invitation was extended to Comenius to visit England and pursue his encyclopaedic studies. 'O if only some blessed means of retirement had befallen me five years ago', mused Comenius in 1641 to Hartlib over his inability to accept the offer (Hartlib papers, 7/84/1A–4B, translated by W. S. Hitchens). It was perhaps in answer to such apparent enthusiasms that Comenius sent the manuscript sketch of pansophical method which Hartlib published, with the assistance of Joachim Hübner (Fundanius), in Oxford in 1637 under the title of *Conatuum Comenianorum praeludia* ('Preludes to Comenian endeavours').

Hartlib circulated copies of this pamphlet widely in England and abroad to elicit critical comment and raise public awareness and finance for the exciting possibilities it contained. Hartlib's surviving papers indicate that he was not disappointed on either count. His accounts for the period from 1637 to 1639 provide us with a roll-call of those who were inspired to subscribe to the cause; his papers contain the (sometimes critical) comments of those who chose to respond. For Comenius, however, such developments must have been a cause for concern. A private manuscript had, without its author's permission, been published and circulated. Years later Comenius glossed over the difference as best he could, but in the meantime he defended the work against the criticism of some members of the Unitas Fratrum in a pamphlet published in Poland in 1638 under the title *Conatuum pansophicorum dilucidatio* ('The dawn of pansophic endeavours'). The only surviving copy of this edition was recently found among a book of tracts in the British Library, it presumably being the one that Comenius had sent to Hartlib. The latter published it in London in 1639 as an appendix to the *Preludes* under the new title, the *Pansophiae prodromus* ('Precursor of pansophy'), and translated it into English as *A Reformation of Schooles* in 1642.

By then Hartlib's invitations to Comenius had borne fruit. Comenius arrived in London on 21 September 1641 and stayed with Hartlib for eight months, before leaving in June 1642 just ahead of the start of the civil war. Hartlib had hoped to provide a place where Comenius could pursue his pansophic ambitions, and he promoted the reform of Chelsea College as a location for the 'universal college of the learned' which Comenius envisioned on the basis of the second book of Bacon's *Advancement of Learning*. That was sketched out in the *Via lucis* ('The way of light'), the treatise that he wrote while in London at this date, outlining the reform of society through a process of learning that he described by means of analogy, metaphor, and parable, especially using the image of light. Comenius was evidently perceived as the dean of the reformed college, which would be devoted to the pursuit of intellectual correspondency of the kind already advocated by Joachim Hübner and Hartlib as the best way to advance universal learning. But it would have required an act of the privy council to rewrite the college's foundation charter, and an act of parliament to replenish the foundation, and neither was forthcoming in the wake of the outbreak of the rebellion in Ireland. In his surviving letters back to the brethren in Leszno, Comenius recorded his disappointment that so few English people that he met spoke adequate Latin and his astonishment at seeing sermons recorded in shorthand. It is not surprising that his valedictory letter of 10 June 1642 to his friends in England should refer to the 'public unrest' which had provided nothing of the 'quiet' from political and military turmoil that he had sought in his visit to London in the first place (Hartlib papers, 7/75A–B). But three months before he left, Samuel Hartlib, John Dury, and Comenius signed a 'fraternal covenant' (that he had apparently drafted) on 3 March 1642. By this solemn private pact they committed one another to spend the rest of their lives in a godly promotion of three defined objectives. These were the procuring of religious peace, the education of young people to Christian truth, and the complete reformation of ways of learning. It was a pact that would underwrite their relationship for the rest of their lives.

Subsequent career and later works Comenius, who had also entertained offers from Richelieu's agents to come to France in April 1642, had been lured from London by the prospect of patronage from the wealthy Dutch merchant and arms manufacturer Louis de Geer. On his journey through the Netherlands in July 1642, he met René Descartes at Endegeest, near Leiden—a signal non-meeting of minds, if the surviving account is to be trusted. From 1642 to 1648 Comenius settled in Elbing (Elbląg), which was in Royal Prussia, subject theoretically to the Polish king but in practice fully controlled by the Swedish empire, and sought influence with Queen Kristina and the Swedish chancellor, Axel Oxenstierna. He did some teaching in the local Gymnasium and refined his method of language instruction, published as the *Methodus linguarum novissima* ('The latest method of [learning] languages') in 1648. However, in the second half of the 1640s Comenius became suspicious of the Swedish Lutheran theologians, and his curriculum proposals were not accepted as part of the Swedish school ordinances of 1649. As the German phase of the international conflict begun in 1618 neared its close, probably in 1644, he began to write his most ambitious work, the *De rerum humanarum emendatione consultatio catholica* ('General discourse on the emendation of human affairs') or *Consultatio*. With the enthusiasm of his patron waning and the patience of the Swedish chancellor wearing thin, thanks in part to Comenius's role in a failed religious colloquy at Toruń (the *Colloquium charitativum* of 1645) and the fact that the issue of the Czech exiles had proved no more than a small pawn in the diplomatic negotiations in Westphalia, in July 1648 Comenius returned to Leszno, where he became the leading senior of the Unity of Brethren.

The decade from 1648 to 1658 was a sequence of defeats and catastrophes for Comenius that he interpreted in an increasingly millennial light. His second wife died in 1648, leaving him with four children, the youngest of whom, Daniel, was two years of age and the eldest of whom, Alžběta (*b.* 1628), married in 1649 his long-suffering amanuensis, Petr Jablonský (Peter Figulus; 1619–1670). In the same year Comenius himself married Jana (Johana) Gajusová, the daughter of Jan Gajus, a Czech protestant pastor in Kampen. The peace of Westphalia of 1648 ignored the exiles from Czech lands, and the brethren became an orphaned protestant minority that Comenius failed to persuade (at the Synod of Leszno, 1650) to merge with one of the larger protestant confessions. Seeing the possibility of a new protestant patron—and potential anti-Habsburg millennial saviour—in the revived fortunes of György II Rákóczi, the prince of Transylvania, he moved to Sárospatak in 1650 and was charged with reforming the prince's prestigious Latin school there. If his efforts on the ground were only partially successful, this was more than compensated for by a stream of writings. The pictorial version of his language teaching method, the *Orbis sensualium pictus* ('The world in pictures')—written in Sárospatak but finally published in Nuremberg in only 1658—and his dramatized version, the

Schola ludus ('The school on stage'), were but a small fraction of the works that emerged from his Transylvanian interlude. He returned to Leszno in 1654 as the crisis in the Polish kingdom reached its climax. In April 1656 Polish Catholic troops occupied the town and burnt it to the ground as a bed of protestant 'heretics'. Comenius and his family were spared, but he lost his library and many unpublished works, including his sermons, the *Consultatio*, and his dictionary of the Czech language. Afflicted by the 'endless dissipation of my mind' that this turmoil provoked, Comenius asked his son-in-law Peter Figulus to seek the support of the son of his former patron, Laurens de Geer, and it was the latter who invited Comenius to Amsterdam, where he spent the rest of his life.

Comenius's productivity in these last years was remarkable. The city of Amsterdam elected him an honorary professor at its Gymnasium (known as the Athenaeum) and he responded by assembling in chronological order the writings that would best represent his search for a right educational method and demonstrate its practical results. The result, the *Opera didactica omnia*, was published by the city council with a date of 1657 (in reality, early 1658). He set about rewriting the *Consultatio*, the first two volumes of which (the *Panegersia* or 'Universal awakening' and *Panaugia* or 'Universal dawning') were read by de Geer, who had them printed. In the preface Comenius addressed himself to the community of learning of his day, enlisting its support for a profound reform of the organization of human affairs to ensure that a right philosophy, religion, and politics could lead to harmony and enlightenment, rather than division and chaos. The remaining five parts of the work, which set Comenius's pansophic, educational, and linguistic concerns into this broader context, remained among the manuscripts that were arranged by his young assistant, K. V. Nigrin, after his death. Their existence was known in the eighteenth century to (among others) Johann Gottfried von Herder, a Comenius admirer. But their exact provenance was discovered by the Ukrainian philologist Dmytri Čyževskij while researching in the archives of the orphanage library in Halle, near Leipzig, in 1934–5, and it was only in 1966 that they received their first edition in Prague under the auspices of the Czechoslovak Academy of Sciences. Comenius's forays against Cartesianism and Socinianism in his later years led to various sharp polemics and disagreements with the Unity of Brethren. He increasingly linked his yearning for universal reform of all humanity with a millenarian belief in the imminent coming of the kingdom of Christ. In 1657 he published *Lux in tenebris* ('Light in darkness'), a Latin rendition and interpretation of the dream-cycles and prophecies of the Silesian Christoph Kotter, Kristina Poniatowska, a prophetess of gentle birth and Polish descent, and his fellow Moravian and one-time student, Mikuláš Drabík. The work predicted a swift and dramatic end to the Habsburg Antichrist, but it attracted derision from anti-chiliast Calvinist theologians, such as the French theologian Samuel Maresius (Desmarets) at Groningen. His last major work, the

'Clamores Eliae' ('The pleas of Elijah') remained in manuscript. Comenius died in Amsterdam on 15 November 1670, and about a week later he was buried in the Walloon church at Naarden.

Comenius's reputation   Comenius's reputation did not flourish during the Enlightenment. When he dispatched four copies of the *Via lucis*, finally published in 1668, to its dedicatee, the Royal Society of London, the gift was politely acknowledged but quietly put on one side. Although his language textbooks continued to be widely used, his broader pedagogy was criticized, and in the eighteenth century his pansophic vision and attempt at universal reform were derided. Nineteenth-century Czech nationalism and twentieth-century international organizations have resurrected the memory of 'that incomparable Moravian'. UNESCO declared 1992, the 400th anniversary of his birth, as 'the year of Comenius', but the magnificent critical edition of his works, directed by the Institute of Philosophy of the Czech Academy of Sciences, remained incomplete and the majority of his writings still awaited translation into English at the beginning of the twenty-first century. It is as a remarkable representative of the universalist tendencies observable in Renaissance thought from Nicholas of Cusa onwards that Comenius is at his most complex and least intelligible to modern readers.

M. GREENGRASS

Sources *Dramata mesta: dejinami Uherského Brodu a jeho obyvatel* (Uherský Brod, [n.d.]) · F. Vyskocil, *Casopis Matice Moravsk*, 111 (1992), 95–111 · G. Menk, *Die Hohe Schule Herborn in ihrer Frühzeit (1584–1660)* (Wiesbaden, 1981) · H. Hotson, *Johann Heinrich Alsted, 1588–1638: between Renaissance, Reformation, and universal reform* (2000) · *Neue Deutsche Biographie* · F. Hofmann, 'Der enzyklopädische Impuls J. H. Alsteds und sein Gestaltwandel im Werke des J. A. Komenský', *Comenius: Erkennen—Glauben—Handeln*, ed. K. Schaller (1985), 22–9 · G. Menk, 'Johann Amos Comenius und die Hohe Schule Herborn', *Acta Comeniana*, 8 (1989), 41–59 · H. Hotson, 'Irenicism and dogmatics in the confessional age: Pareus and Comenius in Heidelberg, 1614', *Journal of Ecclesiastical History*, 46, 432–56 · N. Rejchrtov, *Bohemia*, 32 (1991), 368–79 · V. Cekota, *Studia Comeniana et Historica*, 19 (1989), 195–9 · L. Schmid, *Studia Comeniana et Historica*, 14 (1984), 65–9 · V. Urbànek, *Studia Comeniana et Historica*, 26 (1996), 123–36 · M. Kyralov, *Studia Comeniana et Historica*, 18, supplement (1988), 151–9 · A. Johns, *The nature of the book* (1998) · D. Cram and J. Maat, 'Comenius, Dalgarno and the English translations of the Janua linguarum', *Studia Comeniana et Historica*, 26 (1996), 148–60 · M. Greengrass, 'The financing of a seventeenth-century intellectual: contributions for Comenius, 1637–1641', *Acta Comeniana: Internationale Revue für Studien über J. A. Comenius und ideengeschichte der frühen Neuzeit*, 11/35 (1995), 71–87, 141–57 · Comenius to Morian, 7 March 1641 NS, University of Sheffield, Hartlib papers, 7/84/1A–4B · University of Sheffield, Hartlib papers, 7/75A–B · D. Capkovà and D. Pavlikovà, *Studia Comeniana et Historica*, 23 (1993), 26–34 · V. Dvorák, 'K ceste svetla', *Studia Comeniana et Historica*, 26 (1996), 137–44 · printed letter of Comenius to his English supporters, 10 June 1642, University of Sheffield, Hartlib papers, 7/84/1A–4B · J. Kumpera, *Studia Comeniana et Historica*, 26 (1996), 421–5 · K. Stormbom, 'Komensky und die Schul-organisation im Schwedischen Reich (Schweden, Finnland, Estland) im 17. Jahrhundert', *Studia Comeniana et Historica*, 20 (1990), 152–9 · J. Cach, *Studia Comeniana et Historica*, 19 (1989), 99–106 · J. Pánek, *Comenius: teacher of nations* (Prague, 1991) · M. Spinka, *J. A. Comenius, that incomparable Moravian* (1943) · private information (2004) [V. Urbanek]

Archives National Library, Prague · University of Sheffield Library, corresp. | Leszno, Poland, Unitas Fratrum papers
Likenesses W. Hollar, engraving, 1652, BM [*see illus.*] · engraving, repro. in Comenius, *Reformation of Schooles* (1642) · engraving, repro. in *Opera omnia didactica* (1657), frontispiece

Comerford, John (*c.*1770–1832), miniature painter, was born in Kilkenny, Ireland, the son of a flax-dresser. He acquired some of his knowledge of painting by copying pictures in Kilkenny Castle, then one of the finest collections of portraits in Ireland, where he would have seen works by Sir Godfrey Kneller and Sir Peter Lely. He was educated at the Dublin Society's drawing schools during the mid-1780s and on 13 May 1790 was recommended for a certificate testifying to his 'extraordinary merit in drawing from the flat' (*Proceedings of the Royal Dublin Society*, 26, 1789–90, 122). On 7 April 1791 he received a silver medal in the first class for drawing a single figure from nature (ibid., 27, 1790–91, 81). Comerford divided his time between Kilkenny and Dublin. An advertisement appeared in Finn's *Leinster Journal* on 13 September 1797: 'Likenesses in Oils and Miniature by J. Comerford who has arrived in Kilkenny for a short time at Mr. Comerford's opposite the Tholsel.' In 1799 Comerford met George Chinnery and afterwards adopted a variation of Chinnery's style of miniature painting. Encouraged by Chinnery, he abandoned oil portraiture and concentrated on miniature painting for the rest of his career. Working in watercolour on ivory, using loose brushstrokes, Comerford's miniatures are relatively large and are well drawn. The features of his sitters are modelled using brown shading with a hint of blue in the darkest areas. A representative example of his miniature style is his portrait of *Judge Walter MacGuire*, painted in Dublin in 1818 (V&A, MacGuire loan). Chinnery helped to organize the Society of Artists of Ireland exhibition held in 1800, in which Comerford first exhibited in Dublin. A review of Comerford's work stated: 'Comerford seems to play with his art in all the strength, the ease and the variety of the most vigorous and commanding genius' (*Dublin Evening Post*, 11 May 1802). Comerford lived with the Chinnerys at 27 Dame Street, College Green, Dublin, from 1800. In 1815 he moved to 2 Leinster Street, and shortly before his death he moved to 28 Blessington Street.

When Comerford sent miniatures to the exhibition at the Parliament House in 1802, his work was praised again and he was referred to as 'bursting at once from provincial retirement into the full blaze of public notice' (*Dublin Evening Post*, 17 June 1802). He continued to exhibit miniatures at the Society of Artists of Ireland exhibitions in 1800, 1801, 1802, 1804, and 1810, and at the Irish Society of Artists in 1812 and 1813. In 1811 he was elected to the committee of the Irish Society of Artists and became its vice-president. In 1804 and 1809 he exhibited three portraits at the Royal Academy in London. From 1800, when Comerford first exhibited, until 1823 exhibitions were held by a plethora of societies of artists in Ireland such as the Society of Artists of Ireland, who were continually re-forming as different groups. In 1823 the granting of a charter to the Royal Hibernian Academy did not go without opposition,

led by Comerford, who strongly disagreed with the granting of a charter of incorporation for the formation of an academy of artists.

According to T. J. Mulvany, Comerford accumulated a considerable fortune:

> although of sufficiently prudent turn of mind to amass a very handsome fortune, having left, it is said £16,000 after him, [he] still enjoyed the fruits of fortune during his life and as easy circumstances rendered too great devotion to his profession unnecessary, he delighted to relax in the Society of his friends, among whom were included all the distinguished artists of the day. (Gandon and Mulvany, 152–4)

Among these were the history painter Vincent Waldré (*c.*1742–1814) and William Ashford (1746–1824), the first president of the Royal Hibernian Academy. Comerford often collaborated with Thomas Sautell Roberts (*c.*1760–1826), adding the figures or portraits to Roberts's landscapes, as in, for example, *View of Powerscourt, with a Portrait of Captain Taylor of the Engineers* and *View in the Valley of Glencree, with a Portrait of the Earl of Hardwicke, Lord Lieutenant* (exh. Dublin, 1802).

The miniaturist Samuel Lover (1797–1868) was greatly influenced by Comerford, whom he met in the early 1820s, and by whom he was encouraged to paint miniatures early in his career. His pupil John Doyle (1797–1868) started his career as a miniaturist before becoming a highly successful caricaturist. Thomas Clement Thompson (1778x80–1857) was also taught to paint miniatures by Comerford.

While on a visit to T. J. Mulvany at Lucan, co. Dublin, in 1829 Comerford had a seizure. His life was saved by Dr Fergusson of Leixlip and he lived to resume his profession for three more years. He died on 25 January 1832 at his home in Blessington Street, Dublin, leaving an only daughter, Mary, to whom he bequeathed £500 a year. A prolific miniaturist, Comerford's work is easily identified as he usually signed and dated his portraits in full. The National Gallery of Ireland has a large collection of his work; others are in the Victoria and Albert Museum and at Kenwood House, London.
        PAUL CAFFREY

Sources P. Caffrey, *John Comerford and the portrait miniature in Ireland, c.1620–1850* (1999) · P. Caffrey, 'John Comerford', *Irish Arts Review*, 4/3 (1987), 42–7 · P. Caffrey, 'Irish portrait miniatures, c.1700–1830', PhD diss., Southampton Institute, 1995 · W. G. Strickland, *A dictionary of Irish artists*, 1 (1913), 194–202 · J. Gandon and T. J. Mulvany, eds., *The life of James Gandon* (1846), 152–4 · *The life of Sir Martin Arthur Shee* (1860) · *Proceedings of the Royal Dublin Society*, 21 (1784–5), 91 · *Proceedings of the Royal Dublin Society*, 26 (1789–90), 122 · *Proceedings of the Royal Dublin Society*, 27 (1790–91), 81 · *Proceedings of the Royal Dublin Society*, 56 (1820), 35 · A. M. Stewart, ed., *Irish art loan exhibitions, 1765–1927*, 1 (1990), 139–41 · B, 'Biographical sketch of Mr Cuming', *Walker's Hibernian Magazine* (June 1811), 330 · D. Foskett, *Miniatures: dictionary and guide* (1987), 512–13 · B. S. Long, *British miniaturists* (1929), 77 · D. O'Brien, *Miniatures in the XVIIIth and XIXth centuries, an historical record* (1951), 57–8 · *Leinster Journal* (13 Sept 1797) · *Dublin Evening Post* (11 May 1802) · *Dublin Evening Post* (17 June 1802) · A. Le Harivel, ed., *National Gallery of Ireland: illustrated summary catalogue of drawings, watercolours and miniatures* (1983)
Archives NG Ire., some ephemeral materials
Likenesses W. Bewick, chalk drawing, BM; repro. in Caffrey, 'John Comerford', 42

Wealth at death £16,000: Gandon and Mulvany, *Life of James Gandon*

Comerford [Quemerford], **Nicholas** (*c*.1540–*c*.1599), Jesuit, was the son of Patrick Comerford of Waterford and his wife (*née* Walsh). Nicholas was the first of sixteen Jesuits of that name who lived between 1590 and 1640. He was educated at the school of Peter White in Kilkenny, and subsequently in Oxford, where, according to Anthony Wood, he took his degree in arts in 1562 'after he had spent at least four years in pecking and hewing at logic and philosophy' (Wood, *Ath. Oxon.*, 1.200).

After returning to Ireland, Comerford was ordained priest, but soon felt obliged to leave the country because of persecution. He went to Louvain in 1565 and gained a doctorate in divinity on 23 October 1576. His fellow countryman Peter Lombard marked the occasion with a Latin poem, *Carmen heroicum in doctoratum Nicolai Quemerfordii*. In 1577 Comerford was reported by Sir William Drury, lord president of Munster, as come recently out of Louvain, with James Archer and others, and preaching 'all the way between Rye and Bristol against our religion'. Subsequently, Drury spoke of him as one of 'the principal agents of the pope' (Hogan, 74).

Comerford and Archer left Ireland in 1580 or 1581. Comerford entered the Society of Jesus at Madrid in 1581. Afterwards he lectured in different colleges in Spain. In 1589 he was mentioned as being in Bayona, Spain, and the following year in Lisbon. There is no mention of him after 1590. He is not in the Irish Jesuit catalogue for 1609. He is reputed to have died about 1599. According to Richard Stanihurst's *Descriptio Hiberniae* of 1577, Comerford wrote 'a learned and pitty treatise' entitled 'Answers to certain questions propounded by the citizens of Waterford'. He is also said to have written many learned tracts on philosophical and theological subjects, some sermons, and a poem in Latin, *Carmina in laudem comitis Ormondiae*.

THOMAS J. MORRISSEY

Sources E. Hogan, *Distinguished Irishmen of the sixteenth century* (1894) · J. A. Stephenson, 'Menology of the Irish province of the Society of Jesus', Irish Jesuit Archives, Dublin · H. Foley, ed., *Records of the English province of the Society of Jesus*, 7/1 (1882), 52 · Wood, *Ath. Oxon.*, 2nd edn, 1.200 · *CSP Ire.*, 1589–90

Comfort, Alexander [Alex] (**1920–2000**), physician and writer, was born on 10 February 1920 at 21 Palmerston Crescent, Edmonton, Middlesex, the only son of Alexander Charles Comfort (1882/3–1975), an education officer for the London county council, and his wife, Daisy Elizabeth, *née* Fenner (*d.* 1948), a teacher of modern languages. He was brought up in New Barnet. From Highgate School he won a classical scholarship to Trinity College, Cambridge, but he read medicine, obtaining first-class honours in part I of the natural science tripos in 1940 and second-class honours in the pathology division in 1941. After clinical training at the London Hospital, he qualified MRCS and LRCP and graduated MB in 1944. During the war he was a conscientious objector—'a "pure" pacifist of the other-cheek school', according to George Orwell (*Collected Essays*, 180)—though he would surely have been rejected

Alexander Comfort (1920–2000), by Dellenback, 1961

for military service through having lost four fingers of his left hand as a schoolboy while manufacturing fireworks in his garden for George V's silver jubilee. He obtained his London PhD in biochemistry in 1949 (he received a London DSc in gerontology in 1963). On 16 September 1943 he married Ruth Muriel Harris (1916/17–2000) of Loughton, Essex, daughter of Alfred Harris, master printer. At the time of their marriage she was working as a children's care organizer. They had one son, Nicholas.

Following his childhood accident Comfort's father took him on a voyage to Argentina and Senegal. Comfort's account of this, *The Silver River*, was published by Chapman and Hall in 1938 while he was still at school. His first two novels, *No Such Liberty* (1941) and *The Almond Tree* (1943), appeared while he was a medical student. These writings were precursors of a many-sided life, and of sustained literary productivity. There followed other novels and volumes of poetry. Comfort became well known among the wartime and post-war poets; Orwell, with whom Comfort exchanged polemics in both prose and verse over the latter's opposition to the war and the war leaders, wrote of him as belonging to the group of 'Eliot, Herbert Read, Auden, Spender, Dylan Thomas, Henry Treece … Robert Bridges, Edmund Blunden, D. H. Lawrence' (*Collected Essays*, 329). But poetry did not remain a main activity for Comfort, though it emerged at intervals, and movingly in his last years.

After a lectureship in physiology at the London Hospital (1948–51), during which he wrote his first textbook, *First Year Physiological Technique* (1948), Comfort worked in the department of zoology at University College, London

(1951–73), where he was associated with P. B. Medawar and J. B. S. Haldane and became director of research in gerontology from 1966 to 1973. His *Biology of Senescence* (1956) became a standard work, remarkable also for the quality of his writing. Later he was president of the British Society for Research on Ageing, and first president of the geriatrics and gerontology section of the Royal Society of Medicine (at which he endowed a lecture and prize in memory of his father, and to which he left a substantial legacy).

Comfort's pacifism and anarchism were expressed as an embattled anti-militarism, rooted in the belief that resistance to an aggressive state must lie in disobedience. In 1961 he spent a short time in prison, along with Bertrand Russell and others, after a sit-down protest as a member of the Committee of 100; this was a militant group which grew out of the Campaign for Nuclear Disarmament, of which he was a founder. His political views were reflected in some of his fiction, but were argued more explicitly in the social criticism in which he challenged infringements of personal liberty, and particularly what he saw as the guilt-inducing constraints of religious, social, and sexual convention; this involved him in much controversy. He was a frequent broadcaster, and appeared in *The Brains Trust*.

In 1973 Comfort left his wife, Ruth, and moved to California with Jane Tristram Henderson (*d.* 1991), daughter of a tea merchant. She became his second wife later that year. In California he joined an unconventional think tank, the Center for the Study of Democratic Institutions at Santa Barbara, later holding academic appointments at Stanford University (1974–83), the University of California at Irvine (1976–8), and at the Neuropsychiatric Institute in Los Angeles (1980–91).

California in the 1970s was a good place and time for Comfort to concentrate on his long-standing concern to foster a frank and guilt-free attitude to sex, reflected in his earlier writings such as *Sexual Behaviour in Society* (1950), *Sex and Society* (1963), and *The Anxiety Makers* (1967). Not without trepidation he produced the book for which he became famous, *The Joy of Sex* (1973), featuring memorable drawings (based on photographs) in which a bearded middle-aged man and his younger partner illustrated the varied modes of love making. *More Joy* followed in 1974 and *The New Joy of Sex* in 1991. Some 12 million copies of these works were sold, in many languages. Initially *Joy* appeared with Comfort's name as editor, implying that the text had been 'medically vetted' rather than written by him, so worried was he about possible adverse reaction. He need not have worried: the book fitted its time, both as reflecting the new freedom and openness in sexuality, and as sanctioning it. Later he worried about AIDS, and, in characteristic phrase, urged that certain practices should 'go on hold' (*The Times*, 28 March 2000).

The last phase of Comfort's professional life was bold and surprising. He reinvented himself as a geriatric psychiatrist, and obtained a post as such at Brentwood Veterans' Hospital in Los Angeles (1978–81). Although he was without formal training in psychiatry, his lifelong interest in

ageing, his great intelligence, and his sympathy for psychiatry fitted him well for this new role, for which he further equipped himself (characteristically) by writing a good short textbook: *Practice of Geriatric Psychiatry* (1980). He remarked that the best way to learn about a subject is to write a book on it. He was subsequently consultant at Ventura County Hospital, California (1981–91).

Throughout his life Comfort continued to write and to broadcast. All his writing, including the didactic, was characterized by clarity and elegance of style, and his origins as a classicist remained evident in his fiction and poetry, and in rich allusion in other writings. The titles of his books (leaving aside the many articles) took up several inches of his entry in *Who's Who*. One of the last, *Imperial Patient* (1987), imaginatively and humorously told the story of a fictional personal physician to the emperor Nero, portraying the latter as misunderstood and even sympathetic—typically, for Comfort, going against the accepted grain. There were many works of social commentary and criticism, and there was a translation in 1964, soon after a stay at the Statistical Institute in Calcutta, of an Indian guide to love making, *The Koka Shastra*. How even a polymath and fast learner like Comfort managed quickly to acquire sufficient Sanskrit is unclear. Poetry, often lyrical, terse, and elliptical, occasionally polemical, sometimes of great power, also continued to appear, but less than in earlier years. The main collections were: *A Wreath for the Living* (1943), *Elegies* (1944), *The Signal to Engage* (1947), *Haste to the Wedding* (1961), *Poems for Jane* (1979), and *Microcosmos* (1994). Had his interests and activities not ranged so widely, Comfort might well have been known as a major poet; at the end of the war he was seen as destined for such a role, but his poetry became displaced by other activities.

While maintaining his connection with California, in the mid-1980s Comfort returned to England, settling in Cranbrook in Kent (near the geriatrician Lord Amulree). He continued his new clinical activities as a locum in the south of England. But in 1991 he suffered the first of three strokes that left him disabled and wheelchair-bound. His wife, Jane, died soon after the first stroke. After a period of living in a supported flat in Highgate he moved to a nursing home in Northamptonshire, near his only child, Nicholas, a political journalist, and his family. He died on 26 March 2000, of myocardial infarction, gastro-intestinal haemorrhage, and cerebral atherosclerosis, at the Horton Hospital, Banbury, and was buried at Comforts Wood, Swattenden Lane, Cranbrook, Kent. He was survived by his son. The Irish poet Robert Greacen wrote an affectionate elegy for him; a special issue of *Experimental Gerontology* had appeared as a Festschrift in 1998.   TOM ARIE

Sources D. Goodway, 'Introduction', in A. Comfort, *Writings against power and death*, ed. D. Goodway (1994) · *The Times* (28 March 2000) · *The Independent* (30 March 2000) · *The Guardian* (28 March 2000) · *Daily Telegraph* (28 March 2000) · *New York Times* (29 March 2000) · *Freedom* (22 April 2000) · *Experimental Gerontology*, 33/1–2 (1998) · *The collected essays, journalism and letters of George Orwell*, ed. S. Orwell and I. Angers (1968), vol. 2 · *WWW* · personal knowledge (2004) · private information [N. Comfort, J. Wedgwood, A. N. Exton

Smith] • b. cert. • m. cert. • d. cert. • A. E. Salmon, *Alex Comfort* (Boston, MA, 1978) • G. Talese, *Thy neighbour's wife* (New York, 1980)

Archives State University of New York, Buffalo, corresp. and literary papers • UCL, literary corresp. • UCL, papers on political and other subjects with corresp. • University of Indiana, Kinsey Institute

Likenesses Dellenback, photograph, 1961, News International Syndication, London [*see illus.*] • A. Stones, bust, priv. coll. • photograph, repro. in *The Times* • photograph, repro. in *The Guardian* • photograph, repro. in *Daily Telegraph* • photograph, repro. in *The Independent*

Wealth at death £481,332—gross; £469,753—net: probate, 5 Oct 2000, *CGPLA Eng. & Wales*

Comgall mac Domangart (*d. c.*538). *See under* Dál Riata, kings of (*act. c.*500–*c.*850).

Comgall mac Sétnai (511/16–602). *See under* Ulster, saints of (*act. c.*400–*c.*650).

Comgán mac Dá Cherda (*d.* 645). *See under* Munster, saints of (*act. c.*450–*c.*700).

Commán mac Fáelchon (*d.* 747). *See under* Connacht, saints of (*act. c.*400–*c.*800).

Commerell, Sir John Edmund (1829–1901), naval officer, born in London on 13 January 1829, was the second son of John Williams Commerell of Strood Park, Horsham, and his wife, Sophia, daughter of William Bosanquet. He entered the navy in February 1842 and was at once sent out to China, where he experienced the realities of war. Later he was in the *Firebrand* with Captain James Hope and took part in the operations in the Paraná, including the engagement with the batteries at Obligado on 20 November 1845, when the chain was cut by the boats of the *Firebrand*, a gallant achievement, which passed without official recognition. He was promoted lieutenant on 13 December 1848. Commerell married, in 1853, Mathilda Maria, fourth daughter of Joseph Bushby of Halkin Street, London.

As lieutenant of the *Vulture* Commerell was in the Baltic in 1854 and took part in the operations in the Gulf of Bothnia, in 1855 was in the Black Sea and Sea of Azov, and on 29 September was promoted commander of the gun-vessel *Weser*, employed in the Sea of Azov. A few days later, on 11 October, he landed with a small party, made a hazardous march inland, and set fire to a large store of forage and corn. This service was important and dangerous, and the Victoria Cross was awarded to Commerell and two of his seamen. In 1859 he was off China in the *Fury* and commanded a division of the seamen landed for the unsuccessful attack on the Taku (Dagu) forts. Although repulsed, the determined courage in the face of insurmountable difficulties was recognized, and Commerell was promoted captain on 18 July. In 1866 his services while in command of the *Terrible*, laying the Atlantic cable, were rewarded with a CB civil division. In 1869 he commanded the *Monarch*, which in December carried across the Atlantic the remains of George Peabody, the American philanthropist and founder of the 'Peabody dwellings'. In 1870 Commerell received the military CB, and in February 1871, with a broad pennant in the *Rattlesnake*, was appointed commander-in-chief on the west coast of Africa. In the

Second Anglo-Asante War, in August 1873, while reconnoitring up the River Pra, he was dangerously wounded by a musket shot in the lungs, which compelled him to invalid. In March 1874 he was created a KCB, and he attained his flag on 12 November 1876. In the following year he was sent out to the Mediterranean as second in command, at the special request of Sir Geoffrey Hornby, with whom his relations were most cordial and who highly commended his ability and loyalty. In November 1882 he went out as commander-in-chief on the North American station, where he remained nearly three years, returning in autumn 1885.

In 1880 Commerell had unsuccessfully contested Southampton, but in the 1885 general election, and again in 1886, he was elected Conservative MP for Southampton, and zealously for the next two years endeavoured to awaken the country to the necessity of strengthening the navy. He was thus largely instrumental in bringing about the Naval Defence Act of 1889, though he was not then in parliament, having resigned his seat in July 1888 on being appointed commander-in-chief at Portsmouth. He had already been promoted admiral in April 1886, and had been made a GCB at Queen Victoria's jubilee in June 1887. At Portsmouth in 1889 he commanded at the naval review and received Kaiser Wilhelm II, who afterwards wrote him an autograph letter on presenting him with a sword.

Commerell was always popular at court; he was naval aide-de-camp to the queen from 1872 to 1877, and was her groom-in-waiting from 1874 to 1879 and again from 1891. On the death of Sir Provo Wallis he was, at the queen's request, promoted on 13 February 1892 admiral of the fleet, though not the senior admiral. In January 1899, at the age of seventy, he was placed on the retired list, and he died at his home, 45 Rutland Gate, London, on 21 May 1901; his wife survived him. An officer of great experience in amphibious and riverine warfare, Commerell was one of the leaders of the intellectual and material renaissance of the Royal Navy that began in the early 1880s.

J. K. LAUGHTON, *rev.* ANDREW LAMBERT

Sources A. C. Dewar, ed., *Russian war, 1855, Black Sea: official correspondence*, Navy RS, 85 (1945) • Mrs F. Egerton, *Admiral of the fleet: Sir Geoffrey Phipps Hornby, a biography* (1896) • *Navy List* • *The Times* (22 May 1901) • *Annual Register* (1901) • *WWW*, 1897–1915 • *WWBMP*, vol. 2 • Kelly, *Handbk*

Archives BL, letters to Sir Austen Layard, Add. MSS 39015–39032 • NMM, Hornby MSS

Likenesses M. M. Cookesley, oils, Admiralty, Portsmouth • Lock & Whitfield, woodburytype photograph, NPG; repro. in T. Cooper, *Men of mark: a gallery of contemporary portraits* (1883) • Spy [L. Ward], caricature, chromolithograph, NPG; repro. in *VF* (3 Aug 1889) • T. [T. Chartran], caricature, watercolour sketch, NPG; repro. in *VF* (24 Dec 1881)

Wealth at death £21,664 17s.: administration with will, 1901, *CGPLA Eng. & Wales*

Commius (*fl.* 57–50 BC), king of the Atrebates, was a native of Gallia Belgica, probably of the tribe of the Atrebates, and an agent of Julius Caesar. He is first mentioned in Caesar's narrative of the Gallic wars (iv.21) after the battle on the Sambre in 57 BC when Caesar appointed him king of the Atrebates, one of the tribes defeated in that engagement. Caesar was favourably impressed by his courage and diplomatic abilities, and accorded him several privileges. Commius possessed influence over some of the tribes of southern Britain, presumably through personal contacts. When Caesar (then in western Belgica among the Morini) was contemplating an expedition to the island in 55 BC, he sent Commius as a legate to Britain to forewarn the British tribes of the invasion and to persuade them to join Caesar's cause. Commius crossed to Britain with British legates who had earlier been sent to Caesar, taking with him a guard of thirty horsemen. When he sought to carry out his commission he was seized and put in chains, but during Caesar's expedition of the same year he was returned to his Roman overlord. Commius seems to have remained in Britain, for during Caesar's second expedition, in 54 BC, it was through his agency that Cassivellaunus submitted to Caesar.

In 53 BC, as many Gaulish chieftains began to threaten revolt against Rome, Caesar put Commius in command of a cavalry squadron to watch over the Menapii in western Belgica. In the great revolt of the Gauls in the following year, Commius deserted to the side of his countrymen, commanding his own Atrebates and a substantial force of Bellovaci; he himself was endowed with high military authority among the Gauls and took a leading part in the relief of the stronghold of Alesia (south-east of Dijon). Already before this one of Caesar's officers, Gaius Volusenus Quadratus, had tried to entrap Commius by inviting him to a friendly meeting at which the Gaul was to be killed. Although wounded by a sword-blow on this occasion, Commius was able to escape and return to his command of Gaulish forces in the north. In 51 BC Caesar renewed his operations against the Atrebates and Bellovaci. Commius sought help from the Germans east of the Rhine, returning with a cavalry force. But the Gauls fared badly in this campaign and Commius had to take refuge for a time among the Germans. Late in 51 BC he returned, hoping to continue the struggle, but by now the Atrebates had surrendered and only small raiding operations against Roman supply trains were possible. Again Volusenus Quadratus tried to capture Commius, this time by hunting him down. On one occasion the two came face to face, but this time Volusenus was wounded and Commius again made his escape. Soon afterwards, however, Commius submitted to Marcus Antonius, saying that he would accept any agreement provided that he should never again come into the presence of a Roman.

Shortly after this it is reasonably certain that Commius returned once more to Britain, where a coinage bearing his name was current in the region of modern Hampshire, Sussex, and adjacent areas. An undated episode reported by Frontinus may be linked with his final departure from Gaul. Pursued to the coast by Caesar, Commius hoisted his sails while still in harbour, thereby deluding his pursuers that he had already set sail and thus escaping. It is not known how long he continued in power in Britain. He did, however, found a dynasty from his base within the British

Atrebates. Three other kings in Britain struck coins bearing their names along with the filiation 'son of Commius': *Tincommius in what is now Hampshire and Sussex, *Verica in Sussex and Surrey, *Eppillus in Kent [see under Roman Britain, British leaders in (act. 55 BC–AD 84)]. Commius has a strong claim to recognition as the most successful king of Iron Age Britain. His prestige owed much to his earlier alliance with Caesar, partly through the glamour of association, partly through the advantage of seeing the Roman military machine at work. Had he not decided upon separation from Rome, or had he lived a few decades later, Commius would have made an effective client-king on the frontiers of empire.   MALCOLM TODD

Sources J. Caesar, *C. Iuli Caesaris De bello Gallico*, ed. T. R. Holmes, [2] (1914), 14–15; [4] (1914), 13–14, 17, 21; [5] (1914), 13–14; [6] (1914), 3; [7] (1914), 45–7, 49 • Frontinus, *The 'Stratagems' and 'Aqueducts of Rome'*, ed. and trans. C. E. Bennett, M. B. McElwain, and C. Herschel (1950), ii; xiii.11 • R. D. Van Arsdell, *Celtic coinage of Britain* (1989) • B. Cunliffe, *Iron age communities in Britain*, 3rd edn (1990)

Common, Alfred (1880–1946), footballer, was born on 25 May 1880 at his parents' home, 27 North Milburn Street, Sunderland, the son of Robert Ridley Common, a riveter, and his wife, Sarah Ann Towers. He played for South Hilton juniors and Jarrow before signing for his home town team in 1897 as a goalscoring centre forward or outside right. In November 1901, not long after he had broken into the Sunderland first team, he was transferred to Sheffield United for a fee of £325. He played a vital part in Sheffield United's run to the cup final of 1902, in which he scored in the first, drawn, game and made the pass for the winning goal in the replay. There is some suggestion that homesickness led to his return to Sunderland in 1904 for £520. The directors of Sheffield United must have indulged in some hand-wringing at the profit Sunderland were to make only seven months later.

Common will always be remembered for the fact that he was the first footballer to cost £1000. That was the sum which Middlesbrough paid Sunderland to take him to Teesside in February 1905. Some members of the Football Association (FA), most notably J. C. Clegg, had long believed that the practice of 'buying and selling players is unsportsmanlike and most objectionable in itself, and ought not to be entertained by those who desire to see the game played under proper conditions' (Green, 407–8). Common's transfer provoked an attempt to bring the market for players under some control, and the FA actually made a rule, to come into effect from 1 January 1908, that no club should be entitled to pay or receive any transfer fee, or other payment exceeding £350 upon or in respect of the transfer of any player. It lasted for three months. It was so obviously being ignored by the clubs that it had to be withdrawn.

The signing of Common was part of a last-ditch strategy to save Middlesbrough from relegation and Common's goals helped to do the trick. He was also appointed club captain. The club was later to be convicted by the FA of paying illegal bonuses to players during their successful cup run in 1904 and the relegation battle of 1905. None of the players was suspended but eleven out of the twelve directors were.

Common appeared twice for England while at Sheffield United, scoring two goals. He was also selected to play centre forward against Wales in 1906 while a Middlesbrough player. It was at Middlesbrough that he played for a time with Steve Bloomer. Common was an aggressive and robust forward with an eye for goal. At 5 feet 8 inches and 13 stone he was a tough proposition in the penalty area, and scored 65 goals for Middlesbrough in 178 appearances. In 1910 he moved south to Woolwich Arsenal, this time on a free transfer because Middlesbrough had no money to pay the £250 benefit which he had been promised at the beginning of that season. By then he was probably past his best and was certainly troubled by weight problems. He would often trail in last on training walks and took to returning in the afternoons to wrestle and shadow-box in an effort to shed the unwanted pounds. But he still had one last hurrah and one last move to make. In December 1912 he was transferred to Preston and was a member of the team which won the second division championship in 1913.

Common left football in 1914 and returned to the northeast to become a licensee in Darlington, first at the Cleaver Hotel in Skinnergate and then spending eighteen years at the Alma Hotel, Cockerston, until his retirement in 1943. He was something of a local celebrity, in part owing to a combination of his sporting exploits and his jovial and loquacious character. His ruddy face seemed straight out of a Christmas pantomime. He died eleven months after his wife, on 3 April 1946 at his home, 326 Coniscliffe Road, Darlington.   TONY MASON

Sources *Northern Echo* (26 Feb 1992) · *Northern Echo* (29 April 1992) · B. Joy, *Forward Arsenal!* (1952) · *Darlington and Stockton Times* (11 Aug 1984) · P. Young, *Football in Sheffield* (1962) · A. Appleton, *Hotbed of soccer* (1961) · G. Green, *The history of the Football Association* (1953) · b. cert.

Likenesses group portraits, photographs (with team members), Coloursport · photographs, repro. in C. Lloyd, *Local colour*

Wealth at death £1679 6s. 8d.: administration, 13 Sept 1946, *CGPLA Eng. & Wales*

Common, Andrew Ainslie (1841–1903), astronomer and astronomical photographer, was born on 7 August 1841 at Oxford Street, St Andrew, Newcastle upon Tyne, one of two sons of Thomas Common, a surgeon and descendant of the Scottish border family of Comyn, and his wife, Mary Hall. Recollections from his brother indicate that Common had a youthful interest in astronomy: when he was ten his mother borrowed a telescope for him from Dr Bates of Morpeth. Financial constraints during childhood, due to the death of his father, curtailed his education and forced him to seek employment from an early age. In 1864 he fell out with his relatives and left for London, where he considered emigrating to Australia. By chance he met his uncle, Matthew Hall, who gave him a position in his sanitary engineering firm. Through his engineering talent Common made rapid progress in the company of Matthew Hall & Co., allowing him, on 18 July 1867, to marry Anne Matthews (1838x40–1911) of Gayton in Norfolk,

daughter of Abraham Matthews, a farmer. After Hall's death in 1878 Common took over the company which he managed until his retirement in 1890. Common's improved position allowed him to move to 63 Eaton Rise, Ealing, in Middlesex, where he lived for the remainder of his life, along with his wife and family of three daughters and one son.

Common's childhood interest in astronomy was not seriously resumed until 1874, when he established his first observatory, whose dome housed an equatorially mounted 5½ inch refracting telescope. With this refractor he first attempted celestial photography and in 1876 he was elected a fellow of the Royal Astronomical Society. Two years later, after considering making one himself, Common ordered an 18 inch silver-on-glass mirror from George Calver of Chelmsford which he built into an instrument of his own design. He subsequently used that reflecting telescope to observe the faint satellites of the planets Mars and Saturn. Experience with the reflector convinced him of the superiority of glass over speculum (metal) mirrors. Common then ordered a 36 inch mirror from Calver as he wished to resume his work on astronomical photography using the very slow film then available. He applied his extensive engineering skills to devise an unconventional fork mounting for the larger telescope. The design was innovative in that most of the telescope's mass was carried on mercury bearings. He likewise devised an electric clock control to improve the driving of the instrument during the long exposures necessary in celestial photography. To avoid constructing an expensive observatory dome the telescope was housed in a rotating run-off shed, a design prescient of that later used for large reflecting telescopes. Common initially used the instrument to continue his observations of planetary satellites and the nebulosity around the Pleiades star cluster. Yet his main energies were devoted to trying to photograph the bright Orion nebula; a first attempt in January 1880 ended in total failure. The following year he managed to take one of the two first good photographs of a bright comet (1881.b). Common achieved the feat on the same night that his fellow amateur Henry Draper photographed the Great Comet from New York, but their subsequent rivalry was curtailed by Draper's sudden death in 1882. After further improvements to the telescope guiding he managed on 30 January 1883 to expose a plate on the Orion nebula for 37 minutes. The splendid photograph revealed details invisible on the most carefully rendered hand drawings of the nebula. In recognition of Common's pioneering work he was awarded the Royal Astronomical Society's gold medal in 1884. He later obtained 90 minute exposures of the Orion nebula and successfully photographed the planets Jupiter and Saturn. In taking his nebula images, Common pioneered the technique of completing his exposures over several nights. As a photographic innovator, in 1887 he was invited to attend the first international conference on astronomical photography held at the Paris observatory. Although not directly involved in the proposed Carte du Ciel sky survey, he worked with Jules Pierre Janssen of the Meudon observatory on related projects.

Encouraged by his success Common resolved to build a 60 inch reflecting telescope to continue his work. To make space in his garden for the new reflector, in 1885 he sold the 36 inch reflector to Edward Crossley, a wealthy Halifax merchant. The instrument was little used there, but Crossley virtually gave it to the Lick Observatory in California, where James Keeler modified it and then achieved superb photographs of faint nebulae, thereby opening up a branch of astronomy. In building his largest telescope Common decided to grind and polish the mirror himself and to this end he erected a workshop adjacent to his house. Although the telescope was complete by 1889, the mirror produced unsatisfactory images and, despite several attempts at refiguring, it continued to display oval stars. To rectify the problem Common ordered a new glass disc from France and due to his earlier experience was able to produce an acceptable mirror in a mere three months. The mounting for the larger telescope was similar to the earlier reflector, except that water was employed to float the polar bearings. Apart from photographs of the Orion and Dumbbell nebulae and the Pleiades, Common made little use of the new telescope. It was difficult to use and the encroachment of London had lightened the once dark skies of Ealing. He offered to give the instrument to the Oxford University observatory, but Professor H. H. Turner had no funds to house or operate it. In 1904 the reflector was sold to Harvard College observatory in America, where it proved a failure until it was remounted and moved to their outstation in south Africa. Common's skill in mirror making was next applied to providing 36 and 30 inch mirrors for the Kensington Solar Physics Observatory, along with similar ones for the Royal Observatory, Greenwich, and the Helwan observatory in Egypt. Likewise he mastered the difficult art of making optically flat mirrors up to 20 inches in diameter. They were supplied to the Royal Society, the university observatory, Cambridge, and the National Physical Laboratory. The mirrors were mainly incorporated into heliostats and coelostats, new types of instruments that were important on solar eclipse expeditions to observe the sun. Later Common travelled with an official group to Norway to observe the 1896 solar eclipse, but his efforts were thwarted by clouds.

Common was an active member of the scientific community, acting as treasurer for the Royal Astronomical Society between 1884 and 1895 and as president from 1895 to 1897. For his work on celestial photography he was elected to the Royal Society in 1885 and sat on the council from 1895 to 1897. Until his death he served on the board of visitors for the Royal Observatory, Greenwich. During 1891 he was awarded an honorary LLD by the University of St Andrews and in 1900 he was elected president of the astronomy section of the British Association for the Advancement of Science.

In later years Common was distracted from his scientific work by his involvement with the British Aluminium Company, being one of its first directors. He subsequently became involved with the Ealing firm of Ottaway & Co. in developing improved optical gunsights for the British army and navy. In 1902 Percy Scott RN described Common's work as having increased the fighting efficiency of the navy's battleships fourfold. On 2 June 1903, while still pursuing this work in his study at home, Common died suddenly of a heart attack and was later cremated at Golders Green, Middlesex.

K. L. JOHNSON

Sources H. H. T., *PRS*, 75 (1905), 313–18 · *Monthly Notices of the Royal Astronomical Society*, 64 (1903–4), 274–8 · J. Ashbrook, *The astronomical scrapbook: skywatchers, pioneers, and seekers in astronomy*, ed. L. J. Robinson (1984) · H. C. King, *The history of the telescope* (1955) · P. S. Remington, 'The Crossley reflector', *Sky and Telescope*, 58 (1979), 307–11 · J. Darius, *Beyond vision* (1984), 40–41 · *Journal of the British Astronomical Association*, 13 (1902–3), 319 · b. cert. · d. cert. · d. cert. [Anne Common]

Archives Matthew Hall & Co. · Museum of Science and Industry, Manchester · RAS, letters to Royal Astronomical Society
Likenesses W. Nicholson, lithograph, RAS · portrait, Matthew Hall plc, London
Wealth at death £15,015 2s. 11d.: probate, 12 Aug 1903, *CGPLA Eng. & Wales*

Common, John (1778–1868), agricultural engineer, was born in High Buston, Warkworth, Northumberland, on 25 January 1778, the second child in the family of five sons (one died in infancy) and four daughters of Robert Common of High Buston, a millwright and cartwright from a family of skilled mechanics, and his wife (probably Jane Wilson of Alnwick).

Common followed his father's profession and assisted Henry Ogle, a schoolteacher of Newham, in improving a reaping machine design about 1803. His plans, from which two models were made, substituted a clipping or shearing action for Ogle's rotary one. In 1811 a full-size version was demonstrated secretly at night and appeared to 'answer well', and in 1812 a model was sent to the Society of Arts by Hugh, Earl Percy (later third duke of Northumberland). However, the society made no award of its reaping machine premium as the invention was 'incomplete' without proper trials. A second full-size machine, with a reel to bring the standing corn to the knives, and rollers to deliver the cut corn to the ground, was demonstrated in 1812 before witnesses. Common decided to discontinue further experiments because of the trouble and cost, and he passed the patterns to Thomas Brown and his son, ironfounders of Alnwick, who emigrated to New York state with the designs in 1824.

In 1851 Common claimed that imported American reaping machines, manufactured by Cyrus Hall McCormick, were 'exactly like the one I had made 40 years before'. His supporters subsequently asserted that the Browns had passed Common's patterns to McCormick, but there is no evidence that the American, working in an isolated part of Virginia from 1831, ever encountered them before his reaper improvements of ten years later. Common's achievement was to demonstrate a reaping machine that foreshadowed McCormick's, employing a reciprocating action of the knives. But he failed to persevere with his invention; nor was the era of relatively abundant labour supply, and of machine breaking, propitious for its development, whereas McCormick perfected his reaper at a time favourable to its adoption by farmers in North America and Europe.

Common gained recognition for other inventions, including a Society of Arts silver medal for a double-drill turnip sower of 1818. Common married Mary (1778/9–1847), daughter of John Leithead of Widdrington, in 1804. Two of their five sons and one of their four daughters died in infancy. He continued as an agricultural machine maker and a cartwright for the Northumberland estate until an advanced age, and he died at his home in Denwick, near Alnwick, on 28 June 1868.

JOHN S. CREASEY, rev.

Sources *Alnwick Journal* (15 Aug 1859) · *Alnwick Journal* (15 Aug 1860) · *Alnwick Journal* (July 1868) · R. F. J. Common, *The history of the invention of the reaping machine* (1907) · W. T. Hutchinson, *Cyrus Hall McCormick: seed-time, 1809–1856* (1930) · *Transactions of the Society of Arts*, 36 (1818), 24–9 · *Journal of the Society of Arts*, 26 (1877–8), 419–21, 479–80 · duke of Northumberland's Collection of MSS, Alnwick Castle · parish register (copies), Northumbd RO · d. cert.
Likenesses photograph (in old age), repro. in *Newcastle Weekly Chronicle* (13 Nov 1926)

Common, John William [Jack] (1903–1968), novelist and essayist, was born on 15 August 1903 at 44 Third Avenue, Heaton, Newcastle upon Tyne, the only son and second of the four children of John Common, engine driver, and his wife, Isabella, *née* Johnson. He had two younger sisters, Lilian and Jessie; his elder sister died young. After attending Chillingham Road School, Heaton, where he showed a talent for writing and developed a lifelong love of Shelley, he went on in 1917 to Skerry's Commercial College, Newcastle. This, however, led only to an unsatisfying job in a solicitor's office, followed by intermittent casual employment. By 1924 he was a vigorous debater at the Newcastle Socialist Society in the Royal Arcade, then the location of the pioneering People's Theatre, with its stimulating performances of Shaw, O'Casey, and Pirandello. Plans for a degree course at Durham University came to nothing, but Common was by now submitting articles (typed on his old Monarch) to the literary magazines. John Middleton Murry at *The Adelphi* gave him encouragement, and in 1928 (against his father's wishes) Common made his way to London to earn a precarious living by freelancing in left-wing literary circles. He rose to be editor of *The Adelphi* in 1935–6.

Common's writing was warm, ironic, and intensely political in a non-abstract way, while being occasionally garrulous and couched in a quirky style which strove to combine proletarian directness with intellectual rumination. Without employing dialect, he conveyed something of the cadences of his local speech. He won admirers throughout the 1930s as a writer with a genuine proletarian viewpoint, as distinct from the purveyors of middle-class Marxist fiction. He inspired, prefaced, and edited the compilation *Seven Shifts* (1938), in which seven working men told of their experience. In the same year he published a collection of his own essays, *The Freedom of the Streets*, which was a continual spur to thought with its wry

humanity and subtle analysis of working-class attitudes. Common showed why a propensity for speculative thinking might be a profitable asset to a middle-class child, but led to endless friction at a lower level of society; or why a bright proletarian youth might wilfully fondle his inhibitions, loath to sully his innocence by joining the responsible decision-making class. V. S. Pritchett considered *The Freedom of the Streets* to be the most influential book in his life, and George Orwell heard

> the authentic voice of the ordinary man, the man who might infuse a new decency into the control of affairs if only he could get there, but who in practice never seems to get much further than the trenches, the sweatshop and the jail. . (*New English Weekly*, 16 June 1938)

For his part, the clear-eyed Common saw Orwell, whom he had first met at the *Adelphi* offices, as something of a sheep in wolf's clothing (in pubs the barmen always called Orwell 'sir'). The two remained friends, however, corresponding and occasionally meeting when Common was running the village shop in Datchworth, Hertfordshire, about 10 miles from Orwell's Wallington cottage. The impractical Orwell asked Common's advice on setting up his own shop. At this time Common and his partner, Mary Anderson (1901–1942), a childhood friend from Newcastle who went south to join him, had a son, Peter; another son, Robert, was born later. Though they never married, touching love letters survive from their courtship. Common was poor enough by now to be subsidized by Orwell on occasion, and when the latter was in Morocco in 1938 Common and Mary Anderson looked after the Wallington cottage.

At some time during the Second World War Common moved to Frating Community Farm in Essex, where pacifists contributed to the war effort by farming. Mary died in 1942 from cancer, and Common began living with Constance Helena (Connie), *née* Sambidge (1902–1979), another Newcastle friend of his youth. Their daughter Caroline Alison (Sally) was born in 1944 (she was sixteen when her parents eventually married). Twin daughters, Mary and Charmian, were born in 1946. Meanwhile Common took part in a number of wartime radio broadcasts, including a lively debate, *What Matters?*, broadcast on 19 June 1942, which featured two opposing sets of speakers representing, roughly, suburbia and 'the streets'. Common remarked: 'I like a good argument' (BBC written archive). After the war he was engaged in writing film scripts including *Good Neighbours* (1946), about a community scheme in a Scottish town; he also travelled to Newfoundland on another film assignment. The family changed residence several times, ending up in a council house at 32 Warren Hamlet, Storrington, Sussex, with Common trying to make ends meet by working at a mushroom nursery, while toiling over scripts and reviews at night, and writing for himself in between. He was acutely oppressed by financial insecurity—and the lack of beer and tobacco.

In 1951 Turnstile Press published Common's best-known book, the autobiographical *Kiddar's Luck*, in which he vividly described his childhood on the streets of

Edwardian Tyneside, as seen through the lens of his adult socialism. There were four chapters on his life before five years of age—a feat of detailed memory—while his mother's alcoholism and the overbearing father whom he at length dramatically defied formed the dark background to the vigorous, at times bravura, narrative. The book found praise as a slice of Geordie naturalism, a convincing depiction of 'the other England', which so beguiled the imagination of contemporary intellectuals. On the other hand, its irony and subtly bitter universality went largely unrecognized. In *The Ampersand* (1954) Common took the story further, but his publishers went into liquidation two years later. Neither book was a commercial success, and Common did not complete the trilogy with his long-promised 'Riches and Rare', a novel set in Newcastle at the time of the general strike.

In 1956 Common embarked upon a two-year stint as guide to Chastleton House in the Cotswolds, a position obtained for him through Sir Richard Rees, a friend from *Adelphi* days. Predictable disagreements with the owner, Alan Clutton-Brock, put an end to an arrangement whereby Common had been able to get some writing done in the winter months. In 1958 a friend from Frating days, Irene Palmer, was instrumental in obtaining a rented Georgian house at 14 St John Street, in the centre of Newport Pagnell. There Common spent hours working on books for film treatment reviews in the 'garden' (a cemetery), walking with Connie in the countryside they both loved, and reading to his children. His daughter Sally later recalled listening to Shelley and ʿUmar Khayyam in the Fitzgerald translation, whose atheistic stance Common was at pains to emphasize. He had always been interested in astronomy (his Uncle Robin was a flat-earther), and Fred Hoyle's theory of an endlessly self-renewing universe, which dispensed with a creator, was attractive.

Though not a tactile person, Common was not a stern parent and never struck his children. He had small, feminine hands, badly stained with nicotine, and, Geordie-fashion, left domestic work to his wife. He was not a joiner or an activist, nor did he encourage his children to be so. He did, however, blossom in the right setting, often in pubs (his favourite was The Bull in Newport Pagnell), where he enjoyed political arguments with self-taught thinkers like himself. Another favourite haunt was the nearby working men's club on Silver Street, where he took his slippered ease at the bar. He was a connoisseur of beer and was described by his friend Tommy McCulloch as 'fairly jolly' at this period, though he retained his hatred of the 'bulky bourgeoisie'—and kept his Newcastle accent (private information). Lawrence Bradshaw used Common's brow as a model for his bust of Karl Marx in Highgate cemetery, saying that he found there a similar patience and understanding.

Too old to be an angry young man of the 1950s, Common could not sustain a career in writing. His political attitudes were by now out of fashion, and when he sent the manuscript of *In Whitest Britain* (1961) to his friend Eric Warman, Warman replied in a letter of 7 June 1961 that he was sorry such a 'bloody good writer' could not achieve success. Nevertheless there was too much 'class distinction' in the book, and the downtrodden, golden-hearted workman was a dated 'leading cliché' (Jack Common MSS). Thus Common, perhaps the finest chronicler of the English working class to follow Robert Tressell, spent his last years in Newport Pagnell writing film treatments at poor rates. He died there of lung cancer on 20 January 1968 and was cremated at Bedford on 24 January. He was survived by his wife and children, and left a mass of unpublished material, now held in the Robinson Library of the University of Newcastle upon Tyne.   ALAN MYERS

Sources private information (2004) · J. Common, *Kiddar's luck* (1951) · J. Common, *The ampersand* (1954) · Jack Common MSS, U. Newcastle, Robinson L., special collections · S. Chaplin, 'A farewell to Jack Common', *Sunday Times* (12 May 1968) · K. Armstrong, 'Memories of Jack Common', *Northern Review*, 1 (spring 1995), 89–93 · *The collected essays, journalism, and letters of George Orwell*, ed. S. Orwell and I. Angus, 1: *An age like this, 1920–1940* (1968), 371–3 · R. Colls, 'Cookson, Chaplin and Common: three northern writers in 1951', in K. D. M. Snell, *The regional novel in Britain and Ireland, 1800–1990* (1998), 164–200 · b. cert. · d. cert. [Constance Common]
Archives BBC WAC · U. Newcastle, Robinson L., corresp., diaries, and literary papers |SOUND BL NSA
Likenesses eighty-four photographs, U. Newcastle, Robinson L., Jack Common MSS, P 111 · photograph, U. Newcastle, Robinson L., Jack Common MSS, P 165

Comper, Sir (John) Ninian (1864–1960), architect, was born on 10 June 1864 at 44 Bonaccord Street, Aberdeen, the fourth child and first son of the seven children of the Revd John Comper (1823–1903), rector of St John's Episcopal Church, and his wife, Ellen (1828–1908), the eldest daughter of John Taylor, corn merchant of Hull, and his wife, Anne. Comper's parents were both English, and although he was by birth a Scot and never lost his love of the country his professional life was to be spent in London.

Background, education, and early career The Comper family had lived at Pulborough, in Sussex, since the Norman conquest and were yeoman farmers; the Revd John Comper's romantic belief that the family were Bretons, of Huguenot ancestry, has no substance in fact. Comper's father was a schoolmaster who had gone to Scotland in 1848 on the recommendation of Samuel Wilberforce, bishop of Oxford, to read for holy orders in the episcopal church. Influenced by the Tractarian movement, he became friends with Alexander Penrose Forbes, bishop of Brechin (who ordained him in 1852), the hymnologist John Mason Neale, and other leaders of the Anglo-Catholic revival. He went on to become rector of St Margaret's, Aberdeen, which became the most advanced church within the Scottish Episcopal church. Neale was one of Comper's godfathers and Anglo-Catholicism was the motivation and mainspring of his work as an architect; indeed, it was for this cause that most of it was executed.

In 1874 Comper went to Trinity College, Glenalmond, where he was brutally bullied. He left in 1880, and in 1882, after drawing for a term at the Ruskin School, Oxford, he became a voluntary assistant to C. E. Kempe, the glass painter and church craftsman, while continuing to draw

Sir (John) Ninian Comper (1864–1960), by Walter Stoneman, 1950

at the South Kensington School of Art. He was taken to see Bodley and Garner's unfinished St Michael's, Camden Town (1876–81), by Father George Congreve and he claimed that it was to the beauty of proportion and whiteness that he owed his conversion to architecture. In 1883 he was articled to G. F. Bodley, whom he was proud to call his master and whose work made a lasting impression on him.

In their mature work Bodley and Garner designed in the Decorated Gothic style of the fourteenth century, bringing it to a point of refinement that was in some ways an advance on the original. Comper's early work, notably the vaulted chapel of St Nicholas added to his father's church, St Margaret's, Aberdeen (1888–90), the chapel and extensions for the community of St Margaret, built on the Spital in Aberdeen (1891), and the conventual church of the Holy Name, Malvern Link, Worcestershire (1893), are fluent exercises in his masters' manner.

In 1888 Comper entered into partnership with William Bucknall, an improver in Bodley and Garner's drawing office who had been articled to E. R. Robson, architect to the Board of Education. The partnership was unequal but balanced: Bucknall was a pedestrian architect, but he was a good draughtsman and constructor, while Comper had the greater artistry, originality, and imagination but lacked constructional skills. He always needed assistants, and after the partnership had been dissolved in 1905, Comper was assisted by his nephew Arthur Bucknall, by Ernest Jago, formerly chief draughtsman to J. F. Bentley, by W. A. Forsyth, later by his eldest son, Sebastian, and

finally by his great-nephew John Bucknall. On 6 August 1890 Comper married William Bucknall's sister Grace (1868/9–1933) at an elaborate medievalist ceremony at St Barnabas, Pimlico; they had four sons and two daughters.

Comper's Perpendicular Gothic In preparation for his marriage ceremony Comper had studied medieval manuscripts in the British Museum. The illuminations demonstrated to him that the Gothic altars designed by Bodley and Garner, with their overpowering reredoses, were foreign to the essential simplicity of the medieval originals. It was from this time that Comper's work was informed by liturgical principles in which the altar became the determining feature and focus of church planning. But he always insisted that his work was not purely archaeological but was subordinate to a quest for beauty which, at this stage of his development, he found fully embodied in late Gothic art and architecture.

Comper increasingly came to derive inspiration from English Perpendicular architecture of the fifteenth century. The Perpendicular revival had been started by J. D. Sedding at St Clement, at Boscombe, Hampshire (1873–93). Comper brought to the revival a purist's attention to historical accuracy, modelling his work on the Perpendicular churches of East Anglia, which he visited in 1894–5. His late Gothic preferences were reinforced by studying Flemish primitive panel paintings, initially in the National Gallery, then on a visit to Belgium in 1894. To this was added a study of late Gothic religious art on the Rhine to Mainz in 1896, on a journey which took him to Nuremburg, Rothenburg, Würzburg, and Xanten, and with which he combined an enthusiasm for Wagner in a season at Bayreuth.

The first fruits of Comper's research are found in an authentically designed Gothic altar with riddle posts and a hanging pyx for the chapel of St Matthew's clergy house, Westminster (1892), followed by another in the restoration of St Wilfrid's, Cantley, Yorkshire (1892–4). It was in restorations that Comper's early work was most fully expressed: informed by medieval inventories, he changed stripped, barnlike shells into unified works of art, accomplished by furniture, embroidery, and textiles, base and precious metalwork, painted glass, and decoration. Most complete of all his reconstructions was the restoration of St Mary's, Egmanton, Nottinghamshire (1897), for the seventh duke of Newcastle.

Nineteenth-century churches were remodelled in the same way. Between 1890 and 1900 Comper's work in the lady chapel of Downside Abbey, Somerset (1896–1910), in the crypt of St Mary Magdalene, Paddington (1895), and St Barnabas, Pimlico (1891–1901), introduced an interpretation of English church art and liturgical worship based on scientific principles which had not been attempted since the days of A. W. N. Pugin and George Gilbert Scott the younger (both of whom in terms of authenticity Comper surpassed). Comper's work was intended to fulfil the rubrics of the Book of Common Prayer and apply them to the modern age. What appeared to some to be retrogressive antiquarianism was essentially a radical attempt to restore to the Church of England a continuity with the medieval past and reunite it with the historic Catholic faith. It was Comper's artistry and knowledge which made his experiments acceptable to the educated.

Comper's brilliance as a church furnisher was recognized from the beginning of his practice. The virtuosity of his restorations and furnishing schemes made many regard him more as a church craftsman than an architect and builder, yet his work was architecturally conceived. As a craftsman he was an innovator. From 1886 he became associated with the school of embroidery of the Sisters of Bethany, Clerkenwell, and under his direction the *or nué* technique of embroidery was introduced, leading the school to produce the finest church embroidery in northern Europe. His textiles were dyed by Sir Thomas Wardle, of Leek, in Staffordshire, and effected a transformation of ecclesiastical colour. His experiments in painted glass employed glass of strong but delicate tone on white grounds decorated with yellow stain. He revived the medieval practice of making blue glass in clay, rather than iron, pots using sand and seaweed. The result of these experiments may be seen in the series of windows of abbots and kings in the north aisle of Westminster Abbey (1909–61). From 1903 he signed his windows with a wild strawberry. Comper's ecclesiastical design was not influenced as strongly as Bodley's had been by the aesthetic movement; he declined, too, to follow the free expression of the arts and crafts movement and established an independent line of his own founded upon perfected late medieval precedent.

Comper designed only fifteen churches and his only major secular commission was the Welsh national war memorial, Cardiff (1924–8). His early work came to fulfilment in St Cyprian's, Clarence Gate, St Marylebone (1902–3). Here he built a developed version of the late medieval parish church; but the intention behind it was to build a quintessential Anglican church of the twentieth century. 'Its design', he wrote in a service paper for the consecration, 'neither seeks, nor avoids, originality; still less is its aim to reproduce any period of the past, but only to fulfil these and other needs which are ours today, and to do so in the most beautiful manner of all' ('On the significance of the building', quoted in 'Further thoughts on the English altar, or, Practical considerations on the planning of a modern church', 1933, 32).

Comper's mature style: 'unity by inclusion' In 1900 Comper read George Gilbert Scott the younger's *An Essay on the History of English Church Architecture prior to the Separation of England from the Roman Obedience* (1881), which had a far-reaching influence on his work and thought. In that same year he visited Rome, and in 1905 he went on to visit Sicily and the Mediterranean; in 1906 he visited Greece. These journeys made a profound impression on him and encouraged him to develop an inclusive approach to architecture which synthetized many decorative and architectural styles. In particular it was the Sicilian amalgam of Gothic, Greek, and Saracenic discovered in the Palermitan mosaic churches that led to the evolution of his second period, which he described as 'unity by inclusion'. He moved from seeing the late middle ages as a golden age in comparison

with which other centuries were either immature or decadent to concluding that both the Christian centuries and their classical inheritance had a valid application to an understanding of tradition as a vital, rather than static, force. Comper had discovered the debt owed by Christian art to Greece, and through travel and an exploration of Platonist philosophy he came to believe that the highest expression of beauty can be achieved only by inclusion, not exclusion.

No other English church architect of the twentieth century endeavoured to penetrate so deeply to the core of Western civilization by studying the church art and architecture of Europe in order to find there spiritual values for his own time. Comper's conversion to primitive models did not open a new period of mimesis. His understanding of the Christian tradition was accretive and in his fresh and sparkling use of precedent he vitalized tradition and made it distinctive of an English style. The figure of the Pantokrator became a necessary iconographical constituent; but he translated it from a stern, bearded Christ into a Hellenistic, beardless representation inspired by the early Christian images of the Good Shepherd.

The first expression of the fusion of styles is in Comper's restoration of Wimborne St Giles, Dorset (1908–10). It is indebted to the French Renaissance and has affinities with the English early seventeenth-century amalgam of classical and Gothic. This was followed by St Mary's, Rochdale, Lancashire (1908–12), in which the debt to Greece is more evident and where Comper first designed a figure of the Pantokrator executed in shallow relief above the rood. The altar screen of Wymondham Abbey, Norfolk (1913–33), is the most developed statement of his new synthesis in church furniture. It was in St Mary's, Wellingborough, Northamptonshire (1904–31), that the theory of unity by inclusion was given fullest architectural application. Here he combined English Perpendicular Gothic on a continental scale, using a French plan, with a classical arcade and furniture and Spanish Plateresque *rejas* of black iron. The altar stands beneath a classical ciborium, and the church is planned around it. The Majestas hangs above the rood screen, suspended from a lierne vault with fan pendants. But the aesthetic success of St Mary's lies in an exquisite use of Mediterranean colour, burnished gilding, and hangings of rose-red silk contained within white walls combined with ochre-coloured Northamptonshire ironstone. It is, perhaps, the most beautiful church built in England in the twentieth century. John Betjeman considered Comper to be the most delicate colourist and daring church planner of his time. What Voysey and Baillie Scott had done for houses, he believed, Comper had achieved for churches and so secured a place among the moderns. Yet Comper was strongly opposed to modernism and claimed for St Mary's, Wellingborough, in a paper, 'Further thoughts on the English altar, or, Practical considerations on the planning of a modern church' (1933), that 'Only to its contemporaries does it owe nothing' (p. 32).

A journey to Algeria in 1924 took Comper to see the ruined fifth-century church at Tébessa, which persuaded him of the suitability of Constantinian church planning for modern, centrally planned churches. As early as 1912 he had brought forward the high altar of the Grosvenor Chapel, Mayfair, and for the first time opened a direct visual relationship with the worshippers in the nave. He now repudiated the Gothic altar, insisting on a classical ciborium as a necessary part of the Christian altar; he also broke new ground at the conventual church of All Saints, London Colney, Hertfordshire (1924–7), and then in St Philip's, Cosham, Portsmouth, Hampshire (1937), by designing from the altar outwards. Here he anticipated the planning of churches which was brought to fruition on the continent after the Second World War and applied universally since the Second Vatican Council (1962–5).

Although few and infrequent, Comper's writings had great influence. He published three liturgical papers: 'Practical considerations of the Gothic or English altar and certain dependent ornaments' (1893); 'The reasonableness of the ornaments rubric illustrated by a comparison of the German and English altars' (1897); and 'Further thoughts on the English altar, or, Practical considerations on the planning of a modern church' (1933). These were followed by his mature reflections published in *Of the Atmosphere of a Church* (1940) and *Of the Christian Altar and the Buildings which Contain it* (1950). His early papers underpinned the research of Percy Dearmer and his popularizing attempt to establish a medievalist English use for the Church of England, while his later compositions influenced the theory of radical bodies such as the New Churches Research Group. Comper was dismayed by the plagiarism of his early work by Dearmer's Warham Guild and the encouragement of this development by the Central Council for the Care of Churches under the secretary, F. C. Eeles. Comper had become the most influential Anglican church architect of his time. His foremost public commissions were the Warrior's Chapel in Westminster Abbey (1925–31) and the parliamentary war memorial window in Westminster Hall (1952).

Character and appearance In 1938 Comper met John Betjeman. They formed a firm friendship and from that time until his death Betjeman became his principal advocate. His work was represented through Betjeman's eyes, and it was in reaction that Nikolaus Pevsner adopted an antagonistic stance and consistently dismissed Comper's work in *The Buildings of England*, thereby inflicting lasting damage to his reputation. It was to Betjeman's advocacy that Comper owed his knighthood in 1950. But Betjeman could mock as well as admire, and there was an ambivalence in his regard. It was Comper's personal charm in old age as much as his work that attracted him and others whom Betjeman brought into his life. From youth he had been afflicted by an oversensitive disposition, the result of a sense of frustration combined with a perfectionist sensibility. He was tormented by artistic touchiness and could be a difficult and formidable antagonist with a teasing sense of humour. But in sympathetic company he relaxed: his cultivated manners and exquisitely modulated voice, coupled with his powers as a raconteur of *la fin de siècle* (he had known Beardsley and his circle, Swinburne's sister

Isabel, the aesthetic company of Bodley and his patrons, and had moved in the society of the Souls), enchanted a later generation. With his friend and patron Charles Lindley Wood, second Viscount Halifax, he shared a passionate desire for the reunion of the Church of England with the Roman Catholic church.

Comper was an aesthete, and he dressed with an understated elegance. In youth he had red hair; but it turned white in middle life and from 1905 he wore a well-trimmed goatee beard and exchanged rimless pince-nez for gold-rimmed spectacles. A portrait of Comper (which he himself disliked) was painted in 1921 by his cousin Beatrice Bright and hangs in the National Portrait Gallery. Although happily married, Comper disliked women and felt carefree and more confident in the company of men. He had a Greek appreciation for the youthful male form, and this was represented by an over-delicacy of expression in his figure work and painted glass. He held that the ideal of male beauty was embodied in the ballet dancer Vaslav Nijinsky, and the oriental colouring of Leon Bakst's costume designs for the Ballets Russes influenced his later textile designs.

Death From the start of his marriage in 1890 Comper lived in Norwood, Surrey, first at 5 Chapel Road, then from 1894 at 158 Knight's Hill and from 1905 at 5 Gipsy Road. After the dissolution of his partnership with William Bucknall his drawing office (which he insisted on calling his study) was moved from 35 Old Queen Street, Westminster, to 228 Knight's Hill, where it remained until 1946. In 1912 he finally moved to The Priory, Beulah Hill, a stuccoed late Georgian 'gothick' house with an avenue, large garden, woodland, and a lake; here he lived until his death at the Hostel of God, Clapham Common, on 22 December 1960. His ashes were buried in the north aisle of Westminster Abbey beneath his windows of abbots and kings.

ANTHONY SYMONDSON

Sources *The Times* (23 Dec 1960) · P. Anson, 'The work of John Ninian Comper: a pioneer architect of the modern liturgical movement', *Pax*, 27 (1937), 177–84 · J. Betjeman, 'A note on J. N. Comper: heir to Butterfield and Bodley', *ArchR*, 85 (1939), 79–82 · J. Betjeman, 'Architecture', *Edwardian England, 1901–1914*, ed. S. Nowell-Smith (1964) · A. Symondson, *The life and work of Sir Ninian Comper, 1864–1960* (1988) · A. Symondson, 'John Betjeman and the cult of J. N. Comper', *Journal of the Thirties Society*, 7 (1991), 3–13, 52 · A. Symondson, 'Art needlework in Ireland: Sir Ninian Comper and the Royal Irish School of Art Needlework', *Irish Arts Review Yearbook*, 10 (1994), 126–35 · A. Symondson, 'Theology, worship, and the late Victorian church', *The Victorian church: architecture and society*, ed. C. Brooks and A. Saint (1995), 192–222 · A. Symondson, 'Unity by inclusion: Sir Ninian Comper and the planning of a modern church', *Journal of the Twentieth Century Society*, 3 (1998), 17–42 · J. Wiseman, 'John Comper: a memoir', *Church principles, or, The scriptural teaching of the British churches* (1904), xiii–xxxviii · *John Betjeman: letters*, ed. C. Lycett Green, 2 vols. (1994–5) · b. cert. · m. cert. · d. cert. · S. Bucknall and A. Symondson, *Sir Ninian Comper: an introduction and gazetteer* (2003) · G. Stamp, *An architect of promise: George Gilbert Scott junior (1839–1897) and the late Gothic revival* (2002)

Archives Derbys. RO, corresp. relating to work on St James's, Buxton · RIBA BAL, corresp. and papers, incl. professional papers | CUL, corresp. with Lord Hardinge

Compton, Lord Alwyne (1825–1906), bishop of Ely, born at Castle Ashby on 18 July 1825, was the fourth son of Spencer Joshua Alwyne *Compton, second marquess of Northampton (1790–1851), and his wife, Margaret (*d.* 1830), daughter of Major-General Douglas Maclean Clephane of Torloisk. Lady Marian Alford [*see* Egerton, Marianne Margaret, Viscountess Alford (1817–1888)] was his sister. He was educated at Eton College and matriculated from Trinity College, Cambridge, in 1844, graduating BA as fourteenth wrangler in 1848. He was ordained deacon in 1850 and priest in 1851. On 28 August 1850 he married Florence Caroline (*d.* 1918), eldest daughter of Robert Anderson, a clergyman in Brighton, and his wife, Caroline Dorothea, daughter of John Shore, first Baron Teignmouth. They had no children.

After serving as curate of Horsham Compton was appointed in 1852 by his brother, who had recently become third marquess, to the rectory of Castle Ashby, the chief family seat. He held this benefice for twenty-six years. In 1857 Compton was elected one of the proctors in convocation for the diocese of Peterborough, and was re-elected on four successive occasions until he became an *ex officio* member of the lower house, through his appointment in 1875 by William Connor Magee, bishop of Peterborough, to the archdeaconry of Oakham. From the first he took an active interest in the business of convocation, and became after a few years one of its leading members; he was elected prolocutor on 30 April 1880, and held the office for nearly six years. Meanwhile, in 1879, Compton was nominated by Lord Beaconsfield to the deanery of Worcester. At Worcester he promoted the common good of the city and county, and entered into the friendliest relations with his neighbours of all classes. He also made changes in the arrangements for the triennial musical festivals in the cathedral with a view to securing greater reverence in the performances. After seven years at Worcester he was appointed by Lord Salisbury to the see of Ely on the death of James Russell Woodford, being consecrated on 2 February 1886. In 1882 he had been made lord high almoner, and he retained this office until his death.

Compton increasingly won the respect and affection both of the clergy and the laity of his diocese during his episcopate of nearly twenty years. Although his sermons made no pretensions to oratory either in form or delivery, or to originality of thought, they were often impressive from their simplicity, directness, and sincerity.

In his theological views Compton was an old-fashioned high-churchman, but in his practice he was tolerant. He published charges in 1889, 1893, 1897, and 1903. At his primary and second visitations he expressed disapproval of the practice of evening communions on the grounds that it was a departure from the long-received custom of the church. But there was no diminution in the cordiality of his relations with the incumbents, whom he sought vainly to persuade to discontinue the practice. He felt that

men of an opposite school, whose views were more advanced than his own, had likewise a place in the Church of England, and he was ready to protect them fearlessly, so far as they seemed to him to be within their rights, at the same time as he discountenanced excesses in ritual.

Compton's chief intellectual interest outside his clerical duties lay in the study of architecture and archaeology, and he was a good draughtsman, especially of the details of architecture. He rendered a valuable service to historical students by collecting all the documents connected with the see which had been stored in different places, having them arranged and catalogued by an expert, and publishing the catalogue. He finally placed them in a building, once the gaol of the bishops of Ely in the days when they had civil jurisdiction, which he turned into a diocesan registry and muniment rooms.

In July 1905, on the completion of his eightieth year, Compton resigned his see and settled at St Martin's House, Canterbury. He died there on 4 April 1906, and was buried in the churchyard of St Martin's, which his garden bordered. V. H. STANTON, *rev.* H. C. G. MATTHEW

Sources *The Times* (5 April 1906) · *Manchester Guardian* (11 April 1906) · Venn, *Alum. Cant.* · personal knowledge (1912)
Archives LPL, letters to Edward Benson
Likenesses J. H. F. Bacon, oils, 1903, NPG · E. Clifford, portrait (in middle age); formerly in family possession, 1912 · S. P. Hall, group portrait, watercolour (*The bench of bishops, 1902*), NPG · photograph (*Anglican bishops*), NPG
Wealth at death £19,128 13*s.*: probate, 7 June 1906, *CGPLA Eng. & Wales*

Compton, Denis Charles Scott (1918–1997), cricketer and footballer, was born on 23 May 1918 at 20 Alexandra Road, Hendon, Middlesex, the youngest of three children of Henry (Harry) Ernest Compton, a manufacturing chemist's counterman, and his wife, Jessie Anne Duthie. Both parents resided at Woodford in Essex before moving to Hendon, where Harry Compton established himself as a painter and decorator. Denis's brother, Leslie Harry, followed Denis as a Middlesex cricketer and preceded him as an Arsenal and England footballer. His sister, Hilda, was a natural athlete.

The sporting proclivities of the children derived from their father. Harry Compton was captain of the old boys' cricket team of Bell Lane elementary school, Hendon, and from Denis's earliest years took him to the games to score and, when the chance came, to play. Denis also attended the Bell Lane school; at ten he was in his school team, and at twelve he was scoring runs against an adult team which had to be encouraged by his father to bowl as well and fast as they could. Captain of his school team at both cricket and football, he next captained North London Schools at Lord's against the South, making 88. Aged fourteen he led the London Elementary Schools against a team of public schoolboys, also at Lord's, made 114, and helped to bowl out the opponents for an easy victory. Happily Sir Pelham Warner saw the game and in the spring of 1933 a contract was offered by MCC at the standard ground boy rate of 25*s.* Denis's mother was sceptical until the Arsenal Football

Denis Charles Scott Compton (1918–1997), by unknown photographer, 1949

Club manager, the famous Herbert Chapman, signed the boy on, so providing employment all the year.

As with most batsmen destined to reach the top branches of the tree, success arrived at precocious speed. Compton's first appearance for Middlesex came in the Whitsuntide match of 1936 against Sussex at Lord's. Success in that before a full house was followed after a few weeks by his first hundred, and G. O. Allen was soon wondering whether to take the eighteen-year-old prodigy to Australia with MCC that winter. As it was, the first of Compton's seventy-eight test appearances came in the last test of the following summer (1937) against New Zealand. Against Australia in the first test of 1938 at Trent Bridge he made the fourth hundred of a then record total of 658 for eight declared.

It was, however, at Lord's in the second innings of the second test of the series that Compton played what in the minds of the best judges was the defining innings of his life. On a pitch made treacherous by rain and sun England, having lost five wickets for 76, faced probable defeat if he failed. In this situation Compton confronted the fire of McCormick and the spin and lift of O'Reilly with a mastery of technique and coolness of judgement which would have been remarkable in the most mature of batsmen, let alone a young man of twenty. His 76 not out enabled Hammond to declare and put Australia under pressure to draw

the match. Compton made seventeen hundreds in tests, yet he always regarded this as his best innings. Henceforward, it seemed, that strong hint of genius would be frustrated only by misfortunes outside his control.

Compton was lucky in those pre-war years in being a member of a strong side, second only to Yorkshire, led by a dashing captain of his own adventurous spirit in R. W. V. Robins: lucky also from 1937 onwards, when Bill Edrich of Norfolk arrived at Lord's to form with him what became one of the most famous partnerships of cricket history. He was fortunate also in the influence of successive head coaches of MCC. The first of them, George Fenner, saw that his cricket was essentially instinctive. 'I shouldn't say I coached him', he would demur. 'Let's just say I didn't spoil him' (West, 24). Pat Hendren, the Middlesex senior professional, and Archie Fowler, who took over from Fenner, reacted similarly.

Crowds took to Compton warmly from the start because he communicated an obvious enjoyment of the game. With his dark good looks went an appealing, carefree spirit. Driving over Vauxhall Bridge he was once told by a fellow motorist who was listening to the radio that the day's cricket in the test at the Oval, in which he was playing, had already started. People forgave an uncertain regard for time and place—which unfortunately grew no better with the years, as wives, tour managers, friends, and all concerned would unanimously agree.

In 1939 Compton improved on the previous years' records with 2468 runs at an average of 56: there were eight hundreds, including his first in a Lord's test, 120 against West Indies made in only 2 hours 20 minutes in a scintillating partnership of 248 with Len Hutton. The latter, batting slowly until Compton joined him, suddenly began to match him stroke for stroke, the roundhead donning for once the plumes of the cavalier. It was to be seven years before these brightest of English stars batted again together. Hutton on the resumption had to improvise with a left arm shortened by a physical training accident. Much luckier, Compton had seen the last two years of his service with the Royal Artillery in India, where he took good advantage of some first-class cricket, playing for Holkar in the Ranji trophy tournament.

Twelve seasons remained to Compton after the war. He reached the peak of his fame in the first four, after which his cricket was impeded by permanent trouble with his right knee. There was one operation which kept him off the field for half the 1950 summer. A more serious one entailed removal of the kneecap in 1955 following regular manipulations to increase the flexion. At the end of the 1957 summer, aged thirty-nine, the pain and frustration demanded his retirement. His record, when the restrictions of the last eight years are considered, is extraordinary: in 515 matches 38,942 runs, average 51.85, with 123 hundreds: in 78 tests 5807 runs, average 50.06, with 17 hundreds. There were 416 catches, 49 in tests. His slow left-arm bowling, little used before the war, was at times, when he developed wrist spin and a well-disguised googly, an important factor. He took 622 wickets, all told, at 32 runs apiece. He was too expensive to be a success in tests, though he might have won one.

As an outside-left Compton was a member of the famous Arsenal teams of the 1930s. He played eleven times for England in wartime internationals. Afterwards, though the MCC tours of 1946–7 and 1948–9 restricted his football, he remained an Arsenal player. He had a powerful left foot and the same flair for the occasion which characterized his cricket. Thus, despite the suspect right knee (from which a ligament had been removed following a pre-war collision with a goalkeeper), he was picked for the cup final of 1950 against Liverpool. In this, the last game he ever played, Peter West tells in *Denis Compton: a Cricketing Genius* how his subject considered he had played poorly in the first half. Tom Whittaker, the Arsenal manager, gave him a transforming slug of brandy at the interval, and Denis and Leslie were able to add cup winners' medals to the league winners' medals they had won in 1947–8.

The impact of Compton's cricket now touched new heights of hero-worship. Society found an antidote in sport to war-weariness and austerity, and here was a young man who not only played supremely well but so manifestly relished what he was doing and the pleasure he was giving. 'Let's enjoy this!' he was saying as one county attack after another suffered at his hands. Gerald Brodribb in *Champions of Cricket* has estimated that in his innings exceeding 50 (of which there were 300) his average rate of progress was about 47 runs an hour. B. J. Wakley estimated Don Bradman's rate as 42. Brodribb names only five truly great batsmen who scored faster: Woolley, Trumper, Macartney, Ranjitsinhji, and Duleepsinhji.

Almost inevitably there were brief periods when the machinery failed to synchronize. At the height of the summer of 1946 Compton made four 0s in a row, all at Lord's, yet he still averaged 61 for the season, with ten hundreds. The other blackspot, much more calamitous, encompassed the 1950–51 series in Australia, when he averaged 7.57 in the tests and in the remaining matches 92.11. In between these extremes—and, of course, afterwards less copiously—the runs flowed in abundance both at home and overseas. Against Australia at Adelaide he made a hundred in each innings. In England neither his aggregate of 3816 runs (average 90.85), made in the hot dry summer of 1947, nor his eighteen hundreds for the season, made the same year, has ever been approached. No Englishman has ever scored as many runs in a home series as his 753 in the tests against South Africa. In fact Bill Edrich, his comrade-in-arms, lagged only a little behind him in that memorable summer. He too exceeded with 3519 runs (average 80) Tom Hayward's previous record total. The runner-up, however, suffered the normal eclipse of the second best: 1947 went down in history as Compton's year.

It was as a result of his prodigious fan mail and of certain commercial offers that Compton accepted the suggestion of a businessman, Bagenal Harvey, to help manage his affairs. Harvey became the first prominent sporting entrepreneur. Theirs was a long association, one of the early fruits being the famous Brylcreem advertisement. This became something of a standing joke, for the smiling figure on the hoardings usually batted without a cap and his hair was often conspicuously untidy.

Of all Compton's test hundreds the writer would give pride of place to his 184 in the test against Australia at Trent Bridge in 1948. It was stretched over six and a half hours and ten separate periods of play, most of them in an eerie, yellow light. In a gallant though vain effort to save the game there was scarcely a false stroke, certainly not a chance. Later in that series at Headingley his wrist spin would probably have reversed the result had not one stumping chance and two slip catches off him been missed at the outset of the winning partnership between Morris and Bradman.

Unfit for the first four tests against Australia in 1956, Compton was picked for the last and bowed out with an innings of 94 which Sir Donald Bradman, now a *Daily Mail* reporter, rated as the best of the series. A second visit to South Africa the following winter proved a tour too far. Back home, however, he ended his professional career with a sparkling 143 against Worcestershire at Lord's.

In the 1958 new year honours Compton was appointed CBE. He wrote on cricket for the *Sunday Express* with regular help from R. J. Hayter for forty years, and in the 1950s commented on tests for BBC television. In contrast with his philosophy as a cricketer he was apt to sound a forthright, sometimes almost a fierce note as a critic: he was very much *laudator temporis acti*. He served for many years as a director of Royds public relations company.

Compton was married three times. His first marriage, on 1 March 1941, to Doris Yvonne Rich (*b.* 1920/21), a dancer, daughter of Bernard Stewart Rich, a schoolmaster, was dissolved. They had one son. In 1951 he married Valerie Platt, of Isipingo, Natal, whom he first met in Durban during the 1948–9 tour of South Africa. There were two sons of the marriage, which was dissolved in 1960. On 23 September 1975 he married Christine Franklin Tobias (*b.* 1943/4), daughter of Benjamin Franklin Tobias, company director, with whom he had two daughters. Compton became president of Middlesex in 1990–91 and remained so almost to his death. His name was fittingly perpetuated at Lord's when in 1991 the new open stands at the nursery end were named after Compton and Edrich, one either side of the sightscreen. Edrich had died, but Compton was present on the spot where as a boy he had first watched sixty years previously. The president of MCC, Lord Griffiths, escorted him back to the pavilion to his last standing ovation. He died in hospital at Windsor, Berkshire, on 23 April 1997, survived by his third wife. A memorial service was held in Westminster Abbey on 2 July.

E. W. SWANTON

Sources E. W. Swanton, *Denis Compton: a cricket sketch* (1948) · J. Allen, *Denis Compton: our greatest all-round sportsman* (1949) · I. Peebles, *Denis Compton: the generous cricketer* (1971) · P. West, *Denis Compton: a cricketing genius* (1989) · T. Heald, *Denis Compton* (1994) · *Daily Telegraph* (24 April 1997) · *The Independent* (24 April 1997) · *The Times* (24 April 1997) · D. Compton, *End of an innings* (1958) · N. Cardus, *Wisden* (1958), 78–93 · b. cert. · m. cert. [Doris Rich] · m. cert. [Christine Tobias]

Archives FILM BFI NFTVA, sports short no. 2, 1954 · BFI NFTVA, 'Maestro', 9 Jan 1981 · BFI NFTVA, *Sporting legends*, 18 May 1997 · BFI NFTVA, 'Dennis Compton: 70 not out', 4 May 1998 · BFI NFTVA, documentary footage · BFI NFTVA, news footage · BFI NFTVA, sports footage | SOUND BL NSA, current affairs recordings

Likenesses photographs, 1938–56, Hult. Arch. · photograph, 1949, Empics Sports Photo Agency, Nottingham [*see illus.*] · photographs, repro. in Swanton, *Denis Compton*, 16, 18

Compton, Sir Edmund Gerald (1906–1994), civil servant, was born on 30 July 1906 in Valparaiso, Chile, the elder son and second of the six children of Edmund Spencer Compton (1875–1932), merchant, and his wife, Beatrice (1882–1969), daughter of Edward Moyna, of Sandymount, Ireland. The family returned to England at the beginning of the First World War so that Compton's father could fight in the war, in which he won an MC, and eventually settled at Pailton House, Pailton, near Rugby. Compton won a scholarship to Rugby School, where he had a career of considerable distinction and whose governors he later chaired. From there he won a scholarship to New College, Oxford, where he gained a second in classical moderations in 1927 and a first in *literae humaniores* in 1929.

Compton passed third into the home civil service in 1929 and, after brief periods in the Ministry of Labour and the Colonial Office, transferred to the Treasury in 1931. One of his contemporaries there, Thomas Padmore, later recalled: 'At once I realised that he was a very good civil servant indeed and entirely straightforward' (*The Independent*). Compton's apprenticeship in the Treasury included a spell as private secretary to Duff Cooper when the latter was financial secretary. On 9 June 1934 he married Betty Tresyllian (1912–1987), daughter of Hakewill Tresyllian Williams JP DL of Churchill Court, Kidderminster. She was active in many charitable causes and was made CBE in June 1978. They had a son and four daughters.

In 1940, when Winston Churchill appointed Lord Beaverbrook minister in charge of the new Ministry of Aircraft Production, Compton was seconded from the Treasury as his private secretary. 'The Beaver' was not a conventional minister, nor an easy man to work for, but Compton looked back on this phase of his career as stimulating and enjoyable. In 1942 Compton returned to the Treasury, as an assistant secretary. Though there were interludes in other divisions, for the next sixteen years he was more often than not in the home finance division, which was concerned with monetary policies and controls, at various levels: he was promoted under-secretary in 1947 and third secretary (the equivalent of deputy secretary in other departments) in 1949. His mastery of this aspect of the Treasury's responsibilities was displayed in the evidence that he gave in 1957–8 to the Radcliffe committee on the working of the monetary system. In this field the relationship between the Treasury and the Bank of England was of crucial importance, and Compton made it his particular business to foster good relations with the bank. His relations with the then chief cashier, Leslie O'Brien (later governor of the bank) were especially close and friendly.

Compton (who was appointed CB in 1948 and KBE in 1955) must have expected to stay in the Treasury until his retirement and could legitimately have aspired to be considered as a potential permanent secretary, but in 1958 his career took an unexpected turn when he was appointed comptroller and auditor-general, the parliamentary watchdog on the expenditure of government departments. If he was disappointed to leave the Treasury this was never outwardly apparent. In terms of rank and pay the comptroller and auditor-general rated as a permanent secretary; his move was thus a promotion. He brought to his new duties his characteristic energy, zest, and capacity for hard work, much experience of the work of government departments, an eagle eye for what needed to be investigated, and immense thoroughness in pursuing an investigation. But his thoroughness and his strong sense of fairness made sure that, though his inquiries may have been unwelcome to the departments affected, they were not resented as superficial or unfair. He also brought to his task his own well-honed skill in drafting, which made his reports to parliament all the more telling. He reported first and foremost to the public accounts committee of the House of Commons, and especially to its chairman. Harold Wilson chaired the committee from 1959 until he became leader of the Labour Party, in 1963. He was greatly impressed by Compton; he told Tam Dalyell MP, when the latter became a member of the committee in 1962, that Compton was one of the shrewdest, cleverest, and nicest men in Whitehall, from whom he had learned a great deal about how government operated in Britain.

When the Labour government (1964–70) decided to create a new office of parliamentary commissioner for administration (or ombudsman) Wilson, as prime minister, saw Compton's qualities as indispensable for the first holder of that office. Accordingly in 1966, the year when Compton expected to retire, he was designated first parliamentary commissioner for administration for Great Britain, and held the office from 1967 until 1971. The thoroughness and fairness that he had displayed as comptroller and auditor-general, and his insistence on staying strictly within his terms of reference, ensured that the office quickly developed the necessary authority and became permanent. It also led to Compton's appointment in 1969 as ombudsman for Northern Ireland as well. That in turn led to his being called upon, after he had retired, to chair a committee of inquiry into alleged maltreatment of prisoners suspected of belonging to the IRA. The committee found that the methods of interrogating prisoners amounted to 'physical ill-treatment', and compensation amounting to some £150,000 was awarded to the prisoners concerned.

In retirement Compton (promoted KCB in 1965 and GCB in 1971) undertook various other public duties, including chairmanship of the Local Government Boundary Commission (1971–8) and of the BBC Complaints Commission (1972–81), and reports on the staffing and administration of the House of Commons and on medical services in the armed forces. He had always been active in the Church of England, and from 1965 to 1973 he chaired its central board of finance. For forty years (1946–86) he also chaired the Irish Sailors' and Soldiers' Land Trust. The trust had been set up after the First World War to honour pledges given by Sir John French, when recruiting in Ireland for men to join the armed forces, that those who joined up would have housing provided for them after the war. By the time of Compton's retirement nearly all the beneficiaries of the trust (and their widows) had died, the cottages built for them by the trust had been sold, and the trust itself was being wound up.

Compton was a small man with a warm, friendly, and lively personality, of great charm, and of unfailing courtesy—qualities that generally enabled him to get his way without creating enemies. He was also a man of wide interests, and all his life he kept up his Greek and Latin. But his special passion was music. He was a competent amateur violinist, playing in a Treasury string quartet, three of whose members had knighthoods; the quartet was irreverently but affectionately known as the 'Knights of the Catgut'. He was a lifelong member of the Bach Choir, and had regular weekly gatherings of family and friends to sing at his home. He was a member of the board of governors of the Royal Academy of Music from 1965 to 1981, and was chairman from 1975 to 1981. Towards the end of his life he suffered from cancer of the prostate; he died of renal failure and iron deficiency anaemia at his home, Flat 1, 80 Elm Park Gardens, Chelsea, London, on 11 March 1994. He was survived by his five children. A memorial service was held at St Margaret's, Westminster, on 12 July 1994.   ROBERT ARMSTRONG

Sources *The Times* (14 March 1994) · *The Times* (13 July 1994) · *The Independent* (14 March 1994) · *WWW, 1991–5* · Burke, *Peerage* · personal knowledge (2004) · private information (2004) · b. cert. · m. cert. · d. cert.
Archives SOUND BL NSA, performance recording
Likenesses photograph, repro. in *The Times* (14 March 1994) · photograph, repro. in *The Independent*
Wealth at death £286,934: probate, 3 June 1994, CGPLA Eng. & Wales

Compton, Edward [*real name* Edward Compton Mackenzie] (1854–1918), actor and theatre manager, was born on 14 January 1854 at 16 Charing Cross Road, London, the fifth of the nine children of Charles Mackenzie, known as Henry *Compton (1805–1877), an actor, and Emmeline Montague Compton (1823–1911). He was educated at the academy run by the Revd J. Gaitskell, formerly the classmaster of the Kensington proprietary grammar school. His first stage appearance was at the Bristol New Theatre, on 22 September 1873, in the small role of Long Ned in F. Boyle's *Old London*. In April 1874 he joined the Francis Fairlie Touring Company, playing parts in Alfred Kempe's *East Lynne*, C. R. Munro's *Progress*, and Sheridan's *The School for Scandal*. Then followed stock seasons in Bristol, Glasgow, Kilmarnock, Liverpool, and Birmingham. He made his first appearance in London at his father's benefit at Drury Lane on 1 March 1877, playing Alfred Evelyn in the first act of Bulwer-Lytton's *Money*. He also appeared in his father's second benefit in Manchester, on 27 March 1877.

Compton appeared briefly with companies organized by H. J. Byron and by Mrs Hermann Vezin. For two years from 22 October 1877 he toured with a company organized

by Ellen Wallis, appearing as Cassio, Malcolm, Romeo, Florizal, and Benedick, as Charles Surface in *The School for Scandal*, and as Claude Melnotte in Bulwer-Lytton's *The Lady of Lyons*. On 23 April 1879 he played Claudio in *Much Ado about Nothing* at the dedication of the Shakespearian Memorial Theatre at Stratford upon Avon. During the same year, through Tinsley Brothers, London, he and his brother Charles published their *Memoir of Henry Compton*.

Edward Compton next joined the Adelphi Theatre, London, and accepted the invitation of its star, Adelaide Neilson, to accompany her on her next American tour. The company sailed on 27 September 1879. They played in New York, Boston, and New Orleans before concluding performances in San Francisco on 17 July 1880. The tour was a critical and financial success, netting in excess of £15,000. However, it was also physically exhausting for the star and for her company.

On 28 July 1880 the Neilson company sailed from New York, bound for London. Miss Neilson then continued on to Paris to rest and to prepare her trousseau for her planned marriage that September to Edward Compton. While driving in the Bois de Boulogne on the morning of Sunday 15 August 1880 she was suddenly stricken with a ruptured aneurysm, and she died several hours later. The service and burial took place at Brompton cemetery on 20 August 1880.

By the terms of her existing will, Miss Neilson made several specific bequests, among them a gift of £2000 to Compton. Although he briefly returned to the Adelphi company following his fiancée's death, the gift allowed him to create and equip his own touring repertory troupe, the Compton Comedy Company, which, for the next thirty-five years, presented Shakespearian plays and old English comedies throughout the United Kingdom. The company made its first appearance at Southport on 7 February 1881.

As his leading lady Compton selected Virginia Frances *Bateman (1853–1940) [see under Bateman, Hezekiah Linthicum], who had recently finished an engagement at her mother's New Sadler's Wells Theatre, playing Miss Hardcastle in Oliver Goldsmith's *She Stoops to Conquer*, Lydia Languish in Sheridan's *The Rivals*, and Lady Teazle in *The School for Scandal*.

On 12 June 1882 Compton and Virginia Bateman were married at St Peter's parish church, Brighton. They had five children: the novelist Sir Edward Montague Compton *Mackenzie (1883–1972) and the actors Frank Compton (1885–1964), Viola Compton (1886–1971), Ellen Compton (1891–1970), and Fay *Compton (1894–1978).

By 1891 the Compton Comedy Company had toured for ten years, having given approximately 3000 performances in the British provinces—most notably *The School for Scandal* a total of 398 times, Thomas Holcroft's *The Road to Ruin* 367 times, T. W. Robertson's *David Garrick* 391 times, *The Rivals* 287 times, and *She Stoops to Conquer* 234 times. Believing the time was right for the company to move to London, and realizing that a vehicle by a celebrity author would make an impression, Compton, at the urging of his wife, wrote to Henry James to request that he turn his popular novel *The American* into an actable drama. James agreed, but recorded in his notebooks that 'The field is common, but it is wide and free … And if there is money in it that will greatly help' (*Complete Notebooks*, 53).

The American was first presented by the Compton Comedy Company on 3 January 1891 in Southport, with Edward Compton playing Christopher Newman, the American. The première succeeded beyond the author's reserved expectations, as he gleefully described to his sister the 'big universal outbreak at the end for "author, author, AUTHOR!"' (*Henry James: Letters*, 3.320).

Compton secured the Opera Comique for the first London presentation of *The American* on 26 September 1891. Again he played Christopher Newman, but now cast his sister-in-law Mrs Crowe (Kate Bateman) as the Marquise de Bellegarde, and a young American, Elizabeth Robins, as the heroine, Claire de Cintré. Although the celebrity-studded first-night audience may have anticipated a new dawn of English drama from the facile pen of so eminent a novelist as James, they were to be disappointed by heavy-handed melodrama, convoluted twists of plot, uneven pacing, and painfully poor performances by several members of the cast. As one critic described the scene:

> The audience was much amused and rather interested by the first act, less amused and more interested by the second, still less amused and rather less interested by the third, and not at all amused and barely interested by the fourth. Then the curtain came down, the people kindly clapped their hands as a means of stretching themselves, the actors appeared and bowed, … and those in front of the curtain went away rather bored and much disappointed, while those behind departed full of false hope. (*Pall Mall Gazette*, 28 Sept 1891, 2)

Despite a well-publicized visit by the prince of Wales and some tinkering with the production, *The American* closed on 4 December 1891, after only sixty-nine performances, handing its manager a great disappointment and a heavy financial loss. Edward's son Sir Compton Mackenzie described his father's reaction:

> He realised that it was not his destiny to be a leading London actor–manager and went back to the provinces where he was so much loved, and where in a white wig instead of a toupee and with patches instead of a false moustache he would be making much more money and doing far more for British drama than by trying to establish himself in London. (Mackenzie, *My Life and Times*, octave 2, 22)

While the Compton Comedy Company continued to tour the British provinces, Compton, in association with Milton Bode, acquired proprietary interest in several provincial and suburban theatres. In August 1915, as plans were under way for a return of the company to London at the Shaftesbury Theatre, he became ill and plans were suspended. He died at his home, 54 Avonmore Road, London, of throat cancer, on 16 July 1918.

Two months later, as Mrs Virginia Compton prepared to relaunch the company on an autumn tour, one theatre critic commented:

> it would be impossible, without much delving into the past, to give the list of the famous actors and actresses who learnt their early stagecraft under Mr. Edward Compton's banner. His work rivals that of Sir Frank Benson, and he was a man

just as much loved … we shall miss him. (*Bristol Times and Mirror*, 28 Sept 1918)

The Compton Comedy Company continued to tour the provinces until 26 July 1923, when financial losses could no longer be borne, and it was disbanded.

GAYLE T. HARRIS

Sources J. H. Barnes, *Forty years on the stage* (1914) · L. H. Powers, *The complete notebooks of Henry James*, ed. L. Edel, new edn (1987) · *Henry James: letters*, ed. L. Edel, 3: *1883–1895* (1980) · C. Mackenzie, *My life and times*, 10 vols. (1963–71), vols. 1–2 · L. Warwick, *The Mackenzies called Compton* (1977) · W. Winter, *The wallet of time: containing personal, biographical, and critical reminiscence of the American theatre*, 2 vols. (1913); facs. edn (1969) · *Daily Bristol Times and Mirror* (3 Aug 1880) · *Bristol Times and Mirror* (28 Sept 1918) · *The Era* (5 Sept 1880) · *Pall Mall Gazette* (28 Sept 1891) · *Pall Mall Gazette* (20 Oct 1891) · *The Times* (17 Aug 1880) · Theatre Museum, London, various playbills for Sadler's Wells · IGI
Archives Theatre Museum, London, Theatre Girls Club collection | Folger, Augustin Daly MSS · U. Texas, Sir Compton Mackenzie MSS
Likenesses Robinson & Thompson, photograph, NYPL, Performing Arts collection · photographs, priv. coll.
Wealth at death $350,000: 31 Aug 1918, *Boston (MA) Transcript* · $285,000: 2 Oct 1918, *Variety*

Compton, Fay [*real name* Virginia Lilian Emmeline Compton-Mackenzie] (**1894–1978**), actress, was born at 54 Avonmore Road, Fulham, London, on 18 September 1894, the fifth and youngest child and third daughter of Edward *Compton (1854–1918), actor and manager (whose real surname was Mackenzie), and his wife, the actress Virginia Frances *Bateman (1853–1940) [*see under* Bateman, Hezekiah Linthicum], daughter of the actor Hezekiah Linthicum *Bateman, of Baltimore, Maryland. Her elder brother was Sir (Edward Montague) Compton *Mackenzie (1883–1972), the author.

Educated at Leatherhead Court School, Surrey, and in Paris, Fay Compton's professional début was at the Apollo Theatre, London, in August 1911, acting and singing with the Follies, a troupe created by Harry Gabriel *Pélissier (1874–1913), a comedian who had a rare talent for revue. Before the programme opened, and after a seven-week engagement, she was married to Pélissier on 16 September at the age of sixteen. The marriage lasted only two years, for he died on 25 September 1913, aged thirty-nine, leaving an infant son.

In November 1913 his young widow got the small part of Devise in a comedy called *Who's the Lady?* at the Garrick Theatre, which ran for 180 performances, and she went on to appear in various musical comedies, one of them (*Tonight's the Night*, in December 1914) in New York. From the first this red-haired beauty was an assured professional; no actress of her time was more versatile. She earned an early reputation by performing in the works of J. M. Barrie; but she went on to every type of play, from Shakespeare to romantic drama, high and light comedy, farce, and even as principal boy in pantomime.

Fay Compton had a small part in the revival at the Savoy Theatre by H. B. Irving of *The Professor's Love Story* (1916). She starred in Barrie's *Peter Pan* at the New Theatre at Christmas 1917. In April 1920, at the Haymarket, which would always be her favourite theatre, she experienced

Fay Compton (1894–1978), by Dorothy Wilding, 1920s

her first real triumph when she played the title role in *Mary Rose*, Barrie's fantasy of the girl who vanishes on a Hebridean island and returns after many years as a ghost. She acted the ghost scenes with an enchanted stillness. Now recognized as a leading lady, presently she had a long and improbably contrasted sequence of West End parts, among them the runaway wife in *The Circle* by W. Somerset Maugham (March 1921), Phoebe Throssel in *Quality Street* by Barrie (August 1921), and two characters in the complex and long-running *Secrets* (1922), in which she had to alter her age several times.

During 1923 Fay Compton moved to the declining Ruritanian drama, as Princess Flavia in a revival at the Haymarket of Anthony Hope's *The Prisoner of Zenda*. She was happy as Lady Babbie in Barrie's *The Little Minister* (revived at the Queen's in November 1923); less so as Yasmin in James Elroy Flecker's *Hassan*, directed by Basil Dean at His Majesty's where she succeeded Cathleen Nesbitt in the spring of 1924. In February 1925 she had her first major classical opportunity: to appear at the Haymarket as Ophelia to the American John Barrymore's *Hamlet*, a performance of which the critic James Agate wrote: 'She was fragrant, wistful, and had a child's importunacy unmatched in my time.'

In spite of the number of her later parts (more than eighty in several genres) Fay Compton never quite recaptured her early brilliance. At the Haymarket (1925) she had the voice and technique for the Lady in the felicitous dialogue of a comedy set in a Regency inn, *The Man with a Load of Mischief* by Ashley Dukes. In April 1926 she was aptly cast

as the girl in a man's world in *This Woman Business* by Benn Levy. With a generous professionalism which seldom failed, she employed in very many plays her stage sense, her emotional powers, and her swift comedy. Twice more she was Ophelia, opposite Henry Ainley at the Haymarket (1931) and John Gielgud in the final performances (1939) at the Lyceum, and afterwards in Helsingør (Elsinore), Denmark. She was often in Shakespeare, notably several times at the Old Vic in London where she appeared as Regan (1940) in Gielgud's *King Lear* which was guided by Harley Granville-Barker. She also appeared in such long-running West End plays as *Autumn Crocus* (1931), *Call it a Day* (1935), *Blithe Spirit* (1941), *No Medals* (1944), and *Bonaventure* (1949). Her last Barrie role was the Comtesse in *What every Woman Knows* (Old Vic, 1960). She acted in small parts at the opening at the Chichester festival (1962) and the Yvonne Arnaud Theatre, Guildford (1965), and she was much applauded for her Aunt Ann in the television serial of *The Forsyte Saga* (1967). In 1975 she was appointed CBE.

Fay Compton's second husband, the actor Lauri De Frece (*b.* 1880), died in 1921 when he was only forty-one, and on 14 February 1922 she married Leon Fred Quartermaine (1876–1967), with whom she had acted in *Quality Street*. Her third marriage was dissolved in 1942, and in that year she married, on 20 July, the actor Ralph Champion Shotter (*b.* 1907), whose stage name was Ralph Michael; this marriage was dissolved in 1946. There were no children of these last three marriages.

It was only towards Fay Compton's last decade that a strenuous life told on her and her memory wavered. She will be remembered most as Barrie's Mary Rose, from her youth, and over nearly fifteen years, in various productions, as the supreme Ophelia of her time. Fay Compton died at her home, 10 Eaton Gardens, Hove, Sussex, on 12 December 1978.   J. C. TREWIN, *rev.* K. D. REYNOLDS

Sources F. Compton, *Rosemary: some remembrances* (1926) · J. Agate, *The contemporary theatre* (1925) · J. Parker, ed., *Who's who in the theatre*, 6th edn (1930) · F. C. Mackenzie, *As much as I dare* (1938) · personal knowledge (1986) · b. cert. · m. cert. · d. cert.
Archives FILM BFI NFTVA, news footage · BFI NFTVA, performance footage | SOUND BL NSA, performance footage
Likenesses D. Wilding, photograph, 1920–29, priv. coll. [*see illus.*] · photograph, repro. in Mackenzie, *As much as I dare* · photograph, repro. in P. Noble, *British theatre* [1946]
Wealth at death £10,844: probate, 1 March 1979, *CGPLA Eng. & Wales*

Compton, Henry (1631/2–1713), bishop of London, was born at Compton Wynyates, Warwickshire, the sixth and youngest son of Spencer *Compton, second earl of Northampton (1601–1643), and his wife, Mary (*d.* 1654), daughter of Sir Francis Beaumont of Coleorton, Leicestershire.

Youth and education Compton's father and brothers were active royalists when civil war came, and the ten-year-old Henry was present in the royalist camp at Edgehill, where his father and brothers were involved in the fighting. His father was killed refusing to surrender at the battle of Hopton Heath on 19 March 1643 and thereafter there is considerable uncertainty about Compton's whereabouts. The family seat was garrisoned by parliamentarians in June 1644 and his mother was forced to compound for the

Henry Compton (1631/2–1713), by John Riley, c.1680–85

family's estates. Compton later boasted that he had drawn his sword in defence of the constitution but whether this was in the context of the first civil war or subsequently is not clear. He is known to have attended Uppingham grammar school for a while.

On 9 February 1652 Compton was granted a licence to travel abroad and may have done so. But within less than two years he had returned, for on 12 December 1654 he matriculated at Queen's College, Oxford, as a nobleman. Cromwellian Oxford may not have been congenial to him, for he left without taking a degree and seems to have gone on his travels again, visiting France and Italy. According to one source he enlisted under the duke of York (the future James II) in Flanders in this period. A number of things make this unlikely. Compton never subsequently seems to have had a good relationship with York, which is odd if they had been former comrades in arms. Beyond this there is a conversation reported between them, possibly dating from 1686, from which Compton's claim to have drawn his sword for the constitution comes. If this related to service in the 1640s, Compton would hardly have needed to remind his commanding officer of the 1650s of that fact. The whole conversation actually suggests that Compton's military experience came as news to York, who remarked that he spoke more like a colonel than a bishop.

Military and ecclesiastical careers When the Restoration dawned a military career did indeed seem more likely than an ecclesiastical one for the young Compton. By 16 February 1661 he was commissioned as a cornet in the troop of the Royal Horse Guards, of which two of his brothers were captain and lieutenant. He rose to the rank of lieutenant himself in November. He found time to be admitted as an MA at Cambridge in this year but the next

year, in August 1662, he was sent to Tangier in a military capacity. However, in 1663 he left the army for good and on 25 February 1664 was granted a pass to travel to France. In July he wrote to Archbishop Sheldon, asking to have his pass extended to stay on the continent as 'it may conduce to confirm my health' (Bodl. Oxf., MS Tanner 47, fol. 184).

At thirty-two Compton was something of a rootless cavalier (this is certainly what he looks like in an early portrait of him as a young man). His education, as Burnet later remarked, lacked 'exactness': indeed, it had been highly spasmodic (*Burnet's History*, 2.99). Yet he had travelled widely, gaining a cosmopolitan outlook and an awareness of the wider European scene. His direct observation of the Roman Catholic church abroad seems to have fuelled the strongly anti-Catholic tendency which was so evident in his later career.

Compton finally returned to England in the spring of 1666 and at once came under the influence of John Fell, then dean of Christ Church, Oxford. It was he who persuaded Compton to enter Christ Church as a canon commoner, being incorporated MA on 7 July 1666. Fell also persuaded Compton to be ordained, which took place in the summer of 1666. He was immediately in line for significant ecclesiastical preferment, with a reversion on the next vacant canonry at Christ Church. In 1667 the king made him master of St Cross Hospital at Winchester, to which Bishop George Morley instituted him on 18 November. He came into the canonry at Christ Church even before he had acquired suitable Oxford degrees, receiving his warrant on 29 April 1669 and the degrees BD and DD in May and June respectively. He was then made subdean of Christ Church. Despite his lack of academic background Compton seems to have taken to his new role with relative ease. He made a brief oration at the opening of the Sheldonian Theatre in July 1669, which was well received. In December 1670, when the young prince of Orange—the future William III—visited Oxford, Compton was assigned the task of guiding him through the Church of England liturgy at morning prayer in Christ Church: an episode not without a certain piquancy in the light of their future relationship. Contemporaries were agreed that Compton was not a good preacher but, according to one of his earliest biographers, he moderated well in divinity disputations at this time.

The only shadow over an otherwise promising ecclesiastical career was cast by Compton's financial difficulties, which were already severe by 1670. The profits from St Cross were disappointing and the living at Llandinam in Montgomeryshire in Wales, to which he had been appointed in 1666, does not seem to have made much difference. He owed money to Sir Joseph Williamson, who also acted on behalf of his other creditors. Other livings were added: Cottenham in Cambridgeshire, to which Archbishop Sheldon nominated him in April 1671, and Witney in Oxfordshire, to which Bishop Morley presented him in November 1674. Compton seems to have regarded these livings simply as financial assets but they failed to solve his money problems. A combination of aristocratic excess and genuine generosity meant that his finances were never to be in a healthy condition, even after he became a bishop.

Bishop of Oxford Compton's elevation to the episcopate as bishop of Oxford in succession to Nathaniel Crewe, which was finalized in November 1674, seems to have been entirely due to the earl of Danby's influence. Compton must have caught the eye of the king's new lord treasurer as just the sort of well-born Anglican royalist upon whose support he intended to build his regime. And Compton would not let him down. He was consecrated in the chapel at Lambeth Palace by Archbishop Sheldon and four diocesan bishops from the province of Canterbury on 6 December 1674. His new see was not lucrative: Compton himself estimated its value at just over £343. He was allowed to retain his position at St Cross, his Christ Church canonry, and the living at Witney *in commendam*, in recognition of this, given his still shaky financial situation. In July 1675 he was appointed to the court post of dean of the chapels royal, which gave him some influence over the education of the young princesses Mary and Anne. Further promotion came in December 1675 when he was appointed bishop of London, a post he would hold until his death. Danby's patronage obtained for him the further honour of elevation to the privy council the following January, even before he had done homage for his appointment to London.

Bishop of London Compton very soon showed himself to be a highly effective bishop at both the political and the pastoral level. He immediately began to use his place at court and on the council to lobby against the influence of Roman Catholics there, making sure the princesses were prepared for confirmation in the Church of England, in the face of the duke of York's opposition. Charles II tolerated Compton's zeal as harmless and because 'it helped to lay the jealousies of the church party' (*Burnet's History*, 2.100). Compton had a significant role in the great church party project of 1676: the ecclesiastical census, known to contemporaries as the Bishops' Book but which has come to be known as the Compton Census. It was designed to demonstrate once and for all to a sceptical king that nonconformists were too few to be worth wooing politically and so strengthen Danby's Anglican royalist regime. Incumbents and churchwardens were to be asked to estimate the relative strengths of conformists, Roman Catholics, and protestant dissenters in their parishes. Sheldon wrote to Compton on 17 January 1676 to set the process in motion in the province of Canterbury; just four days later Compton forwarded the instructions to the relevant diocesans. From the resultant figures from the parishes he estimated that the proportion of conformists to nonconformists throughout the country was twenty-three to one. Compton supported and to some extent supplanted the ailing Archbishop Sheldon in his political role. Compton came to act as organizer of the bishops in the Lords, reminding Sheldon in January 1677 of the need to warn bishops to send in their proxies in good time if they could not attend in person.

When Sheldon died later that year Compton was strongly tipped to be his successor, although Compton himself purported to support Archbishop Richard Sterne of York for the job, perhaps hoping to be *his* successor at Canterbury before very long. That Compton was not appointed to Canterbury may be attributed to a number of factors: Danby's lack of enthusiasm (despite professions to the contrary), Charles II's indifference to him, and the duke of York's already passionate hostility. York had even opposed Compton's elevation to London, doubtless already aware of his protestant credentials, and Compton in post had fulfilled York's worst fears, with his interference in his daughters' religious education and his crusade against influential Roman Catholics at court. But 1677 was not an entirely disappointing year for Compton. On 4 November he had the joy of helping the prince of Orange through another piece of Church of England liturgy when he presided at his wedding to the young Princess Mary, a great boost to the protestant cause both at home and abroad.

However, Compton was much more than merely a court prelate tied up with high politics. He was also a remarkably conscientious diocesan bishop. He conducted visitations of his diocese in person throughout his tenure, going in person to the parishes concerned. From January 1678 he developed the idea of conferences for the clergy throughout his diocese, where pastoral and practical issues could be discussed. These took place not only at the urban core of the diocese but in the outlying rural areas as well, convened by rural deans, with reports of proceedings and lists of absentees returned to Compton personally.

But Compton's political involvement made him vulnerable to the growing instability of the times. When the Popish Plot scare broke out in the autumn of 1678 Compton had a prominent role in investigating the alleged conspiracy. He was an energetic member of the privy council committee charged with looking into it. He ordered that English Roman Catholics who attended mass at ambassadors' houses be arrested. In early November he even backed the earl of Shaftesbury's motion in the Lords that the duke of York be removed from the court and council. Not surprisingly this lost Compton favour at court but it did not protect him from rumours that he was a closet papist himself. Danby's fall from power was a grievous blow to Compton, considering how closely he had previously been associated with him.

Perhaps aware of his own political isolation, Compton softened his line towards the duke of York over the course of the exclusion crisis (1679–81). In October 1680 he voted for York to stay in England, and in November he joined the other bishops present in voting down the Exclusion Bill in the Lords. In the same month he brought some words spoken against the duke of York and in favour of the duke of Monmouth to the attention of the privy council. By February 1681 he was firmly back in favour and was appointed to the commission for ecclesiastical promotions, designed to control church patronage and keep it in loyal hands. But Compton's position within the tory reaction, which characterized the years down to 1685, has been the subject of some controversy both at the time and since. In 1682 and 1683 he was criticized for his supposed friendliness and liberality towards nonconformists by some hardline Anglicans. He could certainly *sound* friendly towards individual dissenters, such as Richard Baxter in the 1670s, but his friendliness does not seem to have extended to taking action in their favour. He could hardly be described as liberal about nonconformity in the early 1680s. In March 1683 he wrote to every incumbent in his diocese complaining that churchwardens had been remiss in their presentations especially about absentees from holy communion, and the parish registers of Hillingdon testify to 300 communicants over the following Easter period: 'alarmed to their duty by an order from Henry Lord Bishop of London' (J. S. Burn, *The History of Parish Registers*, 2nd edn, 1862, 186). And the 'shameful disuse of public baptism' was one of the main topics that Compton prescribed for one of his clergy conferences at this time (Sykes, 26).

Where a generous and flexible attitude did show through was in Compton's approach to continental protestants, especially those who were experiencing persecution. He had solicited the opinions of certain European protestant divines about their differences with the Church of England, and in 1677 translated a work of André Lortie as *A Treatise of the Holy Communion*. Compton was the natural choice to spearhead fund-raising and other practical initiatives on behalf of protestant refugees in July 1681 and he worked tirelessly on their behalf, sometimes having to battle against a distinct lack of enthusiasm among his episcopal colleagues. He even found himself compelled to mediate in the internal disputes of the exiled French churches resident within his own diocese. His commitment to international protestantism was very clear. But as the new reign loomed in 1685, Compton's commitment to tory principles was equally clear. He drew up a loyal address to the new king, James II, and sent a copy of it to his rural deans so that the clergy of London diocese might speak with one voice. He presented it in person along with the clergy of the capital within one week of the accession, although it took a while for the outlying archdeaconries to catch up with their copies. It spoke pointedly of 'our religion established by law dearer to us than our lives' (Carpenter, 79). In the general election Compton mobilized rural deans on behalf of loyal candidates and at the coronation in April he attended personally upon the queen.

Opposition to James II and the revolution However, it did not take long for the old feud between Compton and James to resurface. The *casus belli* for the new round of conflict was James's employment of Roman Catholic officers in the army, contrary to the Test Act of 1673. In the second session of parliament on 18 November, Compton made a long, calm, and deferential speech which nevertheless criticized the king's flouting of the law as endangering the whole constitution. He claimed to speak for his episcopal colleagues, a claim endorsed when those bishops who were present in the Lords stood up in solidarity with him when he had finished. As a result of his boldness Compton

was removed from his posts as dean of the chapels royal, clerk of the closet, and member of the privy council.

Compton was soon openly opposing other aspects of royal policy, notably the plans to curtail anti-Catholic preaching, either by suppressing afternoon lectures or by issuing instructions to preachers. James did not follow through the first of these options but he most emphatically pursued the latter and it was from this that his next confrontation with Compton arose. John Sharp, dean of Norwich and rector of St Giles-in-the-Fields, London, indulged in some anti-Catholic remarks in his preaching. James responded on 17 June 1686 by ordering Compton to suspend him. Compton demurred on the ground that Sharp could not be suspended without first being heard (although he had privately persuaded Sharp to desist from preaching for the present). As a result Compton was summoned before the recently created ecclesiastical commission on 9 August and was granted until 31 August to prepare his case. His counsel maintained that Compton had obeyed the king as far as he legally could. Nevertheless the verdict for his suspension was delivered on 6 September by an admittedly divided commission. The harsher sentence of deprivation was not imposed, so Compton's episcopal revenues remained untouched, though more perhaps out of a fear of a challenge at common law than from any clemency on the part of the commissioners.

Compton at once became a protestant martyr. Princess Mary wrote to him expressing her sympathy and his treatment was said to be widely resented. He continued to guide his clergy from behind the scenes, dividing his time between London and the country, indulging his favourite pastime of gardening. His episcopal duties were taken over by three of his colleagues.

Only with James II's showdown with the seven bishops over the reading of the declaration of indulgence in churches in 1688 did Compton again become prominent in public life. He approved their petition and indeed, with typical impetuosity, may well have been responsible for having it published, which raised the stakes on all sides. Compton visited the seven in the Tower of London and may well have been present at their trial.

In his next political action, however, Compton went way beyond what his episcopal colleagues could have contemplated in signing the invitation to William of Orange to intervene militarily in England. In this he joined his former mentor, Danby, who had recruited him to the conspiracy. Rash and impetuous though this undoubtedly was, it was not the bolt from the blue that it might at first appear. Compton had remained in touch with the court at The Hague, initially with his former protégée Princess Mary but latterly with William directly. They shared concern at the developing situation in England: it was through Compton that William expressed his concern for the seven bishops. According to Danby, it was his treatment at the hands of the ecclesiastical commission in 1686 that led him to reconsider his commitment to the traditional doctrine of passive obedience.

William was not perhaps as circumspect as he might

have been in covering Compton's tracks: he mentioned the action taken against Compton by the ecclesiastical commission in his declaration of reasons for intervening in England. He also mentioned an invitation from lords spiritual and temporal (in fact, Compton was the only spiritual one to have signed the invitation). Not surprisingly James became suspicious and invited Compton to a private meeting on 31 October. Compton was out of London at the time. When the two did meet soon afterwards he gave the king a deceptive answer implying that he was innocent: 'I am quite confident that there is not one of my brethren who is not as guiltless as myself in this matter' (Macaulay, 1.562). In this he was not necessarily motivated solely by personal cowardice (others might have been implicated) and even if he had been, a certain lack of courage in the face of the potential penalty for treason in seventeenth-century England is hardly so reprehensible. Compton successfully stiffened his fellow bishops in resisting James's repeated calls for an abhorrence of William's invasion, though they could hardly have guessed the reason for his resolve. He had ignored both the lifting of his suspension by the ecclesiastical commission at the end of September and the abolition of the commission itself on 5 October, neither resuming his episcopal duties nor offering any thanks. He bided his time. Those who had signed the invitation to William had pledged themselves to join him as soon as possible after he landed. Perhaps by agreement with his fellow conspirators, Compton remained in London, keeping a low profile, offering protection to Princess Anne, should she wish to escape. She took up the offer and was escorted out of London by the fully armed bishop and others, reaching Castle Ashby, the earl of Northampton's seat, on 28 November, going thence to Nottingham and then to Oxford, where Princess Anne was reunited with her husband, Prince George, on 15 December.

Compton's bearing arms in the context of the revolution became notorious but requires careful scrutiny. In the context of governmental breakdown and military disintegration it was perhaps prudent to have some weapons about his person. Where Compton appears to have overstepped the mark was in continuing to bear arms and indeed in revelling in military command after he had joined up with forces quite capable of protecting the princess without his assistance. He even rode into the tory centre of Oxford in martial style, which was to fly in the face of Anglican scruples about involvement in armed resistance to the lawfully constituted government and to store up for himself charges of hypocrisy when he returned to the traditional position of passive obedience in due course. He further compounded his insensitivity to Anglican scruples by convening a meeting in Princess Anne's presence at which those present were invited to enter into an association to take revenge should the prince of Orange be harmed by Roman Catholics. Many tory peers and gentry present refused to sign.

Compton was closely identified with William and Mary in the ensuing constitutional struggle. On 21 December he presented a congratulatory address from his clergy to William and before the end of the year celebrated holy communion for him. Early in January 1689 he controversially instructed his clergy to omit prayers for the prince of Wales, James II's son, born the previous June, whom many supporters of the revolution believed to be an impostor. He was isolated from the overwhelming majority of his fellow bishops, who favoured a regency. And not surprisingly it was Compton who preached the sermon following the offer of the crown to William and Mary. Next day he was made a privy councillor and dean of the chapels royal again. He was also to be groom of the stole. On 20 February he led the London clergy in procession to offer a congratulatory address to the new sovereigns, whose coronation he was to preside at in April. He was a keen supporter of the regime and its emphasis on moral reformation. William's letter of 1689 to him ordering the clergy to read the statutes against vice was published and itself became part of the regime's propaganda campaign.

The reign of William and Mary After the spring of 1689 Compton seems hard to place politically. This reflects in part the complexity of the post-revolution political scene but also the fact that he was increasingly motivated by a personal agenda. He appeared to support comprehension for nonconformists within the Church of England, conscientiously presiding over all eighteen sessions of the special commission in October, but was then involved in getting Dr William Jane, a protégé, made prolocutor of the lower house of convocation, which further reduced comprehension's already slim chances of being accepted. Jane was a hardline opponent of comprehension, who had even queried the legality of the comprehension commission. The alternative and pro-comprehension candidate was John Tillotson, the front runner for the archiepiscopate of Canterbury in preference to Compton, pending William Sancroft's removal for failing to take the oaths to William and Mary. In 1690 Compton was said to have 'influence over most of the Whig party' (*CSP dom.*, 1690–91, 210), while on the contrary Gilbert Burnet saw him as a consistent tory. Queen Mary was soon complaining of Compton and other high-churchmen conspiring with her sister Anne against her at court; while Thomas Comber, dean of Durham, hoped that Compton might get the lesser prize of the archbishopric of York and so help engage the tory clergy of the northern province to the revolutionary government.

Compton made no attempt to hide his disappointment at being passed over for Canterbury. He attended neither Tillotson's consecration nor his admission to the privy council in 1691 and was still reluctant to be involved in court business at the end of that year. It appears that neither of the new sovereigns wanted him as archbishop, William motivated perhaps by an uncomfortable awareness of his debt to Compton in the revolution, perhaps also by personal dislike. When Canterbury fell vacant again in 1694–5 Compton's expectations were not as great, and any disappointment was less obvious. He remained politically loyal to the regime, although increasingly alienated from its ecclesiastical preferences and priorities.

Whatever his disappointments Compton continued to work conscientiously as a diocesan and in support of the charitable causes to which he was committed. The clergy conferences and visitations continued. He even managed to conduct a visitation of St Paul's between 1696 and 1698, giving the cathedral new statutes which laid down the basic pattern of worship there for the next century. He also took seriously his spiritual oversight of the American colonies, which he exercised as bishop of London, supporting Thomas Bray in his work there as his commissary in 1699–1700. Compton also backed Bray's brainchild of the Society for the Propagation of the Gospel, which was founded in 1701.

The reign of Anne Compton's political fortunes revived considerably when William was succeeded by Anne, with whom he had enjoyed such a close relationship over the years. He was appointed lord high almoner in 1702 and gained some influence over church appointments. In 1708 he gave pastoral support to the queen on the death of Prince George (he had presided at their wedding twenty-five years before). He clearly supported the high-church and tory programme in this period: the revival of convocation, the clamp-down on occasional conformity, the rallying cry that the church was in danger. Both Francis Atterbury and Dr Sacheverell were protégés. And in 1710 he presented an address to the queen congratulating her on her change of ministry from whigs to tories.

Whigs delighted to exhume evidence of inconsistency and hypocrisy in the light of his later political stance. But it is possible to exaggerate the shift in Compton's views over the years. The impression given by some accounts of the period written then and since of an almost radical bishop becoming reactionary in old age is misleading. His views on most subjects throughout his career were the conventional ones for a churchman of the period. It was the intensity of his anti-Catholicism, compounded by a personal feud with James II, which marked him out from his episcopal colleagues in the 1680s and drove him to actions that they could not countenance. But Danby's right-hand man on the episcopal bench in the 1670s was hardly an incongruous opponent of occasional conformity in the 1700s. The religious complexion of the regime was a critical factor for Compton. Impetuous man that he was, it was not surprising that he should conspire against a Catholic regime at one stage in his career and advocate obedience to a protestant one at another. Burnet was right to detect a certain consistency in his loyalties over a considerable period, although paradoxically it was Burnet who bowled him out publicly for eliding his active role in the revolution, when discussing the rights and wrongs of passive obedience in the Lords in 1705.

After years of good health Compton deteriorated physically, suffering from gout and stones. In 1711 he was seriously ill. In the following year he had a fall, but recovered enough to undertake another taxing visitation. But his health declined again and he died calmly, aged eighty-one, at his episcopal residence at Fulham on 7 July 1713. At his own request he was buried without pomp in the churchyard and with the simplest of memorials within the parish church at Fulham on 15 July. This was typical of the man: he had a real humility which even an opponent like Burnet could recognize. The truth was too that there was little money left for anything grander, even had he wanted it. He had written a begging letter to the earl of Oxford as recently as October 1712, being as ever strapped for cash. Neither the proceeds of the see of London nor the £1000 salary which Compton latterly enjoyed as a commissioner of trade and plantations could offset the effects of his lack of financial management and his impetuous generosity. He had no wife and children to support; no doubt his financial difficulties would have been even greater if he had. At death, little remained apart from his magnificent library, which was split between St Paul's and Colchester corporation.

It is possible, with Burnet, to see Compton as a weak man influenced by others. And yet there can be little doubt that he was one of the most effective diocesan bishops in this period. In many ways a shy and private man, there is seldom displayed an insight into his inner thoughts. Several works were published under his name, sometimes without his consent (such as *Episcopalia*, a collection of letters to his clergy, in 1686). But they seldom shed much light on his personal life, being largely of an official nature, with few clues as to his deeper motivations. The works of others which he translated betray his absorption with anti-Catholicism (such as Gregorio Leti's *Life of Donna Olimpia Maldachini* from the Italian in 1666 and Fulgentio Micanzio's *Jesuits' Intrigues* from the French in 1669).

The surviving portraits in later life are not much more help, although they convey the impression of a man of effectiveness and drive in the public realm, with clear facial features and directness of expression. Botany was a great interest, and he planted his gardens at Fulham with 'a greater variety of curious exotic plants and trees than had at that time been collected in any garden in England' (*DNB*), most obtained from his correspondents in North America. He never married, despite occasional gossip that he would. His household became a sort of surrogate family to him and he inspired great loyalty among his chaplains. Compton was hospitable and his personal generosity to individuals was prodigious.

Compton's legacy in many areas of church and state was significant. Such were the variety and multiplicity of his involvements that his lasting influence defies neat summary. But places as far apart as St Paul's Cathedral and the American colonies were in his debt. His conscientious rule left the diocese of London in a much better spiritual state than it had been when he took over. Indeed, he presided over something of a religious revival there, which had far-reaching consequences in following decades. He struggled to maintain the international contacts of the Church of England at a time when it was in danger of turning inwards and forgetting the wider world and the broader protestant cause. Finally, however mixed the feelings of his contemporaries, Compton's active role in bringing about the revolution was long remembered and celebrated—an example of a certain reckless courage which has not always characterized the political stances of the Church of England's senior bishops.

ANDREW M. COLEBY

Sources E. Carpenter, *The protestant bishop, being the life of Henry Compton* (1956) • *Burnet's History of my own time*, ed. O. Airy, new edn, 1 (1897) • *The life and times of Anthony Wood*, ed. A. Clark, 5 vols., OHS, 19, 21, 26, 30, 40 (1891–1900) • H. Compton, *Episcopalia* (1686) • *Memoirs of Sir John Reresby*, ed. A. Browning, 2nd edn, ed. M. K. Geiter and W. A. Speck (1991) • N. Sykes, *From Sheldon to Secker* (1959) • A. Kippis and others, eds., *Biographia Britannica, or, The lives of the most eminent persons who have flourished in Great Britain and Ireland*, 2nd edn, 1 (1778) • Bodl. Oxf., MSS Tanner • J. Walsh and others, eds., *The Church of England, c.1689–c.1833* (1993) • T. Claydon, *William III and the godly revolution* (1996) • R. Beddard, 'The church of Salisbury and the accession of James II', *Wiltshire Archaeological and Natural History Magazine*, 67 (1972), 132–48 • T. B. Macaulay, *The history of England from the accession of James II*, new edn, 2 vols. (1877) • A. Whiteman and M. Clapinson, eds., *The Compton census of 1676: a critical edition*, British Academy, Records of Social and Economic History, new ser., 10 (1986) • *DNB* • GEC, *Peerage*, new edn, 9.679–81 • Desmond, *Botanists* • M. Hunter, *The Royal Society and its fellows, 1660–1700: the morphology of an early scientific institution*, 2nd edn (1994), 12 • will, PRO, PROB 11/535, sig. 190 • memorial, Fulham parish church
Archives LPL, corresp. and MSS; letters | BL, letters to Lord Hatton, Add. MS 29584 • BL, Sloane MSS, MSS • BL, letters to Warley, Add. MS 27997 • Bodl. Oxf., corresp. with Sancroft, etc. • Bodl. RH, letters to Society for the Propagation of the Gospel • CUL, letters to J. Strype • LPL, corresp. relating to Society for the Propagation of the Gospel • TCD, corresp. with W. King
Likenesses D. Loggan, line engraving, 1679, BM, NPG • J. Riley, oils, c.1680–1685, Castle Ashby, Northamptonshire [*see illus.*] • G. Bower, silver medal, 1688, NPG • G. Kneller, oils, c.1712, NPG; repro. in Carpenter, *The protestant bishop* (1956) • I. Beckett, mezzotint (after J. Riley), BM, NPG • G. Kneller?, oils, Christ Church Oxf. • J. Riley, oils, Queen's College, Oxford • oils (as young man), Compton Wynyates, Warwickshire; repro. in Carpenter, *The protestant bishop*
Wealth at death see will, PRO, PROB 11/535, sig. 190

Compton, Henry [*real name* Charles Mackenzie] (1805–1877), actor, was born on 22 March 1805 at Huntingdon. He was the sixth of the eleven children of John Mackenzie and his wife, formerly Mrs Elizabeth Symonds; the families of both his parents provided numerous distinguished members of the medical profession. After an education at Huntingdon and at a boarding-school at Little Baddow in Essex, Charles was apprenticed to a maternal uncle, a cloth merchant in Aldermanbury, near London. Unhappy in mercantile pursuits and yearning for life on the stage, he was retrieved after running away twice, but, on his third attempt to abscond, in 1826, his family accepted the inevitability of his career on the stage.

Mackenzie's earliest histrionic attempts consisted of imitations of the 'At Homes' of Charles Mathews, with which, as with the acting of John Liston, he was impressed. His first engagement, obtained through an agent, was at Lewes. He then played at Leicester as Richmond and Macduff. He appeared briefly at Cromer, and

then was employed for twelve months as a member of the Bedford circuit. It was during this period that he adopted Compton as his stage name, borrowed from one of his grandfather's wives.

In 1828 Compton was at Daventry, and it was here that he apparently began to specialize in low-comedy roles. Shortly thereafter he appeared at Hammersmith. Three years' experience on the Lincoln circuit was followed by a long and successful engagement on the York circuit. In Leeds he was a special favourite. His first London appearance was at the English Opera House (Lyceum) on 24 July 1837, as Robin in *The Waterman*. After playing several parts there successfully Compton was transferred on 7 October 1837 to Drury Lane, where his Master Slender gave promise of the reputation he was to earn in Shakespeare. Tony Lumpkin, Gnatbrain in *Black-Eyed Susan*, Silky in Thomas Holcroft's *The Road to Ruin*, Bailie Nicol Jarvie, and the First Gravedigger in *Hamlet* followed. His chief successes at the Lyceum and at Drury Lane were Mawworm in Isaac Bickerstaff's *The Hypocrite*, Marrall in Philip Massinger's *A New Way to Pay Old Debts*, and Dr Ollapod in George Colman's *The Poor Gentleman*. While he was at Drury Lane in 1839, a young actress named Emmeline Montague made her London début as Juliet, with Compton taking the role of the Apothecary.

Following the termination of the 1839 season at Drury Lane, Compton went in 1840 to the Theatre Royal, Dublin, whence he returned on 10 December 1841 with the reputation of being the best Shakespearian clown of his epoch. Having been engaged by W. C. Macready, he appeared at Drury Lane in 1843–4, and after visiting Manchester, Liverpool, and Dublin he transferred his services to the Princess's, where he performed as Touchstone on 11 November 1844. He remained at the Princess's for three years. In 1847 he was at the Olympic, where also he remained three years. Polonius, Sir Peter Teazle, Launcelot Gobbo, and Foresight in Congreve's *Love for Love* were among the parts he took at Drury Lane; at the Princess's and the Olympic he played a round of 'legitimate' characters. When the Olympic was burnt down, Compton migrated to the Strand, and in 1853 he began his longest and best-remembered engagement, with J. B. Buckstone at the Haymarket. During his stay at the Haymarket he created Blenkinsop in Tom Taylor's *An Unequal Match*, Sir Solomon Frazer in the same author's *The Overland Route*, De Vaudray in Westland Marston's *A Hero of Romance*, and Captain Mountraffe in T. W. Robertson's *Home*.

On 21 December 1848 Compton and Emmeline Catherine Montague (*d.* 1911) were married. Thereafter the new Mrs Compton appeared at Windsor Castle in a small role in *The Merchant of Venice* (28 December 1848), several times at the Strand (during the summer of 1849), and in a performance at Devonshire House of Bulwer-Lytton's *Not so Bad as we Seem*, before Queen Victoria and Prince Albert (May 1851). She then retired from the stage to devote herself to her growing family. The Comptons resided at 19 Charing Cross Road, where most of their children were born.

Henry Compton left the Haymarket to play at the Princess's Theatre, Manchester, on 15 August 1870, and afterwards at the Olympic (3 September 1870), in Taylor's *Handsome is that Handsome does*, and on 7 October 1871 appeared in H. J. Byron's *Partners for Life*, with which H. J. Montague opened the Globe Theatre. In the noteworthy Bateman–Irving revival of *Hamlet*, which opened at the Lyceum on 30 October 1874, he resumed his old character of the First Gravedigger with great success. With the Vezin–Chippendale touring company he played several of his old characters. His last appearance on the stage was at the Prince of Wales's Theatre, Liverpool, on 14 July 1877, as Mawworm in *The Hypocrite* and Pangloss in two acts of Colman's *The Heir-at-Law*.

When it was known that Compton was ill with cancer and that his family was in serious financial straits, two benefit performances were accorded him. The first, at Drury Lane on 1 March 1877, was notable for the appearances of Henry Irving, Joseph Jefferson, Sir Arthur Sullivan as orchestra leader, W. S. Gilbert in an excerpt from *Trial by Jury*, and Compton's son, Edward *Compton, in his father's roles. The benefit realized in excess of £3250, thought by its organizers to be extraordinarily successful. The second benefit, at Manchester on 27 March 1877, was nearly as generous.

Henry Compton died after a long and painful illness on 15 September 1877 at Seaforth House, 12 Stanford Road, Kensington, London.

JOSEPH KNIGHT, *rev.* GAYLE T. HARRIS

Sources C. Compton and E. Compton, eds., *Memoir of Henry Compton* (1879) · C. Mackenzie, *My life and times*, 10 vols. (1963–71), vol. 1 · *The Era* (4 April 1877) · *The Eugenics Review* (April 1925) · *The Sketch* (22 July 1896) · *Sunday Times* (24 Dec 1848) · *Sunday Times* (31 Dec 1848) · *ILN* (24 May 1851) · *Theatrical Journal* (12 May 1849) · *Theatrical Journal* (5 July 1849) · private information (1886)
Archives Folger
Likenesses H. Watkins, albumen print, 1856–9, NPG · London Stereoscopic Co. and W. Walker & Sons, cartes-de-visite and woodburytype photograph, NPG · Sem [T. F. D. Crocker], portrait, Folger, USA; repro. in Crocker, *Sem's pantheon of celebrities of the day* · photographs, Folger · photographs, Theatre Museum, London · photographs, NYPL, New York · photographs, L. Cong. · prints, BM, NPG · prints, caricatures, Harvard TC
Wealth at death under £4000: probate, 27 Oct 1877, *CGPLA Eng. & Wales*

Compton, Sir Herbert Abingdon Draper (1776–1846),

judge in India, was the only son of Henry Compton (*d.* before 1804) of Hartbury, Gloucestershire. He was a relation of Sir Walter Abingdon Compton, fifth and last baronet (*d.* 1773), of Hartbury. About 1790 he arrived in India and in August 1791 he became an ensign in her majesty's 74th regiment, then stationed in the Madras presidency. He served with the 74th in the war of 1790–92 against Tipu Sultan of Mysore and was promoted lieutenant on 17 October 1793, but in April 1796 he resigned from the army and articled himself in an attorney's office in Madras. On 16 October 1798 he married Mary Anne, the daughter of John (Jean) Carere (*d.* 1780), a Swiss protestant who had joined the Madras medical service in 1764 after defecting from the service of Muhammad Yusuf, governor of Madura.

In 1802 Compton was appointed junior counsel to the East India Company in Madras. He returned to Britain in 1805 and was called to the bar at Lincoln's Inn on 22 November 1808, having meanwhile supported his family by writing for newspapers, principally *The Pilot*. Mary had given birth to a son, Herbert, in September 1803. She cannot have lived for many years after this, for in February 1810 another son, Charles Francis, was born to Compton by a wife whose given names were Maria Elizabeth.

In 1809 the court of directors licensed Compton to return to Madras as an advocate, and in 1811 he again became counsel for the company. In 1814 he was granted permission to move to Bengal, and on 15 June 1815 he was enrolled as an advocate of the supreme court of Calcutta. By then he was again a widower, and on 26 July 1815 he married Sarah Cherry, daughter of Edward Mullins of Calcutta. The artist George Chinnery was a witness to their union in St John's Church. They had at least four children, among them Thomas Abingdon Draper (1820–1862), a future Bombay civilian and judge of Sholapur. In 1816 Compton was appointed standing counsel to the company in the Calcutta supreme court, and in 1820 he became sheriff of Calcutta. In 1822 he was appointed advocate general of Madras, a position which a former incumbent, Alexander Anstruther, had enthusiastically recommended him for a decade previously. In March 1828 he was readmitted to the Calcutta bar, and in 1831, after a brief retirement in Britain, he was appointed chief justice of Bombay and knighted. He finally retired from India in 1839. Throughout his career, government and private clients alike praised his ability, common sense, local knowledge, and integrity. He was the recipient on several occasions of gifts of plate from grateful clients, including a handsome silver service presented by the leading Indian inhabitants of Bombay on his departure in 1839.

Compton died at his house in Hyde Park Gardens, London, on 15 January 1846. He was remembered in Indian legal circles as a self-made man who had worked his way up by exceptional talent. After his death his daughter Mrs Skirrow gave a portrait of him by Ramsay Reinagle to the Oriental Club in Hanover Square. In the words of the club's historian, it shows 'a handsome man, with good nose and forehead', his whiskers 'very small', and his hair 'thick and grey' (Baillie, 221).   KATHERINE PRIOR

Sources personal records, BL OIOC, O/6/16, 689–698 · *GM*, 2nd ser., 25 (1846), 207 · A. F. Baillie, *The Oriental Club and Hanover Square* (1901) · E. Cotton, *Memories of the supreme court at Fort William in Bengal, 1774–1862* (1925) · W. P. Baildon, ed., *The records of the Honorable Society of Lincoln's Inn: admissions*, 2 (1896) · H. D. Love, *Vestiges of old Madras, 1640–1800*, 4 vols. (1913) · D. G. Crawford, ed., *Roll of the Indian Medical Service, 1615–1930* (1930) · writers' records; ecclesiastical records; cadet records, BL OIOC · ecclesiastical records, BL OIOC, N/2/2, fol. 334; N/1/9, fol. 264 · *The Times* (17 Jan 1846), suppl. 1 · W. A. Shaw, *The knights of England*, 2 vols. (1906) · PRO, WO 12/8064 · PRO, WO 76/485, fols. 17, 31
Likenesses R. R. Reinagle, oils, exh. RA 1832, Oriental Club, London

Compton, James, third earl of Northampton (1622–1681),

playwright and translator, was born on 19 August 1622, the eldest of the six sons of Spencer *Compton, the second earl (1601–1643), and his wife, Mary (*d.* 1654), daughter of Sir Francis Beaumont. William *Compton and Henry *Compton were his brothers. In 1633 James entered Eton College, and in February 1636, while visiting Cambridge in the train of the young elector palatine, received the MA as *filius nobilis*. A year later he was admitted at Queens', where in 1615 his father had played before James I in Ruggles's comedy *Ignoramus*. His name appears below the only verse contribution from the college to the university's celebration of the birth of Princess Anne in 1637 (*Synodia*, sig. A3).

In September 1640 Compton was recalled from travel or military service in the Low Countries to stand as knight of the shire for Warwickshire. In April 1641 he voted against Strafford's attainder and the next year served as messenger between the parliament and Charles at York. Deprived of his seat after Edgehill, he fought at Hopton Heath (19 March 1643), where his father died, Cropredy Bridge (June 1644), and Banbury (October 1644), and in April 1645 was routed by Cromwell at Islip. He was present at Naseby in June, and after commanding 1500 horse in Wales retired to Oxford. In February 1646 he began the process of compounding, and his fine of £21,455, reduced on appeal by one third (BL, Add. MS 34253, fols. 42, 44), was discharged by December 1651. He later claimed to have lost £50,000 in the wars, an early sacrifice being his library of some 250 books, confiscated in 1643 from Crosby Hall, Bishopsgate, and sold for £57 3s. 6d. (PRO, SP 20/7, fols. 17–20). In July 1647 he married Isabella (1622–1661), younger daughter of Richard Sackville, third earl of Dorset (d. 1624), and his wife, Lady Anne *Clifford, then countess of Pembroke, who was active in promoting the match. They had six children, only one of whom, Alethea, survived into adulthood.

During the interregnum, when he was several times imprisoned, Northampton occupied his leisure by writing or translating plays and other works that lay unidentified in manuscript at his Northamptonshire seat of Castle Ashby until 1978 (BL, Add. MSS 60276–60282). He was modest about his own literary talents, describing himself to his neighbour Lord Hatton in 1645 as one who had studied 'but slightly and truantlyke' (BL, Add. MS 29570, fol. 30). Rugged translations of Seneca's *Agamemnon* and *Hercules furens*, which omit the choruses, may be early work (Add. MSS 60276, 60277). A taste for Italian literature, evident in his confiscated library, produced his best effort in this field, a racy adaptation of Machiavelli's comedy *La Mandragola*, relocated from Renaissance Florence to Commonwealth London (Add. MS 60278). His rendering of three scenes from *Don Sancho d'Aragon* (1649) into heroic verse makes him one of the earliest English translators of Corneille also (ibid.). The same impulse that moved him to translate the story of the martyred Christian convert Hermenegildus from the Latin (1620) of the Jesuit Nicholas Caussin led him to compose an original piece on the much handled subject of Mariamne, wife of Herod the Great (Add. MSS 60276, 60280). Altogether more accomplished is his blank-verse drama on Leontias, king of Cyprus, in which a close acquaintance with Shakespeare is apparent. A five-act play on the usurper Caracalla and an unfinished

draft of a drama about Strafford (Add. MS 60281) form a link with his few directly political writings which include a brief prose account of Charles I and two unfinished verse satires (Add. MSS 60282, 60276). In the 1650s and early 1660s Northampton acted as patron to actors and dramatists, and was the dedicatee of printed works by Holland, Glapthorne, and Hemings, as well as the recipient of three manuscript plays by his particular protégé Cosmo Manuche (Add. MSS 60273–60275).

At the Restoration Northampton became lord lieutenant of Warwickshire and recorder of Coventry. Within three years of his first wife's death in 1661 he married Mary (d. 1719), eldest daughter of Baptist *Noel, third Viscount Campden, with whom he had three sons and two daughters. In May 1663 he was elected fellow of the Royal Society. He attended the House of Lords punctiliously until 1669, and sporadically thereafter, his most notable action there being the introduction in December 1667 of a bill calling for the perpetual banishment of Clarendon, which Pepys called 'mighty poor I think, and so doth everybody else'. The last decade of his life saw a burst of public activity as privy councillor (1673–9), constable of the Tower (1675–9), and a lord of trade (1677). Northampton died at Castle Ashby on 15 December 1681 and was buried on 29 December at Compton Wynyates. Lely's portrait of him in armour was bequeathed as an heirloom to Ashby by his widow in 1719.   W. H. KELLIHER

Sources H. Kelliher, 'A hitherto unrecognised cavalier dramatist: James Compton, third earl of Northampton', *British Library Journal*, 6 (1980), 158–87 · W. P. Williams, 'The Castle Ashby manuscripts', *The Library*, 6th ser., 2 (1980), 392–412 · W. B. Compton, *History of the Comptons of Compton Wynyates* (1930) · Venn, *Alum. Cant.*, 1/1–4 · *Synodia*, Cambridge University (1637) · GEC, *Peerage*, new edn · Keeler, *Long Parliament* · BL, Add. MSS 60276–60282 · BL, Add. MS 34253, fols. 42, 44 · PRO, SP Car. I, ccclxviii, 87 · PRO, SP 20/7, fols. 17–20

Archives BL, literary and other papers, Add. MSS 60273–60285 · Castle Ashby, Northamptonshire, papers

Likenesses P. Lely, oils, Castle Ashby

Compton, Spencer, second earl of Northampton (1601–1643), army officer, was born in May 1601 and baptized on 28 May at St Michael Bassishaw, London, the eldest son of Sir William Compton (d. 1630) of Compton Wynyates, Warwickshire, later first earl of Northampton, and his wife, Elizabeth (d. 1632), daughter and later heir of Sir John *Spencer (d. 1610) of Canonbury, Middlesex. He was admitted to Queens' College, Cambridge, in 1614, created MA in 1615, and made knight of the Bath in November 1616. His father having become president of the council of Wales, he too was made a councillor (12 November 1617); and following his father's elevation to the peerage as earl of Northampton on 2 August 1618 he was styled Lord Compton. Granted a licence to travel in 1619, Compton was elected MP for Ludlow two years later, his path probably smoothed by his office in the marches. Soon after 20 October 1621 he married Mary (d. 1654), daughter of Sir Francis Beaumont of Coleorton, Leicestershire, and first cousin of the royal favourite George Villiers, marquess of Buckingham. They had two daughters and six sons,

Spencer Compton, second earl of Northampton (1601–1643),
by Henry Paert the elder, 1680s–90s (after Cornelius Johnson and
Sir Anthony Van Dyck)

including James *Compton (1622–1681), William *Compton (1625–1663), and Henry *Compton (1631/2–1713).

Appointed in 1622 master of the robes to Prince Charles, Compton accompanied Charles and Buckingham to Madrid in 1623 on the mission to woo the Spanish infanta, but he became ill during the venture. On the accession of Charles as king he retained his court office and in April 1626 was summoned to the House of Lords as Baron Compton. Following his father's death on 24 June 1630, he succeeded as second earl of Northampton. Although the extravagant first earl left debts of over £10,000, this made a relatively small dent in family fortunes (enhanced by the inheritance of Elizabeth Spencer), and the second earl's income in the 1630s from estates in Warwickshire, Northamptonshire, London, and six other counties was over £6000 a year. He assumed his father's lord lieutenancy of Warwickshire and took on the same position in Gloucestershire, but was often absent from the midlands, leaving local administration to deputy lieutenants; this record was to tell against him later. A close friend of the king, he attended him in Scotland in 1633. He subsequently fought in the European wars, serving in George Goring's regiment at the siege of Breda in 1637, attending the prince palatine and Prince Rupert at The Hague that July, and joining the palatine's forces at the battle of Vlotho in 1638.

On his return to England, Northampton became master of the great wardrobe to the king. As a courtier personally loyal to the crown rather than a man of definite, discernible political views, he raised troops for the bishops' wars

of 1639 and 1640. After the defeat of the royal army at Newburn in August 1640 Northampton supported the petition of the twelve peers for the summoning of parliament, but he never wavered in his opposition to the Scots, even opposing the raising of levies to pay their army of occupation. Against a background of opposition to royal policy in Warwickshire and campaigning by his political rival Robert Greville, Lord Brooke (who had a much higher profile locally), Northampton managed to get his son, James Compton, returned for one of the county seats at both elections of 1640. However, though he signed the parliamentary protestation of 1641, he was replaced as lord lieutenant of Warwickshire by Lord Brooke on 11 February 1642.

That summer Northampton was quick to side with the king. He joined the court at York and on 13 June 1642 signed the engagement in defence of the king; with eight other peers he was impeached for his absence from parliament. Charles appointed Northampton to the commissions of array for Warwickshire, Northamptonshire, Gloucestershire, and Gloucester. Concentrating his energies on the first, Northampton issued on 25 June 1642 the royal commission in Coventry, where he had been recorder since 1640, but he not only failed to raise any support but also prompted Brooke into holding five musters around the county for parliament. Northampton was at the centre of efforts to seize the Warwickshire magazine, and was able to assemble trained bands at four places between 28 July and 1 August. On 30 July he confronted Brooke and a convoy of artillery at Warmington Hill on the southern edge of the county.

A day of negotiations saw the artillery deposited at nearby Banbury, Oxfordshire, with each side promising three days' notice to the other of any attempt to remove it, but a week later, during Brooke's absence in London, Northampton secured it. Having marched on the king's orders to Warwick, he took the town and laid siege to the castle, Brooke's seat, but an unexpectedly energetic defence by Sir Edward Peyto, support for Brooke from below the ranks of the gentry, and eventually the arrival of a parliamentarian army meant that, notwithstanding a visit by Charles to the area on 20 August, Northampton was unable either to overwhelm the castle and keep Warwick or to take the other key local town, Coventry. On 22 August, the day that Charles raised his standard at Nottingham, Northampton's forces were defeated about 10 miles east of Warwick at Southam by John Hampden and Brooke. Northampton then joined the king's field army, fighting at Powick Bridge on 23 September and at Edgehill a month later. By the end of November the earl and three of his sons had captured Banbury, where they survived a siege at the end of December.

Commissioned lieutenant-general of royalist forces in Warwickshire and Northamptonshire in February 1643, Northampton took advantage of Brooke's absence on campaign in Staffordshire to establish garrisons throughout Warwickshire. While Brooke was killed in an attack on Lichfield, its fall to the parliamentarians placed the rest of Staffordshire under threat, and Northampton was ordered to assist his counterpart Henry Hastings. The two joined forces at Coleshill and marched to Stafford, the next target for parliamentarian commanders Sir John Gell and Sir William Brereton. Early on Sunday 19 March the royalist generals dashed out of Stafford with their horse while their foot followed behind. On Hopton Heath they found Gell and Brereton's army and launched an immediate attack. After several charges the parliamentarians were driven from their positions and their artillery captured. During the fighting Northampton had been unhorsed and surrounded by the enemy. Offered quarter, he reportedly 'scorned to take quarter from such base rogues and rebels as they were' (Clarendon, *Hist. rebellion*, 2.476), and was killed by a blow to the head from a halberd. The retreating parliamentarians carried his body from the field and Gell later used it as a bargaining counter in an attempt to retrieve the lost artillery. When the offer was refused, Northampton was buried at All Hallows Church, Derby; he was subsequently reburied at Compton Wynyates. His wife, Mary, who survived him, died in London on 18 March 1654 and was also buried at Compton. Their son James succeeded as third earl of Northampton.

MARTYN BENNETT

Sources GEC, *Peerage* · A. Hughes, *Politics, society and civil war in Warwickshire, 1620–1660* (1987) · Venn, *Alum. Cant.* · Clarendon, *Hist. rebellion* · P. R. Newman, *Royalist officers in England and Wales, 1642–1660: a biographical dictionary* (1981) · F. Wortley, *Character and elegies* (1646) · P. Tennant, *Edgehill and beyond* (1992) · D. Lloyd, *Memoires of the lives … of those … personages that suffered … for the protestant religion* (1668) · *The poems of John Cleveland*, ed. B. Morris and C. Witherington (1967) · E. Warburton, *Memoirs of Prince Rupert and the Cavaliers* (1849)
Archives Castle Ashby, Northampton, accounts as master of the robes | Northants. RO, Finch Hatton MS 133
Likenesses C. Johnson, oils, 1633, Castle Ashby House, Northamptonshire · C. Johnson, oils, 1634, Knole, Kent · H. Paert the elder, oils, 1680–99 (after C. Johnson and A. Van Dyck), NPG [*see illus.*]

Compton, Spencer, earl of Wilmington (*c.*1674–1743), prime minister, was the sixth son of James *Compton, third earl of Northampton (1622–1681), his third son with his second wife, Mary (*d.* 1719), the eldest daughter of Baptist Noel, third Viscount Campden. He was educated at St Paul's School, enrolled at the Middle Temple in 1687, and was admitted a commoner at Trinity College, Oxford, in 1690. Although he failed in an attempt to enter parliament in 1695, he was returned for Eye, Suffolk, at a by-election in June 1698. Among his whig brethren he cut a slightly odd figure, coming from a family of high-church tories (his uncle was Henry Compton, bishop of London), but a violent quarrel with his elder brother George, fourth earl of Northampton, had turned him to the whigs. He was a dull and uninspiring speaker in the Commons and his gifts were limited to a mastery of rule and precedent. By the early years of Queen Anne's reign he had none the less established himself among the more prominent whig politicians, and among his Kit-Cat Club confrères enjoyed a particular rapport with the young Robert Walpole. In the

Commons he chaired the elections and privileges committee from 1705 until 1710, a role usually considered a stepping stone to the speakership.

In 1707 Compton was given office as paymaster of pensions and appointed treasurer to the queen's consort, Prince George. His support for the Marlborough–Godolphin ministry was invariably assiduous, though as a faithful lord treasurer's whig he was least enthusiastic towards the admission of junto whigs to office late in 1708. Difficulties with his electoral patron, Lord Cornwallis, precluded his re-election for Eye in 1710, but, having been one of Henry Sacheverell's severest persecutors at the impeachment trial earlier in the year, he took no steps to secure election elsewhere. The incoming tory ministers nevertheless retained him in his paymaster's office until 1713, though probably out of consideration for his many family connections among the tories.

During this hiatus in his career Compton acquired an estate near Eastbourne in Sussex, and in 1713 he re-entered parliament for the Sussex borough of East Grinstead. At the accession of George I he was said to have been resentful at not receiving immediate recognition from senior whigs in the new ministry, particularly as he had several times been tipped for high office in the preceding reign. After the general election early in 1715, however, during which he was chosen a knight of the shire for Sussex, he became treasurer to the prince of Wales (the future George II), and, on reassembling in March, the Commons unanimously adopted him as speaker. He was sworn of the privy council on 6 July 1716. Despite certain shortcomings, his unflawed knowledge of precedent and the rulings of previous speakers suited Compton particularly well for the role, and he presided over the house with characteristic punctiliousness for the next twelve years. His innate formality and hauteur lent dignity to proceedings, though John Hatsell has suggested that his notions of maintaining order were somewhat lax, and reported an anecdote that Compton would rebuke MPs who called on him to quieten noisy debates and who insisted on a right to be heard with the words, 'No sir, you have a right to speak, but the House have a right to judge whether they will hear you' (Hatsell, 2.108). His successor, the renowned Speaker Onslow, described him as 'very able … in the chair, but [he] had not the powers of speech out of it' (*Buckinghamshire MSS*, 516). At the ministerial split in 1717, to which the prince of Wales's quarrel with his father had in a major way contributed, Compton, as head of the prince's household, joined the Townshend–Walpole group in opposition and thus found himself in the unusual predicament of having to fulfil his duties as speaker while technically in opposition to the king's ministers. Yet he achieved this feat until the reconciliation of 1720 without incurring the least hint of displeasure.

Compton's loyalty to Walpole had been unswerving during the years of the whig schism, but their differing situations were accentuated after the ministerial reconstruction of 1721 which brought Walpole to power. While Walpole could realistically expect to remain at the helm under George I, the prince's appreciation of Compton's efficient management of his household led him often and openly to declare that he had no intention of retaining Walpole when he himself became king and that Compton would replace him. For the time being, Walpole did what he could to keep Compton out of ministerial politics by promoting his re-election to the speaker's chair in 1722; he also pandered to his avaricious instincts by having him appointed paymaster-general, one of the most lucrative offices in the administration. Compton was reputed to have made £100,000 during his tenure of the post between 1722 and 1730. Moreover, in May 1725 he was included in Walpole's newly revived knighthood of the Bath. At the news of George I's death in May 1727 the new king ordered Walpole to take his instructions from Compton. But, on finding himself suddenly encumbered with affairs of state, Compton lost his nerve and needed Walpole's assistance even in the preliminary task of drafting George II's declaration to the privy council. Over the next few days his limited acumen became painfully apparent, and was ultimately confirmed in royal eyes by the ungenerousness of his proposals for Queen Caroline's income compared with those produced by Walpole. At an interview with the king, at which Walpole was also present, Compton reportedly broke down, declaring that the burden of leading the king's administration would be far too great for him. In later years he would gloss over these events by claiming that 'affairs abroad were in so bad [a] situation that [he] durst not be premier minister' (Egmont Diary, 1.375). Compton thereafter bore an unremitting sense of grievance against Walpole for having inflicted on him so public a humiliation.

The king's continuing regard for Compton ensured the latter's retention in the ministry as paymaster, though by the end of the year Walpole was fully aware that he was involved in the growing 'confederacy' of discontented whigs now ranged against him. On 8 January 1728 Compton was created a peer and took the title of Baron Wilmington in the county of Sussex. He was later to claim that Walpole had 'forced it upon him' in the belief that Compton 'had conceived too strong hopes of being [his] superior ever to serve in the House of Commons quietly under him, and that it might be dangerous, consequently, to suffer him in the chair of the new parliament' (Hervey, 1.39). Wilmington's slow-burning hatred of Walpole was never extinguished. Over the next few years he was one of several prominent members of the administration who, while outwardly supporting ministerial measures, privately maintained a dialogue with leading opposition whigs and tories. At the time of the parliamentary crisis over the French refortification of Dunkirk early in 1730, in which Walpole's majority in the Commons became seriously endangered, he was widely recognized as head of a coterie of senior whigs poised to take over whenever Walpole should fall from favour. During the subsequent reshuffling of Walpole's ministry in April, Wilmington was appointed lord privy seal, a surprise choice generally assumed to have been the king's, as against the known wishes of his first minister. Thus brought into the 'inner' or 'effective' cabinet of ministers, Wilmington formally

took office on 14 May, and six days later was promoted in the peerage to the earldom of Wilmington. He was made a DCL at Oxford University on 5 August. Towards the end of December he was appointed lord president of the council, a post which placed him in charge of the administrative apparatus of the privy council.

Wilmington was described by Lord Hervey in his *Memoirs* as:

> a plodding, heavy fellow, with a great application, but no talents. … He was always more concerned for the manner and form in which a thing was to be done than about the propriety or expediency of the thing itself; and as he was to execute rather than project … so he was much fitter for a clerk to a minister. Whatever was resolved upon he would often know how properly to perform, but seldom how to advise what was proper to be resolved upon.   (Hervey, 1.24)

In the House of Lords he barely ever spoke but never wavered from the ministerial line. His name was associated with a re-emergence of the old anti-ministerial faction in the summer of 1732, and during the excise crisis of March–April 1733 he and his kinsman the duke of Dorset threatened to resign their posts in protest against the proposed dismissals of other courtiers who opposed the scheme in parliament. Wilmington was won back by Walpole apparently with a renewed promise of the Garter. He received this on 12 June and was installed at St George's, Windsor, on 22 August. He had largely ceased by this stage to enjoy the close confidence of the king, though their continuing friendship kept him in office. At a time when a number of prominent peers had openly committed themselves to opposition, Wilmington's failure to follow suit rendered him odious in the eyes of leading opposition luminaries, one of whom, Lord Chesterfield, wrote in June 1734 that 'the President is as contemptible and subservient as ever' (Letters, 2.281).

Wilmington's next few years were spent quietly in the performance of his ministerial duties until the beginnings of dissension within the cabinet early in 1739 over policy towards Spain inspired fresh rumours of his intention to resign. Although by the summer of 1740 he and Dorset were regarded as titular leaders of one of three main ministerial factions, he avoided participation in the cabinet quarrels over strategic objectives in the war against Spain and continued at least outwardly to support Walpole. He did not refrain, however, from connivance with several of Walpole's enemies during the election campaign in the spring of 1741. Denying any personal ambition for himself, he once more became explicit in his censure of Walpolian power, and to acquaintances he privately expressed his view that 'the true interest of England was to have no chief minister … that every great office should be immediately dependent on the king and answer for itself' (Egmont Diary, 3.250). Behind the scenes he advocated a new broadly constructed ministry that included opposition elements, believing that the king's power would be preserved thereby from future encroachment by particular ministers or factions. He took his part among the cabinet council members who towards the end of January 1742 quietly advised George II of the impossibility of conducting essential supply business in the Commons if Walpole continued in office; on 2 February Wilmington was summoned by the king and appointed in Walpole's place as first lord of the Treasury.

From the first it was understood that Wilmington, now somewhat elderly and ill with the stone, would hand the effective work of managing the Treasury to a new chancellor of the exchequer. Although he was not at all qualified by political ability for this most senior of ministerial positions, his appointment bore all the marks of the calculation and shrewdness of others. The leading ministerialists Lord Hardwicke and the duke of Newcastle (quite possibly with Walpole's own connivance) had carefully manoeuvred William Pulteney, Walpole's chief opponent and his obvious successor, into rejecting the Treasury, all along smoothing the way for Wilmington as their desired choice. As the holder of a senior if largely non-powerful cabinet position, he was sufficiently far removed from Walpole, as well as being acceptable to the king. It was not until Wilmington had taken office, however, that his own 'broad bottom' views came into play and caused disturbance. Placing himself at odds with those who had been instrumental in his appointment, he joined the duke of Argyll and his sympathizers in demanding a new ministry that included leading tories in addition to former dissident whigs; but when on 13 February Wilmington found that Carteret had been appointed secretary of state (and effective head of the administration) without any prior consultation with himself, he confronted George II with a threat of resignation, dismayed that the ministry was being reconstructed substantially on its old narrow footing and with so many of Walpole's supporters still dominating the field. As ever, royal persuasion worked its effect on Wilmington and he remained in office. His own stewardship as premier was distinctly lacklustre, and in the time that was left to him he was no more than a ministerial figurehead presiding over a group of ministers among whom Lord Carteret, due to his influence with the king, was the real controlling force.

Wilmington died on 2 July 1743 at his house in St James's Square, London, and was buried at Compton Wynyates, Warwickshire, the resting place of many of his forebears. It had already been planned to replace him at the Treasury with Henry Pelham later in the year. Although he was unmarried, Wilmington was understood to have fathered several illegitimate children, one of whom was the wife of James Glen, for whom in 1739 Wilmington procured the governorship of South Carolina. He left his entire estate, most of it in Sussex, including his seat, Compton Place, Eastbourne, to his nephew James Compton, fifth earl of Northampton.　　　　　　　　　　　　A. A. HANHAM

Sources 'Compton, Hon. Spencer', HoP, *Commons, 1690–1715* [draft] • R. R. Sedgwick, 'Compton, Spencer', HoP, *Commons, 1715–54* • GEC, *Peerage* • J. Hatsell, ed., *Precedents of proceedings in the House of Commons*, 4th edn, 2 (1818), 108 • *The manuscripts of the earl of Buckinghamshire, the earl of Lindsey … and James Round*, HMC, 38 (1895) • *Manuscripts of the earl of Egmont: diary of Viscount Percival, afterwards first earl of Egmont*, 3 vols., HMC, 63 (1920–23), vol. 1, pp. 93–4, 280, 357, 375, 443, 452; vol. 2, pp. 33, 156–7; vol. 3, pp. 28, 247–52, 254,

259 • John, Lord Hervey, *Some materials towards memoirs of the reign of King George II*, ed. R. Sedgwick, 3 vols. (1931) • *The letters of Philip Dormer Stanhope, fourth earl of Chesterfield*, ed. B. Dobrée, 6 vols. (1932) • W. Coxe, *Memoirs of the life and administration of Sir Robert Walpole, earl of Orford*, 2 (1798), 519–20; 3 (1798), 201 • P. King, *The life and letters of John Locke*, 2 vols. (1830) • P. D. G. Thomas, *The House of Commons in the eighteenth century* (1971) • J. B. Owen, *The rise of the Pelhams* (1957) • J. H. Plumb, *Sir Robert Walpole*, 2 vols. (1956–60) • Walpole, *Corr.*

Archives BL, corresp. and papers, Add. MSS 45733, 48982, Add. Ch 41290–41297 • L. Cong., papers • PRO | BL, letters to duke of Newcastle, Add. MSS 32688–32700 • priv. coll., Townshend MSS • V&A NAL, letters to Lady Sundon

Likenesses G. Kneller, oils, c.1710, NPG; copy, Castle Ashby, Northamptonshire • G. Kneller, oils, c.1725, Castle Ashby, Northamptonshire • studio of G. Kneller, portrait, c.1726, speaker's apartments, Palace of Westminster

Compton, Spencer Joshua Alwyne, second marquess of Northampton (1790–1851), patron of science and the arts, was born on 2 January 1790 at Erlestoke Park, Wiltshire, the second son of Charles Compton, ninth earl and first marquess of Northampton, and Mary, only daughter of Joshua Smith, MP for Devizes. Educated privately by Edward Meyrick at Ramsbury, Wiltshire, he entered Trinity College, Cambridge, in 1808, where he studied mainly mathematics under George Frederick Tavel, his tutor. As a nobleman he proceeded to his MA in 1810 after only six terms in residence and without taking any examination. He subsequently received two honorary degrees (LLD, Cambridge, in 1835, and DCL, Oxford, in 1850). At Cambridge he acquired and cultivated wide intellectual tastes in science, literature, and the fine arts, and formed enduring friendships with such contemporaries as George Peacock, Adam Sedgwick, Thomas Musgrave, John Frederick William Herschel, and William Empson.

In May 1812, shortly after the assassination of Spencer Perceval, the prime minister (and a relative), Lord Compton (as he styled himself) succeeded him as MP for Northampton and remained there until he lost the seat in the general election of 1820. Although his immediate relatives were all high tories, he soon showed his independence: a maverick tory, he would on occasion vote with the whigs and oppose his own party, which censured him as impractical and crotchety. Preferring direct to indirect taxation, he opposed the repeal of the property tax in 1816; and he supported Wilberforce's attempts to secure the total abolition of slavery in Africa, and James Mackintosh's work as a criminal law reformer. By 1819 he was at odds with both the foreign and home secretaries (Castlereagh and Sidmouth); the former accused him of 'turning his back on himself'. His whiggish tendencies were ascribed to the influence of his wife, Margaret Maclean Clephane, eldest daughter and heir of Major-General Douglas Maclean Clephane, whom he married on 24 July 1815. She was a poet, a great favourite of Sir Walter Scott, a good musician, and an accomplished artist. Although her poetry was praised by Wordsworth for its simplicity, pathos, and energy, it was never published, but was edited after her death by her husband, and printed privately in 1833. Theirs was a happy marriage and they had four sons and two daughters.

Spencer Joshua Alwyne Compton, second marquess of Northampton (1790–1851), by David Octavius Hill and Robert Adamson, 1844

From 1820 to 1830 Compton and his wife lived in Italy, often in Rome, where they not only pursued connoisseurship but also protected victims of despotism in Lombardy and Naples. Compton succeeded his father as marquess of Northampton on 24 May 1828, but remained in Italy until his stay was ended by domestic tragedy: after the birth of their sixth child, on 14 March 1830, his wife died suddenly on 2 April. Northampton returned to England, and thereafter lived mainly at Castle Ashby, Northamptonshire. After 1830 the rich, aristocratic widower began to transform himself into one of the 'good and the great' in polite cultural life. He was dutiful as a politician (supporting constitutional change in the early 1830s, and in 1832 announcing an unsuccessful bill to repeal the law under which an MP, if made a minister, had to vacate his seat and seek re-election), but he was not as active in the House of Lords as he had been in the Commons. Instead he devoted himself to the advancement of literature, the fine arts, archaeology, and, especially, science.

Northampton gained some recognition as a minor poet, but his major venture in literature was to initiate and oversee *The Tribute* (1837), a miscellany of poems published by subscription for the benefit of Edward Smedley, who was poor and severely ill. Northampton subscribed for twenty copies, but was offended when his assistant, Monckton Milnes, suggested he should read some proofs.

From 1849 until his death Northampton was president of the Royal Society of Literature. In the field of antiquities and archaeology he was a minor performer and a major organizer. He was an accomplished draughtsman, and had a fine collection of Etruscan vases, but his forte was office holding: he was a trustee of the National Gallery and of the British Museum, and president of the Architectural Society of the Archdeaconry of Northampton. He was twice president of the Archaeological Institute of Great Britain and Ireland (in 1845–6 and in 1850–51) and was responsible for its name, which he coined after the British Archaeological Association (founded in 1843) had split in the spring of 1845, when a small faction seceded. He presided at the association's meeting in the summer and suggested, as an affordable concession, that its own title be changed to Archaeological Institute in order to prevent the seceding party (which retained the title of Association) from feeling aggrieved; characteristically he refrained from attacking the secessionists.

It was this ability to avoid faction fighting and malice and to promote tactful reconciliation which facilitated Northampton's most notable achievement: in 1838 he was elected president of the Royal Society of London, which office he held until his resignation in 1848. Although he was not a leading scientist he had a sustained interest in geology, on which he published three short papers. His large collection of minerals (including Comptonite found near Vesuvius) and fossils at Castle Ashby was renowned. Conversation there was often focused on geology. Once his daughter, Marian [see Egerton, Marianne Margaret, Viscountess Alford], later a well-known artist, revealed her exasperation with a long discussion about a motto for the Geological Society of London: her solution was to have for its crest a mole with the motto 'I bore'. To the end of his life Northampton remained a zealous hammerer for fossils: in 1849 his unflagging efforts astonished an Arundel chalk-pit worker who remarked 'That man doan't work for his living; if he went on that gate he could do nought next day' (Owen, 1.340). Northampton's house parties at Castle Ashby were useful rehearsals for the fashionable soirées he gave as president of the Royal Society in the large town house in Piccadilly which he inherited in the summer of 1838. He came to be president through his commitment to the British Association for the Advancement of Science (founded in 1831). In 1836 he became a nationally prominent cultural figure when his popular manners, oratory, and good humour made him a resounding success as president of the association, even though he was a last-minute substitute for the president-elect. Subsequently he was in great demand. In 1837 he became a vice-president of both the Royal Society and the Geological Society (having been an absentee president of the latter in 1820–22), and in the autumn of 1838 he replaced the duke of Sussex as president of the Royal Society, one wag commenting that the society had descended from royalty to the nobility. He remained deeply involved in the association's affairs, serving as its president in 1848 and ensuring that the Royal Society and the association acted in amity. As president of the Royal Society he was distinguished by his kindness, courtesy, good humour, patience, responsibility, and tact, as well as by his splendid hospitality, mastery of continental languages, and cultured mind. He avoided being a tyrant, a cipher, or a tool; but his reign saw one scandal and some great changes within the society. In 1845 a royal medal was awarded illegally to T. S. Beck, which led *The Lancet* to denounce the society's council as 'the last Old Sarum of the scientific world' and Northampton (who admitted the council's error, though he was not personally involved in its irregularity) as an autocrat. Although he was not an innovator by temperament or conviction, Northampton did not oppose reform when it was widely supported. In 1847 the age of the almost exclusively scientific Royal Society began, largely as a result of the efforts of William Grove and Leonard Horner: each year only fifteen fellows were to be elected from a list drawn up by the council. Northampton acquiesced in such changes but deplored what he regarded as the ill-mannered and offensive conduct of the reformers. Early in 1848 he showed his chagrin by resigning as president, thoughtfully giving the reformed society nine months in which to find a successor.

For several years Northampton was afflicted by an illness which caused him to spit blood. He was deeply affected by the death of his son-in-law, Lord Alford, on 3 January 1851, and was discovered dead in bed on the morning of the 17th, at Castle Ashby, where he was buried on the 25th.   JACK MORRELL

Sources GM, 2nd ser., 35 (1851), 425–9 • *The Times* (22 Jan 1851) • *Abstracts of the Papers Communicated to the Royal Society of London*, 6 (1850–54), 117–20 • *The Athenaeum* (1845) • *The Athenaeum* (25 Jan 1851), 110–11 • GEC, *Peerage* • M. B. Hall, *All scientists now: the Royal Society in the nineteenth century* (1984) • J. Morrell and A. Thackray, *Gentlemen of science: early years of the British Association for the Advancement of Science* (1981) • W. B. Compton, *History of the Comptons of Compton Wynyates* (1930) • J. A. Secord, *Controversy in Victorian geology: the Cambrian–Silurian dispute* (1986) • R. Owen, *The life of Richard Owen*, 2 vols. (1894)
Archives Castle Ashby, Northamptonshire, corresp. and papers | Bodl. Oxf., corresp. with Sir Thomas Phillipps • GS Lond., letters to Roderick Impey Murchison • NL NZ, Turnbull L., letters to Gideon Algernon Mantell • RS, corresp. with Sir John F. W. Herschel; letters to Sir John W. Lubbock • TCD, corresp. with Sir William Rowan Hamilton • Trinity Cam., corresp. with William Whewell • U. St Andr. L., letters to James Forbes • W. Sussex RO, letters to fifth duke of Richmond
Likenesses J. S. Copley, oils, exh. RA 1803 (with his father), Castle Ashby, Northamptonshire • H. Raeburn, oils, *c*.1815, Castle Ashby, Northamptonshire • D. O. Hill and R. Adamson, photograph, 1844, NPG [*see illus.*] • T. and H. W. Phillips, oils, exh. RA 1847, RS • C. Cook, stipple (after daguerreotype by Claudet), BM, NPG

Compton [Compton Carleton], **Thomas** (1592–1666), Jesuit, was born in Cambridgeshire, the son of Richard Compton and Anne Fludd. The Comptons were a well-to-do Catholic family and the name Compton (or Compton Carleton) figures prominently in lists of early seventeenth-century Jesuits. Like some of his brothers Thomas Compton went to the continent in order to become a priest; he stayed at the English Jesuit college at St Omer from 1606 until 1611. Together with his brother Henry he subsequently moved to the English College at

Madrid. In June 1614 all the English students were transferred to Valladolid in order to continue their studies at the College of St Alban. After three years at Valladolid, Thomas Compton was ordained priest. He was received into the Society of Jesus at Liège in September 1617. The two years of his noviciate at Liège were followed by further studies in France, which prepared him for a teaching career at the Jesuit colleges of St Omer and Liège. During the years 1622–6 he taught a number of basic subjects, such as grammar, syntax, poetry, and rhetoric, at St Omer. On 21 May 1628 he completed his training as a Jesuit by being professed of the four vows at Liège, where he became professor of philosophy and theology and prefect of studies. Apart from a short stay at St Omer in 1631 he remained at Liège for the rest of his life. The contradictory information in Foley about the date of his ordination and his whereabouts in 1625 must be due to his being confused with another member of the Compton Carleton family (Foley, 7.154).

In his entry on Compton, Southwell praises him for his great gifts as a teacher. These gifts are discernible in the handbooks on philosophy and theology that he published. *Philosophia universa* (Antwerp, 1649) is a well-organized treatment of the main branches of philosophy; *Prometheus Christianus* (Antwerp, 1652) surveys the field of moral philosophy on the basis of nineteen 'disputationes' and contains an address to Compton's pupils at Liège; and *Cursus Theologici tomus prior/tomus posterior* (Liège, 1659–64) is a monumental two-volume theological handbook of more than 1000 pages. The many subsequent editions of his works and two posthumous publications dealing with Aristotelian philosophy testify to his reputation. He died at Liège on 24 March 1666.   J. BLOM and F. BLOM

Sources H. Foley, ed., *Records of the English province of the Society of Jesus*, 7 (1882–3), 153–4, 1424 • Gillow, *Lit. biog. hist.*, 1.546–7 • P. Ribadeneira, *Bibliotheca Scriptorum Societatis Jesu*, ed. N. Southwell (1676), 761–2 • T. M. McCoog, *English and Welsh Jesuits, 1555–1650*, 2 vols., Catholic RS, 74–5 (1994–5) • G. Oliver, *Collections towards illustrating the biography of the Scotch, English and Irish members, SJ* (1838), 176–7 • E. Henson, ed., *The registers of the English College at Valladolid, 1589–1862*, Catholic RS, 30 (1930), 119 • E. Henson, ed., *The English college at Madrid, 1611–1767*, Catholic RS, 29 (1929), 85, 307

Compton, Sir William (1482?–1528), courtier, was the son and heir of Edmund Compton of Compton, Warwickshire; he was described as eleven years old and more on his father's death in 1493. According to Dugdale he became a page to Prince Henry, duke of York, and in due course a deep and lasting friendship grew between them. In 1510, a year after Henry's accession to the throne, Compton was first described as groom of the stool, and he served until 1526 as one of the king's most important and intimate personal servants, jousting with the king (nearly losing his life in 1510), keeping the king's linen, holding and disbursing large sums of money for the king's daily purchases. Compton was often entrusted with delicate tasks by Henry: enquiring on his behalf how far the fifth earl of Northumberland's marriage plans had gone, arranging for the king to meet a mistress, arresting the duke of Buckingham. He served in the military campaign of 1513 (he was knighted after the capture of Tournai in September) and on the Scottish borders in 1523.

Compton did enormously well out of the king's service, holding many offices; he became constable of several royal castles in the midlands, including Warwick, Sudeley, Kenilworth, and Fulbrook, and was variously bailiff, keeper, receiver, and steward on crown lands, taking what Wolsey, after Compton's death, described as 'excessive fees' (PRO, SP 1/49, fol. 75). He leased or received crown lands on a notable scale, ruthlessly exploiting his royal favour in disputes with Margaret Pole, countess of Salisbury, Edward Stafford, third duke of Buckingham, and Richard Grey, third earl of Kent, and embezzled jewels and gilt plate properly the king's. He bought up lands aggressively, possibly pressurizing a reluctant Buckingham to sell him a series of manors in 1520, and possibly being committed for a short time to the Fleet prison following complaints by Sir Henry Grey. By the end of his life he had built up a landed estate, centred on the south midlands, whose gross income in 1524–5 was £1689. It provided the basis for the peerage granted by Queen Elizabeth to Sir William's grandson Henry Compton. The latter's descendants, the marquesses of Northampton, have continued to live in the picture-book early Tudor country house built by Sir William Compton at Compton Wynyates in Warwickshire.

Compton does not appear to have played much part in the government of the realm and the administration of the localities. His posts as JP in Hertfordshire (1511–14), in Leicestershire, Northamptonshire, Warwickshire, and Worcestershire (all from 1511), and in Somerset (from 1513), and as sheriff (notably sheriff of Worcestershire for life from 1516), measure his standing rather than describe his activities. Polydore Vergil believed that Compton's favour with the king made Cardinal Wolsey fearful, so much so that in 1523 he had Compton dispatched to the wars on the Scottish borders so that in his absence Wolsey 'might gradually cause him to be hateful to Henry' (*Anglica historia*, 308–9). But military service was a natural step in the evolution from upstart courtier to landed magnate. Possibly Wolsey was responsible for Compton's resignation as groom of the stool in 1526, as part of the reforms known as the Eltham ordinances, but since Compton was then appointed usher of receipts in the exchequer and granted a licence allowing him to wear his hat in the royal presence, and since there is no sign that he lost his influence with the king, perhaps he did not regret the loss of a post too humble for the magnate he had now become.

There is nothing to suggest that Compton was interested in the concerns of government—that he was for or against war with France, or that he had views on taxation or on how Ireland should be governed or the church reformed—nor did he attempt to build up any kind of personal following or to displace Cardinal Wolsey. Lord Herbert of Cherbury, Henry VIII's biographer in the 1640s, summed him up well as 'being more attentive to his profit, than publique affairs' (Herbert, 8). In 1512 Compton married Werburga, widow of Sir Francis Cheyne and

daughter of Sir John Brereton and his wife, Katherine, sister and heir of Sir William Berkeley. That he received several manors as a royal gift suggests that the king may well have played a part in the marriage. Wolsey in his capacity of legate later cited Compton for living in adultery with Lord Hastings's wife and for having taken the sacrament to disprove it. He died of sweating sickness in June 1528, leaving a son, Peter, aged six. G. W. BERNARD

Sources G. W. Bernard, 'The rise of Sir William Compton, early Tudor courtier', *EngHR*, 96 (1981), 754–77 · LP Henry VIII, vols. 1–4 · PRO, state papers domestic Henry VIII, general series, SP1/49 · PRO, special collections, ministers' and receivers' accounts, SC6/Henry VIII/5878 · W. Dugdale, *The antiquities of Warwickshire illustrated*, rev. W. Thomas, 2nd edn, 2 vols. (1730) · *The Anglica historia of Polydore Vergil, AD 1485–1537*, ed. and trans. D. Hay, CS, 3rd ser., 74 (1950) · Edward, Lord Herbert of Cherbury, *The life and raigne of King Henry the Eighth* (1649) · W. B. Compton, sixth marquess of Northampton, *History of the Comptons of Compton Wynyates* (1930)
Likenesses stained-glass window (of Compton?), Balliol Oxf.
Wealth at death £1689—gross landed income, 1524/5: PRO SC 6/Henry VIII/5878

Compton, Sir William (1625–1663), army officer, was born at Compton Wynyates, Warwickshire, the third son of Spencer *Compton, second earl of Northampton (1601–1643), and his wife, Mary Beaumont (d. 1654), daughter of Sir Francis Beaumont. He was educated at Eton College (1634–6), and in his eighteenth year joined his father's royalist regiment, and served with it at the taking of Banbury on 8 August 1642. He led his men in three attacks, and had two horses shot under him during the fighting. Upon the surrender of the town and castle he was made lieutenant-governor under his father, and brought over many to the king's interest. He was knighted at Oxford on 12 December 1643. William and his elder brother James *Compton, third earl of Northampton, worked together uneasily. James blamed William for the capture of the family home, Compton Wynyates, on 9 June 1644 because he had refused to accept James's nominated governor, placing an inexperienced colleague in command. In July 1644 Banbury was besieged by parliamentarian forces from Northamptonshire, Warwick, and Coventry, but Compton resisted the leaguer for three months in what was regarded as a heroic and inspiring defence until his brother, Northampton, raised the siege on 26 October. Compton remained as governor of Banbury until after the king left Oxford, when he was ordered to surrender the garrison, which he did on 8 May 1646, receiving good terms: all officers were allowed to keep their horses, swords, goods, and money, and were given safe conduct.

A landowner in Kent, in 1648 Compton became embroiled in the Kentish rebellion, serving as major-general under George Goring, earl of Norwich. After the defeat at the battle of Maidstone and the failure to gain access to London, Norwich's shrinking army turned towards Essex. When rebellion broke out at Chelmsford on 4 June parliament moved quickly to pardon the rebels on condition they did not support Norwich. The earl dashed to Chelmsford to enlist the rebels' support, leaving Compton in command at Bow Bridge, where he cut

Sir William Compton (1625–1663), by Henry Paert the elder
(after Sir Peter Lely, c.1655)

communications between London and Essex. On 8 June
Norwich and Compton led their forces to Brentwood,
where they joined the Essex rebels, and thereafter Compton's role was overshadowed by the military leadership of
Sir Charles Lucas, who led the forces to Colchester to raise
support. The royalists became trapped in the town when
Fairfax and the New Model made a lightning march to the
county, enduring siege from 13 June until 28 August. By
the end of July they, and the townspeople, were reduced
to eating cats and dogs. Upon surrender Compton was not
singled out for court martial, unlike Lucas and others,
who were shot. Oliver Cromwell is said to have referred to
him as 'the sober young man, and the godly cavalier', and
he escaped with a fine of £600.

Even so, Compton was involved in royalist conspiracies
from the inception of the republic, and in 1650 was felt to
be crucial to Kent royalists' plans to seize Dover Castle.
About 1651 he married Elizabeth Alington (d. 1671), widow
of William, Baron Alington of Horseheath, Cambridgeshire, and sister of Sir Lionel Tollemache, who was married to Elizabeth Murray, countess of Dysart, one of the
principal female intriguers of the period. Thereafter he
resided in Cambridgeshire. From May 1654 onwards he
was one of the six men who comprised the Sealed Knot,
the secret organization which aimed to co-ordinate royalist risings. In 1655 he promised the Knot's reluctant support for Penruddock's rebellion, although no practical
assistance was provided. Despite this Compton had to stay
away from his Cambridgeshire home throughout the
summer. Eventually he surrendered voluntarily to the
government through the mediation of his brother-in-law

Sir Lionel Tollemache. He was held only briefly, but thereafter the authorities kept records of his movements. He
may have remained quiescent during 1656, but in the following year was embroiled in the Knot's discussions with
the Leveller John Wildman. Compton played no major
role in the plotting of the marquess of Ormond and Daniel
O'Neill in early 1658, but in April he was arrested and
placed in the Tower with fellow Knot members Sir Richard
Willys and Colonel John Russell. Upon their release in July
all three were warned by secretary Thurloe to expect no
quarter if they were involved in future plots. Compton
seems to have taken this to heart and his involvement in
the conspiracies surrounding Booth's rising appear to
have been minimal, even though his brother, the earl of
Northampton, was briefly engaged in support for the
national rising.

With the Restoration Compton was returned to parliament for the borough of Cambridge (11 March 1661), and
appointed master of the ordnance by Charles II. He was a
fairly active MP in the early sessions of the Cavalier Parliament. He died suddenly in Drury Lane, London, on 18
October 1663, and was buried at Compton Wynyates,
where a monument was erected to his memory. Pepys
recorded his shock at the death of 'one of the worthiest
men and best officers of state now in England'. Compton,
Pepys thought, was 'of the best temper, valour, abilities of
mind, integrity, birth, fine person and diligence of any
man he hath left behind him in the three kingdoms'
(Pepys, 4.338–9).

THOMPSON COOPER, rev. MARTYN BENNETT

Sources B. Whitelocke, Memorials of English affairs, new edn, 4
vols. (1853) · Clarendon, Hist. rebellion · Pepys, Diary · P. E. Tenant,
Edgehill and beyond (1992) · M. A. E. Green, ed., Calendar of the proceedings of the committee for compounding … 1643–1660, 5 vols., PRO (1889–
92); repr. (1967) · M. A. E. Green, ed., Calendar of the proceedings of the
committee for advance of money, 1642–1656, 3 vols., PRO (1888); repr.
(1967) · CSP dom., 1661–4 · J. Vicars, The burning-bush not consumed
(1646) · J. Vicars, Gods arke overtopping the worlds waves (1646) ·
W. Dugdale, The antiquities of Warwickshire illustrated (1656) · W. C.
Metcalfe, A book of knights banneret, knights of the Bath and knights
bachelor (1885) · W. Dugdale, The baronage of England, 2 vols. (1675–
6) · D. Underdown, Royalist conspiracy in England, 1649–1660 (1960) ·
GEC, Peerage · E. R. Edwards, 'Compton, Sir William', HoP, Commons, 1660–90
Archives PRO, Black, docquets of letters patent, 1837, SP
29/68–19
Likenesses P. Lely, oils, c.1655, Ham House, Richmond, London ·
H. Paert the elder, oils (after P. Lely, c.1655), NPG [see illus.] · monument, Compton Wynyates church
Wealth at death properties in Cambridgeshire and Kent; home
in Drury Lane, Westminster

Comrie, Alexander (1706–1774), theological writer, was
born on 16 December 1706 in Perth, the son of Patrick
Comrie, an attorney, and Rachell Vause. His parents
wanted him to follow his great-grandfather Andrew Gray
and his mother's stepfather, George Hutcheson, into the
Presbyterian ministry. As a youth, Comrie was catechized
by Ebenezer and Ralph Erskine, and greatly influenced by
the writings of Thomas Boston.

Comrie postponed his studies at the age of twenty

because of financial hardship. He went to the Netherlands, where he worked for A. van der Willigen, a Rotterdam merchant. Three years later he enrolled at Groningen University, where he studied under Anthonias Driessen and Cornelius van Velsen. In 1733 he transferred to Leiden to study philosophy under W. J. 's-Gravensande. He was awarded a doctorate in philosophy in 1734 after completing a critical study of the thought of Descartes, entitled *De moralitatis fundamento et natura virtutis.*

Comrie was then elected minister of the parish of Woubrugge, where he was pastor for thirty-eight years until 1773, the year before his death, faithfully working among people who deeply appreciated his zeal for the Calvinist faith of the Dutch Second Reformation church. He married three times: first, on 15 August 1737, to Johanna de Heyde (1710–1738), who died shortly after giving birth to their only child, Rachel Cornelia (1738–1774); second, to Maria van der Pijll (*d.* 1764) on 25 April 1741; and finally to Catharina de Reus (1722–1809) on 2 December 1766. Rachel Cornelia Comrie married Gerhardus Boufy from Schiedam, but died aged thirty-six, only two months before Comrie's own death.

Comrie was even more influential as a writer than as a preacher. Like Voetius, he aimed to unite and promote Reformation doctrine, scholastic methodology, and scriptural piety through his writing. He took on four major tasks, the first of which was to help church members progress in reformed, experiential truth, to which end a collection of his sermons was published in 1749 (*Verzameling van leerredenen*). Secondly, he devoted several treatises to the doctrine of faith and its relationship to justification and assurance. He wrote a book on various biblical terms that describe faith, published as *Het A.B.C. des geloofs* in 1739 (translated as *The ABC of Faith*, 1978); a major work on the scriptural properties of saving faith (*Verhandeling van eenige eigenschappen des zaligmakenden geloofs*, 1744); a commentary on the first seven Lord's days of the Heidelberg catechism (*Stellige en praktikale verklaaring van den Heidelbergschen catechismus*, 1753); and an extended tract on justification of sinners by direct imputation (*Brief over de rechtvaardigmakinge des zondaars*, 1761). His distinction between the principle or habit (*habitus*) of faith and the exercise or act (*actus*) of faith served as the foundation of his doctrine of faith. By emphasizing the principle of faith, he promoted divine grace as the sole cause of faith. He taught that the principle of faith is exercised by knowledge, assent, and trust.

To promote puritan piety, which was his third objective, Comrie translated several important volumes from English into Dutch. These included Thomas Shepard's *The Ten Virgins*, Walter Marshall's *Gospel Mystery of Sanctification*, Thomas Boston's *The Covenant of Grace*, and George Hutcheson's *Brief Exposition of the Twelve Small Prophets*. Finally, Comrie defended reformed theology against neonomianism, Arminianism, and rationalism. By focusing on the habit of faith, Comrie aimed to prevent Calvinism from lapsing into neonomianism, which taught that the gospel is a 'new law' (*neonomos*) that a sinner must obey by faith, and that this obedience, together with the righteousness

of Christ, is the ground of justification. In opposition to Arminianism, Comrie, with Nicolaus Holtius, produced two volumes of dialogues against efforts to reconcile Calvinism and Arminianism by departing from the doctrinal standards of the Dutch Reformed church (*Examen van het ontwerp van tolerantie*, 1753–9). He also wrote against ministers and professors who were advocating rationalism, including Antonius van der Os (*Aanspraak aan Antonius van der Os*, 1753) and Jan van den Honert (*Banieren van wegen de waarheid opgeregt tegen den Heer Jan van den Honert*, 1753).

Van der Os, minister of Zwolle, had declared that no church confessions had power to decide in matters of faith, for the scriptures were the true rule, and each man was at liberty to receive them according to his individual interpretation. He also argued that the Synod of Dort did not mean to set forth truth for all time, but only until further light should be obtained. Van den Honert questioned the fundamental doctrine of justification by faith, which Comrie felt involved the surrender of all that Luther and Calvin had taught on the subject. Despite the strenuous opposition of Comrie and his friends, rationalism advanced steadily among the clergy and professors. But the people of the Netherlands for the most part remained faithful to the gospel that Comrie preached. Today his name is still recognized and his books are still read in the Netherlands by those who advocate reformed, experiential faith. Comrie spent the last months of his life as a pastoral assistant in Gouda, where he died on 10 December 1774, and was buried.

JOEL R. BEEKE

Sources J. H. R. Verboom, *Dr. Alexander Comrie, predikant van Woubrugge* (1964) · A. G. Honig, *Alexander Comrie* (1892) · J. R. Beeke, *Assurance of faith: Calvin, English puritanism, and the Dutch second reformation* (1991), 281–320 · C. Graafland, 'Alexander Comrie', in W. van't Spijker, *De nadere reformatie: beschrijving van haar voornaamste vertegenwoordigers* (1986), 315–48 · A. Kuyper, 'Alexander Comrie: his life and work in Holland', *Catholic Presbyterian*, 7 (1882), 20–29, 192–201, 278–84 · G. Thomas, 'Alexander Comrie: contender for the faith', *Banner of Truth*, 65 (Feb 1969), 4–8 · G. Thomas, 'Alexander Comrie: contender for the faith', *Banner of Truth*, 66 (March 1969), 29–35 · J. M. Banfield, introduction, in A. Comrie, *The ABC of faith*, trans. J. M. Banfield (1978), 1–15 · C. Graafland, *De zekerheid van het geloof: een onderzoek naar de geloofsbeschouwing van enige vertegenwoordigers van reformatie en nadere reformatie* (1961), 218–33 · R. A. Flinterman, 'Alexander Comrie', *Biografisch lexicon voor de geschiedenis van het Nederlands protestantisme*, ed. D. Nauta and others, 3 (Kampen, 1988), 76–8 · J. W. Verschoor, 'Het geloof bij Brakel en Comrie', *Onder Eigen Vaandel*, 3 (1928), 272–94 · J. W. Verschoor, 'Over de rechtvaardigmaking bij Brakel en Comrie', *Onder Eigen Vaandel*, 10 (1935), 182–201 · S. van der Linde, 'De Godservaring bij W. Teellinck, D. G. à Brakel en A. Comrie', *Theologia Reformata*, 16 (1973), 193–205 · A. Vergunst, 'Comrie on faith', *Insight Into* (June 1983), 3–7 · J. de Boer, *De verzegeling met de Heilige Geest volgens de opvatting van de nadere reformatie* (1968) · W. Van Gorsel, *De ijver voor Zijn huis: de Nadere Reformatie en haar belangrijkste vertegenwoordigers* (Groede, 1981), 108–15 · G. H. Kersten, *Reformed dogmatics*, trans. J. R. Beeke and J. C. Weststrate, 2 vols. (1980–83) · 'Alexander Comrie', *Biographisch woordenboek van protestantsche godgeleerden in Nederland*, ed. J. P. de Bie, J. Loosjes, and L. A. van Langeraad, 6 vols. (The Hague, 1903?–1949), vol. 2, 184–92 · W. Steven, *The history of the Scottish church, Rotterdam* (1832, 1833)

Likenesses portrait, repro. in Honig, *Alexander Comrie*, inside cover

Comrie, Leslie John (1893–1950), astronomer and computer, was born on 15 August 1893 at Pukekohe, near Auckland, New Zealand, the son of John Alexander Comrie and his wife, Helen Lois Smith. His father was a farmer, and both the Comrie and Smith families originally came from Scotland. Comrie never forgot the country of his birth; his hospitality to any New Zealander, particularly a serving member of the forces, was renowned. After attending Pukekohe East School (1900–07) and Auckland grammar school Comrie entered Auckland University College in 1912, where he took his MA degree in 1916 with honours in chemistry. In spite of deafness, which became increasingly acute in later years, he served with the New Zealand expeditionary force in the First World War and was wounded, losing a leg. After the war he took up astronomy and computation, subjects in which he had become interested in Auckland. He went as a research student to St John's College, Cambridge, was elected to an Isaac Newton studentship in 1921, and was awarded his PhD degree in 1924 for a thesis on the occultation of stars by planets.

From Cambridge Comrie proceeded to the United States, where he taught astronomy and computing, first at Swarthmore College, Pennsylvania, and then at Northwestern University, Illinois. He returned to England in 1925 to enter the nautical almanac office, rising to become deputy superintendent in 1926 and superintendent in 1930. In 1920 he married Noeline Dagger, of New Zealand; the marriage was dissolved in 1933 and in the same year he married Phyllis Betty, daughter of H. D. Kitto, of Stroud, Gloucestershire. There was one surviving son of the first marriage and one of the second.

Within ten years Comrie revolutionized the work of the nautical almanac office: his greatest achievement was the complete revision, almost single-handed, of the *Nautical Almanac* for 1931—it had been essentially unchanged since 1834. In a paper presented to the Royal Astronomical Society he proposed the use of a fixed frame of reference for the computation of orbits of comets and minor planets and later provided the necessary data in the office's publications; this may well be his most lasting contribution to astronomy. He introduced new methods, computing techniques, and calculating machines, and transformed the office into the most efficient computing organization of its time; he widened its international responsibilities, and laid the foundation for its expansion to fulfil them.

Comrie left the office in 1936 to found the Scientific Computing Service Ltd, a professional organization catering for large-scale numerical computation, particularly in scientific and mathematical fields. He rapidly built up a powerful team of experienced computers, whose resources were fully stretched by the demands of government departments during the Second World War. During and after the war he worked extremely long hours, and after a strenuous tour of Australia and New Zealand he suffered a stroke, which impaired his speech but left him with an active mind.

Comrie was the foremost computer and table maker of his day. He entered the field when the large majority of computing was done by the aid of logarithms and lived to see in operation the first of the automatic digital computing machines. Although he played no direct part in the design of these machines, his influence over a period of thirty years prepared the way for this advance. During this period he was the acknowledged leader in all aspects of computing and table making. His application of commercial mechanical calculating machines to scientific work enabled more rapid and accurate computation than was previously possible. He set new standards of precision, of numerical accuracy, and of presentation which are incorporated in a series of mathematical tables of unsurpassed merit. The greatest of these, in which Comrie compressed a lifetime's experience, is *Chambers's Six-Figure Mathematical Tables* (2 vols., 1948–9). He also compiled *Hughes' Tables for Sea and Air Navigation* (1938), the finest navigational tables of their type ever produced, together with many other minor tables and descriptions of computational techniques. His work was recognized by his election in 1950 as FRS.

Proud, sensitive, and inclined to be intolerant and critical of others, Comrie could not understand, or forgive, lack of appreciation of his work by those not possessing his energy, precision, or thoroughness. This personality led to constant friction with administrative authority and his break with the Admiralty in 1936, and the same unduly critical attitude led to some difficult personal relationships. However, he was also extremely generous, particularly in giving his own time and energy to helping others, endured severe physical handicaps with patience, and gave his friendship wholeheartedly. After a second stroke Comrie died, on 11 December 1950, at his home, 131 Maze Hill, Greenwich.   D. H. SADLER, *rev.* JOHN BOSNELL

Sources personal knowledge (1959) · private information (1959) · H. S. W. Massey, *Obits. FRS*, 8 (1952–3), 97–107 · W. H. M. Greaves, *Monthly Notices of the Royal Astronomical Society*, 113 (1953), 294–304 · R. C. Archibald, *Mathematical table makers: portraits, paintings, busts, monuments, bio-bibliographical notes* (1948), 221–2 · *DSB* · M. Croaken, *Early scientific computing in Britain* (1990) · J. A. N. Lee, *Computer pioneers* (1995), 209–12 · *WWW* · d. cert.
Archives Bodl. Oxf., corresp. relating to British Association mathematical tables committee · CUL, papers · Royal Observatory, Edinburgh, corresp. relating to satellites
Likenesses photograph, repro. in Massey, *Obits. FRS*, facing p. 97 · photograph (aged thirty-nine), repro. in Archibald, *Mathematical table makers* · photograph, repro. in *Scripta Mathematica*, 11 (1945), following p. 216 · photograph, Astromischen Gesellschaft; repro. in *Porträtgalerie der Astromischen Gesellschaft* (Budapest, 1931)
Wealth at death £17,048 0s. 10d.: probate, 29 July 1952, *CGPLA Eng. & Wales*

Comyn, Alexander, sixth earl of Buchan (d. 1289), baron and administrator, was the eldest son of William Comyn, earl of Buchan (d. 1233), and his second wife, Marjory, in her own right countess of Buchan. Alexander, who became earl of Buchan after his mother's death about 1244, was a member of a large family, with two brothers, William and Fergus, and three sisters: Elizabeth, who married William, earl of Mar; Idonea, who married Gilbert de la Hay; and Agnes, who married Philip Meldrum. He was also half-brother to: Richard; Walter *Comyn, lord of Badenoch, who became earl of Menteith on his marriage to Isabella, daughter and heir of Maurice, earl of Menteith, in 1233 or 1234; William, a clerk; David, who married Isabel de Valognes, lady of East Kilbride; and Jean, who married William, earl of Ross.

Alexander Comyn's control over the earldom of Buchan was exercised through key castles at Kingedward, Dundarg (Aberdour), Cairnbulg (Philorth), Rattray, Slains, and Ellon. Ellon was the legal centre of the earldom; Deer Abbey (founded by his father c.1219) the religious centre; Kelly, with its enclosed park for hunting, the domestic centre; and Newburgh the main burgh. He also had considerable landed power outside Buchan, including a manor house on the banks of the River Tay, near Scone, lands in Fife, and Mortlach, which with its important castle of Balvenie, Banffshire, formed an important link with the lands of the Badenoch branch of the family. In addition, his marriage to Elizabeth, one of three daughters and coheirs of the great Anglo-Scottish magnate Roger de Quincy (d. 1264), brought him estates in Fife, Galloway, Dumfriesshire, and Lothian, as well as much land in England, especially in the midlands. Having bought the office of constable in 1274 or 1275, Earl Alexander also added the constable lands in Perth, Clackmannan, Inverness, and Cowie, near Stonehaven, to his landholding. He was thus one of the great Anglo-Scottish barons. He was not entirely an absentee landlord in England and appeared at Shepshed, his important administrative centre in the midlands, in 1282, but he conducted his English business chiefly through attorneys and increasingly through his sons John (in Leicestershire and Warwickshire) and Roger (in Northamptonshire). Earl Alexander's interests were essentially Scottish (and especially northern Scottish)—his religious patronage included the foundation of two almshouses in Buchan (at Newburgh and Turriff) and benefactions to Deer Abbey, Arbroath, Lindores, Inchcolm, Scone, and St Andrews.

Alexander Comyn had appeared in the Scottish royal circle by 1240, and he was prominent in Comyn party activities under the leadership of his half-brother Walter Comyn, earl of Menteith, in the disturbed years 1242–58, participating in the hounding of the Bissets, potential rivals in the north, between 1242 and 1244. Alexander II sought to curb the power which the Comyn party thus displayed by appointing Alan Durward to be justiciar of Scotia, an increasingly important office of state. The Durwards, too, were rivals of the Comyns in northern Scotland, and Alan's attempt to strengthen his political position during the minority of Alexander III after 1249 was regarded by the Comyns as a threat to their political leadership. However, the Comyns gained control of Scottish government in 1251 following the intervention of Henry III, and Earl Alexander's prominence in the Comyn party was shown by his appointment as justiciar of Scotia from 1253. He thus followed his father, who had held this office from c.1205 to 1233. After his removal from office, with the rest of the Comyn government, following an anti-Comyn coup in 1255, Earl Alexander participated in the Comyn counter-coup of 1257 and appeared again as justiciar of Scotia in the treaty made by Comyn supporters with the Welsh princes in 1258. He retained this office when a compromise government, made up of both Comyn and opposing elements, was established in 1258, and he remained one of the crown's leading advisers until his death in 1289. He also became the political leader of the Comyn party after Earl Walter of Menteith's death in 1258. Earl Alexander contributed greatly to the strengthening of royal authority in the south-west and north of the Scottish kingdom. He had a military role in 1263 against the Norwegian threat and contributed to the reorganization of royal control in the south-west and north, taking the offices of sheriff of Wigtown, sheriff of Dingwall, and baillie of Inverie (Knoydart) between 1263 and 1266, while in 1282 he was dispatched by Alexander III on important (though unspecified) business to the remote parts of the Scottish isles.

After 1258 Earl Alexander, who dominates witness lists to Alexander III's acts, was the leader of a responsible aristocratic community in effective support of the crown. In 1281 he participated in negotiations for the marriage between Alexander III's daughter, Margaret, and Erik, king of Norway, and in 1284 affirmed the recognition of the child of this marriage, the Maid of Norway, as Alexander III's heir presumptive. Following Alexander III's death in 1286, the earl, who had been involved in the minority of Alexander III and was behind plans for an emergency council in 1260–61 when Queen Margaret went to England for her confinement, was the most experienced of the six guardians elected to govern the country on behalf of the absent Maid of Norway. Earl Alexander died in 1289, after 10 July. He had a large family, four sons—John *Comyn (d. 1308), his successor, who married Isabel, daughter of Colban, earl of Fife; Roger; Alexander, who married Joan Latimer; and Master William, provost of St Mary's, St Andrews—and five daughters: Marjory (or Marjorie), who was married to Patrick *Dunbar, seventh earl of Dunbar [see under Dunbar, Patrick, eighth earl of Dunbar or of March (1285–1369)]; Emma, who was married to Malise *Strathearn, earl of Strathearn; Elizabeth, who married Gilbert de *Umfraville, earl of Angus; Elena, who was married to William Brechin; and another, married to Nicholas de Soulis.

ALAN YOUNG

Sources A. Young, 'The earls and earldom of Buchan in the thirteenth century', *Medieval Scotland: crown, lordship and community: essays presented to G. W. S. Barrow*, ed. A. Grant and K. J. Stringer (1993), 174–202 · A. A. M. Duncan, *Scotland: the making of the kingdom* (1975), vol. 1 of *The Edinburgh history of Scotland*, ed. G. Donaldson (1965–75) · J. Robertson, ed., *Collections for a history of the shires of Aberdeen and Banff*, Spalding Club, 9 (1843) · J. Robertson, ed., *Illustrations of the topography and antiquities of the shires of Aberdeen and Banff*, 2, 3, Spalding Club, 17, 29 (1847–57) · W. Bower, *Scotichronicon*, ed. D. E. R. Watt and others, new edn, 9 vols. (1987–98), vols. 5–6 · C. Innes and P. Chalmers, eds., *Liber s. Thome de Aberbrothoc*, 2 vols., Bannatyne Club, 86 (1848–56) · J. Dowden, ed., *Chartulary of the abbey of Lindores*, Scottish History Society, 42 (1903) · *CDS*, vols. 1–5 · *Chancery records* · Rymer, *Foedera*, new edn · J. Stevenson, ed., *Documents illustrative of the history of Scotland*, 2 vols. (1870)

Archives NA Scot. · NL Scot.

Wealth at death 100 livres p.a. from manor of Whitwick: *CDS*, vol. 2, p. 421

Comyn, John. *See* Cumin, John (*d.* 1212).

Comyn, John [*called* Red Comyn], **lord of Badenoch** (*d.* *c.*1277), magnate, was the son of Richard Comyn (*d.* 1244x9), and was also nephew (and heir) to Walter *Comyn, earl of Menteith (*d.* 1258), and nephew to Alexander *Comyn, earl of Buchan (*d.* 1289). John had two brothers, William and Richard. He was twice married, his first wife being Eva, his second Alicia (probably de Lindsay, of Lamberton).

John Comyn had inherited important lands in Tynedale in Northumberland and in southern Scotland (in Dumfriesshire, Roxburghshire, and Peeblesshire) by *c.*1250, and the lordships of Badenoch and Lochaber in northern Scotland after 1258. The Tynedale and southern Scottish lands had been acquired by John's great-grandfather Richard (*d.* 1178), who founded the family's secular fortunes through favour with the Scottish royal family. Richard's son, William, extended the family's landed acquisitions northwards through the lordships of Lenzie and Kirkintilloch (*c.*1200), the earldom of Buchan (*c.*1212), and the lordship of Badenoch (*c.*1229) for his son Walter (the future earl of Menteith). William had two wives and two large families. The earldom of Buchan, which he acquired through marriage to his second wife, Countess Marjory, was inherited by Alexander, the eldest son of this marriage. The Tynedale and southern Scottish lands, with the Badenoch lordship, descended to John Comyn through Walter Comyn, the eldest surviving son of William Comyn's first marriage. After Walter's death in 1258, John gained the headship of the senior, Badenoch, branch of the family and became the first Red Comyn. This sobriquet, derived from the heraldic colour of the Badenoch branch of the family, was handed down to his successors as head of the senior branch, to his son John *Comyn, known as the Competitor (*d.* *c.*1302), and to his grandson, another John *Comyn (*d.* 1306). Comyn failed, however, to inherit the earldom of Menteith after first accusing the countess and her new husband, Sir John Russell, of poisoning Earl Walter in 1258, and then forcing them to resign the earldom. The compromise decision reached by the king and a Comyn-dominated council in 1260–61 was to give the earldom to Walter Stewart (*d.* *c.*1296).

John Comyn had been a regular member of a Comyn 'party' under the leadership of Walter Comyn, earl of Menteith, his uncle, in the politically disturbed years 1242–58, when the power of the Comyns in the north was threatened by the Bisset and Durward families, and their political dominance of the aristocratic community was threatened by Alexander II's appointment of Alan Durward as justiciar of Scotia *c.*1244. John Comyn personally participated in the hounding of the Bissets in 1242 and with other members of the Comyn following made a bond of good behaviour in 1244. The death of Alexander II in 1249 and the minority of Alexander III (*r.* 1249–86) intensified the rivalry between the Comyns under Earl Walter and their opponents, especially Alan Durward, for political leadership in Scotland. When the Comyns regained control of Scottish government, with English help, in

1251, John Comyn was part of this government. When they lost this leadership in 1255, John Comyn participated in the kidnapping of the young Alexander III and his queen during the successful counter-coup of 1257, and was named as justiciar of Galloway in the Comyn-led confederation of nobles which made a treaty with the Welsh princes in 1258.

The decision to curb John Comyn's power in 1260–61, by not allowing him to succeed to the earldom of Menteith, was an acknowledgement by the magnates, including fellow Comyns, that John's reputation for bellicose behaviour was substantially true. Fordun regarded him as 'a man prone to robbery and rashness' (*Chronica gentis Scottorum*, 2.293). The setback of 1260–61 probably explains why John Comyn appeared irregularly in the royal circle during the 1260s. Instead he sought advancement and adventure in England. He was in the English royal household in 1262, 1264, and 1265, and fought for Henry III at the battle of Lewes in 1264, where he was captured. The English records from 1260 to 1275 testify to the rich rewards available. Comyn received a confirmation of his important Tynedale lands in 1262 and permission to fortify his Northumberland manor house at Tarset in 1267. He was given numerous privileges in the royal forests, a yearly fee of £50, and in 1266 was promised (though never received) 300 librates of land 'for his faithful service' (*CPR, 1258–66*, 551).

Comyn's military expertise featured further in Scottish record. In 1269 he upset the earl of Atholl by building a castle at Blair in Atholl. The matter was settled by the king and his council. It seems that two great castles of Badenoch and Lochaber, namely Lochindorb and Inverlochy—with Ruthven a possible third—were also founded by John Comyn and that, with Blair, they formed part of a strategic castle building plan in the north. Comyn featured prominently as justiciar of Galloway in a royal expedition against Man in 1275.

John Comyn, who was a benefactor to Melrose Abbey and to the churches at Durham and Glasgow, died *c.*1277. He left five sons: John the Competitor, who married Eleanor (Marjory), sister of John de Balliol, the future king of Scots; William, lord of Kirkintilloch; Alexander; another John (*d.* *c.*1295); and Robert (*d.* 1306). According to Andrew Wyntoun, he had four daughters (the *Scots peerage* mentions a fifth), who married Richard Siward, Geoffrey Mowbray, Alexander of Argyll, and Andrew Murray, father of the Andrew *Murray who died in 1297. **ALAN YOUNG**

Sources A. Young, 'Noble families and political factions in the reign of Alexander III', *Scotland in the reign of Alexander III, 1249–1286*, ed. N. H. Reid (1990), 1–30 · *CDS*, vols. 1–2 · [C. Innes], ed., *Liber sancte Marie de Melros*, 2 vols., Bannatyne Club, 56 (1837) · C. Innes, ed., *Registrum episcopatus Glasguensis*, 2 vols., Bannatyne Club, 75 (1843); also pubd as 2 vols., Maitland Club, 61 (1843) · Andrew of Wyntoun, *The orygynale cronykil of Scotland*, [rev. edn] ed. D. Laing, 3 vols. (1872–9) · A. Theiner, *Vetera monumenta Hibernorum et Scotorum historiam illustrantia* (Rome, 1864) · *Johannis de Fordun Chronica gentis Scotorum / John of Fordun's Chronicle of the Scottish nation*, ed. W. F. Skene, trans. F. J. H. Skene, 2 vols. (1871–2) · *Scots peerage*, vol. 5 · W. Bower, *Scotichronicon*, ed. D. E. R. Watt and others, new edn, 9 vols. (1987–98), vol. 5 · *Chancery records*
Archives NA Scot. · NL Scot. | PRO

Comyn, Sir John [*called* Sir John Comyn the Competitor, Red Comyn], **lord of Badenoch** (*d. c.*1302), magnate and claimant to the Scottish throne, was the eldest son of John *Comyn (*d. c.*1277) and his first wife, Eva. Between about 1270 and 1275, he married Eleanor (called Marjory in Scottish sources), sister of John de Balliol [*see* John], the future king of Scots, and he was also brother-in-law to Alexander *MacDougall, lord of Argyll (*d.* 1310), making a formidable Comyn–MacDougall alliance in the north. John Comyn inherited the headship of the Comyns' senior, Badenoch, branch and became the second Red Comyn. His landed power included: Badenoch and Lochaber, with chief castles at Ruthven, Lochindorb, and Inverlochy; influence in Atholl, possibly including the castle at Blair Atholl; Bedrule and Scraesburgh, Roxburghshire; Dalswinton, with its castle, in Dumfriesshire; Findogask and Ochtertyre in Perthshire; Machan in the Clyde valley; and Lenzie and Kirkintilloch in Dunbartonshire after his brother William's death (after *c.*1290). He also had charge of the castles of Jedburgh and Clunie from Alexander III; and in England he had Tarset and Thornton in Tynedale, Northumberland, and Ulseby in Lincolnshire. He was religious patron to Inchaffray, Cambuskenneth, and Coupar Angus abbeys.

John Comyn was knighted by Alexander III in 1270, and was present in the royal circle at Selkirk in 1276. He swore to observe the marriage settlement between Margaret, Alexander III's daughter, and King Erik of Norway at Roxburgh in 1281, and in 1284 acknowledged the child of this marriage, Margaret, the Maid of Norway, as heir presumptive to Alexander III. When Alexander III died in 1286, Comyn was elected one of the six 'guardians' of the realm. He was chosen, according to John Fordun, as one of three guardians from south of the Forth, though his power was probably greater in the north. As guardian, Comyn was active in government business at Edinburgh (principally), Roxburgh, Haddington, Stirling, Perth, and Berwick between 1287 and 1291. In 1289 the guardians sent him, together with Robert (V) Brus (*d.* 1295) and the bishops of St Andrews and Glasgow, to negotiate with the English king's representative concerning the return of the Maid of Norway to Scotland, and Comyn was among the prelates and barons who confirmed the resulting treaty of Birgham in July 1290. By then John Comyn, as one of four surviving guardians, had become head of a Comyn 'party', following the death of his great-uncle and fellow guardian, Alexander *Comyn, earl of Buchan, in 1289. He was responsible, in 1290, for informing Edward I about the arrival of the Maid of Norway in Orkney, and in the same year was paid £100 out of £200, of the king's gift.

After the Maid's death in Orkney (October 1290), Comyn himself became one of thirteen 'competitors' for the Scottish throne, though his brother-in-law, John de Balliol, and Robert (V) Brus were the two strongest candidates. Comyn claimed descent from Donald III (*d.* 1099?), whose granddaughter Hextilda (married to the Richard Comyn who died in 1178) was the mother of John's great-grandfather. Comyn's claim significantly stated that he would not prejudice the claims of Balliol, his brother-in-law. He had already shown strong support for Balliol, and the list of Balliol's forty auditors was dominated by Comyn family and supporters. Indeed, in 1290–91 the 'appeal of the seven earls' accused John Comyn, with Bishop William Fraser of St Andrews (*d.* 1297), of trying to make Balliol king by a 'coup'. Comyn's claim, soon withdrawn and dismissed in the final judgment (17 November 1292), was, no doubt, intended to safeguard a possible future bid after Balliol became king in 1292. The failure of the Balliol line could have given Comyn's descendants through Eleanor de Balliol a double claim.

Under Balliol's kingship, John Comyn naturally figured prominently in Scottish politics and when, by 1295, King John's leadership had proved ineffective, John Comyn was one of the council of twelve elected to take government out of John's hands. In 1295 he was sent to France to negotiate a treaty which was ratified in 1296, and after John renounced Edward I's overlordship in the latter year, Comyn was regarded as the English king's enemy and his Northumberland lands were confiscated. After the Scottish defeat at Dunbar, Comyn made submission at Montrose in July 1296 and was sent into exile with his family to the English king's manor of Geddington, where he was allowed to hunt fox, hare, and wild cat in the royal forest. Following the outbreak of revolt in Scotland under William Wallace, Comyn was sent by Edward I in 1297 to bring order to Scotland. He was commanded to assist Brian Fitzalan in the custody of the kingdom, and especially to defend the castle at Roxburgh; and he was also instructed to quell the rising in Moray, but appears soon to have joined the Scots, because late in 1297 his Tynedale lands were to be taken again into the king's hands. It is probable that Comyn contributed cavalry to the Scottish army at Falkirk in 1298, as Fordun reports that 'the Comyns' envied Wallace and deserted the Scottish army at the battle. But that it was John's son, John *Comyn the younger (*d.* 1306), who was chosen guardian with Robert Bruce, earl of Carrick, the future king, in 1298, suggests that John Comyn the elder was either too ill or unfit for office, or possibly discredited. He died, *c.*1302, at his castle of Lochindorb and was succeeded by his son, John, who married Joan de Valence, cousin of the English king.

ALAN YOUNG

Sources J. M. Thomson and others, eds., *Registrum magni sigilli regum Scotorum / The register of the great seal of Scotland*, 11 vols. (1882–1914) · J. Stevenson, ed., *Documents illustrative of the history of Scotland*, 2 vols. (1870) · W. A. Lindsay, J. Dowden, and J. M. Thomson, eds., *Charters, bulls and other documents relating to the abbey of Inchaffray*, Scottish History Society, 56 (1908) · D. E. Easson, ed., *Charters of the abbey of Coupar-Angus*, 2 vols., Scottish History Society, 3rd ser., 40–41 (1947) · W. Fraser, ed., *Registrum monasterii S. Marie de Cambuskenneth*, Grampian Club, 4 (1872) · *Scots peerage*, vol. 5 · W. Bower, *Scotichronicon*, ed. D. E. R. Watt and others, new edn, 9 vols. (1987–98), vols. 5–6 · *Johannis de Fordun Chronica gentis Scotorum / John of Fordun's Chronicle of the Scottish nation*, ed. W. F. Skene, trans. F. J. H. Skene, 2 vols. (1871–2) · Rymer, *Foedera*, new edn · Chancery records · Andrew of Wyntoun, *The orygynale cronykil of Scotland*, [rev. edn], ed. D. Laing, 3 vols. (1872–9)
Archives BM · NA Scot. · NL Scot. | PRO

Comyn, Sir John, lord of Badenoch (d. 1306), magnate, was the son and heir of John *Comyn, known as the Competitor (d. c.1302), and his wife, Eleanor (Marjory in Scottish sources), sister of John de Balliol, later king of Scots. He married Joan de Valence, daughter of William de *Valence, earl of Pembroke (d. 1296), a cousin of Edward I, and had three children—John (d. 1314), Elizabeth (married Richard Talbot), and Joan (married David, earl of Atholl). He was known as 'the younger' or 'the son' until he inherited his father's extensive estates—the last reference to him as 'the son' appears to have been in 1301. He was made a knight by King John (de Balliol) probably soon after 1292.

John Comyn had received the gift of the important manors of Walwick, Thornton, and Henshaw in Tynedale by c.1295 but on his father's death he inherited wide-ranging and vast estates in the Scottish highlands (Badenoch and Lochaber), in Roxburghshire (Bedrule and Scraesburgh), in Dumfriesshire (Dalswinton), in Perthshire (Findogask and Ochtertyre), in the Clyde valley (Machan), in Dunbartonshire (Lenzie and Kirkintilloch), and in Atholl. Lands in England included important estates in Tynedale (Tarset and Thornton) and Lincolnshire (Ulseby). The castles of Lochindorb, Ruthven, Inverlochy, and Blair Atholl made a formidable defence to his power in northern Scotland, while the castle of Dalswinton, and probable castle sites at Machan and Kirkintilloch, added weight to his influence further south. Apart from this substantial landed base, John Comyn inherited powerful family support and a long tradition of involvement at the centre of Scottish politics. His family links— John *Comyn, earl of Buchan (d. 1308), who dominated north-east Scotland, was his cousin, King *John was his uncle, and William, earl of Pembroke, was his brother-in-law—had a significant influence on his key role at the forefront of Scottish political affairs from 1296 to 1306.

As a relative of John de Balliol, and one of the leading supporters of his kingship, John Comyn the younger took a prominent role when open rebellion broke out in Scotland against English overlordship in 1296. On 26 March, with seven Scottish earls, he crossed the Solway from Annandale (which had been given to him by King John), burning villages to the suburbs of Carlisle itself before trying unsuccessfully to take the city by storm. He was also present when Hexham Priory was burnt two weeks later, before retreating northwards on news of Edward I's imminent arrival, and he helped to capture Dunbar Castle on 22 April. However, this castle was forced to surrender to Edward I on the 28th, John Comyn having been handed over as a hostage to the English king on the previous day. His wife, Joan, was already in England, having been given letters of safe conduct to go to London as soon as her husband came out in open rebellion. In September 1296 she was given lands worth 200 marks in Tynedale for her support. Along with other Scottish nobles taken into captivity at Dunbar, John Comyn was taken to England where he became a prisoner at the Tower of London. In 1297 he promised to go with the king overseas, and to serve him

well and faithfully against the king of France, but by 1298 he was back in Scotland.

The years 1296 to 1298 had been significant for the Badenoch branch of the family. Not only did they have their valuable Northumberland lands confiscated, but the Comyn leadership of the Scottish political community, little challenged since the mid-thirteenth century, no longer went unquestioned after the enforced absence of the chief members of the family from 1296 to 1298. James Stewart (d. 1309), Bishop Robert Wishart (d. 1316), and William Wallace (d. 1305) came to the fore in these years, and Wallace became sole guardian early in 1298. By then John Comyn was once more in opposition to Edward I, as is indicated by the English king's peremptory command on 26 March of that year to Comyn's wife, Joan, to come to London with her children without delay. After the defeat of an English army at Stirling Bridge by William Wallace and Andrew Murray (d. 1297) on 11 September 1297, Edward I had taken the Scottish threat more seriously. He set up headquarters at York in the summer of 1298, and on 22 July defeated the Scots at the battle of Falkirk. John Comyn probably contributed cavalry to the Scottish forces, led by Wallace. According to the fourteenth-century Scottish historian John Fordun, Wallace's defeat was caused by the flight of the cavalry, and he blamed the Comyns for this. However, it is more probable that panic rather than cowardice was the cause of defeat, and it seems unlikely that the Comyns were blamed at the time. Following his defeat, Wallace resigned as guardian, and between July and December 1298 John Comyn the younger and Robert Bruce, earl of Carrick, the future king, were elected joint guardians of Scotland. It is possible that there had been tension between the Comyns and Wallace, who had risen to prominence in their absence. And there was certainly tension between John Comyn and Robert Bruce, probably resulting from the Bruce claim to the Scottish crown, and the strong Comyn championing of Balliol's kingship, during the Great Cause.

These resentments came into the open at a council held at Peebles on 19 August 1299, when an argument over claims to William Wallace's lands led to a brawl between Comyn and Bruce supporters, in the course of which 'John Comyn leaped at the earl of Carrick and seized him by the throat' (Barrow, 107). The bishop of St Andrews, William Lamberton (d. 1328), was elected as guardian alongside Comyn and Bruce to help preserve unity in government, but this unity lasted only until May 1300, when Bruce was forced from office. At a parliament held in Rutherglen on 10 May, Comyn argued with Lamberton, saying that he would no longer serve with him. Another reorganization of the guardianship led to the preservation of unity with Comyn and Lamberton remaining in office, but being joined by Sir Ingram de Umfraville, an ally of the Comyns and Balliol's kinsman. This alliance appears to have dissolved between December 1300 and May 1301, with John Soulis (d. c.1310) appearing as sole guardian at that time. It seems, from official record sources, that Comyn resigned for a short time, although, according to John Fordun, John

Comyn remained in office continuously from 1298 to 1304, with John Soulis being associated with the guardianship by John de Balliol's express wish in 1301 and 1302. John Comyn was sole guardian in the autumn of 1302, however, when Soulis went with an embassy to France. Early in 1303 Comyn's leadership of the Scottish political community was again apparent, since on 24 February he was 'leader and captain' of the Scottish army which defeated an English force at Roslin. After this victory the Scots, led by Comyn, described by the chronicler Bower as chief guardian of Scotland, and Simon Fraser (d. 1305), harassed the English king's officers as well as the English king's supporters in southern Scotland. They were still active in the autumn of 1303 when they raised Lennox, causing Margaret, countess of Lennox, to ask Edward I's help against John Comyn. Edward's retaliation had already started in the summer of 1303. He marched north to assert English authority, and in October 1303 stayed for a while at Lochindorb, a castle at the heart of John Comyn's northern power base.

A combination of the peace made between France, hitherto Scotland's ally, and England on 20 May 1303, and the realization that the Scots could not muster an army big enough to match the English in pitched battle, led to all the leading Scottish magnates, except William Wallace, Simon Fraser, and John Soulis, submitting to Edward I on 9 February 1304. John Comyn, no doubt in his capacity as sole guardian, negotiated conditions for surrender on behalf of the community of Scotland. Negotiations had begun between the earl of Ulster, the royal commander in the west of Scotland, and Comyn on 6 February. Comyn refused to surrender unconditionally. He demanded firstly an amnesty and restoration of estates for those who had fought against Edward, and secondly that the Scottish people should be 'protected in all their laws, customs and liberties in every particular as they existed in the time of King Alexander III' (Barrow, 130). There was no disinheritance, but not all of Comyn's demands were met—the good old days of Alexander III could not be restored, and varying degrees of exile were imposed on the leading men. Robert Wishart, bishop of Glasgow, for instance, was initially required to leave Scotland for two to three years; in addition, John Comyn, Alexander Lindsay, David Graham, and Simon Fraser were ordered to capture William Wallace and hand him over to Edward. Edward I took over the government of Scotland, appointing his nephew, John of Brittany (d. 1334), as lieutenant of Scotland. John Comyn was one of a council of twenty-two Scots (including Robert Bruce) appointed to advise the new lieutenant.

The savage execution of William Wallace on 23 August 1305 may have raised the level of indignation in Scotland at English overlordship. This forms the background to the infamous murder of John Comyn by Robert Bruce in the Greyfriars Church at Dumfries on 10 February 1306 and Robert Bruce's inauguration as king of Scots six weeks later. According to tradition, first recounted by Scottish chroniclers of the fourteenth and fifteenth centuries, Bruce and Comyn, rivals and the two most powerful nobles in Scotland, made an agreement that Bruce should take the Scottish crown and Comyn should take Bruce's lands in return. Comyn, however, betrayed Bruce and told Edward I of Bruce's plans. After being confronted with his treachery in the church at Dumfries, Comyn quarrelled with Bruce and was murdered along with his uncle, Robert.

More contemporary, though still biased, English accounts give a different angle to the murder, and the narrative of Walter of Guisborough deserves some precedence. According to Guisborough, Bruce feared that Comyn would hinder him in his attempt to gain the Scottish crown, and sent two of his brothers, Thomas and Nigel, from his own castle at Lochmaben to Comyn's castle at Dalswinton, 10 miles away, asking Comyn to meet him at the Greyfriars Church, Dumfries, to discuss 'certain business'. It seemed that Bruce wanted to put a plan to Comyn, no doubt involving the revival of Scottish kingship with Bruce on the throne. After initially friendly words, Bruce turned on Comyn and accused him of treacherously reporting to Edward I that he, Bruce, was plotting against him. It seems probable that their bitter antagonisms of the past were instantly revived and that in a heated argument mutual charges of treachery were made. Bruce struck Comyn with a dagger and his men attacked him with swords. Mortally wounded, Comyn was left for dead. Comyn's uncle, Robert, was killed by Christopher Seton (d. 1306) as he tried to defend his nephew.

According to tradition in both Scotland and England, John Comyn was killed in two stages, with Bruce's men returning to the church to finish off the deed. According to Bower, Bruce returned to Lochmaben Castle and reported to his kinsmen James Lindsay and Roger Kirkpatrick 'I think I have killed John the Red Comyn' (Bower, 6.311). Bruce's men returned to the church to make sure that the deed was done, with Roger Kirkpatrick, according to a wholly fabulous tale, exclaiming 'I mak siccar'.

What is clear is that Comyn's rivalry with Bruce must have been intense since 1286. The Comyns had suppressed Bruce rebellions in 1286 and 1287, and were strong supporters both of John de Balliol's candidature for the Scottish crown in the Great Cause, 1291–2, and of Balliol's kingship after 1292. John Comyn represented a long tradition of Comyn leadership of the Scottish political community during most of the thirteenth century. He was a major obstacle to Robert Bruce's ambitions, especially as he could make a double claim to the Scottish crown himself, as heir to John de Balliol as well as in his own right. Contemporary English sources like Guisborough emphasize John Comyn's refusal to support Robert Bruce's treachery by overturning the lawful sovereign, Balliol.

The importance of John Comyn's murder was soon recognized in both Scotland and England. Edward I's initial response was phlegmatic, but by 5 April he had appointed Aymer de Valence (d. 1324), Comyn's brother-in-law, as his special lieutenant in Scotland with wide-ranging and drastic powers against Bruce and the alliance between the English and the remaining members of the Comyn family continued until the battle of Bannockburn in 1314. In Scotland, Bruce was forced to follow up the murder by destroying the Comyn power base in the north before being fully assured of his kingship. A civil war thus accompanied the Anglo-Scottish war. In 1306 Edward I ordered Joan de Valence to send her son, John, John Comyn's son and heir, to England where he was to be in the care of Sir John Weston, master and guardian of the royal children. His father's vast landholding was divided up among Bruce's supporters. This John Comyn lost his life, and any hope of retrieving the vast Scottish inheritance of the Comyns of Badenoch, at the battle of Bannockburn, when he fought on the side of Edward II. ALAN YOUNG

Sources G. W. S. Barrow, *Robert Bruce and the community of the realm of Scotland*, 3rd edn (1988) · N. Reid, 'The kingless kingdom: the Scottish guardianships of 1286–1306', *SHR*, 61 (1982), 105–29 · R. Nicholson, *Scotland: the later middle ages* (1974), vol. 2 of *The Edinburgh history of Scotland*, ed. G. Donaldson (1965–75) · W. Bower, *Scotichronicon*, ed. D. E. R. Watt and others, new edn, 9 vols. (1987–98), vol. 6 · *CDS*, vol. 2 · *The chronicle of Walter of Guisborough*, ed. H. Rothwell, CS, 3rd ser., 89 (1957) · J. Stevenson, ed., *Chronicon de Lanercost, 1201–1346*, Bannatyne Club, 65 (1839) · J. Barbour, *The Bruce*, ed. W. W. Skeat, 2 vols., STS, 31–3 (1894) · *Scalacronica, by Sir Thomas Gray of Heton, knight: a chronical of England and Scotland from AD MLXVI to AD MCCCLXII*, ed. J. Stevenson, Maitland Club, 40 (1836) · *Johannis de Fordun Chronica gentis Scotorum / John of Fordun's Chronicle of the Scottish nation*, ed. W. F. Skene, trans. F. J. H. Skene, 2 vols. (1871–2)

Comyn, John, seventh earl of Buchan (c.1250–1308), magnate, was the son of Alexander *Comyn, earl of Buchan (d. 1289), and Elizabeth, third daughter of Roger de Quincy, earl of Winchester (d. 1264). He probably succeeded to the title in 1289, aged about forty. Earl John's territorial interests are reflected by his service as sheriff of Banffshire in 1289 and of Wigtownshire in 1290. He played a prominent role during the interregnum, holding a number of royal castles before they were handed over to King Edward and the Competitors in 1291 and petitioning King Edward in 1292 not to renege on the promises made at Birgham. At some point thereafter, Earl John resigned all or part of his lands in Galloway to his cousin, *John, king of Scots, in return for lands in north-east Scotland.

As relations between England and Scotland deteriorated, Buchan played a major role in the patriotic government, leading the Scottish force which raided south of the border in the spring of 1296. King Edward duly confiscated his manor of Whitwick in Leicester. After the collapse of Scottish resistance at the battle of Dunbar, Earl John was present at King John's enforced abdication in July 1296, himself submitting at the same time. Although initially required to live in England south of the Trent, he was sent back to north-east Scotland in June 1297 in order to halt the activities of Andrew Murray (d. 1297), with the help of the bishop of Aberdeen and Gartnait, son of the earl of Mar. They made only a pretence of action, and Buchan soon came out actively on the patriotic side, perhaps taking part, albeit ineffectively, in the battle of Falkirk in 1298.

Having taken his place once more at the heart of Scottish government, Earl John attended a meeting at Peebles in August 1299, where disagreement broke out between members of the pro-Comyn and pro-Bruce factions, prompting John *Comyn the younger (d. 1306) to seize the earl of Carrick, and Buchan himself to attack William Lamberton, bishop of St Andrews. The Scots settled their differences, however, when news came that Buchan's younger brother, Sir Alexander Comyn, was ravaging the north of the country with Lachlan Mac Ruairidh, a freebooting north-western magnate.

In February 1300 Earl John, as justiciar of Scotland, heard cases pertaining to his office in Aberdeen, despite the fact that his brother, Sir Alexander, later claimed that he had also held the area, but for King Edward. A few months later Buchan had gone south, missing a parliament held at Rutherglen in May 1300 because he was 'away in Galloway to treat with the Gallovidians', many of whom tended to side with the English even against their overlord, King John, who was also lord of Galloway. The parliament was postponed until 17 December so that Earl John could attend (Sayles, 245–50). Later that same year, he led a Scottish force which was compelled to flee from the English army at the River Cree. In 1301, however, Buchan and Sir John Soulis, stationed at Loudoun in Ayrshire, were more successful in preventing King Edward's force, at Glasgow, from joining up with his son's army in west Ayrshire.

At some point thereafter, Buchan went to France; when he returned in 1304 he submitted to Edward, along with most of the rest of the Scottish magnates. Under the statesmanlike settlement of Scotland in 1305, Earl John was appointed to serve on the council of the new lieutenant of Scotland, John of Brittany. However, this settlement was disrupted in 1306 by Robert Bruce's rebellion. The murder of John Comyn the younger forced Buchan into the English camp against King Robert. In late 1307 Robert went up to the north-east with the express intention of destroying Comyn power in the area, and Buchan's forces were routed at Inverurie in 1308. The king then ravaged the area in the so-called 'herschip' of Buchan. Although the earl was afterwards appointed Edward II's joint warden of the western marches (Annandale, Carrick, and Galloway), his days of active service in Scotland were over and he died in England between 11 August and 31 December 1308.

Although he was rarely successful in military activities, which perhaps explains why he was never a guardian, Buchan had administrative abilities which served the patriotic government well. But his marriage to Isabel Macduff [*see* Buchan, Isabel (b. c.1270, d. after 1313)], daughter of Colban, earl of Fife, produced no children and ended unhappily when she deserted him in 1306 in order to place the crown on King Robert's head, as was her family's right. Isabel, captured in the Bruce camp after the battle of Methven, was then imprisoned by King Edward in a cage in Berwick Castle. She was released in 1313 into the custody of Henry de Beaumont, who had married Buchan's niece and coheir, Alicia. Alicia was the daughter of Sir Alexander Comyn; though her husband called himself earl of Buchan, there is no evidence that he ever gained entry to the Buchan lands in Scotland, which eventually became a Stewart earldom.   FIONA WATSON

Sources CDS, vols. 1–5 · J. Stevenson, ed., *Documents illustrative of the history of Scotland*, 2 (1870) · Rymer, *Foedera*, new edn, vol. 1 · *Scots peerage*, vol. 2 · M. E. C. Bruce, *Family records of the Bruces and Cumyns* (1870) · W. Gibson-Craig, ed., *Facsimiles of national manuscripts of Scotland*, 2 (1870) · G. W. S. Barrow, *Robert Bruce and the community of the realm of Scotland*, 3rd edn (1988) · F. Palgrave, ed., *Documents and records illustrating the history of Scotland* (1837) · [W. Rishanger], *The chronicle of William de Rishanger, of the barons' wars*, ed. J. O. Halliwell, CS, 15 (1840) · *Johannis de Fordun Chronica gentis Scotorum*, ed. W. F. Skene (1871) · [C. Innes], ed., *Liber sancte Marie de Melros*, 2 vols., Bannatyne Club, 56 (1837), vol. 1 · GEC, *Peerage* · G. O. Sayles, 'The guardians of Scotland and a parliament at Rutherglen in 1300', *SHR*, 24 (1926–7), 245–50

Comyn, Sir Robert Buckley (1792–1853), judge, was born at the vicarage, White Hart Lane, Tottenham, Middlesex, on 26 June 1792, the third son of Thomas Comyn (1746/7–1798), vicar of Tottenham and chaplain of the Royal Hospital, Chelsea, and his wife, Harriet Charlotte *née* Stables. He was educated at Merchant Taylors' School, London (1807–9), and became a commoner of St John's College, Oxford, in 1809, matriculating on 12 April. That year he was admitted to Lincoln's Inn, where his paternal grandfather, Stephen Comyn, had qualified as a barrister. He graduated BA in 1813 (MA 1815, DCL June 1842) and was called to the bar on 24 November 1814. In 1817 he published *A Treatise on Usury*, which Holdsworth has described as 'a good clear summary of the law' with 'useful discussions and explanations' on the statutes of usury (Holdsworth, *Eng. law*, 13.494).

In January 1825 Comyn was appointed a puisne judge of the supreme court of Madras and was knighted on 9 February. In December 1835 he was promoted chief justice of Madras. A leader in local literary circles, from 1835 until 1842 he was the president of the Madras Literary Society. He was also a subscribing member of the Society for Promoting Christian Knowledge. He published *A Treatise on the Law of Landlord and Tenant* (1830) and *History of the Western Empire from … Charlemagne to … Charles V* (2 vols., 1837). The fruit of his leisure hours at Madras, the history is extensively footnoted and contains over fifty genealogical tables, suggesting that Comyn had taken a copious library to India. It is a lively and engaging narrative, and Comyn appears to have hoped that it would be received as a precursor to William Robertson's well-known *History of the Reign of the Emperor Charles V* (1769). It appeared in an English edition in 1841, whereupon its author was commended in the *Monthly Review* for his 'industry, enlargement of views, correct and very often vivid colouring,—condensation, grasp, and a statesmanlike eloquence' (*Monthly Review*, 566). In spite of the reviewer's earnest exhortations, however, Comyn published no more historical works.

In 1842 Comyn returned to Britain. He was made a bencher at the Middle Temple in 1843 (he had been admitted there in January 1819), and in autumn 1848 he acted as a reader at the inn. He died at his house, 9 New Street, Spring Gardens, London, on 23 May 1853, and was the last person to be buried in the vaults of the Temple Church, London. He does not appear to have married.

KATHERINE PRIOR

Sources DNB · J. B. Williamson, ed., *The Middle Temple bench book*, 2nd edn, 1 (1937) · Foster, *Alum. Oxon.* · *GM*, 1st ser., 68 (1798), 177 · *GM*, 2nd ser., 40 (1853), 92–3 · Mrs E. P. Hart, ed., *Merchant Taylors' School register, 1561–1934*, 1 (1936) · *Monthly Review*, 4th ser., 3 (1841), 566–75 · *Madras Almanac* (1826–42) [annual edns] · *VCH Middlesex*, vol. 5 · Holdsworth, *Eng. law*, vol. 13 · W. P. Baildon, ed., *The records of the Honorable Society of Lincoln's Inn: admissions*, 2 (1896) · W. A. Shaw, *The knights of England*, 2 vols. (1906) · Boase, *Mod. Eng. biog.*
Archives BL OIOC, Elphinstone collection, papers of John, thirteenth Lord Elphinstone, MS Eur. F 87

Comyn, Walter, earl of Menteith (d. 1258), magnate, was the second known son by his first marriage of William Comyn who, in right of his second wife, Marjory, became earl of Buchan c.1212 and who died in 1233. Walter had three brothers—Richard, the eldest (d. 1244x9), David (married Isabel de Valognes, lady of East Kilbride), and William, a clerk—and one sister, Jean (married William of *Ross, second earl of Ross [*see under* Ross family (*per.* c.1215–c.1415)]). By his father's second marriage, Walter had three half-brothers—Alexander *Comyn, earl of Buchan (d. 1289), who married Elizabeth de Quincy, William, and Fergus—and three half-sisters—Idonea (married Gilbert de la Hay), Agnes (married Philip Meldrum), and Elizabeth (married William, earl of Mar). Walter Comyn became earl of Menteith on his marriage to Isabella, daughter and heir of Maurice, earl of Menteith, between 30 June 1233 and 9 January 1234. The support of such a large family network was to be a key factor in Earl Walter's political influence between 1235 and 1258.

Walter Comyn's first appearance on record was as witness to two royal charters (between 1211 and 1214) of William the Lion (r. 1165–1214) to Arbroath Abbey. It is a testimony to the political influence of his father, who was justiciar of Scotia c.1205–c.1233 and sheriff of Forfar c.1195–c.1212, that Walter Comyn appeared regularly at the royal court in the later years of William the Lion and throughout the reign of Alexander II (r. 1214–49). By 1221 Comyn not only attended Alexander II on his marriage at York to Joan, sister of King Henry III, but was also one of twelve Scottish noblemen who swore on the Scottish king's behalf to observe the terms of the marriage settlement agreed with the king of England. From 1220 to 1229 Walter Comyn appeared with increasing regularity and prominence in the witness lists of Alexander II's charters. His elder brother Richard, who was still alive in 1244, had received the family estates in north and east Scotland, and devoted himself to these. But between 1229 and 1234 Walter came into possession of the lordship of Badenoch (the highland region based upon Strath Spey), given to him by Alexander II, perhaps as a reward for his father William Comyn's success in quelling the rebellion of Gillescop MacWilliam in Moray in 1229–30. It is clear that Alexander saw the Comyns, in the persons of William and Walter, as playing a key role in reinforcing royal authority in the north, through their possession of Badenoch; the lordship included Lochaber, and occupied a strategic position dominating the principal passes from the north and west highlands into the Tay basin. Following the death of William Comyn in 1233, his son Walter assumed the leadership of the Badenoch (now the senior) branch of the family. His status received an additional boost by January 1234 when he became earl of Menteith on his marriage to Isabella of Menteith. In 1235 Earl Walter's trusted role as crown agent in the north was extended to the south-west, when he was given responsibility for bringing Galloway to order after Alexander II had defeated rebels there. Comyn's role as premier magnate in Scotland was shown at York in 1237 when he alone took a formal oath on the king of Scotland's soul to observe the treaty (the treaty of York) which Alexander II had entered into with Henry III.

Earl Walter was the dominant force in Scottish politics from 1237 to his death in 1258. In 1242 he and his family took action against members of the Bisset family, accused of murdering Patrick, earl of Atholl, an ally of the Comyns. His dominance was seen to be a threat by both Alexander II and Henry III in 1244, when Henry marched north with an army, forced a treaty of friendship from the Scottish king, and received a bond of good behaviour from Earl Walter as one of the leaders of two well-defined groups of Scottish magnates which had emerged by that time. Earl Walter and other Scottish nobles were accused of fortifying castles on the borders. Comyn himself strengthened the castle at Tarset in Northumberland, while Nicholas de Soulis and either Aymer or John Maxwell built castles at Hermitage (Liddesdale) and Caerlaverock (Nithsdale). Earl Walter was also suspected of harbouring the exiled Geoffrey de Marisco, whose son William had plotted to murder Henry III in 1238. Thus in 1244 Earl Walter and his following (forty-one names in all) had to swear that they were neither linked with attacks on the English king's lands in Ireland, nor had given shelter to the English king's enemies. The promotion of Alan Durward (d. 1275) as justiciar of Scotia in 1244, and therefore as head of government, was aimed at curtailing Earl Walter's political power. The nature of the earl's following, however—a tightly knit family group, strong in numbers and influence, based on the three main branches of the Comyn family (the Badenoch, Buchan, and Kilbride lines) and their connections—ensured that Earl Walter was not eclipsed after 1244.

This became apparent in the minority crisis following Alexander II's death in 1249. Earl Walter successfully thwarted Alan Durward's attempt to formalize his position as head of government during the minority. He emerged once again as the dominant Scottish magnate and it was through a joint Comyn and clergy invitation that Henry III intervened in Scottish political affairs in 1251—an intervention sealed by the marriage of Henry III's daughter, Margaret, to the young Alexander III (r. 1249–86) at York—replacing the Durward-led government by a Comyn-dominated one. Earl Walter, perhaps surprisingly, did not become the justiciar of Scotia, the most important government office, but he ensured that his leading supporters were in all the key positions; Alexander Comyn, earl of Buchan, became the justiciar. The years 1251 to 1255 saw Walter Comyn's government successfully deny Henry III's attempts to influence affairs in Scotland through his two appointed guardians to the young Scottish king and queen, Robert de Ros (d. c.1270) and John de Balliol. Henry III intervened again in 1255, supporting Alan Durward's counter-coup, and replacing Comyn leadership with a council of fifteen which would serve for seven years. Alan Durward, who became justiciar of Scotia, was prominent in the new government. His fear of Earl Walter's continuing power in 1255 was obvious in his attempts to discredit the Comyns and reduce their influence by renewing his claim to the earldom of Mar. Comyn and his party refused to put their names to the document setting up the 1255 council, and having failed to convince Henry III that he should intervene once more on their behalf, they kidnapped the young king at Kinross in 1257 and thus regained control of government. For once lacking general support within Scotland, Earl Walter tried to bolster his position by allying his supporters, largely restricted to the Comyn family itself, with Llywelyn of Wales and his supporters in 1258. The cautious terms of the treaty indicated Earl Walter's reluctance to act unconstitutionally and against the wishes of the Scottish king. But it was also significant that Henry III was no longer in a position to intervene, as he was beset at home by opposition from the baronial reform movement, and in fact ceased to control the English government after 12 June. Indeed, without external interference compromise was soon reached, when in September 1258 a new council of ten was agreed upon in Scotland. This included four Comyn supporters headed by Walter Comyn, and four Durward supporters.

Walter Comyn was still the leading political figure in Scotland when he died in late October or early November 1258, apparently as a result of a fall from his horse. Messengers came to Henry III at St Albans on 22 November specially to report his death. Matthew Paris described him as 'the most powerful earl in Scotland' (Paris, *Chron.*, 5.724). In Scotland, even the largely anti-Comyn chronicler, John Fordun, described him as a 'man of foresight and shrewdness in council' (*Chronica gentis Scottorum*, 2.289). To the Comyn party, fear of loss of power was reflected in Walter Comyn's nephew and heir, John *Comyn, seizing (but holding for a short time only) the earldom of Menteith from Walter's widow and her new husband, Sir John Russell, an English knight, amid accusations that Walter Comyn had been poisoned. A visible witness to Earl Walter's importance was his foundation c.1238 of the Augustinian priory of Inchmahome, set on the largest of three islands in the Lake of Menteith, close to a probable chief residence on the adjacent island of Inchtalla. Patronage was also given to Scone and Arbroath abbeys.

Earl Walter's significance in a critical period of Scottish history prompted a number of extreme views about his role. To the influential but monarchocentric fourteenth- and fifteenth-century chroniclers John Fordun and Walter Bower, Walter Comyn was the unprincipled leader of an over-mighty faction, threatening the monarchy itself. Yet Comyn had been a key royal agent in the north (1229 onwards) and in the south west (1235). His leadership of the Scottish political community was, except in 1257–8, largely with the support of the Scottish nobility and church. Alternatively Walter Comyn has been portrayed as the leader of a 'native' party. Yet, though he restricted the influence of the guardians appointed by Henry III between 1251 and 1255, he did not pursue nationalistic policies. He recognized, like his opponents in Scotland, the political necessity of Henry III's support during the minority crisis of Alexander III. ALAN YOUNG

Sources D. E. R. Watt, 'The minority of Alexander III of Scotland', *TRHS*, 5th ser., 21 (1971), 1–23 · A. Young, 'The political role of Walter Comyn, earl of Menteith during the minority of Alexander III of Scotland', *Essays on the nobility of medieval Scotland*, ed. K. J. Stringer (1985), 131–49 · A. A. M. Duncan, *Scotland: the making of the kingdom* (1975), vol. 1 of *The Edinburgh history of Scotland*, ed. G. Donaldson (1965–75) · *CDS*, vols. 1–4 · *Johannis de Fordun Chronica gentis Scotorum / John of Fordun's Chronicle of the Scottish nation*, ed. W. F. Skene, trans. F. J. H. Skene, 2 vols. (1871–2) · A. O. Anderson and M. O. Anderson, eds., *The chronicle of Melrose* (1936) · W. Bower, *Scotichronicon*, ed. D. E. R. Watt and others, new edn, 9 vols. (1987–98), vol. 5 · Paris, *Chron.*, vols. 4–5

Comyns, Barbara. *See* Carr, Barbara Irene Veronica Comyns (1907–1992).

Comyns, Sir John (*c.*1667–1740), judge and legal writer, was the eldest surviving son of William Comyns of Lincoln's Inn, barrister, and his wife, Elizabeth, daughter of Matthew Rudd, of Little Baddow, Essex. The Comyns or Cummins were a well established Essex family. He was admitted a student at Lincoln's Inn in May 1683, probably commencing his law studies in 1684, since he also matriculated at Queens' College, Cambridge, in 1683. He was called to the bar in 1690, and practised in king's bench until 1705, when he took the degree of serjeant-at-law (8 June) and moved to common pleas practice. He was junior MP for Maldon in the tory interest from 1701 to 1708, and from 1710 to 1715, when he was unseated on petition. In 1711–12 he acted as temporary chairman of the elections committee.

After 1715 Comyns was by his own account 'discarded by all but the Tories' (HoP, *Commons*, 569); in 1719 he acted for high-church defendants accused of riot and vagrancy for making a charity collection without a begging licence ('Trial of the Rev. Wm Hendley and others', *State trials*, 15.1407). In 1722 Comyns was again returned to parliament for Maldon, standing at the solicitation of Sir Robert Raymond, who had crossed to the government in 1717 and risen with Sir Robert Walpole. Raymond was also responsible for Comyns's appointment (on 7 September 1726) as a baron of the exchequer, when he was also knighted. In January 1736 he was transferred to the common pleas, and two years later (in July 1738) was appointed lord chief baron of the exchequer by Lord Hardwicke. Comyns was married three times, on 21 April 1693 to Anne Gurdon (*d.* 1705), on 20 October 1708 to Elizabeth Courthope, and in 1726 to Anne Wilbraham; a son from his first marriage predeceased him and he left no children. He died on 13

Sir John Comyns (*c.*1667–1740), by George Vertue, 1744

November 1740, and was buried in the parish church of Writtle, near Chelmsford. His estate of Highlands, Widford, near Chelmsford, passed to his nephew, John Comyns. Comyns's tory background is visible to only a limited extent in his judicial work: he was less inclined to favour the tithe-payer over the tithe-owner than Sir Geoffrey Gilbert and Sir Thomas Pengelly, and more willing than some contemporary judges to use patriarchalist arguments in gender-related litigation. On the other hand, like other, mostly whig, contemporary judges, he made considerable and quite sophisticated use of civil and canon law sources, and displayed explicit commitment both to freedom of contract and of disposition of property, and to strict construction against the crown of criminal law and procedure.

Two legal works were published after Comyns's death. His *Reports of Cases Adjudged in the Courts of King's Bench, Common Pleas, and Exchequer* was translated from the original law French by his nephew and heir, John, and published in one volume in 1744. A second edition by Samuel Rose appeared in 1792. The *Reports* tracks Comyns's career, covering mainly king's bench cases to 1705, mainly common pleas cases to 1726, exchequer cases to 1736, common pleas to 1738, and exchequer again to 1739. Those from his judicial work in the exchequer are much fuller and more valuable than the earlier reports. A translation of Comyns's *Digest of the Laws of England* was published in five instalments between 1762 and 1767, and a supplement in one volume was added by 'a gentleman of the Inner Temple' in 1776. Subsequent editions appeared in 1800 and 1822, and an American version in New York and Philadelphia in 1824–6. The *Digest* clearly originated as a student abridgement or commonplace. Its quality is variable, with the section on pleading exceptionally well developed; its legal thought is generally conservative. These features led to the work's acquiring high authority in the period of tory ascendancy on the bench in the late eighteenth and early nineteenth century; thus, for example, Lord Ellenborough described the *Digest* as a 'book of very excellent authority' (*Kingdon v. Nottle*, 1813).

M. MACNAIR

Sources HoP, *Commons, 1715–54* · P. Mirant, *The history and antiquities of the county of Essex*, 2 vols. (1763–8) · Venn, *Alum. Cant.*, 1/1 · *State trials*, vol. 15 · W. Bunbury, *Reports of cases in the court of exchequer*, 2nd edn (1793) [145 ER Bunbury] · G. Maule and W. Selwyn, *Reports of cases … king's bench*, 1 (1814)
Likenesses G. Vertue, line print, BM, NPG; repro. in J. Comyns, *Reports of cases* (1744), frontispiece [*see illus.*] · bust on monument, Writtle parish church · oils, Lincoln's Inn, London

Conall Crandomna (*d.* 660). *See under* Dál Riata, kings of (*act. c.*500–*c.*850).

Conall mac Comgall (*d.* 574). *See under* Dál Riata, kings of (*act. c.*500–*c.*850).

Conall Cóel mac Máele Coba (*d.* 654). *See under* Cellach mac Máele Coba (*d.* 658).

Conamail mac Faílbi (*d.* 710). *See under* Iona, abbots of (*act.* 563–927).

Conan (IV), duke of Brittany (*c.*1135–1171), magnate, son of Alan the Black, earl of Richmond (*c.*1100–1146), and Bertha, daughter of Conan (III), duke of Brittany, was brought up in England. Quarrels over his inheritance led to his spending much of his life under the shadow of Henry II. A minor when his father died in 1146, Conan's right to the honour of Richmond was first clearly recognized 'in the year in which peace was made between Stephen, king of England, and Henry, count of Normandy [that is, November 1153 – October 1154] when by the grace of the said king and count the heritage of my parents was restored to me', as his first known charter acknowledges (Jones, 'The house of Brittany')—a rare recorded instance of the execution of the settlement agreed at Winchester between Stephen and Henry. As his style in this document, 'earl of Richmond', indicates, at this point Conan's status in Brittany was less certain. Shortly before he died in 1148, Conan (III) had disowned his only son, Hoël, in circumstances that have never been satisfactorily explained, allowing Bertha to succeed. Her second husband, Eudo, vicomte of Porhoët, began to exercise ducal power *iure uxoris*, probably with the intention that his rule should end on Conan's majority. However, Hoël, who retained the county of Nantes until his death in 1156, eventually disputed Eudo's authority, while a late fifteenth-century source alleges that Conan himself invaded the duchy in

1154, though this seems unlikely. But in the ensuing confusion over the Breton succession and Eudo's own personal ambitions, the Angevins, who had long coveted Nantes, were able to seize it, and Henry II finally invested his younger brother, Geoffrey, as count. Almost contemporaneously, in September 1156, the king permitted Conan, who was now of age and had been restoring order to his English lands following his minority and depredations during King Stephen's last years, to cross the channel and challenge his stepfather for possession of the county of Rennes, which soon fell to him. Shortly afterwards Eudo was captured by Raoul de Fougères. On his release he briefly served Louis VII of France while Conan was recognized as duke. But baronial unrest remained endemic, especially after Eudo (*d.* 1179) returned to the duchy and formed alliances with other dissident nobles; Conan's reliance on Henry II's support against his domestic enemies was lifelong.

When Geoffrey of Anjou, count of Nantes, died in July 1158, Conan quickly seized the county—the only time he openly opposed his patron. Henry II retaliated by temporarily confiscating Richmond and crossing to France where Conan hurried to appease him at Avranches (September 1158), when he surrendered Nantes. He displayed little opposition thereafter: it seems certain that his marriage to Margaret, sister of Malcolm IV, king of Scots, in 1160 was sanctioned, if not arranged, by Henry. Conan also spent much time between 1156 and 1164 in England. Many of his surviving charters concern administration of Richmond, notably relations with his burgesses at Richmond and Boston, or show him resolving disputes with and between his leading vassals and officers, such as the one between Roald the Constable and Richard de Rollos over the constableship of Richmond. He was also a generous patron of English abbeys associated with his honour, among them Fountains, Jervaulx, Easby, St Mary's York, Kirkstead, and Rufford, and the priories of Denny, Durham, and Marrick. He was frequently at court and witnessed a number of Henry II's charters, most notably being present at the Council of Clarendon in January 1164, though a charter issued at Wilton soon afterwards in favour of the abbey of Mont-St Michel seems to mark his last known visit to England.

In the interim a dispute with his uncle, Henry, count of Tréguier, led him to confiscate the latter's county of Guingamp, which from the early 1160s became the main centre of Conan's power, more of his surviving charters being sealed there than at any other place. But continuing domestic unrest, especially long-running feuds with Jean of Dol-Combour and Guihomar de Léon, and the persistent intrigues of his stepfather, Eudo of Porhoët, undermined his rule and probably his health as well. On 31 July 1166 he was with Henry II at Angers when the body of St Brioc was translated to the abbey of Sts Serge and Bacchus. This may have been the occasion when Conan finally agreed to betroth his only daughter and heir, *Constance, to Henry's fourth son, Geoffrey, and to relinquish rule in Brittany as the price for more help against his enemies, keeping only personal control of Guingamp and some lands in the diocese of Quimper. With his wife he continued to issue charters for favoured abbeys, especially Breton ones, including St Melaine de Rennes, St Georges de Rennes, Bégard, St Sulpice-la-Forêt, and Ste Croix de Quimperlé. The priory of Ste Croix de Guingamp also received donations from Conan and Margaret, while he founded the abbey of St Maurice de Carnoët (c.1167) and retained close links with the monks of Mont-St Michel and Savigny. He still occasionally visited Henry II (he was with him at Angers again on 24 March 1168 and probably at Avranches in 1170), but real power in Brittany had been in Henry II's hands for several years before Conan's death on 20 February 1171, when the duchy passed to his daughter, Constance. His widow married Humphrey (III) de Bohun, constable of England, and on her death in 1201 was buried at Sawtry Abbey, Huntingdonshire; Conan himself was probably buried at Bégard Abbey.　　　MICHAEL JONES

Sources charter of 1153–4, Archives de la Loire-Atlantique, Nantes, Registre de l'honneur de Richemond, E 116 · GEC, *Peerage* · W. Farrer and others, eds., *Early Yorkshire charters*, 12 vols. (1914–65), vol. 4 · J. Everard, *Brittany and the Angevins: province and empire, 1158–1203* (2000) · H. Guillotel, 'Les origines de Guingamp', *Mémoires de la Société d'Histoire et d'Archéologie de Bretagne*, 56 (1979), 81–100 · M. Jones, 'La vie familiale de la duchesse Constance: le témoignage des chartes', *Bretagne et pays celtiques, langues, histoire, civilisation: mélanges offerts à la mémoire de Léon Fleuriot, 1923–1987*, ed. G. le Menn and J.-Y. le Moing (Rennes, 1992), 349–60 · M. Jones, 'The house of Brittany and the honour of Richmond in the late eleventh and twelfth centuries: some new charter evidence', *Forschungen zur Reichs-, Papst- und Landesgeschichte: Peter Herde zum 65. Geburtstag*, ed. K. Borchardt and E. Bünz, 1 (Stuttgart, 1998), 161–73 · J. Le Patourel, 'Henri II Plantagenêt et la Bretagne', *Mémoires de la Société d'Histoire et d'Archéologie de Bretagne*, 58 (1981), 99–116 · J. Everard and M. Jones, eds., *The charters of Duchess Constance of Brittany and her family, 1171–1221* (1999)
Archives Archives de la Loire-Atlantique, Nantes, Registre de l'honneur de Richemond, E 116

Conant, John (1608–1694), college head, was born on 18 October 1608 at Yettington, Bicton, in south-east Devon, the eldest son of Robert Conant and his wife, Elizabeth Morris; the family had lived for several generations in Devon. His uncle of the same name, rector of Limington in Somerset, recognized an aptitude for learning in the young Conant and placed him first in the free school at Ilchester, Somerset, and then under the instruction of the schoolmaster Thomas Branker. His uncle gave him additional instruction. In 1627 his uncle took him to Oxford, where he was enrolled on 18 February as a commoner of Exeter College, of which the elder John Conant had been a fellow between 1611 and 1620. At Exeter the younger Conant's tutor was Lawrence Bodley, nephew of the benefactor of the Bodleian Library. Conant quickly gained a mastery of Greek, disputing publicly in that language, and also excelled in Hebrew, Syriac, and Arabic. His precocity was recognized by John Prideaux, the anti-Arminian rector of Exeter, who commented that he found nothing difficult. John Conant graduated BA on 26 May 1631, and proceeded MA on 12 January 1634; on 30 June 1632 he was chosen a probationer of Exeter College, and on 3 July 1633 made a fellow. He was ordained deacon and tutored pupils until 1642, when the disruption of Oxford by civil war caused him to depart, leaving behind valuable books which he never regained.

Conant planned to join his uncle at Limington, but by the time he arrived his uncle, a supporter of the parliamentary cause, had gone to London. There his uncle preached to the House of Commons on 26 July 1643, calling on it to reform the church, and was a member of the Westminster assembly (not the nephew, as some sources assert). Conant remained for a while at Limington, preaching and carrying out parish duties, until so menaced by royalist troops that he joined his uncle in London and began to assist him in the parish of St Botolph, Aldersgate, but he soon took up residence at Harefield, Middlesex, in the family of Lord and Lady Chandos, whom he served as chaplain. Lady Chandos, the daughter of Henry Montagu, earl of Manchester, was in particular his patron, awarding him an annual stipend of £80, much of which he used to relieve the needy of the parish, and provide them with bibles and schooling. Meanwhile, for several years he gave a weekday lecture at nearby Uxbridge. On 20 December 1645 he was offered the rectory of Whimple, Devon, by the committee for plundered ministers, but refused it. When in 1647 subscription to the solemn league and covenant was required of college fellows, Conant refused to take it, resigning his fellowship at Exeter by a letter from Harefield dated 27 September 1647.

When the rector of Exeter died in 1649 a majority of the fellows wanted Conant's uncle for the position, but the elder Conant wished to remain at the parish of St Thomas, Salisbury, and urged his nephew for the post; the nephew was duly elected on 7 June 1649, and admitted to the office on 29 June 1649. Conant was soon confronted with the question of affirming his loyalty to the parliamentary government by taking the engagement, which was made mandatory for members of colleges in October 1649. Conant took it, but declared to the commissioners that in doing so he did not necessarily approve of all that the government had done, and that he was not abridging his liberty to declare allegiance to any other future power that God might put over him.

Conant was an ideal choice for rector, and took up his duties with alacrity. He found the college deeply in debt and deficient in discipline, and remedied both, enforcing strict observance of the college statutes. He also catechized the college servants and attended the academic exercises and daily prayers of the college. In weekly instruction to the undergraduates he refuted Socinianism and Roman Catholicism and drew on such standard works of reformed scholasticism as Johannes Wollebius's *Compendium theologiae Christianae* and Johannes Piscator's *Aphorismi doctrinae Christianae*. He led a study of biblical prophecy for more advanced students, using Thomas Parker's *The Visions and Prophecies of Daniel Expounded* (1646), a book by a New England minister which asserted that the pope was the antichrist. Conant's leadership at Exeter attracted large numbers of students, including some from abroad. He was awarded the DD on 31 May 1654.

While rector of Exeter, John Conant preached regularly

at three nearby parishes: at All Saints' he preached every Friday morning at seven o'clock for more than ten years, developing a complete body of divinity for his auditors; at St Michael's he preached almost every Sunday for several years; and at St Mary Magdalen's he preached every other Sunday for half of each year. He also preached frequently as vicar of Kidlington, near Oxford, which was annexed to the rectory of Exeter. Conant declined the rectory of Ewelme in Oxfordshire, which was also attached to the college. In August 1651 he married Elizabeth Reynolds (*d.* 1707), youngest daughter of Edward *Reynolds (1599–1676), then rector of Braunston, Northamptonshire, and a leader of those more moderate puritans usually designated presbyterians; the couple had six sons and six daughters. In October 1652 Conant was presbyterially ordained to the ministry at Salisbury, where his uncle, who may have participated in the ceremony, was then living.

In September 1654 Conant was appointed regius professor of divinity at Oxford. To fulfil the duties of that office he lectured twice a week, basing his lectures on the biblical annotations of Hugo Grotius, whose philological scholarship was much admired even by those who rejected his Arminianism. As compensation for the sequestered income of his divinity chair, in 1657 Conant was awarded by Oliver Cromwell the income from the rectory of Abergele, Denbighshire, much of which, however, he returned to its resident vicar and to the poor of the parish. Conant never published any of his theological lectures, and later destroyed his notes for them. But there are indications of his theological position: for example, a letter from John Warner, a critic of Baxter's *Aphorisms of Justification*, claimed that Conant praised certain theological distinctions Warner had used in refuting Baxter. Orthodox Calvinists had been disturbed by Baxter's book.

On 9 October 1657, shortly after Richard Cromwell succeeded his father as chancellor of Oxford University, he named John Conant as vice-chancellor. Before then Jesus College bursars' accounts show him handling payments to the university by 1654. As vice-chancellor Conant restored many traditional usages, such as the wearing of caps and hoods, which had been considered popish by his predecessor John Owen. He also opposed the grant of a university charter to Durham College, going to London in 1659 with Seth Ward and John Wilkins to help thwart it. And just as he had enforced discipline in Exeter College, he now sought to do so in the whole university. He was also instrumental in procuring in 1659 the enormous library of John Selden for the Bodleian.

Conant welcomed the Restoration, silencing in January 1660 a Baptist preacher at Balliol who denounced the coming changes, and, with a deputation of university notables to the court, on 15 June 1660 presented the king with a book of congratulatory verses composed for the occasion by members of the university. He also made a speech in Latin before the king. But he lost his professorship, as the deprived Robert Sanderson was reinstated. In August 1660 he was removed from the vice-chancellorship. In the summer of 1662 the new vice-chancellor, the Laudian Richard

Baylie, questioned him for preaching against Arminianism and for denying that original sin was taken away by baptism. His lecture at All Saints' was suppressed at about the same time.

Conant was one of the twelve presbyterian leaders who sought compromise with the bishops at the Savoy conference in 1661, but he was dissatisfied with the results of the conference, and could not accept the Act of Uniformity, even though his father-in-law, who was then appointed Bishop of Norwich, did. Conant's son and biographer of the same name thought that his father would have been offered the bishopric of Exeter if he had conformed. On 2 September 1662 Conant was deprived of his last Oxford office, rector of Exeter, for not subscribing to the liturgy of the Church of England. One year later (30 September 1663) he was summoned along with others before the chancellor, the earl of Clarendon, and accused of holding an illegal conventicle in his house. Conant eventually removed to Northampton, where in 1666 he took the 'Oxford oath', rejecting armed opposition to the king and promising not to press for changes in church or civil government. There he apparently did not preach illegally, but attended the services of the established church. After reflecting on the issue of conformity, and comparing the Book of Common Prayer with ancient liturgies, Conant conformed, and was ordained priest by his father-in-law on 20 September 1670. Conformists praised him for persuading others to conformity (both John Tillotson and George Bull spoke well of him), but he was still trusted by such moderate dissenters as Richard Baxter, who thought that Conant and other peaceable persons on both sides could have easily settled the matters separating the church and dissent. Conant was falsely rumoured to be the author of an eirenic tract, *Persuasive to Peace and Unity* (1672).

With conformity and reordination preferment was open to Conant, and he became the vicar of All Saints', Northampton, on 15 February 1671. He remained there, at an annual income of £100, even though other positions were offered him. Various persons, including the secretary of state, Joseph Williamson, and the mathematician John Wallis, both of whom had known him at Oxford, sought further preferment for him. Even when All Saints' Church, along with much of the town (but not Conant's residence), was destroyed by fire in September 1675, he refused to accept other positions, but remained at his post, preaching for a while at St Peter's, Northampton. A letter of Conant's describing the fire was included in his son's biography of him. In addition to his vicarage, on 8 June 1676 he was installed archdeacon of Norwich, appointed by his father-in-law. On 3 December 1681 he was made a prebend of Worcester Cathedral by the king at the urging of the earl of Radnor, a former pupil. But some royalists resented these favours shown to Conant and accused him of keeping a conventicle, preaching seditious sermons, and giving communion to his congregation while they were seated.

At Northampton, Conant kept special days of humiliation and prayer, and appears to have been a model pastor, visiting the spiritually troubled, comforting the sick, preaching sermons on practical godliness, and dispensing charity out of his own resources. His charity also extended to New England and to French protestants. One volume of his sermons was published in 1693; it bore the title *Sermons Preached on Several Occasions*, and was reprinted in a second corrected edition in 1699. Other sermons were published under the same title as volumes two to six, in 1697, 1698, 1703, 1708, and 1722. John Williams, a native of Northamptonshire educated at Oxford while Conant was there, and a royal chaplain who became bishop of Chichester in 1696, was instrumental in bringing about the publication of the first five volumes, and Digby Coates, principal of Magdalen Hall, Oxford, of the sixth. In a preface to the first volume Conant told the parishioners of All Saints', whom he was too infirm to serve any longer, that he hoped the publication of 'plain and practical sermons', which he had formerly preached to them, would further their 'spiritual welfare'.

Conant's general outlook is clear from his published sermons and from twenty-five volumes of sermons in manuscript (Bodleian Library). They exemplify the practical and compassionate divinity common to later seventeenth-century moderate Calvinists: repentance, conversion, holiness, and an earnest longing for 'experimental' knowledge of Christ are stressed, while predestination, justification by faith, and the reformed order of salvation are presupposed. Pastoral concerns are foremost, with warnings about hell as well as against melancholy and excessive scrupulosity. The devout are not to inquire into God's decrees, but to do their duty. Conant was also concerned about scoffers at religion and disturbed by misbelief: among the latter, Lutheran consubstantiation, Quaker pharisaism, Roman Catholic idolatry, and Pelagian (that is, Arminian) denial of free grace in justification are mentioned. His sermons also touch on social issues, asserting that the rich must take responsibility for the poor, and condemning the code of honour demanding revenge. He saw special providences in such events as the fire at Northampton.

Contemporaries described Conant as thin and short in stature. In 1686 he became completely blind. He died on 12 March 1694 and was buried in the rebuilt church of All Saints', Northampton, where he was commemorated by a monument and Latin epitaph.

John Conant (1653/4–1723), biographer, was the eldest son of John Conant and Elizabeth Reynolds. He matriculated from Trinity College, Oxford, on 8 February 1670, aged sixteen, and graduated BA in 1673. Elected a fellow of Merton College, Oxford, in 1676, he was active in the business of his college and proceeded MA on 29 January 1678. He took the LLD on 22 June 1683, moved to London, and became a member of Gray's Inn. He became a successful advocate at Doctors' Commons. In 1693 he was considered for, but not elected, warden of Merton. He married Mary West, daughter of John West, and inherited his father-in-law's property at Hampton Poyle, Oxfordshire, in 1696, though engaged in lawsuits over the property with her

brother John West the younger. When his health deteriorated he moved to Kidlington in Oxfordshire, where he died on 23 August 1723. He wrote a biography of his father that remained in manuscript until publication in 1823.

DEWEY D. WALLACE, JUN.

Sources J. Conant, *The life and times of the Reverend and Venerable John Conant* (1823) · DNB · Calamy rev. · Wood, *Ath. Oxon.*, new edn, 2.397–9 · *Calendar of the correspondence of Richard Baxter*, ed. N. H. Keeble and G. F. Nuttall, 1 (1991), 311; 2 (1991), 91–2, 144, 149 · C. W. Boase, ed., *Registrum Collegii Exoniensis*, new edn, OHS, 27 (1894), cxxi–cxxvi, 95, 103, 111 · *The life and times of Anthony Wood*, ed. A. Clark, 1–3, OHS, 19, 21, 26 (1891–4) · CSP dom., 1675–6, 24, 33, 205–6, 318; 1681, 563–4, 603 · *Reliquiae Baxterianae, or, Mr Richard Baxter's narrative of the most memorable passages of his life and times*, ed. M. Sylvester, 1 vol. in 3 pts (1696), pt 3, p. 13 · Foster, *Alum. Oxon.* · J. Prince, *Danmonii orientales illustres, or, The worthies of Devon*, 2nd edn (1810), 230–34 · G. C. Brodrick, *Memorials of Merton College*, OHS, 4 (1885), 122–3, 295

Archives BL, Add. MS 15669, fol. 230 · BL, Harley MSS 3998, 7190, 297 · Bodl. Oxf., MS Rawl., C. 945.425 · Bodl. Oxf., sermons and theological notes, Add. MSS 29247–29271 · LPL, Lambeth MS '1656', fol. 84

Likenesses line engraving, BM, NPG

Wealth at death over £1200, plus property: will

Conant, John (1653/4–1723). *See under* Conant, John (1608–1694).

Conant, Roger (*bap.* 1592, *d.* 1679), settler in America, was baptized on 9 April 1592 at East Budleigh, Devon, youngest of eight children of Richard Conant and Agnes Clarke. (Claims that the Conant family was of Huguenot origin have not been documented.) He apparently followed his older brother Christopher to London in the first decade of the seventeenth century, for on 20 January 1620 these two men signed a bond for their brother John, upon his entry to the rectory of Lymington, Somerset, as 'Christopher Conant, grocer, and Roger Conant, salter, both of the parish of St. Lawrence, Jewry, London', suggesting that Roger had completed an apprenticeship in the Salters' Company (Conant, 99); a fourth brother, Robert, was father of John Conant (1608–1694), rector of Exeter College, Oxford.

On 11 November 1618 Conant married Sarah (*c.*1598–1660×78), daughter of Thomas Horton and his second wife, Catherine Satchfield, at St Ann Blackfriars, London. This marriage brought him into an extensive kinship network which included such prominent puritan ministers as William Gouge, Ezekiel Culverwell, Lawrence Chadderton, and William Whitaker. Roger Conant and Sarah Horton had ten children, the first two born in England and the last eight in New England. He sailed to New England in 1623 or 1624, and apparently resided briefly at Plymouth and Nantasket. In 1625 the Revd John White of Dorchester, an associate of Conant's brother John, hired Roger Conant to manage the settlement of the Dorchester Company at Cape Ann in Massachusetts Bay. Within a year, as the leader of the so-called 'old planters', he moved the settlers to nearby Naumkeag, which was soon renamed Salem. In 1628 John Endicott, leader of the first party of settlers dispatched by the Massachusetts Bay Company of London, arrived in Salem and supplanted Conant. No later than the end of 1636, and probably some years earlier, Conant had joined the church at Salem.

Combined with his association with White and the likely influence upon him of his many puritan kinsmen by marriage, it would appear that he was at least sympathetic with the puritan movement, if not an ardent advocate.

After Endicott's arrival Conant faded steadily into the background. In 1632 he represented Salem at the Massachusetts Bay general court, and in 1637, 1638, and 1639 he was a magistrate at the Essex county quarter court, but during the remaining forty years of his life he served only in lesser offices, such as Essex county petit jury (on at least ten occasions) and Salem town selectman (for about thirteen years), as well as various minor county and town committees. He was certainly a trusted leader during his early years in New England, but his steady slide down the scale of officeholding suggests that his leadership capabilities were not that strong. Along with the other old planters he received substantial grants of land in that part of Salem which in 1668 was set off as the town of Beverly, Essex county; he died there on 19 November 1679. The inventory of his estate, taken on 24 November, totalled £258 10s., of which £198 was real estate, comprising several parcels totalling about 250 acres.

ROBERT CHARLES ANDERSON

Sources C. K. Shipton, *Roger Conant: a founder of Massachusetts* (1945) · F. O. Conant, *A history and genealogy of the Conant family in England and America* (1889) · R. C. Anderson, ed., *The great migration begins: immigrants to New England, 1620–1633*, 1 (Boston, MA, 1995) · R. C. Anderson, 'The Conant connection [pt 1]', *New England Historical and Genealogical Register*, 147 (1993), 234–9 · R. C. Anderson, 'The Conant connection [pt 2]', *New England Historical and Genealogical Register*, 148 (1994), 107–29 · W. Hubbard, *A general history of New England from the discovery to MDCLXXX* (Cambridge, MA, 1815) · G. F. Dow, ed., *The probate records of Essex county, Massachusetts*, 3 (1916–20), 335–7
Wealth at death £258 10s.: Dow, ed., *Probate records of Essex county Massachusetts*, vol. 3, pp. 335–7

Concanen, Matthew (1701–1749), writer and lawyer, was born in Ireland. Nothing is known of his parentage, education, or early life beyond Shiels's statement that he 'was bred to the Law' (Cibber, 5.27). He showed early literary ambitions with a comedy, *Wexford Wells*, written in 1719, acted in November 1720 at the Smock Alley Theatre (perhaps by command of Charles O'Hara, Lord Tyrawley), and printed in Dublin in 1721. His *Meliora's Tears for Thyrsis*, a conventional pastoral on the death of Thomas, Baron Southwell, and *A Match at Football*, a mock-heroic poem in three cantos, dedicated to Richard Bettesworth, were both published in Dublin in 1720. These and a number of shorter poems appeared in Concanen's *Poems on Several Occasions* (1722), dedicated to the duchess of Grafton, wife of the lord lieutenant.

About this time Concanen and his friend James Sterling moved to London, intending to take up journalism. According to Shiels they decided by the toss of a halfpenny that Sterling should oppose and Concanen defend the whig government (Cibber, 5.27), but Concanen had already sought patronage from at least four prominent whigs in Ireland. *Miscellaneous Poems* (1724), edited by Concanen, included work by Swift, Parnell, Sheridan, Delany, Brown, Ward, Concanen, and others, and was dedicated to

the whig Viscount Gage. Other poems by Concanen appeared in Richard Savage's *Miscellaneous Poems and Translations* (1726).

Concanen had praised Pope and expressed some obligation to Swift in his earliest writings, but some of the essays which from 1725 he wrote in the *London Journal* and the *British Journal* (reprinted in his *The Speculatist*, 1730) attacked those two writers. His co-belligerents included his friend Lewis Theobald and the then obscure William Warburton, but, fortunately for Warburton's later cultivation of Pope, his remark, in an ingratiating letter to Concanen on 2 January 1727, that Pope borrowed 'for want of genius' (Nichols, *Illustrations*, 2.195) was never made public. Joseph Warton believed that Warburton secretly assisted Concanen in one of his anti-Pope publications, *A Supplement to the Profound* (1728). Pope believed, probably correctly, that Concanen was the editor of *A Complete Collection* (1728), a republication of satirical replies to the Pope–Swift *Miscellanies*, and duly crushed him in *The Dunciad* (1728) and the apparatus of *The Dunciad Variorum* (1729). Swift ridiculed him in *On Poetry: a Rhapsody* (1733).

There are songs by Concanen in the *Musical Miscellany* (1729) and a few new poems by him in a miscellany, *The Flower-Piece* (1731), which he edited. With his friend Edward Roome and the whig politician Sir William Yonge he revised Richard Brome's *The Jovial Crew* as a comic opera; it opened at Drury Lane on 8 February 1731 and ran for sixteen performances with Concanen receiving the profits. He was now writing in the *Daily Courant* and was a pensioner of Walpole, according to Bolingbroke, who was one of its main targets. Concanen's last publications were a quibbling attack on Pope in *A Miscellany on Taste* (1732) and a pro-Walpole *Review of the Excise Scheme* (1733).

Concanen was a barrister. On 29 June 1732, through the interest of the duke of Newcastle, he was appointed attorney-general of Jamaica, upon which Warburton wrote him an obsequious congratulatory letter (BL, Egerton MS 1955, fol. 2). He arrived in Spanish Town on 1 March 1733 and lived there for ten years, performing his duties with credit. As a member of the island's council (the upper legislative house, consisting of twelve members) from April 1733 he resisted the arbitrary actions of successive governors. He was suspended from the council by governor Edward Trelawny in May 1740 but remained attorney-general, and, in September 1742, reluctantly under governor's orders, prosecuted Admiral Sir Chaloner Ogle for alleged assault upon Trelawny.

Concanen married in Jamaica; his wife was an opulent widow or planter's daughter, perhaps both (Warburton, 218; Cibber, 5.31). They had no children, but Concanen fathered three illegitimate sons with an unknown partner or partners. His successor as attorney-general was appointed on 24 December 1743, after which, at some unknown date, Concanen returned to London, became a member of Serjeants' Inn and, it seems, lived in affluent retirement from politics and literature until he died of consumption on 22 January 1749. At the end he was perhaps living in Crane Court, Fleet Street, because this is where papers of his were later found, including the letter containing Warburton's imprudent sneer at Pope. By the time this letter was published in 1766 Warburton had shamelessly redrawn the picture of his relationship with Concanen, whom he now painted as a sponger and scoundrel (Warburton, 218). Concanen was survived by his wife, who married the Hon. Mr Hamilton, and by his three natural sons.

JAMES SAMBROOK

Sources R. Shiels, *The lives of the poets of Great Britain and Ireland*, ed. T. Cibber, 5 (1753), 27–31 • Nichols, *Illustrations*, 2.189–204, 845–8 • M. Concanen, *A match at football, or, The Irish champions* (1721), preface • *Journal of the commissioners for trade and plantations*, [vols. 6–7] (1928–30) [Jan 1729 – Dec 1741] • *CSP col.*, vols. 39–45 • will, 22 Jan 1749, PRO, PROB 11/767, sig. 6 • *The tryal of Sir Chaloner Ogle* (1743) • *GM*, 1st ser., 2 (1732), 877 • *GM*, 1st ser., 19 (1749), 44 • A. Pope, *The Dunciad*, ed. J. Sutherland (1943), vol. 5 of *The Twickenham edition of the poems of Alexander Pope*, ed. J. Butt (1939–69); 3rd edn [in 1 vol.] (1963); repr. (1965) • *The poems of Jonathan Swift*, ed. H. Williams, 2nd edn, 3 vols. (1958) • [W. Warburton], *Letters from a late eminent prelate to one of his friends*, ed. R. Hurd, 2nd edn (1809), 218–19 • P. Seary, *Lewis Theobald and the editing of Shakespeare* (1990) • J. V. Guerinot, *Pamphlet attacks on Alexander Pope, 1711–1744* (1969) • A. C. Burns, *History of the British West Indies* (1954) • M. Concanen, *The speculatist* (1730)

Wealth at death £3300; plus landed property in Jamaica, household goods, and plate: will, PRO, PROB 11/767, sig. 6

Conches, Ralph de. *See* Tosny, Ralph de (*d.* 1102?).

Conches, William de (*c.*1085–*c.*1154), grammarian and commentator on classical texts, derived from Conches in south-east Normandy. The most important source for his life is the *Metalogicon* of John of Salisbury, who studied under William between 1138 and 1141. John says that William followed Bernard of Chartres's old-fashioned method of teaching, which centred on the careful exposition of ancient texts; the implication is that he was probably Bernard's pupil. The question of where William taught is much debated. John's account makes it clear that it cannot have been on the Mont-Ste Geneviève. Paris itself is a probable location, because John seems to have studied with other masters at the same time, and only in Paris would this have been possible. However, in spite of the arguments put forward by Southern, some historians think that when John says that he left the Mont-Ste Geneviève to be taught by William, he cannot have meant just that he went into Paris, of which the Mont was a suburb, and they point to allusions in William's writings that suggest that he was a teacher at Chartres. John also says that eventually William gave up his teaching, because students preferred quicker and more fashionable methods of instruction. Instead he formed a connection with the court of Geoffrey the Handsome, duke of Normandy from 1144 to 1149. Not only is William's *Dragmaticon* presented in the form of a dialogue with the duke, but he also gave tuition to the duke's sons. In the *Dragmaticon* William says that he had taught others for twenty years or more, which would put the beginning of his teaching to *c.*1120, or perhaps slightly later. In 1979 Southern argued for an earlier date, but this seems impossible, since William was still teaching publicly when John of Salisbury studied with him. Alberic of Trois-Fontaines, chronicling the death of King Stephen in 1154, says that 'in his time' William had great celebrity—a comment that suggests that William died shortly before or after 1154.

The writings of William de Conches reflect his three linked interests in grammar, ancient texts, and natural science. His strictly grammatical work took the form of a commentary on Priscian's *Institutiones grammaticae*, the standard text for advanced grammatical work in the middle ages. It exists in two recensions, one covering books 1–16, the other the whole work (1st recension: Florence, Biblioteca Medicea Laurenziana, MS San Marco 310; 2nd recension: Paris, Bibliothèque Nationale, MS Lat. 15130). According to William himself, the first recension was written in his youth (probably *c.*1120–25), the second in old age (probably late 1140s to 1150s). William was able to draw on the eleventh-century *Glosule* to Priscian, but he greatly modified and extended their analysis in the direction of providing a universal grammar.

Expounding ancient texts was part of a grammarian's work. William de Conches interested himself especially in the few ancient and late antique Platonic and Neoplatonic texts then available. He commented on Boethius's *De consolatione philosophiae*, on Macrobius's commentary on Cicero's *Somnium Scipionis*, and on Plato's *Timaeus* in Calcidius's translation (*Glossae super Platonem*, ed. E. Jeauneau, 1965). There is also mention by William of a commentary he intended to write on Martianus Capella's *De nuptiis Mercurii et Philologiae*; a manuscript at Florence (Biblioteca Nazionale, MS Conv. soppr. I, 1, 28) probably contains material based on it. William's commentaries are remarkable for the extent to which they treat Platonic texts as sources where the Christian scholar, by unravelling metaphorical language, can discover important truths.

William's work as a commentator was closely linked to his interest in natural science, since Macrobius's commentary on the *Somnium Scipionis* and the *Timaeus* were both rich in scientific discussion. In the *Philosophia mundi* (ed. G. Maurach, 1980), William begins by briefly considering God before talking about the elements, the stars, the seas, and the earth, and then human beings—how they are conceived, their senses, and their souls. It is a plan which, very roughly, might have been suggested by the *Timaeus* itself. The *Philosophia* exists in two recensions, in one of which some of the more daring points are put in more guarded language. In the *Dragmaticon* (printed as *Dialogus de substantiis … a Vuilhelmo Anoponymo philosopho* by G. Gratarolus, Strasbourg, 1567; repr. 1967), William treats the same topics in dialogue form, sometimes developing his earlier ideas and abandoning former certainties for a more complex and tentative approach. Besides ancient texts such as the *Timaeus*, Macrobius, and Seneca's *Quaestiones naturales*, other material translated from the Arabic influenced William's scientific speculations, especially, in his discussion of the elements, Constantine the African's *Pantegni*.

From internal cross-references, the order of William's compositions must have been: commentary on Boethius, commentary on Macrobius, *Philosophia*, commentary on Priscian (1st version)—almost certainly all before 1130;

commentary on *Timaeus*, *Dragmaticon* (1144–9), commentary on Priscian (2nd version). In the course of his career William became increasingly reluctant to propose ideas that might be considered heterodox. For instance, he gradually moved from asserting the identity between Plato's 'world soul' and the Holy Spirit, as he did in his commentary on Boethius, to proposing the identification as a possible view, and finally to omitting it entirely in the *Dragmaticon*. Indeed, in his preface to that work, William explicitly renounces a number of the more daring theological ideas put forward in the *Philosophia mundi*. He may have been influenced by a letter written to Bernard of Clairvaux by Guillaume de St Thierry about 1141, attacking William's orthodoxy and describing his errors as worse than Peter Abelard's. But Bernard, who had conducted a vigorous campaign against Abelard at Guillaume de St Thierry's prompting, was not this time incited into action—perhaps because William de Conches showed himself willing to abandon his contentious positions.

A florilegium of ancient ethical texts, the *Moralium dogma philosophorum* (ed. J. Holmberg, 1929), has often been attributed to William, but almost certainly wrongly. Historians have been misled into thinking there is positive evidence for the attribution by additions made by the early thirteenth-century reviser of the treatise, Bartolomeo da Recanati. Moreover, it is very unlikely that the *Moralium dogma* was written before the late 1150s, by which time William was almost certainly dead.

JOHN MARENBON

Sources E. Jeauneau, 'Note sur l'école de Chartres', *Studi Medievali*, 3rd ser., 5 (1964), 821–65; repr. in E. Jeauneau, *Lectio philosophorum: recherches sur l'école de Chartres* (Amsterdam, 1973), 3–49 · E. Jeauneau, 'Gloses de Guillaume de Conches sur Macrobe: note sur les manuscrits', *Archives d'Histoire Doctrinale et Littéraire du Moyen Âge*, 27 (1960), 17–28 · G. Maurach, ed., *'Philosophia mundi': Ausgabe des 1. Buchs von Wilhelm von Conches' 'Philosophia' mit Anhang, Übersetzung und Anmerkung* (1974), 4–7 · D. Elford, 'William of Conches', *A history of twelfth-century western philosophy*, ed. P. Dronke (1988), 308–27 · *Ioannis Saresberiensis Metalogicon*, ed. J. B. Hall and K. S. B. Keats-Rohan (Turnhout, Belgium, 1991) · A. Vernet, 'Un remaniement de la *Philosophia* de Guillaume de Conches', *Scriptorium*, 1 (1947), 243–59 · R. A. Gauthier, 'Les deux recensions du *Moralium dogma philosophorum*', *Revue du moyen âge Latin*, 9 (1953), 171–260 · P. Courcelle, 'La consolation de philosophie' dans la tradition littéraire (1967), 408–10 · P. Dronke, *Fabula* (1974), 167–83 · E. Jeauneau, *L'âge d'or des écoles de Chartres* (1995) · R. W. Southern, *Platonism, scholastic method and the school of Chartres* (1979) · R. W. Southern, 'The schools of Paris and the school of Chartres', *Renaissance and renewal in the twelfth century*, ed. R. L. Benson, G. Constable, and C. D. Lanham (1982), 113–37, esp. 129–30 · R. W. Southern, *Scholastic humanism and the unification of Europe*, 1 (1995), 73–4, 214–21

Archives Biblioteca Medicea Laurenziana, Florence, MS San Marco 310 · Biblioteca Nazionale, Florence, MS Conv. soppr. I, 1, 28 · Bibliothèque Nationale, Paris, MS Lat. 15130

Condé, Jean [John] (**1765–1794**), printmaker, was the son of a stonemason in Paris, and his wife, Louise Crantin. His name first appears in the 'registre des élèves' of the École des Beaux-Arts in Paris on 20 March 1781: 'Jean Condé, Peintre natif de Paris, âgé de 15 ans ½, protégé par M. Pierre [the painter Jean-Baptiste Marie Pierre], demeurans enclos de Ste Geneviève, chez son père Tailleur de pierre au Bâtiment de Ste Geneviève' (Paris,

Jean Condé (1765–1794), attrib. Richard Cosway, *c.*1794

École des Beaux-Arts, MS 823, fol. 64). During September of that year it was noted that he was a pupil of the engraver Lempereur, and in March 1782 of Boizot. Further references are made in the same source up until 1786. In October 1785 he won the third medal in the painting category of the competition organized by the Académie Royale de Peinture et de Sculpture. That work is now preserved in the collection of the École des Beaux-Arts. In a similar competition held during January 1787 Condé won the second medal, and at this time he became a pupil of Jacques-Louis David.

In 1787 Condé travelled from Paris to London with the print publisher John Boydell. His plans to work in London are likely to have been encouraged after David had met Richard and Maria Cosway on their visit to Paris from August to October 1786. In autumn 1787 he enrolled as a student at the Royal Academy Schools in London; by the end of that year he had won a silver medal for a drawing after the life, and he won a similar medal in 1792. Early in 1788 he returned to Paris and showed off his prize to David, who wrote to Maria Cosway: 'Condé showed me the medal which England had awarded him; this decision gives me a fair idea of London's Academy. Here, a man such as Condé, coming from nowhere, would not even have been allowed to enter the competition' (Daniell, vi). Condé also brought back to David a present for his master of one of the engraved portraits after Richard Cosway of *George, Prince of Wales* (almost certainly that engraved in stipple by L. Sailliar in 1787), a gift which David held in high esteem.

In the eight years up until his premature death, Condé enjoyed a successful career as an engraver; there are forty-six portraits known to have been engraved by him. He enjoyed a particularly close business relationship with Cosway, who may have painted his portrait in miniature (now untraced). Condé reproduced seventeen of Cosway's elegant and refined compositions in stipple; they are engraved in pale delicate tints, using stipple, sanguine, or aquatint. He also enhanced the compositions by enclosing them in frame-like borders, called glomisages after the French engraver Jean-Baptiste Glomy, who had first designed them. Among the ten portraits by Cosway that Condé engraved were those of *Mrs Fitzherbert* (1792), *Madame Du Barry* (1794), *George, Prince of Wales* (1795), and the diplomatist and wit *Caleb Whitefoord* (1806), and the seven subject compositions by Cosway he reproduced include the pair of *Andromache and Ascanius* and *Polindo and Albarosa, docet amor* (all 1791), *Minerva Directing the Arrows of Cupid*, and *Queen Margaret of Anjou and her Son* (1795). The account book belonging to Condé's brother Pierre [*see below*], covering the years 1795 to 1821, which is currently untraced, noted the sales to various London printsellers of his engraving after Cosway as well as after other artists. The volume also contained three pencil drawings by Jean, which were probably portraits. Pierre charged different prices for different types of impressions: for example, for Jean's engraving of *Mrs Fitzherbert*, the prices were 8s. (ordinary), 12s. (half-coloured), and 16s. (coloured and proof). Jean engraved portraits of celebrities for *The European* and other magazines and produced engravings after portraits of actors after De Wilde, or from the life, for *The Thespian* magazine. Among the other artists whose work he engraved were Banks, Opie, Romney, Reynolds, Russell, and Stuart. In 1791 he engraved from his own drawing a portrait of *Mademoiselle La Chevalière d'Eon de Beaumont*, a notorious transvestite then resident in London, as *Minerva*. In the lettering for this print he styled himself as a French artist, who designed this print 'as a monument of English generosity and French gratitude'. Condé also made portrait drawings, a number of which he engraved. He died, possibly at Richmond, Surrey, in July 1794, leaving money in hand to the value of £52 10s. The valuation of his household furniture, engraved plates, drawings, prints, and tools amounted to £162. He was owed about £80 on various accounts, principally from some of the leading London print publishers, such as Bovi, Colnaghi, Dickinson, Harding, Macklin, and Thompkins (among other publishers of his prints were Bell, Boydell, Fores, Lay, and Sewell), and his own debts amounted to £93, which included accounts for his lodgings at Richmond and bills due to Mr Layton, printer in colours. The final balance of the estate was £177 6s. 7d. As Jean neither married nor had children, this sum was divided up between his brother Pierre, who was administrator of his estate, another brother, Matthieu, his sister Louise, and their mother.

Jean's brother **Pierre Condé** (1767/8–1840), printmaker and miniature painter, also born in Paris, moved to London a year after his elder brother and enrolled as a student at the Royal Academy Schools between 28 November 1788 and 24 March 1789, giving his age as twenty-one. After the death of his brother, Pierre engraved in stipple eleven of Richard Cosway's portrait and subject compositions. These included stipple-engravings after portraits of the fashionable mesmerist *J. B. de Mainauduc* (1798) and the composer *J. L. Dussek* (1800), as well as an etched memorial

to the collector *Robert Udny* (1802). He also engraved portraits after various other artists, notably Edridge, Gainsborough, Hoppner, Lawrence, Northcote, and Opie.

Condé later worked as a portrait miniaturist, and he exhibited his work at the Royal Academy from 1806 to 1824. During this period and up until the end of his life he lived at six successive London addresses, four of which were in the West End and the last two in Camden Town. A rare extant example of his portrait miniatures is that of *Dr Plender*, signed and dated 1812 on recto and verso (Dumas Egerton Trust collection on loan to the Scot. NPG). Two oval portrait miniatures in pencil on paper are known: a portrait of the painter *James Northcote*, from which Condé's engraving was published in 1795, and a *Self-Portrait*, exhibited at the Royal Academy in 1811, are now untraced.

The Condé account book included copies of letters by Pierre, mainly to clients, including Lady Athlone in 1804, Lady Holland in 1808, and Lady Petre in 1820. Pierre, who appears to have been somewhat touchy in character, evidently had great difficulty in extracting payment from some of his clients; in later life, unmarried and childless, he seems to have been poor. He expressed the wish that after his death Mr Knock of Jeffreys Street, Camden Town—to whom, in September 1835, he had sold his gold watch for £7—should accept any special prints engraved by his late brother Jean and by himself, and that Mr Knock also choose prints out of his portfolio 'as a small testimony of his gratitude for his kindness and friendship to my father and brother and myself'. Pierre Condé died in Camden Town, London, in 1840. STEPHEN LLOYD

Sources private information (2004) [Philippe Bordes] · registre des élèves, École des Beaux-Arts, Paris, MS 823 · F. B. Daniell, *A catalogue raisonné of the engraved works of Richard Cosway* (1890) · G. C. Williamson, *Richard Cosway, RA* (1905) · Graves, *RA exhibitors* · G. C. Williamson, 'Jean and Pierre Condé, *The Connoisseur*, 33 (Aug 1912), 241–9 · *Engraved Brit. ports.* · *Catalogue of the well-known and valuable collection … the property of Francis Wellseley* (1820) [sale catalogue, Sotheby, Wilkinson, and Hodge, London, 28 June 1820] · S. C. Hutchison, 'The Royal Academy Schools, 1768–1830', *Walpole Society*, 38 (1960–62), 123–91, esp. 149–50 · P. Bordes, *Le serment du jeu de paume de Jacques-Louis David* (1983) · P. Bordes, 'Jacques-Louis David's anglophilia on the eve of the French Revolution', *Burlington Magazine*, 134 (Aug 1992), 482–90 · A. Cahen, 'Les prix de quartier à l'Académie Royale de Peinture et de Sculpture', *Bulletin de la Société de l'Histoire de l'Art Français* (1993) · admon, PRO, PROB 6/171, fol. 138v [Jean Condé] · will, PRO, PROB 11/1940, sig. 86 [Pierre Condé]

Archives École des Beaux-Arts, Paris, registre des élèves, MS 823 · Bodl. Oxf., account book

Likenesses attrib. R. Cosway, watercolour on ivory miniature, c.1794, repro. in Williamson, *Cosway*, 40; formerly in Sir H. Howarth collection [*see illus.*]

Condé, Pierre (1767/8–1840). *See under* Condé, Jean (1765–1794).

Condell, Henry (*bap.* 1576?, *d.* 1627), actor and editor of Shakespeare's first folio, was probably born in East Anglia. The only Henry Condell so far discovered at a suitable date in that part of England was the son of a Robert Condell of St Peter Mancroft, Norwich, a fishmonger, and his wife, Joan, *née* Yeomans, of New Buckenham, a market town not far from Norwich. Henry Condell, presumably their son, was baptized at St Peter on 5 September 1576: the theatrical Condell mentions in his will a deceased 'Cosen Gilder of New Buckenham'.

At some point Condell must have become stage-struck, perhaps when a small troupe employed by Ferdinando Lord Strange, and including Augustine Phillips and John *Heminges, visited Norwich on 15 September 1593. On 24 October 1596, at St Laurence Pountney, near London Bridge, he married Elizabeth (d. 1635), the only child of John Smart of the Strand, a gentleman and man of property: soon, if not immediately, the couple became fellow parishioners of the Heminges family at St Mary Aldermanbury, which had strong links with the theatre. Both Heminges and Condell served as churchwarden—Heminges signing the register twice as second warden and three times as first, and Condell twice in 1617 as second warden. Nine children were born to the Condells there between 1599 and 1614, of whom only three survived infancy: Elizabeth, the third daughter of that name, baptized on 26 October 1606; Henry, baptized on 6 May 1610 (d. 1630); and William, baptized on 26 May 1611.

Condell is known to have played in *Every Man in his Humour* and *Every Man out of his Humour*, written for the Chamberlain's Men by Ben Jonson, in 1598 and 1599. In 1603 James I acceded to the English throne and the Chamberlain's Men became the King's Men; in their first licence, dated 19 May, Condell is named after Shakespeare, Richard Burbage, Phillips, and Heminges. In the next, dated 27 March 1619, he is third after Heminges and Burbage and in fact came second, Burbage having died before the patent was in force. The King's Men, like the Chamberlain's Men, never provided lists of members or cast-lists: however, Condell is known to have acted in four more plays by Jonson—*Sejanus*, *Volpone*, *The Alchemist*, and *Catiline*—between 1603 and 1611, in addition, presumably, to all of Shakespeare's. He also played the Cardinal in the first performance of John Webster's *The Duchess of Malfi*, put on at Blackfriars probably in spring 1614; at a revival about 1621, when he was busy editing the Shakespeare folio, he was replaced by Richard Robinson—who married Richard Burbage's widow, Winifred, in 1622.

In the retrospective list of twenty-six 'Principall Actors' in all Shakespeare's plays in the first folio (the word 'actor' meaning all theatre men, not just performers) Condell is eighth. He was perhaps the principal player after Burbage, for when Phillips died in 1605 he left a will listing all members and associates of the company, beginning with Shakespeare and Condell and bequeathing them each a 30s. gold piece to buy a ring in his memory—a very common bequest at the time.

Condell and Heminges were uniquely qualified to edit Shakespeare's plays for the folio: they were the last surviving members of the original Chamberlain's Men established in 1594. They dedicated the folio to William, third earl of Pembroke, and Philip, earl of Montgomery and fourth earl of Pembroke, declaring that they had so much favoured the plays in performance and the author in his lifetime that the new volume 'ask'd' to be theirs. The editors' sole aim was to 'keepe the memory of so worthy a Friend, & Fellow alive, as was our SHAKESPEARE'—the 'our' emphasizing their admiration and love. It is sometimes supposed that the printers and publishers of the folio were also its editors, but they could not have matched Condell and Heminges in their long professional and personal association with the playwright—closely involved in each play from conception and casting, through rehearsals, to performance.

The scope and methods of the editors' attempts to 'collect' and 'gather' (their words) sources of information are the subject of ceaseless and highly conjectural study and debate. Their main source would have been Shakespeare's 'foul papers', the current term for an author's original manuscript, when available, as distinct from 'fair copies' (a phrase still in use)—these probably made by professional scribes. The term for the manuscript stage-text was 'the book': the 'book-keeper' or 'book-holder', who was also the prompter, had to submit an authentic acting version to the master of the revels (as agent of the lord chamberlain) for endorsement: without the 'approved book' no performance was possible.

Individual plays could be bought and sold, and eighteen of Shakespeare's plays were printed in quarto before publication of the thirty-six in the folio. The folio provided eighteen more hitherto unpublished texts, plus (according to the editors) 'perfect' texts of imperfect quartos. Without their efforts the world would have been deprived of plays including *The Tempest*, *Measure for Measure*, *As You Like It*, *Twelfth Night*, *Julius Caesar*, *Macbeth*, and *Antony and Cleopatra*.

In promoting their volume the editors claimed to have devoted much 'care, and paine' to correcting 'diverse stolne, and surreptitious copies, maimed, and deformed by the frauds and stealthes of injurious impostors' and to have restored the rest 'absolute in their numbers' as Shakespeare had 'conceived' them. E. K. Chambers once observed that an epistle is an advertisement rather than an affidavit: perhaps a little grudgingly he conceded that 'genuine pains' were taken to secure reliable texts. From 1608, when the King's Men were able to move into their walled and roofed Blackfriars playing-place, everything of value would have been kept there for safety, and everything in the open-air second Globe—apart from the theatre itself—survived the fire during a performance in 1613. Their rivals, the Admiral's Men, were 'utterly undone' when in 1621 their only playhouse, the open-air Fortune (close to the Barbican site) was 'burnt downe in two howres & all their apparrell & play-bookes lost' (*The Letters of John Chamberlain*, ed. N. E. McClure, 1939, 2.415).

Like many men who had done well in the capital, Condell acquired a country house in later life. A number of riverside villages, upstream from London and Westminster, were especially popular: the Condells chose Fulham in Middlesex on the north bank. Both died there, but were buried at St Mary Aldermanbury, Henry on 29 December 1627, Elizabeth on 3 October 1635: they are entered in the register as 'Mr Condell' and 'Mrs Cundell', a mark of status. (The 'u' sometimes appearing in the name probably indicates its pronunciation.) As a man of extensive properties and part ownership of the Globe and Blackfriars, Condell appointed four overseers of his will, including Heminges and Richard Burbage's elder brother Cuthbert; he expressed the wish to be buried 'decentlie in the night tyme' (Honigmann and Brock, 156–60). His well-to-do widow wished no part of her estate to be 'prodigally spent, nor lewdly wasted' by her son William (ibid., 182–6). She bequeathed her executors, Burbage and Thomas Seaman, £10 each for their pains, and wished Seaman to have all her books—including, no doubt, a copy of the Shakespeare folio.

St Mary Aldermanbury was destroyed in the fire of London and rebuilt by Sir Christopher Wren, but almost destroyed again in 1940 by enemy air attack which flattened much of this part of the City. The site is now a garden, with a bust of Shakespeare surrounded by flowering trees and shrubs. Inscriptions on the base recall the achievement of the two former long-term parishioners who, with no thought of profit or fame, collected Shakespeare's dramatic writings and gave them to the world: 'they thus merited the gratitude of mankind'. MARY EDMOND

Sources E. K. Chambers, *William Shakespeare*, 2 vols. (1939), vol. 2, pp. 72, 75, 77, 170, 228–30 • Norfolk RO • M. Eccles, 'Elizabethan actors, I: A–D', *N&Q*, 236 (1991), 38–49, esp. 44–5 • parish register, St Mary Aldermanbury, GL, MS 3572/1 [burial], 29 Dec 1627 • parish register, St Laurence Pountney, 24 Oct 1596, GL, MS 7670 [marriage] • E. A. J. Honigmann and S. Brock, eds., *Playhouse wills, 1558–1642: an edition of wills by Shakespeare and his contemporaries in the London theatre* (1993)
Wealth at death obviously a man of means; theatre interests, and props, some derived from wife; also country house at Fulham

Condell, Henry (*bap.* 1757, *d.* 1824), musician and composer, was born in London and baptized at St Martin-in-the-Fields, London, on 15 December 1757. He was the son of John Condell (*d.* 1779), a Covent Garden box-keeper, and his common-law wife, Ann Wilson. His father had previously been married to Jane Wilcox (*d.* 1752) and they had two children, John (*fl.* 1779–1784) and Charlotte (*d.* 1759).

Condell gave his first public performance on 23 May 1771 as soloist in a harpsichord concerto at Covent Garden Theatre. On 25 May 1773 he played his own harpsichord concerto for his father's benefit at the same venue. He was elected a member of the Royal Society of Musicians on 1 March 1778 and between the years 1793 and 1818 served as a member of its governing body, the court of assistants. By 1783 he was engaged as a member of the King's Theatre opera band and he played at the Pantheon with the same ensemble in 1790–91. In his *Musical Directory for the Year 1794* Joseph Doane lists him as a performer at the Concerts of Antient Music and the Professional Concerts (1794). He continued at the King's Theatre from 1800; Sainsbury describes him as 'a good violinist' (Sainsbury, 1.169) there. Condell's compositions included several songs, a piano sonata (1806?), harpsichord duets (published after 1810), and overtures to Michael Kelly's new operas—*A House to be* *Sold* (Drury Lane, 17 November 1802), *The Hero of the North*, and *Love Laughs at Locksmiths* (Haymarket, 25 July 1803)—and William Dimond's *Hero of the North* (19 February 1803). He also wrote music for Fawcett's ballet *The Enchanted Island* (Haymarket, 20 June 1804) and for several stage plays and compilations. In 1811 he gained a prize at the Catch Club for his glee 'Loud Blowe the Wyndes'.

Condell was a member of the committee that arranged the Royal Society of Music's annual concert at St Paul's in 1815. He left the King's Theatre in 1818, and by early December 1823 the news was shared with the Royal Society of Musicians that he was too unwell to attend meetings. He died at Cave House, Battersea, after a severe and lingering illness, on 24 June 1824. He is said to have had a wife and a daughter, Jane, but it seems that both predeceased him. His will, dated 5 April 1821, included annuities and jewellery bequeathed to friends and relations. His instruments and music collection were sold at auction by W. P. Musgrave on 30 March 1825.

W. B. SQUIRE, *rev.* FIONA M. PALMER

Sources Highfill, Burnim & Langhans, *BDA*, vol. 3 [Henry Condell and John Condell] • A. Loewenberg, 'Condell, Henry', *New Grove* • C. Price, J. Milhous, and R. D. Hume, *Italian opera in late eighteenth-century London*, 1: *The King's Theatre, Haymarket, 1778–1791* (1995) • *Violins, tenors, violoncellos and flutes ... with vocal and instrumental music ...late the property of Mr Condell* (1825) [sale catalogue, W. P. Musgrave, London, 30 March 1825] • [J. S. Sainsbury], ed., *A dictionary of musicians*, 2 vols. (1825); repr. (New York, 1966) • L. Baillie and R. Balchin, eds., *The catalogue of printed music in the British Library to 1980*, 62 vols. (1981–7), vol. 3, p. 201 • A. M. Clarke, *Fiddlers, ancient and modern: a biographical dictionary of fiddlers* (1895), 47 • IGI • J. Doane, ed., *A musical directory for the year 1794* [1794]
Likenesses J. Opie, portrait?
Wealth at death annuities of £30; diamond ring, silver watch; also three sums of 19 guineas; plus £29 p.a. ground rent for his property in New James Street, Oxford Road: 'Condell, Henry', Highfill, Burnim & Langhans, *BDA*, 3.437

Conder, Charles Edward (1868–1909), artist, was born on 24 October 1868 in London, the son of James Conder, a civil engineer, who in 1870 took his family to India, where he had a post as railway engineer. Mrs Conder died there in 1873, and Charles, aged five, was returned to England for private schooling. At fifteen he was sent to Sydney, New South Wales, where he entered the lands department of the colonial civil service with a view to the profession of a trigonometrical land surveyor. He disliked the work and soon abandoned it. His predilection was for art, and from an early age he drew and painted from nature. He obtained what art education he could by drawing from life at evening classes in Sydney, by study at the National Gallery of Victoria in Melbourne, and by painting in the country with other Australian artists. During August 1889, with Arthur Streeton and Tom Roberts, he contributed to a small exhibition in Melbourne, 'Sketches and impressions'. In 1890, at the Society of Victorian Artists, he showed several paintings, most of which were realistic; but among them was an imaginative work, *The Hot Wind*, which attracted notice: a nude female figure in the foreground of a sun-baked landscape, vigorously blowing into flame the ashes of a fire. Another of those pictures, *Departure of the SS 'Orient'*, was purchased for the National Gallery of New South Wales in Sydney. An uncle thereupon provided the means for studying painting, and in 1890 Conder returned to England, though Paris was his destination.

In Paris, Conder worked intermittently in the studio of Fernand Cormon and at the Académie Julian, but, always impatient of school routine, followed his own lines and studied the work of artists around him. Louis Anquetin especially influenced him and, to some extent, Honoré Daumier and Toulouse-Lautrec. In March 1891 he and William Rothenstein exhibited together at the gallery of the Paris dealer Thomas, at 43 boulevard Malesherbes; their work was reproduced in *L'Art français*. In March 1896, at the Paris gallery of Samuel Bing, noted for the influence of his Japanese collections, Conder exhibited panels on silk for the boudoir and a few designs for fans, which inaugurated his most original contributions to art. His first fan design was in oils on a wooden panel, executed about 1895. Elected an associate member of the Société Nationale des Beaux Arts in 1893, he quickly won a reputation for the originality and charm of the work which he exhibited at the society's salon.

In 1899 Conder settled in England. He joined the New English Art Club and contributed to the *Yellow Book*. From September 1897 he was one of those who exhibited regularly at the Carfax Gallery in Ryder Street, St James's, London. For the first time his art brought a fairly regular income. In 1901 he married Stella MacAdams, *née* Maris (d. 1912), a Canadian widow, and they settled at 91 Cheyne Walk, Chelsea, thereafter their permanent home. Stella created a stable domestic life, but the excesses of Conder's earlier years had undermined his health.

Conder preferred working chiefly from his exceptionally retentive memory. His paintings seemed to develop without method or scheme, but once an idea gripped him he could not rest until he had carried it through. A number have not survived because he was careless about materials, brushes, and colours. Of a few lithographs, made at Rothenstein's urging, the best are eight dated 1899, six of which are scenes from Balzac and two are fanciful subjects. A single etching by Conder is known, a drypoint, of which Rothenstein owned a print. Conder painted much in oils, his subjects being chiefly landscapes often romantically and imaginatively treated, seashore scenes, modern watering-places with gaily dressed crowds, and an occasional portrait in a decorative style. But his most characteristic works are the dainty watercolour drawings which date between 1895 and 1905, painted after a fashion of his own on panels of white silk, many shaped for fans. The delicate tones of their colour agree perfectly with the frail texture of the material. The subjects are dreamlike fancies which, while far removed from reality, reflect modern life. The colour and general character of his landscape backgrounds were derived entirely from the scenery at Chartamelle on the River Seine, but the scenery of Normandy also influenced his designs. His art has been compared with that of Antoine Watteau, but it is never constructive like that of the French master and is usually more elusive in subject.

Conder exerted a strong influence on contemporary art. His draughtsmanship was sometimes faulty, but he is appreciated for the Arcadian delicacy of his work and as one of the carriers of French influence to England in the late years of the nineteenth century. Conder died on 9 February 1909 at the Holloway Sanatorium, St Ann's Heath, Virginia Water, Surrey, and was buried in the cemetery in Virginia Water. His widow died on 18 April 1912.

F. W. GIBSON, rev. MARY LAGO

Sources J. Rothenstein, *The life and death of Conder* (1938) • J. Rothenstein, *A pot of paint* (New York, 1929); repr. (1970) • W. Rothenstein, *Men and memories: recollections of William Rothenstein*, 2 vols. (1931–2), vol. 1, pp. 55–364 • J.-E. Blanche, *Portraits of a lifetime*, ed. and trans. W. Clement (1938), 80–83 • D. S. MacColl, 'The paintings on silk of Charles Conder', *The Studio*, 13 (1898), 232–9 • C. Ricketts, 'In memory of Charles Conder', *Burlington Magazine*, 15 (1909), 8–15 • *CGPLA Eng. & Wales* (1910) • d. cert. • private information (1912)

Archives Harvard U., Houghton L., Rothenstein MSS • U. Glas. L., letters to D. S. MacColl

Likenesses W. Rothenstein, oils, 1892, Toledo Museum of Art, Ohio • W. Rothenstein, charcoal and chalk drawing, 1893, Tate collection • W. Rothenstein, oils, 1893, Tate collection • H. Toulouse-Lautrec, lithograph, 1893, Aberdeen Art Gallery • attrib. F. H. Evans, prints, c.1895–1896, NPG • C. E. Conder, self-portrait, oils, c.1895–1900, Man. City Gall. • W. Rothenstein, oils, 1896, repro. in J. Rothenstein, *The life and death of Conder* • W. Rothenstein, pencil drawing, 1896, NPG • W. Rothenstein, pastel drawing, 1897, AM Oxf. • C. E. Conder, self-portrait, oils, before 1899, Carlisle City Art Gallery • W. Orpen, chalk drawing, c.1900, V&A • C. Ricketts, group portrait, oils, c.1903 (*A fancy dress party*), Carlisle City Art Gallery • J.-E. Blanche, oils, 1904, Tate collection • M. Beerbohm, caricature, Indian ink, watercolour, and red chalk drawing, 1905, AM Oxf. • C. E. Conder, self-portrait, chalk drawing, 1905, NPG • J.-E. Blanche, portrait, repro. in Blanche, *Portraits of a lifetime* • W. Orpen, pencil, pen and ink, watercolour, and wash drawing, NPG

Wealth at death £2500: probate, 1 March 1910, *CGPLA Eng. & Wales*

Conder, Claude Reignier (1848–1910), army officer and explorer of Palestine, born at Cheltenham on 29 December 1848, was the son of Francis Roubiliac Conder (1815–1889), a civil engineer, and his wife, Anne Matilda Colt (1823–1890). Josiah *Conder, his grandfather, married a granddaughter of the sculptor Louis François Roubiliac.

After spending eight years of his youth in Italy, Conder passed from University College, London, to the Royal Military Academy at Woolwich, where he distinguished himself in surveying and drawing. He was commissioned lieutenant in the Royal Engineers on 8 January 1870, and after two years at the School of Military Engineering at Chatham was selected with the assent of the military authorities to continue a scientific survey of western Palestine, which had been begun by engineer officers under the auspices of the Palestine Exploration Fund some seven years earlier.

In July 1872 Conder took charge of the survey party at Nablus in Samaria and began by measuring a base line, about 4 miles long, near Ramlah on the road from Jaffa to Jerusalem. The triangulation was carried gradually over the whole country. After three years the greater part of the country west of the Jordan had been surveyed and a mass of information about the topography and archaeology of the country collected, while many places mentioned in the Bible and previously unknown had been identified. Conder also devoted himself to the languages of the country and to the decipherment of ancient inscriptions, to which he brought abundant ingenuity.

An attack on Conder and his party by the inhabitants of Safed, a town in the hills north-west of the Sea of Galilee (July 1875), in which Conder and others of the party were seriously injured, temporarily suspended the survey. Conder was sufficiently recovered to return to England in October 1875, after having surveyed 4700 square miles of western Palestine. The plotting of the maps from the field survey data and the preparation of the descriptive *Memoirs* were then started. A map, on a scale of one inch to the mile, was printed at the Ordnance Survey office, Southampton, and, with seven volumes of *Memoirs*, was issued by the committee of the Palestine Exploration Fund in 1880. Conder had been helped in the survey work by C. F. Tyrwhitt-Drake and in both the survey and the subsequent work by H. H. Kitchener, later Earl Kitchener of Khartoum; but it was Conder's name that was chiefly associated with the survey, which won wide acclaim for its contribution to the history, geography, and linguistic understanding of the region.

On 12 June 1877, at Guildford, Surrey, Conder married Myra Rachel, the eldest daughter of Lieutenant-General Edward Archibald Foord (*d.* 1899) of the Royal (Madras) Engineers. He returned to regimental duty in May 1878, and was employed for three years on the new defences of the Forth and stationed in Edinburgh. He continued his studies of the history and archaeology of the Holy Land and adjacent countries. In 1878 he published his first book, *Tent Work in Palestine*, illustrated with his own drawings. It gives a popular account of the survey operations and of the customs of the Palestinians, of various Bible sites, and of the topography of Jerusalem. In 1879 he published *Judas Maccabaeus and the Jewish War of Independence* and, in collaboration with his father, *Handbook to the Bible*. These works were popular, and went through several editions.

In the spring of 1881 Conder resumed his work for the Palestine Exploration Fund in the country east of the Jordan. Near the lake of Hims in the valley of the Orontes, he discovered the remains of the ancient city of Kadesh; then, going south and crossing the Jordan, a base line was measured between Heshbon and Medeba. Conder devoted special attention to the many prehistoric stone monuments in the district, photographing, describing, and making plans of them. His progress was impeded by the Turks, but he acted with great discretion, and managed to complete the survey of about 500 square miles.

On 8 January 1882 Conder was promoted captain, and in March and April he conducted princes Albert Victor and George of Wales (later George V) on a tour through Palestine. He wrote a report on the sacred harem at Hebron and another on the princes' Palestine tour (*Palestine Exploration Fund Quarterly Statement*, 1882).

After his return home in June 1882, Conder joined the expedition to Egypt, under Sir Garnet Wolseley, to suppress the rebellion of Arabi Pasha. He was appointed a deputy assistant adjutant and quartermaster-general on the staff of the intelligence department. In Egypt his knowledge of Arabic and of Eastern people proved most useful. He was present at the action of Qassasin, the battle of Tell al-Kebir, and the advance to Cairo, but then, suffering from typhoid fever, he was invalided home. For his services he received the war medal with clasp for Tell al-Kebir, the khedive's bronze star, and the fourth class of the order of the Mejidiye. On his return to good health he began plotting the survey and preparing the memoir of eastern Palestine. In 1883 he published *Heth and Moab*, a popular account of his second expedition to Palestine.

On 10 November 1883 Conder took command of a depot company at Chatham. A year later, as deputy assistant adjutant and quartermaster-general in the intelligence department, he joined the staff of Major-General Sir Charles Warren in the Bechuanaland expedition to South Africa, and the topographical work was entrusted to him. Having declined an offer of a land commissionership in South Africa, he returned to the command of his company at Chatham in October 1885. While there he published some important works: *Syrian Stone Lore* (1886), *The Canaanites* (1887), and *Altaic Hieroglyphs and Hittite Inscriptions* (1887), where he proved his philological acumen and ingenuity.

On 1 July 1887 Conder went to Plymouth to work at the Ordnance Survey, and from 1888 to 1895 he was at Southampton in charge of the engraving department. He assisted Sir Charles Wilson, then director-general of the Ordnance Survey, with the publications of the Palestine Pilgrims Text Society, of which Sir Charles was the director. In 1891 he published *Palestine*, a résumé of the history and geography of the country, and in 1893 he wrote *The Tell Amarna Tablets*, a translation and description of cuneiform characters written about 1480 BC from Palestine and Syria to the king of Egypt; they throw much light on the connection between the countries.

Conder had been promoted major on 1 July 1888. After superintending the construction of the new defences for the naval base of Berehaven in 1894, in 1895 he directed public works for the relief of distress in Ireland. He was promoted lieutenant-colonel on 12 August 1895 and appointed commanding royal engineer at Weymouth. In his five years there he wrote some of his most important works, notably *The Latin Kingdom of Jerusalem* (1897) and *The Hittites and their Language* (1898), while engaged on technical work at the naval base at Portland. He was promoted brevet colonel on 12 August 1899, and a year later was placed on half pay. Until his retirement on 2 November 1904 he was employed with the Ordnance Survey in Ireland. Thereafter he lived at Cheltenham, where he died, at his home, St Oswald's, Tivoli Road, on 16 February 1910, following a stroke a month earlier. He left a widow, a daughter, and a son.

Conder was a prolific author of both scholarly and popular works. Although his linguistic theories were contested even in his own lifetime, his reputation as a great explorer and surveyor has endured.

R. H. VETCH, rev. ROBIN A. BUTLIN

Sources Y. Ben-Arieh, *The rediscovery of the Holy Land in the nineteenth century* (1979) · W. Besant, *Thirty years' work in the Holy Land of the Palestine Exploration Fund* (1895) · F. G. Bliss, *The development of Palestine exploration* (1906) · B. Tuchman, *Bible and sword* (1956) · *The Times* (17 Feb 1910) · C. M. Watson, 'Colonel C. R. Conder', *Royal Engineers Journal*, new ser., 11 (1910), 283–8 · *GJ*, 35 (1910), 456–8 · *Palestine Exploration Fund Quarterly Statement* (April 1910) · C. C. Close, 'Claude Reignier Conder, 1848–1910, and the survey of Palestine', *Empire Survey Review*, 7 (1944), 234–40 · G. A. Smith, *The historical geography of the Holy Land* (1894) · d. cert. · *CGPLA Eng. & Wales* (1910)

Archives BL, papers relating to survey of western Palestine, Add. MS 69848 · Israeli and Jewish National Library, Jerusalem · Palestine Exploration Fund, London, papers relating to Palestine exploration · RIBA BAL, report on remains at Baalbek | NL Scot., letters to Blackwoods, MSS 4373–4698

Wealth at death £1070 13s. 1d.: probate, 26 Feb 1910, *CGPLA Eng. & Wales*

Conder, James (1761–1823), numismatist and antiquary, the youngest of seven sons of John *Conder DD (1714–1781), Independent minister, and his wife, Susan, daughter of John Flindell, leatherseller of Ipswich, was born at Mile End, Middlesex, on 22 October 1761. He was educated at the dissenters' academy at Ware and under Mr French, a Unitarian minister. At the age of nineteen he moved to Ipswich, where his brother John was working for Flindell (whom he later succeeded). Conder married, on 1 January 1790, Mary Foster (1758–1836), third daughter of George Notcutt, haberdasher, of Ipswich, and his wife, Thomasin Moore, and set up as linen draper in Tavern Street. He sold this business to Shepherd Ray in 1808, and reopened in the Buttermarket, Ipswich, in partnership with his wife's widowed sister Elizabeth Goddard as Goddard and Conder, haberdashers and snuffsellers.

As well as mainstream coins Conder built up an unrivalled collection of trade tokens produced by firms as advertisement and as change at a time when small copper coins were in short supply. In the mid-1790s he issued several tokens advertising his drapery warehouse, the most striking designed by the eminent medallist John Milton (d. 1805). Conder's enthusiasm ran to the lengths of contriving rarities by altering or breaking dies after striking small numbers of coins, and to the publication in 1798 and 1799 of a catalogue of all known tokens issued in the British Isles and the colonies 'within the last twenty years', a work sold at Bucklersbury in London by his elder brother Thomas. Although his projected history of nonconformism in Suffolk came to nothing, Conder's help is acknowledged by Walter Wilson in the preface to his *Dissenting Churches* (1808), and by Benjamin Brook in his *Lives of the Puritans* (1813).

Conder's interest in Suffolk topography brought him the friendship of the Revd James Ford (1779–1850), who wrote a eulogistic obituary of Conder over the initials J. F. in the *Gentleman's Magazine*. Conder's collection of prints and drawings to illustrate the county's history was celebrated, a model for those of G. R. S. Nassau and W. S. Fitch. His ownership of the manuscript copy of the Suffolk collections made c.1655 by Matthias Candler (now Society of Antiquaries MS 667) caused much confusion in nineteenth-century literature when cited as the Conder MS. He played a principal part in founding the Ipswich Friendly Society in 1810 and was generous in its support.

Conder died after a sudden illness on 22 March 1823 in the Buttermarket, Ipswich, and was buried six days later in the grounds of the Independent meeting-house in Tacket Street where the family worshipped. His brother-in-law the Revd Charles Atkinson, who was minister there, preached the sermon. The eldest of his seven children, James Notcutt Conder, took his father's place with his aunt in the business until her death in 1830 in the timber-framed house distinguished by its fine carved cornerpost, 8 feet high, at the corner of St Lawrence Lane and the Buttermarket. It is perhaps ironic that when in 1863 the house was demolished a hoard of over a hundred silver pennies of Ethelred the Unready, some minted in Ipswich, was discovered under the staircase; as they were 5 feet deep one can probably rule out the possibility that Conder hid the coins there for posterity. Conder's widow lived with her daughter Mary Nash in Wymondham, Norfolk, until her death in 1836, when she was buried beside her husband.

J. M. BLATCHLY

Sources *GM*, 1st ser., 93/1 (1823), 648–50 · H. R. Lingwood, 'Worthies of Ipswich no. 17', *East Anglian Daily Times* (14 Oct 1933) · *Ipswich Journal* (1803–23) · *Ipswich Journal* (31 Oct 1863) · M. E. Notcutt and M. P. Sartin, *The Notcutt family history, 1515–1989* (1989) · *IGI* · Register of Independent meeting-house, Tacket Street, Ipswich

Likenesses G. Rowe, lithographs, pubd 1821, Suffolk RO, Ipswich

Wealth at death under £800: will, proved 11 June 1823

Conder, John (1714–1781), Independent minister and tutor, was born on 3 June 1714 at Wimpole, Cambridgeshire, the son of Jabez Conder (d. 1727) and Elizabeth Linkern (1688/9–1730). He came from old nonconformist stock as both his father and grandfather served as minister to an Independent congregation at Croyden in Cambridgeshire. John was sent to school first with the Revd Mr Hicks, a Latin master at Potton, Bedfordshire. On the sudden death of his father from a riding accident in 1727, he was transferred to the grammar school at Hitchin, where he boarded first with Francis Robinson, who died suddenly from smallpox, and subsequently with the headmaster, Mr J. Newman. Conder's recovery from the same smallpox seems to mark a new seriousness in life, leaving behind 'wild' colleagues who enticed him into 'habits of idle-gossiping, card-playing and other vanities' (*Evangelical Magazine*). He was initially a reluctant scholar, and cherished the hope of following former generations of Conders in farming. After leaving school he proceeded to Dr Parsons's academy at Clerkenwell and from there to the academy run by the King's Head Society, under the direction of Dr Thomas Ridgley and Dr John Eames, then situated at the Plasterers' Hall, Moorfields.

Conder started his ministerial career in Cambridge, at

Hog Hill Independent Church on 23 November 1738, and was ordained there on 27 September following. Restoring harmony to a divided congregation, he reportedly gave instruction to three future bishops of the Church of England: Edmund Keen, William Markham, and Bielby Porteus. An encounter with a highwayman on the road to Peterborough became an evangelistic opportunity: Conder's goods were returned, but his assailant was soon recognized and apprehended. The highwayman was sentenced to death; Conder, who was diligent in visiting him in prison, believed he died a converted man. On 8 March 1744 he married Susan (d. 1785), daughter of John Flindell, leather seller, of Ipswich; they had seven sons.

During his Cambridge pastorate Conder penned *A Serious Address to all Sober Christians of every Denomination among Protestant Dissenters … on the Important Subject of a Gospel Ministry* (1753); this brought him to the attention of the managers of the King's Head Society, who in October 1754 appointed him theological tutor in place of Dr Zephaniah Marryat and boarding tutor at their academy as it moved from Moorfields to Mile End in the following year. To these duties he added the merchant's lecture at Pinners' Hall from October 1759, and on 21 May 1760 he became assistant to the increasingly enfeebled Thomas Hall, minister at Little Moorfields (later the Pavement); he succeeded him on his death in 1762. When the academy moved to Homerton in 1770 Conder ceased to be boarding tutor, residing in Hackney instead. From 1778 William Bennet was his assistant at the Pavement.

In occupying a major London pulpit while fully engaged in running an academy, Conder had double work imposed upon 'his Head, Heart and Hands' (Winter, 36). In so doing, his great aim was to provide a scholarly evangelical ministry for the churches at a time when there appeared to be much heterodoxy. Thus in both pulpit and study he affirmed the importance of evangelical doctrine; after searching the scriptures 'with the closest attention and care' he could attest its truth with 'full assurance of faith'; 'it was the darling theme of his ministrations to recommend Christ in his person, office, work, and grace unto poor sinners' (Webb, 26). He stressed the importance of the nonconformist tradition, but was not sectarian, for even among dissenters he discerned too much party spirit both within and between denominations. Concern for unity was not, however, to be at the expense of doctrine; indeed he lamented the 'general disrelish and disuse of the several great doctrines of Scripture and the reformation' (J. Conder, *A Serious Address to All Sober Christians … on the Important Subject of a Gospel Ministry*, 1753, 14) by younger divines, which he identified as the major reason why, under their leadership, once flourishing congregations languished. Critical that insufficient scrutiny was undertaken of those offering themselves for ministry, he even included Philip Doddridge within the terms of his censure. Scrutiny of academic capacity was not enough, for vocational aptitude for the evangelical ministry had also to be probed. Although goodness was a necessary prerequisite, Conder argued that not every good man was qualified to undertake a gospel ministry, which required

that candidates be 'partakers of the evangelical grace of regeneration', a conviction shared, he believed, by traditional Calvinists, moderate Calvinists, and Arminians alike (ibid., 22).

Addressing the Society for the Reformation of Manners in 1763 Conder affirmed the importance of the Reformation in securing that 'liberty, civil and religious, which is the boast and the glory of Britons', but argued that the Reformation needed to be earthed in the lifestyle of each individual. Furthermore the maintenance of civil order was an important ministry, for which all Christians had a responsibility, for by their lives they either advanced Satan's kingdom or curbed it. Since governors and magistrates were God's standing representatives in maintaining order, they needed to be appointed wisely. For their part, Christian ministers were called upon 'both to preach down and live down the vice and immoralities of the times' (J. Conder, *A Sermon Preached before the Society for the Reformation of Manners*, 1763, 16).

Without prior knowledge on his part, Conder was awarded a DD by the University of Aberdeen. The sudden death of his son William, aged nineteen, in 1769 was a trauma from which he never fully recovered. A paralytic stroke, which he survived only a few weeks, occasioned his death in Hackney on 30 May 1781. Conder was buried at Bunhill Fields the Tuesday following, his self-composed epitaph reading: 'Peccavi, Resipui, Confidi, Amavi, Requiesco, Resurgam. Et ex gratia Christi, ut ut indignus, regnabo.' He was survived by his wife. Of his children, Thomas was a cartographer and bookseller and the father of Josiah Conder (1789–1855), hymn writer and doyen of nonconformist journalists, and James *Conder (1761–1823) a haberdasher who made a name for himself as a numismatist. J. H. Y. BRIGGS

Sources *Evangelical Magazine*, 3 (1795), 393ff. · R. Winter, *A sermon preached at the meeting house in Little Moorfields … May 21, 1760* (1760) · J. Webb, *God's faithfulness a sure ground of hope and comfort to believers, a sermon occasioned by the death of John Conder* (1781) · C. Surman, index, DWL · *DNB*

Archives CUL, declaration of faith · DWL, lectures and MSS

Likenesses S. Webster, oils, 1775, DWL · portrait, repro. in *Evangelical Magazine*, 393

Conder, Josiah (1789–1855), bookseller and writer, was born in Falcon Street, Aldersgate, London, on 17 September 1789, the son of Thomas Conder (1746/7–1831), a map engraver and bookseller, and his wife, Elisabeth. His grandfather Dr John Conder was president of Old College, Homerton. In 1795 Josiah contracted smallpox, and the severity of the disease entirely destroyed his right eye. He was educated under the Revd Mr Palmer at Hackney, and at the early age of ten contributed essays to the *Monthly Preceptor*.

At thirteen Conder left school and entered the bookselling business of his father, at 30 Bucklersbury, London, where in his leisure he carried out a system of self-education. To the eleventh number of *The Athenaeum* (1806), edited by Dr Aikin, he contributed some lines entitled 'The Withered Oak', and about this time he became acquainted with James Montgomery and Ann Taylor. His poetical contributions to various periodicals being well received, in 1810 he published an anonymous volume entitled *The Associate Minstrels*, to which Ann and Jane Taylor and others contributed. It reached a second edition within three years.

In the autumn of 1811 his father retired from the business for health reasons, and Josiah Conder took it over. On 8 February 1815 he married Joan Elizabeth, second daughter of Roger Thomas of Southgate, Middlesex, and granddaughter on her mother's side of Louis François Roubiliac, the sculptor. They resided at his new shop at 18 St Paul's Churchyard until 1819, when he disposed of the business to B. J. Holdsworth. They had four sons and one daughter. Conder had become proprietor of the *Eclectic Review* in 1814, and he retained the management of this periodical until 1837, when he transferred it to Dr Thomas Price, having during his editorship supported the dissenting interest. He was a great letter-writer, and kept up a correspondence with James Montgomery, Robert Southey, Revd Robert Hall, Revd John Foster, and other literary men of the day. In 1818 he brought out a work in two volumes, entitled *On Protestant Nonconformity*, of which a second edition appeared in 1822. In 1824 he entered into an agreement with James Duncan of Paternoster Row to edit the afterwards well-known series of the Modern Traveller, undertaking in the first instance to furnish the volume on Palestine only. Ultimately he compiled the whole set of thirty volumes (1825–9), having assistance in only one or two of them. The series was successful, despite the fact of its editor's never having left his native country. On the establishment of the *Patriot* newspaper in 1832 to represent the principles of evangelical nonconformity, Conder became its editor, an office which he held for twenty-three years.

Conder was one of the most industrious of men. Throughout his life he worked long hours for the support of himself and his family, yet he found time to act as a preacher, and to keep up an extensive correspondence on religious and literary topics. He was a prolific writer, editor, and compiler. Some of his works in these roles include: *Thomas Johnson's Reasons for Dissent* (1821); *Memoirs of Pious Women, by Gibbons and Burder* (1823); *The Star in the East with other Poems* (1824); *The Law of the Sabbath* (1830; new edn, 1852); *Wages or the Whip* (an essay on free and slave labour, 1833); *The Congregational Hymn-Book* (1834; another edn, 1836); *Narrative of a Residence in South Africa, by T. Pringle, with a Sketch of the Author* (1835); *An Analytical Sketch of All Religions* (1838); and *The Psalms of David Imitated by I. Watts, Revised by J. Conder* (1851).

Conder wrote steadily until 9 November 1855, when he fell ill from jaundice, from which he never recovered. He died at his home, 28 Belsize Road, St John's Wood, London, on 27 December 1855, and was buried in Abney Park cemetery on 3 January 1856.

G. C. BOASE, rev. REBECCA MILLS

Sources E. R. Conder, *Josiah Conder: a memoir* (1857) · Watt, *Bibl. Brit.*, vol. 1 · IGI · GM, 2nd ser., 45 (1856), 205–6 · J. Harris, *The divine net: a discourse on the death of J. Conder* (1856) · *Eclectic Review*, 9 (1857), 244
Archives Suffolk RO, Bury St Edmunds, corresp. and papers | Sheff. Arch., letters to James Montgomery
Likenesses B. R. Haydon, group portrait, oils, c.1840 (*The Antislavery Society Convention, 1840*), NPG

Conder, Josiah (1852–1920), architect and artist, was born on 28 September 1852 at 22 Russell Grove, Brixton, Surrey, the second son of Josiah Conder (1822–1864) and his wife, Eliza, *née* Willsher (1820–1899). Josiah Conder senior, who may have been a banker, left the family impoverished at his death. Conder won a scholarship to Bedford Commercial School, which he attended between 1865 and 1868. On his return to London he enrolled at South Kensington School of Art and also at University College, London. There seems little doubt that his choice of a career was influenced by Thomas Roger *Smith (1830–1903), a relative, who was lecturer (1871–81) and later professor of architecture (1881–1903) at University College, London. Smith also ran, independently, an architects' office, where Conder went to work. Later Conder was employed in the architectural office of William Burges (1827–1881). Burges was the foremost medievalist in the architectural profession and, since the London exhibition of 1862, which featured a display of Japanese craftwork, had developed a keen interest in Japan.

In 1876, at the age of twenty-four, Conder won the Soane medallion for a design for a country house. Probably because of this on 18 October 1876 he signed a contract with the imperial Japanese government to serve in Tokyo, at the Imperial College of Engineering as professor of architecture. The Imperial College of Engineering was a remarkable, innovative, pioneering institution, founded under the auspices of the ministry of public works in 1872. It remained independent until 1886, when it became the faculty of engineering in the Imperial University, Tokyo. This college was, between 1872 and 1886, under the direct personal supervision of the new young Meiji leaders and thus Conder had direct access to the new source of power in Japan. His work in Japan involved him in teaching the first generation of architects in the Western tradition and in acting as architect to the new energetic and innovative Japanese government. Because of William Burges's medievalism, Conder arrived in Japan receptive to it and to its culture. He taught his students to admire and be proud of the great Japanese temples and castles. Nevertheless, Conder's basic teaching was geared to European, rather than Asian, architecture, as his examination papers indicate. For example the 1884 final examination included the questions 'Give a brief history of the architectural styles in Italy mentioning special examples' and 'Sketch carefully, and in proper proportion, a Grecian Doric entablature, an early English Gothic capital and a vaulting rib, a Perpendicular window, and a Renaissance window' (*Josiah Conder*, 171).

Conder organized the teaching of his students in exemplary fashion: they wanted to learn about Western architecture, and did so. His pupils, including Kingo Tatsuno (1854–1919), Tatsuzo Sone (1853–1937), Tokuna Katayama

(1854–1917), Yorinaka Tsumaki, and George Shimoda (1866–1931), became important Western-style architects. Several of the buildings they designed are still in use today. Conder himself designed the Rokumeikan, a famous italianate building, used as a social club in early Meiji Japan but later pulled down. He also designed other public buildings, none of which survives. In his later years he concentrated on designing fine houses for wealthy Japanese patrons: several survive. In 1884 the emperor honoured him with the order of the Rising Sun, fourth class, and in 1894 the order of the Sacred Treasure, third class, and official rank of honorary *chokunin*.

In 1881 Conder made a commitment to Japanese art by becoming a pupil of Kyosai Kawanabe (1831–1889), nicknamed the Demon of Painting, who taught Conder at the latter's home each Saturday. These were family occasions. Painter and architect became close friends and they travelled on painting expeditions together to Nikko and Kamakura, places of pilgrimage and great beauty within reasonable distance of Tokyo. Kyosai had originally resisted the new regime, which required co-operation with the foreigners, but with the passage of time and the friendship with Conder, his attitude changed.

Conder's publications included *The Flowers of Japan and the Art of Floral Arrangement* (1891), *Landscape Gardening in Japan* (1893), *The Floral Art of Japan* (1899), and *Paintings and Studies by Kawanabe Kyosai* (1911), as well as articles on aspects of Japan in *Transactions of the Royal Institute of British Architects*, *The Builder*, *Transactions of the Asiatic Society of Japan*, and elsewhere.

Conder settled in Japan, and married Mayeba (Maenami) Kume; they had no children. Kume died on 10 June and Conder on 21 June 1920, and they were both buried at Gokokuji Temple, Tokyo. Conder had a daughter, Helen Aiko, who in 1906 married Commander William Lennart Grut of the Swedish navy.   OLIVE CHECKLAND

Sources *Josiah Conder* (1977) · O. Checkland, *Britain's encounter with Meiji Japan, 1868–1912* (1989) · W. H. Coaldrake, *Architecture and authority in Japan* (1996) · T. Kinoshita, 'Josiah Conder: the father of modern Japanese architecture', MA diss., Royal Holloway College, Egham, Surrey, 1996 · *WWW*, 1897–1915
Archives University of Tokyo
Likenesses photographs, repro. in *Railway Station Gallery Catalogue* (1997) · statue, possibly University of Tokyo

Conder, Peter John (1919–1993), ornithologist and conservationist, was born on 20 March 1919 at 81 Thornton Avenue, Streatham, London, the son of John Reynolds Conder, a shipbroker, and his wife Edna Frances, *née* Benson. Conder's interest in birds began with egg collecting, an activity he later opposed. He was educated at Cranleigh School, Surrey; he won a prize when in the junior school for completing a bird diary, and his basic training in ornithology came through the school ornithological society and one of his schoolmasters, Marston Henniker-Godley. Conder recalled sneaking from the school dormitory for early morning bird-watching expeditions. After leaving school he was sent to Lausanne to learn French and spent six weeks in Newfoundland on a British Schools Exploring Society expedition. In the spring of 1938 he

became a clerk in the voucher department of the advertising agency of Samuel Herbert *Benson (1854–1914), his maternal grandfather and one of the pioneers of advertising in England.

As war approached Conder joined the Territorial Army and was commissioned into the Royal Corps of Signals. When the British expeditionary force was sent to France in 1939 his unit was part of the 51st Highland division, and in June 1940 he was captured at St Valery-sur-Somme. During almost five years' incarceration his interest in ornithology helped him to survive. For him the wild birds that flew freely in and out of the camp were objects of hope. He spent part of this period in Eichstatt in Bavaria, where he watched migrants passing over and studied the breeding behaviour of goldfinches, later publishing the results in *Ibis* in 1948. He made notes of his observations on any paper he could find. The camp guards became accustomed to the lone bird-watcher wandering around the camp and constantly taking notes, an activity that gave him the opportunity to record the routine of his captors and thus to provide intelligence for escape attempts.

After demobilization Conder did not relish spending the rest of his working life in an advertising agency and he resigned within a month of returning to S. H. Benson. In 1947, after a short period at the British Museum (Natural History), he became warden of Skokholm bird observatory, where he studied wheatears, the subject of his monograph *The Wheatear* (1990). On 12 January 1952 he married Patricia Neale (b. 1919/20), daughter of John Freeman Higginson, an outfitter, of Tenbury Wells, Worcestershire. In 1954 he became assistant secretary of the Royal Society for the Protection of Birds (RSPB) at the society's headquarters in London. His responsibilities were varied and Conder, who always claimed to be an amateur, described himself as a jack of all trades, dealing with reserves, prosecutions, and protection work.

The RSPB, which had 20,000 members and few staff, moved from its London office to a country house in Bedfordshire in 1961. The move produced a financial surplus and the consequent opportunity to expand. When Conder became director in 1963 he appointed specialist staff to deal with nature reserves, research, education, publications, film, and financial administration. The competent, enthusiastic team he created built on the opportunities they had, so that when Conder retired thirteen years later membership had risen to over 200,000 and there had been some spectacular conservation achievements. The society had been a major contributor to the successful campaign to stop the use of organochlorine pesticides; ospreys had become established once more as a breeding species in Britain; and the society's list of nature reserves was added to each year. Perhaps more important was the growing realization of the significance of research to successful nature conservation, an applied science that was beginning to be taken seriously by government.

Conder himself took most pride in the campaign against pesticides but, almost certainly, his greatest achievement was to lay the foundations that made the

RSPB one of the world's leading voluntary nature conservation organizations. His greatest disappointment was the failure of the RSPB and the Society for the Promotion of Nature Reserves (later the Wildlife Trusts) to merge in the 1970s. The result, he felt, would have created a really influential organization.

Although a relatively shy man, Conder was able to communicate his passion for nature and its conservation both in writing and orally. His retirement at fifty-seven, at a time when the RSPB was growing, showed his understanding of the need for leaders not to outstay their usefulness, though one of his staff wrote that 'he could have easily gone for another 10 years and would have had the loyal support of his staff' (*The Independent*, 18 Oct 1993).

In the 1976 new year's honours Conder was appointed OBE. He was awarded the RSPB's gold medal in 1976 and an honorary MA from the Open University in 1977. He spent his retirement writing, birdwatching, and travelling, sometimes as a tour leader, sometimes as a consultant to overseas conservation organizations, and sometimes on holiday. He spent much of the year in Comberton, Cambridgeshire, and was a regular visitor to Alderney for over twenty years. He died at Arthur Rank House, Cambridge, on 8 October 1993 after suffering from cancer. He was survived by his wife, one son, and a daughter.

NICHOLAS HAMMOND

Sources J. Samstag, *For the love of birds* (1988), 77–9 · *The Times* (12 Oct 1993) · R. Porter, *The Independent* (18 Oct 1993) · R. Scott, 'Peter Conder, OBE, Hon MA (1919–1983)', *British Birds*, 87 (Feb 1994), 70–72 · b. cert. · m. cert. · d. cert.
Archives CUL, corresp. with Sir Peter Markham Scott · Royal Society for the Protection of Birds Archives, Sandy, Bedfordshire
Likenesses photograph, repro. in *The Times* · photograph, repro. in *The Independent*
Wealth at death £109,936: probate, 1994, *CGPLA Eng. & Wales*

Conduitt, John (1688–1737), politician, of Cranbury Park in Hampshire, was the son of Leonard and Sarah Conduitt, and was baptized at St Paul's, Covent Garden, London, on 8 March 1688. He was admitted into Westminster School as a king's scholar in June 1701, and in June 1705 matriculated at Trinity College, Cambridge. After leaving the university he travelled in Europe. In 1711 he was judge-advocate with the British forces in Portugal, and in the following year he was made captain in a regiment of dragoons serving in that country. On 26 August 1717 he married Catherine Barton (*d.* 1739), the niece of Sir Isaac Newton and the reputed mistress of the late Charles Montagu, earl of Halifax. The couple had one daughter.

In June 1721 Conduitt was elected, on petition, whig member for Whitchurch, Hampshire, which he represented during the 1720s as a loyal supporter of Walpole's government. At this time he was also performing the duties of master of the Royal Mint for his wife's uncle, and on Newton's death on 20 March 1727 Conduitt succeeded him in this position. Soon after, Conduitt drew up a memorial sketch for Fontenelle, who was producing Newton's eulogy for the French Académie des Sciences. The finished work was not satisfactory to Conduitt, who criticized Fontenelle for having 'neither abilities nor inclination to do

justice to that great man, who has eclipsed the glory of their hero, Descartes'. He resolved to write Newton's life and began to gather information. Though the biography was never written, Conduitt collected a wealth of material, including Newton's famous comparison of himself to 'a boy playing on the sea-shore and diverting myself in now and then finding a smoother pebble or a prettier shell than ordinary while the great ocean of truth lay all undiscovered before me'.

In his post at the mint Conduitt wrote the clear and much praised *Observations on the Present State of our Gold and Silver Coins* (1730), posthumously published in 1774. The chief objects of the memoir, drawn up at a time when gold was falling in value and silver rising, were to advocate the coinage of the latter metal in preference to the former, and to recommend a reduction in the weight of the silver currency.

By the early 1730s Conduitt had become a relatively prominent parliamentary speaker, defending the government on a number of issues, including Walpole's maintenance of the Septennial Act. In 1734 he was re-elected to his seat but chose to represent Southampton. Two years later (12 January 1736) he introduced a successful bill repealing an early seventeenth-century act against conjuration and witchcraft. He died on 23 May 1737 and was buried in Westminster Abbey on the right-hand side of Sir Isaac Newton. His wife, Catherine, who died in 1739, was buried with him. Their daughter married on 8 July 1740 Viscount Lymington, the eldest son of the first earl of Portsmouth; their son succeeded as second earl of Portsmouth.

PHILIP CARTER

Sources P. Watson, 'Conduitt, John', HoP, *Commons* · *GM*, 1st ser., 7 (1737), 316 · Venn, *Alum. Cant.* · C. E. Challis, ed., *A new history of the royal mint* (1992) · *Old Westminsters* · *DNB* · I. Bostridge, *Witchcraft and its transformations, c.1650–c.1750* (1997)
Likenesses J. S. Tanner, silver medals, BM

Condy, Henry Bollmann (*bap.* 1826, *d.* 1907), chemical manufacturer, was born at Sloane Street, London, and was baptized on 20 August 1826 at St Luke's, Chelsea, the son of George Thomas Condy, barrister and newspaper proprietor, and his wife, Charlotte, the daughter of Colonel Foot of the Scots Greys. He was educated at Brompton Grammar School and later at the Royal College of Chemistry at Oxford Street, London.

In 1843 his mother inherited from Dr Bollmann, a Hungarian chemist, the chemical manufactory of C. Foot & Co. which had been founded at Battersea in 1816. Mrs Condy maintained the business until her son's education was complete, whereupon he took over. The chief products were acetic acid, acetate salts, mineral acids, albumen, pharmaceuticals, and other chemicals. Condy eliminated unprofitable product lines and made significant improvements to production methods, for which he took out fifteen patents over the period from 1852 to 1888. On 19 October 1850 Condy married Eleanor Chrisse at St Dunstan-in-the-East, London. They had three sons and one daughter.

Condy's interest in hygiene and disinfection was evident in sales of 'ozone water', in his patents dealing with the preparation and use of chlorine and of highly oxidized compounds of manganese, and in his authorship of five short books on the topic between 1860 and 1867. It was because of this interest that he was awarded a Red Cross medal for services rendered to the sick and wounded during the Franco-Prussian War. Solutions of sodium manganate and permanganate, patented in 1856 and 1876, were marketed as 'Condy's fluid', and the derived solid as 'Condy's crystals'. These were widely used as disinfectants and the crystals in particular for treatment of snakebite after Dr Lacerda recommended potassium permanganate for this purpose in 1881.

Imitators who marketed potassium permanganate as 'Condy's crystals' (and solutions of it as his fluid) were the subject of litigation which reached its height in Australia at the turn of the century. Although successful, it failed to change the popular belief that Condy's crystals are potassium permanganate. Other litigation between Condy and A. D. Mitchell, who had joined the firm in 1870, led at first to estrangement and then to reconstitution of the company as Condy and Mitchell Ltd, with Mitchell and Condy's eldest son, H. J. Bollmann Condy, as managing directors. From this point the elder Condy gradually withdrew from the business while continuing his interests in industrial chemistry, foreign travel, and horse-riding. He died at his home, 4 The Leas, Folkestone, on 24 September 1907. IAN D. RAE, rev.

Sources Chemist and Druggist (5 Oct 1907) · Chemist and Druggist (12 Oct 1907) · Chemist and Druggist (13 June 1908) · Chemist and Druggist (31 July 1909) · The Times (28 Nov 1877) · Australasian J. of Pharmacy (Nov 1901) · H. B. Condy, patents, 1852–88 · m. cert. · d. cert.
Wealth at death £10,623 10s. 1d.: probate, 4 June 1908, CGPLA Eng. & Wales

Condy, Nicholas (1793–1857), landscape painter, was baptized on 2 April 1793 at Withiel, Cornwall, the son of Nicholas Condy of Mevagissey and his wife, Elizabeth Thomas. He had at least two siblings: John Thomas Condy (bap. 1791 at Mevagissey) and Ann Condy (bap. 1795). He was gazetted to the 43rd regiment as an ensign, on 9 May 1811, and served in the Peninsular War. On 3 October 1814 he married Ann Trevanion Pyle (1792–1860), the daughter of Captain Mark Oates of the marines, at Stoke Damerel, Devon. On 24 February 1818 he was promoted lieutenant, and that same year he retired on half pay. He afterwards lived in Plymouth, where he devoted himself to becoming a professional painter.

Condy produced chiefly small watercolours on tinted paper, about 8 inches by 5 inches, which he sold at prices ranging from 15s. to 1 guinea. He painted many shore scenes with figures and craft in the background, mostly local to Plymouth; he favoured 'rather garish red and greens', and his technique has been described as 'somewhat impressionistic', and 'very appealing' (Mallalieu, Watercolour artists, 65).

In the 1830s Condy associated with the Society of Plymouth Artists and Amateurs, which is said to have met fortnightly in the city. Between 1830 and 1845 he exhibited two landscapes at the Royal Academy, four at the British Institution, and a single work at Suffolk Street. He

also exhibited two works at the Liverpool Academy in 1853, An Interior—Children Buying Sweets and A Cornish Cottage. His best-known painting is The Old Hall at Cotehele on a Rent-Day, which was purchased by the earl of Mount Edgcumbe. Condy later published Cothele, on the Banks of the Tamar (c.1850), illustrated with seventeen lithographed plates.

Condy died on 8 January 1857 at his home, 10 Mount Pleasant Terrace, Plymouth, having suffered paralysis in the last four years of his life, and was buried in St Andrew's churchyard, Plymouth. He was survived by his wife. His son, **Nicholas Matthews Condy** (1818–1851), who has often been confused with his father, was born at Union Street, Plymouth. He was educated at Exeter and was intended for the army or navy, but preferred instead to become a painter. He settled in his native town, where he both practised and taught painting. Between 1842 and 1845 he exhibited three sea-pieces at the Royal Academy. These gave hopes of his becoming a distinguished artist, but he died suddenly and prematurely at The Grove, Plymouth, on 20 May 1851. He was survived by his wife, Flora Ross, the third daughter of Major John Lockhart Gallie, of the 28th regiment. G. C. BOASE, rev. MARK POTTLE

Sources Wood, Vic. painters, 2nd edn · E. H. H. Archibald, Dictionary of sea painters (1980) · Mallalieu, Watercolour artists · private information (2004) · T. Fawcett, The rise of English provincial art (1974) · E. Morris and E. Roberts, The Liverpool Academy and other exhibitions of contemporary art in Liverpool, 1774–1867 (1998) · Bryan, Painters (1886–9) · N&Q, 6th ser., 11 (1885), 17 · Smith's Plymouth Almanac (1885) · d. cert.

Condy, Nicholas Matthews (1818–1851). See under Condy, Nicholas (1793–1857).

Conesford. For this title name see Strauss, Henry George, Baron Conesford (1892–1974).

Coney, John (1786–1833), draughtsman and engraver, was born in Ratcliff Highway, London, and was apprenticed to an architect, but he never followed the profession. Among his early studies were pencil drawings of the interior of Westminster Abbey. In 1805 he exhibited the first of ten works at the Royal Academy, a Perspective View of Lambeth Palace, from 39 Craven Street, Strand. His first publication was a work entitled A Series of Views Representing the Exterior and Interior of Warwick Castle (1815). The plates were drawn and etched by himself.

Coney was next employed for fourteen years by Harding to draw and engrave a series of exterior and interior views of the cathedrals and abbey churches of England, intended to illustrate the new edition of Sir William Dugdale's Monasticon Anglicanum, edited by Sir Henry Ellis (1846). In 1829 he began to engrave cathedrals, town halls, and other buildings in France, the Netherlands, Germany, and Italy, with descriptions in four languages. These were published in London in 1832. The next important work, also engraved and designed by himself, was The Beauties of Continental Architecture (1843), which included twenty-eight plates and fifty vignettes. Coney was employed by the architect Charles Cockerell to engrave a large view of Rome, and he also engraved some drawings of the Law

Courts, Westminster, for Sir John Soane. In addition to the above-mentioned works he was the author of *English Ecclesiastical Edifices of the Olden Time* (1842, the plates of which were previously used in Dugdale's *Monasticon*) and *Original Drawings of London Churches* (1820). Coney died of an enlargement of the heart in Leicester Place, Camberwell, on 15 August 1833. Prints and drawings by him are in the British Museum and the Victoria and Albert Museum in London, the National Gallery of Ireland in Dublin, Manchester City Galleries, and the Nottingham Castle Museum. L. A. FAGAN, *rev.* DENNIS HARRINGTON

Sources Bryan, *Painters* · Bénézit, *Dict.*, 4th edn · Thieme & Becker, *Allgemeines Lexikon* · G. Meissner, ed., *Allgemeines Künstlerlexikon: die bildenden Künstler aller Zeiten und Völker*, [new edn, 34 vols.] (Leipzig and Munich, 1983-) · Graves, *RA exhibitors* · A. M. Hind, *A history of engraving and etching*, 3rd edn (1923) · Mallalieu, *Watercolour artists*

Congal Cáech (d. 637), high-king of Ireland, was killed at the great battle of Mag Roth in 637; the date of his birth is unknown and even his parentage is uncertain. He appears in the annals from 626 until his death in 637, and in the regnal list of the province of Ulster he is given a reign of ten years. He is also included in the regnal list of Dál nAraidi, whose principal kingdom was Mag Line, the valley of the Antrim Water on the east side of Lough Neagh. By the end of the seventh century Dál nAraidi had expanded along the east side of the River Bann as far as Coleraine, but this may only just have started in Congal's day. The genealogies of Dál nAraidi either place Congal in different places or omit his name altogether: he may have belonged to another kingdom among the Cruithni, a group of peoples, including Dál nAraidi, along the east side of the River Bann from Coleraine in the north to Louth in the south. Congal Cáech was the last king of Tara until Brian Bóruma, three and a half centuries later, not to belong to the Uí Néill. All the regnal lists of Tara, even the *Baile Chuind* of the late seventh century, omit his name. What confirms his status is the near-contemporary law-tract *Bechbretha* ('bee-judgements'). This is concerned with Congal Cáech because, it claims, he was blinded in one eye by bees (hence the epithet Cáech, 'One-Eyed' or 'Squinting'), and this physical defect caused him to be removed from the kingship of Tara. The law-tract implies that Congal Cáech was deprived of the kingship of Tara before he was defeated and killed by Domnall mac Áeda (d. 642), the next king of Tara, at the battle of Mag Roth in 637. Whether Congal was blinded by a bee-sting is doubtful: there may be examples of such a phenomenon but, if so, they are exceedingly rare. What is perhaps more likely is that Congal had a bad reaction to a sting close to his eye, and his enemies used this as a pretext to drive him from the high-kingship.

Although the annals do not attest Congal's position as high-king, they make it possible to see how he might have attained this position. The context was feuding among the Uí Néill, between the sons of Áed Sláine, rulers of Brega, and their cousins, the rulers of Mide, between two branches of Cenél nEogain and between Cenél nEogain and Cenél Conaill. All the main branches of the Uí Néill

were at each others' throats in the early 630s. Even as late as his defeat and death at Mag Roth, Congal had allies among the Cenél nEogain and probably among the Uí Néill of Mide. In 626 Congal Cáech was defeated by Domnall mac Áeda, king of Cenél Conaill. Adomnán uses language which suggests, but does not say outright, that Domnall mac Áeda became king of Tara after this battle; this is, however, unlikely since his predecessor, Suibne Mend of Cenél nEogain, was still ruling until he was killed by Congal Cáech two years later, in 628. A likely explanation of Congal's attainment of the kingship of Tara is, therefore, that the feuds of the Uí Néill temporarily made it easier for many of them to accept an overlord from outside their kindred. After the killing of Conall mac Suibni of Mide in 635 the Uí Néill of Brega became more powerful than their rivals of Mide, and also they then gave their support to Domnall mac Áeda of Cenél Conaill, already the most powerful king among the Uí Néill and the man who was to defeat and kill Congal Cáech in 637. This alliance may have resulted in Congal's enemies seizing the pretext of the bee-sting to remove him from the high-kingship, perhaps in 636. The fatal battle at Mag Roth in 637 may then have been his attempt to regain a high-kingship of which he had already been deprived, at least in the view of his enemies. T. M. CHARLES-EDWARDS

Sources *Adomnán's Life of Columba*, ed. and trans. A. O. Anderson and M. O. Anderson, rev. edn, rev. M. O. Anderson, OMT (1991) · W. Stokes, ed., 'The annals of Tigernach [8 pts]', *Revue Celtique*, 16 (1895), 374-419; 17 (1896), 6-33, 119-263, 337-420; 18 (1897), 9-59, 150-97, 267-303, 374-91; pubd sep. (1993) · *Ann. Ulster* · G. Murphy, 'On the dates of two sources used in Thurneysen's *Heldensage*: 1. *Baile Chuind* and the date of *Cin Dromma Snechtai*', *Ériu*, 16 (1952), 145-56, esp. 145-51 · T. M. Charles-Edwards and F. Kelly, eds., *Bechbretha* (1983) · W. M. Hennessy, ed. and trans., *Chronicum Scotorum: a chronicle of Irish affairs*, Rolls Series, 46 (1866) · M. A. O'Brien, ed., *Corpus genealogiarum Hiberniae* (Dublin, 1962) · K. Meyer, ed., 'The Laud genealogies and tribal histories', *Zeitschrift für Celtische Philologie*, 8 (1910-12), 291-338 · F. J. Byrne, *Irish kings and high-kings* (1973)

Congal Cendmagair (d. 710), high-king of Ireland, was of the Cenél Conaill. His father was Fergus Fánat (d. 654), who took his name from the Fanad peninsula lying between Mulroy Bay and Lough Swilly. Cendmagair, modern Kinaweer, lies at the head of Mulroy Bay in the parish and barony of Kilmacrenan, north Donegal.

Congal's grandfather was the high-king *Domnall mac Áeda (d. 642) and he succeeded to the high-kingship on the death of his cousin, the high-king *Loingsech mac Óenguso, in the great battle of Corann (an area covering part of counties Sligo and Mayo) against the Connachta on Saturday 12 July 704. These reigns provided a brief period of glory for the Cenél Conaill. Both branches of the northern Uí Néill, the Cenél Conaill and the Cenél nEogain, had tried to expand south into Connacht. In Congal's reign, in 707, Indrechtach, son of Dúnchad Muirsce, king of Connacht, was killed by the Cenél nEogain king Fergal mac Máele Dúin, Fergal mac Loingsig of the Cenél Conaill, and Conall Menn of the Cenél Cairpri. In 707 Congal made a hosting to Leinster and gained its submission. A poem associated with this expedition suggests that he spent some time there employing a scorched-earth policy. The entry in the annals of the four masters recording that in this year Congal also marched against the Cenél nÉogain, killing Máel Dúin mac Máele Fithrich, must either be misplaced or relate to another individual, because this latter king had died in 681.

There is no information about Congal's marriage relationships. His known sons are: Donngal, who died in 731; Flann Gohan, who was killed in the defeat of the Cenél Conaill king Flaithbertach mac Loingsig by Áed Allán mac Fergaile of the Cenél nÉogain in 732; Conaing, killed by Áed in a battle in the following year; and possibly Fergus, who died in 757. It is less certain that a Feradach who died in 687 was his son. Congal himself died suddenly, of a fit, in 710.   CHARLES DOHERTY

Sources Ann. Ulster • W. M. Hennessy, ed. and trans., Chronicum Scotorum: a chronicle of Irish affairs, Rolls Series, 46 (1866) • AFM • S. Mac Airt, ed. and trans., The annals of Inisfallen (1951) • D. Murphy, ed., The annals of Clonmacnoise, trans. C. Mageoghagan (1896); facs. edn (1993) • T. M. Charles-Edwards, 'Irish warfare before 1100', A military history of Ireland, ed. T. Bartlett and K. Jeffery (1996), 26–51 • D. Mac Giolla Easpaig, 'Placenames and early settlement in county Donegal', Donegal history and society: interdisciplinary essays on the history of an Irish county, ed. W. Nolan, L. Ronayne, and M. Dunlevy (1995), 149–82

Congalach mac Máele Mithig [Congalach Cnogba] (d. **956**), king of Brega and high-king of Ireland, was the son of Máel Mithig mac Flannacáin (d. 919), king of Brega, and Ligach (d. 922), daughter of the high-king Flann Sinna mac Máele Sechnaill. Congalach was a dynast of Síl nÁeda Sláine, part of the powerful Uí Néill confederation, whose lands in the ancient region of Brega are now within Meath and co. Dublin. The name Congalach Cnogba derives from his residence at Knowth (Cnogba) in east Meath.

Congalach became king of Brega about 929 and the early years of his reign were occupied by local affairs. In 939 he defeated a vassal people known as the Gailenga at the River Blackwater and in 942 he killed two rivals, the sons of the former king of Brega. He moved beyond his kingdom in 944 when he allied with the king of Leinster named Bróen mac Máele Mórda for a successful raid on the viking stronghold of Dublin. In that same year the high-king Donnchad mac Flainn died and Congalach advanced his own claims to the high-kingship, the first in his dynasty since the eighth century. He was opposed by Ruaidrí ua Canannáin, from the northern family of Cenél Conaill, and for the next six years the two competitors battled against each other. Congalach allied with Olaf Cuarán (or Sihtricson) of Dublin, and they fought Ruaidrí's forces at Conailli (in Louth) in 945. Ruaidrí carried the fight to Congalach in 947 with an attack on Slane, where Congalach and Olaf were defeated. This seems to have been a personal alliance with Olaf, not with the vikings of Dublin, for the some time king of Dublin named Blacaire son of Guthfrith fought Congalach in 948, which resulted in a victory for Congalach and death for Blacaire. In 949 Congalach led his troops northwards raiding Uí Meith and Fernmag. The following year, Congalach's rival Ruaidrí ua Canannáin was slain by the vikings, during a campaign

lasting for half a year against Congalach and his neighbours. The vikings were fighting for themselves, not for Congalach, and his hostilities with Dublin continued that same year, 950, when the vikings raided his lands and burned the belfry of Slane. Also in 950, Congalach led an army across Munster, and attacked Dál Cais, slaying two nobles named Echthigern and Donngus mac Cennétig. In the following year, a second expedition, using a fleet, saw the province submit to his lordship.

The support of the clergy was crucial for any successful prince and in 951 Congalach sought ecclesiastical favour when he released the monastery of Clonard from secular dues. A new rival, the future high-king Domnall ua Néill, won the submission of Bréifne in 955. Congalach continued, however, with his subjugation of neighbouring provinces, and he led an expedition to Connacht in that year, with mixed success. In 956 he turned his attentions to Leinster and presided over the Óenach Carmáin (fair of Carman), a visible sign of his claim to lordship of the province. This outraged the men of Leinster who sent news of his route to the vikings of Dublin. His former ally Olaf set an ambush, and Congalach was slain with his retinue at a place known only as 'Tech Guigrand', located somewhere near the River Liffey. He was buried at Monasterboice. Congalach had two wives: Eithne (d. 953), daughter of Fergal mac Domnaill, whose son was Muirchertach (d. 964); and Deichter, daughter of Béollán mac Ciarmaic, whose son was Domnall (d. 976). Two daughters were Dirbail (d. 1013), the wife of Conchobar of Uí Failgi, and Muirenn (d. 979), who was the abbess of Kildare.

BENJAMIN T. HUDSON

Sources Ann. Ulster • K. Meyer, 'Das Ende von Baile in Scáil', Zeitschrift für Celtische Philologie, 12 (1918), 232–8 • J. MacNeill, 'Poems by Flann Mainistrech on the dynasties of Ailech, Mide and Brega', Archivium Hibernicum, 2 (1913), 37–99 • M. C. Dobbs, ed. and trans., 'The Ban-shenchus [3 pts]', Revue Celtique, 47 (1930), 283–339; 48 (1931), 163–234; 49 (1932), 437–89 • J. H. Todd, ed. and trans., Cogadh Gaedhel re Gallaibh / The war of the Gaedhil with the Gaill, Rolls Series, 48 (1867) • M. A. O'Brien, ed., Corpus genealogiarum Hiberniae (Dublin, 1962) • AFM • F. J. Byrne, Irish kings and high-kings (1987) • D. Ó Corráin, Ireland before the Normans (1972) • T. W. Moody and others, eds., A new history of Ireland, 9: Maps, genealogies, lists (1984)

Congallus I. See Comgall mac Domangart (d. c.538) under Dál Riata, kings of (act. c.500–c.850).

Congallus II. See Conall mac Comgall (d. 574) under Dál Riata, kings of (act. c.500–c.850).

Congallus III. See Conall Crandomna (d. 660) under Dál Riata, kings of (act. c.500–c.850).

Congleton. For this title name see Parnell, Henry Brooke, first Baron Congleton (1776–1842); Parnell, John Vesey, second Baron Congleton (1805–1883) [see under Parnell, Henry Brooke, first Baron Congleton (1776–1842)].

Congreve, Richard (1818–1899), positivist, was born at Leamington Hastings, Warwickshire, on 4 September 1818, the third son of Thomas Congreve, a farmer, and his wife, Julia. After attending the school run by his uncle Walter Bury in Boulogne, he spent five years (1832–7) at Rugby School, acquiring the moral earnestness, religious latitudinarianism, and political Liberalism characteristic of its headmaster, Dr Thomas Arnold. In 1837 Congreve entered Wadham College, Oxford, on a scholarship; he earned his BA with a first class in *literae humaniores* in 1840, and proceeded MA in 1843. His social idealism found expression at the Oxford Union, of which he was president in 1841, and in 'the Decade', a debating society which included his Rugby contemporaries Arthur Hugh Clough and Matthew Arnold. Congreve took clerical orders in 1843, was elected a fellow of Wadham in 1844, and after a period as an assistant master at Rugby, returned to Wadham in 1848 as a tutor. In the following years he was active in the struggle for university reform with A. P. Stanley, Benjamin Jowett, Mark Pattison, and Goldwin Smith, colleagues he at times found insufficiently ardent.

Congreve's impatience with compromise on many issues accounts for his attraction to the systematic ideas of Auguste Comte. After the revolution of 1848, Congreve visited the philosopher in Paris several times and was encouraged by him to study the positivist philosophy, polity, and religion in relation to British history and politics. Determining to do so free of Oxford's constraints, Congreve resigned his fellowship in June 1854 and moved to Wandsworth, Surrey, planning to earn his living by tutoring. Marriage in the same year to his cousin Maria, daughter of J. Bury, a Coventry surgeon, provided unquestioning devotion that helped him withstand the coming storm of criticism.

Maria Congreve's family in Warwickshire had known George Eliot, and when she and George Henry Lewes settled in Wandsworth in 1859 they became friends of the Congreves and gave moral and financial support to the positivist mission. Congreve could also count on encouragement from three former Wadham pupils—Frederic Harrison, John Henry Bridges, and Edward Spencer Beesly. Early fruits of his positivist studies were his tendentious notes to a new edition of Aristotle's *Politics* (1855); his endorsement of temporary dictatorship in modern Europe in *The Roman Empire of the West* (1855); and two anti-imperialist pamphlets, *Gibraltar* and *India* (1857). Comte, who had urged him to write the first, demanding Britain's immediate surrender of Gibraltar to Spain, was so gratified by it that in 1857 he appointed Congreve head of his British disciples. They were, however, few in number, and all subject to ridicule. Undeterred, Congreve published a translation of Comte's *Catéchisme positiviste* in 1858, expounding the 'religion of humanity', and in 1866 earned membership of the Royal College of Physicians, solely as a prerequisite for the positivist priesthood. Meanwhile he was drawing fire for supporting the trade unions' struggle for legal status, and advocating Irish independence, a liberal foreign policy, and parliamentary reform.

In written controversy Congreve could hold his own, but when he delivered an important series of public lectures on positivism in 1867 even his friend George Eliot found his delivery 'chilling'. Although also aware of his limitations, in 1870 Harrison, Bridges, and Beesly, with others now calling themselves positivists, leased a small hall at 19 (now 20 Rugby Street) Chapel Street, off Lamb's Conduit Street, London, as a meeting-place and accepted Congreve's leadership. He moved to nearby Mecklenburgh Square, and soon began administering Comte's version of baptism. There were hymns and invocations to Humanity and pronouncements on political issues. By 1877 Congreve had completed volume four of the British positivists' four-volume translation of Comte's *Système de politique positive*. Given all this activity, he was understandably irritated by the slackness of Comte's successor in Paris, Pierre Laffitte. By declaring his independence from the Paris leader in 1878, Congreve precipitated a schism in his own movement that had been long brewing. He remained at Chapel Street while his most distinguished followers, Harrison, Bridges, and Beesly, opened their own centre, Newton Hall.

Following the schism, Congreve introduced additional rituals, justifying T. H. Huxley's jibe that positivism was 'Catholicism minus Christianity'. But he eschewed sacerdotal garb: his photographs in his *Historical Lectures* and the third volume of his *Essays Political, Social and Religious* (both edited by his wife in 1900) show a benevolent-looking, patrician gentleman. In his last years he wrote largely on religious subjects, and despite chronic bad health, led his small congregation until his death at Home Lodge, Worsley Road, Hampstead, London, on 5 July 1899. His widow stayed on at their last address, 55 Palace Gardens, Kensington, until her death in 1915. Only then did the rival positivist congregations unite.

MARTHA S. VOGELER

Sources Foster, *Alum. Oxon.* · Boase, *Mod. Eng. biog.* · *The Times* (8 July 1899), 9e · *The Athenaeum* (15 July 1899), 99 · C. Kent, 'Congreve, Richard', *BDMBR*, vol. 2 · J. E. McGee, *A crusade for humanity: the history of organized positivism in England* (1931) · W. M. Simon, *European positivism in the nineteenth century* (1963) · C. Kent, *Brains and numbers: élitism, Comtism and democracy in mid-Victorian England* (1978) · M. S. Vogeler, *Frederic Harrison: the vocations of a positivist* (1984) · *The George Eliot letters*, ed. G. S. Haight, 9 vols. (1954–78) · *Correspondance générale et confessions: Auguste Comte*, ed. P. E. de Berrêdo Carneiro and P. Arbousse-Bastide, 6–7 (Paris, 1984–7)
Archives BL, corresp. and papers, Add. MSS 43842–43844, 45227–45264 · Bodl. Oxf., corresp. and papers · Maison d'Auguste Comte, Paris, Comte archives, corresp. | BL, positivist MSS · LPL, corresp. relating to appointment at Rugby School · Maison d'Auguste Comte, Paris, Comte archives, letters to Auguste Comte · NL Scot., corresp. with Sir Patrick Geddes
Likenesses photograph, repro. in R. Congreve, *Historical lectures*, ed. M. Congreve (1900) · photograph, repro. in R. Congreve, *Essays political, social, and religious*, ed. M. Congreve (1900), vol. 3
Wealth at death £5597 18s.: probate, 30 Oct 1899, *CGPLA Eng. & Wales*

Congreve, Sir Walter Norris (1862–1927), army officer, was born at Chatham on 20 November 1862, the eldest son of Captain William Congreve JP DL of Congreve Manor, Staffordshire, and his wife, Fanny Porcher Townshend, of Wincham Hall, Cheshire. Congreve's father was a regular soldier in the 9th and 29th foot, who later became chief constable of Staffordshire. Among Congreve's military ancestors were two distinguished eighteenth-century artillerymen, Lieutenant-General Sir William Congreve, and his namesake, who developed the Congreve rocket.

Walter Congreve was educated at Harrow School and

Pembroke College, Oxford, matriculating in 1881 but leaving without graduating after apparently wounding a senior member of the college with an air rifle. Congreve had been commissioned in the North Staffordshire militia and, in 1883, resolved to enter the regular army. Passing through the Royal Military College, Sandhurst, where he shared rooms with Douglas Haig, Congreve was commissioned into the rifle brigade as lieutenant on 7 February 1885. Congreve served with the 4th battalion in India and, on returning with it to England in 1889, he became assistant adjutant for musketry. On 3 June 1890 he married Cecilia Henrietta Dolores Blount La Touche, the daughter of Charles Blount La Touche, a captain in the Bombay army. Congreve's work on musketry brought him some recognition and he was promoted to captain on 6 December 1893. After further regimental service in India and England, he was appointed district inspector of musketry at Aldershot on 1 January 1898.

On the outbreak of the Second South African War, Congreve was appointed to the 4th brigade staff, but was then attached to the headquarters of General Sir Redvers Buller as press censor. On 15 December 1899, during Buller's attempt to force the Tugela River at Colenso, Colonel Charles Long's artillery brigade advanced within close range of Boer riflemen and came under sustained, heavy fire. Buller called for volunteers from his own staff to help rescue the twelve guns abandoned in the open by their surviving crews. Congreve volunteered together with two aides-de-camp, Captain H. N. Schofield and Lieutenant Frederick (Freddy) Roberts, only son of Field Marshal Lord Roberts VC.

Galloping forward with two limbers over half a mile of open plain, Congreve was hit in his right leg, with other bullets passing through his clothing, and thrown when his horse was killed. After lying in a hollow for several hours without water under a sun 'which I have never felt hotter even in India' (Congreve diary, priv. coll., 15 Dec 1899), Congreve managed to bring in the mortally wounded Roberts. Taken prisoner by the Boers, the wounded were released after their equipment was removed. For his gallantry, Congreve was awarded the Victoria Cross as were three others, including a posthumous award for Freddy Roberts. Subsequently, Congreve's eldest son, William, killed on the Somme in July 1916, was also awarded the VC. There have been only three cases of the VC being awarded to both father and son: Roberts, Congreve, and Sir Charles and John Gough.

After recovering from his wound, Congreve briefly joined the irregular corps, Kitchener's horse, as adjutant before becoming brigade major of 18th infantry brigade in March 1900 and seeing action at Poplar Grove and Driefontein in the advance upon Bloemfontein. In November 1900 Congreve became, first, deputy assistant adjutant-general and, then, assistant military secretary at headquarters under Roberts and his successor, Lord Kitchener. Promoted to a regimental majority on 12 December 1901, Congreve received a brevet lieutenant-colonelcy for his war services in December 1901. In November 1902 he joined the personal staff of the duke of Connaught, commanding in Ireland, receiving the MVO in 1903 and accompanying Connaught as private secretary in May 1904 when the duke was appointed inspector-general to the forces.

Receiving his brevet colonelcy in June 1905, Congreve returned to regimental duty. Promoted to substantive colonel in July 1908, Congreve remained on half pay until appointed to command the school of musketry at Hythe in September 1909. In December 1911 Congreve, now a CB, took command of 18th infantry brigade with rank of brigadier-general, though troubled by frequent asthma attacks. In March 1914 he was one of many officers who supported Hubert and John Gough at the time of the Curragh incident. With the outbreak of the First World War, Congreve took his brigade to France in September 1914, commanding it on the Aisne and then at First Ypres. Promoted to major-general on 18 February 1915, Congreve remained with his brigade until taking over command of 6th division in May 1915. His division did not see any major action before Congreve was selected to command the new 13th corps in November 1915, receiving the rank of temporary lieutenant-general in June 1917.

A man of great physical and moral courage, it became quickly apparent that Congreve was supremely a fighting general, incurring great risks in visiting the front line. As a subordinate later put it, Congreve was 'a most adventurous man … and infinitely preferred walking out in full view and quite close to the enemy than anything else. He simply asked for trouble' (Stanley, 112–13). Indeed, Congreve was the only corps commander wounded during the war, having his left hand shattered by a shell while visiting his artillery near Vimy Ridge in June 1917: in his typically laconic style, he simply recorded of the event, 'A shell came down & cut off my left hand all but some bits' (Congreve diary, 12 June 1917). The hand was amputated.

As a corps commander, however, Congreve had mixed fortunes. With many practical qualities and great personal charm, he was not a deeply read or scientific soldier despite his university education. Allotted to Sir Henry Rawlinson's Fourth Army in the spring of 1916, Congreve was not regarded as 'dashing enough' by Rawlinson (Congreve diary, 5 April 1916) when he objected to the initial operational plan for the Somme. As a result, Sir Henry Horne's 15th corps took the major role on 1 July 1916, with two of Congreve's five divisions taken from his direct control. Ironically, it was 13th corps, operating on the extreme right of the British advance in co-operation with the French, which enjoyed the greatest success on that otherwise disastrous day, reaching the Montauban Ridge. Congreve complained to Haig, in whom he had little confidence, about his treatment. Generally, Congreve found Haig disingenuous in his dealings with him, though the official historian, Sir James Edmonds, later claimed that Haig had always shrunk from dismissing corps commanders like Congreve whom he believed inefficient. Congreve was then entrusted, however, with the innovative night attack by the Fourth Army on 14 July and, indeed, appears to have been the originator of the operational concept. The death of his son William on 20 July was a grievous blow, and Congreve succumbed to cholera nostras on 10 August, returning to his command only in late September.

Transferred to Hubert Gough's Fifth Army, Congreve commanded 13th corps during the actions around Arras in the spring of 1917. He found Gough more congenial than Rawlinson and, in turn, Gough admired Congreve's qualities:

> Very spare and lightly built, a frame giving evidence of the fragility of his constitution, a firm and very English countenance, with an indomitable and courageous will, a character which could remain outwardly unmoved at times of great personal sorrow or of immense responsibility and danger, an energy which made him active of body in spite of ill-health, there were few generals in the British Army who surpassed him as a commander. (Gough, 151)

Following the loss of his hand, Congreve, who in 1917 was created KCB for his services, returned to the Fifth Army to command 7th corps as a substantive lieutenant-general on 1 January 1918. Congreve's corps took the full brunt of the major German offensive on 21 March 1918. His decision to defend the front line strongly rather than deploy in depth cost 7th corps heavy casualties from the outset. Under mounting German pressure, Congreve's position was further undermined by the withdrawal of the Third Army from the Flesquières salient on his left, opening a crucial gap between 7th and 5th corps. Under a German aerial bombing attack on his headquarters, Congreve had continued to dine, unmoved by the explosions. Always in fragile health from his frequent bronchial attacks, however, and never having fully recovered from the loss of his son, Congreve was clearly stretched to the limits of his mental and physical endurance during the offensive. The strain was evinced by Congreve's contradictory orders to 16th division on 26 March, which led to its collapse, and the removal of Major-General Franks from command of 35th division on the same day for refusing what would have been a disastrous attempt to reoccupy the line of the Ancre, which had already been abandoned.

Gough was removed from command of the Fifth Army on 7 April and, on the same day, Congreve was transferred to command 10th corps, then resting behind the lines. Then, on 15 May, he was ordered home, Haig refusing to see him. Subsequently, Congreve was one of the more vociferous of Gough's friends in urging him to defend the reputation of the Fifth Army.

Congreve remained on half pay until August 1919, when he was sent to command British forces at Haifa, taking over the command of all British forces in Egypt and Palestine on 14 October 1919. It was a period of unrest in the Middle East and, displaying the casual antisemitic views of many of his colleagues, Congreve feared Zionist influence in the region. It might be added that Congreve was also greatly prejudiced towards socialists and Irish nationalists and cheerfully professed to disliking Arabs, Jews and Syrian Christians equally: 'they are all alike, a beastly people, the whole lot of them not worth one Englishman' (Congreve to Wilson, 1 April 1920, Wilson MSS, HHW 2/52A/16). None the less, Congreve's command was judged

a success and, much as he disliked Palestine, he was sorry to leave an Egyptian climate that suited him. Promoted to general on 25 November 1922, 'Squib' Congreve, as he was known to Henry Wilson, returned to southern command at Salisbury in April 1923 and was appointed aide-de-camp to the king in March 1924. Congreve had also become colonel commandant of the 1st battalion, rifle brigade, in 1922, as well as an honorary fellow of Pembroke College, Oxford. A fearless horseman, though he gave up hunting as a result of a growing distaste for blood sports, Congreve was very much a countryman. He derived much pleasure, therefore, from his appointments as both JP and deputy lieutenant of Staffordshire.

Despite his failing health, Congreve accepted the governorship of Malta in June 1924. He proved a popular governor, dying at the military hospital, Imtarfa, Valletta, on 28 February 1927. He was buried at sea between Malta and Gozo, in what is now called the Congreve Strait. It had been intended to give Congreve a baronetcy at the time of his death, and this was awarded to the second of his three sons, Geoffrey, in 1927.   IAN F. W. BECKETT

Sources I. H. Thornton and P. Fraser, *The Congreves—father and son* (1930) · IWM, Henry Wilson papers, HHW 2/52A/16 · T. Travers, *The killing ground* (1987) · J. Bourne, 'British generals in the First World War', *Leadership and command: the Anglo-American military experience since 1861*, ed. G. D. Sheffield (1997), 93–116 · F. C. Stanley, *The history of the 89th brigade, 1914–18* (1919) · A. Farrar-Hockley, *Goughie* (1975) · H. Gough, *The Fifth Army* (1931) · K. Jeffery, ed., *The military correspondence of Field Marshal Sir Henry Wilson, 1918–22* (1985) · T. Travers, *How the war was won: command and technology in the British army on the western front, 1917–1918* (1992) · J. M. Bourne, 'The BEF on the Somme: some career aspects, part I', *Gunfire*, 35 (1994), 2–14 · T. Moreman, 'The dawn attack, Friday 14 July 1916', *Journal of the Society for Army Historical Research*, 71 (1993), 180–204 · R. Prior and T. Wilson, *Command on the western front* (1992) · T. Norman, ed., *Armageddon road: a VC's diary, 1914–16* (1982) [the letters of Billy Congreve, VC (son)] · *DNB* · m. cert. · *CGPLA Eng. & Wales* (1927) · *British Historical Society*, 51/20 (2000), 34

Archives priv. coll., MSS · Staffs. RO, MSS | IWM, corresp. with Sir Henry Wilson | FILM IWM FVA, documentary footage

Likenesses F. Dodd, charcoal and watercolour drawing, 1917, IWM · miniature, Royal Green Jackets Museum, Winchester · photographs, repro. in Thornton and Fraser, *The Congreves*

Wealth at death £20,628 7s. 4d.: probate, 30 Sept 1927, *CGPLA Eng. & Wales* · £12,455 2s. 5d.: further grant, 18 Nov 1927, *CGPLA Eng. & Wales*

Congreve, William (1670–1729), playwright and poet, was born on either 24 or 31 January 1670 in Bardsey Grange, Yorkshire, the son of William Congreve (1637–1708) and his wife, Mary (1636?–1715), daughter of Mary, *née* Bright, and Walter Browning (d. 1636). Congreve's mother was the great-granddaughter of Dr Timothy Bright (1549/50–1615), author of *A Treatise of Melancholie* (1586) and *Characterie: an Arte of Shorte, Swifte, and Secret Writing by Character* (1586). She grew up in the household of her mother's second husband, Dr George Roe (d. 1651), of Doncaster, within easy distance of her cousins the Lewises of Ledstone Park, near Marr. It was to one of these, John Lewis (d. 1671), a successful merchant knighted by Charles II and created a baronet after the Restoration, that the Congreves owed their tenancy of Bardsey Grange. William Congreve senior was the second son of Richard Congreve (1609–1689) of Stretton

William Congreve (1670–1729), by Sir Godfrey Kneller, 1709

Hall, Staffordshire, and Anne, *née* Fitzherbert, of Norbury, Derbyshire. Congreve was described as 'the only surviving son' in information supplied to Giles Jacob's *Poetical Register* in 1719 (p. 41), and there is evidence of only one sister.

Early years and education The Congreve family was in London by 22 September 1672 when William's sister Elizabeth was buried at St Paul's, Covent Garden. The following year Congreve's father secured a passport to the Low Countries to purchase coach horses for the duke of York. In 1674 he was granted a commission as lieutenant in the army in Ireland and moved with his family to join the garrison at the seaport of Youghal. This was the home of Richard Boyle, second earl of Cork and first earl of Burlington. Congreve's father was to manage part of the earl's estates at Youghal and Lismore Castle from about 1690, after he was discharged from a commission as captain in the earl of Danby's volunteer regiment. Congreve later dedicated his first play, *The Old Batchelor*, to Charles, the second earl of Burlington and third earl of Cork, acknowledging 'the particular Ties, by which I am bound to your Lordship and Family'.

William senior was transferred in 1678 to Carrickfergus, where he joined his uncle Christopher Congreve (1622–1706). Both men were with companies quartered at Kilkenny by late 1681. Since children of those in service to the duke of Ormond, lord lieutenant of Ireland, were entitled to the free privileges and benefits of Kilkenny College, Congreve, then almost twelve, may have entered there at once. His portrait, signed 'W. D. Claret' (but possibly by Wolfgang William Claret) and painted about this time, shows a twelve-year-old of slight figure but determined chin, with blue eyes and curly brown hair. Dr Henry Rider, a graduate of Trinity College and later bishop of Killaloe, was then headmaster, in charge of about sixty students, who briefly included Jonathan Swift while Congreve was there (Swift left in April 1682). Congreve began his long and close friendship with Joseph Keally at Kilkenny College, when Keally joined the school in 1685. Dr Edward Hinton, the Greek scholar who succeeded Rider as headmaster in 1684, must have been instrumental in developing Congreve's considerable competence in Greek.

Congreve matriculated at Trinity College, Dublin, on 5 April 1686 'annos natus Sexdecim' ('aged sixteen'; TCD, 'Catalogus omnium studentium'). His tutor there, and Swift's, was the learned St George Ashe, mathematician, member of the Royal Society, later bishop of Cloyne, of Clogher, and of Derry. The presence in Congreve's library of such volumes as the 1684 editions of John Dryden's *Essay of Dramatick Poesy* and François Hédelin's *The Whole Art of the Stage* suggests that his interest in writing for the stage might have been an early one. The flourishing theatre in Dublin at the time probably contributed as well. Congreve's career at Trinity College was evidently cut short with the exodus of protestants from Ireland—his name is deleted from the college buttery book in January 1687 and does not appear thereafter, although in 1696 Trinity College conferred the degree of MA on Congreve. He may have left with his parents for England and Stretton Hall in Staffordshire in March 1689.

Early writings, 1689–1691 Congreve probably wrote *Incognita*, 'an Essay', he says, 'began and finished in the idler hours of a fortnight's time' ('Dedication'), during this stay in Staffordshire, and it was there he met Katherine Leveson, to whom he dedicated the book. A little later, in a 'slow Recovery from a Fit of Sickness' and still 'very much a Boy', he wrote a draft of his first play, *The Old Batchelor* (Congreve, *Amendments*, 39). At some time before 21 March 1691, when he was admitted to the Middle Temple to study law, Congreve moved to London, lodging first in nearby Crane Court in the home of William Brookes. He was evidently able to put his knowledge of the law to good use later, but, like those of Sir George Etherege, William Wycherley, and Thomas Shadwell before him, his inclinations were decidedly towards theatre and poetry, and he was never called to the bar.

In February 1692 Congreve made a muted entrance into the London literary world with the publication of *Incognita* under the pseudonym Cleophil. The more public declaration of his arrival as a talented new writer appeared in the first week of June 1692 in Charles Gildon's *Miscellany*: he contributed imitations of two Horatian odes, two other poems, 'The Message' and 'The Decay: a Song', signed with his initials, and the irregular ode to Arabella Hunt 'Upon a Lady's Singing' signed 'Mr. Congreve'. Were it not for Leonora's song in *Incognita* ('Ah! Whither, whither shall I fly', which was set to music by John Eccles) this would be the earliest evidence of Congreve's love of music and of his capacity for the most minute attention to it. He also assisted Dryden in his edition of the satires of Juvenal and

Persius, supplying a translation of Juvenal's eleventh satire, published in 1693 but probably completed by early 1692, and he paid a classically informed compliment to Dryden in his 'Poem to Mr. Dryden on his Translation of Persius'.

Writings, 1692–1699 It was in this context that Congreve was taken up as a promising young dramatist. Two of his cousins, who had served with Thomas Southerne in Princess Anne's regiment of foot, had introduced Congreve to the older dramatist, and it is likely that Southerne in turn made Congreve acquainted with Dryden. Congreve completed a draft of *The Old Batchelor* at some time before August 1692. Southerne's recollection was that when Dryden read it, he

> sayd he never saw such a first play in his life, but the Author not being acquainted with the Stage or the town, it woud be pity to have it miscarry for want of a little Assistance: the stuff was rich indeed, it only wanted the fashionable cutt of the town.   (BL, Add. MS 4221, fol. 341)

Later in August Congreve went off to Ilam in Derbyshire to revise the play in light of suggestions made by these more experienced friends. Congreve describes the setting there in a letter to his friend Edward Porter on 21 August 1692:

> I have a little tried, what solitude and retirement can afford, which are here in perfection. I am now writing to you from before a black mountain nodding over me and a whole river in cascade falling so near me that even I can distinctly see it. (Hodges, *Letters*)

Kneller painted such a background into his much copied kit-cat portrait of Congreve in 1709.

Samuel Foote recorded that when Congreve eventually brought his finished comedy to the players

> he read it so wretchedly ill, that they were on the point of rejecting it, till one of them good naturedly took it out of his hands and read it; when they were so fully persuaded of its excellence, that for half a year before it was acted he had the privilege of the house. (*Table-Talk*, 133)

The Old Batchelor opened on 9 March 1693 at the Drury Lane Theatre for an exceptionally long run. The play was acted with a good cast that included Thomas Betterton and Thomas Doggett, as well as Elizabeth Barry, Elizabeth Bowman, Anne Bracegirdle, and Susanna Mountfort who, 'when they appeared together, in the last scene of the Old Batchelor, the audience was struck with so fine a groupe of beauty, and broke out into loud applauses' (Davies, 3.391). Congreve had recently provided a song for Southerne's *The Maid's Last Prayer*, 'Tell me no more I am deceiv'd', which Henry Purcell had set to music; it was Purcell's music that accompanied the songs in *The Old Batchelor*. The play's immediate success was described by the earl of Burlington to Congreve's father:

> Your sons Play was Acted on Thursday last & was by all the hearers applauded to bee the best that has been Acted for many yeares. Monday is to bee his day which will bring him in a better sume of money than the writters of late have had, for the house will bee so full that very many persons of Quality cannot have a Seate all the places having been bespoken many days since. (*Complete Works*, 4)

The crowds that had come to see and hear the play were of course eager to read it, and the first edition was reprinted twice by the end of the month: 'indeed the Wit which is diffus'd through it, makes it lose but few of those Charms in the Perusal, which yield such Pleasure in the Representation' (*London Gazette*, 23–7 March 1693).

There are no obvious single sources for *The Old Batchelor*, nor for any of Congreve's other plays. Nevertheless there is evidence of Congreve's wide reading in echoes of texts ranging from Plato, Epictetus, and Aesop, down to Cervantes and Scarron, and clearly he had read and heard Shakespeare, Ben Jonson, Francis Beaumont, and John Fletcher, and his fellow dramatists Dryden, Etherege, and Wycherley. This range and originality are also evident in Congreve's other writings.

Towards the end of March 1693, Dryden's *Examen poeticum* was advertised as then being prepared for the press. The poem on Arabella Hunt is reprinted in it, together with the two imitations of Horace from the 1692 *Miscellany*. To those Congreve added a further 'paraphrase' of Horace. He also included extended translations from the last book of the *Iliad*, including Priam's lamentation as well as the lamentations of Hecuba, Andromache, and Helen. In his dedication to the volume, Dryden drew attention to Congreve's work: 'I am sure my Friend has added to the Tenderness which he found in the Original; and, without Flattery, surpass'd his Author.' Certainly by this time, with his prose narrative, his comedy, his verse, and his verse translations, Congreve was judged by many to be Dryden's rightful literary successor, although he lacked the political connections to be named poet laureate. Dryden expressed his own regret in verse:

> Oh that your Brows my Lawrel had sustain'd,
> Well had I been Depos'd, if You had reign'd!
> The Father had descended for the Son;
> For only You are lineal to the Throne.
> ('To my dear friend Mr. Congreve', ll. 41–4)

Production of this first play was soon followed by *The Double Dealer*, which Congreve may have begun drafting even as *The Old Batchelor* went into performance. Again, Dryden and other friends must have read or heard the play before it was performed. He mentioned to William Walsh on 12 December 1693 that he had written 'To my dear friend Mr. Congreve, on his comedy, call'd, the Double-Dealer' before the play had been acted (*Letters of John Dryden*, 62). It is unclear exactly when *The Double Dealer* was first performed—it was possibly in November 1693—but it had much the same cast as *The Old Batchelor*. Dryden goes on in his letter to Walsh to describe how the play was

> censured by the greater part of the Town: and is defended onely by the best Judges, who … are commonly the fewest. … The women thinke he has exposed their Bitchery too much; & the Gentlemen are offended with him; for the discovery of their follyes.

After the enthusiasm that had greeted his first play, the poor reception of *The Double Dealer* was particularly disappointing for the young dramatist, who had carefully constructed his play to remain true to 'the three Unities of the Drama' ('Dedication'), with a plot tailored to fit his moral. Although Congreve must have been encouraged by a royal command performance for Queen Mary in the following

January, his unhappiness with his general audience was all too clear in the dedication (to his patron Charles Montagu, later first earl of Halifax) published with the first edition of the play in 1694. Congreve removed this uncharacteristically intemperate attack on his 'Illiterate Criticks' from subsequent editions.

For some time a dispute had been developing between the actors and the patentees of the Drury Lane Theatre. The loss in 1692 of three of the most popular actors—William Mountfort (murdered), Anthony Leigh (died), and James Nokes (retired)—and a subsequent drop in audience numbers did not help matters. The company's debts were increasing with the expensive productions given to Purcell's operas, and then in 1693 a realignment led to a whole new managerial approach, unwelcome to the senior actors. The result was that most of the more experienced actors revolted, led by Thomas Betterton. Early in 1695 Betterton, Bracegirdle, Barry, and others secured a licence from the lord chamberlain to reopen the Lincoln's Inn Theatre in the tennis-courts there. The composer John Eccles, already associated with Congreve, became master of the music. Congreve had written *Love for Love* by the end of 1694, and it had been read and accepted for production at the Theatre Royal in Drury Lane. Nevertheless Congreve delayed signing a contract until the outcome of the dispute was clear, and so was able to transfer his play to the new company. Even though a couple of the actors Congreve might well have cast remained with the Drury Lane Company, *Love for Love* brilliantly opened the Lincoln's Inn Theatre on 30 April 1695: 'Extraordinary well Acted, chiefly the Part of *Ben* the Sailor [by Thomas Doggett], it took 13 Days Successively' (Downes, 44).

The play was dedicated to the earl of Dorset, who, as lord chamberlain, had helped secure the patent for Betterton's company. According to Colley Cibber the success of *Love for Love* brought Congreve not only the usual profits from the play itself, but the offer of a full share in the new playhouse (Cibber, 161). The run of recorded performances at both theatres testified to the continued popularity of *Love for Love* through the eighteenth century, matched only by that of *The Old Batchelor*, and it has continued to be the most often produced of Congreve's works. On stage, it is his most wholly successful play, dramatic in the pace and shape of its action, with wit and varied comic turns.

When the critic John Dennis sent some notes on Ben Jonson's comedies for his comments, Congreve replied with a letter dated 10 July 1695. The timing of his remarks makes them particularly pertinent to the characters in *Love for Love*, which had opened only a few months before. His letter was first published as an essay 'Concerning humour in comedy' in Dennis's *Letters upon Several Occasions* (1696). Here Congreve extends the meaning of humour beyond mere affectation to include a bias of the mind and complexity of character, giving humour an edge that the superficially 'humorous' representation of vanities and fopperies might otherwise lack. The letter explains his compassion in exculpating those whose physical condition was none of their own fault, his amused and tolerant exposure of others' affectations and follies, and

his severity in judging those whose vicious conduct was deeply prejudicial to the social harmony secured by true wit and exemplified in the resolution of comedy.

Almost as soon as the new theatre had been opened and *Love for Love* performed, Congreve was seriously at work on his first tragedy, *The Mourning Bride*, his major poetic work of the 1690s. It opens memorably to Godfrey Finger's 'soft Musick' and the line: 'Musick has charms to sooth a savage Breast'. Act III concludes just as memorably with Zara's speech:

Heav'n has no Rage, like Love to Hatred turn'd,
Nor Hell a Fury, like a Woman scorn'd.

The Mourning Bride was first performed at the Lincoln's Inn Theatre, probably on 27 February 1697, and was an instant success. Hopkins records the audience melting 'with Pity at the moving Strains' (Hopkins, 'Epistle … to Mr. Yalden'); Samuel Wesley wrote of Congreve's ability to move his audience (S. Wesley, *Epistle to a Friend Concerning Poetry*, 1700, 19); Charles Gildon confirms that 'This Play had the greatest Success, not only of all Mr. *Congreve*'s, but indeed of all the Plays that ever I can remember on the English stage, excepting none of the incomparable *Otway*'s' (Gildon). Written in irregular blank verse, following Dryden in his tragedies *Don Sebastian* (1689) and *Cleomenes* (1692), *The Mourning Bride* was so popular that it gave rise to two authorized and two pirated editions in 1697, and a third edition in 1703. Congreve continued to work on the verse, revising the metre and making extensive cuts for the 1703 edition. The play remained a favourite through the eighteenth century: the role of Zara was a speciality of the tragic actress Sarah Siddons in the 1780s and 1790s. Smollett adapted parts of Act III for his graveyard scenes in *Ferdinand Count Fathom*, and Jefim Schirmann claims the tragedy is the first work of English literature to be translated into Hebrew.

The pamphleteer Jeremy Collier was addressing serious abuses in late seventeenth-century theatre when he wrote his *Short View of the Immorality and Profaneness of the English Stage* (1698). He was not alone in recognizing what Congreve himself called the 'licentious Practice of the Modern Theatre' ('Dedication', *The Mourning Bride*). But Collier heavy-handedly drove his argument well beyond reform of the theatre to its destruction, attacking in particular Dryden, Congreve, and John Vanbrugh. Congreve followed several others—John Dennis (*The Usefulness of the Stage*) and Vanbrugh (*A Short Vindication of 'The Relapse' and 'The Provok'd Wife'*) among them—in his reply. His *Amendments of Mr. Collier's False and Imperfect Citations*, published on 12 July 1698, set down basic principles, and easily refuted Collier's more foolish accusations, but Congreve was not at his best as a controversialist and, overall, his was not the most effective response to Collier.

Congreve's more considered reply was perhaps *The Way of the World*, a play that has sustained the highest literary reputation of all his work for its sheer verbal wit, its complex design, and its half-dozen brilliantly written and actable scenes. In his dedication of the first edition to Ralph Montagu, earl of Montagu, Congreve pays tribute to the quality of Montagu's company and the ambience of

Boughton House, where he had spent the summer of 1699, and suggests that he wrote the play 'immediately after'. It is more likely—given the care and time he usually spent over his work and noting the comment by the historian John Oldmixon in the spring of 1699 that Congreve was 'giving the World a new Comedy' (J. Oldmixon, *Reflections on the Stage*, 1699, 173)—that he began writing *The Way of the World* soon after finishing his own *Amendments of Mr. Collier's False and Imperfect Citations* in 1698, and worked on it for at least eighteen months after that. Despite its modern acclaim, *The Way of the World* had a mixed reception after its first performance on 5 March 1700. Congreve himself wrote 'that it succeeded on the Stage, was almost beyond my Expectation; for but little of it was prepar'd for that general Taste which seems now to be predominant in the Pallats of our Audience' ('Dedication'). But in Dryden's view 'Congreves New Play has had but moderate success; though it deserves much better' (Dryden to Mrs Steward, 12 March 1700). *The Way of the World* was Congreve's last major comedy, although he, Vanbrugh, and the poet William Walsh collaborated to translate one act each of a comedy based on Molière. The result was *Squire Trelooby*, which was performed at the Lincoln's Inn Theatre in 1704, but never published.

Music and theatre, 1700–1710 It would be wrong to imagine that Congreve left the stage then for a life of sinecured leisure after Jeremy Collier's envenomed attack on him and the alleged failure of *The Way of the World* in 1700. Instead he was already moving on to develop his long interest in writing words for music by devoting himself to the musical stage. A significant prelude to this activity was his role in providing the libretto to *The Judgment of Paris* for the music prize contested in March–June 1701 by John Eccles, Godfrey Finger, Daniel Purcell, and the relatively unknown John Weldon, who was awarded the prize much to everyone's surprise. (A re-enacted competition in the Royal Albert Hall on 13 August 1989 justly gave the first prize to Eccles.) Congreve wrote to his friend Keally on 26 March 1701 describing in detail the first performance in the old Dorset Garden Theatre, with Eccles's music, more than eighty-five performers, and the stage 'all built into a concave with deal boards; all which was to increase and throw forward the sound'. On this occasion the principals were Anne Bracegirdle playing Venus ('performed to a miracle' said Congreve (Hodges, *Letters*, 20–21)), Mary Hodgson as Juno, and Elizabeth Bowman as Pallas. Hodgson was the only professional singer of the three, perhaps an indication of the importance Congreve, like Dryden before him, accorded to actors as singers. In tribute to its eminently settable nature—the fruits of his ten-year apprenticeship in the art of writing for music—Congreve's libretto has proved a continuing attraction to other composers, including Johann Wolfgang Franck, Giuseppe Sammartini, and Thomas Arne.

The depth of Congreve's commitment to the theatre after 1700 is perhaps best seen in his collaboration with Vanbrugh in both planning and writing for the new Queen's Theatre in the Haymarket. Plans must have been formed before June 1703, when Vanbrugh reported to the publisher Jacob Tonson, who acted as secretary to the Kit-Cat Club, that land had been purchased with money raised from twenty-nine benefactors, many of them fellow Kit-Cat Club members; he hoped that the corner-stone might be laid by midsummer day, with business commencing in December. The theatre was to be built to Vanbrugh's design, with a large orchestra, a deep proscenium, and a stage with machinery capable of spectacular scenic effects. There is every reason to believe that the partners hoped to open with an opera worthy of Purcell's precedent (*Dido and Aeneas*), designed to revive and develop a specifically English operatic tradition: Congreve's *Semele*, set to music by John Eccles.

The foundation stone was laid on 18 April 1704 by the duke of Somerset and the countess of Sunderland, one of the duke of Marlborough's daughters and Henrietta Godolphin's younger sister. In December 1704 Congreve and Vanbrugh were granted Queen Anne's royal licence for a new company (Hodges, *Letters*, 110–11). Vanbrugh's commission to design Blenheim Palace was awarded about the same time, and must have distracted him from the management of the new theatre, perhaps leaving more of that work to Congreve. The first event to take place in the unfinished theatre was a recital by an Italian singer, one 'Segniora Sconiance' before Queen Anne in November 1704 (*Diverting Post*, 2 Dec 1704). In the end it was not Congreve's and Eccles's English opera, but Jakob Greber's *Gli amori d'Ergasto* that formally opened the Queen's Theatre on 9 April 1705. Congreve was obliged to supply the epilogue, and it is a telling one:

> To Sound and Show at first we make pretence,
> In time we may regale you with some Sense,
> But that, at present were too great Expence.

Greber's opera was, says John Downes, 'Perform'd by a new set of Singers, Arriv'd from *Italy*; (the worst that e're came from thence)'. He adds in a revealing sequence, as if such had indeed been the plan, that 'had they Open'd the House at first, with a good new *English* Opera, or a new Play; they wou'd have preserv'd the Favour of Court and City, and gain'd Reputation and Profit to themselves' (Downes, 48). Congreve wrote to Keally on 15 December 1705 that he had 'quitted the affair of the Hay-market. You may imagine I got nothing by it' (Hodges, *Letters*, 38–9). Soon after, the lease of the Queen's Theatre was taken up by Owen Swiney. *Semele* evidently was not performed during Congreve's lifetime, although it was reported to be ready for rehearsal in 1707 (*Muses Mercury*, 1707, 10–11). It was published with Congreve's *Collected Works* in 1710, but its first performance was not until 10 February 1744 with a slightly modified libretto and in a new setting by Handel, rather than with Eccles's original score.

Collected Works and later writings Not surprisingly after all his set-backs, Congreve wrote to Keally on 29 November 1708: 'Ease and quiet is what I hunt after. If I have not ambition, I have other passions more easily gratified' (Hodges, *Letters*, 53). In his disappointment, Congreve, like Ben Jonson before him, turned to his readers and prepared his works for publication: his comedies, his tragedy, his poetry, his masque, and his opera *Semele*. He had already begun collecting and revising his poetry by January 1707 when the *Muses Mercury* announced that 'Mr. Congreve is preparing an Edition of all his Miscellany Poems, in one Volume, … with the Addition of several New Pieces.' Their preparation preceded and perhaps suggested the larger collected works. The volume is testimony to Congreve's skill in lyric—including sung lyric, pastoral, and verse epistle—and to his ability, in translation and imitation, to make accessible in English a range of classical poets as diverse as Homer, Juvenal, and Ovid. Among them are 'The Mourning Muse of Alexis', a poem written on the death of Queen Mary in 1694 for which he received £100 from the king, and 'The Tears of Amaryllis for Amyntas', on the death of John, marquess of Blandford, in 1703.

Most of his plays, in quarto format, had been rushed into publication in the 1690s to meet demand, but now Congreve collaborated closely with his publisher Jacob Tonson to ensure that they were presented in their proper scenic form. (Congreve had lodged with Tonson in the mid-1690s, before moving to the house of Frances, *née* Bracegirdle, and Edward Porter in Arundel Street and then Surrey Street.) In 1710 *The Works of Mr. William Congreve* was published in three handsome octavo volumes, the plays edited to the neo-classical standard that Congreve had observed in composing them. In 1719–20, when the *Works* were next reprinted by Tonson, a smaller format was chosen that allowed Congreve to introduce centred speech headings.

Congreve never entirely stopped writing, although in later life, hampered by poor vision and health, he wrote much less. Swift mentioned to Stella in 1711 that Congreve had written *The Tatler*, no. 292, 'as blind as he is, for little Harrison' (Swift, *Journal*, 13 Feb 1711). Heeding Dryden's request that he 'be kind to his Remains' ('To my dear friend Mr. Congreve', l.73), Congreve provided the elegant and affectionate dedication to Dryden's *Dramatick Works* in six volumes, published by Tonson in 1717. He managed *Two Tales*, translated into verse from La Fontaine (1720), possibly the prose squib 'The Game of Quadrille' (c.1726), the political poem 'A Ballad of Quadrille' (1727), and one of his finest poems, his *Letter to Cobham* (1728), written not long before his death.

Anne Bracegirdle and Henrietta, duchess of Marlborough
Congreve did not marry. Instead he formed close alliances, first, with Anne Bracegirdle, for whom he wrote major parts in all his plays, including Angelica in *Love for Love* and Millamant in *The Way of the World*. She retired from the stage in 1707, and they remained friends for the rest of Congreve's life: he left her £200 and her sister Frances Porter £50 in his will, written in 1726. Much of the last decades of his life was spent in the sustaining company of Henrietta, Lady Godolphin and (from 1721) second duchess of Marlborough (1681–1733), whom he had probably met by 1703. He had written 'The Tears of Amaryllis'—dedicated to her father-in-law Lord Godolphin—on the death of her brother the marquess of Blandford in the same year, and her mother Sarah, first duchess of Marlborough, was by then complaining of the company her

daughter was keeping. Congreve left the largest part of his estate to Henrietta, naming her husband as executor, but this was in fact Congreve's discreet provision for his daughter, Mary (1723–1764), born to Henrietta on 23 November 1723. His intention becomes clear when Congreve's will is read with Henrietta's, in which she bequeaths to Mary 'all Mr Congreves Personal Estate that he left me' as well as her 'Fine Brilliant Diamond Neck-lace which cost Five Thousand Three hundred Pounds And also the fine Diamond Ear-Rings with Diamond Drop's to them which cost Two thousand Pounds'. Henrietta was reported to have told Edward Young that these jewels had been purchased with money Congreve had left her; the collets of the necklace may have been engraved with Congreve's initials (Hodges, *Letters*, 268–9). Though not specified in either will, Congreve's library also passed to Mary, who became duchess of Leeds when she married in 1740. The library remained at Hornby Castle in the Leeds family until it was auctioned by Sothebys in June 1930.

Government posts and later years
Aside from earning income from his writing, Congreve held various government posts, most of them, according to Thomas Southerne, through the intervention of his patron, Charles Montagu (BL, Add. MS 4221, fol. 341). After the success of *The Old Batchelor* Congreve was made one of eleven commissioners of the malt lottery on 23 April 1693, for which he seems to have received about £100. From 1695 to 1705 he was one of the commissioners for regulating and licensing hackney coaches, a post worth £100 a year. This was supplemented by his £48 salary as customs collector at Poole from 1700 to 1703. He was one of the commissioners for wine licences (£200 per annum) from 1705 to 1714, and then undersearcher of the London port in 1714, when he deputized one Joshua White, whom he mentioned in his will. Although a spurious letter has Lady Mary Wortley Montagu writing to Pope about Congreve 'enjoying leisure with dignity in two lucrative employments' (*Correspondence of Alexander Pope*, 1.423) and Southerne says that the post was worth £620, it was persistently recorded as £12 per annum in Treasury documents (Hodges, *Congreve, the Man*, 98n.). At any rate his civil service pay and perquisites were notably meagre for the first twenty years (Swift wrote that 'Congreve scarce could spare / A shilling to discharge his chair' ('Libel on Dr Delany', 1730, ll. 41–2)), but clearly improved after 1714 when he became secretary of Jamaica, a post that brought in about £700 a year, and was confirmed until his death. It is uncertain how much time and work these jobs involved. Three previous commissioners for hackney coaches had resigned when the stipend was reduced from £200 to £100, which suggests that that post may have been more demanding than a simple sinecure. The office for licensing wine was only a few minutes' walk from where Congreve lived in Surrey Street, and at least one wine licence signed by him is still extant (Hodges, *Letters*, 39n.). On 26 June 1706 Congreve wrote to his friend Keally complaining that business had been 'full of vexation and without any good consequence' (ibid., 42), which might have

referred to his civil service work. Although he was officially released from the obligation of residing in Jamaica after he became secretary, his appointment of a controversial deputy, one Samuel Page, certainly meant that he had to involve himself for a time in disputes between Page and the governor of Jamaica, Archibald Hamilton.

Ill health and death Evidently Congreve enjoyed good health when he was young—Swift says that he 'had the misfortune to squander away a very good constitution in his younger days' (Swift to Pope, 13 Feb 1729, *Correspondence of Jonathan Swift*, 3.311–12), giving weight to Congreve's claim that he once could 'jump one-and-twenty feet at one jump upon North-hall Common' (Congreve to Keally, 6 May 1712, Hodges, *Letters*, 67)—but he was afflicted through most of his life by gout and poor eyesight. As early as 1692 Congreve had alluded to his failing vision, and many of his letters refer to his incapacitating fits of gout. Swift wrote to Stella in October 1709 that Congreve

> is almost blind with cataracts growing on his eyes, and his case is, that he must wait two or three years, until the cataracts are riper, … and then he must have them couched; and besides he is never rid of the gout, yet he looks young and fresh, and is as chearful as ever.   (Swift to Stella, October 1710, Swift, *Journal to Stella*, 1.69–70)

Richard van Bleeck's portrait of Congreve, dated 1715, shows a man in quiet contemplation, holding a manuscript copy of two plays by his friend Vanbrugh. The downcast eyes suggest both Congreve's modesty and his faulty eyes. In his last poem, written to Lord Cobham less than a year before his death, Congreve describes himself

> retir'd without Regret,
> Forgetting Care, or striving to forget;
> In easy Contemplation soothing Time
> With Morals much, and now and then with Rhime,
> Not so robust in Body, as in Mind,
> And always undejected, tho' declin'd …
> (ll. 71–6)

Late in September 1728 Congreve's coach accidentally overturned. Although it was reported in the *Daily Post* on 1 October that 'he received no Hurt, having been immediately let Blood', he probably suffered some internal injury, for he complained later of a violent pain in his side. Congreve died at the Porters' house in Surrey Street on Sunday 19 January 1729. Henrietta arranged the funeral for the following Sunday, 26 January, when Congreve's body was interred in Westminster Abbey. The pall was supported there by the duke of Bridgewater, Henrietta's husband the earl of Godolphin, Lord Cobham, Lord Wilmington, the Hon. George Berkeley, and Brigadier-General Churchill, according to contemporary report. Congreve's memorial in the abbey is a medallion carved after a portrait by Kneller, with an epitaph beneath, written by the duchess of Marlborough.

Reputation Congreve's reputation suffered after the publication of Voltaire's *Letters Concerning the English Nation* in 1733. The young Voltaire, who clearly admired Congreve for raising 'the Glory of Comedy to a greater Height than any English Writer before or since his Time', had paid Congreve a visit in the late 1720s. By then Congreve was ill and nearly blind. Misinterpreting Congreve's modesty and irony in suggesting that his dramatic works were only trifles and that he should be visited 'upon no other foot than that of a Gentleman, who led a Life of Plainness and Simplicity', Voltaire wrote in the same famous letter that he 'was very much disgusted at so unseasonable a Piece of Vanity' (Voltaire, *Letters Concerning the English Nation*, 1733, 188). The English text has continued unaltered to this day, but a more mature Voltaire took the first opportunity to amend his French text. In the Amsterdam edition of 1738–9 he expunged the passages critical of Congreve's character, leaving only unqualified praise of his work. Voltaire's original theme was ignorantly taken up by Samuel Johnson, who began his life of Congreve with the disparaging suggestion that Congreve had lied about his birth in Yorkshire; he went on to recount the Voltaire story, and could find little to praise in Congreve's work. Even so, Johnson believed that one scene in *The Mourning Bride* (II.i) surpassed 'the whole mass of English poetry', and he expressed grudging admiration for a man who could count among his friends 'every man of his time whom wit and elegance had raised to reputation' (S. Johnson, *The Lives of the English Poets and a Criticism on their Works*, 3 vols., 1779–81).

Another continental, Luigi Riccoboni, who visited Congreve about the same time as Voltaire, found in him a man of 'Taste joined with great Learning', one who was 'perfectly acquainted with Nature' (Riccoboni, 175). Those who knew Congreve better describe a man of candour, wit, good nature, and compassion. Charles Hopkins, writing in 1697, observed:

> Nor does your Verse alone our Passions move,
> Beyond the Poet, we the person Love.
> In you, and almost only you; we find
> Sublimity of Wit, and Candour of the Mind.

Pope dedicated his translation of the *Iliad* to Congreve 'as a memorial of our friendship occasioned by his translation of this last part of Homer' (Pope to James Craggs, 1 Oct 1719, *Correspondence of Alexander Pope*). Swift wrote to Pope of 'our dear friend Mr. Congreve, whom I loved from my youth, and who surely, beside his other talents, was a very agreeable companion' (13 Feb 1729, *Correspondence of Jonathan Swift*, 3.311). Sir Richard Temple built a monument to Congreve at Stowe to commemorate both the poet's 'elegant, polished Wit' and the friend's 'candid, most unaffected Manners'. Indeed in the very first sentence he ever published—the opening lines of Cleophil's address to Katherine Leveson in *Incognita*—Congreve announced the values by which, implicitly, he would both write and live: 'A Clear Wit, sound Judgement and a Merciful Disposition'.

The Way of the World has often been considered the culmination of Restoration comedy. Along with Wycherley and Etherege, Congreve is almost universally regarded as one of the three pre-eminent writers of comedy of his time. As *The London Stage* and E. L. Avery's *Congreve's Plays on the Eighteenth-Century Stage* (1951) amply prove, Congreve's plays had a long and distinguished history through the eighteenth century, and by no means vanished with the alleged triumph of 'sentimental comedy'.

C. Y. FERDINAND and D. F. McKENZIE

Sources J. M. Treadwell, 'Congreve, Tonson, and Rowe's *Reconcilement*', *N&Q*, 220 (1975), 265–9 · J. Vanbrugh, *A short vindication of 'The relapse' and 'The provok'd wife', from immorality and prophaneness* (1698) · *The correspondence of Jonathan Swift*, ed. H. Williams, 5 vols. (1963–5) · W. Van Lennep and others, eds., *The London stage, 1660–1800*, pt 1: *1660–1700* (1965) · E. L. Avery, ed., *The London stage, 1660–1800*, pt 2: *1700–1729* (1960) · *The correspondence of Alexander Pope*, ed. G. Sherburn, 5 vols. (1956) · L. Riccoboni, *Historical and critical account of the theatres in Europe* (1741) · J. Schirmann, 'The first Hebrew translation from English literature', *Scripta Hierosolymitana* (1967), 3–15 · will, PRO, PROB 11/621, fols. 354r–356r · will, Henrietta, duchess of Marlborough, PRO, PROB 11/677, fols. 139v–141r · BL, Add. MS 4221, fol. 341 [Thomas Southerne's recollections of William Congreve] · 'Catalogus omnium studentium admissox in collegium … ab anno 1637', TCD [MS copy of lost original] · E. L. Avery, *Congreve's plays on the eighteenth-century stage* (New York, 1951) · G. Barlow, 'From tennis court to opera house', PhD diss., U. Glas., 3 vols., 1983 · C. Cibber, *An apology for the life of Mr. Colley Cibber* (1740) · J. Collier, *A short view of the immorality and profaneness of the English stage* (1698) · W. Congreve, *Amendments of Mr. Collier's false and imperfect citations* (1698) · *The complete works of William Congreve*, ed. H. Davis (Chicago, 1967) · *The works of William Congreve*, ed. D. F. McKenzie [forthcoming] · T. Davies, *Dramatic miscellanies: consisting of critical observations on several plays of Shakespeare*, 3 vols. (1783–4) · J. Dennis, *Letters upon several occasions written by and between Mr. Dryden, Mr. Wycherly, Mr. —, Mr. Congreve, and Mr. Dennis* (1696) · J. Dennis, *The usefulness of the stage to the happiness of mankind, to government, and to religion* (1698) · J. Downes, *Roscius Anglicanus, or, An historical review of the stage* (1708) · *The letters of John Dryden*, ed. C. E. Ward (Durham, NC, 1942) · *The poems of John Dryden*, ed. J. Kinsley, 4 vols. (1958) · *The table-talk and bon-mots of Samuel Foote*, ed. W. Cook (1902) · [C. Gildon], *The lives and characters of the English dramatick poets … first begun by Mr Langbain* [1699] · J. C. Hodges, *William Congreve, the man: a biography from new sources* (New York and London, 1941) · *William Congreve: letters and documents*, ed. J. C. Hodges (1964) · C. Hopkins, 'An epistle … to Mr. Yalden in Oxon., dated from London-Derry, 3 August 1699', *Poetical miscellanies: the fifth part* (1704), 185–6 · [G. Jacob], *The poetical register, or, The lives and characters of the English dramatick poets*, 2 vols. (1719–20) · J. Swift, *Journal to Stella*, ed. H. Williams, 2 vols. (1948) · *The poems of Jonathan Swift*, ed. H. Williams, 3 vols. (1937)

Archives Bodl. Oxf., letters | BL, letters to E. Porter and Mrs Porter, Add. MS 4293, fols. 54–64 · NRA Scotland, priv. coll., letters to J. Keally

Likenesses W. D. Claret, oils, 1682, repro. in Hodges, *William Congreve, the man* · attrib. G. Kneller, oils, c.1685, Christies, 5 May 1950, lot 108; copy, NPG [photographic negative 5892] · H. Tilson, oils, c.1694–1695, repro. in Burcheall & Sadleir, *Alum. Dub.* (1924) · studio of G. Kneller, oils, c.1695, repro. in A. Crookshank and D. Webb, *The paintings and sculptures in Trinity College Dublin* (1990) · G. Kneller, oils, c.1695–1696, NPG; repro. in D. C. Taylor, *William Congreve* (1931) · miniature, oils on vellum, c.1700, Royal Collection; repro. in G. Reynolds, *The sixteenth and seventeenth century miniatures in the collection of her majesty the queen* (1999) · pear wood, c.1700, Yale U. CBA · H. Howard?, oils, c.1704–1705, repro. in Hodges, *Congreve, the man* · H. Howard?, miniature, 1708, repro. in Hodges, *Congreve, the man* · G. Kneller, chalk sketch on brown paper, c.1708, Courtauld Inst.; repro. in J. D. Stewart, 'Some drawings by Sir Godfrey Kneller', *Connoisseur* (1964) · G. Kneller, oils, 1709, NPG [*see illus.*] · studio of G. Kneller, oils, c.1709, NPG · J. Smith, mezzotint, 1710 (after G. Kneller, 1709), BM, NPG · R. van Bleeck, oils, 1715, Stedelijk Museum Vanderkelen-Mertens, Leuven; repro. in D. F. McKenzie, 'Richard van Bleeck's painting of William Congreve as contemplative, 1715', *Review of English Studies*, 51 (2000), 46–61 · F. Bird, relief sculpture memorial plaque, 1729 (after G. Kneller, 1709), Westminster Abbey; repro. in K. A. Esdaile, *English church monuments, 1510 to 1840* (1946) · W. Kent, stone relief, 1736, Stowe, Kent; repro. in G. Bickham, *The beauties of Stowe* (1750) · J. Hopwood, engraving, 1808 · bronze medallion, 1819, Handel House Museum, London · T. Chambars, engraving (after G. Kneller, 1709), repro. in *The works of Mr. William Congreve*, 3 vols. (1761) · J. Cheere, bronze bust, Castle Museum, York · T. Cook, engraving, repro. in *The poetical works of William Congreve* (1778) · Cooper, engraving (after G. Kneller, 1709), repro. in *Memoirs of celebrated persons composing the Kit-cat Club* (1821) · J. Faber, mezzotint (after G. Kneller, 1709), repro. in *The Kit-cat Club: done from the original paintings of Sir Godfrey Kneller* (1735) · F. Kyte, mezzotint (after G. Kneller, 1709) · P. H., engraving, repro. in *The dramatic works of William Congreve*, 2 vols. (1773) · R. B. Parkes, engraving (after G. Kneller, 1709), repro. in C. Cibber, *An apology for the life of Mr. Colley Cibber*, ed. R. W. Lowe, new edn, 2 vols. (1889) · W. Ridley, engraving, repro. in *The poetical works of William Congreve* · M. Vandergucht, engraving (after G. Kneller, 1709), repro. in *Familiar letters of love and gallantry*, 2 vols. (1718) · M. Vandergucht, engraving (after G. Kneller, 1709), repro. in G. Jacob, *The poetical register* (1719–20) · bronze bust (*Regency*), repro. in auction catalogue for sale of 28 November 1989

Wealth at death £5000–£12,000, including £3000 of old South Sea annuities; other parts of personal estate include a cane, a diamond ring, a Kneller portrait of Henrietta, and an enamelled miniature of Henrietta: wills of William Congreve, with four codicils, proved 21 Feb 1729, and Henrietta, duchess of Marlborough, proved 19 May 1736, in Hodges, *William Congreve: Letters and documents*

Congreve, Sir William, second baronet (1772–1828), rocket designer, was born on 20 May 1772, perhaps at Homerton, Hackney, Middlesex (where he was baptized), the eldest son of Captain-Lieutenant (later Lieutenant-General Sir) William Congreve, first baronet (1743–1814), Royal Artillery, and his first wife, Rebecca, daughter of Fleet Elmstone RN. The younger William attended Newcome's school, Hackney, a fashionable private school for the sons of noblemen and gentlemen, where Thomas Creevey was his fellow pupil; Wolverhampton grammar school; the Revd John Tucker's 'seminary for young gentlemen' at Hever Court, Singlewell, near Gravesend, Kent; and Trinity College, Cambridge. Admitted to Trinity College in 1788, he matriculated in 1789 and was a scholar in 1792. He read mathematics and at the 1793 tripos was placed among the junior optimes; he graduated BA in 1793 and MA in 1796. He may also have attended the Royal Military Academy at Woolwich and, possibly, in the early 1790s, Gray's Inn, London.

Little is known of Congreve's early career. In 1803 he was a volunteer in the London and Westminster light horse, and was a London businessman who published a polemical newspaper, the *Royal Standard and Political Register*, which was tory, pro-government, and anti-Cobbett. Following George Cranfield Berkeley's successful libel action against it in 1804, Congreve seems to have withdrawn from publishing and applied himself to inventing. During the threat of French invasion, as a member of the Society for the Improvement of Naval Architecture, he proposed in 1804 an oar-powered, iron-armoured floating battery; but it was never constructed. He also proposed a large flotilla of mortar boats to destroy the Boulogne invasion flotilla and attack enemy ports.

About this time there were experiments with war

Sir William Congreve, second baronet (1772–1828), by James Lonsdale, c.1812

rockets in several countries, notably France and Ireland. Congreve always denied that he had invented war rockets, attributing their origin to Mughal antiquity. Influenced by their use against the British in India and by the unsuccessful experiments at Woolwich of Lieutenant-General Thomas Desaguiliers (chief firemaster from 1748 to 1780), and backed by his father, who was comptroller of the royal laboratory at Woolwich from 1789 to 1814, Congreve in 1804, at his own expense, began experimenting with rockets at Woolwich. He developed rockets of different calibres and warheads. Through his father he gained official backing, and his rockets were manufactured at the Royal Arsenal there. In September 1805, at the Woolwich marshes, he demonstrated his rockets to William Pitt, the prime minister, and other ministers.

Congreve's father knew the prince of Wales (later the prince regent and George IV) and the duke of York and was liked by them. Congreve had approached the prince, who became his friend and patron, and a keen partisan of his rockets. Thomas Creevey wrote that 'Congreve … took to inventing rocketts for the more effectual destruction of mankind, for which he became patronised by the Prince of Wales' (Creevey Papers, 1905, 147), and Earl Grey privately alleged that 'the rockets were to be the great instruments of security in the new park against the mob' (Brougham, 2.59). Congreve's claim, in his dedication to George IV in his Treatise on the … Congreve Rocket System (1827), that 'the Rocket System not only owes its existence but its present state of perfection to the patronage of His Majesty' was more than a courtier's sycophancy: royal favour was crucial to his career.

Congreve's rockets were rushed into production at Woolwich. His role was essentially in their development and manufacture, though in the early years of their production he sometimes directed their use in combat. They were first used in Sir Sidney Smith's naval attack on Boulogne in November 1805, which Congreve accompanied. With bad weather, the attack failed, and this was followed in Britain by much criticism of rockets. In 1806 Congreve replaced paper-cased by iron-cased rockets. The latter were used, directed by Congreve, in Captain E. R. Owen's attack on Boulogne in October 1806 and were considered by the British to be successful, though apparently with insufficient evidence of the damage inflicted. In September 1807 Congreve directed the successful rocket bombardment of Copenhagen. Rockets were also used elsewhere. Although the duke of Wellington continued to be unimpressed—in November 1810 he wrote that he was 'no partisan of Congreve's rockets' (Dispatches, 6.591)—they were used in the Peninsular War. In March 1811 Congreve was elected a fellow of the Royal Society.

Also in 1811 Congreve, who apparently never held a British regular commission, was commissioned lieutenant-colonel in the Hanoverian artillery—an honorary rank; later he was promoted to major-general. His Hanoverian rank was resented by Royal Artillery officers, who did not consider him a professional soldier. In February 1811 he was appointed an equerry to the prince of Wales, on whose accession in 1820 he became equerry to the king. In September 1812 he visited Liverpool to become a parliamentary candidate—his opponent Henry Brougham wrote that 'Congreve, the rocket-man, stands on the Prince's interest!' (Brougham, 2.57)—but withdrew for lack of support. In October, through the prince regent's influence, Congreve was elected—in fact appointed by the proprietor, the nabob Sir Mark Wood—an MP for the notorious pocket borough of Gatton in Surrey. As MP he supported the tory government, opposed Roman Catholic relief, and spoke little; in 1816 he vacated the seat in favour of Wood's son. In December 1812 his father was made a baronet.

In October 1813 the Royal Horse Artillery 'rocket brigade' (commanded by Captain Richard Bogue) fought with notable success at the battle of Leipzig—the only British troops present. Following this, Tsar Alexander I of Russia awarded Congreve the knighthood of the order of St Anne, and belatedly in 1821 Charles XIV of Sweden awarded him the order of the Sword. Congreve claimed that he had been offered, but declined, command of the rocket corps 'with rank in the Regiment of Artillery' (Congreve, Details of the Rocket System, 9). Rockets were successfully employed in the Anglo-American War of 1812–14. In 1814 Congreve joined Wellington's army in southern France. The use of rockets continued to be controversial, criticized by some officers and by writers in the press: in July 1814 the Morning Chronicle denounced their manufacture as 'tomfoolery'. However, Congreve and his supporters continued to extol their achievements and potential.

In April 1814 Congreve succeeded his father as baronet, afterwards taking over his father's official appointments, which he held almost until his own death in 1828. He was the only head of the royal laboratory in the nineteenth century who was not a Royal Artillery officer. In 1821 he was paid £360 (with housing) as comptroller of the royal laboratory and £101 5s. as superintendent of the royal military repository. He organized the impressive firework displays in London for the peace of 1814 and for the coronation of George IV in 1821. In 1816 he accompanied Grand Duke Nicholas (later Tsar Nicholas I) on his tour of England, and in that year, according to W. A. Shaw's *Knights of England*, was made a KCH.

Congreve continued to experiment with rockets. In 1815 he made his most important change to their configuration, moving the guidestick from the side to the centre, so increasing accuracy. He experimented to produce a stickless, spinning rocket, but never satisfactorily solved the problem. He had developed not just war rockets but a weapon system, which he called 'the Congreve Rocket System', and claimed that the rocket was 'ammunition without ordnance ... the soul of artillery without the body' (Hogg, 1.520). Rockets were envisaged as not merely supplementing, but superseding, conventional artillery, and as having immense potential for future war. He claimed that the rocket was 'an arm by which the whole system of military tactics is destined to be changed' (*Treatise*, 42).

Self-important and an avid publicist for himself and his rockets, Congreve repeatedly asserted—notably in *The Details of the Rocket System* (1814) and *A Treatise on the ... Congreve Rocket System, as Compared with Artillery* (1827)—the advantages of rockets over conventional artillery: these included recoillessness, lightness and portability, volume and rate of fire, moral effect, and economy, with an 'immense saving' over artillery. He asserted the rockets' 'most important property of universal application' (*Treatise*, 38) and, in the longer term, did not want specialized army rocket units, except for the heaviest rockets, but rather the extensive use of rockets by cavalry and infantry. He advocated massed rocket bombardment: 'in all cases, I lay the greatest stress upon the use of this arm in *great quantities*' (ibid., 78). He envisaged rockets of half a ton to a ton, for bombarding fortifications, and advocated naval use of rockets, supplementing but not replacing conventional ordnance, particularly for coastal bombardment and on steam vessels: 'the late introduction of steam navigation opens a new field for naval warfare—by its combination with heavy rockets' (ibid., 21).

Congreve designed naval gun-mountings which were on sale to merchant vessels, but apparently not much used. He designed a lighter 24-pounder which the navy adopted and used to upgun vessels to counter the heavily armed United States warships, and a gunsight which also was adopted by the navy. In 1828 he proposed a steam-powered, iron-armoured floating battery for, if required, forcing the Dardanelles; the controller of the navy rejected it as impractical.

In 1818, through the prince regent, who had an apparently strong electoral influence in Plymouth, and backed by the government, which had Admiralty influence there,

Congreve, a 'Carlton House man', was elected an MP for Plymouth; he continued such until his death. His father had begun the royal military repository, the artillery museum collection at Woolwich. Congreve improved it and, through the prince regent, secured the erection in 1820 of John Nash's Rotunda, which still houses the Museum of Artillery and contains the best collection of Congreve rocketry.

Congreve lived with a mistress (formerly Creevey's) and had at least two illegitimate sons. In December 1824 he married, at Wessel, Prussia, Isabella Carvalho (or Charlotte), a young woman of Portuguese descent and widow of Henry Nisbett McEnvoy. They had two sons and a daughter.

Called by the press the 'ingenious Mr. Congreve' (Winter, 28), he made various inventions—including an improved process of gunpowder manufacture, a hydro-pneumatic canal lock and sluice, a colour-printing process, a rolling-ball clock, and a 'perpetual motion machine'—and took out at least eighteen patents. When Drury Lane Theatre in London was rebuilt after a fire in 1809, he designed its anti-fire water system. He also invented a rocket-propelled whaling harpoon, which was a commercial failure. From about 1822, following Henry Trengrouse's initiative, he experimented in adapting his war rockets to ship-to-shore lifesaving rockets, but gave this low priority and died before he could perfect the system. Others developed lifesaving rockets much more successfully, and in the nineteenth century rockets apparently saved more lives than they destroyed. Among his varied publications were *A Concise Account of the Origin and Progress of the Rocket System* (1807) and works on cash payments and currency.

In addition to his official appointments, Congreve had his own private rocket factory at West Ham, London, and he supplied the East India Company. In later years he was prominent in various industrial ventures, such as gas companies, which were mostly unsuccessful. He was chairman of the Equitable Loan Bank, and director of the Arigna Iron and Coal Company, the Palladium Insurance Company, and the Peruvian Mining Company. As a director of the Arigna company he was apparently involved in fraud; in 1826 the case went to court, with Congreve among those accused. Ill, he went to the south of France, beyond British jurisdiction. The case dragged on and not until May 1828, shortly before Congreve's death, did the lord chancellor rule that the transaction concerned was 'clearly fraudulent' and was intended to profit Congreve and others. Congreve suffered from a 'palsy of the limbs' and became paralysed in the lower part of his body. He stayed in a private hotel at 24 place Ste Scarbes, Toulouse, and died on 15 May 1828. The following day he was buried, with military honours, in the protestant and Jewish cemetery of Terre Cabade, Toulouse. In April 1835 his widow married Charles Fenton Whiting; she died on 5 November 1872. Congreve was succeeded as baronet by his son, William Augustus Congreve (b. 1827), who was last heard of in Sydney, Australia, in 1860 when he intended going to the

Fiji islands; in 1882 he was legally presumed dead. Following his death the baronetcy became extinct.

Congreve rockets, though erratic and inaccurate, were used by British forces in numerous campaigns, and similar rockets were adopted by other states. In Britain Congreve rockets were declared obsolete in 1866, but Hale rockets, derived from them—though overtaken and marginalized by artillery development—were used in colonial campaigns to the end of the century. Congreve had 'created the world's first rocket weapons system' and 'initiated the modern process of research and development in rocketry' (Winter, xiii–xiv).   ROGER T. STEARN

Sources J. R. J. Jocelyn, 'The connection of the ordnance department with national and royal fireworks, including some account of … Sir William Congreve (2nd baronet)', *Journal of the Royal Artillery*, 32 (1906), 481–503 · F. H. Winter, *The first golden age of rocketry* (1990) · *GM*, 1st ser., 98/2 (1828) · W. Congreve, *A treatise on the … Congreve rocket system, as compared with artillery* (1827) · W. Congreve, *The details of the rocket system* (1814); repr. (1970) · P. A. Symonds and D. R. Fisher, 'Congreve, William', HoP, *Commons* · D. R. Fisher, 'Plymouth', HoP, *Commons* · Burke, *Peerage* (1879) · *The Creevey papers*, ed. H. Maxwell, 3rd edn (1905); rev. edn, ed. J. Gore (1963) · O. F. G. Hogg, *The Royal Arsenal: its background, origin, and subsequent history*, 2 vols. (1963) · E. J. Becklake and D. Millard, 'Congreve and his works', *Journal of the British Interplanetary Society*, 45 (1992), 281–4 · H. P. Brougham, *The life and times of Henry, Lord Brougham*, ed. W. Brougham, 2 (1871) · *The correspondence of George, prince of Wales, 1770–1812*, ed. A. Aspinall, 6: 1806–1809 (1969) · *The letters of King George IV, 1812–1830*, ed. A. Aspinall, 1 (1938) · W. A. Shaw, *The knights of England*, 1 (1906) · J. Scoffern, *Projectile weapons of war, and explosive compounds*, 3rd edn (1858); repr. (1971) · W. Y. Carman, 'Sir William Congreve, 1741–1814', *Journal of the Society for Army Historical Research*, 51 (1973) · R. St G. G. Bartelot, 'A concise history of the Rotunda Museum, 1778–1978', *Journal of the Royal Artillery*, 105 (1978), 104–14 · Venn, *Alum. Cant.* · J. R. Tanner, ed., *Historical register of the University of Cambridge … to the year 1910* (1917) · H. Strachan, *From Waterloo to Balaclava: tactics, technology and the British army, 1815–1854* (1985) · T. H. B. Oldfield, *The representative history of Great Britain and Ireland*, 6 vols. (1816) · *The dispatches of … the duke of Wellington … from 1799 to 1818*, ed. J. Gurwood, new edn, 6: *Peninsula, 1790–1813* (1838) · J. Kane, *List of officers of the royal regiment of artillery from the year 1716 to the year 1899*, rev. W. H. Askwith, 4th edn (1900) · L. H. Thornton and P. Fraser, *The Congreves* (1930) · Boase, *Mod. Eng. biog.* · A. D. Lambert, *The last sailing battlefleet: maintaining naval mastery, 1815–1850* (1991) · R. Gardiner and A. Lambert, eds., *Steam, steel and shellfire: the steam warship, 1815–1905* (1992) · R. T. Stearn, '"Congreve, the rocket-man": Sir William Congreve, second baronet', *Soldiers of the Queen*, 86 (1996), 11–18

Archives Royal Arch. · Royal Artillery Institution, Woolwich, London, papers, incl. of his father · Sci. Mus., papers relating to hydro-pneumatic canal locks · Staffs. RO, corresp. and memo | Hunt. L., letters to Grenville family

Likenesses P. Reinagle, oils, *c*.1782 (with his father), NG Ire.; repro. in Winter, *First golden age* · J. Lonsdale, portrait, *c*.1809, NPG; repro. in Winter, *First golden age* · J. Lonsdale, oils, *c*.1812, NPG [*see illus.*] · J. Gilbert, J. F. Skill, and E. Walker, group portrait, pencil and wash drawing, *c*.1856 (*Men of science living in 1807–8*), NPG; repro. in R. Walker, *National Portrait Gallery: Regency portraits*, 2 vols. (1985)

Conin. *See* Baíthéne mac Brénainn (*d*. 598) *under* Iona, abbots of (*act*. 563–927).

Coningham, Sir Arthur (1895–1948), air force officer, was born in Brisbane, Australia, on 19 January 1895, the eldest of the three children of Arthur Coningham (1863–1939), variously a chemist, tobacconist, bookmaker, and book salesman, who played cricket once for Australia against

Sir Arthur Coningham (1895–1948), by Howard Coster, 1940s

England, in 1894–5, and his wife, Alice Stamford Dowling (1869–1959), who emigrated to Australia from Devon in 1885. The family fled to New Zealand following two widely publicized trials in Sydney in 1900 and 1901; the first jury failed to agree, but the second acquitted a Catholic priest of the Coninghams' charge that he had fathered Alice's second child.

After two years at Wellington College, New Zealand (1909–10), where he excelled only at shooting, Coningham worked as a general hand on sheep farms. He enlisted in the 5th Wellington regiment on 10 August 1914 and took part in an expedition that captured German Samoa on the 29th. Following his return to Wellington in April 1915 he joined the Canterbury mounted rifles, sailed with the 4th reinforcements on the 17th, and arrived at Anzac Cove early in June. His health, undermined in Samoa, collapsed: sunstroke, dysentery, and typhoid put him in hospital until September, when he was sent home and discharged, unfit for further service, in March 1916.

During April, however, Coningham sailed for England at his own expense and in August was admitted to the Royal Flying Corps, commissioned as a second lieutenant, and taught to fly. He graduated from the Central Flying School (CFS) at Upavon on 25 November 1916 and joined 32 squadron on the western front in December. He now became known as Mary, a nickname worn down from the original Maori (then thought suitable for any New Zealander) and made sure his friends used it; except officially, he never again answered to Arthur.

After seven months of intense activity, earning promotion to captain and two decorations (DSO, MC), Coningham was invalided back to England in August 1917 and spent three months in hospital, suffering from 'stress of service'. He returned to the western front in command of 92 squadron in July 1918. At the armistice he had flown 176 patrols, personally destroyed nine enemy aircraft, shared in the destruction of four, damaged at least four, and driven away scores.

Coningham was awarded a DFC in June 1919 and granted a permanent commission as a flight lieutenant in August. His flying skills were displayed at the RAF's first aerial pageant at Hendon in July 1920, and in October he returned as an instructor to the CFS, Upavon. He again performed brilliantly at Hendon in 1921. In February 1922 he went to Mosul, Iraq, to join 55 squadron, of which he took command in July 1923, on his promotion to squadron leader. In February 1924 he arrived in Cairo to undertake air staff duties. By 1925 interest was growing in the possibility of opening up Africa to civil aviation. On Air Ministry orders Coningham therefore led three DH 9a two-seater biplanes from Helwan (near Cairo) to Kaduna in Nigeria and back during October and November—a round trip of about 6500 miles. He was awarded an AFC on 1 January 1926 to mark the first east–west crossing of Africa by air. The value of that route for sending aircraft to Cairo from Britain and the United States would be fully realized during the Second World War.

In December 1926 Coningham was appointed a squadron commander at the Cadet College, Cranwell. From there he returned again to the CFS (now at Wittering, near Stamford) in July 1930, this time as deputy commandant. Promoted wing commander in July 1931 he was sent to Khartoum as senior airman at Sudan defence force headquarters. He married Nancy (Nan) Muriel Brooks (1903–1985) in Alexandria in July 1932, six months after the death of her first husband, Sir Howard Frank (1872–1932), the head of a famous property-dealing company. She had two sons from her first marriage and one daughter from her second. Coningham returned to England in March 1935 and spent four years in Coastal Area (Command from July 1936) in various appointments around Southampton Water and was promoted to group captain in January 1937.

In July 1939 Coningham took command as an air commodore in York of 4 group, Bomber Command. He began the task of converting a nominal weapon (five squadrons of men untrained in night operations, flying inadequate Whitley bombers) into one that might become a dangerous weapon. Promoted again, to air vice-marshal in September 1940, his future as a 'bomber baron' seemed assured by July 1941, as his group enlarged and its training and equipment improved.

At that very moment, Coningham was whisked off to Cairo to command 204 group, at the request of Air Marshal Tedder, the newly appointed head of Middle East air command. Notice of his appointment as CB (for Bomber Command service) followed him, and in September he set up his first joint headquarters when the Eighth Army was formed. In October 204 group became the western desert air force, to match that army's status.

Coningham came to be regarded by Tedder (in Liddell Hart's words) as 'the real hero' of the desert war. His powers of inspiration, his tactical awareness (emphasizing the need to win air superiority before attempting close co-operation with ground forces), and his ability to act sensibly in numerous crises also attracted the admiration of senior American airmen, especially during the Tunisian campaign (November 1942 – May 1943). But he had no grasp of logistics—the science of planning and carrying out the movement and maintenance of forces—so Tedder provided him in February 1942 with an able assistant in Air Commodore Thomas Elmhirst. Supported in Cairo by experts handling specific problems, the whole organization was presided over by Tedder, who had the ear in London of two officers whom Churchill respected: Sir Charles Portal (chief of the air staff) and Sir Wilfrid Freeman (his vice-chief).

Unfortunately, Coningham and General Montgomery (appointed to command the Eighth Army in August 1942) became estranged in November over what seemed to airmen the army's tardy pursuit of Rommel after the battle of El Alamein. Personal relations between Coningham (supported by Tedder) and Montgomery worsened, but all three usually agreed on the basic issue that air power must be independent of army (or navy) control—an issue that divided commanders in all services and on all sides throughout the war.

Coningham was knighted (KCB) in November 1942. Having been promoted air marshal in February 1943 he was appointed to command British and American tactical air forces in Tunisia under the direction of an American airman (General Spaatz), who was, in turn, directed by Tedder as head of Mediterranean air command; all of them were subordinate to General Eisenhower as supreme allied commander. During 1943 he established himself as a key member of the Anglo-American team which achieved victory in Tunisia, conquered Sicily, and successfully invaded Italy. He returned to England in January 1944.

As head of the 2nd Tactical Air Force, Coningham was part of an even larger allied team, led by Eisenhower with Tedder as his deputy, charged to liberate occupied Europe and destroy Nazi Germany. The stakes were high, the options various, the enemy cunning, and the commanders forceful men, used to obedience. Among the ensuing quarrels, that which caused Coningham's exclusion from the planning and execution of the Arnhem operation (September 1944) led to an avoidable disaster. Although the allied commanders co-operated more than they quarrelled, notably during Hitler's Ardennes offensive (December 1944), which caught them all off guard, it may have been as well that their resources were abundant and that by 1944 the Soviet Union had gravely weakened German power.

Away from the debating table, Coningham recognized that the fight for air superiority, his first priority, was in fact his least worry. He had many experienced combat pilots, but few who were skilled in ground attack. That role, he foresaw, would become a constant task all the way from Normandy to Berlin, and squadrons must be equipped and trained—as in his earlier campaigns—to move forward rapidly.

In July 1945 Coningham received the DSM, an American decoration, was appointed head of Flying Training Command, and elected commodore of the RAF yacht club. He spent three weeks in the United States in September as guest of the United States Army Air Forces. He was knighted again (KBE) in January 1946 and granted the freedom of Brussels, his favourite city, in April. Although he was required to retire in August 1947, the Air Ministry accepted his plea that it be officially recorded that he left the RAF at his own request. Coningham died early on 30 January 1948, when an Avro Tudor IV airliner named *Star Tiger*, in which he was travelling as a passenger to Havana, Cuba, crashed into the sea north-east of Bermuda.

A big, handsome man, Coningham loved company, gossip, dancing, and parties that went on until morning, although he never smoked and drank little. An outstanding pilot and navigator, he also excelled at polo, sailing, and shooting, though never at cricket. A superb combat record enhanced a natural talent for leadership, never more evident than when danger threatened; his determination to reach high rank was less evident.

VINCENT ORANGE

Sources V. Orange, *Coningham* (1990) · [Lord Tedder], *With prejudice: the war memoirs of marshal of the Royal Air Force, Lord Tedder* (1966) · J. Terraine, *The right of the line: the Royal Air Force in the European war, 1939–1945* (1985) · F. C. Pogue, *The supreme command* (Washington, DC, 1954) · R. G. Davis, *Carl A. Spaatz and the air war in Europe* (1993) · *Air support* (Air ministry, 1955) · B. F. Cooling, ed., *Case studies in the development of close air support* (1990) · A. Coningham, 'The development of tactical air forces', *Journal of the Royal United Service Institution*, 91 (1946), 211–26 · P. Chamberlain, 'A short history of no. 32 squadron, RFC/RAF, 1916–18', *Cross & Cockade USA*, 22/1 (1981), 39–70 · H. H. Russell, 'History of 92 squadron', *Journal of the Society of World War I Aero Historians*, 7/1 (1966), 1–15 · *Report of the court investigation regarding the loss of Tudor IV aircraft 'Star Tiger' G-AHNP on 30 January 1948* (1948) · Zero, *The secret history of the Coningham case* (1901) · AusDB · DNB
Archives FILM BFI NFTVA, documentary footage · BFI NFTVA, news footage · IWM FVA, actuality footage · IWM FVA, news footage |SOUND IWM SA, oral history interview · IWM SA, recorded talk
Likenesses W. Stoneman, photograph, 1930, NPG · H. Coster, photograph, 1940–48, NPG [see illus.] · photograph, 1941 (with Cross), repro. in Orange, *Coningham* · photograph, 1942 (with Montgomery), repro. in Orange, *Coningham* · photograph, 1945 (with Elmhirst), repro. in Orange, *Coningham* · photograph, 1945, Hult. Arch. · W. Stoneman, photograph, 1946, NPG · R. Dobson, portrait, priv. coll. · H. A. Freeth, drawing, repro. in P. Guedalla, *Middle East, 1940–1942* (1944) · W. Rothenstein, drawing
Wealth at death £5451 1s. 7d.: probate, 16 Dec 1948, CGPLA Eng. & Wales

Coningham, James (1669/70–1716), Presbyterian minister and tutor, of unknown parents, was described as 'Anglus' when he graduated MA from Edinburgh University on 27 February 1694. His first ministry was at Penrith, Cumberland, at a new Presbyterian meeting established as a result of a lectureship supported by Dr Thomas Gibson of Hatton Garden, London. Subsequently, the Congregational Fund Board made a grant of £5. He was ordained in August 1694 as a licentiate of the Church of Scotland. While at Penrith he began to prepare students for the nonconformist ministry. He married Agnes Cookson (*bap.* 1671), daughter of William and Alice Cookson, at St Andrew's, Penrith, on 30 July 1694. There is evidence that locally he became a figure of some note. In 1696 he rode to London 'in a monstrous large cloth hat' to present the Cumberland Association to King William (J. Coningham to R. Thoresby, 14 Sept 1699, Thoresby MSS), and he was involved in promoting the reformation of manners. He corresponded with the Leeds antiquarian Ralph Thoresby concerning natural curiosities, making a number of donations to Thoresby's museum. He is said to have been the author of *A critical essay on modern medals, with some reflections on the taste and judgment of the ancients* (1704).

In May 1699 Richard Stretton suggested Coningham as a suitable successor to Timothy Manlove as minister of the Mill Hill Chapel at Leeds, but in 1700 Coningham accepted the call to Cross Street, Manchester, as co-pastor with John Chorlton and to assist in the academy there. Little is known about what was taught, but the surviving manuscript notes of one student, John Turner (1689–1737), in his Bible provide evidence for the study of Semitics. Coningham was said to be 'admirably well fitted for the Work … his Learning was very considerable' (Wright, 23). His most celebrated student was Samuel Bourn the younger. After Chorlton's death in August 1705, unsuccessful attempts by his congregation were made to obtain Samuel Benyon, tutor and minister at Broad Oak. Coningham's situation became increasingly uncomfortable. He was prosecuted for conducting an academy without a licence, and experienced much hostility locally as a dissenter. It was, however, the doctrinal divisions within his own congregation which persuaded him to accept the call to London from the congregation at Haberdasher Hall following the death in 1712 of their minister, Richard Stretton. There his ministry was much more comfortable, but his health was broken and he died on 1 September 1716 in his forty-seventh year. He was buried in Bunhill Fields, London.

DAVID L. WYKES

Sources S. Wright, *The blessedness of them that die in the faith and work of their Lord. A sermon occasion'd by the death of the late Reverend Mr James Coningham, A. M. Preach'd to his affectionate afflicted people, September 9th, 1716* (1716), 23–4 · T. Baker, *Memorials of a dissenting chapel* (1884), 17–20, 140 [incl. bibliography] · J. H. Colligan, *History of the Penrith Presbyterian Church* (1908), 7–8 · G. E. Evans, *Record of the provincial assembly of Lancashire and Cheshire* (1896), 113 · B. Nightingale, *The ejected of 1662 in Cumberland and Westmorland: their predecessors and successors*, 2 (1911), 1278, 1401 · H. McLachlan, *English education under the Test Acts: being the history of the nonconformist academies, 1662–1820* (1931), 115–17 · 'Early nonconformist academies: VI', *Transactions of the Congregational Historical Society*, 5 (1911–12), 73–5 [incl. list of students] · W. Wilson, *The history and antiquities of dissenting churches and meeting houses in London, Westminster and Southwark*, 4 vols. (1808–14), vol. 3, pp. 134–6 · B. Nightingale, *Lancashire nonconformity*, 6 vols. [1890–93], vol. 5, pp. 91–3 · M. Henry, diary, 1 Jan 1704/5–31 Dec 1713, Bodl. Oxf., MS Eng. misc. e. 330, fols. 9v, 10r, 18r, 25r, 53v · H. McLachlan, *Essays and addresses* (1950), 183–4 · J. Evans, 'List of dissenting congregations and ministers in England and Wales, 1715–1729', DWL, MS 38.4, p. 71 · J. H. Turner,

T. Dickenson, and O. Heywood, eds., *The nonconformist register of baptisms, marriages, and deaths* (1881), 248, 270 · James Coningham to Ralph Thoresby, 14 Sept 1699, Richard Stretton to Thoresby, 30 May 1699 and 10 Feb 1700, W. Yorks. AS, Leeds, Yorkshire Archaeological Society, Thoresby MSS 5, 16 · BL, Birch MSS, G. Larkham to J. Coningham, 11 June 1698, Add. MS 4276, fol. 22*r* · BL, Birch MSS, T. Doolittle to J. Coningham, 14 Dec 1699, Add. MS 4275, fol. 193*r* · *IGI* · *DNB* · D. Laing, ed., *A catalogue of the graduates … of the University of Edinburgh*, Bannatyne Club, 106 (1858) · J. A. Jones, ed., *Bunhill memorials* (1849), 34

Archives W. Yorks. AS, Leeds, Yorkshire Archaeological Society, Thoresby MSS

Wealth at death see administration, PRO, PROB 6/92, fol. 174*v*

Coningsburgh, Edmund (*d.* 1479×81), archbishop of Armagh, was apparently English in origin, though nothing certain is known of his background. He attended the University of Cambridge, where he had taken the degree of bachelor of canon law by 1448. He also attended an unidentified foreign university and became doctor of canon law by 1469. He became rector of St Leonard, Foster Lane, London (12 January 1448), vicar of South Weald, Essex (13 October 1450), and rector of Copford, also in Essex (3 November 1451), receiving a papal dispensation to hold an additional incompatible benefice on 26 July 1452.

In 1455, and frequently afterwards, Coningsburgh was employed in university business at Cambridge. He was one of the syndics for building the philosophical and law schools in 1457. It appears that he was a proctor in the court of the bishop of Ely. He may have been originally a member of Corpus Christi College; certainly he occupied chambers there from 1468 to 1473. In 1469 he and Walter Buck, master of arts, had a joint commission from Bishop William Grey of Ely to visit Rome as that prelate's proxies. During that year he is recorded as warden of the English hospice of St Thomas in Rome. He became rector of St James, Colchester, on 1 January 1470. On 10 August 1471 Edward IV addressed a letter of congratulation on his election to Pope Sixtus IV, and sent his councillor, James Goldwell, bishop of Norwich, and Coningsburgh to Rome as envoys. In 1471–2 Coningsburgh was vice-chancellor of the University of Cambridge.

On 5 June 1475 Coningsburgh was appointed archbishop of Armagh by papal provision and was consecrated in Rome by English bishops in early 1477. However, his predecessors had left the archdiocese of Armagh in debt to Italian bankers for 1100 florins, and the pope was concerned that this debt should be cleared. As a result, Coningsburgh was forced to leave his bulls of provision in the hands of the bankers as surety for his promise to repay the loan in two instalments over three years. The pope also, on 13 June 1477, appointed Octavian del Palaccio, a Florentine priest and doctor of canon law, as papal nuncio and governor of the archdiocese in matters both spiritual and temporal, until Coningsburgh had paid off the debt.

However, Coningsburgh and Alfred Cornburgh, an esquire of the body to Edward IV, were given a commission from the king on 21 June 1477 to hear and determine all controversies, suits, and debates depending between any of the great men or peers of Ireland; and on 3 July Coningsburgh had the temporalities of the see, then in the

king's hands, restored to him, along with permission to recover any other property of the archdiocese which might have been lost. Edward was at this time attempting to re-establish control over Ireland after his estrangement from his brother the duke of Clarence, lieutenant of Ireland since 1472. Royal influence outside the pale was virtually non-existent and Coningsburgh's arrival at Dundalk in August 1477, armed with these powers, seems to have been a major plank in Edward's strategy.

However, when Coningsburgh met with the dean and chapter of Armagh there on 5 September 1477, they demanded to see his bulls of provision. Since he was unable to produce them, they refused to grant him permission to exercise his office, citing canon law, and instead he took up residence in Drogheda. By late September Octavian had arrived and presented his papal rescript, which was accepted by the dean and chapter.

On 10 November Octavian and Coningsburgh met, and Coningsburgh, unable to maintain his position, resigned as archbishop, appointing the nuncio as proctor and commissary in return for an annual pension of 50 marks. He returned to England, where he became a suffragan of the bishop of Ely, but he and the king were not content, and on 2 May 1478 Edward renewed the grant of temporalities to Coningsburgh. Nothing resulted from this, however, and Octavian was consecrated as archbishop of Armagh at some point between 30 September 1479 and 31 January 1480. Nothing more is known of Coningsburgh, save for the payment of £1 to the University of Cambridge in respect of a debt of £2, in 1481 by his executors. Claims that he was a suffragan of the bishop of Norwich in 1502 are unsupported, and the likelihood is that he died between 1479 and 1481.

Coningsburgh was the last of a succession of Englishmen appointed to the see of Armagh by the king, the previous two of whom had been responsible for the debt that dominated his short tenure there. Owing to this situation, Coningsburgh was unable to make any impact on the problems of the province of Armagh, and it remained for Octavian to pay off the debts and improve the condition of the diocese over the next few years. Perhaps the most significant aspect of this short interlude is that it was the pope's concerns and wishes that prevailed over those of Edward IV.   MARCUS B. S. FLAVIN

Sources A. Gwynn, *The medieval province of Armagh, 1470–1545* (1946), 6–11 · Emden, *Cam.*, 156, 673 · *Statute rolls of the parliament of Ireland: Edward IV*, 2 vols. (1914–39), 2.495, 547 · Rymer, *Foedera*, 1st edn, 12.44, 45, 58 · *CSP Venice, 1202–1509*, 130 · S. G. Ellis, *Tudor Ireland: crown, community, and the conflict of cultures, 1470–1603* (1985), 60–61 · E. B. Fryde and others, eds., *Handbook of British chronology*, 3rd edn, Royal Historical Society Guides and Handbooks, 2 (1986) · S. M. Leathes, ed., *Grace book A* (1897), 146

Wealth at death £1 paid by executors to University of Cambridge in respect of debt of £2: Leathes, ed., *Grace book*

Coningsby, Sir Harry (*fl.* 1633–1665), translator, was the son of Sir Thomas Coningsby of North Mimms, Hertfordshire, and his wife, Martha (*d.* 1677), daughter of William Button of Alton, Wiltshire. He was admitted to Middle Temple in February 1633. The family was descended from Sir Humphrey Coningsby, a judge under Henry VIII. This lineage made the vicissitudes the family endured during the civil war, as a result of their loyalty to the crown, even harder to bear. Sir Thomas had been high sheriff of Hertfordshire in 1638 and 1642. Having been arrested at St Albans early in 1643 while endeavouring to execute a commission of array for Charles I, Sir Thomas was imprisoned by Cromwell and had to pay so substantial a fine that the family were financially crippled. In 1658 the decision was taken to sell the North Mimms estate, which Sir Thomas had settled on Martha and her son on 13 February 1640, on the occasion of Harry's marriage to Hester, daughter of James Cambell, an alderman of London. Harry and his mother retired to their other estate of Weild or Wold Hall, Shenley, Hertfordshire.

Although Harry was knighted in 1662, the trauma of the decline in family fortunes remained with him, and it was doubtless for this reason that he decided to publish privately his own translation of Boethius, as *The Consolation of Philosophy: a Metrical Translation by Harry Coningsby* (1664). In a manuscript letter, dated 30 March 1665, in the British Museum copy of this rare work, Coningsby addresses the son of the new owner of North Mimms, Sir Thomas Hide, and asks him to accept a copy of the translation so that some part of the family may remain in the house. His decision to translate this work by Boethius parallels his father's translation into English of Justus Lipsius's 'Discourse on constancy', no doubt undertaken in response to seven years of imprisonment in the Tower of London. His decision to include with his translation a short essay on his father's unhappy career demonstrates that this was the chief impetus for Sir Harry's work: to understand 'for what cause it was the storm came upon him and ruined him' (Corser, 430). Sir Harry's only son died young. Each of his three daughters married: the eldest, Genevieva, married Thomas Aram of Gray's Inn, London. The second, Marth-Agnes, married Sir William Hickes of Ruckholt, Essex, while the youngest, Theophania, married Edward Bushes of Rocks Bushes in 1670.

ELIZABETHANNE BORAN

Sources T. Corser, *Collectanea Anglo-poetica, or, A … catalogue of a … collection of early English poetry*, 4, Chetham Society, 77 (1869), 427–31 · R. Clutterbuck, ed., *The history and antiquities of the county of Hertford*, 1 (1815), 443–4 · H. Chauncy, *The historical antiquities of Hertfordshire* (1700), 462–4 · H. A. C. Sturgess, ed., *Register of admissions to the Honourable Society of the Middle Temple, from the fifteenth century to the year 1944*, 1 (1949) · letter, 30 March 1665, BL; in Boethius, *The consolation of philosophy: a metrical translation by Harry Coningsby* (1664)

Coningsby, Humfrey (1567–1610/11), collector of poems and traveller, was born about February 1567, probably at Neen Sollars, Shropshire, the only son of John Coningsby and his wife, Anne, daughter of Thomas Barnaby of Bockelton, Worcestershire. He matriculated at Christ Church, Oxford, after 27 November 1581, aged fifteen. He was related to Thomas Coningsby (1550–1625) of Hampton Court, Herefordshire, whose wife, Philippa, was the daughter of Sir William Fitzwilliam and his wife, Anne, sister of Sir Henry Sidney. Thomas Coningsby accompanied Philip Sidney on his European tour in 1573. In 1604 Sir

Thomas Coningsby sent letters to Robert Sidney, Lord Sidney, 'by my cousin Humfrey Coningesby' (*De L'Isle and Dudley MSS*, 3.99).

Humfrey Coningsby was the owner and compiler of an important Elizabethan poetical miscellany (BL, Harleian MS 7392 (2)). It consists of a collection of courtly poems by writers such as Queen Elizabeth, Edward Dyer, Arthur Gorges, the earl of Oxford, Walter Ralegh, and Philip Sidney, as well as pieces printed in *The Paradyse of Dynasty Devises* (1576), some topical poems, and a large number of poems which appear to be unique to the manuscript. Coningsby's name and signature occur several times in the manuscript: many of the poems have his initials or H. Con. written after them, while other ascriptions indicate some concern with the correct attribution of their authorship. At Oxford, c.1581–1583, and at the inns of court in London in 1584, the manuscript circulated among his friends who included the antiquary St Loe Kniveton (d. 1628), Edward Evans, and Richard Allott, the compiler of *Englands Parnassus*. Thomas Coningsby may have been the source for the courtly poems in his cousin's miscellany.

Humfrey Coningsby was a traveller who left England in April 1594 and during the next four or more years visited much of Europe, including France, Germany, Sicily, and Italy. A second journey took him to Bohemia, Poland, and Hungary where he served under the emperor Rudolph II at the siege of Strigonium. He then went on to Greece, into Asia, and stayed for thirteen months in Turkey. After he returned to England, his next visit was to Spain. He set off, finally, from London on 10 October 1610 for Venice, was never heard of again, and was pronounced dead in 1611. In his will made on 10 November 1608 he left his books, his best lute, and his pictures to Thomas: other bequests included 'a white hower glasse of sea horse toothe' and 'Three greate Venetian lookinge glasses' (PRO, PROB 11/148). His fine tomb in the church at Neen Sollars was set up in 1624 by his half-sister Joyce Jefferies; its inscription supplies most of what is known of his life. He was unmarried: his heir was his sister, Catherine, who married Edward Freeman of Evenlode, Worcester.

H. R. WOUDHUYSEN

Sources J. Webb, 'Some passages in the life and character of a lady resident in Herefordshire and Worcestershire during the civil war', *Archaeologia*, 37 (1857), 189–223, esp. 189–93 · will, PRO, PROB 11/148, fols. 292r–295r · H. R. Woudhuysen, *Sir Philip Sidney and the circulation of manuscripts, 1558–1640* (1996) · *Report on the manuscripts of Lord De L'Isle and Dudley*, 6 vols., HMC, 77 (1925–66) · BL, Harley MS 7392 (2) · tombstone, Neen Sollars church

Coningsby [Conyngesby], **Sir Humphrey** (d. 1535), judge, was born about the end of Henry VI's reign at Rock, Worcestershire, the son of Thomas Coningsby (d. 1498) and Katherine Waldyff. The family derived its name from Coningsby in Lincolnshire, though Thomas's father had settled at Neen Sollars in Shropshire. Humphrey Coningsby began practice as an attorney of the common pleas, and is named in warrants of attorney in 1474; in 1476 he was deputy for the sheriff of Worcestershire. From 1480 to 1493 he was third protonotary, surrendering the office on 24 November 1493 in favour of John Caryll on terms that

Caryll would pass it on to Humphrey's son (which he did). He was also clerk of assize on the western circuit. During the 1480s he became a bencher of the Inner Temple. There was a copy of his reading in Lord Somers's library, but it has not been discovered. He may already have been nominated as a serjeant when he gave up the protonotaryship. At any rate he was one of the nine graduands who, after a long delay, were created serjeant in November 1495. His clients included Queen Elizabeth, the duke of Buckingham, and Peterborough Abbey. In 1500 he became one of the king's serjeants, and on 21 May 1509 the first justice of the king's bench appointed by Henry VIII. He was knighted by 1509. There survives in Westminster Abbey 'A remembrans made by Humfrey Conyngesby for the kynges matters at Yorke', written as an assize judge in preparation for the Lent circuit of 1501. By 1532 he had apparently become incapable of sitting, and an attempt seems to have been made to replace him without discontinuing his salary. However, the salary was discontinued and Walter Luke formally appointed in his place on 28 November 1533, Coningsby being compensated with a lease of the manor of Rock.

Coningsby was a justice of the peace for Hertfordshire from 1493, and was perhaps already of Aldenham, where he acquired Penne's Place as executor of Ralph Penne (d. 1485), a relative of his first wife, Isabel Fereby. Isabel died in the 1490s and was buried in the Whitefriars next to the Temple. In 1513 he was to found a chantry chapel of the Blessed Virgin Mary and St George at Copthorne Hill in Aldenham. About 1499 he married Alice, daughter and heir of Sir John Franceys, widow of John Worsley and William Staveley (d. 1498); she died in 1500. As his third wife, Coningsby in 1504 married Anne, daughter and heir of Sir Christopher Moresby of Cumberland, widow of James Pickering (d. 1498); she died in 1523. Coningsby had come into his patrimony at Rock by 1509 at the latest, and probably by 1504, when he was added to the commission of the peace for Worcestershire. In 1510 he built the south aisle and steeple of Rock church, where a painted window once portrayed him in a scarlet gown with his family; and in 1513 he founded Rock School.

Coningsby died on 2 June 1535, having requested burial in the Whitefriars, Rock, or Aldenham, depending on the place of his death. He left two surviving sons, both by his first marriage, and five daughters (Elizabeth, Amphelice, Margaret, Jane, and Elizabeth). From his eldest son, Thomas, who predeceased him, was descended the Earl Coningsby (the peerage, created in 1719, was extinct in 1729). His second son, William *Coningsby, followed in his footsteps as a bencher of the Inner Temple, protonotary of the common pleas, and justice of the king's bench. His daughter Elizabeth married Sir John *Fitzjames, chief justice of the same court. J. H. BAKER

Sources G. O. Bellewes, 'The two Coningsbys', *The Genealogist*, new ser., 26 (1909–10), 212–17, esp. 212–14 • E. W. Ives, *The common lawyers of pre-Reformation England* (1983), 457–8 • Baker, *Serjeants*, 165, 264–5, 606 • Sainty, *King's counsel*, 12 • Sainty, *Judges*, 28 • *LP Henry VIII*, 1, nos. 221, 2055(53); 6, nos. 299(ii, x), 1370, 1371; 7, no. 263 • *VCH Hertfordshire*, 2.153 • *Fourth report*, HMC, 3 (1874), 194 • N. H. Nicolas, ed., *Privy purse expenses of Elizabeth of York: wardrobe accounts of Edward the Fourth* (1830), 101 • PRO, CP 40 • PRO, C 142/57/1

Coningsby, Sir Thomas (1550–1625), soldier, was born on 9 October 1550, the second son of Humphrey Coningsby (1516–1559) of Hampton Court, Herefordshire, and Anne Englefield. His father's death was quickly followed in 1561 by that of his elder brother, Edward, leaving Thomas heir to substantial estates in Herefordshire and Worcestershire. Through his mother he was connected to the Englefield family of Berkshire, whose landed wealth and tradition of royal service (especially in the law) mirrored that of the Coningsby family. Nothing is known of Thomas's childhood or education, although he may have followed his late brother into wardship under Sir Edward Rogers (d. 1568), comptroller of the household to Elizabeth I.

Coningsby was probably already associated with the earl of Leicester by the time he began to cut a figure at court in 1571: he and his sister and brother-in-law were linked in a property transaction with John Hubaud, a Herefordshire neighbour and one of Leicester's most important servants, in 1564. Coningsby was granted a licence to travel abroad for three years in 1572 and subsequently accompanied Leicester's nephew, Philip Sidney, in Vienna and northern Italy in 1573–4. He married Sidney's first cousin, Philippa Fitzwilliam (d. c.1617), probably after his return to England. By 1577 Coningsby was resident in Herefordshire and anxious to establish his influence over county affairs. In that year he provoked a dispute with the agents of Robert, earl of Essex, then still a minor. He soon became a deputy lieutenant and began to clash with the leading figure in the county, Sir James Croft, comptroller to the queen. The rivalry between Croft's supporters and those of Coningsby became increasingly bitter and violent during the 1580s, resulting in affrays, threats, lawsuits, and sharp competition for local offices. Coningsby received high-level support in his challenge to Croft from Leicester, who had turned against the comptroller in the 1570s.

After Leicester's death in 1588, Coningsby found a new patron in the earl of Essex, Leicester's stepson. Essex's support may explain how Coningsby became a gentleman pensioner extraordinary in 1589. Croft's death in 1590 allowed Coningsby to engineer Essex's election as steward of Hereford and Leominster, where Essex employed him as his deputy. Essex's political clout stifled local opposition to Coningsby and his friends for a decade. In 1591 Coningsby joined Essex's expedition to Normandy, serving as commissary of musters. During this campaign he kept a daily journal of events between 13–14 August and 24 December. At least two incomplete copies of this journal survive. On 8 October 1591 Coningsby was one of twenty-four new knights made by Essex 'upon a fair green in the sight of' Rouen (Coningsby, 27). He was paid as muster-master until 15 March 1592. Either upon his return or shortly before he left for France, he became a gentleman pensioner in ordinary. On 27 September 1592, as part of the celebrations for Elizabeth's visit to the university,

Coningsby was created master of arts at Oxford, along with many other friends of Essex.

In 1593 and 1597 Coningsby was elected to parliament as senior knight of the shire for Herefordshire, an honour previously monopolized by Croft. However, the grip on the county of Coningsby and his friends was never complete and was exposed to challenge by Essex's fall in February 1601. Although he managed to succeed Essex as steward of Leominster, Coningsby failed to find a powerful new patron at court. Despite going to extraordinary and illegal lengths, he and his allies could not prevent Sir John Scudamore from becoming steward of Hereford. Coningsby himself barely retained his status as senior knight in a bruising parliamentary election later in 1601. With the accession of James I he resigned as a gentleman pensioner and turned to his relative Sir Robert Sidney, whose office as chamberlain to Queen Anne allowed him to force an unwilling Sir Herbert Croft to share the office of receiver for the queen's lands in Herefordshire with Coningsby in 1604. Although he was appointed to the council in the marches of Wales in 1617 (fully thirty-five years after Philip Sidney first raised the prospect) and doggedly asserted his rights at Leominster, Coningsby largely conceded dominance in county affairs to the Croft–Scudamore interest during the Jacobean period.

Coningsby's health was often poor and his thoughts apparently turned to ensuring the survival of his family line. Only one of his many sons, Fitzwilliam, born in the late 1590s, survived to adulthood. Three daughters married into allied Herefordshire families, a fourth remained unmarried at her father's death and a fifth, Sidney, was 'defective'.

In 1614 Sir Thomas established Coningsby's Hospital for old soldiers and serving-men on the remains of the old Blackfriars in Hereford. The leader of these servitors was 'to be called Corporal Coningsby, and by no other surname' (Price, 219–20). Sir Thomas's Calvinist faith is illustrated by his regulations for the hospital of July 1617, which stipulated that the chaplain must be a preacher, and that the company of inmates must march to the cathedral in file behind the chaplain carrying the Bible. Coningsby wrote his extraordinary and bombastic will in 1616, revising it several times before his death at his home at Hampton Court, Herefordshire, on 30 May 1625. The will and first codicil of September 1617 emphasize his utter rejection of vain ceremonies and his confidence in his own resurrection. He was buried next to his wife at Hope church, Herefordshire.   PAUL E. J. HAMMER

Sources PRO, SP 12, 14 · PRO, C 66 · PRO, C 115 · HoP, *Commons, 1558–1603*, 1.638–40 · *Calendar of the manuscripts of the most hon. the marquis of Salisbury*, 24 vols., HMC, 9 (1883–1976) · *The manuscripts of his grace the duke of Rutland*, 4 vols., HMC, 24 (1888–1905) · *Report on the manuscripts of Lord De L'Isle and Dudley*, 6 vols., HMC, 77 (1925–66) · T. Coningsby, 'Journal of the siege of Rouen, 1591', ed. J. G. Nichols, *Camden miscellany, I*, CS, 39 (1847) · R. Poole, 'A journal of the siege of Rouen in 1591', *EngHR*, 17 (1902), 527–37 · J. M. Osborn, *Young Philip Sidney* (1972) · A. T. Butler, ed., *The visitation of Worcestershire, 1634*, Harleian Society, 90 (1938) · will, PRO, PROB 11/148, fols. 291v–296r · W. J. Tighe, 'The gentleman pensioners in Elizabethan politics and government', PhD diss., U. Cam., 1984 · J. Price, *An historical account of the city of Hereford* (1796) [repr. 1971] · PRO, E351/244 · W. J. Tighe, 'Courtiers and politics in Elizabethan Herefordshire: Sir James Croft, his friends and his foes', *HJ*, 32 (1989), 257–79

Archives BL, journal of Essex's expedition to Normandy, Harley MS 288, fols. 253–79 · Bodl. Oxf., journal of Essex's expedition to Normandy, MS Eng. hist. c. 61, fols. 5v–9r

Likenesses attrib. G. Gower, oils, 1572, NPG · portrait; formerly at Cashiobury House, Hertfordshire, 1887

Wealth at death approx. £10,000: PRO, PROB 11/148, fols. 291v–296r

Coningsby, Thomas, first earl of Coningsby (1657–1729), politician, was born on 2 November 1657, the only son of Humphrey Coningsby (*d.* 1671), of Hampton Court, Herefordshire, and his wife, Letitia, daughter of Sir Arthur Loftus of Rathfarnham Castle, co. Dublin. He entered Lincoln's Inn in 1671; his call to the Irish bar on 5 May 1691 suggests that he was called to the English bar previously, but there is no record of the event. In 1675 (licence, 18 February 1675) he married Barbara (*c.*1658–1697), daughter of Ferdinando Gorges of Eye Manor, Herefordshire, and Barbados, 'a notorious slaver' (Ferris). The marriage was arranged without the consent of his mother, and while it did not end in divorce as often asserted, it was a tempestuous union, although this did not prevent the couple from having three sons and four daughters.

In October 1679 Coningsby entered the House of Commons as member for Leominster, Herefordshire, which he represented continuously until the election of 1710. Although his family had been royalists during the civil war Coningsby's father-in-law was a cousin of Anthony Ashley Cooper, first earl of Shaftesbury, and Coningsby became a supporter of Shaftesbury and of the exclusion of James, duke of York, from the succession to the throne. He was returned again in the 1681 parliament where he was named to ten committees including one charged with preparing an address on exclusion. His political alliance with his neighbour John Scudamore, second Viscount Scudamore, was threatened when Scudamore learned of an affair between Coningsby and Frances (*née* Cecil), Lady Scudamore (*d.* 1694). The couple eloped, but were confronted by Scudamore's men who forced Lady Scudamore's return to her husband at pistol point. Coningsby sat for Leominster again in 1685, despite being advised not to do so without the support of Henry Somerset, first duke of Beaufort, a leading tory. During the 1685 parliament he was believed to have taken part in the debate on the army that followed the suppression of Monmouth's rising, but the speech against standing armies credited to him by Anchitell Grey may have been made by another member, Thomas Christie. He was an active member of the convention in 1689; in March, during the debate on the coronation oath, he proposed that William III and Mary II should swear to uphold 'the Doctrine of the Protestant Religion established by Law' (Grey, 9.193), which wording was adopted by parliament. Later in 1689 he spoke in the debate which held John Shales, supply officer, responsible for the failure of the duke of Schomberg's Irish campaign on the grounds that he had mismanaged the transport of troops and equipment.

Ireland Coningsby's wholehearted support of William's administration helped recommend him for office; his kinship to Henry Sidney, Viscount Sydney, one of William's closest advisers, was no doubt also important. In June 1690 Coningsby was appointed joint paymaster-general of the army which William was about to take to Ireland. His colleague was Charles Fox, son of Sir Stephen Fox; Fox managed business in London while Coningsby looked after requirements in the field. He accompanied the army to Ireland, and was by the king's side on 30 June 1690, the eve of the battle of the Boyne, when Jacobite gunners wounded William in the shoulder. Coningsby staunched the wound with his handkerchief, and so won William's personal gratitude. Following William's failure to take Limerick, and before the king returned to England from Waterford, on 2 September 1690 Coningsby was appointed a lord justice of Ireland, in charge of the civil government of Ireland, including the management of the militia, pending the appointment of a lord lieutenant or a lord deputy. The appointment was controversial as according to Gilbert Burnet Coningsby already had a reputation as 'a vicious man' whose 'parts were very indifferent' (Simms, *Jacobite Ireland*, 189). Immediately afterwards Coningsby and his fellow lord justice, Viscount Sydney, left Waterford for the army headquarters at Cullen, near Tipperary, where they discussed future plans with the army's commander, Count Hendrik Trajectinus van Solms-Braunfels, and his successor, Godard van Reede-Ginckel. They then travelled north to Dublin where, on 15 September 1690, they were sworn in as lords justices. On 27 September they wrote to Hans Willem Bentinck, earl of Portland, in London, to advise him on the management of the Commons, suggesting that he rely on a broad coalition of non-Jacobite parties. Both Coningsby and Sydney probably sought to ensure that they were remembered in English politics, but it was the senior partner, Sydney, who was recalled to London in December to become a secretary of state.

For ten days Coningsby had sole charge of the government of Ireland, but on 23 December he was joined as lord justice by Sir Charles Porter, lord chancellor of Ireland, who had briefly held office under James II. They governed Ireland together until August 1692; Porter's role may have been to moderate Coningsby's hostility towards the Irish and Catholics, and encourage a form of compromise, while Coningsby, a member of the Irish protestant Loftus family on his mother's side, represented the protestant interest. For the first half of their tenure their task was to assist Ginckel in ridding Ireland of the Jacobite army which had been raised by James II's lord lieutenant, Richard Talbot, duke of Tyrconnell. While Ginckel won a series of victories Coningsby concentrated on the political offensive, advertising the generous terms offered by William

Thomas Coningsby, first earl of Coningsby (1657–1729), by Thomas Bate, 1692

and Mary to Catholics while attempting to avoid alienating protestant support. Following the capture of Galway on 21 July 1691 Coningsby joined Ginckel at Nenagh, where for nearly a fortnight they discussed the terms to be agreed with the Jacobites when they surrendered Limerick. After the cessation of hostilities at Limerick, on 1 October 1691, Coningsby and Porter joined Ginckel outside the city. There Coningsby and Ginckel's secretary, George Clarke, worked late into the night on the proposed settlement. They rejected the 'long scroll' of suggested terms, drawn up by Jacobite bishops and lawyers, which would have granted Irish Catholics political and religious liberty and restored landholdings to the settlement of Charles II's reign, and completed a draft of the military and civil articles. The military articles offered the Jacobite army the opportunity to leave for service under Louis XIV, the freedom to return to their homes and live peaceably under William, or to fight for William's army. The civil articles were controversial as a clause seen and agreed to by the Irish, offering protection to all those defended by the Irish army in the counties of Limerick, Cork, Clare, Kerry, and Mayo, was omitted in the version transmitted to the English government. Clarke's copy of the draft shows that the clause existed before Coningsby's arrival; Coningsby claimed that he and Clarke had removed the clause, and although his case was supported by the English privy council the clause was approved and applied by the Irish parliament. The treaty of Limerick divided the protestant community: when Coningsby and Porter returned to Dublin they heard on successive Sundays sermons from Anthony Dopping, bishop of Meath, condemning the treaty, and from William Moreton, bishop of Kildare, endorsing it.

Encouraged by the government in London, and in particular by Daniel Finch, second earl of Nottingham, secretary of state, Coningsby and Porter set about restoring the connived toleration of Catholics and dissenters that had existed under Charles II, while preserving the broad hegemony of Church of Ireland protestantism. Their policy was set forward in a proclamation by Mary II, but was frustrated by the opposition of dominant figures in the Irish ecclesiastical establishment. These included Bishop Dopping, Robert Fitzgerald, and Sir Francis Brewster, who were helped by their country whig allies in the English parliament at Westminster, led by Goodwin Wharton, who by the English Irish Oaths Act of 1691 restricted all places in the government of Ireland to Anglicans.

In January 1692 Coningsby and Porter began to restore estates to those who came under the provisions of the treaty of Limerick. This was one of the most successful and conciliatory aspects of Williamite policy in Ireland, leading to about 1200 successful claims by 1699, principally from Catholics. In February 1692 Coningsby learned that Sydney was returning to Ireland as lord lieutenant, and in March was told by Sydney that he was to be made an Irish peer with responsibility for the management of the Lords in the coming parliament. On 5 March King William signed the warrant for Coningsby's Irish peerage and also

one appointing him an Irish privy councillor once he ceased to be a lord justice.

Sydney's parliament met in Chichester House, Dublin, on 5 October 1692, and the same day Coningsby took his seat as Baron Coningsby of Clanbrassil, co. Armagh. Between then and the prorogation of parliament on 3 November Coningsby was active in the Irish Lords, where he chaired the grand committee on new means of raising revenue, and was one of only two peers to attend every sitting of the house. It was rumoured that Sydney prorogued the parliament lest Coningsby might be impeached by critics of the treaty of Limerick. Immediately after the prorogation he was sent to London by Sydney to report on proceedings in parliament, but Lady Coningsby remained in Dublin until after 11 March 1693.

Manager in the Commons for William III In London Coningsby resumed his place as member for Leominster in the House of Commons at Westminster, where he was soon called on to vindicate the actions of the Irish administration. The army in Ireland had been accused of extorting money from property owners. Coningsby admitted that there were 'great misdemeanours committed by the army in Ireland' but that 'power then was in the general of the army and not in the civil power' (*Parliamentary Diary of Narcissus Luttrell*, 252). Coningsby thereby transferred the blame for the army's misconduct to Ginckel, nimbly distancing the civil administration of Ireland from William's continental generals. In December 1692, following the sudden death of William Harbord, Coningsby was appointed to the lucrative office of vice-treasurer of Ireland on the nomination of Sidney Godolphin, baron and later first earl of Godolphin, then first lord of the Treasury. His appointment emphasized his position as the principal government spokesman on Ireland in the Commons, but also exposed him to further criticism. Early in 1693 he came again under attack in the English parliament from those who were critical of the terms of Limerick. The attack on 22 February was led by Goodwin Wharton, who produced Irish witnesses, including Brewster, but after two days' debate Coningsby 'spoke very largely in vindication of himself and very much to the satisfaction of the house' (*Parliamentary Diary of Narcissus Luttrell*, 447).

In April 1693 Coningsby was appointed a member of the English privy council. As a member both of the Irish and of the English privy councils he was in a key position for nearly thirty years on the two bodies which, under the terms of Poynings' law, controlled the drafting of all Irish legislation. The same month he was promised a royal pardon for anything which he may have done amiss in Ireland. But in June 1693 his critics returned to the attack. On 24 June Richard Coote, first earl of Bellamont (who was also a member of the Commons at Westminster), and James Hamilton of Tullymore asked the privy council in London to delay his pardon, and on 16 December Bellamont attempted a full scale impeachment of Coningsby and Porter for high treason. On 22 December witnesses were heard, their evidence was discussed on 29 December, on 20 January 1694 Coningsby and Porter replied, and on 24 January the Commons decided that there was no case to answer. They reserved as an exception the condemnation at the Irish privy council of Gaffney, a Dublin farmer involved in the murder of a soldier who had been hanged on Coningsby's orders without a proper trial, but allowed that Coningsby's action was extenuated by the circumstances of the time. Coningsby became known as 'Gaffney's hangman'.

By this time Coningsby had become a member of an inner cabinet of ministers and confidential advisers to William III that met to formulate policy and plan the management of parliament. In September 1694 he joined William in Flanders, where they discussed the appointment of a lord lieutenant of Ireland. Queen Mary, whose mother, Anne Hyde, was a kinswoman of Lady Coningsby's father, died on 28 December 1694, and in political changes that followed Coningsby lost the vice-treasurership of Ireland to his mother's kinsman, Charles Boyle, Viscount Dungarvan. He did not attend the parliament which met under Henry Capel, Baron Capel of Tewkesbury, lord deputy, in Dublin in August 1695, but concentrated on his role as a government manager in the English Commons. In December 1697 he successfully, but narrowly, won a vote on his motion that the Commons should debate the question of supply only and not the speech from the throne as a whole, thereby helping the government preserve a substantial land force in peacetime.

Coningsby's first wife had died shortly before 9 November 1697. In March 1698 it was reported that his government colleague Richard *Jones, earl of Ranelagh, paymaster-general of the forces, had returned home to find 'My Lord Coningsby in bed with [Ranelagh's] wife. At which sight he said nothing, but withdrew very civilly, and went downstairs about his business. What consequences this is like to have is not yet talked of' (Hastings MSS, 2.288). Whatever the truth behind the gossip the upshot may have been Coningsby's second marriage, about 23 April 1698, to Lady Frances Jones (1674–1715), Ranelagh's younger daughter, following which the new Lady Coningsby was disinherited by her father. They had one son, who died after choking on a cherry stone in 1708, and two daughters.

In 1698 government changes following the end of the Nine Years' War included Coningsby's reappointment as vice-treasurer of Ireland, and in October he attended parliament in Dublin. In January 1699 he led the government side in the English Commons on the Disbanding Bill, successfully opposing the measure which would have reduced the size of the army to 7000 men. In December he had to support in the English Commons the bill which deprived him of the Irish estates, including Feltrim and Portmarnock, which he had been granted six years before.

Lord treasurer's whig In the latter part of William's reign Coningsby seems to have followed Godolphin in establishing connections with John Churchill, earl and later duke of Marlborough. James Brydges found him with Godolphin and others at Marlborough's house in October 1700

when Marlborough was expecting to be appointed secretary of state. The alliance helped maintain Coningsby's position as a leader of the government side in the Commons following the accession of Queen Anne in 1702. He remained an intermediary on Irish affairs. In 1703 he attended the Dublin parliament called by James Butler, second duke of Ormond, as lord lieutenant. During discussions of the shaping of the Irish Penal Bill by the English privy council in December 1703 and January 1704 he argued for the further underpinning of the dominant role of Church of Ireland protestants, and has been credited with making the bill much harsher towards Catholics and protestant dissenters than had been intended by the Irish politicians who drafted it. His own suspicion of Catholicism, moderated by pragmatism in the 1690s, now harmonized with the wishes of Anne and Nottingham to strengthen Anglicanism across the queen's dominions. He was suspicious of high-churchmen, and in 1705 told the Commons that 'The greatest danger to the Church … came from the pulpits themselves' (Holmes, *Trial*, 46). During the debates on the Regency Bill in the 1705–6 session Coningsby attacked the bill's tory opponents as enemies of the protestant succession. He attended the 1707 Dublin parliament.

Coningsby was reckoned one of the foremost 'lord treasurer's whigs', working for Godolphin, Anne's lord treasurer, by managing parliamentary business. During the 1708–9 session of what had become the British parliament he negotiated with opposition whigs to ensure that a recruiting bill to keep the army supplied with troops passed the Commons. He was one of the supporters of John Dolben's motion in the Commons on 12 December 1709 that the house take into consideration the sermons of Henry Sacheverell as seditious pamphlets, and in the debate of 14 December 1709 urged that the bookseller and printer be called to the Commons to account for themselves as well. He was a member of the committee that drew up the articles of Sacheverell's prosecution, and in February 1710 was part of the group that managed the trial on the third article, that in alleging that the Church of England was in danger under the Godolphin–Marlborough administration Sacheverell had placed parliament in contempt and slandered the queen. Following Sacheverell's trial he was in the thick of the attack by ministers on the influence that Abigail Masham had with the queen. The queen's determination to shape a new ministry that included Robert Harley, and Coningsby's attachment to Godolphin, led to his departure from office. Coningsby had inherited a dynastic feud with Harley in Herefordshire, and blamed Harley for weakening the administration following his resignation in 1708. On 8 July Coningsby received 'a letter from My Lord Dartmouth, that [the queen] had no more occasion for my service' (Ellis, 18).

Revival and decline Coningsby, out of office and faced with the ascendancy of the high-church party and opprobrium directed towards the prosecutors of Sacheverell, chose not to stand for parliament in 1710. Like many other whigs he returned from the political wilderness at the accession of George I, whose proclamation he signed in 1714. He was retained as part of George's privy council, reduced from eighty under Anne to thirty-two, and was made lord lieutenant of Herefordshire in November 1714, and lord lieutenant of Radnorshire the next month. He used the lieutenancies to reduce the local influence of the Harley family. At the 1715 election he was reinstated as MP for Leominster. In April 1715 he was one of the secret committee which inquired into the conduct of the negotiators of the treaty of Utrecht. His tough handling of Matthew Prior, who was confined on suspicion of treason, inspired Prior to revenge in the composition of *The Viceroy*, in which Prior revived the charges brought against Coningsby in the abortive impeachment twenty years before. In July 1715 Coningsby carried the articles of impeachment of Robert Harley, by then earl of Oxford, up to the Lords. He spoke on behalf of the Septennial Bill in 1716, and was rewarded for his services to the whig cause on 18 June 1716 when he was created Baron Coningsby of Coningsby, Lincolnshire.

In July 1716, before George I left for Hanover, Coningsby submitted to the king his 'Account of the state of political parties during the reign of Queen Anne', in which he blamed Charles Talbot, duke of Shrewsbury, and the Triennial Act for many of the troubles of the two previous reigns, and gave his personal account of the events which led to the dismissal of Harley in 1708 and of Godolphin in 1710. Historians in the nineteenth and early twentieth centuries undervalued the document, as Coningsby was viewed as an egotistical minor figure who exaggerated his own importance; it was also unfinished, as Coningsby declared his intention of taking his account up to 1716 but ended in 1710. However, his claim that Marlborough came very close to siding with Harley in 1708 against Godolphin is supported by other accounts. Coningsby himself claimed that he had kept the Marlborough–Godolphin alliance together, after threatening Marlborough that the 'lord treasurer's whigs' would oppose Harley as chief minister in the Commons. Coningsby's ill feeling towards Lord Oxford and the tories continued to shape his political activity. In 1717 he deliberately withdrew from the Lords before Oxford was discharged. In December 1718, during the debate on the Bill for Strengthening the Protestant Interest, which would have repealed the Occasional Conformity and Schism Acts, he compared Francis Atterbury, bishop of Rochester, to a biblical false prophet, Balaam. This attempt at wit backfired when Atterbury observed that 'Balaam was reproved by his ass, but that he was never reproved by anyone but the Lord Coningsby' (Bennett, 221) and a contemporary lampoon nicknamed him the 'Rochester Pad'. He was created earl of Coningsby on 30 April 1719.

Coningsby had become obsessed with his property and with extending his rights as lord of the manors of Marden and Leominster. His conviction that his father-in-law had abused his estate in his youth may have contributed towards the exclusion of his grandson and heir male from succession to his British peerages. In 1717 he protected his estates by a tripartite indenture, placing them in the hands of trustees but ensuring they would benefit his daughters from his second marriage, Margaret (d. 1761), created Viscountess Coningsby of Hampton Court in 1717, and Frances (bap. 1709, d. 1781). The settlement was confirmed by his will in 1724. Meanwhile he attempted to eject freeholders from their properties in Marden and Leominster, arguing that they were his copyhold tenants. On being unable to prove his case in chancery he published a pamphlet maligning lord chancellor Macclesfield, and as a result in January 1721 was stripped of his lieutenancies and imprisoned in the Tower of London for six months, where he was visited by the Marlboroughs.

Coningsby attempted to remain active in politics despite his disgrace. In November 1721, to Charles Spencer, third earl of Sunderland, he proposed that Sunderland form a coalition with moderate tories and force a general election in which Robert Walpole would be outflanked. After Marlborough's death in 1722 he proposed marriage to the widowed duchess on 20 November; however, the duchess regarded him as deranged, and rejected him. His fall was completed when Leominster corporation persuaded the duke of Chandos to put their case against Coningsby's encroachments before the privy council; the council found in Leominster's favour, and Coningsby was expelled from the privy council on 7 November 1724. He died at Hampton Court on 30 April 1729, and was buried at Hope under Dinmore, Herefordshire, on 9 May 1729. He was succeeded in his Irish barony by his grandson Richard, second and last Baron Coningsby, who survived only until that December, and in his earldom and estate by his daughter Margaret, on whose death in 1761 the title became extinct; Hampton Court then passed to his younger daughter Frances, the wife of Charles Hanbury *Williams (1708–1759). A. E. STOKES

Sources PRO NIre., De Ros MSS · *CSP dom.*, 1690–1702 · W. Troost, 'William III and the treaty of Limerick', PhD diss., University of Leiden, 1983 · J. G. Simms, *The Williamite confiscation in Ireland, 1690–1703* (1956) · J. G. Simms, *Jacobite Ireland* (1969) · J. Cornforth, 'Hampton Court, Herefordshire', *Country Life* (22 Feb 1973), 450–53, (1 March 1973), 518–21 · register book of letters of Sir Charles Porter and Thomas Coningsby, lords justices of Ireland, 1 June 1691–31 May 1692, BL, Add. MS 30149 · H. Horwitz, *Parliament, policy and politics in the reign of William III* (1977) · G. Holmes, *British politics in the age of Anne* (1969), rev. edn (1987) · G. Story, *An impartial history of the wars in Ireland with a continuation thereof in two parts* (1693) · E. Hamilton, *The backstairs dragon: a life of Robert Harley, earl of Oxford* (1969) · T. J. Kiernan, *History of the financial administration of Ireland to 1817* (1930) · J. P. Ferris, 'Coningsby, Thomas', HoP, *Commons, 1660–90* · A. N. Newman, 'Coningsby, Thomas', HoP, *Commons, 1715–54* · A. Grey, ed., *Debates of the House of Commons, from the year 1667 to the year 1694*, new edn, 10 vols. (1769), vol. 9 · *The parliamentary diary of Narcissus Luttrell, 1691–1693*, ed. H. Horwitz (1972) · J. G. Simms, 'Williamite peace tactics, 1690–1', *Irish Historical Studies*, 8 (1952–3), 303–23; repr. in J. G. Simms, *War and politics in Ireland, 1649–1730* (1986), 181–201 · J. G. Simms, *The treaty of Limerick* (1966); repr. in J. G. Simms, *War and politics in Ireland, 1649–1730* (1986), 203–24 · J. G. Simms, 'The making of a penal law (2 Anne, c. 6), 1703–4', *Irish Historical Studies*, 12 (1960–61), 105–18; repr. in J. G. Simms, *War and politics in Ireland, 1649–1730* (1986), 263–76 · G. V. Bennett, *The tory crisis in church and state, 1688–1730* (1975) · H. Ellis, ed., 'Lord Coningsby's account of the state of political parties during the reign of Queen Anne', *Archaeologia*, 38 (1860), 1–18 · G. Holmes and W. A. Speck, 'The fall of Harley in 1708 reconsidered', *EngHR*, 80 (1965), 673–98 ·

The parliamentary diary of Sir Richard Cocks, 1698–1702, ed. D. W. Hayton (1996) • M. Prior, *The history of his own time* (1740) • *Report on the manuscripts of the late Reginald Rawdon Hastings*, 4 vols., HMC, 78 (1928–47), vol. 2, p. 288 • D. H. Somerville, *King of hearts: Charles Talbot, duke of Shrewsbury* (1962), 185 • F. Harris, *A passion for government: the life of Sarah, duchess of Marlborough* (1991) • F. G. James, *Lords of the ascendancy: the Irish House of Lords and its members, 1600–1800* (1995) • GEC, *Peerage* • G. Holmes, *The trial of Doctor Sacheverell* (1973) • private information (2004) [King's Inns, Dublin]

Archives BL, papers, Add. MSS 30149, 57861–57862, 70064 • PRO NIre., corresp., DOD 638 | Belfast City Council, account book of Charles Fox and Thomas Coningsby • BL, 'Political parties during the reign of Queen Anne', Lansdowne MS 885 • BL, corresp. with Charles Fox, Add. MS 51335 • BL, letters to Sarah, duchess of Marlborough, Add. MS 61463, fols. 57–70b • BL, letters to E. Southwell, Add. MS 21553, fols. 63, 65; Add. MS 28569, fol. 101 • TCD, corresp. with George Clarke; corresp. with William King • U. Nott. L., letters to first earl of Portland

Likenesses T. Bate, oils, 1692, Ulster Museum, Belfast [*see illus.*] • G. Kneller, group portrait, oils, 1722 (with his daughters), Tower of London; repro. in *Country Life* (22 Feb 1973), 453 • L. F. Roubiliac, marble statue on monument (with his family), Hope under Dinmore church, Herefordshire; repro. in F. C. Morgan, *Country Life* (26 April 1973), 1166 • oils (as vice-treasurer of Ireland), Royal Hospital, Kilmainham, Dublin

Wealth at death vice-treasurership of Ireland worth £8000 to £10,000 p.a.

Coningsby [Conyngesby], **William** (d. **1540**), judge, was the second (and eldest surviving) son of Sir Humphrey *Coningsby (d. 1535), justice of the king's bench, and his first wife, Isabel Fereby. He was educated in the 1490s at Eton College, and then at King's College, Cambridge, where he was resident from 1497 to 1501; he proceeded to the Inner Temple in the early 1500s. He was appointed a justice of the peace for Hertfordshire as early as 1504, and was perhaps then resident in his father's home at Aldenham. About 1514 he married Beatrice (d. 1543), daughter of Thomas Thoresby of Lynn, Norfolk, and widow of William Trew (d. 1510/1512). Coningsby then moved to Lynn, where he served as a county magistrate from 1514, as recorder of Lynn from 1524, and as member of parliament for Lynn in 1536. In 1510 he succeeded John Caryll as third protonotary of the common pleas under the terms of an agreement made with his father in 1493; but the scheme to pass on to him at the same time the clerkship of assize on the western circuit failed when the assize judges declined to co-operate.

Coningsby continued as protonotary until 1539, when he was nominated for the coif. He became in 1518 a bencher of his inn, and gave a second reading, in 1526, on the first chapter of the Statute of Merton. He is mentioned in the 1530s as the steward of Clackclose hundred, and as steward of courts in Norfolk for the priories of Thetford and Lewes. In 1536 he acquired the lucrative post of attorney-general of the duchy of Lancaster, which he occupied until 1540. He was committed to the Tower in February 1540, with other law officers, for advising on a method of settling land that would have seriously damaged the revenue from wardships; but this disgrace did not prevent his being given the coif in June 1540 and then, on 5 July following, the office of justice of the king's bench in succession to John Port. But these advancements came

too late to be enjoyed. He died on 10 September 1540, a week after making his last will, and was buried in St Nicholas's Church, Lynn.

Coningsby owned a house in Woollen Street, Lynn, probably in right of his wife. In 1524 he purchased the manors of Wallington and Thorpland, Norfolk, and thereafter made his principal seat at Eston Hall in Wallington. He had one son, Christopher, slain at the battle of Pinkie in 1547, and four daughters. His granddaughter Elizabeth married Sir Francis Gawdy, chief justice of the common pleas.

J. H. BAKER

Sources HoP, *Commons, 1509–58*, 1.681–2 • G. O. Bellewes, 'The two Coningsbys', *The Genealogist*, new ser., 26 (1909–10), 212–17, esp. 214–17 • R. Somerville, *History of the duchy of Lancaster, 1265–1603* (1953), 408 • Emden, *Cam.*, 154 • Baker, *Serjeants*, 168, 506 • F. Blomefield and C. Parkin, *An essay towards a topographical history of the county of Norfolk*, [2nd edn], 11 vols. (1805–10), vol. 7, pp. 411–13 • J. Caley and J. Hunter, eds., *Valor ecclesiasticus temp. Henrici VIII*, 6 vols., RC (1810–34), vol. 1, p. 331; vol. 3, p. 313; vol. 4, p. 274 • will, PRO, PROB 11/28, sig. 13 • wife's will, PRO, PROB 11/29, sig. 23 • inquisition post mortem, PRO, C 142/62/37

Conington, Francis Thirkill (1828–1863), chemist, was born on 3 January 1828, the third son of Richard Conington, incumbent of a chapel of ease at Boston, Lincolnshire. John *Conington, professor of classics, was his elder brother. He was educated at Rugby School from 1842 to 1846, in which year he was awarded a Lincolnshire scholarship to Corpus Christi College, Oxford. He graduated BA, taking a second-class degree in classics in 1850, held a fellowship at his college from 1849 until his death, and proceeded MA in 1853.

After spending part of 1851–2 abroad as a travelling tutor, Conington was in 1853 appointed vice-principal and classics master of the new Pulteney College, Bath. He resigned this post in 1855, moved to London, where he lodged with his brother at 11 South Square, Gray's Inn, and studied chemistry for two years at University College. His *Handbook of Chemical Analysis* (1858), based on Heinrich Will's *Anleitung zur chemischen Analyse*, was considered a useful student text. Conington was for a time scientific examiner in the school of natural sciences at Oxford, and it was during one of his examining sessions that he first suffered symptoms of the pulmonary disease from which he died, at Wide Bargate, Boston, on 20 November 1863. Summarizing his character, an obituarist remarked on his varied accomplishments and excellent taste, shrewdness, and humour, which gave pleasure to his many friends (*JCS*).

THOMPSON COOPER, rev. ANITA MCCONNELL

Sources Foster, *Alum. Oxon.* • *GM*, 3rd ser., 16 (1864), 130 • *JCS*, 17 (1864), 435–6

Wealth at death under £4000: probate, 20 Feb 1864, CGPLA Eng. & Wales

Conington, John (1825–1869), classical scholar, was born at Boston, Lincolnshire, on 10 August 1825, the eldest son of the Revd Richard Conington and his wife, Jane, daughter of F. Thirkhill. In 1836 he was sent to Beverley grammar school and two years later to Rugby School, where his housemaster was G. E. L. Cotton and the headmaster was Thomas Arnold.

Conington was a precocious child, who was able to

recite 1000 lines of Virgil to his father before the age of eight, and his near-sightedness and preference for the company of adults made him unhappy in what his biographer describes as the 'primaeval roughness' of Rugby. In his later years there he won the praise of Arnold and was, for a time, head of his house.

On 30 June 1843 Conington matriculated at University College, Oxford, but almost immediately obtained a demyship at Magdalen. He went up in October 1843 and became the pupil of the Revd William Linwood of Christ Church. In the Hilary term of 1844 he won the two most prestigious undergraduate classical prizes: the Hertford and the Ireland scholarships. His main interests lay in ancient literature and language, but although he did not find the study of ancient history or philosophy particularly stimulating he nevertheless obtained a first class in *literae humaniores* in December 1846. He had by then returned to University College (with a scholarship in March 1846), having decided against taking holy orders and realizing that he would be unlikely to obtain a lay fellowship at Magdalen. He won the Chancellor's prizes for Latin verse (1847), for an English essay (1848), and for a Latin essay (1849). In February 1848 he was elected to a fellowship at University College, and in the same year, at the age of only twenty-three, produced an edition of Aeschylus's *Agamemnon* which gained Fraenkel's approbation a century later for its 'fine interpretations and ... instinctive grasp of certain delicate shades of poetry which is characteristic of [his] later work' (Fraenkel, 1.51). His much praised conjecture in line 717 does not appear in this edition, but in *Terminalia* (1851).

Since virtually all academic preferment in Oxford was still restricted to those in holy orders, Conington decided to read for the bar. He had been prominent in the union as an undergraduate, becoming secretary in 1845, president in 1846, and librarian in 1847. He obtained the Eldon law scholarship in 1849, but, disliking London and the study of law, he returned to Oxford after six months. In the union some had seen him as a political radical and his biographer describes him as showing 'a warm sympathy with the spirit of free enquiry in theology' (Smith, xxxiii). Not everyone agreed about his radicalism. 'Conington', someone is reported to have exclaimed, 'write about the working classes! They are only a large generalisation from his scout' (*DNB*). Conington was interested in the continental revolutions of 1848, and became prominent in the movement for university reform which resulted in a royal commission and the act of 1854. He was a member of a liberal group which included Goldwin Smith (his original collaborator in editing Virgil whose appointment as secretary to the commission caused him to abandon the project), H. J. S. Smith, A. P. Stanley, Benjamin Jowett, and H. H. Vaughan. In 1849–50 he wrote a series of articles on university reform for the *Morning Chronicle*, and produced several pamphlets at Oxford. He advocated many of the changes which were brought about by the act of 1854, especially the opening of fellowships to competition, the restriction of the number of fellowships limited to clergymen, and the establishment of professorships.

Conington was himself the first holder of the Corpus professorship of Latin, to which he was elected in 1854. (He had been an unsuccessful candidate for the chair of Greek at Edinburgh in 1852.) In the long vacation of 1854 he appears to have suffered some sort of spiritual crisis in which, according to his biographer, H. J. S. Smith, 'for some weeks he was agitated and unstrung by [an] overwhelming consciousness of the immediate presence of the terrors of the unseen world'. The result was 'the fixed determination to make the obligations of religion ... the sole governing principle of his life' (Smith, xxxiii).

Mark Pattison, in a famously acid passage in his *Memoirs*, writes of Conington's being '"converted" ... by the terrors of hell. He attended chapel assiduously, refused to read anything but religious books on Sunday ... or to dine out on that day ... he began to broach Conservative sentiments, as well in politics as in University affairs, and very soon ranged himself with the followers of Dr Pusey' (Pattison, 249). Pattison's venom may have infected some other accounts; this change of political and theological stance is mentioned but not given such prominence in the writings of Conington's friends such as his pupil and successor but one in the Corpus chair, Henry Nettleship, and H. J. S. Smith.

Conington was perhaps a somewhat surprising choice as first holder of the Corpus chair. At the time of his election he had not published any edition of a Latin work, and a contemporary noted with surprise his limited grasp of German. He showed little interest in the recent advances made in classical scholarship on the continent or in the developing study of ancient history, and his understanding of the importance of earlier English classical scholars (such as Richard Bentley) was limited. Apart from a handful of reviews and essays and the important editions of Virgil and Persius, his chief publications were translations, readings from which often formed the basis of his public lectures. Within Latin literature his interest was limited to a very few authors, and he showed little interest in the history or practice of textual criticism, as is shown by his excessively conservative attitude to the text of Virgil.

Conington's translations have not stood the test of time, and include some strange choices of medium: he turned the *Aeneid* into ballad form (1866), a continuation of P. S. Worsley's Homer into Spenserian stanzas (1868), and Horace's *Satires* and *Epistles* into heroic couplets (1869). Nevertheless, Conington's critics were unfair in judging his production of translations as mere laziness: a genuine interest in attending to 'each word, not merely to the general force of an expression, but to the various constituents which make up the effect produced by it on a thoroughly intelligent reader' (*Miscellaneous Writings*, 1.220) is the most important characteristic which informs his translations, essays, reviews, and editions.

Conington is best remembered for the commentary on Virgil which he began in 1852 and continued to revise throughout his life. The last of its three volumes was partly written by Nettleship, who later revised the first two volumes and added useful essays. Other revisions were undertaken by F. Haverfield. It is the fullest commentary on the whole of Virgil in English, and remains very valuable (especially on the *Aeneid*) for its clear explanatory notes and citations of parallel passages. Conington's edition of Aeschylus's *Choephoroe* (1857) drew warm praise from Fraenkel (52) for the 'quiet and noble language' of its notes; more important was his edition and translation of Persius, which was completed by Nettleship and published in 1872. This contains detailed notes on the subject matter and remained the standard English work on the poet for over a century.

Despite his cadaverous appearance—he was known as the 'sick vulture', and Tuckwell (104) recalls his 'extraordinary visage with its green-cheese hue, gleaming spectacles [and] quivering, protrusive lips'—Conington was a noted conversationalist, an assiduous letter-writer, and an important influence on the small groups of undergraduates whom he cultivated, who included T. H. Green, Nettleship, and J. A. Symonds. Although he had no interest in scenery, he took a daily walk during term (giving favoured undergraduates a regular day on which to accompany him) and led a reading party each summer. Many of his former pupils expressed deep gratitude for his friendship, but Nettleship noted 'his intense craving for human sympathy as an impulse which materially injured his mental development, and diverted his powers from objects more worthy of them' (Nettleship, 1.xxii). In later life he spent the vacations looking after his aged mother in Boston, his father having died in 1861, and his brothers in 1863 and 1868. Conington died at Boston, Lincolnshire, on 23 October 1869 after a short illness caused by a malignant pustule on the lip, and was buried three days later at Fishtoft, Lincolnshire. The Conington prize for a classical dissertation was founded in his memory in 1871.

RICHARD SMAIL

Sources H. J. S. Smith, 'Memoir', in *Miscellaneous writings of John Conington*, ed. J. A. Symonds (1872) · M. Pattison, *Memoirs*, ed. Mrs Pattison (1885) · G. D. Boyle, *Recollections* (1895) · W. Tuckwell, *Reminiscences of Oxford* (1900) · W. R. Ward, *Victorian Oxford* (1965) · C. O. Brink, *English classical scholarship: historical reflections on Bentley, Porson, and Housman* (1986) · E. Fraenkel, ed., *Aeschylus: Agamemnon*, 3 vols. (1950) · K. Lake, ed., *Memorials of William Charles Lake, dean of Durham, 1869–1894* (1901) · H. Nettleship, *Lectures and essays*, ed. F. Haverfield, 2 (1895) · P. G. Naiditch, 'Classical studies in nineteenth-century Great Britain as background to the "Cambridge ritualists"', *The Cambridge ritualists reconsidered: First Oldfather Conference* [Urbana-Champaign, IL 1989], ed. W. M. Calder (1991), 123–52

Archives Bodl. Oxf., letters to Mark Pattison; letters to H. H. Vaughan · NL Scot., letters to William Blackwood & Sons · NL Scot., letters to Alexander Campbell Fraser · NL Wales, letters to Sir George Cornewall Lewis

Likenesses A. Macdonald, drawing, 1918, CCC Oxf.

Wealth at death under £12,000: resworn probate, April 1871, CGPLA Eng. & Wales (1869)

Conington [Conyngton], **Richard** (d. 1330), Franciscan friar and theologian, is of unknown origins. He is first mentioned in July 1300 when, along with John Duns Scotus, Robert Cowton, and nineteen other Oxford Franciscans, he was presented (unsuccessfully) to Bishop John Dalderby of Lincoln by the Franciscan provincial minister,

Hugh of Hartlepool, for licence to hear confessions; only eight licences were granted. As an advanced student in theology he participated in disputations at Oxford in or shortly after 1300. He lectured on the *Sentences* at Oxford as a bachelor of theology *c*.1302–3, and was the Franciscan regent master (DTh) at Oxford *c*.1306. He subsequently lectured on scripture as Franciscan regent master at Cambridge. His lost commentary on the penitential psalms, whose opening words, according to Bale, were 'Saepius dum sedebam solitarius', was probably a result of his teaching as master at Oxford or Cambridge. In 1310 he was elected provincial minister for the Franciscan order in England, a position he apparently held until 1316. He died at Cambridge in 1330 and was buried there in the Franciscan convent.

Although a contemporary and co-religious of Duns Scotus, Conington often favoured the positions of theologians of the previous academic generation, particularly the views of Henri de Gand, who died in 1293. John Baconthorpe, a Carmelite friar and younger contemporary, as well as an anonymous author in Vatican City, Biblioteca Apostolica Vaticana, MS Vat. lat. 869, described Conington as a disciple (*discipulus*) of Henri, which R. L. Poole interpreted to mean Conington had studied under Henri at Paris, but which Doucet read as implying only that Conington followed in Henri's intellectual footsteps. It is likely that Conington was among the select group of Franciscans sent to Paris for part of their initial theological training, which would have been in the early 1290s, but his training would have come primarily through Franciscan masters. Several of Conington's quodlibetal questions and disputed questions have survived from his teaching at Oxford or Cambridge.

While he was in attendance at the Council of Vienne (1311–12) as provincial minister, Conington wrote a treatise on apostolic poverty, *Beatus qui intelligit* (ed. Heysse, 1930), which he followed in 1322 with a second treatise, *Responsiones ad conclusiones domini papae* (ed. Douie, 1931), which was critical of the views Pope John XXII expressed on this issue in the bull *Ad conditorem canonum* of the same year. He is also credited by Leland and Bale with a defence, *De Christi Dominio*, of John XXII against the attacks of William Ockham, and by Leland with a commentary on the *Quadragesimale* of Pope Gregory the Great. Conington was widely cited by contemporaries who, in addition to Baconthorpe, included William Alnwick, Robert Walsingham, William of Nottingham, Peter Thomas, and John Reading. Contemporary citations from his lost commentary on the *Sentences* may eventually help identify it.

W. J. COURTENAY

Sources Joannes Bacho [J. Baconthorpe], *Doctoris resoluti Jo. Bachonis … quaestiones in quatuor libros sententiarum, et quodlibetales*, 1 (Cremona, 1618), in 1 Sent., dist. 4, a. 1 · Biblioteca Apostolica Vaticana, Vatican City, MS Vatican lat. 869, fols. 31r, 32r, 35r · DNB · A. G. Little and F. Pelster, *Oxford theology and theologians*, OHS, 96 (1934), 63–4, 260–61, 344, 359 · 'Richard de Conington, *Tractatus de paupertate*', ed. A. Heysse, *Archivum Franciscanum Historicum*, 23 (1930), 57–105, 340–60 · D. L. Douie, 'Three treatises on evangelical poverty by Fr. Richard Conyngton, Fr. Walter Chatton and an anonymous from MS V. iii. 18 in Bishop Cosin's library, Durham',

Archivum Franciscanum Historicum, 24 (1931), 341–69 • D. L. Douie, *The nature and the effect of the heresy of the Fraticelli* (1932), 149, 202–4 • F. Pelster, 'Franziskanerlehrer um die Wende des 13. und zu Anfang des 14. Jahrhunderts in zwei ehemaligen Turiner Hss. nach Aufzeichnungen von Kardinal Ehrle', *Gregorianum*, 18 (1937), 291–317 • V. Doucet, 'L'oeuvre scolastique de Richard de Conington', *Archivum Franciscanum Historicum*, 29 (1937), 396–442 • J. R. H. Moorman, *The Grey friars in Cambridge, 1225–1538*, The Birkbeck Lectures (1952), 58, 94–7, 144, 165 • Emden, *Oxf.*, 1.477
Archives Biblioteca Apostolica Vaticana, Vatican City, MS Ottoboni lat. 1126, fols. 1r–4v • Biblioteca Apostolica Vaticana, Vatican City, MS Ottoboni lat. 1126, fols. 4v–16v qq. 1–17 • Biblioteca Apostolica Vaticana, Vatican City, MS Vatican lat. 1012, fols. 128r–128v q. 5 • Biblioteca Apostolica Vaticana, Vatican City, MS Vatican lat. 4871, fols. 2ra–2vb • Biblioteca Medicea Laurenziana, Florence, Plut. XXXVI, Dext. cod. 12 • Staatsbibliothek, Munich, MS Clm 8717, fols. 91va–92va • Universitätsbibliothek, Leipzig, MS 470, fols. 69vb–72vb qq. 1–5

Conlaíd (d. 518/520). *See under* Brigit (439/452–524/526).

Conn Cétchathach (*supp. d.* 157), legendary high-king of Ireland, flourished, if he existed at all, many generations before the beginning of documentation in medieval Ireland, and he therefore cannot be dated with any hope of accuracy. The genealogies show him as one of seven sons of Feidlimid Rechtaid, king of Tara (the title of the high-kings of Ireland), and his mother was said anachronistically to be the daughter of the king of Scandinavia. He was claimed as ancestor by three prominent peoples in the northern half of Ireland: the Connachta (whence the name of the later province of Connacht), the Airgialla of Ulster, and the Uí Néill, the most powerful dynasty in Ireland between the sixth and tenth centuries. It is not surprising that when medieval scholars began to think of Ireland in terms of a division between north and south, they called the former 'Conn's Half'. The notion of this dichotomy seems to reflect the politics of the eighth century. One tale explains it thus: Éogan Mór (otherwise Mug Nuadat, supposed ancestor of the Éoganachta dynasties of southern Ireland) seized the province of Munster from the three kings who had formerly held it. One of the dispossessed kings was given troops by Conn, but was defeated. Conn himself then fought with Éogan, but was defeated in ten battles. The result was the division of Ireland from Galway Bay to Dublin Bay.

Conn was said to have been born at Tara, a site with pagan associations, the symbolic seat of those who claimed the kingship of Ireland in the middle ages. At his birth three great rivers sprang up, and three lakes (Lough Neagh, Lough Rea, and Lough Leane), and three famous trees. This may be connected with the concept that the king was the bringer of fertility. However, it has been suggested—notably by T. F. O'Rahilly—that Conn was originally a god. One meaning of his name is 'sense, wisdom', and there is a prominent figure in Welsh mythology called Pwyll, whose name means the same. If this is not coincidence, it would appear that both heroes have their source in a single pre-Christian, pan-Celtic personage. Conn seems to have a divine role in what is perhaps the earliest text to mention him, the late seventh-century *Baile Chuinn*

Chétchathaig ('The frenzy (or vision) of Conn Cétchathach'), a series of obscure and poetic utterances prophesying the kings of Tara who would come after him.

However, an updated version of this text written some centuries later shows Conn as human, not divine. The prophecy is given by Lug (who was undoubtedly a Celtic deity), although Conn is the one to whom it is spoken. Of Conn himself, Lug prophesied that he would participate in a hundred battles; this is evidently an attempt to explain his epithet (which may be translated as 'Hundred-Battler'). Lug listed these battles, but the total is well short of the target. However, the early modern historian Geoffrey Keating quotes a stanza which says that Conn fought a hundred battles against the Munstermen, a hundred against the Ulstermen, and sixty against the Leinstermen.

The genealogies disagree on the number and names of Conn's children. The most significant of his progeny was Art Óenfher, high-king of Ireland, his son with the daughter of the king of Scotland Aífe ingen Alpín. Among his other wives was Lenabair, the daughter of Catháer Már, ancestor of the ruling dynasties of Leinster. A Leinster genealogical source claims that while Catháer ruled at Tara, Conn ruled at nearby Kells, and that there was complete peace between them.

There is a brief tale about Conn's death, reputedly in 157. He was in a state of enmity with his brother, Eochaid, who had fled to the Ulstermen. Conn sent envoys to the kings of Ulster to get assurances from them about his brother. However, the envoys found Eochaid alone, and took the opportunity to murder him, which was regarded as an outrage by his hosts. A peace was made, but one of the kings, Tipraite, did not accept it and fled to Scotland. He and his men returned after three years, veiled and in women's garb. They came across Conn alone at Tara and Tipraite slew him.   PHILIP IRWIN

Sources T. F. O'Rahilly, *Early Irish history and mythology* (1946), 281–3 • O. Bergin, ed. and trans., 'The death of Conn of the Hundred Battles', *Zeitschrift für Celtische Philologie*, 8 (1910–12), 274–7 • E. Curry, ed. and trans., *Cath Mhuighe Leana, or, The Battle of Magh Leana* (1855) • V. Hull, ed. and trans., 'Eogan Mór and Conn Cétchathach', *Zeitschrift für Celtische Philologie*, 19 (1931–3), 59–61 • M. Dillon, *The cycles of the kings* (1946), 11–14 • G. Murphy, 'On the dates of two sources used in Thurneysen's *Heldensage*: 1. *Baile Chuind* and the date of *Cin Dromma Snechtai*', *Ériu*, 16 (1952), 145–56 • R. Thurneysen, 'Baile in Scáil', *Zeitschrift für Celtische Philologie*, 20 (1933–6), 213–27, esp. 218–21 • M. A. O'Brien, ed., *Corpus genealogiarum Hiberniae* (Dublin, 1962), 70, 130 • M. C. Dobbs, ed. and trans., 'The Ban-shenchus [pt 2]', *Revue Celtique*, 48 (1931), 163–234, esp. 176 • G. Keating, *The history of Ireland*, ed. and trans. P. S. Dinneen, Irish Texts Society, 8 (1908), 267

Conn na mBocht (d. 1060), ecclesiastical leader, was 'head of the Céili Dé [Culdees, literally "servants of God"] and anchorites of Clonmacnoise', though he is sometimes mistakenly called bishop of Clonmacnoise on the basis of a misinterpretation of an entry in *Chronicum Scotorum* for the year 948. His death is likewise sometimes given as 1031, on the basis of an entry in the annals of the four masters, mistakenly assumed to be an obit. His name is the eponym of the Meic Cuinn na mBocht family, one of the best documented in early medieval Ireland below the top ranks of royalty, though two versions of their dynastic origin are recorded, one linking them with Uí Chellaig, the royal family of Brega, the other, perhaps more likely, with the Mugdorna Maigen of Airgialla. They are occasionally called Muinter Gormáin, after the abbot of Louth who died on pilgrimage in Clonmacnoise in 758, or Cenél Torbaig, after the latter's famous son, Torbach (d. 808), abbot of Armagh and the person for whom the Book of Armagh was written.

Torbach's son Áedacán was abbot of Louth but died in Clonmacnoise in 835, and the family were thereafter firmly fixed at Clonmacnoise, Áedacán's grandson Luchairén being the first member of Conn na mBocht's ancestry specifically recorded as one of its scribes. Successive members of the family held prominent posts there, Conn's great-grandfather Dúnadach (d. 955) being bishop, and his grandfather Dúnchad being 'lector of Clonmacnoise, and its anchorite afterwards, head of its rule and history' (AFM, s.a. 1005). Although Conn's own father, Ioseph (d. 1024), was described simply as anmchara Cluana mic Nóis ('confessor [literally "soul-friend"] of Clonmacnoise'; AFM, s.a. 1022), there is more than enough evidence to demonstrate that the family had a long tradition as scribes and historians, a tradition that extended beyond Conn. The latter's grandson, for instance, was the principal scribe of Lebor na hUidre, containing the oldest text of the Táin, where an entry requests 'a prayer for Máel Muire mac Céilechair, grandson of Conn na mBocht, who copied and searched out this book from various books' (Lebor na hUidre, fol. 37b). The family probably also maintained the annals at Clonmacnoise, which would account for the detailed and flattering entries about them recorded through the ages.

Conn himself was head of the Céili Dé, who, when they first appeared in the eighth century, were individuals or groups subject to a monastic rule, apparently with observances stricter than those of others; but by the eleventh century the term is synonymous, or nearly so, with the monastic poor, na boicht, individuals inhabiting monastic lands who may or may not have taken vows of poverty. In Armagh, the person charged with looking after the poor was called cenn bocht, 'head of the poor' (Ann. Ulster, s.a. 1074, 1077), a title also given to Conn's son and successor at Clonmacnoise, from which it may be assumed that Conn had served the same function.

The Four Masters state that 'the reason he was called Conn na mBocht is because of the number of poor that he used to feed habitually' (AFM, 807), and the evidence suggests that he enjoyed considerable wealth since the annals of the four masters records for 1031 that he was 'the first to assemble a herd for the poor of Clonmacnoise' (though O'Donovan oddly translates this as 'the first that invited a party of the poor'), and presented twenty cows of his own to it. They were maintained at Ísel Chiaráin (Twyford, Westmeath), a church situated quite some distance north of Clonmacnoise, which had been in its possession for many generations and was by tradition the location of St Ciarán's first settlement in the area. It became the possession of Conn's family in the eleventh century: a verse

couplet in the annals of the four masters for 1031, on the subject of Conn, seems to have Ísel Chiaráin in mind when it refers to do chill, 'your church', while the same source for 1089 records that it 'was purchased for ever by Cormac Mac Cuinn na mBocht' (Conn's grandson) from the abbot of Clonmacnoise and the king of Mide. The annals of Clonmacnoise, in describing an event that belongs to 1072, likewise mention 'the family of Moyle-kyeran mc Con ne mboght in Isillkyeran and the poore of that house'. The same source calls it 'Isill Kieran or the hospitall of St. Queran', which is perhaps an indication of one of the functions the family served there.

These notices seem to confirm that, under the stewardship of Conn and his immediate successors, Ísel Chiaráin, once an important possession of Clonmacnoise, was transformed into an independent church, run by a hereditary ecclesiastical family, and, by virtue of its 'purchase' from both king and abbot, exempted from secular and ecclesiastical authority and taxation. This must have been largely Conn's achievement since, although the annalists are almost totally silent about him, they view him as an apical figure and are very anxious to link others to him by either ancestry or descent. The verse couplet commemorating him gives some idea of his status: 'O Conn of Cluain, thou wert heard from Ireland in Scotland; O head of dignity, it will not be easy to plunder thy church' (AFM, s.a. 1031). He died, as 'the glory and dignity of Clonmacnoise', in 1060 'at an advanced age' (AFM, s.a. 1060). A tombstone with the inscription 'Or[óit] do Chuinn' ('a prayer for Conn') was still visible when George Petrie visited Clonmacnoise in the mid-nineteenth century.

Conn had at least five sons: Célechair Mugdornach, who died as bishop of Clonmacnoise in 1067; Máel Chiaráin (d. 1079), abbot of Clonmacnoise, who paved two roads there and whose inscribed gravestone Petrie also recorded; Máel Finnén, who predeceased his father in 1056 but who was deemed important enough for his obit to record his genealogy, whose son Cormac later held the abbacy or vice-abbacy, and whose gravestone Petrie also noted; Gilla Críst, 'the best cleric's son that was in Ireland in his time, the glory and ornament of Clonmacnoise' (AFM, s.a. 1085); and Máel Ísu (d. 1103).

SEÁN DUFFY

Sources AFM · Ann. Ulster · D. Murphy, ed., The annals of Clonmacnoise, trans. C. Mageoghagan (1896); facs. edn (1993) · W. M. Hennessy, ed. and trans., Chronicum Scotorum: a chronicle of Irish affairs, Rolls Series, 46 (1866) · W. Stokes, ed., 'The annals of Tigernach [8 pts]', Revue Celtique, 16 (1895), 374–419; 17 (1896), 6–33, 119–263, 337–420; 18 (1897), 9–59, 150–97, 267–303, 374–91; pubd sep. (1993) · R. I. Best and O. Bergin, eds., Lebor na hUidre / Book of the dun cow (1929) · Christian inscriptions in the Irish language, ed. M. Stokes, 2 vols. (1872) · J. V. Kelleher, 'The Táin and the annals', Ériu, 22 (1971), 107–27, esp. 125–6 · B. Ó Cuív, 'Boicht Chorcaige', Celtica, 18 (1986), 105–11 · A. Kehnel, Clonmacnoise: the church and lands of St Ciarán (1997)

Conn, George (d. 1640), diplomat, was the son of Patrick Conn of Auchry, near Turriff, Aberdeenshire, and Isabella Chyn of Esselmont. He was raised as a Catholic and educated at Douai, the Scots College at Paris, and in Rome before entering the University of Bologna. He served as tutor to the son of the duke of Mirandola before joining the household of Cardinal Monalto in Rome in the summer of 1623. Monalto left him a substantial legacy six months later. Conn then entered the service of Cardinal Francesco Barberini, nephew to Urban VIII, accompanying him on diplomatic missions to France and Spain. He joined the Franciscan order and became a canon of St Lawrence in Damaso and secretary to the congregation of rites.

In 1624 Conn published *Vita Mariae Stuartae Scotiae reginae*, which he dedicated to the pope. This hagiographic biography became the main source for Lope de Vega's *Corona tragica* (Madrid, 1627) and also inspired Giovanni Battista Ciampoli's *Poesia in lode dell'inchiostro dedicata al Signior Georgio Coneo* (Rome, 1626). Encouraged by his success Conn published *De duplici religionis apud Scotos* with the Vatican Press in 1628. The first book of this work traced the history of Christianity in Scotland from the Roman period down to the beginnings of the Reformation, while the second narrated the contest between Scottish Catholicism and heresy from the 1540s until the early seventeenth century. It closed with a flattering reference to the book's dedicatee, Cardinal Barberini, as a patron and protector of Scottish Catholics.

In 1633 Queen Henrietta Maria nominated Conn to the College of Cardinals in a letter to Barberini transmitted by Sir Robert Douglas. Charles I knew about and tacitly supported the proposal as a means of reopening communications with the Vatican. Barberini foresaw difficulties with the nomination and it was decided to defer action while dispatching an agent to England to assess the situation there, including the prospects that Charles himself might convert. Gregorio Panzani, who was chosen for this assignment, sent back encouraging reports of the desires of the king and other leading figures at the English court for reunion with Rome. The Vatican decided to send a more senior representative and in late spring 1636 selected Conn, largely thanks to active lobbying by Henrietta Maria's favourite, Wat Montagu, who was visiting Rome at the time after converting to Catholicism.

Conn arrived in England on 17 July 1636. Like Panzani he was accredited to the queen rather than the king, to whom he presented himself on 24 July. But he was also immediately welcomed by other leading personalities of the court, including the protestant earls of Pembroke and Holland. He quickly established a close relationship with the king, whom he often encountered in the queen's apartments. Charles confided in Conn his belief that the French were trying to use his wife to serve their own interests, quizzed him about Catholic doctrines, and engaged him in genial arguments over points of theology.

The intimacy between the king and the papal agent aroused jealousies but also enhanced Conn's influence with both protestant and Catholic courtiers. Conn adroitly used his position not only to probe English attitudes and lobby for concessions but to build a Catholic party. He soon became less sanguine than Panzani over the immediate prospects for reunification, since he realized that Charles and Archbishop William Laud would demand concessions that the Vatican was unwilling to grant. He therefore concentrated on softening enforcement of the penal laws and negotiating changes in the wording of the oath of allegiance to make it less objectionable to Catholics. He was largely successful in the first goal and obtained substantial concessions with respect to the oath, although these failed to satisfy the Vatican. Meanwhile he attempted to discover the religious attitudes of English bishops and leading members of the court and to persuade any who seemed well disposed to Rome to convert.

Panzani had commented before Conn's arrival that a successful papal agent to the English court must be especially adept at working through women, and this proved prophetic. Although Conn was assisted in his proselytizing by the queen's confessor, Father Philip of Sanquhar, and the indefatigable Montagu, whose return to royal favour he helped arrange, his most effective allies were the queen and the countess of Arundel. In 1637–8 several other prominent women at court converted and joined his campaign, among them Olivia Porter, the wife of Charles's pro-Spanish bedchamber servant Endymion Porter, and the formerly puritan Lady Newport. These 'Amazons who … day and night employ their uttermost endeavours for the dignity of the apostolic see', as Barberini appreciatively described them (*Various Collections*, 5.121), were further reinforced in 1639 by the arrival of the pro-Spanish French duchess of Chevreuse and the queen's mother, Marie de' Medici. The growth of Catholicism at court caused considerable scandal, as did the increasingly ostentatious worship by English subjects at chapels maintained by the queen and the ambassadors of Catholic states, and in Conn's own Long Acre house, where eight masses were celebrated daily.

Conn regarded the crisis provoked by the new Scottish prayer book of 1637 as an opportunity to make Charles reliant on Catholic support against puritan opponents. He took every opportunity to contrast Catholic loyalty with puritan disobedience, urged the king to lift restrictions on Catholics owning arms so they would be in a better position to defend him, and hinted that the pope's friendship might restrain France and Spain from trying to profit from Britain's internal problems. He helped to organize the collection of a voluntary 'contribution' by Catholics to aid the king in the first bishops' war and encouraged Scottish Catholic nobles at the English court to organize military resistance to the covenanters. He became involved as well in discussions of a possible loan from the pope and military assistance from Spain.

These efforts provoked a fierce reaction. Rumours circulated that Conn had brought the new Scottish prayer book from Rome and that he was hearing the confessions of the king. He was also the victim of internal rancour within the English Catholic community. Moderate Catholics with unrealistic expectations of the concessions Rome would offer to achieve reunification with England blamed him for taking a rigid stance. Many secular priests regarded him as an ally of the Jesuits. Damaging leaks of information and false accusations from disgruntled Catholics further inflamed English opinion. Conn's failure to win the coveted promotion to the cardinalate also undermined his prestige within the British Catholic community and with the king.

By spring 1639 Conn's health was failing and his doctors concluded that he would not survive another winter in England. Barberini therefore reluctantly recalled him to Rome. Conn left England in late summer, shortly after the arrival of his successor, Rossetti, with renewed hope that he would shortly be made a cardinal, but he died on 10 January 1640 without the coveted prize; he was buried in Rome and a monument to him was erected in the church of St Lawrence, Damaso. Henrietta Maria and her allies continued his efforts to build a Catholic party at Whitehall and exploit the Scots crisis to win religious concessions from Charles. Conn played a significant, if indirect, role in creating the climate of religious polarization and fierce suspicion of popery at court that made civil war possible. R. MALCOLM SMUTS

Sources G. Albion, *Charles I and the court of Rome* (1935) · C. M. Hibbard, *Charles I and the Popish Plot* (1983) · *DNB* · PRO, PRO 31/9/124 · BL, Add. MS 15390 · *Report on manuscripts in various collections*, 8 vols., HMC, 55 (1901–14), vol. 6 · *CSP Venice, 1636–9*, 5, no. 24 · G. B. Ciampoli, *Poesia in lode dell'inchiostro dedicata al Signior Georgio Coneo gentilhuomo scozzese* (Rome, 1626) · *The Popes nuntioes, or, The negotiations of Seignior Panzani* (1643)
Archives Archivio Vaticano, Vatican City · BL, Add. MS 15390 · PRO, PRO 31/9/124

Connacht, saints of (*act. c.*400–*c.*800), holy men and women believed to have been buried within the province of Connacht, flourished in the period of the fifth century to the eighth. The province ruled by the Connachta, a group of dynasties claiming to be distantly related, had few outstanding saints. The only one of the front rank was Brendan of Clonfert [*see below*]; and even he came from the Altraige of west Kerry, where his other principal church, Ardfert, ministered to his own people. The importance of Connacht for hagiography lies elsewhere than among the major saints, such as those who came to be designated in the genealogies of the saints and other sources as 'the twelve apostles of Ireland'. Because of the account of St Patrick's circuit round Ireland written by Bishop *Tírechán *c.*690, there is a large amount of information on the minor saints of Connacht who were believed to be of early date. Among them are several whose cults appear to have collapsed for political reasons. Elsewhere it is usually the successful cults that yield evidence; the particular interest of Connacht is, therefore, its failed saints. Another feature of significance, however, is its group of late arrivals. Most major Irish saints belonged to the sixth century; in Connacht, however, two considerable saints, Commán of Roscommon and Garald (Gerald) of Mayo, belonged to the eighth.

Early saints Connacht contains the only Irish site, 'the Wood of Voclut', later Caill Fochlad in north co. Mayo, securely associated with St Patrick in his own writings. An early church, Domnach Mór, was adjacent to Caill Fochlad; moreover Bishop Tírechán was a native of the kingdom to which Caill Fochlad and Domnach Mór belonged, and a member of its dynasty, Uí Amolngada. Domnach Mór, however, was later supplanted by Killala (Cell Alaid) as the chief church of the Uí Amolngada; hence the eclipse of the cult of the saint whose bones were said by Tírechán to lie at Domnach Mór, **Mucnoe** [Mucneus] (*fl. c.*500). His feast day was not recorded in any of the Irish martyrologies, whereas **Muiredach mac Echdach** (*fl.* early 6th cent.) of Killala had his feast day, 12 August. The latest of the major martyrologies, that of Donegal, says that Muiredach belonged to an Uí Néill dynasty, Cenél Lóegairi, whose main lands lay around Trim, far to the east of Connacht's eastern boundary, the Shannon. Tírechán, however, in the late seventh century, placed Muiredach a little to the east of the Uí Amolngada, in the coastal strip along the southern coast of Sligo Bay and thus within the kingdom of Uí Fhiachrach Muaide. This raises the possibility that the replacement of Domnach Mór by Killala as the chief church of the Uí Amolngada to the west of the Moy may have owed much to the influence of the Uí Fhiachrach Muaide, since they were the most powerful dynasty of northern Connacht. Muiredach may also have been thought by Tírechán to be the eponymous saint of Inishmurray, Inis Muiredaig in Sligo Bay, although the patron saint of the island monastery was **Laisrén** [Mo Laisse] **mac Decláin** (*fl.* 6th cent.), whose feast day was 12 August and who was affiliated in the genealogies of the saints to the Westmeath people, Corcu Roíde. Laisrén also had a mainland base at Aughris (Echross), close to where Tírechán placed Muiredach.

Mucnoe was said by Tírechán to have been the brother of a more important saint, **Céthech** [Caetiacus, Cethiachus] (*fl.* 5th cent.), bishop, whose feast day was 16 June. Céthech's name suggests that he may, in reality, have been a Briton (it is probably a nickname, Welsh *coediog*, 'woody') but for Tírechán, *c.*690, Céthech belonged to the Uí Ailella, an important but declining royal dynasty of north-eastern Connacht. Tírechán's evidence suggests that the Uí Ailella had been powerful within Mag nAí, the most fertile area of all Connacht, between Elphin and Roscommon. Céthech's main church was at Cell Garad, on the southern edge of Mag nAí (earlier Brí Garad, now Oran from the name of the holy well, Uarán Garad, marked by the remains of a round tower and a church). From Tírechán's time onwards, the Uí Ailella were confined to the area between Elphin and Collooney in co. Sligo. Their loss of power in Mag nAí may be the explanation of an anecdote in the Book of Armagh, which tells a story of disobedience. Céthech and another early saint, Sachellus, were said to have ordained bishops and consecrated churches without Patrick's permission. Patrick summoned them to Armagh; and, although they did penance, he declared that 'Your churches will not be great' (Bieler, 122–3).

Sachellus (*fl.* 5th cent.), like Céthech, was a bishop; as Céthech was identified with his supposed father's people, the Uí Ailella, and, in a subordinate way, with his mother's people, the Saírige, a minor group close to Duleek, far to the east, so Sachellus and his church, Baislec, were identified with the Ciarraige nAí, a major client-kingdom within Mag nAí. Sachellus, very possibly another early

British missionary, was listed by Tírechán among Patrick's bishops. Baislec—in Ireland a rare name for a church, borrowed from Latin *basilica*—had been, earlier in the seventh century, the recipient of a special gift from Armagh, a share of its relics of Peter, Paul, and Laurence. The implication appears to be that Armagh then had high hopes of an alliance with Baislec, and thus with its saint, Sachellus. Late in the seventh century, however, these hopes were dashed, probably by the reduction of the Ciarraige nAí to close dependence on the rising dynasty of Uí Briúin Aí.

Early Connacht saints' cults were, then, liable to be eclipsed for political reasons. Only Céthech among those already mentioned found a place in the martyrologies, and only his church, Cell Garad, retained any importance in the post-viking period, as shown by the remains of its round tower. Yet his principal advantage seems to have lain in his possession of the famous well Uarán Garad. Two early saints' cults, however, from north-eastern Connacht survived better. **Brón mac Icni** (d. 512), the saint of Caisel Irrae near the town of Sligo, was claimed by Tírechán as another of Patrick's bishops. His feast day of 8 June is in the martyrologies; he is also mentioned in the Middle Irish genealogical collections among a list of bishops, but no pedigree is given. Already in Tírechán's day, Brón's church claimed to possess a tooth of St Patrick—a rare early example of an Irish corporeal relic. It was later enshrined, received a hereditary guardian, and survived long enough to be one of the most valued relics of the entire province of Connacht as late as the seventeenth century; it is preserved in the National Museum. Brón's church and cult thus remained firmly entrenched in a limited area, the peninsula west of the town of Sligo, defended by his Patrician relic.

The cult of **Béoáed mac Ocláin** (d. 520/524), bishop, is broadly similar to that of Brón, but without the Patrician connections of the latter. His feast day is 7 or 8 March. His church of Ard Carna lay within Mag Luirg, an area to the south of Lough Key and north of Elphin. The site, some 4 miles east of the town of Boyle, is marked by the modern Church of Ireland parish church. According to the saints' genealogies, where his father's name is given as Olcán, Béoáed belonged to the Corco Loígde of west Cork. His church and cult were of major but not dominant importance within the kingdom of Mag Luirg, ruled by a branch of the Uí Ailella, 'the Sons of Erc'. But, whereas the main line of the Uí Ailella were on good terms with the heirs of Patrick, the Sons of Erc were not. Not only did their early bishop, Béoáed, have no Patrician allegiance, but they later received an important Columban church at Assylin. **Cormac** [Corbmac] **mac Eogain** (*fl.* 6th cent.) was given a saint's life by John Colgan in his *Acta sanctorum ... Híberniae* (1645) on the basis of a genealogical tract in the late-medieval Book of Lecan (Royal Irish Academy, Dublin, MS 23 P 2). The tract is on a saintly family said to be descended from a collateral branch of the Éoganachta, the ruling dynasties of Munster. The most distinguished member of the family was not, however, Cormac, but his supposed brother, Béccán (d. 690) of Cluain Ard Mo Béccóc, Toureen Peacaun (co. Tipperary). Colgan's life takes Cormac to

Connacht and settles him at the mouth of the River Moy (co. Mayo), but the chronological details are quite inconsistent with the annalistic obit for Béccán. The date of Cormac's death is unknown, his feast day uncertain.

The major saints of the Connachta Béoáed appears to have been among the last of the early (that is, late fifth- and early sixth-century) saints who founded early episcopal churches within local kingdoms (*tuatha*). Most major saints belonged to the next two generations. The outstanding saint of Connacht was **Brendan of Clonfert** [Brénainn mac Findloga, Brendan the Navigator] (d. 577), whose feast day is 16 May and who is associated with Clonfert in Galway and Ardfert in Kerry. The previous saints have all been mentioned, at best, in the martyrologies, except that Béoáed's generosity was celebrated in a Middle Irish poem; Brendan, however, was celebrated in a series of lives as well as in the *Navigatio sancti Brendani*. The relationship and dates of the texts have been disputed, but they indubitably bear witness to an enduring and widespread cult. Although Clonfert was the resting-place of his body, the cult far transcended the kingdom of the Uí Maini, within which Clonfert lay. Indeed, the fourteenth-century text 'The customs of Uí Maini' shows that other, more local saints, such as **Grellán of Cráeb Grelláin** (*fl.* 5th–6th cent.), whose feast day is 10 November and whose crozier was carried into battle before the army of the Uí Maini, were then as, or even more, important locally, as also was the cult of St Brigit, already entrenched in the area by the mid-seventh century.

Brendan belonged to the Altraige, a minor client people of the area north-west of Tralee. The *Navigatio*, probably written in the eighth century, claimed Brendan for the Éoganacht, apparently intending the Éoganacht Locha Léin, centred around Killarney, the overkings of west Munster. Later, however, as the power of the Éoganacht Locha Léin declined, Brendan was claimed by the increasingly powerful neighbours of the Altraige, Ciarraige Luachra (who gave their name to Kerry). The point of change is marked by a propaganda document known as the West Munster Synod (or Macc Ardae's Synod), probably written in the late eighth or early ninth century. It was designed to rally ecclesiastical support for a move to curtail yet further the powers of the king of the Éoganacht Locha Léin. In this text, Brendan is still 'moccu Altai' (that is, a member of the Altraige), as he had been about a century earlier in Adomnán's *Vita Columbae*, but he was said to swear an oath on behalf of the Ciarraige Luachra. His southern church, Ardfert, was now within the power of the Ciarraige Luachra and he had become a Ciarraige saint. The true local affiliation of Brendan was thus partially obscured, since his cult and church were of sufficient importance as to attract the rapacity of the leading kings of west Munster. The various Latin lives seem to derive from an original which ascribed Brendan to the Ciarraige Luachra. Yet his connection with the Altraige is still recorded in the Middle Irish life. Moreover the Connacht connections of the Altraige were to be repeated a century later in the person of **Mo Chua** [Crónán] **mac Bécáin** (d. 694), the patron saint of Balla in modern co. Mayo, the most important church of the kingdom of Cerae. His cult, celebrated with a feast day on 30 March, was reinforced by a Middle Irish life, and the enduring significance of his church is attested by the remains of a round tower.

The *Navigatio* combined together Clonfert, Brendan's principal Connacht church, and Ardfert. He appears to have set out on his journey from Clonfert but to have completed it by coming to the land of his fathers, namely Ardfert and Altraige. Indeed, the text has Brendan die shortly after his return and fails to mention that he had left Ardfert, thus insinuating that he died at his southern church and not at Clonfert. Another indication of the Munster provenance of the *Navigatio* and its Éoganacht links is an episode in which Brendan and his companions visited an island called 'the island of Ailbe's community'. Since *Ailbe [see under Munster, saints of] was the principal patron saint of Emly, the leading Éoganacht monastery, the inclusion of the incident flattered the honour of the Éoganachta as a whole, and not just the Éoganacht Locha Léin.

The importance of the links with the Éoganacht Locha Léin did not, however, exclude Clonfert. Not only did the *Navigatio* begin Brendan's journey at Clonfert, but the latter's connection with Munster endured after the saint's death. **Cumméne Fota** [Cumain mac Fiachnai, Cummian] (*c.*591–662), whose feast day is 12 November, was the most distinguished of Brendan's successors. Whereas his designated successor, **Móenu** [Moínenn] (*d.* 572), bishop of Clonfert, whose feast day is 1 March and who predeceased Brendan, was probably a Briton, Cumméne Fota is said to have belonged to the Éoganacht Locha Léin. This gives some colour to the notion that Ardfert was already controlled by the Éoganacht Locha Léin in the mid-seventh century; Cumméne Fota's abbacy may thus reflect an enduring bond between Brendan's two principal foundations, giving the opportunity for a member of a west Munster dynasty, Éoganacht Locha Léin, to become abbot of Clonfert and successor of Brendan. Cumméne is likely to have been the author of the penitential of Cummian which had a wide influence, not only in Ireland, but also in England and Francia. His life is late, but there are several early stories in which Cumméne Fota plays a role, notably the ninth-century love story of two poets, Liadain and Cuirithir.

Whereas Brendan's *Navigatio* is likely to have been of Munster provenance, having probably been written at Ardfert itself, his lives are more concerned with Connacht. Not only is it made quite clear that Brendan's 'place of resurrection' was Clonfert, but the saint is said to have had angelic guidance on his rule in Mag nAí, by the eighth and ninth centuries the principal kingdom of the Uí Briúin, the ruling dynasty of the Connachta. While the saint's early years were moulded by his association with his foster father, Bishop Erc, whose presumed diocese may well have been the kingdom of Ciarraige Luachra, one of the principal characters of his Connacht career was **Iarlaithe** [Jarlath] **mac Loga** (*fl.* 6th cent.), patron saint of Tuam (Tuaimm dá Gualann), whose feast day is 25 or 26 December. This concern would fit a twelfth-century date,

when, for example, the abbot of Clonfert and the archbishop of Tuam were among the three envoys of Ruaidhrí Ua Conchobair, king of Connacht, who concluded the treaty of Windsor in 1175 with Henry II. Yet if the original life lying behind the extant versions were as late as the twelfth century, it might have been expected that less attention would be given to Brendan's Munster background, since the rulers of Munster and Connacht were then inveterate enemies. Moreover, the life preserves the memory of Brendan's foundation on the island of Tiree, under Norse control since *c.*800.

Eighth-century saints Cumméne Fota died shortly before the great plague of 664–5. One of the particular interests of Connacht for hagiography is the unusual importance of two eighth-century saints. The first was **Commán mac Fáelchon** [Mo Chommóc] (*d.* 747), patron saint of Roscommon, whose feast day was 26 December. Commán belonged to the Sogain, a vassal people, one of whose territories lay to the south of Roscommon. Although his pedigree gave him no special advantage, Commán's church was placed to best advantage, on the southern edge of Mag nAí and thus close to the Uí Briúin Aí. Roscommon rapidly became one of the most favoured churches of the Uí Briúin, as shown by the succession of laws of Commán promulgated in the second half of the eighth century. These edicts were proclaimed in the province of Connacht by the combined authority of the provincial king of the Connachta (by then almost always of the Uí Briúin) and of a leading churchman. To judge by these laws or edicts (*cánai, rechtgai*), Roscommon occupied a more central position than Clonfert enjoyed in the affairs of Connacht in the two generations before the viking attacks began at the end of the eighth century. It was also more central than an Uí Briúin church close to the Shannon, Cluain Coirpthe, the church of **Berach mac Amargin** (*fl.* late 6th–early 7th cent.), whose feast day was 15 February, and who, unlike Commán, was himself said to belong to the Uí Briúin, but to a not particularly powerful branch, Cenél nDobtha.

Surprisingly, no life of Commán survives, whereas there is a life of the other principal eighth-century Connacht saint, the Englishman **Garald** [Garalt, Gerald] (*d.* 732) of Mayo. Mayo had been founded by Colmán, bishop of Northumbria from 661 to 664, and founder also of Inishbofin off the west coast of Connacht. Mayo was intended for Colmán's English monks, who had followed him from Northumbria. It remained an English community, as indicated by its Irish name, Mag nÉo na Saxan ('Mayo of the English'), by letters to the community written by Alcuin (*d.* 804), and by its inclusion within the province of York for the purposes of the legatine synod of 786. Garald, however, was remembered more by the Irish than by the English: his feast day is given variously as 12 or 13 March in the martyrologies of Tallaght, Gorman, and Donegal; his life was included in a late medieval collection deriving from the Shannon borderlands of Connacht. Its highly confused chronology and anachronisms suggest a late date, but it helps to add to the evidence for the enduring importance of the church of Mayo after the viking period, an importance attested by the remains of a round tower. Moreover the English character of the early community was evidently remembered as late as the post-Norman period.

Female saints Connacht, like other provinces of Ireland, had its share of local cults of female saints. **Athracht ingen Thaláin** (*fl. c.*500), whose feast day is 11 August, was said by Tírechán to have received the veil from St Patrick. She was the principal saint of the Gregraige Locha Techet (Lough Gara), on the borders of Roscommon and Sligo. Her church was Killaraght (Cell Athrachtae) on the east side of the lough, but another important site was her well, Toberaraght, on the west side. Her cult sites thus straddled this minor kingdom. Another local saint attached to St Patrick by Tírechán, and thus believed to be of early date, was **Lallóc** (*fl.* 5th cent.) of Senles, or Ard Senlis, whose feast day was 6 February. Her church is represented by the modern townland of Kildalloge (Cell Lallóc) in the parish of Kiltrustan on the west slopes of Slieve Baune, northeast of Roscommon. To judge by Tírechán she was the major saint of a small vassal kingdom lying on the eastern edge of Mag nAí. On the other hand, the church of **Cairech Dergain** (d. 577/579), whose feast day is 9 February, lay in a much more powerful kingdom. She was the patron saint of the church of Cloonburren, almost opposite Clonmacnoise but a little further down the Shannon. Her church thus lay within the important kingdom of the Uí Maini. In spite of the rival attractions offered them by such cults as those of Brendan of Clonfert, Ciarán of Clonmacnoise, and Brigit of Kildare, Cairech Dergain retained a particular role for the women of the Uí Maini; according to their fourteenth-century customs, the queen of the Uí Maini owed seven garments each year to Cairech Dergain and a penny was owed by every girl. In this case, therefore, a female saint was not the principal saint of a minor kingdom, but became a saint specifically for the women of a much larger kingdom.   T. M. CHARLES-EDWARDS

Sources *Ann. Ulster* · S. Mac Airt, ed. and trans., *The annals of Inisfallen* (1951) · *AFM* · W. M. Hennessy, ed. and trans., *Chronicum Scotorum: a chronicle of Irish affairs*, Rolls Series, 46 (1866) · D. Murphy, ed., *The annals of Clonmacnoise*, trans. C. Mageoghagan (1896); facs. edn (1993) · W. Stokes, ed., 'The annals of Tigernach [8 pts]', *Revue Celtique*, 16 (1895), 374–419; 17 (1896), 6–33, 119–263, 337–420; 18 (1897), 9–59, 150–97, 267–303, 374–91; pubd sep. (1993) · R. I. Best and H. J. Lawlor, eds., *The martyrology of Tallaght*, HBS, 68 (1931) · *Félire Óengusso Céli Dé / The martyrology of Oengus the Culdee*, ed. and trans. W. Stokes, HBS, 29 (1905) · *Félire húi Gormáin / The martyrology of Gorman*, ed. and trans. W. Stokes, HBS, 9 (1895) · M. O'Clery, *The martyrology of Donegal: a calendar of the saints of Ireland*, ed. J. H. Todd and W. Reeves, trans. J. O'Donovan (1864) · K. Meyer, ed., 'The Laud (610) genealogies and tribal histories', *Zeitschrift für Celtische Philologie*, 8 (1911), 291–338, 418–19 · M. A. O'Brien, ed., *Corpus genealogiarum Hiberniae* (Dublin, 1962) · P. Ó Riain, ed., *Corpus genealogiarum sanctorum Hiberniae* (Dublin, 1985) · W. W. Heist, ed., *Vitae sanctorum Hiberniae ex codice Salmanticensi nunc Bruxellensi* (Brussels, 1965) · C. Plummer, ed., *Vitae sanctorum Hiberniae* (1910) · C. Plummer, ed. and trans., *Bethada náem nÉrenn / Lives of Irish saints*, 2 vols. (1922) · W. Stokes, ed., *Lives of the saints from the Book of Lismore*, 2 vols., Anecdota Oxoniensia (1890) · F. J. Byrne, *Irish kings and high-kings* (1973) · A. Gwynn and R. N. Hadcock, *Medieval religious houses: Ireland* (1988) · E. Hogan, ed., *Onomasticon Goedelicum, locorum et tribuum Hiberniae et Scotiae* (1910) · J. F. Kenney, *The sources for the early history of Ireland* (1929); repr. (1979) · Lord Killanin and M. V. Duignan, *Shell guide to Ireland* (1962) · T. W. Moody and others, eds., *A new history of Ireland*, 9: *Maps, genealogies, lists* (1984) · C. Plummer, 'A tentative catalogue of Irish hagiography', *Miscellanea Hagiographica Hibernica* (1925) · R. Sharpe, *Medieval Irish saints' lives: an introduction to the 'Vitae sanctorum Hiberniae'* (1991) · C. Plummer, 'Some new light on the Brendan legend', *Zeitschrift für Celtische Philologie*, 5 (1905), 124–41 · C. Selmer, 'The vernacular translations of the *Navigatio sancti Brendani*: a bibliographical study', *Medieval Studies*, 18 (1956), 145–57 · Bede, *Hist. eccl.*, 3.25–6 · L. Bieler, ed. and trans., *The Patrician texts in the Book of Armagh*, Scriptores Latini Hiberniae, 10 (1979) · Tírechán, 'Collectanea', *The tripartite life of Patrick, with other documents relating to that saint*, ed. W. Stokes, 2, Rolls Series, 89 (1887), 302–31

Connachtach (d. 802). See under Iona, abbots of (act. 563–927).

Connad Cerr (d. c.629). See under Dál Riata, kings of (act. c.500–c.850).

Connard, Philip (1875–1958), painter, was born in Southport, Lancashire, on 24 March 1875, the son of David Connard, house painter, and his wife, Ellen Lunt. After elementary school he was briefly apprenticed to his father, but, having wider ambitions, he attended evening classes and eventually won a national school scholarship in textile designing which took him to the National Art Training School, South Kensington, in 1896. With a prize of £100 from the British Institute he went next to Paris where he spent a few months studying under Jean-Paul Laurens and Benjamin Constant. On his return to London he found small jobs as an illustrator and soon afterwards became a master at the Lambeth School of Art.

Meanwhile Connard had begun to submit work to open exhibitions. His début at the New English Art Club caught the attention of Henry Tonks and P. Wilson Steer who proposed him for membership in 1909. He staged his first solo exhibition at the Baillie Gallery, London, in 1904 and this was generally praised. That year he married Mary (d. 1927), daughter of Archdeacon Collyer, with whom he had two daughters. A further solo exhibition of Connard's work was held at the Leicester Galleries, London. His next line of work was portraiture, and he joined the National Portrait Society. His portraits, though sound, were not especially distinguished; until the thirties his chief reputation derived from Romantic and decorative landscapes in oils. Throughout this period Connard's work was compared with that of his mentors. Marion Hepworth Dixon observed for instance that in decorative pictures of picnics and masquerades Connard adopted costumes of the mid-Victorian era, 'like many of his Chelsea brethren' (Dixon, 276). In these stylized compositions, harlequins, pierrettes, and exotic birds appear, the last being derived from careful sketches which he produced at London Zoo. Important decorative commissions included murals in the royal doll's house room at Windsor Castle. He painted two panels for the main ballroom at Delhi, and for the liner *Queen Mary* he executed a decorative panel 26 feet by 14 feet on the subject of England. Examples of his work were acquired by many public galleries including the Tate Gallery, London, and the Luxembourg Gallery, Paris.

During the First World War, Connard served in the Royal

Field Artillery as a captain, but was invalided out after the battle of the Somme in 1916 and at the end of the war became an official artist to the Royal Navy. There are more than forty of his works in the Imperial War Museum.

Between the wars Connard developed new strands in his work, painting a series of monumental river scenes with semi-classical nude bathers of which *Summer* (1922; Tate collection) was purchased under the terms of the Chantrey Bequest. A further example of this type, *Apollo and Daphne* (RA), was accepted as his diploma picture in 1925 when he was elected Royal Academician. Jessica Walker Stephens, referring to his work at this time, described Connard's attempt to revive the era of Watteau as a 'forceful aesthetic' (Stephens, 308).

Painting expeditions with Steer encouraged Connard to take up watercolour and he was elected to the Royal Society of Painters in Water Colours in 1934. Though perhaps more highly appreciated in his lifetime than now, his watercolours form an elegant and lyrical contribution to the English watercolour tradition. By this time he had purchased Cholmondeley Lodge, overlooking the Thames at Richmond, Surrey, and there he painted many riverside scenes which were unlike his earlier works, being far more realistic in style. His evocative landscape *Winter at Richmond* (Tate collection) was the subject of another Chantrey purchase in 1939. He became keeper of the Royal Academy Schools in 1945, a post he held until 1949, and he was made CVO in 1950. In 1933 he had married secondly Georgina York, of Twickenham, who figured in many of his later interior paintings.

Connard was a man of equable and pleasant disposition though on certain issues his friends were apt to find him obstinate and pig-headed. He was a faithful member of the New English Arts Club, where he often met friends such as Sir William Orpen and F. Derwent Wood. An excellent raconteur, he could set the table in a roar with his Lancashire stories.

Connard continued to paint silvery grey landscapes of the river at Richmond up until his death at the Nightingale Nursing Home, Twickenham, on 8 December 1958.

H. B. GRIMSDITCH, rev. KENNETH McCONKEY

Sources F. Wedmore, 'Philip Connard', *Art Journal*, new ser., 29 (1909), 73–8 · M. H. Dixon, 'The paintings of Philip Connard', *The Studio*, 57 (1912–13), 269–80 · J. W. Stephens, 'The paintings of Philip Connard, ARA', *The Studio*, 85 (1923), 303–11 · *Watercolours and drawings by Philip Connard* (1975) [exhibition catalogue, Studio One Gallery, Oxford] · CGPLA Eng. & Wales (1959) · G. Popp and H. Valentine, *Royal Academy of Arts directory of membership: from the foundation in 1768 to 1995, including honorary members* (1996)
Likenesses W. Stoneman, photograph, 1930, NPG · P. Connard, self-portrait, oils, NPG · G. Lambert, pencil drawing, priv. coll.
Wealth at death £7801 2s. 10d.: probate, 29 Jan 1959, CGPLA Eng. & Wales

Connaught and Strathearn. For this title name *see* Arthur, Prince, first duke of Connaught and Strathearn (1850–1942).

Connell, Amyas Douglas (1901–1980), architect, was born at Eltham, Taranaki, New Zealand, on 23 June 1901, the second of the six children of Nigel Douglas Connell, a photographic artist, and his wife, Gertrude Matilda Weber. He was educated at Stratford Boys' High School, Taranaki (1912–16), and New Plymouth Boys' High School. In 1919 he was articled in Wellington to the architect Stanley Fearn, a vernacular traditionalist, for three years. In 1924 Connell and his later architectural partner Basil Ward (1902–1976), who had been articled to J. A. Louis Hay in Napier, worked their passage to Britain. Here they continued their professional studies (1924–6) at the then Beaux-Arts-influenced Bartlett school of architecture, University College, London.

Both Connell and Ward had come in contact with progressive artistic tendencies in New Zealand: Connell's parents had been influenced by *fin de siècle* artistic movements and Hay had introduced Ward to the work of the Vienna Secessionists, the Chicago school, and Frank Lloyd Wright, while also insisting on the need to master 'the styles'. This last was a lesson which was thoroughly absorbed by both Ward and Connell as, in 1926, Connell won the Rome prize in architecture and Ward the Jarvis prize—clear evidence of their skills in draughtsmanship and the conventions of Beaux-Arts design; as Connell put it a year or two before his death, 'I could draw a Corinthian column blindfold with one hand tied behind my back' (private information). By this time, however, both had begun to show an interest in avant-garde architecture in Europe. In 1925 they spent a weekend in Paris, visiting the Universal Exhibition—where they were particularly impressed by Le Corbusier's Esprit Nouveau Pavilion—and scouring bookshops for publications on the new architecture. Subsequently they used their scholarships not only to study Renaissance architecture in Rome but to help further their firsthand knowledge of European modernism. Thus it was not surprising that Connell's first significant building, High and Over (1928–9), a reinforced concrete-framed house in Amersham for Bernard Ashmole, the director of the British School at Rome, was in the modern idiom. The house is now considered one of the key markers of the evolution of the modern movement in Britain.

Connell was joined in practice by Ward (who had married Connell's sister) in 1930 and the two architects went on to develop a more unorthodox constructional system, using reinforced concrete now in shell-type monolithic structures, in a house at Haslemere for Arthur Lowes-Dickinson and some smaller houses, including a group of speculative houses at Ruislip, Middlesex. In 1933 they were joined by Colin Lucas (1906–1988), who had studied architecture at Cambridge University and established his building firm Lucas, Lloyd & Co. in 1928. Lucas had experimented with similar methods of reinforced concrete construction and had established his modernist credentials in the design of houses such as Noah's House at Bourne End, Buckinghamshire (1930), and the Hopfield at Wrotham, Kent (1933), as well as through his membership of Unit One, which included artists such as Paul Nash and Ben Nicholson and the critic Herbert Read.

From 1933 until the Munich crisis Connell, Ward, and

Lucas's work, which was largely domestic, continued to develop their modernist idiom. Their designs were characterized by thin concrete walls, large glazed surfaces, prominent staircases, and a sometimes striking use of colour. Formally their buildings combined some of the vocabulary of Le Corbusier's work of the 1920s with the spatial ambiguities of the Dutch De Stijl movement. Practically all of these met with initial opposition, whether from the owners of neighbouring properties, or estate surveyors, local councils, and planning authorities. A particular case in point was the house at 66 Frognal, Hampstead, London (1936–8), where the client, Geoffrey Walford, a solicitor, took the case to the High Court and won, and the house was built virtually as originally designed. It was described at the time by Sir Robert Tasker MP as 'one of the greatest acts of vandalism ever perpetrated in London' (Sharp, *Connell, Ward and Lucas*, 12).

The partnership dissolved with the approach of the Second World War. After the war Lucas joined the London county council's architects' department, where he became a group leader in the housing section, and Ward became a partner in Ramsey, Murray, White, and Ward, and first Lethaby professor of architecture at the Royal College of Art. After a brief period with the Ministry of Works, Connell worked independently in Tanganyika and, later, in Kenya, where he established a new practice, Triad. He designed the Kenya legislative council building (with H. Thornley Dyer; 1952 and 1963), the Aga Khan Hospital (1956–63), and the crown law offices (1960), all in Nairobi. Climatic conditions, combined with the issue of representing Kenya's post-independence identity, stimulated in his later work an interest in the architectural traditions of tropical and subtropical areas and in decoration.

Connell's significance is as a pioneering British modernist, particularly in his work with Ward and Lucas: he was a tenacious advocate of the cause of modern architecture, through his buildings, through his membership of the MARS (Modern Architectural Research) Group, and in public debate—the latter memorably in the confrontation with Sir Reginald Blomfield, *For and Against Modern Architecture*, broadcast by BBC radio in 1934 and printed in *The Listener*. His work in Africa remains to be evaluated in the context of post-war colonial and post-colonial architecture. He was a man of striking appearance and he showed great consideration towards others, but he was intolerant of the untruthfulness which he considered to characterize much contemporary architecture. He was twice married: his first wife, whom he married on 22 January 1931, was Maud Elizabeth Marjorie Hargroves, the daughter of a manufacturer's agent, Joseph Henry Hargroves. After they were divorced, Connell married Margaret Helen Stroud, probably in the late 1950s. Creative and energetic to the end, he continued to work full-time until a few days before his death, on 19 April 1980, at the Whittington Hospital, Camden Town, London. His second wife and a son survived him.   CHARLOTTE BENTON

Sources D. Sharp, ed., *Connell, Ward and Lucas: modern movement architects in England, 1929–1939* (1994) · 'Connell, Ward and Lucas,

1927–1939', *Architectural Association Journal*, 72 (1956), 94–115 · private information (2004) · *DNB* · M. Emmanuel, ed., *Contemporary architects* (1994) · D. Sharp, 'Connell, Ward, and Lucas', *Macmillan encyclopedia of architects*, ed. A. K. Placzek, 4 vols. (1982) · m. cert. [Maud Hargroves] · d. cert.

Archives priv. coll. | RIBA, Ove Arup MSS, Ar01–2
Wealth at death £4352: probate, 8 Sept 1980, *CGPLA Eng. & Wales*

Connell, James [Jim] (1852–1929), socialist and writer of 'The Red Flag', was born on 27 March 1852 in McCormack's Yard, Kilskyre, Crossakiel, co. Meath, Ireland, the eldest of thirteen children born to Thomas Connell, farm labourer, and his wife, Ann Shaw. It is likely that he was born O'Connell, as other family members, including his brother Canon O'Connell of Scarborough, carried this version of the name. Biographical details of his parents and siblings are scarce, but a brother was known to have been active in the Irish Bakers', Confectioners' and Allied Workers' Amalgamated Union.

Connell's father moved his family to Birr, King's county, in 1862, where he worked as a groom or gamekeeper for the earl of Rosse. James acquired a love of the land, developing a lifelong interest in poaching and in land agitation. In 1870 he moved to Dublin and worked as a docker. Here he fell under the influence of the socialist John Lange (or Laing), and debated theoretical matters on Sunday rambles with the Free Literary Union. Here he met, among others, Fred Ryan, pioneer socialist and later secretary of the Socialist Party of Ireland. In January 1875 he emigrated to London, where he quickly became involved in socialist and Irish nationalist politics. He married an English woman, Catherine Angier, in Poplar, London, on 2 September 1882; they had one child, Norah, and separated when she was thirteen.

Connell's first political activity was in the Irish Republican Brotherhood, being sworn in at Birr in 1870. He also claimed to have founded the first London branch of the National Land League of Great Britain in Poplar in 1879 and to have served on its executive. The league was, in fact, inaugurated on 25 March 1881 under the presidency of Justin McCarthy, with the intention of informing British workers about the Irish land question and their 'community of interests' with Irish tenant farmers. Connell claimed original membership of the Social Democratic Federation (SDF), remaining active for ten years, although he 'never cared for the management'. He was certainly an associate of H. M. Hyndman, and wrote for *Justice*, the SDF party organ, on a regular basis. In September 1890 he stood unsuccessfully for the SDF in Finsbury, failing to attract the Irish vote, which went to the Liberal, and being attacked by T. P. O'Connor's *Star*. Later he became a member of the Independent Labour Party. In 1888 he was named before the commission on Parnellism and crime as an 'advocate of treason, sedition, assassination and violence' (Boyd, *Irish Trade Unions*, 58). Long political activity gave him contact with nearly all the leading trade union and labour movement figures of his day, many regularly visiting him to enjoy his lively company and gift for conversation.

Connell's source of income is unclear: he had various jobs, including some journalism, and had a regular entry in the *Labour Yearbook* as a speaker on socialism, Darwinism, philosophy, and the game laws. Francis Williams recalled Connell's famous discourse on evolution, entitled 'From protoplasm to man', being so erudite that 'he was never known in the course of a two hours' talk to get beyond the introduction' (Williams, 103). From 1909 until his death he was secretary of the Workingmen's Legal Aid Society, based in Chancery Lane, London, providing advice on compensation and other claims. He was well known in Fleet Street, and was visited in his favourite haunt, the Golden Cross in the Strand, by many trade union and Labour leaders. He was 6 feet 1, and wore a black sombrero, a flowing Inverness cape, and bright red scarf; his theatrical manner led many to think he was a Shakespearian actor. He successfully published a series of pamphlets: *Brothers at Last: a Centenary Appeal to Celt and Saxon*; *Socialism and the Survival of the Fittest* (3rd edn, 1908); *The Truth about the Game Laws* (which was published by the Humanitarian League despite their objections to his trapping and poaching, which latter once resulted in Connell being fined in Croydon court); and *Confessions of a Poacher* (1901). This last sold 80,000 copies in several editions by C. A. Pearson, having first appeared in serial form in *Titbits*. He always kept dogs and was inseparable from his favourite lurcher, Nellie, his companion on frequent walks and poaching expeditions.

In the Christmas issue of *Justice* in 1889 Harry Quelch published Connell's song 'The Red Flag'. It was written, he claimed, on a fifteen-minute train journey from Charing Cross to New Cross, and was intended to raise working-class morale and as a celebration of the London dock strike. It was inspired by Connell's knowledge of and commitment to international working-class struggle, as the verses attest. Originally set to the popular air 'The White Cockade', Adolphe Smythe Headingley in 1895 rearranged it to the tune 'Maryland', or 'Der Tannenbaum', with which tune it was principally sung thereafter. Connell hated the change, and George Bernard Shaw dismissed the new air as being like 'a funeral dirge to the eels' (Boyd, 'In search of Jim Connell'). Labour Party leader James Ramsay MacDonald liked neither the song nor its author, and in 1925 the *Daily Herald* held a competition with a £50 prize to find a new, better Labour anthem. Judged by Hugh Roberton, founder of the Glasgow Orpheus Choir, and John McCormack, the Irish tenor, over 300 entries failed to produce a winner. Connell was delighted. Although Connell makes no reference to it, a poem 'The Red Flag' by the Chartist poet Alfred Fennell, first published in the *Red Republican* in 1850, may have provided the original inspiration. Connell's 'Red Flag' was sung at the conclusion of Labour Party and Trades Union Congress conferences, and raised the rafters of the House of Commons when sung by the 393 victorious Labour MPs after the 1945 general election.

Connell wrote many other songs and poems published in the left-wing press. He was on the staff of Keir Hardie's *Labour Leader*, where his material regularly appeared. His work also appeared in Ireland: James Larkin published 'The Blackleg' in the *Irish Worker* on 22 November 1913, and the *Voice of Labour* printed 'The Minor' on 16 August 1918. A collection, *Red Flag Rhymes* (n.d.), was republished in several editions. 'The Red Flag' is the only generally surviving Connell piece, and appears as a standard entry in all socialist song collections. He retained an interest in Irish affairs, actively generating support in Britain for the Dublin workers during the 1913 lockout and returning for occasional meetings, such as that of the Ballinlough Land Back to the People Committee at Crossakiel on 30 August 1918.

Connell died at 390 High Street, Catford, Lewisham, on 8 February 1929 from bronchitis. He was cremated on 14 February at Golders Green crematorium. The *Daily Herald* obituary (9 February 1929) noted that he was 'essentially a man of the people', and that he described himself as 'educated under a hedge for a few weeks' and as a 'sheep farmer, dock labourer, navvy, railwayman, draper, lawyer of a sort and all the time a poacher'. Veteran labour leader Tom Mann conducted the secular funeral proceedings, and he told the crowd Connell was 'no meek and mild platitudinarian' and that his songs 'inspired thousands— possibly millions'. Connell departed to the strains of 'The Red Flag', sung to both his original and the adopted airs. In 1989 Gordon Brown MP unveiled a plaque in Stondon Park, Forest Hill, London—Connell's last address—as Lewisham borough council commemorated the sixtieth anniversary of Connell's death, and in 1997 a permanent memorial was erected in his birthplace under the aegis of the Kells Heritage Committee. FRANCIS DEVINE

Sources A. Boyd, 'The man who wrote "The red flag"' [BBC radio broadcast, 27 Jan 1962] · A. Boyd, 'In search of Jim Connell', priv. coll. · A. Boyd, *Jim Connell: author of 'The red flag'* (2001) · J. Connell, 'How I wrote "The red flag"', *The Call* (6 May 1920) · J. McDonnell, 'We'll keep the red flag flying here', *Obair* (May 1984), 5–6 · J. McDonnell, *Songs of struggle and protest* (1986) · P. O'Donovan, *Jim Connell and 'The red flag'* (1985) · A. Boyd, *The rise of the Irish trade unions, 1729–1970* (1972) · F. Williams, *Fifty years' march: the rise of the labour party* [n.d.] · C. D. Greaves, *The life and times of James Connolly* (1961) · m. cert. · d. cert. · *Daily Herald* (9 Feb 1929) · *Daily Herald* (15 Feb 1929)
Archives SOUND A. Boyd, 'The man who wrote "The red flag"', BBC radio broadcast, 27 Jan 1962

Connell, Sir John (1765–1831), lawyer and judge, was born in Glasgow on 4 September 1765, son of Arthur Connell, merchant in Glasgow and lord provost of that city, and his wife, Magdalen Wallace. Educated at Glasgow University, he was admitted a member of the Faculty of Advocates in 1788. He married a daughter of Sir Ilay *Campbell of Succoth, baronet, lord president of the court of session. In 1795 he was appointed sheriff-depute of Renfrewshire, and in 1805–6 he was procurator, or law adviser, for the Church of Scotland; he enjoyed an extensive practice in church causes. In 1816 he was appointed judge of the court of Admiralty, an office which he held until 1830, when that court was abolished. Some time before 1821 he was knighted. Connell was the author of two books, on the tithes and stipends of the Scottish parochial clergy (1815), and on Scottish law and the parish (1818). Connell died suddenly on 13 April 1831 at Garscube, the seat of his brother-in-law, Sir Archibald Campbell.

W. G. BLAIKIE, rev. ERIC METCALFE

Sources J. Kay, *A series of original portraits and caricature etchings … with biographical sketches and illustrative anecdotes*, ed. [H. Paton and others], new edn [3rd edn], 2 (1877) · minutes, Library of the Faculty of Advocates, Edinburgh · private information (1887) · parish register (births), 4 Sept 1765, Glasgow **Archives** NL Scot., memorandum and letters to Lord Melville | NL Scot., corresp. with Archibald Constable **Wealth at death** £3465 3s. 8½d.: inventory, 1831, NA Scot., SC 70/1/45, p. 75

Connellan, Owen (1800–1869), Irish scholar, was born in co. Sligo, the son of a farmer who claimed descent from the chiefs of Bunnyconnellan in Mayo, and through them from Laoghaire MacNeill, king of Ireland. He studied Irish literature, and worked for more than twenty years as a scribe in the Royal Irish Academy, where he copied a great part of the large collections of Irish writings known as the books of Lecan and of Ballymote. After the visit of George IV to Ireland in 1821, Connellan was appointed Irish historiographer to the king, a post which he also held throughout the reign of William IV. In 1849, shortly after its establishment, Connellan was made professor of Irish at Queen's College, Cork, where he remained until his death in Dublin in 1869.

Connellan wrote a number of grammatical analyses of the gospels and a dissertation on the Irish language. His views on its evolution were somewhat eccentric; he admired Sir William Betham, whose *Etruria Celtica* he believed had proved that the Irish and Etruscan languages were identical. In 1844 he published a *Practical Grammar of the Irish Language*, which is of value as a record of the idiom and pronunciation of Irish in the north of Connaught. His edition of *The Annals of Ireland, Translated from the Original Irish of the Four Masters* (1846) was superseded by that of John O'Donovan (1860). His most important work was a translation of the *Imtheacht na tromdháimhe, or, The Proceedings of the Great Bardic Institutions* (1860).

NORMAN MOORE, rev. MARIE-LOUISE LEGG

Sources Boase, *Mod. Eng. biog.* · A. M. Brady and B. Cleeve, eds., *A biographical dictionary of Irish writers*, rev. edn (1985) · private information (1886)

Connellan, Thaddaeus [Thaddeus] (d. **1854**), lexicographer, was the author of a number of successful works on the Irish language, including *An Irish and English Spelling Book*, which had reached a nineteenth edition by 1848; *An English–Irish Dictionary, Intended for the Use of Schools* had originally appeared in 1814. He also produced translations of parts of the Bible into Irish, and was a Hebrew scholar: his 1823 edition of *The Proverbs of Solomon* contained English, Irish, and Hebrew versions, as well as a Hebrew grammar. Connellan, about whom nothing otherwise is known, died at Sligo on 25 July 1854.

[ANON.], rev. MARIE-LOUISE LEGG

Sources Boase, *Mod. Eng. biog.* · T. Cooper, *A new biographical dictionary: containing concise notices of eminent persons of all ages and countries* (1873)

Connelly [*née* Peacock], **Cornelia Augusta** (1809–1879), Roman Catholic nun and educational reformer, was born on 15 January 1809 at 1 Filbert Street, Philadelphia, USA, the youngest of the six surviving children of Ralph Peacock (c.1767–1818), a merchant and land speculator who had emigrated from Yorkshire, and his wife, Mary (1768–1823), the daughter of Jacob Swope, a German doctor, and widow of John Bowen, an English sugar planter in Jamaica. Cornelia had three brothers, two sisters, and a half-brother and half-sister. An orphan at fourteen, she was adopted by her childless half-sister, Isabella, who had married into the wealthy Episcopalian Montgomery family. Cornelia was brought up a Presbyterian but was baptized in the Episcopalian church in 1831. Well educated in Philadelphian upper-middle-class tradition, she had become, in one bishop's words, 'a woman of great intellectual powers' (McCarthy, 28). On 1 December 1831 she married the Revd Pierce *Connelly (1804–1883), a recently ordained Episcopalian minister. They moved immediately to Pierce's new parish in Natchez, Mississippi. Their five children were born between 1832 and 1840.

In December 1833, at Pierce's prompting, the Connellys began a serious exploration of Catholicism. Pierce resigned his parish in August 1835, sold their house, and moved with his family to Rome for further study, Cornelia having been received into the Catholic church at New Orleans prior to embarkation. She believed her husband would also become a Catholic and then live out his life as a layman. In Rome, however, he petitioned not only to be received but also to be considered for ordination. Canon law allowed this if both partners willingly agreed to live separate and chaste lives. Pierce was received in 1836 but, with him no nearer ordination after a year's stay during which Cornelia met the pope and many leading English Catholics, they returned to Natchez in 1838, having lost much of their investment during a financial recession. They resettled less comfortably off in Grand Coteau, Louisiana. Here their fourth child died in infancy and their third of multiple burns aged two and a half.

This time of suffering was the turning point in Cornelia's long and gradual transition from minister's wife and mother living on the plantation frontier of Mississippi to Catholic nun and founder of a Roman Catholic religious congregation in England. As a paid music teacher at the Sacred Heart Convent, she now experienced her first sustained exposure to the life of religious sisters and Catholic education. She and Pierce took a mutual private vow of celibacy in October 1840 after his final decision to seek ordination, and her diary for September 1841 records her decision to pursue her vocation as a nun. Their vow was made canonically binding on 1 April 1844, when they signed a deed of perpetual separation before Vatican witnesses in Rome. A period of living with the Sacred Heart nuns in Rome led her to conclude by February 1845 that she had no call to enter their society.

Encouraged by the prominent Catholic layman Lord Shrewsbury, Nicholas Wiseman, Cardinal Fransoni, and, finally, Pope Gregory XVI, she agreed to found a new religious congregation in England rather than America. Cardinal Wiseman, archbishop of Westminster, saw her as the right woman to establish an educational congregation suitable for middle-class English converts wanting to become nuns. After three months in Paris living with the Sisters of the Assumption she moved to England in August 1846. Pierce, who had been ordained in July, was already there as assistant chaplain to Lord Shrewsbury. Up to this point the two younger children had lived with Cornelia, but as she began her noviciate they were sent to boarding-schools.

In October, Cornelia and three other women opened the first convent of the Holy Child Jesus in Derby, where they taught in poor schools. On 21 December 1847 she made her vows and was installed by Wiseman as the superior-general of the Society of the Holy Child Jesus, the first new native congregation of women to be founded in England since the Reformation. Its work was educational, ranging from poor schools and industrial schools for young working women to day and boarding-schools for the middle classes, and, from 1856 to 1864, teacher training. Her educational ideas and the pedagogy of her schools and college were expressed in the *Book of the Order of Studies in the Schools of the Sisters of the Holy Child Jesus* (1863). The society's mother house was moved to St Leonards in Sussex, from which new houses and schools were opened in London, Liverpool, Preston, and Blackpool during the 1850s. Their first American house was founded in Pennsylvania in 1862 and that in France in 1869. In 1863 Connelly was given the ruins of the Old Palace at Mayfield, Sussex, the former synod hall of the archbishops of Canterbury, by the duchess of Leeds. In its day the largest remaining medieval hall in England, its restoration was a point of pride among English Catholics. On completion in 1873 it became the noviciate and later the mother house. Mother Connelly was recognized by many as a courageous woman and outstanding educator. Her determination to act firmly and to listen to her conscience, even when it did not accord with the advice of clergy, did not always win her friends. Her position was also adversely affected by external criticisms and the publicity which stemmed from a course of action taken by Pierce Connelly. Unable to accept the reality of matrimonial separation, he initially sought a key role in the society and then, turning against the Catholic church, used it in a public anti-Catholic campaign. From 1848 onwards he used the children in an attempt to control Cornelia, exercising his legal right to refuse her access and removing them from the country. He followed this with an unsuccessful court action for the restitution of conjugal rights, 1848–58. The many forms of suffering which Cornelia experienced, as well as her vigour and fortitude, showed in the constitutions which she drew up for her society. These were never approved by Rome in her lifetime. She died at the convent at Mayfield on 18 April 1879 of chronic nephritis and was buried in the chapel there.

After her death her rule was approved and her reputation re-examined. In 1992 she received the title Venerable, the first step towards canonization. SUSAN O'BRIEN

Sources R. Flaxman, *A woman styled bold: the life of Cornelia Connelly* (1991) · J. Marmion, 'Cornelia Connelly's work in education, 1846–1879', PhD diss., University of Manchester, 1984 · C. McCarthy, *The spirituality of Cornelia Connelly* (1986)
Archives NRA, corresp., papers, engagement diary, and notebook · Society of the Holy Child Jesus, Rome, archives · Society of the Holy Child Jesus, Mayfield, East Sussex, Provincialate Archives | Birmingham Archdiocesan Archives, corresp., and papers of Connelly's husband, Pierce Connelly · Sacra Congregaziona di Propaganda Fide, Rome, Propaganda Fide archives
Likenesses A. Dominguez, photograph, 1836, Ana Dominguez Studio, Summit, New Jersey · photograph, 1860, Society of the Holy Child Jesus, Mayfield, East Sussex

Connelly, Pierce (1804–1883), apostate Episcopal priest and anti-Catholic pamphleteer, was born on 9 August 1804 in Philadelphia, Pennsylvania, the eldest of four sons of Henry Connelly, a cabinet-maker, and his second wife, Elizabeth Pierce. He married Cornelia Peacock [*see* Connelly, Cornelia (1809–1879)] on 1 December 1831; they had two children who survived to adulthood, Adeline and Pierce Francis (the latter became a sculptor in Italy and the United States). Brought up as a Presbyterian, Connelly became an Episcopalian at the University of Pennsylvania (BA 1821, MA 1824). He read theology under William White, bishop of Pennsylvania, and was ordained deacon (1826) and priest (1828).

Appointed rector of Trinity parish, Natchez, Mississippi, in 1831, Connelly read anti-Catholic pamphlets, met the royalist exile scientist Joseph Nicolas Nicollet, and decided that Roman Catholicism taught slaves to be docile more effectively than Anglicanism. He resigned his cure in 1835, moved to Rome, and was converted on Palm Sunday (27 March) 1836. (His wife had converted in December 1835.) The international financial crisis of 1837, which ushered in the 'hungry forties', forced their return to the United States, where they taught school in Grand Coteau, Louisiana, from 1838 to 1842. Connelly believed that he had a vocation to the priesthood, and convinced Cornelia that they should give up sexual relations. They returned to Rome in 1843 and received a papal decree of separation; Pierce was re-ordained and Cornelia entered a convent. During this time, the family was 'reconstituted' once a week for the children to play in their parents' presence.

In 1846 the Roman Catholic bishop Nicholas Wiseman asked Cornelia to start a religious order to educate middle-class girls. Simultaneously, John Talbot, sixteenth earl of Shrewsbury, asked Pierce to become his assistant chaplain at Alton Towers. Both moved to England that summer, but Connelly soon grew frustrated. Wiseman did not give him the respect he wanted, nor was he permitted to visit Cornelia as he had in Rome. Moreover, Cornelia had found her vocation as founder of the Society of the Holy Child Jesus, and no longer obeyed Pierce. When he learned that Wiseman was moving Cornelia and the order from Derby to St Leonards, he took refuge in December 1848 with Henry Drummond at Albury Park, Surrey. Drummond, an anti-Catholic tory banker, supported Connelly for the following six years. Hoping to show that Roman Catholicism was a marriage wrecker, Drummond convinced Connelly to sue his wife for restitution of conjugal rights. Connelly eventually lost his case, for it was clear that he had exercised his free choice to convert, become celibate, and end their marriage. Throughout, the case of *Connelly v. Connelly* (court of arches, 1849; judicial committee of the privy council, 1851) fed the newspaper-reading public with tales of sex, greed, and power.

Connelly wrote anti-Catholic pamphlets, publishing some under the pen-names 'Pascal the Younger' and 'Pen Cler Jocelyn'. His petition to the House of Commons in connection with his court case was so prurient and libellous that it was printed 'for the use of Members only'. He perhaps inspired one of the most notorious anti-Catholic slurs ever uttered in the house, when Drummond declared in 1851 that convents were 'either prisons or brothels' (*Hansard 3*, 115.266). Some of his pamphlets charged that priests slept with nuns, that casuist moral theology condoned crimes, and that Roman Catholicism was essentially persecutory and dictatorial. His *Reasons for Abjuring Allegiance to the See of Rome: a Letter to the Earl of Shrewsbury* (1852) entered the anti-Catholic canon, appearing on both sides of the Atlantic and remaining in print into the twentieth century.

Debarred from preferment in the Church of England, to which he now adhered, Connelly moved to the continent, wrote for the *Daily Telegraph* (using the pen-name 'Thorough'), and in 1867 founded St James's Episcopal Church in Florence, for American visitors who did not wish to attend the English chapel. He developed bronchial pneumonia at the age of seventy-nine, and died on 16 December 1883.

Pierce Connelly had a pointed chin, broad forehead, long nose, and large ears set high on his prematurely bald head, which characteristics, several observers remarked, gave him an impish appearance. His career illustrates the public role of converts in Victorian denominational controversies, and gives an insight into the milieu of the anti-Catholic campaigner. D. G. PAZ

Sources D. G. Paz, *The priesthoods and apostasies of Pierce Connelly: a study of Victorian conversion and anti-Catholicism* (1986) · R. Flaxman, *A woman styled bold: the life of Cornelia Connelly, 1809–1879* (1991) · D. G. Paz, *Popular anti-Catholicism in mid-Victorian England* (1991) · M. C. Gompertz, *The life of Cornelia Connelly, 1809–1879: foundress of the Society of the Holy Child Jesus* (1922) · bap. cert. · private information (1883)

Archives Birmingham Archdiocesan Archives · Mississippi department of archives and history, Jackson, Trinity Episcopal Church records · NL Scot., Minto MSS · Society of the Holy Child Jesus, Mayfield, East Sussex, archives

Connemara. For this title name *see* Bourke, Robert, Baron Connemara (1827–1902).

Connock, Edward (*d.* 1617), merchant and East India Company servant, is of unknown parentage. He had experience of Levantine trade and politics as secretary to the ambassador in Constantinople. The East India Company was considering expansion into Persia, having gained a foothold at Surat on the west coast of India in 1612. After a new fleet from England arrived off Surat in September 1616, Connock, the fleet's 'cape merchant', was chosen by the Surat factors as chief factor for a pioneering Persian venture. He and a group of merchants sailed on the *James* in early November 1616 with a small consignment of cloth, reaching Jask (south of Hormoz) on 4 December. After sundry frustrating delays Connock obtained an audience with Shah Abbas at his military encampment in western Persia in July 1617 and excitedly reported that he had secured trade privileges far exceeding his original brief. Meanwhile the other merchants had conveyed their goods to Shiraz, then Esfahan, the Persian capital, and made a start at setting up 'factories' (trading depots).

Sir Thomas Roe, James I's ambassador to the court of the Mughal emperor Jahangir in India, disapproved of the whole idea of the East India Company's expansion to Persia on political grounds (he was apprehensive about the Portuguese and Turkish reaction) and distrusted Connock, whose name he also renders variously as Connaught or Connocht. The situation was exacerbated by the acrimonious relationship between Connock and his second in command, Thomas Barker, of whom Roe approved—'a sober man and of good stayd judgment' (Foster, *Embassy*, 430 n. 3)—as well as by differences of opinion between Roe and the chief factor at Surat, Thomas Kerridge, who in turn had a high regard for 'Connok' (*Letters Received*, 4.195). Connock's blunt, ambitious, and energetic nature seems to have attracted as much criticism as praise from his contemporaries. Thomas Doughty, an officer on the *James*, judged him to be 'very forward, and … had rather hazard your ship, goods and men than be disappointed of his employment' (*Letters Received*, 5.102).

Connock was unable to make much further progress. He died on 24 December 1617 in the village of Gatan, a day's journey from Jask. Edward Monnox wrote to inform the company of his death, explaining that he died 'a professed Romish catholic, chiefly troubled for want of a confessor and other rites of that his blind religion' (*Letters Received*, 6.283), and that Connock was full of remorse for having berated a Portuguese friar who had sought to persuade the shah of Persia that English traders should be excluded from the region. Despite rumours of poisoning, the climate and living conditions were perilous and most of Connock's party were already ill by this time; several others also died. It subsequently emerged that he had left heavy debts. In a rather testy letter Roe instructed Barker and Monnox that 'whatsoever goods, monies or debts may bee found of the said Edward Connaught may bee seazed or recovered to the use of his Creditors and for the satisfaction of the Honourable Compagnie' (Foster, *Embassy*, 465). JENNY MARSH

Sources F. C. Danvers and W. Foster, eds., *Letters received by the East India Company from its servants in the east*, 6 vols. (1896–1902), vols. 4–6 · *The embassy of Sir Thomas Roe to the court of the great mogul, 1615–1619*, ed. W. Foster, 2, Hakluyt Society, 2nd ser., 2 (1899) · W. Foster, *England's quest of Eastern trade* (1933), 299–303; repr. P. Tuck, ed., *The East India Company, 1600–1858*, 1 (1998) · R. W. Ferrier, 'The trade between India and the Persian Gulf and the East India Company in the 17th century', *Bengal Past and Present*, 89 (July–Dec 1970), pt 2, 189–96 • N. Steensgaard, *The Asian trade revolution of the seventeenth century: the East India companies and the decline of the caravan trade* (1974), 326–31

Connolly, Brian Francis (1945–1997), rock singer, was born on 5 October 1945 at 106 Aikenhead Road, Glasgow. He was apparently abandoned by his mother, a hotel waitress, soon after birth and raised by a nurse and her husband, who gave him the adoptive surname McManus, first in Lanarkshire and later in Middlesex, where he attended Harefield secondary school. After leaving home he changed his surname back to Connolly, which he learned had been that of his mother. At one time he planned to join the merchant navy, but rock music was always his first love. In 1966 he joined the group Wainwright's Gentlemen, which also featured the drummer Mick Tucker (*d*. 2002). Two years later Connolly and Tucker broke away to form Sweetshop, along with the bassist Steve Priest and the guitarist Frank Torpey, who was later replaced by Andy Scott. They made several unsuccessful singles before shortening their name to Sweet.

A new record deal with RCA teamed Sweet with the producer Phil Wainman and the writers Nicky Chinn and Mike Chapman, who wrote their first four singles, on which Connolly was backed by session musicians. All were hits—the most successful, 'Co-Co', reaching number two in 1971. Initially allowed to write and play only on the B-sides, the band demanded greater input and subsequently performed on the A-sides as well. Their biggest seller, 'Blockbuster', topped the charts for five weeks in 1973, while the next three, 'Hell Raiser', 'Ballroom Blitz', and 'Teenage Rampage', all reached number two. By this time Sweet had become one of the leading proponents of the glam rock movement, which was characterized by glittery, colourful stage costumes and outrageous make-up. Connolly—with his trademark shoulder-length, feather-cut blond hair—was the visual focus of the group, who were banned from some venues for the suggestive nature of their stage performance, which was considered unsuitable for family audiences. Although their following was confined largely to the teenage market, they longed to be taken seriously by an older age group. But with their attempts to break into the more critically respectable album market with 'Sweet Fanny Adams' and 'Desolation Boulevard' they were less successful than with their singles.

Diminishing chart success and disagreements with Chinn and Chapman, who wrote all the hits up to and including 'Turn it Down' in 1974, led to Sweet assuming full musical control of their output, which they henceforth wrote and produced themselves. The single 'Fox on the Run' reached number two in 1975, and in the United States their records outsold those of their British contemporaries T. Rex and Slade. After two less successful years in Britain and a new contract with Polydor in 1977, a subsequent single, 'Love is Like Oxygen', reached the British and American top ten in 1978, their last to do so.

Relations between Connolly and the other band members deteriorated owing to his heavy drinking and to musical differences; at one stage he claimed that they were deliberately recording backing tracks in a key which he found impossible to sing. He left in February 1979 to pursue a solo career, but his subsequent releases fared badly and his health worsened, culminating in several heart attacks in 1981 which he was fortunate to survive. The group continued as a trio without him, disbanding in 1982. Scott later revived it with new personnel for well-received live performances, billed as Andy Scott's Sweet in competition with a rival outfit led by Connolly. Attempts to re-form the group with all four original members came to nothing.

On 7 March 1972 Connolly married Marilyn Bernadette Walsh, a hairdresser, and they had two daughters. They divorced in 1986 and in 1991 he married Denise Anne Hough (*née* Barron), a nursery school proprietor, this union being dissolved in 1994. Thereafter he lived for a time with Jean Dibble, a nursery school proprietor, with whom he had a son.

In his last years Brian Connolly was accorded considerable respect as one of the most influential and dynamic vocalists of the glam rock era but, though he had long since stopped drinking on medical advice, his appearances on stage and television testified to his failing health. In particular he suffered from a muscular disease which meant he had to be helped on and off stage. He played his last concert in December 1996. After a suspected stroke he was admitted to Wexham Park Hospital at Slough in January 1997, and died from chronic liver disease on 9 February. His funeral was held on 17 February at the Holy Name Catholic Church, Old Mill Lane, Denham, Buckinghamshire, and his cremation was at Harefield crematorium.

JOHN VAN DER KISTE

Sources *The Independent* (11 Feb 1997) • *The Times* (11 Feb 1997) • *Daily Telegraph* (11 Feb 1997) • *The Guardian* (11 Feb 1997) • *Record Collector* (March 1997) • P. Robertson, interview with Nicola Connolly, *Hello!* (Feb 1998) • C. Roney, 'Home SWEET home', www.thesweet.com, Sept 2000 • www.u-net/~thesweet/, Sept 2000 • memorial, Holy Name Catholic Church, Denham, Buckinghamshire • private information (2004) [Nicola Connolly, daughter] • m. cert. [Marilyn Bernadette Walsh] • m. cert. [Denise Anne Hough] • d. cert. • b. cert.
Archives FILM BBC WAC • BFI NFTVA, documentary footage
Likenesses photograph, Nov 1973 (*Sweet trolley*), Hult. Arch. • photograph, 19 Jan 1978 (*Return of the Sweet*), Hult. Arch. • photographs, repro. in www.thesweet.com

Connolly, Cyril Vernon (1903–1974), writer and literary reviewer, was born on 10 September 1903 at Whitley Villa, Whitley, Coventry, the only child of Major Matthew William Kemble Connolly (1872–1947), of Bath, an expert on snails and shells, stamps, and potted meats, and his wife, Muriel Maud Vernon (*d*. 1964), of Clontarf, Ireland, eighth and youngest child of Edward Vernon and his wife, Jane Brinkley. The Vernons were of the Anglo-Irish ascendancy, having moved to Ireland in the reign of Charles II with the duke of Ormond. Connolly's paternal grandfather, Matthew Connolly, had been an admiral, and was from a family of naval and army officers; he had married

Brackenbury scholar in history at Balliol, he went down with a third.

Having briefly tutored a schoolboy in Jamaica, Connolly became secretary to the elderly man of letters Logan Pearsall Smith, who gave him a small allowance; another literary mentor, Desmond MacCarthy, provided him with his first reviewing assignments, on the *New Statesman*. Although poor, he was able to continue his travels, becoming a devotee of Montparnasse in its headiest period; and his earlier attachments to handsome Etonians, such as Bobby Longden and Noel Blakiston, gave way to a frantic and worldly heterosexuality, which he afterwards maintained. He was famously ugly, in a way that women seemed to find irresistible.

In 1928, in Paris, Connolly met Jean Bakewell (1910–1949), a vivacious, rather wild American art student, aged eighteen, from a wealthy Pittsburgh (Connolly liked to say Baltimore) family. In 1930 they were married, living initially in the south of France, and through much of the 1930s in Chelsea. They kept exotic pets, had no money problems, were unable to have children, travelled widely, and became fat; from the late 1930s, when both took other lovers, their marriage broke down.

Connolly reviewed during the 1930s in the *New Statesman*, but his ambition was to become a great novelist, or at least create a literary masterpiece. He wrote a short and daring novella about drifters living in the south of France, *The Rock Pool*, which was rejected by Faber but issued in 1936 by the Obelisk Press in Paris. Opinions differ widely on whether this, Connolly's only completed novel, shows that he had the ability to produce fiction. During his later lifetime it was widely admired; since his death it has been equally widely disparaged. It seems likely, however, that the book's chequered course in England, where it was reissued as late as 1947, cast a blight over his many later attempts to write novels.

Connolly made a surer reputation with *Enemies of Promise* (1938). This work is part literary criticism, part general observations on the life of the writer, part childhood autobiography, part astute assessment of the precocity forced on English children by public schools. It is given unity by its enquiry into how 'to write a book that will hold good for ten years afterwards'. It is almost universally recognized as having anatomized this complex subject brilliantly, although the *bons mots* are mixed with pretension, and the link between the parts is more implicit than firmly drawn.

The third work on which Connolly's reputation is generally thought to rest is *The Unquiet Grave* (1944), a book of *pensées*, some coined by himself, others drawn from his favourite, mainly French, authors. Compiled during the year he turned forty, when he was cut off by the war from the continental civilization he loved, and suffering unhappiness because of his separation from his wife, it contains many melancholy autobiographical reflections.

The final pillar of Connolly's reputation is his editorship, from December 1939 to January 1950, of the literary magazine *Horizon*, which had the backing of the wealthy Peter Watson and, initially, the editorial assistance of

Cyril Vernon Connolly (1903–1974), by Augustus John, 1945

Harriet Kemble, the daughter of a rector of Bath who dissipated a large fortune on the restoration of Bath Abbey and other munificence.

Connolly was born in Coventry because his father was stationed there, and his early life followed the vagaries of military posting in an age of empire. His first memories were of Wynberg, South Africa, which he visited twice, aged five and six. However, Major Matthew Connolly was retired on half-pay in 1912 and, returning to England, bought the Lock House, outside the village of Frimley in Surrey; this was Connolly's first (almost his only) settled home, but it was let during the war, and in the early 1920s his home life was clouded by his parents' separation.

Connolly attended St Cyprian's preparatory school, Eastbourne, from 1914 to 1918, and Eton College, as a king's scholar, until 1922. He memorialized both in *Enemies of Promise*. His portrait of the dominating headmistress at St Cyprian's, Mrs Vaughan Wilkes, critical yet admiring, contrasts with the unreservedly bitter account of her given by George Orwell in 'Such, such were the joys …'. At Eton, Connolly attained membership of the élite society Pop; social success, romantic friendships, and an initiation into the Latin and Greek classics, and French and English literature, combined to make Eton the golden age of his life. Oxford, from 1922 to 1925, was a disappointment, although it added the new interest of travel; a

Stephen Spender. In the first number, Connolly announced, in defiance of the war, 'our standards are aesthetic ones, politics are in abeyance'. To maintain such a stance was difficult, but, paradoxically, it gave the magazine a prestige which it could never have attained had it been more piously committed to the home front. Connolly, a famously slothful man, passed the mornings in bed and in his bath, but he had a bevy of beautiful female assistants in the office (one, Lys Lubbock, was his mistress), and, when in attendance, was a shrewd editor. He helped to launch such authors as Angus Wilson and Denton Welch, and the magazine consolidated his fame.

Connolly was briefly literary editor of *The Observer* during the war, and from 1950 until his death was, with Raymond Mortimer, chief literary critic of the *Sunday Times*. His later books were largely collections of his journalism, of which he published four (*The Condemned Playground*, *Ideas and Places*, *Previous Convictions*, *The Evening Colonnade*), and three other volumes (*The Missing Diplomats*, *Les pavillons*, *The Modern Movement*) represented the rare gleanings from commissions he never completed. He was married twice in later years: from 1950 to 1955 to Barbara Olive *Skelton (1916–1996), from whom he was divorced; and on 26 August 1959 to Deirdre Craven (*b.* 1931/2), the daughter of Patrick William Dennis Craig and granddaughter of Viscount Craigavon, the first prime minister of Northern Ireland, with whom he had a son and a daughter. In his last years, he lived at Eastbourne, the complexities of his emotional life unabated, his debts and choice collections accumulating, his dreams of a masterpiece unfulfilled. He died of heart disease at St Vincent's Clinic, Ladbroke Terrace, London, on 26 November 1974 and was buried in Berwick churchyard, Sussex.

Since Connolly's death, there have been published: *A Romantic Friendship* (1975), a collection of his early letters to Noel Blakiston; *Shade those Laurels* (1990), a partially written novel completed by Peter Levi; two biographies of him; a diary, supported by a memoir by David Pryce-Jones; and a two-volume selection of his works edited by his son Matthew. Connolly was a chevalier of the Légion d'honneur, FRSL, CBE, and CLit.

Innumerable contemporaries sought to describe, with more or less prejudice, Connolly's greed, his sloth, his gourmandizing, his inconsistency and melancholy. He criticized every aspect of himself more severely than they could, and was among the wittiest men of his time. No other figure straddles the divide between criticism and creation so convincingly, or is more poignantly the epitome of failed promise; few have been equally so celebrated in both their lives and their works.

C. A. R. HILLS

Sources J. Lewis, *Cyril Connolly: a life* (1997) · C. Fisher, *Cyril Connolly: a nostalgic life* (1995) · D. Pryce-Jones, *Cyril Connolly: journal and memoir* (1983) · private information (2004) · C. Connolly, *Enemies of promise* (1938) · *A romantic friendship: the letters of Cyril Connolly to Noel Blakiston* (1975) · b. cert. · m. cert. [D. Craven] · d. cert.
Archives Ransom HRC, corresp. and literary papers · University of Tulsa, Oklahoma | Bodl. Oxf., corresp. with Birrell and Garnett Ltd · Bodl. Oxf., corresp. with Jack Lambert; biographical essay by Lambert · CUL, letters to Oliver Simon · NYPL, Berg collection, MSS · Tate collection, corresp. with Lord Clark · UCL, corresp. with George Orwell |FILM BBC |SOUND BBC
Likenesses H. Cartier-Bresson, bromide print, 1939, NPG · A. John, drawing, 1945, priv. coll. [*see illus.*] · D. Farson, bromide print, *c.*1953, NPG · F. Topolski, portrait, NPG
Wealth at death £41,989: probate, 8 Oct 1975, *CGPLA Eng. & Wales* · debts of £27,000: Fisher, *Cyril Connolly*

Connolly, James (1868–1916), socialist and Irish revolutionary, was born on 5 June 1868 at 107 Cowgate, Edinburgh, the youngest of three sons (there were no daughters) of Irish immigrants John Connolly (1832/3–1900), manure carter of Edinburgh, and his wife, Mary (1832/3–1890), daughter of James McGinn, labourer of Edinburgh. Brought up in the slums of Cowgate, Connolly left St Patrick's School at ten and became in turn printer's devil, bakery hand, and tiling factory worker. In 1882, falsifying his age and name, he joined the army, serving in Ireland and possibly elsewhere; hating it he deserted in 1889 at a time when both his mother and father were seriously ill. On 13 April 1889 he married Lillie Reynolds, a domestic servant from a protestant Wicklow family, whom he had met in Dublin. They had one son and six daughters.

From childhood Connolly had read voraciously; in the army he learned about history, politics, economics, and socialism. In April 1889 he joined the Socialist League in Dundee, then moved back to Edinburgh, where he worked as a night-soil man. He read deeply in socialist literature, even learning some French and German, and applied Marxist theory to his twin preoccupations of Irish nationalism and social inequality. A member of the Scottish Socialist Federation (SSF) from 1890 and the Independent Labour Party from shortly after its foundation in 1893, his powerful mind fed off political discussion. His published branch reports as secretary of the SSF showed that direct, trenchant writing came naturally to him; effective public speaking took longer. As a youth he had difficulty in overcoming physical handicaps that included bow legs, short sight, and a stammer, later cured. He was not tall, but was described by Daniel Figgis as 'sturdy of frame and broad of brow[;] he suggested, and his northern accent conveyed, the thought of a realist who lived to slay illusions' (Figgis, 87).

In 1894 Connolly lost his job and in 1895 failed as a cobbler, but his reputation in socialist circles throughout Scotland as an organizer and propagandist (he wrote a column in a local left-wing paper as 'R. Ascal'), speaker and campaigner (he stood in two local elections) was high and brought him an offer in 1896 from the Dublin Socialist Club to be their paid organizer for £1 per week. The salary was rarely forthcoming and Connolly had to do labouring work, but his energy was boundless; he created the Irish Socialist Republican Party (ISRP) to spread his message that socialism and nationalism were complementary and incompatible with sectarianism. Despite opposing cross-class alliances he formed a friendship with Maud Gonne, who helped to make him an early convert to female suffrage, and together they organized flamboyant anti-monarchical and anti-imperialist protests. But despite demonstrations, public meetings, numerous articles, pamphlets, poetry, and proletarian songs, and a newspaper called the *Workers' Republic* (which frequently collapsed), he won few converts, for romantic nationalism was in the ascendant: 'Ireland without her people is nothing to me', he wrote in frustration in 1900. And in international socialist circles, the ISRP was censured for calling for independence from Britain as well as a socialist revolution.

Connolly was pro-Boer and opposed to home rule, a cause which he regarded as middle class and capitalist. These views had lost him friends in Britain, though he made many speeches there in 1901, leading to an invitation to go to America on a speaking tour under the auspices of Daniel De Leon's Socialist Labor Party (SLP), which had given occasional financial help to the ISRP. De Leon, who believed that a socialist party should be as 'intolerant as science' (Dudley Edwards, 40), hoped that Connolly would win Irish-American recruits for the SLP and return to Ireland ideologically purer and more evangelistic. Connolly's speaking tour from September 1902 to January 1903 took him from New York to California and Canada, and though he disliked the individualism of the United States he found the trip exhilarating and raised some money for his party. On his return to Ireland what a colleague called his 'confoundedly disagreeable integrity and incorruptibility' (John Carstairs Matheson to Connolly, 2 March 1907, Dudley Edwards, 45) resulted in a disastrous split in the ISRP. To support his family, which had been living in grinding poverty in a squalid tenement, he first worked for the new Socialist Labour Party in Scotland, but seeing that it had no future he had to emigrate in 1903 to the United States—bitterly claiming to have been driven out of Ireland by socialists.

During seven years in America Connolly's many jobs included agent for an insurance company, lathe operator, and union organizer. An activist in socialist, Irish, and Italian circles, in 1905 he was a co-founder of the syndicalist Industrial Workers of the World, in 1907 founder of the Irish Socialist Federation, in 1908 of *The Harp* newspaper, and in 1908–9 a paid organizer for the Socialist Party of America. When he left, after numerous rows with American socialists—De Leon ultimately dubbed the atheist Connolly a Jesuit agent; Connolly alleged De Leon was 'purposely doing the work of the capitalist class' (Connolly to Matheson, 8 Nov 1900, Dudley Edwards, 63)—though the class struggle was still his main concern he had developed a new sympathy with cultural and political nationalism. Though still irascible he was mellowing, and had matured into a thinker of depth, breadth, and originality, and an orator of force and passion.

Back in Dublin in 1910 Connolly published a brilliant pamphlet—*Labour, Nationality and Religion*—refuting clerical assertions that Catholicism and socialism were incompatible, and his masterpiece, *Labour in Irish History*, which, although marked by economic determinism and his hatred of the middle-class nationalist tradition, was a ground-breaking application of international thinking to the Irish situation and deeply influenced the thinking of Patrick Pearse. Briefly national organizer of the Socialist Party of Ireland in 1910, Connolly, in 1911, became Ulster district organizer of the Irish Transport and General Workers' Union. Although he had some success as a union representative, increasing membership was an uphill struggle, because of both the sheer poverty of the workers and the rampant sectarianism that meant that most recruits were Roman Catholics. Indeed, while in innumerable speeches (some later printed in 1915 in pamphlet form as *The Reconquest of Ireland*) Connolly stressed the suffering of protestant workers under capitalism, he never understood unionism or the fears of Ulster protestants.

In 1912 Connolly was a founder of the Independent Labour Party of Ireland, and by persuading the Irish trades union conference to back the labour movement he created the conditions from which the Irish Labour Party later developed—one of his most practical achievements. When in 1913 the Dublin Employers' Federation staged a lock-out to prevent workers joining the trade union Connolly returned to Dublin to rally the workers, but poverty defeated them in February 1914. In October James Larkin, whose personality cult Connolly deplored and whom he found an almost intolerable boss, left Ireland and Connolly became his highly efficient successor as general secretary of the union, editor of the *Irish Worker*, and military commander of the Irish Citizen Army, set up in November 1913 as a morale-boosting drilling scheme for locked-out workers. Appalled by the outbreak of war in 1914 Connolly launched a massive anti-recruitment drive. Its failure, combined with the dreadful suffering of the Dublin poor, drove him to join forces with the revolutionary nationalist Irish Republican Brotherhood. His influence was evident in the egalitarian wording of the proclamation declaring an Irish republic published on Easter Monday 1916. Connolly directed operations in the General Post Office capably and courageously, for the last two days with a shattered ankle. After the surrender on 29 April he was court-martialled on 9 May and shot (while seated, being unable to stand) at Kilmainham gaol, Dublin, at dawn on 12 May 1916. He was first interred at the gaol; his final resting place is at Arbour Hill cemetery, Dublin. He was survived by his wife.

Connolly was the fifteenth and last of the rebels to be executed, the killing of an injured man having resulted in a public outcry. His status as a patriotic martyr was at once assured, but an appreciation of his politics took rather longer to develop: socialists disapproved of his participation in an essentially bourgeois nationalist revolution and nationalists disapproved of his socialism. The labour movement in Ireland subsequently developed along broadly non-Marxist lines, and it was only when his writings were rediscovered by civil rights activists in Northern Ireland during the 1960s that his significance as a socialist thinker began to achieve wide recognition.

RUTH DUDLEY EDWARDS

Sources R. Dudley Edwards, *James Connolly* (1981) · C. D. Greaves, *The life and times of James Connolly* (1961) · D. Howell, *A lost left: three studies in socialism and nationalism* (1986) · A. Morgan, *James Connolly: a political biography* (1988) · D. Figgis, *Recollections* (1927) · b. cert. · m. cert.

Archives NL Ire., corresp. and papers | TCD, letters relating mainly to SDF internal politics and his lecture tour
Likenesses portraits (posthumous; after photographs), Services Industrial Professional and Technical Union, Liberty Hall, Dublin

Connor [*formerly* O'Connor], **Bernard** (*c.*1666–1698), physician and writer on Poland, the son of Bernard O'Connor, born in co. Kerry, Ireland, was descended from the O'Connor Kerry family, lords of Kerry. As a Roman Catholic, he was prohibited from attending school or university, and was therefore taught privately by tutors. Of his life in Ireland almost nothing is known, but *c.*1686, when he was about twenty years old, he went abroad to further his education. He is said to have studied medicine about 1690 at the universities of Montpellier and Paris (N. F. J. Eloy, *Dictionnaire historique*), but no confirmation of this has been found in the records of those institutions. There is, however, evidence that he attended the University of Rheims and took the degree of doctor of medicine there on 18 September 1693. (The date 18 September 1691, given in the records of the Royal College of Physicians, is less likely.) While in France, he published in 1693 in Paris a paper describing a spondylitic skeleton, entitled *Lettre écrite à Monsieur le Chevalier Guillaume de Waldegrave, premier médecin de sa majesté britannique.*

Through contact with the French royal court, O'Connor was entrusted with the care of the sons of Jan Wielopolski, crown chancellor of Poland, who had died in 1688. With them he set out late in 1693 on a journey to Italy, where he visited Rome and, on about 13 December 1693, ascended Vesuvius. He met several prominent Italian physicians. He and his Polish companions then passed through Venice, Padua, Innsbruck, and Vienna, on their way to Warsaw, where, following their arrival in mid-1694, King Jan III Sobieski appointed O'Connor his personal physician. Being commanded to confer with certain other physicians concerning a disease of the king's sister, O'Connor immediately diagnosed an abscess of the liver and said she could not live long, whatever her treatment. The others made light of her condition, but within a month she was dead and confirmation of the diagnosis by post-mortem enhanced his reputation. However, since the king was sixty-four years old and in poor health, O'Connor's situation was uncertain. It was therefore with relief that he accepted the task of attending Princess Teresa Kunegunda, the king's daughter, on her journey to Brussels to join her husband, the elector of Bavaria. Soon after the arrival of the royal equipage in Brussels on 12 January 1695 the care of the electress's health was taken over by her husband's physician and O'Connor set sail for England, where he landed in February 1695. He became a member of the Church of England, changed his name to Connor, and soon had friends in high places, including Hans Sloane. At a meeting of the Royal Society on 6 March 1695 Connor presented several natural curiosities, including seeds and minerals collected in Poland and a specimen of *plica polonica* (a matted condition of the hair). He then moved to Oxford, where he stayed for about three months, lecturing to members of the university on anatomy and related matters and attending to the publication of four scientific papers under the collective title *Dissertationes medico-physicae* (1695), including a Latin version of his account of a spondylitic skeleton, now addressed to John Radcliffe. By 20 June he was back in London and attending a meeting of the Royal Society, where he presented a copy of his newly printed *Dissertationes*. While in Oxford he had attracted the attention of Robert Gorge (or Gorges) of St John's College, who reported to Sir William Trumbull, member of parliament for the university and a privy councillor, first that Connor, having pretended to be a Pole, had revealed himself to be an Irishman hostile to the English cause in Ireland; and later, that he was believed to be a French spy. However, this did not hinder Connor's admission on 27 November 1695 as a fellow of the Royal Society and, on 6 April 1696, as a licentiate of the Royal College of Physicians. From January to March 1696 he lectured three times a week in the library of St Martin-in-the-Fields on the fabric and operations of the human body, and that summer he repeated these lectures in Cambridge.

Public interest in Polish affairs resulting from the death of King Jan III Sobieski (17 June 1696) and the election of his successor provided the stimulus for the publication of Connor's *History of Poland*, which he had begun while still in Poland. His medical activities left him little spare time, however, and it was only with the assistance of his friend John Savage (1673–1747) that he managed to prepare this book for the press. The second volume was, in fact, composed by Savage from Connor's notes. *The History of Poland, in Several Letters to Persons of Quality* (2 vols., 1698) is an imposing work of over seven hundred pages, based strictly on identified sources and embodying a valuable eyewitness account of Poland in the late seventeenth century. Connor's most controversial work, however, was his *Evangelium medici, seu, Medicina mystica: de suspensis naturae legibus, sive, De miraculis* (1697), which set out to explain miracles by the principles of medical knowledge.

In October 1698 Connor, who was now living in Brownlow Street, in the parish of St Giles-in-the-Fields, Middlesex, fell ill with a fever. On 27 October he made his will and the next day sent for the rector, William Hayley, who, accepting that he was a true penitent member of the Church of England, gave him communion. But Connor was later visited by an Irish Roman Catholic priest, who spoke to him in Irish and, it appears, gave him extreme unction.

Connor died on 30 October 1698 and was buried at St Giles-in-the-Fields on 3 November. Judging that in his dealings with the Catholic priest Connor had no longer known what he was doing, Hayley gave him burial as a member of the Church of England. Connor's will directed that his property, including his house and furniture, be sold and the proceeds paid to his nearest relatives. It mentions, in particular, a diamond ring, which was to be sold and the proceeds given to his youngest sister. Not having been witnessed, the will had to be proved before a judge, at which point the executors Charles Connor (the doctor's cousin) and William Lilley renounced their rights in favour of Connor's father, who on 6 October 1699 was given administration.   GERALD STONE

Sources R. H. Dalitz and G. C. Stone, 'Doctor Bernard Connor: physician to King Jan III Sobieski and author of *The history of Poland* (1698)', *Oxford Slavonic Papers*, new ser., 14 (1981), 14–35 · B. S. Blumberg and J. L. Blumberg, 'Bernard Connor (1666–1698), and his contribution to the pathology of ankylosing spondylitis', *Journal of the History of Medicine and Allied Sciences*, 13 (1958), 349–66 · W. Hayley, *A sermon preached in the parish church of St Giles in the Fields at the funeral of Bernard Connor, M. D. who departed this life, Oct. 30. 1698, with a short account of his life and death* (1699) · J. O'Hart, *Irish pedigrees, or, The origin and stem of the Irish nation*, 5th edn, 1 (1892) · N. F. J. Eloy, *Dictionnaire historique de la médecine ancienne et moderne*, 4 vols. (Mons, 1778), vol. 1 · will, PRO, Prob. II/452

Connor, Charles (*c.*1788–1826), actor, was born in co. Cork, the son of James Connor. He was educated at Trinity College, Dublin, where he was admitted in 1805 at the age of seventeen. He is believed to have played Euphrasia in *The Grecian Daughter* while still at school, and to have acquired some popularity at the Dublin theatre before travelling to England. There he made his début as an actor at Bath about 1807, as Fitzharding in *The Curfew*. Connor's first appearance in London did not take place until 18 September 1816, in the character of Sir Patrick McGuire in Oulton's *The Sleep Walker*. From this period until 14 June 1826, when as Kenrick in Colman's *The Heir-at-Law* he took a benefit and made his last recorded appearance, he played a round of characters at Covent Garden. These consisted of Irish types, servants, villains, and similar roles, the most prominent being Sir Callaghan in Charles Macklin's *Love à la Mode*, Foigard in Farquhar's *The Beaux' Stratagem*, Sir William Davison in an adaptation of Schiller's *Mary Stuart*, Julio in Barry Cornwall's *Mirandola*, Dennis Brulgruddery in the younger Colman's *John Bull*, and Filch in *The Beggar's Opera*. He also played characters in various adaptations of Scott's novels. The original parts assigned him included Terry O'Rourke, otherwise Dr O'Toole, in *The Irish Tutor*, written expressly for him, at Cheltenham and Covent Garden in 1822; and Dr O'Rafferty in *Cent per Cent*, in 1823. He also played Sir Lucius O'Trigger in *The Rivals*.

Connor's wife (whose name is unknown) was also on the stage and is said to have acted at the Haymarket as Grace Gaylove in Colman's *The Review*. She performed at Covent Garden, taking the roles of Manse Hedrigge in *The Battle of Bothwell Brigg* (May 1820), in which Connor was Graham of Claverhouse; the Duchess of York in *Richard III* (March 1821); and Servia in Sheridan Knowles's *Virginius* (December 1821), to her husband's Appius. A benefit was given for her at the English Opera House (Lyceum) after her husband's death. Connor died suddenly of heart disease on 7 October 1826 while crossing St James's Park to his home in Pimlico, and was buried on 13 October 1826 at the New Church, Chelsea. A Roman Catholic, he was survived by his wife and two children. Connor had a good face, figure, and voice, and, while his career in London cannot be regarded as a great success, he was fairly popular in the roles he performed.

JOSEPH KNIGHT, *rev.* NILANJANA BANERJI

Charles Connor (*c.*1788–1826), by unknown engraver [as Dr O'Toole in *The Irish Tutor*]

Sources Adams, *Drama* · *The biography of the British stage, being correct narratives of the lives of all the principal actors and actresses* (1824) · *GM*, 1st ser., 96/2 (1826), 566 · Hall, *Dramatic ports.* · Genest, *Eng. stage* · Burtchaell & Sadleir, *Alum. Dubl.*
Likenesses coloured etching (as Earl of Montrose), NPG · etching, BM, NPG [*see illus.*] · plate, repro. in *Oxberry's Dramatic biography* (1826) · prints, Harvard TC

Connor, Edric Esclus (1913–1968), actor and singer, was born on 2 August 1913 in the village of Mayaro, Trinidad, the son of Edwin Connor, shoemaker and small farmer. At sixteen he won a scholarship from the Trinidad government railway to study engineering at the Victoria Institute, Port of Spain, where he won the Stephen gold medal for mechanical engineering. In his spare time he studied Caribbean folk singing. During the war he worked on the construction of the American naval air base in Trinidad and saved enough money to move to Britain. In 1944 he left Trinidad, intending to continue his engineering studies at South-east Essex Technical College, but he carried with him some notes on Caribbean folk music. He had already presented a series about Caribbean folk music on Radio Trinidad and on his journey to Britain he carried letters of introduction to the BBC. Two weeks after his arrival he made his début on BBC radio in *Calling the West Indies*, a

Edric Esclus Connor (1913–1968), by unknown photographer

programme for listeners in the Caribbean. His appealing voice and charming personality made a deep impression.

From 1945 to 1947 Connor was featured in the popular music series *Serenade in Sepia* with Evelyn Dove, and its success led to a television version in 1946. In the early postwar years he became a popular television personality in BBC music and variety programmes, but perhaps his most important appearances were those involving the promotion of Caribbean music and dance. In 1951 he organized many concerts for the Trinidad All Steel Percussion Orchestra during its ten-week stay, including its début at the Festival of Britain celebrations at London's South Bank. He married a Trinidadian law student, Pearl Cynthia Nunez (*b.* 1924), in London on 26 June 1948. Many years later she described her husband as

> a contained, disciplined person. Charming and soft-spoken. He was rarely agitated. He always gave the impression of being at ease. He was an independent man who believed in pulling his weight. He was an avid student. A self-made person. He read widely. He had a great collection of books on all sorts of subjects. He embraced literature, music and so on. (Bourne, 98)

In 1952 Connor made his film acting début in *Cry, the Beloved Country*, based on Alan Paton's novel about apartheid in South Africa. During the next decade, he played featured roles in a number of British and American productions, including the harpooner Daggoo in *Moby Dick* (1956) and Balthazar in *King of Kings* (1961). In 1958, when Paul Robeson turned down the role of Gower in Shakespeare's *Pericles* for the Stratford Memorial Theatre, he

recommended Connor for it. Connor thus became the first black actor to appear in a Shakespeare season at Stratford upon Avon. This proved to be one of the high points of his career in the theatre.

Though Connor succeeded in almost everything he set out to do, there were some doors that remained firmly closed. As his wife, Pearl, explained:

> He took the opportunity to go to America and train in opera. He had this marvellous baritone, and in America he learned about technique … [but] in those days they had no room for people like Edric. It wasn't even thought about at that time, that a black actor from the Caribbean could ever perform in the opera houses of Britain. Yet, though he sung the roles of Amonasro in *Aida* and King Boris in *Boris Godunov* in Europe, Edric was never asked to sing at Covent Garden. It was very frustrating for him. (Bourne, 105–6)

Connor also wanted to become a television producer and director at a time when no black person could be found behind the camera, except as a scene shifter. His wife recalled: 'He trained with the BBC. This gave him a qualification but, after he completed his training, he wasn't given the opportunity to direct in film or television. Not one BBC assignment came his way' (Bourne, 108). Determined to become a film-maker, in the early 1960s he directed a series of short films about the Caribbean which he funded himself with help from the British Film Institute. They included *Carnival fantastique*, a documentary about the famous Trinidad carnival. Connor was Britain's first black film director, but he faced opposition from people in the film industry who categorized him as a singer, and would not take him seriously. In the early 1960s Connor and his wife were instrumental in forming the Negro Theatre Workshop, a company of thirty black actors.

Connor suffered a stroke and died at the National Hospital, St Pancras, London, on 16 October 1968. As a Caribbean performer in Britain he had been a trailblazer, an artist touched with greatness, and an inspiration to those who followed. His wife recalled:

> He saw himself as an ambassador for Trinidad … we black people were being judged all the time so we felt we had to show our best … but he died much too young. He hadn't achieved everything he wanted to do. But he moved into this country and took every opportunity he had here … to make a lasting mark so that those who came after him would know that it was possible. (Bourne, 112)

STEPHEN BOURNE

Sources S. Bourne, 'Edric Connor: a man for all seasons', *Black in the British frame: black people in British film and television, 1896–1996* (1998), 92–114 · m. cert. · d. cert. · *CGPLA Eng. & Wales* (1969)
Likenesses photograph, 1945, BBC Photograph Library; repro. in Bourne, *Black in the British frame*, after p. 116 · group portrait, photograph, 1951, Hult. Arch. · R. Gough, photograph, 1954, Hult. Arch. · photograph, 1958, BFI; repro. in Bourne, *Black in the British frame* · V. Wilmer, photograph, 1961, Hult. Arch. · photograph [*see illus.*]
Wealth at death £1263: probate, 23 June 1969, *CGPLA Eng. & Wales*

Connor, George Henry (1822–1883), dean of Windsor, eldest son of George Connor, master in chancery in Ireland, was educated at Trinity College, Dublin, where he graduated BA in 1845 and proceeded MA in 1851. He was ordained deacon in 1846 and priest in the following year. After officiating for some time at St Thomas's Chapel, Newport, Isle of Wight, he was curate at St Jude's, Southsea, and subsequently at Wareham, Dorset. He married in 1852 Maude Worthington, eldest daughter of John Worthington of Kent House, Southsea, with whom he had two sons and several daughters. His daughter Emily Henrietta married Ernest Wilberforce, successively bishop of Newcastle and Chichester.

Connor was appointed vicar of Newport, Isle of Wight, in 1852. Here it was due to his initiative and energy that the parish church was rebuilt at a cost of £22,000. The foundation stone was laid by the prince consort. He also built a vicarage and some almshouses, and effected improvements in the schools. He became acquainted with Queen Victoria, then living chiefly on the Isle of Wight, and he was for years honorary chaplain and chaplain-in-ordinary to the queen, chaplain to the governor of the Isle of Wight, and official and commissary of the archdeaconry of Wight. Following the death of G. V. Wellesley, dean of Windsor and an important conduit between the queen and her prime minister, W. E. Gladstone, the queen appointed Connor to the vacant deanery in October 1882, without consulting Gladstone. This was a serious, if characteristic, error. Connor left Newport amid the general regret of his parishioners. He had no sooner entered on his new duties than his health broke down. He was not, in fact, suited to the pressures of so prominent a deanery. He preached once in St George's Chapel, and several times in the private chapel. It taxed his strength severely to be present on the occasion of the christening of Princess Alice of Albany on 26 March. He died on 1 May 1883 at the deanery, Windsor. J. M. RIGG, *rev.* H. C. G. MATTHEW

Sources The Times (2 May 1883) · G. K. A. Bell, *Randall Davidson, archbishop of Canterbury*, 2 vols. (1935) · O. Chadwick, *The Victorian church*, 2 (1970) · d. cert.

Wealth at death £4177 15s. 9d.: probate, 6 June 1883, *CGPLA Eng. & Wales*

Connor, Sir **William Neil** (1909–1967), journalist, was born in London on 26 April 1909, a twin son of William Henry Connor, a protestant Ulsterman and Admiralty clerk, and his wife, Isobella Littlejohn, a telegraphist, from Aberdeenshire. Connor went to a primary board school, then to a local private school, and finally to Glendale grammar school in Wood Green. He left at sixteen and attended a crammer in the hope of getting into the navy, only to be rejected because his eyesight was not good enough. He then did one or two clerical jobs which did not appear to be leading him anywhere until he became bookkeeper at Arks Publicity, a small firm which helped to nourish the talent of the actor Alec Guinness and the cartoonist Philip *Zec. There Connor found himself writing odd bits of advertising copy and discovered that he had some gift for the pen.

At the age of twenty-three Connor got a job as a copywriter with a leading advertising agency, J. Walter Thompson, where he met Basil Nicholson, inventor of the remarkable concept of 'night starvation' and the strip cartoon used to advertise Horlicks, the particular milky beverage which would relieve it. Connor and Zec then collaborated with Nicholson on a general-knowledge strip plagiarizing Ripley's eternal 'Believe it or not?' series. All three eventually found their way to employment on the *Daily Mirror*.

At that time H. G. Bartholomew had begun to convert the *Mirror* from a respectful servants'-hall picture paper to a brash, demagogic tabloid. Hugh Cudlipp, who was also to play a leading part in the revolution, joined the paper on the same day as Connor in August 1935. In 1936 Connor married Gwynfil Mair Morgan; they had two sons and one daughter.

Bartholomew asked Connor to try his hand at a column. When the pen-name Cassandra was suggested, Connor looked it up, and he later wrote:

> I was a bit surprised to discover that I had changed my sex; was the daughter of the King of Troy; that I could foretell in the stars when the news was going to be bad; … and that I was going to come to a sticky end by being efficiently murdered by Clytaemnestra. (Connor, 35)

The column appeared two or three times a week as and when there was room. Connor soon showed a talent for robust invective and his column became what has been called 'the whipping post, stocks and ducking stool for jacks-in-office, muddling magistrates, indiscreet politicians and erring judges' (*The Times*, 7 April 1967). The column varied. It could contain hard-hitting political comment, attacks on government departments and individuals, lavish praise of individuals, and dithyrambic essays on cats or on homely dishes such as cabbage and herring cooked in a particular way. Whatever it was, it was always Connor and it had a tremendous audience.

In Connor's denunciation of the wicked and praise of the virtuous, it was often possible to catch echoes of the Presbyterian pulpit beneath which Connor had regularly sat throughout his youth. About his religion he was publicly ambiguous although he was a deeply spiritual man and regularly read his Bible and prayer book. Matthew Arnold's 'Dover Beach' was never far from his thoughts.

The youthful Connor, a tall, slender young man, was effaced by the later man, who was plump and red-faced, with thinning hair. It was remarked that he belonged to a bohemian race of journalists which had almost disappeared, a generation which read prodigiously, drank heartily, and argued endless hours away at the bar counter. Connor at this period did not suffer fools gladly either in his column or in his personal encounters. He participated in a brief revival in London of a fashion for contrived rudeness as an antidote to the smoothness and alleged effeteness of the establishment. It was all pose. Connor was basically a kindly man, as his colleagues with troubles found out.

Cassandra was an early critic of Nazism and was convinced that Hitler meant war. But when war came he and the *Mirror* aroused Churchill's anger. In a letter to Cecil King, already a director of the *Mirror*, the prime minister complained of the work of a writer 'dominated by malevolence' (*The Times*, 7 April 1967). Cassandra had in fact described a government reshuffle as a game of musical chairs 'being played to a funeral march … Ours' (ibid.). King replied that Cassandra was not malevolent but was known as 'a hard hitting journalist with a vitriolic style' (ibid.). Throwing vitriol, Churchill observed, was one of the worst of crimes.

Churchill expressed an opinion that the *Mirror* papers generally were written in a spirit of hatred and malice against the national government. Then Zec did a cartoon showing a torpedoed sailor, his face blackened with oil, lying on a raft in an empty ocean. The draft caption had been 'Petrol is dearer now'. Connor said it could be better dramatized by bringing in the penny rise. The caption as printed on 6 March 1942 was: '"The price of petrol has been increased by one penny"—Official' (Connor, 61).

This aroused more wrath. The *Mirror* argued that the object of the cartoon was to show that petrol cost lives as well as money and should not be wasted. The government's interpretation was that it suggested the sailor's life had been put at risk to raise the profits of the oil companies. There was a serious threat from Herbert Morrison to close the *Mirror* down, even an investigation of its ownership. The paper weathered the storm but tempered its criticism.

On 27 March 1942 Connor wrote:

This is the last wartime column you will read by Cassandra … I campaigned for Churchill and my support was early and violent. But since he came to power I have distrusted many of his lieutenants—and I have said so with scant respect for either their position or their feelings … [The government] are far too glib with the shameful rejoinder that those who do not agree with them are subversive—and even traitors. … I cannot and will not change my policy.

Connor concluded grandiloquently: 'I propose to see whether the rifle is a better weapon than the printed word. Mr. Morrison can have my pen—but not my conscience. Mr. Morrison can have my silence—but not my self-respect' (Connor, 63–5). Connor then joined the army. He spent a good deal of the war with Cudlipp in Italy producing the forces paper *Union Jack*, in spirit not unlike a miniature *Daily Mirror*.

On his return to the *Mirror* in September 1946 Connor's journalism became deeper and more mature. He drove himself hard, travelled widely, went regularly to the United States, and covered in his highly personal style some historic events: the trials of Eichmann, General Salan, and Jack Ruby, who shot J. F. Kennedy's assassin; the enthronement of Pope John; Churchill's funeral; the Korean War. He interviewed, among many others, President Kennedy, Senator McCarthy, Billy Graham, Charlie Chaplin, Adlai Stevenson, Ben-Gurion, Archbishop Makarios, and Marilyn Monroe. Of course the writing had to have more splashes of melodrama and sentiment than the fastidious writer of later years would have wished. But that was the limitation of popular journalism. He only once ran into serious trouble, when he was successfully sued for libel by Liberace in 1959.

In his last years Connor, who had developed diabetes, suffered much ill health. His knighthood in 1966, an inspiration of Harold Wilson, gave him and all his friends great delight; and he enjoyed the irony of its bestowal on a lifelong professional critic of the establishment. He died in London on 6 April 1967, at St Bartholomew's Hospital.

JOHN BEAVAN, *rev.*

Sources *The Times* (7 April 1967) · R. Connor, *Cassandra: reflections in a mirror* (1967) · personal knowledge (1981) · private information (1981) · *WWW* · *CGPLA Eng. & Wales* (1967)
Archives HLRO, Aitken MSS, corresp. with Lord Beaverbrook · King's Lond., Liddell Hart C., corresp. with Sir B. H. Liddell Hart
Wealth at death £24,235: probate, 13 June 1967, *CGPLA Eng. & Wales*

Conny, Robert (*c.*1645–1713), physician, son of John Conny, surgeon, and twice mayor of Rochester, was a member of Magdalen College, Oxford, and proceeded BA on 8 June 1676, MA on 3 May 1679, BM on 2 May 1682, and DM on 9 July 1685, on which occasion he 'denied and protested', because the vice-chancellor caused one Bullard, of New College, to be presented LLB before him. After being made a candidate of the Royal College of Physicians in 1692, he was employed by the Admiralty as physician to the sick and wounded landed at Deal. He was admitted as a fellow of the Royal College of Physicians in 1693. Conny married Frances, daughter of Richard Manley. He contributed a paper, 'On a shower of fishes', in the form of a letter to Robert Plot, to *Philosophical Transactions*, vol. 20, and is said to have been a successful physician, and to have improved the practice of lithotomy. He died on 25 May 1713 and was buried in Rochester Cathedral, where a monument was erected to his memory.

[ANON.], *rev.* MICHAEL BEVAN

Robert Conny (*c.*1645–1713), by Edward Luttrell, 1707

Sources Munk, *Roll* · Wood, *Ath. Oxon.* · A. Wood, *The history and antiquities of the University of Oxford*, ed. J. Gutch, 2 (1796), 964
Likenesses E. Luttrell, mezzotint, 1707, BM, NPG [*see illus.*] · J. Faber junior, mezzotint, 1722 (after oil painting by A. Vanderhagen), BM · A. Vanderhagen, oils, Bodl. Oxf. · oils, Magd. Oxf.

Conolly, Arthur (1807–1842?),

army officer in the East India Company, was born on 2 July 1807, third of the six sons of Valentine Conolly (d. 2 Dec 1819) of 37 Portland Place, London, who made a rapid fortune in India at the close of the eighteenth century, and his wife, Matilda (d. 29 Nov 1819). He was educated at Rugby School (1820–22). A shy and sensitive boy, Conolly was not suited to public-school life, and he suffered there. After leaving Rugby he entered Addiscombe College on 3 May 1822, but resigned on receiving a cavalry cadetship. He travelled to Bengal the same year. Reginald Heber, newly consecrated bishop of Calcutta, was a fellow passenger, and had a profound influence on the young Conolly, who in January 1824 was made cornet in the 6th Bengal native light cavalry, to which his brother Edward Barry Conolly [*see below*] was appointed later. Arthur became lieutenant in the regiment on 13 May 1825 and captain on 30 July 1838.

Being in England on sick leave in 1829, Conolly obtained leave to return to India through central Asia. He left London on 10 August 1829, travelled through France and Germany to Hamburg, then continued by sea to St Petersburg, where he stayed a month, and then travelled via Tiflis and Tehran to Asterabad. There he disguised himself as an Asian merchant, with a stock of furs and shawls, hoping to reach Khiva. He left Asterabad for the Turkoman steppes on 26 April 1830, but when the little caravan to which he attached himself was about halfway between Krasnovodsk and Kizil Arvat he was seized by nomads and robbed. The Turkomans were undecided whether to kill him or sell him into slavery. Tribal jealousies in the end secured his release, and he returned to Asterabad on 22 May 1830, from where he travelled to India by way of Mashhad, Herat, and Kandahar, visiting Sind, and finally crossing the Indian frontier in January 1831. He published a lively narrative of the journey—reflecting his bright, hopeful temperament—*A Journey to Northern India* (1834). He also contributed papers entitled 'The overland journey to India' to *Gleanings in Science* (1831). After an interview with Lord William Bentinck at Delhi, Conolly rejoined his regiment, and when stationed at Cawnpore appears to have acquired the lasting friendship of the eccentric Jewish convert Dr Joseph Wolff, then travelling as a missionary in India.

In 1834 Conolly joined the political department and was appointed assistant to the government agent in Rajputana, and in 1838 returned home on furlough, hoping to marry. Disappointed, he sought relief in further professional activity. Russian movements in central Asia were causing anxiety in England, and Conolly proposed to the home government to remove the pretext for Russian advances by negotiating with the principal Uzbek chiefs in order to stop the carrying off of Russian and Persian subjects into slavery. He was provided with letters of recommendation to Lord Auckland, then governor-general

Arthur Conolly (1807–1842?), by James Atkinson, c.1840

of India, by the Board of Control in London, together with £500 for an overland journey. Conolly left London on 11 February 1839, visited Vienna (where he had an interview with Prince Metternich), Constantinople, and Baghdad, where he first met Major Henry Rawlinson, and reached Bombay in November 1839, proceeding from there to Calcutta. The time appeared favourable, and Conolly was sent on to Kabul, where in the spring of 1840 he joined the staff of Sir William Macnaghten, the British envoy with Shah Shuja. One of Macnaghten's brothers had married Conolly's sister.

Passionately religious and enthusiastic, and supporting the abolition of central Asian slavery, Conolly held hopes, which he admitted were somewhat 'visionary', for the political regeneration of central Asia and the ultimate conversion of its people to Christianity. Macnaghten and Conolly in April 1840 planned—the initiative apparently largely Conolly's—that Conolly should go to Turkestan on an ill-defined mission to urge the Uzbek states to combine against Russia, under the leadership of Kokand; initially there was no plan to visit Bukhara. The plan was modified, and in September 1840 Conolly went to Khiva, and in 1841 to Kokand. In Bukhara the amir, Nasrullah, had since December 1838 kept prisoner a British envoy, Colonel Charles Stoddart. The amir, apparently suspicious of Conolly's activities in Kokand, invited him to Bukhara. Conolly, as this apparently fitted his hopes of an Uzbek confederation, went to Bukhara, arriving in October 1841.

In December 1841 the amir, suspicious of British policy and presumably encouraged by British failure in Afghanistan, imprisoned Conolly with Stoddart. Disillusioned, Conolly's views changed, and he came to favour Anglo-Russian co-operation in Turkestan, in the interests of civilization. Conolly was a voluminous and rapid writer. On his travels he noted all he said and did in his journal, a practice he continued even in his dungeon at Bukhara.

Five letters, all written in February and March 1842, forming the main portion of Conolly's prison journal, survived his captivity. The last direct news of him alive was in a letter he sent to his brother, then a hostage at Kabul, early in 1842, in which he described the sufferings of Stoddart and himself. For four months they had no change of clothing; their dungeon was foul, insanitary, and infested with vermin. Stoddart was reduced to a skeleton. They had with difficulty persuaded one of their guards to represent their wretched condition to the amir, and were at that time awaiting his reply, having committed themselves to God in the full belief that unless quickly released death must soon end their sufferings. Nevertheless, he wrote, 'We are resolved to wear our English honesty and dignity to the last' (Yapp, 413). The amir had them murdered, probably in June 1842.

The British government being apparently unwilling to act, a committee was formed in London in 1842, on the initiative of Captain John Grover, to obtain the release of the Bukhara captives, and a sum of £500 so collected supplied the funds to dispatch Dr Wolff on a mission to Bukhara. Wolff, after perilous investigations there, concluded that Conolly, with Stoddart and other victims, after enduring fearful agonies in prison, had been cruelly killed some time in 1843, and that the instigator of this was the pretended friend of the English, Abdul Samut Khan, *naib* or prime minister of Nasir Allah Bahadur, amir of Bukhara.

Although Conolly had undoubted courage and a sense of duty, some of his contemporaries considered him over-enthusiastic and lacking in balance. Sir Alexander Burnes, for example, considered him flighty. Many years later Conolly's prayer book, in which he had written a last record of his sufferings and aspirations when a prisoner, was left at his sister's house in London by a mysterious foreigner, who simply said that he came from Russia. The details were published in Sir John Kaye's account of Conolly in *Lives of Indian Officers* (1867).

Three of Conolly's brothers lost their lives in the Indian service.

Edward Barry Conolly (1808–1840) was captain, 6th Bengal light cavalry, and at the time of his death was in command of the escort of the British envoy at Kabul. He was shot at Tootundurrah, in Kohistan, north of Kabul, while a volunteer with Sir Robert Sale, in the attack on the fort there on 29 September 1840. He had made many contributions to the *Journal of the Asiatic Society of Bengal*.

John Balfour Conolly (d. 1842) was a cadet of 1833; he became lieutenant, 20th Bengal native infantry, and was afterwards attached to the Kabul embassy. He died of fever while a hostage in the Bala Hissar, Kabul, on 7 August 1842.

Henry Valentine Conolly (1806–1855), of the Madras civil service, entered Rugby School in the same year as his brother Arthur, and was appointed a writer on the Madras establishment on 19 May 1824. He became assistant to the principal collector at Bellary in 1826, and after holding various posts—including deputy secretary to the military department, Canarese translator to the government,

cashier of the government bank, and additional government commissioner for the settlement of Carnatic claims—he was appointed magistrate and collector at Malabar, a post he held for many years. Conolly, who was married, was murdered in his house on 11 September 1855 by some Mopla fanatics in revenge for his role in outlawing their *thungai*, or saint, a religious leader who had been deported to Jiddah a few years before for sedition. Shortly before his death Conolly was made a provisional member of the council of the Madras government.

H. M. CHICHESTER, *rev.* JAMES LUNT

Sources J. W. Kaye, *Lives of Indian officers*, 2 (1867) • F. Maclean, *A person from England* (1958) • *Calcutta Review*, 15 (1851) • *Hart's Army List* • J. Grover, *The Bokhara victims* (1845) • A. Conolly, *Journey to northern India*, 2 vols. (1834) • P. Macrory, *Signal catastrophe: the story of a disastrous retreat from Kabul, 1842* (1966) • J. A. Norris, *The First Afghan War, 1838–1842* (1967) • P. Hopkirk, *The great game: on secret service in high Asia* (1990) • J. Wolff, *Mission to Bokhara* (1845) • A. Burnes, *Travels into Bokhara*, 3 vols. (1834); repr. (1973) • J. Lunt, *Bokhara Burnes* (1969) • Lady Sale, *A journal of the disasters in Affghanistan* (1843) • M. E. Yapp, *Strategies of British India: Britain, Iran and Afghanistan, 1798–1850* (1980)
Archives BL, diary and extracts from letters, Add. MS 38725 • BL OIOC, diaries, MSS Eur B 29, D 161 | BL, letters and reports to Sir J. C. Hobhouse and William Cabell, Add. MS 61945 • U. Durham L., archives and special collections, letters to Viscount Ponsonby
Likenesses J. Atkinson, watercolour drawing, c.1840, NPG [*see illus.*] • R. Thorburn, watercolour on ivory miniature, Scot. NPG

Conolly, Edward Barry (1808–1840). *See under* Conolly, Arthur (1807–1842?).

Conolly, Erskine (1796–1843), poet, was born at Crail, Fife, on 12 June 1796, the son of Daniel Conolly and Janet Fowler. He was educated at the burgh school of his native town, and was afterwards apprenticed to a bookseller at Anstruther. Subsequently he began business on his own account in Colinsburgh, but not succeeding to his satisfaction, he went to Edinburgh. There, after serving for some time as clerk to a writer to the signet, he obtained a partnership with a solicitor, and after his partner's death succeeded to the whole business.

Conolly wrote many poems and songs, including 'Mary Macneil', his best-known song, which appeared in the *Edinburgh Intelligencer* on 23 December 1840. No edition of his collected works was ever published. He died at Edinburgh on 7 January 1843.

T. F. HENDERSON, *rev.* S. R. J. BAUDRY

Sources M. F. Conolly, 'Conolly, Erskine', *Dictionary of eminent men of Fife* (1866), 126 • C. Rogers, *The modern Scottish minstrel, or, The songs of Scotland of the past half-century*, 3 (1856), 220–21 • J. G. Wilson, 'Conolly, Erskine', *The poets and poetry of Scotland*, 2 (1877), 175–6 • IGI

Conolly, Henry Valentine (1806–1855). *See under* Conolly, Arthur (1807–1842?).

Conolly, John (1794–1866), physician and alienist, was born at his grandmother's house in Market Rasen, Lincolnshire, on 27 May 1794, the second of three sons of Jonathon Conolly, an impecunious Anglo-Irish gentleman of no fixed pursuits, and of his wife, Dorothy Tennyson (1761–1816), a distant relative of the family of the future poet laureate. After his father's premature death about 1799 John was separated from his brothers and boarded

John Conolly (1794–1866), by William Walker (after Sir John Watson-Gordon, exh. RA 1851)

out 'like an inconvenient superfluity' (Leigh, 211–15) with an elderly relative in Hedon, Yorkshire. Here he passed a barren and wretched childhood, receiving a Dickensian education at the local grammar school. His mother moved to Kingston upon Hull in 1803, supporting herself by opening a boarding-school for young ladies, and married a French émigré who taught languages, a Mr Stirling. In 1807 young John came to live with them, learning French and acquiring a rudimentary general education from his stepfather. At eighteen he secured an ensign's commission in the Cambridgeshire militia, and he spent the closing years of the Napoleonic wars in Scotland and Ireland.

Conolly's military career ended with Napoleon's defeat and he returned to Hull shortly before his mother's death in 1816. There, on 6 March 1817, he married Elizabeth Collins (1784–1866), the impoverished daughter of the recently deceased Sir John Collins, a naval captain. They left immediately for a cottage near Tours on the Loire, where his older brother, William, was already engaged in the practice of medicine. A year later, with a young daughter, Eliza (b. 1818), and with his own meagre capital rapidly diminishing, Conolly urgently needed a stable source of income. Like many middle-class men of his generation he chose a career in medicine. He is said to have matriculated at Glasgow University in 1818, although there is no mention of him in the *Matriculation Albums*, and did so at Edinburgh University in 1819, from where he graduated MD in 1821, having written a thesis 'De statu mentis in insania et melancholia'. At Edinburgh he was strongly influenced by

Dugald Stewart, and served as one of the four annual presidents of the Royal Medical Society.

Lacking the social and intellectual capital essential for metropolitan practice, Conolly moved to Lewes and then Chichester, but was unable to establish himself in what was by now an increasingly overcrowded and competitive profession. His vivacity and charm made him a favourite of the local notables as a social companion, but his lack of faith in his own remedies and his deficiencies as a clinician meant that when ill his well-to-do acquaintances preferred to consult his friend and rival, John Forbes. Shortly after the birth of his second child, his son Edward Tennyson (1822–1908), Conolly therefore moved again, this time to the small town of Stratford upon Avon. Here he enjoyed moderate success, taking a leading role in establishing a dispensary for the sick poor, being elected to the town council, and twice serving as mayor—a well-worn path for a young practitioner trying to make his way. He also assisted James Copland in editing the *London Medical Repository*. Reflecting his earlier interest in insanity, and as a supplement to his still meagre income, he obtained an appointment as inspecting physician to the lunatic houses for the county of Warwick, a position that required only that he accompany two justices of the peace on their annual inspection of the county's half dozen madhouses. Still, in his best year his income did not exceed £400, barely sufficient to sustain a professional man with a growing family, now including another daughter, Sophia Jane (1826–1888). Suddenly, however, the intervention of two patrons from Conolly's Edinburgh days, George Birkbeck and Lord Henry Brougham, offered him the chance to substitute the rewards of a London teaching and consulting practice for the dull routines of provincial general practice. His sponsors, among the prime movers in establishing the new University of London, and, like Conolly, members of the Society for the Diffusion of Useful Knowledge, secured Conolly's appointment as professor of the nature and treatment of diseases, a position he took up in October 1828.

In its early years the medical school at the new university was on a shaky financial footing. There were, besides, recurrent clashes between the medical staff and the new warden, Leonard Horner, for whom Conolly developed a particular antipathy. In this uncertain environment he proved incapable of succeeding, turning out to be a poor lecturer and showing himself once again incapable of attracting upper-class patients to his private practice. Conolly's attempts to pioneer clinical instruction in the treatment of mental disorders at a London asylum were repeatedly rebuffed. Nor was his book on the subject, *An Inquiry into the Indications of Insanity* (1830), a critical success, perhaps in part because he broke with emerging orthodoxy to argue that asylum treatment was actively harmful in most instances, and where absolutely unavoidable should be provided only in publicly funded institutions whose governors would not be tempted to put their own financial interests before the needs of their patients. Increasingly in debt, and now with a fourth child, Anne Caroline (1830–1911), Conolly evidently despaired of his prospects in London. On 4 December 1830 he abruptly and impetuously resigned his professorship, retreating once more to the provinces. Quickly finding that he could not resume his Stratford practice he was forced to move to Warwick, where for the next seven years he struggled to make his way, joining the new Provincial Medical and Surgical Association (later the British Medical Association) and co-editing, with John Forbes, the *Cyclopaedia of Practical Medicine*. Again he had little success as a clinician, and again he responded by impulsively seeking a radical change, applying in 1838 (much to the consternation of his friends) for the vacant post of superintendent of the Hanwell County Asylum in Middlesex. His progressive politics and active espousal of working-class education offended conservative members of the Middlesex bench, however, and he narrowly lost the election to an army surgeon, J. R. Millingen.

Little to this point suggested that Conolly would become more than an obscure historical footnote, let alone the most famous alienist of his generation. Within a year, however, Millingen's regime at Hanwell had proved a catastrophic failure, and when the magistrates demanded his resignation, Conolly secured the post that had previously eluded him. Within months of his arrival in the autumn of 1839 he became the focus of national and even international attention, following his announcement that all forms of mechanical restraint—chains, manacles, strait-jackets, and the like—had been destroyed, and replaced by a purely moral suasion and discipline. The new system of non-restraint was initially controversial. Many of Conolly's fellow alienists insisted that restraint was essential in the therapeutics of mental disorder. Others rallied to the abolitionist cause, however, notably *The Times* and Thomas Wakley, the crusading editor of *The Lancet*. When Lord Ashley (leader of the parliamentary forces pressing for lunacy reform) was also won over, success was assured—as was Conolly's own position at the head of the newly emerging group of experts in the treatment of the mad. Elected a fellow of the Royal College of Physicians in 1844, he was subsequently the recipient of an honorary DCL from Oxford University, and was fêted at the annual gathering of the Provincial Medical and Surgical Association in 1850.

Such extraordinary praise and recognition suggest that Conolly's achievement had a symbolic significance for the Victorian bourgeoisie that extended far beyond its contribution to the welfare of the mad. Confronted by the threats of Chartism and a militant working class, surrounded by the all but inescapable evidence of the devastating impact of industrial capitalism on the social and physical landscape, and themselves the authors of a new poor law assailed by its critics as the very embodiment of inhumanity and meanness of spirit, the Victorian governing classes could at least find a source of pride in the generous and kindly treatment now accorded to the lunatic. By demonstrating that even the irrational and raving could be reduced to docility, and without resort to force, Conolly appeared to have richly earned his audience's applause.

Oddly enough, non-restraint was not Conolly's innovation at all. The approach had been pioneered in 1838 in a small provincial asylum in Lincoln by an obscure house surgeon, Robert Gardiner Hill. Conolly visited Lincoln before taking up his appointment at Hanwell and noted his admiration of Hill's system in the visitors' book. In later years, however, he and his metropolitan allies systematically obscured Hill's claims as the originator of the system, arousing the latter's largely impotent fury.

Despite his inability to manage his own financial affairs with even a modicum of skill, Conolly proved an able administrator of the huge pauper establishment at Hanwell, a ramshackle and overcrowded poor law asylum that prefigured the overgrown 'museums of madness' that were to constitute the Victorians' response to the problems posed by the lunatic. Despite its dismally low cure rate and continuous overcrowding, his asylum was widely regarded as a splendid advertisement for lunacy reform, and Conolly himself, once publicly opposed to segregating the insane into specialized institutions save as a last resort, now became one of the most vigorous advocates of an expanded network of asylums.

Conolly's lectures in *The Lancet*, 'On the construction and government of lunatic asylums', were republished as a monograph in 1847. Even before their appearance, however, Conolly's connections with Hanwell had been sharply attenuated. In 1844 the Middlesex magistrates, always inclined to meddle in the administration of their asylum, decided to divide the task of running Hanwell, restricting Conolly's responsibilities to the medical treatment of the patients, and entrusting primary authority over the day-to-day administration of the asylum to a layman and retired army officer, John Godwin. Viewing these arrangements as an intolerable affront, Conolly had promptly resigned, accepting, as a face-saving gesture for both sides, a subsequent appointment as visiting physician (a position he would eventually relinquish in 1852).

Forced to seek an alternative means of earning his livelihood, Conolly's situation was made the more desperate by pressing domestic worries. His wife, Elizabeth, had simply disappeared from public view at about the time he took up his initial appointment at Hanwell. There have been published suggestions, based on purely circumstantial evidence, that she may herself have become insane. Certainly, she lived apart from him for much of her life, her death occurring four months after his, on 19 July 1866, while being cared for in lodgings in Hill Street, Knightsbridge, London. Besides whatever financial and emotional strain his wife's circumstances may have represented, Conolly's children constituted a continuing and even a growing financial burden. Though his oldest daughter, Eliza, had married an impoverished missionary to China, William Goodall, in 1842, his other two daughters were still his dependants, as was his feckless son, Edward Tennyson. Sophia Jane married Conolly's fellow alienist, Thomas Harrington Tuke, in 1852, but her departure from the household was more than offset when her wayward brother fathered an illegitimate child, and then six more children after his marriage in 1855, all the while failing to find gainful employment and remaining essentially dependent upon paternal largesse.

Despite the fierce attacks Conolly had made as a young man on the practice of 'trading in lunacy', he thus had little alternative but to enter the mad-business. Securing a licence to open his Hanwell residence, The Lawn, as a private asylum for the reception of up to six 'insane ladies', he supplemented his income from this source with appearances as an expert witness, both in criminal cases where the insanity defence was raised, and in chancery court inquisitions in lunacy, where the sanity of sundry socially prominent people was litigated. Not always scrupulous about observing the technicalities of the lunacy laws, Conolly was on occasion successfully sued for damages for false imprisonment. Nor did he make an impressive expert witness, being excoriated as all too prone to consign the immoral or merely eccentric to the ranks of the insane.

During his years in private practice, Conolly wrote a lengthy monograph on *The Treatment of the Insane without Mechanical Restraints* (1856). His model of asylum practice had by this time become the ruling orthodoxy, particularly in the expanding county asylum system, and his standing as the doyen of alienists was recognized by his election in 1859 as president of their professional society, the Association of Medical Officers of Asylums and Hospitals for the Insane (a post he had previously held in 1844). By 1860 he had largely abandoned private practice for retirement. He worked intermittently on *A Study of Hamlet* (1863)—a book devoted to demonstrating that the prince was indeed mad—and enjoyed the flattering attentions of a small group of ambitious young alienists who gathered regularly at his house. One of their number, Henry Maudsley (1835–1918), a cold and cynical man who would soon succeed Conolly as the leading English alienist, married his daughter Anne Caroline in January 1866.

For several years Conolly's health had been deteriorating. It now worsened sharply. On 4 March 1866 he suffered a series of seizures, culminating in a massive stroke that led to his death the next day at The Lawn, Hanwell. He was buried at Kensington Hanwell cemetery, Ealing, Middlesex.   ANDREW SCULL

Sources A. Scull, C. MacKenzie, and N. Hervey, *Masters of Bedlam: the transformation of the mad-doctoring trade* (1996) · H. Maudsley, 'Memoir of the late John Conolly', *Journal of Mental Science*, 12 (1866), 151–74 · R. Hunter and I. Macalpine, editorial introduction, in J. Conolly, *An inquiry into the indications of insanity* (1964) · R. Hunter and I. Macalpine, editorial introduction, in J. Conolly, *On the construction and government of lunatic asylums* (1968) · R. Hunter and I. Macalpine, editorial introduction, in J. Conolly, *The treatment of the insane without mechanical restraints* (1973) · D. Leigh, *The historical development of British psychiatry* (1961) · E. Burrows, 'Alienists' wives: the strange case of Mrs. John Conolly', *History of Psychiatry*, 9 (1998), 291–301 · d. cert. · d. cert. [Elizabeth Conolly]
Archives UCL, letters; letters to Society for the Diffusion of Useful Knowledge | Yale U., Beinecke L., letters to T. J. Pettigrew
Likenesses G. M. Benzoni, marble bust, 1866, RCP Lond. · T. S., wood-engraving, 1866, Wellcome L. · T. M. Baynes, lithograph (after T. Kirkby), Wellcome L. · Maull & Polyblank, photograph, Wellcome L. · W. Walker, mezzotint (after J. Watson-Gordon, exh. RA 1851), BM, NPG [*see illus.*] · portrait, repro. in Scull, MacKenzie, and Hervey, *Masters of Bedlam* · wood-engraving, NPG; repro. in *ILN* (31 March 1866)
Wealth at death under £3000: probate, 30 April 1866, *CGPLA Eng. & Wales*

Conolly, John Balfour (d. 1842). *See under* Conolly, Arthur (1807–1842?).

Conolly [*née* Lennox], **Lady Louisa Augusta** (1743–1821), noblewoman and philanthropist, was born on 24 November 1743, the fifth of the seven surviving children of Charles *Lennox, second duke of Richmond and Lennox (1701–1750), and his wife, Sarah (1706–1751), daughter of William *Cadogan, Earl Cadogan. Louisa spent her early years at Goodwood House, Sussex, but occasionally visited London, where she and her sister Sarah [see Napier, Lady Sarah] became favourites of George II. Following the deaths of her parents Louisa, Sarah, and their younger sister Cecilia were sent to Carton, co. Kildare, and placed under the guardianship of their older sister Emily *Fitzgerald, countess of Kildare. Louisa remained there until her marriage, on 30 December 1758 at the age of fifteen, to Thomas *Conolly (1738–1803), owner of the adjoining estate of Castletown, co. Kildare, and reputed to be the richest man in Ireland (in the 1770s his rentals came to £25,000 p.a.). Mary Delany recorded that, in order to marry Conolly, Louisa had turned down Garrett Wesley, second baron of Mornington, for a man who had 'double his fortune and perhaps half his merit' (Fitzgerald, *Emily, Duchess of Leinster*, 63). This was a harsh judgement, however; though the couple had no children (they adopted Louisa's niece Emily Napier c.1785) their union was happy and Louisa was to devote considerable time and effort to enhancing Castletown House and demesne, the largest in Ireland at that time, and to charitable endeavours within the locality.

In 1758 Castletown was a sturdy but undecorated structure, unfinished inside, with no hothouses, nurseries, or landscaping. Over the next twenty-five years Louisa presided over the installation of a new staircase, paved hall, plastered walls (some by Paul and Philip Lafranchini), a print room, and the famous long gallery, decorated in the fashionable Pompeiian style, for the completion of which Louisa brought over from England Thomas Riley, pupil of Joshua Reynolds. She also had the garden redesigned, with the largest cedar in Ireland and the biggest vine (after Hampton Court) in the British Isles. Castletown and the Conollys' Dublin town house cost between £2500 and £3000 p.a. to run and became famous centres of entertaining. By the end of the eighteenth century eighty-two people regularly dined at Castletown: sixty in the servants' hall, twelve in the steward's room, and ten in the parlour. Castletown became an almost living symbol of the protestant ascendancy in Ireland. It was reputed that the devil himself had eaten there, and was discovered only when Thomas Conolly noted his cloven hoofs and was compelled to send for the local priest to get rid of him.

Despite his wealth and social position Conolly refused to take a title in case his independence was compromised.

Lady Louisa Augusta Conolly [Lennox] (1743–1821), by Allan Ramsay, 1759

Nevertheless when his brother-in-law John Hobart, second earl of Buckinghamshire, was made lord lieutenant of Ireland in 1776 Louisa found herself besieged with people seeking favours. She declared: 'If I had the appointing of all Lord Buckinghamshire's family and the naming of all his tradesmen, I could not satisfy one half of the requests made to me' (Fitzgerald, *Lady Louisa Conolly*, 101). However, when many of those condemned to death during Buckinghamshire's lieutenancy approached her to plead for their reprieve she refused to let herself become involved.

While Louisa was not reckoned to be the beauty her sisters Emily and Sarah were, she was still handsome, being tall and well built, despite suffering from mild deafness following illness in 1769. In the 1750s the countess of Kildare said of her: 'I really think that in my life I never knew or heard of anything equal to the sweetness and gentleness of her disposition! She is indeed as yet quite an angel' (Tillyard, 110). Louisa had a strong religious faith and family correspondence shows that it was usually she who attempted to heal rifts in the Richmond and Leinster family circles. In the wider world, two or three times a year during the warmer months Castletown demesne was decked out for fêtes for servants, locals, and work people or for grander affairs in aid of charitable institutions. In

later life Louisa started to visit labourers and their families who lived in Celbridge, the village on the Castletown estate.

Her concern for the estate workers led Louisa to feel that local involvement in the Irish rising of 1798 was a personal betrayal. In 1795 she had gone to each house in Celbridge and asked every householder to desist from becoming involved in the current political problems. She also made a list of those who pledged support in the outbreak of trouble. Unfortunately this useless test of loyalty served only to identify her with the government forces, a perception that was heightened when she permitted the army to search Castletown for weapons in March 1798. In the following month she again visited each home in Celbridge, trying to persuade the inhabitants to give up their arms. On 26 May 1798 200 rebels with pikes marched across Castletown lawn. They locked the gates at either side of the park, sent word that they would harm no one, then left to join the rebel army. Louisa put Castletown into a state of defence and commenced a journal of the rebellion, which she stopped a few days later, as it was 'too full of misery to continue' (Tillyard, 388).

Louisa was further brought into the events of 1798 when her nephew Lord Edward Fitzgerald was arrested in May for treason. His mother, the duchess of Leinster, was in England at the time, so Louisa contrived to visit him on his deathbed. She reported how she knelt at the feet of the lord lieutenant, John Jeffreys Pratt, second Earl Camden, to entreat him to grant her access to her nephew, but was refused. However, the lord chancellor, John FitzGibbon, first earl of Clare, took her to the prison and there she comforted Lord Edward. Three hours after her departure he died. Louisa arranged his funeral, held in the dead of night to prevent riots, in St Werburgh's Church, Dublin. To the end she never believed him to be guilty of treason but instead to have been led astray by the enthusiasms of others. Conolly shared his wife's disenchantment with the deterioration of Irish politics in the 1790s. He largely withdrew from politics, except for giving disinterested advice on the possibility of an act of union. On 27 April 1803 he died of influenza while being held in Louisa's arms.

Louisa devoted her widowhood to relieving the plight of the poor. This entailed massive investment on the estate, despite the fact that her husband had left substantial debts; indeed in 1808 it was proposed to sell Castletown as a barracks, but the government felt that the asking price of £38,000 was too high. In 1813 she built a church in Celbridge, at the gates of the Castletown estate, which had separate seating for the girls of the female charter school that she supported. Then, aged seventy, she embarked on a trip to the Netherlands and Brussels, where she investigated various charitable institutions. In 1814, following her return, she expanded Celbridge's local educational establishment into an industrial school devoted to teaching boys carpentry, shoemaking, tailoring, and basket making, while girls learned domestic husbandry and economy. By May 1820 the interdenominational school provided an education for 300 children, staggered in groups of 75.

On her estate Louisa constructed workshops, breweries, and bakeshops, interested herself in a chip-hat factory at Celbridge, and built a giant press for extracting oil from beech nuts, almonds, and walnuts. She designed every building erected at Castletown, and all the materials came from the demesne. Following the Napoleonic wars she employed as many workers on the estate as possible; it was said that Castletown was like a small town of the feudal ages, and that Louisa was the lady of the castle.

When Louisa died at Castletown in August 1821, aged seventy-seven, after suffering an abscess on the hip, the local people sought permission to view her body before it was buried, and hundreds of people from all over the country attended her funeral. A few weeks later the Roman Catholic men of Celbridge sent her niece and adopted daughter, Emily Napier, an address, signed by seventeen men on behalf of the whole parish, containing a tribute to Louisa's religious tolerance and practical liberality. The estate was inherited by Conolly's nephew Thomas Pakenham.　　　　　　　　　　ROSEMARY RICHEY

Sources S. Tillyard, *Aristocrats: Caroline, Emily, Louisa and Sarah Lennox, 1740–1832*, new edn (1995) · B. Fitzgerald, *Lady Louisa Conolly, 1743–1821: an Anglo-Irish biography* (1950) · E. O. Blackburne, *Illustrious Irishwomen* (1877), vol. 2 · B. Fitzgerald, *Emily, duchess of Leinster, 1731–1814: a study of her life and times* (1949) · R. W. Bond, ed., *The Marlay letters* (1937) · *GM*, 1st ser., 13 (1743), 612

Archives TCD, papers | BL, Holland House MSS · Bodl. Oxf., Napier MSS · Irish Georgian Society, Dublin, Bunbury letterbook · NL Ire., letters to her sister Emily, duchess of Leinster · Suffolk RO, transcripts of Bunbury letter-book · Terling Place, Waltham, Essex, Strutt MSS

Likenesses A. Ramsay, oils, 1759; priv. coll. [*see illus.*] · J. Reynolds, oils, 1764, repro. in Tillyard, *Aristocrats*; priv. coll. · Healy, oils, 1768 (with husband), repro. in Tillyard, *Aristocrats*; priv. coll. · portrait, 1768 (with gamekeeper), repro. in Tillyard, *Aristocrats*; priv. coll. · portrait, 1770–79, repro. in Tillyard, *Aristocrats*; priv. coll. · portrait, 1780–89, repro. in Tillyard, *Aristocrats*; priv. coll.

Wealth at death £10,000 from father's will, 1750; lands at £6178 p.a. in rent to provide for widow's jointure from marriage settlement, 1758; husband left her Castletown for life and a jointure of £2500 p.a. in 1803

Conolly, Thomas (1738–1803), politician, was born probably in Castletown, co. Kildare, Ireland, the only son of William Conolly (*d.* 1753), MP for Ballyshannon from 1727 until his death in 1753, and Lady Anne Wentworth (*d.* 1797), eldest daughter of Thomas Wentworth, first earl of Strafford of the second creation. The fortunes of the Conolly family in Ireland had been founded by William Conolly (1662–1729), speaker of the Irish House of Commons. He left all his property to his nephew, Thomas Conolly's father. Thomas had four sisters, Catherine, countess of Rosse; Frances, Viscountess Howe; Caroline, who married John Hobart, second earl of Buckinghamshire, and whose daughter, Amelia, later married Lord Castlereagh; and Anne, who married George Byng of Torrington.

After schooling at Westminster (1750–54), Conolly married on 30 December 1758 Louisa Augusta Lennox [*see* Conolly, Lady Louisa Augusta (1743–1821)], third daughter of Charles *Lennox, second duke of Richmond (1701–1750),

Thomas Conolly (1738–1803), by Anton Raphael Mengs, 1758

and his wife, Sarah Cadogan (*d.* 1751). She was the sister of Emily, duchess of Leinster, and Caroline Fox, Lady Holland. In 1759 Conolly was elected MP for Malmesbury in the British House of Commons, and in 1761 for Londonderry County in the Irish House of Commons, which seat he held until May 1800, resigning just before the union. He showed little ability in either house, but from his wealth and connections possessed influence in Ireland, where he held various offices, such as lord of the Treasury, commissioner of trade, and lord lieutenant of the county of Londonderry, and where he was sworn of the privy council in 1784. After sitting for Malmesbury until 1768, and for Chichester, through the influence of his father-in-law, from 1768 to 1780, in the British House of Commons, he gave up his seat in that house, and took up residence permanently at Castletown.

Conolly declared himself to be a whig, but his whiggism was frequently put to the test. In 1774 the Presbyterians of co. Londonderry, including his tenants at Newtownlimavady, were incensed by his support of the Vestry Act, and threatened to oppose him in the 1776 election with an independent candidate. Conolly came to terms with the dissenters. The independent withdrew and he was re-elected for the county of Londonderry. In 1775 he had embraced the cause of the American colonists, but he remained ambivalent towards the Irish volunteer movement, supporting its reform programme in general but becoming nervous when it seemed to impinge on the interests of the Irish aristocracy. In 1788 he was prominent in the revolt of the Irish House of Commons against the ministry, and was one of the members deputed to offer the prince of Wales the regency without any restrictions whatever. This independence lost him his seat at the Board of Trade, but his influence remained so great that he was one of the ten chief persons in Ireland to whom Cornwallis broached the first idea of a legislative union with England in 1798. Cornwallis, in his dispatch of 27 November 1798, wrote that he had consulted seven leading peers, the attorney- and solicitor-general, and Conolly on the subject, and that 'Mr. Conolly had always been a decided friend to an union, and was ready to give it his best assistance' (C. Cornwallis, *Correspondence*, ed. C. Ross, 1859, 2.450). Conolly threw himself warmly into the debates on the question, doubtless under the influence of Castlereagh, who had married his niece Lady Amelia Anne Hobart, and several times spoke in favour of the measure, which, however, extinguished his own political importance.

On the passing of the union Conolly decided to abandon politics, for, though he might easily have been returned for Londonderry to the united parliament, he preferred to hand over the seat to Colonel Charles Stewart, Castlereagh's half-brother. He retired to Castletown in 1800, where he began to suffer acute depression, partly a reaction to the events of the rebellion of 1798 and to a lawsuit with his sisters and Lord Howe, the executors of his mother's will, over settlements due to them out of his English estates. He left Castletown in the summer of 1801 and spent some time in Brighton and London in an attempt to recover his health. He died on 27 April 1803 at Castletown, where he was buried. He was succeeded by his nephew, George Byng, MP for Middlesex, who inherited the estates in Ireland and Castletown. His widow, Lady Louisa Conolly, lived until 1821, and helped to educate her nephews, the children of her sister Lady Sarah Napier, who resided near Castletown.

Although his inheritance made Conolly the richest man in Ireland and the most influential in parliamentary terms, he never used these advantages effectively in politics. Almost alone among the great figures of the protestant ascendancy, he ended his life without a peerage, preferring to be respected as 'Squire Conolly', a conscientious landlord and master of foxhounds. Jonah Barrington, in his *Historic Anecdotes*, devoted some pages to Conolly, in which he criticized his attitude to the union rather unfavourably, and thus analysed the causes of his influence:

> Mr. Conolly had the largest connection of any individual in the commons house. He fancied he was a whig because he was not professedly a tory; bad as a statesman, worse as an orator, he was as a sportsman pre-eminent. ... He was nearly allied to the Irish minister [Castlereagh] at the time of the discussion of the union, and he followed his lordship's fortune, surrendered his country, lost his own importance, died in comparative obscurity, and in his person ended the pedigree of one of the most respectable English families ever resident in Ireland. (Barrington, 265–7)

H. M. STEPHENS, *rev.* A. T. Q. STEWART

Sources E. M. Johnston-Liik, *History of the Irish parliament, 1692–1800*, 6 vols. (2002) • S. Tillyard, *Aristocrats: Caroline, Emily, Louisa and Sarah Lennox, 1740–1832*, new edn (1995) • *Correspondence of Emily, duchess of Leinster (1731–1814)*, ed. B. Fitzgerald, 3 vols., IMC (1949–57) • *The manuscripts of his grace the duke of Rutland*, 4 vols., HMC, 24 (1888–1905) • *Report on the manuscripts of Mrs Stopford-Sackville*, 2 vols., HMC, 49 (1904–10) • *Report on the manuscripts of the marquess of Lothian*, HMC, 62 (1905) • L. Boylan, 'The Conollys of Castletown', *Quarterly Bulletin of the Irish Georgian Society*, 11/4 (1968), 1–46 • PRO NIre., Castlereagh MSS • E. M. Johnston, *Great Britain and Ireland, 1760–1800* (1963) • R. B. McDowell, *Irish public opinion, 1750–1800* (1944) • R. B. McDowell, *Ireland in the age of imperialism and revolution, 1760–1801* (1979) • T. Bartlett and D. W. Hayton, eds., *Penal era and golden age: essays in Irish history, 1690–1800* (1979) • J. Barrington, *Historic anecdotes and secret memoirs of the legislative union between Great Britain and Ireland* (1809) • *GM*, 1st ser., 73 (1803), 596

Archives NRA, priv. coll., corresp. • priv. coll., corresp. • PRO NIre., estate papers • TCD, corresp., family and estate MSS | Bodl. Oxf., Napier MSS • NL Ire., Leinster MSS • PRO NIre., corresp. with Lord Castlereagh • PRO NIre., corresp. with George Lenox-Conyngham

Likenesses A. R. Mengs, portrait, 1758, NG Ire. [*see illus.*] • J. Reynolds, oils, 1759, probably NPG; repro. in Tillyard, *Aristocrats* • J. Collyer, stipple, pubd 1796 (after R. Bull), NG Ire. • W. Sedgwick, stipple, pubd 1796 (after miniature by R. Bull, exh. RA 1796), NG Ire. • J. Collyer, stipple, pubd 1800 (after R. Bull), NPG • R. Healy, oils, repro. in Tillyard, *Aristocrats* • F. Wheatley, group portrait, oils (*The Irish House of Commons 1780*), Leeds City Art Gallery

Wealth at death left Castletown to Louisa for life plus £2500 p.a. jointure; £10,000 to children of her sister; but there were huge debts, income tax arrears, and interests on loans; Sir Thomas Pakenham, father of heir, said heir would receive nothing from property: Johnston, *History of the Irish parliament*

Conolly, William (1662–1729), speaker of the Irish House of Commons, was born in Ballyshannon, co. Donegal, Ireland, the eldest of the three children of Patrick Conolly and his wife, Jane, and brother of Patrick and Jane. Tradition has it that Conolly's father was either a publican or a blacksmith. This is unlikely, however, since William and his father are named on the list of Irish protestants whose land was declared forfeit by the Jacobite parliament of 1689. It is more likely that the Conollys were a minor Catholic gentry family who converted to Anglicanism some time before 1660. William Conolly studied law in Dublin, qualified as an attorney, was attached to the court of common pleas in 1685, and was land agent to Captain James Hamilton between 1692 and 1700. He was elected to the Irish House of Commons as MP for Donegal borough (1692–3 and 1695–9). In 1694 he married Katherine Conyngham, daughter of Sir Albert Conyngham and sister of Henry Conyngham of Mount Charles, co. Donegal. This marriage connected Conolly to the most important families in west Ulster. William and Katherine were childless but he was said to have had an illegitimate son who died in 1727, aged eight (PRO, C 110/46/528).

Conolly's career was founded upon successful land speculation. He used Katherine's dowry of £2300 to buy his first estates in co. Meath, and made his fortune during the 1690s by buying and acting as agent for the sale of forfeited Jacobite estates. The acquisition of an estate in Limavady gave him a valuable electoral interest in co. Londonderry, where he was collector of the revenue (1697–1729) and sat as MP from 1703 until his death. He rose to national prominence during the party conflict of the early 1700s, when he emerged as a leading figure in the Irish whig party. The whig lord lieutenant, Thomas, earl of

William Conolly (1662–1729), by Pierre Fourdrinier, in or after 1729 (after Charles Jervas, c.1720)

Wharton, appointed him a revenue commissioner and an Irish privy councillor in 1709. In 1710, however, he was dismissed by the tory duke of Ormond, and, he was removed from the privy council the following year.

Following the return to power of the whigs in 1714 Conolly was restored to the privy council and revenue board and was persuaded to stand as the government's candidate for speaker of the Irish House of Commons. He was elected unanimously on 12 November 1715 and quickly became a leading figure in the management of the Commons. He formed close relationships with the duke of Grafton, lord justice in 1715–16, and chief secretaries, Charles Delafaye and Martin Bladen. His hitherto friendly relationship with the lord chancellor, Lord Brodrick, first Viscount Midleton, however, rapidly deteriorated. Previously regarded as leader of the Irish whig party, Brodrick resented Conolly's emergence as chief manager or 'undertaker' of the government's parliamentary business. Brodrick's fortunes temporarily recovered with the appointment of his ally, the duke of Bolton, as viceroy in 1717. Conolly, however, continued to support the court in parliament and was appointed as a lord justice when Bolton left for England. A dispute between Brodrick and the ministry over Sunderland's Peerage Bill allowed Conolly to resume his position as chief undertaker when Bolton returned to Ireland in 1719. The speaker's position was strengthened with the appointment of the duke of Grafton as viceroy in 1720. Conolly's influence was so great during Grafton's viceroyalty that he was described as 'Prime Minister' (Wake MSS, 14, fol. 48). However, this viceroyalty witnessed the greatest crisis in Anglo-Irish

relations in the first half of the eighteenth century when opposition to 'Wood's halfpence' made the normal means of managing the Irish parliament impracticable. The intensity of popular opposition to the copper halfpence forced the normally loyal Conolly to desert the government in order to retain his political credibility in Ireland.

The replacement of Grafton by John, second Baron Carteret, in 1724 seriously threatened Conolly's position as chief undertaker. An ally of the Brodricks, Carteret was unlikely to place much faith in the speaker's loyalty and his investigations into the government's accounts provoked rumours that Conolly would soon be dismissed. For a year after his arrival in Ireland, Carteret remained aloof from both Conolly and Brodrick, and he provoked the latter's resignation as lord chancellor in April 1725. However, after having lost control of the House of Commons soon after the start of the parliamentary session of 1725 Carteret turned to Conolly to be his parliamentary manager. With Brodrick's resignation Conolly's position was stronger than ever and his dominant position in parliament was secure until his death. Re-elected as speaker in the first session of George II's parliament, he served until he collapsed in the Commons on 26 September 1729; he resigned as speaker on 13 October. A contemporary wrote on 25 October that Conolly 'has a great looseness that can't be stop'd has been twice blisterd for it. is something better this day, but its thought cannot live' (PRO, C 110/46/728–9). Conolly died at his house in Capel Street, Dublin, on 30 October 1729 and was buried at Celbridge, co. Kildare. After his wife's death Conolly was succeeded by his nephew, William Conolly.

Conolly remains an elusive figure in terms of his personality. His rival, Brodrick, repeatedly accused him of sycophancy. Jonathan Swift was even more scathing:

> There was a fellow in Ireland called Conolly, who from a shoe-boy grew to be several times one of the chief Governors, wholly illiterate, and with hardly common sence. a Lord Lieutenant told the first K. George, that Conolly was the greatest subject he had in both Kingdoms, and truly this Character was gotten and preserved by Conolly's never appearing in England, which was the only wise thing he ever did except purchasing sixteen thousand pounds a year. (*Correspondence*, 3.493–4)

Other contemporaries, normally government supporters, gave a more positive assessment. The English-born bishop of Derry, William Nicolson, described Conolly as 'a person of wonderful parts and temper' (BL, Add. MS 6116, fols. 91–2). Conolly was certainly adept at keeping in with those in power, realizing that political power in Ireland depended upon retaining the backing of the ministry in London. During the whig schism of the early years of George I's reign he kept close connections with the Townshend–Walpole faction while also maintaining a good relationship with the earl of Sunderland, who protected the speaker during Bolton's viceroyalty. Recognizing, but affecting to despise, Conolly's skill in this respect, Brodrick complained that he was 'a happy man who by wishing well to and acting for one set of men renders or keeps himself gracious with the other' (Midleton MSS, 4, fols. 92–4).

The true significance of Conolly's career is that between 1715 and 1729 he established a precedent for the government of Ireland for most of the eighteenth century. The first of the great 'undertakers' who dominated Irish politics until the 1760s at least, he set the pattern for his successors. As speaker, chief revenue commissioner, and lord justice he normally controlled the proceedings of the Commons, had unrivalled access to revenue patronage, and directly communicated with the British ministry. His career illustrates the relatively open nature of the early eighteenth-century Irish élite. Of relatively humble origins, he single-handedly established an Anglo-Irish dynasty and was reputed on his death to be the wealthiest man in Ireland, allegedly worth £17,000 p.a. (*Letters ... Boulter*, 1.267). The physical manifestation of Conolly's career is his great house at Castletown, co. Kildare.

PATRICK MCNALLY

Sources L. Boylan, 'The Conollys of Castletown', *Quarterly Bulletin of the Irish Georgian Society*, 11/4 (1968), 1–46 · 'Introduction', PRO NIre., Castletown MSS · P. McNally, *Parties, patriots and undertakers: parliamentary politics in early Hanoverian Ireland* (1997) · D. W. Hayton, 'The beginnings of the "undertaker system"', *Penal era and golden age: essays in Irish history, 1690–1800*, ed. T. Bartlett and D. W. Hayton (1979), 32–54 · *The correspondence of Jonathan Swift*, ed. H. Williams, 3 (1963), 493–4 · P. McNally, 'Wood's halfpence, Carteret and the government of Ireland, 1723–26', *Irish Historical Studies*, 30 (1996–7), 354–76 · D. W. Hayton, 'Walpole and Ireland', *Britain in the age of Walpole*, ed. J. Black (1984), 95–119 · S. J. Connolly, *Religion, law, and power: the making of protestant Ireland, 1660–1760* (1992) · D. Hayton, 'Two ballads on the county Westmeath by-election of 1723', *Eighteenth-Century Ireland*, 4 (1989), 7–30 · Viscount Midleton to Thomas Brodrick, 11 Nov 1717, Surrey RO, Midleton MSS, 4, fols. 92–4 · William Nicolson to William Wake, 31 Oct 1719, BL, Add. MS 6116, fols. 91–2 · T. Godwin to W. Wake, 16 Jan 1723, Christ Church Oxf., Wake MS 14, fol. 48 · Owen Gallagher to Oliver St George, 14 Dec 1727, PRO, C 110/46/528 · Owen Gallagher to Oliver St George, 25 Oct 1729, PRO, C 110/46/728–9 · *Letters written by ... Hugh Boulter ... to several ministers of state*, ed. [A. Philips and G. Faulkner], 2 vols. (1769–70); repr. (1770), vol. 1, p. 267
Archives PRO NIre. · PRO NIre., letters, T 3161/12 | Irish Georgian Society, Castletown, co. Kildare, Ireland, Castletown MSS [microfilm copies in NL Ire.] · NL Ire., letters to Jane Bonnell · PRO, state papers Ireland · TCD, corresp. with William King
Likenesses P. Fourdrinier, line engraving, in or after 1729 (after C. Jervas, *c.*1720), NG Ire. [*see illus.*] · C. Jervas, portrait, *c.*1729, Castletown, co. Kildare · T. Carter, mezzotint, NG Ire. · T. Carter, monument, Celbridge church, co. Kildare · P. Fourdrinier, line engraving, AM Oxf., BM, NG Ire.
Wealth at death approx. £17,000 p.a.: *Letters written by his excellency*, vol. 1, p. 267; Owen Gallagher to Oliver St George, PRO, C 110/46/732–3

Conquest [*formerly* Oliver], **George Augustus** (1837–1901), actor and playwright, was born at a house adjoining the old Garrick Theatre, Leman Street, Goodman's Fields, London, on 8 May 1837. He was the eldest son of Benjamin Oliver (1805–1872), an actor and theatre manager, and his wife, Clarissa Ann, *née* Bennett, a dancer and ballet mistress. Benjamin Oliver, who used professionally the surname Conquest (which George adopted formally by deed poll in 1883), was manager of the Garrick Theatre, where in 1837, as a child in arms, George made his first appearance on the stage, in the farce *Mr and Mrs White*. He played there, while a child, in such pieces as *Peter the Waggoner*,

Isabella, or, The Fatal Marriage, and *The Stranger*. He was educated at the *collège communal*, Boulogne, where he was a contemporary of the eminent French actor Benoît Coquelin, and learned to speak fluent French. He was intended to be a violinist, but from his earliest years he resolved on the profession of acrobatic pantomimist. Before he left school he made numerous adaptations from the French for his father, who in 1851 became manager of the Grecian Theatre in City Road. His first play, *Woman's Secret, or, Richelieu's Wager*, was produced at the Grecian on 17 October 1853.

At Christmas 1855 Conquest appeared as a pantomimist for the first time, in his own pantomime *Harlequin Sun, Moon, and the Seven Sisters*, and at Easter 1857 he made his first notable success in this class of work as Hassarac, in Henry Spry's *The Forty Thieves*. In the same year he married Elizabeth Ozmond, and at Christmas he appeared as Pastrano Nonsuch, a 'flying pantomimist', in *Peter Wilkins and the Flying Indians*, which he wrote in collaboration with Spry. Conquest later effectively adapted Charles Reade's novel *It is Never too Late to Mend*, which ran for six months at his father's theatre, and in which he appeared as Peter Crawley. In 1861 he distinguished himself as Prince Pigmy in *The Blue Bird in Paradise*.

On his father's death in 1872 Conquest became manager of the Grecian and continued to fill leading parts there. In 1881 he joined Paul Merritt as co-lessee and manager of the Surrey Theatre, of which he was sole lessee and manager from 1885. His only appearances in the West End of London were at the Gaiety Theatre, in 1873, in *Snaefell*, and at the Globe, in 1882, in *Mankind*, where he showed his melodramatic power to good effect in the part of Daniel Groodge. Off the stage, he suffered from an impediment of speech, which disappeared when he was acting. He visited America in 1880, and opened his tour with *The Grim Goblin* at Wallack's Theatre, New York, on 5 August. While performing there in *Flying Fairy and Phantom Flight* he sustained severe injuries through the breaking of trapeze ropes, caused, it was stated, through the treachery of a rival.

Conquest was best known as an acrobatic pantomimist. He produced no fewer than forty-five pantomimes, and played in as many as twenty-seven. He impersonated animals with much popular approval, his most famous part being that of Zacky Pastrana, the man-monkey, in *For Ever*. He is said to have invented the method of 'flying' by means of 'invisible' wires. It was his boast that as a pantomimist he had broken every bone in his face and body. In his performance of the title role in *The Devil on Two Sticks* he employed no fewer than twenty-nine 'traps'—one 'vampire' and twenty-eight ordinary. He retired from the stage in 1894, but his three sons, George, Fred, and Arthur, all successfully adopted their father's calling, both as actors and acrobatic pantomimists.

Of the hundred and more plays, for the most part original melodramas or adaptations from the French, of which Conquest was the author, several were written in collaboration, and of these the more successful were *Velvet and Rags* (1874), *Mankind* (1881), and *For Ever* (1882), written with Merritt, and *Sentenced to Death* (1875), *Queen's Evidence* (1876), and *The Green Lanes of England* (1878), written with Henry Pettitt. His last play, *The Fighting Fifth*, written with Herbert Leonard, was produced at the Surrey Theatre in October 1900.

Conquest died from heart disease at his home, 'Hillsboro', 49 Brixton Hill, London, on 14 May 1901, leaving a fortune of over £70,000, and was buried at Norwood cemetery on 17 May.   J. PARKER, *rev.* NILANJANA BANERJI

Sources *The Era* (18 May 1901) · *The Era* (25 May 1901) · *Daily Telegraph* (15 May 1901) · P. Hartnoll, ed., *The concise Oxford companion to the theatre* (1972) · Adams, *Drama* · P. Hartnoll, ed., *The Oxford companion to the theatre* (1951); 2nd edn (1957); 3rd edn (1967) · C. Scott, *Thirty years at the play* (1890) · *The life and reminiscences of E. L. Blanchard, with notes from the diary of Wm. Blanchard*, ed. C. W. Scott and C. Howard, 2 vols. (1891) · C. E. Pascoe, ed., *The dramatic list*, 2nd edn (1880) · Hall, *Dramatic ports.* · d. cert. · personal knowledge (1912)
Likenesses A. Ellis, woodburytype photograph, *c.*1895, NPG · caricatures, woodcuts, Harvard TC; repro. in *Entr'acte* (1877–83) · carte-de-visite, NPG · engraving, repro. in *The Era* (18 May 1901) · engraving, repro. in *The Theatre* (Sept 1895)
Wealth at death £71,781 9s. 6d.: probate, 8 June 1901, CGPLA Eng. & Wales

Conquest, John Tricker (*bap.* **1789**, *d.* **1866**), man-midwife, was baptized on 25 November 1789 at Clover Street Independent Chapel, Chatham, Kent, the son of a Dr Conquest of Chatham. He entered medical training at an early age, qualifying as MRCS at the age of eighteen. He was appointed assistant surgeon to the military medical depot, Chatham, and to the Royal Marines, Brompton. Conquest graduated MD at Edinburgh in September 1813, and became licentiate of the Royal College of Physicians in December 1819. He commenced practice in London in 1814 and offered four courses of lectures on midwifery annually at his house, 4 Aldermanbury Postern, London, for a fee of 3 guineas. The lectures also covered the diseases of children and forensic medicine. In a few years he moved to 13 Finsbury Square, and in 1825 became lecturer on midwifery in the medical school of St Bartholomew's Hospital, succeeding Robert Gooch. Conquest was said to be an unpopular lecturer, and was persuaded to resign in 1834. Although holding several hospital posts, he was never appointed FRCP. He built up an extensive obstetric practice, and his posts included that of physician to the City of London Lying-in Hospital, the London Female Penitentiary, and the London Orphan Asylum, and consulting physician to the Stoke Newington and Stamford Hill Dispensary.

In 1820 Conquest's *Outlines of Midwifery*, intended as a textbook for students, was published. By 1854 it had passed through six editions and had been translated into several languages. In 1848 he published his popular *Letters to a Mother on the Management of Herself and her Children in Health and Disease*, which reached a fourth edition by 1852. The book covered the care of women in pregnancy and infant rearing, and also strongly advocated the use of chloroform in childbirth. Conquest's diverse interests included homoeopathy and the subject of the abuse of money, and he produced a revised edition of the Bible. Conquest was involved in the establishment of the City of

John Tricker Conquest (*bap.* 1789, *d.* 1866), by Maxim Gauci (after R. W. Warren)

London School and was honorary secretary to the Hunterian Society. In 1829 he presented a substantial collection of obstetrical preparations to the museum of St Bartholomew's Hospital. After retiring from practice, and following several years of deteriorating health and seclusion, he died, unmarried, at his home, The Oaks, Plumstead Common, Kent, on 24 October 1866.

                                                    HILARY MARLAND

Sources *BMJ* (10 Nov 1866), 519 · *BMJ* (17 Nov 1866), 564–5 · 'J. T. Conquest', *The Lancet* (3 Nov 1866), 511 · Munk, *Roll* · V. C. Medvei and J. L. Thornton, eds., *The royal hospital of Saint Bartholomew, 1123–1973* (1974) · P. Branca, *Silent sisterhood: middle-class women in the Victorian home* (1975) · CGPLA Eng. & Wales (1867) · DNB · IGI
Archives St Bartholomew's Hospital, London, collection of obstetrical preparations
Likenesses M. Gauci, lithograph (after painting by R. W. Warren), Wellcome L., iconographic collections [*see illus.*] · M. Gauci, lithograph (after T. Snellgrove), BM
Wealth at death under £40,000: probate, 18 May 1867, CGPLA Eng. & Wales

Conrad, Joseph [*formerly* Józef Teodor Konrad Korzeniowski] (**1857–1924**), master mariner and author, was born on 3 December 1857 at Berdyczów in Ukraine.

Early years Conrad was the only child of Apollo Korzeniowski (1820–1869); named on Conrad's marriage certificate as 'Joseph Theodore Apollonius Korzeniowski', writer and patriot, and his wife, Ewelina (or Ewa, *née* Bobrowska; 1832–1865): members of the Polish *szlachta*, a fusion of gentry and nobility. Nałęcz was the heraldic name of the Korzeniowski coat of arms. In a series of partitions (1772, 1793, and 1795) Poland had been annexed by Prussia and Austria–Hungary to the west and by Russia to the east, so that, by the time of Conrad's birth, the country had virtually disappeared from the map of Europe. His father and mother, dedicated Polish patriots, conspired against the oppressive Russian authorities. Apollo, who advocated the liberation of the serfs as well as national

Joseph Conrad (1857–1924), by George Charles Beresford, 1904

independence, was arrested; and in 1862 he and his wife were sentenced to exile in the remote Russian province of Vologda; their four-year-old son accompanied them. Ewa died of tuberculosis within three years. Apollo, who himself was suffering from this disease, died after four years as a widower; and his funeral, on 26 May 1869, became a huge patriotic demonstration: the Poles had not forgotten the ruthless suppression of the 1863 uprising. Conrad's uncle, Tadeusz Bobrowski, an astute landowner, became the orphan's guardian, and sustained him morally and financially for many years. To this Polish upbringing may be traced Conrad's later preoccupation with the themes of isolation, embattled honour, and political disillusionment.

Maritime career Conrad's education, of which the record remains incomplete, was irregular. His father had given him lessons; he apparently attended a preparatory school in Kraków and (briefly) a *Gymnasium* in Lwów (Lemberg); and private tuition was provided by Izydor Kopernicki and Adam Pulman. He certainly loved literature of travel and exploration, and this encouraged him to dream of becoming a seaman.

In 1874 the sixteen-year-old Conrad left Poland for Marseilles in France. There, for several years, he gained maritime experience, sailing the Atlantic as a passenger in the *Mont-Blanc* and as a steward in another barque, the *Saint-Antoine*. He later intimated that during this period he participated in a gun-running expedition for Colombian conservatives, and he also claimed to have smuggled arms in the two-masted *Tremolino* to Spanish legitimists. In 1878 Conrad attempted suicide with a pistol, wounding himself in the chest, for he was in debt after gambling at Monte Carlo. A related factor may have been the recognition that, as a Russian subject, he could legally serve on French vessels only with the permission of the Russian consul; and, since he was liable for imperial military service, such permission was unlikely to be granted. Subsequently in that year, therefore, he travelled to England

and entered the British mercantile marine. Initially employed humbly on a coasting vessel, the *Skimmer of the Sea*, he next found a berth on the wool clipper *Duke of Sutherland*, which plied between London and Sydney. During the following sixteen years, making numerous voyages on ships ranging from elegant three-masters to rusty steamers, he rose in rank: third mate, second mate, master. In 1886 he not only gained his master's certificate but also took British nationality. His voyages and the landfalls (in Bombay, Singapore, Celebes, Borneo, Mauritius, and other locations) were often to be commemorated in his eventual works, which pay tribute to maritime heroism in an era when deaths at sea were an everyday occurrence. He was shipwrecked when the decrepit barque *Palestine* caught fire and sank near Sumatra, an event to be romantically recalled in the tale 'Youth'; and his experiences as captain of the sailing ship *Otago*, plying between Bangkok, Melbourne, and Mauritius, provided bases for 'The Secret Sharer', 'A Smile of Fortune', and *The Shadow-Line*. A depressing African journey into the Congo Free State in 1890, when he travelled overland and in a paddle-steamer, would be recollected and powerfully transformed in his masterpiece 'Heart of Darkness'. (Having witnessed colonialist corruption, he later aided Roger Casement and E. D. Morel in their international campaign against the cruelty of the Belgian regime to Africans.) Increasingly, as steam superseded sail and as vessels became larger and more efficient, Conrad encountered difficulty in finding employment commensurate with his qualifications, and his maritime career petered out in 1894. Subsequent attempts to return to sea proved unavailing. A large bequest from Tadeusz Bobrowski, however, facilitated his change of career.

Literary career until 1900 In his spare time Conrad had been working on his first novel, *Almayer's Folly*. On the advice of W. H. Chesson and Edward Garnett, this was accepted by the publisher T. Fisher Unwin and published in 1895. Reviews were numerous, often lengthy; and, though they were mixed, praise predominated. *The Spectator*, noting the atmospheric power of this work set in Borneo, prophesied that Conrad might become 'the Kipling of the Malay Archipelago' (19 Oct 1895, p. 530). Before that first publication, Conrad had begun *An Outcast of the Islands*, which appeared in 1896; again, the reviews included sufficient high praise to confirm him in the choice of the literary career. He had established a strong identity as a writer of exotic, adventurous fiction who brought to the material a sophisticated, ironic, sceptically reflective mind, acute political awareness, and distinctive stylistic virtuosity. His recurrent themes were human isolation, beleaguered solidarity, the vanity of romantic aspirations, the myopia of racial prejudice, and the recognition that loyalty to one principle may entail treachery to another.

Then came several false starts. Conrad began *The Sisters*, of which only the opening was ever finished, and *The Rescuer* (later *The Rescue*), a novel which proved so difficult that he took more than twenty years to complete it. In 1896–7 he published in magazines the highly uneven quartet of tales ('Karain', 'The Lagoon', 'The Idiots', and the satiric masterpiece 'An Outpost of Progress') which, with the cumbrously analytic story 'The Return', comprises the volume *Tales of Unrest* (issued in 1898).

On 24 March 1896 Conrad married Jessie Emmeline George (1873–1936), a typist, daughter of Alfred Henry George, bookseller. Their two sons, Borys and John, were born in 1898 and 1906, during the period when Conrad was the tenant of Pent Farm, near Hythe in Kent. Jessie proved to be resourcefully supportive to her highly strung and temperamental husband, although her subsequent memoirs gave telling glimpses of his sometimes neurotic, irascible, and demanding conduct. Conrad's friends and acquaintances during the first decade of his literary career included Edward Garnett (the most perceptive and persuasively enthusiastic of his reviewers), Edward Sanderson, H. G. Wells, Stephen Crane, John Galsworthy, and Ford Madox Hueffer (who changed his surname to Ford in 1919). A particularly sustaining friendship was with R. B. Cunninghame Graham, the aristocratic socialist and adventurer. William Blackwood, the proprietor of *Blackwood's Edinburgh Magazine*, proved to be a crucially generous publisher.

> Garnett describes thus the Conrad of this time:
>
> My memory is of seeing a dark-haired man, short but extremely graceful in his nervous gestures, with brilliant eyes, now narrowed and penetrating, now soft and warm, with a manner alert yet caressing, whose speech was ingratiating, guarded, and brusque turn by turn. I had never seen before a man so masculinely keen yet so femininely sensitive. (Garnett, vii)

The major phase Conrad's major phase as a writer extends from 1897 to 1911. It includes *The Nigger of the 'Narcissus'* (serialized and published as a book in 1897), 'Youth' (serial, 1898), *Lord Jim* (serial, 1898–9; book, 1899), 'Heart of Darkness' (serialized 1899), *Youth* (a volume containing 'Youth', 'Heart of Darkness', and 'The End of the Tether', 1902), *Typhoon* (serial and book, 1902), *Nostromo* (serial and book, 1904), *The Secret Agent* (serial and book, 1907), 'The Secret Sharer' (serial, 1910), and *Under Western Eyes* (serial and book, 1911). This is a period of astonishing range and richness. With *Under Western Eyes* he even dared to challenge (and arguably surpassed) Dostoyevsky's *Crime and Punishment*. 'Heart of Darkness' or *Nostromo* alone would have sufficed to earn Conrad an enduring reputation; but this immense sequence of works (so richly descriptive and morally complex) confirms his stature as one of the greatest fiction-writers—and probably the greatest political novelist—in English.

Although Conrad's prose was occasionally marred by grammatical or idiomatic lapses (particularly into inadvertent Gallicisms), generally his command of styles ranging from the colloquial to the lyrical was audaciously effective. A colourful passage of rhythmic, assonantal and alliterative 'prose poetry' that became renowned (and would be parodied by E. M. Forster) was the description of the burning ship in 'Youth':

> Between the darkness of earth and heaven she was burning fiercely upon a disc of purple sea shot by the blood-red play of gleams; upon a disc of water glittering and sinister. A

high, clear flame, an immense and lonely flame, ascended from the ocean, and from its summit the black smoke poured continuously at the sky. She burned furiously; mournful and imposing like a funeral pile kindled in the night, surrounded by the sea, watched over by the stars. A magnificent death had come like a grace, like a gift, like a reward to that old ship at the end of her laborious days. (*'Heart of Darkness' and other Tales*, 124–5)

More to the taste of comparatively recent readers were the sardonic anti-imperialistic descriptions in 'Heart of Darkness'; for example:

> Once, I remember, we came upon a man-of-war anchored off the coast. There wasn't even a shed there, and she was shelling the bush. It appears the French had one of their wars going on thereabouts. Her ensign drooped limp like a rag; the muzzles of the long six-inch guns stuck out all over the low hull; the greasy, slimy swell swung her up lazily and let her down, swaying her thin masts. In the empty immensity of earth, sky, and water, there she was, incomprehensible, firing into a continent. (ibid., 151–2)

Conrad learned to combine sharp realism with calculated ambiguity and thematic orchestration. His mastery of perspectives enabled him to present a suffering individual now as the vital centre of the universe and now as of no more value than a drop of water in the ocean. Repeatedly the tensions in his own nature found expression in renderings of a close interaction between a central character and a subversive figure, as in the relationships between Marlow and Jim, Marlow and Kurtz, the captain and Leggatt, or Razumov and Haldin. He relished the 'psychopolitical', portraying events which were simultaneously psychological and political, illustrated by the derangement of Kurtz or the subtle corruption of Gould. Traditional values suffered trial by ordeal, and sometimes failed their tests. If his originality delighted such connoisseurs as Wells (for a while), Garnett, Cunninghame Graham, and Arnold Bennett, it sometimes baffled other early readers and reviewers. Nevertheless, Conrad was fortunate in the timing of his literary career.

The fact that so many of Conrad's works were serialized is a reminder that, in various respects, this was a golden age for story-tellers. The expansion of education in Victorian England had created a vast literate public; and numerous periodicals, many of them publishing or reviewing fiction, came into existence to meet the needs of this enlarged readership. Technological advances made books cheaper to produce; commercial advertising and publicity became widespread; and international copyright agreements (notably the Chace Act of 1891) guaranteed payment for works published abroad. Frequently, Conrad was paid several times for a single item. (Even the complex and technically challenging novel *Nostromo* first appeared in a popular magazine, *T. P.'s Weekly*.) Yet, although Conrad's reputation steadily burgeoned, so did his debts. His chronic prodigality was aided by loans from friends (notably John Galsworthy and William Rothenstein); donations came from the Royal Literary Fund (£300 in 1902, £200 in 1908) and from the Royal Bounty Special Service Fund (£500 in 1904); and in 1910 he was awarded a civil-list pension of £100 per annum. Above all, James Brand Pinker, his literary agent from 1900, advanced huge sums in the hope that the author would one day be financially prosperous. By 1909 Conrad's debts totalled £2250, at a time when the average annual earnings of a doctor were about £400. Not surprisingly, his letters are often jeremiads: he complains about his physical ailments (notably gout), his mental state (he was long afflicted by depression), and the daily struggle to wring from his imagination works of integrity while the debts mount. 'I had to work like a coalminer in his pit quarrying all my English sentences out of a black night', he told Garnett (*Collected Letters*, 4.112). The completion of *Under Western Eyes* was marked by a breakdown in which for days he lay in bed conversing with the imaginary characters.

To accelerate the flow of marketable writing, Conrad had collaborated with Ford Madox Hueffer on some inferior works: *The Inheritors* (1901), *Romance* (1903), and 'The Nature of a Crime' (first published in Hueffer's *English Review* in 1909). This collaborator and amanuensis was also paid for his contribution to Conrad's largely autobiographical *The Mirror of the Sea* (variously serialized; book, 1906), although only Conrad's name appeared on the title-page. The relationship between the two writers deteriorated and became recriminatory in 1909. Eventually Ford, who gained renown with *The Good Soldier*, would commemorate the collaboration in lively but unreliable volumes of reminiscence.

Remarkable non-fictional work of this period includes Conrad's letters to Cunninghame Graham, a sequence in which he expresses, often with fine rhetorical panache, his most pessimistic views of human nature and the human situation. For instance, in a letter of 1898, he declares:

> The mysteries of a universe made of drops of fire and clods of mud do not concern us in the least. The fate of a humanity condemned ultimately to perish from cold is not worth troubling about. If you take it to heart it becomes an unendurable tragedy. If you believe in improvement you must weep … Life knows us not and we do not know life—we don't even know our own thoughts. (*Collected Letters*, 2.16–17)

A letter to the *New York Times*, published in 1901, has a quotably contrasting emphasis: 'The only legitimate basis of creative work lies in the courageous recognition of all the irreconcilable antagonisms that make our life so enigmatic, so burdensome, so fascinating, so dangerous—so full of hope' (ibid., 2.348–9). An important essay is 'Autocracy and war' (first published in two periodicals in July 1905, later included in *Notes on Life and Letters*). Here Conrad predicts not only the First World War (as an outcome of aggressive Prussian militarism) but also the Russian Revolution, which, he says, will result only in a new tyranny that will endure for many years. He expresses, furthermore, a bleak recognition that democracy is dominated by commercialism. 'And democracy', he declares, 'which has elected to pin its faith to the supremacy of material interests, will have to fight their battles to the bitter end' (*Notes*, 107).

Transition: 1911–1919 The period from 1911 to 1919 was in two senses a period of transition for Conrad. First, while some of its novels and tales are impressive, others indicate a marked decline in his powers. Second, sales of his work increased sufficiently to end his struggles with debt and ensure his prosperity.

In order, the main publications of this phase of Conrad's artistic life are: *A Personal Record* (1912, originally *Some Reminiscences*), by far the more interesting of his two books of autobiographical reflections; *'Twixt Land and Sea* (1912, three previously published tales, including 'The Secret Sharer'); *Chance* (serialized in the *New York Herald* in 1912 and published as a book early in 1914); *Victory* (serial and book, 1915); *Within the Tides* (1915, four of his more trivial previously published tales); and *The Shadow-Line* (serial, 1916–17; book, 1917).

The short stories in the collections are remarkably uneven in quality, ranging from 'The Secret Sharer', a vivid and enigmatic tale which has elicited a wealth of interpretation, to 'The Inn of the Two Witches', a trite piece reminiscent of Wilkie Collins's 'A Terribly Strange Bed'. Of the novels, numerous critics concur in regarding *The Shadow-Line* as one of Conrad's best: echoing Coleridge's 'Rime of the Ancyent Marinere', this is a subtly allegoric depiction of the stresses on a young captain whose first command is a disease-ridden and apparently accursed sailing-ship. *Victory* is much more problematic for the critics, some seeing it as one of the Conradian masterpieces, others seeing it as a flawed and embarrassingly melodramatic work. It employs a remarkable range of source materials: notably the Bible, Shakespeare's *The Tempest*, Milton's *Comus*, Schopenhauer's bleak doctrines, A. R. Wallace's *Malay Archipelago*, Anatole France's *Le lys rouge*, Villiers de l'Isle Adam's *Axël*, H. G. Wells's *The Island of Doctor Moreau*, Stefan Żeromski's *Dzieje grzechu*, and particularly *The Ebb-Tide* by Robert Louis Stevenson and Lloyd Osbourne. Conrad had always been resourceful in assimilating heterogeneous materials; but, in this case, arguably, the materials do not effectively cohere, and the paradoxical themes lack persuasive embodiment.

In this transitional phase, the publication which most deeply affected Conrad's fortunes was *Chance*. Aided by a substantial publicity campaign for the serial in the *New York Herald* (which insisted that Conrad was now writing with women in mind) and by zealous marketing by Alfred Knopf in the USA, this novel sold well: surprisingly so, in view of its technical intricacy, which caused even Henry James to complain of the excessive elaboration. One explanation of *Chance*'s success is that the feminist debate was then highly topical. During this novel, though Marlow makes various misogynistic comments, modes of male chauvinism are sardonically depicted, and centrality is given to a young woman's struggles through oppression to maturity. (Incidentally, in 1910 Conrad had signed an open letter to the prime minister, Herbert Asquith, advocating female suffrage.)

In January 1914 *Chance* was published in book form; within two years there were numerous reprints. In the same month *Lord Jim* was reissued in a large popular edition: 15,000 copies at a shilling each. Soon, almost all of Conrad's earlier works were being reprinted. Pinker was able to obtain advances for *Victory* of £1000 for the serial rights (in *Munsey's Magazine*) and £850 for the book. Even a short, occasional essay, 'Tradition' (a tribute to British merchant seamen in time of war), earned £250 in 1918 when published in Lord Northcliffe's *Daily Mail*. Since 1912 John Quinn, a manuscript collector based in New York, had been purchasing Conrad's manuscripts on a regular basis: an astute investment. T. J. Wise, a diligent bibliographer and alleged forger, was another eager purchaser. Hollywood film producers recognized that within the stylistic and thematic subtleties of the novels lay popular cinematic materials: dramas of violence and sexual intrigue set in exotic locations. In 1919 motion picture rights to four Conrad works would be bought for over £3000 (at a time when an attractive four-bedroom house in London might cost £1000). At last Conrad was amply wealthy, and his debts to the ever-generous Pinker were cleared.

Decline In the closing years of Conrad's life, as collected editions were issued by Doubleday in New York, by Heinemann, Gresham, and Dent in London, and by Grant in Edinburgh, Conrad's main publications were: *The Arrow of Gold* (serial, 1918–20; book, 1919); *The Rescue* (serial, 1919–20; book, 1920); *Notes on Life and Letters* (1921, a collection of essays and occasional pieces); and *The Rover* (serial and book, 1923). Posthumously published volumes were *Suspense* (unfinished, but both serialized and issued as a book in 1925); *Tales of Hearsay* (an uneven collection, 1925); and *Last Essays* (1926). All four novels of this late phase are disappointing. *The Rover* is relatively concise, but in the others the narrative too often meanders, romantic values are too largely endorsed, and there is too little of the salt of scepticism. Understandably, the author's energies were flagging. As 'modernism' emerged strongly in the works of James Joyce, Virginia Woolf, and D. H. Lawrence, so Conrad, who had once been boldly innovative, was now regressing. While his writing lost its bite, however, public adulation increased. In 1919 Conrad had moved into Oswalds, a large and elegant Georgian house at Bishopsbourne, near Canterbury. On a visit to the United States, where he lectured and gave a reading in 1923, he was lionized: 'To be aimed at by forty cameras held by forty men that look as if they came out of the slums is a nerve-shattering experience', he wrote to his wife (Najder, *Joseph Conrad*, 475–6). Later, he courteously declined a knighthood offered by Britain's first Labour prime minister, Ramsay MacDonald. His health deteriorated, and on 3 August 1924 he died of a heart attack at his home.

After a service in Canterbury at the Roman Catholic church, St Thomas's, Conrad was buried in the public cemetery on Westgate Court Avenue. The gravestone bears the words which he had chosen as the epigraph for *The Rover*:

Sleep after toyle, port after stormie seas,
Ease after warre, death after life, does greatly please.

These are the words uttered in Spenser's *Faerie Queene* by 'a man of hell, that cals himself Despaire'. Though Conrad

was buried with Catholic obsequies, the inscription is a reminder of the radical scepticism which gives so much power to his writings; and, furthermore, by providing a reminder of Peyrol in *The Rover*, who lives and dies by his work as a seaman, the words appropriately recall the dual career of Conrad, the seaman turned writer, who was still toiling at his creative writing in the season of his death.

Subsequent reputation Although Conrad's literary reputation seemed to flag in the 1930s, after the Second World War interest in his work surged. The praise given by F. R. Leavis in *The Great Tradition* (1948) heralded a diversity of academic studies, critical, biographical, and scholarly, while numerous paperback editions extended his popular readership. The formerly widespread notion that Conrad was primarily a nostalgic writer of the age of sail (a notion based largely on *The Nigger of the 'Narcissus'*, 'Youth', and *The Mirror of the Sea*) was superseded by recognition of his moral sophistication and of his proleptic power: repeatedly, it appeared, he had anticipated subsequent psychological, political, and philosophical findings. Critics found Freudian, Jungian, existentialist, and 'absurdist' features; the texts seemed to solicit and reward a diversity of critical approaches. Appropriately, given the international topics of his novels, his fame grew internationally. By the 1990s, for example, he was served by the Joseph Conrad societies of the United States, the UK, France, Italy, Scandinavia, and Poland; intensive scholarly work (accelerated by electronic communications) proceeded in locations as diverse as Lubbock (Texas), Amsterdam, Cape Town, and Tokyo; and his writings had been translated into more than forty languages, from Albanian and Korean to Swahili and Yiddish. While his texts were studied in schools and universities, film adaptations had brought his works to audiences of millions. Gene M. Moore (in *Conrad on Film*, 1997) listed eighty-six versions on film, television, and video. Of these, the most spectacular was Francis Ford Coppola's *Apocalypse Now* (1979), a lavishly free adaptation of 'Heart of Darkness' to the Vietnam War. The same novella was adapted several times for the theatre. Operas inspired by Conrad's texts have been composed by Tadeusz Baird, John Joubert, Richard Rodney Bennett, and Romuald Twardowski.

Conrad's cultural influence can be detected in the works of numerous eminent figures. Bronisław Malinowski declared: 'Rivers is the Rider Haggard of anthropology; I shall be the Conrad' (Firth, 6); indeed, he almost became the Kurtz of anthropology when, working among the Papuans, he ominously echoed Kurtz's 'Exterminate all the brutes!' (This became 'Exterminate the brutes!' in Malinowski's *Diary*, 69.) Bertrand Russell, whose friendship with Joseph Conrad was so intense that he gave the name Conrad to his elder and younger sons, recorded in his *Portraits from Memory* the recognition that the novelist had proved politically wiser than the philosopher. T. S. Eliot's *The Waste Land*, which originally took its epigraph from 'Heart of Darkness', contains some Conradian themes and details, while 'The Hollow Men' takes its title, its epigraph, and its subject from that African tale. Graham Greene regretted that some of his early work, particularly *Rumour at Nightfall*, had been deleteriously influenced by *The Arrow of Gold*; but Greene's greatest debt is probably to *The Secret Agent*, for 'Greeneland' (that seedy, corrupt terrain) has clear affinities with the murky, debased city of Conrad's novel; and indubitably *The Secret Agent* has contributed many features to *It's a Battlefield*. Probably Conrad's peripatetic life helped to shape Greene's. When Greene voyaged up a Congo tributary to research *A Burnt-Out Case*, 'Heart of Darkness' was in his hand.

Conrad's range is indicated by the diversity of other writers influenced by him: among them Virginia Woolf, Malcolm Lowry, Jorge Luis Borges, John Le Carré, Siegfried Lenz, William Golding, V. S. Naipaul, George Steiner, Howard Brenton, and Gabriel García Márquez. Thomas Mann and André Gide paid him handsome tribute. *L'étranger*, by Albert Camus, offered a *reprise* of the central paradox of *Lord Jim*, the contrast between the subjective view and the judicial view of a scandalous action; and Camus remarked that Clamence in *La chute* was 'a less brilliant Lord Jim' (*New York Times Book Review*, 24 Feb 1957, 36). In the United States, numerous major writers, including Eugene O'Neill, Ernest Hemingway, Scott Fitzgerald, William Faulkner, and even William S. Burroughs, admired and learned from his writings. Another American admirer was Orson Welles, who planned films of 'Heart of Darkness' and *Lord Jim*, and twice adapted 'Heart of Darkness' for radio. His cinematic masterpiece, *Citizen Kane*, has various Conradian affinities. 'I think I'm made for Conrad', he declared; 'I think every Conrad story is a movie' (Welles and Bogdanovich, 320). Among African writers (though Chinua Achebe vehemently denounced Conrad as a racist), the acclaimed novelist Ngugi wa Thiong'o based his vivid novel, *A Grain of Wheat*, largely on the plot and themes of *Under Western Eyes*; and Conradian elements have been traced in Tayeb Salih's *Season of Migration to the North*. In the late twentieth century, Conrad was criticized by various feminists, Marxists, and post-colonial writers; and the ensuing controversies naturally tended to enliven and increase his readership. While cultural changes seemed to reveal some ideological flaws in his works, his moral intensity exposed by contrast posterity's capacity for decadence and ideological hypocrisy. Zdzisław Najder wrote in 1997: 'Conrad identified problems and perils which are still with us today. We need him' (*Conrad in Perspective*, 187).

Conrad was a versatile intermediary between the Romantic and Victorian traditions and the innovations of modernism. He was romantic in his interest in adventurous individuals and in his keenly sensuous responsiveness to the beauty, power, and immensity of the natural environment. He was Victorian in his registration of the burdens of thought in an era when science offered bleak vistas; Victorian, too, in his recognition of the magnitude of imperial enterprises, and in his high valuation of an ethic of work and duty. Poland had nourished his concern with the claims of honour and of fidelity to causes which

might seem lost, while his favoured French authors (Flaubert, Maupassant, Anatole France) had strengthened his habits of sceptical and ironic analysis. His sense of individualism sometimes modulated towards a modernistic relativism or even, occasionally, solipsism; and modernistic, too, were his sense of the absurdity of moral beings in a non-moral universe, his profound scepticism about the value of industrial society and its acquisitive imperialisms, and his belief that many people were myopic participants in destructive processes. Frequently, his works enact the difficulties of maintaining a humane morality when that morality lacks supernatural or environmental support. The passage of time, while predictably revealing various limitations, has largely vindicated his technical audacity and his political pessimism. 'Heart of Darkness', which offered a forewarning of the Hitlerian demagogue, seems virtually inexhaustible in its recessive ambiguities and paradoxes. *Nostromo*, in its epic scale and panoramic scope, has proved to be an audaciously penetrating study of economic imperialism. Its view of history, Albert Guerard once remarked, is 'skeptical and disillusioned, which for us today must mean true' (Guerard, 177). Technically, Conrad was resourceful in applying such devices as the time-shift, delayed decoding, covert plotting, symbolic imagery, transtextual narratives, and the unreliable intermediary narrator; he submitted dramatic and sometimes even melodramatic topics to sophisticated reflective scrutiny. The effect of the technical devices was usually to multiply ironies and, broadly, to accentuate possible divisions between appearance and reality.

Conrad found that when he adapted *The Secret Agent* for the stage, removing the narrative flesh to expose the underlying plot, what emerged was a rather grisly skeleton; similarly, many of the film adaptations of his texts have tended to make prominent the melodramatic incidents while silencing the voices of eloquent and sophisticated narrators. Lord Jim, after all, is significant less by virtue of his own character than by the kaleidoscopic multiplicity of the comments that he provokes from other characters and particularly from Marlow; while the technique of delayed decoding (which depicts an effect while delaying or withholding its cause) involves us intimately with Jim's fate. In 'Heart of Darkness', Kurtz's last words ('The horror! the horror!') have their strange ambiguity amplified by Marlow's commentary, so that they seem to sum up, without resolving, major paradoxes of the tale. Perhaps 'the horror' is Kurtz's own corruption; perhaps it is death; perhaps it is the irrational universe; but no interpretation is certain. In *Nostromo*, the suicide of Martin Decoud is described with resonant power. When he shoots himself, he sinks into the Placid Gulf, 'whose glittering surface remained untroubled by the fall of his body'; and the death of this sceptic bears critical reflections which themselves are memorably sceptical: 'In our activity alone do we find the sustaining illusion of an independent existence as against the whole scheme of things of which we form a helpless part' (*Nostromo*, 361). Certainly, Conrad carried a large freight of pessimism which sometimes invited parody (and, in *A Christmas Garland*,

Max Beerbohm wittily accepted the invitation); but it was counterbalanced by the author's creative energy and adventurous range, and even by that guarded love of life which was implicit in his love of searchingly crafted prose.

Through Conrad's 'Author's notes' and other non-fictional (or purportedly non-fictional) writings, as well as through his posed photographs in which he generally appears gravely dignified, he projected the image of Joseph Conrad as patrician weathered sage, as the much-travelled mariner-turned-author who had earned his right to comment wryly, ironically, sceptically, but yet humanely, on human endeavours. At his best, he was a vivid, eloquent, and wise writer who, arguably, provided both warnings and guidance for posterity, and who, indisputably, produced powerfully evocative renderings of individuals enmeshed in historical toils. His long odyssey, as a Polish exile and mariner who eventually gained eminence as a British novelist, displayed exemplary courage, fortitude, and nobility. He is one of those authors who can provide sustenance for a lifetime. We may recall Bertrand Russell's words in *Portraits from Memory*, which, though a little too plaintive, offer an appropriate emphasis:

> Conrad, I suppose, is in process of being forgotten. But his intense and passionate nobility shines in my memory like a star seen from the bottom of a well. I wish I could make his light shine for others as it shone for me. (Russell, 85)

CEDRIC WATTS

Sources Z. Najder, *Joseph Conrad: a chronicle* (1983) · C. Watts, *A preface to Conrad*, 2nd edn (1993) · *The collected letters of Joseph Conrad*, ed. F. R. Karl and L. Davies, 2 (1986) · *The collected letters of Joseph Conrad*, ed. F. R. Karl and L. Davies, 4 (1990) · Z. Najder, *Conrad in perspective* (1997) · Z. Najder, ed., *Conrad's Polish background* (1964) · C. Watts, *Joseph Conrad: a literary life* (1989) · A. Guerard, *Conrad the novelist* (1958) · B. Russell, *Portraits from memory* (1956) · J. Conrad, *'Heart of Darkness' and other tales*, ed. C. Watts (1990) · J. Conrad, *Nostromo*, ed. C. Watts (1995) · J. Conrad, *Notes on life and letters* (1921) · G. M. Moore, ed., *Conrad on film* (1997) · B. Malinowski, *A diary in the strict sense of the term* (1967) · O. Welles and P. Bogdanovich, *This is Orson Welles* (1993) · R. Firth, ed., *Man and culture: an evaluation of the work of Bronislaw Malinowski* (1957); repr. with corrections (1960) · E. Garnett, ed., *Letters from Conrad, 1893 to 1924* (1928) · m. cert. · d. cert.
Archives Duke U., Perkins L., corresp. and papers · Harvard U., Houghton L., Congo travel journal · Indiana University, Bloomington, Lilly Library, papers · Kent State University, Kent, Ohio, Center for Conrad Studies · National Library of Poland, Warsaw · Polish Academy of Sciences, Kraków · Polish Social and Cultural Association Ltd, London, Joseph Conrad Study Centre · Ransom HRC, literary MSS and letters · Yale U., Beinecke L., papers | BL, corresp. with William Archer, Add. MS 45291 · Dartmouth College, New Hampshire, letters relating to R. B. Cunninghame Graham · Harvard U., Houghton L., letters to Sir William Rothenstein · McMaster University, Hamilton, Ontario, letters to Bertrand Russell · NL Ire., letters to Roger Casement · NRA, priv. coll., corresp. with John Galsworthy · NYPL, Berg collection · Polish Library, London, letters to John Galsworthy · Ransom HRC, letters to Norman Douglas · Rosenbach Museum and Library, Philadelphia · U. Leeds, Brotherton L., corresp. with T. Fisher Unwin · UCL, letters to Arnold Bennett | FILM BFI NFTVA, 'The modern world: ten great writers', 17 Jan 1988
Likenesses photograph, 1873, Ransom HRC · photograph, 1893, Yale U., Beinecke L. · E. Heath, oils, 1898, Leeds City Art Gallery · W. Rothenstein, pastel drawing, 1903, NPG · G. C. Beresford, photographs, 1904, NPG [*see illus.*] · W. Cadby, photograph, 1914, NPG · A. L. Coburn, photogravure, 1916, NPG; repro. in *More men of mark* (1922) · W. Rothenstein, pencil drawing, 1916, NPG · photograph, 1916, priv. coll. · P. Anderson, chalk and wash drawing, 1918, NPG · C. Moore-Park, lithograph, 1922, V&A · J. C. Annan, photograph, 1923, U. Texas, Gernsheim collection · T. R. Annan & Sons, photograph, 1923 · M. Bone, etching, 1923–5, FM Cam. · J. Epstein, bronze bust, 1924, NPG · W. Tittle, etching, 1924, NPG · W. Tittle, oils, 1924, NPG · W. Tittle, oils, 1924, U. Texas · print, 1926 (after D. Low), NPG · D. Low, caricatures, pencil drawings, NPG · photograph, Yale U., Keating collection · photographs, Hult. Arch. · postcard (with his son), NPG
Wealth at death £20,045 5s. 8d.: probate, 7 Nov 1924, *CGPLA Eng. & Wales*

Conroy, Sir **John Ponsonby**, first baronet (1786–1854), courtier, was born on 21 October 1786 at Maes-y-castell, Caerhun, Caernarvonshire, the eldest of the five sons and one daughter of John Ponsonby Conroy (1759–1797), barrister, and his wife, Margaret, daughter of Francis Vernon Wilson, who were both Irish-born. Educated by tutors and at the Royal Military Academy, Woolwich, he was commissioned into the Royal Artillery in 1803.

On 26 December 1808 Conroy married Elizabeth (1790–1864), daughter of Major-General Benjamin Fisher and Charlotte Clarke, and niece of Dr John Fisher, bishop of Salisbury, who had tutored Edward, duke of Kent. They had four sons, one of whom died young, and two daughters. Conroy believed his wife to be the duke of Kent's natural child, and this fantasy may have accounted for his arrogance towards Queen Victoria. Through his wife's connections, he became equerry to the duke of Kent on the latter's marriage to Princess Victoire of Leiningen in 1818. Conroy was an organizer of genius. He made it possible for the duke and his wife, in the eighth month of pregnancy, to rush back from Germany to Kensington Palace for the birth, putting up the royal cavalcade at his home in Shooter's Hill, Kent, on the way. When the duke died suddenly in 1820, Conroy became comptroller of the duchess of Kent's household; alone in a hostile environment, she came to place great reliance on him.

At first Conroy shared his influence on the duchess with her brother, Prince Leopold of Saxe-Coburg-Saalfeld, but after Leopold ascended the Belgian throne in 1830, Conroy ruled supreme. He survived the 'Cumberland plot' in 1829, when a rumour said to have been started by Ernest, duke of Cumberland, circulated, to the effect that the duchess of Kent was Conroy's mistress. This was intended to discredit the duchess and have Princess Victoria removed from her care, and even, Conroy feared, killed. He established the 'Kensington system', with the intention of seeing Victoria educated as heir presumptive to the crown, her mother created regent if the king died before Victoria was eighteen, himself appointed Victoria's private secretary with a peerage, and a rival court developed at Kensington, cut off from the tory politics and lax morals of William IV, who referred to Conroy as 'King John'. Victoria had no youthful companionship except Conroy's daughters and no personal champion but her German governess, Baroness Lehzen, Conroy's implacable foe. In order to make Victoria known to the people, and to enhance his own importance, Conroy took her around the country on semi-royal tours, after the last of which, in 1835, she succumbed to typhoid. While she was still on her sickbed, Conroy tried to force her to appoint him as her personal secretary when she became queen. Afterwards she told Lord Melbourne: 'I resisted in spite of my illness'.

As William IV lay dying, Conroy's final desperate attempt to coerce Victoria failed. On her succession to the throne on 20 June 1837, she dismissed him from her household. But he continued to serve her mother, and was partly responsible for the fate of the duchess's lady-in-waiting, Lady Flora Hastings, who died of a tumour while suspected of being pregnant by Conroy. The duchess, too, was reported to be Conroy's mistress, though without conclusive evidence. However, he cannot be absolved of mismanaging her funds and those of Princess Sophia, Victoria's aunt and Conroy's 'spy', from whom he also received gifts and money amounting to £148,000.

In 1839 Wellington persuaded Conroy to resign from the duchess of Kent's household and go abroad for a time. He had a Guelphic knighthood, an honorary DCL from Oxford, and foreign honours. He was created baronet in 1837, but Sir Robert Peel refused him the Irish peerage promised him by Melbourne. 'JC' was not the arch-villain Victoria painted, but the victim of his own inordinate ambition. He died at his home, Arborfield Hall, near Reading, Berkshire, on 2 March 1854. He was succeeded in the baronetcy by his eldest son, Edward.

ELIZABETH LONGFORD, *rev.*

Sources Conroy MSS, Balliol Oxf. · K. Hudson, *A royal conflict: Sir John Conroy and the young Victoria* (1994) · E. Longford, *Victoria RI* (1964) · M. Charlot, *Victoria, the young queen* (1991)
Archives Balliol Oxf., corresp. and papers | BL, corresp. with Sir Robert Peel, Add. MSS 40385, 40545 · BL, letters to Sir George Smart, Add. MS 41777 · Lambton Park, Chester-le-Street, Durham, Lambton MSS, letters to first earl of Durham · priv. coll., corresp. with A. R. Drummond · U. Southampton L., corresp. with Lord Palmerston, etc. · W. Sussex RO, letters to duke of Richmond
Likenesses H. W. Pickersgill, oils, 1836, NPG; repro. in Hudson, *Royal conflict* · A. Tidey, oils, 1836, NPG; repro. in Hudson, *Royal conflict* · W. J. Ward, mezzotint, pubd 1839 (after W. Fowler), BM, NPG · H. T. Ryall, mixed engraving, pubd 1840 (after H. W. Pickersgill), BM · photograph, *c.*1850, Balliol Oxf.; repro. in Hudson, *Royal conflict* · sculpture, Birr Castle, co. Offaly; repro. in Hudson, *Royal conflict*
Wealth at death debts of approx. £40,000: Hudson, *Royal conflict*

Conry, Florence [Flaithri Ó Maoil Chonaire] (d. 1629), Roman Catholic archbishop of Tuam, probably born in Cloonahee, co. Galway, was the son of Fithil Ó Maoil Chonaire and Ónora. The Ó Maoil Chonaires appear frequently as poets, historians, and clergymen in the Irish annals; Flaithri's grandfather Muirgheas mac Paidin Ó Maoil Chonaire was a renowned scribe, antiquary, poet, and teacher. Apparently self-educated, Conry practised his forefathers' arts before leaving Ireland while still young to become one of the first students of the University of Salamanca in Spain. There, he joined the Franciscans in 1584 and developed a reputation for erudition. He could speak Gaelic, English, Latin, Italian, and Spanish.

About 1592 Conry began to act in Madrid on behalf of

certain Irish chieftains led by Hugh Roe O'Donnell who hoped that Philip II of Spain would support their plans to rise against English rule in Ireland. In 1598 he may have gone to Ireland on behalf of Philip II to treat with the insurgents, and he is said to have made many journeys between Ireland and Spain at this time. In September 1601 he sailed to Ireland with the Spanish expeditionary force sent to support the insurgents, but following the disastrous battle of Kinsale he left with Hugh Roe O'Donnell, whose confessor he was, sailing from Castlehaven, co. Cork, on 6 January 1602. On reaching Spain, the two hastened to the royal court to plead unsuccessfully for further military and financial support. O'Donnell died a broken man at Simancas on 9 September with Conry at his side. Conry redoubled his efforts to secure Spanish aid, and eventually King Philip III agreed to send money and arms to the insurgents' leader Hugh O'Neill, earl of Tyrone. In April 1603 Conry accompanied two ships carrying arms, supplies, and money to Ireland. However, on arrival he found that the insurgents had already surrendered, and he returned to Spain without even disembarking.

Over the next three decades Conry was probably the single most influential figure within the hard-line Gaelic opposition to English rule in Ireland. In April 1604 he was appointed special adviser to the Spanish council of state for dealing with Irish refugees. This enabled him to channel Spanish patronage towards those Irish exiles who shared his views. He went to the Spanish Netherlands in 1605, probably to liaise with influential members of the growing Irish community there. An Irish regiment had been set up within the Spanish army at Flanders, and it was hoped that it would one day lead a Spanish invasion of Ireland. Conry was back in Spain by May 1606, when he spoke before the general chapter of the Franciscan order at Toledo of the plight of the Catholics in Ireland. The chapter members were sufficiently impressed to elect him head of the Irish Franciscans, a major breach of precedent as this post had hitherto been in the gift of the Irish chapter. He also persuaded the general chapter to assent to the establishment of a college for educating Irish Franciscans at Louvain in the Spanish Netherlands. He fully intended to return to Ireland to carry out his duties as Irish provincial, but was preoccupied for over a year with the new foundation, named St Anthony's College. After securing King Philip's support for the project, in 1607 he went to Louvain, where the college rented its first premises in May. Difficulties in securing enough financial support for the college led to further delays, but by August he was preparing to sail for Ireland.

However, Conry was overtaken by events. Had he gone to Ireland he would almost certainly have relied on the protection of Tyrone, but in autumn 1607 the earl, fearing arrest for treason, fled the country. It was probably on hearing this that Conry changed his plans. On 22 October he met Tyrone and Rory O'Donnell, earl of Tyrconnell, at the Irish college at Douai. The following year he accompanied them to Rome, where Tyrone hoped to secure Spanish aid for an invasion of Ireland, but Spain was trying to improve its relations with England and refused him permission to even come to Spain. The earl's desperation grew when King James VI and I announced plans for a plantation of Ulster in 1609. There was little the pope could do about events in Ireland, but he did feel obliged to accede to Tyrone's pleas that his friends be advanced within the church. Hence on 30 March 1609, near Rome, Conry was consecrated archbishop of Tuam, in his native Galway. There was no question of Conry ever going to Ireland to take up this position because of the danger this would entail, but under his distant leadership the Counter-Reformation tightened its grip on Connaught.

In June 1609 Tyrone sent Conry to Madrid with the terms of a proposed reconciliation with James. Conry arrived in October 1609, but found the Spanish unreceptive. They preferred to keep Tyrone in reserve, in case relations with England deteriorated at a future date. Only in June 1610 did Philip give Tyrone permission to attempt a reconciliation, but by then James's government was committed to a plantation of Ulster. Conry remained at Madrid, where he was granted a pension of 50 ducats a month in July 1610. That year the command of the Irish regiment in Flanders fell vacant, prompting a struggle between the Gaelic Irish and Old English factions within the regiment. Conry was determined to prevent an Old Englishman from gaining the command. Indeed, throughout his career, he bent his influence toward ensuring that only Gaelic Irish were promoted to key positions within the Spanish army and in the Catholic church. He regarded the Old English as too loyal to the English crown and spoke bitterly of how Old English priests had preached against Tyrone during his uprising. For their part, the Old English resented the manner in which a so-called northern clique of Gaelic clergy and soldiers drawn mostly from Connaught and Ulster monopolized the favour of the king of Spain and to a lesser extent that of the pope. The Old English regarded Conry as an extremist and had been outraged by his promotion to the archbishopric of Tuam.

In May 1611 Philip appointed Eoghan Roe O'Neill, a nephew of Tyrone and Conry's protégé, sergeant-major and effective head of the Irish regiment. Through his lobbying at Madrid, Conry was playing a crucial role in developing the next generation of Gaelic opposition to English rule in Ireland. Although Conry usually had his way with the Spanish in matters of patronage, he had less success with the pope. Here he faced formidable opposition in the form of the Old English archbishop of Armagh, Peter Lombard, who strongly advocated a policy of appeasing the English in the hope of better treatment for Catholics in Ireland. As theological adviser to the Holy See, Lombard always had the pope's ear and had a major influence on the appointment of bishops to Ireland in the 1610s and early 1620s.

On 1 March 1614 Conry wrote an open letter to the Catholic members of the 1613–15 Irish parliament, berating them for their cowardice in voting for Tyrone's attainder. A year later, as relations between England and Spain momentarily soured, he pressed vigorously but unavailingly for a Spanish invasion of Ireland. He briefly visited

Rome in summer 1616 to pay his respects to the fading Tyrone and was with the earl for his death on 21 July. That year he published *Desiderius*, a devotional work written in Irish. At some point he also produced two works on Irish history which remained in manuscript and a quatrium on a rather farcical dispute between the poets of the north and of the south of Ireland, but after his return to Madrid he decided to devote himself to the study of the works of St Augustine. He had first become interested in Augustinian theology in 1610, and during the course of his life he is said to have read all of St Augustine's works seven times, being particularly interested in those works pertaining to the Pelagian heresies and the doctrine of grace. Like many other advocates of the saint, he strongly supported the doctrine of the immaculate conception, which he discussed in his *De S. Augustina sense circa Beatae Mariae Virgines conceptionem* (1619). His high-profile support for the then novel doctrine earned him the approbation of Philip III.

In 1618 Conry was sent by the king to Brussels to advise on negotiations between Spain and England for a marriage between the prince of Wales and Philip's daughter. Before leaving Madrid, he presented a pamphlet to the king on the persecutions suffered by the Irish Catholics. Once the negotiations in Brussels had concluded, he settled in Louvain, where the Irish College was now prospering. In 1619 he persuaded the college to send a mission to the Hebrides in Scotland. At Louvain he continued his studies of Augustinian theology and became acquainted with Cornelius Jansen, then head of the Dutch College in Louvain. Given that they were neighbours and shared a common interest in Augustinian theology, it is unsurprising that they should have been on friendly terms. However, the claims often made that Conry had a major bearing on Jansen's subsequent theological development are untrue. Jansen had little regard for Conry's writings on the doctrine of grace and did not reveal his own highly controversial opinions on the matter to the Irishman. By late 1621 Conry had completed a work on the fate of infants who die before they can be baptized. The pope had banned the publication of any unlicensed works on the highly sensitive topic of the doctrine of grace, but eventually permission was forthcoming for *De statu parvulorum*, which appeared in 1624. It met with a favourable response, particularly from the universities of Louvain and Douai in the Spanish Netherlands.

In autumn 1626 Conry left Louvain for Madrid as a representative of John O'Neill, earl of Tyrone, and Albert O'Donnell, earl of Tyrconnell. Spain and England had been at war since 1625 and hopes were high among the Irish that Spain would invade Ireland once again. In January 1627 Conry presented documents to King Philip IV of Spain proposing that the two earls jointly lead a Spanish expedition to liberate Ireland. The plan envisaged the division of Ireland between the two earls, who would act as captains-general of Ireland and create an interim republic administered in consultation with the Catholic nobility, including the Old English, until an agreed candidate for the kingship of Ireland could be found. Ireland would then become a monarchy under the protection of the

Spanish crown. However, the invasion plans were ultimately shelved. While in Madrid, Conry also defended the University of Louvain from the criticisms of the Jesuits.

Conry died at the convent of San Francisco in Madrid on 18 November 1629. Despite his request that he be buried in the Irish College at Louvain, his body was initially interred at San Lorenzo. However, in 1654 his remains were transferred to Louvain and were buried in the sanctuary of the Irish College on 23 March 1654. Eleven years after his death his theological works were dragged into the controversy surrounding the publication of Jansen's *Augustinius*. In a bid to gain more credibility, the Jansenists tried to associate Conry with their own views by including *De statu*, which had not been censored by the pope, as a supplement to the 1640 and subsequent editions of *Augustinius*. Conry's supporters responded by arranging the publication of his *Peregrinus* (1641), *De flagillis* (1644), and *De gratia Christi* (1646). These theological works made clear that Conry would not have agreed with Jansen's doctrines. Conry's fascination with the works of St Augustine was quite typical for an Irish clergyman of his era. The strict, puritanical brand of Catholicism associated with St Augustine struck a chord with many of the Irish clergy. However, virtually all of them, Conry included, combined this puritanism with total obedience to the pope.

TERRY CLAVIN

Sources *Father Luke Wadding: commemorative volume*, ed. Franciscan Fathers dún Mhuire, Killiney (1957) · M. K. Walsh, *An exile of Ireland* (1996) · J. Casway, *Owen Roe O'Neill* (1984), 20, 22–5, 30–32, 34 · F. O'Byrne, 'Florence Conry, archbishop of Tuam', *Irish Rosary*, 31/2 (1927), 845–7, 896–904; and 32/1 (1928), 346–51, 454–60 · *Galway Archaeological Society Journal*, 8/4, 193–204; 23 (1948), 83–92 · F. Conry, *Desiderius*, ed. T. F. O'Rahilly (1941) · C. P. Meehan, *Fate and fortunas* (1868), 69, 164, 395–7 · *Report on Franciscan manuscripts preserved at the convent, Merchants' Quay, Dublin*, HMC, 65 (1906), 2, 79, 97, 102, 104–6, 119, 124 · H. Grainne, *The Irish military community in Spanish Flanders* (1992), 136, 142–3 · J. J. Silke, *The Spanish intervention in Ireland* (1970), 148, 161, 166–7 · B. Jennings, *Wild geese in Spanish Flanders* (1964), 155, 209, 212–15, 217–19 · M. Walsh, 'The last years of Hugh O'Neill', *Irish Sword*, 7 (1965–6), 5–14, 136–46, 327–37

Cons, Emma (1838–1912), social reformer and theatre manager, was born in London on 4 March 1838, the second daughter in the family of seven children of Frederick Cons (1810–1870), piano-case maker for Broadwoods, and his wife, Esther Goodair (d. 1882), daughter of a Stockport mill owner. She attended a school run by the mother of the painter Henry Holliday, and then went to the art school in Gower Street, London. She continued her education at the school run by Caroline Southwood Hill, but when her father became too ill to work in 1852 she left school. She was employed by the Christian socialist, co-operative Ladies' Guild, which trained girls in glass painting until its closure in 1856.

Emma Cons had been drawn into social reform circles while at Mrs Hill's school, where she had met Octavia Hill (the schoolmistress's daughter), John Ruskin, Charles Kingsley, and F. D. Maurice. Through Octavia Hill she became involved in the management of working-class

housing projects, as a volunteer. Ruskin, meanwhile, employed her in 1856 to work on the restoration of illuminated manuscripts. During a visit to Switzerland she noticed that the work of watch engraving was carried out by women, and, taking the view that this was ideal work for women, when she returned to England she apprenticed herself to a watch engraver, together with a group of female friends. After completing their training the women established a co-operative watch engraving business in Clerkenwell, but they encountered great hostility from male competitors, who intercepted the messenger who brought the women work and injured him so severely that the manufacturers became uneasy at supplying them with further orders. With insufficient work, the co-operative was eventually forced to close. Her next employment also brought Cons into conflict with established male employees. She was the first woman to be hired by the stained-glass manufacturers Powells of Whitefriars, and the men deliberately sabotaged her work until Arthur Powells's personal intervention ended the persecution. One of her most important commissions at Powells was to work on the restoration of the stained-glass windows in the chapel of Merton College, an assignment which kept her in Oxford for two years in the early 1860s.

Alongside her paid employment Emma Cons continued to work as a volunteer in Octavia Hill's housing projects, looking after properties in Drury Lane and Marylebone. In 1865 Hill had bought three tenements in Paradise Place with money provided by Ruskin, and the following year bought more properties in Freshwater Place. From the beginning Cons was an active worker in the enterprise. Although there were differences in their styles of management, Hill appreciated the qualities which Cons brought to the work; she gave an account of Emma Cons's activities at a housing project near Drury Lane: '[she] enrols her own volunteer workers, founds her own classes, clubs, savings, banks, keeps her own accounts, supervises all the business and personal work, and reports to the owners of the courts direct' (Darley, 148). Housing management involved Emma Cons in every aspect of maintenance, including dealing with workmen. She thought nothing of instructing an obstreperous workman in the art of house construction, and her close friend Henrietta Barnett wrote:

> I can visualise her now: mounting ladders, mixing colours, ordering and laughing at the men, who when too inexperienced, backward, or perhaps indolent, would show resentment at, or disinclination for the job, were made ashamed and also encouraged by seeing Miss Cons seize the brush and give an excellent lesson on distempering, painting or washing down. (Barnett, 3)

By 1870 she had become manager of the Central London Dwellings Improvement Company. In 1879 she initiated the South London Dwellings Company, which bought a property between the Lambeth and Kennington roads that Cons transformed into model dwellings, known as Surrey Lodge. She turned two of the cottages into one, and this became her own permanent office and home, which she shared with her sisters Ellen and Eliza.

Emma Cons also became an active member of the temperance movement, believing that the only way to discourage men and women from resorting to the gin palace was to provide an alcohol-free alternative. She opened her first 'coffee tavern' in Drury Lane, providing all the social facilities of the public house with non-alcoholic refreshments; the scheme, which acquired the financial backing of several wealthy aristocrats, grew to encompass about fifty establishments throughout London. Cons was to apply the principles of the coffee tavern to the more general reform of working-class entertainment, which centred on drink and the music-hall. She was convinced that there was a close link between working-class recreation, alcohol, and domestic violence, of which she had seen a great deal in her work in housing management. She believed firmly that the only way to solve the problem was to provide 'purified' entertainment, from which both indecency and alcohol had been eliminated. In 1879 she formed the Coffee Music Hall Company with the specific object of providing such entertainment, and in the next year the company leased the Victoria Theatre on the Waterloo Road (widely known as the Old Vic) as the venue for Cons's experiment with 'purified' entertainment. Formerly an insalubrious music-hall, in an area surrounded by gin palaces, public houses, and criminal haunts (and, incidentally, close to Surrey Lodge), the Old Vic was transformed by a £3000 refurbishment, renamed the Royal Victoria Coffee Music Hall, and opened for business on 27 December 1880, with an offering of wholesome entertainment and alcohol-free refreshments.

Inevitably, the venture ran into immediate financial difficulties, as Emma Cons had greatly overestimated the ability or willingness of the citizens of Lambeth to sit through a performance of elevating entertainment washed down with nothing stronger than tea or coffee. In May 1881 the theatre closed, but after an energetic fund-raising campaign Cons reopened it in October, with a programme of music-hall style entertainment, science lectures, ballad evenings, and temperance meetings. Another financial crisis ensued, and in 1884 the industrialist and Liberal MP Samuel Morley responded to Emma Cons's plea for assistance and bailed the theatre out. The Old Vic could not withstand a further crisis, and Cons and the board of governors launched an appeal to raise the £17,000 necessary to buy the theatre's freehold. With the help of the charity commissioners and private sponsors, including the duke of Westminster, the appeal was successful, and the freehold was purchased in 1891.

Cons had wanted the Royal Victoria Coffee Music Hall to offer both entertainment and education, and the regular science lectures, given by many eminent scientists, had been a success. Following a request from three members of the audience for a series of evening classes to be set up, she founded the first part-time educational institution for working men and women in south London, which she named Morley College after her benefactor. The earliest classes were held in rooms running beneath the Old Vic's stage, and she officially opened the college on 28 September 1889. It remained under the aegis of the theatre until the 1920s, when it was moved to Westminster Bridge Road.

Although remembered chiefly for her work in providing 'rational recreation', Emma Cons was active in many other fields. She 'was one of the founders of the first Women's Horticultural College at Swanley in Kent … [and] she found time to travel to Armenia, to report on the Armenian atrocities'; she established a silk factory for the Armenian refugees in Cyprus on her journey home (Baylis and Hamilton, 281). She was a member of the London Society for Women's Suffrage, serving as vice-president in 1908–11. A lifelong champion of women's rights, she was a constitutional suffragist. She was a member of the executive committee of the Women's Liberal Federation, and vice-president in 1892, and served on its temperance committee in 1894.

In 1889 Cons was appointed an alderman by the newly formed London county council, and as such was caught up in the acrimonious debates and legal cases over women's capacity to act as councillors, along with Jane Cobden-Unwin and Lady Margaret Sandhurst, who had both been elected to the council. Exploiting legal loopholes, Cons and Cobden-Unwin succeeded in holding on to their places on the council (although they both underwent a year of enforced inactivity to prevent their unseating), and in 1890 Cons resumed her place on six committees (asylums, housing, industrial schools, parks, sanitation, and theatre) and a number of subcommittees. She explained her commitment to the cause of women councillors thus:

> I believe that for such work as ours women are not only qualified but needful, and I desire to defend their franchise as far as lawfully I may … those duties are to me a trust, not only for women but for the whole community. (Hollis, 313)

She remained on the council until its term was up, but, with all women, was disqualified for standing for re-election.

By the end of the century Emma Cons's health was suffering from the range of her commitments, and in 1899 she invited her niece, Lilian *Baylis, to take over the management of the Old Vic. She retained an active interest in the theatre for the rest of her life, but it was Baylis who transformed its repertoire. Emma Cons died at a friend's home, Chippens Bank, Hever, Kent, on 24 July 1912, and her ashes were scattered in the surrounding woods.

JUDI LEIGHTON

Sources L. Baylis and C. Hamilton, *The Old Vic* (1926) · R. Findlater, *Lilian Baylis, the lady of the Old Vic* (1975) · L. Baylis, 'Emma Cons—woman pioneer', *Woman Cleric* (Dec 1925) · P. Hollis, *Ladies elect: women in English local government, 1865–1914* (1987) · *Annual Report* [London Society for Women's Suffrage] (1912) · H. Barnett, 'Introduction', typescript for a projected biography, University of Bristol, Theatre Collection, Emma Cons Archives · G. Darley, *Octavia Hill* (1990) · W. T. Hill, *Octavia Hill* (1956) · F. Briant, 'Emma Cons', *Woman's Leader* (6 Dec 1929) · *DNB* · d. cert. · University of Bristol, Theatre Collection, Emma Cons Archives

Archives University of Bristol, Theatre Collection · University of Bristol Library

Likenesses M. J. Healy, pencil and watercolour drawings, NG Ire. · portrait, University of Bristol

Wealth at death £3374 10s.: probate, 28 Sept 1912, CGPLA Eng. & Wales

Const, Francis (1752–1839), legal writer, was born on 2 October 1752, the son of Francis Const (*fl.* 1721–1793) and Catherine Potticary, who married on 9 September 1753. He wrote some dramatic epilogues and prologues and had numerous theatrical acquaintances, including Frederick Reynolds, John Kemble, Stephen Storace, Thomas Harris, Charles Burney, and Richard Brinsley Sheridan. As executor of Ann Martindale he possessed, as a life interest, an eighth share in the Covent Garden Theatre.

Const was called to the bar at the Middle Temple on 7 February 1783 and lived at 5 Pump Court in the Middle Temple from at least 1799 until his death. He edited several editions of Edmund Bott's *Laws Relating to the Poor* and was chairman of the Middlesex magistrates and the Westminster sessions; the latter office he held until his death, in Rickmansworth, on 16 December 1839. He was buried at Kensal Green cemetery. Const acquired a fortune of £150,000 by speculation during his early life and left legacies to many of his friends and servants; his principal beneficiary was his nephew Henry Beaumont Coles.

[ANON.], *rev.* ALANNAH TOMKINS

Sources GM, 2nd ser., 13 (1840), 212 · will, PRO, PROB 11/1922, sig. 83 · *The Times* (6 June 1823), 4 · register, Mayfair, St George's Chapel, LMA [marriage], 9 Sept 1753 · [W. Holden], *Holden's triennial directory* (1799) · [W. Holden], *The triennial directory of London ... for 1817, 1818, 1819* (1817–19) · tablet inscription, Kensal Green cemetery, coffin 2284, catacomb B, vault 83, compartment 16

Likenesses B. Marshall, oils, 1806, Genesee County Museum, Munford, New York, Gallery of Sporting Art · C. Turner, mezzotint, pubd 1806 (after B. Marshall), BM, V&A · C. Turner, mezzotint, pubd 1824 (after J. Jackson), BM

Wealth at death £150,000: GM; will, PRO, PROB 11/1922, sig. 83

PICTURE CREDITS

Clegg, Sir (John) Charles (1850–1937)—© Empics

Clementi, Sir Cecil (1875–1947)—© National Portrait Gallery, London

Clementi, Muzio (1752–1832)—© National Portrait Gallery, London

Clementina [Maria Clementina Stuart] (1702–1735)—Museo del Prado, Madrid; photograph © National Portrait Gallery, London

Clements, Michael (b. in or before 1735, d. c.1797)—© National Maritime Museum, London

Clerk, Sir Dugald (1854–1932)—Scottish National Portrait Gallery

Clerk, Sir John, of Penicuik, first baronet (1649/50–1722)—in the collection of Sir John Clerk of Penicuik House

Clerk, John, of Eldin (1728–1812)—Currier Funds, 1933.8

Clerk, Josiah (bap. 1639?, d. 1714)—by permission of the Royal College of Physicians, London

Clerke, Agnes Mary (1842–1907)—© National Portrait Gallery, London

Clery, Sir Cornelius Francis (1838–1926)—© National Portrait Gallery, London

Cleveland, John (bap. 1613, d. 1658)—© National Portrait Gallery, London

Clibborn, Stanley Eric Francis Booth- (1924–1996)—photograph provided by the Bishop of Manchester's Office

Cliff, Clarice (1899–1972)—Leonard Griffin

Clifford, Anne, countess of Pembroke, Dorset, and Montgomery (1590–1676)—National Trust Photographic Library / Geoffrey Shakerley

Clifford, George, third earl of Cumberland (1558–1605)—© National Maritime Museum, London

Clifford, Sir Hugh Charles (1866–1941)—© National Portrait Gallery, London

Clifford, John (1836–1923)—© National Portrait Gallery, London

Clifford, (Sophia) Lucy Jane (1846–1929)—© National Portrait Gallery, London

Clifford, Thomas, first Baron Clifford of Chudleigh (1630–1673)—private collection

Clifford, William Kingdon (1845–1879)—Estate of the Artist / © The Royal Society

Clinton, Edward Fiennes de, first earl of Lincoln (1512–1585)—© National Portrait Gallery, London

Clinton, Elizabeth Fiennes de, countess of Lincoln (1528?–1589)—National Gallery of Ireland

Clinton, George (1739–1812)—Collection of the City of New York, courtesy of the Art Commission of the City of New York

Clinton, Sir Henry (1730–1795)—courtesy of the Director, National Army Museum, London

Clinton, Henry Pelham Fiennes Pelham-, fourth duke of Newcastle

under Lyme (1785–1851)—Palace of Westminster Collection

Clinton, Henry Pelham Fiennes Pelham-, fifth duke of Newcastle under Lyme (1811–1864)—© National Portrait Gallery, London

Clitherow, Sir Christopher (1577/8–1641)—photograph by courtesy Sotheby's Picture Library, London

Clive, Catherine (1711–1785)—reproduced by permission of the Marquess of Bath, Longleat House, Warminster, Wiltshire, Great Britain

Clive, Robert, first Baron Clive of Plassey (1725–1774)—National Trust Photographic Library / John Hammond

Clodd, Edward (1840–1930)—by permission of the E. O. Hoppé Trust, Curatorial Assistance, Inc., Los Angeles; collection National Portrait Gallery, London

Close, Sir Charles Frederick Arden- (1865–1952)—© National Portrait Gallery, London

Close, Francis (1797–1882)—© National Portrait Gallery, London

Close, Ivy Lilian (1890–1968)—Stockton-on-Tees Museum Heritage Service

Clotworthy, John, first Viscount Massereene (d. 1665)—© National Portrait Gallery, London

Clough, Anne Jemima (1820–1892)—The Principal and Fellows, Newnham College, Cambridge

Clough, Arthur Hugh (1819–1861)—© National Portrait Gallery, London

Clough, Blanche Athena (1861–1960)—Newnham College, Cambridge / photographer Michael Manni Photographic

Clough, Richard (d. 1570)—private collection

Clouston, Arthur Edmond (1908–1984)—© National Portrait Gallery, London

Clover, Joseph Thomas (1825–1882)—reproduced by kind permission of the President and Council of the Royal College of Surgeons of England. Photograph: Photographic Survey, Courtauld Institute of Art, London

Clowes, Butler (d. c.1788)—© Copyright The British Museum

Clowes, William (1779–1847)—reproduced by kind permission of William Clowes Ltd

Clowes, William (1780–1851)—© National Portrait Gallery, London

Clutterbuck, Henry (1767–1856)—© National Portrait Gallery, London

Clutterbuck, Richard Lewis (1917–1998)—© News International Newspapers Ltd

Clutterbuck, Robert (1772–1831)—© National Portrait Gallery, London

Clyde, James Avon, Lord Clyde (1863–1944)—© National Portrait Gallery, London

Clynes, John Robert (1869–1949)—© National Portrait Gallery, London

Cnut (d. 1035)—The British Library

Coates, Eric (1886–1957)—© National Portrait Gallery, London

Coates, (Joseph) Gordon (1878–1943)—© reserved; collection National Portrait Gallery, London

Coats, Thomas (1809–1883)—Paisley Museum and Art Galleries, Renfrewshire Council

Cobb, John Rhodes (1899–1952)—© National Portrait Gallery, London

Cobb, Richard Charles (1917–1996)—© Deborah Elliott; collection National Portrait Gallery, London

Cobbe, Frances Power (1822–1904)—© reserved; Cobbe Collection Trust

Cobbett, William (1763–1835)—© National Portrait Gallery, London

Cobden, Richard (1804–1865)—© National Portrait Gallery, London

Cobham, John, second Lord Cobham of Cobham (d. 1355)—reproduced by courtesy of H. M. Stutchfield, F.S.A., Hon. Secretary of the Monumental Brass Society

Cobham, Sir Alan John (1894–1973)—© National Portrait Gallery, London

Coborn, Charles (1852–1945)—Mander & Mitchenson Theatre Collection

Coburn, Alvin Langdon (1882–1966)—© Alvin Langdon Coburn

Cochran, Sir Charles Blake (1872–1951)—© National Portrait Gallery, London

Cochrane, Sir Alexander Forrester Inglis (1758–1832)—Scottish National Portrait Gallery

Cochrane, Douglas Mackinnon Baillie Hamilton, twelfth earl of Dundonald (1852–1935)—© National Portrait Gallery, London

Cochrane, Thomas, tenth earl of Dundonald (1775–1860)—private collection; photograph National Portrait Gallery, London

Cockburn, Adam, of Ormiston, Lord Ormiston (c.1656–1735)—Scottish National Portrait Gallery

Cockburn, Sir Alexander James Edmund, twelfth baronet (1802–1880)—© National Portrait Gallery, London

Cockburn, Sir George, eighth baronet (1772–1853)—© National Maritime Museum, London, Greenwich Hospital Collection

Cockburn, Henry, Lord Cockburn (1779–1854)—Scottish National Portrait Gallery

Cockcroft, Sir John Douglas (1897–1967)—© National Portrait Gallery, London

Cockerell, Charles Robert (1788–1863)—Ashmolean Museum, Oxford

Cockerell, Sir Christopher Sydney (1910–1999)—Getty Images – Hulton Archive

Cockerell, Sir Sydney Carlyle (1867–1962)—© Fitzwilliam Museum, University of Cambridge

Cockerell, Sydney Morris (1906–1987)—photograph by Philip Sayer

Codrington, Sir Edward (1770–1851)—© National Portrait Gallery, London

Codrington, Sir Henry John (1808–1877)—© National Maritime Museum, London, Greenwich Hospital Collection

Codrington, Sir William John (1804–1884)—© National Portrait Gallery, London

Cody, Samuel Franklin (1861–1913)—Getty Images – Hulton Archive

Coffin, Albert Isaiah (1790/91–1866)—Wellcome Library, London

Coffin, Robert Aston (1819–1885)—Archbishop's House, Southwark; by courtesy of the Saint Austin Press, London; photograph National Portrait Gallery, London

Cogan, Alma Angela Cohen (1932–1966)—© Derek Allen; collection National Portrait Gallery, London

Cogan, Thomas (1736–1818)—© National Portrait Gallery, London

Coggan, (Frederick) Donald, Baron Coggan (1909–2000)—© Eve Arnold / Magnum Photos; collection National Portrait Gallery, London

Coghill, Nevill Henry Kendal Aylmer (1899–1980)—© National Portrait Gallery, London

Cohen, Arthur (1829–1914)—© National Portrait Gallery, London

Cohen, Sir Bernard Nathaniel Waley-, first baronet (1914–1991)—© National Portrait Gallery, London

Cohen, Harriet Pearl Alice (1895–1967)—© National Portrait Gallery, London

Cohen, Henry, Baron Cohen of Birkenhead (1900–1977)—© Charlotte & Stephen Halliday; by kind permission of the Royal Society of Medicine, London

Cohen, Sir Robert Waley (1877–1952)—© National Portrait Gallery, London

Coia, Giacomo Antonio (1898–1981)—RIBA Library Photographs Collection

Coiley, John Arthur (1932–1998)—Science & Society Picture Library

Cokayne, George Edward (1825–1911)—The College of Arms

Coke, Sir Edward (1552–1634)—by kind permission of the Earl of Leicester and the Trustees of the Holkham Estate. Photograph: Photographic Survey, Courtauld Institute of Art, London

Coke, Sir John (1563–1644)—reproduced by kind permission of Lord Ralph Kerr, Melbourne Hall

Coke, Lady Mary (1727–1811)—private collection

Coke, Thomas (1747–1814)—© National Portrait Gallery, London

Coke, Thomas William, first earl of Leicester of Holkham (1754–1842)—by kind permission of the Earl of Leicester and the Trustees of the Holkham Estate. Photograph: Photographic Survey, Courtauld Institute of Art, London

Colborne, John, first Baron Seaton (1778–1863)—© National Portrait Gallery, London